ISBN 978-0-364-59221-2
PIBN 10155824

THE

HOLY BIBLE; B

CONTAINING

THE OLD AND NEW TESTAMENTS,

ACCORDING TO THE AUTHORIZED VERSION;

WITH EXPLANATORY NOTES, PRACTICAL OBSERVATIONS,
AND COPIOUS MARGINAL REFERENCES,

BY THE LATE REV.

THOMAS SCOTT,

RECTOR OF ASTON SANDFORD, BUCKS.

A NEW EDITION,

WITH THE AUTHOR'S LAST CORRECTIONS AND IMPROVEMENTS; AND
EIGHTY-FOUR ILLUSTRATIVE MAPS AND ENGRAVINGS.

VOLUME V.

LONDON:

JAMES NISBET AND CO., 21, BERNERS STREET.

MDCCCLXVI.

PALESTINE
IN THE TIME OF
OUR SAVIOUR

London Published for the Proprietors of Scotts Bible by Fortheins Vire Intosh & Sons

THE

NEW TESTAMENT

OF

OUR LORD AND SAVIOUR JESUS CHRIST.

INTRODUCTION.

THE church, from the earliest antiquity, has called this part of Scripture on which we now enter, ' The New Testament,' or ' The New Covenant:' for the word (διαθηκη) may be translated either way, as it signifies sometimes a stipulation between two or more contracting parties.; at others, the absolute appointment of a person, in those matters that are entirely at his own disposal; and more rarely, a last Will and Testament, by which a man appoints his heirs, and the way in which the inheritance is to be obtained and enjoyed. (*Note, Heb.* ix. 15—17.) It is called, ' The ' *New* Testament' in contra-distinction to ' the *Old* Testament:' not as if the one contained only the old covenant of works, and the other the new covenant of grace; for the contrary has already been abundantly shewn: but because the New Testament gives an account of the abrogation of the old dispensation, and of the introduction of a new and better dispensation. The Mosaick law, the national covenant made with Israel, and the Levitical priesthood, formed as it were an edition both of the covenant of works and of the covenant of grace: (*Note, Ex.* xix. 5:) but at the coming of Christ, the end being answered, this was antiquated and abrogated; and the Christian dispensation, containing clearer light and greater encouragement, not attended with burdensome ceremonies, or clouded by types and shadows, or restricted to any place or nation, formed a new edition of the covenant of grace; yet so that unbelievers continue, as of old, under " the ministration of death," the covenant of works. This dispensation therefore is compendiously called, ' The New Covenant,' or ' The New Testament,' with reference to the death of Christ the Mediator.

The history, contained in this part of Scripture, is an exact counterpart of the prophecies, promises, and types of the Old Testament, in respect of its grand Subject, the great Redeemer and his kingdom and salvation. An enlightened student of the Old Testament, before the coming of Christ, must have expected exactly such events, and such changes in the outward state of the church, as the New Testament records: and the sole reason, why the Jews in general, and the apostles in particular for a time, did not expect such events and changes, is this; " their under-" standings were not opened to understand the scriptures." A careful and constant examination of the sacred volume, diligently comparing one part with another, renders this clear and manifest: insomuch that it is possible, and perhaps not very difficult, to form a connected narrative of all the grand outlines of the history, contained in the New Testament, from the very words of the Old Testament. The person of the Redeemer as Emmanuel, his descent in human nature from Judah, and from David when the family was reduced to poverty and obscurity; his miraculous conception,

INTRODUCTION.

his birth at Bethlehem, his character, miracles, and doctrine; the reception given him by his countrymen, the unparalleled contempt and enmity shewn him, the manner and all the circumstances
of his death and burial, even to minute particulars; the end and design of his sufferings and death,
his resurrection, ascension, the pouring out of the Holy Spirit, the conversion of vast multitudes,
the obstinate unbelief and opposition of the Jewish nation, the tremendous judgments of God on
them for these crimes; the abrogation of the ceremonial law, the destruction of Jerusalem and
the temple, the calling of the Gentiles, the glorious triumphs of Christianity, and indeed the
state of the church through all intervening ages till the consummation of all things, might be related in the words of the prophets, only by substituting in a few instances the past for the future
tense. To so astonishing a degree do the two divisions of the sacred scriptures confirm and illustrate each other! And let it here be observed in general, that the writers of the New Testament
always quote and refer to the several books of the Old, as divinely inspired, as " the oracles of
" God," as " the scripture that cannot be broken;" and never as if they supposed any part of it to
be the words of uninspired men, however eminent and excellent. But the New Testament does
not rest its claim, to be received as a divine revelation, on the Old Testament, and the evidences
by which it is confirmed. While Christ and his apostles appealed to the ancient scriptures, and
shewed " that thus it was written and thus it must be;" they confirmed their instructions, and
combated the prejudices of their hearers, by the most undeniable miracles, wrought in the open
face of day, before great multitudes of all characters, and challenging the investigation of the most
powerful, sagacious, and inveterate of their enemies. Indeed it is utterly inconceivable, that
Christianity could have made its way in the world, by the obscure persons who propagated it, and
against the immense opposition made to it, except it had been thus confirmed, beyond the possibility of any denial.

The prophecies also of our Lord and of his apostles, interspersed, as we shall see, through the
books of the several writers of the New Testament, and fulfilled through all succeeding ages, form
a demonstration of its divine authority, which gathers clearness and energy by revolving centuries.
A variety of other proofs, external and internal, might be mentioned: but these hints may here suffice to shew, that the New Testament stands on its own basis; and not merely on the ground of
the Old Testament, as some have assumed.

The writers of the New Testament speak of themselves and of each other, as divinely inspired.
(*Rom.* x. 14—17. xvi. 25, 26. 1 *Cor.* i. 21. ii 7. 10. vii. 40. *Eph.* iii. 3—5. 1 *Thes.* ii. 13. 2 *Pet.* iii.
15, 16. 1 *John* iv. 6.)—If, then, any persons should be inclined to think, that, provided they be regarded as wise and good men, it is not so absolutely necessary to vindicate their divine inspiration;
let them first consider, whether laying a groundless claim to divine inspiration, be not such an im-
peachment of any writer's probity and veracity, as to render him unworthy of credit in all other
things?—And again, if the writers of the New Testament were not divinely inspired, where is our
standard of faith and practice? How can we know, what the doctrine of Christ was? How shall
we distinguish it from all false doctrine?

The several books, which now form the New Testament, were early received by the Christian
church, as of divine authority. The greatest part of them are quoted by the most ancient Christian writers, and appealed to as the standard of truth. A large proportion of the New Testament
might be collected from writers, who lived in the first two centuries. They formed catalogues of
the several books, and wrote comments on them; both the orthodox and the heretical appealed

B 2

INTRODUCTION.

to them; lectures on several parts of them are still extant; nay, the enemies of Christianity uniformly mention them, as the authentick books of Christians.—So that there is the most complete proof, that all the books now collected in the New Testament were received and read in the assemblies of Christians, before the end of the second century; except the epistle to the Hebrews, that of James, the second of Peter, the second and third of John, that of Jude, and the Revelation of John; and that these, or most of them, were extant and well known, though not universally received as divinely inspired.—Some reasons may be given, why the Christian church hesitated respecting these books, when they come under our consideration: but this only proves, that the persons concerned were cautious, even to an extreme, and therefore not likely to be imposed on by spurious productions.

'From the same tradition we, with the strongest evidence of reason, may conclude, that these...
'Scriptures...were handed down...uncorrupted in the substantials of faith and manners. ...These re-
'cords being once so generally dispersed through all Christian churches, though at a great distance
'from each other, from the beginning of the second century; ...so universally acknowledged...by
'men of curious parts and different persuasions; ...being multiplied into divers versions, almost from
'the beginning; ...being so constantly rehearsed in their assemblies; ...so diligently read by Chris-
'tians, and so rivetted in their memories, that Eusebius mentions some who had them all by heart; ..
'and lastly, so frequent in their writings, ...as now we have them; it must be certain from these con-
'siderations, that they were handed down to succeeding generations pure and uncorrupt.' *Whitby.*

As the notion is very common, that we cannot be *sure,* concerning the correctness of the Scriptures at present, after so many centuries; especially as learned men are frequently speaking of the different readings, found in manuscripts or versions; in addition to the above important quotation the following remark may afford some satisfaction. During nearly two hundred years, our present translation of the scriptures has been extant, and persons of various descriptions have made new translations of the whole, or of particular parts; and scarcely any writer on these subjects fails to mention, in one way or other, alterations which he supposes would be improvements. It may then be asked, how can unlearned persons know, that our translation may be depended on, as in general faithful and correct? Let the enquirer however remember, that episcopalians, presbyterians, and independents, baptists and pædobaptists, Calvinists and Arminians; persons, who maintain eager controversies with each other in various ways, all appeal to the same version, and in no matters of consequence object to it. This demonstrates, that the translation on the whole is just; and also that it is impossible for any party covertly to deviate from it, while so many eager opponents are incessantly watching over one another. The same consideration proves the impossibility of the primitive Christians corrupting the sacred records; while hereticks, Jews, and pagans, stood ready to expose with virulence every deviation; nay, other churches would have protested against the alterations, which any particular church attempted to make.—In fact, if all the different readings, (most of which are of little authority,) were without exception adopted as far as this would be practicable, the rule of truth and duty would remain entirely the same: so that this is merely an artifice, by which the enemies of the gospel perplex the minds of those, who cannot or will not examine the subject.—' Who can imagine, that God, who sent his Son...to declare this
' doctrine, and his apostles by the assistance of the Holy Spirit to indite and speak it, and by so
' many miracles confirmed it to the world, should suffer any wicked persons to corrupt and alter any
' of those terms on which the happiness of mankind depended? ...It is absurd to say, that God re

B 3

INTRODUCTION.

' pented of his good will and kindness to mankind, in vouchsafing the gospel to them; or that he
' so far maligned the good of future generations, that he suffered wicked men to rob them of all
' the good intended to them by this declaration of his will !' *Whitby.* (*Note, Prov.* xxii. 12.)

It should also be observed, that no other books were received by the primitive church, as a part
of divine revelation. Very many other compositions were sent forth, bearing the names of the apostles or primitive teachers : but, on careful examination, all except those which now form the New
Testament, were rejected as spurious. And this shews, with how scrupulous caution the canon of
Scripture was fixed. The four gospels were very early received, as the writings of the evangelists
whose names they bear. They are mentioned distinctly by the fathers of the second century, as
books well known by the name of gospels, and as such were read by Christians, at their assemblies every Lord's day.—Several other gospels were published, and some gained a temporary credit; but they are either not mentioned in the approved writings of the primitive Christians, or
mentioned with disapprobation.

It is well known, that the word *Gospel* signifies *glad tidings :* (God's-spel, or God's good tidings,
Dr. Johnson :) and the original word has precisely the same meaning. The inspired writers of
those histories, which we call ' The Gospels,' give distinct views of those things, which relate to
the birth, life, miracles, discourses, sufferings, death, resurrection, and ascension of our Lord and
Saviour Jesus Christ; connected with some account of his forerunner, John the Baptist, and of his
apostles and primitive disciples. Their accounts, as might have been previously supposed, vary
from one another : each of them recorded more fully those particulars, which most suited his purpose, or which had most affected his mind : for the most complete superintending inspiration did
not supersede the use of the writer's memory, judgment, and understanding; but rather served to
assist, direct, and exalt it. And thus, while these variations shew, that they did not write in concert; (for in that case the appearance of disagreement would certainly have been avoided;) they
tend to corroborate the evidence of the divine authority of their histories : as their actual coincidence, and the easy manner in which their apparent variations may be reconciled, form a strong
presumptive proof that they were under a supernatural guidance, and cannot satisfactorily be accounted for in any other way.—' Industry, ingenuity, and malice have, for ages, been employed,
' in endeavouring to prove the evangelists inconsistent with each other ; yet not a single *contra-*
' *diction* has hitherto been proved on them. ... But one thing is fact. These four men ...have done,
' without appearing to have intended it, what was never performed by any authors before or since.
' They have drawn a perfect human character, without a single flaw. They have given the his-
' tory of one, whose spirit, words, and actions, were in every particular, exactly what they ought
' to have been ! who always did the very thing that was proper, and in the best manner imagina-
' ble ; who never once deviated from the most consummate wisdom and ... excellency, and who in
' no instance let one virtue ... entrench on another ; but exercised all in perfect harmony and exact
' proportion. ... This subject challenges investigation, and sets infidelity at defiance. Either these
' men exceeded in genius and capacity all the writers who ever lived, or they wrote under the spe-
' cial guidance of divine inspiration.' *Answer to Paine's Age of Reason, by the author.*

N. B. Whatever notice may be taken in this edition, of a critical nature, with relation to the
original Greek words, or to the Septuagint, will be placed at the end of each note and distinguished from it; so that it may be omitted, if judged proper, in family reading.

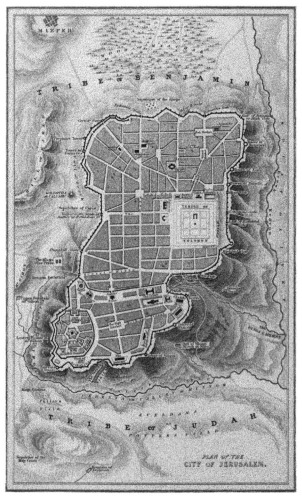

PLAN OF THE
CITY OF JERUSALEM.

London: Published for the Proprietors of Scott's Bible by Wertheim Macintosh & Hunt
24 Paternoster Row and 23 Holles Street, Cavendish Square

THE GOSPEL

ACCORDING TO

St MATTHEW.

LITTLE is known concerning the writer of this gospel, except what he has recorded of himself.—(x. 3. *Notes*, ix. 9 —13.) He is generally supposed to have written his history, about eight years after our Lord's ascension, and before any other part of the New Testament was extant. It is certain that it was published at a very early period.—Many have contended, that this gospel was written in Hebrew, and that we have only a translation of it in Greek. But learned men have satisfactorily shewn, that this is a mistake; and that the apostle wrote his gospel in Greek, as we now have it; though they seem willing to allow, that he also gave a Hebrew or Syriack version of it, for the use of his countrymen. The reader, who wishes to examine the subject, will find it fully discussed in Dr. Whitby's preface.

St. Matthew is supposed to be distinguished from the other evangelists, by the frequency of his references to the Old Testament. He also records more of our Lord's parables, than the others do; and, on the whole, seems more observant of the order in which events occurred. He begins his history with the genealogy of Christ, in the line of Joseph, the husband of Mary his mother: and relates some circumstances concerning his miraculous conception, birth, and infancy. He gives us a brief account of the ministry of John the Baptist; and records the baptism and temptation of Christ, and his entrance on his publick ministry. He then proceeds with the narrative of his miracles and discourses, till at length he fully records the manner of his crucifixion, death, and burial; and, having borne witness to his glorious resurrection, and appearance to his disciples, closes his history with some most important words, which the Lord Jesus is supposed to have spoken immediately before his ascension into heaven.

Year of the World 4000.

CHAP. I.

The genealogy of Christ in the line of Joseph, from Abraham and David, 1—17. His miraculous conception, by the Holy Ghost, of the virgin Mary : and the doubts of Joseph, to whom she was espoused, removed by an angel ; who directs him to take her home, and to call the Son born of her, Jesus, 18—21. This is shewn to accord with the prediction of

Isaiah, 22, 23. Joseph obeys, and Jesus is born, 24, 25.

THE book of the generation of Jesus Christ, the son of David, the son of Abraham,

NOTES.

CHAP. I. V. 1. 'The book of *Genesis*,' or *the Beginning*, that is, the original of the heavens and the earth, stands first in the Old Testament; and the same word, in the Greek, introduces the history contained in the New Testament: but here it signifies the generation, or stock and race of Him, who, as God, created all things, and at length appeared in human nature to redeem mankind from sin and misery. This promised Saviour had been long foretold, as the son of Abraham, and of David; and therefore the inspired writer, having mentioned his

name JESUS, and his office or appointment, as the CHRIST, the MESSIAH, the Anointed of God, proceeded to declare that he was the son of Abraham and of David, in order to introduce the subsequent genealogy, by which that claim would in part be authenticated. (*Marg. Ref.*)—The whole New Testament, however, shews, that this was not considered, as the only or the main proof that Jesus was the Son of David. For the genealogies are not once referred to in this argument; but the appeal is made to the ancient prophecies, and to his own miracles, and to his resurrection from the dead. (*Acts* xiii. 23. 31—37. *Rom.* i. 3, 4. 2 *Tim.* ii. 8.)

B 5

2 [a] Abraham begat Isaac, and [b] Isaac begat Jacob, [c] and Jacob begat Judas and his brethren,

3 And [e] Judas begat Phares and Zara of [f] Thamar, and Phares begat Esrom, and Esrom begat [h] Aram,

4 And Aram begat [i] Aminadab, and Aminadab begat [m] Naasson, and Naasson begat Salmon,

5 And [o] Salmon begat Booz of [p] Rachab, and [q] Booz begat Obed of Ruth, and [s] Obed begat Jesse,

6 And [t] Jesse begat David the king, and David the king begat [x] Solomon of [y] her that had been the wife of [z] Urias,

7 And Solomon begat [a] Roboam, and Roboam begat [b] Abia, and Abia begat [c] Asa,

8 And Asa begat [d] Josaphat, and Josaphat begat [e] Joram, and Joram begat [f] Ozias,

9 And Ozias begat [d] Joatham, and

Joatham begat [e] Achaz, and Achaz begat [f] Ezekias,

10 And Ezekias begat [g] Manasses, and Manasses begat [i] Amon, and Amon begat [l] Josias,

11 And [n] Josias begat [k] Jeconias and his brethren, [l] about the time they were carried away to Babylon:

12 And after they were brought to Babylon, [m] Jeconias begat Salathiel, [n] and Salathiel begat Zorobabel,

13 And Zorobabel begat Abiud, and Abiud begat Eliakim, and Eliakim begat Azor,

14 And Azor begat Sadoc, and Sadoc begat Achim, and Achim begat Eliud,

15 And Eliud begat Eleazar, and Eleazar begat Matthan, and Matthan begat Jacob,

16 And Jacob begat [o] Joseph the husband of Mary, [p] of whom was born Jesus, [q] who is called Christ.

17 So all the generations from Abraham to David *are* fourteen generations; and from David until the carrying away into Babylon *are* fourteen generations; and from the carrying away into Babylon unto Christ *are* fourteen generations.

V. 2—17. Various difficulties have been started, in respect of this genealogy; but a few general remarks may suffice, to shew them to be comparatively of small consequence. It is evident, that the genealogy of Joseph, and not of Mary, is given in these verses. That of Mary is traced back to Adam by St. Luke, as it will be shewn hereafter. (*Note*, Luke iii. 34—38.) Joseph was supposed by the Jews to be the father of Jesus, and he was his father-in-law: it was therefore proper, that his descent from David should be ascertained. Probably, this genealogy was copied from the publick registers of the nation, which were well known; and this may account for some omissions and variations, which are found in it on comparing it with the history of the Old Testament.—The other children of Abraham are not mentioned with Isaac, nor is Esau who was the twin-brother of Jacob, and elder than he: for their descendants were not interested in " the covenants of promise." But the children of Judah are mentioned, as their posterity constituted the chosen people of God; and Zara twin-brother of Phares is inserted, because part of the tribe of Judah descended from him. The names of four women are found in it, being all remarkable characters: Thamar, of whom, by incest with her father-in-law, the greatest part of the tribe of Judah descended; (*Notes*, Gen. xxxviii;) Rachab, or Rahab, who seems to have been the same as had been a harlot, and an inhabitant of Jericho, but through faith was preserved from the destruction of that city; (*Notes*,

Josh. ii. vi;) for no other woman of that name is mentioned in scripture: Ruth, the Moabitess; and Bathsheba, who had been the wife of Uriah, with whom David had committed adultery. This might intimate that Christ was " made in the likeness of sinful flesh," and came to save the Gentiles and the vilest of sinners. Three kings, the immediate descendants of Athaliah, by Joram the son of Jehoshaphat, viz. Ahaziah, Joash, and Amaziah, are passed over without notice. Perhaps it was found so in the genealogies; and they who compiled them, aiming to reduce the number of genealogies, from David to the captivity, to fourteen, as well as that from Abraham to David, thought these descendants of that wicked woman, by an unhallowed fatal marriage, might most properly be omitted. But some think, that Matthew was directed to leave them out for similar reasons.—In some manuscripts it is found, " Josiah begat Jehoiakim, and Jehoiakim begat Jeconias:" and it is certain that Jeconias was *grandson* to Josiah, and the father or grandfather of Salathiel; nor does it appear that he had any brethren, for his uncle Zedekiah succeeded him, when he was carried to Babylon.—From Jeconiah, who was carried captive to Joseph the husband of Mary, were also fourteen generations: and at that time the illustrious house of David was so reduced, that its rights, in the line of Solomon, centred in a poor carpenter: at least he was that descendant, whom the Lord chose to stand in the place of a legal father to the promised Messiah; that so this expected Prophet, Priest,

B 6

18 ¶ Now ᶠ the birth of Jesus Christ was on this wise : When as his mother Mary was espoused to Joseph, before they came together, she was found with child ᵍ of the Holy Ghost.

19 Then Joseph ʰ her husband, being ⁱ a just *man*, and not willing to make her ᵏ a publick example, ˡ was minded to put her away privily.

20 But, ᵐ while he thought on these things, behold, ⁿ the angel of the Lord appeared unto him ᵒ in a dream, saying, ᵖ Joseph, thou son of David, ᵠ fear not to take unto thee Mary thy wife ; for, ʳ that which is ˢ conceived in her is of the Holy Ghost.

21 And ᵗ she shall bring forth a

and King, might spring up " as a tender Plant out of a dry " ground."—The marginal references contain nearly all the information, which can be obtained on the subject of this genealogy.—It is probable, that some names are omitted between Salmon and David. (*Note, Ruth* iv. 18—22.) And either the marginal addition of Jakim or Jehoiakim, must be admitted; or Jeconias, in the twelfth verse, must be considered as the *son* of Jeconias mentioned in the eleventh: for otherwise the fourteen generations are not completed.—' Perhaps interpreters might save themselves ' the trouble of giving a reason of many things contained ' in this catalogue, by saying, St. Matthew here recites it, ' as he found it in the authentick copies of the Jews; who ' doubtless had preserved some known and approved ge- ' nealogy of their descent from Abraham, the father of ' their nation, in whom they so much gloried, and from ' whose loins, they expected the promised Messiah.' *Whitby.* It is conceded, that this genealogy does not prove that Jesus was " the son of David ; " but merely, that Joseph the husband of Mary, and the father-in-law of Jesus, was descended from David. But the customs of the Jews, in genealogies, required this genealogy of Jo- seph to be produced : and it leaves the proof, arising from Mary's descent from David, as stated by St. Luke in full force ; and that is perfectly conclusive. For if " Jacob the " son of Matthan the son of Eleazar, begat Joseph," (15, 16), Joseph could be " the son of Heli, the son of Mat- " thal, the son of Levi." (*Luke* iii. 23, 24.)

V. 18, 19. In ' the Gospel according to St. Luke,' we find a variety of circumstances which are here omitted : but this succinct narrative was deemed sufficient to intro- duce that history of Christ, which was first given to the church. His mother Mary, a virgin of the house of David, had been contracted or betrothed to Joseph; but they had not completed the intended marriage, when it was found that she was with child. By a most extraor- dinary miracle, she had, continuing a virgin, conceived by the power of the Holy Spirit; that the promised Saviour might be " the Seed of the woman," in the strictest sense; and though truly man, our Brother and Redeemer, yet not be conceived and born in sin. (*Notes, Gen.* iii. 14, 15. *Is.* vii. 14. *Jer.* xxxi. 21, 22.) But Mary's espousals, before the time of her miraculous conception, sheltered her character from injurious suspicions; and a pious and ᵖrudent person was thus engaged to afford her assistance, in the care of her son Jesus. When Joseph, who was now considered as the husband of Mary, found that she was pregnant, and probably heard from her an account of the vision which she had seen ; (*Luke* i. 26—38;) and per- haps learned such circumstances from Zacharias and Eliza- beth, as tended to confirm her narration; he was at a loss

how to act on so extraordinary an occasion. He might not be able to give full credit to what he had heard; and yet be unwilling to suspect a person, whom he so much valued, of having been false to him, and then of form- ing so strange a story to cover her guilt. But being *a just*, or a conscientious, godly man, he was neither willing in such circumstances to complete the marriage, nor yet to expose her to publick disgrace and punishment; for, according to the law, she would have been condemned to be stoned as an adulteress, if she had been proved guilty of incontinency after having been betrothed: and if he had declared his reasons for putting her away, without proceeding further against her, it would have exposed her character to lasting disgrace. He therefore purposed pri- vately, (that is, before two witnesses,) to give her a bill of divorcement, and to put her away, without assigning his reasons for so doing.—Some have thought, that reverence of Mary, when he found she was with child by the Holy Ghost, deterred him from marrying her : but, though this might increase his perplexity, it is plain from the angel's answer to his objections, that they were not of this kind. (20, 21.)

To make her a publick example. (19) Παραδειγμαλισαι.— Παραδειγμαλιζοιλας, " putting to open shame." *Heb.* vi. 6. See *Sept. Jer.* viii. 22. *Ez.* xxviii. 17.

V. 20, 21. Whilst Joseph meditated on these matters, he fell asleep; and in his dream he was favoured with a vision of a holy angel, sent from God to direct him how to act. The angel addressed him as " The son of David," as one of that illustrious family, and probably the legal heir of its dignities. Perhaps few persons regarded him, in his reduced condition, on that account, and he himself might think little of such a neglected distinction. He had been afraid of acting contrary to his duty, reputation, in- terest, or peace, if he should proceed to complete his marriage with Mary, though considered as his legal wife : but the angel shewed him, that these fears were unneces- sary; for it would be profitable and proper forᵗ him to take her home to him, as the Lord had so ordered matters for wise and important reasons. The child, with which he knew her to be pregnant, was indeed conceived in her by the miraculous operation of the Holy Spirit ; and would prove a Son, of which she would in due time be delivered; and then he, as the husband of Mary, and the supposed and legal father, was directed to call him JESUS.—It has been before observed, that the word JESUS is the same as *Joshua,* or *Jehoshua,* only framed to the Greek pronun- ciation and *termination.* Joshua, who brought the tribes of Israel into the rest of Canaan, was originally called *Oshea ; (Num.* xiii. 8 ;) but it was afterwards changed into *Jehoshua,* by an addition of the first syllable of the divine

son, and ᵉ thou shalt call his name JESUS: ᵇ for he shall save his people from their sins.

22 Now all this was done, ¹ that it might be fulfilled which was spoken of the Lord by the prophet, saying,

23 Behold, ᵏ a virgin shall be with child, and shall bring forth a son, and

ʰ they shall call his name ¹ Emmanuel, which being interpreted is, ᵐ God with us.

24 Then Joseph being raised from sleep ⁿ did as the angel of the Lord had bidden him, and took unto him his wife;

25 And knew her not till ° she had ᵖ brought forth her first-born son: ᵖ and he called his name JESUS.

name, JEHOVAH; perhaps intimating, that not Joshua of himself, but JEHOVAH by him, would complete the deliverance of Israel. (*Note, Num.* xiii. 16.) As this name was given to the promised Messiah, it signified, as it has been sufficiently proved, JEHOVAH THE SAVIOUR, or JEHOVAH-SALVATION; and it was given him, because " he " shall save his people from their sins." He delivers all, who believe and obey him, from the guilt, condemnation, dominion, and pollution of all their sins; and finally, he will save them from the very existence and from all the effects of sin, when " death shall be swallowed up in " victory," and sorrow in everlasting felicity. (*Marg. Ref.* h.)

V. 22, 23. This seems to be the evangelist's observation on these extraordinary events: yet it is probable, the angel shewed Joseph, that this child was He, to whom all the prophets bare witness. The prophecy has already been explained. (*Note, Is.* vii. 14.) The child to be born of a *virgin* could have no human father.—The solemn introduction, in the prophecy, " The Lord himself will give thee " a sign:" and the call to attention, and even admiration, in the word " Behold,"—" Behold, the LORD himself,"— imply that some extraordinary and unprecedented event was intended: but the marriage of a virgin, and a son being born of her, in consequence of her marriage, are events of common occurrence, and could not, with the least propriety, have been announced in this manner. This prophecy was in the strictest sense fulfilled, when the Virgin Mary's Son was called Jesus: for, JEHOVAH-SALVATION, and IMMANUEL, GOD WITH US, are expressions of similar signification. If God be with us sinners in Jesus Christ, he is " become our Salvation."—But the Saviour has been known to vast multitudes, through successive generations, and been peculiarly dear to them, by his name EMMANUEL: and he will be so, to the end of time, yea, to all eternity.—*They shall call.* (23) ' Thou shalt call :' *Sept. Is.* vii.]4; which accords to the Hebrew. Some copies read it so here.

V. 24, 25. This heavenly vision fully satisfied the mind of Joseph, and, rendering implicit obedience, he delayed not to take Mary home to him as his wife; providing thus for her reputation and comfort in her present circumstances, as far as it was in his power: but he had no conjugal intercourse with her, " till she had brought forth " her first-born Son." Some reference in this expression might be had to Christ, as the " First-born of every crea- " ture," the Heir of all things, and " in all things having " the pre-eminence :" but it seems rather to relate to the law of Moses, concerning the first-born male being consecrated to God. (*Marg. Ref.* o.) Jesus being called Mary's *first-born* Son does not prove, that she had more children

afterwards: nor did it seem good to the Holy Spirit to gratify men's foolish curiosity, about the terms, on which Joseph and Mary afterwards lived together. They who have contended for, and those who have denied, Mary's perpetual virginity, have alike wandered in the pathless regions of uncertain and useless conjecture. It is true, that some of the zealous champions for the affirmative, intended to give some support to their antichristian worship of the Virgin Mary, and their antichristian admiration of virginity and celibacy: but we want no additional proof that God alone ought to be worshipped, and that " mar- " riage is honourable in all, and the bed undefiled."

PRACTICAL OBSERVATIONS.

V. 1—17.

The Lord proves his people's faith and patience by long delays; but his promises stand sure, and will all be fulfilled in due season: nor can we have the least ground for doubting the rest; as that grand promise, of the incarnation of his beloved Son, to be our Surety and atoning Sacrifice, has been exactly verified.—In reviewing the generations of men, who have lived on earth, how vain, transitory, and worthless do all things here below appear! We pass as shadows over the plain, and move on as к pageant over the stage: and except we have a nobler and more enduring inheritance in heaven, it would have been better for us if we had never been born, whatever distinctions we may have possessed on earth. We may also profitably observe the fluctuations in outward circumstances, and the discordant characters, of those who appear in the same genealogy: hence we should learn to expect our happiness from God, and in heaven; and not to flatter our minds with empty hopes concerning our posterity, of whom we cannot know whether they will be rich or poor, wise or foolish, holy or unholy, honourable or dishonourable, happy or miserable. When the Son of God was pleased to assume our nature, he came as near to us, in all the circumstances of our fallen condition, as consisted with his being perfectly free from sin: and whilst we read some of the names in his genealogy, we should not forget how the Lord of glory stooped, to save the most guilty and depraved of the human race. How absurd then must it be, then to reproach others with the crimes of their ancestors, or to glory in the virtues or honours of their own!

V. 18—23.

We should often recollect the circumstances, in which the Son of God made his entrance into this lower world; that we may learn to despise the distinctions of rank, birth, or affluence, when compared with the real dignity which piety and holiness confer. A poor obscure virgin,

в 8

BETHLEHEM.

Gen. xxxv 19. Judg. xvii. 7; xix. 1. Ruth i. 1. 2
1 Sam. xvi. 4; xvii. 12. 2 Sam xxiii. 14–16. 2 Chron. xi. 6.
Mic. v. 2. Matt. ii. 1–8, 16. Luke ii. 4, 11, 15. John vii. 42.

CHAP. II.

Wise men from the east, guided by a star, come to Jerusalem, enquiring for " him, who was born King " of the Jews," 1, 2. Herod, being alarmed, learns that Christ should be born at Bethlehem, and sends the wise men thither, 3—8. The star guides them to Jesus, whom they honour and worship; and, being warned by God, they return home another way, 9— 12. Joseph is directed to go, with the child and his mother, into Egypt, 13—15. Herod murders the children at and near Bethlehem, 16—18. After

Herod's death, Joseph returns from Egypt, with Jesus a i. 25. Luke ii. 4 and Mary, and goes to dwell at Nazareth, 19—23.
—7.
b 5. Mic. v. 2.
Luke ii. 11, 15.
John vii. 42.

NOW when ª Jesus was born in ᵇ Bethlehem of Judea, in the days ᶜ of Herod the king, behold, there came wise men ᵈ from the east to Jerusalem, 2 Saying, Where is he that is ᵉ born King of the Jews? for we have seen ᶠ his star in the east, and are come to ᵍ worship him.

c 3. 19. Gen. xlix. 10. Dan. ix. 24, 25. Hag. ii. 6—9.
d 4. 1 Kings 1ª. 30. Job i. 3. Ps. lxxii. 9—12. Is. xi. 10. Is. l. &c.
e xxi. 5. Ps. ii. 6. Is. ix. 6, 7. xxxii. 1, 2. Jer. xxxii. 5. Zech. ix. 9. Luke ii. 11. xix. 38. xxiii. 3. 38. John i. 49 xii. 13. xviii. 37. xix. 12—15, 19.
f Num. xxiv. 17. Is. lx. 3. Luke ii. 32.
g 10, 11. Ps. xlv. 11. John ix. 38. xx. 28. Heb. i. 6.

a 1. 78, 79.   Rev. xxii. 16.

espoused to a carpenter, was chosen to be the honoured mother of him, " by whom kings reign," and before whom they must all appear in judgment ! Doubtless he could have assumed our nature in an imperial palace, as well as in an obscure cottage, or rather a humble stable. But his dignity and honour were of a more exalted and heavenly nature, and like his " kingdom, which is not of this world." Indeed " that honour, which cometh from God only," is seldom unattended with humiliating and distressing trials. She, whom God pronounced " highly favoured, and blessed " among women," was in danger of being suspected of the most atrocious crimes, by him whose opinion and affection must have been more regarded, than those of any other person ; nay, of being exposed to the deepest infamy and most terrible punishment. Let us not then expect to escape calumnies and suspicions, even as to those things in which we act most conscientiously, or from those persons whom we most love and esteem. But, being careful to keep a clear conscience, let us leave it to the Lord to protect our characters : and if appearances should at any time be against us; let us not be over anxious to vindicate ourselves, but keep on in the path of duty, and wait till he shall justify us from unmerited reproaches. In this way he will in due season appear for us : and if in the mean time we meet with severe mortifications, let us remember that we need them, " as thorns in the flesh," to keep down our pride, which would otherwise tarnish all our endowments and services.—In dubious cases, it behoves a pious man to deliberate with great attention ; and to choose the lenient rather than the severer judgment or measures : and though we ought by no means to connect ourselves with persons, whose conduct would be likely to expose our characters to disgrace ; yet we should not judge by appearances : and we are sometimes liable to scrupulous fears, when our duty, interest, credit, and comfort require us to proceed. But he, who desires to know, that he may do, the will of God, and uses proper means of instruction, shall not be left to fall into any fatal error. We cannot now expect immediate revelations, or angelick interpreters of the mind of God ; but we may discover it, as it stands revealed in his word, and be thus enabled to proceed with confidence and comfort.—But whilst we make observations on the circumstances of this extraordinary conception and birth; let us not overlook the end, for which the Son of God was manifested in our nature. Men may pervert and abuse, or they may object to the sacred truths of God's word ; but surely none can be encouraged to continue in sin, by a free and gracious salvation *from*

sin ! None can have evidence, that they are the people of Christ, who are not now saved from the dominion of their sins, and are not seeking continually for deliverance from the remaining power and pollution of them. Every time that we name the sacred name of JESUS, we should be reminded to rely on him for this complete salvation ; that we may be delivered from guilt, and from sin, and saved in him, " the LORD our Righteousness," " with an everlast- " ing salvation." Then may we rejoice that " God is " with us," as our reconciled Friend and Portion, in every place, and in all the circumstances of mortal life. EM- MANUEL will be our Strength and Song in all our tribulations, and in the hour of death : we shall daily experience the fulfilling of the scriptures, and be enabled to proceed with comfort in the path of unreserved obedience ; and all our perplexities and troubles will soon terminate in glory, honour, and immortal felicity.

NOTES.

CHAP. II. V. 1, 2. Herod was an Edomite by descent, though proselyted to the Jewish religion. He obtained the kingdom of Judea by favour of the Romans, and by means of much war and bloodshed. He reigned in prosperity for about thirty-five years : but his whole administration was tarnished with the most horrible cruelties. Among many others, he put to death his wife Mariamne, and two of his own sons. He was seventy years of age ; but as full of ambition and jealousy, and as prompt to every act of tyranny and cruelty, as ever, at the time when these *wise men* came to enquire about the birth of Christ. The original word is *Magoi*, or Magians : *Magoi*, and words derived from it, are used in the New Testament in a bad sense : (*Acts* viii. 9. 11. xiii. 6. 8. Gr.) yet there was a sect of philosophers, and indeed of religionists, who were called by this name; and who seem to have come nearer to many truths of revealed religion, than almost any other of the heathen. Probably, these were men of some eminence and learning, belonging to that sect.—An opinion at that time prevailed throughout all the east, that an extraordinary person was about to arise in Judea, who would acquire the dominion over the nations ; which doubtless originated from a partial acquaintance with the writings of the ancient prophets, and from the Jews dispersed in great numbers in all these countries.—These sages, or wise men, no doubt, expected this event, and were looking out for some intimations of its taking place : and, it is probable, that they were also favoured with di-

C

3 ¶ When Herod the king had heard *these things,* ᵇ he was troubled, and all Jerusalem with him.

4 And when he had gathered all ᶦ the chief priests and ᵏ scribes of the people together, ᶦ he demanded of them where Christ should be born.

5 And they said unto him, ᵐ In Bethlehem of Judea: for thus it is written by the prophet,

6 And ⁿ thou Bethlehem, *in the* land of Juda, art not the least among the princes of Juda: for out of thee shall come ° a Governor, that shall ° rule my people Israel.

vine intimations of its speedy approach, and shewn something of the Redeemer's real glory, and the nature of his kingdom.—It is not agreed of what country they were. Many think, that they came out of Arabia: and from the opinion, that the prophecy of David was fulfilled by them, (Ps. lxxii. 9, 10,) the absurd popish legend, that they were three kings, seems to have arisen.—The remoter regions of Arabia extended far to the south of Judea: and the queen of Sheba, called "the queen of the "south," (xii. 42,) is by many supposed to have come from thence. (Note, 1 Kings x. 1, 2.) The Magians resided chiefly in Persia, and in countries still further to the east; and it is not improbable, that these Magi came from those regions.—An extraordinary luminous appearance in the heavens, which they noticed, induced them to this journey, as they assuredly gathered from it, that One was born to be "the King of the Jews." But they could not reasonably have drawn this conclusion, unless God, who thus excited their attention, had also in some other way explained it to them; perhaps by a supernatural dream. Being thus excited and instructed, they hesitated not to take a long and expensive journey, in order to pay their early homage and worship to the new-born "King of the "Jews," who, as they understood, would in due time reign over the nations. Probably they supposed, that the inhabitants of Jerusalem were well acquainted with the event, and therefore they directed their course thither; and openly made enquiry concerning him, who was "born" to be "King of the Jews," (yet perhaps with some application to the chief priests and elders of the nation,) declaring both what they had seen, and for what purpose they were come.—This was an early intimation of the calling of the Gentiles into the church of Christ, even when the Jews would neglect him, and be rejected by him; and it was a call to them to consider Jesus, as their long-expected, promised Messiah.—'Christ, a poor child laid ' in a crib, and nothing set by of his own people, received ' notwithstanding a noble witness of his divinity from hea-' ven, and of his kingly estate from strangers.' Beza.— It is plain, that these wise men did not arrive at Bethlehem, till after the presentation of Christ at the temple. (Notes, 9—12. Luke ii. 36—39.)—It is likely, that Joseph and Mary purposed settling at Bethlehem, and had procured some house or lodging there, in which they at this time resided.

V. 3—6. Though Herod was very old, and had never shewn much affection for his family; yet, being a suspicious tyrant, he no sooner heard of "the King of the "Jews," than he began to be haunted with the dread of a rival. He neither understood the spiritual nature of the Messiah's kingdom, nor yet considered that a new-born infant was not likely to give him any disquietude: so that

he was greatly troubled at the tidings. The citizens of Jerusalem also, not having formed any proper judgment of the blessings to be expected from the Messiah, were put into general consternation: they had witnessed so many of Herod's cruelties, whenever a competitor was suspected, that they seem to have dreaded new scenes of confusion and bloodshed; and thus were troubled at that event, which should have given them the highest satisfaction. Herod however, by a strange mixture of regard to the word of God, and contempt of it, supposing that the ancient prophecies were about to be fulfilled, and yet hoping to defeat them, framed a plan for that purpose! And first he convened "the priests and scribes," or the heads of the twenty-four courses with the high priest as their stated superior, and the professed interpreters of the law, that he might know assuredly from them, at what place the promised Messiah was to be born; intending to use this information to direct the wise men where to find him, and then by their means devising to discover and cut him off: and thus by one blow to render abortive all the purposes and prophecies of God, from the beginning! To this question they returned a very proper answer; referring in confirmation of it, to a prophecy, which has been already considered. (Note, Micah v. 2.) The text is here quoted something differently, than it stands in our version of that prophet, especially it is here said "Thou art not the "least, &c." Some propose reading the clause in Micah interrogatively, "Art thou little among the thousands of "Judah?" It is, however, plain that the sense, rather than the exact words of the Old Testament prophecies, is quoted in many places of the New Testament; and that though these quotations are often taken from the Septuagint, yet that is not uniformly, nor exactly adhered to.—' And thou ' Bethlehem, the house of Ephratha, art one of the least ' to be among the thousands of Judah: out of thee shall ' one come forth to me, to be for a ruler of Israel.' Sept.— ' Though thou be a small town; yet thou shalt be famous ' and noble, through the birth of the Messiah, who shall be born in thee.'

. "Bethlehem in the land of Judah," (6) as distinguished from another Bethlehem. (Josh. xix. 15.)—The word princes is here substituted for thousands. ' The people was dis-' tributed by thousands, so many in a town or city: not ' that the number was so to continue; but (as ... in our ' hundreds, which were at first an hundred families pre-' cisely,) only in relation to the first distribution.' Hammond.

Rule. (6) Ποιμανεῖ, feed. (marg.) Rev. xix. 15. Gr.— He shall rule, as a shepherd does his flock; who in feeding, rules, and in ruling, feeds. Sometimes however the word is used, where either ruling or feeding is exclusively meant. It frequently occurs in the Sept.—' Kings are fitly called ' feeders and shepherds of the people.' Beza.

c 2

7 Then Herod, ' when he had privily called the wise men, enquired of them diligently what time the star appeared. 8 And he sent them to Bethlehem, and said, ' Go, and search diligently for the young child; and, when ye have found *him*, bring me word again, ' that I may come and worship him also.

9 When they had heard the king, they departed: and, lo, ' the star which they saw in the east, went before them, till it came and stood over where the young g child was.

10 When they saw the star, ' they rejoiced with exceeding great joy.

11. And when they were come into the house, " they saw the young child with Mary his mother, and fell down and ' worshipped him: and when they had opened their treasures, ' they ' presented unto him gifts, gold, ' and ' frankincense, and myrrh.

12 And being ' warned of God in a dream, that they should not return to Herod, ' they departed into their own country another way.

V. 7, 8. Herod, having learned the place of Christ's birth, next conferred with the wise men, that he might exactly discover from them the time when the star first appeared, from which he meant to compute or conjecture the age of his infant Rival. Having learned this, he dismissed them with directions to go to Bethlehem, exhorting them diligently to search for the young Child in that city; assured that under the divine direction they would certainly find him: and then requiring them to bring information of it, that he might render him the same honours which they intended. Thus far he employed some degree of absurd policy; but surely it was attended with a judicial infatuation : for otherwise he would either have sent messengers along with the wise men, to conduct them and shew them respect; or he would have ordered spies to follow them, who, when they had found the Child, might suddenly have surprised and slain him. But to leave the whole success of his design to these strangers, so that it must miscarry, if they suspected his sincerity, or did not choose to give him information, was a very feeble measure for so experienced a politician, who was not used to do works of impiety or cruelty by halves. Nor was it less wonderful, that neither piety, nor curiosity, nor other motives of any kind, induced a single Jew to accompany the wise men on this pious research, when Bethlehem was not more than seven or eight miles from Jerusalem! But the dread of Herod's cruel indignation, as well as disregard to all spiritual concerns, seem to have thrown them all into a kind of stupor on the occasion.

Enquired ... diligently. (7) Ηκριβωσε. 16.—Ακριβως (from the same root,) is rendered *diligently*; 8. *Acts* xviii. 25 : *circumspectly*; *Eph.* v. 15 : *perfectly*; 1 *Thes.* v. 2.—It means also *exactly, accurately.* See *Acts* xviii. 26. xxii. 8. xxiii. 15. 20. xxiv. 22. xxvi. 5. Gr. (' Quidam deducunt ' παρα το τις ακρον βαινω, quòd ab imo ad supremum ascen- ' datur: quod est exquisitæ perfectæque diligentiæ.' *Scapula.*)

V. 9—12. Notwithstanding the ignorance and inattention of the Jews, the eastern sages prosecuted the design of their journey, by setting out for Bethlehem : and to recompense their pious and believing constancy, the star, which they had seen in their own country, again appeared to them; and, going before them, became stationary just above the house where Jesus was. Hence it appears, that it was no star, (properly so called,) or planet, or comet;

but a luminous meteor in our atmosphere; which at a distance looked like a star, and which was formed by God for that purpose, and could descend so low, as to mark out a single house in the midst of the city: as the cloudy pillar pointed out the spot, where Israel was to encamp in the wilderness.—It is evident, that Joseph and Mary resided at this time in Bethlehem; and that from thence they fled into Egypt.—When the wise men saw the star, they were assured of success in their undertaking; and therefore they rejoiced exceedingly, (the original is peculiarly emphatical,) and entered the house, which doubtless was a very different abode, from what they had expected for " the King of the Jews ; " and having seen the infant Jesus with his mother, they were not offended by his mean circumstances, but acknowledged him as their Lord and King, prostrating themselves before him and worshipping him : and, opening the treasures, which they had brought with them for that purpose, they presented him with the choicest productions of their country, even " gold and " frankincense, and myrrh." Some have supposed, that the frankincense and myrrh were intended as an acknowledgment of his deity, as the gold was of his royalty : and this was the opinion of the fathers in general. We may, however, conclude, that the Lord, who directed and prospered their journey, gave them also some measure of knowledge concerning those things, which related to the person and offices of this new-born King ; that their woi ship was of the same nature with that of other believers in every age ; and that their abundant joy arose from a persuasion, that they had found the salvation of God for their souls, as well as " the King of the Jews."—Having obtained the purpose of their journey, they meant to report their success at Jerusalem, before they went home : but the Lord warned them, in a dream, not to return to Herod ; and so they took a more direct way, and defeated his impious project. Probably, when they arrived in their own country, they spread the report of what they had seen, heard, and learned ; and this would be a preparation for the future preaching of the gospel in those regions. ' Not- ' withstanding the homeliness of the place, and the mean ' appearance of the parents, ... they, acknowledging some ' more than human majesty in that child, fell down and ' worshipped him, and presented unto him the most pre- ' cious gifts which their country yielded.' *Bp. Hall.*— ' The very valuable presents which the Magi offered, not-

c 3

13 ¶ And when they were departed,
behold, [c] the angel of the Lord appeareth to Joseph in a dream, saying,
[d] Arise, and take the young child and
his mother, and flee into Egypt, and
be thou there [e] until I bring thee word:
[f] for Herod will seek the young child
to destroy him.
14 When he arose, [g] he took the
young child and his mother by night,
and departed into Egypt;
15 And was there [h] until the death
of Herod: [i] that it might be fulfilled
which was spoken of the Lord by the
prophet, saying, [k] Out of Egypt have
I called my son.

c 19. i. 20. Acts v. 19. x. 7. 22. xii. 11. Heb. i. 13, 14.
d x. 23. Rev. xii. 6. 14.
e 19, 20. Josh. iii. 13. 17. iv. 10. 18. Dan. iii. 25, 26. Acts xvi. 36.
f 16. Ex. i. 22. ii. 2, 3. Acts vii. 19. Rev. xii. 4.
g 20, 21. i. 24. Acts xxvi. 19.
h 19. Acts xii. 1—4. 23, 24.
i 17. 23. i. 22. iv. 14, 15. viii. 17. xii. 16—18. xxi. 4. xxvi. 54. 56. xxvii. 35. Luke xxiv. 44. John xix. 28. 36. Acts i. 16.
k Ex. iv. 22. Num. xxiv. 8. Hos. xi. 1.

16 ¶ Then Herod, [l] when he saw
that he was mocked of the wise men,
[m] was exceeding wroth, and sent forth,
[n] and slew all the children that were in
Bethlehem, and in all the coasts thereof,
from two years old and under, [o] according to the time which he had diligently enquired of the wise men.
17 Then was [p] fulfilled that which
was spoken by Jeremy the prophet,
saying,
18 In [q] Rama was there a voice
heard, [r] lamentation, and weeping, and
great mourning, [s] Rachel weeping *for*
her children, and [t] would not be comforted because they are not.

l Gen. xxxix. 14. 17. Num. xxii. 29. xxiv. 10. Judg. xvi. 10. Job xli. 4.
m Prov. xxvii. 3, 4. Dan. iii. 13. 19, 20.
n Gen. xlix. 7. 2 Kings viii. 12. Prov. xxviii. 15. 17. Is. xxvi. 21. lix. 7. Hos. x. 14. Rev. xvii. 6.
o 7.
p 15.
q Jer. xxxi. 15. *Ramah.*
r Jer. iv. 31. ix. 17—21. Ez. ii. 10. Rev. viii. 13.
s Gen. xxxv. 16—20.
t Gen. xxxvii. 30. 33—35. xlii. 36. Job xiv. 10.

'withstanding they found the child in so mean a condition, 'shewed the strong ideas, with which they were impressed 'of his dignity.' *Gilpin.*

Warned of God. (12) Χρηματισθέντες. See on *Acts* xi. 26.

V. 13—15. The Lord easily defeated the subtle malice of Herod, who was determined if possible to destroy his supposed Rival: and an angel in a dream, directed Joseph without delay to flee into Egypt, with the young Child and his mother, and there to wait till he had orders to return. Accordingly he was "obedient to the heavenly vision," and arose immediately, and that very night set out on his journey. Thus "the King of the Jews" was driven as an exile out of the land: "he came to his own, and "his own received him not;" but he was driven to seek shelter in a country, which had ever been most hostile to the people of God. It now appeared, how wisely the Lord had ordered it, in engaging so prudent and pious a person as Joseph, by his espousals to Mary, to afford her his assistance in these difficult circumstances. And the oblations of the eastern sages would prove a very seasonable supply, to enable the holy family to bear the expenses of so long a journey, and of their maintenance in a foreign country. In this exiled state they remained till the death of Herod, which seems to have taken place a few months after.—The evangelist adds, "That it might be fulfilled, which was "spoken by the prophet, saying, Out of Egypt have I "called my Son." (*Note, Hos.* xi. 1.) Many prophecies seem to have had a double meaning, both respecting the church, and Christ the Head of the church. And there appears to have been a particular intention of Providence in Christ's going into Egypt, that he might come up at the divine call from the same place, whence the nation of Israel had been brought.—Every circumstance favours the conclusion, that Joseph was warned to flee into Egypt, immediately after the departure of the wise men; and that he considered the case to be so urgent, as not to admit of the least delay.—Numbers of Jews were settled in Egypt, which would render his situation more comfortable, than it would otherwise have been.—'Herein was fulfilled, ... in a higher 'degree, that which was spoken by Hosea. ... That which 'he spake of the people of Israel, which were the sons of 'God by choice and adoption, was now fulfilled in him, 'who was the natural and eternal Son of the Father.' *Bp. Hall.*—'These words can import no less, than that the 'calling of Christ out of Egypt was by God intended as a 'completion of these words; and that till he was called 'thence, they had not their full and ultimate completion.' *Whitby.*

Out of Egypt, &c. (15) This is rendered in the LXX, "Out of Egypt have I called his children:" but the Evangelist gives the sense of the Hebrew.

V. 16—18. Herod, after waiting for some time, found that the wise men did not return to him; and, supposing their conduct to arise from suspicion or contempt, he deemed himself greatly dishonoured by it. Thus his jealousy, disappointment, and indignation concurred in working him up to a degree of rage, which bordered on madness: and, determining to make sure, as he thought, of the destruction of his hated competitor, he sent forth, as it is probable, some of the soldiers that composed his guard, and slew all the male children, that were found in Bethlehem and the dependent villages, which were under two years of age; taking large measure enough, but having respect to the time, at which the wise men informed him they had first seen the star. Thus the date of Christ's birth was publickly marked; and the pretensions of all others to be the Messiah, as born at Bethlehem about the same time, were cut off. This event formed another accomplishment of the prophecy of Jeremiah, which we have already considered. (*Note, Jer.* xxxi. 15—17.)—Rachel, who lay buried betwixt Rama and Bethlehem, (*Gen.* xxxv. 16—20,) might be poetically represented on this occasion to weep inconsolably for the slaughter of her children. Doubtless many of the descendants of Joseph and Benjamin were murdered, as well as those of Judah, in this massacre. It may be observed, that the Evangelist does not say "That it might be fulfilled;" but "Then "was fulfilled." It was a fulfilment of the words, though not the event immediately predicted.—Imagination can better conceive, than the pen can describe, the horrors of so brutal a scene, and the anguish of the tender mothers over their infant offspring, torn from their arms, and butchered before their eyes: it is doubtless almost impossible to form an idea of any wickedness more completely diabolical. Indeed some have objected to the authenticity of the narrative on this ground; but the following account

NAZARETH.   Matt. ii. 23. Luke i. 26; ii. 51, 52.

19 ¶ But when *Herod was dead, behold, *an angel of the Lord appeareth in a dream to Joseph in Egypt,

20 Saying, *Arise, and take the young child and his mother, and go into the land of Israel: *for they are dead which sought the young child's life.

21 And *he arose, and took the young child and his mother, and came into the land of Israel.

22 But when he heard that Archelaus did reign in Judea, in the room of his father Herod, *he was afraid to go thither: notwithstanding, *being warned of God in a dream, he turned aside *into the parts of Galilee:

23 And he came and dwelt in a city called *Nazareth; that it might be fulfilled which was spoken by the prophets, *He shall be called a Nazarene.

---

of Herod's last purpose and deed, will satisfy the reader that there was nothing too vile for that wretched man to perpetrate. 'Knowing the hatred the Jews had for him, 'he concluded aright, that there would be no lamentation 'at his death, but rather gladness and rejoicing all the 'country over. To prevent this he framed a project and 'resolution in his mind, which was one of the horridest, 'and most wicked, perchance, that ever entered into the 'heart of man. For, having issued out a summons to all 'the principal ... Jews of his kingdom, commanding their 'appearance at Jericho, (where he then lay,) on pain of 'death, at a day appointed ; on their arrival thither he 'shut them all up in the circus, and then sending for 'Salome his sister, and Alexas her husband, commanded 'them, that as soon as he was dead, they should send in 'the soldiers upon them, and put them all to the sword. 'For this, said he, will provide mourning for my funeral 'all over the land, and make the Jews in every family 'lament my death, whether they will or no : and when he 'had adjured them hereto, some hours after, he ... died. But 'they, not being wicked enough to do what they had been 'made solemnly to promise, rather chose to break their ob-'ligation, than to make themselves the executioners of so 'bloody and horrid a design.' *Prideaux.*—Nor need it be wondered at, that Josephus does not record the slaughter of the infants ; for he evidently chose to make the best of Herod's bad character, though in many things he could not conceal its infamy : and he never without reluctance mentioned any circumstances, which led him to give his thoughts of Christianity. Yet he could not but know, that Matthew had recorded it as a known matter of fact ; and, as he never contradicted or disputed it, he may be said to have tacitly allowed the truth of it. As, however, internal and external evidences sufficiently demonstrate the evangelist's divine inspiration, we need no corroborating testimony to confirm the fact.

In Rama, &c. (18) This quotation is not made from the LXX ; but is an exact translation of the Hebrew.

V. 19—23. In a few months after Herod had perpetrated the massacre of the infants, he ended his life and cruelties together, in a manner almost too shocking to be related : he endured such excruciating, lingering, and loathsome diseases, as rendered him intolerable to himself and others also. Just before his death, he caused Antipater, his son and the heir apparent of his kingdom, to be executed on some groundless suspicion.—An angel was sent to Joseph to admonish him to go back with the young child and his mother, into the land of Israel, as they were dead who had sought the young child's life. Perhaps An-

tipater had concurred with Herod in attempting to destroy Jesus. Joseph, however, immediately returned into the land of Judah : but finding that Archelaus, the son of Herod, had obtained from the Romans the government of that part of the country in which Bethlehem was situated ; and perhaps learning that he was of a jealous cruel disposition; he feared to settle there : but, being further admonished of God, he went into Galilee, in the northern part of the land, which was under the rule of Philip who was of a more quiet temper ; and fixed his residence at Nazareth, where we find from St. Luke that he had formerly dwelt. The sacred historian, on this occasion, adds, " That it might be fulfilled which was spoken by the pro-" phets, He shall be called a Nazarene."—He 'does not 'cite any particular prophet for these words, as he had done, '(15. 17. i. 22), ... but only what was spoken by the prophets 'in general ;... he took not the words from the prophets, but 'the sense only. ... Most of the prophets speak of Christ, 'as of a person that was to be reputed vile and abject, de-'spised and rejected of men. ... (Ps. lxix. 9, 10. Is. liii. 3.) '...Now the Nazarene was a name of infamy put upon Christ 'and Christians, both by the unbelieving Jews and Gentiles. '... This title ... they always gave by way of contempt to 'our Jesus, because he was supposed to come out of this 'city : yea, his very going to dwell there was one occasion 'of his being ... despised and rejected by the Jews. (John 'i. 46. vii. 52.) ... The angel sent him to this contemptible 'place, that he might thence have a name of infamy and 'contempt put upon him, according to the frequent inti-'mations of the prophets.' *Whitby.*—Others consider the word *Nazarene,* as of the same import with *Nazarite;* and as derived from נזר, to *separate.*—The same word is used of Joseph, who was *one separated from his brethren.* (Gen. xlix. 26. Deut. xxxlii. 16. Heb.)—' As Joseph was by his 'brethren sold into Egypt ; so is Christ by the persecution 'of Herod driven thither: As Joseph was " separated from " his brethren," and cast out from among them ; so was 'Christ, for fear of Archelaus, separated from his own 'tribe of Judah, and constrained to dwell in Nazareth of 'Galilee, whose name may denote that flight or separation.' *Hammond.*—The Nazarites, or *separated ones,* were peculiarly consecrated to God: and, if we allow any thing typical in that remarkable appointment, we cannot but recollect, that Jesus was " holy, harmless, undefiled, and " separated from sinners ; " and that " for our sakes he " sanctified himself," or consecrated himself to God to be our atoning Sacrifice.—Indeed he did not observe the law of the Nazarite, and on that account was not called a Nazarite : yet to mark him out, as the Antitype of this

c 5

CHAP. III.

John the Baptist's preaching. and manner of life; and the prophecy fulfilled in him, 1—4. Multitudes resort to him, and are baptized, 5, 6. His bold and solemn address to the Pharisees and Sadducees, 7—10. His testimony concerning Christ, 11, 12. Jesus is baptized; the Holy Spirit descends on him; and the Father, by a voice from heaven, declares him to be his beloved Son, 13—17.

---

typical order, he dwelt at Nazareth during the greatest part of his life; and so was called "the Nazarene," which is a word of a similar meaning. Sampson was "called a "Nazarite from the womb:" (*Judg.* xiii. 5:) and he was a remarkable type of Christ, both as delivering his people by his own strength, without their help; and as triumphing over his and their enemies even by his death.—Many, however, derive the word Nazareth, from נצר, *a branch;* and suppose those prophecies to be referred to, in which Christ is promised under the title of THE BRANCH.—'The ' appellation, which is given him of a Nazarene, however ' it be objected to him by way of reproach, is rather a ' notable proof of his answerableness to that prediction of ' the prophets; especially that of Isaiah, who by "the root ' "of Jesse," whence he should come, describes Bethlehem, ' the dwelling of Jesse, for the place of his birth; and by ' that *Netzar,* (or *Branch,*) which should arise from that ' root, meant to allude to the place of his abode and edu- ' cation.' *Bp. Hall.*—It should, however, be noted that the צ in the word נצר a *branch*, is perhaps never represented in Greek, by any other letter than Σ.—The interpretation given by Dr. Whitby, is, to me at least, by far the most satisfactory.

PRACTICAL OBSERVATIONS
V. 1—8.

It is often found, that they, who live at a distance from the means of grace, are led to use double diligence; and thus first get acquainted with Christ and his salvation.— But neither natural science, nor abstruse speculations, nor curious arts, can avail in this great concern. The sacred scripture must be searched, with attentive diligence, obedient faith, and fervent prayer. This is "a light shining " in a dark place:" and those who follow this sacred direction, will spare no labour or expense in enquiring after Jesus, our Prince and Saviour; they will desire to render him honour and submission; they will devote their talents to his service, and not be reluctant to avow their expectations from him and obligations to him. But, alas! should eastern sages, or strangers from distant nations, come to many of those cities where Christianity is now professed, purposely to enquire after Christ and his religion; how little satisfaction would they find from the rulers and teachers of the church! and how much would they be surprised at the ignorance and inattention of those who have the best opportunities of instruction, respecting the truths and duties of their holy profession! Such enquirers would not indeed excite much consternation or uneasiness, either to princes or people: but they would probably occasion great astonishment; and even incur the contempt and derision of those, who never bestowed any pains in acquainting themselves with him, whose disciples they profess to be. There are but few places, where so much regard would be shewn them, as that princes and teachers should assemble, in order to consider and answer their enquiries: and even if this were done, it would per-

haps be found rather to arise from profane policy, than from a cordial desire to promote the knowledge of Christ and his salvation!—The scripture must needs be fulfilled; and they who are acquainted with the Bible, and who believe that all things have been, are, and will be, according to the testimony of that blessed book, are likely to find the right way, and to point it out to others: and all who are related to Christ, and submit to him as the Governor " of his people," however little they may be in other respects.—But let us beware of a dead faith. It is plain from facts, that a man may have a prevailing persuasion of many truths; and yet hate them virulently, because they interfere with his ambition, interests, or sinful indulgence. Such a belief will give him uneasiness, and strengthen his resolution of opposing the cause of God! and so great is the inconsistency of human nature, that a man may deliberately form projects to defeat those purposes, which he cannot but perceive are from God; and may vainly hope for success in his impious and infatuated attempts! Indeed this is the enmity, malignity, and misery of Satan from age to age. But "he who " sitteth in heaven will laugh " at these puny enemies, yea, "the LORD will have them in derision: yet will he " speak to them in his wrath, and vex them in his sore " displeasure." He can easily infatuate or crush them when he sees good: yet they often for a time impose upon the unsuspecting simplicity of pious men; and by pretending to join them in honouring Christ, draw them in to forward their base designs.

V. 9—15.

The Lord will guide with his counsel those, who follow the teaching of his word, and wait on him for further light: he can help them even by means of ungodly men, who know more than they practise; and none shall ever seek his face in vain.—Every indication of obtaining an interest in Christ, will give a sincere and very great joy to the humble enquirer after him: he will not be stumbled at finding the Saviour or his disciples in obscure cottages, after having in vain sought them in palaces and populous cities; he will never fear honouring the Lord of glory too much, or being too entirely devoted to his service. Thus our Father, who knows what his children have need of, uses some as his stewards to supply the wants of others; and he will provide for them in every emergency, though the provision should come from the ends of the earth.—But let us remember, that this event was an indication, that Jesus was "the Light of the Gentiles, as well as the " Glory of Israel:" and, whilst we are thankful for our mercies, let us recollect, that if we do not honour and worship him as our Lord and Saviour, who now reigns on his glorious throne, these eastern sages will rise up against us too in judgment: for they came from far, to worship him as an infant in the arms of his mother.—But if we sincerely follow his guidance, he will by various interpo-

c 6

IN ª those days came, ᵇ John the Baptist, ᶜ preaching in ᵈ the wilderness of Judea,

2 And saying, ᵉ Repent ye; ᶠ for the kingdom of heaven is at hand.

sitions direct our conduct; and he has unnumbered methods of defeating the most subtle and best concerted machinations of his enemies.

V. 16—23.

It is impossible to assign any limits to the wickedness of the human heart, when furious passions and great authority combine; and when sinners are become callous by habit, and daring by impunity in atrocious crimes. The near approach of death, instead of weakening the ambition, malice, or cruelty of such men, seems to render them more in haste to seize the fleeting moment for perpetrating their enormities: as if they were afraid of not treasuring up wrath enough; or as if they would set death, and even God himself, at defiance! No wonder therefore that they are unmoved with compassion for bleeding infants, and inconsolable parents, and that they seem to take delight in " lamentation, weeping, and great mourning," occasioned by their cruelties: yet are they more wretched by their own vile passions, than they can render others.—It is well for the world, that the triumphing of overgrown monsters in wickedness commonly proves short; and sometimes their miseries on this side the grave give a specimen of the dire effects of thus waging war, as it were, both against God and man. But, having observed the necessity of avoiding the beginnings of iniquity and impiety, if we would be secured from these horrid extremes, let us avert our eyes from such scenes, to contemplate the reception which the Lord of glory met with, when he condescended to ' visit us in great humility;' and from these his early persecutions and sufferings, learn what usage we must expect, if we are the children of God, in this " world which " lieth in wickedness;" and at what a price all our hopes and comforts were purchased for us by our Surety: As the early honours which he received proved the occasion of his perils and fatigues; so those who belong to him cannot reasonably expect to be honoured by God, without meeting with trouble and contempt from men. Let it suffice us to be as our Master, hoping to have the promises of scripture fulfilled to us, as the prophecies were in him. But we must not expect much solid comfort even from near and dear relations; as our children are far more frequently the occasions of care and deep distress, than of abiding satisfaction: yet we should not " refuse to be comforted," when they are taken from us. For though they die, as sinners, according to the righteous sentence of God, and not in the peculiar circumstances of these infants, who may be considered as a kind of martyrs for Christ; yet we may comfortably conclude, that when they cease to be with us on earth, they are only gone before us to heaven, through " the second Adam," the Lord of life and salvation.— Wherever Providence allots us the bounds of our habitation, we must expect to share the reproach of Christ, and to be branded with some opprobrium for his sake: yet, if this be because we are consecrated to God through him, and copy his example of truth and righteousness, we may

glory in the distinction; assured that " as we suffer with " him, we shall also be glorified together."

NOTES.

CHAP. III. V. 1. St. Matthew entirely passes over John's parentage and birth, and the remarkable circumstances which attended them. (Notes, Luke i.) Indeed, we are scarcely informed of any thing relating to the childhood and youth, either of Christ or of his forerunner; though we might have expected to find many curious and interesting particulars concerning them: as the one was born wholly without sin, and the other " filled with the " Holy Ghost from his mother's womb."—Some think, that John entered on his publick ministry about his thirtieth year; but others, who assign a longer time to his ministry before the baptism of Jesus, must conclude that he began to preach at an earlier age; as Jesus, who was only six months younger, was baptized when thirty years old.— John had spent his youth in retirement; and doubtless in contemplation, and such devout exercises as were suited to prepare him for his extraordinary work: he had attained an uncommon degree of deadness to the world, of holy fortitude, zeal, humility, and devotedness to God, and of every grace and gift, which could qualify him for usefulness: and his mortified spirit and conduct were peculiarly suited to that severe ministry of the law, and that work of humiliation and reformation, by which he was to prepare the Jews for receiving their expected Messiah. But, as he was a priest, and the son of so distinguished a person as Zechariah; as his birth had been miraculous and greatly noticed, and he was himself so very excellent and remarkable a person; he could not be very obscure in his retirement. Probably, his reputation was considerable, before he entered on his publick work, which might conduce to the exceeding popularity of his ministry. He was called the Baptist, or the *Baptizer*, because he admitted the Jews into the number of his disciples by the external rite of baptism, as a sign or profession of repentance. He did not go up to Jerusalem, but opened his ministry in the wilderness, or the least populous part of the country. He came preaching, and as a herald proclaiming, the near approach of the Messiah, their expected King.— ' By " those ' " days " is meant, at that time when Jesus remained as ' yet an inhabitant of Nazareth.' *Beza.*

Preaching.] Κηρυσσων. (From κηρυξ *a herald.* 1 Tim. ii. 7. 2 Tim. i. 11. 2 Pet. ii. 5. Gr.) ' Proclaiming a matter in ' an open place, in the hearing of a multitude, that many ' may take notice of it.' *Leigh.* See Hos. v. 8. Joel i. 14. *Sept.*

V. 2. The Jews thought that the blessings of the Messiah's kingdom belonged to them exclusively; and as they expected temporal deliverance from the Romans, with victory, prosperity, and pre-eminence, they were disposed to prepare for his coming, by levying armies and making insurrections. But the preaching of John was simply, " Repent ye, for the kingdom of heaven is at hand;"

3 For this is he that was spoken of ᵉ by the prophet Esaias, saying, The voice of one crying in the wilderness, ʰ Prepare ye the way of the Lord, make his paths straight.

4 And the same John had ¹ his raiment of camel's hair, and a leathern girdle about his loins ; ᵏ and his meat was locusts and ¹ wild honey.

5 Then ᵐ went out to him Jerusa-

(marginal references col. 1) g Is. xl. 3. Mark i. 3. Luke iii. 3—4. John i. 23. h Is. lvii. 14, 15. Mal. iii. 1. Luke i. 17. 76.

(marginal references col. 2) i xi. 8. 2 Kings i. 8. Zech. xiii. 4. Mal. iv. 3. Mark i. 6. Luke i. 17. k Rev. xi. 3. 22. l 18. Lev. xi. 22. Deut. xxxii. 13. 1 Sam. xiv. 25—27.

m iv. 25. xi. 7—12. Mark i. 5. Luke xvi. 16. John iii. 23. v. 35.

which doubtless he enlarged on, explained, and applied to his hearers. " The kingdom of heaven " signifies the gospel-dispensation ; which is so called, because " the " God of heaven " then began to set up that kingdom, which will at length fill the earth. (*Marg. Ref. f.—Notes, Dan.* ii. 34, 35. 44, 45. vii. 9—14.) It is the kingdom of God and of heaven, set up among men, in opposition to the power of the devil, " the god " and " prince of this world ; " and in the person of Christ, the Son of God, who " was " manifested to destroy the works of the devil." Into this kingdom sinners enter by faith in Christ : then their rebellions are pardoned, they return to their allegiance, become willing subjects, and are admitted to enjoy all the immunities and privileges of the kingdom. These are all of a heavenly nature ; they come from heaven, and prepare the soul for heaven, and at length issue in the felicity of heaven ; which sometimes also is meant by " the kingdom " of heaven." " The kingdom of heaven " ᶠ signifies the ' gospel-dispensation, in which subjects were to be gathered ' to God by his Son, and a society formed, which was to ' subsist, first in more imperfect circumstances on earth, ' but afterwards was to appear complete in the world of ' glory. In some places, the phrase more particularly sig- ' nifies ... the state of it on earth ; ... and sometimes only the ' state of glory. ... It is plain, that the Jews understood it of ' a temporal monarchy, which God would erect ; the seat ' of which, they supposed, would be Jerusalem, which ' would become, instead of Rome, the capital of the world. ' And the expected Sovereign of this kingdom, they learned ' from Daniel to call " the Son of Man." ... Both John the ' Baptist then, and Christ, took up this phrase, ... and gra- ' dually taught the Jews to affix right ideas to it ; though ' it was a lesson they were remarkably unwilling to ' learn. This very demand of repentance shewed, that it ' was a spiritual kingdom ; and that no wicked man ... could ' possibly be a genuine member of it.' *Doddridge.*—" The " kingdom of heaven " is a term peculiar to St. Matthew's gospel ; but " the kingdom of God " in the other parts of the New Testament seems perfectly synonymous.—This " kingdom of heaven " was at hand : the King was about to appear, to collect followers, to finish his work, to ascend his throne, to abrogate the legal dispensation, to terminate the national covenant of Israel, to admit the Gentiles into the church, and to introduce the Christian dispensation. If the Jews then meant to share the blessings of it, they must prepare for them by repentance : they must no longer trust in outward distinctions, and, comparing their tempers and conduct with the law of God, they must judge and condemn themselves, be sorry and humbled for their sins, and turn from them all, to the love and service of God.— The word rendered " repentance," implies a total revolution in the mind, a change in the judgment, dispositions, and affections, another and better bias to the soul. Without this repentance the people could not understand the nature of the kingdom of heaven ; nor could they welcome

Christ, become his subjects, or desire his salvation. (*Marg. Ref. e.*)

Repent ye.] Μετανοειτε. *Post factum sapere ; quasi resapere.* Beza. *Mutare mentem in melius.* ' After a thing ' then at length to be wise.' ' To return to a sound mind.' (*Ex μετα post, et νοεω intelligo.*)

V. 3. The ministry of John fulfilled a prophecy that has been already considered. (*Note, Is.* xl. 3—5.) John was " a voice," which conveys the mind of the speaker, and then vanishes : he declared the mind of God concerning his Son, and then was seen no more ; for his ministry was of short continuance. He proclaimed Christ, as the Son of God, the King of Israel, and the Saviour of the world ; (*Notes, John* i. 29—34. iii. 27—36 ;) and thus " he prepared the way of the LORD," of JEHOVAH, for so the word is in Isaiah ; and he made his paths straight. As pioneers level the road for a monarch, who is about to march his army through deserts, mountains, or morasses ; so John's preaching, by humbling the proud, detecting the hypocrites, counteracting the prejudices of the people, rectifying their judgment, and raising their minds from low and grovelling pursuits, to aspire after things truly great and excellent, prepared the Jews for the reception of Christ.—" Make straight the paths of our God." *Sept.*

V. 4. (*Note,* 2 *Kings* i. 8.) We need not be very accurate in determining what John's food and raiment were. It is probable, that his outward garment was made of camels' hair, woven into coarse rough cloth ; and that this was girded about him with a piece of undressed leather. His food (that is, frequently, as it may be supposed,) consisted of locusts : these were allowed as clean by the law, and they are often eaten in the eastern regions at this day. To this was added the honey, which the bees made in the uncultivated parts of the land, and which was found in great plenty.—The finer parts of camels' hair is indeed formed into a soft and delicate stuff ; but it is manifest, that a coarse and rough garment, made of the long hair of the camel, and wrought in a rude manner, is intended. And the critical pains of learned men, to prove that a plant or pulse was meant, by the word translated " locusts," seem to have been labour in vain. (*Marg. Ref.*)—It is more to the purpose to observe, that this extraordinary man, who was " great in the sight of the Lord," was very homely in his attire, and frugal in his diet ; faring as a poor person, desiring neither abundance nor delicacies, but taking any thing which came to hand in his retirement, to satisfy his wants ; being wholly intent on matters of a more important and spiritual nature. As he could live on little, and was inured to hardship, he was independent of the rich and great, and might be the more direct and plain in his reproofs of them : so that this circumstance seems to have had a considerable effect, in forming the other parts of his character.

V. 5, 6. Through a divine influence on the minds of

c 8

lem, and all Judea, and all the region round about Jordan.

6 And " were baptized of him in Jordan, ° confessing their sins.

7 ¶ But when he saw many of ° the Pharisees and Sadducees come to his baptism, he said unto them, ⁴ O generation of vipers, ⁵ who hath warn-

men vast numbers were induced to resort to John in the wilderness, from all parts of Judea, and from Jerusalem ; so that the whole city and country, as it were, went out to him ; and he was especially attended by the inhabitants of those regions, which lay on each side the river Jordan ; where, after a time, he commonly exercised his ministry. He became at length so celebrated, that the Jews of all ranks and parties flocked to him : and when they were brought to confess their sins, and to profess repentance, and a purpose of submitting to the Messiah who was at hand, and leading a new life, they were baptized by John, *in*, or *at*, the river Jordan. The law of Moses prescribed " divers washings " or baptisms, in which water was used in different ways, as an emblem of the purging of the soul from the pollution of sin, in order that the priests or people might attend on the service of God with acceptance. (*Note, Heb.* ix. 8—10.) By degrees it became customary in the Jewish church to baptize those, who were proselyted to their religion from the Gentiles, both male and female, as well as to circumcise the males : this denoted, that they deemed them unclean in themselves, and not meet to join the congregation of the Lord, till they were washed from the filthiness of their gentile state. The prophets also often alluded to this emblem of the soul's being cleansed from sin ; and some passages of the New Testament intimate, that both the cleansing from guilt by the blood of Christ, and from pollution by the Spirit of Christ were comprised under this outward sign ; yet the latter is more generally intended. (*Marg. Ref.* n, o.) But, though baptism had been before in use, John was singular in baptizing all his disciples, notwithstanding they had before been Jews, and without distinction of previous character ; thus intimating, that by nature and practice they were all polluted, and could not be admitted among the true people of God, except washed from their sins, in the fountain which the Messiah was about to open. This was done by express divine direction : (*John* i. 33 :) but, though his use of baptism was introductory to the appointment of that ordinance, to be the initiatory sacrament and seal of the new dispensation, as circumcision had been of the old ; yet we should not consider it as the same with Christian baptism : but rather as an institution *for the time being*, and an introduction to the change which was gradually to take place, when the old dispensation should be abrogated, and the new one substituted and openly established. Baptism, as used by John, was not intended to supersede circumcision ; for it does not appear, that he baptized any but circumcised persons : except as he baptized the women among the Jews, which is no where mentioned, though it is highly probable. We cannot suppose, that he " baptized in the name of the Father, and of the " Son, and of the Holy Ghost," or that Jesus was thus baptized ; nay, the contrary is manifest : (*Notes, Acts* xix. 1—6 :) and probably Christ's disciples did not use that peculiar form of Christian baptism, till after the ascension

of their Lord.—It is also evident, that some *at least*, who had received John's baptism, received Christian baptism also when admitted into the church of Christ : for it cannot be supposed, but that several of the multitude, who heard Peter on the day of Pentecost, had been John's disciples : yet he exhorted them all to be baptized in the name of Jesus, and the three thousand who gladly received the word were thus baptized. (*Acts* ii. 38—41.) John's baptism and Christian baptism, therefore, were not exactly the same ; and inferences from the one respecting the other are inconclusive. It does not appear, that any but adults were baptized by John ; for circumcision still continued in force, as the initiatory ordinance and seal of the covenant ; and therefore we never read that he baptized households, as the apostles did. Adult Jews, professing repentance and a disposition to become the Messiah's subjects, were the only persons whom John admitted to baptism.—Water was the outward sign ; but whether the rite was administered by immersion, or not, is incapable of decisive proof. The use of water is essential, because that is the universal purifier : the quantity and mode of application, seem to be merely circumstances, varying as occasion may require. The inward and spiritual signification is exactly the same as that of circumcision, which is spoken of as the " cir- " cumcision of the heart ; " that is, *regeneration* and *sanctification* by the cleansing power of the Holy Spirit : and the Jews were taught, by John's use of baptism, that their outward advantages would never qualify them to enjoy the blessings of the Messiah's kingdom, except their hearts were washed from the love and pollution of sin ; since they were by nature polluted, born in sin, and " the chil- " dren of wrath," even as the Gentiles were.

Were baptized. (6) Εϐαπλιζονlo.—Βαπλιζω is derived from ϐαπlω, *to dip* or *immerse* ; (*Luke* xvi. 24. *John* xiii. 26. *Rev.* xix. 13 ;) but is not synonymous with it ; as the use of the word and its derivatives clearly shews. (xx. 22, 23. *Mark* vⁱⁱ. 4. x. 38, 39. *Luke* iii. 16. xi. 38. xii. 50. *Acts* i. 5. *Heb.* ix. 10.) ' It is taken more largely for any ' kind of washing, rinsing, or cleansing, even where there ' is no dipping at all.' *Leigh.* The word was adopted from the Greek authors, and a sense put upon it by the inspired writers, according to the style of scripture, to signify the use of water in the sacrament of baptism, and in many things of a spiritual nature, which stood related to it. Some indeed contend zealously, that *baptism* always signifies *immersion ;* but the use of the words *baptize,* and *baptism,* in the New Testament, cannot accord with this exclusive interpretation. On the other hand, some, arguing perhaps too much from modern habits, have been sufficiently decided for the opposite interpretation. But the writer, after many years' consideration and study, has above given the outline of his own conclusions : and would only add, that vastly too much eagerness and acrimony have been employed in disputes on the subject ; and far too little attention to the instruction suggested by this ordi-

a Rom. v. 9. ed you to *flee from the wrath to
1 Thes. i. 10.
2 Thes. i. 9. come?
Heb. vi. 18. Rev.
vi. 16, 17.　　8 Bring ¹ forth therefore " fruits
t xxi. 28—30. 32.
Is. i. 16, 17. * meet for repentance.
Luke iii. 8. 10—
14. Acts xxvi.　9 And ˣ think not to say within
20. Rom. ii. 4—
7. 2 Cor. vii. 10, 11. 2 Pet. i. 4—8.　u Gal. v. 22, 23. Eph. v. 9. Phil. i. 11.
* Or, answerable to amendment of life. Jer. vii. 3—7. xxvi. 13. xxxvi. 3.　x Mark
vii. 21. Luke iii. 8. v. 22. vii. 39, xii. 17.

yourselves, ⁷ We have Abraham to our y Ex. xxxiii. 24.
Luke xvi. 24.
father: for I say unto you, that ᶻ God John viii. 33.
39. 40. 53. Rom.
is able of these stones to raise up chil- iv. 1. 11—16. Ix.
7, 8. Gal. iv. 22
dren unto Abraham.　　　　　　—31.
z viii. 11. 12.
10 And ᵃ now also ᵇ the axe is laid Luke xix. 40.
Acts xv. 14
Rom. iv. 17. 1 Cor. i. 27, 28. Gal. III. 27—29. Eph. ii. 12, 13.　a Mal. iii. 1—3, iv.
1. Heb. iii. 1—3, x. 28—31. xii. 25.　　　b Luke iii. 9. xxiii. 31.

---

nance, and to the practical improvement which might be
made of the administration of it, for the benefit of all
concerned, both at the time and afterwards.—*In Jordan.*]
Εν Ιορδανη.—The various ways in which the prepositions εν
and εις, which are employed on this subject, are rendered
in English in our authorized version on other subjects,
must convince every one who examines it, that no weight
can be laid upon them in controversial discussions; though
the sound of the words may influence a mere English reader.
V. 7—10. The Pharisees were the strictest sect of the
Jews, and made the greatest profession of religion: and
the most reputable of their scribes and elders belonged to
it. Some of them seem to have been decent formalists of
moral character, but inflated with spiritual pride, and full
of contempt of others. They laid the chief stress on
external observances, often in minute matters, and according to their own traditions and inventions; so that, neglecting the weightier matters of the moral law, and the
spiritual meaning of the legal ceremonies, they dealt
largely in ostentatious austerities and mortifications. But
others of them were the most detestable hypocrites imaginable, who made their reputation for extraordinary sanctity, the cloke of exorbitant avarice, and the occasion for
enormous oppression and iniquity.—The Sadducees were
the scorning infidels of the time: they professed to receive
some parts of the sacred writings, and to reject others;
but they paid no proper regard to any of them. They
did not believe the resurrection of the dead: and, as they
did not allow the existence of angels, or spirits, they could
not hold the immortality of the soul, or the future state of
retribution; nay, it is hard to conceive, how they could
believe the being of a God. . Some of them, at least, seem
to have been mere philosophizing atheists; and the rest
downright sceptics, who treated every thing relating to
God and eternity, as doubtful and disputable, and consequently with a contemptuous indifference.—Considering all
the rewards promised in the law as referring to this world,
they counted prosperity a proof of the divine favour, and
poverty or distress an evidence of a man's being accursed
of God; and thus they pretended, that to relieve the indigent and miserable was an attempt to counteract God's
purposes, and therefore sinful. A very convenient opinion
for a hard and selfish heart!—It is not clear, whether
transient convictions, or a regard to reputation, brought
these Pharisees and Sadducees to desire John's baptism;
but they evidently came with wrong views, and an improper disposition. The Sadducees were as proud of their
superior discernment, as the Pharisees of their superior
sanctity; and with as little reason: but neither of them
were prepared, by repentance and humiliation before God,
to welcome the mercy and spiritual blessings of the Messiah. Instead, therefore, of sanctioning their characters,
or courting their favour, John plainly, and even roughly,
addressed them as a " generation of vipers," a race of

subtle, designing men, of poisonous principles and practice, dangerous to all around them, the genuine children
of the old serpent, the most hopeless part of the nation.
(*Marg. Ref.* q.) He enquired of them with astonishment,
" Who hath warned you to flee from the wrath to come?"
No doubt they deserved the wrath of God, which was about
to come on the nation in this world, and on all unbelievers
in the future and eternal state: but it could hardly be expected that such hypocrites and infidels would think of
fleeing from it, without some extraordinary warning. Was
this warning therefore from God? Or was it only from
man? If, however, they truly repented, they might be
admitted to his baptism: but then they must "bring forth
" fruits meet for repentance," in humility, meekness, patience, faith, love, equity, truth, mercy, and every good
work; in newness of life proceeding from newness of
heart; else the outward sign would be of no advantage to
them. (*Notes, Luke* iii. 7—14.) And they must not take
encouragement, or any longer glory, because they were
the descendants of faithful Abraham: for though the promises were made to him and to his Seed, yet God could
raise up children to Abraham from the very stones before
their eyes, or from the poor Gentiles, whom they equally
disregarded; seeing all believers would be acknowledged
as the spiritual seed of Abraham, and made heirs according to the promise. Instead, therefore, of expecting to
appropriate the blessings of the Messiah's reign, because
of their descent from Abraham; they must observe, that
all these distinctions were about to be abolished: God was
about to come into his vineyard, and to lay the axe to the
root of every tree; and all, without exception, which did
not bring forth the good fruits of a sober, righteous, and
godly life, the " fruits meet for repentance," would be cut
down and cast into the fire, without regard to external privileges, except as these tended to aggravate their guilt and
condemnation.—' Nothing stoppeth up the way of mercy
' and salvation against us, so much as the opinion of our
' own righteousness.' *Beza.* And next to this, perhaps,
the opinion, that the gospel is a mild dispensation, making
allowance for sin in those who profess it, and not requiring
that strict holiness which was before demanded, is the
most fatal.—' Abraham sits next the gates of hell, and
' doth not permit any wicked Israelite to go down into it.'
Talmud.—Do not many Christians seem to countenance a
similar opinion, concerning those who are of their sect,
or zealously contend for their sentiments? And is not this
the case among Protestants, as well as among Papists?

Meet for, &c. (8) Αξιος, rendered *worthy; Luke* iii. 8;
and in many other places. Those things which become repentance, are consistent with it, expressive of it,
and so evince that it is genuine, are. manifestly intended; and not what is *deserving,* in any sense of the
word.—*Repentance.*] Μεθανοιας. 11. (*Α μεθανοιω.* See on
verse 2.)

o 2

unto the root of the trees: therefore every tree which bringeth not forth good fruit is hewn down, and cast into the fire.

11 I indeed baptize you with water unto repentance; but he that cometh after me is mightier than I, whose shoes I am not worthy to bear: he shall baptize you with the Holy Ghost, and with fire:

12 Whose fan is in his hand, and he will throughly purge his floor, and gather his wheat into the garner;

but he will burn up the chaff with unquenchable fire.

13 ¶ Then cometh Jesus from Galilee to Jordan unto John, to be baptized of him.

14 But John forbad him, saying, I have need to be baptized of thee, and comest thou to me?

15 And Jesus answering said unto him, Suffer it to be so now: for thus it becometh us to fulfil all righteousness. Then he suffered him.

16 And Jesus, when he was baptized went up straightway out of the

---

V. 11, 12. John baptized the people with water; calling them to repentance, and making baptism their outward profession of it, and the avowed beginning of a new life. But Jesus, who came after John in order of time, but was immensely superior to him in dignity, authority, and excellency, insomuch that John was not worthy to loose, or carry, his sandals, or to perform the lowest menial service for him, would baptize them, "with the "Holy Ghost and with fire." The descent of the Holy Spirit on the day of Pentecost, in the form of fiery tongues lighting on the apostles, with the effects produced, on their minds and by their ministry, was a remarkable fulfilment of this prediction: yet this baptism "by the Holy Spirit "and by fire," was vouchsafed comparatively to few of those who believed in Christ; but the language of John evidently denotes a general benefit. (Marg. Ref. e—h.—Note, Acts i. 4—8.)—The Saviour, whose forerunner John was, would communicate to his disciples the divine Sanctifier, as purifying water, to wash away their internal pollutions; and as refining fire, to consume all their dross, and the remains of their corrupt affections; to kindle in their hearts the holy flame of divine love and zeal; to illuminate their minds with heavenly wisdom, and to convert their whole souls into his own pure and holy nature. At the same time, to use another emblem, he would come to his visible church, which then consisted of a few believers mingled with many hypocrites and wicked persons, as the husbandman to his heap of threshed corn,—with his fan in his hand: and as the husbandman, easily and exactly, separates between the wheat and the worthless chaff, by winnowing the heap; so Christ, by his doctrine, his convincing Spirit, his omniscience, his providential dispensations, and at the last judgment, would exactly separate believers from unbelievers. And, as the husbandman gathers the wheat into his granary, and burns up the worthless chaff; so would Christ take care of believers, and execute vengeance on unbelievers. This immediately related to the reception of the pious Jews into the Christian church, and the terrible judgments about to be executed on the rejected Jewish nation; but it is equally applicable to the constant tendency of the gospel, and to the final condition of the righteous and the wicked.—The expression "unquenchable fire," as fully proves that the wicked will never be released from the place of torment; as "their

"worm that never dieth" does that they will never be annihilated. (Marg. Ref. i—n.—Notes, Mark ix. 43—50.)

V. 13—15. After John had, during some time, exercised his ministry, Jesus came to be baptized by him. Being free from sin, he could not repent; and he needed no forgiveness, regeneration, or newness of life. He was not capable of those ends of baptism, for which it was administered to others: but he would honour it, as the ordinance of God; and he would use it as a solemn introduction to his most sacred work and offices, of which John's testimony, the descent of the Holy Spirit upon him, and the voice from heaven, were so many notifications. John, being aware of his divine dignity and excellence, by immediate revelation, (Note, John i. 30—34,) hesitated to comply with this proposal; declaring, that he needed to be baptized of Christ with the baptism of the Holy Spirit, and to be purged by him from his sins; and he could not but be surprised, that Jesus should come for this purpose to him, who was his servant, and a poor sinful man. But Jesus, allowing the truth of his words, intimated that it was proper that he should permit it to be so; "for," says he, "it becometh us to fulfil all righteousness." We never find that Jesus spake of himself in the plural number; and it must therefore be allowed, that he meant John also, and all the servants of God, in a subordinate sense. It became Christ, as our Surety and our example, perfectly "to fulfil all righteousness:" and it becomes us to walk in all the commandments and ordinances of God, without exception; and to attend on every divine institution, according to the meaning and intent of it, as long as it continues in force. Thus far Christ's example is obligatory: but as John's baptism, not being exactly the same as Christian baptism, is no longer in force; the example only proves, that Christian baptism should be honoured and attended on. Controverted points, however, cannot thus be settled. Christ's example does not bind us to do exactly as he did: for he was circumcised, kept the Passover, and observed the seventh day Sabbath, according to the dispensation under which he lived: but we are not required to do these things.

It becometh. (15) Πρεπον εστιν. 1 Cor. xi. 13.—Πρεπω. Eph. v. 3. 1 Tim. ii. 10. Tit. ii. 1. Heb. ii. 10. vii. 26.

V. 16, 17. All other persons, whom John baptized, "confessed their sins;" but Jesus "went up straightway

water: " and, lo, the heavens were opened unto him, ' and he saw the Spirit of God descending like a dove, and lighting upon him:

17 And, ' lo, a voice from heaven, saying, ' This is my beloved Son, in whom I am well pleased.

" from the water."—And immediately, while he was praying, (*Note, Luke* iii. 21, 22,) " the heavens were opened;" and the Holy Spirit " descended like a dove," the emblem of purity, gentleness, and love; and " lighted upon him," probably both in the form, and with the hovering motion, of a dove. This extraordinary appearance was seen by John, as well as by our Lord; but it is not said that any of the people were present. (*Note, John* i. 30—34.)— This visible descent of the Spirit upon Christ, was a token of his being endued with his sacred influences without measure, to qualify him, as Man, for every part of his meditatorial work; and to be communicated to his people from him, as the Head of the church. (*Marg. Ref.* x.) —At the same time, a voice was heard from heaven, God the Father himself acknowledging Jesus as his beloved Son, in whose person, character, righteousness, and mediation, he was well pleased, and fully satisfied. And thus it was intimated, that those who would find acceptance with the Father, must hear, believe, and obey his beloved Son, and ask all blessings in his name, and for his sake.—At the baptism of our Lord, there was a manifestation of the three persons in the sacred Trinity, acting in their proper relations, according to the œconomy of our redemption. The Father appointing and sealing the Son to be the Mediator; the Son solemnly accepting the designation, and entering upon his work; and the Holy Spirit descending on him, as through his mediation communicated to his people, to apply his salvation to their souls.—' It is worthy of remark, what an assemblage of circumstances present themselves to our notice on opening the New Testament; all suited to fix our attention, and raise our expectations, respecting the extraordinary character, to whom we are about to be introduced. Here, as in every part of the gospel, *facts* are simply related, without any studied remarks to awaken our attention: but what *facts* are they! In the small compass of the first three chapters; we have the genealogy of Jesus traced back to David and Abraham; the miraculous conception; the repeated interposition of angels; the wise men conducted to the scene of these transactions by an extraordinary star; the fulfilment of prophecies traced in each circumstance; a forerunner (himself the subject of repeated prophecy,) coming to prepare the way of the Lord; and finally, the miraculous appearance, and the voice from heaven, at the baptism of Jesus, announcing him to be " the beloved Son of God." What impressions are these things suited to make! Yet they are introduced, apparently without any design, on the part of the writer, to strike or to affect : they come in of course, as facts which the truth of history required to be related.'

PRACTICAL OBSERVATIONS.

V. 1—6.

The most eminent and useful servants of God often grow up in retired situations, and exercise their ministry In places remote from the busy scenes of life : but wherever stationed, God will bring those to attend on them,

whom he purposes to save by their labours ; and he can as easily convene large congregations in the desert, as in populous cities.—The world at large, with all its inhabitants, is " the kingdom of the wicked one;" except as " of darkness into the kingdom of his dear Son." And all these will soon be received into the realms of felicity, where their King now reigns in glory: but those who remain strangers or enemies to this deliverance, and consequently subjects of Satan, will have their portion with their prince, in the region of darkness and despair. This kingdom of God and heaven is " come nigh to us : " but unless it be set up in our hearts, we shall not enjoy its blessings : nor can we understand the nature, excellency, and glory of it, except we be broken in spirit with godly sorrow, and humbled in true repentance; taught to hate sin, and to long for deliverance both from its punishment and pollution. The preachers of salvation, therefore, must introduce their message of rich mercy and plenteous redemption, by " the ministration of condemnation," and by shewing sinners the nature and necessity of " repentance, and of works meet " for repentance." Thus prophets and apostles, as well as John the Baptist, " prepared the ways of the LORD," and led sinners to welcome his salvation and submit to his authority: and thus even the King of glory, when he humbled himself to be " a Preacher of righteousness," prepared the way for erecting his spiritual kingdom, and for rendering himself precious to the hearts of his hearers.— Modern *deviations* then from this good old way, will not be found *improvements* upon it : and if repentance were more fully and clearly preached, " the Lamb of God, that " taketh away the sin of the world," would not so often be pointed out in vain ; nor would men so much neglect or pervert the gospel, as they do where this is slightly and superficially attended to.—They, who preach repentance, the mortification of worldly lusts, and the renunciation of worldly interests and indulgences, will commonly have success, in some measure proportioned to the degree, in which they exemplify their own doctrine. And if they seem nearly as much alive to the pursuit of wealth, or as desirous of the pleasures and decorations of life, as other men, their declamations will have little influence ; for their hearers will consider their conduct as a comment on their sermons. Nor can ministers in general be sufficiently independent, to be faithful to all men and in all cases, unless they learn to be content with mean accommodations, and to be frugal and simple in their expenses. Indeed, it is no disgrace, but an honour, to the servant of God, to appear as a poor man, and as willing to be poor, in his attire, his table, his furniture, and every thing belonging to him. Those who have not superior wisdom, piety, or holiness, may want external appendages to preserve them from neglect and contempt: but " the man of God," who is devoted to him and " furnished for every good work." has a more valuable distinction, and needs them not.—But how small a portion of those, who attend on the most faithful preachers, become the true disciples of Christ.

CHAP. IV.

Christ, being led by the Spirit into the wilderness, fasts forty-days; is tempted by the devil; overcomes him by the word of God, and is ministered to by an-

gels, 1—11. He dwells at Capernaum, and fulfils a prophecy of Isaiah, by preaching in Galilee, 12—17. He calls Peter, Andrew, James, and John, to follow him, 18—22. He teaches in the synagogues, and heals the diseased; so that, his fame being spread abroad, he is followed by great multitudes, 23—25.

Many are attracted by novelty, or go because others do; and many are brought under transient convictions. They attend on divine ordinances, make confessions of sin, and profess to be disciples; but they have not the true repentance and living faith of real Christians, and in time of temptation they fall away.

V. 7—12.

The servant of God must not judge of men, according to outward rank, profession, or reputation; but according to their characters, estimated by the rule of scripture. None are further from the kingdom of heaven, than formalists, who are proud of their own supposed goodness; and infidels, who are elated with an idea of their superiority to vulgar prejudices, and of their pre-eminent knowledge and sagacity. Little do such men suspect, that they are much more emphatically " the children of the wicked " one," and better serve his cause than the vilest of the profligates whom they disdain; or that they are likely to receive still deeper damnation. Loud indeed are their clamours, of bigotry, uncharitableness, and fanaticism, when they read such declarations: yet they will find them true, except (which is not likely,) they should take warning and " flee from the wrath to come:" and let it be carefully observed, that all the miseries, and multiplied triumphs of death, which are the effects of God's displeasure against the sins of men, are entirely distinct from, and not worthy to be compared with " the wrath to come." Happy are they, who take the alarm, and flee for their lives, without loitering, or turning aside! for whether they have heretofore been Pharisees, Sadducees, or publicans, they will not be rejected by the gracious Saviour. Yet, unless we " bring forth fruits meet for repentance," our profession of Christianity will no more avail us than the relation of the unbelieving Jews to Abraham profited them. The Lord is able to raise up true disciples to Christ, from among those who have not yet heard of his name; and he will never spare any man who works iniquity, (nay, who does not work righteousness, on account of his creed, his sect, or his forms of godliness: for " now is the axe laid to the " root of the trees; and every tree," not only which bringeth forth bad fruit, but " which bringeth not forth good " fruit, shall be hewn down, and cast into the fire."—But our hearts cannot be made productive of this good fruit, except the regenerating Spirit of Christ graft the good word of God on them. ' No outward forms can make us ' clean;' no ordinances, by whomsoever administered, or after whatever mode, can supply the want of " the bap- " tism of the Holy Ghost and of fire:" this alone can produce that purity of heart, and those exalted and holy affections, which uniformly " accompany salvation." All professed Christians, who are destitute of this inward seal of the covenant, are but chaff amidst the wheat: and our Lord has " his fan in his hand, and he will throughly purge " his floor." He employs various methods in this world

for that purpose; but the grand separation will be in the day of judgment, when " he will gather the wheat into his " garner, and burn up the chaff with unquenchable fire."

V. 13—17.

The most eminent saints have always been the most humble; they have had the most abasing thoughts of themselves, and the most exalted apprehensions of the glory and excellency of Christ; they have felt their need of his atoning blood and sanctifying Spirit, more than others; and have thought the meanest place in his service too high and honourable for them. We need no further proof of this, when we hear him, who " was filled with the Holy " Ghost from his mother's womb," and who was " the " greatest of all that had been born of woman," declare himself unworthy to bear Emmanuel's shoes. Let us compare and contrast his character and language, with those of self-sufficient Pharisees and Sadducees, ancient and modern; and of those especially, who spend their lives in derogating from the honour of Christ, that they may exalt themselves. But " before honour is humility;" yea, the Lord honours those who honour him: and whilst we admire the self-abasement of our Surety, " in fulfilling all " righteousness" for our justification, even when it made him appear as if he had been a sinner; let us learn to copy his example, and to honour God, by worshipping him in all his institutions; and to seek his grace in the use of all appointed means. Thus we may wait for the " supply of " the Spirit of Christ," to make us fruitful in the works of righteousness, to evince our union with him, and to be in us " the Spirit of adoption, witnessing with our spirits, " that we are the children of God," accepted in " his be- " loved Son in whom he is well pleased." But let us remember, that the Spirit of Christ resembles the gentle, loving dove, and not any fierce bird of prey: furious contests therefore cannot spring from his influence; nay, they banish him from our hearts and assemblies, they weaken the evidences of our adoption, and mar our comfort. " For " the fruit of the Spirit is love, joy, peace, long-suffering, " gentleness, goodness, faith, meekness, temperance;" and by abounding in these, we best glorify the God of our salvation, to whose service we were devoted, when " bap- " tized in the name of the Father, and of the Son, and of " the Holy Ghost," to whom be glory for evermore. Amen.

NOTES.

CHAP. IV. Good chronologists compute, that Christ was born four years before the time of the Æra, from which we at present calculate. The chapters are here, however, dated according to the vulgar Æra; and as he was thirty years of age at his baptism, that event is dated after Christ twenty six, and the computation is proceeded with on the same principle, as far as the date of events can be ascertained.

ᵃ Mark i. 12, 13. Luke iv. 1, &c. Rom. viii. 14. THEN ᵃ was Jesus led up ᵇ of the Spirit into the wilderness, ᶜ to be tempted of the devil.

ᵇ 1 Kings xviii. 12. 2 Kings ii. 16. Ez. iii. 12. 14. viii. 3. xi. 1. 24. xl. 2. xliii. 5. Acts viii. 39. 2 And when he had ᵈ fasted forty days and forty nights, ᵉ he was afterward an hungred.

ᶜ Gen. iii. 15. John xiv. 30. Heb. ii. 18. iv. 15, 16. 3 And when ᶠ the tempter came to

ᵈ Ex. xxiv. 18. xxxiv. 28. Deut. ix. 9. 18. 25. xviii. 18. 1 Kings xix. 8. Luke ii. 2. e xxi. 18. Mark xi. 12. John iv. 6. Heb. ii. 14—17. f Job i. 9—12. ii. 4—7. Luke xxii. 31, 32. 1 Thes. iii. 5. Rev. ii. 10. xii. 9—11.

him, he said, ᵍ If thou be the Son of God ʰ command that these stones be made bread.

4 But he answered and said, ⁱ It is written, ᵏ Man shall not live by bread alone, ˡ but by every word that proceedeth out of the mouth of God.

g iii. 17. Luke iv. 3, 9. h Gen. iii. 1—5. xxv. 29—34. Ex. xvi. 3. Num. xi. 4—6. Ps. lxxviii. 17—20. Heb. xii. 16, 17. i 7, 10. Luke iv. 8, 12. Rom. xv. 4. Eph. vi. 17. k Deut. viii. 3.

l xlv. 16—21. Ex. xvi. 8. 15, 35. xxiii. 15. 1 Kings xvii. 12—16. 2 Kings iv. 42—44. vii. 1, 2. Hag. ii. 16—19. Mal. III. 9—11. Mark vi. 38—44. viii. 4—9. John vi. 5, &c. 31, &c. 63.

V. 1, 2. After the glorious things, recorded in the close of the foregoing chapter, we might have expected, that Jesus would be openly acknowledged as the Messiah, by the whole Jewish nation: but a very different scene here opens to our view. Immediately after the descent of the Holy Spirit upon him, "he was led up by the Spirit "into the wilderness, to be tempted of the devil." He might be disposed for retirement, in order to pour out his soul in prayer and praise, and by fasting and holy exercises to prepare for his most arduous work: yet was he especially led forth by the Spirit, to conflict with the devil, the false accuser, the adversary of God and man. Many expositors think, that this took place in a desert near Jordan, within the promised land; and tradition favours the opinion: yet it is more probable, that it was in the wilderness of Sinai, where Moses, and after him Elijah, had fasted forty days and nights. (Marg. Ref. d.—Note, Mark i. 12, 13.)—Christ went forth to be tempted: as our Surety, our Champion, our David, he went to meet that great "Go-"liath, who had" so long "defied the armies of the living "God," and had never found one able wholly to prevail against him; and in his success the interests of all his people were involved.—Satan assaulted the first Adam in paradise, and prevailed with him to eat the forbidden fruit, when he might without offence have regaled his appetite with rich variety: but "the second Adam" met the enemy in a howling wilderness, and thus gave him his full advantage; and he was pleased to sustain by miracle an entire fast of forty days and nights, that nothing might interrupt the interesting conflict. Satan could not but know, that this was "the Holy One of God,' and for what end he came into the world: but, from that furious enmity, with which he constantly opposes the purposes of God, though always baffled, his was desirous of assaulting him. Perhaps, he had some presumptuous expectation of success: he knew that, as Man, Jesus was like unto us in all things, except sin; and if he could gain the least advantage, the whole plan of redemption would be frustrated. As he had therefore put it into the heart of Herod, to attempt murdering Jesus in his infancy; so he now attempted to draw him into sin: and if he could not do this, yet he should have the hellish pleasure of giving him uneasiness. For our Lord "suffered being tempted:" in proportion to his perfect holiness, his soul would be the more distressed by the detestable suggestions of the enemy; and that which preserved him from defilement, exposed him to suffer: but to this he willingly submitted, that he might have an experimental sympathy with his people under their temptations, and be able to succour them.—It is probable, that Satan renewed his temptations, from time to time, during the whole forty days, continually interrupting Christ's holy

meditations with his hateful suggestions; (Luke iv. 2;) but we are not informed of what passed during this season. After this long suspension, his appetite of hunger again returned, in a place where no sustenance could be procured by ordinary means: and probably no trial is more acute than that of extreme hunger, without prospect of relief. The tempter therefore chose this crisis for his most subtle and vehement assault.

V. 3, 4. Satan seems to have before acted as an invisible tempter, suggesting thoughts to the mind of Christ, as he does to those of his people: but now he assumed a visible form; not terrifying, but as a friend, perhaps professing to be "an angel of light." In this assumed character, he proposed to him, that if he were indeed "the "Son of God, he should command the stones before him "to be made bread." The subtlety of the tempter appears in the plausibility of the temptation. He did not urge him to create a feast for indulgence; but merely to change a stone into a loaf for his necessity, and to shew that he was indeed the Son of God: and where was the harm of this, when he was ready to perish with hunger?—Some think, that the temptation was chiefly intended to make him question, whether he were indeed the Son of God: but this seems rather to have been assumed, as a kind of principle, on which other things were to be grounded; in something of the same manner, as when Eve was tempted by the serpent: and the same temptation is implied, "Ye "shall be as Gods," self-sufficient, and independent. (Notes, Gen. iii. 1—5.)—He might here address Christ, as in a way of surprise. 'What! art thou the beloved Son of God, and left in this waste desert to perish with hunger! Can it be possible! Is this the love of the Father! Wait no longer on him for a supply, which has been too long delayed, and of which there is no prospect. The case is urgent, and the power inherent in thee; exert thyself, and shew thy divinity, by commanding these stones to become bread.' This seems to have been the tempter's meaning ; but to work a miracle, to satisfy the craving of the appetite, would have implied hard thoughts of God, distrust of his providence and promise, and a disposition to leave the direct path of duty, and to use improper means of relief; like him, who said, "This evil is of the LORD; why should "we wait for the LORD any longer?" We must recollect that Christ, as Man, was bound to obey the whole law; and every thing, which would have been in the least sinful for us in similar circumstances, would have been inconsistent with the very end of his coming into the world. The gift of miracles, in Christ, was in many respects a talent: and it was necessary while he "fulfilled all right-"eousness," and set us a perfect example in all other respects, that he should employ this talent wholly for the

5 Then the devil ᵐ taketh him up into ⁿ the holy city, and setteth him ᵒ on a pinnacle of the temple,

6 And saith unto him, If thou be the Son of God, cast thyself down: ᵖ for it is written, ᵠ He shall give his angels charge concerning thee: and in ʳ their hands they shall bear thee up, ˢ lest at any time thou dash thy foot against a stone.

7 Jesus said unto him, ᵗ It is written again, ᵘ Thou shalt not tempt the LORD thy God.

8 Again ᵛ the devil taketh him up into an exceeding high mountain, ˣ and sheweth him all the kingdoms of the world, and the glory of them;

9 And saith unto him, ʸ All these things will I give thee, ᶻ if thou wilt fall down and worship me.

10 Then saith Jesus unto him, ᵇ Get thee hence, ᶜ Satan: for it is written, ᵈ Thou shalt worship the LORD thy God, and him only shalt thou serve.

11 Then ᵉ the devil leaveth him, and, ᶠ behold, angels came and ministered unto him.

Marginal references (left): m Luke iv. 9. John xix. 11. n xxvii. 53. Neh. xi. 1. Is. xlviii. 2. Dan. ix. 16. o 2 Chr. iii. 4. p 4. 2 Cor. xi. 14. q Ps. xci. 11, 12. Luke iv. 9—12. Heb. i. 14. r Job i. 7. v. 23. Ps. xxxv. 7. 20. s Jo xxi. 16. 42. xxii. 31, 32. Is. viii. 20. t Ex. xvii. 2. 7. Num. xiv. 22. Deut. vi. 16. Is. vii. 12. u Deut. vi. 16. Ps. lxxviii. 18. 41. 56. xcv. 9. civ. 14. Mal. iii. 15. Acts v. 9. 1 Cor. x. 9. Heb. iii. 9. v Luke iv. 5—7.

Marginal references (right): x xvi. 26. Esth. i. 4. v. 11. Ps. xliii. 16. 17. Dan. iv. 30. Heb. xi. 24—26. 1 Pet. i. 24. 1 John ii. 15, 16. Rev. xi. 15. y Rev. xiii. 4. John xii. 31. 2 Cor. iv. 4. z 1 Sam. ii. 7, 8. b 1 Sam. ii. 7. 8. Ps. lxxiii. 11. cxlii. 7, 8. Prov. viii. 15. Jer. xxvii. 5, 6. Dan. ii. 37, 38. iv. 32. v. 18, 19. 26—29. John xiii. 3. xvii. 2. xix. 11. Rev. xix. 16. c 1 Cor. x. 20, 21. 1 Tim. iii. 6. Rev. xii. 9. xxii. 8, 9. b xvi. 23. Jam. iv. 7. 1 Pet. v. 9. d Chr. xxi. 1. Josh. xxiv. 14. 15. 1 Sam. vii. 3. f Ps. xci. 11, 12.

Job i. 6. 12. ii. 1. Ps. cix. 6. Zech. iii. 1, 2. d Deut. vi. 13, 14. x. 20. Josh. xxiv. 14. 1 Sam. vii. 3. Luke iv. 8. e Luke iv. 13. xxii. 53. John xiv. 30. f 1 Tim. iii. 16. Heb. i. 6. Rev. v. 11, 12.

---

purposes for which it was entrusted; *viz.* to confirm his mission and doctrine, to honour the Father and to do good to men: and not at all to accommodate or relieve himself. For this is the precise difference between *holiness* and *selfishness*, in the use of the various gifts of God. It would have been the duty of a prophet in such a situation, to wait patiently, and not to attempt working a miracle for his own relief, without some immediate intimation from God: and therefore Jesus would by no means attend to such an insidious proposal; but answered the tempter by a plain text of scripture. (*Note, Deut.* viii. 3.) The life of man depends on God, and not on food: God can sustain life without food, but food cannot sustain life without his blessing. To rest upon his promise, and to obey all his precepts, and thus to commend our lives to his keeping; and to suffer any extremity, rather than break his commands, or question the truth of his word, by which alone our lives and souls are secured, and on which they must live, constitutes our duty. This reply therefore repelled the temptation, and the tempter was overcome by " the " sword of the Spirit."—The quotation here is *almost* ver*batim* from the Septuagint; but it likewise exactly agrees with the Hebrew text.

Command. Εντ.—Comp. *2 Cor.* iv. 6. Gr. with *Gen.* i. 3. 6, &c. *Sept.*

V. 5—7. The devil, finding Christ immoveably stedfast in confiding in his heavenly Father, changed his method of assault. He conveyed him (doubtless by his own permission, in whatever way it was effected,) into Jerusalem, which had long been called " the holy city;" and there he placed him on a pinnacle of the temple, perhaps on the top of the high porch, or steeple, that was at the east end of it; which, as well as the other parts, was surrounded by a battlement, to prevent any from falling: (*Deut.* xxii. 8 :) and then he proposed to him, being the Son of God, " to cast himself down from thence." This was a publick situation, and he might thus at once prove himself the promised Messiah; and it would also, as the tempter meant to insinuate, be the highest evidence of his confidence in God. Our Lord had produced scripture to refute the former temptation; the tempter therefore supported this with a quotation from the sacred oracles. (*Note, Ps.* xci. 11, 12.) Whether the words adduced were understood as a promise to believers, or a prophecy relating to Christ,

Satan suggested, that they ensured his safety: for if angels were charged with believers, to keep them from dashing their foot against a stone; much more would the Son of God be borne up by them, that he should not be injured by the fall. But he omitted the words, " in all thy ways," knowing that an ostentatious casting himself from this battlement was none of the ways marked out for Christ, (or for any believer,) in which he might depend on divine protection.—Satan could tempt Christ to cast himself down, but he could not cast him down, for his power was limited. Perhaps he presumed, that he should thus induce Jesus to terminate his own life: at least compliance with this proposal, would have been a needless, nay, an ostentatious method of shewing how entirely God protected him, and an unwarranted requisition of a miracle to be wrought in his preservation. Our Lord, therefore, answered the enemy by another quotation of scripture, (*Deut.* vi. 16,) which plainly forbids men to tempt the Lord God.—Some indeed contend, that this expression denotes *diffidence*, rather than *presumption*, and they produce several texts to prove it: but the meaning in every place seems to be, ' putting the power, truth, and love of God to an unnecessary trial; refusing to believe him, without further evidence than he chooses to give; dictating to him what he should do; questioning whether he could do this or the other, and resolving not to be satisfied that he could unless he did; neglecting proper means, running into needless danger, making improper requisitions, expecting unwarranted interpositions.' Thus, if our Lord had cast himself from the temple, he would have demanded, as it were, a needless miraculous publick attestation to his character as " The " Son of God;" and have put himself into circumstances of extreme danger, in expectation of a divine interposition, for which in such a case he could have no warrant: and this would have been " to tempt the LORD," and a violation of the command in the plain meaning of it.—St. Luke mentions this temptation last; but St. Matthew seems to have observed the order of time, in his narration. —*A pinnacle.* (5) Το πτερυγιον, the *pinnacle*. (*Note,* 1 *Kings* vi. 2, 3.) The quotations in the sixth and seventh verses exactly agree with the LXX; except as in the former of them the order of the words is changed: but the LXX exactly translate the Hebrew.

V. 8—11. The devil seems at length to have despaired

12 ¶ Now [g] when Jesus had heard
that John was [*] cast into prison, he departed into Galilee;
13 And, [h] leaving Nazareth, he came
and dwelt in [i] Capernaum, which is
upon the sea-coast, in the borders of
[k] Zabulon and [l] Nephthalim:
14 That [m] it might be fulfilled which
was spoken by Esaias the prophet,
[n] saying,
15 The land of Zabulon, and the
land of Nephthalim, *by* the way of the
sea, beyond Jordan, [o] Galilee of the
Gentiles:
16 The people [p] which sat in darkness saw great light; and to them,
which sat in the region [q] and shadow
of death, light is sprung up.
17 From [r] that time Jesus began to
preach, and to say, [s] Repent: for the
[t] kingdom of heaven is at hand.
18 ¶ And Jesus, [u] walking by the

g Mark i. 14. vi. 17. Luke iii. 20. iv. 14. 31. John iv. 43. 54.
* Or, *delivered up.* A. D. 31.
h Luke iv. 30, 31.
i xi. 23. xvii. 24. Mark i. 21. John iv. 46. vi. 17. 24. 59.
k Josh. xix. 10—16. *Zebulun.*
l Josh. xix. 32—39. *Naphtali.*
m i. 22. ii. 15. 23. viii. 17. xii. 17. & 21. xxvi. 54. 56. Luke xxii. 37. xxiv. 44. John xv. 25. xix. 28. 36, 37.
n Is. ix. 1, 2.
o Josh. xx. 7. xxi. 32. 1 Kings ix. 11. 2 Kings xv. 29.
p Ps. cvii. 10—14. Is. xlii. 7. lx. 1—3. Mic. vii. 8. Luke i. 78, 79. ii. 32.
q Job iii. 5. x. 22. xxxiv. 22. Ps. xliv. 19. Jer. xiii. 16. Am. v. 8.
r Mark i. 14.
s iii. 2. ix. 13. x. 7. Mark i. 15. Luke v. 32. ix. 2. x. 11—14. xv. 7. 10. xxiv. 47. Acts ii. 38. iii. 19. xi. 18. xvii. 30. xx. 21. xxvi. 20. 2 Tim. ii. 25, 26. Heb. vi. 1.
t xi. 12. xiii. 11. 19. 24. 47. xxv. 1.
u Mark i. 16—18.

of success, by any covert, plausible temptation: he therefore resolved openly to make one bold effort, grounding all his hope of success on the vastness of the recompence, which he meant to propose as the price of transgression. To give the better colour to his artifice, he took the Lord Jesus to the top of an exceedingly high mountain, and thence "shewed him the kingdoms of the world, and the "glory of them." This must have been an illusion upon the imagination, over which Satan seems to have peculiar influence: for it is naturally impossible that all the kingdoms of the world could be seen at once; as by far the greatest part of them must be beneath the visible horizon. They were, however, presented to the mind of Christ, as if he had seen them with his eyes; and fully beheld all the wealth, magnificence, and honour, which appear glorious in the eyes of men. And Satan impudently avowed, that all these were absolutely at his disposal; and that he was so pleased with Jesus, that he was ready to put him into immediate possession of them, provided he would do homage for them, by one *single* prostration, one *transient* act of worship.—Doubtless Satan is permitted to use worldly things as his baits, with which to allure his votaries: but nothing could be more audaciously false, than to pretend that God had receded from his providential government of the world, in order that the devil might absolutely dispose of it as he pleased; especially as he was addressing him, "by whom kings reign:" and nothing could be more arrogant, than to require the incarnate Son of God to worship him. Whatever disguise this ambitious spirit had before assumed, (for we suppose him to be the great leader of the whole army of apostate angels,) he was now made manifest, and his diabolical designs also: Christ therefore addressed him by his name, "Satan," the adversary of God and man, and commanded him to depart immediately; for it was written "Thou shalt worship the "LORD thy God, and him only shalt thou serve." (*Marg. Ref.* a.)—The Saviour in this spake as Man, to whom it was absolutely forbidden to worship any other, than God only.—Thus the great enemy was baffled, and left the Redeemer; ceasing for a season to renew his temptations. And then holy angels came, as it were to congratulate him on his victory, to do him honour, and to minister to his wants.

Thou shalt worship, &c. (10) 'From these words, compared with other like scriptures, it appears, that Christ is 'not a creature; because the worship and service due to 'God alone, cannot be duly given to a creature, that being 'to own him equal in dignity with God; and the sin of 'idolatry chiefly consisting in giving that worship to a 'creature which is due only to the God of heaven. And 'therefore *religious adoration* and service ... cannot be given 'duly, or without idolatry to Christ, provided that he be 'only a creature. Seeing then God doth require, "that '"all men should worship the Son, even as they worship '"the Father;" and "when he brought the First-born '"into the world, said, Let all the angels of God worship '"him;" and seeing this is the character of Christians, that 'they "serve the Lord Christ;" it is certain that he 'cannot be a creature only, but must be truly God.' *Whitby.*—*Thou shalt worship.*] Προσκυνησεις.—In both the texts where this command occurs, (*Deut.* vi. 13. x. 20,) the LXX have, 'Thou shalt *fear* (φοϐηθηση) the Lord, &c.'

V. 12—17. Not long after John had baptized Christ, he gave offence to Herod the Tetrarch: and, being cast into prison, he terminated his ministry, and after some time ended his short but useful life. It is, however, evident that Jesus had entered upon his ministry, and become eminent, a considerable time before John was cast into prison. (*Notes, John* i. 29—51. ii. 1—12. iii. 22—36. iv. 1—3.) But at that time he began to preach more fully and openly, in the northern part of the land. He had perhaps been at Jerusalem at some solemn feast, when this account was brought to him; and he immediately departed for Galilee: and then leaving his habitation at Nazareth, (Joseph perhaps being dead, as we read no more of him,) he took up his ordinary abode at Capernaum, a city upon the borders of the two lots assigned to the tribes of Zabulon and Nephthalim, upon the coast of the sea of Galilee, or Tiberias. This was done in order to fulfil a remarkable prophecy of Isaiah. (*Notes, Is.* ix. 1, 2.) Thus, in Galilee of the Gentiles, that is, bordering on the Gentiles, where such darkness had prevailed, that it was "the region of "the shadow of death," the glorious light of the gospel sprang up and shone forth, when Jesus began to preach the same doctrine, which John had preached in another part of the land. (*Notes,* iii. 1, 2.) Stronger language could not be employed in describing even the deplorable ignorance of the Gentiles.—This part of Galilee was not far distant from Tyre: and Solomon had given Hiram, king of Tyre, twenty cities in that neighbourhood. (1 *Kings* ix. 11.)

The people, &c. (16) The quotation is made by translating the Hebrew, with no variation, except the omission of a clause not immediately requisite for the Evangelist's argument; and substituting *sitting* for *walking*. It differs more from the LXX; but not materially.

V. 18—22. Jesus had a considerable time before this,

SEA OF CHINNERETH—SEA OF GALILEE—LAKE OF GENNESARET—
SEA OF TIBERIAS.

Numb. xxxiv. 11.   Josh. xii. 3; xiii. 27.
Matt. iv. 18,   Luke v. i.   John vi. 1; xxi. 1.

sea of Galilee, saw ʳ two brethren, Simon called Peter, and Andrew his brother, casting a net into the sea: ˢ for they were fishers.

19 And he saith unto them, ᵗ Follow me and ᵇ I will make you fishers of men.

20 And ᶜ they straightway left *their* nets, and followed him.

21 And going on from thence, he saw ᵈ other two brethren, James *the* son of Zebedee, and John his brother, in a ship with Zebedee their father, mending their nets; and he called them.

22 And ᵉ they immediately left the ship and their father, and followed him.

23 ¶ And ᶠ Jesus went about all Galilee, ᵍ teaching in their synagogues, and preaching ʰ the gospel of the kingdom, ⁱ and healing all manner of sickness and all manner of disease among the people.

24 And ᵏ his fame went throughout all ˡ Syria: and they brought unto him ᵐ all sick people that were taken with divers diseases and torments, and those which were ⁿ possessed with devils, and those which were ᵒ lunatick, and ᵖ those that had the palsy; and he healed them.

25 And there ᵠ followed him great multitudes of people from Galilee, and from ʳ Decapolis, and from Jerusalem, and from Judea, and from beyond Jordan.

---

heen acknowledged as the Messiah by Andrew and Peter; but, it seems, they had not been required to forsake their ordinary employments, and to follow him constantly, with a view to the ministry and apostleship. (*Notes, John i.* 35—42.) Simon and Andrew were partners, and were employed in casting their net: but Jesus called them to leave it and to follow him, and assured them they should be "fishers of men." They would be employed in bringing men out of the world and its vanities, to Christ and salvation, by means of the gospel; even as they had been, in bringing the fishes out of the sea with their nets: and they would need the same kind of skill, self-denial, endurance of hardships, assiduity, regard to times and opportunities, and patience, which they had been used before to exercise. This call was accompanied with such power, that without delay they left all and followed him.—And, going on, he saw two other brethren who were diligently employed in another way; and at his call they left all, even their aged father, to follow Christ, trusting in Providence for a precarious subsistence in this new employment.—Zebedee probably acquiesced in the will of the Lord concerning his sons: though not called to this service, but allowed to have in his former occupation.—The miraculous draught of fishes, related by St. Luke, probably took place about this time, either before, or soon after, the events here recorded. (*Marg. Ref.—Note, Luke v.* 1—11.)—*A net.* (18) Αμφίβληστρον.—*A large cast-net.* (Ex αμφι *circum,* et βαλλω *jacio.*)

V. 23—25. Jesus, having procured these attendants, not from the schools or palaces of Jerusalem, but from the fisher-boats of Galilee, went about preaching the gospel in the synagogues, or places of worship, which were something like our parish-churches. Wherever he went, he confirmed his divine mission by a variety of benevolent miracles; which were emblems of the healing efficacy of his doctrine, and the influences of the Spirit that accompanied it. So that his fame spread abroad into the adjacent region of Syria, as well as into all the parts of the land

of Israel: multitudes therefore brought their sick unto him, and he healed them all, at the same time instructing them in the way of salvation. We shall have a better opportunity of discussing many subjects, relating to these diseases, possessions, lunaticks, &c. wnen we come to particular instances: only observing, that this beneficent display of our Lord's divine power, both marked the gracious design of his undertaking, and excited the attention of the people to his doctrine. (*Marg. Ref.* f, g, h—r.)—It should, however, be noticed, that persons possessed with devils, are here expressly distinguished from lunaticks; and they could not then be exactly the same, as some sceptical learned men seem to think.—' It seems strange to find ' men, at this distance of time, questioning the truth of ' that, which neither Pharisees nor Sadducees then doubted ' of, or ever did object against the pretensions of Christ ' and his apostles to cast out devils.' *Whitby.—Gospel of* ' *the kingdom.* (23) *Marg. Ref.* h.—*Lunatick.* (24) Σεληνιαζομενος. xvii. 15.—(From σεληνη, *the moon.*)

PRACTICAL OBSERVATIONS.

V. 1—4.

Retirement, fasting, meditation, and devotion, are suitable preparations for the important work of the ministry; and they, who are led ' by the Holy Spirit to take this ' office upon them,' will seek communion with God, and a blessing from him, in the use of every means of grace. Yet we must not yield to discouragement, if, when we thus seek to commune with God, we should be peculiarly assaulted by the temptations of the devil. That subtle enemy often leaves the negligent and slothful unmolested: but when we seek to glorify God and do good, or to enjoy communion with him, Satan will be sure to assault us, as far as he is permitted: and the Lord is often pleased to permit him to do this, either to counterbalance our comforts, or to prove the reality and power of our grace. The enemy also knows how to avail himself of outward circumstances; and whether we be full or hungry, he can vary his temptations accordingly.—The Lord could, if he

CHAP. V.

Christ shews who are happy, 1—12. His disciples, as " the salt of the earth and the light of the " world," and as resembling " a city set on a hill " and a candle in a room, must be bright examples in

good works, 13—16. He came not to destroy, but to fulfil and establish, the law, 17—20. The sixth commandment, vindicated from corrupt glosses, and spiritually expounded and enforced, 21—26; and the seventh, 27—32; and the third, 33—37. Exhortations, to suffer wrong patiently, 38—42; to love our enemies, 43—47; and to aim at perfection, 48.

saw good, suspend the cravings of our appetites; but, as this is not his ordinary method, they are guilty of presumption, who attempt such degrees of abstinence as render their appetites more unruly, and thus expose themselves to temptation: yet the trial of our faith and love sometimes consists in bearing patiently the cravings of nature, rather than remove them by committing the least sin.—Satan is too skilful to assault established believers, in the full exercise of faith and love, at the first, with temptations to evident and gross iniquities. He is most dangerous to them when most plausible, and when his temptations seem to be good and friendly hints, tending to something profitable without evident criminality. He often, in a very specious manner, tempts men to unbelief, or harasses their minds with groundless fears and perplexities. He suggests to the poor or afflicted, that if they were indeed the children of God, surely they would not be left to such sufferings, or to experience such straits; thus insinuating hard thoughts of God, as if he were unkind or unfaithful: or he excites them to affect a sort of independence even of God, by attempting, in a sinful manner, to supply their own wants. Sometimes he affrights the mind with gloomy prospects of still greater difficulties; and represents trusting in the Lord, with scrupulous conscientiousness, as leading to distress and ruin. By his emissaries he persuades men, that some compliances must be made and deviations admitted, or else they must starve: or he tries to embolden them to venture on some convenient or gainful sin, because they are the children of God, and there is no danger of their being cast off for it. In these and numberless other ways, he tempts us to impatience, distrust, or sinful expedients of deliverance from trouble; and, in opposition to our principles, to prefer sin to suffering. And having a party within us, we too often listen to his soothing flatteries, and are induced to dishonour our profession, or at least to honour it less than we ought to do. But " the sword of the Spirit " is that warranted weapon, which Satan cannot stand against; and it is our wisdom to answer all suggestions with, " Thus it is " written." " Let God be true, and every man a liar: " our dependence is wholly on the Lord: his word of promise is our stable support, his precept is our infallible rule. By these men live: and whilst we lean on an express promise, and obey the plain precept, we must be safe, whatever appearances may be against us. " Our Father " knoweth what things are good for; " and sooner all nature shall recede from its course, than any of his promises shall fail of accomplishment.

V. 5—7.

When Satan sees men staying their hearts on God in stedfast faith, and adhering to their duty in the midst of difficulties, determined rather to suffer than to seek relief by sin; he can change his ground and tempt them to neg-

lect proper means, or to thrust themselves uncalled into dangers and difficulties, expecting the Lord to help them out. Taking advantage of their reverence for the scripture, he knows how plausibly to support these suggestions by texts, which seem to give countenance to this unwarranted confidence. " The LORD will provide; " and therefore the believer needs not defraud, or break the sabbath, in order to a maintenance : but Satan will tempt him further to infer, that he may be negligent, improvident, or extravagant; and that even in this case God has engaged to provide for him.—The children of God shall be kept from final apostasy; and therefore they need not be dejected by the consciousness of their own weakness, or by the prospect of strong temptations : but the enemy will suggest, that they need not watch and pray; that they may venture into perilous situations; that they may ostentatiously court difficulty, and thrust themselves into danger, and then expect their heavenly Father to preserve them.—Satan and his instruments have a peculiar advantage in such cases, by partial or distorted quotations of scripture, when the comfort or privilege is separated from the character or duty annexed. The believer shall be preserved " in all his " ways: " but by keeping out of danger by the concluding words, Christians are often seduced out of their way, and expect to be preserved in places and companies where they have no business : and many persons are deluded into a false persuasion that they are believers, by such mutilated quotations. But let all men beware of thus mangling scripture; and be upon their guard against those, who produce part of a text, and leave out some emphatical words, which contradict the end for which they quote it. Godly men may do this in the heat of argument, or through inattention : but they follow a hateful precedent, and it tends to great mischief, and is a powerful engine in the hands of those who oppose the truth.—Let us also recollect that the tempter has no objection to holy places, as the scene of his assaults; nay, he often chooses them for the sake of plausibility: but he delights in high places, to which he would gladly exalt those of whose labours he is afraid, that he might cast them down with the more fatal fall; and he peculiarly urges men to presumption and ostentation.—The perversion of scripture made by numbers should not induce us to neglect it; but by plain texts, used in their obvious meaning, we must answer temptations grounded on its misapplication.—We should ever remember, that we trust in the Lord, when we expect his protection in the path of duty; but tempt him, if we wilfully deviate from it, presuming on his care of us.

V. 8—11.

The believer should not despond, if assaulted by the most horrible temptations to infidelity, blasphemy, suicide, or any other dreadful crime : as Christ himself was tempted to ambition, and even to worship the devil. The more

E 2

a iv. 25. xiii. 2.
Mark iv. 1.
b xv. 30. Mark iii.
19. John vi. 2, 3.
c iv.18—21.x 2—4.
Luke vi. 13—16. **A**ND ^a seeing the multitudes, ^b he went up into a mountain: and when he was set, ^c his disciples came unto him.

2 And ^d he opened his mouth, and taught them, saying,

d xiii. 35. Job. iii.
1. Ps. lxxviii.
1, 2. Prov.
viii. 6 xxx.
s 9. Acts viii. 35. x. 34. xviii. 14. Eph. vi. 19.

such suggestions pain us, the less likely they are to defile us; even as bad language fails to pollute us, in proportion as it wounds our ears and grieves our hearts.—By long observation and deep penetration, our enemy knows how powerfully the prospect of authority, honour, and greatness, with such glories as the kingdoms of the earth contain, attract the minds of men. It was indeed a vain presumption in him to suppose, that the holy heart of our divine Redeemer could be thus allured. But we are all by nature prone to seize on such supposed advantages; to forget, that the Lord alone disposes of them; to mistake these illusions of the imagination for substantial good, and to render Satan any service, which may be required as the price of obtaining them. Alas! we find but very few men who, in all instances, decidedly and with indignant abhorrence, silence every proposal of this kind. Yet " what is " a man profited, if he gain the whole world, and lose his " own soul ?" Conscious therefore of our weakness, we should pray that we may not be " led into temptation," and be thankful to be kept out of the way of it : for numbers, who seemed to run well, have given up religion for a very small portion of the world; and many believers have been greatly hindered and pierced with bitter anguish, by yielding to these alluring suggestions. (*Note*, 1 *Tim.* vi. 6—10.) Let us then beware of covetousness and ambition; store our minds with the precious words of God; and remember to " worship the LORD, and serve him " alone," and not attempt to divide our heart between him and Mammon, which will be as ruinous as more gross idolatry.—Where temptations are strong, and the evil proposed evident, we must not parley for a moment: for the soul that deliberates is already vanquished.—Whilst we admire the condescension and patience of the incarnate Son of God, in suffering himself to be conveyed from place to place by this foul fiend, that as our Surety he might conquer him: let us learn to copy his example, and to pursue his victories, taking encouragement from the consideration, that our exalted Redeemer, ' knows what ' sore temptations mean,' and that " he suffered being " tempted, that he might be able to succour them that are " tempted." Let us observe the honourable issue of his conflict : how angels ministered to him, who refused Satan's counsel to supply his own wants; and how " all " power in heaven and earth is given to him," who refused the proffer of " all the kingdoms of the world, and " the glory of them." If we resist the devil he will flee from us, and the Lord will give his angels charge over us likewise: and if we refuse honours and preferments purchased by Sin, we shall obtain a kingdom in heaven that cannot be moved. Let us then " fight the good fight of " faith, and lay hold on eternal life."

V. 12—25.

Our services and trials are alike short. When one instrument is laid aside, the Lord calls forth others; and when such as have been useful are taken to their rest, we should redouble our diligence in the cause of God.—Those

places are highly favoured, where the pure gospel is preached. Till that blessing is vouchsafed, the people " sit in darkness and the shadow of death." This was the case of the Jews, as well as the gentiles ; and is, even at this day, that of nominal Christians in very many places, as well as of Jews, Pagans, and Mohammedans : but when the word of truth is faithfully declared, they " see a great " light : " may all such " walk in the light, as the chil- " dren of the light;" and may that blessed light be vouchsafed to all the regions of the earth!—All who preach the gospel must deliver the same message, and call men to repentance, that they may share the blessings and bring forth the fruits of salvation.—Next to the duties of religion, honest industry is most valuable : they are more likely to become useful ministers of Christ, who have spent their youth in laborious, self-denying occupations; than they who, professing to be students, waste their time in worldly pleasures, and contracting habits of dissipation, sloth, delicacy, and self-indulgence : and even shepherds, husbandmen, or builders may stand as fair to take good care of the Lord's flock, husbandry, or building, as these fishers, to become " fishers of men ; " provided he is pleased to call them to it. However, let none despise instruction, learning, or preparation for the ministry. Christ himself became the tutor of those, whom he sent forth to preach his gospel; and having taught them heavenly wisdom from his own lips as well as by the holy Spirit, he gave them the knowledge of languages by miracle, that they might be fully qualified for their work.—When he speaks to the heart, men leave all and follow him : and even the demand of parents, on our care and attention, is subordinate to his right to our services, and to be relinquished if he command.—When ministers are not employed in casting their nets, they should be ocupied in mending them : and they will find work for all their time, and abundant need of patience and assiduity.—We do not now experience the Saviour's miraculous healing power in our bodies ; but if we be cured by medicine, the praise is equally his due : and he is the physician of our souls; and if we come to him and follow his directions, he will at length perfectly heal all our maladies.—We cannot draw others to attend the gospel, by miracles of love ; but if we abound in acts of ordinary charity, we shall recommend the truth : and perhaps many may, by these means, be induced to attend on that word, by which their souls will be healed of spiritual lunacy, and Satan dispossessed, who " now " holds them captive at his will;" and thus the name of our God and Saviour will be glorified by us, and others have to bless him in our behalf.

NOTES.

CHAP. V. V. 1, 2. At the close of the last chapter, we read, that the divine Redeemer was surrounded with multitudes, whose diseases he healed: here we find him instructing them in the great concerns of their souls. He " preached to them the gospel of the kingdom : " repentance was his first subject; and on this, as to men's need

* 4—1. xi. 6. xiv.
16. xxiv.46. Ps. l.
1.ii.12. xxxii.1,2
xli. 1. lxxxvi. 12
cxii. l. cxix. 1, 2. cxxviii. 1. cxlvi. 5. Prov. viii. 32. Is. xxx. 18. Luke vi. 2 ; &c. xi. 28. John
xx. 29. Rom. iv. 6—9. Jam. i. 12. Rev. xix. 9. xxii. 14. f xi. 25. xviii. 1—3. Lev. xxvi. 41,
42. Deut. viii. 2. 2 Chr. vii. 14. xxxiii. 12. 19. 23. xxxiv. 27 Job xlii. 6. Ps. xxxiv. 18. li. 17.
Prov. xvi. 19 xxix. 23. Is. lvii. 15. lxi. l. lxvi. 2. Jer. xxxi. 18—20. Dan. v. 21, 22. Mic. vi. 8.
Luke iv. 18. vi. 20. xviii. 14. Jam. i. 10. iv. 9, 10. g iii. 2. viii. 11. Mark x. 14. Jam. ii. 5.

3 **Blessed** *are* [d] the poor in spirit; [e] for their's is the kingdom of heaven.

4 Blessed [h] *are* they that mourn; [h] for they shall be comforted.

Ps. vi. 1—9. xlvi.
1—5. xxx. 7—
11. xxxiii. 3—7.
li. 1—5. lxix.
20, 30. cxvi. 3—7. cxxvi. 5, 6. Is. xii. 1. xxv. 8. xxx. 19. xxxv. 10. xxxviii. 14—19. li. 11,
12. lvii. 18. lxi. 8. lxvi. 10. Jer. xxxi. 9—12. 16, 17. Ex. vii. 16. ix. 4. Zech. xii. 10—14.
xlii. 1. Luke vi. 21. 25. vii. 38. 50. xvi. 25. John xvi. 20—22. 2 Cor i. 4—7. vii. 9, 10.
Jam. i. 12. Rev. vii. 14—17. xxi. 4.

of it, and the effects which it produces, he enlarged in the following practical sermon, which is the longest publick discourse of Christ that is recorded.—He had before preached in the synagogues, as he often did afterwards; but probably no building could contain the multitudes at this time assembled; and therefore he ascended a mountain. Being thus elevated above the people, he sat down according to the custom of the Jewish teachers, and in that posture he instructed them. Those disciples, whom he had called to a more constant attendance on him, seem to have sat next him, and the multitude around them. But the apostles were not at this time chosen; and they, who professed to believe in him as a teacher sent from God, are frequently called disciples : so that the interpretation must not be restricted, by an exclusive application to the case of his more constant attendants. Thus seated and surrounded, the divine Teacher, with the utmost solemnity, taught them as follows.—The expression " opened his mouth " seems intended to convey an idea of the peculiar gravity, deliberation, and distinctness of the Speaker, and of the importance of that which was spoken.

V. 3. (*Notes, Luke* vi. 20—26.) Expositors generally observe, that these Beatitudes, as they are called, were calculated to rectify the mistaken notions and expectations of the Jews, respecting the Messiah's kingdom : but, as all their prejudices originated from those corrupt propensities, which were common to them with other men ; so these maxims of heavenly wisdom are equally adapted to remove false notions of excellency, honour, and felicity, in other men of all nations and ages.—All men seek happiness : but none, except those who are taught by the Spirit of God according to his word, know in what it consists, or how it may be obtained and enjoyed. The beatitudes may therefore be considered as the Christian paradoxes ; for they place happiness in such dispositions of mind, and in such circumstances, as men generally deem incompatible with it. All the declarations of scripture, shewing who are the blessed, or happy, have reference to our state and character as sinners : but some point out those benefits, by which we become entitled to happiness ; (*Note, Ps.* xxxii. 1, 2;) and others those dispositions, or that conduct, which are conducive to the enjoyment of it. (*Marg. Ref.*)—Such short aphorisms require peculiar care in explaining them ; and they commonly admit of limitations, according to other parts of scripture. In general it may be observed, that the beatitudes do not refer to any *natural* tempers, which may bear some resemblance to those intended ; but to *holy* dispositions, produced by divine grace, rectifying the obliquities of fallen nature : and that where one of them *really* exists, all the others do, though perhaps not equally prominent.—In the first place Christ declares that " the poor in spirit " are happy. " Poverty of " spirit " is very different from poverty in outward circumstances. Many poor persons are proud, ungodly, dishonest, and profligate, and far from happiness : while some of the rich are humble, pious, and holy, and therefore happy.—Voluntary poverty cannot be meant. ' It is ' assuredly the duty of all men, who would attain this ' bliss, to be " poor in spirit : " whereas it cannot be the ' duty of all Christians to turn monks and friars mendi- ' cant to this end : for then all other Roman Catholicks ' must be excluded from the kingdom of heaven. ...By ' " the poor in spirit " our Saviour understands the man of ' a true, humble, lowly spirit ; this being the usual expres- ' sion, by which the scriptures ... represent the humble ' man. ...They who are thus poor in spirit are blessed, ' because their humility, rendering them teachable, sub- ' missive, contented, and obedient, prepares them to enter ' into Christ's kingdom ; ... and seeing they who are thus ' holy shall be also happy, they must be also meet to enter ' into the kingdom of glory hereafter.' *Whitby.*—This is widely different from a mean, abject, and grovelling disposition ; and implies much more, than patience in poor and afflicted circumstances.—We are all poor in respect of God and heavenly things ; destitute of righteousness, holiness, strength, and wisdom ; deep in debt without any thing to pay ; under condemnation, foolish, enslaved, helpless, polluted, and vile. Yet very few know this to be their case and character : and amidst all this deep poverty, men in general are of a haughty, self-sufficient, and independent spirit ; which precludes them from obtaining relief, and being made partakers of " the unsearchable riches " of Christ." Happy then is he, who knows, or is willing to know, how poor he is ; who feels his indigence, dependence, and unworthiness ; who is humbled and ashamed before God, as a lost sinner, that cannot demand or purchase salvation, or do any thing towards it ; but must be a supplicant, and a debtor to grace for it, and for all that pertains to it. If this man be rich, learned, or noble, his heart will be weaned from dependence on such distinctions, and rendered lowly, courteous, and affable : if poor, he will be patient, contented, and thankful. He is prepared for exercising repentance, and faith in Christ ; and will gladly welcome his salvation, and give up every thing, that he may enter " the kingdom of heaven." He has the temper of the kingdom, and is prepared for the obedience and privileges of it ; and all the blessings of it are his, certainly, exclusively, and eternally : they are provided for such persons, and appropriated to them, and none but they value, seek, or enjoy them. They are therefore *happy*, in the present sense and the hope of heaven ; and their humble and lowly frame of mind tends to a peaceful enjoyment of life, and to confidence in God, communion with him, and the participation of the consolations of his Holy Spirit.

V. 4. The next blessing is, by the Lord Jesus, declared to belong to those that mourn ; not those who *have mourned*, but those who *are mourning*. The world deems the gay, the dissipated, the jovial, and the prosperous, happy ; and men turn aside from religion as a misery, because of the mourning connected with it. The Jews also expected nothing but festivity and carnal rejoicing, under the reign of the Messiah ; but when he came, he pronounced the

l xi. 29. xxi. 5.
Num. xii. 3. Ps.
xxix. 20. xxv. 9.
Jer. 32. marg.
cxlvii. 6, cxlix. 4.
iil. 12. 1 Tim. vt. 11.
k Ps. xxv. 13, xxxvii. 9. 11. 22. 29. 34.   Is. lx. 21.   Rom. iv. 13.

5 Blessed *are* [l] the meek; for [k] they shall inherit the earth.

l s. xl. 4, xxix. 19. lvi. 1.   Zeph. ii. 3.   Gal. v. 23.   Eph. iv. 2.   Col.
iii. 12.   1 Tim. vi. 11.   2 Tim. ii. 25.   Tit. iii. 2.   Jam. i. 21. iii. 13.   1 Pet. iii. 4. 15.

l Ps.xlii.1.2.lxiii.1.
2. lxxxiv.2.cxl3.a.
Am. viii. 11—13.
xxxx ii.bit. vi.21.
m.xvi.1. vi.27.
l. 5.John vi. 27.
m Ps. iv. 6, 7. xvii.
15. lxiii. 3. lxv. 4.   Cant. v. 1.   Is. xxv. 6. xli. 17, 18. xlv. 3. xlix. 9, 10. lv. 1—3. lxv. 13.
lxvi. 11, 12.   John iv. 14. vi. 48—58. vii. 37, 38.   Rev. vii. 16, 17.

6 Blessed *are* they which do hunger and thirst after righteousness; [m] for they shall be filled.

mourners happy.—All kinds of mourning cannot be intended, "for the sorrow of the world worketh death:" many are afflicted, and grow hardened under it; many "sorrow as men without hope," and spend their lives in rebellious murmurs, and die of vexation, or become their own executioners. The mourning which springs from "poverty of spirit," brokenness of heart, and tenderness of conscience, must especially be meant. A serious, considerate disposition, a readiness to recollect, confess, and be sorry for sin, with the "godly sorrow that worketh" true "repentance;" habitual watchfulness over the present temper and conduct, as well as a frequent humble recollection of past offences, producing remorse of conscience and self-abhorrence; a continual dependence on the mercy of God in Christ Jesus for acceptance; and an application for his sanctifying Spirit to cleanse away the remaining evil that is mourned over, seem primarily intended. But afflictions, and frequent mourning under the Lord's correcting rod, as far more salutary than prosperity, as pledges of his love, and means of humiliation and sanctification, are included: which, when they are properly submitted to and improved, tend to blessedness. And finally, a disposition to sympathize in the sorrows and troubles of our fellow Christians, and fellow sinners, must also be meant.—Such mourners as these are happy; their very tears and sighs have pleasure mixed with them, and prepare them for consolation: they shall be comforted with a sense of pardoning mercy, and with peace, hope, and joy in the Holy Ghost; and thus they shall anticipate the everlasting consolation prepared for them, when "God "shall wipe all tears from their eyes." (*Marg. Ref.—Note, Ps. cxxxvi. 5, 6. P. O.—Notes, Is. xxv. 6. Rev. vii. 13—17, v. 17.*)

Shall be comforted.] Παρακληθήσονται. (Hence Παρακλητος the Comforter.) The verb is often rendered *exhort*, as well as *comfort*. It means *encouraging exhortation, encouragement exciting to exertion.*

V. 5. Humiliation before God, indifference about the world, sorrow for sin, and a succession of trials and afflictions, soften the heart, and render it *meek*, that is, gentle, forbearing, forgiving, teachable, and submissive; which seems to be the disposition intended in this beatitude. There is a constitutional quietness of spirit, springing from love of ease, from defect in sensibility and firmness, and from the predominancy of other passions, which should be carefully distinguished from holy meekness. The natural temper is timid and pliant, easily deterred from good, and persuaded to evil; it leads to criminality in one extreme, as impetuosity of spirit does in another; it is often found in ungodly men; and it sometimes forms the grand defect in the character of pious persons, as in the case of Eli, and of Jehoshaphat. Divine grace operates in rendering such men more firm, resolute, and vigorous; as it does in rendering men of an opposite temper more yielding and quiet. The "meekness," to which the blessing is annexed, is not *constitutional*, but *gracious;* and men of the most vehement, irascible, and implacable dispositions, by looking

to Jesus, through the grace of God, learn to curb their anger, to cease from resentment, to avoid giving offence by injurious words and actions, to make concessions, and forgive injuries. They become gradually more teachable, guidable, patient of counsel and contradiction, and calm in their spirit and conduct, from a principle of conscience, and by faith and prayer.—Whatever a man's previous disposition may have been, this meekness, which has regard both to the authority of the law and to the grace of the gospel, entitles him to the blessing. The temper itself is that of happiness: submission, resignation, peace, and love are its essence; contention, murmurs, and a thousand mischiefs and miseries are avoided by it: and it is said that "the meek shall inherit the earth." This, as it stands in the Old Testament, (*Note, Ps. xxxvii. 10, 11,*) is spoken with reference to the promised land, the type of heaven; of which this meekness proves the possessor an heir, and for which it forms an essential qualification. But it also implies, that the meek, however poor in the world, have more actual comfort than any other persons; as if the whole of it were their inheritance. They are more beloved and respected, in their families and connexions; and are commonly left more undisturbed by their neighbours: they have more peace of conscience, tranquillity of mind, communion with God, and consolation from his Spirit, than other men: and facts in general contradict the declamations of those, who contend that such a temper and conduct will expose a man to intolerable injuries and evils in the world.—Abraham is called the "heir of the world:" and all believers are his children; and if "Christ be our's," all things are ours, both in this world and the next. (*Marg. Ref.*)

Meek.] Πραεις. xxi. 5. 1 Pet. iii. 4.—*Num.* xii. 3. *Ps.* xxv. 9. xxxvii. 11. *Sept.* Hence πραΰτης· *Jam.* i. 21. iii. 13. 1 Pet. iii. 15. (A πραυς. xi. 29. Whence πραΰτης· 2 Cor. x. 1. Gal. v. 22. et al.)

V. 6. The appetites of hunger and thirst, if not satisfied, are universally felt to be most craving and uneasy: they cannot be amused, bribed, or put off, with any other object than meat and drink; and this must be had, if possible, at any price, and by any hardship or peril. The desire of riches, honours, pleasures, knowledge, &c. when very vehement, are often described by metaphors taken from this; which denote both the eagerness of men in seeking, and their pleasure in obtaining, the desired object. But those who hunger and thirst after these things, can only obtain a temporary gratification, and are liable to eternal dissatisfaction. They alone are happy, "who hunger and "thirst after righteousness:" that is, after God, and his favour, his image, and the holy felicity to be enjoyed in his service; who know the nature, excellency, and value of such blessings; who choose and seek them in the first place; who subordinate all other interests and pleasures to them; who will not put up with any thing short of them; who value every thing in proportion as it tends to the acquirement of them; who are dissatisfied with every attainment hitherto made; who are more grieved, that

E 5

a vi. 14, 15. xviii. 33
—35. 2Sam. xxvi.
26. Job xxxi. 16
—22. Ps. xviii. 25.
xxxvii. 26. xli. 1—4. cxii. 4, 5, 9.　Prov. xi. 17. xix. 21. xix. 17.　Is. lvii. 1, 2. lviii. 6—12.　Dan. iv. 27.　Mic. vi. 8　Mark xi. 25, 26.　Luke vi. 35, 36.　Eph. iv. 32. v. 1, 2.　Col. iii.
12.　Jam. iii. .7.　o Hos. i. 6. ii. 1. marg. 23.　Rom. xi. 30, 31.　1 Cor. vii. 25.　2 Cor.
iv. 1.　1 Tim. i. 13. 16.　2 Tim. i. 16—18.　Heb. iv. 16. vi. 10.　Jam. ii. 13.　1 Pet. ii. 10.

7 Blessed ᵃ *are* the merciful; ᵒ for they shall obtain mercy.

8 Blessed ᵖ *are* the pure in heart;

p xviii. 26—28.
1 Chr. xxix. 17
—19. Ps. xviii.
26. xxiv. 4. li.
6. 10. lxxiii. 1.　Prov. xxii. 11.　Ez. xxxvi. 25—27.　Acts xv. 9.　2 Cor. vii. 1.　Tit. i. 15.　Heb. ix. 14. x. 22.　Jam. iii. 17. iv. 8.　1 Pet. i. 22.　q Gen. xxxii. 30.　Job xix. 26,
27.　1 Cor. xiii. 12.　Heb. xii. 14.　1 John iii. 2, 3.

ᵠ for they shall see God.

they are not more holy, than because they are poor, sick, or neglected; and who long above all things for perfect holiness and happiness in the favour and service of God. The new covenant is so constituted, that persons of this character cannot fail to seek and find the righteousness, after which they hunger and thirst: for the Holy Spirit, who excited this spiritual appetite, will lead them to Christ, that it may be satisfied; they will accept of his salvation, and receive from his fulness of grace; they will obtain a measure of the desired felicity on earth; and when all others will be torn from the objects of their choice, then, and not before, they " will be filled;" that is, as firmly established in the enjoyment of the divine love, and as entirely perfected in holiness, as they can desire: and this shall continue for ever; " they shall hunger no more, " neither thirst any more." (*Rev.* vii. 16.)—' The right-
' eousness here mentioned is by some thought to be " the
' " righteousness of faith," by which we being justified, or
' freed from the guilt of sin, have peace with God; and
' this undoubtedly is a fit matter of our spiritual thirst and
' hunger: but yet I think this cannot be the proper import
' of the words: 1. Because the word ... *righteousness* bears
' no such sense in the gospel, but only in the epistles of
' St. Paul: 2. Because the Jews, to whom Christ speaks,
' had no idea of this righteousness, no apprehension that
' their Messiah was to die, and much less that they should
' be justified by his death: and therefore had Christ spoken
' of this righteousness, none of them could have under-
' stood his meaning.' *Whitby.*—It is not necessary, to give an unreserved approbation to every clause in this quotation, in order to perceive, that the general argument is conclusive, against this systematical interpretation of the beatitude, and against a similar explanation of some other passages in our Lord's discourses.

Shall be filled.] Χοῥασθησονται. ' Satisfied, so as to desire ' nothing more.' (xv. 33. 37. Gr.) It is derived from Χοῥος, *Grass*, or *herbage*: and it is a figure taken from cattle in a good pasture, fed till they are satisfied and graze no longer.

V. 7. Connected with the preceding holy tempers, is that of *mercy*, or compassion, tenderness, and love: an aversion to every thing harsh, cruel, oppressive, or injurious; a propensity to pity, alleviate, or remove the miseries of mankind; an unwillingness to increase personal emolument or indulgence, by rendering others uneasy; a willingness to forego personal ease, interest, or gratification, to make others comfortable and happy: this seems the general meaning of the word *merciful.*—There is, however, a natural propensity of this kind, which should be carefully distinguished from the gracious disposition. This is not expansive, habitual, general: it is profuse to some, and cruel to others; it does not spring from proper motives, it is not directed to proper ends, nor governed by any regard to the divine law; it is often joined with impiety, injustice, excessive indulgence, and even tyranny, in other parts of a man's conduct; and in short, it is a sort of *instinct*, which is stronger in some men than others, and

has no connexion with true religion. But the mercy, to which the blessing is annexed, has respect to the authority, law, and glory of God, and to the grace of the gospel; it is learned by looking to the cross of Christ, and the mercy of God to sinners through him; it is uniform in its exercise, and seeks the good both of men's bodies and souls; it extends to the vile, the injurious, and the obscure, and to every one of the human species, however distinguished, as far as he falls under its sphere of action. It is con nected with humility, faith, self-denial, equity, piety, and universal conscientiousness; and it induces a man, from love to God and hope in his mercy, to love, compassion-ate, and do good to all men, as he has time and opportunity: not allowing himself to injure any; but wishing and praying for the happiness of those, whom he cannot reach or help.—Such persons are happy, for they shall " obtain mercy." All are sinners, and need mercy: these are penitent, believing sinners, and are interested in the mercy and grace of the covenant. The Lord will compassionate and be kind to them, according to their conduct towards their brethren; they shall be pardoned, supported, and comforted, through life and in death; and then shall enjoy " the mercy of our Lord Jesus Christ unto eternal " life." But, on the contrary, " they shall have judgment " without mercy, who have shewed no mercy."—Even in this world, the exercise of mercy and beneficence constitutes one of the most delightful employments, of which our nature is capable; as they best know, who have the most decidedly made the experiment. (*Marg. Ref.*)

Obtain mercy.] Ελεηθησονται. From the same root as ελεημονες. They pity, and they shall be *pitied*; they *forgive* and relieve, and they shall be *forgiven* and *relieved.*

V. 8. Men are apt to think those happy, who have it in their power to gratify every ambitious, covetous, or sensual inclination, without restraint or limitation: and probably the carnal Jews expected abundant indulgences of this kind under the reign of their Messiah. But, on the contrary, Jesus pronounces those happy, who are " pure " in heart;" in whose souls all carnal, sensual, and sinful desires are so mortified and subdued, that they do not seek the gratification of them; who are inwardly replenished with holy inclinations and affections, and influenced by the fear and love of God, in their habitual conduct. The believer's understanding is in part purified from darkness, his judgment from error, his will from rebellion, his affections from enmity, avarice, pride, and sensuality; his memory and imagination from the depraved thoughts and recollections, which once occupied them; and his leading aim is to glorify God, obey his will, enjoy his favour, and do good. This is indeed imperfect in this world: but the remainder of sin and pollution forms his burden and grief, and the object of his detestation; which is one peculiar and distinguishing effect and evidence of purity of heart. In proportion as any one is purified through faith, he is pre-pared for discoveries of God to his soul on earth, and favoured with them: and when he shall be perfected in holiness, he shall with open face behold the manifested

9 Blessed ' *are* the peace-makers; ' for they shall be called the children of God.

10 Blessed ' *are* they which are persecuted for righteousness' sake; ' for their's is the kingdom of heaven.

11 Blessed are ye ' when *men* shall revile you, and persecute *you*, and shall say all manner of evil against you ' falsely, ' for my sake.

12 ' Rejoice, and be exceeding glad; ' for great *is* your reward in heaven; ' for so persecuted they the prophets which were before you.

13 ¶ Ye are ' the salt of the earth: but ' if the salt have lost his savour,

---

glory of God; and adore, admire, and be unspeakably happy in the beatifick vision to all eternity. (*Marg. Ref.*)

V. 9. The Jews expected a Messiah, who would lead them forth to war, revenge, victory, and dominion: and mighty warriors and conquerors have always been admired, and celebrated, and congratulated, as honourable and happy; though their mad ambition has rendered the earth a scene of misery, discord, and confusion. But our great Peace-maker pronounced the peace-makers happy; such as are peaceable in their own conduct, and labour to promote peace in families and communities; such as use their influence, to prevent or terminate wars, law-suits, feuds, domestick broils, and religious controversies; such as do all in their power, to promote the reconciliation of sinners unto God, and to induce them to live in harmony and peace with one another. These are happy persons, though they receive little thanks from the furious disputers either of the world, or of the church. They bear the image of God, and copy his example; they are evidently reconciled, regenerated, and adopted: he owns them as his children, and will before the whole world avow their relation to him: many will " call them the children of God " here, and all will know them to be so at last. They shall have much comfort in their loving endeavours on earth, and shall obtain eternal felicity in heaven; that is, if indeed they act from a regard to the authority, example, and glory of God, and to his reconciling love in Christ Jesus. (*Notes*, 1 *Thes*. iv. 9—12. *Jam.* iii. 17, 18.—Comp. *Col.* i. 20. *Jam.* iii. 18. Gr.)

V. 10—12. The Jews expected to be honoured, and paid court to, under the reign of the Messiah: and we all naturally annex the idea of happiness to honour, respect, and favour; and are apt to imagine that a conscientious conduct will certainly ensure them to us. But Christ declared those to be happy, " who were persecuted for right-" eousness' sake." If men suffer, under a profession of religion, for their crimes or follies, or for their obstinate attachment to unscriptural or antiscriptural tenets and practices, without general conscientiousness; they cannot be included in this blessing. But when those who fear God, and rely on his mercy through Christ, suffer for conscience' sake; though they may err in the matter for which they suffer, they must not be excluded: for they act from proper motives, and under a covenant of mercy. Yet the more evidently men suffer, for adhering to the plain truths and precepts of the scripture, the more clearly are they interested in this blessing.—It is here taken for granted, that believers must meet with injurious treatment

in this world. (*Note*, 2 *Tim.* iii. 10—12.) The wicked hate the holy image of God, and those who bear it; his holy truth, and those who profess and preach it; his holy law, and those who obey and stand up for its obligation and authority; and his holy ordinances, and those who attend on them. They accuse true Christians of bigotry, spiritual pride, fanaticism, hypocrisy, sedition, misan. thropy; they invent all kind of calumnies of them, and fasten opprobrious names on them. If then we adhere to the truths, precepts, and ordinances of Christ, and refuse to comply with any thing contrary to our consciences; we must prepare to endure derision, reproach, slander, or more severe treatment, from ungodly men. But the kingdom of grace and glory belongs to those who, on such accounts, meet with and patiently endure persecution: they suffer for the sake of Christ and righteousness; and " all manner of " evil is spoken of them *falsely*," because they belong to the Lord. Instead, therefore, of dejection and complaints, they should count themselves happy, that the enemies of God see and hate his image in them: (*Note*, 1 *Pet*. iv. 12 —16:) yea, they should rejoice and exult for joy, in the prospect of the great and glorious recompence, which is prepared for them; remembering, that they are in this conformed to the most approved and honoured servants of God, in every age and in every part of the world. Nor can any eminence, in all those holy dispositions before de-scribed, (which combine to form the Christian character, are " the fruits of the Spirit," and constitute the image of Christ,) preserve any man from this hatred of the world; nay, they will expose him to it, so long as men in general remain the servants of Satan: for even Christ himself, the only perfect character which ever appeared on earth, was exposed to the greatest contempt and enmity of the world. But these holy tempers will teach a man to bear up under such trials, to overcome evil with good, to pass comfort-ably through them, and to derive good from them all. (*Marg. Ref.*)

Falsely. (11) Ψευδομενοι, *lying*. Marg. Being liars, and false accusers, like Satan, διαϐολος, " the accuser of " the brethren."—*Be exceeding glad.* (12) Αγαλλιασθε. *Luke* i. 47. x. 21. *John* v. 35. viii. 56. 1 *Pet*. iv. 13. ' It signifies exceeding great joy, such as we use to express ' by outward signs, as leaping or dancing.' *Leigh*. (Ex αγαω *valde, et* ἁλλομαι, *salio*.)

V. 13. Salt is the grand preservative from corruption in the material world, and it gives a seasoning to all our viands: but, if it loses its saltness, and becomes insipid, it is the most worthless of all substances; being unfit even

e John v. 35. xii. 34. Rom. ii. 19. 20. 2 Cor. xi. 14. Eph. v. 6— 14. Phil. ii. 15. 1 Thes. v. 5. f Gen. i. 20. ii. 1. l Gen. xi. 4—8. wherewith shall it be salted? it is thenceforth good for nothing, but to be cast out, and to be trodden under foot of men.

Rev. xxi.14, &c. g Mark iv. 21, 22. Luke viii. 16, 17. xi. 33. * A measure containing about a pint less than a peck. h Lu. xxv. 37. Num. viii. 2. i Prov. iv. 18. 1a. viii. 8 1a. i.—3. Rom. xiii. 11— 14 Ye are °the light of the world. 'A city that is set on an hill cannot be hid.

15 Neither 'do men light a candle, and put it under °a bushel, but on a candlestick; and ᵇit giveth light unto all that are in the house.

.4. Eph. v. 8. Phil. ii. 15, 16. 1 Thes. ii. 12. v. 6—8. 1 Pet. ii. 9. 1 John i. 5—7. 10. 23. vi. 18. 16 Let 'your light so shine before men, ᵏ that they may see your good

k vi. 1—5. 16. xxiii. 5. ᵐActs ix. 36. Eph. ii. 10. 1 Tim. ii. 10. v. 10, 25. Tit. ii. 7. 14. iii. 1. 7, 8. 1a. Heb. x. 24. 1 Pet. ii. 12. iii. 1, 16.

works, 'and glorify ° your Father which is in heaven.

17 ¶ Think not that I am come ° to destroy the law or the prophets: I am not come to destroy, ° but to fulfil.

18 For ° verily I say unto you, 'Till heaven and earth pass, one jot or one tittle shall in no wise 'pass from the law, till all be fulfilled.

Col. ii. 16, 17. Heb. x. 5—12. p 26. vi. 2. 16. viii. 10. x. 15. 28. 42. xi. 11. xiii. 17. xvi. 28. xvii. 20. xviii. 3. 18. xix. 23. 28. xxi. 21. 31. xxiii. 36. xxiv. 2. 34. 47. xxv. 12. 40. 45. xxvi. 13. 34. Mark III. 28. vi. 11. viii. 12. ix. 1. 41. x. 15. 29. xi. 23. xii. 43. xiii. 30. xiv. 9. 18. 25. 30. Luke iv. 2½. xi. 51. xii. 37. xiii. 35. xviii. 17. 29. xxi. 32. xxiii. 43. John q 1. 51. iii. 3. 5. 11. v. 19. 24, 25. vi. 26. 32. 47. 53. viii. 34. 51. 58. x. 1. 7. xii. 24. xiii. 16. 20, 21. 38. xiv. 12. xvi. 20. 23. xxi. 18. q xxiv. 35. Ps. cii. 26. 1a. li. 6. Luke xvi. 17. xxxi. 33. Heb. i. 11, 12. 2 Pet. iii. 10—13. Rev. xx. 11. r Ps. cxix. 89, 90. 152. 1a. xl. 8. 1 Pet. i. 25.

---

for the dunghill, as it is rather conducive to sterility than fruitfulness. The disciples and ministers of Christ are scattered about, as salt, in different parts of the world; that their doctrine, conversation, examples, labours, and prayers, may stop the progress of sin and impiety, and be instrumental in seasoning men's minds with grace and holiness: but if they be unsound in doctrine, unholy in life, or vain and carnal in conversation; they disgrace their profession, are a scandal to their Master, prejudice the minds of men against the truth, or seduce them into error; and so they become the most worthless and wretched of mankind. Every approach to this renders a Christian or a minister unfit to be "the salt of the earth," and deducts from his value and usefulness. This was peculiarly applicable to the primitive professors and teachers of Christianity: as they were sent forth to season the whole world, as it were, with their holy doctrine, lives, and labours.

Lost his savour.] 'The word μωρανθη has a peculiar ' beauty and strength here, and might literally be rendered, ' "if it be infatuated," or *grown foolish;* alluding to the ' common metaphor, in which sense and spirit are ex- ' pressed by salt; ... as we call a flat lifeless discourse *in-* ' *sipid.*' Doddridge. (*Marg. Ref.*)

V. 14—16. The same instruction is here conveyed under another image. Christ is the true "Light of the "world:" but his disciples and ministers, shining by the light of knowledge and holiness derived from him, are, in a subordinate sense, "the light of the world" also; and diffuse his truth and salvation around them, where otherwise darkness and wickedness must reign undisturbed. Their profession, character, and doctrine, render them conspicuous; as "a city set upon a hill, they cannot be hid:" men will look at them, and make observations on all their words and actions, in order to form a judgment of their religion from what they see. Indeed, God intends that they should be thus conspicuous and observed, that they may communicate their light around: as we do not light a candle to conceal it, but that it may be placed conveniently to lighten the room. It is, therefore, their bounden duty, and should be their grand object, so to recommend the truth which they openly profess, by their pious and edifying conversation and behaviour, that men "may see their good works" which flow from faith and love, and thus be induced to glorify their God and Father. (*Notes,* 1 Pet. ii. 11, 12.) For the holy examples and abundant good works of true Christians, soften men's prejudices, win on them to attend

to the truth, and are instrumental to their conversion, by which they glorify God, and become his worshippers and servants.—This should be the aim and effect of their general conduct; though they must not do any particular action " to be seen of men," or seek their own glory in any thing. (*Note,* vi. 1—4.)—Those disciples, who were intended for the apostolical office, might primarily be meant, but every minister and Christian is concerned. (*Marg. Ref.—Note, Phil.* ii. 14—18.)

V. 17, 18. Various opinions seem to have prevailed, about the changes which would take place under the Messiah: and many, who supposed Jesus to be the Messiah, and had heard some parts of his doctrine, were ready to conclude that he meant wholly to set aside the ancient religion, and to establish an entirely new one in its place; which idea tended to mislead some and prejudice others. But he assured them, that he had not "come to destroy the " law or the prophets;" or to teach any thing inconsistent with the true meaning of their sacred writings, which would still continue in force as a part of divine revelation. His design was not to "destroy, but to fulfil." It was evident from Moses and the prophets themselves, that the ritual law was "a shadow of good things to come:" and Christ was come to fulfil the intent of it, and to hold forth the truths and blessings typified by it, in a plainer and more intelligible manner. The moral law he came to fulfil, by perfectly obeying it as the Surety of his people, in his life, sufferings, death, and doctrine; to establish it in its fullest honour and authority; and to make the most effectual provision for men's loving and obeying it. (*Note, Rom.* iii. 29—31, v. 31.) So that, as long as the world endured, not the least word, or letter, or point, or comma, (so to speak,) of the whole law, should by any means lose its authority, or fail of answering the end for which it was given: and the moral law would, to the end of time, continue the standard of sin and holiness to all men, and the believer's rule of duty; for Jesus came to *accomplish* the design of the introductory dispensation, and not to *counteract* or *subvert* it.—' Christ came not to bring any ' new way of righteousness and salvation into the world: ' but to fulfil that in deed, which was shadowed by the ' figures of the law, by delivering men through grace from ' the curse of the law; and moreover to teach the true use ' of obedience which the law appointed, and to grave in ' our hearts the force of obedience.' *Beza.*—' The ' phrase' (" till all be fulfilled,") ' occurs, importing the

19 Whosoever therefore 'shall break one of 'these least commandments, and 'shall teach men so, he shall be called 'the least in the kingdom of heaven: but whosoever shall 'do and teach *them*, the same shall be called great in the kingdom of heaven.

20 For I say unto you, That except your righteousness shall 'exceed *the righteousness* of the scribes and Pharisees, 'ye shall in no case enter into the kingdom of heaven.

21 ¶ Ye have heard that 'it was said 'by them of old time, 'Thou shalt not kill; 'and whosoever shall kill shall be in danger of the judgment:

22 But 'I say unto you, 'That whosoever is angry with 'his brother 'without a cause, shall 'be in danger of the Judgment: and 'whosoever shall say to his brother, 'Raca, shall be in danger of "the council: but whosoever shall say, Thou "fool, shall be in danger of "hell-fire.

'performance of what was typified by the law, and foretold by the prophets, xxiv. 34. *Mark* xiii. 30. *Luke* xxi. '32.' *Whitby.* The fulfilment therefore of legal types, and of the prophecies of the Old Testament, concerning the Messiah and his kingdom, must be intended, as well as the establishment of the moral law in full honour and authority. In another passage, (*Luke* xxii. 16, Gr.) a still more emphatical word is employed, in a similar connexion; which fully confirms the above interpretation.

V. 19. The Scribes and Pharisees made many frivolous distinctions, between great and small commandments; as the papists do between mortal and venial sins: yet all the law is enacted by the same divine authority, and no part of it can in that sense be of small obligation; though some parts may respect more important matters than others. But if a man, professing to be the disciple of Jesus, by a misconstruction of his doctrine, should encourage himself in allowed disobedience to the holy law of God, though in a matter of the least importance; and, by false doctrine or assumed authority, should teach others the same: whatever his station in the church, or reputation among men, might be, he should be called by Christ himself, " the least " in his kingdom;" either no true disciple at all, or one of the most inconsistent and mean of the whole company. On the other hand, he whose practice and doctrine tend to induce men to keep the commandments of God, from proper p c es and for evangelical purposes, will be accounted highright in the kingdom of heaven," however men may disesteem him; and the King will approve, employ, and prefer him.—This most conclusively shews, that all views of evangelical truth, which verge in the smallest degree to antinomianism, are utterly inconsistent with the true doctrine of Christ. These are indeed as antichristian, as popish dispensations and indulgences: they lead to the same place by another road; they relax man's obligation to obey God; and so dishonour that law, which Christ came into the world and died on the cross to magnify and make honourable.

V. 20. The Scribes were the most learned teachers of the law, and of the traditions of the elders, among the Jews; and most of them were Pharisees. Their learning related chiefly to those external matters, in which the pharisaical righteousness consisted; and the Scribes and Phari-

sees made the highest profession of religion, and were accounted peculiarly strict, both in their instructions and practice. But our Lord, in setting up his kingdom, declared that he would not acknowledge any one as his subject, whose righteousness did not exceed their righteousness. And, in fact, a new creation to holiness, and the effect of that change on a man's temper and conduct, constitute a righteousness of heart and life far more excellent, than that of the Scribes and Pharisees; even as much as heaven is higher than the earth. Without repentance and faith we cannot enter Christ's kingdom; these produce hatred of sin, and love of God and man; thus the believer is "taught by the " grace of God, to deny ungodliness and worldly lusts, and " to live soberly, righteously, and godly in this world;" and without this he cannot enter into the kingdom of heavenly glory. Nay, how late in life soever a man is converted, and becomes a true believer, he actually possesses a far better personal righteousness, before he enters heaven, than that of any formalist in the world.—The Scribes and Pharisees ' seem to have taught, that the precepts of the ' law extended only to the outward actions; that a zeal in ' the ceremonial parts of religion would excuse moral de-' fects and irregularities; and that some important ritual ' leges were inseparably connected with a descent from ' Abraham. ... It has been commonly said by the Jews, ' that if but two men were to enter into the kingdom of ' heaven, one of them would be a Pharisee, and the other ' a Scribe.' *Doddridge.* It may be added, that the zeal and strictness of the Scribes and Pharisees, both in doctrine and practice, was chiefly shewn about their own traditions, by which they " made void the law of God ;" or about minute observances, by which they covered over their neglect of judgment, mercy, and faith, or the love of God and man. And in this they have been imitated by vast multitudes in all succeeding ages.

V. 21, 22. To illustrate his meaning, the divine Teacher proceeded to vindicate several of the commandments of the moral law, from the corrupt and partial interpretation put upon them by the Scribes; which tended to shew, that their rule of righteousness itself was beneath even the actual attainments of his disciples. " It had been " said by," or to, " them of old time, Thou shalt not kill." (*Marg.—Note, Ex.* xx. 13.) God had of old given the law;

p viii. 4. xxiii. 19.
17. 1 Sam. xv.
22 1s. i. 10–17.
Hos. vi. 6. Am.
v. 21—24.
q Gen. xli. 9. xlii.
21, 22. 1. 15–17.
Lev. vi. 2—6. 1 Kings ii. 44. Lam. iii. 20. Ez. xvi. 33. Luke xix. 8.

23 Therefore if ᵖ thou bring thy gift to the altar, and there ᑫ rememberest that thy brother hath ought against thee;

r xviii. 16—17
Job xiii. 6. Prov.
xxv. 9. Mark ix.
50. Rom. xii.
17, 18. 1 Cor. vi.
7, 8. 1 Tim. ii.
8. Jam. iii. 13—
18. v. 16. 1 Pet.
i. 19.
s xxiii. 23. 1 Cor. xi. 20.

24 Leave 'there thy gift before the altar, and go thy way: first be reconciled to thy brother, ᵉ and then come and offer thy gift.

iii. 7, 8.

and the tradition of the elders had made this gloss upon it, "Whosoever shall kill shall be in danger of the judgment:" by this it was implied, that nothing, except actual murder, was prohibited; and that this was to be avoided mainly from the dread of the capital punishment to be inflicted by the magistrate. Thus they explained away the extensive spiritual import of the command; and led the people to overlook the awful curse of God denounced against transgressors. But Christ, the great Lawgiver and Judge, speaking with less terror, but not less authority, than when he delivered the commandments from mount Sinai, declared that "whosoever was angry with his brother without cause, " would be in danger of the judgment." All *excessive* anger must be proportionably "without cause;" and all that settles into revenge, or vents itself in words and actions, contrary to the law of loving our neighbour as ourselves. We ought to be angry at sin in ourselves and others, and to shew our disapprobation of it, according to our relation to the offender: (*Note, Mark* iii. 1—5, *v.* 5:) we should seek his humiliation and reformation by proper means; but not his hurt in any respect, at least not in our private capacity.· Inferiors, servants, juniors are all brethren in this sense: and he that is angry at another without cause, or above cause, "shall be in danger of the judgment:" it is a sin deserving of a punishment more terrible, than that inflicted by the ordinary courts of justice on the murderer; and consequently it calls for deep repentance, and needs the mercy and forgiveness of the new covenant. Moreover, whosoever uses contemptuous or opprobrious language in the heat of his passion, calling his brother ' an ' empty worthless fellow,' or ' a wicked, and abandoned ' profligate,' and such like, would be in danger of punishment, proportionally more severe, according to the degree of virulence or malignity contained in such revilings. The different courts of justice, and the different kinds of punishment in use among the Jews, are supposed to be referred to, in these expressions. By one court, it is said, the criminal was condemned to be beheaded ; by another stoned ; and by another, burned in "the valley of the son " of Hinnom," which was considered as a sort of type or emblem of the fire of hell. Of this punishment the conduct above described was deserving, and to this the criminal would be exposed, according to the degree of his crime, unless repentance and forgiveness intervened.—This shews both the need ·which all have of the gospel, and the strictness of the believer's rule of duty. (*Marg. Ref.*) ' These words, *vain* and *foolish*, when they are used by ' men assisted by the Spirit of God, or speaking by virtue ' of their office, out of a spirit of charity, and an ardent ' desire to make men sensible of their folly, do not make ' men obnoxious to this guilt; ... (*Gal.* iii. 1. *Jam.* ii. 20;) ' ... but only then when they proceed from causeless anger, ' ... and ill will towards them.' *Whitby.*—' Minerva, in ' *Homer*, forbids Achilles striking Agamemnon ; yet gives ' him leave to reproach him, and counsels to contumelious ᵈ words.' *Hammond.*—This is heathen or *classical* morality!

In danger of. (21) Ενοχος. ' The word signifies to be ' held fast, as a bird when taken in a snare ; or a male-' factor when arrested, ... or a condemned man, when ... fet-' tered against the day of his execution.' *Leigh.* xxvi. 66. *Mark* iii. 29. 1 *Cor.* xi. 27. *Heb.* ii. 15. *Jam.* ii. 10 (Ab ενεχομαι *obstringor* ; *Gal.* v. 1 : hocque ex ιν et εχω.)— *Raca.* (22) ' An empty man, *cerebro vacuus, mente* et ' *judicio carens.*' Leigh. (Der. from the *Heb.* רן, *vacuus,* *inanis.*)—*Thou fool.*] Μωρε. vii. 26. xxiii. 17. 19. 1 *Cor.* iv. 10. 2 *Tim.* ii. 23.—Hence μωραινω. 13. *note.*—(' Quasi ' μηωρος, εx μη non, et ωρα cura ; ... vel quasi μη ορων non ' *videns,* sc. *animo.*' Schleusner.)—*Hell fire.*] Την γεενναν τυ πυρος. The original word is Hebrew, or Syriack, and signifies *the valley of Hinnom.* There idolaters burned their children to Molech : and, after this abominable practice was put a stop to, the valley was by every means rendered as filthy and vile as possible, and a fire was there constantly burning to consume the rubbish carried thither; and at length, it is reported, that it became a place of execution for criminals.—' Hence this place, being so ' many ways execrable, ... it came to be translated to signify ' the place of the damned, as the most accursed, execrable, ' and abominable of all places.' *Mede.*—The word is frequently used in the New Testament ; and always for hell, or the place of final punishment and misery. (29, 30. x. 28. xviii. 9. xxiii. 15. 35. *Mark* ix. 43. 45. 47. Gr.)· (*Note, Is.* xxx. 88.)

V. 23, 24. Attention to expensive externals was often used by Jews of old, as well as by papists and others, in later ages, as a compensation or dispensation· for injustice ; and this the selfish priests encouraged, as it tended to their profit. But if any one of Christ's disciples, should bring an oblation to the altar of God ; and, even after he arrived there, should recollect that his brother had any just cause of complaint against him ; he must not presume to offer his sacrifice, till he had gone, without delay, and made restitution for the injury done, or acknowledgement of the offence committed ; and, by all proper means and reasonable concessions, sought forgiveness and reconciliation. Nor must he, on this account, omit or long postpone his intended sacrifice ; but leave it before the altar, and return as soon as this previous matter was settled, and then offer it in confidence of acceptance with God. This is spoken of, in the language of the dispensation then in force : but it is equally applicable to Christian ordinances, especially to the Lord's supper. Restitution to the injured, (where practicable,) and concessions to those whom we have offended, as well as forgiveness of injuries, are requisite preparatives to the profitable and comfortable attendance on that sacred ordinance : but to neglect attendance for want of this preparation, is excusing disobedience to God, by injustice and malice towards man. The rule is, " First be reconciled to thy brother, and then come and " offer thy gift."

Be reconciled. (24) Διαλλαγηδι. Used here only in N. T.—1 *Sam.* xxix. 4. *Sept.* (Εx δια et αλλασσω.)

ꜰ 2

25 Agree ᵗ with thine adversary quickly, ᵘ whiles thou art in the way with him; lest at any time the adversary deliver thee to the judge, ˣ and the judge deliver thee to the officer, and thou be cast into prison. 26 Verily I say unto thee, ʸ Thou shalt by no means come out thence, till thou hast paid the uttermost farthing.

27 ¶ Ye have heard that it was said by them of old time, ᶻ Thou shalt not commit adultery: 28 But ᵃ I say unto you, ᵇ That whosoever looketh on a woman to lust after her, ᶜ hath committed adultery with her already in his heart.

29 And ᵈ if thy right eye * offend thee, ᵉ pluck it out, and cast it from thee: ᶠ for it is profitable for thee that one of thy members should perish, and not that thy whole body should be cast into hell.

30 And if thy right hand ᵍ offend thee, cut it off, and cast it from thee: for it is profitable for thee that one of thy members should perish, and not that thy whole body should be ʰ cast into hell.

V. 25, 26. The rule of the preceding verses naturally introduced the case of those, who were exposed to lawsuits, as having injured their neighbours. In such circumstances, it would be a man's prudence and duty, quickly to compromise the matter with his legal opponent, though the terms might appear rigorous, and to settle the business ere it came before the magistrate; lest, being found culpable, he should be cast into prison for costs and damages, and continue there till the last farthing were paid.—But under this prudential counsel, a far more important instruction is couched. Our injurious conduct towards men, (as well as our other sins,) renders us liable to the wrath of God, who is our Adversary at law. We are on the way to his judgment-seat; our time may be short; a way of reconciliation is revealed; and we should avail ourselves of it immediately. If this be neglected, the cause will come to a trial, the sinner will be condemned by the Judge, delivered to the executioners of vengeance, and cast into the prison of hell: and, seeing that he can never make satisfaction to offended justice, or pay all his debt, (especially as new crimes will continually enhance the score,) so he must not expect to be enlarged any more for ever.—' Here ' it is insinuated, how much more it concerns us in time to ' repent of our offences against God, and to endeavour to be ' reconciled unto him, lest we be cast into the infernal ' prison.' *Whitby.* (*Note, Luke* xii. 58, 59.)—*Agree.* (25) Ισθι ευνοων *Be disposed to be friendly.* ' Be desirous of ' agreement.' Eυ and νυς *the mind.*—*Adversary.*] Αντιδικω, properly, *an opponent in a trial at law. Luke* xviii. 3. 1 *Pet.* v. 8. (Ex αντι et δικη, *judicium.*)

V. 27, 28. The Pharisees interpreted the seventh commandment, merely as a prohibition of actual adultery with a married woman: but Christ shewed, that its spiritual import reached to the thoughts and desires of the heart. For instance, if a man should allow himself to gaze at a woman, *in order* that thoughts of a criminal intercourse might be excited, or till they were; he would be deemed an adulterer in his heart, and deserve the punishment denounced against adulterers: and his guilt would be still more aggravated, if he indulged the licentious imagination, and actually purposed or devised means for gratifying his desires; though he should by any means be prevented. We cannot suppose, that this prohibits a man from looking at a woman whom he may lawfully marry, with such a predilection as to desire to possess her in marriage. The inclination for that which is not sinful, can only become sinful by being inordinate; but it may be, and alas! commonly is, attended with such things as are greatly polluting and criminal. (*Note, Ex.* xx. 14.)—' The ' expositors of the law said, If a man sees a woman, whom ' he loves better than his wife; let him divorce his wife ' and marry her.' *Jerom.* This is a specimen of *Rabbinical* morality! (*Marg. Ref.*)—*To lust after.* (28) Επιθυμησαι. The word marks a *strong desire,* but it is used in a *good,* as well as a *bad* sense. (*Luke* xxii. 15. *Rom.* vii. 7. xiii. 9.)

V. 29, 30. This exact subjection of the sensual inclinations, this victory over the most potent desires of the heart, (especially when habit and constitution have concurred to enslave men,) must be attended with painful exertions, and the sacrifice of what has been highly valued. But, though it be as painful, and as sensible a loss, as " plucking out a right eye, or cutting off a right hand " would be, it must be done. " The flesh with the affec- " tions and lusts must be crucified," the strongest cor- " ruption conquered; and every appetite and inclination governed, in subjection to the authority of God, and in subserviency to his glory, the welfare of society, and the good of a man's own soul. If then the eye, or hand, or any other part of the body, could be so necessary an occasion of sin, that the temptation could by no other means be overcome, and that would certainly effect it; it would be a man's duty and wisdom to part with it, whatever anguish he endured, or how much soever the loss might be felt: as it would be advantageous for him to lose one of his limbs, or organs of sense, rather than be cast with them all into hell. But, though the members of the body are the instruments of sin, yet it proceeds from the lusts of the heart: if these be mortified, and every idolized object renounced, there will be no need to injure the body; and without this it would be of no use.—This mortification of sinful passions may be excessively painful; but if men consent to lose their limbs, by excruciating operations, to save their lives; what ought they to shrink from, when it becomes requisite to the salvation of their souls? It must be also added, that the most watchful and self-denying government of every sense and appetite, is implied in this admonition.—It is worthy of observation, that Jesus always took it for granted, that there is a future

31 It hath been said, ¹Whosoever shall put away his wife, let him give her a writing of divorcement:

32 But ᵏI say unto you, That ¹whosoever shall put away his wife, saving for the cause of fornication, causeth her to commit adultery: and whosoever shall marry her that is divorced, committeth adultery.

33 ¶ Again, ye have heard that it hath been said by them of old time, ᵐThou shalt not forswear thyself, but shalt perform unto the LORD thine oaths:

34 But I say unto you, ⁿSwear not at all; neither by °heaven, for it is God's throne;

35 Nor by ᵖthe earth, for it is his footstool; neither by Jerusalem, for it is ᵠthe city of the great King:

36 Neither ʳshalt thou swear by thy head, ˢbecause thou canst not make one hair white or black.

37 But ᵗlet your communication be,

Marginal references (left column):
i ᵛⁱᵘ.⁷. Deut. xxiv. Jer. iii. 1. Mark x. 2—4.
k 28. Luke ix. 30.
l xix. 8, 9. Mal. ii. 14—16. Mark x. 2—12. Luke xvi. 18. 1 Cor. vii. 4.
m Ex. xx. 7. Lev. xix. 12. Num. xxx. 2,&c. Deut. v. 11. Ps. l. 14. Isxvi. 11. Ec. v. 4—6. Nah. i. 15.

Marginal references (right column):
n Deut. xdii. 21 —23. Ec. ix. 2.
o Jam. v. 12. xciii. 22. Is. lvi. 16. Isvi. 1.
p Ps. xcix. 5.
q 2 Chr. vi. 6. Ps. xlviii. 2. lxxxvii. 2. Mal. i. 14. xliii. 16—21.
r xxiii. 16—21. 2b.
s vi. 27 Luke xii. 2b.
t 2 Cor. i. 17—20. Col. iv. 6. Jam. v. 12.

---

state, a resurrection of the body, and a hell into which the wicked will be cast: and that he continually realized these things to men's minds, and called their attention to them. (*Marg. Ref.* f—h.)—' The greatest part of Christ's 'auditors, were poor people who lived by their daily labour; 'and to these the loss of a right hand would be a much 'greater calamity than that of a right eye: so that there 'is a *gradation* and force in this passage, beyond what has 'generally been observed.' *Doddridge.* (*Notes,* Mark ix. 41—50.)

Offend.] Σκανδαλιζει, derived from σκανδαλον, a stumbling block, or a bridge in a trap.—The word literally signifies cause to stumble, in this and many other places in the New Testament. A stone is placed in the way, over which a man falls, and is lamed or killed; or a trap, in which he is taken: thus, whatever occasions sin is a stumbling stone, or a trap.—*Is profitable.*] Συμφερει, rendered *expedient*; 1 Cor. x. 23.

V. 31, 32. It has been shewn, (*Note, Deut.* xxiv. 1—4,) how the Jews mistook and perverted the *judicial* law, which permitted and regulated divorces, and was intended to render them less frequent and injurious: so that, when Christ appeared, they were exceedingly common upon the most frivolous pretences. Having therefore mentioned the seventh commandment, our Lord took the occasion to determine this matter by his authority: and he decláred that whosoever should "put away his wife," except for fornication committed before marriage, but concealed till afterwards, or for adultery after marriage, (for the general word is supposed to imply both,) would expose her to a strong temptation to commit adultery by marrying another man, and he would be accessary to her sin; and the man, who should marry her who was put away, would commit adultery, her former husband being still living.—It seems evident, that divorces for adultery, on either side, should be allowed to the injured party, if required, and without any tedious or expensive process. Some contend that the adulterous divorced person should not be allowed to marry again: this perhaps would be consistent with justice; yet it can scarcely be expected, that they who violate conjugal fidelity, will be very scrupulous in a single state; and therefore more harm than good would result from the regulation, which is not found in scripture. It may likewise be observed, that the allowance for divorcing the adulteress seems to imply, that the law for putting to death criminals of this class, was not to be considered as indispensable, under the New Testament. (*Notes,* xix. 3—12.)

Writing of divorcement. (31) Αποστασιον, properly di-

vorcement; but here used for βιβλιον αποστασια. xix. 7. *Mark* x. 4.—*Deut.* xxiv. 3. *Sept.* (Ab αφιραμαι discedo: whence αποστασια defectio, apostasy.) ' It is a biblical word, unknown 'to the Latin and Greek writers.' *Leigh.*

V. 33—37. The Scribes explained the third commandment, according to the tradition of the elders, as merely prohibiting gross perjury, especially the breach of promissory oaths, or vows to the Lord: and they allowed common swearing, except the names of God were expressly mentioned. (*Note, Ex.* xx. 7.) But Christ commanded his disciples not to swear at all. Many examples in the New Testament prove, that swearing on solemn and important occasions is not unlawful: (2 Cor. i. 23. 1 Thes. ii. 5:) and there seems no reason to conclude, that oaths in a court of justice, or on any other occasion which fairly requires them, are wrong; provided they be taken with reverence of the majesty, omniscience, and justice of God, and be exactly consistent with truth and equity. Yet the multiplication of oaths in our judicial, commercial, and ecclesiastical transactions, and the irreverent manner in which they are administered, occasion immense guilt; and are an enormous evil, even exceeding all calculation. (*P. O. Jer.* xxiii. 9—32.) A pious man, however, though he disapproves of the manner in which oaths are administered, needs not disquiet himself when called on to take them, if he can otherwise do it with a clear conscience; for he is only answerable for his own conduct. But all oaths taken without necessity, on trivial occasions, or in common conversation, must be inconsistent with this prohibition; as well as all the expressions, which are in common use, to answer the purpose, and, as it were, to evade the guilt, of an oath. The Jews, who scrupled to swear on such occasions by JEHOVAH, would swear by heaven, or by the earth, or by Jerusalem, or by their own heads. But all these oaths implied an appeal to God, because of their relation to him: "heaven is his throne," where he reveals his glory as the Ruler of the world; and the earth is, so to speak, "the footstool" of that throne; Jerusalem was "the holy city," where the temple, the earthly palace of the great King, was erected: even the heads of the persons concerned were more the Lord's than their own: for, while the continuance of life, understanding, and senses depended on him; they themselves could not change the colour of one single hair by their own exertion.—The whole creation is the Lord's, and therefore to swear by any part of it, implies an appeal to the great Creator and Judge. Thus when men swear by their lives, their souls, their faith, or by all that's good, they

xlii. 19. xv. 19. John viii. 44. Eph iv. 25. Col. iii. 9. x Ex. xxi. 22—27. Lev xxiv. 19, 20. Deut. xix. 19. y Lev. xix. 18. 1 Sam. xxiv. 10 —15. xxvi. 8—11. 34. xxvii. 8—10. Job xxxi.29—31. Prov.xx.22 xxiv. 29 Rom. xii. 17. 29. l Thes. v. 15. Heb. xii. 4. Jam. v. 6. 1 Pet. iii. 9. a 1 Kings xxii. 24. Job xvi. 10. Is. b. 6. Lam. iii. 30. Mic. v. 1. Luke vi. 29. xxii. 64. 1 Pet. ii. 20—23.

Yea, yea; Nay, nay: for whatsoever is more than these ᵘ cometh of evil.

38 ¶ Ye have heard that it hath been said, ˣ An eye for an eye, and a tooth for a tooth:

39 But I say unto you, ʸ That ye resist not evil: but ᶻ whosoever shall smite thee on thy right cheek, turn to him the other also.

a Luke vi. 29 1 Cor. vi. 7. b xxvii. 32. Mark xv. 21. Luke xxiii. 26. c xxv Deut. xv. 7—14. Job xxxi. 16—20. Ps. xxxvii. 21. 25, 26. cxii. 5—9. Prov. iii. 9, 10. xix. 17. &c. Isai. lviii. 6—12. Dan. iv. 27. Luke vi. 30—38. xi. 41. xiv. 12—14. Rom. xii. 20. 2 Cor. ix. 6—15. 1 Tim. vi. 17—19. Heb. vi. 10. xiii. 16. Jam. i. 27. ii. 15, 16. 1 John iii. 16—18.

40 And ᵃ if any man will sue thee at the law, and take away thy coat, let him have thy cloke also.

41 And whosoever shall ᵇ compel thee to go a mile, go with him twain.

42 Give ᶜ to him that asketh thee, and from him that would borrow of thee turn not thou away.

---

virtually swear by the Lord, and appeal to him to confirm their testimony. Such expressions ought not to be used; much less should conversation be intermingled with the sacred names of God, Lord, or Christ, as mere expletives, or notes of admiration; or with bad wishes; or even good wishes or prayers, as ' God bless us,' ' Lord have mercy ' on us,' and such like; when there is no seriousness or solemnity upon the mind, and when they are words without meaning, but not without profaneness.—It is remarkable, that even the writings of the most admired Pagan authors are interlarded with oaths, by Jupiter, by Hercules, or others of their idols; and some professed Christians affect to use this Pagan language: but if an oath is a solemn act of worship, and if the devil was worshipped under these Pagan idols; such expressions imply an act of worship to Satan, though they who use them may mean no such thing. It ought to suffice a Christian, seriously and constantly to affirm or deny, and with decided repetition if necessary: all that is more than this, in ordinary cases and conversation, cometh of evil, of the evil one, or of the evil of our corrupt nature. Men are so deceitful, that they fear trusting each other without the security of oaths: they have suspicions of each other; or the speaker is of a suspicious character, and fears lest his bare word should not be taken; or he swears to conceal his bad designs. But Christians should endeavour so to speak and act, that their word may be deemed as satisfactory as another man's oath. Indeed, though the whole necessity for oaths arises from the selfishness and deceitfulness of man; yet the worse men become, the less they are restrained by them; and the better they are, the less need there is for them.— ' This clause contains a demonstration, that the thirty- ' fourth verse is to be explained with the limitation pro- ' posed: for it is evident that oaths were in some cases ' not only allowed, but required, by the Mosaick law. (Ex. ' xxii. 11. Lev. v. 1. Num. v. 19. 21. Deut. xxix. 12. 14.) ' So that, if Christ's prohibition had here referred to swear- ' ing in solemn and judicial cases, he would in these words ' have charged the divine law with establishing an immo- ' rality.' Doddridge.—The term rendered " communica- " tion," is (λογος) word, or discourse, and limits the pro- hibition to conversation and social intercourse : so that to extend it to judicial and publick transactions, is not warranted by the passage itself. (Note, Jam. v. 12.)

V. 38—42. (Ex. xxi. 24, 25. Lev. xxiv. 19, 20.) The law referred to was a judicial regulation, and the magistrate's rule in deciding causes; declaring the utmost punishment which he might inflict, when nothing less would satisfy the offended party: yet the Scribes explained it, as if it had authorized private revenge, and had even

required people to demand or exact this severe retaliation. But Christ declared, that the moral law required the reverse of this vindictive spirit and conduct. His disciples are not allowed to " resist evil," or the injurious party, either by violent opposition, or litigious law-suits.—In the present state of human nature, there is little need to enumerate exceptions and limitations to such general rules : self-love will suffice, and more than suffice. The preservation of life, or liberty, or important property, authorize, and in many cases require, a man to stand in his own defence, at the peril of the illegal assailant: but in ordinary cases, it is better to give way, and yield to insults and injuries, than to repel them by force, or legal process; and it does not accord with the spirit of Christianity, to put the life and soul of man in competition with a sum of money, however great, when there is no reason to fear further violence. In smaller matters, however, the case is quite clear. If a man give a disciple of Christ a contemptuous or painful blow on the cheek; it is his duty and wisdom to imitate his Master, and take it patiently: nay, rather to turn the other, and expose himself to further insult, than to begin a contest, by returning the blow, sending a challenge, or commencing a law-suit; even though he should be ridiculed and despised for his want of spirit and courage, through his obedience to his Lord. If a man be sued at law, and injuriously deprived of his coat, or outer garment, which, though of small value, he could ill spare; he had better suffer himself to be defrauded of his cloke also, than be involved in the temptations and evils of seeking legal redress. (Notes, 1 Cor. vi. 1—8.) Indeed, in cases of great importance, other duties may require a man to avail himself of the protection of the law: justice to his creditors, and to the publick, and even to his family, may engage him to defend his estate, and to give a check to the exorbitancy of unreasonable men ; and a Christian may prosecute a criminal, out of love to publick justice, though not from private revenge. Yet, there are generally men of the world enough to deal with such depredators; and a disciple of Christ seldom has occasion to waste his time, or embarrass the loss of his temper, about them.—Under various pretences also, unreasonable men may require Christ's disciples to attend them about business, publick or private, but if they should insist upon a man's going a mile out of his way to serve them, it would be better to go two than quarrel about it: and it would be expedient rather to give or lend, to those who injuriously required it, than to refuse with harshness or apparent selfishness: and much more to give, or to lend, where there is need, and a prospect of doing good.—It is self-evident, that many and great

F 5

43 ¶ Ye have heard that it hath been said, "Thou shalt love thy neighbour, " and hate thine enemy: 44 But I say unto you, 'Love your enemies, bless them that curse you, do good to them that hate you, and pray for them which despitefully use you, and persecute you; 45 That ᵉ ye may be the children of your Father which is in heaven: ʰ for

he maketh his sun to rise on the evil and on the good, and sendeth rain on the just and on the unjust. 46 For 'if ye love them which love you, what reward have ye? do not even the ᵏ publicans the same? 47 And if ye 'salute your brethren only, ᵐ what do ye more *than others?* do not even the publicans so? 48 Be ⁿ ye therefore perfect, ° even as your Father which is in heaven is perfect.

---

limitations and exceptions must be admitted in the last instance: for no man could go on giving and lending to every one, who should ask him; but he must consider his own ability and the nature of the case, and act accordingly: and therefore, we must suppose that limitations and exceptions are implied in the other admonitions, which must be judged of, according to the general law of " loving our neighbour as ourselves." The grand and obvious instruction is this, ' Suffer any injury for the sake of peace, when no duty requires the contrary; and commit your interests and concerns to the Lord's keeping.'—The case of those, who were compelled by authority, to accompany and convey the baggage of travellers, sustaining a publick character, is supposed to be meant in the forty-first verse. Even if the case were oppressive, yet the person compelled were legally exempted, compliance would be preferable to a contest.

Smite thee, &c. (39) 'Ραπισει. xxvi. 67. Whence ραπισμα. John xviii. 22. xix. 3. Der. from ραπις, a rod or staff, but which also means a slipper, with which contumelious blows were sometimes given.—Compel. (41) Αγγαρευσει. xxvii. 32. Mark xv. 21. The word is originally Persian. Angari. were post-masters, who might take men's cattle, or them selves, at pleasure, for the publick service.

V. 43—48. The Scribes explained the great law of loving our neighbours, with restriction to their own nation, sect, family, or friends; nay, they added, (in the form of a precept,) " and hate thine enemy:" and it is remarkable, that the best heathen moralists made large concessions, in this matter, to the malignity of the human heart. But the true spirit and intent of the law reaches to enemies and persecutors, on which the example of Christ himself forms the best comment. (Notes, Luke x. 25—37.) He therefore authoritatively commanded his disciples to " love their ene- " mies," to regard them with compassion and benevolence; to return good words and kind wishes to their revilings and imprecations, and beneficent actions to their injuries; and to pray for their conversion and best good, even when oppressed, persecuted, and tortured by them. Thus they would evidence themselves to be the children of God, by bearing his image and copying his example; for he sends the ordinary blessings of providence upon the evil, as well as on the good, though their crimes are direct enmity and rebellion against him. As, however, there are various favours, which he bestows only on his people; so our peculiar friendship, kindness, and complacency, may and ought to be restricted to the righteous: yea, gratitude to benefactors, and predilection for special friends, consist very well with this general good-will and good conduct

towards enemies and persecutors.—Even publicans, and the most ungodly men, knew how to behave, with civil respect and kindness, to their friends and relations: but Christians, considering their superior knowledge, obligations, encouragements, assistances, and motives, must do " more than others:" else what has grace done for them? What evidence have they of conversion? What recompence can they expect from their Lord, for that of which wicked men are capable? They cannot indeed attain to perfection, but it is their duty to aim at it: the *perfect* law is their rule and standard; the *perfect* holiness and love of God, their pattern; they should aim high, and seek to be " perfect, even as their Father which is in " heaven is perfect." These concluding verses evidently prove, that our Lord's spiritual exposition of the law was intended, both to shew the people their need of mercy and salvation, and also to teach his disciples the strict rule of duty: and all that, in which they come short of it, or deviate from it, is sin, and needs deep repentance, continual forgiveness through his blood, and grace to enable them for more exact obedience.—The publicans ' had the over- ' sight of tributes and customs: a kind of men, that the ' Jews hated to death; both because they served the Ro- ' mans in those offices, (whose yokeful bondage they could ' hardly away withal;) and also because these toll-masters ' were for the most part given to covetousness.' Beza.— ' These words, "Thou shalt hate thine enemy," are not ' found in the law of Moses; though nothing is more ' common in the Jewish canons; ... which affords a strong ' argument, that Christ here is not correcting, or adding to ' the moral precepts of the law; but opposing the corrupt ' interpretations of the Scribes and Pharisees. ... A neigh- ' bour is every one, with whom we have any dealing: ... ' so the word must signify in the tenth commandment, if ' we do not leave the Israelite free to covet the wife of his ' Gentile.' Whitby.

Despitefully use. (44) Επηρεαζοντων. Luke vi. 28. 1 Pet. iii. 16. Der. perhaps from Αρης, Mars, the heathen god of war. It signifies primarily to assault in a hostile manner; but is used for calumniating; which is making a hostile assault on a person's character. " The scourge of the " tongue."—" Swords are in their lips."

PRACTICAL OBSERVATIONS.

V. 1—12.

The great end of preaching is, that men may hear and be made wise unto salvation. When multitudes willingly attend, it is seasonable for the minister to preach, and time and place are not very material circumstances: a church

F 6

prayer, 5—8. The Lord's prayer, 9—13. Those who
seek forgiveness must forgive, 14, 15. Cautions and
rules about fasting, 16—18. Treasure to be laid up

or chapel is most convenient, and the Lord's day the most favourable time; but a mountain or a field will be a holy place. or any day holy, if the Lord vouchsafe his presence and blessing. The preaching of the gospel was shewn to be a most honourable employment, by our Lord's own condescending example: and happy are they, who enter upon it at his call, act in it from the same principles, and preach the same doctrines, as he did. But it behoves us to speak with great seriousness, and a deep sense of the weight and difficulty of the work; and in a simple dependence on the Lord, for assistance, acceptance, and a blessing.—The true gospel is exceedingly *practical*, far more so than any other doctrine whatever; and numbers so mistake in this matter, that they would certainly condemn Christ himself as *legal*, if they could hear his sermons, without knowing who the preacher was.—True religion is so inseparably connected with happiness, that none can be happy without it, in this world or in the next; or fail of happiness, if they duly attend to it. But how different are the character and circumstances of the b'essed, as stated by our Lord, from what the carnal mind would have imagined! None, who have not faith and experience, will be persuaded, that " the " poor in spirit," the mourners, the meek, those who long earnestly for righteousness, the merciful, the pure in heart, the peacemakers, and the persecuted, are the only happy persons in the world. Let us learn to consider this as a compendious description of a healthy constitution of mind, and a safe and happy condition in life; and to consider the opposite dispositions and passions, as distempers, spoiling all true enjoyment, and by no means counterbalanced by the friendship of the world. Let us not suppose, that some men possess one, some another, of these holy dispositions; but remember, that they all combine to form the image of Christ, and the temper of a true Christian; and that where any one is absolutely wanting, all the rest are mere counterfeits. Let us also examine, whether we ourselves do actually possess these Christian graces: let us seek them, and the increase of them, from the Giver of every good gift: let us take the annexed promises as encouragements to aspire after higher attainments; assured of proportionate happiness, as the subjects and heirs of the kingdom of heaven, and as the children of God, till we shall be admitted into " his presence, where is fulness of joy, and " pleasures at his right hand for evermore." Let us never envy the ambitious, the high-spirited, the gay, the injurious, or vindictive, the avaricious, the sensual, or the unmerciful; the scourges of the earth who take away peace from it, or any other of the sons of madness and mischief: let us not covet their transient applause and prosperity in this evil world: let us not be disquieted with the contempt, reviling, and persecution, which we meet with, whilst we do all the good that we can to all, and no evil to any. Happy will it be for us to suffer for Christ's sake, and in that cause for which he shed his precious blood; for "great " will be our reward in heaven." But let us be careful to give no just cause to the revilings of the ungodly, and to avoid all ostentation or bitterness under the cross: let us consider what prophets and apostles endured, and how they

behaved under their trials; and especially let us " look " unto Jesus, lest we be weary and faint in our minds," and yield to impatience and recriminations under our lighter trials. (*Notes, Heb.* xii. 1—3.)

V. 13—16.

We ought most carefully and frequently to consider the vast importance of the Christian character; recollecting that we are " the salt of the earth, and the light of the " world:" many eyes will be upon us; many will derive good or harm from their observations on our conduct. We should then endeavour to stem the torrent of impiety and wickedness, to diffuse the savour and light of divine truth, and " to adorn the doctrine of God our Saviour;" " letting our light shine before men," that our good works, as living sermons, may convince our fellow sinners of the excellency of religion, and so conduce to the glory of God and the benefit of mankind. On this account also, the Christian must by no means conceal his sentiments: for God does not enlighten the minds of his people, that they should put the light under a bushel, but that they should hold it forth for the benefit of others. Nor are they required, or even allowed, to retire into cloisters or deserts, or any secret recesses, or to bury themselves in obscurity; but to fill up their stations in families, in society, and in the church, so as to glorify God in the sight of men. We should therefore seek to shine, by professing and adorning the gospel, in our circle, whether large or small, that we may answer the end, for which God has " called us out of darkness into his marvellous light." (*Note*, 1 *Pet.* ii. 9, 10.)

V. 17—20.

Let no man perversely suppose, that Christ allows his people to trifle with any command of God. While he fulfilled the types and prophecies of the Old Testament;— while he honoured the moral law and the exhortations of the prophets, by his obedience to death upon the cross;— how impious must it be to suppose, that he purchased for men the licence of indulging their lusts with impunity! No; till the consummation of all things, " not one word " shall pass from the law, till all be fulfilled." No sinner partakes of Christ's justifying righteousness, till he condemns himself as a transgressor of the law, and repents of his evil deeds; and the goodness and mercy, revealed in the gospel, lead the believer to still deeper repentance and self-abhorrence. All unbelievers will be condemned for their transgressions of this law; but it is the Christian's rule of duty, nay, it is written in his heart, and he delights in it, and longs to obey it. Let us then equally beware of antinomian licentiousness, and of pharisaical self-righteousness: these are Scylla and Charybdis, the fatal rock and whirlpool; and we need " the Lord the Spirit " to pilot us between them. But the clear and full exposition of the holy law of God, and the scriptural application of it to the heart and conscience, form the best preservative from these fatal extremes. They, indeed, who inculcate more soothing doctrines, will best please those who say, " Speak

F 7

in heaven, 19—21. The single eye, 21—23. God and Mammon cannot both be served, 24. Solicitude about worldly things, being vain, needless, and inju-

rious, should be shunned; and " the kingdom of God " and his righteousness " sought in the first place, 25 —34.

" smooth things ; " but they are certainly the least of those that belong to the kingdom, if indeed they at all belong to it : while those who enforce obedience, by example and doctrine, " shall be called great in the kingdom of God ; " nor will any man enter heaven, who has not in this world become more holy in heart and life, than Scribes and Pharisees ever were.

V. 21—32.

We ought most attentively and reverently to consider, how important the Lord Jesus judged the right understanding of the moral law; and how fatal consequences followed from superficial or erroneous views of it. While we, therefore, view the strictness, spirituality, and reasonableness of its precepts, as expounded by our divine Teacher; let us impartially compare our past and present lives, our tempers, affections, thoughts, words, and actions, with this perfect rule: then we shall find every self-confident hope expire, and plainly perceive, that " by the works " of the law no flesh shall be justified in the sight of God: " and then Christ and his salvation will become precious to our souls. Whether we look to our conduct towards those who have injured us, or towards those whom we have offended ; towards our superiors or inferiors, relatives, friends, or servants; the state of our heart, or the government of our passions; to what we have done, or what we have not; we shall see great cause for humiliation, and need of forgiveness : and when we consider that we must be made holy according to this standard, in order to the enjoyment of God and heaven; we shall as evidently perceive our need of the powerful influences of the Holy Spirit, and learn to value the ordinances of God, through which his sacred assistance is obtained.—Thus it will also appear most evident, that strict justice to men, as well as humiliation before God, is indispensably necessary, to our acceptably approaching the throne of grace, or the Lord's table: and we shall frequently be led to examine, whether any of our brethren have just cause of complaint against us, that we may remove every impediment to our comfortable communion with our heavenly Father.—When we further weigh, with serious attention, the importance of eternity, and the shortness and uncertainty of our lives; we shall perceive the propriety and necessity of making our peace with God without delay, and shall learn to value and imitate our blessed Peace-maker, who will shortly appear, as the Judge and Avenger of all the impenitent workers of iniquity. Mature reflection on our situation in this world, will reconcile us to that self-denying and painful mortification of our evil propensities, and strict government even of all the bodily appetites, to which we are indispensably called : we shall see that mercy couched under the apparent harshness of the requirement; that our safety, advantage, and felicity, are consulted ; and that the grace and consolations of the Spirit will render it practicable and even comfortable. And, would we be preserved from gross iniquities, our hearts must be kept with all diligence, and our eyes, and all our senses and faculties, forbidden to rove after those things which lead to transgressions : and the strictest rules of purity and self-denial will be found,

by experience, the most conducive to true and solid comfort even while in this present world.

V. 33—42.

How excellent are all the commandments of God ! Yet how spiritual and extensive! Who can deny, that such a union of reverence towards the glorious God, and inviolable veracity and integrity towards men, as our Lord's prohibition of swearing, and his rule for our intercourse with each other, imply, is most reasonable and valuable ? Indeed all the commands, which require the exact government of the tongue, with meekness, patient endurance of injuries, love of enemies, yielding to the injurious, and doing good to our persecutors, though contrary to corrupt nature and the maxims of an evil world, have an evident excellency in them ; and are calculated to form a character of real dignity, and bearing a great resemblance to the divine purity, patience, beneficence, and mercy : and doubtless they, who act according to these rules, will both have most peace and comfort themselves, and be the greatest blessings to their families, neighbours, and the community. Were these precepts universally obeyed, the greatest part of the evils in the world would be annihilated : wars, murders, lawsuits, domestic discords, frauds, oppressions would cease : unavoidable evils would be mitigated, and rendered more as it were, descend from heaven to dwell on earth, and drive their hateful opposites down to hell, from whence they came. Thus it would be, if all men were Christians, and well understood and practised their holy religion. (*Note, Rev. xx. 4—6.*)

V. 43—48.

Our motives, encouragements, and manifold advantages, suffice for considerable attainments in all things. More may be expected from those, who are " redeemed by God " by the blood of Christ," than from other men ; more will be found in them, notwithstanding inward and outward impediments; and whenever they suffer themselves to be outdone, or even equalled, in what is outwardly good and commendable, by such as are strangers or enemies to the gospel, they forget their principles and degrade their character. Let us all then beg of God to enable us to prove ourselves his children, by copying his example of goodness and mercy, even to the vile and injurious ; not " being overcome of evil, but overcoming evil with good: " let us learn to reverence an oath, as well as to pay the Lord our vows : let us aim to establish such a reputation for truth and integrity, that we may be readily believed, when " our communication is yea, yea, nay, nay; " that we may not be tempted to any of that language which savours of evil. In short, let us be " followers of God, " as dear children, and walk in love, even as Christ loved " us, and gave himself a sacrifice " for our sins : and, following after higher degrees of holiness, let us expect, as our gracious and glorious reward, to be at length made " perfect, even as our Father who is in heaven is per- " fect."

TAKE [a] heed that ye do not your [b] alms before men, [c] to be seen of them; [d] otherwise ye have no reward [e] of [f] your Father which is in heaven.

2 Therefore [g] when thou doest *thine* alms, [h] do not sound a trumpet before thee, [i] as the hypocrites do, [k] in the synagogues and in the streets, that they may have [l] glory of men. [m] Verily I say unto you, They have their reward.

3 But when thou doest alms, [n] let not thy left hand know what thy right hand doeth;

4 That thine alms may be in secret:

NOTES.

Chap. VI. V. 1—4. The religion of the Pharisees was distinguished from that of Christ, by its *motives*, as much as by its *rule*. Our Lord therefore next proceeded to warn his disciples against hypocrisy and ostentation, in external duties. He began by admonishing them, not to perform " their *righteousness*," (*marg.*) or good works, " to be seen of men." Thus some ancient copies and approved versions read it, as a general word, including the several particulars which follow. Christians should " let " their light so shine before men, that others may see their " good works, and glorify their Father;" yet they ought not to do their works, in order " to be seen of men." Their general conduct should be so exemplary, as to constrain others to see an excellency in their religion: but every action should spring from humility, the fear and love of God, and regard to his acceptance and glory; and not from a desire of being noticed and commended. (*Notes*, v. 14—16. xxiii. 5—7.) This our Lord illustrated, by mentioning some of those religious services, in which hypocrites are most tempted to ostentation and vain glory; and in which Christians should most consult secrecy, as far as it is consistent with other duties. He therefore instructed his disciples, that when they gave alms, or contributed to charitable or pious purposes, they should shun notoriety as much as possible. The hypocrites, of that time, bestowed as much pains to publish their liberality, in the synagogues, publick assemblies, and even streets, as if they had caused it to be made known by sound of trumpet; for they sought, as their primary object, the applause of men, and to be accounted excellent persons. Not but that they made a merit before God of their services, and expected them to compensate for their sins, and purchase heaven: but, had not the praise of men been principally aimed at, they would not have been so earnest in proclaiming their liberality; and therefore this praise would prove their sole reward. But the disciple of Jesus must " not let his left hand know what his right hand " doeth:" he should act as secretly as the case will admit, and not think of it himself, or indulge self-complacency; he must not desire that his charity should be known, or spoken of; but rather that it should be concealed, that he may be satisfied of having acted out of regard to the will and favour of his heavenly " Father who seeth in secret," and not from desire of worldly applause: and in this case, his Father, seeing both the action and motive to be good, will graciously accept and publickly recompense them, especially at the day of judgment.—Circumstances vary, and require variations in our outward conduct; there are

VOL. V.

many charities, which can scarcely be promoted, without some degree of publick notoriety; and frequently a leading person may be called to excite those who are backward, by a useful example. Yet no duty is more liable to be made an occasion for vain glory than this : and many designs, very beneficial to others, are supported by a liberality, which almost entirely springs from this corrupt principle. The heart is deceitful : and when men *love* to have their names inserted among the subscribers to publick charities, but are not equally liberal in private ; when they *love* to speak and hear of their own beneficence, and are not willing to do much without the credit of it ; it is too plain how the case stands with them.—In general, private charities, if not more useful, are more unequivocal : and the less reward we receive from man, the more we may expect from our gracious God ; provided we act from evangelical principles.—Our Lord here takes it for granted, that his disciples will give alms, more or less, according to their ability ; and that every good work done from proper motives will be rewarded by our God and Father. (*Notes*, x. 40—42. *Heb.* vi. 9, 10.)

To be seen. (1) Θεαθηναι. *To behold with fixed attention.* 'To be looked at, or seen, with peculiar attention, or ad- ' miration.' *Beza.* (*John* i. 14. 1 *John* i. 1.) From this verb, the word Θεατρον, *a spectacle, a theatre,* is derived. (1 *Cor.* iv. 9.) Θεαομαι is a theatrical word.—*Alms.* (2) Ελεημοσυνην. Der. from ελεεω to *pity*, (See on v. 7,) and that from ελεος, *mercy.* The word implies the genuine motive, as well as the direct act of giving to the poor and afflicted. (*Luke* xi. 41. *Acts* iii. 2, 3. x. 2—4. xxiv. 17.)—*Sound a trumpet.* Σαλπισης. 1 *Cor.* xv. 52. (From σαλπιγξ. *A trumpet.* 1 *Cor.* xiv. 8. xv. 52.) 'It not being apparent from any ' of their writings, that it was customary with the Jews to ' " sound a trumpet" when they distributed their alms : ' this seems only a proverbial expression, for making a thing ' known or publick, as both Jews and Gentiles were used ' to do by sound of trumpet ; ... using it in their triumphs, ' and before they began to act their tragedies.' *Whitby.* The spectators of theatrical exhibitions of every kind, were commouly called together by sound of trumpet.—*Hypocrites.*] Υποκριται. (From υπο and κρινω to *judge.*) *Stage-players.* —' Men who carry themselves with other faces than their ' own, as these do on the stage.' *Leigh.* The word is derived from the profession of actors on a stage, who *personate* characters, which do not belong to them, and which, when the *publick* exhibition is over, they cease to assume, among those who know them in *private* life. This they do, in order to obtain profit and honour ; and hypocrites in religion assume in publick a false character, for similar purposes.

G

l 6. 18. Ps. xvii. 3. xix. 21. Luke xix. l—3. 12. Jer. xvii. 10. xxiii. 24. Heb. iv. 13. Rev. ii. 23. — m x. 42. xxv. 34—40. 1 Sam. ii. 30. Luke xiv. 14. 1 Cor. iv. 5. Jude 24. — n vii. 7. 8. ix. 38. xxi. 22. Ps. v. 2. lv. 17. Prov. xv. 8. Is. liv. 6. 7. Jer. xxix. 12. Dan. vi. 10. ix. 4 &c. Luke xviii. 1. John xvi. 24. Eph. vi. 18. Col. iv. 2. 3. 1 Thes. v. 17. Jam. v. 15. 16. — o 2. xviii. 14. Job xxvii. 8—10. Is. i. 15. Luke xviii. 10, 11. xx. 47. p xxiii. 6. Mark xii. 38. Luke xi. 43. q 2. Luke xiv. 12—14. r xiv. 23. xxvi. 36—39. Gen. xxxii. 24—29. 2 Kings iv. 33. Is. xxvi. 20. John i. 48. Acts iv. 40. ix. 9. 30.

and thy Father which ¹ seeth in secret himself shall ᵐ reward thee openly.

5 ¶ And ⁿ when thou prayest, ᵒ thou shalt not be as the hypocrites *are:* ᵖ for they love to pray standing in the synagogues, and in the corners of the streets, that they may be seen of men. ᵠ Verily I say unto you, They have their reward.

6 But thou, when thou prayest, ʳ enter into thy closet, and when thou

s John xx. 17 Rom. viii. Eph. iii. 14. — t 1 Kings xviii. 26—29. Ec. v. 2, 3. 7. Acts xix. 34. — u xxvi. 39. 42. 44. —54. Dan. ix. 18, 19. — x 22. xviii. 17. — y 32. Ps. xxxviii. 9. lxix. 17—19. Luke xii. 30. Phil. iv. 6.

hast shut thy door, ˢ pray to thy Father which is in secret; and thy Father ᵗ which seeth in secret shall reward thee openly.

7 But when ye pray, ᵘ use not vain ᵗ repetitions, as ˣ the heathen *do:* for they think that they shall be heard for their much speaking.

8 Be not ye therefore like unto them; for ʸ your Father knoweth what things ye have need of before ye ask him.

V. 5. The hypocrites, in our Lord's days, were very ostentatious in their devotions. Not contented with frequenting the synagogues, to join in publick worship, they resorted thither to offer those prayers which ought to have been made in secret; and they stood and prayed in the view and hearing of all the people: nay, it seems, that they stopped in the corners of the streets, or where two ways met, to perform their devotions; professing, perhaps, that it was the stated time, and they must not on any account omit or postpone the duty. They however contrived this, on purpose " to be seen of men," that all might know how devout they were, and applaud and confide in them accordingly. This reputation indeed many of them acquired, and reaped the benefit of it; (*Note,* xxiii. 14;) but they must expect no other reward.

Verily.] Αμην from ןמא, which in Niphal signifies, *to be firm, certain, true, worthy of credit.* Among other derivatives from this root is ןמא, as it occurs in many places of the Old Testament, and is generally retained in our Translation. (*Num.* v. 22. *Deut.* xxvii. 15, &c. *Jer.* xxviii. 6.)—In one place, (*Is.* lxv. 16,) it is rendered as a substantive : " He that blesseth himself " in the earth, shall bless himself in the God of truth; " and he that sweareth in the earth, shall swear by the " God of truth (ןמא יהלאב) :" or *the true God:* τον Θεον τον αληθινον. Sept. The apostle uses the word remarkably when he says, " All the promises of God in him are yea, " and in him amen." 2 *Cor.* i. 20. (εν αυτω το ναι, και εν αυτω το αμην. See *Rev.* i. 7. *Gr.*)—Our Lord assumes it as his own title or name, *Rev.* iii. 14: " These things saith the " Amen, the true and faithful Witness." (Ταδε λεγει Ο Αμην, κ. τ. λ. not το Αμην, as in the words of the apostle. —' But it very often passes into a particle, which, being ' placed at the beginning of a sentence is the language of ' one *asserting, confirming,* and thus even *swearing:* and it ' means, *truly, certainly, verily, undoubtedly.* The doubled ' Αμην, which has the place of a superlative, and more ' stengthens the asseveration, *most truly, most certainly,* ' occurs very frequently in the gospel of John.' *Schleusner.* Αμην ' is the same with αληθως, as appears by comparing ' *Luke* ix. 27, with *Matt.* xvi. 28, and *Mark* ix. 1.' *Leigh.* Christ alone used the word " Verily " in *this manner.* (v. 18. 26. viii. 10, &c.) It is an exceedingly strong affirmation, especially when doubled, and is never thus employed, except to confirm matters of great importance, which men are backward to believe; *John* i. 52, iii. 3. 5. 11. v. 19. 24, 25. vi. 26. 32. 47. 53, &c. and perhaps not very different

from the expression in the Old Testament, " As I live, " saith the LORD."

V. 6. The Christian, when he prays alone, (for *private* and *social* worship,) is to be distinguished from *publick* and *social* worship,) is to be retired as possible : he should go into his closet, or chamber, or any secret place, and shut the door, that he may not be overheard or disturbed; and there pour out his heart before God, as into the bosom of his loving Father; only desiring to be noticed and accepted by him, who seeth the secret recesses of the heart, as well as the most retired corner of the house. Such prayer God will accept, answer, and reward : yea, it shall be openly declared before men and angels, as an evidence of a man's humility, faith, and unfeigned piety; and graciously recompensed accordingly.—Here, likewise, circumstances may demand a different conduct : Daniel saw it right to be very open in his devotions, as not afraid or ashamed, in most perilous times, of being known to pray to his God; and in some cases this exposes a man to contempt and the cross, which it may be his duty to bear for the Lord's sake. They who are constant in private devotions, cannot entirely conceal it from their families; and generally they should not studiously desire to do it.—A field, a garden, or a mountain, may be as retired as a closet; they are consecrated by Christ's own conduct; and wherever the heart can be lifted up to God, without men's observing it, the Christian may properly offer his prayers; though in the most publick concourse of cities, camps, or courts. (*Note, Neh.* ii. 4.)

V. 7, 8. It is evident, that this rule is not transgressed, by using repetitions from the fulness of the heart; when, earnestly craving some special mercy, men know not how to give over, or to proceed to another subject. (*Note,* 2 *Cor.* xii. 7—10.) These are not " vain repetitions," but like those which Christ himself made in the garden; and both he and his most eminent servants have undoubtedly used many repetitions. (*Marg. Ref.* u.) But such repetitions are meant, as Baal's priests used during several hours, for which Elijah even derided them. (*Notes,* 1 *Kings* xviii. 26—29.) These were common among the Pagans, as learned men have clearly shewn : and the church of Rome has imitated them, in their numerous Pater-nosters and Ave-Marias, which the people are taught to use, without either meaning or devotion; and which they number, in performing their penance or task, by counting strings of beads.—But many others are, in a measure, faulty in the same way, in private and social worship; both of those

^{r Luke xi. 1, 2.} 9 After *this manner therefore* in heaven, *Hallowed be thy name.*
a I. 6. 14, 15. v. pray ye: *Our Father* *which* art
16. 45. 48. vii.
11. x. 2v. xxvii.
2v. 39. 42. 1s. lxiii. 16. lxiv. 8. Luke xv. 18, 19. 21. John xx. 17. Rom. i. 7. viii. 15.
Gal. i. 1. iv. 6. 1 Pet. i. 17. b xviii. 9. 2 Chr. xx. 6. Ps. cxv. 3. 1s. lvii. 15. lxvi. 1.

in heaven, *Hallowed be thy name.* ^{c Lev. x. 3. 2 Sam.} vii. 26. 1 Kings
viii. 43. 1 Chr. xvii. 24. Neh. iv. 5. Ps. lxxii. 18, 19. cxi. 20.—22. cxiii. 2, 3. 1s. vi. 3. xxxvii. 20. Ez. xxxvi. 23. xxxvii. 28. Hab. ii. 14 Zech. xiv. 9. Mal. i. 11. 14. Luke ii. 14. xi. 2. 1 Tim. vi. 16. Rev. iv. 11. v. 12—14.

---

who use forms, and of those who pray extempore. It is not uncommon for men to employ the most words, when they have the least meaning; and to spend the time in vain repetitions, even when the affections, and perhaps the very thoughts, are otherwise employed. This is an imitation of the heathen, who thought to excite their deities to help them, by the multiplicity of their words. But Christians should have more honourable thoughts of their omnipresent, omniscient, omnipotent, and merciful Father, who knoweth what they need and desire, before they begin to ask him, and is disposed of himself to give them all they want. He requires his children to pray, that they may more sensibly feel and acknowledge their indigence and dependence; that their desires and expectations may be excited; and that they may thus be brought into a proper frame of mind, to receive the blessing, and render him the praise. All copiousness in prayer must no more be condemned, than all repetitions; for Christ continued whole nights in prayer: and there are so many things to be asked, for ourselves, and for others, near and far off, that if our hearts be in a spiritual frame, we may pray for a long time together, without formality or unmeaning repetition. But where these begin, devotion ends.—' Cicero denies God's ' omniscience, declaring that he did not think, that God ' himself could know things casual and fortuitous. The ' heathen thought it not fit to allow of a God so curious ' as to attend to all things, or take care of all things, or ' to think all things belonged to him : and they thought it ' as well impossible, as unsufferable, in the God of the ' Christians, that he should diligently inspect the manners, ' actions, words, and secret thoughts of all men, and be ' every where present with them.' *Whitby.*—This observation illustrates the propriety and energy of the instructions, given in these verses. If philosophical heathens entertained such mean thoughts of the supreme Being; what must have been the delusion and superstition of the ignorant multitude, when they exclaimed, vociferously and incessantly, " Great is Diana of the Ephesians!" or, " O " Baal, hear us!"

Use not vain repetitions. (7) Μη βατ7ολογησητε. Used here only. Some derive the word from a poet called *Battus,* who was noted for unmeaning verbosity: *words* without *ideas.* In a popish Psalter, addressed to Jesus, the word Jesu, is repeated fifteen times together, with only *have mercy upon us, help us,* intervening; and ending thus, ' Give me here my purgatory.'—*Heathen.*] Εθνικοι. xviii. 17.—From εθνος a nation.

V. 9. We now enter on the consideration of that prayer, which Christ repeatedly taught his disciples; and which perhaps contains more important instruction, than can any where else be found in so few words.—Some expositors argue, that it was only intended for the use of the disciples, before the introduction of the Christian dispensation. But neither Matthew, nor Luke, who recorded it after that dispensation was more fully opened, give any such intimation. We are not indeed directed in this prayer, to present all our petitions in the name of Christ, and through his merits and intercession; for it was not proper explicitly

to declare this at that time.—No doubt the form has been greatly misused, by *unmeaning* repetitions, to the exclusion of real prayer; and it is often repeated, even by Protestants, with very little understanding, and not without some degree of superstition. But, perceiving these mistakes, some pious persons have run into the opposite extreme, and have improperly objected to the use of it, and even in a measure have overlooked the abundant instruction contained in it.—On this occasion our Lord introduced the prayer by saying, " After this manner pray " ye:" in St. Luke's gospel we read, " When ye pray, " say." It may often be *proper* to use the very words, but it is not always *necessary;* for we do not find that the apostles thus used it : but we ought always to pray, after the *manner* of it; that is, with that reverence, humility, seriousness, confidence in God, zeal for his glory, love to mankind, submission, and earnestness about spiritual things, which it inculcates; avoiding vain repetitions, and using grave and comprehensive expressions. Nor can we offer one petition, warranted by the word of God, which is not virtually comprised in these few instances.—Christ instructed his disciples especially, though in the hearing of the multitude; and he had before frequently spoken to them of God, as " *their* Father " ther in heaven," whom they were called upon to glorify, from whom they were to expect their reward, and who knew what things they had need of. Under this endearing character he here teaches us to address him in prayer. He is the Father of all living creatures, being the Author and Preserver of their existence ; of all rational creatures, as " the Father of spirits ;" and especially of men, whom he continues to provide for, and do good to, notwithstanding their transgressions. But, though he has always been as a Father to us, we have rebelled against him ; and by joining the arch-apostate, and becoming like him, we are in state and character " the children of the wicked one." Yet, under a dispensation of mercy, through the divine Mediator, our God is still revealed as a reconciled Father, who is ready to receive his rebellious offspring, whenever they are willing to return to his worship and service. As soon as the sinner " comes to himself," and purposes to return to God by faith and prayer; he is taught to approach him as a kind Father, and not as an inexorable Judge and Avenger; that he may come before him with encouragement. So that this endearing appellation teaches the mourning penitent to pray with hope, and the established believer, with filial confidence; as well as to regard the glory of his Father, and to seek for all the dispositions of dutiful children.—The expression, " which art " in heaven," reminds us of the sovereign and universal authority, power, and majesty of God ; and of his justice, holiness, greatness, and felicity : for heaven is the high, holy, and happy place, the throne of God, and the region of pure delight. This then instructs us to come before God, with deep humility, and adoring reverence of his majesty and condescension ; with abstraction of mind from external objects and carnal imaginations; with spiritual desires and large expectations, and aspiring to the purity

^{G 3}

10 ^d Thy kingdom come. ^e Thy will be done in earth, ^f as *it is* in heaven. 11 Give ^g us this day our daily bread.

and felicity of his heavenly worshippers.—The first petition is, "Hallowed be thy name," or, ' Let thy name be sanctified, and had in honour.' The name of God signifies his being and perfections, even all that is implied in the appellations by which he is known among men. (*Note, Ex.* xxxiv. 5—7.) We are taught to pray *in the first place*, that this name of God may be known, loved, adored, and glorified. We desire in this petition, for ourselves, that happiness which is to be enjoyed in the service and favour of God; that we may so behold his glory, as to love, adore, and honour him; and that he may be glorified in and by us for ever. We also pray, that the Lord would, in the same manner, make himself known to others around us, till all nations know and " worship him in spirit and truth," as the God of salvation, and as revealed to us in his word. —So that this is a prayer, that all atheism, infidelity, idolatry, impiety, superstition, ignorance, and false religion, may be banished from the earth; that God would make himself known, in his mysterious nature, and incomprehensible glory and grace, to all nations; that He, and He alone, as one God in three persons, may be worshipped and honoured, spiritually and acceptably, all over the whole earth, and by every one of the human species. (*Marg. Ref.* c.—(*Note,* xxviii. 19, 20.)—*Hallowed.*] *Ἁγιασθήτω. John* xvii. 17. 19. 1 *Cor.* vii. 14. *Heb.* x. 29.—*Gen.* ñ. 3. *Ex.* xx. 8. *Lev.* x. 3. *Sept.* (From ἅγιος *holy,* or a *saint.*)

V. 10. The next petition has given rise to the opinion, that this prayer was only suited to the first opening of the Christian dispensation, which is frequently called " the " kingdom of God," and " the kingdom of heaven." (*Note,* iii. 2.) But, so long as any part of the earth remains under the power of sin and Satan, this petition must be proper; nay, till the whole kingdom of grace shall be swallowed up in the kingdom of glory. In order that " the " name of God may be hallowed," the kingdom of the Messiah must come, and be established on earth in its energy and efficacy. This petition therefore implies, first an earnest desire, that this kingdom of God may be set up in our own hearts, reducing all within us to entire subjection to Christ our King: then, that it may be set up in the hearts of our children, relatives, servants, friends, neighbours; that ' all, who call themselves Christians, may be ' led into the way of truth' and holiness; that the true gospel may be every where preached, " with the Holy " Spirit sent down from heaven " to render it efficacious; and that " all kings may fall down before " the Redeemer, that " all nations may do him service: " and in short, that sin, and Satan, and all his party may be banished out of the world, and shut up in hell, never more to defile or disturb the creation or kingdom of God. Every thing relating to the sending forth, qualifying, and success of ministers, to the conversion of sinners, to the peace and purity of the church, to the subversion of antichristian powers, and the bringing of Jews, Pagans, and Mohammedans into the church, is implied in this petition.—' We ' therefore in this petition ... pray, that all men may be- ' come subjects to the kingdom of God erected by Christ;

' that the knowledge of the Christian faith may come to ' all nations; that " the kingdoms of this world may be ' " the kingdoms of our Lord Christ; "... " all kings and ' " nations, people and languages doing him service; "... ' " of the Jews," and by the " fulness of the Gentiles; " ' that the Christian religion may obtain every where, as ' well in reality as profession; the minds of all men being ' subdued " to the obedience of faith," and they shewing ' forth the virtues of it in their lives.' *Whitby.*—To this is annexed, " Thy will be done in earth, as it is in heaven." The will of God may be considered, either with respect to his commandments, or his providence: strictly speaking, his providential will is done in earth equally as in heaven; but that submission, acquiescence, and satisfaction in it, which angels feel and express, may be intended. Yet the use commonly made of this clause, as if it exclusively meant resignation to the will of God, greatly limits and enervates its weighty and extensive import.—The inhabitants of heaven do the will of God, universally, perfectly, harmoniously, without weariness, and with ineffable delight: and we are taught to pray, that all the inhabitants of the earth may imitate and emulate their example; that the whole race of men, becoming the disciples and subjects of Christ, may renounce all sin and wickedness, and obey God's commandments, with constancy, harmony, and alacrity, as angels in heaven do; that an end may be put to all injustice, oppression, fraud, violence, bloodshed, intemperance, licentiousness, ungodliness, selfishness, malice, and contention; and that righteousness, truth, goodness, mercy, purity, love of God and of each other, may fill the earth, even as they fill heaven. And what a change would this be! What an extensive petition is this!—At the same time we are taught to pray, that all men may rejoice in the sovereignty and glory of God; and be contented and satisfied with his appointments respecting them, without envy or ambition; but rejoicing to see others honoured, prospered, and happy; even as the inhabitants of heaven do. And, whilst we request so many and great blessings for others, we are taught to ask this obedient, submissive frame of mind for ourselves, and to seek for it and aim at it, in our whole conduct. (*Note, Rev.* xx. 4—6.)

V. 11. Having " in the *first* place sought" those things, which pertain to " the kingdom of God and his righteous- " ness," and prayed for the display of his glory, and the best good of men, all over the earth; we are next directed to ask of God those things, which pertain to our bodies and this present life.—Many indeed explain this petition, as if spiritual blessings, even " the Bread of life, which " came down from heaven to give life unto the world," was meant; and some even interpret it of the sacramental bread in the Lord's supper. But the supply of our temporal wants seems immediately intended. " Bread " is one principal part of the things, which are needful for the body, and it is often put for the whole; by the use of this word, therefore, we are taught to ask only things that are necessary, without craving superfluities; and to refer it to

o 4

ʰ Ex. xxvii. 7. 1 Kings viii. 30. ²⁴ 39. 50. Ps. xxvii. 1, 2. cxxx. 8, 4. Ex. l. 18. Dan. ix. 19.
12 And ʰforgive us our ¹debts, ᵏ as we forgive our debtors.
13 And ¹ lead us not into tempta-
Acts xiii. 38. Eph. i. 7. 1 John i. 7—9. 1 xviii. 23—27, 34. Luke vii. 40—42. xi. 4. k 14, 15, xviii. 21, 22. 28—35. Neh. v. 12, 13. Mark xi. 25, 26. Luke vi. 37. xvii. 3, 4. Eph. iv. 32. Col. iii. 13. l xxvi. 41. Gen. xxii. 1. Deut. viii. 2. 16. Prov. xxx. 8, 9. Luke xxii. 31, 32. 40, 46. 1 Cor. x. 13. 2 Cor. xii. 7—9. Heb. xi. 38, 37. 1 Pet. v. 8. 2 Pet. ii. 9. Rev. ii. 10. iii. 10.

tion, but ᵐdeliver us from evil: For ⁿ thine is the kingdom, and the power, and the glory, for ever, °Amen.
m 1 Chr. iv. 10. Ps. cxxi. 7, 8. Jer. xv. 21. John xvii. 15. Gal. i. 4. 1 Thes. k 16. 2 Tim. iv. 18. n 10. Ex. 17, 18. Heb. ii. 14, 15. 1 John iii. 8. v. 18, 19. Rev. vii. 14—17. xxi. 4. xv. 18. 1 Chr. xxix. 11, 12. Ps. x. 16. xlvii. 2. 7. cxiv 10—13. Dan. iv. 25, 34, 35. vii. 18 1 Tim. i. 17. vi. 15,—17. Rev. v. 13. xix. 1. o xxviii. 20. Num. v. 22. Deut. xxvii. 15, &c. 1 Kings i. 36. 1 Chr. xvi. 36. Ps. xli. 13. lxxii. 19. lxxxix. 52. cvi. 48. Jer. xxviii. 6. 1 Cor. xiv. 16. 2 Cor. i. 20. Rev. i. 18. iii. 14. xix. 4. xxii. 20.

our heavenly Father, to determine what things are necessary, according to our station in life, our families, and various other circumstances. All Christians, whether rich or poor, are instructed to ask this provision from God: for all depend upon him for it, should receive it as his gift, give him thanks for it, and use it to his glory; whether it come from their estates, commerce, husbandry, professions, labour, or skill; or from the liberality of other men. We are taught to ask it for the day; (perhaps with reference to the manna, which Israel received fresh every day;) and this instructs us to beware of covetousness, to be moderate, and contented with a slender provision, and to trust God from day to day. We ask it as " *our* bread," which may intimate, that we must expect it in the way of honest and industry: for all that is gotten by fraud, or any kind of sin, is " the wages of unrighteousness," and the maintenance given, so to speak, by Satan to his servants. Whilst we seek our daily bread from God, we must diligently use all lawful means of obtaining it, and be provident, industrious, and frugal: but we must reject, with abhorrence, all that might be gotten by means inconsistent with piety, equity, truth, and charity; and never expect to be supported in sloth or extravagance. (*Note,* Prov. xxx. 7—9.) —' Lord, give us, day by day, that which shall be sufficient, ' for the remainder of our lives.' *Whitby.* This accords with the clause, as found in the gospel by St. Luke, " Give " us day by day our daily bread."

Daily.] Επιουσιον. *Luke* xi. 3. (Comp. of επι and ουσια *existence, substance, subsistence.*) ' Ο επι τη ουσια ημων αρμοζων, ' ἡ ὁ καθημερινος. That which is fitting to our subsistence; ' or, that for every day.' *Suidas.* 'Αρτον επι τη ουσια και συστασει ' ημων αυταρκη. Bread sufficient for our subsistence and ' support.' *Theophylact.*—' A new word, and not heard ' of among the Greeks, but framed, as it seems, by the ' Evangelists, and used only in the Lord's prayer.' *Schleusner.*

V. 12. Whilst we seek from day to day, from our heavenly Father, so many and great blessings, we must not forget, that we have forfeited our claim to them by sin, and are deserving of his heavy indignation. But " there is " forgiveness with him : " and therefore we are taught to pray for forgiveness, as often as for daily bread; not only of our former sins, but of our renewed offences in thought, word, and deed, in heart and life, of omission and commission, in our conduct towards God and man. By these we contract debts continually. We receive our being and all our powers and possessions from God, to whom they all ought to be devoted in perfect love; by our failure in this we contract a debt, which we cannot pay, but which needs continual remission. (*Note,* Luke vii. 40—43.)— Being taught to ask forgiveness every time we pray, we are thus reminded to exercise constant watchfulness, self-examination, humiliation, faith and hope in the mercy of God through Christ, and patience, and forgiveness of others : for we are required to add, " as we forgive our

" debtors." We ought to forgive others, as we expect forgiveness from God : their failures of duty to us constitute a small debt contracted by them, like our great one in failing of our duty to God. (*Marg. Ref.—Notes,* xviii. 23—35.) True repentance and genuine faith always produce a disposition to forgive others : habitual malice and revenge are proofs of impenitence : if a believer be betrayed into an unchristian spirit in this respect, he must not expect the comfort of forgiveness, or communion with God ; but frowns, rebukes, and corrections, till reduced to a better temper. We are therefore, thus reminded frequently to examine ourselves in this particular, with special impartiality, lest, in praying for the pardon of our sins, we should in fact call for wrath instead of mercy to our souls : at the same time we are reminded to pray for the humble, gentle, forgiving spirit, thus emphatically required of us.— The use of the word *debts,* is not to be understood of pecuniary debts, which the debtor is able to pay, and the creditor cannot well afford to lose : yet where our debtors are in the same circumstances respecting us, as we are in respect of God ; that is, when they have it not in their power to pay us, and would be ruined, or greatly distressed, if we rigorously insisted on it ; then we must remit the debt, as we hope for God to remit ours.—' This ' petition supposeth, ... that we ... are sinners, and want ' God's mercy in the pardon of our offences against him ; ... ' that these our sins, should God deal with us according to ' the merit of them, must render us obnoxious to his just ' displeasure ; ... for seeing every sin is a transgression of ' God's holy law, it must render us guilty, till by an act ' of grace we have obtained the remission of it : and, ... ' being the first spiritual petition we make for ourselves, it ' shews how much we are concerned to obtain it ; our hap- ' piness depending wholly on the favour of God, and our ' misery on his displeasure.' *Whitby.*—' It is hardly pos- ' sible to imagine a more effectual expedient, to promote ' the forgiveness of injuries, than this of making it a part ' of our daily prayers, to ask such pardon from God, as we ' impart to our offending brother.' *Doddridge.*

V. 13. The disciples of Christ are next instructed to pray, that the Lord would " not lead them into temptation." (*Note,* Gen. xxii. 1.)—God never puts evil into our hearts, or stirs it up there by any positive influence : in the former respect, " a man is tempted by his own lust; and enticed," in the latter, by Satan or wicked men. (*Note,* Jam. i. 13 —15.) But Providence may lead us into such circumstances, as have a tendency to give our inward corruptions, and the temptations of Satan and his agents, peculiar advantage against us. This the Lord sometimes does, to prove the reality or p e of our grace, the sincerity or hypocrisy of our profession, or the remaining prevalency of sin. But, conscious of our own weakness and depravity, fearing to offend God, dishonour the gospel, grieve our brethren, stumble others, or wound our own consciences, we ought to pray, continually and most earnestly, " not to

p 12. vii. 2. xviii.
21—35. Prov.
xvi. 18. Mark
xi. 26, 26. Jam.
ii. 13. 1 John
iii. 10.

14 For ᵖ if ye forgive men their trespasses, your heavenly Father will also forgive you:

15 But if ye forgive not men their trespasses, neither will your Father forgive your trespasses.

" be led into temptation ; " beseeching God to mortify our sinful propensities, to restrain the malice and power of the tempter, to keep us out of difficult and trying circumstances, to proportion our strength to our day, and never to permit us to be " tempted above what we are able." Thus we are instructed to hate and dread sin, whilst we hope for mercy ; to distrust ourselves ; to rely on the providence as well as grace of God, to keep us from it ; to shun temptation as much as we can ; to watch over our own hearts ; to be habitually prepared to repel the assaults of the tempter, and to take care not to become tempters to others. Alas ! immense harm often comes to us, by overlooking this needful request. (*Note,* xxvi. 40, 41.)—The concluding petition is, " But deliver us from evil." Some expositors render it " from the evil one ; " which, indeed, is a literal translation : but why should we confine the interpretation? We are taught to pray for deliverance from all kinds, degrees, and occasions of evil ; from the malice, power, and subtlety of the powers of darkness ; from this evil world, and all its allurements, snares, tempters, and deceivers ; from the evil of our own hearts, that it may be subdued, and finally extirpated ; from the evil of suffering ; from the final wrath of God ; from terrible or injurious temporal calamities ; from the terror and sting of death ; from the power of death, by a glorious resurrection ; from all evil natural and moral ; from sin and all its consequences, by the complete restoration of both body and soul to holiness and happiness, glory and immortality, in the enjoyment of the divine favour, and in the beatifick vision for evermore. It is a prayer, that whatever temptation, persecution, or affliction may overtake us, we may be preserved through all ; and finally obtain eternal life and felicity, by the mercy and grace of God in Jesus Christ.—To this is added a concluding doxology, " For thine is the kingdom, and " the power, and the glory for ever. Amen." That *kingdom,* for the coming of which we pray, is his ; all *power* and *authority* are his ; and he is able to set it up in our hearts, and in the world, in defiance of all opposition : and his will be the GLORY to all eternity ; so that this may be considered as a reason why our prayers should be answered, and an encouragement that they will. Or it may be understood, as an expression of our cordial joy and satisfaction that the kingdom, power, and glory are the LORD's ; as becomes the children of our Father in heaven : and our desire and purpose to give him all honour, worship, love, praise, thanksgiving, and obedience for evermore ; and our ardent wish that all others might do the same.—To all this we are taught to set our confirming and entire assent, by the word " Amen," *So be it :* ' Let all this be so established and completed to the glory of God, and we desire no more.' (*Marg. Ref.* o.)—What now is there in this prayer, which is not purely evangelical, and suited to the case and wants of every Christian, and every congregation? What can be more liberal, comprehensive, or energetick? What is wanting? or what redundant? What more fraught with glowing zeal for the honour of God, expansive love to mankind, and fervent thirstings after all the blessings of salvation? What can be more replete with

important instruction? It only wants to be better understood, and used with correspondent affections, to constitute such devotion, as would almost emulate the worship of heaven.—' This clause ' (the concluding doxology,) ' is not ' in St. Luke, nor in many copies of St. Matthew : yet ' there are sufficient reasons for receiving it as a part of the ' Lord's prayer ; as being in the Syriack version, and owned ' in the Greek liturgies, and being in most ancient copies : ' ...and ...because it is very unlikely that the holy fathers ' of the Greek church should presume to add their own in- ' ventions, to a form of our Lord's own composing. But ' it is probable, that our Lord, delivering this form twice, ' upon different occasions, might add this clause at the first ' time, and leave it out at the second ; and that the Latin ' copies, which are full of errors, might leave it out in ' both, lest the evangelists should seem to differ in a matter ' so considerable.' *Whitby.*—It is so perfectly *scriptural,* and so replete with instruction, that the internal evidence of its authenticity is unanswerable. (*Notes,* 1 Chr. xxix. 10— 19. *Ps.* xxi. 13. *Rev.* xi. 15—18.)

Temptation.] Πειρασμον. xxvi. 41. *Luke* iv. 13. viii. 13. xi. 4. xxii. 28. 40. 46. *Acts* xx. 19. 1 *Cor.* x. 13. *Gal.* iv. 14. 1 *Tim.* vi. 9. *Jam.* i. 12. 1 *Pet.* i. 6.—*Evil.*] Τε πονηρο. v. 37. xiii. 19. 38. *Luke* xi. 4. *Eph.* vi. 16. 2 *Thes.* iii. 3. 2 *Tim.* iv. 18. 1 *John* ii. 13, 14. iii. 12. v. 18, 19.

V. 14, 15. Our Lord, by this declaration, calls our attention most powerfully to the clause in the twelfth verse, " as we forgive our debtors ; " and, by substituting " tres- " passes " for " debts," still further illustrates his meaning. We cannot suppose, that forgiveness of those who injure us, can in any degree merit the forgiveness of God ; or that he will pardon the impenitent and unbelieving, because out of a natural facility of temper they forgive others, without any due regard to his authority and glory. The persons addressed are professed disciples : when " their " hearts do not " in this respect " condemn them, they " have confidence towards God," though conscious of much unworthiness ; but if their hearts condemn them, their confidence will be abated : (*Note,* 1 John iii. 18—24 :) and if they utterly fail in this, their hypocrisy is manifested. (*Notes,* xviii. 21—35.)—' To this true remission it is re- ' quisite, that our minds be wholly freed from all desires ' of revenge, or of returning evil [for evil] : ...that we do ' not rejoice in any evil that befalls our brother ; (*Prov.* ' xxiv. 17 ;) ...that we do not so retain the evil done to us, ' in our memory, as ...to upbraid him with it ; ...that we ' be still inclined to shew kindness to him, and be still ' ready to help and do him good. ...So far we must go on ' in our forgiveness of all persons, at all times, even though ' they do not *ask forgiveness.* When this is done sincerely, ' then we are to admit our offending brother into friendship ' and familiarity again ; ...our heart must be toward him ' as formerly it was. ...This remission must be without ' delay, ...seeing we pray ...for forgiveness at present ; and ' if we do not thus forgive, we cannot say " Forgive as we ' " forgive." It must be ...entire, ...even of the most ' heinous crimes ; ...otherwise ...we pray that our greatest ' crimes may not be forgiven. It must be extended to our

ᴏ ꜰ

16 ¶ Moreover ⁴ when ye fast, ʰ be not, as the hypocrites, of a sad countenance: for they disfigure their faces, that they may appear unto men to fast.

17 But thou, when thou fastest, ᵗ anoint thine head, and wash thy face;

18 That thou ᵘ appear not unto men to fast, but unto thy Father which is in secret: and thy Father, which seeth in secret, ˣ shall reward thee openly.

19 ¶ Lay ʸ not up for yourselves treasures upon earth, where moth and rust doth corrupt, and where thieves break through and steal:

20 But ᶻ lay up for yourselves treasures in heaven, where neither moth nor rust doth corrupt, and where thieves do not break through nor steal:

21 For ᵃ where your treasure is, ᵇ there will your heart be also.

ᶜ brother, though he doth frequently offend; (*Luke* xvii. ⁴ 3;) for we pray daily to God for the remission of our ⁴ daily sins.' *Whitby.*—The term brother is frequently used on this subject : but it is evident, that we are not only required thus to forgive our brethren in Christ; but also our bitterest persecutors, for Christ's sake.

Trespasses.] Παραπτωμαία. *Falls, crimes, offences.* xviii. 35. *Rom.* iv. 25. v. 15. 16—20. 2 *Cor.* v. 19. *Eph.* i. 7. ii. 1. (A παραπιπτω, seu potius παραπίπτω.)

V. 16—18. Our blessed Lord, having given these copious instructions concerning prayer, proceeds to caution his disciples against ostentation in another religious duty. The Pharisees fasted often, but in a hypocritical and self-righteous manner : even in their *private* fasts, they used to appear abroad with gloomy countenances, and with such sordid and slovenly neglect of their persons, as gave every body to understand how they were employed. They assumed this appearance, to keep up their credit, and to gain applause for their extraordinary sanctity : and this would be their sole reward; for God would not accept these vainglorious services. But Christ's disciple (who is supposed on some occasions to fast, as well as to give alms and pray,) should avoid all ostentation, when thus humbling himself before God; and in his family, or when called from home, be as cheerful, and as decent in his attire, as at other times : that he may not appear to men to fast, but be satisfied with the notice and acceptance of God his Father, who is present in the secret chambers of his worshippers, as well as in their publick assemblies; and who will graciously and openly reward such unfeigned expressions of humiliation for sin, mortification of the flesh, desires after holiness, and abstraction from worldly pleasures, for the sake of communion with him. ' The word rendered " a sad countenance," is properly, the look of a ' wild beast ; a lion, or a bear robbed of her whelps, grim ' and ghastly.' *Leigh.* That rendered " disfigured," seems to imply, the neglect of usual attentions to the hair, &c. and the covering of the face, as mourners used to do. (2 *Sam.* xix. 4. 24.) Thus the face, or usual form of it, *disappeared.*

Of a sad countenance. (16) Σκυθρωποι· (ex σκυθρος torvus, et ωψ vultus :) *Luke* xxiv. 17.—*Gen.* xi. 7. *Dan.* i. 10. *Sept.*—*Disfigure.*] Αφανιζωσι. (Ab. αφανης quod ex α priv. et φαινω ostendo, appareo.) 19. 20. *Acts* xiii. 41. *Jam.* iv. 14.—*Have.*] Απεχωσι. ' It signifies so to have received ' their portion ... that they cannot ask, and ought not to expect any t..ing more.' *Quot. in Leigh.*

V. 19—21. The Pharisees aimed to be seen of men,

not only to obtain applause and reputation, but to gratify their covetousness : and therefore our Lord next warned his disciples against this destructive evil. As a Christian is a pilgrim on earth, and a citizen of heaven, he in this world wants merely subsistence, or, so to speak, travelling expenses; but he needs " a treasure in heaven." He ought not therefore to " lay up for himself a treasure on earth : " for this must shortly be left to others; and all things here below, however idolized or valued, are liable to decay and waste. Moths eat and spoil the garments of those who have rich wardrobes; nay, even metals are corroded by rust ; and thieves break into the houses of the rich, to seize their treasures, and often to attempt their lives. (*Note, Jam.* v. 1—6, *vv.* 2, 3.) However wealth be secured, it is uncertain ; and far more constantly a source of vexation and disappointment, than of solid comfort. (*Note,* 1 *Tim.* vi. 6—10.) Such things are not the Christian's *treasure:* the acquisition of them should not be his object; he should be contented without them; and if they be entrusted to him, he should neither store them up for himself, nor spend them on himself, but lay them out in doing good. (*Notes, Luke* xii. 15—21. xvi. 1—13. .9—26.) Heavenly things are his treasure : these he should prize and seek, in diligent faith and prayer, and in the improvement of his talents. They are not liable to decay or uncertainty, nor can he be robbed or deprived of them. This is likewise, in all respects, of the greatest importance : for if a man's treasure be laid up on earth, his heart will be earthly; and all his thoughts, affections, projects, conduct, and conversation will be earthly. But, if heavenly things be chosen as a man's most valuable treasure, his heart will be heavenly, he will continually be thinking about spiritual matters ; his very soul will be, as it were, in heaven. This will give a heavenly savour to all his discourse, and the whole tenour of his actions ; (*Note, Phil.* iii. 20, 21 ;) preserve him from, or strengthen him against, those temptations which ruin worldly men ; and quicken him in every part of duty.— Before fashions changed, as they have done for some time past in this part of the world, wardrobes formed a considerable part of the riches laid up by worldly men, and left to their heirs : and this is the case, in the eastern regions, to this day.

Rust. (19, 20) Βρωσις. (A βρωσκω.) It signifies—1. *The act of eating* ; 1 *Cor.* viii. 4. 2 *Cor.* ix. 10.—2. *The food. John* iv. 32. *Rom.* xiv. 17. *Heb.* xii. 16.—3. *That which eats or corrodes.* Such are the vermin that destroy the corn, and the rust which corrodes metals.—*Corrupt.*] Αφανιζει. See on 16.

o 7

22 ¶ The ^clight of the body is the eye; if therefore thine eye be ^dsingle, thy whole body shall be full of light. 23 But if ^ethine eye be evil, thy whole body shall be full of darkness. ^fIf therefore the light that is in thee be darkness, how great is that darkness!

24 ¶ No man can ^gserve two masters: for either he will hate the one, and love the other; or else he will hold to the one, and despise the other. Ye cannot serve God and ^hMammon.

25 Therefore ⁱI say unto you, ^kTake no thought for your life, what ye shall eat, or what ye shall drink; nor yet for your body, what ye shall put on. ^lIs not the life more than meat, and the body than raiment?

V. 22, 23. The preceding truths are here illustrated by an apt similitude. The actions of the whole body are directed, according to the light received by the eye: when that organ is *single*, or clear, and perceives objects as they really are, the whole body has light, and the man moves with safety and propriety: but if the eye be evil, and see things confusedly, and without distinction; he stumbles as in the dark, and is continually liable to lose his way, or run into danger. Thus an enlightened understanding, perceiving objects according to their real nature and value, enables a man to form a proper judgment, to make a wise choice, and to conduct himself aright, respecting them. But a darkened mind, leading to a mistaken estimate of things, produces an erroneous choice; and the more earnestly the deluded person proceeds, the further he wanders from the way. If then, that which is supposed by any one to be his *chief wisdom*, be indeed *folly*;—if his first principle be an error;—" the light that is " in him is darkness," and how intense and fatal must that darkness be!—This immediately relates to men's practical judgment of earthly and heavenly things. The worldly man mistakes in his first principle, and therefore all his reasonings and calculations must be erroneous; and the further he goes, the more fatally he is bewildered. But it is equally applicable to false religion. When that which a man deems extraordinary illumination, whether from philosophy or enthusiasm, is a mere delusion, his very light is thick darkness from the bottomless pit; all his inferences and proceedings lead him further from God, from truth, and from holiness, and plunge him still deeper into error, prejudice, spiritual pride, and the snare of the prince of darkness. This is an awful, yet a common case : how very carefully then should we examine our leading principles, by the word of God, and with earnest prayer for the teaching of his Holy Spirit! *(Marg. Ref.—Notes, Is.* viii. 20. *Luke* xi. 33—36.)

Single. (22) 'Απλὰς. *Luke* xi. 34. 'Απλῶς, *liberally. Jam.* i. 5 :—ἀπλῶς. *Rom.* xii. 8. 2 *Cor.* i. 12. *Eph.* vi. 5.

V. 24. A man may do some service to two masters, but he cannot devote himself to the service of more than one; now God requires the whole man, and will not share the heart with the world. When the two masters, and their interests, are in full opposition to each other, the impossibility of serving both of them is evident. This is the case in respect of God and the world : they are two opposites; he who loves and holds to the world, as his master, will be an enemy and despiser of God; and he who loves and cleaves to the service of God, will renounce the friendship and despise the frown of the world. So that we cannot " serve God and Mammon." (*Note, Luke* xvi. 9—13.) *Mammon* is the Syriack word for riches, and seems here used as the name of an idol : the covetous man is an idolater, and therefore he is no true servant or worshipper of God, who is jealous, and will endure no rivals. By a proper arrangement of our worldly concerns, in subordination and subserviency to religion, we may render them a part of God's service; as worldly men make their religion a part of the service of Mammon : but the two opposite services cannot be attended to.—' We love ' Mammon more than God, when we pursue it by unlawful ' ...means; by a lie, as Ziba and Gehazi; by...oppression, ' theft, violence, or by false testimony : for in all these ' cases, we despise God's authority to obtain Mammon. ... ' When our labour or concernment in these temporals doth ' cause us to...be remiss in our duty to God; ...and when ' we cannot part with them for his sake, but choose rather ' to ... quit our interest in spiritual than in temporal bless- ' ings ; ...then we certainly cleave to them more than God; ' and him we do comparatively despise.' *Whitby*. (*Marg. Ref.* g.—*Notes, Rom.* vi. 16—23.)

Hold to.] Αντεξίλαι. *Luke* xvi. 13. 1 *Thes.* v. 14. *Tit.* i. 9.

V. 25. The anxious fear of want, and the solicitude about a future provision, often as much ensnare the poor, as the love of wealth does the rich. Therefore Christ expressly enjoined his disciples to " take no thought for their " lives, &c." There is a care about temporal things, which is a duty, according to a man's station in the world. He should mind diligently, and with prudent contrivance, his proper business ; he should provide for himself and family, as far as honest industry will go; he should calculate his income, and form his plan to live within the bounds of it, that he may not needlessly be embarrassed with debts; he should see that no bounty of Providence be wasted or lavished; he should make such arrangements as he is able, for those demands which will be hereafter made on him; he should spare needless expense, that he may not want, or be constrained to beg, in sickness, or old age; and he even may, and in some cases ought, to make a moderate provision for his family, if he can do it consistently with justice, piety, and charity : yet there is much danger lest these cares be extended beyond due bounds. No one ought, however, to be solicitous about events, or anxious how he shall be provided for *in future.* This is the Lord's part; and when any take it on themselves, they distrust and dishonour him, become their own tormentors, and are often tempted to sinful methods of making provision for themselves, or their families. This is the *care,* or *solicitude,* which is prohibited. The Christian, trusting in God and

G 8

26 Behold " the fowls of the air: for they sow not, neither do they reap, nor gather into barns; yet ᵏ your heavenly Father feedeth them. Are ye not much better than they?

27 Which of you ° by taking thought can add one cubit unto his stature?

28 And ᵖ why take ye thought for raiment? Consider ᑫ the lilies of the field, how they grow; they toil not, neither do they spin:

29 And yet I say unto you, That ʳ even Solomon in all his glory was not arrayed like one of these.

30 Wherefore, If God so ˢ clothe the grass of the field, which to-day is, and to-morrow is cast into the oven, shall he not much more clothe you, ᵗ O ye of little faith?

31 Therefore take no thought, saying, " What shall we eat? or, What shall we drink? or, Wherewithal shall we be clothed?

32 (For ˣ after all these things do the Gentiles seek:) ʸ for your heavenly Father knoweth that ye have need of all these things.

33 But ᶻ seek ye first ᵃ the kingdom of God, and ᵇ his righteousness; ᶜ and all these things shall be added unto you.

34 Take therefore ᵈ no thought for the morrow; ᵉ for the morrow shall take thought for the things of itself. ᶠ Sufficient unto the day is the evil thereof.

---

attending to his duty, must not be anxious about the continuance or support of his life; he must neither be greatly concerned about the measure of his supplies, nor the manner in which they are to be obtained. The Author of his life, and the Former of his body, having done greater things for him, should be depended on for the less; and food and raiment should be sought and expected from him, in the use of lawful means exclusively.

Take no thought.] Μη μεριμνᾶτε. 27. 28. 31. 34. *Luke* xii. 11. 1 *Cor.* vii. 32—34. *Phil.* ii. 20. iv. 6. (Der. from μεριμνα. xiii. 22. *Mark* iv. 19. *Luke* viii. 14. xxi. 34. 2 *Cor.* xi. 28. 1 *Pet.* v. 7.—Comp. of μερίζω, to divide, and νες the mind.)

V. 26—32. This great Householder (so to speak,) of the universe, "openeth his hand, and filleth all his creatures with his bounty: the birds of the air, which are so gay and cheerful, are provided for by his care without any of their own; for they are not able to use any means for their sustenance. And surely the believer is far more valuable in the sight of his heavenly Father, both as a rational creature and as a spiritual worshipper, than the birds of the air! Indeed such cares are altogether vain. No man could add a cubit to the height of his stature, if he were ever so solicitous about it, and therefore no man thinks of it: and in fact no anxious care can add to the length of men's lives, or to their health, comfort, or prosperity. It is equally absurd to be anxious about raiment: even the lilies of the field, which are incapable of adorning themselves, are far more beautifully decorated, than Solomon, or any earthly monarch, in his royal robes. And has the Lord, with such profusion, adorned the very vegetables, that will so soon be cut down, withered, dried up, or burned; and will he not suitably clothe the Christian? Or should *he* be desirous of such adornings, as are surpassed by the flowers of the field? This must arise from weakness of faith, respecting the truths and promises of God, which will expose a man to just rebukes. Solicitous and distrustful enquiries about temporal things may consist with the character of those who know not God; who con-

sequently must count the world their portion, and who rely on their own foresight for obtaining the good things of it: but Christians have a nobler Portion and a better Provider. "Their Father knoweth what they want;" and he has sufficient power, truth, goodness, and love to them, to send what is best for them: their anxiety is then entirely superfluous.—The clause, "a cubit to his stature," is by many learned men understood to mean, 'an addition to the length of a man's life.' The original word for "stature" certainly often means *age;* but it is used in Greek authors for *stature,* or the size of plants, &c. and probably no instance can be given from any author, of a *cubit* being used as a measure of time.—Fuel is very scarce in the eastern parts of the world: and the stalks of lilies, and other large flowers, when withered, would be very useful in heating ovens, and for similar purposes.—A few passages have been quoted from the writings of heathen philosophers, to shew, that some of them used the same arguments against *carefulness,* which our Lord here employs: but they are brought from those writers, who lived after Christianity was established; and it is highly probable, that they were derived from the New Testament, by those, who thence took materials to improve that philosophy, with which they opposed the gospel: and in this they have had many followers.

Stature. (27) 'Ηλικιαν. · *Luke* ii. 52. xii. 25. xix. 3. *Eph.* iv. 13. *Heb.* xi. 11.

V. 33, 34. The blessings of the Messiah's kingdom, the righteousness in which his subjects are justified, the grace by which they are sanctified, and the good works in which they should walk, are intended by " the kingdom of " God, and his righteousness." Our Lord, therefore, calls his disciples to seek admission into this kingdom by repentance and faith, and every means of grace; and to press forward to the full participation of its privileges, and conformity to the law and example of their righteous King; and also to seek the purity, peace, prosperity, and enlargement of the kingdom, the honour of their Prince, and the good of their fellow subjects. These must be

CHAP. VII.

Cautions against rash judgment, 1—5. Things holy are not to be cast to dogs, 6. Encouragements to prayer, 7—11. The rule of doing as we would be done to, 12. The strait gate and narrow way, and the wide gate and broad way, 13, 14. A warning against false prophets, who may be known by their fruits, 15—20. No gifts or miracles will avail the workers of iniquity at the day of judgment, 21—23. The parable of the house built on a rock, 24, 25; and that on the sand, 26, 27. Christ concludes; and the people are astonished at his doctrine, 28, 29.

sought "in the first place," as the first object, with the first of their affections and time; beginning the year, the month, the week, and the day, with this business, and ordering all things in subserviency to it. Then their bountiful Father will add all those things, which pertain to this present life, without their anxious carefulness : but they who reverse this order, take the way to ruin themselves, in respect of this world and that which is to come.—The Christian should not be careful even about the very next day; for it may never arrive *to him*: and if it do, it will bring its supports and supplies with it, and thus, as it were, "take thought for itself." This should be considered as a merciful appointment of his heavenly Father. He knows, that every day brings more trouble and suffering, than men can well bear; he therefore allows and *commands* his children to "cast all their care" about the future on him. And if any will, notwithstanding, be so absurd as to load themselves with a heavy burden which does not belong to them, and then groan under self-imposed sorrows; they torment themselves, as well as dishonour God, by their folly and unbelief.—This is also applicable to spiritual things. The Christian, while watching, praying, and attending to his duty, is authorized to trust the Lord to give him grace sufficient for future trials and temptations, as well as food sufficient for future temporal wants : and in both cases, "sufficient for the day is the evil thereof."

PRACTICAL OBSERVATIONS.

V. 1—8.

How various are the ways in which the evil of our hearts leads us aside from "simplicity and godly sincerity!" Hypocrites corrupt their duties by selfish motives; on which account profligates and infidels excuse their neglect of religion : but Christians must attend on every good work, and every means of grace, from right principles, and with a holy intention; and the less they seek reward and honour from men, the more confidently may they expect them from God.——What discoveries will be made at the last day! Many an admired character will then be detected as a vainglorious hypocrite, in his charities, devotions, and austerities. But, at that solemn season, the secret charities and fervent prayers of true believers, who earnestly seek the good even of their bitterest enemies; and all their secret self-denial, and mortification of their sinful propensities, arising from love to God and holiness, will be openly proclaimed and rewarded. Whilst the most specious part of an ungodly man's character is held forth to view, and his crimes and corrupt motives are studiously concealed; and whilst the infirmities of a pious man are noticed, and his good works, and holy affections and purposes, are veiled with the mantle of humility; the real difference may be but feebly discerned : but when the whole shall be made known, all the world will see the one to be meet for heaven, and the other justly deserving of his awful doom. Let us then remember, in every thing, to act as before " our Father " who seeth in secret;" and as desiring no reward, but that which he will graciously bestow on his beloved children, for all " their work and labour of love." (*Note*, 1 *Cor.* iv. 3—5, *v.* 5.)

V. 9—18.

It is peculiarly important, that we should accurately examine, in what frame of mind our prayers and supplications are offered; and learn daily from Christ how to pray with acceptance, and confidence of success. If we truly desire the glory and favour of God, and deliverance from guilt, temptations, and sin, above all other things; we may be sure that he will answer our prayers. If he have taught us to forgive our brethren for his sake, we may be assured of his ready forgiveness of our sins, though many and aggravated : if we desire to have him for our Father, in Christ Jesus, and to possess the spirit, and act in the character, of his children; we may come near to him, and call upon him, and confide in him as our Father : and those who refuse to do this at present, must shortly be constrained to appear before him as their awful Judge. But let all beware of malice and revenge; for whatever a man may profess, if he do not forgive others, even his most implacable enemies, God has not forgiven him; and will not forgive him, if he continue of this rancorous disposition.—A morose and gloomy countenance is no part of religion, nor any ornament to the profession of it; and it often covers a proud, hypocritical heart : but real humility, sorrow for sin, and deadness to the world, should be accompanied by a decent and unaffected cheerfulness in the sight of men, springing from gratitude to God, reliance on him, and the hope and earnests of his heavenly glory.

V. 19—24.

We should peculiarly watch and pray against covetousness : " treasures on earth " can little profit dying creatures : yet we are in danger of losing them before we die; and they are only certain, as sources of anxiety, snares, and vexations. But there is an inheritance which is " incor- " ruptible, undefiled, and that fadeth not away, reserved " in heaven for" true believers: for this let us labour with all diligence, that we may secure it, and increase our portion in it, whatever be neglected or renounced for the sake of it.—Anxiety about the world cannot consist with a heavenly mind; for " where the treasure is, there will the " heart be also." Yet multitudes fatally err in this matter; they see all things through a vitiated eye, in which phantoms appear realities, and realities phantoms: thus they wander on in darkness, and know not at what they stumble. So that, after all the warnings which Christ has given, they through unbelief, persist in a vain attempt to " serve God and Mammon." May the Lord preserve us from such false principles and fatal mistakes!

н 2

JUDGE [a] not, that ye be not judged. 2 For [b] with what judgment ye judge, ye shall be judged: and with [c] what measure ye mete, it shall be measured to you again. 3 And [d] why beholdest thou the mote that is in thy brother's eye, [e] but con-siderest not the beam that is in thine own eye? 4 Or how wilt thou say to thy brother, Let me pull out the mote out of thine eye; and, behold, a beam *is* in thine own eye? 5 [f] Thou hypocrite, [g] first cast out the beam out of thine own eye; and

---

V. 25—34.

While we are careful to " choose the good part," to find the right way, to know the state of our souls, and to attend to our present duty, we should not be anxious about future consequences.' Let us rely on our heavenly Father, to support the lives and nourish the bodies, which he has given us; and not trouble ourselves, whether our provision be plenteous, or mean and scanty. Our " *lives* are more " than meat, and our *bodies* than raiment;" what then are our *souls*, which the divine Saviour has redeemed with his precious blood? Whilst we feast on his spiritual provisions, and are adorned with the robes of righteousness and salvation; we cannot surely doubt his truth and love, which are engaged to feed and clothe us! Will he provide for the fowls, and adorn the fading flowers, and yet starve his beloved children? How unreasonable and shameful is our unbelief! We need his merciful rebuke, and should pray continually to him to " increase our faith;" and leave it to Gentiles and unbelievers, to perplex themselves about concerns so far inferior. Let us " seek first the kingdom of " God, and his righteousness," assured that " all things " else shall be added to us;" for our Father knows what things we want. Thus we shall be encouraged for every duty, and relieved from our fruitless anxieties. We shall indeed find, that " sufficient for the day is the evil of it;" and that we have no need to anticipate future possible pains and sorrows: but we shall also find, that the day will bring its own comforts and supports with it.—All these rules and precepts of our gracious Lord will be known by our experience, if true believers, to conduce to our present comfort, as well as to our future benefit; when we shall have done with temptation, be delivered from evil, and employed in praising him, whose is " the kingdom, the " power, and the glory, for ever. Amen."

NOTES

CHAP. VII. V. 1, 2. These verses do not forbid the magistrate to judge, and pass sentence on criminals; or the rulers of the church to censure and exclude such members as disgrace their profession; or Christians to " with-" draw from every brother that walks disorderly :" for these are duties expressly enjoined in scripture. (*Notes*, 2 *Thes.* iii. 6—15.) In like manner, it cannot be supposed, that our Lord intended to forbid his disciples to form a judgment of men's state and character, according to their avowed principles and visible conduct: for in this very chapter he directs us to judge by this rule; (*Note*, 15—20;) and indeed, many duties to others absolutely require us to form some judgment, both in respect of their state, and their actions. But we ought not to be officious, rash,

or severe, in forming our judgment; nor hasty in declaring it. We are not bound to believe an infidel, or a profligate, to be a true Christian : but we should judge as favourably as we can, where the fundamentals of Christianity are professed, and not disgraced by an inconsistent conduct. We ought to put the best construction on doubtful actions, and never ascribe apparently good ones to bad motives, without full proof; to shun curious enquiries into men's conduct, and injurious suspicions; and steadily to avoid giving our opinion, to any man's disadvantage, without some duty require it of us: we should not censure or anathematize those who differ from us; or condemn whole sects and societies of men, except as the scripture evidently condemns them. We should, as far as we can, shun every thing, which savours of malevolence or spiritual pride : for the opinion, which a Christian must form concerning the heart of man, and the state of the world, though he do not needlessly apply it to individuals, will give sufficient offence; and it ought not to be increased, by rash and harsh judgments in particular cases.—He, who is habitually propense to this self-sufficient, presumptuous, and censorious judging of others, gives them great cause to suspect, that he is devoid of true grace himself, and exposed to " judgment without mercy" from God. If a Christian give into so evil a spirit and practice, he may expect sharp corrections ; nay, both the world and the church will commonly judge of men, according to their method of judging others.—Thus in every sense it is verified, " that with what " measure we mete, it will be measured to us again." (*Marg. Ref.—Note*, *Jam.* iv. 11, 12.)

V. 3—5. These verses shew, that while Christ addressed his disciples as the children of God, he yet warned them that there might be hypocrites among them.—If a man, whose eyes were closed with some obstruction or disease, (which like a beam was evident to all, and which entirely prevented him from seeing any object distinctly,) should affect curiously to spy out some little particle in another man's eye, and officiously offer to remove it; he would render himself ridiculous. His attention ought to be directed to the disordered state of his own eyes, and his endeavours used to remedy it, before he offered his assistance to his brother.—Thus, while Christians should watch over one another, and point out and remedy even small mistakes in each other's principles and practice; the man who presumes to reprove every defect of others, when his own spirit and conduct are notoriously wrong, only proves his own officiousness and hypocrisy. He, who would become a wise and faithful reprover or minister, must begin at home; and first " take heed to himself, and to his doc-" trine," temper, and conduct: when these are become unexceptionable, he may with propriety, authority, and

H 3

then shalt thou see clearly to cast out the mote out of thy brother's eye.

6 ¶ Give not ᶠ that which is holy unto the dogs, neither ᵇ cast ye your pearls before swine, lest they trample them under their feet, ⁱ and turn again and rend you.

7 ¶ Ask, ᵏ and it shall be given you; ˡ seek, and ye shall find; ᵐ knock, and it shall be opened unto you:

8 For ⁿ every one that asketh, re-ceiveth; and he that seeketh, findeth; and to him that knocketh, it shall be opened.

9 Or ᵒ what man is there of you, whom if his son ask bread, will he give him a stone?

10 Or if he ask a fish, will he give him a serpent?

11 If ye then, ᵖ being evil, know how to give good gifts unto your children, q how much more shall your Father ʳ which is in heaven, give ˢ good things to them that ask him!

hope of success, offer his help to his brethren, in rectify-ing their judgments and promoting their sanctification : yet he will do it with humility, prudence, tenderness, and can-dour.—But alas! it is observable, that, in *spiritual optricks*, a beam in the eye generally renders a man quick sighted in discerning other men's faults, and blind only to his own.—It is probable, that our Lord alluded to some proverbial expressions, familiar to his hearers ; the knowledge of which would throw more light on the subject, than any criticism on the original words can do.—' There was a pro-' verbial speech among the Jews, in and before Christ's ' time, (set down afterwards with some variation in the ' Talmud, thus,) They, which say to others, *Take out the* ' *small piece of wood out of thy teeth*, are answered, *Take* ' *out the beam out of thine eyes :* to check the importunity ' of those, who are always censuring and condemning ' others for small matters, ... when they themselves are ' guilty of those things, which are much more to be re-' prehended.' *Hammond.*

V. 6. As every man is not qualified or authorized to be a reprover ; so every offender is not the proper subject of reproof. (*Notes*, Prov. ix. 7—9. 9.) To persevere in giving counsel or instruction to some men would be as im-proper, as to throw the holy things, which were the food of the priests, unto unclean dogs ; or to cast " pearls before " swine." The emblems here used, compared with other scriptures, may be supposed to denote hardened scorners, licentious or covetous professors, fierce and untractable op-posers, or manifest apostates. (*Marg. Ref.*) Many truths, and many instances of the Lord's goodness to us, which are precious to the humble and teachable, are not proper to be communicated to scoffers, or those who pervert sa-cred things : they will only be emboldened or exasperated by them, to greater ungodliness, and to shew more impious rage and contempt. They will trample under foot, with disdain, all that can be said of experimental religion, or communion with God ; as swine would tread pearls in the mire, regardless of their value : and they will be so enraged at holy warnings, reproofs, and counsels, that, like fierce dogs, they will be ready to turn again and tear their friendly reprover.—The rule may also be extended to the preaching of the gospel among those, who obstinately contradict and blaspheme : and certainly the admission of openly wicked and ungodly persons to the Lord's supper, and into the sacred ministry, is a too common and most grievous vio-lation of it.

V. 7—11. (*Note, Luke* xi. 5—13.) Many important and arduous duties had been inculcated ; and great wisdom and grace would be requisite for the practice of them, without turning aside, or running into extremes, on the right hand or on the left. Our Lord, therefore, next di-rected and encouraged his auditors, to seek help, and counsel, and every blessing, in earnest prayer, and the use of other means of grace ; assuring them that every one, who thus asked, sought, and knocked at mercy's gate, would be successful.—But is there no such thing as asking, and not receiving ? Undoubtedly there is ; yet not in the sense here evidently intended. A man may ask in vain, when he addresses himself to an idol, or tutelary saint, in-stead of the living God : he may ask for what the Lord has never promised ; or without feeling any need or de-sire of the mercy which he craves ; he may offer proud and hypocritical prayers ; he may pray for exemption from punishment, whilst he wilfully cleaves to sin ; he may ask for temporal and spiritual blessings, without using other proper means of obtaining them ; or he may come in his own name, in contempt of the appointed Mediator, or in the name of other imaginary mediators. A man may seek the world *first*, and then attend to religion, as far as it consists with his worldly interests and pursuits ; he may seek salvation, in a way of his own devising, or in a more smooth and flattering method than that of the gospel ; or he may begin to seek, when " the Master of the house " hath risen up and shut to the door:" (*Note, Luke* xiii. 22 —30, v. 25 :) nay, a man may knock at mercy's gate, when he is in a fright, and leave off when his fears have sub-sided. But he who comes as a sinner to a merciful God, through the divine Advocate, for all the blessings of salva-tion, in sincerity, and with earnest prayer, waiting and persevering, as having hope in this way, and none in any other ; he who seeks spiritual blessings in the first place, without delay, and in the use of all appointed means ; and he who knocks and waits at mercy's gate, resolved to find admission, or to perish knocking, will be sure at length to succeed. The promise is absolute and express ; " Every " one that asketh receiveth, &c." Supplicants of this kind sometimes receive, and find admission, without delay ; always in due time : nor will their previous character, how-ever bad, preclude them from the benefit ; for he who opened the way of access, has taught them to come in it ; and " he giveth to all men liberally, and upbraideth not." (*Note, Jam.* i. 5—8, v. 5.) Indeed, (as our Lord has added,)

12 Therefore *all things whatsoever ye would that men should do to you, do ye even so to them : *for this is the law and the prophets.

13 ¶ Enter ye in °at the strait gate:

*for wide *is* the gate, and broad *is* the way, *that leadeth to destruction, and many there be which go in thereat :

14 °Because strait *is* the gate, *and

---

it would be most dishonourable to God to suppose the contrary, after all the displays which he has given of his fatherly compassion to sinners. For what man would put off his hungry child, when importunately asking food of him, with a useless stone instead of a loaf, or a noxious serpent instead of a fish? He would not deserve the name of a father, or even of a man, who could act in such a manner. If therefore men, who are all corrupt and selfish, and who cannot give to their children without lessening their own store, and often straitening themselves, are yet instructed by natural affection to give salutary and useful gifts to their children; how much more shall our heavenly Father, whose goodness and riches are infinite, give *good things,* even all things which pertain and conduce to salvation, to every one who humbly asks them from him? Christ does not say, " to his children," lest the trembling supplicant should be disconcerted by the apprehension, that he was not one of them ; but he says, " to them that " ask him :" thus the very act of asking may give the assurance of being heard, and of receiving the desired mercy. —It is observable, that our Lord assumed it as the principle from which he argued, that even the disciples, as well as others, were *evil.* ' " What man is there among you," ' in all this numerous assembly, " who, if his son, &c."— ' This seems to be the emphasis of τις εστιν εξ ὑμων ανθρωπος. ' Young preachers will, I hope, observe, how much life ' and force it adds to these discourses of our Lord, that ' they so closely are directed, through the whole of them, ' as an immediate address to his hearers; and are not loose ' and general harangues in the manner of those *Essays,* ' which are now grown so fashionable in pulpits.' *Doddridge.*

Being evil. (11) Πονηροι οντες. (See on *Note,* vi. 13.) This is a most energetical attestation of the Truth himself, to the doctrine of man's natural depravity and wickedness.

V. 12. The example of the truth and mercy of God, the encouragement afforded, and his readiness to pardon, assist, and accept us, constitute the primary argument, with which this rule is enforced, and form its connexion with the preceding verses. It is not only enacted as a strict and holy law ; but it is proposed to believers, as their rule of duty ; with abundant motives and encouragements ; that by observing it, they may glorify God, and shew their gratitude for his mercy : and it is worthy of our consideration, that moral precepts, thus enforced, are very different from the same rules of action, when prescribed by human moralists, without *authority, sanction, efficacious motive,* or *promise.*—This precept has generally been admired, and called *the golden rule:* it is indeed equivalent to that of " loving our neighbour as ourselves," and contains the substance of the second table of the law, and of all the exhortations and instructions of the prophets, *on that subject :* for it would be absurd to suppose our Lord meant, that it contained all that was written concerning

the love of God, or all the types and prophecies of a Saviour. —' This rule, being given as the sum of the law and the ' prophets, ... can never duly be so construed, as to subvert ' any of the laws and orders established by them. ...There- ' fore ir admits these limitations. What I desire ... agree- ' ably to ... the principles of the Christian religion, should ' be done, or not done to me, that I must do, or not do ' to others. It therefore will not follow... that if Socrates ' would lend his wife to a friend, that friend should do the ' like to him; because that ... is opposite to ..." the law and ' " the prophets."...A criminal ...would not have the judge ' condemn him ; ...yet a judge ... must not forbear to con- ' demn ; ... since this would take away vindictive justice, ' and let offenders go unpunished. ...The rule ... requires ' not the master to obey his servants, because he would ' have them obedient to him : but to be as obedient to his ' master as he can reasonably expect they should be to ' him ; and to treat his servants as kindly, ... as ... he could ' reasonably desire to be treated by his master. And so in ' the relations of father and children ... &c.—This rule must ' not be extended to every thing which a man may do law- ' fully. ... A poor man would desire that some very wealthy ' person would give him out of his estate enough to make ' him rich : though were this rich man poor, he would be ' glad, if somebody would shew the same kindness to him ; ' yet he is not obliged by this rule, though lawfully he ' might do it, to make this poor man rich.' *Whitby.* Certainly we are not required to do to others, whatsoever we might *unreasonably* desire them to do, if we were in their case. But, judging according to the rule of duty in all its latitude, and by the feelings of our own minds, we should suppose ourselves to be precisely in the situation of our neighbour ; and then impartially enquire, how we might *reasonably* expect him to behave towards us, if he were exactly in our situation. Every man, at first sight, must perceive, that this would lead to universal justice, truth, goodness, gentleness, compassion, beneficence, forgiveness, and candour; and exclude every thing of an opposite nature. If we honestly proceeded in this way, we should seldom need a casuist, to teach us how we ought to act towards our neighbours, in any possible relation or circumstance. But alas! even most professed Christians content themselves with doing to others as they *are* done by; instead of doing those things to others, which they *would* that others should do to them.—' This maxim will be a proper ' monitor, in common conversation ; ... in negociation and ' commerce ; ... in cases where others need our compassion ' and kindness ; in censures and reflections on others ; ... ' in provocations ; in the several relations of life ; ... and in ' religious differences ; ...and the use of such words as ' Schismaticks and Hereticks.' *Evans's Christian Temper.*

V. 13, 14. Our Lord's audience consisted of unestablished disciples, and of the multitude ; and both needed to be excited to greater earnestness in the concerns of their

н 5

narrow *is* the way, which leadeth unto life, and few there be that find it. 15 ¶ Beware of false prophets, which come to you in sheep's clothing, but inwardly they are ravening wolves.

16 Ye shall know them by their fruits, Do men gather grapes of thorns or figs of thistles? 17 Even so every good tree bringeth forth good fruit; but a corrupt tree bringeth forth evil fruit. 18 A good tree cannot bring forth evil fruit, neither can a corrupt tree bring forth good fruit.

souls: for which purpose, he next gave them this important exhortation and solemn warning.—Our passage through life is represented as a journey of the eternal world: and, as there are two places, to which men are removed at death; so there are two roads, one to destruction, the other to heavenly happiness. The gate, at which men enter into " the broad road," is very wide, even as wide as the whole fallen race of Adam: for we enter at it, when we are born sinners into a sinful world; and we proceed on that road as long as we live in an unconverted state. As it is *broad*, it has in it various paths, suited to men's different humours and inclinations. The covetous and the spendthrift; the infidel, the profligate, and the hypocrite; the Antinomian and the Pharisee; the sons and daughters of levity and giddy dissipation; grave designing politicians, and proud philosophers; decent moralists, and infamous debauchees, have their several paths and their select companies: they mutually despise and condemn each other, yet they all help to keep one another in countenance, by agreeing to oppose the holy ways of the Lord. In this " broad way," men walk without trouble, contrivance, or even intention: whilst they are pleasing or forgetting themselves, they make progress in it; nay, even when they are wasting their time in sleep or loitering: and as it is thronged by the many, and especially by the rich, wise, noble, and honourable of the world; and as many of its paths are fashionable and creditable; numbers have no suspicion whither it leads, and are highly displeased with those who give them warning: thus at length they fall into destruction. But, when a man hears and believes the voice of Christ, speaking by his word and his ministers, he discovers whither this way tends, and feels the necessity of getting out of it; he makes a stand, and determines to proceed no further; and he learns, that by repentance, faith in Christ, and conversion to God and holiness, he may get into another way which leads to life. But " the gate is strait:" sinful pleasures, prospects, interests, and connexions must be relinquished. A man must lay aside his encumbrances, his pride, and darling lusts; he must be humbled, stripped, and emptied; he must break loose from those who would retain him, and force his way through those who would impede his course; he must deny himself, take up his cross, resist temptation, mortify the flesh, endure reproach, earnestly use all the means of grace, and carefully accept of Christ in all his characters and offices; or he cannot get in at this strait gate. After he has entered, " the way is narrow," and, as it were, beset with thorns. It is the direct way of implicit faith and obedience: a Christian cannot pick and choose his path as men do in the broad road; but must go straight forward, turning neither to the right nor to the

left: if he do at all turn aside, he will be scourged back again into the narrow path. When he meets an enemy, he must face and overcome him; when he comes to a mountainous difficulty, he must climb over it; if the road be rough, he must still keep in it; and no persecution or tribulation must divert him from it. Therefore, " few " there be that find " this way to life. Most men either neglect religion entirely, or rest in forms or notions; or are deluded into some of those more soothing, flattering, and fashionable species of religion, which " Satan, transformed into an angel of light," and " his ministers, " transformed into ministers of righteousness," propose to them, when uneasy about their souls. They are deterred by the difficulties to be encountered, in entering at the strait gate and treading the narrow way, and by the dread of being thought singular and precise; and they hope to get to heaven at an easier rate: for they do not know or imagine, that this narrow way has its peculiar joys and consolations, which abundantly compensate for its difficulties and trials. Therefore, Christ warned his hearers and all men, to " enter in at the strait gate," without delay and with all earnestness; and to fear nothing so much as being left without: for, though the entrance is difficult, and found only by few; yet all who resolutely attempt it will succeed; and it leads to eternal life, whilst all other ways lead to destruction.—It is surprising how much this plain declaration of Christ has been overlooked by his professed disciples; and how much pains have been taken to soften the apparent asperity of it, and to explain away its evident meaning.—It cannot be inconsistent with the rule of not judging others, to suppose that most men are in " the way to destruction," and to warn and exhort them " to enter in at the strait gate ; " when such words as these are found in the scripture, and too plainly commented upon by the worldly and ungodly lives of the multitudes around us. (*Notes*, 1, 2. *Luke* xiii. 22—30.)—In all ages hitherto, the real disciple of Christ has been a singular and unfashionable character; and all, who have sided with the majority, have gone on in the broad road to destruction. (*Notes, Eph.* ii. 1—3.)

Broad. (13) Ευρυχωρος, (ex ιυρυς *latus, et* χωρα *regio*,) Spacious, roomy.—Used here only.—*Narrow.* (14) τεθλιμμενη. Θλιβω. *Mark* iii. 9. 2 *Cor.* i. 6. 2 *Thes.* i. 6. *Heb.* xi. 37. It is opposed to ευρυχωρος, as if it were τενχωρος; not a spacious, but a straitened way.

V. 15—20. False prophets were the most dangerous enemies to true religion, under the old dispensation; and false teachers have been the same, in all ages and places where Christianity has been professed. (*Marg. Ref.* b, c.) Nothing so much prevents men from entering in at the strait gate, and becoming true Christians, as the carnal-

19 Every tree that ¹ bringeth not forth good fruit is hewn down, and cast into the fire.

20 Wherefore ᵐ by their fruits ye shall know them.

21 ¶ Not every one that ⁿ saith unto me, Lord, Lord, ° shall enter into the kingdom of heaven; but he ᵖ that

doeth the will of ᑫmy Father which is in heaven.

22 Many will say ʳto me in that day, Lord, Lord, ˢ have we not prophe-sied in thy name? and in thy name have cast out devils? and in thy name done many wonderful works?

23 And then will I profess unto them, ᵗ I never knew you: ᵘ depart from me, ye that work iniquity.

soothing, and flattering doctrine of those, who oppose or pervert the truth. (*Note*, xxiii. 13.) Our Lord, therefore, warned the people to "beware of false prophets." These would come in sheep's clothing; that is, with great appearances of sanctity, and love to men's souls: but inwardly they would be greedy, fierce, and implacable, like "ravening wolves:" they would "teach things which "they ought not, for filthy lucre's sake," and be ready to devour all who opposed their pernicious principles. (*Notes*, lvi. *Is.* 9—12. *Mic.* iii. 5—7.) They might "be "known by their fruits;" that is, by the nature, tendency, and effects of their doctrine, especially as exemplified in their own spirit and conduct, for they would certainly betray themselves, by their selfishness or self-sufficiency, their arrogance or ambition, their eagerness for disputation or persecution, their vehement passions, or embittered resentment, or by some part of their habitual temper and conduct; being evidently contrary to the mind of Christ, and the disinterested humility, meekness, purity, and love, which characterize his true disciples and ministers.—He who regards Christ's words, will no more expect real good from following unchristian teachers, than he would hope to "gather grapes from thorns, or figs from thistles." In fact they commonly infect all, over whom they acquire influence, with their own corrupt principles, their spiritual pride, their selfishness, their wrath and malignity. A good tree may indeed be expected to yield good fruit; but a corrupt tree, in the nature of things, must bring forth evil fruit. The habitual conduct of a truly pious man must be good; and the tendency of his example, converse, and instructions must be beneficial: but the habitual tenour of an unconverted man's actions must be evil, and the effects of his example and doctrine pernicious, however it may be disguised. As, therefore, the Judge will shortly decide upon the characters of professed Christians by this rule; and "every tree, that bringeth not forth good fruit shall be "hewn down, and cast into the fire;" (*Note*, iii. 7—10;) so we ought to judge, as well as we are able, by the same rule at present. "By their fruits we must know them," and not by their "fair speeches;" nor can they be supposed to be really leading others in the way to heaven, who are manifestly themselves treading the contrary road.— The decent, friendly, and fascinating manners of some, who teach doctrines plainly contrary to scripture, have been thought by many an almost insuperable objection to interpreting the clause, "By their fruits ye shall know "them," of the character and actions of false prophets; and no doubt Satan will endeavour, for the credit of his cause, and to give energy to delusion, that "his ministers

"should be transformed as ministers of righteousness." Yet, in the very passage whence this quotation is made, the apostle declares, that "their end shall be according to "their works." (*Note*, 2 *Cor.* xi. 13—15.) The virtue, or amiableness, for which many Heresiarchs have been celebrated, will not bear examining by the law of God. It consists principally of such "things as are highly es-"teemed among men;" and is perceived to be connected with habitual disregard of many duties, and indulgence in many evils, when judged of by the word of God. The enlightened Christian will be enabled to see through the sheep's clothing, and detect the concealed wolf by careful investigation.

Corrupt. (17. 18) Σαπρον. xii. 33. xiii. 48. *Luke* vi. 43. *Eph.* iv. 29.

V. 21—23. Christ on this occasion spake, not only as avowedly the King of Israel, the promised Messiah; but with the dignity and authority of the Judge of the world, and the Arbiter of every man's eternal state, from whose decision there could be no appeal: and when we compare this language of conscious majesty and power, with his lowly appearance and external circumstances, and the neglect and contempt to which he was exposed, the contrast is peculiarly striking.—It is implied, that they, who do not acknowledge him as their Lord and Master, do not even *professedly* in the way to heaven: and it is declared, that even of his professed disciples and subjects, who acknowledge him for their Ruler, Teacher, and Saviour, and openly avow their relation to him, some will be excluded from the kingdom of heavenly glory, as not having been true subjects of his kingdom of grace; and that those "who do the "will of his heavenly Father," shall be finally and eternally saved.—It is here indispensably necessary to distinguish between the will of God, the Creator and Lawgiver, concerning his rational creatures; and his will, as it concerns us fallen and condemned sinners. The law of "loving "him with all our hearts," "and our neighbour as our-"selves," without the least allowance for failure, and sanctioned with the most awful curse, is, in the former sense, "the will of God." This "shuts up all men under sin" and condemnation; but God is now become the Saviour of sinners. What then, in revealing himself to sinners as a God of salvation, is his will concerning them? for this is here exclusively spoken of. As "the God and Father "of our Lord Jesus Christ," it is his will, that we should repent, forsake and hate all sin; believe, submit to, love, and obey his only begotten Son; love one another, and walk in all his ordinances and commandments with an upright heart. His first requirement, in this view, is, "This

ᴍ 7

24 ¶ Therefore * whosoever heareth these sayings of mine, and doeth them, I will liken him unto ʸ a wise man, ᶻ which built his house upon a rock. 25 And ᵃ the rain descended, and the floods came, and the winds blew, and beat upon that house; and it fell not: ᵇ for it was founded upon a rock.

26 And every one that heareth these sayings of mine, ᶜ and doeth them not, shall be likened unto a foolish man, which built his house upon the sand: 27 And ᵈ the rain descended, and the floods came, and the winds blew, and beat upon that house; and it fell: and great was the fall of it.

x 7, 8. 13, 14. v. 3, &c., 26—82. xii. 50. Luke vi. 47—49. xi. 28. John xiii. 17. xiv. 15. 21—24. xv. 10. 14. Rom. ii. 6—9. Gal. v. 6, 7. vi. 7, 8. Jam. i. 21—27. ii. 17—26. 1 John ii. 3. iii. 22—24. v. 3—5. Rev. xxii. 14, 15. *y* Job xxviii. 28. Prov. x. 8. xiv. 26. Jam. iii. 13—18. *z* 1 Cor. iii. 10, 11. Mal. iii. 3. Acts xlv. 22. 1 Cor. iii. 13—15. Jam. i. 12. 1 Pet. i. 7. *a* Ex. xiii. 11, &c. *b* xvi. 18. Ps. cxxv. 1, 2. Eph. iii. 17. Col. ii. 7. 1 Pet. i. 5. 1 John ii. 19.

c Prov. xiv. 1. Luke vi. 49. Jam. ii. 20. *d* xii. 43—45. xiii. 19—22. Ex. xlii. 10—16. Heb. x. 26—31. 2 Pet. ii. 20—22.

" is my beloved Son, in whom I am well pleased; hear ye " him." When this is complied with, all else follows: without it, all else is in vain. Obedience in all things is sincerely attempted, and habitually performed, in the general tenour of the true believer's life, from the time that he comes as a sinner to accept of Christ's salvation. In this sense he does the will of God; though he is far from being able to do his will, as the absolute Governor of the world, in such a manner as to be justified by the works of the law. But hypocrites do not sincerely attend to this will of God; and therefore they shall never enter heaven. Nay, the Lord declares, that many " in that day," (the solemn day of final account and retribution,) even of such as have preached the gospel, prophesied in his name, wrought miracles, cast out devils, will be rejected by him, because they were " workers of iniquity." Not only a single Balaam who prophesied, or a single Judas an apostle, will be thus condemned; but *many* will plead in vain their profession, gifts, and services, and the miracles which they have wrought in the name of Jesus Christ. He will then disavow all knowledge or approbation of them, as his disciples or servants; he knew them as hypocrites, but he did not *accept* them: he " never knew them," they were all along hypocrites, and workers of iniquity. (*Note,* 2 Tim. ii. 19.) They, therefore, will be constrained to depart from the holy Saviour, (whose name they had used and profaned,) with other workers of iniquity, to their own place, under the most aggravated condemnation; (*Note,* xxv. 41—46;) for in departing from Christ, the Light and Life of men, they must sink into darkness and despair.

V. 24—27. To impress more deeply the preceding solemn declaration, our Lord closed his discourse with a most affecting comparison. Doubtless, he is the Rock, the only sure and tried Foundation, on which the church, and every believer's soul and hope are built, and " other foundation " can no man lay." (*Note,* 1 Cor. iii. 10—15.) But this is not the subject: for the false foundation, not of the infidel or Pharisee, but of the hypocritical disciple, is detected. The persons, of whom Christ spake, are not hearers of Plato, of Seneca, of ancient philosophers, of Jewish Rabbies, or of modern deists and moralists : but they " hear his saying," and " call him, Lord, Lord ; " and thus they profess to build for eternity, a house, or refuge, in which they may be safe in every approaching season of dismay or danger. All else are even still further from the true Foundation.—One of the characters, here described, resembles a wise man, who digs deep, bestows pains, removes the rubbish, finds the rock, and on it lays firmly the foundation of his house; and then he proceeds to raise the superstructure, with good materials and sound workmanship, till it is completed. In this he takes up his abode:

and soon after, storms arise, the winds blow, the rains descend, the floods swell, and the house is vehemently beaten on; but it stands secure, amid the fury of the tempest, because " founded on a rock." This wise builder is the true Christian : he comes to Christ, hears his words, and believes them : instructed by the Saviour as his Prophet, he trusts in his righteousness, atonement, and mediation. He submits also to him as his Lord, and obeys his commandments from love to his name : he consults him as his Physician, and follows his directions, to obtain the health and sanctification of his soul. In short, he says, " Lord, what wouldest thou have me to do? " and he aims to render unreserved obedience. Thus he builds upon the Rock, in " faith working by love; " his soul is upheld by the power and grace of the divine Redeemer ; everlasting arms support him amidst the temptations, tribulations, and persecutions of life, and in the hour of death ; and he will be safe, as in a castle, amidst the convulsions of expiring nature, and during all the solemnities of the day of judgment.—But there is another builder, a foolish man, who professes to build on the same Rock; but, for want of care and pains he lays his foundation beside it, upon a quicksand : on this he erects a specious edifice, which greatly resembles the other, and which the superficial observer thinks equally stable ; and perhaps it may have even a fairer exterior : but when it is assailed by storms and floods, it falls with a terrible ruin, and the disappointed builder perishes in it. This is the deluded professor of the gospel, who perhaps bears and assents to its doctrines, and learns to speak and dispute about them ; nay, associates with Christians, adopts their creed, and possesses gifts, joins in sacred ordinances, and seems to be one of them ; but his " knowledge puffeth up," his faith is dead, and he is not obedient. What he does externally, according to the commands of Christ, is done from corrupt, selfish motives, and not from willing subjection to his authority; so that he disobeys, where interest, inclination, or reputation require it : his hope is a delusion, he is " a worker of iniquity ; " and so builds on the sand without a foundation. This is a common, unsuspected, but fatal delusion : there are many, of various descriptions and discordant sentiments, who thus " hear Christ's sayings, and do them not." Their profession may perhaps stand the lighter gusts of temptation, in times of outward peace and prosperity : but the tempests of fierce persecution would make dreadful havock among these edifices ; and the storms of death and judgment will sweep them away, and leave all who take refuge in them, in the deepest ruin, contempt, and misery. (*Marg. Ref.* d.)—It is argued by some expositors, that our Lord, by the words, " Whosoever heareth these sayings of mine, &c." shews, that this sermon contains all things needful for salvation :

N B

4 ch. 54. Ps. xlv.
2 Mark l. 22.
vi. 2. Luke iv.
22. xix. 48. John
vii. 15, 46

28 ¶ And it came to pass, when Jesus had ended these sayings, [a] the people were astonished at his doctrine;

29 For he taught them as one [f] having authority, [g] and not as the scribes.

f v. 20. 28. 32. 44. xxi. 23—27 xxviii. 18. Deut. xviii. 18, 19 Ec. viii. 4. Ja. i. 4. Jer. xxiii. 28, 29. Mic. iii. 8. Luke xxi. 15. Acts iii. 22, 23. vi. 10. Heb. iv. 12, 13.
g xv. 1—9. xxiii. 2—6. 15—34. Mark vii. 5—13. Luke xx. 8. 46, 47.

and many conclude, that the doctrinal parts of the New Testament are not so needful and important, as these practical instructions. But, most certainly, the unchangeable God never meant to recommend one part of his revealed will, by disparaging another. And who have ever, in any age, uprightly and unreservedly obeyed these sayings of our Lord, except those, who have firmly believed the doctrines of the gospel, as more clearly and fully revealed in the apostolical epistles? This sermon, doubtless, contains the grand outlines of *Christian practice;* and none who, on *Christian principles,* observe to do according to it, will come short of salvation. But *Christian principles,* or *doctrines,* must in many particulars be more fully learned from other parts of the sacred oracles.

V. 28, 29. The multitudes, who heard this interesting discourse, were astonished at the wisdom, weight, and energy of Christ's doctrine, and the majesty and authority with which he enforced it. They perceived, that his important instructions had a commanding influence on their understandings, consciences, and affections, which forced their conviction and approbation; and that he spake in a very different manner from their scribes, who only inculcated ceremonial observances, external duties, and their own traditions, or those of some renowned Rabbi, in a dry, disputational, and uninteresting manner.

PRACTICAL OBSERVATIONS.

V. 1—6.

Whilst we are careful not to " call evil good," or " dark- " ness light;" we should also guard against a censorious spirit, the offspring of pride and petulance; or we shall prepare bitterness for ourselves, and may expect sharp rebukes from God, and harsh censures from man. But why should we, who have so much to be humbled for and to rectify in our own conduct, officiously expose our brother's faults, which perhaps are far less heinous than our own? Rather let us seek for more self-knowledge, a sounder judgment, deeper humility, and grace to walk more circumspectly; that, if we have the opportunity, we may have ability, influence, and tenderness, to counsel, caution, and reprove our brethren, with propriety and efficacy.—How unfit must unconverted men be for the ministry! Yet how many such enter into that arduous office, and attempt to take motes out of the eyes of others, without " consider- " ing the beam that is in their own cye!" The minister of Christ is indeed a reprover by office; and must " rebuke " with all authority." It is therefore peculiarly needful for all, who aspire after that office, to begin by " casting the " beam out of their own eye, that they may see clearly to " cast out the mote out of their brother's eye." And all engaged in the work, should be very careful not to expose themselves to be retorted upon with, " Thou hypocrite, " first cast out the beam out of thine own eye." It should, however, be observed, that a discernible *mote* in a man's eye, does not disqualify him from casting out a *beam* from another man's eye : yet many harden themselves in gross sins, or wholly neglect the cautions and reproofs of their ministers, because they see, that they also are liable to

VOL. V.

imperfections!—But prudence and fortitude, as well as a good cause and a good intention, are requisite for the performance of the office of a reprover: we should expect to meet with unreasonable men, who will scoff at the most precious truths, and rage against the most just and friendly warnings; and we ought therefore to prepare for enduring contempt and persecution, with meekness and firmness : and we shall often be constrained to let the proud and impious scorner alone, lest we should drive him to further extremities of madness and blasphemy. But, if holy counsels and warnings should not be thrown away on these hardened offenders; how deplorable is it, when the most sacred ordinances and offices of the church are left open to their profanation, if they choose to do it " for filthy lucre's sake!" Surely this is in the worst sense to " give that which is holy to the dogs, and " to cast pearls before swine!"

V. 7—12.

Amidst all the evils which we witness, and all the wants, weakness, and folly which we experience, let us give ourselves unto prayer. Thus let the sinner seek reconciliation to God, and the believer, all that he needs for his honourable and comfortable walk with him : but let us seek and pray with earnestness, importunity, and resolute perseverance, and with a believing expectation of success. For the promise is express, that " every one that asketh re- " ceiveth :" if therefore men say, that they do ask, seek, and knock, and yet evidently do not obtain, but remain enslaved to their sins ; we must conclude, that they either deceive themselves, or mean to deceive others. " Let " God be true, and every man a liar:" if men have not, it is " because they ask not; or because they ask amiss," and from some carnal and corrupt motive. We should, therefore, seek wisdom, knowledge, grace, strength, and every good thing, in this appointed way, without regarding objectors or despisers. Let us begin, and go on to the end, resting on the promises; and they will carry us safely through, as they have done immense numbers who are now in glory. Let us never suppose, that our heavenly Father would erect " a throne of grace," appoint a Mediator, open a new and living way of access in so wonderful a manner, command us to pray, and incline our hearts to it; and then at last refuse to hear, or give us what would be useless or pernicious, instead of " the Bread of life " and the blessings of salvation. Far be it from us to listen to such suggestions of the enemy; or suspect our merciful God of conduct, which would be a disgrace to one of the sinful race of men! Assured, therefore, of his willingness to " give good things to all that ask him," let us copy the example of his equity, truth, and goodness; and " what- " soever we would that men should do unto us," let us study to " do the same to them;" " not rendering evil for " evil, or railing for railing," but " doing good against " evil, and overcoming evil with good."

V. 18—20.

We ought constantly to keep in mind the awful truth,

I

CHAP. VIII.

Christ cleanses a leper, 1—4; heals a Centurion's servant, and predicts the calling of the Gentiles and rejection of the Jews, 5—18: heals Peter's wife's mother, 14, 15, and many others, fulfilling a prophecy of Isaiah, 16, 17: shews in what spirit he ought to be followed, 18—22: calms the tempestuous sea by his word, 23—27: and casts out devils from two possessed men; suffering them to go into the swine, 28—32. The Gergesenes desire him to leave them, 33, 34.

WHEN he was ᵃ come down from the mountain, ᵇ great multitudes followed him.

2 And, ᶜ behold, there came ᵈ a leper and ᵉ worshipped him, saying, Lord, ᶠif thou wilt, thou canst make me clean.

3 And Jesus ᵍ put forth *his* hand, and touched him, saying, ʰ I will; be thou clean. ⁱ And immediately his leprosy was cleansed.

4 And Jesus saith unto him, ᵏ See thou tell no man; but go thy way, ˡ shew thyself to the priest, and offer

---

that " wide is the gate, and broad the way, which leadeth " to destruction, and many there be who go in thereat." If we would serve God, we must be singular, as well as resolute, in religion. We " must be born again, or we " cannot see the kingdom of God;" we must believe in Christ, and be in him new creatures, and lead sober, right-eous, and godly lives, or we cannot be saved: and facts de-monstrate that so " strait is this gate, and narrow this way," that " few there be that find them." Yet " every one " that seeketh, findeth, and to him that knocketh," the gate shall " be opened;" and, though the way has its diffi-culties, and is painful to the flesh, yet it has its comforts, " which a stranger intermeddleth not with." The entrance is commonly more arduous than the further progress, to those who set out resolutely: and the hope of heaven, and " joy in the Holy Ghost," combine to render it " the way " of pleasantness and the path of peace."—But let all, who would tread this narrow way, beware of those who " prophesy smooth things,".who invent easier ways to heaven, and more pleasing to corrupt nature. Such are " ministers of Satan transformed into ministers of right-" eousness:" these " beguile unstable souls," and preju-dice them against the pure religion of Christ, and those who teach it. Whatever specious appearances they assume, they are actuated by ambition, vain-glory, avarice, or some corrupt principle, and are " wolves in sheep's clothing." The disciple of Christ, who keeps his Master's character and precepts in view, as the standard of his judgment, will generally see through them. " By their fruits he will " know them " from the faithful servants of his Lord, and will not expect to " gather grapes or figs, from thorns or " thistles." He is fully aware, that a good tree cannot habitually bring forth evil fruit, any more than a corrupt tree can bring forth good fruit; and, looking forward to the time, when " every tree that bringeth not forth good " fruit shall be hewn down, and cast into the fire," he will keep at a distance, lest he should be deceived by them.— But alas! most men establish other rules of judgment than the word of God: and a confident tone, a voluble tongue, zeal for some parts of religion in opposition to others, or new notions plausibly dressed up and defended, go much further, than a Christian spirit and conversation, and the plain, faithful preaching of the whole doctrine of the gospel: so that " many follow the pernicious ways" of deceivers, " by reason of whom the way of truth is evil " spoken of." (*Note,* 2 *Pet.* ii. 1—3.)

V. 21—29.

We must " cease from man," if we would hear the de-cision of our future Judge: he assures us, that " not every " one who calls him Lord, Lord, shall enter the kingdom " of heaven, but he only that doeth the will of his hea-" venly Father." Let us remember, that real grace is far more valuable, than the most splendid accomplishments, and even than the gift of prophecy and miracles. If the most admired and useful minister on earth had no better evidence of his conversion, than his abilities and success as a preacher, he would " preach to others and be himself a " cast-away;" whilst the meanest believer in his audience, would be received into the mansions of felicity. Let us then take warning by our Lord's solemn admonitions, and " examine ourselves whether we be in the faith," and whe-ther we have that love, without which all other attainments are nothing. (*Notes,* 1 *Cor.* xiii.) Let us beware not only of infidelity, profligacy, and self-righteousness; but of a dead faith, a formal profession, a perversion of the gospel. Let no man imagine, that he builds on the one tried Foun-dation, who only hears the words of Christ, but does not obey them. Alas! he builds upon the sand, as fatally as the open enemy of evangelical truth: his edifice may rise fair and magnificent; but it will fall when he most wants it: and then his folly will be manifest, his ruin most tre-mendous. May the Lord make us wise builders for eter-nity: may we come to Christ, hear and believe his word, and shew our faith by our works of conscientious, unre-served obedience. Then we may be sure, that " nothing " shall ever separate us from the love of Christ ;" and may look forward, with joyful expectation of smiling in the agonies of death, and triumphing when the world shall be one common conflagration.—Finally, may the Lord send forth many preachers, who may declare the same great truths and precepts as Christ did, and with some good measure of his energy, influence, and authority: may the lives and examples of all preachers of the gospel, give a sanction to their doctrine, for the conviction of their hearers; and may they, whose " word is as fire, and as the hammer " that breaketh the rocks in pieces," every where supplant those, who still continue to teach after the formal, lifeless manner of the Scribes and Pharisees of old.

NOTES.

CHAP. VIII. V. 1—4. In commenting on those mira-cles, parables, or discourses, which are recorded by more

the gift that Moses commanded, *for a testimony unto them.

5 ¶ And when Jesus was ᵃ entered into Capernaum, there came unto him ᵇ a centurion, beseeching him,

6 And saying, Lord, ᵖ my servant lieth at home sick of the ᵠ palsy, grievously tormented.

7 And Jesus saith unto him, ʳ I will come and heal him.

than one of the evangelists, I purpose to be more particular where they first occur, and to reserve only the additional circumstances and variations, to be considered in the other gospels; except where the other evangelists are more full and copious in their narrative.—The harmony of the evangelists has given immense trouble to many expositors, and yet several things remain in great uncertainty. As it is, therefore, a matter of far more difficulty than importance to us, I shall not perplex the reader with conjectures, or attempt exactness in this respect; for we are much more concerned in knowing what Christ said and did, than at what time, or in what order he said and did it. In general, Matthew is supposed to pay more regard to the order of time in his narration, than Mark or Luke. John perhaps was more observant of the regular succession, in his history, than any of the other evangelists: but he chiefly recorded those things, which had not been mentioned by them.—Matthew, however, seems to fix the date of this miracle to the time immediately following the sermon upon the mount, and while Christ was yet surrounded by the multitudes.—The case of the lepers, and the remarkable laws concerning them, have been considered. (Notes, Lev. xiii. xiv.) The leprosy seems to have been commonly inflicted by the immediate hand of God, and not curable by medicine: it excluded a man from publick ordinances, and from most of the employments and comforts of society; and it was an emblem of the guilt and dominion of sin, which exclude men from communion with God and his people, and, unless removed, must exclude them from heaven. This poor leper was probably convinced, by the report which he had heard of the miracles and doctrine of Jesus, that he was the Messiah, of whom he had read in the books of the prophets: and therefore believing that he could cleanse him, and hoping that he would, he applied to him in this most humble and reverential manner; and his believing expectation was immediately answered. . Holy men and holy angels used to decline such worship, as an honour by no means to be paid to them; (Marg. Ref. e;) but Christ never intimated his disapprobation of any who rendered it to him: on the contrary he approved of it in the most decisive manner; which shews that he was conscious of having an undeniable right to divine honour and worship. The touch would have rendered another man ceremonially unclean: but Christ acted as a Priest, and more than a priest; and whilst he cleansed the leprosy, he could not contract defilement from it. It is probable, from the charge of secrecy given to the man, that Jesus took him aside from the multitude to cleanse him. This seems to have been done, in order to avoid all appearance of ostentation in his miracles, which could not but be known sufficiently: perhaps he would not needlessly exasperate his enemies, and excite them to hasten their designs against his life, before the appointed time. But, that the cure might be authenticated, and, as it were, registered; as well as that honour might be put

upon the ordinances of the Mosaick law, which was still in force, Christ ordered the man to go, and shew himself to the priest, and offer the appointed sacrifices; which would bring the priests acquainted with the miraculous cure wrought by him, and might be a testimony to them that he was the promised Messiah.—ᶜ Christ, in healing of ᶜ the leprous with the touching of his hand, shewed that ᶜ he abhorreth no sinners that come to him, be they never ᶜ so unclean.' Beza.

Worshipped. (2) Προσεκυνει. (Ex προς et κυνεω osculor.) iv. 9, 10. xiv. 33. xviii. 26. Acts x. 25. Rev. xix. 10. xxii. 8.—I will, &c. (3) ᶜ Here shines forth the divine ᶜ power of Christ; that he could do so great things only ᶜ by his command. So also Moses says, the world was ᶜ created by God, saying, "Let there be light; and there ᶜ "was light."' Woltzogenius in Whitby.—Be thou clean.] Καθαρισθῃ. Be thou cleansed.

V. 5—7. A centurion was the captain of a hundred men, in the Roman legions: these were not composed of the lowest of the people, but of reputable citizens; and therefore a centurion was considerably higher in rank than a captain in our armies.—It is probable, that this man was of good family and fortune; he was a soldier, educated a heathen, and a Roman: and most of his countrymen, and fellow soldiers, exceedingly despised the Jews and their religion. Yet, his not being cast by Providence in that part of the Roman empire, (probably without his own choice,) his prejudices had been obviated, he had become acquainted with the scriptures, and was evidently a humble and spiritual worshipper of the God of Israel, though not a proselyte to the Mosaick law. He had also conceived the highest esteem of the people of God, and affection for them: and by his good conduct, for some considerable time, he had overcome the prejudices of the Jews against him as a gentile, and as an officer in the army which held their nation in subjection. (Note, Luke vii. 1—10.) · His tender concern likewise about his servant, when sick, should be considered as the effect of his religion; by which he had probably won over some of his domesticks also to the worship of God. He had, no doubt, before this heard of the miracles and doctrine of Christ, and perhaps of a similar miracle wrought on the nobleman's son; (Notes, John iv. 46—54;) and he had conceived the most exalted ideas of his dignity and excellency, as the promised Messiah and the King of Israel: so that when his servant, whom he much valued, was seized with a palsy, which not only disabled him from his business, but filled· him with extreme pain; he hoped for his cure by a miracle, 'and applied to Jesus for that purpose.—We learn from St. Luke, that he did not come himself, at least not at the first; but that he humbly sent the elders of the Jews, and afterwards his friends: yet some think, that at last he came also himself. Nothing however is more common, than for men to be said to do those things, which others do at their instance, and in their stead.

I 3

8 The centurion answered and said, Lord, [e] I am not worthy that thou shouldest come under my roof: [f] but speak the word only, and my servant shall be healed.

9 For I am a man under authority, having soldiers under me: and I say to this man, [u] Go, and he goeth; and to another, Come, and he cometh; and to my servant, [x] Do this, and he doeth it.

10 When Jesus heard it, [y] he marvelled, and said to them that followed, [z] Verily, I say unto you, [a] I have not found so great faith, no, not in Israel.

11 And I say unto you, [a] That many shall come from the east and west, and shall [b] sit down with Abraham, and Isaac, and Jacob, [c] in the kingdom of heaven.

12 But [d] the children of the kingdom shall [e] be cast out into outer darkness: there shall be weeping and gnashing of teeth.

13 And Jesus said unto the centurion, [f] Go thy way; [g] and as thou hast [c] believed, so be it done unto thee. [h] And his servant was healed in the self-same hour.

Centurion. (5) Ἑκατονταρχος. (Ex ἑκαλον, *centum,* and αρχος *princeps.*)—*My servant.* (6) Ὁ παις μυ. Generally παις, ὁ και ἡ, means a *son,* or *daughter.* ii. 16. xvii. 18. xxi. 15. *Luke* ii. 43. *Acts* iii. 26. iv. 27. 30. But here, and in some other places, it evidently means a *servant. Luke* xii. 45. Gr. but a servant of a superior order, and in special favour. In a few instances, it may be doubted, which it denotes. xii. 18. *Luke* i. 54. 69. *Acts* iv. 25.—*Sick of the palsy.*] Παραλυλικος. iv. 24. ix. 2. 6. *Mark* ii. 3—5. 9, 10. (Der. from παραλυω, *dissolvo, debilito.*) This disease is not mentioned in the Old Testament.

V. 8, 9. The centurion, surprised perhaps at our Lord's condescension, and prompt attention to his request, so contrary to the general spirit and conduct of the Jews; and deeply conscious of his own sinfulness, regarded himself as unworthy to receive a visit from so holy and eminent a person; and considered his house, (the residence of a gentile,) an improper place for him to enter.—When we remember, that Christ appeared in all respects as a poor Jew, " who had not where to lay his head;" and that this man was a Roman, of that victorious nation to which the Jews were subject, and one that lived in affluence; we shall perceive that his humble reverence of Christ was, in every respect, extraordinary.—He added, that it was in no wise necessary for Jesus thus to demean himself, for he could remove the disease by a word spoken at a distance. This he illustrated by his own case : he was only an inferior officer, subject to the authority of his tribune and his general : yet, having a company of soldiers under his command, he found them prompt to obey his orders, whether delivered on the spot, or sent to them at a distance ; and, in like manner, his servant implicitly obeyed his word : much more then would diseases obey the command of him, who was " the King of glory" and " the Lord of all." We can hardly conceive of a higher expression of confidence in the power of Christ, as " the Son of God," and as possessed of unlimited authority, than this was.—' If I, who am sub-
' ject to the power of another, have so much power over
' my servants, that they instantly do whatever I would
' have them : how much more shall all things which those
' requirest be done at thy command, who art subject to
' the power of none! And how can we deny him to be
' God, in whom shines forth that divine power, which God
' exerted in the creation of the world; and at whose word

' all things that he commandeth must be done; and who
' is subject to the power of none?' *Woltzogenius* in *Whitby.*

V. 10—12. ' Christ, by setting before them the exam-
' ple of the uncircumcised centurion, and yet of an excel-
' lent faith, provoketh the Jews to emulation, and ... fore-
' warneth them of their casting off, and the calling of the
' Gentiles.' *Beza.*—Our Lord might have commended many things in the centurion's character and conduct; but he specially expressed an entire approbation of his unwavering faith, as one surprised at it, considering all the disadvantages under which, as a Gentile, he had laboured. Thus he emphatically instructed the people, that he best approved of those, who formed the most exalted apprehensions of him, and expected the most from him : and that they could not honour him more than was right, and due to him. He affirmed, that he had not found such strong faith, even in Israel, where it might have been most expected; no, not so much as among his own disciples ! and hence he took occasion to declare, that many of the benighted Gentiles, from the distant parts of the earth, would, by faith in him, become fellow-heirs with Abraham, Isaac, and Jacob, of that heavenly felicity, to the enjoyment of which they had attained; whilst the Jews, " the children of the kingdom," who had so long enjoyed the peculiar privileges of God's people, to whom the gospel was first to be preached, and who supposed themselves exclusively entitled to the blessings of Messiah's kingdom, would be excluded from the church, and left in a dark and wretched condition : and that numbers of them would be shut out of heaven, and left to final wickedness, misery, and despair; where they would in vain weep, and gnash their teeth in rage and anguish, recollecting what happiness they had lost, and what ruin they had incurred, by their unbelief and folly.—The future state must exclusively be meant. ' It cannot be said, with any propriety, either that
' the holy patriarchs share with Christians, in the present
' privileges of the gospel-state; or that the Jews weep and
' wail, on account of their being excluded from them.' *Doddridge.*

Gnashing. (12) Βρυγμος· (a ᵭρυχω, *frendeo, Acts* vii. 54 :) xiii. 42. 50. xxii. 13. xxiv. 51. xxv. 30. *Luke* xiii. 28.

V. 13. The centurion seems by this time to have joined the company : our Lord therefore addressed *him :* and it

I 4

14 ¶ And when Jesus was come
[i]into Peter's house, he saw his [k]wife's
mother laid, and sick of a fever.
15 And he [l]touched her hand, and
the fever left her: and she arose, [m]and
ministered unto them.
16 ¶ When [n]the even was come,
[o]they brought unto him many that
were possessed with devils: [p]and he
cast out the spirits with *his* word, [q]and
healed all that were sick:
17 That [r]it might be fulfilled which
was spoken by Esaias the prophet, saying, [s]Himself took our infirmities, and
bare *our* sicknesses.
18 ¶ Now when Jesus [t]saw great
multitudes about him, he gave commandment to depart [u]unto the other
side.
19 And [x]a certain scribe came, and
said unto him, Master, [y]I will follow
thee whithersoever thou goest.
20 And Jesus saith unto him, The
foxes have holes, [z]and the birds of the
air *have* nests; but [a]the Son of man
hath not where to lay *his* head.
21 And [b]another of his disciples
said unto him, Lord, [c]suffer me first
to go and bury my father.
22 But Jesus said unto him, [d]Fol-
low me; [e]and let the dead bury their
dead.

i 20. xvii. 25. Mark i. 29. Luke iv. 38, 39.
k 1 Cor. ix. 5. 1 Tim. iii. 2. iv. 3. Heb. xiii. 4.
l 3. ix. 20. 29. xiv. 36. xx. 34. 2 Kings xiii. 21. Is. vi. 7. Mark i. 41. Luke viii. 54. Acts xix. 11—13.
m Luke iv. 38, 39. John xii. 1—3.
n Mark i. 32—34. Luke iv. 40, 41.
o iv. 24. ix. 2. Mark ii. 3. Acts v. 16.
p xii. 22. Mark i. 25—27. 34. v. 8. ix. 25. Acts xix. 13—16.
q xiv. 14. Ex. xv. 26.
r i. 22. ii. 15. 23.
s Is. liii. 4. 1 Pet. ii. 24.
t i. Mark i. 35—38. Luke iv. 42, 43. John vi. 15.
u xiv. 22. Mark iv. 35. v. 21 vi. 45. viii. 13. Luke viii. 22.
x Ezra vii. 6. Mark xii. 32—34. Luke ix. 57, 58. 1 Cor. i. 20.
y Luke xiv. 25—27. 33. xxii. 33, 34. John xiii. 36—38.
z Ps. lxxxiv. 3. civ. 17.
a Ps. xl. 17. lxix. 29. cix. 22. Is. liii. 2, 3. Luke ii. 7. 12. 16. viii. 3. 2 Cor. viii. 9.
b Luke ix. 59—62.
c xix. 29. Lev. xxi. 11, 12. Num. vi. 6, 7. Deut. xxxiii. 9, 10. 1 Kings xix. 20, 21. Hag. i. 2. 2 Cor. v. 16.
d iv. 18—22. ix. 9. John i. 43.
e Luke xv. 32. Eph. ii. 1. 5. v. 14. Col. ii. 13. 1 Tim. v. 6.

was found, that the servant was perfectly cured, at the time when he spake the words.

V. 14, 15. This miracle was wrought on the sabbath-day, after our Lord and his disciples returned from the synagogue. (*Mark* i. 29—31. *Luke* iv. 38, 39.) It seems, that Peter and his brother Andrew had a house at Capernaum; that Peter's wife's mother was one of the family; and that our Lord lodged there, when in that city. In his absence, she had been seized with a violent fever, which confined her to her bed: but Jesus, on his return, went to her, and rebuked the fever; (as a man would do his servant, who was going beyond his orders; *Note*, 8, 9;) which immediately obeyed his word and left her. Thus she was able, without delay, to arise, and wait upon him and his disciples, being, in a moment, perfectly restored to full health and strength! This is well known to be wholly different, from the experience of those who, in an ordinary way, recover from violent fevers: for extreme debility universally succeeds to the paroxysm of the disease.

Sick of a fever. (14) Πυρεσσουσαν, *Mark* i. 30. (A πυρετος, 15, hocque a πυρ, *ignis*.)

V. 16, 17. (*Marg. Ref.*) The Jews began their sabbaths in the evening, at sun-set, and ended them at the same time the next day. The people were restrained, by regard to the sabbath, from bringing their sick and demoniacks, till it was over: but the miracles which Christ had wrought, being noised abroad, might induce them thus to throng to him in the evening: and Jesus, not complaining of weariness from the labours of the day, or of the unseasonableness of the hour, restored all the demoniacks to the perfect use of their faculties, and to mental composure: as well as healed all the other sick persons. Thus the prophecy of Isaiah was fulfilled: (*Note, Is.* liii. 4—6:) for though the prophet more directly predicted the sufferings of Christ on the cross for our sins; yet all the labours, fatigues, and sorrows of his whole life, were willingly submitted to out of compassion to sinners, and formed a part of his humiliation as our Surety. Sickness, and the power of the devil, are effects of sin; and he suffered to deliver us from sin and all its consequences. So that, in thus denying himself, that he might relieve demoniacks and sick persons, for the confirmation of the gospel, he might truly be said, "to take our infirmities and bear our sick-"nesses;" that is, to endure pain and uneasiness himself, in order to deliver others from them. 'He himself bears our 'sins, and travails in pain concerning us.' *Is.* liii. 4. *Sept.*

V. 18—20. When great multitudes were gathered about Jesus, and it might have been supposed, that he would instruct them; he either perceived, that they were indisposed to profit, and that he had taught them as much as they could at that time receive and digest; or he meant to put their sincerity to the trial, and to procure leisure for necessary relaxation: he therefore gave orders to his disciples to cross the sea of Tiberias. On this occasion, a scribe, or interpreter of the law and the traditions, (*Marg. Ref.* x,) came to him, offering to become his constant follower. He seems to have been convinced that Jesus was the Messiah, and to have admired his discourses: and, having imbibed some confused ideas of his dignity and authority, he probably built his hopes of future preferment and consequence, on joining him at so early a period; perhaps expecting, that Christ would gladly accede to his proposal, seeing he was as yet only followed by unlearned fishermen, and others of low rank in life. But, probably, our Lord saw that he was actuated by ambition and carnal motives, and that he had not counted his cost: he therefore discouraged his proposal, intimating that it would not answer his expectations: for though the meanest of the wild beasts and birds of the air had their abode, to which they retired for repose and safety; yet he "the "Son of man, during his humiliation in human nature, "had not where to lay his head," even when wearied with labour, and needing the refreshment of sleep. His disciples, therefore, must expect to be equally destitute, to endure hardship, and to be recompensed by spiritual advantages alone.—It is likely, that this intimation sufficed, and induced the scribe to abandon his design. (*Note, Luke* ix. 57—62.)

V. 21, 22. Another person also, who had followed Christ as his disciple, was called to a more constant attendance on him, that he might be sent forth to preach his gospel; but for the present he desired to excuse himself, requesting leave to attend on the funeral of his father, who was just deceased: for Christ's answer seems to imply that this was his request; and not that he might stay with an aged parent till his death, as some explain it. But our

23 ¶ And when he was 'entered into a ship, his disciples followed him. 24 And, behold, 'there arose a great tempest in the sea, insomuch that the ship was covered with the waves: 'but he was asleep.

25 And his disciples came to *him*, and awoke him, saying, Lord, 'save us; we perish.

26 And he saith unto them, 'Why are ye fearful, O ye of little faith? Then he arose, 'and rebuked the winds and the sea; and there was a great calm.

27 But the men 'marvelled, saying, What manner of man is this, that even the winds and the sea obey him?

28 ¶ And 'when he was come to the other side, into the country of the ' Gergesenes, there met him two possessed with devils, 'coming out of the tombs, exceeding fierce, 'so that no man might pass by that way.

29 And, behold, they cried out saying, 'What have we to do with thee, Jesus, ' thou Son of God? art thou come hither to "torment us before the time?

Lord perceived that he had some reluctance to the self-denying service appointed for him, which might have been increased by going to bury his father, and associating with his relations: and at the same time he purposed to shew, that all personal and relative concerns must give place to his command, and our attachment to him and his cause. He therefore would not grant his request: but ordered him to leave that care to his relatives, who were dead in sin, and incapable of spiritual services; (*Marg. Ref.* e;) but could order every thing needful for the burial of the dead, and would give due attention to it.—' *The dead*, in scrip-' ture, often signify ... those, who in a spiritual sense are ' so, by being "alienated from the life of God," and ' " dead in trespasses and sins."—Here then Christ teach-' eth, that when we are called by him to the promotion of ' the gospel, and the salvation of men's souls, we must ' not suffer earthly business, which may be done as well by ' others, who are unfit to be employed in spirituals, to give ' us the least hindrance from setting instantly upon that ' work.' *Whitby*.

V. 23—27. The Evangelists Mark and Luke relate this and what follows in a different connexion. Christ, however, having entered the ship, or fisher-boat, which the disciples had provided, set sail, being accompanied by some other small vessels: (*Note, Mark* iv. 35—41:) but instead of the fair voyage, which probably they expected, they were overtaken with a terrible storm : so that the ship was speedily covered with the waves, and apparently ready to sink ; yet amidst all this confusion and distress, Jesus lay fast asleep. His human nature, like our's in every thing but sin, was wearied with incessant fatigue; and he willingly yielded to sleep, foreseeing the storm, that his power might thus be more noticed. But the disciples, trembling lest they should be swallowed up by the waves, and having no resource but in his power, came and awoke him ; saying " Lord, save us, we perish." Considering all which they had seen of his power, this was compara-tively weak faith ; and their fears were evidences of much remaining unbelief. It was impossible, that the vessel which carried him could sink ; and, in his divine nature, he was as able to restrain the winds and waves, when his human nature lay asleep, as to cure the paralytick by a word spoken at a distance. Having therefore first rebuked them, as men " of little faith ;" he next, with the autho-

rity of the Lord and Governor of the creation, rebuked the winds and waves ; (as a master would rebuke a company of unruly servants ;) and at his omnipotent word, the winds suddenly ceased to blow, the tempestuous sea (contrary to its nature,) immediately became smooth, and a perfect calm succeeded. This filled the disciples with the greatest astonishment ; and they said to each other, " What man-" ner of Person is this?" (Ποταπος εςιν ᵶτος ;) ' No doubt he is more than man ; for with divine " authority, he " commands even the winds, and waves, and they obey " him !" '—Thus the tempest, which threatened their de-struction, was over-ruled to the increase of their faith, and admiration of the majesty and power of their Lord. (*Marg. Ref.* m.)—' It being so often made the property of God, ' to still the raging of the sea ;...it is not to be wondered ' at, that Christ's disciples should conceive there must be ' a divine power in him, who could perform such things.' *Whitby*.

A *tempest*. (24) Σεισμος. (A σειω, *moveo, concutio*.) It is generally rendered *earthquake* ; xxiv. 7. xxviii. 2. *Acts* xvi. 26. It means a sudden *commotion* or *shaking* of any kind ; *Jer.* x. 22. xxiii. 19. xlvii. 3. *Ez.* iii. 12. xxxvii. 7.- xxxviii. 19. *Nah.* iii. 2. *Sept.—O ye of little faith.* (26) Ολιγοπιϛοι. (Comp. of ολιγος *little* and πιϛις *faith*.) vi. 30. xiv. 31. xvi. 8. *Luke* xii. 28. A word peculiar to the New Testament.

V. 28, 29. The country of the Gergesenes included in it the region of Gadara. It seems to have been inhabited chiefly by Jews, but surrounded by Gentiles, who mixed much with the inhabitants.—The other evangelists on this occasion mention but one demoniack ; probably, because one was more remarkable than the other, both before and after his cure ; but they do not say that there was no more than one : this therefore is no real disagreement. (*Notes, Mark* v. 1—20. *Luke* viii. 26—39.)—The circumstances of this narration (like those of several others,) plainly prove the reality of possessions by evil spirits ; for such things were said and done by these demoniacks, and such events took place in consequence of their dispossession, as one would think no man could ascribe to lunacy, who was himself in his sober senses. But a main point of modern Sadduceism consists in denying the existence or agency of apostate spirits ; and they carry on their designs best in the dark, and maintain their empire most successfully, by promoting this kind of infidelity. Some however, who are

ɪ 6

x Lev. xi. 7.
Deut. xiv. 8.
Isv. 4. Isvi. 3.
Mark v. 11.
Luke viii. 32.
xv. 15, 16.
y Mark v. 7. 12.
Luke viii. 30—
33. Rev. xii. 12.
xx. 1, 2.
z 1 Kings xxii. 22.
Job i. 10—12. ii.
3—6. Acts ii. 23.
iv.28. Rev. xx. 7.

30 And there was a good way off
from them ˣ an herd of many swine,
feeding.
31 So ʸ the devils besought him,
saying, If thou cast us out, suffer us to
ᶻ go away into the herd of swine.
32 And he said unto them, ᵃ Go.

And when they were come out, they
went into the herd of swine: and, behold, ᵇ the whole herd of swine ran violently down a steep place into the sea,
and perished in the waters.
33 And ᵇ they that kept them fled,
and went their ways into the city, and

a Job i. 12—19. ii.
7. 8. Mark v. 13
Luke viii. 33.

b Mark v. 14—16.
Luke viii. 34—
36. Acts xix. 15
—17.

---

not sceptical in other respects, are unwilling to admit the
reality of these possessions. But it cannot be thought,
that Satan and his angels want power or malice to distract men's minds and torment their bodies, as well as to
tempt them to sin, if God were pleased to permit them;
nor can it be ascertained how far they have influence in
producing or increasing diseases, which affect both body
and mind. Even, if they do not in any instance immediately cause lunacies, or other maladies, it cannot be denied
upon scriptural principles, that they may take the advantage of the disordered state of the body, to disturb and
terrify the mind, and to augment the effects. (Notes, Job
i. 6, 7. ii. 6.) But when Christ was " manifested to destroy
" the works of the devil," there was a peculiar propriety
and wisdom, in leaving that great enemy of God and man
at greater liberty; that he might shew his power and
malice, and the tendency of his efforts to render mankind
miserable, and to destroy them: and that Christ might
have the fuller opportunity to shew his superior power and
authority; to give conclusive evidence of the existence of
these spirits, in opposition to the infidelity of the Sadducees; and to evince the beneficent intention of his gospel.—' Some are of opinion,...that these were only per-
' sons afflicted with strange maladies : but this cavil may
' be evidently confuted. ...The scriptures...make a plain
' and evident distinction, betwixt ...curing diseases, and
' casting out devils. (iv. 24.) ...This will be farther evident
' from many circumstances, relating to the devils being
' cast out. (Mark i. 34. Luke iv. 41. viii. 27. 33.) Now
' to make all these sayings the effects of a disease, or to
' conceive that Christ spake thus to a disease, is too great
' an evidence of one that is himself diseased. ...Christ
' sometimes puts questions to these demons, asking their
' names, &c. The demoniacks were of such strength that
' no chain or fetters could bind them. ...The diseased per-
' sons could not fear being destroyed, tormented, sent out
' of the country, or into the abyss, by Christ.' Whitby.—
Some persons argue, as if the Evangelists wrote under the
influence of Jewish prejudices, nay, as if our Lord spake
and acted, on these occasions, with some regard to them !
But this argument is suited entirely to subvert the authority of the inspired writers, and most awfully reflects on
the conduct of Christ. Where Jewish opinions were the
effect of error and prejudice, he never faded most decidedly to oppose and counteract them. (Notes, xv. 3—6. Acts
xvi. 16—18.)—Having premised these remarks, the exceeding fierceness of these demoniacks calls for attention :
for they could not be confined, but wandered in the tombs,
or solitary places, without the cities and villages, and were
the terror of the country, so that " no man could pass by
" that way." Yet, when they saw Christ, the evil spirits
knew and dreaded him; and, using the men's organs of
speech, (as Satan of old spake by the serpent,) they cried

out aloud,' " What have we to do with thee, Jesus, thou
" Son of God?" They expected no benefit from him, they
declined all contest with him, they desired to have nothing
to do with him.—' O thou Jesus, the Son of the ever-living
' God, it is our great misery, that we are fallen into thy
' hands. What wilt thou now do with us? Dost thou
' mean now to accomplish our full torture before the day
' of judgment?' Bp. Hall. Thus owning that their doom
was fixed, but desiring longer respite and liberty for mischief.
V. 30—32. Swine were unclean animals by the Mosaick
law, and the very touch of them, when dead, defiled a man;
(Note, Lev. xi. 31—33, v. 31;) yet the Gadarenes fed them
in great numbers, to sell to their Gentile neighbours. The
evil spirits, therefore, being reluctant to quit a region,
where their influence had been so entire, formed a subtle
plan of prejudicing the inhabitants against Jesus, that they
might be induced to reject his instructions. Aware of the
value which was put upon the swine because of the gain
arising from them, they requested permission to possess
those animals : and he, probably to punish the avarice of
the Gadarenes, to give a decisive proof of the reality of
possessions, and to shew the destructive rage and power
of evil spirits, as well as the limits assigned to their influence, permitted them. Immediately, therefore, they impelled the swine to such fury, that the whole herd rushed
from a precipice into the sea, and was drowned:—It is surprising, that any should have thought this permission,
either a ground of objection against our Lord's conduct,
or requiring a laboured vindication. Had not his almighty
power restrained the evil spirits, they would have destroyed,
not only the demoniacks, but also the guilty owners and
feeders of the swine : so that his mercy was truly wonderful
and adorable, in protecting the persons of the Gadarenes,
and permitting only the destruction of that property which
they kept from avarice, and by living under constant temptation to violate the law, and almost under a necessity of
continually contracting ceremonial uncleanness. But the
objection reminds us of one most important fact; viz.
that the enemies of Christianity always throw the blame
on our holy and beneficent religion, of all the mischief
which the devil and wicked men have taken occasion from
it to perpetrate; forgetting, that they would have done
vastly more mischief, had its restraints been removed. Indeed, if permitting be not clearly distinguished from commanding or causing; it will be impossible to avoid im-
puting to the just and holy God, the sins of all his rebellious creatures, which is the most detestable blasphemy
that can be conceived. (Marg. Ref.)—A steep place. (32)
Τῳ κρημνῳ. Mark v. 13. Luke viii. 33.—A precipice, or,
overhanging cliff.
V. 33, 34. It must be supposed, that the keepers were
exceedingly affrighted, as well as astonished, at this strange

1 7

told every thing, and what was befallen to the possessed of the devils.

34 And, behold, the whole city came out to meet Jesus: and when they saw him, ° they besought *him* that he would depart out of their coasts.

c 20. Deut. v, 26. 1 Sam. xvi. 4. 1 Kings xviii. 17. Job xxi. 14. xxii, 17. Mark v. 17, 18. Luke viii. 28. 37—39. Acts xvi. 39.

---

event; and having reported it in the city Gadara, the inhabitants in general came to Jesus : not however to receive instruction, implore protection, or crave miraculous assistance. Probably, their guilty consciences made them dread his power; and the loss of the swine no doubt highly displeased them : yet, not venturing to attempt violence against so extraordinary a person, they presented one single request to him, namely, " that he would depart out " of their coasts ;" which was in fact to say, " What have " we to do with thee, Jesus, thou Son of God ? " This proved them to be under the power of Satan, fully as much as the demoniacks had been, but in another and more criminal sense.—' Where men live like swine, there doth not ' Christ tarry, but devils.' *Beza.*

PRACTICAL OBSERVATIONS

V. 1—4.

The various diseases of our bodies, which entered by sin and end in death, are faint emblems of those which disorder our souls, and must issue in final misery, unless cured by the heavenly Physician : for all other help is totally unavailing. But men feel sickness, and desire deliverance from it; and willingly incur expense, and use unpleasant means, to procure it : while few are sensible of their misery as sinners, or bestow proper pains to obtain a cure!—Were the divine Saviour to return to the earth, and renew his beneficent miracles; he would again be surrounded with multitudes, earnestly beseeching him to relieve their pains and heal their diseases: but he is ever present with us, ready to save us from sin, and to make us holy and happy : yet alas! few are willing to come to him for it; though he confers his benefits, " without " money or price ; " though he never refuses aid to any that ask it, and effectually heals all who wait upon him ! —Those are blessed afflictions, which bring us acquainted with Christ, and cause us to seek salvation from him. If we have discovered that we are polluted with spiritual leprosy, and are humbled on that account; we need not fear being disappointed, in seeking to Christ to cleanse us, however inveterate our maladies have become. He did not indeed take our nature upon him, on purpose to cleanse leprous bodies, but leprous souls: we need not then say, " If thou wilt ; " for we may as fully rely on his willingness as on his power. Let us then wait on him with humble supplications, confessing how vile and miserable we are, and adoring his power and grace : in due time he will speak the word, " I will, be thou cleansed ; " and the effect will as surely follow as when he said, " Let " there be light, and there was light." Nor should we conceal our obligations to his cleansing power ; but rather proclaim them to his glory, that other lepers may hear, and apply to him also.—We should likewise copy the example of his humility, and learn to do good to the mean and to the wretched, without ostentation.—But if men purpose to honour and obey their Benefactor, they must attend on all the ordinances of God : when, in the judgment of faithful ministers, they are indeed cleansed from the guilt

and dominion of their sins, they should, at the Lord's table, offer their spiritual sacrifice of praise and thanksgiving, and join themselves to his people; and this will turn to a testimony, for the instruction of their neighbours also ; and even for the edification and encouragement of the ministers of Christ.

V. 5—13.

Eminent examples of faith and piety are sometimes met with, where least to be expected : and, when those who have religious advantages, and even the ministers of religion, turn away from Christ; soldiers and others, whose education and mode of life cast them at an apparent distance from the gospel, embrace and adorn it. In this the sovereignty of grace is displayed : and often those removals, to which men are most reluctant,· or which have been most casual, or made from secular motives, are over-ruled by Providence, to bring them acquainted with the word and people of God.—Where true religion governs the heart, it regulates the life, and renders men exemplary in relative duties : and thus it promotes domestick comfort, while it glorifies God and saves the soul.—Pious, faithful, and affectionate servants are great and important blessings from the Lord, and ought to be very dear to us : and surely, if we have the benefit of their service, when in health ; we should not desert them in their sickness, or neglect to procure for them all the relief and solace in our power.—True piety is always connected with deep humility: the more we know of God, and of his law and truth, the more carefully we examine our hearts and lives, according to this rule ; and the more we commune with God, and are sensible of our obligations to him, the deeper will be our self-abasement, and the more unreservedly shall we " sit " down in the lowest place," and subscribe even to those degrading opinions which others have formed of us, perhaps out of prejudice and mistake. But, if we proportionably " know the grace of our Lord Jesus Christ," we shall not be discouraged : for we shall perceive that he is ever ready to help the most unworthy. He is " the same " yesterday, to day, and for ever : " he is still ready to hear all our petitions : and though we are consciously unworthy that he should come under our roof, or dwell in our hearts; yet he will come at our desire, and bring salvation with him. At his powerful word, the strongest evil habits and propensities are subdued, as palsies and fevers were of old ; and then strength, liberty, victory, peace, and holiness succeed. The more we honour his power and grace, the more evident tokens of his approbation and favour shall we receive ; and the answer of our prayers will generally bear proportion to the degree of our genuine faith.—What cause have we, in these distant western regions, to rejoice, that we are called by his gospel to enter into his family, to walk with him, and ere long to " sit down with Abraham, and " Isaac, and Jacob, in the kingdom of heaven ! " But let us also remember, that we *now* are " the children of the " kingdom : " let us take warning by the example of the benighted, wretched Jews : let us " not be high-minded, " but fear,'· lest any of us should fall from our height of

1 8

CHAP. IX.

Jesus returning to Capernaum, 1, heals one sick of the palsy, 2—8; calls Matthew from the receipt of custom, 9; justifies himself for eating with publicans and sinners, 10—13; and his disciples for not fasting like the Pharisees, 14—17; is intreated by a ruler to heal his daughter, 18, 19; heals a woman of an inve-terate issue of blood, 20—22; raises the ruler's daugh-ter, 23—26; gives sight to two blind men, 27—31; and casts a devil out of a dumb man, 32. The people wonder, but the Pharisees ascribe it to the prince of the devils, 33, 34. Jesus compassionates the multi-tudes, and preaches to them; and charges his disci-ples to pray, that labourers might be sent forth into the harvest, 35—38.

privilege, through unbelief, and be cast into that outer " darkness, where shall be weeping and gnashing of " teeth; " whilst the Lord shall replenish his church by the conversion of the heathen, or of the most abject sin-ners in our communities.

V. 14—22.

Those, who are confined from publick ordinances by sickness, or by any other real hindrance, and to whom this is an affliction, may expect the Saviour's gracious presence with them in retirement, and that he will soothe their sor-rows, and abate their pains.—When our maladies are cured, even by ordinary methods, we should arise and minister to Christ and his people; giving him praise as our Healer, and dedicating our health and strength to his service: and when he rebukes and removes the fever of our sinful pas-sions, we shall delight in doing his will. He never deems any hour unseasonable, at which we come to him to de-liver us from temptation or trouble: nor should we excuse ourselves from helping others, because it is late, or we are fatigued, when the case is urgent and the opportunity favourable.—Whilst we rejoice in the salvation of Christ; let us remember the pain, labour, and suffering, which he endured, when " himself took our infirmities, and bare " our sicknesses " and sins: that we may not grudge labour, and weariness, and expense in doing good to others.—But let us contrast the divine majesty and glory of our Redeemer, with the external poverty and destitute condition, to which he voluntarily submitted. Was he weary, and without a place where he might recline his sacred head? Was he even more destitute than " the foxes, " or the birds of the air ? " And shall we absurdly aim to render his religion subservient to our secular interests and preferments; and to preach or profess the gospel in order to grow rich or great? Shall we deem honour, excellence, or happiness to be connected with affluence, splendour, and indulgence? Shall we pay court to the wealthy because of their wealth, or despise the poor on account of their po-verty? Shall we " seek great things for ourselves ; " or be discontented with mean accommodations, though far better than our Saviour's were? God forbid ! His disciples must not only profess a readiness " to follow him whithersoever " he goeth ; " but they must be ready to accompany him, by sea and land, through storms and tempests, through poverty, hardship, reproach, and persecution : otherwise they will never hold out to the end. If he requires our service, even the most endeared relative affections, and such things as would otherwise have been our duty, must give place. Enough will be found to attend on other employments, and to take care of the ordinary affairs of families and com-munities: but he, who is called to follow Christ, and preach his gospel, must leave " the dead to bury their " dead ; " and not allow secular concerns to take him off from his high and important work.

V. 23—27.

Even when following Christ in the path of duty, we may expect to meet with tribulations, nay, to be menaced with impending destruction. Satan will then especially en-deavour to obstruct our course, or dismay our souls, by raising some tremendous storm; and the Lord may see good to permit him, for our humiliation and the trial of our faith. But, though the Saviour seems to sleep, and disregard his church and the believer, when conflicting with the winds and waves of temptation or persecution, and apparently ready to be overwhelmed; yet his presence in-fallibly secures their safety : and he only purposes to excite their more earnest prayers for deliverance, and their more simple and entire dependence on him for it. Even weak faith will induce us to cry out, " Lord, save us, we perish : " but our terrors in danger, comparatively small, often prove our faith to be little, which at other times has seemed to be strong; nay, Christ often accounts that little faith, of which we had a far higher opinion. He will not leave the weak believer to perish : but he will rebuke him for his unbelieving fears; and shew his disapprobation of his conduct, when he dishonours him by distrusting his truth and love : and he leads men into perilous circum-stances, both to detect the weakness of their faith, and the greatness of his own power, whom winds and waves, and all creatures implicitly obey; and thus increase and in-vigorate their faith, and excite their admiring and adoring love.

V. 28—34.

The power and malice of apostate angels might justly alarm and dismay us, were it not for the superior power and grace of our Redeemer. We bar our doors, with great care, against a few ruffians of our own species; but we seldom reflect that there are legions of devils, which have constant access to us, against whose assaults we have no method of defence : and whilst they are able, if permitted, to distract our minds, disorder, torment, or kill our bodies, or destroy our possessions, their only delight is in misery and destruction. In what an awful situation then are they, who by daily listening to their temptations, provoke God to give them up to their power and malice! And what cause have we for gratitude, for being preserved, during the unconverted part of our lives!—But the believer, in the path of duty, needs not fear these roaring lions and wolves, being safe under the watchful care of the almighty Shepherd. They cannot break that hedge of protection, which is placed about his people; nay, they cannot enter even a swine without his leave. (Note, Job i. 9—11.) They can tempt sinners to destroy themselves, yet they have no power to destroy them. Spiritual possession by these unclean spirits is, however, most to be dreaded : their influence tends to make men miserable and mischievous, the burden of their families, and the nuisance or terror of

K

AND [a] he entered into a ship, and passed over, and came into [b] his own city.

2 And, behold, [c] they brought to him a man sick of the palsy, lying on a bed: and Jesus [d] seeing their faith, said unto the sick of the palsy; [e] Son, be of good cheer; thy sins be forgiven thee.

3 And, behold, [f] certain of the scribes said within themselves, [h] This man blasphemeth.

4 And Jesus [i] knowing their thoughts

said, [k] Wherefore think ye evil in your hearts?

5 For [l] whether is easier to say, Thy sins be forgiven thee; or to say, [m] Arise, and walk?

6 But that ye may know, [n] that the Son of man hath power on earth to forgive sins, (then saith he to the sick of the palsy,) [o] Arise, take up thy bed, and go unto thine house.

7 And he arose, and departed to his house.

8 But [p] when the multitudes saw it, they marvelled, [q] and glorified God,

---

society. Under their fascinating delusions, the poor sinner imagines that religion can only make him uneasy: and if he have some notions of the truth, and suppose " Jesus " to be the Son of God," nay, if he have any dread of future torment; he will yet have nothing to do with the Saviour, but shuns the gospel, " lest it should torment " him before the time." But Jesus gives deliverance to such wretched slaves, and makes them willing to be his servants, whenever he sees good, notwithstanding all the opposition of the powers of darkness. (Note, Ps. cx. 3.)— Even " devils believe and tremble ; " nay, they can become supplicants to Christ, to be exempted from torments or permitted to do mischief! Let none then trust in notions, dead faith, or selfish prayers ; or in any thing short of " faith that worketh by love."—There is nothing, be it ever so base and filthy, which men will not do for money ; (Note, 1 Tim. vi. 6—10, vv. 8—10;) and nothing more prejudices the mind against the gospel, than its interference with the pursuit of riches by unlawful means. The covetous prove, that they are possessed by Satan, and enemies to Christ, equally with the most abandoned depredators or debauchees. Nay, perhaps, confirmed avarice is more rarely extirpated, than any other distemper of the soul. All that such men hear of the power and grace of Christ, only excites fears and anxiety about their ungodly gain : they want to rid the country of him and his ministers, that they may possess and increase their wealth without fear of consequences ; and they copy the example of the Gadarenes, who loved their swine better than the Saviour, or their own souls. From such possession and insanity, good Lord, deliver us!

NOTES.

CHAP. IX. V. 1. This verse should have been placed at the end of the foregoing chapter, being the conclusion of the narrative there recorded. (Note, Mark ii. 1, 2.)— Capernaum, not Nazareth, was at this time our Lord's own city. (Note, iv. 12—17.)—' Bethlehem brought him forth, ' Nazareth brought him up, and Capernaum was his dwell- ' ing place.' Theophylact.—The miracle next recorded was indeed wrought at Capernaum ; but it appears from the other Evangelists to have taken place before our Lord's voyage to Gadara.

V. 2—8. (Notes, Mark ii. 3—12. Luke v. 17—26.)

This miracle is much more fully recorded by the other evangelists ; and the more particular consideration of it is therefore postponed. Mark records several miracles more circumstantially than Matthew does; from which it is evident, that he did not extract his gospel from Matthew, as some have supposed. (Preface to Mark.) Matthew seems in this place to record several miracles, wrought at different times, in one continued narration; as in other places he relates many parables, without mentioning any of the miracles, which our Lord wrought at the same time.

Son.] ' Son, is a title of condescension and tenderness, ' by which superiors addressed their inferiors.' Doddridge. (Marg. Ref. e.) ' Thou art come hither, in desire and ' confidence of cure; I will give thee more than thou ' askest ;...an happy restitution to a good estate of soul ; ' thy palsy is healed, thy sins (the cause of it,) are for- ' given thee.' Bp. Hall.—Some think, that our Lord re- mitted only the temporal punishment of this man's sins; and the chief argument, which they use in confirmation of this opinion is, that the apostles cured diseases ; so that this could be no proof of authority to forgive sins, as to the eternal punishment. But the apostles healed dis- eases, in the name of Christ ; and they forgave sins by the authority of Christ: (xvi. 19. John xx. 23 :) and he did both, in his own name and by his own authority. If the pa'sy was the temporal punishment of this man's sin, the healing of it alone was the remission of that punishment; and the authoritative language, which offended the Phari- sees, was superfluous. But if sin, in every sense, was for- given to the paralytick, as a true believer, his cure sealed that pardon, and gave him the comfort of it. It also proved the most important point in contest, between Christ and the scribes, namely, that he was the Son of God ; and that even as the Son of man, in his deepest humiliation, all judgment was committed to him ; and he was autho- rized to pardon and save any sinner, in the most summary manner, even as he pardoned and saved the thief upon the cross.—' By remitting the sin, ...he manifestly shewed ' who he was : for if none can remit sins but God, and ' yet our Lord did remit them and cure the man, it is ma- ' nifest, that he was both the Word of God, and the Son ' of man, receiving power of remission of sins from his ' Father, as God and Man.' Irenæus.—' The Jews here say,

K 2

which had given such power unto men.

9 ¶ And as Jesus passed forth from thence, he saw a man ʳ named Matthew, sitting at the receipt of custom: and he saith unto him, ˢ Follow me. And he arose and followed him.

10 And it came to pass, ᵗ as Jesus sat at meat in the house, behold, ᵘ many publicans and sinners came and sat down with him and his disciples.

11 And when the Pharisees saw it, they said unto his disciples, ʸ Why eateth your Master with publicans and sinners?

12 But when Jesus heard that, he said unto them, ᶻ They that be whole need not a physician, but they that are sick.

13 But ᵃ go ye and learn what that meaneth, ᵇ I will have mercy and not sacrifice: for I am not come ᶜ to call the righteous, ᵈ but sinners to repentance.

ᵉ that it was proper to God to forgive sins; and this Christ ᵉ denies not; but only proves, that the Son of man had ᵉ this power also, leaving them to make the inference.' *Whitby.*

Thoughts. (4) Ενθυμησεις· (ab ɛνθυμεω ex ɛν et θυμος *animus:*) xii. 25. Heb. iv. 12.—Rendered *device; Acts* xvii. 29—*Easier.* (5) Ευκοπωτερον (ex ɛυ *bene* et κοπος *labor:*) xix. 24. Mark ii. 9. x. 25· Luke v. 23. xvi. 17. xviii. 25.

V. 9. (*Marg. Ref.—Note, Mark* ii. 13—17.) Matthew here gives an account of the manner, in which he himself was called to follow Christ. He had also the name of Levi; it being common for men to be known by more names than one. Probably, Matthew was his name when a publican; for he always calls himself by it, and Levi, that given him by way of honourable distinction, when he became a follower of Christ; for the other evangelists generally call him so. Thus Saul, when he became an apostle, was named Paul. Matthew was originally a publican, or a collector of the taxes and customs. These were generally farmed out to the best bidder, by publick sale; and those who hired the revenues of a large district, used to let them out in subdivisions to inferior publicans, who were assisted by the Roman soldiery in collecting them.—The Jews were very averse to the Roman government, out of mistaken principles of conscience, as well as from love to independence: and they deemed it very criminal for their countrymen to follow this employment; so that nothing but the love of gain could induce them to engage in it. In general the publicans from among the Jews were persons of immoral character: and many of them increased the odium against the order, by exacting more than their due, and enforcing their demands by military violence. The office itself therefore rendered men infamous; though they were not all so avaricious and iniquitous, as this opinion of them implies. Matthew was employed in this ensnaring and disgraceful occupation; and was sitting in his office, when Jesus spoke to him. His hands were full of business, perhaps his head of calculations, and his heart of covetousness: for it is not certain, that he had previously paid any regard to the doctrine of Christ. But, when our Lord commanded him to follow him, such a power accompanied the word, as influenced him to renounce immediately his lucrative employment, and to become his constant attendant, that he might be made a preacher of the gospel. So that he arose without delay; and, leaving his business to his partners or assist-

ants, he went after Jesus, and never returned to his former occupation. *Receipt of custom.*] Τελωνιον (ab τελωνης, ex τελος *tributum,* et ωνεομαι *emo :) Mark* ii. 14. *Luke* v. 27.

V. 10—13. Matthew probably made a final settlement of his affairs; and then made an entertainment, to which he invited Jesus and his disciples, with many publicans, and others of his former acquaintance. (*Luke* v. 29.) This he seems to have done, in hopes that they too might derive benefit from our Lord's discourse; and accordingly, Christ without hesitation sat down to table with the company. But the Pharisees, who were constantly watching for some objection against him, enquired of his disciples, why their Master acted so inconsistently with his character, as a prophet, as to sit at meat with men of so vile a character: and he justified his conduct by an apt similitude. Persons in health have no occasion for a physician: but the sick are glad of his advice, and willing to follow his prescriptions; and it is his proper business, to go among them, though their diseases may render their company unpleasant, or even dangerous. Thus, none but humbled sinners know how to value a Saviour, or profit by his help. Those, who are in health do not want a physician. This is the case with any of our fallen race: but they who *suppose* their souls to be in health, do not welcome the spiritual Physician; his attendance would be thrown away, and be irksome to them. This was the case of the Pharisees: they despised Christ, because they were whole in their own estimation: but the poor publicans and sinners evidently wanted instruction and amendment; and his compassion led him to go among them, as a Physician, to bring health and cure to their souls. He therefore told the objectors to go and learn the meaning of the passage in their scriptures, which taught them, that God preferred acts of mercy to their brethren, even to the external worship prescribed in the law. (*Note, Hos.* vi. 6.)—Indeed he, the Messiah, did not come into the world, to call the *righteous* that they might share the privileges of his kingdom: if any were truly righteous *of themselves,* they could not want his salvation; and they, who proudly thought themselves to be so, would not accept of it. But he came to call *sinners* to participate the blessings of his kingdom: not by encouraging them in sin; but by exhorting, encouraging, and inducing them to repent, and forsake it.

Sinners. (10) 'Αμαρτωλοι (ab αμαρτια *peccatum:) Luke* v. 8. xv. 17. xix. 27. *Rom.* v. 8. *Gal.* ii 15. 17.—*I will have*

14 ¶ Then came to him 'the disciples of John, saying, 'Why do we and the Pharisees fast oft, but thy disciples fast not?

15 And Jesus said unto them, 'Can the children of the bride-chamber mourn, as long as the bridegroom is with them? but the days will come, when the bridegroom shall be taken from them, 'and then shall they fast.

16 No man putteth a piece of 'new cloth unto an old garment; 'for that which is put in to fill it up, taketh from the garment, and the rent is made worse.

17 Neither do men put new wine into 'old bottles: else the bottles break, and the wine runneth out, and the bottles perish: but they put new wine into new bottles, and both are preserved.

18 ¶ While he spake these things unto them, 'behold, there came a certain 'ruler, and 'worshipped him, saying, 'My daughter is even now dead: but 'come and lay thy hand upon her, and she shall live.

19 And Jesus 'arose and followed him, and so did his disciples.

20 And, 'behold, a woman which was diseased with 'an issue of blood twelve years, came behind him, and 'touched the 'hem of his garment:

21 For she said within herself, 'If I may but touch his garment, I shall be whole.

22 But Jesus turned him about, and when he saw her, he said, 'Daughter, be of good comfort; 'thy faith hath made thee whole. And the woman was made whole 'from that hour.

23 And when Jesus came 'into the

b xvii. 19. John iv. 55. Acts xvi. 18.　c 18, 19. Mark v. 35—37. Luke viii. 40—51

---

mercy and not sacrifice. (13) Ελεον θελω και ου θυσιαν.—Ελεος θελω η θυσιαν. *Sept.* The Evangelist's version is more literal.

V. 14, 15. (*Marg. Ref.*) John was at this time in prison; and his afflicted circumstances, as well as his mortified character, and the nature of his introductory dispensation, led those who were peculiarly attached to him, and not willing to become Christ's disciples, to observe frequent and strict fasts, as the Pharisees also professed to do: and when they saw Jesus and his followers occasionally go to feasts, (though they seem in general to have lived in a very spare and frugal manner,) they concluded that they never fasted. They therefore enquired of Jesus, why his disciples neglected this part of strict religion, as they supposed it to be: but he, referring them to John's testimony concerning him as "the Bridegroom" of the church, reminded them, that such austerities would be unsuitable to the present circumstances. (*Note, John iii. 27—36, v. 29.*) It would be unseasonable for the companions of a bride groom to fast, during the days allotted for the nuptials, which were usually spent in festivity: but if any calamity tore him from them their joy would be turned into mourning, and their feasting into fasting. In like manner, it would be improper for his disciples to fast, whilst they had the comfort of his presence: but he should soon be taken from them, by his crucifixion, and at length by his ascension: and then they would meet with hardships and trials which would render fasting seasonable; nor would they fail to join it with their other religious exercises.

V. 16, 17. Our Lord here referred to some rules of prudence among men. It was not usual to take a piece of woollen cloth, which had never been scoured, or prepared, and to join it to an old garment: because its rough and unpliant sides would not suit the soft old cloth; but would rather tear it further, and make the rent worse. Nor was it usual for men to put new wine into old *leathern*

bottles, which were going to decay; for in this case the bottles would burst, through the fermenting of the wine, and so both be wasted: whereas, by putting the new wine into strong new bottles, both might be preserved. Thus, in those occasional duties, which were not essential to religion, but rather helps to things excellent, discretion should be used, and a proportion observed between the degree of a man's knowledge, experience, and stability, and the self-denial required of him: otherwise they might tend to discouragement, or to fatal mistakes. Hopeful persons might be disheartened, by premature impositions; or led to rest in them and make a self-righteousness of them, and thus become more fatally deluded than ever. So that great caution, prudence, and tenderness were requisite, in dealing with young converts about such matters as, though useful, were not indispensable; that their former habits and sentiments might not be too violently and hastily crossed; and that they might not receive forbidding ideas of the service of their gracious Lord: but opportunities should be waited for, and duties of this kind gradually inculcated as they were able to bear them.

New. (16) Αγναφ. See the margin. (Ex α priv. et γναπτω *purgo fullorum modo:*) whence γναφευς *fullo;* Mark ix. 3.—*Rent.*] Σχισμα (ab σχιζω *scindo, divido;* xxvii. 51. John xix. 24.) John vii. 43. ix. 16. 1 Cor. i. 10. xi. 18. xii. 25.—Hence *schism.*

V. 18—26. *Notes, Mark v. 21—43. Luke viii. 40—56.*

Ruler. (18) The person who superintended the concerns of the synagogue, and directed the worship there performed. In some places, at least, there were several rulers of the synagogue; but one was chief over the others. Some think, that these rulers were also magistrates, and presided over courts of justice in their several cities, which were subordinate to the Sanhedrim, or great council at Jerusalem.—*Worshipped.*] In the other gospels, it is, "Fell down at his feet." (*Marg. Ref. o.*)—*Even now*

ruler's house, and saw ᵈ the minstrels and the people making a noise;

24 He said unto them, ᵉ Give place; for the maid is ᶠ not dead, but sleepeth. ᵍ And they laughed him to scorn.

25 But when ʰ the people were put forth, he went in, ⁱ and took her by the hand, and the maid arose.

26 And ⱼ the ᵏ fame hereof went abroad into all that land.

27 ¶ And when Jesus departed thence, ˡ two blind men followed him, crying, and saying, ᵐ Thou Son of David, ⁿ have mercy on us.

28 And when he was ᵒ come into the house, the blind men came to him: and Jesus saith unto them, ᵖ Believe ye that I am able to do this? They said unto him, Yea, Lord.

29 Then ᑫ touched he their eyes, saying, ʳ According to your faith be it unto you.

30 And ˢ their eyes were opened; and Jesus ᵗ straitly charged them, saying, See that no man know it.

31 But they, when they were departed, ᵘ spread abroad his fame in all that country.

32 ¶ As they went out, behold, they

---

dead.] "She lieth at the point of death," *Mark.* "She "lay a dying," *Luke.*—The ruler's daughter was not dead when he left her; but he feared that she would die before Jesus could reach his house.

Hem. (20) Or *fringe. Note, Num.* xv. 38—40.

Faith hath made thee whole, &c. (22) Or, "Thy faith "hath saved thee; and the woman was saved, &c." (Σωθησομαι. 21. Σεσωχε σε σωθη. 22. *Luke* vii. 50. *Acts* iv. 12. xvi. 30, 31.)—The word signifies preservation, or deliverance, from temporal evils or dangers, to health, or peace, or eternal happiness; according to the context. The power of Christ was the efficacious cause of the woman's recovery; but her faith, by inducing her to apply to him, secured to her that benefit, from which unbelief excluded many.

Minstrels. (23) ' This custom of instruments at fu' nerals was heathen, and came in but late among the ' Jews. ... The ancient Jewish custom was, that...the la' mentation was not begun with musical instruments, but ' only voices of old women, who, in a sad modulation, ' strove to extort lamentation from those that were present.' *Hammond.* (*Marg. Ref. d.*)

Not dead, &c. (24) ' These words of Christ were ' plainly spoken to those, who were preparing for her in' terment, and performing the funeral rites belonging to it; ' and therefore only intimate, that she was not so dead as ' to need their assistance; he being come to awake her, ' as out of a sleep.' *Whitby.* (*Marg. Ref. e—g.*)—*They laughed him to scorn.*] Κατεγελων αυτον. *They derided him.*

V. 27—29. The displays of the power of Christ were varied, in almost every conceivable way of beneficence; but he wrought no miracles of vengeance: for even the destruction of the swine, merely *by his permission,* was doubtless intended in mercy, and conducive to much good. All his miracles were likewise emblems of the salutary efficacy of his truth and grace on the souls of men: and nothing is more emphatically descriptive of man's state by nature, than *blindness.* The mind involved in ignorance or error, through the subtlety of Satan, and the influence of corrupt passions and prejudices, continues impenitent, unbelieving, and unholy: but when the understanding is enlightened, to see things as they really are; the sinner repents, returns to God, and gladly accepts of his salvation. —The prophets had expressly and repeatedly foretold, that

the Messiah should open the eyes of the blind: (*Marg. Ref.* s:) and this is the first instance recorded, in which Jesus proved himself to be the Messiah, by fulfilling those prophecies.—It appears from the narrative, that these blind men met him, immediately after he came out of the ruler's house; and by accosting him as the "Son of "David," they acknowledged him to be the promised Saviour and King of Israel. Thus they shewed, that they were acquainted with the scriptures: and it is probable, that they rested their hope of recovering sight, on the prophecies above mentioned, as well as on the report of his extraordinary miracles which Jesus had already performed. He did not, however, see good *publickly* to attend to their importunate cries, having already abundantly excited the astonishment of the multitude.—But they, not bearing to be disappointed of a cure, followed him into the house; (probably that of Andrew and Peter;) and there, apart from observation, he drew from them an unwavering confession of their faith in his power to perform the miracle, and then answered their believing expectations and earnest desires.—No one except Jesus, ever performed a miracle of this kind. (*Marg. Ref.*)

V. 30. Our Lord gave this decided and authoritative charge, not only to avoid all appearance of ostentation; but also that he might not needlessly excite the opposition of his enemies, or furnish them with plausible accusations against him; and that the people might not be induced to make commotions, as owning him for the Messiah, and desirous of making him a king.

Straitly charged.] Ενεβριμησατο. *Mark* i. 43. xiv. 5. *John* xi. 33. 38.—A vehement commotion of mind is primarily implied by this verb; which is often the commotion of anger, but frequently that of pity, or earnest persuasion and exhortation.—' The word ... is rendered by Phavorinus, ' ... to charge, to command, to appoint with authority. ... By ' Hesychius, to command, or charge with a threat. ...It is a ' rational earnestness and vehemence, not a passionate.' *Hammond.* (*Note, Mark* i. 40—44.)

V. 31. The joy, gratitude, and amazement of the men, who had recovered their sight, rendered them incapable of refraining themselves, and regardless of the injunction given them. Their motives and purpose were doubtless good; yet their conduct cannot be justified.

V. 32, 33. It seems, this man was dumb, not from

ᴋ 5

brought to him ᵃa dumb man possessed with a devil.

33 And when the devil was cast out, ᶠthe dumb spake: and the multitudes marvelled, saying, ¹It was never so seen in Israel.

34 But ᵏthe Pharisees said, He casteth out devils through the prince of the devils.

35 ¶ And ᵇ Jesus went about all the cities and villages, teaching in their synagogues, and preaching the gospel of the kingdom, and healing every sickness

and every disease among the people.

36 But ᶜ when he saw the multitudes, he was moved with compassion on them, because they ᵉfainted, and ᵈwere scattered abroad, ᵈas sheep having no shepherd.

37 Then saith he unto his disciples, ᵉThe harvest truly is plenteous, ᶠbut the labourers are few:

38 ᵍPray ye therefore ʰthe Lord of the harvest, ᶠthat he will send forth labourers into his harvest.

any natural defect, but by the power of an evil spirit; and that this was generally allowed to be the case. When the evil spirit was cast out, he was immediately capable of speaking: and the spectators of these multiplied and stupendous miracles, were so astonished, that they declared the like had never been seen even in Israel, where prophets had often wrought many and great miracles, in confirmation of their testimony.—'This reflection was perfectly 'just: for no one of the prophets, that we read of in the 'Old Testament, appears to have wrought so many bene- 'ficent miracles, in his whole life, as our Lord did in this 'one afternoon.' *Doddridge.*—Perhaps this may admit of some doubt, or exception; but the remark is well worthy of attention. It is not recorded, that either prophet or apostle, in any one instance, enabled the dumb to speak. It was expressly predicted that the Messiah would do this: and it was therefore performed by Jesus only; as exclusively and directly marking him out to be the Messiah. (*Note, Is.* xxxv. 5—7.)

V. 34. The Pharisees, not able to deny the reality or the greatness of the miracle, and fearing, not without cause, lest the people should thence conclude that Jesus was the Messiah; declared that it was not wrought by a divine power, but by that of the prince of the devils: for, Jesus being in league with that arch-apostate, whom all the other fallen angels thought as their leader, availed himself of this authority, in casting out evil spirits, that he might give a sanction to his false doctrine.—What answer Christ at this time made to this most malignant charge, we know not; but on another occasion he very fully confuted and exposed it. (*Notes*, xii. 22—37.)

V. 35. *Synagogues.*] The temple was the centre of the worship appointed for Israel by the law, and no sacrifices might be offered elsewhere: but in process of time, it was found necessary that other places set apart for publick prayer and instruction. For these purposes synagogues were built, and after the captivity, they became general in all the cities and villages; and probably they were proportionably more numerous, than churches and chapels are with us. Learned men think, that forms of worship were statedly used, on certain days in the week, as well as on the sabbath-days; and the scriptures, divided into portions, were constantly read in them: so that they were very useful in keeping the people from idolatry. The Levites and Scribes might commonly officiate in them, but this service was not restricted to them: they had stated

rulers and officers, but no regular pastors or teachers; so that competent persons occasionally gave exhortations, as they were disposed or desired to do it: and the case was the same in other nations, where the Jews resided. Christ therefore went round the country teaching in the synagogues, and no one attempted to interrupt or hinder him. —'It was the manner among the Jews, for divers men to 'contribute their talents, to the exposition of the lesson 'which was read. ... This ordinarily belonged to the sons 'of the prophets, who were brought up in learning the 'law: and at thirty years old might be made doctors; and 'they continued under that name, or the order of scribes, 'till they obtained the Spirit of prophecy. In proportion 'to which was the difference in the Christian church, be- 'twixt the evangelist, and the doctor, or teacher; the first 'telling them good news, and planting the gospel; the 'other watering, or instructing them further in it.' *Hammond.*—It is, however, plain that others, besides scribes or doctors, were allowed and invited to expound the scriptures, and give exhortations in the synagogues. (*Marg. Ref.*) And the gospel was generally planted by the apostles, and apostolical men; not by inferior ministers.

Synagogues.] Συναγωγαι. (ex συν et αγω: to gather together.) The word was first used by the LXX for the *congregation,* or the company assembled. (*Ex.* xii. 6. 19. 47.) But at length it was appropriated to the *place of con* vention. Thus εκκλησια, a word of similar import, first and more properly meant the assembled company; but gradually became the word used for the building in which it assembled.

V. 36—38. Great multitudes resorted from distant places to hear our Lord's instructions: and they appeared not only languishing in soul, for want of better teaching than they had hitherto received; but also ready to faint with hunger and fatigue, by continuing long at a distance from their habitations. In both senses, they were scattered " as sheep having no shepherd." There were many priests, Levites, and scribes all over the land; but they were idol-shepherds: (*Note, Zech.* xi. 15—17:) and Christ had compassion on the people, as " perishing for " lack of knowledge." In the prospect, therefore, of the vast multitudes which would in a short time, both from Jews and Gentiles, be gathered into the church, he declared, that a plenteous harvest was growing in the field, which would require many active and industrious labourers to reap it; but there were very few who deserved that cha-

K 6

CHAP. X.

Christ sends out twelve apostles, with power to work miracles, 1. Their names, 2—4. They must not go to Gentiles or Samaritans, but to Israel, 5, 6. He instructs them, both as to their preaching and

racter. It was, therefore, at that time especially, the duty of the disciples, to pray most earnestly to the Lord of the harvest to send forth labourers, that is, able, faithful, diligent, and effective ministers, into the harvest.—Christ himself is " the Lord of the harvest," and in the next chapter we read that he sent forth labourers: but it is probable that the disciples did not understand him to speak of himself, on this occasion.—The expression translated, " send forth," literally signifies, " thrust forth," and implies the powerful impulse of God upon the heart, which would be necessary to overcome the diffidence and reluctance of humble and able men, to enter on that important work, especially when it would expose them to many perils and hardships.—' Word for word, *cast them out ;* for ' men are very slow in so holy a work.' *Beza.*—' From ' this discourse ... we learn these things, worthy to be re- ' garded by all the pastors of Christ's flock. (1.) That he, ' who doth not instruct his flock in " the sincere milk of ' " the word," and acquaint them with the things belong- · ing to their eternal peace, from an heart full of love to ' God, and to the souls committed to his charge, deserves ' not the name of a true shepherd: for the want of these ' things, in the scribes and Pharisees, made Christ com- ' plain, that the Jews were " as sheep without a shepherd." ' (2.) That when the harvest is great, and there be many ' ... ready to receive instruction, we should be the more ' diligent and laborious to afford it them. (3.) That in ' such cases, when either we are not called to the work, or ' are placed in another station, we should pray fervently, ' that God would raise up men, fitted for their instruction, ' and zealous for his glory and the good of souls.' *Whitby.* —This last remark is peculiarly applicable to the present times, and the efforts made in order to evangelize the heathen. (*See a Sermon, preached before the Missionary Society* in 1804, *on this text, by the Author.*)

Fainted. (36) Ησαν εκλελυμενοι· (εκ et λυομαι, solvor:) xv. 32. *Mark* viii. 3. *Gal.* vi. 9. *Heb.* xii. 3. 5.—2 *Sam.* iv. 1. *Is.* xiii. 7. *Jer.* xii. 5. *Sept.* They were sinking under fatigue, and want of food ; as a man sinks under a heavy burden, or when worn down with labour.—*Scattered.*] Εῤῥιμμενοι. xxvii. 5. *Luke* iv. 35. xvii. 2. *Acts* xxvii. 29.—' Men are here said to be εῤῥιμμενοι, who are ' wholly neglected by their teachers, and not imbued with ' a suitable knowledge of divine instruction.' *Schleusner.*

PRACTICAL OBSERVATIONS.

V. 1—8.

Our gracious Lord will not continue his presence or ordinances, with those who despise them and are weary of them ; for in every place he finds abundant opportunities of shewing mercy.—They who feel themselves miserable through sin and its effects, and who believe that he, and he only, can deliver them, will submit to any inconveniences in applying to him : and, as they are glad of direction and assistance from their stronger brethren, they should be ready to help them, according to their ability and opportunity.—Christ can see faith in *the heart ;* yet he

loves to point it out in those effects, by which it becomes manifest to us also: and when the most sinful and afflicted of the human race earnestly press through difficulties, that they may seek his salvation, they should be " of good " cheer; " for he addresses them as his children, and forgives their sins.—It would be far better to have a pardon, and to be left to languish under incurable disease, till death release us ; than to be cured of our sickness, and left under the guilt and power of our sins, to " treasure up wrath " against the day of wrath:" yet, if the sin be forgiven, deliverance from pain and sorrow will in due time follow, and consolation in the mean while be afforded us.—Even Jesus could not do good so unexceptionably, but that proud scribes would censure him, and even accuse him of blasphemy: let us then never expect to escape calumny, or be deterred from duty by the fear of it.—The Lord, who knows men's hearts, often hears them say such things within themselves, concerning him and his gospel and service, as they would be afraid or ashamed to avow: but he will as certainly call them to a strict account for their evil surmises, as for their wicked words and works.—When at Christ's command, the paralytick arose, and carried home that bed on which he had been brought in a helpless condition ; the authority of Christ to pardon, and the man's forgiveness, were at once demonstrated : and when sinners are enabled, at his word, to renounce customary iniquities, and to delight in obeying God's commandments, they too may know that their crimes are all blotted out. Thus men come to Christ, burdened and enslaved by their sins: but when he heals them, and enables them to walk at liberty in newness of life, all who witness and love the surprising change, are led to adore his power and grace, and to glorify God on their account.—But as Jesus, in his humiliation, had power *on earth* to forgive sins, (which was an act of divine authority,) so, now that he reigns in glory, his mediatorial commission reaches no further ; and they who leave the earth unpardoned, must sink into condemnation for ever.

V. 9—17.

Many eminent servants of God have been called, not only from low occupations, but from scenes of gross iniquity.—The word of Christ appears as powerful, in overcoming avarice or pride, as in rebuking the winds and waves, or in casting out legions of devils.—Those, who have experienced the power of his grace, will compassionate their former companions in sin, and devise means, and willingly incur expense, to bring them into the way of instruction.—We must not associate with ungodly men, out of love to their vain conversation ; but we may from good will to their souls. We should, however, remember that our good Physician had the power of healing inherent in him, and was in no danger of taking infection ; but it is not so with us : we should therefore consider our own constitution, so to speak ; and not needlessly go into unwholesome air, lest in attempting to do good to others, we get injury to ourselves. Let us rather enquire, whether we have discovered our sickness, and have learned to value our Physician, and to follow his directions. For there are

K 7

A. D. 30.   MATTHEW.   A. D. 30.

conduct, 7—15. He forewarns them of persecutions, and suggests motives of comfort and constancy, 16—

39. He promises blessings to those who should receive them, 40—42.

yet many stout-hearted Pharisees, who are whole in their own estimation, and are more disposed to carp at his words and works, than to wait on him for the healing of their souls. But, if we be humbled sinners, and desire his salvation, let us remember that he delights in mercy, and that he " came not to call the righteous, but sinners to re-" pentance:" and let us learn to copy his mercy, and use all proper means, to bring even the vilest of sinners to repentance, and faith in the Saviour.—How prone is the human heart to self-preference and censoriousness! Let us beware of this leaven, which corrupts those things which are good in themselves, and turns even an act of devotion into an abomination. Whilst therefore we judge for ourselves, as in the sight of God, at what seasons the presence and consolations of the heavenly Bridegroom call us to thankful joy and praise, and when his absence, through our sins or for our humiliation, requires us to join fasting with our confessions and supplications; let us not presume to judge or prescribe to others, or prefer ourselves to them on such accounts. There are indeed matters in religion so indispensable, that sinners must be urged to them, without delay or reserve: but there are others, which in due time and manner may be inculcated; but which hopeful persons cannot receive at present, and which are not needful, and might prove injurious to them. And much mischief has been done, both in respect of doctrines, external observances, and austerities, by " putting new wine into " old bottles;" but " wisdom is profitable to direct," and should be sought from God.

V. 18—26.

Rulers and superior persons are sometimes brought to Christ, by those afflictions, which admit of no remedy from their secular distinctions and possessions: and when the greatest feel their need of him, and know his power and dignity, they will abase themselves as much before him, as the meanest.—Even amiable and dutiful children are often the source of much care and sorrow to their parents: but the best remedy, in respect both of their lives and souls, is to apply to Christ in their behalf; as life and death, temporal, spiritual, and eternal, are entirely at his disposal.—How various are the distresses and humiliating diseases, to which sin has subjected our species! And in how many ways does true faith operate, amidst the fears, diffidence, shame, remaining ignorance, and infirmity, of those that are made partakers of it! Yet if we do but touch, as it were, the hem of Christ's garment by living faith, our most inveterate maladies will be healed; but there is no other remedy: and we need not fear his knowing those things concerning us, which are our grief and burden, and which we should not wish to disclose to any earthly friend. We must not, however, desire to conceal our obligations to his power and grace: our comfort and his glory are concerned in their being made known; and when he sees the humble believer ready to sink with shame and terror, he will, by some encouraging token, shew his acceptance and special love. But he often delays to bring intended relief, till things come to an extremity: thus he proves our faith and patience, and renders the mercy doubly welcome, and our gratitude and admiration more abundant.—They,

who treat his words with contempt, and expect nothing from his power, are not meet persons to witness his glory. —Even death, to those whom he loves, is only a sleep: they will shortly awake at his word; and as our deceased Christian friends will share with us this joyful resurrection, we should not " sorrow as men without hope," though we expect not their return to us in this world. And if this single instance, of Christ's raising one that was newly dead, so increased his fame; what will be his glory, when " all that are in the graves, shall hear his voice, and come " forth, that have done good to the resurrection of " life, and they that have done evil to the resurrection of " damnation!"

V. 27—38.

Still we are astonished with the lustre of the Redeemer's power and love. Let sinners then copy the example of these blind men: let them stand before the Son of David, though they cannot behold him; and let them beseech him to have mercy upon them, and open their eyes to see his glory and preciousness, his truth and will: let them persist in following him with their intreaties, and in due time he will notice and help them. In this and in every other respect, we need to cry unto him daily to " increase our " faith;" that we may believe assuredly, that he is both able and willing to do every thing for us, which pertains to our salvation. If faith be not wanting in us, love and power will not be wanting in him; but he will say, " Ac- " cording to your faith be it unto you:" and instead of being deprived of so great a pleasure, we shall be sent forth to proclaim " his praises, who hath called us out of dark- " ness into his marvellous light."—While sinners remain under the power of Satan, they are deprived of the best use of the gift of speech, and cannot speak to any good purpose; but when Christ delivers them, their " mouths " are opened to shew forth his praise." We should therefore bring those to him, who are not willing to come of themselves; and intreat him for those, whom Satan so possesses, that they will not pray for themselves.—But nothing can convince those who indulge pride and malice, that the humbling doctrines of scripture are the truths of God: they will believe any absurdity rather than the divinely authenticated Scriptures; and the injurious reflections, which they cast on those, who are diligently employed in doing good to their fellow creatures, shew the enmity of their hearts against a holy God. We should therefore go on in our work, without regarding them: and, as to this day vast multitudes are " as sheep not having a " shepherd," we should compassionate them, and do all that we can to help them. The harvest that is yet to be reaped, (and ere long, according to the prophecies,) is very plentiful; the real labourers are, alas! extremely few: we should therefore pray earnestly and constantly to the Lord of the harvest, to raise up and send forth many, who will " labour in the word and doctrine," and in bringing souls to Christ; instead of labouring to advance, enrich, and indulge themselves. This is a duty too much neglected: but when God shall stir up the hearts of Christians every where to attend to it, we may expect the dawning of those happy days, when the gospel shall be known and believed all over the earth.

AND when he had **called unto him his twelve disciples, **he gave them **power **against unclean spirits, to cast them out, and to heal all manner of sickness, and all manner of disease.

2 Now the names of the twelve **apostles are these; the first **Simon, who is called Peter, and **Andrew his brother; **James the son of Zebedee, and John his brother;

3 **Philip, and Bartholomew; **Tho-mas, and **Matthew the publican; **James the son of Alpheus, **and Leb-beus, whose surname was Thaddeus;

4 **Simon the Canaanite, **and Judas Iscariot, who also betrayed him.

5 These twelve Jesus **sent forth, and commanded them, saying, **Go not into the way of the Gentiles, and into any city **of the Samaritans enter ye not:

6 But **go rather to **the lost sheep of the house of Israel.

NOTES.

CHAP. X. V. 1—4. It is generally supposed, that the apostles had been called to a constant attendance on Christ, a considerable time before, as persons intended for some important service. (*Notes, Mark* iii. 13—19. vi. 7—12.) At length they were solemnly appointed; and endued by their Lord with the power of casting out unclean spirits, and healing diseases in his name, to confirm their doctrine; and sent forth, by two and two, into different parts of the land, to prepare the people to receive him. The word "apostle" signifies a *messenger*, and as such it is given to Christ himself. (*Heb.* iii. 1.) They were his *messengers*, sent forth to proclaim his kingdom; and after his resurrection, they were especially selected to bear witness of that event. They were twelve in number, probably with reference to the twelve tribes of Israel. A catalogue of their names is here given, in which some things require consideration. Simon is first mentioned, both in this and other places: his original name signifies *hearing*. But our Lord, when Simon first came to him, named him Cephas, or Peter, from the word which signifies a *rock*, or a *stone;* denoting that he would prove a firm and stedfast man, and stable in professing and supporting the truth of the gospel. (*Marg. Ref. d.—Note, John* i. 35—42.) He is first mentioned, not as having authority over the other apostles, which some vainly pretend : but because he was the elder of the first two brothers, who were called to a constant attendance on Christ; and because his abilities, zeal, and disposition, combined in rendering him a principal and conspicuous character among them. His brother Andrew was sent out along with him. James, whom Herod slew, (*Note, Acts* xii. 1—4,) and John the Evangelist, his brother, were sent forth together : they were the two next who were called to follow Christ. Philip and Bartholomew, of whom we know less, were put together. Thomas, who is commonly called Didymus, or the *Twin*, was joined with Matthew the converted publican. James the son of Alpheus, who wrote the epistle, was joined with Lebbeus, or Thaddeus, the same person who is elsewhere called Jude, or Judas : the names here given him are supposed to signify *hearty* or *cordial*, to distinguish him from the other Judas, who was a hypocrite. (*Note, Mark* iii. 13—19.) The latter was joined with Simon the Cananaite, or

the man of Cana, as some explain it; though others suppose the word to be equivalent to *Zelotes*, or the *zealous*, by which he is elsewhere distinguished. (*Acts* i. 13.) The other Judas is always called Iscariot, which is generally supposed to mean " the man of Carioth : " yet some think, that it is derived from a word signifying *suspension*, and refers to the manner of his death. He professed himself Christ's disciple, and his apparent conduct did not contradict that profession : the Lord was therefore pleased to call him to be his constant attendant, and at length to make him one of his apostles, though he knew his hypocrisy; that thus the scripture might be fulfilled by his treachery and apostasy; for he " also," or *even*, " betrayed " him."—Some think that Bartholomew was the same, as St. John calls Nathaniel. (*Marg. Ref. h.*)—Our Lord's " giving power " to his apostles, and enabling them to work miracles, and, after his resurrection and the descent of the Holy Spirit, communicating the same powers to those on whom they laid their hands, was justly considered by the ancient fathers, as a striking proof of his Deity; and as absolutely unparalleled in the history of mankind, true or fabulous, sacred or profane. God put of his Spirit on those whom Moses had appointed ; but Moses did not *give* them power. The spirit of Elijah rested on Elisha, in answer to Elijah's prayer ; but Elijah did not *give* him power. (*Notes, Num.* xi. 16, 17. 25. *2 Kings* ii. 9—11.)

V. 5, 6. When Christ sent forth the apostles, he gave them a charge, or special warnings and instructions, many of which had reference to the whole of their future ministry. In these he forbad them, at that time, to go among the Gentiles, or to any place which bordered on them, or into any city of the Samaritans. He had indeed once preached, with great success, in a city of Samaria ; (*John* iv. 28—42 ;) yet his personal ministry, and that of his apostles before his ascension, were chiefly confined to the Jews; that they might not be prejudiced by a contrary conduct, or have any pretence for rejecting the gospel . for the change intended was to be effected gradually, and the obstinate unbelief of the Jews would make way for the calling of the Gentiles. The apostles therefore were commanded to " go rather to the lost sheep of the house of Israel." The term, " lost sheep," intimated, that the Israelites, though by profession the flock of God, had in general wandered from him, were destitute of faithful

7 And as ye go, [a] preach, saying, [x] The kingdom of heaven is at hand. 8 [y] Heal the sick, cleanse the lepers, raise the dead, cast out devils: [z] freely ye have received, freely give. 9 [a] Provide [b] neither gold, nor silver, nor brass in your purses, 10 Nor [b] scrip for your journey, neither [c] two coats, neither shoes, nor yet [1] staves: [d] for the workman is worthy of his meat. 11 And into whatsoever city or town ye shall enter, [e] enquire who in it is worthy; [f] and there abide till ye go thence. 12 And when ye come into an house, [g] salute it. 13 And if the house be [h] worthy, let your peace come upon it: but if it be not worthy, let your peace return to you. 14 And [i] whosoever shall not receive you, nor hear your words; when ye depart out of that house or city, [k] shake off the dust of your feet. 15 [l] Verily I say unto you, [m] It shall be more tolerable for the land of So-

---

shepherds, and in danger of perishing; even as the Samaritans and Gentiles were. (*Marg. Ref.—Note,* ix. 36—38.)

V. 7, 8. (*Note,* iii. 2.) The apostles were ordered in every place to preach, or *proclaim* as heralds, in the most earnest and publick manner, the same grand doctrine which John the Baptist had done, and which Christ himself began with preaching: for their ministry was, at this time, introductory to the open establishment of the Messiah's kingdom. In confirmation of their mission, they were empowered to work miracles, and even to raise the dead. This latter clause indeed is wanting in some manuscripts, but it is found in the earliest. Yet it is not recorded, that the apostles raised any dead persons, before the descent of the Holy Spirit; and probably they did not: but the charge, at this time given, evidently referred to the subsequent, as well as to the introductory part of their ministry. They were especially and expressly prohibited to make any personal advantage of these miraculous powers, as if they would sell the gift of God for money; (*Note, Acts* viii. 18 —24;) but must confer the benefit freely, as they had received it.—They who urge this text against the preachers of the gospel receiving a maintenance for their labour, evidently pervert it, and set it against the plainest declarations of the New Testament. It is, however, greatly to be desired, that a more decided superiority to "the love "of filthy lucre" were generally observable among the ministers of Christianity.—Doubtless Judas preached and wrought miracles, as well as the other apostles: and, probably for his credit's sake, he resisted the temptation of making any gain of his miraculous powers; at least he was not suspected by the other apostles. (*Note,* vii. 21—23.)

Freely. (8) Δωριαν. *John* xv. 25. *Rom.* iii. 24. 2 *Cor.* xi. 7. *Gal.* ii. 21. 2 *Thes.* iii. 8. *Rev.* xxi. 6. xxii. 17.—*Gen.* xxix. 15. *Is.* lii. 3. *Sept.* 'This particle, in the sacred 'books, is used in a two-fold sense, namely, both of a 'benefit conferred of mere liberality; and of an injury in- 'flicted by iniquity, on one that does not deserve it, either 'for no cause, or for no just cause.' *Leigh.*

V. 9, 10. The command "freely to give," and the prohibition to "provide," or *possess,* money to bear expenses, should be compared together. The apostles (and doubtless all other ministers,) were required to be eminently disinterested; yet they must trust God for support, even in those places where they were strangers. They were not allowed to carry with them either money, or provisions, in a scrip or bag; or clothes, or shoes; or a superfluous staff, in case any thing should happen to that with which they walked: for the Lord engaged to provide for their wants, by disposing those, to whom they went, to supply them. This they might conscientiously take, as the labourer is worthy of his maintenance; and more they must not covet. —The word rendered " purses" signifies *girdles :* it was customary for travellers to carry money for ordinary occasions, in a pocket, or fold, within their girdles.—' The ' ministers of the word must cast away all cares, that might " hinder them the least.'—" Provide neither gold, &c." That is ' for this journey, ... that they might feel some taste ' of God's providence ; for at their return, the Lord asked ' them, whether they lacked any thing by the way. *Luke* ' xxii. 35.' *Beza.*—' " He is worthy of his food ; " not of ' dainties ; for it becomes not a teacher to fare deliciously.' *Theophylact.* (*Note,* 1 *Tim.* v. 17, 18.)

V. 11—15. The apostles were directed to enquire, when they arrived at any city or town, what persons resided there, of good repute for piety and integrity; and to address them with the first proposal of the gospel : and, in case they received and entertained them, they must abide with them, if convenient, till they left the place : that they might not appear to be capricious, dissatisfied with their accommodations, or desirous of going from house to house, to partake of entertainments. When they entered any house, they must salute those who resided in it, in the customary manner, wishing that the peace and blessing of God might be communicated to them, and proposing the gospel of peace and salvation. And if the family, or any in it, were pious persons, disposed to welcome the gospel, the blessing would rest on them, and the messengers of Christ would further instruct and pray for them: but where this was not the case, the prayers and endeavours of the apostles would return in blessings on themselves.— It is generally said, that the imperative mood is here used instead of the future tense; but it seems also to imply a direction to ministers, how to act in such cases.—When, however, their gracious proposal met with an obstinate rejection, on leaving the place they must " shake off the " dust of their feet." (*Marg. Ref.* k.) It is recorded that the Jews, on returning from heathen countries, thus shook off the dust that clave to them; as afraid of bringing any pollution into the holy land, and as renouncing all connexion with idolaters : so that the conduct of the apostles

dom and Gomorrha, * in the day of judgment, than for that city.

16 ¶ Behold, I send you forth * as sheep in the midst of wolves: be ye therefore * wise as serpents, * and * harmless as doves.

17 But ' beware of men; ' for they will deliver you up to the ' councils, and they will * scourge you in their synagogues;

18 And ye shall * be brought before governors and kings for my sake, ' for a testimony against them and the Gentiles.

19 But * when they deliver you up, * take no thought how or what ye shall speak: for ' it shall be given you in that same hour what ye shall speak.

20 For it is not ye that speak, ' but the Spirit of * your Father which speaketh in you.

21 And * the brother shall deliver up the brother to death, and the father the child: and ' the children shall rise up against their parents, and cause them to be put to death.

22 And ye ' shall be hated of all men * for my name's sake; ' but he that endureth to the end shall be saved.

in this respect, would be understood to be a decided protestation against the conduct of the persons concerned; and a declaration, that they considered them equally criminal and exposed to divine wrath, with the Gentiles themselves.—To this injunction our Lord added, in the most solemn manner conceivable, that it would be more tolerable even for the inhabitants of Sodom and Gomorrah, in the day of judgment, than for those of such a city. Their obstinate impenitence and unbelief, amid such abundant opportunities of instruction and conviction, would evince a more determined enmity against God, than was manifested by all the gross abominations of Sodom, for which it had been visited with tremendous vengeance: and though they might escape punishment in this world, yet " in the " day of judgment " and final retribution, their doom would be more intolerable. (*Marg. Ref.*)

V. 16—18. Our Lord next taught the apostles to prepare for persecution. He sent them forth as harmless, defenceless sheep, into the midst of rapacious and cruel wolves, who would neither want will nor power to devour them, except as they were divinely protected. It would therefore behove them to unite the caution and sagacity, of which serpents have ever been the emblem, with the simple, inoffensive, pure, and loving temper of the dove: that they might avoid every thing, which could needlessly exasperate, or give an advantage to their enemies; all intermeddling with secular matters not belonging to them; and all rashness, violence, appearance of evil, or selfishness.—' This is to be wise as serpents; '...to be circumspect in declining their snares, and giving them no just ' occasion to afflict us; and to be harmless as doves, is to ' offend no man by word or example; and so to give them ' no cause to do evil to us.' *Theophylact.*—Circumstanced as the apostles would be, their most determined courage and patience ought to be tempered with prudence; nor must they be rendered unsuspecting, even by the consciousness of integrity and benevolence. On the contrary, they ought to " beware of men," as of enemies more implacable and fierce than wolves or tigers, and also most treacherous and insidious. No dependence therefore must be placed on their engagements; no regard pa to their flatteries, or professions of respect and friendship; no expec-

tations formed of any thing, but injurious treatment of every kind and from all quarters.—It was needful therefore that the apostles should count their cost, and prepare to face danger and endure affliction. For they would certainly be apprehended, and delivered up, as criminals, to the publick councils of the nation, and condemned to be scourged in the synagogues, where their consistories about ecclesiastical affairs were held; nay, they would at length be brought before the Roman governors, and the kings of the nations, for their attachment to the name and cause of Christ. Thus they would have an opportunity of declaring his gospel in their hearing, which, being neglected, would turn to a " testimony against them."

Harmless. (16) Αχεραιοι. *Rom.* xvi. 19. *Phil.* ii. 15. Some derive the word, from *a* priv. and κερας *a horn:* but this derivation is not satisfactory to the best Greek scholars; and indeed animals without horns, as lions and tigers, are by no means the most innoxious. It seems to be derived from *a* priv. and κεραω *to mix,* and to mean *simple, sincere, candid, without guile,* and *without* malignity.—*A testimony against them.* (18) Μαβτυριον αυτοις.—*A testimony unto them.*

V. 19, 20. The apostles were unlearned men, brought up in obscurity, and not used to speak before publick assemblies or earthly potentates: they might therefore fear, lest they should dishonour the cause, by 'impropriety of conduct and language. But they had no need to be solicitous on that account; for, as they were not called to plead their own cause, but that of their Lord, he would immediately suggest to them what they should speak: and thus their answers would not so much be their own thoughts or words, as those of the Holy Spirit of their heavenly Father, speaking by them. (*Marg. Ref.* c.)—The case here supposed was extraordinary; and neither the direction nor the promise is applicable to ordinary cases. Yet every minister and Christian is authorized to expect assistance adequate to the occasion, whatever it be.—*Take no thought.* (19) Μη μεριμνησητε. See on *Note* vi. 25.

V. 21, 22. The apostles might imagine, that their harmless, holy, and prudent conduct, their beneficent miracles, and the glad tidings of the Messiah's advent, would conciliate the favour of great numbers. But Christ assured

23 But ^k when they persecute you in this city, flee ye into another: for verily I say unto you, Ye shall not ^l have gone over the cities of Israel, ^l till the Son of man be come.

24 The ^m disciple is not above *his* master, nor the servant above his lord. 25 It is enough for the disciple that

he be as his master, and the servant as his lord. ⁿ If they have called the Master of the house ^o Beelzebub, how much more *shall they call* them of his household!

26 ^p Fear them not therefore: ^p for there is nothing covered, that shall not be revealed; and hid, that shall not be known.

them, that they would, on the contrary, experience the most rancorous enmity even from near relations: for the gospel, being contrary to the prejudices, pride, and lusts of men; interfering with their worldly interests and projects; and opposed by those evil spirits, which " work in " the children of disobedience ; " would certainly occasion vehement convulsions in cities and nations, and excite the jealousy of rulers; it would throw men into different parties, and produce violent controversies, and at length furious persecutions. Then the enemies of the truth would forget the ties of consanguinity and affinity; brethren would apprehend and accuse one another, and procure each other's death; parents, regardless of natural affection, would prosecute their own children to death; and even children, in violation of all their duties and obligations, would rise up against their own parents to procure their execution: nay, the preachers and professors of Christianity would be hated by men of all nations, sects, and characters, for the sake of Christ; yea, by all men, except those who were won over to embrace the gospel. This would expose them to such dangers, and sufferings, as would violently tempt them to apostatize. But those who continued to cleave to the Lord, and held out to the end, would be preserved from all real damage, and recompensed with everlasting felicity; whilst apostates would be finally ruined and lost. (*Marg. Ref.*)

Cause to be put to death. (21) Θανατώσουσι. *Rom.* viii. 13.—*Kill them.*' For the iniquitous prosecutor in a capital cause, is the real murderer.

He that endureth. (22) 'Ο ὑπομείνας. See on *Note, Heb.* xii. 2, 3. v. 3.—*Note, Jam.* i. 12. The word implies not only *suffering*, but being *tried*, and *standing the trial*, as gold does the fire. This trial hypocrites cannot endure, but true believers do. Judas did not " endure unto the " end ;" but the other apostles did. ' He that endureth ' to the end of these days of persecution from the unbe- ' lieving Jews, shall be saved from the dreadful destruction ' coming on them.' *Whitby.* This may perhaps be implied ; but surely,' endurance to the end of life, and everlasting salvation, are principally intended.

V. 23. The open manner, in which Christ warned his apostles concerning the persecutions which awaited them, emphatically evinced a consciousness of authority, and of influence over their hearts, and of power to support and recompense them.—They must in no wise conceal or palliate their message, in order to avoid persecution : yet they ought not rashly to expose themselves, or to rush into danger ; but when persecuted in one city, to flee to another, and there preach the gospel. This would often drive them from apparent scenes of usefulness ; yet it would prove no injury to the common cause, for they would not have gone

over all " the cities of Israel, till the Son of Man should " come."—' This phrase ... signifies, either his coming ' with the Roman army to destroy the Jews ; ... or else his, ' coming to the final judgment: and seeing the apostles' ' were none of them to live till the final judgment, it seems ' necessary to understand this of his coming to avenge his ' quarrel on the Jewish nation.' *Whitby.*—The apostles met with no persecutions, till after the day of Pentecost ; so that subsequent events must be intended, and the destruction of Jerusalem by the Romans seems especially pointed out.—Persecution prevented the apostles from preaching the gospel throughout the whole land, so fully as they might otherwise have done. The conversion of the Gentiles, after a time, found many of them other employment: and when the judgments of God on the Jews took place, several cities of Israel had not been visited, or statedly instructed, by the preachers of the gospel.

V. 24—26. The disciple is not generally regarded as a person of greater dignity or excellency than his *teacher*, or the servant than his master ; nor ought he to expect greater respect and deference : but never were disciples or servants so inferior to their Lord and Master, as Christ's were. If then, they met with injurious usage and opprobrious language, in the course of their ministry, they should remember, that the great Master of the family, notwithstanding his divine excellency, wisdom, holiness, and beneficence, had been called Beelzebub, as if he were " the prince of the devils," or in league with him : and it ought to satisfy them, his domesticks, to be as their Lord, and treated in the same manner ; considering their immense inferiority and great unworthiness. They were, therefore, exhorted not to fear those, who might load them with reproachful names or false accusations, or charge them with base motives or designs : for a time would soon come, when all secrets would be disclosed ; and then their characters, principles, motives, and intentions would be made known, and fully justified; and the malignity and wickedness of their accusers detected and put to shame. —' These words (26), are capable of two good senses. Let ' not the dread of these persecutors affright you from ' preaching ... the gospel, as despairing of success : for ' though at present it seems to be hidden from the world, ' and it is like to be obscured a while by the calumnies of ' the Jews and others ; I will cause it to shine through all ' the world, and dissipate all the clouds they cast over it, ' and break through all obstacles, and will render it mighty ' to " cast down every high thought, &c." (2 *Cor.* x. 5.) ' Or thus: Fear not the calumnies, with which they shall ' load you ; ... for I will make the innocency and excel- ' lency of your doctrine as clear as the light ; and your in- ' tegrity in the dispensing it, and your patience in suffering

27 What ⁱ I tell you in darkness, that speak ye in light; and what ye hear in the ear, ʲ that preach ye upon the house-tops.

28 And ᵏ fear not them which kill the body, but are not able to kill the soul: but rather ˡ fear him, which is ᵐ able to destroy both soul and body in hell.

29 ¶ Are not ⁿ two sparrows sold for a ° farthing? ᵖ and one of them shall not fall on the ground without your Father.

30 But ᑫ the very hairs of your head are all numbered.

31 Fear ye not therefore, ʳ ye are of more value than many sparrows.

32 Whosoever therefore shall ˢ confess me before men, ᵗ him will I confess also before my Father which is in heaven.

' for it, to redound to your praise, ... throughout all ages, ' and especially at the revelation of the Lord from heaven.' Whitby.

Master. (24) Διδασκαλον. (A διδασκω, doceo.) *Luke* ii. 46. *John* iii. 2. 1 *Cor.* xii. 28. *Eph.* iv. 11. 2 *Tim.* i. 11. It signifies more properly a *teacher*, than a *commander*. As used of Christ, it means *The teacher;* and is used by his opponents, as well as his disciples.—*Them of his household.* (25) Τις οικιακος. 36. (Ab οικος;.) *Domestick* servants especially, as distinguished from servants employed in the field, or at a distance.

V. 27, 28. The apostles could not be cut off, till they had finished their testimony: they ought therefore to be very bold and zealous in declaring, in the most publick manner, those truths which Christ had taught them privately, as by a whisper in their ears: and even to proclaim them from the tops of the houses; according to the usage of the Jews, concerning those things which they desired to make known to all the neighbourhood. This indeed would expose them to much enmity, and even endanger their lives: but if their persecutors should be permitted to proceed as far as possible; they could only kill the mortal body, a little before the time, when it would otherwise die of disease or natural decay: for they could by no means destroy the immortal soul, either by terminating its existence, or preventing its immediate and final felicity. The tortures, which might thus be endured, would indeed be dreadful to nature; yet they would not be comparable to the misery which God was able to inflict, in the destruction of both body and soul in hell. The apostles and other servants of Christ ought not, therefore, to fear the impotent malice of man, but the omnipotent, everlasting, and righteous indignation of God; which they would certainly incur, if they apostatized for fear of persecution, or failed to fulfil their important ministry.—' These words ... ' contain a certain evidence, that the soul dies not with the ' body, but continues afterwards in a state of sensibility. ' ... That which ... men can do to the body, ... they cannot ' do to the soul. ... They who, by killing the body, make ' the soul also to perish, till the reunion and revivescence ' both of body and soul, do also kill the soul : ... and they ' who by killing the body, render the soul ... insensate, ... ' do also kill the soul. For it is not easy to conceive, how ' a ... thinking and perceiving being can be more killed, ' than by depriving it of all sensation, thought, and per- ' ception; the body itself being killed, by a total priva- ' tion of ... sense and motion. ... It remains, that the soul ' doth not perish with the body, nor is it reduced into an

' insensible state by the death of it.' Whitby.—The language also strongly exposes the impotent rage of those; who by brutal treatment of the insensate body, try to do more, than merely to *kill* the object of their hatred : for this after all *does nothing* ; nor ought any thing of this kind to give the least uneasiness to the mind of any one.

V. 29—31. The apostles might expect, that their enemies would at length kill their bodies; but even this could not possibly be effected, without the permission of their almighty Father. His providence watched over all creatures, even the meanest of them. Sparrows, for instance, were so inconsiderable, that two were usually sold for a farthing : yet not one of them could fall to the ground and die, either by a natural or violent death, except by his immediate interposition. Even the very hairs of his people were all numbered and registered : every thing was deemed important that related to them, and especially to those who were employed to spread his gospel. In every way, the apostles, and the other servants of God, were unspeakably more valuable than many sparrows : it could not therefore be supposed, that their Father and Friend would permit any enemy to do them real harm. (*Marg. Ref.*)

A farthing. (29) Ασσαριν· (der. from *as*, a Latin word adopted into the Greek :) *Luke* xii. 6. 'The tenth part of ' a denarius, or drachma; about three farthings of our ' money.' *Schleusner* and *Leigh.*

V. 32, 33. For the further encouragement of the apostles, and of others in every age who should be exposed to persecution for Christ's sake ; he declared, that every one who boldly acknowledged him, and professed his truth in the face of danger and opposition, without turning aside from fear or shame, shall be abundantly recompensed : for he would confess and own him as a disciple, a friend, a brother, in the presence of his Father; especially in the day of judgment and final separation betwixt his people and his enemies. But, on the other hand, whosoever shall be induced by worldly motives to deny or disown Christ, or renounce his service, would, at that most awful crisis, be denied by him before his Father, and left to perish with his enemies; notwithstanding his former profession, gifts, or station in the church.—Every denial of Christ cannot be here intended ; for Peter denied him, yet repented and was pardoned : that only can be meant, which is persisted in. In like manner, every confession of Christ cannot be entitled to the blessed recompence here promised ; but that only which is the genuine and constant language of faith and love. (*Marg. Ref.*) The majesty and conscious dignity and authority of this declaration, made by a

33 But whosoever shall ᵈ deny me before men, him will I also deny before my Father which is in heaven.

34 ¶ Think not ᵉ that I am come to send peace on earth: I came not to send peace, but a sword.

35 For I am come ᶠ to set a man at variance against his father, and the daughter against her mother, and the daughter-in-law against her mother-in-law.

36 And ᵍ a man's foes shall be they of his own household.

37 He ʰ that loveth father or mother more than me, is not worthy of me: and he that loveth son or daughter more than me, is ⁱ not worthy of me.

38 And he that ᵏ taketh not his cross and followeth after me, is not worthy of me.

39 He ˡ that ˡ findeth his life shall lose it: and he that loseth his life for my sake shall find it.

40 ¶ He ᵐ that receiveth you, receiveth me, ⁿ and he that receiveth me, receiveth him that sent me.

l Thes. iv. 8.　*n* John v. 23. xii. 44—49. Phil. ii. 10, 11. 1 John ii. 22, 23. 2 John 9.

---

poor and despised Man, "who had not where to lay his "head;" conveys such a testimony of his Deity, as cannot be answered, in any way consistent with allowing the excellency of his character.

V. 34—36. The gospel, beyond doubt, in its genuine tendency, is suited to reconcile men to God and to each other; and if all men were consistent Christians, peace must be universal. But "the world lieth in wickedness," and under the wicked one: Christians must profess the truth, in opposition to all error; and obey their Lord, in opposition to all the maxims, customs, fashions, and vices of the world: and the end of Christ's coming was to set up a heavenly kingdom in the midst of Satan's empire, and built upon its ruins. Where no true religion is found, men may avoid theological disputes, whatever else they quarrel about; for they are essentially of one party, and their notions and observances admit of what some have called an *intercommunity:* but where the standard of the cross is erected, and sinners enlist under the Redeemer's banner; they are no longer "of the world," but of another kingdom, the laws, maxims, motives, and interests of which, are diametrically opposite to those of "the god" and "prince of this world." This must offend Satan and his servants; and the most harmless disciples, and ministers of Christ, will in consequence be reproached, calumniated, opposed, and persecuted: and when the enemy can excite the princes of this world to oppose the gospel, the sword of religious wars, of massacres, and of persecution, will be sent forth. Thus the wolves devour the inoffensive sheep, and then throw the blame on them as the authors of the quarrel!—Whenever men *called* Christians have persecuted others, it must have arisen from their not being real Christians, or from their not understanding the religion which they professed: for patient, meek endurance of persecution, and courageous profession and obedience in the midst of it, are the characteristics of true Christianity. In the present state of human nature, however, it must be expected, and our Lord foretold, that the gospel would give occasion to furious and bloody conflicts; so that even families would be divided into parties, and men would treat their nearest relatives as their worst enemies: and this has in fact been the case, in every nation, city, town, or village, where the true gospel of Christ has been successfully preached. (*Marg. Ref.* e—g.)—It has been shewn, that instead of the happy and prosperous days, which the Jews expected when the Messiah came; the

most fierce and bloody contests, which ever embroiled that or perhaps any other nation, followed his coming, till judgment came upon them to the uttermost. But this was no otherwise the consequence of his coming, than as their rejection of Christ provoked God to give them up to judicial infatuation; for they did not in the least quarrel about Christianity: this cannot therefore be considered, as the true interpretation of these verses.—The passage refers to the prophecy of Micah: (vii. 6:) but cannot be looked upon as a quotation. (*Notes,* 21, 22. *Gen.* iii. 14, 15. *Luke* xii. 49—53.)

To set at variance. (35) Διχασαι ' (a διχα, *divisim:* into two parts:) *To divide into two parts or parties.* Used here only in N. T.

V. 37—39. When matters should come to such extremities, that a man must lose the comfort and favour of his nearest relations, and incur their enmity, unless he renounced or disobeyed Christ; he, who was found to love father or mother, son or daughter, more than Christ, would be deemed unworthy of the privileges of his kingdom. Nay, he that refused to carry his cross, (as malefactors used to do, when they were led to be crucified,) and to suffer death rather than renounce Christ and the gospel, would be judged unworthy to be called a disciple of such a Master; seeing he would not follow his example of patient suffering, for the cause of God and truth. He therefore, who thus saved his life from imminent peril, whilst he thought himself a gainer by finding the life of his body, would lose all the true comfort and usefulness even of this life, and also the life of his precious soul: but he that lost his temporal life for Christ's sake, would find it amply made up to him by everlasting life in heaven. (*Notes,* xvi. 24—28. *Mark* viii. 32—37. *Luke* ix. 18—27.)—It is manifest that in these verses our Lord claims, and demands from all his disciples, that supreme and entire love, with which the law requires us to love the Lord our God. This he never would have done, had he not been "One with the "Father;" and had not our love of him, as Emmanuel, been the proper evidence and effect of our returning, by repentance and faith, to that love of God with the whole heart and soul, from which we as sinners have departed. —No mere creature could have made such a claim, without becoming the rival of God, who "will not give his "glory to another:" but "he," and he only, "that ho- "noureth the Son, honoureth the Father that sent him."

V. 40—42. Christ here concludes this most solemn and

41 He * that receiveth a prophet in the name of a prophet shall receive a prophet's reward; and he that receiveth a righteous man in the name of a righteous man shall receive *a righteous man's reward.

42 And whosoever shall give to drink unto * one of these little ones, *a cup of cold *water* only in the name of a disciple, verily I say unto you, *He shall in no wise lose his reward.

interesting address, by assuring the apostles, that he should consider himself immediately concerned in the reception, which was given to them : insomuch that those who should entertain them, out of love to their message and a disposition to obey it, would be recompensed in the same manner, as if they had welcomed Christ himself to their houses and to their hearts : and they, who thus received him as their Saviour, in fact received the Father himself to be their God and Portion.—Indeed, at any time, he that should entertain a prophet, or a holy messenger of God, as such, and for the sake of him that sent him, would be recompensed, in answer to the benedictions and prayers of the prophet, with a reward fit to be conferred even upon the prophet himself : and in like manner, he that should receive " a righteous man," a true disciple of Christ, out of love to his character and his master, would receive a reward meet to be bestowed on a righteous man. Yea, if any man should give to one of the meanest of Christ's disciples a cup of water to drink, because he was regarded as a disciple, having no other means in his power by which to testify his love : even this inconsiderable service should by no means pass unnoticed, or without a gracious recompence.—' How great soever your persecutions are, and ' how dangerous ... soever it be to profess to be a follower ' of Christ ; yet shall no man have reason to fear the enter- ' taining of you : for the same. protection which awaits ' you, and the same reward that attends you, shall await ' those that ... receive you. It shall be, as if they had 'en- ' tertained not only angels, but Christ, and God himself. ... ' He that doth support and enable a prophet to do his ' work that sent him, shall receive the same reward that ' he should if himself had been sent to prophesy.' *Hammond.*—This, ' as it is a great incitement to others to ex- ' press their kindness to Christ's ministers, and faithful ' servants ; so it is also to his ministers to apply them- ' selves to his service with a ready mind, and with the ' utmost diligence, in execution of their pastoral charge.' *Whitby. (Marg. Ref.)*

PRACTICAL OBSERVATIONS.
V. 1—6.

The Lord never encourages us to pray for any thing, which he is not ready to bestow in answer to our prayers. " From his fulness," ministers, in every age, receive their ordinary qualifications, even as the apostles did their miraculous powers : he is our Head of authority and influence, the Fountain of honour, wisdom, power, and holiness ; and all true ministers have their commission and instructions from him, in whatever way they obtain their outward designation to that office. Though they cannot miraculously cure men's bodies ; yet, by the power of Christ,' they are healers of souls, and deliverers from the bondage and possession of the devil.—Whatever a vain world may think, the names of Christ's apostles are far

more justly honourable, than those of the most powerful monarchs, the most illustrious conquerors, or the most celebrated philosophers or legislators, which are renowned in the records of mankind : and it in no degree deducted from their true honour, that some of them had been fisher. men, and that one had been a publican. They all were sinners, saved by grace alone ; and they spake and acted as those who were conscious of it : and having been deeply humbled for their sins, and made joyful in the Salvation of God, they were full of love to their Lord and Saviour ; and longed above all things to recommend him to their fellow- sinners on every side. This is the grand peculiarity of that minister, who is ' moved by the Holy Ghost to take the ' office upon him :' but many have the outward appoint- ment, who are strangers and enemies to this inward deter- mination and desire.—Indeed, there was one traitor among the apostles, whose infamy is indelible ; and this will at last humbled for the case of all, who, bearing this sacred office, habitually " seek their own, not the things of Jesus " Christ."—At present, Providence must direct us where to exercise our ministry ; for every restriction is now taken off, and we are authorized " to preach the gospel to every " creature." There 'are lost sheep in every land, as well as " of the house of Israel ;" and we must seek them out, wherever scattered in this wicked world, that they may be brought home to " the Shepherd and Bishop of our " souls."

V. 7—15.

It is always needful to introduce the gospel, by " preach- " ing repentance towards God," as well as " faith in our " Lord Jesus Christ:" for his kingdom never was, nor ever can be, set up in a proud, carnal, and impenitent heart.— Nothing can be more important to usefulness, than to avoid all appearance of a mercenary disposition. Many, who profess great things in various ways, with some ambiguous reference to the power of Christ and faith in his name, stand detected, in the judgment of every cautious en- quirer, by this single mark : ' They make their pretensions a very lucrative trade, and turn what they wish should be believed to be the gift of God, into ready money.' But of all employments, by which men grow rich, live in splen- dour or luxury, or aggrandize their families, none is more infamous than that of a hireling minister : and it is pecu- liarly honourable, when they, who have other means of decent subsistence, preach the gospel to the poor as freely as they have received it. Yet those who are not in circum- stances to do this, may very lawfully and honourably re- ceive a maintenance for their services ; for " the labourer " is worthy of his meat : " and if they be sent to places, where they have but little prospect of support, they should go on in their ministry with simplicity and diligence, cast- ing all their care upon the Lord. He will no doubt pro- vide what is really needful : and they will generally see his hand in the way in which they are supplied ; and taste his

CHAP. XI.

Jesus continues to preach in the cities, 1. John the Baptist sends his disciples to enquire of him, whether he is the Messiah, or whether another were to be expected; whom Jesus refers to the miracles wrought by him, 2—6. His testimony to John, 7—15. The perverseness of the people concerning both John and Jesus illustrated, 16—19. He upbraids the impenitency of those, who had witnessed most of his mighty works; and denounces woes against Chorazin, Bethsaida, and Capernaum, 20—24. He adores the wise and holy sovereignty of the Father, in revealing his truth; and declares his own personal and mediatorial power and majesty, 25—27. He invites and instructs the weary to come unto him for rest, 28—30.

love in their temporal provision, even more than those do who have greater abundance: nor need they scruple to receive what is thus conferred; as it will not deduct from the independence and true dignity of the ministerial character.—The preacher of the gospel is the ambassador of peace, and his commission reaches the vilest sinners; yet he should associate with the most pious and conscientious persons in every place: for though proud self-righteous morality or religion indisposes men to receive the gospel; yet the fear of God possessing the heart, is a real preparation for the embracing of it.—Ministers should manifest steadiness and consistency in their conduct, an evident indifference about outward accommodation, and moderation in all things. Their demeanour should be expressive of benevolence; and their friendly language, fervent prayers, and pious discourse, should be substituted in the stead of those hollow compliments and flatteries, by which so many hide their selfishness.—Diligent labours in the cause of Christ are never in vain; and the prayers of his servants for others will surely bring down blessings on themselves. Their goodwill, however, must not degenerate into timidity: the whole counsel of God must be declared; and they, who will not attend to the gracious message, must be shewn in the most decisive manner, by words and deeds, that their conduct is abhorred, and their state considered most dangerous and deplorable. This will generally be done to better effect, by declining to associate with them, and by shewing a determination to have no fellowship in their perishing, sinful pleasures and pursuits.—The gospel, though not at present confirmed with miracles wrought by the preachers, is so authenticated by external and internal evidence; and, when faithfully declared, so manifests its divine authority to every man's conscience; that all who reject it "hate the light because their deeds are evil." So that, even when enemies of the truth are free from great enormities in their visible conduct, their doom will be more dreadful in a future state, than that of the inhabitants of Sodom. This should be seriously laid to heart by all who hear the gospel, lest their privileges should only serve to increase their future condemnation. (*Marg. Ref. m. v.* 15.)

V. 16—33.

The ministers of the gospel should advert to their character and situation, and count their cost: they are " sent " forth as sheep in the midst of wolves;" let them then remember to be harmless and gentle, as lambs and doves, not resisting evil, nor retorting reproaches and injuries. Let them study to temper zeal and boldness with prudence and discretion; and so to act, that their enemies may find no plausible pretext for their malignity. But this " wisdom " is from above," and must be sought by earnest prayer, or it will degenerate into a time-serving caution. Yet, did

they perfectly unite " the wisdom of the serpent and the " harmlessness of the dove," they could not escape the hatred and contempt of men.—Those who decidedly take the Lord's part against an ungodly world, will be opposed, reviled, ensnared, and evil entreated by men in general. The most excellent servants of Christ, in all ages hitherto, have been imprisoned, scourged, and put to death, as malefactors; and they have been " brought before kings and " rulers," for no other crime, than bearing the name and preaching the gospel of Christ! In this way the Lord often brings truth to the hearing of those, who would otherwise have continued strangers to it; yet alas! this testimony commonly turns *against* them.—The work of the ministry requires study, preparation, and diligence: yet should the upright servant of Christ be suddenly called to declare his message, or bear testimony to the truth, before the princes of the earth; he need not be anxious how or what he should speak, but confide assuredly on Him, who has promised to give his people " a mouth and wisdom, " which all their enemies shall not be able to gainsay or " resist."—Opportunities of doing good may be expected in every place; we are not therefore required to stay among enraged persecutors: yet nothing must cause us to neglect our work, or conceal our relation and obligations to Christ. If then we be ready to faint or murmur, on account of the difficulties which we meet with, we should look to our Lord and Master: for we sinners surely should be willing to experience the same treatment from the world, which the divine Saviour did. And yet we none of us are reviled, insulted, or made to suffer as he was. Let us then pray for deliverance from the fear of man: and if we are falsely accused, let us wait for the Lord's coming, " who will " bring to light the hidden things of darkness, and make " manifest the counsels of all hearts, and then shall every " faithful servant " have praise of God." Let us boldly profess and plainly declare his truth, without regard to consequences. And even if we should be called to seal our testimony with our blood, we should fear apostasy far more than the most agonizing tortures: for " man can " only kill the body," and cannot hurt the soul; but the Lord " is able to destroy both body and soul in hell." " If " any man draw back, he will have no pleasure in him;" and he only, " who endureth unto the end, shall be saved." The Saviour is likewise able to support and comfort us under the sharpest sufferings, and to protect us in the most extreme perils; and without Him, the believer's Father and Friend, who has loved him with an everlasting love, the most trivial event cannot take place.—Let us then boldly confess Christ, and simply obey him before men; assured that he will own us poor sinners, as his brethren, before his Father's throne. But woe be to them, who are ashamed of him and his words among their fellow creatures, or deny him before his enemies; for Christ will disown them at

AND it came to pass, when Jesus had made an end of *commanding his twelve disciples, ᵇhe departed thence to teach and to preach in their cities.

2 ¶ Now *when John had heard ᵈin the prison the works of Christ, *he sent two of his disciples,

3 And said unto him, ᶠArt thou he that should come, or do we look for another?

4 Jesus answered and said unto them, Go and shew John again those things which ye do hear and see:

5 The ᵍ blind receive their sight, ʰand the lame walk, ¹the lepers are cleansed, ᵏand the deaf hear, ¹the dead are raised up, ᵐand the poor have the gospel preached to them.

6 And ⁿblessed is *he*, °whosoever shall not be offended in me.

that solemn season, when eternal happiness or misery will be awarded by his omnipotent word.

V. 34—42.

How desperate must be the enmity of the carnal heart against God, when the gospel of grace and peace excites, in those to whom it is proposed, the most rancorous malice, dissolving all the bonds of relative and social life, and prompting to the most unnatural murders and massacres! and when the most excellent and beneficent of the human race, who deserve to be universally revered and loved, become the objects of general contempt and hatred! To this day, the zealous believer's most inveterate foes are often " those of his own household."—We should, however, remember, that we also are " by nature children of wrath, " even as others;" and if we now love the truth, the cause, and the servants of Christ, all the praise is due to him who " hath made us to differ " by his special grace. This consideration should teach us to bear our cross, patiently and meekly; and to pity and pray for our deluded adversaries.—No personal or relative regards must interfere with our love to the divine Saviour, or with any requisite expressions of it; for he will not endure a rival in our hearts. And let us ask ourselves, Can father or mother, son or daughter, do us the service at that awful period, which He can? Have they done so much to deserve our love? Or are they so worthy of it? Surely our own hearts will declare us unworthy of him, if we prefer any earthly object to him! Surely we ought to be willing to bear our cross, and even to be crucified for him, as he was for our sins! How then can we expect to be counted worthy of his friendship, if we refuse to bear our lighter tribulations for his sake. And doubtless he is able to compensate all our losses for his cause; insomuch that if we lose our lives by cleaving to him, we shall never perish; but have eternal life and felicity as his most gracious recompence. Let us then abide in him, and shew our love to him by kindness to his people and ministers, welcoming their message, and " esteeming them very highly in love for " their work's sake;" satisfied that nothing which we do, from upright principles and pure motives, to the least of his disciples, shall fail of a proportionable and most liberal reward.

———

NOTES.

Chap. XI. V. 1. This verse should have been annexed to the close of the preceding chapter, as it relates

to the same subject; for the events, afterwards recorded, seem to have occurred at a different time.—When the apostles were gone forth, our Lord did not remit his labour, but continued to go from place to place, to instruct the people, and to perform beneficent miracles among them.

V. 2—6. John had continued for a considerable time in prison: and some think his faith in Jesus as the Messiah was in a measure staggered; seeing he took no notice of him, used no means to deliver him, and did not so much as *openly avow* himself to be the Messiah. But this is not at all likely. It is, however, evident that his disciples were, in general, far from being satisfied that Jesus was the Messiah: they were jealous for their master's honour, and did not clearly apprehend the nature of the Messiah's kingdom; they objected to the unreserved and social manner, in which Jesus and his disciples lived; and they were very backward to acknowledge him: so that John seems to have intended to procure them some decisive testimony from Christ himself, which might terminate their hesitation. Hearing therefore the report of his miracles, he sent two of his disciples to enquire of him, whether he were the Messiah, or not: this was the purport of the question.—The words translated, " He that should come," are literally, " He that cometh," or *is coming*. ('Ο ερχομενος.) —ᶜ This was in those days the common stile for the Messias. So he is stiled by John himself; ... " He that " " cometh after me :" (iii. 11 :) so by the multitude ;... ᶜ " Blessed is he that cometh in the name of the Lord ;" ᶜ (xxi. 9 ;) or the " King that cometh." (*Luke* xix. 38.) ᶜ *Whitby.* The question therefore shews, that all the Jews in general were decided in the opinion, that the Messiah was at hand ; and that if Jesus were not He, another was immediately to be expected : yet almost eighteen hundred years have now elapsed, and no other is come, they themselves being judges : how then can they evade the inference, that Jesus of Nazareth was indeed the promised Messiah ?—To the question, however, thus proposed, our Lord answered, rather by actions than by words: probably, lest an explicit reply should give his enemies a handle against him. He therefore wrought many miracles in the presence of John's messengers ; and ordered them to report to him what they had witnessed, as well as what they had heard ; and especially to shew him, that the poor and lowly had the gospel preached to them : these heard glad tidings, and received the report, whilst the rich, learned, and powerful, rejected Christ and his doctrine.—This ex-

M

p Luke vii. 24—
30.
q iii. 1—3. 5. xxi.
25. Mark i. 3—
5. Luke iii. 3—
7. viii. ix. John
i. 58. v. 35.
r Gen. xlix.
2 Cor. i. 17, 18.
Eph. iv. 14. Jam.
i. 6.
s iii. 4. 2 Kings i.
8. Is. xx. 2.
Zech. xiii. 4.
1 Cor. iv. 11.
2 Cor. xi. 27.
Rev. xi. 3.
t iii. 14. xiv. 5.
xvii. 12, 13. xxi.
24—26. Mark ix.
11—13. Luke i.
15—17. 76.
u Is. xl. 3. xlii.
Mal. iii. 1. Iv. 5.
Mark i. 2. Luke
vii. 26, 27. John
i. 23.

7 ¶ And as they departed, ʳ Jesus began to say unto the multitudes concerning John, ˢ What went ye out into the wilderness to see? ᵗ A reed shaken with the wind?

8 But what went ye out for to see? ᵘ A man clothed in soft raiment? Behold, they that wear soft *clothing* are in kings' houses.

9 But what went ye out for to see? ᵛ A prophet? yea, I say unto you, and more than a prophet.

10 For this is he, ʷ of whom it is written, Behold, I send my messenger before thy face, which shall prepare thy way before thee.

11 Verily, I say unto you, Among them that are ˣ born of women there hath not risen ʸ a greater than John the Baptist: notwithstanding, ᶻ he that is least in the kingdom of heaven is ᵃ greater than he.

12 And ᵇ from the days of John the Baptist until now, the kingdom of heaven ᶜ suffereth violence, and the violent take it by force.

x Joh. xiv. 1, 4.
Ps. ii. 7. Eph.
ii. 3.
y iii. 11. 1 Sam.
ii. 3. Luke i.
15. vii. 26. John
v. 35.
z v. 19. Is. xxx.
20. Zech. xii.
& Luke ix. 48.
1 Cor. vi. 4. xv.
9. Eph. iii. 8.
a John xiii. 36. x.
41. Rom. xvi.
25, 26. Col. i.
26, 27. 2 Tim.
i. 10. Heb. xi.
40. 1 Pet. i. 10.
b xxi. 23—32.
Luke vii. 29,
30. xiii. 24. xvi.
16. John vi. 27.
Phil. ii. 12.
c Or, is gotten by
force, and they
that thrust men
take, &c.

---

actly accorded to the prophecies concerning the Messiah; but was contrary to the conduct of deceivers, who, out of carnal policy, generally address themselves to the great and powerful. John had wrought no miracle: and this rendered Christ's miracles the more decisive evidence; especially as they were predicted by the same prophet, who had also foretold John's preparatory ministry, the contempt, opposition, and ill-usage, which the Messiah would meet with, and his humiliation, sufferings, and death. All these considerations tend to shew the wisdom and propriety of our Lord's answer.—He added, " Blessed is he, who " shall not be offended in me." The prejudices of the people against a poor, afflicted, and suffering Messiah were so strong, and his doctrine and manner of life were so contrary to those of the Scribes and Pharisees, that most of them would be stumbled by what they saw and heard, and be induced to reject him; notwithstanding John's testimony, the ancient prophecies, his own miracles, and the abundant evidence which he gave of his divine authority. Yet they only would be happy, who should overcome all these prejudices, and receive him as the Messiah; and all these, whatever their previous character had been, would certainly be so. (*Marg. Ref.* o.)

Do we look for, &c. (3) Προσδοκωμεν, *Luke* xii. 2 *Pet.* iii. 12. Rendered *were in expectation; Luke* iii. 15.—*The dead are raised up.* (5) The widow's son at Nain had been raised just before. (*Luke* vii. 11—21.)—*Have the gospel preached unto them.*] Ευαγγελιζονται. This use of the verb seems to imply, both the *imparting* and the *reception* of the glad tidings. The poor were preached unto, and they heard the gospel gladly, which the superior persons rejected.—*Offended.* (6) Σκανδαλισθη. (See on *Note,* v. 28, 29, v. 29.)

V. 7—11. John came as Christ's forerunner, and large multitudes attended his ministry, and received his baptism; yet very few gave due attention to the grand object of his preaching. His testimony was, therefore, of very great importance, with those who regarded him as a prophet; and our Lord's demand, or enquiry, was suited to excite them to attentive consideration. Surely, they had not gone into the wilderness merely to see the reeds and rushes shaken by the wind; or to hear a man preach who was as easily shaken as they, by every gust of rumour or prejudice, or every change of outward circumstances! John was a man of a very different spirit: he had acknowledged Jesus as the Messiah, and he still persisted in his testimony: why then did they not regard him? They had in-

deed gone forth, in great numbers, as men throng to gaze on a royal procession: but they could not expect to see in the desert, a man clothed in soft, or *delicate* and *sumptuous* raiment. Such persons were rather found in kings' palaces; and the people knew John to be a plain rough man, meanly clad, and mortified to all these vanities. (*Note,* iii. 4.) What then was their object? They would doubtless answer, that they went out to see and hear a prophet, sent from God to instruct and reform them: and John was " a prophet, and more than a prophet," being the very person of whom Malachi had prophesied; and not *predicting* the Messiah, but pointing him out as already come.—In the passage referred to, JEHOVAH, speaking of the coming of Christ, says, " my face," and " before me:" but it is here quoted, as the language of the Father to the Son, and he therefore says, " before *thy* face," and, " thy way be- " fore *thee:* " so that to prepare the way of Christ, was " to prepare the way of the LORD, of JEHOVAH;" for " He " and the Father are One."—Our Lord added, that of all born of women, (that is, of all mere men,) there had not arisen a greater than John the Baptist; not one more holy, zealous, faithful, and humble; not one, who was employed in a more high and honourable service; not one who had been favoured with clearer views of evangelical truth; not one, who had been thus distinguished by being himself the subject of prophecy. And yet, " the least in the kingdom " of heaven was greater than he." The least of the apostles, or New Testament prophets, who were called to establish the Messiah's kingdom, would be further enlightened in the knowledge of his person, obedience, atonement, and mediation; and be employed in a more distinguished service, and more abundantly endued with the Holy Spirit, than John had been; and would possess miraculous powers, which John did not. If we extend the passage to all faithful ministers of the gospel, or to all true believers, (as many do,) it can only relate to their superior excellency of the new dispensation, and the more distinct views of the nature and glory of the gospel, with which they are favoured: for, in respect of personal excellence and usefulness, few believers or ministers have been found greater than John, or indeed equal to him. (*Marg. Ref.*)—But the first interpretation is most satisfactory.

Soft. (8) Μαλακοις. *Luke* vii. 25. ' The apostle, 1 *Cor.* ' vi. 9, transferreth it to the mind.' *Leigh:* where it is rendered " effeminate."

V. 12. With the ministry of John, the New Testament

13 For 'all the prophets and the law prophesied until John.

14 And 'if ye will receive it, 'this is Elias which was for to come.

15 He 'that hath ears to hear, let him hear.

16 ¶ But, 'whereunto shall I liken this generation? 'It is like unto children sitting in the markets, and calling unto their fellows,

17 And saying, 'We have 'piped unto you, and ye have not danced; we have mourned unto you, and ye have not lamented.

18 For 'John came neither eating nor drinking, and they say, 'He hath a devil.

19 The Son of man 'came eating and drinking, and they say, Behold, a man gluttonous, and a wine-bibber, 'a friend of publicans and sinners. 'But wisdom is justified of her children.

20 ¶ Then 'began he to 'upbraid the cities wherein most of his mighty works were done, 'because they repented not:

21 'Woe unto thee, Chorazin! woe unto thee, 'Bethsaida! 'for if the

---

dispensation began to be introduced, and "the kingdom of "heaven" to be preached: and, whilst the careless, the formal, the moral, and the learned in general, disregarded it; persons of the worst characters (who might previously have rather been expected violently to plunder men's houses,) with great earnestness sought admission into the Messiah's kingdom: so that it seemed to suffer violence, and "the "violent seized it by force:" and they, who were supposed not to have the least right to these blessings, obtained possession of them; while the scribes, Pharisees, priests, and rulers, who considered the benefits of the Messiah's coming as their own unalienable inheritance, were excluded, and the publicans and harlots entered before them.

Suffereth violence.] Βιάζεται. Rendered *Presseth into it;* Luke xvi. 16. In Luke the middle verb is used *actively:* but in the present instance it is translated *passively;* and the context confirms the translation. The persons intended were so deeply convinced and so strongly excited, by our Lord's preaching the kingdom of God; that they vehemently broke through every hindrance, to their entrance into it. (Α Cια vis.)—*The violent.*] Βιασται. (Α Cια.) Not used elsewhere in the New Testament.—*Take it by force.*] Αρπαζωσιν. John vi. 15. x. 28, 29.

V. 13—15. All the prophets, and Moses in the law, both by types and express predictions, *foretold* the coming of the Messiah as a *future* event: but John declared him to be at hand, and even pointed him out as *already come.* And, if the people would receive and believe this open declaration, John was indeed the very person, who had been predicted under the name of Elijah, as sent to prepare the way of the Messiah. This information highly concerned all men; and every one, who was capable of hearing, was bound to listen to it, as a truth immediately connected with his duty and happiness. (*Marg. Ref. f.*)—This is the obvious meaning of the concluding sentence, which is often repeated: and the limitation of it, to those who have 'an inward hearing ear,' in the most direct manner tends to prevent the effect, which is most evidently intended; namely, to excite universal attention.

V. 16—19. Our Lord next exposed the perverseness of the Jews, by an apt similitude. They resembled sullen children; who, being out of temper, quarrel with all the attempts of their fellows to please them, or to induce them to join in those diversions, for which they met in the market-places. Their companions aimed to engage them by piping a cheerful tune; but they peevishly refused to dance to it: and if they represented a more doleful scene, and imitated the mournful strains used at the houses of the dead, they refused to lament. Such a capricious and sullen disposition is often observed in children, and thought deserving of sharp rebukes and corrections; yet in a matter of infinite importance, the people of that generation copied it! The Lord employed different means to bring them to repentance, and to prepare them for the blessings of the gospel; but they opposed and objected to all. John the Baptist came in a very abstemious and austere manner, as a mortified recluse, who would not join their feasts; and they said, 'he is melancholy, lunatick, and possessed with a devil.' The Son of Man (the Messiah, the most honourable of the sons of men,) came in a more free and social manner. He ate and drank such things as were set before him, without any peculiar austerity; and he partook of their entertainments as circumstances required: yet instead of being pleased by his condescending, courteous, and social demeanour, they, with a mixture of malevolence and absurdity, called him "a glutton and a wine-bibber;" and because he went among publicans and notorious sinners, to reform them, they accused him of loving their characters and company. But the divine wisdom, displayed in these appointments, and in all others, would be perceived, approved, and adored by the children of wisdom; that is, by all who are born and taught of God, and thus made wise unto eternal salvation.—All these are both taught and inclined by grace, to adore the "depth of "the riches both of the knowledge and wisdom of God," in those dispensations and purposes which they do not understand; to give him credit for wisdom, and justice, and goodness, where they do not perceive them; and to understand many of his designs and appointments, which to others appear perplexed and unsuitable. (*Notes, Rom.* xi. 33—36. 1 Cor. ii. 14—16.)—*Gluttonous.* (19) This is stronger than the original: Φαγος και οινοποτης, "An eater, "and a drinker of wine."

V. 20—24. Our Lord, having exposed the perverseness of the Jews in general, upbraided some of those cities in

mighty works, which were done in you, had been done in Tyre and Sidon, they would have ⁱ repented long ago in sackcloth and ashes.

22 But I say unto you, ᵏ It shall be more tolerable for ᵇ Tyre and Sidon at ᶜ the day of judgment, than for you.

23 And thou ᵈ Capernaum, ᵉ which art exalted unto heaven, shalt be brought down to hell: for if the mighty works which have been done in thee, had been done ᶠ in Sodom, it would have remained until this day.

24 But I say unto you, That it shall

be ᶠ more tolerable for the land of So-dom in the day of judgment, than for thee.

25 ¶ At that time, ᵇ Jesus answered and said, ⁱ I thank thee, O Father, ᵏ Lord of heaven and earth, ˡ because thou hast hid these things from the wise and prudent, ᵐ and hast revealed them unto babes.

26 Even so, Father; ⁿ for so it seem-ed good in thy sight.

27 All things ᵒ are delivered unto me of my Father: and ᵖ no man know-

which he had wrought most of his miracles, because their inhabitants continued still impenitent. After having de-nounced a woe on Chorazin and Bethsaida, two cities in Galilee, to which he had frequently resorted; he declared, that if such miracles as they had witnessed had been wrought in Tyre and Zidon, those wealthy, luxurious, com-mercial cities, the destruction of which the prophets had repeatedly denounced; the inhabitants would long before have shewn the most expressive signs of deep repentance and humiliation.—We are not competent to solve every difficulty in this subject, or fully to understand it: it suf-fices, that Christ knew the hearts of the impenitent Jews, to be more hardened in rebellion and enmity, and less susceptible of suitable impressions from his doctrine and miracles, than those of the inhabitants of Tyre and Zidon would have been; and therefore their final condemnation would be proportionably more intolerable.—And, as to Capernaum, which was a prosperous city, where he had chiefly resided after his entrance upon his publick ministry; it had been, as it were, exalted to heaven by extraordinary privileges: but these would only tend to sink the inhabit-ants deeper into hell; for if the mighty works, there per-formed, had been wrought in Sodom, it might have stood and prospered even to that day. The people of Capernaum must therefore expect a heavier doom, at the day of judg-ment, than even the vile inhabitants of Sodom. (*Marg. Ref. f.—Notes,* x. 11—15. *Luke* x. 13—15.)—It is pro-bable, that many inhabitants of these favoured cities pro-fessed to *believe* in Christ; yet they did not " repent and " do works meet for repentance:" and our Lord, by up-braiding them for not *repenting*, emphatically shewed the inefficacy of an impenitent faith.

V. 25, 26. The sovereignty of God, in vouchsafing more abundant means of instruction to one city or country, than to another which was better disposed to attend to them, might excite objections; to which perhaps Jesus *answered*, when he adored the divine conduct in a similar concern. He addressed the Father, as the Proprietor and Governor of the universe, who " doeth whatsoever pleaseth " him " in heaven and earth: and he thanked or *adored* him, and professed an entire acquiescence in his wisdom, equity, and goodness, which were worthy of all adoration and praise; in that he was pleased to conceal the mysteries of the kingdom of heaven from learned scribes and the

wise men of the nation, and at the same time to reveal them to the poor and unlearned; to men of weak capaci-ties and mean education; to those, who were despised for their ignorance and inexperience, but who were also sim-ple, humble, and teachable as children. This he had done, " because it seemed good in his sight," for wise and gra-cious reasons which he was not pleased to assign. (*Note, Eph.* i. 9—12.) God did not, by any *positive influence,* hide the proofs of Christ's mission from the wise and prudent: they had their scriptures in their hands; they saw or heard of his miracles, and heard, or might have heard, his doc-trine: but they were blinded by pride and carnal prejudi-ces; and he was pleased to give them up to be judicially blinded, among other reasons perhaps, in order that the success of the gospel might evidently appear to be the effect of divine power, and not of human wisdom and sagacity. (*Note, 2 Cor.* iv. 7.) But there was a *positive in-fluence* employed, in making known the truth to the minds of the apostles and disciples. (*Note,* xvi. 17.) ' " The ' " wise and prudent " here, are not men truly and spiritu-' ally wise; but men possessed with carnal, worldly wis-' dom, and with a swelling conceit of their proficiency in ' wisdom; both which indispose men to embrace true spi-' ritual wisdom: and from these God is therefore said to ' have hid the wisdom of the gospel, because he permitted ' them to continue in that self-conceit and worldly mind-' edness, which caused them to reject it, as being not ' agreeable to their inclinations and mistaken sentiments. ' ...The " babes " are those humble modest persons, who, ' having a low esteem of their own wisdom, give them-' selves up to the divine wisdom; and, being free from ' carnal and worldly affections, ... are fitted to embrace it ' when it is revealed. It being therefore suitable to the ' wisdom and good pleasure of God, who " resists the ' " proud, but giveth grace unto the humble," to make ' known his will to persons so prepared to receive it, our ' Lord adds, " for so it seemed good in thy sight." ' *Whitby.* (*Note,* v. 3.)

I thank thee. (25) Εξομολογουμαι σοι. *I confess to thee.* iii. 6. *Luke* x. 21. *Rom.* xiv. 11. xv. 9. *Rev.* iii. 5.—2 *Sam.* xxii. 50. 1 *Chr.* xvi. 4. *Sept.*—*It seemed good.* (26) Ευδοκια. *Luke* ii. 14. x. 21. xii. 32. *Eph.* i. 5. 9. *Phil.* ii. 18. 2 *Thes.* i. 11.

V. 27. This verse contains a very remarkable declara-

eth the Son, but the Father   ⁴ neither knoweth any man the Father, save the Son, and *he* to whomsoever the Son will reveal *him*.

28 ᵉ Come unto me, ᶠ all *ye* that labour and are heavy laden, ᶠ and I will give you rest.

29 Take ʰ my yoke upon you, ᶦ and learn of me : ʲ for I am meek and lowly in heart : ᵏ and ye shall find rest unto your souls.

30 For ˡ my yoke *is* easy, and my ᵐ burden is light.

---

tion, of our Lord's personal and mediatorial dignity. The Father had " delivered all things into his hands," even all power, authority, and judgment over all creatures. (*Notes,* xxviii. 18. *John* iii. 27—36, *vv.* 35, 36. v. 20—29.) None knew Jesus, as the Son of God, but the eternal Father; even as none knew the Father, except the Son : neither could any man truly know the Father, except as the Son revealed his nature and glory to him; for this was entirely committed to him as Mediator, in respect of all the sinful race of men. This represents the Son as co-equal with the Father, and as incomprehensible : and it completely demonstrates, that those who reject the teaching of the Lord Jesus, as the Son of God, and do not depend on him " to " reveal the Father " to them, cannot know any thing aright of that One, true, and living God, whom they profess to worship.—' There is no true knowledge of God, nor ' quietness of mind, but only in Christ alone.' *Beza.* All the worship therefore of the Jews since the nation rejected and crucified their Messiah, of Mohammedans, of modern deists, and of all unbelievers, is in fact rendered to an imaginary deity; " the God and Father of our Lord Jesus " being to them " the unknown God." (*Marg. Ref.* q.— *Note, Luke* x. 21, 22.)

Delivered.] Παρἐδὀθη. xxvii. 2. *Rom.* iv. 25. vi. 17 : rendered *betray;* x. 4. xxvi. 45 : *deliver up;* xxiv. 9. *Rom.* viii. 32 : *committed himself;* 1 *Pet.* ii. 23 : *give; Eph.* v. 25.—*Will reveal.*] Βυλήσεται ... αποκαλύψαι, *willeth to reveal.* 1 *Cor.* xii. 11. 1 *Tim.* ii. 8. *Tit.* iii. 8.—*Reveal.*] Comp. xvi. 17. 1 *Cor.* ii. 10. *Eph.* i. 17.

V. 28—30. The divine Saviour, having thus declared his dignity and authority, invited all those " who laboured " and were heavy laden " to come to him.—In some sense this includes all men : for worldly men labour like slaves, and burden themselves with fruitless cares and disquietudes about increasing wealth, or acquiring honour and pre-eminence. The dissipated and sensual labour hard, and are " heavy laden," in pursuing pleasures and diversions. The slave of Satan, and of his own lusts and passions, is the veriest drudge on earth; and if he attempt by his own strength to break loose, he labours in vain. The superstitious labour in the very fire, and are heavy laden with self-imposed burdens. The ceremonial law caused the people much labour, and laid heavy burdens on them, compared with those of the gospel. They, who endeavour to " establish their own righteousness," are equally burdened and wearied in vain. The convinced, trembling, broken-hearted sinner labours under great discouragement, and is heavy laden with guilt and terror: and the tempted and afflicted believer has his labours and burdens also. In short every " heart knows its own bitterness;" but Christ invites all, who in any respect " labour and are heavy laden," to come to him, for rest to their souls : though such as

laboured under a deep sense of guilt, or were heavy laden with the burdens imposed on them by the scribes and Pharisees, seem especially intended. Christ alone gives this invitation : prophets, apostles, and ministers direct men to go to the Saviour; the Father speaking from heaven, and the Spirit speaking in the heart, concur in the same instruction.—Men come to Jesus, when, feeling their guilt, misery, and inability to help themselves, and believing his love and power to help them, they seek to him in fervent prayer, and rely and wait on him for salvation. All who thus come to him, receive *rest* as his gift, they are released from bondage and condemnation ; relieved from anxious cares, fears, and superstitions; and obtain peace, satisfaction, and comfort in their hearts and consciences. (*Note, Jer.* vi. 16, 17.) But, coming to him, they must take his yoke upon them, and submit to his authority, as their Lord and Master. (*Note,* vii. 24—27.) They must also learn of him, as their Teacher and Counsellor, all things relating to their acceptance, comfort, and obedience ; especially the true knowledge of God the Father. (*Notes,* 27. *John* xvii. 1—3.) To encourage them in this, he assures them, that he is " meek and lowly in heart." Some explain this of the lesson which he teaches, even imitation of his meekness and lowliness : and doubtless this is necessary, and tends to inward rest and peace; for the storms, which rend the cedars on the lofty mountains, leave the lilies unmolested in the lowly valleys. But it is rather to be understood of our Lord's character, as a Teacher and Ruler : he does not govern with rigour, or treat his scholars with harshness; but he deals gently with them, bears with their ignorance and incapacity, condescends to their weakness and infirmity, rejects no willing scholar, and accepts the willing servant, notwithstanding all his numerous mistakes, defects, and incidental faults. In his school and service, therefore, men " find rest to " their souls," and there only. Nor need they fear his yoke : most of his commandments indeed are the same, for substance, with the moral law, and all coincide with it : but that " law is holy, just, and good ;" and obedience tends to proportionable felicity. As it is put by the Saviour, as his yoke, upon the believer, it is deprived of its condemning power; it is enforced by evangelical motives, encouragements, and promises of assistance and gracious recompence ; it is made easy by love and divine consolations ; and a correspondent disposition is wrought in the heart by regenerating grace. Indeed this obedience requires self-denial, and exposes a man to difficulties in many cases ; but all this is a hundred-fold compensated, even in this world, by inward peace and joy. So that Christ's yoke is easy and pleasant in itself; as well as when compared with the yoke of Satan, sin, superstition, or self-righteousness, which those who reject the yoke of the Re-

M 5

CHAP. XII.

The disciples pluck ears of corn to eat, on the sabbath, 1. Christ vindicates them from the charge of breaking the sabbath, 2—8; heals the withered hand of one in the synagogue; and shews it lawful to do good on the sabbath, 9—13. The Pharisees seek to kill him; he withdraws, yet works miracles, and so fulfils a prophecy of Isaiah, 14—21. He casts out a devil from a dumb and blind man, 22, 23; confutes the charge of the Pharisees, of casting out devils by Beelzebub, 24—30; and shews the sin against the Holy Ghost to be unpardonable, and that every idle word must be accounted for, 31—37. He rebukes those who sought a sign, and will give none but that of Jonah, 38—40. The Ninevites, and the queen of the south, will condemn that generation, 41, 42. By a parable he shews their awful state, 43—45. His disciples are his most endeared relations, 46—50.

deemer must bear. Indeed *the burden* of corrections, tribulations, temptations, and persecutions, to which Christ's service may expose us, would sink us, if we were left to ourselves; yet being counterpoised with internal supports, it proves " *light*, and is but for a moment, and works out " for us a far more exceeding and eternal weight of glory." (2 *Cor.* iv. 17. Gr.) So that every way his " yoke is easy, " and his burden light." (*Marg. Ref.*)

Come. (28) Δυ̃τε. iv. 19. xxii. 4. xxv. 34. *et al.*—*Heavy laden.*] πεφορ'ησμενοι. (A φορ'ιος *onus*, seu φορ'ιον *idem*, xxiii. 4.) *Luke* xi. 46.—*I will give … rest.*] Αναπαυσω. xxvi. 45. *Mark* vi. 31. *Luke* xii. 19. 1 *Cor.* xvi. 18. 2 *Cor.* vii. 13. *Philem.* 7. *Rev.* vi. 11.—*Rest.* (29) Αναπαυσιν. xii. 43. *Rev.* iv. 8. xiv. 11.—*Ps.* cxvi. 7. *Sept.*

PRACTICAL OBSERVATIONS.

V. 1—6.

Our divine Redeemer was unwearied in his arduous labour of love: surely then, we " should not be weary of " well doing; for in due season we shall reap, if we faint " not."—The dispensations of Providence, in laying aside and removing eminent ministers, at the very time when we should suppose they were peculiarly wanted, appear very mysterious: but God will not permit any servant in the least to interfere with the glory of " his beloved Son:" and he will shew all men, that, though he may please to employ them in carrying on his designs, he can do without them.—Patience, in a prison or a sick room, glorifies the Lord, as well as the most active services: but, when we cannot do what we would, we should still attempt, as we can, to direct the judgment and confirm the faith of those who regard our words; and Christ will surely and greatly honour those, who thus humbly serve and honour him.—What multitudes in these lands allow that the Saviour is already come, and that they look for no other; yet, alas! how few accept of his salvation, and bow to the sceptre of his grace!—Those things, which men see and hear, if compared diligently with the scriptures, would direct them to the true religion, and determine in what way salvation is to be found. Though outward miracles are no longer wrought; yet the effects produced, where the gospel is faithfully preached to the poor, in opening their eyes, directing their walk, delivering them from their sins, and from the power of Satan, and teaching them to lead a spiritual and holy life, abundantly prove, that it is " the " power of God to the salvation " of those who believe: and the contempt with which the rich, the proud, the worldly wise, and the self-righteous regard this doctrine and these effects, forms an additional demonstration of the truth of the scripture; for is it not written, that " the " preaching of the cross is foolishness to them that perish?"

But men are as apt to be offended with the doctrines, and preachers, and professors of the gospel now, as they were formerly with the lowly estate of the Redeemer: their proud and carnal prejudices are contradicted by them, and they are glad of any pretext for rejecting what they hate. Happy then is that man, whatever his past character has been, or present circumstances are, who neither stumbles at any of these things, nor yet at the call to submission, repentance, self-denial, and unreserved obedience; but, notwithstanding all, cordially believes and embraces the gospel.

V. 7—15.

Alas! how unsatisfactory an account can many give, of what they go to see or hear, when they frequent places of worship, or are throng to attend on faithful preachers! They go to satisfy curiosity, or to trifle away their time: but instead of resorting together to see the shaking of a reed, or " a man clothed in soft raiment; " they often mean rather to exhibit their own elegant and fashionable apparel, and to compare it with that of their neighbours! —For " soft rainment" is not at present confined to the palaces of kings; but all endeavour to wear it, whether they can or cannot afford it: and far more of it appears in worshipping assemblies, than consists with the scriptural precepts, with the glory of God, the interests of families, the good of the poor, or the prosperity of souls. The Lord, however, will call on those who go to hear his word, to give an account of their motives in so doing, as well as those who absent themselves for the reasons of their neglect. We should therefore attend, in order to hear the messengers of the Lord, who come to prepare the way, that his kingdom may be set up in our hearts: and as, in some respects, the least of faithful ministers, who now preach the gospel, is greater than all who came before the introduction of that dispensation; it behoves us to " give " the more earnest heed to the things which we have heard, " lest at any time we should let them slip." (*Note, Heb.* ii. 1—4.) Considering our superior light and information, " what manner of persons ought we to be in all holy con- " versation and godliness!"

In every age " the kingdom of heaven suffereth vio- " lence, and the violent take it by force." The most atrocious transgressors, who " strive to enter in at the strait " gate," who wrestle in prayer, and are in earnest about their souls, outstrip their more moral and decent neighbours, who are supine, dilatory, and lukewarm. They who are determined, at all adventures, to find admission, will surely succeed: but such as postpone the concerns of their souls to worldly interest, pleasures, and diversions, will be found to come short of it; as well as those who seek salvation in any other way, than " by repentance

| a Mark ii. 23—28. Luke vi. 1—5. b Deut. xxiii. 25. | AT that time Jesus ⁵ went on the sabbath-day through the corn; and his disciples were an hungred, and began ᵇ to pluck the ears of corn, and to eat. | 2 But when the Pharisees saw *it*, they said unto him, ᶜ Behold, thy disciples do that which is not lawful to do upon the sabbath-day! | c 10. Ex. xx 9—11. xviii. 12. xxxi. 15—17. xxxv. 2. Num. xv. 32— Mk. Ia. lviii. 13. Mark iii. 2—5. Luke vi. 6—11. xiii. 10—17. xxiii. 56. John v. 9—11. 16, 17. vii. 21—24. ix. 14—16. |

" towards God, and faith" in his beloved Son. To him, both " Moses, and all the prophets," and John the Baptist, and all the apostles and evangelists " bear witness, " that whosoever believeth in him, shall receive remission " of sins." This we must attest, whether men will receive it or not; and call on all, " who have ears to hear," seriously to attend to it.

V. 16—24.

Natural depravity causes even sensible men to act with childish folly, in the most important concerns of their immortal souls. Their cavils are often at the same time most futile and malignant; their dislike to the message of Christ dictates objections to the messengers; something they have to urge against every one, however excellent and holy. Being determined to be displeased, they put a bad construction on their best actions: their self-denial and abstraction from the world arise from melancholy or misanthropy; their cheerfulness from levity; their benevolent sociableness, from intemperance or love of good cheer; their endeavours to reform the profligate are ascribed to a congeniality of disposition, and to dislike of morality and goodness; their different natural tempers, or methods of doing good, are but varied modes of mischief: and, in short, men will censure any thing and every thing, in order to excuse themselves from joining the servants of Christ, in mourning for sin, or in seeking happiness from God, and improving their talents in glorifying God, and doing good to mankind. In vain we hope to escape the perverse and unreasonable calumnies of such men, as said that John the Baptist was a demoniack, and " the holy One " of God " " a gluttonous man and a wine-bibber, a " friend " and companion " of publicans and sinners." These are the children of unbelief and folly: but wisdom's children welcome the messengers of God, an I bless him for them, and for their different gifts and endowments; and they admire and adore the divine wisdom even in those things, at which ungodly men cavil to their own eternal ruin.—Our blessed Lord will never upbraid the trembling penitent with any of his iniquities: but he will sharply rebuke and awfully condemn those, who continue impenitent under the means of grace. He knows the different degrees of enmity and obduracy, which possess the hearts of unbelievers, and will proportion their final punishment accordingly: but it will be far more tolerable for pagans in the day of judgment, than for wicked professors of Christianity.—The Lord, in wise and righteous sovereignty, sends the gospel to whom he pleases; yet he punishes none more than they deserve, and rejects none that seek teaching and salvation from him. But it behoves those, who have been exalted even to heaven, with outward advantages, to fear lest they should sink the deeper into hell, through their abuse of them: and there can be no doubt, that multitudes of the inhabitants of this favoured land will perish with deeper condemnation, than those of Tyre, and even than those of Sodom and Gomorrah.

V. 25—30.

Whilst the eternal Son, with all his holy angels, and his redeemed people, adore and praise the Father and Lord of all, for hiding the mysteries of redeeming love " from the wise and prudent, and revealing them to " the unlearned, even " to babes, because it so seemeth good in " his sight;" the proud and impenitent blaspheme his holy appointments, and treat such declarations with the most pointed scorn and detestation. Thus the wise and prudent of this world often illustrate and demonstate the truth which they oppose: they shew that nothing but divine teaching can make known divine things, in their real nature and glory: and they evince the propriety of the Lord's leaving them to be blinded by their prejudices; seeing their arrogance and enmity more than equal their superior knowledge and sagacity.—But all things are given into the hands of our Redeemer: we cannot know either the Father or the Son, except by the teaching of the holy word, and the Holy Spirit: we can know nothing of the one, apart from the other: and as none can " know the Father, but " the Son, and he to whom the Son will reveal him;" so he must know the most in this matter, who sits at Christ's feet with the greatest docility and simplicity, to hear and believe his words.—The Redeemer's mercy and condescension equal his majesty; and he invites the labouring and burdened sinner to come to him for rest. Why then should any labour for that which is not bread, or seek rest from any other quarter? Let us come to him daily for deliverance from wrath and guilt, from sin and Satan, from all our cares, fears, and sorrows: let us learn of him as our Prophet, rely on him as our Priest, bear his yoke as our King, and copy his example of meekness and lowliness of heart. And, whatever impiety or infidelity may object,— whatever the world, the flesh, and the devil may suggest, —we shall find " his yoke easy and his burden light;" his service perfect freedom and rest to our souls; and that " in " keeping his commandments, there is great reward."

NOTES.

CHAP. XII. V. 1, 2. Matthew seems to fix the date of this transaction, immediately *after* the events recorded in the preceding chapter; but the other evangelists record it in an earlier part of our Lord's history. (*Notes, Marl* ii. 23—28. *Luke* vi. 1—11.)—The Jewish writers say, that it was not customary for the people to taste food, till after the service at the synagogue: but this must be one of " the traditions of the elders;" for the scripture never mentions it; nor is it, on this occasion, once hinted at.— In going to the synagogue on the sabbath, or in returning from it, the disciples being hungry, plucked the ears of corn, rubbed them in their hands, and ate. The law allowed them to take the produce of any man's field or vineyard, in this manner, as they passed through it. (*Note, Deut.* xxiii. 24, 25.) But the Pharisees, who, as has been very probably supposed, were deputed by the chief priests

M 7

3 But he said unto them, ᵈ Have ye not read ᵉ what David did, when he was an hungred, and they that were with him;

4 How he entered into the house of God, and did eat ᶠ the shew-bread, which was not lawful for him to eat, neither for them which were with him, but only for the priests ?

5 Or have ye not read in the law, how that, ᵍ on the sabbath-days the priests in the temple ʰ profane the sabbath, and are blameless ?

6 But I say unto you, ¹ That in this place is one greater than the temple.

7 But ᵏ if ye had known what *this* meaneth, ¹ I will have mercy, and not sacrifice, ye would not have ᵐ condemned the guiltless.

8 For ⁿ the Son of man is Lord even of the sabbath-day.

9 ¶ And when he was departed thence, ° he went into their synagogue:

10 And, behold, there was a man ᵖ which had *his* hand withered. And they asked him, saying, ᑫ Is it lawful

---

and rulers to watch the conduct of Jesus and his followers, condemned this action as a profanation of the sabbath; considering it as in some respects equivalent to reaping and threshing the grain; and intending to involve Jesus also under the same accusation.

On the sabbath-day. (1) Τοις σαϐϐασι, *on the sabbath.* By comparing this whole passage (2. 5. 8. 12,) with the parallel passages in Mark and Luke, it clearly appears, that the plural of σαϐϐας, and the singular σαϐϐατον are used indiscriminately, for the seventh day of the week. Luke mentions the particular sabbath on which this event occurred. (*Luke* vi. 1. 6.)

V. 3, 4. In answering the charge of the Pharisees, our Lord first referred them to the conduct of David, when he fled from Saul: intimating, that they were very deficient in the knowledge of the scriptures, though they prided themselves on their learning in this respect, and despised the common people. They allowed that David was a prophet, and " the man after God's own heart :" yet in circumstances of urgent necessity, he had not scrupled to infringe the injunction of the ritual law, by eating the shew-bread and giving it to his attendants ; though the law required that none but the priests should eat of it. (*Marg. Ref.* f.) He had indeed been blamed, and had condemned himself, for other parts of his conduct; yet this was never deemed criminal, the necessity of the case being allowed as a sufficient reason, for dispensing with a ceremonial institution. Why then should Jesus's disciples be condemned, even if they had deviated from the exact letter of the law, to satisfy the cravings of their hunger? (*Notes, Ex.* xx. 8—11.)—' It is a small thing to say, it is lawful for us to ' eat the bread removed from the table; it would be lawful ' for us, in this extreme necessity, even to eat the bread now ' sanctified on the table, if there were no other.' *Kimchi* in *Whitby*.

The shew-bread. (4) Τῃς αρτῃς τῃς προϑεσιως. *Mark* ii. 26. *Luke* vi. 4.—Ἡ προϑεσις των αρτων. *Heb.* ix. 2.—*Panes expositionis : expositio panum.* (*Note, Lev.* xxiv. 5—9.)—*But only.*] Ει μῃ. *Luke* iv. 26, 27. *John* xvii. 12. *Rev.* ix. 4.

V. 5, 6. Our Lord next shewed his accusers, that in some cases, the exact rest of the sabbath must be dispensed with, or the ritual observances must be neglected: for the priests, at the temple, performed a great deal of labour on the sabbath, in preparing the sacrifices, and tending the fire on the altar; which work, being done by

others, or in another place, would certainly have been a violation of the law : yet it was allowed that they were blameless in what they did. (*Note, John* vii. 19—24, *vv.* 22—24.) And, whether the Pharisees would regard it or not, there was before them One " greater than the temple ;" even the true Temple, " in which the fulness of God dwelleth " bodily,"—the human nature of EMMANUEL; and therefore in attending and obeying Him, the strict rest of the sabbath might be dispensed with. (*Marg. Ref.*)—' All ' that work, done by priests, ... was ... for the service of ' the temple : whereas the service done by the disciples to ' their Lord, was ... to one much greater than the temple, ' both in respect of dignity, as being a divine person, and, ' ... as being ... sanctified even in his human nature, by the ' inhabitation of the Spirit, and of the fulness of the God-' head in him.' *Whitby*.

Profane. (5) Βεϐηλωσι. *Acts* xxiv. 6.—*Neh.* xiii. 18. *Ez.* xliii. 7, 8. *Sept.*—Βεϐηλος. 1 *Tim.* i. 9. iv. 7. 2 *Tim.* ii. 16. *Heb.* xii. 16.

V. 7, 8. The passage here referred to, has been before considered. (*Notes,* ix. 10—13. *Hos.* vi. 6.) Had the Pharisees understood what was meant, when God declared, that he required mercy rather than sacrifice, " they would " not have condemned the guiltless :" for, relieving the disciples' hunger, in subserviency to their attendance on Jesus in his labours of love, was an act of mercy sufficient to justify so trivial a deviation from the exact rest of the sabbath. And in conclusion he added, " The Son of Man is " Lord even of the sabbath :" He, the Messiah, was Lord and Ruler of his church, in this and every other particular. Thus he intimated that, as the Son of God, he had at first instituted the sabbath ; that he gave the law from mount Sinai; and that he had lost none of his authority by his humiliation, but should make such alterations in the time and circumstances of observing this sacred rest, as it became him, the great Law-giver, in respect of his own institutions.—It cannot be supposed, that Christ would so frequently have discussed this subject, and shewn what works were lawful on the sabbath-day, without allowing of any other exceptions ; if it had not been intended that the institution, for the substance of it, should continue in full force under the Christian dispensation.

V. 9—13. When Jesus had silenced the Pharisees, he departed : and on another sabbath he entered into one of their synagogues ; when the same subject was again brought forward. (*Notes, Mark* iii. 1—5. *Luke* xiii. 10—

to heal on the sabbath-days? ' that they might accuse him.

11 And he said unt) them, 'What man shall there be among you, that shall have one sheep, 'and if it fall into a pit on the sabbath-day, will he not lay hold on it, and lift *it* out?

12 How much then * is a man better than a sheep! Wherefore * it is lawful to do well on the sabbath-days.

13 Then saith he to the man, Stretch forth thine hand. And he stretched *it* forth ; ' and it was restored whole like as the other.

14 ¶ Then the Pharisees ' went out, and 'held a council against him, how they might destroy him.

15 But when Jesus knew *it*, * he withdrew himself from thence : ⅃ and great multitudes followed him, and he healed them all ;

16 And ' charged them, that they should not make him known:

17 That ⁴ it might be fulfilled which was spoken by Esaias the prophet, * saying,

18 Behold ' my Servant, ' whom I have chosen; ʰ my Beloved, in whom my soul is well pleased: 'I will put ₈ my Spirit upon him, ᵏ and he shall shew judgment to the Gentiles.

19 He ' shall not strive, nor cry; neither shall any man hear his voice in the streets.

20 A ᵐ bruised reed shall he not break, and smoking flax shall he not quench, ⁿ till he send forth judgment unto victory.

21 And ° in his name shall the Gentiles trust.

17.) As a man whose hand was withered attended at the synagogue : the Pharisees, ever watching to find matter of accusation, asked our Lord, whether it was lawful to heal on the sabbath. This general question, if meant to include the enquiry, how far the various labours attending cures by medicine were consistent with hallowing the sabbath, was not without difficulty; for while many things, generally practised in this respect, are works of necessity and mercy, others doubtless might very well be postponed.—It seems, therefore, from the other evangelists, that Jesus answered in the first instance by another and more simple question, "Is it lawful to do good on the "sabbath-day?" He would, however, neither be diverted from his purpose of mercy by their objections, nor yet give them tnat ground of accusation for which they sought : and he therefore asked them, whether, if a single sheep should fall into a pit on the sabbath, any one of their company, strict as they professed to be, would omit to pull it out, either from regard to the value of his property, or out of compassion to the animal. Yet this would be attended with labour, whilst his healing miracles were performed without any. But how much more valuable is a rational creature, possessed of an immortal soul, than a mere animal ! And how much more requisite, according to the law of love, to bring immediate relief to the distresses of the one, than the other! Wherefore, it must be consistent with the divine law to perform those actions of mercy and love on the sabbath-day, which were evidently good in themselves, and ornamental to piety. Having thus silenced them, he ordered the man to stretch forth his withered hand ; and by the power attending his word, the man found his hand immediately and perfectly restored.

V. 14—21. The Pharisees, not being able to answer our Lord's reasoning, and exasperated by being put to shame; as well as anxious for their authority, and the credit

of their traditions; took counsel together, by what means they might destroy him, or find some plausible accusation against him, that he might be condemned to death as a deceiver or blasphemer. But Jesus, aware of their design, (as "his time was not yet come,') thought proper to retire from that place : yet, being followed by great multitudes of the people, he continued to heal all the sick who were brought to him; strictly charging them at the same time not to speak of his miracles, nor to let the Pharisees know where he was. (*Note*, ix. 30.) Thus he evidently fulfilled the prophecy of Isaiah concerning the Messiah. (*Note*, *Is.* xlii. 1—4.) The passage has already been explained : but it may here be added, that the gentle, lowly, compassionate, condescending, and beneficent nature of Christ's miracles and personal ministry, devoid of ostentation and severity; and his perseverance in the midst of opposition, without engaging in contentious disputation ; as well as the general effects and success of his gospel, and his kind and tender dealing with weak, discouraged, and tempted believers, in all ages, are described in it. In the prophecy of Isaiah, we read, " He shall bring forth judgment unto " truth ; he shall not fail, nor be discouraged, till he have " set judgment in the earth, and the isles shall wait for his " law ;" which is here rendered "till he send forth judg- " ment unto victory, and in his name shall the Gentiles " trust." When the cause of the gospel, and that of our Lord's servants against his enemies, shall be tried, and " judgment shall be brought unto truth ;" they will also be made victorious ; when the Gentiles learn to trust in his name, they also "wait for his law ;" and when all nations shall thus trust in him, judgment will be set or established in the earth.—Flax was used in lamps: smoking flux may therefore be equivalent to an expiring lamp.— ' He that stretcheth not forth his hand to the sinner, and ' he that beareth not the burden of his brother, breaks the

p Ix. 22. Luke xi. 14. 22 ¶ Then was brought unto him one possessed with a devil, blind and q Mark vii. 33. Ix. 17—26. dumb: and he healed him, insomuch r Ps. li. 18. Is. that the blind and dumb both spake xxix. 18. xxxii. 3, 4. xxxv. 5, 6. and saw.
Acts xxvi. 18. s Ix. 33. xv. 30, 31. 23 And all the people were amazed, t Ix. 27. xv. 22. and said, Is not this the Son of Da- xxi. 9. xxii. 42, 43. John iv. 29. vid?
vii. 40—42. u Ix. 34. Mark iii. 24 But when the Pharisees heard 22. Luke xi. 15. it, they said, This *fellow* doth not cast

out devils, but by Beelzebub the * Gr. Beelzebul, and so 27. prince of the devils. x Ix. 4. Ps. cxxxix. 2. Jer. xvii. 10.
25 And Jesus knew their thoughts, Am.   iv.   13. Mark ii. 8. John and said unto them, Every kingdom ii. 24, 25. xxi. 17. 1 Cor. ii. 11. divided against itself is brought to de- Heb.   iv.   13. Rev. ii. 23. solation; and every city or house di- y Is. Ix. 21. xix. 2, 3. Mark iii. vided against itself shall not stand. 23—26. Luke xi. 17, 18. Gal. v. 26 And if Satan cast out Satan, he 15. Rev. xvi. 19. z John 16, 17. is divided against himself: how shall xiv. 30. xvi. 11. 2 Cor. iv. 4. Col. then his kingdom stand? i. 13. 1 John iv. 19. Gr. Rev. ix.
11. xii. 9. xvi. 10. xx. 2, 3.

'bruised reed: ... and he that despiseth the small spark of 'faith in little ones, quenches the smoking flax.' *Jerome.* The evangelist quotes the last clause of this passage from the Septuagint, and no more. In many things the prophet's meaning is mistaken or obscured in that version; as it is evident from the annexed translation, which is literal: but Matthew gives the meaning of the Hebrew, yet not attending to literal exactness; which in an inspired writer was the less necessary.—'Jacob, my servant, I will 'uphold him; Israel my elect, my soul hath accepted him: 'I have given (or put,) my Spirit on him. He shall 'bring forth judgment to the Gentiles. He shall not cry 'aloud, he shall not relax; neither shall his voice be heard 'without. He shall not crush a bruised reed, and smoking 'flax' he shall not quench, but shall bring forth judgment 'unto truth. He shall shine forth and shall not be broken: 'until he place judgment in the earth; and in his name 'shall the Gentiles hope.' *Sept.*—Thus the whole is ascribed to Israel as a nation, instead of being understood of the Messiah.—The Septuagint, though highly venerable, has acquired disproportionate reverence, from the notion, that the writers of the New Testament confine themselves to it in their citations: but in fact, they quote it, only when it accords to the Hebrew, or gives the sense of it without material alteration.
The Gentiles trust. (21) Comp. *Ps.* cxlvi. 3. *Jer.* xvii. 5. *Rom.* xv. 12. *Eph.* i. 12.
V. 22—24. It is probable, that this miracle was wrought sometime after what is before recorded. (*Note, Luke* xi. 14—26.)—An evil spirit having deprived a man of sight and speech, the power of Christ ejecting the evil spirit perfectly restored him.—'As it is not said, that Christ 'gave this man · his hearing, it is plain he was not deaf, 'and indeed it appears worthy of remark, that we hardly 'ever meet with entire blindness and deafness in the 'same person.' *Doddridge.*—This miracle seems to have astonished the people, in an uncommon degree; and it led them to conclude that Jesus must be the Messiah, the Son of David; which exasperated the Pharisees, and made them fear, that he would finally prevail: yet they could not deny the reality of the miracle; and therefore they malignantly renewed their accusation, that he cast out devils, by the concurrence of Beelzebub the prince of the devils, with whom he had formed an alliance. (*Notes,* ix. 32—34.) 'This they did, not only from an apprehension, 'that if this belief prevailed, it might bring the power of 'the Romans upon them: (*John* xi. 48 :) but chiefly, be- 'cause it put an end to their credit with, and authority 'over, the people; they being still represented by our

'Lord, as blind guides and the worst of hypocrites.' *Whitby.* The term employed on this occasion (οὗτος) is very properly rendered " this fellow," as expressive of contempt and aversion.—Beelzebub is the same as Baal-zebub, the god of Ekron in Philistia. (2 *Kings* i. 3.) The name signifies, *the lord of a fly*: but the Greek word here used (βεελζεβουλ) signifies *the lord of a dunghill.*—' The 'heathens fabulously write of the temple of Hercules and 'Jupiter, that the Deity kept the flies from them; ... the 'Jews say of their temple, that a fly was not seen in the 'slaughter-house.' *Whitby.* ' The god of the Ekronites 'was called *Baal-zebub*, either for the plenty of flies with 'which his temple abounded, or because they sought help 'from that idol, against the flies with which they were 'troubled. This name the Israelites after, for the con- 'tempt of that idol, gave to the prince of the devils.— ' *Beelzebul*, signifies *the god of dung.' Leigh.* He is called Satan in our Lord's answer (26).
Dumb. (22) Κωφος. ' 1.' Proprie : *obtusus, hebes :* à κοπίω. ' Sic legitur apud *Homerum*, Il. λ'. v. 390, κωφον βελος, *telum* ' *obtusum.*—2. Qui *sensum amisit, nihil sentiens,* &c.' Schleusner.—It is rendered *dumb;* ix. 32, 33. xv. 30, 31. *Luke* i. 22. (answering to σιωπων, 20,) xi. 14: *deaf;* xi. 5. *Mark* vii. 32. 37. ix. 25. *Luke* vii. 22.—Δωπκωφον και κωφον. *Sept.* rendered, " The dumb or deaf." *Ex.* iv. 11. Zacharias appears to have been *deaf* as well as *dumb :* (*Note, Luke* i. 21—25 :) but no other instance occurs in the N. T. in which it clearly embraces both ideas.
V. 25, 26. It seems that the Pharisees *privately* circulated this opinion ; that " Jesus knew their thoughts," and took occasion to argue the case with them. Probably they grounded their opinion on his disregard to their traditions, and his supposed violation of the sabbath : but he rested his argument on the evident tendency and effect of his doctrine and example, to render men wise and holy, to deliver them from the power of sin and Satan, and to make them servants and worshippers of God ; for these were such, that, as far as his cause prevailed, Satan's kingdom must be subverted. As, therefore, these fallen spirits are too politick and sagacious to assist in ruining their own cause ; and as every kingdom or family, which is divided into parties contending against each other, must be weakened, desolated, and ruined ; so it was evident, that if Satan aided Jesus in casting out devils, the infernal kingdom was divided against itself ; and how then could it any longer subsist ?—Nothing can be more conclusive than this argument.
Is brought to desolation. (25) Ερημωται. (ab ερημος, *desertus :*) *Luke* xi. 17. *Rev.* xvii. 16. xviii. 16.
x 2

27 And if I by Beelzebub cast out devils, ᵇby whom do your children cast them out? therefore ᵇ they shall be your judges.

28 But if ᶜ I cast out devils by the Spirit of God, ᵈ then the kingdom of God is come unto you.

29 Or else ᵉ how can one enter into a strong man's house, and spoil his goods, except he first bind the strong man? and then he will spoil his house.

30 He ᶠ that is not with me is against me, and he that ᵍ gathereth not with me scattereth abroad.

31 Wherefore I say unto you, ʰ All manner of sin and blasphemy shall be forgiven unto men: ᶦ but the blasphemy against the Holy Ghost, shall not be forgiven unto men.

32 And ᵏ whosoever speaketh a word against the Son of man, it shall be forgiven him; ᶦ but whosoever speaketh against the Holy Ghost, ᵐ it shall not be forgiven him, neither in this world, neither in the *world* to come.

V. 27, 28. It is plain that there were those, who made it their business to expel evil spirits from possessed persons; (*Acts* xix. 13—16;) and that some of them were countenanced by the Pharisees. Now these exorcists might be left to determine the cause betwixt Jesus and his accusers: if they asserted, that he " cast out devils by the " prince of the devils," they could not prove that their own children, or disciples, cast them out by any other power. And if they ascribed the exorcisms of these persons to the assistance of God; how could they doubt of those effected by Jesus being the same, when they were every way so vastly superior: and when his life was so indisputably holy, and his instructions so scriptural, and of so excellent a tendency? It was also undeniable, that if he " by the Spirit of God cast out devils, then the " Kingdom of God was come unto them." He was certainly the promised Messiah, and they who opposed or rejected him, would do it at their peril.—' You doubt not ' but your exorcists, who use the name of God, the God ' of Abraham, &c. do cast out devils by virtue of that ' name: it will then be matter of your condemnation, ... to ' pass such an unjust censure on me.' *Whitby.*—Christ ' uses this as an argument *ad homines;* that they who them-' selves professed to cast out devils by the God of Abraham, ' had no reason to say, that he did it by the prince of ' devils.' *Hammond.*

By the Spirit of God. (28) " By the finger of God." *Luke* xi. 20. (*Note, Ex.* viii. 18, 19.)

V. 29, 30. The case might be illustrated by an apt similitude. How could any one enter into a strong man's house, whilst he was on his guard, and plunder his property at his pleasure, unless he first overpowered and bound the strong man? Thus it was evident, that Jesus by his divine power was able to subdue and limit the power of Satan; or he never could rescue the bodies and souls of men from his oppression. And, as he came to " destroy " the works of the devil," so the cause would admit of no neutrality. Every one, who should refuse to join him against the cause of Satan, would be adjudged an enemy; and all who would not concur with him in rescuing sinners from the devil's kingdom, and bringing them into the kingdom of God, whatever pains they might take in any other way, would do worse than lose their labour; for all their contrivances, knowledge, and religious observances, would tend to their own loss and that of others, and they would finally lose their own souls.

Scattereth abroad. (30) Σκορπιζει. *Luke* xi. 23. *John* x. 12. xvi. 32. 2 *Cor.* ix. 9.—' Σκορπιζω, proprie, spargo se-' mina, dissemino.' Schleusner.

V. 31, 32. (*Marg. Ref.*) Scarcely any thing, in the whole scripture, has given more discouragement to weak Christians than this passage, and a few others coincident with it. (*Notes, Mark* iii. 22—30. *Luke* xii. 8—10. *Heb.* vi. 4—6. x. 26, 27. 1 *John* v. 16—18.) Almost every humble and conscientious believer, at one time or other, is tempted to think that he has committed the unpardonable sin; and the interpretations which many have given, without properly adverting to the context, have frequently tended to increase these apprehensions and difficulties. In general we are sure, that they who indeed repent, and believe the gospel, have not committed this sin, or any other of the same kind: for repentance and faith are inseparably connected with forgiveness; and they are the special gift of God, which he would not bestow on any man, if he were determined never to pardon him. On the other hand, without repentance and faith, no man can be forgiven, though he have not committed this sin.—It is probable, that this matter was left in some measure of obscurity, to deter men from presumptuously venturing near the brink of so dreadful a precipice.—The words were addressed immediately, as a solemn warning, to the proud and malignant Pharisees. Our Lord first declared, that " all manner " of sin and blasphemy should be forgiven unto men;" perhaps tacitly comparing the happy situation of men under a dispensation of mercy, with that of apostate angels for whom there is no forgiveness. But, though this was a general rule, it admitted of one exception; for " the " blasphemy against the Spirit should never be forgiven." Whoever had spoken, or should speak, blasphemous words against " the Son of Man," might repent and be pardoned; but whoever should thus speak against the Holy Spirit, could never be pardoned, either in this world or the next. It does not hence follow, that any sin which is not forgiven here, will hereafter be forgiven: the expression at most only shews, that some of the Jews had notions of this kind, as well as the papists and other professed Christians: but it seems to be no more than a form of speech common among the Jews, when they asserted strongly that any thing should never be done. The circumstances, in which this declaration was made, should carefully be adverted to. The Pharisees had spoken most blasphemous words against Christ and his miracles, which

N 3

33 ¶ Either [n] make the tree good,
[o] and his fruit good; or else make the
tree corrupt, and his fruit corrupt: for
the tree is known by *his* fruit.
34 O [p] generation of vipers, [q] how
can ye, being evil, speak good things?
[r] for out of the abundance of the heart
the mouth speaketh.
35 A [s] good man out of the good
treasure of the heart bringeth forth
good things: [t] and an evil man out of
the evil treasure bringeth forth evil
things.
36 But I say unto you, That [u] every
idle word that men shall speak, they
shall give account thereof in the day
of judgment.
37 For by thy words thou shalt be
[x] Justified, and by thy words thou shalt
be condemned.

n xxiii. 26. Ez. xviii. 31. Am. v. 15. Luke xi. 39, 40. Jam. iv. 8.
o iii. 8—10. vii. 16—20. Luke iii. 9. vi. 43, 44. John xv. 4—7. Jam. iii. 12.
p iii. 7. xxiii. 33. Luke iii. 7. John viii. 44. 1 John iii. 10.
q 1 Sam. xxiv. 13. Ps. x. 6, 7. lii. 2—5. liii. 1. lxiv. 3—5. cxx. 2—4. cxl. 2, 3. Is. xxxii. 6. lix. 4. 14. Jer. vii. 2—5. Rom. iii. 10—14. Jam. iii. 5—8.
r Luke vi. 45.
s xiii. 52. Ps. xxxvii. 30, 31. Prov. x. 20, 21. xii. 6. 17—19. xv. 4. 23. 28. xvi. 21—23. xxv. 11, 12. Eph. iv. 29. Col. iii. 16. iv. 6.
t 34.
u Ec. xii. 14. Rom. ii. 16. Eph. v. 4—6. Jude 14, 15. Rev. xx. 12.
x Jam. ii. 21—25.

were indeed wrought by the power of the Holy Ghost, but not under the immediate dispensation of the Spirit. They had gone as far in impiety as they could, without finally excluding themselves from forgiveness. They had spoken "blasphemy against the Son of Man," and ascribed his miracles to the power of the devil; but still they might be pardoned, and one further method would be used to convince them. In a short time, He, the promised Messiah would be crucified, and then rise from the dead and ascend into heaven; when, being exalted to the right hand of the Father, he would send forth the Holy Spirit upon his apostles and disciples, enabling them to perform various wonderful works in his name, in proof of their testimony concerning his resurrection and ascension. Whosoever therefore should blaspheme this last and most complete attestation to Jesus, as the promised Messiah, and, from determined enmity to him and his kingdom, deliberately ascribe the operations of the Holy Spirit to Satan; —that man would be given up to final obduracy and impenitency, and thus never be pardoned, but sink into final perdition.—'You have represented me as a wine-bibber, a 'friend of publicans and sinners, and as one who casts out 'devils by Beelzebub: and you will still go on, after all 'the miracles which I have done among you, to represent 'me as a false prophet, and a deceiver of the people: but 'notwithstanding, all these grievous sins shall be forgiven 'you, if that last dispensation of the Holy Ghost, which 'I shall after my ascension send among you, shall prevail 'with you to believe in me. But if, when I have sent the 'Holy Ghost, to testify the truth of my mission and my 'resurrection, you shall continue in your unbelief, and 'shall blaspheme the Holy Ghost, and represent him also 'as an evil spirit; your sin shall never be forgiven, nor 'shall any thing be further done to call you to repentance.' *Whitby*.—None therefore could commit this sin, who did not witness the effects of the pouring out of the Holy Spirit on the apostles: nor were all degrees of opposition to these operations, thus finally destructive. Peter does not seem to have concluded, that Simon Magus had sinned beyond the reach of mercy, when he offered to buy the power of conferring the Holy Ghost. (*Note, Acts* viii. 18—24.) Yet it is clear, that some kinds of apostasy, when attended with very peculiar circumstances of aggravation, through love of this world, and enmity to the truth, were equivalent to it; and in every age many provoke God to leave them to final impenitence. But there must be great opportunity of information, much inward conviction, determinate sinning against the light of a man's own conscience, deliberate enmity to the truth, and an obstinate opposition to it in defiance of evidence, to constitute this kind of impiety. They, who most fear having committed it, are generally at the greatest distance from it; while such as are thus given up, are perhaps universally either callous in presumption or enmity, or absolutely and outrageously desperate, of which we sometimes meet with awful instances: but the trembling, contrite sinner has "the witness in himself," that neither of these is his case. —The Jews, to this day ascribe the miracles of Jesus, the reality of which they do not deny, especially his casting out devils, to *enchantment;* that is, to the power of Satan.

Blasphemy. (31) Βλασφημια. (A βλασφημεω, 'quasi βλαπτω 'την φημην' *alterius famam lædo.*' Schleusner.) It is rendered *blasphemy;* xv. 19. xxvi. 65. *Mark* ii. 7. *John* x. 33. *Col.* iii. 8. *Rev.* xiii. 1. *et al: evil-speaking; Eph.* iv. 31: *railing;* 1 *Tim.* vi. 4. *Jude* 9. Injurions words in general are denoted; which when they are spoken of men, are called *evil-speaking;* but when they are supposed to relate to God, to Christ, or to the Holy Spirit, the original word *blasphemy* is retained. It is not however always evident, which is the proper rendering of the word; as may be seen by the above references, and especially by comparing *Eph.* iv. 31. with *Col.* iii. 8.—*In this world.* (32) Εν τουτῳ τῳ αιωνι. xiii 22. *Luke* xvi. 8. *Rom.* xii. 2. 1 *Cor.* i. 20. 2 *Cor.* iv. 4. *Eph.* vi. 12.

V. 33—37. (*Notes,* iii. 7—10. vii. 15—20.) Our Lord next shewed the Pharisees his knowledge of the evil of their hearts. They were proud, carnal, malicious, ungodly men; yet they made high professions of piety and sanctity! Let them, therefore, either seek the renewal of their souls to holiness by the grace of God, or let them give up their pretensions to religion. (*Notes, Ez.* xviii. 30—32. *Jam.* iv. 7—10.) If the tree were made good, good fruit would be produced; otherwise they might as well allow the tree to be corrupt, of which the fruit was notoriously bad; seeing the quality of the tree is known, not by its appearance, leaves, or blossoms, but by its fruit. Thus the Pharisees were detected by their malignant opposition to the holy character and doctrine of Jesus, and to his beneficent miracles. Indeed their words sufficiently determined the state of their hearts, and shewed them to be a "generation of vipers," the progeny of the old serpent: how then could they speak good and holy things, habitually and consistently? For out of the abundance of the thoughts, and desires of the heart, the mouth naturally speaks. If any one be humble, pious, spiritual, a lover of God and man; his memory, judgment, and affections become a treasury of good things, from which he brings forth edifying conversation, pious observations, candid opinions,

38 ¶ Then certain of the scribes and of the Pharisees answered, saying, ʸ ᵡᵛⁱ. ¹—⁴. ᴹᵃʳᵏ ⁷ Master, we would see a sign from thee. ⁴⁸. ¹ ᶜᵒʳ. ¹. ²². 39 But he answered and said unto ᶻ ᴵˢ. ˡᵛⁱⁱ. ³. ᴹᵃʳᵏ ᵛⁱⁱ. ³⁸. ᴶᵃᵐ. ⁱᵛ. them, An evil and ᵃ adulterous gene-⁴. ration seeketh after a sign ; and there ᵃ ᵡᵛⁱ. ⁴. ᴸᵘᵏᵉ ᵡⁱ. ²⁹, ³⁰. shall ᵇ no sign be given to it, but the sign of the prophet Jonas.

ᵇ ᴶᵒⁿ. ⁱ. ¹⁷ 40 For ᵇ as Jonas was three days and three nights in the whale's belly ; ᶜ ᵡᵛⁱ. ²¹. ᵡᵛⁱⁱ. ²³. ᶜ so shall the Son of man be three ᵡᵡᵛⁱⁱ. ⁴⁰. ⁶³, ⁶⁴. ᴶᵒʰⁿ ⁱⁱ. ¹⁹. days and three nights ᵈ in the heart of ᵈ ᴾˢ. ˡᵛⁱⁱⁱ. ⁹. ᴶᵒⁿ. ⁱⁱ. ²—⁶. the earth.

41 The ᵉ men of Nineveh shall ᶠ rise ᵉ ᴸᵘᵏᵉ ᵡⁱ. ³². in Judgment with ᶠ this generation, and ᶠ ⁴² ⁱˢ. ˡⁱᵛ. ¹⁷. ᴶᵉʳ. ⁱⁱⁱ. ¹¹. ᴱˢⁱᵛ. ³¹. ᴿᵒᵐ. ⁱⁱ. ²⁷. shall condemn it : ʰ because they re-ᴴᵉᵇ. ᵡⁱ. ⁷. pented at the preaching of Jonas ; ᵍ ⁹. ⁴³. ᵡᵛⁱ. ⁴. ᵡᵛⁱⁱ. ¹⁷. ᵡᵡⁱⁱⁱ. and, ⁱ behold, a greater than Jonas is ʰ ᴶᵒⁿ. ⁱⁱⁱ. ⁵—¹⁰. here ! ⁱ ⁶. ⁴². ᴶᵒʰⁿ ⁱⁱⁱ. ³¹. ᵛⁱⁱⁱ. 42 The ᵏ queen of the south shall ⁵³—⁵⁸. ᴴᵉᵇ. ⁱⁱⁱ. rise up in the Judgment with this ge-ᵏ ¹ ᴷⁱⁿᵍˢ ᵡ. ¹. &ᶜ. ² ᶜʰʳ. ⁱᵡ. neration, and shall condemn it : for &ᶜ. ᴸᵘᵏᵉ ᵡⁱ. ³¹. ᴬᶜᵗˢ ᵛⁱⁱⁱ. ²⁷, she came from the uttermost parts of ˡ ᴵ ᴷⁱⁿᵍˢ ⁱⁱⁱ. ⁹. ¹². the earth to ˡ hear the wisdom of So-²⁸. ⁱᵛ. ²⁹. ³⁴. ᵛ. ⁷². ᵡ. ⁴, ⁷. ²⁴. lomon ; and, ᵐ behold, a greater than ⁱˢ. ᵛⁱⁱ. ¹⁴. ˡᵘᵏᵉ ⁱ. ⁶, Solomon is here ! ⁷. ᴶᵒʰⁿ ⁱ. ¹⁴. ¹⁸. ᴾʰⁱˡ. ⁱⁱ. ⁶, ⁷. ᴴᵉᵇ. ⁱ. ²—⁴.

---

equitable decisions, and whatever can conduce to the glory of God and the good of mankind. But wicked men have within them a treasury of pride, malice, impiety, and self-ishness, from which they naturally educe evil things : nor can they, at all times, avoid venting their avarice, arro-gance, envy, or enmity against true religion ; and speaking boasting, reproachful, and injurious language. Thus the Pharisees betrayed themselves ; and, however they might deem this a light matter, Christ assured them, that every idle or useless word, which in no way tended to their own comfort or benefit, or that of others, or to the glory of God ; (the great ends, for which man is endued with the gift of speech ;) much more all pernicious, polluting, and impious words, must be " given an account of at the day of " judgment :" and at that solemn season, they will be deem-ed decisive evidences of a man's character and the state of his heart ; according to which a person professing religion will be justified as a true believer, or condemned as a hypo-crite ; and all men will be adjudged pious or impious, holy or unholy, as their habitual conversation has been. ' Dis-' course tending to innocent mirth, to exhilarate the spirits, ' is not idle discourse ; as the time spent in necessary re-' creation is not idle time.' Doddridge.

Abundance. (34) Περισσευματος redundantia. (A περισσευω, abundo, redundo, supersum. Eph. i. 8.) Mark viii. 8. Luke vi. 45. 2 Cor. viii. 14.—Idle. (36) Αργον. (Ex a priv. et εργον quasi αεργος.) xx. 3. 6. 1 Tim. v. 13. Tit. i. 12. 2 Pet. i. 8.—A word that produces no good effect, and is not suited to produce any.—Shalt be condemned. (37) Καλα-δικασθηση. (Ex. καλα et δικαζω jus dico. ' Καλα hic valet ' contra.' Leigh.) 7. Luke vi. 37. Jam. v. 6.

V. 38—40. The Scribes and Pharisees, persisting in their enmity, were dissatisfied with the evidences of our Lord's divine mission, arising from his miracles and the fulfilment of prophecy in him : and they desired a sign from heaven ; perhaps meaning some such tremendous dis-plays of the divine glory, as their fathers had seen on mount Sinai ; or somewhat like that which took place when, at the word of Joshua, " the sun stood still in the " midst of heaven, and hasted not to go down about a " whole day." Josh. x. 12—14.—' None of them can say, ' I command that a fire shall come down from heaven ; ' none of them can say, I command the sun to stand still.' R. Crooll. To this our Lord answered, that they were a wicked and adulterous generation of Israel, unfaithful to their covenant with God ; and, hating the truth, they pur-

posed to cloke their enmity under this unreasonable and presumptuous request : but that no sign should be given them, except that of Jonah ; who, having remained three days in the whale's belly, was brought forth alive by the power of God, to preach to the Ninevites. In like man-ner, He, the Son of man, having been slain, and buried in a sepulchre hewn out of a rock, and covered with a great stone, as if in the heart of the earth, would be brought forth alive after three days, or on the third day : (Note, 1 Sam. xxx. 11—15 :) for so the phrase here used signifies, according to the manner of speaking in use among the Jews. Then he would be proved to be alive by many in-fallible demonstrations ; and those who did not receive him for the Messiah, would be left to final unbelief and de-struction.—' It is a received rule among the Jews, that a ' part of a day is put for the whole ; so that whatsoever is ' done in any part of the day, is properly said to be done ' that day. ...(1 Kings xx. 29. Esth. iv. 16. v. 1.) ...' When " " eight days were accomplished for the circumcision of " " the child, &c."... yet the day of his birth and of his cir-' cumcision were two of these eight days. ... Since then our ' Saviour was in the grave all Friday-night and Saturday ; ' seeing he was in the grave all Saturday-night, and part of ' the morning of the day following, ... he may, according ' to the Hebrew computation, be truly said to have been ' " three days and three nights in the heart of the earth." Whitby. (Note, Eph. iv. 7—10.)

Adulterous. (39) Μοιχαλις, (a μοιχος, adulter,) xvi. 4. Mark viii. 38. Rom. vii. 3. Jam. iv. 4. 2 Pet. ii. 14.— ' Perhaps μοιχαλις γενεα, may here be more rightly trans-' lated, a spurious race, the offspring of adultery.' Schleus-ner.—Whale. (40) Κηλος, used here only in the N. T.— Gen. i. 21. Jon. i. 17. ii. 10. Sept. (Note, Jon. i. 17.)

V. 41, 42. The Ninevites had repented at the preach-ing of Jonah, though he wrought no miracles, and though his conduct in many things tended to prejudice them ; and he gave them little instruction, or encouragement to repent. They would, therefore, rise up in judgment with that generation of Israel to whom Christ came, and con-demn them : their repentance in such unfavourable circum-stances would expose the aggravated guilt of the Jews, in continuing impenitent amidst all the miracles, instruc-tions, warnings, and invitations of Christ, attended by his most holy example : for it was most evident, that a far more eminent and excellent person than Jonah was in the midst of them. (Notes, xi. 20—24. Jon. iv. 1—4.)—In like

x 5

43 ¶ When ªthe unclean spirit is gone out of a man, ᵇhe walketh through ᶜdry places, ᵈseeking rest, and findeth none.

44 Then he saith, I will return into ᵉmy house from whence I came out; ᶠand when he·is come, ᵍhe findeth it empty, swept, and garnished.

45 Then goeth he, and taketh with himself ʰseven other spirits ⁱmore wicked than himself; and they enter in and dwell there: ʲand the last *state* of that man is worse than the first. ᵏEven so shall it be also unto this wicked generation.

46 ¶ While he ˡyet talked to the people, behold, *his* mother and ᵐhis brethren stood without, desiring to speak with him.

47 Then one said unto him, Behold, thy mother ˙and thy brethren stand without, desiring to speak with thee.

48 But he answered and said unto him that told him, ⁿWho is my mother? and who are my brethren?

49 And he stretched forth his hand towards ᵒhis disciples, and said, Behold my mother and my brethren!

50 For whosoever shall ᵖdo the will of my Father which is in heaven, ᑫthe same is my brother, ʳand sister, ˢand mother.

---

manner the queen of Sheba would appear against them, to their deeper condemnation; for she came from a remote region to learn heavenly wisdom from Solomon; whereas they had a far greater and a more excellent person in the midst of them, than even Solomon was. (*Notes,* 1 *Kings* x. 1—9.) He likewise went from place to place to instruct them, without their own labour or expense: yet they rejected him, and sinned in contempt of his instructions!— There is vast dignity and propriety in this declaration of Christ concerning himself, when we consider him as the incarnate Son of God; but on the supposition that he was a mere man, the words must impress the mind in a very different manner. (*Marg. Ref.*)—'God ... having promised 'to Solomon such wisdom, that, as there was none like 'him before, ... so should there after none like unto 'him; (1 *Kings* iii. 12;) he that was greater in wisdom 'than Solomon, must be more than a man.' *Whitby.*

V. 43—45. Our Lord next describes the danger of the unbelieving Jews, under a parable, formed on the case of a demoniack. He supposes the evil spirit (called *unclean,* because all sin is *uncleanness* in the judgment of a holy God,) voluntarily ceasing to possess one, who had been thus in his power; and this, lest he should be violently expelled. Yet he finds it greatly against his will; and, as he cannot obtain permission to possess any other person, he wanders about disconsolate, in dry or desert places, "seeking rest and finding none." At length therefore he attempts to recover possession of him from whom he had departed: and on his return, he finds his former dwelling empty, (without any possessor to oppose his entrance,) "swept and garnished," or ready prepared for his reception. On this discovery he goes, and fetches seven, or several other, evil spirits, more malignant than himself, (for it seems, that even some demons are more wicked than others,) and they take up their abode in the man, and the possession becomes more dreadful and incurable than ever. Thus our Lord declared it would be with that generation. The powers of darkness, disturbed by the doctrine and miracles of Christ and his apostles, as well as by the ministry of John the Baptist, would for a time recede from the Jews, and seek rest among the Gentiles, in those dry lands where no water of life had hitherto been found. (*Marg. Ref.* p.—*Note, Ps.* lxiii. 1—4, v. 1.) But, being pursued by the faithful and successful preaching of the gospel, and finding no rest there, they would return to repossess that unbelieving generation of Jews: and meeting with no opposition, other evil spirits, more numerous and more malignant than formerly, would take possession of them, and they would become more hardened, than before the preaching of "the kingdom of heaven" among them. In this view the parable is a prophecy of the rejection of the Jews, and their awful state of enmity to the gospel to this day.—But it is also applicable to the case of individuals, who hear the word of God, are convinced of its truth, and in part reformed, but not truly converted: the unclean spirit indeed retires, but Christ is not welcomed to "dwell "in the heart by faith." The evil spirit hankers after his old abode, and waits his opportunity of returning: on examination, he finds his habitation empty, swept, and garnished or furnished, for the reception and entertainment of unclean spirits, by a preparation of heart to comply with their suggestions. Thus, instead of one evil spirit, seven take up their abode in the man, and "his last state becomes "worse than the first:" he becomes, perhaps, a more decent, plausible, or presumptuous enemy of God; but sevenfold more callous and inveterate than before.—This was doubtless the case with great numbers, who had heard John the Baptist, Jesus, and the apostles, with attention, but who afterwards relapsed into wickedness: and it is the case of many, in all places where the gospel is faithfully preached. (*Marg. Ref.—Note,* 2 *Pet.* ii. 20—23.)

Dry. (43) Ανυδραν. (Εx ωτυ, et ὑδωρ.) *Without water.* Luke xi. 24. 2 *Pet.* ii. 17. *Jude* 12.—*Ps.* lxiii. 1. *Is.* xli. 19. xliii. 19, 20. *Sept.*—*Empty.* (44) Σχολαζοντα · (a σχολη, *otium:*) 1 *Cor.* vii. 5.—*Ex.* v. 8. 17. *Sept.*

V. 46—50. It appears from the other Evangelists, that the earnestness and assiduity of Jesus, in teaching the people, notwithstanding the ºopposition of the Pharisees, gave disquietude to his friends and brethren, or near relations, (perhaps the children of Joseph by a former wife, or his cousins;) some of whom did not believe in him.

м 6

CHAP. XIII.

The parable of the sower, 1—9. The reason why

Jesus taught by parables, 10—17. The parable explained, 18—23. The parable of the tares, 24—30; of the grain of mustard-seed, 31, 32; of the leaven, 33. The scripture fulfilled in Christ's teaching by

(*Marg. Ref.* a) They wanted him to desist, supposing that he exceeded all the bounds of prudence: and they seem to have engaged Mary to concur in the design; which was doubtless reprehensible, as it implied sentiments of him, derogatory to his perfect wisdom and excellence. (*Notes, Mark* iii. 20; 21. 31—35. *Luke* viii. 19—21.) They therefore came when he was teaching the people; and, not being able to approach him for the multitude, they sent to desire to speak with him. But Jesus, aware of their intention, answered by enquiring, who his mother and brethren were: intimating, that even they had no right to interfere, nor any authority over him in respect of his important work; that his spiritual affection to his disciples was greater than any natural affection, which he bare to his relations; that his love to men's souls had the greatest influence over him; that even his mother was nearer to him as a true believer, than on account of her natural relation; and that his brethren would have no advantage from him, if they were not also believers. He therefore stretched forth his hands over his disciples, as expressing his cordial and endeared affection for them: and he declared that they were his mother and his brethren; that he bare them all the regard due to those near relations; and that he would honour and provide for them, even as a dutiful son would behave towards his beloved parent; or a man, when advanced to superior circumstances, would, if he acted properly, do to his poorer brother. Not only would he admit those present, to these high and valuable privileges; but whosoever, of any age or nation, should do the will of his heavenly Father, by hearing, believing, and obeying him as his Saviour, he would in life, death, judgment, and for ever, be honoured and blessed; even as the brother, sister, or mother of him, who is " the Lord " of all," and " the King of glory." (*Notes,* vii. 21—23. *John* xix. 25—27.)

PRACTICAL OBSERVATIONS.

V. 1—13.

They who follow Christ must be ready, when called to it, to endure hunger or submit to mean fare; and to be reproached, and falsely accused, for their close attendance on him and his ordinances: but they should leave the Lord to plead in their behalf, and he will do it effectually.— Such professed Christians, as are most destitute of the power of godliness, are often most tenacious of forms even to a scrupulous minuteness; especially when they can make use of them, to support their credit or authority, to cloke their iniquity, or to oppose the upright servants of the Lord. Many of this description seem never to have read the scriptures: for they severely censure, in living disciples, the very things, for which holy men of old were not blamed: and at the same time they profess to hold the latter in high estimation; because they have the sanction of general opinion, are no longer the subjects of envy or competition, and give them no opposition or uneasiness in their ungodly practices. They will also condemn those things in persons of another party, which they overlook or

excuse in those of their own.—Whilst " the Lord of the " sabbath," who is far greater than the temple, and all external institutions, authorizes those labours on his holy day, which are necessary, and conducive to the real good of ourselves or others, or subservient to piety and charity; he doubtless most strictly binds us from all other secular employments. The exercise of mercy, rather than sacrifice, allows us on some occasions to omit attendance on publick ordinances, and to make needful provision for our health and food : yet surely when domesticks are confined at home, and families rendered a scene of hurry and confusion, " on the Lord's day," in order to furnish a feast for visitants, who can then spare their time, more conveniently than on other days, for social indulgence, the case is very different! In censuring things of this kind, we need not fear " condemning the guiltless."—They, who are unable to labour for their bread, are sometimes capable of attending on the ordinances of God: and in this way, they may expect comfort under their calamities, or deliverance from them. But alas! there are numbers, who frequent places of worship in order to start objections, or to find matter of accusation, against the servants of God; and many a good question is proposed from very base motives. We cannot, like our Lord, discern the thoughts of such objectors: yet we must go on with our duty; endeavouring by meekness, benevolence, an irreproachable conduct, and unanswerable arguments, to obviate or silence their malicious insinuations.—Men will do more to save a trifle of their own property, than to relieve their neighbours: and some will even refuse to infringe the rest of the Lord's day, by visiting the afflicted, who would not decline labour if they were likely to lose the lives of their cattle! " The Lord's day," however, is especially the time for healing the souls of men: and whilst the helpless sinner hears the voice of Christ, and endeavours to obey it; he feels and manifests, that he has received power to do those things, of which before he was utterly incapable; and becomes, by his holy example, a witness of the Saviour's power and love, and of the blessed effects of his gospel.

V. 14—21.

The more abundant good is done by the gospel, the greater opposition proud Pharisees and enemies will excite against it : and the more clearly it is proved to be from God, the more determined will be their malice, if left to themselves; for their sinful dispositions and practices, and their worldly credit and interests are all at stake. We should not, however, needlessly exasperate them; but should give place, as far as it is consistent with continued endeavours to do good.—Whilst we take encouragement, from the condescending mildness of our gracious Lord, the chosen Servant and well-beloved Son of the Father, in all our weakness, and amidst our manifold corruptions and temptations; we should also pray, that his " Spirit may " rest upon us," and enable us to copy his example; that we may avoid all severity, ostentation, and boasting; that we may " study to be quiet, and to mind our own busi-

N 7

parables, 34, 35. That of the tares explained, 36—43. The parable of the hid treasure, 44; of the Pearl of great price, 45, 46; of the net cast into the sea, 47—50; and of the house-holder, 51, 52. Christ's countrymen are offended in him; his remark on it, and subsequent conduct, 53—58.

" ness;" and be gentle to those that are bruised with afflictions and temptations, or whose feeble faith and hope are like an expiring taper. Thus we should endeavour, as often as opportunity is given us, " to strengthen the hands " that hang down, and to confirm the feeble knees;" and thus look to him, in behalf of ourselves and others, to " bring forth judgment unto victory;" expecting and earnestly praying also for the time, when all the Gentiles shall trust in his name, and wait for his law.

V. 22—30.

In every way, we see illustrations of the power and malice of our formidable enemies, and of the superior power and mercy of our great Deliverer. When he rescues the poor sinner from the oppression of the devil, the blind see the glory, and the dumb sing the praises, of our God. The changes effected by the power of divine grace form a continued proof, that Jesus is " the Son of David" and " the Son of God," and that " the gospel is the power " of God unto salvation." This should induce all men to submit to Christ: but it has a contrary effect on many, even among professed Christians, who dare to ascribe the evident effects of divine power and holiness, to the vilest motives, to enthusiasm, or even diabolical delusion! He, who knows men's thoughts, has taught us how to answer such objections: for the evident tendency and effects of the gospel are such, that if Satan could possibly patronize it, he must subvert his own kingdom. In this respect, the enemies of all good might teach Christians a useful lesson; for they exhibit to them an instructive example: hateful and hating as they are, they are too subtle to divide against themselves, so as to subvert their own kingdom; but, whilst they agree together in them, they tempt Christians to divide into parties, and to quarrel with each other, to the irreparable injury of the common cause!—But let us observe, that there are two grand interests in the world; all that side with Christ, against the kingdom of Satan, are his friends; but none else: and when unclean spirits are cast out by the Spirit of God, in the conversion of sinners to a life of faith and obedience, " the kingdom of God is " come unto us." For these powerful enemies, like strong men, possess the sinner's heart, armed with his lusts, errors, and prejudices, and all his faculties and abilities : nor could they be expelled, did not One come upon them with superior power, who is able to bind them at his will, take away from them their usurped possessions, and employ the convert, with all his talents, in his service and to his glory. All they, who refuse to concur, or do not rejoice, in such a revolution as this, are against Christ ; and " he that " gathereth not with him scattereth." Alas! what pains do many take in thus scattering abroad, and in ruining themselves and others, by promoting systems of human invention, in opposition to the gospel of God our Saviour!

V. 31—37.

In various ways, men sin against the clearest evidence of truth, and even against their own consciences ; till, by resisting the Holy Ghost, they provoke God to give them

up to final obduracy and impenitence.—Let all then be afraid of every approach to this fatal conduct : let sinners regard the voice of the Lord without delay, lest he should " swear in his wrath, that they shall never enter into his " rest : " yet, let no trembling penitent yield to Satan's suggestions, to suppose, that the sinful words and works of the days of his ignorance, which he now recollects with shame and contrition, or any of his sins when first brought under convictions, were of this malignant nature. " All " manner of sin and blasphemy " shall certainly be forgiven to the true believer; and " him that cometh to Christ, " He will in no wise cast out." Indeed we might any of us have been left under condemnation, and the power of sin : but if " God hath given us repentance to the acknow-" ledging of his truth," we are evidently escaped " from " this snare of the devil," and should not yield to discou-raging fears.—It is vain, however, for men to think that the tree is made good, when the fruit is evidently evil; or to expect good fruit from an evil tree: we should there-fore daily seek to have our hearts cleansed by divine grace, and stored with the good treasure of divine truth and holy affections; that whilst numbers are corrupting, deceiving, or injuring others, with the evil things which they speak; we may be enabled continually to bring forth seasonable, pious, and edifying discourse from the abundance of our hearts. We should consider this as a matter of great im-portance ; for our Judge has declared, that men shall give an account of every idle word at the last day. If there were nothing else to be, at that awful season, produced against us, this alone would suffice to leave us without excuse. We ought then continually to examine ourselves, and seek forgiveness for the past; and keep a constant watch over ourselves, and bridle our tongues, and improve the gift of speech, as a most important talent, that we may for the future habitually speak such words, and such alone, as consist with the Christian character, are suited to " minister grace unto the hearers," and may be produced as proofs of our faith and love in the day of judgment.

V. 38—50.

Men are more disposed to dictate to the Lord, and to demand those kinds and degrees of evidence, which he sees proper not to give, than to obey his call to " repent, " and do works meet for repentance." The Ninevites therefore, and many from the remotest regions of the earth, who, by some faint report of the gospel, have been led to enquire after Christ and his salvation, will rise up in judg-ment against unbelievers in this age and nation also, and condemn them. For one far more honourable and emi-nent in wisdom than Solomon, or than all the ancient and modern sages, yea, than all prophets and apostles, is in the midst of us, making all who come to him wise unto eternal salvation, by his word, and by his Holy Spirit. Let us then learn of him, and seek to have his kingdom set up in our hearts : then the enemy will no more be able to regain possession of us, however he may threaten or harass us.—But let none rely on convictions, or external reformation : for every heart indeed is the residence of un-

THE same day went Jesus out of the house, and ᵃ sat by the sea-side.

2 And ᵇ great multitudes were gathered together unto him, ᶜ so that he went into a ship, and sat; and the whole multitude stood on the shore.

3 And he spake many things unto them ᵈ in parables, saying, Behold, ᵉ a sower went forth to sow:

4 And when he sowed, some *seeds* fell by ᶠ the way-side, and the fowls came and devoured them up:

5 Some fell upon ᵍ stony places,

where they had not much earth: and forthwith they sprang up, because they had no deepness of earth:

6 And ʰ when the sun was up, they were scorched; and, ⁱ because they had no root, they withered away.

7 And some fell ᵏ among thorns; and the thorns sprang up and choked them.

8 But other fell into ˡ good ground, and brought forth fruit, ᵐ some an hundred-fold, some sixty-fold, some thirty-fold.

Side notes:
ᵃ Mark ii. 13, 14.
ᵇ iv. 25. xv. 30.
Gen. xlix. 10. Luke viii. 4—8.
ᶜ Mark iv. 1. Luke v. 3.
ᵈ 10—13. 34, 35. xxi. 1. xxiv. 32. Judg. ix. 8—
20. 2 Sam. xii. 1—7. Ps. xlix. 4. Ezek. xvii. 2. &c.
ᵉ 1—7. Ez. vii. 2.
xx. 48. xxiv. 37. &c. Mic. ii. Hab. ii. 6. Mark iii. 23. iv. 2, 13.
Luke viii. 10.
ᶠ Mark iv. 3—9. John xvi. 25. marg. Luke viii. 5—8.
ᵍ 18, 19.
ʰ 20. Ex. xl. 19. xxvi. 26. Am. vi. 12. Zech. vii. 12.
ʰ 21. Ja. xlix. 10.
Jam. i. 11, 12. Rev. vii. 16.
ⁱ 26, 27. Luke viii. 13. Eph. iii. 17. Col. i. 23. li.
ᵏ Ja. Gen. iii. 18.
Jer. iv. 3, 4. Mark iv. 18, 19.
ˡ 23. Luke viii. 15.
Rom. vii. 18. m Gen. xxvi. 12.
John xv. 8. Gal. ii.
v. 22, 23. Phil. i. 11.

---

xxv. 34—46. P. O. 31—46.)

clean spirits; those excepted, which are become the temple of the Holy Spirit, by faith in Jesus Christ. These enemies will therefore watch their opportunities, when convictions and terrors are vanished, and inclinations after former indulgences revived : and, finding no effectual opposition, they will re-enter, strengthen the garrison, and render the man more entirely their slave, than ever. Such characters cannot but be noticed, with mingled grief and horror, by those who carefully observe the state of congregations, where the gospel is faithfully dispensed.—What encouragement does our Redeemer give us to follow him wholly, to attend on his instruction, to trust in his mercy, and, by obeying him, to do the will of God our Father! Earthly relatives often fail of the duties incumbent on them : but He is such a Relation and Friend as men would have been, had sin never entered ; indeed far more desirable. Whatever there is peculiar, in the affection or regard of the different endeared relations of life, all centres in the love of Christ to his true disciples; yea, to the poorest, weakest, and most sinful of them. Whatever credit, comfort, or advantage could be derived from a loving brother, father, husband, or son, who was advanced to the highest state of earthly dignity and authority; this, and far more, may we confidently expect from Christ, in life, death, judgment, and to eternity. Let us then cease from men, and cleave to him ; let us look upon every Christian, even in the lowest condition of life, as the beloved brother, or sister, or honoured mother, of the Lord of glory; and let us love, respect, and be kind to them for his sake, and after his example, and count this our privilege and delight : remembering his words, " For as much as ye did it to the " least of these my brethren, ye did it unto me." (*Notes,* xxv. 34—46. P. O. 31—46.)

NOTES.

CHAP. XIII. V. 1, 2. It is evident that the events, recorded in the latter part of the preceding chapter, took place on the same day, on which our Lord spake some of the parables contained in this : but Luke relates the concluding incident *after* the parable of the sower. (*Notes,* xii. 46—50. Luke viii. 4—21.)—When Jesus came to the sea-side, a very great number of people collected together. 'He therefore went into a fisher-boat, or little ship, close to 'the land, that he might be less incommoded, and better 'heard, by the people. ' If the shore were elevated, as it

'probably might be, and formed a kind of semicircular 'bay; the people might range themselves round it, and 'hear with great advantage.' *Gilpin.*

V. 3—8. (*Note, Judg.* ix. 8—15.)—Parables are a kind of pictures of spiritual things which we are slow to understand, under the similitude of external objects with which we are more fully acquainted : so that, when we have got the key, we perceive more of their nature by a single glance, than we could otherwise learn by laboured descriptions, or multiplied distinctions.—This parable of the sower seems to be a prophetical history of the effects produced by the gospel, in all places to which it should be sent.—A husbandman is represented, as sowing good seed ; for every man sows that kind of grain which he hopes to reap. But as he sowed, part of the seed fell by the way-side, a road lying across the field : here the ground was trodden, and the seed left uncovered, and so the birds picked it up. Another part fell on ground, where a rock was covered with a very shallow soil : this part of the seed being only just covered, soon sprang up, and looked very promising ; but when the summer-sun, in its noon-day heat, shone full on it, the soil was dried up beneath the root, and so it was scorched and withered. Another portion fell on ground, which had not been cleared from thorns and weeds : this sprang up, and grew till harvest ; but the thorns and weeds smothered and choked it, so that it could not ear, or yield any increase. But the rest fell into good ground, fertile and well prepared by tillage and manure, and this produced an abundant increase; some of it yielded thirty times as much as was sown, some sixty, and some even a hundred times as much. (*Note, Gen.* xxvi. 12.) This alone answered the sower's purpose, and recompensed his toil. (*Notes, Mark* iv. 1—20. *Luke* viii. 4—15.)

Parables. (3) Παραϐολαις· der. from παραϐαλλω, to cast, or place things one against another, and so compare them. (Εx παρα, juxta, et ϐαλλω jacio.)—*Sprung up.* (5) Εξανετειλε. (Comp. of εξ, ανα, and τελλω, to arise, unused.) Only here and *Mark* iv. 5, in the N. T.—*Gen.* ii. 9. *Ps.* cxii. 4. *Sept.* —*Were scorched.* (6) Εκαυματισθη. (Α καυμα, *æstus: Rev.* vii. 16. xvi. 9 : hocque à καιω ardeo.) *Mark* iv. 6. *Rev.* xvi. 8, 9.—*Thorns.* (7) Ακανθας. (Ab ακη, cuspis, acies.) ' It is ' taken not only for thorns, but likewise for briars and ' brambles, and any thing that hath pricks.' *Leigh.* 22. vii. 16. xxvii. 29. *Heb.* vi. 8.—*Gen.* iii. 18. *Sept.* (*Note, Gen.* iii. 17—19.)—*Choked.*] Απεπνιξαν, *suffocated. Luke*

9 Who ᵃhath ears to hear, let him hear.

10 ¶ And the disciples came, and said unto him, ᵇWhy speakest thou unto them in parables?

11 He answered and said unto them, ᵖBecause it is given unto you to know ᑫthe mysteries of the kingdom of heaven, but to them it is not given.

12 For ʳwhosoever hath, to him shall be given, and he shall have more abundance: but whosoever hath not, ˢfrom him shall be taken away even that he hath.

13 Therefore speak I to them in parables: ᵗbecause they seeing see not; and hearing they hear not, neither do they understand.

viii. 33. Not elsewhere in the N. T. Συνεπνιξαν, Mark iv. 7: συμπνιγονlαι, Luke viii. 14.

V. 9. (Note, xi. 13—15.) This address was suited to call the attention of all present to the parable; and to shew them, that some peculiarly interesting instruction was intended by it.

V. 10, 11. The multitudes, who heard this parable delivered in publick, did not understand it, and probably few at that time enquired further about it. But the disciples, after the assembled company had been dismissed, came to our Lord in private, desiring to be informed, why he thus taught the people, and what was the meaning of the parable. He had doubtless several reasons for adopting this method of instruction, which is peculiarly suited to assist the memory, and engage the attention; and which communicates information and conviction to the teachable, in the most simple and compendious way. (Notes, Prov. i. 1—6.) 'Hereby it was visible who were ... "the sons of " "wisdom," who had a cordial love to divine things, and ' an inflamed desire after them; and thought it worthy of ' their care and pains to search them out, and so were per- ' sons fitly qualified for the reception of gospel-light. It ' was the custom of the disciples of the Jewish doctors, ' when they understood not the meaning of their parables, ' to go unto their Rabbies, to enquire the meaning of ' them; as did our Lord's disciples ask of him. ...And this ' Christ's hearers might have done, had they not been in- ' disposed to receive the doctrine which he taught, and ' chosen rather to be held in error by the Scribes and ' Pharisees. ...Such lessons ... are best remembered; ... for ' the time spent in unfolding them, makes the idea more ' fixed and lasting.' Whitby.—' This happened after Christ ' had upbraided and threatened the neighbouring places, ' from whence doubtless the greatest part of the multi- ' tude came: (xi. 20—24:) and it is not improbable, that ' the ... Pharisees, who had so vilely blasphemed him this ' very morning, might with an ill purpose have gathered ' a company of their associates ... about Christ to ensnare ' him.' Doddridge.—The reason, however, which our Lord here assigned, is replete with instruction, warning, and encouragement. "It was given to" the disciples "to know " the mysteries of the kingdom of heaven, but not to " others;" that is, not at that time, for it might afterward be given to them also.—A mystery, in the scriptural use of the term, signifies, a subject in religion, of which we can know little or nothing, except by revelation, and nothing more than is revealed. This knowledge is received by faith only, and must be used as a principle in all our other reasonings; but itself must not be disputed, as if it were the subject of reason and argument. There are many mysteries respecting the kingdom of heaven: and it is given to

Christ's true disciples to know or understand them, as far as it is needful; and to them alone. Those who in humble faith take him for their Teacher, by attending to the instructions of his word, and seeking the teaching of his Spirit, attain to this knowledge; but the proud, unteachable, and unbelieving do not: for no man can know them, except from the great Prophet of the church.—But his special choice and effectual calling made those persons his disciples, rather than others of their countrymen, and this brought them to learn of him.

Mysteries. (11) Μνηρια. (' Alii ab Hebraico רֶסַ res ' abscondita deducunt; alii vero Græco μυειν claudere; oc- ' cludere, abscondere, aut μυνϑαι sacris initiari, originem ' debere existimant.' Schleusner.) Rom. xi. 25. xvi. 25. 1 Cor. xiii. 2. Eph. i. 9. iii. 3. 4. 9. 1 Tim. iii. 9. 16.

V. 12. It is an invariable rule in the kingdom of Christ, that " whosoever hath, to him shall be given, and " he shall have abundance:" that is, say many expositors, ' he who improves what he has.' Yet if our Lord meant so, why did he not thus express himself, either here or in other places? (Marg. Ref. r, s.) There is no doubt a truth in this way of stating it; for no man improves either natural powers, or external advantages, without the special grace of God: yet it is a truth often misunderstood and perverted. The obvious meaning is, that one of the special gifts of God to his people is an earnest of others: so that he, who has faith and grace, shall receive further communications of knowledge, wisdom, holiness, and every blessing of salvation, till he has a great abundance; whereas he, who has not faith and grace, shall at last be deprived of all his other attainments and advantages, in which he trusted and gloried. The plain inferences from which are, that he who desires these blessings must seek them from Christ, or he never can have them; and he that has received them, must bless the Lord for making him to differ, and trust him to perfect his own good work. (Notes, Mark iv. 23—25. Luke viii. 16—18.)—' Whosoever, ' through my goodness and mercy, hath any measure of ' grace wrought in him; that man, in the effectual use of ' those means which I afford him, shall have yet more: ' but whosoever hardeneth his heart to refuse those gracious ' offers, which are made to him, it is and shall be just with ' God, to take away from him those gracious offers, which ' are made to him; it is and shall be just with God, to ' take away from him those helps, and tenders of means, ' and previous dispensations, which are made to him.' Bp. Hall.

V. 13. Our Lord spake in parables to the people, because they refused to improve their faculties and advantages: for they hated the truth through love of sin, and closed their eyes to the light by proud and carnal preju-

o 2

14 And in them is fulfilled ⁷ the prophecy of Esaias, which saith,· By hearing ye shall hear, and ·shall· not understand; and seeing ye shall ·see, and shall not perceive.

15 For this people's ᶻ heart is waxed gross, and *their* ⁷ ears are dull of hearing, and ᵃ their eyes they have closed; lest at any time they should see with *their* eyes, and hear with *their* ears, and should understand with *their* heart, ᵃ and should be converted, ᵇ and I should heal them.

16 But ᶜ blessed *are* your eyes, for they see ; and your ears, for they hear.

·17 For·verily I say unto·you, ᵈ That many·prophets and righteous *men* have desired·'to· see *those· things*·which ye see, and have not seen *them ;* ·and to hear *those things* which ye hear, and have not heard *them.*

18 ¶ ᵉ Hear ye therefore· the parable of the sower.

19 When any one heareth ᶠ the word of the kingdom, ᵍ and understandeth *it* not, then cometh ʰ the wicked· *one,* and catcheth away ·that ·which · was sown in his heart. ¹ This is he which received seed by the way-side.

dices. They saw his miracles, but could not see that he was the Messiah ; and heard his doctrine, without acknowledging that it was the voice of God : and it was his sovereign will to leave many of them to final obduracy and unbelief. (*Notes,* 16, 17. *Deut.* xxix. 4. *Is.* xlii. 18—20.)

V. 14, 15. (*Marg. Ref.*) The prophecy referred to seems to have had a peculiar respect to the times and persons here spoken of. (*Note, Is.* vi. 9, 10.) They would have the fullest opportunity of learning the way of salvation ; yet they should not understand it, nor perceive in Jesus the fulfilment of the ancient prophecies. Because their hearts were become *gross,* or *fat,* (that is, stupid and insensible,) through pride, avarice, hypocrisy, and unbelief; so that their ears were stopped against the report of the gospel, and they purposely closed their eyes against the light, because they hated it : (*Note, John* iii. 19—21 :) and therefore God judicially left them to be blinded ; so that it became impossible for them to understand or believe the doctrine of salvation, or to be converted, that their souls might be healed : for had they been converted, they must have been pardoned and healed ; or, saved, and renewed unto holiness.—There seems throughout to be a special reference to the malevolent Pharisees and their adherents. (*Notes,* xii. 22—45.) 'The prophets are in other places 'said, to perform the thing, which they only foretel.' *Bp. Lowth.*—'That we might not suspect this grossness of 'heart and heaviness of ears was the effect of nature, and 'not of choice ; he subjoins the fault of the will, " their " " eyes have they closed." ' *Jerome.*

By hearing, &c. (14) The quotation is made almost exactly in the words of the LXX. The meaning is, indeed, the same with the Hebrew, as to the ·substance : but both the evangelist and the Septuagint render that, *as relating the fact,* which the Hebrew gives *imperatively,* " Make this people's heart fat,' &c. It is observable, that the passage is not once quoted *imperatively* in the New Testament.—In John it is quoted, " He hath blinded, &c." In Romans, " God hath given them, &c." (*Notes, John* xii. 37—41, *vv.* 40, 41. *Acts* xxviii. 23—29. *Rom.* xi. 7—10.) *Is waxed gross.* (15) Επαχυνθη. (Παχυνω, *pinguifacio, obesum reddo,* à παχυς, *pinguis.—*Παχυνομαι, *pinguifio, obesus fio vel sum.*) *Acts* xxviii. 27. Not elsewhere in the N. T.—*Deut.* xxxii. 15. Sept.

V. 16, 17. (*Marg. Ref.*) The disciples, notwithstand-

ing remaining ignorance, mistakes, and prejudices, had already been taught of God, to see and hear many things relative to his kingdom : and thus their eyes and ears were blessed, by this sanctifying influence and its happy effects ; they were employed in a proper and· profitable manner, and further light and instruction would continually be added. Their advantages were peculiarly valuable : for " many prophets and righteous persons," from the beginning of the world, had desired to see the times in which they lived, and the miracles which they witnessed, and to hear the Messiah's instructions which they daily heard ; yet they were not allowed to possess these desired privileges. They looked forward to the Redeemer, who was in due time to appear, and rested their hopes on him : they had their light from this Sun, before he arose above the horizon ; and they longed to see him already risen :·but this was reserved as a peculiar blessing for the apostles, whose light was proportionably more distinct and clear. (*Notes, Luke* x. 23, 24. *Heb.* xi. 13—16. 39, 40. 1 *Pet.* i. 10—12.)

V. 18, 19. After this encouraging and instructive introduction, our Lord proceeded to expound the parable to his disciples.' " The Sower " represented the Saviour himself, in his personal ministry, or as speaking by his apostles and faithful ministers. The *seed sown* is " the " word of the kingdom," " the word of God." Every kind of preaching is by no means sowing this seed: if men teach mere morality, metaphysical speculations, enthusiastical delusions, human traditions, false doctrines; as the seed is congenial to the soil of fallen human nature, an increase may be expected. But it must be of the same kind with the seed: for the good fruit of repentance, faith, piety, and holiness can be produced from " the word of " the kingdom " alone. This word, by those discoveries which it makes to us of God and ourselves, of sin and holiness, of Christ and eternity, is as properly in the heart, *a seed* of all true godliness, as the grain of wheat is, in the fruitful soil, of the future crop of wheat. But as the earth must be prepared to receive the seed, by a principle of fertility, and by proper culture ; so the heart must be suitably disposed, or the word of God will not yield any increase. Many hearers of the gospel, where most scripturally preached, are like " the way-side: " their hearts are no more suited to the holy word of God, than the high

o 3

k 5, 6
1 1 Sam. xi. 18—
16. 2 Chr. xxiv.
2. 4. 14. Ps.
lxxviii. 34—37.
cvii.12,13.Ia.lviii.
2 Ez. xxxviii. 31,
32. Marg iv. 16,
17. vi. 20. John v. 35. Acts viii. 13. Gal. iv. 14, 15.

20 But he that ᵏ received the seed into stony places, the same is he that heareth the word, and ˡ anon with joy receiveth it ;

21 Yet hath he not ᵐ root in him- self, but ⁿ dureth for a while: ° for

m 6. vii. 27, 23, 26,
27. Job xix. 28
Prov. xii. 3, 12
Luke vi. 19.
John vi. 26. 61—65. 70, 71. xv. 6—7. Acts viii. 21—24. Gal. v. 6. vi. 15. Eph. iii. 17
2 Pet. i. 8, 9. 1 John ii. 19, 20. n xx. 22. xxiv. 13. Job xxvii. 8—10. Ps. xxxvi. 3
Hos. vi. 4. Rom. ix. 7. Phil. i. 6. 1 Pet. i. 5. o v. 10—12. x. 57—39. xv. 24—26
Mark iv. 1F. viii. 34—56. xiii. 12, 13. Luke iv. 23—25. xiv. 26—35. xxi. 12—18. John xii.
25, 26. Gal. vi. 12. 2 Tim. iv. 10. Heb. x. 36—39. Rev. ii. 13.

road, continually beaten by passengers, would be to re- ceive the seed-corn. They are worldly, proud, prejudiced, and careless : they hear, but understand not, as they have no desire to understand. They attend from curiosity, or custom, or worse motives, out of the midst of secular en- gagements and conversation : whilst the word is sounding in their ears, they are often employed in thoughts about their diversions, pursuits, or schemes, the persons and ob- jects around them, or the appointments which are to suc- ceed the tedious hour : or they come in order to object, deride, or revile ; but without expectation or desire of pro- fiting. They therefore understand nothing of the true meaning, excellence, or importance of what they hear : and those evil spirits, who are sure to form an attentive part of every congregation, where the gospel is truly preached, (having more employment there, and being more in danger of losing their servants, than at the places of dissipation or debauchery ;) are ready immediately to catch away the word out of the mind of such hearers, by sug- gesting more pleasing ideas, by engaging them in vain speculations or frivolous conversation, or by exciting pride and evil passions ; or to excite disgust at the plain truths of God's word, or against something in the style and manner of the preacher. Thus the best sermons make no im- pression and produce no effect ; such hearers are neither convinced, nor informed, but remain as ignorant, infidel, careless, profligate, and ungodly as before. ' This industry ' of Satan to snatch the word out of our hearts, as it dis- ' covers his enmity against the progress of the gospel, so ' doth it highly commend the excellence and efficacy of it : ' for were it not of great importance to preserve it there, ' he would not be so industrious to snatch it thence ; and ' were it not, when there, a powerful instrument to work ' within us that " faith which purifies the heart ;" why doth ' he do this, lest we should believe ? Why is it then that ' men do call this quick and powerful word, this word of ' life, a dead letter ? And when they daily by experience ' see, that the persuasions of themselves and others are ' often prevalent, why do they think that God's can be of ' no effect, without a miracle ? ' *Whitby.*—No man can *persuade* another to that which *his heart is totally set against ; and before regeneration, the heart is totally set against the gospel.* If regeneration be called *a miracle* in the concluding clause ; our Lord's words answer the question, " Except a man be born again, he cannot see " the kingdom of God." But if the learned writer meant something else than regeneration, let those who expect miracles answer him.—The quotation, this excepted, which seemed to require notice, is of great importance.

The *wicked one.* (19) 'Ο πονηρος.—'Ο Σαλανας, *Mark* iv. 15. 'Ο διαβολος, *Luke* viii. 12. (*Note, 2 Cor.* iv. 3, 4.)

V. 20, 21. Other hearers of the gospel resemble the " stony places." They are instructed concerning salvation by grace, through faith, the privileges of the believer, and the felicity of heaven : and without humiliation or change of heart, without abiding conviction of their own guilt

and depravity, the evil of sin, the vanity of the world, their need of a Saviour, or the excellence of holiness, they eagerly endeavour to appropriate the comforts of the gospel they take up a superficial view of religion, and becom confident that all the blessings of which they hear belong to them. This delusion fills them with unsanctified joy, and excites other high and false affections : but they do not manifest godly sorrow, brokenness of heart, tender- ness of conscience, or consistency of conduct. There is, however, in these professors of the gospel great appear- ance of zeal and earnestness, and many pious persons think highly of them ; which tends still more to enhance their joy and confidence. Thus they seem to make more progress than the humble, contrite, and conscientious Christian ; and often exceed him in fluency and forward- ness of speech, and in boldness for the truth, when in no immediate danger. Yet their hearts are proud and worldly : they therefore " endure for a while ; " even so long as their profession conduces to procure them consideration and ad- vantage ; or, at least, does not materially interfere with their secular interests, or require peculiar self-denial. But " when persecution or tribulation," for the sake of the word, arises ; like a scorching sun, it destroys the root of their religion, and then the blade withers. Some heavy trial must be sustained if they cleave to the Lord, or some advantage may be had by forsaking him ; or they are proved by circumstances of peculiar temptation : and, having " no " root in themselves," not being rooted and grounded in the love of Christ, as the only and most precious Saviour of perishing sinners, they are not willing to forsake all, and bear their cross for him. Thus " they are offended," and stumble ; they find some pretence for renouncing or disguising their profession, or they turn aside to a more lax and easy religion, according to which they can " serve " God and Mammon." Many such hearers are doubtless found in every congregation, and in these easy days some of them may continue for a long time : but should perse- cution arise, they would drop off, as the leaves from the trees in autumn.—ᶜ He receives the word with joy, and ' is much affected with it, though afterwards he is offended ' at it : whence also it appears, that it is not enough to ' render us good Christians, that we at present are some- ' what affected with the word, and receive it with some ... ' delight, ... unless it doth produce sincerity and constancy, ' in our obedience to all its precepts, even those which are ' most grievous to flesh and blood.' *Whitby.*—ᶜ The ' sowing of the seed on the stony ground denoteth him, ' that at the first hearing, receives the gospel with all ' greediness and joy ; looking on the smoother part of ' it ; but for want of an *honest* heart, a good soil where ' it may take root, ... they last but a little while.' *Hani- mond.*

Dureth for a while. (21) Προσκαιρος εστιν. (Εκ προς et καιρος, *tempus.*—Προς καιρον πιστευσι, *Luke* viii. 13.) *Mark* iv. 17. 2 *Cor.* iv. 18. *Heb.* xi. 25.—*Offended.*] Σκανδαλιζδαι. See on *Note*, v. 29, 30.

o 4

when tribulation or persecution ariseth because of the word, by and by he ' is offended.

22 He also that received ' seed among the thorns, is he that heareth the word ; and ' the care of this world, and ' the deceitfulness of riches, ' choke the word, and he becometh unfruitful.

23 But he " that received seed into the ' good ground, is he that heareth the word, and understandeth it ; which also ' beareth fruit, and bringeth forth, ' some an hundred-fold, some sixty, some thirty.

24 ¶ Another parable " put he forth

V. 22. Another set of hearers resemble ground, over-run with thorns or noxious weeds. They receive the word into a heart crowded with anxious cares, or covetous de-sires : they are alarmed, and then quieted ; they acquire knowledge, have thoughtful seasons, purpose to be Christ-ians, perhaps assent to an orthodox creed, and make a plausible profession of religion ; and continue even to the end to impose on themselves and others. But they aim to serve two masters : their great concern is about the world ; they eagerly pursue riches, are solicitous to obtain a competency, to advance their families, and to make a re-putable figure among their neighbours. If in lower cir-cumstances, their chief care is about a present and future provision for themselves and their families. Or perhaps being of another turn of mind, the pleasures of the world, and the desire of pomp, luxury, or authority, predominate ; while religion is only a secondary concern to quiet con-science, to exclude the fear of hell, to keep up the hope of heaven, or to maintain the good opinion of Christians and ministers ; whose approbation, or tacit connivance, often confirms them in this delusion. · In this soil the seed seems to grow ; but it is smothered by " the cares of this " world and the deceitfulness of riches : " for wealth seems to promise many advantages ; and men of some serious-ness often pursue it, under the self-flattering idea, that they shall by means of it be enabled to do the more good ; and in both respects they find in the event, that they have been deceived. The love of riches imposes on their judg-ments, and deludes them into multiplied methods of in-creasing them, some of which are fraudulent ; it induces them to procrastinate their intended earnestness about re-ligion ; and allures them into endless encumbrances, in-fectious connexions, sinful compliances, and conformity to the world. These are the thorns, which grow up and choke the word ; so that it becomes unfruitful, or brings nothing to perfection. (Notes, 1 Tim. vi. 6—10, vv. 8—10. 17, 18.)—This is the most unsuspected and fatal dan-ger in great commercial cities, and in times of outward peace and prosperity ; and it is to be feared, that very many are thus deceived, and lose their own souls, in at-tempting to gain more of this present world.

Of this world.] Τ8 αιωνος τ8τ8. See on Note, xii. 31, 32, v. 32.—Choke.] Συμπνιγει. (' Ex συν et πνιγω, fauces com-' primendo neco, suffoco.' Schleusner.—xviii. 28. Mark v. 13.) Mark iv. 7. 19. Luke viii. 14. 42.—Comp. on Note, 3—8, v. 7.—Unfruitful.] Ακαρπος. (Ex α priv. et καρπος, fructus.) Mark iv. 19. 1 Cor. xiv. 14. Eph. v. 11. Tit. iii. 14. 2 Pet. i. 8. Jude 12.

V. 23. Though so much of this precious seed seems thrown away ; yet it will not all " return void," or fail to " prosper in that for which it is sent." (Note, Is. lv. 10,

11.) Some of it falls on good ground, even in an " honest " and good heart," sincerely desirous of learning the truth and will of God, in order to believe and obey them. This " preparation of heart is from the LORD : " and the want of the honest and good heart is the only reason, why the gospel occasions the condemnation of any who hear it. When the heart is influenced by the fear of God, and a desire of his favour ; when it is humble and contrite ; when forgiveness and grace are valued more than worldly objects ; when sin is hated and dreaded, and deliverance from it earnestly desired ; when a man is thus disposed to " buy the truth " at any price, and to become Christ's dis-cipie at all adventures ; then the ground is prepared for the good seed, and nothing can prevent its growth and in-crease. He, whose heart is thus prepared, will hear the word of God with earnest prayer to be taught by the Holy Spirit, and to be delivered from prejudice and error ; he will receive it with reverence, humility, and docility ; he will gradually understand more and more of its nature, excellency, authority, and tendency ; he will receive it into a broken heart, by " faith working by love," and " overcoming the world ; " and he will, as it were, cover it over by meditation and prayer. Satan can by no means take it out of this man's heart : when it springs up, it will strike deep root, so that persecutions and afflictions, which scorch and wither the seed sown upon the rock, will serve to ripen this for the harvest : the cares, interests, and pleasures of the world will be subordinated and mo-derated, with reference to the welfare of the soul ; and when they seem ready to injure the believer, or to mar his fruitfulness, he will bestow pains to root them up, as thorns and weeds, lest they should deprive him of his ex-pected increase. Thus the seed will produce a plenteous crop, and he, in whose heart it grows, will " bring forth " fruit with patience," and perseverance in well-doing even to the end. All, who thus receive the good seed, will manifest their holiness of heart by holy actions ; their piety, justice, truth, goodness, mercy, temperance, and meekness, will glorify God, adorn the gospel, and do sub-stantial benefit to mankind. They will not all be alike fruitful ; but all will yield a rich increase of those " fruits " of the Spirit," which are the effects and evidence of true repentance and faith in Christ. These alone are valued by the Sower of the seed, and the Giver of the increase.—In all congregations, where the true word of God has been preached hitherto, there have been these four sorts of hearers ; and no others are conceivable. So that we may consider the parable as a remarkable prophecy, the accom-plishment of which continually proves the truth of the sacred scripture.

V. 24—30. The kingdom of heaven, or the gospel-

unto them, saying, The kingdom of heaven is likened unto a man which sowed good seed in his field:

25 But while men slept, his enemy came and sowed tares among the wheat, and went his way.

26 But when the blade was sprung up, and brought forth fruit, then appeared the tares also.

27 So the servants of the householder came, and said unto him, Sir, didst not thou sow good seed in thy field? from whence then hath it tares?

28 He said unto them, An enemy hath done this. The servants said unto him, Wilt thou then that we go and gather them up?

29 But he said, Nay; lest while ye gather up the tares, ye root up also the wheat with them.

30 Let both grow together until the harvest: and in the time of harvest I will say to the reapers, Gather ye together first the tares, and bind them in bundles to burn them; but gather the wheat into my barn.

31 ¶ Another parable put he forth unto them, saying, The kingdom of heaven is like to a grain of mustard-seed, which a man took, and sowed in his field;

32 Which indeed is the least of all seeds: but when it is grown, it is the greatest among herbs, and becometh a tree; so that the birds of the air come and lodge in the branches thereof.

33 ¶ Another parable spake he unto them: The kingdom of heaven is like unto leaven, which a woman took, and hid in three measures of meal, till the whole was leavened.

dispensation, resembled also a man that sowed good seed in his field. But whilst his servants, who were set to watch the field, were asleep, an enemy came privily, sowed seed of another nature, and then went away. When, however, the seed had grown so much as to approach maturity, it was plain that there were tares among the wheat. It is not certainly known what is meant by the word rendered *tares;* but it is evident, that the pulse at present called *tares,* or *vetches,* was not intended: otherwise the tares might early and certainly have been known, and eradicated without danger; and if permitted to grow till harvest, they would have been too valuable to be burnt. Some useless, noxious weed must therefore be signified, which could not so easily be distinguished from the blade of the wheat.— When, however, the servants expressed their concern and surprise, that the crop should thus be marred, they were told that "an enemy had done this." Nor would their Lord permit them to pull them up, lest through error or inadvertency they should root up the wheat also. Though injurious to the crop, it was best that both should grow together till the harvest; and then he would give previous orders to the reapers, to separate the tares, and bind them in bundles for fuel, as well as to take care of the wheat. (*Note,* 36—43.)

Tares. (25) Ζιζανια. 'A kind of bad and hurtful 'plant, which spoiled the corn in Palestine, and is un-'known in these days.' *Quot.* in *Leigh.*—'A kind of 'plant very well known in Palestine; the seed of which 'was not unlike wheat, and the plant growing from it had 'the same greenness and stalk as wheat; but it brought 'forth no fruit, or certainly not good fruit.' *Schleusner.* —It is used in this chapter only.—*Was sprung up.* (26) Εξλαστησε. *Mark* iv. 27. *Heb.* ix. 4. *Jam.* v. 18.—*Gen.* i. 11. *Num.* xvii. 8. *Sept.*—*Bundles.* (30) Δεσμας. (A δεω seu δεσμεω, *ligo.*) It does not occur elsewhere in N. T.— *Ex.* xii. 22. *Sept.* where it answers to אגדה, rendered *bunch* there, and *bundle, Am.* ix. 6, *marg.*

V. 31, 32. A grain of mustard-seed is one of the least seeds that men sow in the field: yet in deep and rich soils it will produce a plant of very great size; so large, that they who have not seen it, have seldom an adequate conception of the propriety of the similitude. 'There was a 'stalk of mustard-seed in Sichin, from which sprang out 'three boughs, of which one was broke off, and covered 'the tent of a potter, and produced three cubs of mustard.' *R. Simeon.*—'A stalk of mustard-seed was in my field, 'into which I was used to climb, as men do into a fig-'tree.' *R. Calipha* in *Whitby.*—The author has seen plants of mustard, in the deep and rich soil of some low lands in Lincolnshire, larger than most shrubs, and almost like a small tree. Probably, in the eastern countries, it is the largest plant from the smallest seed, which has yet been noticed. This rendered it peculiarly fit to represent the gospel-dispensation; which from very small beginnings, when its poor, unlearned, unarmed, and despised preachers had all the power, wealth, learning, wickedness, and false religion in the world against them, soon grew so large as to overspread whole nations, and to subvert the deep-rooted foundations of ancient idolatry, as well as to take the place of the Mosaick dispensation; and which ere long will fill the whole earth.—It also illustrates the effect of the gospel in any place, where it is fully and faithfully dispensed. It begins in "a day of small things:" but as one after another is converted, the examples, prayers, and endeavours of this company, render it prevalent, and it diffuses its influence all around. (*Marg. Ref.—Notes, Is.* ix. 6, 7. *Dan.* ii, 34, 35. 44, 45. *Luke* xiii. 18—21.)

V. 33. (*Luke* xiii. 20, 21.) Leaven is generally used in scripture, as the emblem of *corrupt doctrine,* or *wickedness;* (*Notes,* xvi. 5—12. 1 *Cor.* v. 6—8. *Gal.* v. 7—12, *v.* 9:) yet here it represents the truth and grace of God. This circumstance should warn men not to overstrain the emblems and parables of scripture, or apply them without careful discrimination.—Leaven has a peculiar taste, which is

o 6

34 All ʸ these things spake Jesus unto the multitude in parables; and without a parable spake he not unto them: ·.

35 That ᶻ it might be fulfilled which was spoken by the prophet, saying, ᵃ I will open my mouth in parables; ᵇ I will utter things which have been kept secret ᶜ from the foundation of the world.

36 ¶ Then ᵈ Jesus sent the multitude away, ᵉand went into the house: and his disciples came unto him, saying, ᶠ Declare unto us the parable of the tares of the field.

37 He answered and said unto them, ᵍ He that soweth the good seed ʰ is the Son of man;

38 The ⁱfield is the world; ᵏ the good seed are the children of the king-

dom; but the tares are ⁱthe children of the wicked *one*;

39 The ᵐ enemy that sowed them is the devil; ⁿ the harvest is the end of the world; ᵒ and the reapers are the angels.

40 As therefore ᵖthe tares are gathered and burned in the fire: so shall it be in the end of this world.

41 ᵠ The Son of man shall send forth his angels, ʳand they shall gather out of his kingdom all ˢ things that offend, ᵗ and them which do iniquity;

42 And shall ᵘ cast them into a furnace of fire: there shall be ᵛ wailing and gnashing of teeth.

43 Then ˣ shall the righteous shine forth as the sun ʸ in the kingdom of their Father. ᶻ Who hath ears to hear, let him hear.

---

communicates by fermentation to the whole mass of moistened flour, however large it may be; provided it remain in it long enough to diffuse itself. Thus the word of God, when received into the heart by the teaching of the Holy Spirit, gradually changes the judgment, affections, conduct, and conversation. Though these were before carnal, sensual, proud, selfish, envious, and ungodly; they now receive a heavenly savour: the thoughts, desires, pursuits, and discourse gradually become humble, and holy, and spiritual; the Christian learns to attend to his worldly affairs, possessions, comforts, and relative duties after a heavenly manner; and this change is progressive, till perfected in heaven.—The former parable represents the kingdom of heaven as set up in the world; this shews us the nature of it as it is set up in the heart.

V. 34, 35. (*Notes, Ps.* xlix. 1—4. lxxviii. 2.) That, which the Psalmist spake of himself, when instructing the people under the influence of the Holy Spirit, was also fulfilled, when Christ taught the people by parables: for under these dark sayings he actually set before them, in the most effectual manner, those deep mysteries, which had been kept secret from the beginning; which neither prophets nor patriarchs had fully understood; and which many would afterwards remember to have heard from him, when the event had in part developed their meaning. (*Marg. Ref.*)

Will utter. (35) Ερευξομαι. Used here only in the N. T.—*Lev.* xi. 10. *Ps.* xix. 2.—Ανοιξω εν παραβολαις το ϛομα μμ, φθεγξομαι προβλημαλα απʼ αρχης. 'I will open my mouth in parables, I will utter problems (or difficult questions,) ' from the beginning.' *Sept.*

V. 36—43. After our Lord had spoken the preceding parables, he dismissed the multitude and retired into a house; where his disciples applied to him to explain the parable of the tares, as that seems most of all to have perplexed them. He therefore informed them, that " the " Son of Man," the Messiah, was the Sower of the

good seed; that is, personally, and by his ministers: and this implied also, that he is the Lord and Proprietor of the field. This represented " the world," throughout which the word of God was to be preached under the gospel. "The good seed" (or those converts produced from it,) is " the children of the kingdom," true believers, the loyal subjects of Christ, and heirs of heaven: but the produce of the bad seed are " the children of the " wicked one;" hereticks, hypocrites, antichristians, antinomians, and enthusiasts, of every description.—As the parable of the sower represents what is wrong in the visible church, (even where the true gospel is faithfully preached,) through the subtlety of Satan and the depravity of the human heart; so that of the tares represents the fatal effects of false teachers and seducers, drawing men off from the truth, or prejudicing them against it.—The counterfeit characters, above mentioned, are the genuine produce of false doctrine and distorted views of Christianity, which " Satan, transformed into an angel of light," by his ministers of various descriptions, propagates in the world: even as true believers are the produce of the real gospel, attended by the influence of the Holy Spirit. The devil, the enemy of Christ and of men, sows this seed by his servants, in order to deceive souls and disgrace the gospel; he does it " by night," and privily; he is most successful when least suspected, and when ministers and Christians are most unwatchful. (*Notes, Acts* xx. 29—31. 2 *Pet.* ii. 1—3.) The produce of this corrupt seed is not immediately discovered, but gradually detected. And though gross transgressors, and such as openly oppose the fundamentals of the gospel, ought to be separated from the society of the faithful; yet many of " the children of " the kingdom " are so defective, and many of " the chil- " dren of the wicked one " so plausible, that an exact discrimination cannot be made by human discernment; and by attempting too much, true believers may be rejected, stumbled, or discouraged. Much less must separation by

44 ¶ Again, the kingdom of heaven is [a] like unto treasure hid in a field; [b] the which when a man hath found he hideth, and, [b] for joy thereof, goeth and selleth all that he hath, and [c] buyeth that field.

45 ¶ Again, the kingdom of heaven is [d] like unto a merchant-man [e] seeking goodly pearls;

46 Who, when he 'had found [f] one pearl of great price, [g] went and sold all that he had, and bought it.

---

persecution be attempted; by which far more of the wheat has been eradicated, than of the tares, in all cases, in which the officious servants, contrary to their Lord's express command, have employed that unhallowed means. In general they must be let alone till the harvest. This will be at " the end of the world: " for though death will separate them as to their souls, yet the grand and publick separation will be at the day of judgment. Then the holy angels will be employed, as the reapers in this harvest, by the Son of Man, the incarnate Saviour and Judge, whose creatures, worshippers, and servants they are. These will gather together all the wicked, throughout the whole world; and especially all heretical and hypocritical professors of the gospel, who have caused scandals and wrought iniquity, from every part of the church, in order to their destruction; even as the tares are bound up in bundles to be burned: and they shall be cast into hell, as into a furnace of fire, where will be doleful lamentations and gnashing of teeth in rage and despair. When the tempters were tempted, the deceivers and the deceived, and those who have associated together, and encouraged each other in delusion and iniquity, shall be consigned to the same punishment, and, with desperate enmity, shall charge their destruction upon each other; then these tares will, as it were, " be bound in bundles to be burned." But at that time " the righteous," " the children of the kingdom," will shine forth in the image of Christ, with the lustre of the unclouded noon-day sun, " in the kingdom of their " Father; " being made unspeakably glorious, excellent, wise, and happy.—These are truths universally interesting, and infinitely important: and every man in the world is concerned to attend to them, as he values the salvation of his soul.

Of the wicked one. (38) Τα πονηρα. See on *Notes,* 18, 19, v. 19. vi. 13.—*The end of the world.* (39) Συνλελεια τα αιωνος. 40. 49. xxiv. 3. xxviii. 20.—Επι συνλελεια των αιωνων. Heb. ix. 26.—*The end of this world.* (40) Εν τη συνλελεια τα αιωνος τελε.—Συντελεια, (ex συν et τελος,) Neh. ix. 31. Job xxvi. 10. Jer. iv. 27. Dan. xii. 4. 13. *Sept.*—*Shine forth.* (43) Εκλαμψωσιν. (Εκ εκ et λαμπω. Dan. xii. 3. *Sept.*) Not elsewhere in the New Testament.

V. 44. The nature of " the kingdom of heaven," as it is set up in the world and in the heart, and as it is counteracted by human depravity and by false doctrine, has been shewn: here, its *privileges and blessings,* and *the way in which we obtain admission into it,* are illustrated. In this view, " the kingdom of heaven " is like an immense " treasure, concealed in a field." Many walk over this field, without knowing that it contains such a treasure: but when a man has been fully convinced of this, he conceals his discovery, in order that no one may prevent his intended acquisition; and, with great joy at the prospect of speedily being enriched, he goes and sells all his property, that he may purchase the field and every thing con-

tained in it. This represents the invaluable blessings of the gospel, which suffice to render us rich and happy to all eternity: these are contained in the sacred scriptures; yet multitudes have access to the sacred oracles, without being aware of the unsearchable riches which they contain. But when a man is brought to a proper sense of his own character, state, and wants, and becomes in earnest about eternal life; he begins to search the word of God with greater diligence and care: and thus discovering the treasure, he resolves at any rate to obtain it. His joy at this discovery is indeed moderated by fear of coming short, and he uses every precaution against it. He renounces all hopes, claims, pursuits, interests, or pleasures, which are incompatible with salvation. Nothing indeed can be *given* as the *price* of this salvation, yet much must be *given up* for the sake of it. This is implied by *purchasing* the field. The person, who is thus decided, does not conclude that salvation belongs to him, because he has heard and assented to the gospel. He rejoices, that he has found such a treasure, even before he can call it his own; but he knows that he must go to the price of the whole religion of the scriptures, and receive Christ, in all respects, if he would be saved and enriched by him.—Thus he enters the kingdom, and obtains possession of its privileges: and when he has purchased the field, and begins to examine the treasure; he finds it like a mine of gold, which is more and more rich, the longer it is wrought, and the more deeply it is penetrated. (*Marg. Ref.—Notes,* Prov. ii. 3—5. xxiii. 23.)

V. 45, 46. This parable is nearly of the same import as the preceding: but the former represents all spiritual blessings, as they are communicated to us through the scriptures; this exhibits them, as they are laid up in Christ, to whom the scriptures direct us for them.—Every man is " a merchant seeking goodly pearls: " all men seek happiness, and each deems his favourite object a precious jewel. But when the convinced sinner discovers the glory and preciousness of Christ, as the all-gracious Saviour of the lost; he sees Him to be indeed " the Pearl of great price," and all things else comparatively worthless. Whatever it may cost him, he is determined to purchase this invaluable Pearl, which will surely enrich the possessor to all eternity: and if he obtain not this prize, he sees that eternal misery is his portion. He " therefore counts all things but loss " and dung that he may win Christ; " and being determined rather to part with riches, reputation, liberty, or pleas and hopes, but those that arise from his person, undertaking, sufferings, and mediation; he obtains admission into the kingdom, and to the participation of all its blessings. (*Marg. Ref.—Notes,* Eph. iii. 8. *Phil.* iii. 8—11.)

Merchant-man. (45) Ανθρωπω εμπορω. *Rev.* xviii. 3. 11. 15. 23. Not elsewhere in the New Testament.—*Of great price.* (46) Πολυτιμον. (Εξ πολυς et τιμη, *pretium.*) John xii. 3. Not elsewhere in the New Testament.

47 ¶ Again, the kingdom of heaven is like unto ᵇ a net that was cast into the sea, ᶜ and gathered of every kind;

48 Which, when it was full, they ᵈ drew to shore, and sat down, ᵉ and gathered the good into vessels, but cast the bad away.

49 ᶠ So shall it be at the end of the world: ᵍ the angels shall come forth, and sever the wicked from among the just;

50 And shall cast them into the furnace of fire: there shall be ʰ wailing and gnashing of teeth.

51 ¶ Jesus saith unto them, ⁱ Have ye understood all these things? They say unto him, Yea, Lord.

52 Then said he unto them, Therefore every ᵖ scribe *which is* instructed unto the kingdom of heaven, is like unto a man *that is* an householder, ᑫ which bringeth forth out of his treasure *things* new and old.

53 ¶ And it came to pass, *that* when Jesus had finished these parables, ᵗ he departed thence.

54 And ᵘ when he was come into his own country, ˣ he taught them in their synagogue, insomuch that ˣ they were astonished, and said, Whence hath this *man* this wisdom, and *these* mighty works?

55 Is not this ʸ the carpenter's son? is not his mother called Mary? ᶻ and his brethren, James, and Joses, and Simon, and Judas?

V. 47—50. This parable seems to comprise the meaning of the parables of the sower and the tares, under an allusion to those things, about which several of the apostles had been most conversant. The means, used for replenishing the Messiah's kingdom, would resemble the casting of a large net into the sea, which being filled and drawn to shore, would be found to contain valuable fishes, and such as were worthless; either of a bad sort, or out of season, or dead and putrid. These the fishermen would at last separate, gathering the good into their vessels, and throwing the bad away. Thus multitudes profess Christianity, and worship in the visible church, as long as they live: but at the last, the angels of Christ executing his decisions, as Judge of the world, will make an exact discrimination between the good and the bad; gathering true believers into heaven, and casting worthless professors of the gospel, as well as other wicked men, into the place of final punishment.

Net. (47) Σαγηνη, *Verriculum.* ' A kind of fishing-net, ' which drags every thing before it.' *Schleusner.* Used here only in the New Testament; but it occurs several times in the LXX.—*Vessels.* (48) Αγγεια. xxv. 4. Not elsewhere in the New Testament.—*Bad.*] Σαπρα, *putrida, corrupta, prava.* (A σηπω, *putrefacio, corrumpo.*) vii. 17, 18. xii. 33. *Luke* vi. 43. *Eph.* iv. 29.—*Furnace.* (50) Καμινον. 42. *Rev.* i. 15. ix. 2.—*Gen.* xix. 28. *Dan.* iii. 6. Sept.

V. 51, 52. Our Lord seems to have spoken these latter parables to his disciples, apart from the multitude; and he demanded of them, whether they understood the things intended by them. To which they answered, (perhaps too confidently,) that they did: yet it is probable, that they had a general apprehension of his meaning, as there was no immediate reference to his sufferings and death; for it is evident, that they were far more ignorant and prejudiced in respect of his priestly office, than about any other subject. He therefore concluded the whole with another parable, immediately relating to their office in the church. The Scribes were the teachers of the Jews at that time; and the apostles, and other ministers, were to be the teachers under the Christian dispensation. Every one of

VOL. V.

them, therefore, ought to be " a scribe well instructed " in all things pertaining to " the kingdom of heaven." This he represented to them under the similitude of a householder, who has a large family to provide for: such a one will take care to have a stock of provisions in hand for their supply, to which he will be adding continually what he judges to be needful or useful. Thus the people would depend on the apostles, and on other ministers of Christ, as " stewards of the mysteries of God," who were appointed to dispense to them the provision for their souls. They should therefore carefully treasure up, in their memory and heart, all that they had learned; and add to their fund of knowledge continually, deriving fresh instruction from all they heard, saw, or experienced. Then they would be able to bring forth old truth, with new observations, illustrations, and exhortations; and to lead the people forward in knowledge, as they made progress themselves. Some reference may also be had to the old and new dispensations.—' They ought to be diligent, who ' have not only to be wise for themselves, but to dispense ' the wisdom of God to others.' *Beza.*

Instructed. (52) Μαθητευθεις (a μαθητης, bocque a μανθανω:) xxvii. 57. xxviii. 19. *Acts* xiv. 21.

V. 53. (*Mark* iv. 34, 35.) St. Mark expressly fixes our Lord's crossing the sea of Tiberias to go over to the Gadarenes, to the evening of the day, on which he spake the parable of the sower: so that, on finishing his parables, he sailed thither, and left the people to reflect on them.

V. 54—58. On another occasion, Jesus went to Nazareth, (called his own country, because he was there brought up,) and he taught in the synagogue; thus giving the inhabitants an additional opportunity of hearing his doctrine, and seeking the benefit of those miracles, concerning which they must have heard many surprising accounts. (*Notes, Luke* iv. 16—30.) And indeed the authority and wisdom, with which he spake, astonished his former neighbours; and led them to enquire, where he had obtained this wisdom and miraculous power. But, as they were acquainted with his low parentage, education, and manner of life; and knew that he had neither been educated under

P

56 And his sisters, are they not all with us? Whence then hath this *man* all these things? **57** And **b** they were offended in him. But Jesus said unto them, 'A prophet is not without honour, save in his own country, and in his own house. **58** And **d** he did not many mighty works there, because of their unbelief.

---

the scribes, nor authorized by the chief priests; they perversely objected those things to him, which were in fact the most evident proofs that he was sent by God.—Probably, they did not know, that he was born at Bethlehem, and of the family of David.—By comparing several passages in the gospels, (*Marg. Ref.* y—a,) it appears, that Mary, the wife of Cleophas, was the sister of Mary, the mother of Jesus; and that James and Joses were her sons. According to the common way of speaking, being such near relations, they are called brethren, especially as they seem to have lived much together; and it is probable, that the others here mentioned were either the children of Cleophas and Mary, or some others standing in the same near relation to our Lord. But some think that they were Joseph's children by a former wife. They were, however, well known at Nazareth, as persons in a low and poor condition, who were nearly related to Jesus; and this proved an occasion of stumbling to the proud and prejudiced inhabitants.—On this occasion our Lord observed, that "a " prophet was not without honour, except in his own " country, and among his own relations." Those, who have most known and conversed with the man, are least disposed to respect the prophet. He is thought to take too much upon him, in authoritatively addressing their consciences; they are displeased with his pretensions, and the credit which he acquires; and various circumstances of no importance, respecting his former occupations and appearance, recur to their memory, and prejudice them against all he says.—The unbelief of the Nazarenes, however, precluded them from sharing the benefit of our Lord's power and grace: few came to him for healing, and he did not think it consistent with his wisdom and dignity, to obtrude his miracles and presence upon them: so he retired, and left them to their prejudices; and, as far as we can find, he went among them no more. (*Notes, Mark* vi. 1—6.)

Country. (54) Πατρίδα· (a πατηρ :) 57. *Mark* vi. 1. 4. *Luke* iv. 23, 24. *John* iv. 44. *Heb.* xi. 14.—*Carpenter's.* (55) Τε τεκτονος. *Mark* vi. 3. Not elsewhere in the New Testament.—Τεκτων σιδηρε, 1 *Sam.* xiii. 19 : ξυλων και λιθων, 2 *Sam.* v. 11 : χαλχε, 1 *Kings* vii. 14. Τεκτοσι, 2 *Kings* xxii. 6. *Sept.* In general, *an artificer,* or *worker :* but like εη, to which it usually answers in the LXX, it is used καΐ εξοχην for a *worker in wood,* a *carpenter.*—*Offended.* (57) Εσκανδαλιζοντο. See on *v.* 29, 30.—*They were offended in him.*] ' They considered him as guilty of an ... ' usurpation, in assuming the character of a prophet, much ' more in aspiring to the title of the Messiah.' *Campbell.*

PRACTICAL OBSERVATIONS.

V. 1—17.

Our divine Teacher orders every thing in that manner, which best tends to the edification of the humble, teachable, and attentive disciple; but at the same time he leaves occasions of falling, in the way of the careless, the cap-

tious, the self-sufficient, and presumptuous.—We not only have his word to instruct us; but, when we meet with difficulties, we are allowed and required to call on him in private, for the teaching of his Holy Spirit: and to those, who thus wait on him, " it is given to know the " mysteries of the kingdom of heaven," which are concealed from all others under an impenetrable veil. We should therefore fear above all things an unteachable disposition, the result of ignorance, pride, and the carnal mind. To persons of this temper, the things of the Spirit of God appear foolishness; and by deriding, reviling, and opposing them, they provoke the Lord to leave them under the power of strong delusions, to their final perdition. Such men may have excellent abilities, and profound erudition, and many valuable advantages : but not having humble faith and love, all else will soon be taken from them, or turn to their unspeakable detriment. But the meanest and most illiterate believer is happy : his senses and faculties are blessed, they are employed to good purpose, and are " instruments of righteousness unto God." Under the Christian dispensation, we all enjoy that blessed light, and hear that joyful sound, which " prophets and " righteous men" of old desired to see and hear, and were not able : and if we have grace to make a proper use of our advantages, more knowledge and wisdom will be given us, and we shall have abundance. But do any desire these blessings, who cannot ascertain that they have received them ? Let them wait on the Lord for his teaching, and search the scriptures with prayer : let them not close their own eyes and ears, and then God will not close them; but let them remember that the purposes and promises of God are perfectly consistent, and that " every one that asketh, " receiveth." As for those who harden themselves against the truth : they can have no reason to complain, if God leave them to their perverse choice; till they be so blinded, that they can neither see, nor hear, nor be converted and healed.

V. 18—23.

The good seed of divine truth should be sown in every part of the field, all over the world; though it can only bear fruit upon the good ground. But let all, who presume to preach, be careful to sow the "word of the " kingdom," and to keep this good seed free from every intermixture : let them sow it liberally, and " be instant " in season, out of season," " whether men will hear or " forbear." For these things they are accountable; but not for success, except as they prevent it by their own misconduct : nor should they be surprised or discouraged, if many hear in vain, or to bad purpose ; for this was the case, when our Lord himself condescended to preach the gospel.—We should, however, especially look to ourselves, that we may ascertain what sort of hearers we are. We ought to beg of God to prepare our hearts, as good ground ; to teach us the value of his word ; to deliver our minds from pride and prejudice ; to preserve us from wandering

P 2

CHAP. XIV

Herod supposes Jesus to be John the Baptist risen from the dead, 1, 2. An account of John's imprisonment and death, through the resentment of Herod, Herodias, and her daughter, 3—12. Jesus departs to a desert place, and miraculously feeds the multitudes, 13—21. He retires to a mountain to pray, having sent the disciples away in a ship, 22—24. He comes to them walking on the sea, 25—27. Peter obtains leave to come on the water, begins to sink, and is preserved, and rebuked, 28—31. Jesus enters the ship, the storm ceases, and the disciples worship him as the Son of God, 32, 33. Landing at Gennesaret, he heals all the sick, who touch the hem of his garment, 34—36.

thoughts and vain imaginations; and to impress us with a serious and earnest desire to learn of him, all those things which pertain to salvation. For want of thus " giving " earnest heed," many hearers of the pure gospel " receive " the seed by the way-side:" thus Satan immediately catches it out of their hearts, and no good effect can follow. (*Note, Heb.* ii. 1—4.) Though this may not be altogether the case with us, yet we should be humbled by the recollection, that it too often is, and has been so. It is the great object of our enemy to deprive us of the blessing, totally or in part; and it ought to be our's to disappoint him. Having therefore gone to hear the word, with a mind prepared by recollection and devotion; and having attended on it with serious and humble reverence; we should seek to preserve it in our hearts, by retirement, meditation, prayer, or pious conversation.—But there are more plausible paths to ruin, than those of the careless, the infidel, or the profligate: numbers of those, who are greatly affected, and who are led to make a high profession of the gospel, with much confidence, joy, and violent zeal, are found by the event to have " had no root in themselves:" for without deep humiliation, reverential fear of God, and a solemn sense of eternal things, the evil of sin, and the lost estate of our souls; high affections resemble the joy of a madman, who deems all the magnificent edifices which he sees to be his own. Nothing can so grow in an unhumbled heart, as to stand the noon-day sun of tribulation and persecution, in all their varied forms: many, when thus tried, go out from among God's people, because not of them; whilst some upright Christians are ready to stumble at the truths of God, because such men seem to be exceptions to them. But if this superficial religion will not stand present trials, how will it endure in the day of judgment?—Let us, however, beware of the *thorns*, as well as of the *rock:* many a man has " a name to live," whom God sees to be dead in sin; many deep convictions, and serious purposes are choked by " the love of the " world, and the things that are in the world:" (*Note,* 1 *John* ii. 15—17:) thus no fruit is brought to perfection. Such professed Christians often draw their hope of heaven from the gospel; but their present comfort is derived from the world. The kingdom of God and his righteousness are placed *last:* (*Note,* vi. 32, 33:) and the getting, keeping, and spending of deceitful riches, or anxiety about secular affairs, rob them of their time, and at last of their souls; for unless the gospel render us fruitful, it will never bring us to glory. Let us then continually watch and pray against these fatal delusions; and keep at a distance from every degree of this pernicious attachment to worldly objects. Let us be instant in prayer for that " honest and " good heart," which is the only soil, in which the good seed will spring up, and grow, and ripen with a rich increase. This is the grand distinction betwixt the Christian and all other men: and the preachers of the gospel do as

much towards ensuring success to their labours, when employed in earnest prayer to the Lord thus to prepare the people's hearts for the seed, as when faithfully dispensing the word of life; and in this part of the work, all that love the souls of men may afford them effectual assistance. Nor let it be forgotten, that there are different degrees of fruitfulness among true Christians, to which their own present comfort, and future glory, will be proportioned: we should therefore " abide in Christ, that we may bring " forth much fruit," " even an hundred fold," that God may be glorified, and that all may know whose disciples we are. (*Note, John* xv. 6—8.)

V. 24—30. 36—43.

Besides the dangers to which men are exposed, through the deceitfulness of their own hearts, and the subtlety of Satan, even where the good seed is sown; there is also another sort of dangers, from the bad seed, which the enemy is continually endeavouring to sow in the same field. Though the servants be watchful, this enemy will find time to work; but his chief advantage arises from their drowsiness, and unsuspecting inattention. No wonder then that so many spring up in the visible church, whose pernicious heresies, unchristian spirit, or immoral conduct, prove them to " be the children of the wicked one." The enemies of the gospel indeed charge all their pernicious sentiments, and enormous crimes, on the truth itself: this answers Satan's end; for many are thus prejudiced, and perish. But the servants of Christ know that they spring from seed of another kind; and often wonder, as well as grieve, to find tares where wheat was sown. This brings them to complain to their Lord, and to ask counsel from him; and he shews them, " that an enemy hath done " this."—It is indeed our duty to counteract, by all proper means, the effects of these fatal delusions; yet we may be too officious, in attempting to make a complete separation. This exceeds our ability; and if we attempt it, we shall be in danger of rooting up the wheat along with the tares. Thus the devil has often succeeded, in bringing in furious controversies and accursed persecutions, under pretence of opposing and eradicating heresies; to the unspeakable detriment and reproach of the Christian church. Indeed, both must in general be left to grow together unto the harvest; and perfect purity must not be expected till we come to heaven. At length, however, an awful separation will be made: and then the angels of our glorious Judge will gather out of his kingdom " all that offend and " work iniquity, and cast them into a furnace of fire, where " shall be wailing and gnashing of teeth." What a dreadful event will this be to the hypocrite and the deceiver, who will perish miserably with all those, who have been stumbled, prejudiced, deceived, and hardened by them! But, what a blessed event will this be for the true believer, who will then " shine forth as the sun in the kingdom of his

[a] Mark vi. 14—16.
vii. 1b. Luke ix.
7—9. xxli. 31.
32. xviii. 8—12.
15. Acts iv. 27.
[b] Luke iii. 1.
[c] xi. 11. xvi. 14. Mark viii. 28. John x. 41.

AT that time [a] Herod the [b] tetrarch heard of the fame of Jesus,

2 And said unto his servants, [c] This is John the Baptist; he is risen from the dead; and therefore mighty works [*] do shew forth themselves in him.   [*] Or, are wrought by him.

"Father!" May this be our happy case, and may increasing numbers consider these things for their good!

V. 31—35. 44—50.

In attempting to do good by scriptural means, and in dependence on the grace of our Lord, we have firm ground of hope, that from small beginnings a large increase will arise, perhaps after our decease: the grain of mustard-seed, which we have sown and deemed to be lost, may at length spring up and become a tree; the leaven, which lay inactive in the hearts of the hearers, may be gradually diffusing its influence, till the whole lump be leavened; and thus several may hereafter appear to be cast into the very mould, and transformed into the very temper, of the gospel, of whom perhaps we have now but faint hopes, or with whom we have no acquaintance. We ought not, therefore, either in this case, or in respect of individuals, or ourselves, " to despise the day of small things." (*Note*, *Zech.* iv. 8—10.) As eternal life is set before us in the scripture, like " a treasure hid in a field;" may we highly prize and diligently search that sacred book, that we may become acquainted with its invaluable contents, and do what we can to communicate the blessing to all others likewise. Let us also be very circumspect, that we do not come short of the felicity to which it directs us. And as all the salvation of God is laid up in Christ, our great Prophet, Priest, and King; let us fix our attention on him, as the great subject of the sacred word; and determine by the grace of God, to part with all that we have, that we may be made possessors of this inestimable treasure. What worthless pebbles are all worldly things, compared with this " Pearl of great price!" Why then should we hesitate to give up all for him? Why not count all loss, that we may win Christ? He who is willing to do this, will never come short of his Salvation, though he may often fear it; but he that prefers any thing to Christ, will not obtain his " unsearchable riches," though he may often be confident that he shall. Numbers of this description are enclosed in the gospel-net; and besides those multitudes of professed Christians, concerning whose character no competent judge can be deceived; the " fishers of men," will find themselves mistaken in some, of whom they hoped better things, when the grand discrimination shall be made. Yet they have abundant encouragement to go on with patience and diligence in their work: for " he that " winneth souls is wise;" and in this respect, they will also find at last, that " their labour was not in vain in the " Lord."

V. 51—58.

We should often imagine to ourselves, that our Teacher enquires of us, whether we " have understood all these things." And we should endeavour to be able, on good grounds to answer him, " Yea, Lord." If we would be " scribes " instructed unto the kingdom of heaven," we must be always learners. Our place is at Christ's feet; we must daily learn the old lessons over again, and new lessons also: and we must seek to have an increasing fund of knowledge and wisdom, the result of study, experience, and observation; that we may render old subjects attractive and interesting, by new elucidations and applications.

Let none wonder if faithful and able ministers are regarded with contempt and enmity, even where they labour most to do good, or where they might be supposed to possess the greatest influence. Men are seldom disposed to be taught, by their neighbours or relations, or by their equals or inferiors. Even the wisdom, power, holiness, and beneficence of Christ, did not preserve him from the most illiberal prejudices and contempt, in his own city and among his own relations. It is a general case, that the truths spoken are at first disregarded, in proportion as the speaker is known, even where there is no reason for it in his character and conduct; for the carnal heart is glad of any pretence for rejecting the spiritual word of God. Thus, whilst the servant of the Lord loses his labour, and is treated with contempt, men lose the benefit of the gospel, yea, lose their own souls; and the power and grace of the Saviour are of no avail as to them, " because of their unbe- " lief."

NOTES.

CHAP. XIV. V. 1, 2. (*Marg. Ref.*) John was not cast into prison, till some considerable time after Jesus had entered on his publick ministry. (*Notes*, *John* iii. 22— 36. iv. 1—4.) It is supposed, that John lay above a year in prison; and some time must have passed after his death, before Herod could conclude that he was risen again, to perform the miracles of which he heard. We may therefore suppose that more years had elapsed after Christ's baptism, than harmonizers in general can make out.—Herod is called " the tetrarch," and afterwards " the king" (9). He was the son of Herod the great, whose dominions were divided into four parts among his sons after his decease; as the word *tetrarch* implies: Judea, one fourth in this division, soon fell under the rule of a Roman governor as a province of that empire; and other alterations shortly took place. Herod, however, who was surnamed Antipas, was allowed to hold his tetrarchy; in which he was as much a king, as his father had been, only his dominions were smaller. Some think, that he was a Sadducee, because what is called the leaven of the Sadducees, is elsewhere called the leaven of Herod. (xvi. 6. *Mark* viii. 15.)—It is most wonderful, that Herod and his courtiers should not have known of our Lord's preaching and miracles, at an earlier period; especially as he spent most of his time in Galilee.—Some think, that Herod had been absent at Rome, during the former part of our Lord's ministry; but if this were so, his nobles and counsellors had not all been absent likewise. Others think, that he at this time attended to the report, because Christ had just sent forth his disciples, to work miracles in his name.— But the supposition, that Jesus was John the Baptist risen from the dead, implies that Herod had never heard of him before, or known that such a person existed; for how could he, who had lived about thirty years in Galilee, be John the Baptist, who a short time before had been put

P 4

d Iv. 12. Mark vi.
17. Luke iii. 19.
20. John iii. 23.
24.
e Luke iii. 1.
f Lev. xviii. 16.
xx. 21. Deut.
xxv. 5.
g Sam. xii. 7.
1 Kings xvi. 19.
2 Chr. xxvi. 18.
19. Prov. xxviii.
1. Is. viii. 20.
Mark vi. 18.
Acts xxiv. 24, 25.

3 For 'Herod had laid hold on John, and bound him, and put *him* in prison for Herodias' sake, 'his brother Philip's wife.

4 For John said unto him, 'It is not lawful for thee to have her.

5 And 'when he would have put

f Mark vi. 19, 20. xiv. 1, 2. Acts iv. 21. v. 26.

him to death, he feared the multitude, 'because they counted him as a pro-phet.

6 But when Herod's 'birth-day was kept, 'the daughter of Herodias 'danced 'before them, and pleased Herod.

h xxi. 26. 32.
Mark xi.30—32.
Luke xx. 6.
i Gen. xl. 20.
Esth. i. 2—9. ii.
18. Dan. v. 1—4.
Hos. vii. 5, 6.
k Mark xi. 21—23.
xxii. 24.
l Esth. i. 10—12.
* Gr. in the midst.

to death? In fact, nothing can solve the difficulty, but the consideration of the general disregard which persons in high rank shew to the concerns of religion; and the astonishing ignorance in which most of them remain, of what goes forward in that respect.—At this time, however, the fame of our Lord's miracles was so widely circulated, the subject attracted so general attention, and so many opinions prevailed concerning it; that Herod, inattentive as he had hitherto been, could no longer remain in ignorance, but was constrained to form a judgment on these extraordinary events. Thus circumstanced, neither his immoral character, nor his Sadducean principles, could preserve him from dismay, on recollecting his conduct in beheading John the Baptist; and, without much examination, he was led to concur with those, who said it was John risen from the dead. John had indeed wrought no miracle; but Herod, supposing that God had raised him to life again, concluded that he had also endued him with miraculous powers, to confirm his ministry. Nor could this haughty prince conceal, from his own servants, his terrors and convictions; fearing probably that John, thus risen, would soon come and avenge his death on his murderers.

Tetrarch. (1) Τέραρχης. (Ex τετρας, quaternarius numerus, à τισσαρις vel τετλαρις quatuor, et αρχη imperium.) 'He 'who rules over the fourth part of any kingdom, with un-'limited and royal power, though he does not use the 'name of king. ...Thessaly, before the times of Philip of 'Macedon, had been divided into four provinces, each of 'which was called a Tetrarchy.' Schleusner.—Mighty works do shew forth themselves. (2) 'Αι ὃυ αμιις ενεργυσιν.—'Δυνα-'μις, potentia, facultas, vis efficiendi aliquid; et æque de 'facultatibus ingenii ac de viribus corporis usurpatur.' Schleusner.—It is rendered virtue; Mark v. 30. Luke vi. 19. viii. 46; power; Matt. xxii. 29. Acts vi. 8. x. 38. 1 Cor. v. 4. 2 Cor. xii. 9. xiii. 4, et mult. al. and mighty work; Mark v. 5.—The plural is frequently used for the mighty works themselves, wrought by this power: but here it appears to have the same meaning as the singular, viz. the power, or energies, by which, as Herod had heard, Jesus performed his miracles. See Matt. vii. 22. xi. 20. xiii. 54. Acts ii. 22.—Ενηργυσιν does not seem to signify simply, " do shew forth themselves." Ενεργεω, (ex εν et εργον opus,) neither signifies " to shew forth," nor can it be properly rendered either passively or reciprocally, according to the use of it in the New Testament. It is transitive or absolute; 1 Cor. xii. 6. 11. Gal. ii. 8. iii. 5. Eph. i. 11. 20. ii. 2.—These are the only instances in which the active verb occurs, except the parallel passage, Mark vi. 14.—" These powers " (which Herod had heard were displayed by Jesus in his miracles, and which he supposed to be possessed by John as risen from the dead,) " efficaciously work by him," or " are active in him." Herod as a Sadducee, under the momentary impression,

lost sight of his principles, that there was no resurrection, nor angel, nor spirit, into whatever agency he ultimately resolved the δυναμις, powers, which wrought the effects.

V. 3—5. The Evangelist, having mentioned Herod's opinion respecting Jesus, made a digression to relate John's imprisonment and death. We learn from a parallel passage, (Notes, Mark vi. 14—29,) that Herod had taken much notice of John, and attended to his instructions with apparent satisfaction, and " done many things" at his instance, regarding him as a holy man of God: but this did not satisfy John, so long as he retained Herodias, his brother's wife.—Josephus says, that Herodias was granddaughter to Herod the great : and consequently, she was niece both to her former husband Philip, and to Herod with whom she at this time lived. Herod had divorced his own wife in order to take her; and her husband Philip was still living, as well as the daughter whom he had by her. So that no connexion could be more contrary to the law of God, and to all decorum, than this was. John therefore, being a prophet, and no courtier, plainly reproved Herod, having been brought near to him, on whom otherwise he perhaps would not have obtruded himself; and declared that it was not lawful for him to retain Herodias : and it is probable, many would think, that he should for a time at least, have connived at this irregularity; as kings and princes generally deem themselves privileged in these respects. But John knew nothing of reserves or exceptions, being an Elijah in intrepidity and faithfulness. His conduct, therefore, greatly offended Herod, and Herodias still more : so that John was cast into prison, and by the instigation of Herodias, (who was another Jezebel,) Herod was desirous of putting him to death; and that contrary to his own conscience, for he feared him as a holy and righteous man. He was, however, restrained by fear of the people, who regarded John as a prophet; and Herod dreaded lest they should make an insurrection, should he proceed to extremities. These motives induced him for a time to resist the importunity of Herodias, though he kept John still in prison: while Herodias retained her malice, and waited her opportunity of wreaking her vengeance on him, considering his reproof of Herod as an insult on her character; as well as interfering with her ambitiou and inclination.—When he would. (5) Θελων, purposing, willing.

V. 6, 7. At length Herod celebrated his birth-day, entertaining his nobles with great magnificence; and Herodias's daughter, (whose name was Salome, and who probably possessed all exterior accomplishments,) contrary to general custom, came and danced before all the company, in order to honour the guests and grace the entertainment. (Note, Esth. i. 10—12.) This so delighted Herod, who might be heated with wine, that he rashly and impiously promised her, with repeated oaths, that he would give her

7 Whereupon [m]he promised with an oath to give her whatsoever she would ask.

8 And she, [n]being before instructed of her mother, said, [o]Give me here John Baptist's head in [p]a charger.

9 And [q]the king was [r]sorry: nevertheless for [s]the oath's sake, and them which sat with him at meat, he commanded it to be given her.

10 And he sent, [t]and beheaded John in the prison.

11 And his head was brought in a charger, [u]and given to the damsel: and she brought it to her mother.

12 And his disciples came, and [x]took up the body, and buried it, and went and told Jesus.

13 ¶ When [y] Jesus heard of it, he departed thence by ship into a desert place apart: and when the people had heard thereof, they followed him on foot out of the cities.

14 And Jesus [z]went forth, and saw a great multitude, [a]and was moved with compassion toward them, and he healed their sick.

15 And when it was evening, [b]his disciples came to him, saying, This is

---

whatever she asked, though equal in value to half his kingdom. Thus profusely would he reward a worthless dance; whilst a prison and death were the recompence of " the man of God," who honestly sought the salvation of his soul!

V. 8—11. On this proposal, Salome retired to consult her mother, how the most advantage might be made of it: and, revenge getting the better of all other passions, Herodias persuaded and urged her daughter (who must have been reluctant to give up all those objects, which would be desirable to her youthful mind,) to demand the head of John the Baptist without delay, in a charger, or large dish! When Herod heard this strange request, he was sorry: probably not so much from desire of preserving John's life, as from fear of consequences, and checks of conscience; and as some think, from considering the execution as a bad omen on his birth-day. But, though he was in some sense sorry, that the demand had been made so suddenly and on this occasion; yet, pleading his oath and his regard for his guests, he commanded the immediate execution of John. Herod's oath was rash and profane in the extreme; and when it was found to involve such consequences, it became absolutely unlawful to observe it: he ought to have repented of his impiety, and with abhorrence to have rejected Salome's application. Nor was it very honourable to his guests, to suppose that they would be offended, if he refused to murder this holy man, through a rash engagement at a banquet, in their presence. Had Salome demanded the execution of some esteemed chieftain among them, who had displeased Herodias, they would doubtless have arisen to oppose the demand with one accord: (Note, 1 Sam. xiv. 45, 46:) but probably John was obnoxious to many of them, as well as to Herodias. Accordingly he was suddenly and speedily dismissed to his eternal rest; and his head, reeking in its blood, was brought as a strange present to Salome, and by her given to her mother, who is reported to have treated it with indignant barbarity. It was customary for the heads of criminals to be thus brought to those who condemned them, in order to certify that they were really put to death; and this horrid spectacle could only gratify the malevolence even of a female! Thus by a mysterious providence, this most eminent man of God was cut off, in the prime of life and fitness for usefulness, to gratify the malice of an incestuous adulteress, to recompense the vain exhibition of a giddy young female, by the orders of a rash, perhaps intoxicated prince, and to humour the companions of his revels! But they could not long enjoy this impious and cruel triumph. It is recorded that Salome had her head cut off by the ice, that was, Herod was shortly after engaged in a disastrous war on account of Herodias; he was at length expelled his territories, and they both died in exile in a distant land: and, as it is recorded, hated by and hating one another.

Being before instructed. (8) Προβιβασθεισα (προβιβαζω protrudo, ex προ et βιβαζω, *venire facio:*) *præmonita, instigata. Acts* xix. 33. Not elsewhere in the New Testament.—*Ex.* xxxv. 28. *Deut.* vi. 7. *Sept.—In a charger.*] Επι πινακι, *patinâ.* 11. *Mark* vi. 25. 28: rendered *platter; Luke* xi. 39. —*For the oath's sake.* (9) Δια τις ορκις, plural—*oaths* : so *Mark* vi. 26.

V. 12. When John's disciples heard of his death, they came, and were allowed to take his body: and, having honourably buried it, they went to inform Jesus of what had taken place, and probably many of those concerned became his followers.

V. 13, 14. This seems to refer, not to our Lord's hearing of John's death, but of Herod's supposition, that he was John the Baptist risen from the dead: being a continuation of the subject from the second verse.—About the same time the apostles returned to him; (*Marg. Ref.* y ;) and Jesus, to avoid observation, as well as to give them some relaxation, departed in a small vessel into an unfrequented place, on the shore of the sea of Tiberias. But the people, hearing which way he bent his course, followed him by land, to a great distance from their cities and villages. And when he saw them, he did not object to the intrusion, but compassionately healed all the sick persons, whom they had been able to bring along with them; as well as taught the people many things. (*Notes, Mark* vi. 30—46.)

On foot. (13) Πεζη (*subaudi* οδφ a πεζος.) A journey made by land, and not in a ship; for it takes in other ways of travelling by land, as well as walking. *Mark* vi. 33. Not elsewhere in the New Testament.—*Sick.* (14) Αρρωςας. (Ex α priv. et ρωννυμι, *corroboro.*) *Mark* vi. 5. 13. xvi. 18. 1 *Cor.* xi. 30.

V. 15—21. This miracle is recorded by all the evan-

a desert place, and the time is now past: send the multitude away, that they may go into the villages, and buy themselves victuals.

16 But Jesus said unto them, They need not depart; give ye them to eat.

17 And they say unto him, We have here but five loaves, and two fishes.

18 He said, Bring them hither to me.

19 And he commanded the multitude to sit down on the grass, and took the five loaves, and the two fishes, and, looking up to heaven, he blessed, and brake, and gave the loaves to his disciples, and the disciples to the multitude.

20 And they did all eat, and were filled: and they took up of the fragments that remained twelve baskets full.

21 And they that had eaten were about five thousand men, beside women and children.

22 ¶ And straightway Jesus constrained his disciples to get into a ship, and to go before him unto the other side, while he sent the multitudes away.

23 And when he had sent the multitudes away, he went up into a mountain apart to pray: and when the evening was come, he was there alone.

24 But the ship was now in the midst of the sea, tossed with waves; for the wind was contrary.

25 And in the fourth watch of the night, Jesus went unto them, walking on the sea.

26 And when the disciples saw him walking on the sea, they were troubled, saying, It is a spirit; and they cried out for fear.

27 But straightway Jesus spake unto them, saying, Be of good cheer; it is I, be not afraid.

---

gelists, without any material variation. (Mark vi. 35—44. Luke ix. 12—17.—Notes, John vi. 1—21.)—When Jesus had taught the multitude, till the day began to decline; some of the apostles stated that, as the time was past, it would be proper to dismiss the people, that they might reach the neighbouring villages before night, and thus procure lodging and victuals. But Jesus answered, that they need not depart; for the disciples ought to give them food.—On examination, they found, that no more than five loaves, (barley-loaves,) and two fishes, could be procured for the whole company. But Jesus ordered this small provision to be brought; and having, with up-lifted eyes, returned thanks, and prayed for a blessing on it, which we may suppose to have been his constant custom; (Marg. Ref. g;) he began to break and distribute the bread and the fishes to the disciples, that they might dispense it to the multitude: and it is probable, that the portion given to each, continued to increase, by his creating power, as they dispensed it, till the whole multitude was sufficed! He then ordered them to gather together the fragments, that nothing might be lost; when they found they had twelve baskets full left, which seems to have been far more than they had at first: and, on these broken pieces of barley-bread and dried fish, we may suppose that Jesus and his disciples made afterwards many a contented and thankful meal.—As the men were placed on the grass, by hundreds and by fifties, (Note, Mark vi. 30—46, v. 40,) it appeared that five thousand men had thus been fed, besides women and children; who probably were arranged in a separate company.—' There was more real grandeur ' displayed by the Master of this feast, than by Ahasuerus ' in that royal feast, which was intended to shew " the ' " riches of his glorious kingdom and the honour of ' " his excellent majesty." ' Henry.

To sit down. (19) Ανακλιθηναι, reclinare, discumbere. viii. 11.—Ανακλινω, reclinare facio; Luke ii. 7. ix. 14, 15. xii. 37.—Were filled. (20) Εχορλασθησαν See on v. 6.—Baskets.] Κοφινας. See on xv. 37.

V. 22—24. (Marg. Ref.) The multitudes, concluding Jesus to be the promised Messiah, purposed to make him their King; (John vi. 15;) and as the apostles might be disposed to concur, our Lord constrained them to put to sea without him: he then dismissed the people, who retired quietly to their own homes. Instead however of resting after his fatigues, he himself retired to a mountain to pray. (Marg. Ref. n.) He had no sins to be pardoned or subdued: but he had manifold and immense services, temptations, and sufferings before him, through which he was to pass, as Man, in dependence on the power, truth, and love of God; he had the cause of his disciples, and that of his church to plead; his delight was in communion with the Father; and he acted as our Surety and Example. So that when the evening was come, or the day closed, he was on a mountain alone; and there he continued, during the greatest part of the night. In the mean time the disciples met with tempestuous weather and a contrary wind. —' We must sail even through mighty tempests; and ' Christ will never forsake us, so that we go whither he ' hath commanded us.' Beza.

Tossed. (24) Βασανιζομενον· viii.·6. 29. Mark v. 7. vi. 48. Luke viii. 28. 2 Pet. ii. 8. Rev. xi. 10.—' Βασανος· ' proprie : examen quodcunque : ... speciatim ; examen metal-' lorum, et inquisitio per tormenta.' Schleusner.

V. 25—27. The fourth watch of the night began three hours before sun-rise; and during these three hours, Jesus came to the disciples, perhaps after day-break.—' Note, ' that to walk on the sea is made the property of God, ' " who alone spreadeth the heavens, and treadeth upon

28 And Peter answered him and said, Lord, if it be thou, ᵇ bid me come unto thee on the water.

29 And he said, Come. And when Peter was come down out of the ship, ᶠ he walked on the water, to go to Jesus.

30 But ᵍ when he saw the wind ʰ boisterous, he was afraid; and beginning to sink, he cried, saying, ᵃ Lord, save me.

31 And immediately Jesus ᵇ stretch-ed forth his hand, ᶜ and caught him, and said unto him, ᵈ O thou of little faith, wherefore didst thou ᵉ doubt?

32 And when they were ᶠ come into the ship, the wind ceased.

33 Then they that were in the ship came and ᵍ worshipped him, saying, ʰ Of a truth thou art the Son of God.

34 ¶ And ⁱ when they were gone over, they came into the land of ᵏ Gennesaret.

35 And when the men of that place

' " the waves of the sea." Job ix. 8.' Whitby.—' The pic-
' ture of two feet, walking on the sea, was an Egyptian
' hieroglyphick for an impossible thing.' Doddridge. It
was, no doubt, an attestation, that He was the God of
nature, the Lord of the creation ; and also an emblem of
his power over all the troubles and persecutions which disquiet his church.—The disciples, however, cried out for
excess of terror ; supposing that what they saw was either
the apparition of some deceased person, foreboding evil,
or an apostate spirit coming to do them some mischief.—
' That the Jews had then an opinion of hurtful spirits
' walking in the night is evident from the seventy, who
' render, " from the pestilence walking in darkness," (Ps.
' xci. 6.) from the fear of the devils, that walk in the night.'
Whitby.—To allay their terror Jesus spake to the disciples
with his usual voice, assuring them that it was he, their
Lord and Friend.

They were troubled. (26) Eἰαραχθησαν. (Ταρασσω, agito,
turbo ; to put into commotion as water is moved. John v. 4.
7.—Is. xxiv. 14. Ex. xxxii. 7. Sept.—' Metaphorice ad
' omnem vehementiorem animi commotionem et perturba-
' tionem transfertur.' Schleusner.) ii. 3. Luke i. 12. xxiv.
38. John xi. 33. xii. 27. xiii. 21. xiv. 1. Gal. i. 7.—A spirit.]
Φανΐασμα* (à φανΐαζω apparere facio : φανΐαζομαι, appareo,
Heb. xii. 21 : quod à φαινω, ostendo:) spectrum; an apparition. Mark vi. 49. Not elsewhere in the New Testament.
V. 28—32. Peter, from the first, appears a man of
integrity, who had very exalted thoughts of Jesus, and a
cordial affection to him ; but of a sanguine temper, and
not deeply acquainted with his own heart : he was therefore always most forward to speak, to propose, to object,
and attempt. When he saw Jesus walking on the sea, he
found himself excited to a very high confidence, and he
desired permission to come to him on the water ; probably,
expecting a commendation of the strength of his faith.
But our Lord, to show him his weakness, and to teach all
his disciples many useful lessons, bade him come ; and
Peter without hesitation attempted to walk on the unstable
waves ! Indeed, as long as his faith was fixed upon the
divine power of Christ, he was actually enabled to do it ;
but the boisterousness of the elements soon drew off his
attention, and staggered his faith, and then he began to
sink. Yet still he relied on his Lord for deliverance in
this extreme danger ; and, in answer to his application,
Jesus caught him by the hand, and brought him safe to
the vessel, at the same time rebuking him, as one of little

faith.—' By faith we tread under our feet even the tempests
' themselves ; but yet by the virtue ' (or power) ' of Christ,
' who helpeth that virtue, which he of his mercy hath
' given.' Beza.—Peter's doubting did not relate to his own
acceptance, or final salvation, but to the power of Christ
to preserve him from sinking amidst the violence of the
storm. (Note, viii. 23—27.)
To sink. (30) Καΐαποϊιζεσθαι, in mare submergi. (Ex.
καΐα, et ποϊιζω, quod à ποϊος, mare.) xviii. 6. Not elsewhere in the New Testament. (31) O thou of little faith.]
Ολιγοπιστε. vi. 30. viii. 26. xvi. 8. Luke xii. 28. In no other
place in the New Testament.—Didst thou doubt?] Εδιΐασας;
(ex δις bis, et ἱϊημι, vel ῥαω sto.) ' Properly : to stand where
' two ways meet, not knowing which to follow.' Schleusner.
xxviii. 17. Not elsewhere in the New Testament.—Ceased.
(32) Εκοπασεν. Mark iv. 39. vi. 51.—Gen. viii. 1. Jon. i.
11, 12. Sept.—' Proprie : quiesco, gravi defatigatus labore :
' à κοπος, labor.' Schleusner.
V. 33. The apostles, who seem to have been more impressed with this, than any of our Lord's preceding miracles, came with one accord, and prostrated themselves
before him in adoration, declaring that " of a truth he was
" the Son of God :" nor did he in the least decline the honour which they rendered to him.—It does not appear, that
any, except the apostles and those who belonged to the
vessel, were present. To suppose additional mariners, or
heathen mariners, on board this fisher-boat, the property
of fishermen, on an inland lake in Galilee ; in order to explain away this confession to Christ, as if it only meant a
son of a god, according to pagan notions, and as made by
the gentiles alone ; strikingly shews, how unwilling many
learned men are to admit the obvious conclusion : but
even, on this supposition, the words cannot admit that
construction. See Bp. Middleton on the Greek Article, p.
228—231. (Note, Mark xv. 34—39, v. 39.)
Thou art the Son of God.] Θεν υιος εἰ* both nouns without the article. xxvii. 43. Luke i. 35. Rom. i. 4.—' It is
' plain from these proofs, that the presence or absence of
' the article, does not determine the phrase to be used in
' a higher, or a lower sense.' Bp. Middleton on the Greek
Article, p. 181.
V. 34—36. ' Gennesaret is ... the title of the whole pro-
' vince, which contained in it the lake so called.' Hammond.—It is likely, that our Lord landed not far from
Capernaum, which some think was situated in the land of
Gennesaret, for he very soon went to that city. (John vi.

[l iv. 24. 25. Mark l. 28—34. il. 1. &c. iii. 8—10. vi. 56.] had knowledge of him, [¹] they sent out into all that country round about, and brought unto him all that were diseased;

36 And besought him that they might [m] only touch the [n] hem of his garment: and as many as touched were made [o] perfectly whole.

[m ix. 20, 21. Mark iii. 10. Luke vi. 19. Acts xix. 11, 12.
n xxiii. 5. Re. xxviii. 33, &c. Num. xv. 38, 39
o John vii. 23. Acts iii. 16. iv. 9, 10. 14—16.]

---

24. 59.) As the inhabitants had previous knowledge of Jesus, they flocked to him with their sick, who only desired leave to touch the *hem*, or *fringe*, of his garment; and, as this was done in faith and expectation, they were all immediately and perfectly healed.—' In that, that Christ ' healeth the sick, we are given to understand, that we ' must seek remedy for spiritual diseases at his hands; and ' that we are bound, not only to run ourselves, but also ' to bring others, to him.' *Beza.*

The *hem*. (36) Τε κρασπιδα. ix. 20. xxiii. 5. *Mark* vi. 56. *Luke* viii. 44.—*Num.* xv. 38, 39. *Deut.* xxii. 12. *Sept.* —*Were made perfectly whole.*] Διεσωθησαν. *Luke* vii. 3. *Acts* xxiii. 24. xxvii. 44. xxviii. 4. 1 *Pet.* iii. 20.—Comp. *Mark* vi. 56. Gr.

PRACTICAL OBSERVATIONS.

V. —5.

The terror and reproaches of conscience, which the most daring offenders cannot absolutely shake off, are both a demonstration of future judgment, and an anticipation of their future misery. Those who rebel against the light of the sacred oracles, and that of their own convictions; and who quarrel with religion and its ministers (contrary to their own better judgment,) for the sake of some favourite iniquity, which they are determined to retain; are frequently given up to judicical hardness of heart: and companions in licentiousness often tempt each other to revenge and murder.—When the servants of Christ, by faithful reproofs, interfere with the sensual, interested, or ambitious schemes of abandoned transgressors; their resentment sometimes proves more powerful even than their other most domineering passions: not only are *men* on these occasions regardless of equity, humanity, or truth; but *women* may be wrought up to such a pitch of fury and vengeance, as to thirst for blood, more than for any of those objects, to which they would otherwise be most addicted. Yet " the man of God," being fully aware of these consequences, must, if fairly called to the service, rebuke the greatest with all authority. In doubtful matters indeed, tenderness and caution, as well as prudence, are requisite: but when men in the most exalted stations live in evident violations of the divine law, and attempt to compromise by religious professions and observances, we must in no degree abet their delusion, by connivance or silence; but must fairly discharge our consciences, by declaring their conduct to be absolutely unlawful and inconsistent with all religion. They must be clearly warned, that this is "the " right hand, which they are required to cut off," if they would save their souls from hell. Indeed, the servants of God will thus incur the reproach of rudeness and bigotry; and, even from the more timid Christian, the censure of imprudence and want of courtesy: and if those, whom they thus counsel and reprove in love, do not profit by their faithful admonitions, they will certainly be offended, and perhaps exasperated to persecution. Yet the Lord will honour them and bear them out: nor can their most

powerful or enraged enemies proceed any further than he sees good: and even the fear of man, though it in many cases " bringeth a snare," often restrains wicked men from acting out all the evil that is conceived in their hearts.

V. 6—12.

When malice is harboured, opportunities will be found to gratify it: and we have little ground, from scripture, to favour those festive occasions, which are so highly celebrated in this vain world. (*Gen.* xl. *P. O. latter part.*) When reflection is dissipated, and conscience stupified by clamorous mirth, and when the passions are inflamed by sensual indulgence, men easily accede to insidious proposals, or form rash engagements; and, by yielding to the present emotion, ensure future and bitter repentance.—It seems a *general* rule among the rich and great, (though it has some honourable exceptions,) to reward men in an inverse proportion to the *value* of their services: so that no liberality is too great to be lavished on those, who minister to indulgence and dissipation; useful employments are far more parsimoniously encouraged; and endeavours to save their souls are recompensed by reproaches, contempt, or persecution.—The vile occasions and impious manner, in which oaths are often used, form also another proof of the contempt of God and religion which generally prevails. But, how lamentable is the case of those young persons, whose parents are their tempters to impiety and vice; and who are urged on to the greatest enormities, even by regard to parental counsel and authority! Yet thousands have been thus tutored for destruction by those, who were the instruments of their wretched existence, and whose guilt and punishment must be still immensely more aggravated.—Hasty measures are seldom wise: and could we see the predominant inclinations of many, who appear gentle, tender, and modest; we should be as much shocked, as if we had heard Salome's request, that the head of John might be brought to her in a charger.—Men may be sorry, in doing those things, which they are resolved to proceed with; for they grieve, that they must venture so much to gratify their inclinations: but they find, or pretend, some reason for getting over their scruples; and in this way they often more impose on themselves, than on others.— Rash oaths and bad companions are above all things to be avoided: but if men are entangled by them, they ought rather to infringe the sinful oath, and to affront their wicked associates, than to add sin to sin, and ruin their own souls. —The only wise God may see good, to let the lives of his most valuable servants fall a sacrifice to the humours and passions of his vilest enemies: but death can never find them unprepared, or prevent them from finishing their work and testimony; and the *manner* of leaving this world is of small moment, when the conscience is at peace, hope assured, and God their Comforter; the more speedily, the less their sufferings commonly are. But how different will be the hour of death, and the season of righteous retribution, to their impenitent persecutors!—Whoever is cut off,

Q

CHAP. XV.

Jesus reproves the Scribes and Pharisees, for setting their traditions above God's commandments; and exposes their hypocrisy, 1—9. He warns the people against their doctrine, and shews the source and nature of defilement, 10—20. He tries the faith, and heals the daughter, of a woman of Canaan, 21—28; heals great numbers at the sea of Galilee, 29—31; and again feeds the multitude by miracle, 32—39.

THEN [a] came to Jesus [b] Scribes and Pharisees, [c] which were of Jerusalem, saying,

2 Why do thy disciples [d] transgress the tradition of the elders? for they wash not their hands when they eat bread.

[a] Mark vii. 1, &c.
[b] v. 20. xxiii. 2.
[c] 1), &c. Luke v. 30. Acts xxiii. 9.
[c] Luke v. 17. 21.
[d] Mark vii. 2. Gal. i. 14. Col. ii. 8. 20—23. 1 Pet. i. 18.

---

the Lord Jesus still lives to take care of his cause; and when we have paid our tribute of respect and affection to his deceased servants, we must apply to him for support, and for directions about redoubled diligence in his service.

V. 13—21.

We should, indeed, give place to the resentment of persecutors, and shun ostentation: but we must not refuse to do good for fear of trouble or reproach, or for the sake of ease and indulgence.—In promoting the welfare of souls, we should have consideration and compassion for the bodies of men also, and endeavour to relieve their wants, and redress their inconveniences. Yet, even disciples are prone to excuse themselves, and to leave this to others, on various pretences, especially on that of poverty. But our Lord frequently, as it were, says to us, "They need not de-" part; give ye them to eat:" and a little, properly managed, and brought to him for his blessing, will go further than it is commonly supposed. He does not, in general, give his disciples a great fund to begin with: but he disposes them to make a proper use of a little; and when this is done in " the obedience of faith," it increases in their hands, and they are rather enriched, than impoverished, by liberality.—Those who serve Christ must not covet delicacies: he uses his power to *feed*, not to *feast*, his people: and whilst the rich recollect how he and his disciples fared, they should learn to spare from their own expenses to feed his poor; and the poor should learn to be contented with their mean food, which is seldom less luxurious, than that with which the Saviour of the world was pleased to satisfy his hunger.—We should all learn to thank God, and to crave his blessing, at our meals; and to avoid all profusion and waste: remembering that our Lord would not suffer the fragments of this miraculous provision to be lost; and considering that frugality is the proper source of liberality.—But we see also, in this miracle, an emblem of " the " Bread of life, which came down from heaven," to sustain our perishing souls: the provisions of his gospel appear to the carnal eye mean and scanty; yet they suffice for the whole multitude, who ' feed on him, in their hearts, ' by faith, with thanksgiving:' and his ministers may go forth confidently, to break the bread of life to their auditories; assured that it will increase in their hands, and supply the wants of all who hunger; and that whilst they feed others, they will also enrich themselves.

V. 22—36.

Even in those places, to which the Lord has evidently appointed us, we may expect storms and difficulties: but when we have not the sensible comfort of his presence amidst our conflicts, we may by faith realize his watchful eye over us, and his intercession continually made in our

behalf; and rest assured, that in due time he will come to our relief. We should enjoy far more comfort, did we more zealously copy his example, in the days of his humiliation; and were more careful not to omit fervent, constant prayer, on account of any engagements or interruptions.—We are sometimes troubled at those incidents, which denote our deliverance; but our Lord beholds our fears, and will make himself known for our encouragement: and, whatever danger or trouble may assail or alarm us, in life or at death, considering that all power is in our Redeemer's hands, and all events are ordered by his appointment, we may comfortably hear him say to us in every one of them, " It is I, be not afraid."—We find it hard to be very humble without dejection, or animated without self-complacency: but our faith is irregular, when we look off from him, and view the greatness of opposing difficulties and perils, we begin to fall: yet if we feel ourselves sinking ider trouble or temptation, or into destruction, and earnestly apply to him, he will stretch out the arm of his power to deliver us. But he will rebuke the weak believer, though he will not leave him to perish: and when we vainly expect a commendation of our wisdom and strength, we commonly are convicted of weakness and folly, and incur rebukes and chastisements.—We ought indeed to doubt, and to examine ourselves, whether we be true disciples or not: but we never should doubt the power of Christ to save and help all those, who call upon him.— The dangers, trials, and humiliations of the believer, will eventually render the Saviour more glorious in his eyes, and precious to his heart.—Were men more acquainted with him, and with the distempered state of their souls, they would flock to him, that they might experience his healing influence; for all who touch him, though with a feeble trembling faith, shall in due season be made perfectly whole: and, whilst we consider all these wonders of his divine power and love, shall we refuse to adore him, or to acknowledge, that " of a truth He is the Son of " God?" Or shall we neglect to do what we can, to bring others to him for the healing and saving of their souls?

NOTES.

CHAP. XV. V. 1, 2. The report of our Lord's miracles seems to have given great uneasiness to the Scribes and Pharisees at Jerusalem; and some of them had come

q 2

vii. 3—4. Mark vii. 6—8, 13. Is. 10. v. 17. 19. Is. vii. 20. Rom. iii. 31. **3** But he answered and said unto them, 'Why do ye also transgress the commandment of God by your tradition?

g xix. 19. Ex. xx. ; Lev. xix. 3. Deut. v. 16. Prov. xxiii. 22. Eph. vi. 1. **4** For 'God commanded, saying, 'Honour thy father and mother: and,

h Ex. xxi. 17. Lev. xx. 9. Deut. xxi. 18. 21. xxvii. 16. Prov. xx. 20. xxx. 17. 'He that curseth father or mother, let him die the death.

i xxiii. 16—18. Am. vii. 13—17. **5** But 'ye say, Whosoever shall say *k Mark vii. 16—. Acts iv. 19. v. 29.* to his father, or his mother, 'It is a *Acc. Prov. xx. Lev. xxvii. 9. 20. Mark vii. 11, 12.* gift, by whatsoever thou mightest be profited by me;

l 1 Tim. v. 3, 4. 8. 16. **6** And 'honour not his father or his mother, he shall be free. *m Ps. cxix. 126, 127. 139. Jer. viii. 8, 9. Hos. iv. 6. Mal. ii. 7—. 9. Mark vii. 13. Rom. iii. 31.* "Thus have ye made the commandment of God of none effect by your tradition.

in order to watch his conduct, and to seek for matter of accusation against him. But not finding that he, or his disciples, neglected any part of the divine law, they objected to him his disregard of " the tradition of the elders." It was pretended by them, and still is by modern Jews, that these traditions were originally received from God, by immediate revelation, and were of equal authority with the written law; and that they had been delivered down, by word of mouth, from one to another, through successive generations. Thus the Scribes, who were the supposed repositories and interpreters of them, had the power of altering them, and imposing them on the people, according to their conveniency: in the same manner as the Church of Rome long maintained its usurped authority, by dictating to the whole western church under similar pretensions; and as it still maintains that usurpation, through many populous regions.—' Whosoever despiseth the washing of hands, is ' worthy to be excommunicated, he comes to poverty, and ' will be extirpated out of the world.'...' He that eats bread ' with unwashen hands, does as bad as if he committed ' whoredom.'...' R. Aquiba, being in prison, and not ' having water enough to drink, and to wash his hands, ' chose to do the latter, saying, It was better to die with ' thirst, than transgress the traditions of the elders.'...' The ' religious of old did eat their common food in cleanness,... ' and they were called Pharisees. And this is a matter of ' the highest sanctity, and the way of the highest religion, ' that a man separate himself, and go aside from the vul- ' gar; and that he neither touch them, nor eat or drink ' with them: for such separation conduceth to the purity ' of the body from evil works, the purity of the body con- ' duceth to the cleansing of the soul from evil affections, ' and the sanctity of the soul conduceth to the likeness of ' God.'...' Whosoever hath his seat in the land of Israel, ' and eateth his common food in cleanness, and speaks the ' holy language, and recites his phylacteries morning and ' evening; let him be confident, that he shall obtain the ' life of the world to come.' *Jewish writers,* quoted by *Whitby.*

The tradition. (2) Την παραδοσιν. (' Παραδοσις· traditio, ' actus tradendi: etiam per meton. ipsa res quæ traditur.' Schleusner.—A παραδιδωμι.) *Mark* vii. 3. 13. 1 *Cor.* xi. 2. *Gal.* i. 14. *Col.* ii. 8. 2 *Thes.* ii. 15. iii. 6.

V. 3—6. (*Note, Deut.* iv. 2.) All additions to the laws of God are an infringement of his legislative authority; and a presumptuous imputation on his wisdom, as if he had omitted something necessary which man could supply; and, in one way or other, they always clash with the divine precepts: so that an attachment to human traditions necessarily leads men, in some circumstances, or in some respects, to disobey God; and it is evident that our Lord had expressly taught his disciples to disregard them.

Doubtless they, at this time, observed the ceremonial distinction of meats, and other divine appointments. Jesus therefore answered the Scribes by asking them, " Why do ye also transgress the commandment of God by your " traditions?"—' The words of the Scribes are lovely, ' above the words of the law, and more weighty than the ' words of the law or the prophets.' *Quotation in Whitby.* —Our Lord then selected one instance, in proof of this charge. The law, delivered from mount Sinai, and written on the tables of stone by God himself, contained this command: " Honour thy father and thy mother." ' By ' honour is meant all kind of duty, which children owe to ' their parents.' *Beza.* (*Note, Ex.* xx. 12.) And in the judicial law, he had commanded, that " he who cursed father " or mother, should be put to death." (*Marg. Ref.* g, h.) —Now it must be as wicked to do evil to parents, or to withhold the good due to them, as to wish that evil might befall them; especially as the latter might be done in a sudden passion, and the former must be deliberate and habitual. Yet the Scribes had decided, by their traditions, that in case a son should say to his parents, however aged, poor and distressed, that he had vowed to the treasury whatever he could spare, and by which he might have assisted them; and should thus excuse himself from shewing respect, gratitude, or kindness to them, leaving them in indigence, whilst he lived in plenty; he must not only not be required, but he ought not to be suffered, to do any thing for them: it being, probably, expected from him to p t money from time to time into the treasury, (of which the Scribes and Priests had the charge,) by way of compensation for his omission. Thus, from a vain pretence of piety, they directly repealed God's law, and rendered it " of none effect by their traditions:" and, as this was only one instance out of very many, their traditions must be disregarded and opposed, in order that the law of God might be honoured and obeyed.—' If a man can answer ' his parents, when they need any relief, and tell them, I ' have bound myself with an oath, that I will not do any ' thing to the relief of my father or mother: or, as some ' understand it, O father, that by which thou shouldst be ' relieved by me, is a gift already devoted to God, and ' cannot without impiety be otherwise employed; and by ' this piety to God I may be as profitable ... to thee; for ' God will repay it to me and thee in our needs: he is ' under obligation not to give it to his father. ... A father, ' being in want, reqnires relief from his son: the son an- ' swers, that he hath vowed he will not; so that to him ' it remains not lawful to relieve him; and the Pharisees ' approve of this practice; that he may thus evacuate his ' duty to his parent: and though quite contrary to the ' precept of honouring and relieving them, yet it was by ' them thought obligatory to the frustrating of that com-

7 Ye *hypocrites, *well did Esaias prophesy of you, saying,

8 This people *draweth nigh unto me with their mouth, and honoureth me with *their lips; *but their heart is far from me.

9 But *in vain they do worship me, *teaching for doctrines the commandments of men.

10 And *he called the multitude, and said unto them, *Hear, and understand:

11 Not *that which goeth into the mouth defileth a man; *but that which cometh out of the mouth, this defileth a man.

12 ¶ Then came his disciples, and said unto him, *Knowest thou that the Pharisees were offended, after they heard this saying?

13 But he answered and said, *Every plant which my heavenly Father hath not planted, shall be rooted up.

14 *Let them alone: *they be blind leaders of the blind. *And if the blind lead the blind, both shall fall into the ditch.

'mandment. And many cases are set down, wherein it 'doth so, in Maimonides, and the Rabbins.' Hammond.— The pretence of devoting to God the property thus withheld from the parent, as the occasion of the oath, seems implied.—' A man may be so bound by them,' (that is, by vows,) ' that he cannot, without great sin, do what God ' had by his law required to be done. So that if he made ' a vow, which laid him under a necessity to violate God's ' law that he might observe it, his vow must stand, and ' the law be abrogated.' Jewish canon from Pocock.—This specimen is sufficient to lead any reflecting person to conclude, that human traditions and the law of God cannot subsist together; but the prevalence of the former must inevitably lead to make void the latter: and this consideration shews the reason of our Lord's most decided opposition to the system of tradition. (Notes, Mark vii. 1—13.)

He that curseth. (4) 'Ο κακολογων maledicens. Mark vii. 10. ix. 39. Acts xix. 9.—Ex. xxi. 16.—Καχως ιπη. Lev. xx. 9. Sept.—Let him die the death.] Θανατω τελευτατω. Mark vii. 10.—Τελευθησει θανατω. Ex. xxi. 16.—Θανατω θανουσθω. Ex. xxi. 15. Lev. xx. 9. Sept.—Ye have made of none effect. (6) Ηκυρωσατι. (' Ακυρου, ab a priv. et κυρος, plena auctoritas: unde Κυριος, dominus.' Schleusner.) Mark vii. 13: rendered disannul; Gal. iii. 17.

V.—7—9. In concluding this reply, our Lord declared the Scribes and Pharisees to be hypocrites, whose character the prophet had well described. They approached God in his ordinances with good words, and honoured him with fair professions; but their hearts were estranged from his holy character, law, and service, through pride, avarice, and wickedness: so that their very worship was vain, and unprofitable to themselves; even as their instructions were to the people, whilst they taught them the traditions of men, instead of the word of God. The passage in the prophet seems to refer as much to the deluded people, as to their false teachers. (Note, Is. xxix. 13 —16.)

This people, &c. (8) Comp. Is. xxix. 13. Sept.—Μαδην δε σεβονται με, is added in the LXX, not being in the Hebrew; and it is here retained.—In vain.] Ματη. Mark vii. 7. Not elsewhere in the New Testament.

V. 10, 11. When Jesus had thus answered the Scribes, he saw good to caution the people also against their delu-

sions. He therefore called them around him, and exhorted them carefully to hear, that they might understand, his words: and he assured them, that the defilement, of which they ought to be afraid, did not arise from what entered the mouth as food; but from those evil words, which proceeded out of their mouths, as the result of the wickedness of their hearts.—This was an intimation of the inferior value of ceremonial observances, and of their speedy abolition: it cogently instructed the hearers, that real pollution was not an adventitious matter from without, but the genuine produce of man's fallen nature; and that the tongue was one main instrument, in bringing forth and propagating it.—' A man may bring guilt upon himself, ' by eating what is pernicious to his health, or by excess ' in ... food or liquor; and a Jew might have done it by ... ' eating what was forbidden by the ... law ; ... yet, in all ' these instances, the pollution would arise from the wick- ' edness of the heart, and be just proportionable to it.' Doddridge.—' It is evident that, in our Lord's judgment, ' the whole multitude was capable of understanding those ' things, which the Pharisees did not, and by which the ' traditions ... were overthrown.' Whitby.

Defileth. (11) Κοινοι. (' Κοινοω, proprie : communico, ' aliquod commune reddo.—Metaphorice polluo, contamino.' Schleusner.) Mark vii. 15. Acts x. 15. xxi. 28. Heb. ix. 13. Rev. xxi. 27.—All things not sanctified or set apart for God, or by him, were common; and what was thus common, was unclean; ceremonially as to the ritual law, and really as to the moral law. (Note, Tit. i. 14—16.) What is not " sanctified by the word of God and prayer," or not done from regard to God, continues to be common and unclean even under the gospel.

V. 12—14. When our Lord had spoken these words, he retired: and the disciples came to him, apparently with much concern, to inform him, how greatly the Pharisees were offended, or stumbled, by his direct attack on their traditions. To this he answered, that " every plant which " his heavenly Father had not planted, should be rooted " up:" meaning, that the teaching and traditions of the Scribes and Pharisees, not being from God, must be destroyed to make room for true religion; and it was therefore proper to expose them before all the people. But the words are a universal rule, in respect to teachers, doctrines, observances, and every thing relative to re-

15 Then answered Peter and said unto him, ' Declare unto us this parable.

16 And Jesus said, ' Are ye also yet without understanding?

17 Do not ye yet understand, ' that whatsoever entereth in at the mouth goeth into the belly, ' and is cast out into the draught?

18 But ' those things, which proceed out of the mouth, come forth from the heart; and they defile the man.

19 For ' out of the heart proceed ' evil thoughts, murders, adulteries, fornications, thefts, false witness, blasphemies:

20 These are the things " which defile a man: ' but to eat with unwashen hands defileth not a man.

21 ¶ Then Jesus went thence, ° and departed into the coasts of ° Tyre and Sidon.

22 And, behold, ° a woman of Canaan came out of the same coasts, and cried unto him, saying, ' Have mercy on me, O Lord, *thou* ° Son of David: ' my daughter is grievously vexed with a devil.

23 But " he answered her not a word. And his disciples came and besought him, saying, ° Send her away; for she crieth after us.

24 But he answered and said, ' I am ' not sent but unto the lost sheep of the house of Israel.

25 Then ' came she and ' worshipped him, saying, ' Lord, help me.

26 But he answered and said, ' It is °

ligion: all, which is not from God, has no authority or excellency, and cannot be of long duration; and true godliness can never prosper, till these weeds and suckers be extirpated, which draw away the nourishment from its root.—As to the Scribes and Pharisees, they must be *let alone;* (*Note*, vii. 6;) for, whilst they presumed to guide others, they were most ignorant and deluded themselves: and they would fall into the pit of destruction with their obstinate followers, as a blind leader of a blind man falls with him into a ditch, or into some mischief.— ' Regard not what they say or do, ... seeing they say and ' do it out of the blindness of their minds. ... Sometimes ' the vulgar are obliged not to believe, or comply with, ' the rules of their ecclesiastical superiors; because it is ' their duty never to follow them into the ditch.' *Whitby*.

Shall be rooted up. (13) Εκριζωθησεται (ex εκ et ριζα, *radix:*) xiii. 29. *Luke* xvii. 6. *Jude* 12.—*Leaders.* (14) 'Οδηγοι (ex 'οδος, *iter, via,* et αγω, *duco:*) xxiii. 16. 24. *Acts* i. 16. *Rom.* ii. 19.—*Lead.*] 'Οδηγεω. *Luke* vi. 39. *John* xvi. 13. *Acts* viii. 31. *Rev.* vii. 17.—*Ps.* xxv. 5. lxxxvi. 11. *Sept.*—*Ditch.*] Βοθυνον. xii. 11. *Luke* vi. 39.

V. 15—20. Peter, hearing this answer, in the name of all the apostles, desired of Christ an explication of the parable; for probably it seemed to them contrary to the Mosaick law, as well as to the traditions of the Scribes. And Jesus, having reproved their dulness, proceeded to shew them, that their food (if not unlawful or lutemperate,) could not by any contracted pollution defile them: for it entered not into the heart, and had no effect on the state of the soul; but it went into the stomach, and all which was unsuitable to nourish the body, was carried off by a regular process of nature, without communicating any sinful defilement. But those things, which proceeded out of the mouth, came from the heart: when lies, impiety, blasphemy, or wickedness were uttered, corrupt nature expressed itself; and this defiled a man in the sight of God. Indeed from the same corrupt source all kind of wickedness proceeded; such as polluting, malicious, proud, or covetous imaginations, and corrupt, perverse reasonings

against God and true religion; and even murders, adulteries, and every species of lewdness, injustice, and impiety. These crimes were indeed perpetrated by the body, but they were conceived in the heart, and proved its desperate wickedness: *this* rendered men loathsome and filthy in God's sight; and not eating their meals with unwashen hands. Such things related only to natural decency, and were no part of religion.

Yet. (16) Ακμην.—Και ακμην τυ χρονε τ'δι' *At this crisis of time*—after all that you have heard and seen.—Used here only in the New Testament.—Ακμη *cuspis.*—*Blasphemies.* (19) Βλασφημιαι. See on xii. 31.

V. 21—24. After this offence given to the Scribes, our Lord retired to the most remote part of the land, in the borders of Tyre and Zidon; and, though he used proper means for concealing himself, his coming was soon known. (*Mark* vii. 24.) For a woman of Canaan, a Syro-phenician, (probably descended from the ancient Canaanites, a remnant of whom had taken shelter in Tyre and the adjacent regions,) heard of his miracles; having before this renounced idolatry, and become a worshipper of the true God. Doubtless she had become acquainted with the scriptures of the prophets, probably by means of the Greek translation; and, comparing what she read with what she heard, was fully satisfied that Jesus was the promised Messiah. Having therefore this opportunity, and being in distress, she made earnest supplication to him; calling him Lord, and addressing him as " the Son of David." But he heard her with silence, and apparent neglect, intending to prove and manifest the strength of her humble faith. The disciples however, pitying her distress, or wearied with her importunity, requested him to grant her petition and dismiss her; and, in her hearing, he replied, that he was not sent to the Gentiles, but to " the lost " sheep of the house of Israel."

Of Canaan. (22) Χαναναια. (A Χανααν' *Acts* vii. 11. xiii. 19.) Not elsewhere in the New Testament.—'Ελληνις, Συροφοινισσα τω γενει' *Mark* vii. 26.

V. 25—28. The answer of our Lord, above-mentioned,

q 5

... not meet to take the children's bread, and to cast it to dogs.

27 And she said, 'Truth, Lord: yet the dogs eat of the crumbs which fall from their master's table.

28 Then Jesus answered and said unto her, O woman, 'great is thy faith: 'be it unto thee even as thou wilt. And her daughter was made whole from that very hour.

29 ¶ And Jesus departed from thence, 'and came nigh 'unto the sea of Galilee; and 'went up into a mountain, and sat down there.

30 And 'great multitudes came unto him, having with them those that were lame, blind, dumb, maimed, and many others, and cast them down at Jesus' feet; and he healed them:

31 Insomuch that the multitude wondered when they saw "the dumb to speak, 'the maimed to be whole, 'the lame to walk, and the blind to see: 'and they glorified the 'God of Israel.

32 Then 'Jesus called his disciples unto him, and said, 'I have compassion on the multitude, because they continue with me now 'three days, "and have nothing to eat: and I will not send them away fasting, 'lest they faint in the way.

33 And his disciples say unto him, 'Whence should we have so much bread in the wilderness, as 'to fill so great a multitude?

34 And Jesus saith unto them, 'How many loaves have ye? And they said, Seven, and a 'few little fishes.

35 And he commanded the multitude 'to sit down on the ground.

36 And he took the seven loaves and the fishes, 'and gave thanks, and brake them, and gave to his disciples, and the disciples to the multitude.

37 And they did 'all eat, and were filled: and they took up of the broken meat that was left, 'seven baskets full.

---

so far from offending this humble suppliant, excited her to redouble her expressions of reverence, falling down before him, and intreating him to help her. To this he answered, apparently with harshness, and in a manner which seemed to preclude all hope, that it would be improper to rob the children of their bread, in order to feed the dogs. (Note, vii. 6.) Thus the Jews used, proudly and contemptuously, to distinguish themselves from the Gentiles: and the woman might, and if she had not been a very humble believer, she would have taken great offence; disdaining the title of dogs, and altering her opinion of One, who had treated her most respectful address, in a manner so contrary to her expectation. But, being conscious of personal unworthiness, and recollecting her Gentile extraction, and above all, filled with the highest sentiments of the dignity, wisdom, and excellency of Christ; she submitted patiently and meekly to the mortifying distinction; and by a peculiar ingenuity turned it into a cogent argument in support of her petition. 'Truth, Lord,' as if she had said, 'I am a vile sinner of the Gentiles, and have no claim to the privileges of God's people; but the dogs eat the fragments of a plentiful table, without the least disadvantage to the children: and thy power and mercy are so large, that thou canst heal my daughter, without in the least deducting from the blessings intended for thine Israel.'—Our Lord's purpose was now answered; and having openly commended the greatness of the woman's faith notwithstanding all her disadvantages, he assured her that her daughter was healed, and in a manner which intimated that all her other desires were, or would be, granted.

Meet. (26) Καλον *good, becoming.*—*The dogs.*] Τοις κυναριοις. τα κυναρια, *catelli.* (Dim. à κυων.) Little dogs, as lap-dogs, &c. distinguished from large dogs, as mastiffs, &c.—*Mark* vii. 27. 28.—*Crumbs.* (27) Ψιχιων. *Frustula, fragmenta.* Mark vii. 28. Luke xvi. 21.

V. 29. *Notes, Mark* vii. 31—37.

V. 31. *Maimed.*] It is generally allowed, that the word here used, in its primary meaning signifies such persons as have been deprived of their limbs; and the restoration of them may be considered as one of the most stupendous effects of our Lord's creating power. 'The word '(κυλλος,) which we render maimed, does in the strictest 'propriety,...signify one whose hand or arm had been cut 'off; (*Mark* ix. 43;) but it is sometimes applied to those 'who were only *disabled* in those parts....It is reasonable 'to suppose, that among the many maimed, who were 'brought on these occasions, there were some whose limbs 'had been cut off; and I think, hardly any of the miracles 'of our Lord were more illustrious and amazing, than the 'recovery of such.' *Doddridge.*—'Men that had lost their 'limbs.' *Hammond.*

Dumb.] Κωφος. See on xii. 22.—*Maimed.*] Κυλλους. xviii. 8. 'Κυλλος, *mutilatus corpore, quem Latini debilem* 'dicunt. ...Κυλλος, *opponitur* τῳ δυο χειρας εχονθι, *Mark* ix. '43.' *Schleusner.*—It does not occur elsewhere in the New Testament.—*Glorified.*] 'They all, whether Jews or Gentiles, acknowledged this to be a wonderful work of mercy, 'wrought by the God of Israel, and such as no other god 'was able to do.' *Hammond.*

V. 32—38. (*Notes, and P. O.* xiv. 13—21.) The multitudes on this occasion continued with our Lord three days, or till the third day, so that they must have lodged out of doors two nights, which might be done in those warm climates without any great inconvenience: but it shews the earnestness, with which they listened to his un-

38 And they that did eat were four thousand men, beside women and children.

39 And ʰe sent away the multitude, and took ship, and came into the coasts of Magdala. ᵍ xiv. 22. Mark viii. 10.

structions.—It appears wonderful, that the disciples should renew their objection, when Christ had declared his compassionate purpose of feeding the multitude; especially as their provision was something larger, and the number present not so great, as before. The word rendered *baskets* is different from that, so translated, in the preceding chapter (κοφινους); and the same distinction is made in the original, in all the places where either of these miracles is mentioned. Some think, that the word in this place signifies a larger basket than the other, but others suppose exactly the contrary.

I will not. (32) Ου θελω. ʻ I do not will or purpose, to send them away fasting.ʼ—*In the wilderness.* (33) Εν ερημια, scil. χωρα. *Mark* viii. 4. *2 Cor.* xi. 26. *Heb.* xi. 38.—*To sit down.* (35) Αναπεσειν. Comp. xiv. 19. Αναπιπτω (ex ανα et πιπτω,) *discumbo, recumbo, renupinus jaceo. Mark* vi. 40. *Luke* xvii. 7. *John* xxi. 20.—*Baskets.* (37) Σπυριδας xvi. 10. *Mark* viii. 8. 20. *Acts* ix. 25.—In 2 *Cor.* xi. 33, σαργανη is substituted for σπυρις.

V. 39. ʻ Dalmanutha, (*Mark* viii. 10,) was a partic ʻ cular place within the bounds of Magdala.ʼ *Lightfoot.*

Took ship.] Ενεβη εις το πλοιον " he went into the ship." Some small vessel which was waiting, and in which probably he and his disciples had come thither.

PRACTICAL OBSERVATIONS.

V. 1—9

The most virulent enemies of vital godliness are often extremely tenacious of their own inventions in religion, by which they dress up a vain pageant to amuse their consciences, and to impose on the ignorant.—The disciples of Christ are fully justified in disregarding the traditions of men, however sanctioned, by the contrariety of those traditions, in many things, to the holy law of God. How thankful ought we to be for the *written* word, when *oral* traditions are so liable to error, perversion, and uncertainty! —Never let us for a moment imagine, that the religion of the Bible can be improved by any possible additions, doctrinal or practical : but common sense will teach a candid enquirer, to distinguish between those circumstances of worship, which each society *must* order for itself, though none have a right to impose on others ; and those inventions, which corrupt the purity, destroy the simplicity, and deform the spiritual beauty, of religious worship.—We should peculiarly advert to our Lord's marked attention to the due performance of relative duties, especially that of children to their parents. *No* forms, notions, subscription to charities, building churches or chapels, or any thing else, which looks like faith, zeal, or piety, can prove that man a true Christian, who neglects to " honour his father and " mother," or to supply their wants according to his ability. To dispense with this, or other duties, on such grounds, would be as unscriptural, as to say, " It is a gift, by what- " soever thou mightest be profited by me." Indeed temporal death is not now inflicted on him, who curses his parents : yet a far more dreadful punishment will be awarded hereafter to all disobedient children, if they continue impenitent ; and they must expect no comfort or blessing

from God even in this present world.—Alas! too many " draw near to God with their mouth and honour him with " their lips, whilst their hearts are far from him," and thus prove that they worship him in vain. And this is the case, not only among those, who " teach for doctrines the com- " mandments of men ; " but even with many who profess evangelical religion, yet neglect relative duties, and evidently commit iniquity, and are fraudulent in their dealings, and oppressive to their dependents.

V. 10—20.

When professed teachers of religion contradict the word of God ; it often becomes necessary, not only to answer their objections and arguments, but to point out their errors and expose their ignorance to the people ; and to call on *them* to hear and understand the truth. It is not, however, generally expedient for *us* to bring any decided charge of hypocrisy against our opponents, in the manner which became the heart-searching Saviour : yet we must, by no means, put either the honour of the clerical order, or our own reputation, in competition with the glory of God and the salvation of souls. But when Scribes and Pharisees are offended with plain truth ; timid disciples will be disquieted, and almost disposed to think that their bolder brethren have gone too far, even though in other things they honour them : especially when they see those exasperated, whom they had hopes of conciliating. We should however remember, that nothing in religion is of any value, except what God himself has planted ; nothing will endure in the soul, but the regenerating work of the Holy Spirit ; nothing should be admitted into the church, or be suffered to abide there, but what is of heavenly extraction : and therefore, if hypocrites be detected, false teachers offended, and professed friends changed into avowed enemies, by an open declaration of the truth, we ought not to be disconcerted ; for " the trees of righteous- " ness" will grow more fruitful, when such noxious plants are rooted up. If men quarrel with the word of Christ, we must " let them alone," and not " cast pearls before " swine : " yet it is grievous to reflect how the blind have, in every age of the church, undertaken to lead the blind ; and what numbers are thus continually plunging together into the pit of destruction ; in which the blind leader sinks the deepest, in proportion to the degree of his pride, enmity, and presumption. Yet, as God has sometimes opened the eyes of such blind guides, and changed them into faithful teachers ; we should remember still to pray *for* them, as well as *against* their wickedness.—In all our difficulties we should apply to Christ for instruction : and though he rebuke us for our want of understanding, yet he will continue to teach us, and his reproofs will tend to our humiliation and increased attention. When he teaches, he will certainly convince men, that their sin and pollution originate from themselves, and not from external causes. (*Note, Jam.* i. 13—15.) He will shew them " the deceit- " fulness and desperate wickedness" of the human heart : and whilst they perceive that all the wickedness of every kind, which has filled and corrupted the earth, has been

q 7

CHAP. XVI.

Jesus rebukes the hypocrisy of the Pharisees and Sadducees, who required a sign from heaven; and refuses to give any but the sign of Jonas, 1—4. He warns the disciples against the leaven of the Pharisees and Sadducees, explains his meaning, and reproves the disciples for unbelief and want of understanding, 5—12. The opinions of the people concerning him, 13, 14. Peter's confession commended, 15—17. The foundation of the church, and the power of the keys,

18—20. *Jesus foretels his death and resurrection, and rebukes Peter for dissuading him from suffering, 21—23. He shews, that his disciples must deny themselves, and suffer, in prospect of a future reward, 24—27. The speedy establishment of his kingdom, 28.*

a v. 20. ix. 11. xii. 14. xv. 1. xvii. 15. 34. xxiii. 2. xxvii. 62.
b 6. 11. iii. 7. 8. xxii. 23. Mark xii. 18. Luke xx. 27. Acts iv. 1. v. 17. xxiii. 6—8.
c xix. 3. xxii. 18.
d xii. 38, 39. Mark viii. 11.
e xii. 78, 39. Mark viii. 11—13. Luke xi. 16. 29, 30. John vi. 30, 31. 1 Cor. i. 22.

THE ^a Pharisees also, with the ^b Sadducees, came, and ^c tempting desired him that he would shew them ^d a sign from heaven.

2 He answered and said unto them,

---

the genuine produce of depraved nature, and that it would have been tenfold greater but for merciful restraints; they will be led to see and feel, that all this exists in their own hearts, and might be educed from them by suitable temptations. He will teach them to trace all the streams, of their own actual transgressions, to this corrupt fountain; to watch the evil thoughts which rise within; to humble themselves for these defilements, and to seek to be cleansed from them, in " the Fountain which he hath opened for " sin and for uncleanness ;" to consider inward sanctification as far more important than all forms and notions; and to perceive that even truth is no further valuable to them, than as it tends to purify their hearts and consciences.

V. 21—28.

Our divine Saviour is " the same yesterday, to day, and " for ever ;" and still he sees good to vary the expressions of his love to those who wait on him. Sinners of every nation and description are alike welcome to his salvation, and he will in no wise cast out those who cry to him for mercy. Yet, he can veil the compassions of his heart under a frowning countenance ; not only to humble and prove those whom he loves, but also to shew the strength of their faith and the depth of their humility. In some cases, the disciples may *seem* more compassionate than their Lord : but when the folly and selfishness of their pity, and the wisdom and mercy of his frowns and delays, come to be compared, the case will appear far otherwise ; and the event will prove that " he is rich in mercy to all them that " call on him." Let then such as seek help from him, and receive no gracious answer, increase their importunity, and endeavour, with heavenly skill, to turn even their unworthiness and discouragements into arguments, with which to plead before his mercy-seat. Let sinners submit without reserve to every humiliating charge, and rely on his mercy. Thus, whilst they allow that they are not " worthy of the crumbs from his table," they may expect to be supplied with children's food : for he cannot be impoverished by his bounty to the most atrocious transgressors. Indeed true faith gathers strength by trials, as healthy bodies do by exercise ; and when the Lord has sufficiently proved the waiting soul, he will honour faith and humble perseverance, and abundantly answer every believing prayer.—We should intreat him for our children, relations, and neighbours ; especially when, through the oppression of the devil, they are incapable of seeking help for themselves : and we should never fail to intercede with him for discouraged souls.

V. 29—39.

' Who can describe the sentiments of these happy crea-

' tures, who, without any dangerous or painful operation, ' found themselves in a moment restored, beyond all the ' efforts of nature, and beyond all the prospects of hope! ' With what pleasure did the ear, which had been just ' opened, listen to the pleasing accents of his instructive ' tongue! How did the lame leap around him for joy ! ' And the maimed extend their recovered hands, in grate-' ful acknowledgments of his new-creating power ! Whilst ' the voice of the dumb sang forth his praises in sounds ' before unknown ! And the eye of the blind checked the ' curiosity, which would have prompted it to range over ' the various and beautiful objects of unveiled nature, to ' fix its rapturous regards on the gracious countenance of ' Him that had given it the day ! Let us further reflect, ' with what correspondent pleasure must our Lord survey ' these grateful and astonished creatures, while his bene-' volent heart took its share in all the delight which he ' gave. These trophies of his greatness ! how unlike to ' those of the field, the monuments of desolation and ' slaughter !' *Doddridge.*—With what raptures then will they, whose souls have been restored to holiness by his healing grace, for ever contemplate and adore their divine Benefactor, and meditate on the price which he paid for their redemption ! And how will he for ever behold them with immense complacency, and " delight over them to do " them good !" Let us then wait on him to open our eyes that we may behold his glory ; to enable us to walk in his ways and to do his will; and to teach us to shew forth his praises, that the Father may be glorified in him, and in us, during life, and for ever. And let us copy his example of love, according to the ability which he has given us, delighting to do good and to communicate felicity.— Whilst we are willing to endure hardship, in attending to the concerns of our souls; we may be sure that our gracious Lord will compassionate us under all our troubles, and supply what he sees needful for our temporal support. —But alas ! how soon do even believers forget his interpositions in their behalf! How often do we repeat our objections against self-denying and expensive duties, though we never yet were losers by them ! And how frequently do our unbelieving doubts revive, under even lighter trials, after we have been delivered out of greater ! Lord, " increase our faith " and pardon our unbelief ; and still renew thy mercies towards us; teaching us to live upon thy fulness and bounty, for all things pertaining to this world and to that which is to come.

NOTES.

CHAP. XVI. V. 1—4. (*Notes, Mark* viii. 10—13. *Luke* xii. 54—57.) No two descriptions of bad men could

q 8

e Luke xii. 54—56.
• When it is evening, ye say, *It will be* fair weather; for the sky is red:

3 And in the morning, *It will be* foul weather to-day; for the sky is red

f vii. 3. xv. 7. and lowring. ꞌO *ye* hypocrites, ye can
xvii. 16. xxiii. discern the face of the sky; but can
15. Luke xi. 44
xiii. 15.

g iv. 23. xi. 5. ye not *discern* ꝼ the signs of the times?
1 Chr. xii. 32.
h xii. 39, 40. Mark 4 A ʰ wicked and adulterous gene-
viii. 12, 38. Acts
ii. 40. ration seeketh after a sign; and there

i Jon. i. 17. Luke shall no sign be given unto it, ꞌbut the
xi. 29, 30.
k xv. 21. Gen. ꞌj. sign of the prophet Jonas.　ᵏ And he
2. Hos. iv. 17.
ix. 12. Mark v. left them, and departed.
17, 18. Acts
xviii. 6. 5 ¶ And when his disciples ꞌwere
1 xv. 39. Mark
viii. 13, 14. come to the other side, they had for-

m Luke xii. 15. gotten to take bread.
n 12. Ex. xii. 15—
19. Lev. ii. 11. 6 Then Jesus said unto them, ᵐ Take
Mark viii. 15.
Luke xii. 1. heed, and beware of ⁿ the leaven of
1 Cor. v. 6—8.
Gal. v. 9. 2 Tim. ᵒ the Pharisees and of the Sadducees.
ii. 17.

p Mark viii. 16— 7 And ᵖ they reasoned among them-
18. ix. 10. Luke
ix. 46. selves, saying, ꝗ *It is* because we have
q xv. 16—18. Acts
x. 14. taken no bread:

8 *Which* ꞌ when Jesus perceived, he r John ii. 24, 25.
said unto them, ꞌO ye of little faith, xiii. 50. Heb. iv.
13. Rev. ii. 23.
why reason ye among yourselves, be- s vi. 30. viii. 26.
xiv. 31. Mark
cause ye have brought no bread? xvi. 14.

9 Do ꞌ ye not yet understand, nei- t xv. 16, 17. Mark
vii. 18. Luke
ther remember *the five loaves of the xxiv.
25—27.
Rev. iii. 19.
five thousand, and how many baskets u xiv. 17—21.
Mark vi. 38—
ye took up? 44. Luke ix. 13
—17. John vi. 9

10 Neither ꞌ the seven loaves of the —13.
four thousand, and how many baskets v xv. 34—38.
Mark viii. 5—9.
ye took up? 17—21.

11 How ʸ is it that ye do not under- y Mark viii. 40.
vii. 21. Luke
stand, that I spake *it* not to you con- xii. 55. John
vii. 48.
cerning bread, that ye should beware
of the leaven of the Pharisees and of
the Sadducees?

12 Then understood they how that
he bade *them* not beware of the lea-
ven of bread, ᶻ but of the doctrine z xv. 6—9. xxiii.
13. &c. Acts
of the Pharisees and of the Saddu- xxiii. 8.
cees.

---

be much more opposite to each other, in principles and
conduct, than the Pharisees and Sadducees; yet they were
alike enemies to Jesus! (*Note*, iii. 7—10.)—ꞌThe wicked,
ꞌwho otherwise are at defiance one with another, can agree
ꞌwell together against Christ: but do what they can,
ꞌChrist beareth away the victory, and triumpheth over
ꞌthem.' *Beza*.—They could find no objection against his
conduct and doctrine, but what he answered to their confusion: and they therefore came insidiously to make trial
of his power, again "desiring a sign from heaven," to
satisfy them that he was the Messiah, of which they
pleaded, that his other miracles were not a sufficient proof.
(*Note*, xii. 38—40.) The descent of the Holy Spirit on
him at his baptism, and the voice of the Father declaring
him to be his beloved Son, were *signs* from heaven; yet
the Pharisees and Sadducees required some further evidence: and probably they intended to mention some particular sign, or appearance in the heavens, without which
they could not be convinced; purposing thus to make trial
of his power. To this our Lord answered, that they were
able to form conjectures what kind of weather it was likely
to be, from their observations on the clouds and sky, which
were generally found right: and, if they had not been hypocrites in these enquiries, they might as easily, and far
more certainly, have discerned "the signs of the times."
The sceptre was now departing from Judah; Daniel's seventy weeks were terminating; John the Baptist's ministry,
as the predicted forerunner of the Messiah, evidenced his
approach; and all the prophecies were fulfilling in his character, doctrine, and miracles: so that it was plain that
these were the times of the Messiah, and that the nation
was about to be given up for rejecting him. Having therefore again reproved them as a wicked and " adulterous
" generation," (*Marg. Ref.* h,) and refused them any other
sign but that of Jonas, the type of his death and resurrection, he left them to their perverseness.—ꞌO ye hypocrites,
ꞌcan ye prognosticate fair or foul weather, by the face of

ꞌthe sky? ...and can ye not, by those clear predictions of
ꞌthe prophets, and the miraculous demonstrations of my
ꞌpower, discern the time of my coming?' *Bp. Hall*.—
ꞌIt was never known, that any one, pretending to be a
ꞌprophet, laid the foundation of the truth of his preten-
ꞌsions, upon his being despised and rejected, and even
ꞌcrucified as a deceiver, by them to whom he was sent,
ꞌand among whom he performed all his miracles; and
ꞌupon what should be done by others at his death; and
ꞌupon what should do after his resurrection.' *Whitby*.
Yet this our Lord did repeatedly and openly, so that even
his enemies were well aware of it! (xxvii. 63.)

Fair weather. (2) Eὐδία. (Ex ευ et διὰ the accus. of
Ζιυς, *Jupiter*, and figuratively *the air*, or heaven; as the
Latins say, *sub die*, and *sub Jove*.) Opposed to χειμων.—
Used here only in the New Testament.—*Is red*.] Πυῤῥάζει
is red like fire. 3. (A πυρῥος, *rubens*, quasi *colorem ignis
habens*: *Rev.* vi. 4. xii. 3: idque à πυρ ignis.) Used here
only in the New Testament, and supposed never to occur
in any other author than Matthew.—*Foul weather*. (3)
Χειμων. Propriè, *hyems*; xxiv. 20. *Mark* xiii. 18. *John* x.
22. 2 Tim. iv. 21. ꞌMetaphoricè, *tempestas, pluvia, nu-
ꞌbila et procellosa*, qualls esse solet in hyemis tempore.'
Schleusner.—*Acts* xxvii. 20.—*Ezra* x. 9. *Job* xxxvii. 6.
Sept.—It is opposed to ευδια, in *ver.* 2.—*Lowring*.] Στυγνα-
ζων· *tristis sum, mæror*. *Mark* x. 22.—Not elsewhere in
the New Testament.—*Adulterous*. (4) Μοιχαλις. See on
xii. 39.

V. 5—12. The disciples, engaged by more important
concerns, had forgotten to take bread; and the fragments
of their late miraculous meal being consumed, they had
only one loaf remaining. Whilst uneasy on this account,
Jesus, with reference to what had lately passed, warned
them most cautiously to "beware of *the leaven* of the Pha-
" risees, and of the Sadducees," and Herodians; (*Mark*
viii. 15;) meaning their hypocrisy, infidelity, corrupt doctrine, vain traditions, and proud enmity against the truth,

13 ¶ When Jesus [a] came into the coasts of [b] Cesarea Philippi, he asked his disciples, saying, ' Whom do men say that [d] I, the Son of man, am ? 14 And they said, Some *say that* thou art [e] John the Baptist: some, [f] Elias, and others, Jeremias, or one of the prophets. 15 He saith unto them, [f] But whom say ye that I am? 16 And Simon Peter answered and said, [h] Thou art the Christ, the Son of [i] the living God.

17 And Jesus answered and said unto him, [k] Blessed art thou, [l] Simon Bar-jona : [m] for flesh and blood hath not revealed *it* unto thee, [n] but my Father which is in heaven. 18 And I say also unto thee, That [o] thou art Peter ; and [p] upon this rock

---

which soured and corrupted all they did. But the disciples supposed, that he referred to their want of bread, and that he cautioned them against obtaining any from the Pharisees or Sadducees, as if they polluted every thing which they touched; and this troubled and perplexed them. Our Lord therefore, knowing of what they were discoursing, reproved their weakness of faith ; seeing they might confidently have relied on his power to provide for them, if they had properly understood and kept in mind the miracles which they had recently witnessed, in the feeding of the multitudes with so small a provision, and in the quantity that was left. He also reproved them for not understanding, that he had reference to matters far more important than the leaven of bread, which, as he had before taught them could not defile men. (*Notes*, xv. 15—20. *Mark* viii. 14—21.)

Baskets. (9) Κοφινος.—*Baskets.* (10) Σπυριδας. See on xv. 37.

V. 13—16. Cesarea Philippi is supposed by some, to have been the same place, which had anciently been called Laish, or Dan ; (*Note, Judg.* xviii. 7—10 ;) and it lay in the northern extremity of the land, within the Tetrarchy of Philip, Herod's brother. Philip had rebuilt this city, and called it Cesarea, in honour of Tiberias Cesar, the Roman Emperor ; and had added his own name to it, to distinguish it from another Cesarea, a much greater city, in a more southern part of the land, which king Herod rebuilt and called thus, in honour of Augustus Cesar. (*Note, Acts* xxiii. 33—35.)—Our Lord seems to have gone thither, for the sake of retirement and discourse with his disciples : and he enquired of them, what sentiments the people entertained and expressed concerning him, who appeared as " the Son of man " among them, but who gave abundant proof that he was a very extraordinary person. To this they answered, that some, who had but lately heard of his miracles, supposed that John the Baptist was risen again ; (*Note,* xiv. 1, 2 ;) others thought he was Elijah, the forerunner of the Messiah ; and others imagined he was one of the ancient prophets risen again. —Numbers thought Jesus a deceiver ; but those who esteemed him more highly, had very inadequate apprehensions of his real dignity.—He then asked them what *their* sentiments of him were : and this was evidently the drift of the former question. To which Peter, with his usual promptitude, replied, in his own name and in that of his brethren, They were assured that he was the promised Messiah, and " the Son of the living God."—The apostles had, not long before, worshipped Christ, as " the Son of

" God :" (*Note,* xiv. 33 :) and their repeated confessions, to the same effect, shew what their habitual judgment was on this subject. Some think, that they only meant to say that he was the Messiah ; whereas it is obvious they thus shewed, that in this respect they understood the true meaning of the prophecies concerning the Messiah. (*Notes, Ps.* ii. 7—12. *John* vi. 66—71. ix. 35—38. xi. 20—27.)

V. 17. When Peter had made this confession of his faith, our Lord immediately pronounced him *blessed*, or a happy man ; as this knowledge and faith were not the effect of natural sagacity, or human instruction, but of revelation from the Father. Others had enjoyed the same outward means ; but were not yet brought to believe in Jesus, " as the Christ the Son of the living God ;" and the teaching of God alone, had made him differ from his unbelieving countrymen : his faith and knowledge were of a spiritual and saving nature, and therefore he was blessed. Peter was, at this time, greatly ignorant of many evangelical truths, and even prejudiced against them : he did not understand the plan of " redemption by the blood of " Christ ;" he was but little acquainted with his own heart, and with spiritual things ; he had a variety of carnal and vain expectations ; he was afterwards left to make many gross mistakes, yea, even to commit grievous sins, and to incur rebukes and chastenings ; and he had many persecutions to endure, and was at length to die a martyr by a most painful death : yet he was " blessed ;" because he was regenerate, and an upright believer in Christ : having received these introductory benefits, more would in due time be given ; (*Note,* xiii. 12 ;) and his everlasting happiness was sure.—" Revealed," does not seem, in this place, to mean the immediate communication of knowledge by inspiration ; for that would not have ensured Peter's happiness : (*Note,* vii. 21—23 :) but the removing of those proud and carnal prejudices which *veiled* the hearts of others, that they could not understand what was in itself most plain. (*Notes,* 1—4. xi. 25, 26. 2 *Cor.* iii. 12— 16.) Peter was " taught of God ;" and " his understand- " ing " as to this subject was " opened to understand the " scriptures."

Flesh and blood.] Σαρξ και αιμα. Man ; human nature, our bodies as existing and acting in the world.—1 *Cor.* xv. 50. *Gal.* i. 16. *Eph.* vi. 12. *Heb.* ii. 14.—*Revealed.*] Απεκαλυψε (εκ απο et καλυπῖω, tego:) x. 26. xi. 27. *Luke* ii. 35 xvii. 30. *Rom.* i. 17. *Gal.* i. 16. *et al.*

V. 18. This confession gave our Lord an occasion, with reference to the name which he had before given the apostle, (*Note, John* i. 35—42, v. 42) to declare, that " on

A 2

q Zech. vi. 12, 13. ¶ I will build 'my church ; 'and the
Cor. iii. 9.
Heb. iii. 3, 4.   r xviii. 17. Acts ii. 47, viii. f. Eph. iii. 10. v. 25—27. 32. Col. i.
18. 1 Tim. iii. 5, 15.   s Gen. xxii. 17. 2 Sam. xviii. 4. Ps. lxix. 12. cxxvii. 5.
Prov. xxiv. 7. Is. xxviii. 6. 1 Cor. xv. 55? marg.

I will build 'my church ; 'and the gates of hell ' shall not prevail against ' it.

Ps. cxxvi. 1, 2.
Is. ffe. 17. John
x. 27—30. Rom.
viii.33—39. Heb.
xii. 28. Rev. xi. 15. xxi. 1—4

" this rock he would build his church." Peter's confession contains that fundamental truth, respecting the Person and offices of Christ, upon which, as on a rock, he would build his church : and on this foundation it should stand so sure, that no machinations or efforts, of devils or of men, could ever subvert it ; though they should meet in council to form devices against it, and unite all their forces, and lead them forth to assault it. Nor could the powers of death, or the entrance into the eternal world, destroy the hope of those who should build on it : but one generation of believers should be raised up, as others were removed to heaven, to profess these great truths even to the end of time ; and the whole company would be made more than conquerors, and be saved by the belief of them, to all eternity.—The word translated " rock," is of a similar meaning with the name of Peter, but it is not the same word. Nothing however can be more absurd, than to suppose that Christ meant, that the person of Peter was the rock, on which the church should be builded ; except it be the wild notion, that the bishops of Rome have since been substituted in his place! " Their rock is not as our " Rock, our enemies themselves being judges." Without doubt Christ himself is the Rock and tried Foundation of the church, and woe be to him who attempts to lay any other : (Note, 1 Cor. iii. 10—15 :) but Peter's confession is this Rock doctrinally. The profession of the truths implied in it constitutes a man a member of the visible church ; the vital belief of them constitutes a member of the real church, however he may err in other matters : but nothing less than this can entitle any one to the name of a believer. Against these doctrines, the power and policy of Satan and his servants have in every age been directed ; both by exciting furious persecutions, " bringing in damnable here- " sies," and employing the ingenuity of plausible infidels. The Deity of Christ as " the Son of the living God," and his human nature as " the Son of Man," have by turns been opposed ; and his unction to his prophetical, his priestly, and his kingly office, has been explained away by different descriptions of deceivers. Yet the church, established on the person of Christ, as Emmanuel, the Prophet, Priest, and King of his redeemed people, still subsists ; and it will assuredly, ere long, gain a decided victory over all its adversaries of every name, on earth or in hell.—Those protestant writers, who contend that Peter, and he alone, was meant as the rock ; and that this was a peculiar reward for his singular confession of Christ ; explain themselves to mean, that Peter was honoured to lay the first foundation of the Christian church, both among the Jews and the Gentiles ; and perhaps our Lord might refer to this peculiar distinction. (Acts ii. x.) But to lay a foundation, and to be a foundation, are widely different things ; and certainly Peter was the foundation of the church, in no other sense, than the rest of the apostles were. (Marg. Ref. p.—Notes, Eph. ii. 19—22. Rev. xxi. 9—21, v. 14.)—Much pains have also been taken, to shew that " the gates of hell," or Hades, the invisible world, do not mean, according to the common interpretation, the power and policy of the devil, and of his angels and servants ; but merely death, as the entrance into Hades ; and that a

resurrection of all true believers to eternal life is especially intended. But Christ came, not only " to overcome death, " but him that hath the power of death, that is, the devil," and this at last brings in the substance of the more usual and far more ancient interpretation.—' Hades here ... signi- ' fies death, or grave, or destruction, and by consequence ' Satan also, who hath the power of these. ... Gates may ' signify first, power, ... which consists in arms, ... which ' were usually kept over the gates of the cities : secondly, ' counsel, contrivance, stratagems, policy ; because they ' were wont to sit in council in the gates : thirdly, worldly ' authority borrowed by Satan from his instruments, the ' heathen powers of the world, because judgment was wont ' to be exercised in the gates. ...Not all the power,... ' policy, ...authority ...in the world, no not death or grave, ' (which are proverbially irresistible, Cant. viii. 6,) nor ' Satan himself shall be able to destroy this fabrick. ... ' " The church" signifies particular persons, (believers, ' true faithful Christians,) of which the church consists, or ' ... the whole congregation and society of men. ...Though ' Christians shall die, yet death shall have no dominion over ' them : Christ shall break open those bars.—As it refers ' to the church in complexo, that is, to the whole congre- ' gation of Christian professors ; so it signifies a promise ' from Christ, that it shall never be destroyed so as to perish ' totally, but whatever change it undergoes in the world, ' it shall again lift up the head, and have as it were its re- ' surrection : which promise is performed, if, as it decays ' ...in one ... part, it revive and flourish in another.' Ham- mond. The original word signifies any assembly of people, for whatever purpose, or in whatever way collected : but in the New Testament it is generally used in the senses above given.—Considered as a prophecy, this has been most wonderfully accomplished, during almost eighteen hundred years ; during a vast proportion of which, the professed friends of the church have combined with her avowed enemies to destroy her, by power and policy, by persecution and heresies, and by every imaginable way ; but all in vain. —" The gates of hell " have not prevailed, and shall not prevail against her.—" Heaven and earth shall pass away, " but Christ's words shall not pass away."—Let it be re- marked, that our Lord says, " I will build, &c." but the church is " God's building and his church." (1 Cor. iii. 9.)

Peter.] Πέτρος.—Rock.] Πέτρα. vii. 24. xxvii. 60. Luke viii. 6. Rom. ix. 33.—'Η δε πέτρα ην ὁ Χριστος' 1 Cor. x. 4.— Church.] Εκκλησιαν, Acts vii. 38. xix. 32. 39. Heb. ii. 12. —' Ab εκκαλεω, evoco, convoco, ut Heb. קהל : generatim notat ' quemcunque cœtum, è promiscuâ multitudine convocatum ; ' sive sit confusus, sive ordinatus, sive sit politicus, sive sacer. ' —Suid. Εκκλησιαν συναγωγην οχλω.' Schleusner.—The word συναγωγη is used for the congregation by the LXX, though generally for the place of assembling in the New Testament, as church is now commonly used for the sacred building. —The word εκκλησια, however, was as it were adopted and consecrated by the sacred writers to signify the whole body of Christians ; as in xviii. 17. Acts ii. 47. 1 Tim. iii. 15. Heb. xii. 23 : or any particular assembly or company of them : 1 Cor. i. 2. Philem. 2.—Gates of hell.] Πυλαι ᾁδκ. The clause does not occur elsewhere.—On ᾁδης, see Notes,

a 3

a Acts ii. 14, &c.
x. 34, &c. xv. 7.
x Is. xxii. 22.
Rev. i. 18. iii. 7.
ix. l. xx. 1—3.
y xviii. 18. John
xx. 23. 1 Cor. v.
4. 5. 2 Cor. ii.
10. 1 Tim. iv. 8.
Rev. xi. 6.

19 And I will ª give unto thee ˣ the keys of the kingdom of heaven: ʸ and whatsoever thou shalt bind on earth shall be bound in heaven; and whatsoever thou shalt loose on earth shall be loosed in heaven.

z viii. 4. xvii. 9.
Mark viii. 30.
ix. 9. Luke ix.
21. 36.
a John i. 41. 49.
xx. 31. Acts ii.
36. 1 John ii. 22.
v. 1.
b xvii. 22, 23. xx.
17—19, 28. xxvi.
2. Mark viii. 31.
ix. 31, 32. x. 33
—34. Luke ix. 22, 81, 44, 45. xviii. 31—34. xxiv. 6, 7. 26, 27. 46.

20 Then ª charged he his disciples, that they should tell no man that he was ª Jesus the Christ.

21 ¶ From that time forth ᵇ began Jesus to shew unto his disciples, how ᵇ that he must go unto Jerusalem, and

---

Ps. xvi. 8—11. *Acts* ii. 25—32.—*Shall not prevail.*] Οὐ κατισχυσουσιν (ex κατα, contra, et ισχυω, valeo:) *Luke* xxiii. 23.—Ισχυσι κατ αιων· *Acts* xix. 16.

V. 19. Our Lord next stated the authority, with which Peter would be invested. He had spoken in the name of his brethren, as well as in his own; and doubtless this related to them as well as to him: (xviii. 18:) but he might be especially addressed, as he first preached the gospel, after Christ's ascension, both to the Jews, and to the Gentiles; thus opening the kingdom of heaven, as it were, to them both, in which it was impossible that any successor could share with him.—Keys were an ancient emblem of authority. (*Rev.* iii. 7, 8. *Note, Is.* xxii. 20—25.) The expression doubtless immediately related to the authority, which the apostles possessed, as the representatives of Christ, and the principal ministers of his kingdom. (*Note, John* xx. 19—23, *v.* 23.) They were endued with the Holy Spirit, that they might infallibly declare his truth to mankind, and determine what was binding on the conscience, and what not; to shew what persons ought to be admitted into the church, or excluded from it; to decide on the characters of those whose sins were forgiven, or the contrary: and whatever in these, and similar respects, they bound or loosed on earth would be bound or loosed in heaven. The apostles themselves had not an infallible insight into the characters of men, and they were liable to mistakes and sins in their own conduct. But they were infallibly preserved from error, in stating the way of acceptance and salvation, the rule of obedience, the believer's character and experience, and the final doom of unbelievers, hypocrites, and apostates. In such things their decision was absolute, and ratified in heaven, as all will find at last, even they who now despise it. In this respect, their apostolical authority continues in their doctrine, as transmitted to us in the New Testament: but all other ministers, of whatever rank, name, or age, can do no more than declare the doctrine of the apostles, and apply it to particular cases; by preaching the word, administering divine ordinances, admitting men into the visible church, or excluding them from it, or by personal encouragement and warning. As far as they proceed according to the scripture in these things, their decisions are warranted, and ratified in heaven: but not when they mistake, either in doctrine, or in its application to particular persons or characters. As no man can see another's heart; and as no man has any inherent power to forgive sin, or the contrary: so all pretensions *absolutely* to absolve, or to retain men's sins, claim more than even apostolical authority: for surely none will maintain that any man can be made a true believer, or a hypocrite, by the erroneous decision of another concerning him.—' We say, that Christ ' hath given to his ministers power, to bind, to loose, to ' open, to shut, and that the office of *loosing* consisteth in ' this: either (1,) that the minister, by the preaching of

' the Gospel offereth the merits of Christ and full pardon ' to such as have lowly and contrite hearts, and do un- ' feignedly repent themselves; pronouncing unto the same ' a sure and undoubted forgiveness of their sins, and hope ' of everlasting salvation: or else, (2,) that the same mi- ' nister, when any have offended their brother's minds, ' with some great offence or notable and open crime, ' whereby they have, as it were, banished, and made them- ' selves strangers from, the common fellowship, and from ' the body of Christ, then, after perfect amendment of ' such persons, doth reconcile them, and bring them home ' again, and *restore them* to the company and unity of the ' faithful.—We say also, that the minister doth execute ' the authority of binding and shutting, (1,) as often as he ' shutteth up the gate of the kingdom of heaven against ' unbelieving and stubborn persons, *denouncing* unto them ' God's vengeance and everlasting punishment. Or else, ' (2,) when he doth shut them out from the bosom of the ' church by open *excommunication.*—Out of doubt, what ' sentence soever the minister of God shall give *in this* ' *sort,* God himself doth so well allow it, that whatsoever, ' here on earth is loosed and bound, God himself will loose ' and bind, and confirm the same in heaven.—And, touch- ' ing the keys, wherewith they may either open or shut the ' kingdom of heaven, we, with Chrysostom say, they may ' be the *knowledge of the scriptures:* with Tertullian we ' say, the *interpretation of the law,* (or word of God,) and ' with Eusebius, we call them *the word of God.' Bp. Jewel.*

V. 20. Our Lord having opened these things in confidence to his disciples, charged them not to speak to others concerning his being the Messiah. Let them collect it from the fulfilment of prophecy, and from his miracles and doctrine; but the time for an explicit declaration of it was not yet come.

V. 21—23. It is probable, that the apostles were at this time fully expecting their Lord's appearing in external glory, as " the King of Israel: " but, on the contrary, he began to shew them more openly than before, that he must go up to Jerusalem, to suffer many things from those in authority, and even to be put to death; but that on the third day he should rise again. (*Notes,* 17—19. *Mark* x. 32—34. *Luke* xxiv. 26—31.) Thus he proceeded to bring them acquainted with his *priestly* office; and to prepare their minds for those trying scenes, which they were about to witness. But Peter, who had overlooked all those prophecies which related to the Messiah's sufferings, and who probably was elated by the commendation bestowed on him, took him aside, or *by the hand,* and with a mixture of affection and ignorance, expressed to him his desire and hope, that it should not be so with him. The words are rendered by some, ' Spare thyself,' by others ' Mercy be unto thee;' or ' I hope and pray thou wilt be more favourably dealt with, and that this shall not happen to thee.' Our version, however, seems very fairly

B 4

suffer many things of the elders and chief priests and scribes, and be killed, and be raised again the third day.

22 Then Peter took him, and 'began to rebuke him, saying, ' Be it far from thee, Lord: this shall not be unto thee.

23 But he turned, and said unto Peter, ' Get thee behind me, ' Satan: thou art an offence unto me; for thou savourest not the things that be of God, but those that be of men.

24 Then said Jesus unto his disciples, ' If any man will come after me, let him deny himself, ' and take up his cross, and follow me.

25 For " whosoever will save his life shall lose it: and whosoever will lose his life for my sake, shall find it.

26 For " what is a man profited, if he shall ' gain the whole world, and lose his own soul ? ' or what shall a man give in exchange for his soul ?

27 For ' the Son of man shall come in the glory of his Father, ' with his angels ; ' and then he shall reward every man according to his works.

28 Verily I say unto you, ' There be some standing here, which shall not ' taste of death, till they " see the Son of man coming in his kingdom.

---

to give the true import of them. Thus Peter soon shewed how unfit he was to be the rock, on which the church was to be builded. Accordingly Christ turned, and rebuked him in the very terms which he had used in repelling the devil's temptations. (Luke iv. 8.) Some wish to soften the apparent harshness of the expression: but doubtless Christ intended to shew, that on this occasion Satan spake by Peter, and used him (without Peter's intention,) as an instrument in tempting Jesus to shun the cross. It was therefore proper to recognize Satan, as well as Peter, in the suggestion. Satan tempted Christ by Peter, as he did Eve by the serpent, and Adam by Eve. Thus Peter was " an offence," or stumbling-block, to Jesus : for in this instance he spake as a carnal man, who did not properly value, or relish, the spiritual excellency of divine things; but was more disposed to prize and choose the things of men, such as ease, indulgence, honour, and riches, than to understand the doctrine of redemption and the glory of God in it.

Be it far from thee. (22) Ἱλεως σοι (ab ιλαω, propitius, clemens sum:) Heb. viii. 12.—Jer. xxxi. 34. xxxvi. 3. Sept. —' Ἱλεως σοι est vox abominantis et dehortantis, latinè red-' denda : Deus meliora! Absit hoc! Deus hoc avertat!' Schleusner.—In the LXX, it represents חָלִילָה . 2 Sam. xxiii. 17. 1 Chr. xi. 19.—Offence. (23) Σκανδαλον offendiculum, obstaculum in viá positum. xviii. 7. Luke xvii. 1. Rom. xi. 9. xiv. 13. 1 Cor. i. 23. Gal. v. 11.—Lev. xix. 14. Sept.— Thou savourest.] Φρονεις. (' Φρονεω, proprie sapio, hoc est ' intelligo, scio, et video, quæ bona sint et appetenda; quæ- ' que fugienda et mala : à φρην, mens.' Schleusner.) Mark viii. 33. Rom. viii. 5. xii. 16. xiv. 6. 1 Cor. iv. 6. Gal. v. 10. Phil. iii. 16. Col. iii. 2.

V. 24—28. Our Lord next proceeded to remind the apostles, what they must expect in following him. (Note, x. 37—39.) He was, indeed, shortly to enter into his glory: but if any of them purposed to come thither after him, and to share the privileges of his kingdom; he must first learn from his example to " deny himself, take " up his cross," and follow him : he must habituate himself to give a flat denial to the most clamorous solicitations of his pride, ambition, avarice, and carnal self-love ; and to inure every selfish and sensual inclination to submission.

(Note, Luke ix. 18—27, v. 23.) He must also be prepared in mind, to take up and carry his cross, as a condemned person, to the place of execution ; determined rather to be nailed to it, and there expire, than to renounce his Lord, who had thus suffered an excruciating and ignominious death for his sins. And if any man should determine to save his life, even by denying Christ, he would certainly forfeit the eternal life of his soul ; which was ensured to those that should lay down their lives for his sake. To this, Jesus subjoined two most interesting questions, which are supposed to have been proverbial among the Jews. What would that man be profited, who should gain the possession of the whole world, all its riches, power, and splendour, but at the same time should in doing it lose his own life ? Or what could be deemed an adequate price to be given a man in exchange for his life, if that should be lost or forfeited ? If then all worldly things were worthless when compared with temporal life ; how forcibly must the same argument conclude in respect of the soul, and its state of eternal happiness or misery ! If a man should save his life, and gain the whole world, by apostasy from Christ, and thus lose the happiness, and ensure the destruction of his soul, where would be his gain ? (Note, Mark viii. 32—37, v. 36, 37.) Or, with what would he endeavour to redeem his forfeited felicity, or to rescue his soul from deserved misery? The Saviour indeed, at this time, appeared as " the Son " of man," in a state of humiliation, and was about to set them an example of constancy in holy obedience and of patient suffering even unto death. But he assured them, that he would at length appear "in the glory of his Father," displaying the divine perfections of power, wisdom, justice, truth, and mercy; exercising sovereign authority over all creatures; and attended with the holy angels as his servants: then he would graciously reward his disciples for all their self-denying services and patient sufferings for his sake, and execute righteous vengeance on his enemies ; thus rendering to believers and unbelievers, according to their works. And though this event was distant, yet verily some there present would certainly be preserved from death, notwithstanding all persecutions, till they saw him come to set up his kingdom in a glorious manner. This referred especially to the destruction of Jerusalem, and the aboli-

CHAP. XVII.

The transfiguration of Christ, who discourses with Moses and Elias, before Peter, James, and John, 1—8. He charges them not to make it known; and in-

structs them concerning the coming of Elias, 9—13. He casts out an evil spirit, and reproves the unbelief of the people and of his disciples, 14—21. He foretels his death and resurrection, 22, 23; and pays tribute with money obtained by miracle, 24—27.

---

tion of the Mosaick dispensation, when Christ came in his kingdom to destroy his most inveterate enemies. *Will come.* (24) Θιλη...ελθειν *willeth to come. Will come* is simply the future, and *will* merely an auxiliary; but θιλει implies much more. Thus θιλη...σωσαι in the next verse. The same remark holds good of many other places. See *John* vii. 17. *Gr.—Let him deny himself.*] Απαρνησασθω ἱαυτον. xxvi. 34, 35. *Luke* xii. 9.—' *To deny* ' *himself*, in the New Testament is taken for him, who re' nounces himself, and all the advantages of this life; so ' that he is prepared to despise and lose all his most valu' able possessions, and even his life, for the profession of ' the Christian religion. ...The discourse is not concerning ' *vice (vitiositate)* which is to be renounced, as not a few ' persons think; but concerning the advantages of this life, ' of which the follower of Christ must be prepared to suffer ' the loss with an undisturbed mind.' *Schleusner.* (*Note, Phil.* iii. 8—11.)—*Life.* (25) Ψυχην. (à ψυχω, spiro:) rendered *soul;* 26.—Ψυχη is used in different senses: 1. As signifying *persons; Acts* ii. 41. vii. 14. xxvii. 37. *Rom.* xiii. 1 : 2. *Life;* vi. 25. *Acts* xv. 26. xx. 10. 24. *Rom.* xi. 3. xvi. 4 : 3. *Soul, or eternal life;* x. 28. xi. 29. 1 *Cor.* xv. 45. *Heb.* x. 39. xiii. 17. 1 *Pet.* i. 9, &c.—*Lose.* (26) Ζημιωθη. (à ζημια, mulcta, pœna:) *Mark* viii. 36. 1 *Cor.* iii. 15. *Phil.* iii. 8 : rendered *be·cast away; Luke* ix. 25.—Opposed to κερδησει.—*In exchange.*] Ανταλλαγμα· commutatio, pretium redemptionis. *Mark* viii. 37. Not elsewhere in the New Testament.—*Ruth* iv. 7. *Job* xxviii. 15. *Jer.* xv. 13. Sept. —*Works.* (27) Την πραξιν. (Α πρασσω.) Πραξις· factum, negotium, officium: rendered *deed; Luke* xxiii. 51 : and *office; Rom.* xii. 4.—Πραξις· res gestæ, vita, vivendi ratio : rendered *deeds; Acts* xix. 18. *Rom.* viii. 13.—Πραξεις των αποστολων " The Acts of the Apostles."

PRACTICAL OBSERVATIONS.

V. 1—12.

Ungodly men, of discordant sentiments and parties, are united under one common head, and engaged in one common opposition to the cause of Christ: and infidels, Pharisees, and time-servers, often postpone their subordinate controversies, that they may join their subtlety and influence in opposing the word of God. Men frequently discover great ingenuity and sagacity, they make accurate observations, and deduce just inferences, in matters of a temporal nature: yet when they turn their minds to religious subjects, they seem incapable of understanding the plainest truths, which run counter to their interests, passions, and prejudices. And many are constrained to act on probable evidence, in their most important secular concerns, who perversely demand demonstration in every thing relating to Religion, nay, refuse to be satisfied with demonstration itself! But Christ will convict such disingenuous prevaricators : and, in the mean time, it is commouly best for us to leave them, and not to waste our time, or give them a handle, by disputing with them.— We ought not indeed allowedly to neglect our temporal

concerns, in attending to those of our souls : yet if any are betrayed into it occasionally, through great earnestness about spiritual things, they need not fear but the Lord will provide for them. Our main concern should be, to beware of false teachers and false doctrine; and to avoid the leaven of hypocrisy, pride, and infidelity, which diffuse their baneful influence on every side : yet even disciples are sometimes more anxious concerning the supply of their wants, than about keeping at a distance from error and sin. This arises from weakness of faith, and will expose them to rebukes.—Should the Lord interrogate us, under many of our despondings, concerning our past experience of his power, truth, and love; he would soon shew us, what cause we have to be ashamed of our present distrust and solicitude; and force us to confess, that we did not properly understand and remember his former interpositions in our favour. But it is well, if we learn to profit by our own dulness and mistakes, and are made more attentive to his instructions.

V. 13—20.

We often *foolishly* want to know what men say of us, expecting perhaps some flattering report; and this commouly tends to our vexation, or acts as a temptation to resentment or discontent : but our blessed Lord had *wise*, holy, and important reasons for making a similar enquiry; and we ought to imitate his manner of grafting instructive observations on every topick of conversation.—There are various opinions concerning the Lord Jesus ; and they, who think the most honourably of him, come nearest to the truth : but none can be his true disciples, who hesitate to confess, " that he is the Christ, the Son of the living " God," or who labour to explain away the meaning of such emphatical words. Happy are they, who confess this from an understanding and believing heart! Whatever may be their present errors and infirmities, or their future trials and temptations, they certainly are specially favoured by the Lord : for human teaching *alone* has not given them this knowledge of the truth, but it is the gift of their heavenly Father, and an earnest of further favours.—We should learn to make candid allowances for enquirers who seem to have an honest and teachable spirit, but are yet strangers to many important truths : for not the doctrines known and believed, but the origin, nature, and effects of their faith and knowledge, distinguish the true disciples from other men.—The Person and work of Christ, the Son of God, is the Rock, on which alone the church is built ; and hell the powers of darkness plot and rage, let infidels and hereticks revile and menace as they please, they will never be able to subvert this foundation, or to destroy one soul which rests his hope upon it.—We have not at present such authority as was entrusted to the apostles, and none can forgive sins but God only; yet let no man despise the declarations and censures of faithful ministers : for, as far as they agree with the word of God they are ratified in heaven; whether they pronounce the penite :t

¹ Mark ix. 2. AND ¹ after six days Jesus taketh ᵇ Peter, James, and John his brother, and bringeth them up into ᶜ an high mountain apart,

2 And was ⁴ transfigured before them: and ᵉ his face did shine as the sun, and his ᶠ raiment was white as the light.

—15. Rev. i. 13—17. x. 1. xix. 12, 13. xx. 11.

and believing to be fully pardoned, or the unbelieving and hypocritical to remain under the wrath of God.

V. 21—28.

We ought not so to regard one part of the Redeemer's character, as to overlook another; but should keep in view at once, the depth of his voluntary humiliation and sufferings as our great High Priest, and the height of his exaltation as our glorious King. In like manner, we should connect our view of the believer's privileges with that of his duty, and of the cross which he must bear in the way to glory. But it often happens, that men speak so excellently of one part of Christianity, as to be entitled to commendation; and yet betray their ignorance and carnal prejudices, when they give their sentiments on other subjects, and so lay themselves open to deserved rebukes. Those who would dissuade us from self-denying duties, or set us against the cross, which lies in our path, and would counsel us to turn aside, in order to shun it, ought in that respect, to be considered as adversaries : and in all carnal counsellors we should recognize the voice of Satan, whose policy is to tempt us by those whom we love, and who are in other things most worthy of our esteem. We must not parley with such as " are an offence to us," but decidedly reject their solicitations; shewing them, that their false tenderness springs from their " savouring," not the " things of God, but those of men."—But what repeated instructions do we need, to teach us to deny ourselves, and to copy the example of our suffering Redeemer; and to convince us, that every disciple must have the spirit of a martyr, whether it ever be put to the trial, or not!—If life is so valuable, that the whole world is a paltry compensation for the loss of it, and unworthy to be given in exchange for it, what words can describe, or computation reach, the worth of an immortal soul? It is the noblest work of God below, formed at first in his own image, possessed of vast and most valuable powers, capable of most exquisite happiness or misery, and intended for eternal existence. Such an invaluable treasure every man is possessed of; but how few seem sensible of its preciousness, or of the danger of losing it! This loss consists in the final and eternal forfeiture of the favour of God, in deprivation of his image, and banishment from his presence, in the regions of darkness, misery, and despair.—The souls of all men are in themselves thus lost, by transgression of the holy law of our Creator; yet, through the mercy of the Lord Jesus, none will eventually perish, but the impenitent and unbelieving. Could any man therefore obtain the whole world, and the sure enjoyment of it during a thousand years, as his recompence for neglecting the salvation of the gospel; he would, through the countless ages of eternity, curse his own folly, in making so mad a bargain. Yet millions lose their souls for the sake of the most trivial gain, or the most worthless indulgence, nay, from mere sloth and negligence! for whatever the object be for which men refuse or forsake Christ, that is

the price at which Satan purchases their souls. But alas! we are all propense to believe the soothing lies of that cruel murderer and his emissaries, and to disbelieve the alarming truths of God and his ministers : we are disposed to procrastinate, or to take it for granted that all is well, when it is far otherwise; and therefore men lose their souls for " a thing of nought."—But what can they give in exchange for them? Alas! death reduces the wealthiest sinner to the level of the meanest beggar, and he has nought to give. The dying transgressor however wealthy, cannot, with all his treasure, perhaps acquired by iniquity, purchase one hour's respite, in order to seek the mercy of his offended God. The whole world in this case is of no " be let alone for ever," by all who neglect the precious ransom which the Saviour once paid, when " he gave him-" self for us, to redeem us from all iniquity, and to purify " us to himself, a peculiar people, zealous of good works." Let us then learn to value our souls, and Christ as the Saviour of ruined souls; and to despise every glittering bait, and every formidable danger, by which Satan would allure or fright us from our only refuge. Let us fear coming short of this salvation, and continually anticipate the season, when " the Son of Man shall come in the glory of " his Father, and all his holy angels with him, to reward " every man according to his works :" for he will mercifully recompense the fruits of his own grace in us, and all our losses and sufferings for his sake : " but, if any man " draw back, his soul will have no pleasure in him." Though our trials must come first; yet they will soon be over : we shall speedily behold our once suffering Saviour in his glory, and our transient taste of death will introduce us into " his presence where is fulness of joy, and plea- " sures at his right hand for evermore."

NOTES.

CHAP. XVII. V. 1, 2. (Marg. Ref.) The evangelists Matthew and Mark, place this event six days after the discourse of the preceding chapter, as six whole days intervened : but St. Luke, taking in both the day of the discourse, and that of the transfiguration, says that it was eight days after. (Luke ix. 28.)—Our Lord retired to a mountain apart to pray, where he spent the night, as he did on some other occasions : (Note, Luke vi. 12 :) tradition reports that it was Tabor, a lofty mountain to the north of Galilee. He was pleased to take with him Peter, James, and John, but not the other apostles, because it " seemed good in his sight ; " for we cannot assign any other satisfactory reason. The same apostles had witnessed the resurrection of Jairus's daughter, and they afterwards attended him in his agony in the garden. (xxvi. 37. Mark v. 37.) There was a competent number to prove the fact, and more were unnecessary. While engaged in prayer " he " was transfigured," or metamorphosed, before them. The apostles saw their Master daily in " the form of a Servant," and as the Son of Man : but on this occasion, they " be-

n 7

3 And, ᵉ behold, there appeared unto them ᵇ Moses and ⁱ Elias, talking with him.

4 Then ᵏ answered Peter, and said unto Jesus, Lord, ⁱ it is good for us to be here: if thou wilt, let us make here three tabernacles; one for thee, and one for Moses, and one for Elias.

5 While he yet spake, ᵐ behold, a bright cloud overshadowed them: and behold ⁿ a voice out of the cloud, which

said, ᵒ This is my beloved Son, ᵖ in whom I am well pleased; ᑫ hear ye him.

6 And when the disciples heard it, ʳ they fell on their face, and were sore afraid.

7 And Jesus came and ˢ touched them, and said, ᵗ Arise, and be not afraid.

8 And when they had lifted up their eyes, ᵘ they saw no man, save Jesus only.

" held his glory, as of the Only begotten of the Father," and had such a discovery of him " in the form of God," as they were able to sustain. (Note, Phil. ii. 9—11.) His disguise was, as it were, laid aside, and he appeared like himself: " the Sun of Righteousness," " the Light of the " world," shone forth, from behind those clouds which commonly obscured his splendour. " The fashion of his " countenance was altered," and " did shine like the sun:" and his very " raiment became white as snow, so as no " fuller on earth could whiten it;" (Mark ix. 3;) yea, " white as the light," and resplendent as lightning. This appearance of Christ, as Man, would give the apostles some faint conception of the divine glory, which he had with the Father before his incarnation, and which was always inherent in him, though he saw good to veil it under external meanness. It would serve to interpret to them the meaning of their own confession, " thou art the Son " of the living God:" it was intended to support their faith, at that approaching season, when they would witness his crucifixion: and it would give them an idea of his heavenly glory after his ascension; and of the glory prepared for them also, when changed by his power to be like him, even in respect of his glorified body. (Notes, 1 Cor. xv. 45—49. Phil. iii. 20, 21.)

Was transfigured. (2) Μεταμορφώθη. Mark ix. 2. Rom. xii. 2. 2 Cor. iii. 18.—' Μεταμορφοομαι, novam formam sumo, ' personam plané aliam induo, transfiguror, transformor ; ex ' μετα, trans, et μορφοω, formo, à μορφη, forma.' Schleusner. Μορφη. Mark xvi. 12. Phil. ii. 6, 7.

V. 3. (Marg. Ref.) In addition to the personal glory which our Lord at this time manifested, there appeared Moses and Elijah conversing with him, on the subject of the painful and ignominious death, which he was shortly to suffer at Jerusalem. (Notes, Luke ix. 28—36, v. 31.) The apostles, hearing at least part of this conversation, probably understood from it, that the persons whom they saw were Moses and Elijah. Elijah was taken up alive into heaven, and doubtless appeared in his glorified body : how Moses appeared is no proper subject for our enquiry ; but, as Christ rose " the first fruits " of all who rise to die no more, there is no ground for the notion, that the body of Moses was raised for the very purpose.—This scene was suited to give the apostles a realizing apprehension of the invisible world, and of the present felicity of departed believers, to which they would immediately be admitted, if " faithful unto death." These two eminent

persons attended on Jesus, as servants on their Lord, coming, as it were, on purpose to do him homage ; glorious indeed, but with glory far beneath His ; as the planets are less resplendent than the noon-day sun, from whom they derive their lustre, and by whose beams they are eclipsed. Moses was the great lawgiver of Israel, and Elijah the chief of the prophets; but they both came, to lay down their commissions and their honours at the Redeemer's feet ; in whose person, and obedience unto death, the moral law was magnified, the ceremonial types were fulfilled, the prophecies were accomplished, and the end of all preceding dispensations answered. Thus Moses and Elijah bare witness to the apostles, that Jesus was their Lord also; and that by his coming, the time of the law and the prophets was terminated, and that of the gospel introduced. (Notes, Mark ix. 2—10. John i. 16—18. 1 Pet. i. 10—12.)

V. 4. With this glorious scene before their eyes, the apostles were heavy with sleep, either overpowered by the splendour, or drowsy through weariness : (Luke ix. 32 :) but when they were awaked, Peter, delighted and surprised to see his beloved Master " appear in glory " and receive such honour, instead of hearkening to the discourse, broke out into an exclamation, that it was most pleasant and desirable for them to continue there, and not to go down any more to meet those sufferings, of which he was so reluctant to hear. (Marg. Ref. 1.—Note, xvi. 24—28, vv. 22, 23.) He therefore proposed to erect on the mountain three tents, for Jesus, Moses, and Elijah : but in this he knew not what he said. (Mark ix. 6. Luke ix. 33.) That sacrifice was not yet offered, without which his sinful soul could not have been saved ; and most important services were appointed to him and his brethren, for the glory of God, and the good of the church, in all succeeding ages. Peter on this occasion also " savoured the things of " men," and was not meet for the spiritual felicity to which he aspired ; and he seems to have forgotten the other disciples who were left below, from a regard to his own present ease and comfort. He however scarcely understood the meaning of his own proposal, which was rather the language of his feelings, than of his understanding. (Notes, John xiii. 36—38, v. 37. 2 Pet. i. 12—18.)

V. 5—8. While Peter was speaking, " a bright cloud " overshadowed them ;" an emblem of the divine presence and glory, but so veiled as to suit their mortal state :

9 And as they came down from the mountain, *Jesus charged them, saying, Tell the vision to no man, *until the Son of man be risen again from the dead.

10 And his disciples asked him, saying, *Why then say the scribes that Elias must first come?

11 And Jesus answered and said unto them, Elias truly shall first come, *and restore all things:

12 But I say unto you, That Elias is come already, *and they knew him not, *but have done unto him whatsoever they listed: *likewise shall also the Son of man suffer of them.

13 Then *the disciples understood that he spake unto them of John the Baptist.

14 ¶ And *when they were come to the multitude, there came to him a *certain* man, *kneeling down to him, and saying,

15 Lord, *have mercy on my son; *for he is lunatick, and sore vexed: *for oft-times he falleth into the fire, and oft into the water.

16 And I brought him to thy disciples, *and they could not cure him.

17 Then Jesus answered and said, *O faithless and perverse generation, *how long shall I be with you? how

yet it was not like the tremendous display from mount Sinai at the giving of the law, nor like the thick darkness by which the Lord took possession of the temple; but "a "bright cloud," denoting the introduction of a clearer and more encouraging discovery of the divine glory by the gospel. (*Marg. Ref.* m.) From this cloud, a voice was distinctly heard, which coincided with the testimony borne to Jesus at his baptism; the eternal Father declaring "him to be his well beloved Son, in whom he was well "pleased." (*Note*, iii. 16, 17, *v.* 17.) To this was added a command to them to "hear him," to receive his instructions in obedient faith, even in preference to Moses and the prophets, whose *external* appointments he would supersede or alter. This glorious vision astonished and terrified the apostles; and they fell prostrate in adoration and dismay, and lay till Jesus came to encourage them: when arising and looking around, they found that the vision was departed, and their Lord left alone with them in his usual appearance; save that, it is probable, some lustre still continued in his countenance, even after they went down from the mount. (*Marg. Ref.* n—u.—*Notes*, Mark ix. 2—10, *vv.* 7, 8. *Luke* ix. 28—36, *vv.* 34—36.)

V. 9. As Jesus came down, the next day, to the other apostles and the people, he charged those with him, not to mention the instructive and animating scene which they had witnessed, till after his resurrection from the dead: for before that event it would not have obtained credit; and it was, for the present, rather intended for their own support and encouragement, than for the conviction of others. It seems, that the other disciples were included in this general charge, so that it must not be mentioned even to them.—(*Marg. Ref.* x, y. Mark ix. 9, 10.—*Note*, 2 Pet. i. 16—19.)

The vision.] Τὸ ὅραμα, ab ὁραω, *to see.*—'Α εἶδον. *Mark* ix. 9. Οὐδὲν ὧν ἐωρακασιν. *Luke* ix. 36.

V. 10—13. The apostles, being fully convinced that Jesus was the promised Messiah, and that he would speedily set up his glorious kingdom, were nevertheless unable to reconcile these things with the doctrine of the scribes; that Elias, or Elijah, "must first come;" especially as it was grounded on an express prophecy in Malachi. (*Marg. Ref.* z—a.—*Notes*, Mal. iii. 1—4, v. 1. iv. 2—6.)—Perhaps they supposed that the appearance of Elijah on the mount

was intended; and, in that case, why must they conceal it? To this our Lord replied, that it had doubtless been predicted that Elijah would come, and restore, or regulate, all things, in order to prepare the way for the Messiah's kingdom; but that in fact he had come, and the people and scribes had not known or believed him, and at length he had been put to death by the malice of his enemies: and in like manner they would also persecute and slay their promised Messiah, as it had been predicted by the prophets. —By this the disciples more clearly perceived, that John the Baptist had been foretold under the name of Elijah, because of the similarity of his disposition and ministerial labours. (*Notes*, xi. 7—15.)—'He shall *finish*, or *perform*, 'establish, settle all things; both perform all that was pro-'phesied of Elias at his coming, and close and shut up 'the first state of the world, that of the Mosaical œcono-'my, making entrance, as a harbinger, on the second, 'that of the Messias. In this sense it is that it is said, '"the law and the prophets were until John," noting him 'to be the conclusion and shutting up, finishing and 'closing, of that state; and that was to be the office of 'Elias, under whose name John was prefigured.' *Hammond.*—'The Scribes and Pharisees "have done to him '"whatsoever they listed," rejecting his baptism, (*Luke* 'vii. 30,) and refusing to believe his doctrine, (xxi. 25,) '... or to own him as a prophet from God, saying that '"he had a devil." ... And it is probable, that both 'they and the Sadducees did this, because he had 'styled them "a generation of vipers." (iii. 7.) And 'though we do not read that they gave occasion either to 'his imprisonment or to his death; yet may we reasonably 'conceive, that they, who thus thought and spake of him, 'were well pleased at it; ... it being not for fear of them, 'but only of the multitude who accounted him as a pro-'phet, that Herod, for a season, was restrained from kill-'ing him.' *Whitby* on Mark ix. 13.—(*Marg. Ref.* b—e. *Notes*, iii. 1—3. *Mark* ix. 11—13. *Luke* i. 11—17. 76—79. *John* i. 6—9. 19—29.)

Shall restore, &c. (11) Αποκαταστησει. (Ex ἀπο, and Καθιστημι.)—*In pristinum statum restituet.* xii. 13. *Mark* iii. 5. viii. 25. *Luke* vi. 10. *Acts* i. 6. *Heb.* xiii. 19.—*Ex.* iv. 7. *Sept.*

V. 14—18. *Notes*, Mark ix. 16—27. *Luke* ix. 37—

long shall I suffer you? Bring him hither to me.

a xii. 22. Mark i. 34, x. 8. Ix. 25. —27. Luke iv. 39, 36, 41. viii. 29. Ix. 42. Acts xvi. 18. xix. 15—15.
18 And Jesus *c* rebuked the devil, and he departed out of him: and the child was cured *f* from that very hour.

p ix. 22. xv. 28. John iv. 37, 53.
19 Then *q* came the disciples to Jesus apart, and said, Why could not we cast him out?

q Mark iv. 10. Ix. 28.
r 17. xii. 20, 31.
s xxi. 21. Mark xi. 23. Luke xvii. 6. 1 Cor.
20 And Jesus said unto them, *r* Because of your unbelief: for verily I say unto you, *s* If ye have faith as *t* a grain of mustard-seed, ye shall say unto this mountain, Remove hence to yonder place; and it shall remove; and *u* nothing shall be impossible unto you.

t Luke xvii. 6. 1 Cor.
u Mark ix. 23. Luke xvii. 6.
x xii. 45.
y 1 Kings xvii. 20, 21. Dan. ix. 3. Mark ix. 29. Acts xiii. 2, 3. xiv. 23. 1 Cor. vii. 5. 2 Cor. xi. 27. Eph. vi. 18.
21 Howbeit *x* this kind goeth not out *y* but by prayer and fasting.

z xvi. 21. xx. 17, 18. 20, 31. x. 33. 34. Luke ix. 22. 44. xviii. 31—34. xxiv. 6, 7. 26, 46.
22 And while they abode in Galilee, Jesus said unto them, *z* The Son of

---

man shall be *a* betrayed into the hands of men;

a xxiv. 10. xxvi. 16, 46. Acts vii. 52. 1 Cor. xi. 23.
23 And *b* they shall kill him, and *c* the third day he shall be raised again. *d* And they were exceeding sorry.

b Ps. xxii. 16, 22, &c. Is. liii. 7.
c 16—12. Dan. ix. 26. Zech. xiii. 7.
c Ps. xvi. 10. John ii. 19. Acts ii. 23
24 ¶ And *c* when they were come to Capernaum, they that received *e* tribute-*money* came to Peter, and said, Doth not your Master pay tribute?

c —8l. 1 Cor. xv. 3, 4.
d John xvi. 6. 20, 22.
e Mark ix. 33.
25 He saith, *f* Yes. And when he was come into the house, Jesus prevented him, saying, What thinkest thou, Simon? of whom do the kings of the earth take custom or tribute? of their own children, or of strangers?

in value fifteen pence. Ex. xxx. 13. xxxviii. 26.
f iii. 15. xxii. 21. Rom. xiii. 6, 7.
g 1 Sam. xvii. 25.
26 Peter saith unto him, Of strangers. Jesus saith unto him, Then are the children free.

44.—*Kneeling.* (14) *Marg. Ref. g.*—*Lunatick.* .(15) Σεληνιαζεται. (A σεληνη, luna.) That is, one whose malady has paroxysms at certain seasons of the moon. (See on iv. 24.) This is the case in some kinds of madness and epilepsy.—No doubt this youth had an epilepsy; of which an evil spirit taking advantage, produced all those extraordinary and distressing effects, which are more fully recorded in the other gospels.—*Faithless.* (17) The scribes and multitude were chiefly meant in this rebuke; yet the disciples, and even the father of the child, shewed a very reprehensible degree of unbelief on this occasion. (*Marg. Ref. m.*—*Notes,* 19, 20. John xxi. 24—29, v. 27.)—*Shall I suffer you?* Ανεξομαι. Mark ix. 19. Luke ix. 41. Acts xviii. 14. 1 Cor. iv. 12. 2 Cor. xi. 1. 4. 19, 20. 2 Thes. i. 4.—*Note,* Num. xiv. 11; 12.)

V. 19, 20. The apostles had doubtless in some instances cast out devils; but being baffled at this time, they enquired the reason of their disappointment. To this Jesus replied, that it was wholly owing to their unbelief. Perhaps they had been discouraged in the attempt, by an apprehension of the difficulty of the case: they had not, however, that simple and entire reliance on the power and promise of Christ, which was requisite. For if this had been the case, though their faith had been small, and apparently inadequate to the effect, like a grain of mustard-seed, they might, had that been necessary, have removed the mountain before them; as nothing could be impossible to the almighty power, which faith engaged on their side. —'By "faith as a grain of mustard-seed;" (xiii. 31;) ... 'some understand a faith that groweth and increaseth as 'a grain of mustard-seed. ... Christ elsewhere, for "the '"removing of a mountain," ... (xxi. 21,) requires ... '"faith in God," (Mark xi. 22, 23,) which seems to signify 'an excelling faith, "faith without doubting." ... St. Paul 'reckons faith able "to remove mountains," as the 'strongest faith. (1' Cor. xiii. 2.) ... According to this ex-'position the sense runs thus, Did your faith increase, 'according to the examples of God's power you have had 'before your eyes; as the grain of mustard-seed grows up

---

' to be the greatest of all herbs, so would your faith trans-' mount and grow superior to all difficulties.—A remover ' of mountains seems only to import ... a doer of those ' things which are exceeding difficult, and beyond the ' power of nature to perform.' *Whitby.*—Both these ex-pressions seem to have been taken from proverbs com-mouly used at that time, and therefore more fully under-stood by our Lord's hearers, than they are by us. 'Thus ' the Rabbies say, The globe of the earth is but as a *grain* ' *of mustard-seed,* when compared with the expanse of the ' heavens.' *Doddridge.* (*Marg. Ref. s*—u.)

V. 21. This seems clearly to intimate, that there are different orders of evil spirits, some more powerful and malignant than others; (xii. 45;) and that these could not be cast out, except by persons who were much engaged in fasting and prayer. As success depended on the strength and simplicity of faith; "fasting and prayer" may be con-sidered as proper means for increasing humility, zeal, com-passion, and those holy affections of the soul, with which vigorous and simple faith must be intimately connected: and the spirit of the instruction is equally applicable to us, in our personal conflicts and publick services.—'Because ' devotion is apt to grow dull and faint, there must be an ' exercise of fasting and abstinence, to put an edge upon ' it, and to stir it up.' *Bp. Hall.* (*Marg. Ref.*—*Mark* ix. 29, 30.—*Note,* ix. 14, 15.)

V. 22, 23. *Marg. Ref.*—*Notes, Mark* ix. 30—32. x. 32—34. *Luke* ix. 45. *John* xii. 34—36, v. 34.—*While they* *abode,* &c. (22) Αναστρεφομενων αυτων.—"While they went " from place to place in Galilee," (Παρεπορευοντο δια της Γαλιλαιας. *Mark* ix. 30.) Or " had their conversation, " &c." 2 *Cor.* i. 12. *Eph.* ii. 3. 1 *Tim.* iii. 15. *Heb.* x. 33. xiii. 18. 1 *Pet.* i. 17. 2 *Pet.* ii. 18.

V. 24—27. The tribute here mentioned seems to have been the half-shekel a-piece, which was collected to de-fray the expense of the service of the sanctuary. (*Marg.* —*Notes, Ex.* xxx. 11—16. 2 *Kings* xii. 4, 5. *Neh.* x. 32, 33.) This at first was collected occasionally, as wanted; but we are informed by Josephus, that in his time it was

s 2

xv. 12—14. Rom. xiv. 21. vv. 1—3. 1 Cor. viii. 9, 13. ix. 19—22. x. 32, 33. 2 Cor. vi. 3. 1 Thes. v. 22. Tit. ii. 7, 8. ii. 10. Heb. ii. 7, 8.

27 Notwithstanding, ʰ lest we should offend them, go thou to the sea, and cast an hook, ¹ and take up the fish

ⁱ Gen. l. 28. 1 Kings xvii. 4. Ps. viii. 8. Jon. i. 17.

that first cometh up; and when thou hast opened his mouth, thou shalt find *a piece of money: ᵏ that take, and give unto them for me and thee.

* Or, a stater, half an ounce of silver, value 2s. 6d. k 2 Cor. viii. 9. Jam. ii. *.

paid annually, by all above twenty years of age.—Peter, when asked if his master did not pay this tribute, answered at once, that he did; knowing him to be ready for every act of piety and equity. But Jesus, preventing his mention of the subject by shewing that he knew what had passed, asked him, of whom kings were accustomed to levy taxes; whether of their own children, or of strangers. *Children*, in this connexion, must be understood literally; and *strangers* must mean the children of others: for kings generally collect taxes from their subjects, though their own families be exempted. By this question he intimated that as "the Son of God," the Lord of the temple, (and in this character the Jews ought to have recognized and welcomed him,) he had no right to contribute to the expenses there incurred, for the benefit of those, who in themselves were strangers and enemies.—' Our Saviour's argument, ' why he should not pay this tribute, as being the Son of ' that King to whom it was paid, holds not with reference ' to the other tribute paid to Cæsar, he being not the Son ' of Cæsar, but of God.' *Whitby*.—Lest, however, any should take offence at his refusal, as if regardless of the temple-worship, he waved his privilege: and, as he had no money, he ordered Peter to cast a hook into the sea, which was close by; and assured him that in the mouth of the first fish which he caught, he should find a piece of money, containing a shekel of silver, which would suffice for them both.—' By which example Christ teacheth us to ' avoid the scandal and sinister suspicions of men, though ' they be groundless, with some detriment to ourselves, ' especially when we have not means to convince them. ... ' The scandal of the Pharisees, proceeding not from igno-' rance but pure malice, he is not thus concerned to avoid. ' (xv. 12.)' *Whitby*. (*Marg. Ref.* h.)—The external poverty of Christ, contrasted with this display of divine glory, must sensibly affect every considerate mind. By whatever means this piece of money was lodged in the mouth of the fish, *omniscience* alone could discover it there, and *omnipotence* ensure its being first brought to Peter's hook. Had Jesus so pleased, all the treasures in the depths of the sea, and in the heart of the earth, might with equal ease have been laid at his feet. His poverty was therefore voluntary, as our suffering Surety; to take away the reproach of an indigent station, and to reconcile his people to it, as best and safest for them.—The other disciples, it is probable, paid the tribute, either in the several cities where they had lived, or at some other time. —*A piece of money*. (27) " A stater." *Marg*. The stater was equal to two Didrachmas; (24, *marg*.) or of the same value as a shekel.

PRACTICAL OBSERVATIONS.

V. 1—13.

Discoveries of the Redeemer's divine majesty greatly assist us, in rightly understanding the motive, the benefit, and the glory of his abasement. Could we now behold that sacred countenance, which once, for our sins, was disfigured with blood and spitting, we should view it more resplendent than the meridian sun. We should see the Saviour no longer " crowned with thorns," insulted with the purple robe, and nailed to the cross between two robbers: but " arrayed with light as a garment," and surrounded with the adoring throng of prophets, apostles, saints, and angels, emulating each other, who should most rapturously celebrate his praises: yea, we should hear the eternal Father, from the inaccessible light in which he dwells invisible, proclaim the honours of the Redeemer as his coequal Son, and regard himself as glorified in all the adorations rendered to him. (*Notes, John* v. 20—23, v. 23. *Phil*. ii. 9—11, v. 11.) But alas! how dull and drowsy are our minds, when we would contemplate such subjects!—If, however, by faith we get a glimpse of our Redeemer's glory, and our hearts glow with love and joy ; we find our heaven begun, and we are ready to say, "It is " good for us to be here;" and we want always to continue in that pleasant frame of spirit, and to spend our lives in contemplation. But we know not what we say or do: even in this there is a large proportion of carnal self-love; some knowledge indeed of the essence of felicity; but great ignorance of what is needful to fit us for it, and of the situation in which we are placed during our continuance here. These glimpses and foretastes are vouchsafed to prepare us for tribulations, and to support us under them; but we must pass through varying experiences in our way to glory, and spend our lives in self-denying services, for the honour of Christ and the benefit of his people.—We know not what we shall at last be: yet we are assured, that when the Saviour shall appear we shall be like him ; and as our bodies must be changed by his omnipotence, so must our souls be transfigured and transformed by his renewing grace. This should be our grand *personal* object, whilst we wait for the time, when he " will receive " us to himself, that where he is there we may be also." In order to this, we must obediently hear him, as our Prophet and King ; trust in him as the great Mediator, " in " whom " the Father " is well pleased;" and wait for the communication of his grace, in fervent prayer, and retirement from the hurry of this vain world.—But we could not now endure the refulgence of the divine glory: not only the terrors of mount Sinai, but the glories of mount Tabor, would overwhelm us; save for the gracious interposition, and encouraging words, of the incarnate Saviour.—After sweet seasons of communion with God, we must return to our several employments: yet the Saviour will be with us, if we rely on his promises and are observant of his precepts; and we should ever keep in mind his death and resurrection, and anticipate the time, when we shall behold him in glory, and be for ever with him.—But even with the scriptures in our hands, how apt are we to overlook the accomplishments of them ' And how little in comparison has yet been effected, in bringing fallen sinners unto God, by the labours of all his servants! Men knew not the Son of the Father; but crucified and slew him; and we need not wonder, if they treat his disciples and ministers in the same manner.

s 3

CHAP. XVIII.

Jesus teaches humility, by the emblem of a little child, 1—4. He inculcates attention to his " little " ones," and watchfulness against stumbling others, or falling ourselves, 5—10. He illustrates his care of his people, by the parable of a lost sheep, 11—14; shews how to act towards an offending brother, 15—17; assures the apostles that what they bind or loose shall be bound or loosed in heaven, 18; gives special promises to those who unite in prayer, or meet in his name, 19, 20; and enforces the constant forgiveness of injuries, by a parable of a king, and his dealings with a servant, who was deeply indebted to him; yet was not influenced by his readiness to forgive him, to forgive his fellow-servant, 21—35.

AT ᵃthe same time came the disciples unto Jesus, saying, ᵇWho is the greatest ᶜin the kingdom of heaven ᵈ

2 And Jesus called ᵈa little child unto him, and set him in the midst of them,

3 And said, ᵉVerily I say unto you, ᶠExcept ye be converted, ᶠand become as little children, ye shall not ʰenter ᶦ into the kingdom of heaven.

4 Whosoever therefore shall ʲhumble himself as this little child, the same is ᵏgreatest in the kingdom of heaven.

a Mark ix. 33.
b xxiii.
xxiii. 11. Mark
iv. 36. 3.
45. Luke xx 46
—48. xxii. 24.—
27. Rom. xii. 10.
Phil. ii. 3.
c iii. 2. v. 19, 20.
vii. 21. Mark x.
14, 15.
d xix.
1 Kings iii. 7.
Jen. i. 7. Mark
ix. 36, &c.
e v. 18. vi. 2. 5. 16.
John i. 51. iii. 3.
xiii. 1b. Ps. &.
13. Is. vi. 1b.
Mark ix. 13.-
Luke xxii. 32.
xxviii. 27. Jam.
v. 19, 20.
3 hark x. 14, 15.
Luke xviii. 16,
17. 1 Cor. xiv.
20. 1 Pet. ii.2.
f 1.
i xxiii. 12.
h ark x. 43.
h v. 20. xix. 23.
Luke xiii. 24. John iii. 5.
Ps. cxxxi. 1, 2.
Luke xviii. 16. 1 Pet. v. 5.
Acts xiv. 22. 2 Pet.
i. 11.
Luke iv. 48.
k i. xx. 26.

V. 14—27.

Manifold are the troubles of body and mind, personal and domestick, to which we are liable, by the power of Satan, and for our sins: but, through the goodness of our God, hitherto we have not been destroyed, though sorely vexed and endangered; and if our troubles bring us humbly to seek help from Christ, they will eventually be " for " our profit." We may do right in applying to disciples, and they may be desirous to help us, though often unable: nothing, however, but our unbelief and disobedience, can preclude us from finding relief in Christ: yet he will sharply rebuke us, if we remain faithless and perverse amidst abundant opportunities of instruction and conviction. Should we enquire the reason of our ill success, in our conflicts with sin and temptation, and our endeavours to do good; the answer would still be, " Because of your " unbelief." Wonderful is the power of holy faith; and nothing is impossible to those who go forth in the Redeemer's name, to obey his commands and promote his cause. But our faith will commonly be strong, and our efforts successful, in proportion as we seek the victory " by " fasting and prayer;" and it especially behoves us to make a fair trial of this method, as to those particular conflicts in which we have been most foiled; and those services, respecting which we deplore our want of success.— What a varied scene of outward debasement, and of divine glory, was the life of our Redeemer! Yet all his humiliation made way for his resurrection and final exaltation. Let us then " endure the cross," despise riches and worldly honours, and be contented in poverty, if that be his will concerning us. Let those who are rich learn to be poor in spirit, and not to trust in riches, or to despise the poor, lest they be found to have reproached their Saviour, as well as their Maker. (Notes, 1 Tim. vi. 16—19. Jam. i. 9— 11. ii. 5—7.)—We should always be ready to wave our privileges and exemptions, rather than give offence. Yet we seldom follow the dictates of our own minds, without enquiring the will of God, but we fall into some mistakes, even in things apparently most obvious.—Even the poor believer should be ready to pay tribute and custom, for the credit of the gospel, and trust in the Lord to defray the expense: and " the fishers of men," though needy, may go on cheerfully in their work, trusting in the Lord to

supply their wants : for he will, when necessary, bring to their net, such as shall be both able and willing to contribute to the support of his cause.—But how glorious are the privileges, and how noble the freedom, of the children of the King of kings! To these privileges we strangers are admitted by faith in Christ; and " if the Son make us " free, then shall we be free indeed." (Note, John viii. 30 —36.)

NOTES.

CHAP. XVIII. V. 1—4. It appears from the other evangelists, that our Lord first enquired of the disciples, about what they had disputed by the way : and for some time they remained silent, being afraid to mention the subject. But at length, sensible that he knew their thoughts, they plainly asked him, which of them was to be the greatest in the kingdom, he was about to establish. (Marg. Ref. a—c.—Mark ix. 33—37. Luke ix. 46—50, vv. 46— 48.) No doubt they had respect to a supposed secular kingdom, and its dignities and preferments, to the chief of which they all aspired, each resting his claim on a different ground: so that the dispute originated from error, ambitious, and emulation ; and had no reference to growth in grace, and real eminence in the spiritual kingdom on earth, or to a proportionate degree of glory in heaven.— Had our Lord intended to confer any pre-eminence in authority on Peter, or on any of his successors, he would doubtless at this time have given some intimation of it ; but, on the contrary, he treated all such pretensions with the most decided disapprobation. For having " called a " little child unto him, he set him " before them, solemnly assuring them, that " except they were converted, and " became as little children, they could not enter his king- " dom ;" and that he, who should humble himself like the little child, would eventually be found the most excellent and honourable person.—Children, when very young, shew little disposition to claim precedence, or to aspire after authority: they willingly associate with their inferiors, are regardless of external distinctions, and devoid of malice and gnile : they are docile, simple, submissive to authority, willingly dependent on their parents, and disposed to credit what they say. No doubt, they soon begin to shew other propensities, and other ideas are early inculcated on most of them and imbibed by them ; but these are the obvious characteristicks of childhood, and suffice to render " little

ᵛ ᵗ

5 And whoso shall ¹receive one ᵐsuch little child in my name ᵐreceiveth me.

6 But whoso shall ⁿoffend one of these ᵒlittle ones which believe in me, it were better for him that a mill-stone were hanged about his neck, and *that* he were drowned in the depth of the sea.

7 Woe ᵖunto the world because of offences! ᵠfor it must needs be that offences come; ʳbut woe to that man by whom the offence cometh!

8 Wherefore ˢif thy hand or thy foot offend thee, cut them off, ᵗand cast *them* from thee: it is better for thee to enter into life halt or ᵘmaimed, rather than having two hands or two feet to be cast into ˣeverlasting fire.

9 And if thine eye offend thee, pluck it out, and east *it* from thee: it is better for thee to ʸenter into life

" children " proper emblems of the humble, unambitious, submissive, and dependent spirit, which is the essence and the excellence of genuine Christianity. Though not *inno-cent*, strictly speaking, they are comparatively *harmless :* as the young, even of the most ferocious animals, are at first innoxious, but soon begin to discover the nature of that stock from which they spring. (*Marg. Ref.* d, e.— *Notes, Mark* x. 13—16, *v.* 15. 1 *Pet.* ii. 1—3.) In general, therefore, little children are apt emblems of those quali-ties, which are the effects of regeneration : and though all the apostles, except Judas, were at this time regenerate and " converted," in the general sense of the word; yet they all needed a very great change, in respect of their ambition and carnal emulation. It was also proper to shew them, that in their present temper they were not only unfit to be the " greatest in the kingdom of heaven," but even unmeet for the meanest station in it; and that the lust of dominion was as contrary to Christianity, as any kind of immorality. (*Notes,* xx. 20—23. xxiii. 11, 12. *Luke* xxii. 24—27. 1 *Pet.* v. 1—4.)—' He requires them, to fit them ' for this kingdom, to become as to these things like little ' children, who are absolutely free from all contrivances ' and designs of this nature, never concerned in the least ' for empire and dominion over others, or for increase in ' wealth, or great possessions; and know not what a post ' of honour, or what wealth means : this, saith our Lord, ' being that which will remove all that obstructs your en- ' trance into my kingdom, and make you the most eminent ' subjects of it. ...This frame will render him willing to ' minister even to the meanest of my members.' *Whitby.* —As this is the spirit of the kingdom, they who are most lowly, and most indifferent about consequence and pre-eminence, and most willing to be little, inferior, and neg-lected, must be the greatest; and not they who have the greatest abilities, most splendid gifts, or most exalted sta-tions in the church.

The kingdom of heaven. (1. 3, 4.) *Note,* iii. 2.—*Ye be converted.* (3) Στραφητε.—*Ye be changed* or *turned.* xvi. 23. xxv. 16.—See on xiii. 15.—*Notes, Luke* xxii. 31 —34, *v.* 32. *Acts* iii. 19—21, *v.* 19. xxvi. 16—18. 1 *Thes.* i. 9, 10, *v.* 9.—Επιστρεφω is used in all these places.

V. 5, 6. " The little ones," include the meanest of those who come to Christ, and (as far as man can discern) believe in him and belong to him : especially such as, whether mi-nisters or private Christians, being peculiarly humble and " poor in spirit," are the greatest in his sight, though often most slighted by men. (*Marg. Ref.*—*Notes,* 10, 11. 14. v.

3. *Zech.* xiii. 7.) These are the most evident and distin-guished representatives of the meek and lowly Saviour; and whoever shall receive them, (that is, embrace in love, entertain, or be kind to them, and hearken to instruction from any one of them,) will, in the person of a mean and obscure person, receive Christ himself, and be accepted and recompensed accordingly. (*Marg. Ref.* l, m.—x. 40— 42. xxv. 34—40.) But he who wilfully injures, deceives, or ensnares one of them, is guilty of so great a crime, and, without repentance, will be exposed to so terrible a punishment, that it would be better for him to have a large mill-stone tied about his neck, and to be cast into the sea, as it was the custom sometimes in executing notorious cri-minals : and indeed, every one ought to dread stumbling or grieving humble disciples, more than the most terrible death. (*Marg. Ref.* n, o.—*Notes,* 7—9. xxvi. 21—24.)— The word rendered " offend," signifies *cause to stumble.* It is used both for those who fall and perish, and for those who fall and rise again.—All the disciples were " offended," when Christ was betrayed to his enemies; and Peter espe-cially : but says the Saviour, " I have prayed for thee, that " thy faith fail not." (*Notes,* xxvi. 30—35. *Luke* xxii. 31— 34, *v.* 32.) The conduct however of those, who contemptu-ously, maliciously, or even heedlessly, did such things as tended to the destruction of their weak brethren, would not be in the least excused, because the special grace of God might prevent the futal consequences. The men of Lystra, who stoned Paul and left him for dead, were his murderers, in the sight of God, though he was pleased to restore his apostle to life and health.—All attempts there-fore to prove or disprove disputed points of doctrine from such passages, are foreign to the purpose of the sacred historians.

Offend. (6) Σκανδαλιση. See on v. 29, 30.—*Mill-stone.*] Μυλος ονικος, " a mill-stone turned by an ass." *Luke* xvii. 2. Hand-mills were most common in those days : a mill turned by an ass, was one of the largest size; for wind-mills and water-mills are of much later invention.— *Drowned.*] Καταποντισθη. Used only here and xiv. 30.— *Depth.*] Πελαγει. Used only here and *Acts* xxvii. 5.

V. 7—9. Our Lord here proceeded to speak more gene-rally concerning " offences : " meaning, not only the in-juries and snares, by which men would discourage and en-tangle his disciples, and bring guilt upon themselves; but all those evils within the church, which prejudice men's minds against his religion, or any of its doctrines, true ministers, and disciples. The scandalous lives, and shame-

₅ 5

s xvi., 29. Luke
ix. 24, 25.
a 5. 14. xii. 20. Ps.
xv.4. Zech.iv.10.
Luke x.]6.Rom.
viir. 1—3. 10. 13
—15. 21. xv. 1.
l Cor. viii. 8.—11.
ix. 22. xl. 22. xvi. 11. 2 Cor. x. l. 10. Gal. iv. 13, 14. vi. l. 1 Thes. iv. 8. 1 Tim. iv. 12.

with one eye, ᵉrather than having two eyes to be cast into hell-fire.

10 Take ᵃheed that ye despise not one of these little ones; for I say unto

you, That in heaven ᵇtheir angels do always ᶜbehold the face of my Father which is in heaven.

b l. 20. li. 13. 19.
xxiv. 31. Gen.
xxviii. l, 2.
2 Kings vi. 16,
17. Ps. xxxiv. 7.
xci. 11. Luke
c 2 Sam. xiv. 28.

xvi. 22. Acts v. 19. x. 3. xii. 7—11. 23. xxvii. 23. Heb. l. 14.
l Kings xxii. 19. Esth. l. 14. Ps. xvii. 15. Luke i. 15.

---

less oppressions, cruelties, and iniquities, of men called Christians, their divisions and bloody contentions, their idolatries and superstitions, are, at this day, the great "offences" and *causes of stumbling*, to Jews, Mohammedans, and Pagans, in all the four quarters of the globe; they constitute one grand hindrance to the labours of missionaries; and they furnish infidels, of every decription, with their most dangerous weapons against the truth. The acrimonious controversies, agitated among those who agree in the principal doctrines of the gospel, and their mutual contempt and revilings, together with the extravagant notions and wicked practices found among them, excite strong prejudices in the minds of great multitudes against *evangelical* religion; and harden the hearts of hereticks, Pharisees, disguised infidels, and careless sinners, against the truths of the gospel. In these, and in numberless other ways, it may be said, "Woe unto the "world because of offences:" for the devil, the sower of these tares, makes use of them in deceiving the nations of the earth, and in murdering the souls of men. In the present state of human nature " it must needs be, that "offences should come;" and God has wise and righteous reasons for *permitting* them: yet we should consider it as the greatest of personal afflictions, or causes of sorrow and shame, to be accessary to the destruction of souls; and an awful woe is denounced against every one, whose delusions or crimes thus stumble men, and set them against the only method of salvation. If this is done wilfully, and is not repented of, the offender's punishment will be most tremendous: and believers ought to dread occasional falls far more than death; and submit to any present loss or self-denial, rather than cause others to fall. *(Marg. Ref.* p—r.—*Notes,* 2 *Sam.* xii. 14. *Luke* xvii. 1—4. *Rom.* ii. 17—24, v. 24. 2 *Pet.* ii. 1—3, v. 2.) In this connexion, therefore, our Lord introduced again a warning and counsel, which have already been considered; *(Marg. Ref.* s—u. y. —*Note,* v. 29, 30;) and which here intimate, that they, who for the sake of temporal interest or indulgence, or from regard to any friend or relative, or to avoid loss or self-denial, wilfully cause others to stumble; have reason to suspect themselves of hypocrisy, and to fear lest they should perish through their own unmortified lusts, and so *fall* into perdition themselves, as well as prove *scandals* to their profession.—We ought not to forget, that there was a Judas in the company, to which this warning was addressed.—' The *necessity* here mentioned is therefore only ' conditional, on supposition of the wickedness of men not ' hindered, the subtlety and malignity of Satan, and the ' self-denial required of all who would embrace the gospel; ' whence nothing could be expected, but that many should ' be *scandalized* at, and be unwilling to embrace, the gos-' pel upon these terms, and many who had once embraced ' it should fly off from it.' *Whitby.* To maintain any other kind of *necessity,* is not Christian *predestination,* but heathen *fatalism.*—We cannot for a moment suppose, that any will enter halt or maimed into heaven: but even if

that could be, it would be infinitely preferable, to being " cast into *everlasting fire.*" *(Marg. Ref.* x. z.—*Notes,* xxv. 41—46, *vv.* 41. 46. *Mark* ix. 43—50. *Rev.* xx. 11— 15, v. 15.)

Offences. (7) Σκανδαλων. See on xiii. 41. xvi. 23.—*It must needs be.*] Αναγκη εσιν. *Philem.* 14.—Ανενδικτον εσι. *Luke* xvii. 1.

V. 10, 11. The same heresies, divisions, and scandals, which cause numbers to stumble to their ruin, frequently mislead and ensnare unestablished believers also; and thus tend as much to their destruction as any thing can do. *(Marg. Ref.—Notes, Rom.* xiv. 13—18, *vv.* 13. 15. 19—23, *vv.* 19—21. 1 *Cor.* viii. 7—13.) Such as are strong, or think themselves so, are apt to undervalue and *despise* weak, wavering, and unconfirmed disciples, when they see them mistaken or perplexed in their judgments; and liable to be discouraged or drawn aside, by example, authority, persuasion, or plausible reasonings: yet these things may often be the effect of deep humility, combined with weak natural abilities and insufficient instruction. Our Lord therefore cautioned his disciples, not to aspire after being the *greatest,* and not to despise the *least,* of those who professed themselves his disciples. The persons, whom he addressed, were ministers, and the admonition is therefore especially directed to all their successors in that sacred function; who are, alas! very apt to pay far more regard to the eminent, the wise, and the strong, (not to say the *wealthy,*) than to the poor, the ignorant, and the weak of the flock. *(Notes, Rom.* xiv. 1—6. xv. 1—3. *Gal.* vi. 1—5.) In enforcing this exhortation, our Lord assigned some peculiar reasons for it: and first, he declared that " their " angels do always behold the face of his Father which is " in heaven." The holy angels always behold the face and enjoy the favour of the eternal God, and approach him as his most exalted and honourable worshippers. Yet " they ... are all sent forth to minister to the heirs of " salvation;" and weak and trembling believers seem to be their special charge. They do not think their attention to the new convert, or to the discouraged, poor, or despised Christian, any degradation from their dignity, or any interruption of their felicity: nay, it seems, as if they enjoyed special tokens of the divine approbation, when thus employed. And should their brethren on earth despise those whom angels delight to attend on! *(Marg. Ref.* b, c.—*Note, Heb.* i. 13, 14.)—Again, " the Son of Man," whom they knew to be the Son of God also, came into the world " to save that which was lost: " he did not despise them, " even when " dead in sin," and when strangers or enemies. Did he then stoop so low to save them, and should his disciples and ministers despise those weak brethren, whom he was bringing home to himself?—' For ' Christ, that came to reduce [bring back] those, that are ' gone astray from the ways of God, must ... require the ' same of you; to be most diligent and industrious to re-' duce the meanest person upon earth, that is in a course ' of any danger of ruin to the soul.' *Hammond.* (Marg

11 For [d] the Son of man is come to save that which was lost.

12 [e] How think ye? [f] If a man have an hundred sheep, and one of them be gone astray, doth he not leave the ninety and nine, and goeth into the mountains and seeketh that which is gone astray?

13 And if so be that he find it, verily I say unto you, [h] he rejoiceth more of that *sheep*, than of the ninety and nine which went not astray.

14 Even so [i] it is not the will of [k] your Father which is in heaven, that one of these little ones should perish.

15 ¶ Moreover [m] if thy brother shall trespass against thee, [n] go and tell him his fault between thee and him alone: if he shall hear thee, [o] thou hast gained thy brother.

16 But if he will not hear thee, then [o] take with thee one or two more, [p] that in the mouth of two or three witnesses every word may be established.

17 And if he shall neglect to hear them, [q] tell *it* unto the church: but if he neglect to hear the church, [r] let him be unto thee as [s] an heathen man and [t] a publican.

Ref. d.—*Notes, Ex.* xxxiv. 11—16. 23—31. *Luke* xix. 1—10, *v.* 10.)

That which was lost. (11) Το απολωλος· (The præter tense.) *Luke* xv. 6. 24. 32. xix. 10.

V. 12, 13. In illustrating this subject, our Lord added a parable, with an appeal to the understandings and hearts of his hearers. If a man had a hundred sheep in his pasture, and one of them should go astray, would not this wandering sheep more occupy his attention, than all the rest? Would he not go to the mountains to seek it, until he found it? And would he not, in that case, express more joy on account of it, than for all those which had never gone astray?—This shews, the exposed, helpless condition of perishing sinners, who, having wandered from God, are liable to be destroyed by Satan, and to fall into hell; even as sheep, when they have wandered from the fold or pasture, are exposed to devouring beasts, or to fall into a pit and perish.—It moreover shews, that the good Shepherd knows his flock, even before they are brought into his fold; that he seeks them before they seek him; and that he rejoices in saving them from all enemies and dangers. And surely his ministers, and all his disciples, ought to concur in this design; to rejoice at the appearance of a sinner's conversion; to encourage and help the weak; and not to despise, grieve, or stumble them. (*Marg. Ref.—Notes, Ps.* xxiii. 1—3, *v.* 3. cxix. 176. *Is.* liii. 4—6. *Ez.* xxxiv. 2—6. 11—16. *Luke* xv. 3—7. P. O. 1—10.—*Notes, John* x. 14—18. 1 *Pet.* ii. 18—25, *v.* 25.)

Gone astray. (12) Πλανηθη. Πλαναω. *To seduce, or cause to err.* xxiv. 4. *John* vii. 12. In the passive. *To be deceived.* 1 *Cor.* xv. 33. *Gal.* vi. 6. *Tit.* iii. 3. *Jam.* i. 16. *To err. Heb.* iii. 10. *Jam.* v. 19.

V. 14. From this striking comparison, our Lord shews the care which the Father takes of the weakest of his true people. The disciples of Christ ought therefore to copy the example of angels, of the Son of God, and of the Father himself, respecting them; and not that of proud Pharisees. (*Marg. Ref.—Notes, Luke* xv. 1, 2. 8—10. 22—32. *John* vi. 36—40. x. 26—31.)—'God is very 'unwilling that any, the meanest person upon earth, 'should be lost, that might, by any care or methods of 'ours, be recovered to piety.' *Hammond.* 'The weaker 'a man is, the greater care we ought to have of his salva-

'tion, as God teacheth us by his own example.' *Beza.* (*Note,* 1 *Tim.* ii. 3, 4.)

V. 15—17. Contentions among Christians tend exceedingly to set the world against the gospel: (*Note, Luke* xvii. 3, 4:) and as they must arise, in this present state, among persons, who are sanctified only in part, and who are liable both to give cause for anger, and to be " angry " without cause" themselves; our Lord next prescribed some rules for stopping the progress, and preventing the consequences of them, which could seldom fail of being effectual, if honestly and exactly followed. In case a man should be injured by a brother, a professed Christian; he ought not to go and complain of it to others, (as is commonly done, perhaps upon rumour ;) thus inflaming his own resentment, and wounding his neighbour's reputation: but he ought to go privately; and in a gentle, yet plain and convincing manner, to state the matter, and shew him the unreasonableness of his conduct. (*Marg. Ref.* m, n.—*Notes, Lev.* xix. 17. *Prov.* xxv. 8—10.) If this produces a proper effect, (as it generally will with a true Christian,) and he sees and acknowledges his fault; then the offending brother is won over, gained and recovered from the tempter; and, instead of an open breach, a cordial reconciliation takes place, and love is continued, nay increased. (*Marg. Ref.* o.—*Note, Jam.* v. 19, 20.) But if this private application fail of success, and the offender persist in his injury, and refuse reasonable terms of agreement; the offended party is next ordered to take with him one or two other Christian friends, who may hear and bear witness to the facts which are alleged, and the terms of accommodation proposed; that they may be reported to the church on more unexceptionable testimony. And if these witnesses determine the person to be faulty, and approve of the concessions required; and he refuse to hearken to them, and persist in his injury: it will then be necessary to declare the matter more openly, not to the world, but "to the church;" (i. e. to the ministers and disciples of Christ;) that the injurious party may be solemnly censured and reproved by them. (*Marg. Ref.* p, q. —*Notes,* 1 *Cor.* v. 1—5, *v.* 5.) And if he still refuse to submit, he ought thenceforth to be considered " as a hea- " then man, and a publican ;" and should be shunned by all pious Christians, that he may be ashamed; and excluded

a xvi. 19. John
xx. 23. Acts xv.
28, 29. 1 Cor. v.
4, 5. 2 Cor. ii.
10. Rev. iii. 7.

18 Verily I say unto you, "Whatsoever ye shall bind on earth shall be bound in heaven; and whatsoever ye

x xvi. 22. Mark
xi. 24. John xv.
7. 16. Acts i. 14.
ii. 1, 2. iv. 24.
31. vi. 4. xii. 5.
Eph. vi. 18—20.
Phil. i. 19. Jam. v. 14—16. 1 John v. 14—16. Rev. xi. 4—6.

shall loose on earth shall be loosed in heaven.

19 Again I say unto you, "That if

two of you shall agree on earth, as touching any thing that they shall ask, 'it shall be done for them of my Father which is in heaven.

y John xiv. 13, 14.
xvi. 23, 24.

z Gen. xliii. 10.
John xx. 19. 26.

1 Cor. v. 4.
1 Thess. i. 1.

20 For where 'two or three are gathered together in my name, 'there am I in the midst of them.

a xxviii. 20. Ex.
xx. 24. Zech. ii.
b. John viii. 58.
Rev. i. 11—13.
b l. xxi. 3

---

from their communion, till he give tokens of repentance.
—It would be absurd to restrict these rules to any particular form of church-government and discipline; yet they certainly suppose the existence of government and discipline among the disciples of Christ, and the exclusion of disorderly persons, from those societies to which they immediately belong: and they are capable of being reduced to practice, under different forms of church-government; though they are, alas! in great measure, neglected by all. (Marg. Ref. r—t.—Notes, 18. 1 Cor. v. 9—13. 2 Thes. iii. 6—9. 14, 15.)

Tell him his fault. (15) Ελεγξον αυτον. Luke iii. 19. John iii. 20. viii. 46. xvi. 8. Eph. v. 11. 13. Rev. iii. 19.— Ps. cxli. 5. Sept.—'It signifieth such reproving of a bro-
' ther, as is by evincing and convicting him with evident
' arguments and reasons, that he hath done him wrong.'
Leigh.

V. 18. In confirmation of this procedure, our Lord added a solemn assurance, that such decisions would be ratified in heaven; whether they expelled the unruly person from communion, or received the penitent by reversing the sentence. This supposes, that the persons concerned decided according to truth and equity: for a groundless sentence of excommunication, or absolution, cannot possibly make any alteration in a man's state or character: all such decisions being merely declaratory. This has been entirely overlooked, in all those scandalous perversions of church-censures, which are the real cause of that relaxation, or rather destitution of discipline, which now so generally prevails. (Marg. Ref.—See on Note, xvi. 19.)—Our Lord spoke to the apostles, and to all of them. The absolute authority given them was inseparably connected with their immediate inspiration: and all their successors, pretended or real, from the conclave at Rome, to an independent church-meeting, are concerned in the promise; just so far as their decisions, whether they bind or loose, accord to the doctrines, precepts, and rules, transmitted to us from the apostles; and no further.—'Nor shall you only in
' these cases, have power as Christians, to loose your re-
' penting, and bind your obstinately offending brother;
' but, as you are my apostles, to whom I have promised
' my Spirit, "to teach you all things, and lead you into
' "all truth;" ... whatsoever things ye shall bind on
' earth, or shall declare to be forbidden on pain of my dis-
' pleasure, shall render them indeed obnoxious to my wrath:
' and whatsoever things ye shall loose on earth, (though
' once required by divine authority, of those who owned
' the law of Moses,) shall be loosed in heaven; and men
' shall be allowed to do them, without incurring my dis-
' pleasure. And in this sense, this promise is the founda-
' tion of our obligation to believe and obey all the com-
' mands and doctrines of the apostles, and of the cessation
' of the ritual precepts of the law of Moses.' Whitby.—

Authority, to the extent of the words used by our Lord, many have claimed, but God never gave it to any, except his inspired apostles: and in this view, the promise is our Lord's full attestation to all the writings, which by them, and under their inspection, were given to the church and to posterity, as the infallible "oracles of God."

V. 19, 20. It is here supposed, that all such transactions, as those above mentioned, would be conducted with prayer for direction, and for the humiliation of the offender: and in this case not only might an answer be expected, when many should concur; but even when two persons should agree to present their joint request on earth, the eternal Father, whose throne is in heaven, would surely regard and answer it. Some interpret this, of those miraculous interpositions, by which the censures of the church were sometimes followed and confirmed in the primitive times; or restrict it to the apostles, in the execution of their important office: and, as they were immediately addressed, this might be especially intended. (Notes, 1 Cor. iv. 18—21, v. 21. v. 1—5, v. 5. 2 Cor. xiii. 1—4. 7—10. 1 Tim. i. 18—20:) yet, it seems to be also a general promise encouraging social prayer, especially in arduous cases. (Marg. Ref. x, y.) When such prayers are presented in faith, and the petition of them is conducive to our good, and to the glory of God, we are every where warranted to expect a favourable answer: and limitations must have been implied, even in the days when miracles were wrought. —To this our Lord added, that when two or three were assembled in his name; that is, in dependence on his promise, in obedience to his command, out of love to him, and regard to his glory, for prayer or other acts of worship, to hear his word, or to regulate those things, which pertain to the peace and purity of his church; " there," says He, " I AM, in the midst of you:" He says not I will be, but I am, referring to his divine presence, at all times and in all places; and to his special presence by the influences of his Spirit, to communicate blessings to his people, whenever or wherever they wait upon him for them.— Two or three of his true disciples may be thus met together, in ten thousand different places all over the earth, at the same time: this must therefore be allowed to be a direct assertion of his omnipresent Deity; and cannot, on any other supposition, be rendered consistent with propriety. (Marg. Ref. z, a.—Notes, xxviii. 19, 20, v. 20. Ex. iii. 14. xx. 21—25, v. 24. John viii. 54—59, v. 58. Rev. iii. 1—3, v. 1.)

If two of you shall agree. (19) 'The prayer of faith
' being not only effectual for the recovery of the sick, but
' for the remission of his sins. (Jam. v. 14, 15.) This
' exposition ... restrains these words to one particular, viz.
' the pardon of the penitent; whereas it is περι παντος πραθ-
' μάτος, concerning any thing that they shall ask.' Whitby.
—Shall agree.] Συμφωνησωσιν, (ex συν, et φωνη,) of different

s 8

21 ¶ Then came Peter to him, and said, Lord, how oft shall my brother sin against me, and I forgive him? till seven times?

22 Jesus saith unto him, I say not unto thee, Until seven times; but, Until seventy times seven.

23 Therefore is the kingdom of heaven likened unto a certain king, which would take account of his servants.

24 And when he had begun to reckon, one was brought unto him which owed him ten thousand talents:

25 But forasmuch as he had not to pay, his lord commanded him to be sold, and his wife and children, and all that he had, and payment to be made.

26 The servant therefore fell down, and worshipped him, saying, Lord, have patience with me, and I will pay thee all.

27 Then the lord of that servant was moved with compassion, and loosed him, and forgave him the debt.

28 But the same servant went out, and found one of his fellow-servants, which owed him an hundred pence; and he laid hands on him, and took him by the throat, saying, Pay me that thou owest.

29 And his fellow-servant fell down at his feet, and besought him, saying, Have patience with me, and I will pay thee all.

30 And he would not: but went and cast him into prison, till he should pay the debt.

---

voices to form one concert, or symphony. Συμφωνια. *Luke* xv. 25.—*To agree by consent.* xx. 2. 13. *Luke* v. 36. *Acts* v. 9. xv. 15. Συμφωνος. 1 *Cor.* vii. 5. Συμφωνησις. 2 *Cor.* vi. 15.

V. 21, 22. As our Lord had intimated, that his disciples must bestow much pains to preserve or restore peace with their offending brethren, Peter wanted to be informed, how often they were required to renew their forgiveness of injuries, to such as repeated the offence. And, perhaps with reference to the traditions of the elders, he asked whether they were to proceed as far as seven times. To this our Lord answered, that they ought to forgive, not only to the seventh time, but "to seventy times seven:" meaning an indefinite number; even as often as men renew their offences, or as God renews his pardons to believers. (*Marg. Ref.—Note, Luke* xvii. 3, 4.)—' The determination ' of the Rabbins in this case, runs thus, that three offences ' are to be remitted, but not the fourth: and this they ' gather from those words, "For three transgressions, and ' "for four, I will not turn away my wrath." (*Am.* i. 3.) ' St. Peter puts the three and the four together, as perhaps ' others of their doctors did; and asks, whether he must ' forgive " till seven times." ' *Whitby.*

V. 23—27. To illustrate the subject Jesus spoke a parable. "The kingdom of heaven," or the Lord's method of dealing with men, in that kingdom which was about to be set up under the Messiah, (*Note,* iii. 2,) might be compared to that of a king, who required his servants to render their accounts of the sums which they had received, and the way in which they had employed them. This represents God himself, as calling men to account for the use, which they have made of their abilities and advantages; especially, as by his conduct in this respect, the true Christian is distinguished from the hypocrite. (*Notes,* xxv. 14—30. *Luke* xvi. 1—12.)—The king in this enquiry soon met with one, who, having been high in office and very unfaithful, owed him ten thousand talents, which by the lowest computation amounts to nearly two millions sterling. (*Marg.* and *Marg. Ref.—Tables.*) This represents our immense obligations to God, and our exceedingly great guilt as transgressors of his law, which is also increased by the neglect or abuse of his gospel: all indeed are deeply indebted, but some far more than others. (*Note, Luke* vii. 40—43.)—As the servant was wholly unable to pay this very great debt, his lord commanded, that he, and his wife and children, should be sold for slaves, and his substance confiscated, according to the custom of those countries, in order that payment might be made. (*Marg. Ref.* h.—*Notes, Ex.* xxi. 2. 2 *Kings* iv. 1—5. *Is.* l. 1—3, *v.* 1. *Dan.* vi. 24.) This represents the strictness of the law and justice of God, and the dreadful punishment to which sinners are righteously exposed; from which they cannot deliver themselves, and in which their connexions are often involved.—The servant, terrified by this sentence, in the most submissive posture, craved time and patience, and promised that he would at length discharge the whole debt: this may shew the terrors and convictions, to which men are subject from a view of the severity of God's justice, and that general hope of mercy by which they seek relief; but the engagement, "I will pay thee all," seems an intended intimation of an unhumbled and self-confident spirit. (*Notes,* 28—30, *v.* 29. *Luke* vii. 40—43, *v.* 42. *Rom.* x. 1—4.)—The lord, however, of that servant is induced, by compassion, to set him at liberty and to remit the debt; knowing well that he would never be able to pay it: this represents the Lord's readiness to forgive all true penitents; and the false conclusions which many thence draw concerning their sins being pardoned, though they be not truly penitent. (*Marg. Ref.* k.)—*Take account,* &c. (23) Συναραι. *To reckon.* 24. xxv. 19. Not used elsewhere.—*Have patience,* &c. (26) Μακροθυμησον. 29. (Εκ μακρος and θυμος.) *Be long-suffering. Luke* xviii. 7. *Rom.* ii. 4. 1 *Cor.* xiii. 4. 1 *Thes.* v. 14. *Heb.* vi. 15. *Jam.* v. 7, 8.

V. 28—30. This person, who had experienced such extraordinary lenity, went out, and met with a fellow-servant, who owed him a trifling debt of a hundred denarii, or a little more than three pounds sterling: and, laying hold of him by the throat, (in a fierce and insolent man-

T

31 So when his fellow-servants saw what was done, * they were very sorry, ° and came and told unto their lord all that was done.

32 Then his lord, after that he had called him, said unto him, ° O thou wicked servant, I forgave thee all that debt, because thou desiredst me:

33 Shouldest not thou also have had compassion on thy fellow-servant, ° even as I had pity on thee?

34 And his lord was wroth, ° and delivered him to the tormentors, till he should pay all that was due unto him.

35 So likewise shall my heavenly Father ° do also unto you, if ye ° from your hearts forgive not every one his brother their trespasses.

---

ner, as if he meant to strangle him,) insisted upon immediate payment: and even when the other used the very same words to him, which he had used to his lord, he would not wait, but cast him into prison till he should pay the debt: though his debtor might very well in a short time have paid this small debt which he owed; but he himself could never have discharged the immense sum due to his prince. This shews the selfishness, severity, and unrelenting spirit of many who profess religion; and their pertinacious resentments, the result of pride, hardness of heart, and malevolence: for even their views of the gospel, and their forced confessions, serve to exasperate them, instead of softening and meliorating their tempers. Such men deal with their neighbours in so severe a manner, that if God mete to them by the same measure, as no doubt he will, " judgment without mercy" must be their portion. (*Notes*, vii. 1, 2. *Jam*. ii. 8—13, *v*. 13.)—' This seemeth ' to bear hard on those unmerciful and unchristian cre- ' ditors, who cast poor men, who they know have nothing ' to pay, into prison for their debt; ... so rendering their ' brother's state more miserable, and their debt from him ' as desperate as ever. For sure, he that bid us " lend, ' " hoping for nothing again," will not allow us to im- ' prison, where nothing can be hoped for : and it is to be ' feared, that men so unmerciful may find but little mercy ' at that day. For if it be a crime that will then be ob- ' jected to our condemnation, that we did not visit Christ- ' ians when in prison; what will it be to cast them into ' prison?' *Whitby.* (*Marg. Ref.*)—Ten thousand talents were six hundred thousand times as much as the hundred *denarii*, calculating by Roman talents; (*Marg.*) by the Jewish talent, they were more than double that sum. (*Tables.*)

Took him by the throat. (28) Επνγε. Πνγω, *suffoco. Mark* v. 13. Αποπνγω, xiii. 7. Συμπνγω. 22. *Mark* iv. 7. 19. Πνικτον. *Acts* xv. 29. xxi. 25.

V. 31—35. When the fellow-servants saw this trans- action, " they were grieved" to see a man, who had so merciful a master, thus cruel to one who was in his power; and they came to inform their lord of all these things. This shews, that real Christians are grieved and shocked at the misconduct of professed believers, more than at the wickedness of those who do not make any pretensions to religion; and that they complain to God of the dishonour thus done to his gospel.—The lord then called the ser- vant, and, having reproached him, for acting in so direct and marked an opposition to his merciful example; and shewn the wickedness of his character, and the unreason- ableness of his conduct, he, with deep indignation, deli- vered him over to the executioners of justice, to be con-

fined and punished by them till he had paid the whole debt; and as he was not able to pay it, he could never obtain deliverance. (*Marg. Ref.* o—s.—*Notes*, vii. 21—23. xxv. 24—30.)—' God's pardons here in this life are not ' to us absolute, ... but, according to the petition in our ' Lord's prayer, answerable to our dealings with others, ' and so conditional, and are no longer likely to be conti- ' nued to us, than we perform that condition.' *Hammond.* Where then is the " blessedness of him, whose iniquities " are forgiven?" (*Notes*, *Ps.* xxxii. 1, 2. *Rom.* iv. 6—8. 14—17.) " He that heareth my words and believeth in " him that sent me," saith our Lord, " hath everlasting " life, *and shall not come into condemnation*, but is passed " from death unto life." (*Notes*, *John* v. 24—27, *v*. 24. vi. 36—40. x. 26—31. *Rom.* viii. 1, 2. 28—39.)—*Circum- stances* in parables do not always admit of minute applica- tion. In the parable of the prodigal son, the elder brother, who was evidently the representative of the Pharisees, is spoken of as heir of all his father's property. (*Note*, *Luke* xv. 25—32.) Our Lord frequently addressed men, accord- ing to what they thought of themselves, and not according to their real character. The servant, in this parable, bears no one mark of a humble penitent : and none but humble penitents are true believers, or really pardoned; though many others think themselves so. The general tenour of scripture excludes the supposition, that God actually for- gives men, and then afterwards imputes guilt to them to their final condemnation. (*Notes*, *Ps.* ciii. 11—13. *Jer.* xxxi. 33, 34. *Mic.* vii. 18—20. *Heb.* viii. 7—13, *v*. 12.) But men will at last be dealt with, not according to their confidence; but according as their conduct, especially to- wards their offending brethren, has evidenced the reality of their faith and love, or the contrary. This is our Lord's own inference from it: whatever men's profession may be, God will deliver them as " wicked servants" to the tor- mentors, to be punished according to their sins with exact justice; if they " do not from their hearts," which he especially regards, " forgive their brethren their trespasses." No doubt, if true believers are betrayed into any degree of this unchristian spirit, they will experience frowns, re- bukes, and chastenings : but to suppose that a real Christ- ian can be habitually of this unmerciful and malignant temper and act according to it, (*Marg. Ref.* t, u.—*Notes*, vi. 12. 14, 15. *Luke* vi. 37, 38. xvii. 3, 4. *Eph.* v. 30—32. *Col.* iii. 12—15. *Jam.* ii. 8—13, *vv.* 12, 13,) directly mili- tates against the design of the parable, and of the whole scripture; and is calculated to encourage selfish, revenge- ful, and hard-hearted professors of evangelical doctrine, who are the scandal of the gospel, and as unlike Christ as the grossest libertine or drunkard in the world.

T q

CHAP. XIX.

Jesus journeys towards Judea, and heals the sick, 1, 2; answers the Pharisees concerning divorces, and his disciples on the expediency of marriage, 3—12; receives little children, 13—15; discourses with a rich young man, concerning eternal life, and detects his love of wealth more than that of God, 16—22; shews the difficulty of a rich man's salvation, 23—26; and makes gracious promises to those, who renounce worldly objects for his sake, 27—30.

PRACTICAL OBSERVATIONS.

V. 1—6.

Pride and ambition are so deeply rooted in our fallen nature; that they remain, and often break forth, even in those who are " born of God." Hence so many contentions in the church : not only among those nominal Christians, whose religion is merely an occasion of aspiring to distinction and influence ; but even among real disciples, who are tempted to seek pre-eminence above their brethren, after they have given up their prospects of worldly honour and greatness! (*Notes, Prov.* xlii. 10. *2 Cor.* xii. 7—10, *v.* 7. *Phil.* ii. 1—4, *v.* 3.) Such ambitious plans and desires, however, are peculiarly contrary to the spirit of the gospel, and to the character of Christ ; and are productive of envy, discord, and other fatal consequences. In this, as well as in other respects, we need to be daily more and more " renewed in the spirit of our mind," that we may " become as little children, simple," humble, and willing to be " the least of all and the servants of all." If we have not some measure of this disposition, and yet think ourselves the subjects of Christ, we are awfully deceived : and he, who has made the greatest proficiency in self-abasement, is in fact the greatest in the kingdom of grace, and will shine the brightest in the kingdom of glory. We ought therefore daily to reflect and meditate on this subject, and to examine our own spirits respecting it, that we may be more and more cast into the mould of the gospel, and that we may learn to behave properly towards our fellow Christians ; esteeming and honouring those whom the Lord honours, and being afraid of injuring or grieving, or in any way stumbling, any of his little ones, however feeble, poor, or obscure.

V. 7—14.

What miseries come upon the world, through the scandals which prevail in the church! This warning should indeed render men very careful, not to admit prejudices against Christianity, or any peculiar doctrines, from the misconduct of those who profess them ; but to examine what Christianity is, in its nature and tendency, as it stands in the scripture. Yet alas! few will adopt this method. While, therefore, we mourn over the evils which we cannot remedy, we should be careful not to add to them ; and should fear death far less than dishonouring the gospel, and causing souls to stumble and perish by our misconduct. We ought constantly to associate the idea of the Redeemer's glory, with that of our own salvation ; and to mortify every inclination, and renounce every interest, which may throw a stumbling-block in the way of others, even as if it endangered the loss of our own souls. This disposition is a proper evidence that we are true believers : but how dreadful will be the disappointment of selfish or self-indulgent persons, who, taking it for granted that they are safe, and not caring about the souls of their neighbours, prove the occasion of their ruin ; and will at last sink themselves into the unquenchable and everlasting fire of hell, under the guilt of those sins, and the power of those darling sinful inclinations, which they refused here to relinquish and mortify ? We should then keep at a great distance from this and every extreme, and labour to remove those offences which prejudice men against the gospel : remembering, that those persons are peculiarly entitled to our prayers, and to every degree of countenance which we can give them, who attempt, by any proper means, to terminate the cruel oppressions which are the reproach of the Christian name ; or to reform corruptions, and heal divisions, within the church.—Numbers, who have been in some degree awakened to a concern about their souls, stumble and perish by the misconduct of professed disciples ; and weak Christians are greatly harassed and perplexed by them. We ought therefore seriously to consider, what effects our conduct may have upon persons of these descriptions : and by no means to despise the scruples and mistakes of our weak brethren, or endanger their comfort and progress from selfish motives. Ministers, especially, are called upon to watch over the weak, feeble, and discouraged, and the young unestablished convert, to " comfort the feeble minded," and to be gentle, and compassionate, and long-suffering towards them. And shall any of us refuse attention to those, unto whom the blessed angels delight to minister ; whom the Son of God came to seek and save ; and concerning whom " it is the " Father's good pleasure, that not one of them should " perish ? " This would be the more inexcusable in us, seeing we all have been " as lost sheep," and have been ransomed by the blood, and brought back by the tender care, of our good Shepherd ; who delights more in saving lost sinners, than even in the worship of those holy angels, who never went astray ; and who receives, as it were, a new accession of joy and glory, by every one that is brought back to his fold. Let us then remember from what a dreadful state we have been saved, and copy the pattern of our gracious Benefactor ; and let us study to be gentle, harmless, and useful, as behoves " the sheep of his pasture."

V. 15—22.

How careful should all Christians be, to preserve the peace, as well as the purity, of the church! Many deem themselves injured, when in reality they have no cause to complain : and others have recourse to slander and litigation, and almost every other expedient, instead of trying the method which Christ has expressly enjoined to all his disciples ; and few, in any place, have uniformly followed these directions of our common Lord. Various corrupt maxims, customs, and reserves, prevent even conscientious men from speaking privately to their offending brethren, and from referring their disputes to the arbitration of pious Christians : hence jealousies, resentments, contentions, and even frivolous lawsuits, among professors

T 3

AND it came to pass, [a]*that* when Jesus had finished these sayings, he departed from Galilee, and came into the coasts of Judea beyond Jordan:

2 And [b]great multitudes followed him; and he healed them there.

3 ¶ The Pharisees also came unto him, [c]tempting him, and saying unto him, [d]Is it lawful for a man to put away his wife for every cause?

4 And he answered and said unto them, [e]Have ye not read, [f]that he, which made *them* at the beginning, made them male and female,

5 And [g]said, For this cause shall a man leave father and mother, and shall [h]cleave to his wife; [i]and they twain shall be one flesh?

6 Wherefore they are no more twain, but one flesh. What therefore [k]God hath joined together, let not man put asunder.

2. 1 Cor. vii. 10—14. Eph. v. 28. Heb. xiii. 4.

[marginal references left column:]
a Mark x. 1. John x. 40.
b Iv. 23—25. ix. 35, 36. xii. 15. xiv. 35, 36. xv. 30, 31. Mark vi. 55, 56.
c xvi. 1. xxii. 16—18. 35. Mark x. 2. xii. 13—15. Luke xi. 53, 54.
John viii. 6. Heb. iii. 9.
d v. 31, 32. Mal. ii. 14—16.

[marginal references right column:]
e xii. 3. xxi. 16, 42. xxii. 31. Mark ii. 25. xii. 10, 26. Luke vi. 3. x. 26.
f Gen. i. 27. v. 2. Mal. ii. 15.
g Gen. ii. 21—24.
h Ps. xlv. 10. Mark x. 6—9. Eph. v. 31.
i Gen. xxxiv. 3. Deut. iv. 4. xi. 22.
20, 21, 22. 1 Sam. xviii. 1. 2 Sam. i. 26. 1 Kings xi. 2.
k Ps. lxviii. 18. Rom. xii. 9. 1 Cor. vi. 16. vii. 2, 4. Prov. ii. 17. Mal. ii. 14. Mark x. 9. Rom. vii.

---

of the gospel; and hence mutual criminations, and appeals in print to the world against each other, to the scandal of religion, and the insulting triumphs of its enemies! Surely we ought not to harbour so injurious an opinion of a professed Christian, as to think, that he would not endure to be mildly expostulated with, when he had evidently done wrong! Surely we should prefer gaining, recovering, and conciliating our offending brother, to obtaining a victory over him, or exposing his character! And certainly he who has done injustice, and will not be induced to make moderate concessions and amends, by private expostulations, or by the united judgment of Christians and ministers; has no right to be treated as a believer, till he "repent and do works meet for repentance." Harsher means should never be adopted, till milder have been tried without success. No man should think himself a competent judge in his own cause: nor should any Christian seek legal redress, till it is evident, that no other means can procure that justice, which it is requisite should be done him. Indeed the abuse of discipline, through the pride and corrupt passions of men, has so prejudiced the minds of numbers against it, that it is grievously fallen into disuse: yet, in whatever way the faithful ministers of Christ, and consistent believers, concur to shew their decided disapprobation of an offender's conduct, on *scriptural grounds*, by withdrawing from his society, or objecting to communion with him in holy ordinances, it ought to be deemed a very solemn matter: for whatsoever is thus bound or loosed on earth, shall be ratified in heaven, however the offender may despise the protest.—In all our undertakings we should seek direction by prayer; and we cannot too highly value the promises of God to this effect: all the general concerns of families and churches, should be conducted with social as well as secret prayer: nor should we ever censure or rebuke any man, without at the same time praying for his humiliation and salvation.—Whenever we meet in the name of Christ, in our families, or in publick ordinances, at any time, or in any place, we should realize his presence in the midst of us; that we may both be impressed with awe of his holy, heart-searching eye upon us, and encouraged to expect abundant blessings from him.

V. 23—35.

While we sinners live so entirely on mercy and forgiveness, how backward are we to forgive the repeated offences of our brethren! Yet let us not think, that any provo-

cation can authorize us to harbour resentment, or seek revenge. This we can never suppose, if we consider duly, how many and aggravated our former and later transgressions have been, against our Creator and daily Benefactor; and how ready he is to forgive us, when we repent and seek his face. If he enter into judgment with us, our debt will be found immensely large; all the terrible curses of the law will be adjudged to be our righteous desert; and it will be in vain for us to say, "Have patience with me, "and I will pay thee all." This the humbled sinner will perceive, and he will rely only on free abounding mercy, through the ransom of the death of Christ: in this way, his sins will be "blotted out," and "buried in the depths "of the sea;" and his gentle, forgiving, and compassionate spirit and conduct towards those who have injured him, or are dependent on him, will prove him a partaker of the Spirit and mind of Christ. But the unhumbled professor of the gospel will often betray himself, by a harsh, unforgiving, and unrelenting behaviour to his debtors, his servants, the poor, and especially to those who have offended him. Such men scandalize the cause, and grieve true believers: but they deceive and destroy themselves; and their offended Lord will shortly deliver them, as "wicked servants," to the executioners of his vengeance, and the everlasting punishment prepared for the workers of iniquity. (*Note*, xxv. 41—46.) Let us then examine ourselves, whether in *from our hearts* we forgive every one "his brother his trespasses." Let us frequently ask ourselves, whether our conduct towards poor debtors, supplicants, or such as have affronted us, resembles the merciful conduct of our Lord towards us: and let us seek more and more for the renewing grace of God, to teach us to forgive others, even as we hope for forgiveness from him.

NOTES.

Chap. XIX. V. 1, 2. This seems to have been our Lord's final departure from Galilee, previous to his crucifixion: but he took a large compass in his journey, and passed through the districts, which lay east of Jordan. (*Marg. Ref.—Note, Luke* xiii. 22—30, *v.* 22.)

V. 3—6. 'The school of Hillel taught, that a man 'might put away his wife for any cause, because this di- 'vorce was permitted, "if she found not grace in his eyes." '(*Deut.* xxiv. 1.)—The son of Sirach saith, 'If she go not 'as thou wouldst have her, cut her off from thy flesh, ' 'give her a bill of divorce, and let her go.' (*Ecclesias.*

v 4

7 They say unto him, ¹ Why did Moses then command to give a writing of divorcement, ᵐ and to put her away? 8 He saith unto them, Moses ⁿ because of the hardness of your hearts ° suffered you to put away your wives: ᵖ but from the beginning it was not so. 9 And I say unto you, ⁱ Whosoever shall put away his wife, ʳ except it be for fornication, and shall marry another, committeth adultery: and whoso

---

ᶜ xxv. 26.) And Josephus saith, ' The law runs thus, He
' ' that will be disjoined from his wife, for any cause what-
' ' soever, as many such causes there are, let him give her
' ' a bill of divorce.' And he confesseth, that he himself
' put away his wife, after she had born him three children,
' because he was not pleased with her behaviour. But the
' school of Shammah determined on the contrary, that the
' wife was only to be put away for adultery ; because it is
' said, " Because he hath found some uncleanness in her."'
Whitby. (Notes, v. 31, 32. Ex. xx. 14. Mark x. 2—12.
Luke xvi. 16—18.)—These Pharisees had probably heard,
that Jesus opposed their decisions concerning divorces;
and they were desirous of drawing something from him,
which they could represent as contrary to the law of
Moses. With this insidious design, they questioned him,
" whether it were lawful for a man to put away his wife
" for every cause." That is, on account of any thing in
her temper, or person, or for any infirmity, which rendered
her disagreeable. (Note, Deut. xxiv. 1—4.) To this he
replied by referring to the history of the creation, and the
original institution of marriage ; intimating, that this was
the standard by which all transactions in this important
concern ought to be regulated, as every deviation was an
abuse consequent on man's depravity. The Creator first
formed Adam, and from his side took the rib of which the
woman was made : from this one man and one woman,
the whole human species had descended. When the Lord
brought the woman, Adam acknowledged her as a part of
himself ; and it was added, (either by Adam as immediately
inspired, or by Moses,) that " for this cause," in all future
ages, " a man should leave father and mother," foregoing
many of the comforts, and relinquishing many of the duties, of these endeared relations, and " cleave to his wife,"
as a part of himself. Thus these two would constitute, as
it were, one body, never more to be separated, except by
God himself, who in this appointment of marriage had
joined them together ; but to have ever after the same interests, and to share each other's comforts or sorrows, even
as the members of the same body do.—When marriage
was instituted, sin and death had not entered : the sinful
cause of separation afterwards mentioned, and the natural
dissolution of the union, were therefore not referred to :
but they have since been specified, and resemble the
cutting off of a mortified limb, and the separation of the
parts of the body by death. In all other respects the union
is to be considered as indissoluble. It is observable, that
Christ inserts the word " twain," which is not in the original institution, but is added by the LXX, purposely, as
it seems, to obviate all misconstruction of his meaning.
(Marg. Ref. c—g.—Notes, Gen. ii. 21—25.)—The apostle
warning the Corinthians against fornication, says " He
" that is joined (ὁ κολλωμενος) to an harlot, is one flesh."
Hence some have endeavoured to prove, that nothing more
is essential to marriage, than carnal knowledge ; and that

every woman is in fact the wife of him, who first knows
her ; from which the most detestable inferences have been
deduced. But if this were so, such a crime as simple fornication could not exist, nor such a character as a harlot;
for every female must either be a virgin, a wife, an adulteress, or a widow.—The apostle, however, could not mean
this : for the woman of whom he spake is supposed to have
been previously a harlot, not a virgin : (Note, 1 Cor. vi. 12
—17, vv. 15—17 :) and surely none will say, that when a
man becomes one " flesh with a harlot," they are " joined
" together by God, and man must not put them asunder!"
—The Lord brought Eve to Adam, and gave her to him,
and thus joined them together in marriage, previous to
their connubial intercourse : and some established and attested recognition, as well as the consent of parties, is
absolutely needful to honourable marriage, and to distinguish those who live in that state, from the " adulterers
" and fornicators whom God will judge."—The pernicious
effects, which the author has witnessed, of the licentious
sentiments above stated, and the sanction which they have
received from the names of those who have supported
them, and from their plausible reasonings, (which seem
very convincing to a sensual mind, when under powerful
temptation,) render these hints peculiarly needful.—It may
also be added, that they, who from erroneous religious motives, either separate themselves from their wives or husbands, or counsel others to do so ; whatever specious arguments they may use, most evidently act in direct violation of Christ's command.
For this cause, &c. (5) The quotation is very nearly from
the LXX ; in which ἡ δυο is added to the original ; and is
preserved in every quotation in the New Testament.—
Shall cleave, &c.] Προσκολληθησεται. Mark x. 7. Acts v.
36. Eph. v. 31.—Gen. ii. 24. Sept. Ex προς ετ κολλαω, ad-
hæreo. Luke x. 11. xv. 15. Acts v. 13. viii. 29. ix. 26. x.
28. xvii. 34. 1 Cor. vi. 16, 17. Α κολλα, gluten.—' The Greek
' word importeth, to be glued unto, whereby is signified
' that strait knot which is between man and wife, as if
' they were glued together.' Beza.—Joined together.]
Συνεζευξεν. Mark x. 9. Not elsewhere used.—Put asunder.]
Χωριζετω. Mark x. 9. Acts i. 4. xviii. 1, 2. Rom. viii. 35.
39. 1 Cor. vii. 10, 11. 15. Philem. 15. Heb. vii. 26.
V. 7—9. We find from St. Mark, that our Lord,
asked the Pharisees, what Moses had commanded them ;
(Mark x. 4 ;) and to this they answered, that he had " com-
" manded to give a bill, &c." (Mark x. 4, 5.)—' Because
' politick laws are constrained to bear with some things,
' it followeth not that God alloweth them.' Beza. (Notes,
Ex. xxi. 2. Deut. xxiv. 1—4.)—Our Lord then shewed
them, that this was not a command, but a permission : they
were " suffered " without punishment by the magistrate,
to put away their wives; because they were so hard-hearted,
that they would otherwise have used them ill, or even
murdered them ; so that this permission was a stigma on

ᴛ 3

marrieth her which is put away, 'doth commit adultery.

10 His disciples say unto him, 'If the case of the man be so with his wife, it is not good to marry.

11 But he said unto them, " All men cannot receive this saying, save they to whom it is given.

12 For there are some eunuchs, which were so born from their mothers' womb ; and there are some eunuchs, ˣwhich were made eunuchs of men; and there be eunuchs, ʸ which have made themselves eunuchs for the kingdom of heaven's sake. He that is able to receive it, let him receive it.

---

the national character, a testimony against the depravity of human nature, a *judicial* regulation, and a departure from the original institution of marriage, and the meaning of the moral law. The general scope of this reasoning is equally applicable to polygamy. (*Marg. Ref.* l—o.— *Note*, 3—6.)—A question has been raised, and copiously disputed, whether those who, according to this permission, put away their wives, or married others, committed sin against God. But it is a question, in which we are little concerned.—In a state of sinless perfection, such things would not have been even desired. Some, no doubt, were very criminal in availing themselves of the permission, and were adulterers in the sight of God. Others might have stronger reasons and better motives for their conduct: and whatever was sinful in those true believers, who allowed themselves in the practices thus tolerated or connived at, was no doubt forgiven by the special mercy of God, on their general repentance.—Our Lord however added, that *thenceforth* whosoever should put away his wife, except for unchastity, (which violates the marriage-covenant, and destroys as it were the very nature of it,) and should marry another woman, would be adjudged an adulterer; as that man also would, who should marry the divorced woman. Whatever *injustice* there might be in the divorce, it could not be "adultery against" the divorced woman, if the man and woman were not put entirely upon a level in this respect: so that, under the Christian dispensation, it is as much adultery for the husband to take another woman, as for the wife to take another man. (*Marg. Ref.* q—s.—*Notes*, *Mal.* ii. 13—16. *Mark* x. 2— 12, *vv.* 11, 12. *Luke* xvi. 16—18, *v.* 18. 1 *Cor.* vii. 1—5.) —Some argue, that as adultery was punishable by death according to the law of Moses, and the betrothed virgin was considered as the wife of that, to whom she was contracted, and included in this law ; the word rendered " for- " nication' should be here understood in its usual sense, *exclusively:* so that the reason, why the woman may have been guilty of fornication *might*, nay *must*, be divorced, was this : ' She was in fact another man's wife, and to retain her would be to live in adultery.'—This, however, increases the difficulty: for the woman who was detected at her marriage of unchastity before her espousals, was likewise condemned to die: so that, supposing these three laws rigorously executed, no woman detected, after marriage, of previous fornication could escape death ; and, according to this opinion, no man might marry her, who pleaded guilty of that crime, because she was already another man's wife. (*Notes, Lev.* xx. 10—19, *v.* 10. *Deut.* xxii. 13—27.)—For in that case none could be spared, but she who confessed her guilt, and no man on this supposition might marry her: and surely it is very absurd to suppose, that a word, constantly used in an ill sense through

the whole scripture, should here be considered as synonymous with *marriage:* for unless the woman who had committed fornication was, by so doing, married to her paramour, the whole argument falls to the ground.—Did not many lay hold of such unguarded concessions, in reputable writers, to support or palliate a most licentious system, which is secretly doing immense mischief; learned men might possess their peculiar notions undisturbed, at least by the author.—In fact, these laws were seldom rigorously executed under the Old Testament : being *judicial* regulations, they were not intended for the new dispensation, as of divine obligation ; and concerning this our Lord was authoritatively laying down injunctions.—The word rendered " fornication " is in many places used as a general term ; so that, undoubtedly, the common interpretation is the true one.—' Note also hence, that according to either ' interpretation, where it is lawful to put away the wife, it ' is so to marry again.' *Whitby*.

The hardness, &c. (8) Τὴν σκληροκαρδιαν ὑμων. (Ex σκληρος et καρδια.) *Mark* x. 5. xvi. 14.—It occurs frequently in the LXX. (*Note, Mark* x. 2—12, *v.* 5.)—*For fornication.* (9) Επι πορνεια. *v.* 32. 1 *Cor.* v. 1. vi. 13. 18. vii. 2. *Eph.* v. 3. *Col.* iii. 5. 1 *Thes.* iv. 3.—(*Note, v.* 31, 32.)

V. 10—12. The disciples had imbibed the prejudices of their countrymen : they supposed, that the regulations made by their Lord, would in many cases render marriage a source of perpetual uneasiness; and they concluded, that it would be most prudent, and conducive to happiness, to continue unmarried. To this Jesus replied, that all men were not capable of complying with such a restriction; as continence in this absolute sense was a special gift of God to some, and not to others: for seeing it was his plan, that the human species should be continued, and that men should generally marry for that purpose; he had so constituted them, that many could not live, conscientiously and comfortably, in a single state. Indeed some were born with such a temperament of body, that they were all their lives devoid of those inclinations, to which others are subject: some were mutilated in infancy, through the avarice or policy of men : and others were successful in their endeavours to subdue their natural inclinations, that they might more entirely dedicate their time and talents to the service of God, and have less encumbrance in so doing. And if any man found himself disposed to that kind of life, and capable of it; it might " be good for him not to " marry," as he might be more useful in promoting the kingdom of heaven among men. Thus our Lord intimated to the apostles, that, whatever they chose for themselves, they must impose no restrictions on others in this matter. (*Marg. Ref.—Notes,* 1 *Cor.* vii. 1—9. 25—28. *P. O.* 1—9. 25—28. 32—40.)—' That which all men ' may obtain by prayer, temperance, and fasting, ... can-

13 ¶ Then were there [*] brought unto him little children, that he should put *his* hands on them, and pray: [a] and the disciples rebuked them.

14 But Jesus said, [b] Suffer little children, and forbid them not, to come unto me: [c] for of such is the kingdom of heaven.

15 And [d] he laid *his* hands on them, and departed thence.

16 ¶ And, behold, [e] one came, and said unto him, Good Master, [f] what good thing shall I do, that I may have [g] eternal life?

17 And he said unto him, Why callest thou me good? [h] there is none good but one, *that is,* God: [i] but if thou wilt enter into life, keep the commandments.

18 He saith unto him, [k] Which? Jesus said, [l] Thou shalt do no murder, Thou shalt not commit adultery, Thou shalt not steal, Thou shalt not bear false witness,

19 [m] Honour thy father and *thy* mother; and, [n] Thou shalt love thy neighbour as thyself.

20 The young man saith unto him, [o] All these things have I kept from my youth up: [p] what lack I yet?

21 Jesus said unto him, [q] If thou wilt be perfect, [r] go *and* sell that thou hast, and give to the poor, and thou shalt have treasure in heaven; and [s] come *and* follow me.

22 But when the young man heard that saying, [t] he went away sorrowful; [u] for he had great possessions.

' not be called a *special gift*, or a gift proper to some.' *Whitby.*

Cannot receive. (11) Ου ... χωρουσι. 12. John ii. 6. viii. 37. xxi. 25. 2 Cor. vii. 2.—*Eunuchs.* (12) Ευνυχοι. (Ex ευη et εχω.) *Keepers of the bed. Acts* viii. 27. 34. 36. 38, 39.—*Made eunuchs.*] Ευνυχισθησαν.—*Made themselves eunuchs.*] Ευνυχισαν ιαυλης. Not elsewhere used in the New Testament.

V. 13—15. Several instances occur of those, who applied to Christ in behalf of their afflicted relations and friends: but these persons brought their " little children," or *infants,* to him, in order that he might lay his hands on them, and pray for them, or bless them. As it was evident that they were in health, and too young to receive instruction; the disciples thought that the parents gave their Lord needless trouble, or that it would be beneath him to notice infants: and they therefore " rebuked those " who brought them." (*Mark* x. 13.) Yet the conduct of the parents was evidently an expression of high regard to Jesus, and an earnest desire of spiritual blessings on their children: he therefore was " much displeased" with the disciples, for discouraging the application; and directed them to " suffer the little children to come to him " without molestation; " for, of such," added he, " is the king- " dom of heaven."—He might in part be displeased with the disciples, for so soon forgetting that instructive discourse which has been considered : (*Notes,* xviii. 1—6 :) and doubtless he meant to encourage parents to seek a blessing from him, on their children, from their earliest infancy; and to teach the children to seek to him, as soon as they can understand his words. But the expression " of " such is the kingdom of heaven," seems to mean, that little children are admissible into the visible church, under the New Testament dispensation, as they had been under that of Moses. Christ did not indeed order these infants to be baptized; for Christian baptism was not then explicitly instituted as the initiatory ordinance, and circumcision was still in force. (*Note,* xxviii. 19, 20.) Yet the passage seems to give considerable sanction to that method of bringing children to Christ, that they may be admitted among the subjects of his visible kingdom : and we must think those disciples at present mistaken, who object to it, sometimes with arguments, which would have equally held good against infant-circumcision, or against " bringing " infants to Christ that he might touch them." Indeed, the expression may also intimate that the kingdom of *heavenly glory* is greatly constituted of such as die in their infancy. Infants are as capable of regeneration, as grown persons: and there is ground to conclude, that all those who have not lived to commit actual transgressions, though they share in the effects of the first Adam's offence, will also share in the blessings of the second Adam's gracious covenant; without their personal faith and obedience, but not without the regenerating influence of the Spirit of Christ.—What a topick of expostulation would this transaction give the ministers of Christ, if these parents afterwards brought up their children in an unchristian manner, or set them a bad example ! or with the children, if they renounced that Saviour, who had so condescendingly taken t'em in his arms and blessed them ! In what a variety of ways, might instructions and admonitions, both to the parents and the children, have been grounded upon it; and what a sweet subject of converse would it afford to the parents, in afterwards instructing the children ! What a plea in prayer for them ! And might not infant-baptism be improved to similar purposes, did all, who approve and contend for it, bestow true pains to make it a means of grace to themselves and those concerned ? (*Marg. Ref,* —*Note, Mark* x. 13—16.)

Little children. (13, 14) Παιδια.—Και τα ςρεφη, *Luke* xviii. 15.

V. 16—22. We learn from St. Luke, that the young person here mentioned was a " ruler:" (*Luke* xviii. 18 :) he was also a person of great decency and amiableness in his moral character, and had serious thoughts about religion, and an honourable opinion of Christ. He therefore

x Luke. vi. 10—12.
viii. 10—18. John
xxxi. 24, 25. Ps.
xliv. 6, 7. 16—
19. Prov. xi. 28.
xxv. ii. 9. Mark
x. 28 Luke xii.
15—21. xvi. 13,
14. 19—28. xviii.
24. 1 Cor. i. 26.
1 Tim. vi. 9, 10.
Jam. i. 9—11. ii.
6, v. 1—4.
xxiii. 24. Jer. xiii. 23.

23 Then said Jesus unto his disciples, Verily I say unto you, *That a rich man shall hardly ᶠenter into the kingdom of heaven.

24 And again I say unto you, ᵍ It is easier for a camel to go through the

y v. 20. xviii. 3. xxi. 31. John iii. 3, 5. Acts xiv. 22.   z 26.   Mark x. 24, 25. Luke xviii. 25. John v. 44.

eye of a needle, than for a rich man to enter into the kingdom of God.

25 When his disciples heard it, they were exceedingly amazed, saying, ᵃ Who then can be saved?

26 But Jesus beheld them, and said unto them, With men this is impossi-

a xxiv. 22. Ma.k xiii.31. Luke xli. 25, 24. Rom. a 19 al. 5—7.

---

came "running;" and kneeling down to him, (Mark x. 17,) he called him "good Master," or Teacher; and with great apparent earnestness and docility enquired, "What "good thing shall I do, that I may have eternal life?" The question at first sight may seem equivalent to the enquiry of the trembling jailor, "What must I do to be "saved?" (Marg. Ref. f, g.—Notes, Luke x. 25—29. Acts xvi. 29—34, v. 31.) But our Lord saw that his judgment was erroneous, and his heart unhumbled and carnal: h: therefore first objected to his giving him, whom he supposed to be a mere Man, the title of good: as all mere men are evil in themselves: and none is strictly and absolutely good, but the one living and true God, the Fountain and Perfection of goodness and excellency. The remark was the more needful, as the Rabbies affected this title: and it intimated, that the enquirer was not properly sensible of the depravity of his own heart, or of the dignity of the person whom he thus addressed, to whom the title of "good" belonged, in a far higher sense than he supposed. He then directed him to keep the commandments of God, if he purposed "to enter into life," by the good things which he should do. This answer was doubtless intended to meet the young man's case: for the knowledge of the holy and spiritual law of God is the proper cure of a self-justifying spirit, as it tends to discover the deficiencies and defilements of all human obedience: (Marg. Ref. i.— Notes, Rom. iii. 19, 20· vii. 9—12. Gal. ii. 17—21, v. 19:) but probably he expected some external observances and austerities to have been superadded by our Lord, in order to complete his righteousness. (Notes, Rom. ix. 30—33, v. 32. x. 1—4, v. 3.) He therefore ignorantly replied, by enquiring, which of the commandments he was to keep: whereas, a perfect obedience to all of them is the indispensable condition of life, according to the covenant of works; and "cursed is every one, that continueth not in "all things, written in the book of the law, to do them." (Note, Gal. iii. 10—14.) In order therefore to his conviction, or detection, our Lord pointed out to him the commandments of the second table, and summed them up in the rule of "loving his neighbour as himself." But he, regardless of the first table, and ignorant of the spiritual import of the precepts adduced, answered, that "he had "kept them all from his youth." He could mean the letter alone, and that he was free from the grosser violations of it: for doubtless he had infringed several of them, even in his outward conduct; and though he was very far from "loving his neighbour as himself." On his further asking "What lack I yet?" our Lord, to discover to him and others, the evil which lay concealed under these plausible appearances, told him, that he yet lacked one thing; and that if he would be perfect, he must go and sell his estate, distribute the money among the poor, and come and follow him; and then he should have a far better treasure in heaven. (Marg. Ref. k—s.—Notes, Mark x. 17—31,

vv. 17. 19. 21. Luke xviii. 18—30.) This was acting like a skilful physician, who was aware of the patient's disorder, and determined to apply the medicine directly to it. It served at once to prove him far distant from the righteousness of the law, and from the state of mind and heart required by the gospel. Not to enlarge on the love of God with all the heart and soul; had he "loved his "neighbour as himself," and believed Jesus to speak with divine authority, he would readily have disposed of his wealth, at his command, in relieving the afflicted, when at the same time it would have ensured his own felicity: and had he been a humbled sinner, earnestly seeking mercy and eternal life, as the gift of God through the divine Saviour, he would readily have left all to follow him. But the event proved, that his wealth was more valued by him, than either God, or his neighbour; than Christ, a heavenly treasure, or even his own soul. Doubtless it was his duty to yield a prompt obedience to this command: yet our Lord knew that he would not, and it is evident he intended it as a touchstone, by which to discover him to himself. For when he heard that saying, all his pleasing prospects at once vanished, and he departed "sorrowful, for he had great possessions." Though reluctant to give up the hope of eternal life, yet he would not at that time renounce his riches for the sake of it. (Marg. Ref. t, u.)—We cannot decide what he afterwards did: he might at length be brought to a more spiritual frame of mind. Certainly all that Christ said to him was suited to humble and convince him; and some would infer his subsequent conversion from the words of St. Mark, who says that Jesus loved him: though this may only mean, that he saw a natural amiableness, which excited in him, as man, a peculiar regard. (Note, Mark x. 17— 31, vv. 21, 22.)—The reference to the ten commandments accords both to the Hebrew and the LXX; except as the fifth commandment is placed last, and part of it omitted.

If thou wilt, &c. (17. 21) Ει θελεις. "If thou willest," or determinest. (Note, John vii. 14—17, v. 17.)—Have I kept, &c. (20) Εφυλαξαμην. Mark x. 20. Luke xviii. 21. John xvii. 12. 1 Tim. vi. 20. 2 Tim. i. 12. ʻThe Sept. ʻ usually useth it, pro suprema circumspectione custodire.ʼ Leigh.—Sorrowful. (22) Λυπυμενος. Σλυγνασας and λυπημενος both used Mark x. 22. Περιλυπος, Luke xviii. 23.

V. 23—26. This incident afforded our Lord an occasion of shewing the extreme peril of riches. He observed, as one in astonishment, "That a rich man shall hardly "enter into the kingdom of heaven," or become his true subject and disciple. (Notes, iii. 2. John iii. 3—5.) And he added, with affectionate application to the apostles as his children, that it "was easier for a camel to pass through "the eye of a needle, than for a rich man to enter into "the kingdom of heaven." (Marg. Ref. x—z.—Notes, Mark x. 17—31, v. 24.) Some would read a cuble, in-

τ 8

ble; ᵇ but with God all things are possible.

27 Then answered Peter and said unto him, Behold, ᶜ we have forsaken all, and followed thee; ᵈ what shall we have therefore?

28 And Jesus said unto them, Verily I say unto you, That ye which have followed me, ᵉ in the regeneration ᶠ when the Son of man shall sit in the throne of his glory, ᵍ ye also shall sit upon twelve thrones, judging ʰ the twelve tribes of Israel.

29 And ᶦ every one that hath forsaken houses, ᵏ or brethren, or sisters, or father, or mother, or wife, or children, or lands, for ˡ my name's sake, shall receive ᵐ an hundred-fold, and shall ⁿ inherit everlasting life.

30 But ᵒ many that are first shall be last, and the last shall be first.

(marginal references, column 1:) ᵃ Gen. xviii. 14. Num. xi. 23. Job xlii. 2. Jer. xxxii. 27. Zech. viii. 6. Mark x. 27. Luke i. 37. xviii. 27. ᶜ ix. 30—32. ix. 7. Deut. xxxiii. 9. Mark i. 17—20. ii. 14. x. 28. Luke v. 11. 27, 28. xiv. 33. xviii. 28. ᵈ xx. 10—12. Luke xv. 29. 1 Cor. i. ᵉ Is. lxv. 17. lxvi. 22. Acts iii. 21. 2 Pet. iii. 13. Rev. xxi. 5. ᶠ xvi. 27. xxv. 31. 2 Thes. i. 7—10. Rev. xx. 11—15. ᵍ xx. 21. Luke xxii. 28—30. 1 Cor. vi. 2, 3. 2 Tim. ii. 12. Rev. ii. 26, 27. iii. 21.

(marginal references, column 2:) ʰ Ex. xv. 27. xxiv. 4. xxviii. 21. Lev. xxiv. 5. Josh. iii. 12. 1 Kings xviii. 31. Ezra vi. 17. Rev. vii. 4. xii. 1. xxi. 12—14. ᶦ xvi. 25. Mark x. 29, 30. Luke xviii. 29, 30. ᵏ viii. 21, 22. x. 37, 38. Luke xiv. 26. Phil. iii. 8. ˡ v. 11. x. 22. Luke vi. 22. John xv. 21. Acts ix. 16. 1 Pet. iv. 14. ᵐ 2 Chr. xxv. 9. ⁿ xiii. 8. 23. ᵒ viii. 11, 12. xx. 16. xxi. 31, 32. Mark x. 31. Luke viii. 29, 30.

---

stead of a *camel*: but it seems to have been a proverbial expression, signifying extreme difficulty, or apparent impossibility.—Riches powerfully tend to increase pride, covetousness, and self-indulgence: they purchase flatterers, and exclude faithful reprovers; they prejudice the mind against the humbling truths and self-denying precepts of Christ; and they increase the number and force of those obstacles which must be broken through, and the supposed value of those objects which must be renounced, if a man would become a disciple of Christ. Far more in proportion of the poor, than of the rich, are converted, and enter the kingdom of grace and of glory; and the conversion of a very wealthy man seems the peculiar triumph of almighty grace. (*Notes*, Luke xii. 15—21. xvi. 9—15. 19—23. xix. 1—10. 1 *Tim.* vi. 6—10, *vv.* 9, 10. 17—19. *Jam.* i. 9—11. ii. 5—7.) The disciples, however, who were poor and felt their own difficulties, and probably thought that the rich had more advantages for religion than themselves, were exceedingly astonished at this saying, and exclaimed, " Who then can be saved ? " But Jesus, to shew them he did not mean that all rich persons must be lost, but to warn them against the desire of such dangerous distinctions, assured them, that " with men indeed it was " impossible, but with God all things were possible." (*Marg. Ref.* b.)

Hardly. (23) Δυσκολως. *Mark* x. 23. *Luke* xviii. 24. Not used elsewhere—*Easier.* (24) Ευκοπωτερον ex εν et κοπος, labor. See on ix. 5.

V. 27, 28. The young ruler's departure from our Lord, and his observation upon it, led Peter to recollect, that he and the other apostles had actually left all to follow him; and it seems to have excited some degree of self complacency. (*Marg. Ref. c.*—*Notes*, iv. 18—22. ix. 9.) With his usual forwardness, he therefore reminded Jesus of this, and enquired what reward they should receive. Indeed Peter's " all " had been only a few fishing nets, a boat, and other things of small value: yet they were the means of obtaining a decent maintenance; and the same faith, which induced him to renounce them for Christ's sake, would have led him to make larger sacrifices, if he had been called to it, as he afterwards was. Our Lord, therefore, overlooked what was wrong, and assured the apostles, that they, " who had followed him in the regeneration," should at length be advanced and honoured in a peculiar manner. If we join the expression, " in the regeneration," to the preceding clause, it may mean the regenerating work of the Holy Spirit on their hearts, disposing them to obey his call. But it may, and probably should, be

joined to the subsequent clause; and then it refers to the time, when the apostles would receive their full recompence, even " when the Son of man shall sit on the " throne of his glory." (xxv. 31.) Then he will make all things new; and they will be his assessors in judgment; the world and the church will be judged according to their doctrine; and they will appear distinguished in an especial manner from all their brethren in Christ. (*Notes*, xvi. 19. xviii. 18. 1 *Cor.* iii. 10—15.) Some reference may perhaps be had to the establishment of the Christian church, and the condemnation of the Jewish nation in consequence of their ministry: but the day of judgment seems immediately intended. Judas was at this time one of the number; but he had never truly left all and *followed* Christ: when " he by transgression fell," another was appointed in his place, and the number twelve was continued, with reference to the twelve tribes of which Israel was originally constituted.—' In the day of the great restoration of all ' things, when the elect shall enter on a new life of un- ' speakable glory, even in that great and dreadful day, ' when " the Son of Man shall sit upon his throne of ma- ' " jesty, to judge the quick and the dead;" then shall ' ye, my apostles, who are now despicable and mean, have ' the honour to sit upon several thrones, to second and ' assist this awful act of final judgment, on the rebellious ' tribes of Israel.' *Bp. Hall.* (*Marg. Ref.* d—h.—*Notes*, xxv. 31—33. *Luke* xxii. 28—30. 1 *Cor.* vi. 1—6.)

Regeneration. (28) Παλιγγενεσια. *Tit.* iii. 5. Not elsewhere used.

V. 29, 30. Though a peculiar dignity would be reserved to the apostles; yet every one, who had forsaken or should forsake any temporal possession, or relative comfort, for the sake of Christ and of the gospel, would " receive an hundred-fold " increase of happiness for it, even in this life, (notwithstanding the persecutions, to which he would be exposed,) as well as inherit eternal life at last. (*Notes*, *Mark* x. 27—31, *v.* 30. *Luke* xviii. 18—30, *v.* 30.) This must be understood especially of divine consolations, which commonly most abound when great sacrifices are made, or great hardships endured, for conscience' sake; and which are a hundred-fold better, than all earthly comforts and possessions; as they best know who have most experienced them. But those providential interpositions may also be included, by which the Lord often makes up, in outward comforts of a far more valuable nature, all the losses and privations voluntarily incurred by his true disciples, in adhering to him, and obeying his commands: for evidently the promise has respect

CHAP. XX.

Jesus speaks a parable of labourers sent at different hours into a vineyard, and applies it, 1—16. He

foretels his own death and resurrection, 17—19; rejects the request of the mother of James and John in behalf of her sons; and represses the indignation and ambition of the other apostles, 20—28; and gives sight to two blind men, 29—34.

to all times and places. ' A full content of mind, the ' comforts of an upright conscience, the joys of the holy ' Ghost, increase of grace, and hopes of glory; and shall ' have God for their Father, and be rich towards God, and ' have Christ for their Spouse, and all good Christians ' bearing that warm affection to them, which will render ' them more closely united to, and more affectionately ' concerned for them, than those who were allied to them ' by the strictest bonds of nature.' *Whitby.* (*Marg. Ref.* i—n.—*Notes, Rom.* v. 3—5. 1 *Cor.* iii. 18—23, *vv.* 21— 23. 2 *Cor.* i. 1—7, *vv.* 3—6. *Phil.* i. 21—26. 1 *Pet.* iv. 12—16.)—To this our Lord added, " But many, that are " first shall be last, and the last first." He doubtless referred to the moral and amiable young man, who was found on trial to be " further from the kingdom of heaven," than many publicans and harlots, who became " first," when he was cast behind : but the rule has reference to a variety of cases. Prodigals often repent, and get before decent moralists: the Gentile converts obtained the priority to the Jewish nation : splendid hypocrites apostatize, and open persecutors become preachers of the gospel : and those, who have been the grief and reproach of families and neighbourhoods, sometimes become their chief credit and blessing; whilst plausible characters are by this very circumstance rendered more inveterate against the truth. (*Marg. Ref. o.—Notes,* xx. 1—16. xxi. 28—32.)

PRACTICAL OBSERVATIONS.

V. 1—12.

We are again called to follow, with our meditations, the divine Saviour, as " he went about doing good," and " endured the contradiction of sinners against himself : " let us not fail to look earnestly unto him, that we may not be wearied in well-doing, by the ingratitude and perverseness of our fellow sinners.—Human depravity has deranged the appointments of the all-wise Creator, and perverted them to the introduction of accumulated misery; and the unjust oppressors share the consequences with those, whom they cruelly oppress : but the gospel is intended to soften the hard heart, and meliorate the harsh spirits of men; as well as to regulate their passions and subdue their iniquities. When it is really embraced, its sacred energy renders men affectionate relatives and faithful friends: it teaches them to " bear with the infirmities," and " to bear the burdens," of those with whom they are connected; and to consider their interest, peace, and happiness, more than their own indulgence or convenience. This will reduce marriage, in good measure, to its original institution ; and teach the parties concerned to regulate their conduct respecting it by the law of God, and not by their own humour, passion, or caprice. The true Christian will consider his wife, as the gift and appointment of the Lord ; and his union with her as God's ordinance : he will learn to love her as his own flesh; and no more want a separation, on every gust of passion or incidental uneasiness, than he would desire to have his limb cut off, or his

flesh mangled, every time he feels pain or weariness. This he regards as a desperate and most painful remedy, in case of an incurable gangrene. He will consider the regulations of the divine law, as the dictates of wisdom and love, and every deviation as a source of temptation and disquietude, and the bane of domestick felicity: and he will perceive, that this view of the marriage-union, as indissoluble, and as an inseparable conjunction of interests and comforts till death, gives the most effectual motives to persevering endeavours for mutual peace and harmony. (*Notes, Eph.* v. 22—33. 1 *Pet.* iii. 1—7.) Should a Christian even be united with an unconverted person, (which is indeed a heavy affliction,) he will see it best to take it up as his cross, and to submit to the will of God in thus correcting him ; endeavouring to extract good from it, and expecting grace sufficient to support him under it : this he will perceive to be far preferable to any irregular method of dissolving the union. As to ungodly persons, it is proper, that their passions should be so restrained by human laws, formed according to the law of God, that they may not prove injurious to the peace of society. It does not indeed follow, that " if the case of " unbelievers." (*Notes, Prov.* xviii. 22. xix. 13, 14. xxxi. 10—12.) As to the rest, our gracious Lord has imposed upon us no rigorous restrictions ; but has left each of his disciples to choose that state of life, in which he can serve God, and mind the concerns of his soul, with most comfort and least distraction : and his condescending and considerate statement of this difficult subject forms a proper example for his people to imitate, in their conduct towards one another.

V. 13—15.

The training up of children in true religion, is one grand design of God in marriage ; and it behoves all men to have respect to this in every step they take about it. And all Christians should, by faith and prayer, bring their children to the gracious Saviour, at their birth, and even before it, that he may bless them with all his spiritual blessings. Whether they deem it right to devote their infant-offspring to him in baptism, or form other conclusions on that controverted subject ; they should certainly agree, in giving them up to him, and bringing them up for him. In attending to these important duties, we may take encouragement from the very rebuke which Christ gave his disciples, and from his readiness to grant the desire of these parents for their children : nor can we much doubt, that he really received and blessed them, as the lambs of his flock. Whilst we teach our children, as they become ca-

v 2

a iii. 2. xiii. 24.
31. 33. 44. 45.
47. xxii. 2 xxv.
1. 14.
b ix. 37. 88. xxi. 33—43.   Cant. viii. 11, 12.   Is. v. 1, 2.   John xv. 1.

c xxiii. 37. Jer.
xxv. 3, 4.
d Mark xiii. 34.
1 Cor. xv. 58.
Heb. xiii. 21.   2 Pet. i 5—10.

FOR a the kingdom of heaven is like unto b a man *that is* an householder, which went out c early in the morning to hire d labourers into his vineyard.

pahle of learning, how ready the condescending Son of God is to answer their lisping petitions, and to accept of them as his disciples; we may be well satisfied, that he has taken to his heavenly kingdom such of them as have died in infancy: for doubtless the covenant is made with the believer, for the good of this part of his offspring in an especial manner. If then Christian parents have their beloved branches cropt in the bud, they cannot surely have cause to complain ; or to think much of their pain, care, or trouble, when they are made the instruments of God in raising up children to him, who may inherit his everlasting kingdom.

V. 16—22.

It is necessary that we inculcate on those who are put under our care, not only a decency of moral conduct, and an external regard to religion, but an attention to the gospel as the only remedy for lost sinners : otherwise they may appear very amiable, serious, and earnest about eternal life ; yea, they may shew some respect to Christ and his precepts ; and yet never know their need of his precious salvation. Many abstain from gross vices, through pride, and regard to character, interest, health, or outward peace; but remain entirely inattentive to their obligations towards God, and rest in the outward letter of the commandments, which respect their neighbours : and they are ready to say, " All these have I kept from my youth ; " when ten thousand instances of disobedience, in thought, word, and deed, are marked against them in the book of God, to be produced to their conviction and confusion at the day of judgment.—Indeed, no man can enter into life, who does not habitually aim to keep the commandments of God ; and wilful, customary transgression will prove many professors of the gospel to be further from the kingdom of heaven, than even this ruler. But " there is none right-" eous, no not one : " it is therefore proper sometimes to task self-sufficient enquirers ; and when they proudly ask, " What lack I yet? " to point out to them more and more of their duty, according to the spiritual and extensive law of God. This may lead them into an acquaintance with their own weakness and depravity, and detect the secret pride and worldliness of their hearts; and so prepare the way for their understanding and welcoming the gospel of free salvation. Not only does the law require us (if Providence call us to it,) to part with our substance, or even our lives, for the glory of God, and the good of our neighbours: but except a man be ready to forsake all that he has for Christ's sake, he cannot be his disciple, or be saved according to the gospel. No unregenerate man will comply either with the precept of the law, or the requisition of Christ, when he is fairly put to the trial. In this manner, numbers " forsake him, loving this " present world: " they have their convictions and desires, but the sacrifice insisted on is too valuable ; therefore they depart sorrowful, perhaps trembling. This is peculiarly the case with those who have great possessions, and who live in trying times. Few in comparison of the numbers of those " who call Christ, Lord, Lord," seem prepared

for obedience, should he require them to " sell all and " give to the poor, and come and follow him, that they " may have a treasure in heaven." Many refuse, at his express command, to part with the most trivial interest or indulgence: many will not give even a moderate proportion of their goods to the poor, notwithstanding all the promises made to those, who do this out of faith, and love to Christ. It behoves us then to try ourselves in these matters, for the Lord will ere long put us to the trial ; and then, if found wanting, we must abide the eternal and awful consequences.

V. 23—30.

Nothing more fully proves men's want of true faith, than their eagerness to be rich, though Christ has spoken in so alarming a manner, concerning the additional dangers, to which riches expose their precious souls. Yet how few are there who do not labour to be rich, and to enrich their children? Who does not associate the idea of wealth with that of felicity? Who that has riches does not confide in them as a substantial advantage? And who that is poor is not tempted to envy the wealthy? But experience fatally confirms the declarations of Christ; and proves that this earnestness is like toiling to build a high wall, to shut themselves and their children out of heaven: for in this manner, many " that will be rich, fall into " fatal snares," and involve their families in every kind of ruinous temptation, to their everlasting perdition. (*Note,* 1 *Tim.* vi. 6—10.) Such assertions will not only offend unbelievers : even disciples will be astonished at them, and be ready to think that none then can be saved. Indeed, not many of the rich and honourable of the earth are called, but the people of God are generally found among the poor; and the difficulties in the way of the wealthy sinner's conversion are so many, and so insurmountable by man, that we should have no hope of him, except as we know that " with God all things are possible." And, blessed be his name, he surprises us with some demonstrations of the omnipotence of his grace, even in these degenerate days: here and there, a very wealthy person is brought forth, and appears eminent for humility, simplicity, spirituality, and fruitfulness: some of this kind are even found among those, who are *growing rich* from inferior circumstances ; but none among those, that " *will* be " rich," or who trust, idolize, or love riches. What we here read, however, should surely make us willing to be poor, to beware of covetousness, and to pity and pray for the rich ; as we would for men at sea in a violent storm, whom nothing but an extraordinary interposition of God could save, from being swallowed up by the tempestuous waves : and in all our labours of love, we may still apply this rule, even to the most abandoned and hardened, that " with " God all things are possible." But whether a man have a kingdom, or only a fishing-boat ; if he be duly humbled as a sinner, and earnestly seek eternal life from the Saviour, he will, at his call, leave all and follow him; and if he be allowed to keep his substance, he will learn to use it in his service. Indeed, mixtures of self-preference often tarnish our conscious integrity, and our gratitude to him

v 3

2 And when ᵉ he had agreed with the labourers for ᵉ a penny a day, ᶠ he sent them into his vineyard.

3 And he went out about ᶠ the third hour, and saw others ʰ standing idle in the market-place,

4 And said unto them, ⁱ Go ye also into the vineyard, ᵈ and whatsoever is right I will give you. And they went their way.

5 Again he went out about the sixth and ninth hour, ᵐ and did likewise.

6 And about ⁿ the eleventh hour he went out, and found others standing idle, and saith unto them, Why stand ye here all the day idle?

7 They say unto him, ᵒ Because no man hath hired us. He saith unto them, ᵖ Go ye also into the vineyard; ᵠ and whatsoever is right, that shall ye receive.

8 So ʳ when even was come, the lord of the vineyard saith ˢ unto his

steward, Call the labourers, and give them *their* hire, beginning from the last unto the first.

9 And when they came that *were* hired about the eleventh hour, ᵗ they received every man a penny.

10 But when the first came, they supposed that they should have received more; and they likewise received every man a penny.

11 And when they had received *it*, ᵘ they murmured against the goodman of the house,

12 Saying, These last have ᵛ wrought *but* one hour, and thou hast made ʸ them ˣ equal unto us, which have ᶻ borne the burden and heat of the day.

13 But he answered one of them, and said, ᵃ Friend, ᵇ I do thee no w o g: didst not thou agree with me for a penny?

14 Take *that* ᵇ thine *is*, and go thy way: I will give unto this last, even as unto thee.

"who hath made us to differ:" yet our gracious Lord accepts his own work, and pardons our evil; and if we here follow him with simplicity, he will at length cause us to inherit " a crown of glory that fadeth not away." Nay, he has promised most abundantly to recompense us, for all that we give up for his sake; so that it is only like sowing seed, with the assurance, even in this world, of reaping an hundred-fold; as well as of eternal life in that which is to come. May he then give us faith to lay hold of his promise, and rest our hope on him; and then we shall be prepared for every service or sacrifice. But let us neither trust in promising appearances, or in outward profession; nor despair of such as are fallen the deepest into immorality, impiety, or infidelity: seeing " many of the first shall be " last, and the last first;" and the chief of sinners may, for what we know, become most eminent in faith and holiness.

NOTES.

CHAP. XX. V. 1—16. This parable was intended to illustrate the equity of the Lord's dealings, even when " the first are placed last, and the last first." (xix. 30.) In this respect, " the kingdom of heaven" resembles a householder, when he hires labourers to work in his vineyard. He goes very early in the morning, according to the custom at that time, and in some places at present, to some known place, whither those who desired to be employed used to resort, " to hire labourers;" and, bargaining with certain persons at the usual price of a *denarius* a day, (about seven pence halfpenny, or eight pence, *Note, Rev.* vi. 5, 6;) he sends them immediately to work. But he also goes afterwards about nine o'clock, at noon, at

three in the afternoon, and about an hour before sun-set; and he finds persons unemployed, whom he sends into his vineyard, with a general assurance, that he would give them what was right or equitable. When even was come, he gives order to his steward to pay the labourers: and as those who were sent to the work at the latest hour are paid first, and receive a full day's wages: the others, especially those who had gone to work early in the morning, expect to receive more: and, being disappointed, they murmur as if injustice were done them. But the master shews, that they were not injured; that they had their whole due, while the others had more than their's; that it was reasonable for him to dispose of his own property as he saw good; that their objections arose from envy and selfishness, excited by his goodness; and that he certainly should continue his bounty to the others, notwithstanding their murmurs. And then our Lord assured the disciples, that thus " the last shall be first, and the first last; for many " be called, but few chosen."—In interpreting the parable, the grand scope ought principally to be adverted to. The church, as represented by a vineyard, the employment of the servants, and their wages, with several other particulars, are only circumstances: (*Marg. Ref.* a—f:) the main scope of the parable respects the dealings of God with men according to the gospel, and vindicates him from the charge of injustice and partiality.—'As some ... careful 'householder, that has hired labourers, at a set rate, into 'his vineyard; calling in other workmen at the latter end 'of the day, is pleased to give an equal retribution to those 'that came latest into the vineyard, with those that came 'at first; making good his promise and agreement with 'the first, while he is bountiful unto the latter; cannot

v 4

15 Is ᶜ it not lawful for me to do what I will with mine own? ᵈ Is thine eye evil, ᵉ because I am good?

16 So ᶠ the last shall be first, and the first last : ᶠ for many be called, but few chosen.

17 ¶ And ʰ Jesus going up to Jeru-

c xi. 26. Ex. xxxiii. 19. Deut. vii. 6—8. 1 Chr. xxviii. 4. 5. Jer. xxvii. 5—7. John xvii. 2.
Rom. ix. 15—24. xi. 5, 6. 1 Cor. iv. 7. Eph. i. 11. ii. 1. 5. Jam. i. 18. xv. 9. xxviii. 54. Prov. xxiii. 6. xxviii. 22. Mark vii. 22. Jam. v. 9. iv. 1—4. Acts xiii. 45.
d Deut.
e Jon.
f viii. 11, 12. xix. 30. xxi.31. Mark x. 31. Luke vii. 47. xiii. 28—30 xv. 7. xvii. 17, 18. John xii. 19
g vii. 13. xxii. 14. Luke xiv. 24. Rom. viii. 30. 2 Thes. ii. 13, 14.
h Mark x. 32—34. Luke xviii. 31—34. John xii. 12.

' be challenged to have done any wrong to the first, in his ' liberality to the last : even so God, the great Master of ' this earthly family, having called some more early to the ' service and profession of his name, some later; if he ' shall give a like gracious remuneration to all, cannot ' justly be excepted against ; since, if some have cause to ' magnify his bounty, yet no man has cause to complain.' *Bp. Hall.*—Some expositors refer the different hours of the day, to several periods in the history of the church from the beginning ; and others, to the times when a remnant of the Jews, and afterwards the Gentiles, were brought into the Christian church : but it is very difficult, at least, to make the circumstances of the parable in any measure accord to these events. With more plausibility and utility, they may be applied to the conversion of sinners, at the earlier and later stages of human life : for thus indeed one man does serve the Lord longer than another does. (*Marg. Ref. g*—*o*.) Yet this must not be strained too far : for it would be absurd to suppose, that any real Christians, at the great day of account, will murmur at the appointments of the Judge, or boast of their own services. It is, there-fore, rather a description of the state of the visible church ; and an illustration of the maxim, " The last shall be first, " and the first last," in all its bearings. Many outwardly embrace Christianity, who are not made humble and spi-ritual : many real Christians, who have been early con-verted, and preserved from outward vices, do not, for a time, understand the case of their fellow-servants who are called at a later hour. Men are apt to over-rate their own services, and to derogate from those of their neighbours. Innumerable objections are started against the methods of divine grace : the Jews could not endure the admission of the Gentiles, to share all the privileges of the people of God ; though there was no difference, save that they were called at a later period into the vineyard : the elder brother thought himself wronged, when the prodigal was welcomed home : (*Note* and *P. O. Luke* xv. 25—32 :) the Pharisees were offended at Christ's attention to publicans and harlots : (See on *Note*, xix. 29, 30.—*Notes*, ix. 9—13. *Luke* vii. 37—39. xv. 1, 2 :) and the freeness of salvation to " the chief of sinners," has always stumbled moralists and formalists, who boast of having " borne the burden " and heat of the day." But such objections are easily answered : the Lord punishes none above their deserts ; and recompenses, in one way or other, every service which is performed for him : he does no injustice to any, by shewing extraordinary grace to some : and he will, at the close of the day, if not before, convince all the world of his own equity, truth, and goodness, and of the pride, ignorance, and selfishness of these murmurers. He will prove his right to " do what he will with his own," to the full satisfaction of his friends, and the final confusion of every one, whose " eye is evil because he is good." He will fulfil his largest promises to each believer, in whatever period of the church, or in whatever time of his life, he becomes " a labourer in the vineyard : " and he will shew,

that in real grace, as well as in privilege and consolation, many who are latest converted, exceed those who have been longer in the service of Christ. But the concluding sen-tence evidently shews, that professors of religion in general were especially intended, and that they were addressed ac-cording to *their own opinion of themselves*, and not accord-ing to the *real state of their souls*. (*Marg. Ref.* u—d.)—There is a parable, not wholly dissimilar, in the Jewish Talmud ; and some *Christian* expositors seem to think, that our Lord took this from what was then extant of it ; but *omitted* some things, which they seem to think *ought to be added* in order to a right understanding of the sub-ject : especially, that the labourers, who came late into the vineyard, were so diligent, that in a short time they performed as much, as the others had done in the whole day ; and were " chosen," because known to be men of remarkable industry. This is supposed to be necessary in order to make the parable consist with every man being rewarded according to his works. But Dr. Doddridge has very justly called the parable of the Talmudists, ' an *insipid* ' *imitation* : ' and we may add, that it is a perversion of the parable before us, in opposition to the grand principles of the gospel. The *nature and motives* of our works, and not merely the *quantity*, must be taken into the account at the great day ; and the reward be made accordingly : (*Notes*, xxv. 34—40. *Rom.* ii. 4—11. 2 *Cor.* v. 10—12 :) but this is not the immediate subject of the parable, which has above been fully shewn.

Householder. (1) Ανθρωπω οικοδεσποτη· *Master of a house or family.* 11. x. 25. xiii. 27. 52. xxi. 33. xxiv. 43. *Mark* xiv. 14. *Luke* xii. 39. xiii. 25. xiv. 21. xxii. 11.—*When he had agreed.* (2) Συμφωνησας. 16. See on xviii. 19.—*Hour.* (3) Ωρα. A twelfth part of the time, from the rising to the setting of the sun. At the equinox, the third hour answered to nine o'clock in the forenoon ; the sixth, to noon ; the eleventh, to five in the afternoon.—*Steward.* (8) Επιτροπω.—*To one entrusted.* (Ab επιτρεπω.) *Luke* viii. 3. *Gal.* iv. 2. *Επιτροπη. Acts* xxvi. 12.—*They murmured.* (11) Εγογγυζον. *Luke* v. 30. *John* vi. 41. 43. 61. vii. 32. 1 *Cor.* x. 10. *Jude* 16.—*The heat.* (12) Τον καυσωνα. *Luke* xii. 55. *Jam.* i. 11.—*Called,* &c. (16) Κλητοι, sometimes means *invited*, or favoured with the means of grace ; and at others *effectual vocation.* (*Marg. Ref.* f, g.—*Notes*, xxii. 1—14. *Rom.* viii. 28—31. 2 *Thes.* ii. 13, 14.)—Multitudes are called in the former sense, who at last appear to have been at best, only plausible hypocrites. ' But they who ' be endued with so excellent a gift ' (as predestination to ' life) ' be called according to God's purpose by his Spirit in ' due season, they through grace obey the calling ; they ' be justified freely, they be made the children of God by ' adoption ; they be made like the image of his only be-' gotten Son Jesus Christ ; they walk religiously in good ' works ; and at length by God's mercy they attain to ever-' lasting felicity.' *17th Article.*—*Chosen.*] Εκλεκτοι. " The " Elect are few."

V. 17—19. (*Marg. Ref.*) ' Humanly speaking, it was

y 5

salem took the twelve disciples apart in the way, and said unto them,

18 Behold, we go up to Jerusalem; and the Son of man shall be betrayed unto the chief priests and unto the scribes, and they shall condemn him to death,

19 And shall deliver him to the Gentiles to mock, and to scourge, and to crucify him: and the third day he shall rise again.

20 ¶ Then came to him the mother of Zebedee's children with her sons, worshipping him, and desiring a certain thing of him.

21 And he said unto her, What wilt thou? She saith unto him, Grant that these my two sons may sit, the one on thy right hand, and the other on the left, in thy kingdom.

22 But Jesus answered and said, Ye know not what ye ask. Are ye able to drink of the cup that I shall drink of, and to be baptized with the baptism that I am baptized with? They say unto him, We are able.

23 And he saith unto them, Ye shall drink indeed of my cup, and be baptized with the baptism that I am baptized with: but to sit on my right hand, and on my left, is not mine to give, but it shall be given to them for whom it is prepared of my Father.

' much more probable, that Jesus should have been pri-
' vately assassinated, or stoned, as was before attempted,
' ...than that he should have been thus solemnly con-
' demned, and delivered up to crucifixion. ...But " all
' " this was done that the scriptures might be fulfilled." '
Doddridge.—' Christ goeth to the cross necessarily, but
' yet willingly.' Beza. (Notes, xvi. 21—23. Mark ix. 30
—32. x. 32—34.)

They shall deliver, &c. (19) Παραδωσουσιν. The same verb just before translated betrayed (18). It was as much treason for the rulers and priests to deliver up their King into the hands of Pilate, to be crucified; as it had been in Judas, to deliver him up into their hands.

V. 20—23. Perhaps Zebedee, the father of James and John, was dead before this time, or he was not so constant a follower of Christ as his wife was; so that she is mentioned as " the mother of Zebedee's children." (Note, iv. 18—22, vv. 21, 22.)—At their desire, in their name, and with them, she prostrated herself before Christ, and besought him to grant her one request; seeming to expect, that he would engage his word before the petition was made. (Notes, 1 Kings ii. 14—20. iii. 5—14. Esth. v. 1—3.) When required to propose it, she asked that her two sons might have the chief places of honour and authority in his kingdom. (Marg. Ref. x.) Our Lord had just before been discoursing of his sufferings, death, and resurrection; but the apostles were too blinded by carnal prejudices, in that particular, to understand his meaning. They were, however, continually expecting that he would appear in his glory; and probably Salome (Marg. r,) had respect to the twelve thrones which he had promised to the apostles; (xix. 28;) the two principal of which she wished to engage for her sons; being emboldened to make such a request, by the special favour which our Lord had shewn to them. But Jesus told her and them, that they knew neither the nature, nor the consequences, of their request: for the chief preferments which he had to bestow, would expose those who obtained them to the largest share of suffering. He therefore demanded, whether they were able to drink of his cup, and to be baptized with his bap-

tism. He was about to be betrayed, condemned, scourged, mocked, and crucified: and were they prepared to drink after him of this cup, and to be initiated into his service by this baptism? Either they did not duly attend to the meaning of the question, or they had too great a confidence in themselves, when they answered, that " they " were able." He assured them, however, that they would be called thus to follow him, through sufferings and persecutions, and that they would be enabled to endure them for his sake: but that the highest honours of his kingdom were not now to be disposed of by him, to gratify the ambition of any favourite: in this sense, they were not his to give, as Mediator, " save to those, for whom they had " been prepared of the Father; " for that concern had been previously determined, in perfect harmony between the Father and the Son.—The words in Italicks, " it shall " be given," rather obscure the meaning, and may well be spared.—James was the first of the apostles who suffered martyrdom: John survived all the rest, and is not supposed to have died a violent death. He, however, endured hardships and persecutions, stripes, contempt, and suffering, from the enmity of the world, for the sake of Christ and the gospel; and thus it may be said, that he drank of Christ's cup, and was baptized with his baptism.—Our Lord might indeed, by a strong figure of speech, be said to have been immerged in sufferings, when he endured the wrath of God as the propitiation for our sins; but the lighter afflictions of the apostles, connected with abundant joys and consolation, must be allowed, in this sense, to have been another and a far milder kind of baptism than his. (Marg. Ref. a—d.—See on iii. 6.—Notes, xxvi. 42—46, v. 42. Mark x. 35—45, vv. 35—40. Luke xii. 49—53, v. 50. John xviii. 10—14, v. 11. Col. i. 24.)— ' None of Christ's disciples imagined, he had promised the ' supremacy to Peter, by those words, " Thou art Peter:" ' for then neither would these two persons have desired it, ' nor would the rest have contended for it afterwards. Luke ' xxii. 24.' Whitby.—It is prepared. (23) 'Ητοιμασαι. " It " has been prepared." xxii. 4. xxv. 34. Mark x. 40. John xiv. 2. Eph. ii. 10. Heb. xi. 16.

u 6

24 And when the ten heard it, 'they were moved with indignation against the two brethren.

25 But Jesus ᵍ called them unto him, and said, Ye know that ʰ the princes of the Gentiles ' exercise dominion over them, and they that are great exercise authority upon them.

26 But ᵏ it shall not be so among you: but whosoever will be great among you, let him be your ' minister;

27 And whosoever will be chief among you, ᵐ let him be your servant:

28 Even as the Son of man ⁿ came not to be ministered unto, but to minister, ° and to give his life a ransom ᵖ for many.

29 ¶ And ᑫ as they departed from Jericho, a great multitude followed him.

30 And, behold, 'two blind men sitting by the way-side, when they heard that Jesus passed by, cried out, saying, ˢ Have mercy on us, O Lord, thou Son of David!

31 And the multitude ᵗ rebuked them, because they should hold their peace: ᵘ but they cried the more, saying, Have mercy on us, O Lord, thou Son of David!

32 And Jesus stood still, and called them, and said, ˣ What will ye that I shall do unto you?

33 They say unto him, ʸ Lord, that our eyes may be opened.

34 So ᶻ Jesus had compassion on them, and ᵃ touched their eyes: and immediately their eyes received sight, ᵇ and they followed him.

V. 24—28. The other apostles were as ambitious of the chief places in the kingdom, as James and John, notwithstanding our Lord's former discourse on this subject. They were therefore angry with the two brothers, for taking an undue advantage in this contested point. (Marg. Ref. f.) But Jesus, aware of their resentment and ambition, was pleased to argue the case with them. He shewed them the difference between his kingdom, and the kingdoms of the nations. "The princes of the Gentiles" indeed were ambitious of lordly authority, in order to gratify their love of domineering, and of being flattered and had in honour; and every inferior ruler copied their example: but this resulted from false notions of greatness, and from the pride of the human heart. Such a conduct, however, might consist with the character of conquerors and tyrants, and rulers who know not God: but it was wholly unsuitable to the governors of God's people, and most of all to the spiritual pastors of his flock. It must not be at all the case with them: instead of aspiring to dominion, and "lording it over God's heritage;" he, who would indeed be "great among them," must become the menial servant of the whole company; and stoop to the lowest and most laborious employments, in order to be the more useful. This humility, self-abasement, and diligence would at length render·him the chief: whilst a contrary conduct would tend to a man's disgrace and degradation. (Marg. Ref. g—i.—Notes, xviii. 1—4. Mark x. 35—45, vv. 42—44. Luke xxii. 24—27. 2 Cor. i. 23, 24. 1 Pet. v. 1—4.) Of this way to be chief in the kingdom, he had and would set them an example: he appeared among them as "the "Son of man," not to assume external authority, and "to "be ministered to" by courtiers and dependents: but to be a Servant to them, and to all who would require of him any thing conducive to their good. And, after spending his days in this manner, he was about to lay down his life, as a ransom for the souls of multitudes, even of all that

should ever believe in his name; "suffering once for sins, "the just for the unjust, that he might bring us to God." (Marg. Ref. n—p.—Notes, John i. 29. 1 Tim. ii. 5—7. Heb. ix. 27, 28. 1 Pet. iii. 17, 18. 1 John ii. 1, 2.)—This does not prove, that Christians must not be kings or rulers; but it fully demonstrates, that they must not be ambitious and tyrannical. Government and discipline are also necessary to the church: but lordly power, the pride of life, dominion over conscience, and the spirit of persecution, are not necessary to its rulers, under any form of government; nay, totally incompatible with the spirit of the gospel, though alas! too common in most ages and places.

They were moved with indignation. (24) Ηγανακτησαν. (Ex αγαν, valde, et αχθος, dolor.) xxi. 15. xxvi. 8. Mark x. 14. 41. xiv. 4. Luke xiii. 14.—Exercise dominion over. (25) Κατακυριευσιν. Mark x. 42. Acts xix. 16. 1 Pet. v. 3.—Gen. i. 28. Ps. x. 10. Sept.—Exercise authority upon.] Κατεξ-ουσιαζουσιν. Mark x. 42. See Luke xxii. 25.—Ransom. (28) Λυτρον. Mark x. 45. Not elsewhere used.

V. 29—34. Marg. Ref.—Notes, Mark x. 46—52.

PRACTICAL OBSERVATIONS.

V. 1—16.

The pride of the human heart, and its enmity to the sovereignty of God, render it very difficult to convince men of the justice and goodness of his dispensations: yet nothing can be more certain, than that "he is righteous in "all his ways, and holy in all his works." This may be evidently proved, in respect of those parts of his plan, with which we are acquainted; if we impartially judge of them, according to the rules established in human society, for the conduct of men towards subjects, servants, and dependents, and for the disposal of their p o e e y.—In every age, the great Owner of the vineyard comes, by his ministers, to "hire labourers;" and he condescends to take those, who have been rebels against him and servants to

CHAP. XXI.

Jesus enters Jerusalem on an ass's colt, amidst the acclamations of the multitudes, 1—11. He drives the buyers and sellers out of the temple; heals the blind and lame; and answers the objections of the priests,

12—16. He causes the barren fig-tree to wither; and shews the disciples the power of faith and prayer, 17—22. He silences those who demand by what authority he acted, 23—27: and exposes the wickedness, and predicts the doom, of the priests and rulers, by a parable of two sons, 28—32, and by that of a vineyard let out to husbandmen, 33—46.

another master; and, having pardoned and reconciled them, he sends them into his vineyard, to labour in their several stations, to promote the common cause of his church. Those who are early in life called by his grace, and yield themselves to his service, are peculiarly favoured; for " his yoke is easy, and his burden is light." (*Note*, xi. 28—30.) They may deem themselves happy, in being preserved from doing mischief, and from forming bad habits and connexions: and in being early habituated to do good, and associated with " the excellent of the earth." (*Note, Ec.* xii. 1.) Yet those who have wasted their youth in vanity and sin, are invited to enter the Lord's service at a later period: and the case of those who have not before heard the gospel, but have loitered, " because no man " hath hired them," is far more hopeful, than that of such as have long withstood the invitations of the word, and the convictions of their own conscience. We are, however, authorized even to the eleventh hour, to remonstrate with those who " stand all the day idle," and call upon them to enter the Lord's vineyard; assuring them, that " what- " ever is right, that they shall receive." To the end of life, it is written over mercy's gate, " Knock, and it shall " be opened:" but life is uncertain, and it is madness for men to procrastinate, when they know not how soon death may for ever bar the door, and leave them to everlasting and unavailing lamentations and despair.—Whether men enter early in the morning, or the eleventh hour, they will spend the subsequent part of their lives in " the work " of the Lord;" and thus evince the sincerity of their repentance, faith, and love; and prove their interest in " the gift of God, which is eternal life, through Jesus " Christ our Lord."—The exceeding riches of divine grace excite loud murmurs amongst proud Pharisees and nominal Christians; for many are called into the visible church, who do not belong to " the remnant according to the elec- " tion of grace:" and many perform outward services to God, who have never humbly submitted to his righteousness, his sovereignty, and his authority. All their performances are therefore leavened with self-preference: and their objections to the Lord's gracious dealings with publicans and prodigals, their boasts, and their complaining of " the burden and heat of the day," betray the mercenary or the slave; and savour not at all of " the spirit of " adoption," the loving temper of a child, who keeps his father's commandments, and counts them not grievous. (*Note,* 1 *John* v. 1—3, *v.* 3.) First or last, the mouths of all such objectors will be stopped; and it will be well for them if it be in this world: for the Lord will, at the great day of retribution, prove to the whole universe, the equity of his procedure; and silence all who murmur against him for " doing what he will with his own," though they assume that privilege themselves, with what he has entrusted to them. Then it will appear, that many, who were first in morality and profession, were in their hearts at enmity

with God: whilst the late convert will, in many instances, be shewn to have " loved much," and to have been humble and diligent, in proportion to the greatness of his obligations and unworthiness. Let us then remember, that we are all condemned criminals; and that our wise and righteous Sovereign does no one any injustice, and that he dispenses his unmerited favours as he sees good: let us forego every proud claim, and seek salvation as a free gift: and let us never envy or grudge; but always rejoice, and praise God, for every display of his mercy to the vilest of our fellow sinners.

V. 17—23.

A believing view of our once crucified, and now glorified Redeemer, is the great antidote to a proud, self-justifying disposition. When we consider what need there was of the humiliation and sufferings of the Son of God, in order to the salvation of sinners; and when we recollect the willingness, meekness, constancy, and patience, with which the Redeemer endured the insults and cruelty of men and the wrath of God for us; we cannot but feel our self-sufficiency abate, and be sensible of the unspeakable freeness and riches of divine grace in our salvation.—Yet with what strange indifference, do even disciples sometimes read, hear, or speak of these interesting topicks! especially when Satan tempts them to aspire after " the honour that " cometh from man."—If we ask such things as are truly good for us or others, God will not refuse our request: but when we pray, under the influence of pride, avarice, or any other passion, we " know not what we ask;" we mistake poison for food or medicine; and if he loves us, he will withhold from us what we foolishly crave.—If we would at last be conformed to our glorified Lord, we must be willing here to have fellowship with him in his sufferings; we must pass through tribulations and reproach; we must drink in some measure of his bitter cup, and experience some degree of his afflictive baptism: yet how light, and mingled with comfort, are our sharpest trials, compared with the unmixed agony and anguish which he endured for us! Possessing a good hope of being admitted to the felicity of heaven, we shall be satisfied with the thought, that it will be " according as it is prepared for " us by our heavenly Father." And, even in this world, it becomes us indeed to be earnest about growth in grace, and diligence and fruitfulness, the redemption of our time and the improvement of our talents, and usefulness in the lowest station in the church; but not about pre-eminence among our brethren.

V. 24—34.

Alas! how have ambition and envy moved professed Christians to indignation against each other, and sown contentions among brethren, in every age! And what enormous mischiefs have arisen, from church-rulers and pastors exercising dominion after the manner of the kings, nay, tyrants of the nations; or indeed with more atro-

v 8

AND [a] when they drew nigh unto Jerusalem, and were come to Bethphage, unto [b] the mount of Olives, then sent Jesus two disciples,

2 Saying unto them, 'Go into the village over against you, and straightway ye shall find an ass tied, and a colt with her: loose them, and bring them unto me.

3 And if any man say ought unto you, ye shall say, 'The Lord hath need of them; and straightway he will send them.

4 All 'this was done, that it might be fulfilled which was spoken by the prophet, saying,

5 Tell ye [b] the daughter of Sion, Behold, 'thy King cometh unto thee, meek, and sitting upon an ass, and a colt the foal of an ass.

6 And the disciples went, and did as Jesus commanded them;

7 And brought the ass and the colt, and put on them their clothes, and they set him thereon.

NOTES.

cions pride, cruelty, and iniquity! (P. O. Rev. xviii. 9—19.) Carnal men thus seek to be the greatest: but those Christians and ministers are in reality the chief, and most honourable, and will be deemed so by all competent judges, who stoop the lowest, labour the most diligently, and suffer with most entire meekness and patience, in seeking to do good to their brethren, and to promote the salvation of souls. They most resemble him, "who came not to be "ministered unto, but to minister, and to give his life a "ransom for many;" and will be most honoured by him to all eternity. Yet, so deceitful is the heart, that those who sincerely avow the determination of leaving all for Christ's sake, and in hope of an eternal and gracious recompence; and who have actually given up many things on these accounts; may yet, like the apostles on this occasion, have secret expectations of honour and importance among their brethren; which various circumstances detect, and which should always be watched against. But a humble sense of our own indigence, unworthiness, and misery, and exalted apprehensions of the Saviour's power and grace, are in some respects the standard of human excellency, and the source of human felicity. However poor, ignorant, weak, and sinful that man may be, who thus humbly seeks to Christ for help, he will be earnest in proportion as his applications are discouraged; he will cry the more vehemently, when men would require him to "hold his peace;" and the Lord will at length attend to him and answer his petitions; he will compassionate his sorrows, open his eyes, supply his wants, and forgive his sins; and thus enable him to join the number of his followers, and "to shew forth his praises, who hath called "him out of darkness into his marvellous light."

CHAP. XXI. V. 1—5. Several events, especially the resurrection of Lazarus from the dead, intervened before those recorded in this chapter, which occurred no more than five days before our Lord's crucifixion. (Notes, John xi. xii. 1—11.) In his last journey to Jerusalem, he lodged at Bethany; and then proceeded on the road towards the city, to the extremity of that village, or rather to a part of the mount of Olives, which lay between it and Bethphage. (Marg. Ref. a, b.) From thence he sent two of his disciples to the village over against them, perhaps to Bethphage; informing them, that in a certain

place, which he described, they would find a she-ass tied, and her colt with her, and ordering them to "loose them "and bring them" to him: and if any man objected, as he foresaw the owners would, they were directed to say, "The Lord hath need of them:" "The Lord of all;" and not merely our Lord. The owners might have heard of Jesus under that title: but it undoubtedly implied a high claim of authority over them and their's. He likewise assured the disciples, that they would find the persons concerned entirely willing to send them away, with the ass and her colt, being fully satisfied with their answer. (Marg. Ref. c—e.—Note, Mark xi. 1—11, vv. 1—3.) —'The other evangelists make mention only of the colt, 'because our Saviour sat on him only. ... Note also here, 'a wonderful instance of Christ's prescience in the minutest 'matters. 1, You shall find a colt; 2, on which no man 'ever sat; 3, bound, with his mother; 4, in bivio,' (" a "place where two ways meet," Mark xi. 4;) '5, as you 'enter into the village; 6, the owners of which shall at first 'seem unwilling that you shall unbind him; 7, but when 'they hear "the Lord hath need of him," they will let 'him go.' Whitby.—In the whole of this transaction our Lord had respect to a prophecy concerning the Messiah, (Note, Zech. ix. 9, 10, v. 9,) which described him as meek, and coming to Zion as her "King, riding on an ass, even on "a colt the foal of an ass." The kings of Israel and Judah were forbidden to multiply horses, or to use them in war; for this would make way for worldly confidences: it was therefore a proper characteristick of Zion's King, to come "riding on an ass," to denote the spiritual nature of his kingdom. Asses were then frequently used to ride on, though not so much as in preceding ages: yet this was an emblem of our Lord's external poverty and humiliation; and an open declaration, that he was Zion's predicted King and Saviour. (Marg. Ref. f—l.—Note, Deut. xvii. 16.) The quotation is a more literal translation of the Hebrew text than the Septuagint is, in which the Greek word for an ass is not used, but more general terms, (ὑποζύγιον, πωλον νεον;) though two different words, both signifying an ass, or asses, or an ass, and a colt the son of asses, are found in the Hebrew. Perhaps they did not choose to state explicitly to the magnificent Grecians, famed for beautiful horses, that Zion's glorious King should come to his royal city riding on an ass's colt.

V. 6, 7. The disciples went, without hesitation, on this

X

8 And a very great multitude spread
their garments in the way; ₚ others
cut down branches from the trees, and
strawed *them* in the way.

9 And the multitudes that went
before, and that followed, cried, saying, 'Hosanna to the Son of David:
' blessed is he that cometh in the
name of the Lord: Hosanna ' in the
highest!

10 And when he was come into Jerusalem, ' all the city was moved, saying, " Who is this?

11 And the multitude said, * This is
Jesus the prophet ' of Nazareth of Galilee.

12 And Jesus ' went into the temple of God, ' and cast out all them that
sold and bought in the temple, and '
overthrew the tables of the ' money-
changers, and the seats of them that
sold ' doves,

13 And said unto them, ' It is written, 'My house shall be called the
house of prayer; but ' ye have made it,
a den of thieves.

---

service, and found every circumstance accord to what their
Lord had foretold; which could not fail to impress their
minds with a deep conviction of his divine knowledge and
power, and help to prepare them for that trying scene
which was about to open. When, therefore, they had
brought the ass and the colt to Jesus, they threw their
loose upper garments upon them instead of saddles. But
he was pleased to be seated on the *unbroken* colt; and by
his miraculous energy to render it tractable and steady,
amidst the acclamations of the multitude, which were sufficient to render unruly even an animal, that had been
accustomed to the road. This seems to have been an emblem of his power, in rendering the hearts of sinners submissive to his will in the midst of the temptations of this
world; and notwithstanding their natural pride, obstinacy,
and carnal affections.—*Thereon*, or, *on them;* that is, on
the garments; for he rode on the colt only. (*Marg Ref.*
—*Note, Mark* xi. 1—11, *v. 7.*)

V. 8—11. When our Lord's intentions of entering
Jerusalem, in this humble kind of triumph, became known;
the multitudes which attended him, (being doubtless increased by continual accessions,) began to spread the way,
on which he was to pass, with their garments, and to strew
on each side green branches cut from the trees; or to carry
palms in their hands, as it was usually done at the feast of
tabernacles. Thus they shewed their joy, and attempted
to honour him, by such methods as were used upon the
accession of kings to the throne, or on the triumphal return of victors to their capital cities. It was owing, in
great measure, to the miracle of Lazarus's resurrection,
which took place not long before, that the people came
thus to meet Christ and welcome him to Jerusalem: (*Note,
John* xii. 12—19:) and he was pleased to accede to it,
both as an avowal of his character, and in order to accele-
rate his crucifixion, now that "his time was come." The
multitudes, on this occasion, acknowledged him as the
Messiah, who was come in the name of JEHOVAH, to
assume the kingdom over Israel: and with loud acclamations they cried, Hosanna to the Son of David. "Hosanna,"
signifies, "Save, I pray," and may be deemed nearly equivalent to "God save the King." They wished prosperity
and blessings on him and on his kingdom, with " peace in
" heaven, and glory in the highest;" either the peculiar
favour and friendship of heaven, to render his kingdom
glorious above all other kingdoms; or that God might
through him be at peace with Israel, and be glorified with

the most exalted praises of men and angels. Some of the
multitude might use one expression, and some another;
but all meaning the same for substance; namely, to welcome him as the promised Messiah, and to wish peace and
prosperity to his kingdom. (xxiii. 39.) Part of them were
true disciples: numbers might be favourably disposed, and
act under an immediate impulse: and many might scarcely
advert to the meaning of their own words; only joining
with the rest, as it is customary on such occasions. No
wonder therefore, that when his disciples and favourers
were intimidated and retired, and persons of another character came to head the multitude, they as loudly cried out,
" Crucify him, crucify him." (*Note, xxvii.* 19—23.) They
were perhaps likewise disappointed, as to their expectations of a temporal kingdom immediately to be set up:
and they might be willing to atone to their rulers for their
former offence, by joining them against Jesus. For it
gave the latter great umbrage to see the city in such commotion, and every body enquiring who this was, and ready
to receive " Jesus of Nazareth, the prophet of Galilee," as
their promised Messiah. (*Marg. Ref.—Note, Mark* xi.
1—11, v. 10.)—*Hosanna.* (9) *Note, Ps.* cxviii. 25, 26.

V. 12, 13. It appears from St. Mark, that Jesus went
to the temple and surveyed it, the same day on which he
rode into Jerusalem; yet he relates the expulsion of the
traders, as if it had occurred on the next day: hence some
conclude that he expelled them on two days in succession;
as he was departed. (*Mark* xi. 15.) But this is not probable.—When, however, Zion's King entered his royal
city, he did not go to any palace, or senate-house, or court
of justice; but to the temple, to shew the spiritual nature
of his kingdom. There he found some of the precincts,
probably the court of the Gentiles, turned into a market
for cattle, and such things as were used in their sacrifices:
and in part occupied by money-changers, who gave the
current coin in exchange for that of other countries, for the
sake of a premium; or gave money for bills of exchange
or letters of credit, from merchants or bankers in the several countries whence the people came to worship. It
may be supposed, that the persons concerned exacted on
strangers, and thus joined iniquity to profanation: whilst
the priests encouraged these scandalous transactions, doubtless for a share of the booty! Our Lord, therefore, drove
the whole company from the place, as he had before done
when he entered on his ministry; (*Note, John* ii. 13—17;)

x 2

VILLAGE OF BETHANY.

Matt. xxi. 17 ; xxvi. 6.   Mark xi. 1, 11, 12 ; xiv. 3.
Luke xix. 29 ; xxiv. 50.   John xi. 1 ; xii. 1.

14 And the blind and the lame came to him in the temple; and he healed them.

15 And when the chief priests and scribes saw the wonderful things that he did, and the children crying in the temple, and saying, Hosanna to the Son of David; they were sore displeased,

16 And said unto him, Hearest thou what these say? And Jesus saith unto them, Yea; have ye never read, Out of the mouth of babes and sucklings thou hast perfected praise?

17 ¶ And he left them, and went out of the city into Bethany, and he lodged there.

18 Now in the morning as he returned into the city he hungered.

19 And when he saw a fig-tree in the way, he came to it, and found nothing thereon, but leaves only, and said unto it, Let no fruit grow on thee henceforward for ever. And presently the fig-tree withered away.

20 And when the disciples saw it, they marvelled, saying, How soon is the fig-tree withered away!

21 Jesus answered and said unto them, Verily I say unto you, If ye

---

a divine energy attending his words and works, which dismayed every mind, and prevented all opposition. And when the peculiar property of the money-changers, and the sellers of doves, caused them to loiter, he overturned their tables and seats, and constrained them to be gone.— At the same time, he reminded them of the words which God had spoken by his prophets concerning his temple, (*Notes, Is.* lvi. 3—7, *v.* 7. *Jer.* vii. 8—11, *vv.* 10, 11;) that it should be rendered a house of prayer and holy worship, not only to the Jews, but to persons of all nations : whereas, instead of allowing the Gentiles a place to worship in, they had converted the court intended for that purpose into a place of merchandise, which was conducted with such fraud and exaction, that it was become a den of thieves; so that dishonest men were sheltered from justice, within the precincts of the temple, as robbers are in their caves and forests. (*Marg. Ref.—Notes,* Mark iii. 1—4. Mark xi. 15—21.)—The quotation from Isaiah, is in the words of the Septuagint ; which exactly render the original Hebrew. The words of Jeremiah seem rather referred to than quoted.

Money changers. (12) Κολλυβιστων (à κολλυβος, obolus:) *Mark* xi. 15. *John* ii. 15.—*Thieves.* (13) Ληστων xxvii. 44. *Luke* x. 30. *John* xviii. 40. The word more generally and properly denotes *robbers,* than *thieves.*

V. 14—16. The blind and lame persons, who frequented the avenues of the temple, to ask alms of those that entered, came around Jesus on this occasion, and he healed them : thus shewing the benign nature of his authority, and producing as it were the seal of heaven to what he had done. But the chief priests and scribes, instead of being convinced by his miracles, were the more exasperated ; especially when they heard the very children, who had followed him into the temple, crying out, " Hosanna " to the Son of David," as the multitudes had done before. They therefore, in a cavilling manner, enquired whether he heard what they said. To which he answered, in a way which implied that he approved of it, as an honour justly due to him : and he asked them, whether they had never read the words of David, declaring, that " God perfected " his praise, even out of the mouths of babes." (*Ps.* viii. 2.) Thus he intimated, that, as the Son of God, he had caused honour to be rendered to him by these children, while the rulers and priests were endeavouring to disgrace him ; and that it was a specimen of that glory, which he would receive, in all ages, from the humble and despised of the human race. (*Marg. Ref.—Note,* Luke xix. 28—40, *v.* 40.)—The Septuagint is exactly quoted, though it varies from the Hebrew. (*Note, Ps.* viii. 2.)—*Perfected.* (16) Καταρτιζω. *Sarcio, perficio, constituo, adapto, coagmento, instauro.* (Ab αρτιος, *integer, perfectus.*) *Mark* i. 19. *Luke* iii. 5. *Rom.* ix. 22. 1 *Cor.* i. 10. 2 *Cor.* xiii. 11. *Gal.* vi. 1. 1 *Thes.* iii. 10. *Heb.* x. 5. xi. 3. xiii. 21. 1 *Pet.* v. 10. (*Note, Gal.* vi. 1—5, *v.* 1.)

V. 17—20. It does not appear, that any person in Jerusalem offered to entertain Christ on this occasion: at least, he chose to retire to Bethany, from the rage of his enemies, and the acclamations of the people. Accordingly he spent the night there, probably at the house of Lazarus and his sisters : and in the morning, for the sake of retirement, and that he might be early at the temple, or that he might not disturb the family, he went away fasting. He was therefore hungry by the way; and seeing a single fig-tree covered with leaves, he went to it, as though he expected fruit from it. But when he found that there were only leaves, he pronounced a solemn malediction upon it, saying, " Let no fruit grow on thee hence- " forward for ever :" and the next morning, the disciples observed with astonishment, that the fig-tree was entirely dead, and all its verdure withered. . This was an emblem of the Jewish nation, which professed to worship the true God, and seemed to promise fruit; but when Christ came he found none : they therefore fell under his wrath, and their profession and privileges withered ; nor have they produced any of the genuine fruits of righteousness from his time to this present day. (*Marg.* and *Marg. Ref.—Notes,* Mark xi. 12—14, v. 13. Luke xiii. 6—9. Heb. vi. 7, 8.)

Lodged. (17) Ηυλισθη. Αυλιζομαι. *Luke* xxi. 6. *Sept.—Withered away.* (19, 20) Εξηρανθη. Ξηραινω· xiii. 6. *Mark* iii. 3. iv. 6. *Luke* viii. 6.

V. 21, 22. When Jesus observed the surprise of the disciples, he again shewed them the energy of faith, with a special reference to the power of working miracles in his name. Whenever a proper occasion offered of performing a miracle, in support of their doctrine, and they went about it, relying on his power and not doubting of his concurrence ; they would not only be enabled to perform as wonderful works, as that of withering the barren fig-

have faith, and doubt not, ye shall not only do this *which is done* to the fig-tree, but also if ye shall say unto this mountain, Be thou removed, and be thou cast into the sea, it shall be done.

22 And [y] all things whatsoever ye shall ask in prayer, believing, ye shall receive.

23 ¶ And [z] when he was come into the temple, [a] the chief priests and the elders of the people came unto him as he was teaching, and said, [b] By what authority doest thou these things? and who gave thee this authority?

24 And Jesus answered and said unto them, [c] I also will ask you one thing, which if ye tell me, I in like wise will tell you by what authority I do these things.

25 The [d] baptism of John, whence was it? from heaven, or of men? And they reasoned with themselves, saying, If we shall say, From heaven; he will say unto us, [e] Why did ye not then believe him?

26 But if we shall say, Of men; [f] we fear the people: [g] for all hold John as a prophet.

27 And they answered Jesus, and said, [h] We cannot tell. And he said unto them, Neither tell I you by what authority I do these things.

28 ¶ But [i] what think ye? [k] A certain

---

tree; but even the mount of Olives, which they were then passing, might at their word be removed and cast into the sea: that is, nothing which they undertook, would be impossible for them. (*Marg. Ref.* x.—*Notes*, xvii. 19, 20. *Luke* xvii. 5, 6.) To this our Lord subjoined, that they ought not to doubt, but verily to believe, that they should receive whatever they asked in prayer. This too *specially* refers to the case of miracles; but not *exclusively*. Whenever any person offers suitable petitions, in a right manner, and grounded on God's express promise; he ought not to doubt of his power or willingness to grant them, on account either of his own unworthiness, or of any difficulty in the way. (*Marg. Ref.* y.—*Note*, *Mark* xi. 22—26.)

Doubt not. (21) Μη διακριθητε. *Mark* xi. 23. *Acts* x. 20. xi. 12. *Rom.* iv. 20. 1 *Cor.* iv. 7. xi. 29. 31. xiv. 29. *Jam.* i. 6. ii. 4. *Jude* 9. 22.—' Μη διακριθηναι, signifies ' *not to discriminate*, or put a difference. ...*Rom.* xiv. 23. ' So here it may import, If you have such a faith, as puts ' no difference between things you can, and things you ' cannot do, but makes you fully persuaded, you can do ' any thing which tends to the glory of God, and is requi-' site for the promotion of the Christian faith, you shall ' be able to perform the most difficult things : for that is ' the meaning of that phrase to *root up mountains*. (1 *Cor.* ' xiii. 2.)' *Whitby.*

V. 23—27. As our Lord now openly appeared in the character of the Messiah ; the chief priests, and other leading persons of the nation, were exceedingly offended at his teaching, and working miracles in the temple : and especially as he had exposed those corrupt practices, at which they had connived. They thought themselves the source of ecclesiastical authority, and the rulers of the temple; and therefore they came to him in a body, to demand " by what authority he did these things." For they overlooked the divine power of his miracles, which sanctioned all his other actions. The answer of our Lord is a most beautiful model of " the meekness of wisdom." He did not directly assert his divine prerogative, or appeal to his miracles, or reproach them with perverseness and hypocrisy; though he did the latter, on other occasions, in the character of the heart-searching Judge: but he left them on this occasion to condemn themselves. He only

enquired of them, what they thought of John's ministry and baptism; whether these were of divine authority, or merely from man. If they fairly answered this plain question; he would then explicitly inform them by what authority he acted. This enquiry threw them into the greatest embarrassment: they readily perceived the drift of it, and, reasoning among themselves, observed, that if they allowed John to have acted by divine authority, Jesus would certainly enquire of them, " Why did ye not then believe " him ?" This referred not only to his exhortations to " repentance and fruits meet for repentance;" but also to his testimony to Jesus as the promised Messiah, " the " Lamb of God," and " the Son of God :" and this inference they did not know how to evade. On the other hand, if they treated John's baptism as a mere human device, they feared lest the people should stone them; for these were generally persuaded that John was a prophet, and a very eminent servant of God. Being thus pressed on every hand, they were constrained to confess their ignorance or uncertainty ; and thus to allow that they were incompetent to determine who was, and who was not, sent by God; that is, that they were " blind guides," who could only mislead those who depended on them. Our Lord, therefore, refused to give them any answer to their enquiry about his authority ; concerning which John's testimony, his own character, doctrine, and miracles, and the scriptures of the prophets, gave abundant information to every impartial person.—' They could not own the baptism ' of John to be from heaven, but they must also own ' Christ to be the Son of God, and him concerning whom ' God had testified by a voice from heaven, and by the de-' claration of the Holy Ghost upon him, that he was " the ' " beloved Son, in whom he was well pleased : " whence ' these great doctors chose rather to pretend ignorance, ' than to confess that truth which would condemn them.' *Whitby.* (*Marg. Ref.*—*Notes*, *Luke* xx. 1—8. *John* v. 31—38.)—*From heaven.* (25) *Note*, *Dan.* iv. 24—26, v. 26.

V. 28—32. The principal persons, who professed a zealous regard to religion, and who were the apparent supporters of it, among the Jews, were more inveterate enemies to the truth, than the vilest profligates in the nation.

x 4

man had two sons; and he came to the first, and said, ¹Son, go work to-day in my vineyard.

29 He answered and said, ᵐI will not: but afterward ⁿhe repented, and went.

30 And he came to the second, and said, likewise. And he answered and said °I go, sir: and went not.

31 Whether of them twain ᵖdid the will of *his* father? They say unto him, ⁹The first. Jesus saith unto them, ʳVerily I say unto you, That ˢthe publicans and the harlots go into the kingdom of God before you.

32 For John ᵗcame unto you in the way of righteousness, ᵘand ye believed him not; but the publicans and the harlots believed him: and ye, when ye had seen *it*, ˣrepented not afterward, that ye might believe him.

33 ¶ ʸHear another parable: ᶻThere was a certain householder, which planted a vineyard, and hedged it

round about, and digged a wine-press in it, and built a tower, and let it out to ᵃhusbandmen, and ᵇwent into a far country.

34 And when the time of the fruit drew near, ᶜhe sent his servants to the husbandmen, ᵈthat they might receive the fruits of it.

35 And the husbandmen ᵉtook his servants, and beat one, and killed another, and stoned another.

36 Again, he sent other servants more than the first: and they did unto them likewise.

37 But ᶠlast of all, he sent unto them his son, saying, ᵍThey will reverence my son.

38 But when the husbandmen saw the son, they said among themselves, ʰThis is the heir; come, let us kill him, and let us seize on his inheritance.

39 And they ⁱcaught him, and ᵏcast *him* out of the vineyard, ˡand slew *him*.

This Jesus shewed in a parable.—The father of these two sons represents God, as the Creator and Benefactor of all men, and as the special Friend of Israel. The first of the two sons represented the profligate and openly wicked Jews, who were at length brought to repentance, and became the disciples of Christ: and the second son represented the priests, scribes, and Pharisees, who had " a " form of godliness," but proved the greatest enemies to the gospel. Our Lord, therefore, asked their opinion concerning these two sons; " Whether of them twain did the " will of his Father? " And when they could not but acknowledge, that the elder was the more obedient of the two; he applied it to the p a s and harlots, whom they despised and despaired uðíchøt who actually entered into the kingdom of God before them. This was evident in the success of John's ministry: for when John came shewing, by his doctrine and example, " the way of right-" eousness; " the chief priests, scribes, and Pharisees did not believe him: while many of the publicans and harlots received his testimony, and as true penitents embraced the gospel: yet when the former had seen the effects of John's ministry, they continued impenitent and unbelieving; they neither changed their judgment and conduct, nor yet believed John's word, to acknowledge the Messiah whom he had pointed out to them.—Some think, that the rejection of the Jews, and the calling of the gentiles, were also thus intimated. (*Marg. Ref.—Notes*, xix. 29, 30, v. 30. *Luke* xv.)

He repented. (29) Μεταμεληθεις (ex μέλω, et μέλει, curæ est:) 32. xxvii. 3. 2 *Cor.* vii. 8. *Heb.* vii. 21. No where else in the New Testament.

V. 33—39. Our Lord next added a parable, which related to the nation at large; yet with peculiar reference to their rulers and teachers. The vineyard, the fence, the wine-press, and the tower, have been briefly explained, on a similar parable. (*Notes, Is.* v. 1—7.) The oracles of God, the instituted ordinances, and all the means of instruction, and peculiar privileges, vouchsafed to Israel, were intended. These were given them, in order that they might be rendered fruitful in good works; and were especially entrusted to the priests and rulers, for the benefit of the people. But when the Lord was no longer present among them, by external displays of his power and glory, as he had been when the law was promulgated; they forgot their accountableness to him, and acted as if their possessions, and authority, and distinctions, were independently their own, to be employed according to the dictates of their worldly inclinations. They neglected their duty, and were unfaithful to their trust: but from time to time he sent prophets, to call them to repentance, and to direct their attention to the promises of a Messiah who was to come : thus the fruits were demanded in their season. But the rulers and teachers, in every age, had been exasperated by these faithful monitors; and, instead of " repenting and " doing works meet for repentance," they apprehended the servants of JEHOVAH, " beating one and killing another; " and when he sent others, they still treated them as criminals and enemies, out of hatred to their Master and their message. Yet at length the Lord saw it proper to send his only and well-beloved Son, supposing that they would " reverence him." In applying the parable, it is not needful to enquire how far such a measure would have

x 5

40 When the lord therefore of the vineyard cometh, ^m what will he do unto those husbandmen?

41 They say unto him, ⁿ He will miserably destroy those wicked men, ^o and will let out *his* vineyard unto other husbandmen, which shall render him the fruits in their seasons.

42 Jesus saith unto them, ^p Did ye never read in the scriptures, ^q The Stone which the builders rejected, the same is become the Head of the corner: this is the LORD's doing, ^r and it is marvellous in our eyes?

43 Therefore say I unto you, ^s the kingdom of God shall be taken from you, and given to ^t a nation bringing forth the fruits thereof.

44 And ^u whosoever shall fall on this stone shall be broken: ^x but on whomsoever it shall fall, it will grind him to powder.

45 And when the chief priests and Pharisees had heard his parables, ^y they perceived that he spake of them.

46 But when ^z they sought to lay hands on him, they feared the multitude, ^a because they took him for a prophet.

---

been prudent in a householder; for it was doubtless in infinite wisdom, as well as love, that " the Father sent his " Son to be the Saviour of the world." On the other hand, he certainly did not expect, that the Jews would " reverence him;" for he had for ages before predicted how they would reject, abhor, and persecute him. They, however, ought to have adored him and submitted to him; and their usage of one so excellent and honourable, and manifested to be so by all his miracles, his words and conduct, formed the grand aggravation of their atrocious wickedness. For " when they saw the Son, they said " among themselves, Let us kill him, and let us seize on " the inheritance." This described the spirit and conduct of the Jewish rulers, who were, at the very time, consulting together to put Jesus to death, in order to secure their own authority and reputation, and to preserve the nation from the Romans: as if determined wilfully to murder the heir, in order to seize on the inheritance. For these purposes, they apprehended him, cast him out of the vineyard, and put him to death: that is, the priests and rulers apprehended Christ, condemned him, and led him out of Jerusalem to be crucified. (*Marg. Ref.—Notes*, xxiii. 34— 36. *Mark* xii. 1—12. *Luke* xx. 9—18, *vv.* 10—14. *Acts* vii. 51—53. 1 *Thes.* ii. 13—16.)

Went into a far country. (33) Απεδημησεν. Αποδημεω, *Peregre proficiscor,* ... *abesse a populo.* (Αποδημος. *Mark* xiii. 34. ex απο et δημος, populus.) xxv. 14, 15. *Mark* xii. 1. *Luke* xv. 13. xx. 9.—*They will reverence.* (37) Εντραπησονται. Εντρεπομαι (ex εν et τρεπω, verto.— When a man ' turneth within himself.') *Mark* xii. 6. *Luke* xviii. 2. 4. xx. 13. 1 *Cor.* iv. 14. 2 *Thes.* iii. 14. *Tit.* ii. 8. *Heb.* xii. 9.—*Is.* xliv. 11.

V. 40—44. Having spoken the parable, Jesus enquired, what " the Lord of the vineyard would do to these " husbandmen," when he should come to call them to account for their conduct. To this they answered, as not at first fully understanding his meaning, that he would put them to death in some terrible manner, and let out the vineyard to other husbandmen, who would render him the fruits of it in due season. (*Marg. Ref.* m—o.—*Note, Luke* xx. 9—18, *v.* 16.) And to bring this concession home to their consciences, he called their attention to a passage in the Psalms, in which it was foretold, that " the Stone

" which the builders rejected, would be made the Head of " the corner;" that is, the grand ornament, stability, and cement of the whole spiritual temple. (*Marg. Ref.* q, r—*Note, Ps.* cxviii. 19—24, *vv.* 22, 23.) This was about to be fulfilled, in their rejection of him and in his subsequent exaltation: and they would, in consequence, be excluded from all the blessings of his kingdom, forfeit all their privileges, and be visited with terrible calamities; while the Lord would form another Israel, " a holy nation," by the incorporation of Gentile converts among the believing Jews, who would bring forth the fruits of righteousness to his praise and glory. Whoever, therefore, should stumble and fall on this Corner-stone, in unbelief and disobedience, would be broken and perish: yet the ruin of those, on whom " this " Stone should fall," would be still more aggravated; namely, that of such as should be found guilty of crucifying him and persecuting his followers. Some suppose, that the distinction refers to those, who opposed him in his state of humiliation; and such as should persist in their enmity, after his resurrection and exaltation, and the pouring out of the Holy Ghost on his disciples.—The punishment here mentioned may allude to the method sometimes used in executing criminals, by throwing down large stones upon them to crush them at once. (*Marg. Ref.* s—x.—*Notes,* viii. 10—12. xxii. 1—10, *vv.* 6, 7. *Luke* xx. 9—18, *v.* 18.)

The Stone, &c. (42) Exactly from the LXX, which accords to the Hebrew.—*Rejected.*] Απεδοκιμασαν. *Mark* viii. 31. xii. 10. *Luke* ix. 22. xvii. 25. xx. 17. *Heb.* xii. 17. 1 *Pet.* ii. 4, 7. (Εx απο et δοκιμος, *probatus.*)—*Shall be broken.* (44) Συνθλασθησεται. *Luke* xx. 18. Not elsewhere used in the New Testament.—*Grind him to powder.*] Λικμησει. *Luke* xx. 18. Not elsewhere in the New Testament.—*Ita comminuere, ut partes in auras dispergantur. Jer.* xxxi. 19. *Sept.*

V. 45, 46. The chief priests, scribes, and Pharisees, now fully understood his parables: but they were the more exasperated by them; and determined as soon as they could, to apprehend him, and put him to death, whatever the consequence might be: yet they would not do it openly, lest the multitude should excite a tumult, as the people were generally of opinion that he was at least a prophet of God. (*Marg. Ref.—Notes,* xxvi. 3—5.)

x 6

the wedding-garment, 1—14: answers the Pharisees and Herodians about paying tribute to Cæsar, 15—22; the Sadducees about the resurrection and future

PRACTICAL OBSERVATIONS.

V. 1—11.

We should be ready cheerfully to resign whatever we possess, if the Lord require it : for he has a right to dispose of us and our's, for the purposes of his own glory, as he sees best.—There is nothing so mean in itself, but he knows how to employ it in his service: we should not then despise men of weak abilities, or in obscure stations ; and we have no ground for self-complacency, should he be pleased to " have need of us," or to use us as the instruments of his work : nor ought we to wonder, if he at one time employ us, and afterward lay us aside, having no further occasion for us.—As meekness and external poverty distinguished our King, and even marked his triumphal entrance into Jerusalem, how inconsistent must avarice, ambition, and " the pride of life," be with the character of his subjects, and especially of his ministers. Once the divine Redeemer rode, but it was on an ass's colt; at all other times, as far as we can learn, he went on foot, to perform his labours of love ; or sailed in a fishing boat : surely then his disciples and ministers should be content to weary themselves in his service, and to be poor for his sake ; and they should by no means covet or value such distinctions and indulgences, as are more suitable to the kingdoms of this world, than to that of the meek and lowly Jesus.—His servants must unreservedly obey his orders, however opposite to the opinions and fashions of the world ; and in so doing he will order every circumstance for their good, and give them continual experience of his foreknowledge, truth, and love. He has every heart in his .hand ; and he can, when he pleases, dispose the multitude to favour his cause, and to honour his ministers. But, of 'how little value in general is popular applause ! It is the way of the unstable multitude, in every age and nation, to join the cry of the day, whether it be " Hosanna," or " Crucify him : " and even that popularity, which sometimes attends the preaching of the gospel, is little to be depended on. Multitudes hear, and seem to approve ; yet few in comparison become consistent disciples : the applause conferred is frequently injurious to the preacher; his doctrine serves, in numerous instances, merely to condemn the hearers; and it is well, in this case, if he so " declare the whole counsel of God," as to stand clear of the blood of those that perish. It is, therefore, more desirable to be faithful and useful in an obscure situation, than to aspire to notoriety and popularity. But, though many seem earnestly to cry " Hosanna to the Son of David," who prove as inconstant as the winds or waves ; yet surely the peace and prosperity of his kingdom should be the object of our most ardent desires, and fervent prayers ; and we should both labour for ourselves, and encourage all " who " come in the name of the Lord," to promote his interest in the world. And if " we have the mind of Christ," we shall rather resort to " the houses of prayer," when we come to populous cities, than to places of diversion, pleasure, or magnificence ; or even to the houses of those few, in superior stations, who favour his cause.

V. 12—16.

When Zion's king shall come to enlarge his kingdom, he will begin with purging the church from traders and money-changers. Alas! what numbers of these mercenaries frequent and engross the outer courts of the temple! The worship of God, the administration of sacraments, the most sacred functions and engagements, and the cure of souls, are valuable or important in their judgment, only as far as preferment or wealth can be got by them. If Christ should come into many parts of the visible church, how many recesses of iniquity and avarice would he discover and cleanse! And how many things, which are daily practised under the guise of religion, would he shew to be more suitable for " a den of robbers," than for " the " house of prayer ! " (P. O. Rev. xviii. 9—19.) Ingenious and interested men may plead in favour of these abuses, and rulers may connive at them : but it will at length appear, that the covetous and ambitious spirit of such ecclesiastics has been one grand cause of the spread of infidelity, one principal hindrance to the progress of the gospel, and one most powerful engine of the devil, for hardening the hearts and murdering the souls of men : so that, in fact, such brokers and traders in the temple have far more to answer for, than other depredators; who only plunder men's property, or kill their bodies, but do little injury to their immortal souls. May the Lord then come, and drive them out of the church ; and may he stir up the spirit of such as have influence and authority, to check the progress of these sacrilegious profanations.—It is indeed to be feared, that buying and selling, in every way, are often connected with great dishonesty: yet certainly no merchandizing is so iniquitous as that, which is conducted within the e   s of the sanctuary.—No wisdom, holiness, beneficence, or kindness to the poor and afflicted, can silence the clamours of interested men against those persons, who endeavour to put a stop to their iniquitous lucre: nor can we wonder at this, when we recollect, that even the miracles and holiness of the Son of God could procure him no exemption ; but on the contrary drew upon him the more desperate enmity. Those who hate his gospel, because it interferes with their interests, reputation, or authority, will be greatly displeased with such as shew favour to it : but the Lord has often " perfected his praise " out of the mouths of mere children, in age, abilities, learning, or estate; when chief priests, and learned scribes, and rulers professing Christianity, have contradicted and blasphemed.

V. 17—27.

It is best to shun needless altercations with malicious opposers, and to avoid all appearances of ostentation : and the genuine followers of Christ will cheerfully submit to the pinchings of poverty or the cravings of hunger, rather than be deprived of opportunities of usefulness ; though their zeal and love will not prevent them from feeling the inconvenience as sensibly as other men.—But let us be

A. D. 33.   MATTHEW.   A. D. 33.

state, 23—33; and a lawyer concerning the chief commandment in the law, 34—40: and enquires how the Messiah could be David's Son, and yet his Lord, 41—46.

peculiarly afraid of the doom denounced on " the barren " fig-tree." The leaves of profession may impose on men: but the Lord will shortly come, and seek for fruit; and if to the last he finds none, the tree will fall under his curse of everlasting unfruitfulness: and how tremendous the sentence of being left to eternal unholiness and enmity against God! to be eternally contrary to him, and the object of his holy abhorrence and indignation! Such considerations should excite us to more fervent prayer; and lead us to offer all our petitions, in an unwavering reliance on the promises of God, and on the merits of our great Advocate; fully expecting that he will grant our requests, in every thing really good for us. In this way no impediments need discourage us: for we may surmount or remove them all, by the power of faith and prayer. Thus we may go on with our Master's work, without regarding the objections of his enemies.—Those, who are evidently destitute of faith and grace, will often demand of the Lord's servants, by what authority they act. As if men might do mischief in a variety of ways without asking leave of any one, or taking out any licence or commission; but might not endeavour to do good, without obtaining the permission of the enemies of all goodness! No doubt, order and regularity are in general expedient: but even where the external order of the church was of undoubted divine original; when its regular teachers and rulers degenerated, or evidently neglected their duty; God raised up extraordinary persons, to expose their crimes, and to call sinners to repentance, faith, and holiness. It is true, that the sanction of miracles is requisite for those, who would introduce any new revelation: but it cannot be proved from scripture, that these credentials are necessary, to authorize such as only call on their perishing fellow-sinners " to repent and believe the gospel:" and if God evidently honour men in this work, as instruments in reviving true religion, and promoting the salvation of many souls; who are they, that shall deem themselves authorized to call them to account, about the supposed irregularity of their useful labours? (Note, Mark ix. 38—40.) Indeed there have been characters of this kind, in different ages, of whom it would greatly embarrass objectors to give a decided opinion, whether they were sent by God, or ran without being sent; as either conclusion would involve them in perplexing difficulties. Many more, however, will give the eminent servants of God a good word, especially after their death, than are disposed to believe their doctrine, or obey their call to repentance and faith in Christ, and the obedience of faith.

V. 28—32.

The whole human race are like children, whom the Lord has brought up; but they have rebelled against him: only some are more plausible and decent in disobedience, than others. It however often happens, that the daring rebel is brought to repentance and becomes the servant of God, while the decent formalist is hardened in pride and enmity to the gospel. It was by no means peculiar to the days of Christ, that " publicans and harlots entered the kingdom " of heaven, before " proud Pharisees and learned scribes. But it exceedingly aggravates the guilt of such men, when the evident reformation of the vilest transgressors, by the " foolishness of preaching," serves only to render them more outrageous in scorn and opposition. In these circumstances, it is peculiarly incumbent on those, who " come in " the way of righteousness," to exemplify, as well as to explain, the holy tendency of their doctrine.

V. 33—46.

We have parable after parable, to shew us the rage and enmity of the human heart, against the religion of the Saviour. How can we then, if faithful to his cause, expect a favourable reception from a wicked world, or from ungodly professors of Christianity; when the holy prophets, and " the well-beloved Son" of God himself, were thus rejected with contempt, and treated with outrageous cruelty by his professed worshippers? How can we expect to convince or conciliate them, merely with our reasonings and persuasions; when the words of Christ only exasperated those to whom they were addressed, even when they felt the truth of his reproofs, and the energy of his arguments? The awful doom of the hypocritical rulers and unbelieving nation of the Jews, was recorded for our warning. They slew the prophets and " crucified the Lord " of glory:" but they were destroyed with most tremendous vengeance; and " the kingdom of God was taken " from them, and given to a nation bringing forth the " fruits thereof." We now have the vineyard and all its advantages: but do we as a nation render the fruits in due season? Here we must be silent, or answer, No. Yet amidst all our abominations, the monster persecution is chained up by authority: and while this is the case, we still hope for the continuance of our privileges. Numbers, however, " stumble at the word, being disobedient," and thus fall on the Corner-stone and are broken: alas! numbers likewise cause others to stumble by their wicked lives. Some use all their abilities in opposing the gospel and dishonouring Christ, apparently in order to obtain reputation and distinction for themselves: it is to be feared, even many professed builders thus reject the " Head-Stone " of the Corner;" and that some are restrained in their opposition by no higher motive than the fear of man. Alas! few consider, that we are accountable for all our privileges: and shall be the more deeply condemned on account of them, if not made fruitful. Yet, blessed be God, there is a remnant, and we trust an increasing remnant, of such as adorn the gospel by their holy lives: may we be found among them; may we attend to the voice of those whom the Lord sends to reprove or exhort us, in order to our increasing fruitfulness; may we reverence and obey the beloved Son of God; may he become more and more precious to our souls, as the firm Foundation and tried Corner-stone of the church; may we be willing to be despised and hated for his sake; and may we be faithful and obedient even unto death: and so when he shall come to destroy his enemies, we shall " receive a crown of glory " which fadeth not away."

x 8

AND Jesus answered, and spake unto them again by parables, and said, 2 The kingdom of heaven is like unto a certain king, which made a marriage for his son, 3 And sent forth his servants to call them that were bidden to the wedding: and they would not come. 4 Again, he sent forth other servants, saying, Tell them which are bidden, Behold, I have prepared my dinner; my oxen and my fatlings are killed, and all things are ready: come unto the marriage. 5 But they made light of it, and went their ways, one to his farm, another to his merchandise:

6 And the remnant took his servants, and entreated them spitefully, and slew them. 7 But when the king heard thereof, he was wroth: and he sent forth his armies, and destroyed those murderers, and burned up their city. 8 Then saith he to his servants, The wedding is ready, but they which were bidden were not worthy. 9 Go ye therefore into the highways, and as many as ye shall find, bid to the marriage. 10 So those servants went out into the highways, and gathered together all as many as they found, both bad and good: and the wedding was furnished with guests.

NOTES.

CHAP. XXII. V. 1—10. (Notes, Luke xiv. 15—24.) Our Lord, proceeding to shew the priests and people the criminality and consequences of their unbelief, stated the case to them in another parable; for in parables, for two are connected together. "The kingdom of heaven" might, in this respect, be compared "to a king, who made a marriage-feast for his son." The preceding parable represented the sufferings of Christ, and the guilt and punishment of those who put him to death: but this shews the motive of his humiliation, and the effects of it to himself, to his people, and to unbelievers and hypocrites. The union of the Son of God with our race, by assuming human nature; the endeared relation, into which he receives his redeemed church, and every true member of it; the spiritual honours, riches, and blessings, to which they are advanced by this sacred relation; the comforts which they receive from his condescending and faithful love, and from communion with him; and the reciprocal duties of their relation to him, are all intimated by this metaphor. (Marg. Ref. c.)—The abundant and rich provision, which the Lord has made for our perishing souls in the gospel, is represented by a royal feast, made on so important and joyful an occasion, as the marriage of the king's son. (Notes, Prov. ix. 1—6. Is. xxv. 6—8. lv. 1—3.) John the Baptist, the apostles, and the seventy disciples, who first announced the arrival of the promised Messiah, were the servants that went to call to the feast those who had been bidden long before, even the Jews who expected the coming of the Messiah, to save and bless them: yet "they would not come" to him when he appeared, being prejudiced against his holy doctrine and lowly character. (Marg. Ref. d—f.—Note, xxiii. 37—39.) The other servants, sent with the second invitation, when "all things were ready," seem to mark out the apostles and preachers of the gospel, after Christ's ascension into heaven; who shewed, to the Jews first, the nature of the gospel, and

the preparation made for it. (Marg. Ref. g, h.—Notes, Luke xxiv. 44—49. Acts i. 4—8, v. 8. xiii. 42—48. xviii. 1—6.) But the persons thus favoured, having no value for the king or his son, or desire for the feast, or gratitude for the special honour shewn them, treated these urgent and repeated invitations with supercilious contempt; "making light of them," and going to their different employments and interests. And, as the servants may be supposed to have remonstrated with the remnant, on the impropriety and criminality of their conduct; they were enraged, and shewed their enmity against the king, by abusing, wounding, or killing them. This represents the final rejection of Christ and the gospel by the Jewish nation; and the contempt and cruelty, with which they treated the apostles and other ministers of Christ, with the corrupt motives and extreme wickedness of their conduct. (Marg. Ref. k—m.—Notes, xxiii. 34—36. John xi. 47—53. xvi. 1—3. Acts vii. 51—60. xii. 1—4.) When the king heard this, he resolved to send them no more invitations; but, in due time, he made war upon them, destroyed "the murderers, and burned up their city." Thus the Lord sent the Roman armies to execute vengeance on the Jewish nation, and to desolate Jerusalem, for their obstinate contempt of his gospel, and the cruelties exercised towards the ministers of Christ, which completed their guilt in crucifying him. (Marg. Ref. n, o.)—As, however, the persons first invited would not come, and so proved themselves unworthy of the favour shewn them; the king determined to find other guests to partake of his royal banquet: he therefore sent his servants into the publick roads, ordering them to invite all whom they met with, of every rank, description, and character. Accordingly, they collected together a sufficient number, to furnish the wedding with guests. This represented the successful preaching of the gospel to the Gentiles, and the admission to all the privileges of the Lord's people. (Marg. Ref. r—t.—Notes, xiii. 36—43. 47—50. xxi. 40—44.)—' Not all the whole company of them, that are

11 And "when the king came in to see the guests, he saw there a man "which had not on a wedding-garment:

12 And he saith unto him, ' Friend, * how camest thou in hither, not having a wedding-garment? "And he was speechless.

13 Then said the king to the servants, " Bind him hand and foot, and take him away, and cast *him* into " outer darkness: " there shall be weeping and gnashing of teeth.

14 For ' many are called, but few *are* chosen.

15 ¶ Then ' went the Pharisees, and took counsel ' how they might entangle him in *his* talk.

16 And they sent out unto him their disciples with " the Herodians, saying, ' Master, " we know that thou art " true, and teachest the way of God in ' truth, " neither carest thou for any man; for thou regardest not the person of men.

17 Tell us therefore, " What think-est thou? ' Is it lawful to give tribute unto ' Cæsar, or not?

18 But Jesus " perceived their wick-

' called by the voice of the gospel, are the true church
' before God: for, the most part of them had rather follow
' the commodities of this life; and some do most cruelly
' persecute those that call them. But they are the true
' church, who obey when they are called; such as for the
' most part they are whom the world despiseth.'

Bidden. (4) Κεκλημενοις· 8.—See on xx. 16.—*Notes, Rom.* viii. 28—31. ix. 24—29.—*They made light of it.* (5) Αμελησαντες. 1 *Tim.* iv. 14. *Heb.* ii. 3. viii. 9. 2 *Pet.* i. 12. (Εx α neg. et μελει, curæ est.) *Notes,* xxiv. 36—41. *Luke* xiv. 15—24, *vv.* 18, 19. *Acts* xviii. 12—17, *v.* 17. *Heb.* ii. 1—4, *v.* 3. xii. 15—17.) They " who made light " of " the invitation, as well as the persecutors, were " not worthy." None else are put among them.—*Highways.* (9) Διεξοδας των οδων. The passages from one road into another; or places where several roads met. Used here only in the New Testament.

V. 11—14. The preceding part of the parable represented the replenishing of the church with professed Christians : this shews the difference between nominal and real disciples. According to the custom of those times, when princes had large wardrobes, from which, on some occasions, they furnished numbers with suitable apparel; it must be supposed, that a wedding-garment was offered to each guest when he entered the banqueting house : for it could not be expected, that travellers from the high-ways should be properly habited for the royal entertainment, to which they were so unexpectedly invited. One man, however, either proud of his own apparel, or despising the feast, obtained admission without the wedding-garment, and continued unnoticed till the king came in to see his guests; when, being questioned how he came thither, " he was speechless:" which he could not have been, if it had been out of his power to procure a wedding-garment. He was therefore ordered to be excluded and punished, as a despiser of the king and the royal banquet, by being thrown, bound hand and foot, into some dark dungeon without the palace; where weeping and extreme vexation would be his portion, -while the guests were enjoying the feast.—This denotes, that' some, who have not the true and living " faith which worketh by love," are found among the guests at the gospel-feast, and intrude

among the people of God in attending on its most sacred ordinances. It is not material, whether we understand the wedding-garment to mean the imputed righteousness of Christ, or " the sanctification of the Spirit;" for both are alike necessary, and they always go together. No man can obtain either of these blessings, except from Christ and by faith in him : yet those who remain unrighteous and unholy, besides all their other crimes, are chargeable with refusing the blessing when offered them. Such persons often impose on ministers and Christians : but when the King shall come to scrutinize the whole multitude of his guests, he will detect their hypocrisy, silence their excuses, and expose their wickedness. (*Marg. Ref.* u. z—b.—*Notes, Is.* lxi. 10, 11. *Luke* xv. 22—24. *Rom.* iii. 19, 20. 21—26, *v.* 22. 1 *Cor.* i. 26—31, *v.* 30. *Rev.* xix. 7, 8.)—The appellation of " friend," seems to allude to the man's profession, and contains a tacit reproof of his inconsistent character. (*Marg. Ref.* y.)—" The " outer darkness, &c." plainly describes the future portion of all hypocrites of every nation, as well as open unbelievers. (*Marg. Ref.* c, d.—*Note,* viii. 10—12.) This parable our Lord closed, as he had done one before, by observing that many were called, or invited by the gospel, who were not chosen and approved as true disciples. (*Note,* xx. 1—16, *v.* 16.)—' Think not that all, who are ' outwardly called by the sweet invitations of the gospel, ' are made partakers of grace and salvation. God calleth ' all sorts of men, and men of all sorts; and they do ' outwardly answer this voice of God : but his inward and ' effectual calling, and the election of grace, is but of few.' *Bp. Hall.*—' In the small number which come at the call-' ing, there are some castaways, which do not confirm their ' faith with newness of life.' *Beza.*—' The called are many, ' but the elect few.' *Hammond.*

He was speechless. (12) Εφιμωθη. (" Φιμοω signifieth to " muzzle, and is properly used of beasts, as 1 *Tim.* v. 18. ' By a metaphor to bring to silence.' *Leigh.*) 34. *Mark* i. 25. iv. 39. *Luke* iv. 35. 1 *Cor.* ix. 9.—*Deut.* xxv. 4. *Sept.*—*Note,* 1 *Sam.* ii. 9.

V. 15—22. This question was proposed to our Lord, in consequence of a plan formed by the chief priests and rulers, to compass his death The persons sent on this

edness, and said, 'Why tempt ye me, ye hypocrites?

19 Shew me the tribute-money. And they brought unto him 'a penny.

20 And he saith unto them, Whose is this image and 'superscription?

21 They say unto him, Cæsar's. Then saith he unto them, 'Render therefore unto Cæsar the things which are Cæsar's, 'and unto God the things that are God's.

22 When they had heard these *words*, 'they marvelled, and left him, and went their way.

23 ¶ The 'same day came to him 'the Sadducees, 'which say that there is no resurrection, and asked him,

24 Saying, 'Master, 'Moses said, If a man die, having no children, his brother shall marry his wife, and raise up seed unto his brother.

25 Now 'there were with us seven brethren; and the first, when he had married a wife, deceased, and, having no issue, left his wife unto his brother:

26 Likewise the second also, and the third, unto the 'seventh.

27 And last of all the woman died also.

28 Therefore in the resurrection, whose wife shall she be of the seven? for they all had her.

29 Jesus answered and said unto them, Ye do err, 'not knowing the scriptures, 'nor the power of God.

30 For 'in the resurrection they

---

occasion were Pharisees and Herodians. They held contrary opinions, in the controverted point of paying tribute to the Roman emperor. The Pharisees inferred from the law, which forbad them to place a stranger over them as their king; that it was unlawful to obey or pay tribute to the Romans, though forcibly reduced to subjection under them: and this suited the refractory spirit and the pride of the people, and was the more popular opinion. (*Marg. Ref.* o.—*Note, Mark* xii. 13—17.) But the Herodians, (*Marg. Ref.* h,) who were strongly tinctured with Sadducean infidelity, and avowedly attached to Herod's family, made their religion subservient to their politicks, and endeavoured to accommodate it to the humours and interests of their prince: and as he was supported by the Romans, so they argued that tribute might lawfully be paid to them. These contending parties combined to entangle our Lord in his discourse: and, finding that he was open and communicative, they addressed him as " a teacher of right- " eousness," whose knowledge, faithfulness, and disinterested intrepid impartiality, they highly venerated. After this insidious exordium, (which, though most justly deserved by him, was in their mouths, most vile flattery,) they desired him, to inform them, whether *he* thought it lawful to pay tribute to Cæsar, or not; for they were disposed to settle that controversy by his judgment. It seems, that they thought it impossible for him so to answer, as to escape the snare. Had he simply directed them to pay tribute, they would have represented him, not only as an enemy to their liberties, but also, as deciding in opposition to the law of Moses, and requiring unreserved obedience to idolaters. On the other hand, had he declared it unlawful to pay tribute to Cæsar; they would have accused him before the Roman governor, and have delivered him up into Pilate's hands, to be punished for sedition or rebellion. (*Marg. Ref.* i—m.—*Notes, Luke* xx. 19—26, *v.* 20. xxiii. 1—5.) But Jesus gave them to understand, that he was fully aware of their insidious designs: yet, he chose to answer the question, because he intended to graft on it most important instruction. Having, therefore, obtained the coin in which the tribute was paid, and drawn them to acknowledge that it was stamped with Cæsar's image and name; he tacitly inferred that Cæsar was the civil ruler to whom God had subjected them: and therefore, as they derived protection, and the benefits of magistracy from him, (of which the currency of his coinage was an evidence,) they were not only allowed, but required, to render to him both tribute, and civil honour and obedience. (*Marg.* and *Marg. Ref.* q—t. —*Notes, Jer.* xxvii. 4—11. xxix. 4—7. *Rom.* xiii. 6, 7.) At the same time, they must render to God that honour, worship, love, and service, which his commandments claimed, and which were justly due to him; and must not disobey him, out of regard to any earthly sovereign. This answer condemned equally the refractory spirit of the Pharisees, who scrupled civil obedience to the Roman emperors under pretence of religion; and the time-serving Herodians, who made a compliment of their religion to their prince, and conformed to many heathen customs to please him: and it is moreover of universal application, and replete with practical instruction. The conviction conveyed by this most wise, conclusive, and beautiful answer was so delicate a question, astonished, confounded, and disappointed the spies, and they went away unable to take any advantage of his words. (*Marg. Ref.* u. x.— *Note, Prov.* xxvi. 4, 5.)—'Christians must obey their magistrates, although they be wicked and extortioners; but 'so...that the authority of God may remain safe to him, 'and his honour be not diminished.' *Beza.* (*Note, Acts* iv. 13—22, *vv.* 19, 20.)

They might entangle. (15) Παγιδευσωσιν. Used here only in the New Testament. 1 *Sam.* xxviii. 9. *Sept.* It signifies, to take in a snare, as fowlers take birds.—*Ye hypocrites.* (18) —*Note,* vi. 1—4, *v.* 2. ' Christ justly calls these persons ' hypocrites, because they pretended to own him as a *just* ' person, and one who bore no respect to persons; and yet ' came with design to accuse him for an *unjust* decision. ' And...because they... (*Luke* xx. 20,) " feigned them- ' " selves " to be such as they were not.' *Whitby.*

V. 23—33. The Sadducees denied a future resurrection, as well as the immortality of the soul: yet they al-

neither marry, nor are given in marriage, but are ^b as the angels of God in heaven.

31 But as touching the resurrection of the dead, ⁱ have ye not read that which was spoken unto you by God, saying,

32 I ^k am the God of Abraham, and the God of Isaac, and the God of Jacob? ^l God is not the God of the dead, but of the living.

33 And when the multitude heard ^m this, ^m they were astonished at his doctrine.

34 ¶ But ⁿ when the Pharisees had heard that he had put the Sadducees

to silence, ^o they were gathered together.

35 Then one of them, which was a lawyer, asked him a question, tempting him, and saying,

36 Master, ^r which is the great commandment in the law?

37 Jesus said unto him, ^s Thou shalt love the LORD thy God with all thy heart, and with all thy soul, and with all thy mind.

38 This is the first and great commandment.

39 And the second is like unto it, ^t Thou shalt love thy ^u neighbour as thyself.

(marginal references:)
b xiii. 43. Ps. ciij. 20. Zech. jii. 7. Rev. v. 9—11.
xix. 10.
i ix. 3, xii. 3, 7. xxi. 16. 42.
k Ex. iii. 6, .6. Acts iii. 32. Heb. xi. 16.
l Mark xii. 26, 27. Luke xx. 37, 38.
m 22, vii. 28, 29. Mark vi. 2. Luke ii. 47, iv. 22. xx. 39, 40. John vii. 46.
n Mark xii. 28.
o xii. 14. xxvi. 3 —5. 1a. xli. 5.
7. John xi. 47—53. xii. 19.
10. Acts v. 24—.
28. xix. 28—29.
xxi. 28—30.
p Luke viii. 30. x.
25. xi. 45, 46. 52. xiv. 3. Tit. iii. 13.
r 18. Mark x. 2.
s 19, 20. xv. 6. xxiii. 23, 24.
Hos. vii. 12. Mark xii. 28—34. Luke xi. 42.
17. xxx. 6. Mark xii. 29. 30. 3a. Luke x. 27. Rom. vii. 7. John i. 3—5.
t xlix. 19. Lev. xix. 18. Mark xii. 31. Luke x. 27. 28. Rom. xiii. 9, 10. Gal.
u 14. Jam. ii. 8. Luke x. 29—37. Rom. xiii. 9. Gal. v. 14.

---

lowed the divine authority of the books of Moses, and of other parts of scripture. (Marg. Ref. z.—Acts xxiii. 8.) They knew, however, that Jesus taught a contrary doctrine; and they purposed to embarrass him with a difficulty, which probably had perplexed others of their opponents: though the case stated would not have been worth recording, had it not shewn the cavilling, frivolous spirit of infidelity, and given our Lord an occasion of returning a most instructive answer. The whole difficulty lay in determining, to whom the woman would belong in the future world, as seven brothers had married her, and she had born no children to any of them: (Marg. Ref. c, d.—Note, Deut. xxv. 5—10:) but the inference which they meant to insinuate from it, was no less, than the impossibility of a resurrection. This method of arguing by insinuation, from imagined difficulties against authenticated revelation, or even stubborn facts, forms a species of logick for which infidels, ancient and modern, have shewn a peculiar predilection: and indeed it is the best method, which can be taken, of perplexing weak minds, and amusing superficial enquirers. Our Lord therefore first declared, that they "greatly erred," because they did not understand the scriptures; or the power of God, to raise the dead incorruptible, and fitted for a far different life from this. (Marg. Ref. e, f.—Mark xii. 18—27, v. 27.) Among other egregious errors, the Sadducees took no notice of a state of punishment, in the future world; but spake as if those who believed the resurrection thought all men (at least all Jews) to be of one character, and to go to one place.—Our Lord further reminded them, that marriage was intended only for this present world; to replenish the earth, and to repair the ravages that death continually makes among its inhabitants: but that in the future state, as there would be no death, so no marriage; for all the righteous would be made like unto the angels, being "the children of God as well as the children of the resurrection." There the very body will be made spiritual, and all the employments and pleasures will be pure, intellectual, and angelick. (Marg. Ref. a. g, h.—Notes, Luke xx. 27—38, vv. 34. 38. 1 Cor. xv. 12—19. 35—54.)—Having refuted this cavil, our Lord next proceeded to establish the truth of the doctrine which they opposed, from that part of the scripture which they professed to be-

lieve: he therefore referred them to the words of God to Moses, when he spake to him from the burning bush. (Marg. Ref. i, k.—Notes, Ex. iii. 6. 15.) The patriarchs had been dead a considerable time before this appearance of the LORD to Moses: yet he there declared himself to be the God of Abraham, Isaac, and Jacob: now he is " not " the God of the dead," who have sunk into non-existence, " but of the living," who are capable of enjoying his favour. (Marg. Ref. l.—Notes, Luke xx. 27—38, v. 38. Heb. xi. 13—16, v. 16.) The argument seems at first sight more immediately to prove, that the souls of the patriarchs were, at that time, in existence and felicity, than to evince the resurrection of their bodies: but if we consider, that man is constituted of soul and body, we shall perceive that it proves both. For if JEHOVAH gave himself, by an everlasting covenant, to be the God and Portion of any person; it implied that he would finally render him happy, in body and soul, by bringing him to the complete enjoyment of his presence and favour; and this could not be done unless the body be restored from the grave. The whole reasoning shews, that the doctrine of the resurrection, and the future state, is as certainly contained in the Old Testament, when properly understood, as in the New. The resurrection of the wicked is revealed in other places; but the question proposed led Jesus rather to speak concerning that of the righteous.

Shall marry, &c. (24) Επιγαμβρευσει. Ex επι et γαμβρευω, affinitatem contraho. It implies an additional affinity.) It used elsewhere in the New Testament.—Gen. xxxviii. 8. Sept.—Ye do err. (29) Πλανασθε (a πλανη, error, aberratio:) xxiv. 4. Mark xiii. 5. Gal. vi. 7. 2 Tim. iii. 13. Tit. iii. 3. Jam. i. 16. 1 John i. 8. iii. 7.—See on Note, Heb. iii. 7— 13, v. 10.—I am, &c. (32) The quotation is exactly from the Septuagint: except as " the God of thy father," is omitted.

V. 34—39. Marg. Ref.—Notes, Mark xii. 28—34. Love the LORD, &c. (37) ' We are to love God above ' all things ... so as to prize him in our judgments above all ' things, to esteem him more valuable in himself, more ' beneficial to us, than all things else we can enjoy; ac- ' cording to that saying of the Psalmist, "Thy loving ' " kindness is much better than is life itself;" (Ps. lxiii. 3;) ' to esteem him as the only Felicity of our immortal souls:

40 On ˣ these two commandments hang all the law and the prophets.

41 ¶ While ʸ the Pharisees were gathered together, Jesus asked them,

42 Saying, ᶻ What think ye of Christ? whose Son is he? They say unto him, ᵃ The Son of David.

43 He saith unto them, How then doth David ᵇ in Spirit call him Lord, saying,

44 The ᶜ LORD said unto ᵈ my Lord, Sit thou on my right hand, ᵉ till I make thine enemies thy footstool?

45 If David then call him Lord, ᶠ how is he his son?

46 And ᵍ no man was able to answer him a word, ʰ neither durst any man from that day forth ask him any more *questions.*

---

x vii. 12. John i. 17. Rom. iii. 19
b. 1 Tim. i.
y 11. i. 9—21. 15, 34. Mark xii.
z 35. Luke xx. 41.
a ii. 4—6. xiv. 33. xvi. 15—17.
John i. 46. 49. 66. iii. xx. 37.
Phil. ii. 9—11.
b iii. 11. 1 Pet. ii. iii. 11. 1 Pet. i. 12
4—14. Rev. v. 12
a i. 1. xxi. 9. Is. vii. 13, 14. ix. 6, 7. xl. 1—4. Jer. xxiii. 5, 6. Ez. xxxiv. 23, 24. Am. ix. 11. 27, 25.
b 2 Sam. xxiii. 2. Heb. iii. 7. 2 Pet. i. 21.

c Ps. cx. 1. Acts ii. 34. 1 Cor. xv. 25. Heb. i. 13.
d Is. 2. xix. 2.
d John xx. 28. 1 Cor. i. 2. Phil. ii. 8.
e Gen. iii. 15. Ps. ii. 8, 9. xxi. 8. Is. lxiii. 1—3. Luke xix. 27. Rev. xix. 11.
f John viii. 48. Rom. i. 3, 4. iv. *h* Phil. ii. 6—9.
1 Tim. iii. 16.
g xxi. 27. Job xxxii. 15, 16. Is. l. 2—9. Luke xiii. 17, xiv. 6. John viii. 7—9. Acts iv. 14.
h Mark xii. 34. Luke xx. 40.

' their chief and most desirable Good; the only Being, in ' whom is perfect rest, entire complacency, and full satis- ' faction to be found. ...We are to love God above all ' things ... with a superlative affection. ...Our desires must ' be more ardently inclined to his favour, and the enjoy- ' ment of him; we must long, thirst, and pant more after ' him; rejoice more in his favour, than in any thing else; ' be more concerned to retain it, than to secure any worldly ' blessings, and be more satisfied in it than " in marrow ' " and fatness." ... Hence it follows, that we are to love ' all other things only in way of relation, and subordina- ' tion to God. ...Surely, if I love God, so as to love ' nothing which is contrary to him, or which he forbiddeth ' me to love, I can do nothing contrary to the love I owe him. If I love him, so as to prize neither friendship, ' relations, fame, honour, pleasure, riches, life, or any ' temporal concernments, so as to offend him by preserv- ing them; I do not inordinately love them. ...Moreover, ' if I prize nothing in comparison with him in my mind, if ' I cleave to nothing in competition with him in my will, ' if I desire nothing in comparison with him in my affec- ' tions; if I pursue nothing but with relation to his glory, ' and in subordination to his sacred will, how can I be ' wanting in my duty to him? And if I be not wanting in ' my duty to him, how can I sin against him?' *Whitby.*— Did this learned writer really think, that any mere man, during his whole life, ever thus loved God? Or that true Christians, from the time of their becoming such, do thus without failure love God? Or did he suppose, that he himself had always, or for any length of time, thus loved God? If all, who " are willing to justify themselves," would thus explain this first and great commandment; many of them must soon perceive, that " by the works of " the law no flesh shall be justified in the sight of God." Yet, I apprehend, even this comment is not fully adequate to the meaning of the spiritual precept. (*Notes, Ex.* xx. 1—11. *Deut.* vi. 5.)—The quotation of this " first and " great commandment," varies considerably from the Sep- tuagint in words: but accords in meaning with it; as it does with the original Hebrew. Indeed, as the passage is found but once in the Old Testament, and is referred to repeatedly in the New, with variation in words, but not in meaning, it is most manifest that no quotation was in- tended.—The Septuagint seems to be a more literal trans- lation of the Hebrew, than any of those found in the New Testament.

Second. (39) *Marg. Ref.—Note, Lev.* xix. 18.—' If ' the worst, the most despiteful, and most disobliging of ' our enemies must, by the Christian be thus loved, and

' therefore owned as a neighbour, what man can be ex- ' cluded from that appellation?' *Whitby.* (*Notes, Luke* x. 25—37.)

V. 40. The law, duly interpreted, required this love of " God and man; the prophets enforced the law, and foretold " Christ, as the end of the law for righteousness to every " one that believeth:" and the whole of revelation is in- tended to bring fallen sinners, by regeneration, repentance, and faith in the Saviour, to love God supremely, and man, unfeignedly and fervently on earth, and perfectly for ever in heaven. The whole system of revelation will generally be comprehended, in proportion as these two command- ments are understood: perhaps every error in religion arises from inadequate or mistaken views of them; so that the whole may well be said to depend on them. (*Marg. Ref.—Note, Is.* xxii. 20—25, *vv.* 23—25.)

V. 41—46. When Christ had baffled the insidious de- vices of his enemies, and exposed their ignorance, hypo- crisy and malice; he proposed a question to them as they gathered around him. He enquired, what thoughts they had concerning their expected and promised Messiah, and whose Son did they suppose he would be. And, when they answered that he would be " the Son of David;" he asked them, why David, speaking by the Spirit of God, had called the Messiah, Lord, or Governor, seeing he was to be his remote descendant. (*Note, Ps.* cx. 1.) If he would be a mere man, who would have no existence till many ages after David's death, with what propriety could his progenitor call him his Lord? For he could not possi- bly owe him any subjection. If Jesse had lived till David was established in the kingdom, David might, in some- good sense, have been called Jesse's lord, though Jesse's son: but could David, with any propriety be called the lord of Boaz, Judah, Abraham, Noah, and Adam, his pro- genitors? Yet this would be quite as reasonable, as to call the Messiah David's Lord, if he had no existence till a thousand years after David's death. And who, even if existing at that time, could be called David's lord, at the summit of his exaltation, as the Lord's anointed king of Israel, except the Lord of all? The modern Jews, unable to answer this argument, affirm that David did not write Psalm cx: but those to whom Jesus spoke did not attempt such an evasion, or they would not have been silent.— This question, which is equally interesting to modern Socinians, the Pharisees could not answer; and they were so baffled in their endeavours to entangle Jesus, that they never after dared to put another question to him. *{Marg. Ref.* g, h.) Nor can any man solve the difficulty proposed, in a satisfactory manner, except he allow the Messiah to

CHAP. XXIII.

Jesus exhorts the people to regard the scriptural instructions of the Scribes and Pharisees; but not to follow their bad examples, and especially not to imitate their ambition, 1—12. He denounces divers woes on them, for their blindness, hypocrisy, and iniquity, 13—33. He predicts the destruction of Jerusalem, and the calamities of the Jews for their atrocious crimes, 34—39.

be truly and properly " the Son of God;" and, equally with the Father, " David's Lord" at the time when his progenitor thus spake of him; and that at the appointed season he assumed our nature into personal union with the Deity, and so became " God manifested in the flesh," and in this sense " the Son of man," and " the Son of David." To this the Old Testament had given abundant testimony: but the Pharisees, blinded by carnal prejudices, overlooked all that had been said of Immanuel, and of " the mighty " God" becoming " a Child born," and expected a mere man and a temporal deliverer, instead of a divine and spiritual Redeemer.—' Our Lord...always takes it for granted, ' that the writers of the Old Testament were under such an ' extraordinary guidance of the Holy Spirit in their writings, ' as to express themselves with the strictest propriety on ' all occasions.' *Doddridge.* (*Marg. Ref.—Notes, Mark* xii. 35—37. *Luke* xx. 41—44.)

The *Lord said*, &c. (44) From the LXX, who literally translate the Hebrew.

PRACTICAL OBSERVATIONS.

V. 1—14.

Our merciful God has not only provided food, but a royal feast, for the perishing souls of his rebellious creatures: and there is " enough and to spare " of every thing, which can conduce to our present comfort and everlasting felicity, in the salvation of his Son Jesus Christ. Let none then think of religion, as of an unpleasant service, to which they are urged; but as a rich and magnificent feast, to which they are invited: and, whilst believers enjoy peace of conscience, joy in the Holy Ghost, communion with God, and the lively hope of glory; let them not forget at what a price the feast was prepared. " All things " are" now " ready;" the servants are continually employed in inviting guests; and their commission reaches, not only to the utmost limits of the visible church, but " to the highways" of the Gentile world. They are commanded to invite all, " as many as they find, both bad and " good;" to renew their invitations to such as have repeatedly rejected them; and not to be wearied out by disappointments or ill usage, but to address others, and others still, that " the wedding may be furnished with guests." Yet, after all these invitations, numbers perish in their sins: not because they *may not* come; nor, properly speaking, because they *cannot;* but because they " will not." This is the effect of profane contempt of spiritual blessings, inordinate love of worldly objects, carnal dislike to the perfection, law, and government of God, and proud aversion to the humbling salvation of the gospel. From such motives, numbers " make light " of the invitations, and carelessly and ungratefully turn aside to worldly employments, diversions and studies; perhaps pretending want of leisure, or purposing to come at " a more convenient season." Others are enraged at the warnings and expostulations, with which the servants enforce the invitation; and treat them with insult and reproach; or even murder them if

they have it in their power. Thus the gospel of salvation occasions their deeper condemnation, because they hate the light through love of sin: and so God is provoked to give them up to temporal and eternal destruction. Sometimes they, who have been brought up under the gospel, prove the greatest despisers and enemies of it: and the servants, who are sent forth into the high-ways and hedges, have most success, in winning souls to Christ.—No objections will be made to any man, on account of his previous character, who is desirous of admission to this feast: yet no man will actually partake of it, who has not the wedding-garment prepared for lost sinners, who does not seek and obtain an interest in the merits of Christ, or who remains a stranger to converting grace. (*Notes, Rev.* iii. 17—19.) Many find admission among believers, and continue with them to the last, who have not this " wedding-" garment," and whom the King will at length distinguish and separate from his chosen people: then their present pretences will be shewn to be fallacious, and they will have nothing to plead in arrest of judgment, when he shall order them to be " bound hand and foot, and cast into outer " darkness, where shall be weeping and gnashing of teeth." As therefore " many are called, and few chosen;" let us " examine ourselves whether we be in the faith," and seek above all things to be approved of by the King himself, when he shall come in to see the guests.

V. 15—22.

While we carefully shun the hypocrisy and wickedness of the enemies of Christ, we may learn from their words what a minister of God ought to be. By their allowance, and in their unimpassioned judgment, he should be an upright, faithful man, " teaching the way of God in truth;" able and bold " to declare the whole counsel of God;" and not so caring for man, or fearing him, or respecting the person of any man, as to keep back, alter, or soften any part of his message. Who will deny in words, that this ought to be the character of a minister? Yet how few reduce it to practice! Who expects such unpliant faithfulness and unreserved honesty, towards all ranks and descriptions of men, from the ministers of Christ? Who does not censure that man, as rude, uncourtly, and intruding, who flatters no one, connives at no errors or sins, of his patron, his friend, or his prince; and will not disguise his sentiments, to please any party, or for fear of the frown of any man or multitude of men? The nearer any servant of God comes to this character, the more need he will have to pray for " the meekness of wisdom," and to copy the example of his Lord: for, many will seek for matter of accusation against him, that they may re-establish their own reputation by ruining his; and if his boldness be not evidently disinterested, benevolent, humble, harmless, and prudent, he will often be entangled in their snares.—Few subjects are more perilous in this respect, than those, which are in any degree connected with political contests: for it is difficult to touch on them, without

x 6

* st. 10, &c. **THEN** spake Jesus *a* to the multi-
Mark vii. 14.
Luke xii. 1. &c. tude, and to his disciples,
xx. 45.

2 Saying, *b* The Scribes and the Pha- *b* Neh. viii. 4—8.
risees sit in Moses's seat: Mal. ii. 7. Mark
                               xii. 38. Luke xx.
                               46.

---

giving advantage to one party or other, or without verging
to some extreme. Yet ministers must teach the people
their duty, though it should interfere with their own popularity, or incur the displeasure of their rulers : and to this
they should confine their interposition. They must insist
upon men's rendering tribute, honour, and civil obedience,
without reserve, to " the powers that be ; " let Pharisees,
or men of any creed or name, attempt to render religion
the watch-word of sedition, or the cloke of their depreda-
tions on the publick revenue; or indulge their rebellion
against the providence of God, by reviling the persons or
measures of their rulers : and they must equally insist upon
men's " rendering to God the things that are God's," let
Herodians say what they will to prove, that kings are authorized to lord it over the consciences of their subjects,
and to model the gospel and its ordinances, as may best
suit their interest, convenience, or caprice. Nor will it
be very difficult to apply this general rule to particular
cases, provided the heart be upright : except that it will
sometimes expose a man to secular loss or persecution, if
he determines to obey Cæsar as far as his duty to God
will give him leave, and no farther.—But how broad is
the rule of God's commandments! The enlightened soul
can never seriously meditate on any one of them, without
seeing cause to say, " God be merciful to me, and write
" this law in my heart, I beseech thee."

V. 23—33.

Those who are most proud of their reasoning powers,
and most disposed to boast of them, often form the grossest
conceptions of spiritual things : they speak of God, as if
he were altogether such a one as themselves, and of heaven, with carnal ideas and imaginations; so that they are
commonly fighting with shadows, when they start objections to the doctrines of the gospel. If they understood
the plain meaning of the scriptures, or had any proper
ideas of the divine power, they must be convinced of the
futility of their own arguments; which seldom need any
other answer, than a fair statement of the truths which
they oppose. Indeed all our errors result from " not
" knowing the scriptures, and the power of God : " and
this should excite us to redouble our diligence in searching
the sacred oracles, and our earnestness in prayer to be led
into a right understanding of them.—We are continually
reminded what a dying world this is. The history of men
in general resembles the account here given of one family :
death removes one after another, and so terminates all
their carnal hopes, joys, cares, sorrows, and connexions.
(P. O. Gen. v.) How wretched then must they be, who
have all " their good things " here, and can expect nothing
but misery beyond the grave! And how grovelling the
soul of an infidel, who can be content, and even hope, to
die like a beast, for the sake of living " without God in
" the world ! " Yet even of his forlorn hope, he will most
certainly be disappointed.—The whole scripture " warns
" us to flee from the wrath to come," and calls us to expect a far better and happier state; and the thoughts of
that felicity will be the more welcome to the spiritual man,

(however comfortable in his relative connexions,) from the
consideration, that there will be " neither marrying nor
" giving in marriage." For he aspires to a higher state of
existence; and emulates the worship, the holiness, and
the blessedness of angels; compared with which, the most
rational and honourable of earthly comforts are mean and
of no estimation. In that happy world, the God of Abraham will be the Portion of all his believing children ; and
they will, in body and soul, live to him and with him,
and have the unalloyed fruition of that " fulness of joy
" which is at his right hand for evermore."

V. 34—46.

While Pharisees, Sadducees, and Scribes are perplexing
each other, and trying to disconcert us, by curious questions
and frivolous disputes : let us remember that the love of
God with all our heart, and the love of our neighbour as
ourselves, though the ministration of condemnation to the
sinner, is our perfect rule of obedience ; and that " Christ
" is the end of the law for righteousness, to every one that
" believeth." It behoves us sinners, therefore, above all
things, to enquire seriously, what we think of Christ.
What are our views of his person, his priesthood, his atonement, his intercession, his power, truth, and love ? Is he
altogether glorious in our eyes, and precious to our hearts ?
Do we trust in him as the incarnate Son of God, and submit to him as the anointed King of Israel ? Do we seek
him in all his characters and offices ? Do we desire that
" all his enemies should be put under his feet," without
excepting any of our own sinful passions? Do we deem
him entitled to all the service and honour, which we can
possibly render him, and far more ? According to a man's
practical judgment in these matters, are his state and character ; and his conduct will eventually prove this. His
judgment of the perfections, law, and government of God,
of sin and holiness, of this world and the next, of himself, his life past, and present, and of his heart, in short,
of every object around him, will be influenced by his view
of this subject. The temper of his mind will be humble,
meek, patient, compassionate, thankful, spiritual, or the
contrary, according to his thoughts of Christ; and his
whole conduct will be habitually influenced by it. May
Christ then be our Joy, our Confidence, our All: may we
daily see more of his glory and preciousness, and experi
ence more of his love; and may we daily be more conformed to his image, and devoted to his service. Then
our words and works will confute and shame those who
would falsely accuse us, and effectually silence the malicious objections and subtle insinuations of Pharisees,
Sadducees, and Herodians, however distinguished.

NOTES.

CHAP. XXIII. V. 1—4. It is probable, that our Lord
continued still at the temple ; and addressed himself to the
disciples and the multitude, in the presence of " the
" Scribes and Pharisees." These were the stated teachers
and rulers of the nation : in this respect, " they sat in
" Moses's seat ; " for they explained the law of Moses to

Y 7

3 All therefore ' whatsoever they bid you observe, that observe and do; but do not ye after their works; ' for they say, and do not.

4 For ' they bind heavy burdens, and grievous to be borne, and lay them on men's shoulders; but they themselves will not move them with one of their fingers.

5 But ' all their works they do for to be seen of men: ' they make broad their phylacteries, and enlarge the borders of their garments,

6 And ' love the uppermost rooms at feasts, and the chief seats in the synagogues,

7 And greetings in the markets, and to be called of men, ' Rabbi, Rabbi.

8 But ' be not ye called Rabbi: for ' one is your Master, even Christ; and ' all ye are brethren.

9 And ' call no man your father

---

the people, and enforced obedience to it. Whatever therefore, *from this source,* they inculcated, the people ought to attend to and practise. This limitation must be admitted; otherwise their traditions and perversions of the law, and even their opposition to Christ, would have been included; for they taught these to the people. But he evidently meant, that whatever they enforced or required, according to the law of Moses, or the writings of the prophets, was to be obeyed. ' Saith Theophylact, ' All that " ' they require from the books of Moses, or the law of " ' God;' which interpretation must be allowed of. Be- " ' cause Christ elsewhere requires his disciples to " beware " ' of the leaven," that is, the doctrine, " of the Scribes and " ' Pharisees:" (xvi. 6. 12.) and that because " they taught " ' for doctrines the commandments of men," and " by " ' their traditions made void the law of God;" (xv. 6. 9;) ' and " were blind leaders of the blind." (xv. 14.)' *Whitby.* No argument can fairly be formed on this, to prove that men are obliged to follow the instructions, or obey the commands, of any teachers or rulers, further than they consist with the word of God: (*Notes,* xv. 1—14. xvi. 5—12:) yet, on the other hand, the bad character of rulers and teachers should not induce men to disobey their *lawful* commands, or to reject their *scriptural* instructions.—Corrupt as the doctrine of the Scribes was, their works were still worse: and therefore the people were in no respect to imitate them; as they did not even practise their own injunctions. Indeed, by enforcing, under severe penalties, great exactness in ceremonial observances, and in their traditional restrictions and austerities, as well as in moral duties; they " bound up heavy burdens, and laid them on " the shoulders" of the people: but they found out methods of dispensing with whatever was uneasy to themselves, or compounding for it: so that they would not put a finger to assist in moving the load, which they had imposed on others. (*Marg. Ref.—Notes,* xi. 28—30. Gal. vi. 11—14, v. 13.)

They bind. (4) Δισμευυωσι. ' Ligant, ut solent onera ' jumentis ligari, ne decidant.' Leigh. Acts xxii. 4.—Gen. xxxvii. 7. Sept.—*Grievous to be borne.*' Δυσ6αςακτα. Luke xi. 46. Βαςαζω, porto.

V. 5—7. Our Lord further guarded the people against the doctrine and spirit of the Scribes and Pharisees, who were ostentatious hypocrites in all their external observances. (*Marg. Ref.* f.—*Notes,* iii. 1—4. 16—18.)—The Jews understood the words of Moses in a literal sense; (*Marg. Ref.* g.—*Note,* Deut. vi. 7—9;) and therefore used to have scraps of parchment, inscribed with texts out of the law, fastened to their foreheads or wrists: these were called " phylacteries," or *preservatives,* being superstitiously considered as amulets, to protect them from dangers; and the Pharisees, in ostentation of their extraordinary devotion, wore their phylacteries remarkably broad. For the same reason, they enlarged the *fringes,* which they were commanded to wear upon their garments. (*Marg. Ref.* h.) In the same self-exalting spirit, they *delighted* to intrude into the chief seats, when they went to a feast; or to be placed in a conspicuous situation, as very honourable persons, even when they went to the synagogue, professedly to abase themselves in the worship of God. It was also very pleasing to them, to be addressed with great respect, in the places of publick resort, as men of eminent wisdom and piety, under the appellation of Rabbi; a word importing the variety of their learning, and the greatness of their religious knowledge.—' What great holiness they ' placed in putting on these phylacteries, we may learn ' from the Targum on Cant. viii. 3, which introduc- ' eth the Jews speaking thus: ' I am chosen above all " ' people, because I bind my frontals to my head and my " ' left hand; and my parchment is fixed to the right side " ' of my gate or door, so that a third part of it comes up " ' to my bed, that the evil spirits may not hurt me.' ' *Whitby.*—' These rolls of parchment were by them pre- ' pared with a great multitude of ceremonies; and decrees ' made by them, of the creatures of whose skins that parch- ' ment was to be made, and of the knives with which it ' was to be cut, and a great deal more. Being made, they ' fitted and applied them to the foreheads, and to the ' wrists. ...The special use of them was in their prayers.' *Hammond.*

Phylacteries. (5) Φυλακτηρια, (ὰ φυλασσω, custodio,) occurs in this place only.—*Borders.*] Κρασπεδα. Note, ix. 18—26, v. 20.—*Uppermost rooms.* (6) Πρωτοκλισιαν. (Ex πρωτος, et κλινω, accumbo.) Accubitus in primo loco. Mark xii. 39. Luke xiv. 7, 8. xx. 46.—*Chief seats.*] Πρωτοκαθεδριας. (Ex πρωτος et καθεδρα. Consessus. Whence Cathedral.) Mark xii. 39. Luke xi. 43. xx. 46.—*Synagogues.* (n) ' There ' shewing their pride, saith Theophylact, where they ought ' to have taught others humility.' *Whitby.*—*Rabbi.* (7) ' The word signifies one that is above his fellows, and is ' as good as a number of them; and we may see by the ' repeating of it, how proud a title it was.' Beza. (*Marg. Ref.* i, k.—*Note,* Luke xx. 45—47.)

V. 8—10. This instruction seems to have been imme-

upon the earth; for one is your Father, which is in heaven.

10 Neither be ye called masters; for one is your Master, *even* Christ.

11 But he that is greatest among you shall be your servant.

12 And whosoever shall exalt him-self shall be abased; and he that shall humble himself shall be exalted.

13 ¶ But woe unto you, Scribes and Pharisees, hypocrites! for ye shut up the kingdom of heaven against men: for ye neither go in *yourselves*, neither suffer ye them that are entering to go in.

-diately addressed to the disciples, who were warned to shun all approaches to such ostentation, or desire of human applause, as that which disgraced the scribes. Even the apostles, though the most eminent persons who ever appeared on earth, were commanded not to accept of the title of "Rabbi:" because they had one Master, even Christ himself; yet they were all brethren, without any pre-eminence or authority over each other; being all equally dependent on their common Lord, and equally subject to him. This is twice repeated, perhaps to shew how prone men are to forget it. And, as the disciples were not to affect lordly authority or worldly honour; they were required not to "call any man their father upon "earth." This cannot be supposed to forbid men from expressing respect, affection, and gratitude to those, who have been instrumental to their spiritual good; any more than to interfere with the duties of children to their parents. (*Marg. Ref.* o.—*Note*, 1 *Cor.* iv. 14—17.) But Christians are forbidden to look up to any man, as "having dominion "over their faith," as entitled to implicit credence and submission; or as the head of a sect, whose decisions are stamped with authority over men's consciences: nay, they ought to oppose all claims and pretensions of this kind, by whomsoever advanced, or on whatever grounds. If these rules were proper for the apostles and primitive disciples; they must be still more suitable to the case of all other teachers and Christians: and it is evident, that they were given with a prophetick view to the enormous abuses and fatal effects, which have since been witnessed in the Christian church, from the ambition and lust of dominion in some, and the abject subjection of others, to their assumed authority and pretensions to infallibility. The astonishing degree to which these evils have proceeded, especially in the church of Rome, the exorbitant claims, and high sounding titles of ecclesiasticks, and servile submission of the people, are well known: but the same leaven still works; and many things are found, among different bodies of protestant Christians, which by no means comport with these rules, and which do not at all savour of the simplicity and humility of the gospel; or consist with believing and obeying no teacher, church-ruler, learned doctor, or head of a sect, in the least matter, further than he evidently declares the truth and will of Christ, our common Teacher and Lord.—It is observable, that assuming priests of all religions have been ambitions of being called "father," or of some such name; importing rather what they are conscious they ought to have been, than what they really were. The following citations shew to what an exorbitant height the claims of the Rabbies were advanced. —'They declare that the traditions of their fathers were 'equal to the words of the law, and more to be regarded 'than the words of the prophets: that a prophet was not

'to be believed, except he could shew a sign or a miracle: 'but as for these elders or fathers, they were to be believed 'without them. ... (*Deut.* xvii. 11.) ...If a thousand pro-'phets, who were equal to Elias and Elisha, bring one 'interpretation; and a thousand and one wise men pro-'duce one contrary to it; we must incline to the sentence of 'the most, 'and be obliged rather to act according to the sentence of 'these wise men, than of the thousand prophets.' *Whitby.* —These were, in some sense, the schoolmasters of the Romish bishops and clergy, who have exceedingly profited by their instructions. (*Marg. Ref.* l—n. p.—*Notes*, v. 27, 28. 43—48. vi. 9. xv. 7—9. *Luke* xxii. 24—27. *Rom.* ii. 17—24. 2 *Cor.* i. 23, 24. 1 *Pet.* v. 1—4.)

Master. (8) Καθηγητής. 10. (Εχ καδα et ήγεομαι, *duco*.) ' A Guide of the way.' Not elsewhere used in the New Testament.

V. 11, 12. Our Lord further observed, that, if any one was in reality the greatest, he should shew it, by being more active, humble, and condescending than others; and by becoming the willing servant, rather than the domineering lord, of the whole fraternity: for it was the invariable rule of his kingdom, to abase all who should exalt themselves, and to advance all who abased themselves.—' No ' one sentence of our Lord occurs so often as this.' *Doddridge.* (*Marg. Ref.*—*Notes*, xviii. 1—4. xx. 24—28. *Mark* x. 35—45, *v.* 43. *Luke* xiv. 7—11, *v.* 11. xviii. 9—14, *v.* 14.)

V. 13. Our Lord next addressed the Scribes and Pharisees, who stood around him: and, without any reserve, in the character of their heart-searching Judge, he exposed their hypocrisy and wickedness, and denounced sentence against them; as he had before done, in some measure, on another occasion. (*Notes, Luke* xi. 39—52.) He first convicted them "of shutting the kingdom of heaven against "men." They assumed, that they were the authorized teachers of the Jews: yet they used all their influence and authority to set the people against Christ, and to keep them from becoming the subjects of his kingdom. (*Note,* iii. 2.) Thus they wickedly destroyed the souls of numbers, to support their own reputation, dominion, and worldly interest: for, being blinded by their carnal lusts and prejudices, they would neither themselves receive him as the Messiah, nor permit those who seemed disposed to it: and by keeping them out of the heavenly kingdom, which was set up among them, they did all in their power to shut them out of the kingdom of future glory and felicity.— ' They themselves refused to go in; and obstructed the ' entrance of others, by saying, "Have any of the rulers ' " or Pharisees believed on him?" (*John* vii. 48.) ... ' They cavilling at all that he said; ... rejecting him, as not ' of God, because he "kept not the sabbath," (*John* ix. ' 16;) and accusing him of blasphemy, and of "casting

Z

14 Woe unto you, Scribes and Pharisees, hypocrites! "for ye devour widows' houses, and for a pretence make long prayer: ˣ therefore ye shall receive the greater damnation.

15 Woe unto you, Scribes and Pharisees, hypocrites! ʸ for ye compass sea and land to make one ᶻ proselyte, and when he is made, ᵃ ye make him two-fold more the child of hell than yourselves.

16 Woe unto you, ᵇ ye blind guides, which say, 'Whosoever shall swear by the temple, ᵈ it is nothing; but whosoever shall swear by the gold of the temple, ᵉ he is a debtor! ,

, 17 Ye fools and blind; for whether is greater, the gold, ᶠ or the temple that sanctifieth the gold?

18 And, Whosoever shall swear by the altar, it is nothing; but whosoever sweareth by the gift that is upon it, he is ᵍ guilty.

19 Ye fools and blind: for whether is greater, the gift, ᵍ or the altar that sanctifieth the gift?

20 Whoso therefore shall swear by the altar, sweareth by it, and by all things thereon.

21 And whoso shall swear by the temple, sweareth by it, ⁱ and by him that dwelleth therein.

22 And he that shall swear by heaven, sweareth ⁱby the throne of God, and by him that sitteth thereon.

' " out devils by Beelzebub ". (xii. 24;) and by their vain ' traditions, ... putting a bar to the spiritual doctrine of his ' kingdom: thus did they " shut up the kingdom of hea- ' ven against men." ...By excommunicating and mali- ' ciously prosecuting them who owned his doctrine, and ' decreeing that they should be " cast out of the syna- ' gogue." (John ix. 22.)' Whitby.—' Hypocrites can ' abide none to be better than themselves.' Beza. (Marg. Ref.—Notes, vi. 1—4, v. 2. xii. 22—28. xv. 3—6. Luke xi. 52. John vii. 40—53. ix. 19—23.)

V. 14. The Scribes and Pharisees, by pretensions to extraordinary devotion, insinuated themselves into the confidence of the people, and perhaps induced many persons, when they died, to leave them in trust for their widows and households, or families. Thus they got the effects into their hands, and, on one pretence or other, defrauded the widows and orphans of their property; as if they had swallowed up the whole at once, after the manner in which some greedy animals devour their food. But, to avoid suspicion and to silence every complaint, they made long formal prayers; which prevented the deluded people from believing any report to their disadvantage. Thus religion was disgraced by being made the covering of enormous oppression; and God was dishonoured, as if he had been a partner in the robbery! They would therefore have a more tremendous account to give, and be more terribly punished in another world, than other wicked men; yea, than other oppressors, who had not made a profession of piety under the cloke of their iniquity. (Marg. Ref. Is. lviii. 3— 7. lxi. 7—9, v. 8. Jer. vii. 5—11. Luke xx. 45—47.)— Ye devour, &c.] Kαἴεσθιετε, ye eat up. (Kαἴα auget significationem.) Mark xii. 40. Luke xx. 47. 2 Cor. xi. 20. Gal. v. 15. Rev. xi. 5.—Damnation.] Kρμα, judgment. Note, Jam. ii. 8—13, v. 13.

V. 15. The Scribes and Pharisees were very zealous and assiduous, in endeavouring to make proselytes to the Jewish religion, and so to their own sect; not from a desire of promoting the glory of God, or the salvation of souls, but in order to strengthen their party, and to advance their reputation. When, therefore, with great pains,

as if " compassing sea and land," they had brought any one under their tuition, they worked him up to such a degree of ignorant and furious bigotry, and enmity to Christ and his gospel, that he became fit for the most desperate services, to which they could direct him. So that, instead of being benefited by his supposed conversion, he became a more devoted servant of Satan, and more deeply deserving of divine wrath, than before: and as he might be pushed on to such actions as they themselves declined, he became even " two-fold more a child " of hell than themselves;" that is, more openly and outrageously mischievous and blasphemous, in opposing the cause of Christ and in persecuting believers. (Marg. Ref. —Note, Gal. vi. 11—14.)—Proselyte.] Προσηλυτον. (Απο τε προσεληλυθηναι, ' from their coming and adjoining unto ' the Jews.' Leigh.) Acts ii. 10. vi. 5. xiii. 43.—The child of hell.] Τιον γεννης. Note, v. 21, 22. A hebraism, as " Sons of Belial," " Children of wrath," &c.

V. 16—22. Our Lord next exposed the ignorance of these teachers, who had by sinister means obtained immense credit and influence, which enabled them to do the greatest mischief. They taught, that men were not bound by an oath, when they " sware by the temple," or " by " the altar;" yet were guilty of perjury, if they sware falsely by the gold in the sacred treasury, or by the oblations. This decision led the people to a stupid veneration for the latter, in preference to the former, and served the interests of the priests and scribes: but it exposed their folly and blindness in the most evident manner; for the gold and the sacrifices had no other sanctity, than what they derived from the temple and the altar; which must therefore be greater and more honourable, than the oblations on which they conferred a relative sanctity. In fact, these oaths referred to whatever was connected with that which was sworn by: an oath " by the altar " included the gift upon it; and an oath " by the temple," the God whose typical residence it was, as well as the gold that was there consecrated to him: even as when a man " sware " by heaven," he " sware by the throne of God and him " that sat on it."—Our Lord had before disallowed all such

z 2

TOMBS IN THE VALLEY OF JEHOSHAPHAT.

MATT. xxiii. 29; xxvii. 52, 60.   MARK vi. 29.
JOEL iii. 2, 12.

TOMBS OF ABSALOM AND THE KINGS.

23 Woe unto you, Scribes and Pharisees, hypocrites! ᵏ for ye pay tithe of mint and anise and cummin, and have omitted ˡ the weightier *matters* of the law, judgment, mercy, and faith: ᵐ these ought ye to have done, and not to leave the other undone.

24 *Ye* blind guides, ⁿ which strain at a gnat, and swallow a camel.

25 Woe unto you, Scribes and Pharisees, hypocrites! ° for ye make clean the outside of the cup and of the platter, but within they are ᵖ full of extortion and excess.

26 *Thou* blind Pharisee! ⁴ cleanse first that *which is* within the cup and platter, that the outside of them may be clean also.

27 Woe unto you, Scribes and Pharisees, hypocrites! for ye are ʳ like ˢ unto whited ᵗ sepulchres, which indeed appear beautiful outward, but are within full of dead *men's* bones, and of all uncleanness.

28 Even so ᵗ ye also outwardly appear righteous unto men, ᵘ but within ye are full of hypocrisy and iniquity.

29 Woe unto you, Scribes and Pharisees, hypocrites! because ˣ ye build the tombs of the prophets, and garnish the sepulchres of the righteous,

30 And say, If we had been in the days of our fathers, we would not have been partakers with them in ʸ the blood of the prophets.

31 Wherefore ye be ᶻ witnesses unto

oaths: they are profane in common conversation, and not solemn enough on important occasions: but he here shews, that they imply an appeal to God for the truth of what is thus declared or promised. (*Marg. Ref.—Notes*, v. 33—37. *John* ix. 39—41.)

He is a debtor. (16) Οφιλει, rendered " he is guilty," 18,—If the person made a vow, he was bound to perform it, as if paying a debt: if an oath to a falsehood, he was *guilty* of perjury.—*Fools.* (17) Μωροι. See on v. 22.

V. 23, 24. Another instance of the blindness of the Jewish teachers is here adduced. They were very scrupulous in minute externals, but very lax in important matters. They professed to be so tender in their consciences, that they paid tithe even of garden-herbs; but they neglected justice, mercy, sincerity, and fidelity, in their conduct toward man; as well as their most important duties to God. These were the most weighty requirements of the moral law, which must be obligatory under every dispensation: and if they had attended to them, it would then have been proper to observe the more minute requirements of the ritual law: (*Note, Lev.* xxvii. 30—34:) but to be exact in trifles, and devoid of conscience in matters of the highest importance, was egregiously absurd. They " strained a gnat," or *strained a small insect out* of their liquor, lest it should choke them; and yet they could on occasion " swallow a camel." We must suppose this to have been a common proverb ; denoting, that the sins they committed were as much larger than those which they scrupled, as a camel is larger than an insect. (*Marg. Ref.—Notes*, xxvii. 6—10. *John* xviii. 28—32.)

Strain at, &c. (24) Διυλιζοντες.—' *A liquore per linteum* ' *defluente aliquid separare.*' Leigh. Used here only. *Am.* vi. 6. *Sept.—Swallow.*] Καλαπινοντες' ex καλα, et πινω. See on *Note* 13.

V. 25—28. These Scribes and Pharisees, who " trusted " in themselves that they were righteous, and despised " others," and proudly rejected the salvation of Christ, were mere hypocrites. They acted as absurdly, as a man would do, who should carefully wash the outside of his

cup or dish, and yet leave the inside filthy and nauseous, with the remains of his former excesses. They were careful to maintain a decent exterior, and to practise outward duties, as far as human inspection could reach: but they paid no attention to their imaginations, motives, or affections: so that avarice, pride, and sensuality, reigned with uncontrouled dominion in their hearts; and induced them covertly to grasp at wealth by extortion, and to spend it in inordinate self-indulgence. This proved them blind, and ignorant of God, of his law, of true religion, and of themselves: for common sense might have directed them, to begin first with their hearts; and when these had been cleansed from the love of sin, and its gains and pleasures, their external conduct would of course have become clean. Indeed, they only resembled the sepulchres of rich persons, which, being painted and decorated, appeared beautiful to the beholder; yet they contained nothing but dead men's bones, putrid corpses, and such things as were loathsome and polluting. Thus they appeared righteous to their neighbours; but God saw and abhorred their inward and secret wickedness, though varnished over by hypocrisy. (*Marg. Ref.—Notes*, xii. 33—37. *Jer.* iv. 3, 4. 14. *Ex.* xviii. 30—32, v. 31. *Luke* xi. 39, 40. *Jam.* iv. 4—10.)—The touch of a grave communicated a ceremonial uncleanness. (*Notes, Num.* xix. 11. *Ez.* xxxix. 11—16.) The Jews therefore, used to whiten them, with lime, or other materials of that kind: and some learned men are of opinion, that the word *beautiful*, does not refer to the grave when whitened, but when grown over with grass and flowers. But this does not at all agree with the text; for the Pharisees were like *whited* sepulchres, and so appeared beautiful, not like those which were grown over with grass: and to return to our subject, as well as in modern times, those who could afford it, adorned and beautified the tombs of their deceased friends (29).

The platter. (25, 26) Παροψίδος. ' *Vas concavum,* in ' *qua opsonia apponuntur.*' Leigh.—Used here only. Πινακος, *Luke* xi. 39, translated *a charger.* xiv. 8.—*Whited.* (27) Κεκονιαμενος. (à κονια calx.) *Which have been white-washed.* *Acts* xxiii. 3.

V. 29—33. By the just judgment of God, hypo-

Marginal references (left column):
ᵏ Luke xi. 42.
ˡ Is. 13. xii. 7. xxii. 37—40. 1 Sam. xv. 22. Prov. xxi. 3. Hos. vi. 6. Mic. vi. 8. Gal. v. 22, 23.
ᵐ v. 19, 20.
ⁿ vii. 4. xv. 2—6. xix. 24. xxvii. 6—8. Luke vi. 7—9. John xviii. 28. 40.
° xv. 19, 20. Mark vii. 4. Luke xi. 39, 40.
ᵖ 1s. xxviii. 7, 8.
q xii. 33. 1s. 1r. 7. Jer. iv. 14. xiii. 27. Ez. xviii. 31. Luke vi. 45. 2 Cor. vii. 1. Heb. x. 22. Jam. iv. 8.

Marginal references (right column):
ʳ 1s. Iviii. 1, 2. Luke xi. 44. Acts xxiii. 3. ˢ Num. xix. 16.
ᵗ ν. 5. 1 Sam. xvi. 7. Ps. li. 6. Jer. xvii. 9, 10. Luke xvi. 15. Heb. iv. 12, 13.
ᵘ xii. 34, 35. xv. 19, 20. Mark vii. 21—33.
ˣ Luke xi. 47, 48. Acts ii. 29.
ʸ 34, 35. xxi. 35, 38. 2 Chr. xxxvi. 16. Jer. ii. 30. 1 Thess. ii. 15.
ᶻ Josh. xxiv. 22. Job xv. 5, 6. Ps. liv. 6. Luke xix. 22.

c 3

yourselves, ^a that ye are the children of them which killed the prophets.

32 Fill ye up then ^b the measure of your fathers.

33 ^c Ye ^c serpents, *ye* generation of vipers, ^d how can ye escape the damnation of hell?

34 ¶ Wherefore, behold, ^e I send unto you ^f prophets ^g and wise men

and ^h scribes; and *some* ⁱ of them ye shall kill and crucify; and *some* of them shall ye scourge in your synagogues, and persecute *them* from city to city:

35 That ^j upon you may come all the righteous blood shed upon the earth, from ^k the blood of righteous Abel ^l unto the blood of Zecharias, son of Barachias, whom ye slew between the temple and the altar.

Margin/reference notes (left column):
a Acts vii. 51, 52. 1 Thes. ii. 15, 16.
b Gen. xv. 16.
Num. xxvii. 14.
Zech. v. 6—11.
c iii. 7. xii. 34.
Gen. iii. 15. Ps. lviii. 3—5. lxxii. 4. Isa. lvii. 3, 4. Luke iii. 7. John viii. 44. 2 Cor. xi. 3. Rev. xii. 9.
d 14. Heb. ii. 3. x. 29. xii. 25.
e x. 16. xxviii. 19, 20. Luke xi. 49. xxiv. 47. John xx. 21. Acts i. 8. 1 Cor. xii. 3—11. Eph. iv. 8—12. Col. i. 28.
f Acts xi. 27. xiii. 1. xv. 32. Rev. xi. 10.
g Prov. xi. 30. 1 Cor. ii. 6. iii. 10. Col. i. 28.

Margin/reference notes (right column):
h xiii. 52. x. 16, 17. John xvi. 2. Acts v. 40. vii. 51, 52. 58, 59. ix. 1, 2. xii. 2. xiv. 19. xxii. 19, 20. xxiii. 2 Cor. xi. 24, 25. 1 Thes. ii. 16.
i Gen. iv. 8, 6. Num. xxxv. 33.
j Deut. xxi. 7, 8. 2 Kings xxiv. 4.
k xxiv. 4. Isa. xxvi. 21. Jer. ii. 30.
l Gen. iv. 8. Heb. xi. 4. xii. 24.
1 John iii. 11, 12.
2 Chr. xxiv. 21, 22. Zech. i. 1. Luke xi. 51.

'crites, when they must seek to cover their crimes, most
' expose themselves to disgrace.' *Beza.*—It is probable,
that some allusion was in these verses intended to the preceding comparison. Not only did the principal persons
decorate the tombs of their relations, or of distinguished
princes and conquerors; but they especially put themselves
to expense in repairing and " adorning the sepulchres of
" the prophets," whom their ancestors had murdered for
their faithfulness.—They professed exceedingly to disapprove the conduct of these persecutors; and avowed, that,
had they then lived, they would not have concurred with
them. Yet they hated the doctrines and precepts, which
the prophets taught; and rejected, with determined scorn
and enmity, the Messiah whom they predicted; nay, they
were even at that time counselling to put him to death:
In fact, the dead persons no longer gave offence to their
pride, or interfered with their favourite sins; and it increased their reputation, and aided their hypocrisy, to appear as their friends and admirers: but Christ and his disciples greatly offended and exposed them. So that, comparing their profession and conduct together, it was evident, by their own testimony, that they were the genuine
offspring of those who slew the prophets. (*Marg. Ref.*
x—b.—*Notes,* 34—36. *Luke* xi. 46—48, *v.* 48. *Acts* vii.
51—53. 1 *Thes.* ii. 13—16, *v.* 15.) Let them then lay
aside these disguises, and openly proceed to commit those
crimes which they were meditating, and which would " fill
" up the measure of their fathers' " iniquity: for they
were a most subtle and poisonous race of " serpents, a
" generation of vipers," the brood of the old serpent: and
how could such enemies to God, his truth, and salvation,
" escape the damnation of hell," by any of their hypocritical observances or vain pretences?—It is remarkable, that
the most severe and awful things contained in scripture,
were spoken by Jesus Christ himself. (*Marg. Ref.* c, d.
—*Notes,* iii. 7—10. *Gen.* iii. 14, 15.)

Garnish. (29) Κοσμειτε, *adorn, or beautify.*—*The damnation of hell.* (33) Της κρισεως της γεεννης. *The judgment
of hell.* See on *Note,* 14.

V. 34—36. ' By your hatred against me and mine, you
' farther shew your likeness to them' (your fathers) ' in
' dispositions also: so that I foresee, that of those wise
' men which I send to you, some of them you will perse-
' cute, and some you will kill and crucify: and so will
' so far fill up the measure of their sins, that upon you
' may justly fall the punishment, of all the blood of the
' prophets and righteous men shed by your fathers, and
' by you their children in iniquity.' *Whitby.* (*Notes, Ez.*
xviii. 2—4. 19, 20.)—Our Lord here evidently speaks in

his own name, and as acting by his own authority. He
was about to send his apostles and evangelists, as " pro-
" phets, wise men," and " scribes well instructed unto
" the kingdom of God," to declare to the Jewish nation
his truth and salvation: but he foresaw, that the Jews
would put some of them to cruel and ignominious deaths,
and treat the others with great indignity and enmity. For
they would be left to their infatuated conduct, that they
might ripen for the destruction, which the nation had so
long deserved; and that the guilt and punishment of all
the righteous blood, shed from the murder of Abel,
through the different ages of the world, might be laid
upon that generation: because they were about to sanction
and exceed all the wickedness of this kind, which had
ever been committed; and they might justly be made an
example for it to all future generations of the world.
(*Marg. Ref.* e—k. m.—*Notes, Gen.* iv. 3—12. *Luke* xi.
49—51. *Heb.* xi. 4. xii. 22—25, *v.* 24. 1 *John* iii. 11—15.)
—It has been before observed, that there are reasons,
which may induce us to think, that Zechariah the prophet
is here meant. (*Note, Zech.* i. 1.)—But it is objected,
that ' this Zacharias could not be one of the minor pro-
' phets; he living when the temple was in ruins, and
' neither altar, nor temple were set up again.' *Whitby.*
Dr. Hammond makes the same objection.—Now the fact
is, that the altar was set up immediately after the Jews
came from Babylon, (*Ezra* iii. 2,) and the temple was
finished in the sixth year of Darius. (*Ezra* iv. 14, 15.) No
prophecy indeed of Zechariah, is expressly dated later
than the fourth year of Darius: (*Zech.* vii. 1:) but nothing is said of his death; he delivered many important
prophecies, recorded in the latter part of his book, which
are not dated; ... he was a young man, in the second year
of Darius; (*Zech.* ii. 4,) there is great reason to think
that he lived many years afterwards; and certainly some
of his concluding prophecies were exceedingly calculated
to exasperate the hypocritical Jews.—' A second objection
' against this,' (that Zechariah the son of Jehoiada is
' meant,) ' is, that he being slain by Joash so long ago,
' could not fitly be set down as the last of that catalogue
' whose blood brought down judgment on the Jews; it
' being all reason, that beginning so high as righteous
' Abel, the speech should descend much lower than Ze-
' chariah: and it is not easy to give a probable answer to
' ...this.' *Hammond.*—' All the martyrs from Abel to Ze-
' chariah, seems to have been a proverb; and it might na-
' turally arise from observing, that Abel was the first, and
' Zechariah in Chronicles the last eminently good man,
' of whose murder the scripture speaks.' *Doddridge.*

36 Verily I say unto you, ᵐ All these things shall come upon this generation.

37 O ⁿ Jerusalem, Jerusalem, ° thou that killest the prophets, and stonest them which are sent unto thee, ᵖ how often would I have gathered thy children together, ᵠ even as a hen gathereth her chickens under *her* wings, ʳ and ye would not!

38 Behold, ˢ your house is left unto you desolate.

39 For I say unto you, ᵗ Ye shall not see me henceforth, till ye shall say, ᵘ Blessed *is* he that cometh in the name of the LORD.

(Marginal references, as printed:)
ᵐ xxiv. 34. Lu. xi. 21—25. Mark xiii. 30, 31. Luke xxi. 32, 33. — ⁿ Jer. ix. 14. xi. 4. Luke xiii. 34. — ° 30. v. 12. xxi. 35, 36. xxii. 6. 2 Chr. xxiv. 21. 24. Neh. ix. 26. Jer. ii. 30. xxvi. 23. Mark xii. 3—5. Luke xx. 1—14. Acts vii. 51, 52. 1 Thes. ii. 15. Rev. xi. 7. xvi. 6. — ᵖ 2 Chr. xxxvi. 15, 16. Ps. lxxxi. 8—11. Jer. vi. 16, 17. xi. 7, 8. xxv. 3—7. xxxv. 16. xliii. 9—13. xliv. 4. Zech. i. 4. xvii. 8. xxxvi. 7. li. 1. lxii. 7. xci. 4. — ʳ xxii. 3. Prov. i. 24—31. Is. l. 2. Hos. xi. 2, 7. Luke xiv. 17—. — ˢ xxiv. 2. 2 Chr. vii. 20, 21. Ps. lxix. 24, 25. Is. lxiv. 10—12. Jer. vii. 9—14. xxii. 5. Dan. ix. 26, 27. Zech. xi. 1, 2. Mark xiii. 1, 2. Luke xiii. 14. Luke xix. 43, 44. — ᵗ Hos. iii. 4, 5. Luke ii. 26—30. x. 22, 23. xvii. 22. John viii. 21. 24. 56. — ᵘ xxi. 9. Ps. cxviii. 26. Is. xi. 9—11. Zech. xii. 10. Rom. xi. 25, 26. 2 Cor. iii. 14—18.

(*Note, 2 Chr.* xxiv. 19—22.) But here is not the shadow of a proof, that such a proverb was used: and it is worthy of notice, that the Old Testament in general terms speaks of the prophets being murdered; but mentions very few particular instances. In fact, I cannot recollect a single specified instance from Abel to Zechariah, the son of Jehoiada; and but one after him, namely, Urijah, the son of Shemaiah. (*Jer.* xxvi. 20—23.)—This shews, that the silence of the scripture respecting Zechariah, the son of Barachiah, is no conclusive proof that he was not martyred; and the other Zechariah might more properly be called the *first* eminently good man, whom the Jews, as distinguished from the kingdom of Israel, murdered, than the *last*; as we have reason to conclude, that far greater numbers were slain between his time and the Babylonish captivity, than before his days; that is, in Judah.—' When ' Jeremiah introduceth the Jews speaking thus, " Behold, ' " O LORD, &c." (*Lam.* ii. 20;) ' the Targum introduces ' the house of judgment answering, Was it fit for you, ' even in the day of propitiation, to kill a priest and a pro-' phet, as you did Zechariah, the son of Iddo, in the house ' of the sanctuary of the Lord, because he would have ' withdrawn you from your evil ways?' *Whitby.* Whatever the compilers of this Targum meant, it is plain, that a tradition prevailed when it was written, that one Zechariah, the son of Iddo, had been thus slain. Now Zechariah, the son of Barachiah, is repeatedly called the son of Iddo; but Zechariah the son of Jehoiada, is never called so. (*Ezra* v. 1. vi. 14. *Zech.* i. 1. 7.)

V. 37—39. ' He speaketh of the outward ministry : ' and, as he was promised for the saving of this people ; ' so was he also careful for it, even from the time that the ' promise was made to Abraham.' *Beza.*—Jerusalem, which had been the holy city, and ought always to have been so, is here characterized as the cruel murderer of God's prophets and messengers. (*Marg. Ref.* n, o.—*Notes,* iv. 5—7, v. 5. *Is.* i. 21—24. *Ez.* xxii. 3—5. *Zeph.* iii. 1—4.) After this introduction, our Lord proceeds, with immense tenderness and dignity, to declare the miseries, which its inhabitants were bringing on themselves by crucifying him; without taking the least notice of the sufferings, which he himself was so soon to endure. The emblem of " a hen gathering her chickens under her wings" is similar to what is used, with respect of JEHOVAH, in several places of the Old Testament. (*Marg. Ref.* q.— *Note, Ruth* ii. 11, 12.) The hen, having hatched her brood with assiduous attention to her genial warmth, continues to foster them under her wings, and calls them to her for that purpose, when she perceives them in any danger. She exposes herself to the storm in order to shelter them : though timid by nature, she becomes heroick, when defending them from birds of prey : and they are comfortable, as well as safe, under her wings. All nature does not. afford a more apt emblem of the Saviour's tender love,. and faithful care of his redeemed people; but his *power* is also adequate to the confidence reposed in him. He bore the storm of divine justice against our sins, in order to save us from it; and " he suffered being tempted, that " he might succour us when tempted." He calls sinners to take refuge under his tender and compassionate protection; and there he keeps them safe and comfortable, and. nourishes them unto eternal life. He had for ages, by his. prophets, repeatedly invited the children of Jerusalem, or the Jews, to take shelter under his almighty wings, before he came to call them by his personal ministry : " but they " would not come ;" so that their ruin was wholly owing. to their obstinate unbelief and rebellion. (*Marg. Ref.* p.) —Does not this language manifestly shew, that he who used it was truly " the LORD God of Israel," who sent his. prophets to that people?—Many, indeed, during his personal ministry, came to him for spiritual and eternal salvation; and great numbers afterwards did : but the ruin of the nation was absolutely determined; the temple would soon be levelled with the ground, together with the city; and the Jews would be cast out of the church, and. excluded from the blessings of the Messiah's kingdom ;. till they became willing to submit to him who came to them " in the name of the LORD," and to be thankful for his spiritual kingdom and salvation. No doubt but their present dispersion and unbelief, and their future conversion to Christ, are here predicted. (*Marg. Ref.* s—u. —*Notes,* xxi. 8—11, v. 9. xxiv. 1, 2. *Ps.* cxviii. 25, 26. *Is.* lxiv. 9—12. *Dan.* ix. 25—27. *Hos.* iii. 4, 5. *Zech.* xii. 9—14, v. 10. xiv. 1—3. *Luke* xix. 41—44. xxi. 20—24. *Rom.* xi. 11—15. 22—32. 2 *Cor.* iii. 12—16, v. 16.)— With this solemn prophetical warning our Lord closed his. publick ministry, and finally left the temple.—*Ye would' not.* (37) *Notes,* xxii. 1—10, vv. 3. 5. *Ps.* cx. 3. *John* v.. 39—44, v. 40. *Phil.* ii. 12, 13.

PRACTICAL OBSERVATIONS.

V. 1—7.

It has been too common in every age, for those who fill' the highest stations in the visible church, to be strangers and enemies to " the power of godliness;" and to be entirely the reverse of those, to whom they seem to succeed in their sacred functions. We must not, however,. think the worse of the truths and ordinances of God on that account ; but must " observe and do " whatever they scripturally command and teach. Yet we should guard·

CHAP. XXIV.

Christ foretels the destruction of the temple, 1, 2; and the preceding signs and attendant calamities, intermixing counsels and warnings, 3—28; also the subsequent revolutions and miseries, in figurative language, which may be understood of the end of the world, 29 —31. By the parable of a fig-tree, he shews the certainty of the prediction, 32—35. No man knows the day or hour, which shall come suddenly, 36—41. All ought to watch, as vigilant servants who expect their master, 42—51.

---

against their perversions, and not imitate any part of their ungodly conduct: for loose as the principles of such men are, their lives are still worse; and they are far from practising even the scanty measure of duty which they teach. Indeed, if the human inventions and uncommanded austerities, which some of this description enforce, with great rigour, on men's consciences, be taken into the account; they may be said to " bind up heavy burdens, and " grievous to be borne, and to lay them on men's " shoulders:" but their negligence and self-indulgence often evidence, that they disdain to " move them with " one of their fingers;" except as ambition and vainglory lead them to observe some worthless externals " to " be seen of men," and to amuse and dazzle superficial observers, with a splendid superstition; and thus to render appearances of piety subservient to their love of homage, distinction, and authority. How contrary is all this to the humble, unassuming, and self-abasing spirit of Christianity! —He, who is consistently a disciple of Christ, courts privacy for his duties, and delights most to commune with his Father in secret: he steps forth into notoriety with reluctance; and instead of " loving," is pained by, " the chief " places," either in private houses, or in publick congregations; as he is disposed to make choice of the lowest place, and " in honour to prefer others to himself."

V. 8—12.

Who, that looks around him into the visible church, could think that a lowly unassuming spirit was essential to Christianity, and expressly required by its divine Author? Who could suppose, that his disciples were forbidden to be called Rabbi, or Master? To assume, or receive high-sounding pompous titles, to usurp dominion over others, or submit to such usurpation? It is evident that there are " many antichrists," and some measure of this spirit prevails perhaps in every religious society. Much remains to be done, in all parts of the church, before Christians will live together as brethren, the children of one common Father, the disciples and subjects of one common Lord and Master, in the equality of genuine humble love and harmony; and before no one aspires to be greatest, in any other way, than by becoming the servant of the whole fraternity for Jesus's sake. (Note, 2 Cor. iv. 5, 6.) We have all very much to learn, and to unlearn, before we can be completely qualified to form a part of such a company: while we therefore lament the horrid evils, the spiritual tyranny and abject slavery, the damnable heresies, superstitions, idolatries, persecutions, and bloody contentions, which have resulted from the spirit of pride and ambition; let us watch against it in our own hearts: let us aspire after no honour, except that of being accepted by our Master; of being useful to our brethren; and known as " the children of our Father which is in heaven." But let us by no means " call any man Father upon .' earth," or so attach ourselves to any leader or teacher,

as to be more properly his disciples, than the disciples of Christ; and let us believe and follow no man, any further than he follows our common Lord. This well consists with the deepest humility; which must never be lost sight of, if we would be truly wise, honourable, or happy. In proportion as men endeavour to exalt themselves, into consequence and eminence, the Lord will surely abase them; he will save none who continue proud and ambitious; he seldom employs self-sufficient instruments; he will expose to disgrace even his own servants, if they begin to be aspiring, and desirous of honour from men; but he will exalt to real eminence, usefulness, and felicity, those, who are abased as sinners in his sight, and are humbly willing to be despised of men, and to attend to the meanest service of love to his people.

V. 13—25.

It gives great offence, yet on some occasions it is absolutely necessary, to expose the hypocrisy, wickedness, and blindness of false teachers; especially when they have acquired extensive influence, and are eminent for learning, reputation, or authority. In such circumstances, they often mislead very great numbers into fatal errors, and harden them in sin. It does not, indeed, become us to speak in that decisive language concerning their characters, or in that authoritative manner of their state and punishment, which he did, " who knew what was in man," and to whom all judgment belongs. But it is common for such men to lay themselves so open, by their egregious absurdities, or enormous crimes, as to make it obvious that they are " blind guides,"¹ or subtle deceivers, who are going on the broad road, and leading their disciples in the same destructive course.—What discoveries then will Christ make in the great day of account, when he shall strip off the mask from every character, and shew every man exactly as he is!—They, who are appointed by office to guide men into the way of salvation, often use all their influence " to shut the kingdom of heaven " against them: hating the gospel themselves, they instil their proud carnal prejudices into others; and they are most observant of those who seem about to enter, that by reasoning, ridicule, calumny, menaces, flatteries, or promises, they may deter them from becoming the real disciples of Christ. Woe be to such deceivers! they are Satan's agents, and share with that old murderer, in the guilt of destroying immortal souls.—Many enemies of the gospel, nay, professed believers, are notoriously defective in common honesty : for in various ways, there has always been a race of men, who have used religion as a mask, or pretext, to obtain confidence, and to get money. Long prayers, demure countenances, religious phrases and gestures, have gained them the opportunity of " devouring widows' houses; " or of plundering the publick, and practising manifold frauds, impositions, and oppressions; and have for a time screened them from investigation and conviction: but

ᵃ xxiii. 39. Jer. vi.
8. Ez. viii. 6. x.
17—19. xi. 22,
23. Hos. ix. 12. **A**ND Jesus went out, ᵃand departed from the temple: and his disciples came to *him* for ᵇto shew him the buildings of the temple. ᵇ Mark xiii. 1, 2.
Luke xxi. 5, 6.
John ii. 20.

such scandals to all godliness "·shall receive the deeper " damnation," and be more severely punished than robbers of a less sanctimonious cast.—Hypocrites also find their account, in bestowing much pains to make proselytes to their party; while every one whom they win over, becomes more callous in enmity to true religion than before, and even vies with his tutor in pride and bigotry. It is also observable, that new converts to any superstition, or to any sect, are generally more intolerant and vehement, than such as have been brought up in it: for they aim to evince the sincerity of the change, and to vindicate what they have done, and the importance of the contested points, by an·excess of zeal for their new opinions.

V. 26—33.

There is no tracing all the absurdities of " blind " guides," and hypocritical professors of religion. In general, they inculcate a peculiar regard to the *gold* of the temple and to *the oblations;* in which their own interest and credit are more concerned, than in the purity of doctrine, and the due administration of sacred ordinances. They often teach men to trifle with oaths, subscriptions, and solemn engagements; and to disregard important duties, in order to attend on comparatively little matters, which distinguish them from other parties. But they must be " blind guides," who on any pretence, by doctrine or example, teach men to neglect " the weightier matters of " the law," and dispense with the want of justice, mercy, and truth, that they may draw their attention to disputed sentiments, forms, and external observances; and thus " strain at a gnat and swallow a camel." The important matters ought surely first to be attended to: yet the others ought not to be left undone, provided they be agreeable to the word of God.—Too many, who seem to be religious, cleanse only " the outside " by a decent behaviour before men; whilst their hearts are full of covetousness, pride, sensuality, malice, and all uncleanness; their secret actions are infected by these evils, and all their duties corrupted with them. But let us seek to have our " hearts washed " from wickedness, that evil thoughts may not lodge with- " in;" and then our outward conduct will become clean also. Otherwise we shall be like painted sepulchres; and God will at length lay us open, and expose the filthiness contained within to the view of the whole world.—We should, however, at the same time, recollect, that religion must be very valuable, to be thus worth counterfeiting. A hypocrite could not make so good a mask of the appearance, if the reality were not sterling gold, in the secret judgment of men in general. Indeed this appears by the conduct of many wicked men, who hate the living servants of God, yet honour the memories of those who lived in other ages and nations. They are ready to build their sepulchres, or be lavish in their commendation; but not to copy their examples, or to profit by their instructions. Thus, notwithstanding their avowed respect to their memories, and exclamations against their persecutors; they continually testify against themselves, that " they are the chil- " dren of those who killed the prophets;" and their temper

and conduct often evince it to their own consciences: and when the whole shall be made known, the severest language, and most tremendous sentence, of the Judge against them, will appear most just and reasonable; nor will there be any possible way for them of " escaping the damnation " of hell."

V. 34—39.

What a lamentable proof of human depravity does the history of the church exhibit! What men have ever been hated, persecuted, and murdered, like the prophets and apostles of the Lord? And this has been more frequently perpetrated by professed worshippers of God, than by avowed idolaters: so that the guilt of all " the righteous " blood, which hath been shed from the days of Abel," will fall, rather on the visible church, than on the world at large. Jerusalem and her children had a great share of this guilt, and their punishment has been made a signal for a warning to all others. But the Christian church, *so called,* has far exceeded them, the crucifixion of Christ alone excepted; and ere long that generation will arise, on whom the accumulated guilt will fall, of all the blood shed by antichristian persecutors of every name, and in every age. In the mean time the compassionate Saviour stands ready to receive all who come to him, into a state of safety and comfortable rest, as " a hen gathereth her " brood under her wings:" and when even despisers and enemies become willing to receive and prize his salvation, and to say, " Blessed is he, who cometh in the name of " the Lord," they shall see his glory and rejoice in his love. Nothing therefore stands between the chief of sinners and eternal felicity, but their proud, carnal, and unbelieving *unwillingness.* May we then hear his voice, and take shelter under his almighty protection: thus we may pass safe through the trials of life, and the storms of death: and then in the solemn day of judgment, we shall see him " in " the glory of his Father, and all the holy angels," and rejoice in his coming to perfect our redemption, and consummate our felicity.

NOTES.

CHAP. XXIV. V. 1, 2. *(Mark* xiii. *Luke* xxi.) The apostle John does not mention the prophecy contained in this chapter; for it is probable, that he wrote his gospel after the destruction of Jerusalem. (*Preface to the Gospel according to John.*)—Our Lord, having finally departed from the temple, and closed his publick ministry with the awful reproofs and predictions, contained in the close of the preceding chapter; *(Marg. Ref.* a;) the disciples, perhaps adverting to his discourse, came and pointed out to him the buildings of it, as filled with admiration of them. According to Josephus, these were exceedingly magnificent and beautiful, and constructed with the greatest stability; so that it was extremely improbable they should be entirely destroyed, except in a very long course of time: no one, therefore, who was not conscious of speaking with divine authority, would have ventured to deliver such a prediction, as that which follows. (*Note, Luke* xxi. 5.) But the Redeemer, with a peculiar dignity, as one con-

z 7

2 And Jesus said unto them, See ye not all these things? Verily I say unto you, ᶜThere shall not be left here one stone upon another, that shall not be thrown down.

3 ¶ And as ᵈhe sat upon the mount of Olives, ᵉ the disciples came unto him privately, saying, ᶠTell us, when shall these things be? and what shall be ᵍthe sign of thy coming, and of ʰthe end of the world?

4 And Jesus answered and said unto them, ᶦTake heed that no man deceive you:

5 For many shall come ᵏin my name, saying, I am Christ; and shall deceive many.

6 And ˡye shall hear of wars, and rumours of wars: ᵐsee that ye be not troubled; for all *these things* ⁿ must come to pass, ᵒbut the end is not yet.

7 For ᵖ nation shall rise against nation, and kingdom against kingdom: and there shall be ᑫfamines, and pestilences, and earthquakes, in divers places.

8 All ʳthese *are* the beginning of sorrows.

(marginal references)
c 1 Kings ix. 7, 8. Jer. xxvi. 18. Ez. vii. 20—22. Dan. ix. 26, 27. Mic. iii. 12. Luke xix. 44. 2 Pet. iii. 11.
d xxi.1.Mark xiii. 3, 4.
e xvi. 10, 11, 36. xv. 12. xxii. 19.
f Dan. xii. 6—8. Luke xxi. 7. John xxi. 21, 22. Acts i. 7. 1 Thes. v. 1.
g 32, 33, 48. xxiii. 39, 40, 49. xxviii. 20. Heb. ix. 26.
i Jer.xxix.8.Mark xiii.5,6.22. Luke xxi. 8. 2 Cor. xi. 13—15. Eph. iv. 14. v. 6. 2 Thes. ii. 3. 2 Pet. ii. 1.
k 11. 24. Jer. xiv. 14. xxiii. 21. 25. John v. 43. Acts v. 36, 37. viii. 9. 10. Rev. xiii. 8.
l Jer. iv. 19—22. vi. 22—24. viii. 15, 16. xlvii. 6, 7. Ez. vii. 24—26. xiv. 17—21. xxi. 9—15. 28. Mark xiii. 7, 8. Luke xxi. 9.
m Ps. xxvii. 1—3. xlvi. 1—3. cxii. 7. Is. viii. 12—14. xii. 2. xxvi. 3, 4. 20, 21. Hab. iii. 16—18. Luke xxi. 19. John xiv. 1. 27. 2 Thes. ii. 2. 1 Pet. iii. 14, 15.
n xxvi. 54. Luke xxii. 37. Acts xxvii. 24—26.
o 14. Dan. ix. 24 —27.
p 2 Chr. xv. 6. Is. ix. 19—21. xix. 2. Ez. xxi. 27. Zech. xiv. 2, 3. 13. Heb. xii. 27.
q Is. xxiv. 19—23. Acts ii. 19, 20. xi. 28. r Lev. xxvi. 18—29. Deut. xxviii. 59. Is. ix. 12. 17. 21. x. 4. 1 Thes. v. 3. 1 Pet. iv. 17, 18.

---

versant with spiritual and heavenly glories, and regardless of exterior splendour, simply assured the disciples, that "not one stone would be left upon another," of all this magnificent and stately pile of buildings.—When Jerusalem was taken, Titus, the Roman general, desired exceedingly to preserve the temple, either from regard to its sanctity, or as a monument of his victory: but the pertinacity of the infatuated Jews, and the fierce revenge of the soldiers, defeated his purpose. The temple was repeatedly set fire to, contrary to his strict orders and menaces; and at last the fire could not be extinguished: and when it had done its utmost, the residue of the structure was demolished and the materials removed, in order to search for the treasure which was buried under its ruins: so that, in the event, the very foundations were subverted, and the ground on which it stood was plowed up. Thus the prophecy received an exact and literal accomplishment, in less than forty years after it was uttered. (*Marg. Ref.* b, c.—*Note, Luke* xxi. 6.)

V. 3. After our Lord had removed with his disciples to the mount of Olives, where the temple was full in view, they privately asked him some questions concerning the events which he had mentioned: but their meaning is not very clear and explicit. Perhaps they had a general idea, that he would go from them for a time, before he set up his kingdom; that he would at length come in a very glorious manner, according to several intimations which he had given them; that he would then execute the predicted vengeance on his enemies, destroy the temple, terminate that dispensation, and introduce his own glorious reign as the Messiah. Some expositors suppose this to be the meaning of the phrase translated, "the end of the world." (*Marg. Ref.* h.) But it is difficult to determine what opinions the disciples held at this time concerning that subsequent dispensation: and perhaps they scarcely knew the precise meaning of their own questions; for their views were as yet very obscure and perplexed. Some suppose, that they thought the day of judgment, and "the end of the world," would be immediately connected with the destruction of Jerusalem and the temple; and that our Lord did not see good explicitly to undeceive them. Indeed this is not improbable; for the latter part of the chapter is couched in language very applicable to those events; and it is proper for prophecy to be in some measure obscure, till it is accomplished. The general import, however, of their enquiry was, when the events before intimated would take place; and what signs would indicate their approach.

—'Being asked by the disciples, when those things, which ' he had intimated concerning the desolation of the temple, ' should take place; he set before them the order of the ' times, first concerning the Jews, till the destruction of ' Jerusalem; and then concerning men in general, till the ' end of the world.' *Tertullian.* (*Marg. Ref.*—*Notes, Mark* xiii. 1—8, vv. 3, 4. *Acts* i. 4—8, v. 7. iii. 19—21.)

Of thy coming.] Της σης παρουσιας· *Adventus, præsentia.* 27. 37. 39. 1 Cor. xv. 23. 1 Thes. ii. 19. iv. 15. v. 23. 2 Thes. ii. 1. 8. Jam. v. 7, 8. 2 Pet. i. 16. iii. 4. 12. 1 John ii. 28.—*The end of the world.*] Της συντελειας τε αιωνος. See on *Notes,* xiii. 39, 40.

V. 4, 5. Our Lord, in replying, first cautioned the disciples to take heed that they were not deceived: for one sign of the predicted events being about to take place, would be, that many persons would pretend to be " the " Christ," or Messiah; thus coming in his name, and as it were intruding into his office, and fatally deceiving numbers. History informs us of several such false Messiahs, who made their appearance previously to the destruction of Jerusalem.—' Dositheus ... said he was the Christ foretold by Moses; and Simon Magus,... said he appeared ' among the Jews as the Son of God.' *Whitby.*—' In the ' reign of Nero, when Felix was procurator of Judea, such ' a number of these impostors made their appearance, that ' many of them were seized and put to death.' *Bp. Porteus.* These deceivers, promising the Jews deliverance from the Roman yoke, and temporal dominion, drew after them many followers, and excited great insurrections. This exasperated the Romans: numbers perished miserably, and the siege and destruction of Jerusalem were accelerated by these commotions. At the same time, they took off men's attention from the gospel, and occasioned many to perish by " neglecting so great salvation." (*Marg. Ref.*—*Notes,* 23—25. *Luke* xxi. 7—11, v. 8.)

V. 6—8. This next sign related to the external situation of the Jews and the neighbouring nations, when the predicted time drew nigh. Our Lord warned the disciples not to be troubled by the terrible wars, which they witnessed or heard of, so as to leave their stations; supposing that the ruin of the nation would immediately take

ε 8

9 Then ʰ shall they deliver you up to be afflicted, and shall kill you: and ye shall be hated of all nations for my name's sake.

10 And then ⁱ shall many be offended, and shall ᵏ betray one another, and shall hate one another.

11 And ˡ many false prophets shall rise, and shall deceive many.

12 And ᵐ because iniquity shall abound, ⁿ the love of many shall wax cold.

13 But ᵒ he that shall endure unto the end, the same shall be saved.

14 And ᵖ this gospel of the kingdom

---

place. These events must indeed happen, and they would forebode that desolation; but the end of the city and state of the Jews would not yet arrive. Many such wars and bloody contests must take place, both of the Jews against their enemies, and among the surrounding nations; together with famines, pestilences, and earthquakes: yet all these miseries would only resemble the first and slightest pains of a travailing woman, which assuredly presage the approach of more extreme anguish.—An account of the wars, insurrections, tumults, and massacres, which took place in that part of the world, prior to the destruction of Jerusalem, would form the best comment on this passage; together with copious extracts from Josephus and other historians, of several famines and pestilences, which made great havock in many countries; and of terrible earthquakes, in Crete, in Asia Minor, in Italy, and Judea. The latter is thus described: ' By night there broke out a most ' dreadful tempest, and violent strong winds, with the ' most vehement showers, and continued lightnings, horrid ' thunderings, and prodigious bellowings of the earth : so ' that it was manifest, that the constitution of the universe ' was confounded for the destruction of men.' These things can here be no more than hinted at: it suffices to observe, that by the concurrent testimony of ancient historians, and the judgment of modern learned men, the period alluded to was distinguished from all others, which went before and which have followed, by such events as are here predicted. (*Marg. Ref.—Notes, Mark* xiii. 1—8, *v.* 8. *Luke* xxi. 7—11, *vv.* 8. 11.)

Be not troubled. (6) Μη θροεισθε. (Α θρους, *clamor tumultuentium.*) *Mark* xiii. 7. 2 *Thes.* ii. 2.—*The end.*] Τε τελος. 13, 14. *Mark* xiii. 7. *Luke* xxi. 9. 1 *Pet.* iv. 7.

V. 9—14. The persecutions, to which the disciples would themselves be exposed, formed the next sign of the times. (*Marg. Ref.* s.) When these should be excited, many professed believers would be stumbled, and apostatize for fear of suffering: and then to ingratiate themselves with the persecutors, they would become traitors, and bitter enemies to the Christians, and concur in apprehending them and exercising cruelties on them. ' Christ here ' begins to foretel what should happen to the apostles and ' disciples, and to others, before the destruction of Jeru- ' salem : the troubles and persecutions which should come ' upon them, both from their enemies, and seeming friends: ' and what event these persecutions should have on some ' unsound and temporizing Christians, and what deliver- ' ance would be vouchsafed to those who persevered to the ' end.' *Whitby.* (*Marg. Ref.* u.—*Notes,* x. 16—23. xiii. 20, 21. *Mark* xiii. 9—13.) At the same time, many false prophets would appear among the Christians, as distinct from the false Christs above-mentioned, " speaking per-

" verse things to draw away disciples after them." These would deceive many souls, and bring an additional odium on the cause by their corrupt tenets and practices. (*Note,* 2 *Pet.* ii. 1—3.) And, through the prevalence of treachery, injustice, cruelty, and all kinds of wickedness, many who did not openly apostatize, would become lukewarm : they would lose their apparent zeal for the cause, and love to their brethren, and become shy of them, and afraid of shewing them any favour. (*Notes, Rev.* ii. 2—5, *v.* 4. iii. 14—16.) Yet some would continue stedfast in the midst of these multiplied and varied difficulties; and they would be preserved from all real evil, and be saved for ever. (*Marg. Ref.* a.)—Notwithstanding all these commotions and scandals, the gospel would soon be preached through the various nations of the Roman empire, and in the different parts of the then known world; for a witness to them, that the Messiah was come, to be " a Light to " lighten the Gentiles," and " to be for salvation to the " ends of the earth:" and when this should be accomplished, the end of the Jewish church and state would come.—' It appears from the most credible records, that ' the gospel was preached in Idumea, Syria,' and Mesopo- ' tamia, by Jude; in Egypt, Marmorica, Mauritania, and ' other parts of Africa, by Mark, Simon, and Jude; in ' Ethiopia, by Candace's Eunuch and Matthias; in Pon- ' tus, Galatia, and the neighbouring parts of Asia, by Peter; ' in the territories of the seven Asiatick churches, by John ; ' in Parthia, by Matthew ; in Scythia, by Philip and An- ' drew; in the northern and western parts of Asia, by Bar- ' tholomew ; in Persia, by Simon and Jude; in Media, ' Carmania, and several eastern parts, by Thomas; through ' the vast tract from Jerusalem round about unto Illyri- ' cum, by Paul, as also in Italy, and probably in Spain, ' Gaul, and Britain ; in most of which places Christian ' churches were planted, in less than thirty years after the ' death of Christ, which was before the destruction of ' Jerusalem.' *Doddridge.*—' The world and Satan furiously ' raging to no purpose ; the gospel shall be every where ' propagated, and they that constantly believe it shall be ' saved. ...When Jerusalem shall be utterly destroyed, the ' church, so far from being desolated, shall be extended ' to the utmost borders of the earth.' *Beza.* (*Marg. Ref.* b—d.)

Shall wax cold. (12) Ψυγησεται. Used here only.—*The world.* (14) Τη οικουμενη, *habitabilis, id est terra.* (Ab οικεω, *habito.*) *Luke* ii. 1. iv. 5. xxi. 26. *Acts* xi. 28. *Rom.* x. 18. *Heb.* i. 6. *Rev.* iii. 10. It properly signifies the whole *habit able* earth, where *inhabited* or not : but it is sometimes used for the Roman empire : (*Note, Luke* ii. 1 :) and is by many restricted to that sense in this place, perhaps impro perly. (*Mark* xvi. 15. *Col.* i. 6. 23.)

c xxvii. 19. Mark xvi. 15, 16. Luke xxiv. 47. Acts i. 8. Rom. x. 18. xv. 19—71. xvi. 21. 2b, 26. Col. i. 6. d 3. 6. Ex. vii. 5— 7. 10. e Mark xiii. 14. Luke xix. 48. xxi. 20. f Dan. ix. 27. xii. 11. g Ex. xl. 4. Dan. ix. 23, 25. x. 12—14. Heb. ii. 1. Rev. i. 3. iii. 22. h Gen. xix. 15— 17. Ex. ix. 20, 21. Prov. xxii. 3. Jer. vi. 1. xxvii. 11, 12. Luke xxi. 21. 22. Heb. xi. 7. i vi. 25. Job ii. 4. Prov. vi. 4, 5. Mark xiii. 15, 16. Luke xvii. 31—33. k x. 21. Deut. xxii. 6.

e shall be preached in all the world, for a witness unto all nations; d and then shall the end come. 15 When e ye therefore shall see the abomination of desolation, spoken of f by Daniel the prophet, stand in the holy place; (g whoso readeth, let him understand;) 16 Then h let them which be in Judea flee into the mountains: 17 Let him i which is on k the housetop not come down to take any thing out of his house;

l Deut. xxviii. 53—56. 2 Sam. iv. 4. 2 Kings xv. 16. Lam. iv. 3. 4. 10. Hos. xiii. 16. 17, 18. Luke xxi. 23. xxiii. 29, 30. m Ex. xvi. 29. Acts i. 12. n Ps. lxix. 22—28. 1s. iii. 12—16. lxvi. 15, 16. Dan. ix. 26. xii. 1. Joel i. 2. ii. 2. 2 Chr. xv. 8, 9. xiv. 2, 3. Mal. iii. 1. Mark xiii. 19. Luke xix. 43, 44. xxi. 24. 1 Thes. ii. 16. Heb. x. 26—39. o Mark xiii. 20.

18 Neither let him which is in the field return back to take his clothes. 19 And l woe unto them that are with child, and to them that give suck in those days! 20 But pray ye that your flight be not in the winter, m neither on the sabbath-day. 21 For n then shall be great tribulation, such as was not since the beginning of the world to this time, no, nor ever shall be. 22 And o except those days should

---

V. 15—18. "An abomination" is the scriptural term for idols and idolatry, and in various ways these tended to desolate the church: but "the abomination of desolation" here signifies, the Roman armies with their idolatrous standards, encamping on the holy ground, which was supposed to extend to some furlongs distance from Jerusalem, on every side. (Marg. Ref. e, f.—Luke xxi. 20.) This approach of the Roman armies to besiege that city was thus pointed out to the Christians, as the signal for them to retire to a place of safety: and they were exhorted to apply their minds, that they might understand what they read. When this token of approaching desolation was seen, they must without delay escape for their lives, by leaving Judea, and taking shelter in the surrounding mountains: and be so earnest in doing this, that if a man were walking on the flat roof of his house, when the signal was observed, he ought not to go into his house to carry away with him any part of his property; but to go down the nearest way, (which generally was on the outside,) and flee for safety: nay, a man, at work in the field, without his upper garment, must not go and fetch it, lest the delay should cost him his life. ' By the special providence of God, after the ' Romans under Cestius Gallus made their first advance to- ' wards Jerusalem, they suddenly withdrew again, in a ' most unexpected, and indeed impolitick manner; at which ' Josephus testifies his surprise, since the city might then ' have easily been taken. By this means, they gave, as it ' were, a signal to the Christians to retire; which in regard ' to this admonition they did, some to Pella, and others to ' mount Libanus, and thereby preserved their lives.' Dod- dridge.—' These ... admonitions were not lost upon the ' disciples: for we learn from the best ecclesiastical histo- ' rians, that, when the Roman armies approached Jerusa- ' lem, all the Christians left that devoted city, and fled to ' Pella, a mountainous country, and to other places beyond ' Jordan. ...And Josephus also informs us, that when ' Vespasian was drawing his forces towards Jerusalem, a ' great multitude fled from Jericho into the mountainous ' country, for their security.' Bp. Porteus. ' Then the ' Christians fled to Pella, in Peræa, a mountainous country, ' and other places under the government of king Agrippa, ' where they found safety.' Whitby. (Marg. Ref. g—k.— Notes, Mark xiii. 14—23, v. 14. Luke xvii. 33—37. xxi. 20—24.)

The abomination of desolation. (15) Τὸ βδελυγμα της ερημωσεως. Βδελυγμα. (ὰ βδελυσσομαι, abominor.) Mark xiii.

14. Luke xvi. 15. Rev. xvii. 4.—Ερημωσις. Luke xxi. 20. Notes, Dan. viii. 13, 14, v. 13. ix. 25—27, v. 27. xi. 31. The quotation is in the words of the LXX, which accord to the Hebrew.

V. 19, 20. Whatever could prevent or retard the flight of the persons concerned, would increase their peril and calamity. Not only would many pregnant women, and such as gave suck, be prevented from taking proper care of themselves, and of their infants; but mothers during the extremities of the siege would literally kill and eat their own children: so that the blessing of being fruitful, which the Jewish women greatly valued, was turned into the heaviest woe. Our Lord also warned his disciples to pray, that they might not be constrained to flee in the winter; as the inclemency of the weather, the badness of the roads, and the shortness of the days, might retard their course and endanger their lives; nor yet on the sabbath-day, as their own scruples, or the obstructions thrown in their way by the Jews, might have a similar effect.—' The Lord ' shewed mercy to Israel: they should have been carried ' away to Babylon in the tenth month, when all would have ' perished by the winter: but God prolonged the time, and ' they were led away in the summer.' Talmud. (Marg. Ref.— Notes, Hos. ix. 11—14. Luke xxiii. 26—31. Jam. v. 15, 16.)

V. 21, 22. At the predicted season, there would be such tribulations, for extremity, variety, and continuance, as no nation had ever experienced from the beginning of the world, or ever would to the end of it. (Marg. Ref. n.— Notes, Dan. ix. 12. xii. 1. Luke xxi. 20—24, v. 22.) ' For ' indeed all history cannot furnish us with a parallel to the ' calamities and miseries of the Jews: rapine and murder, ' famine and pestilence; within fire and sword, and all the ' terrors of war, without. Our Saviour wept at the fore- ' sight of these calamities; and it is almost impossible for ' persons of any humanity, to read the relation of them in ' Josephus, without weeping too.' Bp. Newton.—' If the ' misfortunes of all, from the beginning of the world, were ' compared with those of the Jews, they would appear ' much inferior upon the comparison.' Josephus. ' Is not ' this precisely what our Saviour says, " There shall be " great tribulation, such as was not from the beginning " of the world to this time, no, nor ever shall be?" It ' is impossible, one would think, even for the most stub- ' born infidel, not to be struck with the great similarity ' of the two passages; and not to see, that the predic- ' tion of our Lord, and the accomplishment of it as de-

be shortened, there should no flesh be saved: but ᵖ for the elect's sake those days shall be shortened.

23 Then if any man shall say unto you, ᑫLo, here is Christ, or there; believe it not.

24 For ʳ there shall arise false Christs, and false prophets, ˢ and shall shew great signs and wonders: ᵗ insomuch that, ᵘ if it were possible, they shall deceive the very elect.

25 Behold, ˣ I have told you before.

26 Wherefore if they shall say unto you, Behold, ʸ he is in the desert; go not forth: behold, he is in the secret chambers; believe it not.

27 For ᶻ as the lightning cometh out of the east, and shineth even unto the west; so shall also ᵃ the coming of the Son of man be.

28 For ᵇ wheresoever the carcase is, there will the eagles be gathered together.

Left margin references: p Is. vi. 13. lxv. 8. 9. Zerb. xiii. 8. 9. xiv. 2. Rom. ix. 11. xi. 25. 31. 2 Tim. ii. 10. q Mark xiii. 21. Luke xvii. 23. 24. xxi. 8. John. r 5. 11. 2 Pet. ii. 1—3. iii. 17. s Deut. xiii. 1, 2. 2 Thes. ii. 9— t 11 Rev. xiii. 13, 14. xix. 20. John vi. 39. x. 28—29. —36. Rom. viii. 2 Tim. ii. 19. 1 Pet. i.5. 1 John v. 18. Rev. xii. 9—11. Rev. xiii. 7, 8. 14. u Mark xiii. 22. Acts xx. 16. Rom. xii. 13. Gal. iv. 15.

Right margin references: x Is. xliv. 7, 8. xlvi. 10, 11. xlviii. 3, 5, 6. Luke xxi. 13. John xvi. 1. y vii. 1. Is. xl. 3. Luke iii. 2, 3. Acts xxi. 38. z Job xxxvii. 3. xxxviii. 35. Is. xxx. 30. Zech. ix. 14. Luke xvii. 24. a xvi. 28. Mal. iii. 2. 1 v. 5. Jam. v. 8. 2 Pet. iii. 4. b Deut. xxviii. 49. Job xxxix. 27—30. Jer. xvi. 16. Am. ix. 1—4. Luke xvii. 37.

'scribed by the historian, are exact counterparts of each 'other, and seem almost as if they had been written by the 'same person. Yet Josephus was not born, till after our 'Saviour was crucified; and he was not a Christian, but a 'Jew, and certainly never meant to give any testimony to 'the truth of our religion.' *Bp. Porteus.*—Eleven hundred thousand Jews are recorded to have perished in this siege; besides the immense numbers who were slain in other parts of the world, about the same time. So that except those days of tribulation had been " shortened, no flesh could " have been saved:" that is, the whole nation must have been extirpated, had these calamities continued much longer. But, as God intended to bring forth " an elect " people" in after ages, of their descendants, he was pleased to shorten those days, and to preserve a remnant of that nation, as a separate people even to this day. (*Marg. Ref.* o, p.—*Notes, Is.* vi. 13. lxv. 8—10.)—Many learned men explain this last clause, of the Jews who had embraced Christianity: but it does not appear, that the continuance of these tribulations, in the smallest degree, tended to exterminate them; indeed it is not known, that any Christians lost their lives by means of them. The Jews therefore, and their descendants, who should in any age of the world embrace Christianity, must be meant by " the elect;" " a " remnant according to the election of grace." (*Notes, Mark* xiii. 14—23, v. 20.)—*Should be shortened.* (22) Εκολοβωθησαν. Κολοβοω, *mutilo, detrunco.* (A κολοΓος, *mutilus.*) *Mark* xiii. 20.—2 *Sam.* iv. 12. *Sept.*

V. 23—25. When these calamities began to take place, the Jews were full of expectations, that the Messiah would speedily appear for their deliverance; and the lower they were reduced, the more readily they listened to every report of this kind : so that many impostors were emboldened to assert their claim to this character, professing to work miracles in support of it. (*Note*, 4, 5.) The artifice of man, and the power of Satan if permitted, can doubtless produce effects which appear miraculous, though they will not bear to be compared with the incontestable miracles, wrought by Christ and his apostles. (*Marg. Ref.* q—s.—*No'es, Deut.* xiii. 1—5. 2 *Thes.* ii. 8—12, vv. 9, 10.) The signs and wonders, wrought by these impostors, would, however, have such a semblance of divine power, as to deceive many, and would be sufficient to impose even upon the elect, were that possible. But, by the decision of Christ, this is *not possible:* " the elect " cannot be fatally and finally deceived; because men and devils cannot defeat the purpose of God, who " hath chosen them unto salva-" tion." Professed Christians in general cannot here be

meant by " the elect ;" for many of these actually were deceived and apostatized. (*Note*, 9—14.) " Their election " of God," and that grace, by which he effected his merciful purposes concerning them, were the security of real Christians; and the same cause would secure from final deception those, whom " God had foreknown" and chosen, but who were not *yet* called to the knowledge of Christ and his salvation. (*Notes, Luke* xxii. 31—34, v. 32. *John* x. 26—31. *Rom.* viii. 28—39. 1 *Thes.* i. 1—4, vv. 3, 4. 2 *Thes.* ii. 13, 14. 1 *Pet.* i. 3—5.)—As the means of preservation, to those who regarded his word, " he told them, " before-hand," what calamities were coming on Jerusalem, and what deceivers would at that time arise. (*Marg. Ref.* x.)—' The delusions of their signs and wonders shall be so ' strong, that the world shall be utterly carried away there-' with; and, if it were possible that the very elect of God ' could be macarried by them, they should also be deceived. ' Were it not more of the grace and mercy of that power-' ful God, who sustaineth them, and that infallible decree ' by which they are ordained to life, than of any power ' and wisdom of their own ; they could not stand against ' these strong delusions.' *Bp. Hall.*—' They will be likely ' to draw many after them, even the most sincere perse-' vering Christians, if it were possible for any deceit to ' work upon them.' *Hammond.*—The arguments against this interpretation, which some learned men have used, go on the erroneous suppositions, that all the elect know themselves to be so ; that there are other methods of " making our calling and election sure," and possessing " the full assurance of hope unto the end," besides vigilance, and diligence in every duty and means of grace ; and that God preserves his elect, without their own willing concurrence, instead of " working in them to will and to " do of his good pleasure;" and so exciting them " to work " out their own salvation with fear and trembling." (*Notes, John* vi. 36—40. *Phil.* ii. 12, 13. 2 *Pet.* i. 10, 11.)—The instances in scripture, in which this expression, " if it be " possible," is used, are not many: but they all imply, that the persons spoken of, at least doubted, whether it would *be possible for them* to obtain their requests, or accomplish their purposes; though the thing might not be in itself impossible. (*Marg. Ref.* t, u, s)

The very elect. (24) Και της εκλεκτης. Εκλεκτος (ab εκλεγομαι, *eligo.*) xx. 16. xxii. 14. *Mark* xiii. 20. 22. 27. *Luke* xviii. 7. *Rom.* viii. 33. xvi. 13. *Col.* iii. 12. 1 *Tim.* v. 21. 2 *Tim.* ii. 10. *Tit.* i. 1. 1 *Pet.* i. 1. ii. 4. 6. 9. 2 *John* 1. 13. *Rev.* xvii. 14.

V. 26—28. The apostles were here cautioned, and in-

29 ¶ Immediately ° after the tribulation of those days ° shall the sun be darkened, and the moon shall not give her light, and the stars shall fall from heaven, and the powers of the heavens shall be shaken:

30 And then shall appear ° the sign of the Son of man in heaven: ° and then shall all the tribes of the earth mourn, and they shall ° see the Son of man coming in the clouds of heaven, with power and great glory.

31 And ° he shall send ° his angels with ° a great sound of a trumpet, and they shall ° gather together his elect from the four winds, ° from one end of heaven to the other.

32 ¶ Now learn ° a parable of the fig-tree: When his branch is yet tender, and putteth forth leaves, ye know that summer is nigh:

33 So likewise ye, ° when ye shall see all these things, ° know that ° it is near, even at the doors.

34 Verily I say unto you, ° This ge-

---

structed to caution the converts to Christianity, to disregard all the reports, which were circulated to this effect; whether they were informed, that the Messiah was in the desert, waiting to be joined by the people, in order to march for the deliverance of Jerusalem; or whether he was said to be in some " secret chamber," among his friends, and about to make his more public appearance. —We find from history that such deceivers actually arose; some collecting followers in the wilderness, and others caballing with their adherents in secret chambers; and that they greatly accelerated and aggravated the ruin of their country.—' Josephus mentions one of these pretenders, ' who declared to the inhabitants of Jerusalem, that God ' commanded them to go up into some particular part of ' the temple, ... and there they should receive the signs of ' deliverance. A multitude of men, women, and children, ' went up accordingly; but instead of deliverance, the ' place was set on fire by the Romans, and six thousand ' perished miserably in the flames, or by endeavouring to ' escape them.' Bp. Porteus.—The Christians, if they had not been fore-warned, might have been deceived on another ground; for they expected their Lord to come, not to deliver, but to destroy Jerusalem; they were therefore reminded that his coming, for this purpose, would not be secret, or local; but like the " lightning, which shineth" at once from east to west; for in his righteous Providence, he would with conspicuous and irresistible energy desolate the whole land. The Roman armies entered Judea by the east, and carried their victorious ravages to the west, in a very rapid and tremendous manner.—Our Lord further added, " wheresoever the carcase is, there will the eagles be gather- " ed together." The Jewish nation, spiritually dead and about to be given up to destruction, was the carcase which was doomed to be the prey of the Roman armies: these were represented by the most ravenous birds of prey, to denote their force and fury; and perhaps because they had eagles for their standards. The history of those times records the multiplied massacres and devastations of the Jews, in different parts of the world; as if they had attracted the destroying sword of the Romans, wherever they resided, or whithersoever they fled for safety. (Marg. Ref.—Notes, Deut. xxviii. 49—57. Job xxxix. 26—30.)

V. 29—31. The language of these verses is suited, and probably was intended, to lead the mind of the reader to the consideration of the end of the world, and the coming of Christ to judgment: yet the clause, " immediately " after the tribulation of those days," restricts the primary sense of them, to the destruction of Jerusalem, and the events which were consequent to it. (Marg. Ref. c, d. —Notes, Is. xiii. 9, 10. xxxiv. 3—7. Jer. iv. 19—27, vv. 23—25. Joel ii. 28—32, vv. 31, 32. Acts ii. 14—21, vv. 19, 20.) The darkening of the sun and moon, the falling of the stars, and the shaking of the powers of the heavens, denote the utter extinction of the light of prosperity and privilege to the Jewish nation; the unhinging of their whole constitution in church and state; the violent subversion of the authority of their princes and priests; the abject miseries to which the people in general, especially their chief persons, would be reduced; and the moral or religious darkness to which they would be consigned. This would be an evident " sign" and demonstration of the Son of man's exaltation to his throne in heaven; whence he would come, in his divine providence, as riding upon " the clouds of heaven, with power and great glory," to destroy " his enemies, who would not have him to " reign over them;" at which events " all the tribes of " the land " would mourn and lament, whilst they saw the tokens, and felt the weight, of his terrible indignation. (Marg. Ref. e—g.—Notes, Dan. vii. 13, 14. Rev. i. 7.) At the same time, he would send forth his angels, (or messengers, the preachers of the gospel, Marg. Ref. i, k,) as with a great sound of a trumpet, proclaiming the year of Jubilee, " the acceptable year of the Lord." Thus he would " gather his elect" into his church, from every quarter, all over the world. (Marg. Ref. l, m.—Note, Is. lxv. 1—3.)—The remarkable appearances in the heavens which attended these transactions, might be alluded to, and the extensive promulgation of the gospel, about the time of the destruction of Jerusalem, was predicted : but the whole passage will have a more literal and far more august accomplishment, at the day of judgment. (Notes, Mark xiii. 24—31. Luke xxi. 25—28.)—Be darkened. (29) Σκοτισθησεται (a σκοτος tenebræ.) Mark xiii. 24. Luke xxiii. 35. Rom. i. 21. xi. 10. Eph. iv. 18. Rev. viii. 12.—Her light.] Φεγγος αυτης. Splendor. Mark xiii. 24. Luke xi. 33.

V. 32—35. Our Lord here answers the former part of the apostles' question, concerning the time when these events would take place (3). In general he assured them, that the approach of them would be as certainly determined, by the signs which he had mentioned, as the approach of summer was by the budding, and the tender

neration shall not pass, till all these things be fulfilled.

35 ¶ Heaven and earth shall pass away, but 'my words shall not pass away.

36 ¶ But of 'that day and hour knoweth no man, no, not the angels of heaven, but my Father only.

37 But "as the days of Noe were, so shall also the coming of the Son of man be.

38 For as in the days that were before the flood, "they were eating and drinking, marrying and giving in marriage, until the day that Noe entered into the ark;

39 And 'knew not until the flood came, and took them all away; so shall also the coming of the Son of man be.

40 Then shall two be in the field; 'the one shall be taken, and the other left.

41 Two *women shall be* 'grinding at the mill; the one shall be taken, and the other left.

42 'Watch therefore; 'for ye know not what hour your Lord doth come.

43 But know this, that if the 'goodman of the house 'had known in what watch the thief would come, he would have watched, and 'would not have suffered his house to be broken up.

44 Therefore 'be ye also ready: for

°ranch, of the fig-tree; and that they would all be accomplished, before that generation had passed away. This absolutely restricts our primary interpretation of the prophecy to the destruction of Jerusalem, which took place within forty years. To this he added, " Heaven and earth " shall pass away, but my words shall not pass away." The performance and effects of his words would be found more stable and durable, than the visible creation; which would at length wax old, and vanish away; but not a tittle of his word would fail of its accomplishment, and the effects of it will subsist to all eternity. This is as applicable to all other words of Christ, without any exception, as to this prediction, and to every part of the word of God. (*Marg. Ref.—Notes, Ps.* cii. 25—28. *Is.* li. 4—6. lv. 10, 11. *Matt.* v. 17, 18. *Heb.* i. 10—12. 2 *Pet.* iii. 10 —13. *Rev.* xx. 11—15.)—'He that shall compare the ' words of our Saviour with those of Josephus, concerning ' the wars of the Jews, cannot but admire the wisdom of ' Christ, and own his predictions to have been divine.' *Eusebius.*—It is indisputable, that the three gospels in which the substance of this prophecy is given, were extant and widely dispersed, a considerable time before the siege of Jerusalem was begun; and that the Christians, believing the words of their Lord, left Judea and were preserved. Probably, none of these three evangelists lived to witness the fulfilment of this astonishing prediction: and some particulars, not here explicitly mentioned, have been fulfilling to this present day. (*Note, Luke* xxi. 20—24, *v.* 24.)

It is nigh, &c. (33) ' I now think it more agreeable to ' this phrase in scripture, to understand ἐγγύς *ille.* " He," ' the Son of man mentioned verse 30, stands at the doors ' ... (*Jam.* v. 8, 9.)' *Whitby.* .

V. 36—41. Some expositors explain those words exclusively of the day of judgment, as being emphatically " that day;" and the context denotes that Christ intended to lead the thoughts of the hearers, and of those who should ever read this prediction, to that solemn occasion: '*Notes,* 42—51. xxv :) but might not this be done, with reference also to the precise day and hour of Jerusalem's destruction? Even this was not declared either to man or angel, so far as we can learn: but the disciples were warned to expect and be ready for its approach, and to mark the signs which had been given them. (*Note, Mark* xiii. 32.) For it would resemble the deluge, in that it was expressly predicted, and some general intimations were given concerning the appointed season when it would take place, with instructions how to escape. Yet men in general would not believe, or take warning: but, being occupied about the employments and satisfactions of life, they would be overwhelmed and destroyed by its unexpected coming; just as the inhabitants of the old world had been by the flood. Even when two persons were in the same place, or about the same business, one of them would be destroyed, and the other escape: as one would be watching and observing " the signs of the times; " and the other carelessly neglecting them.—This is more emphatically applicable to the day of judgment, or the time of death, which is to every one in effect the same thing.—The antediluvians " knew not;" because they would not believe or regard the testimony of God by Noah, that the flood was coming. (*Marg. Ref.—Notes, Gen.* vii. 10—23. *Ex.* ix. 20, 21. *Luke* xvii. 24—37. *Heb.* xi. 7. 1 *Pet.* iii. 19—22.)

The flood. (38, 39) Κατακλυσμος· *an abundant inundation of waters. Luke* xvii. 27. 2 *Pet.* ii. 5. (A κατακλυζω. 2 *Pet.* iii. 6.)—*Gen.* vi. 17. vii. 6. 10. 17. *Sept.—The mill.* (41) Μυλων. A μυλος *mola.* It occurs here only N. T.

V. 42—44. Our Lord, at length, more clearly speaks of his coming to take men away by death, and of his second advent to judge the world. (*Marg. Ref.* b, c.)—The disciples were exhorted to watch, and be on their guard, expecting and preparing for his coming, as they would not know when it would take place. A man, who knew before-hand at what hour a robber would attempt to break into his house, would be found watching and ready to oppose his entrance: but if he knew that the robber would come, and did not know at what hour, it would be his wisdom to watch all night, and no prudent

in such an hour as ye think not the
Son of man cometh.
45 Who then [h] is a faithful and wise
servant, whom his Lord hath made
ruler over his household, [i] to give them
meat in due season?
46 [k] Blessed *is* that servant whom
his Lord, when he cometh, shall find
so doing.
47 Verily I say unto you, [l] That
he shall make him ruler over all his
goods.
48 But and [m] if that evil servant shall
[n] say in his heart, [o] My Lord delayeth
his coming;
49 And shall begin [p] to smite *his* fellow-servants, [q] and to eat and drink
with the drunken;
50 The Lord of that servant shall
[r] come in a day when he looketh not
for *him*, and in an hour that he is not
aware of;
51 And shall [*] cut him asunder, [s] and
appoint *him* his portion with the hypocrites: [t] there shall be weeping and
gnashing of teeth.

h Luke xii. 41—48. xvi. 10—12. xix. 17. Acts xx. 28. 1 Cor iv. 1, 2. 1 Tim. i. 12. 2 Tim. ii. 2. Heb. iii. 5. 1 Pet. iv. 10, 11. Rev. ii. 13.
i xxv. 35—40. Ez. xxxiv. 2. John xxi. 15—17. 1 Cor. iii. 1, 2. Eph. iv. 11—13. 1 Pet. v. 1—3.
k xxv. 34. Luke xii. 37. 43. Phil. i. 21—23. 2 Tim. iv. 6—8. 2 Pet. i. 13—15. Rev. ii. 19. xvi. 15.
l xxv. 21. 23. Dan. xii. 3. Luke xii. 37. 44. xix. 17. xxii. 29, 30. John xii. 26. 2 Tim. ii. 12. 1 Pet. v. 4. Rev. iii. 21. xxi. 7.
m xviii. 32. xxv. 26. Luke xix. 22.
n Deut. ix. 4. xv. 9. 2 Kings v. 26. Is. xxxii. 6. Mark vii. 21. Luke xii. 45. John xiii. 2. Acts v. 3. viii. 22.
o Ec. viii. 11. Ez. xii. 22. 27. 2 Pet. iii. 3—5.
p Is. lxvi. 5. 2 Cor. xi. 20. 1 Pet. v. 3. 3 John 9, 10. Rev. xiii. 7. xvi. 6. xvii. 6. xix. 2.
q vii. 15. 1 Sam. ii. 13—16. 29. Is. lvi. 12. Ez. xxxiv. 3. Mic. iii. 5. Rom. xvi. 18. Phil. iii. 19. Tit. i. 11, 12. 2 Pet. ii. 13, 14. Jude 12.
r 42—44. Prov. xxix. 1. 1 Thes. v. 2. Rev. iii. 3.
* Or, cut him off.
s Job xx. 29. Is. xxxiii. 14. Luke xii. 46.
t viii. 12. xxii. 13. xxv. 30. Luke xiii. 28.

man would go to sleep in such circumstances. Thus it behoved the disciples to watch and be ready at all times; assured, that in every sense the "coming of Christ" would be at a season, and in a manner, not generally expected; and that none could have any well-grounded confidence of being "found of him in peace," who did not habitually watch, and continue patiently in the obedience of faith, hope, and love. (*Marg. Ref.* d—g.—*Notes*, 45—51. xxv. 1—13. *Mark* xiii. 33—37. *Luke* xii. 35—46, *vv.* 35—40. xxi. 34—36. 1 *Thes.* v. 1—3. 1 *Pet.* iv. 7. 2 *Pet.* iii. 10—13. *Rev.* iii. 1—3, *v.* 3. xvi. 12—16, *v.* 15.)

V. 45—51. This exhortation applies to all the professed servants of Christ; but to ministers especially, who are watchmen by office, as well as "stewards of the mysteries of God." "Who then is that faithful and prudent steward," that is constituted over the household of faith, to dispense to each individual his portion in due season; warning, instructing, encouraging, or reproving, according to every man's character, wants, and conduct, by the rule of the word of God, for the honour of his name, and from disinterested love to souls? The servant, who shall be found diligently and humbly employed in this work, when his Lord shall come, will be most happy; for he will be highly honoured and advanced in his glorious kingdom. But if a man, professing to be the servant of Christ, be an unbeliever, actuated by avarice, ambition, or sensuality; if he suppose that his Lord will never come, to call him to an account, or that he shall have time enough to get ready before he comes; and shall thus be emboldened to domineer and tyrannize over his fellow-servants, as a rapacious oppressor, or cruel persecutor; or shall indulge in luxury and excess: "the Lord of that servant" will come to take vengeance on him, when he least expects it; by some tremendous judgment he will cut him off, separating his body and soul; and he will, after death, appoint him his portion with hypocrites, to whom belongeth "greater damnation," and there he will for ever weep and gnash his teeth in anguish and despair.—Whatever reference might here be intended to the case of apostates and hereticks, in the primitive times; luxurious, sensual, domineering, and unprincipled ministers of Christianity are, doubtless, immediately intended—'Mohammed ... mentions seven caverns in hell, 'the deepest and most wretched of which is to be inhabited by hypocrites.' *Doddridge.* (*Marg. Ref.*—*Notes,* xxv. 19—23. *Is.* lvi. 9—12. *Luke* xii. 35—46, *vv.* 42—46. xxi. 34—36. 1 *Cor.* iv. 3—5. 2 *Cor.* v. 9—12. 2 *Tim.* iv. 1—5, *vv.* 1, 2. 1 *Pet.* v. 1—4. 2 *Pet.* iii. 1—4. 10—13. *Rev.* ii. 8—11.)—*Household.* (45) Θεραπειας. *Family; Luke* xii. 42: *healing; Luke* ix. 11. *Rev.* xxii. 2.—*Delayeth.* (48) Χρονιζει (a χρονος, *tempus:*) xxv. 5. *Luke* i. 21. xii. 45. *Heb.* x. 37. *Shall cut him asunder.* (51) Διχοτομησει. (ex διχα, et τεμνω *seco*) *Luke* xii. 46. Not elsewhere in the New Testament.—*Ex.* xxix. 17. *Sept.*

PRACTICAL OBSERVATIONS.

V. 1—8.

The more spiritual our minds are, the less we shall be attracted with external splendour, either in the world, or in the worship of God. If we continually meditate on the revealed glories of his perfections and works; created beauty will feebly affect our minds, except as it leads our thoughts to the uncreated Source of beauty and excellency.—The true temple is built upon "a living Foundation," and consists of "living stones;" and it therefore shall for ever endure "an habitation of God through the Spirit:" but, all other edifices, sacred or profane, will soon be thrown down, and "not one stone of them be left upon "another."—We ought to apply to our great Teacher for instruction, in every matter which perplexes us: but it is more important for us, to be put upon our guard against fatal deceptions; than to be informed of the exact time when prophecies shall be fulfilled, when the world shall end, or when Christ shall come to judgment.—Even true Christians are liable to be drawn into mistakes, injurious to themselves and others, and dishonourable to their profession, by those who come in the name of Christ, and profess to declare the will of God; when they draw men off from attending to his word, and delude multitudes to their destruction.—While we meditate on the extraordinary prophecy in this chapter, with deep conviction of the truth of our divine religion; let us apply it to our edification, by considering the events predicted as typical of far more important transactions.—In the prospect of the approaching season of final retribution, we must grieve, if we be indeed real Christians, to see such innumerable multitudes deceived into a presumptuous hope and fallacious peace. Wars, insurrections, famines, pestilences, earthquakes, which desolate nations, will also excite our

CHAP. XXV.

The parable of the wise and foolish virgins, 1—13.

That of the talents committed to servants of different characters, 14—30; and a most solemn representation of the day of judgment, and of its infinitely important proceedings and consequences, 31—46.

sympathizing concern; yet we should not be too much discomposed at bearing of them; for the Lord is thus carrying on his grand designs, in perfect wisdom, justice, truth, and mercy. (*Notes, John* xiv. 1. 27, 28, *v.* 27.) It is a vain superstition to conclude from such events, that the end of the world is at hand; for they have occurred, again and again, in different ages, to answer some wise and righteous purposes: but we are not competent to know the designs of God, in his mysterious dispensations.— To ungodly men, the most tremendous temporal calamities are but " the beginnings of sorrows:" and the prevalence of impiety is, in fact, a far more awful dispensation than any other judgment.

V. 9—15.

In this evil world, believers must experience, as well as witness, afflictions; not only in common with other men, but many which are peculiar to themselves. If we escape bloody persecution, we must expect to be treated with contempt, loaded with reproach, and hated by the wicked of every description. This sharp trial is often increased, by our being called to weep over such as are fallen, and to tremble for ourselves lest we also should be offended.— Apostates often prove the most treacherous and rancorous enemies of those, with whom they formerly associated: for the evil spirit, which was gone out, has returned with " seven others more wicked than himself; and the " last state of these men must be worse than the first." (*Notes,* xii. 43—45. 2 *Pet.* ii. 20—22.) These things loudly call upon us to pray for ourselves and our brethren; and to dread the least beginning of negligence, in attending on the great concerns of our souls.—But besides the greedy wolves, which are sometimes let loose to waste the flock; men also " arise from among ourselves speaking " perverse things, to draw away disciples after them;" whose pernicious tenets and unholy lives bring still greater scandal on the cause of Christ. (*Note, Acts* xx. 29—31.) When iniquity thus abounds, " the love of *many*," nay, of *most* professors of the gospel, is apt to wax cold; they grow lukewarm and selfish, devoid of heavenly zeal or brotherly affection; and only warm in the fierce disputes and controversies, which they agitate with each other, instead of uniting against their common enemies. Yet, in the midst of all these evils, there is a remnant, who endure every trial, as gold abides the fire; these, and these only, continue unto the end, and are saved, being " kept " by the power of God through faith unto salvation."— Notwithstanding all the efforts of earth and hell, and all the evils which are found within the church; the gospel must be preached in all the world, and with the most glorious success through all nations, before " the end come:" and let us endeavour so to understand the prophecies, which relate to these events, that we may know the duties incumbent on us, according " to the signs of the times," in which we live.—While we remember that the abominations of idolatry, within the Christian church, are sure indications either of approaching desolations, or of spiri-

tual judgments still more to be dreaded; let us learn to separate from the corruptors, and shun all approaches to these corruptions of our holy faith.

V. 16—28.

If the danger of temporal calamities renders it reasonable, for men to leave all and flee for their lives, how proper is it for us to forsake all, " that we may win Christ," and be " delivered from the wrath to come!" He that believes will take warning, and without delay " flee for " refuge to lay hold on the hope set before him;" but the unbeliever, having been often warned in vain, will at length perish without remedy. (*Note,* Prov. xxix. 1.)— If a man would rather save his life, without money or clothes than be slain in going back to fetch them; " what " is he profited, who gains the whole world, and loses " his own soul?" (*Note,* xvi. 24—28, *v.* 26.) We should then avoid even those lawful things, which have an evident or a probable tendency to prevent our eternal good: and we ought to pray earnestly to the great Disposer of all events, ' to keep us from all things hurtful ' to our salvation, and to give us all things that are pro- ' fitable to the same.'—The greatest tribulation, which ever was or ever shall be witnessed upon earth, befell those, who " crucified the Lord of glory," and persisted in rejecting his gospel. " How then shall we escape, if " we neglect so great salvation," as is set before us in his word! The future punishment of unbelievers will doubtless be so dire a tribulation, that all the complicated miseries which have been known on earth, cannot give us an adequate idea of it: nor will the days of that *only evil* be shortened; as none of the elect will be exposed to it, that for their sake it should be mitigated or terminated. Let us then " give diligence to make our " calling and election sure:" then we may know that no enemy or deceiver shall ever prevail against us: and " let us abide in Christ and seek to have his words abide " in us;" that we may be aware of the various methods, which Satan and his instruments will take to impose upon us. If we remember what he " has told us before," we shall not listen to those deceivers, who, having new modelled the gospel, cry out, " Lo, here is Christ! or, " lo, he is there!" when in fact he is to be found only in his word and ordinances, and on his " throne of grace." Such persons, as deal in imposition or pretended miracles, love to perform their exploits in unfrequented deserts, or in secret chambers; for their ambiguous performances shrink from investigation, which real miracles have ever challenged. This suffices to convince the judicious Christian, that he ought to disregard them. In whatever way Christ comes, light, not darkness, is his garment: his operations are conspicuous and illustrious: the establishment of his kingdom will illuminate the earth from east to west, and from pole to pole; and wherever the obstinate enemies of his cause are found, there will the executioners of his vengeance be gathered together, with speed and rapacity like the eagle's.

2 A 7

^{a xxiv.} ^{Luke xxii.—37.} ^{36.} ^{b iii. 2. xiii.²⁴.} ^{31. 39. 44. 45. 47. xx. 1. xxii. 2. Dan. ii. 44.} ^{vi. 1. 8. Rev. xiv. 4.} **T**HEN shall ^b the kingdom of heaven be likened unto ^c ten virgins, ^c Ps. xiv. 14. Cant. i. 3. v. 8. 16. ² which took their lamps, and ³ went ^{d v. 16. Luke xii.35.} ^{36. Phil. ii.15,16.} forth to meet ⁴ the Bridegroom. ^{e 2 Tim. iv. 8.} ^{Tit. ii. 13. 2 Pet.} ^{i. 12—15. iii. 12, 13. f iv. 18. xxii. 2. Ps. xlv. 9—11. 1s. liv. 5. lxii. 4, 5. Mark ii. 19, 20.} ^{Luke v. 34, 35. John iii. 29. 2 Cor. xi. 2. Eph. v. 25—33. Rev. xix. 7. xxi. 2. 9.}

V. 29—35.

Ere long the expected end shall come: then the " sun " shall be darkened, and the moon shall not give her " light, the stars shall fall from heaven," and nature shall seem to expire in convulsions. The tokens of the Saviour's coming will be perceived: he will come with divine power and glory in the clouds of heaven; and " all " the tribes of the earth shall mourn because of him," whom now they despise and disobey. But before he executes his righteous vengeance on his enemies; he will employ his holy " angels to gather his elect " from every part of the earth, as with the sound of a mighty trumpet, that they may " be for ever with the Lord." It is not for us " to know the times and seasons " of this grand event: but we may easily perceive the tokens of our own approaching dissolution. Within the space of thirty or forty years, or probably in a far shorter time, the writer and most of the readers, of these observations, will have done with all things here below, and be fixed in an eternal and unchangeable state. Let this thought induce us to attend more diligently to the words of Christ: and, whilst we meditate on his declarations concerning " the things which " accompany salvation," on his promises, his denunciations, and his discoveries of the final event, respecting the righteous and the wicked; let us still recollect, that " heaven and earth shall pass away, but his word shall " not pass away."

V. 36—51.

After all the warnings and instructions of heavenly wisdom, men in general copy the example of the unbelievers in the days of Noah: they " eat and drink, plant and " build, marry and are given in marriage; " and act in every respect, as if this world were all, or as if they were to live here for ever. Thus death and judgment come upon them unawares, and with as terrible a surprise, as the deluge came upon the inhabitants of the old world: and then, too late, they wish to be with the believer in his derided ark. Even from the same families and religious societies, death is continually taking one to heaven, and another to hell. Men labour and live together, nay, they associate in the same acts of worship: yet they are the subjects of two opposite kingdoms; and at death they are removed to the capital, so to speak, of that kingdom to which they belong. As we therefore know that our Lord will speedily come to take us hence, but cannot know when, or how soon; " let us watch and be sober." To us, at least, " the end of all things is at hand: " and as we should be overwhelmed with confusion, if found, at that solemn season, indulging sloth, or sinful passions, or in the places of fashionable dissipation, and should rather wish to be found in the path of duty, or pouring out our hearts in prayer; so let us never venture on the former, or neglect the latter. " We are not in darkness, that " that day should overtake us as a thief; " therefore, let us as " the children of light," be always expecting the coming of our Lord. (*Note,* 1 *Thes.* v. 4—11)—Above all, the

stewards of the Lord's household should continually be looking to him, to make them wise, faithful, and assiduous in their work; and to enable them to avoid all interested or ambitious pursuits, and worldly pleasures; nay, even all literary avocations, or engagements, not intimately connected with the grand object, that they may wholly give up themselves to their most important work. Blessed will that servant be, however neglected or despised in this vain world, " whom his Lord when he cometh shall find " so doing; " for he will delight to honour that servant, whose pleasure it was to do his Master's work, and seek his glory. But woe be to the presumptuous infidel, the mercenary hireling, the lordly oppressor, or the voluptuous sensualist, in the garb of a priest! The Lord of that evil " servant will come in a day, when he looketh " not for him; " and what will all his preferments, distinctions, and enjoyments do for him, when God shall cut him off, and appoint him " his portion with the hypo- " crites, where shall be weeping and gnashing of teeth ? "

NOTES

Chap. XXV. V. 1—4. This chapter continues our Lord's discourse to his disciples: and the whole of it relates to the general concerns of death and judgment; rather than to the particular events which were coming on the Jewish nation. Towards the close of the foregoing chapter, our Lord made a gradual transition, from the latter to the former of these subjects; and he here more directly enforces the need of constant vigilance, which he connects with the conclusion of the foregoing chapter, by the introductory word " Then." In this respect, " the " kingdom of heaven shall be likened to ten virgins, &c." (*Marg. Ref.* a, b.—*Note,* iii. 2.) The circumstances of the parable were taken from the customs of the Jews, in celebrating nuptials. The bridegroom used to go in the evening to fetch home his bride, by the light of lamps: these were carried by bride-maids, which some say were never fewer than ten; and when they arrived at his house, there was a feast prepared for them and the company.— Christ is the Bridegroom of the church: they who profess his gospel are the companions of his bride, who wait for his coming: and their continuance in this world constitutes the time of their waiting. (*Marg. Ref.* c—f.—*Notes, Ps.* xlv. 13—15. *Cant.* i. 5, 6. viii. 13, 14. *John* iii. 27— 36, *v.* 29. 2 *Cor.* xi. 1—6, *vv.* 2, 3. *Rev.* xix. 7, 8. xxi. 1—4, *v.* 2. 9—21, *v.* 9.) It must not, however, be supposed, that *all nominal* Christians are intended. Those who make a credible profession of the gospel, and act in such a manner as to give real Christians a favourable opinion of them, and so gain admittance into their society, are exclusively meant.—Of the ten here mentioned, " five " were wise, and five were foolish." The foolish had lamps, but " no oil in their vessels," with which to replenish them: that is, they had just as much religion as was necessary in order to make a plausible appearance; but their hearts were not truly sanctified, and stored with holy affections, by the new creating Spirit of God. They

2 And [g] five of them were wise, and
five *were* foolish.
3 They that *were* [h] foolish took their
lamps, and took no oil with them:
4 But the wise took [i] oil in their vessels with their lamps.
5 While [k] the Bridegroom tarried,
[l] they all slumbered and slept.
6 And [m] at midnight there was [n] a
cry made, [o] Behold, the Bridegroom
cometh; [p] go ye out to meet him.
7 Then [q] all those virgins arose, and
trimmed their lamps.
8 And the foolish said unto the
wise, [r] Give us of your oil; [s] for our
lamps are [*] gone out.
9 But the wise answered, saying,
Not so; [t] lest there be not enough for
us and you: [u] but go ye rather to them
that sell and buy for yourselves.
10 And while they went to buy,
[x] the Bridegroom came; and [y] they
that were ready went in with him to
the marriage; [z] and the door was shut.
11 Afterward came also the other
virgins, [a] saying, Lord, Lord, open to
us.
12 But he answered and said, Verily
I say unto you, [b] I know you not.
13 [c] Watch therefore, for ye know
neither the day nor the hour, wherein
the Son of man cometh.
14 ¶ For *the kingdom of heaven is*
[d] as a man travelling into a far country, *who* called his own servants, [e] and
delivered unto them his goods.
15 And unto one he gave five [f] talents, to another two, and to another,
one; to every man according to his

g vii. 24—27. xiii. 19—23. 38—43. 47, 48. xxii. 10, 11. Jer. xxiv. 2 1 Cor. x. 1—5 1 John ii. 19. Jude 5.
h xxiii. 25, 26. Is. xlviii. 1, 2. lviii. 2. Ez. xxxiii. 31. 2 Tim. iii. 5. Heb. xii. 15. Rev. iii. 1. 15, 16.
i Ps. xlv. 7. Zech. iv. 2, 3. John i. 15, 16. iii. 34. Rom. viii. 9. 2 Cor. i. 22. Gal. v. 22, 23 1 John ii. 20 27. Jude 19.
k xxiv. 48. Hab. ii. 3. Luke xii. 45. xx. 9. Heb. x. 36, 37. 2 Pet. iii. 4—9. Rev. ii. 25.
l xxvi. 40. 43. Cant. iii. 1. v. 2. Jon. i. 5, 6. Mark xiv. 37, 38. Luke xviii. 8. Rom. xiii. 11. Eph. v. 14. 1 Thes. v. 6—8. 1 Pet. v. 8.
m xxiv. 44. Mark xiii. 33—37. Luke xii. 20. 38—40. 46. 1 Thes. v. 1—3. Rev. xvi. 15.
n xxiv. 31. John v. 28, 29. 1 Thes. iv. 16. 2 Pet. iii. 10.
o 31. Ps. l. 3—6. xcvi. 13. xcviii. 9. 2 Thes. i. 7—10. Jude 14, 15.
p 1. Is. xxv. 9. Am. iv. 12. Mal. iii. 1, 2. Rev. xix. 7—9.
q Luke xii. 35. 2 Pet. iii. 14. Rev. ii. 4, 5. iii. 2. 19, 20.
r iii. 9. Luke xvi. 24. Acts viii. 24. Rev. iii. 9.
s xiii. 20, 21. Job viii. 13, 14. xviii. 5. xxi. 17. Prov. iv. 18, 19. xiii. 9. xx. 20. Luke viii. 18.
* Or, *going out.* Heb. iv. 1.
t Ps. xlix. 7—9. Jer. xv. 1. Ez. xiv. 14—16. 20.
u Is. lv. 1—3. 6, 7. Acts viii. 22. Rev. iii. 17, 18.
x 6. Rev. i. 7. xxii. 12. 20.
y 20—23. Luke xii. 36, 37. Col. i. 12. 2 Tim. iv. 8. 1 Pet. i. 13.
z Gen. vii. 16. Num. xiv. 28—34. Ps. xcv. 11. Luke xiii. 25. Heb. iii. 18, 19.
a vii. 21—23. Heb. xii. 16, 17.
b Ps. i. 6. v. 5. Hab. i. 13. Luke xiii. 26—30. John x. 27. 1 Cor. viii. 3. Gal. iv. 9. 2 Tim. ii. 19.
c xxiv. 42, 43. Mark xiii. 33—37. Luke xxi. 36. Acts xx. 31. 1 Cor. xvi. 13. 1 Thes. v. 6. 2 Tim. iv. 5. 1 Pet. iv. 7. v. 8. Rev. xvi. 15.
d xxi. 33. Mark xiii. 34. Luke xix. 12, 13. xx. 9.
e Luke xvi. 1—12. Rom. xii. 6—8. 1 Cor. iii. 5. iv. 1, 2. xii. 7—28. Eph. iv. 11. 1 Pet. iv. 9—11.
f xviii. 24. Luke xii. 48. xix. 13, 14.

began wrong, as well as were left without at last. But the wise had "oil in their vessels," as well as the external lamp of profession. (*Marg. Ref.* g—i.—*Notes,* 5—9. vii. 21—27. xiii. 18—23. xxii. 10—14.)

Wise. (2) Φρονιμοι. 4. 8, 9. vii. 24. x. 16. xxiv. 45. *Luke* xii. 42. xvi. 8. *Rom.* xi. 25. xii. 16. 1 *Cor.* iv. 10. x. 15. 2 *Cor.* xi. 19.—*Foolish.*] Μωραι. See on v. 22.

V. 5—9. The delay of the Bridegroom represents the intermediate space, between the real or supposed conversion of professed believers, and the coming of Christ: their slumbering and sleeping intimates the comparative unwatchfulness and inattention, even of many real Christians, as well as of hypocrites, when thoughts of death and judgment are excluded for a season: and it shews that the difference between the two characters in many instances consists more in the state of their hearts, than in their external conduct. (*Marg. Ref.* k, l.—*Notes,* xxiv. 45—51, *vv.* 48, 49. xxvi. 40—46. *Heb.* iv. 1, 2. 2 *Pet.* iii. 1—4. 14—16, *v.* 14.) The coming of the Bridegroom, "at midnight," with a loud summons to the virgins to meet him, represents the unexpected manner, in which Christ calls men out of the world, and in which he will come to judgment; and the surprise thus occasioned to hypocrites. (*Marg. Ref.* m—q.—*Notes, Is.* xxxiii. 14. *Mark* xiii. 33—37. *Luke* xxi. 34—36. 1 *Thes.* v. 1—11.) The conduct of the virgins, when they heard this summons, denotes the earnest enquiries into the state of their souls, and the endeavours to get all ready, to which the apprehensions of immediate death or judgment excite professors of the gospel. This at length discovered the difference between the wise and foolish virgins. The latter, when they came to trim their lamps, found that they were *going out;* nor had they any oil with which to feed them. Thus the hypocrite's religion serves him to make a shew with, whilst he lives; but when he comes to die, and most wants its support and benefit, it goes out, and leaves him to darkness and despair. (*Marg.* and *Marg. Ref.* r, s.—*Notes,* iii. 7—9. *Luke* xvi. 24—26. *Gal.* vi. 1—5, *vv.* 4, 5.) But the wise virgins, when they came to trim their lamps, had oil ready with which to replenish them: thus true Christians, notwithstanding comparative inattention, are *habitually* ready for all events.—The application of the foolish virgins to the wise, for some of their oil, shews that numbers are at last convinced of their ruinous mistake, and earnestly apply to ministers or believers, for their prayers and assistance, in their dire extremity: or it might prophetically expose the vanity of the popish doctrine, concerning works of supererogation, human merits, and priestly absolutions. The answer of the wise virgins implies, that the best Christians know they have nothing to spare, and can give others no effectual help. (*Marg. Ref.* t, u.—*Notes, Ps.* xlix. 6—9.)—*Tarried.* (5) Χρονιζοντος. See on xxiv. 48.—*Slumbered.*] Ενυσταξαν. Νυσταζω, *à* νευω, *capite necto, dormito capite nutans, ...ad somnum proclivis sum. 'Ita enim differt,* νυσταζειν *à* '*καθευδειν, ut hoc de eo dicatur, qui somno libere indulget, gravique consopitur somno.*' Schleusner. 2 *Pet.* ii. 3. Not elsewhere N. T.

V. 10—13. This conclusion of the parable shews the wisdom, and happy effects, of being ready; and the folly and misery of an unprepared state, and of carnal and presumptuous procrastination. The wise virgins, being ready, were admitted to the marriage-feast: but the door was immediately shut; and the others, coming afterwards, were denied admission, and disowned by the Bridegroom, as persons with whom he had no acquaintance. Our Lord then made the same application of it, which he had before done of the subject in the former chapter. (*Marg. Ref.*—*Notes,* vii. 21—23. viii. 10—12. xxiv. 42—44. *Gen.* vii. 16. *Luke* xiii. 22—30, *vv.* 25—27.)

V. 14—18. "The kingdom of heaven," in this respect, might likewise be represented by a man, about to take a journey into a distant country, and entrusting his servants with certain portions of his property, to be employed by

several ability; and straightway took his journey.

16 Then he that had received the five talents went and traded with the same, and made them other five talents.

17 And likewise he that had received two, he also gained other two.

18 But he that had received one, went and digged in the earth, and hid his lord's money.

19 After a long time the lord of those servants cometh, and reckoneth with them.

20 And so he that had received five talents came, and brought other five talents, saying, Lord, thou deliveredst unto me five talents: behold, I have gained besides them five talents more.

21 His lord said unto him, Well done, thou good and faithful servant; thou hast been faithful over a few things, I will make thee ruler over many things: enter thou into the joy of thy Lord.

22 He also that had received two talents came, and said, Lord, thou deliveredst unto me two talents: behold, I have gained two other talents besides them.

23 His lord said unto him, Well done, good and faithful servant; thou hast been faithful over a few things, I will make thee ruler over many things: enter thou into the joy of thy Lord.

them as his agents, or stewards.—Christ, as ascended into heaven, to return in due season to judge the world, is this Master: professed Christians are his servants: " the ta- "lents " represent the powers of body and mind, natural or acquired abilities, time, health, influence, authority, wealth, gifts, privileges, or offices in the church; in short every thing, of which a good or a bad use may be made, or which may be left unemployed. (*Marg. Ref.* d—f.— *Notes,* xxi. 33—39. *Luke* xvi. 1—8. xix. 11—27, *vv.* 12, 13. 1 *Cor.* iv. 1—5. 1 *Pet.* iv. 9—11.) It cannot be sup- posed, consistently with scripture, that the improvement of *natural* powers, by unregenerate men, can entitle them to *regenerating* grace: for all unregenerate men are *carnal,* and " alienated from God;" and therefore wholly indis- posed and unwilling to improve their natural powers, ac- cording to their bounden duty. (*Notes, Rom.* viii. 5—9. 1 *Cor.* xv. 3—11, *v.* 10. *Phil.* ii. 12, 13.) But the sancti- fying influences of the Holy Spirit, producing a holy judg- ment and heart, teach, incline, and enable a man to make a good use of all other things: so that this improvement of talent does not *make men Christians,* but *evidence that they are such;* whilst the contrary conduct evinces the hy- pocrisy of a man's professed faith in Christ.—The five ta- lents given to the first servant, the two to the second, and the one to the third, represent the different proportions in which the great Head of the church, and Lord of the uni- verse, entrusts his servants with various advantages, " as it " seemeth good in his sight." The expression " according " to his several ability," may denote, that every man has that portion, which best suits the station intended for him, in the church and in the community; and which would suffice, if made a good use of, to prove him a useful, honourable, and accepted servant. (*Notes, Rom.* xii. 3— 8. 1 *Cor.* xii. 4—11. 27—31. *Eph.* iv. 11—13.) It should not be concluded from what follows, that they who re- ceive most are always or generally the most faithful: for the contrary is very commonly the case, and the scripture teaches us to expect that it will be so. But our Lord thus shews, that an account must be rendered of the weakest abilities, and smallest advantages, as well as of those which are more eminent and distinguishing: and that it will be no excuse for a man to plead, he had but little en- trusted to him, if he neglects to make a good use of that little. (*Marg. Ref.* g, h.—*Notes, Luke* xvi. 9—12.) For the conduct of the servant, who buried his talent, repre- sents the character of formalists and hypocrites, who make no good use of their abilities, opportunities, and advan- tages; who neglect the duties of their stations; who live to themselves, and are engaged in earthly pursuits; who deem it enough not to do positive evil; and who are desti- tute of zeal and love; and who indulge sloth, or are actuated by envy, discontent, and selfish passions. (*Marg. Ref.* i. —*Note,* 24—30.)—*Traded.* (16) Ειργασατο, *wrought.* Comp. *Luke* xix. 13. 15, 16. Gr.

V. 19—23. " After a long time the Lord of those ser- " vants cometh, and reckoneth with them." Unbelievers either conclude that Christ will never come to judgment; or that event appears to them so doubtful and distant, that it has no influence on their conduct: (*Note,* xxiv. 45—51:) and believers have " need of patience, that, " after they have done the will of God, they may re- " ceive the promise." (*Note, Heb.* x. 35—39, *v.* 36.)— The first servant being called, stated that he had traded successfully with his five talents, and had doubled the sum. This represents the humble and thankful conscious- ness, with which the true Christian will at length reflect on the labours of faith and love, in which he has em- ployed his time, abilities, and providential advantages, in the service of Christ and his church, and which are the infallible evidences of his sincerity. Accordingly, the Master highly commended this " good and faithful ser- " vant;" and assured him of advancement to a post of far higher rank and authority, with immediate admission into " the joy of his Lord," as prepared for his friends, and resembling his own felicity. (*Marg. Ref.* m—p.— *Note, Heb.* xii. 2, 3.) This doubtless relates to the final happiness of believers. Faithfulness, in a lower condition, is, indeed, often here recompensed by advancement to a higher and more honourable service: but hereafter true Christians shall be " made kings and priests unto God,"

24 Then he which had received the one talent came and said, 'Lord, 'I knew thee that thou art an hard man, reaping where thou hast not sown, and gathering where thou hast not strawed:

25 And I "was afraid, and went and hid thy talent in the earth; lo, there thou hast that is thine.

26 His lord answered and said unto him, 'Thou wicked and slothful servant, thou knewest that I reap where I sowed not, and gather where I have not strawed;

27 Thou 'oughtest therefore to have put my money to the exchangers,

and then at my coming I should have received mine own 'with usury.

28 Take 'therefore the talent from him, and give it unto him which hath ten talents.

29 For 'unto every one that hath shall be given, and he shall have abundance: but from him that hath not, 'shall be taken away even that which he hath.

'30 And 'cast ye the unprofitable servant into ''outer darkness: there shall be weeping and gnashing of teeth.

31 ¶ When 'the Son of man shall r

---

and shall reign with their divine Redeemer, in glory and joy inexpressible and inconceivable.—The case of the servant who had received two talents, and the gracious acceptance and recompence with which he met, exactly correspond with the other; and we are thus taught, that inferior endowments and advantages, when faithfully improved, will be as graciously accepted as those which are greater. (*Marg. Ref.* q, r.—*Notes*, xviii. 23—27, *vv.* 23, 24. xxiv. 45—51, *vv.* 46, 47. *Luke* xii. 35—46, *v.* 44. xvi. 1—8, *vv.* 1, 2. xix. 11—27, *vv.* 15—19. *Rev.* ii. 24—28. iii. 4—6. 12, 13. 20—22.)

V. 24—30. The servant, "who had received the one "talent," and had hid it in the earth, gave a widely different account of his motives and conduct, and met with a very different reception. He avowed, that he knew his Lord to be a hard and unreasonable master, who expected more than his servants could perform, or than he had given them the means of effecting; like a man, who should expect to "reap where he had not sown." Being, therefore, afraid of any miscarriage, should he attempt to trade with the money, he had concealed it in the earth; and though it was not increased, yet it was not wasted.—This describes the heart and inward thoughts and reasonings of many decent and plausible hypocrites, and the motives of their slothfulness. They are "carnally minded," and at enmity with the holy character and law of God: they murmur against his providence, sovereignty, and method of salvation: they disbelieve his promises, suppose his service to be perilous, unprofitable, and detrimental: they complain, that he requires more than they are capable of performing, and that he punishes men for what they cannot help: they pervert the doctrines of Revelation to support these conclusions, and confound the want of *inclination* to what is good, with a want of *natural ability.* Thus they excuse their sloth and selfishness, and cast the blame of their misconduct on God; and they suppose their unfruitfulness to be justifiable, because they are not outwardly so immoral as some other persons. (*Marg. Ref.* s—u.—*Notes, Luke* xv. 25—32, *vv.* 29, 30. xix. 11—27, *vv.* 20, 21.)—To these most injurious insinuations of this servant, his Lord answered, that even if the case had been as he stated, he might and ought to have put out his money

on good security, that some increase might have been made of it; and therefore he was, by his own confession, a " wicked and slothful servant." This shews, that such men will be condemned out of their own mouths; as conscious that they might have done better if they would: they will therefore be left without excuse, and will as certainly be condemned for sloth and negligence, as others will be for open infidelity, impiety, or profligacy. ' This ' is not a concession, that the Master was truly so, but ' an argument out of his own mouth to condemn him, for ' not acting suitably to his own hard conceptions of his ' Lord. (*Luke* xix. 22.)' *Whitby.* (*Luke* xv. 31.)—His Lord then ordered the talent to be taken from him, and given to him that had ten talents: on which Christ observed, as he had done before; that it was the rule of his kingdom, to give more and more to every man who had faith and grace, in order that he might be greatly enriched; but that from all others, those things would be taken away which they had not improved, and they would be left under condemnation. (*Marg. Ref.* z—c.—*Notes,* xiii. 12. *Mark* iv. 23—25, *v.* 25. *Luke* viii. 16—18, *v.* 18. xix. 11—27, *vv.* 24—26.) The unprofitable servant was therefore ordered to be cast into outer darkness, misery, and despair. (*Marg. Ref.* d, e.—*Note,* viii. 10—12.)—*Hard.* (24) Σκληρος, ' *durus:* ... metaphorice, ... *severus, austerus,* ' *asper moribus, morosus ... molestus, odiosus.*' Schleusner. *John* vi. 60. *Acts* ix. 5. xxvi. 14.—1 *Sam.* xxv. 3. *Is.* xix. 4.' *Sept.*—Λυπηος. *Luke* xix. 21.—*Slothful.* (26) Οκνηρος. *Rom.* xii. 11. *Phil.* iii. 1. Ab οκνεω, *piger sum. Acts* ix. 38.— *The exchangers.* (27) Τοις τραπεζιταις. ' Α τραπεζα, ' *mensa : abacus ad quem mensarius sedens nummos nu-*' *merat et computat. Argentarius ... fœnerator.*' Schleusner. Used here only.—*With usury.*] Συν τοκω. (Τοκος a τετοκα, *verbi* τικτω, *pario.*) ' *Proprie partus, fœtus:* ... metaphorice ' *fœnus, usura.*' Schleusner. *Luke* xix. 23.—*Deut.* xxiii. 19, 20.—*Notes, Ex.* xxii. 25—27. *Lev.* xxv. 35—37. *Neh.* v. 1—13.—*Unprofitable.* (30) Αχρειον. (Ex a neg. et χρεια, *utilitas.*) *Luke* xvii. 10.

V. 31—33. In order more fully to explain and confirm the foregoing parabolical representations, our Lord next spake one of the most interesting and sublime discourses, which we meet with even in the holy scriptures: and it is

Q 3

come in his glory, and all the holy angels with him, ᵍ then shall he sit upon the throne of his glory:

32 And ʰ before him shall be gathered all nations; and ʲ he shall separate them one from another, as a shepherd divideth *his* sheep from the goats:

33 And he shall set ᵏ the sheep on his right hand, but the goats on the left.

34 Then shall ᵐ the King say unto them on his right hand, ⁿ Come, ye blessed of my Father, ° inherit the kingdom ᵖ prepared for you ᵠ from the foundation of the world:

35 For ʳ I was an hungred, and ye gave me meat; I was ˢ thirsty, and ye gave me drink; ᵗ I was a stranger, and ye took me in;

36 ᵘ Naked, and ye clothed me; I ˣ was sick, and ye visited me; ʸ I was in prison, and ye came unto me.

37 Then shall the righteous answer him, saying, Lord, ᶻ when saw we thee an hungred, and fed *thee?* or thirsty, and gave *thee* drink?

38 When saw we thee a stranger, and took *thee* in? or naked, and clothed thee?

39 Or when saw we thee sick, or in prison, and came unto thee?

40 And ᵃ the King shall answer, and say unto them, Verily I say unto you, ᵇ Inasmuch as ye have done *it* unto one of ᶜ the least of these my brethren, ᵈ ye have done *it* unto me.

---

wonderful, that any person can read it, and yet suppose the Speaker to be no more than man; when there is such a divine authority and dignity in it, as, we may venture to say, could never have, with propriety, been assumed by any mere creature, however exalted. Having previously and by degrees, drawn the attention of the disciples to the great season of retribution, he here spake concerning it in the character of the sovereign Judge. The time will come, when "the Son of man," even he who appeared in human nature, will be manifested in his divine glory, attended by all the holy angels, as his servants and worshippers; and then "he will sit upon the throne of his glory," as the Judge of the world. (*Marg. Ref.* f, g.—*Notes,* xvi. 24—28, v. 27. *Ps.* xcvi. 11—13. *John* v. 20—23. 2 *Thes.* i. 5—10. *Jude* 14—16. *Rev.* xx. 11—15.) On this grand and awful occasion, there will be gathered before his tribunal, not only the disciples, or the Jews, or all professed Christians, but "all nations," all the inhabitants of the earth, being raised from the dead for that purpose: and he will separate the immense multitude, with as much ease and exactness, as "a shepherd divideth the sheep from the goats." For there will not be the least danger of his mistaking any man's character, motives, or state; nor any possibility of opposition, or escape; nor any danger lest any one should be overlooked, or remain disguised before him. (*Note, John* vi. 36—40, vv. 39, 40.)—What less than omnipotence and omniscience can effect such an exact separation of the whole human species?—This being done, he will set the sheep (the proper emblem of his harmless, gentle, useful, and holy people,) on his right hand, in token of their acceptance and honour; and the goats (the emblem of the unholy nature and character of unbelievers,) at his left hand, as rejected and exposed to condemnation. (*Marg. Ref.* h—l.)—*Shall separate.* (32) Αφορισει.—*Divideth.*] Αφοριζει. Αφοριζω (ex απο et ὁριζω, definio, termino. *Acts* ii. 23.) xiii. 49. *Acts* xiii. 2. xix. 9. *Rom.* i. 1. 2 *Cor.* vi. 17. *Gal.* i. 15.

V. 34—40. Then "the King," not only of the Jews, or of the church, but of the whole world, (as our Lord on this occasion called himself,) will address the company at his right hand, as the "blessed of his Father;" his chosen, redeemed, regenerate, adopted, and beloved children, whom he has determined to render most blessed for evermore. (*Marg. Ref.* m, n.) He will call them "to "come to him," that they may behold and share his glory, and concur with him in the judgment about to be given upon the wicked; and that they may "inherit the king- "dom," or that confluence of all honours, riches, felicities, and pleasures, "which had been prepared for them "from the foundation of the world," in the counsels of God's everlasting love and mercy. (*Marg. Ref.* o—q.— *Notes,* 19—23. *Luke* xii. 22—34, v. 32. *Rom.* viii. 14— 17. 1 *Cor.* vi. 1—6, vv. 2, 3. *Jam.* i. 12. ii. 5—7, v. 5.) And in order to shew, that they are indeed the persons for whom this inheritance was prepared, he will next before the whole assembled world make known their good works, as the effect of their faith and love. They had on earth proved themselves his obedient and devoted friends: for they had given him meat when he was hungry, and drink when he was thirsty; when he was a stranger and destitute, they had hospitably entertained him; when in want of raiment, they had clothed him; when sick, they had visited and tended upon him; and when in prison, through oppression or persecution, they had owned him, and had come to enquire into his wants, and to administer to his comforts.—On hearing this, the righteous are represented, as enquiring when they had ever seen him in such circumstances, and relieved him in this manner. For they were not conscious of having done any service worthy of this honourable notice and abundant recompence. To which the King will answer, that "inasmuch as they did it to "the least of these his brethren," (the poor afflicted Christians whom they relieved for his sake, who will be present to bear grateful testimony to "their labour of

41 Then shall he say also unto them on the left hand, Depart from me, ye cursed, into everlasting fire, prepared for the devil and his angels:

42 For I was an hungred, and ye gave me no meat; I was thirsty, and ye gave me no drink;

43 I was a stranger, and ye took me not in; naked, and ye clothed me not; sick, and in prison, and ye visited me not.

44 Then shall they also answer him, saying, Lord, when saw we thee an hungred, or athirst, or a stranger, or naked, or sick, or in prison, and did not minister unto thee?

45 Then shall he answer them, saying, Verily, I say unto you, Inasmuch as ye did it not to one of the least of these, ye did it not to me.

46 And these shall go away into everlasting punishment, but the righteous into life eternal.

"love," and liberal and active kindness, and whom the King of Glory will condescend to own as his brethren,) "they did it unto him." (*Marg. Ref.* r—b.—*Notes*, xii. 46—50. *John* xiii. 31—35, *vv.* 34, 35. xv. 12—16. *Gal.* vi. 6—10, *vv.* 9, 10. *Jam.* i. 27. ii. 14—18.) It is impossible that human language can express greater encouragement to self-denying, assiduous, laborious, and expensive charity to poor Christians, for the sake of our common Lord, than that which is contained in this declaration. We must not, however, by any means, suppose that acts of liberality, from whatever motive, will constitute a man's title to eternal felicity: nor can there be a more fatal delusion, than this too common, but groundless inference from this and a few similar texts. For many who are liberal, humane, and compassionate in some instances, live habitually in the practice of one or other of those sins, concerning which it is expressly said, that "they who do "such things shall not inherit the kingdom of God." (*Notes, Gal.* v. 19—21. *Eph.* v. 5—7.) And as none but believers are "the brethren of Christ;" so love to Christ must be the motive of the liberality and kindness here spoken of. The matter may therefore be thus stated: there is no salvation for a sinner, but by the free mercy of God; no mercy but through the mediation and merits of his beloved Son; no interest in Christ, (at least for those who hear, or might hear or read the gospel, after they are capable of understanding good from evil,) except by faith in him; no justifying faith, but that "which "worketh by love;" (*Note, Gal.* v. 1—6, v. 6;) no love to Christ, which does not imply love to his people, his example, and his precepts; no genuine love to his people, which does not influence a man to do good to them, as he has ability and opportunity, and as he sees them in difficult and necessitous circumstances. But whenever any one is habitually induced to self-denying beneficence to others, especially to such as he thinks disciples of Christ, out of love to his name; he gives an unequivocal proof, that he is a true believer, a justified person, a member of Christ's mystical body. (*Notes, 2 Cor.* viii. 6—9. ix. *Heb.* vi. 9, 10. 1 *John* ii. 7—11. iii. 11—24.) At the same time it is impossible, that this man should be proud of his beneficence, or trust in it; that he should be liberal merely out of ostentation, or to compensate for indulged iniquities, or to atone for former sins: for these things would prove him an absolute stranger to true repentance, and genuine faith, and every evangelical principle of obedience. So that the actions

here mentioned will be produced, as evidences of the excellency and efficacy of justifying faith and the love of Christ; of a person's having been a real believer and one who loved Christ; and to shew that it is in every way proper, the Lord should honour him in heaven, who thus proved himself his zealous friend on earth. (*Notes*, x. 40 —42. *John* xiv. 15—17. 21—24. xxi. 15—17. *Eph.* vi. 21—24, v. 24. 2 *Thes.* i. 3, 4. 5—10, v. 5—7. 1 *Pet.* i. 8,. 9.)—Compassion and good will to men in general, shewn by a decidedly loving and beneficent conduct, and love to enemies and persecutors, for Christ's sake, in obedience to his commandments, and in imitation of his example, are the genuine fruits of justifying faith: but there is a peculiar propriety, in this fruit of love to Christ, shewn in loving his brethren, for his sake, being selected in this concise declaration of the proceedings of the great and decisive day of retribution. Even the poorest Christian manifests the same spirit of love to Christ, by kind actions to his brethren, and to all men for the Lord's sake; which will be also made known at the same time, as the evidences of his living faith and merciful acceptance.—*Prepared.* (34) 'Ητοιμασμενην. See on xx. 23.—*The foundation of the world.*] Καβαβολης τη κοσμου. *Mundi initia, creationem universi notat.* Schleusner. xiii. 35. *Luke* xi. 50. *John* xvii. 24. *Eph.* i. 4. *Heb.* iv. 3. 1 *Pet.* i. 20.

V. 41—46. The Judge next shews the awful reverse.. He declares, that he will address all those "on his left "hand" as "cursed," lying under the curse of the broken law, strangers to the blessings of the gospel, and justly deserving of the final wrath and vengeance of God. He will sentence them to "depart from Him," the only Author of salvation to sinners, and the Fountain of life and felicity to all creatures; for many of them had in their hearts bid him "depart from them, as they desired not the know-" "ledge of his ways." He will doom them "to fire," the dreadful emblem of the wrath of God, as causing the most. excruciating pains, of which we have any conception. This fire will be "everlasting;" which would be an unmeaning addition, if the wicked were not to continue in it eternally. It had been indeed "prepared" originally "for "the devil and his angels," those first apostates from and rebels against God; but as the wicked held with them,. and would not separate from their service, it must be their portion also. (*Marg. Ref.* f—i.—*Notes, Gal.* iii. 6—14. 2 *Thes.* i. 5—10, *vv.* 8, 9. *Rev.* xx. 11—15.)—No doubt. impenitent sinners of every age and nation will then be' Judged; but those, to whom the scriptures are sent, are-

CHAP. XXVI.

Jesus foretels his crucifixion after two days, 1, 2. The chief priests conspire against him, 3—5. A woman pours precious ointment on his head : the disci-ples censure, but Jesus commends her, 6—13. Judas bargains with the chief priests to betray him, 14—16. Jesus eats the passover, and marks out the traitor, 17—25. He institutés the Lord's supper, 26—29 ; and foretels that all his apostles would forsake him, and Peter

chiefly concerned in these previous delineations of the final Judgment, and its process and event; and therefore our Lord represents nothing more, than the ground on which false professors of Christianity will be condemned. It will then be proved against them, that they had no love to Christ, and therefore no true faith in him; seeing they refused to relieve him, when they saw him in necessity and distress, and had ability and opportunity of doing it. ' For so close is the union betwixt Christ and his mem-' bers, that he looks upon the favours conferred on them ' as done to himself, and promises,accordingly a reward for ' them : (*Matt.* x. 42 :) and also threatens punishment to ' them who do neglect, and are injurious to them, as if ' they had been so to him. (45 ... *Acts* ix. 4.)' *Whitby.*— These however, will be as ready to deny or palliate their guilt, as true believers to disclaim all merit in their services: but the Judge will prove his charge, and stop their mouths, by shewing their selfish neglect of his poor disciples, and their refusal to relieve them in their distresses. This alone will be sufficient to evince that they were unbelievers ; even if no injustice or oppression, no open profligacy or secret licentiousness, nor any other gross wickedness should be adduced against them. ' It is not suffi-' cient to preserve us from that dreadful sentence, " De-' " part from me, &c." that we have done no evil, if we have ' been deficient in those acts of charity and mercy we owe ' to the members of Christ's body.' *Theophylact.* Being therefore evidently proved to be under the condemnation of the law, and entitled to no benefit from the gospel : nay, exposed to deeper condemnation for their neglect of it, or their hypocrisy and abuse of their privileges ; they will be left without plea, or the least power of resistance or escape ; and be constrained to " go away into everlast-" ing punishment," whilst the righteous will be received into everlasting life and felicity. (*Marg. Ref.* k—o.—*Notes, Ps.* ix. 17. xxi. 8—12. *Is.* xxx. 14. *Mar's* ix. 43—50. *John* iii. 19—21. 2 *Cor.* v. 9—12, v. 10. *Rev.* xx. 11—15, *vv.* 14, 15.)—The original word is the same in both clauses (αιωνιος) : and he must be blinded by Satan in no ordinary degree, who will risk his immortal soul and its eternal interests on interpreting the same word *temporary* in one clause, and *eternal* in another, of the same verse : and if the *punishment be eternal*, there can be no place for annihilation, or for final restitution. The contrast also between " punishment," and " life," is carefully to be observed. (*Notes, Rom.* v. 20, 21. vi. 21—23.)

PRACTICAL OBSERVATIONS.

V. 1—13.

It is most important for us all, continually to be reminded of death and judgment, and of that discrimination of characters, which will soon be made. Immense multitudes of infidels, profligates, Pharisees, and apostates, are thronging the broad road to destruction : but this is not all; alas ! a large proportion even of those who appear to be followers of Christ, and are externally admitted to ' the

' communion of the saints,' will be found "*foolish* virgins ; " having indeed the lamp in their hands, but no grace in their hearts. With what seriousness, diligence, and fervent prayer, should we then " examine ourselves " whether we be in the faith ! " How afraid of being deceived, where so much is at stake, and so many come short of eternal life ! How earnestly should we seek for heavenly wisdom, and desire to be found upright in the sight of God ; rather than to be approved by our ill-judging fellow-sinners !—It is indeed to be lamented, that whilst the heavenly Bridegroom tarries, even true Christians are too apt to be drowsy and inattentive : yet, notwithstanding all defects on the one hand, and all fair appearances on the other; there is an essential difference between the weakest believer, and the most specious hypocrite. This sometimes appears even here : the unexpected summons of death may throw the Christian into an alarm ; but, proceeding without delay to trim his lamp, the grace which before lay almost dormant, shines forth more bright; and his serious self-examination and fervent prayer bring humility, faith, hope, patience, love, and every holy affection into lively exercise ; so that all around perceive him to be *ready*, and " meet to be a partaker of the " inheritance of the saints in light." On the other hand, the mere professor, in such circumstances, often detects his consciousness of hypocrisy, and impresses the minds of beholders with a gloomy fear, that " his lamp is going " out," and about to be extinguished in utter darkness. We may compassionate such persons, but we can give them little help : we should direct them to him, who sells all the blessings of salvation " without money and without " price : " but the hour is unseasonable, and the time is short ; nor can they well know that their prayers are not the dictates of mere selfishness, and their repentance constrained and insincere. How dreadful then will be the case of those, who do not seek " the things which accom-" pany salvation," till the time is past ! who do not knock, till the door is finally closed ! But, however it may appear at death, assuredly no one will partake of the marriage-supper of the Lamb, who has not in this world " washed " his robes, and made them white " in his atoning blood ; and who is not a partaker of his sanctifying Spirit. Let us then make no delay, but be earnest in our preparation for the feast ; and let us ever be upon our watch, for " we " know not either the day or the hour, when our Lord " cometh."

V. 14—30.

In some respects, " the kingdom of heaven is like unto " a man travelling into a far country, and delivering his " goods unto his own servants." Whatever any one possesses is entrusted to him by the great Lord of all, who will at length call him to an account for the use which he has made of it.' The holy law requires us to devote the whole, in perfect love, to the service of God, and to the benefit of our neighbour ; and denounces its awful curse on every one, who in any instance, or at any time, fails

deny him, 30—35. His agony and prayer in the garden, 36—46. He is betrayed and apprehended, 47—50. A disciple cuts off the high priest's servant's ear; but Jesus forbids all resistance, 51—56. He is arraigned before Caiaphas, falsely accused, condemned, and treated with insult and indignity, 57—68. Peter thrice denies him, with peculiar aggravations; but going out he weeps bitterly, 69—75.

of so doing: but the gospel inwardly teaches and disposes the true believer, to attempt this sincerely, though feebly ; from the time when he begins in any degree to experience " the joy of God's salvation." He believes his word respecting the future judgment and its important consequences; and he gives implicit credit to his promises and threatenings. By faith he perceives his danger as a sinner, and fears and flees from it ; and at the same time he discovers his Refuge, and in hope repairs to it. Having obtained peace with God, and peace of conscience, through the atoning blood of Christ; his " faith works by love," and his language is, " What shall I render to the LORD, " for all his benefits?" This humble love and gratitude, uniting with hatred of sin, contempt of the world, love to the brethren, and compassion for perishing sinners, impels him to devote himself, and all his abilities and advantages, to the service of Christ; and to do good, in his church and in the world, according to his opportunity, and in exact proportion to the vigour of his faith and hope. This obedience distinguishes the real disciple of Christ from every other man: the self-righteous Pharisee, the self-wise infidel, the careless sinner, the formal professor of the gospel, are alike unacquainted with these evangelical principles of devoted diligence, in the service of a crucified Saviour.—It is the real Christian's liberty, privilege, honour, interest, and satisfaction, to be employed, as the Redeemer's servant, and as his instrument in promoting his glory and the benefit of his people: and, " the love of Christ even " constrains him to live no longer to himself, but to him " that died for him, and rose again." (Note, 2 Cor. v. 13—15.) According to the number of his talents, he will become a blessing to others, by his example, influence, conversation, and labours ; by the use, which he makes of his time, money, and abilities; by his relative conduct in his family ; and by serving the Lord, as a minister, magistrate, or private Christian: and whether he has had five talents, two, one, or only a small portion of one ; " he will not " be ashamed, but have confidence before Christ at his " coming." Nay, he may now humbly " rejoice in the " testimony of his conscience ;" and, giving the Lord all the glory, he may look forward to death and judgment, assured of being then received with " Well done, good " and faithful servant ; thou hast been faithful over a few " things, I will make thee ruler over many things, enter " thou into the joy of thy Lord." " Let us not then be " weary of well-doing: for in due season we shall reap, if " we faint not."—But let every one dread the doom of the unprofitable servant: for it is not enough, that men do not spend their Lord's goods upon their lusts, or waste their time and talents in sin ; even those, who " bury them " in the earth," will be left without excuse. Whatever they may profess, they dislike the character and word of the Lord ; they count his service irksome and unprofitable ; they dare not trust his promise, and they are dissatisfied with his providence; and, because they may not have the pre-eminence, or take the lead, and manage things in their own way, they sit down in sullen discon-

tent; and will do nothing, because they cannot do every thing. But many of those excuses and objections, which pass current here, will be refuted and silenced at last; and every unfruitful professor will be condemned out of his own mouth, and consigned to " outer darkness, where is " weeping and gnashing of teeth." For whatever else men may possess, who are destitute of sanctifying grace ; they will soon be deprived of it, and have nothing but the additional condemnation of having been ungrateful for so many mercies. But the most indigent believer is rich, and shall have abundance, and his felicity will be for ever increasing. Let us not then envy sinners, or covet any of their perishing and dangerous possessions.

V. 31—40.

Our gracious Redeemer once " humbled himself and ' " became obedient unto death, even the death of the " cross : " but now he reigns the Sovereign of the world ; and ere long he shall appear in glory, attended by " all " the holy angels" to judge the nations of the earth. Before his tribunal we must all appear ; and every effort to escape, to conceal, to resist, or to prevaricate, will then be entirely unavailing. With infinite ease and exactness, he will " bring to light the hidden things of darkness," and develope the secrets of every heart; he will shew the real motive of every action, and the true character of every individual ; and he will infallibly separate his true disciples, from all other men in the world. (Note, 1 Cor. iv. 3—5.) In that decisive hour, " the King of glory" will not be ashamed to own, as " his brethren, his sisters, or " his mother," the least and meanest of his chosen flock. And, if we would possess a good hope, that he will then address us as " the blessed of his Father," and call us to him, that we may " inherit the kingdom prepared for us " from the beginning of the world;" we must now recognize our Saviour and future Judge, as disguised under the mean attire of these his beloved brethren. When we see a believer, hungry, thirsty, a stranger, or in want of proper clothing; we should suppose that our Saviour himself stands before us, requires us to own our relation to him, and calls upon us to give him food or raiment, or to provide him lodging or entertainment: and we should ask ourselves, whether we can find in our hearts to drive him from our door? (Notes, Cant. v. 2, 3.) And when we hear of pious persons being sick, or in prison, and wanting advice, attendance, or other relief; we should suppose that Jesus is in these circumstances, and sends to us by name to come and " minister unto him." Let us then, renounce our own ease, interest, convenience, indulgence, and decoration: that we may shew our ardent gratitude for his salvation, by abounding in this " work of faith, and labour " of love:" and should we even be mistaken in the character of those, for whom we thus deny ourselves, and love to Christ ; he will certainly accept and recompense our services. (Note, x. 40—42.)—But alas! how little do we see of " these fruits of the Spirit" even among professed Christians! Who does not think, that he should

AND it came to pass, [a] when Jesus had finished all these sayings, he said unto his disciples,

2 Ye [b] know that after two days is [c] *the feast of* the passover, and the Son of man is [d] betrayed to be crucified.

3 ¶ Then [e] assembled together the chief priests, and the scribes, and the elders of the people, unto [f] the palace of the high priest, who was called [g] Caiaphas,

4 And consulted that they might take Jesus [h] by subtlety, and kill *him*.

5 But they said, [i] Not on the feast-day, [k] lest there be an uproar among the people.

---

have counted it an honour, to have entertained Christ when on earth? But how few are willing to *retrench* greatly from their unnecessary expenses, to relieve these his representatives and brethren? Many however will even part with their money, who will not subject themselves to the hardship and inconvenience of visiting the sick, and such as are in prisons, or other recesses of misery and distress; by which means their bounty is distributed at random, does comparatively little good, and will often be shewn to spring, rather from an easy temper, than from a disinterested self-denying love of others for the sake of Christ. But "while we have time, let us" lay ourselves out "in doing good to all men, especially to them that "are of the household of faith:" and, even if we have but little in our power, let us endeavour by that little to shew our good-will, and what we would do if we had more. —They, who most abound in good works, will be the least apt to glory in them: nay, they will be, as it were, surprised at the gracious mention, which will at last be made of them. Yet those services, which the humble believer thought nothing of at the time, and soon entirely forgot, as well as those which were concealed from men, will all be brought to light, and graciously recompensed by our King: not a crust of bread, or a cup of water, given for his sake to a poor brother, shall pass unnoticed; but every instance of this kind will be adduced as an evidence, that the giver was a faithful friend, and a loyal subject, to "the Lord of glory," and a proper person to be numbered with those, whom "he delighteth to honour," and to bless. (*Notes*, x. 40—42. Heb. vi. 9, 10.)

V. 41—46.

What tongue can describe, what words can express, or even convey a faint idea, of the horror and despair of the wicked, when placed at the left hand of their omnipotent and omniscient Judge! While conscious of their guilt, and calling in vain " on the rocks and mountains to fall " on them," they shall behold his awful countenance clouded with an indignant frown; and hear his mouth, which used to invite the weary sinner to come to him, sternly say to them "Depart, ye cursed, into everlasting "fire, prepared for the devil and his angels!" Then all their works will be produced, to demonstrate the justice of the tremendous sentence: and their omissions alone, and selfish neglect of poor Christians, whom they ought to have loved "with a pure heart fervently," for the Lord's sake, whilst they were indulging themselves, or heaping up riches, will prove them unbelievers, and deprive them of all relief from the mercy of the gospel. They may avow, that they would gladly have ministered unto Christ, had they seen him in his humiliation; but, inasmuch as they refused to "do it to his brethren, they "did it not to him." If this alone will prove a man, otherwise moral and decent, to be an enemy of Christ, a "child of the devil, and "a vessel of wrath fitted for de-"struction; where will oppressors, persecutors, blasphem-"ers, and profligates appear?" Yet all resistance to the power of the Judge will be hopeless, even that of united thousands of millions, combined with the devil and his angels: every plea will be refused, "every mouth will be "stopped: the wicked shall be silent in darkness;" "the "wicked shall be turned into hell, and all the nations that "forget God." But the reflection is too tremendous to be dwelt upon. Let us then take warning, flee from the wrath to come, and seek that faith in Christ, which "work-"eth by love" of him and his people and cause, and by obedience to his commandments; that we may abound in all the fruits of righteousness here, and that, when "the "wicked shall go away into everlasting punishment," we may be ' numbered with his saints in glory everlasting.'

NOTES.

CHAP. XXVI. V. 1, 2. Our Lord had closed his public ministry, when he left the temple : he had afterwards given his disciples many important warnings and instructions; and after the sublime representation, which he had made of his future coming to judgment, he informed them of the immediate approach of his sufferings. (*Notes*, xxiii. 37—39, *v.* 39. xxiv. xxv.) After two days the feast of the passover would be celebrated, and then he should be betrayed into the hands of his enemies, and put to death by crucifixion. (*Marg. Ref.* c, d.—*Notes*, 20—24.) He had all along a perfect knowledge of the variety and intenseness of his approaching sufferings, though he met them with the most entire calmness and serenity.—This seems to have been peculiar to him : none of the prophets or apostles knew beforehand, what they should be called to suffer. Even holy Paul says, " I go up to Jerusalem, not know-" ing the things which shall befall me there."—This peculiarity should be carefully noted, when the intrepid and cool courage and resolution of Jesus, in the complete foreknowledge of his unparalleled sufferings, is the subject of our meditation. (*Notes, Acts* xx. 22—24. 1 *Pet.* iv. 1, 2. 2 *Pet.* i. 12—15.)—The contrast between the words of our Lord concerning himself, as "the Son of man," in these verses, and those in the foregoing chapter, "The "Son of man shall come in his glory," is peculiarly worthy of our observation. (*Note*, xxv. 31—33.)

V. 3—5. The members of the Jewish Sanhedrim, the grand council of the nation, being met together at the

2 B 3

6 ¶ Now when Jesus was [1] in Bethany, in the house of [m] Simon the leper, 7 There [n] came unto him a woman having an alabaster-box of [o] very precious ointment, and poured it on his head as he sat at meat. 8 But when his disciples saw it, [p] they had indignation, saying, [q] To what purpose is this waste? 9 For [r] this ointment might have been sold for much, and given to the poor. 10 When Jesus understood it, he said unto them, [s] Why trouble ye the woman? for she hath wrought [t] a good work upon me. 11 For [u] ye have the poor always with you, [x] but me ye have not always. 12 For [y] in that she hath poured this ointment on my body, she did it for my burial. 13 Verily I say unto you, [z] Wheresoever this gospel shall be preached in the whole world, [a] there shall also this, that this woman hath done, be told for a memorial of her.

l xxi. 17. Mark xi. 12. John xi. 1, 2. xii. 1, 2.
m Mark xiv. 3.
n John xii. 2, 3.
o Ex. xxx. 23. 3X. Ps. cxxxiii. 2. Ec. ix. 8. x.
l. Cant. i. 3. iv. 10, 14. Luke vii. 37, 38, 46.
p Sam. xvii. 28.
q 2 Ec. iv. 4. John xii. 4, 5. xiii. v. 17. Am. vii. 5. Hag. i. 3.
r Josh. vii. 20, 21. 1 Sam. xv. 9. 21. 2 Kings v. 20. Mark xiv. 5. John xiii. 8, 6. 1 Pet. ii. 18.
s Job xiii. Mark xiv. 6. Luke vii. 44—50. Gal. i. 7. v. 12. vi. 17.
t Neb. ii. 18. 2 Cor. ix. 8. Eph. ii. 10. Col. i. 10. 2 Thes. ii. 17. 1 Tim. iii. 1. v. 10. 2 Tim. ii. 21. Tit. i. 16. ii. 14. iii. 8, 14. Heb. xiii. 21. 1 Pet. ii. 12.
u xxv. 34—40. 42—45. Deut. xv. 11. Mark xiv. 7. John xii. 8. Gal. ii. 10. 1 John iii. 17.
x viii. 20. xxvii. 30. John xiii. 33. xiv. 19. xvi. 5. 28. xvii. 11. Acts iii. 21.
y 2 Chr. xvi. 14. Mark xiv. 8. John xix. 39, 40.
z xxiv. 14. xxviii. 19. Ps. xcvii. 2, 8. Mark xiv. 9. Luke xxiv. 47. Rom. x. 18. xv. 19. Col. i. 6. 23. 1 Tim. ii. 6. Rev. xiv. 6.
a 1 Sam. ii. 30. Ps. cxii. 6. Mark xiv. 9. 2 Cor. x. 18. Heb. vi. 10.
xvii. 1. Luke xxiii. 56, xxiv. 10. Mark xiv. 6.

palace of the high priest, consulted how they might get Jesus into their power, in order to put him to death. Having deliberated on the subject, they agreed to attempt it by subtlety, or contrivance, and not by open force: and concluded that it would be better to defer it till after the feast of the passover; lest the people, whom they supposed to favour him, should make an insurrection for his rescue, if he were apprehended, while such numbers from all quarters were assembled in the city (Marg. Ref.) But it pleased God to defeat this intention: as it was proper that Christ, the true paschal Lamb, should be sacrificed at that season; and that his death and expiation should be rendered the more extensively known.—'Mai-'monides saith, it was the custom among the Jews to 'punish those who rebelled against the sentence of the 'judge, or the high priest, or were notoriously criminal, 'at one of the three feasts, because then only by reason 'of the publick congress of the people, all might hear and 'fear. (Deut. xvii. 12, 13.) From this received custom 'the fathers of the Sanhedrim seem willing to recede, for 'fear of the multitude; but having so fair an offer 'made by Judas, they embrace that season.' Whitby. 'God himself, and not men, appointed the time in which 'Christ should be crucified.' Beza. (Note, Ps. lxxvi. 10.)

Uproar. (5) Θορυβος. xxvii. 24. Mark v. 38. xiv. 2. Acts xx. 1. xxi. 34. xxiv. 18.—Θορυβεω. Perturbo. Acts xvii. 5.

V. 6—13. St. John fixes the date of this transaction to six days before the passover: (John xii. 1:) and as it is utterly improbable, that it should have occurred twice in so short a time, and with exactly the same circumstances, we must conclude that the other evangelists have related it, out of the order of time in which it happened.—Our Lord was at this time entertained at Bethany, by "Simon "the leper," who had probably been cleansed by him. But Lazarus was a guest, and Martha one who waited on them. Mary, the sister of Lazarus, doubtless was the woman, who anointed him; and the late extraordinary favour conferred on her, in the resurrection of her beloved brother, excited those fervent and grateful affections which influenced her conduct. Having therefore in her possession an alabaster-box of very costly and fragrant ointment, such as was used about the persons of the wealthy, according to the custom of those days; she came in before the company, broke off the top of the box, and poured the ointment on the head of Christ as he sat at meat, anointing his feet also with part of it; so that the house was "filled with the odour of the ointment." (Marg. Ref. l—o.—Note, Mark xiv. 3—9, v. 3.) When the disciples saw this action, they were highly displeased, and enquired, what end could be answered by this "waste of the oint-"ment," which might have been sold for a considerable sum of money; and this would have done much good, if given in alms to the poor. We find that Judas, from bad motives, started the objection; yet it is probable that the other disciples joined in it, in a manner, which was not only discouraging to Mary, but highly disrespectful to Christ. (Note, John xii. 1—8, vv. 3—6.) But he, knowing the simple, humble, thankful, fervent love, and reverential regard to him, from which this action sprang, was pleased to vindicate her from these censures. She had rightly judged, that nothing could be too costly to be used in honouring him; nor any thing wasted which was spent in his service: and, though in general his disciples must shew their love to him by doing good to men, especially their Christian brethren for his sake; (Note, xxv. 34—41;) yet the present circumstances justified a deviation. Why then did they trouble one, who had done a good and acceptable work, in thus honouring him by such means as were in her power, when others were about to betray, insult, and most cruelly use him? They would always have poor persons, whom they might relieve whenever they would: but his personal presence was not long to be continued with them. And, though when Mary knew it not, he was about to be put to death; and this might be regarded as the anointing for his burial, performed a little beforehand; (for they would have no opportunity of performing it afterwards;) in which last expenses, as a testimony of respect to beloved friends, men were not used to be parsimonious. He further assured the disciples, that this action was so acceptable to him, that he would take care it should be reported, as a memorial of her faith and love, to all future ages, and in all places where his gospel should ever be preached.—This may be considered as a most remarkable prophecy: he would influence the evangelists to record this incident, which might appear trivial, among the important actions of his publick life; and take care that it should never be erased, to the end of time. (Marg. Ref. p—a.—Notes, Mark xiv. 3—9, vv. 4—9. John xii. 1—8. vv. 7, 8.)

14 ¶ Then ^b one of the twelve, called ^c Judas Iscariot, went unto the chief priests,

15 And said *unto them,* ^d What will ye give me, and I will deliver him unto you? And they covenanted with him for ^e thirty pieces of silver.

16 And from that time ^f he sought opportunity to betray him.

17 ¶ Now ^g the first *day* of the *feast of* unleavened bread, the disciples came to Jesus, saying unto him,

^h Where wilt thou that we prepare for thee to eat the passover?

18 And he said, ⁱ Go into the city to such a man, and say unto him, ^k The Master saith, ^l My time is at hand; I will keep the passover at thy house with my disciples.

19 And ^m the disciples did as Jesus had appointed them; ⁿ and they made ready the passover.

20 ¶ Now ^o when the even was come, ^p he sat down with the twelve.

Very precious. (7) Βαρυτιμα. Εx βαρυς, *gravis,* et τιμη, *pretium.* Used here only in N. T.—Πολυτελης, *Mark* xiv. 3. Πολυτιμα, *John* xii. 3.—*Waste.* (8) Απωλεια, *destruction, perdition. Mark* xiv. 4. *John* xvii. 12.—*Why trouble ye?* (10) Τι κοπους παρεχετε· *Mark* xiv. 6. *Gal.* vi. 17.—Κοπος, 'abundant labour: ... *fatigatio ex labore:* ... *molestia.'* Leigh. 2 *Cor.* xi. 27. 1 *Thes.* i. 3. iii. 5. *Rev.* ii. 2.

Me ye have not always. (11) ' These words destroy the ' doctrine of transubstantiation: for if Christ were, as to ' soul, body, and divinity, truly in the *host;* that being ' always present with them of Rome, they would have ' Christ always with them.' *Whitby.*—*For my burial.* (12) Προς το ενταφιασαι με.—Εις τον ενταφιασμον. *Mark* xiv. 8. Εις την ημεραν τα ενταφιασμα μα. *John* xii. 7. 'Ενταφιαζειν *est* ' *preparare ad sepulturam; sive involvendo, ... sive ungendo.* ' *Non est idem quod,* θαπτω.' *Leigh. John* xix. 40. Not elsewhere N. T.—*For a memorial.* (13) Εις μνημοσυνον. *Mark* xiv. 9. *Acts* x. 4.—' *Non simpliciter significat memo-* ' *riam; sed pignus aliquod, aut monumentum, quod amicus* ' *apud amicum relinquit, quod illum sui commonefaciat.'* Erasmus *in* Leigh.

V. 14—16. Judas, notwithstanding his plausible conduct and apostolical office, was a hypocrite, and a covetous dishonest man. (*Marg. Ref.* b, c.—*Notes, Mark* xiv. 10, 11. *John* vi. 66—71, *vv.* 70, 71. xiii. 1—5, *v.* 21. 18— 30, *vv.* 27—30.) Knowing therefore, that the chief priests and rulers greatly desired to get Jesus into their hands, without disturbance; he framed the design of conducting their officers to him, in the absence of the people. Probably, he hoped to ingratiate himself, and to obtain further advantages, beyond the present recompence. Perhaps he expected, that Jesus would miraculously liberate himself; and so no fatal consequences would ensue from his treachery. The reproof implied in our Lord's commendation of the woman's conduct, which from base motives he had condemned, seems also to have exasperated him; and thus Satan found access to hurry him forward to the execution of his infamous design. Accordingly, he obtained admission to the chief priests, and proposed to betray his Master to them, demanding what they would give him for that service: and they (loving the treachery, though they doubtless despised and detested the traitor,) offered him thirty pieces of silver, supposed to have been shekels, in value about 3*l.* 15*s.* This was the sum appointed by the law, to be paid for a slave who had been slain by accident. (*Marg. Ref.* d, e.—*Notes,* xxvii. 3—5. *Gen.* xxxvii. 28. *Ex.* xxi. 28—32, v. 32. *Zech.* xi. 12—14.) ' So

' true is that of St. Paul, that Christ took on him "the ' " form of a servant."' *Hammond.* Though the sum was so paltry, Judas bargained to take it, and thenceforth watched for an opportunity to betray him! (*Note, Luke* xxii. 1—13, *vv.* 5, 6.)

Opportunity. (16) Ευκαιριαν. (Εx ευ, et καιρος, *tempus, occasio.*) *Luke* xxii. 6.—Ευκαιρως. *Mark* xiv. 11. 2 *Tim.* iv. 2.

V. 17—19. The person here mentioned, was probably a concealed friend and disciple of Christ, who, he knew, would be glad to accommodate him and his apostles.— ' Christ points out a certain person, as known to him, ... ' whose name and house he does not mention to the disci- ' ples; but divinely foretels, that he would be discovered ' to them, by the events which they would meet with, as ' they entered the city. This was done, in order to con- ' vince the disciples more and more clearly, that nothing ' would happen to their Lord by chance; but that he had ' the most exact foreknowledge of every minute circum- ' stance. Thus they would be confirmed, by this example ' of divine Providence, against the great offence of his ' cross.' *Beza.* (*Marg. Ref.*—*Note, Mark* xiv. 12— 16.)

To such a man. (18) Προς τον δεινα. Not used elsewhere in the New Testament.

V. 20. Without doubt our Lord ate the Passover at the time, which was appointed by the law, and which was customary among the Jews. (*Note, Ex.* xii. 3—10.)—St. Mark says expressly, " when they killed the passover ;" and St. Luke, " when the passover must be killed." (*Mark* xiv. 12. *Luke* xxii. 7.)—The passover was celebrated at the close of the fourteenth day of the month Nisan, and just when the fifteenth day began ; for the Jews reckoned from evening to evening. " The first day of unleavened " bread," strictly speaking, began at the very time when the Jews were eating the paschal lamb: but, in a more general sense, the whole fourteenth day, in which among other preparations for the passover, leaven was put out of their houses, might be so called. (*Notes, Ex.* xii. 15—20.) —' It is a very remarkable circumstance, that our Saviour ' was crucified, and our deliverance from the bondage of ' sin completed, in the same month, and on the same day ' of the month, that the Israelites were delivered from the ' bondage of Egypt, by their departure from that land. ' For the Israelites went out of Egypt, and Christ was put ' to death, on the fifteenth day of the month Nisan.' *Bp. Porteus.*

2 G 2

21 And as they did eat, he said, ⁹ Verily I say unto you, that one of you shall betray me. 22 And ʳ they were exceeding sorrowful, and began every one of them to say unto him, Lord, is it I? 23 And he answered and said, ˢ He that dippeth *his* hand with me in the dish, the same shall betray me.

24 The ᵗ Son of man goeth, as it is ᵗ written of him; ᵘ but woe unto that man by whom the Son of man is betrayed! it had been good for that man if he had not been born. 25 Then ˣ Judas, which betrayed him, answered, and said, Master, is it I? He said unto him, ᶻ Thou hast said. 26 ¶ And ᵃ as they were eating,

Marginal references (left): q 2. 14—16. Ps. iv. 12—14. John vi. 70, 71. xiii. 21. Heb. iv. 13. Rev. ii. 23. r 38. Mark xiv. 19. 20. Luke xxii. 23. John xiii. 22—23. xxi. 17. s Ps. xli. 9. Luke xxii. 21. John xiii. 26—28.

Marginal references (right): t 54. 56. Gen. iii. 15. Ps. xxii. 1—21. lxix. 1—21. lii. l. 5. 6. liii. Dan. ix. 26. Zech. xii. 10. xiii. 7. Mark ix. 12. Luke xxiv 25, 26, 46. John xix. 24. 28. 36. 37. Acts xiii. 27 —29. xvii. 2, 3. xxvi. 22, 23. xxviii. 53. 1 Cor. xv. 3. 1 Pet. i. 11. u Luke xxii. 22. x xviii. 7. xxvii. 3—5. Ps. lv. 15. 23. clx. 6—19. Mark xiv. 21. John xvii. 12. Acts i. 16 —50. y 2 Kings v. 25. Prov. xxx. 20. z 64. xxvii. 11. John xviii. 37. a Mark xiv. 22. Luke xxii. 19.

V. 21—24. When the two disciples had made all ready; at the usual time in the evening, Jesus, and the apostles who were with him, went to the house which he had marked out.—' He seems not to have gone to Jerusa-' lem that morning: so that it is probable he spent most ' of the day in retirement for meditation and prayer.' *Doddridge.*—While they were celebrating the passover, our Lord assured the disciples, that " one of them should " betray him " into the hand of his enemies. Thus he gave Judas to understand, that he was fully acquainted with his conduct, and prepared the minds of the others for the event. This declaration, however, greatly grieved and troubled them. It does not appear, that any of them suspected Judas; they had no reason to suspect each other; they could not suppose that Christ suspected them groundlessly: and, though they did not think themselves capable of so base and ungrateful a treachery; they yet put the question severally, each respecting himself, as anxious to be assured that they were not intended. Our Lord therefore gave a general intimation of the traitor, by observing that he was one, " who dipped his hand with him in the " dish:" probably others of them did this from time to time, but Judas might be doing so at that instant: this, however, was intended to expose the baseness of his conduct, as well as to mark him out to the disciples; and *afterwards* (I apprehend,) Jesus distinguished him more plainly by giving him a sop. (*Marg. Ref.* o—s.—*Notes, Ps.* xli. 9. lv. 12—15. *John* xiii. 18—30, *vv.* 18. 26, 27.) To this he added, that the Messiah was about to be taken off by a violent death; and that nothing would take place, but what had been determined and predicted concerning him: yet that would by no means excuse the traitor's conduct, or lessen the severity of his punishment; for he would be doomed to such misery in another world, that it " would have been good for him if he had never been born." (*Marg. Ref.* t—x.—*Note, Luke* xxii. 21—23.) This could not have been the case, if he should ever be liberated from punishment, and made partaker of eternal happiness: for that would infinitely overbalance all possible *temporary* suffering, whatever its acuteness and continuance might be; and would therefore prove his existence, upon the whole, to be an invaluable blessing.—' The prediction of ' this event, that Jesus should suffer, and by the treachery ' of Judas, did lay on Judas no antecedent necessity of ' doing this action: because it did not lessen the woe due ' to him for it; but only doth suppose in God a know-' ledge, how the will of man, left to his own freedom, will ' determine or incline itself.' *Whitby.* Surely, it implies also, that God determined to leave Judas to himself: and

if this foreknowledge and predetermination, did not interfere with Judas's free agency and accountableness; it does not appear, how any foreknowledge and predetermination to leave men to themselves, can interfere with their free agency and accountableness. It is wonderful that thinking and studious men do not see, that the whole system of prophecy is a direct and full confutation of all objections, *on this ground*, against the doctrine of predestination. The predicted events cannot possibly fail of accomplishment: they must therefore either be absolutely decreed by the allwise God, or there must be some *necessity* which cannot be overcome even by the Deity himself. The first is *Christian predestination*, the latter is *Heathen fatalism:* but neither interferes with man's free agency and accountableness; for he still acts voluntarily, according to the prevailing inclinations of his heart.

That dippeth. (23) 'Ο εμβαψας. *John* xiii. 26. 'Ο εμβαπ-'ημενος. *Mark* xiv. 20. See on *Note*, iii. 5, 6, v. 6.—*In the dish.*] Εν τω τρυβλιω. *Mark* xiv. 20. Not used elsewhere N. T.—*Goeth.* (24) 'Υπαγει. *Mark* xiv. 21. " goeth " to death. (Πορευεται. *Luke* xxii. 22.) *John* vii. 33. viii. 14. xiii. 3. 33. 36. xiv. 4, 5. 28. xvi. 10. 16, 17.

V. 25. At length Judas also enquired, whether he were the person. He probably feared, that his silence would excite suspicion; or he meant to face out the matter, as if unconscious of guilt. The answer of our Lord plainly meant, that he was the traitor: yet, neither the awful sentence denounced on him, nor this additional proof of Christ's knowledge of his heart, had any effect, to prevent him from rushing headlong on his own destruction! (*Marg. Ref.*)—*Thou hast said.*] Συ ειπας. 64. Συ λεγεις. xxvii. 11. *John* xviii. 37.

V. 26—28. When the paschal lamb had been eaten, the Lord's supper was appointed; to be substituted, to be a *commemorative* observance, " without shedding of " blood," of redemption already made, as the passover had been a *prefigurative* ordinance, with " shedding of " blood," of redemption to be made in the fulness of time.—Nothing can be more simple in its nature and use, than this sacred institution; yet nothing has ever been more obscured, perplexed, misunderstood, and perverted, than it has been.—Our Lord, just before his death, " took " bread, and blessed it," with praise and thanksgiving: this he set apart for a sacred purpose, as the representation of his body; and he " brake it," to shew that his body would be wounded, put to great torture, and undergo death, as the sacrifice for sins. He then gave it to his disciples, that each of them might eat of it, as an outward expression of their receiving the atonement and re-

^b Jesus took bread, and ^c blessed *it*, ^d and brake *it*, and gave *it* to the disciples, and said, ^eTake, eat; ^e this is my body.

27 And ^f he took the cup, and gave thanks, and gave *it* to them, saying, ^g Drink ye all of it:

28 For this is ^h my blood of the New Testament, which is ⁱ shed for many for the remission of sins.

b Luke xxiv. 30. I Cor. xi. 23—25.
c Many Greek copies have gave thanks. Matt vi. 41. Acts ii. 46. xx. 7. 1 Cor. x. 16, 17.
d John vi. 31—35, 47—58. x. 4. Gal. iv. 24, 25.
e Ex. v. 4, 5. 1 Cor. xi. 26—29.
f Mark xiv. 23, 24. Luke xxii. 20.
Luke xxii. 20. 1 Cor. xi. 25. Heb. ix. 14—22. x. 4—14. xiii. 20. v. 15. 19. Eph. i. 7. Col. i. 14. 20. Heb. ix. 22, 28. 1 John ii. 2. Rev. vii. 14.
Luke xxii. 20. 1 Cor. xi. 20.
g Ps. cxvi. 13. Cant. v. 1. vii. 2. Is. xxv. 6. lv. 1. 1 Cor. x. 16.
h Ex. xxiv. 7, 8. Lev. xvii. 11. Jer. xxxi. 31. Zech. ix. 11. Mark xiv. 24. 1 Pet. 28. Rom.

conciliation made by his death, and in remembrance of his love and sufferings for them. In like manner " he took " the cup," and, having blessed it and given thanks as before, he gave it to them, and bade them all drink of it: for the wine in that cup represented his blood, as shed to make way for the new covenant; and to ratify it, as valid for their benefit; and especially to atone for their sins, and those of many, even of all of them who should ever believe in his name; in order that they might obtain remission of them.—The language which our Lord used, in instituting this ordinance, is manifestly *figurative*, and cannot admit of a *literal* interpretation; unless any will say, that the *cup* was literally the *blood* of Christ, or the *new covenant*: and this renders it the more wonderful, that any set of men should be so adventurous and absurd, as to require all Christians to believe, in contradiction to their senses and understandings, that the bread in the sacrament, after consecration, becomes the real entire living body of Christ, together with his Deity, and therefore a proper object of divine adoration. (*Marg. Ref. e.—Notes, Ex.* v. 5—10, *v.* 5. *Luke* xxii. 19, 20. 1 *Cor.* x. 1—5, *v.* 4. xi. 23—28, *v.* 25. *Gal.* iv. 21 —31, *vv.* 24, 25.) Indeed the scripture gives no intimation of any peculiar mystery, or even difficulty, in this institution. By comparing the several passages, which relate to this subject, it appears that our Lord commanded his disciples to meet together in his name; and with prayer, praise, and thanksgiving, to break, distribute, and eat bread, the most salutary and universal of all those viands, by which life is sustained; and to pour out and drink wine, the most valuable and refreshing of all cordials. This action was to be performed " in remembrance of him," and of his love and his sufferings for them; and as a representation of " his body broken, and his blood shed" for their sins, in order to purchase the blessings of the new covenant; and of the method, by which they were made partakers of this salvation, even by receiving and ' feeding upon him in ' their hearts, by faith with thanksgiving.' By his body and blood we are doubtless to understand his human nature, as joined in personal union with his Deity: and the separation of the blood from the body, which was the immediate cause of his death, must be understood to include all his expiatory sufferings.—The holiness and dignity of the Redeemer, the depth of his humiliation and the intenseness of his agonies; the immensity of his compassion and condescension; the deplorable condition from which he redeemed his people; the extensive efficacy of his one oblation; the honour and happiness to which he exalts believers; and the discovery made in that great transaction, of the perfect justice and unspeakable love of God, the excellency of his law, the evil of sin, the vanity of the world, and the importance of eternal things; require peculiar consideration and devout meditation, when the death of Christ is contemplated, through the medium of these outward emblems. The bread and wine were, probably,

received by the apostles *sitting*, or *reclining*, and *in the evening*: yet no *command* was given about these things; and therefore the time, place, and posture must be considered as mere circumstances. (*Note, Ex.* xii. 11—14.) —The action of communicating seems to imply an open confession of our guilt and ruined state, as justly condemned criminals, who could have no hope of pardon or salvation, from any thing we could do of ourselves; a profession of our faith, respecting the Person, incarnation, suretiship, and atonement of Christ, and the necessity, reality, and suitableness of his sacrifice and vicarious sufferings; an avowed dependence on this atonement, and the mercy of God, according to the covenant thus mediated; an acknowledgment of our unspeakable obligations to our gracious Benefactor, who laid down his life for us; a strong and open expression of our love and gratitude to him; a sacramental engagement to submit to and obey him, as our beloved Lord and Saviour; and a publick joining of ourselves to him and his people, to walk with them in Christian fellowship, in all sacred ordinances, and devotedness to the Redeemer's service. No man can therefore *sincerely* and *intelligently* partake of this ordinance, who is not self-condemned and penitent; who does not with application to his own case believe the peculiar doctrines of the gospel; who does not apply in secret earnest prayer for an interest in the salvation of Christ; who lives in allowed habitual sin, or the neglect of known duty; whose heart is under the *dominion* of pride, malice, avarice, or any evil propensity; who makes it merely a step to preferment, or a compensation for sin, a covering of his iniquity or infidelity, a self-righteous service, or an excuse for licentiousness: for such men are " guilty of the body and blood " of Christ." But the humble penitent, the trembling believer, who relies on a crucified Saviour, and longs to live to his glory, should fear no snare in this institution: it is his duty and privilege to come to it, as often as he has opportunity; and he will find it to be admirably suited to increase humility, tenderness of conscience, self-examination, watchfulness, the life of faith, hope, love, gratitude, brotherly affection, and every holy disposition and consolation. These are obvious and intelligible effects of devout and frequent communicating; which shew it to be as well suited to strengthen and refresh the soul and its graces, as bread and wine are to nourish and cheer the animal life. They, who are not prepared to receive the Lord's supper, cannot be fit for death and heaven; nay, acceptable prayer cannot be offered without a measure of a similar preparation of heart.—It has been much disputed, whether Judas partook of the Lord's supper, or not; but the controversy seems not to be of great consequence. If he did, his presence gives no encouragement to intruders; but rather solemnly warns every man previously to examine himself as to the state of his soul: nor can it sanction the admission of openly wicked persons; and no discipline can ex-

29 But I say unto you, *I will not drink henceforth of this fruit of the vine, ¹until that day when I drink it new ¹ with you in my Father's kingdom.

30 ¶ And ° when they had sung an hymn, ° they went out into the mount of Olives.

31 Then saith Jesus unto them, ° All ye shall be offended because of me this night : for it is written, ⁴ I will smite the Shepherd, ° and the sheep of the flock shall be scattered abroad.

32 But after ' I am risen again, ' I will go before you into Galilee.

33 Peter answered and said unto him, ° Though all men shall be offended because of thee, ° yet will I never be offended.

34 Jesus said unto him, Verily I say unto thee, ' That this night, before the cock crow, thou shalt deny me thrice.

35 Peter said unto him, ° Though I should die with thee, yet will I not deny thee. ° Likewise also said all the disciples.

clude specious hypocrites. (*Note, John* xiii. 18—30, *v.* 30.) —Some persons have endeavoured to prove the Resurrection of Christ, to be the *chief* doctrine of Christianity, the belief of which constitutes a man a Christian : but it is in fact rather the grand *proof* of all other doctrines, and the evidence that the atonement of his death was accepted. The appointment, however, of this ordinance, " to shew " forth the Lord's death till he come," abundantly evinces the belief of that doctrine to be most essentially distinguishing of a real Christian ; and that a reliance on the atonement of Christ, for remission of sins and all the blessings of salvation, and thus spiritually eating his flesh, and drinking his blood, forms the great peculiarity of the life of faith in the Son of God. (*Marg. Ref.—Notes, John* vi. 52—58. 1 *Cor.* x. 14—17. xi. 23—34.)—Why did our blessed Redeemer, so distinguish this mournful scene?— Why ' should not his followers rather celebrate his mira- ' culous birth, his triumphant resurrection from the dead, ' or his glorious ascension into heaven, than his ignomi- ' nious death? ...Certainly the mode of celebration is ' yet more surprising. ...It is by a *feast*, not by a *fast*. ' It is a celebration of praise and thanksgiving, not of ' mourning. ... It purports to be a feast upon the body and ' blood of him, whose death is commemorated ! ...This ' assuredly, is the most singular commemoration of a ' highly venerated deceased character, that was ever heard ' of in the world, much more that was ever practised ' among the civilized part of mankind ! Familiarity with ' the *ceremony* has laid our attention to it asleep: other- ' wise it must appear most extraordinary. Deny the great ' doctrines of the atonement, and of the communion of ' the soul with the Saviour by faith, and, I conceive, such ' an observance is absolutely inexplicable. But, admit ' these doctrines, and all is easy, all is natural, all is ' in the highest degree significant.' *Sermons on Baptism, Confirmation, and the Lord's Supper, by the Rev. John Scott, Hull.*—The papists who refuse the cup to the laity, and give an *unbroken* wafer, instead of *broken* bread, in these respects also in effect disannul our Lord's institution, and substitute another in its ·place.

V. 29. ' It is not long, that I shall abide with you, ' nor shall I again celebrate this or any the like feast ' among you, till we meet in heaven, and partake of those ' joys, which are wont to be figuratively expressed by new ' wine.' *Hammond.*—' I will no more in this mortal state,

' drink henceforth of this fruit of the vine : but shall re- ' serve myself for a more comfortable draught, sweeter ' than all the new wine earth can afford, which I shall enjoy ' in my Father's kingdom, whereof ye shall be blessed par- ' takers with me.' *Bp. Hall.*—' The passover, which was a ' type of the redemption to be wrought by me, shall be ' fulfilled and completed by my death and resurrection. ' The shadow passes away ; the substance takes place : and ' when you eat this supper in remembrance of me, there ' will I be virtually present amongst you ; and your souls ' ᴗhall be nourished and refreshed by my grace, as your ' bodies are by the bread and wine.' *Bp. Porteus.—Wine* is the scriptural emblem of *gladness; (Notes, Is.* lxii. —15, *v.* 13. *Ps.* civ. 14, 15. *Is.* xxv. 6—8. lv. 1—3. *Zech.* ix. 15—17 ;) but Christ had done with joy and gladness, till after his resurrection : then the kingdom of his Father would be established ; and his gracious presence with his true disciples, in every publick or private act of worship, would fill their hearts with joy, and put *new* songs of praise into their mouths. In this new joy he also would share ; he would " sup with them " on earth, and at length they should " sup with him " in heaven. *(Notes, Is.* lxii. 1—5, *v.* 5. *Zeph.* iii. 14—17. *John* xv. 9—11. *Rev.* iii. 20 —22, *v.* 20.) So that the joy of his disciples in him, and his in them, both in the church on earth, and in the hea- venly state, may be figuratively intended. (*Marg. Ref.— Note, Luke* xxii. 14—18.)—' If you enquire, When did ' Christ thus drink this wine with them ? I answer, he did ' it, not so much by " eating and drinking with his dis- ' " ciples after he arose from the dead, ...as by fulfilling ' " the promise made to them ; I dispose to you a kingdom, ' " as my Father hath done to me ;...and ye shall eat and ' " drink with me at my table in my kingdom :" (*Luke* ' xxii. 29, 30 :) for in what sense soever, they are here ' said to drink with him at his table ; he must also be said ' to drink with them.' *Whitby.*—Our Lord calls the wine, after consecration, " the fruit of the vine."

V. 30—35. After our Lord and the disciples had sung a hymn of praise ; (*Marg.* and *Marg. Ref.* n ;) according to the custom at the conclusion of the paschal supper, (which some think consisted of psalms, from the hun- dred and thirteenth to the hundred and eighteenth, inclu- sive,) he proceeded with the eleven to the mount of Olives; for Judas had previously left them. (*Marg. Ref.* o.— *Notes, John* xiii. 18—38. xiv—xvii.) At this time he so-

36 ¶ Then cometh Jesus with them unto ᵇ a place called Gethsemane, and saith unto the disciples, Sit ye here, ᶜ while I go and pray yonder.

37 And he took with him ᵈ Peter and the two sons of Zebedee, and began to be ᵉ sorrowful and very heavy.

38 Then saith he unto them, ᶠ My soul is exceeding sorrowful, even unto death: ᵍ tarry ye here, and watch with me.

39 And he went a little farther, ʰ and fell on his face, ⁱ and prayed, saying, ᵏ O my Father, ˡ if it be possible, ᵐ let this cup pass from me: nevertheless, ⁿ not as I will, but as thou wilt.

lemnly assured them, that during that very night they would all meet with such temptations, as would stagger their faith in him, and cause them to fall into sin through fear of men; for the prophecy was about to be fulfilled, in which the Lord had declared, that he would " smite the " Shepherd, and the sheep should be scattered." (Note, Zech. xiii. 7.) They had ground, however, to be fully assured that he would rise from the dead; and then " he " would go before them into Galilee." (Marg. Ref. q—t.) —But Peter, instead of noticing these last important words; with much ignorant self-confidence, (as if he had been so strong in faith above all other men, that nothing could possibly move him, and even supposing that Jesus was mistaken respecting him,) declared " that he would " never be offended," even if that should be the case of all others: upon which our Lord solemnly assured him, that before the usual hour of cock-crowing that very night, and before the cock which he should hear, would crow twice, he should thrice deny all knowledge of him. Peter, however, not conscious of any such intention, being honestly and warmly attached to his Lord; not aware of the treachery of his heart, the force of temptation, and the fiery trial that awaited him; and somewhat indignant at being thus suspected, confidently declared, that he would sooner die with him than deny him: in which profession he was joined by the other apostles, who were doubtless unwilling to be outdone in professions of fidelity and cordial attachment. (Marg. Ref. u—a.—Notes, Mark xiv. 17—30, v. 30. Luke xxii. 31—34, v. 34. John xxi. 15—17, v. 15.) This unwarranted self-confidence was the first step towards Peter's shameful fall.—As John relates a similar warning and protestation, previously to the departure of Christ and the disciples from the house, some have supposed that this was a second warning, especially addressed to Peter.

When they had sung an hymn. (30) Ὑμνησαντες' (ὑμνεω, ab ὑμνος. Eph. v. 19. Col. iii. 16.) Mark xiv. 26. Acts xvi. 25.—Ye shall be offended. (31) See on Note, v. 29, 30. —I will smite.] " Smite the Shepherd, and the sheep shall " be scattered." Zech. xiii. 7. ' Ρομφαια εξεγερθητι επι τις ' ποιμενας μμ, και επι ανδρα πολιτην μμ, λεγει Κυριος παντοκρατωρ, ' παταξαλε τις ποιμενας, και εκσπασατε τα προβαια.' Sept. The evangelist neither quoted from the LXX, as it is most evident, nor exactly translated the Hebrew; but gave the plain general meaning of the prophecy.—Shall be scattered abroad.] Διασκορπισθησεται. xxv. 24. 26. Mark xiv. 27. Luke i. 51. xv. 13. xvi. 1. John x. 12. xi. 52. Acts. v. 37.

V. 36—39. The word " Gethsemane " signifies the valley of fatness; and this seems to have been a pleasant and fruitful garden, to which Jesus frequently resorted with his disciples, for retirement, devout conversation, and religious exercises. When he came thither, he left the other apostles at a distance, and took with him those only as witnesses of his agony, who had before witnessed his transfiguration. (Note, xvii. 1, 2.) In their presence " he began " to be sorrowful and very heavy ; " and he complained, " that his soul was exceeding sorrowful, even unto death." The words used, are the most expressive imaginable, and denote the greatest dejection, amazement, anguish, and horror of mind, which can be conceived; the state of one surrounded with sorrows, overwhelmed with miseries, and almost swallowed up with consternation. In this frame of mind, he went a little way from the disciples; and first kneeling down, but afterwards prostrating himself on the earth, he prayed to his Father, that, if " possible, that " cup might pass from him." Some refer this to the present anguish and horror which he felt in his soul, and not to his approaching crucifixion : but, whatever we understand by it, it expressed his strong aversion to suffering, save when the glory of God and the good of man required it; and it shewed that he had all the innocent feelings of our nature, in the most exquisite degree ; that, had it been " possible," that is, consistent with the justice, truth, holiness, and mercy of God, to have mitigated or remitted his sufferings, he would have desired it, as much as we should in similar circumstances: and the subsequent retraction shewed his perfect resignation, and willingness to bear that unspeakable burden, which must otherwise have sunk us into everlasting destruction. (Marg. Ref.— Notes, Mark xiv. 32—46, v. 33. John xii. 27—33. xviii. 10—14, v. 11. Heb. v. 7—10, v. 7.) St. Luke records, that when Jesus was at prayer, an angel was sent to strengthen his mind for the conflict; and that, though the night was cold, his whole frame was agitated to such a degree, " that his sweat became as great drops of blood " falling to the ground." (Note, Luke xxii. 39—46, vv. 43, 44.)—It therefore occurs here to enquire, with diffidence and caution, into the causes of our Lord's agony. He had doubtless a distinct view of all the sufferings which he was about to undergo, with all their aggravations: but then he had all along had the same; yet, he acted and spoke with the most entire serenity, even to the very moment of this extraordinary scene. (Note, i. 2.) Many of his disciples, in different ages, have met the most excruciating tortures, which human, or rather diabolical, cruelty and ingenuity could devise, without any such perturbation ; being supported by inward peace, consolation, and joyful hope: and doubtless Christ was as much superior to them all, in fortitude and constancy, as the heavens are above the earth. We must therefore conclude, that there were some ingredients mingled in his cup, which were not in their's, and some in their's which were not in his. (Notes, xx. 20—23. Ps. lxxv. 8.) To mention the treachery and fate of Judas, or the misconduct of Peter

2 c 6

o 43 xxv. a. Cant.
v. 2. Mark xiv.
37. Luke ix. 22.
xxii. 45.
p 35. Judg. ix. 28.
; Sam. xxvi. 15,
16. 1 King° xx.
11.

40 And he cometh unto the disciples, ° and findeth them asleep, and saith unto Peter, ᵖ What, could ye not watch with me one hour?

q xxiv. 42. xxv
13. Mark xiv
33—37. xiv 38.
Luke xxi. 36
xxii. 40. 46
1 Cor. xvi. 13
2 Pet.

41 ᑫ Watch and pray, that ye ʳ enter not into temptation: ˢ the spirit indeed is willing, but the flesh is weak.

r vi. 13. Luke viii. 13. xi. 4. 1 Cor. x. 13. 2 Pet.
ii. 9. Rev. iii. 10. s Ps. cxix. 4, 5. 24, 25. 32. 35—37. 115—117. 173. 174. Is. xxvi. 6,
9. Rom. vii. 18—25. viii. A 1 Cor. ix. 27. Gal. v. 16, 17. 24. Phil. iii. 12—14.

and the other apostles, or the unbelief of the Jews, as causes of this surprising effect, must fail to give the reflecting mind the least satisfaction.—We must also exclude many of those things, which cause the most exquisite misery to the human mind of which it is capable: for there could be in the holy Jesus no horrors of a guilty conscience, no conflict of sinful passions, no despair as to the final event of his sufferings. It is not indeed possible for us fully to understand or explain this subject: yet we may point out the light, which the scriptures afford us upon it. Christ sustained the character of our Surety, who undertook to be answerable for our sins: accordingly " our " iniquities were laid upon him," and " he was made sin " for us," and " suffered once for sins, the just for the " unjust;" and the scripture ascribes the heaviest of his sufferings to the immediate hand of God ; " It pleased the " LORD to bruise him,... he made his soul a sacrifice for " sin." The sword of divine justice was commanded to " awake against the Shepherd, and smite him;" and " God spared not his own Son." (Notes, Is. liii. 9, 10. Zech. xiii. 7. Rom. viii. 32—34, v. 32.) From these scriptures we may conclude, that the human nature of Christ was, on this occasion, left wholly destitute of all consolatory communications from the Holy Spirit ; though supported by its union with the Deity, to endure the unknown anguish without sinking under it: that he had the most distinct and clear perception of the infinite evil of sin, and of that immensity of guilt which he was to expiate: that he had the most awful view of the divine justice, and the vengeance deserved by the sins of men; and that such a sense of the divine wrath oppressed his inmost soul, as no tongue can express, or imagination conceive. At the same time " he suffered being tempted;" and, probably, all kind of horrible thoughts were suggested by Satan, which tended to despondency, and every other dreadful conclusion ; which would be the more intolerable, in proportion to the perfection of his holiness. (Note, Heb. ii. 16—18.) So that we may be certain, he endured as much misery, of the same kind with that of condemned spirits, as could possibly consist with a pure conscience, perfect love of God and man, and an assured confidence of a glorious event. Probably, some degree of the same darkness and horror oppressed his mind, during the whole subsequent scene, till on the cross he said, " It is finished." Accordingly we do not read, that he uttered any complaint about his outward sufferings, but he most dolefully exclaimed, " My God, my God, why hast thou forsaken me?" —Nor is it at all ' improbable, that his great enemy and ' our's, the prince of darkness, whom he came to over- ' throw, and with whom he maintained a constant con- ' flict through life, and triumphed over by his death, ... ' should exert his utmost power, by presenting real, or ' raising up imaginary terrors, to shake the constancy of ' his soul, and deter him from the great work he had un- ' dertaken. These, and a multitude of other agonizing ' distresses, unknown and inconceivable to us, which might

' necessarily spring from so vast, so momentous, so stu- ' pendons a work, as the salvation of a whole world, ' made a plain distinction between our Saviour's situation, ' and that of any other martyr to the cause of truth ; and ' most clearly prove that there never was a sorrow in every ' respect like unto his sorrow.' Bp. Porteus.—' Christ ' dreaded not death in itself, but the wrath of God against ' sin, the weight of which for our sakes must be sustained.' Beza.
To be ... very heavy. (37) Αδημονειν. ' Αδημενια. Gra- ' vissime angor. Beza. Est ita vehementi objecti discriminis ' metu angi, ut quasi exanimis, et extra te sis.' Leigh.— Mark xiv. 33. Phil. ii. 26.—Exceeding sorrowful. (38) Περιλυπος. ' Aristoteles negat μεγαλοψυχον esse περιλυπον. ' But Christ saith ... that he was περιλυπος, usque ad mortem, ' (" even unto death,") thereby signifying that his soul, ' with all the faculties and powers of it, was sad on every ' side; and as it were, beset and besieged with grief, sorrow ' went round about him.' Leigh. (Mark vi. 26. xiv. 34. Luke xviii. 23, 24.—Gen. iv. 6. Sept.)
V. 40, 41. Notwithstanding the confidence of Peter and his companions, and the injunctions of Christ, in his extreme anguish, that they should watch with him, they were fallen asleep, when he returned ; which occasioned him to rebuke Peter especially, as if surprised at him, that after all he could not " watch with him one hour!" (Note, 30—35.) He therefore exhorted them to watch and pray, not so much on his account, as on their own: lest, through negligence and presumptuous security, they should be drawn into circumstances of peculiar temptation, and overcome by it: for though, by divine grace, they were sincerely willing and ready to adhere to him, even to sufferings and death; yet " the flesh was weak " and frail, and their natural aversion to pain and shame would render them unable to stand their ground in the time of trial, if they did not seek for the powerful assistance of God, to uphold and strengthen them. (Marg. Ref.—Notes, vi. 13. Mark xiv. 37, 38. John iii. 6. Rom. vii. 18—25. viii. 3—9. Gal. v. 16—18, v. 17.)—Most expositors understand the clause as a kind excuse, which the Lord made for their present conduct : but he was never used to excuse any thing wrong in them ; and their sleeping on this occasion was peculiarly unseasonable and criminal. It seems therefore more proper to consider the words, as a caution respecting the future ; and a warning, that self-confidence and neglect of watching and prayer, would leave them defenceless in the time of danger, and that they would fall, notwithstanding their most sincere and determined resolutions to the contrary. Indeed, it is evident, that Peter's confidence in " the willingness of his spirit," and his overlooking " the weakness of the flesh," occasioned his neglect of means, induced him to thrust himself into perilous circumstances, and so made way for his awful fall.—' The words ... are not meant as an excuse, or miti- ' gation of their sins ; but as a motive to their prayer and ' vigilance.' Whitby.—Willing. (41) Προθυμον. Mark xiv.

2 c 7

42 He went away again ' the second time, and prayed, saying, O my Father, if this cup may not pass away from me, except I drink it, thy will be done.

43 And he came and found them asleep again; " for their eyes were heavy.

44 And he left them, and went away again, and ' prayed the third time, saying the same words.

45 Then cometh he to his disciples, and saith unto them, ' Sleep on now, and take *your* rest: behold, ' the hour is at hand, and the Son of man is betrayed into the hands of sinners.

46 Rise, ' let us be going: behold, ' he is at hand that doth betray me.

47 ¶ And while he yet spake, ' lo, ' Judas, one of the twelve, came, and with him a great multitude with swords and staves, from the chief priests and elders of the people.

48 Now he that betrayed him gave them a sign, saying, ' Whomsoever I shall kiss, that same is he; ' hold him fast.

49 And forthwith he came to Jesus, and said, ' Hail, Master; ' and kissed him.

50 And Jesus said unto him, ' Friend, wherefore art thou come? Then came they, and laid hands on Jesus, and took him.

51 And, behold, ʰ one of them which were with Jesus stretched out *his* hand, and drew his sword, and struck a servant of the high priest's, and smote off his ear.

52 Then said Jesus unto him, ' Put up again thy sword into his place: for all ᵏ they that take the sword shall perish with the sword.

53 Thinkest thou that I cannot now pray to my Father, ' and he shall presently give me more than ᵐ twelve ⁿ legions of angels?

54 But ° how then shall the scriptures be fulfilled, that thus it must be?

55 In that same hour said Jesus to the multitudes, ᴾ Are ye come out as against a thief, with swords and staves for to take me? ᑫ I sat daily with you teaching in the temple, and ye laid no hold on me.

56 But all this was done, ' that the scriptures of the prophets might be fulfilled. ' Then all the disciples forsook him, and fled.

---

38. *Rom.* i. 15.—Προθυμια. *Acts* xvii. 11. 2 *Cor.* viii. 11, 12. 19. ix. 2.—Προθυμως. 1 *Pet.* v. 2.

V. 42—46. After this, Christ again left the disciples, and prayed nearly as before; except that he expressed more entirely his resignation to the will of the Father, in respect of his sufferings: but when he came again the second and the third time, he still found them sleeping; for their very sorrow, at what they witnessed and expected, concurred in rendering them heavy for sleep. But when he came the third time, he bade them "sleep on, and "take their rest;" that is, if they were able: for, though his agonies and exhortations had failed to keep them awake, there were those concerned who would do it effectually; as the "hour was at hand," when, as he had foretold, "the Son of Man," the Messiah, was to be "be-"trayed into the hands of sinners." (*Marg. Ref.*)

Heavy. (43) Βεβαρημενοι. *Mark* xiv. 40. *Luke* ix. 32. 2 *Cor.* i. 8. v. 4. 1 *Tim.* v. 16.—Βαρεομαι à ßαρυς, *gravis.*—*Now.* (45) Το λοιπον. As to what remains. Often translated *finally.* 'Behold, now is no time for sleeping; ' for the hour of your and my temptation is at hand. "'Arise," therefore, "and let us be going."' *Whitby.*

V. 47—56. Judas is constantly noted as "one of the "twelve;" for this was the grand aggravation of his guilt. (14)—He had made all ready for the execution of his base purpose; and, knowing the place of Christ's retirement, he led thither an armed multitude from the chief priests and rulers, who were also attended by some of the

principal persons themselves. (*Marg. Ref.* b.—*Note, John* xviii. 1—3, *v.* 3.)—It is probable, that our Lord had been accustomed to welcome the disciples, in the most condescending and affectionate manner, by allowing them to kiss him, when they returned from any service: and Judas agreed by this token to mark him out to the officers, exhorting them to seize and hold him fast; which some think implies, that he expected Jesus would miraculously deliver himself. (*Note, Mark* xiv. 43—50, *v.* 44.) Accordingly, he came up with the utmost effrontery, and, with an address expressive of the highest respect and affection, he "kissed him:" but Jesus, with a meek rebuke of his complicated hypocrisy, treachery, and ingratitude, calling him "friend," or *companion,* as an aggravation of his guilt, demanded, why he was present on this occasion, or why he came thus attended. The officers then approached and apprehended him: and Peter, recollecting his promise, and purposing to shew his readiness to fight in his Master's cause, drew a sword, and, without waiting for orders, aimed a blow at the head of the high priest's servant, and cut off his ear; probably, he was one of the rudest and most forward in the company. (*Marg. Ref.* f.—h. —*Notes, Luke* xxii. 47—53, *vv.* 48. 51. *John* xviii. 10— 14.) But our Lord ordered Peter to put up his sword again, "as all they who took the sword would perish with "the sword." This intimated to the disciples, that their warfare would be of a spiritual nature, and not waged with carnal weapons: (*Note, 2 Cor.* x. 1—6:) it denoted,

57 And 'they that had laid hold on Jesus, led *him* away to Caiaphas the high priest, where the scribes and the elders were assembled.

58 But Peter followed him afar off, unto the high priest's palace, " and went in, and sat with the servants to see the end.

59 Now the chief priests, and elders, and all the council, * sought false witness against Jesus, to put him to death;

60 But 'found none: yea, though many false witnesses came, *yet* found they none. ' At the last came two false witnesses.

61 And said, * This *fellow* said, ' I am able to destroy the temple of God, and to build it in three days.

62 And the high priest arose, and said unto him, ' Answerest thou nothing? what *is* it which these witness against thee?

c xxvii. 12—14. Mark xiv. 60. Luke xxiii. 9. John xviii. 19—23. xix. 9 -11.

that those who are prompt to fight, and avenge their own cause, only bring mischief and death upon themselves ; and perhaps it implied, that the Jews, who now used the Roman sword against him, would soon perish by it. He further added, that he did not want their feeble help : for, if he chose to decline his sufferings, he could speedily obtain from his Father even " more than twelve legions " of angels;" that is, more angels than there were legionary soldiers in the largest Roman armies, or more than seventy thousand angels, to fight for him. (*Marg. Ref.* i—n.) The idea will appear most grand and sublime to those, who consider the execution made in the army of the proud Assyrian, by a single angel in one night's time. (*Note,* 2 *Kings* xix. 85.)—But, in this case, he enquired " how the scriptures could be accomplished," which predicted, that the Messiah must be cut off, and be numbered with transgressors. (*Marg. Ref.* o. r.) Then, addressing those who came to apprehend him, he demanded, why they came out against him with such warlike preparations, as if he had been some desperate robber, at the head of a determined gang, who could not be seized without much danger and difficulty: whereas he had daily appeared among them, as a teacher, unarmed, and unattended except by a few fishermen, and had acted in the most peaceable manner. (*Marg. Ref.* p, q.—*Notes, Mark* xiv. 43—50, *vv.* 48—50. *John* xviii. 17—23.) They had before indeed been secretly restrained from assaulting him: but now " his time was come ;" and all this was ordered and performed, that the scriptures might be exactly accomplished. When, therefore, the disciples perceived, that he intended quietly to yield himself up to the officers, their courage and resolution at once entirely failed, and they all forsook him and fled to save themselves. This conduct can by no means be excused : but thus his words were fulfilled, that they should " all be offended because " of him." (*Note,* 30—35.)—It is remarkable, that our Lord so over-awed the spirits of the assailants, that they never attempted any violence even against Peter, nor offered to apprehend any of the company. (*Notes, John* xviii. 4—9.)

Kissed him. (49) Κατεφιλησεν αυτον.—Καταφιλεω, *valde osculor. Mark* xiv. 45. *Luke* vii. 38. 45. xv. 20. *Acts* xx. 37. Φιλεω, 48. ' Καλα ... significationem auget.' *Leigh.*— *A thief.* (55) Ληστην. See on *Note* xxi. 13.

V. 57—62. The grand council of the Jews was convened at the high priest's palace, at that late hour, waiting to have Jesus brought before them; and thither the officers conducted him bound as a criminal. (*Marg. Ref.* t.) Peter likewise, followed at some distance, to see how matters would terminate : and, having obtained admission into the high priest's palace, he associated with the servants, as a stranger drawn thither from curiosity. (*Note, John* xviii. 15, 16.) This was another false step tending to his fall. By striking the high priest's servant, he had rendered himself obnoxious, and afraid of being detected; and seeing he had not courage openly to attend Jesus as his disciple, he ought by no means to have gone at all : for thus he thrust himself into the midst of enemies, and was forced silently to hear all their scoffs, insults, menaces, and blasphemies; and so " he entered into temptation." (*Note,* 40, 41.)——In the mean time, the council earnestly " sought false witness " against Jesus; as conscious, that they could p e no other, and as desirous of giving their proceedings an appearance of law and justice ; that so, a capital sentence having been pronounced against him by the council, they might apply to the Roman governor to have it put in execution. (*Marg. Ref.* x.)—'The ' professed entertaining of false witnesses against Christ ' will not seem strange, if it be remembered, that among ' the Jews, in actions against seducers of the people, or ' false prophets, it was lawful to say any thing whether ' true or false, no man being permitted to say any thing in ' defence of them.' *Hammond.* This extract from the Jewish writers, shews the blindness and iniquity of their teachers to have been beyond conception great. (*Notes, Ps.* xxxv. 11, 12. *Acts* vi. 9—14, *vv.* 11—13. xxiii. 12— 22. xxiv. 1—9. 10—21, *v.* 13. 1 *Pet.* iv. 12—16.)—But, while many false witnesses appeared against Jesus, the council could find no two persons agreeing in one testimony; without which the law forbade them to put any man to death. (*Marg. Ref.* y.—*Notes, Deut.* xvii. 7. *v.* 6. xix. 15—21, *v.* 15. *Mark* xiv. 53—59, *vv.* 56—59.) At length two persons concurred in testifying, that he had declared himself able to destroy the temple, and to build it again in three days. The words, which our Lord had uttered long before, were widely different from this statement of them ; so that their testimony was *false,* though it had the semblance of truth : yet even these two, did not so agree, as to give any ground to a regular sentence of condemnation. (*Note, John* ii. 18—22.) Indeed it does not appear, in what respect any thing capitally criminal could have been found in these words, had they been actually spoken.—The high priest, however, arose from his place, in great commotion, as if some great crime had

63 But ⁴ Jesus held his peace. And the high priest answered and said unto him, ᵉ I adjure thee by the living God, ᵉ that thou tell us whether thou be ᶠ the Christ, the Son of God.

64 Jesus saith unto him, ʰ Thou hast said: nevertheless I say unto you, ᵍ Hereafter shall ye see the Son of man sitting on ᵏ the right hand of power, and coming in the clouds of heaven.

65 Then ˡ the high priest rent his clothes, saying, ᵐ He hath spoken blasphemy; what further need have we of witnesses? behold, now ye have heard his blasphemy.

66 What think ye? They answered and said, ⁿ He is guilty of death.

67 Then ° did they spit in his face, ᵖ and others smote him with ˙ the palms of their hands,

68 Saying, ᵠ Prophesy unto us, ʳ thou Christ, Who is he that smote thee?

69 ¶ Now ˢ Peter sat without in the palace: and a damsel came unto him, saying, Thou also wast with ᵗ Jesus of Galilee.

70 But ᵘ he denied before them all, saying, I know not what thou sayest.

71 And ˣ when he was gone out into the porch, another maid saw him,

Marginal references: d Ps. xxxvii. 12—14. liii. 7. Dan. iii. 16. Acts viii. 32—33. e 1 Pet. ii. 23. e Lev. v. 1. Num. v. 19—21. 1 Kings xxii. 16. 2 Chr. xviii. 15. Prov. xxix. 24. f Mark xiv. 61. Luke xxii. 66—71. John viii. 25. g xvi. 16. xxvi. 63. 40. 43. 54. Ps. ii. 6, 7. ix. 6. vi. 7. John i. 34, 49, 50. iii. 16—18. v. 18—25. vi. 69. h xx. 36. xix. 7. xxv. 31. Dan. vii. 13. Luke xxi. 27. John i. 50, 51. Acts i. 11. Rom. xiv. 10. 1 Thes. iv. 16. Rev. i. 7. xx. 11. k Ps. cx. 1. i xxvi. 27. xxiv. 30. Acts vii. 55. Heb. i. 3. xii. 2. l Lev. xxi. 10. 2 Kings xviii. 37. xix. 1—3. Jer. xxxvi. 24. Mark xiv. 63, 64. m in. 8 1 Kings xxi. 10—13. Luke v. 21. John x. 33, 36. n Lev. xxiv. 11—16. John xix. 7. Acts vii. 52. xiii. 27, 28. Jam. v. 6. o xxvii. 30. Num. xii. 14. Deut. xxv. 9. Job xxx. 10. Is. l. 6. Mark xiv. 65. Is. l. 6. liii. 3. xv. 19. p v. 39. 1 Kings xxii. 24. Jer. xx. 2. Lam. iii. 30. John xviii. 22. Acts xxiii. 2, 3. 2 Cor. xi. 20, 21. q Or. rods. Mic. v. 1. q xxvii. 39—44. Gen. xxxvii. 19, 20. Judg. xvi. 25—31. r xxvi. 58. Luke xxii. Mark xv. 16, 19. s xxvi. 58. Luke xxii. t ii. 22, 23. u 58. 1 Kings xix. 9, 13. x Mark xiv. 68, 69. Luke xxii. 56. John xviii. 25—27.

been proved; demanding, whether Jesus had nothing to say in his own behalf, when such things were witnessed against him.

V. 63—68. Our Lord remained silent before this iniquitous tribunal ; not merely from perfect meekness and patience, but as our Surety, that we might have an effectual plea before the tribunal of God. The high priest, therefore, at length solemnly " adjured him by the living " God," to declare whether " he was the Christ, the Son " of God," or not. This was the customary method of putting men upon their oath, to which the criminals, or witnesses, were required to answer, as in the presence of God. (Marg. Ref. d—g.) When the matter therefore was thus proposed, our Lord saw good to answer, that indeed Caiaphas had declared the real truth ; and that, notwithstanding his present despised condition, they would see him, as " the Son of man, sitting on the right hand " of power, and coming in the clouds of heaven." This is generally interpreted, of his exaltation, " at the right " hand of the Father," which was manifested by the " pouring out of the Spirit" on his disciples, and the vengeance executed by his power on Jerusalem : but his final coming to judgment seems also to have been intended ; and the members of the council were warned, that they would at length be constrained to stand before his awful tribunal. (Marg. Ref. h—k.—Notes, Dan. vii. 13, 14. Joel ii. 28—32. Luke xxii. 66—71. Acts ii. 33 —36. Heb. i. 3, 4. viii. 1, 2. xii. 2, 3. Rev. i. 7.) The avowal was evidently the very thing which the high priest wanted : and therefore he " rent his clothes," as if in detestation of blasphemy ; enquiring, what further need they had to examine any more witnesses, as they all had " heard his " blasphemy." In consequence therefore, they unanimously pronounced him guilty of a capital crime, and passed the sentence of death upon him ; and the attendants began, by the allowance of the rulers, to insult, buffet, and spit upon him, with the greatest disdain imaginable. Having covered his eyes, they " smote him " with " the " palms of their hands," or rather, " with their rods," (marg.) demanding of him a specimen and proof of his prophetical powers, by declaring the names of those who, one after another, smote him.—Thus they, without in-

tending it, fulfilled several prophecies, the literal accomplishment of which must previously have appeared highly improbable. (Marg. Ref. o, p.—Notes, Is. l. 5, 6. lii. 13— 15, v. 14. Mic. v. 1.)

I adjure. (63) Εξορκιζω. ' Adjuro, id est, interposito jure-' jurando, et Dei auctoritate præcipio, ut intelligas te coram ' Deo consistere, et velut a Deo ipso interrogari.' Beza. Used here only N. T.—Εξ ιχ, et ορκιζω, Mark v. 7. Acts xix. 13.—Thou hast said. (64) Συ ειπας. See on Note, 25.—Hereafter.] Απ᾽ αρτι. Luke xxii. 69, απο τα νυν, from the present time. This implies, that the manifested effects of his exaltation would in a little time be conspicuous : but it did not exclude such as were very remote.—Guilty of death. (66) Ενοχος θανατι. See on Note, v. 21, 22.— Buffeted. (67) Εκολαφισαν.—Κολαφιζω, alapa vel manu cædo. Mark xiv. 65. 1 Cor. iv. 11. 2 Cor. xii. 7. 1 Pet. ii. 20. A κολαφος, a blow with the palm of the hand.—Smote ... with the palms of their hands.] Ερβαπισαν. See on Note, v. 39. —Ραπισμα, ictus bacilli ictus, qui virgā, baculo, vel fuste incutitur. John xviii. 22. xix. 3.

V. 69—75. Every thing, which Peter had seen and heard, from his entrance into the high priest's palace, must have tended to dismay his mind. Whilst in this situation, surrounded with terrors and dangers on every side, and doubtless assaulted by strong temptations from Satan, a young woman challenged him as being a follower of Jesus ; and the dread of immediate detection, with all its imagined consequences, made him entirely forget his promises and resolutions. He was ready to fight for his Master ; but he had not before thought of the ignominious death of a criminal : he was therefore surprised into a denial of Christ, and a declaration, that he knew not what the woman meant by such an assertion. (Marg. Ref. t, u. —Notes, Mark xiv. 66—72, vv. 67, 68. John xviii. 17— 23, vv. 17, 18.) When he was gone out into the porch, or portico, belonging to the palace, perhaps with some thoughts of departing, another maid saw him, and said to those around her, that he certainly had been an attendant of Jesus : accordingly they charged him with it ; (Marg. Ref. x.—Note, Luke xxii. 54—62, v. 58 ;) and he again denied it, declaring with an oath that he did not so much as know him. This, probably, prevented him from at-

and said unto them that were there, | 61. ᵗ This *fellow* was also with Jesus of Nazareth.

ᵃ v. 54—56. Ex. xv. 7. Is. xlviii. 1. Zech. v. 3, 4. viii. 17. Mal. iii. 5. Acts ii. 3, 4. ᵃ 74. Luke xxii. 34. ᵇ Luke xxii. 59, 60. John xviii. 26, 27. ᶜ Judg. xii. 6. Neh. xiii. 24.

72 And again ʰe denied ¹ with an oath, ᵃ I do not know the man.

73 And after a while came unto *him* they that stood by, and said to Peter, ᵇ Surely thou also art one of them; ᶜ for thy speech bewrayeth thee.

74 Then ᵈ began he to curse and to swear, ᵉ *saying*, I know not the man. ᶠ And immediately the cock crew.

75. And Peter ᶠ remembered ·the word of Jesus, which said unto him, Before the cock crow, thou shalt deny me thrice. ʰ And he went out, and wept bitterly.

ᵈ xxvii. 25. Judg. xvii. 2. xxi. 18. 1 Sam. xiv. 24. 28. Mark xiv. 71. Acts xxiii. 12. 14. Rom. ix. 3. ᵉ 1 Cor. xvi. 22. ᶠ x. 28, 32, 33. John xxi. 15—17. Rev. iii. 19. Mark xiv. 30. 68. 72. Luke xxii. 60. John xviii. 27. ᵍ 34. Luke xxii. 61, 62. John xiii. 38.

ʰ xxvii. 3—5. Luke xxii. 32. Rom. vii. 18—20. 1 Cor. iv. 7. Gal. vi. 1. 1 Pet. i. 5.

tempting to go away, though we learn from Mark, that the cock at this time crowed : and in consequence, after another hour, those who stood by came to him, with a relation of Malchus whose ear he had cut off, and with greater confidence declared, that he assuredly was one of them ; for they had seen him with Jesus in the garden, and his Galilean dialect betrayed him as one of his followers. But Peter, now filled with extreme terror, " began to curse " and to swear," or to anathematize himself, as accursed of God and devoted to utter destruction, if he so much as knew the man! While he was using this horrid language, the cock again crowed ; and Jesus, being come into sight, turned and " looked upon him." Thus he was at once brought to recollect the words of Jesus, and his own rash engagements. His whole guilt immediately rushed into his mind ; he without delay left the place, full of the deepest shame, anguish, and remorse; and " wept bitterly" at the remembrance of his profaneness, treachery, cowardice, and ingratitude. (*Marg. Ref.* b—h.—*Notes, Mark* xiv. 66—72, *v.* 72. *Luke* xxii. 54—62, *v.* 61.) —Peter was left thus to fall, in order to give him a deeper acquaintance with his own heart, to abate his self-confidence, and to render him more modest, humble, and compassionate : and his whole subsequent conduct shewed, that he had exceedingly profited by the painful lesson. The event has also proved most instructive in various ways to believers ever since; and if infidels, Pharisees, and hypocrites will stumble at it, or abuse it, they do it at their peril. (*Note,* 2 *Sam.* xi. 27. *P. O.* 14—27.)—' Peter by ' the wonderful providence of God, appointed to be a wit- ' ness of all these things, is prepared to the example of ' singular constancy, by the experience of his own incre- ' dulity.' *Beza.*—' I venture to say, that it is useful to ' proud men to fall into some open and manifest sin, that ' they may be displeased with themselves, as they had al- ' ready fallen by their self-complacency. For Peter, being dis- ' pleased with himself, *wept* in a more salutary manner, than ' he had *presumed,* when pleased with himself.' *Augustin.*
To curse. (74) Καταναθεματίζειν. Used here only N. T. —Καταναθεμα. Rev. xxii. Αναθεμαλίζειν. Mark xiv. 71. ' Κατα significationem auget : ... potest etiam κατα reddi ' per seipsum, Seipsum devovere. Leigh.' Acts xxiii. 12. 14.

PRACTICAL OBSERVATIONS.
V. 1—13.
Amidst the apparently confused, casual, and distressing events, which take place in the world, through the treachery, avarice, ambition, or impiety of mankind ; we should always advert to the " determinate counsel and foreknow- " ledge of God," as bounding, directing, and over-ruling all, for the purposes of his own glory, and the benefit of

those who trust in him. " There are many devices in the " heart of man ;" and ungodly politicians form their plans with profound sagacity, and conceal them with deep dissimulation : yet, contrary to their intentions, they are led to arrange or alter them, in subserviency to the secret counsel of the Lord !—The enmity of the carnal heart against the law, truth, and image of God, is irreconcilable and mortal : it rages with greater violence in hypocrites, than in other men ; but most of all in covetous and ambitious churchmen. Thus power and policy have, in every age, combined against the Person and cause of Jesus ; yet they have not been able to prevail against them. But there has always been a remnant of another character : these are humble, penitent, and believing ; they reverence and love the Redeemer's Person and character ; they deem themselves to be under infinite obligations to him ; they long to express their love and gratitude, and zeal for his glory ; and they count nothing too valuable to be renounced for his sake, or employed in his service. These principles operate differently, as circumstances vary ; but they always produce such actions, as honour Christ, and as he will accept and commend : for he judges of men's conduct by their motives, and will not reject a well-meant service, springing from humble faith and love, though it may appear to us informal. But covetous hypocrites are ready to exclaim, " To what purpose is this waste ? " When they see others liberal in honouring Christ, even the *fraudulent* and *unjust* will plead for *charity,* if they can thus discredit the pious effusions of a believer's fervent love : and too often their plausible pretences seduce injudicious, or less zealous disciples, to censure those services which Christ accepts. But he will plead the cause of his humble followers; and rebuke those, who trouble them for their good works, which they have " wrought for his name's sake." It is his plan, that there should, in every age and place, be poor persons, and poor Christians as his stated representatives, in order to make trial of the faith and love of his disciples ; that whenever they will, they may relieve them for his sake. This is the ordinary method ; but extraordinary expressions of our love and gratitude are sometimes proper ; and these will not be found inconsistent with each other, or materially to interfere with one another.

V. 14—25.
Upright persons, when betrayed into a mistake, will take reproof in good part ; but it often proves the detection of hypocrites : thus the discovery of their secret motives, and the commendation of those whom they dislike, or the actions which they disapprove, exasperate them, and push them forward to still baser attempts : and, while those whom they censured are had in perpetual and ho-

2 p 3

CHAP. XXVII.

Jesus is delivered bound to Pilate, 1, 2. Judas, in remorse, restores the silver, and hangs himself, 3—5. The priests fulfil the scripture, in disposing of the

nourable remembrance, themselves sink into final infamy and misery.—But, with what scrupulous care and vigilance should every one guard against the first workings of avarice, and shun the most minute deviations from strict equity! For when dishonesty, in comparatively little things, has rendered the conscience callous, and given energy to temptation, men become capable of the most shameless injustice without hesitation; and the common question is, " What will ye give me ? " Then the most endeared or sacred ties will be broken, for even paltry filthy lucre, by men who set their consciences and their souls to sale. And by these means, scheming villains, who were at a loss how to accomplish their intended iniquities, are furnished with instruments as detestable as themselves; and they mutually assist, and yet abhor and despise, each other.—But let us follow the steps of our divine Master, whatever man may devise against us. His disciples may enquire when, where, and with what preparation he would have them to attend on his institutions : but they should take it for granted, that he will not countenance neglect in any; as he himself attended on all which were then in force.—Every heart is in his hands : he knows those " hidden ones " who favour his cause, and will graciously visit all who are willing to receive him : and he will take care to procure from them entertainment for his disciples also.—But divine ordinances are seldom administered, even to a few persons, without the intrusion of some hypocrite : and the cause of Christ is often most betrayed by some of those, who seem most entirely to belong to him. This consideration may often make us " exceedingly sorrowful;" and it should always render us very diligent in self-examination.—When a few persons are met for social prayer, religious conversation, or at the Lord's table ; it may probably occur to each of them to suppose, that their heart-searching Saviour is saying to the company, " Verily I say " unto you, that one of you shall betray me." They should not, however, look round on others with suspicion ; but with self-examination and prayer should say, " Lord, is " it I ? " We ought to be the more earnest in this investigation, because the doom of such domestick enemies will be most dreadful; so that it may be said of them especially, that " it would have been good for them, if " they had never been born : " and what heart can conceive the awful and tremendous import of those words! (Note, Ps. xc. 11.)

V. 26—35.

Self-examination and fervent prayers are peculiarly pro-per before " the Lord's supper;" in order, that, as " Christ ' our Passover is now sacrificed for us," we may " keep ' this"ᵗ commemorative " feast, not with the old leaven ' of malice and wickedness, but with the unleavened bread ' of sincerity and truth : " and that we may, every time we partake of it, renew our repentance, our faith in his blood, our consent to his covenant, our lively exercise of

admiring grateful love to him, and love to his people, and our surrender of ourselves to his service, as " bought with, " a price to glorify him with our bodies and our spirits, " which are his." While we contemplate the outward signs of " his body broken and his blood shed for the " remission of our sins;" let us recollect, that the feast was as expensive to him, as if he had literally " given us his " flesh to eat, and his blood to drink ;" that there must be a real (though a spiritual) participation of him, and appropriation of his salvation to our souls, or else we shall have no benefit from his sacrifice; and that by a continued reliance on him, in lively faith, we must be strengthened and recruited for our conflict, our work, and " the race " that is set before us." Let no humble believer then neglect the obedience of faith and love, in respect to this command of his dying Saviour; as safety and comfort should be sought in the way of his precepts. Whilst multitudes profane this sacred ordinance, by a proud, pharisaical, infidel, or licentious attendance; and numbers, by statedly absenting themselves, confess their consciousness that they have no part or lot in the blessings of salvation ; there are many true Christians who are guilty of ingratitude and hard suspicions of the gracious Redeemer, and do great harm to their own souls, by refusing this profession of their faith and love, or by so seldom joining with his people. It may be apprehended that some are alarmed by the case and doom of Judas, and the conscious hypocrite may well be called upon to pause and tremble at the thought : but the feeble Christian should remember, that all the apostles were offended during that very night, in which they had eaten both the passover and the Lord's supper, and that Peter fell in a more dreadful manner; yet their guilt was not unpardonable, nor their fall irrecoverable. Our communicating indeed ought to excite us to redouble our watchfulness : but the fear, of afterwards being overcome by temptation, should never induce any man to neglect obedience to the express command of Christ. Rather we should seek in this affecting ordinance, to enjoy his " love, which is " better than wine;" (Notes, Cant. i. 2. 4 ;) and to anticipate the felicity of heaven, when we shall rejoice with the Saviour, and he with us, unspeakably and eternally.

V. 36—46.

While we with thankfulness take the cup of salvation, let us never forget that cup of wrath, which the Redeemer drank off to the very dregs, for the remission of our sins. If we were not shamefully and surprisingly drowsy in spiritual things, we never could read or meditate about Gethsemane, without the most lively affections, and most instructive recollections. Here let us look attentively, that we may learn to distinguish between the sufferings of a martyr, and those of our atoning Sacrifice. View a poor, frail, sinful man, under the smiles of his reconciled Father, serene and cheerful in the prospect and endurance

dren, he releases Barabbas, and delivers Jesus to be crucified, 20—26. He is mocked, and crowned with thorns by the soldiers, 27—31; crucified between two thieves, 32—38; and reviled by the people and rulers, 39—44. The land is darkened, 45; Jesus calling on God expires, 46—50. The veil of the tem- ple is rent, the earth quakes, the tombs burst open, and the centurion confesses him, as "the Son of "God," 51—54. Certain women witness these scenes, 55, 56. Joseph of Arimathea asks his body and buries it, 57—61. His tomb is sealed by the chief priests, and a watch placed at it, 62—66.

---

of every possible torture: then behold the incarnate Son of God, "the holy, undefiled," "well beloved" of the Father, "in whom he was well pleased," prostrate on the earth, "exceedingly sorrowful even unto death," and "sweating great drops of blood, rolling to the ground;" and with this scene before our eyes, let it be determined, whether he was not then enduring the wrath and tremendous frown of God, as our Surety and the vicarious Sacrifice for our sins. And let the careless and impenitent ask themselves, Did God's own hand inflict these insupportable strokes, in fulfilment of his ancient prophecies, on his "beloved Son," who was more valued by him, than the whole visible creation; and will he break his word, in order to spare a determined rebel and enemy, who takes encouragement to sin from the very persuasion of God being merciful? Most vain and destructive presumption! (Note, Deut. xxix. 19, 20.) Did the load of imputed guilt so weigh down the soul of him, concerning whom it is said, that "He upholdeth all things by the "word of his power?" Into what an abyss of misery unknown then must they sink, whose iniquities are left upon their own heads, a burden far "too heavy for them "to bear!" "How will they escape who neglect so great "salvation?" What a forlorn hope must that of the Pharisee or the infidel be, who expects happiness in his own way, despising that which infinite wisdom has devised, and infinite love effected, at a price which baffles the powers of computation itself! Assuredly it will end in black despair; with the presumption of every one, who perverts the doctrine of a free salvation, as an excuse for indulged wickedness.—But the same scene discovers a cheerful dawn of hope to the trembling, desponding penitent: here we see the infinite hatred of sin of our holy Lord GOD, and his infinite love of sinners; his determination to satisfy his justice, and his delight in exercising mercy. In short, we must resort to Gethsemane, to learn repentance, hatred of sin, humility, hope, love, patience, meekness, and self-denying obedience; and to find comfort under dejection and temptations. Here we see our pattern, our motives, our encouragements; here we learn the vanity of the world, the evil of sin, and our obligations to live devoted to him, and willingly to suffer for his glory, who agonized and died for our salvation. While here we abide, we should beware of drowsiness: when "our souls are sorrowful," we should pour them out in prayer; and when nature would shrink from suffering, and would say, "If it be possible, let this cup pass from me," we should learn to add, "Nevertheless, not as I will, but "as thou wilt." We should also remember, that even our merciful High Priest will "rebuke those whom he "loves:" and if we promise great things, and come evidently short in little things; he will as it were, say to us, "What! could ye not watch with me one hour?" We must all indeed be tempted: yet we should be exceedingly afraid of "entering into temptation," by being drawn

into such circumstances, as give our enemies an opportunity of coming specially near to us, and obtaining their advantage against us. To be secured from this, we should watch and pray without ceasing: for though, in the regenerate, "the spirit is willing" for service or suffering; yet we carry about with us the remains of a carnal mind, our "hearts are deceitful above all things," we are "weak "through the flesh," and should continually be looking to the Lord, to "hold us up that we may be safe." But, after repeated warnings and rebukes, how dull and inattentive do we often remain! This causes our compassionate Lord to employ other means and instruments, to rouse us from our fatal lethargy; and when sharp afflictions or persecutions come upon us, he will, as it were, say to us, "Sleep on now, and take your rest," if you are able: yet, if even then we arise and follow him, he will preserve us from all permanent or fatal evil.

V. 47—56.

While we contemplate the insolence and enmity of those, who assaulted the Prince of Peace, and above all the treachery of Judas, with abhorrence: let us not forget, that such are we by nature, and so should we have acted, if left to ourselves. No enemies, however, deserve such decided execration, as those professed disciples, who "be- "tray Christ with a kiss." It behoves us to learn to copy the meekness and patience of Christ; and very circumspectly to avoid the rashness and cowardice of Peter, and the other apostles. Whatever provocations we meet with from avowed adversaries or false friends, or however we may be tried by the infirmities of inconsistent believers; we should learn of Jesus to "possess our souls in "patience," and to use no weapons, except sound arguments, mild expostulations, kind actions, and fervent prayers. Thus we shall be kept in peace; whilst "they "who take the sword will perish by the sword."—If it should be necessary for us, the prevalent intercession of our heavenly Advocate will procure for us the protection of "legions of angels:" but when our appointed time is come, we must be removed from this present world; yet "the scriptures must needs be fulfilled" in us also, and all the promises belong to every believer in Christ, and shall assuredly be fulfilled in everlasting glory and felicity.

V. 57—68.

Happy are they, against whom their most malicious enemies can allege nothing, except by "false witnesses!" —Persecutors will indeed commonly be more assiduous in doing mischief, than the most diligent Christian in doing good; and they will be sometimes watching to execute their wicked purposes, even when he is neglecting to watch and pray: they will find false witnesses, and invent slanders, to give a colour to their cruel hatred; and pervert the words of those, who plead the cause of God, to a quite contrary meaning: by these methods Jesus has been

WHEN *the morning was come, all the chief priests and elders of the people took counsel against Jesus to ^b put him to death.

a Judg. xvi. 2. 1 Sam. xix. 11. Prov. iv. 16—18. Mic. ii. 1. Luke 2i. xxii. 66. Acts v. 2i.
b xxiii. 13. xxvi. 3, 4. Ps. ii. 2. Mark xv. 1. Luke xxiii. 1, 2. John xviii. 28. Acts iv. 24—28.

2 And when they had ^c bound him, they led *him* away, ^d and delivered him to Pontius Pilate the governor.

3 ¶ Then ^e Judas, which had be-

c Gen. xvii. 9. John xviii. 12. 24. Acts ix. 2. xii. 6. xxi. 33. xxii. 25. 29. xxiv. 27. xxviii. 20. 2 Tim. ii. 9. Heb. xiii. 3.
d xx. 19. Luke xviii. 32, 33. xxiii. 20. Acts iii. 13. xxvi. 14. xiv. 10, 11. 43—46. Luke xxii. 2—6. 47, 48. John xiii. 2. 27. xviii. 3.

persecuted in his followers in every age. But while such men profess to execrate the imagined crimes of those whom they condemn ; their own consciences often protest against the sentence, and they feel that their proceedings are iniquitous. How then will they abide the coming of the Judge, when they shall " see him at the right hand of " power, and coming in the clouds of heaven ? " Let those, therefore, who have the honour to " suffer for his " sake," contemplate his calm behaviour before the council, and his intrepid confession of his true character ; and let them consider the crimes alleged against him, the condemnation passed on him, and the contempt, indignity, and insult which he most patiently and meekly endured. For the Christian cannot *reasonably* expect so much tenderness and compassion, when suffering for the truth, as a thief or murderer might, when punished for his crimes! and if he look to the scene which we are considering, he will perceive, that disdain, cruel mockings, and every expression of abhorrence, are the sure portion of the true disciple, from such men, as spat in the face of the holy Jesus, and buffeted and derided the " Lord of glory." Yet let us boldly confess his name, and bear the reproach ; and he will confess us before his Father's throne : whilst those, who pretend to do service to God, by murdering his saints, will be covered with shame and everlasting contempt.

V. 69—75.

Let all beware of vain-confidence and self-preference. It does not become us to boast, or resolve what we will do : rather let us decline temptation as much as we can, and trust in the Lord alone to uphold us. Let us also avoid rashness, and pray for victory over the fear of man. In all these respects, we need much forbearance from our gracious Lord : though we be not traitors, we are prone to decline the cross ; though we do follow Christ, it is commouly at a great distance ; and it is not unusual for even his disciples to be afraid of being known to belong to him! But when self-confidence induces men to thrust themselves uncalled into perilous circumstances, we may expect to hear of lamentable consequences.—Little do we know how we should act in very difficult situations, if left to ourselves : the snow does not more naturally melt before the fire, than our resolutions vanish when we enter into temptation. Who then can say, what he will do, or what he will not do ? The way of sin is also down-hill ; every step makes way for another still more fatal ; and there is nothing so false, impious, or atrocious, to which we might not gradually be tempted, if the Lord should wholly leave us. " Let him therefore, that thinketh he standeth, take " heed lest he fall," and let us all distrust our own hearts, and rely wholly on God, according to his word.—Let it also be noted, that Peter first lied wilfully : then he committed the most direct perjury to cover his lie : and then he uttered the most horrid execration on himself, equivalent to the worst language of those who delight in cursing.

This is the common progress of men in such cases. He, who ventures on a lie, will almost always, if pressed to it, urged, will wish all manner of evil on himself, if he does not speak truth.—If any have fallen even in the most dreadful manner, let them think of Peter's recovery, and not despair ; and let them recollect the words of Christ, as well as their own sins ; that their tears, confessions, and humiliations may be mingled with hope. And let us all frequently remember our past follies, and manifold instances of ingratitude ; that we may learn watchfulness, humility, caution, and compassion for the tempted and fallen, by the experience of our own numerous mistakes, sins, and recoveries.

NOTES.

CHAP. XXVII. V. 1, 2. The night must have been far advanced, before the transactions recorded in the foregoing chapter were finished : and it was early in the morning, when the chief priests and elders " delivered up " Jesus " to the governor." It is not certain whether they adjourned for a while, or continued together all night. If they had not " taken counsel against him to *put him to* " *death*," they would not have had occasion to apply to Pilate ; for they had still the power of executing lighter punishments : but they were not allowed to inflict death, without the consent of the Roman governor. Perhaps they were the more willing to deliver Jesus up to him, because the Roman punishment of crucifixion was more ignominious and excruciating, than stoning. They therefore bound Jesus, (having probably loosed him during his examination ; or, they confined him more closely than before, as a condemned malefactor,) and delivered him up to Pontius Pilate, the Roman procurator of Judea, in order that he might be put to death by his authority.— ' To ensure success in that quarter, it was necessary to give ' their accusations against Jesus such a colour and shape, ' as should prevail upon the governor to put him to death. ' ...They had condemned him for blasphemy : but this ' they knew would have little weight with a pagan, ... who, ' like Gallio, would " care for none of these things." ... ' They therefore resolved to bring him before Pilate as a ' *state-prisoner*, and to charge him with treasonable and ' seditious practices.' Bp. Porteus. (Marg. Ref.—Notes, *Mark* xv. 1—5. *Luke* xxiii. 1—5.)—*To put ... to death.* (1) Θανατωσαι. x. 21. Rom. viii. 13.

V. 3—5. Whatever Judas's views and expectations had been, when he betrayed his Lord ; he saw his own conduct in a very different light, when he found that Jesus was condemned to die, and was about to be crucified as a malefactor and a slave. (Note, xxvi. 14—16.) Then " he repented " himself ; " yet not with genuine humiliation and godly sorrow, united with faith, hope, and love : but he was sorry that he had committed this one crime ; his conscience was filled with horror and remorse, and his heart with

2 D 6

trayed him, when he saw that he was condemned, ' repented himself, and brought again the thirty pieces of silver, to the chief priests and elders, 4 Saying, ' I have sinned, in that I have betrayed ° the innocent blood. And they said, 'What is that to us? ' see thou to that. 5 And he cast down the pieces of

---

anguish and terror He could not but be sensible of the excellency and holiness of the character of Jesus; probably he was convinced that he was the promised Messiah; the miracles which he had witnessed, and the miraculous powers which he had received, must occur to his memory; and the wisdom, condescension, and love of his Lord, together with his peculiar kindness to him, must on this occasion rush at once on his recollection. Thus being left by God, Satan, who before had tempted him to presumption, now urged him to despair. Yet, before his last fatal determination, perhaps hoping to obtain a reversal of Christ's condemnation, he went to the chief priests and elders, to return " the wages of his iniquity." They were at that time in the precincts of the temple; whether they held their council there, and had not yet delivered up Jesus to Pilate; or whether they had gone thither after he was delivered up to be crucified, in order to perform some hypocritical task of devotion. In their presence, however, Judas acknowledged, that " he had sinned," (Marg. Ref. g.—Note, Ex. x. 16, 17. 1 Sam. xv. 24, 25. 30, 31,) in that he had betrayed an innocent person into their hands, who was by that means likely to be put to death; and he was now fully sensible, that his conduct had been peculiarly base and criminal. This was a most honourable testimony to Christ's character: but though this crime lay with intolerable weight on the conscience of Judas, and he confessed it to man, and dared not to keep the infamous wages of his crime; yet it does not appear that he was at all sensible of the guilt of his hypocrisy, and covetousness, and thefts, and all the other wickedness, committed during the whole course of his past life. The rulers, however, were too malignant and hardened, to be any ways affected by this interesting circumstance; and they coldly declared, that the opinion and conduct of so base a wretch concerned not them; let him look to that himself, for they were determined to put Jesus to death. ' Could they think ' it no sin to hire a man to " betray innocent blood?" Do ' not they confess this money to be " the price of blood?" ' (6) And was it not the very money they gave to purchase ' that blood? And was not the field they bought with it, ' stiled upon this account, " The field of blood?" And ' was not this a lasting testimony of their guilt, whose ' money purchased this blood? And therefore Stephen ' roundly calls them 'οι προδοται, the betrayers and mur- ' derers of that Just One. Acts vii. 52.' Whitby. This answer of the elders and chief priests completed Judas's despair; and, casting down the money, " he departed, and " went and hanged himself." It seems evident that he was his own executioner, by strangling himself; and this account may be reconciled with that of Peter, as recorded in the Acts, by supposing that he suspended himself, in such a place and manner, that the rope, or wood to which it was fastened, brake; and that he fell from a great height, and so burst asunder; this coming to pass by the special purpose of God, to render his body a more terrible spectacle to all beholders, and to cause his death to be the more

remarked. (Marg. Ref. h—k.—Note, Acts i. 16—18.) It admits of little doubt, that Judas's death preceded that of his injured Lord: so speedily did divine vengeance overtake him. Yet the rulers took no notice even of this alarming circumstance!—' It appears to me, that the acquittal or ' condemnation of Jesus never entered into Judas's con- ' templation. ...All he thought of was gain. He had kept ' the common purse, and had robbed it: and his only ob- ' ject was to obtain a sum of money, which he determined ' to have at all events, and left consequences to take care ' of themselves. But when he saw, that his divine Master, ' whom he knew to be perfectly innocent, was actually ' condemned to death, his conscience then flew in his ' face, his guilt rose up before him in all its horrors: ...he ' could no longer bear the agonizing tortures that racked ' his soul, but went immediately and destroyed himself. ... ' The answer of the chief priests...was perfectly natural ' for men of that character. ...Men who had any feeling, ' any sentiments of common humanity, or even of com- ' mon justice, ... would have put an immediate stop to the ' proceedings. ...But this was far from entering into their ' plan. ...All they wanted, was the destruction of a man, ' whom they hated and feared; and whose life and doc- ' trine was a standing reproach to them. ...And yet, to see ' the astonishing inconsistence of human nature, and the ' strange contrivances, by which the most abandoned of ' men endeavour to satisfy their minds; ... these very men, ' ...had wonderful qualms of conscience, about putting ' into the treasury the money, which they themselves had ' given as " the price of blood."—Judas was the constant ' companion of our Saviour's ministry, and witness to every ' thing he said or did. If there had been any plan con- ' certed to impose a false religion on the world, ... Judas ' must have been in the secret. ... His testimony is invalu- ' able, because it is the testimony of an unwilling witness; ' the testimony, not of a friend, but of an enemy.' Bp. Porteus. ' The greatest enemy, with a choice of means ' for detection of fraud and collusion, could not have ' pointed out any thing better calculated to suit his pur- ' pose, than the placing of Judas among the apostles.— ' It was a remarkable provision made by the Lord, for in- ' creasing to the highest point, the value of the testimony ' of the twelve apostles. It was like the water which Elijah ' commanded to be poured around the altar, before the fire ' from heaven descended to consume the sacrifice. Judas ' also, as the other apostles, although in a different way, ' sealed his testimony with his blood.' Haldane on Divine Revelation.

Repented himself. (3) Μεταμεληθεις—See on xxi. 29.— *Innocent.* (4) Αθωον (ex a priv. et θαη, mulcta:) not elsewhere N. T.—*Hanged himself.* (5) Απηγξατο. Not elsewhere N. T.—2 Sam. xvii. 23. Sept. ' Ahithophel ...' went ' " away and hanged himself:" not dying with excess of ' grief and melancholy as some think; since that, in all ' likelihood, would have hindered him from " setting his ' " house in order;" or giving such a solemn charge con-

silver in the temple, ¹ and departed, and went and hanged himself.

6 And the chief priests took the silver pieces, and said, ᵐ It is not lawful for ⁿ to put them into the treasury, because it is the price of blood.

7 And they took counsel, and bought with them the potter's field, to bury strangers in.

8 Wherefore ° that field was called, The field of blood, ᵖ unto this day.

9 Then was fulfilled that which was spoken by Jeremy the prophet, saying, ᵠ And they took the ʳ thirty pieces of silver, the price of him that was valued, whom they ˢ of the children of Israel did value;

10 And gave them for the potter's field, as the Lord appointed me.

11 ¶ And ᵗ Jesus stood before the governor; and the governor asked him, saying, Art thou the king of the Jews? And Jesus said unto him, ᵘ Thou sayest.

12 And when ˣ he was accused of the chief priests and elders, he answered nothing.

13 Then saith Pilate unto him, ʸ Hearest thou not how many things they witness against thee?

14 And he answered him to never a ᶻ word; insomuch that the governor ᵃ marvelled greatly.

15 ¶ Now at that ᵇ feast the governor was wont to release unto the people a prisoner, whom they would.

16 And they had then ᶜ a notable prisoner, called Barabbas.

'cerning it.' Whitby. (Note, 2 Sam. xvii. 23.)—' Proprie ' significat *strangulare*; id est, contrictâ gulâ necare.' Beza.

V. 6—10. When the priests and rulers had leisure, with a scrupulosity worthy of their character, they consulted what was to be done with the money restored by Judas, and determined that it was unlawful to put it into the sacred treasury; having been the price paid for the blood of Jesus, and proving eventually that of Judas also. (Note, xxiii. 23, 24.) Yet they thought it proper to lay it out in some way, which might appear *charitable*: and therefore they purchased with it a piece of waste ground, which had been dug up for clay by a potter, and was of small value; that it might be appropriated to the burial of such persons of other nations as died at Jerusalem; on which account that field was called, " the field of blood," even to the time when Matthew wrote his gospel. (Marg. Ref. m—p. —Note, Acts i. 19.) This fulfilled an ancient prophecy, which is here said to have been spoken by Jeremiah, but which we have already considered in the prophecy of Zechariah. (Note, Zech. xi. 10—14.)—Various conjectures have been formed on the subject: but it is most natural to admit that a trivial error has crept into the text; for the change of a single letter, according to the abbreviated manner in which names are written in the old manuscripts, would suffice to occasion the mistake. The passage is quoted something differently than it stands in the prophecy: but the meaning is, that the thirty shekels, the vile price at which the Jews valued and bargained for the Shepherd of Israel, as if he had been a slave, came into the hands of a potter. This was foretold and exactly accomplished. If this be, as it is by far most probable, intended as a quotation from Zechariah, or a reference to his prediction; the Septuagint must have been wholly disregarded by the Evangelist. This version may be literally translated, as follows: ' They appointed thirty pieces of silver as my ' hire; and the Lord said unto me, Place these in the re- ' fiuer's furnace, and I will see whether it be approved, in ' the manner in which I have been proved by them. And

'I took the thirty pieces of silver, and I brought them ' into the house of the Lord, unto the refiner's furnace.'— It accords much more nearly, though not exactly, to the Hebrew.—*The treasury.* (6) Κορβαναν.—Κορβαν Note, Mark vii. 11, 12.

V. 11—18. ' Little did the governor imagine who it ' was that then stood before him! Little did he suspect, ' that he himself must one day stand before the tribunal ' of that very person, whom he was then about to judge as ' a criminal!' Bp. Porteus.—The rulers of the Jews, knowing how jealous the Romans were of their authority, accused Jesus of advancing claims to the kingdom. Pilate therefore " asked him," saying, " Art thou the king of " the Jews," to which he answered in the affirmative: yet, as Pilate had doubtless heard of the inoffensive demeanour of Jesus and his few followers, he probably thought his pretensions more worthy of derision, than opposition. His prosecutors, therefore, fearing that they should not carry their point, were earnest in laying many things to his charge; which only convinced Pilate that they envied his authority and reputation among the people, as eclipsing their own. Yet when Pilate enquired, whether Jesus had any thing to say in answer to all these accusations, he remained silent! He had no guilt to confess; yet he would not exculpate himself: for he submitted to condemnation, that he might die as a Sacrifice for our sins. This silence, which doubtless was distinguished by a mild and sedate dignity of aspect, the reverse of the sullenness of an obstinate criminal, astonished Pilate. He believed Jesus to be perfectly innocent; and yet he would use neither arguments nor intreaties, to rescue himself from that terrible death, with which he was threatened! The Romans allowed accused persons to answer for themselves. The apostle Paul frequently availed himself of this, and made his defence. (Notes, Acts xxiv. 10—21. xxv. 15—27. xxvi.) Jesus, long accustomed to speak in publick, could not be considered as incapable of pleading his own cause. Pilate was, therefore, exceedingly amazed, to find that he would not avail himself of the opportunity. (Marg. Ref. s—y.—

2 D 6

17 Therefore when they were gathered together, Pilate said unto them,
[b] Whom will ye that I release unto
you? Barabbas, [c] or Jesus which is
called Christ?
18 For [d] he knew that for envy they
had delivered him.
19 ¶ When he was set down on the
judgment-seat, [e] his wife sent unto him,
saying, Have thou nothing to do with
[f] that just man; for I have suffered
many things this day in a dream because of him.
20 But the chief priests and elders
[g] persuaded the multitude that they
[h] should ask Barabbas, and destroy
Jesus.
21 The governor answered and said
unto them, Whether of the twain will
ye that I release unto you? They said, [i]
Barabbas.
22 Pilate saith unto them, [i] What
shall I do then with Jesus, which is
called Christ? *They* all say unto him, [k]
Let him be crucified.
23 And the governor said, [k] Why, [l]
what evil hath he done? [l] But they
cried out the more, saying, Let him be [m]
crucified.
24 When Pilate saw that he could [n]
prevail nothing, but *that* rather a tumult was made, he took water, [m] and [o]
washed *his* hands before the multitude, saying, I am innocent of the
blood of this [n] just person; see ye *to it*.
25 Then answered all the people,
and said, [o] His blood *be* on us, [p] and on
our children. [p]

b 21. Josh. xxiv. 15. 1 Kings xviii. 21.
c 22. Mark xv. 9—12. John xix. 15.
d Gen. xxxvii. 11. 1 Sam. xviii. 7—11. Ps. cvi. 16. Prov. xxvii. 4. Ec. iv. 4. Is. xxvi. 11. Mark xv. 10. Acts v. 17. vii. 9. xiii. 45. Jam. iv. 5.
e Gen. xx. 3—6. xxxi. 24. 29. Job xxxiii. 14—17.
f Prov. xxix. 1. 4. 24. Zech. ix. 9. Luke xxiii. 41. 47. 1 John ii. 1.
g Mark xv. 11. Acts xiv. 18, 19. xix. 23—29.
h Luke xxiii. 18—20. John xviii. 40. xix. 15, 16. Acts iii. 14, 15.
i 17. Job xxxi. 31. Ps. xxii. 6, 9. Is. xlix. 7. liii. 2, 3. Zech. xi. 8. Mark xiv. 55. xv. 12—14. Luke xxiii. 20—24. John xix. 14, 15. Acts xiii. 28.
k Gen. xxxvii. 18, 19. 1 Sam. xix. 3—15. xx. 31—33. xxii. 14—19.
l Acts vii. 57. xvii. 5—7. xxi. 28—31. xxii. 22, 23. xxiii. 10. 12—15.
m Deut. xxi. 6, 7. Job ix. 30, 31. Ps. xxvi. 6. Jer. ii. 27. 35.
n 4. 19. 54. John xix. 4. Acts iii. 14. 2 Cor. v. 21. 1 Pet. iii. 18.
o xxiii. 30—37. Num. xxxv. 33. Deut. xix. 10. 14. Josh. ii. 19. 2 Sam. iii. 28, 29. 2 Kings xxiv. 3, 4. Ps. cix. 12—19. Ez. xxii. 2—4. xxiv. 7—9. Acts v. 28. vii. 52. 1 Thes. ii. 15, 16. Heb. x. 28—30.
p Ex. xx. 5. Ez. xviii. 14, &c.

Notes, Mark xv. 1—5. *Luke* xxiii. 1—5. *John* xviii. 33—36. xix. 8—12. 1 *Tim*. vi. 13—15, *v*. 13.) Pilate was, however, still desirous of releasing him: and as it had become a custom to pardon some condemned Jew, at the feast of the passover, to please the people; he supposed, that this custom would give him the occasion of releasing him; for he concluded that the multitude in some degree favoured him: so that, when they required him to indulge them as usual, he proposed none but Jesus and Barabbas. And, as Barabbas was a noted criminal, who had been guilty of murder as well as robbery, Pilate doubtless concluded, that they would unanimously prefer Jesus to him. (*Marg. Ref*. z—d.—*Notes, Mark* xv. 6—10. *Luke* xxiii. 13—25, *v*. 25. *John* xviii. 37—40. *Acts* iii. 12—16, *v*. 14.)

Notable. (16) Επισημον. *Insignis. Rom*. xvi. 7. Not elsewhere N. T.

V. 19—23. While these things were in agitation, another circumstance occurred, which increased Pilate's perplexity, and his desire to save Jesus: for his wife sent to caution him, by no means to have any hand in the death of "that "*righteous* man," whom he was solicited to condemn; as she had endured much misery, by terrifying dreams respecting him; which made her conclude, that his death would be avenged in an awful manner upon all concerned in it. (*Marg. Ref*. e, f.) In the mean time, the rulers were using all their influence with the people, to induce them to demand the release of Barabbas, and the crucifixion of Jesus: and when Pilate renewed his proposal, he was surprised to find, that Barabbas was unanimously preferred; and that the multitude were clamorous in demanding the crucifixion of Jesus, whom they had called the Messiah; though they could lay no crime to his charge. On other occasions, the condemnation of any Jew, who was not a slave, to this ignominious and cruel death, would have hazarded an insurrection: but the people had been disappointed in their expectations of a temporal kingdom; and many of them seem to have thought, that a Messiah of Jesus's character was worthy only of contempt and crucifixion.—It has, however, often excited wonder, that the multitude, who but a short time before had welcomed him with loud Hosannas, as the "Son of David" and "the "King of Israel," (*Note*, xxi. 8—11,) and who so much favoured his cause, as to render the rulers afraid of openly proceeding against him, should all at once be induced to demand his crucifixion with irresistible vehemence. But a multitude hastily collected is a fluctuating body; and resembles the waters of the sea, which yield to the least impulse of the wind.—Many, who before led the people and favoured the cause of Christ, intimidated by late events, had no doubt retired: others were disappointed, because he would not assume temporal dominion, and raise an army to liberate them from the Romans; and several persons, who had been driven away, by the popular torrent in his favour, when he entered Jerusalem, no doubt at this time came forward, attended by emissaries from the scribes and priests. And those who remember, that in every multitude thus collected, "the most part know not wherefore they are "come together," will readily perceive that a small company of considerable persons (a hundred out of ten thousand,) eager on the contrary part, and skilful in exciting men's passions and prejudices, would soon give a new direction to the populace; and that the change, from *Hosanna* to *Crucify*, was not materially different from other changes, which varying circumstances have made in large companies promiscuously assembled. (*Marg. Ref*. g. l.—*Note, Acts* xix. 23—31.)

V. 24, 25. Pilate was very reluctant to condemn Jesus to be crucified: but the Jews were so bent upon it, that he concluded it would be hazardous to stand out against them; lest they should excite an insurrection, or accuse him to the emperor as disaffected to his authority. His government was also very odious to the Jews, and he was afraid of exasperating them. (*Note, John* xix. 8—12, *v*. 12.) But his struggle, on this occasion, shews the power of conscience in the worst of men; and the horror, which it often feels, (till inured to it,) of wilful deliberate murder. —The whole process resembled the examination of a sacrifice, that it might be proved to be without blemish, far

26 ¶ Then 'released he Barabbas unto them; and when he had 'scourged Jesus, he delivered *him* to be crucified.

27 Then the soldiers of the governor took Jesus into the * common hall, and gathered unto him the whole 'band *of* soldiers.

28 And they 'stripped him, and put on him a scarlet robe.

29 And when they had "platted a crown of thorns, they put *it* upon his head, and a reed in his right hand; and they bowed the knee before him, and mocked him, saying, "Hail, king of the Jews!

30 And ' they spit upon him, and took the reed, and smote him on the head.

31 And after that they had mocked him, they took the robe off from him, and put his own raiment on him, ' and led him away to crucify *him*.

more than the trial of a criminal for condemnation: and it is unprecedented in the annals of mankind, for a person condemned to so dreadful a death, to have been at the very time pronounced " innocent," or righteous, by the person who conducted those that apprehended him (3), by the judge who passed sentence on him, and at length by the very officer who superintended his execution (54); whilst they who clamorously demanded his death, could allege no reason for their conduct. No doubt God providentially ordered all these circumstances, to make it evident, that Jesus suffered for no fault of his own, but merely for the sins of his people.—When, however, Pilate had determined to yield to the desire of the Jews; as a relief to his conscience, and a protestation against their injustice, " he " took water, and washed his hands before them." This was probably a custom among the Romans, as well as the Jews, in averring their innocence of any crime charged on them. (*Marg. Ref.* m.—*Note, Deut.* xxi. 1—9, *vv.* 6—9.) It was a most explicit testimony to Christ's innocency of the crimes charged on him; for Pilate could intend no more, though his words, compared with the reality of the case, may seem to imply that his death would be required of the Jews as his murderers: but it was vain for Pilate to expect thus to free himself from the guilt of " the innocent blood" of " a righteous person;" when he was bound by office to protect him from his cruel enemies. The Jews, however, were more callous than the heathen governor: and while he feebly attempted to clear himself of the guilt, they, by a most horrid imprecation, willingly took it all upon themselves and their posterity! This imprecation has been most awfully answered: as they were willing to bear the guilt of the blood, which they were about to shed; so it actually was avenged on them in the siege and destruction of Jerusalem, when vast numbers were crucified; and doubtless some of these very persons, as well as of their children: and the nation has ever since been exposed to incessant injuries from man, and left as an anathema from God; as still, from age to age, persisting in the sin of their fathers, and justifying it, as the deserved punishment of a deceiver.—
' They put Jesus to death, when the nation was assem-
' bled to celebrate the passover; and when the nation was
' assembled for the same purpose, Titus shut them up
' within the walls of Jerusalem. The rejection of the true
' Messiah was their crime: and the following of false Mes-
' siahs to their destruction was their punishment. They
' bought Jesus as a slave, and they themselves were after-
' wards sold and bought as slaves, at the lowest prices. ...

' They put Jesus to death, lest the Romans." should come,
' " and take away their place and nation;" and the Romans
' did come, and take away their place and nation. And,
' what is still more striking, and still more strongly marks
' the judgment of God upon them; they were punished
' with that very kind of death, which they were so eager to
' inflict on the Saviour of mankind, the death of the cross;
' and that in such prodigious numbers, that Josephus as-
' sures us, there wanted wood for crosses, and room to
' place them in.' *Bp. Porteus.* (*Marg. Ref.* o, p.)—*See ye to it.* (24) Ὑμεῖς ὄψεσθε. 4.

V. 26—31. Barabbas escaped, in consequence of Jesus's condemnation. He deserved death, but was preserved, and the righteous and holy Saviour suffered in his stead. This accords, as to the grand outline, with the method of a sinner's salvation, through the sufferings of Christ.—The Jewish rulers, by using their influence in preserving a murderer from death, took an effectual method of bringing the vengeance of God on the land; though not so effectual, as by crucifying the Son of God. (*Notes,* 11—18, *vv.* 16, 17. *Num.* xxxv. 31—34. *Mark* xv. 6—10, *v.* 7. *Luke* xxiii. 21—25, *v.* 25.)—St. John expressly mentions Christ's being scourged, and crowned with thorns, before Pilate finally passed sentence on him : it is therefore conjectured, that he had been scourged some time before, by orders from Pilate, in hopes that this disgrace and torture would have appeased the rage of the multitude, or softened them into compassion, and so have made way for his release. It is well known that the Romans used to scourge malefactors, just before they were crucified; ' as if the ' exquisite tortures of crucifixion were not sufficient, with- ' out adding to them those of the scourge!' *Bp. Porteus.* Possibly, the scourging might be twice repeated; but it is more probable, that Matthew and Mark introduce this account, not in the exact order of time in which it occurred. It is at least evident, that Pilate made an effort to save Jesus, after he had been scourged, and crowned with thorns: and perhaps the soldiers, after sentence was finally passed, carried still further the indignities which they had before commenced. (*Marg. Ref.* r.—*John* xix. 1—7.)— But, in whatever order these events occurred, the blessed Jesus was at length delivered up, without reserve, to the insults, derision, and cruelty of the soldiers; who, collecting the whole cohort into the praetorium, clothed him with " a scarlet" or *purple* robe, (perhaps a purple vestment with a scarlet robe over it,) such as used to be worn by the Roman generals, being probably one that Pilate had cast off. Thus, they arrayed him in the garments of royalty,

32 And *as they came out, ᵇ they found a man of ᶜ Cyrene, Simon by name: him they compelled to bear his cross.

33 And when they were come unto ᵈ a place called Golgotha, that is to say, A place of a skull,

34 They ᵉ gave him vinegar to drink mingled with gall: and when he had tasted thereof, he would not drink.

35 And ᶠ they crucified him, and ᵍ parted his garments, casting lots : ʰ that it might be fulfilled which was spoken by the prophet, They parted my garments among them, and upon my vesture did they cast lots.

---

as indignantly scorning his claim to be the " King of the " Jews : " and then mingling cruelty with contempt, they platted thorns into a crown for his head, and put a reed, or cane, such as was used to walk with, into his hand instead of a sceptre. Then they bowed their knee in mockery ; and at the same time they spit upon him, and smote the thorns into his temples, by taking the cane and striking him with it upon the head. (Marg. and Marg. Ref. s—y. —See on Note, xxvi. 63—68, v. 67.—Notes, Mark xv. 11 —20, vv. 16. 19, 20. Luke xxiii. 6—12, v. 11.)—We may form some conception of this scene, if we consider the ferocity, haughtiness, and impiety of the idolatrous Roman soldiers ; and how they were let loose on the mild and holy Jesus, to give full scope to their savage and cruel contempt, and to divert themselves with his sufferings, till they were even weary of mocking him. When this at length was the case, they took off from him the insignia of royalty ; and, putting on him his own garments, those who were appointed to be his executioners led him away to crucify him. Had he suffered as a murderer, they would not have thus insulted him ; but would have in some measure pitied his anguish, whilst they executed the sentence of the law upon him.—Another meaning has been sought out for the word rendered thorns, as if bearsfoot, or some inoffensive vegetable, was intended. This criticism, however, has been proved, by the most competent scholars, wholly untenable. But why should the peculiar weed, or plant, of which the contemptuous crown was made, be especially noted, if this had not been a circumstance particularly marking the cruelty of our Lord's enemies, and the variety and intenseness of his sufferings ?

When he had scourged, &c. (26) Ψραγελλωσας. Mark xv. 15. ' Est vox Latina, flagello, unà tantum literâ com-' mutatâ. Φραγελλιον flagellum. John ii. 15.' Leigh.—The common hall. (27) " The governor's house." Marg.—Τo πραιτωριον. (A prætor, Lat.) Mark xv. 16. John xviii. 28. 33. xix. 9. Acts xxiii. 35. Phil. i. 13.—(Note, John xviii. 28— 32, v. 28.)—The band.] Την σπειραν cohortem. Mark xv. 16. John xviii. 3. 12. Acts x. 1. xxi. 31. xxvii. 1. A Roman cohort consisted of about 500 men ; but perhaps a less number is here meant.

A scarlet robe. (28) Χλαμυδα κοκκινην. Χλαμυς· 31. Not elsewhere N. T. ' Paludimentum : ... pallium insigne ' bellicum, et imperatorum ducumque proprium.' Leigh. —Κοκκινος, Coccineus. Heb. ix. 19. Rev. xvii. 3. xviii. 16.—Πορφυραν, Mark xv. 17. 'Ιματιον πορφυρον, John xix. 2.—Of thorns. (29) Ακανθων. ' It is taken not only ' for thorns, but likewise for briers and brambles, and ' any thing that hath pricks.' Leigh. Ακανθινος· Mark xv. 17. John xix. 5.—Gen. iii. 18. Sept.—They bowed the knee.] Γωνυπετωντες. In genua procidentes. Mark i. 40. x. 37.—Τ.... τα γονατα προσκυνων αυτω· Mark xv. 19.

V. 32—34. ' Jesus is led out of the city, that we may ' be brought into the heavenly kingdom. He found no ' comfort any where, that we might be filled with all com- ' forts. He is made a curse, that we may be blessed. He ' is spoiled of his garments, that we might be enriched by ' his nakedness.' Beza.—It was customary for the persons who were sentenced to crucifixion, to carry their crosses, or at least a heavy part of them, to the place where they were crucified. But Jesus had been so harassed, by multiplied fatigues and miseries, that probably he appeared almost exhausted : so that the persons employed might fear lest he should die under the burden, and escape their further cruelties, if they compelled him to bear the cross all the way to Golgotha. It seems at first to have been laid upon him ; but afterwards meeting with Simon, a native of Cyrene, who evidently was suspected of favouring him, they obliged him to bear the cross after Jesus. Perhaps he bare the whole rest of the way; or he carried one end, while Jesus, going before, carried the other. This aptly represented the believer's conformity to his Lord, in bearing the cross, even the scorn and hatred of the world. (Marg. Ref. b, c.—Note, xvi. 24—28, v. 24.) In this manner, they proceeded to a place without the city, called " Golgotha," or " a place of a skull :" being, probably, so called from the skulls and human bones, which were there in abundance ; as it had long been the place of execution and burial for malefactors. (Marg. Ref. d.—Note, Luke xxiii. 32—38, v. 33.)—It was customary to give those, who were about to suffer this lingering and most painful death, a potion to benumb their feelings, composed of wine mingled with myrrh or spices: and some compassionate persons seem to have prepared this cordial, which they offered to Jesus ; but he would not taste it, as his purpose was to suffer death in all its bitterness. But others, full of contempt and malignity, had mingled " vinegar with gall," to render it most nauseous, and offered it to him instead of the spiced wine, which, having tasted, he refused to drink : and thus an ancient prophecy of the Messiah was literally fulfilled. (Note, Ps. lxix. 21.) —Those learned men, who labour to prove, that " the " vinegar mingled with gall " was in fact the same as " the " wine mingled with myrrh," mentioned by St. Mark, seem to have forgotten this remarkable prophecy. (Marg. Ref. e.—Note, Mark xv. 21—24, v. 23.)—They compelled. (32) Ηγγαρευσαν. See on v. 41.

V. 35. The soldiers next proceeded to crucify Jesus. This was performed in the following manner : the sufferer was stripped almost naked, and extended on the wood of the cross, as it lay on the ground; his arms were then stretched out on the transverse beam, and fastened to it by spikes driven through the hands; and the feet were fastened to the upright part of the cross, by spikes driven through

i 54. Mark xv. 39.
k Mark xv. 26.
Luke xxiii. 38.
John xix. 19—24.
l 44. Is. liii. 12.
Mark xv. 27.
28. Luke xxiii.
37. xxiii. 22, 33.
xix. 18. 31—39.
m Ps. xxii. 6, 7.
17. xxxi. 11—13.
xxxv. 15—21.
Isiv. 7—12. 20.
cix. 2, 25. Lam.
i. 12. ii. 15—17.
Mark xv. 29,30.
39. 1 Pet. ii. 22.
n Gen. xxxvii. 19,
20. Rev. xi. 10.
o xxvi. 61. Luke
xix. 29, 30. John
ii. 19—22.
p 54. iv. 3, 6. xxvi. 63, 64.

36 And ¹sitting down, they watched him there:

37 And set up over his head ᵏ his accusation written, THIS IS JESUS THE KING OF THE JEWS.

38 Then were there ¹ two thieves crucified with him; one on the right hand, and another on the left.

39 And they that passed by ᵐ reviled him, wagging their heads,

40 And ⁿ saying, Thou ° that destroyest the temple, and buildest it in three days, save thyself. ᵖ If thou be

the Son of God, ⁹ come down from the cross.

41 Likewise also ʳ the chief priests, mocking him, with the scribes and elders, said,

42 He ˢ saved others, himself he cannot save. If he be ᵗ the King of Israel, let him now come down from the cross, and we will believe him.

43 He ᵘ trusted in God: let him deliver him now, if he will have him: for he said, ˣ I am the Son of God.

44 The ʸ thieves also, which were

q xvi. 4. Luke xii. 31.
r Ps. xxii. 12, 13. Is. xlix. 7. Zech. xi. 8. Mark xv. 31, 32. Luke xxiii. 52. xxiii. 35.
s John ix. 24. xi. 47. Acts iv. 14.
t 37. ii. 2. Luke xix. 38. John i. 49.
u Ps. iii. 2. xiv. 6. xxii. 8. xlii. 10. xxxvii. 10. xl. John iii. 16, 17. v. 17—22, xi.
x 30. 36. xix. 7. 38. Job xix. 7—9. John xix. 7—
Mark xv. 32. Luke xxiii. 39, 40

both of them together. Then the cross was erected, and the foot of it, going into a hole made for that purpose, with a violent jerk, often dislocated some of the bones of the crucified person; who, being suspended in this dreadful posture, hung in most exquisite torture, till at length loss of blood and excess of pain ended his life. It is plain, that Jesus hung in this manner for six hours, before he expired: yet it was thought wonderful that he died so soon; as many lived a whole day and night in this anguish, unless some method were taken to shorten their pains.— When the soldiers (four of whom were employed in it,) had completed the cruel business, they proceeded to part the clothes among them as their recompence; and finding the upper garment, worn by Jesus, to be made of one piece, they cast lots for it: (*Notes, John* xix. 23, 24:) thus several prophecies concerning the Messiah received their accomplishment in Jesus. (*Note, Ps.* xxii. 16—18.)—The quotation is *verbatim* from the Septuagint; which literally gives the meaning of the Hebrew. The whole quotation, however, is wanting in many manuscripts, and ancient versions.

Vesture.] 'Ιματισμον. (Ab ιμαδιον, vestis.) *Luke* vii. 25. ix. 29. *John* xix. 24. *Acts* xx. 33. 1 *Tim.* ii. 9. ' Si stric-' tius interdum sumi debeat, *exteriorem potiùs quàm interi-* ' *orem vestem* denotat.' *Leigh.*

V. 36. The soldiers watched, that none might remove the bodies of the persons crucified, till it was ascertained, that they were dead, and orders were given, that they might be removed.

V. 37, 38. It was usual, at least in remarkable cases, to affix the name and the crime of the crucified person, in writing, on the top of the cross; and Pilate had ordered that it should be written in different languages over his head, " This is Jesus the Nazarene, the King of the Jews:" for God over-ruled his mind thus to attest the truth concerning Jesus, as the Messiah, the King of the Jewish nation, and of the whole Israel of God. (*Marg. Ref.* k.—*Note, John* xix. 20—22.) Yet at the same time two malefactors were crucified with him, and he was placed between them, as if more criminal than either of them; which was no doubt devised in order the more deeply to disgrace him.— ' But this act of malignity, like many instances of the same ' nature, answered a purpose, which the authors of it little ' thought of, or intended. It was the completion of a pro-' phecy of Isaiah, in which ... he says of the Messiah, " He ' " was numbered among the transgressors." ' *Bp. Porteus.*

(*Marg. Ref.* l.—*Notes, Is.* liii. 11, 12. *Mark* xv. 26—28, v. 28.)

V. 39—44. While the holy and divine Saviour was suspended, in this most ignominious and excruciating posture; the multitudes which passed by, knowing for what alledged crime he was crucified, reviled and derided him in every way which they could devise; reproaching him with having spoken of " destroying the temple, and re-" building it in three days;" and calling on him in deri-sion to break loose, and come down from the cross, if he were " the Son of God." (*Marg. Ref.* m—q.—*Notes,* xxvi. 57—62, vv. 60, 61. *John* ii. 18—22.) From an igno-rant and unprincipled rabble such behaviour might the less be wondered at: but the very priests, even the chief of them, and the scribes, the learned men, and rulers of the nation, forgetful of their character, office, education, and authority, and permitting their disdainful rage to overcome all regard to decorum, joined the multitude, and led them on to insult and mock the meek and suffering Jesus. They even reproached him with his miracles; allowing that he saved the lives of others, yet deriding him as unable to save his own. It was indeed an important truth, that if he would save sinners from eternal misery, he could not save himself from these exquisite sufferings and this igno-minious death; but they did not understand this. They treated all the proofs of his being the Messiah with con-tempt, and called upon him, if he were indeed " the King " of Israel, to come down from the cross, and they would " believe in him." (*Marg. Ref.* r—t.—*Ps.* xxii. 11—13. 16—18. *Is.* xlix. 7, 8.) Not that this would have con-vinced them, for his resurrection had no such effect: but, assuring themselves that he could not rescue himself, they grew more hardened in unbelief, and used this cruel sar-casm to increase his anguish. (*Note, Luke* xvi. 27—31.) Nay, they reproached him for his confidence in God, and challenged God himself to deliver him, if he had any de-light in him, seeing he had " called himself the Son of " God." (*Marg. Ref.* u, x.) Probably they did not know, that in this daring impiety, enmity, and blasphemy, they used the very words, which the prophet had put into the mouths of the murderers of the Messiah, a thousand years before! (*Note, Ps.* xxii. 7, 8, v. 8.) To complete this un-paralleled scene, even the thieves who were crucified with him, could find a heart, in the midst of their own agonies and the horrid prospect which lay before them, to join the general voice, and to upbraid the crucified Jesus with his

q x 4

crucified with him. cast the same in his teeth.

2 Mark xv. 25. 33, 34. Luke xx iii. 44, 45. a Is. l. 3. Am viii. 9. Rev. viii. 12. Lu. 2. 45 ¶ Now ² from the sixth hour there was ³ darkness over all the land unto the ninth hour.

46 And about the ninth hour ᵇ Jesus cried with a loud voice. saying, " Eli, Eli, lama sabachthani ? that is to say, My God, my God, why hast thou forsaken me ?

b Mark xv. 34. Luke xxiii. 46. John xiv. 28. 30. Heb. v. 7. c Ps. xxii. l. lxxi. 11.

---

claim to be the Messiah, and " the Son of God." Though they suffered for notorious crimes, they escaped this obloquy and insult, and were regarded as objects of compassion; yet even *they* could look down on Jesus with disdain and derision! The evangelists Matthew and Mark speak, as if both the malefactors had been guilty of this outrage: but it is not certain whether more than one of them be meant. (*Marg. Ref. y.—Note, Luke* xxiii. 39—43.)—We may challenge universal history to furnish another instance, in which any person, expiring under the tortures of a cruel execution, was treated with such derision, contempt, and mockery, by all ranks and orders of men, and even by one at least of his fellow-sufferers. This was reserved for the holy Jesus, " the Brightness of the Father's glory, and " the express Image of his Person," " God manifest in the " flesh:" and this transaction is a full demonstration of apostate man's rancorous enmity to the holy image, truth, and law of his Creator; and a sufficient confutation of all the flattering representations of proud moralists and philosophers, who know more of every thing, than of God and of themselves. Indeed prophets and martyrs, who were renewed to some measure of the same image, and stood up for the same truths, always met with an adequate proportion of the same treatment: but it has been confined to them, and malefactors have almost universally been exempted from it. The perfect patience and meekness of this holy sufferer, in the midst of such provocations, which he was well able to avenge, is also worthy of our peculiar attention. (*Notes, Ps.* xxxv. 13, 14. *Luke* xxiii. 32—38, *v.* 34. 1 *Pet.* ii. 18—25, *v.* 20—23.)

Reviled. (39) Εℂλασφημων. ix. 3. *Acts* xxvi. 11. *Rom.* iii. 8. 1 *Cor.* iv. 13. *Tit.* iii. 2. (Ex Ɵλαπτω, *noceo* et φημι, *loquor.*)—*If he will have him.* (43) Ει Ɵελει αυτον.—'Οτι Ɵελει αυτον. *Ps.* xxii. 8. *Sept.*—" Seeing he delighted in him."

V. 45. It is here supposed, and will hereafter be shewn, that Christ was nailed to the cross at " the third hour," or by nine o'clock in the morning: but this darkness did not begin before the sixth hour, or noon; and it lasted till the ninth hour, or three o'clock in the afternoon. As the moon was then at the full, it could not be an eclipse from a natural cause: and probably it reached no further than the holy land, at least the language of the evangelists implies no more. (*Notes, Mark* xv. 25. 33.) The sun, however, seems to have been entirely obscured, and his beams intercepted; whence arose a most extraordinary and awful gloom. This was an apt emblem of the state of the spiritual world, when " the Sun of Righteousness," and " the Light of men " was under an eclipse; his soul being full of darkness and horror, his character wounded with reproaches and loaded with infamy, and his body ready to expire with torture. It was also an awful indication of the frown of heaven on the Jews and their rulers, who were guilty of this most enormous crime, from which the sun seemed to hide his astonished face, refusing his light to that land where it was committed.—Some infidels have greatly exulted, because Josephus and the Pagan writers

have not mentioned this phenomenon : but none have attempted to deny it, and every writer notices and records only what he sees proper. Josephus, and the Pagan authors, were in general as little disposed to bear a favourable testimony to Christianity, as modern infidels are: the former could not but have heard of it, and his silence may be considered as the effect of his inability to deny the fact, and his unwillingness to admit the proper conclusion; but the heathen authors would probably treat the report with contempt and neglect, as unworthy of regard.—It is deserving of notice, that all the evangelists record the scoffs and insults of the spectators, before they mention this darkness, which, it is probable, for the time alarmed and silenced them.—Many things have been conjectured concerning the intenseness of this gloom; but little can be known : probably it was neither so intense, nor so slight, as different writers, contending with each other, have represented it. There is no proof, that during it, Jesus saw and spoke to his mother and the apostle John, at a considerable distance, as some have supposed: for nothing appears from the narrative, why this might not take place either during the three hours which preceded the gloom, or just before Jesus expired, when it seems to have terminated. (*Notes,* 50. *John* xix. 25—27.)—We have, however, the testimony of three evangelists, authenticated by miracles and prophecy, that such a darkness took place; and we may be sure it was sufficiently intense, to convince considerate persons, that it was an awful token of the wrath of God against the crucifiers of the holy Jesus.

V. 46. At the ninth hour, our Lord, being probably oppressed with a measure of the same inward horror, as when in the garden, cried out aloud, " Eli, Eli, lama sa-" bachthani, that is to say, My God, my God, why hast " thou forsaken me? " (*Note, Ps.* xxii. 1.) The words are not exactly the same as they stand in the original of the psalm referred to, and they are supposed to be quoted in the Syro-Chaldaick dialect; but the meaning is precisely the same. This doleful exclamation of Jesus shewed, that the total want of " the light of God's countenance " on his soul, and the sense of his frown and wrath against him, as our Surety, were far more dreadful than all his complicated outward sufferings; that his confidence in his Father, together with his love, zeal, submission, and every holy affection were unabated and most perfect, even in that dreadful hour; and that there was no cause in him, why he should be thus forsaken, it being wholly through his willing answerableness for the sins of his people. (*Marg. Ref.—Notes,* xxvi. 36—39. *Mark* xv. 34—39, *v.* 34.)—' This he did, in a deep sense of his ' Father's wrath unto mankind, in whose stead he now ' underwent that, which was due for the sins of the whole ' world : while he said, " Why hast thou forsaken me ? " ' implying that God had for the time withdrawn from him ' the sense and vision of his comfortable presence ; and ' while he said, " My God," implying the strength of his

2 z 5

47 Some of thém that stood there, when they heard *that*, said, 'This *man* calleth for Elias.

48 And straightway one of them ran, and took a sponge, 'and filled *it* with vinegar, and put *it* on a reed, and gave him to drink.

49 The rest said, Let be, 'let us see whether Elias will come to save him.

50 Jesus, 'when he had cried again with a loud voice, ʰ yielded up the ghost.

51 And, behold, ' the veil of the temple was rent in twain from the top to the bottom; ᵏ and the earth did quake, and the rocks rent,

52 And the graves were opened; ₖ and ' many bodies of the saints which ᵐ slept arose,

53 And came out of the graves after his resurrection, and went into the ⁿ holy city, and appeared unto many.

' faith, whereby he did firmly apprehend the sure and gra-
' cions aid of his eternal Father.' *Bp. Hall.*—*Eli*, &c.]
יְלֵי יְלֵי לָמָה עֲזַבְתָּנִי. 'O Θεος, ὁ Θεος μᾶ, προσχες μοι, ἱνάϊι ἐγκαθϊ-
λιπες με ; *Ps.* xxii. 1. *Sept.*
V. 47—49. Some of the persons present, who heard
the words of Christ indistinctly, or who were not acquainted
with the language or dialect in which they were spoken,
supposed that he called upon Elias to come and rescue
him: for, as it was understood that Elias was to be the
fore-runner of the Messiah, they probably thought that he
meant thus to assert his claim to that character, even to
the last. (*Marg. Ref. d.*)—About the same time he also
said, " I thirst," being parched through excess of anguish
and torture : and, as a vessel stood by filled with vinegar,
(which being mixed with water, was commonly drunk by
the Roman soldiers,) one of them filled a sponge with
vinegar, and putting it on a reed, or *a stalk of hyssop*,
reached it to him that he might drink : whilst the rest
said, " Let be, let us see whether Elias will come to save
" him.' This seems to have been spoken in derision, and
not from any expectation that Elias would actually come.
(*Notes, Ps.* lxix. 21. *John* xix. 28—30, *vv.* 28, 29.)
V. 50. Perhaps the darkness continued, nearly to the
time, when Jesus said, " It is finished : " and then the
darkness and horror seem to have been removed also from
his mind ; and an inexpressible joy in the sense of his
Father's love, the near approach of his glory, and the
blessed effects of his sufferings, to have filled his soul.
He therefore, immediately after, " cried out with a loud
" voice, Father, into thy hands I commend my spirit."
(*Notes, Luke* xxiii. 44—49, *v.* 46. *John* xix. 28—30, *v.* 30.)
This has been generally supposed to be an indication, that
his strength was unbroken ; and that when he " yielded
" up the ghost," or resigned his spirit, he did it voluntarily, " having power to lay down his life, and power to
" take it again." So that his soul could have left the
body, at the very beginning of his lingering agonies, had
he so pleased, as these were necessary only for the expiation of our sins.—' This view of the case ... suggests an
' illustration of the love of Christ manifested in his death,
' beyond what is commonly observed. Inasmuch as he
' did not use this power to quit his body, as soon as ever
' it was fastened to the cross, leaving only an insensible
' corpse to the cruelty of his murderers : but continued
' his abode in it, with a steady resolution, as long as it
' was proper ; and then retired from it, with a majesty and
' dignity never known, or to be known, in any other death ;

' *dying*, if I may so express it, like " the Prince of life." '
Doddridge.—*Yielded up the ghost.*] Αφηκε το πνευμα.—
Resigned, or *dismissed, the spirit.* Εξεπνευσε, *expired; Mark*
xv. 37. *Luke* xxiii. 46.—Παρεδωκε το πνευμα, *delivered up
the spirit; John* xix. 30.
V. 51—53. At that solemn time, the veil in the temple, which separated the most holy place from the other
part of the sanctuary, was miraculously rent from top to
bottom. This indicated, that the Mosaick dispensation
was now virtually abolished, the types of the Levitical
priesthood accomplished, the way into the holiest laid
open, and the distinction between Jew and Gentile terminated, through that oblation which had just been offered.
(*Marg. Ref. i.*—*Notes, Ex.* xxvi. 31—33. *Heb.* ix. 1—10.
x. 19—22.) As this was the hour of the evening-sacrifice,
some of the priests must have been in the temple burning
incense, at the time when it happened ; and the rest of
them, and even Caiaphas himself, must afterwards have
seen the veil which had been rent : yet this prodigy made
no impression on their hardened hearts, any more than the
other events of that surprising day. This insensibility,
amidst such astonishing miracles, appears to some persons almost incredible, and even beyond what human
nature, depraved as it is, seems capable of. But it should
be considered, that the most alarming and amazing scenes
gradually lose their effect on the mind, when persons become familiar with them. Men live among the dead and
dying, often without terror or reflection : and in an age
when miracles were frequently wrought, many spectators
would by habit grow familiar with them, as men do with
scenes of carnage and desolation ; especially, when the
astonishment, at first excited by witnessing a miracle, was
attended by a conviction which was resisted with deep
aversion, and when every subsequent miracle was followed
by a similar process. The minds of those, who thus
" rebelled against the light," would of course be employed,
with all the ingenuity which they possessed, in accounting
for the wonderful events, without owning the hand of God
in them, or the conclusion to be drawn from them, in favour of the Teacher ; whose doctrine condemned their
conduct, and was contrary to their prejudices, and their
ambition, avarice, and wickedness. Thus the heart and
conscience would gradually become more and more callous,
as if " seared with a hot iron : " and God in awful justice
would give the obstinate rebels up to judicial hardness and
blindness. So that, in an age of miracles, it is highly
reasonable to expect, that the opposers of the truth, thus

2 E 6

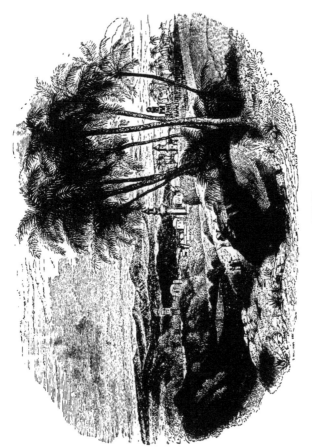

RAMAH, OR ARIMATHEA.

1 Sam. vii. 17; xix. 1. Jer. xxxi. 15. Matt. xxvii. 57. John xix. 38.

o M. viii. 5. Acts
x. 1. xxi. 32.
xxiii. 17. 23.
xxvii. 1. 43.
p Mark xv. 39.
Luke xxiii. 47.
q 2 Kings i. 15.
14. Acts ii. 37.
xvi. 29. 30. Rev.
xi. 13.
r 40. 43. xxvi. 63.
Luke xxii. 70.
Rom. i. 4.
s Luke xxiii. 27,
28. 49, 55. John
xix. 25—27.

54 Now when ° the centurion, and ²³ they that were with him watching P Jesus, ? saw the earthquake, and those things that were done, they ⁴ feared greatly, saying, ' Truly this was the Son of God.

55 And ° many women were there beholding afar off, which followed

Jesus from Galilee, ' ministering unto him ;

56 Among which was ° Mary Magdalene, and ° Mary the mother of ⁷ James and Joses, ᵗ and the mother of Zebedee's children.

57 ¶ When the even was come, ° there came a rich man of ᵇ Arima-

t Luke viii. 8.
u 61. xxvii. 1.
Mark xv. 40, 41.
xvi. 1. 9. Lu 6
xxiv. 10. John
xx. 1. 18.
x Mark xv.47.xvi.
1. John xix. 25.
y xiii. 55. Mark
xv. 40. xvi. 1.
xx. 20, 21.
a Mark xv. 42, 43.
Luke xxiii. 50,
51. John xix. 38
—42.
b 1 Sam. i. 1. vii.
17.

divinely attested before their eyes, should become obdurate and insensible to a degree, which, to those who never witnessed miracles, must be inconceivable. (Notes, Ex. iv. 21. vii. 13. ix. 12. xiv. 3, 4. 2 Thes. ii. 8—12.)—At the time when " the veil was rent," there was also an earthquake, which rent the rocks in the vicinity of Jerusalem, and even opened the sepulchres in a very extraordinary manner : and after the resurrection of Christ, many of the bodies of departed " saints," or holy persons, who had fallen asleep in the faith, arose, came forth out of their graves, entered into Jerusalem, and appeared to several persons who knew them. Probably, they were such believers as had died not long before, and now arose after Christ, as it were, to grace his resurrection. It would, however, be wrong to indulge vain curiosity, by further enquiring who they were : but as they are said to have " appeared to many," and not to have continued with them ; it seems probable, that they also went to heaven, with or after their ascended Saviour. This was a most extraordinary event ; and doubtless it was generally spoken of in Jerusalem by those to whom they appeared. (Marg. Ref. l—n.—Note, 1 Cor. xv. 20—28, v. 20.)—The veil. (51) Καλαπέλασμα. Mark xv. 38. Luke xxiii. 45. Heb. vi. 19. ix. 3. x. 20. A καλαπέλαζω, expando, obtego.—Was rent : ... rent.] Εσχισθη ... εσχισθησαν. Mark i. 10. xv. 38. Luke xxiii. 45. John xix. 24. xxi. 11. Acts xiv. 4. xxiii. 7. Hence σχισμα, ix. 16.—Appeared. (53) Ενιφανισθησαν. Εμφανιζω, conspicuum prabeo, appareo. John xiv. 21, 22. Acts xxiii. 15. 22. xxiv. 1. xxv. 2. 15. Heb. ix. 24. xi. 14.

V. 54. The earthquake, and the other wonderful events which attended the crucifixion of Christ; together with his mild and patient behaviour under his sufferings, and the cheerful confidence, with which he commended his departing soul into the hands of God ; had a powerful effect upon the minds of the Roman soldiers, though the Jewish rulers remained unimpressed. Only four soldiers were employed in nailing Jesus to the cross ; but a considerable number, commanded by a Centurion, watched him whilst he hung there. These were greatly alarmed at what they saw and heard, and " they glorified God," perhaps by confessing their guilt and deprecating his vengeance ; and they acknowledged, that " Truly this was the Son of " God." It is not to be supposed, that the soldiers, who joined with the Centurion in this confession, and who seem to have been the same as had crowned Jesus with thorns and mocked him, should understand the full meaning of these words : yet we may reasonably conclude, that this conviction terminated in the conversion at least of some of them, and perhaps of the very persons who nailed him to the cross ; according to his prayer, " Father, forgive them, " for they know not what they do." (Note, Luke xxiii. 32—38, v. 34.)—Some would interpret the words recorded

by Matthew, " Truly this was the Son of God," by those of Luke, " This was a righteous man." But in fact that expression-is explained by this ; for as Jesus was crucified for saying that he was " the Son of God ;" so, if he were a righteous man and unjustly condemned, he must be " the Son of God." (Marg. Ref. r.)—' Thus Jesus was ' put to death upon pretence of blasphemy; for that he ' gave himself out for the Son of God : but these things ' plainly shew, that he said nothing but truth of himself.' Bp. Hall.—A son of a god, according to the notions of the pagans, say some : but could the officer and soldiers, who crucified Christ, be ignorant, that he was put to death, for averring himself to be " the Son of God ?" Surely then this supposed crime was referred to ; though those who said it, might not well understand their own words.—' He is condemned to death, as a blasphemer, for ' saying, " I am the Son of God ; ' but truly this was the ' Son of God.' (Notes, Mark xv. 34—39, v. 39. Luke xxiii. 44—49, v. 47.)—The Son of God.] Θευ Ϋιος, 63. xiv. 33. Mark xv. 39. Luke i. 35. Rom. i. 4.—Ps. ii. 6. Ϋιος μυ. Sept.—Ϋιος τα Θευ. 40. iv. 3. 6. John xix. 7. In these and some other places, the article is omitted before Ϋιος, when it is used in the highest sense : and Bp. Middleton on the Greek article has shewn, that Θευ Ϋιος, and Ϋιος τα Θευ, are used without any exact discrimination.— ' The Centurion could not fail to know the alledged blas-' phemy, for which our Saviour suffered ; and had he in-' tended in heathen phraseology, to express his admiration ' of our Saviour's conduct, he would not have called our ' Saviour Θευ Ϋιος.' Bp. Middleton, on this verse.

V. 55, 56. Among the witnesses of this melancholy and interesting scene, there were some women who had followed Jesus from Galilee, and had waited on him ; supplying his wants from their substance. (Marg. Ref.— Note, Luke viii. 1—3.) Anxious concern and affection induced them to be present ; and perhaps they stood afar off, for fear of the outrages of the multitude. Words cannot express, nay, imagination fails to conceive, the mixed emotions of love, reverence, gratitude, sorrow, compassion, anxiety, and despondency, which must have agitated their minds on this occasion. We find from John, who also was present, that " Mary the mother of Jesus " was a spectator of the distressing scene ; when " a sword " must indeed have pierced her heart " and inmost soul. (Note, Luke ii. 33—35, v. 35.)

V. 57—61. Joseph lived at Arimathea, or Ramah, the city of Samuel. (Marg. Ref. b.) He was a rich and honourable person; a counsellor, or member of the sanhedrim, and a pious man who had not consented to the proceedings of the rulers against Jesus : for he probably absented himself when this was agitated, finding he could not make any effectual resist-

thea, named Joseph, who also himself was Jesus's disciple:

c *Mark* xv. 44—46. *Luke* xxiii. 52, 53. 58 He went to Pilate, 'and begged the body of Jesus. Then Pilate commanded the body to be delivered.

59 And when Joseph had taken the body, he wrapped it in a clean linen cloth,

d *Is.* liii. 9. 60 And laid it ª in his own new tomb, which he had hewn out in the e *66.* xxviii. 2. *Mark* xvi. 4. *Luke* xxiv. 2. *John* xx. 1. rock; and he rolled ª a great stone to the door of the sepulchre, and departed.

61 And there was ' Mary Magda- f *M.* lene, and the other Mary, sitting over against the sepulchre.

62 ¶ Now the next day that followed ª the day of the preparation, ʰ the chief priests and Pharisees came together unto Pilate,

g *xxvi.* 17. *Mark* xv. 42. *Luke* xxiii. 54—56. *John* xix. 14. 42. n *l.* 2. *Ps.* ii. 1—5. *Acts* iv. 27, 28.

63 Saying, Sir, we remember that 'that deceiver said, while he was yet alive, ᵏ After three days I will rise again.

i *Luke* xxiii. 2. *John* vii. 12. 47. 2 *Cor.* vi. 8. k *xvi.* 21. xvii. 23. xx. 19. xxvi. 61. *Mark* viii. 31. xiv. 58. *Luke* ix. 22. xviii. 33. xxiv. 6, 7. *John* ii. 19.

64 Command therefore, that the sepulchre be made sure until the third

---

ance. He also " waited for the kingdom of God," expecting the Messiah as a spiritual Redeemer, and he had secretly become a disciple of Jesus; but being timid, moving in a high rank in society, and knowing the malignity of the rulers, he had not openly confessed his faith. It pleased God to leave him thus far under the power of his unbelieving fears; because he intended him for a service, from which he might have been precluded, if he had rendered himself obnoxious to the ruling powers. But, when the courage of our Lord's stated followers failed them, he found himself animated to a more decided conduct; and his faith being invigorated by the circumstances attending the death of Christ, he determined no longer to conceal his opinion. He, therefore, " went boldly to " Pilate," and desired leave to take the body of Jesus, that he might give it an honourable interment; and that it might not be buried on the spot, as those of malefactors generally were. Accordingly, when Pilate found by enquiry that Jesus was dead, being convinced of his innocence, he did not hesitate to order that the body should be delivered to Joseph; though he must have known that this would be highly displeasing to the Jewish rulers. Having obtained this permission, and being assisted by Nicodemus, Joseph went and took the body of Jesus from the cross, wrapped it in linen cloth, with a quantity of myrrh, aloes, and other aromaticks, which had been procured for that purpose; and immediately conveyed it into a new sepulchre which he had prepared for himself. This was situated in a garden near the spot, and had been hewn out of the solid rock; and there was only one entrance into it, which he closed with a large stone, when he had deposited the body of Jesus in it. The interment of Christ was thus hastily performed, because the Sabbath was near; and probably Joseph and his friend proposed, afterwards more carefully to embalm the body: at the same time Mary Magdalene and the other Mary before mentioned witnessed the transaction, and formed their plan for testifying their respect to the remains of their beloved and honoured Master. (*Marg. Ref.* a. c—e.—*Notes*, 62—66. *Mark* xv. 42—47. *Luke* xxiii. 50—56. *John* xix. 38—42.) —*Was Jesus's disciple.* (57) Εμαθητευσε τῳ Ιησυ. xiii. 52. xxviii. 19. *Acts* xiv. 21.—*Wrapped.* (59) Ενιλιξεν. *Luke* xxiii. 53. *John* xx. 7.—Ενειλησε, *Mark* xv. 46.—*Had hewed.* (60) Ελατομησε. *Mark* xv. 46. Ex λαϊομος, *lapicida*; quod εx λαας, *lapis*, et τιμνω, *cædo.*—*Rolled.*] Προσκυλισας. *Mark* xv. 46. Not elsewhere *N. T.*—This burial of Christ was

an accomplishment of a remarkable prophecy; (*Note, Is.* liii. 9, 10, *v.* 9;) and it made way for the more complete proof of his resurrection.

V. 62—66. Some think, that this occurred as soon as the sun was set, after our Lord's crucifixion; for at that hour the sabbath entered.—' It is wonderful, that these ' most superstitious men, should not have scrupled to ' violate the rest of the sabbath, by sealing the sepulchre ' and placing a guard.' *Beza.* The day that followed the crucifixion of our Lord was the sabbath, and peculiarly solemn, by reason of the feast of the passover which was then celebrating; and the day, on which he was crucified, was observed as a preparation for it: (*Marg. Ref.*) yet the malicious zeal of the chief priests induced them to come, on that great solemnity, in a body to Pilate, to represent to him, that Jesus (whom they confidently called " that deceiver,") had said repeatedly during his life-time, that he would rise again on the third day. This had always been in connexion with predictions of his violent death; and they in fact had paid more attention to it than the disciples had done. (*Marg. Ref.* k.)—As his friends therefore had been permitted to bury him, the rulers desired that he would give orders to secure the sepulchre " until " the third day;" (which shews what they understood by the words " after three days;") lest his disciples should come in a clandestine manner, steal away the body, spread the report that he was risen, and thus seduce the people into a more fatal error than ever.—It was indeed very unlikely, that the terrified disciples, who in that case could expect no better usage than their Master had just received, would, even if wicked enough, have either courage or inclination for such an imposture. This however was providentially permitted, in order to give the more indisputable demonstration of our Lord's resurrection. Pilate, in answer, observed to them, that they had a body of Roman soldiers at their command, who were stationed near the temple to keep watch there: of these they might take as many as they pleased, and such as they could most depend on; and secure the sepulchre as carefully as they could. Accordingly they went, and placed a strong guard at the sepulchre: affixing their seal to the stone which closed the mouth of it, that there might be no collusion between the soldiers and the disciples. Thus they were themselves satisfied, that they had made it sure by every needful precaution.—' The chief priests, having taken ' these precautions, waited, probably with no small im-

2 R 9

day, lest his disciples come by night, and steal him away, and say unto the people, He is risen from the dead: ¹ so the last error shall be worse than the first.

65 Pilate said unto them, Ye have a watch: go your way, ᵐ make it as sure as ye can.

66 So they went, and made the sepulchre sure, ⁿ sealing the stone, and setting a watch.

m xxviii. 11—15. Ps. lxxvi. 10. Prov. xxi. 30.

n Dan. vi. 17. 2 Tim. ii. 19.

l xii. 45.

' patience, for the third day after the crucifixion, ... when ' they made no doubt they should find the body in the ' sepulchre, and convict Jesus of deceit and imposture.' *Bp. Porteus.*—The number of the soldiers on guard is supposed to have been sixty. (*Notes,* xxviii. 1—8, v. 4. 11—15.)

Deceiver. (63) Πλανος. *2 Cor.* vi. 8. *1 Tim.* iv. 1. *2 John* 7. ' *Non solum errans, sed etiam alios errare faciens.*' *Leigh.*—*Error.* (64) Πλανη. *Rom.* i. 27. *Eph.* iv. 14. *1 Thes.* ii. 3. *2 Thes.* ii. 11. *Jam.* v. 20. *2 Pet.* ii. 18. iii. 17. *1 John* iv. 6. *Jude* 11.—*A watch.* (65) Κκτωδιαν. 66. xxviii. 11. Not elsewhere *N. T.* From the Latin word *custodia.*—*Make it ... sure.*] Ασφαλισασθι· 64. 66. *Acts* xvi. 24. (Ex a priv. et σφαλλω, *everto, fallo.*)

PRACTICAL OBSERVATIONS.

V. 1—10.

Whilst wicked men pursue their *primary* object with unwearied assiduity, and sacrifice rest, indulgence, and every other interest, in order to secure it; let none of the servants of God remain inactive, or shrink from difficulty, in their " work and labour of love."—The advantages attainable by sin, appear in prospect very desirable to the carnal mind; but they contain far more bitterness than satisfaction, when actually possessed.—Men foresee very little of the consequences of their crimes, at the time when they commit them; but they must be answerable for all: and the anguish and remorse of Judas, when he saw that Jesus was condemned, should impress our minds with some idea of what wicked men will feel hereafter, when they shall learn all the fatal effects of their infidelity, impiety, licentiousness, and iniquity. In this world, there is ground of hope for the vilest transgressors: and, when deeply convinced of their guilt, they should be reminded, that their chief danger arises from temptations to despair of God's mercy.—When faith and hope are totally wanting, repentance itself cannot be genuine: and the enemy, who once persuaded his deluded servants, that their sins were small, and that they had nothing to fear, will at length perhaps take occasion, from some special aggravations of their crimes, to represent them to their affrighted imaginations as absolutely unpardonable; that he may drive them to desperate wickedness, or to suicide. For, though he cannot himself destroy them, he has very great influence in urging them thus to plunge themselves beyond the reach of mercy: and God often gives up those especially into his power, who have sinned wilfully against much light and conviction.—Many things, which accompany true repentance, may yet be foud where that is wanting: a deep remorse for atrocious crimes, which have made dreadful inroads on the conscience, an open confession of sin *in some particulars,* and a restitution of the wages of iniquity, will not prove that man truly penitent, who is not humbled for all the sin of his heart and conduct; who does not rely solely on the mercy of God in

Jesus Christ; or who does not learn to hate sin, to love God, to submit to his will, and to " walk in newness of " life." But no warnings can withdraw hardened hypocrites from their purpose: they will treat such, even of their accomplices, as shew remorse for their crimes, with the most disdainful neglect, and concur with Satan in driving them to despair: and, while they are deliberately perpetrating the most atrocious iniquities, they will keep up the appearance of strict devotion, avow the most exact conscientiousness, and affect the praise of beneficence! And God sometimes perpetuates the memory of their crimes, and fulfils the prophecies of his word, by means of those very actions, in which they most deliberately rebelled against him.—Of how small estimation must spiritual excellency be among men, when even Israelites valued the divine Saviour at no more than the price of the meanest slave!

V. 11—18.

Who can reflect on the malice, envy, dissimulation, and murderous rage, of the Jewish priests and rulers; on the prevaricating cowardly injustice of Pilate; on the conduct of the multitude, in preferring a murderer to the holy Jesus, and in clamorously demanding his crucifixion; or on the insults and cruelty of the soldiers, without horror and indignation? But let us not deem these instances any other, than a fair specimen of human nature; let us not imagine that " the Lord of glory" would meet with better usage, if he were now to appear on earth *in disguise,* and to testify concerning his nominal disciples " that their " works were evil," in the same manner that he did of the Jews. Still he would be " despised and rejected of men," and meet with decided opposition; still numbers would pursue him with revilings and cruel mockings: and others would be afraid or ashamed, to acknowledge their relation to him: still there would be found chief priests, scribes, rulers, and Pharisees, whose hypocrisy and ignorance he had exposed, whose consciences he had galled, and whose authority and reputation he had undermined, to persecute him with unrelenting malice and revenge: still there would be ungodly Pilates, who, being persuaded of his innocency, and knowing that he was persecuted from envy, would yet deem it impolitick to risk any thing in his cause; and, after some feeble efforts to stem the torrent, or to throw the blame on others, would prostitute authority to sanction the unrighteous decrees of his enemies: still the unstable multitude would to-day cry " Ho- " sanna," and to-morrow " Crucify him :" still hardened scoffers would divert themselves with his ignominy and anguish; and even wretches would be found, who would try to forget their own misery by reviling him.—But are we not all concerned? Alas! how often is Barabbas preferred to Jesus! When sinners reject his salvation, that they may retain their darling sins, which rob God of his glory, and murder their own souls, and those of other men; they repeat the disgraceful transaction : when the society of

     2 F

CHAP. XXVIII.

Early on the first day of the week, the women go to the sepulchre, 1. An earthquake, and an angel rolling away the stone, terrify the guard, 2—4. The angel declares the resurrection of Jesus to the women, and orders them to tell the disciples, 5—8. Jesus himself appears to them, 9, 10. The priests hire the

pious ministers and Christians is forsaken, for the company of profligates and infidels, the preference is of the same nature: and indeed we are all apt, in some instances and in some measure, to prefer the friendship and interests of this evil world, to the commands, glory, and approbation of the Son of God.—But we must also remember, that "he was wounded for our transgressions :" in this sense we are all chargeable with the guilt of his crucifixion ; and our sins were as the scourge, the thorns, and the nails, by which he suffered. When his disciples act inconsistently with their character, and cause his enemies to revile or deride ; they then deliver up the blessed Jesus to be again mocked, spit on, crowned with thorns, and loaded with every indignity: whilst they, who treat his followers with cruelty and contempt, act over again the part of the Roman soldiers, and the Jewish rulers and people: and when professed Christians openly apostatize, " they crucify " the Son of God afresh, and put him to an open shame." —Embittered persecutors are often so hurried away by their furious zeal, that even infidels can discern the malignant principles, by which they are actuated ; and the people of God may expect more favour from the most avowed profligates, than from hypocrites.

V. 19—25.

The warnings, which God sends, by various means, to deter men from wickedness, will eventually leave many of them the more inexcusable : but what will be the guilt and condemnation of those, who use authority, influence, and ingenuity, to set men against the gospel ; and thus ruin multitudes of immortal souls !—Various and irrational are the means, by which men seek impunity, in acting contrary to their own consciences : they sometimes plead necessity or compulsion ; when nothing but unbelief, fear of man, and regard to worldly interest, compel them : and they often throw the blame on others, vainly hoping to have the *pleasure* or *advantage* of iniquity themselves, and to leave the *punishment* to be suffered by their tempters. But all the water in the ocean cannot wash away the guilt of murder, from those rulers, who, even reluctantly, permit innocent blood to be shed for political purposes ; as it is their bounden duty at all hazards to protect the oppressed.—Such as are bent upon evil, are commonly most clamorous when their conduct is most unreasonable: persecutors are generally most ready to call for the instruments of torture or death, when it is enquired, " What " evil have these persons done ?" and in every case, when arguments are wanting, men are prone to abound in vociferation, in order to silence both their opponents and their own consciences. But, who can reflect without terror at the awful imprecation of the Jewish multitude, and its tremendous accomplishment ? What miseries did they call for on themselves! What a legacy did they leave to even their remote posterity! Yet there is mercy in reserve for a remnant of that nation : let us then pray for them, that at length they " may look to him, whom they " have pierced, and mourn for their sins," in true repent-

ance and with living faith. (*Note, Zech.* xii. 9—14, *v.* 10.) —All, however, who delight in anathemas and imprecations, will find that they rebound upon themselves.

V. 26—44.

Under trivial injuries, we worthless creatures are prone to complain bitterly, and even to retort or retaliate on those who offend us: but the holy and divine Saviour endured the most complicated indignities and cruelties, without a murmur, an angry word, or a menace! In the meekness and dignity of heavenly wisdom, he heard unmoved the false accusations, with which he was pursued ; the preference given to a murderer before him ; the ungrateful people, whose diseases he had healed, and whose wants he had supplied, demanding his crucifixion ; the iniquitous sentence passed on him ; and the sarcasms and cruel derision of the soldiers, the people, the rulers, and even of the malefactors. Without the least impatience, he suffered his sacred body to be torn with the scourge, his head to be wounded with the thorns, and his hands and feet to be pierced: and thus he met the horrors of the most excruciating death, and the shame of being numbered among the worst of criminals, with the most entire resignation to his Father's will, the most ardent love and zeal for his glory, and the deepest compassion even for his cruel murderers. He was also as much superior to fear, as to anger or impatience ; and he supported his most complicated sufferings with a gravity, a sensibility, and a fortitude, equally distant from the ill-timed disgusting levity, which some have shewn in the prospect of immediate death, and the sullen affectation of insensibility which others have displayed: so that all which has been admired in the death of heroes or philosophers, is no more comparable to the setting of this " Sun of Righteousness," than the glimmering taper is to the clear light of day.—But let us especially consider this conduct of the Saviour as our pattern : and recollect that all our fretfulness, peevishness, bitterness, and despondency are indeed acts of rebellion, which could not have been pardoned, but through the shedding of his precious blood. Let us remember, that we are called to *do good*, and *suffer evil*, in this present world ; let us keep a guard over our spirits and at the door of our lips, when we are injured, insulted, and afflicted; let us consider how " light our afflictions" are, and how mixed with consolations, when compared with those of our divine Surety; and let us never expect or desire kind usage from such characters as " crucified the Lord of " glory."

V. 45—50.

Our blessed Redeemer endured all his other complicated sufferings in silent submission : but the frown and wrath of the Father, which he bare for our sins, extorted the doleful exclamation, " My God, my God, why hast thou " forsaken me ?"—What then will be the misery of those, who shall for ever be forsaken by God, and sink under his wrath and absolute despair ! The believer, who has tasted

2 F 2

soldiers to say, that the disciples had stolen the body while they slept, 11—15. Jesus appears to the disciples in Galilee, 16, 17. He sends them to preach the gospel, and baptize all nations; and promises his presence with his church to the end of the world, 18—20.

---

a few drops of the cup, which the Saviour drank off to the very dregs, in the garden and on the cross—who has lost for a season the comfort of communion with God, and dreads lest he should come finally short of his favour, and is oppressed with a sense of his displeasure—can frame some feeble conceptions on this awful subject. Thence he learns to estimate in some degree the immensity of the Saviour's love : thence he acquires deeper convictions of the evil and desert of sin, and of his obligations to him, "who hath delivered us from the wrath to come;" and thence he is led to consider the words, " Depart from me," which unbelievers little regard or dread, as more tremendous even than the unquenchable fire prepared for the devil and his angels.—But, how must adoring angels have been filled with astonishment, when they witnessed their incarnate Lord and Creator thus despised and hated by sinful men! Nothing could more astonish these holy spectators, than the madness and wickedness of his foes ; except it were his patience in bearing with them, when his frown must at once have sunk them into hell; his compassion for the souls of those who were by nature so deeply depraved, in thus agonizing and dying for them; and his power and grace, in thus triumphing over the prince of darkness, even in that deepest scene of his humiliation. Thus were the purposes and prophecies of God accomplished ; thus was his " law magnified," his justice satisfied, and his holiness displayed ; thus was the way opened for us sinners to " the throne of grace" now, and to the kingdom of glory hereafter. Yet, never were the norrid nature and effects of sin so tremendously displayed, from the creation of the world to this time, nor ever shall be, as on that important day, when the beloved Son of the Father hung upon the cross, " suffering once for sin, the " just for the unjust, that he might bring us to God." So great was the wickedness then committed, that the sun might well hide his astonished head, the earth be clothed with sable, and nature herself be thrown into convulsions, as in sympathy with her expiring Lord.—Our God will not grant presumptuous unbelievers those proofs of the truth of his word, which they arrogantly require, and with which they would by no means be satisfied : but he will give to every enquirer such as are proper, in his own time and manner ; and he will deliver, and receive to himself, all those who trust in him, however men may deride their confidence, as his children. Their trials may be sharp, and appear tedious ; and at some times, they may cry " My God, my God, why hast thou forsaken me ?" But they will be enabled at last to say, " Into thy hands I commend my spirit ; for thou hast redeemed me, O LORD, " thou God of truth." (Notes, Ps. xxxi. 5. Acts vii. 54—60, v. 60.)

V. 51—56.

Our divine Saviour has, by dying, deprived death of his terrifick sting, and removed all obstructions to the happiness of his people. He has consecrated the grave, to be the quiet repository of the bodies of his sleeping saints, and has prepared for its future opening again, to restore them immortal and glorious, by his resurrection, as the first fruits of that blessed harvest; that they may for ever inhabit the holy city above, " where is fulness of joy at " his right hand for evermore."—We may also reflect with comfort on the abundant attestations, which were given to the character of the calumniated Jesus; in that all concerned in his death were constrained to say, " This was a " righteous man," " This was the King of Israel," " Truly this was the Son of God :" and we also, " exer- " cising ourselves to have a conscience void of offence," may leave it to the Lord to vindicate our reputation. Let us at the same time always keep our faith fixed on every illustration of that truth, that " where sin hath abounded, " grace much more abounds :" observing that ignorant idolaters are far more frequently brought to glorify God, and confess faith in his Son, than proud Pharisees and hypocrites.—As " God spared not his own Son, but de- " livered him up for us all, how shall he not with him " freely give us all things ?" " Hereby we know his " love " to sinful men : may we then prove our love to him, by crucifying our lusts, and resigning our dearest earthly comforts, at his word, for his glory, or in submission to his providence. In short, let us, not only " afar " off," but as nearly and closely as we can, contemplate this affecting scene ; that our hearts may be melted into godly sorrow, weaned from this world, encouraged in hope, animated by love, admiration, and gratitude ; that we may glory in his cross alone, and be induced to yield ourselves most willingly to his service.

V. 57—66.

The Lord has a chosen remnant among various descriptions of men : and, whilst we find a Judas among the apostles, and a Joseph in the Jewish sanhedrim, we should learn not to condemn whole societies for the crimes, or to sanction them for the good conduct, of an individual, or even of several individuals belonging to them.—The heart-searching Saviour knows even his secret disciples : and though we must not excuse the timidity of such, as for a time are afraid of confessing him before his inveterate enemies ; yet we should make allowances for difficult situations, and approve of conscientiousness and holy singularity, in men surrounded by the worst of examples : nor must we " despise the day of small things." But we should especially adore the mysteries of divine wisdom, in preparing men for particular services in the church ; and the sovereign power of his grace, which sometimes gives courage to the fearful, when the most intrepid are intimidated. Thus he provides for the honour of his name and the support of his cause, and defeats the purposes of his most implacable and potent adversaries.—Let us then be willing to be accounted " deceivers," and to pass " through " evil report and good report," as our Lord did : for if we be upright in the sight of God, all the suspicions and endeavours of men to disgrace us will tend to their confusion, and the manifestation of our integrity ; even as the precautions of the Jewish rulers tended to prove the resurrection of Jesus, and to forward the success of the gospel.

2 F 3

IN [a] the end of the sabbath, as it began to dawn toward the first *day* of the week, came [b] Mary Magdalene and the other Mary to see the sepulchre.

2 And, behold, [c] there was a great earthquake: [d] for the angel of the Lord descended from heaven, and came and rolled back the stone from the door, and sat upon it.

3 His [e] countenance was like lightning, and [f] his raiment white as snow.

4 And for fear of him [g] the keepers did [h] shake, and became as dead men.

5 And the angel answered and said unto the women, [i] Fear not ye: for I know that [k] ye seek Jesus, which was crucified.

6 He is not here; for he is risen, as he said. [m] Come, see the place where the Lord lay:

7 And [n] go quickly, and tell his disciples that he is risen from the dead; and, behold, [o] he goeth before you into Galilee; there shall ye see him: [p] lo, I have told you.

8 And they departed quickly from the sepulchre [q] with fear and great joy, and did run to bring his disciples word.

9 ¶ And [r] as they went to tell his disciples, behold, Jesus met them, saying, [s] All hail. And they came [t] and held him by the feet, and [u] worshipped him.

10 Then said Jesus unto them, [x] Be not afraid: [y] go tell [z] my brethren that they go into Galilee, and there shall they see me.

Margin notes (left):
a Mark xvi. 1, 2. Luke xxiii. 56. xxiv. 1. 22. John xx. 1.
b xxvii. 56. 61.
c xxvii. 51—53. Acts xvi. 26.
• Or, *had been.*
d Mark xvi. 3—5. Luke xxiv. 2—4.
John xx. 1. 12.
• 1 Tim. iii. 16. 1 Pet. i. 12.
e xvii. 2. Dan. x. 5, 6. Rev. x. 1.
xviii. 1.
f Mark ix. 3. xvi. 5. Acts i. 10. Rev. iii. 4, 5.
g 11. xxvii. 65, 66.
h Job iv. 14. Ps. xlviii. 6. Dan. x. 7. Acts iv. 3—7. xvi. 29. Rev. i. 17.
17.
i Is. xxxv. 4. xli. 10, 14. Dan. x. 12, 19. Mark xvi. 6. Luke i. 13, 30. Rev.
k Ps. cv. 3, 4. Luke xxiv. 5. xx. 13—15. Heb. i. 14.

Margin notes (right):
l xii. 40. xvi. 21. xvii. 9, 23. xx. 19. xxvi. 31, 32. xxvii. 63. Mark viii. 31. Luke xxiv. 6—8. 28. John ii. 19.
m Mark xvi. 6.
• John xx. 4—9. xxvi. 32. Mark xvi. 7.
n 10. Mark xvi. 7. xxix. 9, 10. 23—34. John xx. 17.
16.
o 14. 16, 17. xxvi. 32. Mark xiv. 28.
• 16, 17. xxvi. 32. Mark xiv. 28. John xx. 21.
p John xxv. 25. Is.xliv. 8. xlv. 21. John xxix. 29. xvi. 4.
q Ezra iii. 12, 13. Ps. ii. 11. Mark xvi. 8—11. Luke xxiv. 9—11. John xx. 18.
r 16. 17. xxvi. 32. Mark xiv. 28. xxix. 10. John xx. 21.
s Mark xvi. 9, 10. John xx. 14—18.
t John xx. 17. Luke vii. 38. John xii. 3. xx. 27.
u 17. Rev. iii. 9.
x 5. xiv. 27. Luke xxiv. 31—36. John vi. 20.
y 7. Judg. x. 16. Ps. ciii. 8—13. Mark xvi. 7.
z xii. 48—50. xxv. 40. 45. Mark iii. 33—35. John xx. 17. Rom. viii. 29. Heb. ii. 11—18.

· NOTES.

CHAP. XXVIII. V. 1—8. 'Christ having put death
' to flight in the sepulchre, riseth by his own power, as
' straightway the angel witnesseth.' *Beza.*—The Lord
Jesus expired on the afternoon preceding the sabbath: his
body lay in the grave the remainder of that day, during all
the sabbath, and part of the day after, which began at
sun-set: so that he arose early in the morning on the third
day. " In the end of the sabbath," or *after that the sab-*
bath was ended, and the day dawned on the first day of the
week, Mary Magdalene and the other Mary went to see
the sepulchre; and to examine whether it remained in the
same state, in which it had been left on the evening of his
burial; knowing nothing of the guard which had been afterwards placed there. Probably, the women, mentioned by the
other evangelists, followed some time after with the spices.
(*Notes*, xxvii. 62—66. *Mark* xvi. 1—4. *John* xx. 1—10, *vv.*
1, 2.) But before any of them arrived, most astonishing
events had taken place: " a great earthquake " had announced the approaching resurrection of Jesus, and probably thrown the soldiers into consternation; and then an
angel appearing in a most glorious form, " rolled away
" the stone from the door " of the sepulchre, and sat down
on it; which affrighted the soldiers, so that they became
senseless, as if they had been dead: but it is probable,
that at length coming to themselves, they recovered courage enough to flee from the terrifying scene. In the
mean time, the Lord arose from the dead; re-uniting his
human soul to his body by his own divine power, and
leaving the sepulchre as a mighty conqueror over death
and the grave.—When the women therefore came to the
sepulchre, they found the stone rolled from the door.—It
is probable, that Mary Magdalene immediately returned
to the city to inform the apostles: whilst the other women
examined the sepulchre; and at length saw a vision of
angels, one of whom addressed them in the most encouraging manner; bidding them not fear, because, as they

came to seek and honour Jesus who had been crucified,
they had abundant cause for confidence and joy, seeing he
was indeed risen; and inviting them to examine the place
where he had lain, calling him THE LORD, that is, the
Lord of angels as well as men. He then commanded
them to go with all speed to inform the disciples of these
particulars, that they might share the comfort of the glad
tidings, and prepare to meet him in Galilee; where the
whole company would have the inexpressible satisfaction
of beholding him: and as he, an angel of God, had
expressly told them these things, they must not doubt the
truth of them, how extraordinary soever they might appear; or neglect to report them, for fear of being deemed
credulous visionaries. Upon this they immediately departed, with mingled affections of terror and joy, but the
latter seems to have been the most prevalent; and they
ran with haste to carry word to his disciples. (*Marg. Ref.*)
10—12. *John* xx. 1—17.)

In the end of the sabbath. (1) Οψε...σαββατων. Οψε.
Mark xi. 19. xiii. 35.—Διαγενομενα τε σαββατε, *Mark* xvi.
1.—Τη ... μια των σαββατων ορθρε βαθεος, *Luke* xxiv. 1. Πρωι,
σκοιας ἐτι εσης, *John* xx. 1. *Extremo sabbato.* Stephanus.
' *Extremam partem sabbati significat*, scil. *diluculum*, aut
' *tempus diluculo proximum*, *Romanorum more*, *qui a media*
' *nocte*, *non autem Hebræorum*, *qui a vespera diem inchoant.*'
In *Leigh.*—*It began to dawn.*] Επιφωσκεσης. (Ex επι, et φως
lux.) *Luke* xxiii. 54. Not elsewhere N. T.—*Towards the*
first day of the week.] Εις μιαν σαββατων. *John* xx. 1. 19.
Acts xx. 7. 1 *Cor.* xvi. 2.—*Earthquke.* (2) Σεισμος.—See
on viii. 24.—*Appearance.* (3) Ιδεα. Used here only N. T.
Ab ειδω, *video.*

V. 9, 10. As the women were going to the city, Jesus
himself was pleased to appear to them, and congratulate
them on the arrival of that joyful morning; expressing his
ardent good will and affection for them. The original
word means, " Rejoice ye."—And after they had embraced
his feet, and worshipped him with deep humility, pro-

11 ¶ Now when they were going, behold, [a] some of the watch came into the city, and shewed unto the chief priests all the things that were done.

12 And [b] when they were assembled with the elders, and had taken counsel, they gave large money unto the soldiers,

13 Saying, Say ye, His disciples came by night, and stole him *away* while we slept.

14 And if this come to the governor's ears, [c] we will persuade him, and secure you.

15 So [d] they took the money, and did as they were taught: and this saying is commonly reported among the Jews, [e] until this day.

margin refs:
[a] 4. xxvii. 65, 66.
[b] xxvi. 3, 4. xxvii. 1, 2, 62—65. Ps. ii. 1—7 John xi. 47, 48. xii. 10. Acts iv. 5—22. v. 33 34, 40.
[c] Acts xii. 19
[d] xxvi. 15. 1 Tim. vi. 10.
[e] xxvii. 8.

---

found reverence, and joyful love, yet not without some emotions of fear; he encouraged them, and ordered them to proceed on their way to inform his disciples; (whom he very graciously called " his brethren," notwithstanding their desertion of him in his sufferings;) assuring them, that the whole company should have the satisfaction of seeing him in Galilee, at a time and place appointed. (*Marg. Ref.*)—It is obvious to every attentive reader, that there is some difficulty in arranging the various circumstances, recorded by the Evangelists, into one compact narration : and it is plain, they did not write in concert; but the Lord was pleased to direct each of the sacred historians to write those incidents, which most impressed his own mind. When the different accounts have been separately considered, a compendious view will be given of the most approved method, by which they have been shewn to be consistent with each other : and that will be the proper place also, for a brief statement of the complex demonstration afforded us of this important event, on which the truth of Christianity, and all our hopes depend. (*Notes, John* xx. 18. 24—29, *v.* 29.)

All hail. (9) Χαιρετε. ' Apud Græcos tria significat ; ' *gaudete, salvere, et valere.*' Erasmus. *Luke* i. 28. *John* xix. 3. *Acts* xv. 23. *2 Cor.* xiii. 11. *Phil.* iii. 1. iv. 4. *Jam.* i. 1.

V. 11—15. ' The more the sun shineth, the more are ' the wicked blinded.' *Beza.*—' It may be said, that this ac' count is the representation of friends, of those who were ' interested in asserting the reality of the resurrection ; but ' that there is probably another story told by the opposite ' party, ... which may set the matter in a different point of ' view ; and that before we can judge fairly of the question, ' we must hear what they have to say of it. ...This is cer' tainly very proper and reasonable. ...There is, we ac' knowledge, another account given by the Jews ; and ... ' the sacred historians ... tell us what this opposite story ' was.' *Bp. Porteus.*—It should also be observed, that this is the *only* account given of these transactions by the opposite party : at least no other is extant, (nor do we read of any other in ancient writers,) except that which is contained in the verses under consideration.—The Roman soldiers seem to have been the first, who gave intimations of the resurrection of Jesus. Probably, some of them retired to their quarters, or into the city, and dispersed uncertain rumours of what had passed ; while some of the leaders went to make their report to the chief priests and rulers, by whom they were set to watch the sepulchre.—It is not conceivable, but that the latter must have been convinced that the events were miraculous, and afraid that Jesus was indeed risen again as he had predicted : but they had engaged all their credit, and authority, and even safety, in this unequal contest : they could not think of submit

ting or receding ; and there was no other way left, but to conceal, if possible, what had taken place. (*Note,* ii. 3—6.) They therefore deliberated on the subject, and could devise no better project, than to bribe the soldiers to deny the facts which they had reported, and to propagate an absurd falsehood instead of them : and, as the soldiers had no serious convictions, that they were any ways concerned in these transactions; they bargained for a large sum of money, and agreed to accuse the disciples of having stolen the body when they were asleep. At the same time, the rulers undertook to secure them from punishment, if Pilate should be informed that they had slept on duty, which was death by the Roman law. Accordingly, they took the money and said what they were ordered; and this report was circulated with such diligence and success, that it was commonly current among the Jews, when Matthew wrote his gospel ; and no one, as far as we can learn, attempted to disprove it, when thus published to the world. Yet was it a falsehood which confuted itself, and was the most effectual acknowledgment of the obstinacy and malice of those who invented it, that can be imagined. Had all the soldiers been asleep, they could not have known any thing which passed : if some were awake, why did they not alarm the others? Moreover, if they had slept, they would not have dared to mention it : if it had been discovered, the Jewish rulers would certainly have done their utmost to bring them to condign punishment : and had there been the least shadow of probability in the accusation, they would assuredly have prosecuted the apostles, with the most unrelenting vengeance. (*Notes, Acts* iv. 13 —22. v. 27, 28.) For their credit and authority were most deeply concerned : so that this *single omission* was a full demonstration, that they did not believe one word of the report, which they so industriously circulated. It was also improbable in the extreme, that the intimidated apostles and disciples should attempt such an action, which would have been excessively rash, even in the most experienced soldiers : it was still more improbable, that they should succeed ; and if they had, reproach, torture, and death were the whole recompence, which they could possibly have expected. But, in fact, the Jewish rulers were determined not to confess the truth : and as they knew not what to say, they were reduced to the distressing necessity, of circulating one of the most senseless lies, which ever was devised. (*Marg. Ref.*)

Will secure you. (14) Ὑμας αμεριμνες ποιησομεν. Αμεριμνος. 1 Cor. vii. 32. Not elsewhere N. T. (Ex a priv. et μεριμνα, *cura.*) The rulers undertook to secure the soldiers not only from *punishment,* but from fear and *anxiety.—It is commonly reported.* (15) Διεφημισθη. Διαφημιζειν, " To blaze " abroad, &c." *Mark* i. 45. Not elsewhere N. T.

16 ¶ Then ' the eleven disciples ' went away into Galilee, into a mountain where Jesus had appointed them.

17 And when they saw him they ʰ worshipped him: ˡ but some doubted.

18 ¶ And Jesus came and spake unto them, saying, ᵏ All power is given unto me in heaven and in earth.

19 Go ˡ ye therefore, and teach all nations, ᵐ baptizing them in ⁿ the name of the Father, and of the Son, and of the Holy Ghost ;

20 Teaching ° them to observe all things whatsoever I have commanded you : and, lo, ᴾ I am with you alway, even ᵠ unto the end of the world. ʳ Amen.

V. 16, 17. Several appearances of Christ are here passed over in silence; but his meeting with the disciples, by appointment, in Galilee, is particularly mentioned. (*Notes, Mark* xvi. 9—16. *Luke* xxiv. 13—43. *John* xx. 11—23. 24—29, *v.* 29.) Most of the apostles were inhabitants of that district: Jesus had far more disciples in Galilee than in Judea, and was personally known to far greater numbers. Probably, this was the time when he appeared to " above five hundred bre- " thren at once." (*Note*, 1 *Cor.* xv. 3—11, *v.* 6.) The place appointed for this purpose was a mountain, perhaps Tabor, on which he had been transfigured. When the disciples saw him, and were satisfied that he was really risen from the dead, they worshipped him, as " the Son " of God " and " the Lord of all." But there were some who doubted at the first, yet probably they were at length convinced. As all the apostles had before this repeatedly seen him, and as even incredulous Thomas had been fully satisfied of his resurrection ; we cannot understand this of any of *them*, but of some of the five hundred brethren who were gathered together on this occasion.—' This cir- ' cumstance shews the scrupulous fidelity of the sacred ' his orians, who ... fairly tell you every thing that passed, ' on this and similar occasions, whether it appears to make ' for them or against them.' *Bp. Porteus*.

V. 18. It is not certain, whether what is next recorded took place in Galilee, or after the return of the disciples to Jerusalem, and just before our Lord's ascension. He, however, came and conversed with them of those " things, " that pertained to the kingdom of God ; " and informed them, that, in consequence of his humiliation, he was now invested with all authority, in heaven and earth, over angels and men, in regulating the course of providence, and in communicating all spiritual blessings, for the benefit of his church.—' The word here is *authority*, not *power :* ' but it is manifest that these differ from each other ; for ' many are not able to perform those things, which they ' have a right to do ; and on the contrary, many have ' power to do those things, which they have no right to ' do.' *Beza*. (*Marg. Ref.* k.—*Notes*, xi. 27. *John* iii. 27— 36, *vv.* 35, 36. *v.* 20—29. xiii. 1—5, *v.* 3. xvii. 1—3, *v.* 2. *Eph.* i. 15—23, *vv.* 20, 21. *Phil.* ii. 9—11. 1 *Pet.* i. 21, 22. *Rev.* i. 12—20, *v.* 18. xi. 15—18.)—This *authority* is given to Christ, as Emmanuel, as the Son of Man, and as Mediator : but did he not possess all divine perfections, how could he exercise it ? ' He to whom any office is ' committed, must have sufficient power and wisdom to ' discharge that office. Now to govern all things in heaven ' and earth, belongs only to him, who is the Lord and

' Maker of them. ...To have power over death, and to ' be able to raise the dead, is to have that power, which is ' proper to God alone : and to have power over the souls ' of men, and the knowledge of all hearts, belongs to God ' alone.' *Whitby*.

V. 19, 20. After this solemn declaration of his sovereign authority over all creatures, received in human nature from the Father ; our Lord proceeded to give his commission to the apostles especially, but certainly to his other ministers and disciples also, according to their several stations in the church, to propagate his religion " among " all nations, baptizing them in the name of the Father, " and of the Son, and of the Holy Ghost." (*Marg. Ref.* l— n.—*Notes, Ps.* xxii. 27—31. *Mark* xvi. 14—16. *Luke* xxiv. 44—49. *Acts* i. 4—8, *v.* 8.) The apostles were, however, so much under the influence of Jewish prejudices, that they did not understand this commission, as authorizing them to preach to the Gentiles, till a considerable time after the descent of the Holy Spirit! (*Note, Acts* xi. 1—3. 18.) There are two words in this passage, which are translated *teach*, and *teaching* ; but they are of a different meaning. The former means that general instruction, which was necessary to bring men to profess themselves the disciples of Christ ; and the other relates to their more particular subsequent instruction, in all the various parts of Christianity.—As the words might have stood in the same order, if it had been a command to ' go, and convert all ' the nations to Judaism, circumcising them in the name of ' the God of Israel, and teaching them to observe the law ' of Moses ; ' no argument can hence be fairly adduced respecting the *subjects* of baptism. For in this case it would have been understood, that the adult males must be circumcised on a profession of the Jewish religion, and their infant-offspring at the time appointed : and in like manner all adults, admitted into the church from among the Jews and Gentiles, must be instructed in Christianity before they were baptized ; though their infant-offspring might be baptized also : and the case is exactly the same still.—The general nature of baptism has already been explained ; (*Note*, iii. 6 :) but we have here an account of the appropriation of this institution to the Christian dispensation. The apostles and preachers of the gospel, were ordered to baptize those who embraced the gospel, " into " the name " (not *names*) " of the Father, and of the Son, " and of the Holy Ghost." (*Note, Num.* vi. 24—27.) This is a most irrefragable proof of the doctrine of the Trinity ; that is, of the Deity of the Son, and of the distinct personality and Deity of the Holy Spirit : for it would be absurd to suppose, that a mere man, or creature, or a

2 ᴠ 6

mere *modus*, or quality of God, should be joined with the Father, in the one " name," into which all Christians are baptized. To be baptized into the name of any one, implies in the person so baptized a professed dependence on him, and devoted subjection to him : (*Note*, 1 *Cor.* i. 10—16, *vv.* 13—15 :) to be baptized therefore " into the name " of the Father, and of the Son, and of the Holy Ghost," implies a professed dependence on these three divine Persons, jointly and equally, and a devoting of ourselves to them as worshippers and servants. This is proper and obvious, upon the supposition of the mysterious unity of three co-equal Persons in the unity of the Godhead ; but not to be accounted for upon any other principles. Christianity is the religion of a sinner, who relies for salvation from wrath, and sin, and all evil, on the mercy of the Father, through the Person, righteousness, atonement, and mediation of the incarnate Son, and by the sanctification of the Holy Spirit ; and who in consequence gives up himself to be the worshipper and servant of the triune Jehovah, in all his ordinances and commandments ; that, according to the ancient and excellent doxology, ' Glory may ' be to the Father, and to the Son, and to the Holy Ghost : ' as it was in the beginning, is now, and ever shall be.'—Baptism is an outward sign of that inward washing, or sanctification of the Spirit, which seals and evidences the believer's justification. When an adult is baptized, he avows his acceptance of this salvation, and makes this surrender of himself to the service of God his Saviour. When we bring our infant-offspring to be baptized, we express our earnest desire, that they may share the same benefits ; and be the redeemed and accepted worshippers and servants of God the Father, Son, and Holy Spirit : we renew our own profession of faith, and devotedness to this one God in three Persons : and we pledge ourselves to God and his church, to use all proper means, to " bring " up our children in the nurture and admonition of the " Lord ; " in hope of their being made partakers of the inward and spiritual grace of baptism. As far as these things are attended to, they have a most salutary effect both on parents and children ; and this sacrament thus administered helps to keep up the remembrance of the principal doctrines of Christianity, in all places where it is used. (*Note* and *P. O.* xix. 13—15. *Note, Mark* x. 13—16.)—There can be no reasonable doubt, that the apostles and primitive Christians always administered baptism in this very form : and it would be strange to infer their disobedience to so express a command of Christ, from the brevity, with which matters of this nature are recorded in ' the Acts of the Apostles.' Indeed it would be a most daring presumption in any man to alter it, as if he knew better than the Lord himself, in what manner to administer this sacrament.—When our Lord had thus instituted baptism, and directed the apostles in respect of the subsequent instruction of their converts ; (which demands our most careful and obedient consideration, as his parting command to his ministers ;) being about to depart from them as to his visible presence, he said, " Lo, I *am* " with you always, even to the end of the world." He did not say, *to death*, or *to eternity ;* for that might have been restricted personally to the apostles ; but " to the " end of the world : " which must include all succeeding true missionaries and ministers, all congregations and disciples, in every age and nation, even to the consummation of all things. He is with us, in the power of his protecting providence ; by the influences of his teaching, sanctifying, and comforting Spirit ; and in the communication of all spiritual blessings from the favour of his omnipresent Deity : and we should realize him with us, in secret and in social worship, and in our publick assemblies. (*Note*, xviii. 20.) To this, the word *Amen* is affixed, probably by the evangelist, as expressing his desire that it might be so ; and perhaps to lead the reader to convert the promise into a prayer, for himself, and for every part of the church. (*Marg. Ref.*)

Teach all nations. (19) Μαθητευσατε παντα τα εθνη. " Make " disciples of all the nations." See on xxvii. 57.—*Always.* (20) Πασας τας ημερας, " all the days," or " every day."—*Unto the end of the world.*] 'Εως της συντελειας τυ αιωνος. xlii, 39, 40. 49. xxiv. 3. Συντιλεια των αιωνων. *Heb.* ix. 26.

PRACTICAL OBSERVATIONS.

V. 1—10.

Our God can with infinite ease accomplish his promises, by methods which are beyond the expectations of his friends, as well as in defiance of all his enemies.—Let us with joy contemplate the divine Saviour, bursting the barriers of the grave, and triumphing over " the king of terrors " by his glorious resurrection. Thus he proved himself " the Son of God and the King of Israel ; " he evinced the sufficiency and acceptance of his atoning sacrifice ; and he became " the First-fruits of the resurrection," " the First-begotten from the dead," and the Author of spiritual and eternal life to his people. Vain were the precautions of the Jewish rulers ; vain the stone, the seal, the guard of valiant soldiers ! These only served to render the illustrious event more incontestable. But if the earthquake, and a single angel, could so terrify the Roman guards, whose courage has been renowned through every age and nation ; where will the wicked appear, when the same power shall raise the dead, destroy the visible creation, and be displayed to judge the world ? Yet, the humble weeping penitents, who in faith and love " seek Jesus " who was crucified," to be saved through his precious blood, and employed in his service, and to honour him as they are able, need fear none of these things. None can so accuse them, as to compass their condemnation ; because Jesus who died for them is risen again, and " ever liveth " to plead their cause : all holy angels are their friends and guardians, and neither earth nor hell, life nor death, can hurt them. While they behold the place where the dear Redeemer lay, they find themselves gradually reconciled to death and the grave, and inspired with the hopes of a glorious resurrection, and with the joyful expectation, that " when he shall appear, then shall they also appear with " him in glory." (*Note, Col.* iii. 1—4.)—We are now called to rejoice with our risen Lord, as we not long since were to sympathize in his sufferings, and attend his funeral : let us then delight to tell to all around us, that " the Lord " is risen indeed," and is perfected to be " the Author of " eternal salvation to all them that obey him."—The believer, however, will not always be able to divest himself of fear, even when he has the most abundant cause for joy ; and he may think himself highly favoured in this present world, if hope and cheerfulness generally prevail. When we endeavour to obey the word sent us by the servants of our Lord, he will manifest himself unto us, dispel our

fears, confer blessings, and cause us to worship him with adoring love and joyful gratitude: for, notwithstanding his majesty and purity, and our meanness and unworthiness and many offences, he still condescends to call us his " brethren !"

V. 11—20.

The malice of proud persecutors cannot be overcome even by demonstration: nay, avarice itself will expend large sums, to silence the evidence of the truth, and to propagate error; policy will adopt the most foolish measures in such a cause; and reasoning infidels will swallow the most absurd falsehoods with a stupid credulity! We must not impute such things to the weakness of men's understandings; but to the malice of their hearts, and to the judicial blindness to which God gives them up. Thus he leaves them to expose their own cause, and to give a constrained testimony to his truth.—But those who are teachable, and impartially seek to know the ways of God, shall be admitted to clearer and fuller discoveries of the truth, from time to time; and at length their perplexities shall be all removed, by what they see, hear, and experience in their own souls. Being then compassed with such numerous witnesses of our Redeemer's resurrection; let us ever be ready to meet him in all his appointed ordinances, for the fuller establishment of our faith and hope; and to shew forth his praises, and express our admiring, joyful, grateful love, and to hold communion with him, and with his people: and let us often contemplate him, as now possessed of " all power in heaven and earth," for

the benefit of his church. He has sent his gospel into this distant nation, to call us to be his disciples; and most of us have been " baptized in the name of the Father, and " of the Son, and of the Holy Ghost: " let us then examine whether we really possess ' the inward and spiri- ' tual grace, of a death unto sin, and a new birth unto ' righteousness,' by which ' the children of wrath' become ' the children of God.' Let us seek to experience more fully the salvation of our triune God, and to be more entirely devoted to his service and worship; and let us bring up our families, as those who desire more, far more, that they may be genuine Christians, than that they should be rich, learned, or honourable in the world. Let ministers also observe, to act always under the commission, and according to the instructions, of the great " Head of the " church" and " Lord of all: " let them still preach the gospel to all around them, administering sacred ordinances by the rule of the holy scriptures; and teaching the people, not only a few doctrines, but to " observe all things what- " ever Christ hath commanded them." He is not indeed now personally present with us, and miraculous gifts have ceased: but he is yet spiritually among us, to assist and bless us in our studies and labours, publick and private: and he is and will be with all his servants and disciples " alway, even to the end of the world," and till he have gathered them all into his heavenly kingdom, to behold and share his glory and felicity. ' Even so, Lord Jesus, be thou with us, and with all thy people;' and " cause thy " face to shine upon us, that thy way may be known upon " earth, thy saving health among all nations." Amen.

THE GOSPEL

St. M A R K.

St. PETER speaks of Marcus, and calls him " his son;" perhaps implying that Marcus was converted by his ministry, and served with him in the gospel. (*Note*, 1 *Pet.* v. 13.) This Marcus, or Mark, was undoubtedly the writer of the gospel, on which we now enter · but whether he was, or was not, a different person from John surnamed Mark, of whom we read in the Acts of the apostles, and in St. Paul's epistles, (*Acts* xii. 12. xiii. 5. 13. xv. 37—39. *Col.* iv. 10. 2 *Tim.* iv. 11,) must remain doubtful, as the most able and laborious enquirers are divided in opinion on the subject; the celebrated Grotius taking the lead on the one side, and the indefatigable Lardner on the other. —It is, however, generally agreed, that this gospel was written under the immediate inspection of the apostle Peter, and received by the church on his authority.—' St. John had seen the three gospels, and wrote his own as a supple-
' ment to them, as plainly appears in the harmony of the gospels. ... Ecclesiastical history informs us, that Mark's
' gospel had the approbation of Peter, and that Mark was instructed by him. ... Papias conversed with the disci-
' ples of the apostles, about the beginning of the second century. He speaks of the gospels of Matthew and Mark
' as extant, and written by them. Justin Martyr, A. D. 150, mentions the gospels as universally received, and read in
' the congregations in his time. He must have conversed with Christians who were old men, and learned that the
' gospels were extant when they were young. ... Between A. D. 70, and Justin, are the authors called apostolical,
' Clemens, Hermas, Barnabas, Ignatius; these make use of some of the gospels and epistles.' *Jortin :* Remarks on Ec-
clesiastical History.—' Justin Martyr ... cites passages from every one of the gospels, declaring that they contained the
' words of Christ. ... Irenæus, in the same century, not only cites them all by name, but declares, that there were nei-
' ther more nor less, received by the church. ... Moreover, he cites passages from every chapter of St. Matthew and
' St. Luke, from fourteen chapters of St. Mark, and from twenty chapters of St. John. ... Tatianus, who flourished in
' the same century, wrote a harmony of the gospels ; *the gospel gathered out of the four gospels.*' *Whitby :* Preface to
the Four Gospels. It is therefore undeniable, that from the earliest ages of the church, this gospel, and that of St. Luke, though not written by apostles, were received as authentick, and as divinely inspired : and this consideration gives much weight to the tradition, that St. Peter sanctioned it by his apostolical authority, which induced the primi.tive church, without hesitation, to number it among the canonical books of scripture.—Some have considered Mark, as epitomizing or abridging Matthew's gospel ; and he doubtless records many of the same facts, and a few of the same discourses and parables, which are found in it. But he omits many things, and adds others ; and he records some miracles much more fully than Matthew had done, and not without considerable variation : so that there is no reason to suppose, that he intentionally took any thing from Matthew, but that he wrote such things, as were especially brought to his knowledge, and impressed on his mind. The coincidence, therefore, seems to have arisen, rather from the circumstance of the two evangelists writing the history of the same grand and most highly interesting events, than from any design in the one of deducing his materials from the other. The circumstance of the same facts in many instances being repeated in this gospel, and but few of our Lord's discourses introduced, may seem to render the expositor's labour less needful, except in noting variations. But, as it has pleased God to confirm his truth by several witnesses ; it will never be without use to a humble pious enquirer, to re-examine the same important trans-actions, as placed by each evangelist in that point of view, which most affected his own mind : while the inimitable simplicity common to them all, however they vary the narrative, is an internal proof, that they were not left to be carried away by their feelings, or to use any expression unsuitable to the intrinsick dignity of the subject.

CHAP. I.

The gospel is introduced by John the Baptist's ministry, 1—8. The baptism and temptation of Christ, 9—13. John being imprisoned, Jesus preaches in Galilee, and calls Simon and Andrew, James and John, to follow him, 14—20. He casts out an unclean spirit, 21—28; heals Peter's wife's mother, and many sick persons, 29—34; retires very early in the morning for prayer; preaches in the synagogues of Galilee; and cleanses a leper, 35—45.

a Luke l. 2, 3. ii. 10, 11. Acts i. 1.
b John xx. 31. Rom. l. 1.—4. i. John i. 1—5.
c 1 John i. 7. Matt. iii. 17. xiv. 33.
d Ps. xl. 7. Matt. ii. & xxvi. 24. xvii. 81. Luke i. 70.
e Mal. iii. 1. Matt. xi. 10. Luke vii. 27. 78. vii.
f Is.xl.3—5.Matt. iii. 3. Luke iii. 4. —6. John i. 15. 19—34. iii. 28—36.
g Matt. iii. 1, 2 6. Luke iii. 2, 3. Acts x. 37. viii. 24, 2x. xix. 3, 4.
* Or, unto. h Acts xxii. 16.
i Matt. iii. 5, 6. iv.
k John i. 28. iii.
l Lev. xxvi. 40. Josh. vii. 19. Ps. xxxii. 5. Prov. xxviii. 13. Acts ii. 38. 1 John i. 8—10.

THE ª beginning of the gospel of ᵇ Jesus Christ, ᶜ the Son of God;

2 As it is ᵈ written in the prophets, ᵉ Behold, I send my messenger before thy face, which shall prepare thy way before thee.

3 The ᶠ voice of one crying in the wilderness, Prepare ye the way of the Lord, make his paths straight.

4 John ᵍ did baptize in the wilderness, and ·preach the baptism of repentance * for the ᵇ remission of sins.

5 And ⁱ there went out unto him all the land of Judea, and they of Jerusalem, and were all ᵏ baptized of him in the river of Jordan, ˡ confessing their sins.

6 And John was ᵐ clothed with camels' hair, and with a girdle of a skin about his loins; and he did ⁿ eat locusts and wild honey;

m 2 Kings i. 8. Zech. xiii. 4.
Matt. iii. 4.
n Lev. xi. 22.

7 And preached, saying, ° There cometh one mightier than I after me, the latchet of whose shoes I am not worthy to stoop down and unloose.

o Matt. iii. 11. 14. Luke iii. 16. vii. 6, 7. John i. 27. iii. 28—81. Acts xiii. 25.

8 I indeed ᵖ have baptized you with water; but ᑫ he shall baptize you with the Holy Ghost.

p Prov. i. 23. Is. 3. xliv. 3.
q 82. xxxvi. 25.—27. Joel ii. 28.
Acts i. 5. ii. 4. 17. xi. 15. xix. 4—6.
16. xix. 4—6.

9 ¶ And it came to pass in those days, ʳ that Jesus came from Nazareth of Galilee, and was baptized of John in Jordan.

r Matt. iii. 13—15. Luke iii. 21.
Matt.iii.16.John. l. 31—34.

10 And straightway ˢ coming up out of the water, he saw the heavens ᵗ opened, and the Spirit ᵘ like a dove, descending upon him :

s Or, rivers, or, rent. Matt. iii. 16.
t John i. 32.
u Matt. iii. 16. John i. 32. 2 Pet. i. 17, 18.
x Is. 7. Ps. ii. 7.

11 And ˣ there came a voice from heaven, saying, ʸ Thou art my beloved Son, in whom I am well pleased.

x Is. xlii. 1. Matt. xvii. 5. Luke ix. 35. John i. 34.
y Matt. iii. 17. xvii. 5. & xii. 18. 20—23. xix. 4. Co-i. 13.

12 And immediately ᶻ the Spirit driveth him into the wilderness.

z Matt. iv. 1, &c. Luke iv. 1, &c.

13 And he was there in the wilderness ª forty days ª tempted of Satan, and was with the wild beasts : ᵇ and ᶜ the angels ministered unto him.

a Ex. xxiv. 18. xxxiv. 28. Deut. ix. 9. 18.
ix. 11. 18. 25. 1 Kings xix. 8.
b 1 Kings xix. 5. 7. Matt. iv. 11. xxvi. 53. 1 Tim. iii. 16.

NOTES.

CHAP. I. V. 1, 2. Mark, writing after Matthew as it is generally supposed, passed over every thing which related to the birth of Jesus, and began his history with a brief account of John the Baptist's ministry. This was in fact " The beginning of the gospel," the introduction of the New Testament dispensation ; the opening of the glad tidings relating to Jesus Christ the anointed Saviour, the incarnate Son of God ; according as it had been foretold by the prophets. (*Marg. Ref.*)—The history of John the Baptist is stiled " the beginning of the gospel ; " ' because he began his office by preaching repentance as the ' preparation to receive it, and faith in the Messiah as the ' subject of it. (*Luke* xvi. 16.) ... This he styles " the ' " gospel of the Son of God," ... that so we might have ' worthy thoughts both of the gospel, ... and of the Author, ' as being ... so nearly related to the Father.' *Whitby.*

Behold, &c. (2) *Note, Matt.* xi. 7—11, v. 10.—The quotation here is exactly in the words, which Matthew uses ; and except the change of the pronoun *my* for *thy,* is literal from the Hebrew.—I³ⁿ εξαποστελλω τον αγγελον μs, και επιϐλεϸεται οδον προ προσωπs μ. ' Behold I will send out my ' messenger, and he shall look out the path before my ' face.' *Sept.* (*Notes, Mal.* iii. 1—4. iv. 4—6. *Luke* i. 76 —79, v. 76.)

V. 3. (*Notes, Is.* xl. 3—5. *Matt.* iii. 1—3. *Luke* i. 11 —17, vv. 16, 17. 67—80. iii. 1—6.)—' The same is called, ' in the foregoing clause, JEHOVAH. Therefore, as this ' verse is necessarily interpreted of Christ, it is an unde-

' niable proof of his Deity, as of one substance with the ' Father.' *Beza.*—The quotation exactly as in Matthew. Instead of τας τριϐς αυτη, the LXX have τας τριϐς τy Θεy ημων, (" the paths of our God ; ") which accords to the Hebrew.

V. 4—11. (*Marg.* and *Marg. Ref.*—*Notes, Matt.* iii. 4—17. *Luke* iii. 9. 15—18. *John* i. 15. 19—34. iii. 22 —36. *Acts* xix. 5, 6.)—Some infer, from the addition of the word " river," to the name Jordan, that St. Mark wrote especially for the use of those who were strangers to Judea.

For the remission of sins. (4) " Unto." *Marg.* Εις αφεσιν αμαρτιων. *Notes, Luke* iii. 2, 3, v. 3. *John* i. 29.—*In ... Jordan.* (5) Εν τω Ιορδανη. The same preposition is twice translated *with,* in the eighth verse, and once in the twenty-third.—*The latchet,* &c. (7) Τον ιμαντα, &c. *Luke* iii. 16. *John* i. 27. *Acts* xxii. 25.—" Whose shoes I " am not worthy to bear," *Matt.* iii. 11.—*In Jordan.* (9) Εις Ιορδανην, *apud Jordanem.*—*Opened.* (10) " Cloven," or " rent." *Marg.* Σχιζομενς. See on *Note, Matt.* ix.

V. 12, 13. *Marg. Ref.*—*Notes, Matt.* iv. 1—11. *Luke* iv. 1—13.—*Driveth him.* (12) Εκϐαλλει αυτον. (*Note, Matt.* ix. 36—38, v. 38.) The expression may imply the energy of that impulse on the mind of our Lord, by which he was inwardly constrained to retire from society, and to go into the waste howling wilderness, to be " with the " wild beasts." This last circumstance, mentioned by Mark alone, favours the opinion, that he went into that

14 ¶ Now ᵃ after that John was put in prison, Jesus came into Galilee, ᵈ preaching the gospel of the kingdom of God,

15 And saying, ᵉ The time is fulfilled, and ᶠ the kingdom of God is at hand: ᶠ repent ye, and believe the gospel.

16 Now ʰ as he walked by the sea of Galilee, he saw ˡ Simon, and Andrew his brother, casting a net into the sea: for they were fishers.

17 And Jesus said unto them, Come ye after me, and I will make you to become ᵏ fishers of men.

18 And straightway they ˡ forsook their nets, and followed him.

19 And when he had gone a little farther thence, he saw ᵐ James the son of Zebedee, and John his brother, who also were in the ship mending their nets.

20 And straightway he called them: and ⁿ they left their father Zebedee in the ship with the hired servants, and went after him.

21 ¶ And ᵒ they went into Capernaum: and straightway on the sabbath-day ᵖ he entered into the synagogue, and taught.

22 And ᵠ they were astonished at his doctrine; for he taught them as one that had authority, and not ʳ as the scribes.

23 ¶ And there was in their synagogue ˢ a man with an unclean spirit; and he cried out,

24 Saying, ᵗ Let us alone; what have we to do with thee, thou Jesus of Nazareth? art thou come to destroy us? I know thee who thou art, ᵘ the Holy One of God.

25 And Jesus ˣ rebuked him, saying, Hold thy peace, and come out of him.

26 And when the unclean spirit had ʸ torn him, and cried with a loud voice, he came out of him.

27 And ᶻ they were all amazed, insomuch that they questioned among themselves, saying, What thing is this? what new doctrine is this? ᵃ for with authority commandeth he even the unclean spirits, and they do obey him.

---

desert, in which Israel formerly had wandered; and it shews the dreary situation in which he chose so long to continue, and the peculiar advantages which Satan would in that respect possess, in suggesting his horrid temptations. (*Note, Matt.* iv. 1, 2.) ' These forty days, saith ' Dr. Lightfoot, the holy angels ministered to Christ visibly, ' and Satan tempted him invisibly: at the end of them ' Satan puts on the appearance of an angel of light, and ' pretends to wait on him as they did.' *Whitby.* This is adduced, as one instance out of very many, in which learned men ingeniously explain passages in one gospel, without duly attending to the other gospels: for Matthew says, " Then the devil left him, and behold angels came " and ministered to him." (*Matt.* iv. 11.)

V. 14. (*Notes, Matt.* iv. 12—17. *Luke* iv. 14, 15.) From this verse, and the parallel passages, not duly compared with the gospel of St. John, many writers have asserted, that Jesus *began* his ministry, when John had *finished* his: but it is evident, that Jesus had preached, and baptized by the hands of his disciples, for a considerable time, before John was imprisoned. (*Notes, John* ii. iii. 22—36. iv. 1—4.)

V. 15. ' The time fixed by the prophets, especially by Daniel's seventy weeks, has been fulfilled; and the predicted events, which have so long excited the most anxious and sanguine expectation, are on the very eve of being fulfilled.' (*Notes, Gen.* xlix. 10. *Dan.* ix. 24—27. *Hag.* ii. 6—9. *Mal.* iii. 1—4.)—*Repent ye, and believe the gospel.*] Πιστευετε εν τω ευαγγελιω.—" Repent ye, for the kingdom of " heaven is at hand;" *Matt.* iv. 17. Repentance would prepare the heart, for a believing reception of the gospel.

the glad tidings of Messiah's salvation, and this faith would certainly attend, or spring out of, true repentance. (*Notes, Matt.* xxi. 28—32. *Acts* ii. 37—40. iii. 19—21, *v.* 19.)

V. 16—20. (*Marg. Ref.—Note, Matt.* iv. 18—22.) Few passages are more exactly parallel, than these verses and those referred to in St. Matthew: yet, if carefully compared, (especially in the Greek,) it will be found, that they so vary, as to minute things, in several particulars, as to render it clear, that Mark did not intentionally copy Matthew.—" The hired servants," whom Zebedee had as helpers, when his sons were called to a higher employment, are not mentioned by Matthew.

V. 22. *Notes, Matt.* iv. 23—25. vii. 28, 29.

V. 23—28. (*Luke* iv. 33—37.) This miracle is not particularly recorded by Matthew.—As the possessed person was admitted into the synagogue, it may be supposed that the unclean spirit did not harass him at all times; but perhaps took advantage of the paroxysms of bodily disorder, or other circumstances, to renew his more violent assaults. Accordingly, the man was seized upon in this manner, while in the synagogue, and cried out with great vehemence, " Let us alone, what have we to do with thee," &c. Probably, the man was led by satanical influence to fear immediate destruction to himself, instead of expecting the destruction of the power of the unclean spirits, and his own deliverance, from the power of Christ. (*Notes, v.* 2 —17. *Matt.* viii. 28, 29.) No disorder could possibly enable a man to know Jesus to be " the Holy One " of God," who came " to destroy the works of the " devil:" this was doubtless the language of the unclean spirit or spirits, speaking by the organs of the man; and

28 And immediately [b] his fame spread abroad throughout all the region round about Galilee.

29 ¶ And forthwith, when they were come out of the synagogue, they [c] entered into the house of Simon and Andrew, with James and John.

30 But Simon's [d] wife's mother lay sick of a fever; and anon [e] they tell him of her.

31 And he came [f] and took her by the hand, and lifted her up; and immediately the fever left her, and she [g] ministered unto them.

32 ¶ And [h] at even, when the sun did set, they brought unto him all that were diseased, and them that were possessed with devils.

33 And [i] all the city was gathered together at the door.

34 And he healed many that were sick of divers diseases, and cast out many devils; [k] and suffered not the devils to [o] speak, because they knew him.

35 ¶ And in the morning, [l] rising up a great while before day, he went out, and departed into a solitary place, and there prayed.

36 And Simon, and they that were with him, followed after him.

37 And when they had found him, they said unto him, [m] All men seek for thee.

38 And he said unto them, [n] Let us go into the next towns, that I may preach there also : [o] for therefore came I forth.

39 And he [p] preached in their synagogues throughout all Galilee, [q] and cast out devils.

40 ¶ And [r] there came [s] a leper to

Marginal references (left column):
b 45. Mic v. 4. Matt. iv. 24. &c. 41. Luke iv. 14. 37.
c Matt. viii. 14, 15. Luke iv. 38, 39. ix. 58.
d 1 Cor. ix. 5.
e r. 23. John xi. 13.
f v. 41. Acts ix. 4..
g xv. 41. Ps. ciii. 1—3. cxvi. 12. Matt. xxvii. 55. Luke viii. 2, 3.
h 21. ii. 2. Matt. viii. 16, 17. Luke iv. 40.
i 5. Acts xiii. 44.

Marginal references (right column):
k 25. iii. 12. Luke iv. 41. Acts xvi. 16, 17.
o Or, my that they knew him.
l vi. 46—48. Ps. v. 3. cix. 4. Luke iv. 42. vi. 12. xii. 39—46. John iv. 34. vi. 15. Eph. vi. 18. Phil. ii. 5. Heb v. 7.
m 5. Zech. xi. 11. John iii. 26. xii.
n vii. xii. 16. Luke ii. 49. 1—d. Luke ii. 49. iv. 18—21. John ix. 4, 5. xvi. 28.
p 21. Luke iv. 43, 44.
q vii. 30. Luke iv. 44.
r Matt. viii. 2—4. Lev. xiii. xiv. Num. xii. 10—15. Deut. xxiv. 8, 9. 2 Sam. iii. 29. 2 Kings v. 5, &c. 27. vii. 3.
s xv. 8. Matt. xi. 5. Luke xvii. 12—19.

---

probably intending to bring Jesus into the suspicion of a confederacy with Satan by this insidious testimony. (*Note, Acts* xvi. 16—18.) Our Lord therefore imposed silence on him, and constrained him to quit possession : and though 'he shewed his malice, by tearing, or convulsing, the possessed person, and causing him to call out aloud as in extreme anguish ; yet he so entirely left him, that the people were exceedingly astonished at the miracle ; and it greatly increased and extended the reputation of Christ. (*Marg. Ref.* t. x—a.—*Notes,* 34. ix. 16—18.)

Let us alone. (24) Εα. *Luke* iv. 34. (Ab εαω, *sino.*) Not elsewhere N. T.—*What have we,* &c.] Τι ημιν και σοι. " What to us and to thee ? " v. 7. *Matt.* viii. 29.—2 *Sam.* xix. 22. *Sept.*—*The Holy one of God.*] O 'Αγιος τα Θεα. *Luke* iv. 34.—*Marg. Ref.* u.—*Had torn.* (26) Σπαραξαν. ix. 20. 26. *Luke* ix. 39. Not elsewhere N. T.—*They were amazed.* (27) Εθαμβηθησαν. x. 24. 32. *Acts* ix. 6. (Α θαμβος. Pavor, stupor.)—*What new,* &c.] Such astonishing miracles are not wrought in vain : some new discovery of the will of God is intended ; but what can it be? (*Note, Acts* xvii. 19—21)—*The region,* &c. (28) " Throughout all Galilee."

V. 29—31. *Marg. Ref.*—*Note, Matt.* viii. 14, 15.

V. 32, 33. The sabbath ended at sun-set ; and then the people seized the opportunity of bringing the diseased to Jesus, that they might be healed. (*Note, Matt.* viii. 16, 17).

V. 34. *Marg. Ref.*—*Many,* &c.] If on this one evening, after the other miracles of the day, our Lord " healed " *many,*" and " cast out *many* devils ;" how numerous must we conceive the miracles of mercy, wrought by him, to have been, if all had been recorded !—*Suffered,* &c.] (*Note,* 23—28, v. 25.) ' It is not the office of the devil to ' preach the gospel. ... Otherwise Christ might seem to ' have something in common with Satan ; ... who is never ' more to be feared by us, than when he transforms him- ' self into an angel of light.' *Beza.* (*Note, 2 Cor.* xi.

13—15.)—The clause may be rendered, " He suffered not " the devils to say that they knew him." (*Marg.*) ' He ' suffered not the evil spirits to profess their knowledge of ' him ; because he would not have him, who is the father ' of lies, to slander and disgrace the truth by his testi- ' mony.' *Bp. Hall.*

V. 35—39. After a day spent in unremitted labours of love, to a very late hour, our Lord next morning arose " a great while before day," for retirement and prayer. (*Note, Luke* iv. 38—44, v. 42.) But after some time, Peter and some others went after him, and informed him, that all the people of the place sought for him : and it is probable, they were delighted at his increasing popularity. Yet he did not see good, to go among the same people at present ; but went to other places. Perhaps he knew the multitude to be meditating some design, in order to make him King over them.

A great while before day. (35) Εννυχον λιαν. *Much in the night.* (Εκ εν et νυξ, *nox.*) Not elsewhere N. T.—*Followed after him.* (36) Κατεδιωξαν. Not elsewhere N. T. The word seems to denote *pursuing in a hostile manner ;* but it cannot here mean this : yet the interruption might be unwelcome to the holy mind of the Saviour, and constitute a kind of persecution. *Ps.* xxiii. 20. *Sept.*—*Towns.* (38) Κωμοπολεις. Not elsewhere N. T. ' Κωμοπολεις. Towns, saith Dr. Lightfoot, are villages ' which had a synagogue in them ; Κωμαι, villages which ' had none ; Πολεις, towns girt about with walls.' *Whitby.* —*Therefore came I forth.*] " Therefore am I sent," *Luke* iv. 43. ' For that purpose am I sent into the world ' by my Father, with the most extensive designs of useful- ' ness : and therefore came I forth from his more imme- ' diate presence.' *Doddridge.* (*Marg. Ref.* o.)

V. 40—44. (*Notes, Matt.* viii. 1—4. ix. 30, 31. *Luke* v. 12—15. xvii. 11—19.) It is probable, that our Lord noticed something in this man, and some others, which rendered a strict and even stern charge, in this respect,

him, beseeching him, and 'kneeling down to him, and saying unto him, ᵃ If thou wilt, thou canst make me clean.

41 And Jesus, ᵃ moved with compassion, put forth *his* hand, and touched him, and saith unto him, ᶠ I will, be thou clean.

42 And as soon as he had spoken, ᵍ immediately the leprosy departed from him, and he was cleansed.

43 And ʰ he straitly charged him, and forthwith sent him away ;

44 And saith unto him, See thou say nothing to any man: but go thy way, ᵇ shew thyself to the priest, and offer for thy cleansing those things which Moses commanded, for a testimony unto them.

45 But he went out, ᶜ and began to publish *it* much, and to blaze abroad the matter, insomuch that Jesus ᵈ could no more openly enter into the city, but was without in desert places: and they came to him from every quarter.

---

peculiarly needful, to prevent or counteract any impropriety of conduct in them, which might have given some occasion to his vigilant enemies. None but our Lord, ever thus charged those who were miraculously cured, not to speak of it.—*Shew*, &c. (44) A cleansed leper might shew himself to any priest, who resided in the neighbourhood, and thus have his cleansing legally attested : but it was requisite, that the offerings required by the law should be presented at the sanctuary ; so that, either immediately, or in a short time, this man must go up to Jerusalem for that purpose ; and it is most probable, that he went to shew himself to the priests at the temple, without any delay. (*Notes, Lev.* xiv. 1—32.)

He straitly charged. (43) Εμβριμησαμενος.—See on *Matt.* ix. 30.—*He ... sent him away.*] Εξεβαλλεν αυτον. i. 12. *Matt.* ix. 38. xxi. 12. 39. *Luke* viii. 54. xi. 14. *John* x. 4.

V. 45. *Could no more,* &c.] ' This phrase signifies, ' what is unfit, incongruous, or inconvenient to be ' done. ... (*Luke* vi. 42. xii. 7.) ...That which cannot ' justly, or without violation of some law of equity and ' justice be performed. ... (*Acts* x. 47. 1 *Cor.* x. 21.) ... ' That which is not agreeable to the divine economy, ' counsel, or will. ... (*Matt.* xxvi. 42. *John* v. 19. 30.) ... ' That which we cannot do by reason of the trouble of it, ' or because of some other employment which interferes ' with it. ... (iii. 20. vi. 19, 20. *Luke* xiv. 20.) ...That ' which cannot be done, not for want of power in the ' agent, but on account of some defect or fault in the pa- ' tient. (vi. 5, 6.) ... That which cannot be done, by reason ' of some disposition in us, which renders us averse to, ' and unwilling to do any thing, till it be removed. (*Gen.* ' xxxvii. 4. *Jer.* vi. 10. *Matt.* xii. 34. *John* viii. 43. xii. 39. ' xiv. 17. *Rom.* viii. 8.) And so concerning a good disposi- ' tion. (*Matt.* vii. 18. *Acts* iv. 20. 1 *John* iii. 9. *Rev.* ii. ' 2.)' *Whitby.* (*Note,* ii. 18—22, v. 19.) This quotation is peculiarly important, in establishing the distinction between *moral* and *natural* inability, as shewing, that the total want of inclination, or an entire aversion, forms as *real* an impossibility, as to the event, as a total want of physical power ; but an impossibility, which in no degree interferes with our free agency, or responsibility.—' Inso- ' much as Jesus, who purposely shunned the confluences ' and applauses of the people, found it not fit for him to ' enter openly into the city.' *Bp. Hall.—To blaze abroad.*] Διαφημιζειν. See on *Note, Matt.* xxviii. 15.

PRACTICAL OBSERVATIONS.

V. 1—13.

Those characters and actions, which are for a time concealed, through obscurity or humility, are commonly far more excellent, than such as are the subjects of extensive human applause : but when the Lord's time comes, or his work requires it, he makes his approved servants known, and renders their eminence equal to their excellence.—The hearts of sinful men must be prepared, before they can welcome the privileges, and perform the duties, of the kingdom of God : and this is commonly effected by the divine blessing on the scriptural preaching of repentance and conversion.—Ministers should diligently perform their duty in this respect, and in administering divine ordinances ; and thus numbers may be led to confess their sins, and to profess repentance : but without faith in the Saviour, through the regeneration of the Holy Spirit, they cannot be accepted servants or worshippers of God. This all faithful preachers plainly declare : and all believers speak and think humbly of themselves, and honourably of Christ, in exact proportion to the degree of their spiritual discernment and progress in the divine life : (*P. O. Matt.* iii. 13—17. viii. 5—13 :) and when to this they join a holy indifference to all worldly things, they are likely to be extensively useful.—While we rejoice in the perfection of our Surety's obedience, we should copy his example : and by attending on all the ordinances of God, we shall be in the way of receiving more abundant supplies of " the Spirit of adoption," witnessing " with our spirits " that we are the children of God," accepted through " his " beloved Son, in whom he is well pleased." Then should we be exposed to persecutors, fierce as wild beasts, as well as to Satan's temptations, during our continuance in this wilderness ; we may confide in the divine protection and consolation, and expect that angels will delight in ministering to us also, for our Redeemer's sake.

V. 14—28.

One human instrument after another finishes his transient season of usefulness ; but the divine Agent " work- " eth hitherto," and will to the end and for ever : and though apparent delays intervene, yet " when the time is " fulfilled," he will " perfect what concerneth " the church and the believer, according to his holy word.—Those who are labouring, with honesty and harmony, in some mean

CHAP. II.

Jesus heals a paralytick, and shews his authority on earth to forgive sins, 1—12. He calls Matthew; and answers those who blamed him for eating with publicans and sinners, 13—17. He vindicates his disciples, when blamed for not fasting frequently, and accused of breaking the sabbath, 18—28.

AND ᵃagain he entered into Capernaum after *some* days; ᵇ and it was noised that he was in the house.

2 And ᶜstraightway many were gathered together, insomuch that there was no room to receive *them*; no, not

a i. 45. Matt. ix. 1.
b vii. 24. Luke xviii. 35—38. John iv. 47. Acts ii. 6.
c i8. i. 33. 37. 45. iv. 1, 2. Luke v. 17. xii. 1.

employment, are more in the way of being called forth to further usefulness; than such as are disputing, or loitering, under pretence of study and preparation. (*P. O. Ps.* lxxviii. 55—72. *Note, Am.* vii. 15—17. *P. O. Matt.* iv. 12—25.)—The occupation of a minister, though despised by worldly men, ought to be deemed a high preferment, not only by those who may be called to it from the fishing boat, or the flock; but even by such as should leave the highest offices in the community for the sake of it: for the salvation of one soul is a far more important event, than the temporal prosperity even of whole nations. But they " who desire this good work," must be content to forsake all worldly interests and expectations, that they may follow the example, the instructions, and the commandments of Christ; and give up themselves wholly to learn his truth and will, in order that they may teach them to others also. May his powerful word call forth many self-denied, disinterested, laborious, patient, and skilful " fishers of men:" for though many have been, and are now employed; and large numbers of sinners have been, and many still are, brought forth from the course of this evil world into his church; immensely greater numbers continue in their natural estate, destroying each other, and falling a prey to that great leviathan, who takes pastime in this work of destruction.—Many scribes indeed there have been, and are, possessed of human learning, and making worldly preferment their leading object: but our prayer ought to be, that " Scribes, well instructed unto the king- " dom of God," may teach " with authority," in all congregations, after the manner of Christ; and to the conviction and astonishment of such hearers, as have hitherto been taught in a mere formal manner: and this would render our churches more frequented than they now generally are.—But there are too many, even in assemblies for sacred worship, who are slaves to unclean spirits : such may quietly attend, whilst only formal teachers officiate; but if the Lord come with his faithful ministers, and his holy doctrine, and by his convincing Spirit, they begin to cry out, and are ready to say, " What have we to do with " thee, Jesus of Nazareth? art thou come to destroy us?" Satan indeed well knows him to be " the Holy One of " God;" but he very successfully labours to hide this truth from his servants, that he may maintain and extend his empire through their ignorance and prejudice.—The immediate and perfect cure of frantick lunaticks, by a word speaking, would even in our days excite astonishment, and cause men to exclaim, " What thing is this!" Yet a work really greater is frequently wrought, and men treat it with supercilious contempt and neglect. If this were not so, the evident conversion of one notorious profligate to " a sober, righteous, and godly life," by the preaching of a crucified Saviour, would cause all around to enquire " What new doctrine is this," (*new* to them, though *old* in itself; for every thing is *new* to him who

never heard it before,) by which unclean spirits are constrained to depart, and rebels are brought to the willing obedience of children ? Indeed it is in this way, that the fame of Jesus, and the honour of the gospel, do spread abroad in this evil world : and if every one, who professes the doctrines of grace, was but evidently thus dispossessed and changed, they would gradually prevail against all opposition.

V. 29—45.

We ought to supplicate the Saviour for help in all our spiritual and temporal maladies, for ourselves and those belonging to us; and to use our health and strength in ministering to him and his disciples: diligently recommending him to others, as knowing that nothing is too large for his grace, or impossible to his omnipotence.—But when did any one of us spend a single day, as Jesus spent each of his days? Were we like him, we should " rise a great " while before" light, (if health permitted,) rather than be straitened in time for communion with our heavenly Father, when hindered at other hours by urgent engagements : and having had a good sabbath, we should be the more earnest in prayer the next morning, lest the impression should wear off; and that we might obtain a blessing on those especially, who have heard the word of God from us, or with us.—Men may outwardly attend on instruction with diligence, and yet not be prepared to follow Christ fully: but it behoves us to use our opportunities whilst they are afforded us, that we may be established in the faith, in case we should be proved by losing them for a season.—As Christ came to preach the gospel in different places, we should endeavour to attend on every side as we have opportunity.—Let all who are weary of the leprosy of sin, and afraid of its consequences, wait on Christ to be cleansed : for when he speaks the word, (and he will speak it, if we truly believe in him,) the most inveterate evil propensities will be brought under, and evil habits conquered, and sin shall have no more dominion over us. If this blessing be vouchsafed us, let us approve it in our conduct ᵗᵒ the ministers and people of God, by ᵍ walking " in all his ordinances and commandments," as witnesses for Christ in this evil world. Nor ought we to conceal our obligations to the Saviour : for no reasons now exist, why we should hesitate to spread abroad his praises, and the more abundantly sinners flock to him from every quarter, the greater is his honour, and the more complete his triumph and joy.

NOTES.

Chap. II. V. 1, 2. (*Note,* i. 45.) As Jesus had been for some time absent from Capernaum; it is probable, some of the inhabitants began to conclude that he would not return : and those who were sick, or had sick friends and relations, might fear that they had finally missed the opportunity of obtaining cures. So that, the rumour of

so much as about the door: [d]and he preached the word unto them.

3 ¶ And they come unto him, [e]bringing one sick of the palsy, which was borne of four.

4 And when they could not come nigh unto him for the press, [f]they uncovered the roof where he was: and, when they had broken it up, they let down the bed wherein the sick of the palsy lay.

5 When Jesus [g]saw their faith, [h]he said unto the sick of the palsy, [i]Son, thy [k]sins be forgiven thee.

6 But there were certain of the scribes sitting there, [l]and reasoning in their hearts,

7 Why doth this man thus [m]speak blasphemies ? [n]who can forgive sins, but God only ?

8 And immediately, [o]when Jesus perceived in his spirit that they so reasoned within themselves, he said unto them, [p]Why reason ye these things in your hearts?

9 Whether [q]is it easier to say to the sick of the palsy, [r]Thy sins be forgiven thee ; or to say, Arise, and take up thy bed, and walk ?

10 But that ye may know [s]that the Son of man hath power on earth to forgive sins, (he saith to the sick of the palsy,)

11 I say unto thee, [t]Arise, and take up thy bed, and go thy way into thine house.

12 And immediately he arose, took up the bed, and went forth before them all ; [u]insomuch that they were all amazed, and [x]glorified God, saying, [y]We never saw it on this fashion.

his return excited great attention, and such numbers assembled to hear his discourses, or witness his miracles, that the house and the court or space before the door, could not contain the whole company. (Marg. Ref.)

After some days. (1) Δι' ἡμερων. Probably some considerable time had elapsed.—In the house.] Εις οικον. No particular house is specified : probably it was that of Andrew and Peter.—There was no room. (2) Μηκέτι χωρειν. See on Note, Matt. xix. 11.

V. 3—12. (Notes, Matt. ix. 2—8. Luke v. 18—26.) We find from Luke, that certain Pharisees and Scribes had come from all the cities and towns, far and wide, and even from Jerusalem ; doubtless to watch our Lord, and to seek for matter of accusation against him. (Luke v. 17.)—While he was earnestly instructing the people, four persons came, bringing on a bed a man so enfeebled by the palsy, that he could not be otherwise conveyed. Probably, he despaired of a cure from any other quarter, and deeply regretted that he had not applied to Jesus, when before at Capernaum ; but his hope of being healed reviving on our Lord's return to that city ; he was earnestly desirous of being carried to him, and his friends were equally willing to assist him ; though it would be laborious to them, and painful to him. And, when they could not come into the presence of Christ, because of the multitude, being unwilling to postpone the application, lest the departure of Christ should again deprive them of the opportunity, they conveyed the bed to the top of the house. This, it may be supposed, was low, perhaps only one story high, and there was some way up on the outside : (Note, Matt. xxiv. 15—18, v. 17:) but though there might be also an opening in the roof, yet it seems not to have been wide enough to let the bed pass through. They therefore uncovered the roof, and even broke up what was in the way. Thus they let him down through the tiling in his couch, and brought him into the presence of Jesus. Some think, judging from the sight of the houses, and acquaintance with the cus-

toms, in those eastern countries, that he was let down through the battlements, on the outside of the house, into the court-yard : but the language of the evangelists seems incapable of this meaning ; and any injury done to the roof, by breaking it up, might be repaired at a small expense.—When, however, Jesus " saw their faith," (in these evident effects of it, as well as by his intimate knowledge of their hearts, Marg. Ref. g,) he did not, in the first instance, remove the man's disorder ; but, addressing him in the most condescending and affectionate manner, authoritatively pronounced his sins forgiven. (Marg. Ref. k.) This afforded the Scribes the occasion for which they were waiting : and though they did not openly declare their sentiments ; they inwardly thought him guilty of blasphemy, in presuming to do that which was the prerogative of God only. (Marg. Ref. l—n.) But our Lord soon shewed them, that he possessed divine perfection and authority ; for " he perceived in his spirit," or by his own knowledge of their hearts, " the thoughts," or reasonings, which inwardly employed them : and he enquired, " Whether is it easier to say to the sick of the palsy, Thy " sins be forgiven thee, or to say, Arise, take up thy bed, " and walk ? " (Marg. Ref. o—q.) Divine authority was requisite actually to forgive sins ; and omnipotence was needful for the immediate and complete removal of that terrible disorder. Having therefore put the matter upon that issue, he proved his authority as " the Son of man," even " on earth " in his state of humiliation, to forgive sins, by commanding the paralytick to arise, and take up his bed and carry it to his house : and such power accompanied his word, that the man was enabled to do this in the sight of the multitude ; so that they were all astonished, and gave praise to God on his behalf, and acknowledged that they had never seen it on this fashion before. (Marg. Ref. s. x, y.) Thus the man, in his miraculous cure, possessed the fullest evidence that his sins were pa e ; every one, who saw him carry his bed, had a demonstra-

2 G 2

13 ¶ And he went forth again ' by the sea-side; ' and all the multitude resorted unto him, and he taught them.

14 And as he passed by, ' he saw Levi the son of ' Alpheus sitting at the ' receipt of custom, and said unto him, ' Follow me. And he arose, and followed him.

15 And it came to pass, that, ' as Jesus sat at meat in his house, many publicans and sinners sat also together with Jesus and his disciples: for there were many, and they followed him.

16 And when the Scribes and Pharisees saw him eat with publicans and sinners, they said unto his disciples, ' How is it that he eateth and drinketh with ' publicans and sinners?

17 When Jesus heard it, he saith unto them, ' They that are whole have no need of the physician, but they that are sick: ' I came not to call the righteous, but sinners to repentance.

18 ¶ And ' the disciples of John and of the Pharisees used to fast: and they come and say unto him, ' Why do the disciples of John and of the Pharisees fast, but thy disciples fast not?

19 And Jesus said unto them, ' Can the children of the bride-chamber fast, while the Bridegroom is with them? as long as they have the Bridegroom with them they cannot fast.

20 But the days will come, when ' the Bridegroom shall ' be taken away from them, ' and then shall they fast in those days.

21 No man also ' seweth a piece of ' new cloth on an old garment; else the new piece that filled it up, taketh away from the old, and the rent is made worse.

22 And no man putteth new wine into old ' bottles; else the new wine doth burst the bottles, and the wine is spilled, and the bottles will be marred: but new wine must be put into new bottles.

23 ¶ And it came to pass, ' that he went through the cornfields on the sabbath-day; and his disciples began, ' to pluck the ears of corn.

24 And the Pharisees said unto him, Behold, ' why do they on the sabbath-day ' that which is not lawful?

25 And he said unto them, ' Have ye never read ' what David did, when he had need, and was an hungred, he, and they that were with him?

26 How he went into the house of God, in the days of ' Abiathar the high priest, and did eat the shew-

---

tion of the divine power and authority of Christ; others were encouraged to apply to him for health, and salvation; God was glorified; and the malignant Scribes were put to shame and silence.—' Christ, by healing the para-' lytick, demonstrates, that man must, by faith in him ' alone, recover all the strength which he has lost.' Beza.

They uncovered the roof. (4) Απεστεγασαν την στεγην. "They unroofed the roof." The verb not used elsewhere N. T. Στεγη. Matt. viii. 8. Luke vii. 6.—When they had broken it up.] Εξορυξαντες. Gal. iv. 15. Ex ιξ, et ορυσσω, fodio. Not elsewhere N. T.—They let down.] Χαλωσι. Luke v. 4, 5. Acts ix. 25. xxvii. 30. 2 Cor. xi. 33.— Reasoning. (6) Διαλογιζομενοι. Interius ratiocinari: animo versare et cogitare. Luke i. 29. iii. 15. v. 22. xii. 17. John xi. 50. Vel, disserere, verbis inter se disceptare. viii. 16. ix. 33. Matt. xvi. 7, 8. xxi. 25. (Ex δια et λογιζομαι.)—Bed. (11) Κραββατον. 4. 9. 12. vi. 55. John v. 8, 9, 10. 11, 12. Acts v. 15. ix. 33. Grabbatum. A mean bed, a couch.— Amazed. (12) Εξιστασθαι. iii. 21. v. 42. vi. 51. Matt. xii. 23. Luke ii. 47. Acts ii. 7. 12. viii. 13. 2 Cor. v. 13. Extra se esse. Beza. Hence the word Ecstasy.

V. 13—17. (Marg. and Marg. Ref.—Notes, Matt. ix. 9—13. Luke v. 27—32.) Matthew is here called ' Levi

"the son of Alpheus:" but it is doubtful, whether he was brother to James the son of Alpheus, or son to another person of the same name, though the former supposition is by far the most probable. (Marg. Ref. a.—See on Note, Matt. ix. 10—12.)

Sinners. (16, 17.) These "sinners" were not gentiles, as some learned men interpret the word to mean; but Jews of disgraceful character. Our Lord's ministry was almost exclusively among "the lost sheep of the house of "Israel."

V. 18—22. (Notes, Matt. ix. 14—17. Luke v. 33— 39.) ' Superstitious and hypocritical persons rashly place ' the sum of piety, in things of an indifferent nature. ... ' Not considering, what the strength of each person can ' bear, they rashly enact any kind of laws about these ' things without discretion: ... and they make no distinc-' tion between the laws which God made concerning them, ' and laws against things in themselves unlawful. ... And ' they prefer the ceremonial law ... to the moral; when, ' on the contrary, they ought to seek from the latter the ' true use of the ceremonial law.' Beza. (Marg. and Marg. Ref.)

V. 23—26. (Notes, Matt. xii. 1—8.) " Abiathar the

^b Ex. xxix. 33. ^b bread, ^b which is not lawful to eat but for the priests, and gave also to them which were with him?

27 And he said unto them, ^c The sabbath was made for man, and not man for the sabbath:

28 Therefore ^d the Son of man is Lord also of the sabbath.

" high priest." Ahimelech was *high* priest when David took the shew-bread; but Abiathar, his son, was *chief* priest under him, and probably superintended the tabernacle and its stated concerns. Ahimelech was soon after slain; and Abiathar became high priest, and continued in that office for above forty years, till after the death of David. He was much more eminent in the history, than his father had been: and these considerations sufficiently shew the evangelist's reason for inserting his name, rather than Ahimelech's, on this occasion. (*Marg. Ref.—Notes*, 1 *Sam.* xxi. 1—9. xxii. 18—22. xxiii. 1—6. 2 *Sam.* viii. 15—18. 1 *Kings* ii. 26, 27.)

High priest. (26) Αρχιερεως. Αρχιερευς is used either for *high priest* or *chief priest*: but generally in the singular it denotes the high priest; in the plural, the chief priests.

V. 27, 28. The sabbath was originally instituted for the good of man even before the fall: (*Notes, Gen.* ii. 2, 3:) and it was continued and enforced after the fall, as still more needful for men, considered as rational agents, living in society, having many wants and troubles; the creatures and subjects of God, preparing for an eternal state of happiness or misery, and sinners under a dispensation of mercy: but " man was not made for the sabbath," as if his observance of it could be of any service to God; or as if he were required to adhere strictly to the letter of it, to his real detriment. Every regulation therefore respecting it should be interpreted, according to this general rule; so that, when a strict observance of the external rest, according to the prescription, especially of the judicial or ceremonial law, would be injurious to the individual, or to others, in an enlarged and complex view of the subject; " the Lord of the sabbath," now become, by his incarnation, " the Son of man," has granted him a licence to dispense with it; but not on any other account. (*Notes, Ex.* xvi. 22—27. xx. 8—10. xxxi. 13—17. xxxv. 2, 3. *Is.* lviii. 13, 14. *Ez.* xx. 12. *Matt.* xli. 7—13. *Luke* xiii. 10—17. *P. O.* xxiii. 44—56. *Notes, John* v. 10—18. vii. 19—24. xx. 19—23. *Rev.* i. 9—11.)

PRACTICAL OBSERVATIONS.

V. 1—12.

Violent sickness and the fear of death, when united to some hope of recovery, and an apprehension that the opportunity may speedily elapse, render men willing to use various irksome and painful methods of cure; and the failure of one remedy commonly renders them more eager to make trial of another. This indeed is not to be blamed: on the contrary, we should put ourselves to inconveniences and hardship, in attempting the relief of the afflicted and diseased: but it is most to be desired, that their afflictions may bring them to Christ for the salvation of their souls, as well as for a blessing on the means used to recover bodily health: for in that case their afflictions will certainly be either removed or sanctified. Forgiveness of sins, being the fore-runner of all other real blessings, is far more valuable than the removal of any sickness; and the loss of the soul is infinitely more dreadful, than the death of the body: but how very few act, as if they believed these undeniable truths!—(*Notes, Ps.* xxxii. 1, 2. *Matt.* x. 28, 29.) We cannot deliver our fellow-sinners from the maladies of the body, much less from those of the soul: but we may in various ways, be helpful in bringing them to Christ for salvation; and should lose no opportunity, and shrink from no self-denial, in attempting it.—The humbled sinner, who despairs of all help, except from the Saviour, will evince his faith by seeking to him, with all earnestness and without delay; and difficulties will only serve to increase his diligence and resolution. He will not attempt to heal himself, or expect to become better, before he comes to his Physician; but when he receives the blessing of forgiveness, it is accompanied by such a powerful operation of renewing grace on his soul, that he evidently becomes " a new creature; old things " pass away, behold all things become new!" (*Notes, Rom.* vi. 1, 2. 2 *Cor.* v. 17. *Eph.* ii. 4—10, *v.* 10. *Heb.* vi. 9, 10.) When enabled to overcome those evils to which he was before enslaved, and to delight in those duties which he had been incapable of, or had an aversion to, he has " a witness in himself," that he is pardoned and justified in Christ Jesus: for he, who heals the distempered soul, must also have power to cleanse the guilty conscience; and the former is the seal and attestation of the latter.— Whatever proud Pharisees and scribes may say in their hearts, or with their lips, against such instances of our Redeemer's power and grace, the happy change is often so evident, that it cannot be gainsayed: and all impartial judges must see and own, in the conduct of many who profess the gospel, a demonstration of the excellency of the doctrines, and of the efficacy of the grace, which they have received. But if any think, however confidently, that their sins are forgiven, who still remain under the power of their corrupt passions and habits, they deceive themselves and bring a scandal on the gospel; for Christ is glorified in those alone, who glorify him by their conduct, from the time when they profess to believe in his name. Should any assume to forgive sins, who have no power to cure paralyticks, and to bid them " take up their bed and " walk;" they would be justly chargeable with the most presumptuous blasphemy: but the feeblest believer may attempt such things at Christ's command, as otherwise would be impossible to him; for his word is with power, and he will strengthen the willing soul to yield obedience to it. (*P. O. Matt.* ix. 1—8. *John* v. 1—14.)

V. 13—28.

While the faithful servants of Christ, after his example, call on publicans and sinners to forsake all and follow him, and meet with some success in their labour of love; there are many who accuse them of encouraging vice, and of being enemies to morality and goodness: not understand-

CHAP. III.

Jesus restores a man's withered hand in the synagogue, on the sabbath, 1—5. The Pharisees conspire his death : he retires, is followed by multitudes, and heals many, 6—12. He chooses twelve apostles, 13—19. His friends-look upon him as beside himself, 20, 21. He confutes the blasphemous absurdity of the scribes, who ascribe his casting out devils to the power of Beelzebub, 22—30. Those who do the will of God are regarded as his nearest relations, 31—35.

a 1. 27. Matt. xii.
9—14. Luke vi.
6—11.
b 1 Kings xiii. 4.
c John v. 8.
e Ps. xxxvii. 32.
Is. xxix. 20, 21.
Jer. xx. 10.
Dan. vi. 4.
Luke vi. 7. xi.
53, 54. xiv. 1.
xx. 20. John ix.
16.

AND [a] he entered again into the synagogue : and there was a man there which had [b] a withered hand.

2 And [c] they watched him, whether

he would heal him on the sabbath-day ; that they might accuse him.

3 And [d] he saith unto the man which had the withered hand, Stand forth.

4 And he saith unto them, [e] Is it lawful to do good on the sabbath-days, or to do evil ? to save life, or to kill ? [f] But they held their peace.

5 And when he had looked round [h] about on them [f] with anger, being [h] grieved for the [i] hardness of their hearts, he saith unto the man, [l] Stretch forth thine hand. And he stretched it out : and his hand was restored whole as the other.

d Is. xliii. 4. Ps.
xl. 10. Luke vi.
9. John ix. 4.
1 Cor. xv. 58.
g. 14.　　26—30
1 Pet. iv. 1.
e ii. 27, 28. Matt.
　　　10—12.
Luke vi. 9. xiii.
15—17. xiv. 1—
6.
f ix. 34.
g Luke vi. 10. xiii.
15. Eph. iv. 26.
Rev. vi. 16, 17.
h Gen. vi. 6.
Neh. xiii. 8. Ps.
xcv. 10. Is. lxiii.
9, 10. Luke xix.
40—44. Eph. iv.
30. Heb. iii. 10
i Or, blindness. Is.
vi. 10. xlii. 18.—
20. xliv. 18.—
20. Matt. xiii.
14, 15. Rom. xi.
7—10. 25. 2 Cor.
iii.14. Eph.iv.18.
ix. 7. Heb. v. 9
l 1 Kings xiii. 6. Matt. xii. 18. Luke vi. 10. xvii. 14. John v. 8. 9. ix. 7. Heb. v. 9

---

ing that " Christ came, not to call the righteous, but sinners to repentance."—The divine Redeemer himself did not escape such slanders; and we should therefore be willing to bear them, as well as careful not to deserve them. If we be blamed for omitting such things as are not needful or seasonable, or for doing that which is not sinful, we may quietly leave him to plead our cause. But we should attend to every part of our duty, in its proper order and season : and ministers should be cautious, in dealing with the weak but conscientious, that they may not discourage them. They should insist on the habitual practice of all holiness, the observance of the Lord's day, and the attendance on divine ordinances, in subserviency to their real good and that of others : but not be so exact in minute or doubtful externals, as to interfere with the grand concerns of genuine piety, justice, and charity ; or with any thing, which may glorify God, or do good to men. (P. O. Matt. ix. 9—17.)

NOTES.

CHAP. III. V. 1—5. (Notes, ii. 23—28. Matt. xii. 9—13.) When Christ demanded, " whether it was lawful to " do good, or evil, on the sabbath-day ; to save life, or " to kill ; " he referred to the secret intentions of the scribes and Pharisees to compass his death. While they were forming designs of perpetrating the most atrocious murder from the basest motives, in the synagogue, and on the sabbath-day ; they blamed him for doing good, and saving men's lives on that day, even when done in subserviency to the salvation of their souls also ! Their malice and perverseness therefore excited his holy indignation : but their exposedness to misery, through the hardness and blindness of their hearts, caused him also to grieve over them, as well as for the mischief which they did to the people.— Stand forth. (3) " Arise into the midst."

Is it lawful, &c. (4) It seems from St. Matthew's narrative, that the enemies of Christ first " asked him, say-" ing, Is it lawful to heal on the sabbath-days ? " and that he answered them by the question here stated.—' Hence ' it seems to follow, that he who doth not do good to his ' neighbour when he can, doeth evil to him ; it being a ' want of charity, and therefore evil, to neglect any oppor-' tunity of doing good, or shewing kindness to any man in

' misery ; and that not to preserve life when it is in danger, ' is to transgress the precept which saith, " Thou shalt " not kill."' Whitby. (Note, 1 John iii. 16, 17.)

Anger. (5) ' Hence we learn, that anger is not always ' sinful ; this passion being found in him in whom was no ' sin. But then it must be noted, that anger is not pro-' perly defined by philosophers, ορεξις αντιλυπησεως, a de-' sire of revenge, or causing grief to him who hath pro-' voked, or hath grieved us ; for this desire of revenge is ' always evil : and though our Saviour was angry with the ' Pharisees for the hardness of their hearts ; yet he had no ' desire to revenge this sin upon them, but had a great ' compassion for them.' Whitby.—Our Lord's anger was not only not sinful, but it was a holy indignation, a perfectly right state of heart ; and the want of it would have been a sinful defect. It would shew a want of filial respect and affection, for a son to hear, without emotion, his father's character unjustly aspersed. Would it not then be a want of due reverence for God, to hear his name blasphemed, without feeling and expressing an indignant disapproba-tion ? Vengeance belongs to the ruler exclusively : and he may grieve at the necessity imposed on him of thus ex-pressing his disapprobation of crimes ; but it is his duty. Eli ought to have shewn anger, as well as grief, when inform-ed of the vile conduct of his sons ; and to have expressed it by severe coercive measures. (Notes, 1 Sam. ii. 23—34. iii. 11—14.) Thus parents and masters, as well as magistrates, may sin, in not feeling and expressing just displeasure against those under their care : and anger is only sinful, when it springs from selfishness and malevolence ; when causeless or above the cause ; and when expressed by un-hallowed words and actions. (Notes, Matt. v. 21, 22. Eph. iv. 26, 27.)

Withered. (1) Εξηραμμενην. 3. See on Matt. xxi. 19, 20. —To do good. (4) Αγαθοποιησαι. Luke vi. 9. 33. 35. Acts xiv. 17. 1 Pet. ii. 15. 20. iii. 17. 3 John 11.—To do evil.] Κακοποιησαι. Luke vi. 9. 1 Pet. iii. 17. 3 John 11. Κακοποιος. John xviii. 30.

Being grieved. (5) Συλλυπημενος. Simul dolens. Here only N. T. ' There is, unless I am deceived, a certain peculiar ' force in the preposition συν in this place ; it neither im-' plies the same as dolens ' (grieving), ' nor can it be taken ' as the same as compati ' (to sympathize) ; ' ... for these ob ·

g a 2

6 ¶ And [k] the Pharisees went forth,
and straightway took counsel with the
[l] Herodians against him, how they
might destroy him.
7 But [m] Jesus withdrew himself with
his disciples to the sea: [n] and a great
multitude from [o] Galilee followed him,
and from Judea,
8 And from Jerusalem, and from
[p] Idumea, and *from* [q] beyond Jordan;
and they about [r] Tyre and Sidon, a
great multitude, when they had heard
what great things he did, came unto
him.
9 And he spake to his disciples, that
a small ship should wait on him, [s] because of the multitude, lest they should
throng him.
10 For he had healed many, insomuch that they [*] pressed upon him for
to [t] touch him, [u] as many as had plagues.
11 And [x] unclean spirits, when they
saw him, fell down before him, and
cried, saying, Thou art [y] the Son of
God.

k Ps. cix. 3, 4. Matt. xii. 14. Luke vi. 11. xx. 19, 20. xxii. 2. John xi. 53.
l viii. 15. xii. 13. Matt. xxii. 16.
m Matt. x. 23. xii. 15. Luke vi. 12. John x. 39—41. xi. 53, 54. Acts xiv. 5, 6. xvii. 10, 14.
n Matt. iv. 25. Luke vi. 17.
o i. 39. Josh. xx. 7. xxi. 32. Luke xxiii. 5. John vii. 41. 52.
p Is. xxxiv. 5. Ez. xxxv. 15. xxxvi. 5. Mal. i. 2—4. *Edom.*
q Num. xxxii. 33—38. Josh. xiii. 8, &c.
r vii. 24. 31. Josh. xix. 28, 29. Ps. xlv. 12. lxxxvii. 4. Is. xxiii. Ez. xxvi—xxviii.
s v. 30, 31. John vi. 15.
* Or, *rushed.*
t v. 27, 28. vi. 56. Matt. xiv. 36. Acts v. 15. xix. 11, 12.
u v. 29. Gen. xii. 17. Num. xi. 33. Luke vii. 21. Heb. xii. 6.
x i. 23, 24. v. 5, 6. Matt. viii. 31. Luke iv. 41. Acts xvi. 17. xix. 13—17.
y i. 1. Matt. iv. 3. 6. viii. 29. Luke viii. 28.

12 And he [z] straitly charged them,
that they should not make him known.
13 ¶ And [a] he goeth up into a
mountain, and calleth *unto him* whom
he would: and they came unto him.
14 And [b] he ordained twelve, that
they should be with him, [c] and that he
might send them forth to preach,
15 And to have power to heal sicknesses, and to cast out devils.
16 And [d] Simon he surnamed Peter;
17 And [e] James the *son* of Zebedee,
and John the brother of James; [f] and
he surnamed them Boanerges, which
is, The sons of thunder;
18 And [g] Andrew, and [h] Philip, and
[i] Bartholomew, and [k] Matthew, and
[l] Thomas, [m] and James the *son* of [n] Alpheus, and [o] Thaddeus, and [p] Simon the
Canaanite,
19 And [q] Judas Iscariot, which also
betrayed him: and they went [†] into an
house.

z i. 25. 44. Matt. xii. 16. Acts xvi. 18.
a Matt. x. 1, &c. Luke vi. 12—16.
b John xv. 16. Acts i. 24, 25. Gal. i. 1. 15—20.
c Luke ix. 1—6. x. 1—11. xxiv. 47. Acts i. 8.
d i. 16. Matt. xvi. 16—18. John i. 42. 1 Cor. i. 12. iii. 22. ix. 5. Gal. ii. 7—9. *Cephas.* 2 Pet. i. 1.
e i. 19, 20. v. 37. ix. 2. x. 35. xiv. 33. John xxi. 2. 20—25. Acts xii. 1.
f Is. lviii. 1. Jer. xxiii. 29. Heb. iv. 12. Rev. x. 11.
g John i. 40. vi. 8. xii. 21, 22. Acts i. 13.
h John i. 43—45. vi. 5—7. xiv. 8, 9.
i Matt. x. 3. Luke vi. 14. Acts i. 13.
k ii. 14. Matt. ix. 9. Luke v. 27—29. *Levi.* vi. 15.
l John xi. 16. xx. 24—29. xxi. 2. Acts i. 13.
m vi. 3. Matt. x. 3. xiii. 55. Luke vi. 15. Acts xv. 13. xxi. 18. 1 Cor. ix. 5. xv. 7. Gal. i. 19. ii. 9. Jam. i. 1.
n ii. 14. o Matt. x. 3. Luke vi. 16. John xiv. 22. Acts i. 13. *Judas the brother of James.* Jude 1, &c. p Matt. x. 4. Luke vi. 15. Acts i. 13. *Simon Zelotes.* q Matt. xxvi. 14—16. 47. xxvii. 3—5. John vi. 64. 71, 72. xii. 4—6. xiii. 2. 26—30. Acts i. 16—25. † Or, *home.*

'durate men did not *grieve* over their own condition, but 'raged against Christ. Therefore by this word it is signi-'fied, that Christ was indeed greatly offended at their des-'perate wickedness; yet so that he also pitied their misery.' *Beza.*—*Hardness.*] Πωρωσει. (A πωρος, *callosa concretio.*) *Rom.* xi. 25. *Eph.* iv. 18.—Πωροω. vi. 52. *Rom.* xi. 7.—Some read πηρωσις, *blindness* (*marg.*) here and in other places.

V. 6—12. (*Note, Matt.* xii. 14—21, *v.* 14.) The time-serving Herodians had no regard to religion, except in subserviency to politicks: yet they concurred with the superstitious Pharisees in plotting the death of the holy Jesus! (*Marg. Ref.* l.—*Note, Matt.* xxii. 15—22, *v.* 16.)—The word translated "plagues" signifies *scourges*, and implies, that all afflictions are the effects of the divine displeasure against the sins of men, and should be received and improved as salutary corrections. (*Notes, Ps.* xciv. 12—14. 1 *Cor.* xi. 29—34. *Heb.* xii. 4—11.)—When it is said that "unclean spirits fell down before him," it relates to the persons possessed with them; and it forms an undeniable proof of the reality of the possessions, of the power of the evil spirits over these afflicted persons, and of the absolute authority of Christ over them. (*Note, Matt.* viii. 28, 29.)

Took counsel. (6) Συμβουλιον εποιουν. "Made a consulta-"tion," or "a council" (Συμβουλιον ελαβον, *Matt.* xii. 14.) The combination of the leaders of the different sects, convening together, as in council, against Jesus, seems intended.—*From Judea,* &c. (7, 8.) *Marg. Ref.* o—r.—*Should wait on him.* (9) Προσκαρτερη· *Adsit, ut semper præsto sit.* *Acts* ii. 42. 46. vi. 4. viii. 13. x. 7. *Rom.* xii. 12. xiii. 6. *Col.* iv. 2.—*Pressed upon.* (10) "Rushed." *Marg.* Επιπιπτειν. *Irruere, incidere, incumbere.* *John* xiii. 25. *Acts* xx. 10. 37.—*Plagues.*] Μαστιγας. v. 29. 34. *Luke* vii. 21. *Acts* xxii. 24. *Heb.* xi. 36.

V. 13—19. (*Marg.* and *Marg. Ref.*—*Notes, Matt.* x. 1—4.) This appointment of the twelve apostles seems to have occurred some time before they were sent forth to preach. (vi. 7—12.) Jesus chose them "to be with "him," that his daily instructions, conversation, and devotions might prepare them for their most important work.—The surname of "Boanerges" or, "sons of "thunder," given to James and John, doubtless related to the energy and efficacy, with which they addressed men's consciences, to awaken their fears, and to shew them their need of mercy and salvation. (*Notes, Jer.* xxiii. 28, 29. *Heb.* iv. 12, 13.) 'Christ seems to have given them this 'name, from a foresight of the heat and zeal of their 'temper, of which they quickly gave an instance, in their 'desire to call down fire from heaven ... to consume the 'Samaritans. (*Luke* ix. 54.) ... Hence we find in the Acts 'of the Apostles Peter and *John* are the chief speakers 'and actors in the defence and propagation of the gospel: 'and the zeal of *James* and Peter seems to be the reason, 'why the one was slain by Herod, and the other im-'prisoned, in order to the like execution.' *Whitby.* It is evident, that John, as well as James, was naturally of a warm and sanguine disposition: but when this was greatly sanctified, it constituted that fervent, zealous, and affectionate temper, which appears in his writings. Yet numbers, who speak of his *loving* spirit, (I suppose, because he so much inculcates *love*,) as if he had been more lenient, indulgent, and incapable of giving pain by sharp reproofs and awful warnings, than the other apostles, seem to have totally mistaken his character: for no part of the scripture

20 ¶ And the multitude cometh together again, ʳ so that they could not so much as eat bread.

21 And when his ˢ friends heard of it, they went out to lay hold on him: for they said, ᵗ He is beside himself.

22 ¶ And the scribes ᵘ which came down from Jerusalem said, ˣ He hath Beelzebub, and by the prince of the devils casteth he out devils.

23 And he called them unto him, and said unto them ˣ in parables, ʸ How can Satan cast out Satan?

24 And if ᵃ a kingdom be divided against itself, that kingdom cannot stand.

25 And if ᵃ a house be divided against itself, that house cannot stand.

26 And if Satan rise up against himself, and be divided, he cannot stand, ᵇ but hath an end.

27 No man ᵇ can enter into a strong man's house, and spoil his goods, except he will first bind the strong man; and then he will spoil his house.

28 Verily I say unto you, ᶜ All sins shall be forgiven unto the sons of men, and blasphemies wherewith soever they shall blaspheme:

29 But he that shall blaspheme against the Holy Ghost hath never forgiveness, ᵈ but is in danger of eternal damnation:

30 Because ᵉ they said, He hath an unclean spirit.

31 ¶ There came ᶠ then his brethren and his mother, and, standing without, sent unto him, calling him.

32 And the multitude sat about him; and they said unto him, Behold, thy mother and thy brethren without seek for thee.

33 And he answered them, saying, ᵍ Who is my mother, ʰ or my brethren?

34 And he looked round about on them which sat about him, and said, ⁱ Behold my mother and my brethren!

35 For whosoever shall ᵏ do the will of God, the same is my brother, and my sister, and mother.

---

is more suited to give offence to all hypocritical professors of Christianity, than his first epistle; or even to put inconsistent or negligent Christians to a stand, and make them question their own sincerity.

Simon the Canaanite. (18) "Simon called Zelotes." Luke vi. 15. Κανανιτης, derived from the Hebrew root קנא, to be zealous. Ζηλωτης signifying a native of Canaan, begins with χ not κ. Matt. xv. 22. Acts vii. 11. xiii. 19.

V. 20, 21. After Jesus had appointed the apostles, they went into a house: but the multitude assembled so speedily, that they had no time to take refreshment; yet our Lord proceeded to instruct them. His friends, or "kinsmen," (marg.) therefore, deemed him to be too far transported by zeal; and such of them, as did not believe him to be " the Son of God," concluded that he was " be- " side himself," and that he exceeded all bounds of moderation and prudence: they therefore sought to lay hold on him, and, either by importunity or compulsion, to prevail with him to desist from his excessive labours. (Note, 31 —35.)—Many objections indeed have been made to this translation and interpretation: yet I can have no doubt, that it is the real meaning of the passage. Some of Christ's relations or acquaintance might think him " beside " himself," for the same reason that Festus and others did St. Paul; and in their natural affection for him, might purpose to use compulsion, if persuasions would not prevail with him to desist: and even his more pious relatives might possibly be anxious for his health, and judge his labours to be indiscreet, and so concur in the design; for it is thought by many, on very probable grounds, that he had watched all the preceding night, and been laboriously employed all the former part of the day. (Luke vi. 12 —19.)

He is beside himself. (21) Εξεστι. See on ii. 12.—' He ' is fainty, or may fall into a deliquium by spending thus ' his spirits. Gen. xlii. 28. xlv. 26. Josh. ii. 11. Is. vii. 2. ' xxxiii. 3. Sept.' Whitby. It does not, however, appear, that any symptoms of fainting were discernible in Jesus; and the present, not what might be feared as to the future, is evidently intended.

V. 22—30. Notes, Matt. xii. 22—32. Luke xi. 14—26. —Parables. (23) The instances of a kingdom, and a family, divided against themselves, constituted distinct parables, illustrating the subject under consideration.— Forgiven, &c. (28) They are pardonable, and in some instances are forgiven. The expression, " in danger of " eternal damnation" (29), signifies ' exposed to eternal damnation.' (See on Matt. v. 22.)

V. 31—35. (Notes, Matt. xii. 46—50. Luke viii. 19— 21.)—There is scarcely any difference in the import of the passage, from that in Matthew; but he who bestows the pains to compare the words of the two evangelists, must be convinced, that the one did not intend to copy from the other. (Marg. Ref.)

His mother. (31) ' Hence Theophylact taxes her ... of ' vain glory and of guilt, in endeavouring to draw him ... ' from teaching the word. Tertullian pronounceth her ' guilty of incredulity: Chrysostom, of vain-glory, in- ' firmity, and madness, for this very thing.' Whitby.—It is plain, that many of these intimations were suited, and doubtless prophetically intended, to be a scriptural protest against the idolatrous honour, to this day by vast multitudes rendered to Mary, the mother of Jesus. She was, no doubt, an excellent and honourable character, but evidently not perfect: she is intitled to great estimation and high veneration; but surely not to religious confidence

CHAP. IV.

The parable of the sower, 1—9. Why Christ taught by parables, 10—13. The interpretation of the parable, 14—20. Knowledge is given in order to be communicated, 21, 22. A call to hear with attention, 23—25. The parable of seed sown, imperceptibly growing up, and ripening for harvest, 26—29:

that of the grain of mustard-seed, 30—32. Christ teaches only by parables, which he expounds to his disciples, 33, 34. He stills a tempest by his word, 35—41.

AND ²he began again to teach by the sea-side: and there was gathered [a Lu. 18. Matt. xiii. 1, 2]

---

and worship. (*Notes, Luke* ii. 41—52. *John* ii. 1—5.)—*My mother*, &c. (35) *Notes, Matt.* vii. 21—23. xxv. 34 —40. *Luke* xi. 27, 28. *John* xix. 25—27.—The instruction conveyed most emphatically and affectionately, in this observation of our Lord, that we also should consider all, whom we candidly judge to be obedient believers in him, as his brethren, sisters, and mother, and to act towards them as such in all their wants, sorrows, and difficulties for his sake, is generally far too much overlooked, both by readers and expositors; and far too seldom, or too slightly pressed home to the hearts and consciences of professed Christians, who are stewards of this world's good things.

PRACTICAL OBSERVATIONS.

V. 1—19.

Acts of mercy and charity can never be unseasonable; for it is as lawful "to do good" to man, as it is proper to attend on the worship of God, on the Lord's day. But selfish and malicious men, who are projecting wickedness in the midst of formal or ostentatious devotion, are most prone to censure those good works, which they will not imitate: and they are especially glad to find something to condemn in those, who are labouring to promote the salvation of souls, and to shew the vanity of their assumed appearances of religion.—While we steadily persevere in doing good, notwithstanding opposition, we may properly express an indignant abhorrence of wickedness; but it should be connected with compassion for the persons of opposers, and earnest desires of their salvation.—We shall commonly find, that the rage and enmity of proud enemies will increase, in proportion as the power and grace of Christ are glorified; and that unbelievers, of the most opposite sentiments and characters, will combine against the cause of evangelical godliness: but if we be at any time compelled to retire from their persecuting rage, we ought to seek for other scenes and opportunities of usefulness.—What multitudes thronged after Jesus, to hear his word, behold his miracles, and share the beneficent effects of them! Yet how few in comparison were willing to avow their relation to him, when the time of his sufferings arrived! He knew that it would be so, and could form a proper estimate of their inconstancy: but we should be upon our guard ; for popular applause and favour are very dangerous, and are no more to be trusted than the deceitful calm of the unstable ocean.—All our sicknesses and calamities spring from the anger of God against sin ; and the removal of them, or the sanctifying blessing on them for the good of our souls, was purchased for us by the sufferings of Christ. But the plagues and maladies of our hearts are chiefly to be deprecated : he can cure these also by a touch or a word ; and unclean spirits, knowing him to be " the Son of God," are still constrained to obey him. May increasing numbers press to be healed of these

plagues, and delivered from these enemies : may he send forth more and more of such, as have " been with him," and have learned from him to preach his gospel, and to be his instruments in this blessed work : may all his ministers be " Boanerges, sons of thunder," to speak his word with energy and efficacy ; and may no Judas be found among those who presume to declare his sacred truths !

V. 20—35.

If we were as earnest as our Lord, and " instant in season and out of season, in preaching the word," in prayer, and in every good work ; we should count no hour improper, no situation inconvenient, for these labours of love : but we also should find, that our carnal or injudicious friends would be ready to deem us " beside ourselves" and would use all their influence to moderate our ardour and lessen our diligence. Prudence indeed is necessary and commendable ; but it is extremely apt to degenerate into lukewarmness, indolence, and timidity : and zeal like that of Christ, will seldom escape the charge of being excessive and indiscreet, from the more decent part of mankind, or even from professors of the gospel, who can scarcely conceive, that invisible and future things require more earnestness, than our most important temporal concerns. (*Note*, 2 *Kings* ix. 11.) But proud and malignant enemies will not stop here : they will impute the most beneficial effects to the basest motives or causes; and maintain that men are doing Satan's work, acting under his influence, and opposing every thing good, when sinners are evidently brought to repentance and to newness of life. But let them beware, how they ascribe the operations of the Holy Ghost to the power of the devil, or how they deride and revile them : for in so doing they may be guilty of such blasphemy, as shall never find forgiveness, but expose them to eternal damnation. Let the servants of Christ go on with their work, in dependence on his power, and avoiding all contentions with each other, which only weaken the common cause: then they will have an almighty Helper ready to overcome their strong enemy, and to deliver sinners from his hateful dominion. And let all those who hear, believe, and obey the Saviour, according to the will of God the Father, rejoice and glory in their relation to him, who will assuredly own every one of them, " as his brother, his sister, or his mother :" and conduct themselves towards all their fellow Christians, however mean, or however they in some things differ from them, as they would behave, or ought to behave, to Christ himself, if visibly present on earth, in precisely the same circumstances : and this, as they hope to meet him with confidence and joy at the day of judgment.

<hr>

NOTES.

Chap. IV. V. 1—20. (*Marg. Ref.—Notes, Matt.* xiii.

2 n 5

unto him a great multitude, [b] so that he entered into a ship, and sat in the sea; and the whole multitude was by the sea on the land.

2 And he taught them many things by parables, and said unto them [d] in his doctrine,

3 [e] Hearken; Behold, [f] there went out a sower to sow:

4 And it came to pass, as he sowed, some fell by the way-side, [g] and the fowls of the air came and devoured it up.

5 And some fell on [h] stony ground, where it had not much earth, and immediately it sprang up, because it had no depth of earth:

6 But when [i] the sun was up, it was scorched; and because it had [k] no root it withered away.

7 And some [l] fell among thorns, and the thorns grew up and choked it, and it yielded no fruit.

8 And other [m] fell on good ground, and did yield fruit that sprang up, and increased, and brought forth, some thirty, and some sixty, and some [n] an hundred.

9 And he said unto them, [o] He that hath ears to hear, let him hear.

10 ¶ And [p] when he was alone, they that were about him, with the twelve, asked of him the parable.

11 And he said unto them, [q] Unto you it is given to know the mystery of the kingdom of God: but unto [r] them that are without, [s] all these things are done in parables:

12 That [t] seeing they may see, and not perceive, and hearing they may hear, and not understand; lest at any time they should [u] be converted, and their sins should be forgiven them.

13 And he saith unto them, [x] Know ye not this parable? and how then will ye know all parables?

14 The [y] sower soweth [z] the word.

15 And [a] these are they by the way-side, where the word is sown; but, when they have heard, [b] Satan cometh immediately, and taketh away the word that was sown in their hearts.

16 And these are they likewise which are sown on stony ground; who, when they have heard the word, immediately receive it with gladness;

17 And [c] have no root in themselves, and so endure but for a time: afterward, [d] when affliction or persecution ariseth for the word's sake, immediately they are offended.

18 And these are they [f] which are sown among thorns; such as hear the word,

19 And [g] the cares of this world, and [h] the deceitfulness of riches, [i] and the lusts of other things, entering in, choke the word, and it becometh [k] unfruitful.

20 And these are they [l] which are sown on good ground; such as hear the word, and receive it, and bring forth fruit, some thirty-fold, some sixty, and some [m] an hundred.

1—23. Luke viii. 4—15.) 'See, saith Theophylact, how ' rare are good men, and how few are saved! for only the ' fourth part of the seed fell on good ground and was pre-' served. Observe here also the gradation. The seed ' sown in the high way comes not up at all; the seed sown ' upon stony ground comes up, but increaseth not; the ' seed sown among thorns increaseth, but bears no fruit; ' the seed sown on good ground, brings forth fruit to per-' fection.' Whitby.

They that were about, &c. (10) Such as more constantly attended on Christ, as his disciples, along with his apostles.—To them that are without, (11) 'It was customary to the Jews to give this title to the heathens: our ' Saviour therefore by applying it to them, seems to hint, ' that in a short time the kingdom of God would be taken ' from them; and they themselves would be ... " them that ' " were without." ' Whitby. (Notes, 1 Cor. v. 9—13,

v. 13. Col. iv. 5, 6. 1 Thes. iv. 9—12, v. 12. 1 Tim. iii. 7.) —Their sins should be forgiven them. (12) " That I should " heal them," Matt. xiii. 15. The quotation, if intended as such, varies more from the LXX, than that in Matthew. (Note, Is. vi. 9, 10.)—How then, &c. (13) Our Lord here gently reproved the dulness of his disciples, whose minds were in a measure obscured by those prejudices and carnal expectations, with which the unbelieving Jews were entirely blinded; and he intimated, that, as he had many things to teach in parables, they ought to apply their minds to the attentive consideration of them, that they might be able to explain them to others also.—Lusts of other things. (19) Anxious cares in the poor, and deceitful riches in the wealthy, are peculiarly unfavourable to religious improvement: but the eager desire and pursuit of any earthly object has the same effect, whatever a man's outward circumstances may be.—This addition to the parable, as de-

2 H 6

21 ¶ And he said unto them, *Is a candle brought to be put under a *bushel, or under a bed? and not to be set on a candlestick?

22 For *there is nothing hid, which shall not be manifested; neither was any thing kept secret, but that it should come abroad.

23 If *any man have ears to hear, let him hear.

24 And he saith unto them, *Take heed what ye hear: *with what measure ye mete, it shall be measured to you: and unto you that *hear shall more be given.

25 For *he that hath, to him shall be given: and he that hath not, from *him shall be taken even that which he hath.

26 ¶ And he said, *So is the kingdom of God, *as if a man should cast seed into the ground;

27 And should sleep, and rise night and day, and the seed should spring *and grow up, he knoweth not how.

28 For *the earth bringeth forth fruit of herself; *first the blade, then the ear, after that the full corn in the ear.

29 But when the fruit is *brought forth, immediately *he putteth in the sickle, because the harvest is come.

---

livered by St. Matthew, with very many other variations, (more than could be conceived, without accurately comparing the evangelists together in the original,) demonstrate that St. Mark was no copier of St. Matthew, even when he recorded the same actions, miracles, and discourses.—No seed, except "the word of God," "the word "of the kingdom," produces any genuine fruit: for the regenerating and sanctifying grace of God attends no instruction of another kind, which alone can make the heart of fallen man " good ground," and " give the increase:" (*Notes, 1 Cor. iii. 4—9 :*) and when this " good seed" does not yield fruit; the fault lies in the ground alone : " They " had no root in themselves."

V. 21, 22. (*Marg. Ref.—Notes, Matt. v. 14—16. vi. 22, 23. x. 24—28.*) These verses were intended to call the attention of the disciples to the word of Christ. By thus instructing them, he meant to qualify them to be the instructors of others; as candles are lighted, not to be covered, but to be placed on a candlestick, that they may give light to the room. The meaning of his parables and discourses, though at that time concealed from the people, was afterwards to be manifested and spread abroad, in the most extensive and perspicuous manner. ' These words ' being only spoken to Christ's disciples, when he was ' alone with them, and both here and in *Luke* viii. 16, 17, ' subjoined to the explication of this parable, I think it ' best to explain them accordingly; as if Christ had said, ' I give you a clear light, by which you may discern the ' import of this and other parables : but this I do, not ' that you may keep it to yourselves, and hide it from ' others, but that it may be beneficial to you, and by you ' be made beneficial to others. ... And though I give you ' the knowledge of " these mysteries of the kingdom of ' " God " ... *privately ;* I do it not that you may keep them ' so : for " there is nothing (*thus*) hid, which should not ' " be made manifest ;" neither was any thing made secret ' (*by me*), but that it should (*afterwards*) come abroad. ... ' Had Christ's apostles so obscurely delivered or writ the ' gospels, and those other scriptures which contain the ' rule of faith, even in things necessary to be believed or ' done unto salvation, as the Romanists pretend they did ; ' they must have hid this " candle under a bushel," and

' not have manifested it to the world, as Christ here re- ' quires them to do.' *Whitby.* (*Note, 2 Cor. iii. 12—16.*)
V. 23—25. (*Marg. Ref.—Notes, Luke viii. 16—18. Heb. ii. 1—4. Rev. ii. 6, 7.*) The apostles (and indeed all who heard, or read these words,) were exhorted to bow their ears, and apply their minds attentively, to the words of Christ : to take heed " what they heard," and " how " they heard" it; that they might receive in faith and love the truth alone, and all of it; and that they might impart it to others, as well as adorn it by their own lives. For, according to their faithfulness, and correspondent conduct, as his ministers, or the contrary, they would at length be dealt with : and more knowledge, wisdom, and spiritual gifts would be given to those of them, who heard the word in obedient faith and with humble attention; according to that general rule of his kingdom, which we have repeatedly considered. (*Notes, Matt. xiii. 12. xxv. 24—30, v. 29.*)
V. 26—29. This parable, which is not found in any other gospel, represents the manner in which the kingdom of God gains ground in the world. *In this respect,* he who faithfully and diligently preaches " the word of the truth " of the gospel," may be likened to a husbandman, who sows his seed with suitable care and attention, and then leaves it. Accordingly, he sleeps by night, and rises in the morning to attend on his other business ; not being solicitous about the seed, as if the increase depended on his constant attention. In the mean time it springs up, and by imperceptible degrees grows to maturity; and he is so far from managing the process, that he does not comprehend it: for the earth, made fruitful by the Creator's power and goodness, and receiving the influence of the sun, rain, and varying seasons, as ordered by him, spontaneously p the increase. A small blade first appears ; and, rdding the changes of the weather, it sometimes appears more flourishing, and at others seems to wither : yet at length it ears, fills, and ripens; and the husbandman gathers in the crop, which God has given him as the increase of his seed sown. (*Marg. and Marg. Ref.*)—Thus faithful preachers sow " the good seed of the " word," and use the other appointed means of obtaining success; " but God alone gives the increase." When they

30 ¶ And he said, "Whereunto shall we liken the kingdom of God? or with what comparison shall we compare it?

31 It is "like a grain of mustard-seed, which, when it is sown in the earth, 'is less than all the seeds that be in the earth:

32 But when it is sown, it groweth up, and becometh greater than all herbs, and "shooteth out great branches; so that the fowls of the air may "lodge under the shadow of it.

33 And 'with many such parables spake he the word unto them, 'as they were able to hear it.

34 But without a parable spake he not unto them: and 'when they were alone, he expounded all things to his disciples.

35 ¶ And "the same day, when the even was come, he saith unto them, "Let us pass over unto the other side.

36. And when they had sent away the multitude, they took him "even as he was in the ship: and there were also with him other little ships.

37 And 'there arose a "great storm of wind, and the waves beat into the ship, so that it was now full.

38 And he was 'in the hinder part of the ship, asleep on a pillow: 'and they awake him, and say unto him, Master, 'carest thou not that we perish?

39 And "he arose, and "rebuked the wind, and said unto the sea, Peace, be still. And the wind ceased, and there was a great calm.

40 And he said unto them, 'Why are ye so fearful? how is it that ye have "no faith?

41 And they 'feared exceedingly, and said one to another, "What manner of man is this, that even the wind and the sea obey him?

---

have the opportunity of watching the effects of their own labours, they find their hopes and fears continually fluctuate: they meet with disappointments which they can by no means prevent, and success where they had almost given up the hope of it: but much of the good done will generally be unknown at the time, and perhaps become visible after their death. However, the labour of that man, who is faithful and diligent, will not be in vain: the seed finds some hearts prepared by the preventing grace of God to receive it; under the influences of the Spirit it springs up; and from convictions of sin and enquiries after salvation, it grows up into a more solid judgment, deeper experience and humility, and greater simplicity; and thus proceeds to increasing fruitfulness in good works. In this manner, souls are prepared for heaven: and when their measure of services and trials are completed, and they are made ready for the glory and felicity intended for them; the Lord will gather them as the wheat of his harvest into his garner: and they, who have been the instruments of their conversion and sanctification, will at last glorify God for the blessed increase of their patient labours, which perhaps at the time they concluded to be almost entirely unsuccessful. (Note, John iv. 35—38.)—God, by his ministers, sows the seed; and he by ministering angels gathers in the harvest. (Notes, Matt. xiii. 36—43. 1 Cor. iii. 4—9.)

Spring. (27) Βλαϛαιη. Matt. xiii. 26. Heb. ix. 4. Jam. v. 18.—Grow up.] Μηκυνηται. (A μηκος, longitudo.) Here only N. T.—Of herself. (28) Αυτομάτη. Acts xii. 10, " of " his own accord." Not elsewhere N. T.

V. 30—32. 'The kingdom of the Messiah, before his ' death, and burial in the earth, which is called the sowing ' the body in the earth, (1 Cor. xv. 42, 43,) will have only ' a small and insensible increase; but will afterwards spring ' up and become the greatest of all kingdoms.' Whitby. (Notes, Is. ix. 6, 7. Dan. ii. 34, 35. 44, 45.)—No words, conveying precisely the same meaning, can well be more different, than those of the two evangelists Matthew and Mark. (Marg. Ref. d—h.—Note, Matt. xiii. 31, 32. 44, 45.)

Shall we compare. (30) Παραϐαλωμεν. (Εκ παρα et ϐαλλω, jacio.) Acts xx. 15. Hence παραϐολη, a parable.

V. 33, 34. Our Lord taught the people in that manner, which was most suited to their state of mind. They were too much prejudiced to receive and profit by such plain declarations of doctrinal truth, as his apostles afterwards made: but his parables, without giving needless offence, or affording his enemies any advantage, were calculated to excite enquiries, and to prepare the way for fuller and more particular instructions, when the proper season arrived. And he privately expounded all to his disciples; and so prepared the way for that " great plain-" ness of speech," which he intended that they should use. (Marg. Ref. i—l.—Notes, Ps. xlix. 1—4. lxxviii. 2. John xvi. 12, 13. 1 Cor. iii. 1—3. Heb. v. 11—14.)

V. 35—41. (Marg. Ref.—Notes, Matt. viii. 23—27.) All the parables, contained in this chapter, and in the thirteenth of Matthew, seem to have been spoken during the remainder of that day, on which the friends of Jesus were dissatisfied with his unwearied and zealous labours : (Notes, iii. 20, 21. 31—35 :) yet, having persisted in them till the evening, he put to sea, even " as he was," in the ship whence he had preached, and without any peculiar attention to his health, ease, or indulgence, after so great fatigues! Such an example did he set us of enduring hardship, and avoiding all needless regard to ourselves, whilst employed in doing good to the souls of men ! (Note. Phil. ii. 24—30.)

2 u 8 ·

CHAP. V.

Jesus casts out a legion of devils; and suffers them to enter and destroy a herd of swine, 1—13. The owners intreat him to depart: and the man, who had been possessed, desires to be with him; but is sent to declare what Jesus had done for him, 14—20. Jairus intreats Christ to heal his daughter, 21—24. By the way, he heals a woman of an inveterate issue of blood, 25—34. He raises Jairus's daughter to life, 35—43.

Carest, &c. (38) This clause intimates, that the apostles, amidst their terrors, were tempted to censure their Lord, who lay asleep, as if regardless of their danger. *(Marg. Ref. t.—Note, Luke* x. 38—42.)—*That ye have no faith.* (40) Or rather, " that ye have not faith;" that is, faith proportioned to the occasion, and sufficient to exclude these needless terrors.

Storm. (37) Λαιλαψ. *Pluvium, conflictus ventorum. Luke* viii. 23. 2 *Pet.* ii. 17.—Σεισμος. *Matt.* viii. 24.—*It was full.*] Γεμιζεσθαι. xv. 36. *Luke* xiv. 23. xv. 16. *John* ii. 7. *Rev.* viii. 5.—*A pillow.* (38) Προσκιφαλαιον. (Ex προς et κιφαλη, *caput.*) Here only *N. T.—Be still.* (39) Πεφιμωσο. i. 25. *Matt.* xxii. 12. 34. *Luke* iv. 35. 1 *Cor.* ix. 9. 1 *Tim.* v. 18. 1 *Pet.* ii. 16. A φιμος, *a muzzle.*

PRACTICAL OBSERVATIONS.

V. 1—25.

While we lament, that so few of the human species are instructed, according to the pure gospel of Christ; and that so large a majority of those who are thus favoured, derive no real benefit from it; let us " look to ourselves," and to our own hearts, that they be not as fallow ground, or " the " way-side," through carelessness and inattention.—Satan, that " wicked one," is ever active and vigilant, in preventing the success of the gospel: and if men do not immediately secure what they have heard, by meditation, prayer, faith, and obedience; he will immediately take it away from their hearts and memories. Nor will any impressions be *durable*, which are not *deep:* the heart, that is not broken, humbled, and changed, will not be made fruitful; and superficial convictions or affections, and that profession which springs from them, will gradually vanish : this will especially be evident when " persecution and affliction " arise because of the word." We cannot be real Christians, if we " have not *that* root in ourselves," which would withstand the most scorching sun of persecution, should it fall upon us : but many prove, even in the most quiet times, how they would act in more trying circumstances, while " the cares of the world, the deceitfulness of riches, " and the lusts of other things, choke the word, and it " becometh unfruitful." Let us then earnestly beseech the Lord, that, by his new-creating grace, our hearts may become " good ground;" and that the good seed of the word may produce a large increase in our lives, of all those good words and works, " which are through Jesus " Christ to the praise and glory of God." Thus will it appear, that " to us it is given to know the mystery of " the kingdom of God :" while numbers know it not, because of the pride, unbelief, and carnality of their hearts; and so, being given up by God, " they see, but do not " perceive ; they hear, but do not understand ; lest at any " time they should be converted, and their sins be for- " given them."—Unless we understand this parable of the sower, which is so plain and universally interesting, how shall we understand all those parables, under which divine mysteries are couched ? Let us then attend more dili-

gently to instruction, and pray for a humble, teachable disposition, and for the illumination of the Holy Spirit: for we are called to " shine as lights" in this dark world : and though our light is only as the feeble glimmering of a candle, compared with the splendour of " the Sun of right. " eousness;" yet we may hope to receive from him, and to communicate to others, some rays of heavenly wisdom ; provided we do not put our candle under a bushel, but endeavour to let it shine before men, in our profession of the truth, and a conversation consistent with it.—Though no human teaching can make " the natural man receive " the things of the Spirit of God;" yet it is our business, to make known the great truths of the gospel, according to the duties of our respective stations. But, as so many discordant doctrines are propagated on every side ; it is incumbent on us to take heed *what*, as well as *how*, we hear. If we believe, obey, and impart to others, the blessed truths of Scripture, all blessings will be measured to us in great abundance : but woe be to those, who reject, corrupt, or conceal the light, which Christ came into the world to diffuse among mankind ! For all their earthly possessions, admired abilities, and valuable opportunities, shall be taken from them ; and they will be left to eternal contempt, poverty, and misery.

V. 26—41.

In endeavouring to promote the kingdom of God, we should rest satisfied with having done our part, and wait in patient hope on God, that he may do his also: for he reserves to himself the power of giving the increase; and he does it in an incomprehensible manner, that he may secure the whole honour of it to his own great name. We should, therefore, bear up against discouragement, though we do not yet perceive much success in our labours : we ought indeed to redouble our diligence, and become more fervent in prayer ; but, however anxious, we cannot make the seed grow, nor understand why it springs up in one case, and not in another. The effects we may often see, but the cause and method of operation we cannot comprehend. Let us then go on with our work, in cheerful assurance, that " in due season we shall reap, if we " faint not : " and let us seek unto the Lord to give the increase, wherever the word is preached ; and pray, that all Christians may " grow in grace, and in the knowledge " of Christ Jesus," and daily ripen for the glorious harvest. —We should not despise feeble beginnings, either in individuals, or in the diffusing of the light of divine truth in dark places; as " the kingdom of heaven is like the " grain of mustard-seed," and as great consequences often spring from feeble causes and instruments.—These things will not be obvious to others, but Christ will expound them to his disciples : and if we follow him closely, he will afford us his special presence; and he will teach us self-denial by his precepts and his example.—Storms may indeed assail us, and our fears may be great; but faith will apply to him for help, and meet no disappointment.

2 I

v.35. Matt.viii.) **AND** they ' came over unto the
18—34.　Luke⟨
iii. 26.　⟨ other side of the sea, into the country
of the Gadarenes.

2 And when he was come out of the
b Is. lxv. 4. Luke ship, immediately there met him ᵇ out
viii 27.
c 8. i. 23. 26. iii. of the tombs a man ᶜ with an unclean
30. vii. 25. Luke
ix. 42.　spirit,

3 Who had *his* dwelling among the
d ix. 18—22. Dan. tombs, and ᵈ no man could bind him,
iv. 32, 33. Luke
viii. 29.　no, not with chains;

4 Because that he had been often
bound with fetters and chains, and the
chains had been plucked asunder by
him, and the fetters broken in pieces:
e Jam. iii. 7, 8. neither could any *man* ᵉ tame him.

5 And always, night and day, he was
in the mountains, and in the tombs,
f 1 Kings xviii. 28. ᶠ crying, and cutting himself with
Job ii. 7, 8. John
viii. 44.　stones.

6 But when he saw Jesus afar off,
g Ps. lxvi. 3. marg. ᵍ he ran and worshipped him,
lxxii. 9. Luke iv.
41. Acts xvi. 17.
Jam. ii. 19.　7 And cried with a loud voice, and
h i. 24. Hos. xiv.
8. Matt. viii. 29. said, ʰ What have I to do with thee,
Luke iv. 34.

Jesus, *thou* ' Son of the most high i iii. 11. xiv. 61.
God? ᵏ I adjure thee by God, ' that　Matt. xvi. 16.
　　　　　　　　　　　　　　　John xx. 31.
thou torment me not.　　　　　Acts viii. 37. xvi.
　　　　　　　　　　　　　　　17.
8 (For he said unto him, ᵐ Come k 1 Kings xxii. 16.
out of the man, *thou* unclean spirit.)　Matt. xxvi. 63.
　　　　　　　　　　　　　　　Acts xix. 13.
9 And he asked him, ⁿ What *is* thy l Gen. iii. 15.
name? And he answered, saying, My　Matt. viii. 29.
　　　　　　　　　　　　　　　Luke vii. 28.
name *is* ᵒ Legion; for we are many.　Rom. xvi. 20.
　　　　　　　　　　　　　　　Heb.ii.14. 2 Pet.
10 And ᵖ he besought him much ii. 4. 1 John iii.
that he would not send them away out 8. Jude 6. Rev.
　　　　　　　　　　　　　　　xii. 12. xx. 1—3.
of the country.　　　　　　　　m i. 25. ix. 25, 26.
11 Now there was there, nigh unto n Luke viii. 30.
the mountains, a great ᵠ herd of swine xi. 21—26.
feeding.　　　　　　　　　　　o Matt. xxvi. 53.
　　　　　　　　　　　　　　　p 13. vii. 22.
12 And ʳ all the devils besought
him, saying, Send us into the swine, q Lev. xi. 7, 8.
that we may enter into them.　　　Deut. xiv. 8. Is.
　　　　　　　　　　　　　　　lxv. 4. lxvi. 3.
13 And forthwith Jesus ˢ gave them r Matt. viii. 30.
leave. And the unclean spirits went Job i. 10, 11.
out, and entered into the swine; and 32. 2 Cor. ii. 11.
ᵗ the herd ran violently down a steep 1 Pet. v. 8.
place into the sea, (they were about two s 1 Kings xxii. 22.
thousand,) and were choked in the sea. Job i. 12. ii. 6.
　　　　　　　　　　　　　　　Matt. viii. 32.
　　　　　　　　　　　　　　　Rev. xiii. 5—7.
　　　　　　　　　　　　　　　xx. 7.
　　　　　　　　　　　　　　　t John viii. 44.
　　　　　　　　　　　　　　　Rev. ix. 11.

Even, when he seems to slumber, he restrains the violence of the winds and waves, and the fury of wicked men
and apostate spirits: and when he awakes for our help,
he will speak every tempest into a calm, and turn all our
terrors into adoring love and gratitude. But, while
" he careth for us, that we perish not," he will rebuke
our unbelief: and indeed our excessive fears, in little difficulties and dangers, sometimes seem to indicate, that
we have almost no faith; notwithstanding all, that we have
heard, witnessed, and experienced, of his power, truth,
and love, who is " the mighty God and the Prince of
" peace," and who " never faileth those who trust in him."
—Instead therefore of dreading outward dangers, to the dishonour of the Lord; let us reverently, fully, and thankfully adore him, whom " even the winds and seas obey."

NOTES.

CHAP. V. V. 1. (*Matt.* viii. 28.) The region of the
Gergesenes was of larger extent, than that of the Gadarenes, which was included in it.

V. 2—13. (*Notes, Matt.* viii. 28, 29. *Luke* viii. 26—
39.) St. Matthew gives a brief account of *two* demoniacks, who were dispossessed on this occasion: but Mark
and Luke omit the mention of one of them, (who was not,
perhaps, so remarkable either before or after his cure,) to
record that of the other more fully. Many circumstances
therefore here require more particular consideration.—It is
probable, that our Lord had landed, intentionally, near
the place where the demoniack wandered, and was immediately met by him. He was possessed " with an unclean
" spirit," or a *fallen spirit*, impure and unholy, and an
enemy to the authority of God, in whose judgment all
sin is *uncleanness*, and " filthiness of flesh or spirit."

(*Note,* 2 *Cor.* vii. 1.) The words, " unclean spirits," and
" demons," are used as synonymous. (12, 13.) Though
many evil spirits possessed the man, one is first mentioned,
who may be considered as the ruler of the company. The
force, which they exerted by the limbs of the man, was
so great, that his friends could by no means confine him;
for he had repeatedly broken even the fetters and chains,
with which he had been bound, and was so fierce that
none could tame or subdue him. He was therefore left
to wander, night and day, without clothes, among the
solitary tombs, and on the mountains; where he cried hi-
deously, as one in excessive anguish, and cut himself with
stones, by running among them, lying down naked, or in
a frantick manner. (*Marg. Ref.* d—f.—*Note, Dan.* iv.
28—33.) Thus was he most wretched in himself, the
grief of all his friends, and the terror and nuisance of the
neighbourhood: an apt emblem of the more desperate
" children of disobedience," in whom Satan reigns and
works without controul. Yet, as soon as Jesus appeared,
he came and prostrated himself before him in the posture
of a worshipper; (*Marg. Ref.* g, h.—*Note,* iii. 6—12, *v.*
11;) and the unclean spirit, which spake by the man's
organs of speech, earnestly intreated and adjured him by
God, (who had respited them from torment for a time,
and given them permission to tempt and harass the sinful
race of men,) that he would not consign them immediately to the place of punishment; nor even drive them
out of that region, where they had, it seems, hitherto continued unmolested. The permission asked and obtained of
entering into the swine, and the effects of that permission,
in the destruction of the swine, have been already cousi-
dered. (*Note, Matt.* viii. 30—32.) But we here further
learn, that our Lord demanded of the spirit which spake
to him, what his name was: to which he answered, that

14 And * they that fed the swine fled, and told *it* in the city, and in the country. And they went out to see what it was that was done.

15 And they come to Jesus, and see * him that was possessed with the devil, and had the legion, sitting, and clothed, and in his right mind; * and they were afraid.

16 And they that saw *it*, told them how it befell to him that was possessed with the devil, and *also* concerning the swine.

17 And they began * to pray him to depart out of their coasts.

18 And when he was come into the ship, he that had been possessed with the devil * prayed him that he might be with him.

19 Howbeit Jesus suffered him not; but saith unto him, *b* Go home to thy friends, and tell them how great things the Lord hath done for thee, and hath had compassion on thee.

20 And he departed, and began to publish in * Decapolis, how great things Jesus had done for him: and all *men* did marvel.

21 ¶ And when Jesus was * passed over again by ship unto the other side, much people gathered unto him, and he was nigh unto the sea.

22 And, behold, * there cometh one of the *rules* of the synagogue, Jairus by name; and when he saw him, *f* he fell at his feet,

23 And *b* besought him greatly, saying, My little daughter lieth at the

---

it was " Legion;" and that he had this name, because " they were many." A legion is well known to have been a body of Roman soldiers, which at that time consisted of above six thousand men. (*Note, Matt.* xxvi. 47—56, *v.* 53.) This therefore gives us a most tremendous view of the subject; though we determine nothing concerning the precise number, which combined under one head in harassing the·man. For the question was doubtless asked, and the answer extorted, in order to display the number, power, and malice of those unclean spirits, which Sadducees, ancient and modern, have denied; and which most men are apt unwatchfully to disregard. (*Marg. Ref.* q—s.)

With chains. (3) Ἁλυσισιν. 4. *Luke* viii. 29. *Acts* xii. 6, 7. xxi. 33. xxviii. 20. *Rev.* xx. 1.—*Fetters.* (4) Πεδαις, *pedicis. Luke* viii. 29. Not elsewhere *N. T.* (Ε πις, *pes,* et δεω, *ligo.*)—*Plucked asunder.*] Διεσπασθαι. *Acts* xxiii. 10, " torn in pieces." Not elsewhere N. T.—*Broken in pieces.*] Συντετριφθαι. xiv. 3. *Matt.* xii. 20. *Luke* iv. 18. ix. 39. *John* xix. 36. *Rom.* xvi. 20. *Rev.* ii. 27.—*Tame.*] Δαμασαι. Or, *subdue. Jam.* iii. 7, 8. (*Note, Jam.* iii. 7—12, *vv.* 7, 8.)—*Cutting.* (5) Κατακοπτων (ex κατα et κοπτω, *cædo,*) " striking himself against stones." Here only N. T.—*What have I,* &c. (7) See on i. 24.—*I adjure,* &c.] Ὁρκιζω. *Acts* xix. 13. 1 *Thes.* v. 27. Ab ὁρκος, *jusjurandum.*—Εξορκιζω. See on *Matt.* xxvi. 63.

V. 14—20. The success of the stratagem, formed by these evil spirits, to prejudice the covetous minds of the Gadarenes against Jesus, has been considered: (*Note, Matt.* viii. 33, 34:) but we must not overlook the contrary behaviour of the man who was rescued from the demons. (*Note, Luke* viii. 26—39, *vv.* 31, 32. 36. 39.) He was now found sitting, in proper clothing, composed and rational, at the feet of Jesus, (like Mary, *Luke* x. 39,) to hear his instructions: and when our Lord entered the ship to go away, according to the sole request of the Gadarenes, he desired leave to accompany him; being full of gratitude to his Benefactor, and desirous of becoming his stated follower; and perhaps fearing the return of the un-

clean spirits, in case he should be left behind. What a contrast to his own petition while possessed (7), as well as to that of the Gadarenes! But Jesus had another design in the transaction: and he therefore refused to grant his petition; ordering him to return to his friends, and inform them " what great things the Lord," in his tender compassion, " had done for him." Accordingly he departed, and published in Decapolis, a region in which were ten cities, what great things Jesus had done for him: and, as they had been generally acquainted with his former miserable condition, and now saw him perfectly rational, and in good health, they were exceedingly astonished at hearing his thankful account of his deliverance. Thus this very man became the wisest, happiest, and most useful person, in the country; and the herald, or preacher, of Christ to his friends and neighbours! being at the same time a living demonstration of his power and mercy; and no doubt he was made the instrument of procuring a more favourable reception to him and his disciples, when they went among them afterwards. (*Notes,* vii. 31—37.)— " What the Lord hath done for thee" (19), as spoken by Jesus, implied what JEHOVAH, the God of Israel, had done for him : but the connexion with the subsequent words, " how great things Jesus had done for him," if it does not evince the man's views, concerning his Benefactor, (which is not improbable,) at least manifests those of the sacred historian; who, had he been afraid of giving his Lord too much honour, would have expressed himself in a more guarded manner. (*Marg. Ref.* a—c.)

In his right mind. (15) Σωφρονντα. *Luke* viii. 35. *Rom.* xii. 3. 2 *Cor.* v. 13. *Tit.* ii. 6. 1 *Pet.* iv. 7.—Σωφρονεω. ' Sanæ mentis sum. Modestus, et continens sum; prudenter, ' modestè, et temperanter me gero.' Leigh.

V. 21—24. The two miracles, recorded in the remainder of this chapter, were briefly mentioned by St. Matthew; but the particular consideration of them was reserved for this place. (*Note, Matt.* ix. 18—26.)—Our Lord, having returned to Capernaum, was speedily surrounded by a great multitude of people, who were rejoiceo

point of death; *I pray thee,* come and lay thy hands on her, that she may be healed, and she shall live.

24 And *Jesus* went with him; and much people followed him, and thronged him.

25 ¶ And a certain woman, which had an issue of blood twelve years,

26 And had suffered many things of many physicians, and had spent all that she had, and was nothing bettered, but rather grew worse,

27 When she had heard of Jesus, came in the press behind, and touched his garment:

28 For she said, If I may touch but his clothes, I shall be whole.

29 And straightway the fountain of her blood was dried up; and she felt in *her* body that she was healed of that plague.

30 And Jesus immediately knowing in himself that virtue had gone out of him, turned him about in the press, and said, Who touched my clothes?

31 And his disciples said unto him, Thou seest the multitude thronging thee, and sayest thou, Who touched me?

32 And he looked round about to see her that had done this thing.

33 But the woman, fearing and trembling, knowing what was done in her, came and fell down before him, and told him all the truth.

34 And he said unto her, Daughter,

---

to see him again. (*Notes*, ii. 1, 2. *Matt.* ix. 1.)—And not long after, he was addressed by one of the rulers of the synagogue, called Jairus, who seems to have been a person of some distinction in the city. (*Marg. Ref.* f.—*Note, Matt.* ix. 18—26, *v.* 18.) Being in deep distress, he approached Jesus in the most humble manner, and, casting himself at his feet, besought him to accompany him without delay; as his only daughter, only twelve years old, lay at the point of death, and perhaps might even then be dead: (*Marg. Ref.* h, i.—*Note, Luke* viii. 40—56, *v.* 42:) yet he believed, that if Jesus went and laid his hands upon her, she would recover. He seems not to have thought, that Christ could heal her at a distance, or that he could raise her from the dead; though it is probable, this was subsequent to the resurrection of the widow's son at Nain. (*Notes, Ps.* lxxviii. 17—31. 41. *Matt.* viii. 8, 9. *Luke* vii. 11—17. *John* xi. 20—27, *v.* 21. 28—32.) Our Lord, however, readily complied with his request, and set off immediately to go to his house.

Lieth at the point of death. (23) Εσχατως εχει. *Is at the last extremity.* Used here only. See on *Note, Matt.* ix. 18.

V. 25—34. While Jesus was walking to the house of Jairns, thronged by the surrounding multitude, he wrought another most remarkable miracle, the account of which here comes in as a parenthesis. A woman, who had been afflicted for twelve years with an issue of blood, which both exceedingly debilitated her frame, and rendered her ceremonially unclean, took that opportunity of applying for a cure. (*Lev.* xv. 25—29.) She had tried other methods of recovery, and had impoverished herself in procuring tne aid of physicians; but all in vain: nay, her malady grew still worse; so that (unless by miracle) she had no prospect but that of lingering sufferings, terminating in death. The nature of her disorder made her reluctant to mention it, and she hoped to be cured without doing it. She entertained the highest thoughts of Christ's power and sanctity; but her views of his knowledge, and of the manner in which he wrought his miracles, were confused. She therefore concluded that if she did but touch his clothes, even the *border,* or *fringe,* of his garment, (*Note, Num.* xv. 38—40,) she should certainly receive a cure; as if this could have been done by any natural efficacy, without his being conscious of it! In pursuance of this design, she seized the opportunity, when Jesus was surrounded by the multitude, and coming behind him touched his garment: nor was she disappointed; for notwithstanding the misapprehensions and infirmity mixed with her faith, her disorder was instantaneously removed; and her impaired vigour completely restored; and this not by slow degrees, as it is uniformly the case after the removal, by ordinary means, of such long continued diseases.—Had the matter terminated here, she would have come short of the instruction, comfort, and advantage, which the Saviour intended her; he would have been deprived of the honour of so extraordinary a miracle; and many thousands would have been left without the encouraging instructions, to be deduced from the transaction. Our Lord therefore, being conscious that " virtue," or divine energy, was gone forth from him to effect this cure, demanded who " had touched his clothes." When all that were near him denied, that they had touched him, that is, for any particular purpose, or intention to give offence; (for the woman seems to have retired to a little distance;) Peter and the other apostles expressed their surprise, that he should ask the question : for as numbers thronged him, how could it be expected, but that some must touch him, without meaning to offend. But Jesus still insisted on it, that some person had touched him with a special intention, and had received a cure from his power. And the woman, finding that she could not be concealed, and being alarmed lest he should rebuke her intrusion, came trembling, and fell down before him, and in the presence of all the people declared the whole of her case. As the touch of persons, thus diseased, communicated ceremonial pollution, this perhaps increased her fears. But our Lord, so far from shewing any displeasure, addressed her by the affectionate appellation of " daughter;" assured her that her cure was the evidence and happy effect of her faith, by which she had been made whole,

[c] thy faith hath made thee whole; [d] go
in peace, and be whole of thy plague.
35 ¶ While he yet spake, [e] there
came from the ruler of the synagogue's
house, certain which said, Thy daughter is dead; [f] why troublest thou [g] the
Master any further?
36 As soon as Jesus heard the word
that was spoken, he saith unto the
ruler of the synagogue, Be not afraid,
[h] only believe.
37 And [i] he suffered no man to follow him, [k] save Peter, and James, and
John the brother of James.
38 And he cometh to the house of
the ruler of the synagogue, [l] and seeth
the tumult, and them that wept and
wailed greatly.
39 And when he was come in, he
saith unto them, Why make ye this
ado, and weep? the damsel is [m] not
dead, but sleepeth.
40 And [n] they laughed him to scorn.
But [o] when he had put them all out,
he taketh the father and the mother of
the damsel, and them that were with
him, and entereth in where the damsel
was lying.
41 And he [p] took the damsel by the
hand, and said unto her, Talitha, cumi;
which is, being interpreted, [q] Damsel,
I say unto thee, arise.
42 And straightway the damsel
arose, and walked; for she was *of the
age* of twelve years; [r] and they were
astonished with a great astonishment.
43 And [s] he charged them straitly
that no man should know it; and commanded that something should be
[t] given her to eat.

c x. 52. Luke vii. 50. viii. 48. xvii. 19. xviii. 42. Acts xiv. 9.
d 1 Sam. i. 17. xx. 42. 2 Kings v. 19. Ec. ix. 7.
e Luke viii. 49.
f Luke vii. 6, 7. John xi. 21. 32. 39.
g x. 17. Matt. xxvi. 18. John xi. 28.
h 34. ix. 23. 2 Chr. xx. 20. Matt. ix. 28, 29. xvii. 20. Luke viii. 50. John iv. 48—50. xi. 40. Rom. iv. 18—24.
i Luke viii. 51. Acts ix. 40.
k ix. 2. xiv. 33. 2 Cor. xiii. 1.
l Jer. ix. 17—20. Matt. ix. 23, 24. xi. 17. Luke viii. 52, 53. Acts ix. 39.
m Dan. xii. 2. John xi. 11—13. Acts xx. 10. 1 Cor. xi. 30. 1 Thes. iv. 13, 14. v. 10.
n Gen. xix. 14. Neh. ii. 19. Job xii. 4. Ps. xxii. 7. cxxiii. 3, 4. Luke xvi. 14. Acts xvii. 32.
o 2 Kings iv. 33. Matt. vii. 6. ix. 24, 25. Luke viii. 53, 54.
p i. 31. Acts ix. 40, 41.
q i. 41. Gen. i. 3. Ps. xxxiii. 9. Luke vii. 14, 15. viii. 54, 55. John v. 28, 29. xi. 43, 44. Rom. iv. 17. Phil. iii. 21.
r i. 27. iv. 41. vi. 51. vii. 37. Acts iii. 10—13.
s i. 43. iii. 12. vii. 36. Matt. viii. 4. ix. 30. xii. 16. xvii. 9. Luke v. 14. viii. 56. John v. 41.
t Luke xxiv. 30 42, 43. Acts x. 41.

or saved; and exhorted her to be of good comfort, and to go away in peace, and to rest assured that she was now finally delivered from that tedious affliction, with which she had so long been chastened. (*Marg. Ref.—Notes, Matt.* ix. 18—26, *v.* 22. *Luke* viii. 40—56, *vv.* 43. 45.)

Virtue. (30) Δυναμιν, *power. Luke* vi. 19.—*Thronging.* (31) Συνθλιβοντα. 24. (Ex συν et θλιβω, *premo.*) "Fressing "together upon thee."—Not elsewhere *N.* T.—*Hath made ... whole.* (34) Σεσωκε. See on *Matt.* ix. 22.—*Plague.*] Μαστιγος. See on iii. 10.

V. 35—43. The preceding transaction occasioned delay, and thus no doubt increased the anxiety of Jairus: but his trial was much greater, when messengers came to inform him that his daughter was dead. (*Notes, Prov.* xiii. 12. *John* xi. 1—6. 11—16.) When Jesus heard this, he exhorted Jairus not to disquiet himself, "only to believe," namely, that he was able to restore his daughter, and would certainly do it. (*Note,* ix. 16—24.) He then dismissed the multitude, and even all his disciples, except Peter, James, and John; (*Note, Matt.* xvii. 1, 2;) that he might be attended by a competent number of witnesses, and yet keep at the utmost distance from all appearance of ostentation, in that display of his power which he was about to make. (ix. 2. xiv. 33.) When he arrived at the house, he found that the mourners and minstrels had already been called in, as was customary; and while some played mournful tunes, others uttered the most doleful lamentations. (*Marg. Ref.* l.—*Notes, Jer.* ix. 17, 18. *Matt.* ix. 18—26, *vv.* 23, 24.) But Jesus forbad them to weep, and assured them that she was not dead, (so as to continue long in that state,) but was only fallen into a sleep from which she would soon awake. But they, knowing that she was really dead, treated his words with contempt; though they must often have heard of his miracles, and were acquainted with the wisdom and holiness of his character! He therefore put them all out of the room, after he had drawn from them this attestation of her death: and, having none with him, but the parents of the damsel, and his three apostles, he took hold of her hand, and said aloud, as having power over death, and the spirits of the dead, "Talitha, cumi," or, "Damsel, arise;" and immediately she arose and walked, to the inexpressible astonishment of the spectators, and doubtless the exceeding joy and gratitude of her before afflicted parents. (*Notes,* 1 *Kings* xvii. 20—24. 2 *Kings* iv. 33—37. *Luke* vii. 11—17. *John* xi. 41—46. *Acts* ix. 36—43.) Our Lord then commanded them not to mention it to any person. It was sure to be sufficiently known, and in fact the fame of it soon spread abroad very widely. He also directed them to give her something to eat; by which it appeared, that she was recovered to full health: and it was thus intimated, that her life must be preserved as before, by ordinary means; being the same as that of others here on earth, and not like that to which the saints shall be restored by the general resurrection.—It is worthy of observation, that of the three persons, whom Christ is particularly recorded to have raised from the dead, one was the *only* son of a widow, another this *only* daughter of Jairus, and the third, the beloved brother of Martha and Mary: so much compassion, and condescension, did he shew to the feelings of natural affection. (*Marg. Ref.—Note, Luke* viii. 40—56, *vv.* 42. 54, 55.)

Troublest. (35) Σκυλλεις. *Luke* vii. 6. viii. 49. 'Proprie ... dicitur de fatigatione, et lassitudine ex via.' *Beza.* Not elsewhere *N.* T.—*Wailed.* (38) Αλαλαζοντας. Αλαλαζω, *Perpetuo conitu strepo; ejulo; tinnio.* 1 *Cor.* xiii. 1. Not elsewhere N. T.—*Jer.* xxv. 34. xlvii. 2. *Ez.* xxvii. 30. *Sept.*—*They laughed,* &c. (40) "They derided him," *Matt.* ix. 24.—*Talitha, cumi.* (41) This is Syriack, or Chaldee, and not Hebrew.—*Astonishment.* (42) Εκστασει. xvi. 8. *Luke* v. 26. *Acts* iii. 10. x. 10. xi. 5. xxii. 17.—Εξεστησαν εκστασει μεγαλη.—See on ii. 12. iii. 21.

PRACTICAL OBSERVATIONS.

V. 1—13.

This chapter calls us to contemplate the varied glories

CHAP. VI.

Jesus preaches and is despised in his own country,

1—6. He sends out the apostles to preach, with power over unclean spirits, 7—13. The opinions of Herod and others concerning Christ, 14—16. Herod imprisons and beheads John the Baptist, at the insti-

of our Redeemer's power and love; and each of the instances here set before us, may be considered, not only as a miracle, but also as an emblem of his gracious operations on the souls of men.—If a legion of apostate spirits were combined against one man, who can conceive the numbers, which there are in this wicked world, of which their great leader is "the god" and "prince!" (*Notes, John* xii. 27—33, *v.* 31. xiv. 29—31, *v.* 30. 2 *Cor.* iv. 3, 4. *Eph.* ii. 1—3. 1 *John* iv. 4—6. v. 19. *Rev.* xii. 7—12, *v.* 9.) The intention and tendency of all their unremitted efforts are to destroy mankind, both in body and soul, and to render them miserable and mischievous. May these alarming thoughts effectually warn every one of us to flee to that refuge, which God has prepared for us in the kingdom of his beloved Son! (*Note, Col.* i. 9—14, *vv.* 12—14.) —All unconverted sinners are under a far more fatal possession, than that which distracted men's minds and destroyed their health: (though it is owing to the restraining power of God, that we are preserved even from these dire calamities:) but some wicked men seem to be possessed by a Demon, whose name is Legion; their evil propensities and actions are so varied and numerous. Frequently, we see or hear of persons of this kind carried away by their own passions and Satan's temptations, into every scene of pollution and recess of iniquity; so that they *dwell* among those "whose feet go down to "death, whose steps take hold on hell." Neither fear, shame, conscience, nor regard to interest or health, can restrain them: neither the affection and authority of parents, the counsel of friends, the requirements and sanctions of human laws, the feelings of present painful effects of their vices, nor the dread of "the wrath to come," can deter them from their destructive courses. In whatever way they be bound and fettered, their strong corruptions and evil habits break loose from every restriction, and "no "man can tame them." (*Note, Rom.* viii. 3, 4.) Thus they reduce themselves to penury, disease, a prison, or an ignominious death; in the mean time, they are the reproach and grief of their friends, the terror and nuisance of the neighbourhood, and a mortified and pernicious part of the community. Yet, if Jesus be pleased to exert his power, he can bring the most abandoned and hardened of them, to tremble and fall down before him; and thus effect a blessed change in his character and conduct. But the poor sinner, when this work is first begun, often fears that the gracious Saviour means to torment or destroy him; and is ready to cry out, "What have I to do with "thee, Jesus, thou Son of the most high God?" This arises not only from unbelief and error, but also from the artifice of these malignant enemies, who are reluctant to leave those, over whom they have hitherto reigned without a rival. They dare not however resist the power of Christ, who can, if he pleases, consign them to the place of torment: and, knowing this, they on some occasions even become his supplicants, and earnestly beseech and adjure him to respite their punishment, or continue their allowance to tempt and distress the sinful race of men.—But

all the hosts of hell, formidable as they are, cannot destroy one frantick sinner, or so much as possess one swine, except the Redeemer grants them permission. This is a most encouraging thought to the believer: but what comfort can Satan's willing servants derive from it? (*Note, Job* i. 9—12.) Yet, even in respect of them, his power is limited: for the same agency, which hurried the swine into the sea, would have been sufficient for the immediate destruction of their avaricious possessors, had not the power of Christ restrained it. Long suffering and mercy may therefore be recognized in those corrections, by which men are deprived of property; whilst their lives are preserved, and warning is given them to seek the salvation of their souls.

V. 14—20.

Losses and alarms frequently terrify and exasperate sinners, instead of promoting repentance: and those who are determined not to part with iniquitous gain, or to mortify their corrupt passions, are as averse to the gospel of Christ, as unclean spirits themselves are.—But when the most enslaved sinner is delivered by the power of Jesus, from the possession of Satan and the bondage of sin, he will gladly sit at the feet, and hear the word, of his great Deliverer. Being "come to himself," and to "his right mind," he now learns to love and cleave to Christ, and longs to be with him and like him. (*Notes, Phil.* i. 21—26. 1 *John* iii. 1—3.) When these desires grow very vigorous, and are accompanied with an assured hope of heavenly felicity, he is willing "to be absent from the body that he may be "present with the Lord:" no wonder therefore, that he chooses rather to part with father and mother, or the nearest relations and most valued possessions, than to forsake Christ, and lose the benefit and comfort of his instruction, and of communion with him. Words cannot express the blessed change which takes place, when Jesus delivers such wretched slaves of Satan, as have been before described, and numbers them among his saints and servants. Instead of their former abject misery, they now enjoy a felicity before unknown; they henceforth become the ornament and blessing of their families; they are made partakers of a heavenly wisdom, and a glorious liberty; and they are rendered useful in those communities, to which before they were a terror, or a temptation. They go among their friends and neighbours, to bear testimony to Christ; "shewing what great things he hath done for "them, and hath had compassion on them:" and, whilst their conduct evinces the reality and excellency of the change, they often excite great attention, and are made the instruments of inducing even their more orderly neighbours to hearken to the gospel, which before they neglected. (*Notes,* 2 *Cor.* v. 17—21. *Gal.* i. 15—24. 1 *Thes.* i. 5—8. 1 *Tim.* i. 12—16. 2 *Pet.* i. 13—15.) Nay, the Lord sometimes makes choice of such converts for his ministers: and, whilst they publish through cities and countries, what great things Jesus has done for them; their simple testimony confirmed by their characters, ren-

ders them extensive blessings, and sometimes in those places where they were once most mischievous. Indeed, we all seem to be continued in this world of sin and sorrow, after our conversion, chiefly to declare and display, by word and deed, the Saviour's power and grace among our fellow sinners.

V. 21—34.

Our blessed Lord will not obtrude himself on those, who are not disposed to entertain him; nor refuse his presence and salvation to any, whose hearts are prepared to welcome him.—The feeling of distress, for which men can obtain no adequate remedy, from themselves or others, is frequently the means of bringing them to Christ: and thus severe family-trials are sometimes appointed in love, to shew those in affluence especially the vanity of their distinctions; and so lead them to enquire after a better portion, and a spiritual salvation.—Those who are in temporal distress, readily find words to express their meaning and desires: how is it then, that men experience such difficulty in presenting their supplications before God? Certainly, because they have not so distinct an understanding of their wants, nor so deep a feeling of their dangers and miseries.—There are different degrees and exercises of faith, where it is vital and saving; but that which most honours Christ, will be most advantageous to us. The history of his life is an account of his continued earnestness in doing good, without weariness or intermission; so that we know not whether we should most admire his divine power, or his beneficent use of it: and, whilst we derive encouragement from this reflection, let us learn to use our little ability in doing what we can, to alleviate the miseries and promote the benefit of mankind.—And if we look around and make diligent enquiry, we shall find many pious Christians, wasted by disease, pinched by penury, and lodged in cottages, cellars, garrets, or almshouses; whilst stately palaces are often scenes of riot to infidels, profligates, and cruel oppressors. But " the prosperity of fools destroys them," and the afflictions of the righteous conduce to their everlasting felicity.—Men often prove vain helpers, even in temporal calamities, and only add to our sufferings by their efforts to relieve us: yet the aversion of sinners to seek help from God, in this respect, is very conspicuous; for they will try every method of redress, and persevere, after reiterated disappointments, in running to this and the other fellow-creature; yet they will not apply to him, who alone can render means and instruments successful, and who can help us when all other helpers fail! Thus many, through their own obstinacy, or for want of wholesome instruction, waste their time and strength to no purpose, by applying to " physicians of no " value;" from whom they " suffer many things," and get no better, but " rather grow worse." Some run into diversions, and gay company, to pacify an uneasy conscience, or to relieve the dejection of their spirits; many plunge into a hurry of business, into abstruse speculations, or even into intemperance, for the same purpose; and others " go about to establish their own righteous- " ness," or torment themselves by vain superstitions: thus numbers perish miserably. But happy are they who, by

many disappointments, are led to hearken to the report of the gospel, and to expect help from Jesus alone: for even their remaining infirmity and misapprehensions will not prevent their obtaining the desired blessing. (*Note, Matt.* xi. 28—30.)—The example before us may likewise instruct us to receive and encourage those, who seem humbly to rely on Christ for pardon and grace; though in many respects mistaken and defective.—In proportion as our faith in Christ brings peace into our conscience, and destroys the love and power of sin, it is proved to be genuine: and the more singly we depend on him, and expect great things from him; the more evidently we shall find that he is become our salvation. Thus he gradually and effectually teaches his people, by their own experience: he evinces to them his knowledge of their thoughts, their wants, and their difficulties; and he shews his power and love in relieving and helping them. But, whilst we have the benefit, he will secure to himself the glory, of all that he does for us: and he will at length bring to light, in numberless instances, the " virtue that hath gone forth from him," to heal those hidden evils of the heart, under which his people had groaned for years before they sought to him. Yet, while multitudes throng around him, as it were, by crowding the places where the gospel is preached; only here and there one thus " touches him," in humble faith, as the lives of most too plainly testify.—Even the disciples of Christ are, in many instances, apt to express themselves dissatisfied with his words and works, with the dispensations of his providence and grace. This is the effect of remaining pride, ignorance, and unbelief: no believer, to this hour, ever could conceive of his compassion and love half so highly as they deserve; though he sometimes conceals them under a frown or a rebuke. Humble souls, therefore, in seeking to him, are apt to tremble and fear, lest he should abhor or destroy them; whilst his heart yearns with pity, and he is about to say to them, as to his children, " Be of good comfort, go in peace, thy faith " hath saved thee." For he will honour that faith, which honours him, by seeking from him all the blessings which he is exalted to bestow.

V. 35—43.

The Lord will not let any one, who waits on him, be a loser by his kindness to others: his delays are intended to render his favours more precious: he waits for our extremities, that he may manifest his glory, and encourage our faith and hope. He regards no application to him as a *trouble*, and no case can be desperate which he undertakes: we should not therefore yield to fear, but desire and pray to be strengthened in faith, in the most difficult circumstances; and he will then fulfil his word, and all our expectations grounded on it. (*Notes, Rom.* iv. 18—25.) —No wonder that worldly men make a tumult, with wailing and lamentation, when bereaved of those whom they love; for they have no prospect, or a very gloomy one, beyond the grave: but Christians should not " sorrow as " men without hope, for them who sleep in the Lord :" nor should they indulge grief, or affect to be inconsolable, for any loss; as the Lord still lives to be their never-

54. AND he went out from thence, and came into his own country, and his disciples followed him.

2 And when the sabbath-day was come, he began to teach in the synagogue: and many hearing *him* were astonished, saying, From whence hath this man these things? and what wisdom *is* this which is given unto him, that even such mighty works are wrought by his hands?

3 Is not this the carpenter, the son of Mary, the brother of James and Joses, and of Juda, and Simon? and are not his sisters here with us? And they were offended at him.

4 But Jesus said unto them, A prophet is not without honour, but in his own country, and among his own kin, and in his own house.

5 And ¹ he could there do no mighty works, save that he laid his hands upon a few sick folk, and healed *them*.

6 And he marvelled because of their unbelief. And he went round about the villages teaching.

7 ¶ And he calleth unto him the twelve, and began to send them forth by two and two; and gave them power over unclean spirits;

8 And commanded them that they should take nothing for *their* journey, save a staff only; no scrip, no bread, no money in *their* purse:

9 But *be* shod with sandals; and not put on two coats.

10 And he said unto them, In what place soever ye enter into an house, there abide till ye depart from that place.

11 And whosoever shall not receive you, nor hear you; when ye depart thence, shake off the dust under your feet for a testimony against them. Verily I say unto you, It shall be more tolerable for Sodom and Gomorrah, in the day of judgment, than for that city.

---

failing Friend and Comforter. Indeed death is but a sleep to believers; and we shall soon join our deceased Christian friends in that world, where sin and all its effects will be known no more. (*Notes, Prov. xiv. 13—18.*) But our gracious Redeemer, while he rebukes our excessive sorrow, makes kind allowances to the feelings of nature and affection: and, though we cannot now expect to have our deceased children or relatives restored to us; yet we may hope to experience consolations proportioned to our trials.—When sinners ridicule the truths and promises of Christ; they exclude themselves from witnessing or experiencing their gracious accomplishment: for he has the power over death, the grave, and the unseen world; and he will ere long bring forth all the nations of the dead to appear before his awful tribunal, and to hear his powerful word, either calling them to inherit eternal felicity, or bidding them depart into everlasting punishment. (*Notes, Matt. xxv. 31—46! John v. 28, 29. Rev. xx. 11—15.*) May he then raise our ' souls from the death of sin to the ' life of righteousness;' that we may now feed on his spiritual provisions, and walk with him in his holy ways, as the trophies and monuments of his grace; and that when he shall at length "appear, we may also appear "with him in glory." (*Note, Col. iii. 1—4.*)

NOTES.

CHAP. VI. V. 1—4. (*Marg. Ref.—Notes, Matt. xiii. 54—58. Luke iv. 16—32.*) In this account of our Lord's last visit to Nazareth, (as it appears to have been,) we find that the people asked, "Is not this the carpenter?" whence it has reasonably been concluded, that he had wrought with Joseph at this laborious business, during the former years of his life.—Justin Martyr says, that ' being among ' men he made plows and yokes, which are the works of ' carpenters.'—By the Jewish canons, all fathers were bound to teach their children some trade: Jesus was not educated in the schools of human learning; but having " for our sakes become poor," he, " the second Adam," submitted to the sentence denounced on the " first Adam," and ate his " bread in the sweat of his brow." (*Notes, Gen. iii. 17—19. Acts xviii. 1—6.*)

Offended. (3) Εσκανδαλιζοντο. See on *Matt. v.* 29, 30. *Notes, Is. viii.* 11—15. *Matt. xi.* 2—6, *v.* 6.

V. 5, 6. Jesus " could not " with propriety work many miracles at Nazareth, or the people did not give him the opportunity, by bringing their sick to be healed. It seems, however, that there were some exceptions; and therefore he wrought a few miraculous cures. (*Marg. Ref. 1.—Note,* i. 45.) The obstinate and unreasonable unbelief and contempt of the Nazarenes were truly wonderful, when all their advantages are considered: and our Lord is generally spoken of as affected with the scenes around him, according to the nature of them, in the same manner as we should have been; except as sinful emotions are also excited in us, from which he was perfectly free. (*Marg. Ref.* m.)

V. 7—12. *Marg. Ref.—Notes, Matt. x.* 5—15. xi. 20—24. *Luke ix.* 1—6. x. 1—16.—*That men should repent.* (12) Repentance was the main subject of the instructions and exhortations, which the apostles were commanded to use on this occasion, as connected with the approaching kingdom, or reign, of the promised Messiah. (*Notes, Matt. iii.* 2. *Luke xxiv.* 44—49, *v.* 47.)

Sandals. (9) Σανδαλια. *Acts xii.* 8. Not elsewhere N. T. —Ὑποδηματα, *Matt. x.* 10.

12 And they went out, and *preached that men should repent.

13 And they * cast out many devils, and b anointed with oil many that were sick, and healed them.

14 ¶ And c king Herod heard of him; (for d his name was spread abroad;) and he said, That John the Baptist was risen from the dead, and therefore mighty works do shew forth themselves in him.

15 Others said, That e it is Elias. And others said, That it is f a prophet, or as one of the prophets.

16 But when Herod heard thereof, he said, f It is John, whom I beheaded: he is risen from the dead.

17 For h Herod himself had sent forth and laid hold upon John, and bound him in prison for Herodias's sake, his brother i Philip's wife; for he had married her.

18 For John had said unto Herod, k It is not lawful for thee to have thy brother's wife.

19 Therefore l Herodias had a quarrel against him, and would have killed him; but she could not.

20 For Herod m feared John, knowing that he was a just man, and an holy, and n observed him; and when he heard him, he did many things, o and heard him gladly.

21 And p when a convenient day was come, that Herod on q his birth-day made a supper to his lords, high captains, and chief estates of Galilee;

22 And when r the daughter of the said Herodias came in, and danced and pleased Herod, and them that sat with him; the king said unto the damsel, Ask of me whatsoever thou wilt, and I will give it thee.

23 And s he sware unto her, Whatsoever thou shalt ask of me, I will give it thee, unto the half of my kingdom.

24 And she went forth, and t said unto her mother, What shall I ask? And she said, u The head of John the Baptist.

25 And she came in straightway with haste unto the king, and asked, saying, I will that thou give me by and by, in x a charger, the head of John the Baptist.

26 And the king y was exceeding sorry; yet for his oath's sake, and for their sakes which sat with him, he would not reject her.

27 And immediately z the king sent an executioner, and commanded his head to be brought: and he went and beheaded him in the prison,

28 And brought his head in a charger, and gave it to the damsel: and the damsel gave it to her mother.

29 And when his disciples heard of it, a they came and took up his corpse, and laid it in a tomb.

V. 13. Learned men have bestowed some pains to shew, that it was usual with the Jews to anoint the sick with oil, in order to their recovery: and some think, that the apostles complied with this custom, without any direction from their Lord. But this is not at all probable: nor can we suppose that the miraculous effect would have followed, had they acted without orders. Doubtless, in this they observed the directions given them by Christ: and the observance was intended to be an outward sign of his inward operation; which was itself an emblem of healing our souls by the unction of the Holy Spirit. This practice was continued for some time in the church, as the token of a miraculous cure: but it was obvious, that it must be left off, when miracles ceased. Yet the popish ceremony (or sacrament, as they call it,) of 'extreme unction,' seems absurdly to have been derived from it; for that is not used in order to a miraculous cure, but when all hope of recovery is given up. (Note, Jam. v. 14, 15.)

That were sick.] Αρρωστους, Invalidos. xvi. 18. Matt. xiv. 14. 1 Cor. xi. 30. 'Ab α priv. et ρωμη, robur, Roma, απο της ρωμης, quia fuit robusta civitas.' Leigh.

V. 14—29. Marg. Ref.—Notes, Matt. xiv. 3—12. Luke iii. 19, 20. ix. 7—9.—King Herod. (14) Thus his courtiers and flatterers called him, though only a Tetrarch, or governor of Galilee under the Romans; being a fourth part of his father's kingdom. (Notes, Matt. xiv. 1, 2. Luke iii. 1.)—' It is not easy to meet with a more striking instance ' than this, of the force of conscience over a guilty mind, ' or a stronger proof how perpetually it goads the sinner, ' not only with well grounded ... apprehensions of impend-' ing ... vengeance, but with imaginary terrors and visionary ' dangers. ...There is reason to believe that Herod ... was ' of the sect called the Sadducees: ...yet his fears over-' ruled all the prejudices of his sect, and raised up the ' semblance of the murdered Baptist, armed with the ' power of miracles, for the very purpose (as he imagined) ' of inflicting exemplary vengeance upon him for that atro-' cious deed; as well as for his adultery, his incest, and ' all his other crimes. ...Herod had been married a consi-' derable time to the daughter of Aretas, king of Arabia ' Petræa; but conceiving a violent passion for his brother ' Philip's wife, Herodias, he first seduced her affections

2 K

e 7, &c. Luke ix.
10, x. 17.
30 ¶ And * the apostles gathered themselves together unto Jesus, and
d Acts l. I. xv. 16 told him all things, *d* both what they
—21. 1 Tim. iv.
12—16 Tit. ii. had done, and what they had taught.
6, 7. 1 Pet. v. 2.
e L. 45. lil. 7. 20. 31 And he said unto them, *e* Come
Matt. xiv. 13. ye urse ves apart into a desert place,
John vi. 1. ancy rest awhile: for there were many
coming and going, and they had no
leisure so much as to eat.

32 And they departed into a desert place by ship privately.

f 54, 55. Matt. xv. 33 And the people saw them de-
2)—31. John vi. parting, and many *f* knew him, and ran
2. Jam. l. 19. a-foot thither out of all cities, and out-
went them, and came together unto
g Matt. xiv. 14. him.
xv. 32. Luke ix.
11. Num. xv. 2. 34 And Jesus, when he came out,
5. Heb. ii. 17. iv.
15. *g* saw much people, and was moved
h Num. xxvii. 17. with compassion toward them, *h* be-
1 Kings xxii. 17.
2 Chr. xviii. 16. cause they were as sheep not having
Jer. l. 6. Zech.
x. 2. Matt. ix.
36.

a shepherd: *i* and he began to teach *i* *Ie* *tat.* *—s.*
them many things.

35 ¶ And *k* when the day was now *k Matt. xiv. 15.*
Luke ix. 12.
far spent, his disciples came unto him,
and said, This is a desert place, and
now the time *is* far passed;

36 *l* Send them away, that they may *l* iii. 21. v. 31.
Matt. xiv. 23.
go into the country round about, and *xvi. 22.*
into the villages, and buy themselves
bread: for they have nothing to eat.

37 He answered and said unto them,
m Give ye them to eat. And they say *m* viii. 2. 2.
2 Kings iv. 42—
unto him, *n* Shall we go and buy two *44. Matt. xiv.*
16, xv. 32. Luke
hundred *o* pennyworth of bread, and *ix. 13. John vi.*
4—10.
give them to eat? *n Num. xi. 13. 21*
—25. 2 Kings
38 He saith unto them, How many *iv. 2 Matt. xv.*
33. John vi. 7.
loaves have ye? go and see. And when *o Matt. xvii. 28.*
marg.
they knew, they say, *p* Five, and two *p viii. 6. Matt.*
xiv. 17, 18. xv
fishes. *34. Luke ix. 13.*
John vi. 9.
39 And he commanded them to

f from her husband, then dismissed his own wife, and
f married Herodias during the life-time of his brother.—
f The Baptist had the honesty and the courage to reproach
f the tyrant with the enormity of his guilt: ... and forbear
f to do his duty, and to take the consequences. ...Herod
f observed John, that is, listened to him with attention
f and with pleasure: nay, he went further still, " he did
f " many things,"...which John exhorted... him to do. ...
f He perhaps shewed more attention to many of his pub-
f lick duties, more gentleness to his subjects, more com-
f passion to the poor, more equity in his judicial determi-
f nations, more regard to publick worship; and vainly
f hoped, like many other audacious sinners, that this
f partial reformation, this half-way amendment, would
avert the judgments, with which John threatened him.
f But the main point, the great object of John's repre-
f hension, the incestuous adultery in which he lived, *that*
f he could not part with. ...What a picture does this hold
f out to us, of that strange thing called human nature!
f Of that inconsistence, that contradiction, that contrariety,
f which sometimes takes place in the heart of man, un-
f sanctified and unsubdued by the power of divine grace!
f And what an exalted idea does it give of the dignity of a
f truly religious character, like that of John, which com-
f pels even its bitterest enemies to reverence and to fear it!
f and forces even the most profligate, and most powerful,
f to pay an unwilling homage to excellence, at the very
f moment, perhaps, when they are meditating its destruc-
f tion! ...The fate of John might have remained undecided
f for a considerable time, had not an incident taken place,
f which determined it. ...The folly, the rashness, and the
f madness of such an oath,' (as Herod's,) *f* on so foolish
ʳ an occasion, could be exceeded by nothing, but the hor-
ʳ rible purpose to which it was perverted. ... than any other,
f a passion to gratify, stronger perhaps than any other,
f when it takes full possession of the human heart, and
f that was *revenge*. She had been mortally injured, as she
f conceived, by the Baptist:...and she not only felt the

f highest indignation at this insult, but was afraid that his
f repeated remonstrances might at length prevail. ...Herod,
f conceiving himself, most absurdly, bound by his oath to
f comply even with this inhuman demand, ... preferred the
f real guilt of murder, to the false imputation of perjury.
f Herodias " had a quarrel against John : " according to
f the original, " she fastened and hung upon him," and
f was determined not to let go her hold, till she had de-
f stroyed him. ...We are informed by Josephus, that He-
f rod's marriage with Herodias drew on him the resent-
f ment of Aretas, ... the father of his first wife, who de-
f clared war against him, and ...defeated his army with
f great slaughter. This, says the historian, the Jews con-
f sidered as the just judgment of God for his murder of
f John. ...Not long after this, both he and Herodias were
f deprived of their kingdom by the Roman emperor, and
f sent into perpetual banishment: and it is added by
f another historian, that Salome met with a violent and
f untimely death.' *Bp. Porteus.*

As one of the prophets. (15) If not one of the old prophets risen from the dead, his character, preaching, and
miracles, resemble their's.—*Had a quarrel.* (19) " An in-
" ward grudge." *Marg. Εuχεν. Luke* xi. 53. *Εuχω.* ' *Im-*
mineo. ...Significat *summam offensionem, quæ faciat ut*
' *quis omnes captet occasiones quibus alteri noceat.*' Leigh.
Implicor. Gal. v. 1. Not elsewhere N. T.—Heard him
gladly. (20) *Notes, Ex. xxxiii. 30—33, v. 32. Matt. xiii.*
20, 21.—*High captains.* (21) Χιλιαρχοις. *Qui mille viris*
præest. John xviii. 12. Acts xxi. 31. 33.—Half, &c. (23)
Note, Esth. vii. 2—4.—An executioner. (27) " One of his
" guard." *Marg. Σπικυλατωρα. Spiculator, Satelles.* It is
originally a Latin word, being derived from *spiculum,* a
javelin; or rather from *speculator,* a kind of soldier employed to guard the person of the Emperor.

V. 30—46. *Marg. Ref.—Notes, Matt. xiv. 13—21.*
Luke ix. 10—17. *John* vi. 1—21.—*Rest.* (31) Αναπαυεσθε.
xiv. 41. *Matt. xxvi. 45. ... Αναπαυσις.* See on *Matt. xi. 29.*
—Had ... leisure.] Ηυκαιρον. *Acts* xvii. 21. 1 *Cor* xvi. 12.

make ᵇ all sit down by companies upon the green grass.

40 And they sat down in ranks, ᵍby hundreds, and by fifties.

41 And when he had taken the five loaves and the two fishes, ʰ he looked up to heaven, and ⁱblessed, and brake the loaves, and gave *them* to his disciples to set before them; and the two fishes divided he among them all.

42 And they did all eat, ʲand were filled.

43 And they took up ᵏtwelve baskets full of the fragments, and of the fishes.

44 And they that did eat of the loaves were about five thousand men.

45 And ˡstraightway he constrained his disciples to get into the ship, and to go to the other side before ᵐunto Bethsaida, while he sent away the people.

46 And when he had sent them away, ⁿhe departed into a mountain to pray.

47 ¶ And when even was come, the ship was in the midst of the sea, and he alone on the land.

48 And ᵃhe saw them toiling in rowing; for the wind was contrary unto them: and about ᵇthe fourth watch of the night ᶜhe cometh unto them, walking upon the sea, and ᵈwould have passed by them.

49 But when they saw him walking upon the sea, they ᵉsupposed it had been a spirit, and cried out;

50 For they all saw him, and were troubled: and immediately he talked with them, and saith unto them, Be of good cheer: ᶠit is I; be not afraid.

51 And he went up unto them into the ship; ᵍand the wind ceased: ʰand they were sore amazed in themselves beyond measure, and wondered.

52 For ⁱthey considered not *the miracle* of the loaves: for ᵏtheir heart was hardened.

53 ¶ And when they had passed ᵏover, they came into ˡthe land of Gennesaret, and drew to the shore.

54 And when they were come out of the ship, straightway they ᵐknew him,

55 And ⁿran through that whole re-

—Eυκαιρος. 21. Eυκαιρος. xiv. 11. 2 Tim. iv. 2. (Ex ω bene, et καιρος, tempus, opportunitas.) See on 2 Tim. iv. 2.—*Out-went.* (33) Προηλθον. Came before. The people were at the place, before Jesus and his disciples landed.—*Sheep,* &c. (34) Note, Matt. ix. 36—38. —*Two hundred penny-worth.* (37) Διακοσιων δηναριων. Two hundred denarii: each the value of a day's labour in harvest. (*Matt.* xx. 2. Gr.)—*By companies.* (39) Συμποσια συμποσια *symposia, convivia.* (Ex συν, et ποσις, potus.) —*In ranks.* (40) Πρασιαι πρασιαι. Neither συμποσιον nor πρασια is used elsewhere in N. T. The latter word is taken from beds in a garden, to which companies of people, seated in rows, twice the number in rank as in file, would bear some resemblance. Many expositors seem to think, that the whole multitude formed one body, a hundred in rank and fifty in file: but the plural number, ('companies, companies; ranks, ranks,') leads us to conclude, that several distinct companies were formed, but all arranged in the same manner.—*Bethsaida.* (45) Bethsaida was near the place, where Jesus and the disciples then were, and probably to the east of the sea of Tiberias: but learned men are not agreed in respect of its situation. (*Marg. Ref.—Luke* ix. 10.)—*Had sent ... away.* (46) Αποταξαμενος, *valedicens, amandans. Luke* ix. 61. xiv. 33. *Acts* xviii. 18. 21. 2 *Cor.* ii. 13. (Ex απο, et τασσω, *mando.*) The word *implies,* the parting directions and injunctions of one about to leave his family, friends, or servants.— *To pray.*] *Marg. Ref. z.—Note, Matt.* xiv. 22—24, v. 23.

V. 47—52. (*Marg. Ref.—Notes, Matt.* xiv. 22—32.)

Had the disciples duly reflected on the miracle which Christ had wrought, in feeding the multitude; they would not have been so exceedingly amazed at his walking on the waves of the sea, and causing the tempest to subside. But their minds were in part hardened, through remaining unbelief and carnal prejudices; so that they did not make a proper improvement of the miracles which they beheld, nor durably retain the impressions, which at first were made on them. Thus they speedily forgot their conviction of the divine power of their Lord; and this occasioned their astonishment at every renewed display of it. (*Note,* viii. 17—21.) The same words are sometimes used for the remaining, and in a degree *prevailing* evil in true disciples, as for the total dominion of evil in unbelievers. (*Matt.* xvi. 23. *Rom.* viii. 5, 6. 1 *Cor.* iii. 1.) This is not duly attended to by some controversial writers.—' Some ' cheats have pretended to cure diseases miraculously; and ' some have even attempted to raise the dead: yet no im- ' postor, I believe, has ever been so bold as to undertake ' to feed five thousand people at once with five loaves and ' two fishes; or to walk on the waves of the sea.' *Bp. Porteus.*

Hardened. (52) Πεπωρωμενη. viii. 17. *John* xii. 40. *Rom.* xi. 7. 2 *Cor.* iii. 14. Πωρωσις. See on iii. 5.

V. 53—56. *Marg. Ref.—Notes,* v. 14—20. *Matt.* xiv. 34—36.—*Touch.* (56) Perhaps the report of the woman, who had been cured by touching the fringe of Christ's garment, encouraged these afflicted persons to apply to him, by his permission, in this manner.

Drew to the shore. (53) Προσωρμισθησαν. Ex προς, et

gion round about, and began to carry about in beds those that were sick, where they heard he was.

56 And whithersoever he entered, into villages, or cities, or country, [a] they laid the sick in the streets, and besought him that they might [b] touch if it were but [c] the border of his garment; and as many as touched [d] him were made whole.

a Acts v. 15.
b lu. 16. v. 27, 28
2 Kings viii. 61
Luke vii-18. xxii-
51. Acts xix. 12.
q Num. xv. 38.
39. Deut. xxii.
12. Matt. ix. 20.
Luke viii. 44.
* Or, it.

ὅρμος, *statio navalis.* Not elsewhere N. T.—*If it were but.* (56) Κᾳ, *at least. Acts* v. 15. 2 *Cor.* xi. 16.

PRACTICAL OBSERVATIONS.

V. 1—13.

We are taught, by our Lord's example, to renew our endeavours for the spiritual good even of those, who have already treated us with cruelty or contempt, and where danger and contumely may again be expected: and we are reminded that industry, in the meanest and most laborious honest calling, is far more honourable and beneficial, than indolence or dissipation, especially in youth. They therefore, who are placed in inferior situations, should cheerfully go on with their employments; and, if God have work of another kind for them, this will prove no hindrance to their future usefulness. Worldly men indeed despise the most wise and excellent persons, because of their mean extraction, low occupations, or poor relations; or on account of their owr previous familiarity with them, or superiority over them: for unbelief will always find some objection against the truth, and those who are zealous for it: but while their unreasonable prejudices preclude them from the benefit, the servants of God will find others disposed to profit by them.—Indeed the inhabitants of villages are often more ready to welcome the gospel, than those of flourishing and populous cities: if therefore we fail of meeting with acceptance in the latter, we should be satisfied to go and teach poor peasants and cottagers the way of salvation. (*Note, Jer.* v. 3—6.)—The Lord Jesus, the Fountain of all authority in his church, dispenses to every man as he pleases: and he will surely qualify and assist those, whom he commissions to preach his gospel.—Where the truth has hitherto been but little known, it is very desirable that ministers should go forth at least by two and two; that they may have the comfort and benefit of each other's society, counsel, and prayers. (*Note, Ec.* iv. 9—12.)—While faithful preachers earnestly desire and uprightly design to be a blessing to the people; and, content with food and raiment, however mean and scanty, seek " not their's but them ;" they often prove the occasion of deeper condemnation to those, who constrain them to " shake off the dust of their feet for a testimony " against them," by refusing to hear and receive their message.—How heinous a sin must unbelief be, in all who have the adequate means of conviction ; seeing a righteous God will render the final doom of those who refuse the salvation of the gospel, even more intolerable than that of Sodom and Gomorrah ! (*Notes, John* iii. 19 —21. *Heb.* ii. 1—4. xii. 22—25.)—The servants of Christ must go forth in his name, every where " preaching, that " men should repent, and turn to God, and do works " meet for repentance;" and enforcing their exhortations both by the terrors of the law, and by the encouraging truths and promises of the gospel. In this way we may hope that our labours will be blessed, to turn many " from " darkness unto light, and the power of Satan unto God,"

and that we shall be the instruments of healing their souls by the unction of the Holy Spirit.

V. 14—29.

When the truths and honour of Christ are spread abroad, by the successful labours of his ministers; men will make their observations or conjectures respecting them, according to their different humours or prejudices: and then the secret remorse and horror of conscience, which wicked men experience, will often be brought to light. (*Note, Ps.* lxxiii. 18—22.)—No infidel principles, or hardness of heart, or worldly grandeur, can at all times preserve the enemies of God from terrors and anxieties. They are seldom wholly exempt from convictions of their own guilt, and they are often unable to exclude the dread of divine vengeance. They may imprison or murder their reprovers; but this only increases the clamour of their inward monitor and accuser: and any person, who understands and believes the Bible, may predict the consequence of a man's determining to mount, if possible, the summit of prosperity, by whatever means and at any rate: for if he succeed, he will find his desired eminence a most turbulent, anxious, and perilous situation; and unless he have the wisdom and grace to descend speedily into the valley of humiliation, he will soon be cast down into the depths of hell. We may see the reason, why men cannot receive the message of God's ministers, and why they treat them with contempt and enmity: they feel that their example and doctrine is a reproach; their pride is affronted, their consciences are disquieted, and their darling indulgences opposed: and thus they, excited by their associates in iniquity, have an irreconcileable quarrel against the very persons whom they cannot but stand in awe of, as " just and " holy men," whom they have often heard with apparent satisfaction, and at whose instance they have " done many " things." But the frame of men's minds is very different, when they are hearing the word of God, as delivered by a heart-searching awakening preacher, than it is at those times, when they are celebrating luxurious and joyous feasts, indulging their appetites, surrounded with flatterers, and carousing with dissipated companions. (*Note, Dan.* v. 1—4.) Such revels are Satan's opportunities: he waits for them, in order to take his advantage, to push men forward into those enormities, from which they were restrained by remaining scruples, in their more sober hours. Hence it has often been known, that the most atrocious murders have been hastily committed, as it were, to grace a riotous banquet, or to gratify some worthless individual, who had contributed to the luxury or conviviality of the occasion! (*Note,* 2 *Sam.* xiii. 22—29.) Thus the great murderer of men carries his point, and employs his servants in the work of destroying each others' lives and souls.—If the history of persecutions and martyrs could be written, under the guidance of inspiration; it would be found, that thousands of the most valuable lives had fallen a sacrifice to the revenge of some ambi-

CHAP. VII.

The Pharisees find fault with the disciples for eating with unwashen hands; and Jesus shews, that their traditions "make void the law of God," 1—13. He teaches the source and nature of defilement, 14—23; heals the daughter of a Syrophenician woman, 24—30; and a man who was deaf, and had an impediment in his speech, 31—37.

THEN came together unto him [a] the Pharisees, and certain of the Scribes, [ii. 22. Matt. xv. 1. Luke v. 17. xi. 53, 54] which came from Jerusalem.

2 And when they saw some of his disciples eat bread with [*] defiled, that [* Or, common. Act. x. 14, 15.] is to say, with unwashen hands, [b] they [b Dan. vi. 4, 5. Matt. vi. 3—5. xxiii. 25—28.] found fault.

tions and licentious Herodias; or of some base wretch, whose pride had been affronted, and whose success in wickedness had been impeded or endangered by their faithful reproofs. Yet even those who are instigated by such prompters often avow, that their conscience and honour are concerned; and devise to connect oaths, engagements, and regard to friends, to the publick peace, or the good of the church, with the gratification of their iniquitous cruelty and revenge! They can, however, do the faithful servants of God no real harm: he will graciously vouchsafe them another kind of recompence, than they receive from men; and avenge their cause on those, who repay their friendly warnings with indignity and cruelty. But what will be the doom of those, who have instigated even their own children, and nearest relatives, to the most atrocious crimes, in order to gratify their own malignant and hateful passions! (P. O. Matt. xiv. 1—12.)

V. 30—56.

While the enemies of God are triumphing in their short-lived success, and his friends are mourning over the loss of those who have entered into their rest; he will send forth other ministers to spread his gospel, and will protect them in their labours till they be finished.—Every minister must give an account of himself to Christ at last: and it behoves us now to do it continually, before his " throne of " grace;" both concerning "all we have done, and all " we have taught." Thus we shall have the comfort of his gracious acceptance of that which has been right, and obtain his blessing upon our labours: and thus we may seek his merciful forgiveness of what has been wrong, pray that the effects of it may be counteracted, and learn to profit even by our own mistakes and offences.—Our blessed Lord, knowing our frailty, will allow and provide for us seasons of relaxation after fatiguing exertions in his service: that we may be recruited for our work; recollect ourselves respecting the state of our own souls; and receive further instructions from him concerning our future conduct: and if he, by sickness, or any other providential hindrance, lay us aside for a season from our work; we should not think the time wasted, but listen more attentively to his teaching, and seek to profit by the visitation.—Those who know the preciousness of Christ and his salvation, and have learned where he may be found, will break through all hindrances, that they may seek to him: nor will he refuse instruction or assistance to those, who deviate from ordinary rules, in their earnestness to obtain the blessings of salvation. He has tender compassion for them who are "as sheep not having a shepherd;" and such as wait on him, take the best method of obtaining all things needful for soul and body: for, as he died on the cross, that he might feed our perishing souls with " the " Bread of life," he will not fail, in his providence, to give

us food for our bodies also. While we therefore cheerfully and thankfully depend on his power and grace, let us copy his example, in being accessible at all times to those who want our help; in compassionating the temporal afflictions of our neighbours, as well as the lost condition of their souls; and in being always " ready to dis-" tribute, and glad to communicate" to their necessities. In order to this, we should be frugal in our own expenses, that we may have the more to employ in liberality; and we may trust in the Lord to make up, by his blessing, whatever is necessary to our state in life.—We should also learn to connect piety and charity together; and to delight alternately in communion with God, and in doing good to men: and should we meet with storms and difficulties in the path of duty, we may by faith behold our heavenly Advocate pleading our cause, and ready to come to our help, as it were " walking upon the waves," silencing the tempest as he pleases; and allaying our terrors by saying, " Be of good cheer: it is I; be not afraid."—Did we duly regard even our own experience of his power, truth, and love, we should not be so much alarmed at renewed difficulties, or at formidable appearances : our expectations would then be raised higher; and, though our amazement at his renewed interpositions might be less, our admiring gratitude and praise would be greater, than they now are. But we lose much of our comfort, in the watchful care of our Lord, by remaining unbelief, forgetfulness, and hardness of heart.—Did men value the health of their souls as they do that of their bodies, and had they strong faith in the Redeemer's power and grace, they would flock to him from villages and cities, sparing neither trouble nor inconvenience, and beseeching him, that they might be enabled in faith to " touch even the hem of his garment;" for certainly, those who thus apply to him, will be made whole of their most inveterate diseases.—And here again let us learn to be doing good wherever we go, and to seek the salvation of Christ, for others as well as for ourselves.

NOTES.

CHAP. VII. V. 1. ' None do more resist the wisdom ' of God, than they that should be wisest; and that upon ' zeal for their own traditions: for men do not please ' themselves more in any thing than in superstition; ... to ' which hypocrisy is a constant companion.' Beza. It should have been ' a general companion.'—It is probable, the chosen persons of the Pharisees and scribes had been deputed to watch the conduct and discourses of Jesus, in order to find matter of accusation against him; and had come from Jerusalem for this purpose, though they did not avow it. (Marg. Ref.—Note, Matt. xv. 1, 2.)

V. 2. Marg. Ref.—Defiled.] "Common." Marg. Κοιναις. Acts x. 14. xi. 8. Rom. xiv. 14. Tit. i. 4. Heb. x. 29. Κοινου, Acts x. 15. xi. 9.—What was not in the pro-

2 K 5

3 For the Pharisees, and all the Jews, except they wash *their* hands oft, eat not, holding the tradition of the elders.

4 And *when they come* from the market, except they wash, they eat not. And many other things there be which they have received to hold, *as* the washing of cups, and pots, brazen vessels, and of tables.

5 Then the Pharisees and Scribes asked him, Why walk not thy disciples according to the tradition of the elders, but eat bread with unwashen hands?

6 He answered and said unto them, Well hath Esaias prophesied of you hypocrites, as it is written, This people honoureth me with *their* lips, but their heart is far from me.

7 Howbeit in vain do they worship me, teaching *for* doctrines the commandments of men.

8 For, laying aside the commandment of God, ye hold the tradition of men, *as* the washing of pots and cups: and many other such like things ye do.

9 And he said unto them, Full well ye reject the commandment of God, that ye may keep your own tradition.

10 For Moses said, Honour thy father and thy mother; and, Whoso curseth father or mother, let him die the death.

11 But ye say, If a man shall say to his father or mother, *It is* Corban, that is to say, A gift, by whatsoever thou mightest be profited by me; *he shall be free.*

12 And ye suffer him no more to do ought for his father or his mother;

---

per manner purified, and set apart for God, was common or profane, in Israel. (*Note, Ex.* xlii. 15—20, *v.* 20.)—*They found fault.*] Εμεμψαντο. *Rom.* ix. 19. *Heb.* viii. 8. Not elsewhere N. T.

V. 3, 4. (*Note, Matt.* xv. 1, 2.) This evangelist gives a more particular account of these traditional washings, than Matthew did.—The Pharisees and other Jews used not to eat, except " they washed their hands *oft*," or *diligently*, being afraid of having inadvertently contracted defilement. When they returned from the markets, or places of publick resort, they would not eat, except they washed, or were *baptized;* and " they had received," and very tenaciously held, many such things, as " the wash-" ing," or *baptisms,* " of cups, pots," and even of their " tables," or rather *beds*, the couches on which they reclined to meat. If we suppose, that they *always* bathed the whole body, after they returned from the markets, which is not very probable; we cannot conceive that they plunged their couches in water also. The Pharisees blamed Christ's disciples for " eating with unwashen hands;" and not for not immersing their bodies in water : so it seems undeniable, that by the words *baptize* and *baptisms,* a partial application of water was intended, in this, as well as in several other places. (*Notes, Luke* xi. 37, 38. *Heb.* ix. 8—10.)—' A man shall wash his hands in the morning, ' so that it shall suffice him for the whole day; and he shall ' not need to wash his hands as oft as he eats; which ' holds if he do not avert his mind any other way; (that is, ' go abroad, or meddle with business, or go to the mar-' ket, &c.) but if he do so, he is bound to wash his hands ' as oft as there is need of washing.' *Maimonides* in Hammond. This washing is here called *being baptized;* not the hands being baptized, but the persons being baptized. —It is intimated here, that these observances were not peculiar to the Pharisees, but general among the Jews, through the influence of the scribes and elders : and this shews that the conduct of our Lord and his disciples, in this protest, was very marked and pointed. The rites of the ceremonial law they strictly observed; and paid the required tribute, lest they should give offence : (*Notes, Matt.* xvii. 24—27. xxiii. 1—4 :) but as the traditions of the elders undermined the authority of the divine law; our Lord himself openly refused to comply with them, and taught his disciples to do the same. (*Note, Matt.* xv. 3—6.) *Oft.* (3) " Diligently." " With the fist. Up to the " elbow." *Marg.* Πυγμη. *Pugnus, ... manus in pugnum complicata.* ' All interpretations imply diligent and ' accurate care in washing.' *Leigh.* Here only N. T. *Ex.* xxi. 18. *Sept.—Except they wash.* (4) Εαν μη βαπτισωνται. See on *Matt.* iii. 6.—*The washing.*] Βαπτισμις. 8. *Heb.* vi. 2. ix. 10. Βαπλισμα. *Matt.* iii. 7. xx. 22, 23. —*Pots.*] *Marg.* Εστων. 8. Not elsewhere N. T.—*Tables.*] " Beds." *Marg.* Κλινων. *Matt.* ix. 2. 6. *et al.*

V. 5—7. *Marg. Ref.—Notes, Is.* xxix. 13—16. *Matt.* xv. 7—9.

V. 8. *Cups.*] If made of metals; for earthen vessels, if in any way they contracted defilement, must be broken. (*Lev.* xi. 33.)

V. 9. *Full well, &c.*] Do ye not act in a most becoming and pious manner, by thus preferring human traditions to God's commandments ? The guilt and folly of the scribes and Pharisees are exposed by an ironical commendation. (*Note,* 1 *Kings* xviii. 27—29.)—Καλως. 6. 37. *Matt.* xv. 7. *John* viii. 48.—*Reject.*] " Frustrate." *Marg.* Αθετειτε. (Εx α et τιθημι, *pono.*) *Ye put away,* that is, *contemptuously. Luke* vii. 30. x. 16. *John* xii. 48. 1 *Cor.* i. 19. *Gal.* ii. 21. iii. 15. *Heb.* x. 28.

V. 10. *Marg. Ref.—Notes, Ex.* xxi. 15—17. *Lev.* xx. 9. —*Die the death.*] Θανατω τελευτατω. *Let him die by death. Ex.* xxi. 17. *Sept.* A Hebraism. ' Without hope of escaping.'

V. 11, 12. (*Marg. Ref.—Note, Matt.* xv. 3—6.) Corban is a Hebrew word, very frequently used in the Old Testament, for different kinds of sacred oblations.—Some

13 Making ⁴ the word of God of none effect through your tradition, which ye have delivered: and many ⁶ such like things do ye.

14 ¶ And ⁶ when he had called all the people *unto him*, he said unto them, Hearken unto me every one *of you*, and understand:

15 There is ⁶ nothing from without a man, that entering into him can defile him: ⁶ but the things which come out of him, those are they that defile the man.

16 If ⁶ any man have ears to hear, let him hear.

17 And ⁷ when he was entered into the house from the people, his disciples asked him concerning the parable.

18 And he saith unto them, ⁶ Are ye so without understanding also ? Do ye not perceive that whatsoever thing from without entereth into the man, *it* cannot defile him:

19 Because ⁶ it entereth not into his heart, but into the belly, and goeth out into the draught, purging all meats ?

20 And he said, ⁶ That which cometh out of the man, that defileth the man.

21 For from within, ⁶ out of the heart of men, proceed ⁴ evil thoughts, adulteries, fornications, murders,

22 Thefts, covetousness, wickedness, deceit, lasciviousness, ⁶ an evil eye, blasphemy, ⁶ pride, ⁶ foolishness :

23 All these evil things come from within, and ⁶ defile the man.

24 ¶ And ⁶ from thence he arose, and went into the borders of ⁶ Tyre and Sidon, and entered into an house, ⁶ and would have no man know *it :* but he could not be hid.

25 For ⁶ a *certain* woman, ⁶ whose young daughter had an unclean spirit, heard of him, and came and ⁶ fell at ⁶ his feet:

26 The woman was a ⁶ Greek, ⁶ a Syrophenician by nation; and she besought him that he would cast forth the devil out of her daughter.

---

have supposed, that this might be especially meant of a rash vow made by a man in a passion, that he would do nothing more for his parents, but would rather give all that he could spare to the treasury of the temple ; which would be equivalent to cursing them : yet the blind Pharisees had determined that even such a vow ought to be religiously observed ! The words however seem to mean generally, that any man's vow, to devote his substance, or what could be spared, to the Corban, was supposed not only to excuse him from relieving his parents, but to subject him to a dreadful curse, if he did ; to avoid which, he would rather venture on the consequence of breaking the commandment of God. This makes the contrast very striking.

V. 13. *Notes, Is.* viii. 20. *Jer.* viii. 8, 9. *Hos.* viii. 11, 12. *Matt.* v. 17—20. *Rom.* iii. 29—31.—*Many such*, &c.] ' Vows take place even in things commanded by the law, ' as well as in things indifferent : and then any one is so ' bound by them, that he cannot, without great sin, do that ' which is commanded.' *Jewish Canon in Pocock.*

Making ... of none effect.] Ακυρωντες. *Matt.* xv. 6. *Gal.* iii. 17.

V. 14—21. *Marg. Ref.—Notes, Matt.* xv. 10—20.—*Are ye*, &c. (18) *Note*, viii. 17—21.—*Evil thoughts.* (21) Διαλογισμοι πονηροι. *Matt.* xv. 19. *Luke* ii. 35. v. 22. xxiv. 38. *Rom.* i. 21. *Jam.* ii. 4. " Evil thoughts," or *reasonings*, or *imaginations*, spring from the corrupt state of the heart. (*Marg. Ref.* d.—*Notes, Gen.* vi. 5. *Is.* lix. 3—8. *Jer.* iv. 14. *Rom.* i. 21—23. 2 *Cor.* x. 1—6, v. 5.)

V. 22. *Marg. Ref. Covetousness.*] Πλεονεξιαι. (Εx πλεον, *plus*, et εχω, *habeo*.) *Luke* xii. 15. *Rom.* i. 29, 2 *Cor.* ix. 5.

Eph. iv. 19. v. 3. *Col.* iii. 5. 1 *Thes.* ii. 5. 2 *Pet.* ii. 3. 14. (*Note, Eph.* v. 3, 4.) The connexion of this word, with πλεονεξ, *thefts*, both plural, fixes its meaning, and shews that covetousness, in all its forms, makes way for varied kinds of dishonesty.—*Wickedness.*] Πονηριαι, *wickednesses. Mark* xxii. 18. *Rom.* i. 29. *Inveteratam malitiam declarat omnium scelerum matrem.* Beza.—*An evil eye.*] Οφθαλμος πονηρος, a malignant, grudging, envious disposition, often expressed by the eye. (*Marg. Ref.* e.—*Notes, Gen.* xxxi. 1—3. *Matt.* xx. 1—16, *v.* 15.)—*Lasciviousness.*] Ασελγεια. *Rom.* xiii. 13. 2 *Cor.* xii. 21. *Gal.* v. 19. *Eph.* iv. 19. 1 *Pet.* iv. 3. 2 *Pet.* ii. 7. 18. *Jude* 4. *Petulantia, protervia, ... effrænata quædam peccandi libido.* In *Leigh.*—*Wantonness, lasciviousness.'—Pride.*] Υπερηφανια. Here only N. T. Υπερηφανος. *Luke* i. 51. *Rom.* i. 30. *Jam.* iv. 6. (Ex ὑπερ et φαινομαι.) ' He thinks himself above that which he is.' *Leigh. Note, Rom.* xii. 3—5.—*Foolishness.*] Αφροσυνη. 2 *Cor.* xi. 1. 17. 21.—Αφρων. *Luke* xi. 40. (Ex α priv. et φρην, *mens.*) Some understand this of vain glorious boasting ; but whatever evil propensity leads men to act in a foolish, rash, infatuated manner, as if deprived of reason, may be intended. Even excess in eating and drinking by which indeed a man is defiled with what goeth in at his mouth, must be considered as springing from the sensuality of his heart, and its immoderate hankering after animal indulgence. (*Note, Matt.* xv. 10, 11.)

V. 24—30. (*Marg. Ref.—Notes, Matt.* xv. 21—28.) This woman, of Canaan's devoted race, seems to have had no other instruction, than that derived from reading the scriptures of the Old Testament alone. Yet, having heard concerning the miracles and doctrine of Jesus; (iii. 8.

2 κ 7

27 But Jesus said unto her, 'Let the children first be filled: for it is not meet to take the children's bread, and to cast it unto the dogs.

28 And she answered and said unto him, Yes, Lord: 'yet the dogs under the table eat of the children's crumbs.

29 And he said unto her, 'For this saying go thy way; the devil is gone out of thy daughter.

30 And when 'she was come to her house, she found the devil gone out, and her daughter laid upon the bed.

31 ¶ And again, departing "from the coasts of Tyre and Sidon, he came unto the sea of Galilee, through the midst of the coasts of "Decapolis.

32 And they 'bring unto him one that was deaf, and had an impediment in his speech; and they beseech him to put his hand upon him.

33 And 'he took him aside from the multitude, and put his fingers into his ears, and he spit, and touched his tongue;

34 And 'looking up to heaven, 'he sighed, and saith unto him, 'Ephphatha, that is, 'Be opened.

35 And 'straightway his ears were opened, and the string of his tongue was loosed, and he spake plain.

36 And 'he charged them that they should tell no man: but the more he charged them, so much the more great deal they published it,

37 And.' were beyond measure astonished, saying, 'He hath done all things well: 'he maketh both the deaf to hear, and the dumb to speak.

Matt. iv. 24 ;) and doubtless having compared what she heard with the prophecies of the Messiah, she assuredly knew that he was the. Messiah; and without hesitation addressed him in that character !—She was not only a true, but a most eminent believer.—What an inducement to disperse the Bible !

Borders. (24) Μεθορια. (Εχ μετα et ὁρια, *terminus, fines.*) Here only N. T.—*Would have,* &c.] ' Lest he should ' seem industriously to resort to, and converse with hea- ' thens, neglecting the Jews.' *Grotius.—Greek.* (26) "Gen- " tile." *Marg.* Ἑλληνις. *Acts* xvii. 12. *Fem.* of ἱλλην, *Græcus.* Not a full proselyte to the religion of Israel, and therefore regarded as a Gentile.—*Syro-phenician.*] That part of Phe- nicia, which the Syrians had conquered, was called Syro- phenicia.—*Yes.* (28) Ναι. It is rendered in Matthew *Truth :* "Truth, Lord."—It is sometimes a form of assenting, and sometimes of intreating. *Philem.* 20.—' That which the ' proud to reject, that do the humble, as it were, wring ' out.' *Beza.*

V. 31—36. This miracle is no where else recorded. The dispossessed demoniack had declared, through the re- gion of Decapolis, " what great things Jesus had done for " him." (v. 20.) Some persons indeed, long before, at- tended on Christ from that country : (*Matt.* iv. 25 :) but it is probable, that the man's testimony had considerable effect in disposing the people to regard Jesus with greater reverence and expectation, when he went again into those parts. (*Note,* v. 14—20.) They immediately therefore brought unto him a man, who was deaf, and could scarcely speak, intreating him to cure him by laying his hand upon him, as he frequently did: (v. 23. *Note, 2 Kings* v. 9— 12, v. 11 :) but he was pleased on this occasion to vary his method, and to shew that he was not confined to any one. (*Note,* viii. 22—26.) He took the man aside, put his fingers in his ears, and, spitting, touched his tongue. Then " looking up to heaven," to denote that he acted by a divine power, in perfect union with the Father, and " sighing," as sympathizing with the man in misery, and

in a view of the calamities to which men are exposed by sin ; (*Notes, John* xi. 33—46, *vv.* 33. 35. 38. 41,) he said with authority, " Be opened ;" and an immediate cure ensued, to the exceeding great astonishment of the peo- ple, who acknowledged the power, goodness, and excel- lency of his works, in this and other instances. And, though he charged them, as usual, not to publish the miracle, this only proved an occasion to them the more to speak of it. They probably deemed it improper, that his wonderful works should be concealed, through his care in avoiding ostentation. (*Notes, Matt.* ix. 30, 31.)

Had an impediment in his speech. (32) Μογιλαλον. (Εχ μογις, *vix, Luke* ix. 39, et λαλεω, *loquor.*) Here only N. T. —*Is.* xxxv. 6. *Sept.*—*Ephphatha.* (34) This is Syriack, but it varies little from the Hebrew word of the same sig- nification.—*Be opened.*] Διανοιχθητι. 25. *Luke* ii. 23. xxiv. 31, 32. 45. *Acts* xvi. 14. xvii. 3. (Εχ δια, et ανοιγω, *aperio.*) V. 37. (*Note,* 9.) This unreserved commendation im- plied that Jesus was the predicted Messiah, and that the Pharisees and Scribes were highly criminal in opposing him.

PRACTICAL OBSERVATIONS.

V. 1—23.

Those " clean hands and that pure heart," which Christ requires and bestows, are very different from the external decency, and superstitious forms and appearances of sanc- tity, which have distinguished Pharisees in every age. (*Notes, Matt.* v. 8. 2 *Cor.* vii. 1. *Jam.* iv. 7—10.) Their outward purifications and ceremonies can neither purge the conscience from guilt, nor the affections from avarice, ambition, sensuality, or hypocrisy: and if our hearts be purified by faith and grace, we need no human inventions in accession, but " all things will be made clean unto us." Yet formalists commonly find fault with true disciples, for not complying with their superstitions ; and plead his au- thority for them, in order to bear down his cause and per- secute his people !—Men may be very zealous for various plausible and burdensome observances, and exact in at-

2 к 8

CHAP. VIII.

Jesus miraculously feeds the multitudes, 1—9; refuses the Pharisees a sign, 10—13; warns the disciples against their leaven, and that of Herod; and reproves them for dulness of understanding, 14—21; gives sight to a blind man at Bethsaida, 22—26; approves Peter's confession, predicts his own sufferings, and rebukes Peter for objecting to them, 27—33; and teaches self-denial and a willingness to suffer for his sake, 34—50.

 IN those days, ^a the multitude being very great, and having nothing to eat, Jesus called his disciples *unto him*, and saith unto them,

2 I have ^b compassion on the multitude, because they have now been with me three days, ^c and have nothing to eat:

side notes:
a Matt. xv. 32.
b L. 4). v. 19. vi. 34. ix. 22. Ps. viii. lx. Mic. vii.
19. Matt. ix. 36. xiv. 14. xx. 34. Luke vii. 13. xv. 20. Heb. ii. 17. iv. 15.
c Matt. iv. 2—4. vi. 21, 25. John iv. 6—8. 30—34.

3 And if I send them away fasting to their own houses, ^d they will faint by the way; for divers of them came from far.

4 And his disciples answered him, ^e From whence can a man satisfy these men with bread here in the wilderness?

5 And he asked them, ^f How many loaves have ye? And they said, Seven.

6 And he commanded the people ^g to sit down on the ground: and he took the seven loaves, ^h and gave thanks, and brake, and gave to his disciples to set before *them*; and they did set *them* before the people.

7 And they had a few small ⁱ fishes: and he blessed, and commanded to set them also before *them*.

8 So they did eat, ^k and were filled:

side notes right column:
d Judg. viii. 4—6. 1 Sam. xiv. 28—31. xxx. 10—12. Is. xl. 31.
e vi. 52. Num. xl. 21—23. 2 Kings iv. 43—44. vii. 2. P . lxxviii. 19, 20. Matt. xv. 33. John vi. 7—9.
f vi. 38. Matt. xiv. 15—17. xv. 34.
g xiv. 18, 19. xv. 35, 36. Luke ix. 14, 15. xii. 37.
h John ii. 5. vi. 10. vi.41—44. 1 Sam. ix. 13. Matt. xv. 36. xxvi. 26. Luke xxii. 19. John xxi. 13. Rom. xiv. 6. 1 Cor. x. 30, 31. Col. iii. 17. 1 Tim. iv. 3—5.
i Luke xxiv. 41, 42. John xxi. 8, 9.
k Ib. 30. Ps. cvii. 8, 9. cxlv. 16. Matt. xxvi. 26. Luke i. 53. John vi. 11—13. 27 Rev. vii. 16, 17.

---

tending to them; yet remain strangers to true religion, enemies of Christ, and hypocritical worshippers. This must be the case of those zealots, of every denomination, who " reject the commandments of God," and the doctrines of the gospel, " that they may keep their own tradi- " tions:" and all vows or engagements must be antichristian and impious, which allow children to dishonour or neglect their parents; or which authorize men to violate the important and immutable obligations of justice, mercy, and truth. A spiritual understanding of the holy law of God, and of the evil of sin; an acquaintance with the depravity of the human heart, and the defilement, which thence flows into the conduct and conversation; and a discernment of the scriptural way of cleansing a guilty conscience and a polluted heart, will effectually wean a man from these human inventions.—The enlightened Christian will seek the grace of the Holy Spirit, to enable him to repress the evil imaginations and affections of his heart: as he is aware that the very " thought of wicked- " ness is sin;" he will endeavour to mortify and purge out the sensual, malicious, unjust, covetous, envious, proud, and ambitious desires of his heart. He will seek deliverance from all enmity and hard thoughts of God; from all ingratitude, selfishness, and inordinate love even of lawful things. He will pray to be cleansed from every inclination, which is inconsistent with piety, equity, sincerity, purity, and charity: and he will know, that if he be indeed purified from these, and such like inward evils, " which defile the man," he is certainly made partaker of that " holiness, without which no man shall see the " Lord;" and his grand object will then be, to increase more and more in faith and grace, from day to day.

V. 24—37.

While Pharisees are left with decided disapprobation, the blessed Saviour manifests his compassion and love to humble sinners of the Gentiles; and all, who allow themselves to be " unworthy of the crumbs that fall from his table," may confidently call upon him for the food of his beloved

children. Still he goes about to every place, to seek and save the lost: and neither the obscurity of his ministers, nor the opposition of his enemies, can prevent the discovery of his glory and grace. In like manner, it is our business to persevere in doing good, privately and in an unambitious manner; and " our labour of love" will not always be hid or misrepresented.—When sinners apply to Christ, in behalf of themselves and those who are dear to them, earnestly desiring deliverance by him from the oppression of the devil; they may have their faith and humility tried by delays and frowns, and be ready to conclude that the blessings are reserved for others, and will not be vouchsafed to them: but patient and humble waiting on Christ, by faith and prayer, will certainly prevail; nor shall any have cause to say, they have sought his face in vain. Thus one after another obtains the blessing, and declares the Saviour's love to others; and they too seek to him, in their trouble and distress. And though we find a great variety in the cases, the reception, and the manner of relief, of those who came to him, when he was here below; yet, in one way or other, they all obtained the help which they sought. Thus it still is, in the grand concerns of our souls: the compassionate Saviour still opens the deaf ear, and looses the stammering tongue: and when he speaks with divine authority, he opens the understanding and the heart to receive instruction, and the lips to shew forth his praise. (*Notes, Is. xxxv. 5—7. John ix. 4—7.*) Whilst we then admire the grace and excellency of his character, and the power of his works; let us proclaim to all around us, that " he hath done all things " well; he maketh both the deaf to hear, and the dumb " to speak."

NOTES.

CHAP. VIII. V. 1—9. *Marg. Ref.—Notes, Matt.* xv. 31—38.—*Faint, &c.* (3) ' Had there not been such dan- ' ger, Christ had not wrought this miracle; that the people ' might not follow him for loaves: and having done this, ' he straightway leaves them (10), that he might avoid

2 L

and they took up of the broken *meat* that was left seven baskets.

9 And they that had eaten were about four thousand: and he sent them away.

10 ¶ And [1] straightway he entered into a ship with his disciples, and came into the parts of Dalmanutha.

11 And the [m] Pharisees came forth, and began to question with him, [n] seeking of him a sign from heaven, [o] tempting him.

12 And [p] he sighed deeply in his spirit, and saith, [q] Why doth this generation seek after a sign? Verily I say unto you, [r] There shall no sign be given unto this generation.

13 And [s] he left them, and entering into the ship again departed to the other side.

14 ¶ Now the disciples [t] had forgotten to take bread, neither had they in the ship with them more than one loaf.

15 And [u] he charged them, saying, [x] Take heed, beware of [y] the leaven of the Pharisees, and *of* the leaven [z] of Herod.

Side references (left column):
Matt. xv. 39.
[m] ib. 16. vii. 1, 2.
Matt. xii. 38.
xvi. 1—4. xiv. 3.
xvi. 23. xxii. 15.
16. 23. 34. 55.
Luke xi. 53, 54.
John vii. 48.
[n] Luke xi. 16. xii.
54—57. John iv.
48. vi. 30. 1 Cor.
i. 22, 23.
[o] xii. 15. Ex. xvii.
2, 7. Deut. vi.
16. Mal. iii. 15.
Luke x. 25. Acts
v. 9. 1 Cor. x. 9.
[p] iii. 5. iii. 34. ix.
19. ix. 41.
John xi. 33—38.
[q] vi. 6. Luke xvi.
29—31. John
37—43.
[r] Matt. xii. 39, 40.
xvi. 4. Luke xi.
29, 30.
[s] Ps. lxxxi.12. Jer.
xxiii. 33. Hos.iv.
17. ix. 12. Zech.
xi. 8, 9. Matt.vii.
6. xv. 14. Luke
viii. 37. John
viii. 21. xii. 36.
Acts xiii. 45, 46.
xviii. 6.
[t] Matt. xvi. 5.
[u] Num. xxvii. 19
—23. 1 Chr.
xxviii. 9. 10. 20.
1 Tim. v. 21. vi.
13. 2 Tim. i. 14.
[x] Matt. xvi. 6. 11,
12. Luke xii. 1.
[y] Ex. xii. 18—20.
v. 6—8.
Lev. ii. 11. 1 Cor.
v. 6—8.
[z] iii. 6. Matt.
xxii. 15—18.

16 And they [a] reasoned among themselves, saying, It is because we have [b] no bread.

17 And when Jesus [b] knew *it*, he saith unto them, Why reason ye because ye have no bread? [c] perceive ye not yet, neither understand? have ye your heart yet hardened?

18 Having eyes, [d] see ye not? and having ears, hear ye not? and do ye not remember?

19 When I brake [e] the five loaves among five thousand, how many baskets full of fragments took ye up? They say unto him, Twelve.

20 And when [f] the seven among four thousand, how many baskets full of fragments took ye up? And they said, Seven.

21 And he said unto them, [g] How is it that ye do not understand?

22 ¶ And he cometh to [h] Bethsaida; and [i] they bring a blind man unto him, and besought him [k] to touch him.

23 And he took the blind man [l] by the hand, and led him [m] out of the town; and when he had [n] spit on his

Side references (right column):
[a] Matt. xvi. 7, 8.
Luke ix. 46. xxiv.
[b] ii. 8. John ii. 24,
25. xvi. 30. xxi.
17. Heb. iv. 12,
13. Rev. ii. 23.
[c] vi. 52. xvi. 14.
Is. xliii. 17.
Matt. xv.17. xvi.
8, 9. Luke xxiv.
25. Heb. v. H,
12.
[d] iv. 12. Deut.
xxix. 4. Ps. lxix.
23. cxv. 5—8. Is.
vi. 9, 10. xlii. 18
—20. xliv. 18.
Jer. v. 21. Matt.
xiii. 14, 15. John
xii. 40. Acts
xxviii. 26, 27.
Rom. xi. 8.
[e] vi. 38—44. Matt.
xiv.17—21.Luke
ix. 12—17. John
vi. 5—13.
[f] 1—9. Matt. xv.
34—38.
[g] 12. vi. 52. ix. 19.
Ps. xciv.8. Matt.
xvi. 11, 12. John
xiv. 9. 1 Cor. xi.
9. xv. 34.
[h] vi. 45. Matt. xi.
21. Luke ix. 10.
Luke ix. 1. Luke i. 44.
xii. 21.
[i] ii. 3. vi. 55, 56.
v. 27—29. Matt.
viii. 3. 15. ix. 29.
[k] -1 Is. li. 18. Jer.
xxxi.32.Acts ix.
8. Heb. vii. 9.
xviii. 33. Is. xlii.
2.
[m] John ix. 6, 7.
Rev. iii. 18.

---

[f] their attempts to make him a king.' *Theophylact,* quoted by *Whitby.* (*Notes,* vi. 30—46. *Matt.* xiv. 15—24. *John* vi. 1—21.)

Bread. (4) ' This, among the Hebrews, frequently signifies all kinds of food: but here it must be understood ' literally; ... as if the disciples had said; Not even bread ' alone, or any kind of food, can in this place be procured ' to satisfy so large a multitude.' *Beza.*—Our Lord's blessing the fishes, before he ordered them to be set before the company, is here mentioned separately; which shews the importance attached by the evangelist to this blessing.— *About four thousand.* (9) " Four thousand men besides " women and children," *Matt.* xv. 38.

V. 10—13. *Marg. Ref.—Notes, Matt.* xii. 38—40. xv. 39. xvi. 1—4. *John* vi. 30—35.—*Sighed deeply.* (12) *Αναστεναξας.* Here only N. T. *Alte ingemiscens.* (Εξ ανα et στεναζω, *suspiro.*) This was a strong expression of our Lord's holy indignation against the obstinate unbelief and hypocrisy of the Pharisees; as well as of his compassionate concern at seeing them, in this manner, bent on their own destruction, and deceiving the souls of the people. (*Notes,* iii. 1— 5, *v.* 5. *John* xi. 33—40.)—He seems to have left Dalmanutha, without either preaching, or working miracles: for it is probable, that the people in general were greatly prejudiced against him by their false teachers.

V. 14—16. (*Marg. Ref.—Note, Matt.* xvi. 5—12.) ' We must especially beware of them, who corrupt the ' word of God, of what degree soever they be, either in ' the church or the community.' *Beza.* (*Notes, Luke* xii. 1—7. 1 *Cor.* v. 6—8.)

Of Herod. (15) " Of the Sadducees," *Matt.* xvi. 6. 11, 12.—*Note, Matt.* xxii. 15—22.

V. 17—21. ' They who have their minds fixed on ' earthly things, are utterly blind as to heavenly things; ' though they be never so plainly set forth to them.' *Beza.* —Even the disciples were in some degree infected with the same carnal prejudices, which had entirely occupied the minds of the Pharisees and other Jews. Our Lord therefore " rebuked them sharply, that they might be " sound in the faith." He intimated, that their dulness of understanding was marvellous and inexcusable, when all their advantages were considered. Were *their* hearts also so hard and *their* eyes so blind, that his continued instructions could not convince them of his purpose to raise their minds to spiritual and eternal objects, and guard them against false doctrines; and not to occupy them with minute outward distinctions and peculiarities? And could *they* be so unbelieving, as to doubt his power to feed them, after the astonishing miracles which they had so lately witnessed? (*Marg. Ref.—Notes,* 1—9. 32—37, *v.* 33. vi. 30 —46. *Matt.* xiii. 14, 15. xv. 32—38. xvi. 5—12. 21—23. *Rom.* vii. 13, 14. 1 *Cor.* iii. 1—3.)

Hardened. (17) Πεπωρωμενην. See on vi. 52.

V. 22—26. St. Mark alone records this miracle.—This blind man was conducted by his friends to Jesus, when he was come to Bethsaida; yet he seems not to have been an inhabitant of that city. Our Lord, however, was pleased to restore him to sight in an unusual method; perhaps, in order gradually to increase his faith, and to raise his expectation: but it also illustrated the manner, in which he

eyes, and put his hands upon him, he asked him if he saw ought.
24 And he looked up and said, [o] I see men, as trees, walking.
25 After that, he put *his* hands again upon his eyes, and made him look up: and he was restored, [p] and saw every man clearly.
26 And he sent him away to his house, saying, [q] Neither go into the town, nor tell *it* to any in the town.
27 ¶ And Jesus went out, and his disciples, into [r] the towns of Cesarea Philippi: [s] and by the way he asked his disciples, saying unto them, Whom do men say that I am?
28 And they answered, [t] John the Baptist: but some *say* [u] Elias; and others, One of the prophets.
29 And he saith unto them, [x] But whom say ye that I am? And Peter answereth and saith unto him, [y] Thou art the Christ.
30 And [z] he charged them that they should tell no man of him.
31 ¶ And [a] he began to teach them, that the Son of man must suffer many things, and be [b] rejected of the elders, and *of* the chief priests, and scribes, and be killed; [c] and after three days rise again.
32 And he spake that saying [d] openly. And [e] Peter took him, and began to rebuke him.
33 But when he had [f] turned about, and looked on his disciples, [g] he rebuked Peter, saying, [h] Get thee behind

o Judg. ix. 36. Is. xxix. 18. xxxii. 3. 1 Cor. xiii. 9. 11, 12.
p Prov. iv. 18. Matt. xiii. 12. Phil. i. 6. 2 Pet. iii. 18.
q v. 43. vii. 36. Matt. viii. 4. ix. 30. xii. 16.
r Matt. xvi. 13.
s Luke ix. 18, 19.
t vi. 14—16. Matt. xiv. 2. xvi. 14. Luke ix. 7—9.
u ix. 11—13. Mal. iv. 5. *Elijah*. John i. 21.
x iv. 11. Matt. xvi. 15. Luke ix. 20. 1 Pet. ii. 7.
y Matt. xvi. 16. John i. 41. 49. iv. 42. vi. 69. xi. 27. Acts viii. 37. ix. 20. 1 John iv. 15. v. 1.
z 26. vii. 36. ix. 9. Luke ix. 21, 22.
a ix. 31, 32. x. 33, 34. Matt. xvi. 21. xvii. 22, 23. xx. 17—19. Luke ix. 22. xviii. 31—34. xxiv. 6, 7. 26. 44.
b xii. 10. 1 Sam. viii. 7. x. 19. Ps. cxviii. 22. Is. liii. 3. Matt. xxi. 42. Luke xvii. 25. John xii. 48. Acts iii. 13—15 vii. 35. 51, 52.
c Hos. vi. 2. Jon. i. 17. Matt. xii. 40. John ii. 19. 1 Cor. xv. 4.
d John xvi. 25. 29.
e iv. 38. Matt. xvi. 22. Luke x. 40. John xiii. 6—8.
f iii. 5. 34. Luke xxii. 61.
g Lev. xix. 17. 2 Sam. xix. 22. Ps. cxli. 5. Prov. ix. 8, 9. Matt. xvi. 23. Luke ix. 55. 1 Tim. v. 20. Tit. i. 13. Rev. iii. 19.
h Gen. iii. 4—6. Job ii. 10. Matt. iv. 10. Luke iv. 8.

often enlightens the souls of men. (*Notes*, vii. 31—36. *Is.* xlii. 13—17, *v.* 16. *John* ix 4—7.) "He took the blind man "by the hand, and led him out of the town;" not only that he might work the miracle in a more private manner, but probably to mark his disapprobation of the unbelief and wickedness of the inhabitants. (*Note*, *Matt.* xi. 20—24.) He then spat on his eyes, and laid his hands on him; (as intimating that the power came from him, whatever external sign was used;) and enquired, if he could see any thing: and the man answered, that "he saw men, as trees, "walking." He could see the people walking at a distance, and their motion satisfied him that they were men; or else he would not have been able to distinguish them from the trees, which he dimly saw at the same time. "I "see men walking, as trees." Our Lord, having again laid his hands upon his eyes, and made him look up, his sight was completely restored: and he then ordered him to return home, and not enter into Bethsaida, or tell any one there of his being restored; as they were unworthy to receive any more attestations of divine power and goodness, having already withstood so many. (*Marg. Ref.*)

Eyes. (23) Ομματα. Here only N. T. Ab οπτομαι, *video.* —*He looked up.* (24) Αναβλεψας. 25. *Matt.* xi. 5. *Luke* vii. 22. The verb is translated in several places, "he received "sight:" yet it is evident, that it is here rendered properly. (Comp. *Luke* xviii. 43. with *Luke* xxi. 1. Gr.)

V. 27—30. (*Notes*, *Matt.* xvi. 13—20.) 'As the an'cients, with general consent, record that this history was 'dictated by the apostle Peter to Mark; who can believe 'that either Peter, or Mark, would have omitted that ex'pression "Thou art Peter, &c." if they had thought 'that the foundation of the Christian church was placed 'in these words? ...Many praise Christ, who yet rob him 'of his true honour.' *Beza.*—*Charged*, &c. (30) The premature and unreserved avowal of this truth must, without perpetual miracles, have excited the ill-judging multitude to such measures, as would have given the scribes and priests an occasion against Jesus, and even have rendered the Romans jealous of his popularity. It was therefore highly proper, that he should in the most peremptory manner, forbid the disciples to declare openly that he was the Messiah. Let the people gradually collect it, by comparing his miracles and doctrine with the scriptures; as they became better acquainted with the true nature of the Messiah's kingdom and salvation. (*Notes*, *Matt.* xvi. 20. *John* iv. 25, 26.)

The towns, &c. (27) Τας κωμας. Τα μερη, "the parts," *Matt.* xvi. 13.—*Charged*, (30) Επετιμησεν. 32, 33. i. 25. iii. 12. iv. 39. *Matt.* viii. 26. *Luke* ix. 21. *Charged with rebukes.* Διεστειλατο. *Matt.* xvi. 20.

V. 31. *Marg. Ref.*—*Note*, *Matt.* xvi. 21—23, *v.* 21. —*After three days.*] '1. It is ten times expressly said, 'that our Lord rose, or was to rise, "again *the third day*:" '(*Matt.* xvi. 21. xvii. 23. xx. 19. *Mark* ix. 31. x. 34. *Luke* 'ix. 22. xviii. 33. xxiv. 7. 46. *Acts* x. 40:) and so the ex'pression, which is most used, both in our Lord's predic'tions before his death, and in his and his apostles' lan'guage after his resurrection, being this, ...these other 'forms of speech, which are but once or twice found in 'scripture, must be interpreted to accord with it. ...2. Ac'cording to the language both of the Hebrew and the 'Greek, that is said to be done after so many days, months, 'or years, which is done in the last of them. ...(*Deut.* 'xiv. 28. xv. 1. xxvi. 12. xxxi. 10. 2 *Chr.* x. 5. 12.) ... '"After three days they found him in the temple;" (*Luke* 'ii. 46;) that is, on the third day. ...3. The Jews...un'derstood "after three days" to signify no more than *on* '*the third day.* ...For, having told Pilate, that Christ had 'said, "after three days I will rise again;" they desire 'only that a watch might be kept... "till the third day." *Whitby.* (*Matt.* xxvii. 63, 64.)

Be rejected.] Αποδοκιμασθηναι. *Reprobari.* xii. 10. *Matt.* xxi. 42. *Luke* ix. 22. Ex απο et δοκιμαζω, *probo, discerno.*— Δοκιμος. *Rom.* xiv. 18.—Αδοκιμος. 1 *Cor.* ix. 27.

V. 32—37. *Marg. Ref.*—*Notes*, *Matt.* xvi. 21—28. *Luke* ix. 18—27.—*Satan.* (33) 'Jesus calls Peter, Sa'tan, as savouring of the things of Satan; it being only 'Satan, who would not that our Lord should suffer for

ⁱ Matt. vi. 31, 32. Rom. viii. 5—8. me, Satan: for thou ⁱ savourest not the things that be of God, but the things that be of men.

Phil. iii. 19. ᵍGrᵌ Jam. iii. 15—18. ⁱ Pet.

ᵏ vi. 14. Luke ix. 34 And when he had ᵏ called the people *unto him*, with his disciples also,

ⁱ ix. 43—48. Matt. x. 29, 30. xii. 13, 14. xvi. 24 Luke xiii. 24. xiv. 27. he said unto them, ˡ Whosoever will come after me, let him deny himself,

ⁱⁱ Rom. xv. —3. 1 Cor. viii. 13. ix. 19. Phil. iii. 7, 8. Tit. ii. 12. and ᵐ take up his cross, and ⁿ follow me.

ⁿ x. 21. Matt. x. 38. xxvii. 32. John xix. 17. Acts xiv. 22. Rom. vi. 6. viii. 17. 1 Cor. iv. 9—13. xv. 31. Gal. ii. 20. v. 24. vi. 14. 35 For whosoever ⁿ will save his life shall lose it; but whosoever shall lose his life ᵖ for my sake and 2 Tim. iii. 11. 1 Pet. iv. 1 13. Rev. ii. 10. Luke xiv. 26. xvii. 22. John x. 27. xiii. 36, 37. xxi. 19, 20. Heb. xii. 13. 2 Pet. i. 14. 1 John iii. 16. the gospel's, the same shall save it.

ᵒ Eath. iv. 11—16. Jer. xxvi. 20—24. Matt. x. 39. xvi. 25. Luke ix. 24. xvii. 33. John xii. 25, 26. Acts xx. 24. xxi. 13. 2 Tim. ii. 11—13. iv. 6—8. Heb. xi. 35. Rev. ii. 10. 11. vii. 14—17. xii. 11. p Matt. v. 10—12. x. 22. xix. 29. Luke vi. 22. 23. John xv. 20, 21. Acts ix. 16. 1 Cor. ix. 23. 2 Cor. xii. 10. 2 Tim. i. 8. 1 Pet. iv. 12—16. 36 For ᑫ what shall it ʳ profit a man, if he shall gain the whole world, and lose his own soul?

37 Or ˢ what shall a man give in exchange for his soul?

38 Whosoever therefore shall be ᵗ ashamed of me, and of my words, in this ᵘ adulterous and sinful generation, of him also shall ˣ the Son of man be ashamed, ʸ when he cometh in the glory of his Father, with the holy angels.

ᑫ Job ii. 4. Ps. xlix. 17—19. lxxiii. 18—20. Matt. iv. 8—10. xvi. 26. Luke i. 23. xii. 19, 20. xvi. —23. Phil. iii. 7—9. Rev. xviii. 7, 8. Job xxii. 2. Mal. iii. 14. Rom. vi. 21. Heb. xi. 24 —26. Jam. i. 9 —11. r Matt. x. 32, 38. Luke ix. 26. xii. 8, 9. Acts ix. 41. Rom. i. 16. Gal. vi. 14. 2 Tim. i. 8. 12. Heb. xi. 26. xii. 2, 3. xiii. 13. 1 John ii. 23. u Matt. xii. 39. xvi. 4. Jam. iv. 4. x xiv. 62. Dan. vii. 13. Matt. xvi. 27, 28. xxiv. 30. xxv. 31. xxvi. 64. John i. 51. y Deut. xxxiii. 2. Dan. vii. 10. Zech. xiv. 5. 1 Thes. i. 7, 8.' Jude 14, 15. b Matt. xiii. 41.

' the salvation of mankind.' *Theophylact*, quoted by *Whitby*.

Called. (34) The preceding discourse seems to have been delivered to the disciples in the absence of the multitude: but Christ, having an exhortation of universal interest to give, called to him the people, who were at some distance, that they also might hearken, and be instructed by it.

The gospel's sake. (35) This is not found in Matthew. He who loses his life for the sake of the true gospel of Christ, loses it " for Christ's sake:" but if he dies by adhering to " another gospel," the case is far different. It is then of no ordinary importance to determine what is the gospel of Christ, and what is " another gospel." (*Note*, Gal. i. 6—10.)—If, as some learned men think, the word (ψυχή) rendered " soul," (36, 37,) should be translated *life*; it must certainly be the office of the expositor, to shew, that the *life*, or *salvation*, of the soul is meant; else how can he, who " loses his life for Christ's sake," " save " his life ? " (*Note*, *John* xii. 23—26.)

V. 38. (*Notes*, *Is.* li. 7, 8. liii. 2, 3. *Matt.* v. 10—12. x. 32, 33. *Acts* v. 41, 42. 2 *Tim.* i. 6—8. 11, 12. *Heb.* xi. 24—26. xii. 2, 3. xiii. 9—14. 1 *Pet.* iv. 12—16.) That the fear of imprisonment or death should terrify others, as it did Peter, to deny Christ, could not be at all incredible: but that any should " be ashamed " of him, whom all angels worship, and in whom all the inhabitants of heaven glory, must before the event have appeared inconceivable; except to those who had a deep knowledge of human nature, and experience of the deceitfulness of their own hearts. Yet perhaps there is no sin, to which every convert to true Christianity is more powerfully tempted; and no temptation, which induces such large numbers to act, *habitually*, against the light and conviction of their own consciences, in order to escape the reproach and scorn of men, and often of their inferiors, dependents, and domestics! The propriety of this solemn warning is therefore manifest to all, who properly consider what passes under their own observation, in every rank and station in the community, nay even in the church, in countries professing Christianity. For a bold avowal of our dependence on Christ, our expectations from him, and our obligations and devotedness to him, in the language and spirit of the scripture, will not fail, in almost every circle, to expose us to scorn, and to the imputation

of folly or enthusiasm: and the fear lest the Saviour and Judge should at last be ashamed of us, is the proper preservative against yielding to this temptation, in all those who desire above all things " to have confidence, and not be " ashamed before him at his coming." (*Marg. Ref.*— 1 *John* ii. 28.)

Ashamed.] Επαισχυνθη. *Luke* ix. 26. *Rom.* i. 16. vi. 21. 2 *Tim.* i. 8. 12. 16. *Heb.* ii. 11. xi. 16.—*Adulterous.*] Μοιχαλιδι. See on *Matt.* xii. 39.

PRACTICAL OBSERVATIONS.

V. 1—21.

Our compassionate Lord sometimes requires his followers to endure hardship in attending on him; but he relieves them before they faint under their burdens: and we should copy his example, in noticing the difficulties and wants of those around us, that we may obviate or remove them. But his love as much excels ours, as his power and all-sufficiency exceed our weakness and indigence. He will feed his hungry disciples with suitable provision, but they have no reason to expect luxuries from him; for these are generally lavished on the servants of another master.— Yet many professed Christians excuse themselves, on account of their poverty, from relieving the distressed, who would think it a hardship to dine with Jesus and his company, on those provisions which he miraculously supplied! The lively Christian, however, while his soul is feasted with " the hidden manna," will eat his mean morsel with thankfulness, and, by the blessing of God upon it, with better relish than unthankful worldly men do their royal dainties. (*Note*, *Rev.* ii. 17.)—Alas ! what cause have we to groan and sigh because of those around us, who destroy themselves and others, by their perverse and obstinate unbelief, and enmity to the gospel! But we have great cause to be humbled and thankful on our own account; for the Lord has continual reason to reprove us, for our remaining distrust, and carnal apprehensions. How is it, that we no more see the glory of his truths, the privileges of his kingdom, the security of his word, the spirituality of his precepts? How is it, that we so often mistake his meaning, disregard his warnings, and distrust his providence? Alas! these things arise from the remains of that same leaven, which wholly prevails in the hearts of unbelievers. Let us then watch against it : and let us beseech the Lord to remove from us ' all hardness of heart,' and

2 L 4

CHAP. IX.

The transfiguratiol of Christ, 1—10. He shews that John the Baptist is "Elias who was to come," 11—13. He casts out a dumb and deaf spirit, having rebuked the company, and the disciples, for their unbelief, 14—29. He foretels his own death and resurrection, 30—32; reproves the ambition of the disciples, 33—37; forbids them to hinder one, who cast out devils in his name, though he followed not with them, 38—41; shews the guilt of offending weak believers, 42; and warns his hearers to part with all occasions of sin however valued; shewing the eternal doom of the wicked, especially of apostates, in most awful language, 43—50.

AND he said unto them, Verily I say unto you, * that there be some of them that stand here, which shall not b taste of death, till they have seen c the kingdom of God come with power.

a Matt. xvi. 28.
b Luke ix. 27.
b Luke ix. 36. John iii. 9.
c Luke xxi. 31.
John xxi. 23.
Acts i. 6, 7.

2 ¶ And d after six days, Jesus taketh with him e Peter, and James, and John, and leadeth them up into f an high mountain apart by themselves: and he was g transfigured before them.

3 And h his raiment became shining, i exceeding white as snow; so as k no fuller on earth can white them.

4 And there l appeared unto them m Elias with h Moses; and they were talking with Jesus.

5 And Peter answered and said to Jesus, Master, o it is good for us to be here: and let us make three tabernacles; one for thee, and one for Moses, and one for Elias.

6 For p he wist not what to say; for they were sore afraid.

d Matt. xvii. 1, &c. Luke ix. 28, &c.
e v. 37. xiv. 33.
f 2 Cor. xii. 1. Ex. xxiv. 1.
1 Kings xviii. 42.
43. Matt. xiv. 18. Luke vi. 12.
g xvi. 12. Ex. xxxiv. 29—35.
h Is. xxxiii.17. liii.
2. Matt. xvii. 2.
i Luke ix. 29. John i. 14. Rom. xii. 2. 2 Cor. iii. 7—10. Phil. ii. 6
k — 8. lii. 21. 2 Pet. i. 16—18. Rev. i.
l 13—17. xx. 11.
Ps. civ. 1, 2. Dan. vii.9.Matt. xxvii. 3. Acts x. 30.
h Ps. li. 7. Isviii. 14. la. i. 18. Rev. vii. 9, 14. xix. 8
k Mal. iii. 2, 3.
l Matt. xi. 13 xvii. 3, 4 Luke 27, 44 John iv. 39. 40—47. Acts iii. 21—24. 1 Pet. i. 10—12. Rev. xix. 10.
m 2 Kings ii. 11.
o Ps. Elijah.

n Deut. xxxiv. b. 6.　o Ex. xxxiii. 17—23.　Ps. lxiii. 2, 3.　John xiv. 8, 9. 21—23
Phil. i. 23.　1 John iii. 2.　Rev. xxii. 3, 4.　p xvi. 5—8. Dan. x. 15—19.

blindness of understanding; that we may perceive, hear, and remember his truths and precepts, and be thankful for all his multiplied kindnesses to us.

V. 22—38.

The Lord in general illuminates our minds gradually; and he works by means, which are often no more than external signs of his efficacious operation. Thus he sometimes takes a poor blind sinner aside from the multitude, gradually removes the darkness from his understanding, and leads him to some indistinct views of spiritual things. This is his own work; till he perfect it, and we should wait his time. Let then all who desire this blessing, seek for it to Christ, " the Light of the world," in the use of the means appointed by him, and they shall not be disappointed. But while " the blind see out of obscurity," the proud, who reject his teaching, are given up to darkness and delusion; and even the means of instruction are in righteous judgment withdrawn from them.—The Lord will interrogate his followers on their proficiency: and his real disciples are distinguished, by their honourable thoughts of him, and large expectations from him. He will approve of what we are enabled to speak or do in a proper manner: but we continually need to be taught further lessons, or to have our minds stirred up to remembrance, concerning his sufferings for us, and the self-denial which he requires from us. Our minds are by nature very averse to these humiliating and spiritual instructions: and even where some true knowledge, faith, and grace exists, there may be, and often are, much ignorance, error, and remains of " the carnal mind."—As our Lord so sharply reproved Peter for objecting to his sufferings, which the glory of God and the salvation of his people required; we should by this be reminded, that those who would set us against self-denial, for the honour of our Lord, and the good of others, " savour the things that " are of men, and not those that are of God." All people should therefore be called to observe, that they, who would go after Christ to heaven, must " deny themselves,

" take up their cross, and follow him: " and that they only are in the way of eternal happiness, who are willing to venture all, even their very lives, rather than deny Christ, or be ashamed of him in this evil world. Did we duly consider the worth and danger of our precious souls, for which no ransom could be found but the blood of Emmanuel, we should count the whole world contemptible, if the gain of it endangered our salvation; and the loss of life our greatest gain, if laid down for the sake of Christ and the gospel. May we then continually think of that season, when he will " come in the glory of the Father, " with his holy angels," and may we now estimate every earthly object as we shall do on that important day! (P. O. Matt. xvi. 13—28.)

NOTES.

CHAP. IX. V. 1. (Notes, Matt. xvi. 24—28, v. 28.) ' This chiefly refers to the providential appearance of ' Christ for the destruction of Jerusalem. ...Our Lord's ' manner of speaking intimates, that most of the company ' should be dead before the event referred to: yet his as-' cension happened in a few months after.' Doddridge. Some interpret the passage of the successful preaching of the gospel after Christ's ascension, and the powerful establishment of his kingdom by means of it: but the reason assigned in this quotation seems conclusive, for interpreting it of his glorious appearance, in his providence, to remove the great hindrance to the full settlement of the Christian church, by destroying Jerusalem, and terminating the Jewish dispensation. (Marg. Ref.—Notes, xiii. 24—31. Matt. xxiv. 3. 15—18. 26—28. Luke xxi. 25—28. John xxi. 18—23.)

V. 2—9. Marg. and Marg. Ref.—Notes, Matt. xvii. 1—9. Luke ix. 28—36. 2 Pet. i. 16—18.—It is good, &c. (5) Had it been possible for Peter to have gone to heaven directly, with Christ, and Moses, and Elias; all his usefulness would have been prevented. (Notes, John xii. 23—26. xv. 12—16.) But he lived many years amidst conflict and suffering, and died on a cross: yet tens and hundreds of thou

2 L 5

7 And there was ˙ a cloud that over-shadowed them :, and a voice came out of the cloud, saying, 'This is my beloved Son; 'hear him.

8 And ' suddenly, when they had looked round about, they saw no man any more, save Jesus only with themselves.

9 And as they came down from the mountain, " he charged them that they should tell no man what things they had seen, " till the Son of man were risen from the dead.

10 And ' they kept that saying with themselves, questioning one with another ' what the rising from the dead should mean.

11 ¶ And they asked him, saying, " Why say the scribes that Elias must first come ?

12 And he answered and told them, Elias verily cometh first, and ' restoreth all things; and how it is written of the Son of man, that 'he must suffer many things, and be ' set at nought.

13 But I say unto you, That ' Elias is indeed come, ' and they have done unto him whatsoever they listed; as it is written of him.

14 ¶ And ' when he came to his disciples, he saw a great multitude about them, and " the scribes questioning with them.

15 And straightway all the people, when they beheld him, ' were greatly amazed, and running to him saluted him.

16 And he asked the scribes, " What question ye * with them ?

---

sands were saved by his means, to the glory of God by him ! And was not this well worth his while? (Notes, Phil. i. 19 —26. 2 Pet. i. 12—15.)

Shining. (3) Σίλεοντα. Σίλεοω, corrusco. Not elsewhere N. T. Ps. vii. 12. Sept.—Sore afraid. (6) Εκφοβοι. Heb. xii. 21. Not elsewhere N. T. Deut. ix. 19. Sept.—Should tell, &c. (9) Διηγησωνται. v. 16. Εινητε. Matt. xvii. 9.

V. 10. Marg. Ref.—Questioning, &c.] The apostles argued with each other, concerning their Lord's meaning, when he said, " Till the Son of man be risen from the " dead." (9) Not, that they did not believe a future resurrection, or had any peculiar difficulty concerning the common meaning of the words; for they had witnessed some instances of the dead being restored to life: but they were so prepossessed with prejudices against the Messiah's being cut off by death, and so assured that Jesus was the Messiah, that they supposed some figurative sense must be put on his words; for as they erroneously supposed he could not literally die, so he could not literally rise again. (Note, Luke ix. 45.)—Nothing has more tended to induce false interpretations of scripture, than a vain imagination that the literal meaning could not be true, because contrary to some notion, which, though no better than the prejudiced conclusion of a set of men, has been regarded as certain truth : and therefore allegorizing (called spiritual interpretation) must be adopted. But the grand wisdom and discernment of an expositor consists, in knowing what ought to be explained literally, and what must be interpreted figuratively. The papists explaining " This is my body " literally, and others allegorizing the parable, or story, of the good Samaritan, will shew the attentive and judicious reader the importance of this remark. (Notes, Matt. xxvi. 26—28. Luke x. 30—37.)

V. 11—13. (Note, Matt. xvii. 10—13.) ' In answer ' to their other scruple, how the Son of man could die, he ' told them also from the scriptures, how it was foretold, ' that he should suffer many things, &c.' Whitby.

Restore, &c. (12) That is, bring back numbers from ungodliness to the true worship and service of God ; as Elijah had done the Israelites from Baal to Jehovah. (Marg. Ref.—Notes, Mal. iv. 4—6. Luke i. 11—17.)— The thirteenth verse would be more readily understood, if translated as follows :—" Elias is indeed come, as it " is written of him : and they have done to him whatso-" ever they listed." For this is the evident meaning of the words. It was not foretold, that the Messiah's forerunner would suffer martyrdom; and the scribes and priests did not put him to death: but it is plain, that they were well pleased, when he was thus taken off, and the conduct of the nation to so eminent a servant of God, shewed what might be expected from them, against the Saviour whom he preceded.

V. 14, 15. Christ and the three apostles found the rest of the disciples surrounded with a multitude : for some Scribes had taken that opportunity of disputing with them ; hoping perhaps to perplex them, in the absence of their Master. (Marg. Ref. g, h.) But when Jesus appeared, the multitude, who had been listening to the debate, " were greatly amazed," probably by some remains of lustre visible in his countenance ; for no other adequate reason of their surprise can be assigned : and running to him they saluted him again. ' Seeing some remainders of the splen-' dour at his transfiguration in his visage.' Whitby. (Notes, Ex. xxxiv. 29—35. 2 Cor. iii. 7—11.)

Were greatly amazed. (15) Εξεθαμβηθη. xiv. 33. xvi. 5, 6. Not elsewnere N. T. Εκθαμβος. Acts iii. 11.—Dan. vii. 7. Sept.

V. 16—24. (Notes, Matt. xvii. 14—18. Luke ix. 37— 44.) On our Lord's enquiry into the subject, on which the scribes were disputing with his disciples, one of the multitude addressed him in behalf of his son ; who, as he stated it, was possessed with an evil spirit, which deprived him of speech and hearing : and often seized him with

2 L 6

17 And one of·the multitude answered and said, Master, [l] I have brought unto thee my son, which hath [m] a dumb spirit:

18 And wheresoever he taketh him, he [n] teareth him; and he [o] foameth, and [o] gnasheth with his teeth, and pineth away; and I spake to thy disciples that they should cast him out, [p] and they could not.

19 He answereth him, and saith, [q] O faithless generation! how long shall I be with you? how long shall I suffer you? Bring him unto me.

20 And they brought him unto him: and when he saw him, straightway [r] the spirit tare him, and he fell on the ground, and wallowed, foaming.

21 And he asked his father, [s] How long is it ago since this came unto him? And he said, Of a child.

22 And oft-times it hath cast him into the fire, and into the waters, to destroy him: but [t] if thou canst do any thing, [u] have compassion on us, and help us.

23 Jesus said unto him, [x] If thou canst believe, all things are possible to him that believeth.

24 And straightway the father of the child cried out, and said [y] with tears, Lord, I believe; [z] help thou mine unbelief.

violence, dashing him upon the ground, and causing him to foam at the mouth, and " gnash with his teeth;" so that he pined away, as with continued wasting sickness.—This accords very much with the case of persons afflicted with the epilepsy, and hence some have ventured to assert, that it was no real possession: but does it not better become our ignorance, concerning the real causes of these maladies, to allow that at least the symptoms are aggravated by diabolical agency; than to suppose, that Christ, by word and deed, gave the most explicit sanction to a vulgar error, and taught men to ascribe effects to the malice and power of apostate spirits which they had no agency in producing? This irreverence to the word of God, and to the Redeemer's sacred character, is very often the effect of pride and determined infidelity, in which Satan has far more influence, than such persons are willing in any thing to allow him.—In this calamity, the afflicted father had applied to the apostles to cast out the evil spirit; and it is probable, that their failure gave the scribes an occasion of questioning them concerning Jesus, and endeavouring to shew that he was not the Messiah, or even a true prophet. Our Lord therefore answered the father of the youth, with reference to the scribes, the multitude, and even the disciples, who in different degrees were chargeable with very criminal unbelief; and he reproved them all together as an *unbelieving* generation, because they had not more enlarged apprehensions of his power and authority, notwithstanding all the miracles which he had wrought among them: and he enquired, how long he must be with them, to display his glory; and how long he must bear with their perverseness and incredulity; before they would be convinced that he was the Son of God, and that nothing was impossible to his omnipotence. (*Notes, Num.* xiv. 11, 12. *Heb.* iii 7—19.)—He then ordered the demoniack to be brought: upon which the evil spirit exerted his utmost malice and power, and dashed the young man on the ground, tearing him, and constraining him to wallow, or roll upon the earth, and foam in a dreadful manner. The question, " How long is it ago, since this came upon " him?" was probably intended to shew the inveteracy of the case, to put the man's faith to a sharp trial, and to illustrate his own power. (*Marg. Ref.* l—s.—*Note, John* v. 5—9.) The father answered, that he had been so tormented from his childhood: and though he had hitherto been marvellously preserved; yet he had often been cast by the evil spirit into the fire, and into the water, apparently with the purpose of destroying him. So that the case had baffled every attempt hitherto made for his relief: but if Jesus " could do any thing," he intreated him to pity and help them. Our Lord then assured him, that in case " he could believe," the deliverance would certainly follow; seeing " all things were possible to him that believed." The event being thus suspended on the father's faith, so that the son could not fail of a cure except through his default; the former, feeling a vehement struggle in his mind between faith and unbelief, and fearing lest he should throw an impediment in the way, immediately cried out, with great earnestness, and with a flow of tears, " Lord, I " believe, help thou mine unbelief." He could scarcely believe, that Jesus could cast out this powerful and obstinate evil spirit; and yet he concluded, that he could enable him to believe, and inwardly assist him against unbelief! In effect he said, ' Lord, I do believe, and expect help from thee alone; but I am not able to exclude all doubting about it: but do thou first help me against my unbelief, and then deliver my afflicted child from his deplorable calamity.'—Where do we ever read of such an address to any prophet or apostle, in the whole scripture? And who does not perceive, that such a request must have been highly reprehensible, if made to any mere man or creature? (*Marg. Ref.* t—z.—*Notes, Luke* xvii. 5, 6. xxiv. 44 —49, v. 45. 2 *Cor.* xii. 7—10. *Phil.* iv. 10—13, v. 13. *Heb.* xii. 2, 3.)—' " What is wanting to my faith, supply ' " by thy goodness." For that he should hope for an in-' crease of faith from Jesus, and that suddenly, is scarcely ' credible.' *Grotius.*—This translation is wholly *unfaithful;* and the reason assigned for it is the language of direct *unbelief.*

A dumb spirit. (17) Πνευμα αλαλον. 25. vii. 37. Not elsewhere N. T.—*Teareth,* &c. (18) " Dasheth." Marg. 'Ρησσει. ii. 22. *Matt.* vii. 6. ix. 17. *Luke* v. 37. ix. 42. *Gal.* iv. 27.—*He formeth.*] Αφριζει. 20. Not elsewhere N. T.

25 When Jesus saw that the people came running together, *he rebuked the foul spirit, saying unto him, b Thou dumb and deaf spirit, c I charge thee come out of him, and enter no more into him.

26 And the spirit d cried, and rent him sore, and came out of him: and he was as one dead; insomuch that many said, He is dead.

27 But Jesus e took him by the hand, and lifted him up, and he arose.

28 And when he was come into the house, his disciples f asked him privately, g Why could not we east him out?

29 And he said unto them, h This kind can come forth by nothing but i by prayer and k fasting.

30 ¶ And they departed thence, and passed l through Galilee, m and he would not that any man should know it.

31 For he taught his disciples, and said unto them, n The Son of man is delivered into the hands of men, and they shall kill him; and after that he is killed, he shall rise the third day.

32 But o they understood not that saying, and p were afraid to ask him.

33 ¶ And q he came to Capernaum: and being in the house, he asked them, r What was it that ye disputed among yourselves by the way?

34 But they held their peace: for by the way s they had disputed among themselves, who should be the greatest.

35 And he sat down, and called the twelve, and saith unto them, t If any man desire to be first, the same shall be last of all, and servant of all.

36 And u he took a child, and set him in the midst of them: and when he had taken him in his arms, he said unto them,

37 Whosoever shall x receive one of such children in my name, receiveth me: and whosoever shall y receive me, receiveth not me, but him that sent me.

38 ¶ And John answered him, saying, z Master, we saw one casting out

---

Gnasheth.] Τρίζει. Not elsewhere N. T.—Pineth away.] Ξηραίνεται. See on Matt. xxi. 17.—Tare him. (20) Εσπαραξεν. 26. i. 26. Luke ix. 39.—Wallowed.] Εκυλίετο. Not elsewhere N. T. Κυλισμα, wallowing. 2 Pet. ii. 22.

V. 25—27. The multitude assembling, that they might witness the event, our Lord was pleased to rebuke the unclean spirit, and to charge him to come out of the young man, and to enter no more into him. This command the demon was unable to resist: but it filled him with torture and rancour; so that, crying out in a dreadful manner, he grievously tore the youth before he left him; insomuch that the spectators supposed him to be dead: but when Jesus took him by the hand he arose, and was found to be perfectly recovered. (Marg. Ref.—Notes, i. 23—28. Zech. iii. 1—4. Acts xvi. 16—18.)

V. 28, 29. Marg. Ref.—Notes, Matt. xvii. 19—21.

V. 30—32. Our Lord chose at this time to be retired, that he might with the more freedom converse with his disciples, about his approaching sufferings and the event of them. But though no words could be more explicit, than those which he made use of; yet they were so blinded by prejudice, that they could not understand him; and they were ashamed of their ignorance, and afraid to ask him what he meant, lest he should reprove them. (Note, 10.)—'Christ, indeed, with great diligence warns us, that ' we may not be disconcerted by unexpected calamities: ' but the inattentive dulness of men 'is incredible.' Beza. (Marg. Ref.—Notes, 33—37. Luke ix. 45. Luke xx. 1— 10, v. 9.)

V. 33—37. Marg. Ref.—Notes, Matt. xviii. 1—6. Luke ix. 46—50, vv. 46—48. xxii. 24—27.—The house.

(33) Probably that of Andrew and Peter. 'The thing ' itself shews, that the apostles were thinking of an earthly ' kingdom, ... which they dreamed was about to follow : ' and this prevented them from understanding what Christ ' spake, concerning his death and resurrection; their minds ' being pre-occupied with that imagination. ... If there ' were to be any primacy among the apostles, why was ' Christ on this occasion silent respecting it? Or, if he ' had, in the hearing of the others, conferred it on Peter; ' what occasion would there have been for the apostles to ' dispute about it?' Beza.—Servant, &c. (35) 'The ' precedence among my disciples, all that they are capable ' of, that of being governors of the church, brings no ad- ' vantage to him that has it, but to be more the servant of ' other men; more work and business being the only ad- ' vantage of that precedence, which shall befall you and ' your successors.' Hammond. If this were known by all to be the case, or generally believed to be so ; the number of candidates for the distinction of being 'suc- ' cessors to the apostles,' would be exceedingly diminished. (Notes, x. 35—45. Matt. xx. 20—28. Phil. ii. 1—4.)

Whosoever shall receive, &c. (37) Notes, Matt. x. 40 —42. xviii. 5, 6. 10, 11.

V. 38—40. Our Lord's declaration, in the preceding verse, reminded John of what he and his brethren had done, on a former occasion; and which he perhaps now suspected to be blameable. They had met with a person who "cast out devils in the name" of Jesus: but as he did not statedly follow with them, and was not regularly sent forth, as the apostles and seventy disciples had been ; they forbad him to proceed. This was the result of wrong

devils in thy name, and he followeth not us; and we forbad him, because he followeth not us.

39 But Jesus said, ᵃ Forbid him not: for ᵇ there is no man which shall do a miracle in my name, that can ᶜ lightly speak evil of me.

40 For ᵈ he that is not against us, is on our part.

41 For ᵉ whosoever shall give you a cup of water to drink in my name, ᶠ because ye belong to Christ, verily I say unto you, he shall not lose his reward.

42 And whosoever shall ᵍ offend one of *these* little ones that believe in me, ʰ it is better for him that a mill-stone were hanged about his neck, and he were cast into the sea.

43 And ⁱ if thy hand ᵏ offend thee, cut it off: it is better for thee to enter into life ᵏ maimed, than having two hands to go into hell, into the fire that never shall be quenched;

44 Where ˡ their worm dieth not, and ᵐ the fire is not quenched.

45 And if ⁿ thy foot offend thee, cut it off: it is better for thee to enter halt into life, than having two feet to be cast into hell, into the fire that never shall be quenched;

46 Where ᵒ their worm dieth not, and the fire is not quenched.

47 And if ᵖ thine eye ᵗ offend thee, pluck it out: it is better for thee to enter into the kingdom of God with one eye, than having two eyes to be cast into hell-fire;

48 Where their worm dieth not, and the fire is not quenched.

49 For every one shall be salted with fire, ᵠ and every sacrifice shall be salted with salt.

50 Salt ʳ *is* good: but if the salt have lost his saltness, wherewith will ye season it? ˢ Have salt in yourselves, ᵗ and have peace one with another.

---

apprehensions and remaining self-preference. Had not Christ secretly and effectually wrought by the man, he could not have succeeded in his attempt to cast out devils in his name : (Note, *Acts* xix. 13—20 :) they were, therefore, reprehensible in prohibiting him ; especially without so much as asking their Lord's advice. Accordingly, Jesus warned them not to forbid any one on that account: as it was not likely, that he, who wrought undeniable miracles in his name, would easily be induced to disparage and vilify him or his cause; and all who were· not engaged against them were, in the present circumstances, to be considered, as "on their part."—Working miracles in the name of Christ did not indeed prove a man to be a true believer : but, in the contest between the kingdom of God, and that of Satan, it shewed, that, in this instance, a man fought under the banner of Christ, and against his enemies. (*Marg. Ref.—Notes, Num.* xi. 28, 29. *Matt.* xii. 29, 30. *Luke* ix. 46—50, *v.* 50. 1 *Cor.* xii. 1—3. *2 Cor.* xiii. 7—10. *Phil.* i. 15—18. 1 *John* iv. 1—3.)—' God, the ' author of the ordinary vocation, acts in an extraordinary ' manner whenever he pleases : but the extraordinary ' vocation must be tried by the doctrine and the effects.' *Beza.*

Speak evil, &c. (39) Κακολογησαι. See on *Matt.* xv. 4.
V. 41, 42. Instead of prohibiting those, who aided in promoting the common cause, our Lord declared, that he would certainly recompense every one, who gave one of the least among his disciples so much as " a cup of water, " because he belonged to him," the promised Messiah : on the contrary, whosoever injured, grieved, or stumbled the least of his disciples, would commit so grievous a crime, and be in danger of so great a punishment, that the most terrible death would be a much lighter evil, than that to which he would expose himself. (*Marg. Ref.*—

VOL. V.

Notes, Matt. x. 40—42. xviii. 5, 6. *Rom.* xiv. 19—23. 1 *Cor.* viii. 7—13.)
Ye belong to Christ. (41) Χριστυ εστε, " Are Christ's." 1 *Cor.* iii. 23. xv. 23. 2 *Cor.* x. 7.) ' These words explain ' what the phrase " in the name of a disciple," in St. Mat- ' thew signifies.' *Beza.*
V. 43—50. (*Notes, Matt.* v. 29, 30. xviii. 7—9.) These solemn warnings, as here introduced, seem especially to relate to the ambition and carnal expectations of the apostles, which misled them into many mistakes, both in judgment and practice. All such evil propensities must be mortified and " cut off," in order to their " entering " into life," however painful the operation might be. The expressions are here much more strong and varied, than in any of the parallel passages. The hand, the foot, and the eye are separately mentioned, as illustrative of the supposed value of the sacrifices to be made ; and of the resolution, self-denial, and wisdom required in order to make them. (*Marg.* and *Marg. Ref.* i, k. n. p.—*Notes, Gen.* iii. 6. *Deut.* xiii. 6—11. *Luke* xiv. 25—27.) ' I saw ' Philip himself, with whom our contest was for rule and ' dominion, after having lost an eye, having had his hip ' broken, and being lamed in his hand and his leg, dis- ' posed, readily and easily, to part with any part of his ' body, which fortune might choose ; so that, with the re- ' mainder, he might live in glory and honour.' *Demosthenes.* " They do it for a corruptible crown ; but we for an incor- " ruptible." (*Note,* 1 *Cor.* ix. 24—27.)—It is repeatedly said, " *Their worm never dieth,"* as well as that " the fire " is never quenched." (*Note, Is.* lxvi. 24.) Doubtless, remorse of conscience and keen self-reflection constitute this never-dying worm : so that the expression is alike contrary to the ideas of annihilation, and of final restitu- tion to happiness ; for, on either of these suppositions,

CHAP. X.

Jesus teaches in Judea, 1; answers the Pharisees concerning divorces, 2—12; receives and blesses young children, 13—16; instructs and proves the rich young man; shews the danger of affluence; and makes gracious promises to those who forsake worldly objects for his sake, 17—31. He again predicts his own death and resurrection; reproves the ambition of James and John, and the other apostles, 32—45; and gives sight to blind Bartimeus, 46—52.

" *their* worm" would die, and their torturing consciences would cease. And as the fire is doubtless at least an emblem of the wrath of God; its *unquenchableness* must denote, that his justice will never be satisfied, nor his anger turned away from those, who are cast into this fire of hell. (*Marg. Ref.* l, m.—*Notes, Is.* xxxiii. 14. *Matt.* iii. 11, 12. xxv. 41—46. 2 *Thes.* ii. 5—10, *vv.* 8, 9. *Rev.* xxi. 5—8, *v.* 8.)—The sacrifices under the law were commanded to be salted with salt. (*Note, Lev.* ii. 13.) This was primarily an emblem of grace, which renders the sanctified soul meet for the enjoyment of its incorruptible inheritance: but it also represented that " every sacrifice " to the divine justice " would be salted with fire; " the very nature of the punishment, or the righteous vengeance of God, will render the heirs of hell incorruptible: so that their misery will be as endless, as the happiness of the righteous. ' Every wicked man shall be seasoned with fire itself, so ' as to become inconsumable, and shall endure for ever to ' be tormented; and therefore may be said to be " salted ' " with fire," in allusion to that property of salt, which ' is to preserve things from corruption.' *Whitby.*—In concluding this solemn subject our Lord reminded the disciples, that as salt, though valuable in itself to season and preserve other bodies, was yet worthless and irrecoverable when it had lost its saltness; so they would become more vile and hopeless than others, if they were not truly sanctified: for they would be employed in converting and preserving others, and would have none to season them, should they turn aside. It would therefore be incumbent on them, to watch over their own hearts, to mortify their lusts, and laying aside ambition, the fruitful parent of contention, to live at peace with each other. (*Marg. Ref.* r—t.—*Notes, Matt.* v. 13. *Luke* xiv. 34, 35. *Eph.* iv. 1—6. 29—32. v. 1, 2. *Col.* iv. 5, 6.)—' If the teachers them-' selves to whom is committed the administration of the ' divine word, with which men must be seasoned as with ' salt, ... do themselves become insipid,' (not savouring of that holy word, in doctrine, spirit, and practice,) ' what ' remaineth, but either, that the hearers perish, or that ' God should send other teachers ? ' *Beza.*

Into hell. (43) Εις την γεενναν. *Note, Matt.* v. 21, 22, v. 22.

PRACTICAL OBSERVATIONS.

V. 1—13.

Those Christians, who shall live in future times to behold " the kingdom of God come with power," and set up in all parts of the world, will enjoy a peculiar satisfaction, with which others have not been favoured: but though we shall " taste of death " before those happy days arrive; (*Note, Heb.* ii. 5--9, *v.* 9 ;) yet we shall possess a still more exalted felicity, if admitted into those regions, where Jesus continually displays far brighter glories, than even on the mount of transfiguration. The pleasures of that divine vision must be unspeakably great; seeing the glimpses, which we now behold, as " through a glass darkly," sometimes so ravish our minds, that we are ready to cry out, " It is good for us to be here." (*P. O.* 1 *Cor.* xiii. 8—13.) But we should not expect such peculiar consolations to be abiding, in this state of conflict and probation. We must now learn to hear, believe, love, and obey an unseen Saviour; to " walk by faith," and to wait in patient hope. We should seek conformity to him in holiness; and expect ere long to be with him, and like him in body and soul, where prophets and apostles, yea and archangels, vie with each other, who shall most honour, adore, and praise his glorious majesty. In this hope, we may cheerfully pass through life and death; though we be often under a cloud, and ready to question, what the meaning of his words and his appointments can be : and if we consider the way, in which Jesus and his servants have passed through this world to heaven; we shall be the less discouraged, should we be called to suffer many things, or be " set at nought" as the most despicable of mankind ; if so be, that we may by any means attain unto eternal life. (*Note, Phil.* iii. 8—11.)—The enemies of Christ always watch their opportunities of perplexing and disconcerting his disciples : their cavils and objections create much disquietude, to such as neglect to maintain a continual communion with their Lord: and perverse opponents often attack the unestablished, from a consciousness that they can make no impression on those, who are more fully confirmed and experienced. But the Lord will interpose to plead for his friends, and to silence the objections of his adversaries: yet many seem zealously to welcome him and his ministers, who do not cordially believe and obey his gospel.

V. 14—29.

In what varied ways does Satan with his angels attempt to render mankind miserable! Yet his chief success, among those who are favoured with the gospel, entirely arises from their unbelief : for if they had a clear apprehension of the power and grace of the Saviour, who " came to destroy the works of the devil," they would seek to him and obtain deliverance.—When our children or relatives are made wretched, useless, or mischievous, through the destructive influence of Satan ; we should bring them to Christ by faith and prayer, earnestly beseeching him to " have compassion upon us and help us :" and we may do this for them, when they are incapable of receiving our instructions, or determined to disregard all our counsels.—Ministers and Christians may be applied to on such occasions, and their counsel and prayers may be useful : but our dependence must rest on Christ alone; and should they conclude the case to be hopeless, we should still persist in expecting help from his almighty arm. But, alas ! after all the displays which he has made of his power and love, and after all his patient teaching of us, by his word and our own experience, we are prone to form low expectations from him. Yet the things, which to all others are impossible, are easy with him.—Even in the

^a Matt. xix. 1. AND ^a he arose from thence, and cometh into the coasts of Judea, ^b by the farther side of Jordan; and the people resort unto him again: and, as he was wont, ^c he taught them again.

^b John x. 40. xi. 7.

c Ec. xii. 9. Jer. xxxii. 33. John xviii. 20

---

case of those, who from their earliest years have been peculiarly enslaved by Satan, and have contracted various pernicious habits and fatal connexions; by means of which they have, as it were, "often been cast into the fire, and "into the water," and have repeatedly been brought to the verge of destruction; we have abundant encouragement to expect help from the Saviour. He has hitherto bounded the rage of the enemy, and borne with the provocations of the sinner; and he can easily break the power of the former, and glorify himself in the salvation of the latter. Our chief danger, in every thing really good for us, arises from unbelief: "if we can believe, all things "are possible to him that believeth:" and as we shall certainly find a difficulty in exercising such an unshaken faith in the power and grace of Christ, on many occasions; we should apply to him, "as the Author and Finisher of "our faith," to strengthen us against unbelief; that we may not, through our own default, come short of the blessings which we seek, in behalf of ourselves or others. Indeed Satan will be very reluctant to be driven out of those, who have long been his slaves; and when he cannot deceive or destroy the sinner, he will cause him as much trouble and terror as possible: so that when a man is about to experience a most blessed deliverance, he is often more harassed and distressed, than at any other time; and the beginnings of liberty and life resemble the very agonies of death.—Ministers would witness, and be the instruments of, more of those remarkable conversions, if they were stronger in faith, more fervent in prayer, and more entirely mortified to earthly pleasures and pursuits: and should we enquire of Jesus, why we have no more success "in turning sinners from the power of Satan unto "God;" he would probably answer, "Because of your "unbelief;" for this effect cannot be produced "except by "fasting and prayer."

V. 30—50.

While the Saviour teaches most plainly those things, which relate to his love and grace, his sufferings and death, his present glory and future coming to judgment; men in general are so blinded by prejudice, that they do not understand his sayings: and by various hindrances they are frequently deterred from praying for divine illumination. Even disciples are often more ready to dispute with each other, "which shall be the greatest;" than with humble simplicity to sit at his feet, and learn the doctrine of the cross, "by which the world" must be "crucified "to them, and they unto the world:" (Note, Gal. vi. 11 —14:) and we all need repeated rebukes, before we are made willing to seek wisdom by becoming "as little chil- "dren," and to aspire after greatness by stooping to "be "the least of all, and the servants of all." Yet disciples of this character are most dear to their Lord, and will be most honoured by him, as his messengers to mankind: and "whosoever receiveth one of them in Christ's "name, receiveth" both "him and the Father who sent "him."—Pride and bigotry are great hindrances to usefulness: men often think the interests of a party, or the credit of their order, of more importance than the cause of godliness: they are ready, by an assumed presumptuous authority, to forbid others "to cast out devils in the name "of Christ," "because they follow not with them:" and even to grieve when evident good is done, if it be not managed according to their notions of regularity, and by those who are commissioned and sent forth *in their way*. Whereas all who believe, love, serve, and honour Christ are of one side: "he that is not against us is on our part;" and if sinners be brought to repent, to believe in the Saviour, and to lead sober, righteous, and godly lives, we must perceive that the Lord works by the preacher; and who are we, that we should attempt to silence him? While, therefore, we are encouraged to do good to others "for his name's sake," and especially to those who belong to him, assured that such services shall not lose their reward; let us also favour all who appear to be on his side in this evil world, and be glad to shew our concurrence with them: and let us dread, even worse than death, any thing which can tend to injure and grieve them, or hinder their usefulness.—Instead of acrimony against those, who "follow not with us," let us bend all our *severity* against our own evil propensities and habits; not sparing one of them, though it has been as a hand, a foot, or an eye unto us; or however painful we may find the mortification of it. Thus we shall be assured of "entering into life," and be preserved from the most distant fear of being "cast into hell, where *their* "worm dieth not, and the fire is not quenched."—And surely it would be infinitely better to undergo all possible pain, self-denial, and hardship here, and so be for ever happy hereafter; than to enjoy all worldly pleasure for a season, and then to be for ever miserable! (P. O. Matt. xvi. 21—28.) If then the difficulty and pain of mortifying every sinful inclination, and subduing every bad habit, appear to any man very great; if the worldly advantages to be renounced appear very valuable; let him consider the awful alternative. For eternity is before us: incorruptible in holiness and happiness, or in sin and misery, we must be: either sacrifices to God's justice to be "salted with "fire," or living willing sacrifices to his honour, by the sanctification of the Spirit of Christ, and through the redemption of his blood. We have indeed the name of Christians: some of us preach, and many others profess, the truths of the gospel; and we are thus "the salt of "the earth." If we then answer to our character, we shall be useful here and happy for ever: but if we remain destitute of the grace of God, our name, our profession, or our sacred function, will only serve to aggravate our guilt, and increase our condemnation. Let us then lay aside every carnal and ambitious project and pursuit: let us "look diligently, lest any man fail of the grace of God:" and "let us follow after peace and holiness, without "which no man shall see the Lord." (Notes, Heb. xii. 14 —17.)

NOTES.

Chap. X. V. 1. *Marg. Ref.—Note, Matt.* xix. 1, 2.

2 x 3

2 ¶ And ᵈ the Pharisees came to him, and asked him, ' Is it lawful for a man to put away *his* wife? ' tempting him.

3 And he answered and said unto them, ᵉ What did Moses command you?

4 And they said, ʰ Moses suffered to write a bill of divorcement, and to put *her* away.

5 And Jesus answered and said unto them, ' For the hardness of your heart he wrote you this precept:

6 But from ᵏ the beginning of the creation, ' God made them male and female.

7 For ᵐ this cause shall a man leave his father and mother, and cleave to his wife,

8 And they twain shall be ⁿ one flesh: so then they are no more twain, but one flesh.

9 What ° therefore God hath joined together, let not man put asunder.

10 And ᵖ in the house his disciples asked him again of the same *matter*.

11 And he saith unto them, ᑫ Whosoever shall put away his wife, and marry another, committeth adultery against her.

12 And if a woman shall put away her husband, and be married to another, she committeth adultery.

13 ¶ And ' they brought young children to him, that he should touch them; and *his* ˢ disciples rebuked those that brought *them*.

14 But when Jesus saw *it*, ' he was much displeased, and said unto them, " Suffer the little children to come unto me, and forbid them not; ˣ for of such is the kingdom of God.

15 Verily I say unto you, ʸ Whosoever shall not receive the kingdom of God as a little child, he shall not enter therein.

16 And ᶻ he took them up in his

---

d viii. 15. Matt. ix. 34. xv. 12.
xxiii. 15. Luke v. 30. vi. 7. vii. 30. xi. 53, 54. xvi. 14. John vii. 32. 48. xi. 47. 57.
e Mat. ii. 16. iii. 31, 32. xix. 3. 1 Cor. vii. 10, 11.
f vii. 11. Matt. xvi. 1. xxii. 35. John viii. 6. 1 Cor. x. 9.
g Is. viii. 20. Luke x. 25, 26. Gal. iv. 21. v. 23.
h Deut. xxiv. 1—4. Is. l. 1. Jer. iii. 1. Matt. v. 31. xix. 7.
i Deut. ix. 6. xxxi. 27. Neh. ix. 16, 17, 26. Matt. xix. 8. Acts vii. 51. Heb. iii. 7—10.
k Gen. i. 1. 2 Pet. iii. 4.
l Gen. i. 27. ii. 20—28. v. 2. Mal. ii. 14—16.
m Gen. ii. 24. Matt. xix. 5, 6. Eph. v. 31.
n 1 Cor. vi. 16. Eph. v. 28.
o Rom. vii. 1—3. 1 Cor. vii. 10—13.
p See on iv. 10. ix. 28, 33.
q Matt. v. 31, 32. xix. 9. Luke xvi. 18. 1 Cor. vii. 4. 10, 11. Heb. xiii. 4.
r Matt. xix. 13—15. Luke xviii. 15, 16.
s 48. ix. 38. Ex. xxxi. 12, 13. Deut. xxxii. 9—11.
t iii. 5. viii. 33. Luke ix. 54—56. Eph. iv. 26.
u Gen. xvii. 7. 10. —14. Num. xiv. 31. Deut. iv. 37. 1 Sam. i. 11. 22. 27, 28. Ps. lxxviii. 4. cxv. 14. Jer. xxxii. 39, 40. Luke xviii. 15, 16. Acts ii. 39. iii. 25. Rom. xi. 16. 1 Cor. vii. 14. 2 Tim. i. 5.
x Ps. cxxxi. 1, 2. Matt. xviii. 4. xix. 14. 1 Cor. xiv. 20. 1 Pet. ii. 2.
y Matt. xviii. 3. Luke xviii. 17. John iii. 3—6. 16. Deut. xxvii. 8. Is. xi. 11. Luke ii. 28, 34. xxiv. 50, 51. John xxi. 15—17.

V. 2—12. (*Notes, Matt.* xix. 3—12.) ' This seeming ' difference ' (between this account and that in Matthew's ' gospel,) ' may be removed by saying, They first asked ' him, " Why did Moses command? " And then our Sa- ' viour asked them, What were the words of Moses in ' this case? And when they had repeated them, he tells ' them the reason why Moses gave them this permission.' *Whitby.*—It is here added, " If a woman shall put away " her husband, and be married to another, &c." (12) This case, which often occurred among the Romans, and sometimes even among the Jews, (having been introduced by Salome, sister to Herod the great, who sent a bill of divorce to her husband, Costobarus; and her example was followed by Herodias and others,) serves to confirm the conclusion, that our Lord intended to put men and women exactly on the same footing in this matter: so that the same conduct is in the man adultery against his wife, which in the woman is adultery against her husband. (*Marg. Ref.*—*Notes, Matt.* v. 31, 32. *Luke* xvi. 16—18. 1 *Cor.* vii. 1—9.)—' Though this discourse be originally ' about divorce; yet it seems plainly to evince, that poly- ' gamy must be unlawful, under the Christian economy. ' For, from Christ's saying, " He that putteth away his " wife, and marries another, committeth adultery against " her; " it clearly follows, that he, who having not put ' her away, marries another, must be guilty of the same ' crime; seeing he must have at least the same power to ' marry another, when the first is put away, as when she ' is not. ... Since to commit adultery is to violate the bed ' of another person, he that commits adultery against his ' wife, must violate her bed; which no husband can do, ' only by doing that which a husband lawfully might do. ' ...Since then a right to polygamy is a right to marry ' more wives than one, he that hath this right cannot vio-

' late the bed of his first wife, by assuming another to it. ' It must therefore be acknowledged, either that the hus- ' band, under Christ's institution, and by the original law ' of matrimony, had no such right; or that he that mar- ' rieth another, cannot by that commit adultery against his ' first wife.' *Whitby.*—The Old Testament no where sug- gests the idea of a husband committing adultery against his wife. (*Note,* 1 *Cor.* vii. 1—5.)

Hardness of heart. (5) Σκληροκαρδία. See on *Matt.* xix. 8. The original word does not mean *cruelty*, in its primary signification, but an obstinate untractable disposition: yet cruelty to those who stand in the way of a man's self-will, naturally springs from this state of mind and heart.—For remarks on other Greek words in the passage, See on *Matt.* v. 31, 32. xix. 3—12.

V. 13—16. (*Notes, Matt.* xix. 13—15. *Luke* xviii. 15 —17.)—' Christ's shewing his regard in such a manner to ' the children, not only must have been exceedingly pleas- ' ing to the parents; but the memory of this condescension ' might make tender and lasting impressions on the chil- ' dren themselves; and the sight must be very edifying ' and encouraging to other young persons, who might ' happen to be present. ... Nicephorus tells, that the cele- ' brated Ignatius, afterwards bishop of Antioch, was one ' of these infants. Our Lord might reasonably be the ' more displeased with the disciples, for endeavouring to ' prevent their being brought; as he had so lately set a ' child among them, and insisted on the necessity of their ' being made conformable to it.' *Doddridge.*—The lan- guage, in this gospel, is more emphatical than that in St. Matthew: and it must be obvious, that the exhortations and instructions, which might have been addressed both to the parents and the children, and by the parents to their children, as a subsequent improvement of the trans-

2 N 4

arms, put *his* hands upon them, and blessed them.

17 ¶ And when he was gone forth into the way, there came one running, and kneeled to him, and asked him, Good Master, what shall I do that I may inherit eternal life?

18 And Jesus said unto him, Why callest thou me good? there is none good but one, *that is,* God.

19 Thou knowest the commandments, Do not commit adultery, Do not kill, Do not steal, Do not bear false witness, Defraud not, Honour thy father and mother.

20 And he answered and said unto him, Master, all these have I observed from my youth.

21 Then Jesus, beholding him, loved him, and said unto him, One thing thou lackest: go thy way, sell whatsoever thou hast, and give to the poor, and thou shalt have treasure in heaven: and come, take up the cross, and follow me.

22 And he was sad at that saying, and went away grieved: for he had great possessions.

23 And Jesus looked round about, and said unto his disciples, How hardly shall they that have riches enter into the kingdom of God!

24 And the disciples were astonished at his words. But Jesus answereth again, and saith unto them, Children, how hard is it for them that trust in riches to enter into the kingdom of God!

25 It is easier for a camel to go through the eye of a needle, than for a rich man to enter into the kingdom of God.

26 And they were astonished out of measure, saying among themselves, Who then can be saved?

27 And Jesus, looking upon them, saith, With men *it is* impossible, but not with God: for with God all things are possible.

28 Then Peter began to say unto him, Lo, we have left all, and have followed thee.

29 And Jesus answered and said, Verily I say unto you, There is no man that hath left house, or brethren, or sisters, or father, or mother, or wife, or children, or lands, for my sake, and the gospel's,

30 But he shall receive an hundred-fold now in this time, houses and brethren, and sisters, and mothers, and children, and lands, with persecutions; and in the world to come eternal life.

31 But many *that are* first shall be last, and the last first.

---

action, must have been in many respects similar to those, which may be grounded on infant-baptism, when duly improved. The passage therefore, though not a direct proof, has surely a favourable aspect towards bringing our infant-offspring to Christ, seeking his blessing on them, and devoting them to his service, in this sacrament; provided it be done intelligently and uprightly.—" He took them up " in his arms, put his hands upon them, and blessed them." What Christian parent does not beseech him thus to ' embrace his children in the arms of his mercy, to lay his ' hands on them and bless them?" And is not this the language of parents in presenting their children for baptism, if rightly understood and attended to? (*Marg. Ref.* —Notes, Gen. xlviii. 14—16. Is. xl. 9—11. Matt. xviii. 1 —6. 10, 11. John iii. 3—6.)

He was much displeased. (14) Ηγανακτησε. See on *Matt.* xx. 24.—*He took them up in his arms.* (16) Εναγκαλισαμενος. ix. 36. Εκ εν, et αγκαλη, ulna. *Luke* ii. 28.

V. 17—31. *Notes, Matt.* xix. 16—30. *Luke* xviii. 18 —30.—*Good Master.* (17) It is said that the Rabbies

affected this title, which shews the peculiar propriety of our Lord's answer.—*Defraud not.* (19) This is supposed by some expositors to be here substituted, instead of the tenth commandment; yet that is far more extensive in its requirement. (*Notes, Ex.* xx. 17. *Rom.* vii. 7, 8.)—' Surely ' all endeavours to defraud shew a very covetous mind; ' inclining us, against the dictates of our consciences, and ' to the damage of our precious souls, to defraud another ' of his right. ...The word ... signifies also, *to detain,* and, ' keep back a thing *when it is due.* ...And surely they who ' desire thus to detain that which belongs to others, and ' they know they must want, must *covet* to have at their ' time what is another's. ...He pays less than he ought, ' who pays not in due time.' *Whitby.* (*Notes, Ex.* xx. 17. 1 *Tim.* vi. 6—10, *vv.* 8—10.)—*Loved him.* (21) There was a natural amiableness in this young ruler, compared with the base conduct of the Scribes, Pharisees, and many others, which excited our Lord's compassion; and, as he was like us in all things, sin excepted, we may suppose that he felt that tender regard for him, which pious minis-

2 M 5

32 ¶ And [p]they were in the way
going up to Jerusalem; and Jesus
went before them: and [q]they were
amazed; and as they followed, they
were afraid. [r]And he took again
the twelve, and began to tell them
what things should happen unto
him,
33 *Saying*, Behold we go up to Jerusalem;
[s]and the Son of man shall
be delivered unto the chief priests,
and unto the scribes; and they shall
[t]condemn him to death, and shall
[u]deliver him to the Gentiles:
34 And they shall [x]mock him, and
shall scourge him, and shall [y]spit upon
him, and shall kill him; [z]and the
third day he shall rise again.
35 ¶ And [a]James and John, the
sons of Zebedee, [b]come unto him,
saying, Master, [c]we would that thou
shouldest do for us whatsoever we shall
desire.
36 And he said unto them, [d]What
would ye that I should do for you?
37 They said unto him, Grant unto
us that we may [e]sit, one on thy right
hand, and the other on thy left hand,
[f]in thy glory.
38 But Jesus said unto them, [g]Ye
know not what ye ask: can ye [h]drink
of the cup that I drink of? and be
[i]baptized with the baptism that I am
baptized with?
39 And they say unto him, [k]We
can. And Jesus said unto them, [l]Ye
shall indeed drink of the cup that I
drink of; and with the baptism that
I am baptized withal shall ye be baptized:
40 But [m]to sit on my right hand
and on my left hand is not mine to
give; but *it shall be given to them* for
whom it is prepared.
41 And when the ten heard *it*,
[n]they began to be much displeased
with James and John.
42 But Jesus called them *to him*,
and saith unto them, [o]Ye know that
they which [*]are accounted to rule
over the Gentiles exercise lordship
over them; and their great ones exercise
authority upon them.
43 But [p]so shall it not be among
you: but [q]whosoever will be great
among you shall be your minister:
44 And whosoever of you will be
the chiefest, shall be servant of all.
45 For even the Son of man [r]came
not to be ministered unto, but to minister,
[s]and to give his life a ransom
for many.

p Matt. xx. 17. Luke xviii. 31.
q Zech. iii. 8. Luke ix. 51. John xi. 8, 16.
r iv. 34. Matt. xi. 25. xiii. 11. Luke x. 23, 24.
s viii. 31. ix. 31. Matt. xvi. 21. xvii. 22, 23. xx. 17—19. Luke ix. 22. xviii. 31—33. xxiv. 6, 7.
t xiv. 64. Matt. xxvi. 66. Acts xiii. 27, 28. Jam. v. 6.
u xv. 1. Matt. xxvii. 2. Luke xxiii. 1, 2. 21. John xviii. 28. xix. 11. Acts iii. 13, 14.
x xiv. 65. xv. 17—20. 29—31. Ps. xxiii. 6—8. Is. liii. 3. Matt. xxvii. 27—44. Luke xxii. 63—65. xxiii. 11. 35—39. John xix. 2, 3.
y xiv. 65. Job xxx. 10. Is. l. 6. Matt. xxvi. 67.
z Ps. xvi. 10. Hos. vi. 2. Jon. i. 17. ii. 10. Matt. xii. 39, 40. 1 Cor. xv. 4.
a i. 19, 20. v. 37. ix. 2. xiv. 33.
b Matt. xx. 20, &c.
c 2 Sam. xiv. 4—11. 1 Kings ii. 16. 20.
d 51. 1 Kings iii. 5, &c. John xv. 7.
e xvi. 19. 1 Kings xxii. 19. Ps. xlv. 9. cx. 1.
f viii. 38. Matt. xxv. 31. Luke xxiv. 26. 1 Pet. i. 11.
g 1 Kings ii. 22. Jer. xlv. 5. Matt. xx. 21, 22. Rom. viii. 26. Jam. iv. 3.
h xiv. 36. Ps. lxxv. 8. Is. li. 22. Jer. xxv. 15. Matt. xxvi. 39. Luke xxii. 42. John xviii. 11.
i Luke xii. 50.
k xiv. 31. John xiii. 37.
l John xv. 20. Acts xii. 2. Col. i. 24. Rev. i. 9.
m Matt. xx. 23. xxv. 34. John xvii. 2. 24.
n ix. 33—36. Prov. xiii. 10. Matt. xx. 24. Luke xxii. 24. Rom. xii. 10. Phil. ii. 3. Jam. iv. 5, 6.
o Matt. xx. 25. Luke xxii. 25. 1 Pet. v. 3.
* Or, *think good.*
p John xviii. 36. Rom. xii. 2.
q ix. 35. Matt. xx. 26, 27. xxiii. 8—12. Luke ix. 48. xiv. 11. xviii. 14. John xiii. 13—18. 1 Cor. ix. 19—23. Gal. v. 13. 1 Pet. v. 5, 6.
r Matt. xx. 28. Luke xxii. 26, 27. John xiii. 14. Phil. ii. 5—8. Heb. v. 8.
s Is. liii. 10—12. Dan. ix. 24. 26. 2 Cor. v. 21. Gal. iii. 13. 1 Tim. ii. 4—6. Tit. ii. 14. 1 Pet. i. 19.

ters do for some in their congregations, who appear amiable, moral, and benevolent, but whom they do not consider at present as truly religious.—*Take up thy cross.* (21) *Notes, Matt.* xvi. 24—28, *v.* 24. *Luke* ix. 18—27, *v.* 23. "The cross," is some trial or suffering which might be avoided by turning out of the way of duty, but cannot otherwise: as the cross lay in our Lord's path; and he took it up, carried it, and was nailed to it, not turning aside because of it. (*Marg. Ref.* r.)—*Trust in riches.* (24) *Marg. Ref.* b.—*Notes, Job* xxxi. 24—28. *Ps.* lxii. 8—10. 1 *Tim.* vi. 17—19.—The danger consists not in possessing, but confiding in riches; and the difficulty consists in possessing, and not confiding in them.—*With persecutions.* (30) Or, notwithstanding persecutions; nay, in the midst of persecutions; for "where tribulation abounded, con-"solation likewise abounded." The comfort of communion with God, as aided greatly by the communion of the saints, and the fellowship of the Holy Spirit, seems especially intended. (*Marg. Ref.* i—n.—*Notes, Rom.* v. 3—5. 1 *Cor.* iii. 18—23. 2 *Cor.* i. 1—7, *vv.* 2—6.)—The promise indeed cannot be understood literally; but as relating to blessings immensely more than equivalent; among which, kind and valuable Christian friends may be numbered.

Defraud not. (19) Μη αποστερησης. 1 *Cor.* vi. 8. vii. 5. 1 *Tim.* vi. 5. *Jam.* v. 4.—*Ex.* xxi. 10. *Sept.*—*Sad.* (22) Στυγνασας. See on *Matt.* xvi. 3. xix. 22.—*Were astonished.* (24) Εθαμβουντο. 32. i. 27. *Acts* ix. 6.

V. 32—34. (*Notes, Matt.* xx. 17—19.) As our Lord and his disciples were on their last journey to Jerusalem; being aware of the inveterate malice of his enemies, and of their designs against his life, and having heard many intimations of his approaching sufferings, they were exceedingly amazed at his resolution; and followed him with great fear of the dangers, to which they too were likely to be exposed. (*Note, John* xi. 11—16.) He was therefore pleased again more particularly to declare to them the sufferings, which he was shortly to endure; that, witnessing the calm intrepidity with which he met them, they might be prepared for their share of the trial, and be encouraged to expect a happy event. But it does not appear that they properly attended to his words; though they are so plain as to need no interpretation, except the history of their accomplishment. (*Marg. Ref.*—*Notes*, ix. 30—32. *Luke* ix. 45.)

They shall mock, &c. (34) Εμπαιξουσιν. xv. 31. *Matt.* ii. 16. xx. 19. xxvii. 29. 31. 41. *Luke* xviii. 32. xxii. 63. xxiii. 11. 36.—*Shall spit*, &c.] Εμπτυσουσιν. x. 34. xv. 19. *Matt.* xxvi. 67. xxvii. 30. *Luke* xviii. 32.

V. 35—45. *Notes*, ix. 33—37. *Matt.* xx. 20—28.—*In thy glory.* (37) "In thy kingdom," *Matt.* xx. 21.—

t Matt. xx. 29, &c. Luke xviii. 35, &c.
u Luke xvi. 20.
22. John ix. 8. Acts iii. 2, 3.
x Matt. ii. 23.
xxi. 11. xxvi. 71. Luke iv. 16. xviii. 36, 37. John i. 45. vii. 41. 52. xix. 19.
Acts vi. 14.
y Is. ix. 6, 7. xi. 1. Jer. xxiii. 5, 6. Matt. i. 1. ix. 27. xii. 23. xv. 22. xxi. 9. xxii. 42—45. Acts xiii. 22, 23. Rom. i. 3, 4.
Rev. xxii. 16.
v. 25. Matt. xix.
13. xx. 31. Luke xviii. 39.
a vi. 35—2. Gen. xxvii. 34—28. Jer. xxix. 13. Matt. xv. 23—
28. Luke xi. 8—10. xviii. 1, &c. Eph. vi. 18. Heb. v. 7. Heb. ii. 17. iv. 15.

46 ¶ And 'they came to Jericho: and as he went out of Jericho with his disciples, and a great number of people, blind Bartimeus, the son of Timeus, sat by the high-way side " begging.

47 And when he heard that it was x Jesus of Nazareth, he began to cry out, and say, Jesus, y thou Son of David, have mercy on me.

48 And z many charged him that he should hold his peace : a but he cried the more a great deal, Thou Son of David, have mercy on me.

49 And Jesus b stood still, and com-

b Ps. lxxxvi. 13. cxlv. 8. Matt. xx. 32—34. Luke xviii.

manded him to be called. And they call the blind man, saying unto him, c Be of good comfort, rise ; he calleth c John xi. 28. thee.

50 And he, d casting away his gar- d Phil. iii. 7—9. ment, rose, and came to Jesus.   Heb. xii. 1.

51 And Jesus answered and said e M. 2 Cor. i. 7. unto him, e What wilt thou that I should do unto thee ? The blind man said unto him, Lord, that I might receive my sight.   Matt. vi. 8. vii. 7, 8. Luke xviii. 41—43. Phil. iv. 6.
f 54. Matt. ix. 22. 28—30. xv. 28. Luke vii. 50. viii. 48.

52 And Jesus said unto him, Go g Or, saved thee. thy way ; f thy faith hath g made thee whole. And immediately f he received his sight, h and followed Jesus in the way.

g vii. 25. Ps. xxxiii. 9. cxlvi 8. Is. xxix. 18. 35. 5. xlii. 16—18. Matt. xi. 5. xii. 22. xxi. 14. John ix. 5—7. xii. 39.
h i. 31. Luke viii. 2, 3.

Baptism. (38, 39) Marg. Ref. h—k.—Note, Luke xii. 49 —53.—(40.) " It is not mine to give, save to those for " whom it hath been prepared." The original is exactly the same as in Matthew; except as " of my Father" is omitted.—(42—44.) ' They that, among the Gentiles, do ' exercise rule over them, receive advantages from their ' subjects, are served and maintained in all their grandeur ' and splendour by them : but in the authority, which I ' shall confer on you and your successors, it shall be quite ' otherwise : ye shall attend and wait upon them whose ' rulers ye are. And the higher ye are advanced in eccle- ' siastick dignity, the greater burden of office and duty ' shall lie upon you, to attend to the wants of all your in- ' feriors, and to supply them.' Hammond. (Notes, 1 Cor. ix. 13—23. 2 Cor. iv. 5, 6. 1 Pet. v. 1—4.)—(44.) In Matthew, " Let him be your servant :" here, " He shall be " servant of all."

V. 46—52. (Matt. xx. 29—34. Note, Luke xviii. 35— 43.) St. Matthew mentions two blind men, who received sight on this occasion ; probably the other was excited to apply to Jesus by Bartimeus's example, and was much less known. Both Matthew and Mark record the miracle, as wrought when Jesus " went out of Jericho ;" but Luke says, it took place, " when he was come nigh to Jericho," and he afterwards records an event which took place in that city. (Note, Luke xix. 1—10.) He seems, however, only to mean that the miracle was performed when he was near Jericho : for it is not improbable that Jesus staid some days in that neighbourhood ; and this occurred, as he went out of the city during that time, though perhaps he returned thither again.—Our Lord, attended by his disciples and surrounded by the multitude, came to a place, where a man, well known in those parts, " sat by the way-side " begging." This person had no doubt previously heard of him and his miracles ; and believed that he was the promised Messiah, by comparing these reports, with what he had read while he had his eye-sight, or had heard from the prophecies of scripture on that subject. (Notes, Is. xxix. 17—19. xxxv. 5—7.) It is computed by the harmonists, that the man born blind, was restored to sight before this time. (Notes, John ix.)—Enquiring, therefore, what the great concourse of people meant ; he learned that " Jesus

" of Nazareth was passing by :" and immediately he conceived the hope of recovering his sight by miracle. Accordingly, without delay or hesitation, he cried out, saying, " Jesus, thou Son of David, have mercy upon me." Our Lord might perhaps be then engaged in discourse with his attendants : and as Bartimeus was a mean person, and his application appeared rude and clamorous ; " many charged " him to hold his peace." He was, however, too much in earnest in seizing the present opportunity of craving so greatly desired a blessing to be thus silenced : on the contrary, he " cried out a great deal" more loudly and incessantly, " Thou Son of David, have mercy upon me." (Marg. Ref. y—a.—Notes, Gen. xxxii. 24—30. Matt. xv. 21—28.) At length our Lord stood still, and ordered the blind man to be conducted to him ; and some encouraged him to expect a cure, as Jesus had expressly called him. Accordingly, he cast away his upper garment, as in haste, and desiring to be rid of every encumbrance. Thus he came to Jesus, who asked him, " What wilt thou that I should do to " thee ?" He well knew what Bartimeus wanted ; but he chose to hear it from his own lips, as the language of faith, dependence, and expectation. When therefore the man had answered, " Lord, that I might receive my sight ;" Jesus said to him, " Go thy way," or depart in peace ; " thy " faith hath made thee whole :" or, " hath saved thee." His faith procured from Jesus the opening of his eyes, and, there can be no reasonable doubt, the salvation of his soul also. " Immediately he received sight ;" but instead of departing, he joined the multitude, and followed Jesus in the way, for the mercy which he had received ; and all the people joined him in praising God for what had been done. (Marg. and Marg. Ref. b—h.—Note, Matt. ix. 27—29.) —Bartimeus signifies, in Syriack, the son of Timeus. Some think, that he was thus specially mentioned by name, because he afterwards became of note among our Lord's disciples.

As he went out of, &c. (46) Εκπορευομενα αυτα. " He " going forth from Jericho, &c." Εν τω εγγιξειν αυτον εις Ιεριχω. Luke xviii. 35.—' St. Luke saith, that Christ was ' yet near Jericho : but then, so is he, who is gone a little ' way from it, as well as he who is come near to it.' Whitby.

2 м 7

CHAP. XI.

Jesus enters Jerusalem, riding on an ass, amidst the

acclamations of the multitude, 1—11. He curses a barren fig-tree, 12—14; and drives the traders from the temple, 15—19. From the fig-tree being dried

PRACTICAL OBSERVATIONS.

V. 1—16.

Our blessed Lord hath given his ministers an example of being " instant in season and out of season," in " preaching the word," whenever or wherever the people are disposed to hear it; and notwithstanding the perverseness and malice of those who " watch for their halting." —We should expect to be frequently proved with ensnaring questions, from Pharisees and infidels; and we should study to be expert in answering them pertinently, and in " the meekness of wisdom." (Notes, Prov. xxvi. 4, 5. 1 Pet. iii. 13—16.) In general, our appeal must be to the plain testimony of God's word: yet in applying texts of scripture to particular cases, an accurate attention to the meaning and design of the sacred writer is absolutely necessary; and many distinctions must be noted, between temporary appointments or allowances, " because of the " hardness of men's hearts," or with reference to peculiar circumstances; and those truths and precepts, which are of universal and immutable importance and obligation. For it is evident in fact, that almost all errors in doctrine and practice have been grounded on wrong conclusions from detached texts, either misinterpreted, or misapplied to cases to which they have no relation. But the humble, teachable, and unprejudiced, who love the truths and ways of God, and depend on the teaching of the Holy Spirit, will be conducted safe through such difficulties, as are absolutely insurmountable to those, who " lean to their own " understandings."—True religion will teach us our duty in every relation of life, and render us comfortable in ourselves, and blessings to each other in them: so that even those restrictions, which to carnal men appear intolerable, become easy and pleasant to the consistent Christian; and he considers the liberty and indulgence for which others contend, as the source of confusion, debasement, and misery.—Those, " whom God hath joined together," and taught to be helpers and blessings to each other, as having one common inseparable interest here, and as being " heirs " together of the grace of life;" (Notes, Eph. v. 22—33. 1 Pet. iii. 1—7;) if they have children, will bring them, by their united prayers, to Jesus, that he may impart his salvation to their souls: and he will be " much displeased " with all," who would discourage them in so doing; for all men ought to be exhorted to seek his blessing on those with whom they are connected. (P. O. Matt. xix. 1—15.) Even " little children should be suffered " and directed to go to the loving Saviour, as soon as they are capable of understanding his words: they should be assured that he will regard their lisping petitions; and all his ministers should copy his condescension, and attentive regard to the lambs of the flock, the young, the newly awakened, the weak believers, the poor, and the discouraged; that they may be his instruments in gathering them to him, and in leading them to establishment and comfort. (Note, Is. xl. 9—11.)—While we consider the case of children, and remember that " of such is the kingdom of God;" let us

peculiarly attend to our Lord's declaration, that " whoso- " ever shall not receive the kingdom of God as a little " child, he shall not enter therein." No learned scribe, or philosopher, no man of the most distinguished learning, or pre-eminent abilities, can be a true subject of the kingdom of grace here, or an heir of the kingdom of glory hereafter, who will not stoop to receive the instructions and blessings of the kingdom, in the simple teachable spirit, with which a little child learns the first elements of knowledge, from its parent, nurse, or teacher. (Note, Matt. xi. 27.) " If any man therefore be wise in this world, " let him become a fool, that he may be wise" unto salvation: and, as scarcely any thing militates so much against this submission of the understanding to the divine teaching, this exercise of implicit faith in the word of God, and willing dependence on him, and unreserved subjection to his will, in the appointments of his providence and the dispensations of his grace, as the pride of human wisdom; so not many of the wise and learned, any more than of the rich and noble, have hitherto been found among the followers of Christ. (Notes, 1 Cor. i. 26—31. iii. 18—23.)

V. 17—31.

Whatever increases pride, and an attachment to the world, must enhance the difficulty of a man's embracing the gospel. If it were not the fixed determination of God, that " no flesh shall glory in his presence," the case of rulers, scribes, and Pharisees would be more hopeful. Many of them will call Jesus " Good Master;" seem to have serious thoughts about " eternal life;" and approve, and even profess exactly to obey, several of the commandments; but they do not understand the holiness of the divine character, the spirituality and extent of the holy law, the evil and desert of sin, their own deep guilt and depravity, the nature of salvation, or their need of the Redeemer's blood, righteousness, and regenerating Spirit. A sharp trial often proves even their moral goodness to be radically defective, and to be carnal selfishness in a more decent garb: so that self-denying, impoverishing duties no more suit their love of this present world, than the doctrines of grace do their self-complacency. They appear to be very sorry, that they cannot reconcile the service of God and Mammon, and both obey Christ and keep the world: but they cannot think of leaving an earthly treasure, which they have in possession, for the hope of " a " heavenly treasure" in reversion, by " taking up the " cross and following Christ." All these evils are enhanced by increasing wealth: few can possess riches, without loving them and trusting in them; and it is extremely difficult to break the strong bands, which hold a carnal mind to large possessions. So that Jesus speaks to us, " as to children," when he reminds us, " How hardly shall " they that have riches enter into the kingdom of heaven!" And instead of expressing our astonishment, or indulging our speculations, let us learn contentment in a low estate: or if a higher be allotted us, let us watch against confidence in riches, and the love of them, or any thing that

2 M 8

up, he shews his disciples the power of faith, and directs them how to pray, 20—26. He silences the priests and scribes, who questioned his authority, 27—33.

can be purchased with them. (*Note, Prov.* xxx. 7—9.) Let us pray to be enabled to part with every earthly object for Christ's sake; and to use all, which we are allowed to keep, in his service and as his faithful stewards: (*Notes,* and *P. O. Luke* xvi. 1—12 :) and let us be encouraged to pray for the rich especially, and to employ all the means which we can for their good, remembering, " that with " God all things are possible."—But, whatever our circumstances be, we shall be called on to prove the sincerity of our faith and love, by renouncing some temporal advantages for Christ's sake, if we profess to be his followers. The trial in this case may be sharp, but the recollection of having made the required sacrifice will afterwards " turn unto us for a testimony : " and to encourage us in so doing, we are assured of an immense compensation even in this present world, as well as of " eternal life " in that to come." If we have true faith, we shall be satisfied with this security, and expect the promised blessing ; and thus well regulated, holy self-love will be reconciled to self-denial, renunciation of worldly objects, and persecutions for Christ's sake. But such trials lay open men's hearts, and thus the " first become last, and the last first." (*P. O. Matt.* xix. 16—30. *Luke* xviii. 18—43.)

V. 32—45.

Even disciples are often more disposed to be amazed at our Lord's contempt of the world, and patient endurance of poverty, hardship, contempt, suffering, and death for them ; than to consider him, as having " left them an ex-" ample that they should follow his steps : " and though they do follow him, even when danger approaches ; yet they do it fearfully, and with hesitation and reluctance. Indeed when we consider, that the holy Jesus endured every indignity and cruelty, from Jewish priests and scribes, who delivered him up to the insults of gentile rulers and soldiers, as a condemned malefactor ; we cannot expect exemption from reproach and suffering, however prudent, blameless, or benevolent, our conduct may be : but the view of his glorious resurrection and exaltation may encourage our hope of a happy event to all our conflicts.—It is greatly to be lamented, that " honour, glory, " and immortality" in a future world, and obscurity, poverty, contempt, and persecution here, are but ill suited to the desires of most of those who are called Christians: nay sanctification must be considerably advanced in us, before we shall be unreservedly reconciled to them. If Jesus were ready to gratify all our desires ; it would soon appear, that we were aspiring to reputation, authority, popularity, or eminence among our brethren; and that we were unwilling to taste of his cup, or to have any measure of his baptism, if we could by any means avoid it. We should often ask for " we know not what," and should be effectually ruined by having our prayers answered. But he loves us more wisely than we love ourselves; and he will give us what is good for us, not what we foolishly hanker after.—We are indeed often keen-sighted in discerning, and severe in reproving, the vain glory and ambition of our brethren ; but prone to fall into the same faults in our competitions with them : yet our gracious

VOL. v.

Master gently rebukes and corrects us, and gradually represses and subdues our foolish desires of pre-eminence. He teaches us to leave lordly authority, vain distinctions, and the praise of men, to Gentiles and nominal disciples; and to follow him, in aspiring after true greatness, by self-abasement, serviceableness, and a readiness to labour and suffer in any way, however obscure and disregarded, b7 which we improve our talent to the glory of God and the good of the souls of men. (*P. O. Matt.* xx. 17—34.)

V. 46—52.

Whilst enlightened believers are admonished daily to " behold the glory of their Lord," till they are more completely changed into his image ; let sinners be exhorted to imitate blind Bartimeus.—As long as men are favoured with the use of their eyes, how diligent should they be, in searching the scriptures, and storing their memories with them ; that if visited with blindness, they may have something treasured up, on which they may profitably meditate, and with which they may compare what they hear, either from preachers, or concerning them ! And when the Lord deprives any of the use of one sense, how diligent should they be in improving those which they still enjoy ! In these respects, this interesting narrative sets before us an instructive and encouraging example.— If the eyes of men's understandings are not opened to behold the preciousness of Christ, and the beauty of holiness ; they are shut up under a far more dreadful darkness, and precluded from far more delightful prospects and exquisite pleasures, in respect of the spiritual world, than any blind man in respect of the natural. But where the gospel is preached, or the written word vouchsafed, and men are able to read it, Jesus is passing by; and this is the sinner's opportunity. Though he cannot at present understand the doctrine of Christ, or see his glory ; yet let him as a perishing sinner cry after him, " Jesus, thou Son of David, have mercy on me." And if any man attempt to dissuade, deride, and reproach him, or to threaten him into silence, let him take occasion from thence to cry the more earnestly for salvation. In this way the Saviour will notice him ; and his invitations and promises will, as it were, direct him to be called. We too should delight in encouraging enquiring souls, and in exhorting them to " be of good comfort," while they arise and go to Jesus, who calls them by his word, and " will " in no wise cast them out." In seeking to him, all delay must be avoided, and every impediment laid aside ; and he will, as it were, enquire of us, what we would have. We should therefore study to get acquainted with our own wants, and with his promises, that we may our answer ready, and find liberty and earnestness in prayer. We cannot indeed see him, as blind Bartimeus could not, when he sought mercy from him : but he is ever present with us; and by faith we realize that presence, and address our requests to him, which he never fails to answer. Thus faith brings salvation from Christ unto men's souls , and they join the company of his disciples, in shewing forth his praises, and in walking in his most holy ways. (*Notes*, 1 *Pet.* ii. 9—12.)

2 N

AND [a] when they came nigh to Jerusalem, unto Bethphage, and Bethany,
[b] at the mount of Olives, [c] he sendeth
forth two of his disciples,
2 And saith unto them, [d] Go your
way into the village over against you;
and as soon as ye be entered into it,
ye shall find a colt tied, whereon never
man sat; loose him, and bring *him*.
3 And if any man say unto you,
Why do ye this? say ye, [e] that the Lord
hath need of him; [f] and straightway he
will send him hither.
4 And they went their way, [g] and
found the colt tied by the door without, in a place where two ways met;
and they loose him.
5 And certain of them that stood
there said unto them, What do ye
loosing the colt?
6 And they said unto them even as
Jesus had commanded: and they let
them go.
7 And they brought [h] the colt to
Jesus, [i] and cast their garments on
him; and he sat upon him.
8 And many spread their garments
in the way; and others [k] cut down
branches off the trees, and strawed
them in the way.
9 And they that went before, and
they that followed, cried, saying, [l] Hosanna; Blessed *is* he that cometh in
the name of the Lord:
10 Blessed *be* [m] the kingdom of our
father David, that cometh in the name
of the Lord: Hosanna [n] in the highest.
11 And [o] Jesus entered into Jerusalem, and into the temple: and when
he had looked round about upon all
things, and now the even-tide was
come, [p] he went out unto Bethany,
with the twelve.
12 ¶ And [q] on the morrow, when
they were come from Bethany, [r] he
was hungry:
13 And [s] seeing a fig-tree afar off,
having leaves, he came, if [t] haply he
might find any thing thereon: and
when he came to it, he found nothing
but leaves; for the time of figs was
not *yet*.
14 And Jesus answered and said
unto it, [u] No man eat fruit of thee
hereafter for ever. And his disciples
heard *it*.

a Matt. xxi. 1. Luke xix. 29.
b xiii. 3. 2 Sam. xv. 30. Zech. xiv. 4. Matt. xxiv. 3. xxvi. 30. John viii. 1. Acts i. 12.
c *See on* vi. 7. xiv. 13.
d Matt. xxi. 2, 3. Luke xix. 30, 31.
e Ps. xxiv. 1. Acts x. 36. 2 Cor. viii. 9. Heb. ii. 7—9.
f xiv. 15, 1 Chr. xxix. 12—18. Ps. cx. 3. Acts i. 24.
g Matt. xxi. 6, 7. xxvi. 19. Luke xix. John ii. 3—5. Heb. xi. 8.
h Zech. ix. 9. Matt. xxi. 4, 5. Luke xix. 35.
i 2 Kings ix. 13. Matt. xxi. 7, 8. Luke xix. 36. John xii. 12—16.
k Lev. xxiii. 40.
l Ps. cxviii. 25, 26. Matt. xxi. 9. xxiii. 39. Luke xix. 37, 38. John xii. 13. xix. 15.
m Is. ix. 6, 7. Jer. xxxiii. 15—17. 26. Ez. xxxiv. 23, 24. xxxvii. 24, 25. Hos. iii. 5. Am. ix. 11, 12. Luke i. 31—33.
n Ps. cxlviii. 1. Luke ii. 14. xix. 38—40.
o Mal. iii. 1. Matt. xxi. 10—12. 14—16. Luke xix. 41—45.
p Matt. xxi. 17. Luke xxi. 37, 38. John viii. 1, 2.
q Matt. xxi. 18.
r Matt. iv. 2. Luke iv. 2. John iv. 6, 7. 31—33. xix. 28. Heb. ii. 17.
s Matt. xxi. 19. Luke xiii. 6—9.
t Ruth ii. 3. 1 Sam. vi. 9. Luke x. 31. xii. 6, 7.
u 20, 21. Is. v. 5, 6. Matt. iii. 10. vii. 19. xii. 33—35. xxi. 19, 20. 33, 44. John xv. 6. Heb. vi. 4—8. x. 26—31. 2 Pet. ii. 20—22. Rev. xxii. 11.

NOTES.

CHAP. XI. V. 1—11. *Notes, Matt.* xxi. 1—11. *Luke* xix. 28—40. *John* xii. 12—19.—*Ye shall find*, &c. (2) 'The exact knowledge, which our Lord shewed, of so 'many minute and most fortuitous particulars, must surely 'impress the minds of these messengers greatly, and esta- 'blish the faith of his followers. It is observable, that 'many such things occurred a little before his death, which, 'considered in this view, have a peculiar beauty. (xiv. 15, '16. *Matt.* xxvi. 31—35. *Luke* xxii. 10—13.)' *Doddridge.* —*Whereon*, &c.] Mark alone notices this circumstance.—*Why do*, &c. (3) The owners actually made this demand. (5. *Luke* xix. 33.) Thus every occasion of objection was precluded.—*The Lord.*] I cannot recollect one instance, in which this word, (ὁ Κυριος,) with the article, and without either noun or pronoun, is used in speaking of any other person, than Jesus; except when used of the glorious God absolutely.—*The colt.* (7) 'It 'seems to have been a miracle, that such a colt should 'patiently suffer Christ to ride upon him.'—*Blessed*, &c. (10) *Marg. Ref.* m.—*Notes, Is.* ix. 6, 7. *Jer.* xxiii. 5, 6. *Ez.* xxxiv. 23—31. *Hos.* iii. 4, 5. *Luke* i. 26—33, *vv.* 32, 33. 'Let the kingdom be happily begun, and flourish, 'which God is to erect, according to his promise to our 'father David. Let prosperity be from heaven to the 'King Messiah and to his kingdom.' *Whitby.*—*Hosanna.*] *Marg. Ref.* l.—*Note, Ps.* cxviii. 25, 26.

A place where two ways met. (4) Τυ αμφοδυ. Ex αμφι, et ὁδος. Used here only N. T.—*Branches.* (8) Στοιϐαδας. Used here only N. T. Κλαδυς, *Matt.* xxi. 8.

V. 12—14. *Marg. Ref.—Note, Matt.* xxi. 17—20.—*The time*, &c. (13) It is evident, that the fruit, on the common fig-trees, must have been utterly unfit for food, at this early season of the year: for though the fig-tree puts forth its blossom before the leaves; yet the fruit must have been very small at the passover, which is said by the Jewish writers to be five months before the time of ripe figs. (*Note, Matt.* xxiv. 32—35, *v.* 32.) It has been said, that our Lord found only leaves, and no fruit of any kind, and therefore this must have been a barren tree; for if no fruit were at this time set, there could be none that year. But this could be no reason, why he should, when hungry, seek fruit on it to eat; as there could have been none fit for use, however fruitful it might promise to be. The following quotation seems to contain the true solution of the difficulty.—'Let it be noted, 'that St. Mark doth not by these words, "for the time of '"figs was not yet," assign a reason why our Lord found 'no figs upon the tree; but why he went to this one tree, 'which had leaves on it, and so was of that kind of figs, 'which, saith Theophrastus, was αει φυλλον, *semper coman- 'tibus foliis*; a fig-tree, that had always leaves; and why 'he expected to find fruit on that tree, which upon the 'ordinary fig-trees abounding there, he could not expect, 'the time of ordinary figs not being yet. For this kind of

15 ¶ And they come to Jerusalem: ˣ and Jesus went into the temple, and began to cast out them that sold and bought in the temple, and overthrew ʸ the tables of the money-changers, and the seats of them that sold doves ;

16 And would not suffer that any man should carry *any* vessel through the temple.

17 And he taught, saying unto them, ᶻ Is it not written, My house shall be called of all nations, The ᵇ house of prayer ? but ye have made it ᵃ a den of thieves.

18 And the scribes and chief priests heard *it*, ᵇ and sought how they might destroy him: for they ᶜ feared him, because all the people was ᵈ astonished at his doctrine.

19 And ᵉ when even was come, he went out of the city.

20 ¶ And in the morning, as they passed by, ᶠ they saw the fig-tree dried up from the roots.

21 And Peter, calling to remem-brance, saith unto him, Master, behold, the fig-tree which thou ᵍ cursedst is withered away!

22 And Jesus answering, saith unto them, ʰ Have ⁱ faith in God.

23 For verily I say unto you, That ⁱ whosoever shall say unto this mountain, Be thou removed, and be thou ʲ cast into the sea, ʲ and shall not doubt in his heart, but shall believe that those things which he saith shall come to pass ; he shall have ᵏ whatsoever he saith.

24 Therefore I say unto you, ˡ What things soever ye desire when ye pray, believe that ye receive *them*, and ye shall have *them*.

25 And when ye ᵐ stand praying, ⁿ forgive, if ye have ought against any ; that your Father also which is in heaven may forgive you your trespasses.

26 But if ye do not forgive, neither will your Father which is in heaven forgive your trespasses.

' fig-tree, being ever green with leaves, hath, saith Theo-
' phrastus, ἅμα και τον ενον και τον νεον καρπον, old and new
' fruit hanging on it together ; the fruit of the year past
' and present, say the Jewish doctors. Accordingly, Julian
' the apostate, speaking of the fruit of Damascus, saith,
' Some of them were but of a short duration ; ...only the
' fig-tree carries its fruit above a year, and it hangs on with
' the fruit of the following year.' *Whitby.* (Note, *Is.*
xxviii. 1—4, *v.* 4.)—The fig-trees, in England, seem in
general to be of this kind, though the frost kills their
leaves ; but the case in Judea was different : so that the
time of ripe figs, on the ordinary fig-trees, was not come ;
but fruit might have been expected on this tree, because
its leaves shewed it to be of the other species. Thus it
was an apt emblem of the Jewish nation, whose profession
of true religion gave an expectation of fruit ; though
none could have been looked for among the Gentiles.
But as this expectation was not answered, the nation was
rejected, and has ever since continued unfruitful. (*Notes,
Jer.* viii. 13. *Luke* xiii. 6—9. *Heb.* vi. 7, 8. *Rev.* xxii. 10
—12.)

V. 15—17. *Notes, Matt.* xxi. 12—16.—*Would not suffer,*
&c. (16) This circumstance is not mentioned by Matthew ;
and it rather favours the supposition, that Christ purged
the temple two days successively ; and more completely
the second day than before. In order to vindicate the
sanctity of that holy place, and to keep up the distinction
between its sacred services and all kinds of secular business ; he would not suffer any man on whatever pretence
to carry a vessel, or burden, through its courts. (*Marg.
Ref.—Note, John* ii. 13—17.)—*Of all,* &c. (17) It would
be more properly rendered, " for all nations." Not that

all nations would call it so ; but, men out of all nations,
who should come to it, as the centre of the worship of the
true God, uprightly to pray to him, would be accepted,
and such ought to have been encouraged.

The temple. (15, 16) To ἱερον, signifies, the temple,
with all the courts, and adjacent buildings. Ὁ ναος, the
sanctuary, consisting of " the holy place," into which none
but the priests were allowed to enter ; and the most holy
place within the veil.—*Of all nations.* (17) Πασι τοις
εθνεσιν, " to, or *for*, all nations." Exact from *Is.* lvi. 7.
Sept.

V. 18, 19. *Marg. Ref.* b. e.—*Note, Matt.* xxi. 14
—16.

V. 20—26. (*Marg. Ref.—Notes,* 12—14. *Matt.* xxi.
17—22. *Luke* xiii. 6—9.) The apostles were exhorted to
have " faith in God," or, " the faith of God ; " (*marg.*)
that is, a firm confidence in his power and truth, as enabling them to effect those things which they undertook
in his name. This was peculiarly applicable to that faith
required in working miracles. ' These were generally in-
' troduced by some solemn declaration of what was in-
' tended, which was in effect a prediction of immediate
' success. So Peter says, (*Acts* iii. 6,) " In the name of
" Jesus Christ rise up, and walk ; " and, (ix. 34,) " Eneas,
" Jesus Christ maketh thee whole." And in pronounc-
' ing this, the person speaking pawned all his credit as a
' messenger from God, and consequently all the honour
' and usefulness of his future life, on the immediate mira-
' culous energy to attend his words, and to be visibly ex-
' erted on his uttering them. Hence it is, that such a
' firm courageous faith is so often urged on those, to whom
' such miraculous powers were given.' *Doddridge.* This

2 x 3

27 ¶ And they come again to Jerusalem: and, [o] as he was walking in the temple, there come to him [p] the chief priests, and the scribes, and the elders,

28 And say unto him, [q] By what authority doest thou these things? and who gave thee this authority to do these things?

29 And Jesus answered and said unto them, [r] I will also ask of you one [*] question, and answer me, and I will tell you by what authority I do these things.

30 The [s] baptism of John, was *it* from heaven, or of men? answer [t] me.

31 And they reasoned with themselves, saying, If we shall say, From heaven, he will say, [u] Why then did ye not believe him?

32 But if we shall say, Of men; [u] they feared the people: [x] for all *men* [y] counted John, that he was a prophet indeed.

33 And they answered and said unto Jesus, [y] We cannot tell. And Jesus answering, saith unto them, [z] Neither do I tell you by what authority I do these things.

o Mal. iii. 1. Matt. xxi. 23—27. Luke xx. 1—8. John x. 23. xviii. 20.
p xiv. 1. Ps. ii. 1—5. Acts iv. 5—8. 27, 28.
q Ex. ii. 14. Num. xvi. 3. 13. Acts vii. 27, 28. 38, 39. 51.
r Is. iii. 13. Matt. xxi. 24. Luke xx. 3—8.
* Or, *thing*.
s i. 1—11. ix. 13. Matt. iii. Luke iii. 1—20. John i. 6—8. 15—36. iii. 25—36.
t Matt. xi. 7—14. xxi. 25—27. 31, 32. John i. 15. 29. 34. 36. iii. 29—36.
u vi. 20. xii. 12. Matt. xiv. 5. xxi. 46. Luke xx. 19. xxii. 2. Acts v. 26.
x Matt. iii. 5. xxi. 31, 32. Luke vii. 26—29. xx. 6—8. John x. 41.
y Is. vi. 9, 10. xxix. 9—14. xlii. 19, 20. lvi. 10. Jer. viii. 7—9. Hos. iv. 6. Mal. ii. 7, 8. Matt. xv. 14. xxiii. 16—26. John iii. 10. Rom. i. 18—22. 28. 2 Cor. iii. 15. iv. 3, 4. 2 Thes. ii. 10—12.
z Job v. 13. Prov. xxvi. 4, 5. Matt. xvi. 4. xxi. 27 Luke xx. 7, 8. xxii. 66—69. John ix. 27.

ought not, however, to be considered, as the exclusive meaning of the exhortation, which should also be kept in mind in all our expectations and prayers, *grounded on the promises of God*, which will certainly be fulfilled to every believer, in the proper meaning of them, and in the due season; and this we ought to expect, notwithstanding all difficulties and apparent improbabilities. (*Notes, Jam.* i. 5—8. 1 *John* v. 14, 15.) Therefore, "whatever we desire, "according to the will of God," made known by his precepts and promises, we should when we pray for it confidently hope to receive, and go on with our duty as though we had received it.—But if we would thus have confidence in prayer before a holy God, we must have an assured hope of his merciful forgiveness; in order to which we must fully and heartily forgive all that have injured us. (*Notes, Matt.* vi. 12. 14, 15. xviii. 21—35. *Luke* xvii. 3—5. 1 *Tim.* ii. 8—10, *v.* 8. 1 *John* iii. 18—24.)—*Standing* seems to have been a frequent posture in prayer among the Jews; (*Marg. Ref.* m;) though kneeling is far the most sanctioned by the example of Christ and his apostles, and indeed in most parts of the Old Testament.

V. 27—33. *Marg. Ref.—Notes, Matt.* xxi. 23—32. *Luke* xx. 1—8.

PRACTICAL OBSERVATIONS.

V. 1—19.

We should learn from our divine Master to meet sufferings, in a good cause, with constancy and alacrity; and to be bold and open in our profession of the truth, in proportion as its enemies grow virulent and determined in opposition.—The undeniable proofs which he gave during his humiliation on earth, of his knowledge of all events, and his influence over all hearts, should inspire us with implicit confidence, and excite us to unreserved and prompt obedience: for we shall find all his words true and faithful, and he will carry us through all difficulties and reproaches, with which we can meet in his service.—It is a peculiar honour and felicity to be instrumental, in any way, to the display of his glory. His "kingdom is "not of this world," and therefore its external appearance is often mean; and its subjects and ministers must not affect worldly grandeur, or be ashamed of appearing poor, and even despicable in the eyes of carnal men: but "righteousness, peace, and joy in the Holy Ghost," are their privileges, which are of more value than all earthly honours and riches, however abundant. These blessings we should seek for ourselves, in the first place, with decided preference above all other things, and then aim to communicate them to others: and we ought to welcome all those, who "come in the name of the Lord," to promote the peace and prosperity of his kingdom, rejoicing greatly on account of their success in this good work.—While we expect the great Head of the church effectually to purge it from all hirelings and abuses, that it may no more be reproached as "a den of robbers," (P. O. *Rev.* xviii. 9—19,) but may be indeed "a house of prayer" and spiritual worship, "to all nations;" how active should rulers and teachers be, in doing what they can to promote the scriptural administration of his ordinances, the sanctification of his holy day, and the faithful preaching of his word; and to establish and maintain a decided distinction between things sacred and secular! And at how great a distance should all, who love and preach the truth, keep from every appearance of turning their ministry into a lucrative trade!—Alas! that chief priests, scribes, and elders should so frequently be the most inveterate opposers of reformation; from a mistaken regard to their own interests and reputation, which in fact they thus undermine and destroy! Men of this character and spirit set themselves against the truth, for fear of the consequences of its getting ground, when they find the people attentive and impressed. Thus they enter on a contest, from which they cannot recede with credit, and in which they cannot persist without the most fatal consequences: for, though they should for a time be successful, they must in the event be crushed by the power of the exalted Redeemer. (P. O. *Matt.* xxi. 12—16. 33—46.)

V. 20—33.

Alas! how many professed Christians and ministers are barren fig-trees, covered with leaves, raising, and disappointing, the expectations of those who seek fruit from them; and exposing themselves to the doom of being withered, and remaining to all eternity unfruitful under the awful curse of the Lord! We should fear this sentence far more than death, and should rest in no religion which does not render us "fruitful in good works." This will be the sure effect of "faith in God," in proportion as

CHAP. XII.

The parable of the vineyard let out to wicked husbandmen, 1—12. Jesus answers the Pharisees and Herodians about paying tribute to Cæsar, 13—17; the Sadducees, concerning the resurrection, 18—27; and a Scribe, concerning the first commandment in the law, 28—34. He demands of the Scribes, whose Son the Messiah was to be, 35—37; warns the people against the ostentation and hypocrisy of the Scribes, 38—40; and commends a poor widow, who had cast two mites into the treasury, 41—44.

AND [a] he began to speak unto them
by parables. [b] A *certain* man [c] planted
a vineyard, [d] and set an hedge about *it*,
and digged *a place for* the wine-fat,
and built a tower, [e] and let it out to
husbandmen, [f] and went into a far
country.
2 And [g] at the season he sent to the
husbandmen [h] a servant, that he might
receive from the husbandmen of the
fruit of the vineyard.
3 And [i] they caught *him*, and beat
him, [k] and sent *him* away empty.
4 And again he sent unto them another
servant: and at him they cast
stones, and wounded *him* in the head,
and sent *him* away shamefully handled.
5 And again he sent another; [l] and
him they killed, and many others;
beating some, and killing some.
6 Having yet therefore [m] one son,
[n] his well-beloved, he sent him also
last unto them, saying, [o] They will reverence
my son.
7 But those husbandmen said among
themselves, [p] This is the heir; come,
let us kill him, and the inheritance
shall be our's.
8 And they took him, and killed
him, and [q] cast *him* out of the vineyard.
9 What [r] shall therefore the lord of
the vineyard do? [s] He will come and
destroy the husbandmen, [t] and will give
the vineyard unto others.
10 And [u] have ye not read this
scripture, [x] The Stone which the builders
rejected is become the Head of the
corner:
11 This [y] was the Lord's doing, and
it is marvellous in our eyes?
12 And they sought to lay hold on
him, but [z] feared the people; for they
[a] knew that he had spoken the parable
against them: and they left him, and
went their way.
13 ¶ And [b] they sent unto him certain
of the Pharisees, and of the [c] Herodians,
to catch him in *his* words.
14 And when they were come, they
say unto him, [d] Master, [e] we know that

a iv. 2. 11—13. 33, 34. Ez. xx. 49. Matt. xiii. 10—15. 34, 35. xxi. 28—33. xxii. 1—14. Luke viii. 10.
b Matt. xxi. 33—40. Luke xx. 9—15.
c Ps. lxxx. 8—16. Is. v. 1—4. Jer. ii. 21. Luke xiii. 6—9. John xv. 1—8. Rom. xi. 17—24.
d Neh. ix. 13, 14. Ps. lxxviii. 68, 69. cxlvii. 19, 20. Ez. xx. 11, 12. 18—20. Acts vii. 38. 46, 47. Rom. iii. 1, 2. ix. 4, 5.
e Cant. viii. 11, 12. Is. vii. 23.
f xiii. 34. Matt. xxv. 14. Luke xv. 13. xix. 12.
g Ps. i. 3. Matt. xxi. 34. Luke xx. 10.
h Judg. vi. 8—10. 2 Kings xvii. 13. 2 Chr. xxxvi. 15. Ezra ix. 11. Jer. xxv. 4 b. xxxv. 15. xliv. 4. Zech. i. 3—6, vii. 7. Heb. i. 1.
i 1 Kings xviii. 4. 13. xix. 10. 14. xxii. 27. 2 Chr. xvi. 10. xxiv. 19—21. xxxvi. 16. Neh. ix. 26. Jer. ii. 30. xx. 2. xxvi. 20—24. xxix. 26. xxxvii. 15, 16. xxxviii. 4—6. Matt. xxiii. 34—37. Luke xi. 47—51. xiii. 33, 34. Acts vii. 52. 59. 1 Thes. ii. 15. Heb. xi. 36, 37.
k Jer. xliv. 4. 5. 16. Dan. ix. 10, 11. Zech. vii. 9—13. Luke xx. 10—12.
l ix. 13. Matt. v. 12. xxi. 35, 36. xxii. 6. Luke vi. 22, 23. 26.
m Ps. ii. 7. Matt. i. 23. xi. 27. xxvi. 63. John i. 14. 18. 34. 49. iii. 16—18. 1 John iv. 9. v. 11, 12.
n i. 11. ix. 7. Gen. xxii. 2. 12. xxxvii. 3. 11—13. xliv. 20. Is. xlii. 1. Matt. iii. 17. xvii. 5. Luke iii. 22. ix. 35. John iii. 35.
o Ps. ii. 12. John v. 23. Heb. i. 6. Rev. v. 9—13.
p 12. Gen. iii. 15. xxxvii. 20. Ps. ii. 2, 3. xxii. 12—15. Is. xlix. 7. liii. 7, 8. Matt. ii. 3—13. 16. John xi. 47—50. Acts ii. 23. v 28. vii. 52. xiii. 27, 28.
q Matt. xxi. 33. 39. Luke xx. 15. Heb. xiii. 11—13.
r Matt. xxi. 40, 41.
s Lev. xxvi. 15—18. 23, 24. 27. 28. Deut. iv. 26, 27. xxviii. 15, &c. 61. Josh. xxiii. 15. Is. v. 5—7. Dan. ix. 26, 27. Zech. xiii. 7—9. Matt. iii. 9—12. xii. 45. xxii. 7. xxiii. 34—38. Luke xix. 27. 42—44. xx. 15, 16.
t Is. xxix. 17. xxxii. 15, 16. lxv. 15. Mal. i. 11. Matt. viii. 11—13. xxi. 43. Acts xiii. 46—48. xxviii. 23—28. Rom. ix. 30—33. x. 20, 21. xi. 1, &c.
u 26. ii. 25. xiii. 14. Matt. xii. 3. xix. 4. xxi. 16. xxii. 31. Luke vi. 3.
x Ps. cxviii. 22, 23. Is. xxviii. 16. Matt. xxi. 42. Luke xx. 17, 18. Acts iv. 11, 12. Rom. ix. 33. Eph. ii. 20—22. 1 Pet. ii. 7, 8.
y Num. xxiii. 23. Hab. i. 5. Acts ii. 12. 32—36. iii. 12—16. xiii. 40, 41. Eph. iii. 8—11. Col. i. 27. 1 Tim. iii. 16.
z xi. 18. 32. Matt. xxi. 26. 45, 46. Luke xx. 6. 19. John vii. 25. 30. 44.
a 2 Sam. xii. 7, &c. 1 Kings xx. 38—41. xxi. 17—27.
b Ps. xxxviii. 12. lvi. 5, 6. cxl. 5. Is. xxix. 21. Jer. xviii. 18. Matt. xxii. 15, 16. Luke xi. 54. xx. 20.
c iii. 6. viii. 15. Matt. xvi. 6.
d xiv. 45. Ps. xii. 2—4. lv. 21. cxx. 2. Prov. xxvi. 23—26. Jer. xlii. 2, 3. 20.
e John vii. 18. 2 Cor. ii. 17. iv. 2. v. 11. 1 Thes. ii. 4.

it is vigorous and lively. Thus our feeble attempts to do good may be rendered more successful than we could have imagined, by a divine blessing on our labours of love: and though we may not possess superior abilities, or station, influence, or authority; we may yet make a useful stand against the prevalence of impiety and iniquity, by the silent efficacy of fervent, constant prayers, whilst "we "lift up holy hands, without wrath and doubting:" and, provided our petitions be dictated by a forgiving and loving spirit towards men, as well as by zeal for the honour of God, we may in this way, and by a Christian example and conversation, by "a word spoken in due season," and various other similar attempts, be useful; without any one having so much as a pretence for enquiring "by what au"thority we do such things." But should we be called out to more publick services; while we act by the commission and according to the instructions of Christ, we need not greatly regard opposers, and shall not want a ready and pertinent answer to the enquiries of such as presume to interfere; though evidently ignorant of the most obvious and important distinction between those who act by authority from heaven, and those who are only sent forth by man. (P. O. *Matt.* xxi. 17—32.)

NOTES.

CHAP. XII. V. 1—12. *Notes, Is.* v. 1—7. *Matt.* xxi. 33—44. *Luke* xx. 9—18.—*Wine-fat.* (1) 'Υπολήνιον. Here only *N.* T. Ληνον, *Matt.* xxi. 33.—'The word, used 'by St. Matthew, signifies "the wine-press;" that by 'Mark, the cavity under it, in which the vessel was fixed, 'which received the liquor pressed from the grapes.' *Doddridge.*—*Wounded him in the head.* (4) Εκεφαλαιωσαν. Here only *N.* T.—*Reverence.* (6) Εντραπησονται. See on *Matt.* xxi. 27. They will be so overawed, when they see my son, that they will at once be induced to submit and seek forgiveness.—*Heir,* &c. (7) *Marg. Ref.* p.—*Notes, Matt.* ii. 3—6. *John* xi. 47, 48. xii. 47—53. *Acts* iv. 5—12.—*And cast,* &c. (8) "They both slew him, and cast "him out of the vineyard." (*Matt.* xxi. 39.)—See on *Matt.* xxi. 33. 42.

V. 13—17. (*Notes, Matt.* xxii. 15—22. *Luke* xx. 19—26.) 'Judas of Galilee,' (*Acts* v. 37,) 'saith Josephus, '...solicited the people to defection, telling them that God 'was to be their only...Prince, and no mortal to be ac'knowledged such; that the requiring a tax from them, 'if it were paid by them, was a manifest profession of ser-

thou art true, and f carest for no man; f for thou regardest not the person of men, but teachest the way of God in truth: h Is it lawful to give tribute to Cæsar, or not? 15 Shall we give, or shall we not give? But he, i knowing their hypocrisy, said unto them, k Why tempt ye me? bring me a penny, that I may see it. 16 And they brought it. And he saith unto them, Whose is this image and superscription? And they said unto him, Cæsar's.

17 And Jesus answering said unto them, m Render to Cæsar the things that are Cæsar's, n and to God the things that are God's. o And they marvelled at him.

18 ¶ Then p come unto him the Sadducees, which q say there is no resurrection: and they asked him, saying, 19 Master, Moses wrote unto us, If a man's brother die, and leave his wife behind him, and leave no children, that his brother should take his wife, and raise up seed unto his brother. 20 Now there were seven brethren: and the first took a wife, and dying left no seed. 21 And the second took her, and died, neither left he any seed: and the third likewise.

22 And the seven had her, and left no seed: last of all the woman died also. 23 In the resurrection therefore, when they shall rise, whose wife shall she be of them? for the seven had her to wife. 24 And Jesus answering said unto them, r Do ye not therefore err, s because ye know not the scriptures, t neither the power of God? 25 For when they shall rise from the dead, they neither marry, nor are u given in marriage: v but are as the angels which are in heaven. 26 And as touching the dead that x they rise; y have ye not read z in the book of Moses, how in the bush God spake unto him, saying, b I am the God of Abraham, and the God of Isaac, and the God of Jacob? 27 He c is not the God of the dead, but the God of the living: d ye therefore do greatly err.

28 ¶ And e one of the scribes came, and, having heard them reasoning together, and perceiving that he had answered them well, asked him, f Which is the first commandment of all? 29 And Jesus answered him, The first of all the commandments is, g Hear, O Israel, The Lord our God is one Lord: 30 And thou shalt love the Lord thy

---

' vitute; and that it was their duty to vindicate their liberty.
' By which means he raised a great sedition among the
' Jews, and was the cause ... of innumerable mischiefs to
' the nation. Of this sect it is possible they suspected
' Christ to be a favourer, and the rather for his being
' counted a Galilean.' *Hammond.*—' If he said No, the
' Herodians might represent him as an enemy to Cæsar:
' if Yea, the Pharisees might represent him to the people,
' as no friend to the nation.' *Whitby.*—*Shall we give,* &c.
(15) They urged our Lord to answer explicitly.—' Per-
' haps the very circumstance of taking upon him to deter-
' mine such a question, might, by these invidious en-
' quirers, be construed as a pretence to sovereignty.' *Doddridge.*—*Render to Cæsar,* &c. (17) *Marg. Ref.* m—o.
" The meekness of wisdom" was never more beautifully
manifested, than in our Lord's most instructive answer to
so insidious a question: and nothing can be more worthy
of imitation, than this particular in his conduct; that he
always took occasion, even from the most captious and
frivolous questions, and impertinent interruptions, which
would have excited contempt, disdain, or indignation, in
others, calmly to call the attention of the hearers to some

very important observation and instruction. (*Note, Prov.*
xxvi. 5, 6.)—*That they might catch,* &c. (13) Ἵνα αγρευσωσι.
Here only N. T· That they might ensnare him by their
words, as hunters entangled animals in their nets and
toils. Παγιδευσωσι, *Matt.* xxii. 15.
V. 18—27. (*Marg. Ref.*—*Notes, Matt.* xxii. 23—33.
Luke xx. 27—38.) The circumstances of the adduced
case are more particularly related here, than in Matthew:
but the concluding words, " Ye therefore do greatly err,"
as a strong protest against the Sadducees, and their doctrine, is the most remarkable addition. (*Notes, iv.* 23—
25. *Prov.* xix. 27. *Matt.* vi. 22, 23. *Heb.* xi. 13—16.)
Where the narrative in Mark seems most entirely a repetition of that in Matthew; comparing them will fully
shew, that Mark did not copy Matthew.—Indeed the difference of *style,* in the Evangelists, is much more conspicuous in the original, than in our translation, or probably
in any translation.
V. 28—34. St. Matthew informs us, that this " scribe,"
" lawyer," or doctor of the law, was one of the company which convened together to consult in what manner
they should proceed against Jesus; (*Matt.* xxii. 35;)

God with all thy heart, and with all thy soul, and with all thy mind, and with all thy strength. This *is* the first commandment.

31 And the second *is* like, *namely* this, ᵇThou shalt love thy neighbour as thyself. There is none other commandment greater than these.

32 And the scribe said unto him, Well, Master, thou hast said the truth: for there is one God; and there is none other but He:

33 And to love him with all the heart, and with all the understanding, and with all the soul, and with all the strength, and to love *his* neighbour as himself, ᵏ is more than all whole burnt-offerings and sacrifices.

34 And when Jesus saw that he answered discreetly, he said unto him, ˡThou art not far from the kingdom of God. ᵐAnd no man after that durst ask him *any* question.

35 ¶ And Jesus answered and said, ⁿwhile he taught in the temple, ᵒHow say the scribes that Christ is the Son of David?

36 For David himself said ᵖby the Holy Ghost, ᵠThe LORD said to my Lord, Sit thou on my right hand, till I make thine enemies thy footstool.

37 David therefore himself calleth him Lord; ʳand whence is he *then* his Son? ˢAnd the common people heard him gladly.

---

and that he asked the question " tempting him:" yet he was convinced, that Jesus had answered the Sadducees in a satisfactory manner. He was not exempt from the prejudices of the other Scribes and Pharisees: but it is evident, that he had far deeper convictions and juster apprehensions about religion, than the rest of them. To prove Jesus still further, how he was able to resolve difficult questions, and perhaps with some expectation of entangling him in his discourse; he asked him, " which was the " first," or greatest, " commandment in the whole law." The Pharisees, scribes, and teachers of the Jews had several frivolous disputes on this subject, suited to their traditions, and superstitious observances grounded on them. Our Lord, however, took no notice of these controversies, but returned a direct answer to the question: referring the Scribe to the summary of the first table of the law, which Moses had given them, and which has already been fully explained. (*Notes, Deut.* vi. 4, 5.) This he declared to be the " first commandment;" as it is of the highest possible importance and obligation, and as it virtually implies in it all other commandments. He then added, that the rule of loving our neighbours as ourselves was the second in importance, and of a similar nature: this too has been explained. (*Note, Lev.* xix. 18.) He then declared, that there was no other commandment greater than these; as on them depended all the law and the prophets. (*Marg. Ref.* g, h.—*Notes, Matt.* xxii. 34—40, *vv.* 37. 39, 40. *Luke* x. 25—29. *Rom.* xiii. 8—10.) When these two precepts are properly explained and understood, they are found to contain the substance of all, which was commanded in the law, or enforced by the prophets: unless these be properly received and observed, nothing else in religion is of any value; in proportion as they are understood, all other parts of scripture are unfolded in their nature, use, and importance: and whilst the types, predictions, and promises of Christ and the gospel are illustrated, the pardoned and justified believer, loving and obeying these commandments unreservedly, though not perfectly, cannot but attend to every other part of his duty to God and man. (*Notes, Ex.* xx. 1—17. *John* i. 17.

Rom. iii. 19, 20. 29—31, *v.* 31. vii. 9—12. *Gal.* ii. 17—21, *v.* 19.)—This answer of Christ was so satisfactory and convincing, that the Scribe openly declared, he had spoken the truth in a most excellent manner; and that all sacrifices, however numerous and costly, were comparatively of small value. These were typical atonements for transgressions of the moral law; and were of no efficacy, except as they were the expression of repentance, and of faith in the promised Saviour, and as they led to moral obedience. When Jesus, therefore, heard the Scribe answer so discreetly and pertinently, and like a man who understood the nature of true religion, and the spirituality and excellency of the moral law; he declared that " he " was not far from the kingdom of God." Probably, this man afterwards became a disciple of our Lord. (*Marg. Ref.* i—l.—*Notes, Deut.* vi. 4. 1 *Sam.* xv. 22. *Ps.* l. 7—15. *Is.* i. 10—20. *Jer.* vii. 21—23. *Hos.* v. 6. *Am.* v. 21—24. *Mic.* vi. 6—8.)—The quotation, of the first and great commandment, here made, is not exactly either from the Hebrew, or the Septuagint; but contains the evident meaning of the passage. The clause " with all thy mind," or " with all the understanding," is additional; and shews that, in general, all the capacities of the rational soul are intended.

Well. (28. 32) Καλως. See on vii. 9.—*The Lord our God is one Lord.* (29) Κυριος ὁ Θεος ἡμων, Κυριος εἱς ἐστι. It is remarkable, that the word JEHOVAH is not used in this quotation.—*Whole burnt-offerings.* (33) Ὁλοκαυτωμα-των. (Ex ὁλος, et καιω, incendo. *Heb.* x. 6. 8.) Not elsewhere *N. T. Ex.* xxix. 18. *Sept.*—*Discreetly.* (34) Νουιχως. Ex νας, *mens,* et ιχω, *habeo.* Not elsewhere *N. T.*

V. 35—37. *Note, Matt.* xxii. 41—46. *Luke* xx. 41—44.—*Christ,* &c. (35) Or, " The Christ," the Messiah. The question was not asked by our Lord concerning himself, whom most of his hearers were far from allowing to be " the Christ;" but concerning the Messiah, whom they expected.—*By the Holy Ghost.* (36) ' By a divine ' afflatus, or the ' Spirit of prophecy; for elsewhere we ' read, that " God spake by the mouth of David." (*Acts* ' i. 16. iv. 25.) This deserves to be noted by them who

t ir. 2.
u Matt. x. 17.
xxiii.—7. Luke
xx. 4—7.
x Matt. vi. 5.
Luke xi. 43. John
gir9—11
y Jam. ii. 2, 3.

z Ex. xxii. 22.
Mic. ii. 2. iii. 1
—4. Matt. xxiii.
14. Luke xx. 47.
a Matt. vi. 7. xi.
22—24. xxiii. 33.
Luke xii. 47, 48

b Matt. xxvii. 6.
Luke xxi. 1.
John viii. 20.

38 ¶ And he ' said unto them in his doctrine, " Beware of the scribes, " which love to go in long clothing, and *love* salutations in the market-places,

39 And ' the chief seats in the synagogues, and the uppermost rooms at feasts ;

40 Which ' devour widows' houses, and for a pretence make ' long prayers : these shall receive greater damnation.

41 ¶ And Jesus b sat over against the treasury, and beheld how the people cast * money into the treasury : and many that were rich cast in much.

42 And there came a certain poor widow ; and she threw in two mites, which make a farthing.

43 And he called *unto him* his disciples, and saith unto them, Verily I say unto you, ' That this poor widow hath cast more in, than all they which have cast into the treasury :

44 For all *they* did d cast in of their abundance ; but she of her want did cast in all that she had, *even* ' all her living.

* A piece of brass money. Matt. x. 9.

c Ex. xxxv. 21—29. Matt. x. 42.
Acts xi. 29. 2 Cor. viii. 12.
d 1 Chr. xxix. 2—17.
2 Chr. xxiv. 10
—14. xxxi.
16. xxxv. 7, 8. Ezra ii. 68, 69.
Neh. vii. 70—72. 2 Cor. viii. 2, 3.
Phil. iv. 10—17. Luke viii. 43.
xv. 12. 30. xxi. 2—4.

' deny that the Psalms of David were writ by the Spirit of ' prophecy.' *Whitby.* (*Marg. Ref. p.*)—The same preposition is used, as in Matthew, where it is rendered " in " Spirit ; " and in those places also where Christians are exhorted to " pray in the Spirit," or " in the Holy " Ghost." (*Eph.* vi. 18. *Jude* 20. Gr.)—' This implies ' both the existence of David in a future state, and the ' authority of the Messiah in that world, into which that ' prince was removed by death. Else how great a mo- ' narch soever he might be, he could not have been pro- ' perly called David's Lord ; any more than Julius Cesar ' could have been called the lord of Romulus, because he ' reigned in Rome seven hundred years after Romulus's ' death, and vastly extended the bounds of that empire, ' which Romulus had founded.' *Doddridge.* It shews also that the Messiah had authority over David when he wrote the ex. Psalm. (*Marg. Ref. p. r.—Notes, Ps.* cx. 1, 2. 1 *Cor.* xv. 20—28.)

The common people. (37) 'Ο πολυς οχλος. " The great " multitude."—*Gladly.*] 'Ηδεως. vi. 20. 2 *Cor.* xi. 19. xii. 9. 15.—*Marg. Ref. s.*

V. 38—40. *Marg. Ref.—Notes, Matt.* xxiii. 5—7. 14. *Luke* xx. 45—47. *Jam.* iii. 1, 2.

V. 41—44. (*Note, Luke* xxi. 1—4.) Our Lord, being about finally to leave the temple, sat down over against the treasury, into which the people put money to defray the several expenses, incurred by the stated services of the sanctuary. While he there beheld the Jews making their oblations, he observed several rich persons contributing large sums : but at length a poor widow put in two mites ; the exact amount of which is not easily determined, but it could not be less than a farthing, nor so much as a penny, of our money. Upon this, Jesus declared that she had cast in more than all the rest : for the large donations of the rich were only a part of their *superfluities*, and bare a small proportion to the abundance which still remained, for their own expenses and indulgence at present, and in reserve for the future, to them and their heirs : but she had in reality cast in " all her living ; " having nothing left to buy food for herself, save what she might afterwards earn by labour, or procure in some other precarious manner. Doubtless, our Lord saw her heart humble and upright, devoted to God, and desirous to express her affection to his worship ; and that she did not cast in her pittance out of affectation of singularity, or expectation

of being applauded for it, but in dependence on the promises and providence of God, and out of love to his name. Others, in such circumstances, would have pleaded, that so small a sum would be of no use, and that they could not spare it ; nay, many would have derided this poor widow, or dissuaded her from making any oblation : but our Lord approved and commended her conduct ; thus teaching us many important lessons, to direct and encourage us in our several duties.—How applicable it is to the case of weekly small subscriptions from the poor, to Bible societies, doctrines, and Missionary societies, must be obvious to every reflecting reader. (*Marg. Ref.*)

The treasury. (41) Γαζοφυλακιον. (Ex γαζα, thesaurus, et φυλασσω, custodio.) 43. *Luke* xxi. 1. *John* viii. 20.—*Neh.* x. 37. xiii. 5. *Sept.—Mites.* (42) Λεπτα. *Luke* xii. 59. xxi. 2. Not elsewhere N. T.—*A farthing.*] Κοδραντης. *Matt.* v. 26. Not elsewhere N. T. See *Tables.—Of their abundance.* (44) Εκ τε περισσευοντος αυτοις. *Luke* xxi. 4. *Rom.* v. 15. 2 *Cor.* viii. 2. ix. 8. *Eph.* i. 8. *Phil.* iv. 18.—*Want.*] Υστερησεως. *Phil.* iv. 11. Υστερημαλος. *Luke* xxi. 4. ab υστερω, deficio. *Rom.* iii. 23.—*Her living.*] Τον Giον αυλης. *Luke* viii. 14. xv. 12. 30. xxi. 4. 2 *Tim.* ii. 4. 1 *John* iii. 17.

PRACTICAL OBSERVATIONS.

V. 1—12.

We are accountable to God for all those peculiar advantages, which are afforded us in order that we may become fruitful in good works. Our gracious Lord, the Proprietor of the vineyard, waits for the fruits till " the due season ; " but he will by no means dispense with any who do not render them : and as we in this land are even more favoured than the Jews of old, so our doom will be more dreadful if we continue unfruitful. The sacred scriptures in our hands, or in our houses, and the labours of faithful preachers, are so many demands on us, to render the due revenue of glory to God, by the holiness of our lives : and the coming of the beloved Son of the Father, and all his miracles, doctrines, and salvation, were intended to supply us with motives, encouragements, and assistance for fruitfulness. But proud and carnal men, though they profess themselves the worshippers of God, will be exceedingly offended at these truths and warnings : and many rulers and teachers, to whom the vineyard has especially been entrusted, have often been and still are ready to insult,

2 N 8

beat, and murder the servants of God, who came to demand the fruits in their Master's name; nay, they have not shewn reverence even to his Son, but have acted with decided contempt and enmity against him, for the sake of their own credit, authority, and secular interest! Thus have " the builders rejected the Corner-stone" of the temple to their own ruin; and in securing their present advantages, have come short of " the inheritance of " the saints in light," and sunk into the most tremendous state of misery and despair. Let sinners beware of this proud or worldly spirit: and remember, that if they are offended by the faithful reproofs and admonitions of zealous ministers, they would have been far more irritated by those of Jesus Christ, had they lived when he was on earth; and would therefore have concurred with his crucifiers. If provoked to revile or ridicule their teachers, instead of profiting by their labours, they would easily be tempted to ill treat or murder them, were the power in their hands: for when this disposition prevails, the more plain and convincing the truth is rendered, the greater rage and enmity it excites. Let us then regard and profit by the instructions of the servants, as a proof that we really " reverence the beloved Son " of our glorious God: and let us seek grace from him that we " may be filled " with all the fruits of righteousness which are through " Jesus Christ, to the praise and glory of God," that our privileges may be continued to us, and that our souls may be perfected, when wicked professors of Christianity shall be expelled and destroyed for ever. (*P. O. Matt.* xxi. 33 —46. xxiii. 34—39. *Luke* xx. 1—18.)

V. 13—27.

Wisdom, truth, and holiness must excite opposition in this wicked world: for they are equally contrary to open impiety or infidelity, and to hypocrisy, and the love of secular interest and preferment; and thus naturally excite, as it were, an effervescence, whenever they meet with them. But, while men of different, and even opposite sentiments or parties seek to entangle ministers in their words, let these imitate the firmness, meekness, and prudence of the Lord Jesus; and endeavour to graft important instruction on insidious questions, and on frivolous or malignant objections. If all professed Christians did indeed conscientiously " render to Cæsar the ' things that are Cæsar's, and to God the things that are " God's," according to the exhortations of every faithful and wise teacher; and if all who preach the gospel, approved themselves true men, no " respecters of persons, " but teachers of the way of God in truth," they would soon put to shame and silence the ignorant cavils of obstinate adversaries. For though truth and holiness are the real objects of their implacable enmity, our errors and misconduct give them their most *plausible handle* against us. We should then study to " walk with wisdom to- " wards them that are without;" as well as to avoid hypocrisy, which is always known to our heart-searching

Judge. Thus we may pass through this dying world, with a joyful hope of immortal happiness, and of a glorious resurrection: and may expect to be at length made " equal " to the angels;" while Sadducees can only expect at best, to live and die like " the beasts that perish." We should then diligently seek to understand, accurately and fully, the sacred scriptures, and endeavour to enlarge our apprehensions of " the power of God;" that we may be preserved from fatal errors, and have confidence in " the " God of Abraham," and of all believers, as our everlasting Portion and Felicity; that we may " know how to " answer every man" in a conclusive manner, and to avoid all useless altercations, as well as to confute all vain objections. (*P. O. Matt.* xxii. 15—33. *Luke* xx. 19—47.)

V. 28—34.

By pertinent replies to one description of opposers, we may sometimes obtain a more candid hearing from others, who have hitherto been equally estranged from the truth: for we shall find some more teachable than the rest, of those collective bodies to which they belong. A careful attention to the scriptures will also convince us of the very great importance of a deep acquaintance with the spirituality, extent, reasonableness, and excellency of the moral law. Whilst, therefore, many are disputing about nice distinctions in speculative points, or external ceremonies and observances; we should peculiarly hearken to the sacred word, which requires us to " love the LORD our " God with all our heart, and soul, and mind, and strength," and " to love our neighbours as ourselves." Did we thus love the Lord with all our powers and faculties, and to the full extent of them; did we thus supremely admire and delight in his infinite excellences; did we wholly desire his favour and love, as our felicity; were we thus filled with adoring gratitude for his unspeakable goodness to us; and were we completely actuated by zeal for his glory, as in reason and justice we ought to be: what spiritual worshippers and devoted servants of God should we be! and in what should we differ from the inhabitants of heaven? (*Note, Ex.* xx. 2.) Did we " love our neighbours as our- " selves," and in every thing seek their good, and value their comfort and happiness equally with our own; what perfect justice, truth, purity, goodness, compassion, and peace would every where prevail! (*Notes,* and *P. O. Luke* x. 25—37.) This indeed would be far " more than all " whole burnt-offerings and sacrifices." But, because we have not thus loved God and man; because our character and conduct have been, and are, (as far as left to ourselves,) the reverse of this blessed temper and behaviour; therefore we are condemned sinners, we need repentance, we need mercy, and the Saviour's righteousness and atoning sacrifice; we cannot be justified by the works of the law, but must be " saved by grace, through faith," and " by " the sanctification of his Spirit unto obedience." Yet, it really interested in this redemption, we shall love and obey these great commandments, as our perfect rule of duty;

1 AND [a] as he went [b] out of the temple, one of his disciples saith unto him, Master, see what manner of stones, and what buildings *are here!*

2 And Jesus answering said unto him, Seest thou these great buildings? [c] there shall not be left one stone upon another, that shall not be thrown down.

3 And [d] as he sat upon the mount of Olives, over against the temple, [e] Peter, and James, and John, and Andrew, asked him [f] privately,

4 Tell us, [g] when shall these things be? and what *shall be* the sign when all these things shall be fulfilled?

5 And Jesus answering them, began to say, [h] Take heed lest any *man* deceive you:

6 For [i] many shall come in my name, saying, I am *Christ ;* [k] and shall deceive many.

7 And [l] when ye shall hear of wars, and rumours of wars, be ye not troubled : for *such things* [m] must needs be; but the end *shall* not *be* yet.

8 For [n] nation shall rise against nation, and kingdom against kingdom; and there shall be earthquakes in *divers* places, and there shall be [o] famines and troubles : [p] these *are* the beginnings of [q] sorrows.

24. xiii. 21. xxii. 23. xlix. 24. 1. 43. Mic. iv. 9, 10. 1 Thes. v. 3.

---

and daily mourn and be humbled, because our obedience to them is so very defective. Thus a just apprehension of the holy law is generally the first step towards a spiritual understanding of the gospel, and a proper improvement of its glorious truths : and though. many, who contend for the doctrines of free salvation, might have been ready to reprobate the conviction and confession of this Scribe, as self-righteous; we may easily perceive, that our Lord, with perfect wisdom and propriety, allowed him to have " answered discreetly," and as a man of reflection and intelligence; and declared that he was " not far from " the kingdom of God." We may also learn from our Lord's example to commend what is right, and to encorage what is hopeful, in those who differ from us, and are even prejudiced against us.

V. 35—44.

With a proper view of the holy law, a serious recollection of its awful sanction, and a believing prospect of the day of judgment, we shall be prepared to attend reverently to what the scriptures declare, concerning the person and offices of Christ; and shall be led more unreservedly to confess him to be " our Lord and our God ;" to welcome him as " the End of the law for righteousness to every " one who believeth;" (*Note, Rom.* x. 1—4 ;) to obey him as our exalted Redeemer; and to rejoice, that he is seated at the right hand of the Father, to perfect his people's salvation, and to " put all enemies under his " feet."—If " the common people hear these things " gladly," while the learned and distinguished in rank and authority oppose them; we may congratulate the former, however despised and neglected, and pity the latter, in the midst of their renown and splendour: for what will rich or long clothing, salutations in publick assemblies, or " chief rooms in synagogues " and feasts, however now loved and valued, avail men; when the Judge shall prove their devotions to have been the mask of impiety and iniquity, and sentence them to receive the deeper condemnation ?—And let us not forget, that Jesus still watches the treasury, to observe how much, and from what motives, men contribute to it. He approves of liberality in the rich ; and they ought to appropriate a far greater propor-

tion of their wealth to works of piety and charity, than they generally do, or indeed almost ever do; but it should be in simplicity, and not from pride and ostentation. And though their contributions should be encouraged ; they ought not to be flattered into an opinion, that they are meritorious, or that they can atone for their ungodliness or licentiousness, and prove a substitute for repentance, faith, and holiness. Nor should the poor on any account be discouraged or despised in their humble endeavours to shew " the sincerity of their love :" as their small oblations, spared from their hard earned and scanty supply, and from such expenses as are generally deemed needful, are more honourable to God, more evident effects of the power of divine grace, and expressions of patient self-denial and reliance on Providence; as well as, by comparison, a far greater bounty, than the applauded generosity of their superiors. Let then the poor contribute their mite to the relief of the distressed, or to promote the cause of God : and though men may deride or censure them, and those who excite and encourage them to such contributions ; the Lord will approve and graciously recompense them. They will not be impoverished by what they lend in this manner to him ; and their believing and thankful, though feeble efforts to honour him, and to do good to their brethren, will be mentioned with commendation in that day, when all the splendid actions of unbelievers, will be exposed to deserved contempt, as the result of pride, ostentation, enmity to God, and dislike to his holy and humbling salvation. (*P. O. Matt.* xxii. 34—46. xxv, 34—36.)

NOTES.

CHAP. XIII. V. 1—8. (*Marg. Ref.—Notes, Matt.* xxiv. 1—8. *Luke* xxi. 5—11.) ' The disciples joined to-' gether the destruction of the temple, with the last day ' of final judgment, as things which were to take place at ' the same time ; not being fully instructed in the know-' ledge of these secret things : and this gave Christ the ' occasion of discoursing on both in conjunction.' *Beza.* (*Note, Matt.* xxiv. 3.)

All these. (4) ' Thereby is signified the destruction of ' the temple, and, what was implied ... in that, the city

306

9 But ⁴ take heed to yourselves: for they shall deliver you up to councils; and in the synagogues ye shall be beaten: and ye shall be brought before rulers and kings for my sake, ʳ for a testimony against them.

10 And ˢ the gospel must first be published among all nations.

11 But when they shall lead you, ᵗ and deliver you up, ᵘ take no thought beforehand what ye shall speak, neither do ye premeditate; but whatsoever ˣ shall be given you in that hour, that speak ye: for it is not ye that speak, ʸ but the Holy Ghost.

12 Now ᶻ the brother shall betray the brother to death, and the father the son; and children shall rise up against *their* parents, and shall cause them to be put to death.

13 And ᵃ ye shall be hated of all men for my name's sake: ᵇ but he that shall endure unto the end, the same shall be saved.

14 ¶ But when ye shall see ᶜ the abomination of desolation spoken of by Daniel the prophet, standing ᵈ where it ought not, ᵉ (let him that readeth understand,) ᶠ then let them that be in Judea flee to the mountains:

15 And ᵍ let him that is on the house-top not go down into the house, neither enter *therein*, to take any thing out of his house:

16 And let him that is in the field, not turn back again for to take up his garment.

17 But ʰ woe to them that are with child, and to them that give suck in those days!

18 And pray ye that your flight be not in the winter.

19 For ⁱ in those days shall be affliction, such as was not ᵏ from the beginning of the creation which God created, unto this time, neither shall be.

20 And except that the Lord had shortened those days, no flesh should be saved: but ˡ for the elects' sake, whom he hath chosen, he hath shortened the days.

21 And then, ᵐ if any man shall say to you, Lo, here *is* Christ; or, lo, *he is* there; believe *him* not:

22 For false Christs and false prophets shall rise, and shall shew signs and wonders, to seduce, ⁿ if *it were* possible, even the elect.

23 But ᵒ take ye heed: ᵖ behold, I have foretold you all things.

24 ¶ But ⁱin those days, after that

---

⁴ and nation of the Jews, their whole government civil and 'ecclesiastical.' Hammond. (Note, Acts vi. 9—14.)—What manner, &c. (1) Ποᾶτοι. Matt. viii. 27. Luke i. 29. vii. 39. 2 Pet. iii. 11. 1 John iii. 1. (Note, Luke xxi. 5.)—Be thrown down. (2) Καᾶαᾶυθη. " Be dissolved," one part separated from another.—Shall be fulfilled. (4) Σνϊεᾶωϑαι. Της σνντεᾶιας τυ αιωνος, Matt. xxiv. 3.—Troubles. (8) Ταραχαι. John v. 4. Not elsewhere N .T. A ταρασσω, turbor. Ταραχος, Acts iii. 18. xix. 23. The tumults which were excited by the persecuting Jews against the apostles, and by the seditious, against the Romans, which brought dire calamities on immense numbers, and at length ruin on the nation, seem especially intended.

V. 9—13. Notes, Matt. x. 16—22. xxiv. 9—14. Luke xxi. 12—19.—Shall deliver, &c. (9) ' All this was exactly 'accomplished: for Peter and John were called before the 'Sanhedrim; (Acts iv. 6, 7;) James and Peter before 'Herod; (Acts xii. 3;) and Paul before Nero, as well 'as before the Roman governors, Gallio, Felix, and Festus. '(Acts xviii. 12. xxiv. xxv. xxviii.)' Doddridge. (Marg. Ref.)

Ye shall be beaten. (9) Δαρησεϑε. xii. 3. 5. Matt. xxi. 35. Luke xii. 47,48. Acts v. 40. xvi. 37. xxii. 19. 1 Cor. ix.

26. 2 Cor. xi. 20. (Note, Deut. xxv. 2, 3.) Μαντγωσιν, Matt. x. 17.—Premeditate. (11) Μελᾶαᾶε. Acts iv. 25 1 Tim. iv. 15. Not elsewhere N. T.—' I refer this to that 'artificial method of speaking, of which kind, orators de- 'liver many things, for the exercising of their disciples in 'fictitious declamations, which they call μελᾶας (exercises).' Beza.

V. 14—23. Marg. Ref.—Notes, Matt. xxiv. 15—28. Luke xxi. 20—24.—Where it ought not. (14) Jerusalem and all the adjacent country was holy ground, on which nothing which pertained to idolatry was allowed to approach.—The Lord, &c. (20) " Except those days should " be shortened," Matt. xxiv. 22.—The elects' sake, whom he hath chosen. (20) The Christians, who fled out of Judea when these calamities began, cannot here be meant; as the continuance of these desolating judgments on the Jews, had no tendency to extirpate the Christians. That chosen seed, therefore, which was to arise out of the remnant of the Jews, in after ages, is evidently intended. (Notes, Is. vi. 13. lxv. 8—10. Matt. xxiv. 21, 22.)

Luke xxi. 25—33.)—' Our Saviour seems to hold out the de- 'struction of Jerusalem, which is his principal subject, as a 'type of the dissolution of the world. ...By thus judiciously

tribulation, the sun shall be darkened, and the moon shall not give her light;

25 And the stars of heaven shall fall, and the powers that are in heaven shall be shaken.

26 And then shall they see ' the Son of man coming in the clouds, with great power and glory.

27 And then 'shall he send his angels, and ' shall gather together "his elect from the four winds, 'from the uttermost part of the earth to the uttermost part of heaven.

28 Now ' learn a parable of the fig-tree: When her branch is yet tender, and putteth forth leaves, ye know that summer is near:

29 So ye, in like manner, when ye shall see these things come to pass, ' know that it is nigh, even at the doors.

30 Verily I say unto you, ' That this generation shall not pass, till all these things be done.

31 ᵇ Heaven and earth shall pass away; but 'my words shall not pass away.

32 ¶ But ' of that day, and that hour, knoweth no man, no, not the angels which are in heaven, 'neither the Son, but the Father.

33 Take 'ye heed, watch and pray: for ye know not when the time is.

34 For the son of man is 'as a man taking a far journey, who left his house, and gave authority to his servants, ' and to every man his work, ' and commanded ' the porter to watch.

35 ' Watch ye therefore; for ye know not when the Master of the house cometh, at even, or at midnight, or at the cock-crowing, or in the morning;

36 Lest coming suddenly, "he find you sleeping.

37 And what I say unto you, 'I say unto all, Watch.

' mingling together these two important catastrophes, he ' gives at the same time (as he does in many other in- ' stances) a most interesting admonition to his imme- ' diate hearers,. the Jews, and a most awful lesson to all ' his future disciples: and the benefit of his predictions, ' instead of being confined to one occasion, or one people, ' is, by this admirable management, extended to every ' subsequent period of time, and to the whole Christian ' world.' *Bp. Porteus.* (*Notes, Matt.* xxiv. 42—44. xxv. 1—4.)

V. 32. (*Marg. Ref.—Notes, Dan.* vii. 13, 14. *Matt.* xxiv. 36—41, *v.* 36. xxvi. 63—68, *v.* 64. *Rev.* i. 7.) 'That ' day which the Father alone knoweth, is not to be curi- ' ously enquired into; but care should be taken that it '.does not come upon us unawares.' *Beza.*

The Son, &c.] The precise season, either of the day of judgment, or of the destruction of Jerusalem, was no part of the revelation which the incarnate Son of God had received to communicate to his church: it was not revealed to his human nature, by the unction of the Holy Spirit. But we cannot understand many things, which relate to .he mysterious union of his divine and human nature, and ¡ bould not further presume to pry into them.—' "The Son " ¡ is here considered as the Prophet sent into the world, to ¡ reveal the Father's will: and therefore as delivering to ¡ the world, not what the Logos knew or taught, but what ¡ the Spirit of God revealed to him. (*John* iii. 34, 35. v. ¡ 20. xii. 49. xiv. 10.)' *Whitby.*—' This he speaks in his ' human nature, and in his prophetick capacity. This ' point was not made known to him by the Spirit, nor was ' he commissioned to reveal it.' *Bp. Porteus.* (*Note, Rev.* i. 1—4, *vv.* 1, 2.)

V. 33. *Marg. Ref.* 37.—*Notes, Matt.* xxiv. 42—44.

xxv. 10—13. *Luke* xii. 35—46. xxi. 34—36. *Acts* xx. 29 —31. 1 *Thes.* v. 4—11. 2 *Tim.* iv. 1—5, *v.* 5. *Heb.* xiii. 17. 1 *Pet.* iv. 7. v. 8, 9.

V. 34—37. *Notes, Matt.* xxiv. 36—41. 45—51. xxv. 14—30. *Luke* xix. 11—27.—For the Son, &c. (34) The addition in Italicks is not requisite; ". As when " a man takes a far journey, &c." The parable coin- cides with those in Matthew; but is more particular. (*Marg. Ref.*)—*Authority.*] To the superior servants; such as " the stewards of the mysteries of Christ," espe- cially the apostles. (*Notes, Matt.* xvi. 19. 1 *Cor.* iv. 1, 2.) —*Porter.*] *Notes,* 1 *Chr.* xxiii. 3—6. *John* x. 1—5. 1 *Tim.* v. 21, 22. 2 *Tim.* ii. 1, p. iv. 1—5.—Those whe are concerned in admitting members into the Christian church, and especially in the ordination of ministers, and in all appointments respecting them, seem especially in- tended.—*At even,* &c. (35) Nine in the evening, mid- night, three in the morning, and sun-rise.

The porter. (34) Τῷ θυρωρῳ. (Εκ θυρα, *ostium,* et ουρεω, *custodio.*) *John* x. 3. xviii. 16, 17.—*At even.* (35) Oὖϛ. See on *Matt.* xxviii. 1.

PRACTICAL OBSERVATIONS.
V. 1—23.

When we behold the magnificence of flourishing cities, and stately palaces or temples, we should recollect how soon they will all be desolated and come to nothing, through the sin of man; that we may be reminded, how necessary it is for us to have a more permanent mansion in heaven, and to be prepared for the sanctification of the Holy Spirit, sought in the earnest and persevering use of all ' the means of grace.'—If we duly consider how soon all temporal things will pass away, like an empty vision, we

shall find our desires after wealth, grandeur, and prosperity abated: and we shall be less disquieted, *on our own account*, when we hear of wars, earthquakes, famines, and other dreadful judgments; however we may be concerned for the sufferers, and sympathize with them. Such reflections will conduce to reconcile us to the thoughts of contempt, reproach, and persecution: but they will render us also more careful, that " no man may deceive us," or draw us into error, to prevent our being " partakers of Christ," and the blessings of the gospel. Indeed we cannot profess and adorn his holy doctrine, without experiencing many effects of the world's hatred and scorn: but, if we be wearied by our trivial difficulties, what should we be, if we were delivered up to councils and eternal weight them with rage and cruelty; or if betrayed by near relations, and exposed to the sentence of death for our adherence to the truth? (*Note*, *Jer.* xii. 5, 6.)—When the hatred of men, and the fear of hardship and suffering, cause us to shrink or complain, we should remember, that " he that continueth unto the end, the same shall be " saved;" but " if any man draw back, the Lord will have " no pleasure in him."—We should take comfort under our trials for the sake of Jesus, by hoping that our testimony to his truth, and our patience and meekness under the cross, may be of use, even to our persecutors or revilers; and assuredly our " light afflictions, and but for a moment, " will work for us a far more exceeding and eternal weight " of glory." Should any of us be called to appear before the princes of this world in so good a cause; we ought not to be anxious about " what we should speak," or to " premeditate," in a distrustful and disquieting manner: for, in such extraordinary cases, we may expect peculiar assistance, and that the Spirit of God will teach us to plead the cause of his truth with propriety and energy.—The enmity and pride of man's heart, when inflamed by religious bigotry and furious zeal, produce most fatal effects: this should put us upon our guard, and instruct us to pray for the Spirit of wisdom, truth, and love, to dwell in our hearts, and to counteract and mortify our natural depraved propensities, even in our religious pursuits and controversies.—Indeed, when we consider, that brethren, and even parents and children, are capable of hating, betraying, and murdering each other; and that atrocious abominations are often established even in the very sanctuary: (*Notes* and *P. O. Ez.* viii:) we shall see more abundant cause to flee without delay for refuge to Christ, from our own sins, and those of others; and to renounce every earthly object to secure the salvation of our souls. We should also deem every thing an evil, and pray against it as such, which tends to retard our course to heaven: for every unbeliever will soon be overtaken with such misery, as has never been witnessed on earth " from the beginning of the crea-

" tion that God created, unto this time, neither shall be." (*P. O. Matt.* xxiv. 1—28. *Luke* xxi. 1—19.)

V. 24—37.

In all things we ought to remember the Saviour's words: for as sure as the predictions, which related to Jerusalem and the temple, were exactly accomplished; so will all those things come to pass, which are written concerning the eternal happiness of the righteous, and the misery of the wicked in another world. Ere long " heaven and earth " shall pass away," and all the things which we behold will be dissolved; but " the words of Christ shall not pass " away." A firm belief of his truth will be our only and sure support under those trials, which occasion the ruin of all, " but the elect, whom God hath chosen." At length we shall see " the Son of man coming in the clouds of " heaven, with power and great glory," and then all his chosen people will be gathered from among the wicked into his heavenly kingdom. Instead, therefore, of curiously enquiring into " the secret things, which belong to the " LORD;" let us carefully improve the revelation of his will, by " giving diligence to make our calling and elec- " tion sure." (*Notes*, 2 *Pet.* i. 5—11.) We know that the hour of our death cannot be very distant: our Lord, though not present to our sight, beholds our whole conduct, and will shortly come to call us to an account for it. To some of his professed servants he entrusts authority to preach his gospel, to preside in his church, and to be his porters for the admission of proper persons into sacred services and ordinances, and to exclude such as are unfit for them; and to every one of us he gives his proper work, by attending to which we may approve ourselves true believers, and both honour our Lord and serve our generation. (*Note*, *Phil.* i. 9—11.) Happy therefore is that servant, who continues sober, vigilant, and diligent in his place, without interfering with that of other men! He will be prepared for the coming of his Lord, whenever that may be: he will be found awake, and employed in his service, according to the duty of his station; and his gracious recompence will be secure. But it will be an awful surprise to a professed Christian or minister, should he be found sleeping, supine, self-indulgent, and unprepared, by his Lord at his coming; yet this may probably be our case, if at any time we relax our vigilance, or neglect our work. (*Note*, *Heb.* iv. 1, 2.) He therefore speaks to us all, charging and warning us to " take heed " to ourselves," to our duty, or our ministry, and to watch and pray always, " lest coming suddenly he should find us " sleeping." (*P. O. Matt.* xxiv. 29—51. *Luke* xxi. 20— 38.)

a Matt. xxvi. 2.
Luke xxii. 1, 2.
John xi. 53—57.
b Ex. xii. 6—20.
Num. xxviii. 16
—25. Deut. xvi.
1—8.
c Ps. ii. 1—3.
John xi. 47.
Acts iv. 25—28.
d Ps. iii. 3. lxii.
4. 9. lxiv. 2—6.
Matt. xxvi. 4.
e Prov. xiv. 21.
xxi. 30. Lam.
iii. 37. Matt.
xxvi. 5.
f xi. 16. 32. Luke
xx. 6. John vii.
40. xii. 19.
g Matt. xxvi. 6, 7.
John xi. 2. xii.
1—3.
h Cant. iv. 13, 14.
v. 5. Luke vii.
37, 38.
u Or, *pure nard,*
or, *liquid nard.*
i Ec. iv. 4. Matt.
xxvi. 8, 9. John
xii. 4, 5.
k Ex. v. 4—8.
Mal. i. 12, 13.
† Matt. xviii. 28.
marg. John vi.
7.

AFTER * two days was *the feast of* ' have been given to the poor. **m** And
the passover, and of unleavened | they murmured against her.
bread : ' and the chief priests and the | 6 And Jesus said, * Let her alone ;
scribes sought how they might take | why trouble ye her ? she hath wrought
him ' by craft, and put *him* to death. | ' a good work on me.
2 But they said, * Not on the feast- | 7 For ' ye have the poor with you
day, ' lest there be an uproar of the | always, and whensoever ye will ye may
people. | do them good : ' but me ye have not
3 ¶ And ' being in Bethany, in the | always.
house of Simon the leper, as he sat at | 8 She ' hath done what she could :
meat, there came a woman, having an | ' she is come aforehand to anoint my
alabaster-box ' of ointment of * spike- | body to the burying.
nard, very precious ; and she brake the | 9 Verily I say unto you, ' Whereso-
box, and poured *it* on his head. | ever this gospel shall be preached
4 And ' there were some that had | throughout the whole world, *this* also
indignation within themselves, and said, | that she hath done shall be spoken of,
* Why was this waste of the ointment | for " a memorial of her.
made ? | 10 ¶ And * Judas Iscariot, ' one of
5 For it might have been sold for |
more than three hundred † pence, and |

l John xii. 5. 6.
xiii. 29. Eph. iv.
28.
m Ex. xvi. 7, 8.
Deut. i. 27. Ps.
cvi. 25. Matt.
xx. 11. Luke
xv. 2. John vi.
43. 1 Cor. x. 10.
Phil. ii. 14. Jude
16.
n Joh xiii. 7, 8.
ix. liv. 17. 2 Cor
x. 18.
o Matt. xxvi. 10.
p Deut. xv. 11.
Matt. xxv. 35—
46. xxvi. 11.
John xii. 7, 8.
2 Cor. ix. 5.
q John x. 32. xvi.
5. 7, 10. 16. 28.
xvii. 11. xx. 17.
r Deut. xv. 11.
Matt. xxv. 35—
46. Philem. 7.
Jam. ii. 14—16.
1 John iii. 16—
19.
s John xiii* 33.
xvi. 5. 28. xvii.
—9.

11. Acts iii. 17. **r** 1 Chr. xxviii. 2, 3. xxix. 1—17. 2 Chr. xxxi. 20, 21. xxxix. 1—
33. Ps. cxx. 3. 2 Cor. viii. 1—3, 12. * xv. 42—47. xvi. 1. Luke xxiii. 53—56. xxiv. 1—
3. John xii. 7. xix. 32—42. **t** xvi. 15. Matt. xxvi. 12, 13. **u** Num. xxxi.
54. Ps. cxii. 6—9. Zech. vi. 14. **x** Matt. xxvi. 14—16. Luke xxii. 3—6. John
xiii. 2. 30. **y** Ps. xli. 9. lv. 12—14. Matt. x. 4. John vi. 70, 71.

CHAP. XIV. V. 1, 2. *Marg. Ref.*—*Notes, Matt.* xxvi.
1—5. *John* xi. 49—57.

V. 3—9. (*Notes, Matt.* xxvi. 6—13. *Luke* vii. 37—39.
John xii. 1—8.) ' It appears to me more probable, that
' Matthew and Mark should have introduced this story a
' little out of its place ; that Lazarus, if he made this feast,
' (which is not expressly said by John,) should have made
' use of Simon's house, as more convenient ; and that
' Mary should have poured this ointment on Christ's head
' and body, as well as on his feet ; than that, within the
' compass of four days, Christ should have been twice
' anointed with so costly a perfume ; and that the same
' fault should be found with the action, and the same value
' set on the ointment, and the same words used in defence
' of the woman, and all this in the presence of many of
' the same persons : all which improbable particulars must
' be admitted, if the stories be considered as different.'
Doddridge.—Neither Matthew nor Mark says, that this
occurred no more than two days before the passover ; they
only relate it subsequent to some transactions which took
place at that time. It happened when Jesus was at
Bethany : this may be explained to mean any evening from
his arrival on this occasion at Bethany, till the passover ;
and it was no doubt on the first evening, before he entered
Jerusalem riding on the ass's colt.

Sold. (5) Mary had not bought it on this occasion :
but she might have sold it ; as perhaps she had done many
of those ornaments and luxuries, which she had used before she " chose the good part." (*Note, Luke* x. 38—42.)
—*Three hundred,* &c. (5) About 9*l.* 15*s.* sterling. (*Tables.*) A denarius was then a day's wages of a labourer
even in harvest : (*Matt.* xx. 2 :) and therefore equal in
value, though not in weight, to three shillings at least, in
this land at present ; as it would purchase as many necessaries of life.—This would therefore appear a large sum.

The language, concerning the poor (7), " Whensoever ye
" will ye may do them good," and so shew your love and
gratitude to me, should be especially noticed.—Mary " did
" what she could " (8), to express her reverence, love, and
gratitude to Jesus ; whom she regarded as her Lord and
her Saviour, and to whom she considered herself as under
the greatest possible obligations. (*Notes,* 1 *Chr.* xxix. 1—
20. 2 *Cor.* ix. 12—15.) But this is totally different from
the pretensions of many, ' that they do what they can ;'
that is, " to establish their own righteousness," while they
refuse to " submit to the righteousness of God." (*Note,
Rom.* x. 1—4.)

Spike-nard. (3) " Pure, or liquid nard." *Marg. Nap-
δυ πιστικης.* Ναρδυ, *John* xii. 3. Not elsewhere N. T.—From
נרד. *Cant.* iv. 14 : ναρδος. *Sept.* Πιστικης, *John* xii. 3. Not
elsewhere N. T. Various opinions are held of the meaning of this word : probably, it was derived from a Syriack
word, *pistaca,* answering to the Latin word *spicata,* and
denoted the manner, in which the ointment was prepared
from the *spikes,* or small blades, of the plants which
yielded it.—*She brake,* &c.] Συντριψασα. v. 4. Matt. xii.
20. *John* xix. 36. *Rom.* xvi. 20. *Rev.* ii. 27. Some would
render the word *shook ;* supposing it improbable, that the
alabastar box should be thus broken : but perhaps the
ointment was closed up in the vessel, in such a manner,
that it was needful to break the top or cover, in order to
get at it.—*They murmured.* (5) Ενεβριμωντο. See on *Matt.*
ix. 30.—*She hath done what she could.* (8) Ὁ εσχεν αὑτη,
εποιησε. " What she had, she has done." Other ways of
shewing her veneration and affection were not in her possession, or power.—*She is come beforehand.*] Προελαβε.
1 *Cor.* xi. 21. *Gal.* vi. 1. Not elsewhere *N.* T. She has
laid hold of the opportunity by anticipation.—*To the
burying.*] Εις τον ενταφιασμον. *John* xii. 7. Not elsewhere
N. T.

V. 10, 11. (*Marg. Ref.*—*Notes, Matt.* xxvi. 14—16.
Luke xxii. 1—13, *vv.* 3—6. *John* xiii. 1—5.) It is certain,

the twelve, went unto the chief priests, to betray him unto them.

11 And when they heard *it*, ᵇ they were glad, ᵃ and promised to give him money. And ᵇ he sought how he might conveniently betray him.

12 ¶ And ᶜ the first day of unleavened bread, when they ᵈ killed the passover, his disciples said to him, ᵉ Where wilt thou that we go and prepare, that thou mayest eat the passover?

13 And he sendeth forth two of his disciples, and saith unto them, ᵃ Go ye into the city, and there shall meet you a man bearing a pitcher of water: follow him.

· 14 And wheresoever he shall go in, say ye to the good-man of the house, ᶠ The Master saith, Where is the guestchamber, where I shall eat the passover with my disciples?

15 And ᵍ he will shew you a large upper room furnished *and* prepared: there make ready for us.

16 And his disciples went forth, and came into the city, ʰ and found as he had said unto them: and they made ready the passover.

17 ¶ And ᵏ in the evening he cometh with the twelve.

18 And ˡ as they sat and did eat,

Jesus said, ᵐ Verily I say unto you, ᵃ One of you which eateth with me shall betray me.

19 And they began to be sorrowful, ᵃ and to say unto him one by one, *Is it I?* and another *said, Is it I?*

20 And he answered and said unto them, ᵖ *It is* one of the twelve ˑthat ᵠ dippeth with me in the dish.

21 The Son of man indeed ʳ goeth, as it is written of him: ˢ but ˑwoe to that man by whom the Son of man is betrayed! ᵗ good were it for that man if he had never been born.

22 ¶ And ᵘ as they did eat, Jesus took bread, ˣ and blessed, and brake *it*, and gave to them, and said, Take, eat: ʸ this is my body.

23 And he took the cup, and ᶻ when he had given thanks, he gave *it* to them: ᵃ and they all drank of it.

24 And he said unto them, ᵇ This is my blood of the new testament, ᶜ which is shed for many.

25 Verily I say unto you, ᵈ I will drink no more of the fruit of the vine, until that day that I drink it ᵉ new in the kingdom of God.

26 ¶ And when they had ᶠ sung an ᵍ hymn, ᵗ they went out into the mount of Olives.

Marginal references (left column):
ᵃ Hos. vii. 5. Luke xxii. 3.
ᵃ 2 Kings v. 26. Prov. xxviii. 21.
22. Matt. xxvi. 15. 1 Tim. vi. 10. 2 Pet. ii. 14. 15. Jude 11.
ᵇ Luke xxii. 5, 6.
ᶜ Ex. xii. 6, 18. xiii. 3. Lev. xxiii. 5, 6. Num. xxviii. 16 —18. Deut. xvi. 1—4.
ᵈ Matt. xxvi. 17. Luke xxvii. 8.
ᵉ Or, *sacrificed*. 1 Cor. v. 7, 8.
ᵈ Matt. iii. 15. Luke xxii. 8, 9. Gal. iv. 4.
ᵃ Matt. viii. 9. xxvi. 18, 19. Luke xxii. 10—13. John ii. 5. xv. 14. Heb. v. 9.
ᶠ Ex. 17. xi. 3. John xi. 28.
ᵍ 2 Chr. vi. 30. Ps. cx. 3. Prov. xvi. 1. xxi. 1, 2. John ii. 24, 25. xxi. 17. 2 Tim. ii. 19. Heb. iv. 13.
ʰ Acts i. 13. xx.
ˡ Luke xxii. 13. 33. John xvi. 4.
ᵏ Matt. xxvi. 20. Luke xxii. 14.
ˡ Matt. xxvi. 21.

Marginal references (right column):
ᵐ 9. 25. iii. 28. vi. 11. viii. 12. ix. 1. 41. xi. 23. 29. Matt. v. 18.
vi. 2. 16. Luke ix. 24. xi. 51. John i. 51. iii. 5. 11. v. 19. 24, 25. vi. 26. 32. 47. xiii. 20, 21.
26. 23. 47. xiii. 2. Matt. xxvi. 23, John xiii. 26.
ᵖ Ps. xli. 9. lv. 13, 14. John vi. 70, 71. xiii. 21.
p 43. Matt. xxvi. 47. John vi. 71.
ʳ 45. Gen. iii. 15. Ac. ix. 14. 26. Zech. xiii. 7. Matt. xxvi. 54. Luke xxiv. 25, 26, 27. 44. Acts ii. 23. xiii. 27—29. 1 Pet. i. 11.
ˢ —20. Matt. xviii. 7. xxvi. 24.
ᵗ Acts i. 16—20.
ᵘ Matt. xxvi. 26—28.
ˣ 1 Cor. x. 16. 11. 28.
ʸ 1 Cor. xi. 24. 26.
ᶻ Zech. v. 11.
ᵃ 1 Cor. xi. 25—
ᵇ Ex. xxiv. 8. Zech. ix. 11. Heb. ix. 13—23.
ᵈ Ps.cix.13. Matt.
d Ps.cix.13. Matt.
xxvi. 29. Luke xxii. 16—18, 29, 30. ᵉ Joel iii. 18. Am. ix. 13. Zech. ix. 17. xii. 6, 7. Acts xiv. 25. 1 Cor. xiv. 15. Eph. v. 19, 20. Col. iii. 16. Jam. v. 13. Rev. v. 9. ᶠ Or, *psalm*. ᵍ Matt. xxvi. 30. Luke xxii. 39. John xviii. 1—4.

on which day Judas first went to the chief priests; but it is most probable, that it was two days before the passover, when they were consulting how to apprehend Jesus, that they might put him to death. The devil had before this " put it into his heart;" but it may be supposed, that he hesitated for a time, before he carried his design into execution.

V. 12—16. (*Note, Matt.* xxvi. 17—19.) Nothing could be less the object of natural sagacity and foresight, than the events here mentioned. Had the two disciples come to the place specified, rather sooner or later than they did, the " man, bearing the pitcher of water," would either not have arrived, or he would have been gone. But our Lord knew that the owner of a certain commodious house in Jerusalem would, he foresaw that at a precise time of the day, he would send his servant for a pitcher of water; that the disciples would meet him just when they entered the city; that by following him they would find out the person whom he intended; and that by mentioning him, as " the Master," or " the Teacher," the owner of the house would readily consent to accommodate them in an upper chamber. When the disciples found all these circumstances so exactly accord to the prediction, they

could not but be deeply impressed with a conviction of their Lord's knowledge of every event, and his influence over every heart. (*Marg. Ref.—Notes*, xi. 1—11. 1 *Sam.* x. 2—7.)—*Furnished,* &c. (15) That is, with table, couches, and all other things suited to the occasion.

The guest-chamber. (14) Τὸ καϑάλυμα. *Luke* ii. 7. xxii. 11. Probably every householder in Jerusalem, who had it in his power, reserved a room in his house for this purpose, for such of his friends as came up thither to eat the passover. He was their host, and this " guestchamber " was as it were their " inn."—*An upper room*. (15) Ἀνωγεον. *Luke* xxii. 12. Quod *σαω της γης*. Not elsewhere *N. T.*

V. 17—25. *Marg. Ref.—Notes, Matt.* xxvi. 21—29. *Luke* xxii. 14—23.—*Written.* (21) Notes, *Ps.* xli. 9. lxix. 22—28, *v.* 28. cix. 6—20. *Matt.* xxvi. 21—24. *Luke* xxii. 21—23, *v.* 22. *John* xiii. 18—30. *Acts* i. 16—26.—*All ye.* (27) ' Christ foretelleth, how he shall be forsaken of his ; ' but yet that he will never forsake them.' *Beza*. (*Note, John* xvi. 31—33.)

V. 26—31. *Marg. Ref.—Notes, Matt.* xxvi. 30—35. *Luke* xxii. 31—34. *John* xiii. 36—38—*Twice.* (30) ' After ' thou hast heard it once, thou shalt not be admonished

AFTER two days was *the feast of* the passover, and of unleavened bread: and the chief priests and the scribes sought how they might take him, and put him to death.

2 But they said, Not on the feast-day, lest there be an uproar of the people.

3 ¶ And being in Bethany, in the house of Simon the leper, as he sat at meat, there came a woman, having an alabaster-box of ointment of spikenard, very precious; and she brake the box, and poured it on his head.

4 And there were some that had indignation within themselves, and said, Why was this waste of the ointment made?

5 For it might have been sold for more than three hundred pence, and have been given to the poor. And they murmured against her.

6 And Jesus said, Let her alone; why trouble ye her? she hath wrought a good work on me.

7 For ye have the poor with you always, and whensoever ye will ye may do them good: but me ye have not always.

8 She hath done what she could: she is come aforehand to anoint my body to the burying.

9 Verily I say unto you, Wheresoever this gospel shall be preached throughout the whole world, *this* also that she hath done shall be spoken of, for a memorial of her.

10 ¶ And Judas Iscariot, one of

NOTES.

CHAP. XIV. V. 1, 2. *Marg. Ref.—Notes, Matt.* xxvi. 1—5. *John* xi. 49—57.

V. 3—9. (*Notes, Matt.* xxvi. 6—13. *Luke* vii. 37—39. *John* xii. 1—8.) 'It appears to me more probable, that ‘ Matthew and Mark should have introduced this story a ‘ little out of its place; that Lazarus, if he made this feast, ‘ (which is not expressly said by John,) should have made ‘ use of Simon's house, as more convenient; and that ‘ Mary should have poured this ointment on Christ's head ‘ and body, as well as on his feet; than that, within the ‘ compass of four days, Christ should have been twice ‘ anointed with so costly a perfume; and that the same ‘ fault should be found with the action, and the same value ‘ set on the ointment, and the same words used in defence ‘ of the woman, and all this in the presence of many of ‘ the same persons: all which improbable particulars must ‘ be admitted, if the stories be considered as different.' *Doddridge.*—Neither Matthew nor Mark says, that this occurred no more than two days before the passover; they only relate it subsequent to some transactions which took p ace at that time. It happened when Jesus was at Bethany: this may be explained to mean any evening from his arrival on this occasion at Bethany, till the passover; and it was no doubt on the first evening, before he entered Jerusalem riding on the ass's colt.

Sold. (5) Mary had not bought it on this occasion: but she might have sold it; as perhaps she had done many of those ornaments and luxuries, which she had used before she " chose the good part." (*Note, Luke* x. 38—42.) —*Three hundred,* &c. (5) About 9*l.* 15*s.* sterling. (*Tables.*) A denarius was then a day's wages of a labourer even in harvest: (*Matt.* xx. 2 :) and therefore equal in value, though not in weight, to three shillings at least, in this land at present; as it would purchase as many necessaries of life.—This would therefore appear a large sum.

The language, concerning the poor (7), " Whensoever ye " will ye may do them good," and so shew your love and gratitude to me, should be especially noticed.—Mary " did " what she could " (8), to express her reverence, love, and gratitude to Jesus; whom she regarded as her Lord and her Saviour, and to whom she considered herself as under the greatest possible obligations. (*Notes,* 1 *Chr.* xxix. 1— 20. 2 *Cor.* ix. 12—15.) But this is totally different from the pretensions of many, ' that they do what they can ; ' that is, " to establish their own righteousness," while they refuse to " submit to the righteousness of God." (*Note, Rom.* x. 1—4.)

Spike-nard. (3) " Pure, or liquid nard." *Marg.* Ναρδου πιστικης. Ναρδου, *John* xii. 3. Not elsewhere N. T.—From נרד. *Cant.* iv. 14 : ναρδος. *Sept.* Πιστικης, *John* xii. 3. Not elsewhere N. T. Various opinions are held of the meaning of this word : probably, it was derived from a Syriack word, *pistaca,* answering to the Latin word *spicata,* and denoted the manner, in which the ointment was prepared from the *spikes,* or small blades, of the plants which yielded it.—*She brake,* &c.] Συντριψασα. v. 4. *Matt.* xii. 20. *John* xix. 36. *Rom.* xvi. 20. *Rev.* ii. 27. Some would render the word *shook* ; supposing it improbable, that the alabastar box should be thus broken: but perhaps the ointment was closed up in the vessel, in such a manner, that it was needful to break the top or cover, in order to get at it.—*They murmured.* (5) Ενεβριμωντο. See on *Matt.* ix. 30.—*She hath done what she could.* (8) Ὁ εσχεν αυτη, εποιησε. " What she had, she has done." Other ways or shewing her veneration and affection were not in her possession, or power.—*She is come beforehand.*] Προελαβε. 1 *Cor.* xi. 21. *Gal.* vi. 1. Not elsewhere N. T. She has laid hold of the opportunity by anticipation.—*To the burying.*] Εις τον ενταφιασμον. *John* xii. 7. Not elsewhere N. T.

V. 10, 11. (*Marg. Ref.—Notes, Matt.* xxvi. 14—16. *Luke* xxii. 1—13, *vv.* 3—6. *John* xiii. 1—5.) It is not certain,

the twelve, went unto the chief priests, to betray him unto them.

11 [a] And when they heard it, [a] they were glad, [a] and promised to give him money. And [b] he sought how he might conveniently betray him.

12 ¶ And [c] the first day of unleavened bread, when they [*] killed the passover, his disciples said to him, [d] Where wilt thou that we go and prepare, that thou mayest eat the passover?

13 And he sendeth forth two of his disciples, and saith unto them, [e] Go ye into the city, and there shall meet you a man bearing a pitcher of water: follow him.

14 And wheresoever he shall go in, say ye to the good-man of the house, [f] The Master saith, Where is the guest-chamber, where I shall eat the passover with my disciples?

15 And [g] he will shew you a large upper room furnished and prepared: there make ready for us.

16 And his disciples went forth, and [h] came into the city, [i] and found as he had said unto them: and they made ready the passover.

17 ¶ And [k] in the evening he cometh with the twelve.

18 And [l] as they sat and did eat, Jesus said, [m] Verily I say unto you, [n] One of you which eateth with me shall betray me.

19 And they began to be sorrowful, [o] and to say unto him one by one, Is it I? and another said, Is it I?

20 And he answered and said unto them, [p] It is one of the twelve [q] that dippeth with me in the dish.

21 The Son of man indeed [r] goeth, as it is written of him: [s] but woe to that man by whom the Son of man is betrayed! [t] good were it for that man if he had never been born.

22 ¶ And [u] as they did eat, Jesus took bread, [x] and blessed, and brake it, and gave to them, and said, Take, eat: [y] this is my body.

23 And he took the cup, and [z] when he had given thanks, he gave it to them: [a] and they all drank of it.

24 And he said unto them, [b] This is my blood of the new testament, [c] which is shed for many.

25 Verily I say unto you, [d] I will drink no more of the fruit of the vine, until that day that I drink it [e] new in the kingdom of God.

26 ¶ And when they had [f] sung an hymn, [g] they went out into the mount of Olives.

Marginal references (left column): a Hos. vii. 1. Luke xxii. 5. a 2 Kings v. 26. Prov. xxviii. 21, 22. Matt. xxvi. 15. 1 Tim. vi. 10. 2 Pet. ii. 14. 13. Jude 11. b Luke xxii. 3, 6. c Ex. xii. 6, 18. xiii. 5, Lev. xxiii. 5, 6. Num. xxviii. 16—18. Deut. xvi. 1—4. Matt. xxvi. 17. Luke xxii. 7. * Or, sacrificed. 1 Cor. v. 7, 8. d Matt. iii. 15. Luke xxii. 8, 9. Gal. iv. 4. e Matt. viii. 9. xxvi. 18, 19. Luke xix. 30—33. xxii. 10—13. John ii. 5. xv. 14. Heb. v. 9. f x. 17. xi. 2. John xi. 28. g 2 Chr. vi. 30. Ps. cx. 3. Prov. xvi. 1. xxi. 1, 2. John ii. 24, 25. xxi. 17. 2 Tim. ii. 19. Heb. iv. 13. h Acts i. 13. xx. 8. i Luke xxii. 13. 55. John xvi. 4. k Matt. xxvi. 20. Luke xxii. 14. l Matt. xxvi. 21.

Marginal references (right column): m 9. 26. iii. 28. vi. 11. viii. 17. ix. 1. 41. x. 29. Matt. v. 18. vi. 2. 5. 16. Luke iv. 24. xi. 51. John i. 51. iii. 3. 5. 11. v. 19. 24. 25. vi. 26. 32. 47. xiii. 38. xxi. 18. n Ps. xli. 9. iv. 13. 14. John vi. 70, 71. xiii. 21. o Matt. xxvi. 22. Luke xxii. 21—23. John xiii. 22. p 43. Matt. xxvi. 47. Luke xxii. 47. John vi. 71. q Matt. xxvi. 24. John xiii. 26. r Gen. iii. 15. Is. liii. 1, &c. Ps. xxii. 1, &c. Isa. l, 6. liii. iii. 14. liii. Dan. ix. 26. Zech. xii. 7. Matt. xxvi. 54. 56. Luke xxii. 22. 35. 37. Acts ii. 23. iii. 18. iv. 28. xiii. 27—29. s Ps. iv. 18? 7. xxvi. 5—20. Matt. xviii. 7. xxvi. 24—26. t Acts i. 16—20. 25. u Matt. xxvi. 26—29. 19. 26. 1 Cor. x. 16. 17. xi. 23—29. x vi. 41. Luke xxiv. 30. John vi. 23. y 24. Gen. xli. 26, 27. Zech. v. 7. z 1 Cor. x. 4. 20. 1 Cor. xi. 24. Gal. iv. 26. a 22. Luke xxii. 17. Rom. xiv. 6. 1 Cor. x. 16. b Ex. xxiv. 8. Zech. ix. 11. 1 Cor. xi. 25. Heb. ix. 15—22. c x. 45. Rev. v. 9—14. d Ps. cviii. Matt. xxvi. 29. Luke xxii. 16—18. 29, 30. e Joel iii. 18. Am. ix. 13. Zech. ix. 17. f Ps. xlvi. 7. Acts xvi. 25. 1 Cor. xiv. 15. Eph. v. 18—20. Col. iii. 16. Jam. v. 13. Rev. v. 9. † Or, psalm. g Matt. xxvi. 30. Luke xxii. 39. John xviii. 1—4.

---

on which day Judas first went to the chief priests; but it is most probable, that it was two days before the passover, when they were consulting how to apprehend Jesus, that they might put him to death. The devil had before this " put it into his heart;" but it may be supposed, that he hesitated for a time, before he carried his design into execution.

V. 12—16. (Note, Matt. xxvi. 17—19.) Nothing could be less the object of natural sagacity and foresight, than the events here mentioned. Had the two disciples come to the place specified, rather sooner or later than they did, the " man, bearing the pitcher of water," would either not have arrived, or he would have been gone. But our Lord knew that the owner of a certain commodious house in Jerusalem favoured him; he foresaw that at a precise time of the day, he would send his servant for a pitcher of water; that the disciples would meet him just when they entered the city; that by following him they would find out the person whom he intended; and that by mentioning him, as " the Master," or " the Teacher," the owner of the house would readily consent to accommodate them in an upper chamber. When the disciples found all these circumstances so exactly accord to the prediction, they could not but be deeply impressed with a conviction of their Lord's knowledge of every event, and his influence over every heart. (Marg. Ref.—Notes, xi. 1—11. 1 Sam. x. 2—7.)—Furnished, &c. (15) That is, with table, couches, and all other things suited to the occasion.

The guest-chamber. (14) Το καταλυμα. Luke ii. 7. xxii. 11. Probably every householder in Jerusalem, who had it in his power, reserved a room in his house for this purpose, for such of his friends as came up thither to eat the passover. He was their host, and this " guest-" chamber " was as it were their " inn."—An upper room. (15) Ανωγεον. Luke xxii. 12. Quod απο της γης. Not elsewhere N. T.

V. 17—25. Marg. Ref.—Notes, Matt. xxvi. 21—29. Luke xxii. 14—23. —Written. (21) Notes, Ps. xli. 9. lxix. 22—28, v. 28. cix. 6—20. Matt. xxvi. 21—24, Luke xxii. 21—23, v. 22. John xiii. 18—30. Acts i. 16—26.—All ye. (27) ' Christ foretelleth, how he shall be forsaken of his; ' but yet that he will never forsake them.' Beza. (Note, John xvi. 31—33.)

V. 26—31. Marg. Ref.—Notes, Matt. xxvi. 30—35. Luke xxii. 31—34. John xiii. 36—38—Twice. (30) ' After ' thou hast heard it once, thou shalt not be admonished :

27 And Jesus saith unto them, ʰ All ye shall be offended because of me this night: ʲ for it is written, I will smite the Shepherd, and the sheep shall be scattered.

28 But ᵏ after that I am risen, I will go before you into Galilee.

29 But Peter said unto him, ˡ Although all shall be offended, yet will not I.

30 And Jesus saith unto him, Verily I say unto thee, That ᵐ this day, even in this night, ⁿ before the cock crow twice, thou shalt deny me thrice.

31 But ᵒ he spake the more vehemently, If I should die with thee, I will not deny thee in any wise. ᵖ Likewise also said they all.

32 ¶ And ᵠ they came to a place which was named Gethsemane: and he saith to his disciples, Sit ye here, ʳ while I shall pray.

33 And he taketh with him ˢ Peter, and James, and John, ᵗ and began to be sore amazed, and to be very heavy;

34 And saith unto them, ᵘ My soul is exceeding sorrowful unto death: ᵛ tarry ye here, ʷ and watch.

35 And he went forward a little, ˣ and fell on the ground, and prayed that, if it were possible, the hour might pass from him.

36 And he said, ᵃ Abba, Father, ᵇ all things *are* possible unto thee; ᶜ take away this cup from me: ᵈ nevertheless, not what I will, but what thou wilt.

37 And he cometh, ᵈ and findeth them sleeping, and saith unto Peter, Simon, sleepest thou? ᶠ couldest not thou watch one hour?

38 ᵍ Watch ye, and pray, lest ye enter into temptation: ʰ the spirit truly *is* ready, but the flesh *is* weak.

39 And again ⁱ he went away, and prayed, and spake the same words.

40 And when he returned, he found them asleep again; (for their eyes were heavy;) ᵏ neither wist they what to answer him.

41 And he cometh the third time, and saith unto them, ˡ Sleep on now, and take *your* rest: it is enough, ᵐ the hour is come; behold, ⁿ the Son of man is betrayed into the hand of sinners.

42 Rise up, let us go: lo, he that betrayeth me is at hand.

43 ¶ And immediately, ᵒ while he yet spake, cometh Judas, one of the twelve, and with him a great multitude, with swords and staves, from the chief priests, and the scribes, and the elders.

44 And he that betrayed him had

ᵉ but before it crows a second time, thou shalt repeat the fault, nay, thou shalt do it thrice, and every time with new aggravations.' *Doddridge.* (*Note, Matt.* xxvi. 69—75.)

He spake the more vehemently. (31) Εκ περισσου ελεγε μαλλον. I know no English words, which can fully express the emphasis of the original.—The circumstances of Peter's self-confidence, and dreadful fall, are related with peculiar energy by St. Mark, who is supposed to have written his gospel under Peter's immediate inspection; but those of his repentance are more slightly touched on. (*Note,* 66—72.)

V. 32—36. *Marg. Ref.—Notes, Matt.* xxvi. 36—39. *Luke* xxii. 39—46.—*And he said,* &c. (36) 'O Father, I know that all things are possible to thine...almighty power. When I consult with human infirmity, I could incline to wish the removal of this bitter passion: but these weak volitions are not now for me; I do and shall willingly submit my human will, to thy divine will and pleasure.' *Bp. Hall.*—(*Note, John* xii. 27—33.) 'Christ, suffering for us, in that flesh which he took upon him for our sakes, the horrible terrors of the curse of God, receiveth the cup at his Father's hands, which he, being just, doth straightway drink off for the unjust.' *Beza.*

To be sore amazed. (33) Εκθαμβεισθαι. See on ix. 15.—

The hour might pass from him. (35) Παρελθη απ' αυλα η ωρα.—Παρελθετω απ' εμα το ποληριον τυτο, *Matt.* xxvi. 31. Ωρα, 41. *Luke* xxii. 53. *John* ii. 4. xii. 23. 27. xiii. 1. xvii. 1.—*Abba.* (36) A Syrack word signifying *Father,* but in a way of peculiar affection and confidence. (*Notes, Rom.* viii. 14—17. *v.* 15. *Gal.* iv. 5—7, *v.* 6.)

V. 37, 38. (*Marg. Ref.—Note, Matt.* xxvi. 40, 41.) 'Thou, that didst even now express so much kindness and constancy to me (31), art thou able to do so much less? In this state of agony, which I expressed to you, that I was in (34), couldest thou be so little concerned, as to fall asleep when I stayed so little while from you?' *Hammond.*

V. 39—42. *Marg. Ref.—Note, Matt.* xxvi. 42—46.— *It is enough.* (41) Απεχει. *Matt.* vi. 2. xv. 8. *Luke* vi. 24. It is impersonally in this place only, in N. T. Both my charge to you, to watch, and your sleeping are at an end: it is sufficient," you can no longer now be of any service in watching for me.

V. 43—50. *Marg. Ref.—Notes, Matt.* xxvi. 47—56. *Luke* xxii. 47—53. *John* xviii. 1—14.— *Take and lead him away safely.* (44) 'It is probable that Judas thought they could not do this; but that, as Jesus had at other times conveyed himself away, when they attempted to cast him

given them ʼ a token, saying, ʼWhom-
soever I shall kiss, that same is he;
take him, ʼand lead *him* away safely.

45 And as soon as he was come, he
goeth straightway to him, and saith,
ʼMaster, Master; and kissed him.

46 And ʼthey laid their hands on
him, and took him.

47 And ʼone of them that stood by
drew a sword, and smote a servant of
the high priest, and cut off his ear.

48 And Jesus answered and said
unto them, ʼAre ye come out as against
a thief, with swords and *with* staves to
take me?

49 I ʼwas daily with you in the temple teaching, and ye took me not:
ʼbut the scriptures must be fulfilled.

50 And ʼthey all forsook him, and
fled.

51 And there followed him a certain young man, having a linen cloth
cast about *his* naked *body*; and the
young men laid hold on him.

52 And ʼhe left the linen cloth,
and fled from them naked.

53 ¶ And ʼthey led Jesus away to
the high priest: ʼand with him were
assembled all the chief priests, and the
elders, and the scribes.

54 And ʼPeter followed him afar off,
ʼeven into the palace of the high priest:
ʼand he sat with the servants, ʼand
warmed himself at the fire.

55 And the chief priests and all the
council ʼ sought for witness against
Jesus to put him to death; ʼand found
none:

56 For many bare false witness
against him; but their witness agreed
not together.

57 And there arose certain, ᵐ and
bare false witness against him, saying,

58 We heard him say, I will destroy
this temple that is made with hands,
and within three days I will build another ⁿ made without hands.

59 But ⁿneither so did their witness
agree together.

60 And the high priest stood up in
the midst, and asked Jesus, saying,
ʼAnswerest thou nothing? what *is it
which* these witness against thee?

61 But ʼ he held his peace, and answered nothing. Again the high priest
asked him, and said unto him, ʼArt
thou the Christ, ʼ the Son of the
Blessed?

62 And Jesus said, ʼI am: and ye
shall see ⁿ the Son of man sitting on
the right hand of power, and coming
in the clouds of heaven.

63 Then the high priest rent ˣ his
clothes, and saith, What need we any ʸ
further witnesses?

64 Ye ʸ have heard the blasphemy:
what think ye? And they all con-

ʼ down a precipice, (*Luke* iv. 29, 30,) or to stone him,
ʼ (*John* viii. 59. x. 39,) so he would have done now.'
Whitby.—Master. (45) Rabbi, Rabbi. *Gr.—And Jesus,* &c.
ʼ48—50) ʼ As men had knowingly and willingly deserted
ʼ their Creator, become traitors against him, and robbed
ʼ him of his glory: so Christ willingly making satis-
ʼ faction for the unjust, being deserted by his disciples,
ʼ and betrayed by one whom he had admitted to the most
ʼ familiar acquaintance with him, is apprehended like a
ʼ robber; that the punishment might answer to the sin;
ʼ and we, the real traitors, deserters, and sacrilegious rob-
ʼ bers, might be rescued from the snare of the devil.' *Beza.*
A token. (44) Συσσημον. Here only N. T. ʼ Signum quo
ʼ inter duo pluresve convenit tessera, symbolum.' Schleusner.
(Εχ συν, et σημα, a watchword.)
V. 51, 52. It is probable, though not certain, that this
young man was one of our Lord's followers: being, however, awaked by the tumult, he seems to have left his bed,
covered only with a sheet, or loose covering; and to have
followed the company, either out of curiosity, or from
affection to Jesus. He was, on this account at least, suspected to be a disciple; and " the young men," the sol-

diers, or servants, attempted to lay hold on him; so that
he was forced to flee away naked, and escape for his life.
(*Marg. Ref.* c.) But, though the transaction was conducted with such extreme violence, the apostles had been
permitted to escape through the secret influence of Jesus
over the minds of those who apprehended him! (*Note,
John* xviii. 4—9.)
V. 53—59. *Marg. Ref.—Notes, Matt.* xxvi. 57—62.
Luke xxii. 63—65. *John* xviii. 10—16.—*Warmed,* &c. (54)
John xviii. 25. *Notes, Luke* xxii. 39—46, *v.* 44.—*Agreed.*
(56, 59.) Ισαι ισα. 'Their testimonies were not *equal* to the
ʼ charge brought against him; that he was worthy to die; or
ʼ they were not sufficient εις το θανατωσαι αυτον, to cause him
ʼ to be put to death, either not testifying two of the same
ʼ thing, or else not charging him with a crime which de-
ʼ served death by the law.' *Whitby.* Perhaps one testified,
that he had said he was able to destroy the temple, and
the other, that he would actually destroy it. (*Note, John* ii.
18—22.)
V. 60—65. *Notes, Matt.* xxvi. 63—68. *Luke* xxii. 63
—71.—*The Blessed.* (61) Τε Ευλογητε, *nempe* Θευ. *Matt.*
xxvi. 63. *Luke* i. 68. *Rom.* i. 25. ix. 5. 2 *Cor.* i. 3. xi. 31

demned him to be guilty of death.

65 And ' some began to spit on him, and to cover his face, and to buffet him, and to say unto him, Prophesy: and the servants did strike him with the palms of their hands.

66 ¶ And ᵃ as Peter was beneath in the palace, there cometh ᵇ one of the maids of the high priest:

67 And when she saw Peter warming himself, she looked upon him, and said, And thou also wast with ᶜ Jesus of Nazareth.

68 But ᵈ he denied, saying, I know not, neither understand I what thou sayest. And ᵉ he went out into the porch; ᶠ and the cock crew.

69 And a maid saw him again, ᵍ and began to say to them that stood by, This is one of them.

70 And he denied it again. And ʰ a little after, they that stood by said again to Peter, Surely thou art one of them: ⁱ for thou art a Galilean, and thy speech agreeth thereto.

71 But ᵏ he began to curse and to swear, saying, I know not this man of whom ye speak.

72 And ˡ the second time the cock crew. And ᵐ Peter called to mind the word that Jesus said unto him, Before ⁿ the cock crow twice thou shalt deny me thrice. ᵒ And ᵖ when he thought thereon, he wept.

Eph. i. 3. 1 *Pet.* i. 3.—ᵉ Of God, who is worthy of all ᵉ praise.' *Beza.* (*Note*, 1 *Tim.* vi. 13—16.)—*I am.* (62) Εγω ειμι. " I am what thou hast said." Συ ειπας, *Matt.* xxvi. 62. ᵉ These two phrases are of equal import in the Hebrew ᵉ idiom.' *Whitby.*—*To buffet him.* (65) Κολαφιζειν. See on *Note, Matt.* xxvi. 67.—*The palms of their hands.*] 'Ραπισμασιν. *Bacillis.* Beza. *John* xviii. 22. xix. 3. Comp. xv. 19. *Matt.* xxvii. 30.—ᵉ Christ, suffering all kind of reproach ᵉ for our sakes, getteth everlasting glory to them that believe ᵉ in him.' *Beza.* (*Marg. Ref.*—*Notes, Ps.* lxix. 8—12. *Is.* l. 5—9. liii. 2, 3. *Mic.* v. 1.)

V. 66—72. *Notes, Matt.* xxvi. 69—75. *John* xxi. 15—17.—*Thou,* &c. (67) " Thou also wast with the Naza-" rene Jesus." (*Matt.* ii. 23.)—*He denied.* (68) ᵉ A mourn-ᵉ ful example of human weakness; and also an example ᵉ of God's compassion, who giveth to his elect the spirit ᵉ of repentance and faith.' *Beza.*—*Peter called,* &c. (72) ᵉ Peter, remembering what the Saviour had foretold con-ᵉ cerning his denial; and considering how exactly, but ᵉ shamefully, after all his confident engagements to the ᵉ contrary, he had fulfilled the same, was filled with com-ᵉ punction and wept bitterly.' *Whitby.*—ᵉ Peter was suf-ᵉ fered to fall fouler, than any of the rest of the apostles, ᵉ (except Judas the traitor,) that we might be cautioned ᵉ against that extravagant regard which would after-ᵉ wards be demanded to him and his pretended succes-ᵉ sors.' *Clarke.*—ᵉ Peter by the look of Christ, and by the ᵉ crowing of the cock, was awaked as from a deep sleep.' *Beza.*

Understand I, &c. (68) Επισταμαι. More strong than in *Matt.* xxvi. 70.—*The porch.*] Προαυλιον. Ex προ et αυλη. Here only N. T. Πυλωνα, *Matt.* xxvi. 71.—*A maid.* (69) 'H παιδισκη.—Αλλη, *Matt.* xxvi. 71. *Another* maid was certainly meant; yet ἡ παιδισκη, with the article, scarcely admits of being translated " a maid," indefinitely. May it not refer to the maid who was stationed at the door? (*John* xviii. 17.)—*Agreeth thereto.* (70) 'Ομοιαζει, ab ὁμοιος, *similis.* Here only N. T.—*When he thought thereon.* (72) Επιβαλων. Εξελθων εξω, *Matt.* xxvi. 75. (*Marg.*) Some refer the expression to the vehemence, with which Peter rushed forth from the palace, when he heard the cock crow the second time. Our translation supposes,

εις τον ναν, or εν τῳ νῳ αυτᾳ, to be understood. (*Note, Luke* xxii. 54—62.)

PRACTICAL OBSERVATIONS.

V. 1—16.

While numbers combine with implacable enmity against Christ, and employ both power and subtlety to run down his truth, and injure his people; there are a few, though generally in inferior stations, who spare no pains or expense to express their love to him, and to promote his glory. But it is not uncommon for their fervent expressions of zeal and affection to be misunderstood, and censured, even by their brethren, as well as by hypocrites and open enemies. We should not therefore be discouraged, if those whom we love should think our time, labour, or expense wasted, or misapplied; when we are sincerely desirous of honouring Christ and promoting his gospel, and are really employed in some good work for him: and, on the other hand, we should fear giving any molestation to those, who are led to express their love in a different manner than we do.—Happy is he, of whom in these things the Lord says, " He did what he could."—We indeed have not Christ personally present with us, and may have little opportunity of promoting his cause, or ability to do it; but we have " the poor always with us, and whensoever we will " we may do them good:" and if in this, or in any other proper way, we " shew the sincerity of our love" and gratitude to our gracious Redeemer, he will accept our well-meant services, and make them known to the whole world, for a memorial of us; when mercenary hypocrites, as well as avowed enemies, shall sink into shame and everlasting contempt. (*Notes, Matt.* xxv. 34—40. P. O. 31—40. xxvi. 1—13. *John* xii. 1—8. *Notes,* 2 *Cor.* viii. 1—9.) —Our blessed Lord knows every circumstance respecting us before it comes to pass: and if we carefully compare our experience with his words, we shall be more and more convinced, that he is ordering every thing relative to him, in perfect wisdom, truth, and goodness, " according to " the counsel of his own will;" and that even the most painful dispensations will in the event conduce to the good of all who trust in him.—Whatever we possess is

CHAP. XV.

Jesus is bound, and delivered up unto Pilate; and when accused before him, and interrogated by him, he continues silent, 1—5. Pilate, induced by the priests and people, releases Barabbas, and delivers Jesus to be crucified, 6—15. The soldiers crown him with thorns, and cruelly mock him; and then lead him away to the place of crucifixion, 16—24. He is crucified between two thieves, and reviled by the people and the priests, 25—32. The sun is darkened; and Jesus, calling on God, expires, 33—37. The veil of the temple is rent; and the centurion confesses him to be " the Son of God," 38, 39. Certain women are spectators of his crucifixion, 40, 41. Joseph of Arimathea asks Pilate for the body, which having obtained he honourably inters, 42—47.

then best employed, and most profitable to us, when it is most entirely devoted to the Redeemer's service: if we be disposed to admit him, he will come and dwell in our hearts, and will provide for us that we may feast with him: and when we consecrate our houses to him, by family-worship properly conducted, and by hospitably entertaining his disciples, he will .here also manifest his presence with us and bless us. (*P. O. Matt.* xxvi. 14—25.)

V. 17—42.

While we consider the Lord Jesus, (' the very paschal ' Lamb, that was sacrificed for us;' and who has given his body to be broken, and his blood to be shed, that we might live by faith in his name,) as attending on those divine institutions which bring sin to remembrance; that he might " fulfil all righteousness :" let us learn, in copying his example, to beware of hypocrisy, and to fear being counted intruders, or detected as traitors. To be preserved from this, we must " take heed and beware of co-" vetousness," and be diligent in self-examination: not trusting to our own hearts, but still enquiring, when we read of the guilt and misery of hypocrites and apostates, " Lord, is it I?" as more ready to suspect ourselves than any of our brethren. Let us thus " examine ourselves," and then, as frequently as opportunity is afforded us, " let " us eat of that bread, and drink of that cup," which are the appointed symbols of the body and blood of Christ, given for us, to purchase the blessings of the new covenant for our perishing souls. Thus we shall be frequently led to recollect our guilt and danger, our hope and our obligations, and our profession of faith, and love to our Redeemer and his ransomed flock: thus we shall receive renewed pledges of his love to us, and have our affections enlivened, and our strength increased, for his service: thus we shall anticipate the blessed hour, when we shall drink of the fruit of our living Vine with him, for ever new in the kingdom of our Father: and thus we shall also be prepared for bearing our cross, and for drinking of the cup of tribulation, and for tasting death in our passage to glory. (*P. O. Matt.* xxvi. 26—35.)—The great and good Shepherd indeed passed through his unspeakable sufferings, without one false step; but even the principal of his followers have often been offended and scattered, by the comparatively small measure of afflictions allotted to them: and this has been exactly proportioned to the degree, in which they have confided in themselves, and formed their resolutions in their own strength.—Did we indeed properly contemplate the scene exhibited in Gethsemane; did we duly consider the amazement and anguish of the great Redeemer, when " his soul was sorrowful even unto " death," through the load of our guilt which he willingly sustained; did we advert to " his strong crying and tears,"

(*Note, Heb.* v. 7—10, *v.* 7,) and to the victorious resignation of his heart, when he said, " Nevertheless, not as I " will, but as thou wilt :" these reflections would fill our minds with such convictions concerning the evil of sin, the awful justice of God, the love of the Saviour, the vanity of the world, the impotency of men's malice, and the danger and helpless condition of our souls; as would have a powerful effect, in rendering us humble, dependent, thankful, and stedfast, in the hour of trial; and in exciting us to watchfulness and prayer, lest we should be borne down by the force of temptation, or lest we should at last fall under the insupportable wrath of God. But, alas! while unbelievers entirely disregard this interesting and affecting subject, even believers are apt to contemplate it in a drowsy manner; and, instead of being " ready to " die with Christ," they are often unprepared to " watch " with him one hour !" Thus, after repeated warnings, through their own negligence they " enter into tempta-" tion;" and then, through the weakness of the flesh, they fall into sin, notwithstanding the readiness of the spirit, in their better moments. (*Notes, Rom.* vii. 15—21. *P. O.* 15—25.) But let us not attempt to excuse such folly, disobedience, and ingratitude; should Jesus call us to account for it, we should not know what to answer him: and though he will not cast off the true believer for these offences, he will yet sharply rebuke and chasten him, and bring him to condemn himself on account of them. (*P. O. Matt.* xxvi. 36—46. *Luke* xxii. 35—46.)

V. 43—72.

There is an essential difference between the general character of faulty disciples, and that of hypocrites. These often prove traitors, and deliberately join the enemies of Christ in opposing his cause. Having long carried on a trade of iniquity, under the mask of piety, and amid all the means of grace, they grow callous in sin, and treat all religious concerns with an unfeeling familiarity; they conceal their crimes, by attending on ordinances and sacraments; and, whilst they presumptuously call Christ their Lord and Master, and express great affection for him, they betray him into the hands of his implacable enemies. Thus they hasten their own destruction, and " it would " have been better for them had they never been born."— Whilst the enemies of Christ are actuated by the most outrageous malice, and seem to carry every thing their own way, they are under secret restraints, and can only fulfil the scriptures: nor can they move any faster or further, or touch one person more, than the Lord is pleased to permit them. (*Note, Ps.* lxxvi. 10.)—The most enormous wickedness has commonly been committed, under the forms of law and justice, and varnished over by a sem-

2 P 3

AND [a] straightway in the morning the chief priests held a consultation with the elders and scribes and the whole council, and bound Jesus, and carried *him* away, [b] and delivered *him* to Pilate.

2 And Pilate asked him, [c] Art thou the King of the Jews? And he answering said unto him, Thou sayest it.

3 And [d] the chief priests accused him of many things; [e] but he answered nothing.

4 And Pilate asked him again, saying, [f] Answerest thou nothing? behold how many things they witness against thee.

5 But Jesus yet answered nothing; so that [f] Pilate marvelled.

6 ¶ Now [h] at *that* feast he released unto them one prisoner, whomsoever they desired.

7 And [i] there was *one* named Barabbas, *which lay* bound with them that had made insurrection with him, who had committed murder in the insurrection.

8 And the multitude, crying aloud, began to desire *him to do* as he had ever done unto them.

9 But Pilate answered them, saying, [k] Will ye that I release unto you the King of the Jews?

Marginal references (left column):
a Ps. ii. 2. Matt. xxvii. 1, 2. Luke xxii. 66. Acts iv. 5, 6, 25—28.
b x 33, 34. Matt. xx. 18, 19. Luke xxiii. 32, 33. John xviii. 1, 2, 3. John xviii. 28. Acts iii. 13.
c Matt. ii. 2 xxvii. 11. Luke xxiii. —37. xix. 19—22. 1 Tim. vi. 14.
d Matt. xxvii. 12. Luke xxiii. 2—5. John xviii. 29 —31. xix. 6, 7. 12.
e Is. liii. 7.

Marginal references (right column):
g Ps. lxxi. 14. viii. 18. Zech. iii. 8. Matt. xxvii. 14. 1 Cor. iv. 9.
h Matt. xxvii. 15. xxvii. 16. Luke xxiii. 16, 17. John xviii. 30, 40. Acts xxiv. 27. xxv. 9. Matt. xxvii. 16. Luke xxiii. 18, 25.
k Matt. xxvii. 17 —21. John xviii. 30. xix. 4, 5. 14 —16. Acts iii. 13 —15.

Left commentary column:

blance of piety: and while rulers have been ringleaders in the most aggravated perjury, venality, oppression, and murder; they have often paused, and perplexed themselves, in devising how to regulate their conduct by statute and custom, and with the appearance of impartiality! Indeed, when we contemplate the whole body of the rulers and teachers of God's professed people, combined against his holy and beloved Son, and determined at any rate to condemn him to death; and when we view him given up by them as a malefactor, to such insults and cruelties, as the vilest murderer would have been exempted from; we have the clearest demonstration of man's extreme enmity to God, and of God's most free and unspeakable love to man. In the conduct of our suffering Lord, we see the brightest pattern of meekness, patience, fortitude, holiness, and compassion to sinners, that the earth or even the creation at large ever witnessed: we here perceive likewise the desert of sin, the worth of our souls, the foundation of our hope, and the nature of our Christian calling; which is to do good with unwearied perseverance, and to endure evil with fortitude, meekness, and patience, after the example of our gracious Saviour. (*Note,* and *P. O.* 1 *Pet.* ii. 18—25.) Thus may we look forward with comfort to the time, when we "shall see the Son of man, "sitting on the right hand of power and coming in the "clouds of heaven;" and hope to be numbered with his victorious army of glorified saints; when all his persecutors and enemies will be driven away into everlasting destruction.—But when we hear Peter, after all his promises and resolutions, repeatedly denying his Lord with oaths and curses; we may well tremble to reflect on the weakness and depravity even of believers, if left to themselves; we may take occasion from the reflection to admire the mercy and patience of our God; we may be excited to thankfulness, that we have not yet been left utterly to forsake him; and we may confess with shame our manifold instances of *partial* unfaithfulness. Finally, "Let "him, that thinketh he standeth, take heed lest he fall:" and let him that has fallen think of these things, and of his own offences, and return to the Lord with weeping and supplication, with deep repentance, and lively faith; still hoping to receive forgiveness to be restored to "the

Right commentary column:

"joy of God's salvation," and to be henceforth established by his free Spirit. (*Notes,* and *P. O. Ps.* li. 5—13. *Matt.* xxvi. 47—75.)

NOTES.

CHAP. XV. V. 1—5. (*Marg. Ref.—Notes, Matt.* xxvii. 1, 2. 11—18, *vv.* 11—14. *Luke* xxiii. 1—5. *John* xviii. 28 —32.) 'The observation of Theophylact is this: The 'Jews delivered up our Lord to the Romans; and they, for 'that sin, were themselves given up into the hands of the 'Romans.' *Whitby.—*'Christ being publickly bound be-'fore the tribunal of an earthly judge, not for his own 'sins, as it appears out of the mouth of the judge him-'self, but for the crimes of us all, was condemned to the 'cross; that we most guilty creatures being freed from the 'penalty of our sins, might be publickly justified before 'the tribunal of God, and the assembly of his angels.' *Beza.*

Delivered. (1) Παρεδωκαν. xiv. 44. They, as well as Judas, were traitors to their Kings.—*Yet answered nothing.* (5) Ουκέτι ωδεν απεκρινατο.—He answered nothing further, than what was implied in the words "Thou sayest it" (2). (*Note,* 1 *Tim.* vi. 13—16, *v.* 18.)

V. 6—10. (*Marg. Ref.—Notes, Matt.* xxvii. 11—18, *vv.* 15—18. *Luke* xxiii. 13—25. *John* xviii. 37—40.) Besides the notoriously bad character of Barabbas, as a robber, he had been guilty of the very crime, of which the scribes and priests falsely accused Jesus; having joined in or headed an insurrection against the Romans, which had committed murder in the attempt. Yet this man was preferred decidedly before the holy and beneficent Saviour! though the publick demand, that a criminal of this kind should be released, might have given great offence to Pilate, had he not perceived the envy and malice by which the priests and rulers were actuated.

Had made insurrection with him. (7) (Ex σun et τασις, insurrectio.) Here only N. T.—*Who had committed murder, &c.*] 'Οιτινες, κ. τ. λ. plural. The insurgents had committed murder, to which Barabbas was either the principal or an accomplice. (*Acts* iii. 14.)— *Crying aloud.* (8) Αναζοησας. *Matt.* xxvii. 46. *Luke* ix. 38.

10 For he knew that the chief priests had delivered him for envy. 11 But the chief priests moved the people, that he should rather release Barabbas unto them. 12 And Pilate answered and said again unto them, What will ye then that I shall do unto him whom ye call the King of the Jews? 13 And they cried out again, Crucify him. 14 Then Pilate said unto them, Why, what evil hath he done? And they cried out the more exceedingly, Crucify him. 15 And so Pilate, willing to content the people, released Barabbas unto them, and delivered Jesus, when he had scourged him, to be crucified. 16 And the soldiers led him away into the hall called Pretorium; and they call together the whole band. 17 And they clothed him with purple, and platted a crown of thorns, and put it about his head; 18 And began to salute him, Hail, King of the Jews! 19 And they smote him on the head with a reed, and did spit upon him,

him, and bowing their knees worshipped him. 20 And when they had mocked him, they took off the purple from him, and put his own clothes on him, and led him out to crucify him.

21 And they compel one Simon a Cyrenian, who passed by, coming out of the country, the father of Alexander and Rufus, to bear his cross. 22 And they bring him unto the place Golgotha, which is, being interpreted, The place of a skull. 23 And they gave him to drink wine mingled with myrrh: but he received it not. 24 And when they had crucified him, they parted his garments, casting lots upon them, what every man should take. 25 And it was the third hour; and they crucified him. 26 And the superscription of his accusation was written over, THE KING OF THE JEWS. 27 And with him they crucify two thieves, the one on his right hand, and the other on his left. 28 And the scripture was fulfilled, which saith, And he was numbered with the transgressors.

V. 11—20. (Marg. Ref.—Notes, Matt. xxvii. 19—23. 26—31. Luke xxiii. 13—25. John xix. 8—18.)—Worshipped. (19) Marg. Ref. a.—Note, Acts. iii. 2.—Adoration, in the strictest meaning of the word, was paid to many of the Roman emperors; and no doubt the soldiers mocked our Lord's claim to regal authority by the semblance of it.—And when, &c. (20) Before the soldiers had taken off the purple robe, and put on Jesus his own clothing; Pilate brought him forth to the people and priests, saying, "Behold the man." (Note, John xix. 1 —7.)

Moved, &c. (11) Ανσισαν. Luke xxiii. 5. Επησαν, Matt. xxvii. 20.—King of the Jews. (12) "The Christ," Matt. xxvii. 22.—Why, what evil, &c. (14) Τι γαρ κακον; "Why should I crucify him? for what evil hath he "done?" (Acts xix. 35.)—To content, &c. (15) Το ικανον ποιησαι. Quod illis sufficiat. Acta xvii. 9. Gr.—Pretorium. (16) Πραιτωριον. See on Matt. xxvii. 27.

V. 21—24. Notes, Matt. xvi. 24—28, v. 24. xxvii. 32 —36. Luke xxiii. 26—38. John xix. 23, 24.—Wine, &c. (23) This "wine mingled with myrrh," is said to have been prepared by certain honourable women at Jerusalem, who used to send it to such criminals as were led forth to execution.—Christ, being about to drink off the most bitter cup of his Father's wrath against our sins, refused

this solace; being so mindful of his Father's command, as to be unmindful of himself; and only solicitous at once to expiate our sins, even to his latest breath.' Beza. (Note, Matt. xxvi. 29.)

Mingled with myrrh. (23) Εσμυρνισμενον. Here only N. T. (Note, Matt. xxvii. 32—34, v. 34.)

V. 25. The third, &c.] Or about nine o'clock in the morning.—The rulers must have been very early and active in their proceedings, to have gone through so much business, and to have surmounted so many difficulties, by that hour. Indeed in John's gospel, we read of "the "sixth hour;" but this is generally allowed, either to be an error of the transcribers, or to admit of another interpretation; and Christ is commonly supposed to have been nailed to the cross about nine o'clock in the forenoon (Note, John xix. 13—18, v. 14.)—' The darkness began at 'the sixth hour, which yet began not, till after our Lord 'had hung on the cross some considerable time; till after 'the soldiers had divided the garments, the Jews had 'mocked him, and bid him come down from the cross; 'and the discourse had passed between the two thieves 'among themselves, and betwixt the repenting thief and 'our Lord.' Whitby. (Notes, Matt. xxvii. 45. Luke xxiii. 39—43.)

V. 26—28. Marg. Ref.—Notes, Matt. xxvii. 27—34.

29 ¶ And 'they that passed by railed on him, wagging their heads, and saying, 'Ah, thou that destroyest the temple and buildest *it* in three days, 30 Save thyself, and come down from the cross. 31 Likewise 'also the chief priests, mocking, said among themselves with the scribes, "He saved others, himself he cannot save. 32 Let 'Christ, the King of Israel, descend now from the cross, that we may see and believe. 'And they that were crucified with him reviled him. 33 ¶ And 'when the sixth hour was come, there was 'darkness over the whole land until the ninth hour. 34 And 'at the ninth hour Jesus cried with a loud voice, saying, 'Eloi, lama sabachthani?' which is,

being interpreted, My God, my God, 'why hast thou forsaken me? 35 And some of them that stood by when they heard *it*, said, Behold, 'he calleth Elias. 36 And one ran, 'and filled a sponge full of vinegar, and put *it* on a reed, and gave him to drink, saying, Let alone: let us see whether Elias will come to take him down. 37 And 'Jesus cried with a loud voice, and gave up the ghost. 38 And 'the veil of the temple was rent in twain, from the top to the bottom. 39 And when 'the centurion, which stood over against him, saw that he so cried out, and gave up the ghost, 'he said, Truly this man was the Son of God.

John xix. 19—22.—*The superscription of his accusation.*
(26) 'Η επιγραφη της αιλιας αυλα. Επιγραφη. xii. 16. *Matt.* xxii. 20. *Luke* xx. 24. xxiii. 38. Αιλιας. *Matt.* xxvii. 37.
' This is spoken according to the manner of the Romans, ' by whom the title of the crimes for which the criminals ' were condemned, were either carried before them, or ' affixed to the instrument of their punishment.' *Whitby.*
—*He was numbered.* (28) Ελογισθη. " He was accounted " among, &c." xi. 31. *Rom.* iii. 28. iv. 3. viii. 18.—*Transgressors.*] Ανομων. (Εx α priv. et νομος, *lex.*) *Luke* xxii. 37. *Acts* ii. 23. 1 *Cor.* ix. 21. 2 *Thes.* ii. 8. 1 *Tim.* i. 9. 2 *Pet.* ii. 8.—*Εν* τοις ανομοις ελογισθη, *Is.* liii. 12. *Sept.* The word more properly signifies *malefactors*, than " transgressors."
V. 29—32. *Marg. Ref.—Notes, Ps.* xxii. 4—8. *Matt.* xxvii. 39—44. *Luke* xxiii. 39—43.—*Christ*, &c. (32) If he be " Messiah, the King of Israel," let him thus prove it.
Ah. (29) Ουα. Here only N. T.—'*Respondet He-*'*braico* דאָה, et Latinorum *Vah: est vox ... insultantis, ex-probrantis, et lætantis de alieno infortunio.* Schleusner.
V. 33. (*Marg. Ref.—Note, Matt.* xxvii. 45.) ' The ' anger of God, as avenging our sins on our Surety, was ' attested by this horror of darkness. ...It is enquired by ' many, whether this is to be understood of the land of ' Judea, or of the whole earth. Tertullian seems to em-' brace the latter opinion, calling the failure of the sun ' the misfortune of the world, which they had recorded in ' the Roman archives. But I rather agree with those who ' understand it of Jerusalem, and all the neighbouring ' country: for it would be more proper for the prodigy to ' be noted in the archives, if peculiar to Judea. ...While ' the sun enlightened the rest of the earth, and even at ' the noon-day, this one corner of the world, in which so ' horrible a crime was perpetrating, was covered with the ' thickest darkness! ...This miracle may seem to have ' been opposed to one directly contrary; when darkness ' covered the Egyptians, while the sun shone on the Is-' raelites in Goshen. At that time verily, God intimated

' that destruction impended over the Egyptians; and that ' liberty was obtained for his people: but now on the con-' trary, he shewed that, while miserable blindness was ' coming on the Jews, (with which they are punished even ' to the present time,) the heavenly light of the gospel ' would arise on all other nations.' *Beza.* (*Notes, Ex.* x. 21—23. *P. O.* 12—29.)
V. 34—39. (*Marg. Ref.—Notes, Matt.* xxvii. 46—49. 51—54. *John* xix. 25—30.) ' Christ, striving mightily ' with Satan, with sin, and with death, all armed with the ' dreadful curse of God; his body hanging on the cross, ' oppressed with exquisite tortures, and his soul sinking ' in the depths of hell, cries out with a loud voice: and ' though he had received a wound from death, as being ' for a time deprived of life; yet by smiting both things ' above and things beneath, by rending the veil of the ' temple, and extorting a testimony in his favour from his ' executioners, declares to his enemies, who still remained ' obstinate and mocked him, that he was speedily about to ' shew himself a Conqueror, and the Lord of all.' *Beza.*
—It has been supposed, that the vigour with which Jesus cried out just before he expired, being contrary to what is generally observed in such cases, (*Note, Matt.* xxvii. 50,) helped to convince the centurion, that he was " the " Son of God:" but the confidence, with which, in those circumstances, he openly addressed God as his Father, and committed his soul into his hands, seems to have had still greater influence in producing this conviction. (*Note, Luke* xxiii. 44—49, *vv.* 46, 47.)—*My God*, &c. (34) Ελωι, Ελωι, from Ελωιμ, *Elohim*, as Ηλι, from Ηλ, *El*, God. *Matt.* xxvii. 46. 'Ο Θεος, ὁ Θεος μυ, προσχες μοι, ινα τι εγκαλελιπες με; *Ps.* xxii. 1. *Sept.*—*Gave up the ghost.* (37) Εξεπνευσε. See on *Matt.* xxvii. 50.—*The centurion.* (39) 'Ο κεντυριων. 44, 45.—The Latin name *Centurio* is here placed instead of ικαβονταρχος, the Greek name, as in the other gospels: whence some infer, that Mark had lived among Romans, and had got accustomed to their language. But Matthew uses the word κυστωδια. (*Matt.* xxvii. 66. xxviii. 11 ,

40 There were also ¹ women looking on afar off; among whom was ᵐ Mary Magdalene, and ⁿ Mary the mother of James the less, and of Joses, ° and Salome;

41 (Who also, when he was in Galilee, followed him, and ᵖ ministered unto him;) and many other women which came up with him unto Jerusalem.

42 ¶ And now ⁴ when the even was come, (because it was the preparation, that is, the day before the sabbath,)

43 Joseph of Arimathea, ʳ an honourable counsellor, ˢ which also waited for the kingdom of God, came, ᵗ and went in boldly unto Pilate, and craved the body of Jesus.

44 And Pilate ᵘ marvelled if he were already dead: and calling *unto him* the centurion, he asked him whether he had been any while dead.

45 And when he knew *it* of the centurion, ˣ he gave the body to Joseph.

46 And he bought fine linen, ʸ and took him down, and wrapped him in the linen, ᶻ and laid him in a sepulchre which was ᵇ hewn out of a rock, ᵃ and rolled a stone unto the door of the sepulchre.

47 And ᶜ Mary Magdalene, and Mary *the mother* of Joses, beheld where he was laid.

Marginal references (left column):
l Ps. xxxvii. 11.
Matt. xxvii. 55.
56. Luke xxiii. 49. John xix. 25
—27.
m xvi. 9. Matt. xxvii. L. Luke viii. 2. John xx. 11—8.
n 47. xvi. 1. Matt. xiii. 55. xxvii. 56. 61. John xix. 25. 1 Cor. ix. 5. Gal. i. 19. Jam.
o xvi. 1.
p Matt. xxvii. 55. Luke viii. 2, 3.
q Matt. xxvii. 57. 62. Luke xxiii. 50—54.
r x. 23—27. s Luke ii. 25. 38. xxiii. 51.
t xiv. 54. &c. xxiii. 55. &c. Matt. xix. 30. xx. 16. Acts iv. 13. Phil. i. 14.

Marginal references (right column):
u John xix. 31—37.
x Matt. xxvii. 58. John xix. 38.
y Matt. xxvii. 59, 60. Luke xxiii. 53. John xix. 38
z Luke xxiii. 53. John xx. 7.
a xvi. 3, 4. Matt. xxvii. 60. xxviii. 2. John xx. 1.
b xvi. 4. Matt. xxvii. 60.
c 40. xvi. 1. Matt. xxvii. 61. xxvii. 1. Luke xxiii. 55, 56. xxiv. 1, 2.

---

custodia, which is as entirely Latin as κεντυριων.—*This man was the Son of God.* (39) 'Οιτος ην ἱιος Θεu. Because the article is wanting before each of the nouns; some would render the clause, ' A son of a god.' (See on *Matt.* xxvii. 40. 54.) For saying, " I am the Son of God," Jesus had been crucified; but the centurion says, " Truly " he was the Son of God ;" in that sense, most clearly, in which Jesus had said that he was; and for saying it, had been crucified.—His views doubtless were very indistinct on the subject; and so were those of the Jews, and even of the apostles. (*Note, Matt.* xiv. 33.)

V. 40, 41. (*Marg. Ref.—Notes, Matt.* xxvii. 55, 56. *John* xix. 25—27.)—*Of James the less.* (40) Ιαχωβu τu μικρu. *The little*: probably, he was not so tall, as James the son of Zebedee.—*James* the son of Alpheus. *Matt.* x. 3. *Mark* iii. 18. *Luke* vi. 15. *Acts* i. 13. " James the " Lord's brother." *Gal.* i. 19. (*Note, Mark* vi. 1—4, *v.* 3.) —*Jam.* i. 1.—*Ministered.* (41) *Note, Luke* viii. 1—3.

V. 42—47. *Notes, Matt.* xxvi. 57—61. *Luke* xxiii. 50—56. *John* xix. 31—42.—*Honourable counsellor.* (43) That is, a member of the sanhedrim, the highest council of the Jewish nation. Joseph " had not consented to the " counsel and deed of them." (*Luke* xxiii. 51.) But, unless he had been one of the council, he would have had no opportunity of consenting to the counsel and deed of those, who condemned Jesus.—*Boldly.*] ' Certainly the ' confidence of this man was very great: as by asking for ' the body of Jesus, he could not but openly oppose him- ' self to all the Jews, and even to Pilate himself.' *Beza.*— *Any while.* (44) Jesus hung six hours in torture on the cross, yet Pilate marvelled that he died so soon !—His care in ascertaining Christ's death, precluded those objections, which the Jews might otherwise doubtless have started against the reality of his resurrection, seeing his body was conceded for interment to his friends. We do not find, that any, either of the rulers or people, ever pretended that he had not really been dead.

Honourable. (43) Ευσχημων. (Ex ευ, *bene*, et σχημα, *species, habitus. Phil.* ii. 8.) *Acts* xiii. 50. xvii. 12. 1 *Cor.* vii. 35. xii. 24. Ευσχημονως, *Rom.* xiii. 13.—*Counsellor.*] Βελευτης, *Senator*, (à ϐɛλη, *consilium*,) *Luke* xxiii. 50. Not elsewhere N. T.—*Which ... waited.*] Αυτος ην προσδεχομενος.

" He was waiting for," &c. *Luke* ii. 25. 38, *Tit.* ii. 13. *Heb.* x. 34.—*Been any while dead.* (44) Ει παλαι απεθανε. *Matt.* xi. 21. 2 *Pet.* ii. 3. See on *Matt.* xxvii. 59, 60.

PRACTICAL OBSERVATIONS.

V. 1—26.

The sufferings of our meek and holy Redeemer are an inexhaustible source of instruction to the lively believer; and a subject of which, in his best hours, he cannot be weary. The consideration, that no one was ever so universally hated, or so cruelly and contemptuously treated, by men of every rank, profession, or religion, (his own disciples alone excepted,) as the only perfectly wise, holy, and excellent person, who has appeared on earth; leads the serious mind into such views of human depravity and enmity to God, as, being applied to himself, by recollecting that such are we all by nature, tends exceedingly to humiliation before God : while a view of his stupendous love, in delivering up his well-beloved Son to this ignominious and cruel death; not sparing him, but making his soul a sacrifice for the sins of such daring rebels and enemies, must cause the broken heart to overflow with admiration and grateful joy. To believe, that such an atonement was absolutely necessary, in order that a God of infinite mercy might honourably pardon sin, and save sinners, cannot fail to give the mind the deepest impression of his justice and holiness, the excellency of the law which was thus magnified, and the evil of sin which was thus expiated : and it must at the same time destroy all expectations of being saved in any other way; for, " if " righteousness come by the law, then Christ died in " vain." The contemplation of the whole human species, however otherwise distinguished, all lying under deserved condemnation, and exposed to everlasting misery; except as Jesus thus opened the gate of life and salvation to believers, must fill our minds with compassionate concern for all around us, and lead us to look upon the most prosperous sinners, with a mixture of solemn awe and tender commiseration : at the same time it directly tends to crucify us to the world; to reconcile us to its scorn and hatred; to mortify us to its friendship, interests, honours, and pleasures, to heal the diseases of our souls,

CHAP. XVI

An angel informs the women that Jesus is risen, 1
—8. He appears to Mary Magdalene, 9—11; to
two disciples going into the country, 12, 13; and to
the eleven; whom he upbraids for their unbelief, and
commissions to preach the gospel to all the world, 14
—18. He ascends into heaven, 19. The gospel is
every where preached, and confirmed by miracles, 20.

a xv. 42. Matt.
xxviii. 1. Luke
xxiii. 54. 56.
xxiv. 1. John
xix. 31. xx. 1.
b vv. 40, 47. Luke
xxiv. 10. John
xix. 25.

AND [a] when the sabbath was past, [b] Mary Magdalene, and Mary the mo- ther of James, and Salome, had bought

[c] sweet spices, that they might come and anoint him.

c xiv. 3. 8. 2 Chr.
xvi. 14. John
xix. 40.

2 And [d] very early in the morning, the first day of the week, they came unto the sepulchre at the rising of the sun.

d Matt. xxviii. 1.
Luke xxiv. 1.
John xx. 1.

3 And they said among themselves, [e] Who shall roll us away the stone from the door of the sepulchre?

e xv. 46, 47. Matt.
xxvii. 60—66.

4 And when they looked, [f] they saw that the stone was rolled away: for it was very great.

f Matt. xxviii. 2—
4. Luke xxiv. 2.
John xx. 1.

which break forth in envy and eager competition; and to render us contented in poverty and obscurity. (Note, Gal. vi. 11—14.)—But with what earnestness will the man, who firmly believes these truths, seek an interest in this great salvation! With what ardent gratitude will he re- ceive the comfortable assurance, or even the dawning hope, of forgiveness and eternal life, as purchased for him by the sufferings and death of the incarnate Son of God! And with what " godly sorrow" will he mourn over those sins, which he now looks on as having " crucified the " Lord of glory!" Hence that attention to this " one " thing needful," which subordinates all other interests and employments: hence that devoted obedience to Christ, which neither danger nor suffering can move: hence that abhorrence of sin, which renders its indwelling, and occa- sional prevalency, the great burden and deepest distress of a believer's life; and which induces him to the diligent use of every means, which tends to weaken and destroy all evil out of his heart: hence that endeared affection to all those who love and resemble Christ; that desire to re- commend him to all around; and that delight in speaking, hearing, or reading of him, and his love and suffering for sinners: and hence that love to enemies, that patience under afflictions, and that meekness under injuries and provocations, which distinguish the character of consistent Christians from that of all other men. The same views of Christ crucified, gradually reconcile the believer to the thoughts of death; in order that he may behold, love, and praise as he ought, that dear Saviour, who was wounded and pierced to save him from the wrath to come.—Let us then frequently meditate on the interesting scenes, which have so blessed an efficacy in producing these holy and benevolent affections, and in forming our character into a conformity to Jesus, and a meetness for heaven: and let us especially adopt this method, when we are tempted to impatience under trials, or peevishness under contempt and reproach; or when we grow anxious or discontented about worldly things, or are disposed to hanker after sinful indulgences. (P. O. Matt. xxvii. 11—44. Luke xxiii. 1 —31. John xix. 17—30.)

V. 27—47.

Careful meditation on the silence, meekness, and patience of the holy Jesus, amidst all his complicated sufferings, and the varied contempt and cruelty of his numerous ene- mies, must cause us to exclaim, ' Did Jesus thus suffer, and shall I, a wretched sinner, fret or repine? shall I

indulge resentment, or utter reproaches and menaces, because of troubles and injuries?' With this object before us, surely we cannot think it too much to pour out tears for those sins, for which the Son of God shed his precious blood; or to pour out our prayers for those blessings, for which " he poured out his soul unto death, " and was numbered with malefactors;" or to bear hard- ship for him who bore the wrath of God for us. Indeed all we can suffer must be light, compared with his un- known agonies: yet how often are we " weary and faint " in our minds;" instead of being thankful, that we are not in the pit of destruction, as we justly might have been! But did we more constantly contemplate these scenes, we should not only derive peace and comfort from the Saviour's atoning blood; but we should also trans- cribe his character into our lives, and learn more and more to dread and hate all those evil dispositions, which marked the conduct of his persecutors: and we should always find arguments, encouragements, and motives, to live to the glory of " him who died for us and rose again." We also ought to remember, that the hiding of God's face from us is in itself more dreadful, than all that man can do unto us; that we may learn to cry earnestly to him for help and comfort, when insulted and contemned by men. He will not forsake those who trust and call upon him: death, now deprived of his sting, will soon termi- nate the believer's sorrows, as it did the Saviour's; then the way into the holiest will be open to his soul, as it was before to his prayers, and he will be out of the reach of all enemies. His dying words and behaviour may leave a salutary impression on the minds of those who observe them; his memory may perhaps be honoured by those, who despised him when living; the grave will be a quiet and sacred repository to his body, till the joyful resurrec- tion; and thus he will be made " more than conqueror, " through him who loved him," and " washed him from ". his sins in his own blood."—Lord, visit our souls with this salvation, and make us thankful for these thine inesti- mable gifts! (P. O. Matt. xxvii. 45—56.)

NOTES.

CHAP. XVI. V. 1—4. Marg. Ref.—Note, Matt. xxviii. 1—8, v. 1.—Had bought. (1) That is, the evening before the sabbath. (Notes, Luke xxiii. 50—56, vv. 55, 56. xxiv. 1—9.) But some think, that the women bought more spices when the sabbath was ended, that is, after sun-set.—Very early. (2) ' They began their journey to

2 P 8

5 And ᵉ entering into the sepulchre, they saw ʰ a young man sitting on the right side, clothed in a long white garment; ⁱ and they were affrighted.

6 And he saith unto them, ᵏ Be not affrighted: ¹Ye seek ᵐ Jesus of Nazareth, which was crucified: ⁿ he is risen, he is not here: behold the place where they laid him.

7 But go your way, ° tell his disciples and Peter, that he goeth before you into Galilee: ᵖ there shall ye see him, as he said unto you.

8 And ᵠ they went out quickly, and fled from the sepulchre; ʳ for they trembled and were amazed: ˢ neither said

they any thing to any man: for they were afraid.

9 Now when *Jesus* was risen early, ᵗ the first *day* of the week, ᵘ he appeared first to Mary Magdalene, ˣ out of whom he had cast seven devils.

10 *And* she went and told them that had been with him, ʸ as they mourned and wept.

11 And they, when they had heard that he was alive, and had been seen of her, ᶻ believed not.

12 ¶ After that, ᵃ he appeared in another form unto two of them, as they ᵇ walked, and went into the country.

13 And ᵇ they went and told *it* unto the residue: ᶜ neither believed they them.

(marginal references, left column)

ᵉ Luke xxiv. 3. John xx. 8.
ʰ Dan. x. 5, 6. Matt. xxviii. 3. Luke xxiv. 4, 5. John xx. 11, 12.
ⁱ ver. 48, 50. Dan. viii. 17. x. 7—9. 12. Luke i. 12. 29, 30.
ᵏ Matt. xiv. 26, 27. xxviii. 4, 5. Rev. i. 17, 18.
ˡ Rev. cv. 3, 4. Prov. viii. 17.
ᵐ John xix. 19. 20. Acts ii. 22, 23. iv. 10. x. 38 —40.
ⁿ ix. 9. 10. x. 34. Matt. xii. 40. xxviii. 6, 7. Luke xxiv. 4—8. 20—27. 46. 1 Cor. xv.—7.
° ver. 50. 66.—7. Matt. xxviii. 7.
ᵖ xiv. 28. Matt. xxvi. 32. xxviii. 10. 16, 17. John xxi. 1. Acts xiii. 31. 1 Cor. xv. 6.
ᵠ Matt. xxviii. 8. Luke xxiv. 9—11. 22—24.
ʳ b. 6. Luke xxiv. 37.
ˢ 2 Kings iv. 29. Luke x. 4.

(marginal references, right column)

ᵗ John xx. 19.
ᵘ Acts xx. 7. 1 Cor. xvi. 2. Rev. i. 10.
ˣ ver. 40. 47. Luke xxiv. 10. John xx.
ᵉ xix. 72. Matt. ix. 15. xxv. 70. Luke xxiv. 17. John xvi. 6. 20 —22.
ᶻ 13. 14. ix. 19. Ex. vi. 9. Job ix. 16. xxv. xxvi. ix. 11. 23—35. Luke xxiv. 13— 32.
ᵇ Luke xxiv. 34.—Nᵈ.
ᵇ Luke xxvi. 31 John xx. 8. 25.
ᶜ Luke xvi. 31 John xx. 8. 25.

ᵉ see the sepulchre, while it was only twilight, ... and they "came to the sepulchre, ... as the sun began to rise." *Whitby.* (*Notes,* John xx. 1—10. 18.)—*They said,* &c. (3) The women had seen where the body of Jesus was laid, and the very large stone placed at the opening of the sepulchre: (xv. 46, 47:) and this was a difficulty, which they knew not how to remove; yet they proceeded, in hope of finding some to help them, to roll away the stone. Had they known of the guard of Roman soldiers, their trial would have been still greater.

V. 5—8. (*Notes,* Luke xxiv. 1—12.) St. Luke mentions two angels, whom the women saw on this occasion; but Matthew and Mark take notice only of the one who spake to them, and whom they probably saw first.—The angel appeared like a man, in the vigour of youth; and "clothed in a long white garment," the emblem of purity and innocence: but his appearance to the soldiers seems to have been far more majestick and awful; yet the women were affrighted, being aware that he was more than man. —In encouraging and directing them, he especially mentioned Peter, who might otherwise have deemed himself cast off, for his grievous offence in denying his Master. In the subsequent conduct of the women, their amazement and terror are noticed, and not their joy. The former first seized them; but the latter afterward prevailed. The clause however may be rendered, " for terror and *ecstasy* " possessed them ; " and the *ecstasy* may signify, the mingled affections of astonishment and joy, in the greatest excess. (*Marg. Ref.—Note,* Matt. xxviii. 1—8.)

Neither said, &c. (8) They did not stay to speak to any one, till they came to the apostles, and those who were with them.

They were affrighted. (5) Ε εθαμβηθησαν. 6. ix. 15. xiv. 33.—*They trembled and were amazed.* (8) Ειχε ... αυτας τρομος και εκτασις. " Terror and ecstasy held them." Τρομος. 1 Cor. ii. 3. 2 Cor. vii. 15. Eph. vi. 5. Phil. ii. 12. Εκτασις. See on *Note,* v. 42.

V. 9—11. (*Marg. Ref.—Note,* John xx. 11—17.) It is here said, that Jesus had cast out of Mary Magdalene " seven devils," or demons. (Luke viii. 2.) This no doubt refers to a real possession, from which she had mercifully been delivered, in the same manner as the man was

who had the legion : but whether this had been a visitation appointed her, for the sins of her former life, or not, is quite uncertain. (*Note,* v. 2—13.) Indeed all that is generally taken for granted, of her previous bad character and profligate conduct, rests merely on the credit of tradition, which reports that she was " the woman who " was a sinner," of whom St. Luke speaks; (*Notes,* Luke vii. 36—50 ;) for there is no scriptural proof of it, though very much has frequently been built on it. Her surname of *Magdalene,* seems to relate to the place of her nativity, or abode : for the words translated Mary Magdalene, or, " Mary the Magdalene," (Μαρια η Μαγδαλην,) may very properly be rendered " Mary of Magdala," as " Jesus the " Nazarene " is commonly rendered " Jesus of Nazareth." —The mourning of the apostles, and their not believing Mary's report, shew how little they had regarded our Lord's repeated predictions of his resurrection, and how far they were from expecting that event. This must have occurred before the return of the other women from the sepulchre ; for Jesus appeared to them also by the way.ˊ (*Note,* Matt. xxviii. 9, 10.)

Believed not. (11) Ηπιστωσαν. 16. Luke xxiv. 41. *Acts* xxviii. 24. *Rom.* iii. 3. 2 *Tim.* ii. 13. Ex α priv. et πιτις, *fides.*

V. 12, 13. (*Notes,* Luke xxiv. 13—35.) Our Lord was pleased to change his habit or appearance on this occasion, that the disciples might not for a time know who he was. —*Neither believed,* &c. (13) That is, several of the disciples did not fully credit them; though others had been before convinced of Christ's resurrection. But in so extraordinary an event, and among a number of persons, we need not wonder, that some were more deeply impressed by what they heard than others. ' Hence one of the ancients ' says well, *their* doubting is the confirmation of *our* faith : ' and the more difficulty they shewed in believing Christ's ' resurrection, the greater reason have we to believe it. ' For the testimony of them, who believed not themselves ' till after unquestionable conviction, is the more credible ' on that account.' *Whitby.* (*Notes,* Matt. xxviii. 16, 17. 1 Cor. xv. 3—11.)

In another form. (12) Εν ετερα μορφη. Phil. ii. 6, 7. See on *Note,* Matt. xvii. 2.

14 ¶ Afterward ᵈ he appeared unto the eleven as they sat ᵉ at meat, ᵉ and upbraided them with their ᶠ unbelief and hardness of heart, because they believed not them which had seen him after he was risen.

15 And he said unto them, ᵏ Go ye

ᵢ into all the world, and preach the gospel to every creature.

16 He ᶦ that believeth and ᵏ is baptized shall be saved; ᵢ but he that believeth not shall be damned.

V. 14—16. (Notes, Matt. xxviii. 18. Luke xxiv. 36—49. John xx. 19—29. xxi. 1—23.) If we understand this of our Lord's appearing to the apostles, on the evening of the day on which he arose, Thomas was not present: but they might be called the eleven, that being the whole remaining number, though one of them was absent: or some other appearance of our Lord to them might be intended. At this time, Jesus sharply rebuked them, yea, upbraided them, for their unbelief and hardness of heart. (Notes, viii. 17—21. Matt. xi. 20—24. Luke xxiv. 25—31, v. 25. Jam. i. 5—8.) Their ambition, and carnal prejudices and expectations, had closed their minds, so that they did not suitably attend to our Lord's predictions of his death, resurrection, and spiritual kingdom; and therefore they were most unreasonably backward to believe the report of those, who had seen him after his resurrection.—He, however, renewed his choice of them as his apostles, and commissioned them to " go into all the world, " to preach his gospel to every creature." (Note, John xx. 19—23.) Though they did not, at this time, understand the full import of these words; yet they certainly contained an express commission to preach his salvation and kingdom to all the nations of the earth, and to men of every description and character, as far as they were able: and they imply a command to the same effect, to all their successors in the sacred ministry, as far as it is in their power; and to all Christians to aid them according to their several abilities and situations. (Notes, Rom. x. 12—17. Col. i. 21—23. 1 Thes. ii. 13—16. 3 John 5—8.) They were authorized, and commanded, to propose the blessings of the gospel indiscriminately to all men, as far as they had access to them; inviting them to believe in Christ, and calling them to submit to his authority, as the subjects of his mediatorial kingdom. These things they were instructed to enforce in the name and stead of Christ their Lord, by assuring all " who believed and were " baptized," that they should " be saved," that is, with eternal salvation; and by declaring the final and dreadful condemnation of all unbelievers, whatever their character in other respects might be. Doubtless we must understand this solemn declaration, of that true faith which receives Christ in all his characters and offices, and for all the purposes of salvation, and which produces a proper effect upon the heart and life; and not of a mere assent, a dead faith, which cannot p ᵗt. Baptism is the outward sign of regeneration, and rᶦf is also that profession of faith in Christ, which is required of all who embrace Christianity. (Notes, Matt. xxviii. 19, 20. Acts ii. 37—40. Rom. x. 5—11. 1 Pet. iii. 21, 22.) But if men truly believe in Christ, profess openly faith in him, and partake of his sanctifying Spirit, they will doubtless be saved: even should they

have no opportunity of being baptized with water, or should they fall into any mistake, about the external mode of administering that ordinance: and if men both believe and are baptized, it does not follow from the order of the words in the text, that the baptism is invalid, because it was previous to believing; for no set of Christians rebaptize those, who have been baptized in their own way, because it afterwards appears that they were not true believers at the time, though it be hoped that they have since become so. On the other hand, unbelievers must be condemned: for they remain under the sentence of the holy law which they have broken; and they are also guilty of neglecting the salvation of the gospel, and of despising all the divine perfections displayed in it, from pride of heart, self-will, enmity to God, and love of sin and the world. (Notes, John iii. 19—21. 27—36, vv. 35, 36. 1 John v. 9—13.)— ' They who hence conclude, that infants are not capable ' of baptism, must also hence conclude, that they cannot ' be saved: faith being more expressly required to salva- ' tion than to baptism. ... In the second clause baptism is ' omitted : because it is not simply the want of baptism, ' but the contemptuous neglect of it, that makes men ' guilty of damnation ; otherwise infants might be damned ' for the mistakes, or the profaneness, of their parents.' Whitby. (Notes, John iii. 3—8.)—The words, perhaps, may more correctly be rendered, " He that shall believe " and be baptized," &c.—It is the aorist, or indefinite participle : but it cannot here mean the past; and it cannot exclusively denote the present; for it looks forward to the end of time.

Afterward. (14) Ὕστερον, postea, vel postremo. This seems to imply a later appearance of Jesus to the apostles, than that on the evening of his resurrection.—Upbraided them.] Ωνειδισε. xv. 32. Matt. v. 11. xi. 20. xxvii. 44. Luke vi. 22. Jam. i. 5. Ονειδος, probrum. Luke i. 25.— Unbelief.] Απιτιαν. vi. 6. ix. 24. Rom. iii. 3. iv. 20. Heb. iii. 12. 19.—Hardness of heart.] Σκληροκαρδιαν. See on Matt. xix. 8.—To every creature. (15) Παση τη κτισει. " To the whole creation :" that is, as St. Paul explains it, which is " under heaven." Col. i. 23. Gr.— Shall be damned. (16) Κατακριθησεται, condemned. x. 33. Matt. xii. 41, 42. xx. 18. xxvii. 3. John viii. 10, 11. Rom. ii. 1. viii. 3. 34. 1 Cor. xi. 32. Jam. v. 9. 2 Pet. ii. 6.— The words damned and damnation, are sometimes used in our translation, where the original words mean simply judge or judgment; which weakens its effect when it should be used. (Note, 1 Cor. xi. 29—34, v. 29.) In this place, however, eternal judgment is manifestly intended; and " condemnation " will then be damnation, eternal damnation. (Notes, Matt. xxv. 41—46. 2 Thes. i. 5— 10, vv. 8, 9 Rev. xx. 11—15.)

17 And "these signs shall follow them that believe: "In my name shall they cast out devils; "they shall speak with new tongues;

18 They 'shall take up serpents; "and if they drink any deadly thing it shall not hurt them; 'they shall lay hands on the sick, and they shall recover.

19 ¶ So then, 'after the Lord had spoken unto them, 'he was received up into heaven, "and sat on the right hand of God.

20 And 'they went forth, and preached every where, 'the Lord working with them, and confirming the word with signs following. Amen.

V. 17, 18. The Lord Jesus was about to be removed from his apostles, and they were sent forth into the world, to preach his gospel in the face of opposition and persecution: but to encourage them in this arduous and perilous undertaking, he assured them of extraordinary miraculous powers, and protection. And not only so, but that when any believed on him through their word, they also would be endued with power from on high; enabling them to cast out devils, to speak with tongues, and to take up serpents without being injured by them. And, at times when the art of poisoning was almost cultivated as a science, and it might be expected that their enemies would endeavour in this way to destroy them; they were also assured, that " if they drank any deadly thing it should not hurt " them:" and that they should be enabled to heal the sick, by laying on of hands, both for the comfort of their friends, and to demonstrate the truth of their doctrine. (*Marg. Ref.*—*Notes, Acts* ii. 4—11. x. 44—48. xix. 5—20. xxviii. 3—6.) It is not said, that all who ever should believe, would be enabled to work miracles; or that none, except those who had saving faith, would perform them: (*Notes, Matt.* vii. 21—23. 1 *Cor.* xiii. 1—3:) but that " these signs would follow them that believed," that is, would be manifestly displayed among them.

Deadly thing. (18) Θανασιμον, *mortiferum*, à θανατος, *mors.* Here only N. T.

V. 19, 20. We shall have a future opportunity of considering Christ's ascension and exaltation, and the ministry of the apostles. (*Notes, Luke* xxiv. 50—53. *Acts* i. 1—12.) Wherever they went, the Lord, their risen, ascended, and exalted Saviour, " wrought with them;" both by the power of his Spirit upon the hearts of the people, and by " confirming their words with signs follow-" ing." The addition of the word " Amen," may denote the Evangelist's earnest desire, that the same powerful and gracious presence of Christ, and the same success, might still attend the preaching of the gospel in every place. (*Note, Matt.* xxviii. 19, 20.)

Working with them. (20) Συνεργατος. *Rom.* viii. 28. 1 *Cor.* xvi. 16. 2 *Cor.* vi. 1. *Jam.* ii. 22.—*Confirming.*] Βεβαιωντος. *Rom.* xv. 8. 1 *Cor.* i. 6. 8. 2 *Cor.* i. 21. *Heb.* ii. 3. xiii. 9. (*Notes, John* xv. 26, 27. *Heb.* ii. 1—4, *vv.* 3, 4.)

PRACTICAL OBSERVATIONS.

V. 1—11.

When we deny ourselves, and voluntarily incur trouble and expense, from love to Christ and zeal for his glory, we shall be accepted, even though our endeavours should prove unsuccessful: and when we proceed in the path of duty, as far as we can; those difficulties, which we were ready to look upon as insurmountable, will often be removed by means, of which we had no expectation.—Those whose hearts are right before God, may yet be greatly mistaken in their judgment and purposes; and they will be often disquieted, when they have abundant reason to rejoice. Indeed, those who believe, love, and seek " Jesus, " who was crucified and is risen," should not in any possible circumstances give way to disconsolate sorrow, or gloomy fears. Evil men and apostate angels cannot hurt them : and holy angels are their faithful friends, and delight to minister to their comfort, because they are the objects of the Lord's peculiar love and favour. Even after they have been overcome by temptation, and have acted inconsistently, yea very basely; yet when they are contrite and deeply penitent, the gracious Saviour will mingle encouragement with their humiliation, lest they " should " be swallowed up of over-much sorrow;" and a trembling Peter shall be especially mentioned, that he may not be tempted to despondency. But alas! how slowly do we admit the consolations, which the word of God holds forth to us! and how difficult is it to believe, that the Lord will specially favour those, over whom Satan has heretofore peculiarly domineered! Yet he sometimes employs such trophies of his victory over the powers of darkness, to bear tidings of his complete salvation and abundant grace to those who mourn and weep; that the very example of the messenger may evince the truth of the message; and prove that Jesus lives, and " is able to save to the uttermost all " them that come to God through him." (*P. O. Matt.* xxviii. 1—10.—*Notes, 2 Cor.* v. 18—21. 1 *Tim.* i. 12—16.)

V. 12—20.

In whatever way the Lord is pleased to confirm his truth, our faith is apt to be weak and wavering : and therefore, while he comforts his people, by " manifesting himself to " them as he doth not to the world," he often sees it needful to rebuke and correct them for " their hardness of " heart," in distrusting his faithful promises, as well as in not obeying his holy precepts. Yet he will " heal the " backslidings " of his people, and " love them freely," and again employ them in his service.—The commission, given by Christ to his ministers, extends to " every creature," throughout the world; so that wherever a human being is found, we are expressly commanded to propose to him the gospel of Christ, whatever reception he may give it, Our instructions likewise, as preachers of the gospel, contain not only truths, promises, encouragements, and precepts, but also most awful warnings and sanctions : so that we as much preach the gospel, when we declare in the

name of God, that " he who believeth not shall be " damned," as when we proclaim, that " whosoever be- " lieveth " in Jesus " shall be saved." However men may now despise, or dispute against, such solemn denuncia- tions, or deride and revile those who insist on them; they will doubtless be fulfilled in their most tremendous mean- ing, upon all who hear and reject the gospel. We indeed do not now profess to work miracles in confirmation of our instructions : but the scriptures are irrefragably proved to be of divine original ; and this will render all those inexcusa- ble who despise or neglect them. The effects also pro- duced, wherever the gospel is faithfully preached and truly believed, in changing the tempers, characters, and con- versation of mankind, form a constant proof, that the gospel is " the power of God unto salvation :" (*Notes,*

Rom. i. 13—16, *v.* 16. *P. O.* 16—21. 1 *Cor.* i. 20—25 :) and indeed they, who truly believe in Christ, will be de- fended against all the assaults of the serpent and his seed, and rendered more than conquerors over them ; and be preserved from the fatal effects of those poisonous and dreadful heresies, which he is continually propagating in the world. (*P. O. Matt.* xxviii. 11—20. *Luke* xxiv. 36—53.) May then our ascended and glorified Redeemer send forth very many faithful ministers, every where to preach his gospel ; and may he work with them and confirm his word " by signs following ;" even " by opening men's eyes, and " by turning them from darkness to light, and from the " power of Satan unto God, that they may receive for- " giveness of sins, and an inheritance among all that are " sanctified, by faith in him." Amen.

THE GOSPEL

St. L U K E.

THIS evangelist was the companion of the apostle Paul, in all his labours and sufferings during many years, probably till he suffered martyrdom: (xxviii. 7—10. *Col.* iv. 14. 2 *Tim.* iv. 11. *Philem.* 24.—*Notes, Acts* xvi. 6—12, *v.* 10.˙ xx. 1—6. xxvii. 1, 2:) and, as he wrote " the Acts of the Apostles" also, which conclude with a brief account of St. Paul's imprisonment at Rome; we may be sure, that he had the apostle's sanction to what he did; and we may infer with great probability, that this gospel was written some time before that event.—It certainly was extant at an early period, and was from the first received by the church as of divine authority. (*Introduction to the New Testament.*)— It is not certainly known, of what country St. Luke originally was, or when he was converted to Christianity. He never once mentions himself, except as he uses the first person plural, when writing several parts of St. Paul's history: and nothing is recorded of him, till we find him among the companions of that apostle: for Lucius of Cyrene seems to have been another person. (*Acts* xiii. 1.) Origen and Epiphanius say, that he was one of the seventy disciples: and in that case he must have been an eye-witness of many of the transactions which he records; yet he seems to say the contrary. (*Note,* i. 1—4.) The more general tradition however is, that he was a Syrian, and that he first became acquainted with Christianity at Antioch.—He is called by the apostle Paul, " the beloved physician;" and some report, that he had practised in this profession at Rome, having been taken thither for that purpose. It is known, that the physicians, among the Romans, were generally the servants, or slaves, of the great men: and it is thought, that, having been rewarded with his liberty, he received a name from his patron, as was often the case, and then, returning to Antioch in Syria, he became acquainted with St. Paul, embraced Christianity, was appointed to the ministry, and from that time attended in his travels. But Paul never calls him " his son," as he does Timothy and Titus: it is therefore probable that he was previously converted.—It is also uncertain, whether he was a Jew by birth, a proselyte, or a gentile convert. The language of St. Paul seems to favour the latter opinion: for having mentioned several persons, who saluted the Colossians, he adds, " Who are of the circumcision. These only ' are my fellow-workers unto the kingdom of God, which have been a comfort to me." Yet he directly speaks in high terms of Epaphras, and calls " Luke, the beloved physician:" and as he could not mean to say, that these persons had not been a comfort to him, it seems to follow, that they were not of the circumcision. (*Note,* Col. iv. 9— 4.) It is indeed a general opinion, that none of the sacred books of the New Testament were written by gentile converts, however eminent many of them were as preachers of the gospel. But the scripture lays down no rule of that kind: it is probable that the book of Job was written by Elihu, who was not of the nation of Israel; (*Preface to Job;*) and certainly Nebuchadnezzar wrote the fourth chapter of Daniel.—The sanction of the apostle, and the early and unanimous reception of St. Luke's writings, as divinely inspired, and a part of the canon of Scripture, are alone sufficient to satisfy any reasonable person: and it is remarkable, that in recording our Lord's words, when he foretold the destruction of Jerusalem, he adds some particulars, not expressly mentioned in the other gospels, which, taken with the extraordinary accomplishment of them during above seventeen hundred years, form an internal demonstration, that he wrote " as he was moved by the Holy Ghost." (*Note,* xxi. 20—24.)—This gospel contains many parables, discourses, miracles, and events, which had been omitted by the preceding evangelists; and several, recorded by them, are here passed over. The history begins with the circumstances preceding and attending the birth of John Baptist, and that of Jesus himself; and it closes with a fuller account of what passed between our Lord's resurrection and ascension, than Matthew or Mark had given.—St. Luke is supposed to have been a man of learning, previous to being endued with spiritual gifts. His style is more pure and classical than that of the other evangelists; though free from the Hebrew or Syriack idiom, which some make an objection to his being a Gentile convert: yet it fully proves, that he had studied the Septuagint, and was conversant with Hellenists. The simplicity of the manner, however, in which he sets before the mind, as in a picture, the wonderful events which he records; and the talent which he manifests of fixing the attention and exciting the affections of his readers, by the most artless narrative; are so exquisite, that many have thought him, as a writer, capable of standing the competition with the most celebrated historians of Greece itself. (*Note,* vii. 11—17.)

CHAP. I.

The preface, and dedication to Theophilus, 1—4. An account of Zacharias and Elisabeth, 5—7. The angel Gabriel appears to Zacharias in the temple, and promises him a son in his old age, who would be singularly eminent and useful, 8—17. He is chastised for unbelief, by being struck dumb, 18—23. Elisabeth conceives, and hides herself, 24, 25. The angel appears to the virgin Mary; and assures her that she should become the mother of the Messiah, the King of Israel, by the power of the Holy Spirit, 26—33. Her humble faith and acquiescence, 34—38. She visits Elisabeth, and is saluted by her : she prophesies, and praises God, 39—56. The birth, circumcision, and naming of John the Baptist, 57—63. Zacharias, restored to the use of speech, prophetically praises God, 64—79. The manner in which John spent his youth, 80.

FORASMUCH as many have taken in hand to set forth in order a declaration of ᵃ those things which are most ᵃ John xx. 31. Acts i. 1—3. 1 Tim. iii. 16. 2 Pet. L 16—19. surely believed among us,

2 Even as they delivered them unto us, which from the beginning were ᵇ eye-witnesses, ᶜ and ministers of the word ; ᵇ xxiv. 48. John xv. 27. Acts i. 3. 8. 21, 22. iv. 20. x. 39—41. Heb. ii. 3. 1 John i. 1

3 It ᵈ seemed good to me also, having had perfect understanding of all things from the very first, to write unto thee ᵉ in order, ᶠ most excellent Theophilus, ᵈ Acts xxvi. 16. Rom. xv Eph. iii. 7, 8. Col. i. 23—29. ᵉ Acts xv. 19. 25. 2K. 1 Cor. vii. 40. xvi. 12. ᶠ 1. Ps. xl. 5. 1. 21. Ep. xli. 4. Acts xl. 4

4 That thou ᵍ mightest know the certainty of those things, wherein thou hast been instructed. ᵍ Acts i. 1. xxiii xxvi. 25. Gr. ᵍ 1 John xx. 31. 2 Pet. L 15, 16.

NOTES.

CHAP. I. V. 1—4. Matthew and Mark are supposed to have written before Luke ; but they could not be called " many :" and the former of them at least wrote from his personal knowledge, as well as under the guidance of the Holy Spirit ; while the persons here mentioned had written from *report*. We must therefore understand the evangelist of some compilations, which have been lost very long since ; for publishing and circulating authentic narratives, would soon discredit spurious ones : yet the persons who made them seem to have meant honestly, and those heretical gospels, which were propagated during the primitive times were not intended.—We hence learn, however, that several persons had undertaken to publish orderly narratives of those things, which were " most " surely believed" by Christians, or as ʹ most fully proved ʹ to them,' or ʹ most certainly performed among them ;' for either the evidence by which they were attested, or the conviction which arose from the evidence of their having been accomplished, may be intended. These writers had collected their information from the testimony of those, who had " from the first been eye-witnesses" of the miracles, life, death, resurrection, and ascension of Jesus, and who were ministers of the gospel to declare them unto others : the apostles seem especially intended. Most expositors suppose the second verse to point out the manner, in which the evangelist had derived his information : yet it is directly connected with the first verse, and precedes the writer's first mention of himself. The histories referred to, however, had not been compiled with sufficient accuracy ; and the evangelist was led to consider it as a service allotted him, to form a more exact and regular work of this kind : as he had accurately investigated the subject, and acquired a complete acquaintance with it, from the beginning of the gospel, in the conception and birth of John the Baptist ; evidently by information and testimony, and not as an eye-witness.—This history he addressed to Theophilus, for his more full instruction in Christianity. Theophilus signifies, *A lover of God*: he appears to have been a person of rank and authority; for the title, " Most " excellent," is the same in the original, which is else-

where addressed to the Roman governors. (*Marg. Ref. f.— Note, Acts* xxvi. 24—29, *v.* 25.) The title was given to Theophilus with greater propriety : but as St. Paul uses it to Festus, this fully proves, that Christianity does not forbid us to give this kind of customary honour to persons in authority, whatever their character or religion may be.— The word rendered " instructed," relates to the initiatory instruction in the first principles of Christianity, in which the converts were afterwards to be more fully taught and established.—ʹ St. Luke thought not what was delivered by ʹ word of mouth only, even by the eye-witnesses and mini- ʹ sters of the word, sufficient to give Theophilus a knowledge ʹ of the certainty of these things, without writing the gospel. ʹ ... He held it not unlawful, or unfit, for a layman, or any ʹ Christian, to read the scriptures ; nor such a one insuffi- ʹ cient, by thus reading, to understand the things in which ʹ he had been instructed.' *Whitby.*—ʹ The very circum- ʹ stance of the number of such narratives, at so early a ʹ period, is itself an evidence, that there was something in ʹ the first publication of the Christian doctrine, which ... ʹ excited the curiosity, and awakened the attention, of ʹ persons of all ranks and denominations; insomuch, that ʹ every narrative, which pretended to furnish men with ʹ additional information, concerning so extraordinary a ʹ personage, as Jesus, seems to have been read with ʹ avidity.' *Campbell.*

Forasmuch. (1) Επιδηπερ, *quoniam.* Here only N. T : επιδη, *often.—Have taken in hand.*] Επιχειρησαν. *Acts* ix. 29. xix. 13. Ex επι, et χειρ, *manus.—To set forth.*] Ανατάξασθαι. Here only N. T. Ex ανα, et τασσομαι, *to place in due order.—A declaration.*] Διηγησιν. Not elsewhere N. T.—*Which are most surely believed.*] Πεπληροφορημενων. *Rom.* iv. 21. xiv. 5. 2 Tim. iv. 5. 17.—*Eyewitnesses.* (2) Αυτοπται. Here only N. T. Ex αυτος, et οπτομαι, *video.—Having had perfect understanding.* (3) Παρηκολωθηκοτι. *Mark* xvi. 17. 1 Tim. iv. 6. 2 Tim. iii. 10. —ʹ Cunctis ab initio exacta diligentia pervestigatis.' Eras- ʹ mus. Accurata omnium ab initio ratione habita.' Heinsius. One that followed another step by step, to note and mark his course.—*From the very first.*] Ανωθεν. Sometimes rendered " from above." (*John* iii. 31. *Jam.* i. 17. iii. 15. 17.) It is however often used in another sense. (*John*

LAND of MORIAH
or
ENVIRONS of JERUSALEM

London Published for the Proprietors of Bagster's Works by Wertheim, Macintosh & Hunt.
24 Paternoster Row and 23 Holles Street, Cavendish Square.

5 THERE was in the days of Herod, the king of Judea, a certain priest named Zacharias, of the course of Abia: and his wife was of the daughters of Aaron, and her name was Elisabeth.

6 And they were both righteous before God, walking in all the commandments and ordinances of the Lord blameless.

7 And they had no child, because that Elisabeth was barren; and they both were now well stricken in years.

8 And it came to pass, that while he executed the priest's office before God in the order of his course,

9 According to the custom of the priest's office, his lot was to burn incense when he went into the temple of the Lord.

10 And the whole multitude of the people were praying without, at the time of incense.

11 And there appeared unto him an angel of the Lord standing on the right side of the altar of incense.

12 And when Zacharias saw him, he was troubled, and fear fell upon him.

13 But the angel said unto him, Fear not, Zacharias: for thy prayer is heard; and thy wife Elisabeth shall

---

iii. 3. 7. *Acts* xxvi. 5. *Gal.* iv. 9.) No doubt Luke wrote under the superintending inspiration of the Holy Spirit: yet this word cannot properly be adduced as a proof of it, nor does it at all imply, that he had his information " from " above," without the intervention of the ordinary methods of information.—*In order.*] Καθεξης, *ordine, distincte, cohærenter, Acts* iii. 24. xi. 4. xviii. 23.—*Most excellent.*] Κρατιϛε. *Acts* xxiii. 26. xxiv. 3. xxvi. 25.—*Hast been instructed.* (4) Κατηχηθης. (Ex καλα, et ηχεω, sono.) *Acts* xviii. 25. xxi. 24. 1 *Cor.* xiv. 19. Hence the words *catechism* and *catechize.*

V. 5—7. Zacharias ' was not, as some have imagined, ' high priest. ... Zacharias was chosen by lot to burn in- ' cense: the high priest did it by the right of succession, ' and burned it in the Holy of holies, into which Zacharias ' entered not. ... Zacharias was priest of the course of ' Abia; whereas the high priest was of no course at all. ... ' These several courses began on the sabbath-day, and ' continued to serve till the next sabbath.' *Whitby.* (*Notes,* 2 *Kings* xi. 5—9. 1 *Chr.* xxiii. 2—6. xxiv. 10. *Ezra* ii. 36—39.)—St. Luke begins his history with the parentage and birth of John. His father Zacharias was a priest of the order of Abia, or Abijah; (*Marg. Ref.* i;) and his wife Elisabeth also was descended from Aaron. They were exemplary persons, being " righteous before " God," and not merely in the sight of men; (*Marg. Ref.* k—m;) being accepted as true believers, and approving themselves to him by a conscientious conduct in his sight: so that they habitually walked in an upright and regular course of obedience to all the moral commandments of the law, and in an attendance on all the ordinances of his instituted worship; and thus acted in a most blameless and irreproachable manner, as to the general tenour of their conduct. Doubtless they, as sinners, were justified and saved in the same way as others: but they were eminent examples of piety and integrity, and cordially concurred together in every part of the service of God.—They had no children: and as Elisabeth had been barren in her younger years, it was not to be expected, that she should bear children in her old age. This was thought a very heavy affliction by the Jews: yet Zacharias gave no coun-

tenance to the practice of polygamy or divorce, by taking another wife. (*Notes, Gen.* xvi. 1—6.) The latter of these, especially, was common at that time: yet the pious Jews generally disapproved it. (*Notes, Matt.* v. 31, 32. xix. 3—12.)

Of the course, &c.] Εξ εφημεριας. Ex επι, et ημερα, dies. Here and 8, only N. T.—*Ordinances.* (6) Δικαιωμασι. *Rom.* i. 32. ii. 26. v. 16. 18. viii. 4. *Heb.* ix. 1. 10. *Rev.* xv. 4. xix. 8. The word is used in different senses: but the institutions of the ritual law of Moses, seem here exclusively meant.

V. 8—10. ' The law required, that the priest should ' burn incense morning and evening, upon the altar of in- ' cense, placed before the veil of the most holy place. ' (*Ex.* xxx. 6—8.) But because they who thus served ' in every course were many, it was necessary that they ' should by lot choose the man, who was to perform that ' service for that week; and so the Jews say they did.' *Whitby.*—According to the law and custom, Zacharias was employed to burn incense on the golden altar within the sanctuary; and at the same time a great number of people were collected without, in the courts of the temple, silently offering up their prayers and supplications. This was an apt and constant type of Christ's intercession in heaven; through which the prayers of believers, in every part of the outer court of the church on earth, ascend with acceptance before God. (*Marg. Ref.* r, s —*Notes, Ex.* xxx. 1—10. *Rev.* viii. 1—6.)

To burn incense. (9) Θυμιασαι. Here only N. T.—*The temple.*] Τον ναον. This word generally means the sanctuary: but ιερον includes the courts and out-buildings.—*Of incense.* (10) Τε θυμιαματος. 11. *Rev.* v. 8. viii. 3, 4. xviii. 13.—*Ex.* xxx. 1. 7. *Sept.*

V. 11—17. While Zacharias was officiating within the sanctuary, he was surprised by the appearance of an angel, probably in a splendid form, at the right hand of the altar of incense. This vision greatly alarmed him, though he was a man of approved piety: but the angel encouraged him not to be afraid, for he was come to assure him, that his prayers were heard and answered.—Zacharias and Elisabeth had doubtless often prayed for children; but it

 h 60—63. ib. 21. Gen. xvii. 19. 1s. viii. 3. Hos. i. 4. 6. 9, 10. Matt. xi. 21. c 58. Gen. xxi. 6, 7. Prov. xv, 20. xxiii. 15, 16, 24. 25. d vii. 28. Gen. xii. 2. xlviii. 19. Josh. iii. 7. iv. 14. 1 Chr. xvii. 8. xxix. 12. Matt. xi. 9—12. John v. 35. e vii. 33. Num. vi. 2—4. Judg. xiii. 4—6. Matt. xi. 18. f Zech. ix. 15. g Ps. xvii. 9. Jer. 1. 5. Gal. i. 15. h 76. Is. xl. 3—5. xlix. 6. Dan. xii. 3. Mal. iii. 1. iv. 5. Matt. i. 1—6. i 16. John i. 18. 23—30. iii. 28. k Mal. iv. 5. Matt. xi. 14. xvii. 11, 12. Mark ix. 11—13. John i. 21—24. Rev. xx. 4. xvi. 20. 2 Kings i. 4—6. 16. Elijah: Matt. iii. 4. 7—12. xiv. 4. Mal. iv. 6.	**bear thee a son, and** ᵇ**thou shalt call his name John.** 14 And ᶜthou shalt have joy and gladness; and many shall rejoice at his birth. 15 For he shall be ᵈgreat in the sight of the Lord, ᵉand shall drink neither wine nor strong drink; and he shall be ᶠfilled with the Holy Ghost, ᵍeven from his mother's womb. 16 And ʰmany of the children of Israel shall he turn to the Lord their God. 17 And he shall go ⁱbefore him ᵏin the spirit and ˡpower of Elias, to ᵐturn the hearts of the fathers to the children, ⁿand the disobedient ᵒto the

wisdom of the just; ᵒto make ready a people prepared for the Lord. 18 And Zacharias said unto the angel, ᵖWhereby shall I know this? ᵠfor I am an old man, and my wife well stricken in years. 19 And the angel answering said unto him, ʳI am Gabriel, that stand in the presence of God; and am sent to speak unto thee, ˢand to shew thee these glad tidings. 20 And, behold, ᵗthou shalt be dumb, and not able to speak, until the day that these things shall be performed, ᵘbecause thou believest not my words, ˣwhich shall be fulfilled in their season.	o 1 Sam. vii. 5. 1 Chr. xxix. 18. 2 Chr. xxix. 36. Ps. x. 17. lxxviii. 8. Am. iv. 12. Acts x. 33. Rom. ix. 23. 1 Tim. ii. 9. Col. i. 12. 2 Tim. ii. 21. 2 Pet. iii. 11— 14. 1 John ii. 28. p 34. Gen. xv. 8. xvii. 17. xviii. 12. Judg. vi. 36 —40. Is. xxxviii. 22. q 7. Num. xi. 21 —23. 2 Kings vii. 2. Rom. iv. 19—21. r Dan. viii. 16. ix. 21—23. Matt. xviii. 10. Heb. i. 14. s 10. t 22. 62. 63. Ex. iv. 11. Ez. iii. 26. xxiv. 27. u 45. Gen. xviii. 10—15. Num. xx. 12. 2 Kings vii. 2. 19. 20. Is. vii. 9. Matt. xxi. 32. Rev. iii. 19. x Rom. iii. 3. 2 Tim. ii. 13. Tit. i. 2. Heb. vi. 18.

must be supposed, that they had for some time given up the hope of having any, and had submitted to the will of God, concluding that these prayers would not be answered. The angel's words, however, may refer to the prayers which Zacharias had then been offering up, in behalf of himself and his people, and for the coming of the promised Redeemer : or, in general, his prayers were accepted, and would all in due season be answered. As a proof of this, his wife Elisabeth, even in her old age, would bear him a son, whose name he should call John, *the grace,* (or *favour*) *of the LORD:* for he would be an honour and blessing to his father, a gracious answer to his prayers, and a pledge of the divine favour: so that he would have great joy and gladness in him; and many would rejoice at his birth, as anticipating the great usefulness of his future life. For, though he would be a plain man, and appear mean in his person and attire; yet he would be " great in the " sight of the Lord," and according to his estimation of characters; being eminent for wisdom and piety, and a blessed instrument in glorifying him and doing good to men. As a token of his entire devotedness to God, he would be a perpetual Nazarite from his birth; *(Marg. Ref.* e.—*Notes, Num.* vi. 1—21. *Judg.* xiii. 2—5, *vv.* 4, 5 ;) and be likewise " filled with the Holy Ghost from his mother's " womb." Though " conceived in sin," like other men, yet a saving change would be wrought in his soul by the regenerating Spirit of God, even at or before his birth ; which would appear in his eminent wisdom and piety from his earliest youth. *(Marg. Ref.* f, g.) In due time he would be brought forth, as a zealous preacher and a successful reformer, in converting many of the descendants of Israel, from their hypocrisy, impiety, or infidelity, to the true worship and service of the LORD their God : and he would go " before Him, in the spirit and power of " Elijah," with intrepidity, zeal, sanctity, and a mind mortified to all earthly interests and pleasures, like that illustrious prophet. Thus he would turn the " hearts of " the fathers *with* the children," or persons of every age and situation in society, to lay aside their party-disputes or domestick contests, and to unite in repenting of their sins, and attending on the great duties of true religion. The

disobedient and rebellious would thus be brought back to the wisdom of their righteous progenitors ; or rather induced to attend to the wisdom of that Just One, who was coming among them : that they might become a people prepared, by humiliation and genuine repentance, to welcome in true faith the salvation, and become the subjects, of the LORD, even of Jesus Christ. *(Note, Mal.* iv. 4—6.) —John went before Christ, as his forerunner, to prepare the people for him ; yet THE LORD THEIR GOD is the antecedent to the pronoun " Him,"—" Shall he turn to the " Lord their God ; and he shall go before him, &c." so that the angel's address was evidently calculated to induce the belief, that Christ was the Lord God of Israel ; and must have been improper, and suited to mislead us, on any other supposition. *(Marg. Ref.* h—o.—*Notes,* 76—79. iii. 4 —6. *Is.* xl. 3—5. *Mal.* iii. 1—4. *John* i. 30—34. iii. 27 —36, *vv.* 28, 29.)—Dr. Campbell renders the clause, " he " shall go before *them ;*" without the least intimation in the notes of any different reading, or even conjectural alteration.—ᶜ *John,* in Hebrew *Johanan,* which occurs ' nearly thirty times in the Old Testament, is derived from ' *JEHOVAH* and *Chen,* and properly signifies *the grace and* ' *favour of the* LORD.' Doddridge.
He was troubled. (12) Εταραχθη. See on *Matt.* xiv. 26. —*Gladness.* (14) Αγαλλιασις. 44. *Acts* ii. 46. *Heb.* i. 9. *Jude* 24. An exceedingly great joy, with exultation, and the outward expressions of it. *Ps.* li. 8. *Sept.* Ab αγαλ-λιαω, or αγαλλιαομαι, *præ gaudio exulto.* 47.
V. 18—20. *(Notes,* 34—38. *Gen.* xvii. 17, 18. xviii. 9 —12.) When the angel had delivered this gracious message, Zacharias, reflecting upon the great improbability of having a son by his wife in their old age, and not duly considering the power of God, " staggered at the promise " through unbelief." *(Marg. Ref.* p, q.—*Note, Rom.* iv. 18—22.) He therefore required some further sign, by which he might know that this would be performed : whereas the very appearance of the angel, whose presence had so alarmed him, was a sufficient sign that the promise sent by him would be accomplished. The angel therefore informed him, that he was Gabriel, who stood before God, and ministered unto him, and of whom he must have read

21 And the people ¹ waited for Zacharias, and marvelled that he tarried so long in the temple.

22 And when he came out he could not speak unto them: and they perceived that he had seen a vision in the temple; for ¹ he beckoned unto them, and remained speechless.

23 And it came to pass, that as soon as ¹ the days of his ministration were accomplished, he departed to his own house.

24 And after those days his wife Elisabeth conceived, and hid herself five months, saying,

25 Thus ¹ hath the Lord dealt with me, in the days wherein he looked on me, ¹ to take away my reproach among men.

26 ¶ And in ¹ the sixth month ¹ the angel Gabriel was sent from God unto ¹ a city of Galilee, named Nazareth,

27 To ¹ a virgin espoused to a man, whose name was Joseph, of the house of David; and the virgin's name was Mary.

28 And the angel came in unto her, and said, ¹ Hail, *thou that art* ¹ highly favoured, ¹ the Lord *is* with thee: ¹ blessed *art* thou among women.

29 And when she saw *him*, ¹ she was troubled at his saying, ¹ and cast in her mind ¹ what manner of salutation this should be.

30 And the angel said unto her, ¹ Fear not, Mary: for thou hast found favour with God.

31 And, behold, ¹ thou shalt conceive in thy womb, and bring forth a son, ¹ and shalt call his name JESUS.

32 He ¹ shall be great, and shall be called ¹ The Son of the Highest: and the Lord God shall ¹ give unto him the throne of his father David:

33 And ¹ he shall reign over ¹ the

---

in the prophecy of Daniel; (*Dan.* viii. 16. ix. 21;) and that he was sent from heaven on purpose to declare to him these glad tidings. But, as he had doubted the truth of his words, and had demanded a sign in confirmation of them, notwithstanding so many eminent persons had been born of parents, who had long been childless, as Isaac, Jacob, Joseph, Samson, and Samuel; a sign would be given him, which would at the same time be a rebuke of his unbelief: for he would thenceforth be no more able to speak, till the promise had received its accomplishment; (*Note*, 21—25;) yet that would certainly take place in its appointed season. (*Marg. Ref.* r—x.)

To shew thee these glad tidings. (19) Ευαγγελισασθαι σοι *τaùta.—Dumb.* (20) Σιωπων. xviii. 39. xix. 40.

V. 21—25. The interview between the angel and Zacharias, as above related, would not take up much time: but the mind of Zacharias must have been occupied and agitated by a variety of reflections and emotions; so that he continued in the temple, some time after the angel had left him, perhaps employed in devotion. In the mean while the people waited for him, probably to dismiss them with the customary blessing, (*Notes*, Num. vi. 23—26,) being surprised on what account he continued in the temple beyond the usual time. But when he came out he was unable to speak to them; and they perceived by his signs " that he had seen a vision." Thus he remained speechless, or deaf and dumb, for this was doubtless the case with him. (61—63.) He was, however, able to burn incense according to his office; and he continued at the temple, till the time of his appointed ministration was expired, when he returned to his own house: and soon after Elisabeth finding herself pregnant, " hid herself five months." She kept at home and much alone, either that she might be preserved from contracting any ceremonial defilement,

as the child to be born to be was to be a perpetual Nazarite; or that she might not seem to be lifted up with the favour conferred on her; or rather, that she might have the more leisure for meditation, prayer, and thanksgiving, on this extraordinary occasion. For she observed, as in admiration, that " thus," in so unexpected a way of grace and favour, " the Lord had dealt with her," at the time, when he was pleased to take away the reproach of barrenness, under which she had hitherto lain among her neighbours and acquaintance; (*Notes*, Judg. xi. 34—40. *Is.* iv. 1;) in that he had promised to make her, in a marvellous way, the mother of a son, of whom so great things had been spoken.—Doubtless, Zacharias had by writing made known to her the purport of the angel's message. The time of her close retirement continued five months, for in the sixth month Mary went to visit her: yet it is probable, she lived much at home and in retirement during the whole of her pregnancy.

That he tarried so long. (21) Εν τω χρονιζειν αυτον. xii. 45. Matt. xxiv. 48. xxv. 5. *Heb.* x. 37.—*A vision.* (22) Οπτασιαν, (ab οπτομαι *video* ;) xxiv. 23. *Acts* xxvi. 19. 2 *Cor.* xii. 1.—*He beckoned.*] Ην διανευων. Here only *N. T.*—*Speechless.*] Κωφος. See on *Matt.* xii. 22.—*Ministration.* (23) Της λειτουργιας. 2 *Cor.* ix. 12. *Phil.* ii. 17. 30. *Heb.* viii. 6. ix. 21.—*Num.* iv. 24. viii. 22. A λειτουργεω. Hence Liturgy.

V. 26—33. The Evangelist next proceeds to relate the miraculous conception of Jesus. In the sixth month of Elisabeth's pregnancy, the angel Gabriel was sent from God to Nazareth, to the Virgin Mary, whose espousals to Joseph have already been considered. (*Notes*, Matt. i. 18 —25.)—It is remarkable that the name " Elisabeth" was the same with *Elisheba*, the wife of Aaron; and that of " Mary," the same with that of *Miriam* his sister. (*Ex.* vi. 23. xv. 20, 21.)—When the angel came to Mary in her

house of Jacob for ever; and of his kingdom there shall be no end.

34 Then said Mary unto the angel, ^f How shall this be, seeing I know not a man?

35 And the angel answered and said ^z unto her, ' The Holy Ghost shall come upon thee, and the power of the Highest ^a shall overshadow thee; therefore also ^a that holy thing, which shall be born

of thee, shall be called ^b The Son of God.

36 And behold, ^c thy cousin Elisabeth, she hath also conceived a son in her old age : and this is the sixth month with her who was called barren.

37 For ^d with God nothing shall be impossible.

38 And Mary said, ^e Behold the handmaid of the Lord ; be it unto me ac-

(marginal references, left column)
f Judg. xiii. 8.—
12. Acts ix. 6.

z 27. 31. Matt. i.
20.
a Job xiv. 4. xv.
16. xxv. 4. Ps.
li. 6. Eph. ii. 3.
Heb. iv. 15. vii.
26—28.

(marginal references, right column)
b 22. Ps. ii. 7.
Matt. xiv. 33.
xxvi. 63. 64.
xxvii. 54. Mark
i. 1. John i. 34.
49. xx. 31. Acts
viii. 37. Rom. i.
4. Gal. ii. 20.
c 24—26.
d xviii. 27. Gen.
xviii. 14. Num.
xi. 23. Job xiv.
5. Jer. xxvii. 17.
27. Zech. viii.
6. Matt. xix. 26.
Mark x. 27.
Phil. iii. 21.
e 2 Sam. vii. 25—
29. Rom. iv. 20,
21.

---

retirement, (probably in a glorious form,) he addressed her by saying, " Hail, thou that art highly favoured of the " Lord, &c." That is, ' Rejoice on account of the honour intended thee, and on which I now congratulate thee ; for thou art highly favoured of God, not only as an accepted believer, but as the mother of the long expected Messiah : " the Lord is with thee," therefore, in a special manner, and in this respect, thou art happy above other women, and distinguished from them all.' (*Marg.* and *Ref.*) The Papists have unaccountably turned this salutation of the angel into an act of adoration ; and the word for " highly " favoured," having been rendered in the Vulgate, " full of " grace," they have thus addressed the Virgin Mary with idolatrous worship, and very great numbers do so to this day : nay, this act of devotion, such as it is, often precludes the use of the Lord's prayer, or of any other prayer to God, or at least is far more frequently repeated than any other ! But there is no expression in this address, but what might properly be used by a superior to an inferior, in Mary's situation ; and doubtless it was thus intended : for a greater absurdity can scarcely be devised, than to suppose that the angel Gabriel came down from heaven, to worship a poor sinful mortal here on earth, as Mary well knew herself to be !—This extraordinary appearance and salutation, however, disquieted her mind : she was not only alarmed at the angel's presence ; but was greatly perplexed about the meaning and consequences of so uncommon an address. But the angel calmed her fears, and assured her, that she had " found favour with God," and would shortly conceive and bear a Son, whom she was directed to call JESUS. He would be great, above all whoever appeared on earth, being called, and acknowledged to be, " the Son of the Highest ;" as being one in nature and perfection with the " Lord God " who would in due time exalt him, in his mediatorial character, to the throne of David, his father as to his human nature ; and on that throne he would reign " over the house of Jacob," and over the true Israel of God, not only for a few years, as David and his successors had done, but for ever ; so that " of his kingdom there should be no end." (*Marg. Ref.* t—x.—*Notes*, 2 Sam. vii. 12—16. *Ps.* ii. 4—9. lxxxix. 19—37. *Is.* ix. 6, 7. *Dan.* ii. 34, 35. 44, 45. vii. 13, 14. 1 *Cor.* xv. 20—28. *Rev.* xi. 15—18.)—*His father David.* (32) *Marg. Ref.* r. ' The virgin must therefore be of the ' house of David ; for seeing the angel told her, she should ' not have this Son by the knowledge of a man, it was ' not Joseph's but Mary's being of the house of David, ' which made David his father.' *Whitby.*
. *Espoused.* (27) Μεμνηστευμενη. ii. 5. *Matt.* i. 18.—Thou that art *highly favoured.* (28) Κεχαριτωμενη. *Eph.* i. 6. Not

elsewhere N. T. Αχαρις, *gratia.* 30.—*She was troubled.* (29) Διεταραχθη. Here only N. T. Δια, et ταρασσω, 12.—*Of* the Highest. (32) Υψιστς. 35. vi. 35. *Mark* v. 7. *Acts* xvi. 17.

V. 34—38. " How shall this be ? " is very different from, " Whereby shall I know this ? " (18) The latter implies a doubt of the truth of the prediction ; the former merely asks direction. Mary's question seems entirely the language of faith and humble admiration. She probably meant to enquire, what her conduct ought to be respecting her espousals with Joseph, and in other res ects. (*Note, Judg.* xiii. 8.) She seems to have understoopit, as implying that she was to conceive miraculously ; but she desired further information : she, however, asked no sign for the confirmation of her faith, as Zacharias had done. The angel therefore, in replying, merely told her that she would conceive by the Holy Spirit descending upon her : in this manner " the power of the most High would over-" shadow her ; " and the Infant would be formed in her womb by his creating energy, and under his special protection. Thus the promised Seed would properly be " made " of a woman," and partaker of human nature, without the pollution of sin, which is common to all others descended from fallen Adam. (*Notes, Gen.* iii. 14, 15. *Job* xiv. 1—6. *v.* 4. *Is.* vii. 14. *Jer.* xxxi. 21, 22. *Gal.* iv. 4—7.) This child might therefore be called " that holy thing," or *holy child :* and even in respect of his human nature, he should be acknowledged to be " the Son of God ;" as well as in his divine nature, and his mysterious Person as " God manifest in the flesh."—The Man, Christ Jesus; being called " the Son of God," because conceived by the operation of the Holy Spirit, is a full proof of the Deity of that sacred Agent.—In order more fully to establish Mary in her believing expectation of this great event, the angel informed her, that Elisabeth had conceived *a son* in her old age ; and was at that time in the sixth month of her pregnancy, though she had long been deemed barren ! Elisabeth was cousin to Mary, by the mother's side, though a daughter of Aaron in the father's line : for the families of David and Aaron frequently intermarried ; and this affinity shadowed forth the union of the kingly and priestly office, in the person of the Messiah.—Mary's conception in virginity was more evidently miraculous, than Elisabeth's in her old age : but nothing was, or could be, impossible to the power of God. (*Note, Gen.* xviii. 13—15.) —When Mary heard this, she did not at all waver in her belief of what the angel had told her : and though she could not but fear, that her pregnancy might expose her to many suspicions, or injurious reflections, and painful trials, and indeed to very great danger ; she humbly and

2 A 2

cording to thy word. And the angel departed from her.

39 ¶ And Mary arose in those days, [f Josh. x. 40. &c.] and went [into] the hill-country with haste, into a city of Judah;

40 And entered into the house of Zacharias, and saluted Elisabeth.

41 And it came to pass, that when Elisabeth heard the salutation of Mary, [g] the babe leaped in her womb: and Elisabeth [h] was filled with the Holy Ghost.

42 And she spake out with a loud voice, and said, [i] Blessed *art* thou among women, and [k] blessed *is* the fruit of thy womb.

43 And [l] whence *is* this to me, that the mother of [m] my Lord should come to me?

44 For, lo, as soon as the voice of thy salutation sounded in mine ears, [n] the babe leaped in my womb for joy.

45 And [o] blessed *is* she [o] that believed: for there shall be a performance of those things which were told her from the Lord.

46 ¶ And Mary said, [p] My soul doth magnify the Lord,

47 And my spirit hath rejoiced in [q] God my Saviour.

48 For he hath [r] regarded the low estate of his handmaiden: for, behold, from henceforth [s] all generations shall call me blessed.

s 26. 42. xi. 27. Gen. xxx. 13. Mal. iii. 12.

---

implicitly resigned herself to the divine will, saying, ' Behold here I am, the handmaid and servant of the Lord; let it be to me according to thy word.' Probably, the miraculous conception immediately took place; and the angel having executed his commission departed from her. (*Marg. Ref.* a. b. d. e.)

Shall overshadow. (35) Επισκιασει. ix. 34. *Matt.* xvii. 5. *Mark* ix. 5. *Acts* v. 15.—*Ex.* xl. 35. *Sept.*—*Holy thing.*] To ... αγιον. Παιδιον, or ζρεφος, *child*, or *infant*, may be understood.—*Thy cousin.* (36) Ἡ συγγενης. 58. 61. ii. 44. *Mark* vi. 4. The word is used for remote relations, as well as more strictly for " cousins."—*Shall be impossible.* (37) Αδυνατησει. *Matt.* xvii. 20. Not elsewhere N. T.—*Gen.* xviii. 14. *Deut.* xvii. 8. 2 *Chr.* xiv. 11. *Sept.*

V. 39—45. Soon after this vision, Mary, being in haste to communicate with Elisabeth, took a long journey from Nazareth to the hill-country of Judea, perhaps to Hebron, for that purpose. (*Marg. Ref.* f.) Being arrived she saluted Elisabeth, and probably congratulated her on the unexpected favour conferred on her: but no sooner did Elisabeth hear her voice, than she felt the infant leap in her womb in a very extraordinary manner; even as if he had been conscious of the presence of the mother of the great Redeemer, whom he was appointed to precede. At the same time, " Elisabeth was filled with the Holy " Spirit," and under his prophetical influence, she pronounced Mary and " the Fruit of her womb," to be most blessed, as peculiarly honoured by the most high God. (*Marg. Ref.* h—k.) Though Elisabeth was superior in age, in station, and in reputation; yet she considered Mary as so distinguished a person, by being chosen to be the mother of the Messiah, that she was filled with admiration, at being favoured with a visit from her, in addition to all her other mercies. (*Marg. Ref.* l.—*Note, Matt.* viii. 8, 9.) She acknowledged the child which was to be born of her, to be " her Lord " and the Lord of all: (*Marg. Ref.* m. —*Note, Matt.* xxii. 41—46:) and she declared, that the infant in her womb, exulted for joy under the impulse of the Holy Spirit, and as a kind of homage to his Lord. (*Note, Gen.* xxv. 22, 23.) Indeed Mary was peculiarly happy, in that she had so readily and implicitly believed

the divine message; by which means she had honoured God, and had received her mercies unmingled with rebukes; for the promise would surely and exactly be accomplished.—There was in this a reference to Zacharias's unbelief, and the painful rebuke under which he lay; but the subject was touched very gently, as it was proper from the mouth of Elisabeth.—It is remarkable, that Mary, though young and inexperienced, so readily believed a far more difficult promise, than that about which Zacharias, an aged priest and an experienced believer, had hesitated. (*Marg.* and *Marg. Ref.* o.—*Note,* 18—20.)—It does not appear, that Elisabeth knew the circumstances of Mary's vision, or her faith in the divine message, except by the Spirit of prophecy: for it may be concluded from the narrative, that she thus addressed Mary, before she had time to inform her of these matters. The words of Elisabeth, and all the circumstances of her interview with Mary, must have had a powerful effect in establishing the faith, and in enlarging the expectations, of the latter: and the favour and testimony of persons, so highly respected as Zacharias and Elisabeth, would powerfully operate to prevent any injurious reflections on her character. (*Note, Matt.* i. 18, 19.)

The hill-country. (39) Την ορεινην. 65. Not elsewhere N. T.—*Josh.* xi. 21. *Sept.* See also *Josh.* xxi. 10, 11.— *Leaped.* (41) Εσκιρτησε· εσκιρτησεν εν αγαλλιασει. 44. vi. 23. Not elsewhere N. T.—*Gen.* xxv. 22. *Ps.* cxiv. 4. 6. *Sept.* —*Blessed,* &c. (42) Ευλογημενη ... ευλογημενος. 28. (Ex ευ, *bene,* et λεγω, *dico.*) *Quam vel quem oportet benedicere : laudabilis.*—*Blessed is she,* &c. (45) Μακαρια. *Beata.* vi. 20, 21, 22. x. 27, 28. *Matt.* v. 3—11. *Rom.* iv. 7, 8. 1 *Tim.* i. 11. vi. 15.—*A performance.* (45) Τελειωσις, ἁ τελειου, *perficio. Heb.* vii. 11. Not elsewhere N. T.

V. 46—55. (*Notes,* 1 *Sam.* ii. 1—3.) Mary, being greatly animated with holy affections by Elisabeth's address, and likewise under the immediate influence of the Spirit, breaks out, as in a transport of joy, admiration, and gratitude; declaring, that her soul did most ardently extol and praise the Lord, and dictate to her tongue, while she celebrated his perfections and extolled his wonderful works; yea, " her spirit " within her ex-

2 B 3

49 For ' he that is mighty " hath done to me great things; ² and holy *is* his name.

50 And ' his mercy *is* on them that fear him from generation to generation.

51 He hath ' shewed strength with his arm: ' he hath scattered the proud in ' the imagination of their hearts.

52 He hath ' put down the mighty from *their* seats, and exalted them of low degree.

53 He hath ' filled the hungry with good things; ' and the rich he hath sent empty away.

54 He ' hath holpen his servant Israel, in remembrance of *his* mercy;

55 As ' he spake to our fathers, to

---

ulted and " rejoiced in God her Saviour." By this it is evident, that she confessed herself a sinner, who needed a Saviour, and who could no otherwise rejoice in God, than as she was interested in his salvation through the promised Messiah. (*Marg. Ref.* p, q.—*Notes, Is.* xii. 2. xlv. 15—17. *Tit.* ii. 13. iii. 4—7.)—It is also supposed by many, that by " God my Saviour " she meant that divine Person who was about to receive his human nature from her. (*Note, Matt.* i. 20, 21.) She however added, that the Lord had graciously condescended to regard the " low " estate of his handmaid," who was very poor, obscure, and despised in the world, though descended from the stock of David; when it might have been expected that the Messiah would assume his human nature, from one of more illustrious station, and more honoured among men. (*Marg. Ref.* r.—*Notes, Gen.* xxxii. 9—12. 2 *Sam.* vii. 18, 19. 1 *Cor.* l. 26—31.) It was therefore greatly to be admired, that so mean a person should be thus distinguished; for indeed every generation to the end of time would count her happy beyond all other women: as the almighty God, who disposes of his favours as he sees good, had " done great things for her," such as had never before been heard of or experienced: and as his name was holy, and his perfections infinite, so she could not doubt of his accomplishing his promises, and fulfilling his work of mercy, purity, and righteousness, which he had thus begun. Indeed his mercy had always been extended towards " those who feared him," his humble worshippers and servants, in every generation, and would be to the end of the world; and was only withheld from the proud, impenitent, and unbelieving. (*Marg. Ref.* s—y.— *Notes, Ex.* xxxiv. 5—7. *Ps.* ciii. 15—18.) He had, in former ages, often shewn his power, in protecting and delivering his people; and in scattering the numerous armies, or formidable confederacies, of his haughty enemies; confounding them even in those sagacious schemes, which they had framed according to the imaginations, or reasonings, of their hearts. (*Marg. Ref.* z—c.—*Notes,* 1 *Sam.* ii. 4—8. *Job* v. 8—16. 2 *Cor.* 1—6.) Thus he had dethroned, or ruined, proud and prosperous monarchs, as Pharaoh, Sennacherib, Nebuchadnezzar, and Belshazzar; and had exalted such persons as were of low estate and of humble minds, as Joseph, David, and Daniel. (*Note, Ps.* cxiii. 7—9.) He had also been used to satisfy the poor and hungry with the bounty of his v e e, whilst the rich were impoverished and reduced to deep distress: and this was an emblem of the methods of his grace, in abas-

ing the proud and exalting the humble; and in feasting, enriching, and comforting those, who hungered and thirsted for spiritual blessings; whilst the self-wise and self-righteous were left destitute of all real good, and sent away to their souls. (*Marg. Ref.* d, e.—*Notes,* vi. 21—26. xviii. 9—14. *Ps.* cvii. 8, 9.) Thus he had, in former ages, helped his people Israel, when they humbly cried to him, and succoured them in extreme distress: and thus he was about to help them at that time, by fulfilling his promises concerning the Messiah, when they were sunk very deep in depravity, and in abject subjection to their enemies. This would be done " in remembrance of his *mercy*," according to his former unmerited kindness to that nation; and in accomplishment of his promises, which he had graciously made to their fathers; especially to Abraham, with relation to himself and his posterity; and that Seed in particular, " in whom all the nations of the earth should " be blessed." (*Marg. Ref.* f, g.—*Notes,* 67—75. *Gen.* xii. 1—3. xxii. 16—18. xlix. 9, 10. *Mic.* vii. 18—20. *Heb.* vi. 13—15. xi. 39, 40.)

Doth magnify. (46) Μεγαλυνει. 58. *Matt.* xxiii. 5. *Acts* v. 13. x. 46. xix. 17. 2 *Cor.* x. 15. *Phil.* i. 20.—*Hath rejoiced.* (47) Ηγαλλιασε. x. 21. *John* v. 35. viii. 56. *Acts* ii. 26. xvi. 34. 1 *Pet.* i. 8. iv. 13. *Rev.* xix. 7. Αγαλλιασις, 14.—*The low estate.* (48) Την ταπεινωσιν. *Acts* viii. 33. *Phil.* iii. 21. *Jam.* i. 10.—*Gen.* xvi. 11. xxix. 32. xxxi. 42. xli.-52. *Ps.* cxxxvi. 23. *Is.* liii. 8. *Lam.* i. 3. 7. 9. *Sept.* The word is uniformly used for a low and afflicted condition, and not for the grace of humility, or lowliness.— And it is certain, that Mary did not mean to commend her own humility, (as ' lowliness,' used in the Prayer Book, may seem to imply,) but to shew her low and impoverished condition, and that of David's family, when God so noticed her.—*Shall call me blessed.*] Μακαριουσι με. *Jam.* v. 11. Not elsewhere N.T.—See on 45.—*Ps.* lxxii. 17. *Sept.* —*He that is mighty.* (49) Ὁ Δυνατος. Here only in this sense N. T.—*Great things.*] Μεγαλεια. *Acts* ii. 11. Not elsewhere N. T.—*Ps.* lxxi. 19. *Sept.*—*He hath scattered.* (51) Διεσκορπισεν. See on *Matt.* xxv. 24. 26.—*The proud.*] Ὑπερηφανους. Ex ὑπερ, super, et φαινομαι, appareo. *Rom.* i. 30. 2 *Tim.* iii. 2. *Jam.* iv. 6. 1 *Pet.* v. 5. Ὑπερηφανια. *Mark* vii. 22.—*The mighty.* (52) Δυναστας. *Acts* viii. 27. 1 *Tim.* vi. 15. Not elsewhere N. T.—1 *Sam.* ii. 8. *Sept.*—*He hath holpen.* (54) Αντελαβετο. *Acts* xx. 35. 1 *Tim.* vi. 2. Not elsewhere N. T. Συναντιλαμβανεται, *Rom.* viii. 26.

2 R 4

Abraham, and to his seed for ever.
56 And Mary abode with her about
three months, and returned to her own
house.
57 ¶ Now [h] Elisabeth's full time
came that she should be delivered; and
she brought forth a son.
58 And [i] her neighbours and her
cousins heard how the Lord had shewed
great mercy upon her: [k] and they rejoiced with her.
59 And it came to pass, that [l] on the
eighth day they came to circumcise the
child; and they called him Zacharias,
after the name of his father.
60 And his mother answered and
said, [m] Not *so;* but he shall be called
John.
61 And they said unto her, There is
none of thy kindred that is called by
this name.
62 And [n] they made signs to his
father, how he would have him called.
63 And he asked for [o] a writing-
table, and wrote, saying, His name is
John. And they marvelled all.
64 And [p] his mouth was opened immediately, and his tongue *loosed,* [q] and
he spake, and praised God.
65 And [r] fear came on all that dwelt
round about them: and all these [*] sayings were noised abroad throughout all
[s] the hill-country of Judea.
66 And all they that heard *them*
[t] laid *them* up in their hearts, saying,
What manner of child shall this be!
[u] And the hand of the Lord was with
him.

h 13. ii. 6, 7. Gen. xxi. 2, 3. Num. xxiii. 19.
i 25. Ruth iv. 14—17. Ps. cxiii. 9.
k 14. Gen. xxi. 6. Is. lxvi. 9, 10. Rom. xii. 15. 1 Cor. xii. 26.
l ii. 21. Gen. xvii. 12. xxi. 3, 4. Lev. xii. 3. Acts vii. 8. Phil. iii. 5.
m 13. 2 Sam. xii. 25. Is. viii. 3. Matt. i. 25.
n 22.
o Prov. iii. 3. Is. xxx. 8. Jer. xvii. 1. Hab. ii. 2.
p 20. Ex. iv. 15, 16. Ps. li. 15. Jer. i. 9. Ez. iii. 27. xxix. 21. xxxiii. 22. Matt. ix. 33. Mark vii. 32—37.
q Ps. xxx. 7—12. cxviii. 18, 19. Is. xii. 1. Dan. iv. 34—37.
r vii. 16. Acts ii. 43. v. 5. 11. xix. 17. Rev. xi. 11.
* Or, *things.*
s 39. Josh. x. 6. 40.
t ii. 19. 51. ix. 44. Gen. xxxvii. 11. Ps. cxix. 11.
u 80. ii. 40. Gen. xxxix. 2. Judg. xiii. 24, 25. 1 Sam. ii. 18. xvi. 18. 1 Kings xviii. 46. Acts xi. 21.

V. 56. After these things, Mary continued with Elisabeth till the time of her delivery drew near, and then returned to Nazareth. Probably, she left the house of Zacharias at this time, that she might not be in the way of being too much noticed, when so many would be coming to see him and Elisabeth, and to congratulate them on the birth of a son in their old age: but we may be sure, that the communications between these two favoured and pious women, while together, would be peculiarly delightful and edifying to each other.—After Mary's return home, those events seem to have occurred which have already been considered, concerning the difficulties and conduct of Joseph in respect of her. (*Notes, Matt.* i. 18—21.)

V. 57—66. The neighbours and relations of Elisabeth had, no doubt, previously heard of her pregnancy: but when the Lord had "magnified his mercy," in making her the joyful mother of a son, they "rejoiced with her," and congratulated her on so unexpected a blessing. (*Marg. Ref.* h—l.) On the eighth day many assembled to attend on the circumcision of the child, according to the law: and as it was customary to give children their names at that time, (perhaps with reference to Abram's being called Abraham, when circumcision was appointed,) some of them proposed that the child should be called Zacharias. (*Notes, Gen.* xvii. 4—12. xxi. 1—7.) We find no instance in the ancient scriptures of any person in Israel, who was called after the name of his father: but it was then become customary; (as in the case of Herod, and his descendants;) and these relations meant it out of respect to Zacharias, especially as he was far advanced in years. But Elisabeth would by no means agree to this, declaring that he should "be called John;" at which they expressed their surprise, as none of the family had been so named. Zacharias, being deaf and dumb, probably spent his time in retirement and devotion, patiently expecting the termination of his chastisement: (*Notes,* 18—25:) and having given Elisabeth all needful information and instructions concerning the heavenly vision, he seems hitherto to have left the whole matter to her. But the difference of opinion, between her and her friends, caused them *by signs* to apply to him to determine it: and he, in the same manner, desiring a writing-tablet, wrote that the child's name was John, that being a settled point which was by no means to be disputed.—'*God is gracious,* which is the import of 'that name, is a name very fit for him, who was to be 'the first preacher of the kingdom of grace, and who was 'to point out him, from whose "fulness we receive grace '"for grace." (*John* i. 16.)' *Whitby.* (*Marg. Ref.* l—o. —*Notes,* 11—17. *John* i. 15—17.)—At this the company was astonished, not having hitherto been acquainted with the particulars of Zacharias's vision; but the time appointed for his correction being now expired, he immediately recovered the gift of speech, and used it in praising God. Probably, he returned thanks to him, for his goodness and faithfulness in the birth of his son, acknowledging the righteousness of the rebuke under which he had lain, and praising the mercy of God, in restoring to him the use of his tongue. It is supposed that the prophetical hymn which follows was spoken at the same time; but this is not certain.—Zacharias seems also on this occasion, to have made publick all the circumstances of the vision that he had in the temple; whence a solemn awe and fear fell on all the neighbours, respecting the event of these extraordinary transactions: and, while they were rumoured abroad through the adjacent country, all who heard them, carefully observed and remembered them, expecting great things from a child, whose birth had been attended by so many wonders. In the mean time John grew up under the immediate protection of God, and the powerful influence of his grace: so that his knowledge and piety, far beyond his years, evinced that the Lord was with him in a peculiar manner. (*Marg. Ref.* p—u.—*Notes,* 80. ii. 40. *Judg.* xiii. 25.)

Neighbours. (58) Περιοικοι. Here only N. T. Περιοικουντας. 65.—*They rejoiced with her.*] Συνεχαιρον. xv. 6. 9. 1 *Cor.* xii. 26. xiii. 6. *Phil.* ii. 17, 18.—*They made signs.* (62) Ενενευον. *Nutu significabant.* Here only N. T. Δια-

67 ¶ And his father Zacharias was filled with the Holy Ghost, and prophesied, saying,

68 ' Blessed *be* the Lord God of Israel; for 'he hath visited and redeemed his people,

69 And hath raised up 'an Horn of salvation for us 'in the house of his servant David;

70 As he 'spake by the mouth of his holy prophets, 'which have been since the world began;

71 That 'we should be saved from our enemies, and from the hand of all that hate us;

72 To 'perform the mercy *promised*

to our fathers, 'and to remember his holy covenant;

73 The 'oath which he sware to our father Abraham,

74 That he would grant unto us, 'that we, being delivered out of the hands of our enemies, might serve him without fear,

75 In ' holiness and righteousness before him all the days of our life.

76 And thou, child, 'shalt be called the prophet of the "Highest: for 'thou shalt go before the face of the Lord to prepare his ways;

77 To 'give knowledge of salvation unto his people, 'by 'the remission of their sins,

---

νευων. 22.—*A writing-table.* (63) Πινακιδιον. Here only N.T.

V. 67—75. When Zacharias had recovered the gift of speech, he was also filled with the Holy Spirit, and uttered the following prophecy, concerning the kingdom and salvation of the Messiah. (*Note,* 46—55.)—He began with blessing and praising "the Lord God of Israel," especially, for again visiting his people in mercy, after having for a long time left them without inspired prophets; and having begun that work of redemption, which had so long been predicted and expected, in the birth of him, who was to be the fore-runner of the Messiah; which was a certain proof that he himself would shortly appear. (*Marg. Ref.* y, z.) So that, speaking of the Saviour as already come, according to the language frequently used by the prophets, he declared that God had "raised up an Horn of salvation "for" his people. (*Marg. Ref.* a.—*Notes,* 1 *Sam.* ii. 10. 2 *Sam.* xxii. 2, 3. *Ps.* cxxxii. 17.) The horn, which is the ornament, and weapon of protection and annoyance of every enemy, in many animals, is an apt emblem of the divine Saviour; "the glory of his people," their Defender against every assailant who makes them, "in all things more "than conquerors."—This salvation God had "raised up "in the house of his servant David," even Jesus, the Son of the virgin Mary. (*Marg. Ref.* b.—*Notes, Ps.* lxxxix. 1—4. 19—37. *Is.* vii. 14. ix. 6, 7. xi. 1. *Jer.* xxiii. 5, 6.) His birth, character, and salvation would accomplish the predictions of the holy prophets, from the beginning of the world; all of whom, in one way or other, gave intimations of the promised Messiah; and assured the people of God, that by him they should be "saved from their "enemies," and protected against all those wicked men and apostate spirits, who hated them and sought their destruction. So that the coming of this Saviour was intended to "perform" the mercy, which God had been bestowing on their ancestors for ages past; and to accomplish the gracious and faithful covenant, which he had entered into with believers under all preceding dispensations; from the first promise made to fallen Adam: and

which he had ratified to Abraham by a solemn oath, in behalf of himself and all his spiritual seed; the blessings of which were also shadowed forth under external signs and advantages, secured to his natural posterity. (*Marg. Ref.* c—h.—*Notes,* xxiv. 25—31. 44—49, *vv.* 44—46. *Gen.* xxii. 16—18. 2 *Sam.* xxiii. 5. *Is.* lv. 1—3. *John* v. 45—47. *Acts* x. 36—43. *Heb.* vi. 13—20. 1 *Pet.* i. 10—12. *Rev.* xix. 9, 10.) This promise, covenant, and oath, engaged to all believers, deliverance from the power of Satan, sin, the world, death, and every enemy, as well as redemption from the curse of the holy law and the righteous vengeance of God: that, being safe under his protection, and partakers of his mercy and grace, they might worship and serve him, as under his immediate eye, "without "fear" of being destroyed by their foes, or cast off by him, "in all righteousness and holiness" during the remainder of their lives in this world; and so at length inherit eternal felicity in heaven. (*Marg. Ref.* i, k.)

Prophesied. (67) Προεφητευσε. *Matt.* xi. 13. xv. 7. *Acts* xxi. 9. 1 *Cor.* xi. 4, 5. xiv. 3, 4. 24.—*Blessed.* (68) Ευλογητος. See on *Mark* xiv. 68.—*Hath visited.* Επεσκεψατο. 78. vii. 16. *Matt.* xxv. 36. 43. *Acts* vi. 3. vii. 23. xv. 14.—*Redeemed.*] Εποιησε λυτρωσιν. "Has wrought "redemption." Λυτρωσις, ii. 38. *Heb.* ix. 12. Not elsewhere N. T.—*Since the world began.* (70) Απ' αιωνος. *Acts* xv. 18.—*That we should be saved.* (71) Σωτηριαν. "Salvation." 69.77. xix. 9. *John* iv. 22. *Acts* iv. 12, *et al.* —*Without fear.* (74) Αφοβως. 1 *Cor.* xvi. 10. *Phil.* i. 14. *Jude* 12.—*In holiness.* (75) Εν οσιοτητι. *Eph.* iv. 24. Not elsewhere N.T. Όσιος. *Acts* ii. 27.

V. 76—79. Zacharias next addressed himself to his son, though at that time a child, declaring, that he had the singular honour of being that "prophet of the most "high God," who was appointed to "go before the face "of the Lord," even of Christ, "to prepare his ways." (*Marg. Ref.* l—n.—*Notes,* 11—17. *Matt.* xi. 7—15.) The grand object of his preparatory ministry would be, to give the "knowledge of salvation," by the sure testimony and faithful promise of God, "to his people," through the

2 R 6

78 Through ‘the *tender mercy of our God; whereby the ʳ Day-spring ᵍ from on high hath visited us,

79 To 'give light to them that sit in darkness, ᵏ and *in* the shadow of

death, 'to guide our feet into the way ᵗ of peace.

80 ¶ And ᵘ the child grew, and waxed strong in spirit, ˣ and was in the deserts till the day of ʸ his shewing unto Israel.

19, 20.

full remission of all sins to every one who believed in Christ; and by this assurance to call men to repent, and accept of this inestimable blessing, that they might have the experience of it in their own souls, and know themselves to be partakers of it. (*Notes,* 1 John v. 9—13.) All these benefits would come to them " through the tender " mercy," or bowels of compassion, of Israel's God ; who, pitying the misery of perishing sinners, had caused this Day-spring from heaven to visit them, ushering in the appearance of " the Sun of righteousness," and the evangelical dispensation. (*Marg.* and *Marg. Ref.* o—q.—*Notes, Is.* lx. 1—3. *Mal.* ii. 2, 3. 2 *Pet.* i. 19. *Rev.* xxii. 16, 17.) Thus, light would be afforded to sinners, whether Jews or Gentiles, whose ignorance, guilt, and misery, resembled the darkness of a dungeon, in which condemned criminals are confined; and whose dreary situation was like the dark shade of death and hell. (*Marg. Ref.* r, s.—*Notes, Matt.* iv. 12—17. *Acts* xxvi. 16—18.) Then would their minds be enlightened, and their path marked out; they would see their danger and their refuge; they would be inspired with hope and encouragement; they would be directed into the way of peace with God, with their consciencs, and with each other; and would learn to walk in those holy and happy paths, which lead to everlasting peace and felicity, and are an earnest of them. (*Marg. Ref.* t.—*Notes, Is.* lix. 3—8. *Rom.* iii. 9—18. v. 1, 2.)—This was evidently a very remarkable prophecy, describing the nature, privileges, and effects of the salvation of the gospel; and foretelling the success of Christianity both among the Jews and Gentiles. Probably, it was much circulated, and attended to, among Zacharias's friends, and the pious remnant of the nation.

Of the Highest. (76) Ὑψιϛu. See on 35.—*The tender mercy.* (78) Σπλαγχνα ελεος, *viscera misericordiæ :* σπλαγχνα, *interiora vitalia. Acts* i. 18. 2 *Cor.* vi. 12. vii. 15. *Phil.* i. 8. ii. 1. *Col.* iii. 12. *Philem.* 7. 12. 20. 1 *John* iii. 17: answering to בְּרַחֲמֵי, *Prov.* xii. 10. *Sept.* (*Note, Ps.* ciii. 6—8.)—*The day-spring.*] Ανατολη, *oriens. The east.* xiii. 29. *Matt.* ii. 1. 9. viii. 11. xxiv. 27. *Rev.* vii. 2. xvi. 12. xxi. 13.—*Jer.* xxiii. 5. *Zech.* iii. 8. vi. 12. *Sept.* Our version properly " Branch." Ανατελι ὑμιν ...Ἡλιον δικαιοσυνης. *Mal.* iv. 2. *Sept.*—*To guide.* (79) Κατευθυναι. 1 *Thes.* iii. 11. 2 *Thes.* iii. 5.

V. 80. As John grew in stature, his understanding and judgment matured: and he gave indications not only of superior natural abilities, and energy of mind; but also of strong faith, vigorous holy affections, great fortitude and resolution in the cause of God, a superiority to grovelling desires and pursuits, and a victory over the fear and love of the world. Thus did he ripen for usefulness: but whether his parents died whilst he was young, or whether they were specially directed by God in this matter; he seems neither to have received an education from the Jewish Scribes, nor attended on any *sacerdotal* services at the

temple; but to have lived privately in the most retired and unfrequented part of the country, being given up to meditation, devotion, and mortification, till the time when he openly appeared among the people as the Messiah's forerunner. (*Marg. Ref.*—*Note,* 57—66.)

Waxed strong.] Εκραδαιυτο· (à κραδος, *robur :*) ii. 40. 1 *Cor,* xvi. 13. *Eph.* iii. 16. Κρατιος, 1 *Pet.* v. 6.—*Shewing.*] Αναδιξεως. Here only *N. T.* Ab αναδιικνυμι. x. 1. *Acts* i. 24.

PRACTICAL OBSERVATIONS.

V. 1—7.

Those things, which we are required " most surely to " believe," are most abundantly proved to be of divine original; and if our faith were as strong, as the truths and promises are certain, we should continually rejoice in them. For the great transactions, on which our hopes depend, have been recorded, not only by such as " from the be- " ginning were eye-witnesses and ministers of the word ;" but by those who were guided by the inspiration of God ; this was attested by the miracles which they wrought, and by the prophecies interwoven with their histories, and fulfilled from age to age in the most evident manner. We should therefore endeavour to get acquainted with the " certainty of those things, which are most surely believed" by all true Christians, and to obtain a more exact knowledge of them; and also labour to bring our friends and neighbours to an established faith in them. This is the way to approve ourselves to be indeed " Lovers of God," and to fill up our station in the community to his glory. Thus we shall evidently be " righteous before him," and not merely in the opinion of our fellow mortals : and an habitual tenour of conscientious and blameless obedience, to all the commandments and ordinances of the Lord, forms the best proof of our gracious justification, and the best ornament of " the doctrine of God our Saviour." (*Note, Tit.* ii. 9, 10.) This is peculiarly needful and becoming in those, who sustain the office of ministers: and it is a singular felicity, when married persons are of one heart in the worship and service of God. Yet some alloy to our comfort must be expected in every situation ; and this consideration should reconcile us to our own trials ; as we probably should be no gainers, could we exchange condition with those whom we are most apt to envy. But those who " grow in grace" as they advance in years, and who steadily attend to their proper employment, may hope for increasing peace and comfort in the eve of life. (*Notes, Ps.* lxxi. 17—24. xcii. 13—15.)

V. 8—25.

While by faith we view our great High Priest in the temple above, continually presenting the prayers of believers before his Father's throne, with the fragrant incense of his intercession ; and are encouraged to join our peti-

2 R 7

CHAP. II.

Joseph and Mary go to Bethlehem, to be enrolled there, according to the decree of Augustus, 1—5. Jesus is there born and laid in a manger, 6, 7. An angel makes this known to shepherds: and the heavenly host praise God in their hearing, 8—14. The shepherds, finding it to be as the angel had said, report these transactions, and glorify God, 15—20. Jesus is circumcised, 21; and presented at the temple,

---

tions to those of multitudes all over the earth, who every hour are approaching the mercy-seat by this " new and " living Way:" (*Note, Heb.* x. 19—22:) let us also recollect how terrifying, to our frail sinful nature, the appearance of visitants from the world of spirits has always been; that we may be thankful for the *invisible* ministry of angels, and that the Lord sends his messages to us by men like ourselves, whose "terror cannot make us afraid." (*Notes, Job* iv. 12—16. xxxiii. 1—7.) We need, however, fear no evil, but may expect glad tidings from heaven, when we are found in the path of duty: and if our prayers be accepted, all blessings will in due time be communicated. Nor should delays in this respect be construed into denials; many prayers which we have been offering during years which are past, for ourselves and others, may be abundantly answered after we are gone to heaven. We ought not indeed to be anxious about having children; for we know not whether they would be cause of "joy and " gladness," to us and to others, or the contrary: since it is obvious, that numbers seem to live only to render the world more wicked and miserable than it would otherwise have been; and then they die in such a manner, that we cannot but think it would have been " better for them if " they had never been born." Yet it is a peculiar favour to have children, for whose birth many shall have cause to rejoice, as instruments of God in doing good to others, and being themselves heirs of eternal life and happiness. In seeking such distinguishing blessings for those who belong to us, we should carefully observe the difference between *a great man in the world's esteem*, and one who is " great " in the sight of the LORD." The mighty conquerors, potentates, and statesmen, and all who have been renowned as philosophers, or men of exalted genius; as well as all the sons of affluence, ostentation, and magnificence, are mean and obscure persons, in the judgment of God, compared with a poor prophet or minister, who is filled with wisdom and zeal; who is superior to the smiles and frowns of the world; who wants none of its honours, advantages, or pleasures; and whose only employment and joy it is to bring sinners to repentance, to " turn the dis- " obedient to the wisdom of the just," and to call on men to believe in Christ, and prepare for his coming to judge the world. Some measure of this kind of greatness we may desire for our children; and with that view we should early devote them to God, and bring them up for him : and, as some have been " filled with the Holy Spirit from " their mother's womb;" we should hope and pray that our's may thus be changed, in early youth, by divine grace; and we ought to instruct them in the truth, as soon as they are capable of knowing good from evil. Nor should we forget, that early and constant temperance, and indifference about worldly pleasures, are proper indications of future eminence and usefulness; that the increase of true godliness tends to the termination of contentions in families, churches, and communities; and that *nominal* Christians in general need conversion to the real worship and service

of God, as much as the heathen; even as Israelites by birth did of old.—Even real believers are not always alike strong in faith: when they lose sight of the power, truth, and love of God, and perplex themselves with difficulties and impediments, they are apt to dishonour him by unbelief: thus the glad tidings and precious promises of his word become the occasion to them of sin and correction; the very messengers of his mercy are constrained to give them intimations of his displeasure; the accomplishment of his promises are attended by rebukes; and their mouths are stopped in silence and confusion, when otherwise they would have been praising God with the voice of joy and gratitude. It is good, however, even under divine chastisement, to go on with our work, as far as we are able: for thus our afflictions may be mitigated and sanctified, and returning mercies will be preparing for us. But when we are peculiarly favoured, we should shun all ostentation: and every interposition of the Lord, to take away reproach or trouble, should remind us to court retirement, that we may meditate on his goodness and truth, pour out our thanksgivings before him, and seek his gracious teaching and assistance, in order to a due improvement of his mercies.

V. 26—38.

Whilst we contemplate the peculiar honour which was conferred on the Virgin-mother of our Lord, we should remember that angels rejoice over every sinner who repenteth; they deem those " highly favoured" in whose hearts "Christ dwells by faith," and are ready to congratulate each believer on so important a blessing. (*Notes,* ii. 8—14. *Eph.* i. 3—8.) Happy indeed must they be, among the sons and daughters of Adam, to whom the Lord is graciously reconciled, and with whom he is present by his sanctifying Spirit! They may indeed be troubled and perplexed by many things, of which they read and hear; and they can scarcely raise their hopes so high, as to expect the blessings intended for them: but they shall, in due season, be raised above their fears, and assured that they have " found favour with God," as most nearly related to " the Saviour of the world." (*Notes, Matt.* xii. 46—50. xxv. 34—40. *P. O.* 31—40.) Let us then rejoice in his personal and mediatorial exaltation; for he now reigns not only " over the house of Jacob ;" but over " angels, principalities, and powers in heavenly places," as " the Son of God" and " the Son of David." Let us seek to be, and to approve ourselves, the subjects of " his " kingdom of which there shall be no end :" and if we meet with sufferings in the way to the full enjoyment of our privileges and felicity; let us remember how Jesus was abased, impoverished, reproached, rejected, and crucified, before he entered into his glory. We should therefore entirely rely on the promises of God, carefully observe his directions, and diligently keep his commandments: for, waiting on him in this manner, the Holy Spirit, by whose operation the human nature of Jesus, " the First-born " among many brethren," was formed in the Virgin's

2 a 3

with the accustomed sacrifice of the poor, for the purifying of Mary, 22—24. Simeon's prophecy concerning him, 25—35: and that of Anna, 36—38. He grows, and increases in wisdom, 39, 40. At twelve years of age he goes with his parents to Jerusalem, and hears and asks questions of the doctors in the temple, 41—50. He returns to Nazareth, and is subject to his parents, 51, 52.

---

womb, will gradually renew his image on our souls, that we too, in a subordinate sense, may be " the sons and " daughters of the Lord almighty." (*Notes*, 2 *Cor.* vi. 14 —18, *v.* 18. vii. 1.)—In all our conflicts and temptations we should still remember, that " with God nothing shall " be impossible ; " and when we read and hear his promises, we should turn them into prayers, saying, " Behold the " servant of the Lord, let it be unto me according to this " thy word."

V. 39—56.

Those who are experienced in the things of God, will delight in each other's company ; they will take pleasure in speaking together of " what the Lord hath done for their " souls," and in joining in grateful praises and fervent prayers ; they will value each other's pious counsels, cautions, and exhortations ; and not decline that labour, which is requisite, in order to this ' communion of the ' saints.'—The influences of the Spirit of God effectually counteract that emulation and ambition, to which we are naturally prone, and through which we forget our own mercies, by repining at the superior honour conferred on others. His holy consolations raise us above the petty disparities of external rank and station : in proportion to his sacred illumination, we feel our own unworthiness, learn thankfulness for every favour, and rejoice in the gifts and graces bestowed on others : and thus " in honour pre- " ferring them to ourselves," we deem ourselves highly distinguished by the company of those believers, whom, under another influence, we should, perhaps disdainfully, have looked down upon as our inferiors. (*Notes*, *Rom.* xii. 9—16, *vv.* 10. 16. *Phil.* ii. 1—4.) Indeed, true honour consists in our relation and conformity to Christ : we ought therefore to rejoice in the company of those, who are evidently thus dignified ; and to commend that faith and obedience, which tend in a measure even to reflect disgrace on our own less honourable conduct, or on that of such as are most dear to us. Yet humble believers will appropriate no glory to themselves ; but will take occasion, from congratulations and commendations, to " magnify the Lord," and to " rejoice in him" as their " God and Saviour," with their whole heart and soul. Notwithstanding every other distinction, they must have been for ever miserable without this salvation : their thankfulness will therefore always be connected with a humble sense of sinfulness, and of his mercy, who has looked down with pity on their low estate, and raised them to the hope of everlasting happiness. Indeed, the almighty God " whose name is holy," might have been expected to do great things *against us* guilty and polluted criminals : but he has greatly glorified even his holiness, in extending mercy to all them that fear him, in every age and nation. Proud infidels and Pharisees, and presumptuous sinners of every description, will be " scattered" by this powerful arm, and disappointed in the vain " imaginations of their " hearts ;" and haughty potentates will be cast down from their thrones, into everlasting shame and misery : but the broken-hearted sinner, who abases himself before God,

shall be exalted ; and our gracious Lord will satisfy the desires of the poor in spirit, who long for spiritual blessings ; whilst the rich and self-sufficient shall be " sent " empty away." This is the true reason, why so many frequent those ordinances in vain, from which others go away abundantly satisfied, and rejoicing in the goodness of the Lord. For he still helps his true Israel, nor shall the believing seed of Abraham be ashamed for ever.

V. 57—66.

We should trace back every rill of comfort to the full fountain of the Lord's mercy, which he is continually magnifying. Delays often render the benefit doubly precious, by increasing our admiration and gratitude : and it is beautiful, when believers so behave, that all their neighbours cordially rejoice in the tokens of the divine favour towards them.—When the promises of God are performed, as well as while we are waiting for them, we should keep close to his ordinances : nor should we be influenced by any counsels, expostulations, or examples, to deviate in the least from his commandments ; but should study, by every method, to perpetuate the remembrance of his mercies to us. At the removal of our chastisements, our mouths should be open to shew forth the praises of the Lord : thus it will be known, that we approve the justice of the correction, as well as admire the mercy which has terminated it ; and that we have derived benefit from our sufferings. We ought likewise to observe the dealings of God with our neighbours, and wait the event of his dispensations with attentive expectation : and when our children grow up healthy, and improve in the exercise of their faculties ; we should ascribe it to the good " hand of the " Lord upon them," and take occasion to intreat him to give them also his heavenly grace and wisdom.

V. 67—80.

What multiplied praises, in heaven and earth, did the Saviour's advent occasion ! Shall not we also unite in blessing " the LORD God of Israel, who hath thus visited " and redeemed his people ?" We are as deeply concerned in the " raising up of this Horn of Salvation," and in the redemption which he made for sinners with his blood, as the Jews of old were. The predictions of holy prophets being fulfilled in Christ, confirm the truth of the scriptures to us, as well as to them ; the covenant and oath of God to Abraham, were intended to give us " a strong " consolation, who have fled for refuge to lay hold on the " hope set before us." Even John the Baptist's ministry still calls on us to repent, and welcome our incarnate Prince and Saviour : the whole scripture gives assurance of salvation to all believers, " by the remission of their sins :" and " through the tender mercy of our God, this Day- " spring from on high hath visited " these distant nations, to give light to us benighted pagans, who " sat in dark- " ness and the shadow of death." But let us remember, that this salvation implies " a deliverance from our ene- " mies, and from all that hate us ;" that, being set at

ᵃ From the ac-
count called
Anno Domini,
the fourth year.
iii. l. Acts xi. 28. xxv. 11. 21. Phil. iv. 22.

AND it came to pass in those days, that there went out a decree from ᵃ Cæ-sar Augustus, that ᵇ all the world should be ᶜ taxed.

2 (*And* this ᶜ taxing was first made

ᵇ Matt. xxiv. 14.
Mark x.v. 9.
xvi. 15. Rom. l.
3.
ᶜ Or, *enrolled*.
c Acts v. 37.

---

liberty from bondage, as well as from condemnation, we " may serve God without fear," under the influence of the Spirit of adoption, " in holiness and righteousness before " him all the days of our " future " lives." Is this then the salvation we desire? Do we experience its power in our nearts and consciences? Do we use the light of the gospel " to guide us into the ways of peace" and purity? If this be our case, we may be thankful and joyful, and expect complete victory over Satan, sin, and death, and an abundant entrance into heavenly felicity. Let us then take encouragement from the " knowledge of salvation," brought to us in the holy scriptures, to repent, and mortify every sin : let us assert our Christian liberty by being the diligent servants of God, whose ' service is perfect freedom ;' let us fear nothing but sin and temptation, and the consequences of them ; let us pray that the light which shines around us, may shine into our hearts, and appear in our lives ; and let us " follow peace with all men," and seek peace with God and our own consciences. If it be the will of the Lord that we should live in obscurity, let us the more diligently seek to grow " strong in the grace of " Jesus Christ:" and let those who are preparing for public usefulness, live retired and mortified to the world; employing their time in useful studies, attended by searching the scriptures, by meditation, and devotion, till the Lord shall open their way to some proper service for the benefit of his people, and the enlargement, purity, and peace of his kingdom.

NOTES.

Chap. II. V. 1. It had been predicted many ages before, that the Messiah should be born at Bethlehem ; (*Notes, Mic.* v. 2. *Matt.* ii. 3—6 :) yet the mother of Jesus resided at Nazareth, at the distance of sixty or seventy miles from that city; and she continued there till far advanced in her pregnancy. She was not, however, directed to go up to Bethlehem ; indeed that would have appeared too much the effect of design. But Augustus Cæsar, the Roman emperor, being left to follow the dictates of his own ambition, rapacity, or policy, issued an edict, that an account should be taken of the number and degree of all the subjects in his extensive empire ; (*marg.*) which in a vain-glorious style was then commonly called, " all " the world," or the whole habitable earth ; (*Marg. Ref.* b ;) because it contained all the most civilized and best cultivated regions which were then known. Some interpreters indeed suppose, that only the whole land of Israel, which was then governed by king Herod, and which was soon after divided into several distinct provinces, was included in this edict ; and that it was issued on account of some umbrage that Herod had given Augustus. But this gives a very restricted interpretation of the word translated " all the world ;" of which no indisputable instances have been produced.—' Such an account used to be taken of the ' citizens of Rome every fifth year, and they had officers ' on purpose appointed for it, called censors. Their busi-' ness was to take an account, and make a register, of all

' the Roman citizens, their wives and children, with the ' age, qualities, trades, offices, and estates, real and personal, ' of all of them. Augustus first extended this to the pro-' vinces. ...Three times, during his reign he caused the like ' description to be made. ...The second is the description, ' which St. Luke refers to. The decree concerning it was ' issued out ... three years before that in which Christ was ' born. So long had the taking of this ... survey been carry-' ing on through Syria, Cœle-syria, Phœnicia, and Judea, ' before it came to Bethlehem. ...Joab was nine months ' and twenty days in taking an account only of ten of the ' tribes of Israel, and of no more in them, than of the men ' that were fit for the wars. (*2 Sam.* xxiv. 8.) ...And when ' a survey ... was ordered by William the Conqueror to be ' taken for England only, I mean that of the Doomsday-' book, it was six years in making. ... No payment of any ' tax was made, (on this survey,) till the twelfth year after ; ' till then Herod, and after him Archelaus, his son, reign-' ing in Judea. ... But when ... Archelaus was deposed, ' and Judea put under the command ... and government ' of a Roman procurator, then first were taxes paid the ' Romans for that country. ...If it be asked, for what ' reason then was this survey or description of Judea ' made, if no taxes were then to be paid upon it ? The ' answer is, he was then at work on the composure of ' a book, containing such a survey and description of the ' whole Roman empire, as that which our Doomsday-' book doth for England. In order whereto his decree for ' this survey ... was made to extend to the depending king-' doms, as well as the provinces of the empire : that he ' might have a full account of both, for the thorough com-' pleting of the work. ... However, taxes were by the ' people of the provinces only paid to the Romans, and ' those of the dependent kingdoms to their own proper ' princes ; ... the people paid their taxes to their princes, and ' the princes paid their *tribute* to the Roman emperors.' *Prideaux.*—It is plain from this account, that the sceptre was at least departing from Judah, when Christ was born. (*Note, Gen.* xlix. 10.)

A decree.] Δογμα. *Acts* xvii. 7. *Eph.* ii. 15. *Col.* ii. 14.— *Dan.* ii. 13. iii. 10. 29. *Sept.—Augustus.*] Αυγυστα.—Here only N. T. Σεβαστος, *Acts* xxv. 21. 25. xxvii. 1. which answers to the Latin word " Augustus." *Note, Acts* xxv. 21. —*All the world.*] Πασαν την οικημενην. *Universa habitabilis,* nempe *terra.* iv. 5. xxi. 26. *Matt.* xxiv. 14. *Acts* xi. 28. xvii. 6. 31. xix. 27. xxiv. 5. *Rom.* x. 18. *Rev.* iii. 10. xii. 9. xvi. 14.—*Is.* xiv. 17. 26. *Sept. Note, Jer.* xxv. 26.—*Taxed.*] Απογραφεσθαι. 3. 5. *Heb.* xii. 23. Not elsewhere N. T. Απογραφη. 2. *Acts* v. 37.

V. 2. ' It is added, that this was " the first enrolling,'' ' to distinguish it from another ; (*Acts* v. 37 ;) the same ' which Josephus and Eusebius speak of, and place under ' Cyrenius also ; but differing from this here. As for Cy-' renius having rule over Syria at this time, that is to be ' taken in a looser, not stricter sense. Not that Cyrenius ' was there now the standing governor under the Romans : ' but sent by the emperor particularly on this occasion,

2 ʀ 2

ᵈ lb. 1. Acts xiii. 7. xviii. 12. xxiii. 26. xxvi. 3. when Cyrenius was ᵈgovernor of Sy-ria.)

ᵉ 4. 3 And all went to be taxed, ᵉevery

ᶠ i. 26. 27. iii. 23.
ᵍ Ir. 16. Matt. ii. one into his own city.

2a. John i. 46.
ᵇ Gen. xxxv. 19. 4 And ᶠJoseph also went up from

xlviii. 7. Ruth i. 19. ii. 4. iv. 11. Galilee, out ᵍof the city of Nazareth,
17. 21, 22. I Sam. xvi. 1. xvii. 12. into Judea, ʰunto the city of David,
58. xx. 6. Mic. v. 2. Matt. ii. 1. which is called Bethlehem, (because
John vii. 42. he was of the house and lineage of

ⁱ i. 27. iii. 23—31. Matt. i. 1—17. David,)

5 To be taxed with ᵏMary his ᵏ Deut. xxii. 23—27. Matt. i. 18, 19.
espoused wife, being great with child.

6 And ˡso it was, that while they ˡ Ps. xxxiii. 11. Prov. xix. 21.
were there, ᵐthe days were accom- ᵐ ver. 2.
plished that she should be delivered. ⁿ i. 57. Rev. xii. 1—5.

7 And ⁿshe brought forth her first- ᵒ Is. vii. 14. Matt. i. 25. Gal. iv. 4.
born son, ᵒand wrapped him in swad- ᵒ 11, 12. Ps. xxii. 9. Is. liii. 2, 3.
dling-clothes, and laid him in a manger; Matt. viii. 20. xiii. 55. John ii. 14. 2 Cor. viii. 9.
because there was no room for them in ᵖ x. 34. Gen. xlii. 27. xliii. 21. Ex. iv. 24.
ᵖthe inn.

'to take an inventory of this part of the empire. So saith
'Suidas,...out of some ancient author: Cæsar Augustus,
'desiring to know the strength and state of his dominions,
'sent twenty chosen men,...one into one part, another
'into another, to take this account, and Publius Sulpitins
'Quirinius had Syria for his province.' *Hammond.*—'Justin
'Martyr calls this Cyrenius the first procurator of Cæsar
'in Judea; namely on this account, that he was sent to
'make this survey, in Judea and Syria, even during the
'life of Herod the great.' *Beza.*—Saturninus was the resident governor of Syria at this time, and Tertullian says,
that this survey was entrusted to him: and it is doubted
by learned men, whether the words rendered " was
" governor" were ever used in that sense, which the
above interpretation requires.—' When Judea was put
'under ... a Roman procurator, then first were taxes paid
'to the Romans for that country; Publius Sulpitius
'Quirinius, who is in Greek called Cyrenius, being go-
'vernor, that is, president of Syria. ...There were two dis-
'tinct particular actions, in this matter, done at two dis-
'tinct and different times; the first, the making the de-
'scription or survey, and the second the levying the tax
'thereupon. And what is in the first verse of the second
'chapter of St. Luke, is to be understood of the former of
'these, and what is in the second verse, only of the latter.
'And this reconciles that evangelist with Josephus; for it
'is manifest from that author, that Cyrenius was not go-
'vernor of Syria, or any tax levied on Judea, till Archelaus
'was deposed. ...And therefore the making of this de-
'scription cannot be that which was done while Cyrenius
'was governor of Syria: but the other particular, that is,
'the laying and levying the tax thereon certainly was.'
Prideaux.—' This was the first enrolment made by Quiri-
'nius, governor of Syria.' *Lardner.* This very learned
author, who has fully discussed the subject, supposes that
there were two enrolments made by Quirinius; and that he
is called the governor of Syria, though not then advanced
to that dignity, because he was afterwards thus distinguished : and there seems no objection to this conclusion,
except the testimony of Tertullian, above mentioned, which
is far from being entitled to implicit credence.—The second
enrolment, or the levying of the taxes on the Jews, after
the deposition of Archelaus, excited most dreadful commotions, and was an introduction to those seditions and
insurrections, which at length brought destruction on Jerusalem, and unspeakable calamities on the Jews.

  Was governor.] Ἡγεμονευοντος. iii. 1. Ab ηγεομαι, duco.
Not elsewhere N. T.

  V. 3—7.] Thus it pleased God to take occasion, by the

determination of a heathen prince, to accomplish his own
purposes and predictions, in the most natural and simple
manner: for, as all persons were required to resort to the
city, to which the family had belonged; it became incumbent on Joseph and Mary, being the lineal descendants of
David, to go to Bethlehem for. this purpose. If, as some
think, Mary's situation might have excused her from so
long a journey; it must be supposed, that she was divinely
directed not to avail herself of that excuse.—When they
arrived at Bethlehem; it is probable, that they were obliged
to wait some time, before it came to their turn to be enrolled : in the interval Mary was delivered of her first-born
Son; (*Marg. Ref.* f—n.—*Note, Matt.* i. 24, 25;) and was
so strengthened, as to be able herself to wrap him in such
clothes, as she could there procure, and to " lay him in a
" manger" instead of a cradle.—' By her doing this her-
'self, it is thought that her labour was without the usual
'pangs of child-birth.' *Whitby.*—As the city was then
crowded with strangers, many of whom were doubtless in
superior circumstances, and as Joseph and Mary were poor
people; " there was no room for them in the inn," nor
was any person disposed to give them a hospitable reception. Thus " the Saviour of the world," " the Lord of
" glory," made his first appearance (as Man) in a stable,
or some kind of out-building, and his first bed in a manger!
This was an emblem of the reception which he was to meet
with on earth, and of the external poverty and debasement,
in which he would pass through life. (*Marg. Ref.* o, p.)—
It is probable. that Jesus also would be enrolled, and thus
his birth at Bethlehem authentically registered.—It is generally supposed, that there was only one inn of the superior sort at Bethlehem, which was at this time an inconsiderable place: and many think, that the word rendered
" stable," does not mean a place exclusively allotted to
cattle; but an inferior sort of receptacle for poor travellers,
in which they and the animals, which brought them, were
accommodated meanly, under the same roof.—Certainly,
the customs, in those countries, differed widely from our
manners; and some notice should be taken of this: but
a large proportion of what has been copiously written on
this subject, has arisen from a carnal notion, that so mean
a nativity did not become " the Lord of glory." (*Note,*
2 *Cor.* viii. 6—9.)

  Espoused. (5) Μεμνηστευμενη. See on i. 27.—*Great with
child.*] Εγκυω, *gravida.* Here only N. T. Ex εν et κυω.
Αποκυησιν, *Jam.* i. 18.—*Wrapped him in swaddling-clothes.*
(7) Εσπαργανωσιν. 12. Here only N. T.—*Ex.* xvi. 4. Sept.
—*Manger.*] Φατνη. 12. 16. xiii. 15. Not elsewhere N. T.
—*The inn.*] Τῳ καλαλυματι. See on *Mark* xiv. 14.

8 ¶ And there were in the same country shepherds ⁴ abiding in the field, keeping ⁵ watch over their flocks by night.

9 And, ⁶ lo, the angel of the Lord came upon them, ⁷ and the glory of the Lord shone round about them; ⁸ and they were sore afraid.

10 And the angel said unto them, ⁹ Fear not: for, behold, ¹⁰ I bring you good tidings of great joy, which shall be ⁶ to all people.

11 For ⁷ unto you is born this day ⁸ in the city of David, a Saviour, ᵇ which is Christ, ᶜ the Lord.

12 And this *shall be* ᵈ a sign unto you; Ye shall find the babe wrapped ⁶ in swaddling-clothes, lying in a manger.

13 And suddenly there was with the angel ⁶ a multitude of the heavenly host praising God and saying,

14 ⁶ Glory to God in the highest, ⁶ and on earth peace, ᵇ good-will to-wards men.

15 ¶ And it came to pass, as the angels were gone away from them ⁶ into heaven, the ⁷ shepherds said one to another, ᵏ Let us now go even unto Bethlehem, and see this thing which is to come to pass, which the Lord hath made known unto us.

16 And they came ¹ with haste, and ᵐ found Mary and Joseph, and the babe lying in a manger.

17 And when they had seen *it*, ˢʰᵉᵖʰᵉʳᵈˢ the

V. 8—14. 'As Abraham and David, to whom the pro-
'mise of the Messiah was first made, were shepherds;'
(Moses likewise might have been added, *Note, Ex.* ii. 21;)
'so was the completion of this promise first revealed to
'shepherds. ...These flocks being kept in the field, the
'shepherds watched severally in their courses, to preserve
'them from thieves, and wild beasts; and had there little
'cottages erected for that purpose.' *Whitby.*—The birth of
our Lord was attended with circumstances of external indigence and meanness: but it was also marked with a dignity and majesty, far surpassing all the pomp of kings, and
the splendour of palaces and retinues; and suited to pour
contempt on all human grandeur.—It was proper that so
important an event should be announced with peculiar
solemnity, and angels were the heralds of the new born
Saviour: but they were not sent to the rulers of the nation,
or to the priests, Scribes, and Pharisees: on the contrary,
some poor, humble, industrious shepherds were favoured
with the first tidings of Emmanuel's birth. (*Note, Matt.*
ii. 1, 2.) These were spending the night, or part of it, in
the field, keeping watch over their flocks, to defend them
from robbers and beasts of prey; and probably there was
a number of them, who watched by turns. (*Marg. and
Marg. Ref.* q.) While they were thus employed, a holy
angel suddenly appeared, and "the glory of the Lord,"
even of his manifested presence, surrounded them. (*Marg.
Ref.* r, s.) This threw them into great consternation; but
the angel encouraged them not to fear, for he was come
to bring them good tidings, which would be the source of
great and lasting joy to them, and 'to all people:' for
to them, as men, as sinners, and as believers, was born
on that day, at Bethlehem, a Saviour from wrath, Satan,
sin, and death, who was indeed the promised and expected
Messiah, Israel's anointed Prophet, Priest, and King; nay,
"the Lord of glory," "the Lord of all," "the Lord from
"heaven," "God manifest in the flesh." (*Marg. Ref.* u—
c.—*Notes, Is.* vii. 14. ix. 6, 7.) This great and invaluable
blessing to mankind, this glorious new-born Prince and

Saviour, they might find "wrapped in swaddling-clothes,
"and lying in a manger:" and they might surely know
him by this sign; for probably no other babe could be
found at Bethlehem in so mean a situation. *No sooner*
had the angel finished this address to the poor shepherds,
than he was visibly joined by "a multitude of the heavenly
"host," or of the *angelick armies*; who, being filled with
inexpressible admiration of the love of God, and the display of all his glorious perfections, in this surprising transaction, audibly celebrated his praises with triumphant acclamations, saying, "Glory to God in the highest, &c."
implying that this was the grand display of the divine glory,
and superior to all others which they had ever witnessed.
(xix. 38.) They therefore called on all the inhabitants of
the highest heavens, to praise God in their loftiest strains
of adoration: for now peace was prepared for the earth,
which had so long lain in a state of rebellion, enmity, discord and misery: peace inward and outward, with God
and with each other, would be found on earth, through
the gracious work of the divine Peace-maker, whom the
Father, out of "good-will to men," fallen men, had provided and sent among them. (*Marg. Ref.* d—f.—*Notes,
John* iii. 16. *Rom.* v. 7—10. *Eph.* i. 3—8. ii. 14—18. iii.
9—12. 1 *Pet.* i. 10—12. *Rev.* v. 11—14. xx. 4—6.)—' So
rich and free is the good-will of God to fallen men; and
such blessed peace, external and internal, will eventually
be produced on earth; that the glory of God will be more
displayed and adored, in this, than in all his other works.'
—This seems the purport of these angelick praises; but
the abrupt, sententious manner, in which they were delivered, whilst it rendered them more suited to their fervent acclamations, increases the difficulty of unfolding the
full meaning of each expression. (*Note, Ps.* lxxxv. 10—13.)

Abiding in the field. (8) Αγραυλουντες. Here only N. T. Ex
αγρος, *ager,* et αυλιζομαι, *stabulor, dego.*—*In the highest.* (14)
Εν υψιστοις. xix. 38. *Matt.* xxi, 9. *Mark* xi. 10.—*Job* xvi. 19.
Sept.—*Good-will.*] Ευδοκια. See on *Matt.* xi. 26.

V. 15—20. When the angels had rendered their joyful

ⁿ "they made known abroad the saying which was told them concerning this child.

18 And all they that heard *it*, °wondered at those things, which were told them by the shepherds.

19 But ᵖMary kept all these things, and pondered *them* in her heart.

20 And the shepherds returned, ᑫglorifying and praising God for all the things that they had heard and seen, as it was told unto them.

21 ¶ And when ʳeight days were accomplished for the circumcising of the child, ˢhis name was called JESUS, which was so named ,of the angel before he was conceived in the womb.

22 And when ᵗthe days of her purification, according to the law of Moses,

were accomplished, they brought him to Jerusalem, to present *him* to the Lord;

23 (As it is written in the law of the Lord, "Every male that openeth the womb shall be called holy to the Lord ;)

24 And to offer a sacrifice according to that which is said in the law of the Lord, ˣA pair of turtle-doves, or two young pigeons.

25 ¶ And, behold, there was a man in Jerusalem, whose name *was* Simeon: and the same man *was* ʸjust and devout, ᶻwaiting for the consolation of Israel: ᵃand the Holy Ghost was upon him.

26 And ᵇit was revealed unto him by the Holy Ghost, that he should not

---

adorations of God, and benevolent congratulations to men, on this most happy occasion, the vision disappeared: and the shepherds, conferring together on the wonders which they had witnessed, determined to go immediately to Bethlehem; where they were soon enabled to find Mary, Joseph, and the new-born Saviour, exactly in the situation which had been described. Having witnessed this instructive scene, they publickly reported the whole transaction, and the assurance given them that this child was " the Saviour," even " Christ, the Lord." This excited the astonishment of all who heard it: but most of them seem to have speedily forgotten it. (*Marg.* and *Marg. Ref.* i—o.) Mary, however, carefully observed, and meditated on, all these wonderful incidents, which were so suited to enlarge her expectations and enliven her holy affections: and the shepherds returned to their humble employment, with joyful, thankful hearts, glorifying and blessing God for his distinguished favours to them. (*Marg. Ref.* p, q.—51.)

Kept, &c. (19) Συντηρει. *Mark* vi. 20. Διετηρει, 51.—*Pondered.*] Συμβαλλουσα. (Εκ συν, et βαλλω.) xiv. 31. *Acts* iv. 15. xvii. 18. xviii. 27. xx. 14.—The word is peculiar to St. Luke, and in this place seems to imply, a careful and persevering consideration of all circumstances, relating to these interesting events; with a diligent comparison of each part with all the rest. (1 *Cor.* ii. 13.)

V. 21. Our blessed Saviour was not conceived or born in sin, and did not need that mortification of a corrupt nature, or that renewal unto holiness, which were signified by circumcision. (*Marg. Ref.* r.—*Notes*, i. 57—66. *Gen.* xvii. 9—12.) But he was " made under the law," and, both as our Surety and Example, he was subjected to all its institutions. (*Note*, *Gal.* iv. 4, 5.) This painful ordinance was, *in his case*, a pledge given of his future perfect obedience to the whole law, (*Gal.* v. 3,) in the midst of sufferings and temptations, even unto death for us; and it was an entrance on that vicarious work which he finished on the cross.—The name JESUS has already been explained. (*Note*, *Matt.* i. 20, 21.)—*Eight.*]

' That is, not when the eighth day was ended, but when ' it was come.' *Whitby.* This illustrates the expression " after three days," as used concerning our Lord's resurrection. (*Note*, *Mark* viii. 31.)

V. 22—24. (*Marg. Ref.—Notes*, *Ex.* xiii. 2. 11—16. *Lev.* xii. 2—5.)—At the end of forty days, Mary went up to the temple, to offer the appointed sacrifices for her purification: for though in her case, there were not the same reasons for that observance, as in that of other women, yet she claimed no exemption. Joseph also attended her, taking the holy child Jesus; because, being a first-born Son, he was to be presented to the Lord and redeemed according to the law.—*A pair*, &c. (24) *Note*, *Lev.* xii. 6—8. ' This, being the oblation appointed only for the poor, ' discovers the poverty of Joseph and Mary, that they ' could not reach to a lamb of the first year, the offering ' which they who had ability were to make.' *Whitby.*—*Every male*, &c. (23) The quotation is not made either from the Septuagint or the Hebrew: but the general meaning of several texts is condensed into one. (*Marg. Ref.* u.)

Of her purification. (22) Τη καθαρισμη αυτης. v. 14. *Mark* i. 44. *John* ii. 6. iii. 25. *Heb.* i. 3. 2 *Pet.* i. 9.—1 *Chr.* xxiii. 28. *Neh.* xii. 45. *Sept.*—' The ancient reading was ' αυτων' (*their*) :...' nor is there any fear of ascribing any ' moral impurity to the holy Jesus, by allowing this read- ' ing; since this purgation imports only a compliance with ' a ceremonial law, in order to their admittance into the ' congregation of God's people ; to which Christ, being " made of a woman, made under the law," was to sub- ' mit, that he might " fulfil all righteousness;" on which ' account also, he was made relatively holy, by being con- ' secrated to the Lord, according to the law concerning " every male that openeth the womb." ' *Whitby.—The womb.* *Rom.* iv. 19. Not elsewhere N. T.—*Ex.* xiii. 2. *Sept.*

V. 25—32. The Jewish priests and scribes remained ignorant of the birth of the promised Messiah, till some time after this. (*Notes*, *Matt.* ii. 1—12.) But there was

e Ix. 2 Ps. ' see death, before he had seen ⁴ the Lord's Christ.

27 And he came ⁵ by the Spirit into the temple: and when ⁶ the parents brought in the child Jesus, ⁷ to do for him after the custom of the law,

28 Then ⁸ took he him up in his arms, ⁹ and blessed God, and said,

29 Lord, ᵏ now lettest thou thy servant depart in peace, ˡ according to thy word;

30 For ᵐ mine eyes have seen thy Salvation,

31 Which ⁿ thou hast prepared before the face of all people;

32 A °Light to lighten the Gentiles, ᵖ and the Glory of thy people Israel.

33 And ᑫ Joseph and his mother marvelled at those things which were ʳ spoken of him.

34 And Simeon ᶠ blessed them, and said unto Mary his mother, Behold, this *child* is ˢ set for the fall ᵗ and rising again of many in Israel; and ᵘ for a sign which shall be spoken against; ˣ

35 (Yea, ᵞ a sword shall pierce through thy own soul also;) ᶻ that the thoughts of many hearts may be revealed.

---

a small remnant, who had more spiritual views and expectations; and to them it pleased God to give intimations of what had taken place. Among these was Simeon; concerning whom many vain conjectures have been formed by those, who would represent the eminent believers mentioned in the Bible, as persons who stood very high in the world's esteem: but we know no more of him than what is here recorded. He was strictly just and upright in his whole conduct, and a devoted worshipper of God: yet he did not rest in these attainments; but expected the coming of the Messiah, as " the consolation of Israel," and the source of all their hopes and comforts. (*Notes,* 36—38. *Acts* x. 1, 2.) Simeon was likewise endued with the Spirit of prophecy; (which had begun to be restored, after a suspension of nearly four hundred years, from the days of Malachi;) and by immediate inspiration he was assured, that he should not die, till " he had seen the Lord's " Christ," or Anointed, the promised Messiah. Thus, under the guidance of the Holy Spirit, he came to the temple, at the very time when Joseph and Mary presented Jesus there; and so he witnessed the first accomplishment of a very remarkable prophecy concerning him. (*Note, Hag.* ii. 6—9.) Seeing, therefore, the infant Redeemer, and knowing who he was by the inspiration of the Holy Spirit, he " took him in his arms," and " blessed God " for his mercies to him and to his people; expressing himself willing, nay desirous, to die, seeing the Lord now " let " him depart in peace," having favoured him with the sight of " his Salvation." (*Marg. Ref.* y—g.—*Notes, Is.* xii. 2. xlv. 8. 15—17. 20—25. *Hos.* i. 6, 7. *Zech.* ix. 9, 10. *Matt.* i. 20, 21. *Acts* iv. 5—12. *Tit.* ii. 13,14. iii. 4— 7.) The Lord Jesus himself is here called " the Salvation " of God," because the whole salvation of a sinner centres in his person, as " God manifest in the flesh;" all the purposes and promises of salvation had reference to him; he obtained all the blessings of it by shedding his blood; they are all treasured up in him, and dispensed by him to believers; and they are all applied, through the operation of the Holy Spirit, who is given to us through his in'ercession.—Thus Simeon acknowledged Jesus " as God's " Salvation, which he had prepared before the face of all " people;" as the Lord intended to exhibit him publickly, before all nations, by the preaching of the gospel: for, as

" the Light of the world," (*Notes, Is.* ix. 2. xlii. 5—7. xlix. 5, 6. lx. 1—3. *John* i. 4—9. iii. 19—21. viii. 12. xii. 34—36,) he was intended to illuminate all nations by his doctrine and grace, and also to be " the Glory of his " people Israel." The chief honour of that nation consisted in having given birth to this glorious Saviour; and all true believers deem their relation to him their grand distinction, and learn to glory in him alone. (*Marg. Ref.* k.m— p.—*Notes, Rom.* iv. 4, 5. *Phil.* iii. 1—7, *v.* 3.)—No doubt the Spirit of prophecy opened to Simeon's enlarged view, the glorious and blessed consequences, both to Israel, and the gentiles, in all subsequent generations, arising from the birth of the child which he held in his arms: and joyfully anticipating these glories and blessings, he counted himself to have lived long enough upon earth, and was ready for the society, worship, and joy of heaven, to join the songs of " the heavenly host," who had before sang at his birth, " Glory to God in the highest, and on earth " peace, good will to men." (14)—' It is wonderful that, ' after so many clear prophecies, in the Old Testament, of ' the calling of the Gentiles, the Jews should have been all ' so blind, as to imagine God had no kindness for them.' *Whitby.*—It is likewise worth enquiring, in this view, how far the bulk of professed Christians also may be blinded by prejudice, concerning many things as plainly revealed in the New Testament.

Devout. (25) Ευλαβης. *Acts* ii. 5. viii. 2. Not elsewhere *N. T.* Ευλαβεομαι, *Acts* xxiii. 10. *Heb.* v. 7.—*Waiting.*] Προσδεχομενος. See on *Mark* xv. 43.—*Revealed.* (26) Κεχρηματισμενον. See on *Acts* xi. 26.—*Lord.* (29) Δεσποτα. *Acts* iv. 24. 2 *Tim.* ii. 21. 2 *Pet.* ii. 1. *Jude* 4. *Rev.* vi. 10. *Plur.* 1 *Tim.* vi. 1, 2, &c.—*Lettest...depart.* (19) Απολυεις. vi. 37. xiii. 12. *Matt.* i. 19. xviii. 27. xxvii. 21. *Acts* v. 40. xvi. 35, 36.—' It ' signifies, a release from a sorrowful and dark prison, ' such as this wretched life certainly is.' *Victor Strig.* in *Leigh.* The forgiveness of sin, and deliverance from sin, are also implied, and an entrance into perfect peace, and felicity: else death would not be such a release.—*To lighten.* (32) Εις αποκαλυψιν. *In patefactionem rei opertæ. Rom.* ii. 5. viii. 19. xvi. 25. *Gal.* i. 12. *Eph.* i. 17. iii. 3. 2 *Thes.* i. 7. 1 *Pet.* i. 7. 13. iv. 13. *Rev.* i. 1.

V. 33—35. While Joseph and Mary were astonished

36 ¶ And there was one Anna, 'a prophetess, the daughter of Phanuel, of the tribe of ᵃAser; ᵇshe was of a great age, and had lived with an husband seven years from her virginity:

37 And she *was* a widow of about fourscore and four years, ᶜwhich departed not from the temple, ᵈbut served God with fastings and prayers night and day.

38 And she ᵉ coming in that instant ᶠgave thanks likewise unto the Lord, and spake of him to all them that ᵍ looked for redemption in ᵍJerusalem.

39 ¶ And when they had ʰperformed all things according to the law of the

[marginal references:]
Ex. xv. 20. Judg. iv. 4. 2 Kings xxii. 14.
Acts ii. 18. xxi.
9. 1 Cor. xii. 1.
a Gen. xxx. 13.
Asher. Rev. vii. 6.
b Job v. 26. Ps. xcii. 14.
c Ex. xxxviii. 8. 1 Sam. ii. 22. Ps. xxiii. 6.
xxvii. 4 lxxxiv.
4. 10. xcii. 13.
cxxxv. 1, 2. Rev. iii. 12.
d Ps. xxii. 2. Acts xxvi. 7. 1 Tim. v. 5. Rev. vii. 15.

[second set:]
f 27.
2 ... 22. 1. 46. &c.
64, &c. 2 Cor.
i. 5. Eph. i. 3.
1b. xxiii. 51.
xxiv. 21. Mark
xv. 43.
g Or, Israel.
21—24.
Deut. xii. 32.
Matt. iii. 15.
Gal. iv. 4, 5.

at the words which Simeon addressed to the Infant in his arms; he blessed them also, praying for them and expressing his satisfaction in their felicity. (*Marg. Ref.* r.) He then assured his mother, that her Son was placed for " the fall and rising again of many in Israel." Many of them would reject, despise, persecute, and crucify him, through the pride and enmity of their hearts against the truth; thus they would fall into sin and under condemnation, and this would terminate in the temporal ruin of the nation, as well as in the perdition of many souls: but, at the same time, numbers of those who had sunk deep into error, profligacy, and impiety; yea, many who at first rejected and persecuted him, would at length repent, and by faith in him would obtain pardon, and so be raised up again to " walk in newness of life." Yet he would be set " for a sign which should be spoken against," the very butt of contradiction and opposition, to all orders and descriptions of men. His external meanness, his holy character, his humbling doctrine, and his spiritual salvation, proved equally offensive to the Pharisees and Sadducees; and interfered as much with the reputation, interests, and authority of the hypocritical priests and scribes, as with the carnal prejudices of the nation in general. Notwithstanding the distinguished honour conferred on Mary, she must expect to witness such things, from the cruelty and enmity of the people and rulers against her Son, as would, like a sword, pierce her soul with the most exquisite anguish. This must have been emphatically the case, when she stood by the cross on which he suffered. (*Notes*, *Ps.* xlii. 9, 10. *John* xix. 25—27.)—It is also probable that she was exposed to persecution among the primitive Christians: and some of the ancients report that she at length died a martyr; but this must be allowed to be uncertain.—The event of the ministry of Jesus, and of the dispensation which he came to introduce, would also be that " the thoughts of many hearts would be revealed," or " the imaginations and reasonings which secretly occupied men's minds detected. The plausible characters of numbers would thus be shewn to be leavened with pride, malice, covetousness, and hypocrisy; while the humility, faith, and piety of others, who had been disregarded, would thus be brought forth and made manifest. (*Marg. Ref.* s—y.)—*This*, &c. (34) ' Neither look that he shall ' be applauded of all; yea rather, he shall be as a common ' mark, whereat the arrows of contumely and reproach ' shall be generally shot, throughout the world: and his ' name and religion shall be sure to receive opposition and ' contradiction, every where. And thereby men shall be ' tried, and occasions shall be given them, to shew either ' the truth or falsehood of their hearts, towards his name ' and profession.' *Bp. Hall.* (*Notes, Is.* viii. 11—15. 1 *Pet.* ii. 7, 8.)

The fall. (34) Πτωσιν. *Matt.* vii. 27. Not elsewhere N. T.—*Rising again.*] Αναστασιν, *resurrectionem. Matt.* xxii. 23. 28.—*Rom.* vi. 5. 2 *Tim.* ii. 18. *Heb.* xi. 38. *Rev.* xx. 5, 6.—*Which shall be spoken against.*] Αντιλεγομενον. xx. 27. *John* xix. 12. *Acts* xiii. 45. xxviii. 19. 22. *Rom.* x. 21. *Tit.* i. 9. ii. 9.—*Is.* l. 5. *Sept.*—*A sword.* (35) 'Ρομφαια. ' Proprie, telum, *seu* jaculum longum nationis ' *Thraciæ;* item, *genus gladii oblongi.*' Schleusner. *Rev.* i. 16. ii. 12. 16. vi. 8. xix. 15. 21.—*The thoughts.*] Διαλογισμοι. See on *Mark* vii. 21. ' It ... signifieth more than ' thoughts, even reasonings, disputations, discourses, done ' with weighing and poising things.' Leigh. " That rea- " soning out of many hearts may be revealed."—*May be revealed.*] Αποκαλυφθωσιν. See on *Matt.* xvi. 17.

V. 36—38. The Lord was pleased to confirm Simeon's testimony to Christ, by that of Anna. She was a prophetess, and probably known to be so. (*Marg. Ref.* z.)—Phanuel seems to have been an eminent person of the tribe of Asher. Anna, having lost her husband in the prime of her life, continued a widow to her death. Some think that eighty-four years had elapsed from the death of her husband; others suppose her to have been eighty-four years of age. She resided near the temple, that she might attend on all its sacred ordinances; and, having no relative engagements to occupy her attention, she spent her whole time in the worship and service of God: and, joining frequent fastings with her constant prayers and supplications, for herself and her people, she employed the day, and often part of the night also, in these religious exercises; not desisting from them even on account of the infirmities of advanced age. (*Marg. Ref.* a—d.—*Notes, Dan.* ix. 2, 3. x. 2, 3. 1 *Tim.* v. 5, 6.) This devoted person came into the temple at the same time, when Simeon was speaking concerning Jesus; and she also returned thanks to God for sending the promised Saviour, and for favouring her with a sight of him: and she spake of him to all the pious remnant, with whom she was acquainted, and who waited for a spiritual redemption in Jerusalem: for most of the citizens were looking only for a temporal prince and deliverer. (*Marg. Ref.* f, g.—*Note,* 25—32.)

Served God. (37) Λατρευουσα. i. 74. iv. 8. *Acts* xxiv. 14. *Phil.* iii. 3. 2 *Tim.* i. 3. *Rev.* vii. 15. xxii. 3.—*Gave thanks.* (38) Ανθωμολογειτο. Here only N. T. Εx αντι, et ομολογεομαι. *Matt.* vii. 23. x. 32. See on *Matt.* xi. 25, 26. She confessed in concert with Simeon to the Lord Christ, (τψ Κυριψ,) and spake of him. Some think, that she addressed the infant Jesus, as Simeon had done.

V. 39. After these remarkable occurrences, and the completion of all things respecting Jesus and Mary, according to the law, Joseph and Mary left Jerusalem; and it is said that " they returned ... to Nazareth:" but St.

2 s 7

i 4. Matt. ii. 22,
23.

k 52. Judg. xiii.
24. 1 Sam. ii.
18, 26. iii. 19.
Ps. xxii. 9, 10.
ia. liii. 1, 2.
l 1. 80. Eph. vi.
10. 2 Tim. ii. l.
m 47. Is. xi. 1—3.
Col. ii. 2, 3.
n Ps. xiv. 2. John
30. 14. Acts iv.

o Ex. xxiii. 14—
17. Deut. xii. 5
—7. 11. 16. xvi.
1—8. 1 Sam. i.
3, 21.
A. D. 8.
p Ex. xii. 14. Lev.
xxiii. 5, 6. Num.
xxviii. 16. John
ii. 13.

q 2 Chr. xxx. 21
—23. xxxv. 17.

r Ps. xlii. 4. cxxii.
1—4. Is. ii. 3.

s 44. 45. 1 Kings
xii. 5, 12. Matt.
xii. 40. xvi. 21.
xxvii. 63, 64.

Lord, [i] they returned into Galilee, to their own city Nazareth.

40 And [k] the child grew, and waxed [l] strong in spirit, [m] filled with wisdom: and [n] the grace of God was upon him.

41 ¶ Now his parents [o] went to Jerusalem every year at [p] the feast of the passover.

42 And when he was twelve years old, they went up to Jerusalem, after the custom of the feast.

43 And when they had [q] fulfilled the days, as they returned, the child Jesus tarried behind in Jerusalem; and Joseph and his mother knew not *of it.*

44 But they, supposing him to have been [r] in the company, went a day's journey; and they sought him among *their* kinsfolk and acquaintance.

45 And when they found him not, they turned back again to Jerusalem seeking him.

46 And it came to pass, that [s] after three days they found him in the tem-

ple, sitting in the midst of [t] the doctors, [u] both hearing them, and asking them questions.

47 And all that heard him, [x] were astonished at his understanding and answers.

48 And when they saw him, they were amazed: and his mother said unto him, Son, why hast thou thus dealt with us? behold, thy father and I have sought thee sorrowing.

49 And he said unto them, How is it that ye sought me? wist ye not that I must be about [y] my Father's business?

50 And they [z] understood not the saying which he spake unto them.

51 And he went down with them, [a] and [b] came to Nazareth, [b] and was subject unto them: but his mother [c] kept all these sayings in her heart.

52 And [d] Jesus increased in wisdom and [e] stature, [e] and in favour with God and man.

t v. 17. Acts v. 34.

u Is xlix. 1, 2. l.
4.

x iv. 22, 32. Matt.
vii. 28. Mark i.
22. John vii. 15.
46.

y 48. Ps. xl. 8.
Mal. iii. 1, 2.
Matt. xxi. 12.
John ii. 16, 17.
viii. 29.

z ix. 45. xviii. 34.

a 89.
b Matt. in. 15
Mark vi. 3.
Eph. v. 21. vi.
1, 2. 1 Pet. ii.
21.

c 19. Gen. xxxvii.
11. Dan. vii. 28.

d 40. i. 80. 1 Sam.
ii. 26.
e Or. age.
Prov. iii. 3, 4.
Acts vii. 9, 10.
Rom. xiv. 18.

Luke passes over the coming of the wise men, and the flight of the holy family into Egypt; for it is evident, that this return to Nazareth did not occur till some time afterwards. Probably they returned to Bethlehem, supposing that Jesus was there to be educated. After some time the wise men arrived, and then, by the divine monition, they fled into Egypt, and on their return went to reside at Nazareth. (Notes, Matt. ii.)

V. 40. Jesus grew in strength and stature like other children; and at the same time " waxed strong in spirit." (Note, i. 80.) It was manifest, that as the faculties of his human soul unfolded, all holy affections and dispositions became proportionably vigorous : he was also filled with wisdom and knowledge, and all his words and actions were regulated in perfect conformity to the divine law, so that the special favour of God evidently rested on him.—As to the manner, in which the indwelling Deity gradually communicated knowledge, wisdom, and holiness to the human nature of Christ, we must confess that we know nothing. " Without controversy great is the mystery of " godliness, God was manifest in the flesh." (Note, 1 Tim. iii. 16.) That, as Man, his wisdom and knowledge could not be infinite, or incapable of increase, we know: but how the union was formed, or the communications imparted, we cannot, in the smallest degree, comprehend or explain. (Marg. Ref.)

V. 41—52. These verses contain all, which the Spirit of God has seen good to record, concerning the childhood and youth of the divine Saviour: though we should have expected fuller information; and desired a more adequate gratification of our curiosity, on so extraordinary a subject. Joseph, his father-in-law, and Mary his mother, used to go up to Jerusalem every year at the feast of the

passover. (Marg. Ref. o, p.—Notes, Ex. xxiii. 14—18. Deut. xvi. 1—17. 1 Sam. i. 3. 19—22.) Perhaps Joseph went up at the other great feasts: but, though the women were not required, Mary, and many others who loved the ordinances of God, used to attend at the feast of the passover. And when Jesus was twelve years old, he went up with them; for it seems to have been the custom for young persons to accompany their parents at that age. When the days of unleavened bread 'were expired, they set out on their return home: and as great numbers came to Jerusalem from every part of the country, they journeyed in a great company, for mutual security: so that they departed without the child Jesus, who stayed behind; being engaged with the sacred ordinances and conversation, which attended the observation of the festival. Perhaps there was some culpable inattention in Joseph and Mary: for they took it for granted that he was in the company, among some of their neighbours and relations, who doubtless greatly delighted in his conversation, so that they travelled a whole day's journey before they missed him. But when in the evening the several families separated for the night, they could not find him : and they returned to Jerusalem, with great anxiety and under many apprehensions. At length, however, after two days, spent in journeying and returning, on the third day, probably towards night, they found him : not in the house of any acquaintance, nor in such places as young people generally frequent ; but in some court, or chamber, of the temple, sitting amidst the doctors or teachers of the law; diligently hearkening to their discussions and instructions, modestly proposing questions to them on various subjects, and pertinently answering the enquiries which were put to him : and this he did with such wisdom and

CHAP. III.

The time when John the Baptist entered on his ministry, 1, 2. His preaching and exhortations, 3—

14. His testimony to Jesus, 15—18. He is put in prison by Herod, 19, 20. Christ is baptized and receives testimony from heaven, 21, 22. His genealogy is traced back to Adam, 23—38.

propriety, that all who heard him were astonished and delighted with him. (*Marg. Ref.* s—x.)—Thus he was pleased to emit some beams of his heavenly light and glory, even in his early youth; both to raise the expectation of the Jews, and to give a proper example to young people, for the regulation of their enquiries, employments, and behaviour.—The common expression by which he is represented, as ' disputing with the doctors,' is calculated to give wrong ideas on the subject, and very contrary to those which naturally present themselves to the mind on reading this account. ' Not one word is said of his *dis-*' *puting*, by the evangelist, ... but only of his asking some ' questions, and answering others, which was a very usual ' thing in these assemblies, and indeed the very end of ' them. All was no doubt conducted with the utmost mo-' desty and decorum. And if he ' (Jesus) ' were with ' others at the feet of these teachers,' (where learners generally sat, x. 39. *Acts* xxii. 3,) ' he might be said to be ' " in the midst of them," as they sat on benches of a se-' micircular form, raised above their auditors and disci-' ples.' *Doddridge.* It is indeed astonishing, that any one should conceive of the child Jesus as placing himself among the teachers, on the same seat; or of his being allowed to do it, and so to enter on disputes with them! —When, however, Joseph and Mary saw Jesus, they were exceedingly surprised; and his mother, in a way of gentle rebuke, enquired of him, " Why he had thus dealt with " them ; " adding " Behold, thy father and I have sought " thee *sorrowing*," or in great anguish of mind. To this he answered by enquiring " wherefore they sought him : " did they not know, that he must be engaged in his Fa-" ther's business ? " i. e. in those places, and in those things, which related to his worship and service. In this he had been, and must at all times be, employed ; this they would have known, had they duly attended to the various prophecies, and to the words of the angel Gabriel, concerning him : and with this no regard to any earthly relation must be allowed to interfere. (*Marg. Ref.* y.) This expression also intimated that he was in every sense " the Son of God." However, neither Joseph nor Mary at that time fully understood his meaning, having still many prejudices, and much darkness upon their minds, as to those subjects: yet Mary carefully remembered, and deeply meditated on, all these sayings of her Son. (*Note,* 15—20, *v.* 19.) But, though in this one instance he shewed the superior obligation of his great work, to any authority, even that of a parent; yet he went down to Nazareth, and was in every thing else subject, not only to Mary, but to Joseph also : and it is probably reported, that he earned his livelihood by working as a carpenter, in making plows and yokes, till his entrance on his publick ministry. (*Note, Mark* vi. 1—4.)—He still continued to increase in wisdom, as well as in stature; and was, as Man, proportionably more worthy of the divine favour, as well as more dear to all who knew him. (*Marg.* and *Marg. Ref.* d, e.—*Note,* 40.— 1 *Sam.* ii. 26.)

The company. (44) Συνοδια. Here only N. T.—*Neh.* vii. 5. *Sept.* Εκ συν, et ὁδος, *via, iter :* συνοδευοντες, *Acts* ix.

7.—*They were amazed.* (48) Εξεπλαγησαν. ix. 43. *Matt.* vii. 28. xiii. 54. xix. 25. xxii. 33, *et al.*—*Sorrowing.*] Οδυνω-μενοι. (Ab οδυνη, *cruciatus.*) xvi. 24, 25. *Acts* xx. 38. Not elsewhere N. T.—*About my Father's business.*] Εν τοις τε Πατρος μω, in my " Father's house ; " " in those things," or places, " which are my Father's."—*Increased.* (52) Προκοπτε. *Rom.* xiii. 12. *Gal.* i. 14. 2 *Tim.* ii. 16. iii. 9. 13.

PRACTICAL OBSERVATIONS.

V. 1—7.

The omniscient God foresees and permits the innumerable volitions of free agents, and over-rules them for the accomplishment of his own righteous purposes : and thus he performs his prophecies and confirms his truth, even by wicked men, and by events which seem to us most casual. But who would have expected, that " the Lord " of glory," whom " all the angels of God worship," when he became a Child and was " made of a woman," would have been lodged in a stable, or laid in a manger ? Yet this was but a faint shadow of " his grace, who though " he were rich, yet for our sakes became poor, that we " through his poverty might be made rich." (*Notes, John* xiii. 1—5. 2 *Cor.* viii. 6—9, *v.* 9. *Phil.* ii. 5—8. *Heb.* ii. 10—13.) He well knew how wealth and magnificence glitter in our eyes, and fascinate our vain minds; how unwilling we are to be poor, and to be meanly lodged, clothed, or fed ; how we desire to have our children decorated and indulged; how apt the poor are to envy the rich, and to repine at their own condition ; how prone the rich are to disdain the poor, and how backward to " condescend " to men of low estate." He was aware what deference would be paid, even by his ministers and disciples, to the wealthy and the noble ; and what an *improper* distinction would be made between them and the indigent, even in religious societies and places of worship. (*Note, Jam.* ii. 1—4.) Too much of these evils are every where to be seen: and they must have been much more predominant, had our Lord appeared on earth, attended with outward splendour and magnificence. But his condition, from his birth in a stable to his death upon the cross, was suited to expose the vanity of outward distinctions, and to ennoble and dignify poverty and all its mean attendants. When we by faith view the incarnate Son of God lying in a manger, we cannot but feel a check given to our vanity and ambition, and our coveting and envying ; our souls must in some degree grow more weaned from the world : we cannot, with this object before our eyes, " seek great " things," for ourselves or our children ; or disdain the poor believer : we cannot flatter the rich or honourable, or refuse respect to those, who are the most apt representatives of our poor and suffering Redeemer : and we should be more effectually delivered from such errors in judgment and practice, did we more fully " ponder these things in " our hearts."—But while, with admiring gratitude, we contemplate the Saviour's condescension, in thus enduring all to which sin had exposed us, from his birth to his death, let us not forget to copy the meekness and patience of his virgin-mother : she willingly endured fatigue, cou-

s ii. 7.
xxiii. 1—4. 24. NOW in the fifteenth year of the late being governor of Judea, *and c 19. ix. 7. xxiii.
2b. Gen. xlix. reign of *Tiberius Cæsar, *Pontius Pi- Herod being tetrarch of Galilee, and *—11.
10. Acts iv. 27.
xxiii. 36. xxiv. 27. xxvi. 30.

tempt, and neglect, and contentedly was lodged in a stable;
and she met the pains of child-birth in that incommodious
situation, without complaining of the unkindness of the citizens of Bethlehem.—If any persons, when performing
the tender duties of the parental character, should be ready
to complain, that their beloved offspring are not provided
for as they could wish; let them think of Mary, wrapping
her holy babe in swaddling clothes, and laying him in the
manger: this will silence the rising murmur, or change it
into admiring praise. And, whilst we contrast her conduct with that of those, who at that time shut their doors
against the most excellent and honoured persons who ever
visited the city, that they might entertain the sons and
daughters of pride and affluence; let us learn to "use
"hospitality without grudging," especially to poor believers; and, instead of feasting the rich with ostentatious
expense, let us entertain Christ in the person of his
poor disciples. Thus we shall approve ourselves "fol-
"lowers of God, as dear children," and ensure a gracious
recompense at the "resurrection of the just." (*Note*, xiv.
12—14. *P. O.* 12—24.)

V. 8—14.

We should learn to judge and act as holy angels do:
they did not regard the holy family the less, for being
lodged in a stable: nay, the humility and abasement, which
veiled the Saviour's glory as he lay in the manger, made it
in their eyes more admirable; and he never appeared so
honourable and excellent, according to their judgment,
as in that situation, except when he hung expiring upon
the cross for our sins, and praying for his crucifiers. These
blessed spirits were perfectly satisfied to announce his
birth to poor shepherds in the field, rather than to such
as inhabited palaces, or even to those who were lodged in
the precincts of the temple: for humble and simple piety,
and honest industry, are more approved by the inhabitants
of heaven, than all the dignities and wisdom of the world.
(*Note*, Heb. i. 13, 14.) The angels delight in contemplating the mysteries of redeeming love; and in celebrating
the praises of God, for those displays of his glory, in
which they are not personally interested: and they still,
as it were, proclaim in our ears, "To you is born a Sa-
"viour, who is Christ, the Lord." These then ought to be
glad tidings to all who hear them, and they will give
great joy to all who believe them: for in them all our
hopes centre, and from them all our comforts flow.—What
an auspicious morning was that, which brought so great
a blessing to lost mankind! How joyful was that day,
which first conveyed the sound of the gospel to our ears!
But most happy for us the hour, in which we were enabled to believe in Christ for the salvation of our souls.
Unless this has been vouchsafed, we can have no reason
to celebrate the nativity of Jesus with rejoicings; for that
event will enhance the guilt and condemnation of unbelievers: and if real Christians deem it proper to commemorate it, at a season set apart for that purpose; they
will not do it with bacchanalian revels or luxurious feast-
ings; but with more abundant thanksgivings to God, and

liberality to the poor. They will join their feeble lispings
to the songs of angels, and with adoring, grateful acclamations repeat, "Glory to God in the highest, on earth
"peace, good-will towards men:" they will employ their
prayers, examples, and endeavours, to give glory to God,
by doing what they can to make known the gospel to those
who sit in darkness all over the world, by seeking the
peace of his church, and by copying his good-will to men;
and thus they will ripen for the joys of heaven, by their
worship and services here on earth.

V. 15—24.

When we are favoured with peculiar discoveries of the
glory of the Lord, and of his love to us, we should excite
one another to a more unreserved attention to his directions; we should examine more fully those things which
he has made known to us, and seek to have our faith confirmed by experience; we should endeavour to report to
others, what he has taught us concerning the divine Saviour; and, pondering such things in our hearts, we should
return from holy ordinances to our secular employments,
glorifying God for all we have heard and experienced.—
While we trust in the perfect righteousness of our divine
Surety, we ought to copy his example; seeking the true
circumcision of the heart, the genuine purification from
the pollution of sin, and the dedication of body and soul
to God, which were shadowed forth in the ancient types
and institutions of the Mosaick law. We ought also to
present our children to the Lord, who gave them to us;
desiring that he would redeem them from sin and death,
make them holy to himself, and number them with "the
"church of the first-born, whose names are written in
"heaven:" and such poor services, if they be the fruit of
a humble and upright heart, will not be rejected. (*Notes*,
Matt. xix. 13—15. Mark x. 13—16.)

V. 25—40.

Professing to depend on the salvation of the Lord, and
to "wait for the consolation of Israel;" justice, truth,
and mercy, as well as piety, should adorn our conduct:
and if the Holy Spirit rest upon us, our feet will be directed to the courts and ordinances of the Lord. In this
way we shall experience the fulfilment of the promises:
and if we embrace, as it were, the Saviour, in the arms of
faith, hope, and love, we shall meet death bereaved of his
sting, and be willing to leave this world and go to heaven;
provided our work be done, and God be pleased to dismiss
us to his heavenly rest. (*Note*, Heb. iv. 3—11.) Blessed
be his name, that this Salvation "is prepared before the
"face of all people," and that this Light hath lightened
our Gentile land: may we become a part of the true
Israel, who glory in Christ alone! (*Note, Phil.* iii. 1—7,
v. 3.)—But let us not look merely on one side of this subject. This blessed gospel eventually occasions the fall of
many professed Christians, who neglect, despise, or pervert
so great salvation: as well as causes the rising again of
many, who were sunk deep into guilt and impiety. Still
Jesus, and his doctrine and people, are placed for a "sign,

2 T 2

^{d Matt. xiv. 3.} ^{Mark vi. 17.} ^e his brother Philip tetrarch of Iturea and of the region of Trachonitis, and ^{• John xi. 49—51. xviii. 13, 14. 24.} ^{Acts iv. 6.} Lysanias the tetrarch of Abilene, 2 [•] Annas and Caiaphas being the high priests, ^f the word of God came unto John the son of Zacharias,[,] ^g in the wilderness.

3 And he came into all ^h the coun-

^{f 1. 59—62. Jer. 1. 2. ii. 1. Ez. i. 3. Hos. i. 1, 2. g Joe. 1. 1. Mic. i. 1. Zeph. i. 1. g 1. 80. iii. 2. 3 Matt. iii. 1. xi. 7. Mark i. 3 7. Mark i. 3 John i. 28. iii. 26}

^{John i. 23. h Matt. iii. 5, 6. Mark i. 5. John i. 28. iii. 26}

"that is every where spoken against;" still his truth and holiness are contradicted and blasphemed; still the preaching of his word is the touch-stone of men's characters, and often brings to light the secret pride, enmity, and wickedness of their hearts; still they, who are blessed by their relation to Jesus and union with him, must expect to witness and experience such things in this evil world, as will wound and distress their souls; and still they must prepare to endure contradiction, reproach, and contempt, because they resemble their blessed Saviour.—We should be careful how we indiscriminately condemn practices, or modes of life, because many have disgraced them: for who can refuse a tribute of commendation to the pious Anna? When the relative and social duties have been attended to, or as far as consists with a due performance of them, it is very proper to spend the decline of life especially, in retirement and devotion: and to serve God with fastings and prayers, day and night, as connected with deep humility, and a readiness to welcome Christ and his Salvation, and to speak of him to all who wait for his redemption, must be allowed to be essentially different, from the proud austerities, and hypocritical devotions of self-righteous Pharisees, ancient and modern. But, whether zeal against the latter has not led many persons to *overlook* and even *despise* the former, instead of considering them, *in similar circumstances*, as models for imitation, is a question which ought seriously to be examined. They, however, who are most mortified to the world, and abstracted from it, or abundant in every good work from proper principles, will with one consent bear testimony to Christ, " as the end of the law, for righteousness to every " one that believeth." (*Note, Rom.* x. 1—4.)

V. 41—52.

Let us not pass over unimproved the only authentick record, which we have of our Redeemer's conduct in his youth. When we had read that he " waxed strong in " Spirit, filled with wisdom, and that the grace of God was " with him;" (alas! most of us may say, ' How contrary to my youthful years; in which I grew in sin and folly, as I grew in stature, and as the powers of my mind unfolded!') we might have expected to hear many extraordinary things concerning him: yet nothing is related, of such matters as are commonly reported about promising children. We are, however, informed that the ordinances and temple of God were his delight; and that, in Jerusalem, nothing so much attracted his attention, as the instructions of the publick teachers of the divine law. (*Note, Matt.* xxiii. 1—4.) These things we ought to deem most worthy of our regard: thus young persons should employ their early days; seeking the knowledge of divine truth; attending on the ministry of the gospel; proposing such enquiries to their seniors and instructors, as may tend to the increase of knowledge; and studying to be able, with pertinency and propriety to answer such questions as may be put to

them. From the earliest youth, every one should deem the service of God his great business: and the glory of his name, and the duty owing to him, must be allowed a pre-eminence, even above that of children to their parents; and must be attended to, even when it interferes with their inclination and satisfaction. In all things else the blessed Saviour has left an example to young persons, of unreserved subjection, not only to their own parents, but even to those who are by any means entrusted with a kind of parental authority; and he has also taught them patient industry and contentment in a mean condition. These, when connected with piety and humility, are proper evidences of an increase of true wisdom, and of having obtained favour with God: and they have a tendency to render the possessor dear to his fellow creatures also; especially to those who most deserve estimation, and whose friendship is a privilege. Let us then endeavour to keep the sayings of Jesus in our hearts, and to transcribe his example in our life.

NOTES.

CHAP. III. V. 1. In the interval, between the birth of Jesus, and the entrance of John the Baptist on his publick ministry, various changes had taken place in the government of Judea, and the adjacent countries. Augustus Cæsar, having admitted his nephew Tiberius to a share in the imperial authority, died about three years after: and Tiberius was at that time in the fifteenth year of his reign, from his appointment as the colleague of Augustus. Not long after the death of Herod the great, his dominions were divided into four distinct governments, under the Roman emperor. Pontius Pilate had just been appointed procurator of Judea. Herod Antipas, the son of king Herod, held as tetrarch the government of Galilee; his brother Philip, that of Iturea and Trachonitis, to the west of Herod's district; and Lysanias (who seems not to have been of Jewish extraction) held the government of Abilene, to the north of Galilee on the borders of Syria. *Being governor.*] 'Ηγεμονευοντος. See on ii. 2.—*Being tetrarch.*] Τετραρχουντος. Here only. A τηραρχης. See on *Matt.* xiv. 1.

V. 2, 3. The ecclesiastical affairs of the Jews were at this time fallen into great disorder, and the high priesthood was disposed of at the will of the ruling powers, from secular motives, without regard to the regular succession; and frequently the high priest was deposed, and another substituted in his place: so that in some instances it appeared more like an annual office, than one held during life. It cannot be supposed, that there were, strictly speaking, two high priests at the same time: but in the New Testament the same word (αρχιερευς) is used for *the high priest*, and *the chief priests* who were the heads of the twenty-four courses: being singular when the high priest is intended, and plural when used for the chief priests. The two persons, therefore, whom the Roman governor considered as the chief of the priests; and whose names

try about Jordan, ¹preaching the baptism of repentance for the remission of sins;

4 As it is written in the book of the words of Esaias the prophet, saying, ᵏThe voice of one crying in the wilderness, ˡPrepare ye the way of the Lord, make his paths straight.

5 Every ᵐvalley shall be filled, and every mountain and hill shall be brought low; ⁿand the crooked shall be made straight, and the rough ways shall be made smooth;

6 And °all flesh shall see the salvation of God.

7 Then said he to the multitude that came forth to be baptized of him, ᵖO generation of vipers, who hath warned you ᑫto flee from the wrath to come?

8 Bring forth therefore ʳfruits ˢworthy of repentance; and begin not to

---

stood as such in the publick registers, may be intended. From the time of the Maccabees, the high priesthood had been held by persons, who also exercised a kind of regal authority. And when the nation was subdued under the Roman governors; the " ruler of the people," (*Acts* xxiii. 5,) and the president of the sanhedrim, was the high priest, or a chief priest. Now Annas had been high priest, in the ordinary sense of the word, but had been deposed by the Roman governor: yet it seems, that he still continued " ruler of the people" and president of the sanhedrim; while, after several other changes, Caiaphas his son-in-law had been appointed by Pilate high priest, to officiate at the temple. So that an irregularity had arisen out of the confusion of the times: and the ruler or prince under the Romans, though a chief priest, was a distinct person from the high priest: Annas being the one, and Caiaphas the other. Thus St. John ' mentions the carrying of Christ ' to Annas first, as to an officer of principal authority ' among them, who sent him bound to Caiaphas, who ' " was the high priest that year," (*John* xviii. 13, 14. ' 24. *Acts* iv. 6,) and so continued all the time of Pilate's ' procuratorship.' *Hammond.*—Some indeed suppose that Annas was high priest, and Caiaphas acted as his deputy: but no deputy of the high priest was allowed to officiate, except when the high priest was sick, or by some means incapacitated, and it does not appear that Annas was either: and the above statement seems satisfactorily to solve the difficulty, of two persons being considered as chief or high priests, one as " the ruler of the people," and the other as performing the office of high priest at the temple. Thus " the sceptre was departing from Judah," and consequently Shiloh was at hand, at the time when " the word of the Lord " came to John," as to the prophets of old; (*Note, Gen.* xlix. 10;) and when by immediate inspiration he was directed to go into the country about Jordan, and " to preach the " baptism of repentance for the remission of sins."—From these words we learn that John preached the necessity of repentance, in order to the remission of sins; and that the baptism of water was an *outward* sign of that inward cleansing and renewal of heart, which attend or spring from true repentance: so that if the baptized persons were really partakers of this inward humiliation and cleansing, they would certainly receive forgiveness of sins through the Saviour, who was about to appear: for they would then be prepared to welcome and participate the privileges and blessings of his spiritual redemption and kingdom. (*Marg. Ref.* g—i.—*Notes, Matt.* iii. 1, 2. 5, 6. 11, 12. *Mark* i. 4—11.)—*The word*, &c. (2) ' These are the very ' words used of the prophets of the Old Testament. (*Jer.*

' i. 2. 4. 11. *Ez.* i. 3. vi. 1. vii. 1. xii. 1. xiii. 1. xiv. 2. 12 :) ' and it is so said of the rest. Shall we then think that ' this forerunner of the Messiah spake the words of the ' Lord, as did the prophets of the Old Testament; and ' that the prophets and apostles of the New Testament, on ' whom the Holy Ghost descended, to enable them to teach ' the mind of Christ to all future ages of the church, should ' not speak and write, what they delivered as the rule of ' faith, by like divine assistance?' *Whitby.*—Nothing can be determined concerning the time of our Lord's baptism, from the date of John's beginning to preach. I believe there are no *data*, from whence to conclude the age of John at that time. (*Notes, Num.* iv. 3. viii. 25, 26. 1 *Chr.* xxiii. 24—28.) Probably, he preached and baptized longer, before our Lord entered on his ministry, than some harmonists have allotted him. Nothing, however, can be more frivolous, than an objection started by some against the narrative of the evangelists, because the thirtieth year of our Lord's age, (*Note*, 23,) being supposed coincident with the fifteenth of Tiberius's reign, according to their computation, would fix the birth of Christ, subsequent to the death of king Herod. But John might come forth in the fifteenth of Tiberius; and Jesus might not be baptized till the seventeenth or eighteenth, without the least inconsistency with any thing taught or recorded in scripture. V. 4—6. (*Marg. Ref.* k—o.—*Notes, Is.* xl. 3—5. *Matt.* iii. 4. *Mark* i. 1—3.) This quotation is nearly according to the Septuagint, though it does not exactly accord to it. Instead of the words, " The glory of the LORD shall be " revealed, and all flesh shall see it together;" (*Is.* xl. 5 ;) the clause from the Septuagint is here added, " All flesh " shall see the salvation of God." (*Note, Is.* lii. 9, 10.)— The glory of God is specially shewn in Christ, " the sal- " vation of God ;" and it shall at length be made known to all mankind.—The word in the Hebrew is JEHOVAH. " Prepare ye the way of JEHOVAH, &c."

Valley. (5) Φαραγξ, *Barathrum; i. e. profunda atque prærupta terræ cavitas, seu hiatus.* Here only N. T.—*Is.* xl. 4. *Sept.*—*Crooked.*] Σκολια. *Acts* ii. 40. *Phil.* ii. 15. 1 *Pet.* ii. 18.—*Is.* xl. 4. *Sept.*—*Rough.*] Τραχυαι. *Acts* xxvii. 29. Not elsewhere N. T.—*Deut.* xxi. 4. *Is.* xl. 4. *Sept.*—*Shall be made smooth.*] Εις ιδας λειας. Here only N. T.—Εις πεδια. *Is.* xl. 4. *Sept.*—*The salvation.* (6) Το σωτηριον. ii. 30. *Acts* xxviii. 28. *Eph.* vi. 17.—*Is.* xl. 5. *Sept.*

V. 7—9. (*Marg. and Marg. Ref.*—*Note, Matt.* iii. 7— 10.) ' What in St. Matthew (*Matt.* iii. 7) is said to have ' been spoken to the Pharisees and Sadducees, is here said ' to have been spoken τοις οχλοις, to the multitude coming

say within yourselves, ' We have Abraham to *our* father: for I say unto you, That God is able ' of these stones to raise up children unto Abraham.

9 And * now also the axe is laid unto the root of the trees : every tree therefore which bringeth not forth good fruit is hewn down, and cast into the fire.

10 And the people asked him, saying, 'What shall we do then?

11 He answereth and saith unto them, ' He that hath two coats, let him impart to him that hath none;

and he that hath meat let him do likewise.

12 Then ' came also publicans to be baptized, and said unto him, Master, what shall we do?

13 And he said unto them, ' Exact no more than that which is appointed you.

14 And * the soldiers likewise demanded of him, saying, And what shall we do? And he said unto them, ' Do violence to no man, neither ' accuse *any* falsely; ' and be content with your ' wages.

' forth to be baptized; partly, because it was spoken to ' the Pharisees mixed with the multitude, and in their audi-' ence; and agreed to them, not only as being generally ' of one of these two sects, but being also an adulterous ' generation, degenerated from the seed of Abraham, to be ' the seed of the serpent.' *Whitby.*—The warning here given seems to have been principally addressed to the Sadducees and Pharisees : though the people, being in general infected with the same leaven, were likewise in some measure included. (*Note, Matt.* xxiii. 29—33.)—*Begin not,* &c. (8) ' Do not attempt to plead, as you generally do, your relation to Abraham; for it will not at all avail you.' (*Notes, John* viii. 30—47.)

V. 10—14. While the Pharisees, Sadducees, priests, scribes, and rulers, generally neglected John's exhortations; the common people enquired of him " what they " must do," in order " to bring forth fruits worthy of re-" pentance." To this he answered in general, by inculcating a disinterested love to their neighbours. Not only ought the rich to be very liberal; but every one who possessed two coats, when one would serve his present purpose, was directed to give the other to some poor man who had none ; and he that had food for the present, to impart a portion of it to him that had none, without any solicitude about the future. (*Marg. Ref.* y—*Note,* 1 *John* iii. 16, 17.) It may not be proper, to interpret such general rules, *strictly* and *literally :* but, however explained, unless they be supposed to mean nothing, they certainly require a far greater degree of liberality in the rich, and even in the poor, according to their present ability, towards their still more indigent neighbours, than is almost any where practised among Christians.—The whole scripture forbids us to consider such duties as a meritorious condition, or qualification for coming to Christ : but as none can or will accept of his salvation, or become subjects of his kingdom, without true repentance ; so the evidences and effects of this repentance are here marked out : and in the performance of these duties, the humble penitent must wait for the comforts and blessings of free salvation, and not in the neglect of them, or in the practice of his former sins. (*Notes, Is.* i. 16—20. *Acts* v. 1—8, *vv.* 2. 4.)—In like manner John answered the more particular enquiry of the publicans, or the farmers of the publick taxes. (*Notes, Matt.* v. 43—48. ix. 9.) He did not require them to renounce their employment ; but to act in it with scrupulous

integrity ; not using either force or fraud to enhance their profits, by exacting more than their legal due. This implied that many of them were guilty of such exactions ; but it seems also to allow that these might be entirely avoided, and that the employment was not unlawful in it-self. (*Marg. Ref.* z, a.—*Note,* xix 1—10, *vv.* 2. 8.)—That repentance cannot be sincere, which does not induce men to make restitution of iniquitous gain, as far as they have ability and opportunity : yet John seems not in the first instance to have insisted on this, for it is a subject which often involves complicated questions ; but the same principic, which induces men to forego all unjust gain, will at length lead them to make restitution as far as they are able. (*P. O.* xix. 1—10. *Notes, Num.* v. 7, 8. *Eph.* iv. 28.) —There were also some soldiers who, under convictions of sin, enquired what they must do. The Jews, in those days, sometimes served in the Roman armies, and John did not direct them to quit that ensnaring situation, which probably could not have been done without extreme difficulty, and causing much displeasure to their rulers : but he ordered them to behave in a harmless and quiet manner in their station; not terrifying or injuring any one, and not bearing slanderous testimony against any person in order to obtain his property, or to flatter their superiors and court their favour; but to be content with their wages and provisions. (*Marg.* and *Marg. Ref.* b. d.)—We should consider these answers, as prescribing the *present duty* of the enquirers, and as forming an *immediate touchstone* of their sincerity : for it would be most absurd to conclude, that an external performance of these duties would purchase an indulgence to continue in other sins, or profit those who neglected the salvation of Christ. But they, who yielded prompt obedience in these things, would afterwards be more fully instructed in the nature of the kingdom and salvation of Christ. (*Note, Matt.* xxviii. 19, 20. 1 *Thes.* iv. 1—5.)

Exact. (13) Πρασσετε. xix. 23. *Acts* xix. 19. Generally, *to do, to practise, to commit.* Xenophon repeatedly uses the word in this sense of *exacting.* See Schleusner on πρασσω.—*That which is appointed.*] Το διατεταγμενον. viii. 15. *Matt.* xi. 1. *Acts* vii. 44, *et al.* : Ex δια et τασσω. *Acts* xiii. 48.—*The soldiers.* (14) Στρατευομενοι. 1 *Cor.* ix. 7. 2 *Cor.* x. 3. 1 *Tim.* i. 18. 2 *Tim.* ii. 4. *Jam.* iv. 1. 1 *Pet.* ii. 11.— *Do violence.*] Διασειστε. Here only. Ex δια et σειω, *moveo, quatio* : threatenings and violence are intended.—

15 ¶ And as the people were in expectation, and all men ⁱmused in their hearts of John, whether he were the Christ or not;

16 John answered, saying unto *them* all, ᵉI indeed baptize you with water; but one mightier than I cometh, the latchet of whose shoes I am not worthy to unloose: ᶠhe shall baptize you with the Holy Ghost, ᵍand with fire:

17 Whose ʰfan *is* in his hand, and he will throughly purge his floor, ⁱand will gather the wheat into his garner; ᵏbut the chaff he will burn with fire unquenchable.

18 And ˡmany other things in his exhortation preached he unto the people.

19 ¶ But ᵐHerod the tetrarch, being reproved by him for Herodias his brother Philip's wife, and for all the evils which Herod had done,

20 Added yet ⁿthis above all, that he shut up John in prison.

21 ¶ Now when all the people were baptized, it came to pass, °that Jesus also being baptized, ᵖand praying, ᵠthe heaven was opened:

22 And the Holy Ghost descended° in a bodily shape like a dove upon him, ᵠand a voice came from heaven, which said, ʳThou art my▸beloved Son, in thee I am well pleased.

23 ¶ And Jesus himself began to be about ˢthirty years of age, ᵗbeing (as was supposed) the son of Joseph, which was *the son* of Heli,

24 Which was *the son* of Matthat,

Accuse...falsely.] Συκοφαντησητε. xix. 8. Not elsewhere N.T. Εχ συκον, *ficus,* et φαινω, *indico.* ' *Indico illos, qui ficus Athenis* ' *in aliam regionem exportabant, absque vectigali impenso.*' Schleusner.—Lev. xix. 11. Job xxxv. 9. Ps. cxix. 122. 134. Sept. False or invidious accusations are evidently intended.— Hence the word *Sycophant.*—*Be content.*] Αρκεισθε. Matt. xxv. 9. John vi. 7. xiv. 8. 2 Cor. xii. 9. 1 Tim. vi. 8. Heb. xiii. 5. 3 John 10.—*Wages.*] Οψωνιοις. Rom. vi. 23. 1 Cor. ix. 7. 2 Cor. xi. 8.

V. 15—17. Whilst John in this manner taught the people; his holy life and his faithful instructions, (though he wrought no miracles,) induced many to enquire whether he were not the Christ; and they were in suspense in their own minds, and disputed or reasoned with each other about this matter; (*marg.*) till John, who sought no glory to himself, but only to Jesus, assured them that the Messiah was at hand, and was a far more honourable and excellent Person than he.—Some expositors seem to interpret " the baptism of the Holy Ghost and of fire," almost exclusively of the descent of the Holy Spirit on the apostles, and of the miraculous powers thus communicated: but it seems rather to refer to his penetrating, purifying, and transforming influences in the hearts of true Christians, of which those miraculous operations were an earnest and emblem. (*Marg. Ref.*—*Notes, Matt.* iii. 11, 12. *John* i. 19 —28. x. 40—42. *Acts* i. 4—8.)

Mused. (15) Διαλογιζομενων. i. 29. xii. 17. Matt. xvi. 7, 8. Mark ii. 6. viii. 16. ix. 33. John xi. 50. Α διαλογισμος. See on ii. 35.

V. 18. *Preached, &c.*] Ευηγγελιζετο, " preached the " gospel." John's testimony to Jesus, as " the Lamb of " God, that taketh away the sin of the world," as " the " Son of God," as " the Bridegroom " of the church, and as " baptizing " with the Holy Ghost," fully answers the import of this appropriate term. (*Notes, John* i. 29—34. iii. 27—36.)—John was a preacher of the gospel; though many consider his ministry in another light. (*Marg. Ref.*)

V. 19, 20. (*Marg. Ref.*—*Notes, Matt.* xiv. 3—11. *Mark* vi. 15—29.)—Herod's persecution of so eminent a servant of God, was a more direct act of hostility against God, than his most atrocious licentiousness; and so filled up the measure of his crimes. (*Marg. Ref.*—*Notes,* xiii. 31— 33. xxiii. 6—12.)

V. 21, 22. *Notes, Matt.* iii. 13—17.—*Praying, &c.* (21) ' It is observable, that all the three voices from heaven, by ' which the Father bare witness to Christ, were pronounced ' while he was praying, or very quickly after it.' *Doddridge.* (ix. 28. 35. *John* xii. 27, 28.)—*Bodily, &c.* (22) Σωματικω, 1 Tim. iv. 8. Not elsewhere N. T. Σωμαλικως. Col. ii. 9 It is evident that this was an appearance, resembling a material substance, descending on Christ, as a dove lights on the ground; probably in the shape, as well as after the manner, of a dove. The emblem has before been considered.

V. 23. Jesus " began to be about thirty years of age," at his baptism ; or perhaps he began his publick ministry, by being baptized of John, when he was about thirty years old. Some understand the clause to mean, that he was ruled, or was in subjection to Joseph and Mary, for about thirty years.—He was however about thirty years of age when he entered on his ministry. (*Note,* 2, 3.) This single decision of an inspired writer outweighs all the specious conjectures of learned men, concerning the duration of our Lord's ministry : and if he was crucified in the year A. D. 33, it must have lasted longer than they generally allow ; for he would be thirty years old A. D. 27. (*Note, Matt.* iv, *beginning.*) But the word *about,* and the *decimal number,* concur in warranting an opinion, that he might be rather above thirty at this time.

Began to be.] Αρχομενος. 8. xiii. 25. xiv. 18. xv. 14. Matt. iv. 17. Mark vi. 7. John xiii. 5. Acts i. 1.—Gen. ii. 3. Sept.—*As was supposed.*] Ως ενομιζετο. ii. 44. Matt. v. 17. x. 34. xx. 10. Acts vii. 25. viii. 20. xiv. 19. xvi. 13. 27. xvii. 29.

V. 24—38. (*Marg. Ref.*) There seems no reason to doubt, that the following is the genealogy of Jesus in the line of Mary : (*Note, Matt.* i. 2—17 :) but as the names of men alone, or chiefly, stood in publick registers ; so the name of Joseph, not that of Mary, must have been in-

which was *the son* of Levi, which was *the son* of Melchi, which was *the son* of Janna, which was *the son* of Joseph,

25 Which was *the son* of Mattathias, which was *the son* of Amos, which was *the son* of Naum, which was *the son* of Esli, which was *the son* of Nagge,

26 Which was *the son* of Maath, which was *the son* of Mattathias, which was *the son* of Semei, which was *the son* of Joseph, which was *the son* of Juda,

27 Which was *the son* of Joanna, which was *the son* of Rhesa, which was *the son* of Zorobabel, which was *the son* of Salathiel, which was *the son* of Neri,

28 Which was *the son* of Melchi, which was *the son* of Addi, which was *the son* of Cosam, which was *the son* of Elmodam, which was *the son* of Er,

29 Which was *the son* of Jose, which was *the son* of Eliezer, which was *the son* of Jorim, which was *the son* of Matthat, which was *the son* of Levi,

30 Which was *the son* of Simeon, which was *the son* of Juda, which was *the son* of Joseph, which was *the son* of Jonan, which was *the son* of Eliakim,

31 Which was *the son* of Melea, which was *the son* of Menan, which was *the son* of Mattatha, which was *the son* of Nathan, which was *the son* of David,

32 Which ˣ was *the son* of Jesse, ʸ which was *the son* of Obed, which was *the son* of Booz, which was *the son* of Salmon, which was *the son* of Naasson,

33 Which was *the son* of ᶻ Aminadab, which was *the son* of Aram, which was *the son* of ᵃ Esrom, which was *the son* of ᵇ Phares, which was *the son* ᶜ of Juda,

34 Which was *the son* of Jacob, ᵈ which was *the son* of Isaac, which was *the son* of Abraham, which was *the son* of ᵉ Thara, which was *the son* of Nachor,

35 Which was *the son* of ᶠ Saruch, which was *the son* of Ragau, which was *the son* of ᵍ Phalec, which was *the son* of ʰ Heber, which was *the son* of ᶦ Sala,

36 Which was *the son* of Cainan, which was *the son* of Arphaxad, which was *the son* of ᵏ Sem, which was *the son* of ˡ Noe, which was *the son* of Lamech,

37 Which was *the son* of ᵐ Mathusala, which was *the son* of Enoch, which was *the son* of Jared, which was *the son* of Maleleel, which was *the son* of Cainan,

38 Which was *the son* of Enos, which was *the son* of Seth, ⁿ which was *the son* of Adam, which was *the son* ᵒ of God.

serted. It had been said that Jesus was " supposed " to be the Son of Joseph; which may refer to the legal constitution, as well as to the common opinion of the Jews, as he was born of Mary after she was married to Joseph. Joseph's father was called Jacob : (*Matt.* i. 16 :) but marrying the daughter of Heli, and being perhaps adopted by him, he was called his son, and as such his name seems to have been inserted in the publick registers; and so the pedigree is carried backward in the line of Nathan to David, and from him to Adam, " who was the son of God," as created by him in his own image, though he soon lost it by sin. Some of the same names indeed occur, which are in Joseph's genealogy : but as different persons often bear the same name, it seems needless to perplex ourselves about so common a case.—Indeed Joseph could not, in the *male line*, be descended both from Solomon and Nathan. Yet the arguments urged to prove, that this is Joseph's genealogy, not Mary's, are formed on the supposition that the female line was excluded.—Cainan (36) is not found in the Hebrew text in any of the genealogies, but only in the Septuagint. It is probable, the evangelists transcribed the registers, as sufficiently exact for their purpose, and

as more generally suited to command attention, than if they had even rendered them more accurate.—The interpretation of this genealogy as that of Mary, and in the line of Nathan, is objected to, on the supposition that the Messiah was to descend from Solomon ; which in this case he did not. But it is no where said, that he was to descend from Solomon: but merely, that he was to be the Son of David, and spring " from the root of Jesse." Solomon was an eminent type of Christ, and is spoken of as such : but it is not said, to David, " In Solomon shall thy seed " be called ;" as to Abraham, " In Isaac shall thy seed be " called." (*Notes*, 2 *Sam.* vii. 12—16. *Ps.* lxxii. lxxxix. 19—37. *Jer.* xxii. 28—30.)

PRACTICAL OBSERVATIONS.

V 1—18.

While the people of the world are eagerly contending for transient honours, or employed in the pursuit of earthly vanities ; the servants of God grow up in obscurity : but when the Lord has prepared them for usefulness, he will bring them forth and employ them.—The true doctrine of the holy scriptures is equally calculated to encourage the

CHAP. IV.

Jesus fasts forty days, being tempted by the devil, and overcomes all his temptations, 1—13. He preaches in Galilee with great renown, 14, 15. He goes to Nazareth: and while his words excite admiration, the citizens are so offended, that they seek to kill him; but he avoids them by miracle, 16—30. He casts out an unclean spirit, 31—37; heals Peter's wife's mother, 38, 39; and works many other miracles, 40, 41. He preaches through the cities of Galilee, 42—44.

AND ᵃ Jesus, being ᵇ full of the Holy Ghost, returned from Jordan, ᶜ and was led by the Spirit into ᵈ the wilderness,

2 Being ᵉ forty days ᶠ tempted of the devil. And in those days ᵍ he did eat nothing: and when they were ended, ʰ he afterward hungered.

t Matt. iv. }. 14. 16. iii. 22.
ie. vi. 2—4. lvi. 1. Matt. iii. 16.
John i. 32. iii. 34. Acts i. 2. x. 38.
e ii. 27, ; 1 Kings xviii. 12. Ez. iii. 14. Mark i. 12.
Acts viii. 39.
d 1 Kings xix. 4. Mark i. 12.
e Ex. xxiv. 18. xxxiv. 28. Deut. ix. 9. 18. 25.
1 Kings xix. 8.
g Exch. iv. 16.

Matt. iv. 2.   f Gen. iii. 15. 1 Sam. xvii. 16. Heb. ii. 18.
Jon. iii. 7.   h Matt. xxi. 18. John iv. 6. Heb. iv. 15.

---

humble, and to abase the proud: when faithfully and successfully dispensed, "the valleys are exalted and the "hills brought low," and every obstacle is removed to make way for Christ to reveal his salvation, and set up his kingdom in the hearts of sinners. But many attend the preaching of the gospel, and come to sacred ordinances, who are no better than "a generation of vipers:" they should therefore be dealt with very plainly, nay, sometimes roughly; that they may be "warned to flee from the wrath "to come," and made sensible that it is vain to rely on forms, notions, or external privileges, without "repent-"ance and fruits meet for repentance." Some indeed seem to think, that God would have no church on earth, if their sect or company were cast off: but he would sooner form children to Abraham from the very stones of the street, than accept or save hypocrites and wicked professors of the gospel. These are trees, at whose root the axe is laid, to cut them speedily down that they may be "cast into the fire;" because amidst all their advantages, they bring forth no good fruit: yea, they are light worthless chaff, to be driven, as with a whirlwind, into the unquenchable fire of hell. Men should therefore not only ask, What "must we do to be saved?" but also enquire particularly concerning the proper evidences and effects of saving faith and true repentance; the duties of their stations, and the way in which they must wait for the consolations of the gospel: and ministers should enter into the detail, and be exact and particular in answering these enquiries. In general our repentance, faith, and love of God our Saviour, must be evinced by love to our neighbours and brethren: and surely our clearer discoveries, of the unspeakable mercy of the Lord Jesus to our sinful souls, ought not to render us more niggardly in relieving the distresses of our fellow-sinners: yet the rule laid down by this "man of God" would be deemed extremely rigorous, if we now should attempt to insist upon its being strictly observed. Thus much, however, we must say: "He who soweth liberally, shall reap also liberally;" and that "God loveth a cheerful giver." (*Notes,* 2 *Cor.* viii. 1 —15.)—It is not generally advisable for men to quit their stations in the community, provided they are not directly criminal: for though they be attended with peculiar temptations; yet they may also afford them peculiar advantages for shewing the excellency of the gospel, and the power of divine grace, by a blameless deportment in them; and there are many employments, that have no existence without the present state of the world, and a person may conscientiously serve God in them. Men should first be cautioned against the peculiar temptations of their respective

employments; and warned to avoid the sins, and to give up the iniquitous gains, which generally attend them: (*Note, Ex.* xxii. 25—27:) and when they are prevailed upon to make these sacrifices for conscience' sake, their hearts are prepared to welcome the salvation of Christ, and to receive instructions in every thing belonging to the doctrine, experience, and practice of Christianity: and eminent holiness, so far from rendering a man proud, will proportionably abase him in his own esteem, render him regardless of his own glory, and make Christ more precious to his heart and glorious in his eyes.

V. 19—38.

The faithful servants of God will be sure to make themselves enemies, among the proud and licentious; and contempt, reproach, and persecution are the general recompence of their honest reproofs. Yet those who thus injure them add a *greater evil* to all their other sins, and one expressive of more determined enmity to God and holiness, than any of the rest.—While, after the example of our righteous Surety, we are pouring out our hearts in prayer, and honouring the ordinances of God, we may expect to have the heavens, as it were, opened to pour down blessings on our heads. Indeed *all good things* may be said to be comprised in the Spirit of adoption communicated to us, to glorify the Saviour, and to be the pledge and earnest of eternal felicity. (*Notes,* xi. 5—13, *v.* 13. *Matt.* vii. 7 —11, *v.* 11.) If our souls be renewed, by his sacred influences, to a conformity with Christ, in purity, meekness, and love; we shall thus be evinced to be the children of our Father, with whom *for his sake* he will be well pleased, though in ourselves we are most unworthy: and thus also we shall be qualified for every service to which we are called. These are privileges worthy of our estimation.— "All flesh," as descended from the first Adam, is indeed "as grass," and "withers as the flower of the field;" but he who partakes of "the Spirit of life" from the second Adam, has that eternal happiness "which by the gospel "is preached to us." (*Note,* 1 *Cor.* xv. 45—49.)

NOTES.

CHAP. IV. V. 1—13. *Marg.* and *Marg. Ref.*— *Notes, Matt.* iv. 1—11. *Mark* i. 12, 13.—*Led by,* &c. (1) *Note, Rom.* viii. 14—17.—*He did eat,* &c. (2) Jesus not only abstained from some kinds of food, or for a certain portion of each day, as fasting is often understood; but he ate nothing all those days.—*Man shall not live,* &c. (4) 'He suffered thee to hunger, and then "fed thee with 'manna," (a light aerial sort of food,) giving thee as 'great strength from that, as from the bread and flesh

2 т 8

3 And the devil said unto him, 'If thou be the Son of God, command this stone that it be made bread.

4 And Jesus answered him, saying, ᵏ It is written, 'That man shall not live by bread alone, but by every word of God.

5 And the devil, ᵐ taking him up into an high mountain, shewed unto him all the kingdoms of the world ⁿ in a moment of time.

6 And the devil said unto him, ᵒ All this power will I give thee, ᵖ and the glory of them: for that is delivered unto me, ᵠ and to whomsoever I will I give it.

7 If thou therefore wilt ʳ worship me, all shall be thine.

8 And Jesus answered and said unto him, ˢ Get thee behind me, Satan; ᵗ for it is written, Thou shalt worship the Lord thy God, and him ᵘ only shalt thou serve.

9 And he ᵛ brought him to Jerusalem, and set him ʷ on a pinnacle of the temple, and said unto him, ˣ If thou be the Son of God, cast thyself down from hence:

10 For ʸ it is written, ᶻ He shall give his angels charge over thee, to keep thee;

11 And in *their* hands they shall bear thee up; lest at any time thou dash thy foot against a stone.

12 And Jesus answering, said unto him, It is said, ᵇ Thou shalt not tempt the Lord thy God.

13 And ᶜ when the devil had ended all the temptation, he departed from him for a season.

14 ¶ And Jesus ᵈ returned in the power of the Spirit into Galilee: ᵉ and there went out a fame of him through all the region round about.

15 And ᶠ he taught in their synagogues, ᵍ being glorified of all.

16 ¶ And he came ʰ to Nazareth, where he had been brought up: and, ⁱ as his custom was, he went into the synagogue on the sabbath-day, ᵏ and stood up for to read.

17 And there was delivered unto him ˡ the book of the prophet Esaias: and when he had opened the book, he found ᵐ the place where it was written,

18 The ⁿ Spirit of the Lord *is* upon me, because he hath ᵒ anointed me ᵖ to preach the gospel to the poor; he hath sent me ᵠ to heal the broken-hearted, ʳ to preach deliverance to the captives, ˢ and recovering of sight to the blind, to set at liberty them that are ᵗ bruised,

19 To ᵘ preach the acceptable year of the Lord.

'thou didst eat in Egypt: and this he did providing 'it miraculously every day, "that he might teach "" thee" (by this example) "that man doth not live by "" bread alone, but by every word of God," every thing 'that he shall please to command to give him nourish-'ment. So that, though I am now hungry, as they were; 'I have no need to work a miracle myself to satisfy my 'hunger; seeing I know by this example, that God, though 'he suffer his children to want bread, yet will command 'some other thing to keep them alive, and will himself 'rather work a miracle, than they shall want nourishment.' *Whitby.* (Notes, *Deut.* viii. 2, 3.)—*In a moment*, &c. (5) This circumstance is noted by St.Luke alone: and it confirms the opinion, that the whole was an illusion of the senses, effected by "the prince of the power of the air." (*Note, Eph.* ii. 1, 2.)—*That is delivered*, &c. (6) A most direct falsehood spoken by "the father of lies;" who, in this and similar ways, has alway deceived the children of men. (*Notes, Gen.* iii. 1—5.)—*A pinnacle*. (9) To πτερυγιον· *the pinnacle*. The porch of the temple. (*Note*, 1 *Kings* vi. 1, 3.)—*All the*, &c. (13) 'Christ being tempted by 'Satan, first to distrust God, then to covet riches and 'worldly good, and thirdly to vain confidence, thrice con-

VOL. V.

'quers him by the word of God. ... Hardly any kind of 'temptation will be found, which may not be referred 'either to distrust of God, the desire of perishing things, 'or vain ostentation.' *Beza.*—' If this enemy of mankind 'omitted no season of tempting Christ; we have reason 'to believe, he will omit no opportunity of tempting us.' *Whitby.*

Were ended. (2) Συντελεσθεισων. 13. *Matt.* vii. 28. *Mark* xiii. 4. *Acts* xxi. 27. *Rom.* ix. 28. *Heb.* viii. 8.— *The Son of* God. (3) Ὑιος τȣ Θεȣ. See on *Matt.* xiv. 33. xxvii. 54.—*In a moment.* (5) Εν τιγμη. Here only *N. T. Is.* xxix 5. *Sept.*—*For a season.* (13) Αχρι καιρȣ. 'Till the time of his passion; ...that was his hour. (*Luke* 'xxii. 53. *John* xiv. 30.)' *Whitby.*

V. 14, 15. (*Marg. Ref.*—Notes, *Matt.* iv. 12—25.) "The power of the Spirit" may here refer, either to the impulse upon our Lord's own mind; to the miracles which he wrought in confirmation of his doctrine; or to the energy, which attended his word to the hearts and consciences of the hearers.

Being glorified. (15) Δοξαζομενος. ii. 20. *John* vii. 39. xii. 16. 23. 28. xiii. 31, 32. xvii. 1. *Acts* iii. 13.

V. 16—19. When our Lord had made a circuit through

2 U

20 And he closed the book, ᵉ and he gave it again to the minister, ᶠ and sat down. ᵍ And the eyes of all them that were in the synagogue were fastened on him.

21 And he began to say unto them, ʰ This day is this scripture fulfilled in your ears.

22 And all bare him witness, and ᵃ wondered at ᵇ the gracious words, which proceeded out of his mouth. And they said, ᶜ Is not this Joseph's son?

23 And he said unto them, Ye will surely say unto me this proverb, ᵈ Phy-sician, heal thyself: ᵉ whatsoever we

---

the other parts of Galilee, he came at length to Nazareth, where he had spent his former life : ' that he by his exam-' ple might teach us, saith Theophylact, first to tench and ' do good to those of our own family and abode.' *Whitby.*
—On the sabbath-day, according to his constant custom in every place, he resorted to the Synagogue; that he might join in the publick worship there performed, and embrace the opportunity of instructing the people: (*Marg. Ref.* h, i :) and, either because he had been used to join in their stated worship, and perhaps sometimes to officiate as a reader; or because of the reputation, which he had acquired by his miracles and doctrine in other places; they gave him a roll containing the prophecy of Isaiah, that he might read the scriptures to them, which was always a part of their stated service. (*Marg. Ref.* k—m.) When therefore he had unrolled the parchment, he read a por-tion, which has already been considered. (*Note, Is.* lxi. 1—3.) Perhaps it was a part of one of the lessons ap-pointed for the day.—"The day of vengeance of our God," (which the prophet connected with "the acceptable year " of the LORD,") seems not to have been insisted on by Jesus; that the Nazarites might have the less pretence for rejecting him, when his whole discourse breathed nothing but mercy and compassion. (*Marg. Ref.* n—u.)—The passage, as here quoted, does not exactly accord either to the Hebrew or to the Septuagint: yet it does not vary materially from either.—The " recovering of sight to the " blind " is here added, not being either in the Septuagint, or our Hebrew Bibles: and it seems an allusion to the wretched state of those prisoners, whose eyes had been put out, when they were thrown into the dungeon, and loaded with fetters which " bruised" their limbs. No other deliverer except the Lord Jesus, could restore to a redeemed captive, the sight of which he had been deprived.

When he had opened. (17) Αναπτυξας. Here only N. T. *Judg.* viii. 25. 2 *Kings* xix. 14. *Sept.* Πτυξας, 20.—*To preach the gospel.* (18) Ευαγγελιζεσθαι. The word gospel is used in rather different meanings, both in the subse-quent part of the New Testament, and in modern divi-nity : sometimes signifying the publication of Christianity, or the coming and kingdom of the Messiah, in general; at other times, the glad tidings of salvation, as distin-guished from other parts of revealed truth.—*The broken-hearted.*] Συντετριμμενος την καρδιαν. ix. 39. *Matt.* xii. 20. See on *Mark* xiv. 3.—Συντριμμα, *Rom.* iii. 16.—*Them that are bruised.*] Τεθραυσμενος. Here only N. T. *Ex.* xv. 6. *Deut.* xxviii. 33. *Is.* xlii. 4. *Sept.*

V. 20—22. Having chosen the foregoing words as the subject of his discourse, Jesus gave the book into the hands of the minister, (or stated servant of the synagogue, who took care of those matters,) and sat down, as teach-ers used then to do. (*Marg. Ref.* x, y.) ' He stood up to

' read (20) and closing the book, he sat down. Here ' Christ conforms to the ceremonies of the Jewish doc-' tors, who in honour of the law and prophets, stood up ' when they read them. ... And he sits down to teach.' *Whitby.* The report of his miracles and doctrine, when compared with this remarkable prophecy, caused the people to fix their eyes upon him, with the greatest ex-pectation and attention. Indeed he began by explicitly declaring, that the words, read to them, had been that " day fulfilled in their ears;" which implied that he was the promised Messiah of whom the prophet spake: and doubtless he explained the words, as referring to the spi-ritual redemption which he came to effect in behalf of enslaved sinners, and earnestly exhorted and persuaded his hearers to seek these important blessings. In short, he spake with such energy, wisdom, and affection, that, notwithstanding their strong prejudices, they " bare wit-" ness to him," that he had discoursed in an excellent manner, and exceedingly admired the " words of grace," and tender compassion for the miseries of sinful men, which he had delivered with much propriety and authority.
—Yet the recollection of his mean birth, and of the dis-advantages of his education and previous manner of life, proved an insuperable stumbling block : and, instead of inferring, that he had his wisdom and utterance imme-diately from heaven, they rejected his claim to be the Messiah, and seem even to have doubted of the reality of the miracles, which it was reported that he wrought. (*Notes, Matt.* xi. 2—6. xiii. 54—58. *Mark* vi. 1—6.)—' It does not appear to me likely, that persons of every ' kind were rashly admitted to speak publickly in the syna-' gogues; but that this was the ordinary office of the ' scribes and lawyers; the Levites for this purpose having ' been dispersed into many places. ... But, moreover, that ' certain persons, as invited by the rulers of the synagogue, ' sometimes officiated, besides this settled order, appears ' from *Acts* xiii. 15. ... The majesty and the miracles of ' Christ every where procured him a hearing.' *Beza.*

He closed. (20) Πτυξας. Here only N. T.—*Were fast-ened.*] Ατενιζοντες. xxii. 56. *Acts* i. 10. iii. 4. 12. vi. 15. vii. 55. 2 *Cor.* iii. 7. 13.—*The gracious words.* (22) Τοις λογοις της χαριτος. " The words of the grace, &c." ' which, ' it is probable, may refer to the agreeable manner of ' Christ's discourse, as well as to the matter of it.' *Dod-dridge.* That our Lord's elocution was peculiarly becom-ing, majestick, solemn, impressive, and persuasive, can scarcely be doubted. In every sense, " he spake as never " man spake :" and this would excite the additional asto-nishment of those, who knew the meanness of his birth and education. It may, however, be questioned, whether χαρις ever has this meaning in the N. T.

V. 23—32. The thoughts of the Nazarenes were fully

f John ii. 3, 4. iv.
25. vii. 3, 4.
Rom. xi. 34, 35.
2 Cor. v. 16.

have heard done in Capernaum, [f] do also here in [g] thy country.

g Matt. xiii. 54.
Mark vi. 1.

24 And he said, Verily I say unto

h Matt. xiii. 57.
Mark vi. 4. 5.
John iv. 41. Acts
xii. 3. 18—22.

you, [h] No prophet is accepted in his own country.

i x. 21. Is. iv. 8.

25 But I tell you of a truth, [i] Many

Matt. xx. 16.
Mark vii. 25—
29. Rom. ix. 15.
30. Eph. i. 9. 11.

widows were in Israel in the days of

j 1 Kings xvii. 1.
xviii. 2. *Elijah*.
Jam. v. 17.

Elias, [j] when the heaven was shut up three years and six months, when great famine was throughout all the land: 26 But u t none of them was

k 1 Kings xvii. 9.
&c. *Zarephath*.
Ob. 20.

Elias sent, [k] save unto Sarepta, *a city* of Sidon, unto a woman *that was* a widow.

27 And many lepers were in Israel

l 1 Kings xix. 19
—21. *Elisha*.

in the time of [l] Eliseus the prophet;

m Matt. xii. 4.
John xiii. 12.

and none of them was cleansed, [m] sav-

n 2 Kings v. Job
xxi. 22. xxxiii.
15. xxxvi. 25.
Dan. iv. 35.

ing [n] Naaman the Syrian. 28 And all they in the synagogue, when they heard these things, [o] were filled with wrath,

o vi. 11. xi. 53.
54. 2 Chr. xvi.
10. xxiv. 20, 21.
Jer. xxxvii. 15.

29 And rose up, [p] and thrust him out of the city, and led him unto the [q] brow of the hill, whereon their city was built,

16. xxxviii. 6.
Acts v. 33. vii.
54. xxii. 21—23.
1 Thes. ii. 15.
16.

[r] that they might cast him down head-long.

p John viii. 37. 40.
59. xv. 24, 25.
Acts vii. 57, 58.
xvi. 23, 24. xxi

30 But he, [s] passing through the midst of them, went his way.

q Or. *edge.*
r 2 Chr. xxv. 12.
Ps. xxxvii. 32, 33.
John viii. 59. x.

31 And [t] came down to Capernaum, a city of Galilee, [u] and taught them on the sabbath-days.

39. xviii. 6, 7.
Acts xii. 18.
s Matt. iv. 13.
Mark i. 21.

32 And [x] they were astonished at his doctrine; for his word was with power.

t John iii. 40. 17.
xvi. 1—8, 10.
xvii. 1—8, 10,
1, 2, 6, 7. 19—21
4, xxi. 1, 2, 28.

33 ¶ And [z] in the synagogue there was a man, which had a spirit of an unclean devil, and cried out with a loud voice,

24.
u 38. Jer. xxiii.
24. Mark i. 22.
22. John vi. 63.
xiv. 24, - 25.
2 Cor. iv. 2. x.
4, 6. 1 Thes. i.
5. Tit. ii. 15.
Heb. iv. 12, 13.
z Mark i. 23.

---

known to our Lord: and he intimated, that he was aware they were disposed to use the common proverb, "Physi-"cian, heal thyself," with relation to him: intimating, that if indeed he were able to perform miraculous cures, he ought to have begun with healing the diseases of his old neighbours; or at least that he ought now to do such miracles among them, as it was reported he had wrought at Capernaum, if he expected any regard from them. Thus they were disposed to dictate to him, or to cavil at his ministry, because he did not comply with their unreasonable demands, or pay court to them : nay, they spake as if they had a *just* claim to his miraculous cures in preference to others. (*Marg. Ref.* d—g.) He therefore now first applied to them that proverb, which has already been considered : (*Marg. Ref.* h.—*Notes, Matt.* xiii. 54—58. *John* iv. 43—45 :) for having known him in a situation, externally inferior to that of many present, they could not endure to be warned and instructed by him, or admit of his superiority over them. But he further observed, that he had a right to dispense his favours as he saw good; and that in working miracles at other places rather than at Nazareth, he did the same as the ancient prophets had done. For in the terrible famine, which took place in the days of Elijah, (*Notes,* 1 *Kings* xvii.) that prophet was not sent to relieve any of the poor destitute widows of Israel, but to a widow of Gentile extraction alone : and, in like manner, Elisha cleansed none of the lepers of Israel; but exerted his miraculous power on Naaman, a Syrian. (*Notes,* 2 *Kings* v.) So that, if he had not only given Capernaum the preference to Nazareth, but had even neglected the Jews, and conferred his favours on the Gentiles, they could not have objected to his conduct, without condemning these two prophets. But, while their prejudices and unbelief were the real reasons, why they were not favoured equally with other cities; this declaration of our Lord, that he had a right to work his miracles where he pleased, exceedingly enraged them, as if it had been an inexcusable injustice! (*Marg. Ref.* i—o.) They therefore forgot the holiness of the day, and the religious purposes for which they were assembled; and, rising up

with one consent, they thrust him out of the synagogue, and even out of the city; hurrying him away to the brink of a precipice, that they might cast him down and dash him to pieces. But he miraculously eluded their attempt; and, passing unobserved through the midst of them, went to Capernaum, where he proceeded to teach the people with surprising authority and energy. (*Marg. Ref.* p—u. —*Notes, Matt.* viii. 28, 29. *John* viii. 54—59, v. 59. x. 32 —39, v. 39.)—' When they heard Christ declaring them ' *unworthy* of the benefit of those miracles, which he had ' done at Capernaum, and ... plainly intimating, that this ' gospel should chiefly be received among the Gentiles, ' they, in a furious zeal, seek to destroy him.' *Whitby.* The inhabitants however, of the cities, in which our Lord's miracles were principally wrought, were expressly declared by him to be *unworthy* of them : (x. 13—15. *Note, Matt.* xi. 20—24 :) yet their prejudices were not so strong as those of the Nazarenes, nor were they disposed to persecute him ; and there were more believers among them, than at Nazareth. In fact, the indignation shewn on this occasion, was excited by the doctrine of the divine sovereignty. "May I not do what I will with my own ?" May I not confer *unmerited favours* on whom I will, without doing injustice to those who do not share them ? The doctrine, which is supported against all objections by these questions, offended the men of Nazareth; as it ever did, and ever will, offend those, who " have not submitted to " the righteousness of God." (*Notes, Matt.* xx. 1—16, *vv.* 13—15. *P. O.* 1—16.—*Notes, Rom.* ix. 15—21.) Surely. (23) Πάντως. Omnino: utique: nimirum. Acts xviii. 21. xxi. 22. Rom. iii. 9. 1 Cor. v. 10. xvi. 12.— Save. (26.) Ει μη. 27. John xvii. 12.—(Note, John xvii. 11, 12.)—*The brow,* &c. (29) Της οφρυος. Here only N.T. —*Lev.* xiv. 9. *Sept.* ' Omne quod prominet, et editum est.' Schleusner.—*Cast down headlong.*] Το κατακρημνισαι. Here only N. T.—*Passing,* &c. (30) *Marg. Ref.*—*Notes,* 2 *Kings* vi. 18 —20.

V. 33—37. *Marg. Ref.*—*Notes, Mark* i. 23—28. v. 2 —13.—See on *Mark* i. 24.—*The Holy One,* &c. (34)

2 v 3

34 Saying, †Let *us* alone: [y]what have we to do with thee, *thou* Jesus of Nazareth? [z]art thou come to destroy us? I know thee who thou art; [a]the Holy One of God.

35 And [b]Jesus rebuked him, saying, Hold thy peace, and come out of him. And when the devil had [c]thrown him in the midst, he came out of him, and hurt him not.

36 And [d]they were all amazed, and spake among themselves, saying, [e]What a word *is* this! for with authority and power he commandeth the unclean spirits, and they come out!

37 And [f]the fame of him went out into every place of the country round about.

38 ¶ And [g]he arose out of the synagogue, and entered into Simon's house: and Simon's wife's mother was taken with a great fever; [h]and they besought him for her.

39 And he stood over her, [i]and rebuked the fever; and it left her. And immediately she arose, [k]and ministered unto them.

40 ¶ Now [l]when the sun was setting, all they that had any sick with divers diseases brought them unto him; [m]and he laid his hands on every one of them, and healed them.

41 And devils also came out of many, [n]crying out, and saying, [o]Thou art Christ, the Son of God. And he, rebuking *them*, suffered them not to [*]speak: for they knew that he was Christ.

42 And [p]when it was day he departed and went into a desert place; [q]and the people sought him, and came unto him, [r]and stayed him, that he should not depart from them.

43 And he said unto them, [s]I must preach the kingdom of God to other cities also; for [t]therefore am I sent.

44 And [u]he preached in the synagogues of Galilee.

† Or, *Away.* viii. 37. Acts xvi. 39.
y 41. viii. 28. Matt. viii. 29. Mark i. 24. 34. v. 7.
z Gen. iii. 15. Heb. ii. 14, 15. 1 John iii. 8. Rev. xx. 2.
a i. 35. Ps. xvi. 10. Dan. ix. 24. Acts ii. 27. iv. 27. Rev. iii. 7.
b 39. 41. Ps. i. 16. Zech. iii. 2. Matt. viii. 26. xvii. 18. Mark iii. 11, 12. Acts xvi. 17, 18.
c ix. 39. 42. xi. 22. Mark i. 26. ix. 26. Rev. xii. 12.
d Matt. ix. 33. xii. 22, 23. Mark i. 27. vii. 37.
e 32. x. 17—20. Mark xvi. 17—20. Acts xix. 12—16.
f 14. Is. iii. 13. Matt. iv. 23—25. ix. 26. Mark i. 28. 45. vi. 14.
g Matt. viii. 14, 15. Mark i. 29—31. 1 Cor. ix. 5.
h vii. 3, 4. Matt. xv. 23. John xi. 3. 22. Jam. v. 14, 15.
i 35. viii. 24.
k viii. 2, 3. Ps. cxvi. 12. 2 Cor. v. 14, 15.
l Matt. viii. 16, 17. Mark i. 32—34.
m vii. 21—23. Matt. iv. 23, 24. xi. 5. xiv. 13, 14. Mark iii. 10. vi. 5. 55, 56. Acts v. 15. xix. 12.
n 34. Mark i. 34. iii. 11.
o Matt. viii. 29. xxvi. 63. John xx. 31. Acts xvi. 17, 18. Jam. ii. 19.
* Or, *say, that they knew him to be Christ.*
p vi. 12. Mark i. 35. John iv. 34.
q Matt. xiv. 13, 14. Mark i. 37. 45. vi. 33, 34. John vi. 24.
r viii. 37, 38. xxiv. 29. John iv. 40.
s Mark i. 14, 15. 38, 39. John ix. 4. Acts x. 38. 2 Tim. iv. 2.
t Is. xlii. 1—4. xlviii. 16. lxi. 1—3. John vi. 38—40. xx. 21.
u 15. Matt. iv. 23. Mark i. 39.

Ο ἁγιος τȣ Θεȣ. 'When this word is used, in the New 'Testament, with the article, in the singular, and ap'plied to a person; the application is always to God, or to 'Christ.' *Campbell.*—*The fame.* (37) Ηχος. *Acts* ii. 2. *Heb.* xii. 19. Not elsewhere N. T. Ηχεω, xxi. 25. 1 *Cor.* xiii. 1.

V. 38, 39. *Marg. Ref.*—*Note, Matt.* viii. 14, 15.

V. 40—44. *Marg. Ref.*—*Notes, Matt.* viii. 16, 17. *Mark* i. 32—39.—*When it was day.* (42) Γενομενης ... ἡμερας. This may be rendered, "When the day was "coming on."—Πρωι εννυχον λιαν "A great while before "day." *Mark* i. 35.—*Stayed him,* &c.] Κατειχον. viii. 15. xiv. 9. 1 *Cor.* vii. 30. xi. 2. 2 *Cor.* vi. 10. 1 *Thes.* v. 21. *Philem.* 11. They held him fast, or *earnestly detained him.*

PRACTICAL OBSERVATIONS.

V. 1—15.

When we return from sacred ordinances, replete with those spiritual affections which are excited by the Holy Spirit, it is good to retire for prayer and meditation: and should Satan even take that opportunity of harassing us, we shall possess many advantages for repelling his assaults.—Fervent devotion, or sharp conflicts, may render us for a time regardless of the concerns of our animal life, and this may conduce to our earnestness and success: but the cravings of nature will again return; and then the devil will tempt us to impatience, to irregular methods of obtaining a supply, or to excessive indulgence: we ought therefore to be especially upon our guard, after remarkable seasons of abstraction, and communion with God. The enemy knows how to make his advantage of all the peculiarities of our situation; and it is our wisdom and duty to study them ourselves, that we may be prepared for the assault, and have our answer ready to every suggestion.—To whatever sin we are tempted, the scripture, well understood, supplies us with spiritual armour of proof, with which to baffle the tempter. Let us remember in all our straits, that "man doth not live by bread only, but by "the word of God also;" that all Satan's promises and pretences are illusion and deceit; and that, as far as he is *permitted* to have any influence, in disposing of the "kingdoms of the world and the glory of them," he uses them merely as baits, by which to ensnare ambitious and carnal men to their destruction. We should therefore reject every opportunity of sinful gain or advancement, with decision and abhorrence, as a price offered for our souls; (*P. O. Matt.* xvi. 21—28;) and seek our riches, honours, and happiness, in the worship and service of God only. Thus, as his beloved children, angels will have it in charge to "keep us in all our ways," and we shall be preserved from turning aside through presumptuously or ostentatiously "tempting the Lord our God."—As seasons of peculiar consolation are commonly transient, so are those of distressing temptation, especially when the enemy is vigorously resisted. But though he "depart for "a season," we shall never be out of his reach, till we are removed from this evil world. Yet when, in the strength and after the example of our Redeemer, we have obtained a decisive victory, we may hope for a respite, and an opportunity of applying ourselves, with composure and diligence, to our proper work. (*P. O. Matt.* iv. 1—11.)

V. 16—31.

When we meet with acceptance for a time, in our endeavours to do good; we should expect some change or alloy. Indeed fame and honour do not belong to us, but

CHAP. V.

Jesus teaches the people from Simon's ship, 1—3; who, by his direction and power, takes a large draught of fishes, 4—7. Simon, James, and John, follow him, 8—11. He cleanses a leper, 12—15; withdraws for prayer, 16; heals a paralytick, and silences the objections of the scribes and Pharisees against his forgiving sins, 17—26; calls Levi, and justifies his own eating with publicans and sinners, 27—32, and vindicates his disciples, for not fasting, at present, after the manner of the Pharisees, and John's disciples, 33—39.

AND it came to pass, that, ª as the people pressed upon him to hear the word of God, he stood by ᵇ the lake of Gennesaret,

2 And saw two ships standing by the lake: but the fishermen were gone out of them, and were ᶜ washing *their* nets.

3 And he entered into one of the ships, ᵈ which was Simon's, and prayed him that he would thrust out a little

a viii. 45. xii. 1. Matt. xl. 12. Mark iii. 9. 24.
b Num. xxxiv. 11. Chinnereth. Josh. xii. 3. Chinneroth. Matt. xiv. 34. Mark vi. 53.
c Matt. iv. 21. Mark i. 19.
d Matt. iv. 18. John i. 41, 42.

---

to the Lord; nor can we reasonably hope to escape that reproach and contempt, which our Redeemer continually experienced: yet this ought not to damp our ardour, or dismay us from constancy in our attempts to be useful. It should be our custom, as it was our Saviour's, to resort, on " the Lord's day " *at least,* to the assemblies of his people, to join in his worship and attend to his truth: and whether we read, hear, or preach the word of God, we should enquire diligently into its meaning, and then apply it to our own case, or to that of others. " The Spirit of " the LORD," who anointed the Saviour for his work, and who has revealed him in the scriptures, must also discover him to our hearts, in all his gracious characters and offices: we ought, therefore, to seek this blessing, by fervent prayer, in behalf of ourselves and others, especially when attending on " the means of grace," or when about to use them. Under this blessed influence we shall perceive, that the message of the gospel is indeed " glad tidings to the poor" and humble: the divine Redeemer came on purpose to " bind up the broken in heart," and to give peace to the wounded conscience; to rescue the wretched captives of Satan; to bring them forth into the blessed light of divine truth; and to open their blinded eyes, that they may behold and rejoice in the light, and be delivered from all the galling chains of their own destructive lusts; and thus to admit them " to the glorious liberty of the children of " God." Let sinners then attend to the Saviour's invitation, in " the acceptable year of the Lord," when liberty is thus proclaimed to " those that are bruised :" let them seek to him for this blessed deliverance, that this scripture may not only be fulfilled in their ears, but in their hearts and experience; while victory, peace, consolation, and the fruits of righteousness, are the results of their faith in the incarnate Son of God.—But many will attend to the gospel, and express their approbation of the things which are spoken; yea, many will give the Lord himself good words, who will not give him their hearts. Some prejudice intervenes, to furnish an objection against the humbling doctrine of the cross: and, while the word itself excites their proud and carnal enmity; men lay the blame on something in the conduct or manner of the speaker, that they may not be self-condemned in neglecting his message.—Many seem to think themselves entitled almost exclusively to the favour of God; yet they will not seek it *in his appointed way:* when, therefore, others enjoy the privileges which they have forfeited, they are greatly offended. In vain do we shew, that God has asserted his undoubted right to " do what he will with his own ;" that

he has frequently passed by formalists, to save pagans and profligates; and that he always dispenses his favours, in that manner, which tends most to display his own glory, and especially the riches of his unmerited grace and mercy. Instead of being silenced, they are the more exasperated by such representations; and their enmity to God often shews itself in revilings, outrages, and persecutions against his servants. But he, who avoided the assaults of his enraged enemies, till his appointed hour arrived, will uphold and protect all his ministers, till they have " finished their " testimony."

V. 32—44.

If the ministers of Christ be persecuted from one place and driven to another, let them still boldly proceed in declaring to " all men every where" the way of salvation. The word which they speak, being attended with the power of their Lord, will be made effectual to convince, alarm, and convert some of their hearers. No case can be desperate if Jesus see good to work; even those in their assemblies, who are most evidently possessed of " unclean " spirits," may be delivered from them, and made illustrious monuments of his grace and power : and, though the devil may create great distress, to such as Christ is rescuing from his dominion, he cannot do them any real harm. We ought therefore to spread abroad the fame of the Saviour in every place; to beseech him for those who are diseased in body or mind; and to use our influence in bringing sinners to him, that his powerful hands may be laid upon them for their healing. Thus relying on his power, truth, and love, for ourselves, and those who are more immediately connected with us, we should seek to promote the preaching of his " gospel in other cities also," and in other regions, even to the ends of the earth. For though his personal ministry was confined to one place at a time, yet he may continue *with us,* by his word and Spirit, and extend the same blessings to other nations also; till, throughout all the earth, those who now are the worshippers and servants of Satan, shall acknowledge him as " the " Christ the Son of God," and find " redemption through " his blood, the forgiveness of their sins, according to " the riches of his grace, wherein he hath abounded to- " wards us in all wisdom and prudence." (*Note, Eph.* i. 3—8, *vv.* 6—8.)

NOTES.

CHAP. V. V. 1—11. (*Notes, Matt.* iv. 18—22. xiii. 1, 2. *Mark* i. 16—22.) This is generally supposed to be a more particular account of the manner, in which

2 v 5

from the land. And *he sat down, and taught the people out of the ship.

4 Now when he had left speaking, he said unto Simon, *Launch out into the deep, and let down your nets for a draught.

5 And Simon answering said unto him, Master, *we have toiled all the night, and have taken nothing: *nevertheless at thy word I will let down the net.

6 And when they had this done, *they inclosed a great multitude of fishes: and their net brake.

7 And they beckoned unto *their* partners, which were in the other ship, that they should come and help them.

And they came, and filled both the ships, so that they began to sink.

8 When Simon Peter saw *it*, *he fell down at Jesus' knees, saying, *Depart from me, for *I am a sinful man, O Lord.

9 For *he was astonished, and all that were with him, at the draught of the fishes which they had taken:

10 And so *was* also *James and John, the sons of Zebedee, which were *partners with Simon. And Jesus *said unto Simon, Fear not; *from henceforth thou shalt catch men.

11 And when they had brought their *ships to land, *they forsook all, and followed him.

Andrew and Peter, James and John, were called to be the constant followers of Christ, in order to their appointment to the apostolical office. Andrew indeed is not mentioned; but it is probable that he was present. The exact order of the history is not, on that supposition, observed. Some of the company might be employed in " mending their nets" after washing; and others in " washing their nets," by casting them from the shore into the lake. All of them had become acquainted with Jesus some time before; were called his disciples, and even baptized those who became his followers; and probably had attended him to Jerusalem, and returned with him through Samaria into Galilee: (*Notes, John i. 35—42. ii. 1—5. iii. 22—24. iv. 1—9 :) yet they seem to have followed their ordinary employments, from time to time, till on this occasion they became his constant attendants, which was after John the Baptist had been " cast into prison." (*Note, Matt. iv. 12—17, v. 12.)—Jesus had hitherto, generally, preached in the synagogues; but now such numbers thronged around him, that those places of worship could no longer contain them. Being, therefore, on the bank of the lake of Gennesaret, or the sea of Tiberias, attended by a vast concourse of people, who pressed on him to hear " the word of God ; " (*Marg. Ref.* a, b ;) he saw two small fishing vessels near the shore, but the fishermen had just left them : accordingly he entered that vessel which belonged to Peter, and desiring him to thrust it a little from the land, he sat down, and thence instructed the people. (*Marg. Ref.* c—e.—*Note, Matt.* xiii. 1, 2.) Having finished his instructions, he directed Peter to push out his boat into the deep water of the lake, and there to let down his nets for a draught of fishes. To this Peter answered, that having toiled during the whole night, the proper time for fishing, they had taken nothing: at his word, however, they would make another attempt; though there was no human probability of success. But, beyond expectation, they inclosed immediately so large a number of fishes, that the net brake in some places with the weight of them: yet by the assistance of their partners in the other ship, they secured them all; and with them both their boats were filled so much, that they were ready to sink. (*Marg. Ref.* f—k.—*Notes, John* xxi. 1—14.) This display of the power and know-

ledge of Jesus so astonished Peter, that he was overpowered with awe and consternation: and being conscious of his own sinfulness, as well as impressed with a scose of Christ's holiness and majesty; he very humbly, but ignorantly, desired him " to depart from him," being afraid of some fatal consequence from his presence with so great a sinner. (*Marg. Ref.* l—n.—*Job* xlii. 1—6, v. 6. *Is.* vi. 5—8. *Matt.* viii. 5—9.) Indeed he seems to have been so astonished, that he scarcely knew what he said : though he spake according to the notions, which have generally been entertained of sinful man's danger, from the power and presence of a holy God, or of those whom he especially approves and favours. (viii. 37. *Notes, Deut.* v. 22—29. *Judg.* xiii. 18—23. 1 *Sam.* vi. 19—21. 2 *Sam.* vi. 8, 9. 1 *Kings* xvii. 18.)—The miracle itself was emblematick of many things relative to the preaching of the gospel, and especially of Peter's great success on the day of Pentecost. (*Note, Acts* ii. 41.)—When Christ had encouraged him and his companions, and assured them, that he purposed to employ them in bringing sinners by his gospel to the obedience of faith, they did not hesitate to leave all and follow him. (*Marg. Ref.*—*Note, Matt.* xix. 27, 28.)

Pressed upon him. (1) Επικεισθαι. xxiii. 23. *John* xi. 38. *Acts* xxvii. 20. 1 *Cor.* ix. 16. *Heb.* ix. 10.—*Launch out.* (4) Επαναγαγε. 3. Rendered " to thrust out."—*The deep.*] To Cαθος. *Matt.* xiii. 5. *Rom.* viii. 39. xi. 33. 1 *Cor.* ii. 10. *Eph.* iii. 18.—*Mic.* vii. 19. *Sept.—A draught.*] Αγραν. 9. Here only N. T.—*Master.* (5) Επιστατα. viii. 24. 45. ix. 33. 49. xvii. 13.—Luke alone uses this word.—*Ex.* i. 11. v. 14. 2 *Kings* xxv. 19. 2 *Chr.* ii. 2. *Sept.* Ab εφιστημι, præficio.— *They inclosed.* (6) Συνεκλεισαν. *Rom.* xi. 32. *Gal.* iii. 22, 23. Not elsewhere N. T.—*Brake.*] Διερρηγνυτο. viii. 29. *Matt.* xxvi. 65. *Acts* xiv. 14.—*Their net* " was rent," in some places.—*They beckoned.* (7) Κατενευσαν. Here only N. T. Εννευον,. i. 62.—*Partners.*] Μετοχοις. *Heb.* i. 9. iii. 1. vi. 4. Μιλοχη, 2 *Cor.* vi. 14.—*They began to sink.*] Ωςε Cυθιζεσθαι αυτα.—" So that they were near to sink," or *in danger of sinking.* 1 *Tim.* vi. 9. Not elsewhere N. T.— *Partners.* (10) Κοινωνοι. *Matt.* xxiii. 30. 1 *Cor.* x. 18. 20. *Philem.* 17. *Heb.* x. 33. 1 *Pet.* v. 1. 2 *Pet.* i. 4.—*Thou shalt catch men.*] Εση ζωγρων. 2 *Tim.* ii. 26. Not elsewhere N. T. (*Note, 2 Tim.* ii. 24—26.)

12 ¶ And it came to pass, when he was in a certain city, behold, ª a man, ª full of leprosy; who, seeing Jesus, ª fell on *his* face, and ª besought him, saying, Lord, ª if thou wilt, thou canst make me clean.

13 And he put forth *his* hand, and touched him, saying, ªI will; be thou clean. And ª immediately the leprosy departed from him.

14 And ª he charged him to tell no man: but go, ª and shew thyself to the priest, ª and offer for thy cleansing according as Moses commanded, ª for a testimony unto them.

15 But ª so much the more ª went there a fame abroad of him: ª and great multitudes came together to hear, and to be healed by him of their infirmities.

16 And ª he withdrew himself into the wilderness, and prayed.

17 ¶ And it came to pass on a certain day, as he was teaching, ª that there were Pharisees and doctors of the law sitting by, which were come out of every town of Galilee, and Judea, ª and Jerusalem; and ª the power of the Lord was *present* to heal them.

18 And, behold, ª men brought in a bed a man which was taken with a palsy; and they sought *means* to bring him in, and to lay *him* before him.

19 And when they could not find by what *way* they might bring him in, because of the multitude, ª they went upon the ª house-top, and let him down through the tiling, with *his* couch, into the midst before Jesus.

20 And when ª he saw their faith, he said unto him, 'Man, thy sins are forgiven thee.

21 And ª the Scribes and the Pharisees began to reason, saying, Who is this which speaketh ª blasphemies? ª Who can forgive sins but God alone?

22 But when Jesus ª perceive₄ their thoughts, he answering said unto them, ª What reason ye in your hearts?

23 Whether ª is easier to say, Thy sins be forgiven thee; or to say, Rise up and walk?

24 But that ye may know ª that the Son of man hath ª power upon earth to forgive sins, (he said unto the sick of the palsy,) ª I say unto thee, Arise, ª and take up thy couch, and go unto thine house.

25 And ª immediately he rose up before them, and took up that whereon he lay, and departed to his own house, ª glorifying God.

26 And they were all amazed, ª and they glorified God, ª and were filled with fear, saying, We have seen strange things to day.

27 ¶ And after these things he went forth, ª and saw a publican, named Levi, sitting at the receipt of custom; and he said unto him, ª Follow me.

28 And he ª left all, rose up, and followed him.

29 And Levi ª made him a great feast in his own house; and there was a great company of publicans, and of others, that sat down with them.

30 But ª their Scribes and Pharisees murmured against his disciples, saying, Why do ye eat and drink with publicans and sinners?

1, 2. xxii. 11. xix. 7. Is. lav. 5. Matt. xxi. 28—32. Mark vii. 3.

V. 12—15. *Marg. Ref.—Notes, Matt.* viii. 1—4. *Mark* i. 40—45.—*A certain city.* (12) The confines of the city are intended, for the lepers were not suffered to live in towns. It is uncertain, whether Capernaum, or some other place in Galilee, be meant.

V. 16. *He withdrew.*] Ην ὑποχωρων. ix. 10. Not elsewhere N. T. "He was withdrawing," or separating himself. He frequently went aside from the multitude, for those exercises of devotion in which his soul delighted. (*Notes*, vi. 12. *Prov.* xviii. 1, 2. *Mark* i. 35—39.)

V. 17. *Marg. Ref.—The power,* &c.] ' " The power " " of the Lord was present to heal them;" who came to ' be healed of their infirmities. (15) and not the Pharisees

' and lawyers. ... So, (*Ps.* xcix. 8.) " Thou answeredst " " them," Moses and Aaron, " and tookest vengeance " " of their inventions," that is, the inventions of the peo-" ple.' *Whitby.* (*Note, Ps.* xcix. 8.)

V. 18—26. *Marg. Ref.—Notes, Matt.* ix. 2—8. *Mark* ii. 1—12.—*The house-top.* (19) Το δωμα. xii. 3. xvii. 31. *Matt.* x. 27.—*The tiling.*] Των κεραμων. Here only N. T.— Couch.] Το κλινιδιον. (24) Here only N. T.—Τον γραβϐατον. *Mark* ii. 4. 9.—*Strange things.* (26) Παραδοξα. Here only N. T. "Things beyond all expectation;" or so wonderful, that we could not have thought of them.—Hence *Paradox.*

V. 27—32. (*Marg. Ref.—Notes, Matt.* ix. 9—13. *Mark* ii. 13—17.) Matthew says of himself, " He arose

3 ß 7

31 And Jesus answering, said unto them, 'They that are whole need not a physician, but they that are sick. 32 I 'came not to call the righteous, but sinners to repentance. 33 ¶ And they said unto him, *Why do the disciples of John fast often, 'and make prayers, and likewise the disciples of the Pharisees; but thine eat and drink? 34 And he said unto them, Can ye make *the children of the bride-chamber fast while the *bridegroom is with them? 35 But the days will come, 'when the Bridegroom shall be taken away from them, 'and then shall they fast in those days.

36 ¶ And he spake also a parable unto them, *No man putteth a piece of a new garment upon an old: if otherwise, then both the new maketh a rent, and the piece that was taken out of the new, agreeth not with the old. 37 And no man putteth new wine into *old bottles; else the new wine will burst the bottles, and be spilled, and the bottles shall perish. 38 But *new wine must be put into new bottles; and both are preserved. 39 No man also, having drunk old wine, straightway desireth new; for he saith, *The old is better.

" and followed him :" but Luke says of him, " He left " all." Matthew only says, "Jesus sat at meat : " but Luke says of him, " He made a great feast." ' True saints love ' not to speak of their own excellences : but it is fitting ' that those who see them, should not be silent concerning ' them.' *Milner.—A feast.* (29) Δοχην. xiv. 13. Not elsewhere N. T.—*Gen.* xxi. 8. xxvi. 30. *Sept.*

V. 33—38. *Marg. Ref.—Notes, Matt.* ix. 14—17. *Mark* ii. 18—22.—*No man,* &c. (36—38.) Perhaps the impropriety of attempting a coalition between the religion of the Pharisees, and even that of John's disciples, when they did not become the disciples of Jesus, may be meant. True religion has been for substance the same, since the revelation of a Saviour to fallen man. Even the ritual law, and the whole Mosaick dispensation, were intended to answer special purposes only for a season ; (*Notes, Rom.* v. 20, 21. *Gal.* iii. 19—22 ;) and the traditions of the elders, with the ceremonies of the law, and many uncommanded plausible austerities, formed the religion of the strictest sect of the Jews, in our Lord's days, to which many of John's disciples, (as distinct from Christ's,) seem in great measure to have conformed. But Jesus came, to introduce another and better dispensation, than even that of Moses, which was " waxing old and ready to vanish away ; " (*Notes, Heb.* viii. 8—13, *v.* 13 ;) as well as to vindicate the moral law, from the corrupt glosses and traditions of the Pharisees. He would not, therefore, allow his disciples to attempt a coalition between his religion, and that of the Pharisees. Fasting, as far as obligatory and useful, would form a part of the new dispensation, and not be disgraced by the superstition, hypocrisy, and spiritual pride which then attended it. But, as things were at that time, it would be as absurd to retain any part of the old system, and to graft Christianity upon it, as to put new undressed cloth on an old worn-out garment; or new fermenting wine, into old leather-bottles. Thus the Jews, " going " about to establish their own righteousness," and to shore up the old building by props and buttresses, refused to build on the Foundation which God himself had laid. (*Note, Rom.* x. 1—4.) This attempt at a coalition between the old and new dispensations, or rather between the reli-

gion of the Pharisees and that of Jesus, was the grand fault of the Judaizing teachers of Christianity, against whom St. Paul so zealously contended, especially in his epistle to the Galatians. They wanted to mend the pharisaical religion, which was as an old worn-out garment, with the gospel; and to put the new wine of the gospel into the " old bottles," of the antiquated ceremonies of the Mosaick law, and the traditions of the elders.—This interpretation has never before been proposed, as far as I know, and I suggest it with diffidence ; having never been satisfied with the interpretation generally given.

V. 39. As old wine is more valued, and deemed more wholesome and pleasant, than new, which is still in a state of fermentation ; and as those who have been used to the former cannot readily be brought to relish the latter, but will still prefer the old wine; so the substantials of religion, which have been the same, from the first revelation of mercy to fallen man, are far more valuable than the austerities, traditions, or peculiarities, of any party, or even than the ceremonial observances of the Mosaick law; and they, who have been habitually conversant with the former, will not easily be brought to pay great regard to the latter ; but will deem repentance, faith, and holiness far preferable to them all. The Christian dispensation was new, compared with the Mosaick covenant ; yet the religion contained in it is as *old wine*; it is that of Abel, Enoch, Noah, Abraham, &c. with only circumstantial variations. (*Notes, Heb.* xi.)—The verse, however, is generally explained to mean, that men cannot at once change their modes and habits of life, but must gradually be inured to those kinds and degrees of self-denial, which are not immediately necessary; as persons that have been used to old wine must be gradually brought to relish the new: and therefore Jesus did not think proper to impose such austerities on his disciples at once, but gradually to train them up to self-denial, hardship, and suffering.—*Better.*] Χρησοτερος. vi. 35. *Rom.* ii. 4. *Eph.* iv. 32.

PRACTICAL OBSERVATIONS.
V. 1—15.

When multitudes " press to hear the word of God," it

CHAP. VI.

Jesus vindicates his disciples from the charge of breaking the sabbath, 1—5. He shews it lawful to do good on the sabbath; and restores a withered hand, 6—10. His enemies are filled with madness, 11. He spends the night in prayer, 12; appoints the twelve apostles, 13—16; heals divers diseased persons, 17—19; pronounces blessings and woes, 20—26; and teaches love to enemies, meekness, liberality, mercy, and candour, 27—38. He shews, by parables, that knowledge is indispensably needful in teachers, and holiness in reformers, 39—42. The tree is known by his fruit, 43—45. The parable of the wise and the foolish builders, 46—49.

becomes expedient to exceed ordinary measures of diligence, in teaching them. On these rare and important occasions, every day is seasonable, and every place proper, for preaching the gospel; and the common maxims, by which such matters are regulated at other times, are superseded by far more weighty considerations.—Whatever is employed in the service of Christ, becomes holy by its relation to him: thus our houses, possessions, employments, and even refreshments, may be sanctified to us, by being rendered subservient to his glory. (*Notes*, 1 *Cor.* x. 29—33, *v.* 31. *Col.* iii. 16, 17.)—We are often called upon to renounce temporal advantages for his sake; but we are seldom, even in these things, eventually losers by him. Obedience to his word, and dependence on his power and blessing, will in every respect ensure all desirable success; but especially in the great concerns of religion. The minister, who has toiled long, under great discouragement, and with no apparent success, must not give up his hope or cease from his labour, but at the word of his Lord he must, again and again, " let down the net." Such delays sometimes lead to more signal success, by increasing humility, simplicity, and fervency of spirit in prayer: and thus the unsuccessful endeavours of many years may be amply recompensed by the blessing of God even on a single sermon! It would indeed be more encouraging to see some fruit of our labours, from time to time; and when this is not witnessed, it may well cause us to enquire, whether there be nothing in our spirit, conduct, or doctrine, which prevents usefulness: and whether we use *all* proper means of attaining it, and use them in simple dependence on the divine blessing for success: yet the effect may at length be equally great, when we long labour, diligently and patiently, as it were in the dark. Let then the " fishers of " men " persevere in their work, without yielding to discouragement, or growing remiss in it: let them seek the salvation of souls alone, and not court applause; or fish for preferments, honours, and secular advantages: let them stand prepared to relinquish every worldly object at the call of Christ, that they may follow him more closely, and give themselves up wholly to their ministry: let them be helpers of each other in the work, as *partners*, and not *rivals*; and let them not fear but " from henceforth they shall " catch men."—The more fully the Lord displays his excellent glory and majesty to us, the viler shall we appear in our own eyes: yet this should not induce us to say, " De- " part from me, for I am a sinful man, O Lord; " but rather to intreat him to come and " dwell in our hearts " by faith," that he may transform and cleanse them. As we are all full of the leprosy of sin, so when we hear of Jesus, we should humbly and earnestly beseech him, saying, " Lord, if thou wilt, thou canst make *me* clean: " nor need we fear a repulse, as this work is his delight and glory. Thus being saved from the guilt and power of our

VOL. V.

sins, we may diffuse abroad his fame, and be in some measure instrumental in bringing others to hear him, and to be healed of their infirmities.

V. 16—32.

In tracing the example of our divine Saviour, we find that he interchanged publick services and retired devotion; and that the sole business of his life was to glorify God by doing good to men, and to commune with his Father. Thus our several duties should in succession occupy our time; and piety and charity should be connected in our habitual and persevering conduct. A life thus spent will best manifest our faith in Christ, and evince that he has both pardoned our sins and healed our souls. When professors of the doctrines of grace thus copy their Lord's example, they will effectually confute the malicious cavils and perverse reasonings of opposing Scribes and Pharisees: and, being enabled by divine grace to delight in the holy service of God, which no man by nature can do; they will not only glorify him themselves, but excite others to do the same. Indeed when " the power of the Lord is " present to heal " men's souls; when the avaricious are induced to forego their lucrative employments, because unlawful; and profligate persons are taught to live sober, righteous, and godly lives, by hearing the despised gospel of Christ; mere spectators must sometimes be astonished, and allow that they have witnessed " strange things," which they did not expect, and cannot account for.—As Jesus " came not to call the righteous, but sinners to re- " pentance," we too should be ready to go among them, as far as we have a prospect of doing them good; and especially to direct them to the only Physician of distempered souls: and if we well know our own sinfulness, and the power and grace of the divine Redeemer, we shall not disdain or despair of any.

V. 33—39.

Let all, who would prosper in the divine life, attend chiefly to the grand essentials of religion: for when externals and circumstantials are magnified above their real importance, censoriousness, bigotry, and divisions are the invariable consequences.—Because humble Christians practise their self-denial, and perform their devotions, in secret, and without ostentation, Pharisees may sometimes be ready to conclude that they neither fast nor pray at all. But every part of our duty has its proper season and proportion, as stated in the scriptures; and it should have the same in the conduct of our lives: the gracious presence of our Beloved makes a feast to our souls, so long as it is continued to us; but when our sins provoke his departure or his frown, we are called to mourn and fast, as well as pray. The Lord, however, trains up his people gradually for the trials and hardships allotted them; and, in perfect wisdom

2 X

AND it came to pass on ᵃ the second sabbath after the first, ᵇ that he went through the corn-fields; ᶜ and his disciples plucked the ears of corn, and did eat, rubbing *them* in *their* hands.

2 And certain of the Pharisees said unto them, ᵈ Why do ye that which is ᵉ not lawful to do on the sabbath-days?

3 And Jesus answering them said, ᵉ Have ye not read so much as this, ᶠ what David did, when himself was an hungred, and they which were with him;

4 How he went into the house of God, and did take and eat the shewbread, and gave also to them that were with him; ᵍ which it is not lawful to eat but for the priests alone?

5 And he said unto them, ⁱ That the Son of man is Lord also of the sabbath.

6 ¶ And ᵏ it came to pass also on another sabbath, that ˡ he entered into the synagogue and taught: ᵐ and there was a man whose right hand was withered.

7 And the Scribes and Pharisees ⁿ watched him, whether he would heal on the sabbath-day; ᵒ that they might find an accusation against him.

8 But ᵖ he knew their thoughts, and said to the man which had the withered hand, ᵠ Rise up, and stand forth in the midst. And he arose, and stood forth.

9 Then said Jesus unto them, I will ask you one thing; ʳ Is it lawful on the sabbath-days to do good, or to do evil; ˢ to save life, or to destroy it ?

10 And, ᵗ looking round about upon them all, he said unto the man, ᵘ Stretch forth thy hand. And he did so: and his hand was restored whole as the other.

11 And ˣ they were filled with madness; ʸ and communed one with another what they might do to Jesus.

---

and tenderness, he proportions their services to their strength: we should therefore copy his example, in dealing with the weak in faith, the young convert, or the tempted discouraged believer.—Those who have been used to drink the " old wine " of divine consolations, and of a close walk with God, have not only lost their relish for earthly joys ; but they will not easily be brought to attend to those novel inventions and human additions to religion, which are most ostentatious and shewy, but far less valuable and satisfactory, than a life of humble faith, and devoted obedience to the commandments of our Lord and Saviour.

NOTES.

CHAP. VI. V. 1. *Second Sabbath*, &c.] Some render the original words, " the second prime sabbath ; " supposing, that the day of Pentecost was meant, and that it fell on the sabbath-day. The three great feasts were, in many respects, observed as sabbaths; (*Marg. Ref.* a ;) for the first day of unleavened bread began in the evening, after the close of the fourteenth day of the first month, about the time when the passover was eaten. (*Notes, Ex.* xii. 15—20.) But when either the first day of unleavened bread, or the day of Pentecost, or the first day of the feast of Tabernacles, fell on a sabbath, it was reckoned peculiarly sacred. When the first day of unleavened bread fell thus, it was called ' The first prime sabbath : ' the Pentecost falling thus, was called ' the second prime sabbath :' and the first day of the feast of tabernacles, in this case, was called ' the third prime sabbath.' This is the opinion of Grotius, Hammond, and many learned expositors.—But others render the words, " The first sabbath, after the second day " of unleavened bread." From this day, seven weeks were numbered, and then the Pentecost, or the feast of weeks, was observed. ' The first sabbath, from this second day ' of unleavened bread, was called δευτεροπρωτον, the second ' δευτεροδευτερον, the second sabbath from that day ; the ' third, δευτεροτριτον, the third sabbath from that second day, ' and so on till they came to the seventh sabbath from that ' day, that is, the forty-ninth day, which was the day of ' Pentecost. ... Epiphanios expressly says, our Lord's dis' ciples did this, on the sabbath following the first day of ' unleavened bread.' *Whitby*. If this interpretation be adopted, the ears of corn plucked by the disciples, must have been *barley*: for the wheat was not ripe till some time after. And, though the offering of wave-loaves, for the first-fruits, at the feast of Pentecost, (*Note, Lev.* xxiii. 15—21,) shews that some of the harvest was then gathered in ; yet it does not follow, but that some might remain in the fields, unreaped, at the same time.—It should be observed, that in case there was no likelihood of any barley being fit to cut, at the time when the passover would otherwise have been celebrated ; a moon, or month, was intercalated, and so the beginning of the first month was fixed to the subsequent new moon : and by the passover all the other feasts were regulated.—These are the most probable opinions on this subject, which is evidently of greater difficulty than importance.—*Rubbing.*] Ψωχοντες. Here only N. T.

V. 2—11. *Marg. Ref.—Notes, Matt.* xii. 1—21. *Mark* ii. 23—28. iii. 1—5.

An accusation. (7) Κατηγοριαν. *John* xviii. 29. 1 *Tim.* v. 19. *Tit.* i. 6.—*Madness.* (11) Ανοιας. (Ex α priv. et νες; *mens.*) 2 *Tim.* iii. 9. Not elsewhere N. T. (*Notes, Ps.* ii. 1—3. *Ec.* ix. 1—3, v. 3. *Acts* xxvi. 9—11.)

12 ¶ And it came to pass in those days, 'that he went out into a mountain to pray, and 'continued all night in prayer to God.

13 And 'when it was day, he called unto him his disciples: and of them he chose 'twelve, whom also he named 'apostles:

14 'Simon (whom he also named Peter) and 'Andrew his brother, 'James and John, 'Philip and Bartholomew,

15 'Matthew and 'Thomas, 'James the son 'm of Alpheus, and 'Simon called Zelotes,

16 And 'Judas the brother of James,

'and Judas Iscariot, which also was the traitor.

17 ¶ And he came down with them, and stood in the plain, and the company of his disciples, 'and a great multitude of people out of all Judea and Jerusalem, and from 'the sea-coast of Tyre and Sidon, 'which came to hear him, and to be healed of their diseases;

18 And they that were 'vexed with unclean spirits: and they were healed.

19 And the whole multitude 'sought to touch him: 'for there went virtue out of him, and healed them all.

20 ¶ And 'he lifted up his eyes on his disciples, and said, 'Blessed be ye

---

V. 12. Our Lord spent the whole night, preceding the appointment of his apostles, alone upon a mountain, " in " prayer to God." Some think, that the original words signify " an oratory of God," or small building erected for retirement and devotion; and the construction of the original best suits that rendering. Jesus, however, doubtless was engaged in prayer during the whole night, whilst his disciples seem to have gone to their rest as usual.—' Christ, ' by choosing his twelve apostles, not without long and ' fervent prayer, shews what piety is needful in ecclesias- ' tical elections, or in the choice and ordination of mi- ' nisters.' Beza. (Marg. Ref.—Notes, Acts xiii. 1—3. 1 Tim. v. 21, 22. 24, 25.)

Continued all night. (12) Ην διανυκτερευων. Here only N.T. Εx δια, et νυξ, nox.—In prayer to God.] Εν τη προσευχη τη Θεω.—Acts xvi. 13.

V. 13—16. Marg. Ref.—Notes, Matt. x. 1—4. Mark iii. 13—19.

He chose. (13) Εκλεξαμενος. Mark xiii. 20. John vi. 70. xiii. 18. xv. 16. 19. Acts i. 2.

V. 17—19. Marg. Ref.

The sea-coast. (17) Της παραλιου.—Here only N. T. Παρα, et αλις, mare.—That were vexed. (18) Οι οχλουμενοι. Acts v. 16. Not elsewhere N. T. Ab οχλος, turba.— Virtue. (19) Or, power. Δυναμις. viii. 46. Mark v. 30.— The word commonly rendered virtue, (αρετη, from Αρης, Mars, the fabled god of fortitude, as virtus from vir,) does not occur in the gospels, or in the Acts of the apostles: but only, Phil. iv. 8. 1 Pet. ii. 9. 2 Pet. i. 3. 5.

V. 20. ' The question here raised by interpreters, whe- ' ther this sermon be the same which we find men- ' tioned Luke the sixth, or only like a sermon spoken at ' another time and place, is of some concern for the ' right understanding of the words: for if the sermon be ' the same in both gospels, and it were spoken only once ' by Christ, though it be set down twice by the evange- ' lists; the words of one evangelist must be interpreted ' in a sense agreeable to the other, or else they cannot ' both be true. Whereas, if our Lord spake the words ' recorded by St. Luke, at any other time and place, than

' the discourse related by St. Matthew was delivered at, we ' may give different interpretations to their words: and ' that this was so seems highly probable. 1. Because St. ' Luke omits so many things recorded by St. Matthew, as ' parts of this discourse, viz. from the thirteenth to the ' thirty-ninth verse of the fifth chapter, all the sixth chap- ' ter; and from the sixth to the sixteenth verse of the ' seventh chapter; that is, he omits the greatest part of ' this sermon: ... and also added many woes. 2. ... St. ' Matthew doth sufficiently inform us, that his sermon was ' delivered before the healing of the leper; for " as Christ ' " came down from the mount, the leper came to him; " ' (Matt. viii. 2;) whereas St. Luke ... gives us the story of ' the leper first, and the history of Christ's sermon after.... ' Again, St. Luke reckons Matthew among those whom ' Christ had chosen to be of the twelve; and (17) he ' adds, that Christ went down with them, and preached ' the following sermon: whereas the sermon mentioned ' by St. Matthew was preached long before his calling to ' be one of Christ's disciples. ... Lastly, St. Matthew's ' sermon was preached on the mount by our Lord, calling ' his disciples up to him; whereas St. Luke informs us, that ' our Lord came down with his disciples from a mount, ' and stood in the plain, and from thence preached what ' he recorded.' Whitby on Matt. v. 1.—' Here being but ' four of the eight beatitudes mentioned, (Matt. v. 1—13,) ' and not one of these being delivered in the same words ' which are there used; as it is certain this must be ano- ' ther sermon than that on the mount, and spoken to ' other auditors; so it is only probable, not necessary, that ' they should bear the same sense.' Whitby.—The thirty- ninth, fortieth, and forty-fifth verses are not found in the sermon on the mount, but for substance in other parts of St. Matthew's gospel. (Notes, 39, 40. 43—45.)—Some however think, that the circumstance of a plain being here mentioned, and a mountain by St. Matthew, is not of much weight: ' our Lord, say they, might come down from the mountain with his disciples, and finding a large multitude assembled in the plain, he might reascend the mountain so far, as to be placed advantageously for being

a xii. 32. xiii. 36.
xiv. 15. Matt. v.
3. 10. Acts xiv.
22. 1 Cor. iii. 21
—23. 2 Thes. i.
5. Jam. i. 12.
b 25. 1. 53. Ps.
xliii. 4. 2 cxiii.
6. Is. iv. 1.
1 Cor. iv. 11.
2 Cor. xi. 27.
xii. 10.
c Ps. xvii. 15. lxiii.
1—6. lxv. 4. cxii.
9. Is. xxv. 6.
xliv. 3, 4. xlix.
9, 10. lxv. 13.
lxvi. 10. Jer. xxxi. 14, 25.
f 25. Ps. vi. 6—8.
18. lxi. 1—3.
xi. 35. xvi. 20, 21.
1 Pet. 1. 6—8.
cxxvi. 1, 2. Is.
John vii. 7. xv.
18, 19, 1 Pet. iii.
34. xii. 42.

poor; a for your's is the kingdom of God.

21 Blessed are b ye that hunger now; c for ye shall be filled. Blessed are d ye that weep now; e for ye shall laugh.

22 Blessed are ye f when men shall hate you, and when they g shall separate you from their company, and shall

h xxi. 17. Matt.
x. 18. 22. 39.
Acts ix. 16.
1 Cor. iv. 10, 11.
i Acts v. 41. Rom.
v. 3. 2 Cor. xii.
10. Col. i. 24.
Jam. i. 2.
k 1. 41, 44. 2 Sam.
vi. 16. Is. xxxv.
6. Acts iii. 8.
xiv. 10.
l 35. Matt. v. 12.
vi. 1, 2. 2 Tim.
i. 5—7. 2 Tim.
ii. 12. iv. 7, 8.
Heb. xi. 6. 26.
1 Pet. iv 13.
Rev. ii. 7. 10,
17. 26. iii. 5.
12. xxii. 7.
m 1 Kings xviii. 4.
Neh. ix. 26. Jer. ii. 30. Matt. xxi. 35, 36. xxiii. 31—37. Acts vii. 52.
Heb. xi. 36, 37.
lxxiii. 8—12. Prov. i. 32. Jer. v. 4—6. Am. iv. 1—3. vi. 1—6.
v. 1—6. Rev. xviii. 6—8.

reproach you, and cast out your name h as evil, b for the Son of man's sake.

23 i Rejoice ye in that day, and k leap for joy; for, behold, l your reward is great in heaven: m for in the like manner did their fathers unto the prophets.

24 But n woe unto you that are rich! o for ye have received your consolation.

---

heard by the people, and his disciples might go and seat themselves around him. Both the evangelists agree that a mountain was near; both agree, that Christ had been healing considerable numbers just before he delivered this discourse. St. Luke says, that he had been praying all night in the mountain: we may naturally suppose, in the higher and more retired part of it; that he then came down, and healed the numerous afflicted persons; and that seeing the multitudes he proceeded to teach them. And after both sermons we find him entering into Capernaum, and healing the centurion's servant.—Thus different persons view the subject very differently: but the circumstance of St. Matthew's gospel recording the sermon on the mount, not only before his own appointment to the apostolical office, but before he relates how he was called from the receipt of custom to follow Christ, seems of great weight: and several passages appear to require so different an interpretation than that which has been given of what are thought parallel passages in St. Matthew, that I scarcely know how to expound them, without adopting Dr. Whitby's conclusion; though I would by no means be confident in so controverted a point.—It seems probable, that the sermon recorded by St. Luke, being delivered at another time, and to another audience, than the sermon on the mount; our Lord saw good to inculcate the same general and important truths, with such variations, as his perfect knowledge of his hearers required.

Blessed, &c.] (Note, Matt. v. 3.) ' Christ teaches, ' against all the philosophers, especially the Epicureans, ' that the chief felicity of man is laid up no where on ' earth, but in heaven; and that persecution for righteous- ' ness' sake, is the way by which we must attain to it.' Beza.—All the true disciples of Christ are " poor in " spirit;" most of them are " the poor of this world;" and many become poor by forsaking all for his sake and the gospel, or parting with all from zeal for his glory: but though he knows their poverty, he declares " that they " are rich," " having nothing and yet possessing all " things;" " poor, yet making many rich." (Note, 2 Cor. vi. 3—10, v. 10.) Poverty indeed has advantages in respect of religion : but the blessing here pronounced, belongs to no poor persons, except those who are Christ's true disciples, and " heirs of the kingdom, which God hath pre- " pared for them that love him." (Note, Jam. ii. 5—7.) Voluntary poverty, without any call to it, is no where commanded; and it has generally been a self-righteous rival to true Christianity, and cannot here be intended.

(Marg. Ref. z, a.) It was peculiarly proper, that a special blessing should be pronounced on poor disciples, who have many trials to endure; but the rich, if " poor in spirit" and crucified to the world, are not excluded from it. (Note, Jam. i. 9—11.)

V. 21—23. (Marg. Ref.—Notes, Matt. v. 4 6. 10— 12.) It is probable, that many present were kept at a great distance from their necessary food, by attention on our Lord's instructions: and thus their natural hunger might be the effect of their " hungering after righteous- " ness;" which would ensure their being satisfied, in due time, with divine consolations and a holy felicity. Many might also be weeping for sin, or through affliction; but being Christ's disciples they must be accounted happy, for they would surely rejoice in due time. (Notes, Ps. cxxvi. 5, 6. 2 Cor. vi. 3—10. vii. 9—11.) Indeed they would shortly be hated, excommunicated, excluded from the company of their former friends, reproached as if guilty of the most atrocious crimes, and loaded with hard names, and with infamy and disgrace, for their profession of his truth and obedience to his commandments: but instead of being dejected on these accounts, they ought to " exult with exceeding joy;" being assured that the contempt and hatred of the world, thus incurred, would be a decisive evidence of their acceptance with God, and the greatness of their future recompence; for their fathers had behaved in exactly the same manner to the prophets of old, whom God had sent among them.—' Blessed are ' they, who patiently suffer poverty, hunger, grief, and per- ' secution for the sake of Christ; that they may obtain that ' kingdom, and that reward in heaven, he hath promised ' to his faithful servants.' Whitby. (Notes, Is. lvii. 7, 8. lxvi. 5, 6. 2 Thes. i. 3—10. Jam. v. 9—11. 1 Pet. iv. 12 —16.)

Ye shall be filled. (21) Χορτασθησεσθε. See on Matt. v. 6.—Ye shall laugh.] Γελασετε. 25. Here only N. T. Γελως, Jam. iv. 9.—Shall separate. (22) Αφορισωσιν. Matt. xiii. 49. xxv. 32. Acts xiii. 2. xix. 9. Rom. i. 1. 2 Cor. vi. 17. Gal. i. 15. ii. 12. Απο, et οριζω termino, ab ορος, terminus.—Leap for joy. (23) Σκιρτησατε. See on i. 41.

V. 24—26. Perhaps some persons, who were rich and lived in plenty and luxury, had come to make remarks on our Lord's preaching, and to deride what they heard; and these might here primarily be addressed. (Note, xvi. 14, 15.) But in general, he intended to shew his disciples the danger of riches, worldly indulgences, and all those

25 Woe unto ᵖ you that are full! for ye shall hunger. Woe unto you ᵗ that laugh now! ᵠ for ye shall mourn and weep.

26 Woe unto you ʳ when all men shall speak well of you! for ˢ so did their fathers to the false prophets.

27 ¶ But I say ᵗ unto you which hear, ᵘ Love your enemies, ᵛ do good to them which hate you,

28 ᵂ Bless them that curse you, and pray for them which ᵇ despitefully use you.

29 And ᶜ unto him that ᵈ smiteth thee on the *one* cheek, offer also the other; ᵉ and him that taketh away thy cloak, forbid not *to take thy* coat also.

30 Give ᶠ to every man that asketh

of thee ; ᵍ and of him that taketh away thy goods ask *them* not again.

31 And ʰ as ye would that men should do to you, do ye also to them likewise.

32 For ⁱ if ye love them which love you, ᵏ what thank have ye ? for sinners also love those that love them.

33 And if ye do good to them which do good to you, what thank have ye ? for sinners also do even the same.

34 And ˡ if ye lend *to them* of whom ye hope to receive, what thank have ye ? for sinners also lend to sinners, to receive as much again.

35 But ᵐ love ye your enemies, and do good, and lend, hoping for nothing again : and your reward shall be great, ⁿ and ye shall be the children of the Highest : ° for he is kind unto the unthankful, and *to* the evil.

36 Be ye therefore ᵖ merciful, as your Father also is merciful.

---

ruinous advantages which men so eagerly pursue ; and of that pride and self-sufficiency which are commonly increased by outward prosperity. They who were not made partakers of better riches than these coveted possessions, would soon have " received their consolation," be left finally destitute, and exchange their mirth and laughter, for weeping, wailing, and gnashing of teeth. (*Marg. Ref.* n—s. —*Notes*, xii. 15—21. xvi. 22—26. *Matt.* xix. 23—26. 1 *Tim.* vi. 6—10, *vv.* 9, 10. *Jam.* i. 9—11.)—As it could not be expected, that his disciples, who decidedly adhered to his holy doctrine and commandments, would be generally commended in this evil world ; he likewise pronounced a woe on " those, of whom all men spake well." (*Note*, 2 *Tim.* iii. 10—12.) This might especially be intended of teachers : as the false prophets had been thus generally applauded by the Jews in former ages ; so it might be inferred, that those teachers, who were generally commended, even by men of bad or doubtful character, had, in like manner, soothed men's consciences, and encouraged them in some measure in their sins.—ᶜ He that ' will be pleasing to all, must speak things grateful to all : ' now that cannot be good, which is grateful to bad men. ' Thus the false prophets, whom the Jews commended, ' spake to them " smooth things," (*Is.* xxx. 10,) they ' " prophesied lies," " because the people loved to have ' " it so ;" ... " they strengthened the hands of evil doers," ' (*Jer.* xxiii. 14,) " and daubed with untempered morter." ' (*Ez.* xiii. 10, 11.)' *Whitby*. (*Marg. Ref.* t, u.—*Notes*, 1 *Kings* xxii. 13, 14. *Is.* xxx. 8—11. *Jer.* v. 30, 31. *Ez.* xiv. 10—16. *John* vii. 3—10. *Rom.* xvi. 17—20. 2 *Pet.* ii. 1—3.)

Have received. (24) Απεχετε. *Matt.* vi. 2. 5. 16. *Philem.* 15.—*Gen.* xliii. 23. *Num.* xxxii. 19. *Sept.*—*That are full.* (25) Οἱ εμπεπλησμενοι. i. 53. *John* vi. 12. *Rom.* xv. 24.— *Ex.* xv 9. *Ps.* cvii. 9. *Jer.* xxxi. 25. *Sept.*

V. 27—36. *Marg. Ref.*—*Notes*, *Matt.* v. 38—48. vii. 12. *Rom.* xii. 17—21. 1 *Pet.* ii. 18—25. iii. 8—12.

Ask ... again. (30) Απαιτει. xii. 20. Not elsewhere N. T.—*Deut.* xv. 2, 3. *Neh.* v. 7. *Sept.*—ᶜ Do not exact even what has been taken away by fraud or violence, if it would distress the person concerned to repay thee : rather lose it, if consistent with other duties, than demand it by a legal process.' (*Marg. Ref.* g.—*Note*, 1 *Cor.* vi. 1 —6.)—*What thank*, &c. (32. 34) Ποια ὑμιν χαρις εστι ; 1 *Pet.* ii. 20, 21. " What grace is it to you ? "—ᶜ What evidence have you that you are partakers of the grace of God ? What reason can you give for your hope, that your persons and services are accepted ? '—Mere nature can produce mutual affection between men of similar character, and a reciprocal intercourse of good offices ; notwithstanding that they are in a state of enmity against God, and under the dominion of selfish passions : for they either gratify a natural instinctive inclination in this way ; or they seek their own ease, interest, pleasure, or reputation, by such attachments and friendly actions, without regard to the glory, will, or favour of God. Τινα μισθον εχετε ; ... τι περισσον ποιειτε ; *Matt.* v. 46, 47.—*Hoping for nothing again.* (35) Μηδεν απελπιζοντες. Here only N. T. ᶜ *Ut nihil inde speretis.*' *Vulgate.* ᶜ *Opponitur τω επελπιζειν. Schleusner.* (*Notes*, *Deut.* xv. 4—10.) Or, expecting nothing from man in return ; but trusting that God will make up your loss, if you do it in dependence on him and in obedience to his command.—*Ye shall be the children*, &c.] Εσεσθε ὑιοι τω Ὑψισυ. See on i. 32.—'Ονως γινησθε ὑιοι, &c. *Matt.* v. 45. (*Note*, *John* xv. 6—8, *v.* 8.)— *The unthankful.*] Τυς αχαριστυς. 2 *Tim.* iii. 2. Not elsewhere N. T.—Ονη ... ινχαριστησαν, *Rom.* i. 21.—*Merciful.* (36) Οικτιρμων. *Jam.* v. 11. Not elsewhere N. T. Οικτιρμος, *Rom.* xii. 1. *Phil.* ii. 1.—*Ex.* xxxiv. 6. *Neh.* ix. 17 31. *Sept.*

2 Y 5

37 ¶ [a] Judge not, and ye shall not be judged: condemn not, and ye shall not be condemned: [b] forgive, and ye shall be forgiven:

38 Give, [c] and it shall be given unto you; good measure, pressed down, and shaken together, and running over, shall men give into your [d] bosom. For [e] with the same measure that ye mete withal, it shall be measured to you again.

39 And he spake a parable unto them, [f] Can the blind lead the blind? [g] shall they not both fall into the ditch?

40 The [h] disciple is not above his master: but every one [i] that is perfect shall be as his master.

41 And [k] why beholdest thou the mote that is in thy brother's eye, [l] but perceivest not the beam that is in thine own eye?

42 Either how canst thou say to thy brother, Brother, let me pull out the mote that is in thine eye, when thou thyself beholdest not the beam that is in thine own eye? [m] Thou hypocrite, [n] cast out first the beam out of thine own eye, and then shalt thou [o] see clearly to pull out the mote that is in thy brother's eye.

43 For [p] a good tree bringeth not forth corrupt fruit; neither doth a corrupt tree bring forth good fruit.

44 For every tree is known by his own fruit: [q] for of thorns men do not gather figs, nor of a bramble-bush gather they [r] grapes.

45 A [s] good man out of the good [t] treasure of his heart bringeth forth that which is good; [u] and an evil man out of the evil treasure of his heart bringeth forth that which is evil: [v] for of the abundance of the heart his mouth speaketh.

46 ¶ And [w] why call ye me Lord, Lord, and do not the things which I say?

47 Whosoever [x] cometh to me, [y] and heareth my sayings, [z] and doeth them, I will shew you to whom he is like.

48 He is like a man which built an house, and digged deep, [a] and laid the foundation on a [b] rock: and when [c] the flood arose, the stream beat vehemently upon that house, and could

---

V. 37, 38. (*Notes, Matt.* vii. 1, 2. *Rom.* xiv. 2—4.) Those who are kind and liberal to others from evangelical motives, and according to the rules of God's word, commouly meet with much unexpected favour and kindness from individuals of their brethren, and often from strangers; which tend to counterbalance the enmity, ingratitude, and contempt of the world at large: and, as the Lord has all hearts in his hands, this may confidently be expected by those, who lay themselves out in doing good for his sake. On the contrary, they who are harsh, unmerciful, unforgiving, or niggardly, in their conduct to others, may expect similar treatment both from God and man. (*Marg. Ref.—Notes, Matt.* v. 7. vi. 12. 14, 15. xviii. 21—35. *Jam.* ii. 8—13.)

Pressed down. (38) Πεπιεσμενον.—Here only N. T.— *Mic.* vi. 15. *Sept.—Shaken together.*] Σεσαλευμενον. 48. vii. 24. xxi. 26. *Matt.* xxiv. 29. *Acts* iv. 31. *Heb.* xii. 26.—*Running over.*] Ὑπερεκχυνομενον.—Here only N. T. —*Joel.* ii. 24. *Sept.*

V. 39, 40. ' Unskilful instructors destroy themselves and others; for as the master is, so will the disciple be.' *Beza.* It cannot be expected that the scholar will excel his teacher: but the complete disciple will be as his teacher, to whom he has implicitly attached himself; and not wiser or better than he. If, therefore, men follow blind guides, in their religious enquiries, they must continue in ignorance, or be deluded into error: so that it is of the greatest importance for them to take care on what teachers they attend; lest their greatest diligence, and highest attainment, should leave them short of the saving knowledge of God and of themselves.—Some, however, explain the latter verse to mean, that the genuine disciple of Christ would be like him, and be prepared to endure the cross for his sake; yet the former is the more obvious interpretation, and more suited to the context. (*Marg. Ref.* —*Note, Matt.* xv. 12—14.)

Perfect. (40) Κατηρτισμενος. See on *Matt.* xxi. 16.

V. 41, 42. *Marg. Ref.—Note, Matt.* vii. 3—5.

V. 43—45. *Marg. Ref.—Notes, Matt.* vii. 15—20. xii. 33—37. *Gal.* v. 19—26. *Jam.* iii. 7—12.

V. 46—49. (*Marg. Ref.—Notes, Matt.* vii. 21—27.) How large a proportion of professed Christians, of all parties and creeds, fall under condemnation, when judged by this most solemn and unspeakably interesting passage! " Weighed in this balance, they are found wanting." They " call Christ Lord, Lord, and do not the things which he says." " They hear, and do not." Nay, immense numbers, of jarring sentiments in other respects, agree in this, to make the mercy of God published in the gospel, a plea for neglecting strict obedience; and an encouragement, not to repent, but to continue in the neglect of many duties, and the commission of many sins, provided they be not grossly immoral ! ' If, say they, we are to be judged by the law, we should be condemned, no

not shake it; for it was founded upon a rock. 49 But he ¹ that heareth and doeth not, is like a man that without a found-ation built an house upon the earth; ᵘ against which the stream did beat vehemently, ˣ and immediately it fell; ʸ and ᶻ the ruin of that house was great.

doubt: but God is merciful, Christ came to save sinners, we are Christians, and under the new covenant; and there is no need to be so strict, or to disquiet ourselves about the event.' (*Note, Jam.* ii. 8—13.) Thus countless multitudes, who exclaim vehemently against the supposed antinomian tendency of the doctrines of grace, and the antinomian principles of some that profess to believe them, are themselves practical antinomians. They sin on, because God is merciful, and habitually neglect self-denying obedience, because Jesus came to "save us from our sins." (*Note, Rom.* vi. 1, 2.) This will most awfully appear, at the day of judgment; and the question, with which the passage begins, will suffice to stop the mouths of millions, and to leave them silent in darkness and despair. (*Note, Rom.* iii. 19, 20.)

Digged deep. (48) Εσκαψε και εβαθυνε.—Σκαπτω. xiii. 8. xvi. 3. Not elsewhere N. T.—Βαθυνω. Here only N. T. Βαθος, *depth.—The flood.*] Πλημμυρας. Here only N. T. —*Shake it.*] Σαλευσαι. See on 38.—*The ruin.* (49) Το ρηγμα. Here only N. T. From ρηγνυμι, to break.

PRACTICAL OBSERVATIONS.

V. 1—19.

The Lord Jesus will vindicate his disciples, against the false and frivolous accusations of their enemies; but he will not allow them to neglect his ordinances and commandments: yet how often do nominal Christians take occasion, from his concessions respecting the sabbath, to spend this holy day in sloth, indulgence, worldly employments, or vain company and dissipation! (*Notes, Ex.* xx. 8—10. *Is.* lviii. 13, 14.) This, however, neither consists with his authority and glory, as "the Lord of the sab- "bath;" nor yet with the real good of man, for whose advantage it was instituted. Let us then follow our Saviour to the places of publick worship, on that day of sacred rest; or rather, let us meet him in his house and at his table; (*Note, Matt.* xviii. 19, 20;) and imitate him in devoting it to the various duties of piety and charity, to the care of our own souls and of those that are connected with us; and in endeavouring to preserve the lives, or alleviate the miseries, of our brethren around us. And if, after all, the enemies of true religion be "filled with "madness," and consult to injure us; let us retain and give ourselves up to fervent prayer, and "continue in- "stant in it," according to the difficulty and importance of our work and station.—Serious consideration and earnest prayer should precede the appointment of men to the sacred ministry: and all concerned in so momentous a work, should observe and copy the example of Christ, when he ordained his apostles. Those, who have thoughts of being thus employed, should retire seriously to examine their motives, and to seek the divine direction, assistance, and blessing; and all Christians should join in prayer "to the Lord of the harvest, that he would send "forth labourers into his harvest," and that there may no

more be any covetous treacherous Judas, among those who sustain that sacred character. But, in this and in every other particular, at how great a distance do the disciples follow their Lord! Thousands of the votaries of pleasure frequently pass whole nights in the pursuit of it: but how rare for a Christian, or a minister, even in the most important and arduous circumstances, to devote a single night to retired prayer and supplication, or even to abridge himself of any considerable measure of his sleep for that purpose!—Men regard the diseases of their bodies as greater evils than those of their souls; but the scripture teaches us to form a contrary judgment: for if we could have access to Jesus, and obtain from him the most perfect cure of every disease, and the greatest degree of health and long life, which fallen man ever possessed; without deliverance from the guilt, power, and pollution of sin, by the efficacy of his blood, and the energy which proceeds from him, we must be miserable to all eternity. Yet how few in proportion earnestly apply to him for this inestimable benefit! (*P. O. Matt.* ix. 1—8.)

V. 20—26.

We may easily discover that there is but little faith among professed Christians; while we observe how eagerly they seek happiness, in those things on which Jesus has pronounced a woe; and how they shun those circumstances, in which he declares that true happiness may be found. Yet poverty, scanty subsistence, affliction, and contempt, when connected with humility, godly sorrow, faith, and an earnest desire after the blessings of salvation; conduce more even to present comfort, than all the riches, splendour, luxury, and carnal mirth of ungodly men. (*Note,* 1 *Tim.* vi. 6—10.) The former tends to weaken all those evil propensities, which the latter more and more inflames: and a peaceful conscience, a submissive will, a contented mind, communion with God, well regulated affections, and the hope of heaven, will render a Christian more happy in a cottage or a dungeon, than a prince can be in a palace, with a guilty conscience, a proud heart, a stubborn will, furious passions, and the fear of death and all its terrifying consequences. (*Notes, Ps.* xxxvii. *Matt.* v. 4, 5. 7, 8. *P. O.* 1—12.) To the poor, humble, and despised believer the kingdom of heaven exclusively belongs: there his best desires will be eternally satisfied, his tears will be changed for triumphant songs of joy, and "his "reward will be great" in the blessed society of the holy prophets and apostles; and in that of the incarnate Son of God, who passed the same way to his glory. On the other hand, when a few fleeting years are gone, the rich luxurious sinner will "lift up his eyes in hell," at the utmost distance from all consolation, and his unsatisfied desires will there for ever torment him: the giddy mirth of the dissipated will be turned into bitter weeping; and the laughter of the scorner will terminate in doleful wailings and lamentations. May these reflections be made effectual, by the Spirit of God, to rectify our judgments,

CHAP. VII.

Jesus commends the faith, and heals the servant, of a centurion, 1—10. He raises a widow's son at Nain, 11—17. He sends back the messengers of John the Baptist, with an account of his miracles, 18—23; bears testimony to John, 24—30; and exposes the perverseness of the people, respecting both John, and himself, 31—35. He is entertained by a Pharisee, 36.

A woman of previous bad character washes and anoints his feet, 37—39. He justifies to the Pharisee his conduct towards her by a parable; and shews that she loved much, and that her many sins were pardoned, 40—50.

NOW [a] when he had ended all his [a Matt. vii. 28, 29] sayings in the audience of the people, [b] he entered into Capernaum. [b Matt. viii. 5—13.]

and to direct our choice to " that good part which shall " never be taken from us ;" and teach us to prefer the reproach and the cross of Christ, to all the temporal pleasure of sin, or the applause of an ungodly world. (*Note, Heb.* xi. 24—26.) Nor ought any one to be disquieted, when he hears worldly men, who teach smooth doctrines and " prophesy deceits," applauded on every side; even if this be attended with invidious, slanderous, and malicious reflections on those, who are less complaisant to the fashions and customs of a wicked world. Thus the false prophets, whom God abhorred, were generally applauded even by his professed worshippers; whilst the true prophets, who " declared his whole counsel," were hated, reproached, and persecuted, as if they had been the basest of mankind. But it is unspeakably better to have the blessing of God, amidst man's contumely and execration, than to be abhorred by him while " all men speak well of " us."

V. 27—36.
We should be careful that our faithfulness, in professing or preaching the truth of God, be not leavened with moroseness or resentment. Our attention ought, therefore, to be continually directed to those precepts, which require us to " love our enemies," and to pray for our revilers and persecutors : and the bolder and more decided we are in the cause of God, the more pliant and passive we ought to be in our own concerns. (*Note, Rom.* xv. 1 —3.) We should in many things recede quietly from our due, and meekly submit to injuries and provocations: and at the same time we ought to persevere in " doing to " others, as we *would* they should do to us," and in unwearied acts of kindness to the most perverse and ungrateful of our enemies. Such a conduct will evince us to be " the " children of the Highest, who is kind unto the unthankful " and evil ;" and ensure a large and gracious recompence from him : and it will prove the superior excellency of our doctrines above all other systems ; and the efficacy of the sanctifying grace on which we profess to depend. Whereas, if Christians love those alone who love them, and do good to such as do good to them; in what are their religion and principles discriminated from those of heathens, who do the same ? Let us then " do good and lend, hoping for " nothing again ;" and let us aim to be merciful to the miserable and the guilty, even according to the mercy of our heavenly Father to us poor perishing sinners. (*P. O. Matt.* v. 33—48. *Rom.* xii. 17—21.)

V. 37—49.
To avoid giving needless offence, we should carefully abstain from all rash and rigorous decisions about men's motives, state, and character. Our great business is to judge ourselves; and not to judge another's servants, who

must stand or fall to their own Master. (*Notes, Rom.* xiv. 2—4. 10—12.) We should never be backward to forgive any kind or degree of injury, as we hope to be forgiven by God for Christ's sake : and we may rest satisfied that we shall not be losers in the event, by the most liberal and abundant kindness to others, according to our measure of ability, and as far as consists with other duties : for it shall assuredly be " measured to us, by the same measure with " which we mete to others," whether that be more large or more scanty.—These extensive and most excellent precepts, as well as the evangelical principles connected with them, are overlooked or explained away by " blind guides," of whom every one ought to beware ; for they are falling into the ditch together with their followers, in great multitudes, continually, on every side of us. And as " the " disciple is not above his Master," let us be indeed the disciples of Christ alone : that, following his instructions and example, and regarding no man further than he declares the truth and bears the image of Christ, we may grow up into conformity to him, till at length we become " perfect even as our Master is perfect." Let us also seek to subdue our own evil tempers, and break off our sins, before we set up for censors or reformers of others ; lest Jesus should check our officiousness by saying, " Thou " hypocrite, cast out first the beam out of thine own eye, " and then shalt thou see clearly to cast out the mote that " is in thy brother's eye." As then the tree is known by its fruits, may the truth, as taught by Jesus and his apostles, be grafted in our hearts, that we may be fruitful in every good word and work; and that instructive discourse may be as natural to us, as corrupt conversation is to ungodly men. In vain do we call Christ, " Lord, Lord," or even call on him to rescue us from condemnation, if we do not the things which he says. May we then wisely come to him, hear his words, and " do them ;" that we may with diligence " dig deep," to lay the foundation of our hope upon a Rock. Thus when unbelievers of every name, whether they reject, despise, oppose, or pervert the gospel, shall be driven with all their presumptuous confidences into everlasting ruin ; we shall dwell securely, weather out every storm, and have at last " a building of God, an " house not made with hands, eternal in the heavens." (*P. O. Matt.* vii. 13—29.)

NOTES.
CHAP. VII. V. 1—10. (*Notes* and *P. O. Matt.* viii. 5—13.) ' Thus is Christ said to have " preached peace " ' to the Ephesians, which personally he did not, but by his ' apostles. ... Notwithstanding, St. Luke, willing to add ' one evidence more of the centurion's humility, from the ' reason of his not going personally unto Christ, chooses ' rather to set it down exactly as it was, in each circum-

2 B 2

2 And a certain 'centurion's servant, who was dear unto him, 'was sick, and ready to die. 3 And when he heard of Jesus, he sent unto him the elders of the Jews, 'beseeching him that he would come and heal his servant. 4 And when they came to Jesus, they besought him instantly, saying, That he was 'worthy for whom he should do this: 5 For 'he loveth our nation, 'and he hath built us a synagogue. 6 Then 'Jesus went with them. And when he was now not far from the house, the centurion sent friends to him, saying unto him, Lord, 'trouble not thyself; 'for I am not worthy that thou shouldest enter under my roof: 7 Wherefore neither thought I myself worthy to come unto thee: 'but say in a word, and my servant shall be healed. 8 For I also am a man set 'under authority, having under me soldiers; and I say unto 'one, 'Go, and he goeth; and to another, Come, and he cometh; and to my servant, Do this, and he doeth it. 9 When Jesus heard these things, 'he marvelled at him, and turned him about, and said unto the people that followed him, I say unto you, I have not found so great faith, no, 'not in Israel. 10 And they that were sent, returning to the house, 'found the servant whole that had been sick. 11 ¶ And it came to pass the day after, that 'he went into a city called Nain: and many of his disciples went with him, and much people. 12 Now when he came nigh to the gate of the city, behold, there was a dead man carried out, 'the only son of his mother, and she was 'a widow: and much people of the city was with her. 13 And when the Lord saw her, 'he had compassion on her, and said unto her, 'Weep not. 14 And he came and touched the 'bier: and they that bare him stood still. And he said, 'Young man, I say unto thee, Arise. 15 And he that was dead sat up, and began to speak. 'And he delivered him to his mother. 16 And there came 'a fear on all: and 'they glorified God, saying, That 'a great prophet is risen up among us; and, That 'God hath visited his people. 17 And 'this rumour of him went forth throughout all Judea, and throughout all the region round about.

'stance, than only in brief ... as St. Matthew had done.' *Hammond.*—The centurion's liberal affection for the worshippers of the true God, shewn in building them a synagogue at his own expense, is also added by St. Luke, as what had peculiarly tended to soften the prejudices of the Jews, and to conciliate their favour towards him. " And he himself has built the synagogue for us."—The favour shewn an officer in the army, by which the conquerors held the nation in subjection; and the earnestness, with which the elders pleaded the cause of an uncircumcised Gentile, is not the least wonderful circumstance in the narrative. It attests in the strongest manner the excellency of his character; and shews the power of persevering good and kind behaviour, to overcome the prejudices of those who witness them, and share the benefit.

Dear unto him. (2) Εντιμος αυτω. xiv. 8. Phil. ii. 29. 1 Pet. ii. 4. 6.—1 Sam. xxvi. 21. *Sept.*—*Instantly.* (4) Σπουδαιως. Tit. iii. 13. Not elsewhere *N. T.*—*Hath built us a synagogue.* (5) Την συναγωγην ωκοδομησεν ημιν. "He hath built the synagogue for us:" probably there was only one at Capernaum.

V. 11—17. It does not appear that our Lord ever went to Nain, except on this occasion. It is supposed to have been distant about twelve or thirteen miles from Capernaum; and he seems to have taken this journey, on purpose to perform the compassionate miracle here recorded. For when he came, with numerous attendants, to the entrance of the city, he met a company of people carrying a dead man out to bury him. He was the only son of a widow woman, who, it may well be supposed, had been the support and comfort of her declining years; and every circumstance tended to render her affliction peculiarly distressing: and, as the funeral was attended by great numbers, the miracle which ensued would be more fully attested, and generally known. When our Lord, therefore, saw the afflicted widow following the corpse, he " had com-" passion on her," and bade her weep no more: he then touched the bier on which the body lay, for those who carried it stood still, perhaps with some degree of expectation, as the rumour of his other miracles must have reached them. Upon which he said, as one possessed of divine authority and power, " Young man, I say unto thee, arise;" and immediately he that had " been dead sat up, and began to

18 ¶ And [i] the disciples of John
shewed him of all these things.
19 And John calling *unto him* [k] two
of his disciples, sent *them* to Jesus,
saying, [l] Art thou he that should come?
or look we for another?
20 When the men were come unto
him, they said, John Baptist hath sent
us unto thee, saying, Art thou he that
should come? or look we for another?
21 And in that same hour he cured
many of *their* infirmities and [m] plagues,
and of evil spirits: and unto many
that were blind he gave sight.
22 Then Jesus answering, said unto
them, Go your way, and tell John
what things ye have seen and heard:
[n] how that the blind see, [o] the lame
walk, [p] the lepers are cleansed, [q] the
deaf hear, [r] the dead are raised, [s] to
the poor the gospel is preached.
23 And [t] blessed is *he*, whosoever
shall not be offended in me.
24 ¶ And when the messengers of
John were departed, he began to speak
unto the people concerning John,
[u] What went ye out into the [x] wilderness for to see? [y] a reed shaken with
the wind?
25 But what went ye out for to see?

i *See on* Matt. xi. 2—6.—John iii. 26.
k x. 1. Josh. ii. 1. Mark vi. 7. Acts x. 7, 8. Rev. xi. 3.
l Gen. iii. 15. xxii. 18. xlix. 10. Deut. xviii. 15—18. Ps. cx. 1—4. Is. vii. 14. ix. 6, 7. xi. 1. xl. 10, 11. lix. 20, 21. Jer. xxiii. 5, 6. Dan. ix. 24—26. Mic. v. 2. Hag. ii. 7. Zech. ix. 9. Mal. iii. 1—3. iv. 2. John iv. 25.
m 1 Kings viii. 37. Ps. xc. 7—9. Mark iii. 10. v. 29. 34. 1 Cor. xi. 30—32. Heb. xii. 6. Jam. v. 14, 15.
n 21. xviii. 35—43. Job xxix. 15. Ps. cxlvi. 8. Is. xxix. 18, 19. xxxii. 3, 4. xxxv. 5, 6. xlii. 6, 7. 16. lxi. 1—3. Jer. xxxi. 8. Matt. ix. 28—30. xxi. 14. John ix. 30—33. Acts xxvi. 18.
o Matt. xv. 30, 31. Acts iii. 2—8. viii. 7. xiv. 8—10.
p *See on* v. 12—15. xvii. 12—19.
q Is. xliii. 8. Mark vii. 32—37.
r *See on* 14, 15. viii. 53—55.
s iv. 18. Zeph. iii. 12. Jam. ii. 5.
t ii. 34. Is. viii. 14, 15. Matt. xi. 6. xiii. 57, 58. John vi. 60—66. Rom. ix. 32, 33. 1 Cor. i. 22, 23. ii. 14. 1 Pet. ii. 7, 8.
u *See on* Matt. xi. 7, 8.
x i. 80. iii. 2. Matt. iii. 1—5. Mark i. 4, 5. John i. 28.
y Gen. xlix. 4. 2 Cor. i. 17—20. Eph. iv. 14. Jam. i. 6—8. 2 Pet. ii. 17. iii. 17.

[z] A man clothed in soft raiment? Behold, they which are gorgeously ap-
parelled, and live delicately, [a] are in
kings courts.
26 But what went ye out for to see?
[b] A prophet? Yea, I say unto you,
[c] and much more than a prophet.
27 This is *he* of whom it is written,
[d] Behold, I send my messenger before
thy face, which shall prepare thy way
before thee.
28 For I say unto you, [e] Among
those that are born of women, there is
not a greater prophet than John the
Baptist: [f] but he that is least in the
kingdom of God is greater than he.
29 And all the people that heard
him, and the publicans, [g] justified God,
[h] being baptized with the baptism of
John.
30 But the Pharisees and lawyers
[*] rejected [i] the counsel of God [†] against
themselves, being not baptized of him.
31 ¶ And the Lord said, [k] Whereunto then shall I liken the men of
this generation? and to what are they
like?
32 They [l] are like unto [m] children
sitting in the market-place, and calling one to another, and saying, We

z 2 Kings i. 8. Is. lix. 17. Matt. iii. 4. 1 Pet. iii. 3, 4.
a 1 Kings x. 5. Esth. iv. 2. v. 1. viii. 15. Matt. vi. 29.
b i. 76. xx. 6.
c xvi. 16. *See on* Matt. xi. 9—14.—John iii. 26, &c. v. 35.
d i. 16, 17. 76. Is. xl. 3. Mal. iii. 1. iv. 5, 6. John i. 23.
e i. 14, 15. iii. 16.
f ix. 48. x. 23, 24. Matt. xi. 11. xiii. 16, 17. Eph. iii. 8, 9. Col. i. 25—27. Heb. xi. 39, 40. 1 Pet. i. 10—12.
g 35. Judg. i. 7. Ps. li. 4. Rom. iii. 4—6. x. 3. Rev. xv. 3. xvi. 5.
h iii. 12. Matt. xxi. 31, 32.
* Or, *frustrated* xiii. 34. Jer. viii. 8. Rom. x. 21. 2 Cor. vi. 1. Gal. ii. 21.
i Acts xx. 27. Eph. i. 11.
† Or, *within.*
k Lam. ii. 13. Matt. xi. 16. Mark iv. 30.
l Prov. xvii. 16. Is. xxviii. 9—13. xxix. 11, 12. Jer. v. 3—5. *See on* Matt. xi. 16—19.
m Zech. viii. 5

" speak, and Jesus delivered him to his mother," that he might still live to be a comfort to her. (*Marg. Ref.* t—c.)—The evangelist has left us to conceive of the emotions of her heart on this occasion, to which no words could possibly do justice: but he informs us, that an awe and fear of the divine power of Jesus fell upon the spectators: and that they " glorified God" for his mercy, and thanked him for having " visited his people," and raised up such a prophet among them. (*Marg. Ref.* d—h.—*Notes, Mark* v. 35—43, *vv.* 41—43. *John* xi. 41—46. *Acts* ix. 36—43.) But though the rumour of this extraordinary miracle spread even to Judea, and through all the adjacent regions, yet we do not find, that any one expected a similar miracle in the case of Jairus's daughter. (*Note, Mark* v. 22—24.)—'What can exceed the beautiful simplicity of these verses? In particular, that simple, yet touching enumeration, which occurs in the twelfth verse, is a pure classical beauty. Common writers either overlook such circumstances, and fail to arrange them in the delicate order which gives them their effect; or they dwell so much on them, as to excite weariness and disgust. A similar instance occurs in the contrast towards the close of this chapter. (44—46.) Few minds are so acute in their first perceptions, as thus to catch every circumstance which properly enters into a parallel, or a contrast, and to exclude all fanciful agreements and oppositions; and few who catch them can thus exhibit them without parade. This clearness of conception, united with such simple and unembarrassed communication, is, I conceive, true classical excellence. St. Luke particularly abounds in these instances. Those petulant criticks, who spurn him away from a comparison with Xenophon, can only support their sentence by maintaining that his Greek is not Attick.—The walk to Emmaus may challenge a comparison with any work of any master.—St. Luke leaves the mind full of pictures, produced, not by height of colouring, but by exquisite and simply natural description.—Thus it is especially with the first two chapters of this gospel, and the first chapters of the Acts of the Apostles. These paint themselves, on the fancy and memory, on every perusal.'

There was a dead man carried out. (12) Εξεκομιζετο τεθνηκως. " One who had died was carried out." Εκκομιζομαι. Here only N. T.—*The only son.*] Υἱος μονογενης. ix. 38. *John* i. 14. 18. iii. 16. 18. *Heb.* xi. 17. 1 *John* iv. 9.—*The bier.* (14) Της σορυ. Here only N. T.

V. 18—35. *Marg. Ref.—Notes, Matt.* xi. 1—19.—*John.* (18) ' John from the prison sends his unbelieving ' disciples to Christ himself, to be confirmed: that, hear- ' ing and seeing him, they might by him be instructed, ' from whom they had otherwise fled, out of a preposter- ' ous emulation.' *Beza.*—*In that same,* &c. (21) What a view does this verse give us of the number and variety

have piped unto you, and ye have not danced; we have mourned to you, and ye have not wept.

n i. 15, Jer. xxi. 6—16 Matt. iii. 4. Mark i. 6.

33 For John the Baptist ⁿ came neither eating bread nor drinking wine;

o Matt. x. 25.

and ye say, ° He hath a devil.

John viii. 48, 52. x. 20. Acts ii. 13. p v. 29, xi. 87. xiv. I. John xii. 2.

34 The Son of man is come ᴾ eating and drinking; and ye say, Behold, a

gluttonous man, and a wine-bibber, ᑫ a friend of publicans and sinners!

q xv. 2. xix. 7. Matt. ix. 11.

35 But ʳ 'wisdom is justified of all her children.

r 29. Prov. viii. 32 —36 Hos. xiv. 9. Matt. xi. 19. 1 Cor. ii. 14, 15.

36 ¶ And one of the Pharisees desired him that he would eat with him.

ˢ And he went into the Pharisee's house, and sat down to meat.

s 34. xi. 37. xiv. 1

---

of our Lord's miracles! The word rendered " gave," seems to express how highly gratifying the gift of sight was to those who had been blind; and in what a gracious and kind manner our Lord bestowed it, as taking pleasure in imparting so welcome a gift.—*Blessed.* (23) ' He adds ' this, to correct the preposterous emulation of John's dis-' ciples, who envied the honour of Jesus, as eclipsing that ' of John : ... but again, lest any should suppose that he ' meant to censure John himself, he subjoins a commend-' ation of his office, which he places in the middle between ' the prophets and his own coming (28). ... The predic-' tions of the prophets are compared with John's pointing ·out Christ to the people; and that again with the exhibition given of him in the gospel. At the same time it is ' shewn, that as much as the second discovery excelled the ' first, so much did the third excel the second.' *Beza.*— *And all,* &c. (29, 30.) It is not evident, whether these verses are a continuation of Christ's discourse, or the evangelist's remark upon the effects producᵉd by it: our translation favours the latter supposition, yet the most approved expositors incline to the former.—If they were the words of Christ, they called the attention of his hearers to the effects produced by John's ministry. The common people, and even the publicans, and others of bad moral character, had been induced by it " to justify God;" for they acknowledged the justice of the punishment, which was denounced against them for their sins; and their need of repentance, forgiveness, and a change of heart and life: and, professing these things, they had received his baptism, and had regarded, in some measure, his testimony to Jesus as the promised Messiah. But the Pharisees and Scribes generally rejected his ministry, and were not baptized by him; and thus they rendered " the counsel of " God," in sending him to prepare the way of Christ, of none effect, as far as they were concerned; and they despised the warnings and denunciation which John addressed to them. (*Marg.* and *Marg. Ref.* i.—*Note, Matt.* xxi. 28—32.) Hence the people might infer that their pride and hypocrisy were more adverse to spiritual religion, than the ignorance or profligacy of others, or even of the publicans; that they might be expected to be the inveterate enemies to Jesus, whose forerunner John was; and that all must be cautioned not to follow such blind guides.—If, however, we understand the passage, as the words of the evangelist, it implies, that the common people, and even the publicans, approved of Christ's honourable testimony to John, and expressed themselves to be well satisfied with the wisdom, justice, and goodness of God, displayed in that dispensation; to which they were the more inclined, as they had been baptized of John. But the Pharisees and Scribes, who in general had refused his baptism, were displeased with our Lord's testimony to him, as it implied a severe

censure on their conduct : (*Note, Matt.* xxi. 23—27 :) and thus they persisted in their opposition to the counsel of God, to their own great loss and danger; proving themselves to be none of " wisdom's children," by all of whom her appointments are justified and approved (35).—' In ' rejecting John's baptism, they are said to " reject the " " counsel of God towards them ; " that is, his gracious ' design of calling them by him to that repentance, ' which could alone exempt them from the wrath to come; ' and by that refusal declared they approved not of God's ' counsel, as just and righteous, in calling such unblame-' able persons as they were, and such zealots for the law, ' to repentance, that so they might escape the ruin threat-' ened by John. For thus Eleazar, one of them, speaks, ' after the destruction of the Jews, that though all the rest of ' the Jews perished, ... we alone ought to be preserved, ' as having not sinned against God, nor been guilty of any ' fault, and who were teachers to others. Christ tells us, ' that they " were confident in themselves, that they were " " righteous," ... and represents them by the elder son, ' saying, " I never transgressed at any time thy command-" " ment." (xv. 29.) They therefore judged it an incon-' gruous thing, to call such righteous persons to repent-' ance; and threaten them with ruin who were so dear to ' God. But the publicans and common people were ' conscious to themselves of sins, sufficient to expose them ' to divine judgments; and therefore they approved of this ' counsel God sent to them by his messenger; and de-' clared him righteous, both in calling them to repentance, ' and threatening his judgments if they did neglect it.' *Whitby.*—It is probable, that many of the Scribes and Pharisees who came to John, hearing his exhortations and warnings, declined his baptism, or at least that the rest of the body stood aloof from him. (*Note, Matt.* iii. 7—10.)

He gave sight. (21) Εχαρισατο το βλεπειν. 42, 43. *Acts* xxv. 11. 16. xxvii. 24. 1 *Cor.* ii. 12. *Gal.* iii. 18. *Phil.* i. 29. *Philem.* 22.—*The messengers.* (24) Των αγγελων. 27. 2 *Cor.* xii. 7. *Jam.* ii. 25.—*Mal.* iii. 1. *Sept.*—*Being baptized.* (29) Βαπτισθεντες. " Having been baptized." 30.

V. 36. When our Lord had concluded his discourse, a Pharisee, named Simon, who was present, invited him to eat with him. This man seems to have been considerably impressed with what he had seen and heard ; but his prejudices were strong, and he was yet in suspense whether Jesus was, or was not, a prophet. It is probable, therefore, that he invited him to his house, in order the more narrowly to observe and scrutinize all his words and actions: and he seems to have had others about him in the same state of mind. (49. *Notes,* xi. 37, 38. xiv. 1.—6.) Our Lord, however, was always ready to shew a friendly and sociable disposition, and to embrace every occasion of

37 And, behold, a woman in the city, ¹ which was a sinner, when she knew that *Jesus* sat at meat in the Pharisee's house, ² brought an alabaster-box of ointment,

38 And stood at his feet behind *him* ³ weeping, and began to ⁴ wash his feet with tears, and did wipe *them* with the hairs of her head, and kissed his feet, ⁵ and anointed *them* with the ointment.

39 Now when the Pharisee, which had bidden him, saw *it*, ⁶ he spake within himself, saying, ⁷ This man, if he were a prophet, ⁸ would have known who, and what manner of woman, *this is* that toucheth him; for she is a sinner.

---

doing good: he therefore accepted the invitation, and, having entered his house, he immediately sat down to meat; or, reclined on the couch, according to the custom of the Jews at that time. For the Pharisee, as it appears, considering Jesus as a poor man, and having no proper sense of his real excellency and dignity, did not shew him even the customary tokens of respect or affection. (44—46.)

V. 37—39. While our Lord was at the Pharisee's table, a woman, an inhabitant of the city, who was of known bad character, having formerly been a harlot, as it is generally supposed, came into the room.—Tradition reports that this was Mary Magdalene, but there is no scriptural proof of it: and indeed what is said of Mary Magdalene, or Mary of Magdala, in other places, renders it improbable; as she is spoken of, rather as one, who had been remarkably *afflicted*, than peculiarly *wicked*. (*Note, Mark* xvi. 9—11.)—This woman, however, had heard our Lord's instructions with great attention; and had been led to a deep conviction of her guilt and danger, and to unfeigned repentance: and, being thus prepared to receive the truth, she seems to have believed him to be the promised Messiah, a spiritual Redeemer, the Saviour of sinners. She therefore longed to hear more of his convincing and encouraging instructions, and also to express her love and gratitude to him: and, in the fulness of her heart, she followed him into the Pharisee's house, having taken with her an alabaster-box of valuable ointment, which probably she had been accustomed before to use for other purposes. Coming thus behind him as he reclined at meat, his presence and conversation so affected her, with a remembrance of her former sins, and with a sense of his grace and mercy, that she wept abundantly : and, as his feet were bare, (his sandals having been put off,) she *rained tears* plenteously upon them, wiping them at the same time with her neglected dishevelled hair : and kissing them, in the most humble, respectful, and affectionate manner, she anointed them with the ointment. But when the Pharisee saw this interesting scene, instead of rejoicing in these tokens of her repentance, he confined his thoughts entirely to her former scandalous character; and began to form a disadvantageous opinion of Jesus, because he allowed such a woman to approach him: for reasoning in his heart on the subject, he inwardly formed the conclusion, that if Jesus were a prophet, he would have known her character, and consequently would have driven her from his presence, as he himself and his brethren the Pharisees would have done. (*Notes,* xv. 1, 2. xviii. 9—14. *Is.* lxv. 3—7. *Matt.* ix. 10—13.)—It is most surprising that many persons, (among whom have been several remarkable for learning and diligent investigation,) should

have supposed that St. Luke here records the same event, which the other evangelists relate, concerning Mary, the sister of Lazarus. (*Notes, Matt.* xxvi. 6—13. *Mark* xiv. 3—9. *John* xii. 1—8.)—' This woman was " a woman of ' " that city," either of Nain or Capernaum, the only cities ' here mentioned; whereas Mary, the sister of Lazarus, ' was of ... the village of Bethany. ... After the collation, ' which is not stiled a supper, our Lord " went through ' " every city and village, preaching the kingdom of God;" ' (viii. 1;) whereas, after he raised Lazarus, " Jesus walked ' " no more openly." (*John* xi. 54.) And lastly, Mary's ' unction was made for Christ's interment, and but six ' days before his last passover, when he continued in ' Bethany and Jerusalem. (*Mark* xi. 11.)' *Whitby.*— ' This was in one of the Pharisees' houses, not in Simon ' the leper's, nor ... in Bethany. The Pharisee objected ' against Christ for this; not Judas, or one of the disci- ' ples: and the objection was not the unnecessary expense, ' as there, but that Christ would let a sinner be so kind to ' him, if he knew it; or if he did not, that he was no ' prophet. And then the discourse between Christ and ' Simon, ... is far distant from that in the other gospels, of ' anointing him for his burial : ... which also contains an- ' other circumstance in it, that that of Mary's was imme- ' diately before his death, Judas going out immediately to ' betray him.' *Hammond.*—To this it may be added, that it is hardly conceivable, a supper should have been made for Jesus, after Lazarus was raised from the dead, at which Lazarus was a guest, and Martha waited, and which was evidently done in honour of Christ ; while the person who entertained the company doubted of his being a prophet, because the sister of Lazarus his guest, and of Martha who waited, was permitted to touch him. And it is equally inconceivable that the Jews should throng to the house of " Martha and Mary to comfort them concerning their bro- " ther;" if the character of Mary had been so infamous, that it was enough to induce suspicion against one, who was so eminent for his miracles and doctrine, that he permitted her to touch him.—There is every reason to think, that Mary, the sister of Lazarus and Martha, was, like her brother and sister, in all respects, a person of approved character, even among such as did not receive Jesus as the Messiah : and though the circumstances of the alabaster-box, the anointing of our Lord's feet, and wiping them with her hair, and " the leper" being called Simon, as well as " the Pharisee," seem at first glance to give some plausibility to the opinion ; yet the more carefully the connexion of the narrative, the time, the place, the discourse, the woman's motive, the commendation bestowed on each, and indeed the whole account, is considered, the more complete must be the reader's conviction, that two entirely dif-

2 Y 4

40 And Jesus ^d answering said unto him, Simon, I have somewhat to say unto thee. And he saith, ^e Master, say on.

41 There was ^f a certain creditor which had two debtors; ^g the one owed five hundred ^h pence, ⁱ and the other fifty.

42 And ^k when they had nothing to pay, ^l he frankly forgave them both. Tell me therefore, which of them will love him most?

43 Simon answered and said, ^m I suppose that *he* to whom he forgave most. And he said unto him, ⁿ Thou hast rightly judged.

44 And he turned to the woman, and said unto Simon, ^o Seest thou this woman? I entered into thine house: ^p thou gavest me no water for my feet;

but she hath washed my feet with tears, and wiped *them* with the hairs of her head.

45 Thou ^q gavest me no kiss; but this woman, since the time I came in, hath not ceased to kiss my feet.

46 Mine head ^r with oil thou didst not anoint; but this woman hath anointed my feet with ointment.

47 Wherefore, I say unto thee, ^s her sins, ^t which are many, are forgiven; for ^u she loved much: but to whom little is forgiven, *the same* loveth little.

48 And he said unto her, Thy sins are forgiven.

49 And they that sat at meat with him began to say within themselves, ^x Who is this that forgiveth sins also?

50 And he said to the woman, ^y Thy faith hath saved thee: ^z go in peace.

---

ferent persons, and two distinct transactions are intended.—The apostle John indeed records, that Mary anointed Christ's "feet:" but St. Luke never intimates, that this woman anointed "his head," as two evangelists do of Mary. This was more suited to the respectful and affectionate freedom of one long honoured with the Saviour's friendship, than with the weeping trembling diffidence of a new convert, whose life had been notoriously scandalous.

A sinner. (37) Ἁμαρτωλος. 34. 39. v. 8. xiii. 2. xv. 10. xviii. 13.—See on *Matt.* ix. 10. The word commonly marks a person of immoral character, and is seldom used for a truly penitent, believing, and justified person, except by the person himself in humble confession. (*Note,* xv. 1, 2.)—*To wash,* &c. (38) Βρεχειν της ποδας. 44. *Matt.* v. 45.—*Ps.* vi. 6. *Sept.*—*Wiped,* &c.] Εξεμασσε. *John* xi. 2. xii. 3. xiii. 5. Not elsewhere *N. T.*

V. 40—43. Whilst Simon imagined he had obtained a decisive proof that Jesus was not a prophet, our Lord answered to his inmost thoughts in such a manner, as sufficiently evinced that he was far more than a prophet. (*Notes, John* ii. 23—25. xxi. 15—17. 1 *Cor.* xiv. 20—25, *vv.* 22—25. *Heb.* iv. 12, 13. *Rev.* ii. 20—23, v. 23.) Had he directly attacked the Pharisee upon the subject of his wicked and unreasonable pride, and unfeeling disdain of the poor weeping penitent, (as we should have been apt to do,) he would probably have been only hardened and irritated by it: but the manner, in which Jesus addressed him was admirably suited to convince, without affronting, him. He first rivetted his attention, by intimating that he had something of importance to say to him; and he stated a case to him, desiring his opinion upon it.—The "Creditor" in this parable evidently represents God himself; the "two debtors," one of whom owed him ten times as much as the other, denote different descriptions of sinners, who are all guilty, but in various degrees, and who have no power, in any measure, to pay their debt, or atone for their own sins. (*Notes, Matt.* xviii. 23—35.) As therefore two

debtors, thus circumstanced, and then freely forgiven, would love their kind creditor, in some proportion to the sum remitted to them; so pardoned sinners may be supposed to love their gracious Lord, in proportion to the degree of their guilt, or rather to that of their own estimation of it. This case being proposed to Simon in the form of a question, he could not but allow, that the debtor who had been freely pardoned the larger sum, would, in all probability, have the deeper sense of his obligations, and the more lively impression of his benefactor's liberality.—The longer men live in sin, the more advantages they abuse, and the more mischief they do, the greater is their actual guilt: yet pride, and ignorance of God, of the evil of sin, and of themselves, impose on many to think their debt small, when it is indeed very large. But the convictions, which spring from divine illumination, always lead men to consider themselves as great sinners; and when they attain to a comfortable sense of forgiveness, by the free mercy of God in Christ Jesus, their love and gratitude are proportioned to the degree of their humiliation. (*Notes,* 2 *Cor.* v. 13—15. *Eph.* iii. 8.)—*Master,* &c. (40) *O teacher, speak.*—Considering the state of Simon's mind; this address seems not only *hypocritical,* but *sarcastical.*

A creditor. (41) Δανειη. Here only *N. T.*—2 *Kings* iv. 1. *Ps.* cix. 11. *Prov.* xxix. 13. *Sept.*—*Debtors.*] Χρεωφειλεται. xvi. 5. Not elsewhere *N. T.*—*Job* xxxi. 37. *Prov.* xxix. 13. *Sept.* Ex χρεως, *debitum,* et οφιλετης, *debitor. Matt.* xviii. 24.—*He frankly forgave.* (42) Εχαρισατι. 43.—See on 21.—*I suppose.* (43) Ὑπολαμβανω. x. 30. *Acts* i. 9. ii. 15. Not elsewhere *N. T.*

V. 44—50. Our Lord approving of Simon's answer, proceeded to apply it to the case in question: and turning to the weeping penitent, he said, "Seest thou this woman?" Simon had indeed noticed her with disdain, and thought that her presence even polluted his house; but he had not duly considered her tears of godly sorrow, and her expressions of grateful love. Our Lord, therefore, in the most

CHAP. VIII.

Our Lord preaches, attended by his apostles ; and

beautiful manner, contrasted her conduct with that of the Pharisee. The latter had not even treated him with ordinary respect: when he came into his house, he had not so much as brought him water, with which to wash his feet; he had not welcomed him with a friendly kiss; nor given him oil, which was cheap and plentiful, to anoint his head, according to the customs on such occasions. (*Marg. Ref.—Gen.* xxix. 13. *Notes, Gen.* xviii. 3—8, *v.* 4: *Ps.* ii. 10—12, *v.* 12.) But this despised woman had "washed his feet "with her tears, and wiped them with her hair;" she had incessantly kissed his feet from her first entrance into the room, and had anointed them with costly and fragrant ointment. Therefore, though her sins had been very many and aggravated, even far more and greater than Simon supposed, they were all "forgiven, for she loved much." Many expositors would render it, "*Therefore* she loved "much," though they allow this use of the Greek particle to be very uncommon. But there seems no occasion for the alteration: and in fact no indisputable instance of its being used in this sense has ever been produced.—Her love was not the *cause* of her forgiveness, which is ascribed to her faith (50), but it was an *evidence* of it; for it proved the sincerity of her repentance and faith in Christ, from which her forgiveness might with certainty be inferred. (*Notes, Matt.* x. 37—39. *John* xxi. 15—17. 1 *Cor.* xvi. 22—24, *v.* 22. 2 *Cor.* v. 13—15. *Eph.* vi. 21—24, *v.* 24. 1 *Pet.* i. 8, 9.)—Indeed, if her love to Christ had arisen from the assurance that her sins were forgiven ; there would have been no occasion for him repeatedly to assure her that they were : but he pointed out the effects of her fervent love, both to comfort her drooping heart, and to silence her rigorous judges. The word, rendered "wherefore" (47), signifies *On account of which,* or, *For the sake of which,* and seems at least to induce as much difficulty as that translated "for." But the verse may perhaps be thus paraphrased, as it stands in the context:—' Observing these effects of this woman's love and gratitude, it is reasonable on account of them, as evidences of her repentance and faith, to conclude, that her numerous sins are pardoned : because it is plain that "she loveth much ;" and so the depth of her repentance, and the sincerity of her faith, are put beyond all doubt. (*Note,* 1 *John* iv. 19.)—Whereas, did she think her guilt but small, yet supposed that it was pardoned ; her love would be so little, and the effects so indecisive, that her real character might still continue doubtful.' Thus our Lord intimated, that the Pharisees, forming such an erroneous estimate of their own character, could not properly value salvation by grace, or love the gracious Saviour of lost sinners : and were it possible, that in this state of mind, they should be pardoned ; they could only "love a little," and give him the formal cool reception, that Simon had done : instead of shewing, by every action, the fervent love and gratitude of this deeply humbled penitent.—It is plain, that our Lord addressed Simon, according to his own thoughts of himself, and not according to the real state of the case, when he seemed to allow that he "loved a little". This was frequently his manner ; (*Note,* xv. 25—32 ;) and there was something in

it very conciliating, though plain and faithful.—He certainly did not treat all Pharisees alike ; or pursue every one, whose heart was not right before God, with all that severity, which he expressed against those, who combined with their self-righteousness the most detestable hypocrisy and enormous wickedness. Some preachers and authors have perhaps too much overlooked this.—Having stated these things, our Lord more expressly declared to the woman " that her sins were forgiven : " and, regardless of the murmurs which this excited, he again encouraged her with the assurance that " her faith had saved her," and that she might "depart in peace" with God and her conscience, for all the blessings of his gospel belonged to her. (*Notes, Matt.* ix. 2—8. *Mark* ii. 3—12.)

Kiss. (45) Φιλημα. xxii. 48. *Rom.* xvi. 16. 1 *Cor.* xvi. 20.—*Wherefore.* (47) 'Ου χαριν. *Gal.* iii. 19. *Eph.* iii. 14. *Tit.* i. 5. 1 *John* iii. 12.—*They that sat at meat with him.* (49) 'Οι συνανακειμενοι. xiv. 10. 15. *Matt.* ix. 10. xiv. 9. *Mark* ii. 15. xiv. 10. 15. *John* xii. 2.—Συν, ανα, et κειμαι, *jaceo.*—*Thy faith hath saved thee.* (50) 'Η πιστις σου σεσωκε σε. Here these words must relate to eternal salvation. (*Note, Acts* iv. 5—12, *v.* 12.)

PRACTICAL OBSERVATIONS.

V. 1—17.

The grace of God is communicated to some of every rank and order in the community ; and where it prevails, it influences men to a conscientious and affectionate performance of the various duties of their several relations in domestick life. When masters and servants behave properly, in their respective situations, from the fear of God, they become dear to each other. (*Note, Gen.* xxxv. 8. *P. O.* 1—15.)—Those who love the Lord will love his people also, and will be disposed to employ their wealth or influence in promoting his worship: and such as are most worthy in the opinion of competent judges, will most honour Christ, and be most sensible of their own unworthiness.—When we have received benefits which we are unable to return ; justice, as well as gratitude, requires us to beseech the Lord very earnestly in behalf of our benefactors, especially when they are under trials and afflictions: and we are most likely to obtain the greatest favours from him, when we are most sensible that we do not deserve the least. To him all things are alike easy ; all creatures obey his word ; and he never fails to answer the expectation of that faith, which honours his power and love.— Our blessed Redeemer's heart is susceptible of pity, on account of all the distresses to which we are exposed. The weeping widow, and bereaved parent, are the peculiar objects of his compassionate regard : and, though he no longer restores their deceased relatives ; yet the power which formerly effected this, can now repair every breach, dry up every tear, and cause every bleeding heart to rejoice. While many, therefore, glory in a worthless sensibility, or weep over imaginary woe with an unmeaning sympathy, and leave real misery to pine in neglect ; let the Christian joyfully copy the compassion of his Lord ; let

2 Y 6

dient disciples are his most beloved relations, 19—21. He calms a violent tempest, 22—25; and casts out the legion, 26—39. He heals the woman who had an issue of blood, and raises Jairus's daughter, 40—56.

him look out for those objects of distress, which often lie concealed from the superficial observers of mankind; and endeavour to soothe the aching heart, to relieve the indigent, and to comfort the afflicted. In this way, he will most reasonably hope for comfort, under the troubles of life, and in the hour of death, from the stroke of which no period of age, or vigour of health, can secure him: and thus he may also look forward with joyful expectation to the time, when the Redeemer's powerful voice shall call forth all that are in the graves, either to " the resur-" rection of life, or to the resurrection of damnation." (*Notes, John* v. 24—27. xi. 20—27.)—All the displays of the glorious power and majesty of the Lord, should make us fear coming short of his salvation; and all ̣ṿis kindness to us, or to others, should excite us to glorify him, especially for " visiting his people " and raising up a great Redeemer among them.

V. 18—35.

As the beneficent miracles of Christ, above all things, proclaimed him to be the Son of God and the promised Messiah; so the effects of his gospel, in enlightening, reforming, and changing the hearts of sinners, is still a most important evidence of the divine excellency of our holy religion. Ministers ought therefore to be peculiarly earnest in " preaching the glad tidings of salvation to the poor," and in seeking a blessing on their doctrine; that all may see its salutary effects in the sober, righteous, and godly lives of those who favour it.—Every individual should enquire into his own motives, in going to hear the word of God, and ask himself whether he derives any benefit from it; for the true minister is a messenger sent by the Lord Jesus, to prepare the way before him, and to bring sinners to receive and obey him. But, while numbers are offended with the truths and precepts of Christ, and " re-" ject the counsel of God against themselves," from perverse prejudices of diverse kinds; may we study to approve ourselves to be " the children of wisdom," by attending to the instructions of the sacred oracles, and adoring those mysteries and dispensations, which proud infidels and Pharisees deride and blaspheme. (*P. O. Matt.* xi. 1—24.)

V. 36—43.

Those who seek to do good to souls, must meekly bear with the perverseness of opposers, and avoid all affected moroseness; and they should endure personal slights, in order to have access to sinners, and obtain a hearing from them.—None can perceive the preciousness of Christ, or the glory of the gospel, except the broken-hearted. But while these cannot sufficiently express their self-abhorrence on account of their sins, or their admiration of his mercy and grace; the self-sufficient will not only be disgusted with them, but will even think the worse of the gospel for giving encouragement to them! and men of this character often feel a deeper enmity against Christ, and his ministers and disciples, than they choose to avow. But did they know the real state of mankind and of their own souls, they must perceive the folly and wickedness of their objections: for " all," without exception, " have sinned, " and come short of the glory of God." (*Notes, Rom.* iii. 21—26, *vv.* 21—23. *Gal.* iii. 10—14. 19—22.)—By per-

verting his bounty, and using even the faculties of our souls, and the members of our bodies, which he has created, as well as his other gifts, in violating his commands instead of devoting them to his service; and by refusing him the love and worship due to him, we have contracted a debt, of which we cannot in any possible way discharge the smallest part: nay, it must continue to increase as long as we live in this world; for who can render unto God all that obedience during one day, which is due on every day? Or who can perform one service, which is free from every defect or alloy of sin? Without free forgiveness, we can none of us escape the wrath to come: and this, our gracious Saviour has procured by his atoning blood, that he might freely bestow it on every one who believes in him.

V. 44—50.

He who is convinced of his own great sinfulness, and expects pardon and all the blessings of salvation, as " the " gift of God in Jesus Christ," will in proportion become humble, patient, contented, teachable, and obedient. Above all other things, he will learn to love the Saviour, in every part of his character, and to value him in all his offices: he will desire his favour, be thankful for his mercy, and zealous for his glory; he will become earnest, constant, and diligent, in endeavours to please him and to recommend his salvation; he will love his ordinances, commandments, and disciples; and value every talent in proportion as it enables him to express his love to Jesus and his cause. Thus it often happens, that " the chief of sinners," having been brought to repentance, and made joyful by a free forgiveness and salvation, become more zealous and active in obedience than other believers: " they love much, because " much hath been forgiven them;" and they labour much because they love much. In the case of others, deep humiliation will always be connected with a proportionable love and willing obedience, when it is accompanied with a good hope that all their sins are pardoned. The scanty formal services, therefore, of too many prove, either that they have no proper sense of their guilt, and no just views of the preciousness of Christ, and the redeemed sinner's obligations to him; or that they " love little," because they suppose that " little has been forgiven them." But when a real and vigorous love to Christ springs from sorrow for sin, and hope of forgiveness through him, and is expressed by such methods as a man's situation admits of; we may from it safely infer that his " sins though many are for-" given;" and may thus give him great encouragement, without in the least palliating his guilt: and when the witnessing Spirit makes it evident to the believer's conscience, that he does indeed love Christ; he may know more certainly that " his sins are forgiven," than if an angel from heaven had told him so. Let who will object, and murmur at these things, Christ will assert his authority of thus forgiving sin, and of bidding the weeping penitent " de-" part in peace," as partaking of salvation through faith in his name.—But may not we with shame confess, that while we hope that our many and great offences are freely pardoned, we yet comparatively love but little? If this be the case, we should seek for more heart-affecting views of our own vileness, and of Christ's preciousness: we

AND it came to pass afterward, [a] that he went throughout every city and village, preaching, and shewing [b] the glad tidings of the kingdom of God: [c] and the twelve *were* with him.

2 And [d] certain women, which had been healed of evil spirits and infirmities, Mary called Magdalene, [e] out of whom went seven devils,

3 And [f] Joanna, the wife of Chuza, Herod's steward, and Susanna, and many others, which ministered unto him [h] of their substance.

4 ¶ And [i] when much people were gathered together, and were come to him out of every city, he spake by a parable:

5 A [k] sower went out to sow his seed: and as he sowed, some [1] fell by the way-side; and it was trodden down, [m] and the fowls of the air devoured it.

6 And some fell upon [n] a rock; and as soon as it was sprung up, it withered away, because it lacked moisture.

7 And some fell among [o] thorns; and the thorns sprang up with it, and choked it.

8 And [p] other fell on good ground, and sprang up, and bare fruit [q] an hundred-fold. And when he had said these things he cried, [r] He that hath ears to hear, let him hear.

9 And his disciples asked him, saying, [s] What might this parable be?

10 And he said, [t] Unto you it is given to know the mysteries of the kingdom of God; but to others in parables, [u] that seeing they might not see, and hearing they might not understand.

11 Now the parable is this; [v] The seed is the word of God.

12 Those [y] by the way-side are they that hear: [z] then cometh the devil, and taketh away the word out of their hearts, lest they should believe and be saved.

13 They on the rock *are they*, which, when they hear, [a] receive the word with joy; [b] and these have no root, [c] which for a while believe, and in time of temptation fall away.

14 And that which fell among thorns are they, which, when they have heard, go forth, [d] and are choked with cares, and riches, and pleasures of *this* life, [e] and bring no fruit to perfection.

15 But that on the good ground are they, which, [f] in an honest and good heart, having heard the word, [g] keep *it*, and [h] bring forth fruit with patience.

---

should " give diligence to make our calling and election " sure ; " and strive to get deeper impressions of our obligations to Jesus, and expectations from him : that we may stand at a greater distance from the proud spirit of the Pharisee ; that we may more simply trust and rejoice in the Saviour alone ; and so be prepared to obey him more zealously, and more cordially to recommend him to our fellow-sinners on every side, and be made more meet for the society and songs of heaven. (*Notes*, and *P. O. Rev.* v. 8—14. vii. 9—17.)

NOTES.

CHAP. VIII. V. 1—3. *Marg. Ref.*—Mary called Magdalene, &c. (2) *Notes*, vii. 37—39. *Mark* xvi. 9—11.— Joanna, &c. (3) Some have conjectured that " Chuza, " Herod's steward," was the nobleman, or courtier, whose son Jesus had healed. (*Notes, John* iv. 43—54.) Doubtless, it was by his consent that his wife accompanied Jesus, when journeying to preach the gospel.—As our Lord chose to be " poor for our sakes," and did not work miracles for his own support ; these pious women, who had been under the greatest obligations to him, in respect both to their souls and bodies, being also in good circumstances, were glad to communicate, from their substance, to the maintenance of him and his disciples, as well as personally to attend him : and he was pleased to stoop thus low, for an example to his servants and disciples in similar circumstances. It does not appear that any *men* shared this honour " of ministering to Christ of their substance."

Of their substance. (3) Απο των ὑπαρχοντων αυταις. xi. 21. xii. 15. 33. 44. xiv. 33. xvi. 1. xix. 8. *Matt.* xix. 21. xxiv. 47. xxv. 14. *Acts* iv. 32. 1 *Cor.* xiii. 3. *Heb.* x. 34.

V. 4—15. *Marg. Ref.*—Notes, *Matt.* xiii. 3—23. *Mark* iv. 1—20.—*It was trodden*, &c. (5) 'This is not mentioned ' by St. Matthew, or St. Mark, and seems to signify a great ' contempt of the divine seed.' *Whitby.*—Believe, &c. (12) The inseparable connexion of faith with salvation, and of unbelief with damnation, is here strongly marked ; and it is considered as well known to the enemy of our souls, who therefore uses all possible methods to prejudice men against the true gospel of Christ, or to render them inattentive to it. (Note, 2 Cor. iv. 3, 4.)—*Perfection.* (14) Whatever is by any means destroyed, before it arrives at its full growth, and before it is fit for use, is not brought

16 ¶ No man, when he hath lighted a candle, covereth it with a vessel, or putteth it under a bed; but setteth it on a candlestick, that they which enter in may see the light.

17 For nothing is secret, that shall not be made manifest; neither any thing hid, that shall not be known and come abroad.

18 Take heed therefore how ye hear: for whosoever hath, to him shall be given; and whosoever hath not, from him shall be taken even that which he seemeth to have.

19 ¶ Then came to him his mother and his brethren, and could not come at him for the press.

20 And it was told him by certain, which said, Thy mother and thy brethren stand without, desiring to see thee.

21 And he answered and said unto them, My mother and my brethren are these which hear the word of God, and do it.

22 ¶ Now it came to pass on a certain day, that he went into a ship with his disciples; and he said unto them,

Let us go over unto the other side of the lake. And they launched forth.

23 But as they sailed, he fell asleep: and there came down a storm of wind on the lake; and they were filled with water, and were in jeopardy.

24 And they came to him, and awoke him, saying, Master, master, we perish. Then he arose and rebuked the wind, and the raging of the water; and they ceased, and there was a calm.

25 And he said unto them, Where is your faith? And they being afraid wondered, saying one to another, What manner of man is this? for he commandeth even the winds and water, and they obey him.

26 ¶ And they arrived at the country of the Gadarenes, which is over against Galilee.

27 And when he went forth to land, there met him out of the city a certain man which had devils a long time, and ware no clothes, neither abode in any house, but in the tombs.

28 When he saw Jesus, he cried

---

to perfection: and all in religion, which comes short of fruitfulness in good works, according to the time and opportunities vouchsafed, is like the corn that withers before it be ripe. (Note, xxiii. 39—43.)—*Honest,* &c. (15) Καλη. *Notes, Jer.* xvii. 9, 10. *Ez.* xi. 17—20. *John* iii. 3—8. *Rom.* vii. 18—21. ' From these words it is manifest, that some ' good dispositiou of heart is requisite, to render the word ' truly and durably fruitful.' *Whitby.* This no man has by nature, but by grace only. " God worketh in us to will " and to do." (*Notes, John* i. 10—12. *Acts* xvii. 10—15, *vv.* 11, 12. *Phil.* ii. 12, 13. *Jam.* i. 15—17.) ' O God, ' from whom all holy desires, all good counsels, and all ' just works do proceed, &c.' *Col. Even. Liturgy.*

It was trodden, &c. (5) Κατεπαθη, xii. 1. *Matt.* v. 13. vii. 6. *Heb.* x. 29.—*Moisture.* (6) Ικμαδα. Here only *N. T.* —*An hundred fold.* (8) Ἑκατονταπλασιονα. *Matt.* xix. 29. *Mark* x. 30. Not elsewhere *N. T.*—*Should believe and be saved.* (12) Πιτευσαντες σωθωσιν. " Lest believing, they " should be saved."—*Bring no fruit to perfection.* (14) Ου τελεσφορουσι. Here only *N. T.*—Εx τελος, *finis,* et φερω, *fero.* —*With patience.* (15) Εν ὑπομονη. xxi. 19. *Rom.* ii. 7. v.3, 4. viii. 25, et al. In perseverance: " He that continueth to the " end shall be saved." (*Notes, Matt.* x. 21, 22, *v.* 22. *Rom.* ii. 7—11, *v.* 7.)

V. 16—18. *Marg. Ref.—Notes, Matt.* v. 14—16. *Mark* iv. 21—25.—*He seemeth to have.* (18) Either to himself or others. (*Marg.*) This is here added, which is not found in the parallel scriptures. (*Notes, Matt.* xiii. 12. xxv. 24— 30, *v.* 29.)—Whatever of natural genius, learning, wealth,

authority, influence, religious knowledge, spiritual gifts, or even power of working miracles any man had; if he has not saving and sanctifying grace, he only seems to have it, and it will soon be torn from him.—' Heavenly good things ' are lost by parsimony, and increase by liberality.' *Beza.*

V. 19—21. (*Marg. Ref.—Notes,* xi. 27, 28. *Matt.* xii. 46—50. *Mark* iii. 31—35.) ' This might be intended as ' an awful intimation to some of his near relations, to take ' heed how they indulged that unbelief, which so long ' after prevailed in their minds.' *Doddridge.* (*Note, John* vii. 3—10.)

Come at him. (19) Συντυχειν. Here only *N. T.*—*By certain, which said.* (20) Λεγοντων, supply τινων.

V. 22—25. *Marg. Ref.—Notes, Matt.* viii. 23—27. *Mark* iv. 35—41.—*Where is,* &c. (25) The disciples had faith, but it was not in exercise, when most wanted: as if a soldier should leave his arms in his tent, when he marched out to battle. ' Where is your sword ? Where is your ' shield ? ' must be the general question. (*Marg. Ref.* a.)

They launched forth. (22) Ανηχθησαν. *Acts* xiii. 13. xvi. 11. xxi. 1. xxvii. 12.—*He fell asleep.* (23) Αφυπνωσε. Here only *N. T.*—*Were in jeopardy.*] Εκινδυνευον. *Acts* xix. 27. 40. 1 *Cor.* xv. 30.—*Master.* (24) Επιστατα. See on v. 5. Κυρι *Matt.* vii. 25. Διδασκαλε *Mark* iv. 38.

V. 26—39. *Notes, Matt.* viii. 28—34. *Mark* v. 1—20. —*The deep.* (31) ' The abyss, the prison, in which many ' of these fallen spirits are detained; and to which some, ' who may, like these, have been permitted for a while to ' range at large, are sometimes by divine justice and power

out, and fell down before him, and with a loud voice said, ᵇWhat have I to do with thee, Jesus, *thou* Son of God most high? ¹I beseech thee torment me not.

29 (For he had ᵏcommanded the unclean spirit to come out of the man. For often-times it had ¹caught him; and he was kept bound with chains, and in fetters; and he brake the bands, and was driven of the devil into the wilderness.)

30 And Jesus asked him, saying, ᵐWhat is thy name? And he said, ᵐLegion: because ⁿmany devils were entered into him.

31 And ᵒthey besought him that he would not command them to go out into ᵖthe deep.

32 And there was ᑫthere an herd of many swine feeding on the mountain: and they ʳbesought him that he would suffer them to enter into them. And ʳhe suffered them.

33 Then went the devils out of the man, and entered into the swine: ˢand the herd ran violently down a steep place into the lake, and were choked.

34 When they that fed *them* saw what was done, ᵘthey fled, and went and told *it* in the city, and in the country.

35 Then they went out to see what was done; and came to Jesus, ˣand found the man, out of whom the devils were departed, ʸsitting at the feet of

Jesus, ᶻclothed, and in his right mind: and they were afraid.

36 They also which saw *it* told them by what means he that was possessed of the devils was healed.

37 Then the whole multitude of the ᵉcountry of the Gadarenes round about, ᵃbesought him to depart from them: for they were taken with great fear. ᵇAnd he went up into the ship, and returned back again.

38 Now the man, out of whom the devils were departed, ᶜbesought him that he might be with him: but Jesus sent him away, ᵈsaying,

39 Return to thine own house, and shew how great things God hath done unto thee. And he went his way, ᵉand published throughout the whole city how great things Jesus had done unto him.

40 ¶ And it came to pass, ᶠthat when Jesus returned, ᵍthe people gladly received him; for they were all ᵇwaiting for him.

41 And, behold, ʰthere came a man named Jairus, and he was ᵏa ruler of the synagogue; ˡand he fell down at Jesus' feet, ᵐand besought him that he would come into his house:

42 For he had ⁿone only daughter, about twelve years of age, ᵒand she lay a dying. ᵖBut as he went the people thronged him.

43 And a woman ᑫhaving an issue of blood ʳtwelve years, which ˢhad spent

---

' remanded.' *Doddridge.* (*Marg. Ref.* p.)—' The first request of the devil to Christ was, " I beseech thee, torment me not." " Art thou come to torment me before my time?" (*Matt.* viii. 29;) expressing the devil's fear, that by this coming of Christ, he should presently be cast into the chains of hell; ... and confined to those torments, which he thought belonged not to him till the day of judgment: and the next was in plain words not to send him into hell.' *Hammond.* (*Marg. Ref.* i. o.)—*He suffered them.* (32) ' But why did Christ grant this to them ? Partly to shew himself the sovereign Lord of all; partly to punish the Gadarenes for their manifest contempt of the divine law; and finally to shew the folly of ungodly men, in preferring their filthy swine to their own salvation.' *Beza.*

They arrived at. (26) Κατεπλευσαν εις. " They sailed unto." Here only N. T.—*Ware no clothes.* (27) Ἱματιον ουκ ενεδιδυσκετο. xvi. 19. Not elsewhere N. T.—*It had caught.* (29) Συνηρπακει. *Acts* vi. 12. xix. 29 xxvii. 15.—*He brake.*]

Διαρρησσων. See on v. 6.—*The bands.*] Τα δεσμα. xiii. 16. *Acts* xvi. 26, *et al.* A δεω, ligo.—*The deep.* (31) Την αβυσσον.—(Εκ α priv. et ζυσσος, *fundus.*) *Rom.* x. 7. *Rev.* ix. 1, 2. xi. 7. xvii. 8. xx. 1.—*Gen.* i. 2. *Deut.* xxxiii. 13. *Sept.*—*Healed.* (36) Εσωθη, " was delivered," or " saved." The man was *rescued* by superior power from the legion of evil spirits; and not merely *healed* of a disease.—*Published.* (39) Κηρυσσων, " preaching " or proclaiming as a herald.— *The whole city.*] Ολην την πολιν. Gadara was one of the cities of Decapolis, part of which lay on the one side, and part on the other side, of the sea of Tiberias. Gadara suffered great extremities from the Romans, under the command of Vespasian.

V. 40—56. *Marg. Ref.*—*Notes, Matt.* ix. 18—26. *Mark* v. 21—43.—*One only daughter.* (42) This affecting circumstance is not mentioned by the other evangelists. (*Note,* vii. 11—17.)—*Neither could be healed,* &c. (43) The force and inveteracy of this afflicted woman's disease baffled all the skill of the physicians: so that, besides all addi-

all her living upon physicians, neither could be healed of any,◦

44 Came 'behind *him*, and ◦ touched the border of his garment: ◦ and immediately her issue of blood staunched.

45 And Jesus said, Who touched me? When all denied, Peter and they that were with him said, Master, ◦ the multitude throng thee, and press *thee*, and sayest thou, Who touched me?

46 And Jesus said, Somebody hath touched me: ◦ for I perceive that virtue is gone out of me.

47 And when the woman saw that she was not hid, ◦ she came trembling, and falling down before him, ◦ she declared unto him before all the people, for what cause she had touched him, and how she was healed immediately.

48 And he said unto her, ◦ Daughter, be of good comfort: ◦ thy faith hath made thee whole; ◦ go in peace.

49 While ◦ he yet spake, there cometh one from the ruler of the synagogue's *house*, saying to him, Thy

daughter is dead; ◦ trouble not the Master.

50 But when Jesus heard *it* he answered him, saying, Fear not: ◦ believe only, and she shall be made whole.

51 And when he came into the house, ◦ he suffered no man to go in, ◦ save Peter, and James, and John, and the father and the mother of the maiden.

52 And ◦ all wept, and bewailed her: but he said, Weep not; ◦ she is not dead, but sleepeth.

53 And they ◦ laughed him to scorn, ◦ knowing that she was dead.

54 And ◦ he put them all out, and ◦ took her by the hand, and called, saying, ◦ Maid, arise.

55 And ◦ her spirit came again, and she arose straightway: ◦ and he commanded to give her meat.

56 And her parents were astonished: but ◦ he charged them that they should tell no man what was done.

---

tional sufferings, from the medicines, and the means in vain used for her recovery, the expense had added poverty to her calamities; and her case appeared altogether hopeless, as to this world. The extreme distress to which several of those, who were healed by our Lord, had been previously reduced, and the length of time during which they had suffered, are frequently noted by the sacred writers; both to illustrate his tender compassion of our miseries, and our desperate condition as sinners, without his most gracious and powerful interposition. (*Marg. Ref.*) —*All out*, &c. (54) All the multitude; all but the apostles and the parents of the damsel.—*Her spirit*, &c. (55) This expression, thus used of one before dead, strongly implies, that at death the immortal soul exists separately, but returns and is re-united to the body, when raised from the dead. (*Note*, 1 *Kings* xvii. 21, 22.)—*Commanded*, &c.] The life of the damsel, though restored by miracle, was to be preserved in the usual manner. This shewed, that she was recovered to health also; and that she wanted food, which during her extreme illness had not been the case.

Had spent all her living. (43) Προσαναλωσασα ὁλον τον ϐιον. Προσαναλισκω, *insuper impendo*. Here only N. T. 'Ολον τον ϐιον. See on *Mark* xii. 44.—*Staunched*. (44) Εϛη, *stood*. —*Throng*. (45) Σινεχουσι. 45. iv. 38. xii. 50. xix. 43. xxii. 63. 2 *Cor*. v. 14. *Phil*. i. 23.—*Bewailed*. (52) Εκοπτοντο. xxiii. 27. *Matt*. xi. 17. xxiv. 30. *Rev*. i. 7. xviii. 9.

PRACTICAL OBSERVATIONS.

V. 1—25.

The ministers of Christ should copy his example of assiduity and earnestness, in " preaching the glad tidings of " the kingdom of God;" and in submitting to any hard-

ship or degradation in outward circumstances, which may conduce to the success of the gospel: and those who are profited by their labours, ought to imitate these pious women; and to use their substance in ministering unto Christ, by supporting his indigent servants and disciples, as occasion may require, and according to their ability. In this way, as well as in many others, they may " bring forth " fruit with patience," and evince that the grace of God has indeed made their hearts " honest and good," and prepared them to receive the good seed of his word; for it has taken effectual root, and will certainly ripen to a glorious harvest. Indeed we should aim, by every method, to discriminate our character and conduct, from those of careless hearers, of superficial and temporary professors, and of " such as are choked with the cares, riches, and " pleasures of this life, and bring no fruit to perfection." (*P. O. Matt*. xiii. 1—23.) It is not enough for us, " not " to hold the truth in unrighteousness;" we should desire to " hold forth the word of life," and to shine in our several circles, as a lighted candle in the room, for the benefit of all around. (*Note*, *Phil*. ii. 14—18.) Thus professing and recommending the truths of the gospel by our conduct and conversation, we shall receive more and more from our gracious God; while many " who seemed " to have" knowledge, abilities, and possessions, not having had grace to make a proper use of them, will shortly be deprived of all; and their poverty, folly, and worthlessness, which were before kept secret, shall be made known to the whole world. Happy are they, " who hear the word " of God, and keep it!" These are the Redeemer's beloved friends and relations; every storm which arises, every peril that dismays them, will tend to excite their

CHAP. IX.

Jesus sends forth the twelve apostles, 1—6. Herod desires to see him, 7—9. The apostles return; Jesus retires with them, but the multitudes follow him, 10, 11. He feeds them by miracle, 12—17. The different opinions concerning him, and Peter's confession, 18—21. He foretels his death, and warns his disciples to prepare for self-denial and sufferings, 22—27. His transfiguration, 28—36 : he heals a demoniack, 37—42; again foretels his death 43—45; checks the ambitious disputes of his disciples, 46—48; will not allow them to forbid any, who "cast out devils in his "name," 49, 50; reproves the fiery zeal of James and John against the Samaritans, who would not receive them, 51—56; and answers some, who were not disposed to follow him unreservedly and immediately, 57—62.

a vi.13—16. Matt.
x. 2—5. Mark
iii. 14—19. vi.
7—13.
b x. 19. Matt. x.
1. xvi. 19. Mark
vi. 7. xvi. 17,
18. John xiv.12.
Acts i. 8. iii. 16.
iv. 30. ix. 34.
c x. 11. xvi. 16.
Matt. iii. 2. x.
7. xiii. 19. xxiv.
14. Mark i. 14,
15. xvi. 15.
Heb. ii. 3, 4.
d x. 4. xxii. 35.
Ps. xxxvii. 3.
Matt. x. 9, 10.
Mark vi. 8, 9.
2 Tim. ii. 4.

THEN [a] he called his twelve disciples together, and [b] gave them power and authority over all devils, and to cure diseases.

2 And he sent them [c] to preach the kingdom of God, and to heal the sick.

3 And he said unto them, [d] Take nothing for *your* journey, neither staves, nor scrip, neither bread, neither money; neither have [e] two coats apiece.

4 And [f] whatsoever house ye enter into, there abide, and thence depart.

5 And [g] whosoever will not receive you, when ye go out of that city, [h] shake off the very dust from your feet for [i] a testimony against them.

6 And they departed, and went through the towns, [k] preaching the gospel, and healing every where.

7 ¶ Now [l] Herod the tetrarch heard of all that was done by him: and [m] he was perplexed, because that it was said of some, that John was risen from the dead;

8 And [n] of some, that Elias had appeared; and of others, that one of the old prophets was risen again.

9 And Herod said, [o] John have I beheaded: but who is this, of whom I hear such things? [p] And he desired to see him.

e iii. 11. v. 29.
xii. 28.
f x. 5—8. Matt.
x. 11. Mark vi.
10. Acts xvi. 15.
g 48. x. 10—12,
16. Matt. x. 14,
15. Mark xi. 11.
ix. 37. Acts xiii.
51. xviii. 6.
h 53—56. Neh. v.
13.
i y. 14. Matt. x
15.
k 1, 2. Mark vi.
12, 13. xvi. 20.
Acts iv. 30. v.
15.
l Job xviii. 11, 12.
Ps. lxxiii. 19.
Matt. xiv. 1—
12. Mark vi. 14
—28.
m xxi. 25. Is.xxii.
5. Mic. vii. 4.
n 19. Matt. xvii.
10. Mark vi. 15.
21.
o 7.
p xiii. 31, 32.
xxiii. 8.

---

fervent prayers; and their Lord will awake for their help and deliverance, and cause the trial to terminate in their increasing admiration of his power and love. Yet, at times, even true believers seem to have mislaid their faith, or to have left it behind them: as they have so many anxious fears about the event, even when they are following Christ in the path of duty; concerning which alone we ought to be solicitous. (*P. O. Matt.* viii. 23—27. xii. 38—50. *Mark* iv. 1—25.)

V. 26—56.

Our own observation and experience may convince us, that the effects of sin, and of Satan's malice, fill the earth with misery : but let us advert to the varied displays of the Redeemer's power to counteract this fatal tendency. If he have delivered our souls from the power of the devil, and brought us "to sit at his feet, in our right mind," to hear his word, and to desire to be with him : he will preserve us from falling again under the dominion of sin ; he will remove or sanctify our bodily sicknesses, and give us the comfort of his forgiving love; he will support us under domestick afflictions, and do us good by them; he will deliver us from the fear of death, and at length make us "more "than conquerors" even over this "king of terrors." Let us then declare what great things our God and Saviour has done for us; let us commit all our concerns into his hands, and apply to him for help in all our difficulties; and let us endeavour to imitate his compassion and unwearied activity in doing good.—But, woe be to them, who desire Jesus "to depart from them," through fear of worldly loss, or from love to sin ! He will not stay with those who thus slight him, and perhaps may return to them no more; for others are glad to receive him, being "waiting for him :" and none but Jesus can save them from the wrath of God, or the power of Satan ; or give

them effectual help in the time of trouble, 'in the hour 'of death, and in the day of judgment.' (*P. O. Matt.* viii. 28—34. ix. 18—26. *Mark* v. 1—43.)

NOTES.

CHAP. IX. V. 1—6. (*Marg. Ref.—Notes,* x. 1—12. *Matt.* x. 1—15. *Mark* vi. 7—13.) The apostles had both the *power* of working miracles, and *authority* over evil spirits, immediately given them by Christ himself; in whom it was originally inherent, as One with the Father, as "God manifest in the flesh;" as well as given to him as our Mediator. (*Note, Matt.* xxviii. 18.) The miracles of *mercy*, wrought by them, proved their doctrine to be the word of God, and illustrated its benign and salutary tendency : and their holy doctrine, calling men to repent of sin and turn to God, and welcome the Saviour promised in the scriptures, demonstrated that their miracles were wrought by the power of God, whose word they established. (*Notes, Deut.* xiii. 1—5. *Matt.* xii. 25—30.)—*Thence, &c.* (4) Remain in the same house, if convenient, till ye depart from that city.

V. 7—9. (*Marg. Ref.—Notes,* iii. 19, 20. *Matt.* xiv. 1—12. *Mark* vi. 14—29.)—Herod was perplexed and uneasy, at the report of Christ's miracles ; and concurred in the opinion of those, who said that "John was risen from "the dead ;" yet he desired to see him, in order to ascertain the truth of this opinion, or in hopes to disprove a report which gave him much alarm. (*Notes,* xiii. 31—33. xxiii. 6—12.)

He was perplexed. (7) Διηπορει. xxiv. 4. *Acts* ii. 12. v. 24. x. 17.—*Dan.* ii. 3. *Sept.* ' Proprie de viatoribus di- ' citur, cum non pateat, quo progrediantur ... πορον μη ευρισ- ' κυσι ... hesitare, incertum esse, ... ambigere.' Schleusner.

224

10 ¶ And *the apostles, when they were returned, told him all that they had done. And 'he took them, and went aside privately into a desert place, belonging to the city called *Bethsaida.

11 And the people, ' when they knew it, followed him; *and he received them, and spake unto them *of the kingdom of God, and healed them that had need of healing.

12 And 'when the day began to wear away, then came the twelve, and said unto him, *Send the multitude away, that they may go into the towns and country round about, and lodge, and get victuals: *for we are here in a desert place.

13 But he said unto them, *Give ye them to eat. And they said, 'We have no more but five loaves and two fishes; except we should go and buy meat for all this people?

14 For they were about five thousand men. And he said to his disciples, *Make them sit down by fifties in a company.

15 And they did so, and made them all sit down.

16 Then he took the five loaves and the two fishes, *and looking up to heaven, 'he blessed them, and brake, and gave to the disciples to set before the multitude.

17 And they did *eat, and were all filled: *and there was taken up of fragments that remained to them, twelve baskets.

18 ¶ And it came to pass, 'as he was alone praying, his disciples were with him; and he asked them, saying, *Whom say the people that I am?

19 They answering said, 'John the Baptist: but some say, Elias: and others say, That one of the "old prophets is risen again.

20 He said unto them, But *whom say ye that I am? Peter answering said, *The Christ of God.

21 And 'he straitly charged them, and commanded them to tell no man that thing;

22 Saying, *the Son of man must suffer many things, and be rejected of the elders, and chief priests, and scribes, and be slain, and be raised the third day.

23 And he said to them all, 'If any man will come after me, let him *deny himself, and take up his cross 'daily, and follow me.

24 For whosoever *will save his life shall lose it: but whosoever will lose his life for my sake, the same shall save it.

25 For *what is a man advantaged, if he gain the whole world, and lose himself, or 'be cast away?

26 For 'whosoever shall be ashamed of me, and of my words, *of him shall the Son of man be ashamed, *when he shall come in his own glory, and in his Father's, and of the holy angels.

27 But 'I tell you of a truth, There be *some standing here, which shall not *taste of death till they 'see the kingdom of God.

V. 10—17. (Marg Ref.—Notes, Matt. xiv. 13—21. Mark vi. 30—46. John vi. 1—21.)—' They shall lack ' nothing that follow Christ; no, not in the wilderness.' Beza.

Lodge. (12) Καταλυτωσι. xix. 7.—Gen. xxiv. 23. Josh. ii. 1. Sept. Καταλυμα, diversorium. ii. 7.—Victuals.] Επισιτισμον. Here only N. T.—Make them sit down. (14) Κατακλινατε. xiv. 8. xxiv. 30. Not elsewhere N. T.

V. 18—27. Notes, Matt. xvi. 13—28. Mark viii. 27—38. ix. 1.—Whom say ye, &c. (20) ' Though the world ' fluctuates amidst various errors, the truth must not on ' that account be despised; but rather the knowledge of ' it should be the more diligently sought, and the pro-' fession of it made with the greater constancy.' Beza.—Deny himself. (23) Self-denial, among other things, re-

quires us to renounce all those advantages, and risk all those sufferings, which arise from the favour or enmity of men.—' Although the yearning bowels of a tender mother, ' pleaded as motives to induce me to break the least com-' mand of the holy Jesus; though the authority of civil, ' natural, or ecclesiastical superiors should tempt me to do ' what Christ forbids; though this authority should allure ' me with proffers of the highest honours or rewards, or ' should endeavour to affright me with the severest me-' naces; yet if all these considerations should prevail with ' me to gratify myself and them, by doing that which my ' own conscience, and God's word, assures me will be ' displeasing to my Saviour, or opposite to his commands; ' it is evident that I regard myself, or them, more than I

28 ¶ And it came to pass, ʳ about an eight days after these ˢ sayings, ʰ he took Peter, and John, and James, and went up ᶦ into a mountain to pray.

29 And, as he prayed, ᵏ the fashion of his countenance was altered, and his raiment *was* white *and* glistering.

30 And, behold, there talked with him two men, ᶦ which were Moses and ᵐ Elias;

31 Who ⁿ appeared in glory, and ° spake of his decease, which he should accomplish at Jerusalem.

32 But Peter, and they that were with him, ᵖ were heavy with sleep: and when they were awake, ᑫ they saw his glory, and the two men that stood with him.

33 And it came to pass, as they departed from him, Peter said unto Jesus,

Master, 'it is good for us to be here: 'and let us make three tabernacles; one for thee, and one for Moses, and one for Elias: not knowing what he said.

34 While he thus spake, ᵗ there came a cloud, and overshadowed them; 'and they feared as they entered into the cloud.

35 And there came a voice out of the cloud, saying, ᵛ This is my beloved Son; ʸ hear him.

36 And when the voice was past, Jesus was found alone. ² And they kept *it* close, and told no man in those days any of those things which they had seen.

37 ¶ And it came to pass, ᵃ that on the next day, when they were come down from the hill, much people met him.

' do my Saviour, and therefore am unworthy of him, and ' cannot be sincerely his disciple.' *Whitby.* This learned writer proceeds in the same energetick manner, to shew particularly, how self-denial requires the same decision and firmness against solicitation, allurements, and upbraiding complaints, from wives, children, and other relations, where obedience to Christ is concerned : as well as to deny the cravings of our own pride, ambition, love of money, pleasure, ease ; by willingly enduring reproach, contempt, poverty, imprisonment, or tortures, nay death itself, when these things cannot be shunned, except by denying, disobeying, or dishonouring our Redeemer. (*Notes,* xiv. 25—27. *Matt.* x. 34—39.)—*Daily.*] ' Great is the emphasis ' of this word, which indeed implies, that as day succeeds ' day, so would one cross follow another.' *Beza.*—*Lose himself,* &c. (25) This must mean final perdition. (*Marg. Ref.* x, y.)—" His own soul." *Matt.* xvi. 26. *Mark* viii. 36.—*In his own glory,* &c. (26) This, as distinguished from " the glory of the Father," denotes the glory of Christ, as Mediator, exercising all divine perfections through the medium of his human nature, in accomplishing and perfecting the grand purposes of his incarnation. (*Note, Matt.* xxv. 31—33. *John* v. 20—29. 1 *Cor.* xv. 20 —28. 2 *Thes.* i. 5—10. *Rev.* xx. 11—15.)

Alone. (18) *Καλαμονας. Mark* iv. 10. Not elsewhere *N. T.*—*Ps.* cxli. 10. *Jer.* xv. 17. *Sept.*—Apart from the multitude.—*One of the old prophets.* (19) Προφητης τις των αρχαιων. 8. *Matt.* v. 21. 27. 33. *Acts* xv. 7. 21. xxi. 16. 2 *Pet.* ii. 5.—*Be cast away.* (25) Ζημιωθης. See on *Matt.* xvi. 26.

V. 28—36. (*Marg. Ref.*—*Notes, Matt.* xvii. 1—9. *Mark* ix. 2—10. ' Lest the disciples should be offended ' at his humiliation in the flesh, Christ teaches them that ' it was voluntary, withal shewing them for a space his ce- ' lestial glory and majesty.' *Beza.*—*His decease.* (31) (*Note, John* xiii. 1—5.) The subject of the conversation on the holy mount, mentioned only by this evangelist,

shews that the atonement made by the death of Christ, was the great object to which Moses and the prophets, rightly understood, directed mankind. They, as well as John the Baptist and the apostles, in fact say, " Behold the " Lamb of God, which taketh away the sin of the world." (*Marg. Ref.* o.)—Feared, &c. (34) " They," (the disciples) " feared, when those men," Moses and Elijah, " en- " tered the cloud." *Campbell.*—The cloud overshadowed the disciples also ; and at that time Moses and Elijah disappeared.—*Hear him.* (35) This is the first and great command of God *to sinners by the gospel,* without obedience to which all else is vain. (*Notes, John* vi. 28, 29. 1 *John* iii. 18—24.)

The fashion. (29) Το ειδος. See on iii. 22.—*Was altered.*] Ἑτερον, " another." — *Glistering.*] Εξαστραπτων. Here only *N. T.* ... *Ex.* i. 7. *Nah.* iii. 3. *Sept.*—Ab awaken the most tender sympathy in the reader. (*Note,* vii. 11—17.)—*Lo,* &c. (39) " And, behold, a spirit " seizeth him, and suddenly *the youth* crieth out, and *the* " spirit teareth him till he foameth, and bruising him, " hardly departeth from him." In this rendering, (which is literal, except as the proper nominative to each verb is added instead of the relative,) what the evil spirit, and what in consequence the youth did, are distinguished : and this is of considerable importance, in order to shew more clearly that it was a real possession.—*The mighty power.* &c. (43) Or, " the majesty of God," which was displayed by Jesus in this miracle, according to what he says,

9 z 6

.38 And, behold, a man of the company cried out, saying, Master, I beseech thee, [b] look upon my son; [c] for he is mine only child :

39 And, [d] lo, a spirit taketh him; and he suddenly crieth out; and it teareth him that he foameth again, and bruising him hardly departeth from him.

40 And I besought thy disciples to cast him out; [e] and they could not.

41 And Jesus answering, said, [f] O faithless and [g] perverse generation! [h] how long shall I be with you, [i] and suffer you? [k] Bring thy son hither.

42 And as he was yet a coming, [l] the devil threw him down and tare him. And Jesus rebuked the unclean spirit, and healed the child, [m] and delivered him again to his father.

43 And they were all [n] amazed at the mighty power of God. But while they wondered every one at all things which Jesus did, he said unto his disciples,

44 Let [o] these sayings sink down

into your ears: [p] for the Son of man shall be delivered into the hands of men:

45 But [q] they understood not this saying, and it was hid from them, that they perceived it not: and they feared to ask him of that saying.

46 ¶ Then there [r] arose a reasoning among them, which of them should be greatest.

47 And Jesus, [s] perceiving the thought of their heart, [t] took a child, and set him by him;

48 And said unto them, [u] Whosoever shall receive this child in my name, receiveth me : and whosoever shall receive me, receiveth him that sent me : for [v] he that is least among you all, the same shall be great.

49 And John answered and said, [w] Master, [x] we saw one casting out devils in thy name; and we forbad him because he followeth not with us.

50 And Jesus said unto him, [y] For-

" He, that hath seen me, hath seen the Father."—*Snk deep*, &c. (44) Or, " Place these things in your ears : " ' Let them still sound in your ears, and let no subsequent events cause you to forget them ; for a very different scene will soon open.'—' We have no reason to promise ourselves ' tranquillity ; seeing they, who at one time extol Christ, ' not long after crucify him.' *Beza.* (*Marg. Ref.* o, p.)

Mine only child. (38) Μονογενης ... μοι. See on vii. 12.—*Suddenly.* (39) Εξαιφνης. ii. 13. Mark xiii. 36. *Acts* iv. 3. xxii. 6.—*That he foameth.*] Μετ αφρυ, " with " foam." Here only *N. T.*—*Tare him.* (42) Συνεσπαραξεν. Here only *N. T.* " Threw him down, and at the same " time tare him." Σπαρασσω. See on *Mark* ix. 20.— *The mighty power.* (43) Τη μεγαλειοτητι. *Acts* xix. 27. 2 *Pet.* i. 16. Not elsewhere N. T.—*Jer.* xxxiii. 9. *Sept.* Μεγαλεια. i. 49.

V. 45. ' They understood the words ; but knew not ' how to reconcile them with their own traditions, that ' their Messiah should live for ever, or with the great ' things they expected from him : and therefore in after ' ages, they' (the unbelieving Jews,) ' invented the dis- ' tinction of Messiah Ben Joseph, who was to die, and ' Messiah Ben David, who was to triumph, and live for ' ever.' *Whitby.* (*Notes, Mark* viii. 17—21. ix. 30—32. x. 32—34. 2 *Cor.* iii. 12—16.)

It was hid.] Ην παρακεκαλυμμενον. Here only N. T. —*Ex.* xxii. 26. *Sept.*—*That they perceived it not.*] 'Ινα μη αισθωνται.—" That they might not apprehend it." ' There ' is no impropriety in supposing that predictions were in- ' tentionally expressed, so as not to be perfectly under- ' stood at the time; but so as to make an impression, ' which would secure their being remembered, till the

' accomplishment should dispel every doubt.' *Campbell.* Certainly the translation here given is more literal than our version.

V. 46—48. (*Marg. Ref.*—*Notes, Matt.* xviii. 1—6. *Mark* ix. 33—37. 41, 42.) ' Their words, spoken among ' themselves, could not escape him, who knew their ' thoughts, or *reasonings.*'—*The same shall be great.* (48) Or, " greatest ; " as some understand it : but indeed " the " least" true Christian " shall be great," above all the great ones of the earth, and equal to the angels in heaven. (xx. 36.)

V. 49, 50. *Marg. Ref.*—*Note, Mark* 38—40.—*Forbid,* &c. (50) ' In extraordinary cases, we should not rashly ' either condemn, or approve.' *Beza.* This is an observation of no little importance : for on the one hand precipitate and harsh condemnations of extraordinary appearances of a revival in religion, when it afterwards appears, that God was eminently prospering his gospel, by those who followed not with these rash censurers, are very common : and so on the other, is an indiscriminate sanctioning of all that is done or observed on these occasions, as *divine*; when the event shews, that human infirmity and depravity, and Satan's artifice, in various ways, concurred to disgrace, if possible, and stop the good work of the Holy Spirit. To wait, to examine and observe, and impartially to distinguish between what is scriptural, and what is unscriptural, in these extraordinary events; and not to give an opinion, till the whole be maturely weighed, so as to leave but little danger, either of condemning the work of God, or of sanctioning the delusions of the devil, is a chief point of heavenly wisdom.

Master. (49) Επιστατα.—Διδασκαλε, *Mark* ix. 38.

bid *him* not; ^a for he that is not against us is for us.

51 ¶ And it came to pass, when the time was come ^b that he should be received up, ^c he stedfastly set his face to go to Jerusalem,

52 And ^d sent messengers before his face: ^e and they went and entered into a village of ^f the Samaritans, to make ready for him.

53 And ^g they did not receive him, because his face was as though he would go to Jerusalem.

54 And when his disciples, James and John, saw *this*, they said, Lord, ^h wilt thou that we command ⁱ fire to come down from heaven, and consume them, even as Elias did?

55 But he turned, ^k and rebuked them, and said, ^l Ye know not what manner of spirit ye are of.

56 For ^m the Son of man is not come to destroy men's lives, but to save *them*. ⁿ And they went to another village.

Margin references (left column):
a xi. 23. Matt. xii. 30. Mark ix. 41. 1 Cor. xii. 3.
b xxiv. 51. 2 Kings ii. 1–3, 11. Mark xvi. 19. John vi. 62. xvii. 1, 5, 13. xvii. 11. Acts i. 2, 9. Eph. i. 20. iv. 8–11. Tim. iii. 16. Heb. vi. 20. xii. 2. 1 Pet. iii. 22.
c xii. 50. Is. l. 5–7. Acts xx. 22–24. xxi. 11–14. 1 Pet. iv. 1.
d vii. 27. x. 1.
e Mal. iii. 1.
f Matt. x. 5. 2 Kings xvii. 24. Ezra iv. 1–4. John iv. 4, 9. 40–42.
g 46. John iv. 4, 9. 40–42.

Margin references (right column):
h 2 Sam. xxi. 2. 2 Kings x. 16. 31. Jam. i. 19, 20. iii. 14–16.
i 2 Kings i. 10–14. Acts iv. 29. 30. Rev. xiii. 13. 1 Sam. xxiv. 4. —7. xxvi. 8–11. 2 Sam. xix. 22. Job xxxi. 29–31. Prov. ix. 8. Matt. xvi. 23.
k Num. xii. 3.
l Num. xvi. 15. Job iii. 10. xxxi. 30. xxxv. xxvi. 4. 1 Kings. Jer. xvii. 9. Matt. xxvi. 33. xii. 4, 51. John xvi. 9. Acts xxiii. 3–5. xxvi. 9–11. Jam. iii. 10.
m Pet. iii. 9. xix. 10. Matt. xviii. 11. xx. 28. John iii. 17. x. 10. xii. 47. 1 Tim. i. 15.
n vi. 27–31. xxii. 51. xxiii. 34. Matt. v. 39. Rom. xii. 21. 1 Pet. ii. 21–23.

V. 51—56. The evangelist seems, in the conclusion of this chapter, to have recorded several detached incidents of similar import, which occurred at different times: it is not therefore needful to conclude, that the remainder of his gospel relates to events, which took place during Christ's last journey from Galilee to Jerusalem, or subsequent to it.—The expression here is very remarkable: " When the time was come that he should be received up," (*Mark* xvi. 19. *John* vi. 60, 61. xvi. 25—30. xvii. 4, 5,) which relates to his ascension to his glory in heaven, " he " stedfastly set his face to go up to Jerusalem." He had " the joy set before him " continually in his eye, and his sufferings and crucifixion were regarded merely as preparatory steps to it: and therefore he stedfastly and constantly set his face to go up to Jerusalem, though he perfectly knew all that there awaited him; nor would he be induced by any persuasions to defer his journey. (*Marg. Ref.* b.—*Notes, Acts* xx. 22—24. xxi. 7—14.) As he went along, he sent some of his disciples as messengers before him, to make things ready for his reception, in the several places through which he passed: but when they came to a village of the Samaritans, the inhabitants would not entertain him in their houses, or admit him into the village; because they found by his route that he was on his journey to Jerusalem. They had doubtless heard of his miracles and doctrine; (*Notes, John* iv. 5—42;) and probably were displeased at his protesting against their schismatical worship on mount Gerizim, by going up to Jerusalem to worship. This repulse so excited the indignation of James and John, that they desired permission to call for fire from heaven upon the Samaritans; as Elijah (perhaps near the same place) had done on those who were -sent by king Ahuziah to apprehend him: not doubting that it would be sent at their command. (*Notes, 2 Kings* i. 9—14.) They did not however consider the immense difference of the two cases. The Samaritans were indeed highly blameable; but their conduct was the effect rather of national prejudices and bigotry, than of determined enmity to the word and worship of God: and though they refused to entertain Christ and his disciples; they did not attempt to persecute or murder them, according to the conduct of idolatrous Ahaziah towards the prophet Elijah: so that there was no occasion for so terrible a judgment, either to vindicate the honour of God, or to secure his servants from their enemies. Neither were the disciples aware of the different dispensation about to be intro-

duced, which would chiefly be characterized by miracles of beneficence. Above all, they were not duly sensible of the prevailing state of their own hearts: they supposed themselves to be actuated by zeal for the honour of their Lord; but pride, ambition, resentment, and bigotry, in reality instigated them to make so improper a proposal. (*Note, 2 Kings* x. 15, 16.) For when the inhabitants of Nazareth behaved far worse to Jesus, than these Samaritans did, they had not thought of calling for miraculous judgment; (*Note,* iv. 23—30;) but the Nazarenes, and others who slighted or injured Jesus, were *Jews*, and therefore the disciples were more disposed to bear it from *them*, than from the despised and detested Samaritans.—Elijah on the contrary was actuated by a zeal for the honour of God, and a regard to the real good of his people, who were about to be ruined by the abominable idolatries and persecutions of Ahab's family: so that they, whom the fire from heaven consumed at his word, fell sacrifices to the justice of God, and their death greatly conduced to the benefit of Israel; whereas had these Samaritans been destroyed, they would have been sacrificed to the disciples' prejudices and resentment, and the consequences would have been injurious to both Jews and Samaritans.—Our Lord, therefore, sharply rebuked the disciples, assuring them, that " they knew not what manner of spirit they " were of:" they were not aware under what influence they spake, or what dispositions predominated in their hearts; for they desired to destroy the lives of their enemies, instead of overcoming them with persevering kindness. Whereas he, " the Son of man," was come to preserve and restore men's lives, as well as to save their souls; his miracles were uniformly acts of mercy; his gospel was not to be propagated by fire and sword, but by more rational and beneficent means; and the effects of it would be to terminate these furious contests, as far as it truly prevailed. Accordingly, without any dispute with the Samaritans, he led the disciples forward to another village.—What our Lord said, against calling for fire from heaven upon the Samaritans, is still more forcibly conclusive against every kind and degree of persecution. The Samaritans were really schismaticks and hereticks, and they openly rejected Christ himself. Whatever, therefore, has been urged, concerning the tendency of penalties and severities, to reclaim hereticks and schismaticks, or to prevent others from joining them, and to preserve the unity of the church, or the honour of its ministers; indeed,

2 I 8

57 ¶ And it came to pass, that as • they went in the way, * a certain man said unto him, Lord, I will follow thee whithersoever thou goest.

58 And ᵖ Jesus said unto him, ᵠ Foxes have holes, and birds of the air ᵣ have nests; but the Son of man hath ˢ not where to lay *his* head.

59 And he said unto another, ᵗ Follow me. But he said, Lord, ᵘ suffer me first to go and bury my father.

60 Jesus said unto him, ' Let the dead bury their dead; ˣ but go thou and preach the kingdom of God.

61 And another also said, Lord, I will follow thee: ʸ but let me first go bid them farewell which are at home at my house.

62 And Jesus said unto him, ᶻ No man having put his hand to the plow, and looking back, is fit for the kingdom of God.

---

every topick, which persecutors, whether popish or protestants, have urged, or can urge, on this subject, is shewn by our Lord's answer to be perfectly nugatory; and they who plead for the necessity of secular authority to promote religion, " know not what manner of spirit they are " of." It is also to be considered, that it is one thing to appeal to God, and wait his decision, whether he will miraculously interpose, which was all that the apostles required; and another, and a widely different thing indeed, to take the cause out of his hands, and to execute vengeance on opposers, by the arm of man, and according to his sentence, without any possibility of certainly knowing, whether God does or does not approve what we are doing: one thing to call for fire from heaven, and another to kindle fires on earth, to consume men branded as hereticks. (*Note,* 2 *Cor.* xiii. 7—10.)

That he should be received up. (51) Της αναληψεως αυτ. Here only N. T.—Ανηληφθη, *Mark* xvi. 19.—2 *Kings* ii. 11. *Sept.*—*He stedfastly set.*] Εσηριξε. xvi. 26. xxii. 32. *Rom.* i. 11. xvi. 25, *et al.*—*Jer.* xxi. 10. *Ex.* vii. 2. *Sept.*—*Messengers.* (52) Αγγελας. See on vii. 24.—*Lives.* (56) Ψυχας. See on *Matt.* xvi. 25.—The destruction of the *lives* of these Samaritans, by fire from heaven, must have been the destruction of their *souls* also; at least in the opinion of those, who were desirous of calling for this judgment upon them. But Jesus came to *save,* and not to *destroy* the souls of men.

V. 57—62. (*Marg. Ref.*—*Notes,* Matt. viii. 18—22.) Some of these incidents seem to have occurred early in our Lord's ministry: but the last we have not before met with. The desire of this person to go home, and bid farewell to his friends, and to settle his temporal concerns, before he attached himself to Christ as his constant follower, was no doubt the effect of a wavering and undetermined state of mind: Jesus therefore answered his request, by applying to his case a proverbial expression, which seems to have been frequently used. If a man should " put his hand to the plow," and then look behind him, he could not make his furrows straight, and of a proper depth; thus no one could be expected to transact any business in a particular manner, if his attention were fixed on some other object. No man therefore can be fit to be a preacher of the gospel, whose heart hankers after those worldly interests or pleasures, which he has left behind; and who looks back with a desire of recovering them, even when outwardly employed in the work of the Lord. The proverb applies to the subjects, as well as to the ministers, of " the kingdom of God; " but the latter seem especially intended. (*Notes,* xiv. 28—33. xvii. 32—

37. 1 *Kings* xix. 19—21. *Acts* xiii. 13—15. xv. 36—41. *Jam.* i. 5—8.)

Bid ... farewell, &c. (61) Αποταξασθαι. (Ex απο, et τασσω, *statuo, ordino.*) xiv. 33. *Mark* vi. 46. *Acts* xviii. 18. 21. 2 *Cor.* ii. 13. ' Not simply to bid farewell; but having ' given orders what thou wouldest have done, to dismiss ' any one, and bid him farewell.' *Leigh.*—' *Permitte ut* ' *prius res meas domesticas curem, aut mandem domesticis* ' *meis aliqua.*' Heinsius in *Schleusner.*—*Fit.* (62) Ευθετος. (Ex εν et θετος, *positus.*) xiv. 35. *Heb.* vi. 7. Not elsewhere N. T.

PRACTICAL OBSERVATIONS.
V. 1—27.

The Lord Jesus is the Fountain of power and authority, to whom all creatures must in one way or other be subjected: and if he accompany the word of his ministers with efficacy, to deliver sinners from Satan's bondage; they need not fear but he will procure them needful sustenance: and more they ought not to desire. They should always shew a kind attention to the temporal comforts of mankind, while they seek their eternal salvation; and when this is attended with an evident indifference to their own ease and accommodation, it tends much to conciliate good-will: if they can therefore, by ordinary means, or any thing to relieve the distresses, and heal the diseases, of those among whom they labour, it may help to promote the success of their ministry. But when truth and love, in this manner, go hand in hand, and the message of God is yet rejected and despised; it will leave men most inexcusable, and every circumstance will turn to a testimony against them. (*P. O. Matt.* x. 1—15.)—The increase of faithful ministers, and the success of the gospel, frequently cause great perplexity and distress to those, who set themselves to oppose the cause of God: and they, who have shed innocent blood, will often have their guilt brought to remembrance, with renewed and increased terror and dismay, as long as they live; yea, except they truly repent, and seek and find mercy, to all eternity. (*Note, Gen.* xlii. 21, 22.)—While the blessed Jesus consults the benefit and comfort of his disciples, and readily receives all who come to him; healing the souls of those who feel their need of it and seek it from him, and feeding all who hunger for the " Bread of life;" let us learn to communicate liberally to the necessities of our brethren; and even if poor ourselves, to share our mean and scanty morsel with those, who are in more urgent and immediate want. By the blessing of God, a little will *in this use of it* go far, and we shall never by so doing be impoverished. —After our Lord's example also, ministers, parents, and

CHAP. X.

Jesus sends out seventy disciples, to work miracles and preach: and pronounces a woe against Chorazin, Bethsaida, and Capernaum, 1—16. The seventy return with joy at their success; and Christ instructs them in what they should rejoice, 17—20. He adores the Father, for revealing his gospel to the simple only;

and declares his own personal and mediatorial authority and glory, 21, 22; and the happiness of his disciples, 23, 24. A lawyer enquires what he must do to inherit eternal life; and Jesus refers him to the law of God, 25—28; and shews him by the example of a good Samaritan, who is his neighbour, 29—37. He commends Mary's attention to his doctrine, and reproves Martha, who was " cumbered about much. " serving," 38—42.

heads of families should pray *with*, as well as *for*, those who are entrusted to their care: and their retired conversation should be attended by social devotions, which will often render it as profitable as publick ordinances.—Those who are established in one important doctrine of the gospel, will be prepared to understand others connected with it: and those truths which relate to the person, the sufferings, and the mediatorial kingdom of Christ, form the very substance or centre of true religion. In meditating on his crucifixion, and the glory which ensued, we shall best learn " to deny ourselves and to bear our cross *daily:*" we shall thus be induced to renounce the friendship and venture the enmity of the world: we shall, in this glass, see the folly and madness of seeking the largest temporal advantages, with the hazard of " losing ourselves " and being cast away;" and we shall get the victory over that foolish and wicked shame, which causes so very many to forsake and disobey Christ, against the convictions of their own consciences; though he has expressly declared, that " he will be ashamed" of all such, " when he shall " come in his own glory, and in his Father's, and of the holy " angels." (*P. O. Matt.* xiv. 6—21. xvi. 21—28.)

V. 28—45.

To form some faint conception of the Redeemer's glory, now in heaven, and at his future appearance to judge the world, let us contemplate him upon the mount, when " the fashion of his countenance was altered, and his rai-" ment was white and glistering," like the lightning. With this scene before our eyes, we may meditate with advantage on " his decease which he accomplished at Jeru-" salem;" and thence follow him with our thoughts to his present exaltation in heaven, where he is surrounded by his saints, who there appear with him in glory, and expatiate in his praises. This may reconcile us to our present trials, and prepare us for the stroke of death; that we may go to behold and share that glory, one glimpse of which has sometimes made those favoured with it to say, " It is good for us to be here." But we must now walk by faith, and hear obediently the words of the beloved Son of God; treasuring up every comfortable experience of his love, and every discovery of his majesty and excellency, to be our support in " the days of darkness." Thus we may maintain a successful conflict with the enemies of our souls: and in the exercise of a vigorous faith, we may hope to be instrumental in rescuing some of our fellow sinners from their destructive influence. But if we would be useful to others, we must seek to have our own minds delivered from every prejudice: and when we find ourselves unable to understand the words of Christ; we should not fear or neglect to ask him, and to consult his more experienced servants, concerning them. (*P. O. Matt.* xvii. 1—13. *Mark* ix. 1—13.)

V. 46—56.

Alas! our reasonings and discussions (instead of being directed to mutual edification) are too often mere disputes, " which of us should be the greatest." This may be, and in general is, very speciously disguised: but applause, popularity, and precedency, are vastly too much aimed at, by professed Christians, and even by ministers. These thoughts of our foolish hearts Jesus perceives; and a little child is his constant emblem, by which to teach us simplicity and humility. But if indeed we be his disciples, we need not be ambitious of further honour: for not only are apostles, prophets, and evangelists distinguished persons; but the least of the whole company of believers, though insignificant among his brethren as an infant, and as much disregarded by them in all their concerns, is and shall be great, as a child and friend of God, an heir of heaven, and a future companion and compeer to the angels before the throne. " Such honour have all his " saints:" and as every one, who in any place or form, successfully preaches " repentance towards God and faith " towards our Lord Jesus Christ," is instrumental in bringing the slaves of Satan to partake of these glorious and everlasting privileges; surely we should not presume to forbid those, " who cast out devils in Christ's name, be-" cause they follow not with us!" lest he rebuke us for our officiousness, and remind us that " he who is not " against us is for us."—But, while we are zealous, courageous, and patient to endure hardship in the work of the Lord; let us also look well to our own spirits, lest we be betrayed into dishonourable measures, and disgrace the cause which we mean to promote. It is easy for us to say, " Come, see my zeal for the LORD," and obvious for us to think, that we are remarkably faithful in his cause; when, in fact, we are inflamed with resentment, impatient of contradiction, seeking our own honour, and doing great harm instead of good. (*Notes, Jam.* i. 19—21. *P. O.* 19 —27. *Notes,* and *P. O.* iii. 13—18.) Nay, we may be so zealous against the errors, prejudices, superstitions, and bigotry of others, as to fall into the same evils ourselves; and so to sanction all their calumnies and injuries. How strange is it, that the professed disciples of Christ, who thus decidedly blamed the proposal of calling for fire from heaven to consume their adversaries, should think of kindling fires on earth for that purpose! or of promoting the gospel, and destroying schismaticks and hereticks, by wars and massacres! " Fire from heaven" might indeed have proved the doctrine to be true, and thus might have in some measure tended to the conviction of opposers: but fire and faggot, can only prove the diabolical malice and cruelty of those who use them; and if the truth itself were supported by such means, it would reasonably become suspected of being from beneath. Yet many, who

AFTER [a] these things the Lord appointed other [b] seventy also, and sent them [c] two and two before his face, [d] whither he himself would come.

2 Therefore said he unto them, [e] The harvest truly *is* great, but [f] the labourers [g] *are* few: [h] pray ye therefore [i] the Lord of the harvest, that he would send forth labourers into his harvest.

3 Go your ways: behold, [k] I send you forth as lambs among [l] wolves.

4 Carry [m] neither purse, nor scrip, nor shoes: [n] and salute no man by the way.

5 And [o] into whatsoever house ye enter, first say, Peace *be* to this house.

6 And if [p] the son of peace be there, your peace shall rest upon it: if not, [q] it shall turn to you again.

7 And [r] in the same house remain, eating and drinking such things as they give: [s] for the labourer is worthy of his hire. Go not from house to house.

8 And into whatsoever city ye enter, and [t] they receive you, [u] eat such things as are set before you;

9 And [x] heal the sick that are therein; and say unto them, [y] the kingdom of God is come nigh unto you.

10 But into whatsoever city ye enter, and they receive you not, [z] go your ways out into the streets of the same, and say,

11 Even the very dust of your city, which cleaveth on us, we do wipe off against you: [a] notwithstanding, be ye sure of this, that the kingdom of God is come nigh unto you.

12 But I say unto you, [b] That it shall be more tolerable in that day for Sodom, than for that city.

---

a Matt. x. 1.
b Num. xi. 16. 24
—26.
c Acts xiii. 2—4.
Rev. xi. 3—10.
d 17. 76. iii. 4—
6. ix. 52.
e Matt. ix. 37 38.
John iv. 35—38.
l Cor. iii. 6—9.
f Matt. xx. 1.
Mark xiii. 34.
1 Cor. xv. 10.
2 Cor. vi. 1.
Phil. ii. 25. 30.
Col. i. 29.
1 Thess. ii. 9.
v. 12. 1 Tim.
iv. 15. 18. 16.
x. 17. 18. 2 Tim.
ii. 3—6. iv. 5.
Philem. 1.
g 1 Kings xviii. 22.
xxii. 6—8. Is.
lvi. 9—12. Ez.
xxxiv. 2—6.
Zech. xi. 5. 17.
Matt. ix. 36.
Acts xvi. 9. 10.
Phil. ii. 21.
Rev. xi. 2. 3.
h 2 Thes. iii. 1.
i ix. 1. Num. xi.
17. 29. Ps.
lxviii. 11. Jer.
iii. 15. Mark vi.
15. 20. Acts viii.
4. xi. 19. xiii. 2.
4. xx. 28. xxii.
21. xxvi. 15—18.
1 Cor. xii. 28.
Eph. iv. 7—12.
1 Tim. i. 12—14. Heb. iii. 6. Rev. ii. 1.
k Ps. xxii. 12—16. 21. Ez. ii. 3—6. l Matt. x. 16. 22. John xv. 20. xvi. 2. Acts ix. 2. 16. 1 Zeph. iii. 3. Matt. vii. 15. John x. 12. Acts xx. 29. m ix. 3. xxii. 35. Matt. x. 9. 10. Mark vi. 8. 9. n ix. 59, 60. Gen. xxiv. 33. 56. 1 Sam. xxi. 8. 2 Kings iv. 24. 29. o xix. 9. 1 Sam. xxv. 6. Is. lvii. 19. Matt. x. 12. 13. Acts x. 36. 1 Cor. v. 18—20. Eph. ii. 17. p 1 Sam. xxv. 17. Eph. ii. 2, 3. v. 6. 1 Pet. i. 14. Gr. q Ps. xxxv. 13. 2 Cor. ii. 15, 16.

r xx. 4. Matt. x.
11. Mark vi. '0.
Acts xvi. 15. 34.
40.
s Deut. xii. 12
18. 19. Matt. x.
10. 1 Cor. ix. 4
—15. Gal. vi. 6.
Phil. iv. 17, '8.
1 Tim. v. 17, 18.
2 Tim. ii. 6
3 John 5—8.
t 10. ix. 48. Matt.
x. 20. 40. John xiii
20.
u 1 Cor. x. 27.
x ix. 2. Matt. x.
8. Mark vi. 13.
16.
y 11. xvii. 20, 21.
Dan. ii. 44. Matt.
iii. 2. iv. 17. x.
7. Mark vi. 12.
z ix. 5. Matt. x.
14. Acts xiii.
51.
xviii. 6.
a x 9. Deut. xxx. 11
—14. Acts xiii.
26. 40. 46. Rom.
x. 8. 21. Heb. i.
3.
b Lam. iv. 6. Ez.
xvi. 48—50.
Matt. x. 15. xi.
24. Mark xi. n.

---

seem upon the whole to be upright, are led to indulge the same spirit in another way: and their sarcasms and calumnies, against those who differ from them, with other bitter fruits of pride and resentment, too plainly shew, that "they know not what manner of spirit they are of." Many controversial books, many religious conversations, nay, many sermons, demonstrate to the impartial judge, that very much indeed is wrong in the temper of the parties concerned; though they are not at all aware of it. (*Note, Ex.* xx. 16.) It behoves us therefore to beg of the Lord, that he would convince us of our sin; and that he would rather rebuke and sharply chasten us, than leave us to indulge unchristian tempers; and thus to act contrary both to his precepts, his example, the end of his coming into the world, and the tendency of his holy religion. (*P. O. Matt.* xviii. 1—6. *Mark* ix. 30—50.)

V. 57—62.

In following Christ, we should count our cost: worldly riches and pleasures cannot reasonably be expected in his service, who, when on earth, "had not where to lay his head:" and in that cause, for which he shed his blood, we should be ready to renounce all secular interests, and to forego even relative comforts and endearments, that we may preach or promote the kingdom of God.—No man is fit for the ministry of the gospel, whose eye and heart are fixed on worldly objects: for he will either leave his work to return to them; or he will neglect it, and do it in an improper manner, by hankering after them. This should be seriously laid to heart by all, who intend to engage in that important service, as well as by those who are already employed in it. Many lay hold of this sacred function, while their affections are fixed upon the riches, honours, and pleasures of the world; nay, while they are

scheming to render their ministry itself subservient to the gratification of avarice, ambition, or sensuality! But no one would employ a man to plow his lands, who neglected his work, or performed it in so heedless and unskilful a manner, as these men do their sacred services: as therefore they are not fit for the work of the kingdom of God on earth, they will assuredly not be found meet for the inheritance of the kingdom of God in heaven. (*P. O. Matt.* viii. 14—22.)

NOTES

CHAP. X. V. 1—12. (*Note,* ix. 1—6.) St. Luke alone records the appointment of the seventy disciples, who in number answered to the elders, which had been constituted by Moses, (*Notes, Num.* xi. 11—30,) and seem to have been intended as assistants to the apostles both at the present, and after our Lord's ascension. Many of the first preachers of the gospel no doubt were of this company: but the traditions on this subject are little to be depended on. Some expositors conjecture that the evangelist himself was one of them: but this seems altogether unfounded. (*Preface to this Gospel.*) The seventy disciples were sent forth by two and two, to go, in different circuits, to the several places which Jesus intended to visit; that they might prepare the inhabitants for his reception, as his personal ministry among them would be very short. The instructions given them were nearly the same, as those which had been delivered to the apostles. (*Marg. Ref.* k—q.— *Notes, Matt.* x. 7—18.) As an intimation of the still greater things, which would afterwards be wrought among them, he began by repeating an exhortation, which has been already explained. (*Marg. Ref.* e—i.—*Note, Matt.* ix 36— 38.) He also ordered them "to salute no man by the "way;" that is, as their time was short and precious, and their work important, they must be altogether intent upon

13 Woe 'unto thee, Chorazin! woe unto thee, Bethsaida! 'for if the mighty works had been done 'in Tyre and Sidon 'which have been done in you, they had a great while ago 're-pented, sitting in sackcloth and ashes.

14 But 'it shall be more tolerable for Tyre and Sidon at the judgment, than for you.

15 And thou, 'Capernaum, 'which art exalted to heaven, shalt be 'thrust down to hell.

16 He that 'heareth you, heareth me; and he that 'despiseth you, de-spiseth me; and he that despiseth me, 'despiseth him that sent me.

17 ¶ And the seventy 'returned again with joy, saying, Lord, even the devils are subject unto us through thy name.

18 And he said unto them, 'I be-held Satan as lightning fall from hea-ven.

19 Behold, 'I give unto you power to tread on serpents and scorpions, and over all the power of the enemy; 'and nothing shall by any means hurt you.

20 Notwithstanding 'in this rejoice

it; and not loiter or trifle, out of a needless regard to ceremony or personal regards. (Note, 2 Kings iv. 29—31.) —The labourer. (7) Note, 1 Tim. v. 17, 18. Appointed. (1) Ανεδιξεν. Acts i. 24. Not elsewhere N. T. —Purse. (4) Βαλαντιον. xii. 33. xxii. 35, 36. Not else-where N. T.—The son of peace. (6) 'O υιος ειρηνης. Eph. ii. 2. 1 Pet. i. 14. It signifies one, who was disposed to welcome the message of peace, with which the seventy disciples were sent.—Shall rest.] Επαναπαυσεται. Rom. ii. 17. Not elsewhere N. T.—It shall turn ... again.] Ανα-καμψει. Matt. ii. 12. Acts xviii. 21. Heb. xi. 15.—We do wipe off. (11) Απομασσομεθα. Here only N. T. Εξιμασσε, vii. 38.—Come nigh, &c. (9. 11) Ηγγικεν. Notes, Ex. ii. 3—5. Acts xiii. 42—48.

V. 13—15. (Note, Matt. xi. 20—24.) A more toler-able doom, at the day of judgment, is widely different from eternal salvation: yet the former is all that is favourable, which our Lord speaks concerning the gentiles. (Note, Rom. ii. 12—16.)

More tolerable. (14) Ανεκλοτερον. Matt. x. 15. xi. 22. 24. Mark vi. 11.—Ab ανεχω, tolero. ix. 41.—Shall be thrust down. (15) Καταβιβασθηση. Matt. xi. 23. Not elsewhere N. T.—Deut. xxi. 4. Josh. ii. 18. Jer. li. 40. Sept.

V. 16. (Marg. Ref.—Notes, Matt. x. 40—42. John xii. 44—50. 1 Thes. iv. 6—8.) To reject an ambassador, or to treat him with contempt, is an affront to the prince who commissioned and sent him, and whom he represents. (Notes, 2 Sam. x. 3, 4. 2 Cor. v. 18—21.) The apostles and seventy disciples were the ambassadors and represen-tatives of Christ; and they who rejected or despised them, in fact rejected and despised him. Christ himself was the Apostle of his Father, his Ambassador to men, and " the " Effulgency of his glory;" so that to reject or despise him, was to reject and despise the Father that sent him. None would despise the apostles, or messengers, of Christ, ex-cept those who despised him; and they were despised for his sake: nor would any despise Christ, but they who de-spised the Father who sent him. The Jews " saw and " hated both him and his Father." (Notes, 1 Sam. viii. 6—9. John xv. 17—25.)—The miraculous powers, exercised by these primitive messengers of Christ, rendered their case peculiar: but in every age Jesus " is despised and rejected " of men," by the contempt poured on his faithful and ex-emplary ministers; and in despising him, men shew their contempt of God, and their enmity against him.—De-spiseth.] 'O αθετων. vii. 30. John xii. 48. 1 Cor. i. 19. Gal. ii. 21. iii. 15. 1 Thes. iv. 8. Heb. x. 28. Jude 8. (Ex α et τιθημι, pono.) To put away, or reject with contempt.

V. 17—20. It does not appear, that our Lord expressly promised the seventy disciples the power of casting out unclean spirits. When, therefore, they returned to him, (doubtless at a time and place appointed for them,) they told him with a joyful surprise, that not only diseases, but even devils, had been " subject to them through his " name!" Our Lord, however, pointed out far more valu-able blessings to be conferred on his disciples. He ob-served, that " he beheld Satan as lightning from hea-" ven." Satan had thus instantaneously been cast down from heaven, on his original apostasy; and his usurped dominion on earth, with the idolatrous worship which he had devised to establish, was about to be thrown down in the same sudden and surprising manner, by means of the gospel preached to the nations; in which work the seventy disciples would in a short time be employed: so that their success, in casting out devils, was only an emblem of a far more decisive victory, which they and their coadjutors and successors would, by his power, obtain over Satan, the ruler of the whole multitude of evil spirits. (Marg. Ref. p, q.—Notes, John xii. 27—33. 2 Pet. i. 4—9. Rev. xii. 7—12.) The circuit which they had made, and the effects which they had witnessed, were only earnests of their future services and successes; for which, he their Lord promised to qualify them, by giving them " power to tread on ser-" pents and scorpions, &c." to crush the old serpent and his seed, and to withstand the power of every enemy of God and his church; so that neither temptations, afflictions, nor persecutions should eventually hurt them. (Marg. Ref. r, s.—Notes, Gen. iii. 14, 15. Ps. xci. 13. Mark xvi. 17, 18. Rom. xvi. 17—20. Rev. xx. 1—3.) Yet they ought not so much to rejoice, that evil spirits were subjected to them; but rather that " their names were written in " heaven," as the people of God, and the heirs of his king-dom: for many workers of miracles would at last be con-demned as wicked men; (Note, Matt. vii. 21—23;) but no true believer would come short of eternal life. (Marg. Ref. t, u.—Notes, Is. iv. 3, 4. Phil. iv. 2, 3, v. 3. Heb. xii. 22—25, v. 23. Rev. iii. 4—6, v. 5. xiii. 8—10, v. 8. xx. 11—15, vv. 12, 15.)—It cannot be supposed that Christ

not, that the spirits are subject unto you; but rather rejoice, because " your names are written in heaven.

21 In that hour ˣ Jesus rejoiced in spirit, and said, ʸ I thank thee, O Father, ᶻ Lord of heaven and earth, that ᵃ thou hast hid these things from the wise and prudent, and hast ᵇ revealed them unto babes: ᶜ even so, Father; for so it seemed good in thy sight.

22 ᵈ All ᵉ things are delivered to me of my Father: ᶠ and no man knoweth who the Son is, but the Father; and who the Father is but the Son, and ʰe to whom the Son will reveal *him*.

23 And he turned him unto *his* disciples, and said privately, ' Blessed *are* the eyes which see the things that ye see:

24 For I tell you, That ᵏ many prophets and kings have desired to see

those things which ye see, and have not seen *them;* and to hear those things which ye hear, and have not heard *them.*

25 ¶ And, behold, ᵇ a certain lawyer stood up, and tempted him, saying, 'Master, what shall I do to inherit eternal life?

26 He said unto him, ᵏ What is written in the law? how readest thou?

27 And he answering said, ˡ Thou shalt love the Lord thy God with all thy heart, and with all thy soul, and with all thy strength, and with all thy mind; ᵐ and thy neighbour as thyself.

28 And he said unto him, ⁿ Thou hast answered right: ° this do, and thou shalt live.

29 But he, ᵖ willing to justify himself, said unto Jesus, ⁹ And who is my neighbour?

---

meant, by special revelation, to inform all these seventy persons, that they were registered in heaven, as heirs of eternal life. In general, however, none can know this of themselves, except by those evidences, which prove them to be " born of the Spirit," and truly converted. —' Here Woltzogenius says Christ cast out devils by ' a virtue residing in himself; his disciples only in the ' name and by the power of the Lord. Seeing then this ' power accompanied them into all parts of the world; it ' is necessary that Christ's presence should be with them ' every where: now such a presence is a certain indication ' of the Deity. (1 *Kings* viii. 27. *Ps.* cxxxix. 7. *Jer.* xxiii. ' 24. *Am.* ix. 3.)... Satan being ... spoiled of his dominions, ' may be said to " fall from heaven," by a phrase familiar ' both to sacred and profane writers. So of the fall of the ' king of Babylon, the prophet says, " How art thou fallen ' " from heaven, O Lucifer!" (*Is.* xiv. 12.) ...Of the fall ' of the colleague of Antonius, Cicero says,...' Thou hast ' " pulled him down from heaven.' And when Pompey ' was overthrown, he is said by him,... to have fallen from ' the stars.' *Whitby.*

V. 21, 22 (*Marg. Ref.—Notes, Matt.* xi. 25—27.) Our Lord inwardly rejoiced with a holy and spiritual joy, in the prospect of the extensive success of the gospel, the salvation of souls, and the glory which would redound to God, both in those events themselves, and by the instruments by which they would be brought to pass. (*Note, Heb.* xii. 2, 3.)—*No man knoweth who the Son is,* &c. (22) ' This seems not to respect what he was to do or suffer, ' but his nature, excellence, and dignity: as the words fol- ' lowing, " who the Father is," res̹ect his nature, his ' divine excellence and dignity exhibited to us, ... in the ' person of Jesus Christ. (2 *Cor.* iv. 6.)' *Whitby.*—' Who- ' soever seeks the Father without the Son, wandereth out ' of the way.' *Beza.—Rejoiced.* (21) Ηγαλλιασατο. i. 47. See on *Matt.* v. 12.

V. 23, 24. (*Marg. Ref.—Note, Matt.* xiii. 16, 17.) Kings, as well as prophets and righteous persons, had desired to see the promised Messiah, and to hear his doctrine; but they died before he came. David was a prophet, as well as king of Israel: Moses was king in Jeshurun: (*Note, Deut.* xxxiii. 4, 5 :) and Solomon was one of the inspired writers. (*Notes,* xxiv. 44—49. *Heb.* xi. 13—16. 39, 40. 1 *Pet.* i. 10—12.)

V. 25—29. While our Lord was teaching the people, " a certain lawyer," in order to make trial of him, or to ensnare him, asked, " What shall I do to inherit eternal life?" (*Notes, Matt.* xix. 16—22, *v.* 16. *Mark* x. 17—31, *v.* 17. xii. 28—34. *Acts* xvi. 29—34, *vv.* 30, 31.) In answer to this question, Jesus referred him to the law, which the lawyer professed to study and to teach : and when he had quoted the two precepts, of loving God with " all the " heart, and soul, and mind, and strength," and " our " neighbour as ourselves," (*Notes, Lev.* xix. 18. *Deut.* vi. 4, 5 ;) Jesus declared that he " had answered right:" that was indeed the sum and substance of the whole law ; and if indeed he perfectly kept those two commandments, he would acquire a title to eternal life: but it was also implied, that if he had failed, or should fail, of perfect obedience, he could not possibly obtain life *in this way*, but must be condemned by the law as a transgressor. (*Notes, Ex.* xx. 11. *Matt.* xxii. 34—40. *Rom.* iii. 19, 20. *Gal.* iii. 10—14.) Of this he seems to have been aware: and finding himself in danger of being entangled in his own net, yet desiring " to justify himself," he passed by the law of " loving " God with all the heart," and enquired, " Who is my " neighbour?" For the scribes confined this term to their own nation, sect, friends, and connexions, and did not deem themselves bound to love others at all. (*Note, Matt.* xix. 16—22, *v.* 18.) ' Being confident of his having per- ' formed the first part, the duties toward God, by the exact ' observance of the ceremonies of the law, he made no

30 And Jesus answering said, A certain man went down from Jerusalem to Jericho, and fell among thieves, which stripped him of his raiment, and wounded *him*, and departed, leaving *him* half dead.

31 And ' by chance there came down a certain ' priest that way; and when he saw him, " he passed by on the other side.

32 And likewise a Levite, when he was at the place, came and ' looked *on* him, and passed by on the other side.

33 But a certain ' Samaritan, as he journeyed, came where he was: and when he saw him, ' he had compassion on *him*,

31 And ' went to *him*, and ' bound up his wounds, pouring in oil and wine, and set him on his own beast, and brought him to ' an inn, and took care of him.

35 And on the morrow, when he departed, he took out ' two pence, and gave *them* to ' the host, and said unto him, Take care of him: and ' whatsoever thou spendest more, when I come again I will repay thee.

36 Which now of these three, ' thinkest thou, ' was neighbour unto him that fell among the thieves?

37 And he said, ' He that shewed mercy on him. Then said Jesus unto him, ' Go, and do thou likewise.

' question concerning that: but for the second, the love of ' the neighbour, he proposed that other question.'*Hammond.* Thus he, though a lawyer, " was alive without the law;" (*Note, Rom.* vii. 9—12;) and the wisdom of our Lord's discourse with him, as exactly suited to his case, is still further illustrated. (*Note, Prov.* xxvi. 4, 5.) *Thou shalt,* &c. (27) This is not exactly either in the words of the Septuagint, or according to the Hebrew text; but completely gives the meaning of both.

V. 30—37. Our Lord did not give the enquirer a direct answer, but stated a case, and led him to answer himself. This has generally been called *a parable;* but it is related as *a fact*, and probably was so. It is said, that a great number of priests and Levites resided at Jericho, who would frequently go to Jerusalem, and back again; and, as the road lay through a desert, it was greatly infested by robbers. Now a certain man, supposed to be a Jew, being on the road to Jericho, fell into the hands of robbers, who stripped him, and wounded him very much, and " left him half dead." While he lay in this deplorable condition, a priest happened to be going on the road; yet neither natural compassion, nor regard to the duties of religion, induced him to assist his countryman, who lay perishing for want of help: but, either pretending urgent business, or fearing lest he too should fall among the thieves, he " passed by on the other side," regardless of his groans and misery. A Levite also, who travelled that way, came indeed and cast a transient look on him, but gave him no help. At length a Samaritan, in his journey, came to the place: and when he saw the poor man's perilous and pitiable case, he forgot his strong national and religious prejudices, as well as the contempt and hatred, with which the Jews in general treated the Samaritans. Being moved with compassion, he disregarded the hinderance, trouble, danger, and expense, which must be incurred by helping him; he poured the wine and oil, which he carried for his own refreshment, into his bleeding wounds, and bound them up with such linen as he had about him. Having then placed him on the beast, on which he rode, he conveyed him to an inn; and there took care of him during the night, as his surgeon and nurse, even as if he had been his friend and brother; and

on the morrow, when his business required him to depart, he gave the host what money he could spare, and promised to repay him, whatever he should further expend in taking care of him.—*Two pence.* (35) Or *denarii.* The circumstance, that the Samaritan could spare only so small a sum, seems an intimation that he was not affluent.—The direct scope of this parable, or narrative, is evidently fixed by the context: it is a beautiful illustration of the law of " loving our neighbour as ourselves," without regard to nation, party, or any other distinction. The Samaritan alone had acted according to the commandment; and the whole was admirably suited to lead the lawyer to understand the subject. Had a Jew been introduced, as thus relieving a distressed Samaritan, prejudice might have prevented the cordial approbation of a bigotted Jew; but his feelings were deeply interested in the case of the Jew, and he could not but allow, that " he who shewed mercy on " him" was neighbour to him, and fulfilled the duty of that relation. Our Lord then called on him to imitate the Samaritan's conduct; and this conclusion was calculated, by shewing him the extent and spirituality of the law, to convince him that he could not, in this way, " inherit eternal " life," as well as to direct his subsequent conduct. (*Marg. Ref.* r—f.)—Some commentators explain this *supposed* parable almost exclusively of the love of Christ to sinners; but this can be only an instructive accommodation. Man is not only in a *pitiable* state, as if, contrary to his will and without his fault, he had fallen under the power of Satan; without his fault, he was also a *condemned criminal* exposed to the righteous vengeance of God, from which Christ alone can deliver him. The Priest and the Levite *could* have helped the man if they *would*, and were *very wicked* in omitting to do it; but the law of God is " holy, just, and good," though it leaves the sinner to perish. (*Note, Rom.* vii. 7—12.) At the same time Christ has far outdone the good Samaritan: he came into the world *on purpose* to save sinners; their rebellions had been committed *against him*, and they were deserving of his righteous indignation and holy abhorrence: he not only ventured some danger, and incurred some trouble and expense, in rescuing them from *deserved* destruction; but he impoverished and abased himself, and endured the most excruciating tortures, and the most igno-

3 A 6

DEFILE BETWEEN JERUSALEM AND JERICHO.

Luke x. 30.

38 ¶ Now it came to pass, as they serve alone? bid her therefore that she [q] [viii. 14. 1 Cor. vii. 32—35.] went, that he entered into [k] a certain help me. [r] [Phil. iv. 6.] [Ec. vi. 11. Matt.] village: and a certain woman, named 41 And Jesus answered and said, [s] [xi. 35—44.] [xviii. 22. Ps.] Martha, [l] received him into her house. unto her, Martha, Martha, [t] thou art [xxvii. 4. 1xxiii.] [35. Ec. xii. 13.] 39 And she had a sister called Mary, careful and troubled about [r] many [John xvii. 3.] [Gal. v. 6. Col.] [m] which also sat at Jesus' feet, and things; [ii. 10. &c. 1 John] [v. 11, 12.] heard his word. 42. But [u] one thing is needful: and [t] [Deut. xxxv. 19.] [Josh. xxiv. 15.] 40 But Martha was [n] cumbered Mary hath [t] chosen that [v] good part, [22. Ps. xxvii. 13.] [cxix. 80. 111] about much serving, and came to [w] which shall not be taken away from [a] [Ps. xvi. 5, 6. cxlii. 5.] him, and said, Lord, [o] dost thou not her. [x] [viii. 18. xii. 20.] [33. xvi. 2. 2 J.] care that [p] my sister hath left me to [John iv. 14. v. 24. x. 27, 28. Rom. viii. 35—39. Col. iii. 3, 4. 1 Pet i. 4, 5.]

[k] John xi. 1—3. xii. 1—3.
[l] viii. 2, 3. Acts xvi. 15. 2 John 10.
[m] ii. 46. viii. 35. Deut. xxxiii. 3. Prov. viii. 34. Acts xxii. 3.
[n] xii. 29. John vi. 27.
[o] Matt. xiv. 15. xvi. 22. Mark iii. 21.
[p] ix. 55. Jon. iv. 1—4.

minious death, for that end; and he not only brings them a temporary relief, but perfects their everlasting salvation. (P. O. Gen. xxii. 13—24. Notes, Rom. v. 8—10.) In short the blessed Jesus has perfectly fulfilled the law of " lov-" ing our neighbour as ourselves," in such circumstances, as no other person could be placed in. His conduct there-fore is the best interpretation of the commandment, and the best example for our imitation.—Several other accom-modations have been made of the subject : " the oil and " wine " have been considered as representing the blood and Spirit of Christ, by which our souls are healed ; " the " inn," his church ; " the host," his ministers ; and " the " two pence," his sacraments : but these fancies are far more amusing than instructive ; and it may seriously be apprehended, that, by such interpretations, men's thoughts have been very much drawn off from the grand practical inference, " Go, and do thou likewise." (Marg. Ref. h—i. —Notes, John xiii. 12—17. 1 Pet. ii. 18—25.)

Answering. (30) 'Υπολαβων. See on vii. 43.—Half dead.] 'Ημιθανη. Here only N. T.—By chance. (31) Κατα συγκυριαν. Here only N. T. A συγκυρεω, obvenio, accido ; that is, Without intention. The priest was pursuing his own ob-ject ; and his coming to the spot, at this special time, was undesigned in that respect. But that which is accidental, or by chance, as man is concerned, forms a part of the plan and purpose of God. (Note, Ruth iii. 3.)—Passed by on the other side.] Αντιπαρηλθε. 31. Here only N. T. Ex αντι, παρα, et ερχομαι.—As he journeyed. (33) 'Οδευων. Here only N. T. ab οδος, via, iter.—Set him. (34) Επιβιβασας. xix. 35. Acts xxiii. 24. Not elsewhere N. T.—Beast.] Κτηνος. Acts xxiii. 24. 1 Cor. xv. 39. Rev. xviii. 13.—An inn.] Πανδοχειον. Ex παν et ιοχειον, receptaculum. Here only N. T.—Πανδοχευς, the host, 35. Here only N. T.—Took care of him.] Επι-μεληθη. 35. 1 Tim. iii. 5. Not elsewhere N. T. Επι et μελει, curæ est, 40.—Thou spendest more. (35) Προσδαπανησης. Here only N. T.

V. 38—42. On some occasion, when our Lord and his disciples stopped at Bethany, in their way to Jerusalem, and were hospitably entertained in the house of Martha, the sister of Lazarus, the following incident occurred. (Marg. Ref. k, l.) As soon as Jesus was sat down, he en-tered, as usual, on some edifying discourse ; and Mary, de-lighted with the opportunity, " sat at his feet " as a hum-ble disciple to hear his word, and thus to welcome him as her Instructor and Saviour. (Notes, ii. 41—52, v. 46. Prov. viii. 34. Mark v. 14—20, v. 15. Acts xxii. 1—5, v. 3.) But Martha, desirous of shewing her respect and affection to him in another manner, was aiming to provide a suitable entertainment; so that she was hurried and " cumbered

" about much serving." Thus she was likely to lose the opportunity, of obtaining good to her own soul by our Lord's visit ; and she also put herself into an agitation of mind, which was both uncomfortable and sinful. Not being able, however, alone to accomplish her designs, in which she probably too much consulted the credit of her hospi-tality, she was displeased with her sister for not coming to her assistance. She therefore entered the room in haste : and, with some warmth, appealed to Jesus himself ; nay, in some sense expostulated with him, about the supposed impropriety of Mary's conduct ; enquiring, whether it gave him no concern to see her sister so inattentive, as to leave her to serve alone ; and desiring him to direct her to go to her assistance. But the holy and heavenly mind of Christ viewed the case in a far different light : and, addressing Martha, with a tender and compassionate repetition of her name, he observed that she was solicitous and disquieted (as the waters when agitated by a violent storm,) " about " many things," which were not worth her regard : " but " that one thing was needful," which she was at that time led to neglect.—The term needful has reference to some proposed end : many things are needful to the gratification of men's passions ; but the end proposed is, in itself, neither needful nor useful : many things are needful to the conti-nuance of our lives on earth, but that may not be needful, or profitable for us. So that the favour of God is the only thing which is absolutely needful to our final happiness ; the salvation of Christ is absolutely needful for us sinners, in order to the enjoyment of the favour of God ; and a humble, believing, obedient attention to the gospel is ab-solutely needful, in order to our obtaining an interest in the salvation of Christ. Where this " one thing needful " is properly attended to, all other matters will be used, or pursued in subserviency to it ; and whatever may seem to be neglected or lost, by this choice and conduct, present comfort and eternal felicity will be secured.—Our Lord therefore added that " Mary had chosen that good part, " which should not be taken from her." (Notes, xvi. 1— 8. 19—23. Matt. xiii. 12.) It was her wise and happy choice to " sit at his feet, and hear his words ; " she was not to be seduced into a neglect of his instructions, by any secular cares and encumbrances : and as neither life, death, nor eternity would deprive her of her interest in his salva-tion ; so Christ would by no means consent to her being deprived of the present satisfaction of listening to his dis-course, in order to assist in providing a needless plenty and variety, for the refreshment of the bodies, or the in-dulgence of the appetites, of the company.—Though Mar-tha was on this occasion faulty, yet she was a true be-

3 A 7

CHAP. XI.

Jesus teaches his disciples to pray, and encourages

earnestness and importunity by two illustrations, 1—13. He casts out a devil, and exposes the absurdity and malice of those who ascribed the miracle to the power of Beelzebub, 14—26. He shews the blessed-

liever, and did not in her general conduct neglect " the " one thing needful : " we may therefore suppose that this seasonable and affectionate reproof had its proper effect ; and that her conduct, when Jesus afterwards came to her house, was regulated by more spiritual and rational considerations. (*Notes, John* xi. 1—46. xii. 1—8.) ' Not one ' dish only to eat of, as Theophylact, and many of the ' fathers descant here, but the better part, which Mary ' made it her chief care to labour after.' *Whitby.*

Received. (38) Ὑποδεξατο. xix. 6. *Acts* xvii. 7. *Jam.* ii. 25.—*Was cumbered.* (40) Περισπατο. Here only N. T. Ex περι et σπαω, traho.—2 *Sam.* vi. 6. *Sept.—Help me.* (40) Συναντιλαβηται. *Rom.* viii 26. *Note, Rom.* viii. 24—27, v. 26.—*Thou art ... troubled.* (41) Τυρβαζη. Here only N. T.

PRACTICAL OBSERVATIONS.

V. 1—16.

The ministry of the gospel is intended to prepare men to receive Christ, as a Prince and a Saviour; and he will surely come in the power of his Spirit, to all places whither he sends his faithful servants.—The increase of *labourers,* in this blessed work, should excite us " to pray the Lord of " the harvest, to send forth " more and more : for they are very few hitherto compared with the harvest of souls, which shall in due time be gathered in all over the earth; or even in proportion to the extent of the visible church, and the number of mere *loiterers* or " blind guides." (*P. O. Matt.* ix. 27—38.)—At Christ's command we should go forth to preach his gospel, " as lambs among " wolves : " depending on his power, we need not fear their rage; and, copying his example, we should maintain a meek and blameless conduct, in the midst of injuries and provocations. While we disinterestedly seek the peace and salvation of those to whom we are sent; we may conscientiously " eat and drink such things as are set before " us; " for the faithful minister is as justly entitled to a moderate subsistence, as the labourer is to his wages : (*Notes,* 1 *Cor.* ix. 6—18 :) yet we should endeavour to requite those who contribute to our support, as well as to promote the success of the gospel, by our prayers and good offices in their behalf. But if our message be obstinately rejected, we ought, in the most decided manner, to bear testimony against the opposers of it, and withdraw from them : and dreadful will be the case of those, to whom " the kingdom of God hath come nigh," but who have put it from them with contempt and dislike. In this way, numbers. who have possessed, and been proud of, valuable privileges and distinctions, will be " thrust down into " hell; " with more terrible vengeance, than the inhabitants of Tyre, or even of Sodom; for these did not continue impenitent under such abundant means of grace. Nor let any imagine, that this will only be verified in those, who were favoured with the ministry of Christ and his apostles, and rejected it; for it is still true of all the faithful preachers of the gospel, that " he who heareth " them heareth Christ; and he who despiseth them, de- " spiseth Christ, and ... the Father who sent him." (*P. O. Matt.* x. 7—33. xi. 16—24.)

V. 17—24.

Pious and zealous ministers, when evidently made useful, disregard their toil and hardship; and return from preaching the word, to meet their gracious Lord in retirement, with joy and gratitude.—We may be sure that he will always rather exceed his promise, than fall short of it, to all who go forth depending on his help, and observing his directions. As he " was manifested to destroy the " works of the devil," and as, in consequence of his death upon the cross, he foresaw that adversary " falling as " lightning from heaven; " so we may labour and pray, in hope, for the pulling down of his kingdom of ignorance, infidelity, impiety, and vice, all over the earth, through the preaching of the gospel and by the power of our exalted Redeemer. (*Note,* 2 *Cor.* x. 1—6.) Relying on him, we may expect to trample under foot the most potent and malignant enemies, who are like serpents and scorpions, nor can any adversary by any means hurt those, whom Jesus employs, protects, and prospers. But, though we should be thankful for gifts and usefulness, yet we should chiefly seek the assurance of our " names being written in hea- " ven," that we may have a solid ground of rejoicing : for it would be far better to be the most obscure believer, than to have all knowledge, eloquence, and even success in preaching the gospel, and at length to prove " a cast- " away." Let us then beware especially of spiritual pride : by this sin, Satan " fell like lightning from heaven," and from a bright arch-angel became a hateful and miserable fiend : (*Note,* 1 *Tim.* iii. 6 :) pride has been the fore-runner of destruction to many, who " have prophesied, " wrought miracles, and cast out devils in the name of " Christ; " and of many, who for a time have preached with great popularity, and apparent success : and it has tarnished the lustre and terminated the usefulness of others, concerning whose final state better hopes may be entertained. (*Note,* 2 *Cor.* xii. 1—6. *P. O.* 1—10.)—The Lord Jesus " rejoiced in spirit," that it pleased the Father to hide his " mysteries from the wise and prudent, and to " reveal them unto babes; " and he has at all times " re- " sisted the proud, and given his grace unto the humble." The more simply dependent we therefore are on the teaching, help, and blessing of the Son of God, the more we shall know both of the Father and of the Son ; (*Notes, John* xvii. 1—3. 1 *John* ii. 20—25 ;) the more blessed we shall be in seeing the glory, and hearing the words, of the divine Saviour; and the more useful we shall be made in promoting his cause. (*V. O. Matt.* xi. 25—30.)

V. 25—29.

Good questions may be proposed from very base motives : yet we ought seriously to enquire, " What shall we do to " inherit eternal life?" And nothing should be counted difficult or perilous, where such a prize is at stake; especially as it is connected with the awful alternative of everlasting punishment. In answer to this enquiry the blessed

ness of true piety above all external privileges; and warns the impenitent Jews, 27—36. Dining with a Pharisee, he exposes the ignorance, hypocrisy, and wickedness of the Scribes and Pharisees, 37—52 ; who eagerly endeavour to ensnare and accuse him, 53, 54.

Saviour will direct us to the written word, and demand of us, " How readest thou?" Yet the holy law itself cannot answer the question, How *a sinner* may inherit eternal life? It is, however, proper for those " who desire to be " under the law, to hear the law :" and when its extensive, spiritual, and reasonable requirements are fully and scripturally stated, we may safely assure any enquirer, that if he do this he shall live. Indeed the most perfect obedience for the time to come would not discharge any part of the debt, which we have already contracted : yet we know, that no man will ever perform this condition, or be able to claim eternal life, even on this ground; nay, no one will ever love God and his neighbour with any measure of pure spiritual love, who is not made partaker of regenerating grace ; which invariably produces humiliation for sin, and simplicity of dependence on the free mercy of God in Christ Jesus. But the proud heart of man strives earnestly against these mortifying convictions : and every ray of light that breaks in upon the conscience, excites men to other and further endeavours " to justify themselves," even as the approach of danger stirs us up to provide for our own defence. (*Note, Rom.* x. 1—4.) As the nature and effects of the love of God are most out of the way of carnal men, they elude conviction on that account; provided they can flatter themselves that they have not been injurious to their neighbours. Leaving out therefore " the first and great commandment," as if it were actually repealed ; or supposing that they satisfy its requirements by " a form of godliness;" they endeavour " to justify " themselves " in respect of the second, which is like " unto it :" and learned Scribes, ancient and modern, come in to their aid, with a variety of corrupt glosses, perplexing criticisms, and frivolous distinctions, before which the meaning and spirit of the precept seem to evaporate. Thus the most flagrant injustice, treachery, oppression, and inhumanity, are openly vindicated as consistent with the law of God ! Nay, the scripture is ransacked, and quoted for precedents and arguments, in favour of the most horrid cruelties, which rapacious avarice, malignity, bigotry, or ambition can perpetrate! Some difference of climate, or colour, or religious tenets, is pleaded ; as if this bounded the divine command, and excused us for not loving a vast majority of the human species as our neighbours! Or some *Judicial* regulation, made to prevent the fatal effects of that hardness of heart, which no law can change ; or some practices, evidently originating from human selfishness, are adduced, as if they actually repealed the laws of " loving our neighbour as ourselves," and " of doing to " others, as we would they should do unto us." Thus men " render the commandments of God of none effect, " by their traditions " and corrupt reasonings ; and human learning, nay, what is called theology, often rivets those prejudices, which are equally subversive of the law of love, and of the gospel of free grace. We must, however, endeavour by every means to counteract the effects of such destructive errors : and in order to this, apt illustrations, and appeals to the heart and conscience, may be more useful, than abstracted reasonings : and though we must not countenance any corrupt prejudices, yet on many occasions

it is adviseable to oppose them *indirectly*, and to study by what avenue we may best find access to the heart.

V. 30—37

It is most lamentable to observe, to what a degree *selfish-ness* pervades all ranks and orders of men ; and how many excuses they devise, that they may avoid incurring trouble or expense, in relieving the miseries of others. They plead that they are in haste, that their business is urgent or *sacred*, that the attempt is vain or perilous, that they have it not in their power, that others may do it to greater advantage, that " the time is not come." With such pretences great multitudes pass by the wretched and perishing, and avoid looking on them, that they may be excused from assisting them ; especially the countless millions all over the world, who are " perishing for lack of knowledge." Others will give those in urgent misery or danger a transient look and a pitying word, hoping some good Christian will come to their relief, though *they* cannot get time, or are not able to do it. Alas! that many professors and ministers of the gospel are as evidently selfish and unfeeling as any other men! and thus they give up their holy faith and sacred function to the contempt and invectives of infidels; who substitute a proud semblance of benevolence, in the place of repentance, faith in a divine Saviour, love to God, and to man for his sake. The true Christian, however, has the law of love written in his heart : the Spirit of Christ dwells in him, and his image is renewed on his soul : misery will therefore uniformly excite compassion in his breast, wherever it is seen, though in a stranger, an enemy, or one of an opposite sect or party. Thus the Son of God looked down, with compassion, on our deserved and helpless misery, and came to our relief; though he knew that it would expose him to the deepest abasement, and most intense sufferings, to deliver us : thus he is ever ready to pity and help the poor sinner, when stripped of every plea, wounded in his conscience, and without hope of deliverance from any other quarter. In our utmost distress he has come to us, to bind up our broken hearts, to pour his healing balm into our bleeding wounds, and to preserve us from that destruction, into which our enemies had plunged us : by his power and grace he brings us into his church, and there takes care of us and heals our souls ; and he requires his ministers and people, to shew their love to him, by their attention to the weak and discouraged of his flock ; (*Note, John* xxi. 15—17 ;) assuring them of an abundant recompence at his return to judge the world. After this interesting and endearing example of inexpressible love, to which we owe all our hopes and comforts ; every true believer must and will pity and endeavour to relieve the oppressed, and to comfort the wretched ; he will be induced to venture loss, danger, and reproach, in this work and labour of love : the excuses, which satisfy others, and which once satisfied him, will no longer be admitted : he will become the good Samaritan to the poor and afflicted, the ignorant and ungodly, of every name and nation, who come in his way : yea, he will go out of his way to meet with and relieve them, as he has ability and opportunity.

AND it came to pass, [a] that as he was praying in a certain place, when he ceased, one of his disciples said unto him, Lord, [b] teach us to pray, as John also taught his disciples.

2 And he said unto them, 'When ye pray, say, [d] Our Father, [e] which art in heaven, [f] Hallowed be thy name.

[g] Thy kingdom come. [h] Thy will be done, as in heaven, so in earth.

3 [i] Give us [k] day by day our daily bread.

4 And [l] forgive us our sins; [m] for we also forgive every one that is indebted to us. And [n] lead us not into tempta- tion; [o] but deliver us from evil.

And when he considers that Jesus loved him and bled for him, when an enemy and a rebel; and, having shewn him mercy, that he has commanded him " to go and do like- " wise ; " he will love, and do good to, even his enemies, and to the vilest of mankind for Christ's sake. With this view of Christianity before our eyes, have we reason to ex- pect that any, who profess it, will defraud, oppress, en- slave, or persecute any of the human race? If there be an appearance of such practices in some who seem to be Christians, we must either allow that they are not what they profess to be, or that they " know not what manner " of spirit they are of." And can we but wonder, that pro- fessed Christians should discourage, oppose, or " forbid " us, to preach the gospel to the gentiles," and to the Jews " that they may be saved ?" (Notes, Rom. i. 13—16. x. 12—17. 1 Thes. ii. 13—16.)

V. 38—42.

Let us follow Christ, especially in his persevering love to sinners ; let us welcome him into our hearts, and his disciples and ministers into our houses : and let the latter especially be careful to improve the hours of social inter- course in edifying discourse. But we should have more profit in meeting together, as well as larger ability in imi- tating the good Samaritan, if we were not so " cumbered " about much serving." Alas! what time is wasted, and what expenses are incurred, even in the entertainment of the ministers and professors of the gospel, to feast the guests, and to gratify the vanity of those who furnish the repast ; while a scanty surplus remains for the poor, and a small proportion of the opportunity, for religious im- provement! (Note, xiv. 12—14.) Nay, sometimes the persons concerned thus lose their temper also; and are even induced to violate the sabbath, and to constrain their servants to neglect the publick ordinances of God, and perhaps to do the same themselves! If the gracious Saviour were personally present on such occasions, and saw his professed disciples thus " careful and troubled about many " things ; " would he not rebuke them far more sharply than he did Martha? Indeed the delinquents will attempt to vindicate their conduct; and perhaps may be angry, and affect to censure those, who are indifferent to external accommodations, compared with " sitting at Christ's feet," " and hearing his word : " but he will decide the matter against them, and not admit of their plea that these are little things ; much less will he consider such cares and encumbrances as needful.—But it is not in this way alone, that we are apt to be " careful and troubled about many " things." Numbers are wholly given up to a variety of

worldly pursuits and anxieties, to the entire neglect of their souls : and there are none of us, who do not at some times expose ourselves to the rebuke of Christ, for our dispro- portionate solicitude and eagerness about mere trifles, when compared with our attention to the great concerns of eternity. Let us then mind more diligently and entirely, " the one thing needful." ' None but Jesus can do help- ' less sinners good : ' to hear, believe, and obey his gospel, and to have him for our " Wisdom, Righteousness, Sanc- " tification, and Redemption," comprises all that is neces- sary for this world and the next : and without this all the rest will leave us for ever miserable. This good part is by the gospel proposed to our choice : happy then are they, who give it a decided preference to all earthly objects ; for it " shall not be taken from them," through the countless ages of eternity : and to those who choose and seek it in the first place, all things else which can conduce to their present comfort, or their everlasting felicity, shall assuredly be added. (Notes, Matt. vi. 25—34.)

NOTES.

Chap. XI. V. 1—4. Our Lord, it may be supposed, constantly prayed with his disciples, when they were retired together. On one of these occasions, a certain person (perhaps one of the seventy disciples, who might not have heard the sermon on the mount) intreated him to teach them to pray, as John had taught his followers. Probably, John had added to his general instructions on this subject, some comprehensive directory, or form of prayer ; which both served to distinguish his disciples from those of the Pharisees, and to impress upon their minds the important truths which he had inculcated, concerning the Messiah and the spiritual blessings of his kingdom ; and thus to regulate their judgment and devotions, at the same time. This disciple therefore desired Jesus to instruct him and the other disciples to pray, by some similar method : for we cannot suppose, but that he had in general taught them both what to pray for, and in what manner to pray, by his doctrine and daily example. In answer to his request, our Lord again delivered that prayer, which has been fully con- sidered. (Notes, Matt. vi. 7—13.) The variations are immaterial, except the omission of the concluding dox- ology.—Instead of " this day," we here read, " day by " day," or daily ; and sins is substituted for debts (4). But the clause, " When ye pray, say," at least warrants the frequent use of the very words here prescribed, which certainly imply every thing that we can ask for ourselves or others, in respect of this life, and of that which is to come. (Marg. Ref.)— Thy will be done, &c. (2) To pray,

5 And he said unto them, "Which of you shall have a friend, and shall go unto him at midnight, and say unto him, Friend, lend me three loaves;

6 For a friend of mine * in his journey is come to me, and I have nothing to set before him?

7 And he from within shall answer and say, Trouble me not: the door is now shut, and my children are with me in bed; I cannot rise and give thee.

8 I say unto you, Though he will not rise and give him, because he is his friend; yet because of his importunity, he will rise and give him as many as he needeth.

9 And I say unto you, Ask, and it shall be given you; seek, and ye shall find; knock, and it shall be opened unto you.

10 For every one that asketh, receiveth; and he that seeketh, findeth; and to him that knocketh, it shall be opened.

11 If a son shall ask bread of any of you that is a father, will he give him a stone? or if he ask a fish, will he for a fish give him a serpent?

12 Or if he shall ask an egg, will he offer him a scorpion?

13 If ye then, being evil, know how to give good gifts unto your children; how much more shall your heavenly Father give the Holy Spirit to them that ask him?

14 ¶ And he was casting out a

---

that "the will of God may be done, as in heaven, so on "earth," is widely different from saying, in submission to Providence, in some special instance, "The will of the "Lord be done:" (xxii. 42. Acts xxi. 14:) for the former takes in obedience to the will of God, as a lawgiver, and as a Saviour, as well as submission to his providential appointments. (Notes, Matt. vi. 10. vii. 21—23.)—*Indebted*, &c. (4) 'It is carefully to be observed, for the 'due stating of the controversy of Christ's satisfaction, 'that sins are not strictly and properly compared to debts; 'seeing, by sinning we do not so properly contract a '*debt* as a *guilt*, and obnoxiousness to punishment; which 'two things will admit these differences: (1) That, if 'another will pay my debt, the creditor cannot justly re-'fuse his paying it for me, or complain that he is not sa-'tisfied when the whole debt is paid: but let another be 'never so willing to suffer for my offence he can make no 'satisfaction for it, unless the judge be willing to admit 'him to suffer in my stead. Hence, (2) the creditor does 'no act of grace, by admitting the solution of another: 'and if that other pay the whole, he can require no con-'ditions for my discharge. But the ruler against whose 'laws I have personally offended, does me an act of grace, 'in admitting another to suffer in my stead; and so may 'do this only upon some reasonable conditions.' *Whitby.*

V. 5—13. In addition to this comprehensive form of prayer, our Lord encouraged the disciples to be persevering and earnest in their requests, so as to take no denial; the happy effects of which he illustrated by a case, which might occur to them. In those hot countries, it is common, where it can be done safely, to travel in the cool of the evening, and the first hours of the night. Should an unexpected guest, therefore, from his journey come at midnight to the house of one wholly unprepared for entertaining him; the person thus visited would apply to a friend or neighbour to assist him, in affording the weary traveller some refreshment. And though his friend might attempt to put him off, and excuse himself; yet, if he were not easily denied, (as it might be supposed, he would not,) but urged the request, with an importunity which in other circumstances would be reprehensible; he would seldom fail, in the event, to overcome the reluctance of his friend. If then importunity proved so successful with men, notwithstanding their selfishness, and the inconvenience which attends granting a request made at a late hour; how much more will it prevail with God, who delights in mercy, who deems no time unseasonable, who answers every prayer with most perfect ease, and who only delays his favours, in order to make men more earnest and persevering in their supplications! (*Marg. Ref.* p—r.—*Notes*, xviii. 1—8. Gen. xxxii. 24—30.) This illustration our Lord concluded by repeating such exhortations and promises, as have already been considered: (*Marg. Ref.* s—e.—*Note, Matt.* vii. 7—11:) except that, instead of "good things," he here inserts "the Holy Spirit;" by which it is intimated, that this gift to us sinners, since the work of redemption was completed, is the sum or earnest of all good things: for by his influences, we are brought to know God and ourselves, to repent, to believe in and love Christ, to hope, rejoice, and obey; and so are made comfortable and useful in this world, and meet for happiness in the next. (*Marg. Ref.* f.—*Notes, John* xvi. 7—15.) The gift of the Holy Spirit is two-fold: his immediate inspiration made men prophets; his regenerating and sanctifying influences render men *saints*, or holy persons. No sober man can suppose that every one, who prays for the Holy Spirit, will be made a prophet, or enabled to work miracles. His renewing, enlightening, sanctifying, and comforting influences are no doubt exclusively intended. (*Notes, John* iv. 10—15. vii. 37—39.)

Importunity. (8) Την αναιδειαν. Here only N. T. Ex α priv. et αιδως, *pudor: sine pudore.* ' *Qui moleste urget, nec* 'ullo responso aut alio modo abigi potest.' Schleusner.—'According to that saying of the Jews, the impudent man 'overcomes the modest and the bashful, how much more 'God who is goodness itself.' *Whitby.*—*Heavenly*, &c. (13) Εξ κρανυ.—Εν τοις κρανοις, *Matt.* vii. 11.

V. 14—26. (*Marg. Ref.*—*Notes, Matt.* xii. 22—30. 43—45. xvi. 1—4. 2 Pet. ii. 20—22.) "The finger of "God," (20) denoting the power by which Christ wrought

devil, and it was dumb. And it came to pass, when the devil was gone out, the dumb spake; and the people wondered.

15 But some of them said, [b] He casteth out devils through [a] Beelzebub the chief of the devils.

16 And others, [i] tempting *him*, sought of him a sign from heaven.

17 But he, [k] knowing their thoughts, said unto them, [l] Every kingdom divided against itself is brought to desolation; and a house *divided* against a house, falleth.

18 If [m] Satan also be divided against himself, how shall his kingdom stand? because [n] ye say that I cast out devils through Beelzebub.

19 And if I by Beelzebub cast out devils, [o] by whom do your sons cast [p] *them* out? therefore [p] shall they be your judges.

20 But if I with [q] the finger of God cast out devils, no doubt [r] the kingdom of God is come upon you.

21 When [s] a strong man armed keepeth his palace, his goods are in peace:

22 But [t] when a stronger than he shall come upon him, and overcome him, he taketh from him all his armour wherein he trusted, and divideth [u] his spoils.

23 He [u] that is not with me is against me; and he that gathereth not with me scattereth.

24 When [x] the unclean spirit is gone out of a man, [y] he walketh through [z] dry places, [a] seeking rest: and finding [a] none, he saith, [b] I will return unto my house whence I came out.

25 And when he cometh, [c] he findeth *it* swept and garnished.

26 Then goeth he, and taketh *to him* [d] seven other spirits [d] more wicked than himself; and they enter in, and dwell there: [e] and the last *state* of that man is worse than the first.

27 ¶ And it came to pass, as he spake these things, a certain woman of the company lifted up her voice, and said unto him, [f] Blessed *is* the womb that bare thee, and the paps which thou hast sucked.

28 But he said, [g] Yea, rather blessed *are* they that hear the word of God and keep it.

29 ¶ And [h] when the people were gathered thick together, he began to say, [i] This is an evil generation; [k] they seek a sign, and there shall no sign be given it, but the sign of Jonas the prophet.

30 For [l] as Jonas was a sign unto the Ninevites, so shall also the Son of man be to this generation.

31 The [m] queen of the south shall [n] rise up in the judgment with the men

---

b Matt. ix. 34. xii. 24—30. Mark iii. 22—30. John vii. 20. viii. 48. 52. x. 20.
a Gr. *Beelzebul.*
so 18, 19.
i Matt. xii. 38, 39. xvi. 1—4. Mark viii. 11, 12. John vi. 30. 1 Cor. i. 22.
k Matt. ix. 4. xii. 25. Mark iii. 23—26. Rev. ii. 23.
l 2 Chr. x. 16—19. xiii. 16, 17. Is. ix. 20, 21. xix. 2, 3.
m Matt. xii. 26.
n 15. Matt. xii. 31 —34. Jam. iii. 5
o ix. 49. Matt. xii. 27, 28.
p 31, 32. xix. 22. Job xv. 6. Matt. xii. 41, 42. Rom. iii. 19.
q Ex. viii. 19. Matt. xii. 28.
r x. 9, 11. Dan. ii. 44. Acts xx. 28. 2 Thes. i. 5.
s *See on* Matt. xii. 29. Mark iii. 27.
t Gen. iii. 15 Is. xxvii. 1. xlix. 24, 25. liii. 12. Is. lii. John i. 8. 1 John iii. 8. iv. 4. Rev. xx. 1—3.
u ix. 50. Matt. xii. 30. Rev. iii. 15, 16.

x Matt. xii. 43—45.
Job i. 7. ii. 2 1 Pet. v. 8.
Judg. vi. 37—40. Ps. lxiii. 1. Is. xxxv. 6, 7. xli. 17—19. xliv. 3. Ezk. xlvii. 8—11. Eph. ii. 2.
y Prov. iv. 16. Is. xlviii. 22. lvii. 20, 21.
b Mark v. 10. ix. 25.
c 2 Chr. xxiv. 17 —22. Ps. xxxvi. 3. lxxxi. 11, 12. cxxv. 5. Matt. xii. 44, 45. 2 Thes. ii. 9—12. 2 Pet. ii. 10 —19. Jude 6—13.
d Matt. xxiii. 15. Zeph. i. 6. Matt. xii. 45. John v. 14. Heb. vi. 4— 8. x. 26—31. 2 Pet. ii. 20—22. Jude 12, 13.
e vi. 47, 48. viii. 13. cxii. l. cxix. l. —6. cxxviii. 1.
f Is. xlviii. 17, 18. Matt. vii. 21—
g Matt. vii. 21. 2b. xii. 48—50. John xiii. 17. Jam. i. 21—25. 1 John iii. 21— 24. Rev. xxii. 14.
h xii. l. xiv. 25.
i Matt. xii. 38,39. xvi. l. 1 Cor. i. 22.
k 18. vi. 30.
l Matt. xii. 39,40.
m 1 Kings x. 1, 2. 2 Chr. ix. 1.
n Is. liae. 17. Jer. iii. 11. Rom. ii. 27. Heb. xi. 7.

---

his miracles, may refer to the confession of the Egyptian magicians, with respect to the miracles performed by Moses. (*Note, Ex.* viii. 18, 19.) " The Spirit of God," *Matt.* xii. 28.—*A strong man*, &c. (21) The circumstances of the " strong man's being armed," (namely, with the sinner's ignorance, error, prejudices, pride, and lusts,) the confidence which he places in this armour, and the peace in which he retains his possession, till overcome by one " stronger than he," are here added to the parable : and the contrast between " the strong one," and one " stronger " than he," is marked emphatically. (*Note,* 1 *John* iv. 4 —6.)

Thoughts. (17) Διανοηματα. Here only N. T. Ex δια, et νοεω, cogito. Ενθυμησεις, *Matt.* xii. 25.—*Divided.*] Διαμερισθεισα. 18. xxii. 17. xxiii. 34. *Matt.* xxvii. 35. *Acts* ii. 45. Ex δια, et μεριζω, quod à μερις, pars.—*Is come upon.* (20) Εφθασεν. *Matt.* xii. 28. *Rom.* ix. 31. *Phil.* iii. 16. 1 *Thes.* ii. 16. iv. 15.—*A strong man.* (21) Ο ισχυρος.— *A stronger.* (22) Ο ισχυροτερος. iii. 16. xv. 14. 1 *John* ii. 14, *et al.—Armed.* (21) Καθωπλισμενος. Here only N. T. —'Οπλιζομαι, 1 *Pet.* iv. 1.—'Οπλα, *arma.—All his armour.*

(22) Την πανοπλιαν. *Eph.* vi. 11. 13. Not elsewhere N. T.— *Swept.* (25) Σεσαρωμενον. xv. 8. *Matt.* xii. 44. Not elsewhere N. T.—*Garnished.*] Κεκοσμημενον. xxi. 5. *Matt.* xii. 44. xxiii. 29. xxv. 7. 1 *Tim.* ii. 9. *Tit.* ii. 10. 1 *Pet.* iii. 5. *Rev.* xxi. 2. 19.

V. 27, 28. The power and beneficence of Christ's miracles, the authority and excellence of his doctrine, the holiness of his character, and the wisdom of his answers to his malicious enemies, seem to have combined so to fill this woman with admiration, that she could not refrain from crying aloud, that the woman, who had the honour of being his mother, must be peculiarly happy above all others. The answer of our Lord to this, was exactly to the same effect with one on another occasion, which has already been considered. (*Marg. Ref.—Notes, Matt.* xii. 46—50.) ' The blessedness of my mother ariseth not ' from this, that she conceived me, and brought me forth ' into the world : but in order to that, it is necessary for ' her, as well as others, to believe and obey my word. So ' Theophylact.' *Whitby.*

V. 29—32. *Marg. Ref.—Notes, Matt.* xii. 38—42.

of this generation, and condemn them: for she came from the utmost parts of the earth to hear the wisdom of Solomon; and, behold, a greater than Solomon is here.

32 The men of Nineveh shall rise up in the judgment with this generation, and shall condemn it: for they repented at the preaching of Jonas; and, behold, a greater than Jonas is here.

33 No man, when he hath lighted a candle, putteth it in a secret place, neither under a bushel, but on a candlestick, that they which come in may see the light.

34 The light of the body is the eye: therefore when thine eye is single, thy whole body also is full of light; but when thine eye is evil, thy body also is full of darkness.

35 Take heed therefore that the light which is in thee be not darkness.

36 If thy whole body therefore be full of light, having no part dark, the whole shall be full of light, as when the bright shining of a candle doth give thee light.

37 ¶ And as he spake, a certain Pharisee besought him to dine with him: and he went in, and sat down to meat.

38 And when the Pharisee saw it, he marvelled that he had not first washed before dinner.

39 And the Lord said unto him, Now do ye Pharisees make clean the outside of the cup and the platter; but your inward part is full of ravening and wickedness.

40 Ye fools! did not he that made that which is without, make that which is within also?

Were gathered thick together. (29) Επαθροιζομενων. Here only N. T. Ab αθροος *confertus.*

V. 33—36. This was an answer to another cavil, connected with the preceding objection (16). The substance of it has been already commented upon; but the allusion to the light and the eye, seems here to be applied in a different manner, than elsewhere. (*Notes, Matt.* v. 14—16. vi. 22, 23. *Mark* iv. 21, 22.) Our Lord intimated by it, that he should proceed to diffuse the light of his truth, notwithstanding the perverse opposition of the Pharisees; nor would they be able to cover or extinguish that light, which he had kindled for the benefit of mankind. Yet the Pharisees, and others of similar character would remain in darkness, through the prejudices of their wicked hearts; even as men, whose eyes are diseased, see nothing, or nothing as it really is, in the clearest light. It therefore concerned every hearer to be peculiarly careful, that the supposed light, which he followed, was not darkness; or his first principles and practical judgment erroneous. For, as the body is furnished with light for its direction by the eye; so the mind is guided in every operation by the practical judgment: if then their minds were well prepared to receive the benefit of revelation, they would have no more occasion to demand further information; than a man with good eyes is at a loss to distinguish the surrounding objects, " when the bright shining of a candle doth give him " light." (*Marg. Ref.*)—This last verse may be thus understood: " If thy whole body therefore be full of light, " having no part dark; the whole " (*of thy conduct, or, path,*) " shall be full of light, as when the bright shining " of a candle doth give thee light."—'A mind thus en-
' lighteped, and free from all those distempers, which
' darken and make blind the soul, will direct all our facul-
' ties and inclinations, and all the actions of the life aright;
' as a light doth the body, when it walks in a dark night.'
Whitby.

The bright shining of a candle. (36) 'Ο λυχνος τη αςραπη, " a candle by its lightning." x. 18. xvii. 24.—*Doth give ... light.*] Φωλιζει. John i. 9. 1 Cor. iv. 5. Eph. i. 18. iii. 9. 2 Tim. i. 10. Heb. vi. 4. x. 32. Rev. xviii. 1. xxi. 23. xxii. 5. A φως, *lux.*

V. 37, 38. As Jesus was speaking on some other occasion, (for harmonists seem, with probability, to place the following incident in another connexion,) a Pharisee, with apparent respect and earnestness, pressed him to dine with him, and he was pleased to accept of the invitation; yet it is probable, that the Pharisee had purposely collected together many of his brethren to meet Jesus, with a design to ensnare him, of which he was fully aware. This may account for the remarkable sharpness of his reproofs and warnings. (*Notes,* vii. 36. xiv. 1—6.)—The Pharisee, however, expressed his surprise, that Jesus had not first washed according to their traditions; (*Marg. Ref.* b.—*Notes, Matt.* xv. 1, 2. *Mark* vii. 3—8;) and this gave him the opportunity of exposing and condemning their hypocrisy and superstition. (*Note, Matt.* xxiii. 23 24.)

To dine. (37) 'Οπως αριησῃ. John xxi. 12. 15. Not elsewhere N. T. Αρισον, 38.—*Had not washed.* (38) Ου ... εβαπλισθη. " Had not been baptized."—If the verb βαπτιζω means exclusively to immerse; certainly all the company, except Jesus and his disciples, had openly been immersed, and were daily immersed, before dinner; so that it was a matter of astonishment, that our Lord should not be thus immersed.

V. 39, 40. (*Marg. Ref.—Notes, Matt.* xii. 33—37. xxiii. 25—28.) As God, who created the soul, and perfectly knows it, abhors all sin, and requires especially inward purity; nothing can be more irrational and foolish than to suppose, that any external observances can please him, while avarice, pride and ambition, revenge and other malignant passions, or sensual lusts possess the heart.

41 But ^h rather give alms ° of such things as ye have, and, behold, ⁱ all things are clean unto you.

42 But ^k woe unto you, Pharisees! ^l for ye tithe mint and rue, and all manner of herbs, ^m and pass over judgment and the love of God : these ought ye to have done, ⁿ and not to leave the other undone.

43 Woe unto you, Pharisees! ° for ye love the uppermost seats in the synagogues, and greetings in the markets.

44 Woe unto you, Scribes and Pharisees, hypocrites! ^p for ye are as graves which appear not, and the men that walk over *them* are not aware *of them.*

45 Then answered one of the lawyers, and said unto him, Master, thus saying ^q thou reproachest us also.

46 And he said, ^r Woe· unto you also, *ye* lawyers! for ye lade men with burdens grievous to be borne, and ye yourselves touch not the burdens with one of your fingers.

47 Woe unto you ! ^s for ye build the sepulchres of the prophets, and your fathers killed them.

48 Truly ^t ye bear witness that ye allow the deeds of your fathers : ^u for they indeed killed them, and ye build their sepulchres.

49 Therefore also said ^x the Wisdom of God, ^y I will send them prophets and apostles, ^z and *some* of them they shall slay and persecute ;

V. 41. (*Notes, Is.* lviii. 3—12. *Dan.* iv. 27. *Matt.* v. 7. xxv. 34—40.) Pilate washed his hands, as a token that he was pure from the blood of Jesus, when he gave him up to be crucified : and the Pharisees washed their hands, as a profession of holiness and piety, while their hearts were full of rapacity and iniquity. (*Note, Matt.* xxvii. 24, 25.) But the observance in both cases was vain and inefficacious : and the conduct of Zaccheus, who, having made large restitution to all whom he had wronged, gave half of his remaining goods to the poor, was a far better proof of love to God and man, as well as of sincere repentance and faith ; and a far better method of seeking the sanctified and comfortable use of outward things. (*Marg. Ref.—Notes,* iii. 10—14. xix. 1—10.)—Some think our Lord meant, that, as the possessions of many among the Pharisees had been in great measure acquired by oppression and injustice; and as it would have been impracticable, in all cases, to make restitution to the injured persons ; they must dispose of all their ill-gotten and idolized property in alms, before they could expect that God would accept their services, and bless their provisions : and the original expression, with the connexion, and the character of the persons addressed, give considerable probability to this interpretation. Liberality to the poor, however, according to a man's ability, from proper principles, does more towards rendering outward possessions or enjoyments sanctified, than any ceremonial washings can do. Where this is duly attended to, from scriptural motives, and men deduct from their own indulgence to give a portion to their poor neighbours, " Behold, all things are clean " unto them."

Of such things as ye have.] " As you are able." *Marg.* Τα εvovτα.—' *Pro viribus et facultatibus vestris distribuite* ' *eleemosynas ; ut τα εvovτα* positum sit pro *καθα τα εvovτα* ' *χρηματα,* seu ix *των εvovτωv. Schleusner.*

V. 42. *Marg. Ref.—*xviii. 12. *Notes, Matt.* xxiii. 23, 24.

V. 43. *Marg. Ref.—Notes,* xx. 45—47. *Matt.* xxiii. 5—7.

V. 44. (*Marg. Ref.—Note, Matt.* xxiii. 25—28.)—

Some graves or tombs were purposely whitened ; others were grown over with grass, and not seen ; but both were full of dead men's bones, and those who walked where they were, often contracted ceremonial uncleanness. (*Notes, Lev.* xix. 11. 21.) Thus, they who formed an acquaintance with the hypocritical Scribes and Pharisees, were deeply corrupted by them, in their principles and conduct, sometimes before they suspected any harm.

Which appear not.] Αδηλα. 1 *Cor.* xiv. 8. Not elsewhere *N. T.—Ps.* li. 6. *Sept.* Ex α priv. et δηλος, *manifestus.*

V. 45. The lawyers seem to have been a superior order of the Scribes, who were most celebrated as learned men, or most followed as teachers, and gave lectures on the law. This man considered himself and his brethren as superior to all censure or reproof : he wondered therefore, that Jesus should join the Scribes with the Pharisees, in the preceding woe, and charged him with reproaching so honourable a body.

The lawyers.] Των voμικωv; 46. 52. vii. 30. x. 25. xiv. 3. *Matt.* xxii. 35. *Tit.* iii. 9. 13.—*Thou reproachest.*] 'Υβριζεις. xviii. 32. *Matt.* xxii. 6. *Acts* xiv. 5. 1 *Thes.* ii. 2. Ab ύβρις, *contumelia.*

V. 46—48. *Marg. Ref.—Notes, Matt.* xxiii. 1—4, *v.* 4. 29—33.—*Truly,* &c. (48) ' As in your conduct you ' imitate your fathers, truly ye bear witness to them, rather ' than against them ; and in effect approve...the works of ' your fathers : for one would imagine that you erected ' these monuments, not so much in honour of the pro- ' phets as of their persecutors by whom they were so wickedly ' destroyed.' *Doddridge.*

Heavy to be borne. (46) Δυσβασταχτα. *Matt.* xxiii. 4. Not elsewhere N. T. Εx δυς, et βασταζω, tolero.

Eph. iv. 7—13.—*Wisdom.* (49) Some expositors understand " the Wisdom of God," of Christ himself : and as the words which follow are not found in the Old Testament, we may suppose, that he meant, as the Word and Wisdom of God, immediately to reveal to the hearers his wise counsels and purposes respecting them. In the pa-

50 That ^a the blood of all the pro- ^a Gen. ix. 5, 6. Num. xxxv. 33. 2 Kings xxiv. 4. Ps. ix. 12. Ia. xxvi. 21. Rer. xviii. 20—24. phets, which was shed from the found- ation of the world, may be required of ^b this generation; ^b Jer. vii. 29.

51 From ^c the blood of Abel, unto the blood of ^d Zacharias, which pe- rished between the altar and the tem- ple: verily I say unto you, It shall be required of this generation. ^c Gen. iv. 8—11. Heb. xi. 4. xii. 12. ^d 1 John iii. 12. ^d 2 Chr. xxiv. 21. 22. Zech. i. 1. Matt. xxiii. 35.

52 Woe unto you, lawyers! ^e for ye have taken away the key of know- ^e xix. 30, 40. Matt. xxiii. 13. John vii. 47—52. ix. 24—34. Acts iv. 17, 18, v. 40.

ledge: ye entered not in yourselves, and them that were entering in ye ^a hindered. ^a Or, forbad

53 And as he said these things unto them, the Scribes and the Pharisees began ^f to urge him vehemently, and to provoke him ^g to speak of many things; ^f Ps. xxii. 12, 13. Ia. liv. 12. ^g xx. 20, 27. Jer. xviii. 18. xx. 10.

54 Laying wait for him, and ^h seek- ing to catch something out of his mouth, that they might accuse him. ^h Ps. xxxvii.32,33. lvi. 6, 6. Matt. xxii. 15. 18. 35. Mark xii. 13.

rallel passage of St. Matthew, which was spoken at the close of his ministry, our Lord evidently spoke in his own person.

V. 52. (*Marg. Ref.—Notes,* xix. 28—40, v. 40. *Matt.* xxiii.) The Scribes are said to have been distinguished, by the symbolical figure of *a key;* intimating that their proper office was to open and explain the scripture, and to admit men into the knowledge of God, and of his truth and will: (*Notes, Is.* xxii. 20—25. *Matt.* xvi. 19. *Rev.* iii. 7 :) but, instead of using this key aright, they had taken it away, by their corrupt glosses and perverse opposition to the doctrine of Christ: so that they neither entered in themselves, nor allowed the people to enter, even when they were in a measure desirous of doing it. (*Notes, Acts* iv. 1—22.' v. 17—40.)—' For a long season, they, ' who ought to have been the door-keepers of the church, ' have been the chief persons in driving away the people ' from the knowledge of God.' *Beza.*

V. 53, 54. It is no wonder, that these sharp reproofs extremely enraged the hypocritical Scribes and Pharisees; especially as Jesus was guest to a Pharisee, when he thus spake to them: they therefore set on him, all at once, to put him off his guard, with a variety of questions or objections, that he might say something, which should give them matter of accusation against him.—Several of the original words are taken from *hunting;* which is an apt emblem of the vehemence, and rudeness, and artful devices, with which the company sought to entangle Jesus in their nets and toils. (*Marg. Ref.*)

. *To urge him vehemently.* (53) Δεινως ενεχειν. Δεινως, *admodum vehementer. Matt.* viii. 6. Not elsewhere N. T. —Ενεχειν. See on *Mark* vi. 19.—*To provoke him to speak.*] Αποστοματιζειν αυτον. Here only N. T. Ex απο, et στομα, os. ' *Incipiebant Pharisæi eum variis quæstionibus* ' *captiosis exercere, et ad responsa solicitare.*' Schleusner. —*Laying wait for him.* (54) Ενεδρευοντες. *Acts* xxiii. 21. Not elsewhere N. T.—*Josh.* viii. 4. 1 Sam. xv. 5. *Sept.* Ab ενεδρα, *Acts* xxiii. 16.—*To catch.*] Θηρευσαι. *Venari, feras capere.* Here only N. T.

PRACTICAL OBSERVATIONS

V. 1—13.

It is a most valuable effect of preventing grace and mercy, to be made so sensible of our indigence, and our dependence on God, as heartily to desire to pray; and so aware of our own ignorance, and of the difficulty of pray- ing aright, as explicitly to seek for instruction in this most important concern. When we are thus led to beseech the

Lord Jesus to teach us to pray, we use a very proper in- troduction to all our subsequent devotions: but he will do it, in a manner far superior to that of John, or any other of his servants. He will lead us into an acquaintance with our own wants, and the promises of God, and excite in our hearts correspondent desires and affections; and thus he will teach us to pray in humility, reverence, faith, expectation, and earnest importunity: he will give us " the Spirit of adoption," that we may come with confi- dence to God, as " our Father who is in heaven;" and from love to him and zeal for his glory, as well as from " good-will to men," to pray " that his name may be " hallowed, his kingdom" enlarged to all regions, " and " his will done," his commands unreservedly obeyed, and his dispensations cheerfully submitted to, " on earth as in " heaven." From submission to his will, moderation in our desires, and reliance on his providence, we shall thus learn to live willingly dependent on him, " day by day, for " our daily bread." We shall, under this instruction, seek continually for the " pardon of our sins, and learn to for- " give every one who is indebted to us;" and from ab- horrence of iniquity, as well as from dread of its conse- quences, we shall, in humble consciousness of our own weakness, pray " not to be led into temptation, but to be " delivered from evil;" from the evil one, from the evil of this world, and from the evil of our own hearts; that we may be made holy as our God is holy, and be pre- pared for perfect felicity in his favour and presence for ever. (*P. O. Matt.* vi. 9—18.) The teaching of Christ will also encourage and enlarge our hopes. Assured that we are praying for such things as are good for us; we shall persevere, and be importunate, though we seem to meet with a repulse; being satisfied, that " every one that " asketh receiveth." We shall therefore return again and again to the throne of grace, even when we have been baffled by temptation, or proved by delays; and renew and increase our earnestness in asking, seeking, and knocking; especially that we may obtain the Holy Spirit, to enlighten, sanctify, strengthen, and comfort our hearts; and to put us in full possession of the salvation of Christ. (*Note, John* iv. 10—15.) All these blessings our hea- venly Father is far more ready to bestow, on " *every one* " who asketh for them," than any indulgent father can be to give food to his hungry child; and, in this way, we need no more fear being fatally deluded, or finally overcome by our enemy, than a beloved child needs fear, lest his father should " give him a scorpion instead of an egg:" nay, this would be far more likely; because men without exception are evil by nature; and that depravity often triumphs over

3 ▸ 7

CHAP. XII.

Jesus warns his disciples against hypocrisy; and the fear of man in confessing him. He shews the danger of blasphemy against the Holy Ghost, and teaches dependance on him, 1—12. He refuses to act as judge in temporal things; and warns his disciples against covetousness, by the parable of a rich man, suddenly torn by death from all his purposed and expected enjoy-ments, 13—21. He cautions them against anxious cares, and exhorts them to seek spiritual blessings, 22—34, and to be always ready for the coming of their Lord, 35—40. He instructs and warns his ministers, by the parable of a faithful, and of a wicked steward, 41—48. He predicts the divisions which his gospel would occasion, 49—53; reproves those who knew not the signs of the times, 54—56; and counsels the people to seek reconciliation to God without delay, 57—59.

---

even natural affection; but " God is Love," and " de-" lighteth in mercy." (Note, Is. xlix. 14—16.)

V. 14—36.

The goodness of God, in all its varied displays, tends to draw forth man's ingratitude and enmity as far as he is left to himself. Even when divine love was incarnate for the salvation of sinners, his continued and persevering kindness, and pre-eminent excellency, excited the utmost envy and malignity in those persons, whose hypocrisy he exposed, whose selfishness he shamed, and with whose credit, interest, or authority, his doctrine interfered : nay, they ascribed even his most beneficent miracles to diabolical agency! But the tendency of his gospel to humble deity, purity, equity, truth, and love, did then, and does still, confute such blasphemous slanders; and it is even now in a measure accompanied with " the finger of God," to change the willing slaves of Satan into the devoted worshippers and servants of JEHOVAH. As the conversion of a sinner breaks that false peace, which existed in his heart and conscience, whilst the devil reigned there with undisturbed sway, and two conflicting parties are formed within the soul, of which grace is superior and will obtain the complete victory: (Note, Gal. v. 16—18 :) so the strange indifference of men to the concerns of religion is disturbed, wherever the gospel is successfully preached; and two parties are formed, the one for Christ and his cause, and the other in opposition to them; but the former will certainly prevail at length. (Notes, xii. 49—53. Matt. x. 34 —36. P. O. Acts xiv. 1—10.) In this contest, none are allowed to stand neuter: the Lord Jesus calls on every one to join him in destroying the kingdom of Satan; " he that is not for him is against him, and he that ga-" thereth not with him scattereth." Yet we must not hastily conclude, that all who appear to be for him, will " continue to the end." Alas! the unclean spirit for a time goes out of many, who never admit the Saviour to take possession of their hearts : and so the enemy returns to his habitation, and " the last state of those men be-" comes worse than the first." From such a dreadful event, (may every one say,) ' Good Lord, deliver us!' (P. O. Matt. xii. 22—50.)—In order to this, we should endeavour to " hear the word of God, and keep it" by faith and love in our hearts, and by obedience in our lives. Without this we cannot be blessed : for all notions, forms, and outward privileges, which fail of rectifying men's dispositions and regulating their conduct, will lead to their deeper condemnation. Thus multitudes who hear the gospel are proved to be " an evil generation :" they stand out in unbelief against every demonstration of the truth, and continue in sin against the convictions of their own conscience: while many come from distant places through love to the word of God, and bestow great pains under immense disadvantages to become wise unto salvation; and others profit by far inferior means and instruments, who " will rise up in judgment against them and con-" demn them."—But were Christ himself the constant Preacher to any company, and did he daily work his miracles of love among them ; unless his grace also humbled their hearts, and subdued their carnal prejudices, they would not be profited. Instead, therefore, of requiring more evidence and fuller instruction, than the Lord is pleased to afford us; we should " pray without " ceasing," that our understandings may be opened, and our hearts prepared, to profit by the light which we enjoy : and above all things we ought to take heed that the " light " which is in us be not darkness;" for if our leading principles be fallacies, and our affections carnal, our judgment and practice must become more egregiously wrong by all our reasonings and assiduity.

V. 37—54.

The case of these Pharisees and lawyers is an awful but instructive example. Their ambitious desire of pre-eminence, applause, and authority, and their proud and worldly prejudices, led them to place religion in minute but specious observances : this seduced them from the spiritual truth, will, and worship of God, and entangled them more and more in superstition and delusion. They gravely marvelled that Jesus washed not before dinner; yet they did not attempt to cleanse their own hearts from ravening and wickedness ; foolishly forgetting, that " he who made " that which is without, made that which is within also!" They fancied, that external and uncommanded purifications would sanctify their meals ; whilst the demands of justice and charity, as well as the duties of piety, were neglected. That they might appear singularly conscientious, and pay court to the priests, who doubtless flattered them in return, they scrupulously tithed even their garden-herbs ; but at the same time " they passed over judgment " and the love of God." Thus they were exposed to the sharp rebukes of Christ, and engaged in opposition to him : and, with all their sanctimonious gravity and austerity, they became his persecutors and murderers, and fell under his most tremendous indignation, till " venge-" ance came upon them to the uttermost." Alas ! they have had many successors, who have proved themselves to be their children, even as they were proved to be " the " children of those who slew the prophets;" for their conduct has evinced, that the honour, which they affected to render to the memory of deceased saints and martyrs, seemed rather intended for their murderers, than for them.

3 a 8

IN the mean time, when there were gathered together [a] an innumerable multitude of people, insomuch that they [b] trode one upon another, he began to say unto his disciples [c] first of all, [d] Beware ye of the leaven of the Pharisees, [e] which is hypocrisy.

2 For [f] there is nothing covered, that shall not be revealed; neither hid, that shall not be known.

3 Therefore [f] whatsoever ye have spoken in darkness, shall be heard in the light; and that which ye have spoken in the ear in closets, shall be proclaimed upon the [h] house-tops.

4 And I say unto you, [i] my friends,

[k] Be not afraid of them that kill the body, and after that have no more that they can do.

5 But I will [l] forewarn you whom ye shall fear: [m] Fear him, which after he hath killed, hath [n] power to cast into hell; yea, I say unto you, Fear him.

6 Are not [o] five sparrows sold for two farthings? [p] and not one of them is forgotten before God.

7 But [q] even the very hairs of your head are all numbered. Fear not therefore: [r] ye are of more value than many sparrows.

8 Also I say unto you, [s] Whosoever shall confess me before men, him shall

cxix. 46. Matt. x. 32, 33. Rom. x. 9, 10. Rev. ii. 13. iii. 4, 5.

—Proud men deem the word of God to be a *reproach* to them : many would allow the preacher to be severe upon the crimes of others, provided he would be gentle to their's ; and among learned men, haughty ecclesiasticks, and false professors of the gospel, numbers seem to think, that their characters even sanctify their crimes ; so that it is often thought intolerable insolence, for a minister to expose their most flagrant enormities. But the reproach comes from their own consciences; and we must by no means connive at their vices, which are dishonourable to God and ruinous to men, in proportion to the eminence or sacredness of their characters : and when renowned or authorized teachers perplex the truth by their subtilties, and set the people against it by their influence, they become murderers of men's souls, and ought most carefully to be avoided, and decidedly protested against. " Woe unto " them ! for they take away the key of knowledge ; they " enter not in themselves, and those who are entering in " they hinder :" and they are the more dangerous for being " as graves that appear not, of which the men who " walk over them are not aware." But such truths must excite opposition, and many will vehemently urge those who openly declare them, to speak or do something which may give them a handle against them. Such persons therefore as engage in contests of this kind, should be of a blameless conversation, and endued with heavenly wisdom; they should also have a clear call, and a great command of their own temper and spirit: so that few are qualified for these services. But we should all look well to our own hearts, that they may be cleansed and new created : and, while we insist on the great things of the law and of the gospel, we must be careful not to neglect even the smallest matter, which God has appointed.—Finally, the more careful we are " to give alms of such things as we " have," and to deduct from every article of expense for that purpose, the more comfortable, pure, and holy will all our possessions and enjoyments be. (*P. O. Matt.* xxiii. 13—39.)

multitude collected together without; so that they even trampled upon one another, in endeavouring to get near him. The people must have come from very distant places : and our Lord seems to have left the Pharisee's house, and to have spoken the subsequent instructions to his disciples, in the hearing of the multitude, yet in the presence of the company with whom he had before dined. He began by earnestly warning his disciples against hypocrisy, which was " the leaven of the Pharisees," and corrupted all their services. (*Notes*, xi. 44. *Matt.* xvi. 5—12. xxiii. 13—28.)—The folly of hypocrisy is clearly seen, when it is considered that " there is nothing covered which " shall not be revealed, neither hid that shall not be " known ;" and, that it shall be discovered before the Judge himself, and the whole assembled world : so that, no one word, whispered in confidence most secretly, can escape detection. (viii. 17. *Notes, Matt.* x. 24—28. *Mark* iv. 21, 22. 1 *Cor.* iv. 2—5. 2 *Cor.* v. 9—12.)—The solemn warning to " fear him, who after he hath killed hath power " to cast into hell," is here addressed immediately to the *friends* of Christ : for even believers have often been rendered victorious over the dread of man's cruelty, by fear of falling under the wrath of almighty God.—The word, here translated *hell*, always means the place of final and eternal punishment. (*Note, Matt.* v. 21, 22.)—*Farthings*. (6) ' This was a Roman coin, the tenth part of a dena- ' rius, in value about three farthings of our money. Two ' sparrows might be bought for one, and five for two of ' these.' *Doddridge.* (*Note, Matt.* x. 29—31.)

An innumerable multitude. (1) Τῶν μυριαδων· " The ten " thousands." *Acts* xix. 19. xxi. 20. *Heb.* xii. 22. *Jude* 14. *Rev.* ix. 16.—*Is forgotten.* (6) Εστιν επιλελησμενον. *Matt.* xvi. 5. *Mark* viii. 14. *Phil.* iii. 14. *Heb.* vi. 10. xiii. 2. 16. *Jam.* i. 24.

V. 8—10. (*Marg. Ref.—Notes, Matt.* x. 32, 33. xii. 31, 32. *Mark* viii. 38.)—Blaspheming the Holy Spirit is more criminal than denying Christ : many who denied Christ have repented and found mercy; but none that blasphemed the Holy Spirit. (*Note, Matt.* xxvi. 69—75.) —The Deity of Christ, and that of the Holy Spirit, is strongly implied in these verses.—*Angels.* (8, 9) " Before " my Father," *Matt.* x. 32, 33 ; that is, when our Lord

the Son of man also 'confess before the angels of God.

9 But "he that denieth me before men, 'shall be denied before the angels of God.

10 And 'whosoever shall speak a word against the Son of man, it shall be forgiven him: but unto him that blasphemeth against the Holy Ghost, it shall not be forgiven.

11 And 'when they bring you unto the synagogues, and *unto* magistrates and powers, take ye no thought how or what thing ye shall answer, or what ye shall say:

12 For 'the Holy Ghost shall teach you in the same hour what ye ought to say.

13 ¶ And one of the company said unto him, 'Master, speak to my brother, that he divide the inheritance with me.

14 And he said unto him, 'Man, 'who made me a judge or a divider over you?

15 And he said unto them, 'Take heed, and beware of covetousness: 'for a man's life consisteth not in the abundance of the things which he possesseth.

16 And he spake a parable unto them, saying, 'The ground of a certain rich man brought forth plentifully.

17 And he thought within himself, saying, "What 'shall I do, because I have no room where to bestow my fruits?

18 And he said, 'This will I do: I will pull down my barns, and build greater; and there will I bestow all my fruits and my goods.

19 And I will say to my soul, 'Soul, thou hast much goods laid up "for many years; " take thine ease, eat, drink, *and* be merry.

20 But 'God said unto him, 'Thou fool, this night 'thy soul shall be required of thee: 'then whose shall those things be which thou hast provided?

21 So *is* 'he that layeth up treasure for himself, and is not 'rich toward God.

19, 20. lxxviii. 30, 31. Dan. v. 1—6. 25—30. Nah. i. 10. Matt. xxiv. 48—51. 1 Thes. v. 3. p xi. 40. Jer. xvii. 11. *Or, do they require thy soul.* q Eath. v. 11. viii. 1, 2. Job xxvii. 16, 17. Ps. xxxix. 6. xlix. 17—19. lii. 5—7. Prov. xi. 4. xxviii. 8. Ec. ii. 18—22. v. 14—16. Dan. v. 28. 1 Tim. vi. 7. r 33. vi. 24. Hos. x. 1. Matt. vi. 19, 20. Rom. ii. 5. 1 Tim. vi. 18, 19. Jam. v. 1—3. s xvi. 11. 2 Cor. vi. 10. 1 Tim. vi. 18. Jam. ii. 5. Rev. ii. 9.

" shall appear in his own glory, and the glory of his Fa-
" ther, and of the holy angels," to judge the world.
(*Note*, ix. 18—27, *v*. 26.)
V. 11, 12. *Marg. Ref.—Notes*, xxi. 12—19, *v*. 15.
Matt. x. 19, 20. *Mark* xiii. 9—13, *v*. 11.
Ye shall answer. (11) Απολογησησθε. xxi. 14. *Acts* xix.
33. xxiv. 10. xxv. 8. xxvi. 1, 2. 24. *Rom.* ii. 15. 2 *Cor.*
xii. 19.
V. 13, 14. It is evident, that earthly things had the
ascendency in the mind of this man: though he seems to
have had honourable thoughts of Jesus; when he desired
him to require his brother, by authority, as a prophet, or
as the Messiah, to give him that share of the inheritance,
to which he supposed himself entitled. Perhaps, his brother was one of the assembled multitude; and this circumstance might induce the man to propose his request in
so unseasonable a manner.—Our Lord, however, saw
much wrong in his spirit and conduct, and in language,
which implied *reproof*, asked " Man, who made me a
" ruler and a divider over you ?".Who appointed me to
decide causes, or an umpire to divide inheritances? His
" kingdom was not of this world:" (*Note*, *John* xviii. 33
—36 :) he appeared as a Teacher and a Saviour: he was
not commissioned by the Father to take the civil magistrate's office out of his hand; and if he had attempted it,
the people would have enquired of him, as the Israelite
had formerly done of Moses, " Who made thee a prince
" and a judge over us?" (*Acts* vii. 27. 35. *Note, Ex.* ii.

13—15.)—' Christ would not, for three causes, be a judge
' to divide inheritances. First, for that he would not ...
' cherish the carnal opinion, which the Jews had of the
' Messiah. Secondly, for that he would distinguish the
' civil governance from the ecclesiastical. Thirdly, to
' teach us to beware of them, which abuse the shew of
' the gospel, and also the name of ministers, to their own
' private advantage.' *Beza.*—' It is probable, that Christ
' refused to take this office upon him ; ... chiefly, because
' he had but little time remaining, which he could better
' spend in dividing to them the word of life, and promoting
' their eternal interest.' *Whitby.* This reason is at least
very forcible, in all similar cases, with ministers of the
gospel : if they duly consider the shortness and uncertainty
of life, the state of the world, the worth of souls, and
the immense importance and arduousness of their work.
(*Notes, Acts* vi. 2—6. *P. O.* 1—7. *Note,* 1 *Cor.* iv. 1—6.)
A judge. (14) Δικαστην.— *Non quilibet judex dicitur,*
' *sed judex qui lites minores componit.* A δικαζω, *jus dico.*'
Schleusner. *Acts* vii. 27. 35. Not elsewhere N. T. *Ex.*
ii. 14. *Sept.—A divider.*] Μεριστην à μεριζω, *divido.* Here
only N. T.
V. 15—21. Our Lord, according to his usual manner,
took occasion from this improper intrusion, with great
energy, to warn his hearers against every kind or degree of
covetousness, and all approaches to it: as neither the
duration, comfort, credit, usefulness, or happy event of a
man's life, consists in the abundance of his· possessions.

3 c 2

22 ¶ And he said unto his disciples, Therefore I say unto you, 'Take no thought for your life, what ye shall eat; neither for the body, what ye shall put on.

23 The " life is more than meat, and the body is more than raiment.

24 Consider " the ravens : for they neither sow nor reap; which neither have store-house nor barn; and God feedeth them. 'How much more are ye better than the fowls?

25 And ' which of you, with taking thought, can add to his stature one cubit?

26 If ye then be not able to do that

(Marg. Ref. e, f.—Note, 1 Tim. vi. 6—10, vv. 8—10.) To illustrate and enforce this caution, he spoke a parable, replete with instruction. The " rich man," described in it, is not said to have obtained his wealth by fraud or oppression, or to have been a penurious miser. (Note, xvi. 19 —21.) He had an estate ; and, by skilful and diligent culture, it yielded him large crops, so that his affluence increased rapidly : at length, however, he found difficulty about storing his treasures, seeing he had no longer room for them. He therefore determined to build larger barns, and granaries ; and, having thus secured his abundance, to have done with the encumbrance of business, and to give himself up to ease and indulgence, in the liberal use of his riches. (Marg. Ref. k—n.) The character here drawn, is exactly that of a prudent worldly man, who rises from inferior circumstances to great affluence, by assiduous industry and good management; and then retires from business, to spend the latter part of his life according to his own inclinations. But there was no grateful regard to the bountiful providence of God, " who gave him power to " get wealth ; " no consideration of his accountableness for the use of it; (Notes, xvi. 1—13 ;) and no respect to the authority, commandment, favour, or glory of God. There was no proper sense of the instability of human affairs, the uncertainty of life, the vanity of earthly pleasure, the worth of his soul, or the importance of eternity; no thought of happiness to be found in communion with God, in peace of conscience, and the hope of glory ! But the man spake " within himself," as if " eating, drinking, and " being merry " had constituted the chief good of a rational creature; and as if it might be enjoyed here for ever. Neither did he express any regard to his neighbour : his wealth was his own, and he would hoard it for himself, and spend it on himself ; for if he had enquired how many poor persons were destitute of food and raiment, and in various ways needed relief; he might have found a far better way to dispose of his superfluity, and have enjoyed a far superior satisfaction, than what he proposed to himself.—' " What shall I do ? " Give it to the poor, that ' shouldst thou do.' Basil. (Marg. Ref. h, i. 33.)—The whole was the language of a selfish ungodly man, and was intended to expose men of this character, even when not chargeable with gross immorality. However, therefore, this man might glory, that " the might of his hand " had gotten him this wealth," and deem himself wise and happy ; or however he might be envied, respected, or commended by his neighbours ; he was in the judgment of God " a fool," and as such God addressed him. He had foolishly reckoned on many years to come, when he had not a single day to live ! He had provided a large superfluity for a future continuance on earth, which was never to be granted him ; but he had made no provision

for the world to come, into which he was immediately to pass, and in which he was to exist to eternity ! For, on that very " night his soul was required of him," and he must give an account of his ungodliness, selfishness, and covetousness ; " and then whose would those things be, " which he had provided," to the neglect of his soul, and to his everlasting ruin? He could not tell into whose hands his wealth would pass : nor would it be any comfort to him, even for his children or friends to possess it, when he was torn from all which he loved and idolized, and plunged into the pit of destruction; and perhaps they too were preparing by it for the same dreadful end. (Marg. and Marg. Ref. o—q.—Notes, xvi. 22—31. Ps. xxxix. 6. Matt. xvi. 24—28. P. O. 21—28.)—To this parable our Lord added, that " so is every one, who layeth up trea- " sure for himself, and is not rich towards God." All those persons " lay up treasure for themselves," who seek wealth either for its own sake, or for the influence and consequence which it bestows, or to spend in the pride of life and luxurious indulgence ; or in order to aggrandise their families; but who are not rich in faith, in wisdom, and grace, in good works, and a heavenly treasure. (Notes, 22—34, vv. 33, 34. Jam. i. 9—11. ii. 5—7.) Every man of this character is in God's account " a fool ;" his life is vanity and vexation ; his success an empty bubble, or a destructive delusion ; and his end most miserable.

Covetousness. (15) Της πλεονεξιας. See on Mark vii. 22.—A man's life, &c.] Ουκ εν τω περισσευειν τινι η ζωη αυτη εκ των υπαρχοντων αυτω. " Not in the abounding to any " one, is his life of those things which he possesses." Even when any man acquires abundance, his life is not preserved, and made comfortable or useful, or the true life of his soul promoted by his possessions. These blessings must be conveyed to the rich man, in the same way, and from the same sources, as to the poor man, if he at all enjoy them.—Brought forth plentifully. (16) Ευφορησεν. Here only N. T. Ευ, bene, et φερω.—He thought. (17) Διελογιζετο. " He reasoned with himself."—Be merry. (19) Ευφραινω, xv. 23, 24. 29. 32. xvi. 19. Acts ii. 26. vii. 41. Rom. xv. 10. Rev. xviii. 20.—Ex ευ, bene, et φρην, mens.— Thou fool. (20) Αφρον, xi. 40. Rom. ii. 20. 1 Cor. xv. 36. 2 Cor. xi. 16. 19. xii. 6. Eph. v. 17. 1 Pet. ii. 15.—Ex a priv. et φρην, mens. (Notes, Jer. xvii. 11. Matt. v. 21, 22.) —Shall be required.] Απαιτωσιν.—See on vi. 30.—" Shall " they require of thee." The angels, commissioned by God for that purpose.—Who layeth up treasure. (21) 'Ο θησαυριζων. Matt. vi. 19. Rom. ii. 5. 1 Cor. xvi. 2. 2 Cor. xii. 14. Jam. v. 3. 2 Pet. iii. 7. Θησαυρος, 34.—Is not rich.] Μη ... πλωτων. Rom. x. 12. 2 Cor. viii. 9. 1 Tim. vi. 9. 18. Rev. iii. 17, 18.

V. 22—34. (Marg. Ref. t—i.—Notes, Matt. vi. 24— 34.)—It is probable, that our Lord frequently repeated the

s e 3

thing which is least, `why take ye thought for the rest?

27 Consider " the lilies how they grow: they toil not, they spin not; and yet I say unto you, 'That Solomon in all his glory was not arrayed like one of these.

28 If then God so clothe the grass, 'which is to-day in the field, and to-morrow is cast into the oven; how much more will he clothe you, 'O ye of little faith?

29 And 'seek not ye what ye shall eat, or what ye shall drink, neither 'be ye of doubtful mind.

30 For 'all these things do the nations of the world seek after; and 'your Father knoweth that ye have need of these things.

31 But 'rather seek ye the kingdom of God; and all these things shall be added unto you.

32 Fear not, 'little flock; for 'it is your Father's good pleasure to give you " the kingdom.

33 " Sell that ye have, and give alms; 'provide yourselves bags which wax not old, a treasure in the heavens that faileth not, where no thief approacheth, neither moth corrupteth.

34 For 'where your treasure is, there will your heart be also.

35 ¶ Let 'your loins be girded about, and 'your lights burning;

36 And ye yourselves like unto 'men that wait for their lord, when he will 'return from the wedding; that " when he cometh and knocketh, they may open unto him immediately.

37 " Blessed are those servants whom the Lord, when he cometh, shall find watching: verily I say unto you, 'That

---

following instructions: and he here assigns the reason, why he so often inculcated them'; namely, because of the folly and fatal consequences of covetousness in all its forms, and the excessive proneness of the human heart to it, in one or another of them. The disciples were poor, and might think themselves unconcerned in the parable: not considering that the desire of riches, even when the pursuit of them is unsuccessful, is equally criminal, with the covetous acquisition and possession of them.—Some variation from the passage referred to may be noted. "If " ye be not able to do that which is least, &c." (26) Whence we may infer, that the preceding question (25) was proverbial, and was used to shew the inefficacy of being careful about those things, which are not at all in our power. If a man were ever so solicitous about it, he " could not add a cubit to his stature:" why then should men be anxious about other matters, of far greater importance to their comfort and happiness, but which are unconnected with their present duty? For these also would be ordered by the same unerring hand of God, as he saw best, without their being able in the least to alter his appointments. Rich Zaccheus, probably, would have given a large sum to have " added a cubit to his stature." (xix. 3.)—" Fear not, little flock, it is your Father's good " pleasure to give you the kingdom." (32) His disciples are a small flock of harmless defenceless sheep, in the midst of the vast multitudes of this wicked world; but they are dear to him, who has purchased them, and brought them back to his fold: and, as " their Father in-" tends to give them the kingdom" of heavenly glory and felicity, and greatly delights in doing this; so he will certainly provide for them, during their passage through this world to it. They ought therefore to dismiss their fears, and to cast all their cares upon him. 'It is a foolish thing, ' not to look for small things at his hands, who freely giveth us the greatest things.' Beza. (Notes, Ps. lxxxiv.

11, 12. Rom. viii. 32—34.) Instead of burdening themselves in endeavours to accumulate wealth, Christ's disciples ought, when properly called to it, to part with their possessions, and distribute to their needy brethren. When this is done in faith and love, it ensures to them a treasure, of which God himself is the Guardian. In this manner they are secured from putting their " money into " a bag with holes," or into one liable to wear out: (which is an apt emblem of the uncertainty of all earthly possessions :) for their treasure is laid up in heaven, out of the reach of change or danger; and their hearts also become more and more heavenly.—Probably, this instruction influenced the primitive converts, after the day of Pentecost, to sell their estates for the support of their poor brethren. (Marg. Ref. k—p.—Notes, 15—21. xix. 1—10, v. 8. Matt. xix. 16—22, v. 21. Acts iv. 32—35. Jam. v. 1—6.)

Therefore. (22) Δια τυτο. " Because of this:" " for " this reason."—Take no thought.] Μη μεριμνατε. See on Matt. vi. 25.—Be ye of doubtful mind. (29) Μετεωριζεσθε. Here only N. T. The word seems to be taken from the irregular motion of meteors in the air, or the clouds as driven by the winds: thus men's minds are hurried about with various cares and anxieties, by the changing events of life, so long as they want to contrive and manage for themselves, and have not learned to trust God in the path of duty. (Note, 2 Pet. ii. 17.)—That faileth not. (33) Ανεκλειπτον. Here only N. T. Ex ανα, εκ, et λειπω, deficio.

V. 35—46. (Notes, Matt. xxiv. 42—51.) Our Lord here addressed his disciples in respect of diligent attention to their proper work; as he before had done about moderation, indifference, and confidence in God, as to their subsistence. It was the custom of servants, in those days, to gird up their long loose garments by a girdle round their loins, that they might attend to their work with less encumbrance. Thus the disciples were reminded to be

he shall gird himself, and make them to sit down to meat, and will come forth and serve them.

38 And if he shall come ° in the second watch, or come in the third watch, and find *them* so, blessed are those servants.

39 And ° this know, that if the good man of the house had known what hour the thief would come, he would have watched, and not have suffered his house to be broken through.

40 Be ° ye therefore ready also: for the Son of man cometh at an hour when ye think not.

41 Then Peter said unto him, ° Lord, speakest thou this parable unto us, or even to all?

42 And the Lord said, ° Who then is that faithful and wise ° steward, whom *his* lord shall make ° ruler over his household, ° to give *them their* portion of meat ° in due season?

43 Blessed *is* that servant, ° whom his lord when he cometh shall find so doing.

44 Of a truth I say unto you, ° That he will make him ruler over all that he hath.

45 But ° and if that servant say in his heart, My lord delayeth his coming; and shall begin ° to beat the menservants and maidens, ° and to eat and drink, and to be drunken;

46 The ° lord of that servant will come in a day when he looketh not for him, and at an hour when he is not aware, and will ° cut him in sunder, ° and will appoint him his portion with ° the unbelievers.

47 And that servant which ° knew his lord's will, and prepared not himself, neither did according to ° his will, ° shall be beaten with many stripes.

48 But he that ° knew not, and did commit things worthy of stripes, shall be beaten with few *stripes*. ° For unto whomsoever much is given, of him shall be much required; and to whom men have committed much, of him they will ask the more.

---

prepared for active service, by a vigilant frame of mind; and by laying aside *every* needless worldly engagement, and avoiding improper indulgences; as well as strengthened for it by the habitual exercise of faith, hope, and love. (*Marg. Ref.* q.—*Note*, 1 *Pet.* i. 13—16.) And as servants, during the night, when they were waiting for their master's return home, or engaged in any work, kept their " lights burning;" so the disciples were directed to keep the instructions of Christ before them, to make an open profession of his truth, and to hold out the light of a good conversation. (*Marg. Ref.* r.—*Notes, Matt.* v. 13 —16. *Phil.* ii. 14—18.)—Weddings were then generally celebrated at night, and the return of the guests might be uncertain: the servants, therefore, when waiting for their master, must watch, that they might open to him without delay: and by this simile our Lord might allude to his own ascension to heaven, his coming to call his people to him by death, and his return to judge the world; for which the disciples were continually to hold themselves in readiness. (*Marg. Ref.* s—u.—*Notes, Matt.* xxv. 1—13. *Mark* xiii. 33—37.)—To induce them to this constant habitual preparation by the vigilant and diligent performance of their present work, in their several places, he further speaks in language peculiarly suited to excite attention and interest, on the blessedness of those servants whom he should " find " watching," and the danger of being found unprepared .r misemployed. In respect of the former, he says, that " the Lord will gird himself, and make them sit down to " meat, and will come forth and serve them:" that is, the Redeemer, " the Lord of glory," and the " Lord of all," will graciously condescend to employ all his power and au-

thority, in advancing their honour and felicity; in proportion as they have simply devoted all their ability to promote his glory, and do his will. (*Marg. Ref.* x—b.) —In answer to Peter's enquiry, whether they only, or all his disciples, were concerned in these exhortations, promises, and warnings; our Lord intimated, that though the apostles and other ministers, who had authority in his church, were primarily intended, yet that others also were included, according to the different situations and services to which they were called. (*Marg. Ref.* c—o.—*Notes*, xxi. 34—36. *Mark* xiii. 33—37.)—*Unbelievers.* (46) " Hypocrites," in Matthew. Hypocrites are concealed *infidels*, and they will have their portion among avowed infidels.

Girded about. (35) Περιζωσμεναι. 37. xvii. 8. *Acts* xii. 8. *Eph.* vi. 14. *Rev.* i. 13. xv. 6.—*He will return.* (36) Αναλυσει. *Phil.* i. 23. Not elsewhere *N. T.* Αναλυσις, 2 *Tim.* iv. 6.—*Make ... to sit down to meat.* (37) Ανακλινει. See on ix. 14, 15.—*Steward.* (42) Οικονομος, xvi. 1. 3. 8. *Rom.* xvi. 23. 1 *Cor.* iv. 1, 2. *Gal.* iv. 2. *Tit.* i. 7. 1 *Pet.* iv. 10.—*Portion of meat.*] Σιτομετριον. Here only *N. T.*—Σιτομετρεω. *Gen.* xlvii. 12. Sept. Εχ σιτου, *frumentum*, et μετρον, *mensura.*—*Cut him asunder.* (46) Διχοτομημσοι. See on *Matt.* xxiv. 51.

V. 47, 48. Our Lord here further shewed, that his ministers, or professed disciples, would not only be severely punished for gross enormities, but also for *neglecting* or improperly performing their duty; and in proportion to the information afforded them, and the knowledge of their Lord's will which they had acquired. The servant, who knew what his Lord commanded him to do, and yet did not prepare himself for his work, and so did not duly per-

49 ¶ I am *come to send fire on the earth, ʸ and what will I if it be already kindled?

50 But ᶻ I have a baptism to be baptized with : ᵃ and how am I ᵇ straitened till it be accomplished!

51 Suppose ᵇ ye that I am come to give peace on earth? I tell you, Nay; but rather division:

*Or, pained.　　b 49. Zech. xi. 7, 8. 10, 11. 14. Matt. x. 34—36. xxiv. 7—10.

52 For from henceforth ᶜ there shall be five in one house divided, three against two, and two against three.

53 The father shall be divided against the son, ᵈ and the son against the father; the mother against the daughter, and the daughter against the mother; the mother-in-law against her daughter-in-law, and the daughter-in-law against her mother-in-law.

form it, would be severely punished; as servants were when scourged with many stripes: but he who had not received such explicit instructions, or had not attained to such distinct knowledge of his master's will, and was remiss and negligent in his work, would indeed be adjudged deserving of punishment, but not dealt with in so rigorous a manner. This may be considered as a general rule of the Lord's dealing with all his rational creatures. No man is left in such absolute ignorance, except by his own fault, as not to do many things which he knows to be wrong, and to neglect many things which he knows to be right: therefore all are inexcusable, and liable to condemnation and punishment, if they continue impenitent. But in proportion to the degree in which they have the means of instruction, and are actually acquainted with the will of God; their disobedience becomes more aggravated, more direct and deliberate rebellion, and their punishment will be proportionably more severe. (Notes, Rom. ii. 12—16.) Thus likewise will the Lord dispense correction to his offending children, in proportion as they have sinned against light and conviction, or the contrary. For as men expect a proportional return from them, to whose stewardship they have committed much: so will God call every man to account for the use of all the talents entrusted to him; and if he has been unfaithful in the midst of many advantages, he will inflict on him the heavier vengeance. (Marg. Ref. —Notes, xvi. 1—13. xix. 11—27. Matt. xiii. 12. xxv. 14—30. Mark iv. 23—25. Jam. iv. 13—17.) 'This being one 'grand difference betwixt the pastors of the church, and 'other Christians, they must expect a severer punishment, 'as sinning against greater evidence, and knowledge of 'their duty; for "to whom much is given, of them will '"much be required."' Whitby.

Shall be beaten.] Δαρησεται. Matt. xxi. 35. John xviii. 23. Acts v. 40. 1 Cor. ix. 26. 2 Cor. xi. 20.

V. 49—53. The introduction of the gospel would in some respects resemble the kindling of a fire, which should occasion very destructive and wide-spreading desolations. Not that this is the tendency of Christianity, which is most pure, peaceable, and loving: but it would be the effect of the opposition raised against it, by the pride and lusts of men; and of the perversions which many would make of it. Hence would arise furious persecutions, bitter contentions, and multiplied divisions, usurpations, and oppressions: and these things, with the resistance made to them, producing fierce and bloody wars, would diffuse manifold calamities and evils all over the earth. (Marg. Ref. c, d.—Notes, Mic. vii. 5—7. Matt. x. 34—36.)—Infidels have confidently alledged these consequences of the promulgation of Christianity, as so many objections to its divine original;

wilfully forgetting that " thus it was written, and thus it " must be." The prediction of these effects, which no philosophizing or speculative observer would ever have expected from so benign a religion, forms an additional demonstration that it is from God: and every man, who is experimentally acquainted with the human heart, will readily account for them, without charging the least blame on the gospel; nay, he will see, that they are occasioned by its excellency, and must follow from it, so long as men continue proud, carnal, selfish, and alienated from God.— " kindled?"—' What would I, but that it were kindled.' Campbell. (Marg. Ref. x. y.) It may, however, refer to the malignant opposition of the Scribes and Pharisees, and the divisions and contests which our Lord's ministry had already excited: yet, though the fire was indeed already kindled, did he regret that he had been so open in his instructions and sharp in his reproofs? Did they suppose that he was disappointed or disconcerted? Did they imagine that he meant to desist? This was by no means the case: on the contrary, he earnestly desired that this fire should be more completely kindled, by the full and extensive publication of his gospel. But before that could take place, " He had a baptism to be baptized with," far different from that " of water and of the Holy Spirit," by which he had been admitted to the exercise of his prophetical office: for he must endure the most extreme sufferings, shed his blood on the cross, and pour out his soul unto death, before he could enter upon his office within the veil, as the High Priest of his church, and be put in full possession of the mediatorial throne. (Marg. and Marg. Ref. z, a.—Notes, Matt. xx. 20—23.) " But how was he straitened, " till this was accomplished!" It did not consist with the plan laid down for the performance of this work, to preach the gospel more openly or extensively, till this baptism was completed: in the mean time he was exceedingly straitened and limited, in the exercise of his ardent love and zeal; and even longed for that awful and important crisis, which should make way for his exaltation, and the publication of his gospel to all nations, that God might be glorified in the salvation of an innumerable multitude of precious souls; in the same manner, as a pregnant woman desires the approach or increase of her pangs, in expectation of deliverance and of being made a joyful mother. (Notes, Is. liii. 11, 12. John xvi. 16—22. Heb. xii. 2, 3.)

Be... kindled. (49) Ανηφϑη. Acts xxviii. 2. Jam. iii. 5. Not elsewhere N. T.—Straitened. (50) Συνεχομαι. iv. 38. viii. 37. 45. xix. 43. xxii. 63. Acts xviii. 5. xxviii. 8. 2 Cor. v. 14. Phil. i. 23.—Divided. (53) Διαμεμερισμενοι. See on xi. 17. Διαμερισμος, 51.

3 c 6

54 ¶ And he said also to the people, ' When ye see a cloud rise out of the west, straightway ye say, There cometh a shower ; and so it is.

55 And ' when *ye see* the south wind blow, ye say, There will be heat; and it cometh to pass.

56 *Ye* hypocrites, 'ye can discern the face of the sky, and of the earth ; but how is it ᵏ that ye do not discern this time ?

57 Yea, and ' why even of yourselves judge ye not what is right ?

58 When ᵏ thou goest with thine adversary to the magistrate, *as thou art* in the way, ' give diligence that thou mayest be delivered from him ; lest he hale thee to the judge, ᵐ and the judge deliver thee to the officer, and the offi- cer cast thee ⁿ into prison.

59 I tell thee, ° thou shalt not de- part thence, till thou hast paid the very last ° mite.

Marginal references (left):
c 1 Kings xviii. 44, 45. Matt. xvi. 2.
f Job xxxvii. 17
g 1 Chr. xii. 32. Matt. xi.25. xvi. 3. xxiv. 32, 33. h xii. 42—44.Dan. ix. 24—26. Hag. ii. 7. Mal. iii. 1. iv. 2. Acts iii. 24 —26. Gal. iv. 4.

Marginal references (right):
i Deut. xxxii. 29. Matt. xv 10— 14. xxi. 31, 32. Acts ii. 40. xiii. 26—38.
k Prov. xxv. 8, 9. Matt. v. 24—26. xviii. 31, 32. Gen. xxxii. 3—28.
l 1 Sam. xxv.18— 34. Job xxii. 21. xxiii.3, Ps.xxxii. 6. Prov. vi. 1—5. Is.lv. 6. 2Cor. vi. 2.Heb.iii. 7—13. m xiii. 26—28. Job xxxvi. 17, 18. Ps. i. 22.
n Matt. xviii. 34. 1 Pet. iii. 19. Rev. xx. 7.
o xvi. 26. Matt. xviii. 34. xxv. 41— 46. 2 Thes. i. 8. marg.

V. 54—57. (*Marg. Ref.* e—h.—*Notes, Matt.* xvi. 1—4. *Mark* viii. 10—13.) When the people saw a cloud rise in the west, from the Mediterranean sea, they had learned by constant observation to expect copious showers ; and a south-wind from off the sultry deserts was deemed a sure prognostick of heat. In such matters they were sagacious : but the exact accomplishment of types and prophecies, in the doctrine, miracles, and character of Christ, and in the time and circumstances of his appearance, did not suffice to convince them that he was their promised Messiah ! In this, their hypocritical scribes and teachers were most faulty ; and, being blinded by their carnal prejudices, they used their whole influence to mislead the people. Yet, as the case was so very evident, why did not the people see with their own eyes, and judge for themselves what was right, or decide impartially and justly between him and his mali- cious opponents ? (*Marg. Ref.* i.—*Note, Acts* ii. 37—40.)

A shower. (54) Ομβρος. Here only *N. T.*—*Deut.* xxxii. 2. *Sept.*—*Heat.* (55) Καυσων. *Matt.* xx. 12.—*Discern.* (56) Δοκιμαζω. xiv. 19. *Rom.* i. 28. ii. 18. xii. 2. xiv. 22. 1 *Cor.* iii. 13. xi. 28. xvi. 3. *Phil.* i. 10, et al. ' *Proprie est metallo- rum, quæ probantur et explorantur per ignem, an sint bona et pura.* 1 *Pet.* i. 7.' Schleusner.—*Right.* (57) Το δικαιον. " That which is just."

V. 58, 59. This passage, as it is here connected, im- plied a warning to the Jews, and their priests, scribes, and rulers to cease from their opposition to Christ, and to wel- come him as their Prince and Saviour, before it were too late ; otherwise terrible and durable miseries would soon come upon them : but it also inculcated those instructions to individuals, which have been already considered. (*Marg. Ref.*—*Notes, Prov.* vi. 1—5. xxv. 8—10. *Matt.* v. 25, 26.)

Adversary. (58) Αντιδικω. See on *Matt.* v. 25.—*Dili- gence.*] Εργασιαν. *Acts* xvi. 16. xix. 24, 25. *Eph.* iv. 19. *Ab εργον, opus.*—*Be delivered.*] Απηλλαχθαι. *Acts* xix. 12. *Heb.* ii. 15. Not elsewhere *N. T.* (Διαλλαγηθι, *Matt.* v. 24.) It seems to imply deliverance from an enemy by paci- fying him and being reconciled. Ex αττο et αλαττω, *muto.*— *He hale.*] Κατασυρη. Here only *N. T.* Ex κατα et συρω, *traho.* —*The officer.*] Πρακτορι. *Lictori.* Here only *N. T.*—*Mite.* (59) Λεπτον xxi. 2. *Mark* xii. 42. Not elsewhere *N. T.*

PRACTICAL OBSERVATIONS

V. 1—12.

Increasing popularity, and the earnest and diligent at- tendance of multitudes, must not induce ministers to be less plain and faithful in their addresses. This could only

serve to multiply hypocrites ; for even amidst " innumerable " multitudes " of hearers, there is generally but a " little " flock " of true disciples.—All who attend in any degree to religion, need repeated and earnest warnings, " first of " all to beware of hypocrisy : " but they who are most deeply infected with this leaven will be most ready to take offence. Indeed the plainest warnings seldom have a salu- tary effect on those, who are confirmed in hypocrisy ; but they tend to prevent others from venturing on the same destructive course : for those who are under concern about their souls, but not established in the faith, are in various ways tempted to it. Yet, while it assumes many specious appearances, and promises great advantages, it is a most foolish, as well as hateful sin : it can only hide for a mo- ment, what must at length be made known to all ; and it confers a temporary reputation, but leads to " everlasting " shame and contempt." Let us then continually think of that day, when our most secret actions, words, thoughts, and motives, will be· proclaimed before men and angels ; that we may be far more careful to approve our inmost purposes and our most retired conduct, to a heart-search- ing God, than to obtain the good opinion of our fellow- servants.—But if we are the " friends " of Christ, we must also be open and avowed in our religion, and on our guard against the fear of men : were we sure that our enemies would prevail as much as possible, we know that they could only " kill the body : " and after the transient pain occasioned by their cruel hatred, we should be for ever beyond their reach : whereas, should their terror induce us to incur the righteous displeasure of God, we know, that " after he hath killed, he hath power to cast into hell." If we are true believers, we are perfectly safe from every effect of man's enmity, which can prove eventually hurt- ful : and, while we realize the superintending providence of God over the meanest animal, we may be sure, that " even the very hairs of our head are all numbered." Let us then boldly confess Christ before men, in joyful hope of being acknowledged by him before the angels of God ; while they who have denied him for fear of reproach or persecution, will be rejected, and left under the condem- nation to everlasting misery.—But let no trembling peni- tent, who in an unguarded hour has spoken " a word against " the Son of man," doubt of obtaining forgiveness : for this is far different from that determined enmity, which dictates the blasphemy against the Holy Spirit, and which shall never be forgiven, because it will never be repented of. And let no one, who is suffering for Christ's sake, or

3 c 7

called upon to speak in his name amidst his enemies, fear lest he should not by his " Holy Spirit teach him in the " same hour, what he ought to say;" for " they who " trust in him shall never be confounded." (P. O. Matt. x. 16—33. xii. 31—37. Notes, Heb. vi. 4—8. x. 26—34.)

V. 13—21.

Alas! most men are too much immersed in thoughts and contrivances about the world, to value spiritual blessings: and many, even while hearing the gospel, are so distracted in their thoughts about their inheritances, that they would be ready to interrupt the preachers, if they could by their counsel or influence promote their own secular interest! But, as Christ would not attend to these *inferior* concerns, his ministers should avoid similar interruptions to their grand concern; and leave it to others to be " judges and dividers " over the people.—Every opportunity, however, should be embraced of warning men to " take heed and beware of covetousness;" by which almost all men are, one way or other, in some degree seduced. Every reflecting man's experience and observation may convince him of the inefficacy of riches, to promote even the comfort or continuance of this life: yet after all which the Lord has said upon this subject, how few are there among professed Christians, who do not desire to be rich, and to make their children rich! (P. O. Matt. xix. 23—30.) And many are apt to point out to them similar characters, with this in the parable, as models for their imitation, and as proper persons with whom to form connexions! Yet it is, as it were, said to one of them after another, " This night thy soul is required of thee," perhaps when they are saying within themselves, " Soul, " thou hast much goods laid up for many years; take " thine ease, eat, drink, and be merry." And what does it then avail, to have the publick informed, how many tens or hundreds of thousands they have left behind them, or how rich their heirs are made by their decease? (Note, Job xiv. 16—22.)—Indeed it often happens, that after men have spent their lives, without regard to God, to their neighbours, or their own souls, in order to enrich their families; they are even disappointed in this vain ambitiou, their riches are strangely dissipated, and their children reduced to dependence or poverty: for " man walketh " in a vain shew, he disquieteth himself in vain ; he heap- " eth up riches, and cannot tell who shall gather them." As therefore " every one, who layeth up treasure for him- " self," is thus foolish, guilty, and miserable; let us seek the true riches, that we may be approved by God himself as wise men, and made honourable and happy in his presence and in the eternal enjoyment of his favour.

V. 22—34.

If we are the disciples of Christ, and have learned to serve him in our secular employments, and in the use of our possessions, we should peculiarly watch against distracting cares and apprehensions. He who created our bodies, and sustains our lives, and who also feeds the ravens and adorns the lilies, will give us needful food and raiment : and if we have acquired a relish for spiritual pleasures, and know the value of " the beauty of holi- " ness " we shall not crave the luxuries and elegances of life. Yet we often need rebuking for " being of little faith;" and therefore " of a doubtful mind." But it becomes Christians to seek nobler blessings, than the nations of the earth who know not God : they should remember that " their Father knoweth that they have need of " food and raiment, and is both able and willing to bestow them ; and if we seek first the privileges and the righteousness of his kingdom, and desire its peace and prosperity, all other things will surely be added unto us. Indeed, the flock which the good Shepherd has purchased, and collected into his fold, and which he has taught to rely on his powerful and watchful care, to hear his voice, to love his ordinances, and copy his example, is but small; when compared with the vast multitudes around them, who resemble filthy swine, ravening wolves, subtle foxes, or venomous serpents : but they need not fear wanting any good thing, " for it is their Father's good pleasure to give them the " kingdom," and he will withhold no good things from them. (Notes, Matt. xi. 25—27. Eph. i. 9—12. 1 Thes. v. 4—11.) Let us then first examine, whether we belong to this " little flock," and have those dispositions which characterize it : let us also keep close under our Shepherd's care: and let us be thankful, that it was not the Lord's good pleasure to give us worldly treasures, and to leave us destitute of his grace. While others, therefore, are grasping after more and more of earthly, perishing vanities; Christians should excite one another to abound in love and good works : that, willingly expending what they have, in relieving the necessitous and promoting the cause of godliness, they may " provide themselves bags which wax not " old, a treasure in heaven that faileth not :" and this will gradually both enlarge their capacities of enjoyment, and ensure to them a gracious and most glorious recompence. (Matt. vi. P. O. 19—34.)

V. 35—48.

While we cast all our care upon God, in respect of events and consequences, we cannot be too attentive to our duty. We are the servants of Christ, whose coming to remove us by death, or to judge the world, may be very soon, or very sudden : but if " our loins be girded and our " lights burning," we shall have no more reason to dread the summons, than a child has to be alarmed at the arrival of a messenger, who is sent to convey him home to his tender parents: nay, words can never express the delight,

THERE were present at that season some that told him of [a] the Galileans, whose blood Pilate had [b] mingled with their sacrifices.

2 And Jesus answering said unto them, 'Suppose ye that these Galileans [c] were sinners above all the Galileans, because they suffered such things?

3 I tell you, Nay: but, [d] except ye repent, [e] ye shall all likewise perish.

[a] Acts v. 37.
[b] Lam. ii. 20. Ez. ix. 5—7. 1 Pet. iv. 17, 18.
[c] 4. Job xxii. 5—16. John ix. 2.
[d] 5. xxiv. 47. Matt. iii. 2, 10—12. Acts ii. 38—40. iii. 19.
[e] xlix. 42—44. xxi. 22—24. xxiii. 26—30.
Matt. xii. 45. xxii. 7. xxiii. 35—38. xxiv. 21—29.

---

with which our gracious Lord will welcome and bless his faithful servants. If then we are habitually watching and ready, what does it signify to us personally, whether he " come at the second or the third watch ? " For " blessed " are those servants, who ... are found so doing." But as robbers assault the house, when the family has least expectation of them, so death generally surprises a man when he is least thinking of it. We should therefore never remit our watch, to pursue vain diversions, worldly interests, or sensual indulgences; lest our Lord should come at that very time. (Note, Rom. xiii. 11—14.) This indeed applies to every man, but more especially to the ministers of the gospel. They are " the stewards of God's myste- " rie.," and rulers of his household, to " give every one " his portion in due season," and " rightly to divide the " word of truth." Happy then is that faithful and wise servant who delights in his work, and gives himself continually to it; for " his Lord, when he cometh, will make " him ruler over all that he hath : " and how paltry are all other preferments, when compared with " this crown of " glory that fadeth not away ! " (Note, 1 Pet. v. 1—4.) But woe to infidels, and ungodly men, who appear in the garb of ministers! They say in their hearts, " My Lord " delayeth his coming," and so they are emboldened to persecute, oppress, and fleece their brethren, and to indulge in riot and licentiousness : but they will soon be surprised in the midst of their successful impiety, and torn away from all their abused preferments and dignities, " in a " day when they think not of it; " and, they will have their portion with the unbelievers. Those, however, who were thus ungodly, not only with the Bible in their hands, but with the gospel in their mouths; and who knew their Lord's will accurately, and could instruct others in it, yet never prepared themselves, or set about obeying it; will be punished in the most tremendous manner. Indeed the condemnation of heathens, and others who have had but few advantages for knowing the will of God, will be very light, compared with that of wicked professors of Christianity, and of ungodly ministers : " For unto whomsoever " much is given, of him shall much be required." May the Lord then give us grace, to improve our many advantages to the glory of his name ! (Note and P. O. Is. lvi. 9—12. P. O. Matt. xxiv. 36—51)

V. 49—59.

We ought not to be greatly disconcerted at the undesirable effects, occasioned by the preaching of the gospel; or even by the abuse which wicked men make of it. The blessed Jesus persevered in his work, though he saw " the " fire already kindled," and foresaw how far it would communicate its flames: nay, he even longed for the hour of his extremest sufferings, that he might possess the " joy " set before him," and send the gospel through the nations of the earth. We should therefore be bold and zealous in promoting his truth, without shrinking, from fear of con-

VOL. V.

sequences to ourselves or others: for, though afflictions must be endured, divisions excited, and " a man's foes be " those of his own household; " yet sinners will be converted, and God will be glorified.—But if men were as wise for their souls, as most of them are in their temporal concerns, they would know " the signs of the times " and " the day of their visitation : " and though false teachers might attempt to prejudice or mislead them ; they would " even of themselves discern what was right" and just and true, suitable to their wants and conducive to their salvation.—If any man therefore is convinced, that God has a controversy with him concerning his sins; let him without delay seek to him, as " God in Christ, reconciling the " world to himself : " for if death come, before his peace be made with God, his soul will be cast into the prison of hell ; and, as he will never be able to pay his mighty debt, so he must abide as an enemy, and hater, and blasphemer of God, in that doleful place of torment, to all eternity. (P. O. Matt. xviii. 23—35.)

NOTES.

CHAP. XIII. V. 1—3. The Galileans, here mentioned, are supposed to have been concerned in the insurrection made by Judas of Galilee, (Acts v. 37,) who opposed paying tribute to Cæsar, and submitting to the Roman authority. (Notes, xxiii. 1—5. Matt. xxii. 15—22.) When, therefore, they were come to Jerusalem to worship, and were presenting their oblations in the court of the temple ; Pilate sent a company of soldiers, who slew them, and " mingled their blood with their sacrifices." Those, who brought this report to Christ seem to have concluded, that these men were guilty of some dreadful crimes, concealed from men, but thus visited by an awful judgment from God; and that they were far greater sinners, than their countrymen who escaped the destruction : (Notes, John ix. 1—3. Acts xxviii. 3—6:) but our Lord repressed this rash and proud decision on their state and character ; and assured the whole company, that except they repented of their sins, they too would fall under the righteous indignation of God, and perish " in like manner." This is generally supposed to refer to the destruction of Jerusalem, and the slaughter of the Jews by the Romans, for making insurrections against the government: and especially to the havock made among them, in the courts of the temple, while they were offering their sacrifices ; insomuch that the altar was sprinkled with their blood, and a multitude of dead bodies lay round about it. (Marg. Ref.—Notes, Ez. ix. 5—7. 1 Pet. iv. 17—19.)—This shews, that those who brought sacrifices were admitted into the inner court. (Notes, Lev. i. 5—9. 2 Chr. xxiii. 3—10, v. 6.)—' Perhaps ' this story of the Galileans might now be mentioned unto ' Christ, with the design of leading him into a snare, whether ' he would justify, or condemn, the persons that were slain.' Doddridge.

Likewise. (3) 'Ωσαυτως. ' Eodem modo, itidem. Ex

3 D

4 Or those eighteen upon whom the tower 'in Siloam 'fell, and slew them, think ye that they were °sinners above all men that dwelt in Jerusalem?

5 I tell you, Nay: but, ᵇ except ye repent, ye shall all likewise perish.

6 ¶ He spake also this parable: A certain *man* had a ¹fig-tree planted in his vineyard: ᵏ and he came and sought fruit thereon, and found none.

7 Then said he unto the dresser of his vineyard, Behold, these ¹ three years I come seeking fruit on this fig-tree, and find none: ᵐ cut it down; ⁿ why cumbereth it the ground?

8 And he answering said unto him, °Lord, let it alone this year also, till I shall dig about it, and dung *it:*

9 And if it bear fruit, *well;* and ᵖif not, *then* after that thou shalt cut it down.

10 ¶ And ᵠhe was teaching in one of the synagogues on the sabbath:

11 And behold, there was a woman, ʳ which had ˢa spirit of infirmity ᵗeighteen years, and was ᵘbowed together, and could in no wise lift up *herself.*

12 And when Jesus saw her, he ᵛ called *her to him,* and said unto her, ʷ Woman, thou art ˣ loosed from thine infirmity.

' ὡς, *sicut,* et αυτος, *ipse.'* Schleusner. *Matt.* xx. 5. xxi. 30. 36. xxv. 17. 'Ομοιως, 5.

V. 4, 5. Our Lord took occasion to mention another event, doubtless well known to his hearers, but of which there is no account in history, concerning eighteen persons who were slain by the falling of a tower in Siloam. (*Marg. Ref.* f, g.) These were supposed to have been greater sinners than any other inhabitants of Jerusalem; because they seemed to be singled out, by the hand of God himself, for immediate punishment. But Christ assured them that this was not the case; and he renewed his declaration, that except his auditors repented, they would " all like- " wise perish."—This is commonly supposed to refer to the destruction of the Jews in great multitudes, by the casting down of the walls and towers of Jerusalem, when the city was taken: but the sudden and dreadful slaughter of the Jews at that time, seems in general intended; as the immediate hand of God was gone forth against them. —It is observable, that our Lord determines nothing, concerning the character and state of the persons in question: they were sinners, but not greater sinners than many others. (*Note, Num.* xxvii. 1—4.)—No doubt he also intended to warn all men, in every age, that final and eternal ruin would certainly overtake all the impenitent, to whatever nation, society, or party they belonged. Sinners. (4) " Debtors." *Marg.* Οφιλεται. *Notes,* vii. 40—43. xi. 1—4, *v.* 4. *Matt.* vi. 12.

V. 6—9. (*Notes, Is.* v. 1—7. *Matt.* xxi. 17—20. 33— 44.) This parable seems to have been added to enforce the preceding warning. A fig-tree planted in a vineyard, would have every advantage of culture. In three years' time the young trees were expected to bear: (*Note, Lev.* xix. 23—25:) but the owner of this tree is represented, as coming three subsequent years to seek fruit, and as not finding any. It might therefore be concluded to be a barren tree, not fit to occupy the room, or appropriate the nourishment and culture, which might be more profitably employed.—" The dresser of the vineyard," however, intreated that it might be spared for one more year; during which space he would use further means for rendering it fruitful: and then perhaps it would produce fruit, but otherwise it ought to be cut down.—The Jewish nation seems to have been primarily intended: the Lord had long borne with

their unfruitfulness amidst manifold advantages, and the time of his vengeance approached. They would, however, be spared a little longer; that the apostles and preachers of the gospel might make another vigorous and zealous effort to bring them to repentance, faith, and holiness: and if this failed, they must be given up to ruin. For Jerusalem would be destroyed, the ceremonial worship terminated, and the unbelieving Jews cast out of the church, to make way for the calling of the Gentiles.—The parable, however, is equally applicable to the case of all those individuals, who continue unfruitful under the means of grace: though spared from time to time, through the long-suffering of the Lord, they will at length be cut down by death, and cast into hell, " except they repent" and " bring forth fruits " meet for repentance."—Some expositors speak, as if Christ himself was represented by " the dresser of the vineyard;" and indeed the long-suffering of God with sinners is the effect of his mediation: yet he seems rather to be the Owner of the vineyard, who sentences the barren trees to be cut down. Besides, his intercession is never finally in vain: (*Note, John* xvii. 6—10, *v.* 9:) and the language used may describe the fervent prayers and zealous labours of faithful ministers, who earnestly desire to prevent the ruin of the people. (*Marg. Ref.—Notes, Jer.* xiv. 10—22. xv. 1. *Ez.* xiv. 13—21. *Matt.* iii. 7—10.)

The dresser of his vineyard. (7) Τον αμπελουργον. Here only N. T. Εx αμπελος, *vitis,* et εργον, *labor, opus.—Cumbereth.*] Καθαρχει. ' *Quorsum terram inutiliter occupat; seu* ' *partem terræ, quam occupat, inutilem reddit.'* Schleusner. (Εx κατα, et αργεω, *cesso.) Rom.* iii. 31. vii. 2. 1 *Cor.* i. 28. ii. 6. vi. 13. xiii. 8. 10, 11. xv. 24. 2 *Cor.* iii. 14. *Gal.* iii. 17. *Eph.* ii. 15. 2 *Tim.* i. 10.—*Dung it.* (8) Βαλω κοπριαν. xiv. 35. Not elsewhere N. T.—*If it bear fruit.* (9) Καν... ποιηση καρπον. It is an elliptical form of speaking; and implies, that if it then bare fruit, it would be preserved; but not otherwise. There is nothing for " *well"* in the Greek.

V. 10—17. This woman must have attended the worship of God with great difficulty; as she was so bowed together, that she " could in no wise lift up herself," but was forced to go almost double. The calamity, under which she had so long laboured, would in general have been considered as a very remarkable disease, arising from

3 D 2

13 And ᵃ he laid his hands on her: ᵇ and immediately she was made straight, and glorified God.

14 And ᵃ the ruler of the synagogue answered ᵇ with indignation, because that Jesus had healed on the sabbath-day, and said unto the people, ᶜ There are six days in which men ought to work: in them therefore come and be healed, ᵈ and not on the sabbath-day.

15 The Lord then answered him, and said, ᵉ Thou hypocrite, ᶠ doth not each one of you on the sabbath loose his ox or his ass from the stall, and lead him away to watering?

16 And ought not this woman, ᵍ being a daughter of Abraham, ʰ whom Satan hath bound, lo, these eighteen years, ⁱ be loosed from this bond on the sabbath-day?

17 And when he had said these things, ᵏ all his adversaries were ashamed: ˡ and all the people rejoiced for all the glorious things that were done by him.

18 ¶ Then said he, ᵐ Unto what is ⁿ the kingdom of God like? and whereunto shall I resemble it?

19 It is ᵒ like a grain of mustard-seed, which a man took, and ᵖ cast into his garden; ᵩ and it grew, and waxed a great tree; ʳ and the fowls of the air lodged in the branches of it.

20 And again he said, Whereunto shall I liken the kingdom of God?

21 It is ˢ like leaven, which a woman took and hid in three measures of meal, ᵗ till the whole was leavened.

22 ¶ And he went ᵘ through the cities and villages teaching ˣ and journeying towards Jerusalem.

23 Then said one unto him, Lord, ʸ are there few that be saved? ᶻ And he said unto them,

24 ᵃ Strive to enter in at ᵇ the strait gate; ᶜ for many, I say unto you, will seek to enter in, and shall not be able.

25 When ᵈ once the Master of the house is risen up, and hath ᵉ shut to the door, and ye begin to stand without, and to knock at the door, saying, ᶠ Lord, Lord, open unto us; and he shall answer and say unto you, I know ᵍ you not whence ye are;

some known or unknown natural cause: but it was at that time *justly* ascribed to an evil spirit; so that in fact " Satan " had bound her eighteen years." (*Notes, Matt.* viii. 28, 29. *Mark* ix. 16—24.)—Our Lord, seeing her in this afflicted state, called her to him, and by his word, attended with the laying on of his hands, immediately restored her; and, being made straight, she glorified God before all, for this most desirable and unexpected deliverance. (*Note, Ps.* cxlvi. 8.) But the ruler of the synagogue, who evidently hated the doctrine, and envied the honour, of Christ, yet attempted to veil his enmity with the appearance of singular piety; told the people in anger, that they ought to come for healing on other days, and not on the holy rest of the sabbath: as if the woman had come to the synagogue on purpose for a cure; or as if a word and a touch, attended with so powerful and beneficent an effect, could break the sabbath! The malice and hypocrisy of the man were therefore evident, and our Lord severely rebuked him; shewing, that none, even of the Scribes and Pharisees, scrupled to water their cattle on the sabbath-day; though it was attended with some labour, and was necessary only to preserve the animals from the uneasiness of a day's thirst, or the owner from some temporal loss which might result from it: and could it then be questioned, whether it were right to relieve a rational creature, a descendant of Abraham, (probably an heir of his faith,) from her long continued calamity, on that holy day; even if it had been effected by labour? This reply was so satis-

factory and conclusive, that it silenced and put to shame the ruler, and all the other adversaries of Jesus; and caused the people to rejoice in his glorious miracles, as so many proofs of his being the promised Messiah. (*Marg. Ref.—Notes,* xiv. 1—6. *Matt.* xii. 1—13. *Mark* iii. 1—5. *John* v. 10—18. vii. 19—24. ix. 13—16.)

Was bowed together. (11) Ην συγκυπτουσα. Here only N. T.—*In no wise.*] Μη ... εις το παντελες. *Heb.* vii. 25. Not elsewhere N. T.—*Lift up herself.*] Ανακυψαι. xxi. 28 *John* viii. 7. Not elsewhere N. T.—*She was made straight.* (13) Ανωρθωθη. *Acts* xv. 16. *Heb.* xii. 12. Not elsewhere N. T. Εξ ανα, et ορθος, *rectus.—The glorious things.* (17) Ενδοξοις. vii. 25. 1 *Cor.* iv. 10. *Eph.* v. 27.—*Ex.* xxxiv. 10. *Job* xxxiv. 24. *Is.* xii. 4. Sept.

V. 18—21. (*Marg. Ref.—Notes, Matt.* xiii. 31—33. *Mark* iv. 30—34.) The grain of mustard-seed is represented as sown in a good soil, and a select spot; a garden, and not a field.

Garden. (19) Κηπον. *John* xviii. 1. 26. xix. 41. Κηπουρος, *gardener. John* xx. 15.—*Lodged.*] Κατεσκηνωσεν. *Matt.* xiii. 32. *Mark* iv. 32. Εξ κατα, et σκηνοω, *in tabernaculo dego.—Of meal.*] Αλευρου. *Matt.* xiii. 33. Not elsewhere N. T.

V. 22—30. It is probable, that our Lord was now on his last journey from Galilee towards Jerusalem, in which he took a large circuit, and spent considerable time: so that he no more visited the northern part of the land, till after his resurrection. (*Marg. Ref.* u, x.) While he was

26 Then shall ye begin to say, 'We have eaten and drunk in thy presence, and thou hast taught in our streets. 27 But he shall say, " I tell you, I know you not whence ye are : ' depart from me, all ye workers of iniquity. 28 There shall be ' weeping and gnashing of teeth, ' when ye shall see Abraham, and Isaac, and Jacob, and all the prophets in "the kingdom of God, and " you yourselves thrust out. 29 And ° they shall come from the east, and from the west, and from the north, and from the south, and shall

sit down in the kingdom of God. 30 And, behold, ° there are last, which shall be first, and there are first which shall be last.

31 ¶ The same day there came certain of the Pharisees, saying unto him, 'Get thee out, and depart hence : for Herod will kill thee.

32 And he said unto them, Go ye and tell ' that fox, Behold, ' I cast out, devils, and I do cures, to-day and to-morrow, and the third day ' I shall be ' perfected.

33 Nevertheless, " I must walk to-

teaching the people, a person asked him, " Are there few " that be saved ? " Or, " Are the saved few ? " Perhaps the man inferred this from his doctrine, and was prejudiced against him on that account ; or he deemed this inconsistent with the preceding parables. It was, however, a curious question, though it does not appear that the man had any ill design in it. Our Lord therefore did not directly answer him, but took occasion to inculcate a most important exhortation : ' It not being our concern to know ` now many shall be saved ; but how we may be saved.' Whitby. The whole context shews, that no temporal preservation, but deliverance " from the wrath to come," and inheriting eternal life, were meant ; as the subsequent mention of the strait gate fully proves. (Marg. Ref. b, c. —Note, Matt. vii. 13, 14.) " The strait gate " is the passage, from " the broad way to destruction " into " the narrow way to life ; " that is, a sinner's conversion and reconciliation to God, by repentance and faith in Jesus Christ. Many difficulties must occur in thus " passing " from death unto life : " the gate is beset with enemies ; and much must be left behind, broken off, broken through, overcome, and attained, in getting in at it ; yet without this there can be no salvation. They therefore, who would be saved, must " strive to enter in at the strait gate ; " they must struggle with all their force, and employ all their attention and circumspection, as those did who wrestled in the publick games. (Marg. Ref. a.)—" Force your way " in at the strait gate." Campbell.—To excite them to this, Christ, the Saviour and Judge of men, solemnly assured them, that " many will seek to enter in, and shall " not be able." Some seek admission into the favour of God and eternal happiness, without conversion, or faith in the divine Saviour ; others seek the blessing in a slothful manner, or in the use of such means as God has never appointed ; others, with reserves for their worldly interest, reputation, or sinful pleasures, or for avoiding reproach and persecution. In these and similar ways, many come short of salvation ; notwithstanding convictions, temporary seriousness and earnestness, and partial reformation. But, it is by procrastination especially, that men at last " will " seek to enter in, and not be able. While life endures, " the Master of the house," the Lord Jesus, sits, as it were, at mercy's gate, over which it is written, " Knock " and it shall be opened to you : " but at length he rises up, and by cutting off a sinner in his unconverted state, he

" shuts the door" against him, and bars it for ever. (Marg. Ref. d, e.—Notes, Gen. vii. 16. Matt. vii. 7—11.) Many therefore, even of those who then heard Christ, would first " begin to knock " at the gate, and to seek salvation from him, when it was too late ; and whatever presumptuous confidence they had before entertained, or whatever plea they might have to urge, these would in no wise prevail for admission. For though they could truly say, that they had sat at table with him, or welcomed him to their tables, and that he had taught in the streets of their cities ; yet he would disown all acquaintance with them, and drive them from him as " workers of iniquity." (Notes, xvi. 24—26. Matt. iii. 7—10. vii. 21—23. xi. 20—24. xxv. 41 —46.) At that tremendous season, their anguish and misery would be enhanced, by beholding the happiness of patriarchs and prophets, yea, of immense numbers of the Gentiles, from every quarter of the globe ; who would be saved by the promised Messiah, through repentance and faith, whilst they perished through unbelief and impenitence ; for " the first would be last, and the last first." (Notes, Prov. i. 20—33. Is. lv. 6, 7. Matt. viii. 10—12. xix. 29, 30.)—In this address our Lord evidently declared to the people, that their admission into life and happiness, or exclusion from them, entirely and absolutely depended on him alone.

Are there few that be saved ? (23) Ει ολιγοι οι σωζομενοι ; Acts ii. 47. 1 Cor. i. 18. 2 Cor. ii. 15. Rev. xxi. 24.— Strive. (24) Αγωνιζεσθε. John xviii. 36. 1 Cor. ix. 25. Col. i. 29. iv. 12. 1 Tim. vi. 12. 2 Tim. iv. 7. Αγων. Phil. i. 30. Col. ii. 1. 1 Thes. ii. 2. Αγωνια, xxii. 44. The word every where conveys the idea of sharp conflict, with great exertion, and self-denial, and persevering endurance.— Depart from me. (27) Αποστητε απ' εμν. ii. 37. iv. 13. viii. 13. 2 Tim. ii. 19. Heb. iii. 12. Περινοησθε, Matt. xxv. 41.

V. 31—33. Our Lord still continued within Herod's jurisdiction : and his miracles, doctrine, and reputation excited much uneasiness in that wicked prince, who probably menaced him, rather in hope of driving him to a distance, than with any intention of proceeding against him. The Pharisees also, of those parts, wanted to remove him from them ; and therefore they warned him to go thence ; for otherwise Herod had determined to put him to death. But Christ directed them to inform " that " fox," that subtle, insinuating, and mischievous man, (Marg. Ref. r.—Note, Ez. xiii. 1—4,) that he should pro-

day and to-morrow, and the *day* following: * for it cannot be that a prophet perish out of Jerusalem.

34 O Jerusalem, ' Jerusalem, which * killest the prophets, and stonest them that are sent unto thee : * how often would I have gathered * thy children together, * as a hen *doth gather* her

brood under *her* wings, ⁴ and ye would not !

35 Behold, * your house is left unto you desolate : and verily I say unto you, 'Ye shall not see me, until *the time* come when ye shall say, * Blessed *is* he that cometh in the name of the Lord.

---

ceed with his work without regarding him : he must continue to work his miracles of mercy for a very short time longer, as it were " that day and the morrow ;" and then, as " on the third day," he should be perfected by his sufferings, which would complete his work on earth, and make way for his mediatorial exaltation. Nevertheless, though his time was short, he *must need* go openly from place to place, while it lasted : and though he certainly should soon be put to death, yet that would not be by the hands of Herod, in Galilee ; for " it could not be that a prophet " should perish out of Jerusalem." That city had, as it were, an exclusive claim to the guilt and infamy of murdering the prophets of God ; and it was not proper that the great Prophet of the church should lay down his life in any other place.—As John the Baptist and others had been slain elsewhere, it is evident that this sentence must not be taken strictly : it was a general rule, and Jesus, the Messiah, would not be an exception to it.—This message was in fact a defiance sent to Herod : but his wickedness in slaying John the Baptist, contrary to the conviction of his own conscience, being added to all his other crimes, rendered it improper for our Lord to shew him any regard. (*Note*, xxiii. 6—12.)—' I know that subtle tyrant, who ' hath shed the blood of my forerunner, is hunting after ' my death also : but tell him from me, that my times are ' set in the eternal counsel of God, ... and when my pre- ' fixed time is accomplished, for my labours and sufferings, ' I shall, in spite of all the opposition of earth and hell, ' be perfected, and enjoy my full glory.' *Bp. Hall.*— ' The word signifies, I am consecrated to my priestly ' office, by dying a sacrifice for the sins of the world.' *Whitby.* The offering of this sacrifice, however, was itself a most essential part of our Lord's priestly office ; and introductory to the rest, which having finished on earth, he " ascended into heaven," to appear in the presence of God " for us." (*Notes, Heb.* v. 7—10. ix. 11—14. 24—26.)

Herod will, &c. (31) Θελει σε αποκλιναι. *Matt.* xiv. 5. Rather, Herod *willeth*, or *wills*, to kill thee. *Will*, thus used, is merely an auxiliary ; and the clause as here rendered properly means, that Herod would put Jesus to death : but this is far from the real import, which is, " Herod purposes to kill thee." Herod intended to kill Jesus ; but in fact he did not kill him, but Pilate, who purposed no such thing, crucified him.—*I shall be perfected.* (32) Τελωμαι, ii. 43. *John* iv. 34. v. 36. xvii. 4. 23. xix. 28. *Acts* xx. 24. 2 *Cor.* xii. 9. *Phil.* iii. 12. *Heb.* ii. 10. v. 9. vii. 19. 28. ix. 9. x. 1. 14. xi. 40. A τελειος, *perfectus.*—*It cannot be.* (33) Ουκ ενδιχεται. Here only N. T. (Ανενδεκτον ετι, xvii. 1.) Ab εν, et διχομαι, *capio.*— ' Subintelligetur χρημα, ut sit χρημα ενδιχεται, res vel usus ' *admittit*, seu *capit*.' *Schleusnei.*

V. 34, 35. *Marg. Ref.—Note, Matt.* xxiii. 37—39.— *Brood.* (34) Νοσσιαν. Here only N. T.

PRACTICAL OBSERVATIONS.
V. 1—9.

As no place or employment can secure us from the stroke of death, we should always be preparing for it : and instead of considering the sudden or extraordinary deaths of our neighbours or countrymen, as proofs that they were " sinners above other men," we should endeavour to improve them as warnings to ourselves : for when dire calamities are reported, it may be said to sinners of every age and nation, " Except ye repent, ye shall all likewise " perish." Nay, whatever we read in the scriptures, of the misery of the wicked in hell, is intended to speak the same important warning to each of us.—Those who hear the gospel and associate with the people of God, and yet continue impenitent and unconverted, are the barren fig-trees in the Lord's vineyard : from time to time he comes seeking fruit on them ; but finding none, he at length condemns them to be cut down as " cumberers of the " ground ;" that they may no longer disgrace his church in the eyes of those who are without, or prevent the fruitfulness of those within. (*Notes* and *P. O. John* xv. 1—8.) Indeed when faithful ministers behold such barren trees in their congregations, (alas, how numerous are they !) and when they fear that they are about to be cut down, and cast into the fire ; they are led, both by inclination and duty, to pray that they may be spared a little longer, and they desire to use every additional means for their salvation with redoubled assiduity : yet if at last they continue unfruitful, their most affectionate pastors must acknowledge the justice of the sentence, by which they are cut off to make way for more useful characters.—It behoves every one of us to enquire, how long we have been favoured with the means of grace, and borne with by the long-suffering of God ; and to examine, whether we be now bearing fruit to his glory, and the good of men, or be still mere " cumberers of the ground." Such enquiries are peculiarly proper to be made at the beginning of a new year, or the return of any other periodical season. And when any are restored from sickness, and spared a little longer, in answer to the prayers of ministers or Christian friends ; surely they should take their admonitions in good part, and seek to profit by their endeavours ; remembering how short their respite may be, and how soon they may be cut down, if not at length rendered fruitful.—But alas ! many of these despise and revile such as pray and labour for their salvation, and " watch for their souls as " those who must give account, that they may do it with " joy and not with grief ! "

CHAP. XIV.

Jesus, on the sabbath, heals a man who had the dropsy, and justifies himself in so doing, 1—6. By parables he teaches humility, 7—11; and hospitality to the poor, 12—14. The parable of the great supper, 15—24. The necessity of self-denial, and renouncing the world, in order to be the disciples of Christ, inculcated, and illustrated by similes, 25—33. The worthlessness of salt which has lost its savour, 34, 35.

V. 10—21.

We must indeed not rest in means and ordinances, but we should thankfully attend on them. If we would have a blessing from Christ, we must frequent the assemblies of his people, especially on his holy day : and even if we come thither with pain and trouble, we shall not have cause to repent. We are not concerned or competent to determine, what influence Satan has in occasioning or increasing our bodily diseases : but we know, that he has bound our souls with the chain of our own sinful propensities, so that we are not able in any wise to lift up or liberate ourselves : and this has been the case with numbers for many years, while their evil habits have continually been strengthening, and rendering their case more hopeless. But if Jesus speak the word, and put forth his healing power ; even these will immediately be loosed, and their crooked judgments and dispositions rectified : and they will, without delay, be able and willing to glorify God by word and deed. This deliverance is most frequently wrought on the Lord's day : and whatever labour tends to put men in the way of receiving this blessing, or in being instrumental in its being communicated to them, must peculiarly accord to the pious and beneficent intention of that sacred season of rest.—But they, who hate the gospel and its blessed effects, always find some objection to make against every instance of the power of divine grace : and when this is accompanied by a professed exactness in externals ; the hypocrisy of it may often be shewn, by observing that they do things of the same kind for their own secular interest, which they blame others for doing to promote the salvation of souls. But evident good works, connected with a blameless conversation, and defended by convincing arguments, must at length silence the most malicious adversaries, and bear testimony to men's consciences of the power and presence of God with us : and let enemies be never so numerous or malicious, his kingdom will continue to increase in the world, till it fills the whole earth ; and in every renewed soul, till it has perfectly communicated its heavenly savour and nature to all its faculties, dispositions, and affections.

V. 22—30.

When we reflect on the immense multitudes of the human species, it is very awful to consider, how very few of them appear to be in the way of salvation, as that is marked out in the word of God : and the very proposal of the question considered in all its awful importance, causes the soul to recoil appalled from the reflection. Yet let us rather look to ourselves, than waste our time in calculations or curious enquiries about others. It will not avail us how few, or how many, shall be saved, if we be not of that number ; and if we be, we shall at length approve of the appointments of God in this and in every other respect. Nor will the awful truth, that few comparatively have hitherto been saved, prevent our being of the happy number, if we seek salvation as our grand object, according to the oracles of God. Every unconverted sinner should then " strive to enter in at the strait gate," by earnest prayer, by resisting temptations, by avoiding all occasions of committing sin, or silencing his conscience, and hardening his heart, and by attending diligently on every means of grace : and every one of us should continue thus to labour and wrestle, that we may make " our calling and election sure." But with what solemn attention, and application to our own souls, should we hear our Judge declare that " many " shall seek to enter in, and shall not be able !" We are indeed assured that none shall seek the Lord, when and where he may be found, as in Christ, and on a throne of grace, by humble faith and fervent prayer, and at last fail of obtaining the blessing : but let all men beware of a proud, a slothful, a hypocritical, a partial seeking ; and above all of procrastination. How dreadful will be the disappointment of those, who hoped and intended at some future time, to enter the strait gate ; but when deferred the grand concern, from worldly motives, till it became too late, and the door was for ever shut against them ! In vain will they call Christ, Lord, Lord, and intreat him to open to them : in vain will they plead, that they heard his ministers, entertained them at their own tables, and frequented his table : he will utterly disregard their pleas, and refuse all pity to their anguish ; while he shall sentence them " to depart from him, as workers of iniquity," whom he never acknowledged to be in the number of his redeemed people : and even the felicity of those, with whom they formerly associated, as well as that of others whom they disdained, will add poignancy to their misery and despair. As there were such persons among our Lord's hearers, among those whom he fed by miracle, or with whom he sat down to meat ; and as there was a Judas even among his own apostles ; we ought surely to address our congregations in a similar manner ; to put the case, that many of them may at last be found in this awful condition ; and to enforce our warnings and exhortations by such alarming topicks, addressed to them directly, in the second person ; and not merely to speak of such characters in a general way, which may be understood to imply our opinion, that none of them are found in our audience. But especially we ought to examine ourselves, and not to take things for granted by an unwarranted confidence, where such infinite interests are at stake. None, however, ought to yield to despondency, either with respect to himself or others : for, " behold, there are last who shall be " first, and first who shall be last ;" and, though few of our immediate relations or neighbours should appear to be in the way of salvation ; yet there will be others brought from every part of the earth, and the multitude of the saved will in all be found immensely large. (P. O. Matt. vii. 13—29. viii. 5—13.)

V. 31—35.

It does not in general behove us to speak disrespectfully

AND it came to pass, as he went into the house of one of the chief Pharisees to eat bread on the sabbath-day, that they watched him.

2 And, behold, there was a certain man before him which had the dropsy.

3 And Jesus answering spake unto the lawyers and Pharisees, saying, Is it lawful to heal on the sabbath-day?

4 And they held their peace. And he took him, and healed him, and let him go;

5 And answered them, saying, Which of you shall have an ass or an ox fallen into a pit, and will not straightway pull him out on the sabbath-day?

6 And they could not answer him again to these things.

7 ¶ And he put forth a parable to those which were bidden, when he marked how they chose out the chief rooms; saying unto them,

8 When thou art bidden of any man to a wedding, sit not down in the highest room, lest a more honourable man than thou be bidden of him;

9 And he that bade thee and him come and say to thee, Give this man place; and thou begin with shame to take the lowest room.

10 But when thou art bidden, go and sit down in the lowest room; that when he that bade thee cometh, he may say unto thee, Friend, go up higher: then shalt thou have worship in the presence of them that sit at meat with thee.

11 For whosoever exalteth himself shall be abased: and he that humbleth himself shall be exalted.

of any who are invested with authority: yet apostates, persecutors, and crafty dissemblers may, on some occasions, be spoken of in their true characters, that men may beware of them; and we must not flatter the wicked, or fear any man, when performing our bounden duty. We too should " go about doing good," while our appointed span of life endures: and in that case when life expires, we shall be perfected in holiness and felicity.—But how black a mark of human depravity was the extraordinary circumstance, of Jerusalem's being the slaughter-house of God's prophets, and the very place where his beloved Son was crucified! Alas! the visible church has generally been the grand scene of persecution; (Note, Rev. xvii. 6;) and those whom the Saviour has, with persevering tenderness, invited to take shelter under the shadow of his almighty wings, have not only contemptuously refused his kindness, but have hated and persecuted those who brought the invitation! (Note, Matt. xxii. 1—10.) Thus men bring upon themselves swift destruction from the presence of the Lord, as well as the forfeiture of all their privileges: but let us shun this fatal rock, and learn thankfully to welcome and to profit by all those, " who come in the " name of the Lord" Jesus, to invite us to partake of his great salvation.

NOTES.

CHAP. XIV. V. 1—6. (Notes, vii. 36. xi. 37, 38.) Some think, that this chief Pharisee was a ruler also, or one of the Sanhedrim or great council of the nation, but perhaps he was only a person of influence and authority among the Pharisees. He, however, (as well as some others who invited Jesus,) seems to have had an insidious design in entertaining him; and to have combined with several of his brethren in endeavouring to entangle him. But our Lord would not on that account be deterred from

healing a man, afflicted with the dropsy, who probably came thither for that purpose. When they had declined answering his question, respecting the lawfulness of doing this, he took the man by the hand, and having healed him, so that his restoration to health was manifest to all, he sent him away: and then shewed, that compassion for an animal, or regard to their own property, would have induced any of them to far more labour, than what they blamed in him, where the life or comfort of a brother was concerned. This silenced their objections, though it did not subdue their enmity. (Marg. Ref.—Notes, xiii. 10—17. Matt. xii. 1—13. Mark iii. 1—5.)

The chief Pharisees. (1) Των αρχοντων των φαρισαιων. xxiv. 20. John iii. 1. vii. 26. 48. Acts iii. 17. 1 Cor. ii. 8.—Had αρχοντων been used separately, one of the rulers would clearly have been marked out: but as used before των φαρισαιων, our version seems adequately to express the meaning.—Which had the dropsy. (2) Ύδρωπικος. here only. Ab ύδωρ, aqua, et ωψ, facies.—Answer him again. (6) Ανταποκριθηναι. Rom. ix. 20. Not elsewhere N. T.

V. 7—11. The Scribes and Pharisees seem not to have attended even to that semblance of humility, under which numbers veil their pride and ambition, that they may more successfully gratify them: but they openly contended for precedency; probably on the score of their reputation for wisdom, learning, or piety, or on account of their rank and authority: and they chose out for themselves the chief seats, thus claiming the highest respect as justly due to them. (Marg. Ref.—Notes, xx. 45—47. Matt. xxiii. 5—7.) This disgraceful competition, however, though it rose from the same source, was merely a shadow of that spiritual pride and ambition, which has excluded numbers from the kingdom of Christ, produced the most lamentable effects in the visible church, and done immense injury even to many true Christians and ministers. Our Lord therefore, in a mild, yet firm and decisive manner, re-

12 ¶ Then said he also to him that bade him, When thou makest a dinner or a supper, call not thy friends, nor thy brethren, neither thy kinsmen, nor thy *rich* neighbours; lest they also bid thee again, and a recompence be made thee.

13 But when thou makest a feast, call the poor, the maimed, the lame, the blind:

14 And thou shalt be blessed; for they cannot recompense thee: for thou shalt be recompensed at the resurrection of the just.

---

proved the vain-glory of the guests, by a parable addressed, as it were, to each of them, the substance of which was taken from their own scriptures. (*Note, Prov.* xxv. 6, 7.) If any of them were indeed in a marriage-feast, which was the principal festive occasion, let him not aspire to the highest place; lest a more honourable person should be present, whom the master of the feast should deem entitled to the precedency. In this case, being required to give place to his superior, and the intermediate places being occupied, he would be sent with disgrace to take the lowest place. On the contrary, let him go at first to the situation intended for the meanest of the company, as claiming no honour and pre-eminence; and then the master of the house might think it proper to desire him to go up higher, which would procure him respect and deference among the other guests.—Thus the Christian should deem it honour enough for him, a poor sinful and rebellious creature, to be admitted among the redeemed in the lowest form; and not contend for eminent stations, authority, or reputation: for such ambition only tends to disgrace. (*Notes,* xxii. 24—27. *Acts* viii. 18—24.) But he ought, in unaffected humility, to take the lowest station, or the meanest service, preferring others to himself: (*Notes, Rom.* xii. 9—13, *v.* 10. *Phil.* ii. 1—4, *v.* 4:) and in due time he will, in this manner, obtain " the honour which cometh " from God;" and he will have the approbation of angels and men at the day of judgment. For it is an universal rule of the Lord's dealings with every individual, in respect of the various incidents and actions of their lives, that " he abases those who exalt themselves;" and advances " those who abase themselves," as conscious of their actual and comparative worthlessness, and as willing to be little, despised, neglected, and subjected to others. (*Notes,* xviii. 9—14, *v.* 14. *Matt.* xviii. 1—6. xx. 24—28. xxiii. 11, 12. *Jam.* iv. 4—6. 1 *Pet.* v. 5—7.)

The chief rooms. (7) Τας πρωτοκλισιας. 8. See on *Matt.* xxiii. 6.—*Sit not down.* (8) Μη κατακλιθης. ix. 14. xxiv. 30. Not elsewhere N. T. Ex κατα, et κλινω, *recumbo.* —*Sit down.* (10) Αναπισον. xi. 37. xvii. 7. xxii. 14, *et al.* —*Go up higher.* (10) Προσαναβηθι ανωτερον. Προσαναβαινω, here only N. T.—Ex προς, ανα, et βαινω, *eo.*—Ανωτερον. *Heb.* x. 8. Not elsewhere N. T.—*Them that sit at meat with thee.*] Συνανακειμενων. 15. vii. 49. *Matt.* ix. 10. xiv. 9. *Mark* ii. 15. vi. 22. 26. *John* xii. 2. Ex συν, ανα, et κειμαι, *jaceo, recumbo.*—*Exalteth, &c.* (11) Ὑψων. i. 52. x. 15. xiv. 11. xviii. 14. *Matt.* xi. 23. xxiii. 12. *et al.*

V. 12—14. The Pharisee at whose table Jesus was sitting, seems to have been a person of eminence; and had probably prepared an expensive entertainment for the company; though this was on the sabbath-day, and must have been attended with some labour: for perhaps the Pharisees were as ostentatious in their feasts, as in their fasts. Our Lord therefore saw it proper to point out the criminality of the practice: and he counselled his host, when he made a dinner or a supper, not to invite his " friends, or relations, or rich neighbours," but on the contrary to invite the poor, and those who by divers bodily infirmities were incapable of procuring the necessaries or comforts of life (21); a great number of whom might be *feasted* with the same expense, which would be incurred to entertain a few of the rich. In this manner he would " be blessed : ' as his guests could not recompense him, except by their prayers, and he would receive his reward at " the resurrection of the just." It is not to be supposed that Jesus meant, absolutely and universally, to prohibit men from entertaining their wealthy friends, relations, and neighbours; and poor relations are as proper to be invited as other poor persons: yet they, who are most applauded for their useless generosity in this respect, are seldom very eminent for real charity, not always for strict honesty; and our Lord shews his disciples a more excellent way. The profusion occasioned by feasting the rich, serves to gratify a man's vanity and pride, and the sensual appetites of his friends; who in return are tempted to run into similar extravagance, of which the consequences are often very fatal, and it renders a man incapable of relieving the poor, in any adequate degree. Such expenses cannot be incurred from love to God, or regard to his authority; favour, or glory; therefore no recompence can be expected from him: and human applause, or a similar banquet in return, is the only reward of them. (*Marg. Ref.* p, q.— *Notes,* vi. 27—36. *Prov.* xxii. 16. *Matt.* vi. 1—4.) But when a man, from *proper motives,* expends his wealth in relieving the distressed and indigent, he derives the greatest satisfaction imaginable from this use of it, and his gracious Lord will abundantly reward it in another world. It certainly is not meant, that God will " recompense, at the " resurrection of the just," a proud and unbelieving liberality to the poor: but our Lord spoke for the instruction of his disciples in every age; and the less they spend in " conformity to the world," by luxurious feasting of the rich, the more they will have to employ in feeding the poor, and in all those fruits of faith and love, " which are " by Christ Jesus to the praise and glory of God." (*Marg. Ref.* r—t.)—How clearly does it appear, that a future state of retribution was a prominent article of the general or popular creed, among the Jews at this time!

They ... bid thee again. (12) Αντικαλεσωσι. Here only N. T. Ex αντι, et καλεω, *invito.*—*A recompence.*] Ανταποδομα. *Rom.* xi. 9. Not elsewhere N. T.—2 *Chr.* xxxii. 25. *Ps.* xxviii. 4. cxxxvii. 8. *Sept.*—*A feast.* (13) Δοχην. See on v. 9.—*Recompense.* (14) Ανταποδοναι. *Rom.* xi. 35. xii. 19. 1 *Thes.* iii. 9. 2 *Thes.* i. 6. Ex αντι, απο, et διδωμι.

15 ¶ And when one of them that sat at meat with him heard these things, he said unto him, * Blessed is he that shall eat bread in the kingdom of God.

16 Then said he unto him, * A certain man made a great supper, and ' bade many:

17 And sent ' his servant at supper-time to say to them that were bidden, * Come; for all things are now ready.

18 And they * all with one consent began to make excuse. The first said unto him, ' I have bought a piece of ground, and I must needs go and see it: I pray thee have me excused.

19 And another said, I have bought five yoke of oxen, and I go to prove them: I pray thee have me excused.

20 And another said, * I have mar-

ried a wife; and therefore I cannot * come.

21 So that servant came * and shew-ed his lord these things. Then the master of the house, ' being angry, said to his servant, ' Go out quickly into the streets and lanes of the city, and bring in hither * the poor, and the maimed, and the halt, and the blind.

22 And the servant said, Lord, ' it is done as thou hast commanded, * and yet there is room.

23 And the Lord said unto the servant, ' Go out into the high-ways, and hedges, and " compel them to come in, that my house may be filled.

24 For I say unto you, * That none of those men which were bidden shall taste of my supper.

V. 15—24. The person, who made the remark which gave occasion to this parable, seems to have alluded to the satisfactions to be enjoyed in the days of the Messiah, under the figure of " eating bread in the kingdom of " God;" though the thought might occur to him, from what our Lord had spoken of " the resurrection of the " just." " Eating bread " was a common expression for any kind of meal, however plentiful or even luxurious; and it is probable, that the man entertained low and carnal expectations concerning the kingdom of God. (Marg. Ref. u.) Our Lord, therefore, to shew him how little the blessings to be conferred by the Messiah, would prove suited to the taste of the Jews in general, and how generally they would refuse them; thus describing their present and future conduct respecting his gospel, spake the parable here recorded. (Marg. Ref. x—a.—Notes, Prov. ix. 1—6. Is. xxv. 6—8. lv. 1—3. Matt. xxii. 1—14.)—The " great supper " represented the plenteous provision made for the souls of men in the redemption of Christ: the previous invitation denotes the promises and prophecies of his salvation, to the Jews of old; the ministry of John the Baptist, and that of Christ himself and his apostles. The servants being sent to " call those who had been bidden," when " all things were ready," may signify the preaching of the apostles and evangelists after Christ's ascension. The invited persons all " with one consent " desiring to be excused, though on different pretences, may represent the general rejection of the gospel by the Jewish nation, especially by their rulers, teachers, and Pharisees: the servants being then sent forth into " the streets and lanes " of the city," to call in the poor, lame, and blind, may intimate the success of the gospel among the publicans, and common people of the Jews; and among those, who were dispersed in other countries, and the proselyted Gentiles: and when the servants were sent out to " the high " ways and hedges," to fetch in the poor strangers and

travellers, the calling of the Gentiles seems to have been principally intended, with whom the church has since been chiefly replenished; while the Jews who were first invited are, through their unbelief, excluded from it. (Marg. Ref. b—l. n.)—The whole parable, however, may be applied to the preaching of the gospel, and the reception which it meets with, in every age.—The excuses, here stated, were all taken from things lawful in themselves: yet from the manner in which they were attended to, they became the occasion of the greatest contempt being shewn to the feast, and to him who made it. Nothing could be more frivolous than for one man to go to see his estate, and another to prove his oxen, (after they had been bought,) just at the hour when they were invited to the feast; when they might easily have deferred these matters to another time. The man, who pleaded " that he had married a " wife, and therefore could not come," is supposed by some, to have meant that his own marriage-feast was fixed for the same time; but as the marriage was past, the feast also may be supposed to have been over. It shews however, that a carnal mind gives every thing the preference to Christ and his salvation, instead of using all in entire subserviency to them. Indeed all these excuses, thus pointed out, are intended to teach us, that contempt of spiritual blessings, and inordinate attachment to worldly objects, are the real causes of men's negligence and procrastination in religious matters: and the circumstances of those who " desired to be excused," when compared with the poverty of such as were the guests at last, especially shews, that pride and self-sufficiency are incompatible with the faith of the gospel.—The servants were ordered " to " compel " those " from the high ways and hedges to " come in." It would be absurd to understand this of compulsive force, which would be a strange way of bringing men to a banquet, though great numbers have thus explained it! and this proves that scriptural arguments

25 ¶ And [a] there went great multitudes with him: and he turned, and said unto them, 26 If [b] any *man* come to me, and [c] hate not his father, and mother, and wife, and children, and brethren, and sisters, yea, and his own life also, he cannot be my disciple. 27 And whosoever [d] doth not bear his cross, and come after me, [e] cannot be my disciple. 28 For which of you, [f] intending to build a tower, sitteth not down first and [g] counteth the cost, whether he have *sufficient* to finish it? 29 Lest haply, after he hath laid the foundation, and is not able to finish *it*, all that behold *it* begin to mock him, 30 Saying, [h] This man began to build, and was not able to finish. 31 Or what king, [i] going to make war against another king, sitteth not down first, and consulteth, whether he be able with ten thousand to meet him that cometh against him with twenty thousand? 32 Or else, while the other is yet a great way off, he sendeth an ambassage, [k] and desireth conditions of peace. 33 So likewise, [l] whosoever he be of you that forsaketh not all that he hath, he cannot be my disciple.

for persecution are not to be found. It shews also that the objections against the doctrine of 'special grace,' as if inconsistent with free agency, are wholly groundless; unless the inward blessing of God, on proper means, producing willingness where it did not before exist, inclining the heart, and so 'preventing us that we may have a good 'will,' be more inconsistent with free agency, than urgent and pressing invitations to a feast are. (*Notes, Ps.* cx. 3. *Phil.* ii. 12, 13.) It might, however, be supposed that poor travellers, or beggars, would not readily be convinced that the feast was intended for them; and therefore repeated pressing invitations would be peculiarly proper: and thus our Lord would have his ministers use most earnest and affectionate invitations, persuasions, and expostulations, and whatever can convince the understanding, or affect the heart, or give encouragement: especially when they address those who, by the greatness of their guilt, may be tempted to despair of mercy. (*Marg. Ref.* m.)

To make excuse. (18) Παραιτεισθαι. *Excused,* παρητημενον. 19. *Acts* xxv. 11. 1 *Tim.* iv. 7. v. 11. 1 *Tim.* ii. 23. *Tit.* iii. 10. *Heb.* xii. 19. 25. Ex παρα, et αιτεομαι, peto.—*The* \maimed. (21) Αναπηρος. 13. Not elsewhere N. T.—*Captos* membris. ' Herodotus ... Homerum oculis captum, αναπηρον, ' vocat.' *Schleusner.*—*Compel.* (23) Αναγκασον. *Matt.* xiv. 22. *Mark* vi. 45. *Acts* xxvi. 11. xxviii. 19. 2 *Cor.* xii. 11. *Gal.* ii. 3. 14. vi. 12.

V. 25—27. As our Lord journeyed towards Jerusalem, great multitudes flocked about him: but he knew that they had generally very erroneous notions of his kingdom, and were not prepared to submit to the losses and privations, or to encounter the various dangers and difficulties, which certainly awaited his true disciples. If therefore they followed him in their present temper, they would leave him in the time of trial to the discredit of the cause, the discouragement of others, and the ruin of their own souls. He therefore turned himself, and addressed them in a manner, which was apparently calculated to drive them from him: (*Note, Josh.* xxiv. 19:) assuring them, that though they came assiduously to hear him; they could not be his disciples, except they hated their nearest relations, and even their own lives. Men are in general expressly required to honour and to love these relations,

and to take care of their own lives. But this love and regard must be entirely subordinated to the love of Christ; and they must give his favour, will, and glory, a decided preference to the approbation, interests, or comfort of their dearest relatives: so that they may often be required to act towards them, as though they *hated* them; disobeying their injunctions, thwarting their inclinations, rejecting their intreaties, renouncing the comfort of their society or turning it into bitterness by exciting their resentment. (*Marg. Ref.* q.—*Notes, Gen.* xxix. 30, 31. *Deut.* xiii. 6— 11. *P. O. Note,* xxxiii. 9.) Nay, at some times they may be called to be, as it were, cruel to themselves, (in respect of temporal life,) as well as to their friends; exposing themselves to persecution, torture, and death, if they will obey Christ. So that unless they are habitually prepared, by a deep sense of their need of his salvation, and of their immense obligations to him, to venture every consequence, and meet any extremity rather than forsake him, they " cannot be his disciples:" for in that case they will refuse to bear their cross and go after him. (*Marg. Ref.*—*Notes, Matt.* x. 37—39. xvi. 24—28. *Mark* viii. 31—38. 2 *Cor.* v. 16.)

V. 28—33. To shew the very great importance of the subject, our Lord next enquired, whether every man of common prudence did not calculate the expense, before he began to build a tower; that he might form a previous judgment, whether he should be able to complete the work or not. For if a man neglected this: and, having begun to build, was afterwards compelled to leave the edifice unfinished; he would not only lose all his labour and expense, but the building itself would remain a monument of his indiscretion, and excite the derision and mockery of all who beheld it. (*Marg. Ref.* t—x.) Thus, if a man should profess himself a follower of Christ, without considering what losses, trials, self-denial, or sufferings it might expose him to, or how he might be enabled to endure them, his constancy would at length fail; all he had given up or endured would be in vain; and his apostasy would render him contemptible and miserable.—The same might also be illustrated by the case of a prudent king, who would not declare war, or persist in a competition with a more powerful monarch; without considering whether his resources, situation, or alliances were such, as to

3 H 2

^b Matt. v. 13.
Mark ix. 49, 50.
Col. iv. 6. Heb.
ii. 4—8.
34 Salt *is* good: ^b but if the salt have lost his savour, wherewith shall it be seasoned?

35 It is neither fit for the land, nor yet for the dunghill; *but* men cast it out. ^c He that hath ears to hear, let him hear.

^c viii. 8. Is. 44
Matt. xi. 15.
xiii. 3. Rev. ii.
7. 11. 17. 29.

---

give him a reasonable prospect of success: otherwise he would endeavour, whilst his enemy was at a distance, to obtain the best terms of peace that he could. (*Marg. Ref.* y, z.—*Notes, Prov.* xx. 18. xxiv. 3—6. xxv. 8—10.)—To become the disciple of Christ implies a declaration of war against Satan, sin, and this evil world, which are far too powerful for any man to withstand in his own strength: unless a sinner therefore be led to such a conviction of his own weakness, and of the power of his enemies, as to seek help from God, he will never stand his ground: and in all cases, the warfare will be attended with so many hardships, perils, and losses, that if a man be not aware of them, and instructed how to support them, **he** will never be able to " continue to the end." Though it is, therefore, desperate for him to remain in his present state of subjection to his enemies; yet it will rather make the matter worse, for him to take up a mere profession of the gospel, without that sincerity, humility, and entire dependence on Christ, which alone can give him victory in the conflict.—In like manner, " whosoever he be of you," said Jesus, " that forsaketh not all that he hath, he cannot " be my disciple." (*Marg. Ref.* a.) It would not in general consist with a man's *duty*, to leave his business and relatives, or to quit possession of his estate: but he must be prepared for this, whenever the commandment or the providence of God may call him to it. In this way a professed disciple will be repeatedly put to the trial: he will be called on, in steadily acting according to his principles and conscience, to blast his opening prospects of preferment, reputation, or riches; to renounce worldly pleasures; to forego relative comforts and agreeable friendships; and to bear losses, reproaches, and various hardships, for the sake of Christ: and in times of fierce persecution, (such as were at hand when this was spoken,) he may be required to renounce his country, friends, and possessions, to become an exile or a captive, and to part with his liberty or his life; otherwise he cannot follow Christ as his true disciple. (*Notes, Matt.* xvi. 24—28. xix. 16—22. *Phil.* iii. 8—11.)—The judgment and disposition of a martyr every Christian must possess: these will habitually be evinced in inferior concerns; and, when it becomes necessary, God will strengthen him, and enable him to bear the greatest extremities for his sake. Many things may hereafter be expedient and useful, which are not essential to being a Christian: but this decided preference of Christ to the whole world, and to life itself, when placed in competition with him, is the very heart, or the most vital part, of Christianity. (*Notes, Matt.* xiii. 44—46.)

Counteth. (28) Ψηφιζει. *Rev.* xiii. 18. Not elsewhere N. T. A Ψηφος, *calculus. Acts* xxvi. 10. *Rev.* ii. 17.—*The cost.*] Την δαπανην. Here only N. T. A Δαπαναω. xv. 14. *Mark* v. 26.—*To finish it.*] Προς απαρτισμον. Here only N. T. Ab απαρτιζω, *perficio.*—*To mock.* (29) Εμπαιζειν. xviii. 32. xxii. 63. xxiii. 11. 36, *et al.*—*Forsaketh.* (33) Αποτασσεται. See on ix. 61.

V. 34, 35. (*Marg. Ref.*—*Notes, Matt.* v. 13. *Mark* ix. 43—50.) Without that holy and spiritual preparation of

heart above described, professed Christians, or preachers, can only be as " Salt that has lost his savour," which, instead of preserving other bodies from corruption, or giving them a pleasant relish, is itself most incurably tasteless and worthless. Men of this description can be no real credit or advantage to the church, or to the world: and they are commonly more incurable in their presumption and impenitence, than any other sinners. After a temporary profession they generally decline, till they totally apostatize; and they often run into destructive heresies, and endeavour to propagate them; so that they become the most worthless of men: and as this subject is of universal importance, it demands the serious attention of every one " that hath ears to hear." (*Marg. Ref.* c.)—It is evident, that " salt " is here spoken of in popular language, according to the uses which are made of it in common life, and not as a chemist would define it; and that the common opinion, that the residue, when the saline particles were separated, was of no use for manure, or any other purpose, was mentioned merely by way of illustrating the subject.—It is clear, that " salt may lose its savour;" and that true Christians might lose the principle of divine life, unless God have engaged to preserve it: (*Notes,* xxii. 31—34. 1 *Pet.* i. 3—5:) but in respect of all those mentioned in scripture, who became like " salt which hath lost its " savour," some intimation is annexed that there was previously a radical defect: " No root in themselves:" " no " oil in the vessel:" " They went out from us, because " they were not of us." (*Notes, Jer.* xxxii. 39—41. *Ez.* iii. 20, 21. *Matt.* xiii. 20—22. xxii. 11—14. xxv. 1—13. *John* xv. 2. 6—8. 1 *John* ii. 18, 19.)

Have lost his savour. (34) Μωρανθη. *Matt.* v. 13. *Rom* i. 22. 1 *Cor.* i. 20. See on *Matt.* v. 13.—*Shall it be seasoned.*] Αρτυθησεται. *Mark* ix. 50. *Col.* iv. 6.

PRACTICAL OBSERVATIONS.

V. 1—11.

We must not allow even the hospitality of those, who appear friendly, to interrupt us in our duty, or induce us to be unfaithful to the truth, or to the souls of men: though the contrary conduct will probably, on some occasions, draw on us the censure of rudeness or ingratitude.—It requires reiterated and particular instruction, to bring men to understand the proper connexion of piety and mercy, in the observation of the sabbath; and the distinction between real works of necessity, and those which are only made so by habits of self-indulgence: and the " wisdom that is from above " is requisite to teach us such meek yet firm perseverance in well doing, amidst malicious and watchful opposers, as may stop their mouths, even when their hearts are not changed.—Ministers ought to copy Christ, in embracing every opportunity of introducing instructive discourse, in all companies to which they are admitted; and in taking occasion, even from men's follies and mistakes, to make useful remarks whenever any fair opening is given for them.—No disposition of the depraved heart of man is more odious and foolish, or more universal, than pride in its varied exercises. Yet the vain

CHAP. XV.

ambition of honour, which is not a man's due, exposes him to contempt even among competitors for the same distinctions; and they count him as a rival, whom they delight to degrade and mortify: whilst modesty commonly engages respect and attention. It is indeed far more honourable for a man to begin low, and to be unassuming, and to be advanced by the verdict and with the consent of others, than to assume a rank and advance pretensions, to which he is singular in deeming himself entitled, and from which he is likely to be degraded with shame and contempt. But when we know our real character in the sight of God, and are made well acquainted with our own hearts, we shall proportionably be disinclined to aspire at the chief places, either in society or in the church, and shall be contented and thankful for the most obscure; and be made willing to see others honoured, and ourselves neglected and slighted in the comparison. This is in reality a far better way of being made useful and honourable, in the Lord's due time, than to aspire after high-sounding titles, or places of authority, popularity, and precedency; which cannot be coveted, without forgetting what poor, guilty, polluted, weak, and foolish creatures we are. And this forgetfulness tends to abasement and degradation, by the invariable rule of the Lord's dealings with his reasonable creatures.

V. 12—24.

Would any unbiassed observer of mankind have supposed, that Christ had laid down such a rule for the conduct of all his disciples, as we here meet with? (Note, 12—14.) Who almost, whether he can or cannot afford it, does not make expensive feasts for his rich friends and relations? What large sums are often wasted in this manner, compared with the scanty pittance which is given to the poor! Yet what good can be expected from this ostentatious profusion, which is worthy to be put in competition with " a recompence at the resurrection of the " just?" Whilst, therefore, so many prefer the vain commendation or customs of the world, or an interchange of festive indulgence, to the approbation of Christ; let us observe his precept of feasting " the poor, the " maimed, the lame, and the blind," from love to him, and to them for his sake; and let us remember, that it is peculiarly blessed to do good to those who cannot recompense us, and to labour in those services for which we receive nothing from man; (Note, vi. 27—36, v. 35;) for the Lord has engaged himself by promises to recompense us, and his rewards are unspeakably most valuable.—Let us also consider the example of Christ, as it is a comment on this precept: he too has " made a great supper," by dying upon the cross for our sins, that he might rescue us from eternal destruction, and feast us with holy consolations, and substantial, enduring felicity. Was this rich provision made for the wise and the righteous? By no means: but for sinners, rebels, and enemies to God; for the " poor, the maimed, the halt, and the blind." Indeed many are invited; yea, many are ready to say, " Blessed " is he that shall eat bread in the kingdom of God!" But the poor in spirit, the broken-hearted sinner, alone will lish this spiritual feast: (Note, Matt. v. 3:) and while

the servants, from age to age, are employed to invite guests, and to assure " them that all things are ready;" and that pardon, peace, grace, and eternal life are freely bestowed on all, who seek them by faith in the name of Christ: instead of thankfully accepting the invitation; even they, who do not proceed to greater instances of contempt and enmity, " begin with one consent to make " excuse;" and desire leave to continue in sin, at least for some time longer. They have no desire after this feast, or due regard to him who prepared it; and so are not fearful of being excluded: and thus any worldly engagement, amusement, or attachment, suffices as a pretence for " neglecting so great salvation!" Not only do men destroy their souls, for great secular advantages, or by gross outward sins; but they so misplace even lawful things, and act so carnally even in the ordinary affairs of life, that they perish by such matters, as might have been attended to with far superior advantage, had they " sought " first the kingdom of God and his righteousness."—Alas! that men should be so sensibly alive to their little temporal interests, to their credit among neighbours, and to the success of their worldly projects; and yet so careless, where the favour or wrath of God, and eternal happiness or misery, are at stake! But " the god of this world blinds " their minds," and renders them insensible to the awful consequences of their procrastination, till the Lord gives sentence against them : " that," after the repeated invitations which they have rejected, " they shall never taste of " his supper."—These things grieve the hearts of faithful ministers, who go and complain to their Lord, of the folly and perverseness of their hearers : but, though he is angry with obstinate unbelievers, he will not suffer the feast to be provided in vain : if the rich, the learned, the self-wise and self-righteous put it from them with neglect and disdain; he orders his servants to go without delay into the streets and lanes of the city, and bring in thence the publicans and harlots. And as " yet there is abundance " of room" and plenty of provisions; he orders some of them to go without the precincts of the visible church, to bring in the sinners of the Gentiles who have never yet heard of his name, till his house be filled with guests. Oh! that he would be pleased to inspire many ministers with that zeal and love, which would animate them to " compel " sinners to come in;" and to be earnest, affectionate, and solemn, in calling the vilest of transgressors to repentance, and faith in Christ! But alas! some, mistaking God's *secret decrees for their rule of* duty, are thus restrained from exhorting, inviting, and persuading sinners at all: and far greater numbers are contented with a cold unmeaning harangue; as if they did not wish to be thought in earnest, in calling men to that feast, for which, it is to be feared, they themselves have no appetite. (*Note, Prov.* i. 21—33. *P. O.* 20—33. ix. *Matt.* xxii. 1—14.)

V. 25—35.

Though men are bound to use every proper means with all assiduity, earnestness, and perseverance, God alone can prevail with sinners to partake of his salvation. Great multitudes may indeed attend on the gospel; and the op-

THEN [a] drew near unto him all the publicans and sinners for to hear him.

2 And [b] the Pharisees and Scribes murmured, saying, This man receiveth sinners, and eateth with them.

3 And he spake this parable unto them, saying,

4 What [c] man of you, [d] having an hundred sheep, if he lose one of them, doth not leave the ninety and nine in the wilderness, and go after that which is lost, until he find it?

5 And [e] when he hath found it, [f]

a v. 29—32. vii. 29. xiii. 30. Ps. xviii. 27, 28. Matt. ix. 10—13. xxi. 28—31. Rom. v. 20. 1 Tim. i. 15. b ver. 30. v. 30. vii. 34, 39. xix. 7. Matt. ix. 11. Acts xi. 3. 1 Cor. v. 9—11. Gal. ii. 12.

c xiii. 15. Matt. xii. 11. Rom. ii. d Ps. cxix. 176. Is. liii. 6. Jer. l. 6. Ex. xxxiv. 11, 12. 16. 31. Matt. xviii. 12. 13. John x. 1b. 16.26—28. 1 Pet. ii. 25. e xix. 9. xviii. 43. f Is. lxii. 12. John iv. 34, 35. Acts ix. 1—16. Rom. x. 20, 21. Eph. 3.5—6. Tit. iii. 3—7.

---

portunity should be embraced, of warning and instructing them with all plainness and faithfulness : but, unless they are taught of God supremely to value spiritual blessings, and to feel their perishing need of Christ, they will by no means become his true disciples. Indeed by far the greater number of teachers state this matter very conveniently ; and by smooth words induce men to conclude, that they may enjoy the world, and the privileges of the gospel, at the same time : and whilst " many follow their pernicious " ways, by reason of whom the way of truth is evil spoken " of," it is almost become obsolete, (at least very unfashionable, even where some doctrines of the gospel are preached,) to declare the necessity of acting, as if we " hated " our nearest relatives, or our own lives, when we aspire to be Christ's disciples. It is to be feared, many dream that they are interested in the cross of Christ, who were never willing to bear the cross for him ; and who neither renounce their worldly interests, nor mortify their lusts, in order to follow him. But, unless we mean to build a Babel, as an eternal monument of our folly and madness, we must " count our cost " when we take up a profession of the gospel. It may cost us our lives ; and it will inevitably expose us to losses, difficulties, and hardships : and if we be not prepared to give up iniquitous gain, forbidden indulgences, and the friendship of the world ; and to bear ridicule and reproach, the displeasure or loss of friends, and many things of this kind ; how should we be able to forsake all, and lay down our lives for Christ ? (*Note, Jer. xii. 5, 6. P. O. Heb. xii. 4—8.*) But while men shrink from the perils and sufferings of a warfare with sin and Satan ; let them also reflect how dreadful their case must be, if they continue exposed to the wrath of God ! If on any terms they have made their peace with him, they may bear, resist, and overcome every thing, by his grace ; but who can help them against his omnipotent indignation ? These considerations, therefore, should not deter men from following Christ, but stir them up to seek help and grace from him to do it effectually and constantly ; that they may not be as " salt, that has lost its " savour, which is neither fit for the land, nor yet for the " dunghill." May we then seek to be disciples indeed, and be careful not to grow slack in our profession, or afraid of the cross ; that we may be the good salt of the earth, to season all around us with the savour of Christ, and of his heavenly truth !

NOTES.

CHAP. XV. V. 1, 2. Some expositors suppose our Lord to have been at this time beyond Jordan, on the borders of the Gentiles ; that many of them attended his ministry ; and that the term " sinners " is here meant of them : but this is highly improbable ; for " he received " and ate with " the " sinners " here mentioned ; (2.)

but " he was made under the law," and perfectly fulfilled it ; though he disregarded the traditions of the elders : and it was generally considered as a violation of the law, to eat with those who were uncircumcised, and did not observe the distinction of clean and unclean meats. Had he eaten with Gentiles, his apostles would hardly have scrupled it after his ascension, as they most evidently did. (*Notes, Acts x. 9—16. 27—33. xi. 1—3.*) Yet it is probable, that he ate with the Samaritans, when he staid two days at Sychar : and accordingly we find that the apostles readily went among those Samaritans, who embraced the gospel. But these were circumcised, and observed the distinction of meats ; though they were hereticks and schismaticks, and abhorred by the Jews.—Our Lord was " sent to the lost sheep of the house of Israel ; " did he then " come to call the Gentiles " exclusively " to re- " pentance ? " (v. 32.) Was Zaccheus a Gentile ? (xix. 7—9.) Was St. Paul a Gentile before his conversion ? or did Jesus come to save only Gentiles ? (1 Tim. i. 15.)—In fine, the word " a sinner," is applied to our Lord himself: but did the Jews suppose him to be a Gentile ? (*John* ix. 16. 24, 25. 31.)—The publicans, and other notorious sinners, however, in the neighbourhood, with one consent, came to hear our Lord's instructions ; and not merely to gratify curiosity, or to obtain the cure of their diseases. Probably, many of them were touched with a sense of their need of repentance and forgiveness : and our Lord not only instructed them, but sat at table with them, without any scruple, as he had been used to do in other places. This excited the murmurs and reproaches of the Pharisees and Scribes, who observed, with astonishment and indignation, that he acted entirely contrary to their maxims. As these men were generally regarded to be oracles of wisdom and models of piety, their frown was likely to discourage the poor trembling sinners : but to prevent this effect, as well as to check and expose their arrogant spirit ; Jesus vindicated his own conduct, and described the gracious dealings of God with sinners, in three parables ; which all agree in many of the same great outlines, though they place the subject in different lights, to make it the more clearly understood.—' Publicans, gross sinners, and hea- ' thens, were by the Scribes and Pharisees judged unfit to ' be conversed with, even though it were with a design to ' reduce them from their evil courses ; they thinking God ' had cast off the care of them, and had no design to grant ' them " repentance unto life : " ' whence they abhorred ' their company, as thinking it a defilement to be touched ' by them, and never would concern themselves to make ' them better. (v. 30. Matt. ix. 11. Acts x. 28. xi. 18, 19.)' Whitby. (*Notes, vii. 37—50. xix. 1—10. Matt. ix. 10—13.*)

Sinners. (1) Ἁμαρτωλοι. 7. v. 30. vii. 34. 37. xiii. 2. xviii. 13. *John* ix. 24. 31. 1 Tim. i. 15. See on *Matt.* ix. 13.

V. 3—7. " The lost sheep," in this emblem, represents

ʰhe layeth *it* on his shoulders, ᶠrejoic-ing.

6 And when he cometh home, he calleth together *his* ʰ friends and neigh-bours, saying unto them, Rejoice with me; for I have found my sheep which ᶦ was lost.

7 I say unto you, That likewise ʲjoy shall be in heaven over one sinner that repenteth, more than over ninety and nine just persons, ᵏ which need no re-pentance.

8 ¶ Either what woman, having ten pieces of silver, if she lose one piece, doth not light a candle, and sweep the house, ᶦand seek diligently till she find *it ?*

9 And when she hath found *it,* she calleth *her* friends and *her* neighbours, together, saying, ᵐ Rejoice with me; for I have found the piece which I had lost.

10 Likewise, I say unto you, ⁿThere is joy in the presence of the angels of God over ᵒ one sinner that repenteth.

the sinner, as departed from God, and exposed without help to manifold dangers and certain ruin, if not brought back to him; yet is utterly without either power or incli-nation to return. Christ is the Owner, or Shepherd, his chosen and purchased flock, and counts them his pro-perty even when in their sinful state. (*Note, John* x. 14—18.) As a man would leave the rest of his flock, in the pastures of the wilderness, being comparatively safe, to go and seek one lost sheep; so Christ is particularly earnest in bringing home sinners to his church from their perilous wanderings; and he considers this as much his office, or employment, as taking care of those who are already brought back. The owner of the flock sought the lost sheep till he found it, and then " laid it on his shoulders " rejoicing:" thus Christ, by his word and providence, seeks out the lost sinner, and by his Spirit overcomes his unwillingness to return to God; by his power he delivers him from the bondage of sin and Satan, and carries him above the temptations of this evil world: and he rejoices in thus bringing him back to the favour and service of God, by repentance, faith, and true conversion. (*Marg. Ref.* c—g.—*Notes, Ps.* xxiii. 1—3. cxix. 176. *Is.* liii. 4—6. *Ez.* xxxiv. 11—16. 23—31. *Matt.* xviii. 12—14. *John* x. 1—13. 26—31. 1 *Pet.* ii. 18—25, *v.* 25.)—As he, who had found his lost sheep, might be supposed to call on his friends and neighbours to rejoice with him on that account, rather than because the other ninety-nine had not strayed; so our Lord declared, that " there is joy in heaven over " one sinner that repenteth:" the Lord himself rejoices, and all his holy worshippers rejoice with him, on that ac-count; even " more than over ninety and nine just per-" sons who need no repentance."—This may be differently explained. Angels are perfectly righteous and need no re-pentance: yet the repentance of one sinner on earth, taken in connexion with its causes and consequences, redounds more to the glory of God, and therefore causes more joy in heaven, than the continuance of angels in their primi-tive state of rectitude. (*Marg. Ref.* h—k.—*Note, Eph.* iii. 9—12.) Some have been preserved from that degree of outward vice and impiety, to which others have been left: but the conversion of the latter, being more unexpected and surprising, as well as the more signal display of divine power and mercy, may be considered as exciting far louder acclamations of joy and praise, than that of such as com-*paratively* " needed no repentance."—Every Christian at his first conversion, occasioned this joy in heaven; but it

is the cause of renewed joy, when another and another is brought to repentance: and this joy is more sensibly felt and expressed, every time one more is added to the com-pany of the redeemed, than it is on account of " the " ninety and nine" who are already brought home, and have no further occasion for that entire repentance from dead works, which the newly awakened sinner exercises: even as a father rejoices more in the unexpected recovery of one son, who was given over for death, than in the health and safety of his other children, whom yet he loves with equal tenderness.—But doubtless our Lord intended more immediately to address the Pharisees, according to their own opinion of themselves. They proudly fancied that they needed no repentance; yet the conversion of one publican or harlot was far more pleasing and honourable to God, and matter of far greater joy in heaven, than the formality and decency of any number of those, who yet thought themselves exclusively " the sheep of his pasture:" and the publican's tears of godly sorrow, and broken cries for mercy, were far more acceptable, than all their long prayers and ostentatious austerities. (*Notes,* 8—10. 22—32. *Matt.* xviii. 9—14. *Jer.* xxxi. 18—20. *Matt.* xxi. 28—32.)

Rejoice with me. (6) Συγχαρητε μοι. 9. i. 58. 1 *Cor.* xii. 26. xiii. 6. *Phil.* ii. 17, 18.—*Gen.* xxi. 6. *Sept.*—*Which was lost.*] Το απωλολος. 24. 32. xix. 10. *Matt.* xviii. 11.

V. 8—10. The purport of this parable is nearly the same with that of the preceding: it shews the value which Christ puts upon the souls of his chosen people. They are his property, the fruit of his toil and sufferings: and he will use suitable means and render them effectual, to find them out, and bring them home to his church; and then all who love him will be called on to rejoice with him on that account: so that " there is joy in the presence of " the angels of God, over one sinner that repenteth."— The true repentance of a sinner implies his deliverance from eternal misery, and his being made an heir of ever-lasting felicity. It is a trophy of Christ's victory over the powers of darkness, and a blessed effect of his atoning sacrifice. A monument is thus raised up to the glory of divine mercy and grace, which shall continue to all eter-nity: a worshipper of God is added to his church, who will glorify him for ever: a man, before unprofitable and mischievous, and who would otherwise have served the cause of Satan during the rest of his days, is now made the disciple and servant of Jesus Christ, to do his will and promote his gospel, by his example, prayers, endeavours,

3 ᴇ 6

P Matt. xxi. 28—31.

q Deut. xxi. 16, 17. Ps. xvi. 5, xvii. 14.

r 2 Chr. xxxiii. —9. Job xxi. 13—15. xxii. 17, 18. Ps. x. 4—6. lxxiii. 27. Prov. xxvii. 8. Is. i. 4. xxx. 11. Jer. ii. 13. 17—19. Mic. vi. 3. Eph. ii. 12, 13, 17.

11 ¶ And he said, 'A certain man had two sons:

12 And the younger of them said to his father, Father, 'give me the portion of goods that falleth to me. And he divided unto them his living.

13 And not many days after, the younger son gathered all together, 'and took his journey into a far country, and there 'wasted his substance with riotous living.

14 And when he had spent all, there 'arose a mighty famine in that land; and he began to be in want.

15 And 'he went and joined him-

s. xvi. 1. 19. Prov. v. 9—14. vi. 26. xviii. 9. xxi. 17. 20. xxiii. 19—22. xxviii. 7. xxix. 3. Ec. xi. 9, 10. Is. xxii. 13. lvi. 12. xxii. 13. lvi. 12. Am. vi. 3— 7. Rom. xiii. 13, 14. 1 Pet. iv. 3, 4. 2 Pet. ii. 13.

t 2 Chr. xxxiii. 11. Ez. xvi. 27

Hos. ii. 9—14. Am. viii. 9, 10.	u 13. Ex. x. 3. 2 Chr. xxviii. 22. Is. i. 5. Is. l. 1 —13. lvii. 17. Jer. v. 3. viii. 4—6. xxxi. 18, 19. 2 Tim. ii. 25, 26.	Rev. ii. 21, 22.

and the improvement of all his talents during the residue of his life. As then angels love the Lord, and hate iniquity; as they are free from pride, enmity, and envy, and filled with benevolence; they must rejoice exceedingly with the divine Saviour, whenever they are made acquainted with a work of his grace, which is of such immense and everlasting importance, as even the repentance of one single sinner. All true Christians rejoice, and praise God, for the appearance of this happy change in the temper and conduct of any person within the circle of their acquaintance, in exact proportion to the degree of their humility, zeal, and love : these dispositions are perfect in the angels, and the gracious change may be fully certified to them; we may therefore conclude, that their acclamations of joyful praise will be proportionably fervent and rapturous, most honourable to God, and an accession to their own felicity. In this declaration the Pharisees might see, as in a glass, the hatefulness of their own temper and conduct : and nothing could be more suited to give encouragement to the poor sinners, who came to hear our Lord's instructions.—The good Shepherd himself rejoices over the lost sheep when found, and the Father over the returning prodigal ; and therefore some expositors seem to confine the "joy in heaven" to God himself, who rejoices in the presence of his angels. But the good Shepherd called on all his friends to rejoice with him ; and the whole family rejoiced when the prodigal returned : so that, doubtless, angels and "the spirits of just men made perfect," participate the joy of God our Saviour when one sinner repents ; as it is intimated in each of these parables. (Marg. Ref. v.—Notes, 3—7, vv. 6, 7. 22—24.)—' This ' consideration should inflame the zeal, and quicken the ' industry, of the spiritual shepherd, for the conversion of ' sinners; as knowing this is a work so highly acceptable ' to the God of heaven, and that for which he sent " the ' " great Shepherd of the sheep" into the world.' Whitby. (Note, Jam. v. 19, 20. P. O. 12—20.)

Pieces. (8) Δραχμας, 9. " Drachmas." Marg. Here only N. T. Διδραχμα, Matt. xvii. 24.—Diligently.] Επιμελως. Here only N. T. (Επιμελεομαι, x. 34.)—Gen. vi. 5. viii. 21. —That repenteth. (10) Μετανοωντι. 7. x. 13. xiii. 3. 5. See on Matt. iii. 2.

V. 11, 12. (Note, Matt. xxi. 28—32.) The preceding parables chiefly illustrate the importance of a sinner's conversion, in the judgment of God himself, and of his angels and servants : but this further shews the nature of repentance, and the most gracious reception, which the truly penitent, however vile they have been, experience from our merciful God and Father. In those, the exposed and helpless condition of lost sinners is represented ; but in this the rebellion and ingratitude of their conduct is exhibited. Many suppose, that the Jews and Gentiles are re-

presented by the two sons : but the occasion on which the parable was spoken, evidently shews, that the Pharisees were primarily intended by " the elder son ;" and the publicans, and other immoral and irreligious Jews, by the younger. The same distinction between formal and moral persons, and those of more scandalous lives, is found in every country : and the two companies include all, except the remnant of penitent believers. The situation, however, of the idolatrous nations, compared with that of the Jews; and the conversion of the former, with the indignation of the latter, might also be prophetically intended.—The case of " the younger son" is first and more largely described. We are led to consider him, as having been well educated, and kindly treated, by a pious, prudent, and affectionate father, in whose family he had every profitable indulgence : but, without cause, he ungratefully demanded " the por- " tion of goods that fell to " his share. This accords to the foolish and perverse conduct of many children ; who grow weary of the good regulations and subordination of their parents' family, and want to be removed from under their rule and out of their sight ; vainly supposing that they can manage better for themselves, than their parents do for them : and, instead of being thankful for the persevering care and tenderness of their parents in former years, they think themselves entitled to a " portion of goods," as if they had a legal claim to it. But it also aptly describes the temper of sinners respecting God : notwithstanding his providential kindness and the reasonableness of his commands, they cast off all regard to his authority, and endeavour to break loose from the impressions of a religious education, if they have been favoured with one : they count themselves entitled to a large share of worldly possessions, and murmur if not thus indulged ; and they foolishly imagine that they shall best enjoy themselves, when they most regret or rebel against God.—The father's division of his substance, between his sons, may be considered as an illustration of his kindness, and an aggravation of the prodigal's guilt in leaving him : and it shews that God often indulges men in their carnal inclinations, that they may be more inexcusable in rebellion, and may know by experience the folly of their own choice.—It is said that there is a custom, or law, in the east, by which the son may demand his portion, in the life time of his father, who cannot legally refuse compliance. Nothing of this, however, is at all intimated in scripture.

Of goods. (12) Της ουσιας. 13. Here only N. T.—His living. (12) Τον βιον. 30. See on Mark xii. 44.

V. 13—16. It is next stated, that the younger son removed with all his property into a far country, as if he meant to traffick with it ; but in fact that he might receive no more counsel or controul from his father. This represents the prosperous sinner's increasing impiety, and dis-

3 I 7

self to a citizen of that country; and he sent him into his fields *to feed swine.

16 And ʰ he would fain have filled his belly with the husks that the swine did eat: and ˡ no man gave unto him.

17 And ᵏ when he came to himself, he said, ᵇ How many hired servants of my father's have bread enough and

to spare, and I perish with hunger!

18 I ᶜ will arise, and go to my father, and will say unto him, ᵈ Father, ᵉ I have sinned ᶠ against heaven, and before thee,

19 And am ᵍ no more worthy to be called thy son: ʰ make me as one of thy hired servants.

20 And he arose, and came to his

---

regard of God: and the prodigal's "wasting his substance "in riotous living," shadows forth the abuse which men make of the bounty of Providence, by spending it on their lusts, and the manner in which they often ruin their health, and shorten their lives, by excess. (*Marg. Ref.* r, s.) The prodigal is next described, as having "spent all:" and, a famine at the same time prevailing in the land, he was entirely deserted by his companions and flatterers, and began to be destitute. This shews the wasting transient nature of ungodly pleasure and prosperity, and the tendency of sin to produce misery: and also that the Lord often visits the sinner with additional afflictions, especially when he proposes to bring him to repentance. (*Marg. Ref.* t.—*Note, Hos.* ii. 6, 7.)—But the prodigal was at this time too stout-hearted to return home, disgraced and impoverished, and submit to his offended father: and therefore he hired himself as a servant to a person in that distant country, who " sent him into his fields to feed swine." This was a mean employment in itself; but among the Jews, to whom those animals were ceremonially unclean, it might be considered as the greatest debasement imaginable, especially to one who had been brought up in affluence. Yet, as if the hardship and disgrace had been too little, he was scarcely allowed to satisfy the cravings of his appetite with the husks, or mast, the coarse wild fruits, on which the swine fed; though for want of other food, he earnestly desired it: so that he was reduced to the danger even of perishing by hunger.—Thus the sinner, when suffering under the effects of his transgressions, instead of repenting and humbling himself before God, often plunges still deeper into the basest crimes, and sells himself to Satan, that most cruel of masters, to work iniquity of the most scandalous and degrading kind: and yet sometimes can hardly obtain the meanest sustenance; and grows more and more despicable and miserable, having nothing but destruction before his eyes!

Wasted. (13) Διεσκορπισε. xvi. 1. *Matt.* xxv. 24.— *In riotous living.*] Ζων ασωτως. Here only N. T. Ab ασωτια. *Tit.* i. 6. 1 *Pet.* iv. 4. Ex a priv. et σωζω, servo.— *To be in want.* (14) Ὑστερισθαι. xxii. 35. *Matt.* xix. 20. *Mark* x. 21. *John* ii. 3. *Rom.* iii. 23, et al.—*He joined himself.* (15) Εκολληθη. x. 11. *Acts* v. 13. viii. 29. ix. 26. x. 28. xvii. 34. *Rom.* xii. 9. 2 *Cor.* vi. 16. ' Proprie glutino:... a ' κολλα, gluten.' Schleusner.—*The husks.* (16) Των κερατων. Here only N. T.—*Cornicula: sloes: wild fruits.*

V. 17—19. Having viewed the prodigal, in his most abject state of servitude and misery as ready to perish; we are next led to consider his recovery from it. This began " when he came to himself:" he had been infatuated and

frantick, and had acted as a man bereft of understanding, having been blind both to his interest and obligations; but, by means of his afflictions, he was brought to serious consideration, and to form a more just estimate of his own conduct and situation.—' He who lives a sinful life is be- ' sides himself: for, being a rational creature, and having ' a judgment and conscience to direct his actions; he acts ' against his reason, his judgment, and his conscience.' *Whitby.* But in conversion, the Lord opens his eyes, and convinces him of sin; and then he views himself and every object around him in a new light, and so forms a contrary judgment respecting almost every thing, from what he had before done. (*Marg. Ref.* a.)—The first thought that oc curred to the prodigal, when " come to himself," related to the plenty in which his father's menial servants lived, and his own misery, compared even with *their* condition. Though numerous, they had " bread enough and to spare;" whilst he, who once lived as a son in that happy family, and might still have done so had it not been for his own sin and folly, was perishing with hunger at a distance from home! Thus the convinced sinner perceives that his own wickedness has reduced him to a state of misery and extreme peril, from which he cannot escape, except he return to God, whose meanest servant is happier than he. —Accordingly, the prodigal resolved to " arise, and go to " his Father," and, without attempting to excuse or pal- liate his conduct, or cast any blame on others, as is usual in such cases, (*Notes, Gen.* iii. 12, 13. *Prov.* xxviii. 13,) to acknowledge that in his ungrateful disobedience to him, he had sinned against the God of heaven also; that he was not deserving to be admitted into his family as a son: and intreating his father not to leave him to perish, but tó employ him in the work, and to give him the maintenance, of a hired servant. And in forming this resolution he drew his whole encouragement from the recollection of his father's goodness, which at the same time aggravated his own criminality.—In like manner, convinced sinners are led to hope in the mercy of that God, against whom they have rebelled; and are excited to return to him, with un- reserved and ingenuous confessions and earnest supplica- tions: and whenever brought to this spirit, they may ad- dress him as a kind Father, though conscious that they are unworthy to be called his children. (*Marg. Ref.* c—h.— *Notes, Lev.* xxvi. 40—42. 2 *Chr.* xxxiii. 12, 13. *Ps.* li. 3. *Jer.* iii. 12—15. 1 *John* i. 8—10.)

Have bread enough and to spare. (17) Περισσευσιν αρτων. See on *Mark* xii. 44.—*Against heaven.* (18) *Note, Dan.* iv. 20—26, v. 26.

V. 20, 21. According to his determination, the prodi-

father. ¹ But when he was yet a great way off, his father saw him, and had compassion, and ran, ᵏ and fell on his neck, and kissed him.

21 And the son said unto him, ¹ Father, I have sinned ᵐ against heaven, and in thy sight, and am no more worthy to be called thy son.

22 But the father said to his servants, Bring forth ⁿ the best robe, and put it on him; and put ᵒ a ring on his hand, ᵖ and shoes on his feet:

23 And bring hither ⁴ the fatted calf, and kill it; and let us eat and be merry:

24 For ʳ this my son was dead, and is alive again; ˢ he was lost, and is found. ᵗ And they began to be merry.

25 Now ᵘ his elder son was in the field: and as he came and drew nigh to the house, ˣ he heard musick and dancing.

26 And he called one of the servants, and asked what these things meant.

27 And he said unto him, ʸ Thy brother is come: ᶻ and thy father hath killed the fatted calf, because he hath received him safe and sound.

28 And ᵃ he was angry, and would not go in: ᵇ therefore came his father out and intreated him.

29 And he answered and said to his father, ᶜ Lo, these many years do I serve thee, neither transgressed I at

---

gal, not regarding himself bound by his engagement to his cruel master, set out on his journey home; and did not delay, or yield to weariness and discouragement, till he came thither: though in such a case we may conceive how he must be distressed with fears, lest his father should reject or upbraid him; as well as have very many hardships to endure. But when he was yet at a distance, his father, (who is represented as regretting his absence, and longing for his return,) saw and knew him; and, forgetting all his son's provocations, yea, and overlooking his own years and dignity, being full of " compassion," he " ran and fell on his " neck and kissed him;" expressing his joy at his arrival, and his entire reconciliation to him. (Marg. Ref. i, k.—Notes, 2 Chr. xxxiii. 11, 12. 18, 19. Job xxxiii. 27—30. Jer. xxxi. 18—20.) Whilst the son, being made the more ashamed of his own misconduct by his father's kindness, acknowledged his guilt and unworthiness, in the words which he had premeditated: save that he omitted the latter clause; either interrupted by his kind father, or not content-ing it necessary, seeing he was welcomed as a son.—Thus the penitent sinner quits the bondage of Satan, and returns to God by faith and prayer, amidst a variety of fears and difficulties; and the Lord readily meets him with unex-pected tokens of his forgiving love. These conduce still farther to humble his heart, though they inspire him with more confidence of hope, in the mercy of his gracious Lord.—' After sin is pardoned,' (as well as before,) ' it ' becomes the sinner ingenuously to acknowledge and con-' fess it.' Whitby. (Marg. Ref. l, m.—Notes, Ps. xxxi. 3—5. Is. lv. 6—9. lvii. 15, 16. Ez. xvi. 60—63, v. 63.)

Fell on his neck. (20) Επεπεσεν επι τον τραχηλον αυτω. Acts xx. 37.—Gen. xlv. 14. xlvi. 29. Sept.—Kissed.] Κατεφιλησεν. vii. 38. 45.

V. 22—24. While the prodigal was confessing his guilt, the father ordered the servants to bring " the best robe," or " the principal robe;" that he might be clothed as it became his beloved son to be; and to " put a ring on his " hand, and shoes on his feet;" and then to prepare a feast for him and them, that they might rejoice together

over one, who had been as dead, and lost to his family and friends, but was now returned alive and well. (Marg Ref. n—q.—Notes, Is. lxi. 10, 11. Ez. xvi. 9—14. Rom. iii. 21—26, v. 22. xiii. 11—14, v. 14. Gal. iii. 26—29.)—Thus the humbled sinner is clothed in the robe of the Re-deemer's righteousness, made partaker of the Spirit of adoption, prepared by peace of conscience, and believing dependence on the mercy and the grace of the gospel, to walk with pleasure in the ways of holiness; (Marg. Ref. p.—Notes, Deut. xxxiii. 24, 25. Eph. vi. 14—17, v. 15.) He is also feasted with divine consolations; while the whole family of God rejoices at his being restored as a child to his father's house, and recovered ' from the death ' of sin to the life of righteousness.' (Marg. Ref. r, s.—Notes, Eph. ii. 1—10, vv. 1. 4, 5.)

The best robe. (22) Την σολην την πρωτην. " The robe, even " the first." xx. 46. Mark xii. 38. Rev. vi. 11.—A ring.] Δακτυλιον. Here only N. T. Δακτυλος, digitus. Matt. xxiii 4.—Fatted. (23) Σιτευτον. Here only N. T. A σιτον, triticum, frumentum.—Be merry.] Ευφρανθωμεν. 29. 32. See on xii. 19.

V. 25—32. In the subsequent part of this parable the character of the Pharisees is delineated, as to the most pro-minent feature of it. Had they been as righteous as they thought themselves, their conduct towards the publicans and sinners would have been very unreasonable. (Note, 1, 2.) On this ground our Lord took the opportunity of ex-posing their hypocrisy and wickedness.—The elder son is repre-sented as having been in the field employed in labour: but when he returned, and heard the unexpected expressions of festive rejoicing, he enquired the reason; and being told on what account the feast was made," he was angry and " would not go in." This represented the Pharisees, though not them alone. They were exact in external duties, but proud of their goodness; they deemed themselves the pecu-liar favourites of heaven, and could not endure that pub-licans and abandoned sinners should receive any encou-ragement. (Marg. Ref. u—a.—Notes. vii. 37—39. xviii.

d 7. xiv. 21. Mal. any time thy commandment: and *yet
i. 12, 13. iii. 14.
Rev. ii 17. thou never gavest me a kid, that I
might make merry with my friends:
e 37. xviii. 11. 30 But as soon as 'this thy son was
Ex. xxxii. 7. 11.
f 13. 22, 23. come, which hath 'devoured thy living
with harlots, thou hast killed for him
the fatted calf.

31 And he said unto him, 'Son, g xix. 22, 23.
Matt. xv. 13—
thou art ever with me, and all that I 16. Mark vii. 27,
28. Rom. ix. 4.
have is thine. xi. 30.
32 It ʰwas meet that we should make h vii. 34. Hos.
xiv. 9. Jon. iv.
merry, and be glad: 'for this thy bro- 10, 11. Rom. iii.
4. 19. xv. 9—13.
ther was dead, and is alive again; and i 24. Eph. ii. 1—
10.
was lost, and is found.

9—14. xix. 1—10, v. 7.) They abhorred them, not only when living in sin, but even when they appeared penitent: they would not eat with them, and deemed it very criminal in Jesus that he would: and they rejected the gospel with the greater disdain, because such worthless persons were admitted to share its blessings; as the Jews also did afterwards, when the Gentiles were called into the church. Thus, when angels, and the Lord of angels, and all the friends of God, were rejoicing over penitent and pardoned sinners; they envied, murmured, and raged!—The father is next described, as going out to intreat his son to come in; but he answered with boastings and complaints. He had done the work of a servant for many years, and had never at any time disobeyed his father's commandment; yet his father had never given him so much as a kid, that he might feast with his friends: but now that " this his " son," (whom he disdained to acknowledge as a brother," was returned home, after having consumed his wealth, and impoverished the family as far as he could, by debauchery, he " had killed for him the fatted calf!" This represents the condescension of the Lord, in persuading even proud objectors to accept his salvation, and the arrogant manner in which such invitations and persuasions are often received. The Pharisees supposed that there was great merit in their strict and constant services; and, because they were not guilty of the outward scandals which they charged on the publicans, they thought themselves exempt from all blame: yet they had never experienced those joys in religion, to which the penitent sinner professed to be admitted. (Marg. Ref. b—f.—Notes, Matt. xx. 1—16, v. 12. xxv. 24—30, vv. 24, 25.)—It is well known that the Jews in general were of the same spirit, respecting the converted Gentiles; and numbers, in every age, object to the gospel, and its preachers, on similar grounds.—To this proud, rude, ungrateful reply, the father meekly answered, that, as his son, he " was ever with him," sharing the provisions of his family, and continually receiving tokens of his favour: and that he was the acknowledged heir of all his substance, though no feast had expressly been made on his account, because he had never left home. But, that it was meet that they should all rejoice over his " brother," who had so unexpectedly been reclaimed from his evil courses, and restored to the family, as one that was alive from the dead. (Marg. Ref. g—i.)—Some expositors have been greatly perplexed in applying this latter part of the parable: yet the difficulty will vanish, if we advert to the general scope of it. Had it been true, that the Pharisees were the favourites of heaven, and had always been obedient and deserving, their present privileges would have been continued to them, and their future inheritance secure, and undiminished by the favour shewn to the publicans. The same would have been the case with the Jews, notwithstanding the calling of the Gentiles, if they had been indeed the

children of believing Abraham. So that they could not be deprived of the blessing, except they were found among unbelievers and hypocrites. In the mean time it was meet, that all the servants of God should rejoice with him over the repentance and reconciliation of the poor publicans and harlots, by which his name would be glorified, and immortal souls saved. They were of the same nature and nation with the Pharisees, who disdained them; and the less hope there was of their conversion, the more heartily it ought to be rejoiced in. Thus our Lord closed the subject, not seeing good at that time to push the argument further against the Pharisees; whom he left to contemplate, as in a glass, the unreasonableness of their own conduct; that they might be induced to give up their objections, and to apply for a share in the blessings of his gospel: even as the refractory son was invited to come in and partake of the feast. The elder son is not represented to have returned any answer to his father, and it is not said that he went in, or that he did not; we may therefore suppose our Lord to mean, that they ought to be satisfied with this statement of the matter, and that some of them would be so; but that others would remain sullen and untractable, after all that could be said to convince them. ' The elder son, in this parable, representeth not the just, ' or righteous: for they are not angry either that sinners ' do return to God, or that he graciously entertains them ' when they do so; but rather are industrious to bring ' them home to him and rejoice at their return.' Whitby. —With harlots. (30) 'They could never say, that he' (Jesus) ' was a friend to prostitutes: because it does not ' appear, that such persons ever came to Christ, or that he, ' in the way of his ministry, ever came to them.' Dr. Adam Clarke, Note, Luke viii. Dr. Clarke, however, allows, that the ' prodigal son was among harlots.' I trust he did not, in his zealous defence of Mary Magdalene from the unjust charges brought against her, recollect at the moment the conclusions, which might readily be deduced from this statement.—Are the harlots (πορναι) so immensely more criminal and hopeless, than their male associates and often seducers, (πορνοι,) that while one of the latter was selected by our Lord himself for the encouraging pattern of our gracious God's ready mercy to the penitent, however vile their previous character; the former are to be considered merely as the objects of his frown and studied disregard? Musick. (25) Συμφωνιας. Here only N. T.—Dan. iii. 15. Sept. A συμφωντω. v. 36.—Dancing.] Χορων. Here only N. T.—Ex. xv. 20. Judg. xi. 34. xxi. 21. Lam. v. 15. Sept.—Safe and sound. (27) Ὑγιαινοντα. v. 31. vii. 10. Tit. i. 13. 3 John 2: Ab ὑγιης, sanus.—Harlots. (30) Πορνων. Matt. xxi. 31, 32. 1 Cor. vi. 15, 16. Heb. xi. 31. Jam. ii. 25. Rev. xvii. 1. 5. 15, 16. xix. 2.—Gen. xxxiv. 31. xxxviii. 15· 21, 22. Prov. xxix. 3. Sept. I can scarcely doubt

3 F 2

tions deduced from it, 1—13. Jesus reproves the hypocrisy of the Pharisees, who deride him ; and speaks
of the introduction of the gospel, 14—18. The parable of the rich man and Lazarus, 19—31.

that the " woman who was a sinner" (not Mary Magdalene,) had been a harlot, and was infamous on that account. (*Note*, vii. 37—39.) The Samaritan woman, if not
a harlot, was an adulteress. (*Note, John* iv. 16—18.) "The
" publicans and harlots enter into the kingdom of God be-
" fore you." (*Matt.* xxi. 32, 33.)—The statement given
in the note, on which I make these remarks, is certainly
suited to sink those wretched women, of this description,
who may read it, into deep despondency ; and also to discourage efforts for rescuing them from their abject condition.
Nay, it seems to censure the very charities instituted for
that purpose. I hope, therefore, that the learned writer
will, on a revisal, modify the statement which he has
made.

PRACTICAL OBSERVATIONS.
V. 1—10.

When the chief of sinners draw near to hear the gospel,
they should be addressed with compassion, as well as plainness of speech, and never be driven away with contempt
and upbraidings : nor should we shun to go among them
for their good, however the self-wise and self-righteous
may murmur or revile. Nay, it is reasonable for us to bestow peculiar attention to them : as the lost sheep excites
the shepherd's chief regard ; and his labour in seeking, and
joy at finding it, are far greater than he exercises about
the sheep which remain in the pasture. Indeed we " all
" have been as sheep going astray," and he " on whom
" were laid the iniquities of us all," comes to seek us, and
rejoices in bringing us back to his chosen flock : and he
requires all who love him, to rejoice over every instance
of this abundant grace. Let us then leave it to those, who
think that " they need no repentance," to refuse their tribute of joyful praise, on such occasions. We know, if we
be indeed true believers, that there is joy in heaven over
every weeping penitent, more than over ninety and nine
formal professors of Christianity.—But shall the Lord do
so much, and employ so many means and instruments to
bring sinners home to himself ; shall Christians, ministers,
angels, yea, the Lord of angels, judge the repentance of
one sinner a matter of such high importance, and cordial
rejoicing ; and shall sinners themselves not think it worth
while to bestow any pains in seeking the inestimable blessing ! Shall they not desire to cause holy joy in heaven by
repenting, who have excited a malignant joy in hell by
their crimes ? What immense encouragement also does
this assurance give the weeping penitent, in coming to the
compassionate Saviour ! We may likewise conclude, that
the powers of darkness will never rejoice in the final ruin
of those, over whom angels have thus rejoiced : and we
may be excited to employ our labours, and pour out our
prayers with all earnestness, for the conversion of sinners
around us ; for if one only should be rescued by our means
from destruction, and brought into the way of everlasting
felicity, it will incalculably over-pay all the labours of our
whole lives.—Nor should we yield to enfeebling discouragement, when our zealous labours seem apparently but
little successful : for perhaps, while we complain and

grieve, that we " labour in vain, and spend our strength
" for nought ; " and while others may suppose we are
doing little or nothing ; angels are rejoicing over one and
another, by our means brought to true repentance. In
this, as far as we can know it, we are bound to be joyful
and thankful, while we take encouragement to labour and
pray with redoubled earnestness, for more extensive usefulness.

V. 11—16.

Some men evidently run greater lengths in rebellion
and impiety than others ; yet we may all of us discern
several features of our own character, in that of the prodigal son. Have we not counted the service of God a burden, and his commands and restraints grievous ? Have we
not coveted a worldly portion, and secretly desired to be
independent of God ? Have we not gone far from God,
and endeavoured to forget him, when indulging our appetites and passions ? While many have been ruined by
prosperity in sin, may not some of us be thankful, that
we have been afflicted and disappointed ? that our expected enjoyments have been embittered, the materials of
them torn from us, and our own iniquities made to correct
us ? Yet even in this case, have not some of us, have not
numbers, plunged still deeper into wickedness, and become more entirely the servants of Satan, in the very midst
of sufferings ?—Let us also reflect on the fading nature of
earthly enjoyments ; the instability of prosperity ; and the
unfaithfulness and unfeeling selfishness of companions
in vice, who readily leave those to perish, whom they once
flattered and caressed for their own base purposes. And
what a vile master is Satan, who allures men by the hopes
of sensual and worldly pleasure ; and then reduces very
great numbers to the most abject penury, disease, contempt, and wretchedness, leaving them thus to perish un-
pitied and unlamented ! But the change in the prodigal's
situation, when, from the credit and indulgences of his
father's family, he was reduced to " feed swine," and want
even husks to satisfy his hunger, but feebly shadows forth
the fall of man by sin, from the image, favour, and enjoyment of God, to be a condemned rebel, a slave of Satan,
an heir of hell, and " a vessel of wrath fitted for destruc-
" tion." Yet alas ! how few are sensible, that this is their
real state and character !

V. 17—24.

Happy are they, who, by means of any afflictions, are
made to see the madness and folly of their rebellion against
God ! With what new eyes do they then begin to behold
the divine character and law, their own obligations and
conduct, their interest and duty, their state and prospects !
The sinner, when " he is come to himself," is made sensible that he is a wretch undone ; and that the meanest of
those servants of God, whom he formerly despised, is
happy compared with him. He discovers that there is no
hope of escaping destruction, except by repentance, and
returning unto God through Jesus Christ, and by faith in

3 F 3

a Matt. xviii. 23.
24. xxv. 14, &c.
b viii. 3. xii. 42.
Gen. xv. 2. xiii.
19. 1 Chr. xxviii.
1. 1 Cor. iv. 1.
2. Tit. i. 7. 1 Pet. iv. 10.

AND he said also unto his disciples, There was *a certain rich man which had *b* a steward; and the same was ac- cused unto him that he had 'wasted his goods.

c 19. xv. 13. 30.
xix. 20. Prov
xviii. 9. Hos. ll.
8. Jam. iv. 3.

2 And he called him, and said unto

his blood; the riches of whose goodness and mercy give him his sole encouragement to repent, and hope for pardon: he sees and confesses the greatness of his guilt and its manifold aggravations, which before he palliated, excused, or gloried in: he allows himself to be utterly unworthy of those blessings, which from the goodness of God he enjoyed and ungratefully despised; and he is rendered willing to submit to any abasement, or self-denial, if he may be admitted into the number of the Lord's servants, and be preserved from impending destruction. Nor does he rest in recollections, or good purposes to be realized at some future period: (*Note, Ps.* cxix. 57 —63 :) without delay, he arises from sloth, and despondency; he breaks his league with sin; encounters difficulties with resolution and perseverance; " ceases to do evil, " learns to do well;" uses the means of grace, and endeavours to mortify sinful propensities and perform self-denying duties, even upon a peradventure that the Lord may have mercy upon him: and he proceeds in this course, though harassed with fears, lest his sins should be unpardonable, or lest he should finally be rejected. But when our gracious Lord has thus humbled sinners, and led them to justify him by condemning themselves, to submit to his will, and to seek mercy in his appointed way; he will not delay to come to their relief and comfort. He sees all their remorse and anguish, he witnesses their groans and tears, he hears and accepts their broken petitions and confessions; and he never upbraids those, who loathe and abhor themselves. This genuine repentance is increased by every fresh discovery of the Lord's goodness and mercy; every token of forgiveness renders the heart more contrite, godly sorrow more ingenuous, and confessions of guilt more unreserved. Thus a blessed reconciliation takes place, between an offended God and a heinous transgressor of his laws : and while the broken-hearted penitent feels himself unworthy of the least favour, his heavenly Father puts him in full possession of all the blessings of his salvation, " seals him with the Spirit of adoption," and comforts him beyond his largest hopes. Thus he is encouraged, animated, and even constrained by redeeming love, to walk with pleasure in the ways of holy obedience: and his services will be as much superior to those of formal Pharisees, as his joy in the Lord exceeds their conception and experience. Then angels and saints rejoice, that the lost sinner is found, that the dead is raised, and that the rebel is reconciled.—And let it be here hinted, that this is an example, which parents especially are called to imitate in their conduct towards their children; when, having been even very disobedient and profligate, they " come to " themselves," desire to return to their duty, and to obtain forgiveness of the past.

V. 25—32.

How hateful must that disposition be, in a *sinner,* which leads him to repine at an event, that fills all the holy inhabitants of heaven with rejoicing! which excites him to despise and abhor those, for whom the Saviour shed his precious blood, who are the objects of the Father's special choice, and the temples of the Holy Spirit! and which induces a worm on earth to disdain *him* as a brother, whom the God of heaven has numbered among his children. (*Notes, Acts* ix. 17—22, *v.* 17.)—It is very wrong to despair of those, who are living in the most abandoned profligacy and impiety. Who can tell, but that they may be brought to repentance? For " where sin hath abounded, grace much " more abounds." But to disdain those, who actually repent, believe, rejoice in God, and live to his glory, because of those crimes, which are now " buried in the depths of " the sea;" must spring from pride, self-preference, and ignorance of a man's own heart. Where this disposition is habitual and allowed, it far more than counterbalances all external decency of conduct: and he who boasts of his unremitted obedience, as if he " had never transgressed " God's commandments;" who complains of the Lord's dealings with him, as if he were not suitably rewarded; who grudges the favour shewn to returning prodigals, and disdains their company; and who quarrels with the gospel itself, or with those who preach it, for giving them encouragement : this man is of a more hateful disposition, than the profligates whom he abhors, and as far from the spirit of Christ and the temper of angels, as the most abandoned debauchee on earth; however moral he may be, and exact in forms of godliness. But a degree of the same temper may be found in men of a better character. Even believers are sometimes apt to limit the mercies of God, and to give up as hopeless, those who are abandoned to crimes, from which they themselves have been graciously preserved. Many who have been long preserved from any remarkable inconsistency of conduct, seem to have little tenderness for those who have been foiled by temptation, even when they give clear evidence of deep repentance. Others look with suspicion on such of their brethren, however deep their repentance, or however unexceptionable their conduct, who have been reclaimed from very immoral practices ; and sometimes they are even surprised or offended, to see them assured of their acceptance, and rejoicing in the Lord! In these, and numberless other ways, the remains of the Pharisee may be discerned; and every feature of his countenance is most hateful, in one who must be saved by unmerited grace, or else perish for evermore. If a man be a true Christian, his present privileges and future inheritance will not be diminished, by the admission of the lowest profligates to the same felicity : but the prevalence of self-preference, on any ground whatever; of contempt, of envy, and such other malignant tempers, gives proportionable ground to suspect that a man is a stranger to the true grace of God.—But how adorable is the condescension of the Lord, in thus continuing to reason the case with perverse worms of the earth, and in beseeching them to accept the blessings of his salvation! Happy will it be for those, who are at length won over, thankfully to accept of his invitation, and to come to the feast and rejoicing, of which repenting prodigals participate, and in which adoring angels

him, 4 How is it that I hear this of thee? 5 give an account of thy steward-ship; f for thou mayest be no longer steward.

3 Then the steward g said within himself, h What shall I do? for my lord taketh away from me the steward-ship: i I cannot dig; k to beg I am ashamed.

4 I am l resolved what to do, that, when I am put out of the steward-ship, they may receive me into their houses.

5 So he called every one of m his lord's debtors unto him, and said unto

the first, How much owest thou unto my lord?

6 And he said, An hundred * mea-sures of oil. And he said unto him, o Take thy bill, and sit down quickly, and write fifty.

7 Then said he to another, And how much owest thou? And he said, p An hundred q measures of wheat. And he said unto him, Take thy bill, and write fourscore.

8 And the lord commended the p un-just steward, because he had q done wisely: for r the children of this world are s in their generation wiser than t the children of light.

NOTES.

But as for those, who persist in their enmity and con-tempt, their boastings will speedily be silenced, and their portion allotted them "with the devil and his angels;" with whom alone they accord in repining, when "·those "that were dead are alive again, and those who were "lost are found."

CHAP. XVI. V. 1—8. (*Note*, 1 Cor. iv. 1, 2.) This parable was addressed to the disciples, but in the hearing of the Pharisees (14). The "rich man" represented the Lord himself, the sole Proprietor of all things; "the "steward" marked out the man, who is entrusted with worldly riches and misemploys them, or with any thing, of which a good or a bad use may be made; as the mem-bers and senses of our body, especially the tongue; the faculties of our souls, health, strength, genius, learning, eloquence, authority, and influence; as well as our pro-perty, and every part of it, however small. (*Marg. Ref.* a, b.—*Note, Matt.* xxv. 14—18.) Every man is in many things the steward of the Lord: all his possessions and endowments are entrusted to him, that he may with them glorify God and do good to men; and an account will soon be required of the use which he has made of them.— The steward, in this parable, "was accused to his lord "that he had *wasted* his goods;" he had employed his master's property on his own indulgence, or suffered it to be embezzled by others, or wasted it by bad management. Thus men spend their riches in gratifying their appetites, pride, vanity, or curiosity; they lavish them on those who do not want them, and in such expenses as tend to en-courage vice or folly: in short, they do not obey the com-mandments, and seek the honour of God, in using them; and they stand accused of wasting their Lord's property, though they neither amass wealth by rapine and injustice, nor hoard it penuriously; nay, though they obtain a high reputation for generosity: for that must be *wasted*, which is spent to no good purpose. (*Marg. Ref.* c.—*Notes*, xiv. 12—14. xv. 13—16. *Matt.* xxv. 19—30.)—The lord is next described as expostulating with the steward, who could neither deny the charge, nor excuse himself; and was therefore ordered to make out his accounts, and recede from the stewardship. This teaches us, that men will not,

when called to account, be able to vindicate or excuse their waste, or improper expenditure, of worldly things, and that death will shortly turn every man out of his stew-ardship. (*Marg. Ref.* d—f.)—When the steward heard the decisive sentence, of which he knew there would be no reversal; he considered in what manner he might so em-ploy his present advantages, that they would stand him in stead after he had been dismissed from his place: other-wise he foresaw that his case would be very wretched; as he had never been accustomed, and was not able, "to dig," or to get his living by hard labour; and he was ashamed to beg his bread after having lived in credit and plenty. This suggests some idea of the most wretched state of ungodly men, when "put out of their stewardship" by death. (*Marg. Ref.* g—k.)—Accordingly the steward de-vised a plan well suited to his purpose, and consistent with his character; determining to seduce his lord's debtors to concur in defrauding him, for their own advantage. By this measure he could, at his lord's expense, confer an obligation on them; and, being induced to become accom-plices in the fraud, they would be restrained from inform-ing against him: yet if they should refuse to give him assistance in his distress, he would have them in his power, and, as a desperate man who had nothing to lose, he could inform against them, to the great injury of their character and property. Thus he made himself sure, that they would, one after another, entertain him in their houses, or provide for him some other method of subsistence. He therefore called them to him separately, and ordered one of them, to give a note of hand, as we say, for half of what he really owed, instead of one for the whole; and another, with the deduction of one-fifth, and so to the others. (*Marg. Ref.* l—q.)—When this project came to light, his "lord commended the unjust steward;" (not for his *iniquity*, but for his *policy*:) he could not deny that it was a well-concerted plan of providing against the time of approaching distress; and in this respect alone is it pro-posed for our imitation: for our Lord added, that "the "children of this world are in their generation wiser than "the children of light." (*Marg. Ref.* r—t.—*Note, Eph.* v. 8—14.) Worldly men, who make temporal things their primary object, are more prudent in respect of their pre-sent interests, than "the children of light," the people

9 And I say unto you, *Make to yourselves friends *of the *mammon of unrighteousness: that, *when ye fail they may receive you *into everlasting habitations.

10 He that is *faithful in that which is least, is faithful also in much: and *he that is unjust in the least, is unjust also in much.

11 If therefore ye have not been faithful *in the unrighteous *mammon, who will commit to your trust the *true riches?

12 And if ye have not been faithful in *that which is another man's, who shall give you *that which is your own?

13 No *servant can serve two masters: for either he will *hate the one, and love the other; or else he will hold to the one, and despise the other. Ye cannot serve God and mammon.

---

of God, in respect of their eternal concerns. In the choice of their object they are emphatically foolish: but in the selection of means, in assiduity and perseverance, in subordinating every other concern to the favourite pursuit, and rendering every thing subservient to it; in politick contrivances to prevent disappointment, to get over untoward circumstances, and to educe advantages from them; in these and various other particulars, they are exceedingly "wise in their generation:" yea, far wiser even than real believers, who are not so singly given up to the pursui. of their great object, nor so active, sagacious, and unremitting in the choice and use of means, in order to the attainment of it. Much more then, are they wiser than men in general are about their religious concerns; or than professed Christians are in improving their advantages.—'The 'Lord seems in this place to teach us, that the good things 'pertaining to this present life were granted to us by God; 'not that we should, as proprietors, spend them according 'to our own will; but that we should dispose of them, as 'entrusted to us by the Lord, in entire faithfulness. But 'men, especially those to whom the greatest abundance is 'committed, are used to abuse them in luxuriously gratify-'ing themselves and others. Hence it comes to pass, that 'the Lord, no longer enduring this waste, justly determines 'to deprive us, as bad stewards, of our stewardship; either 'by taking our abused goods from us, or calling us, by ter-'minating our lives, to his tribunal. But the proper way 'of averting this doom, procuring the continuance of our 'stewardship, and obtaining the means of greater benefi-'cence, is, to make amends to the poor, by a charitable 'use of them. Thus it will come to pass, that God, per-'ceiving that we more properly use these perishing things, 'will count us worthy of more valuable endowments.' *Beza.*—The name annexed to this quotation, is a sufficient pledge that nothing inconsistent with the doctrines of salvation by grace, and justification by faith alone, was intended. But it proves, that the first reformers considered many practical instructions, and even a kind of language in inculcating them, consistent with these doctrines, of which many at present would scarcely admit.

A steward. (1) Οικονομος. 2. 8. See on xii. 42.—*He was accused.*] Διεβληθη. Here only N. T.—*Had wasted.*] Διασκορπιζων. See on xv. 13.—*Stewardship.* (2) Οικονομιας. 3, 4. 1 Cor. ix. 17. Eph. i. 10. iii. 2. Col. i. 25.—*Is.* xxii. 19. 21. Sept.—*Thou mayest be no longer steward.*] Ου ... δυνηση ὲτι οικονομειν. "Thou canst not any longer perform "the office of a steward." Οικονομειν. Here only N. T. —*To beg.* (3) Επαιτειν. Here only N. T.—*I am put out of,* &c. (4) Μετασταθω. Acts xiii. 22. 1 Cor. xiii. 2.

Col. i. 13.—*Debtors.* (5) Χρεωφειλετων. See on vii. 41.—*Measures.* (6) Βαθυς. (*Marg.*) Here only N. T.—*Measures.* (7) Κορης. (*Marg.*) Here only N. T. See *Tables.*—*Thy bill.*] Σου το γραμμα. 6. *Writing.*—*The unjust steward.* (8) Τον οικονομον της αδικιας. Thus, τον μαμμωνα της αδικιας. 9.—*Wisely.*] Φρονιμως. Here only N. T. *Wiser.*] Φρονιμωτεροι. Ibid. Φρονιμος. See on xii. 42.

V. 9—13. From the preceding parable, our Lord took occasion to counsel his disciples to "make to themselves "friends of the mammon of unrighteousness;" that is, of those worldly riches which men idolize, as if they worshipped a deity called *Mammon;* and in getting, keeping, or spending of which, they commit all kind of unrighteousness. (*Marg.* and *Marg. Ref.* u, x.—*Notes,* Matt. vi. 24. 1 Tim. vi. 6—10, vv. 9, 10.) Some indeed interpret the expression, of the deceitfulness of riches, which impose upon those who expect happiness from them: and the clause, "the Mammon of unrighteousness," afterwards called, "the unrighteous Mammon:" is exactly similar to that before rendered "the unjust steward," which is literally, "the steward of unrighteousness."—The disciples of Christ, however, are directed to use riches, in "making to themselves friends;" that is, to expend them in acts of piety and charity, that many, being benefited by them, may pray for blessings on them as their benefactors. This alludes to the steward's *failing* of his former resources, by being discharged from his place; yet, "hav-"ing made himself friends" by his use of his master's property, he was received into their houses. Thus when the believer "shall fail," and be removed from his stewardship by death; those whom he has made his friends by his charitable assistance, "will receive him into everlasting "habitations." Not that this will in any measure merit that blessed recompence, or that the poor whom he has relieved can have the disposal of it; or that all whom he has relieved were pious persons, or all removed to heaven: but, as the cries of the oppressed and neglected poor will testify against unfaithful stewards to their condemnation: so the prayers of widows and orphans, for their pious benefactors, will testify for them, that they were faithful; and such believers as have died before them, may be considered as standing ready to welcome their benefactors to their everlasting habitations, when they quit this world. But as the most of Christ's disciples were then, and generally are, comparatively poor; they might think themselves unconcerned in this exhortation: and therefore he assured them, that if any man were "faithful in a very little," and consulted the will and honour of his Lord in the use of it, he would as certainly be accepted and rewarded, as if

14 ¶ And the Pharisees also, ¹ who were covetous, heard all these things; and they ᵏ derided him.

15 And he said unto them, ¹ Ye are they which justify yourselves before men, but ᵐ God knoweth your hearts: ⁿ for that which is highly esteemed among men, is abomination in the sight of God.

16 The ᵒ law and the prophets were until John: since time ᵖ the kingdom of God is preached, ᑫ and every man presseth into it.

17 And ʳ it is easier for heaven and earth to pass, ˢ than one tittle of the law to fail.

18 Whosoever ᵗ putteth away his wife, and marrieth another, committeth adultery: and whosoever marrieth her

much had been committed to him ; and the same disposition of mind would also render him faithful, if he should afterwards receive more. On the other hand, he, who was unjust in the least, spending even small sums upon his own vanity and indulgence, or wasting them through improvidence, and thus robbing God and the poor, would as certainly be condemned, as if he had been an unfaithful steward in abusing a larger property ; and the same temper of mind would render him unjust in much, if it were committed to him. Indeed if men were unfaithful in " the " unrighteous mammon, who would commit to their trust " the true riches ? " " The true riches " signify those blessings, which ennoble and satisfy the soul for ever : faith gives the sinner a title to these riches, and grace and grace always render a man proportionably " faithful in " the unrighteous mammon." If therefore a man spend his riches upon himself, or hoard them in avarice ; what evidence can he have that he is an heir of God through Christ ? Or what reason to expect, that God will give him that eternal felicity ?—The verse indeed may signify, that they who were not faithful, as stewards of this world's riches, were improper persons to be made " stewards of " the mysteries of God," to whom are committed the true riches, that they " may make many rich."—If, however, any persons were unfaithful in the things entrusted to them for a time, and of which an account must be rendered ; how could they expect the Lord to give them at last an inheritance to be their own for ever, by an unalienable tenure ? For what prudent man would give an estate to his steward, when he had been dishonest and unfaithful to the trust which had been reposed in him ? (Marg. Ref. a—h.) This application of the parable, our Lord closed by repeating a solemn warning, which has already been considered. (Note, Matt. vi. 24.)—' At least he will at-' tend to the one, and neglect the other.' Campbell.

The mammon, &c. (9) Τᴇ μαμωνα. 11. 13.—See on Matt. vi. 24. Not elsewhere N. T.—Ye fail.] Εκλιπητε. xxii. 32. Heb. i. 12.—Gen. xxv. 8. xlix. 33. Ps. civ. 29. Jer. xlii. 17. 22.—Habitations.] Σκηνας. ix. 33. Matt. xvii. 4. Mark ix. 5. Acts xv. 8. Rev. xiii. 6.—Will hold to. (13) Ανθεξεται. Matt. vi. 24. 1 Thes. v. 14. Tit. i. 9.—' Firmi-' ter teneo ... ne eripiatur, concidat, et pereat.' Schleusner.

V. 14. 15. The Pharisees were addicted to covetousness, in proportion as they desired to be thought exempt from licentiousness. (Notes, 1, 2. Matt. v. 27, 28. 31, 32.) They were " lovers of money," and often got it by extortion and injustice ; and they either spent it in self-indulgence, or hoarded it for themselves, and their families. When therefore they heard our Lord discourse in this manner on the use of riches, they treated his instructions with the utmost derision and contempt ; sneering at him, ' as a vi-' sionary, who did not understand human life, or only ap-' peared to despise the world, because (as they supposed) ' it was out of his reach.' Doddridge. But he calmly replied to their disdain, that they indeed " justified them-" selves " by various plausible pretences, and preserved a fair appearance before men ; but " God knew their hearts," which were full of hypocrisy, pride, and wickedness : and, though their forms, austerities, superstitions, and traditions were highly esteemed " among men," as if they were of great excellency ; yet they were an " abomination in the " sight of God."—This is also the case with a variety of endowments, dispositions, and achievements, which men " highly esteem," but which God abhors : such, for instance, is the thirst for glory, the ambition of conquest, the desire of revenge called a quick sense of honour ; the disposition to grasp after riches as the grand object, if not attended with gross injustice or excessive penuriousness ; and a lavish generosity, though not directed to any valuable purpose. In these and innumerable other instances, God abhors what man highly esteems.

Covetous. (14) Φιλαργυροι. 2 Tim. iii. 2. Not elsewhere N. T. Φιλαργυρια. 1 Tim. vi. 10. Ex φιλος, amicus, et αργυρος, argentum, pecunia.—They derided.] Εξεμυκτηριζον. xxiii. 35. Not elsewhere N. T. Ps. xxii. 7. Sept. Μυκτηριζω. Gal. vi. 7.—Job xxii. 19. Ps. lxxx. 6. Prov. i. 30. xv. 5. 20. Jer. xx. 7. Sept. A μυκτηρ, nares, nasus.—That which is highly esteemed. (15) Το ὑψηλον. Rom. xii. 16. Tᴗηλος. ' Altus ... excellens, magnificus, ... robustus, ... fas-' tuosus. ... Homines qui superbiunt de pictate sua, displicent ' Deo.' Schleusner. (Note, Hab. ii. 4.)—Abomination.] Βδελυγμα. See on Matt. xxiv. 15.

V. 16—18. The Pharisees were very zealous for the ceremonial law, as well as for their own traditions ; and they opposed Christ, supposing that his doctrine was contrary to it : but he intimated to them, that a more spiritual dispensation was about to be introduced. The law, and the p hets who explained and enforced the law, continued inᵖfull force, as the sole rule of faith and practice, till John the forerunner of the Messiah began his ministry : since that time " the kingdom of God had been preached ;" and though the Pharisees opposed it, yet numbers were earnestly pressing into it, and breaking their way through every obstruction, that they might share its invaluable privileges. (Marg. Ref. o—q.—Notes, Matt. xi. 12—15.) They ought not, however, to suppose, that this new dispensation would interfere with the law of Moses ; for it

that is put away from *her* husband,
committeth adultery.
19 ¶ There was a certain [u] rich man,
which was [x] clothed in [y] purple and fine
linen, and fared sumptuously every day.
20 And there was [z] a certain beggar
named [a] Lazarus, which [b] was laid at
his gate, [c] full of sores,
21 And [d] desiring to be fed with
[e] the crumbs which fell from the rich
man's table; moreover, the dogs came
and licked his sores.
22 And it came to pass, [f] that the
beggar died, and [g] was carried by the
angels into [h] Abraham's bosom: [i] the
rich man also died, [k] and was buried;
23 And [l] in hell he lifted up his eyes,
being [m] in torments, and [n] seeth Abraham afar off, and Lazarus in his bosom.

u xii. 16—21. xviii. 24, 25. Jam. v. 1—6. x 1. xv. 13. Job xxi. 11—15. Ps. lxxiii. 3—7. Ez. xvi. 49. Am. vi. 4—6. Rev. xvii. 4. xviii. 7. 16. y Judg. viii. 26. Esth viii. 15. Ez. xvi. 13. xxvii. 7. Mark xv. 17. 20. z xviii. 35—43. 1 Sam. ii. 8. Jam. i. 9. ii. 5. a John xi. 1. b Acts iii. 2. c 21. Job ii. 7, 8. Ps. xxxiv. 19. lxxiii. 14. Is. i. 6. Jer. viii. 22. d 1 Cor. iv. 11. 2 Cor. xi. 27. e Matt. xv. 27. Mark vii. 28. John vi. 12.

f Job iii. 13—19. Is. lvii. 1, 2. Rev. xiv. 13. g Ps. xci. 11, 12. Matt. xiii. 38—43. xxiv. 31. Heb. ii. 14. h Matt. viii. 11. John xiii. 23. xxi. 20. i xii. 20. Job xxi. 13. 30—32. Ps. xlix. 6—12. 16—19. lxxiii. 18—20. Prov. xiv. 32. Mark viii. 36, 37. Jam. i. 11. 1 Pet. ii. 24. k 2 Kings ix. 34, 35. Ec. viii. 10. Is. xiv. 18. xxii. 16. l Ps. ix. 17. xvi. 10. xlix. 15. lxxxvi. 13. Prov. v. 5. vii. 27. ix. 18. xv. 24. Is. xiv. 9. 15. Matt. v. 22. 29. xviii. 9. xxiii. 33. 1 Cor. xv. 55. *marg.* 2 Pet ii. 4. Rev. xx. 13, 14. m 28. viii. 28. Matt. viii. 29. Rev. xiv. 10, 11. xx. 10 n xiii. 28, 29. Matt. viii. 11, 12.

would be "easier for heaven and earth to pass away," than for one tittle of that law to fail of answering its intended purposes. (*Marg. Ref.* r, s.—*Notes, Matt.* v. 17—20.) The ceremonial law would not fail of being accomplished, in that great Antitype which it prefigured; and the moral law would be magnified by his obedience unto death, and established in its full authority by his religion, as well as vindicated from corrupt interpretations. (*Note, Rom.* iii. 29—31, *v.* 31.) But what they contended for as "the "law" was frequently a perversion of it. This our Lord shewed in one instance, which has been before considered; (*Marg. Ref.* t.—*Notes, Matt.* v. 31, 32. xix. 3—9. *Mark* x. 2—12;) for in this matter the real meaning of the *moral* law was contrary to the doctrine, which they grounded on a misinterpretation of a *judicial* regulation, a "*permission* "for the hardness of their heart." So that, while they imposed on the people by an apparent zeal about the law, they were in fact supplanting its authority, and perverting its meaning by their traditions.

Presseth. (16) Βιαζεται. *Matt.* xi. 12. Not elsewhere N. T.—*Tittle.* (17) Κεραιαν. *Matt.* v. 18. Not elsewhere N. T.

V. 19—21. Our Lord here illustrates more fully the guilt, and folly, nay madness, of men's wasting riches on self-indulgence, by a parable or description, which is interesting and affecting in the highest degree: a parable indeed it must be, as to many of its circumstances; yet in its grand outlines it is doubtless continually verified. The "rich man," here described, is not charged with having acquired his wealth by iniquity: and though he was clothed in the most costly attire, and lived in splendour, luxury, and jovial mirth, every day; it is not said, that he ruined his family, or defrauded his creditors. Nor is he accused of being an adulterer, a drunkard, or a blasphemer, or even a glutton, though often called, 'the 'rich glutton.' He is represented as a Jew, "of the "stock of Abraham," and therefore may be conceived to have had "a form of godliness;" and he was so far from being a miser, that he kept a noble house and an elegant table, and it may be supposed entertained his guests in a most hospitable manner. But he was "an unfaithful "steward, who wasted his Lord's goods," neither using them to his glory, nor to the real advantage of mankind. (*Marg. Ref.* u—y.—*Notes,* 1—8. xii. 15—21.) However honourable he might therefore be in the world's estimation (15), he was not deemed worthy of a name in the word of God: while that honour was conferred on "a "certain poor man" who lay at his gate, and was called *Lazarus,* which some explain to mean *Helpless,* and others *God my Helper;* and in either construction it suited both his case and his character. He was without help among men; but he trusted in God, who was his Helper. This man, having no power to labour, was supported by begging. "He could not dig, but to beg he was not ashamed;" and he was laid at the rich man's gate, that he might move his compassion. He was not only destitute, but covered with grievous ulcers; and he "desired to be fed with the "crumbs," or the refuse broken victuals, which fell from the rich man's table, such as were either thrown away or eaten by the dogs. (*Note, Matt.* xv. 25—28, *v.* 27.) It is not indeed said, that none were given him, yet it is strongly implied that his hunger was not satisfied. At the same time he was grievously diseased, and had no surgeon or nurse, to dress, or ointment to mollify, or even garments to cover, his sores; (*Note, Job* ii. 7, 8;) so that "the dogs came, and licked them," as more compassionate than their master, who probably chose to keep them for his pleasure or pride, rather than sustain a poor suffering fellow creature of the same race, as well as of the same nature, with himself.

Clothed. (19) Ενεδιδυσκετο. viii. 27.—*Purple.*] Πορφυρα. *Mark* xv. 17. 20. *Rev.* xvii. 4. xviii. 12.—*Fine linen.*] Βυσσον. *Rev.* xviii. 12. Not elsewhere N. T.—'*Species* '*lini Ægyptiaci, optimi, tenuissimi, mollissimi, et candi-* '*dissimi.*' Schleusner.—*Fared.*] Ευφραινομενος. See on xii. 19.—*Sumptuously.*] Λαμπρως. Here only N. T. Λαμπρος xxiii. 11. *Acts* x. 30.—'*Laute quotidie epulabatur, et* '*splendide.*' Schleusner.—*Beggar.* (20) Πτωχος. 22. xiv. 13. 21. *Poor man.*—*Full of sores.*] 'Ηλκωμενος. Here only N. T. Ab ἑλκος, *ulcus.* 21. *Rev.* xvi. 2. 11.—*To be fed.* (21) Χορτασθηναι. xv. 26. See on *Matt.* v. 6. xiv. 20.—*Licked.*] Απελειχον. Here only N. T.

V. 22, 23. Poor Lazarus was soon delivered from his sufferings, by the friendly stroke of death; and as his body had not been the great object of his care, so no account is given how it was disposed of: the survivors, for their own sakes, would put it somewhere out of the way, where it would sleep till the resurrection. But angels, who are all "ministering spirits sent forth to minister unto the "heirs of salvation," waited round him in his dying hours, and when he resigned his spirit they conveyed it "into "Abraham's bosom." (*Marg. Ref.* f—h.—*Notes, John* xiii. 18—30, *vv.* 23. 25. *Heb.* i. 13, 14.) The joys of heaven are here represented as a feast; Abraham "the "father of the faithful" is placed, as it were, at the head of the table: so that "Abraham's bosom" denotes a place in heaven near to that distinguished patriarch, and intimates that the poor man was an eminent believer, a

24 And he cried, and said, 'Father Abraham, 'have mercy on me; and send Lazarus, that he may dip the tip of his finger 'in water, 'and cool my tongue; 'for I am tormented in this flame.

25 But Abraham said, 'Son, 're-member that thou in thy life-time receivedst 'thy good things, and 'likewise Lazarus evil things: but now he is comforted, and thou art tormented.

26 And beside all this,' between us and you there is a great gulf fixed: so that they which would pass from hence to you cannot; neither can

---

-aint of superior excellency. About the same time the rich man also died, for death is no respecter of persons: and as he had indulged and decorated his body to the neglect of his soul, so he had a funeral suited to his rank. (*Marg. Ref.* i, k.) According to modern customs, in that *silliest of all vanities*, we may imagine his poor lifeless clay lying in state, surrounded with all the appendages of nobility; and then, after a proper time for the display of this ostentation, conveyed with a pompous procession to a magnificent tomb, with great attendance and distinction. We may suppose, that some venal orator would deliver a fulsome panegyrick on his noble birth, honourable titles and achievements, distinguished virtues, and princely generosity; and at length that the sepulchre would be adorned with some inscription replete with adulation. But all this time his soul, all of him that could feel or reflect, was " in hell," in the place of separate spirits, condemned to torment and misery. In this dreadful state " he lifted up his " eyes," which before he had shut against the truth of his case and character, and discovered his own misery when it was become too late to escape it. Among other objects, he is represented as seeing Abraham afar off, and poor despised Lazarus reclining on his bosom, enjoying the most perfect rest and most exquisite satisfaction: and this view of Lazarus's felicity, joined to the dreadful reverse which himself had experienced, must add to his inward anguish and torture. (*Marg. Ref.* l—n.)

He was carried. (22) Απηνεχθηναι αυτον. *Mark* xv. 1. 1 *Cor.* xvi. 3. *Rev.* xvii. 3. xxi. 10.—*Bosom.*] Κολπον. 23. *John* i. 18. xiii. 23.—*In hell.* (23) Εν τω αδη. *Matt.* xi. 23. xvi. 18. *Acts* ii. 27. *Note, Ps.* xvi. 8—11.—*Torments.*] Βασανοις. 28. *Matt.* iv. 24. Not elsewhere *N. T.*

V. 24—26. It is not needful to determine, whether condemned spirits actually know or see what takes place in the realms of bliss: the representation is intended to shew the hopeless misery, to which they are reduced.—The Jews were prone to confide in their relation to Abraham, even though not partakers of his faith: (*Marg. Ref.* o.—*Notes, Matt.* iii. 7—10. *John* viii. 30—40, *vv.* 33. 37. 39:) and when the rich man in hell claimed him for his father, Abraham did not deny the relation, yet shewed him no compassion. The rich man despaired of mercy from God, yet cried to Abraham to have mercy on him; as if Abraham had been more merciful than his Maker, and was either able or willing to favour and help the irreconcileable enemies of God!—This is the only *scriptural* instance of a prayer, offered to a departed saint, and it gives small encouragement to that prevalent species of idolatry.—The wretched supplicant did not expect that Abraham could deliver him out of " that place of tor-" ment," or give him any durable relief in it; but he desired that " Lazarus might dip the tip of his finger in

" water to cool his tongue." A man scorched by intense heat, and parched with exquisite thirst, might crave such a small and momentary alleviation: thus this poor condemned sinner sought a transient abatement of his exquisite misery; being all that he could hope for. His request was the language of despair, and made way for it. His desire that Lazarus might be sent, may either intimate, that he retained his haughty spirit in his deepest misery; or else it implied a conviction that Lazarus had been a benevolent man, who wished him well, and was glad to do any one a service when he had it in his power: or, as some think, he considered Lazarus under obligation to him for his charitable donations. (*Marg. Ref.* p—s.)—Perhaps the particular mention made of the tongue might intimate, that as this member is peculiarly instrumental in promoting wickedness and impiety; so his sufferings were greatly enhanced by the sins, which he had committed in his profane and profligate discourse.—Abraham, however, answered him in such a manner, as entirely to extinguish his expiring hopes. He allowed that he was " his son according to the flesh:" but then he should " remember, that he had received *his* good things." Riches, sensual pleasures, and the pride of life, were the good *things* which he had chosen, in preference to the favour and image of God and heavenly happiness. In this he had been gratified: he had in his life-time received and spent his portion, and he must not expect any more good. In like manner Lazarus had received and endured his evil things: he had feared sin and the wrath of God, more than pain, poverty, or contempt: he had chosen sanctified affliction rather than unsanctified prosperity: he had endured his afflictions patiently, and profited by them; and they were now terminated, and he was comforted in heavenly felicity, whilst the rich man was tormented in the flames of hell. This doom was not awarded to the rich man, because he had possessed worldly riches; for Abraham had been rich: but because he idolized and made an ill use of riches; instead of using them as a steward, and seeking God himself for his Portion. (*Marg. Ref.* u—x.)—To complete the horror of this answer, Abraham assured him, that there was " a great chasm " fixed between the places of happiness and misery: so that if an inhabitant of heaven desired to go to relieve one that was in the place of torment, it would be impracticable; even as it would be for the condemned sinners to leave their prison, and enter the realms of happiness: so that both of them were finally and eternally fixed in their respective states, by the unchangeable decrees of God. (*Marg. Ref.* y.)—Many in different ages have endeavoured, as it were, to fill up or make a bridge over this " great gulf;" and multitudes have wished them success in the enterprize, as this was their only hope of escaping the rich man's doom ·

*they pass to us, that *would come from* thence.

27 Then he said, I pray thee therefore, father, that thou wouldest send him to my father's house:

28 For I have five brethren; that he may testify unto them, *lest they also come into this place of torment.

29 Abraham saith unto him, They *have Moses and the prophets: let them hear them.

30 And he said, Nay, father Abraham: but if one went unto them from the dead, they will *repent.

31 And he said unto him, If they hear not Moses and the prophets, *neither will they *be persuaded though one rose from the dead.

---

but it has and must be for ever as vain, as his expectation of a drop of water from Lazarus.

The tip. (24) Το ακρον. *Matt.* 24. 31. *Mark* xiii. 27. *Heb.* xi. 21.—*Cool.*] Καλαψυξη. Here only N. T.—*I am tormented.*] Οδυναμαι. 25. ii. 48. *Acts* xx. 38. Not elsewhere N. T.—*Flame.*] Φλογι. *Acts* vii. 30. 2 *Thes.* i. 8. *Heb.* i. 7. *Rev.* i. 14.—*A ... gulph.* (26) Χασμα, hiatus, vorago, ... vastum inane. A Χαινω, hisco.' Schleusner. Here only N. T.—*Is ... fixed.*] Εστηρικται. See on ix. 51.

V. 27—31. Abraham's answer put a final period to the rich man's forlorn hope: yet he still claimed Abraham as his father (30); and supposed that, though he could not *mitigate* his torture, he might prevent the *increase* of it. He knew there was a passage open between heaven and earth, though none between heaven and hell: he therefore desired that Lazarus might be sent to his father's house; (supposing that he would gladly go on so benevolent an employment;) for he had five brethren, who were living in the same luxury and magnificence as he had done, and were in the way to the same " place of torment." (*Marg. Ref.* z, a.)—They are represented as thus indulging themselves on earth, while he was in a place of torment. This fully proves the separate state between death and judgment; unless any man can think that our Lord would decorate a parable, in a manner suited to mislead the upright enquirer.—The poor despairing wretch therefore intreated that Lazarus should go, and testify to them concerning the awful realities of the invisible world, and so excite them to repentance, that they might escape the wrath to come. It is intimated in this representation, that the rich man died young: for nothing is said of a family left behind him, and his brethren are supposed to be living together in their father's house, as joint heirs of his estate. We cannot imagine that there is any *charity*, or even *natural affection* in hell: we must therefore either consider this as a mere circumstance, intended to introduce the subsequent instruction; or else we must conclude that they, whose example, discourse, or seductions have led others into infidelity, impiety, and profligacy, will be rendered more miserable hereafter, by the upbraidings of those whose souls they have murdered: they would therefore most willingly prevent their destruction, for fear of an addition to their own intolerable misery. Many admired writers would *now* be willing to publish recantations of their sceptical, heretical, or licentious works: many actors would wish to come upon the stage again, to act a different part from those,. by which they inflamed the passions, and corrupted the principles and morals, of mankind; and many false teachers, to inculcate and defend a more orthodox creed, than they once propagated. For men will be accountable for all the effects of their conduct, however widely they may spread, or durably they may last; even as he who wickedly sets fire to a house, is answerable for the burning of a city, if the conflagration should extend so far.—In answer to this request Abraham observed, that " they had " Moses and the prophets," whom they might " hear" and attend to. In their writings, the future state, the day of judgment, and the way of salvation were declared, and men were warned, exhorted, and invited, as much as it was necessary: so that if they would not hear them, their destruction would be of themselves alone. To this the other replied, that ' surely they would regard one who went to ' them from among the dead,' and be induced to repentance; as the terror of his appearance, and the awfulness of his warnings, especially coming from a person whom they had known in his life-time, would produce a salutary effect upon them. But Abraham closed the conversation, by declaring that if they refused to hear Moses and the prophets, even this would not " persuade them." They might be amazed, affrighted, and restrained by an apparition: but they would not be influenced to renounce sin and the world, to mortify their lusts, to humble themselves before God, to trust his mercy, and devote themselves to his service. Such external demonstrations and alarms would not change their hearts, without which there could be no true repentance; and they had sufficient means of conviction and instruction, if disposed to attend to them. (*Marg. Ref.* b—f.—*Notes*, John v. 39—47. xii. 42, 43.)—It should be recollected that many of those, who witnessed the resurrection of Lazarus, did not believe in Christ by means of that stupendous miracle: the Roman soldiers, who saw many circumstances of our Lord's resurrection, immediately after agreed for hire to propagate the most notorious falsehood; and the Jews persisted in their impenitence, amidst the multiplied demonstrations of that same event! And indeed circumstances occur in every age, which sufficiently evince, that no terrors, arguments, or convictions, can effect true repentance, without the special grace of God renewing the sinner's heart. (*Notes*, 1 *Sam.* xxviii. 11—25.)

He may testify. (28) Διαμαρτυρηται. *Acts* ii. 40. viii. 25. x. 42. xviii. 5. xx. 23. xxiii. 11. 1 *Tim.* v. 21. 2 *Tim.* ii. 14.—' Διαμαρτυρομαι. ... *Attestor* ... *demonstro aliquid idoneis* ' argumentis; comproho; certa fide, tanquam testis, aliquid ' doceo, trado, et divulgo.' Schleusner.—*Will they be persuaded.* (31) Πεισθησονται. xx. 6. *Matt.* xxvii. 20. xxviii. 14. *Acts* v. 26. xix. 26. xxvi. 28. xxviii. 23. 2 *Tim.* i. 5. 12, et al.

PRACTICAL OBSERVATIONS.

V. 1—8.

It is indisputable that the wealthiest of men, and indeed

CHAP. XVII.

Jesus teaches his disciples, carefully to avoid giving

offences, 1, 2; and to forgive one another, 3, 4. Being asked by the apostles to increase their faith, he shews the power of faith, 5, 6; and that man's best obe-

all men, are only stewards to the great Lord of all: yet alas! very few duly consider this; and numbers are continually " accused to him of having wasted his goods." The Lord is also frequently calling on them, in his providence and by his word, and enquiring, " How is it that I " hear such things of you?" and reminding them that ere long, " they must give account of their steward- " ship, and be no longer stewards." If no suitable preparation be made for that solemn event, the consequences will be awful beyond conception: we should therefore *now* seriously enquire, What shall we do, that when " put out of our stewardship," we may be received into a better habitation? The Lord himself has shewn us what we should do: and though we need the *prudent fore-sight*, yet we have no occasion for the *dishonest policy*, of the unjust steward; for the way of acceptance and of duty are plainly marked out for us.—Indeed many seem to say, " I cannot dig, and to beg I am ashamed: " they cannot enter heaven by obeying the law, and are too proud to ask and seek salvation, " as the free gift of God " through Jesus Christ." Nay, they are equally unwilling to " labour for the meat that endureth unto everlasting " life which the Son of Man giveth," or to seek the blessing by fervent prayer. But the believer, though he knows that he can do nothing " himself," will yet " work out " his salvation with fear and trembling; " depending on God alone, " for it is he that worketh in us to will and do, " of his good pleasure." The true believer also shews his faith in Christ by love to his brethren. Instead of " wasting " his Lord's goods," he " makes himself friends with the " mammon of unrighteousness." Thus he attains " a " good hope through grace," that " everlasting mansions " are prepared for him, " when flesh and heart shall fail." But alas! in this respect as well as in very many other instances, " the children of this world are wiser in their ge- " neration, than the children of light: " and though the security and advantage to a man's present comfort, to his family, and in respect of eternity, of communicating gladly and largely to the relief of the necessitous, be demonstrable; yet how scantily do most professed Christians " lend " to the Lord," in comparison of the sums wasted in needless embellishments and indulgence, and in feasting the rich! (*Note,* xiv. 12—14.) It would be well, if " the " children of light" would, on scriptural principles, learn wisdom from the men of the world: and, having chosen their object, would pursue it as singly and constantly, as they do their worthless interests. In this case, what a privilege would wealth be! How much good might be done with it! How much honour would redound to the gospel! How many thanksgivings would be rendered to the Lord! and how many prayers, by those whose souls and bodies were benefited, for the felicity of their benefactors! (*Note,* 2 *Cor.* ix. 8—15.) And with what satisfaction might " the " faithful steward" expect the hour of dissolution, or the coming of his Lord; and anticipate the joy of being then welcomed by such friends to the regions of perfect felicity!

V. 9—18.

Those who are in lower circumstances should not

forget that they too are the Lord's stewards. Something almost all might spare, that is now wasted, with which to prove their faithfulness " in a little: " and this would ensure a gracious recompence, equally with the larger liberalities of our more wealthy brethren. If men spend even their *little* upon themselves, they will surely be condemned as unfaithful stewards, when turned out of their stewardship. But there are very many other things besides " the unrighteous mammon," in which they may prove themselves faithful or unfaithful. Some may say, " Silver " and gold have I none: " yet, being entrusted with a stewardship of the true riches, they may in deep poverty be more useful, than those who are entrusted with great worldly riches; and need not aspire to or desire their advantageous situation. (*Notes,* 1 *Cor.* iv. 1, 2. 2 *Cor.* vi. 3— 10.) But surely they are unfit to be entrusted with " the " true riches," who are " unfaithful in the unrighteous " mammon: " even as they who expect God to give them " the eternal inheritance," though they waste and abuse the talents more or fewer committed to their stewardship, are undeniably indulging a vain and presumptuous confidence. But in vain do men attempt to serve two masters, or to worship God and Mammon: " if the Lord be God" let us decidedly serve him, and devote all we have to his glory, *Josh.* xxiv. 14, 15. 1 *Kings* xviii. 21.)— When ministers, who have the honour to resemble their Lord in poverty, discourse on such topicks, the covetous, whether Scribes, Pharisees, Sadducees, or Herodians, will be sure to deride them, as visionaries and enthusiasts, if they do not revile them in more opprobrious language. But they little think how entirely the servant of God disregards their contempt and ridicule, and pities their ungodly prosperity. Some indeed of this character are zealous professors of evangelical truth: and if ministers preach against covetousness, or reprove them for it, or exhort them to liberality, they " justify themselves " by a variety of ex cuses, and call their selfishness by soft names, and so make the matter out " before men " as well as they can : but God knows the wickedness of their hearts; and when it must be left, when we have reminded them, that " those " things which are highly esteemed among men, are abo- " mination in the sight of God," as is every thing exalted, self-sufficient, or haughty. Persons of this description are commonly the bitterest enemies to the power of godliness: and while those, who know the worth and the danger of their souls, are pressing through difficulties and temptations into the kingdom of God; they are objecting to the doctrine or exhortations of faithful ministers, and explaining away those scriptures which run counter to their sins; " making " void the law " of God by their own notions or traditions, and attempting to prejudice better disposed persons against the truth.

V. 19—26.

It is most astonishing, that any man can read this chapter, and profess to believe it to be " the word of God; " and continue to spend his life in those very courses, of which the consequences are so awfully and expressly declared! Yet, what numbers are there, in our prosperous cities, of these " rich men, who are clothed in purple and fine linen,

A. D. 33.   LUKE.   A. D. 33.

dience has no merit with God, 7—10. He cleanses
ten lepers, of whom one only, and he a Samaritan,
returns to give thanl s to God, 11—19. The spiritual

nature of the kingdom of God, 20—22. The manner
in which it was about to he established, with the ruin
of all who neglected it, 23—37.

"and fare sumptuously every day!" and how many more would there be, if men could attain the objects of their wishes! The most of those, who do not resemble the rich sinner here described, are either restrained by penurious avarice, or by murmuring, envying, and grudging poverty. Multitudes go to the utmost limits of their ability, nay, beyond what they can afford; and then fret continually to see themselves out-done by their more prosperous neighbours!—What person of common sense would deliberately prefer the rich man's lot, in life, death, and eternity, to that of Lazarus? yet how few prefer " suffering affliction with the people of God, to the enjoy-" ment of the pleasures of sin for a season!" (*Note, Heb.* xi. 24—26.) Alas! most men endeavour to disbelieve or forget such declarations, that they may not be disturbed by painful reflections, in their pursuit of worldly gratifications: so that they refuse to " lift up their eyes," till they drop into hell; and then they curse and bewail their own madness and folly, and envy the condition of the meanest beggar, whom here they scorned, loathed, and neglected. But it is vain for him who has no mercy on the poor, to expect mercy from God: and even if his luxury and splendour be not supported by rapine, oppression, and murder; yet, " if any man have this world's good, and " see his brother have need, and shut up his bowels of " compassion from him;" he has no right to call himself the disciple of the blessed Jesus. " Let no man there-" fore deceive himself by vain words."—He who said, " Heaven and earth shall pass away, but my words shall " not pass away," has here stated to us, that when any one dies, his soul immediately is received into heavenly felicity, or cast into the fire of hell; that whilst the bodies of rich sinners are entombed, often with the vain ostentation of the survivors, " they lift up their eyes in hell, being in " torment;" that neither God, nor saints, nor angels, will shew them any more mercy; that even pious parents, who here prayed for and wept over their children, will hereafter approve of their final condemnation; that not the least mitigation of their misery can be obtained, not " a drop " of water to cool the" burning " tongue of those tor-" mented in that flame" can be procured, by all their cries and intreaties; that with the dying sinner's breath all his hopes expire, and an end is put to all " his good things;" and that " a great gulph is fixed," and all escape is rendered for ever impossible.—Plausible objections to these truths, or direct contradictions of them, may be advanced; and those " who speak according to the oracles of God," will be ridiculed and reviled, as melancholy or malevolent men: for numbers feel it *their interest*, (according to the tenour of their present conduct,) that any view of this subject should be true, rather than that of revelation: but when one after another dies, and " lifts up his eyes in " hell," he awfully finds whose words have been accomplished, the Lord's, or those of such as dared to contradict him. Instead therefore of presumptuously speculating on the brink of this tremendous precipice; (like him, who lost his life by attempting to discover the source of the flames of mount Ætna;) let us copy the example of those,

who fled from the gaping earth, " lest it should swallow " them up also." (*Num.* xvi. 34.) If there were only a peradventure of sinking from ungodly self-indulgence into everlasting misery, or of obtaining eternal life by any possible self-denial; a wise man would surely relinquish (if needful) the greatest affluence, submit to abject penury, embrace a dunghill, and endure far severer miseries than those of Lazarus, without a murmur or hesitation. But the matter is as certain as the word of " God who cannot " lie." The rich are not, in common cases, required to leave their estates, or to forego any real comfort of them: nay, the temperance and moderation, commanded them, tend to increase the measure of their actual enjoyment; while the liberal distribution, to which they are exhorted and encouraged, leads to additional pleasures, almost as much superior to the epicure's gratifications, as the felicity of an angel exceeds that of the lowest animal. But should the Lord call us to endure poverty, pain, and sickness, he will not leave us comfortless. It is possible that a believer " may be laid at a rich man's gate full of sores, " and desire " in vain " to be fed with the crumbs from his " table;" but it is not possible, that he should be deprived of the mercy of his heavenly Father. He may be unattended, in pain and sickness, by physicians, friends, or servants: but angels will minister to him, and watch around his dying bed: and the Spirit of God will communicate effectual consolations. And should want or neglect (which rarely happens) shorten his life; he will only be the sooner removed from " his evil things," and introduced to the enjoyment of complete felicity: so that in every possible case, they, and they only, " are blessed, who have the " LORD for their God." (*Note, Ps.* lxxxiv. 11, 12. *P. O.*)

V. 27—31.

It is vain to imagine, that other evidence, or means of instruction, would induce men to repentance, while they neglect " the word of God." Those who have perished in sin could indeed come, and tell such a tale of woe, as would harrow up the soul with horror, or drive men to distraction; and probably some of them would, if at liberty, try in this way to prevent their own increasing misery. The souls also of departed saints could relate astonishing things of their own blessedness, and of the misery of the damned: and sinners on earth or in hell·may fancy, that this would bring men to repentance. But " the testimony " of the LORD is sure, and giveth wisdom to the simple," and is the best and the only means of converting souls, which God has promised to bless and prosper. Though the witness of saints or angels is great, " the witness of " God is greater:" the same things are testified to in the sacred scriptures, which would be told us by " one that " should come from the dead." He that rejects this testimony " makes God a liar," and further proof would be improper: an apparition might produce a greater temporary alarm, but it would not afford so solid and permanent a ground of conviction; and therefore if men " believe " not Moses and the prophets, neither would they be per-" suaded, though one rose from the dead." Instead then,

THEN said he unto the disciples, [a] It is impossible but that offences will come; but woe unto him through whom they come!

2 It were [b] better for him that a millstone were hanged about his neck, and he cast into the sea, than that he should offend [c] one of these little ones.

3 Take [d] heed to yourselves : [e] if thy brother trespass against thee, [f] rebuke him ; and if he repent, forgive him.

4 And [g] if he trespass against thee seven times in a day, and seven times in a day turn again to thee, saying, [h] I repent ; thou shalt forgive him.

5 And the apostles said unto the Lord, [i] Increase our faith.

6 And the Lord said, [k] If ye had faith [l] as a grain of mustard-seed, ye might say unto this sycamine-tree, Be thou plucked up by the root, and be thou planted in the sea, and it should obey you.

7 But [m] which of you, having a servant plowing, or feeding cattle, will say unto him by and by, when he is come from the field, Go and sit down to meat?

8 And will not rather say unto him, [n] Make ready wherewith I may sup, [o] and gird thyself, and serve me, till I have eaten and drunken ; and afterward thou shalt eat and drink ?

9 Doth he thank that servant because he did the things that were commanded him? I trow not.

10 So likewise ye, [p] when ye shall have done all those things which are commanded you, say, We are unprofitable servants : we have done that which was our duty to do.

---

of indulging unwarranted speculations, let every one take heed to the sure word of truth, and pray to God for that new heart and humble spirit, without which all means must prove ineffectual : and let us conclude by seriously enquiring, " What is a man profited, if he gain the whole " world, and lose his own soul ? Or what shall a man give " in exchange for his soul ? " (*P. O. Matt.* xvi. 21—28.)

NOTES.

CHAP. XVII. V. 1, 2. *Marg. Ref.—Notes, Matt.* v. 29, 30. xviii. 1—14. Mark ix. 41, 42. Rom. xiv. 13—23. 1 Cor. viii. 7—13.

Impossible. (1) Ανενδεκτον. Here only N. T. *Quod nunquam contigit.* Ab α priv. et ενδιχομαι. See on xiii. 33. Αναγκη εςιν ελθειν σκανδαλα, *Matt.* xviii. 7.—*It is better.* (2) Λυσιτελει. Here only N. T. *Prodest, utile est, expedit.*

V. 3, 4. ' This contains a strong and important intima- ' tion, how much sin and scandal is occasioned by a severe ' quarrelsome temper in the disciples of Christ : as it not ' only stirs up the corruptions of those, with whom they ' contend ; but leads others to think meanly of a profes- ' sion, which has so little efficacy to soften and sweeten ' the temper of those whom they maintain it.' *Doddridge.— Forgive,* &c. (3) *Notes, Matt.* vi. 12. 14, 15. xviii. 15— 35.—We are required to forgive those who do not repent, so as to pray for them, and to wait for an opportunity of doing them good : but our *friendly intercourse* with such as have been evidently injurious, and obstinately persist in evil, and our confidence in them, or esteem of their cha- racter, must necessarily be in some measure interrupted. (*Marg Ref.—Notes,* vi. 27—38. 1 Sam. xxx. 26—31. *Matt.* v. 43—48. *Rom.* xii. 14—21.)

V. 5, 6. The apostles perceived the excellency, and the difficulty, of the conduct prescribed to them ; and that faith in the divine mercy, grace, and truth was the prin- ciple from which it must proceed : they therefore besought Jesus to " increase their faith." This implied a full per- suasion, that he was able to remove those impediments to the vigorous exercise of faith, which they could not. (*Note, Mark* ix. 16—24, *v.* 24.) True faith is " the gift " of God," and the work of his power : nor can it be con- ceived possible for one mere man, or creature, so to in- fluence the mind of another, b/ any direct act of power, as to produce faith, where it did not before exist, or to increase it when weak and wavering. (*Marg. Ref.* i.— *Notes,* 1 Cor. ii. 3—5. *Eph.* ii. 4—10, *v.* 8. *Heb.* xii. 2, 3.) According therefore to the system of Arians and Soci- nians, our Lord would have reproved the disciples for attributing too much to him : but, on the contrary, his answer evidently implied an approbation of their petition ; and was a further recommendation to them of that power- ful principle, to which " all things are possible."—The idea of a tree being planted, taking root, and growing, in the unstable ocean, is a most emphatical figure to repre- sent to us, that by faith " we may do all things, through " Christ who strengtheneth us." (*Marg. Ref.* k.—*Notes, Matt.* xvii. 19—21. xxi. 21, 22. *Mark* xi. 22—26. 2 Cor. xii. 7—10.)

Increase our faith. (5) Προσθες ημιν πιστιν. " Add to us " faith." Προστιθημι. iii. 20. xx. 11, 12. *Matt.* vi. 27. *Acts* ii. 41.—' Give us faith ; and if we have any true faith, add to it, and increase our faith.'—*Be thou plucked up by the root.* (6) Εκριζωθητι. *Matt.* xiii. 29. xv. 13. *Jude* 12. —*Jer.* i. 10. *Zeph.* ii. 4. *Sept.* Ab εκ, et ριζοω, radices figo.

V. 7—10. The connexion between strong and lively faith with its practical effects, and deep humility, is here pointed out. A man who possessed and maintained a ser- vant would think himself entitled to his services, one after another, through the day ; and yet would not thank him for them at night, or think himself under obligation to him, as for a favour conferred ; even though he had been

q ix. 51, 52. John iv. 4.
r v. 13. xvii. 18. Lev. xiii. 45, 46. Num. v. 2, 3. xii. 14. 2 Kings vii. 3.
s 27. vii. 3. 2 Chr. xxvi. 20, 21.
t xviii. 38, 39. Matt. ix. 27. xv. 22. Mark ix. 22.
u v. 14. Lev. xiii. 2, &c. Matt. iii. 15.
v Matt. viii. 3. John iii. 2. iv. 50—53. ix. 7. xi. 40.
x 17, 18. 2 Chr. xxxii.24—26. Ps. xxx. 11, 12. cvii. 1—4. cviii. 20— 22. cxvi. 12—15. cxviii. 18, 19, 1. xxxviii. 19—22.
John v. 14. ix. 38.

11 ¶ And it came to pass 'as he went to Jerusalem, that he passed through the midst of Samaria and Galilee.

12 And as he entered into a certain village, there met him ten men that were lepers, 'which stood afar off:

13 And they lifted up *their* voices, and said, Jesus, Master, 'have mercy on us.

14 And when he saw *them*, he said unto them, 'Go shew yourselves unto the priests. And it came to pass, that 'as they went, they were cleansed.

15 And , one of them, when he saw that he was healed, turned back, and with a loud voice glorified God;

16 And 'fell down on *his* face at his feet giving him thanks : 'and he was a Samaritan.

17 And Jesus answering, said, Were there not ten cleansed? 'but where *are* the nine ?

18 There are not found that returned 'to give glory to God, ' save this stranger.

19 And he said unto him, Arise, go thy way : 'thy faith hath made thee whole.

20 ¶ And when he was demanded of

y v. 8. Gen. xvii. 3. Matt. ii. 11.
z Matt. x. 35. John iv. 22. Acts x. 25, 36. Rev. iv. 10. v. 14. xix. 4.
a 10.
b ix. 52—56. x. 33. —35. John iv. 9. 21, 22, 39—42.
viii. 48. Acts i. 8. viii. 5, &c. Gen. iii. 9. Ps. cvi. 13. John viii. 7.
b Ps. xxix. 1, 2. l. 23. ix. xiii. 12. Rev. xiv. 7.
c Matt. viii. 10, 11. xv. 24—28. xix. 30. xx. 16. xxii. 42. Matt. iv. 22. Mark v. 34. x. 52.

---

faithful and obedient. Now the Lord has such a property in every creature, as no man can have in another : and he can never be indebted to us for our most constant and unremitted services. The obedience of angels, who " do " all that is commanded them," and that perfectly, leaves them " unprofitable servants" who have only done their duty, without having at all benefited the Lord, or conferred any favour on him. (*Note, Rom.* xi. 33—36.) The services of redeemed sinners therefore, who are under peculiar obligations to obedience, who do no good thing except by his grace, and who " in many things offend all," can never *deserve* recompence, or give any ground for boasting, or in any way be profitable to God. (*Marg. Ref.*— *Notes, Job* xxii. 1—4. xxxv. 4—8. *Ps.* xvi. 2, 3. *Matt.* xxv. 24—30.) A constant succession of services, and an unreserved obedience, with the deepest sense of dependence, unworthiness, and obligation to the Lord, are therefore here most powerfully inculcated. ' It is the duty of ' servants, after they have done their work in the field, to ' minister to their lord as he shall require ; and when they ' have done what he requires, they for that service merit ' not so much as thanks, because they only do their duty. ' If then I treat you more liberally, rather as friends than ' as servants ; if I condescend to " minister unto you," and ' " place you over all that I have ; " (xii. 37. 44 ;) you are ' not to imagine that I am indebted to you, or owe you ' such favours, but rather are to acknowledge, when you ' have done all, that you are still unprofitable servants, ' and only have performed your duty. ... Here Christ de- ' stroys two doctrines of the schools ; the merit of good ' works, and works of supererogation.' *Whitby.*

Ploughing. (7) Ἀροδριωντα. 1 *Cor.* ix. 10. Not elsewhere N. T. Ἀροδρον, *a plow,* ix. 62. *Gird thyself.* (8) Περιζω- σαμενος. See on xii. 37.—*Does he thank,* &c. (9) Μη χαριν εχι. See on vi. 32.—*I trow not.*] Οὐ δοκω. *Matt.* xxvi. 66. *Acts* xxv. 27. 1 *Cor.* vii. 40. xii. 23.— *Which are commanded.* (10) Διαταχθεντα. 10. See on iii. 13.—*Un- profitable.*] Ἀχρειοι *Matt.* xxv. 30. Not elsewhere N. T.

V. 11—19. (*Marg. Ref.* r.—*Notes, Matt.* viii. 1—4. *Mark* i. 40—44.) At some place on the confines of Galilee and Samaria, these lepers met Christ in his last circuit. They were companions in distress, and therefore they associated together ; though one at least of them was a Samaritan. Having heard of our Lord's miracles, they standing at a distance, with loud cries, earnestly begged of him to compassionate their case, and cleanse their leprosy ; having a general belief of his power to perform the miracle. Jesus therefore sent them to the priests, some of whom probably lived in that neighbourhood : and having been cleansed by the mighty power of Christ when at a distance from him, nine of them attested their cleansing before the priests, and then returned home. But one of them, even a Samaritan, being more deeply affected with the mercy vouchsafed him, came back to Jesus, glorifying the God of Israel ; and, returning thanks to his gracious Benefactor, he cast himself prostrate at his feet. The priests would not have attended to the case of a Samaritan, and he could not be admitted to offer the appointed sacrifices at the temple : but he took the proper method of shewing his gratitude. This gave our Lord occasion to remark, as with surprise, that " this stranger" alone had " returned to give glory to God ; " whilst the nine others who had been cleansed, though most, if not all, of them were Jews, had failed of rendering him their thankful acknowledgments. Probably, the Samaritan alone believed in Jesus, as the Messiah, the Saviour of sinners : and this faith, united with a consciousness of his own unworthiness, produced the difference in his conduct. He was therefore dismissed, with the assurance that his " faith had " saved him : " the others obtained the outward cure, he alone got the spiritual blessing. (*Marg. Ref.* s—d.— *Notes,* vii. 44—50. *Acts* iv. 5—12.)—The connexion between " returning " to give thanks to Jesus, and " giving " glory to God," is peculiarly to be observed. It is probable, that the others, at the temple, gave thanks to God for their recovery ; but they disregarded Jesus, their immediate Benefactor. (*Note, John* v. 20—23.)

Through the midst, &c. (11) Δια μεσυ. ' Between the ' confines of both countries.' *Whitby.*—*This stranger.* (18) Ὁ αλλογενης ἱτος. Here only N. T.—*Is.* lvi. 3. lxi. 5. *Sept.*—The Samaritans were generally strangers, or aliens, and not of the stock of Israel. (*Notes,* 2 *Kings* xvii. 24 —41. *John* iv. 19, 20.)—*Hath made thee whole.* (19) Σισωκε σε. vii. 50.

V. 20—23. The Pharisees understood, that the doctrine, miracles, and ministry of our Lord implied a claim to the character of the promised Messiah ; and, according to their notions of temporal victory and dominion, they

the Pharisees, ' when the kingdom of God should come; he answered them and said, The kingdom of God cometh not with * observation.

21 Neither shall they say, 'Lo here! or, Lo there! for, behold,' the kingdom of God is ' within you.

22 And he said unto the disciples, The days will come, ᵇ when ye shall desire to see one of the days of the Son of man, and ye shall not see it.

23 And they shall say unto you, 'See here, or, See there: go not after 'them, nor follow them.

24 For 'as the lightning, that lighteneth out of the one part under heaven, shineth unto the other part under heaven, so shall also the Son of man be 'in his day.

25 But first "must he suffer many things, and be 'rejected of this generation.

26 And 'as it was in the days of Noe, so shall it be also in 'the days of the Son of man.

27 They 'did eat, they drank, they married wives, they were given in marriage, until the day that Noe entered into the ark; and the flood came, and destroyed them all.

28 Likewise also, 'as it was in the days of Lot; they did eat, they drank, they bought, they sold, they planted, they builded:

29 But 'the same day that Lot went out of Sodom, it rained fire and brimstone from heaven, and destroyed them all.

30 Even thus shall it be 'in the day when the Son of man is revealed.

31 In that day, "he which shall be upon the house-top, and his stuff in the house, let him not come down to take it away; and he that is in the field, let him likewise not return back.

32 'Remember Lot's wife.

33 Whosoever 'shall seek to save his life shall lose it; and whosoever shall lose his life, shall preserve it.

34 'I tell you, 'in that night there

---

desired to know from him, " when the kingdom of God " should come." To this he replied, that it would " not " come with observation," and be conspicuous by outward splendour and magnificent displays, like the triumphs of conquerors, or the coronation of kings and emperors; " for behold, the kingdom of God is within you." The Jews expected a kingdom like the kingdoms of this world; und overlooked such things as, according to the prophets, marked out the promised kingdom of the Messiah, which was to be of a spiritual nature, set up in the hearts of men by the power of divine grace. (*Marg.* and *Marg. Ref. e.—Note, Rom.* xiv. 13—18, *v.* 17.) It could not indeed be said to be thus " within " the Pharisees; but it was so, as to many of those whom they despised: and it must be *in* them also thus set up, or they would derive no advantage from it. (*Marg.* and *Marg. Ref.* f, g.)—The establishment of the kingdom of God involved the ruin of its opposers, and the subversion of the Jewish polity: and some think that these events are intepded. (*Notes, Matt.* iii. 2. *Mark* ix. 1.)—To this our Lord added, that his disciples would soon be deprived of his personal presence: and while they longed in vain for one of the days which they now enjoyed, or of those which they waited for, of the Son of man when he should come to set up his kingdom; they would be tempted to follow those seducers, who would then pretend to be the Messiah: but they must carefully reject their solicitations. (*Marg. Ref.* h, i.—*Notes, Matt.* xxiv. 4, 5. 23—28.)

Observation. (20) Παρατηρησεως. Here only N. T. " Out- " ward shew." *Marg.* A παρατηρεω. vi. 7. xiv. 1.—*Within* you. (21) Εντος ὑμων. *Matt.* xxiii. 26. Not elsewhere N. T.—*Ps.* xxxix. 3. ciii. 1. cix. 22. *Cant.* iii. 10. *Is.* xvi.

11. *Sept.*—Several learned men would render the words, " the kingdom of God is *among* you." (*Marg.*) But the preposition εντος never has that meaning in scripture; and scarcely ever in the Greek writers: though εν, which some confound with it, has frequently.

V. 24—31. (*Marg. Ref.* k, l. o—u.—*Notes, Gen.* vii. 16—23. xix. 13—25.) The contemptuous rejection and crucifixion of the Messiah must precede, and make way for, both the establishment of his kingdom, and the destruction of his enemies. (*Marg. Ref.* m, n.—*Notes, Is.* liii. 10—12. *Matt.* xvi. 21—23. xxiv. 26—28. 36—41. *Mark* ix. 30—32.)

The lightning that lighteneth. (24) Ἡ αστραπη ἡ αστραπ-᾽ Ἰωσα. Αστραπη. x. 18. xi. 36. Αστραπτω. xxiv. 4. Not elsewhere N. T.—*Be rejected.* (25) Αποδοκιμασθηναι. See on *Matt.* xxi. 42.—*It rained.* (29) Εβρεξε. See on vii. 38.— Κυριος εβρεξεν, *Gen.* xix. 24.—*Brimstone.*] Θειον. *Rev.* ix. 17; 18. xiv. 10. xix. 20. xx. 10. xxi. 8.—*Gen.* xix. 24. *Sept.*

V. 32. Lot's wife left Sodom; yet lost her life by looking back to those possessions and connexions, which she was called to forsake: and thus she was made a perpetual warning to men in every age, not to allow even a wish for or hankering desire after those sinful interests or indulgences, which religion requires them to renounce, lest they should be drawn aside to destruction. (*Note, Gen.* xix. 26.)—The manner in which our Lord introduces this short but emphatical warning, is suited to excite our deepest attention. (*Marg. Ref.*)

V. 33—37. Our Lord further reminded the disciples, that in the day, when he should be revealed to execute vengeance on the Jews, those professed disciples, who had sought to preserve their lives by forsaking their religion,

shall be ² two *men* in one bed; the one shall be taken, and the other shall be left.

35 Two *women* shall be ᶜ grinding together; the one shall be taken, and the other left.

36 Two ᵈ *men* shall be in the field;

the one shall be taken, and the other left.

37 And they answered and said unto him, Where, Lord? And he said unto them, ᵉ 'Wheresoever the body *is*, thither will the eagles be gathered together.

---

would perish miserably; while those, who were willing to lose their lives for his sake, should be marvellously protected. (*Notes, Matt.* xvi. 24—28. *John* xii. 23—26.) Providence would indeed singularly interpose, " in that " night," in the depth of the distresses which were coming on the Jews, to preserve the remnant of believers who were living among them: insomuch that when two persons were sleeping or working together in the same place, the Romans would seize or kill the one; and the other would escape in some unexpected manner. (*Marg. Ref.*—*Notes, Matt.* xxiv. 26—28, *v.* 28. 36—41.)

Shall preserve. (33) Ζωογονήση. *Acts* vii. 19. Not elsewhere N. T. A ζωον, *vivum, animal,* et γονος, *generatio.*

PRACTICAL OBSERVATIONS.

V. 1—10.

While we adore the awful depths of the divine judgments, in *permitting* such scandals in the church, as harden multitudes in unbelief; and while we allow, that " it is " impossible," without constant miracles, " but that offences " must come;" let us recollect that these considerations do not in the least exculpate those, " by whom they " come." We should therefore fear, more than even a violent and ignominious death, every action, which may prejudice men against the gospel, or stumble so much as one weak believer: and we ought to " abstain from all " appearance of evil," in every case when we can do it without committing *real* evil. We should endeavour to be harmless in all things, and to do good to all men, as we are able; and also " take heed to ourselves" not to yield to resentment against such as injure us. If then our brother has trespassed against us, we should privately and meekly expostulate with him; and if he repent, we should cordially forgive him, and be reconciled to him, without insisting rigorously on satisfaction: nay, if this should be repeated many times in a day, we must not allow our amity to be interrupted by it, provided the private wrong do not involve in it a publick scandal; for thus the peace of the church, the good of souls, and the honour of God and his gospel, may best be promoted, to which all other considerations should be subordinated.—But this strict precept is replete with encouragement to the humble believer. He is often betrayed, more than " seven times a day," into those things, which need repentance and forgiveness; and this consciousness, which covers him with shame, would also sink him into dejection, did he not recollect that his gracious Lord would not require him so constantly to forgive his offending brother, were he not ready also in like manner to forgive his offending children. This will by no means encourage him to sin, but rather " lead him to re- " pentance;" (*Note, Rom.* ii. 4—6;) yet it will support him, in his painful conflict, while he grieves that " he " cannot do the things that he would." (*P. O. Matt.*

xviii.)—When we would imitate the example of our forgiving Lord, or perform any duty which runs counter to corrupt nature; we shall perceive our need of faith, both to realize our motives to obedience, and to lay hold on an almighty Arm for assistance. Then we shall also feel the weakness of our faith, and our inability to strengthen it; and be led to look unto Jesus, both as the Author and the Object of faith; beseeching him to increase that precious grace, on which the exercise of all others depends: nor will the Lord refuse to answer this request.—All men are bound to be the servants of the great Creator, and to devote all their time and powers to him; and are justly condemned, for not doing " all those things which are com- " manded." But as Christians, we are servants to our redeeming God, and bound to obedience by immensely superior obligations. We should therefore serve him in our several places, without intermission: one duty should succeed another, through each of our days; and every personal interest or indulgence should be postponed, and give place to his glory and his command: yet at last we *merit* no reward, and have nothing to boast of; but must still say, " We are unprofitable servants, we have done " that which was our duty to do;" and at the same time we must humbly confess our guilt in every instance, in which we have come short of this perfect obedience. But were it possible for a man to serve God, as Paul did, or even as Gabriel does, and then to become exalted in an opinion of his own worthiness; this would tarnish all, and he would " fall into the condemnation of the devil." How horribly impious then, how sacrilegious must it be, for sinners to boast of their poor polluted services, as if they could atone for their sins, make God their Debtor, purchase heavenly felicity, or even merit for others also!

V. 11—19.

Through pride, ingratitude towards God came into the world. Of the numberless multitudes, who have been created, and are upheld by his power, and who feast upon his bounty; how few are thankful for his goodness! When vice and folly bring sickness on men, and the Lord in mercy again restores their health; most of them immediately use their returning vigour, in adding to their former provocations. (*Note, Ps.* cvii. 17—22. *P. O.* 1—22.) Of the numbers discharged cured from our various hospitals, how few " return to give glory to God," ' not only with ' their lips, but in their lives!' Even of those, who cry unto him in distress, and intreat him mercifully to spare them, how few afterwards " praise him for his goodness," and live to his glory! Of those whom ministers visit in sickness, and who give some indications of repentance, how large a proportion, when they recover in answer to their prayers, live only to disappoint their expectations! In this case it may generally be said, " Were there not

CHAP. XVIII.

The parable of the unjust judge and the importunate widow, shewing that men should pray without fainting, 1—8. That of the Pharisee and the publican, 9—14. Jesus receives and blesses little children, shewing that his disciples should be like them, 15—17. He detects the covetousness of a young ruler; shews the dangers of riches; and promises great re-

wards to those, who forsake things present for his sake, 18—30. He foretels his own sufferings, death, and resurrection, 31—34. He opens the eyes of a blind man, 35—43.

a xi 6—8, xxi. 36. Gen. xxxii. 9—12. 24—26. Job xxvii. 8—10. Ps. iv. 16,17. lxxxvi. 3. marg. cxlii 5—7. Jer. xxix. 12, 13. Rom. xII. 12. Eph. vi. 18. Phil. iv. 6. Col. iv. 2. 12. 1 Thes. v. 17. b Ps. xxvii. 13. Jon. ii. 7. Gal. vi. 9. Heb. xli 3—6.

AND he spake a parable unto them *to this end,* [a] *that men ought always to pray,* [b] *and not to faint ;*

" ten healed ? But where are the nine ?" And of those, who enjoy the best means of grace, and make some general profession of seeking mercy from Jesus ; how few are there, who glorify God by living according to that profession ! All this springs from the want of a broken heart ; a deep sense of their need of free salvation, and a real reliance on Christ, and earnest, frequent, persevering application to him to cleanse them from the leprosy of sin. For when a man is convinced of his guilt and pollution, and that he must for ever be excluded from the company of God and his saints, unless he be cleansed by the divine Saviour ; he will heartily seek mercy, by using the means of grace, and observe the Lord's directions in humble expectation : and when he experiences the comfort of his forgiveness, and the power of his new-creating Spirit, he will glorify God, and most thankfully adore the gracious Saviour. This is the source of gratitude in our sinful hearts ; it springs from deep humility and lively faith, and it produces fervent praises and cheerful obedience. Thus strangers are brought nigh to the Lord ; poor Samaritans put to shame and condemn proud Israelites ; those who have greatly sinned, " love much, because much hath been " forgiven them ;" and whilst they give the whole praise to the Lord, he delights in communicating comfort to them. (*P. O.* vii. 39—50.)—And let us not forget that we cannot " honour the Father," except we honour his beloved Son ; and that when we bow to Jesus in adoring gratitude, we most acceptably give glory unto God.

V. 20—37.

It is not uncommon for men to profess, that they are enquiring after truth, and " waiting for the kingdom of " God ;" while they oppose the progress which it makes among them, and despise those who have it set up *within* them. They are looking for outward splendour, human wisdom, or the success of their own party : but the kingdom of God consists not in meats and drinks, in vestments and temples, in names and forms ; but " in righteousness, " peace, and joy in the Holy Ghost :" and it commonly has the greatest success, when least attended with ostentation ; when unassuming modesty and gentleness characterize the instruments employed ; and when " the word of " truth and the power of God " silently operate, and nothing noisy or shewy attracts notice, or needlessly excites opposition.—Many, who now despise " the days of the " Son of man," and refuse to hearken to his gospel, will at length dolefully wish that they might see one more such day ; but this will for ever be in vain : and, even in this world, those who despise the truth commonly become the dupes of destructive lies, and are given up to strong delusions.—Our blessed Redeemer has finished his sufferings, and ascended into his glory. The generation to

whom he preached, and among whom he wrought his miracles, rejected and crucified him : but his day of vengeance soon arrived ; his powerful indignation, like lightning, suddenly pervaded the whole land, and the Jews were destroyed amidst their carnal security and sensual indulgence, by as tremendous judgments as the deluge, or as the fire and brimstone which consumed Sodom and Gomorrah. Yea, divine vengeance followed even the scattered remnant of them, as eagles resort where the carcases are laid ; and indeed they are in a measure pursued by it to this day. Yet the remnant, who obeyed the word and relied on the promise of Christ, were as remarkably preserved.—But has not the Saviour been rejected by other generations also ? and is there not a still more awful day coming, when he shall appear [*t]o judge the world ? In this we are all interested. Yet alas ! most men live now, as they did in the days of Noah and of Lot ; notwithstanding the warnings given in the word of God, to prepare to meet him in judgment ! They are generally given up to worldly interests or pleasures, as if life had no period, or there were no future judgment. In this course they proceed, till death, like the deluge, or the fire from heaven, sweeps them into destruction : and thus will it also be " in the " day, when the Son of man shall be revealed." But let those, who profess to be Christ's disciples, make haste to escape for their lives ; to get into the ark ; to flee from Sodom ; to renounce all for Christ ; to prepare to meet their God. Let us all " remember Lot's wife ; " that we may no longer hanker after those things which we have left behind, or be tempted to " draw back unto perdition :" let us venture our lives and souls in the Lord's hands ; and fear nothing so much as being deluded into sinful methods of seeking present security : and then we shall certainly be " kept by the power of God, through faith, unto sal- " vation."—The time is speedily coming, when they who have lived together in families, united in the most endeared relations, partners in the same employments, or even partakers of the same religious ordinances, will, in numberless instances, be finally and eternally separated ; while one shall be taken to heaven, and another left to perish for ever in hell. For as the messengers of the Lord's mercy will " gather together his elect from the four " winds of heaven," into his kingdom of complete felicity ; so the executioners of his vengeance will pursue the wicked to every place, whither they may flee to hide themselves, that they may cast them into the furnace of his fiery indignation. " Remember us, O LORD, with the favour " that thou bearest unto thy people : O visit us with " thy salvation." (*Note, Ps.* cvi. 4, 5.)

NOTES.

CHAP. XVIII. V. 1—8. This parable is prefaced by

2 Saying, There was in a *city a judge, which feared not God, neither regarded man:

3 And there was a widow in that city; and she came unto him, saying, Avenge me of mine adversary.

4 And he would not for a while: but afterward he said within himself, Though I fear not God, nor regard man;

5 Yet because this widow troubleth me, I will avenge her, lest by her continual coming she weary me.

6 And the Lord said, Hear what the unjust judge saith.

7 And shall not God avenge his own elect, which cry day and night unto him, though he bear long with them?

8 I tell you, that he will avenge them speedily. Nevertheless, when the Son of man cometh, shall he find faith on the earth?

9 ¶ And he spake this parable unto certain which trusted in themselves, that they were righteous, and despised others:

10 Two men went up into the temple

a brief statement of the instruction intended by it. It was spoken, "that men should pray always and not faint." (*Marg. Ref.* a, b.—*Note,* xxi. 34—36.) Men ought to pray constantly at stated times; to be habitually in that spirit of humble dependence, desire, and expectation, which give life to prayer; to be frequently offering ejaculatory petitions; and to be always ready for prayer, secret, social, or publick, when opportunity is afforded: and they ought not " to faint," or grow slack, through delays, disappointments, difficulties, temptations, persecutions, and conflicts with in-dwelling sin; or even if foiled repeatedly in those conflicts.—Our Lord, in giving this general rule, seems to have had a particular reference to the state of his disciples, under the persecutions which awaited them from the unbelieving Jews, before his coming with power to set up his kingdom, and execute vengeance on their enemies. For this they were exhorted " to pray without fainting." And to encourage them in so doing, he stated the case of a judge, who neither regarded the favour of God, nor feared his wrath; and who cared not for the welfare or the opinion of men, but determined causes, merely as best suited his interest, conveniency, or caprice. (*Note,* 2 Sam. xxiii. 3, 4.) To this man a widow made application for protection against her oppressor; and as often as he appeared in publick, she renewed her suit: but, as he did not regard the wrong done to her, or hope for any profit, or fear any danger from her; he for a time refused to do her justice. At length however he revolved the matter in his mind: and though he seems to have gloried, in disregarding both God and man; yet he determined to defend her, and punish her adversary, lest she should weary, or stun him, with her continual applications. (*Marg.* and *Marg. Ref.* c—i.) Now if an unjust judge might be induced to an action, contrary to his habitual character and inclination, for a person whom he neither loved nor feared, merely by an importunity which he hated; how much more would God, who is perfect in justice, truth, and goodness, answer the persevering prayers of his people, whom he loves, (even those prayers in which he delights,) by fulfilling those promises which he has given for the glory of his name, and by such interpositions as accord to his own holy excellency! (*Note,* xi. 7—13,v. 8.) He might indeed bear with them, and leave them to pray, for a long time, under troubles and discouragements, to prove their sincerity, and to increase

their humility, simplicity, and fervency: but he would doubtless answer them in due time, deliver them from their afflictions, and " speedily" avenge them on their enemies. This will be *speedily;* as it will come soon enough for every good purpose, and in a sudden and unexpected manner. (*Marg. Ref.* k—p.)—The word *elect,* or *chosen,* must, in this connexion, especially mean those who have already been called by divine grace to join the number of fervent supplicants: and the answer to their prayers for deliverance, necessarily implies the infliction of vengeance on their impenitent persecutors. The concluding clause may be differently interpreted: probably our Lord meant, that when he came to deliver the church, and to avenge his people on their Jewish persecutors; he should find but little faith in the land. The Jews would be hardened in unbelief; and the Christians, having been harassed by long persecutions, would be ready to doubt of the performance of his word; while many would draw back to perdition. It may also refer to the general weakness of the faith of his tempted and afflicted people, while they are waiting for him to come to their relief. (*Notes,* Matt. xxiv. 9—14, vv. 10—12. Heb. x. 23—25. 35—39.)—Some think that a great prevalence of infidelity will take place, just before Christ shall come to judge the world; (*Note, Rev.* xx. 7— 9;) as it is probable it will be immediately before the introduction of the millennium.

To faint. (1) Εκκακειν: ' ab εκ ... et κακος, *malus, ignavus, meticulosus, qui pedem refert in certamine.*' Schleusner. 2 Cor. iv. 1. 16. Gal. vi. 9. Eph. iii. 13. 2 Thes. iii. 13.—*Regarded.* (2) Εντρεπομενος. 4. See on *Matt.* xxi. 37.—*Avenge.* (3) Εκδικησον. 5. Rom. xii. 19. 2 Cor. x. 6. Rev. vi. 10. xix. 2. Εκδικησις. 7, 8.—*Adversary.*] Αντιδικα. See on *Matt.* v. 25.—*She weary.* (5) Υπωπιαζη, *contundat, obtundat.* 1 Cor. ix. 27. Not elsewhere N. T. Εκ ὑπο et ωψ *oculus.* *Under the eye.* Taken from the blows given by boxers, under the eye, which blind those who receive them.—*The unjust judge.* (6) Ὁ κριτης της αδικιας. xvi. 8.—*Avenge.* (7) Ποιησει την εκδικησιν. 8. xxi. 22. *Acts* vii. 24. Rom. xii. 19. 2 Cor. vii. 11. 2 Thes. i. 8. Heb. x. 30. 1 Pet. ii. 14. " Vengeance belongeth to God;" but it belongs also to the magistrate, as his vicegerent. (*Notes,* Rom. xii. 17— 21. xiii. 3—5. Rev. vi. 9—11.)—*He bear long.*] Μακροθυμων. See on *Matt.* xviii. 26.

V. 9—14. The persons to whom our Lord spake this

3 H 2

ᶠ vii. 2x, 30. Matt.
xxxi. 31, 33. Acts
xxiii. 6—8. Phil.
xxvi. b.
iii. 5.
a Ps. cxxxiv. 1.
b Matt. 2. Matt.
vi. 5. Mark xi.
25.
x Jer. ii. 63. 35.
Ex. xxxiii. 31.
Mic. iii. 11.
1 Cor. iv. 7, 8.
xv. 9, 10. 1 Tim.
i. 12—16. Rev.
iii. 17.
7 xv. 47. Matt.
iii. 7—10. xix.
16—20. Gal. iii.
10. Phil. iii. 6.
x. 14. 1a i. 15.
xi. 27. x. 1—4.
xxvii. 30—33.

ple to pray; the one ¹a Pharisee, and the other a publican.

11 The Pharisee ᵃ stood, and prayed thus with himself, ᵇGod, I thank thee, that I am not ⁷as other men are, extortioners, unjust, adulterers, or even as this publican.

12 I ˣfast twice in the week, ʸI give tithes of all that I possess.

Jam. ii. 9—12. x xvii. 10. Num. xxiii 4. 1 Sam. xv. 13. 2 Kings
Zech. vii. 5, 6. Matt. vi. l. 5. 16. lx. 14. xv. 7—9. Rom.
1 Cor. i. 29. Gal. i. 14. Eph. ii. 9. 1 Tim. iv. 8. a xl. 42. .Lev.
Num. xviii. 24. Mal. iii. 8. Matt. xxiii. 26, 24.

13 And the publican, ᵇstanding afar off, would not lift up so much as his eyes unto heaven, ᶜbut smote upon his breast, saying, ᵈGod be merciful to me ᵉa sinner.

14 I tell you, This man ᶠwent down to his house ᵍjustified rather than the other: for ʰevery one that exalteth

ᵇ v. 8. vii. 6. 7
xvii. 12. Ezra
ix. 6. Job xliii.
6. Ps. xc. 12. 1x.
vi. 5. Ez. xvi.
63. Dan. ix. 7—
9. Acts ii. 37.
c xxiii. 48. Jer.
xxxi. 18, 19.
2 Cor. vii. 11.
d Ps. xxv. 7, 11
xli. 4. li. 1—3.
lxxxvi. 15, 16.
cxix. 41. cxxx.
3, 4, 7. Dan. ix.
5, 9—11, 18, 19.
Hab. iv. 16
vii. 12. x xv. 18—21. xxiii. 40—43. 2 Chr. xxxiii. 12, 13. 19, 23. Ps. cvi. 6. Is.
16. lxix. 5, 6. Matt. ix. 13. Rom. v. 8. 20, 21. 1 Tim. l. 15. 1 John i. 8—10. f v.
24, 25. viii. 47—50. 1 Sam. l. 18. Ec. ix. 7. g x. 29. xvi. 15. Job ix. 20. xxv. 4.
Ps. cxliii. 2. Is. xlv. 25. Rom. iii. 20. iv. 5, v. 1. viii. 33 Gal. ii. 16. Jam. ii. 21
—25. h i. 52. xiv. 11. Ex. xviii. 11. Job xxii. 29. xl. 9—13. Ps. cxxxviii. 6. Prov.
iii. 34. xv. 33. xvi. 18, 19. xviii. 12. xxix. 23. Is. ii. 11—17. lvii. 15. Dan. iv. 37. Hab. ii.
4. Matt. v. 3. xxiii. 12. Jam. iv. 6, 10. 1 Pet. v. 5.

parable, were confident that they were righteous, accepted of God, and his peculiar favourites; and they "despised "others," "the rest," all others, who did not comply with their rules, as vile and unholy. The Pharisees were especially intended, who relied on exemption from gross immoralities, attendance on the externals of religion, and exact observance of the traditions of the elders.—To these persons our Lord stated, that two men went up to the temple to perform their devotions : the one a Pharisee, one of that sect who were looked upon as examples of piety; the other a publican, one of those who were regarded as the most atrocious of sinners. The Pharisee, full of self-confidence, "stood and prayed thus with himself." Probably he stood apart from the other worshippers, either that he might be noticed, or lest he should be polluted. In this situation he addressed God, thanking him, that he was not as other men, or as "the rest of men," were; enumerating some gross vices, from which he was free, and some supposed duties in which he was exact; and viewing the publican at a distance with contempt and abhorrence. (Marg. Ref. q—z.—Notes, vii. 44—50. Is. lxv. 3—7, v. 5.)—A humble believer indeed will say, "God I "thank thee, that I am not like other men;" (Note, 1 Cor. iv. 6, 7. xv. 3—11, v. 10. Eph. iii. 8;) meaning that the whole difference between him and the worst of those who disgrace civil society, or are cut off from it by the hand of the executioner, is owing wholly to providential restraints, or to the sanctifying grace of God : but at the same time he has very many sins to confess with deep humiliation; he feels himself a guilty, polluted, weak, foolish, indigent creature; he does not generally conclude any one to be viler than he is, all circumstances considered; be pities and prays for the most abandoned, and hopes that they are penitent whenever there are favourable appearances; and he knows, that he is still liable to be tempted to the most atrocious crimes, yea, and overcome by temptation, unless the Lord uphold him. But, "God I thank "thee" was merely a word of course, in the Pharisee's mouth. He spake as if he had not been a sinner, in any respect; and as if he were in no danger at all of falling into temptation and sin. He disdainfully mentioned the publican in particular; as if he were one for whom there was no pardon, or as if it had been impossible that he should repent : and he could not expatiate on his own goodness, without contrasting it with the publican's supposed extortion and injustice. In fact there was neither confession of sin nor petition in his prayer; but he was in his own opinion "rich, and increased with goods, and had "need of nothing." (Note, Rev. iii. 17.) But truly a man

may be exempt from the gross crimes of robbery, extortion, and adultery; and yet be covetous, unmerciful, contentious, revengeful, proud, envious, deceitful; in short, like Satan in all the leading features of his character. He may use uncommanded austerities, "fast twice a week," or more frequently, be scrupulously honest in some particulars even to minuteness; and yet be destitute of "judgment, mercy, "and the love of God:" nay, he may be a hypocrite, a perjurer, and even a sensualist : he may not be "like the "publican;" and yet far worse than he.——But the publican "stood afar off," in some remote corner of the court, as unworthy to come near the other worshippers, and especially to approach that holy man, the Pharisee : and though his burdened conscience and inward distress constrained him to pray, yet he did not presume to "lift up his eyes "unto heaven;" but with down-cast looks, as one overwhelmed with shame, and "smiting upon his breast," as full of self-abhorrence at the recollection of his crimes, only said, "God be merciful to me a sinner." These emphatical words, (which in the original imply the idea of atonement as the ground of forgiveness,) when really the language of the heart, express humiliation for sin, repentance, submission to God's righteousness, faith, and hope of pardon and acceptance. Thus the publican left his cause with God, and "returned home to his house." But our Lord assured those "who trusted in themselves," that he was justified, or counted a righteous person before God, "rather than the other," or in preference to him. (Marg. Ref. b—g.—Notes, Ps. xxxii. 3—5. li. 1, 2. 17. Prov. xxviii. 13. Is. lvii. 15, 16. lxi. 1—3. Matt. iii. 3.) The Pharisee, relying on the merit of his own goodness, and puffed up with an opinion of his singular holiness, remained under the condemnation of the law, and a stranger to the grace of the gospel : but the publican, by confessing his guilt, and crying for mercy as a sinner, became partaker of the blessings of the new covenant of mercy and grace, according to that rule which has before been considered. (Notes, xiv. 7—11.)—Tithes (12) xi. 42. Notes, Lev. xxvii. 30—34. Matt. xxiii. 23, 24. Heb. vii. 4—10.— It does not appear, that the Pharisee meant any thing more than the legal tithes; though some think that he devoted a tenth of his gains to pious and charitable uses : but had our Lord intended, by the words put into the Pharisee's mouth, to convey that idea; he would no doubt have made this point more prominent.

Despised. (9) Ἐξουθενοῦντας. xxiii. 11. Acts iv. 11. Rom. xiv. 3. 10. 1 Cor. i. 28. vi. 4. xvi. 11. Gal. iv. 14. 1 Thes. v. 20.—Pro nihilo habeo; nullifico. It is a very expressive term ; and no doubt was used, as designating one prom·

himself shall be abased; and he that humbleth himself shall be exalted.

15 ¶ And 'they brought unto him also infants, that he would touch them: but when *his* disciples saw *it*, ^k they rebuked them.

16 But Jesus called them unto him, and said, 'Suffer little children to come unto me, and forbid them not; ^m for of such is the kingdom of God.

17 Verily I say unto you, ⁿ Whosoever shall not receive the kingdom of God as a little child, shall in no wise enter therein.

18 ¶ And ^o a certain ruler asked him, saying, ^p Good Master, ^q what shall I do to inherit eternal life?

19 And Jesus said unto him, ^r Why callest thou me good? none *is* good, save one, *that is,* God.

20 Thou ^s knowest the commandments, 'Do not commit adultery, Do not kill, Do not steal, Do not bear false witness, Honour thy father and thy mother.

21 And he said, ^u All these have I kept from my youth up.

22 Now when Jesus heard these things, he said unto him, Yet lackest thou ₓ one thing: ^y sell all that thou hast, and distribute unto the poor, and thou shalt have treasure in heaven; and come, follow me.

23 And when he heard this, ^z he was very sorrowful; for he was very rich.

24 And when Jesus saw that ^b he was very sorrowful, he said, ^c How hardly shall they that have riches enter into the kingdom of God!

25 For it is easier for ^d a camel to go through a needle's eye, than for a rich man to enter into the kingdom of God.

26 And they that heard *it* said, ^e Who then can be saved?

27 And he said, 'The things which are impossible with men, are possible with God.

28 ¶ Then Peter said, ^f Lo, we have left all, and followed thee.

29 And he said unto them, Verily I say unto you, ^h There is no man that hath left house, or parents, or brethren, or wife, or children, for the kingdom of God's sake,

30 Who shall not receive 'manifold more in this present time, and in the world to come life everlasting.

31 ¶ Then he took *unto him* the twelve, and said unto them, ^k Behold, we go up to Jerusalem, 'and all things, that are written by the prophets concerning the Son of man, shall be accomplished.

32 For he shall be ^m delivered unto the Gentiles, and shall be ⁿ mocked, and spitefully intreated, and spitted on:

33 And they shall scourge *him,* and put him to death; ^oand the third day he shall rise again.

---

nent feature in the character delineated. Many on different grounds, may have confidence that they are righteous persons; and something in themselves may be either the *support* or the *evidence* of that confidence: but when any look down with disdain on other men, it is manifest, that their self-confidence is that of the character here described.—*Others.*] Τας λοιπας. Ὡσπερ οἱ λοιποι, 11. The article with λοιποι, implies "the rest," "all others."—*Stood and prayed,* &c. (11) Σταθεις προς ἑαυλον, ταυτα προσηυχετο.—"Standing by "himself, he prayed these things."—*I give tithes.* (12) Αποδεκαλω. xi. 42. Matt. xxiii. 23. Heb. vii. 5.—Gen. xxviii. 22. Deut. xxvi. 12. 1 Sam. viii. 15. 16, 17. Sept.—Be merciful. (13) Ἱλασθητι. Heb. ii. 17. Not elsewhere. Ἱλασμος. 1 John ii. 2. iv. 10.—A sinner.] Τω ἁμαρτωλω.—"The sinner." The Pharisee claimed favour, or reward, as 'the 'righteous man;' the publican sued for mercy as "the "sinner."—*Justified.* (14) Δεδικαιωμενος. vii. 29. 35. x. 29. xvi. 15. Matt. xi. 19. xii. 37. Acts xiii. 39, et al.

V. 15—17. *Marg. Ref.—Notes,* Matt. xix 13—15. Mark x. 13—16.—*Infants.* (15) Βρεφη. i. 41. 44. Acts vii. 19. Παιδια. Matt. xix. 13. Mark x. 13.

V. 18—30. (*Marg. Ref.—Notes,* Matt. xix. 16—30. Mark x. 17—31.) 'Let us not mistake the character of 'this individual. He was unquestionably covetous: for it 'is said of him that he had large possessions, which he 'could not find in his heart to sell, and give to the poor, 'at the command of him whom he professed to reverence 'as the Messiah. Christ detected the covetousness of his 'heart, by his refusal to pursue the course of external con-'duct prescribed to him; and this exposed the deficiency 'of his moral character: for covetousness is immorality of 'the worst kind, according to the gospel.' Christian Observer.—*Manifold more.* (30) 'From the joys of a good 'conscience, and of the Holy Ghost, the sense of God's 'favour, and the hopes of treasures in heaven, and the 'affection of good Christians to him.' *Whitby.*

A ruler. (18) Αρχων. See on xiv. 1.—It is not very probable, that this person was a member of the Sanhedrim: but rather a magistrate in some other court, or a ruler of a synagogue.—*Manifold more.* (30) Πολλαπλασιονα. Here only N. T.

V. 31—34. *Marg. Ref.—Notes,* Matt. xx. 17—19.

34 And ⁹ they understood none of these things: and this saying was hid from them, neither knew they the things which were spoken.

35 ¶ And it came to pass, that ᵃas he was come nigh unto Jericho, a certain blind man sat by the way-side begging:

36 And hearing the multitude pass by, ᵇhe asked what it meant.

37 And ᶜthey told him, that ᵈJesus of Nazareth passeth by.

38 And he cried, saying, ᵉJesus thou Son of David, have mercy on me.

39 And they which went before, ᶠrebuked him, that he should hold his peace: ᵍbut he cried so much the more, Thou Son of David, have mercy on me.

40 And Jesus ʰstood, and commanded him to be brought unto him; and when he was come near, he asked him,

41 Saying, ᵇWhat wilt thou that I shall do unto thee? And he said, Lord, ᶜthat I may receive my sight.

42 And Jesus said unto him, ᵈReceive thy sight: ᵉthy faith hath saved thee.

43 And immediately ᶠhe received his sight, ᶠand followed him, glorifying God: and all the people, when they saw it, gave praise unto God.

2 Thes. i. 10—12. 1 Pet. ii. 9.

Mark x. 32—34.—All things that are written, &c. (31) Marg. Ref. k.—Notes, xxiv. 25—31, vv. 25—27. 44—49, vv. 44, 45.—Understood. (34) Note, ix. 45. Mark ix. 30—32.—Shall be mocked, &c. (32) Εμπαιχθησεται. See on Mark x. 34.

V. 35—43. (Marg. Ref.—Note, Mark x. 46—52.) The beggars, of whom we read in scripture, lived in the place or neighbourhood, where they asked alms, and so were known to be real objects of charity: they also gave a kind of pledge for their good behaviour. This widely differs from the modern case of strolling beggars, who are frequently impostors, and still more generally profligate characters. Except in extraordinary cases, it is in all respects most adviseable to relieve those, who are known by us both as to their wants and conduct: and, provided less be not given in charity, and no extreme case neglected, the refusal of relief to vagrant beggars, is rather a proof of discretion, than an indication of defect in beneficence. If this conduct were generally adopted, the indigent would, in ordinary cases, be compelled to abide where they are known; the sums expended in charity would be far more profitably applied; the interests of morality and religion would be better secured; and the poor themselves would be far more adequately relieved.——Receive thy sight. (42) It is worthy of observation, that giving sight to the blind was peculiar to our Saviour. No instance is recorded in scripture of this miracle having been wrought, either by prophets before his coming, or by his apostles afterwards; nor is it mentioned among the miraculous powers which he conferred on them. In answer to Elisha's prayer, indeed, the Lord smote with a temporary and partial blindness, the men who came to take the prophet; and afterwards, at his request, their eyes were again opened: but this was very different from giving sight to those who were born blind, cr who had become blind by disease. Our Lord was "the Light of the world." "The eyes of the blind being "opened" is frequently mentioned by the prophets, as accompanying the advent of the Messiah; and the literal fulfilment of these predictions was a striking emblem of the effects of his gospel and grace, in enlightening the minds of men. (Notes, Ps. cxlvi. 8. Is. xxix. 17—19. xxxv. 5—7. John ix. 4—7. Acts xxvi. 18—20.) Glorifying God,

&c. (43) These circumstances are added to that which was recorded by Mark.

PRACTICAL OBSERVATIONS.

V. 1—8.

The very great importance of earnest, persevering prayer, and the hindrances, with which we must expect to meet in attending to it, are brought to our minds with peculiar energy, by these repeated exhortations, "to pray always, "and not to faint." (Notes, Eph. vi. 18—20. Col. iv. 2—4. 1 Thes. v. 16—22, vv. 17, 18:) and we may learn how to draw instruction from every object, and every incident, by the animating conclusions deduced from the conduct of "the unjust judge."—Alas! that there should be so many, even in authority, among professed Christians, who "neither "fear God, nor regard man," and who glory in impiety and iniquity! No wonder, when this is the case, that cruel oppressions and unrighteous decrees abound in cities and provinces: but what will such men do, when God shall cite them to his tribunal, to avenge on them the cause of those whom they have injured, "because it was in the "power of their hand to do it?"—Whether importunity, or any other address to their self-love, will induce them to do justice, or not; yet God will surely plead the cause of "his "own elect, who cry night and day unto him, and avenge "them" on all their adversaries. We must not indeed seek vengeance on our enemies, but should pray for their conversion: yet we may, and ought, to desire the deliverance of the church from those, who oppress or corrupt her; even though accompanied with their destruction. Whether we seek to be delivered from temptation, to have our iniquities subdued, and our souls comforted; or while ther we pray for the peace of the church; we shall at length be answered, if we be earnest, importunate, and persevering in prayer: and, however long the Lord "bear with "us," our requests will be granted in the best time, and perhaps when we least expect it. However infidels may deride and defy the threatened judgments of God; or however Christians may be tempted to despond concerning his promises; yet they will be accomplished in the appointed season: and the surprise of terror, on the one hand, and that of joy on the other, will then be nearly equal.

3 H 5

CHAP. XIX.

The conversion of Zaccheus the publican, 1—10. The parable of a nobleman going to receive a kingdom, and entrusting money to his servants ; with the account required of them, and the punishment of his enemies, 11—27. Jesus enters Jerusalem riding on an ass, amidst the acclamations of the multitude, 28 —38. He answers the objection of the Pharisees, 39, 40 ; weeps over the city, and predicts its destruction,

41—44 ; drives the traders from the temple, 45, 46 ; and teaches daily there, while the rulers seek to kill him, 47, 48.

AND *Jesus* entered and passed through ª Jericho.

2 And, behold, *there was* a man named Zaccheus, which was the chief among the publicans ; ᵇ and he was rich.

ª Josh. ii. 1. vi. 1, &c. 26. 1 Kings xvi. 34. 2 Kings ii. 18—22

ᵇ xviii. 24—27. 2 Chr. xvii 5, 6.

V. 9—17.

We ought especially to beware of presenting proud and self-preferring devotions to the Lord. Too many of different descriptions " trust in themselves that they are right-" eous," and take it for granted that they are the peculiar, and almost exclusive, favourites of heaven ; whilst their contempt of others proves the haughtiness and uncharitableness of their hearts. Such men may address the Lord, in a high tone of confidence and familiarity ; they may profess to give him the glory ; they may boast, that they are not like the rest of men, not extortioners, unjust, adulterers, or like the poor Publicans around them ; and glory in their gifts, forms, notions, or austerities : yet it will be proved, that " they have exalted themselves," and therefore God will certainly " abase them : " and all their revilings, calumnies, and rash judgments, will fall on their own heads, and increase their shame and everlasting contempt ; except they be previously humbled in deep repentance, and come with " the Publicans and sinners " whom they disdained, for unmerited mercy through the great atonement. —But " blessed are the poor in spirit, for their's is the " kingdom of heaven." (*Note, Matt.* v. 3.) The man, who abhors and condemns himself ; who approaches God with deep self-abasement, and reverence of his holy majesty ; who looks into his past life, his present conduct, his heart, his duties, with humiliation of soul ; who is ready to think every one better than himself, and must despair were it not for the free salvation brought to his knowledge by the blessed gospel of Christ ; who seeks for mercy, with a trembling heart and with earnest desires, in the way, and through the name, which God has revealed : this man will surely be heard and accepted, when he breathes out, " God be merciful to me a sinner ; " while the Pharisee, with his long prayers or boasted services will remain under condemnation, " the wrath of God abiding on him." This is the path to honour, glory, immortality, and eternal life ; whilst " pride goeth before destruction, and a haughty " spirit before a fall." Let us then take heed, not to glory in ourselves, or to despise others ; let us also be careful not to discourage the weak or the ignorant, or to deter men from coming themselves, or bringing their children, unto Christ ; and let us recollect, that " except we receive " the kingdom of God, as a little child, we shall in no " wise enter therein."

V. 18—43.

The best obedience of mere man, to the holy commandments of God, must leave him under condemnation. We may accost one another as *good*, whether ignorantly, or as a hollow compliment ; but in fact " there is none *good*, no " not one," our glorious Emmanuel alone excepted. The

higher any man's confidence is, that he has kept all the commandments, or any of them, from his youth ; the more clearly does it appear, that he wants understanding as to the spiritual meaning of them ; and that he is a stranger to repentance, to faith, to his own real character and heart, and his need of a gratuitous salvation. (*Notes, Rom.* vii. 7—12.) Men's professed obedience also, when brought to the touchstone, will be found of no value in the sight of God : for the love of the world, in one form or other, lies at the root of their flourishing gourd, and will shortly wither it. Prosperity, authority, and reputation, conduce to feed this ruinous self-flattery, as well as an idolatrous attachment to earthly objects : many, who have serious thoughts, " depart very sorrowful," because they are rich, and unwilling to part with or to distribute their idolized treasures, at the command and for the sake of Christ. So that, it would be impossible for " a rich man to " enter into the kingdom of God," were it not, that " with " him all things are possible."—Men in general are as backward to derive instruction from the humiliation, the crucifixion, and the resurrection of Christ, as the disciples were to regard his declarations concerning those events : and for the same reason ; even because self-love and a desire of worldly objects close their understandings, and warp their judgments. Thus they are left in the dark about the evident meaning of the scriptures ; while they perplex or amuse themselves and others, by endeavouring to find out some hidden sense, which accords better to their pre-conceived opinions. Were it not for this, all would see, that they would best consult their present comfort, as well as their eternal good, by renouncing every earthly possession or enjoyment, at Christ's command and for his sake.— Would we then rightly understand these things, we must come to him, like the blind man, earnestly beseeching him to open our eyes, and to shew us, more and more clearly, the excellency of his precepts, and the preciousness of his salvation : and then, being saved by our faith, we shall learn to follow him, glorifying God : and his other disciples also, witnessing the change, will praise God continually on our behalf. (*Note, Gal.* i. 15—24, *vv.* 23, 24.)

NOTES.

CHAP. XIX. V. 1—10. Zaccheus seems to have farmed the revenue of a certain district : so that he was " the chief among the publicans," in that neighbourhood ; having many others under him, who either rented of him smaller portions, or were employed as his servants to collect the taxes. It is probable, that he possessed considerable property, before he engaged in this employment ; as large securities were required of those, who farmed the taxes under the Roman governors : but he had doubtless

3 H 6

3 And ᶜ he sought to see Jesus, who he was ; and could not for the press, ᵈ because he was little of stature.

4 And he ran before, ᵉ and climbed up into ᶠ a sycamore tree to see him : for he was to pass that *way*.

5 And when Jesus came to the place, ᵍ he looked up, and saw him, and said unto him, ʰ Zaccheus, make haste, and come down ; ⁱ for to-day I must abide at thy house.

6 And ᵏ he made haste, and came down, and received him ˡ joyfully.

7 And when they saw *it*, ᵐ they all murmured, saying, That he was gone to be guest with a man that is a sinner.

8 And Zaccheus stood, and said unto the Lord, ⁿ Behold, Lord, the half of my goods I give to the poor ; and

if I have taken any thing from any man ᵒ by false accusation, ᵖ I restore *him* four-fold.

9 And Jesus said unto him, ᵠ This day is salvation come to this house, ʳ forsomuch as he also is a son of Abraham.

10 For ˢ the Son of man is come to seek and to save that which was lost.

11 ¶ And as they heard these things, he added and spake a parable, because he was nigh to Jerusalem, and because ᵗ they thought that the kingdom of God should immediately appear.

12 He said therefore, ᵘ A certain nobleman went into ˣ a far country, ʸ to receive for himself a kingdom, ᶻ and to return.

13 And he called ᵃ his ten servants,

c h. 7—9. xvii. John vii. 7l.
d xii. 25.
e v. 19.
f 1 Kings x. 27. Is. ix. 10. Am. vii. 14.
g E.zek. xvi. 6 John 7—10.
h Ec. ix. 10. 2 Cor. vi. 1, 2.
i 10. Gen. xviii. 3—5. Acts i. 1—8. Ps. ci. 3. John 17. Heb. xiii. 2.
k 15.Gen. xviii. Rev. iii. 20.
6, 7. Ps. cxix.60, 60. Gal. i. 15, 16.
l v. 29. 1s. lxiv. 5.
Acts ii. 41. xvi. 15, 34.
m v. 30. vii. 34. 39. xv. 2. xviii. 9—14. Matt. ix. 11. xi. 28—31.
n ii. 8—18. xi. 41. xii. 33. xvi. 9. xviii. 22. Acts ii. 41—47. iv. 34, 35. 2 Cor. viii. 7, 8. 1 Tim. vi. 17, 18. Jam. i. 10, 11.
o lii. 14.
p Ex. xxii. 1—4. Lev. vi. 1—5. 2 Sam. xii. 3. 2 Sam. xii. 6. Prov. vi. 31.
q ii. 80. xiii. 30. John iv. 38—42. 1 Cor. vi. 9—11. 1 Pet. ii. 10.
r iii. 16. Rom. iv. 11, 12. Gal. iii. 7, 14 29.
s v. 31, 32. xv. 4—7, 32. Matt. I. 21. ix. 12, 13. xv. 6. xv. 24. xviii. 11. 1 Tim. i. 15 —16. Heb. vii. 25. 1 John iv. 9 —14.
t xvii. 20. Acts i. 6. 2 Thes. ii. 1 —3.
u Matt. xxv. 14—30. Mark xiii. 34—37.
x xx. 9. xxiv. 51. Matt. xxi. 33. Mark xii. 1. xvi. 19. Acts i. 9, 10. Matt. xxvii. 18.
y John xviii. 37. 1 Cor. xv. 25. Eph. i. 20—22. Phil. ii. 9—11. 1 Pet. iii. 22.
z Acts i. 11. xvii. 31. Heb. ix. 28. Jam. i. 1. 2 Pet. i. 1.
Rev. i. 7. a Matt. xxv. 14. John xii. 26. Gal. i. 10. Jam. i. 1.

greatly increased his wealth by his lucrative occupation. (*Marg. Ref.* a, b.)—It does not appear, that he had previously any serious concern about religion : and his contrivance, to get a sight of Jesus was probably the result of curiosity, which the miracle just before wrought on Bartimeus could not fail to increase. In what manner the words of our Lord affected his mind, we cannot tell ; but without all doubt, they were attended with a divine influence, to humble and change his heart, and to make way for true repentance and living faith : he therefore gladly welcomed Christ, and doubtless was further instructed, convinced, and determined, by his discourse. Whilst the Pharisees and others, as usual, murmured at our Lord's thus inviting himself to be the guest of a man " who was " a sinner," (*Note*, xv. 1, 2,) whose employment and character were infamous ; and this in preference to any of the priests or Levites, who resided there ; (*Note*, x. 30—37, *v*. 31 ;) Zaccheus stood forth, in the midst of the company, and, avowing the change which had taken place in his mind and heart, his judgment and disposition, he professed his purpose of immediately devoting half his wealth to charitable uses, and of making four-fold restitution to all those whom he had wronged. The Publicans were used to charge the people more than the real amount of their taxes ; and then if they refused to pay it, they " falsely accused them " to the Romans, as disobedient to their authority : thus they obtained the assistance of the military to enforce their exorbitant demands : (*Marg. Ref.* n, o.—*Note*, iii. 10—14 :) in every instance, in which Zaccheus had thus, or in any other manner, oppressed and injured any man, he was determined to make the utmost restitution required by the law, in case of concealed theft. (*Marg. Ref.* p.)—It has been argued, that he could not have got much of his wealth by extortion ; or his estate would not have sufficed for such a restitution, after half of it had been given to the poor ; especially if he reserved any part of it for himself. But it is more reasonable to suppose, that he did not give half to the poor, till after restitution had been made ; as he could not previously consider his riches as *his own*, even to give away. (*Is.* lxi. 8.) Perhaps he lay under a worse character than he really deserved : yet the transaction seems to be purposely recorded as an illustrious triumph of mercy and grace ; (xviii. 24— 27. *Note, Matt.* xix. 23—26 ;) and the whole narration implies that he was before a man who bore a bad character. —But Jesus, knowing the sincerity and humility of his professed subjection to the gospel, declared, " that salva- " tion was *that day* come to his house : " he and his family had before been estranged from it, but it was now come thither for the benefit of all belonging to it ; " for- " somuch as he also was a son of Abraham," not only according to the flesh, but as being now made partaker of Abraham's faith and privileges, and the promises made to him and his seed. (*Notes, Gen.* xii. 1—3. xvii. 7, 8. xviii. 18, 19. *Jer.* xxxii. 39—41. *Acts* ii. 37—40, *v*. 39. *Rom.* iv. 9—17. xi. 16—21.) This was indeed the very end for which he, " the Son of man," was come into the world, even to " seek out and save the lost." (*Marg. Ref.* s.—*Notes, Matt.* xviii. 10, 11. 1 *Tim.* i. 15, 16.)—' The name of Zac- ' cheus, (which is the same with Zaccai, *Ezra* ii. 9,) shews ' that he was a Jew.' *Doddridge*.

The chief among the publicans. (2) Αρχιτελωνης. Here only N. T.—*Stature.* (3) Ἡλικια. See on *Matt.* vi. 27.— *A sycamore tree.* (4) Συκομωραιαν. Here only N. T. Its fruit resembled the fig.—*To be a guest.* (7) Καλωλυσαι. See on ix. 12.—*If I have taken any thing from any man by false accusation.* (8) Ει τινος τι εσυκοφαντησα. See on iii. 14.— *Four-fold.*] Τετραπλων. Here only N. T.—*That which was lost.* (10) Το απολωλος. xv. 6. 24. 32. *Matt.* xviii. 11.

V. 11—27. Our Lord now drew near to Jerusalem, and his attendants, who were numerous, supposed that he was about to avow himself the Messiah, and to set up his kingdom, in outward authority and majesty : (*Note*, xvii. 20—23 :) but to obviate this erroneous conclusion- he gave them a parabolical representation of what was about to take place in those respects. (*Marg. Ref.*—*Notes, Matt.* xxv. 14—30.) The " nobleman " evidently signifies Christ himself, ascending into heaven to be exalted on the medi-

15 and ^b delivered them ten ^c pounds, and said unto them, Occupy till I come.

14 But ^c his citizens hated him, and sent a message after him, saying, We will not have this *man* to reign over us.

15 And it came to pass, that when he was returned, ^d having received the kingdom, then he commanded these servants to be called unto him, to whom ^e he had given the money, ^f that he might know how much every man had gained by trading.

16 Then came the first, saying, ^f Lord, thy pound hath gained ten pounds.

17 And he said unto him, ^g Well, thou good servant: because thou hast ^h been faithful in a very little, have thou authority over ten cities.

18 And the second came, saying, Lord, ^i thy pound hath gained five pounds.

19 And he said likewise to him, ^k Be thou also over five cities.

20 And another came, saying, ^l Lord, behold, *here is* thy pound, which I have kept laid up in a napkin.

21 For ^m I feared thee, ^n because thou art an austere man; thou takest up that thou layedst not down, and reapest that thou didst not sow.

22 And he saith unto him, ^o Out of thine own mouth will I judge thee, *thou* wicked servant. ^p Thou knewest that I was an austere man, taking up that I laid not down, and reaping that I did not sow.

23 Wherefore then gavest not thou my money into the bank, that at my coming I might have required mine own with ^q usury?

24 And he said unto them that stood by, ^r Take from him the pound, and give *it* to him that hath ten pounds.

25 (And they said unto him, ^s Lord, he hath ten pounds.)

26 For I say unto you, ^t That unto every one which hath shall be given; ^u and from him that hath not, even that he hath shall be taken away from him.

27 But those ^x mine enemies, which would not that I should reign over them, bring hither, and slay *them* before me.

atorial throne, till his coming to judgment. The "ten "servants" denote his professed disciples, who were few, in comparison of the multitudes of his enemies, or of his subjects in the heavenly world. The "pound," given to each of them to "occupy," or trade with, till his return, represents the gifts, abilities, or possessions entrusted to each person; with the means of grace, and encouragements and advantages for improvement, vouchsafed him; in the proper use of which, they prove themselves faithful servants, glorify their Lord, and do good, during their continuance on earth. (*Note*, xvi. 1—8.) The "citizens who "hated him," represent especially the Jewish nation, who hated the doctrine and kingdom of Christ, and did all they could to prevent its establishment. (*Notes*, *Ps.* ii. 1—6.)— It was very common, for ambassadors to be sent to Rome by cities and states, to oppose such as sought there an appointment to be king over them. His "return" after he had received the kingdom, which his enemies could not prevent, had reference to his coming to take vengeance on the Jews: but it also represents the final judgment of all men. The account required, accords almost exactly with what has been already considered: except that, with the same sum entrusted, some servants had gained more, some less; and they were rewarded in proportion, by being appointed rulers under him over the cities of his kingdom; and that the punishment of the avowed enemies of Christ, as well as that of hypocritical professors of the gospel, is represented.—*Went into.* (12) 'This probably refers to the ' history of Archelaus, who after the death of his father,

' Herod the great, went to Rome, to receive from Augus-' tus the confirmation of his father's will, by which he ' had the kingdom of Judea left to him.' *Bp. Porteus.* As, however, considerably more than thirty years had elapsed, since the death of Herod the great, when our Lord spake this parable; and as Archelaus was deposed and banished for his tyranny, after he had reigned ten years; it is not likely that his case was *especially* alluded to. But most of the kings of the east, in those times, were vassals to the Romans; so that the next heir seldom ventured to ascend the vacant throne, without their permission: and, in many instances, it was needful to travel to Rome; and very heavy expenses, and tedious delays, generally preceded even a favourable decision. To this case, which frequently occurred, and was familiar to the hearers, perhaps our Lord intended to make some distant allusion.—' There are ' three sorts of men in the church: first, those who know ' not Christ, and revolt from him: secondly, those, who ' according to their own vocation, diligently and zealously ' use those things which he has given them to his glory, ' and the good of their neighbours: and thirdly, those who ' are benumbed by indolence, and do no good. When the ' Lord shall come, ... he will inflict righteous vengeance on ' the first: he will bless the second in proportion to the ' labours which they have sustained: and he will also ' punish the last as useless; even those who waste an indo-' lent life in deliberation and speculation.' *Beza.*

A certain nobleman. (12) Ανθρωπος τις ευγενης. *Acts* xvii. 11. 1 *Cor.* i. 26.—*Pounds.* (13) Μνας. 16. 18. 20. 24. Here

28 ¶ And when he had thus spoken,
[y] he went before, ascending up to Jerusalem.
29 And it came to pass, [z] when he
was come nigh to Bethphage and
[a] Bethany, at the mount called *the
mount* of Olives, he sent two of his
disciples,
30 Saying, [b] Go ye into the village
over against *you*; in the which, at
your entering, ye shall find a colt tied,
whereon yet never man sat: loose him,
and bring *him hither*.
31 And if any man ask you, Why do
ye loose *him?* thus shall ye say unto
him, Because [c] the Lord hath need of
him.
32 And they that were sent went
their way, and found even as he had
said unto them.
33 And as they were loosing the
colt, the owners thereof said unto them,
Why loose ye the colt?
34 And they said, [d] The Lord hath
need of him.
35 And they brought him to Jesus:
and [e] they cast their garments upon
the colt, and they set Jesus thereon.
36 And as they went, they spread
their clothes in the way.

y ix. 51. xii. 50. xviii. 31. Ps. xl. 6—8. Mark x. 32—34. John xviii. 11. Heb. xii. 2. 1 Pet. iv. 1.
z Matt. xxi. 1, &c. Mark xi. 1, &c. John xii. 12—16.
a Ⅶ. xxi. 37. xxii. 39. xxiv. 50. Zech. xiv. 4 Acts i. 12.
b 22. xxii. 8—13. 1 Sam. x. 2—9 John xiv. 29.
c Ps. xxiv. 1. l. 10—12. Matt. xxi. 2, 3. Mark xi. 3—6 Acts x. 36.
d Zech. ix. 9. John x. 35. xii. 16. 2 Cor. viii. 9.
e 2 Kings ix. 13. Matt. xxi. 7, 8. Mark xi. 7, 8. Gal. iv. 15, 16.

37 And when he was come nigh,
even now [f] at the descent of the mount
of Olives, [g] the whole multitude of the
disciples began to rejoice, and praise
God with a loud voice, for all the
mighty works that they had seen;
38 Saying, [h] Blessed *be* the King
that cometh in the name of the Lord;
[i] peace in heaven, and [k] glory in the
highest.
39 And some of the Pharisees from
among the multitude said unto him,
Master, [l] rebuke thy disciples.
40 And he answered and said unto
them, I tell you, that if these should
hold their peace, [m] the stones would
immediately cry out.
41 ¶ And when he was come near,
he beheld the city, [n] and wept over it,
42 Saying, [o] If thou hadst known,
even thou, at least [p] in this thy day,
[q] the things *which belong* unto thy
peace! [r] but now they are hid from
thine eyes.
43 For [s] the days shall come upon
thee, that thine enemies shall [t] cast a
trench about thee, and compass thee
round, and keep thee in on every side,

f 20. Mark xiii. 3. xiv. 26.
g vii. 16. Ex. xv. 1, &c. Judg. v. 1, &c. 2 Sam. vi. 2—6. 1 Kings viii. 55, 56. 1 Chr. xv. 28. xvi. 4, &c. 2 Chr. xxix. 28—30. 36. Ezra iii. 10—13. Ps. cvi. 12, 13. John xii. 12, 13.
h xiii. 35. Ps. lxxii. 17—19. cxviii. 22—26. Zech. ix. 9. Matt. xxi. 9. Mark xi. 9, 10.
i ii. 10—14. Eph. ii. 14—18. Col. i. 20.
k Eph. i. 6. 12 iii. 10. 21. 1 Tim. i. 17. 1 Pet. i. 12. Rev. v. 9—14. xix. 1—6.
l Is. xxvi. 11. Matt. xxiii. 13. John xi. 47, 48. xii. 10. 19. Acts iv. 1, 2. 10—18. Jam. iv. 5.
m Ps. xcvi. 11. xcviii. 7—9. cxiv. 1—8. Is. lv. 12. Hab. ii. 11. Matt. iii. 9. xxi. 15, 16. xxvii. 45. 51—54. 2 Pet. ii. 6.
n Ps. cxix. 53. 136. 158. Jer. ix. 1. xiii. 17. xvii. 16. Hos. xi. 8. John xi. 35. Rom. ix. 2, 3.
o Deut. v. 29. xxxii. 29. Ps. lxxxi. 13. Is. xlviii. 18. Ez. xviii. 31, 32. xxxiii. 11.
p 44. Ps. xxxii. 6. Is. lv. 6. John xii. 35, 36. 2 Cor. vi. 1, 2.
q i. 77—79. ii. 10—14. x. 5, 6. Acts x. 36. xiii. 46. Heb. iii. 7. x. 26—29. xii. 24—26.
r Is. vi. 9, 10. xxix. 10—14. xliv. 18. Matt. xiii. 14, 15. John xii. 36—41. Acts xxviii. 25—27. Rom. xi. 7—10. 2 Cor. iii. 14—16. iv. 3, 4. 2 Thes. ii. 9—12.
s xxi. 20—24. Deut. xxviii. 49—68. Ps. xxxvii. 12, 13. Dan. ix. 26, 27. Matt. xxii. 7. xxiii. 37—39. Mark xiii. 14—20. 1 Thes. ii. 15, 16.
t Is. xxix. 1—4. Jer. vi. 3—6.

only *N. T.*—*Ex.* xlv. 12. *Sept. Marg.* See *Tables.*—*Occupy.*] Πραγματευσασθε. Here only N. T. Πραγματειαι, 2 Tim. ii. 4. A πραγμα, *res, negotium.*—*Had gained by trading.* (15) Διεπραγματευσατο. Here only *N. T.*—*Hath gained.* (16) Προσειργασατο. Here only N. T. Ex προς et εργαζομαι, *negotior.*—*A napkin.* (20) Σουδαριω. *John* xi. 44. xx. 7. *Acts* xix. 12.—*An austere man.* (21) Ανθρωπος αυστηρος. 22. Here only *N. T.*—Σκληρος, *Matt.* xxv. 24.—*The bank.* (23) Τραπεζαν. "The table." *Matt.* xxi. 12. Τραπεζιτης, *nummularius. Matt.* xxv. 27.—*Usury.*] Τοκῳ, *Matt.* xxv. 27. Not elsewhere N. T.—*Ex.* xxii. 25. *Deut.* xxiii. 19. *Sept.* A fair and adequate profit on money lent for commercial purposes; not gain made by occasion of the necessities of the poor, and by oppressing them. (*Note, Ex.* xxii. 25—27.)—*Would not,* &c. (27) Μη θελησαντας. ...Ου θελομεν, 14. *Notes, Matt.* xxvii. 19—25. *John* xix. 13—18.—*Slay them.*] Κατασφαξατε. Here only *N. T. Note, Ps.* xxi. 8—12.

V. 28—40. *Marg. Ref.*—*Notes,* &c. *Matt.* xxi. 1—11. *Mark* xi. 1—11. *John* xii. 12—19.—*Peace,* &c. (38) *Notes,* ii. 8—14, v. 14. *Ps.* lxxxv. 10—13.—*I tell you,* &c. (40) The numerous miracles, which had been wrought by our Lord, (especially that of raising Lazarus from the dead a short time before,) and the evident fulfilment of ancient prophecies in him, rendered it so manifest that he was the promised Messiah; that if the Jews refused to own and honour him as such, some other method would be taken, which would appear to the Pharisees as strange, as if the very stones should speak, and declare him to be "the King of Israel," and "the Lord of glory." The expression was proverbial; but the calling of the Gentiles seems to have been alluded to. (*Marg. Ref.* m.—*Notes, Hab.* ii. 9—11. *Matt.* iii. 7—10. xxvii. 51—53.)—It is observable, that towards the close of his life, our Lord gradually laid aside that reserve, which he before used. He no longer enjoined silence on those who were healed by him: and in this instance he expressly declared himself to be "the Son of David" and "the King of Israel." His time was now come; and the reasons for his former caution no longer existed.—'When they linger, who 'ought to be the chief preachers and setters forth of the 'kingdom of God; he will raise up others extraordinarily, 'in despite of them.' *Beza.*

They cast, &c. (35) Επιρριψαντες. 1 *Pet.* v. 7. Not elsewhere *N. T. Num.* xxxv. 20. 22. *Josh.* x. 11. 2 *Sam.* xx. 12. *Ps.* lv. 22. *Sept.*—*They set ... thereon.*] Επεβιβασαν. x. 34. *Acts* xxiii. 24.—*They spread,* &c. (36) Υπεστρωννυον. Here only *N. T.*—Εστρωσαν, *Matt.* xxi. 8.

V. 41—44. When Jesus approached Jerusalem, and had a clear view, from the adjacent hills, of its magnificence and prosperity; instead of being alarmed by the prospect of those inexpressible sufferings, and deep indignities which there awaited him, or expressing resentment

u 1 Kings ix. 7, 8.
Mic. iii. 12.
x xiii. 34. Matt.
xviii. 37.
y Matt. xxiv. 2.
Mark xiii. 2.
z 42. i. 68. John
iii.18—21. 1 Pet.
ii. 12.
a Matt. xxi. 12.
13. Mark xi. 15
—17. John ii. 13
—16.
b Deut. xiv. 26.
c Ps. xciii. 5. Is.
lvi. 7. Jer. vii.
11. Ez. xiii. 12.
Hos. xii. 7.
Matt. xxiii. 14.

44 And shall " lay thee even with the ground, and ˣ thy children within thee; and they shall not ʸ leave in thee one stone upon other; ᶻ because thou knewest not the time of thy visitation.
45 ¶ And he ᵃ went into the temple, and began to cast out them that ᵇ sold therein, and them that bought;
46 Saying unto them, ᶜ It is written,

My house is the house of prayer; but ye have made it a den of thieves.
47 ¶ And ᵈ he taught daily in the temple. But ᵉ the chief priests, and the scribes, and the chief of the people sought to destroy him;
48 And ᶠ could not find what they might do: for all the people ᵍ were very attentive to hear him.

d xxi. 37, 38.
Matt. xxi. 23
Mark xi. 27, &c.
Mark xii. 35.
e Matt. xxvi. 3, 4.
Mark xiv. 1, 2.
xiv. 1. John vii
iv. 44. viii. 37—
40. x. 20. xi. 53
—57.
f xx. 19, 20. xxii.
2—4. Matt. xxii.
15, 16.
g 51. honored on
him, Nah. viii.
3. John vii. 46.—
49. Acts xvi. 14.

---

for the base usage which he was about to experience; he foresaw the miseries coming on that ungrateful and persecuting city, by the awful justice of God, with tears of deep compassion: (Note, John xi. 33—40. P. O. 28—40:) saying, as with a wish or ardent desire, expressive of his deep concern, " If thou hadst," or, " Oh! that thou hadst " known, in this thy day," (the time when the city was honoured and favoured, with the presence of her King, Messiah, the Son of God,) " the things, which belonged " to thy peace!" (Marg. Ref. o, p.—Notes, Deut. v. 28, 29. xxxii. 29. Ps. lxxxi. 13. Is. xlviii. 17—19.) But that day was expired, her doom was passed, her eyes were blinded, and every thing conducive to her welfare was judicially kept out of sight. Our Lord therefore concluded with predicting in the most explicit language, the siege and entire destruction of the city, and the dire havock made of its devoted inhabitants; because they knew not the time of their gracious visitation, but rejected, and were about to crucify, their King. (Note, 1 Pet. ii. 12.) ' Christ is not simply delighted with the destruction, ' no not of the wicked.' Beza. The possibility, nay, the actual existence, of an union between awful inflexible justice denouncing sentence against the criminal, and benevolence sympathizing in his misery even to tears, is most affectingly shewn in this passage. So that it stands as an unanswerable refutation of the charges, which are so constantly brought against those, who denounce the vengeance of God on impenitent sinners, as if they must of course be actuated by malevolence. All such accusations involve the Saviour himself, as well as the prophets and apostles, along with modern teachers and professors of Christianity, under one general condemnation. (Notes, Jer. ix. 1, 2. 10, 11. xvii. 15—18. Ez. xviii. 23. xxxiii. 11. Rom. ix. 1—3.)—The language of the original is abrupt and interrupted; and peculiarly suited to shew the deep interest, which the Speaker took in the concerns of those, about whom he was discoursing.—' If after slaying ' so many prophets, and so often refusing the Lord of ' the prophets; in this my last coming to thee, thou hadst ' had any regard to thyself!' Beza.—' When Vespasian ' besieged Jerusalem, his army compassed the city round ' about, and kept them in on every side. And though it ' was judged a great and almost impracticable work, to ' compass the whole city with a wall; yet Titus animating ' his soldiers to attempt it, they in three days built a wall ' of thirty-nine furlongs, having thirteen castles in it; and ' so cut off all hopes that any of the Jews within the city ' should escape. ... Titus having commanded his soldiers ' to dig up the city, this was so fully done, by levelling ' the whole compass of it, except three towers, ... that they ' who came to see it, were persuaded it never would be

' built again.' Josephus, quoted by Whitby. (Marg. Ref. s—z.—Notes, xxi. 20—24. Matt. xxiii. 37—39. xxiv. 1, 2.)
A trench. (43) Χαραχα. Here only N. T.—Is. xxxvii. 33. Jer. xxxiii. 4. Ez. iv. 2. xxvi. 8. Sept.—Compass ... round.] Περικυκλωσωσι. Here only N. T.—Josh. vii. 9. 2 Kings vi. 14. Sept. Ex περι, et κυκλοω, cingo.—Keep thee in.] Συνιξωσι. See on xii. 50.—Shall lay thee even with the ground. (44) Εδαφιωσι.—Here only N. T. Ps. cxxxvii. 9. Is. iii. 26. Hos. x. 14. Nah. iii. 10. Sept.—Visitation.] Επισκοπης. 1 Pet. ii. 12. In another sense, Acts i. 20. 1 Tim. iii. 2.
V. 45—48. Marg. Ref.—Notes, Matt. xxi. 12—16. Mark xi. 15—21, vv. 15—18.
Were very attentive. (48) Εξεκρεμαλο. Here only N. T. —Gen. xliv. 30. Sept. ' They listened to him with so ' great attention and pleasure, that they hung as it were ' on his lips while he spake.' Doddridge.

PRACTICAL OBSERVATIONS.
V. 1—10.

Our Lord illustrates by facts, what he declares in words, concerning the omnipotency of his grace, and the exceeding riches of his pardoning mercy. Many are brought to the places where Jesus dispenses his blessings, without any design of obtaining a share of them: and curiosity, though idle and vain, is often over-ruled to bring men acquainted with the gospel. Whatever puts a sinner, as it were, in the Saviour's way, is a probable means of doing him good. Where the gospel is preached, Jesus " stands " and knocks at the door" of a man's heart, demanding admission, proposing to be his guest, and promising a royal recompence for his entertainment: (Note, Rev. iii. 20—22. P. O. 14—22:) but unless grace prepare the heart, no one will " make haste to receive him joyfully:" when therefore this event takes place, angels rejoice, adoring the Redeemer's condescension, and congratulating the sinner's felicity. (48) Repentance is not to be estimated by terrors or distresses, but by its effects: where it is genuine a new judgment and disposition are produced, a new character is formed, and a new life is entered on. The penitent gladly welcomes the Saviour; and, while he accepts of his free salvation, he devotes himself to his service. If he possess wealth, he will immediately think of becoming a faithful steward: though he may not be called actually to leave all, and follow his Lord; yet he will begin, without any express command, to employ a considerable part of it in charitable uses, according to the degree of his faith and love: and if conscious of having defrauded others, he will not count any thing his own, till he has made ample restitution, accord-

3 I 2

CHAP. XX.

Jesus answers those who demand by what authority he acts, 1—8; speaks the parable of the vineyard let out to wicked husbandmen, 9—18: shews that tribute should be paid to Cæsar, 19—26: confutes the Sadducees, concerning the resurrection of the dead; and puts all his adversaries to silence, 27—40: enquires how Christ was both David's Son, and David's Lord, 41—44; and warns the people against the ambitious and hypocritical Scribes, 45—47.

---

ing to his ability and opportunity. When we see such " fruits meet for repentance," we may conclude, that salvation is come to the sinner's heart, and that he is become " a son of Abraham " by faith in Jesus Christ: and we may cheerfully hope that mercy is intended to his family also. What thanks then do we owe to him, who " came to seek and save the lost! " If we are in the way of salvation, he has ransomed our souls, sought us out, and saved us; and the same way is open even to extortioners and harlots: we should therefore gladly use every scriptural means, or countenance every scriptural endeavour, to promote the preaching of the gospel, to sinners of every description; for all objections to designs of this kind, arise from the dominion, or the remainder, of pharisaical pride and self-preference. (*Note,* and *P. O.* xv. 25—32.)

V. 11—27.

It behoves us carefully to study the nature of the Redeemer's kingdom, that we may understand our present situation, and form just expectations in respect of the future. Our blessed Lord is indeed established on his glorious throne; and it is vain to send a message after him, refusing submission to his authority: yet many, even from professed regard to the honour and worship of God, (like the Jews of old,) speak as if this was left to their option. They seem to think, that they may choose their own way of approaching God, or entering heaven; and determine for themselves by what Judge, or according to what rule, their final doom shall be determined. But these things are immutably settled; and all, who will not have the Saviour " to reign over them," shall be punished as enemies to his Person and kingdom; of which awful doom, the vengeance executed on the unbelieving Jews was an earnest and an example.—He has indeed " received " a kingdom ;" and will certainly " return:" but he is now unseen, except by faith; so that true believers alone act as in his presence, and as expecting and preparing for his coming. (*Notes, Phil.* iii. 20, 21. 2 *Tim.* iv. 6—8. *Tit.* ii. 13. *Heb.* ix. 27, 28. 2 *Pet.* iii. 1—4. 10—13.) Alas! the number, even of his professed servants, is very small, in proportion to that of his enemies; and their ability is often little, compared with the talents and possessions which ungodly men abuse. Yet if, in humble faith, cheerful diligence, and patient hope, they " occupy " with that little, till their Lord comes; their reward shall be exceedingly great, and exactly proportioned to the improvement made: though every faithful servant will allow, that the power, the opportunity, and the will to improve them, were wholly from the Lord; and that " *his* pound hath " gained the ten pounds." (*Note,* 1 *Chr.* xxix. 9—19.) This union of faithfulness, and diligence, and humility, ensures a gracious acceptance: to persons of this character " the Lord when he cometh" will say, " Well, thou " good servant; because thou hast been faithful in a little, " have thou authority over ten cities." Whilst these views

of the Redeemer's abundant grace encourage the humble believer to increasing diligence; hypocrites are deterred from activity by hard thoughts of him, and a persuasion that his service is unprofitable. But, whatever excuses and pleas such men now make for their indolence or avarice, their mouths will soon be stopped; and their unimproved advantages will be taken from them, to enrich the faithful servants. " For unto every one that hath shall be " given, and he shall have abundance; and from him that " hath not, even that he hath shall be taken away from " him." (*P. O. Matt.* xxv. 14—30.)

V. 28—48.

Would we " have confidence before Christ at his " coming," we should now observe his directions, and rely on his promises; and when " the Lord hath need of" ought belonging to us, we should readily devote it to his service.—But what will be the feelings of the multitude of the disciples, when they shall behold their Lord and Saviour return in his glory to judge the world! How will they then " rejoice and praise God, with a loud voice, for " all the mighty works which they have seen ! " In anticipation of this joy, let us now gladly welcome every display of his grace, in the conversion of sinners and the success of his gospel; exulting in the triumphs of our " King, who cometh in the name of the Lord," and rejoicing that " there is glory to God in the highest, peace " on earth, and good will to men."—Those who continue to object to these songs of adoring and thankful praise to the Redeemer, will wail and lament when he shall appear to complete his people's salvation; and if there were none on earth, to adore the display of the divine perfections, in the work of our redemption, " the very stones would cry " out," and upbraid the ingratitude and insensibility of mankind.—But, who can behold the holy Jesus weeping over the city, where his precious blood was about to be shed, in the prospect of the miseries awaiting his insulting murderers; without perceiving that the image of God, in human nature, consists very much in expanded benevolence, and tender compassion to the miserable, even when their miseries are most justly deserved? Surely then, those persons, who take up certain doctrines of the gospel in such a manner, as to have their hearts rendered by them more callous towards their fellow sinners; and who (from topicks grounded on God's *secret* purposes,) object to compassion for perishing sinners, or prayers for men in general, have far more of the Pharisee in them, than of " the mind that was in Christ Jesus!"—But let every one apply his mind to know, " in the day of his visitation," " the things, which belong to his eternal peace :" for though Jesus wept over Jerusalem, yet he did not fail to execute vengeance upon it : and though " he delighteth " not in the death of a sinner, but rather that he should " repent and live ;" yet he will surely accomplish his most awful threatenings on all who " neglect his great salva-

AND it came to pass, *that on one of those days, as he taught the people in the temple, and preached the gospel, the chief priests and the scribes came upon him, with the elders,

2 And spake unto him, saying, Tell us, By what authority doest thou these things? or, Who is he that gave thee this authority?

3 And he answered and said unto them, I will also ask you one thing; and answer me.

4 The baptism of John, was it from heaven, or of men?

5 And they reasoned with themselves, saying, If we shall say, From heaven; he will say, Why then believed ye him not?

6 But and if we say, Of men; all the people will stone us: for they be persuaded that John was a prophet.

7 And they answered, That they could not tell whence it was.

8 And Jesus said unto them, Neither tell I you by what authority I do these things.

9 ¶ Then began he to speak to the people this parable: A certain man planted a vineyard, and let it forth to husbandmen, and went into a far country for a long time.

10 And at the season he sent a servant to the husbandmen, that they should give him of the fruit of the vineyard: but the husbandmen beat him, and sent him away empty.

11 And again he sent another servant; and they beat him also, and entreated him shamefully, and sent him away empty.

12 And again he sent the third: and they wounded him also, and cast him out.

13 Then said the lord of the vineyard, What shall I do? I will send my beloved son: it may be they will reverence him when they see him.

14 But when the husbandmen saw him, they reasoned among themselves, saying, This is the heir: come, let us kill him, that the inheritance may be our's.

15 So they cast him out of the vineyard, and killed him. What therefore shall the lord of the vineyard do unto them?

16 He shall come and destroy these husbandmen, and shall give the vineyard to others. And when they heard it, they said, God forbid.

17 And he beheld them, and said, What is this then that is written, The Stone which the builders rejected, the same is become the Head of the corner?

18 Whosoever shall fall upon that Stone shall be broken; but on whomsoever it shall fall, it will grind him to powder.

"tion." May he then come, and cleanse our hearts by his Spirit, that they may be a holy temple unto the Lord! May he purify his church and his holy ordinances, from all those practices and persons, which pervert or defile them! May his obstinate enemies be disappointed, and not find what to do; while sinners on every side become attentive to his words of truth and salvation! (P. O. Matt. xxi. 1—11. xxiii. 34—39.)

NOTES.

CHAP. XX. V. 1—8. (Marg. Ref.—Notes, Matt. xxi. 23—32.)—'The Pharisees, being overcome with the truth 'of Christ's doctrine, move a question about his outward 'calling, and are overcome by the witness of their own 'conscience.' Beza.

They reasoned with themselves. (5) Συνλογισαντο προ, ἱαυτις. Here only N. T.

V. 9—18. Marg. Ref.—Notes, Matt. xxi. 33—46. Mark xii. 1—12.—The inheritance, &c. (14) It was not at all probable, that the owner of a vineyard would suffer

the murderers of his son to keep the inheritance, if he had power to dispossess and punish them. This circumstance, therefore, pointed out the extreme folly, as well as the detestable wickedness, of the priests and rulers, in that conduct on which they had determined.—He, &c. (16) The scribes allowed, that the husbandmen deserved the most dreadful punishment: but when they found, that our Lord applied it to them, and condemned them according to their own verdict, (as "Nathan said unto David, Thou "art the man,") they said, "God forbid." They neither allowed their guilt, nor apprehended any such consequences from their conduct.—On whom. (18) The persevering opposition of the Roman empire, in all its forms, and in every age, to Christ and his cause, and the final and dreadful destruction of it, may here be predicted, along with the calamities and miseries of the Jews. (Notes, Dan. ii. 34—45. Zech. xiv. 1—3.)—The dreadful punishment of all persecutors is also intimated.

For a long time. (9) Κρονυς ικανυς. A sufficient time, for them to get ready for payment.—Beat. (10) Δειραντες,

19 ¶ And the chief priests and the scribes, ª the same hour, sought to lay hands on him; and they feared the people: for they perceived that he had spoken this parable against them.

20 And ᵇ they watched *him*, and sent forth spies, which should ᵖ feign themselves just men, that they might take hold of his words, that so ᑫ they might deliver him unto the power and authority of the governor.

21 And they asked him, saying, ʳ 'Master, we know that thou ˢ sayest and teachest rightly, neither ᵗ acceptest thou the person *of any*, but teachest the way of God ᵘ truly:

22 Is it ˣ lawful for us to give tribute unto Cæsar, or no?

23 But ʸ he perceived their craftiness, and said unto them, ᶻ Why tempt ye me?

24 Shew me ª a penny. Whose image and superscription hath it? They answered and said, ᵇ Cæsar's.

25 And he said unto them, ᶜ Render therefore unto Cæsar the things which be Cæsar's, and ᵇ unto God the things which be God's.

26 And ᶜ they could not take hold ᵈ of his words before the people; ᵈ and they marvelled at his answer, and held their peace.

27 ¶ Then came to *him* certain of the Sadducees, which deny that there is any resurrection; and they asked him,

28 Saying, Master, ᶠ Moses wrote unto us, If any man's brother die, having a wife, and he die without children, that his brother should take his wife, and raise up seed unto his brother.

29 There were therefore seven brethren: and the first took a wife, ᵍ and died without children.

30 And the second took her to wife, and he died childless.

31 And the third took her; and in like manner the seven also: and they left no children, and died.

32 Last of all the woman ʰ died also.

33 Therefore ¹ in the resurrection, whose wife of them is she? for seven had her to wife.

34 And Jesus answering said unto them, ᵏ The children of this world ˡ marry, and are given in marriage:

35 But they which shall be ᵐ accounted worthy ⁿ to obtain that world, and the resurrection from the dead, ᵒ neither marry, nor are given in marriage:

36 Neither ᵖ can they die any more: for ᑫ they are equal unto the angels: and are ʳ the children of God, being the children of the resurrection.

37 Now that the dead are raised, ˢ

---

11. xii. 47, 48. xxii. 63.—*Entreated him shamefully.* (11) Αἰμασαντες. *John* viii. 49. *Acts* v. 41. *Rom.* i. 24. ii. 23. *Jam.* ii. 6.—*They wounded.* (12) Τραυματισαντες. *Acts* xix. 16. Not elsewhere N. T. A τραυμα, *vulnus*, x. 34.—*God forbid.* (16) Μη γενοιτο. *Rom.* iii. 4. vi. 2. 15. vii. 7, *et al.* (*Note*, 1 *Kings* xxi. 3.) The priests and scribes used this language, not against the case stated in the parable; but against the application of it to them, as about to put to death Jesus, whom they condemned as a deceiver, for speaking of himself as the Son of God.—*Shall be broken*, &c. (18) See on *Matt.* xxi. 42.

V. 19—26. *Marg. Ref.—Notes, Matt.* xxii. 15—22. *Mark* xii. 13—17.—*Spies.* (20) The design of these *spies* 's here more expressly stated, than by the other evangelists: to "deliver him to the power and authority of the go- "vernor." 'The last refuge that false prophets have to 'destroy the true prophets, is to lay treason and sedition to 'their charge.' *Beza.*—'They put to him the question, 'about paying tribute to Cæsar; hoping, that by denying 'it to be due to him from the Jews, they might accuse 'him as an enemy to Cæsar; for they knew, that his de- 'cision of questions, relating only to their law and con-

'troversies, would not offend those Gallios.' *Whitby.*— It would be well, if all who are insidiously watched and questioned, on such subjects, would imitate our Lord's conduct; neither intermeddling with disputable political subjects, nor maintaining a suspicious silence; but plainly shewing, that obedience and tribute should be rendered even to usurpers and heathens, while possessed of authority; except where the higher obligation of obedience to God requires the contrary.

They watched. (20) Παρατηρησαντες. vi. 7. xiv. 1. *Acts* ix. 24.—*Spies.*] Εγκαθετες. Here only N. T.—*Job* xix. 12. xxxi. 9. *Sept.* 'Proprie is dicitur, *qui subsidet in loco ali-* 'quo et insidias facit alteri.' *Schleusner.*—*Should feign.*] Ὑποκρινομενες. Here only N. T.—*Craftiness.* (23) Πανυρ- γιαν. 1 *Cor.* iii. 19. 2 *Cor.* iv. 2. xi. 3. *Eph.* iv. 14. Πανυρ- γος, 2 *Cor.* xii. 16. Ex παν, *omne*, et εργον, *opus.* Πομριαν, *Matt.* xxii. 18. Ὑποκρισιν, *Mark* xii. 15.

V. 27—38. *Marg. Ref.—Notes, Matt.* xxii. 23—33. *Mark* xii. 18—27.—*Children*, &c. (34) 'They are here '... called "the children of this world," who live in this 'world: and not they, that are wholly given to the world, 'as before, xvi. 8.' *Beza.*—*Children of*, &c. (36) 'Par-

even Moses shewed at the bush, 'when he calleth the Lord, the God of Abraham, and the God of Isaac, and the God of Jacob.

38 For he is not "a God of the dead, but of the living: ' for all live unto him.

39 Then certain of the Scribes answering said, Master, ' thou hast well said.

40 And after that, ' they durst not ask him any *question at all.*

41 ¶ And he said unto them, "How say they that * Christ is David's Son? ·

42 And David ' himself saith in the book of Psalms, ' The LORD said

unto my Lord, Sit thou on my right hand,

43 Till I make ' thine enemies thy footstool.

44 David therefore calleth him Lord, 'how is he then his Son?

45 ¶ Then "in the audience of all the people, he said unto his disciples,

46 "Beware of the Scribes, 'which desire to walk in long robes, and love greetings in the markets, and the highest seats in the synagogues, and the chief rooms at feasts;

47 Which "devour widows' houses, 'and for a shew make long prayers. "the same shall receive greater damnation.

' takers of the resurrection: for as they ... shall *live indeed,* who shall enjoy everlasting bliss; so do they ' *rise indeed,* who rise to life: though if this word *re-surrection* be taken generally, it belongeth also to the ' wicked; who shall rise unto condemnation, which is ' not properly *life,* but death.' *Beza.—Equal, &c.*] ' Angel-like.' *Campbell.* To be angel-like, and to be "*equal* " to angels," are certainly very different things.—*Live unto him.* (38) ' The godly do not die, though they ' die here on earth.' *Beza.—'* When it is said, " God " is not the God of the dead," the meaning is, He ' is not the God of them who are to abide in a state of ' death, and never to enjoy "the resurrection of the just;" ' that is, he owns not them for his, who are not to be the ' sons of the resurrection :... and will not be called their ' God, as not having prepared for them an heavenly city. ' *(Heb.* xi. 16.) Hence doth the scripture say of them, ' that "they are passed from death unto life ;" *(John* v. ' 24;) because Christ " will raise them up at the last day." ' *(John* vi. 40.) God here stiles himself the God of Abra-' ham, Isaac, and Jacob; that is, not of their souls only, ' but of their *persons;* in which sense the Jews always ' understood these words : now thus he would be the God ' of the dead, though their souls lived, unless their bodies ' also rose again.' *Whitby.—*God is not the God of the dead : but he is "the God of Abraham, &c." therefore Abraham now lives, as to his soul, and shall awake, as to the body, at the resurrection, like one out of sleep : for, if " God be not the God of the dead ;" all, who have him for their God, " live by him :" Their souls now live, their bodies shall at length arise, and " death be swallowed up " in victory." *(Notes, Rom.* viii. 10, 11. 1 *Cor.* xv. 50 —54.)

Which deny, &c. (27) 'Οι αντιλεγοντες αναστασιν μη ειναι. ... Αντιλεγω. See on ii. 34.—*Without children.* (28) Ατεκνος. 29, 30. Here only N. T.—*Shall be accounted worthy.* (35) 'Οι ... καταξιωθεντες. xxi. 36. *Acts* v. 41. 2 *Thes.* i. 5. Ex καλια, et αξιου, ab αξιος, *dignus.—Equal unto the angels.* (36) Ισαγγελοι. Here only N. T. 'Ως αγγελοι. *Matt.* xxii. 30. *Mark* xii. 25. Ισος, here may be supposed to explain ὡς, iu the other evangelists. vi. 34. *Matt.* xx. 12. *John* v. 18.

Acts xi. 17. *Phil.* ii. 6.—*Live unto him.* (38) Αυτῳ ζωσιν. " For all live by him," or, " in him," or " with him." All who have the Lord for their God, " live by him."—" Be-" cause I live, ye shall live also." " Ye are dead; and " your life is hid with Christ *in God;* when Christ who is " our Life shall appear, then shall ye also appear with him " in glory." *(Notes, John* xiv. 18—20. *Col.* iii. 1—4, v. 4.) Believers, as one with Christ, " never die." *(Note, John* xi. 20—27.)—" They *sleep* in Jesus, and God will " bring them with him." *(Note,* 1 *Thes.* iv. 13—18.) " For whether we live, we live unto the Lord, and whe-" ther we die, we die unto the Lord ; whether we live " therefore or die, we are the Lord's." *(Rom.* xiv. 8.)

V. 39, 40. *(Marg. Ref.)* The Sadducees were finally silenced : but one of the Scribes, being a Pharisee, after this asked our Lord a question ; and his answer to it silenced the Pharisees also. *(Notes, Matt.* xxii. 34—40. *Mark* xii. 28—34.)

V. 41—44. *(Marg. Ref.—Notes, Matt.* xxii. 41—46. *Mark* xii. 35—37.) ' Christ is so the Son of David, ac-' cording to the flesh ; as to be his Lord, being the eternal ' Son of God.' *Beza.*

V. 45—47. *(Marg. Ref.—Notes, Matt.* xxiii. 1—7. *Mark* xii. 38—40.) ' The example of ambitious and ' covetous pastors must be avoided.' *Beza.—'* The clergy ' ... are to be distinguished from the people, and from ' others, not so much by their apparel, as by their learn-' ing; not only by their habit, but by their conversation ; ' not by the adornment of their body, but by purity of ' mind.' *Pope Celestine,* in *Whitby.*

PRACTICAL OBSERVATIONS.

V. 1—18.

Men often profess to enquire into the evidences or doctrines of Revelation ; when they are secretly determined not to submit to its authority, and are, in fact, only seeking plausible apologies for their infidelity and disobedience. But the fear of man, and regard to reputation, deter them from avowing their real sentiments and purposes. Objectors of this character should be answered with pertinence, brevity, and caution. It is doing them too much

316

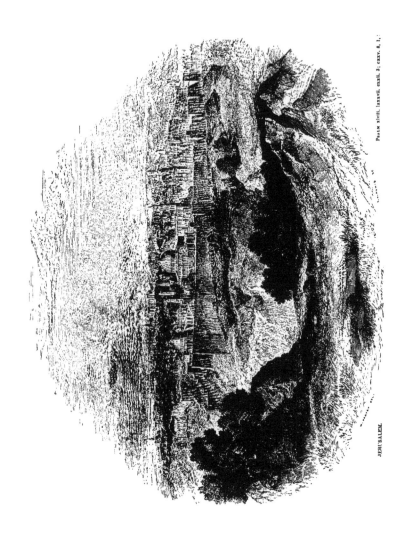

JERUSALEM.

Psalm xlviii, lxxxvii, cxxii, 3; cxxv, 8, 1.

CHAP. XXI.

Christ prefers the widow's two mites to the large offerings of the rich, 1—4. He foretels the destruction of the temple, 5, 6; the signs and calamities which would precede and accompany it, giving suitable exhortations and promises, 7—19; and the destruction and continued desolations of Jerusalem, 20—24. The signs of his coming, 25—33. He exhorts to watchfulness and prayer, 34—36. He daily preaches at the temple; and retires at night to the mount of Olives, 37, 38.

a Mark vii. 11—13. xii. 41—44.
b Jnoh. vi. 19. 24.
1 Kings xiv. 26.
2 Kings xxiv. 13.
2 Chr. xxxvi. 18.
Neh. xiii. 13.
Matt. xxvii. 6.
John viii. 20.

AND he looked up, [a] and saw the rich men casting their gifts into [b] the treasury.

2 And he saw also a certain poor widow casting in thither two [c] mites.

3 And he said, [d] Of a truth I say unto you, That this poor widow hath cast in [e] more than they all:

4 For all these have of their abundance cast in unto the offerings of God: but she of her penury hath cast in [f] all the living that she had.

5 ¶ And [g] as some spake of the temple, how it was adorned with goodly stones and gifts, he said,

6 As for these things which ye behold, the days will come, in the which

* Mark xii. 42.
Mary.
c iv. 25. ix. 27. xii. 44. Acts iv. 27. x. 34.
d Ex. xxxv. 21—29. Mark xii. 43, 44. xiv. 8, 9. 2 Cor. viii. 2, 3. 12. ix. 6, 7.
e viii. 43. xv. 12. Acts ii. 44, 45. iv. 34.
f Matt. xxiv. 1. Mark xiii. 1. Joh. ii. 20.

---

honour, in general, to enter into a formal controversy with them : the best way is to address their consciences by apt illustrations, closely applied ; and so to detect those corrupt affections, or secret sins, which are the real grounds of their dislike to the Bible, but which they endeavour to conceal even from themselves. " They flatter themselves " in their own sight, until their iniquity be found to be " hateful." In this way it may often be shewn, that they resemble in pride, perverseness, ingratitude, enmity to God, and aversion to his holy service, those men who murdered the prophets, and crucified the Son of God ; in order to establish their own authority and reputation, and to live according to their own ungodly lusts without controul.—But it behoves every one of us, who are favoured with the word and ordinances of God, to enquire, whether we make a proper and adequate improvement of our advantages, and act consistently with our professed subjection to the gospel. For awful will the doom, not only of builders that reject him who is " the Head-Stone of " the corner," but of those who profess to " reverence the " Son," and yet render not the fruits of the vineyard in due season. (P. O. Matt. xxi. 23—46. xxii. 15—22.)

V. 19—47.

When ministers succeed in bringing the word of God home to the consciences of obstinate transgressors, these will surely be exasperated : and in return they will watch their opportunity, and assume every disguise, to fasten some charge upon the character of the ministers, or to expose them to the displeasure of the ruler. But " the " wisdom from above" will direct those, who " teach the " way of God truly," to avoid their snares : and they will instruct men in their duty to God, to the king, and to all men, in so clear a manner, that " such as are of the con- " trary part can have no evil thing to say of them."—Ungodly men continually grow more and more like to " their " father the devil, and the lusts of their father they will " do :" but let us seek to be daily " transformed in the " renewing of our minds," that we may be counted worthy to obtain the heavenly inheritance, and be made meet to be partakers of it ; where we shall be " equal to the " angels, as the children of God, and the children of the " resurrection ;" and where " the Lord himself will be our " everlasting Light " and our all-sufficient Portion. " Thi- " ther our Forerunner," the Son of David and his Lord,

" hath for us entered," " who is at the right hand of God," " and shall there remain till " all enemies are put under his " feet." Let us therefore fear being found among his ene- mies ; as all hypocrites, infidels, and profligates most cer- tainly will be : and let us pray to God continually to pre- serve us from pride, ambition, covetousness, and every evil thing ; and to teach us to seek that " honour which " cometh from him alone." (P. O. Matt. xxii. 23—46. xxiii. 1—12.)

NOTES.

CHAP. XXI. V. 1—4. (Marg. Ref.—Note, Mark xii. 41—44.) ' This treasury received the voluntary oblations ' of the worshippers, who came up to the feasts ; and the ' money thrown into it was employed to buy wood for the ' altar, salt, and other necessaries, not provided for in any ' other way.' Doddridge.—It is probable, that the pub- lick sacrifices, and the incense, were bought with this money ; and that part of it was often expended in repair- ing the temple and its out-buildings. The worshippers from a distance might be the principal persons, who cast money into it at the great feasts ; but it does not appear, that it was exclusively intended for them.

Poor. (2) Πτωχραν. Here only N. T.—Ex. xxii. 25. Prov. xxviii. 15. xxix. 7. Sept.

V. 5. Josephus says, that some of the stones of the temple were forty-five cubits long, five high, and six broad ; and that the marble of it was so white, that it ap- peared at a distance like a mountain of snow : and several writers have mentioned various oblations of massy gold, which were affixed to the walls and pillars, besides the immense riches contained in the treasuries.

Goodly.] Καλοις.—' Proprie pulcher, formosus : meta- ' phorice, bonus, ... probatus, optabilis.' Schleusner.—Gifts.] Αναθημασι. Here only N. T. Αναθμα denotes that which is consecrated to the service of God : Αναθεμα, what is de- voted upon a curse to utter destruction. Rom. ix. 3. 1 Cor. xii. 3. xvi. 22. Gal. i. 8, 9.—Lev. xxvii. 28. Sept. Both are derived from ανατιθημι, and include the same general idea of being devoted to God, one as employed in his service, the other as a sacrifice to his justice.

V. 6. Marg. Ref.—Note, Matt. xxiv. 1, 2.—These, &c.] " As for these things, which ye behold, &c." The manner and language emphatically shew the holy indiffer- ence of our Lord to all external magnificence. The dis-

f *there shall not be left one stone upon another, that shall not be thrown down.

7 And they asked him, saying, Master, but ʰwhen shall these things be? and ⁱwhat sign *will there be* when these things shall come to pass?

8 And he said, ᵏTake heed that ye be not deceived; ˡfor many shall come in my name, saying, I am *Christ*; and the time draweth near: go ye not therefore after them.

9 But ᵐwhen ye shall hear of wars and commotions, be not terrified: for these things must first come to pass; ⁿbut the end *is* not by and by.

10 Then said he unto them, °Nation shall rise against nation, and kingdom against kingdom:

11 And great earthquakes shall be in divers places, and famines, and pestilences; and fearful sights, ᵖand great signs shall there be from heaven.

12 But ᑫbefore all these, they shall lay their hands on you, and persecute *you*, delivering *you* up to the synagogues, and into prisons, being brought before kings and rulers for my name's sake.

13 And ʳit shall turn to you for a testimony.

14 ˢSettle *it* therefore in your hearts not to meditate before what ye shall answer.

15 For ᵗI will give you a mouth and wisdom, ᵘwhich all your adversaries shall not be able to gainsay or resist.

16 And ˣye shall be betrayed both by parents, and brethren, and kinsfolks, and friends, ʸand *some* of you shall they cause to be put to death.

17 And ᶻye shall be hated of all men ᵃfor my name's sake.

18 But ᵇthere shall not an hair of your head perish.

---

ciples, not much accustomed to splendour and grandeur, expressed great admiration; and probably were disposed to think, that true religion was closely connected with these externals, or promoted by them. But the spiritual mind of our Lord, in both respects, disregarded them; being wholly occupied by things of a far more sublime and heavenly nature. (*Note, John* iv. 21—24.)

V. 7—11. *Marg. Ref.—Notes, Matt.* xxiv. 3—8. *Mark* xiii. 1—8.—*The time, &c.* (8) The time, when the deceivers would come in the name of Christ; that is, each of them professing to be the promised Messiah.—*Fearful.* (11) Josephus gives a very particular account of many terrible appearances in the heavens; as a comet like a flaming sword waving over Jerusalem, and the appearance of contending armies in the air.—'The great gate of the 'temple, which twenty men could scarcely shut, and 'which was made fast with bolts and bars, was seen ... to 'open of its own accord, to let in their enemies: for so, 'saith he, our wise men construed this omen. ... At the 'feast of Pentecost, when the priests went at midnight 'into the temple to attend their service, they first heard a 'kind of noise, as of a movement from the place, and 'then a voice, saying, ... Let us go hence. ... Four years 'before the war, one Jesus began at the feast of taberna-'cles to cry, ... 'A voice against Jerusalem and the temple; '' a voice against all the people, Woe, woe unto them;' 'and he continued crying thus about seven years. ... 'These things Tacitus, a Roman historian, doth thus epi-'tomize: 'Armies seemed to meet in the clouds. Wea-'pons were there seen glittering; the temple seemed to 'be on a flame, with fire issuing from the clouds, and a 'divine voice was heard, that the Deity was quitting the 'place; and a great motion, as of his departing.'' *Whitby,*

on *Matt.* xxiv. 7, 8. Josephus was a Jew who never embraced Christianity, and Tacitus a learned Gentile who hated and vilified it.—These and many other extraordinary events excited great consternation among the Jews, and were intimations of their approaching miseries. (8) *That ye be not deceived.* Μη πλανηθητε. *Matt.* xxiv. 4. *Mark* xiii. 5. See on *Matt.* xviii. 12.—*Commotions.* (9) Ακαταστασιας. 1 Cor. xiv. 33. 2 Cor. vi. 5. xii. 20. *Jam.* iii. 16. (Ex α priv. et καθιστασις, constitutio in statu suo: idque ex κάθα, et ἱστημι, sto.) *Seditiones; bella intestina.* —*Be not terrified.*] Μη πτοηθητε. xxiv. 37. Not elsewhere N. T.—*Deut.* xxxi. 6: 1 Chr. xxii. 13. Sept. Θροηθης, *Matt.* xxiv. 6.—Πτοησις, 1 Pet. iii. 6.—*Fearful sights.* (11) Φοβητρα. Here only N.T.—*Is.* xix. 17. Sept.

V. 12—19. *Notes, Matt.* xxiv. 9—14. *Mark* xiii. 9—13.—*Turn to you, &c.* (13) 'The persecutions which you endure, being thus exactly foretold, shall still more fully confirm and establish your faith in me.'—*I will, &c.* (15) *Notes,* xii. 11, 12. *Ex.* iv. 11, 12. *Prov.* ii. 6. *Jer.* i. 9, 10. *Matt.* x. 16—20. *Acts* ii. 4. vi. 9—14. *Jam.* i. 5 —8.—In the texts referred to, it is declared, that it belongeth to JEHOVAH alone, to make, or open, man's mouth, or to give wisdom; and the constant language of scripture is, "as the Spirit gave them utterance:" being "filled with the Holy Ghost, he said, &c." Yet Jesus, during his lowest humiliation on earth, in the most express and explicit terms, promised to give his disciples "a mouth "and wisdom, which all their adversaries should not be "able to gainsay or resist." Such texts are seldom adduced in controversies on our Lord's Deity, or on the doctrine of the Trinity; but they are of immense importance in settling them: and the inference from them cannot be evaded in the same manner, which some use, with more

19 In your *patience possess ye your souls.

20 ¶ And when ye shall see Jerusalem compassed with armies, then know that the desolation thereof is nigh.

21 Then let them which are in Judea flee to the mountains; and let them which are in the midst of it depart out: and let not them that are in the countries enter thereinto.

22 For these be the days of vengeance, that all things which are written may be fulfilled.

23 But woe unto them that are with child, and to them that give suck in those days! for there shall be great distress in the land, and wrath upon this people.

24 And they shall fall by the edge of the sword, and shall be led away captive into all nations: and Jerusalem shall be trodden down of the Gentiles, until the times of the Gentiles be fulfilled.

---

plausibility, against express declarations on these subjects. For, the learned and ingenious opponents of these great mysteries of Christianity, have long been employed, in searching for other readings, or specious criticisms, on those texts, which form the grand pillars of our system; but they are not so well prepared to answer unexpected arguments. Most certainly, however, our Lord here promises to perform the *work of God*, which other scriptures declare incommunicably to belong to him; yet the same things are also ascribed to the Holy Spirit: and *unbiassed* common sense will shew any man, what the conclusion must be, according to the sacred oracles.—*To gainsay.*] 'Against which nothing can be said, which has the ap-'pearance of truth.' Grotius.—*Hair*, &c. (18) (*Marg. Ref.* b.) 'This, saith Grotius, is a proverbial expression, 'used 1 *Sam.* xiv. 45. 2 *Sam.* xiv. 11. 1 *Kings* i. 52. *Acts* 'xxvii. 34, signifying that they should sustain no loss, all 'circumstances considered; for to suffer some loss for the 'present, to gain eternal life, is the greatest advantage. '... But I cannot acquiesce in this interpretation; ... be-'cause this proverb, in all the places cited, contains a 'promise, that the persons spoken to should not die, or 'perish in the danger they lay under. ... Christ therefore 'seems to promise, that whatever might befall them at 'other times, yet in these "days of vengeance" upon the 'Jews, or at the time of destruction of the city and of 'the temple, none of those Christians who endured to the 'end should perish in that siege.' *Whitby*. (*Note, Matt.* xxiv. 15—18.)—*In your patience*, &c. (19) The apostles and other Christians were here exhorted to exercise patient resignation to the will of God, patience and perseverance in waiting the performance of his promises, patient continuance in well doing, and meek long-suffering under injuries. (*Notes*, viii. 4—15, v. 15. *Rom.* ii. 7—11, v. 7. *Jam.* v. 7, 8.) This would be " *their* patience," required of them and peculiar to them; by means of it, they would " possess their souls;" they would be enabled to preserve the calmness and cheerfulness of their minds, and thus have a comfortable enjoyment of life amid their troubles; and be kept from violent terrors and unruly passions, and from being driven from their hope in God, and obedience to him, to deeds of desperation. For self-murderers, in one way or other, lose " possession of their souls," whether by insanity or despair; and generally through want of patient submission to the will of God.

Shall turn, &c. (13) Απ⸰θῠσεται. *Phil.* i. 19.—*To me-*
VOL. V.

ditate before. (14) Προμελεταν. Here only N. T. Μελεταω. *Mark* xiii. 11.—*Ye shall answer.*] Απολογηθηναι. See on xii. 11.—*Adversaries.* (15) 'Οι αντικειμενοι.' xiii. 17. 1 *Cor.* xvi. 9. *Gal.* v. 17. 2 *Thes.* ii. 4. 1 *Tim.* v. 14.—*To gainsay.*] Αντιπειν. *Acts* iv. 14. Not elsewhere N. T.—*Resist.*] Αντιπτηναι. *Matt.* v. 39. *Acts* vi. 10. xiii. 8. *Rom.* ix. 19. *Gal.* ii. 11. *Eph.* vi. 13. 2 *Tim.* iii. 8.

V. 20—24. (*Marg. Ref.*—*Notes, Matt.* xxiv. 15—22. *Mark* xiii. 14—23.) St. Luke explains the language of the prophet Daniel, and that of the other evangelists, by saying, " When ye see Jerusalem compassed with armies" (20); instead of saying, " When ye see the abomination " of desolation, &c."—*Midst of it*, &c. (21) That is, Jerusalem, mentioned in the preceding verse.—*Days of vengeance.* (22) *Notes, Lev.* xxvi. 14—40. *Deut.* iv. 25 —28, xxviii. 49—67. *Ps.* lxix. 22—28. *Dan.* ix. 25—27. *Zech.* xi. 1—3. *Mal.* iv. 1.—*Fall*, &c. (24) Eleven hundred thousand Jews are recorded to have fallen in the siege of Jerusalem, besides great multitudes in other places: nearly a hundred thousand were sold for slaves, and reduced to the most abject captivity in distant countries: the remains of that devoted nation have been dispersed as captives, or in a most dependent oppressed condition, throughout the kingdoms of the earth; and yet have been preserved a distinct people for above one thousand seven hundred years! (*Notes, Num.* xxiii. 9. *Jer.* xxx. 10, 11.) This unparalleled event was doubtless intended, among other reasons, that they might be undeniable witnesses, or monuments, of the truth of the scriptures; of that part which they reject, as well as of that which they retain. Jerusalem has ever since been " trodden under-foot," or *governed with despotick sway*, by the Gentiles; by the Romans, Saracens, Mamaluks, Franks, and Turks who possess it to this day. A law was made by the Roman victors, forbidding any Jew to dwell in their ancient inheritance, or to come within sight of Jerusalem : the foundations of the old city were plowed up; a new city was at length builded by the conquerors, called Ælia, and an idolatrous temple was erected in the place where the temple of Jehovah had stood. In the days of Constantine and afterwards, the city was indeed possessed by Christians among others; but they were chiefly the Gentile converts, and the Jews were driven thence with great severity. Julian the Roman emperor, an apostate from Christianity, attempted to rebuild the temple, and to induce the Jews to settle there again, in avowed contempt

3 K

25 ¶ And there shall be ° signs in the sun, and in the moon, and in the stars; and upon the earth distress of nations, ° with perplexity; ° the sea and the waves roaring;

26 Men's ° hearts failing them for fear, and for looking after those things which are coming on the earth; ° for the powers of heaven shall be shaken.

27 And then shall they ° see the Son of man coming in a cloud, ° with power and great glory.

28 And when these things begin to come to pass, then ° look up, and lift up your heads; for your ° redemption draweth nigh.

29 ¶ And he spake to them a parable: ° Behold the fig-tree, and all the trees;

30 When they now shoot forth, ye see and know of your ownselves that summer is now nigh at hand.

31 So likewise ye, ° when ye see these things come to pass, know ye that ° the kingdom of God is nigh at hand.

a Matt. xvi. 27, 28. xxv. 31.

and defiance of this prophecy; but his impious attempt was repeatedly frustrated, by the eruption of balls of fire from the earth, which destroyed his workmen. Great pains were taken some ages after, and many bloody wars, called ' the Crusades,' were waged, in order to rescue this " holy city" from the hands of the infidels, and to establish there a Christian empire: but the success of these ruinous and infatuated wars was always very imperfect and short-lived; and, in general, Mohammedans (who are Gentiles, neither Jews nor Christians,) have had possession of it: the few Christians, who reside there have little more of their religion, than the name, and are most grievously oppressed by the Turks: and the " Jews," as a people, who are especially to be opposed to the Gentiles, have generally been driven from their ancient city, though many may now be found there.—" The times of the Gentiles " seem to signify the times during which the Gentiles are permitted to keep possession of Jerusalem, namely, till the Jews be converted to Christ: then their " times will " be fulfilled;" probably the Jews will be restored to their own land, and vengeance will be taken on those, who oppose their return: (Notes, Ez. xxxiv. 23—31. xxxvi. 25 —38. xxxvii. 25—28. xxxviii. xxxix. Dan. xi. 40—45. Am. ix. 13—15. Zech. xiv:) for these events seem to be predicted, as introductory to the calling of the nations into the church. (Notes, Rom. xi. 15—32, vv. 15—25.) —Or, the times appointed for the calling of the gentiles, or all nations, into the church may be meant. When this is arrived, or just at hand, the Jews will recover their holy city.—This prediction, however, has already been so remarkably accomplished, that it may be said to contain a full demonstration of the truth of the Christian religion. No human or created sagacity could have foreseen such remote events; no conjecture could have been formed of them. It must have previously been supposed, that, if the Jews were dispersed among all nations, they would be incorporated among them. Their preservation as a distinct people, neither Christians nor idolaters, in the midst of their several conquerors and oppressors, being Christians or idolaters, is an event, which has no parallel in the annals of the world; an event that could never have been expected or thought of, if prophecy from the days of Moses had not excited that expectation; an event which is a sure pledge of the accomplishment of all the other prophecies concerning this extraordinary people, as well as a preparation for it. (Note, Hos. iii. 4, 5.)—It is ob-

served by many expositors, that all the three evangelists who recorded these predictions were dead, before Jerusalem was destroyed. This is indeed true, as far as we can learn from history; yet some may doubt of it. But the fulfilment of the prophecy to this present day conveys the most unanswerable proof of its divine original: and I am verily convinced, that if men were as impartial and unprejudiced in their religious enquiries, as they are in mathematical reasonings; no one, who well considered this prediction, and examined its accomplishment, could any more doubt of the truth of the gospel, than learned men do of the Theorems in Euclid.

Armies. (20) Σ᾽ρατοπεδων. Here only N. T. Propriè castra. Ex ϛρατος, exercitus, et πεδον, campus.—The desolation.] Ερημωσις. See on Matt. xxiv. 15.—Shall be led away captive. (24) Αιχμαλωθισθησονται. Rom. vii. 23. 2 Cor. x. 5. Not elsewhere. Αιχμαλωτος. iv. 19.—Trodden down.] Παθουμενη. x. 19. Rev. xi. 2. xiv. 20.

V. 25—28. These expressions, of which some were literally verified in those events, which preceded, attended, and followed the taking of Jerusalem; and others, figurative of the subversion of the Jewish civil and religious establishment; may also be considered as typical of the awful solemnities, which will usher in the appearance of Christ to judge the world. And as the ruin of the Jews procured deliverance to the Christians whom they had persecuted, and was therefore a ground of encouragement to them: so the tremendous events, which make way for the " perdition of ungodly men," will introduce the complete redemption of believers from death and every enemy. —The ruin of the Jewish nation was attended by violent distractions and convulsions in the adjacent regions. (Marg. Ref.—Notes, Matt. xxiv. 29—31. Mark xiii. 24 —31.)

Distress. (25) Συνοχη. 2 Cor. ii. 4. Not elsewhere N. T.—A συναχω. viii. 45. xix. 43.—Perplexity.] Απορια. Here only N. T. Απορεω. Acts xxv. 20. Gal. iv. 20.— Failing. (26) Αποψυχοντων. .Here only N. T. Ex απο, et ψυχω, animus: expirantes.—Looking after.] Προσδοκιας. Acts xii. 11. Not elsewhere N. T.—Gen. xlix. 10. Ps. cxix. 116. Sept.—The earth.] Οικουμενη. See on Matt. xxiv. 12. (Note, Acts xi. 27—30.)

V. 29—33. Notes, Matt. xxiv. 32—35. Mark xiii. 32.

They shoot forth. (30) Προβαλωσι, subaudi κλαδους. Acts xix. 33. Not elsewhere N. T.

3 x 2

32 Verily I say unto you, ᵉ This generation shall not pass away till all be fulfilled.

33 ᶠ Heaven and earth shall pass away; but my words shall not pass away.

34 ¶ And ᵉ take heed to yourselves, lest at any time ᶠ your hearts be overcharged with ᵍ surfeiting and drunkenness and ʰ cares of this life, and so ᶦ that day come upon you unawares.

35 For ᵏ as a snare shall it come on all them that ˡ dwell on the face of the whole earth.

36 ᵐ Watch ye therefore and ⁿ pray always, that ye may be ᵒ accounted worthy to escape all these things that shall come to pass, and to ᵖ stand before the Son of man.

37 ¶ And in ᵠ the day-time he was teaching in the temple; and at night he went out, and abode in the mount that is called the ʳ mount of Olives.

38 And ˢ all the people came early in the morning to him in the temple, for to hear him.

V. 34—36. (*Marg. Ref.—Notes*, xii. 35—48. *Matt.* xxiv. 36—51. *Mark* xiii. 33—37.) Similar exhortations nave been considered in the parallel scriptures, which may be understood as addressed to the primitive Christians, who were waiting for those awful events which had been foretold: but they are equally applicable to those great concerns, in which all men alike are interested.—Every degree of excess in eating, drinking, and other animal indulgences, tends not only to oppress and disorder the body, but to stupify and darken the powers of the understanding, and to render the affections torpid and carnal. So that these sensualities, as well as the cares attending the pursuit of wealth, or anxiety about our temporal provision; and the desire of worldly honours and distinctions, unfit men for religious duties, and make way for the day of evil coming " upon them unawares," and should be most vigilantly avoided. (*Notes,* 1 *Cor.* ix. 24—27, *v.* 27. 1 *Thes.* v. 1—11. 2 *Pet.* i. 10, 11. iii. 10—13.)—The Roman armies invaded Judea and besieged Jerusalem, when they were not expected; and the Jews were every where taken, as " a bird in the snare of the fowler : " in like manner, death surprises most " men that dwell on the face " of the whole earth," in an unprepared state; and so will the day of judgment.

Overcharged. (34) Βαρυνθωσιν. Here only N. T. A ϐαρυς, *gravis.—Surfeiting.*] Κραιπαλη. Here only N. T.—*Of this life.*] Βιωτικαις. 1 *Cor.* vi. 3, 4. Not elsewhere N. T. A ϐιοω, *vitam ago.—Accounted worthy,* &c. (36) Καταξιωθητε. See on xx. 35. That is, meet persons to be thus delivered and accepted. This was to be sought by constant earnest prayer, and must " therefore be the gift of God," and not the worthiness of man.—*Stand,* &c.] *Notes, Rom.* xiv. 2 —4. 2 *Cor.* v. 9—12. *Eph.* vi. 10—13. 1 *John* ii. 26—29. *Jude* 22—25.

V. 37, 38. These verses shew us, in what manner our Lord spent the last days preceding his crucifixion. Early every morning he came to Jerusalem, and spent the day at the temple : and in the evening he retired to Bethany, probably to lodge at the house of Lazarus and his sisters. —The people from curiosity, conviction, or expectation, early resorted to attend on his instructions: yet when he would not assume the outward dignity of the regal character, but suffered himself to be apprehended by his enemies, they turned against him and joined in demanding his crucifixion ! (*Marg. Ref.*)

Came early. (38) Ωρθριζε. Here only N. T.—*Gen.* xix. 2. 27. Sept. Ab ορθρος, *diluculum, mane.*

PRACTICAL OBSERVATIONS.

V. 1—19.

Our gracious Lord particularly notices the small oblations, which spring from the love of his name in the hearts of his poor people ; because men are apt to despise and discourage them : " for man looketh at the outward appearance, but the Lord looketh at the heart." (*P. O. Mark* xii. 35—44.)—The spiritual mind will not be satisfied, except with a city and a temple, the foundations of which cannot be subverted, and the ornaments of which cannot be removed or defaced ; foreseeing the time when " the fashion of this world will pass away."—Instead of curious enquiries and speculations, every wise man will take heed " that he be not deceived," or led to countenance deceivers, and so add energy to delusion, in the great concerns of eternity. (*Note,* 2 *John* 7—11.) Whatever calamities may be in the world, or persecutions in the church, " before the end come ; " we are sure that it will be well with those who serve the Lord, and their very trials shall " turn to them for a testimony." We should therefore " settle it in our hearts " not to be anxious about these matters, or afraid lest we should be put to shame before our enemies : for the divine Saviour will give all his disciples " a mouth and wisdom, which none of " their enemies shall be able to gainsay or resist."—Whatever treachery, cruelty, contempt, or enmity wᵉ may meet with from men of all sorts, for his name's sake, nothing can in the least harm us. Let us then " possess our souls in " patience ;" " knowing that we are hereunto called ; " even to suffer patiently, as well as to be unwearied in doing good. (*P. O. Matt.* xxiv. 1—15. *Mark* xiii. 1—23. *Note,* and P. O. 1 *Pet.* ii. 18—25.)

V. 20—38.

The performance of ancient prophecies is very encouraging, to those who are waiting on God to perform his promises : for if " the days of vengeance " arrived," that all " things which were written might be fulfilled ; " surely the predictions of Zion's prosperity will also be accomplished ; for " God delighteth in mercy."—The scattered Jews around us *unwillingly* preach to us the truth of Christianity, and prove, that " though heaven and earth

CHAP. XXII.

The priests and scribes determine to put Jesus to death, 1, 2. Judas bargains to betray him, 3—6. Two apostles prepare the passover, and Jesus eats it with the twelve, 7—18. He institutes the Lord's supper, 19, 20; points out the traitor, 21—23; checks the ambition of the disciples, and promises them an honourable station in his kingdom, 24—30. He shews Peter, that Satan desired to sift him and his brethren; but that his faith should not fail, though he would thrice deny him, 31—34; and instructs his disciples about their approaching dangers, 35—38. His agony and prayer in the garden, and his warnings to the apostles, 39—46. He is betrayed and apprehended, 47—49; heals him whose ear Peter cut off, 50—53; and is led to the high priest, 54. Peter thrice denies him, but bitterly repents, 55—62. Jesus is mocked, insulted, and condemned, 63—71.

ᵃ Ex. xii. 6—23. Lev. xxiii. 5, 6. Matt. xxvi. 2. Mark xiv. 1, 2. 12. John xi. 55

N OW ᵃ the feast of unleavened bread drew nigh, which is called the Passover.

—37. 1 Cor. v. 7, 8.
ᵇ xix. 47, 48. xx. 19. Ps. ii. 1—4. Matt. xxi. 38. 45, 46. xxvi. 3—5. John xi. 47—53. 57.

2 And ᵇ the chief priests and scribes sought how they might kill him; for they feared the people.

ᶜ John. xii. 70, 71. xiii. 6. xiii. 2 27. Acts v. 3.

3 Then ᶜ entered Satan into Judas surnamed Iscariot, ᵈ being of the number of the twelve.

ᵈ xi. vi. 16. Ps. xli. 9. li. 19. 14. Matt. xxvi. 23. Mark xiv. 18—20. John xiii. 18, 26.

4 And he ᵉ went his way, and communed with the chief priests and captains, how he might betray him unto them.

ᵉ Matt. xxvi. 14. Mark xiv. 10, 11.

5 And they were glad, ᶠ and covenanted to give him money.

6 And he promised, and sought opportunity to betray him unto them, ᵍ in the absence of the multitude.

ᶠ Zech. xi 12, 13
Matt. xxvi. 15
Id. xxvii. 8—4
Acts i. 18. viii.
20. 1 Tim. vi. 9
10. 2 Pet. ii. 3
15. Jude 11.
ᵍ Or, without tumult. Matt. xxvi. 5. Mark xiv. 2.

7 ¶ Then came ᵍ the day of unleavened bread, when the passover must be killed.

ᵍ Ex. xii. 6. 18. Matt. xxvi. 17 Mark xiv. 12.

8 And ʰ he sent Peter and John, saying, ⁱ Go and prepare us the passover, that we may eat.

ʰ Mark xiv. 13—16.
ⁱ i. 6. Matt. iii. 15 Gal. iv. 4, 5.

9 And they said unto him, Where wilt thou that we prepare ?

10 And he said unto them, ᵏ Behold, when ye are entered into the city, there shall a man meet you, bearing a pitcher of water : follow him into the house where he entereth in.

ᵏ xix. 29, &c. 1 Sam. x. 2—7. Matt. xxvi. 18, 19. John xvi. 4. Acts viii. 26—29.

11 And ye shall say unto the goodman of the house, ˡ The Master saith unto thee, ᵐ Where is the guest-chamber, where I shall eat the passover with my disciples?

ˡ xix. 31 34. John xi. 28.
ᵐ xix. b. Rev. iii. 20.

12 And ⁿ he shall shew you ᵒ a large upper room furnished : there make ready.

ⁿ John ii. 25. xxi. 17. Acts xvi 14. 15.
ᵒ Acts i. 13. xx. 8.

13 And ᵖ they went and found as he had said unto them: and they made ready the passover.

ᵖ xxi. 32. John li. 5. xi. 40. Heb. xi. 8.

14 ¶ And ᵠ when the hour was come,

ᵠ Deut. xvi. 6, 7. Matt. xxvi. 2 Mark xiv. 17.

" pass away, the words of Jesus shall not pass away : " and they may also remind us to pray for those times, when neither the literal nor the mystical Jerusalem shall any longer be trodden down by the Gentiles, and when both Jews and Gentiles shall be turned to the Lord. (Note, Rev. xi. 1, 2.)—If we would " lift up our heads, as know-" ing that our redemption draweth nigh," in those seasons when there shall be " distress of nations with perplexity, " the sea and the waves roaring, men's hearts failing them " for fear, and for looking after those things which are " coming on the earth ; " or in the day when " flesh and " heart shall fail ; " or when " the powers of heaven shall " be shaken, and the Son of man shall be seen coming in " a cloud, with power and great glory ; " we must continually be expecting and preparing for those events. Even true Christians have great need to be warned " to take " heed to themselves," that they may not, on any occasion, be drawn into excessive or inexpedient indulgence, or be entangled by worldly cares : otherwise those days may come upon them unawares, which as a snare surprise to their destruction the inhabitants of the earth. May we then watch and pray incessantly, that we may " be ac-" counted worthy to escape " these fatal delusions; and " that we may be found " of Christ, when he cometh, " in peace, without spot and blameless." (Notes, 2 Pet. iii. 11—15.) May we begin, employ and conclude each

of our days, in reading and hearing his word, obeying his precepts, and imitating his example, that whensoever he cometh we may " be found watching ! " (P. O. Matt. xxiv. 16—51. xxv. 1—13. Mark xiii. 24—37. 1 Thes. v. 1—11. 2 Pet. iii. 9—18.)

NOTES.

Chap. XXII. V. 1—13. Marg. Ref.—Notes, Matt. xxvi. 1—5. 14—19. Mark xiv. 10—16.—Then entered, &c. (3) Notes, John xiii. 1—5. 18—30. ' God, by his ' wonderful providence, causeth him to be the minister of ' our salvation, who was the author of our destruction.' Beza.—Money. (5) ' As the priests proposed so small a ' price,' (thirty shekels), ' to express their contempt of ' Jesus; so God permitted Judas, covetous as he was, to ' acquiesce in that mean and trifling sum; (though he ' might easily have raised it higher:) that thus the pro-' phecy of Zechariah might be fulfilled, in which it had ' been particularly specified.' Doddridge—Promised. (6) Ἐξωμολογησε. See on Matt. xi. 25. Ὁμολογέω. Idem dico cum altero, adsentio, consentio. Matt. xiv. 7. Covetous and vile as Judas was, it is hardly conceivable, that he should formally thank the priests for the paltry sum, which they stipulated to give him.
V. 14—18. Jesus assuredly knew, that this passover would bring on immediately his most intense and inexpres-

¶ K 4

he sat down, and the twelve apostles with him.

15 And he said unto them, *With desire I have desired to eat this passover with you before I suffer:

16 For I say unto you, I will not any more eat thereof, until it be fulfilled in the kingdom of God.

17 And he took the cup, and gave thanks, and said, Take this, and divide it among yourselves

18 For I say unto you, I will not drink of the fruit of the vine, until the kingdom of God shall come.

19 And he took bread, and gave thanks, and brake it, and gave unto them, saying, This is my body which is given for you: this do in remembrance of me.

20 Likewise also the cup after supper, saying, This cup is the new testament in my blood, which is shed for you.

21 But, behold, the hand of him that betrayeth me is with me on the table.

22 And truly the Son of man goeth, as it was determined: but woe unto that man by whom he is betrayed!

23 And they began to enquire among themselves, which of them it was that should do this thing.

---

sible sufferings: yet he ardently longed for its arrival, that he might enter on that conflict, which would certainly end in a glorious victory, productive of the most happy consequences to his people to all eternity: and he desired to join with his disciples in that passover " before he suffered;" that he might more fully open his mind to them, and speak such things as would conduce to prepare them also for the trials which were before them. He likewise informed them, that he should no more partake of that sacred feast, till its typical meaning was fulfilled in his atoning sacrifice, the clear revelation of his gospel, and the establishment of his spiritual kingdom. (*Notes, Ex.* xii. 3—14.) Having said this, he took the cup of wine, with which it was customary for the head of the family to begin the paschal supper; and, giving thanks for it and the mercies then commemorated, he directed his disciples to divide it among them; as he should no more drink of the fruit of the vine, till the kingdom of God should come, i. e. till the gospel-dispensation should be introduced. (*Marg. Ref.* x—z.)—*Note, Matt.* xxvi. 29.)—It is probable, that Jesus made the same declaration, at giving the disciples the cup of wine, usually drunk in celebrating the passover; and when he gave them the cup in instituting the Lord's supper. Perhaps he tasted the former, as a part of the *custom*, though not required by the *law*: but he did not partake of the wine, used in appointing the sacramental memorial of his death.

With desire, &c. (15) *Marg.* Επιθυμια επιθυμησα.—Επιθυμια. *Mark* iv. 19. *John* viii. 44. *Rom.* i. 24. vi. 12. vii. 7, 8. xiii. 14. *Phil.* i. 23. 1 *Thes.* ii. 17. iv. 5. 2 *Pet.* ii. 18. 1 *John* ii. 16, 17.—Επιθυμεω. xv.'16. xvii. 22. *Acts* xx. 33. *Jam.* iv. 2. 1 *Pet.* i. 12.—See on *Matt.* v. 28.

V. 19, 20. *Marg. Ref.*—*Notes, Matt.* xxvi. 26—28. *Mark* xiv. 17—30. 1 *Cor.* x. 14—22. xi. 23—34.—*After*, &c. (20) ' This was said, after the paschal supper, to signify that ' this cup pertained not to the solemnity of the passover.' *Whitby.*—' The cup" is here put for the *wine* contained in it; and that is said' to be " the new covenant in my " blood" as representing the blood of Emmanuel. It is astonishing that, amidst language so undeniably *figurative*, one expression should have been so long, so extensively, and so pertinaciously, interpreted *literally*, in contradiction to scripture, to fact, and to common sense.—As we are not under the ritual law, and as nothing in this respect is spoken in the New Testament; it does not appear, that unfermented bread is essential to the Lord's Supper: or that cutting the loaf is improper; though to *break* a portion of it at least seems more scriptural.—The passover was *once* celebrated by anticipation, before the deliverance of Israel out of Egypt; and the Lord's supper, once before our ransom had been paid.

In remembrance of me. (19) Εις την εμην αναμνησιν. 1 *Cor.* xi. 24, 25. *Heb.* x. 3. Not elsewhere N. T.—*Num.* x. 10. *Sept.*

V. 21—23. *Marg. Ref.*—*Note, Matt.* xxvi. 21—24.— *As it was determined.* (22) The other evangelists say, " as " was written of him." It was *written* because it was *determined*: but as Judas betrayed Christ, neither because it was decreed that he should, of which he could ' know ' nothing; nor because it was so written, .which assuredly he did not understand, or attend to, at the time; so neither the one nor the other interfered, in the smallest degree, with his free agency and accountableness, and consequently did not excuse his wicked conduct.—It is surprising, that learned men should allow the system of prophecy to be consistent with man's free agency; and yet think the secret purposes of God inconsistent with it. Of *predicted* events we may know something; and this, in certain cases, may influence our conduct: but of *secret* decrees we can know nothing, previous to the accomplishing of them; and so it is impossible that they should be the motives of our actions, or form any excuse for our sins. And as the predicted event must infallibly take place, for " the scripture can- " not be broken;" this as certainly ensures the predicted conduct, in the persons concerned, if only *foreseen*, as if absolutely *decreed.* The objection therefore, on this ground, is *unreasonable*; but the scriptures must decide which system is : true.—' The decree of Providence, though it ' necessarily take place, yet does not excuse the crime ' of the instrument.' *Beza.*—This Calvin himself would have maintained.

Determined: (22) Ωρισμενον. *Acts* ii. 23. x. 42. xi. 29,

24 ¶ And there was also ·a strife among them, which of them should be accounted the greatest.

25 And he said unto them, ᵐ The kings of the Gentiles exercise lordship over them ; and they that exercise authority upon them are called benefactors.

26 But ᵒ ye *shall* not *be* so: but he that is greatest among you, let him be as the younger ; and he that is chief, as he that doth serve.

27 For whether *is* ᵖ greater, he that sitteth at meat, or he that serveth ? *is* not he that sitteth at meat? but I am among you as he that serveth.

28 Ye are they which have ᵖ continued with me in my temptations :

29 And ᵠ I appoint unto you a kingdom, as my Father hath appointed ʳ unto me ;

30 That ye may ᵗ eat and drink at ᵘ my table in my kingdom, ᵛ and sit on thrones, judging the twelve tribes of Israel.

31 ¶ And the Lord said, ʸ Simon, Simon, behold, ᶻ Satan hath desired *to* have you, that he may ˣ sift *you* as wheat :

32 But ʸ I have prayed for thee, that ᶻ thy faith fail not ; and ᵃ when thou art ᵇ converted, ᵇ strengthen thy brethren.

33 And he said unto him, Lord, ᶜ I am ready to go with thee, both into prison, and to death.

34 And he said, I tell thee, Peter,

2 Cor. l. 4—6. 1 Tim. i. 13—16. Heb. xii. 12, 13. 1 Pet. i. 13. v. 8—10. 2 Pet. i. 10—12. iii. 14, 17, 18. c 2 Kings vii. 12, 13. Prov. xxviii. 26. Jer. x. 23. xvii. 9. Matt. xx. xxi. 13.

---

xvii. 26. 31. *Heb.* iv. 7 : ub ὁριον, *terminus.* Προοριζω. *Rom.* viii. 29, 30.

V. 24—27. 'It is wonderful, Christ should not have answered, that Peter was he to whom all the rest must ' be subject, as a prince or head; if indeed Peter was ' placed in any degree of apostolical authority above the ' rest.' *Beza.*—This competition seems to have been secretly revived among the apostles, even at the last passover. The immediate introduction of "the kingdom of " God " would be considered by them, as implied in what our Lord had before spoken ; and they overlooked all which he had said of his sufferings, as what they could not understand. He, however, saw the same ambition working in their hearts ; and to repress it he had recourse to arguments, similar to those which he had used on a former occasion. (*Marg. Ref.*—*Notes*, ix. 46—50. *Matt.* xviii. 1—6. xx. 20—28. *Mark* x. 35—45.)—*Exercise,* &c. (25) Both the original words, here used, imply arbitrary domineering authority; like that of a slaveholder over his slaves. One of the most ambitious, cruel, and tyrannical of the Egyptian kings was called P*tolemæus Euergetes,* the Benefactor :' but the apostles must not affect to be called benefactors, by assuming state or exercising dominion ; but be ready for the meanest and lowest services, by which they might do real good to others; and this without excepting the senior or most eminent of them.—When our Lord said, that he " was among them as he that " served ;" he seems to have referred to the washing of the disciples' feet, which took place about the same time. (*Notes*, xii. 35—46. *John* xii. 1—8. xiii. 1—17.)

A strife. (24) Φιλονεικια. Here only N. T. Φιλονεικος. 1 Cor. xi. 16. Εx φιλος, et νεικος, *jurgium, rixa.*—*Exercise* lordship. (25) Κυριευσιν. *Rom.* vi. 9. vii. 1. xiv. 9. 2 *Cor.* i. 24. 1 *Tim.* vi. 15. Καλακυριευσιν, *Matt.* xx. 25.—*Exercise* authority.] Εξουσιαζοντες. 1 *Cor.* vi. 12. vii. 4. Not elsewhere N. T. Καλεξουσιαζουσιν, *Matt.* xx. 25.—*Benefactors.*] Ευεργεται. Here only N. T. Εx ευ *bene,* et εργον *opus.*

V. 28—30. Our blessed Saviour would not countenance in the least the worldly ambition of his disciples;

but he saw good to animate them with the prospect of an honour worthy of their most ardent desires. They had followed him, with persevering constancy, through all his humiliating trials, which were about to terminate in his crucifixion ; and they would follow his example, and adhere to him, through all temptations even unto death. As a reward for their faithful attachment, he engaged, as by covenant, to assign them a kingdom ; even as the Father had covenanted to give him a kingdom, when he had passed through his sufferings. He would there admit them to share the glory and felicity of his exaltation ; even as a victorious monarch admits his valiant captains and chosen friends to feast with him at his own table : and he would also make them assessors with him in judgment, especially in passing sentence on the twelve tribes of Israel, who would reject their ministry as they had done his, and put most of them to death as they were about to crucify him (*Notes, Dan.* xii. 2, 3. *Matt.* xix. 27, 28. 1 *Cor.* vi. 1—6, *vv.* 2, 3. *Rev.* xxi. 9—12, *v.* 14.)—Judas could not be intended in this promise ; but as twelve apostles were at first appointed, and as the vacancy would soon be filled up, after he " was gone to his own place," the original number was mentioned.—Some explain this of the authority of the apostles over the Christian church : but, while this authority is most readily allowed to belong to them, and in some respects to them exclusively ; (*Note, Matt.* xvi. 19 ;) some special honour and distinction in the world above, seems to be more directly intended.

Have continued. (28) Εσε οι διαμεμενηκοτες. i. 22. *Gal.* ii. 5. *Heb.* i. 11. 2 *Pet.* iii. 14.—*Ps.* cii. 26. cxix. 90, 91. *Sept.*—*Temptations.*] Πειρασμοις. See on *Matt.* vi. 13.—*I* appoint, &c. (29) Διαλιθεμαι. ... *appointed,* διεθετο. *Acts* iii. 25. *Heb.* viii. 10. ix. 16. x. 16.—' *Testor* ... *testamentum cando, testamento ordino* ... *fœdus pango.* Schleusner. Hence διαθηκη, *fœdus testamentum.*

V. 31—34. Perhaps Peter was here called by his former name, Simon, because in the events referred to, his instability so little accorded to the signification of that which had been given him. (*Notes, Matt.* xvi. 18. *John* i. 35.—

3 x 6

d Matt. xxvi. 34.
74. Mark xiv.
30, 71, 72. John
xiii 38. xviii. 27.
 ᵈ the cock shall not crow this day, before that thou shalt thrice deny that thou knowest me.

e iv. 3. x. 4 Matt.
x. 9, 10. Mark
vi. 8, 9.
f xii. 29—31. Gen.
xlviii. 15. Deut.
viii. 2, 3, 16. Ps.
xxiii. 1. xxxiv.
9, 10. xxxvii. 3.
35 ¶ And he said unto them, ᵉ When I sent you without purse, and scrip, and shoes, ᶠ lacked ye any thing? And they said, Nothing.

g Matt. x. 22—25.
John xv. 20.
xvi. 33. 1 Thes.
ii. 14, 15, iii. 4.
1 Pet. iv. 1.
36 Then said he unto them, ᵍ But now, he that hath a purse, let him take it, and likewise his scrip: and he that

hath no sword, let him sell his garment, and buy one.

h 22. xviii. 31.
xxiv. 44—46.
Matt. xxvi. 54—
56. John x. 35.
xix. 28—30 Acts
xiii. 27—29.
i xviii. 32. Is. liii.
12. Mark xv. 27,
28. 2 Cor. v. 21.
Gal. iii. 13.
37 For I say unto you, That ʰ this that is written must yet be accomplished in me, ⁱ And he was reckoned among the transgressors: for the things concerning me have an end.

k Matt. xxvi. 52—
54. John xviii.
36. 2 Cor. x. 3
4. Eph. vi. 10—
18. 1 Thes. v. 8.
1 Pet. v. 9.
38 And they said, Lord, behold, here are two swords. And he said unto them, ᵏ It is enough.

42.) Our Lord addressed him in particular, and in a very emphatical manner; though the other apostles were in a measure concerned, and the pronoun is plural, *you*, not *thee*. Satan, their adversary, had desired, and earnestly sought permission, and in some degree obtained it, to make his advantage of the approaching time of trial, and to assault them with most violent temptations. Probably he hoped completely to prevail against some of them; or to bring such a scandal on their characters, as might prevent their future usefulness, or grievously discourage and distress them. He wanted " to sift them as wheat;" or to agitate their minds by his inward suggestions, concurring with their outward perils and difficulties, as the wheat is tossed about in the sieve: (*Marg. Ref.* t—x.—*Note, Am.* ix. 7—10:) but, whatever his intentions were, the Lord meant to permit him, by these means, to prove them, and to over-rule it for the increase of their purity. Their distress and peril would indeed be very great, and they would none of them be able to sustain the shock unmoved: but Peter especially would be so violently assaulted, that, if left to himself, he would fall, like Judas, to rise no more. But he, who denounced the traitor's doom before his crime was perpetrated, assured Peter, that " he had " prayed for him, that his faith might not fail." Not fail, as strength does in sickness; but as *life* fails in death. His faith was grievously interrupted in its *exercise and effects*, when he denied his Lord: but the *principle* did not fail in his heart. (*Marg. Ref.* y, z.—*Notes, Rom.* v. 7—10. viii. 32—34. 1 Pet. i. 2—5.) " The Spirit of life" did not finally leave Peter, who was a believer, and whose conduct on a sudden temptation was entirely contrary to his real character, and his habitual purpose; though He no more strove with Judas, who was a hypocrite, and acted according to his true character, which he had hitherto concealed. Peter was speedily brought, in the renewed exercise of *faith*, to mourn for his sin, to hope in God's mercy, and to return to his service; but Judas was left to utter apostasy, despair, and suicide. (*Notes, Matt.* xiii. 20, 21. xxv. 1—4. *Rom.* vii. 15—17.) When Christ had given Peter this intimation of his merciful intentions respecting him; which doubtless afterwards gave support to his faith and hope, under the anguish of his bitter remorse after he had denied his Lord; he commanded him, when thus renewedly " converted, to strengthen his brethren." Accordingly, after his fall and recovery, he was peculiarly earnest in encouraging the disciples to hope for a happy event of their trials; and in animating them boldly to profess and preach the gospel: while the humiliating lessons, which he learned by those events, had a very salutary effect on his own spirit, and tended to qualify him especially for

encouraging and warning the tempted, the fearful, the desponding, or the fallen, even to the end of his days. The discerning reader will perceive the traces of it in his epistles. —Peter, however, was not at this time prepared to attend to his Lord's warnings, being confident of his good intentions, and foolishly disposed to " trust in his own heart." (*Notes, Matt.* xxvi. 30—35. *Mark* xiv. 17—30. *John* xiii. 36—38.)—' It was certainly Peter's advantage that our ' Lord did pray for him: but it was not so much for his ' honour, that he should stand in need of such a prayer, ' beyond all others.' *Lightfoot.* To Peter belonged *shame;* the *honour* was the Lord's.—All need the same intercession of Christ, which is the believer's only security against final apostasy: and who dares to say, that he needs it less than Peter did?—' It is through the prayers of Christ, that the ' elect do never utterly fall away from the faith. ...He ' shews that faith differeth much from a vain security, in ' setting before us the grievous example of Peter.' *Beza.* *Hath* desired. (31) Εξηθησατο. Here only—' Expeto ..., deposco, ut *aliquis mihi dedatur.*' Schleusner. Ex *et* et ταυτω posco.—*That he may sift.*] Τε σινιασαι. Here only N. T.—*Fail.* (32) Εκλειπη. See on xvi. 9.

V. 35—38. To prepare the disciples for approaching trials, our Lord reminded them of their past experience. He had sent them to preach the gospel, without allowing them to make any provision for the journey: yet they had met with persons, in every place, ready to entertain and supply them. (*Marg. Ref.* e, f.—*Note, Matt.* x. 9, 10.) They must now, however, expect to meet with a different reception, and prepare to encounter hardship, opposition, and persecution: insomuch, that it would behove them to take with them such provision as they had; and swords for self-defence would appear more necessary than even their garments. For all the prophecies, concerning the sufferings of the Messiah, were about to be accomplished in him, and to come to a speedy conclusion in his being crucified as a malefactor: and as they would then be " hated " for his sake," and would shortly be sent forth to preach him, the Lord and Saviour of the world; they must count their cost, and prepare to be despised, persecuted, and put to death.—The apostles, on hearing this, having two swords, (which were then frequently worn by travellers to defend them against the robbers,) shewed them to their Lord, by way of expressing their readiness to use them, and of asking permission to go and procure more. But as he said, " It is enough;" (though two swords could not be *enough* to arm eleven persons;) and as he shewed strong disapprobation of Peter's conduct in using the sword: we are sure, that he did not intend to be understood literally, but as speaking of the weapons of their spiritual warfare.—

39 ¶ And [l] he came out, and went, [m] as he was wont, to the mount of Olives; and his disciples also followed him.

40 And when he was at the place, he said unto them, [n] Pray that ye enter not into temptation.

41 And he was withdrawn from them about a stone's cast, [o] and kneeled down, and prayed,

42 Saying, [p] Father, if thou be willing, remove this [q] cup from me: nevertheless [r] not my will, but thine, be done.

43 And there appeared [s] an angel unto him from heaven, [t] strengthening him.

44 And [u] being in an agony, he prayed more earnestly: [x] and his sweat was as it were great drops of blood falling down to the ground.

45 And when he rose up from prayer, and was come to his disciples, he found them [y] sleeping for sorrow,

46 And said unto them, [z] Why sleep ye? rise and pray, lest ye enter into temptation.

l Matt. xxvi. 36—36. Mark xiv. 32—34. John xviii. 1, 2.
m xxi. 37. Mark xi. 11. 19. xiii. 3.
n 46. xi. 4. 1 Chr. iv. 10. Ps. xvii. 5. xix. 13. cxix. 116. 117. 133. Prov. xxx. 8, 9. Matt. vi. 13. xxvi. 41. Mark xiv. 38. 2 Cor. xii. 7—10. Eph. vi. 18, 19. 1 Pet. iv. 7. v. 8, 9 Rev. iii. 10.
o Matt. xxvi. 39 Mark xiv. 35.
p Matt. xxvi. 42. 44. Mark xiv. 36. John xii. 27, 28.
q 17—20. Is. li. 17. 22. Jer. xxv. 15, &c. Matt. xx. 22. John xviii. 11.
r Ps. xl. 8. John iv. 34. v. 30. vi. 38. Heb. x. 7—10.
s iv. 10, 11. Ps. xci. 11, 12. Matt. iv. 6. 11. xxvi. 53. 1 Tim. iii. 16. Heb. i. 6. 14.
t 22. Deut. iii. 28. Job iv. 3, 4. Is. xxxv. 3, 4 Dan. x. 16—19. xi. 1. Acts xviii. 23. Heb. ii. 17.
u Gen. xxxii. 24—28. Ps. xxii. 1, 2. 12—21. xl. 1—3. lxix. 14—18. lxxxviii. 1—18. cxxx. 1, 2. cxliii. 6, 7. Lam. iii. 53—56 Jon. ii. 2, 3. John xii. 27. Heb. v. 7.
x Is. liii. 10. Lam. i. 12. Rom. viii. 32.
y Matt. xxvi. 40. 43. Mark xiv. 37. 40, 41.
z 40. xxi. 34—36. Prov. vi. 4—11. Jon. i. 6.

47 ¶ And [a] while he yet spake, behold, a multitude, and he that was called [b] Judas, one of the twelve, went before them, and drew near unto Jesus to kiss him.

48 But Jesus said unto him, Judas, [c] betrayest thou the Son of man with a kiss?

49 When they which were about him saw what would follow, they said unto him, Lord, shall we smite with the sword?

50 And [d] one of them smote a servant of the high priest, and cut off his right ear.

51 And Jesus answered and said, [e] Suffer ye thus far. [f] And he touched his ear, and healed him.

52 Then [g] Jesus said unto the chief priests, and [h] captains of the temple, and the elders, which were come to him, Be ye come out as against a thief, with swords and staves?

53 When [i] I was daily with you in the temple, ye stretched forth no hands against me: [k] but this is your hour, and [l] the power of darkness.

a Matt xxvi. 46—47. Mark xiv. 41—43 John xviii. 2—9.
b 3—6. Matt. xxvi. 14—16. 47. Mark xiv. 10, 11. 43. Acts i. 16—18.
c 2 Sam. xx. 9, 10. Ps. lv. 21. Prov. xxvii. 6. Matt. xxvi. 48. 50. Mark xiv. 44—46.
d Matt. xxvi. 51—54. Mark xiv. 47. John xviii. 10, 11. Rom. xii. 19. 2 Cor. x. 4.
e John xvii xviii. 8, 9.
f Rom. xii. 21. 2 Cor. x. 1. 1 Pet. ii. 21—23.
g Matt. xxvi 55. Mark xiv. 48, 49.
h 4. 2 Kings xi. 15 John xviii. 12. Acts v. 26.
i xxi. 37, 38 Matt. xxi. 12—15. 23. 45, 46. John vii. 25, 26. 30. 45, &c.
k Judg. xvi. 2—30. Job xx. 5. John xvi. 20—22.
l John xiv. 30. Acts xxvi. 18. 2 Cor. iv. 3—6. Eph. vi. 12 Col. i. 13. Rev. xii. 9—12.

'His meaning was not perfectly comprehended by them: 'and he did not think it necessary, at that time, to open 'the matter further to them.' *Campbell.*—'This whole 'speech is allegorical. My fellow soldiers, you have 'hitherto lived in peace; but now a dreadful war is at 'hand: so that, omitting all other things, you must think 'only of *arms*. ... But when he prayed in the garden, and 'reproved Peter for smiting with the sword, he himself 'shewed what those *arms* were.' *Beza.*—'You may easily 'guess at the reception you are like to meet with, when 'you come in the name and authority of one, who has 'suffered as a malefactor; and yet demand faith and obe- 'dience to him as an almighty Saviour.' *Doddridge.* (*Marg. Ref.* g—k.—*Notes, Is.* liii. 11, 12. *Matt.* xxvi. 47—56. *Mark* xv. 26—28, *v.* 28. *John* xix. 28—30.)

It is enough. (38) Ἱκανον ἐστι. 2 *Cor.* ii. 6. 2 *Tim.* ii. 2.

V. 39—46. *Marg. Ref.*—*Notes, Matt.* xxvi. 36—46. *Mark* xiv. 32—38, *vv.* 36, 37.—*Pray*, &c. (40) Or, "Pray "that ye may not enter into temptation." Let this be your peculiar request, "Lead us not into temptation." (*Note, Matt.* vi. 13.)—'Prayers are a sure succour against the 'most perilous assaults of our enemies.' *Beza.*—*Angel*, &c. (43) The appearance of a holy angel to our Lord, in this conflict with the powers of darkness, and when he was weighed down with the feeling of the wrath of God against our sins, was an intimation of approaching victory. The angel could not *efficaciously* communicate strength, even to his human soul; but he might suggest encouraging topicks: (32. *Note, Is.* xxxv. 3, 4:) and it was doubtless a part of our Saviour's humiliation, and an instance of his condescension, that he was pleased to be thus "strength- "ened" by "a ministering spirit," though "all the angels "of God worship him."—*Drops*, &c. (44) Learned men have adduced some instances of persons who have sweated blood: but it was always in the greatest excess of anguish or terror; and commonly attended by weakness of body.—'Christ by overcoming all the horrors of death, in conjunc- 'tion with the curse of God for our sins, renders death 'friendly and lovely to us.' *Beza.*

Was withdrawn. (41) Απεσπασθη, *Matt.* xxvi. 51. *Acts* xx. 30. xxi. 1.—*Strengthening.* (43) Ενισχυων. *Acts* ix. 19. Not elsewhere N. T.—*An agony.* (44) Αγωνια. Here only N. T. Ab αγων. *Phil.* i. 30. *Col.* ii. 1, et al.—*More earnestly.*] Εκτενεστερον. Here only N. T. Εκτενης. *Acts* xii. 5. 1 *Pet.* iv. 8. Εκτενεια. *Acts* xxvi. 7.—*Great drops.*] Θρομβοι. Here only N. T.

V. 47—53. *Marg. Ref.*—*Notes, Matt.* xxvi. 47—56. *Mark* xiv. 43—52. *John* xviii. 1—9.—*Betrayest thou.* &c. (48) Dost thou make my condescending kindness the occasion of thy base treachery, and persist in the tokens of respect and affection even in the very deed?—*Suffer*, &c. (51) 'Almost all antiquity seem agreed in understanding 'our Lord's expression, as a check to his disciples.' *Campbell.* Having always considered his words as addressed to the officers, desiring them thus far to endure the rash opposition of his disciples, and not to proceed to violence against them; and still thinking it by far the most natural construction, and most obvious meaning; I yet thought it proper to introduce it, by stating what this learned writer asserts to be the general sense of antiquity.—Peter's rash

m Matt. xxvi. 57. 56. Mark xiv. 53. John xviii 12,17,19. n 33, 34. 2 Chr. xxxii. 31.

54 Then "took they him, and led him, and brought him into the high priest's house. "And Peter followed afar off.

o 44. John xviii. 18.

55 And when they "had kindled a fire in the midst of the hall, and were set down together, " Peter sat down among them.

p Ps. i. 1. xxvi. 4, 5. xxvii. 3. Prov. ix. 6. xiii. 20. 1 Cor. xv. 33. 2 Cor. vi. 15 —17.

56 But "a certain maid beheld him as he sat by the fire, and earnestly looked upon him, and said, This man was also with him.

q Matt. xxvi. 69. Mark xiv. 66. 68. John xviii. 17.

57 And "he denied him, saying, Woman, I know him not.

r 58. 34. xii. 9. Matt. x. 33. xxvi. 70. John xviii. 25. Acts iii. 13, 14. 1 & 2 Tim. ii. —12. 1 John v. 9.

58 And after a little while, "another saw him, and said, Thou art also of them. And Peter said, Man, I am not.

s Matt. xxvi. 71. 72. Mark xiv. 69. 70. John xviii. 25.

59 And about the space of one hour after, another " confidently affirmed, saying, Of a truth this *fellow* also was with him; for he is a Galilean.

t Matt. xxvi. 73. 74. Mark xiv. 69, 70. John xviii 26, 27.

60 And Peter said, Man, I know not what thou sayest. And immediately, while he yet spake, " the cock crew.

61 And the Lord " turned, and ' looked upon Peter: 'and Peter remembered the word of the Lord, how he had said unto him, 'Before the cock crow, thou shalt deny me thrice.

62 And Peter went out, ' and wept bitterly.

63 ¶ And ' the men that held Jesus ' mocked him, and smote *him*.

64 And when they had 'blind-folded him, they struck him on the face, and asked him, saying, Prophesy, who is it that smote thee?

65 And many other things ' blasphemously spake they against him.

66 ¶ And ' as soon as it was day, ' the elders of the people, and the

a 34. Matt. xxvi. 74. 75. Mark xiv. 71, 72. John xviii. 27. x x. 41. Mark v. 30.

y Job xxxiii. 27. Is. lvii. 15—18. Jer. xxxi. 18— 20. Hos. xi. 8. Acts ix. 5. z Ez. xvi. 63. xxxvi. 31. 82. xxxix. ii. 11. Rev. ii. 5.

a Matt. xxvi. 34. 75. John xiii. 38.

b Matt. xxvi. 75. Zech. xii. 10. 2 Cor. vii. 9 —11.

c Matt. xxvi. 67. 68. Mark xiv. 65. John xviii. 22.

d Matt. xxvi. 75. —Mic. v. 1. Matt. xxvii. 28—31.

e Judg. xvi. 21, 25. f xii. 10. Matt. xii. 31, 22. Acts xxvi. 11. 1 Tim. i. 13, 14. g Matt. xxvii. 1. Mark xv. 1. h Ps. ii. 1—3. Acts iv. 26—28.

---

courage seemed to render a miracle necessary for his preservation, and that of the other disciples; but, without a previous knowledge of our Lord's character, we could not have expected such a miracle as he wrought on this occasion. Desiring his furious adversaries to " suffer thus far," he immediately and perfectly restored the ear of Malchus. Yet neither this evidence of his power, nor his kindness to so officious an adversary, had any effect in softening them, or withdrawing them from their purpose!—*Captains.* (52) These are supposed to have been the leaders of the priests and Levites, who alternately kept guard at the avenues of the temple. (*Marg. Ref.* h.—*Note, Acts* iv. 1—3.)—*Hour,* &c. (53) That was the hour in which the enemies of Christ were allowed to prevail; because it was the very time, when Satan was to have power to " bruise the heel of the " Seed of the woman," who would at length crush his head. (*Notes, Gen.* iii. 14, 15. *Col.* i. 13—15.)

Shall we smite, &c. (49) Ει παιαξομεν; 50. *Matt.* xxvi. 31. 51. *Mark* xiv. 27. *Acts* vii. 24. xii. 7. *Rev.* xi. 6.—*Captains,* &c. (52) Στρατηγυς τυ ιερυ. 4. *Acts* iv. 1. v. 24. *Notes,* 2 Kings xi. 5—9, v. 9.—*The power of darkness.* (53) 'Η εξυσια τυ σκοτυς. *Acts* xxii. 18. *Col.* i. 13.

V. 54—62. *Marg. Ref.—Notes,* 31—34, vv. 33, 34. *Matt.* xxvi. 57—62. 69—75. *Mark* xiv., 66—72. *John* xviii. 15, 16.—*Man,* &c. (58) A maid challenged Peter, in the second instance, according to Matthew and Mark: yet he here answers to a *man.* But Matthew writes, " She " said to them that were there;" and Mark, " She began " to say to them that stood by." So that the maid gave the information to those around her, and some *man* charged Peter with it. Perhaps several joined, though he answered to one in particular, for St. John writes, " *They* said unto " him, &c." How must these people have been surprised, when they saw (as no doubt some of them did,) this timorous disciple, within the compass of a few weeks, when he was brought with John before the council, not only maintaining the honour of Jesus, but charging the

' murder of " the Prince of life " on the chief men of the ' nation, and warning them of their guilt and danger in ' consequence of it. (*Acts* iv. 5—13.)' *Doddridge.—Looked.* (61) ' What effect that look must have had on ' the heart, and on the countenance of Peter, every one ' may, perhaps, in some degree perceive; but it is utterly ' impossible for any words to describe, or I believe, for the ' pencil of a Guido to express. The sacred writer, there ' fore, judiciously makes no attempt to work upon our ' passions, or our feelings, by any display of eloquence on ' the occasion. He simply relates the fact, without any ' embellishment or amplification.' *Bp.* Porteus.

Were set down together. (55) Συγκαθισαντων. *Eph.* ii. 6. Not elsewhere N. T.—*Confidently affirmed.* (59) Διισχυριζετο. *Acts* xii. 15. Not elsewhere N. T.—*Omnibus viribus contendit.* Ex δια et ισχυριζομαι, ab ισχυς, *robur.*

V. 63—65. (*Marg. Ref.—Notes, Matt.* xxvi. 63—68. *Mark* xiv. 65.) ' It is probable that some insults pre ' ceded, and others yet more violent followed, his being ' solemnly condemned by the Sanhedrim as guilty of death. ' ...They charged Jesus with blasphemy, in asserting him ' self to be the Son of God : but the Evangelist fixes this ' charge on them, because he really was so.' *Doddridge.*

When they had blind-folded. (64) Περικαλυψαντες. *Mark* xiv. 65, rendered " to cover," *Heb.* ix. 4. Not elsewhere N. T.

V. 66—71. (*Notes, Matt.* xxvi. 57—68. xxvii. 1, 2. *Mark* xiv. 65.) From the narrative of the two preceding evangelists it appears, that after the council had condemned Jesus, they separated, and met again early in the morning : and the words here used, " As soon as it was day, &c." seem to refer to this latter meeting of the council. Nor is it improbable, that the high priest should again put the same questions to our Lord, as he had done the night before : both to see, whether he would stand to what he had said; and that such members of the council, as had been absent, might hear his answers.—*Ask,* &c. (68) That is,

3 L

chief priests, and the scribes, came together, and led him into their council, saying,

i Matt. xi. 3—5. xxvi. 63. Mark xiv. 61. John x. 24.

67 [i] Art thou the Christ? tell us. And he said unto them, [k] If I tell you,

k xvi. 31. John 39—47. vii. 48.

ye will not believe:

—45. ix. 27, 28. xi. 25, 26. xii. 57.

68 And [l] if I also ask you, ye will

l xx. 3,—7. xi. 41—44.

not answer me, nor let me go.

m Matt. xxvi. 64. Mark xiv. 62.

69 Hereafter [m] shall the Son of man

sit [n] on the right hand of the power of God.

70 Then said they all, Art thou then [o] the Son of God? And he said unto them, [p] Ye say that I am.

71 And they said, [q] What need we any further witness? for we ourselves have heard of his own mouth.

n Ps. cx. 1. Dan. vii. 13, 14. Matt. xxii. 44. Mark xvi. 19. Acta ii. 34—36. vii. 55, 56. Rom. viii. 34. Eph. i. 20—23. iv. 8—10. Col. iii. 1. Heb. i. 3. viii. 1. xii. 2. 1 Pet. iii. 22.
o Rev. xxii. 1. ix. 41. Ps. ii. 7. 12. Matt. iii. 17. xxvii. 43, 54. John i. 34, 49. x. 30. 36. xix. 7.
p xxiii. 3. Matt. xxvi. 64. Mark xiv. 62. xv. 2. John xviii. 37.
q Matt. xxvi. 65, 66. Mark xiv. 63, 64.

[r] If I demand a reason of your unbelief, or require you to set me at liberty, ye will not.'—Art thou. (70) What Christ said of himself and his exaltation, as "the Son of man," being understood as a declaration that he was the promised Messiah, occasioned the rulers to enquire whether he was "the Son of God:" by which it appears that they expected that the Messiah would be the Son of God: for they charged him with blasphemy, because they would not allow that he was the Messiah.—It is not indeed clear, in what sense they allowed of this term, as applied to the Messiah. (Ps. ii. 7.) But as our Lord used it, they regarded it as "making himself God." (John x. 33.)

PRACTICAL OBSERVATIONS.

V. 1—23.

When sinners have long gone on in wickedness, and done violence to the convictions of conscience under the means of grace, and still listened to temptation; Satan is often permitted to take full and final possession, and to hurry them into such crimes as "bring on them swift de-"struction." (Note, John xii. 1—8. xiii. P. O. 18—30.) This is more likely to be the doom of hypocritical preachers of the gospel, than of any other persons: nor will eminence of rank, gifts, or abilities in the least preserve them from it.—The avarice of false friends sometimes concurs with the malice of open enemies, in contriving plans of persecution; and in getting over the obstacles which they meet with from the fear of man: and, however they despise or hate one another, they are very glad of each other's assistance. The faithful followers of the Lamb may, however, confidently commit their cause to "him who judgeth "righteously:" and, after the example of their Lord, they should attend on the ordinances of God in due season; assured that no plots of their enemies can accomplish more than "was before determined," with a view to the glory of God, and the salvation of their souls. If then the Redeemer "greatly desired" the approach of his last most tremendous sufferings, that he might furnish an everlasting feast for our souls, "by his body broken, and his blood "poured out for us;" with what patience and cheerfulness should we meet those lighter trials, through which we are to follow him to his kingdom above! We should therefore continually remember his love, his sufferings, and our obligations to him, both in that sacred institution which he has appointed, and by our daily meditation on his word; that we may feel the constraining influence of love to him, who died for us to purchase the blessings of the New Testament, which he sealed with his blood.—Let us then only beware of hypocrisy: and though the hand of traitors should be with us, either at his table, or at our own; we shall be free from their woe, and be able to ap-

peal to the Lord, and confide in him with conscious integrity. (P. O. Matt. xxvi. 1—35. Mark xiv. 1—42.)

V. 24—34.

How unbecoming is worldly ambition in a follower of Jesus, who "took upon him the form of a servant," and "humbled himself even to the death upon the cross!" Let us leave it to those rulers of this world who know not God, to lust after dominion, and to retain flatterers, who may compliment them as "benefactors;" whilst their mad ambition fills nations with blood and misery. It is our part to do good by stooping and labouring, and to become "benefactors" indeed, by being servants to all men for Christ's sake, and after his example. (Notes, 2 Cor. iv. 5, 6. Gal. v. 13—15.) Nor are we allowed to aspire after any other pre-eminence in his kingdom, than what springs from deeper humility, with superior diligence and usefulness. Thus following Christ in his "temptations," we too shall obtain a kingdom, even as he has been exalted to his mediatorial throne: and though we shall not have the distinguished honour of the holy apostles; yet we shall be admitted to a "fulness of joy" and "a weight of glory," of which we at present can form no adequate conception. —But in the way to this felicity we must expect to be assaulted and sifted by Satan: if he cannot destroy us, he will endeavour to disgrace, to pollute, or to distress us: and the Lord may see good to permit him to harass us grievously, and even to baffle us in some painful conflicts, that he may the more prove, humble, and sanctify us; and shew the power of his grace in making us at length more than conquerors. (Notes, 2 Cor. xii. 7—10.) It is not owing to our own wisdom and strength, if we be not finally overcome; but to the intercession of our heavenly Advocate, who prays "for his people, as he does "not for the world:" therefore "their faith does not fail;" though it seem to be dead, it revives again; "though they "fall, they are not utterly cast down," for they again look to the Lord and he restores their souls. If we have experience of this conflict, and have been recovered, and as it were converted again, after having been foiled by temptation; we shall both be qualified and disposed to strengthen our brethren, to caution and encourage them for the combat, to address the weak and tempted with tenderness and compassion, and to "restore in the spirit "of meekness such as have been overtaken in a fault." (Note, Gal. vi. 1—5, v. 1.)—But nothing so certainly forebodes a fall, in a professed disciple of Christ, as self-confidence connected with disregard to warnings, and contempt of danger. We may honestly mean what we profess, when we say, "I am ready to go with thee to prison, or to "death;" but it is not so easy to stand our ground in the

3 L 2

CHAP. XXIII.

Jesus is accused before Pilate, who sends him to Herod, 1—7. He is silent before Herod, who mocks him and sends him back, 8—11. Pilate and Herod are made friends, 12. Pilate, convinced of the innocence of Jesus, is yet prevailed on by clamour to give him up to crucifixion, and to release Barabbas, 13—25. Jesus is led away, Simon of Cyrene bearing his cross, 26. To the women and others who bewailed him, he predicts the calamities coming on the Jews, 27—31. He is crucified between two thieves, and prays for his murderers, 32—34 The people, rulers, priests, and soldiers, and one of the thieves, scoff at him, 35—38. The other thief rebukes his companion, and confesses Christ, who promises that he shall "that day be with "him in paradise," 39—43. The land is darkened, the veil of the temple rent, and Jesus, commending his spirit into the hand of his Father, expires, 44—46. The centurion confesses him; and the people with his acquaintance retire, smiting their breasts at what they had seen, 47—49. Joseph of Arimathea asks for the body, and buries it, 50—54. The women prepare spices; but rest on the sabbath, according to the commandment, 55, 56.

AND [a] the whole multitude of them arose, and led him unto Pilate.

2 And [b] they began to accuse him, saying, We found this *fellow* [c] perverting the nation, [d] and forbidding to give tribute to Cæsar, saying, [e] That he himself is Christ a King.

3 And [f] Pilate asked him, saying, Art thou [g] the King of the Jews? And he answered him, and said, Thou sayest it.

4 Then said Pilate to the chief priests, and *to* the people, [h] I find no fault in this man.

Matt. xv. 14. John xviii. 38. xix. 4—6. Heb. vii. 26. 1 Pet. i. 19. ii. 22. iii. 18.

a xxii. 66. Matt. xxvii. 1, 2. Mark xv. 1. John xviii 28.
b Mark xv. 3—5. John xviii. 30.
c 8. 1 Kings xviii. 17. Jer. xxxviii.
4. Am. vii. 10. Acts xvi. 20. xvii. 6, 7. xxiv. 5.
d xv. 20—23. 1 Kings xxi. 10—13. Ps. xxxv. 11. lxii. 4. lxiv. 3—6. Jer. xx. 10. xxxvii. 15—18. Matt. xxvi. 59, 60. Mark xiv. 55, 56. Acts xxiv. 13. 1 Pet. iii. 16—18.
e xxii. 69, 70. Matt.xiv.61, 62. John xix. 12.
f Matt. xxvii. 11. Mark xv.2.John xviii. 33—37. 1 Tim. vi. 13.
g 38—40. Mark xv. 18. 32. John i. 49. xix. 3. 19—21.
h 14. 15. Matt. xxvii. 19. 34.

hour of temptation : and unless we " watch and pray " always," we may be drawn into those things during the course of the day, against which in the morning we were most fully and honestly resolved. (P. O. Matt. xxvi. 26 —35.—Notes, Rom. vii. 18—25. P. O. 14—25.)

V. 35—46.

Our experience of the Lord's faithfulness and goodness, in times past, should animate us to trust his providence and grace for the future : for many of us must say to his praise, that when in obedience to his word, and depending on his promises, we neglected ordinary methods of obtaining temporal provisions, we in the event have wanted nothing. Yet we should not so presume on his care, as to rush needlessly into danger : and we may expect, that as our faith is strengthened it will be more sharply tried than heretofore. We should then be continually preparing and arming for the battle, that we may be " able to stand " in the evil day" of sharp temptation : and we shall find, that a believing acquaintance with the word of God, that " sword of the Spirit," will be more needful for us, in our passage through the enemy's country, than even our ordinary raiment. We cannot expect to escape tribulation and ill usage, in a world which numbered the Lord of glory with the worst of malefactors, if we indeed profess his truth and obey his commandments : but if we pray fervently that we " may not enter into temptation," we shall either be preserved from the severer trials, or be enabled under them to say, " Not my will but thine be done." And surely, when we contemplate the Redeemer " in an " agony, praying more earnestly," and " his sweat like great " drops of blood falling down to the ground," while " he was bruised for our iniquities ; " we shall pray also to be enabled " to resist unto blood, striving against sin," if we should ever be called to it. (P. O. Matt. xxvi. 36— 46. Mark xiv. 17—42.—Notes, Heb. xii. 2—8, vv. 2—4.)

V. 47—71.

Our supineness frequently exposes us to rebukes and chastenings : yet on some occasions, our intemperate zeal betrays us into dishonourable mistakes, even as our timidity does on others. For corrupt nature still counteracts the tendency of grace, and warps our conduct to opposite extremes : we should therefore ask, and *wait* for, the Lord's directions, before we act in difficult circumstances. He will, however, prevent the most fatal consequences of our errors, provided our hearts be upright : yet when we contrast his temper and conduct with our own, we shall always see much to admire, and much to be ashamed of.—Neither the displays of his power, nor those of his love, can intimidate or soften hardened unbelievers ; for such men could treat the divine Saviour, as if he had been a thief or a robber, even when he was working his gracious miracles before their eyes, nay, when healing their wounds ! But their *hour*, and that of " the power of " darkness," was of short continuance ; and such will always be " the triumphing of the wicked."—To whatever part of the scene before us we turn our thoughts ; we shall see proofs of the Redeemer's excellency, and of the deceitfulness and desperate wickedness of the human heart : but especially let us contemplate him, amidst all the insults and cruelties which he meekly endured, looking with compassion on his fallen disciple : that we too may be excited to call our own sins to remembrance, and to renew " that godly sorrow, which worketh repentance unto sal- " vation not to be repented of ; " and to compassionate, and " restore in the spirit of meekness, such as have been " overtaken in a fault ; considering ourselves, lest we also " should be tempted."

NOTES.

CHAP. XXIII. V. 1—5. (Notes, Matt. xxvii. 1, 2. 11—18. Mark xv. 1—5. John xviii. 28—40.) The beginning of this chapter favours the opinion before given, (Note, xxii. 66—71,) that the assembling of the council in the morning, and an examination of Jesus before them, on the same things which had been enquired of during the preceding night, was intended in the verses referred to.— The rulers were determined, if possible, to induce Pilate

5 And ¹they were the more fierce, saying, He stirreth up the people, teaching throughout all Jewry, ᵏbeginning from Galilee to this place.

6 When Pilate heard of Galilee, he asked whether the man were ¹a Galilean.

7 And as soon as he knew that he belonged unto ᵐHerod's jurisdiction, he sent him to Herod, who himself also was at Jerusalem at that time.

8 And when Herod saw Jesus, he was exceeding glad: ⁿfor he was desirous to see him of a long *season*, because he had heard many things of him: ᵒand he hoped to have seen some miracle done by him.

9 Then he questioned with him in many words:ᵖ but he answered him nothing.

10 And the chief priests and scribes stood ᑫand vehemently accused him.

11 And ʳHerod with his men of war ˢset him at nought, and mocked *him*, and arrayed him in a gorgeous robe, and sent him again to Pilate.

12 And the same day ᵗPilate and Herod were made friends together; for before they were at enmity between themselves.

to put Jesus to death: it was therefore necessary for them to accuse him of some crime against the Roman government. Accordingly they said nothing, at first, of his confessing himself to be " the Son of God;" but spake of him in the most disdainful language, as one whom they had found " perverting the nation," not only in their religious principles, but also in respect of their subjection to the Roman authority: and, notwithstanding his unexceptionable answer a few days before, they directly accused him of forbidding the people " to pay tribute to Cæsar!" (*Marg. Ref.—Note, Matt.* xxii. 15—22.)—This shews with what intent they had proposed to him that insidious question, and to what difficulties his answer had reduced them. They were, however, determined to draw this conclusion from his claim to be the Messiah, " the King of the Jews," though in direct contradiction to his own express decision of their question. But though Pilate heard from Jesus himself, that he was " the King of the Jews ;" yet he declared that he was perfectly satisfied concerning his innocence of the charges brought against him. This rendered his accusers still more furious and eager in their prosecution ; fearing a disappointment, and being enraged at the insinuation, that they were seeking the death of an innocent man. They therefore further charged him, with having " stirred up the people" to revolt, by his preaching, throughout all the land: for he had begun in Galilee, and had proceeded, with a multitude of followers, till he arrived at Jerusalem. Probably, they referred to his public entrance into the city a few days before, to which Pilate could not be a stranger; and to his teaching at the temple in contempt of their authority.—Certain impostors had indeed before this arisen in Galilee ; and there, collecting followers and exciting insurrections, had given the Romans considerable trouble ; for which cause the rulers probably supposed Pilate would have been the more jealous of Jesus : (*Note*, xiii. 1, 2 :) but that governor well understood the difference between armed forces, and our Lord's inoffensive followers ; who were formidable to nothing, but the hypocrisy and ambition of the scribes, priests, and Pharisees.

Perverting. (2) Διαστρεφοντα. ix. 41. *Acts* xiii. 8. 10. *Phil.* ii. 15.—*Fault.* (4) Αιτιον. 14. 22. *Acts* xix. 40. Not elsewhere N. T. Αιτιος. *Heb.* v. 9.—1 *Sam.* xxii. 22 *Sept.* —*They were the more fierce.* (5) Οι ... επισχυον. Here only N. T.—*He stirreth up.*] Ανασειει. *Mark* xv. 11. Not elsewhere.

V. 6—12. Pilate evidently desired to decline the necessity of deciding a cause, in which his judgment, and his apparent interest, were likely to interfere with each other. When therefore he learned, that Jesus had lived in the district which Herod governed; he immediately sent him and his accusers to that prince, who was then at Jerusalem, perhaps on account of the passover : and Herod was greatly rejoiced to see Jesus, perhaps desiring to satisfy himself whether he were indeed " John the Baptist risen from " the dead," as he had once supposed. (*Notes*, xiii. 31— 33. *Matt.* xiv. 1, 2.) He had, however, long wished to see him, (having heard many reports concerning his doctrine and miracles,) in hopes of having his curiosity gratified, by beholding some effects of his power in working miracles. But our Lord saw good, not only to disappoint that expectation, but also to keep a profound silence in his presence, not returning any answer either to his multiplied questions, or to the vehement accusations of his enemies. Yet Herod, though doubtless vexed and mortified, did not choose to have any hand in putting him to death, having probably been greatly terrified in his conscience on account of his murder of John the Baptist. He therefore contented himself with treating Jesus as a despicable person, beneath his notice ; except that he joined with his officers and guards in deriding and insulting him. In token of their contempt of his pretensions to be a king, they clothed him with some splendid garment, which had perhaps been worn by Herod ; and he was sent back thus attired to Pilate, that he might dispose of him as he pleased. Probably, the Roman soldiers took the hint, from this insult of Herod and his guard, to clôthe Jesus with a purple robe, and to put on him a crown of thorns.—As Pilate and Herod, the one a Roman, the other a proselyted Idumean, and both very wicked men, governed adjacent regions, we need not wonder that they were jealous of each other, and that causes of enmity arose between them. The mutual respect, however, shewn on this occasion, and their agreement with each other, in treating Jesus with a scornful disregard, brought about a reconciliation.— ' This Herod ... was son to Herod the Great, under whom ' Christ was born ; and uncle to Herod Agrippa, by whom ' James was beheaded and Peter imprisoned, who was eaten

13 ¶ And [a] Pilate, when he had called together the chief priests, and the rulers, and the people,

14 Said unto them, Ye have brought this man unto me, [x] as one that perverteth the people: and, behold, I, having examined *him* before you, [y] have found no fault in this man, touching those things whereof you accuse him:

15 No, nor yet Herod; for I sent you to him; and, lo, nothing worthy of death is done unto him

16 I will therefore [z] chastise him, and release *him*.

17 (For [a] of necessity he must release one unto them at the feast.)

18 And [b] they cried out all at once, saying, ' Away with this *man*, and release unto us Barabbas.]

19 (Who, for a certain [d] sedition made in the city, and for murder, was cast into prison.)

20 Pilate therefore [e] willing to release Jesus, spake again to them.

21 But they cried, saying, [f] Crucify him, crucify him.

22 And he said unto them the third time, ' Why, what evil hath he done? [g] I have found no cause of death in him: [h] I will therefore chastise him, and let *him go*.

23 And they were [i] instant with loud voices, requiring that he might be crucified: and the voices of them and of the chief priests prevailed.

24 And [k] Pilate [*] gave sentence, that it should be as they required.

25 And he released unto them him that [l] for sedition and murder was cast into prison, [m] whom they had desired; [*] but he delivered Jesus to their will.

26 ¶ And as they led him away, [o] they laid hold upon one Simon, [p] a Cyrenian, coming out of the country,

---

' by worms; (*Acts* xii. 2, 3. 23;) and great uncle to that ' Agrippa, who by Paul's discourse was " almost persuaded " to be a Christian." (*Acts* xxvi. 28.) ...Christ's arraign- ' ment before him, when he was sent back uncondemned, ' was a great additional proof of the falsehood of those ac- ' cusations, which the Jews had brought against him as a ' seditious person, and particularly as one who had stirred ' up the people in Galilee.' *Doddridge.* (*Marg. Ref.*)

Jurisdiction. (7) Εξουσιας· *authority, dominion, power.* —*Vehemently.* (10) Εντονως. *Acts* xviii. 28. Not elsewhere. —*Men of war.* (11) Στρατωμασι. *Matt.* xxii. 7. *Acts* xxiii. 10. *Rev.* ix. 16. xix. 14. 19.—*Gorgeous.*] Λαμπραν. *Acts* x. 30. *Jam.* ii. 2. *Rev.* xv. 6. xviii. 14. xix. 8. xxii. 1. 16. A λαμπω, *luceo*.

V. 13—25. *Marg. Ref.*—*Notes*, Matt. xxvii. 19—26. Mark xv. 6—10. John xviii. 37—40. xix. 8—18.—*Unto*, &c. (15) Pilate could not mean, that nothing which Herod had done to Jesus was " worthy of death;" but that Herod's conduct proved, he thought " nothing wor- " thy of death" had been committed by Jesus. Herod's concurrence with Pilate in this judgment seemed of great weight, as Herod was well acquainted with the customs and religion of the Jews.—Pilate purposed therefore to chastise him, in order that he might be deterred from using again those expressions which had given umbrage; and then to release him, according to the custom of the feast, which might render that measure less offensive to the Jewish rulers, as implying that he deserved punish- ment, but was set at liberty by an act of grace.—*Whom*, &c. (25) The decided preference given by the rulers to one who had actually excited sedition, as well as committed murder, was a clear demonstration of their malice against Jesus; and shewed that *this* was indeed their real motive, and not any regard to the Roman authority. The words, " Whom they had desired," are full of energy. (*Marg. Ref.* n.—*Notes*, Jer. viii. 1—3. *Acts* iii. 12—16.)

Perverteth. (14) Αποστρεφοντα. *Matt.* v. 42. xxvi. 52. xxvii. 3. *Tit.* i. 14. *Heb.* xii. 25. Διαστρεφοντα, 2.—*Is done unto him.* (15) Επι πεπραγμενον αυτῳ. " Has been done *by* " him." The dative, instead of the ablative with a preposition, after verbs passive, is frequent in the Latin classicks; the omission of the preposition in this place is an anomaly of the same kind; and the Greek writers often omit the preposition, in expressions entirely simi- lar. Instances of this occur frequently in Demosthenes.— *Chastise.* (16) Παιδευσας. 22. Παιδευω, *educo, pueros doceo.* A παις, *puer.* *Acts* vii. 22. xxii. 3. 2 Tim. ii. 25. Tit. ii. 12.—*Castigo*; 1 Cor. xi. 32. 2 Cor. vi. 9. *Heb.* xii. 6. 10. *Rev.* iii. 19.—*All at once.* (18) Παμπληθει. Here only.— *Away with*, &c.] Αιρε. *John* xix. 15. *Acts* xxi. 36. xxii. 22. —*Spake again to them.* (20) Προσεφωνησε. vi. 13. vii. 32. *Acts* xxi. 40. xxii. 2.—*They were instant.* (23) Επεκειντο. v. 1. *Acts* xxvii. 20.—*Prevailed.*] Κατισχυον. *Matt.* xvi. 18. Not elsewhere.—Every word implies the violence and fierceness, with which the rulers of the Jews urged their demand.

V. 26—31. The multitude of the Jews had indeed been instigated, to demand the crucifixion of Jesus; (*Notes*, Matt. xxi. 8—11. xxvii. 19—23;) yet there were many individuals, who had a sincere regard for him. A great company of these, especially many women, followed him when led away to be crucified, expressing their sympathy and grief by doleful lamentations. But he called on them to mourn for themselves, and for their posterity, rather than for him; as he went to his sufferings most willingly, being assured of a speedy joyful event, and most glorious effects from them: whereas vengeance, beyond example terrible, would shortly come on their city and nation, as the punishment of the enormous wickedness about to be perpetrated. For the days were at hand, when those wo- men would generally be counted most happy, who never had any children; as parents would see their offspring

3 L 5

q Is. 53. xiv. 27. and on him they laid the cross, 'that he might bear *it* after Jesus.

27 And there followed him a great *r* 55. viii. 2. Matt. xxvii. 55, 56. Mark xv. 40. company of people, 'and of women, which also bewailed and lamented him.

28 But Jesus, turning unto them, *s* Cant. i. 5, ii. 7. iii. 5, 10. v. 6. 16. viii. 4. said, 'Daughters of Jerusalem, weep not for me, but weep for yourselves, and for your children.

29 For, behold, 'the days are com- *t* xxl. 28, 24. Matt. xxiv. 19. Mark xiii. 17. ing, in the which they shall say, *u* Deut. xxviii. 53 'Blessed *are* the barren, and the wombs —37. Hos. ix. 12—16. xiii. 16. that never bare, and the paps which never gave suck.

x Is. ii. 19. Hos. 30 Then shall they *x* begin to say to ix. 8. Rev. vi. 16, 1x, 6. *y* Prov. xi. 31. the mountains, Fall on us ; and to the Jer. xxv. 29. Ez. xx. 2—7, xxi. 47. xxii. 31. Dan. hills, Cover us. ix. 26. Matt. iii.

12. John xv. 6. 31 For if they do these things 'in Heb. vi. 8. 1 Pet. iv. 17, 18. Jude 12. a green tree, what shall be done in the *z* xxiii. 87. Is. liii. dry ? 12. Matt. xxvii.

36. Mark xv. 27. 32 ¶ And 'there were also two other 28. John xix. 18. Heb. xii. 2. *a* Matt. xxvii. 33, malefactors, led with him to be put to 54. Mark xv. 22. 23. John xix. 17. death. 18. Heb. xiii. 12, 18.

33 And 'when they were come to the place which is called 'Calvary, *a* Or, *the place of a skull.* there 'they crucified him, and the ma- *b* xxiv. 7. Deut. xxl. 23. Ps. xxii. lefactors: one on the right hand, and 16. Zech. xii. 10. Matt. xx. 19. the other on the left. xxvi. 2. Mark x. 33, 34. John iii.

34 Then said Jesus, 'Father, for- 14. xii. 33, 34. 29. Gal. iii. 13. give them ; for 'they know not what xviii. 22. Acts ii. they do. 'And they parted his rai- 9, 80. xiii. 23. ment and cast lots. 1 Pet. ii. 24. 47, 48. vi. 27, 28. Gen. l. 17. Ps.

35 And 'the people stood behold- cvi. 16—23. Matt. v. 44 Acts ing : and the rulers also with them vii. 60. Rom. xii. 14. 1 Cor. iv. 'derided *him*, saying, He saved others ; *d* —28. iii. 9. let him save himself, if he be 'Christ, xi. 27—24. xxiii. 11. Acts iii. 17. the chosen of God. 1 Cor. ii. 8. 1 Tim. i. 13.

36 And the soldiers also 'mocked *e* Ps. xxii. 18. him, coming to him, and offering him *f* Matt. xxvii. 35, 36. Mark xv. 24. vinegar, John xix. 23, 24. 37 And saying, If thou be the King *g* xxii. 12, 13. 17. Matt. xxvii. of the Jews, save thyself. 39—42. Mark 38 And 'a superscription also was xv. 29—33. xxxvi. 19, 20. written over him in letters of Greek, *h* Ps. iv. 2. xxxv. and Latin, and Hebrew, THIS IS THE 15. 19—25. lxix. 7—12. 20. lxxi. KING OF THE JEWS. 11. Is. xlix. 7. 14.

39 ¶ And 'one of the malefactors *i* Ps. xxii. 7, 8. *k* xxii. 69. John xix. 26—30. Matt. xxvii. 35. Mark xv. 19, 20, 36. John xix. 28—30. *k* 3. Matt. xxvii. 11. 37. Mark xv. 18, 26, 32. John xix. 3, 19—22. 1 Matt. xxvii. 44. Mark xv. 32.

---

cruelly murdered, or enslaved, or dying by famine or pestilence; nay, mothers would even be driven by extreme hunger to eat their own infants. (*Marg Ref.* s—u. —*Notes, Matt.* xxiv. 19, 20.) Then the Jews, who now clamorously demanded his crucifixion, would " begin to " call on the mountains" to hide or crush them ; that they might escape the lingering miseries to which that crime would expose them. This intimated the long duration of their national calamities, and that more dreadful vengeance awaited individuals in another World ; they would then *begin* to call on " the mountains, &c." but they would not speedily cease to do so. (*Marg. Ref.* x.—*Notes, Hos.* x. 7, 8. *Rev.* vi. 15—17.) For if the Romans, at their instigation, and by the permission of God, inflicted so terrible a punishment on him, whose conduct had been perfectly holy, inoffensive, and excellent : what would they, as the executioners of divine vengeance, do to that nation, when they had filled up the measure of their iniquities ; and when the turbulent conduct, repeated insurrections, and obstinate resistance of the Jews, had determined the Romans to destroy them without mercy ? If such a fire were kindled in " a green tree," which was altogether unfit for fuel ; what would be the case in respect of the " dry wood," which was every way ready for the flames ? (*Marg. Ref.* y.—*Notes, Ex.* xvii. 22—24. xx. 45—48.)

Bewailed. (27) Εκοπτοντο. viii. 52. *Matt.* xi. 17. *Rev.* i. 7. xviii. 9.—*Gave suck.* (29) Εθηλασαν. xi. 27. *Matt.* xxiv. 19. *Mark* xiii. 17.

V. 32—38. *Marg. Ref.—Notes, Matt.* xxvii. 27—44. *Mark* xv. 21—28. *Luke* xix. 13—24.—*Forgive,* &c. (34) This prayer seems to have been made, at the time when the soldiers were employed in nailing our Lord's hands and feet to the cross. In the extremity of his anguish and the contumelious cruelty with which he was treated, he seems to have been more concerned for the sin of his murderers, than for his own sufferings. The soldiers, who crucified him, were primarily intended : as Romans, " they knew " not what they were doing ; " and their guilt was far less heinous than that of the chief priests, or that of the people, who had enjoyed fuller means of instruction. (*Note, John* xix. 8—12, v. 11.) Instead of complaints or threats, our Lord pleaded the only extenuation of the guilt of his cruel executioners, in praying for their forgiveness ! In this he acted as our perfect example : yet doubtless his intercession prevailed for those, whom he especially intended. Probably, the soldiers immediately concerned were afterwards converted. (*Note, Matt.* xxvii. 54.) Many of the surrounding multitude also, who had demanded his crucifixion, " not knowing what they did," were doubtless saved in answer to this prayer ; and in some sense, it may be applied to every one who is " justified by faith in his " blood." (*Marg. Ref.* c, d.—*Notes, Acts* vii. 54—60, *v.* 60.)

Calvary. (33) Κρανιον. *Matt.* xxvii. 33. *Mark* xv. 22. *John* xix. 17. The word " Calvary," (*Calvaria,*) is merely a Latin translation of the Greek and Hebrew words. It does not occur in the original, and is taken from the *Vulgate,* or other Latin versions.—*Malefactors.*] Κακηργης. 32. 39. 2 *Tim.* ii. 9. Not elsewhere N. T.—*Prov.* xxi. 15. *Sept.*—' *Malefici, publicè flagitiis insignes, et ad infames* ' *pœnas damnandi,…fures, latrones, sicarii, piratæ, &c.*' Schleusner. Αποαι, *Matt.* xxvii. 38.—*Forgive.* (34) Αφες. *Matt.* vi. 12. 14. ix. 2. 5, 6. xii. 31, 32. *John* xx. 23.— *Derided.* (35) Εξεμυκτηριζον. See on xvi. 14.

V. 39—43. The language of the other evangelists has led many to conclude, that both the malefactors, at first, concurred in reviling our Lord : but others think, that it

which were hanged, railed on him, saying, If thou be Christ, save thyself and us.

40 But the other answering ᵐ rebuked him, saying, ⁿ Dost not thou fear God, ° seeing thou art in the same condemnation?

41 And ᵖ we indeed justly; for we receive the due reward of our deeds:

ᵏ but this man hath done nothing amiss.

42 And he said unto Jesus, ʳ Lord, remember me ˢ when thou comest into ᵗ thy kingdom.

43 And Jesus said unto him, Verily I say unto thee, ᵘ To-day shalt thou be ˣ with me ʸ in paradise.

Marginal references:
w Lev. xix. 17.
x Eph. v. 11.
n xiii. 3. Ps. xxxvi. 1. Rev. xv. 4.
o 2 Chr. xxviii. 22. Jer. v. 3. Rev. xvi. 11.
p xv. 16, 19. Lev. xxiv. 40, 41. Josh. vii. 19, 20. 2 Chr. xxxiii. 12.
Ezra ix. 13. Neh. ix. 3. Dan. ix. 14. Jam. iv. 7. 1 John i. 8, 9.

q 47. xxii. 69, 70. Matt. xxvii. 4. 1 Pet. i. 19.
r xviii. 13. Ps. cvi. 4, 5. John xx.
s 28. Acts xvi. 31. xx. 21. Rom. xi. 19—14. 1 Pet. ii. 6, 7. 1 John v. 1.
t 11—13.
u xii. 8. John i. 49. Rom. x. 9 10.
x xxiv. 26. Ps. li.
6. Is. ix. 6, 7. liii. 10—12. Dan. vii. 13, 14. 1 Pet. l. 11.　10. Job xxxiii. 27—30. Ps. xxxii. 5. l. 15. Is. l. 18, 19. lili. 11. ly. 6—9.　2li. 18. Matt. xx. 15, 16. Rom. v. 20. 1 Tim. l. 1b, 16. Heb. vi. 25.
u xv. 4, 5. 20—24. xix. 9. Ixv. 34. Mic. vii.　x John xiv.　y 2 Cor. xii. 4. Rev. ii. 7.

---

cannot be inferred from their words. In itself indeed it is improbable; especially as the penitent thief neither confessed his own guilt, *in this particular*, nor assigned any reason for so suddenly altering his opinion, when he rebuked his fellow-sufferer. Doubtless, he who was saved had spent a very wicked life, and there is no proof that he was at all penitent, even when nailed to the cross; though his awful situation might possibly have produced many serious reflections in his mind. The most, of what he had previously heard of Christ, must have been from his enemies: but being a Jew, he probably had some general knowledge of the prophecies concerning the Messiah, and he might have heard some reports concerning our Lord's doctrine and miracles. Knowing therefore on what account Jesus was condemned, and witnessing his extraordinary meekness and patience under his sufferings, and his prayer for his murderers; he seems to have been led, under the immediate teaching of the Holy Spirit, to believe that he was the promised Messiah, " the Son of God," and " the " King of Israel;" and perhaps to remember and understand, that he was to be a suffering Redeemer, and be " led as a lamb to the slaughter." Under this conviction he first rebuked his fellow-sufferer for reviling Jesus, saying, " Dost thou not fear God?" As to this life, neither of them could have any thing more to *fear*, than what they were actually suffering: this therefore implied a realizing belief of a future state, and of the cause which his fellow-sufferer had to fear the wrath of God for his crimes, in another world; so that he ought to have been employed in confessing his guilt, and in crying for mercy, and not in reviling an innocent illustrious person who suffered with him. In respect of himself, and the other malefactor, he acknowledged the punishment to be deserved both from God and man; they were indeed " receiving the due re- " ward of their deeds;" but Jesus had " done nothing " amiss." Thus he expressly declared his assurance of our Lord's innocence, as to those things of which he was accused by the Jews, and in his whole conduct ; and that he was indeed " the Son of God," " the King of Israel," who would hereafter " sit on the right hand of the throne of " God:" otherwise, it would have been indeed greatly " amiss' to have advanced such claims. (*Marg. Ref.* l—q. —*Notes, Job* xxxiii. 27—30. *Prov.* xxviii. 13.) Thus fearing God, and being conscious that he deserved his wrath and eternal condemnation; and believing Jesus to be " the " Christ the Son of the living God," though now about to expire on the cross; and that he certainly would possess the promised kingdom, and have the disposal of eternal life and salvation; he humbly besought him to " remem- " ber him, when he came into his kingdom." He had nothing further to fear, or to hope, in respect of this world:

he did not expect Christ to save himself or them in that sense: but he was taught by the Holy Spirit to discern something of the true nature of " the kingdom of God." (*Note, John* iii. 3.) He knew himself to be unworthy of Christ's regard, or of the spiritual and eternal blessings which he had to bestow: yet he earnestly desired to be remembered by him, according to the riches of his mercy; (*Marg. Ref.* r, s.—*Notes, Ps.* cvi. 4, 5. cxix. 132 ;) and he evidently " trusted in Christ" for deliverance from the wrath to come, and for eternal happiness, whatever his views were about the design of his death, or whether he expected that he would rise immediately from the dead, or not. He was humbled in true repentance; he " believed " on Jesus " in his heart unto righteousness," and " he " made confession" of him " with his mouth unto sal- " vation." (*Note, Rom.* x. 5—11.) He was decided in this confession of Christ as the Messiah the King of Israel, when all around were deriding and reviling him; and when even his own disciples dared not to avow themselves, and were stumbled in respect of his promised redemption, and his kingdom. He brought forth all " the " fruits meet for repentance," of which his circumstances could possibly admit. He shewed holy fear of God, humbly confessing his guilt, and thus glorifying him, by submitting patiently to his excruciating sufferings: he exercised faith and hope in Christ, love to his name, and zeal to his honour: and he shewed his love to the soul of his fellow-sufferer, and hatred of his sin, by his faithful reproof, and seasonable expostulation with him. Here was evidently the substance, or embryo, of all Christian graces, which would have been expanded into all the actions of a holy life, had time been allowed. Perhaps he actually more honoured Christ in this short space, than many do, who live a number of years to profess faith in him: and, in short, here were evidently both the title to " the inherit- " ance of the saints in light," and the meetness for it. Our Lord therefore, without delay, and in the most solemn manner, assured him, that " on that very day he should be " with him in paradise." " That day " was then spending apace, and many crucified persons used to hang far longer on the cross, than from the time when Jesus and the two malefactors were suspended, till the close of it: but our Lord predicted both his own death, and that of the penitent thief, before the setting of the sun, when the Jewish day ended; and their immediate entrance into a state of happiness.—The first Adam lost " paradise " by his sin; the second Adam regained it by his obedience unto death, or rather obtained for us a state of far superior felicity in heaven: into this felicity believers are admitted immediately after their death; and this gracious promise would be an exhilarating cordial to the heart of the dying peni-

3 L 7

44 ¶ And *it was about the sixth hour, and *there was a darkness over all the *earth until the ninth hour.

45 And the sun was darkened, *and the veil of the temple was rent in the midst.

46 And when Jesus had *cried with a loud voice, he said, *Father, into thy hands I commend my spirit: and *having said thus, he gave up the ghost.

47 Now when the Centurion saw what was done, *he glorified God, saying, Certainly this was a righteous man.

48 And all the people that came together to that sight, beholding the things which were done, *smote their breasts, and returned.

49 And all his *acquaintance, and *the women that followed him from Galilee, stood afar off, beholding these things.

*Matt. xxvii. 45.
Mark xv. 33.
*Ex. x. 21—23.
Ps. cv. 28. Joel
ii. 31. Am. v. 18.
viii. 9. Heb. iii.
*Or, land.
*Ex. xxvi. 31.
Lev. xvi. 12—16.
2 Chr. iii. 14.
Matt. xxvii. 51.
Mark xv. 38.
Eph. ii. 14—18.
Heb. vi. 19. ix.
8—10. x. 19—22.
*Matt. xxvii. 46.
Mark xv.
*Ps. xxxi. 5. Acts
vii. 59. 1 Pet. ii.
23.
*Matt. xxvii. 60. Mark xv. 37. John xix. 30.

*f 41. Matt. xxvii.
54. Mark xv. 39.
John xix. 7.

*g xviii. 13. Jer.
xxxi. 19. Acts ii.
37.

*h Job xix. 13. Ps.
xxxviii. 11.
*27. 55. viii. 2.
Matt. xxvii. 55,
56. 61. Mark xv.
40, 41. 47. John
xix. 25—27.

---

tent, to support him during the remainder of his agonies, which soon terminated in unspeakable joys. (*Marg. Ref.* u—x.) This was doubtless intended as the grand display of the Redeemer's power and grace, in the view of numberless invisible spectators; and for the instruction of mankind, in all future ages, about those things which relate to the freedom and sovereignty of his mercy, the efficacy of his atoning blood, and the omnipotence of his saving arm. Thus he triumphed over Satan upon the cross, and delivered the prey from the very jaws of that devouring lion, even in the crisis of his deepest humiliation. (*Notes, Col.* ii. 13—15, v. 15. *Heb.* ii. 14, 15.) Thus he communicated life, when he was in the very agonies of death; and he dispensed pardons and disposed of kingdoms, as from a glorious throne, even while hanging on the tree, as a slave and a malefactor! But it is a single instance in scripture, of a death-bed repentance: and, if possible, it is still more absurd, for men to adduce this instance, in proof of their licentious views of salvation by faith alone, to the disparagement of holiness, and of good works as the necessary fruits of saving faith; when this man's faith was connected with real sanctification, and productive of good works. as far as the case could possibly admit of them.—'This thief improved his time at last, in that extraordinary manner, as perhaps no man ever did before, or will hereafter. He then believed Christ to be the Saviour of the world, when one of his disciples had betrayed him, another had denied him, and all of them had forsook him; to be the Son of God, the Lord of life, when he was hanging on the cross, suffering the pangs of death, and seemingly deserted by his Father: he proclaims him the Lord of paradise, when all the Jews condemned him, and the Gentiles crucified him as an impostor and a malefactor. He feared God, acknowledged

'the justice of his punishment, and did with patience submit to it: he condemned himself, and justified the holy 'Jesus, declaring that " he had done nothing amiss." He 'was solicitous, not for the preservation of his body, but 'the salvation of his soul; not only for his own, but the 'salvation of his brother-thief, whom he so charitably re- 'prehends, so earnestly requests not to proceed in his blas- 'phemous language, so lovingly inviteth to the fear of 'God. So that the glory which he did to Christ, by his 'faith and piety upon the cross, seems such as the whole 'series of a pious life in other men can hardly parallel.' *Whitby.*

Which were hanged. (39) Των κριμασθεντων. *Matt.* xviii. 6. xxii. 40. *Acts* v. 30. x. 39. xxviii. 4. *Gal.* iii. 13.— *Gen.* xl. 19. 22. xli. 13. *Deut.* xxi. 23. *Josh.* viii. 29. x. 26. *Sept.—Railed on.]* Εξλασφημει. xii. 10. xxii. 65, *et al.* See on *Matt.* xii. 31.—*Condemnation.* (40) Κριμαδι. xx. 47. xxiv. 20. *John* ix. 39, *et al.* See on *Matt.* xxiii. 14.— *Amiss.* (41) Ατοπον. *Acts* xxviii. 6. 2 *Thes.* iii. 2. Not elsewhere N. T.—*Job* iv. 8. xi. 11. xxxiv. 12. *Sept.* Ab α priv. et τοπος locus. *Out of its place.—Paradise.* (43) Παραδεισφ. 2 *Cor.* xii. 4. *Rev.* ii. 7.—*Is.* li. 3. *Ez.* xxviii. 13. *Joel* ii. 3. *Sept.* 'The thief could only be 'there that day by the presence of his soul. ...The souls 'of men die not with their bodies, but remain in a state 'of sensibility. ...The souls of good men after death 'are in a happy state, a state of joy and felicity.' *Whitby.*

V. 44—49. *Notes, Matt.* xxvii. 45—56. *Mark* xv. 33— 39. *John* xix. 25—37.—*Father,* &c. (46) *Notes, Ps.* xxxi. 5. *Acts* vii. 54—60. Our Lord had just before cried out with a loud voice, saying, " My God, my God, why hast " thou forsaken me?" After that, it is probable, he said, " I thirst;" then, " It is finished;" and finally, " Father, " into thy hands I commend my spirit." (*Marg. Ref.*)— *A righteous,* &c. (47) That is, 'This person was unjustly 'put to death, for saying that he was the Son of God; for " Truly this was the Son of God." '—*All,* &c. (48) Doubtless many of those, who had been prompted to demand the crucifixion of Jesus, were deeply affected by his behaviour on the cross, and by the prodigies attending his death; and we may suppose that their remorse and sorrow, for their concurrence in his death, prepared the way for their believing the gospel, when preached by the apostles at and after the day of Pentecost. But the chief priests, Scribes, and rulers, seem to have felt neither remorse nor sorrow on the occasion!

Was darkened. (45) Εσκοδισθη. See on *Matt.* xxiv. 29.— *I commend.* (46) Παραθησομαι. xii. 48. *Acts* xiv. 23. xvi.

3 L 8

p. Matt. xxvii. 57,
58. Mark xv. 47
—&c.
50 ¶ And, behold, [p] *there was* a man named Joseph, a counsellor; *and he*

1 1. 25. Acts x. 2.
22. xl. 24.
r Gen. xxxvii. 21,
22. xlii. 21, 22.
Ex. xxiii. 2.
Prov. i. 10. 1s.
viii. 12.
s. 1 Sam. i. 1.
o 42. ii. 25. 38
tion, xlix. 18.
Mark xv. 43.
was [q] a good man, and a just:
51 (The same [r] had not consented to the counsel and deed of them:) *he was* of [s] Arimathea, a city of the Jews; who also himself [o] waited for the kingdom of God.

p John xix. 38—
42.
52 This *man* [p] went unto Pilate, and begged the body of Jesus.

q Is. liii. 9. Matt.
xxvii. 59, 60.
Mark xv. 46.
53 And he took it down, [q] and wrapped it in linen, and laid it in a sepul-

chre that was hewn in stone, wherein never man before was laid.
54 And that day was [r] the prepara- *r Matt. xxvii. 62*
John xix. 14. 31
42.
tion, and the sabbath drew on.
55 And [s] the women also, which *s 49. viii. 2. Matt.*
xxvii. 61. Mark
xv. 47.
came with him from Galilee, followed after, and beheld the sepulchre, and how his body was laid.
56 And they returned, [t] and prepared *t xxiv. 1. 2 Chr.*
xvi. 14. Mark
spices and ointments; [u] and rested the *xvi. 1.*
u Ex. xx. 8—10.
xxxi. 14. xxxv.
sabbath-day, according to the com- *2, 3. Lv lviii. 13.*
14. Jer. xv 34,
mandment. *25.*

---

32. 1 *Tim.* i. 18. 2 *Tim.* ii. 2. 1 *Pet.* iv. 19.—*Ps.* xxxi.
5. Sept. Hence Παραδηκη, 2 *Tim.* i. 12.
V. 50—56. *Marg. Ref.*—Notes, *Matt.* xxvii. 57—61.
Mark xv. 42—47, *vv.* 43, 44. *John* xix. 38—42.—*The same,*
&c. (51) Probably Joseph absented himself from the council
when he found that his dissent had no effect.—*The sabbath,*
&c. (54) Literally, "The sabbath dawned:" yet the close
of the sixth day, and the beginning of the seventh, *in the
evening,* is evidently meant.—*Rested,* &c. (56) Even the
embalming of Christ was not so absolutely a work of urgent
necessity, as to authorise, in the judgment of these women,
(which was certainly just,) the interruption of the hallowed
rest of the sabbath.—How unscriptural and injurious is the
too general custom, whether to accommodate the priest or
the people, of making the Lord's day the chosen time of
funerals! by which numbers are kept from the worship of
God, either as concerned, or as curious spectators, and
much positive evil is occasioned. (*Marg. Ref.* u.)
Had not consented. (51) Ουκ ην συγκαταθειμενος.
Here only N. T.—*Ex.* xxiii. 1. 32. *Sept.*—*Was hewn in
stone.* (53) Λαξευτφ. Here only N. T. Ex λαας *lapis,* et ξεω,
polio, sculpo.—*The preparation.* (54) Παρασκευη. *Matt.*
xxvii. 62. *Mark* xv. 42. *John* xix. 14. 31. 42.—*Drew on.*]
Επεφωσκε. *Matt.* xxviii. 1. Not elsewhere N. T. Ex επι,
et φως, *lux.*—*Spices.* (56) Αρωματα. xxiv. 1. *Mark* xvi.
1. *John* xix. 40. Not elsewhere N. T.—*Rested.* (56)
'Ησυχασαν. xiv. 3. *Acts* xi. 18. xxi. 14. 1 *Thes.* iv. 11. Ab
ησυχιος, *quietus.* 1 *Tim.* ii. 2.

PRACTICAL OBSERVATIONS.
V. 1—12.

Envy, malice, cruelty, and calumny are combined in the
character of "the seed of the serpent," who hate and persecute "the Seed of the woman:" and they seldom are
backward to charge their own crimes on those, who are
most evidently innocent of them. No prudence or harmlessness, in word or deed, can secure a man from their enmity and slander: yet an unexceptionable conduct may
drive them into such absurdities and palpable
falsehoods, as serve to expose their own malignity.—When
wicked men are determined to accomplish their iniquitous
and impious pu os s, every check renders them more impetuous; and every intimation, that they are acting wrong,
is considered as an intolerable affront. The Lord, however, conducts all his great designs to a glorious event, by
means of those who are following the evil devices of their
own hearts; in like manner, as all parties concurred in
VOL. V.

proving the immaculate innocency of Jesus, the atonin_
Sacrifice for our sins. (Note, *Matt.* xxvii. 24, 25.)—Even
very wicked men have some reserves in iniquity. There
are lengths to which they are reluctant to proceed, especially without what appears to them an adequate advantage:
yet, while they are restrained by inward terror from some
crimes, they are kept from such actions as they cannot
but approve, by fear of their fellow-creatures, and even of
their inferiors! But profligate professors of true religion
are commonly more hardened than open idolaters; and
they are entitled to less regard from us. Herod desired to
see Jesus, and to witness his miracles, from worthless motives: but our Lord would take no notice of a man, who
had committed most enormous wickedness, in opposition
to the convictions of his own conscience. How careful
then should every one be, not to provoke God to give him
up to final infatuation and insensibility! He, who had
reverenced John the Baptist, knowing him to be a holy man,
and yet at length had beheaded him; (Note, *Mark* vi. 14
—29;) was left to treat the divine Saviour with the utmost contempt, and to join with his brutal soldiers, in deriding and insulting him, to whom John came to bear witness!—We may also observe, that as the enmities of
wicked men are often excited about the veriest trifles; so
their friendships are sometimes grounded on the basest
combinations in wickedness, or cemented by them; or
they spring from coincidence in vicious dispositions and
pursuits. Frequently they agree in little, except in enmity against God, and contempt of Christ and his cause:
death therefore will soon terminate their amity; and perfect hatred, in every sense, will be their final temper and
portion. (*P. O. Matt.* xxvii. 1—25. *Mark* xv. 1—26.)

V. 13—31.

It is not expedient here again particularly to dwell on
that display of man's depravity, and of the justice and
mercy of God; the meekness, patience, fortitude, and love
of the divine Saviour; the evil of sin, the misery of unbelievers, the felicity of true disciples, which the cross of
Christ continually suggests to us. Let us however remark,
that no man will, in all circumstances, be constant to the
dictates of his judgment and conscience, who is not actuated by the fear of God and faith in his word: that they,
who from carnal motives are prevailed on to sanction iniquity by their authority and influence, will by no means
be held guiltless: that wicked men who reject Christ for
tne sake of their destructive lusts, will have what they de-
3 M

CHAP. XXIV.

sired, and have none to blame but themselves for their perverse choice : that many are transiently affected by the recital of the sufferings of Christ, who have no true faith in him or love to him : that sinners have cause to weep incessantly for the calamities, which are coming upon them from the wrath of an offended God; and that it is unspeakably more desirable to remain childless, than to bring up children to be heirs of wrath and misery. How should we then use every means, and especially beseech the Lord continually, for our offspring ; that, whatever be their lot in this life, they may be ' numbered with his ' saints in glory everlasting !'—At the approach of the miseries, reserved for the unbelieving and disobedient, the stoutest despisers will " begin to call on the " mountains to fall on them," and hide them from the wrath of their offended Judge : yet this refuge will be denied to those, who now refuse to flee for refuge to the gracious Saviour : and even his sufferings most energetically preach terror to obstinate transgressors ; for if " these things were done in the green tree, what shall be " done in the dry ?"

V. 32—43.

Who can sufficiently admire the Redeemer's compassionate prayer and plea, for his cruel and insulting murderers! May that prayer be heard for our souls! for we also, when living in sin, concurred with those who crucified him, though we " knew not what we did." But let every reader fear " crucifying him afresh," now he knows better, by continuing in sin and neglecting his salvation. —We should also meditate on this subject frequently; that we may learn to " forgive our enemies, to bless those " who curse us, and to pray for them who despitefully use " us and persecute us ;" that we may be induced to persist in doing good, amidst all the obloquy, outrage, and cruelty, to which we can be exposed; and that we may be shamed out of our resentments and aversions, which are generally excited by very trivial provocations. (P. O. Matt. v. 33—48.)—While the Lord refuses the presumptuous demands of proud Scribes and Pharisees, and leaves insulting scorners to be hardened in their prejudices, for the honour of his wisdom and justice ; he shews, that this conduct does not arise from want either of power or love, by snatching others as " brands from the burning," to " the praise of the glory of his grace." When he pleases, he can at once enlighten the darkest mind, and soften the hardest, humble the proudest, and cleanse the most polluted heart ; and thus plant holy fear, repentance, faith, love, and every heavenly affection, in that breast, which before was occupied by the vilest abominations ! But, if he saves from wrath, he also saves from sin : and the change of nature is the evidence of the happy change.

which has taken place in the state of pardoned sinners. Such monuments of mercy will then become reprovers or counsellors to their former companions in iniquity ; they will justify God in their own sharpest sufferings, and glorify him by ingenuous confessions of their guilt; they will fear and deprecate his wrath, and attain to honourable thoughts of Christ and his salvation ; they will confess him before men, even before those who despise and revile him ; they will humbly rely on him, for deliverance " from the wrath " to come," and for the blessings of his kingdom ; and they will recommend, honour, and obey him, as far as they have opportunity. Beyond doubt, therefore, Jesus will take them under his protection, and make them partakers of his salvation ; he will support them in the agonies of death, and immediately receive them to his glory : and should their passage thither be effected, even by a torturing and ignominious execution, for crimes previously committed ; that very circumstance shall not prevent the comfort of their dying moments, or impede their joyful " entrance into the everlasting kingdom of our Lord and " Saviour Jesus Christ." God forbid that we should attempt to darken the lustre of such displays of the Redeemer's sovereign grace, out of fear lest men should pervert them, and be emboldened to continue in sin. Instances, in some respects similar, occur in every age ; but such evident changes are very rare. The most of those who live strangers to serious religion, die, at best, very ambiguously, and give but feeble hopes to discerning ministers and Christians ; while numbers, like the hardened thief, depart, either despising the Saviour, or despairing of mercy : and the awful instances of this kind, which we sometimes hear of, would effectually prevent the fatal delusion of sinning on in hopes of a death-bed repentance, did not " the god of this world blind " and infatuate the minds of unbelievers. (P. O. 2 Chr. xxxiii. 11—25.)

V. 44—56.

Let us come unto Jesus without delay, and " give dili-" gence to make our calling and election sure;" approaching the throne of grace, through the rended veil, through his atoning blood and prevailing intercession ; that when we die, we may confidently commend our departing souls into his hands, as he did his spirit into the hand of his Father ; (Note, Acts vii. 54—60, v. 60 ;) and by his light pass through that scene, which to unbelievers is encompassed with inexpressible darkness and horror. Let us not content ourselves, with superficially viewing the transactions before us ; with acknowledging Jesus to have been " a righteous man," or with some outward expressions of sorrow and remorse : but let us seek to glorify God by our repentance and conversion; by protesting against the coun-

THE MOUNT OF THE ASCENSION.

Luke xxiv. 50.

NOW [a] upon the first *day* of the week, very early in the morning, [b] they came unto the sepulchre, bringing the spices which they had prepared, and certain *others* with them.

2 And [c] they found the stone rolled away from the sepulchre.

3 And [d] they entered in, and found not the body of the Lord Jesus.

4 And it came to pass, as they were much perplexed thereabout, behold, [e] two men stood by them in shining garments:

5 And as [f] they were afraid, and bowed down *their* faces to the earth, they said unto them, Why seek ye [g] the living among the dead?

6 He is not here, but is risen: [f] remember how he spake unto you when he was yet in Galilee,

7 Saying, The Son of man must be delivered into the hands of sinful men, and be crucified, and the third day rise again.

8 And [h] they remembered his words,

9 And [i] returned from the sepulchre, and told all these things unto the eleven, and to all the rest.

10 It was [k] Mary Magdalene, and Joanna, and Mary *the mother* of James, and other *women that were* with them, which told these things unto the apostles.

11 And their words seemed to them as [l] idle tales, and they believed them not.

12 Then [m] arose Peter, and ran unto the sepulchre; and, stooping down, he beheld the linen clothes laid by themselves, and departed, wondering in himself at that which was come to pass.

13 ¶ And, behold, [n] two of them went that same day to a village called Emmaus, which was from Jerusalem *about* threescore furlongs.

14 And [o] they talked together of all these things which had happened.

15 And it came to pass, that while they communed *together*, and reasoned, [p] Jesus himself drew near, and went with them;

---

sel and deed of those who crucified the Saviour; by a sober, righteous, and godly life; and by filling up our stations in the community, and employing all our talents, in the service of him, who died for us and rose again. Finally, in whatever business we engage, or however our hearts may be affected; nay, whatever be the claim of the most revered and beloved relatives and friends, living or deceased; unless it clearly amount to an act of necessity, piety, or mercy, we should never omit to prepare for the day of sacred rest, and keep it holy, according to the commandment of our God and Saviour. (Note, *Is.* lviii. 13, 14.)

NOTES.

CHAP. XXIV. V. 1—9. *Marg. Ref.*—*Notes*, xxiii. 50—56. *Matt.* xxviii. 1—8. *Mark* xvi. 1—8. *John* xx. 1—17.—*Two*, &c. (4) Mary Magdalene and the other Mary saw only one angel in white, sitting on the stone, which he had rolled from the door of the sepulchre; but the women here mentioned saw no angel till they had entered the sepulchre, when two appeared to them in " gar- " ments, shining as lightning; " for so the word signifies. Probably, two distinct events are intended. (*Note, John* xx. 18.)—*Bowed.* (5) As afraid of looking on the angels, or dazzled with the glory of their appearance.—*Living.*] Or, " Him that liveth." (*Marg.* and *Ref.*—*Notes, John* xiv. 18—20, *v.* 19. *Rom.* xiv. 7—9. *Rev.* i. 12—20, *v.* 18.) The sepulchre was a place for the dead, though none had before been buried there.—*How he spake.* (6) ' The fa- miliar manner, in which the angel speaks of what passed

' between Jesus and them in Galilee, seems to intimate ' that he had been present, though invisible, and heard ' what Jesus said.' *Doddridge.* *Rolled away.* (2) Αποκικυλισμ̇ενον. Matt. xxviii. 2. Mark xvi. 4.—*Gen.* xxix. 8. Sept. V. 10—12. St. Luke gives no intimation that these women saw Jesus himself, in the way to the city; as the women mentioned by St. Matthew did. (*Marg. Ref.*— *Note, Matt.* xxviii. 9, 10.) This confirms the supposition, that the women did not go to the sepulchre all in one company; that they returned at several times, and by different ways; and that some of them were at the sepulchre more than once.—The apostles, however, disregarded in a great measure their report, and deemed it to be the effect of terror, or a warm imagination, and not a reality : for they had no expectation of such an event as their Lord's resurrection. Yet Peter, who is supposed to have been with John at the sepulchre before this, (*Note, John* xx. 1— 10,) hearing, that the women had seen angels, who de- clared that Jesus was alive, went again to the sepulchre; probably expecting to see the angels, and perhaps with. some feeble hope of seeing Jesus also: but on examina- tion he found *only* the linen clothes laid in the tomb, nothing else; so that he departed thence, " wondering in " himself " at these events and reports, of which he could not understand the meaning, nor how they would end; yet not speaking to others concerning them. *Idle tales.* (11) Ληρος. Here only.—*Stooping down.* (12) Παρακυψας. John xx. 5. 11. Jam. i. 25. 1 Pet. i. 12. V. 13—24. Cleopas is supposed to be the same with

3 м 3

16 But ⁹ their eyes were holden, that they should not know him.

17 And he said unto them, What manner of communications *are* these, that ye have one to another, as ye walk, ʳ and are sad?

18 And the one of them, whose name was ˢ Cleopas, answering said unto him, Art thou only a stranger in Jerusalem, and hast not known the things which are come to pass there in these days?

19 And he said unto them, What things? And they said unto him, ᵗ Concerning Jesus of Nazareth, which was a prophet ᵘ mighty in deed and word, before God and all the people:

20 And how ˣ the chief priests and our rulers delivered him to be condemned to death, and have crucified him.

21 But ʸ we trusted that it had been he which should have redeemed Israel: and, beside all this, to day is the third day since these things were done.

22 Yea, ᶻ and certain women also of our company made us astonished, which were early at the sepulchre:

23 And when they found not his body, they came, saying, That they had also seen a vision of angels, which said that he was alive.

24 And certain of them which were with us, ᵃ went to the sepulchre, and found *it* even so as the women had said: but him they saw not.

25 Then he said unto them, ᵇ O fools, and slow of heart to believe all that the prophets have spoken!

26 ᶜ Ought not Christ to have suffered these things, and to enter into his glory?

Alpheus, the father of two apostles, and also nearly related to our Lord himself. (13. *Mark* ii. 14. iii. 18. *John* xix. 25.) Many conjecture that Luke himself was the other: but of this there is no intimation, nor indeed probability. (*Preface to Luke*.)—Emmaus was a village nearly eight miles distant from Jerusalem. (*Tables*.)—These two disciples were conversing earnestly, as they walked, concerning the crucifixion of Jesus, and the reports which they had heard of his resurrection; and probably consulting together what to expect, or to do, in such perplexing circumstances, and reasoning or disputing on the subject. While thus employed, Jesus himself joined them, as if he had been a stranger travelling the same road: purposely assuming a different form than usual; and supernaturally influencing their sight, that they might not know him. (*Note, Mark* xvi. 12, 13.)—Having listened a while to their earnest discourse, he at length enquired into the subject, which engrossed their minds and rendered them so sorrowful. This induced Cleopas to ask, whether he were so entirely a stranger at Jerusalem, that he never had heard of those extraordinary events which had just occurred, and had attracted the attention of all ranks and orders of men in the city, though in different ways? On his further enquiry, they proceeded to inform him of the things, which had taken place in respect of Jesus of Nazareth, who was *at least* a prophet, whose miracles and powerful doctrine abundantly proved, that he was "great in the sight of "God," as well as in the judgment of all the people. Yet at length the chief priests and rulers had apprehended him, and delivered him to the Roman governor, to be condemned to death, and had actually crucified him. But as for them, they had confidently believed him to be the promised Messiah, who had so long been predicted, and whom they expected, to redeem Israel from bondage, and to rule over them in great prosperity: and therefore these events, so contrary to their expectations, had exceedingly distressed and perplexed them; seeing they could not un-

derstand how his crucifixion could consist with his "redeeming his people." Indeed he had spoken some things about rising on the third day, which day was arrived: and some women of their company had exceedingly surprised them; for, having gone early to visit the sepulchre, they could not find his body; and they had also declared that they had seen a vision of angels, who assured them that he was alive: and some men of their company had also gone to the sepulchre, and found that the body was gone; but they had not seen him as risen from the dead.—This account seems to imply, that these disciples came away, before the women "who had seen Jesus" returned to the apostles: though some think that the contrary is intimated in the expression, "Him they saw not;" which may signify that the women reported that they had seen him; but that the disciples thought it was only the appearance of an angel in his form. (*Acts* xii. 15.)—ᵈ But why would 'not Christ be as yet known by them? That they might 'more unreservedly express their sentiments; and that 'they might not rest on the bare authority of a Teacher;' 'but on the arguments which he was about to produce.' *Beza.*

They talked together. (14) Ὁμιλων. 15. *Acts* xx. 11. xxiv. 26. Not elsewhere Ὁμιλια. 1 *Cor.* xv. 33. Hence *Homily.—Were holden.* (16) Εκρατειτο. *John* xx. 23. *Acts* ii. 24. iii. 11.—*Ye have,* &c. (17) Αντιϐαλλετε. Here only—*Sad.*] Σκυθρωποι. See on *Matt.* vi. 16. —*Art thou... a stranger.* (18) Συ... παροικεις. *Heb.* xi. 9. Not elsewhere. Παροικος, *Acts* vii. 6. *Eph.* ii. 19. 1 *Pet.* ii. 11.—*Which should have redeemed,* &c. (21) Ὁ μελλων λυτρουσθαι.—*Tit.* ii. 14. 1 *Pet.* i. 18. Not elsewhere N. T. Λυτρον, *Matt.* xx. 28.—*Early.* (22) Ορθριαι. Here only. Ορθριζω, xxi. 38.

V. 25—31. When the two disciples had stated their subject, and their perplexities to the supposed stranger; he addressed them as one filled with astonishment at their ignorance and dulness. They appeared perfectly devoid

27 And, ⁴ beginning at Moses ° and all the prophets, he expounded unto them in all the scriptures the things concerning himself.

28 And they drew nigh unto the village whither they went: ᶠ and he made as though he would have gone further.

29 But they ° constrained him, saying, Abide with us; for it is toward evening, and the day is far spent. And he went in to tarry with them.

30 And it came to pass, as he sat at meat with them, ʰ he took bread, and blessed *it*, and brake, and gave to them.

31 And ¹ their eyes were opened, and they knew him; and he ° vanished out of their sight.

32 And they said one to another, ᵏ Did not our heart burn within us, while he talked with us by the way, and while he ¹ opened to us the scriptures ʳ

23 And they rose up the same hour, and returned to Jerusalem, ᵐ and found the eleven gathered together, and them that were with them,

34 Saying, The Lord is risen indeed, and ° hath appeared to Simon.

35 And ° they told what things *were done* in the way, and how he was known of them in breaking of bread.

of understanding, and incapable of forming a proper judgment in this great concern. This arose from their prejudices, and their backwardness to believe all those things, which the ancient prophets had spoken concerning the Messiah, and thus made them shrink back from the subject of his crucifixion, and manifest a great unwillingness impartially to consider it. But was it not plain from the writings of the prophets, that the promised Messiah and Redeemer of Israel " must needs " pass through those very sufferings which Jesus had endured, before he entered into his glory? The purposes of God, the predictions of his word, the honour of his name, and the nature of his salvation, concurred in rendering this absolutely necessary. (*Marg. Ref.* c.—*Notes, Matt.* xvi. 21—23. 1 *Pet.* i. 10—12.) To satisfy them of this, and to shew them, that there was nothing in those events, which so much disconcerted them, that ought either to perplex or distress them ; he began with the types and prophecies of the books of Moses, and so proceeded regularly through the several parts of the Old Testament, adducing and expounding those prophecies which related to himself. ' What a sermon this must have been ; where all the pro- ' phecies relative to the incarnation, birth, teaching, mira- ' cles, sufferings, death, and resurrection of the blessed ' Jesus were all adduced, illustrated, and applied to him- ' self, by an appeal to the well known facts, which had ' taken place during his life ! We are almost irresistibly ' impelled to exclaim, What a pity this discourse had not ' been preserved !' *Dr. Ad. Clarke.* As they thus conversed together, they arrived at Emmaus ; and he offered to go further, in order to excite their more earnest invitations : accordingly they " constrained," or *importunately* pressed him, to spend the night with them, (as the evening now approached,) that they might have further conversation with him on those interesting subjects ; to which he consented. But when they sat down to meat, he, though a supposed stranger, acted as head of the family ; so that he " took read, and blessed," and breaking gave it to them, as his custom had been at their ordinary meals : and, the supernatural restraint being at the same time taken from their eyes, they immediately perceived who their instructive Companion was : yet as soon as they were fully

satisfied in this matter, he was pleased to render himself invisible, and to withdraw from them ; but in what manner it does not become us to enquire.—*Ought not,* &c. (26) ' Is it not by those prophets foretold, to be decreed by ' God, that the Messias should be despised by men, and ' slaughtered by them, before he should enter on his ' kingdom?' *Hammond.—Beginning,* &c. (27) ' We ' may hence learn that the Mosaical sacrifices, and espe- ' cially the solemn anniversary expiation, typified the suf- ' ferings of Christ : as also did the oblation of Isaac, and ' the lifting up of the brazen serpent.' *Whitby.*

Fools, &c. (25) Ανοηίοι. *Rom.* i. 14. *Gal.* iii. 1. 3. 1 *Tim.* vi. 9. *Tit.* iii. 3. Εχ a priv. et νεϛ, *mens.* Ανοητοι, not *μωροι.* ' The two words are not synonymous. Μωροϛ is a term of ' great indignation, and sometimes of contempt ; that ' employed here, a term of expostulation and reproof.' *Campbell.* (*Note, Matt.* v. 21, 22.)—Μωροϛ is not used in the whole New Testament, speaking of men, or of an individual, except in the passage referred to, and *Matt.* vii. 26. xxiii. 17. 19 ; though the words *fool* and *fools,* several times occur in our translation.—*Slow of heart.*] Βραδειϛ τη καρδιᾳ. *Jam.* i. 19. Not elsewhere.—*He made as though,* &c. (28) Προσεποιειτο. Here only N. T.—*Prœ me fero.* Εχ προϛ et ποιεω, *facio.*—*They constrained.* (29) Παρεϐιασαντο. *Acts* xvi. 15. Not elsewhere N. T.—1 *Sam.* xxviii. 23. *Sept.* Εχ παρα et ϐιαζομαι. *Matt.* xi. 12.—*He vanished out of ... sight.* (31) " Ceased to be seen of " them." *Marg.* Αφαντοϛ εγινετο. Here only. Ab a priv. et φαινω, *appareo.*

V. 32—35. When the two disciples had considered the circumstances of this most extraordinary event, they peculiarly recollected the effects, which the conversation of their Lord had produced on them : for their affections had been so enlivened, that their hearts seemed to glow in their breasts with hope, joy, love, gratitude, and admiration, while he opened to them the scriptures, and shewed the accomplishment of them, in his sufferings, death, and resurrection. (*Marg. Ref.* k.—*Notes, Ps.* xxxix. 1—4. *Jer.* xx. 7—9.) Being, therefore, earnestly desirous of communicating the glad tidings to their brethren, they set off immediately and returned to Jerusalem ; where they found the apostles assembled together with other disciples ;

36 ¶ And as they thus spake, Jesus himself stood in the midst of them, and saith unto them, ¹ Peace be unto you.

37 But they were ² terrified and affrighted, and supposed that they had seen a spirit.

38 And he said unto them, Why are ye troubled? ³ and why do thoughts arise in your hearts?

39 Behold ⁴ my hands and my feet, that it is I myself. Handle me, and see: ⁵ for a spirit hath not flesh and bones, as ye see me have.

40 And when he had thus spoken, he shewed them *his* hands and *his* feet.

41 And while they yet ˣ believed not for joy, and wondered, he said unto them, ʸ Have ye here any meat?

42 And they gave him a piece of a broiled fish, and of an honey-comb.

43 And he took *it*, ᶻ and did eat before them.

44 And he said unto them, ᵃ These *are* the words which I spake unto you, ᵇ while I was yet with you, ᶜ that all

things must be fulfilled which were written ᵈ in the law of Moses, ᵉ and *in* the prophets, ᶠ and *in* the psalms concerning me.

45 Then ᵍ opened he their understanding, that they might understand the scriptures,

46 And said unto them, ʰ Thus it is written, and thus it behoved Christ to suffer, and to rise from the dead the third day;

47 And ¹ that repentance and remission of sins should be preached in his name, ᵏ among all nations, ˡ beginning at Jerusalem.

48 And ᵐ ye are witnesses of these things.

49 And, behold, ⁿ I send the promise of my Father upon you: ᵒ but tarry ye in the city of Jerusalem, until ye be endued with power from on high.

many of whom, in a mixture of astonishment and exultation, informed them, that " the Lord was risen indeed, and " had appeared to Simon !" thus assuring him that he had forgiven his late denial of him. Then the two disciples related, how he had appeared to them in their journey, and discovered himself to them whilst he was breaking bread. Yet after all this we find that some of the company did not fully believe them, so backward were they to credit this unexpected event ! (*Marg. Ref.* l—o.)

He opened. (32) Διηνοιγεν. 31. 45. *Mark* vii. 34. *Acts* xvi. 14. xvii. 3.—*2 Kings* vi. 17. *Sept.—Gathered together.* (33) Συνηθροισμενους. *Acts* xii. 12. xix. 25. Not elsewhere N. T.—*Ex.* xxxv. 1. *Num.* xx. 2. *Joel* iii. 11. *Sept.—Indeed.* (34) Οντως. xxiii. 47. *Mark* xi. 32. 1 *Cor.* xiv. 25. *Gal.* iii. 21, et al.

V. 36—43. (*Note, John* xx. 19—23.) While the disciples were discoursing on these subjects, Jesus himself, in a miraculous manner, entered the room, and appeared in the midst of them; assuring them, by his salutation, of " peace," or of his entire reconciliation to them, though they had so lately forsaken him; and promising them spiritual peace and every blessing. Yet, after all the preparation which had been made, they were greatly alarmed at his presence, as if they had seen a spirit, or an apparition resembling him. He therefore expostulated with them on their unreasonable incredulity; enquiring, why they thus troubled themselves, and yielded to the intrusion of so many perplexing thoughts and *reasonings :* seeing every circumstance so exactly accorded to his former declarations, and was so well suited to inspire them with joy and confidence To remove all their doubts, he shewed them

the wounds in his hands and feet; and allowed them to touch him, that they might be sure it was not an apparition, but his body really risen from the dead. (*Marg. Ref.* p—a.)—Yet they had been sunk so low in despondency, by his crucifixion; that the fact, however evident, seemed to be too wonderful and joyful to be true; and they still feared lest it should prove an illusion. (*Gen.* xlv. 26—28.) To obviate this still more, Jesus was pleased also to eat before them, " a piece of a broiled fish, and an honey-" comb ;" which some think was a kind of cake, or bread in use among them. Eating might consist with, though it were not needful to, that kind of life to which he was risen.—It is evident from the appeal of our Lord to the *senses* of the apostles, that no greater certainty can in this world be had of any thing, than the testimony of our eyes, ears, and other senses : and that it is unreasonable, in the highest degree imaginable, to require men to believe in direct opposition to them.—It is likewise manifest from our Lord's words, that disembodied spirits, even the spirits of deceased men, do *exist;* whether they ever become visible, or not.

They were terrified. (37) Πτοηθεντες ... γενομενοι. See on xxi. 9.—*Handle.* (39) Ψηλαφησατε. *Acts* xvii. 12. *Heb.* xii. 18. 1 *John* i. 1.—*Gen.* xxvii. 12, 21. 22. *Deut.* xxviii. 29. *Sept.—Any meat.* (41) Τι βρωσιμον. Here only N. Γ. —*Lev.* xix. 23. *Ez.* xlvii. 12. *Sept.* Esculentum, cibus.— *Honey-comb.* (42) Μελισσειν κηριν.—Here only N. T.

V. 44—49. Having thus at length satisfied the minds of the disciples, our Lord proceeded to shew the consistency of these events with his former discourses, as well as with the predictions of the Messiah contained in the several

3 m 6

50 ¶ And he led them out as far as to Bethany: and he lifted up his hands, and blessed them.

51 And it came to pass, while he blessed them, he was parted from them, and carried up into heaven.

52 And they worshipped him, and returned to Jerusalem with great joy;

53 And were continually in the temple, praising and blessing God. Amen.

parts of the scripture: (*Marg. Ref.* a—f.—*Note*, 13—24:) and, as their remaining prejudices alone caused their difficulties, and closed their minds to truths so fully proved and illustrated; he powerfully removed the obstruction, and " opened their understanding," as well as explained the scriptures to them.—' It is one thing to open ... the ' scriptures themselves; and another to open their under- ' standings to perceive them. Christ did the latter, pro- ' bably by giving them now the first-fruits of the Spirit of ' prophecy, which fell more plentifully on them at the day ' of Pentecost.' *Whitby*. (*Marg. Ref.* g.—*Notes, Ps.* cxix. 1S. *Acts* xvi. 13—15. *Rev.* ii. 17.)—Thus at length Jesus convinced them, that nothing had occurred, but what was written by the ancient prophets, and what was necessary for the honour of God in the salvation of sinners. In both respects it was requisite that the Messiah " should suffer, and " rise again on the third day," as he had done; in order that he might live for ever to complete the redemption of his people. (*Marg. Ref.* h.) It was therefore now his purpose, as well as agreeable to the tenour of the scriptures, that " repentance and remission of sins, should be preached " in his name" to men of every nation; that all should be instructed in the nature and necessity of repentance, in order to the forgiveness of their sins; and be taught that these blessings were to be sought by faith in his name, as obtained for sinful men by his atoning sufferings, as the fruit of his intercession, and the effect of his grace. But though all nations were thus to be called upon " to repent " and be converted, that their sins might be blotted out;" yet the inhabitants of Jerusalem must *first* be invited to partake of this spiritual redemption; instead of being excluded, on account of their ingratitude and cruelty to him! ' Making the first overtures of mercy to my murderers! If ' then the sinners at Jerusalem might repent, believe, and ' be saved; none on this side hell need despair.' *Dr. Ad. Clarke*. (*Marg. Ref.* i—m.—*Notes*, xv. 1, 2. 25—32, *v.* 30. *Matt.* xxviii. 18—20. *Mark* xvi. 14—18. *Acts* ii. 22— 24. 37—40. iii. 12—21.) The apostles especially were chosen to be his witnesses, as to the truth and reality of his resurrection, and the doctrine of salvation connected with it. Yet they were not immediately to enter upon their ministry, and adduce their testimony : for he would assuredly, after his ascension into heaven, send them the blessing of the Holy Spirit, which the Father had promised to him as a Mediator, and to his church through him; that, by his powerful energy on the minds of their hearers, they might both be enabled for their arduous service, and rendered successful in it. In the mean time, they were directed to remain at Jerusalem, at a distance from their home and families, among persons with whom they had little acquaintance, and where they apparently had no employment. This, however, they must do, till their commission was ratified, and a marvellous power conferred upon them from on high. (*Marg.*

Ref. n, o.—*Notes, John* xiv. 25, 26. xv. 26, 27. xvi. 7—15. *Acts* i. 4—8.)

Witnesses. (48) ' Christ's resurrection being a matter of ' fact must be proved by the testimony of eye-witnesses, ' who, if they be honest men, and such as suffer the ' greatest prejudices in fortunes, reputation, and life, for ' this testimony, we have the greater reason to believe it: ' for their honesty must render them unwilling to testify a ' falsehood; their interest and prudence would not suffer ' them, without any necessity laid upon them, to testify a ' lie; much more to testify the grossest falsehood, to their ' utmost damage, and without any prospect of advantage. ' But, further, if they confirm this testimony by all kinds of ' signs, miracles, and wondrous powers, exercised by them- ' selves, and others who embraced their testimony; if this ' was done in all places, on all kinds of persons, for a ' whole age, or ages, this renders it impossible that they ' should attest a lie: and therefore Christ bids them stay ' at Jerusalem; till they were empowered by virtue from ' on high, to confirm this testimony. *Acts* i. 8.' *Whitby*. (*Notes, John* xx. 24—29, *conclusion. Heb.* ii. 1—4, *v.* 4.)— *Be endued.* (49) Ενδυσησθε. *Clothed.* xii. 22. xv. 22. *Note, Ps.* cxxxii. 7—9, *v.* 9.

V. 50—53. At the end of forty days after our Lord's resurrection, during which time he had in different places appeared to his disciples, and given them copious instructions for their work; (*Notes, Matt.* xxviii. 11—20. *Mark* xvi. 12—18. *John* xxi. 1—23. *Acts* i. 1—3. 1 *Cor.* xv. 3— 11;) he at length met them at Jerusalem, and went before them to the confines of Bethany : and while with uplifted hands he pronounced blessings upon them, he was marvellously parted from them, and ascended visibly, till a cloud intercepted their sight of him. (*Marg. Ref.* p—r. —*Notes, Mark* xvi. 19, 20. *John* vi. 60—65, *v.* 62. *Acts* i. 9—14.) Thus he was carried up into heaven, " leading " captivity captive," and ascending his glorious throne. that from thence he might bestow all blessings, most freely and liberally, on his chosen people. (*Notes, 2 Kings* ii. 11. *Ps.* lxviii. 18. *Eph.* iv. 7—10. 1 *Pet.* iii. 21, 22, *v.* 22.) When the apostles and disciples had witnessed this august and surprising scene, they prostrated themselves to worship him as " their Lord and their God: " for the adoration was paid after he was taken from them. Then they returned to Jerusalem, not mourning for their loss, but rejoicing in the exaltation of their beloved Lord, and in glad expectation of the performance of his promises. And, while they abode together at Jerusalem, waiting and praying with one accord for the Spirit of power, truth, and holiness; they continually resorted to the temple at the proper times, to join in the worship there performed; and especially in those psalms of praise and thanksgiving, which were sung under the direction of the priests and Levites. (*Marg. Ref.* s—x.—*Notes*, 1 *Chr.* xxv. 1—8.)

PRACTICAL OBSERVATIONS.

V. 1—12.

The Lord " loveth those who love him, and they who " seek him early shall find him." They who humbly desire and pray to be taught his will, and be partakers of his salvation, though at present in error and perplexity, shall at length be directed into a saving acquaintance with his truth.—All our mistakes in religion spring from ignorance or forgetfulness of the word of God : and our judgments will be rectified, when we call to remembrance, and are enabled to understand, what he has revealed and promised. This forms one great use of faithful preaching, for by it men are continually reminded of the words of Christ; and especially they are led to consider those things, which relate to his sufferings, his death, resurrection, and glorification. Many errors in religion are like " seeking the living " among the dead:" yet those who seek happiness from worldly vanities or in sinful pleasures, or who seek salvation from human inventions and superstitions, are most fatally thus employed.—Even where a measure of faith and grace are found, how unbelieving are men on some occasions! not only in those things which are contrary to their prejudices, but in those also that are above their experience, or expectation : these, however attested, seem to be " idle tales, and they believe them not!" Yet a diligent spirit of enquiry will gradually lead to a more clear perception of spiritual things. (*P. O. Matt.* xxviii. 1—10. *Mark* xvi. 1—11.)

V. 13—35.

When Christians travel together, or are any ways employed in company with each other, they should be careful to commune of those things, which relate to their gracious Lord; and to open their difficulties to each other for mutual edification. When thus engaged, they may expect that Jesus himself will be invisibly present : (*Note, Mal.* iii. 13—18, *vv.* 16, 17 :) nay, he will sometimes speak by those, with whom they are not acquainted, or from whom they have no expectations.—When we have carefully investigated the causes of our sorrow and dejections ; we shall perhaps find that those events, which seemed to blast all our hopes, were indeed as necessary to their accomplishment, as the crucifixion of Christ was to the redemption of his people; and that our fears and troubles arose from unbelief alone, and not from want of evidence, security, or information.—Our gracious Lord will reprove his disciples for their folly and ignorance, and their " slow- " ness of heart to believe the scriptures:" for the more diligently we study, and the more fully we understand them, the more evidently will it appear, that the Saviour of sinners " ought to have suffered these things, and to enter " into his glory." We should also keep in mind continually, that every part of scripture testifies of Christ, in some way or other; this we shall perceive, in proportion as we spiritually understand the word of God. (*Note, Rev.* xix. 9, 10.) —When we earnestly desire and intreat his presence with us, he will come and abide with us : and this will render

our conversation, our worship, and even our meals, blessed But our more rejoicing seasons of communion, with him and his saints, are commonly of short duration : yet it may afterwards be exhilarating to remember, how our hearts glowed with heavenly affections, " while he opened to us " the scriptures," as we were reading, hearing, or meditating on them; and how he made himself and his glorious salvation known to us, as we were " breaking bread " in his name.—We should hasten to communicate, to our sorrowing brethren, those discoveries and communications, which have gladdened our hearts; that we may thus mutually strengthen each other's faith, and hope, and assurance " that the Lord is risen indeed," as our experience of his power, truth, and love has abundantly proved (*Notes,* 2 *Pet.* i. 19. 1 *John* v. 9, 10.)

V. 36—53.

When we meet together in the name of the gracious Saviour, he will again and again " manifest himself unto " us, as he doth not unto the world;" (*Note, John* xiv. 21—24 ;) he will speak pardon and peace to our souls, and dispel our terrors and troubles; he will assure us of his love, and " open our understanding to understand the " scriptures." Then we shall see with increasing clearness, that " thus it was written," that redemption is completed, and that " repentance and remission of sins by " faith in his name" should freely " be preached to all " nations." Blessed be God, that ever they were preached in this nation! may we be made partakers of them, and endeavour to diffuse the blessed tidings, further and further, with all our talents and influence, and our whole heart and soul.—As they who crucified the Lord of glory, had the first offers made them of salvation through his blood, what sinners need now despair of mercy? And as thousands of the inhabitants of Jerusalem were in a few weeks converted to him, whose death they had clamorously demanded; why should the ministers of the gospel be discouraged, or cease to labour, pray, and hope for success ; when a short time may cause them to witness as happy a change?—Pardoned rebels, where " sin hath abound- " ed," but grace hath much more abounded," are unexceptionable witnesses to the love and power of our risen Redeemer : yet without the promise of the Father, even the blessed gift of his sanctifying Spirit, we can neither preach nor hear the word of God to good effect. Though we do not expect miraculous powers; we are yet encouraged to wait and pray for his more ordinary, but not less valuable influences, through our risen and ascended Advocate. Let us then plead his promise, worship his name, rejoice in his glory, and wait for his salvation ; and let us continually attend on his ordinances, praise and bless him for his mercies, " set our affections on things above," and expect the Redeemer's return to complete our felicity. Amen. " Even so, Lord Jesus, come quickly." (*P. O. Matt.* xxviii. 11—20. *Mark* xvi. 12—20. *Note, Col.* iii. 1—4.)

THE GOSPEL

ACCORDING TO

St. J O H N.

●

THE several particulars, which the scripture records, concerning the inspired writer of this gospel, may be seen and compared by consulting the annexed references. (xiii. 23—26. xix. 25—27. 35. xx. 2—10. xxi. 2—7. 20—25. *Matt.* iv. 21, 22. x. 2. xx. 20—23. *Mark* i. 19, 20. v. 37. ix. 2. 38—40. xiv. 33. *Luke* ix. 49—56. xxii. 8. *Acts* iii. 1— 11. iv. 13—20. viii. 14. *Gal.* ii. 9. *Rev.* i. 1. 9. x. 9—11.) He was, in many things distinguished among the apostles, and was specially honoured as the bosom-friend of the divine Saviour.—To this information, subsequent histories have added but little; and that little is not entitled to our implicit credit. Some particulars, however, will be mentioned in the prefaces to the other books ascribed to him.—' The ancient tradition, and uniform testimony, both ' of the friends and the foes of Christianity, ... concur in affirming, that this gospel was written by John. In all the ' controversies maintained with Celsus, with Porphyry, and with the emperor Julian, who strained every nerve to un- ' dermine the authority of the gospels; they never thought of controverting, that they were written by those whose ' names they bear. So clear was this point accounted, for ages, even by the most *acute* adversaries of the Christian ' name.' *Campbell.*—It is probable, that this apostle continued in the neighbourhood of Judea, till the time approached for the predicted destruction of Jerusalem. It is recorded, that he then went into Asia; resided some years at Ephesus; was banished to the island of Patmos by the emperor Domitian, but returned to Asia after the death of that emperor; that he lived to be nearly a hundred years of age, and then died a natural death, being the only apostle who escaped martyrdom. On some of these points there are different opinions, of no material consequence, which cannot be discussed in this place. *Preface to the Revelation.*

The general current of ancient writers declare that the apostle wrote this gospel, at an advanced time of life; and yet (strange to say,) many learned moderns are of a different opinion! The question is perhaps of more difficulty than importance: but it appears to me, that several passages become far more interesting, by supposing that it was written, long after the destruction of Jerusalem, and the martyrdom of the other apostles. This evangelist alone mentions Peter as the apostle who smote the high priest's servant, and Malchus as the name of that servant. (*Note,* xviii. 10 —14.) Now it is obvious to conclude, that he disclosed what the others had purposely concealed; because Peter was, at the time when he wrote, out of the reach of all his enemies.—He alone records the resurrection of Lazarus; a miracle so stupendous and notorious, that one can hardly conceive how the other evangelists could pass it over in silence. But the Jews had consulted to put Lazarus also to death. (*Notes,* xi. xii. 9—11.) While Lazarus lived, the memory of the miracle could not be lost in Judea; in other countries, it might be published by word of mouth: but the publick recording of it by the evangelists, while the Jewish priests and rulers possessed authority, might needlessly have exasperated them, and exposed Lazarus and his sisters to much hatred, and even to imminent danger. Profound silence. in the publick writings of the Christians, on this subject, seems therefore to have been observed, till Jerusalem was destroyed, and Lazarus deceased; and then the whole was circumstantially related.—The other evangelists record our Lord's predictions concerning the destruction of Jerusalem and the temple, and the dispersion of the Jews; but this writer is entirely silent in respect of them. Now, can a more satisfactory account of this be given, than by supposing, that many of the predicted events had at that time received their accomplishment? And this, with the consideration, that St. John was appointed in the Revelation to be the prophet of the New Testament, in respect of the church, and the nations as far as connected with it, even to the end of the world, may also account for the circumstance, that we find no express and particular prophecies in this gospel, as in the others.—None of the other evangelists (except by genealogies concerning our Lord's descent from Abraham and David,) go further back, than the

miraculous conception of John the Baptist, the forerunner of Jesus : but this apostle begins his gospel by at once declaring, who the Saviour was, antecedently to his incarnation. This is supposed to have been done, in opposition to certain Hereticks of those early days, some of whom denied our Lord's real Deity, and others his real humanity. The testimonies of John the Baptist also, as here recorded, are far more numerous and explicit, both in respect of the Deity, atonement, and salvation of Christ ; as " the Word made Flesh ;" as " full of grace and truth," " from whose " fulness all receive ; " as " the Lamb of God, that taketh away the sin of the world ;" " the Son of God," " the " Bridegroom of the church, &c." than we have hitherto met with. (*Notes*, i. 6—9. 14—16. 29 30—34, v. 34. iii. 27—36.)—The beginning of our Lord's miracles and ministry from a short time after his baptism, till John the Baptist was imprisoned, (a space perhaps of nearly two years,) is here alone recorded. And one very wonderful miracle, with our Lord's discourse with the scribes, priests, and rulers, and the great council of the nation, concerning it, in the earlier part of his ministry, is here alone transmitted to us. (*Notes*, v.) Indeed scarcely any of the miracles or incidents of our Saviour's life, which the other evangelists recorded, are here repeated ; and in the exceptions, it is evident that the subsequent discourses, as more fully and explicitly declaring the great doctrines of Christianity, (some of which had by the others, been rather generally hinted than fully stated,) required the repetition of the narrative. (*Notes*, vi.)—In short, while this gospel, published long after, by the only surviving apostle, was suited to establish the authority of those which preceded ; it is almost entirely an original narrative, and far more than an appendix to them, as some have very improperly called it. From about the twenty-sixth verse of the sixth chapter, to the end of the eleventh, the whole is entirely new : and even the events, which preceded and made way for our Lord's crucifixion, resurrection, and ascension, though for substance the same, are enriched with such a variety of new and interesting information, as is exceedingly suited to fix the attention and impress the mind of the reader : especially that most affectionate and pathetick discourse of our Lord with his disciples, just before his crucifixion, which occupies the fourteenth, fifteenth, and sixteenth chapters, in which repeated and most express promises of the Holy Spirit are contained ; and his prayer for them, and for his church to the end of time, which closes the whole in the seventeenth chapter. To this prayer I affix no epithet ; as every epithet and every exposition must fall far below such a subject.—Various circumstances respecting his crucifixion, are recorded in this gospel alone, especially his committing his afflicted mother to the care of the beloved John, when about to expire on the cross, in the most affecting manner imaginable.—Our Lord's repeatedly meeting his assembled disciples, " on the first day of the week ; " with the instructive account of Thomas's absence the first time ; his obstinate incredulity ; our Saviour's condescension to him ; and Thomas's conviction, and confession of him as " his Lord and his God," are not mentioned elsewhere. The beautiful account also of Jesus's meeting the disciples, at the lake of Tiberias ; his threefold rebuke of Peter, (who had thrice denied him,) by thrice questioning his love to him, and thrice requiring his to shew his love, by feeding his sheep and his lambs ; with the prediction of the manner, in which this apostle should at length glorify God; the tacit readiness of John to follow in the same path ; and the obscure intimation, that perhaps this might not be the case, is added by this evangelist, in the most artless and affecting language. (*Notes*, xxi. 15—25.)—St. John's style is always plain, simple, and unaffected, and generally perspicuous : and when it appears not so, this will commonly be found to arise from the sublimity of his subject, to which no human language is adequate, rather than from any want of exactness in selecting and arranging his words and expressions.—Learned men have noted several particulars in which the language of this gospel differs from that of the others.—The phrase, " And it came to pass," (Και εγενετο,) so common in the other gospels, never occurs in this. " The WORD," (ὁ Λογος,) and " the only begotten," (ὁ Μονογενης,) as applied to Christ ; and the word, rendered " the COMFORTER," (Παρακλητος,) as a title given to the Holy Spirit, are peculiar to this gospel.—Other things of this kind are pointed out in the notes.—Where the other evangelists say, " The people," or " The multitude," St. John generally says, " The Jews ;" and from this, and his frequent short explanations of Jewish customs and terms, it is supposed, that he wrote his gospel, at a distance from Judea, and at a time and in a place where these subjects were little known. His style is also thought to be ruder, and to abound more with Hebraisms, than the other gospels.—The reader may enter on the perusal of this book, under the full assurance, that it is inexpressibly rich in most important instruction ; and if the commentator do not set its riches before him, the fault is wholly his. But let it be here observed, that in this gospel peculiarly, the teaching of the Holy Spirit, who " glorifies Christ and receives of the things of Christ to shew unto us," is indispensably needful, and must be sought by daily, fervent, and humble prayer.

CHAP. I.

The Word who was in the beginning with God, and was God, is the Creator of all things, has life in himself, and is the Light of men, 1—5. John a witness to that true and only Light, which was unknown to the world which he made, and not received by his own, except by such as were born of God, and these were adopted as his children, 6—13. The Word became flesh, and displayed his glory, as the only begotten of the Father, 14. John testifies to his superior dignity, and fulness whence all receive ; for grace and truth came by him, 15—17. He declares the invisible God to men, 18. Various testimonies of John to the Pharisees, concerning himself and Jesus, 19—28. John points him out as " the Lamb of God," and " the Son of God," who " baptizeth with the Holy " Ghost," 29—34. Two of John's disciples follow

Jesus, 35–-39. Andrew, one of them, brings Peter to him, whom he surnames Cephas, 40—42. Philip is called, who brings Nathanael, 43—45. Jesus declares him to be " an Israelite indeed ·" and he confesses Jesus as " the Son of God and the King of Israel," 46 —49. Jesus promises that he shall see still greater things, 50, 51.

IN ᵃ the beginning was ᵇ the Word, and the Word was ᶜ with God, and ᵈ the Word was God.

2 The same was in the beginning with God.

3 All ᵉ things were made by him ; and without him was not any thing made that was made.

Marginal references:
a Gen. i. 1. Prov. viii. 22, 23. Eph. iii. 9. Col. i. 17. Heb. i. 10. vii. 3. xiii. 8. Rev. xxii. 13.
b 14. 1 John i. 1, 2. v. 7. Rev. xix. 13.
c 16. xvi. 28. xvii. 5. Prov. viii, 22 —30. 1 John i. 2.
d v. 30—33. xx. 28. Ps. xlv. 6. Is. vii. 14. ix. 6. xl. 9—11. Matt. i. 23. Rom. ix. 5. Phil. ii. 6. 1 Tim. iii. 16. Tit. ii. 13. Heb. i. 8. 2 Pet. i. 1. Gr. 1 John v. 7, 20.
e 10. v. 17—19. Gen. i. 1. 2 K. Ps. xxxiii. 6. cii. 25. Is. xlv. 12, 18. Eph. iii. 9. Col. i. 16, 17. b. Prov. viii, 2. Heb. 1. 2, 3. 10—12. iii. 3. 4. Rev. iv. 11.

NOTES.

CHAP. I. V. 1—3. The other Evangelists leave us to collect the Deity of Christ, from his miracles and doctrine, and from the various declarations and displays of his glory and perfections, which they record : but John opens his gospel, with an express avowal and statement of this fundamental truth. He declares, that, " In the beginning " was the Word." (Marg. Ref.) Nothing could precede this, that man can know, but an immeasurable incomprehensible eternity. (Note, Gen. i. 1.) Time began, when the creation was called forth into existence by the Word himself : and " in the beginning, the Word was," that is, from eternity. Criticks have shewn, that there is an important difference between " in the beginning ; " and "from " the beginning : " the context, however, generally fixes the meaning. " The devil was a murderer," or manslayer, " from the beginning ; " but this he could not be, ere man existed. (viii. 44.)—Some imagine that the evangelist referred to the speculations of Plato and his disciples, in the term " the WORD," or the LOGOS, which that philosopher used : but it is not likely that he would at all countenance such speculations, as those of that philosopher, which seem originally to have been borrowed from Revelation, though they were at length so distorted and darkened, as to be little better than atheism.—' The Jews were constantly ' taught in their synagogues, that " the Word of God " ' was the same as God ; and that by " the Word all things " ' " were made : " which undoubtedly was the cause, why ' St. John delivered so great a mystery in so few words, as ' speaking unto them, who at the first apprehension un- ' derstood him. Only that which they knew not was, that ' this " Word was made flesh," and that this Word made ' flesh was Jesus Christ.' Bp. Pearson. The same learned divine, shews, that this way of speaking was in use, before Platonism was at all introduced among the Jews : and Jerom, in his note on Ez. i. 24, says, that the Septuagint translate the words, rendered in our version " the voice of " the Almighty," the voice of the Logos, or second person in the sacred Trinity. The clause, however, is at present wanting in some copies of the Septuagint ; and in others, the words τοῦ λογου, do not appear to be a translation of the original word Shaddai, but of that rendered speech.— " As the voice of a mighty one : when they went, there

" was the voice of speech, like the voice of an host."— ' The word may probably be taken, in its ordinary signifi- ' cation : though we may certainly conclude, that this was ' the appearance of the second person in the sacred Trinity ; ' both because he appears under the resemblance of a man ' (26), and from what hath been said on this subject, upon ' Is. vi. 1.' Lowth. (Notes, Is. vi. 1—4. Ez. i. 15—28.) —It is indeed probable, that the apostle referred to expressions, often made use of by the ancient Jewish writers, who spoke of " the Word," in language not very dissimilar from that of the ancient fathers of the church, and other Christian divines ; who, endeavouring to explain a mysterious subject, and to add further information, to that which the scripture has afforded us, have only darkened it, and laid it open to the objections of infidels. I apprehend, however, that St. John especially regarded the doctrine of the Old Testament, in what he declared. We have in many places observed the clearest intimations of distinct persons called JEHOVAH, in the writings of the ancient prophets ; (Notes, Is. xlviii. 16. Zech. ii. 6—13. iv. 8—10. vi. 14, 15 ;) and Solomon especially speaks of Wisdom, in language very similar to that which John here uses concerning " the Word." (Notes, Prov. viii. 22—34.) But the apostle " spake as he was moved by the Holy Spirit," and could refer to no higher authority than his own : he expressly states the doctrine, as a divine testimony ; and we should endeavour to ascertain his meaning, according to the most simple and obvious interpretation of his words ; and explain occasional intimations on the same mysterious subject by his words, and not his words by other intimations.—The title of " the Word " is peculiar to this Evangelist, at least with but few exceptions ; it may signify Reason, and is nearly equivalent to Wisdom, as speaking by Solomon. Probably, the title is given to Christ ; because by him the perfections, will, and secret counsels of God are made known to man ; especially his hidden and deep thoughts of wisdom and love in our redemption ; even as a man communicates his secret purposes and counsels to others, by his word : and by him exclusively ; for all prophets shine by his light, and report his testimony. ' The plainest reason, why this essential " Son of God " is ' styled " the Word," seems to be this ; that as our words ' are the interpretation of our minds to others, so was this ' " Son of God " sent to reveal his Father's mind to the

3 N 3

r v. 21. 26. xi. 25.   4 In ᶠ him was life; and ᵍ the Life
vii. 6. 1 Cor.
xv. 45. Col. iii.   was the Light of men.
4. 1 John i. 2.
y. 11. Rev. xxii. j.   g 8, 9. vii. 12. ix. 5. xii. 35. 46.   Ps. lxxx,v. 11.   Is. xxxv. 4.
5. xiii. 6, 7. 16. xlix. 6. 1x. 1—3.   Mal. iv. 2.   Matt. iv. 16.   Luke i. 76, 79. ii. 32.   Acts
xxvi. 23.   Eph. v. 14.   1 John i. 5—7.   Rev. xxii. 16.

5 And ʰ the Light shineth in dark-   h 10. 11. 10. 20.
                                         xii. 35—41. Job
ness, and the darkness comprehended   xxiv. 13—17.
                                         Prov. i. 23. 29.
it not.   30. Rom. i. 26.
                                         1 Cor. ii. 14.

'world.' *Whitby.*—It follows, " The WORD was with " God." The apostle had not here mentioned Christ as " the Son of God ;" and therefore he did not say " the " Father," but God. The Word existed, and was with God, when no creature had been produced. (*Notes,* 1 *John* i. 1—4.)—" And the WORD was GOD." Christianity was doubtless intended to deliver the world from idolatry, that principal work of the devil: it would therefore have been the most palpable absurdity, to suppose that one of its divinely inspired teachers should use those expressions, at the opening of his gospel, which were exactly suited to draw the whole Christian church into a new species of idolatry, and which could scarcely fail to have that effect. Yet this must be the consequence of supposing the person, of whom he here spake, to have been a mere creature, however highly exalted. The article is not indeed prefixed to the word rendered " God," but the rules of grammar require that it should be omitted, to distinguish the predicate from the nominative before the verb: and the word is frequently thus used even of God the Father; so that scarcely the shadow of an objection can be drawn from that circumstance. And what can we understand by this testimony, " The Word was God," but that he was possessed of the same divine nature and perfections with the Father; participated the same glory and felicity; and was in every respect as fully entitled to the adoration of all rational creatures which should ever exist, as that God with whom he was ? (*Note,* v. 20—23.) ' " The word God," is used eleven times in this chapter, ' in its proper sense : nor can one instance be produced, ' from the whole New Testament, where, in the singular ' number, it is used in any other sense. Is it then reason- ' able to conceive, that it is here used in that improper ' sense, in which it never is again once used throughout ' this gospel or the whole New Testament, rather than in ' that sense, in which it is continually used in all other ' places ? ' *Whitby.* The only objection to this inference seems to be, that it is incomprehensible : but it should carefully be noted, that those who will not admit of it, avowedly on this account, are driven into hypotheses, the absurdity of which at least is perfectly comprehensible. (*Note,* 1 *Tim.* iii. 16.) Every succeeding generation of opponents hitherto has been induced to give up the system of their predecessors as indefensible, or as less specious than more modern discoveries or explanations : and many from age to age contend each for his own scheme, of getting over the difficulties here thrown in the way ; yet their utmost improvements on the subject scarcely need any other answer, than to compare them with this divine testimony, to which they must be in everlasting opposition.— The inspired writer, however, was equally careful to establish the *personal distinction,* as the eternal Godhead, of the Word ; and therefore he adds again, " The same was " in the beginning with God." Having thus stated the Deity and distinct personality of " the Word," he proceeds to ascribe all the work of creation to him ; as working in perfect union of will and purpose with the Father and the Holy Spirit. (*Notes* Gen. i. 2. 26, 27. *Col.* i. 15—17. *Heb.*

i. 3, 4. 10—12.) In this he is so explicit, as to use a repetition which at first sight may appear needless : " All " things were made by him :" but the word *all* is sometimes used, when absolute universality is not meant; therefore he adds, " without him was not any thing made, " that was made :" or, *not so much as one single being,* for so the original words imply. In what language can the divine power and operation of the great Creator be more emphatically described ? Or what could have been said, better suited to lead every one to adore " the Word," as his omnipotent Maker and Sovereign Lord ? To suppose him to be a mere creature, is to suppose infinite power and perfection communicable to a creature ; and the whole universe standing in the same relation to a creature, as they do to the infinite and eternal God : and to assert that " the Word" was only an instrument or subordinate agent in creation, beside the absurdity of the notion, expressly contradicts the scripture, which says, that " JEHOVAH stretcheth forth the heavens alone, and spread- " eth abroad the earth by himself :" and that " he will not " give his glory to another." (*Notes, Is.* xlii. 8, 9. xliv. 6—8. 24.) Indeed it is self-evident, that " he who built " all things is God," in the strictest and fullest meaning of the word. This doctrine however, is not grounded on any single expression, but on a combination of very many ; and it will therefore appear more and more incontrovertible as we proceed.

In the beginning. (1) Εν αρχη. 2.—*Gen.* i. 1. *Sept.*— The *Word.*] 'Ο Λογος. 14. 1 *John* i. 1. v. 7. *Rev.* xix. 13.

V. 4, 5. The Evangelist here further testifies, that " in " the Word was LIFE;" (even as water is in a fountain or spring, or as light is in the sun ;) whence it issued forth to animate all orders of living creatures, from the most minute to the most exalted. (*Marg. Ref.* f.—*Notes,* xi. 20—27, *vv.* 25, 26. xiv. 4—6, *v.* 6. *Col.* iii. 1—4, *vv.* 3, 4. 1 *John* i. 1. v. 11, 12. *Rev.* xxi. 5—8, *v.* 6. xxii. 1.) " And " the Life was the Light of men :" all the powers of man's understanding, and all the information, communicated to him from every quarter and by every avenue ; all that can be called *light,* natural, intellectual, moral, or spiritual, is from " the Word," and that Fountain of life which is in him : especially he, who is the *Life* of the universe, is become the *Light* of fallen men, to shew them the way to everlasting life and felicity. (*Marg. Ref.* g, h.—*Notes,* 6 —9. viii. 12. ix. 4—7. xii. 34—36. *Mal.* iv. 2, 3. *Luke* ii. 25—32. *Eph.* v. 8—14.)—But " this Light shineth in " darkness :" men " hold the truth in unrighteousness :" the discoveries made of the Creator by the works of creation, as addressed to the natural reason and conscience of men, fail of producing a profitable knowledge of God, because of the depravity of the human heart; (*Note,* iii. 19—21;) and, notwithstanding this light, the world continues enveloped in darkness and wickedness. The light of Revelation, in the former ages of the world, had shone amidst the darkness which it had not dispelled : the Gentiles still continued in almost total darkness ; (*Notes, Rom.* i. 18—32 ;) and the Jews misunderstood, perverted, or neglected the light. Even the Christian Revelation, though

6 ¶ There was ¹ a man sent from God, whose name was ᵏ John.

7 The same came for ¹ a witness, to bear witness of the Light, ᵐ that all men through him might believe.

8 He was not ⁿ that Light, but was sent to bear witness of that Light.

9 That was ᵒ the true Light, which lighteth ᵖ every man that cometh into the world.

10 He ᑫ was in the world, ʳ and the

more complete, still shines as a light in the midst of a dark world, which generally lies in error, ignorance, and wickedness.—For " the darkness comprehended it not," or " did not apprehend it." Fully to comprehend the light which God affords us, concerning himself, his truth, and will, may be impossible to a finite creature; but the perverseness, to which sin and Satan have reduced men, causes them to despise, hate, and reject the light : " they " like not to retain God in their knowledge;" they will not take hold of, or retain, instruction; they do not avail themselves of the light, but close their eyes to it ; so that as to numbers it shines in vain. This is the real, and in some sense the only reason, why Christ, " the Light of " the world," has not by his gospel enlightened all the nations of the earth. But no external revelation can effectually profit an apostate, rebellious creature, except it be attended with an internal operation of the Holy Spirit, preparing the vitiated organ of the human intellect to receive the light, and his heart to welcome and love it: and as it seems to have been the design of infinite wisdom, in leaving the nations during so many ages without revelation, to prove by facts, what a blind guide man's boasted reason is ; so it appears also to be the purpose of God to shew in the same manner, that even Revelation alone will not profit fallen creatures, without the teaching of his Holy Spirit. When these two humiliating truths are undeniably proved, we have ground in scripture to conclude, that God will render the light of revelation effectual by his powerful teaching, to " fill the earth with the knowledge of his " glory, even as the waters cover the sea."—The passage under consideration may be applied to all these particulars. The evangelist's language, however, is very remarkable, and has been considered as the mere effect of inattention to the common rules of grammar. The first verb is present, " shineth ;" the second is the aorist, which generally denotes the past, " comprehended," or " apprehend-" ed." But may he have intended to state, that the light of divine truth still shone, when he wrote, in the midst of a dark world; yet, that during the ages preceding Christ, nay during his personal ministry, this light had been less apprehended and made use of in the world, than it was after his ascension, and the pouring out of the Spirit, and the preaching of the gospel to the Gentiles. Before, it shone dimly among the Jews ; but then it shone far more clearly both on Jews and Gentiles. (Note, Is. lx. 1, 2.)

Comprehended. (5) Καλέλαβέτ. viii. 3, 4. xii. 35. Mark ix. 18. Acts iv. 13. x. 34. xxv. 25. Rom. ix. 30. 1 Cor. ix. 24. Eph. iii. 18. Phil. iii. 12, 13. 1 Thes. v. 4.

V. 6—9. The coming of Christ was intended to make way for a more general diffusion of divine light among men ; and this was introduced by the ministry of John the Baptist. He was " a man sent from God," wise, holy and useful; but the evangelist spake of him in very dif-

ferent language, from what he had used respecting " the " Word, who was in the beginning, was with God, and was " God, and made all things." (Marg. Ref. i, k.—Notes, 1—3. Luke i. 11—17. 76—79.) John came by the express appointment of God, " to bear witness of the Light ;" to announce the coming of " the Light of the world ;" to call men's attention to " the brightness of the rising" of " the Sun of righteousness ;" and to testify of Jesus, that he was to be " a Light to lighten the Gentiles, and to be " for salvation unto the ends of the earth ;" in order " that " all men," (or men of all ranks, characters, and descriptions) might by his testimony be brought to believe in Christ. (Marg. Ref. l, m.—Notes, Is. xlii. 5—7. xlix. 5, 6. Acts xxvi. 16—23.) Nothing can more fully prove the darkness which envelopes men's minds, than the consideration, that when the Light was manifested, it was needful that a witness should be sent from God, to call men's attention to it. Light is its own witness, and renders itself, as well as other objects, conspicuous : but then this presupposes that men have eyes ; that they are not blinded, nor wilfully closed, nor locked up in sleep : for in any of these cases, " the light may shine in darkness, and the " darkness apprehend it not :" and it is for similar reasons, that it is necessary for the preachers of the gospel to proclaim the words of God, and to say, " Awake, thou that " sleepest, and arise from the dead, and Christ shall give " thee light." (Note, Eph. v. 8—14, v. 14.)—John was indeed " a burning and a shining light :" (Note, v. 31— 38, v. 35 :) but " he was not the Light," who came to illuminate a benighted world ; having no light for himself except from Christ, or for others but by reflecting his light. He was merely a witness to " the Word," who was indeed, " that Light, which enlighteneth every man who " cometh into the world." That is, he is the source of all true light, by which any man in the world ever was, is, or shall be enlightened ; all that comes not from him is but darkness, at least it is not profitable light in spiritual things. (Notes, Is. viii. 20. Matt. vi. 22, 23.) We can no more infer from this expression, that Christ gives every individual a measure of spiritual light ; than from one just before (7), that every man actually " believeth in Christ" through John's testimony : both inferences are alike contrary to scripture and to facts.—It may further be observed, that Jesus was the true Light, not only in opposition to the false and delusive light of philosophy, and the perverted light of the traditions of the elders ; but also in distinction from the typical light of the Mosaick ceremonies, and the derived light of prophets and apostles. (Note, 1 John ii. 7—11.)—' With this light he enlighteneth ' every man, namely, who doth receive him (12).' Whitby. —' Which coming into the world, enlighteneth every ' man.' Doddridge. Ὁ φωτίζει παντα ανθρωπον, ερχομενον εις τον κοσμον. iii. 19. xii. 46. 1 Tim. i. 15.

V. 10—13. Before Christ appeared as Man on earth,

3 w 5

xvii. 26. Mat'.
vi 27. 1 Cor. i.
21. ii. 8. 1 John
iii. 1.
t Matt. xv. 24.
Acts iii. 25, 26.
xiii. 26. 46.
Rom. ix. 4. 5.
xv. 8. Gal. iv. 4.
v iii. 32. ix. iiii.
2, 3. Luke xix.
14. xx. 15—18.
Acts vii. 51, 52.
x Matt. v. 45. the
xxiii. 8. Col. i. 2.
y Is. lvi. 5. Jer.
iii. 19. Hos.
i0. Rom. viii. 14, 15. 2 Cor. vi. 17, 18. Gal. iii. 26. iv. 6. 1 John iii. 1. ● Or,
the right, or, privilege. ● ii. 23. iii. 18. xx. 31. Matt. xii. 21. Acts iii. 16.
t John iii. 23. v. 12, 13.

world was made by him, and the world * knew him not. 11 He ᶜ came unto his own, ᵈ and his own received him not.

12 But as many as ᵉ received him, ᶠ to them gave he ᵍ power to become the sons of God, ʰ even to them that believe on his name :

13 Which ⁱ were born, ᵏ not of blood, ˡ nor of the will of the flesh, ᵐ nor of the will of man, but ⁿ of God.

14 And ᵒ the Word was made flesh, and dwelt among us, (and ᵖ we beheld his glory, the glory as of ᵠ the only begotten of the Father,) ʳ full of grace and truth.

a iii. 3. 1 Pet. i.
3. 23. ii. 2.
1 John iii. 9.
iv. 7. v. 1. 4
18.—4
b viii.
Matt. iii.
Rom. ix. 7—9.
c Gen. xxv. 22.
28. xxvii. 4. 33.
Rom. ix. 10—16
d Ps. cx. 3. Rom
ix. 1—5. x. 1—
4. 1 Cor. iii. 6.
Phil. ii. 13. Jam. i. 18. ● iii. 6. Tit. iii. 5. 1 John ii. 28, 29. f 1. ix. vii. 14. Matt.
i. 16. 20—24. Luke i. 31—35. ii. 11. Rom. i. 3. 4. ix. 5. 1 Cor. xv. 47. Gal. iv. 4. Phil. ii. 6—
8. 1 Tim. iii. 16. Heb. ii. 14—17. x. 5. 1 John iv. 2, 3. 2 John 7. g ii. 11. x. 40. xiv.
40. 41. xiv. 9. 1s. 3. iii. 2. ix. 1, 2. Matt. xvii. 1—5. 2 Cor. iv. 4—6. Heb. i. 3. 1 Pet.
ii. 4—7. 2 Pet. i. 17. h iii. 16. iii. 18. Px. ii. 7. Acts xiii. 33. Heb. i. 5. v. 5. 1 John
iv. 9. i 16. 17. 2 Cor. xii. 9. Eph. iii. 8. 18, 19. Col. i. 19. 1 Tim. i. 14—1€.

"He was in the world;" both as he upheld and governed it by his providence, and as he enlightened some of its inhabitants by his word and Spirit. But though the world was made and sustained by him; yet men in general "knew him not," so as to worship, trust, and obey him. (*Marg. Ref.* q—s.—*Notes*, 18. *Phil.* ii. 5—8. *Heb.* i. 1—4. 10—12.) When he appeared in our nature, he came immediately to his own professed people the Jews, whose Lord, King, and Redeemer he had ever been, as a man would come to his own house or estate; whom he had chosen, brought out of Egypt, settled in Canaan, separated and preserved distinct from other nations; and whom he had favoured with his word and ordinances: so that the whole of their constitution was his appointment for their good. Yet, when he came, in the fulness of time, according to their ancient prophecies, his own family received him not, but thrust him from them with contempt and abhorrence, notwithstanding the displays which he made of his Almighty power and divine perfection! (*Marg. Ref.* t, u.) But though the Jews in general rejected and "crucified the Lord of glory;" yet there was a remnant of them, and afterwards an immense number of the Gentiles, who welcomed him as their Redeemer and King. To all these he gave the power, privilege, or legal right, by adoption, of "becoming the children of God;" that, being adopted into his family, and made partakers of his fatherly compassion, care, and affection, they might reverence, love, trust, and obey him, with delight, as his beloved children. (*Marg.* and *Marg. Ref.* x—z.—*Notes, Rom.* viii. 14—17. 2 *Cor.* vi. 14—18, *v.* 18. *Gal.* iv. 4—7, *vv.* 6, 7.) This "receiving of Christ" was indeed equivalent to "believing in his name," that is, to a firm belief of the divine testimony concerning his personal dignity and excellency, the end of his coming into the world, his mediatorial character, and his salvation; with a cordial reception of him as a Saviour, and a reliance on him, for all the blessings which he came to bestow on lost sinners. —These "children of God" "were born" into his family, not by any natural descent from the blood of Abraham; (*Note, Matt.* iii. 7—10 ;) or through the blood of the legal sacrifices; or by their own natural choice, as fallen creatures, whose will, being "the will of the flesh," is carnal and enslaved to sin. (*Notes*, iii. 6. *Rom.* vii. 18—21. viii. 5—9. *Gal.* v. 16—21.) Neither did it arise from the will of man respecting them; as men, who had no children, sometimes chose persons of distinguished excellency, whom they adopted as their heirs: for no man can insure the conversion of his dearest friends or relatives ; no minister can choose who shall, or even conjecture beforehand who will, profit by his ministry; nay, the most unlikely persons are very frequently thus distinguished:

(*Marg. Ref.* b—e :) for they are "born of God," according to his purpose, by an immediate operation of his Holy Spirit, producing in them divine life, a new nature, renewing them to the image of God, and inclining them to choose and delight in the spiritual excellency of the things of God. (*Notes*, iii. 3—8. *Tit.* iii. 4—7. *Jam.* i. 16—18. 1 *Pet.* i. 3—5. 22—25. 1 *John* v. 1—5.) Thus new creatures are formed and brought into the spiritual world, to be nourished up by the word of sound doctrine, to a complete meetness for the inheritance of the children of God in heaven. This new birth is the preparation for receiving Christ, and believing in his name, without which all men would still continue to despise and reject him.—The difference between *regeneration* and *adoption*, as noticed in these verses, deserves peculiar attention. They who are "born of God" receive Christ, and to those who receive him, he gives the "power, or privilege, of becoming the sons of God." The former is regeneration, or a change in their nature ; the latter is adoption, or a change in their state : and when .hus regenerated and adopted, they receive "the Spirit of "adoption." (*Note, Eph.* i. 5—8, *v.* 5.)

Unto his own. (11) Εις τα ιδια. xvi. 32. xix. 27. *Acts* xxi. 6. 1 *Thes.* iv. 11.—*His own.*] Ιδιοι. xiii. 1. *Acts* iv. 23. xxiv. 23.—The former includes the temple, and all things belonging to worship, and peculiar advantages of the nation: the latter denotes exclusively the Jews, as possessing those advantages, and so by profession and right the people of the divine Messiah.—*Power.*] Εξεσιαν. "gative.' *Whitby.—v.* 27. xvii. 2. 1 *Cor.* viii. 9. ix. 4—6. 12. 18.

V. 14. The evangelist next proceeds to shew in what manner "the Word came to his own;" "He was made "flesh," or "became flesh," that is, he assumed man's entire nature, into a personal union with the Deity. "He "was made in the likeness of sinful flesh," he became Man, and subjected himself to all those infirmities which sin gave rise to, as far as this could be done without being polluted by sin. He "became flesh," as he became liable to hunger, thirst, weariness, pain, suffering, and death. He "was God, and with God from the beginning:" at length he became Man, and was with man : he was "in "the form of God," and he "became in fashion as a "man." (*Marg. Ref.* f.—*Note, Phil.* ii. 5—8.) This was effected by the miraculous conception and birth of Jesus the Son of Mary, who was incomprehensibly, yet really and inseparably, one Person with the Eternal Word. We cannot explain this ; nor can we understand the union between the body and soul in our own persons. (*Notes, Gal.* iv. 4—7. 1 *Tim.* iii. 16.) "But the testimony of God is "sure, making wise the simple." This testimony declares

15 ¶ John ᵏ bare witness of him, and cried, saying, This was he of whom I spake, He that cometh after me is preferred before me; for ᶦhe was before me.

16 And ᵐof his fulness have all we received, ⁿand grace for grace.

17 For ᵒ the law was given by

ᵏ See on 7, 8. 29. —34. 31. 35, 36. v. 33—36. Matt. iii. 11. Mark i. 7. Luke iii. 16. l. 1, 2. 30. viii. 58. xvii. 5. Prov. viii. 22. Is. ix. 6. Mic. v. 2. Phil. ii. 6, 7. Col. i. 17. Heb. xiii. 8. Rev. i. 11. 17, 18. ii. 8.

ᵐ xv. 1—5. Matt. iii. 11. 14. Luke iii. 12 — .6. Rom. viii. 9 l Cor. i. 4, 5. Eph. iv. 7—12. Col. ii. 2, 9. 1 Pet. i. 2. n Zech. iv. 7. Matt. xiii. 12. Rom. v. 2. 17. 20. Eph. i. 6, 7. ii. 5—10. iv. 7. 1 Pet. i. 2. o v. 45, 46. 28. Acts vii. 38. xxviii. 23. Rom. iii. 19, 20. v. 20, 21. 2 Cor. iii. 7—10. Gal. iii. 10—13. 17. Heb. iii. 5, 6. viii. 6—12.

" that the Word was made flesh ; " and that he " taberna-" cled among us," as the Shechinah, or divine glory, dwelt in the tabernacle in the wilderness; so that " the Word of " God," yea, " God the Word," condescended to dwell here on earth in human nature, and visibly to display his glory for many years. For he was " full of grace and " truth ; " accomplishing the types, predictions, and promises of the Old Testament; exercising all kind of condescension, compassion, love, and mercy to mankind ; communicating all grace to those who sought to him for it ; and shewing himself ever full of kindness and truth, in the blessed instructions which he continually gave to those around him, concerning the things of God and the eternal world. (Marg. Ref. g—i.—Notes, 17. 1 John i. 1—4.)—This glory was indeed veiled under his external poverty and deep humility, from the view of carnal men : (Notes, Is. liii. 2, 3 :) but the apostles, and others who were enabled to believe in this name, beheld the glory of his power, wisdom, knowledge, holiness, truth, and grace ; and they were assured that they were such as became the character and person of " the only begotten of the Father." (Note, 18.)—Some reference may here also be had to his transfiguration, of which this evangelist was an eye-witness. (Notes, Matt. xvii. 1—8.)

Flesh.] Σαρξ. Acts ii. 30. Rom. i. 3. 1 Tim. iii. 16. Heb. ii. 14.—Gen. vi. 17. Sept.—Dwelt.] Εσκηνωσιν. Rev. vii. 15. xii. 12. xiii. 6. xxi. 3. A σκηνη, tentorium, tabernaculum.—Only begotten.] Μονογενης. 18. See on Luke vii. 12.—Full.] Πληρης. This must agree with Λογος, in the former part of the verse.

V. 15. The evangelist next shews how the things which he had stated accorded to what John the Baptist had testified respecting Jesus. When he first saw him, (for this seems to refer to the time, when Jesus came to be baptized by him,) he proclaimed aloud, that this was the person, whom he had announced to the people as about to appear among them. As to the order of time, and his entrance on his work, " he came after John : " but in every other way he had been, and would be, " preferred before him." Indeed it was most reasonable that he should be thus preferred, " for he was before him." John was the elder man, and it does not appear what sense can be made of this expression (30), except we allow, that Jesus existed before he appeared on earth as Man, whereas John had no previous existence : for if John had only meant to declare the superiority of Jesus, he must, according to all the rules of language, have said " He is before me," not " He was before me." Besides, this would have been no more than a repetition of his foregoing assertion, when it is evidently introduced as a reason for it. (Marg. Ref.—Notes, 19—34. iii. 27—36.)—Preferred, &c.) ' This is ' properly said of those, who are placed in rank before ' others, as masters whom their attendants follow. It ' signifies a more honourable situation, and by consequence, ' superior dignity.' Beza. The parallel passages, where another word is used, confirm this interpretation. (27.

Notes, Matt. iii. 11, 12. Luke iii. 15—17.) Jesus came to John, and was baptized by him, as if he meant to become his disciple : but John gave place to him; assigned him the foremost station ; in the most decided manner, owned him as his Lord ; and pointed him out to his disciples, as the promised Messiah.—Before me.] ' This I ' said, because he indeed was before me, as being " in the " " beginning with God" (2).' Whitby.

Is preferred before me.] Εμπροσθεν μου γεγονεν. " He " became before me." 27. 30.—Ισχυρότερος μου εστιν. Matt. iii. 11. Luke iii. 16.—He was before me.] Πρωτος μου ην. 30. viii. 7. 1 Cor. xv. 45, 46. 1 Tim. i. 15. ii. 13. Rev. i. 11. 17. ii. 8. xxii. 13.

V. 16. This, and the two following verses, are considered by many expositors, as the words of the evangelist resuming his subject from the fourteenth verse ; for they consider the fifteenth merely as a parenthesis, and not as a continuation of John the Baptist's testimony. (Note, 14.) The instruction, however, is the same, and grounded on the same divine authority, whoever be the speaker. John the Baptist and John the Evangelist, the prophets and the apostles. and all believers from the beginning of the world had received all their wisdom, knowledge, strength, and grace from " the fulness of Christ : " and all to the end must receive from the same fulness. For they have nothing of their own, but sin, weakness, folly, and misery : none ever had, or can have any thing from God, but as it is communicated through his Son, the eternal Word ; either in consequence of his engagements, as the Surety of the new covenant, or of his actual incarnation, and the work which he accomplished on earth. In him is the fulness of life, light, wisdom, power, grace, and truth ; " all fulness dwells in him," even " all the fulness of the " Godhead bodily ; " from which alone fallen sinners have been, are, and shall be receiving, by faith, all that renders them wise, strong, holy, useful, or happy. (iii. 34. Notes, Col. i. 18—20. ii. 1—4. 8—10.)—" And grace for grace ; " this may signify, a large abundance of all spiritual blessings, most freely bestowed from the fulness of Christ, even " grace upon grace : " or, that each believer receives a measure of every kind of grace, which is treasured up in Christ for his people, answerable to all his wants, even " grace sufficient for him : " (Note, 2 Cor. xii. 7—10, v. 9 :) or, that by the grace received from Christ, they are renewed into his image, and reflect every holy excellency which appeared in his character; even as the melted wax receives line for line, and letter for letter, the exact impression from the seal which is put upon it. The words of our Lord, " To him that hath shall be given, and he shall " have abundantly," seem also referred to. (Marg. Ref.— Note, Matt. xiii. 12.)

Fulness.] Πληρωμαος. Matt. ix. 16. Mark viii. 20. Rom. xi. 12. 25. xiii. 10. xv. 29. 1 Cor. x. 26. 28. Gal. iv. 4. Eph. i. 10. 23. iii. 19. iv. 13. Col. i. 19. ii. 9.

V. 17. The Jews trusted in Moses, glorying that they were his disciples : (Notes, v. 45—47. ix. 27—34, vv. 27

3 N 7

p xiv. 6. Gen. iii. | Moses, *but* ᵖ grace and truth came by
15. xxii. 18. Ps.
lxxxv. 1, 2. | Jesus Christ.
lxxxix. 1, 2.
xcviii.3. Mic.vii. | 18 No man hath ᑫ seen God at any
20. Luke i. 54,
55. 68.—79. Acts xiii. 34—39. Rom. iii. 21—26. xv. 8—12. 2 Cor. i. 20. Heb. ix. 22. x. 4
—10. xi. 39, 40. Rev. v. 8—10. vii. 9—17.   q vi. 46. Ex. xxxiii. 20. Col. i. 15.
1 Tim. i. 17. vi. 16. 1 John iv. 12. 20.

time: 'the only begotten Son, which r 14. 51. 16—18.
                                   1 John iv. 9.
is ˢ in the bosom of the Father, ᵗ he ˢ xiii. 23. Prov.
                                 viii. 30. Is. xl.
hath declared *him.* ||t. Lam. ii. 12.
                                 Luke xv. 77, 28.
t xii. 41. xiv. 9. xvii. 6. 26. Gen. xvi. 13. xviii. 33. xxxii. 28—30. xlviii. 15, 16. Ex. iii. 4
—6. xxiii. 21. xxxii. 18—23. xxxiv. 5—7. Num. xii. 8. Josh. v. 13—15. vi. 1, 2. Judg.
vi. 12—26. xiii. 20—23. Is. vi. 1—3. Ex. i. 26—34. Hos. xii. 3—6. Matt. xi. 27. Luke x.
22. 1 John v. 20.

—29:) and indeed he was a most eminent prophet of God, the lawgiver of Israel; by whom God gave his people both the moral law, the perfect standard of holiness; and the ceremonial law, which was a shadow of the grace of the gospel. The former, however, is " the ministration of " condemnation " to transgressors; and the latter had no inherent efficacy to take away the guilt or power of sin; and therefore both, as forming along with the *judicial* law, one complex dispensation, were intended to lead men to Christ, and could do nothing to save those who did not believe in him, though excellently fitted to the purpose for which God appointed them. (*Marg. Ref. o.—Notes, Deut.* xxxii. 4. xxxiii. 4, 5. *Rom.* vii. 7—12. *2 Cor.* iii. 7—11.) These " came by Moses; but grace and truth came " by Jesus Christ." All the mercy shewn to sinners in pardoning and justifying them: all the grace by which they are sanctified, and taught repentance, faith, and holiness; all the favour in any way vouchsafed to each individual of the race of fallen Adam from the beginning, " came by Jesus," the promised Messiah. All the faithful promises, given and performed to the church of believers, and all the ancient prophecies and types, had reference to him and were verified in him. He was the Truth of all the shadows, the Substance of all the promises, the Object of all the prophecies, the Centre of all the doctrines, the Source and Standard of truth, and the Medium of communication of all the grace and blessings, which ever were made to fallen man, or conferred on him. (*Notes, v. 39—* 45, *v.* 39. xiv. 4—6, *v.* 6. 1 *Pet.* i. 10—12. *Rev.* xix. 9, 10, *v.* 10.) As soon as Adam sinned, the divine Saviour stepped in, as it were, between him and the avenging sword of justice; and as the promised Seed, " the Seed of the " woman," undertook to be the Surety of a new covenant to his people. He was and is " the real cause for " righteousness to every believer," in every age. (*Notes,* 16. *Gen.* iii. 14, 15. *Rom.* x. 1—4. *Heb.* vii. 20—25. viii. 3—6.) Through him alone sinners have access to God as a Father, acceptance with him or grace from him; and even their repentance, faith, and holiness, come from him alone.—" Grace and truth:" ' As the moral law pointed ' out the disease, which Christ cures: and the ceremonial ' law shadowed forth that which Christ indeed performed: ' therefore *grace* answers, by way of contrast, to the moral ' law; and *truth* to the ceremonial.' *Beza.*—(*Marg. Ref.* p. —*Notes, Ps.* lxxxv. 10—13. lxxxix. 1—4.)

Grace and truth.] Ἡ χαρις και ἡ αληθεια.—" The grace " and the truth," *viz.* which was set forth in the Old Testament from the beginning.

V. 18. As one instance in which " the Truth came by " Jesus Christ; " the sacred writer assures us, that all true and useful knowledge of God was always derived to man through him. No man ever did or can see the divine essence: (*Marg. Ref. q.—Notes,* 1 *Tim.* i. 17. vi. 13—16, *v.* 16:) but all the declarations concerning him, all the discoveries of his Being, perfections, truth, and will, have been made by the Son, who was, is, and ever shall be, with

the Father, as " in his bosom," the object of his entire and ineffable love and delight; knowing his infinite excellency, and sharing all his counsels and purposes, and revealing them to man, as far as it is proper that they should be known by him. (*Notes, Matt.* xi. 27. *Luke* x. 21, 22.)—We have frequently had occasion to observe, that from the beginning every discovery of God to man, and all the visions and displays of Jᴇʜᴏᴠᴀʜ to Adam, Noah, Abraham, Isaac, Jacob, Moses, Joshua, Isaiah, and others, were made by the eternal Son, who afterwards became incarnate, being anticipations of that event: (*Notes,* Gen. iii. 8. xvi. 10, 11. 13, 14. xviii. 33. xxxii. 26—30. xlviii. 16. *Ex.* iii. 2. 14. *Josh.* v. 13—15. *Is.* vi. 1—4. *Hos.* xii. 3—6:) nor can those *appearances* of God be reconciled with this, and similar declarations, on any other principle.—According to this testimony, no man really knows any thing of God to good purpose, as to the mysteries of his nature, and the glory and harmony of his attributes, but he who receives his knowledge by faith in the Son of God.—' From Christ alone all true knowledge ' of God is derived.' *Beza.*—It is, however, doubted by many, who stedfastly maintain the doctrine of our Lord's deity, and of a Trinity of persons in the godhead, whether the title of " the Son of God," relates to any thing more than his human nature, his miraculous conception, and his mediatorial character and work; and the opinion of former orthodox divines on this subject seems to be given up by them as unscriptural. Now it is allowed, that numbers have speculated, explained, and disputed a great deal too much concerning these mysteries, of which we can know no more than is expressly revealed: and it must also be remembered, that such relative terms as Father and Son, when applied to the Deity, can only be used in a figurative sense, or one not comprehensible by us, in order to help our feeble apprehensions: and therefore they must not be made the foundation of any conclusions inconsistent with the eternity, self-existence, and co-equality of " the " Word." Yet I apprehend, that Christ is called in scripture " the only begotten Son of God," and " the Son of " the Father," in *respect of his divine nature;* and that he is the Son of God, by " a generation that none can de- " clare." Various expressions, concerning the love of God in giving his Son for us, seem to refer, not to his giving him to death, *when incarnate;* but to his giving him *to be incarnate* for that purpose. " He spared not his *own Son;*" and this gift was so immense, that the apostle counted all other things to be as nothing in comparison of it. Indeed it does not appear why he should be called " the only be- " gotten Son of God," merely in respect of his human nature; for the formation of Adam, and of all the angels, was a production equally immediate and divine, as that of the human nature of Christ; and " the glory as of the " only Begotten of the Father," (14) evidently relates to his divine, and not to his human nature. (*Notes,* iii. 16. 1 *John* iv. 9—12.)—In short it seems to denote something incomprehensible, and infinitely superior to creation, and

3 N 8

19 ¶ And this is the record of John, when the Jews sent priests and Levites from Jerusalem, to ask him, *a v. 33.—M. Deut. xvii. 9. 11. xxiv. 8. Matt. xxi. 23* Who art thou? *v. 24. Acts xiii. 25. xix. 4.*

20 And he confessed, and denied not; but confessed, I am not the Christ. *y iii. 28—M. Matt. iii. 11, 12. Mark i. 7, 8. Luke iii. 15—17.*

21 And they asked him, What then? Art thou Elias? And he saith, I am not. Art thou that prophet? And he answered, No. *z Mal. iv. 5. Matt. xi. 14. xvii. 10—12. Luke i. 17. a 2b. vii. 40. Deut. xviii. 15—18. Matt. xi. 9—11. xvi. 14.*

22 Then said they unto him, Who art thou? that we may give an answer to them that sent us: what sayest thou of thyself? *b 2 Sam. xxiv. 13.*

23 He said, I am the voice of one *c iii. 28 Matt. iii. 3. Mark i. 3. thou of thyself? Luke i. 16. 17. 76—79. iii. 4—6.* crying in the wilderness, Make straight the way of the Lord, as said the prophet Esaias. *d Is. xl. 3—5*

24 And they which were sent were of the Pharisees. *e iib. 1, 2. vii. 47—B. Matt. xxvii. 15—18. 26. Luke vii. 70. xi. 39—44. 58. xvi. 14. Acts xxiii. 8. xxvi. 5. Phil. iii. 5, 6.*

25 And they asked him, and said unto him, Why baptizest thou then, if thou be not that Christ, nor Elias, neither that prophet? *f Matt. xxi. 23. Acts iv. 5—7. v. 28. g See on 20—22. —Dan. ix. 24—26.*

26 John answered them, saying, I baptize with water: but there standeth one among you, whom ye know not. *h Matt. i'i. 11. Mark i. 8. Luke iii. 16. Acts i. 5. xi. 16. i iii. 10. 11. viii. 19 xvi. 3. xvii. 3.*

27 He it is, who coming after me is preferred before me, whose shoe's latchet I am not worthy to unloose. *k Mal. iii. 1, 2. before iii. 1. l Seeon 15. 30.—Acts xix. 4. m Matt. iii. 11. Mark i. 7. Luke iii. 16.*

---

to every thing of which we have the most remote conception, constituting an equality of nature, and a relation between the eternal Father and the Son, of which that relation among men is but a feeble shadow; yet suited to help our conceptions about it. Perhaps we should never have been informed of the distinction of persons in the Godhead, but on account of the œconomy of the work of redemption: or, to speak more properly, that work seems to have been planned, in order to a display of the glory of God, as well as this distinction of persons, as in the harmony of his attributes. The apprehensions of the most exalted creatures, on such a subject, must be inadequate. Our's must *at present* be also confused and defective. The second person in the sacred Trinity may be spoken of as " the only begotten Son; " as he is appointed, in the eternal counsels, to be the Image, Representative, and Revealer of the invisible God, to man, in every age, and under every dispensation: and our conception of him, as the Son, should doubtless be restricted to his participation of the divine nature, and his representing it to man; so that " he who hath seen the Son, hath " seen the Father also." (*Notes*, xiv. 7—14, *vv.* 7. 9—11. 2 *Cor.* iii. 17, 18. iv. 5, 6. *Col.* i. 15—17. *Heb.* i. 3, 4.) This will appear with increasing evidence as we proceed with this gospel.

In the bosom.] Εις κολπον. See on *Luke* xvi. 22.— *Hath declared.*] Εξηγησαλο. *Luke* xxiv. 35. *Acts* xv. 12. 14. xxi. 19.—Ἀβ εξ et ἡγεομαι, *duco.*

V. 19—28. The evangelist next relates a more publick testimony of John the Baptist to Christ. The chief priests, scribes, and great council of the nation, who regarded themselves as entitled to superintend all concerns of religion, having heard reports concerning John, and his doctrine, baptism, and popularity; sent a deputation to him, to know, who he was, and whether he professed to be the promised Messiah; as he presumed to preach and collect disciples, without authority from them. (*Marg. Ref.* u. x. —*Notes, Matt.* xxi. 23—32. *Luke* vii. 18—35.) To this, John answered in the most explicit manner, that he was not the Messiah. Being further interrogated whether he were Elias, or Elijah, whom the Jews expected to come *personally* from heaven, before the Messiah made his appearance, he declared that he was not. He was not personally Elias, he was not Elias, in the sense of those who proposed the question; though he came " in the spirit " and power " of that zealous reformer: and, though he was " a prophet, yea more than a prophet," yet he was not Jeremiah, or any one of their old prophets risen from the dead, as they expected. (*Marg. Ref.* y—a.—*Notes, Mal.* iv. 4—6. *Matt.* xi. 7—15. xvi. 13—16. xvii. 10—13. *Rev.* xx. 4—6.) When they further demanded who he was, that they might carry some determinate answer to the sanhedrim; by which they were sent; he referred them to a prophecy concerning him, which has been considered. (*Notes, Is.* xl. 3—8. *Matt.* iii. 3.) He was " the voice of " a herald in the desert, calling upon men to prepare the " way of JEHOVAH," who was about to come among them: (*Notes, Luke* i. 11—17. 76—79:) and when, as " a voice," he had signified the mind of the Lord, who spake by him, he should vanish and be no more considered. But the persons sent at this time were Pharisees, and very tenacious of their ancient customs and traditions; and they did not know that this prophecy was parallel to that of Malachi, to which they had referred: they therefore proceeded to demand of John, why he baptized his own countrymen, and made disciples, if he were neither the Messiah, nor Elias, nor an old prophet risen again. To this he replied, that he baptized the people with water, as a profession of repentance, and an outward sign of the spiritual blessings to be conferred on them by the Messiah, who had not indeed yet publickly avowed himself; but he was in the midst of them though they knew him not, and was ready to enter on his work. (*Notes, Matt.* iii. 5, 6. 11, 12.) Indeed this was the Person, who, as he had always declared, " was preferred before him; " being in fact so much John's superior in dignity, authority, and excellency, that he was not worthy to perform the lowest menial service for him. (*Marg. Ref.* b—l.—*Notes*, 15. *Luke* iii. 15—17.)—*That prophet.* (25) ' They evidently distin- ' guished *that prophet,* of whom they enquired, from ' Christ: the opinion, therefore, of Chrysostom, Cyril, and ' Theophylact, does not displease me. They declare that ' the Jews were under an error, ... supposing, ... not only ' that Elias, ... but also that " the prophet like unto Moses," ' being distinct from the Messiah, would come before him. ' This seems to be confirmed by what follows. (vi. 14. vii.

28 These things were done in ᵐ Bethabara beyond Jordan, ⁿ where John was baptizing.

29 ¶ The next day John seeth Jesus coming unto him, and saith,

ʷ x. 40. Judg. vii. 24, *Bethabah.* xii. 5. n Isl. 23.

° Behold the Lamb of God, ᵖ which ᵏ taketh away the sin of the world.

* M. Gen. xxii 7, 8. Ex. xii. 3 &c. Num.xxviii 3—10. 1s. liii. 7.

Acts viii. 32. 1 Pet. i⁰. 19. Rev. v. 6. 8. 12. 13. vi. 1. 16. vii. 9, 10. 14. 17. xii. 11. xiii. 8. xiv. 1. 4. 10. xv. 8. xvii. 14. xix. 7. 9. xxi. 9. 14. 22, 23. 27. xxii. 1—3.　p Is. liii. 11. Hos. xiv. 2. Matt. xx. 28. 1 Cor. xv. 3. 2 Cor. v. 21. Gal. i. 4. iii. 13. 1 Tim. ii. 6. Tit. ii. 14. Heb. i. 3. ii. 17. ix. 28. 1 Pet. ii. 24. iii. 18. 1 John ii. 2. iii. 5. iv. 10. Rev. l. 5.　* Or, *beareth.* Ex. xxviii. 38. Lev. x. 17. xvi. 21, 22. Num. xviii. 1. 23.

' 40, 41.)' Beza. (*Notes, Deut.* xviii. 15—19. *Acts* iii. 22—26. vii. 37—43.) Either " the prophet like unto "Moses," was intended, or one of the ancient prophets as arisen from the dead: for John would hardly have denied, that he was " a prophet." (*Marg. Luke* i. 76.) It is not, however, clear, that any particular prophet was meant : yet it is evident, that the Jews in general paid far less regard to those scriptures, which related to the prophetical and priestly office of the Messiah, than they did to those, which foretold him as a glorious King: and this made way for many of the errors, and carnal expectations, which led them to reject " the Lord of glory."—Bethabara seems to have been the place, where Israel passed over Jordan into Canaan : though some think it was a distinct place, and stream of waters, to the east of Jordan. (*Marg. Ref.* m, n.) Several manuscripts read Bethany : not the place, where Martha, Mary, and Lazarus resided ; but another place of the same name, as it is supposed, near Jordan.

He confessed. (20) 'Ωμολογησε. ix. 22. xii. 42. *Matt.* vii. 23. x. 32. xiv. 7. *Luke* xii. 8.—Εξομολογεω. See on *Matt.* xi. 25.—*Beyond Jordan.* (28) Περαν τυ Ιορδανυ. iii. 26. x. 40. *Matt.* iv. 15. 25. xix. 1. *Mark* iii. 8.—*Gen.* l. 10, 11. *Deut.* iii. 8. 20. 25. *Josh.* i. 15. ii. 10. v. 1. *Sept.* ' Περαν. *Non* ' solum *trans, ultra,* sed etiam *cis, juxta, ad.*' Schleusner. —The preposition evidently admits of either interpretation : but the name " Bethabara" favours the former.

V. 29. The preceding testimony of John is supposed :o have been given, at the time during which Jesus was :e mpted in the wilderness, and just before his return. On .h e next day John saw Jesus coming to him ; and he immediately pointed him out to his hearers, as " the Lamb ' of God.'¹ (*Marg. Ref.*—*Notes, Gen.* xxii. 7, 8. *Is.* liii. 4—7. *Acts* viii. 32—35. 1 *Pet.* i. 17—21, v. 19. *Rev.* v. 5—14. vii. 9—17. xii. 7—12, v. 11. xiii. 8—10, v. 8. xix. 7, 8.) The paschal lamb, in the shedding and sprinkling of its blood, the roasting and eating of its flesh, and all the attendant circumstances, aptly represented the redemption of man by the death of Christ, and the salvation of penitent sinners by faith in his blood : and those lambs, which were sacrificed every morning and evening, as expiations of the sins of Israel, were evident types of " the " Lamb slain from the foundation of the world." (*Notes, Ex.* xii. 3—10. xxix. 38—41. 1 *Cor.* v. 6—8.) The emblem of a lamb might indeed denote the purity, gentleness, harmlessness, and patience of the Redeemer, and his valuableness and usefulness, living and dying ; but it especially marked his fitness to be a spotless sacrifice to God for the sins of his people. He is called " the Lamb of " God ;" as he was a sacrifice which God himself both required, provided, and accepted. As a Lamb he " taketh " away sin," by being made an expiatory oblation, that justice might be satisfied, and yet the sinner pardoned. The lambs, sacrificed according to the law, were appropriated to the nation of Israel : but the atonement of Christ, being of infinite value, extends its efficacy to all

nations, and to every generation of men. A lamb could not " take away sin," except by becoming a sacrifice : and why should John call Christ " the Lamb of God," in this connexion, if he did not really atone for the sins of men, by bearing the punishment due to them ?—' Grotius ' refers this to the reformation of men's lives ; whereas it ' plainly respects the Lamb slain as a piacular Victim, to " redeem us to God by his blood." ...To illustrate this, ' let it be noted, that when a sacrifice was oifered for sin, ' he that brought it laid his hand upon the head of the ' victim, according to the command of God ; (*Lev.* i. 4. ' iii. 2. iv. 4 ;) and by that rite transferred his sins upon ' the victim, who is said to take them upon him, and to carry ' them away. Accordingly, in the daily sacrifice of the ' lamb, the stationary men, saith Dr. Lightfoot, who were ' the representatives of the people, laid their hands on the ' lambs thus offered for them. ... When therefore the Bap- ' tist had said, He baptized them for the remission of ' sins ; he here shews them by what means that remission ' was to be obtained.' *Whitby.*—' We are often told, ' that ... repentance and reformation are fully sufficient to ' restore the most abandoned sinners to the favour of a ' just and merciful God, and to avert the punishment due ' to their offences. But what does the great herald and ' forerunner of Christ say to this ? He came professedly ' as *a preacher of repentance.* ...If then repentance alone ' had sufficient efficacy for the expiation of sin, surely we ' should have heard this from him who came on purpose ' to preach repentance. But what is the case ? Does he ' tell us that repentance *alone* will take away the guilt of ' our transgressions, and justify us in the eyes of our ' Maker ? Quite the contrary. Notwithstanding the great ' stress he justly lays on the indispensable necessity of ' repentance ; yet he tells his followers at the same time, ' that it was to Christ *only,* and to his death, that they ' were to look for the pardon of their sins. " Behold," ' says he, " the Lamb of God which taketh away the sin " " of the world." And again, " He that believeth on " " the Son hath everlasting life ; and he that believeth " " not shall not see life ; but the wrath of God abideth " " upon him." ' *Bp. Porteus.*—Thus the Saviour " taketh " away the sin of the world," by removing every hinderance to the forgiveness of the sin, original and actual, of all men throughout the world, who rely on him by humble faith. Through his atoning sacrifice, it consists with the glory of God to pardon all persons who thus trust in him. On this ground any man may come to " the throne of grace" for all the blessings of salvation, nor does he want any other plea, than that " Christ has died, yea, rather is risen " again, and ever liveth to make intercession for us.' (*Notes, Rom.* viii. 32—34. *Heb.* vii. 23—28, 1 *John* ii. 1, 2.) In virtue of his atonement, Jesus takes away all the guilt of every believer, and " buries it as in the depth of the " sea," giving him peace of conscience and hope in God ; and likewise by that grace, which is vouchsafed to sinners through the same sacrifice, he takes away the power, the

30 This is he, of whom I said, ^q After me cometh a man which is preferred before me; for he was before me.

31 And ^r I knew him not: but that he should be made manifest to Israel, ^s therefore am I come baptizing with water.

32 And John bare record, saying, ^t I saw the Spirit descending from heaven like a dove, and it abode upon him.

33 And ^u I knew him not: but he that sent me to baptize with water, the same said unto me, Upon whom thou shalt see the Spirit descending and remaining on him, ^x the same is he which baptizeth with the Holy Ghost.

34 And I saw and bare record that ^y this is the Son of God.

35 ¶ Again the next day after, John stood, ^z and two of his disciples:

36 And looking upon Jesus as he walked, he saith, ^a Behold the Lamb of God!

37 And the two disciples heard him speak; ^b and they followed Jesus.

38 Then Jesus ^c turned, and saw them following, and saith unto them, What seek ye? They said unto him, Rabbi, (which is to say, being interpreted, Master,) ^d where dwellest thou?

39 He saith unto them, ^e Come and see. They came and saw where he dwelt, and abode with him that day: for it was about the tenth hour.

40 One of the two which heard John speak, and followed him, was ^f Andrew, Simon Peter's brother.

41 He ^g first findeth his own brother Simon, and saith unto him, We have found ^m the Messias, which is, being interpreted, the ^h Christ.

42 And he brought him to Jesus. And when Jesus beheld him, he said, ⁿ Thou art Simon ^o the son of Jona: thou shalt be ^p called Cephas, which is by interpretation ⁱ A stone.

---

love, and the pollution of sin; yea, in due time the very existence of it from the heart. (Notes, Mic. vii. 18—20. Rom. viii. 1, 2.)—This general proposal and declaration of the death of Christ, as a common benefit to all, throughout the whole world, who desire to avail themselves of it, is entirely consistent with a particular purpose of God, in making "his people willing in the day of his power," who would otherwise have perished in pride, impenitence, and unbelief. Accordingly, John called on all his hearers, to "behold the Lamb of God;" to observe, consider, and depend on him to take away their sins, and to baptize them with the Holy Spirit.

Behold.] Ib. 36. 47. xi. 36. xix. 5. 14. Matt. xxv. 20. 22. 25. Jam. iii. 3.—' Proprie de rei præsentis exhibitione et ' demonstratione.' Schleusner.—It bespeaks attentive contemplation, accompanied with surprise or admiration.—Taketh away.] Αιρει. ii. 16. xi. 39. xv. 2. Luke vi. 29, 30. 1 John iii. 5.

V. 30—34. Jesus and John were nearly related, and the mother of Jesus had been intimately acquainted with John's parents; yet it was so ordered in Providence, that John did not personally know Jesus. They lived indeed very distant from each other; for Jesus was brought up at Nazareth in Galilee, John in Judea, probably at or near Hebron; (Note, Luke i. 34—38, v. 36. 39—45;) yet it seems to have been by special design, that they did not become acquainted at the publick feasts. Indeed, when John had borne testimony to Jesus, we do not find that they ever afterwards met together. Had they been long and closely united in friendship, as it might previously have been expected, John's testimony would have been rendered more equivocal and exceptionable: but though

John knew, by immediate revelation, that his ministry and baptism were entirely subservient to Jesus the Messiah's being manifested to the people; yet he seems never to have seen him, till he applied to him for baptism; and then it is evident he was made known to him, by an immediate divine suggestion. But when he saw the Spirit of God "descending and abiding on him," all former intimations were fully ratified to him, and he thenceforth bare open testimony to him, as "the Son of God," and the promised Messiah.—'Christ is proved to be the Son of ' God, by the descent of the Holy Ghost, by the Father's ' voice, and by the testimony of John.' Beza. (Marg. Ref.—Notes, 18. iii. 27—36. Matt. iii. 11—17. Luke iii. 15—17. 21, 22, v. 21.)—He was before, &c. (30) See on Note, 15. Should be made manifest. (31) Φανερωθη. ii. 11. iii. 21. vii. 4. ix. 3. xvii. 6. xxi. 1. 14. Mark iv. 22. 1 Cor. iv. 5. 2 Cor. v. 10, 11. Eph. v. 13. 2 Tim. i. 10. Tit. i. 3. 1 John i. 2. iii. 2. 5. 8. iv. 9, et al.

V. 35—42. The persons here spoken of were John's disciples, before they followed Jesus. While John stood and discoursed with them, Jesus came near them, and John immediately pointed him out to them, as "the Lamb "of God." (Marg. Ref. b.—Note, 29.) Accordingly they followed Jesus, as desirous of becoming his disciples, or of being acquainted with him. To facilitate and encourage their application, Jesus turned to enquire what they sought: and, addressing him by the honourable title of Rabbi, or Teacher, they asked where he dwelt; as they wanted to come to him for instruction. He therefore invited them to accompany him; (for he seems to have had some retired lodging near the place where John preached;) and, as it was but two hours before sun-set, they spent the re

2 o 3

43 ¶ The day following Jesus would go forth into Galilee, and findeth Philip, and saith unto him, Follow me.

44 Now Philip was of Bethsaida, the city of Andrew and Peter.

45 Philip findeth Nathanael, and saith unto him, We have found him, of whom Moses in the law and the prophets did write, Jesus of Nazareth, the son of Joseph.

46 And Nathanael said unto him, Can there any good thing come out of Nazareth? Philip saith unto him, Come and see.

47 Jesus saw Nathanael coming to him, and saith of him, Behold an Israelite indeed, in whom is no guile!

48 Nathanael saith unto him, Whence knowest thou me? Jesus answered and said unto him, Before that Philip called thee, when thou wast under the fig-tree, I saw thee.

49 Nathanael answered and saith unto him, Rabbi, thou art the Son of God; thou art the King of Israel.

mainder of the day in attending to his instructive conversation. (*Marg.* and *Marg. Ref.* c—i.) Some think that the evangelist himself was one of these two disciples, but that is uncertain: however, Andrew, Peter's brother, was one of them; who, being fully convinced that Jesus was the promised Messiah, first brought Peter acquainted with him. This was a considerable time, before they were called to a constant attendance on Christ: (*Note, Matt. iv. 12—22:*) for that took place in Galilee; and this was near Bethabara, or the passage of Jordan. It was, however, on this occasion that Jesus, previously intimating his knowledge of Simon, his family and character, surnamed him Cephas, or Peter, the one being Syriack, the other Greek, and by interpretation meaning *a stone*. (*Marg.* and *Marg. Ref.* k—p.) This denoted the fortitude and firmness, with which he would labour and suffer in the cause of Christ. (*Notes, xxi.—17. Matt. x. 1—4, v. 2. xvi. 17, 18.*)

Rabbi. (38) Ῥαββί. 50. ii. 2. 26. iv. 31. vi. 25. ix. 2. xi. 8. *Matt. xxiii.* 7. *xxvi.* 25. 49. *Mark ix.* 5. xi. 21. xiv. 45.—*Being interpreted.*] Ἑρμηνευομενον. 43. ix. 7. *Heb. vii,* 2.—*Being interpreted.* (41) Μιθερμηνευομενον. *Matt. i.* 23. *Mark v.* 41. xv. 22. 34. *Acts iv.* 36. xiii. 8.

V. 43—46. When the time was arrived, at which our Lord purposed to go forth into Galilee, in order to enter on his publick ministry, he found Philip, and called him to a stated attendance on him. Philip was an inhabitant of Bethsaida, where Peter and Andrew at first resided, though they afterwards removed to Capernaum; and perhaps he was brought acquainted with Jesus by their means. (*Marg. Ref.* q—s.) Philip not long afterwards met with Nathanael, who seems to have been his intimate friend: and in a very earnest manner he informed him, that they had found the promised Messiah, concerning whom Moses and the prophets had written those extraordinary things, which had excited the expectation of him, that generally prevailed; and that Jesus, who had hitherto lived at Nazareth, the son of Joseph, was assuredly the great Redeemer of Israel. But Nathanael, though a Galilean, had so bad an opinion of Nazareth, that he could not think it likely so great a blessing, or indeed "any good thing," could arise from that wicked place. This opinion, as to the general character of the Nazarenes, seems to have been well founded: but it was going too far, to suppose that "no good thing" could thence arise; and this prejudice was calculated to set him against Christ and his doctrine. (*Marg. Ref.* t—z.) Philip, however, very prudently intreated him to go with

him, and judge for himself; and Nathanael, being a candid pious man, readily complied. Philip himself seems not to have known that Jesus was born at Bethlehem, or to have heard of his miraculous conception.

V. 47—51. As Nathanael approached, our Lord at once said concerning him, "Behold an Israelite indeed, in whom "there is no guile:" he is a genuine son of Israel, a servant and worshipper of JEHOVAH, an honest upright person, a man of faith and prayer, a real Israelite; while most of his neighbours have nothing but the name and outward form of Israelites. (*Marg. Ref.* a, b.—*Notes, Gen. xxxii. 27, 28. Ps. lxxiii. 1. Rom. ii. 25—29. Gal. vi. 15, 16. Phil. iii. 1—7.*) "In whom there is no gnile:" his profession of religion was not leavened with hypocrisy; he was the same man before God, as he appeared to be among men: and his general conduct was devoid of insincerity, dissimulation, and dishonesty. In short, he was a sound character, a really upright godly man. (*Note, Ps. xxxii. 1, 2.*)—This decided attestation of Jesus greatly surprised Nathanael; and, with a consistent frankness, he enquired, whence he had his information, or by what means he knew him. To this Jesus replied, that he had seen him, and witnessed what passed, when he was "under the fig-"tree," before Philip called him. Probably, Nathanael was then engaged in devotion, and pouring out his heart with peculiar fervency before God: perhaps he was seeking direction concerning "the Hope and Consolation of "Israel," in some secret retirement, where he knew that no human eye observed him. (*Marg. Ref.* c.—*Notes, ii. 24, 25. Matt. vi. 6. Acts x. 3—8, v. 4.*) This declaration, however, evidenced to his mind, that our Lord knew the secrets of his heart; so that his prejudices vanished at once, and, in astonishment at what he had heard, he confessed with the utmost confidence, that Jesus was "the "Son of God and King of Israel." (*Marg. Ref.* d—f.— iii. 16. iv. 28—30. v. 20—30. ix. 35—38. x. 26—31. xi. 20—27. xx. 30, 31. Ps. ii. 4—12. Matt. xvi. 13—16.) Our Lord, then, in honour of his faith, assured him, that as he had believed by means of this single discovery of his glory, he should be favoured with the sight of still greater things: for "hereafter," or *henceforth*, he would see "the "heaven opened, and angels ascending and descending on "him, the Son of man;" for they would minister to him in human nature as their glorious Lord. This may refer to Jacob's ladder, which typified Christ as the medium of communication between heaven and earth; (*Marg. Ref.*

3 o 4

50 Jesus answered and said unto him, *Because I said unto thee, I saw thee under the fig-tree, believest thou? ʰthou shalt see greater things than these.

51 And he saith unto him, ¹Verily, verily, I say unto you, ᵏHereafter ye shall see heaven open, ¹and the angels of God ascending and descending upon ᵐthe Son of man.

*Luke xxii. 43. xxiv. 4. Acts i. 10. 2 Thes. i. 7—9. 1 Tim. iii. 16. Heb. i. 14. Jude 14. m iii. 13, 14. v. 27. xii. 28, 24. Dan. vii. 13, 14. Zech. xiii. 7. Matt. iii. 6. xvi. 13—16. 27, 28. xxv. 31. xxvi. 24. Mark xiv. 62. Luke xxii. 69.

i—m.—*Notes, Gen.* xxviii. 12—17;) and it may be explained figuratively to signify the whole course of Christ's miracles, till his ascension into heaven, which was testified to the apostles by angels: but perhaps there may also be a reference to his future appearance, with all his holy angels, to raise the dead, and to judge the world.—Some think that Nathanael was also called Bartholomew, and was one of the apostles: and some, that he was the same as Matthias. (*Acts* i. 26.)
Indeed. (48) Αληθως. iv. 42. vi. 14. 55. *Matt.* xiv. 33. xxvii. 54, *et al.—Guile.*] Δολος. *Matt.* xxvi. 4. *Mark* vii. 22. *Acts* xiii. 10. *2 Cor.* xii. 16. *Rev.* xiv. 5.—*Verily, verily.* (52) Αμην, αμην. iii. 3. 5. 11. v. 19. 24, 25. vi. 26. 32. 47. 53, *et al.* See on *Matt.* vi. 5.—*Hereafter.*] Απ' αρτι. xiii. 19. xiv. 7. *Matt.* xxvi. 29. 64. *Rev.* xiv. 13. 'Απτι ... 'cum απο ... reddendum est *ab hoc tempore, post hac, exinde.*' Schleusner.

PRACTICAL OBSERVATIONS.
V. 1—5.
While we carefully avoid the error of those, who seem to place the whole of religion in an exactly orthodox creed; and who sacrifice every Christian temper, and violate the plain precepts of scripture, in zealously and vehemently contending for doctrinal sentiments and expressions; we should, at least, equally beware of the opposite extreme of treating the doctrines of scripture, as speculative points of comparatively little consequence. To the person of Christ, as the Foundation of all true godliness, " bear all " the apostles and prophets witness;" yea, God himself has testified, " that he sent his Son to be the Saviour of " the world." Let us then beware of those, who degrade Him whom the Spirit of truth and holiness delights to glorify: and while we allow " the mystery to be, without " controversy, great " and inexplicable, that " God was " manifest in the flesh;" let us still hold it fast, yea, glory in it, as " the great mystery of godliness," with which all true piety, in the heart and life of sinful man, is inseparably connected. Let us never think of Him, whose name is called " The WORD of God," as any other, than " God " over all, blessed for evermore;" as subsisting before all worlds " with God," and co-equal with yet distinct from the eternal Father. Standing on these plain testimonies of scripture, without indulging vain reasonings or requiring curious explanations; let us avoid with equal caution, those who allow indeed the distinct personality, but deny or interpret away the proper Deity, of " the " Word;" and those who zealously assert his Deity, but seem to lose sight of his distinct personality, and thus unwarily verge to the sentiments which they seem to oppose. It is not for us to comprehend such exalted subjects, or to resolve all questions about them: but we can prove by conclusive arguments, which no infidel ever yet was, or ever will be, able to answer, that the scripture is a divine revelation: and we can fully shew these mysterious doctrines to be contained in the express language of revelation. By faith we receive this testimony, and by grace we derive nourishment from it to our souls. But it is the most unreasonable thing in the world, to reject the testimony of the infinite God, concerning his own mysterious existence; when every process of nature (as we call it) baffles our feeble powers; and when the best philosophers allow, that we can only know that things are so, but cannot comprehend the manner *how*, or the reason *why*, they are so. Indeed he who knows the worth of his soul, the evil of sin, and other things pertaining to our present fallen condition, can see no ground of hope, but in the power, truth, and love of him, " who made all things, and without whom " was not any thing made that was made." This will be his encouragement " to hope and not be afraid, because " God is become his Salvation;" (*Notes, Is.* xii. 1—3, *v.* 2;) and " the Life " is become " the Light of life " to fallen " men." Nothing can be more evident than these truths, as they are revealed in scripture, by which the personal Word of God speaks to us; but this " Light still " shineth in darkness, and the darkness apprehendeth it " not." Every absurd system or detached imagination, and conjecture of soothing error, from the pit of darkness, is preferred to it, as more congenial to the pride and lusts of men: thus " they walk on still in darkness," and neither understand nor value " the Light of the world!" May we then pray without ceasing, that our eyes may be opened to behold this Light, that we may walk in it; and thus be " made wise unto eternal salvation by faith in Jesus " Christ."

V. 6—13.
Many have, in different ages, been " sent from God to " bear witness to the truth," that " all men through them " might believe;" and these have " shone as lights in the " world:" but every one of them has been ready to confess, that all his light was a reflection of the beams of " the Sun of Righteousness," " the true Light, which en- " lighteneth every man that cometh into the world:" and all the boasted illumination, which is set up in opposition to him, will infallibly lead men down to everlasting darkness and despair. But what numbers, not only of his creatures, but even of his professed disciples, refuse to welcome the condescending Saviour of the world! Too wise to submit to his teaching, too proud of their goodness to rely on his merits, too attached to their own will to be subject to his commands, they reject him in each of his offices; or, like Gallio, they " care for none of these " things:" and should he come in person again on earth, he would be despised by numbers, who could see no glory in him, and who would feel no need of him. But there are those at present also, who have other views and desires; who, conscious of their ignorance, guilt, pollution, and slavery to sin and Satan, gladly receive him as their Prophet, Priest, King, Redeemer, Physician, and Saviour; believe his word, and rely on his truth, power, and love. He is to them " the Pearl of great price;" they would " sell

CHAP. II.

. At a marriage in Cana, Jesus turns water into wine, 1—11. He goes to Capernaum, 12; and thence to Jerusalem, where he drives the buyers and sellers out

of the temple, 13—17. He predicts his own death and resurrection, as the proof his authority, 18—22. Many believe in him because of his miracles ; but he does not commit himself to them, as " knowing what " was in man," 23—25.

" all to purchase him;" and, having once received him, they are ever after desirous of renewing and ratifying that important transaction. To this chosen remnant the Saviour gives the glorious privilege of becoming the children of God; and he will surely preserve them, and prepare them for the everlasting inheritance reserved for them in heaven. These happy souls are not found. in one family, sect, or nation; they are not selected by the partiality of ministers or pious friends; they are not chosen because of their previous excellency; but they ·are " born of God." Then they begin to fear God, to mourn for· sin, to believe, to hope, to pray, to perceive the preciousness of Christ, and gladly to embrace his salvation.

V. 14—18.

To unbelievers, there appears in Christ " no form or " comeliness, no beauty that they should desire him : " but all who truly believe, adore the infinite condescension of the eternal " Word, who became flesh to tabernacle " among us." They discern some glimpses of his glory, as of " the only Begotten of the Father, full of grace and " truth :" they value " the unsearchable riches" and inexhaustible fulness, which are laid up in him : (Note, Eph. iii. 8 :) they see that " He ·is the Chief among ten thou- " sand, and altogether lovely;" worthy to be admired, adored, and loved, far beyond all the sons of earth and heaven; and that " from his fulness all have received." They therefore consider prophets, apostles, martyrs, and saints, as so many monuments erected to the Redeemer's glory, and so many encouragements to apply to him, who is able to render them also wise, holy, useful, and happy ; and to furnish them with every kind and degree of grace, which may enable them to " shine as lights in the world," and to live to the glory of his name. Indeed, we ought highly to value every discovery of the perfections, truth, and will of JEHOVAH : his " law is holy, just, and good," and was given for most important purposes ; and we should endeavour to make the proper use of it. But we cannot from it derive pardon, righteousness, or strength : it may recommend, and then teach us to " adorn, the doctrine of " God our Saviour," but it cannot supply the place of it. No mercy comes from God to sinners, but through Jesus Christ ; " no man can come to the Father but by him ;" no man can know God, except as the only begotten Son reveals him. Ignorance, delusion, condemnation, and unmitigated wrath, must be the portion of every man, who rejects the Word and Son of God; the great Substance and Centre of all the promises; and the Life and Soul of all doctrines, ordinances, and precepts whatsoever. (Notes, 2 Cor. iii. 7—11. 17, 18.)

V. 19—34.

Let us regard the testimony of John the Baptist. He was " filled with the Holy Ghost from his mother's " womb;" he was " great in the sight of God," and one of the most excellent of mere men : yet he had nothing

to say " of himself," save that he was the voice of a herald, to proclaim the Saviour's glory; being " unworthy " even to loose the latchet of his shoes." He knew that Jesus was " before him," as the eternal Word; that he would for ever be " preferred before him " and all creatures ; and that he alone could pardon sin, or baptize with the Holy Ghost. He thought he could not enough abase himself, or exalt his Lord: he only desired to prepare his ways, and to manifest him to Israel. Let us then not at all regard those, who exalt themselves and degrade Christ: for their light is darkness, and their wisdom madness, being directly in opposition to the wisdom of God, and " the " Light of the world." But let us especially behold Jesus " as the Lamb of God, who taketh away the sin of the " world." Sin must be taken away, or sinners must be ruined for ever : " God hath provided himself a Lamb for " a burnt offering," through whose infinitely valuable atonement, he can be " just and the justifier of the un- " godly." Let sinners then behold and trust in him : let believers look to him continually for renewing pardon, peace, strength, encouragement, motives, instructions, righteousness ; and a perfect example of holy meekness, patience, and love. (Note, Heb. xii. 2, 3.) Thus guilt will be removed from the conscience, and sin will be taken away from the heart, till no more remain there. And while we look to him for pardon, let us also earnestly seek to be made like him, and to partake of his baptism by the Holy Ghost, that we may abound in all holy fruits to the glory of his name.

V. 35—51.

The ministers of Christ must never desire to make disciples to themselves, but to him : they, who are enquiring after salvation, must hearken to those teachers, who direct them to " the Lamb of God," and distinguish them from all others : and they, who have known him to their comfort and profit, should endeavour to recommend him to others ; that thus each believer may bring his brother, his friend, his children, or his neighbours : and so, these private exertions combining to draw men's attention to the testimony of ministers ; the light may diffuse itself more widely, in families, cities, and countries. (Notes, Is. ii. 2— 5. 2 Thes, iii. 1—5, v. 1.)—All, who desire to profit by the word of God, must beware of narrow prejudices against places, or denominations of men, from which even pious Christians are by no means exempt : they should come, and examine for themselves; and then perhaps they will find good where they expected none.—But let us seek and pray to be " Israelites indeed, in whom there is no guile," truly Christians, approved of Christ himself. Defects and infirmities are found in all ; but hypocrisy and guile belong not to a believer's character. He does not profess one thing with his lips, and think another thing in his heart; he is not a double-minded or deceitful man : it is pecu liar to him, to allow of nothing before God which he dis · avows before men, to pretend to nothing before men, which God knows that he does not aim to perform. He is con-

CANA.

JOHN ii. 1—11; iv. 46—54; xxi. 2.

ᵃ i. 43.
ᵇ Gen. i. 27, 28.
ii. 18—25. Ps.
cxxviii. 1—
Prov. xviii. 22.
xix. 14. xxxi. 10
—12. Eph. v. 30
—33. 1 Tim. iv.
1—3. Heb. xiii.
4.
ᶜ iv. 46. xxi. 2.
Josh. xix. 28.
Kanah.
ᵈ Matt. xii. 19.
Luke vii. 34—
38. 1 Cor. vii.
30, x. 31. Col.
iii. 17. Rev. iii.
20.
ᵉ Matt. x. 40—
41. xxv. 40,
47.
ᶠ Ps. cix. 15. Ec.
x. 19. Is. xxiv. 11. Matt. xxvi. 28, 29.
27. xx. 13. 15. Matt. xv. 28.
2 Cor. v. 16. Gal. ii. 5, 6.

And ᵃ the third day there was ᵇ a marriage in ᶜ Cana of Galilee; and the mother of Jesus was there.

2 And ᵈ both Jesus was called, and ᵉ his disciples, to the marriage.

3 And when ᶠ they wanted wine, the mother of Jesus saith unto him, ᶿ They have no wine.

4 Jesus saith unto her, ʰ Woman, ⁱ what have I to do with thee? ᵏ mine hour is not yet come.

ᵍ xi. 3. Phil. iv. 6.　　ʰ xix. 26,
1 Deut. xxxiii. 9. 2 Sam. xvi. 10. Luke ii. 49.
k vii. 6. 30. viii. 20. xii. 23. xiii. 1. Ec. iii. 1.

5 His mother saith unto the servants, ˡ Whatsoever he saith unto you, do it.

6 And there were set there six waterpots of stone, ᵐ after the manner of the purifying of the Jews, containing two or three firkins apiece.

7 Jesus saith unto them, ⁿ Fill the water-pots with water. And they filled them up to the brim.

8 And he saith unto them, ᵒ Draw out now, and bear unto the governorᵖ of the feast. And they bare it.

ˡ xv. 14. Gen. vi.
22. Judg. xiii
14. Luke vi. 46.
—49. Acts ix. 6.
ᵐ Heb. v. 9. xi. 8.
2—6. Eph. v.
26. Heb. vi. 2.
ix. 10. 19. x. 22.
ⁿ 3. 5. Num. xxi.
3—9. Josh. vi.
3—5. 1 Kings
xvii. 13. 2 Kings
iv. 2—6. v. 10—
14. Mark xi. 2
—6. xiv. 12—17.
ᵒ Acts viii. 26, &c.
ᵖ b. Prov. iii. 5, 6.

---

sciously, as well as by confession, a poor sinner, who has no hope of deliverance from condemnation or pollution, but through the mercy and grace of God in Christ: and whilst he seeks free salvation, he really aims, and desires, and earnestly endeavours to lead a sober, righteous, and godly life; and is continually abased before God, because he "cannot do the things that he would." He "who "seeth in secret" observes and approves this disposition, and hears the retired supplications which it dictates. He marks the humble believer,when beseeching him to teach him his truth and will; and he will evince that he graciously accepts of such petitions. Thus the believer obtains "the "witness in himself," that "Jesus is the Son of God, and "the King of Israel;" and he will attain continually to fuller discoveries of his glory, and larger communications from him; till he learns to "love his appearing," "in "his own glory, and in the glory of the Father, with all "his holy angels, when he will render unto every man "according to his works."

NOTES.

Chap. II. V. 1—5. On the third day after our Lord's interview with Nathanael, or after his return into Galilee, (i. 43. 51,) a marriage was solemnized at Cana, a small town in that neighbourhood, "called Caua of Galilee" to distinguish it from another, in the lot of Ephraim. (11. iv. 46. xxi. 2. Josh. xvi. 8. xix. 28.)—Probably, Mary was nearly related to one of the parties, for she seems to have been present as one of the family: and as Joseph is not mentioned, either on this occasion or afterwards, we may suppose that he died before our Lord entered on his publick ministry.—Jesus had now collected a few disciples, and both he and they were invited to the marriage-feast: and, in order to honour God's institution, as well as to shew the free and social spirit of his religion, he was pleased to accept of the invitation. (Marg..Ref. b. d.) Perhaps, they had not been previously expected, and our Lord's presence might also draw others thither to hear his conversation; so that all the wine provided for the occasion was nearly spent: and it is probable, that the persons concerned were not affluent, nor well able to bear any additional expense. Mary therefore stated the case to her Son, as under some concern about it, and with expectation of his providing a miraculous supply. Some expositors think, that he had before wrought miracles in private, to supply the necessities of the family: but this is highly improba-

ble; and the circumstances of his conception and birth, could not but lead his mother to expect extraordinary things from him, now that he had entered on his publick ministry. But Jesus replied to her in a manner, which shewed that she was in some measure reprehensible, in supposing that her authority or influence was to be employed in directing his conduct as the Messiah. There is not indeed the least disrespect in the word, "Woman," with which he addressed her; as the greatest princesses were accosted, even by their own servants, in the same manner among the ancients: and he afterwards used it, when speaking from the cross with the most endeared affection and tenderness; (Note, xix. 25—27;) yet the whole reply was an evident and intentional discouragement to her, from interposing on such occasions. In this respect, "what had he to do with her," or with any other? None must dictate to him, when or for whom he should work miracles: (Marg. Ref. h—k.—Notes, Matt. xii. 46—50 Mark iii. 20, 21. 31—35. Luke ii. 41—52. 2 Cor. v. 16.) —"My time is not yet come." The time of our Lord's open appearance as the Messiah was not yet completely arrived, and a publick miracle might not have been expedient.—The occasion, on which this miracle was wrought, the miracle itself, and this answer of our Lord to Mary, seem to have been expressly intended, as a prophetical protest against the superstitions and idolatries of the church of Rome; especially against two leading branches of that system, namely, the disparaging and prohibiting of marriage, and the worship of the Virgin Mary. Even to this day there are, very large multitudes who call on her, not to beseech, but to command, her Son, now that he fills the throne of glory; though in his lowest humiliation on earth, he would not allow her even to counsel him in the exercise of his sacred ministry!—Mary, however, did not give up her hope of a miraculous supply, though she saw the propriety of not urging it: she therefore ordered the servants carefully to observe and follow his directions, whatever they might be, or attended with whatever inconvenience. (Marg. Ref. e—i.)

They wanted wine. (3) Ὑστερησαντος τȣ οινȣ. "Wine "failing." Matt. xix. 20. Mark x. 21. Luke xv. 14. xxii. 35. Rom. iii. 23, et al.—Woman. (4) Γυναι. xix. 26. xx. 13. 15. 1 Cor. vii. 16.—What have I to do with thee?] Τι εμοι και σοι; Matt. viii. 29. Mark i. 24. v. 7.—2 Sam. xvi. 10. xix. 22. Sept.

V. 6—11. The Jews had vessels in their houses, in

9 When the ruler of the feast had tasted the water that was made wine, and knew not whence it was, (but the servants which drew the water knew,) the governor of the feast called the

p Gen. xliii. 34. bridegroom,

q Prov. ix. 1—6. Cant. v. 1. 16—18. Luke xvi. 25. Rev. vii. 16, 17. 10 And saith unto him, Every man at the beginning doth set forth good

r 1 Tim. Ex. iv. 9. vii. 10—21. Ec. ix. 7. Mal. ii. 2. 2 Cor. iv. 17. Gal. iii. 16—19. s 50, 51. iii. 2. 36, 48. wine; *r* and when men have well drunk, then that which is worse : *s but* thou hast kept the good wine until

t 1. 14. v. 23. xii. 41. xix. 9—11. 13. Deut. v. 24. Ps. lxxii. 19. xcvi. & Is. xl. 5. 2 Cor. iii. 18. iv. 6. u xi. 15. xx. 30. 31. 1 John v. 13. now.

11 This *t* beginning of miracles *t* did Jesus in Cana of Galilee, and *t* manifested forth his glory ; *u* and his disciples believed on him.

12 After this he went down to *x* Capernaum, he, and his mother, *y* and his brethren, and his disciples ; and they continued there not many days.

x vi. 17. Matt. iv. 13. xi. 23. vi. 3—5. Matt. xiii. 55. y Mark vi. 3. Acts i. 13, 14. 1 Cor. iv. 5. Gal. i. 19.

13 ¶ And the Jews' *z* passover was at hand ; and Jesus went up to Jerusalem,

z 22. v. 1. vi. 4. xi. 55. Ex. xii. 6—14. Num. xxviii. 16—25. Deut. xvi. 1—8. 16. Luke ii. 41.

14 And *a* found in the temple those that sold oxen and sheep and doves, and the changers of money sitting :

a Deut. xiv. 23—26. Matt. xxi. 12. Mark xi. 15. Luke xix. 45. 46.

15 And when he had made a scourge of small cords, *b* he drove them all out of the temple, and the sheep and the oxen ; and poured out the changers' money, and overthrew the tables ;

b xviii. 11. Zech. iv. 6. 2 Cor. ii. 4.

16 And said unto them that sold

---

which they kept water always ready, for the ceremonial washings prescribed by the law ; as well as for the observance of the purifications, enjoined by the traditions of the elders. It is not agreed how much each of these water-pots contained ; but on the lowest computation the six must have held above a hogshead.—Our Lord was pleased to order the servants to fill these vessels with water, by which they became unexceptionable witnesses to the reality of the miracle : and, though they had doubtless a variety of other employments on this occasion, and the order might seem ill-timed and to no purpose ; they obeyed without hesitation, and filled the water-pots " to the brim !" As soon as this was done, Jesus directed them to draw from them, and carry it to " the ruler of the feast ; " and they obeyed without making the least objection, drawing out what they had just before put into the vessels as water, and carrying it to " the ruler of the feast," to set before the guests, as wine ! (*Marg. Ref.* m—o.—*Notes, Josh.* vi. 3—5. *Judg.* vii. 4—8. 16—22. *Ez.* xxxvii. 1—10, *vv.* 4—7. 9, 10.)—" The ruler of the feast" seems to have been a person chosen to maintain order on such occasions, as well as to see that all the guests had what they wanted ; and some think that a Levite or priest was generally chosen for that purpose.—When this person therefore had tasted this fresh supply of wine, without knowing how it was procured ; he found it so excellent, that he expressed his surprise to the bridegroom, at his having acted so differently from what others used to do on such occasions : for it was customary to give them good wine, till they had drunk what was sufficient : and then that which was of a smaller and inferior quality, as most suitable to their situation : whereas he had kept the best wine till the last! The original word, which is rendered " have well drunk," is often used for men's drinking to intoxication ; yet learned men have shewn that it does not necessarily imply that idea, but merely a moderate exhilaration consistent with temperance. (*Note, Gen.* xliii. 34.) It may however be further observed, that the words refer to the *general management of feasts*, and not to *any thing which took place on this occasion ;* where we may be sure, every circumstance was conducted with the utmost regard to temperance and propriety.—The remainder of this wine would be an ample recompence to the new-married persons, for the

entertainment of Jesus and his disciples.—This was the beginning of Christ's miracles, by which he " manifested " his glory :" an expression never used concerning the miracles of any prophet or apostle, and which could not properly have been used ; for they were only instruments, the power being of God and for the display of his glory which belonged to him alone : but Jesus wrought by his own power, as Emmanuel, and displayed his " own glory, " as of the only begotten of the Father, full of grace and " truth."—This miracle, however, was not wrought publickly, or generally made known : yet it served to confirm the faith of the disciples in him, as the Son of God and the promised Messiah. (*Marg. Ref.* p—u.)—*Purifying*, &c. (6) On the largest computation of the contents of these vessels ; it must be evident, that they could not supply a sufficiency of water, for the *immersion* of all the guests, on such occasions, as well as for all other purposes of ceremonial and traditional purification : yet these are called *baptisms ;* which is in fact a demonstration, that *baptism* does not always signify *immersion*. (*Notes,* iii. 25, 26. *Mark* vii. 3, 4. *Luke* xi. 37, 38.)

Water-pots. (6) Ὑδριαι. 7. iv. 28. Not elsewhere.—*Firkins.*] Μετρητας. Here only. See *Tables.—To the brim.* (7) Ἑως ανω. ' *Pro ἑως τυ οιλος ανω μερως.*' *Schleusner.—Draw out.* (8) Αντλησατε. 9. iv. 7. 15. Not elsewhere *N. T.—Governor.* xxiv. 13. 20. 43. *Is.* xii. 3. *Sept.—To the governor of the feast.*] Τω αρχιτρικλινω. 9. Here only. Ex αρχων, princeps, τρις, ter, et κλινη, lectus.—*Have well drunk.* (10) Μεθυσθωσι. *Luke* xii. 45. *Eph.* v. 18. 1 *Thes.* v. 7. *Rev.* xvii. 2.—*Gen.* xliii. 34. *Sept.—That which is worse.*] Τον ελασσω. " That which is less," or *smaller*.

V. 12. (*Marg. Ref.*) This preceded John's imprisonment. Our Lord on this occasion visited Capernaum, and continued a few days there, with his disciples and brethren, before he ascended to Jerusalem to keep the approaching passover : but after John was imprisoned, he went to reside at Capernaum.

V. 14—17. This was evidently a distinct transaction from that which has before been considered : (*Notes, Matt* xxi. 12, 13. *Mark* xi. 15—21 :) for it took place on the first passover, after Jesus entered on his publick ministry ; which he almost began and ended, by purging the temple from the mercenary traders, whom the covetous priests and

doves, Take these things hence; *make not ᵈmy Father's house an house of merchandise.

17 And his disciples remembered that it was written, ᵉThe zeal of thine house hath eaten me up.

18 Then answered the Jews, and said unto him, ᶠWhat sign shewest thou unto us, ᵍseeing that thou doest these things?

19 Jesus answered and said unto them, ʰDestroy this temple, ᶦand in three days ᵏI will raise it up.

20 Then said the Jews, Forty and six years was this temple in building, and wilt thou rear it up in three days⸱

21 But ᶦhe spake of the ᵐtemple of his body.

22 When therefore he was risen! from the dead, ⁿhis disciples remembered that he had said this unto them;

rulers encouraged to make a market-place of its courts. Considering the immense number of sacrifices used at the feast of the passover, it must have been a very large market, which was there held, and a great multitude of people must have been assembled and employed: yet Jesus, appearing as a poor man, at that time but little known, without human authority, without attendants or arms, except a scourge made of the small cords which were used in fastening the parts of the pens, or folds, or in other ways confining the cattle, drove them all before him; overturning the tables of those who exchanged foreign for current coin, and clearing the place of them; though it must be supposed that pride, avarice, resentment, and every corrupt passion, would have disposed them to resistance, if they had not been over-awed and over-powered. (*Marg. Ref.*)—In ordering those who sold doves, to remove them, that they might no longer render " the house " of God a house of merchandize," he expressly called " God his Father;" and that in a manner which evidently implied a claim to be the promised Messiah, " the Son of " God." When the disciples witnessed his courage and vehemency, his holy indignation, and disregard to opposition or reproach, in thus vindicating the courts of the temple from so gross a profanation; and compared them with the general meekness and gentleness of his character, (*Note, Mark* iii. 1—5,) they recollected a passage, in which David, speaking as a type of the Messiah, and uttering many evident predictions of him, had said, " The zeal of " thine house hath eaten me up;" or, ' I am inwardly consumed by an earnest desire to purify thy sacred ordinances and thy holy habitation from every corruption; and can have no ease, till I have taken proper measures for that purpose:' and they readily perceived how applicable it was to the conduct of Jesus on this occasion. (*Note, Ps.* lxix. 8, 9.)—The quotation is exactly in the words of the Septuagint, and as exactly translates the Hebrew.— *Oxen.* (14) No oxen, in the strict meaning of the word, were offered in sacrifice; but bulls, or cows only. (*Note, Lev.* xxii. 18—24.)

The changers of money. (14) Κερμαλιστας. Here only. —Α κερμα. 15. The word means small coins, which were given in exchange for larger.—*A scourge.* (15) Φραγελλιον. Here only.—*Small cords.*] Σχοινων. *Acts* xxvii. 32. Not elsewhere N. T. 2 *Sam.* viii. 2. xvii. 13. *Esth.* i. 6. *Sept.* —*The changers.*] Κολλυζιστων. See on *Matt.* xxi. 12.—*Of merchandise.* (16) Εμποριου. Here only N. T. *Deut.* xxxiii. 19. *Is.* xxiii. 17. *Ez.* xxvii. 3. *Sept.*—Ab εμποριος. *Rev.* xviii. 3.

V. 18—22. We can scarcely conceive of an action more incontestably evidential of a divine energy, or more undeniably right in itself, than the driving of the traders from the temple: yet the Jews (probably the Scribes, priests, and rulers,) demanded of Jesus some sign or attestation from heaven to his mission; seeing he presumed, in defiance of publick authority, to act in this manner. (*Marg. Ref.* f, g.—*Note, Matt.*xxi. 23—27.) In answer to this demand, he said, " Destroy this temple, and in " three days I will rear it up again." Some think that he pointed to his body at the time; but, as his disciples did not understand him till long afterwards, this is not likely. His opponents, however, treated his assertion with derision: forty-six years had elapsed from the time that Herod the king had begun to rebuild, or repair, the temple; and, though a very great number of hands had at some times been employed, it was not yet completed: and would he alone presume to rebuild it, if destroyed, in the short space of " three days?" (*Marg. Ref.* h, i.—*Note, Hag.* ii. 6— 9.)—But he spake, not of the temple which was of man's building, but " of his body," of which the temple was a type. The Jews would proceed in their enmity, till they had, as it were, demolished that temple by his crucifixion; and then on the third day he would raise it up again, and thus give the grand proof of his being " the Son of God," and the promised Messiah.—This explanation of the Evangelist contains two direct proofs of the Deity of Christ: his body was, in an especial sense, " a Temple," in which God dwelt, and in which he displayed his glory: (*Notes, Col.* i. 18—20. ii. 8, 9:) and he declared that he would raise his body from the dead by his own power; yet doubtless " God raised him from the dead." (*Marg. Ref.* k.—*Notes,* x. 14—18, vv. 17, 18. *Acts* x. 36—43, v. 40. *Heb.* xiii. 20, 21. 1 *Pet.* i. 3—5, v. 3. iii. 17, 18, v. 18.)— After his resurrection his disciples remembered and understood this remarkable prediction; and when compared with its exact accomplishment, it confirmed their faith in him as the Messiah, " the Son of God," and in the scriptures that testified of him. His enemies also remembered these words some years after, and by misquoting them bare false witness against him. (*Note, Matt.* xxvi. 57—62.)

This temple. (19) Τον ναον τουτον⸱ (not ιερον, 14.) 20, 21. *Matt.* xxvi. 61. xxvii. 40. *Mark* xiv. 58. xv. 29. Ναω, properly means *the sanctuary,* apart from its courts; and so Jesus meant: but the application of it by the Jews must be understood with some latitude; for a very large proportion of that which Herod caused to be done, was about the out-buildings of the sanctuary.

3 P

° 11. xx. 8, 9. ° and they believed the scripture, and
the word which Jesus had said.

p 111. 2. vi. 14. vii.
31. viii. 30, 31.
xii. 42. 43.
Matt. xiii. 20,
21. Mark iv. 16,
17. Luke viii.
13. Gal. v. 6.
Eph. iii. 16, 17.
Jam. ii. 19, 20.

23 ¶ Now when he was in Jerusalem at the passover, in the feast-*day*,
? many believed in his name, when
they saw the miracles which he did.

24 But Jesus ° did not commit himself unto them, ‘ because he knew all
men,

25 And needed not that any should
testify of man; for he knew what was
in man.

q vi. 15. Matt. x.
16, 17.
r 42. 46, 47. v.
42. vi. 64. xvi.
30. xxi. 17.
1 Sam. xvi. 7.
1 Chr. xxviii. 9.
xxix. 17. Jer.
xvii. 9,10. Matt.
?ix. 4. Mark ii.
8. Acts i. 24.
Heb. iv. 13.
Rev. ii. 23.

V. 23—25. It appears, that our Lord wrought several
miracles at Jerusalem during this passover, and many persons were thus led to believe in him, and own him as a
prophet, or even as the Messiah: but they seem to have
had no proper knowledge of the *spiritual* redemption
which he came to effect, nor any due sense of their need
of his salvation. (*Marg. Ref.* p.—*Note*, iii. 1, 2.) He
did not therefore think it proper to consort much with
them, as if he had confided in their professions; perhaps
knowing that they wanted to make him a king, and thence
take occasion to excite disturbances in the city. For he
knew the secret thoughts and dispositions of their hearts:
he had no need that others should testify to him of any
man's character or intentions; for by his own omniscience
he knew perfectly every man's heart, and all its desires and
counsels. (*Marg. Ref.* r.—*Notes*, viii. 30—36. xvi. 25—
30. xxi. 15—17. *Heb.* iv. 12, 13. *Rev.* ii. 20—23, *v.* 23.)
Commit. (24) Επιστιυν. 21. *Luke* xvi. 11. *Rom.* iii. 2.
1 Cor. ix. 17. *Gal.* ii. 7. 1 *Thes.* ii. 4. 1 *Tim.* i. 11. 2 *Tim.*
i. 12. *Tit.* i. 3.

PRACTICAL OBSERVATIONS
V. 1—11.

We should always endeavour to ensure the divine approbation in all our undertakings. "Marriage indeed is
"honourable among all men," and Jesus sanctioned and
graced that institution by his first miracle, as well as by
his presence: yet the believer cannot expect comfort and a
blessing, unless he engage in it on such principles, and in
such a manner, as may give him confidence in calling on
Jesus, so to speak, to attend on it. (*Note*, Col. iii. 16,
17, *v.* 16.)—We ought not in any thing to affect a superstitious austerity, nor need we scruple to feast with our
friends on proper occasions: yet every social interview
should be so conducted, that we might confidently invite
the Redeemer to join with us, if he were now on earth.
He will at all times be present invisibly, to approve or
condemn our conduct; and all levity, luxury, and excess
must be offensive to him.—If we would have the comfort
of his presence, we must entertain his disciples also; and
our conversation should be such as they delight in. In
this manner we may "use hospitality without grudging;"
and the Lord himself will not suffer us to want. Having
stated our difficulties to him, and submitted to his wisdom,
in respect of the season, manner, and proportion of our
supply, we shall not long be left unprovided for.—But
how ready should we also be to relieve our needy brethren,
and to minister to their comfort; seeing Jesus himself
wrought a miracle, to supply wine on a joyful occasion,
for the refreshment of the company!—If we would have
blessings from his power and love, we must unreservedly
and promptly follow his directions; even though some of
them should seem to us unnecessary or unseasonable.—
What he gives in a special manner to his disciples is always

the best; and his ways are not only unlike those of men,
but far superior to them. (*Note*, *Is.* lv. 8, 9.)—The anger
of God, the curse of his broken law, and our depravity
and guilt, turn the bounties of Providence into occasions
of deeper destruction; but his blessing and the grace of
the gospel convert them all into spiritual advantages, and
give them a peculiar relish. Thus Moses opened his commission to the Egyptians, by changing water into blood;
but Christ began his gracious ministry, by turning water
into wine.—Those whom the world feasts have their best
wine first; and even while they live, every enjoyment
grows more and more insipid; their mirth is soon damped;
and death at length removes them to final misery and despair: (*Note*, *Luke* xvi. 24—26:) but they, whom Christ
entertains at his marriage-supper, have indeed many present comforts, which increase on them here: but their
best wine is kept till last, and they shall drink it for ever
" new in the kingdom of their Father." In all these things
he manifests his glory; and his disciples, who believe in
his name, will be excited more and more to honour and
obey him.

V. 12—25.

Where the presence and doctrine of Christ are not
valued, they will not long be continued: but he always is
present with those who copy his example, by conscientiously attending on the ordinances of God. His power is
principally exerted by a secret influence upon the minds of
men; and to extirpate the corruptions from our hearts,
and from his visible church, (where, alas! they are found
in great abundance,) constitutes the chief part of his present severity. His hand holds the *scourge*, not the avenging *sword*, during the day of his patience; nor will he ever
destroy those who are willing to be cleansed. Zeal for the
honour of the sanctuary and ordinances of God still en-
grosses his mind: his indignation is daily excited by the
abominations of those, who make "his Father's house an
"house of merchandize;" and, unless they repent, he
will at length "make them as a fiery oven in the day of
"his wrath." They, who of old questioned his authority
to purge his temple, and to oppose their wickedness, were
at length enraged by his rebukes to put him to death; but
he raised up the sacred temple of his body by his own
divine power, that in it "all the fulness of the Godhead
"might dwell" for ever. He speedily took dreadful
vengeance on the Jews for their enormous impiety; and
all who despise his authority and warnings, or hate his
gospel, shall perish in like manner. But his disciples will
reverence his words, when they do not fully understand
them; they will treasure them up in their memories, and
wait till the event explains them; and thus their faith will
be continually strengthened, by further evidence of his
truth and love.—Let us above all beware of a dead faith,
or a formal profession; as carnal temporary believers are
not to be trusted, for they often prove most treacherous

CHAP. III.

Nicodemus comes to Jesus by night, 1, 2. Jesus shews him the indispensable necessity of being born again, 3—11. He shews the difference between earthly and heavenly things, 12, 13, and speaks of his own death, and of faith in him, 14, 15. The great love of God, in giving his only begotten Son to redeem the world, 16, 17. Unbelief is the great cause of men's condemnation, 18—21. Jesus baptizes in Judea, and John at Ænon, 22—24. John instructs his disciples who were jealous for his honour, concerning the glory of Christ, the salvation of those who believe in him, and the wrath of God abiding on unbelievers, 25—36.

THERE was a man ᵃ of the Pharisees, named Nicodemus, a ruler of the Jews :

2 The same ᵇ came to Jesus by night, and said unto him, ᶜ Rabbi, ᵈ we know that thou art a Teacher come from God : ᵉ for no man can do these miracles that thou doest, except God be with him.

3 Jesus answered and said unto him, ᶠ Verily, verily, I say unto thee, ᵍ Except a man be born ʰ again, ʰ he cannot see the kingdom of God.

a 10. vii. 47—49.
b vii. 50. xii. 42.
4b. xix. 38, 39.
Judg. vi. 27. 1s.
li. 7. Phil. i. 14.
c 26. i. 38. xx. 16.
Matt. xxiii. 16.
Mark xii. 14.
d v. 36. vii. 31.
xi. 47, 48. xii.
37. xv. 24. Acts
ii. 22. iv. 16, 17.
x. 38.
f See on i. 51.
Matt. v. 18.—
2 Cor. i. 19, 20.
g 5, 6. i. 13. Eph.
ii. 1. Jam. i. 18.
1 Pet. i. 3, 23.
1 John ii. 29. iii.
9. v. 1. 18.
Or, from above.
Jam. i. 17. iii.
17.
17.
h 5, i. 5. xli. 40. Deut. xxix. 4. Jer. v. 21. Matt. xiii. 11—16. xvi. 17.
2 Cor. iv. 4.

---

enemies : and, however men may impose on others or on themselves, they cannot impose on their glorious heart-searching Judge. (*Notes, Matt.* xiii. 20, 21. xxii. 11—14. xxv. 1—13. *P. O.* 1—13.)

NOTES.

CHAP. III. V. 1, 2. The miracles, which our Lord wrought at Jerusalem, and those reported to have been wrought by him in other places, excited the attention of the rulers and Pharisees : and, though prejudiced against him, they were not at this time so inveterate as they afterwards became. Indeed, some of them were of opinion, that he was an extraordinary prophet : and Nicodemus, who was a Pharisee, a teacher, and a ruler of the Jews, or a member of their grand council, was desirous of some conversation with him. But, as he was afraid of being reviled by his brethren, or otherwise subjected to censure and suspicion ; he came by night privately to the house where Jesus lodged, at or near Jerusalem ; and addressed him by the respectful name of Rabbi. This appears the more remarkable, when we consider the obscurity of our Lord's birth and education, and the poverty of his circumstances, and contrast them with the rank and station of Nicodemus.—He also declared that he and others were assured that he was a Teacher sent immediately from God ; as no man could perform such powerful and beneficent miracles, without the presence, favour, and operation of almighty God : and in this conviction, he came to him, that he might learn what were the peculiar doctrines or practices, which he came to inculcate. (*Marg. Ref.—Notes*, v. 31—38. ix. 27—34, vv. 30—33. xiv. 7—14, v. 11. *Acts* x. 36—43, v. 38.)

A teacher come from God. (2) Απο Θευ εληλυθας διδασ-καλος. . " From God thou hast come a Teacher," or " to " be a Teacher." This introduction shews, that Nicodemus expected some very momentous and peculiar instruction from Jesus, who had after a lapse of ages " come " from God as a Teacher," and confirming his doctrine by undeniable miracles.

'. V. 3. The Pharisees, besides a scrupulous exactness in the ceremonies of the law, strictly observed " the traditions " of the elders ;" and thus sought and rested in an external purity, while the heart was full of uncleanness : but our Lord immediately directed the attention of Nico-

demus to the source of internal purity. (*Note, Matt.* xxiii. 25—28.)—It has been already .observed, that the word *Verily*, implies a strong asseveration ; and· in the beginning of a sentence it is peculiar to Christ. (*Note, Matt.* vi. 5.) St. John generally mentions the affirmation··as doubled, which adds a still greater.energy to it. (*Marg. Ref.*—See on i. 52.) We are therefore previously sure, that something of peculiar importance, and very liable to be overlooked, is here intended. If it be allowed that the expression, " born again," is figurative, and therefore ought not to be strained too far in the interpretation : yet surely the figure should be regarded as peculiarly appropriate and significant. Some argue that " to be born " again" means no more than.to be baptized, and they quote the ancient fathers in proof of it. But will any man say, that no one can " see," or " enter into," the kingdom of God (5) ; that is, no one can understand the nature of true religion, become Christ's true disciple, or inherit the happiness of heaven, without the baptism of water ? This is indeed the outward sign ; but surely we must look for something far more spiritual, as the thing signified, than baptism, or any thing which uniformly accompanies it, even when rightly administered.—Others understand it of *reformation :* but outward reformation may be mere hypocrisy ; or it may be the result of worldly and selfish motives, or corrupted by pride and ostentation. · Nay, a man may change one kind of sin for another, or one creed or sect for another, in various ways, and yet remain very " far from the kingdom of God : " in short, ' If regenera-' tion here mean only reformation of life, our Lord, instead ' of making any new discovery, has thrown a great deal of ' obscurity on what was before plain and obvious, and ' known, not only to the Jews, but to the wiser heathens. ' And indeed this is the main article in dispute among ' many. Some think, all things in scripture are expressed ' in condescension to our capacities, so that there is still ' to be conceived in many of them an inexpressible gran-' deur : whilst on the other hand, others suppose, that ' under the pomp and grandeur of the most hyperbolical ' expressions, things of a low and ordinary sense are to be ' understood.' *Owen.* Every one may see how applicable this is to all those interpretations of the new birth, which explain this most energetick expression to signify, either things exceedingly plain, or of a very inferior nature in religion.—Frequent occasions have before occurred of con-

3 P 2

4 Nicodemus saith unto him, ' How can a man be born when he is old? can he enter the second time into his mother's womb, and be born?

5 Jesus answered, Verily, verily, I say unto thee, Except a man be ^k born of water, ^l and of the Spirit, ^m he cannot enter into the kingdom of God.

k 3. iv. xliv. 3, 4.
Ez. xxxvii. 26—
27. Matt. iii. 11.
Kph. v. 26. Tit.
iii. 4—7. 1 Pet.
i. 2   iii.   21.
l   John v. 6—8.   1 i. 13.   Rom. viii. 2.   1 Cor. vi. 11.   1 John i. 29. v. 1.   m Matt.
v. 20. xviii. 3. xxviii. 19.   Luke xiii. 3, 5, 24.   Acts ii. 38. iii. 19.   Rom. xiv. 17.   2 Cor.
v. 17, 18.   Gal. vi. 15.   Eph. ii. 4—10.   2 Thes. ii. 13, 14.

---

sidering the subject; (*Notes*, i. 10—13. *Jer.* xxxii. 39—41, *v.* 39. *Ez.* xi. 17—20. xxxvi. 25—27;) but it may here be expedient to elucidate the propriety of the metaphor. When a child is born into the world, though no new matter is brought into existence, yet "a new creature" is produced; and all its capacities, senses, and limbs, are new, and suited to that new life on which it has entered. Thus when the grace of God changes the sinner's heart, the person indeed is the same; but he becomes a new man, possessed of new capacities, perceptions, affections, and dispositions, and is prepared to make a new use of all his organs, senses, and faculties: he enters, as "a new crea-"ture," into the spiritual world, and becomes capable of employments and satisfactions, to which he was before an utter stranger. (*Notes, Eph.* ii. 4—10, *v.* 10. *2 Cor. v.* 17.) —When an infant is born, it has all the parts of a grown man: but they are in a feeble state, and need nourishment, attention, and time, before they grow to their proper size, and are fitted to perform their appropriate functions in a complete manner. Thus the regenerated sinner has the substance of all right principles and holy dispositions communicated to his soul; but they are in an infantile state, and must grow up gradually, and with care and spiritual nourishment, to maturity: this nourishment is provided, and "the new-born babe," in the spiritual as well as in the natural world, desires, relishes, and thrives upon it. (*Note,* 1 *Pet.* ii. 1—3.)—No man can comprehend how the infant is formed in the womb; nor can any man know how God effects the new-creating change in the sinner's heart. He works by means and instruments in both cases; and in each of them a real creation is effected by his omnipotence.—The birth of the infant precedes the exercise of its senses, and is the necessary introduction to all the actions of future life: so the new birth must precede all the actions of the spiritual life: till that has taken place, the man can neither see, hear, speak, walk, or work, in a spiritual manner. But as, when a living child is born, it will certainly move and act; so when the sinner is "born "again," he will repent, believe, love, obey, and worship. —Whatever be a man's natural abilities, attainments, notions, or profession, our Lord assures us, that "he cannot "*see* the kingdom of God:" he can neither discern its spiritual nature, or the excellence of its blessings and privileges, nor enjoy those blessings. (*Note, Matt.* iii. 2.) This is the unalterable appointment of God; but it has also its foundation in the reason and nature of things. God is perfect in holiness, his law is holy, his gospel is holy, all things relating to true religion are holy and spiritual. This is their glory and excellency: but man by nature is unholy and carnal, and cannot *relish* or even *discern* that excellency. God and his law, with the nature of holiness and happiness, are unchangeable: therefore man must change, or he can never be conformed to them, or be happy in them. (*Notes, Rom.* viii. 5—9. 1 *Cor.* ii. 14—16, *v.* 14.) Every revelation of God requires of sinful man the deepest humiliation; but man is a self-justifying,

self-sufficient creature: he must therefore be inwardly and effectually changed, before he can understand the nature and glory of the gospel. Without this, he can see no excellency in the holiness of God, no goodness or justice in the strict and spiritual precepts and awful sanction of the law, no hatefulness in himself, no malignity deserving damnation in his sins; no preciousness and glory in the way of salvation by Christ, no beauty in conformity to his image and character. Consequently he can neither submit, repent, believe, love, nor obey; but he must remain a rebel and an enemy, and a despiser, hater, or abuser of the gospel: he cannot therefore be a true Christian, or a spiritual worshipper; nor can he have the meetness for the enjoyments and employments of heaven. He may exercise the functions, and participate the satisfactions, of the animal or the rational life; but he must remain *spiritually* dead, and incapable of such satisfactions as angels and saints enjoy in heaven, and as pious men experience on earth: even as a watch, or other curious machine, constructed with three distinct parts, may move on regularly as to two of them, when the third is rendered incapable of further motion, unless it be restored by a skill similar to that of the original maker. (*Note, Gen.* ii. 16, 17.)— Some render the words "born again," *born from above;* and no doubt they admit of that meaning: but it is evident that Nicodemus did not thus understand them.—In short, the new-birth is the beginning of spiritual life, without which we can no more live a heavenly life, than we could an earthly one without being born into this world. (*Marg. Ref.*—*Notes, Jam.* i. 16—18, *v.* 18. 1 *Pet.* i. 3—5, *v.* 3. 22—25.—*Notes,* 1 *John* ii. 26—29, *v.* 29. iii. 7—10, *v.* 9. iv. 7, 8. *v.* 1—5, *vv.* 1. 4. 16—18, *v.* 18.)—'The beginning ' of Christianity is placed in this; that we know ourselves ' not only to be in some measure corrupt, but entirely ' " dead in sin;" so that it is necessary, that our nature, ' as to its qualities, should be created again and anew; ' which can be effected by no other power, than that of ' God, by whom we were at first made.' *Beza.* (*Notes, Eph.* ii. 1—3.)—' Jesus, observing that he (Nicodemus) ' said nothing of the excellency and power of his doctrine, ' to change the hearts and reform the lives of men ... but ' only of his miracles, by which it was confirmed, an- ' swered and said unto him, " Verily, verily, I say unto ' " thee, except a man be born again ;" that is, renewed ' in his mind, will, and affections, by the operations of ' the Holy Spirit, and so become a new creature, ... " he ' " cannot see," that is, enjoy the blessings of " the king- ' " dom of God." ' *Whitby.*

Again.] Ανωθεν. 7. 31. xix. 11. 23. *Matt.* xxvii. 51. *Luke* i. 3. *Acts* xxvi. 5. *Gal.* iv. 9. *Jam.* i. 17. iii. 15. 17. —' It is significant, and imports, that we must go over all ' that is past, and reject it as unprofitable, and begin anew.' *Beza.* Ab origine, a primordiis, denuo. So παλιγγενεσια, *Tit.* iii. 5.

V. 4, 5. Nicodemus, though seriously impressed, seems to have had no distinct view of religion, further than as it

n Gen. v. 3. vi. 5.
12. Job xiv. 4.
xv. 14—16. xxv.
4. Ps. li. 10.
Rom. vii. b. 18.
25. viii. l. 4, 9.
—0. 13. Gal. v. 16—21. 24. Eph. ii. 3. Col. ii. 11.
27. Rom. viii. 5. 9. 1 Cor. vi. 17 Gal. v. 17. 1 John iii. 9.

6 That which is ª born of the flesh is flesh; and ª that which is born of the Spirit is spirit.

o Ez. xi. 19, 20. xxxvi. 26, 27.

7 ª Marvel not that I said unto thee,
ª Ye must be born ª again.

8 The ª wind bloweth where it list-

p 12. v. 26. vi. 61
—63.
q 2. Job xv. 14.
Matt. xiii. 33—
35. Rom. iii. 9—
19. ix. 22—23.
7. Rev. xxi. 27
* Or, from above.
s Ez. xxxvii. 9.
r Job xxxvii. 10—13. 16, 17. 21—23. Ps. cvii. 25. 29. Ec. xi. 4,
Acts ii. 2. iv. 31. 1 Cor. ii. 11. xii. 11.

related to the outward conduct. (*Notes, Luke* xi. 37—40.) He could not, therefore, understand what our Lord intended; but, adverting to the literal meaning of the words, and observing with what earnestness Jesus insisted on the necessity of being "born again;" he enquired, with great surprise, how this could possibly take place; or how, if possible, it could prepare any one for the kingdom of God. To this our Lord replied, in the same emphatical and decisive manner as before, and to the same effect; except as he further declared the Author and nature of this mysterious work. By "the kingdom of God" he doubtless primarily meant the *kingdom of the Messiah*, about which the Jews entertained very carnal and erroneous opinions: but as admission into this is necessary, in order to "enter into "the kingdom of God" in heaven, both may be included. .(*Note, Matt.* iii. 2.) No man "can enter into the king- "dom of God," no one can become a true disciple of Christ and an heir of heaven, without that change, of which the Holy Spirit is the Author, and purifying ferti- lizing water is the outward sign. (*Note, Ez.* xxxvi. 25— 27.) Water was used among the Jews in "divers wash- "ings," or, "baptisms." John used it in his baptism, and Jesus appointed it in his initiatory sacrament. This was the emblem of that spiritual washing, without which no man can be admitted into the true church, as a living mem- ber of the same. As baptism, in the ordinary course of things, is requisite to the outward profession of Christ- ianity; so regeneration is invariably necessary to the pos- session of its privileges, and the performance of its duties. (*Note, Mark* xvi. 14—16.) Except a man "be born of "water, and of the Spirit;" except his heart be purified by that inward washing of the Holy Spirit, of which water has been the constant emblem, "he cannot enter into "the kingdom of God." (*Marg. Ref.*—See on 3. *Note, Tit.* iii. 4—7, *v.* 5.)—'If, under the word *water*, bap- 'tism be especially intended, as that which is the pecu- 'liar sacrament of our regeneration, the sentence must be 'taken, as Christ had respect to the general order of the 'church. Neither yet did he simply bind the grace of God 'to baptism, as if it was, absolutely, and without any ex- 'ception, necessary; seeing he just after ascribes regener- 'ation to the Spirit, without any mention of water. ... 'Thus elsewhere the *Spirit* and *fire* are joined, but the 'order is reversed. "He shall baptize you with the Holy '"Ghost, and with fire." ... *Water* is really present in the 'sacrament of baptism, as an outward sign and seal of the 'spiritual and divine energy, which inwardly cleanses us. 'But *fire*, when joined to the Spirit, cannot be understood 'otherwise than metaphorically. In this place "the Spirit" 'being added to "water," is a declaration of the external 'sacramental baptism; in the other the fire is mentioned as 'an explanation of the divine energy, taken from a corpo- 'real thing.' *Beza.* (*Note, Matt.* iii. 11, 12.)—'Whatever 'ignorance of the precept, or mistake about the nature of 'it, renders not men incapable of baptism by the Holy 'Ghost, can never render them incapable of the salvation

'promised to the baptized....It cannot be purely the want, 'but the contempt, of it, which must condemn us.' *Whitby.*—If, however, baptism and being "born again" be terms of the same meaning, or if the one invariably accompanies the other, so that all who are rightly bap- tized are regenerate, and none else; then all who die un- baptized, even infants, as well as all others, all over the earth, and in every age of the world, without exception, are shut out of heaven! A proposition far more dreadful, than any held by the most unfeeling and presumptuous Supralapsarian Calvinists.

V. 6. To be born again, of parents either Jewish, or Gentile, or Christian, if it were possible, could be of no use to any man: as "that which is born of the flesh," by natural generation from the stock of fallen Adam, "is "flesh," carnal, corrupt, and enmity against God; (*Marg. Ref.*—*Notes, Rom.* vii. 18—25, *vv.* 18. 25. viii. 1—13, *vv.* 1. 3. 4, 5. 8, 9. 12, 13. *Gal.* v. 13—25, *vv.* 13. 15—17. 19—21. 24;) but "that which is born of the Spirit," that which is communicated to the soul from the second Adam, by the operation of the Holy Spirit, "is spirit;" is like its Author, of a spiritual and holy nature, and capable of spiritual and holy exercises and enjoyment.—'Christ takes 'it for granted, as beyond all contradiction, that he must 'be pure, who would be happy with God. By the word '"flesh," therefore, it is meant, that the whole man, as 'the offspring of man, is impure, as well in his mind as 'in his body.' *Beza.* (*Notes, Job* xiv. 1—6, *v.* 4. xv. 14— 16. *Ps.* li. 5, 6.) The clause, "that which is born of the "Spirit, is spirit," cannot mean, that *the rational soul* as distinct from the body, is brought into existence by being "born of the Spirit:" but that the man is raised "from 'the death of sin to the life of righteousness,' and so his renewal to holiness is begun. To understand by "the "flesh," in the first clause, the body exclusively, would wholly destroy the antithesis; and indeed all connexion between the two parts of the verse. And where would be the need of regeneration, or to be renewed "in the spirit "of our mind," if the soul were in itself *spiritual*, and only the body *carnal?* In fact, the soul, or heart, is the more immediate seat and source of sin, and the body only or mainly its instrument. (*Notes, Prov.* iv. 23. *Jer.* xvii. 9, 10. *Matt.* xv. 15—20.) 'It appears to me impossible, to 'clear up either the beauty of the antithesis, or the truth 'of the assertion, on any other interpretation.' *Doddridge.* The subject is of such importance, in order to understand Christianity, that it deserves the most diligent investiga- tion, and a very careful and humble examination of all those parts of scripture which relate to it, with constant, fervent prayer for heavenly wisdom and illumination to understand them.—*That which is born.*] Τὸ γεγεννημένον. 1 *John* v. 4.

V. 7, 8. Nicodemus had no adequate reason to be so greatly surprised at our Lord's declaration, that fallen man of every nation and creed, Jews and Pharisees, as well as Gentiles "must be born again;" as if it were more un-

3 P 5

eth, and thou hearest the sound thereof, but canst not tell whence it cometh, and whither it goeth: *so is every one that is born of the Spirit.

9 Nicodemus answered and said unto him, 'How can these things be?

10 Jesus answered and said unto him, "Art thou a master of Israel, ʸ and knowest not these things?

11 Verily, ʸ verily, I say unto thee, ᶻ We speak that we do know, and testi-

intelligible than many other things, the truth and reality of which no man disputed. The wind, for instance, blows from different points of the compass, and more gently or more furiously, " as it listeth;" that is, so far as man is concerned: but though the sound of it is heard, and the effects of it most manifest; yet no man can "tell whence " it cometh, or whither it goeth." Even to this day, after all improvements in natural science, men can neither account satisfactorily for all the changes of the wind, nor render it at all submissive to their will or command, or counteract its effects. Even so it is with " every one that " is born of the Spirit:" the nature and effects of this change are most manifest; the manner in which it is wrought is inexplicable; and its direction, as to this or the other person, is independent on the will of man, and according to the sovereign pleasure of the great Creator: for the " willing mind " which God approves is produced by it. (Marg. Ref.—Notes, i. 10—13. Phil. ii. 12, 13.) But if man cannot govern or change the wind, or explain those things which relate to it; how can he expect to govern or explain the operations of the Holy Spirit?—As the same word signifies both spirit, and the wind, in the original languages; the similitude has a peculiar propriety, if " being born again" be interpreted of the communication of divine life to " the dead in sin." But if understood of baptism exclusively, or what always accompanies it when rightly administered, there seems nothing appropriate in it. The administration of baptism is evident, and most public, foreseen, and appointed. Every thing relating to it depends on " the will of man," of the baptized person in adults, of parents and sponsors in infants, and of the officiating minister in both cases. But if the thing signified, be intended, the whole depends absolutely on the sovereign will, who commands and governs the winds and waves. (Note, Ex. xxxvii. 1—10.)

Where it listeth. (8) 'Οπυ θελει. Willeth. Rom. ix. 16.— Note, Matt. vi. 33, 34, v. 34.

V.—11. Nicodemus had not been used to hear this new-birth insisted on, by the scribes and priests; nor had he ever made it the immediate subject of his own study, or investigation, or attained to an experience of its nature and effects: he could not therefore understand our Lord's meaning. He was not however willing to reject his instruction, which he had allowed to be confirmed by evident miracles; yet this doctrine, on which he so strenuously insisted, seemed to him inexplicable and impracticable; and he therefore enquired, as a man in perfect astonishment, " How can these things be?" (Marg. Ref. t.) To this our Lord answered, as expressing surprise at his ignorance, by demanding, whether he, as a teacher of God's people, could possibly be unacquainted with this essential and important truth. Not only was the new birth absolutely requisite to the existence of true religion in the

soul of fallen man, as nothing but a worthless form could subsist without it; but it was evidently contained in the scriptures of the Old Testament, and implied in every passage which required spiritual worship, inward holiness, and heavenly affections, from a fallen creature; or promised to give a new heart, or produce a change of heart. (Marg. Ref. u, x.—Notes, Deut. x. 16. xxix. 4. xxx. 1— 10, v. 6. 1 Chr. xxix. 10—19. Ps. li. 10. Jer. iv. 3, 4. xxxi. 31—34. xxxii. 39—41. Ez. xi. 17—20. xxxvi. 25—27.) Jesus then declared, that he and those servants of God, who in every age concurred with him, spake in this respect what they assuredly knew to be true, and testified what they were most intimately acquainted with: yet the Jews in general, and the Pharisees in particular, would not receive their testimony.—Prophets, apostles, and faithful ministers knew this subject from revelation, from their own experience, and from observation of its effects in others: Jesus knew it in a still higher and more sublime manner. (31, 32.)—' There is an implied antithesis, which, ' in my judgment, should be carefully noted. You, saith ' Christ, ... teach things which you do not understand, and ' are believed; we teach a certain and known doctrine; ' and yet ye will not receive our doctrine. ...He joins him- ' self with the prophets, whose writings were so negligently ' read in the synagogues.' Beza.—Some expositors think, that our Lord, in the tenth verse, referred to the language of the Jews about proselytes, whom they spake of, as in- fants new born, &c. but it is not likely that he should lay such stress on any of their traditions or expressions, which on other occasions he decidedly opposed: and the above remark shews what our Lord meant; as Moses and the prophets, which were continually read in their synagogues, joined in his testimony to the necessity of regeneration. So that, even the principal teachers in Israel, who did not understand and teach regeneration, " erred, not knowing the scriptures, nor the " power of God." As " a teacher " of Israel," Nicodemus might know many things concerning the " divers baptisms" of the Mosaick law, the traditionary baptisms of the Pharisees, and even John's baptism. But Christian baptism was not instituted till some time afterwards: and Nicodemus could not at this time be supposed to understand the nature, obligation, and benefits of it. Or, that this baptism was intended to be the initiatory sacrament of Christianity, and indispensably necessary to salvation. Could it then be wonderful, that a " Teacher of Israel" did " not know these things?" or was he deserving of reproof for not knowing, what he never had the means of learning? Our Lord's surprise, and reproving question, must have related to what Nicodemus might have known, and ought to have known. (Notes, 25, 26. Matt. xxviii. 19, 20.)

A master. (10) 'Ο διδασκαλος. 2. This word with the article implies, that Nicodemus was regarded as an eminent teacher, as well as a ruler, of Israel.

3 P 6

tify that we have seen; *and ye re- ceive not our witness.

12 If I have told you ^b earthly things, and ye believe not, how shall ye believe if I tell you *of* °heavenly things?

13 And ^d no man hath ascended up to heaven, ^e but he that came down from heaven, ^f *even* the Son of man, which is in heaven.

14 ¶ And ^f as Moses lifted up the serpent in the wilderness, ^h *even* so must the Son of man be lifted up;

15 That ⁱ whosoever believeth in him should ^k not perish, but have ^l eternal life.

V. 12, 13. The change before described seems here to be meant by "earthly things:" for, as it must be, and continually has been, wrought on earth; so it is *comparatively* easy to be understood and illustrated; and we may reason and discourse about it far better, than about the mysteries which are next spoken of. (*Marg. Ref.* a.) No creature can find satisfaction, without capacities of enjoyment suited to his situation. Pleasure cannot be experienced without appetite and relish, as well as the means of gratification. Every animal must be in its proper element, in order to be easy and comfortable. The fish could not possibly live, and enjoy life, on dry ground, unless its nature should previously be changed. Holiness and spirituality are not the sinner's element: submission to God, and communion with him, are not his desired enjoyments; nay, he has a rooted antipathy against them. Yet happiness is impossible to a rational creature without holiness; and holiness cannot be so much as begun without "being " born again." So that this truth, which men are so apt to deny, and treat as enthusiasm, has as evident a ground in reason, as in scripture. Let it but be granted, that God is perfectly holy; that happiness consists in his favour, presence, image, and service; and that man by nature has no relish for this kind of happiness: and from these premises (which any one must be very hardy to deny,) it demonstratively follows, that " except a man be born " again," he could not enjoy happiness, were he admitted into heaven; but for that reason, among others, he never can enter thither. If men will not therefore believe this doctrine, of which we " that are of the earth, and earthly," can reason so plainly, and illustrate by the nature of animals, and the grafting of trees, (*Miraturque novas frondes, et non sua poma :* ' It,' the grafted tree, ' admires new ' branches, and fruit not its own,' *Virgil,*) and various other apt similitudes; (*Note, Is.* xi. 6—9;) and which is actually witnessed in its effects whenever sinners are converted; how shall they believe what Jesus testifies to them concerning " heavenly things?" namely such as relate to the mysteries of the Trinity, to his own eternal Deity, to his incarnation, and redemption by his blood; which could never have been thought of, had not God revealed them, and which must rest wholly on the testimony of Revelation. We may indeed discern glory and suitableness in them when revealed: but we feel, that they are sublime and mysterious beyond comparison; and though not contrary to our reason, are far above it, and out of its reach and province. The knowledge of these things must be derived, immediately and entirely, from above, and received by faith alone: yet no man has ascended thither to fetch down that knowledge; (*Marg. Ref.* c—f.—*Deut.* xxx. 12. *Notes, Prov.* xxx. 4. *Rom.* x. 5—11 ;) nor can it be received, except from Christ, who came down from heaven,

when he became " the Son of man:" yet even then he " was in heaven," in respect of his divine nature. For the two natures are so inseparably united in his mysterious Person, that as the apostle says, " the church of God, " which he hath purchased with his own blood," so our Lord says " the Son of man which is in heaven," when he was here on earth, because One with the eternal Word and Son of God. (*Notes,* i. 1—3. 14. 18. *Acts* xx. 28.) This language seems incapable of any other interpretation ; and to wrest it to agree with any other doctrine, makes our Lord to speak in the most obscure and unintelligible manner imaginable. Doubtless this was intended as a specimen of those " heavenly things " which he had before mentioned.—' If while I have discoursed...of those ' principles of Christianity, which both our enlightened ' reason and experience can easily make good, thou be- ' lievest not, but findest such difficulties ;...what...pos- ' sibility is there, that thou shouldest believe, when I shall ' tell thee of the great mysteries of salvation, and of those ' high and incomprehensible matters of another world ? ... ' These are things which no man can tell thee, but he that ' has been in heaven; and no man hath been there to see ' them, but he that is now come down from heaven, even ' that Son of man, (that talketh with thee,) who in respect ' of his Deity is still in heaven.' *Bp. Hall.*

Earthly things. (12) Τα επιγεια. 1 *Cor.* xv. 40. 2 *Cor.* v. 1. *Phil.* ii. 10. iii. 19. *Jam.* iii. 15. Ab επι et γη, *terra.*— *Heavenly things.*] Τα επιφρανια. *Matt.* xviii. 35. 1 *Cor.* xv. 40. 48, 49. *Eph.* i. 3. 20. ii. 6. iii. 10. vi. 12. *Phil.* ii. 10. 2 *Tim.* iv. 18. *Heb.* iii. 1. vi. 4. viii. 5. ix. 23. xi. 16. xii. 22. Εx επι et ερανος, *cœlum.*

V. 14, 15. (*Notes, Num.* xxi. 6—9.) This passage in the history of Israel was well known, but the typical meaning seems not to have been at all discovered by the Jews. The promised Messiah was not to be " lifted up" *on earth* to a glorious throne, as they vainly expected ; but to " be lifted up," or *exalted,* by being suspended on an ignominious cross, for the redemption of his people. (*Marg. Ref.* h.—*Note,* xii. 27—36, *vv.* 32. 34.) Moses, the giver of the law, was ordered to make a serpent of brass, like the fiery serpents, yet perfectly innoxious : this he lifted up on a pole in a conspicuous place, that it might be clearly seen by all the people; and especially by those, who looked at it when mortally bitten by the serpents ; and in so doing they were miraculously healed. Thus Jesus, in " the likeness of sinful flesh," in the nature of Adam, by whom sin and death entered into the world, though 'himself perfectly free from sin, was " lifted up " on the cross, to " redeem us from the curse of the law, being made a " curse for us." This " must " take place, or was previously necessary, in order to the completion of the promises and predictions which God had given, and the satis-

16 For "God so loved the world, that he "gave his only begotten Son, *that whosoever believeth in him should not perish, but have everlasting life.

17 For 'God sent not his Son into the world to condemn the world; 'but that the world through him might be saved.

18 He that believeth on him 'is not condemned: but ' he that believeth not is condemned already; because he hath not believed in the name of the only begotten Son of God.

19 And 'this is the condemnation, that Light is come into the world, and men loved darkness rather than light, "because their deeds were evil.

---

faction of his justice in saving sinners. In consequence of his crucifixion, Jesus is set forth in the gospel, as preached throughout the world, that " whosoever be- " lieveth in him, should not perish, but have eternal life." This method, which God has devised in his infinite wisdom, is suited to bring the perishing sinner to expect all his salvation from God, and to give him all the glory of it: to promote humility, dependence, and gratitude; to render him submissive and obedient; and to teach him every salutary lesson, by looking to that one Object, from which he derives his peace, hope, and comfort. (*Marg. Ref.* i, k. —*Notes*, i. 29. *Heb.* xii. 2, 3.) Thus the important change, which takes place in the heart, and is manifested in the life, of every true believer, proves the efficacy of faith in a crucified Saviour, as evidently, as the restored health and vigour of the almost expiring Israelite proved, that his expectation of recovery, by looking to the brazen serpent, was not a vain presumption.—' Justin Martyr, ' Tertullian, and Barnabas say, This was a figure of the ' cross; and that it was a symbol of salvation; he that ' turned to it being preserved from death, not by what ' he saw, but by the Saviour of all men.' *Whitby.* (*Note*, *2 Kings* xviii. 4.)—How strongly do our Lord's words shew the actual state of all men! They must *perish* without a Saviour, and without faith in that Saviour!

V. 16. The whole design of man's redemption originated in the love of God to the world, even to the apostate race of men; to " the whole world, that lieth in wick- " edness," or " in the wicked one." (*Note*, 1 *John* v. 19.) This could not be *approbation*, or *complacency* : for he judged them deserving of his final indignation, and meet objects of his holy abhorrence; and so criminal, that he could not honourably shew them mercy, except by an expedient more suited to expose the desert of their rebellion, than even the eternal punishment of the whole race would have been. (*Notes*, *Rom.* v. 6—10.) The love of God to the world was therefore *good-will*, compassion, benevolence. (*Marg. Ref.* m.) He " so loved the world," that he not only purposed to pardon sin, and to give heaven to those who repented; but (when the honour of his justice and holiness seemed to oppose the exercise of mercy,) " he " gave his only-begotten Son," the co-equal partaker of his divine nature, a person of infinite dignity and excellency, and infinitely beloved by him, compared with whom all worlds were as nothing, to " become flesh," that in our nature he might atone for our sins, by his sufferings and death upon the cross; that, this obstacle being removed, he might forgive, save, and bless with everlasting life, all those of every nation who believe in this divine Saviour, but who must otherwise have perished for ever. (*Marg. Ref.* n, o.—*Notes*, i. 1—3. 14. 18. *Rom.* viii. 32—

34. *Col.* i. 15—17. 1 *Tim.* iii. 15, 16. *Heb.* i. 1—4.) The world, or the race of men, (and not merely the one nation of Israel, for whose sake alone the Jews supposed that the Messiah would come,) is therefore now borne with, as under a dispensation of mercy; sinners in general are called on to believe in Christ, and invited to partake of the blessing; believers without exception are saved. (*Notes*, i. 29. 1 *John* ii. 1, 2. iv. 9—12. v. 11, 12.) But, as true faith springs from regeneration, and as " the Spirit " quickens whom he will;" those alone who are " born " of the Spirit," willingly avail themselves of this most gracious provision : and " known unto God are all his " works from the beginning of the world." (*Notes*, 3—8. i. 10—13, v. 13.)

The world.] Τον κοσμον. 17. 19. i. 9, 10. 29. 1 *John* ii. 2. iii. 13. 17. iv. 9. 14. 17. v. 19.

V. 17, 18. Our Lord further shewed Nicodemus, that God did not send his Son into the world, (at his first coming,) " to condemn," or *judge*, the world, as might previously have been expected, when the approach of so glorious and holy a person was announced to a world of rebels and apostates. This was not the purpose of his incarnation, ministry, and work on earth : on the contrary he came to procure and reveal salvation, that sinners of every nation might be invited to partake of it. Insomuch that the man, who believes in Christ, " is not judged : " he no longer remains under condemnation, and " shall not " come into condemnation," how many or heinous soever his sins have been. (*Marg. Ref.* p—r.—*Notes*, v. 24—27 *Rom.* viii. 1, 2.) But the unbeliever " is condemned al- " ready : " he has rejected the only method of pardon and reconciliation, which God ever revealed; he remains under the sentence denounced by the law, as a condemned criminal reserved for execution; and his guilt is exceedingly aggravated, by his refusal to " believe in the name of the " only begotten Son of God," and by despising the glorious display of the divine wisdom, justice, truth, and mercy made in that method of salvation. (*Marg. Ref.* s. —*Notes*, 19—21. 27—36, *vv.* 35, 36.)—*In the name*, &c. (18) ' Though the name of a person be often put for ' the person himself; yet I think it farther intimated in ' this expression, that the person spoken of is great and ' magnificent; and therefore it is generally used to ex- ' press either God the Father, or our Lord Jesus Christ. *Doddridge.*

To condemn. (17) 'Iva κρινη. " That he should judge." 18. xii. 47, 48. xvi. 11. 1 *Cor.* xi. 31, 32. As " to judge" unpardoned sinners would be " to condemn " them, the translation here does not at all affect the meaning.

V. 19—21. Unbelief is not a mere *speculative mistake* into which an *honest* mind may be led; but it originates

20 For *every one that doeth evil hateth the light, neither cometh to the light, lest his deeds should be *reproved.

21 But *he that doeth truth cometh to the light, *that his deeds may be made manifest, that they are wrought in God.

22 ¶ After *these things came Jesus and his disciples into the land of Judea; and there he tarried with them, *and baptized.

23 And John also was baptizing in Ænon, *near to Salim, because there was *much water there: *and they came, and were baptized.

24 For *John was not yet cast into prison.

---

from the wickedness and enmity to God of the heart of man: so that this is the reason of the unbeliever's condemnation, and the test by which he will be judged; "that Light is come into the world," to shew men the perfections, truth, and will of God, and the way of salvation from wrath and sin. But men, as left to themselves, love ignorance, delusion, idolatry, superstition, or infidelity, in preference to it, because more congenial to the pride, alienation, and rebellion of their hearts, and the secret or open wickedness of their lives. (Notes, i. 4—9. vii. 3—10. viii. 41—47. Rom. viii. 5—9. Heb. iii. 7—19, v. 12.) For every one, who habitually loves and practises any kind of evil, hates and shuns that light which detects and exposes it: thus men keep aloof from the true gospel of Christ, and run into various perversions of it; lest it should disquiet their consciences, interfere with their indulgence in sin, or detect the fallacy of their presumptuous confidence. (Marg. and Marg. Ref. t—x.—Notes, Job xxiv. 13—17. Eph. v. 8—14.) But he, who acts uprightly and conscientiously, and really desires to know and do the whole will of God without reserve, is glad to bring his creed, his character, and whole spirit and conduct, to the Light, that they may be scrutinized by it; that he may be further instructed and directed; and that it may be made manifest that "his works are wrought in God," by virtue of union with him, and grace derived from him, according to his will, for his glory, and as accepted by him. (Marg. Ref. y, z.—Note, Is. xxvi. 12—18, v. 12. 1 Cor. xv. 9—10. 2 Cor. i. 12—14, v. 12. v. 5—8, v. 5. 17. Gal. v. 22—26, vv. 22, 23. Eph. ii. 4—10, v. 10.)—These are important truths of general application: yet they were spoken with a peculiar reference to the case of the Pharisees; and it was thus declared, that the opposition, which would be made by them, to Jesus and his doctrine, arose from the wickedness of their hearts and lives, which could not enure the light of his spiritual ministry. Nicodemus therefore, and those to whom he might report the result of this conference, were warned not to "reject the counsel of God "against themselves."—Some think, that the conduct of Nicodemus, in coming to Jesus by night, as if he "loved "darkness rather than light," is gently reproved.—Thus our Lord set before this "teacher of Israel" the grand outlines of Christian truth; probably he enlarged more fully on the several particulars: and though Nicodemus did not clearly comprehend his meaning, he was gradually led further into the knowledge of the truth, and afterwards grew bolder in making a profession of it. (Notes, vii. 40—53. xix. 38—42.)—Doeth truth. (21) Notes, Ps. cxix. 29, 30. Is. xxvi. 2. 1 Pet. i. 22. 1 John i. 5—7.

The condemnation. (19) Ἡ κρισις. "The judgment." v. 22. 24. 27. 29. 30. xii. 31. xvi. 8. 11. Jam. ii. 13.—Light.] Το φως. "The Light." 20, 21. i. 4, 5. 8, 9. viii. 12. xii. 35, 36.—More than.] Μαλλον η. xii. 43. 1 Tim. i. 4. 2 Tim. iii. 4. Heb. xi. 25.—' Note, μαλλον η is not a ' comparative, as if the workers of iniquity did in some ' measure love the Light, for, verse 20, they are said to hate ' it; but, as in other places, is a negative.' Whitby.—That doeth evil.] Ὁ φαυλα πρασσων. v. 29. Tit. ii. 8. Jam. iii. 16. Not elsewhere.—Should be reproved.] Ελγχθη. See on Matt. xviii. 15.

V. 22—24. Our Lord, soon after this, left Jerusalem, and retired into the cities or villages of Judea, where he preached, and collected followers; and his more stated disciples baptized them. (Note, iv. 1—4.) It is not probable, that they baptized in that form which he afterwards prescribed; but after the manner of John, and as introductory to the more complete establishment of his religion. The place, where John was preaching and baptizing at the same time, is not mentioned elsewhere: there were "many "waters" in it, which rendered it convenient to him, as he still baptized great numbers. (Note, Matt. iii. 5, 6.) This must have preceded any thing recorded of Christ's ministry by the other evangelists. (Note, Matt. iv. 12—17.)—It is remarkable, that we read nothing of the apostles or disciples baptizing, before our Lord's ascension, except in these few passages of John's gospel. Yet the disciples of Jesus are expressly distinguished from those of John: and at this time he "made and baptized more dis-"ciples than John." (iv. 1.) It must then be supposed, that the disciples of Jesus were baptized in his name: and that this baptism discriminated them, not only from those Jews who had not been baptized; but also from those who had been baptized by John as his disciples, yet had not become the professed disciples of Jesus, and received his baptism. But Christian baptism, "into the name of the "Father, and of the Son, and of the Holy Ghost," was at this time not instituted: and as circumcision still continued in force, as the initiatory sacrament of the Abrahamick and Mosaick covenants, the baptism of Jesus was doubtless of adults alone. It appears then to me, that all, who at this time or afterwards, during our Lord's personal ministry, who by means of John's testimony, as in other ways, professed themselves the disciples of Jesus, as the Messiah, the Son of God, in an intelligent manner, were baptized in the name of Jesus: and whether he personally baptized any individuals or not, (for the language may only mean, that in general he did not baptize, but his disciples,) all those above described were thus baptized, though we do not further read of it. Among these we

25 Then there arose a question between *some* of John's disciples and the
Jews [g] about purifying.
26 And they came unto John, and
said unto him, Rabbi, [h] he that was
with thee beyond Jordan, [i] to whom
thou barest witness, behold, the same
baptizeth, [k] and all *men* come to him.
27 John answered and said, [l] A man
can [*] receive nothing, except it be
given him [m] from heaven.
28 Ye yourselves bear me witness,
that [n] I said, I am not the Christ, [o] but
that I am sent before him.
29 He that [p] hath the bride is the
Bridegroom: but [q] the friend of the
Bridegroom, which standeth and heareth him, rejoiceth greatly because of
the Bridegroom's voice. [r] This my joy
therefore is fulfilled.
30 He [s] must increase, [t] but I *must*
decrease.
31 He [u] that cometh from above [x] is
above all: [y] he that is of the earth is
earthly, and speaketh of the earth: [z] he
that cometh from heaven is above all.
32 And [a] what he hath seen and
heard, that he testifieth; [b] and no man
receiveth his testimony.
33 He that hath received his testimony [c] hath set to his seal that God is
true.
34 For [d] he whom God hath sent
speaketh the words of God: [e] for God

g ii. 6. Matt. iii. 11. Mark vii. 2—5. 8. Heb. vi. 2. ix. 10. 13, 14. 23. 1 Pet. iii. 21.
h Num. xi. 26—29. Ec. iv. 4. 1 Cor. iii. 3—5. Gal. v. 20, 21. vi. 12, 13. Jam. iii. 14—18. iv. 5, 6.
i i. 7, 15, 26—36.
k i. 7. 9. xi. 48. xii. 19. Acts xix. 26, 27.
l Num. xvi. 9—11. xvii. 5. 1 Chr. xxviii. 4, 5. Jer. i. 5. xvii. 16. Am. vii. 15. Matt. xxv. 15. Mark xiii. 34. Rom. i. 5. xii. 6. 1 Cor. i. 1. iii. 5. iv. 7. xii. 11. xv. 10. Gal. i. 1. Eph. i. 1. iii. 7, 8. 1 Tim. i. 7. Jam. i. 17. 1 Pet. iv. 10, 11.
* Or, *take unto himself.* Heb. v. 4, 5.
m Matt. xxi. 25. Mark xi. 30, 31.
n i. 20. 25. 27.
o i. 23. Mal. iii. 1. iv. 4, 5. Matt. iii. 3. 11, 12. Mark i. 2, 3. Luke i. 16, 17. 76. iii. 4—6.
p Ps. xlv. 9—17. Cant. iii. 11. iv. 10. Is. liv. 5. lxii. 4, 5. Hos. ii. 19, 20. Matt. xxii. 2. 2 Cor. xi. 2. Eph. v. 25—27. Rev. xix. 7—9. xxi. 9.
q Judg. xiv. 10, 11. Ps. xlv. 14. Cant. v. 1. Matt. ix. 15.
r Is. lxvi. 11. Luke ii. 10—14. xv. 6.
s Ps. lxxii. 17—19. Is. ix. 7. liii. 2, 3. 12. Dan. ii. 34, 35. 44, 45. Matt. xiii. 31—33. Rev. xi. 15.
t Acts xiii. 36, 37. 1 Cor. iii. 5. 2 Cor. iv. 7—11. Col. i. 18. Heb. iii. 3—6.
u 13. viii. 23. Eph. iv. 8—10.
x i. 15. 27. 30. v. 21—25. Matt. xxviii. 18. Acts x. 36. Eph. i. 21. Phil. ii. 9—11. 1 Pet. iii. 22. Rev. xix. 16.
y 12. 1 Cor. xv. 47, 48. Heb. ix. 1. 9, 10.
z vi. 33. 51. xvi. 27, 28.
a 11. v. 20. viii. 26. xv. 15.
b 26. 32. i. 11. Is. liii. 1. Rom. x. 16—21. xi. 2—6.
c Rom. iii. 3, 4. iv. 18—21. 2 Cor. i. 18. Tit. i. 2. Heb. vi. 17, 18. 1 John v. 9, 10.
d vii. 16. viii. 26—28. 40. 47.
e 17. i. 16. v. 26. vii. 37—39. xv. 26. xvi. 7. Num. xi. 25. 2 Kings ii. 9. Ps. xlv. 7. Is. xi. 2—5. lix. 21. lxii. 1—3. Rom. viii. 2. Eph. iii. 8. iv. 7—13. Col. i. 19. ii. 9, 10. Rev. xxi. 6. xxii. 1. 16, 17.

may number the 120, who met at Jerusalem after the day of Pentecost, and most of the 500 brethren to whom he appeared in Galilee. So that after the institution of Christian Baptism, just before our Lord's ascension, those, who had thus been baptized in his name, were not rebaptized. Nor were they considered as unbaptized persons; neither should they be adduced, as a precedent for unbaptized persons being employed in preaching the gospel, and baptizing others, or receiving and administering the Lord's supper.—Most of the apostles and primitive disciples had been baptized both with John's baptism, and with that of Jesus as "the Messiah the Son of the living God:" and the rest had been baptized with Jesus's baptism, which was an anticipation, suited to existing circumstances, of the more complete form, when Baptism became the initiatory sacrament of Christianity, and the sign and seal of regeneration.—Whether either John, or Jesus during his personal ministry, baptized *women*, is no where expressly said: and the argument about the subjects and mode of baptism has no immediate connexion with the subject: for that rests exclusively on those scriptures which relate to baptism, as superseding circumcision, in becoming the initiatory sign and seal of the covenant.—The evangelist here speaks of John the Baptist's imprisonment, as well known; but no where mentions any further particulars, either of that, or of his being put to death by Herod. Had he not been satisfied, that these important facts had been recorded by other divinely inspired writers, he would hardly have passed them over in this manner, after having so particularly insisted on the ministry and testimony of John. This confirms the opinion, that he intended his gospel, as a kind of supplement to the three other gospels, which had before been published.

Much water. (23) Πολλα ὑδατα. "Many waters." *Rev.* i. 15.—Των ὑδατων των πολλων, *Rev.* xvii. 1.

V. 25, 26. This question seems to have been, whether the baptism of John, or that of Jesus, or the traditional or the ceremonial washings, were most efficacious to take away sin. (*Marg. Ref.* g.—*Note*, ii. 6—11, *v.* 6.) Some might argue, that there was no end of innovating, and that they might as well adhere to the Pharisees, as follow either of the new teachers. This would also further excite the jealousy of John's disciples, who complained to their master, that all men came to Jesus to be baptized of him, so that John had lost his influence and popularity by bearing testimony to Jesus. Thus they seem obliquely to have censured our Lord, and to have intimated that John ought to retract the testimony, which he had given in his favour.—Many ancient manuscripts and versions read, "between "John's disciples and a Jew," in the singular: but it does not appear, that this materially alters the meaning of the passage. As the language of the New Testament always distinguishes our Lord's disciples from the other Jews, we cannot suppose that a disciple of Jesus was meant. (*Marg. Ref.* h—k.)

Purifying. (25) Καθαρισμȣ. ii. 6. *Mark* i. 44. *Luke* ii. 22. *Heb.* i. 3. 2 *Pet.* i. 9.—1 *Chr.* xxiii. 28. *Neh.* xii. 45. *Sept.*

V. 27—36. The jealousy of John's disciples for the honour of their teacher, gave him an opportunity, of bearing still fuller and more explicit testimony to our Lord. He laid it down as an universal truth, that "a man can "receive nothing, except it be given him from heaven." (*Marg.* and *Marg. Ref.* l, m.—*Note*, *Jam.* i. 16—18.) Thence he had received his commission, qualifications, and instructions; and he was fully satisfied with the place and work assigned him: (*Note*, *Eph.* iv. 7—10:) but Jesus came with a far superior commission, and for a more important design; and indeed John's ministry was superseded by that of Jesus. John's disciples knew, that he had always expressly declared he was not the Messiah, but merely his servant and forerunner: why then should it trouble them, that superior honour was rendered to him? (*Marg. Ref.* n, o.—*Notes*, i. 19—34.)—Jesus was indeed "the Bride-"groom," who had loved, and would prepare and espouse his church of redeemed sinners to himself, and ennoble, enrich, and bless it for ever by that sacred union, in which he would greatly delight and be glorified. (*Marg. Ref.* p.

giveth not the Spirit by measure *unto him.*

35 The ʳFather loveth the Son, ˢand ᵗhath given all things into his hand.

36 He ᵇthat believeth on the Son hath everlasting life: and he that believeth not the Son shall not ˡsee life; ᵏbut the wrath of God abideth on him.

Notes, Ps. xlv. 9—17. *Cant.* iii. 9—13. iv. 10. *Is.* liv. 4, 5. lxii. 1—5, *vv.* 4, 5. *Hos.* ii. 18—20. *Matt.* ix. 14, 15. *2 Cor.* xi. 1—6, *vv.* 2, 3. *Eph.* v. 22—33, *vv.* 23—27. 29. 32. *Rev.* xix. 7—10.) And John was honoured as " the friend of the " Bridegroom," and employed in collecting disciples; and thus was an instrument in effecting these gracious espousals. He therefore stood and heard his orders, and gladly obeyed them; he rejoiced greatly to hear his voice and to witness his glory; and thus his joy was now complete, in that he had heard and seen the promised Messiah, and found that the people flocked to him. He also knew, that Jesus would continue to increase in honour and influence, for " of his government and peace there would be " no end:" but for himself he must expect to be less and less considered; nor did this at all deduct from his rejoicing in Christ. (*Marg. Ref.* q—t.) He was sensible that this was reasonable and right: for Jesus came from heaven as the Son of God, and was " above all " men, angels, or creatures; while John was of the earth, a mere sinful mortal man, who could only speak in the language of the earth, concerning the more plain subjects of religion; but Jesus came from heaven to speak of heavenly things, in language suitable to their sublime and mysterious nature; as of matters familiar to him, being what " he had " seen and heard." Yet very few, and, as it were, none, compared with the whole nation, received his testimony. Those few, however, who acknowledged him as the Messiah, and profited by his instructions, " set their seal " to the truth of God, in respect of the fulfilment of his ancient prophecies and promises, and publickly declared their assurance that his word was to be depended on, in every possible case, as infallibly sure. (*Marg. Ref.* u—c. —*Notes,* 9—13.) For as Jesus came from the bosom of the Father, his words were indeed the words of God, and implicitly to be credited: and, as the great Prophet of the church, the Father gave him " the Spirit; not by " measure," as to inferior prophets, but in immeasurable fulness, from him to be communicated to all others who were sent by him. (*Marg. Ref.* d. e.—*Notes, Is.* lix. 20, 21. *Eph.* iv. 7—10, v. 7.) Indeed " the Father loved " and delighted in the Son, and in his mediatorial undertaking and work, because they so greatly glorified his name: and therefore he had entrusted to him, as Mediator, all authority and judgment; had committed to him every thing relative to the government of the church and of the world; and had determined that " all fulness should dwell " in him. (*Marg. Ref.* f, g.—*Notes,* v. 20—29. *Col.* i. 18—20.) Thus everlasting life could only be had by faith in him, and might assuredly be thus obtained: whereas every one, whether he were a disciple of the Pharisees, or of John, or whatever his character and profession might be, who " did not believe in the Son of God," or *obey* him, (for so the word is often rendered,) could not see life, or partake of salvation; but the wrath of God must for ever rest upon him; as it does on every sinner till he believe in

Christ. (*Marg. Ref.* h—k.—*Notes,* 14—21. i. 29. *Mark* xvi. 13—16. 1 *Thes.* i. 9, 10.)—' Why do you endeavour ' to add any thing to my condition ? This is the lot of ' all men, that they cannot attain even the least thing of ' themselves; but whatever they have of excellency, they ' must ascribe it to the bounty of God. You must, how- ' ever, confess that you have heard from me, what is His ' pre-eminence, and what is the nature of my ministry, ' namely, that I am sent as the forerunner of Christ. Why ' therefore should you desire me to compare myself with ' him ? Truly it is right and just, that his excellency ' should gradually more and more shine forth, and that I ' should be gradually eclipsed. But nothing could possibly ' occur, more rejoicing to my heart: and so far from en- ' deavouring to prevent your going over from me to him; ' I, on the contrary, diligently warn you, that all your sal- ' vation depends on him alone.' *Beza.*—It was certainly the aim of John to influence his disciples to become the disciples of Jesus; and to convince them, that in no other way could they escape the wrath of God.

Bride. (29) Νυμφην. *Rev.* xviii. 23. xxi. 2. 9. xxii. 17. *A daughter in law, Matt.* x. 35. *Luke* xii. 53.—*Bride- groom.*] Νυμφιος. ii. 9. *Matt.* ix. 15. xxv. 1. 5, 6. 10, *et al.*— *Decrease.* (30) Ελαllσσϑαι.—*Heb.* ii. 7. 9. Not elsewhere N. T.—*Ps.* viii. 5. *Sept.*—*Hath set to his seal.* (33) Εσφρα- γισεν. vi. 27. *Matt.* xxvii. 66. *Rom.* xv. 28, *et al.*—*He that believeth not.* (36) 'Ο απειϑων. *Acts* xiv. 2. xvii. 5. xix. 9. *Rom.* ii. 8. x. 21. xi. 30, 31. 1 *Pet.* ii. 7, 8. iii. 20. iv. 17. —*Απειϑης, Acts* xxvi. 19. *Απειϑεια, Rom.* xi. 30. Ex *a* priv. et πειϑω, *suadeo.* ' The latter phrase explains the ' former, and shews that the faith, to which the promise ' of life is annexed, is an effectual *principle* of sincere and ' unreserved obedience.' *Doddridge.* (*Notes, Heb.* iii. 14 —19. v. 7—10.)

PRACTICAL OBSERVATIONS.

V. 1—5.

Numbers are convinced in their consciences, concerning the truth of many doctrines of Christianity, and of the piety and faithfulness of its ministers, but they dare not avow their sentiments in the face of an ungodly world, or among despisers of the gospel: and, though we must not excuse such as are afraid or ashamed to associate with those, whom they believe to be " sent of God ; " yet we must not hastily reject them, lest we should " quench the " smoking flax : " for by proper instruction and encourage- ment they may at length become more bold and decided.— True religion consists especially in the right state of the heart : and as he, who has life and death at his disposal, has so repeatedly and solemnly assured us, that " except " a man be born again, he cannot see," or " enter into, " the kingdom of God ; " it surely becomes every one seriously to enquire into the meaning of this important de- claration, and earnestly and perseveringly to beseech the Lord to direct him to a proper solution of that enquiry.

CHAP. IV.

Jesus leaves Judea, 1—3. In the absence of his disciples, he discourses with a Samaritan woman concerning the water of life, 4—15 ; brings her sins to remembrance, 16—19 ; shews her the nature of acceptable worship, 20—24 ; and declares himself to be the Messiah, 25, 26. The disciples return, and are surprised to see him thus employed, 27. The woman goes to inform her neighbours, and induces them to come and hear him, 28—30. Jesus shews his disciples his delight in his Father's work ; and the blessed harvest about to be reaped by them, with reference to the Samaritans coming to him, 31—38. The Samaritans believe in him, and he continues among them for two days, 39—42. He returns to Cana ; and heals a nobleman's son who lay sick at Capernaum, 43 —54.

In this way, a man may hear, read, meditate, pray, and wait for a considerable time, before he clearly enters into the meaning ; yet he will gradually and certainly obtain an experimental knowledge of it. But surely, it is the most absurd presumption in the world, to expect future happiness without either knowing what it is to be " born " again," or enquiring further about it ; as if we could enter heaven in defiance of Christ, and by so doing prove his most solemn and repeated declaration to be a falsehood ! (*P. O. Matt.* xxiv. 29—35.) Nor is it safer or wiser, to interpret it of any notion or impression, which leaves a man proud, carnal, and an enemy of God and holiness, even as he was before ; which neither evidences his title to the kingdom, nor gives him any meetness for its holy employments. But " the natural man receiveth " not the things of the Spirit of God ; for they are fool-" ishness to him." (*Note,* 1 *Cor.* ii. 14—16.) To evade conviction therefore, it is common for man to put an absurd construction on the words of those, who " speak " according to the oracles of God," and to draw ridiculous conclusions from them ; and then to enquire, whether this be not very foolish. Whereas the folly lies in the misconstruction and misapplication, and not in the doctrine itself, which appears evident, reasonable, and wise to every teachable enquirer.—The Lord will explain his declarations, but he will not retract them ; nor will he alter the rules of admission into his kingdom, to humour the prejudices of any set of men whatever : and the true baptism is not " that which is outward in the flesh, but " that which is inward, even that of the heart," by the work of the Holy Spirit, " whose praise is not of men " but of God." (*Note, Rom.* ii. 25—29.)

V. 6—11.

Without regeneration, we cannot come to God, or walk with him, or spiritually worship him, or enjoy him. " The " carnal mind," which belongs to us all as " born of the " flesh ," is " enmity against God," so that " they who " are in the flesh cannot please him." But happy were they who are " born of the Spirit," and made spiritually minded : they can discern the things of God, and relish them ; religion becomes their element ; they are made subjects of that " kingdom of God, which is in righteous-" ness, peace, and joy," and heirs of the incorruptible inheritance of heaven. Let it not then be marvelled at, that Jesus has said, " ye *must* be born again :" it is enough that the Author, the nature, the necessity, and the effects of this gracious work are manifest, though the *manner and rule* of it be not known. Can we indeed understand fully how the most ordinary and regular effects in nature are produced ? Can we comprehend all that relates to our natural formation in the womb, and birth into the world ? Or can we change the course which God has established ? One ship is wafted into port, and another dashed upon the rocks, by the wind, as it pleases God. The sailors can neither comprehend the reasons of it, nor repel its effects : but yet they may use means, and employ their skill to avail themselves of a favourable wind, or to retire from the effects of a furious tempest : and we may also use means, and expect the blessing of God on them. It is, alas, true, that there are very many " teachers " in Israel," many professed ministers of Christianity, and those of great repute, who are ready to say, " How can " these things be ? " Nay, they positively declare that they cannot be ; and that all are enthusiasts or hypocrites, who profess them. In an inferior sense, however, we may say with humble confidence, " We testify that which we have " seen," heard, experienced, and observed, whether men will receive or reject our testimony.

V. 12—21.

If more obvious truths be rejected, we need not wonder, that the great mysteries of redemption, by the blood of the incarnate Son of God, are controverted or neglected ; for can men believe that this glorious Person, the Creator of all worlds, atoned for the sins of his enemies by his ignominious death upon the cross ; when they are not sensible, that their carnal hearts must be changed by new creating grace, before they can share with delight the holy joys of heaven ? If they do not believe that, which is as capable of proof, illustration, and comprehension, as *earthly* things in general are ; how can they believe that the Son of man was so " One with the Father," that he was in heaven when teaching here on earth ; and that he actually is present with his people here on earth, now that " he ever liveth to appear in the presence of God for them ?" (*Notes, Matt.* xviii. 19, 20. xxviii. 19, 20. *Acts* iii. 19— 21.) These are " heavenly things," and far out of the reach of all, who judge of God by carnal sense or purblind reason : yet in them is contained the great plan of God for " destroying the works of the devil," and the healing of those who have been mortally wounded with the venom of that old serpent. However infidels, scribes, or Pharisees may deride or revile ; still Christ crucified, when beheld with the eye of faith, brings life and salvation to the soul of perishing sinners ; and there is no other way of escaping everlasting misery. But, if we so look to him as to be saved from wrath ; we shall also be delivered from the power of sin ; restored gradually to spiritual health ; and transformed into the image of that glorious Object which is exhibited in the gospel.—Words can never express, how free and excellent the love of God to a sinful world has been, in " giving his only begotten Son " to be the " propitiation for our sins." Did it ever enter into the heart

394

a Luke i. 76.
ii. xix. 31. 3½.
Acts x. 36.
i Cor. ii. 8, xv.
47. 2 Cor. iv. 5.
Jam. ii. 1. Rev.
xix. 16.
b iii. 22-26.

WHEN, therefore, *the Lord knew how the Pharisees had heard* that Jesus made and baptized more disciples than John,

2 (Though 'Jesus himself baptized not, but his disciples,)

3 He 'left Judea, and departed again into Galilee.

c Acts x. 48. 1 Cor.
i. 12-17.

d iii. 22. x. 40. xi
54. Matt. x. 2.
Mark iii. 7.
e i. 43.

of an earthly prince to give his only son, his beloved, to suffer an ignominious death, in order that he might honourably save the lives of some base traitors, who had aimed to subvert his throne? Yet even this would be little and mean, compared with the love of God to rebellious man. But though our God is so ready to pardon all those who "believe in the name of his only begotten "Son," whom he "sent into the world, not to condemn "the world, but that the world through him might be "saved;" yet his infinite love will lead to the deeper condemnation of all, who continue to "neglect so great sal- "vation." The believer indeed "is not condemned," and "shall not come into condemnation:" but the unbeliever "is condemned already;" the wrath of God abideth on him; and he goes about continually under that awful load, which is sufficient to sink him into everlasting misery. Nor is this unbelief a light or venial matter: it springs from enmity against God, his truth, his law, and his glory; and from love of sin in some form or other. "Men love "darkness rather than light, because their deeds are evil;" but this would not have been so fully proved, if "Light "had not come into the world," and been hated by them. And is it proper that men should hate God, his truth, knowledge, and holiness, and love wickedness and Satan's service, with impunity? They may indeed shelter themselves under some plausible pretext, or varnish it over with some specious appearance; but they have a secret hatred of the truth, because it opposes their favourite iniquities: they wish to disbelieve, and then seek for arguments to satisfy themselves in infidelity. Let us remember it: The Judge has declared, that unbelief springs from this source, and that "every one who doeth truth cometh to the "light, that his deeds may be made manifest that they are "wrought in God." Let us judge ourselves, and bring our characters and conduct to his word, to be assayed by it: let us beseech him to discover to us the secret motives by which we are actuated, and to prevent our being deceived by Satan and our own hearts, and so lead and guide us in the safe and happy way to everlasting life and felicity.

V. 22—36.

The same state of heart and mind, which leads to bigotry and formality in religion, produces also envy, ambition, and jealousy of those who seem to outshine us: but true excellency and sanctifying grace are combined with deep humility, submission to God, and a willing dependence on him. As "a man can receive nothing except it be given "him from heaven," let us seek all our blessings from thence; give God all the glory of whatever we have or do; occupy with our talents as we are able; rejoice in the honour and service of Christ, the condescending Bridegroom of his church; stand for his voice; and seek our happiness in his presence and favour. And should we be laid aside from usefulness, and see others "increase "whilst we decrease," and are eclipsed and obscured by their superior and increasing talent, zeal, and success;

let us pray to be enabled to bear it *meekly*, yea *thankfully*, that Christ may be more honoured by it; and that numbers of such burning and shining lights may be sent forth into every part of the earth, when we are neglected or forgotten, as laid aside, and become as a broken vessel. Let us attend to him, "who cometh from above and is "above all," that we may simply receive heavenly things from his testimony; and neither call any one father or master, nor "lean to our own understanding," as all men "being of the earth are earthly, and speak of the earth." And though few indeed thus "set to their seal that God "is true;" let us seek so to honour his word, that he may seal his salvation to us, by the Spirit of his Son "shedding "abroad his love in our hearts." This is the only way of everlasting life, through faith in the Son of God, whom "the Father loveth, and into whose hand all things are "given;" for there is no salvation for sinners in any other: and 'he that believeth not shall without doubt 'perish everlastingly.'

NOTES.

CHAP. IV. V. 1—4. In many manuscripts and ancient versions, the chapter begins as follows. "When there- "fore Jesus knew that the Pharisees had heard, that he "made and baptized, &c."—Our Lord did not see good to preserve his life by a succession of miracles; and the time was distant, when he purposed to give himself into the hands of his enemies: he therefore avoided every thing, which could needlessly excite their jealousy and indignation. He seems, however, to have continued a considerable time in Judea, preaching and collecting disciples: but this at length gave umbrage to the Pharisees, (the most powerful party in the Sanhedrim,) who heard that he received, by baptism, greater numbers as disciples, than John did; and on hearing this he left Judea to return into Galilee. (*Marg. Ref.* a—e.)—It is observable, that our Lord did not baptize with his own hands. Perhaps he chose to act as the Head of the church, who baptizes with the Holy Spirit, and therefore left his servants to baptize with water: perhaps he saw that disputes would best be prevented by his not baptizing, lest those who had this peculiar distinction should glory in it: and perhaps he meant to shew, that preaching the gospel is in itself a far higher and more honourable employment, than the administration of the *external* signs of the covenant, which have generally been *exalted* too much, by those who have carefully *observed* them. (*Notes, Acts* x. 14—48. 1 *Cor.* i. 1,—19.) It cannot, however, be certainly concluded from this observation, that he never had, in any instance, baptized. It was not his practice, at the time spoken of, or his general custom. Yet he might have baptized a few of his first constant followers, whom he employed afterwards to baptize others. Thus he instituted at first the sacrament of the Lord's supper; but ever after it has been administered by his disciples. (*Note,* iii. 22—24.)—In returning to Galilee, the road lay through Samaria, and Jesus "must needs" go

f Matt. x. 5, 6.
Luke ix. 51, 52.
xvii. 11.

4 And 'he must needs go through Samaria.

5 Then cometh he to a city of Samaria, which is called Sychar, near to 'the parcel of ground that Jacob gave to his son Joseph.

6 Now Jacob's well was there. Jesus therefore, h being wearied with his journey, ' sat thus on the well: and it was about k the sixth hour.

7 There cometh a woman of Samaria to draw water: Jesus saith unto her, ' Give me to drink.

8 (For his disciples were gone away unto the city " to buy meat.)

9 Then saith the woman of Samaria unto him, How is it that thou, being a Jew, " askest drink of me, which am a woman of Samaria? ° For the Jews have no dealings with the Samaritans.

10 Jesus answered and said unto her, ' If thou knewest the gift of God, ¶ and who it is that saith to thee, Give

me to drink; 'thou wouldest have asked of him, and he would have given thee 'living water.

11 The woman saith unto him, Sir, 'thou hast nothing to draw with, and the well is deep: from whence then hast thou that living water?

12 Art "thou greater than our father Jacob, which gave us the well, and drank thereof himself, and his children, and his cattle?

13 Jesus answered and said unto her, " Whosoever drinketh of this water shall thirst again:

14 But whosoever drinketh of the water that I shall give him ' shall never thirst; but the water that I shall give him 'shall be in him a well of water springing up into everlasting life.

15 The woman saith unto him, Sir, " give me this water, that I thirst not, neither come hither to draw.

that way, unless he would go very far about: but he had also secret purposes for taking the road in which Sychar was situated. (Note, Luke vii. 11—17.)

V. 5—9. Sychar is supposed to have been the same as Sichem, or Shechem; and to have been so named from the drunkenness of the inhabitants; for Sichar, or Sychar, signifies drunk, or drunkenness, in Hebrew and Syriack. (Note, Is. xxviii. 1—4.)—In a field which Jacob bequeathed to Joseph, there was a well, which tradition reported to have belonged to Jacob. (Marg. Ref. g.—Notes, Gen. xlviii. 22. Josh. xxiv. 29—32, v. 32.) At this place our Lord arrived at the sixth hour, or about noon, for there seems no reason to suppose that John computed time differently than the other evangelists; (i. 39;) and "being wearied with his journey he sat thus on the side of the well," or near to it; taking the poor accommodations as he found them, though the seat would be uneasy, and perhaps there was no shelter from the meridian sun. (Marg. Ref. h—k.) The Samaritans were not generally disposed to receive the Jews into their houses: (Notes, Luke ix. 51—56:) he therefore did not attempt to go into the town, but sent the disciples to buy some necessary provisions; as if he intended, after making a homely meal by the well's side, to walk forward in the afternoon. In the mean while, a woman came to draw water, and Jesus, being thirsty, condescended to become her suppliant for a draught of it; intending doubtless by this method to engage her in conversation. Accordingly, she expressed her surprise that he, whom she knew by his apparel to be a Jew, should ask water of her, a Samaritan. How could he think of becoming her petitioner? Or how could he expect any favour from her? For the inveteracy between the two nations and sects was so great, that they generally confined all their intercourse to matters of mere necessity, and mu-

tually refused to ask, or perform, any actions of friendship or kindness to each other. (Marg. Ref. l—o.—Note, Luke x. 30—37.) These words are the evangelist's observation, and not the reason assigned by the woman for her question.—' By the traditions of the Pharisees, the Jews ' might buy of them, and therefore Christ's disciples do ' not scruple at this (8); but they were not to borrow ' any thing of them, or receive any kindness from them, ' or drink of their water, or eat of their morsels; for they ' bound them under an anathema, not to eat of the fruit, ' or morsel, of a Cuthæan; and held this as bad as eating ' swine's flesh. But Christ, despising such traditions as ' had no foundation, either in the law of God, or in equity; ' and tended to the impairing the laws of common friend-' ship or humanity, asks drink of this Samaritan woman, ' and eateth with them.' Whitby. (Note, 2 Kings xvii. 41. Neh. xiii. 23—30.)

Sychar. (5) Συχαρ. Here only.—שכר, ebrius. 1 Sam. xxv. 36.—שכר, ebrietas. Ez. xxiii. 33. xxxix. 10.—Being wearied. (6) Κεκοπιακως. " Having laboured." 38. Luke v. 5. 1 Cor. xv. 10, et al. A κοπος, labor.—With his journey.] Εκ της οδοιπορίας. 2 Cor. xi. 26. Not elsewhere. Εκ οδος, via, et πορεω, transeo.—'Οδοιπορεω, Acts x. 9.—To draw. (7) Αντλησαι. 15. See on ii. 8.—Have no dealings with.] Ου συγχρωνται. Here only. Εκ συν, et χραομαι, utor.

V. 10—15. Our Lord did not expressly notice the woman's narrow prejudices; but directed her attention to matters of greater importance. He told her, that, though she should refuse him the small favour which he had asked, because he was a Jew; yet he was ready to confer far greater benefits on her though a Samaritan. Had she known the plenteous mercy and bounty of God, the value and freeness of his Gift to sinful men, (Note, iii. 16,) and her urgent need of it; and had she been apprized of the

2 2 6

b ch. 1. 42, 47, 48.
ii. 24. 25. xvi.
17. Heb. iv. 13.
Rev. ii. 23.
16 Jesus saith unto her, ᵇ Go, call thy husband, and come hither.

17 The woman answered and said, I have no husband. Jesus said unto her, Thou hast well said, I have no husband:

18 For thou hast had five husbands, and he whom thou now hast ᶜ is

c Gen.   xx.   3.
xxxiv. 7.   7. b.
31. Num. v. 29.
Ruth iv. 10, 11.
Jer. iii. 20. Ez.
xvi. 82. Mark x.
12. Rom. vii. 3.
1 Cor.   vii. 10,
11. Heb. xiii. 4.

character, authority, and grace of him with whom she was conversing; she would have made her request to him for "living water:" and if she asked him, he would certainly bestow it on her.—"The gift of God" may either mean in general, his free grace to sinners, or the gift of his own Son to be their Saviour, and procure for them all spiritual blessings : but the *living water* seems especially to mean the Holy Spirit, in his sanctifying and comforting influences, through which his salvation is applied to the soul. (*Marg. Ref.* p—s.—*Notes, Ex.* xvii. 5, 6. *Is.* xliv. 3—5. *Ez.* xxxvi. 25—27. 1 *Cor.* x. 1—5. *Rev.* xxi. 5—8. xxii. 1.) His influences may be compared to water, because of the inexhaustible abundance which is provided; the gratuitous manner in which they are communicated; and their purifying, fertilizing, and refreshing efficacy. This is "*living* water," as it confers, sustains, and perfects, spiritual life; and as it is continually flowing pure from "the Fountain of life" for our use, till we come to the enjoyment of eternal life. All who know the value of these blessings, and the power and grace of Christ, ask him for them; and all who ask obtain them. (*Note,* vii. 37—39.) But the Samaritan woman supposed that our Lord meant "*running* water," which is sometimes called *living* water, both in the scriptures, (Gen. xxvi. 19. *marg. Lev.* xiv. 5. Heb.) and in the heathen poets. (' Donec me flumine vivo ' abluero,' *Virg.*) ' In this sense, the water of springs ' and rivers would be denominated *living,* and that of ' cisterns and lakes,' (or rather ponds,) ' ... dead, be- ' cause motionless.' *Campbell.* She therefore enquired whence he expected to obtain this "living water :" he could not get it out of that well, which was very deep, as he had nothing to draw with; and there was no other well nigh at hand. Yet she seems to have had some idea of his being an extraordinary person, and therefore she addressed him with a degree of respect; intimating that if he spake of some water to be procured in a supernatural manner, she wished to be informed, whether he were more honourable and powerful than the patriarch Jacob, who had used that well and left it to his posterity.—She called Jacob the father of the Samaritans, though they were generally of another race. Our Lord, however, let this groundless claim also pass unnoticed; and observed, that "whosoever drank of that water, would thirst again :" he would soon be as thirsty as ever, and might at length die of thirst, and finally perish. (*Note, Luke* xvi. 24—26.) But the nature of the water of which he spake was such, that "whosoever drank of it, would thirst no more for "ever." (*Marg. Ref.* t—y.—*Notes, Matt.* v. 6. *Rev.* vii. 13—17, v. 16.) He would thirst for more and more of it, but it would be ever at hand to satisfy his desires : it would deliver him from vitiated inclinations, and be "within "him," as a well or fountain of water, springing up in all holy affections and consolations, till perfected in everlasting life : this, as the words must imply, it certainly would be, notwithstanding all possible opposition from the world, the flesh, and the devil.—This language the woman

did not understand : and she answered as one in amazement, or half disposed to ridicule; desiring Jesus to give her some of this extraordinary water, that she might no more feel the inconvenience of thirst, nor have the trouble of fetching water from the well.—*Nothing,* &c. (11) ' Travellers provide themselves with small leathern ' buckets, because the wells in those parts are furnished ' with no apparatus for drawing.' *Thevenot.*—' The well, ' now shewn as Jacob's well, is thirty-five yards deep.' *Maundrell.*

The gift. (10) Την δωρεαν. *Acts* ii. 38. viii. 20. x. 45. xi. 17. *Rom.* v. 15. 17. 2 *Cor.* ix. 15. *Eph.* iii. 7. iv. 7. *Heb.* vi. 4.—Δωρεαν. Used adverbially. xv. 25. *Matt.* x. 8. *Rom.* iii. 24. 2 *Cor.* xi. 7. *Gal.* ii. 21. 2 *Thes.* iii. 8. *Rev.* xxi. 6. xxii. 17.—*Ps.* xxxv. 7. *Sept.*—*Nothing to draw with.* (11) Ουτε αντλημα. Here only. Ab αντλεω, 7.—*Cattle.* (12) Θρεμματα. Here only. A τρεφω, nutrio.—*Never.* (14) Εις τον αιωνα. viii. 51, 52. x. 28. xi. 26. xiii. 8. *Matt.* xxi. 19. *Mark* iii. 29. xi. 14. 1 *Cor.* viii. 13.

V. 16—18. The woman could not understand our Lord's words, because she had no conviction of sin, or thirst after spiritual blessings : yet she would afterwards remember them with great advantage. But to prepare her for receiving the truth, he next "called her sins to remem-"brance;" for this was no doubt part of his design, when he said, "Go, call thy husband, and come hither." She, however, being willing to conceal her shame, endeavoured to evade the subject, by declaring that she "had no hus-"band :" and Jesus allowed the truth of this assertion, in a manner, which shewed that he was fully acquainted with all her past conduct. It is not certain, whether all her five husbands had died, or whether she had been divorced from some of them : but at that time she cohabited with a man who was not her husband. If she had left her husband to live with another man, it could hardly have been said, that "she had no husband;" and if we suppose, that the person with whom she lived was "not her "husband," but the husband of another woman; the words of our Lord will contain such an express declaration, that polygamy was unlawful, and that the secondary wife was in fact an adulteress, as would hardly have been made, without further explanation, on this occasion. So that it is probable, she lived with a man to whom she had never been married according to the custom and order of that age and people. This shews, that a recognition before witnesses, and duly authenticated, is necessary to marriage, and distinguishes it from fornication. (*Marg. Ref.* —*Notes, Ruth* iv. 11, 12. *Matt.* xix. 3—9.)—' Five hus- ' bands from whom thou hast been divorced for thy adul- ' teries.' *Whitby.* This is neither said, nor hinted at, in the narrative : neither is it at all probable. The adulteress was punishable by death, according to the Mosaick law : (*Note,* viii. 3—11, v. 2:) and it is likely, that the Samaritans so far regarded that law, as not to suffer a woman five times convicted of adultery, and divorced for it, to escape with impunity.

not thy husband: in that saidst thou truly.

19 The woman saith unto him, Sir, [d] I perceive that thou art [e] a prophet.

20 Our [f] fathers worshipped in this mountain; [g] and ye say, that in Jerusalem is the place where men ought to worship.

21 Jesus [h] saith unto her, Woman, believe me, the hour cometh, [i] when ye shall neither in this mountain, nor yet at Jerusalem, [k] worship the Father.

22 Ye worship [l] ye know not what: [m] we know what we worship; [n] for Salvation is of the Jews.

23 But [o] the hour cometh, and now is, when the [p] true worshippers shall worship the Father [q] in spirit and [r] in truth: for [s] the Father seeketh such to worship him.

24 God is [t] a Spirit: and they that worship him, [u] must worship him in spirit and in truth.

V. 19, 20. This explicit reference to the woman's past history by an entire stranger, when probably most of it was concealed from all her neighbours, satisfied her that Jesus was a prophet, and she frankly confessed her conviction: (Marg. Ref. d, e:) but to divert the conversation from a subject so disgraceful to her, she requested of him to inform her, whether the Samaritans or the Jews were right in the grand subject of controversy between them. Adhering to the groundless pretence, that the Samaritans were descended from the stock of Israel, she observed that their fathers worshipped on mount Gerizim, the centre of their religion at that time; whereas the Jews contended that they ought to worship at Jerusalem. Abraham and Jacob erected altars at Shechem, which was very near to mount Gerizim; and from that mountain God ordered the blessings to be pronounced, while the curses were spoken from mount Ebal. (Marg. Ref. f.—Notes, Deut. xi. 26—30. xxvii. 1—13. Josh. viii. 30—35.) From these and similar premises the Samaritans inferred, that Gerizim was the place where the temple of God ought to have been built, and his sacrifices offered; and that the Jews were schismaticks and sectarians: and they rejected the greatest part of the Old Testament, perhaps because it so expressly and continually declared, that Zion was the place which God had chosen for his residence. (Marg. Ref. g.) Indeed there was no temple on mount Gerizim, till Sanballat built one there, after the days of Nehemiah. (Notes, 2 Kings xvii. 24—41. Ezra iv. 1—6. 17—24. Neh. xiii. 23—30, v. 28.) This had been destroyed by John Hyrcanus, about one hundred and thirty-one years before Christ; but probably it had been rebuilt, though with less magnificence. The Samaritans, however, thought the example of the patriarchs greatly in their favour; and this woman, notwithstanding her immorality, was eager in the controversy.

V. 21—24. In answer to this, our Lord assured the woman, (if she would " believe him " as a Prophet,) that the time was even then arrived, when all these disputes would be superseded: for neither mount Gerizim, nor Jerusalem, should longer be specially appropriated to the worship of God. (Marg. Ref. h—k.—Note, Mal. i. 9—11, v. 11.) The Samaritans indeed " worshipped they " knew not what:" they knew not the perfections of God; their worship was not regulated according to his commandments; their hope of acceptance was not grounded on his promises; their whole system was a fabrick of

superstition, ignorance, or imposture; a human device without any divine rule or warrant: for they rejected the greatest part of the sacred oracles, and misinterpreted the rest. (Marg. Ref. l, m.—Notes, viii. 54—59, v. 55. xvi. 1—3. Acts xvii. 22—25.) On the other hand the religion of the Jews was from God: they had his oracles entire; a succession of prophets had been sent among them; they worshipped the true God as revealed by his word, in the ordinances which he had instituted, and with a ground of assurance that they would be accepted, provided they were not hypocritical in their services.—Especially the promised Saviour was to arise from among the Jews: to him all the types referred, all the prophets bare witness, and all believers looked and found salvation; and through him all their ordinances became ' means of grace.' (Marg. Ref. p.—Notes, Ps. lxviii. 19, 20. Is. xii. 1—3, v. 2.) Yet the appointed period of that dispensation was come, and thenceforth the true worshippers would not be restricted to any place for their spiritual sacrifices. God was about to be revealed, as the God and Father of the Messiah, and in him the Father of all believers in every nation; and he would seek out immense multitudes " to worship him in spirit " and in truth." For as he is a Spirit, immaterial, holy, omnipresent, and intimately acquainted with the inmost soul of man; so those who acceptably " worship him, " must worship him in spirit and truth." Splendid temples, costly vestments, multiplied sacrifices, and external ceremonies with types and shadows, have nothing in them suited to his nature; and could only be appointed for a time, to be " figures of good things to come." The spirit, or soul, of man, as influenced by the Holy Spirit, must worship God, and have communion with him: knowledge of his perfections, reverential fear, humiliation as creatures and sinners, hope in his mercy and truth, regard to his word, love of his excellency, earnest desires after his favour and image, gratitude for his goodness, delight in his service, zeal for his glory, submission to his will, and cheerful dependence on his grace and providence; these spiritual affections, expressed in fervent prayers, supplications, praises, and thanksgivings, form that worship of an upright heart, in which God delights and is glorified. The redemption of Christ, the ministry of the word, and the work of the Holy Spirit, concur in forming such worshippers, and rendering them accepted: and nothing can be pleasing to God, which has not in it something of this nature.—' Not with carnal sacrifices, but with spiritual

3 q 8

25 The woman saith unto him, I *know that *Messias cometh, (which is called Christ:) *when he is come, he will tell us all things.

26 Jesus saith unto her, *I that speak unto thee am *he*.

27 ¶ And upon this came his disciples and *marvelled that he talked with the woman: yet no man said, What seekest

thou? or, Why talkest thou with her?

28 The woman then *left her water-pot, and went her way into the city, and saith to the men,

29 *Come, see a man, which told me all things that ever I did: is not this the Christ?

30 Then *they went out of the city, and came unto him.

' worship, with those " spiritual sacrifices, which are ac-
' " ceptable to God through Jesus Christ." (1 *Pet.* ii. 5.)
' ...Not in types, but according to the truth contained in
' them ; " for the Law was by Moses, but grace and truth
' " came by Jesus Christ." (i. 17.) ...We must have just
' and awful thoughts of the divine majesty, often repre-
' senting him to our thoughts, as a God of infinite purity
' and justice, as well as of power and wisdom ; one who
' is always present with, and beholds all our secret
' thoughts and actions, in order to a future recompence.
' ...We must endeavour to resemble him, as much as may
' be, in holiness and righteousness, in truth, in goodness,
' and in mercy....And we must worship God from spiritual
' principles, a sincere love, and filial reverence of him ;
' and to spiritual ends, that we may promote his glory, and
' do what is well pleasing in his sight ; and after a spiritual
' manner, serving him with the whole heart, soul, and
' mind, and with a fervency of spirit.' *Whitby.* (*Marg.
Ref.* o—u.—*Notes, Ps.* l. 7—15. li. 17. *Is.* lvii. 15, 16.
lxvi. 1, 2. *Matt.* xv. 7—9. *Rom.* i. 8—12, *v.* 9. xii. 1. *Phil.*
iii. 1—7, *v.* 3. *Heb.* xiii. 15, 16. 1 *Pet.* ii. 4—6.)—The immediate and powerful influences of the Holy Spirit are
indispensably necessary, in forming such worshippers:
(*Notes, Rom.* viii. 14—17. 24—27. *Eph.* vi. 18—20. *Jude*
20, 21:) as it is likewise, that the worshippers should
know, and trust, and approach him, as " the God of sal-
" vation," in and through Christ our Saviour. (*Notes, Rom.*
4—6, *v.* 6. *Rom.* v. 1, 2. *Eph.* ii. 14—18, *v.* 18. iii. 9—12,
v 12. *Heb.* vii. 23—25. xi. 4—6.)

Salvation. (22) Ἡ σωτηρια. " The salvation," predicted,
prefigured, and promised, in every part of the sacred scriptures.

V. 25, 26. The woman did not object to our Lord's
words: yet she seems not to have been fully satisfied ; and
therefore she was disposed to leave the matter undecided,
till the advent of the Messiah, who she expected would
come, and finally determine all these controversies, and
give them more complete instructions. But our Lord,
(not having the same reasons for caution, as he had among
the Jews, who were disposed either to excite insurrections,
or to accuse him to the Romans,) without any reserve informed her, that he was indeed the Messiah : and doubtless a power accompanied his words, which enabled her to
believe in him, and to understand in some measure the
nature of his salvation. (*Marg. Ref.*)—' Christ, leaving
' the proud Pharisees, communicates the treasures of ever-
' lasting life to a poor sinful woman, and a stranger ; re-
' futing the gross errors of the Samaritans, and defending
' the true service of God, which was delivered to the Jews:
' but so that he calleth both of them back to himself, as

' One whom alone all the fathers, and all the ceremonies
' of the law, did regard.' *Beza.*—*Which is called Christ.*
(25) This is evidently the evangelist's remark, to his
readers, who understood Greek and not Hebrew : and not
the words of the woman, who doubtless spake in the language of the country, which was Syriack, or a dialect of
the Hebrew.

He will tell. (25) Αναγγελει. v. 15. xvi. 13, 14. *Mark* v.
14. 19. *Acts* xiv. 27. xv. 4. xvi. 38. xx. 20. *Rom.* xv. 21.
1 *Pet.* i. 12.

V. 27. The disciples themselves had just before been
conversing with the Samaritans, while purchasing provisions ; and on other occasions, intercourse of *that kind*
must have taken place between the Jews and Samaritans :
but that Jesus should enter into free conversation with a
woman, who was an entire stranger, and also a Samaritan,
and appear earnest in it, was very wonderful to them.
(*Luke* vii. 39.) It is not at all likely, that the mere cir
cumstance of conversing with a woman should exclusively
excite this wonder : and as to the absurd and illiberal traditions and maxims of the Rabbies, which some learned
men have adduced on this subject ; it is manifest that they
were wholly disregarded by our Lord, except when he entered his protest against them. The women with whom
he conversed in general were Jewesses, and persons well
known to him and his disciples : but this woman was a
Samaritan, and likewise unknown to them. They had,
however, notwithstanding their strong remaining prejudices, too high a veneration for their Lord, to ask any
questions concerning his motives or intentions.

V. 28—30. In the mean time the woman, being greatly
affected with what she had heard, and with the discovery of
the promised Messiah, left her water-pot, (either through
forgetfulness, being full of other thoughts, or because she
intended to come again to draw water ;) and, hasting to the
city, she excited the attention of her neighbours, by calling
on them to go with her, and see a most extraordinary
Person, who had told her the history of her whole past
life. And was " not this the Christ?" Indeed he had
told her that he was ; but she wished them to go, and
judge for themselves.—Thus she, who left the town an
ignorant, bigotted, and licentious woman, by a miracle of
grace returned thither, as it were, an evangelist, to preach
Christ to her neighbours ; who were so impressed by her
words, and by the power which attended them, that they
went forth in great numbers to meet Jesus ! (*Marg. Ref.*
—*Notes*, 16—18. i. 47—51. *Note* and *P. O. Mark* v. 14—
20. *Note*, 1 *Cor.* xiv. 20—25, *vv.* 24, 25.)

Water-pot. (28) Ὑδριαν. ii. 6, 7.—Probably this vessel was
used for *drawing*, as well as *carrying* the water. Αντλημα, 11.

31 In the mean while his disciples prayed him, saying, ' Master, eat.

32 But he said unto them, ' I have meat to eat ' that ye know not of.

33 Therefore ' said the disciples one to another, Hath any man brought him *ought* to eat?

34 Jesus saith unto them, ' My meat is to do the will of him that sent me, ' and to finish his work.

35 Say not ye, There are yet four months, and *then* cometh harvest? behold, I say unto you, Lift up your eyes, and look on the fields; ' for they are white already to harvest.

36 And ' he that reapeth receiveth wages, and gathereth fruit, unto life eternal: that ' both he that soweth, and he that reapeth, may rejoice together.

37 And herein is that saying true,

' One soweth, and another reapeth.

38 I ' sent you to reap that whereon ye bestowed no labour: ' other men laboured, and ye are entered into their labours.

39 ¶ And ' many of the Samaritans of that city believed on him ' for the saying of the woman, which testified, He told me all that ever I did.

40 So when the Samaritans were come unto him, ' they besought him that he would tarry with them: ' and he abode there two days.

41 And ' many more believed, ' because of his own word;

42 And said unto the woman, Now we believe, not because of thy saying: ' for we have heard *him* ourselves, ' and know that this is indeed the ' Christ, the Saviour of the world.

e Gen. xxiv. 33. Acts xvi. 30—34.
f 34. Job xxiii. 12. Ps. lxiii. 5. cxix. 103. Prov. xviii. 20. Is. liii. 11. Jer. xv. 16. Acts xx. 35.
g Ps. xxxv. 14. Prov. xiv. 10. Rev. ii. 17.
h Matt. xvi. 6—11. Luke ix. 45.
i 34. vi. 33. Ps. xl. 6. Is. lxi. 1—3. Luke xv. 4—6. 10. xix. 10. Acts
k v. 36. xvii. 4. xix. 30. Heb. xii. 2.
. 35. Matt. ix. 37. 38. Luke x. 2.
m Prov. xi. 30. Dan. xii. 3. Rom. i. 13. 1 Cor. iv. 15. 2 Phil. ii. 16. 1 Thes. ii. 19, 20. 1 Tim. iv. 16. 2 Tim. iv. 7, 8. Jam. v. 19, 20.
n 1 Cor. iii. 5—9.

o Judg. vii. 3. Mic. vi. 15.
p Acts ii. 41. iv. 32. v. 14. vi. 7. viii. 4—8. 14
q 1 Pet. i. 7. 2 Chr. xxxvi. 15. Jer. xliv. 4. Matt. iii. 2, 9. vi. 33. xi. 8—10. Acts x. 37, 38, 42. xi. 1 Pet. i. 11. 12.
s 29. 42.
t Gen. xxxii. 26. Prov. iv. 13. Cant. iii. 4. Jer. xix. 8. Luke viii. 38. x. 39. xxiv. 29. Acts xvi. 15.
u Luke xix. 5—10. 2 Cor. vi. 1.
x Rev. iii. 20. Oro. xliv. 19.
y vf. 53. vii. 46.
z Matt. xvi. 28. 29. Luke iv. 32. 1 Cor. ii. 4, 5. Heb. iv. 12.
a Acts xvii. 11, 12.
b 20. i. 29. iii. 14—16. iv. 68, 69. vi. 27. Is. xlv. 22. iii. 10. Luke ii. 11.

ii. 10, 11. 32. Acts iv. 12. Rom. x. 11—13. 2 Cor. v. 19. 1 John iv. 14.

V. 31—34. In this interval, the disciples were earnest with Jesus, to partake of the provisions which they had brought; but he was so much engaged in the labour of love, that he thought no further of his weariness, hunger, or thirst. (*Note,* 5—9, *v.* 6.) He therefore told them, that " he had meant to eat that they knew not of:" and when they did not understand his meaning; he added, " My " meat is to do the will of him that sent me, and to finish " his work." It was the Father's will, that he should labour, preach, work miracles, " fulfil all righteousness," in the midst of difficulties and temptations, and at length " finish his work " on earth, by his sufferings on the cross. This was his " meat:" he had an appetite and a relish for it, and found every part of it a delight and refreshment to his soul, because God was glorified and men were benefited by it. As therefore an opportunity was now afforded him, of being employed in his work, he intimated, that he would postpone eating till afterwards. (*Marg. Ref.—Notes, Gen.* xxiv. 33—36. *Ps.* xl. 6—8. cxix. 44—48. *Jer.* xv. 15—18. *Acts* xx. 32—35.)

Master. (31) 'Ραββί. *Notes,* iii. 2. *Matt.* xxiii. 8—10.— *Meat.* (32) Βρωσις. vi. 27. 55. *Matt.* vi. 19, 20. *Rom.* xiv. 17, *et al.—My meat.* (34) Εμον βρωμα. *Matt.* xiv. 15. 1 Cor. iii. 2. vi. 13, *et al.—To finish.*] Ινα ... τελειωσω. v. 36. xvii. 23. *Acts* xx. 24. See on *Luke* xiii. 32.

V. 35—38. It was indeed about four months to the time of the natural harvest: yet if they looked up and observed the Samaritans coming to hear his doctrine, they would see that the fields were even then white unto a better harvest; which he was about to reap, in consequence of the seed he had just sown by conversing with the Samaritan woman. And they ought to consider, that this kind of harvest was far more important than the other: for not only would the laborious reaper be graciously rewarded with eternal life; but they who were converted by his labours would be as " fruit gathered " into the same

blessedness: and while many, in one way or other, contributed to the sowing the seed, and gathering in the crop; they would all at last rejoice together in the success. This was the good work, in which he meant to employ them, as well as to labour himself: and in their case the proverb, that " one soweth, and another reapeth," which generally was applicable to times of publick calamity, would be happily verified. (*Notes, Judg.* vi. 2, 3. *Is.* lxv. 21—23. *Mic.* vi. 10—15.) He was about to send them out to preach in his name: and the labours of the ancient prophets, and of John the Baptist, and especially his own ministry, would render their work comparatively easy, and they would be abundantly successful: thus they would " enter into others' labours," and reap the harvest which sprang from what others had sown. (*Marg. Ref.—Note, Matt.* x. 36—38.)—This was accomplished after our Lord's ascension, in the conversion of vast multitudes, both of Jews and Samaritans, by their ministry.—The clause, " There are yet four months, and then cometh harvest," seems to have been meant of the *fact,* and not as a *proverb:* but how far it may be made use of to settle the chronology, or harmony, of our Lord's life and labours, must be determined by those, whose studies have been more immediately directed to that object; which after all seems to be of very subordinate consequence.—' In your common ' harvest, you usually say, after your seed is sown, four ' months hence will come the harvest. ...But in this spi- ' ritual harvest it is otherwise; for the seed of the word ' sown in the heart of the woman of Samaria, in your ab- ' sence, hath made the Samaritans already ripe for the har- ' vest.' *Whitby.—Four months.* (35) Τιτραμηνον. Here only.

V. 39—42. Many of the Samaritans were convinced that Jesus was the Messiah, by what the woman had told them concerning him, in which it is probable, many circumstances would be mentioned, illustrative of the subject, which are not adduced in so concise a narrative: (*Notes,* 16—18. 28—30:) and when they had come to him

b Matt. xv. 21—
24. Mark vii. 27,
28. Rom. xv. 8.
c Ex. i. 42. Matt.
iv 14.

43 ¶ Now b after two days, he departed thence, c and went into Galilee;

d Matt. xiii. 57.
Mark
Luke iv. 24.

44 For Jesus himself testified, d that a prophet hath no honour in his own country.

e Matt. iv. 23, 24.
Luke iv. 40.
f ii. 13—16. iii. 2.
g Deut. xvi. 16.
Luke ii. 42—44.
ix. 53.
h 2. Josh. xix. 28.
i Or, courtier, or, ruler.
k Ps. 16. lxxviii. 34. Hos. v. 15.
Matt. iv. 16. xv. 22. xvii. 15.
Luke vii. 2. viii. 42.
k Mark ii. 1—3.

45 Then when he was come into Galilee, e the Galileans received him, f having seen all the things that he did g at Jerusalem at the feast: h for they also went unto the feast.

46 So Jesus came again into h Cana of Galilee, where he made the water wine. And there was a certain i nobleman, k whose son was sick at Capernaum,

l xi. 21. 32. Ps. alvi. 1. Luke vii.
6—8. viii. 41.
Acts ix. 38.
m 41. 42. ii. 18.
xii. 37. xv. 24.
xv. 29. Num.
xiv. 11. Matt.
xvi. 1. xxvii.
42. Luke x. 1st.
xvi. 31. Acts ii.
22. 1 Cor. i. 22.

47 When k he heard that Jesus was come out of Judea into Galilee, he went unto him, and besought him l that he would come down and heal his son : for he was at the point of death.

48 Then said Jesus unto him, m Except ye see signs and wonders ye will not believe.

n Ps. xli. 17.
lxxviii. 10—12.
Mark v. 22. 26, 36.

49 The nobleman saith unto him, Sir, n come down ere my child die.

o xi. 40. 1 Kings xvii. 13—15.
Matt. viii. 13.
Mark vii. 29, 30. ix. 23, 24.
Luke xvii. 14.
Acts xiv. 9, 10.
Rom. iv. 20, 27
Heb. xi. 19.

50 Jesus saith unto him, o Go thy way; thy son liveth. And the man believed the word that Jesus had spoken unto him, and he went his way.

p 50. 53. 1 Kings xvii. 23.

51 And as he was now going down, his servants met him, and told him, saying, p Thy son liveth.

52 Then enquired he of them the hour when he began to amend. And they said unto him, Yesterday at the seventh hour the fever left him:

q Ps. xxxiii. 9.
cxlviii. 20. Matt.
viii. 6, 9. 13.
r Luke xix. 9.
16. 34. xviii. 8.

53 So the father knew that' it was q at the same hour in the which Jesus said unto him, Thy son liveth: r and himself believed and his whole house.

s ii. 1—11.

54 This is again s the second miracle that Jesus did, when he was come out of Judea into Galilee.

and heard his word, notwithstanding their national and religious prejudices, they invited him to stay a while among them for their further instruction. (Notes, 5—9, v. 9. Matt. x. 5, 6. Luke ix. 51—56. Acts i. 4—8. viii. 5—8.) Accordingly he graciously condescended to abide two days with them, and doubtless shewed the evidences of his being the Messiah, and the nature of his kingdom; by means of which many more of them believed, and were fully assured that he was " the Saviour of the world," that is, of all sinners throughout the world, who trust and obey him. This was the more wonderful, as we do not find that Jesus wrought any miracle among them. (Marg. Ref.) —Two days. (40) ' He abode there so long, that he might ' not contemn persons so desirous to learn of him; and ' no longer, that he might not neglect the Jews, even ' to prefer the Samaritans before them: and he com- ' manded his apostles, not to go to any city of Samaria, ' (Matt. x. 5,) because the gospel was first to be preached ' to the Jews.' Whitby.—The Saviour of the world. (42) (Note, 1 John iv.13—17, v. 14.) ' That is, says Mr. Cl——, of ' the Jews; for it is not likely, that the Samaritans thought ' of the salvation of the Gentiles. But why might they ' not think so, who knew, " that in the seed of Abraham ' " were the families of the earth to be blessed?" And ' seeing the Samaritans were not Jews, had they used ' these words in that restrained sense, they excluded ' themselves from this salvation. ... " The world " ... ' never means the Jews in opposition to the Gentiles.' Whitby.

V. 43—45. (Marg. Ref.—Notes, Matt. xiii. 54—58, v. 57. Luke iv. 16—32, vv. 16. 24.) The proverb referred to was a general truth: yet the miracles which Jesus had wrought, and the reputation which he had acquired, at Jerusalem, procured him influence and acceptance, among many of the Galileans who had been at the feast. It is,

however, the general opinion, that Nazareth and its neighbourhood are here called " his own country:" and that this is assigned as the reason, why he went by another road to Cana, instead of going to Nazareth to reside, or even taking that city in his way; for Cana lay north of Nazareth.

V. 46—54. When our Lord was come again to Cana, the son of a certain " nobleman," or courtier, (Marg.) probably of Herod's court, who was sometimes called king, (Note, Mark vi. 14—29, v. 14,) lay dangerously ill at Capernaum, which was at a considerable distance. This courtier, hearing that Jesus was returned, came in person to Cana, and most respectfully intreated him to go with him, and heal his son, who lay at the point of death. (Marg. Ref. i—l.—Notes, 2 Kings iii. 11, 12. v. 9—12. Matt. viii. 5— 9. Luke vii. 1—10.) Upon this, our Lord rebuked the unteachableness of his countrymen, and their neglect of spiritual blessings, by observing that they would not believe in him, except they continually witnessed his power in working miracles, and received the temporal benefit of them: whereas the Samaritans had believed his word without any miraculous confirmation of it. This reproof, of the truth and justice of which the courtier was probably convinced, only influenced him more earnestly to intreat Jesus to go with him, " ere his son died:" for he believed he could recover him if upon the spot; though he does not then seem to have conceived, that he could raise him from the dead, or heal him at a distance. But our Lord, in order to prove and increase his faith, ordered him to return home, as " his son lived," or was recovered and out of danger: and though the man had no proof of this but the word of Jesus, and no instance of this kind seems at that time to have occurred, yet he was enabled to believe it. He therefore set off home without hesitation, and being met by his servants, he found from them, that his son was

CHAP. V.

Jesus goes up to Jerusalem; and at the pool of
Bethesda, on the sabbath day, heals one who had
been diseased thirty-eight years; and orders him to

carry his bed, 1—9. The Jews demand of the man,
who ordered him to carry his bed: Jesus finds him at
the temple, and warns him to sin no more; and he
informs the Jews that Jesus had healed him, 10—15.
They persecute Jesus, 16. He defends himself, as-

instantaneously relieved from his fever, exactly at the time
when Jesus had spoken the word : in consequence of this
both the courtier and his family became the avowed disciples of Christ. (*Marg. Ref.* m—s.)—Some think that this
was Chuza, Herod's steward. (*Note, Luke* viii. 1—3.)—
Our Lord had wrought miracles elsewhere, but this was
the second performed at Cana, and on his return from
Jerusalem. (*Note,* ii. 1—11.)

Nobleman. (46) Βασιλικος, scil. *amp.* 49. *Acts* xii. 20,
21. *Jam.* ii. 8.—A ϲασιλευς, *rex.* Some think, that he was
a near relation, as well as a courtier of Herod.—*He began
to amend.* (52) Κομψοτερον εσχε. Here only.

PRACTICAL OBSERVATIONS.

V. 1—15.

The success of the gospel always exasperates proud
unbelievers, especially Pharisees, and formal teachers and
rulers in the church, however prudently its ministers behave : but it is best in general not to out-brave, but to
give way to, the violence of persecutors, as far as it consists with faithfulness and usefulness.—In all our journeys
we should copy our Lord's example : into whatever place
we come, we should endeavour to render our presence useful ; and we ought always to subordinate our personal accommodations to that superior object.—We should frequently meditate on his " weariness," and his painful,
exposed, and inconvenient situation, when " he sat thus
" at the well ; " few would be cheerfully satisfied to journey, to rest, and to fare as he did. This consideration
may teach the poor, patience and contentment ; and the
rich, self-denial, simplicity, gratitude, and liberality.—But
let us observe where and what the " lost sheep " of Christ
are, when he comes " to seek and save " them ; and how he
meets with them frequently, when they are not at all
thinking of him. If we now believe in his name, after
a careful review of our own character, thoughts, and plans,
when he first began to make himself known to us ; we
shall, many of us at least, be constrained to confess, that
we were as unworthy and unlikely, as much prejudiced
against him, and apparently as far out of his way, as this
poor Samaritan woman was. This illustrates the riches of
his grace, and should excite our humble gratitude. (*Note,
Is.* lxv. 1, 2. P. O 1—10.)—We may also remark, that
bigotry and controversy are extremely inimical to piety and
charity : they indispose men to communicate good, or to
receive it from others : and thus when they should be
praying together, or edifying one another, they are separated by strong antipathy. Nay, those who are agreed in
the most important matters, and only differ about subordinate points, are often most vehement in their animosity !
But, if we " know the gift of God " and the excellency of
Christ, we shall ask of him, and he will give us the blessings of salvation. If we are made wise in the things of
God, we shall gladly take a hint from a stranger, or one
of another sect or sentiment : and they who are like Jesus
will readily counsel or help the meanest, the vilest, or

the most prejudiced of mankind.—Blessed be God, for
" the wells of salvation " and " the water of life ; " and that
we are assured that God will " give his Holy Spirit to all
" who ask him " in the Saviour's name. Indeed men in
general do not value these blessings : they thirst only for
sensual pleasures, worldly honours, wealth, power, or splendour : and how largely soever they drink of these wasting
and polluted streams ; they thirst again and are still dissatisfied, and will thirst for ever, without hope or remedy, unless they now drink the waters of life. But happy are they,
who are " athirst for the living God," and for his image
and favour ! (*Notes, Ps.* xlii. 1—3. lxiii. 1—4. lxxxiv. 1,
2.) The trifles of this world will no more quiet them, than
toys will content a hungry child ; they will be importunate
in prayer for the blessings which Jesus is exalted to bestow : and the more they perceive that " the well is deep,"
and that they cannot draw of themselves ; the more earnest
will they be in beseeching God to assist them by his Holy
Spirit. When they experience his holy consolations, their
thirst after sinful pleasures abates ; the world appears
worthless ; and an abiding change is manifested in their souls ;
he, who began the good work, maintains it and carries it
on ; holy desires, purposes, and affections, spring up in the
heart ; and these are earnests and foretastes of everlasting
life, and will terminate and be perfected in it. (*P. O.* vii.
37—53. *Rev.* vii. 9—17.)

V. 16—26.

In vain do we enlarge on the comforts, privileges, and
security of the new covenant ; in vain do we represent the
preciousness and love of Christ, to the unregenerate, the
unhumbled sinner. He can " see no beauty in him," no
desirableness in his salvation, no need of it ; and he will
not apply for the healing of his soul before he feels his
sickness, nor for the binding up of his heart, till it is
broken by a sense of guilt and danger. (*Notes,* iii. 3—6.
Matt. v. 3.) We should therefore lay open the law as " the
" ministration of condemnation," and endeavour to put
men in remembrance of their crimes, that " their mouths
" may be stopped," and their thoughts turned from other
objects to their own hearts and lives. When the word of
God is faithfully opened, and skilfully divided, it often
reaches the case, as it were, at one stroke ; and thus it
produces both a conviction of sin in the outward conduct,
and a discovery of the evil which lay concealed within.
(*P. O.* 1 *Cor.* xiv. 12—25, *vv.* 24, 25.) Indeed the sinner,
when thus attacked, often employs every imaginable means
to shift off the conviction ; and even religious controversy
is frequently had recourse to for a plausible evasion. When
those subjects are started, which are suited immediately
to detect men's vanity, sensuality, luxury, avarice, or ambition ; they will, as it were, say, ' Come let us talk of
something else. What think you of this or the other
doctrine ? Of this sect, this book, this sermon, or this
preacher ? ' They appear to be religiously disposed, but it
is in order plausibly to escape conviction ; and in fact they

serting his personal and mediatorial dignity and autho- | a voice from heaven, 37, 38, and to the scriptures, 39,
rity, in the most explicit and energetick language, 17 | 40. He exposes their unbelief, ambition, and ungod-
—32: appealing to the testimony of John, 33—35; | liness; and shews, that in disbelieving him, they dis-
to his own miracles, 36; to the testimony of God by | believed Moses also, 41—47.

say, ' any subject but Herodias,' or any thing even about Herodias, except, " it is not lawful for thee to have " her." But the wisdom of the minister consists, in pursuing the convicted culprits through all these windings; and if they escape one net to lay another for them.—When any one shrinks from the *touch*, we may be sure there is a *sore*, and we should take courage to push vigorously our advantages. Indeed it is surprising and lamentable, to observe how the most abandoned persons will dispute about forms and notions.—There is an essential difference between the ordinances of God, and the most specious human inventions: even many called Christians " know not what " they worship," or where salvation is to be found: and let it never be lost sight of, that a sinner cannot worship the " only living and true God," with comfort and acceptance, except as in Christ the God of salvation. We must not, however, over-value external distinctions: as no worshippers can be accepted, who do not " worship God in " spirit and truth;" nor indeed could any other be capable of enjoying felicity in him. As " the Father seeketh " such to worship him;" let us beseech him to make us such by his new creating grace, and let us willingly become his instruments in endeavouring to increase the number and the zeal of these spiritual worshippers, that we may offer " spiritual sacrifices, acceptable to him " through Jesus Christ our Lord:" and, if thus distinguished, let us rejoice and thank our God; for in praising and adoring him we shall find happiness to all eternity!

V. 27—42.

Even wise and good men are very incompetent judges of what it becomes the Lord to do: but reverence will impose silence on them, even when perplexed with the greatest difficulties; and they will deeply abhor such blasphemous objections, as unbelievers often utter, concerning " things which they understand not."—When the heart is much engaged in pursuit of " the Pearl of great " price," outward concerns will sometimes be neglected: and when our affections are greatly excited, we shall naturally be led to call on others to seek those blessings, which we see to be valuable beyond all comparison. Thus, the greatest sinners become witnesses for Christ; and from their own experience, they declare his love and truth to all around them. But no trembling sinners can be more earnest to hear the words of life, than some zealous ministers are (and than all ministers should be) to preach them.—When we consider the Lord Jesus counting his rugged path, his hardships, his labours, and his whole work on earth, till he " finished " it on the agonizing cross, (*Note*, xix. 28—30,) as more pleasant to him than his necessary food; and when we remember that his love and zeal are still unabated, while the exercise of them is attended with no suffering or fatigue; we may confidently seek to him for all the blessings of salvation, and expect them from him. But we should also consider him as our example; and in our inferior services and lighter trials, it should be our " meat to do the will of God, and to finish " his work." This mind of Christ should be in all his dis-

ciples, but in his ministers especially. When the harvest is ripe, the husbandmen endure hardship, heat, thirst, and fatigue, to seize the opportunity of reaping it: and when sinners are disposed to hear the gospel, we should deem the " fields already white for harvest," and disregard personal inconveniences and self-denial, to improve the precious occasion. On the other hand, the husbandman, having sown his seed, waits patiently till " the appointed " weeks of harvest;" and so should we, when we have sown the good seed of the word, though we do not presently see the fruit of our labours. Indeed comparatively small success will render this the most gainful employment in the world. Every soul converted will be the minister's everlasting crown of rejoicing, and be for ever happy with him. Let us then patiently and cheerfully endure " the heat and burden of the day:" for as prophets, apostles, and martyrs have laboured and suffered in sowing that seed, of which we now reap the blessed harvest without their toil and tribulation; so others may reap the crop with joy, of what we now sow, weeping because perhaps it all seems to be thrown away. Faithful ministers often labour long, and with little encouragement, but the seed is not lost; for others enter into their labours, and gather many souls unto Christ: and in that world, where ambition and envy are no more, they will all unite in rejoicing over that success, to which they have been in different ways instrumental. In the mean time then, let us labour (whether sowing or reaping,) in faith, hope, love, and patience.—The chief usefulness of ministers is sometimes found among those, who previously bore the worst characters, and were counted the most hopeless persons. Such are often the instruments of exciting others, by carrying a report of what they have heard and experienced; and the effects of " the quick and powerful word " of Christ, in detecting the thoughts and intentions of their hearts, and bringing to remembrance the sins of their past lives, are the general means by which men are brought to believe. Those, however, who hear and receive the word of God, " have the witness in themselves;" and shall know and be assured that " Jesus is the Christ, the Saviour of the " world." (*Notes*, 1 *John* v. 9—13.)

V. 43—54.

Pride, prejudices, and worldly prosperity concur in keeping men from the Saviour; and those are happy afflictions, personal or domestick, which induce any to enquire after him. Indeed the rich and honourable of the world seldom come to him; till some grievous trial shews them the vanity of their distinctions, and that they need other help than man can give, or wealth can purchase. (*P. O. Matt.* ix. 18—26.) This conviction, and a heart broken for sin, prepare the mind so to see the suitableness of Christ and his salvation to their wants and desires, that signs and wonders are no longer needful, in order to a man's believing and humbly trusting in him. But we must submit to his rebukes, and renew our applications with increasing importunity; we must simply credit his words and follow his directions, if we would have the blessing from him. Then

a ii. 13 Ex. xxiii.
14—17. xxxiv.
23. Lev. xxiii.
2. Deut. xvi. 16.
Matt. iii. 15.
Gal. iv. 4.

* Or, gate. Neh.
iii. 1. xii. 39.
b ix. xxii. 9. 11.

AFTER this a there was a feast of the Jews, and Jesus went up to Jerusalem.

2 Now there is at Jerusalem by the sheep *market* b a pool, which is called in the Hebrew tongue Bethesda, having five porches.

3 In these lay a great multitude of impotent folk, c of blind, halt, d withered, e waiting for the moving of the water.

4 For an angel went down at a certain season into the pool, and troubled the water: whosoever then f first, after the troubling of the water, stepped in, g was made whole of whatsoever disease he had.

c Matt. xv. 30, 31
Luke vii. 22.
d 1 Kings xiii. 4.
Zech. xi. 17
Mark iii. 1....
Prov. viii. 34
Lam. iii. 26.
Rom. viii. 25.
Jam. v. 7.
f Ps. cxix. 60.
Prov. vi. 4, 5.
Ec. ix. 10. Hos.
xiii. 13. Matt.
vi. 33. Luke
xiii. 24—28. xvi.
16.
g 2 Kings v. 10—
14. 1 John i. 7.

14 Ex. xlvii. 8. 9.   Zech. xiii. 1. xiv. 8.   1 Cor. vi. 11.

experience will confirm and strengthen our faith; and we shall find that every event exactly accords with his declarations, and that all things in heaven and earth obey him. In this way, the knowledge of Christ spreads through families, and men find health and salvation to their souls. These miracles never cease : may we and all our's seek to Jesus, and experience them for our good ! ..

NOTES.

CHAP. V. V. 1. This is generally supposed to have been the feast of the passover: (*Marg. Ref.*) yet perhaps none of the evangelists mention all the passovers, which occurred during our Lord's publick ministry. But, subsequent to what was related in the former chapter, several things, recorded by the other evangelists, are supposed to have taken place, before Jesus went up to Jerusalem. He had called several disciples to a stated attendance on him, wrought many miracles, and probably delivered the sermon on the mount. (*Notes, Matt. iv. 12—25. v—vii. Luke iv. 16—44. v. 1—11.)—'He refused not communion with 'a church, which had clogged these festivals with human 'traditions: though perhaps he performed only the rites 'required by the law.' Whitby.

V. 2—4. As the evangelist uses the present tense, saying, "There is at Jerusalem, &c.' it has been conjectured, that he wrote his gospel before the subversion of that city : but this is not decisive; for the pool might remain, even though the porches were laid in ruins; and the spot on which the city stood was called Jerusalem, long after the temples and buildings were destroyed by Titus; and indeed is so to this day. Thus our Lord says, "Jeru- "salem shall be trodden down of the Gentiles, until the "times of the Gentiles be fulfilled." (*Luke* xxi. 24.) Many things are recorded, or reported, concerning this pool; which do not appear deserving of credit. It was situated near "the sheep-market," or the *sheep-gate*, by which great numbers of these animals were driven into the city, to be sold for sacrifices, or for consumption. (*Marg. and Ref.*) The name, "Bethesda," signifies "a house of "mercy;" and it seems to have been given it, on account of the miracles there wrought. The "five porches," or porticos, were probably built on the several sides of the pool, for the accommodation of those who walked there to recreate themselves, or converse with their friends; but they became at length, in great measure, appropriated to the use of those diseased persons, who went thither to be healed. Of these "a great multitude" were collected together; some of them being afflicted or disabled in one way, and some in another. Probably, most of them were deemed incurable by ordinary methods; and therefore they were carried thither, to wait and hope for a miraculous recovery. (*Marg. Ref.* b—e.) For it pleased God (in order to shew that he had not forsaken his people, but that he was about to visit them again in mercy,) to send "an angel," from time to time, to excite a visible and extraordinary commotion in the pool : and whenever this took place, it was found by experience, that the person who first bathed in it after the troubling of the water, was perfectly cured, whatever disorder he had been afflicted with; but that others who bathed afterwards obtained no relief.—Some have thought that this effect was produced only once a year, at the feast of the passover; and others, with more probability, that it occurred every sabbath. But if "the troubling of the water" took place so regularly, that the time might be certainly foreknown; it does not appear that the diseased persons would have had any occasion previously to wait by the pool, as it would have sufficed for them to come at the appointed seasons. (*Marg. Ref.* f, g.)—'An Angel went down at the seasons appointed 'by God, though not fixed or foreknown by men.' Bp. Hall.—The hypothesis of Dr. Hammond, (though supported by the sanction of some of the ancient fathers,) which supposes, that the washing of the numerous sacrifices and the entrails of them, in this pool, had given it a salutary virtue; and that the *angel* was no other than a *messenger*, sent by the priests or rulers, to stir up the water, that this efficacy might be more powerfully exerted; is so unscriptural ar d so irrational, that it is wonderful it should ever have been thought of a *second time*, by any one to whose imagination it might once occur. To mention nothing else, what were the brazen sea, and the lavers, in the courts of the temple provided for, and always replenished with abundance of water; but that the sacrifices (as well as the priests and Levites,) might be washed upon the spot, and not carried out of the holy place, to a distant pool for that purpose?—It is probable, that this miracle was not wrought for any length of time, and perhaps it ceased on this occasion—'This may account for the 'surprising silence of Josephus in a story which made so 'much for the honour of his nation. ...He was himself 'not born when it happened : and though he might have 'heard the report of it, he would perhaps (in the modern 'way) oppose speculation and hypothesis to fact. ...Or, 'if he secretly suspected it to be true, his dread of the 'marvellous, and fear of disgusting his pagan readers, 'might as well lead him to *suppress* this, as to *disguise* the 'passage through the Red Sea, and the divine voice 'from mount Sinai, in so mean and foolish a manner, as 'it is known he does. And the relation, in which this fact 'stood to the history of Jesus, would render him peculi- 'arly cautious·in touching on it.' Doddridge.—This mira-

5 And a certain man was there, ᵇ¹⁴ ˡˣ ¹ ²¹· which had an infirmity ᵇ thirty and eight years.

6 When Jesus saw him lie, ¹ and knew that he had been now a long time in that case, he saith unto him, ᵏ Wilt thou be made whole?

7 The impotent man answered him, Sir, ¹ I have no man, when the water is troubled, to put me into the pool: but while I am coming another steppeth down ᵐ before me.

8 Jesus saith unto him, ⁿ Rise, take up thy bed, and walk.

9 And ᵒ immediately the man was made whole, and took up his bed, and walked: ᵖ and on the same day was the sabbath.

10 The Jews therefore said unto him that was cured, It is the sabbath-day: q it is not lawful for thee to carry thy bed.

11 He answered them, ʳ He that made me whole, the same said unto me, Take up thy bed, and walk.

12 Then asked they him, ˢ What man is that which said untò thee, Take up thy bed, and walk?

13 And he that was healed wist not who it was: for Jesus ᵗ had conveyed himself away, ᵘ a multitude being in that place.

14 Afterward Jesus findeth him ᵛ in the temple, and said unto him, Behold, thou art made whole: ˣ sin no more, ʸ lest a worse thing come unto thee.

---

culous effect seems to have been an emblem of the healing of men's souls by the gospel, and by washing in " the " Fountain opened for sin and uncleanness : " and, compared with the multiplied and continual miracles wrought by our Lord, ' not at distant periods of time, but every ' day ; who not only performed a single cure, but healed whole ' multitudes that resorted to him!' (*Doddridge;*) it might also denote the efficacy of divine grace under the old dispensation, as distinguished from its more extensive effects under the ordinances of the New Testament.

The sheep-market. (2) Τῇ προβάτικῃ. Here only *N. T.* (A προβατον, *ovis, pecus.*)—Neh. iii. 1. 32. xii. 38. *Sept.*— A pool.] Κολυμβηθρα. 4. ix. 7. 11. Not elsewhere. A κολυμβαω, *nato.*—*Porches.*] Σʹβας. x. 23. *Acts* iii. 11. v. 12.—' *Locus* ' *tectus et columnis instructus, sub quo à tempestate et solis* ' *æstu tuti homines stare et ambulare possunt.'* Schleusner. —*At a certain season.* (4) Καʹα καιρον. Rom. v. 6.—*Troubled.*] Εταρασσε. 7. xii. 27. xiii. 21. xiv. 1. *Matt.* ii. 3. *Mark* vi. 50. *Luke* i. 12. *Acts* xv. 24. xvii. 8.—*Troubling.*] Ταραχην. *Mark* xiii. 8.—*Disease.*] Νοσημαῖι. Here only.

V. 5—9. Among the numerous pitiable objects found in this place, our Lord was pleased to notice one especially, who had laboured under disease, perhaps the palsy, " for thirty-eight years." Many persons 'speak as if he had lain by the pool all that time; but that is without foundation, and utterly improbable. When, however, all other means failed, he had been taken thither in hopes of a miraculous cure; and he persevered in waiting, notwithstanding tedious delays and bitter disappointments. This man our Lord selected from the rest, probably because his case was more desperate and lamentable, than that of any other even in this recess of misery; for he well knew how long he had been thus afflicted. In order to excite his attention and expectation, he asked him, " Willest," or desirest, " thou to be made whole? a question which in his case might appear unnecessary, but which aptly represented the proposal of the gospel to those, whose souls have long 'been diseased and disabled by sin. The man replied, that 'being very poor, as well as enfeebled by disease, he had neither friend nor servant to assist him, when the water

was troubled; and had hitherto been precluded from a cure, by " another stepping in before him : "—the language of one, who nearly despaired of relief. But Jesus at once commanded him to " take up his bed, and walk : " and though his disorder was so inveterate, and of so long continuance, it was instantaneously removed, and he was enabled to carry his bed, as a man in perfect health and vigour. This would be the more generally noticed, and excite the greater surprise and the more enquiries, as it occurred on the sabbath-day, when burdens were not allowed to be carried; by which means the power of Jesus would become more extensively known and attended to. (*Marg. Ref.—Notes,* *Matt.* xii. 1—13. *Luke* xiii. 10—17.)—' There is no evil ' so inveterate that Christ cannot cure it.' *Beza.*

Had an infirmity. (5) Εχων εν τη ασθενεια, (Καλησετο. 4.) " Under the power of an infirmity." Ασθενια. xi. 4. *Matt.* viii. 17. *Luke* v. 15. viii. 2, *et al.* Ab α priv. *et* σθενος, *robur.* *Wilt thou,* &c. (6) Θελεις υγιης γενεσθαι. *Rev.* xxii. 17. V. 10—14. The Jews here mentioned seem to have been the Pharisees, scribes, or rulers. They found fault with the man for violating the sabbath-rest by carrying his bed; (*Marg. Ref.* q.—*Notes, Neh.* xiii. 15—19. *Jer.* xvii 19—27 ;) though it was evidently done in honour of God, as manifesting the miraculous cure which had been performed. He therefore replied, that the very person who had made him whole, even he had ordered him to take up his bed and walk. But they, not at all noticing the stupendous miracle, only enquired, who ordered him to carry his bed. It is probable, that they suspected who it was, and were the more excited to opposition by that circumstance. Our Lord, however, had so speedily and silently withdrawn from the place, where multitudes were assembled, that the man was not able to inform them who his Benefactor was. But soon after, probably on the same day, Jesus met him in the temple, whither he had repaired, no doubt to render thanks for his unexpected cure, and perhaps to offer a sacrifice of praise: and Jesus called his attention to the greatness of the unmerited benefit which he had received, and warned him to " sin no more," lest a still worse evil should befall him. This was an intima-

15 The man departed, and told the Jews that it was Jesus which had made him whole.

16 And therefore did the Jews persecute Jesus, and sought to slay him, because he had done these things on the sabbath-day.

17 But Jesus answered them, My Father worketh hitherto, and I work.

18 Therefore the Jews sought the more to kill him, because he not only

had broken the sabbath, but said also that God was his Father, making himself equal with God.

19 Then answered Jesus, and said unto them, Verily, verily, I say unto you, The Son can do nothing of himself, but what he seeth the Father do; for what things soever he doeth, these also doeth the Son likewise.

---

tion, that his most tedious and painful disease had originated from some youthful irregularities, which were well known to Jesus, though committed before his birth as Man. And it was thus implied, that repentance and its genuine fruits would be the best evidence of the sincerity of the man's gratitude. As he had been grievously afflicted for thirty-eight years, we cannot easily conceive of a worse temporal evil, which could afterwards befall him; but doubtless Christ spake of " the wrath to come," which is indeed infinitely worse. (*Marg.* and *Marg Ref.* t—y.)

Had conveyed himself away. (13) Ἐξένευσεν. Here only. ' Propriè, *enato, ex undis emergo*, ... (ex *ex*, et *νεω*, pro quo ' et *νεω* dicitur, *nato*,) ... *clam secedo*. ... *Jesus enim se* ' *subduxerat*.' Schleusner.

V. 15, 16. When the man had thus discovered to whom he owed his cure; he went and told the Jews, (saying nothing of his having ordered him to carry his bed;) and probably he expected, that they would honour his Benefactor. ' Partly out of gratitude to own the author of ' his cure; and partly to excuse himself, as only doing this ' at the command of so great a prophet.' *Whitby.* But on the contrary the Jews prosecuted Jesus, seeking to put him to death as a sabbath-breaker, and it is likely that he was brought before the Sanhedrim, and spake what follows before that assembly. (*Marg. Ref.* 33.—*Note*, i. 19 —28.) This view of the subject makes the discourse peculiarly interesting, and there is a dignity in it which indeed is inexpressible.

V. 17, 18. In answer to the accusation brought against him, our Lord briefly said, " My Father worketh hitherto, " and I work." Thus he called God his Father in a peculiar sense, and claimed the prerogative of acting as God the Father did, without being restricted by rules laid down for his creatures and subjects: for the miracle, which had been performed, was not wrought by human labour, but by the immediate energy of his divine power. God finished the work of creation in six days, and " rested on the se- " venth;" (*Notes, Gen.* ii, 2, 3. *Ex.* xx. 8—10;) but he incessantly works in upholding the universe, and in continning the course of nature by his providential superintendence. In this work the Son concurs, by a union of will and operation, " upholding all things by the word of " his power." (*Note, Heb.* i. 3, 4.) His work also as Mediator was to be conducted by the same unremitted and uninterrupted action, as that of sustaining the universe : this miracle was a part of the work well suited to the sabbath-day; and he claimed the prerogative of carrying it forward on that day as well as on others, even as the Father

conducts his providential operations on every day alike. (*Marg. Ref.* d.)—Unless we suppose this, or something to this purpose, to have been our Lord's meaning, there could be no argument in his plea: for the example of the Creator in " working hitherto," can be no reason why a creature, a servant, a mere man, should do as he pleased on the sabbath-day: nor did any of the prophets ever advance a claim of that kind. The divine power of the miracle proved Jesus to be " the Son of God;" and he insisted on the prerogative of working with and like unto his Father, as he saw good, without giving any account of his conduct. (*Matt.* xii. 8.) These ancient enemies of Christ plainly understood him, (though modern opposers of his Deity cannot!) and were thus rendered more violent in their prosecution; not only charging him with sabbath-breaking, but with blasphemy, in calling God his *own* Father, " and making himself equal with God " in perfection and operation.—' If God my Father, working on the ' sabbath, doth not violate the sabbath; neither do I, when ' I work on the sabbath, violate the sabbath. This con- ' clusion cannot stand, unless the quality of the persons ' of the Father and of the Son be determined. ... " Making " himself equal with God." These are the words of the ' evangelist, not only repeating, but approving, what the ' Jews rightly collected from the words of Christ.' *Beza.* ' The whole nation of the Jews thought God their Father; ' (viii. 41;)...and they could not have accounted it blas- ' phemy to have used that phrase, had they not interpreted ' it in so high and appropriating a sense.' *Doddridge.* (*Marg. Ref.* e, f.—*Notes*, x. 26—39.)

Had broken. (18) Ἐλυε. ii. 19. *Matt.* v. 19. xviii. 18, *et al.* Λυω, *laxo, dissolvo.*—*His Father.*] Πατερα ἰδιον. *Rom.* viii. 32. 1 *Cor.* vii. 2. 4. See on i. 11.—*Equal.*] Ἰσον. *Phil.* ii. 6.

V. 19. In answer to this further charge, Jesus solemnly assured them, that " the Son can do nothing of himself." As the Father and the Son are one in nature and perfec- tions, so they are one in will, counsel, and operation; and it is impossible that the Son can do any thing of himself, apart from what the Father does. But, being intimately acquainted with every thing which the Father does, he co-operates with him in all his works of creation and pro- vidence; so that it is equally proper to ascribe them to the Son, as to the Father: for the Son not only performs *similar* works to those of the Father, but *the same* works, what- ever they be. (*Marg. Ref.* h.)—' Christ did not say, *He* ' doeth *like unto them;* but *the same things in like man-* ' *ner*.' *Beza.* Creation, the resurrection of the dead,

20 For **the Father loveth the Son, and sheweth him all things that himself doeth: and he will shew him greater works than these, that ye may marvel.

21 For **as the Father raiseth up the dead, and quickeneth *them* ; *even so the Son quickeneth whom he will.

22 For *the Father judgeth no man ; but hath committed all judgment unto the Son:

23 That *all *men* should honour the Son, even as they honour the Father. *He that honoureth not the Son, ho-noureth not the Father which hath sent him.

24 Verily, verily, I say unto you, *He that heareth my word, and believeth on him that sent me, hath everlasting life, *and shall not come into condemnation; *but is passed from death unto life.

25 Verily, verily, I say unto you, *The hour is coming, and now is, *when the dead shall hear the voice of the Son of God: and they that hear shall live.

26 For as the Father *hath life in himself, *so hath he given to the Son to have life in himself:

27 And *hath given him authority

our Lord's own resurrection, and many other works of omnipotence, are sometimes ascribed to the Father, at others to the Son, at others to the Holy Spirit : this the marginal references fully prove. (*Marg. Ref.* i.—*Notes*, 20—29. ii. 18—22. *Acts* xvii. 30, 31. 1 *Pet.* i. 3—5. iii. 17, 18, *v.* 18.) As simply the works of God, they may with equal propriety, be ascribed to any one of the three persons in the sacred Trinity ; but the expressions, "of "himself," "seeth," "sheweth," seem to refer to the delegated authority and power of the Son, as Mediator ; and his perfect concurrence with the Father, in accomplishing the glorious plan. of redemption as to every particular.

These also doeth the Son likewise.] Ταυτα και ὁ ἱνος ὁμοιως ποιι. "These also the Son doeth in like manner." 'Ομοιως, ' *Similiter, simili modo, eodem modo* : ab ὁμοιος, *par, æqualis.*' Schleusner.

V. 20—23. The Father most perfectly " loveth the "Son," and communicates in all his counsels with him : so that the Son perceives and fully comprehends all that the Father does, and co-operates in it. Of this the Jews had seen some instances, especially in the exercise of divine power and goodness, by which the impotent person had been healed : but the Father would shew his beloved Son " greater works than these," that by the displays of his divine glory, in the miracles wrought by him, they might be *astonished*, even if they were not induced to believe in him. (*Marg. Ref.* k—m.—*Note*, iii. 27—36, *vv.* 35, 36.) For as God is able to restore the dead to life, of which some examples were recorded in their scriptures; so they should see the Son also by his divine power raising the dead, as an emblem of his restoring to spiritual life, whom he pleases of those who are dead in sin. Indeed all things, relative to the government of the church and of the world, to the final judgment, and to the eternal states of men, were " committed to the Son," as the divine Mediator: insomuch that the Father, in person, " judgeth " no man," and therefore all the texts in which it is said, that " God shall judge the world," must be interpreted of the Son, as one with the Father. (*Marg. Ref.* n—p.— *Notes*, 24—29.) No appeal can then be made to the

Father, from the award of the Son : and this was purposely so constituted, " that all men should honour the " Son, even as they honour the Father ;" submitting unreservedly to him, relying entirely on him, and rendering him all worship, love, reverence, gratitude, and obedience ; which are his due as God, and to which he has in no respect forfeited his claim by becoming " manifest in the " flesh." It is the duty of all men thus to honour both the Father and the Son ; men of all nations, who really understand and obey the gospel, will thus honour the Son, as co-equal with the Father ; and every one who does not *thus* " honour the Son," (whatever he may think,) ho-noureth not the Father that sent him :" for he mistakes his character, rejects the revelation which he has made of himself, rebels against his authority, despises his gospel, and sets up an idol in his place, the creature of his own imagination or fallacious reasonings. (*Marg. Ref.* q, r.— *Notes*, xiv. 7—14. 1 *John* ii. 20—25. *Rev.* v. 11—14.)— Surely Jesus would never have insisted upon " all men " honouring him as they honour the Father," if he had not been conscious, that he was One with the Father in glory and majesty; though he was pleased to veil his glory, and to assume " the form of a servant," that he might become the Saviour of rebellious men. And to refuse him divine honour and worship, because of his infinite grace and condescension, is the height of perverse ingratitude. (*Notes, Phil.* ii. 5—11.)—*Whom he will.* (21) Thus it is also said of the Holy Spirit, " Dividing to every man seve-" rally as he will." 1 *Cor.* xii. 11. Is any thing in the least degree like this spoken in scripture, of prophets, apostles, angels, or archangels ? (*Notes*, xi. 20—27, v. 26. *Deut.* xxxii. 37—39, *v.* 39. 1 *Sam.* ii. 4—8, *v.* 6.)

Quickeneth. (21) Ζωοποιει. vi. 63. *Rom.* iv. 17. viii. 11. 1 *Cor.* xv. 22. 36. 45. *2 Cor.* iii. 6. *Gal.* iii. 21. 1 *Tim.* vi. 13. 1 *Pet.* iii. 18.—Εx ζωος, *vivus*, et ποιεω, *facio.* " Maketh alive."

V. 24—27. Our Lord here declared, more explicitly, his mediatorial authority and character as the Messiah: but he carefully avoided every expression, which the Jews could use as an accusation against him to the Roman governor. He assured them, with the most solemn asseveration, that

e Dan. vii. 13, 14.
2 Phil. ii. 7—11.
Heb. ii. 7—9.
d 20. 20. iii. 7. Acts
iii. 12.
e vi. 39. 40. xi.
25. Job xlx. 25,
26. Is. xxvi. 19.
Ez. xxxvii. 1—
10. Hos. xiii, 14.
1 Cor. xv. 22. 42—54. Phil. iii. 21. 1 Thes. iv. 14—17. Rev. xx. 12.

to execute judgment also, 'because he is the Son of man. 28 'Marvel not at this: 'for the hour is coming, in the which all that are in the graves shall hear his voice,

29 And shall 'come forth; they that have 'done good, unto the resurrection of life; and they that have done evil, unto the resurrection of damnation.

f Dan. xn. 2, 3.
Matt. xxv. 31—
46. Acts xxiv.
15.
g Luke xiv. 14.
Rom. ii. 6—10.
Gal. vi. 9—10.
1 Tim. vi. 18,
19. Heb. xlii.16.
1 Pet. iii. 11.

everlasting life was entirely at his disposal; insomuch that every one, who heard and duly attended to his instructions, and thus believed in the Father as revealed by him, " had eternal life;" the title to it, and the beginning of it. Such a believer would never come into judgment, to be tried and condemned for his sins; but, having passed from a state of spiritual death and exposedness to destruction, into a state of acceptance and peace with God, and the life of faith and grace, he would be preserved from falling again under condemnation, and thus dying without repentance and forgiveness. (Marg. Ref. s—u.—x. 26— 31. xiv. 18—20.—Notes, Rom. viii. 1, 2. 32—39. 2 Cor. v. 13—15. Col. iii. 1—4, vv. 3, 4. 1 John iii. 13—15, v. 14. v. 9—13.) No words can more expressly declare the eventual preservation of all true believers.—Our Lord further assured them that the hour was even then come, " when the dead should hear the voice of the Son of God, " and they that heard should live." This may refer to his raising the dead in several instances by his omnipotent word; but it seems rather to signify his raising those, who were dead in sin, to newness of life, by his doctrine attended by the power of his Spirit. For as the Father had the self-existent Source of life, natural, spiritual, and eternal, to all creatures; so had " he given to the Son to " have life in himself." (Marg. Ref. x—a.—Notes, 1 Cor. xv. 45—49. Rev. xxii. 1.) It is not conceivable that a mere creature can " have life in himself," in the same sense, as the eternal self-existent Father has, and for the purpose of communicating it to others, as it is here evidently meant: but that the Son of God (being according to his divine nature, self-existent, eternal, and One with the Father,) should, as Mediator, have it given to him by covenant, on the condition of his humiliation and expiatory sufferings, " to have life in himself," for the benefit of those, who had forfeited life, who were dead in sin, and doomed to eternal death by the law, and whose Surety he was become, that they might be quickened, pardoned, and saved, consistently with the honour of divine justice and holiness; is very intelligible and important: for this was to " have life in himself," for other purposes and in another manner, than he had as " God over all, blessed " for evermore." (Notes, iii. 2,—36, vv. 35, 36. Matt. xxviii. 18.)—In respect of the same undertaking, the Father had also given him " authority to execute judg- " ment," for the punishment of all his enemies, and the salvation of his people; because he, the Son of God, was also become " the Son of man." (Marg. Ref. b, c.— Notes, Rom. xiv. 7—9. Phil. ii. 9—11.) It is evident that the office of " Judge of all men," must require omniscience, omnipotence, infinite justice, truth, and perfection; these are absolutely incommunicable to any mere creature; and " the Son of man," cannot be conceived capable of having this work absolutely committed to him, and of properly executing it, but upon the supposition that he is also

" the Son of God," and equal with the Father. (Notes 28—30. Matt. xxv, 34—46. 1 Cor. iv. 3—5, v. 5. 2 Cor. v. 9—12, v. 10. 2 Thes. i. 5—10. Rev. xx. 11—15.)

Hath. (24) Εχει, not ίξει, present, not future. vi. 47.

54.—Is passed.] Μεταβεβηκεν. xiii. 1. 1 John iii. 14. Εx μετα, trans, et βαινω, vado.—The Son of man, (27) Τιος ανθρωπου, without the article, a Son of man. ' It occurs ' thus no where in the gospels, except in this passage. ' Judge, as well as the Saviour, of men, should maintain ' be a man.' Campbell. (Note, Acts xvii. 30, 31.)

V. 28, 29. Our Lord next added, that the persons who heard him, had no reason to express such astonishment at what he had said, as it seems was visible in their looks; for the time was approaching, when all the innumerable multitudes of the dead would " hear his voice," calling them to arise and come to judgment; so that wherever their bodies were dispersed and turned to dust, they would immediately be raised up and come forth, either to life, or to damnation, according as their works had been. (Note, Rev. xx. 11—15.) Those who have repented, believed in Christ, and by his grace, have learned to love and obey him during the remainder of their days, are the persons " who have done good." Their good is indeed scanty, defective, and defiled; but they are interested in the covenant of grace, and are acknowledged the heirs of everlasting life: whereas the unregenerate, impenitent, and unbelieving, who go on to the end doing evil, will arise to judgment, condemnation, and everlasting punishment. (Marg. Ref. —Notes, Matt. xxv. 31—46. 2 Cor. v. 9—12, v. 10.) Is it possible to conceive, that Jesus would have used such language as this, had he not intended his disciples to conceive of him as of the almighty God, dwelling in our nature, and " manifest in the flesh?" (Note, xi. 20—27, vv. 25, 26.)—They that have done evil, &c. (29) ' This seems ' to be spoken in opposition to the doctrine of the Pharisees, ' who, saith Josephus, thought the resurrection pertained ' only to the just; and that the wicked, and antediluvian ' sinners, would be excluded from it.' Whitby. The doctrine of a future state has very generally been considered, implicitly, in this light. The reasonings of Pagan philosophers, and of modern deists and moralists, and. of many who admit some of the doctrines of Christianity, as well as the cavils of the Sadducees, against the doctrine of the resurrection, in the question proposed by them to our Lord, go on the supposition, that if men live hereafter, they must of course be happy; (Note, Matt. xxii. 22— 33 ;) and that to prove the immortality of the soul, or to establish the doctrine of a future resurrection, is laying a foundation of hope and comfort to men in general, without much discrimination of character. But this one scripture shews how vain all such reasonings are. (Note, 2 Tim. i. 10.)

Of damnation. (29) Κρισεως. " Judgment," 22. 27.

3 s 2

30 I can of mine own self do nothing: as I hear, I judge; and my judgment is just: because I seek not mine own will, but the will of the Father which hath sent me.

31 ¶ If I bear witness of myself, my witness is not true.

32 There is another that beareth witness of me; and I know that the witness which he witnesseth of me is true.

33 Ye sent unto John, and he bare witness unto the truth.

34 But I receive not testimony from man: but these things I say, that ye might be saved.

35 He was a burning and a shining light: and ye were willing for a season to rejoice in his light.

36 But I have greater witness than that of John: for the works which the Father hath given me to finish, the same works that I do, bear witness of me, that the Father hath sent me.

37 And the Father himself which hath sent me, hath borne witness of me. Ye have neither heard his voice at any time, nor seen his shape.

38 And ye have not his word abiding in you; for whom he hath sent, him ye believe not.

---

30. xll. 31. "Condemnation," 24. iii. 19. "Damnation," *Matt.* xxiii. 33. Certainly "judgment" will be "damna- "tion," to those "who have done evil."

V. 30. (*Note*, 19.) Our Lord here repeats his decla- ration of the entire coincidence of design and operation, between the Father and the Son; and, by using the *first* person instead of the *third* as before, he declared himself to be "the Son of God." It was impossible, that he should do any thing in his work, as Mediator, from any motive, to any end, or by any power, diverse from those of the Father. In executing his judicial authority, he acted, and ever should act, according to the instructions which he had received, with which his own will and wis- dom perfectly harmonized; and in none of his actions did he seek his own will, as man; but that of the Father who had sent him, whom he came to glorify, and who was glorified in his glory. (*Marg. Ref.—Note*, vi. 36—40.)

V. 31—38. If indeed Jesus had claimed such honours and authority, without any proof, except his own testimony to himself; it might have been allowed, that there would be no sufficient reason to receive that testimony: indeed his testimony, in that case, must have been, not only *in- valid*, but *destitute of truth*; for who could be authorized to say such things of himself, without any other proof than his own word? There was however another who bare witness to him, whose witness he supposed they must allow to be true, as he assuredly knew it to be. Some refer this to John's testimony; but it rather means that of the Father, by John, and in various other ways. The rulers of the Jews, the very persons here addressed, had indeed sent unto John; and he had testified to Jesus that he was "the Son of God," and "the Lamb of God, that "taketh away the sin of the world." (*Marg. Ref.* l—p. *Notes*, i. 19—29. 30—34, v. 34.) Yet our Lord did not stand in need of man's testimony, though he mentioned it as well worthy of their serious attention: for, while they sought his life, he would use every means to bring them to accept of his salvation, and those means would be effectual to some of them. Probably, Nicodemus and Joseph of Arimathea were present at the time.—John in- deed had been "a burning and a shining light:" by his holy life, his flaming zeal, his clear instructions, and his patient labours, he had both burned and shined, to warm as well as illuminate them. (*Marg. Ref.* q—t.—*Notes*, i. 6—9.) '"He was the lighted and shining lamp." John's 'ministry was of a peculiar character; he was the single 'prophet, in whom the old dispensation had its comple- 'tion, and by whom the new was introduced: ...till our 'Lord's ministry took place, John may have justly been 'said to have been the light of that generation.' *Campbell.* —Indeed for a season the Jews had attended to him, and seemed glad to have so eminent a man of God among them; but they only amused themselves with his instruc- tions, without reducing them to practice; and at last they rejected his testimony concerning Jesus, and forsook his ministry. But a far higher testimony had been borne to him, as "the Son of God," than that of John, who wrought no miracle: for the works the Father had entrusted to him to perform, which he had already begun in the miracles he had wrought, and which he should remain on earth to finish, notwithstanding their purpose of killing him; these powerful, holy, and beneficent works sufficient- ly attested, "that the Father had sent him," and autho- rized all that he had spoken of his own personal and medi- atorial dignity and authority. (*Marg. Ref.* u, x.—*Notes*, iii. 1, 2. xiv. 7—14, vv. 10, 11. xx. 30, 31.) Nay, the Father himself had borne witness to him, by a voice from heaven, at his baptism, declaring him to be "his beloved Son, in "whom he was well pleased." (*Note*, Matt. iii. 16, 17.) This was such a witness to him, and attended with such a visible display of the divine presence and glory, as neither they nor any of their nation had ever heard or seen, re- specting the most eminent prophets, and indeed the highest that could be imagined · for none could possibly "see the "form and hear the voice" of the Father as a witness, in any other or more evident manner. This seems to be an intimation to them, that all the appearances of JEHOVAH to their ancestors, and his speaking to them, ought to be understood of him as "the Son of God;" for none of them had heard the voice and seen the form of *the Father* at any time. (*Marg. Ref.* y, z.—*Note*, i. 18.) He had indeed spoken to them in his word; but that had no abiding place in their hearts: which was evident, in that they re- fused to believe in him, whom the Father had sent to them according to his ancient promises. (*Marg. Ref.* a, b.— *Note*, viii. 37—40, v. 37.)

39 ⁱ Search the scriptures: for in them ᵏ ye think ye have eternal life, and they are ˡ they which testify of me.

40 And ᵐ ye will not come to me, ⁿ that ye might have life.

41 I ᵒ receive not honour from men.

42 But ᵖ I know you, ᵠ that ye have not the love of God in you.

43 I am ʳ come in my Father's name, and ye receive me not: ˢ if another shall come in his own name, him ye will receive.

44 How ᵗ can ye believe, ᵘ which receive honour one of another, ᵛ and seek not the honour that cometh from God only?

45 Do not think that I will accuse you to the Father: ᵂ there is one that accuseth you, even Moses, ˣ in whom ye trust.

46 For ʸ had ye believed Moses, ye

A burning and a shining light. (35) Ὁ λυχνος ὁ καιομενος και φαινων.—" The lamp, which burneth, and shineth," or " is lighted and shineth." Λυχνος. *Matt.* vi. 22. *Luke* xi. 33, 34. 36. xv. 8. 2 *Pet.* i. 19.—Καιω, *to light. Matt.* v. 15. *To burn.* xv. 6. *Luke* xxiv. 32. *Heb.* xii. 18. *Rev.* viii. 8. xix. 20. xxi. 8.—Φαινων. i. 5. *Phil.* ii. 15. 2 *Pet.* i. 19. 1 *John* ii. 8. *Rev.* i. 16, *et al.*—*To rejoice.*] Ἀγαλλιασθηναι. See on *Matt.* v. 12.—*To finish.* (36) Ἵνα τελιιωσω. See on iv. 34.—*Shape.* (37) Ειδος. *Luke* iii. 22. ix. 29. 2 *Cor.* v. 7. 1 *Thes.* v. 22.

V. 39—44. The Jews supposed that eternal life was revealed to them in their scriptures: nay, they imagined they had it, as it were, in possession; because they had the word of God in their hands. But Jesus exhorted them to " search those scriptures," with more exact diligence and attention ; as all the types and prophecies were fulfilling in his character, actions, doctrine, and miracles ; and as the sacred writings every where testified to him, and fully warranted all which he had spoken of himself, by what they contained respecting the divine dignity and authority of the promised Messiah. (*Marg. Ref.* c. e.—*Notes,* *Luke* xxiv. 25—31. 44—49. 1 *Pet.* i. 10—12. *Rev.* xix. 9, 10.) Or it may be rendered, " Ye do search the " scriptures." They bestowed pains in examining the scriptures, especially with reference to the kingdom of the Messiah : yet they were so blinded by prejudice, that they could not discern the clear and express testimony, which these bore to him ; and therefore, while they expected eternal life, they would not come to him for it, who alone could bestow it upon them. (*Marg. Ref.* g.—*Notes,* vi. 28—35. 41—46. *Matt.* xxiii. 37—39.)—He spoke not this, as if he needed their sanction, or could receive honour from their approbation : he desired not human applause or external grandeur ; nor could he be rendered more honourable, by having priests, scribes, or rulers for his disciples. But he spake thus plainly to them, because he certainly knew that they had no love to iod in their hearts, though they professed to be his zealous worshippers ; and this was the real ground of their rejecting and opposing him. (*Marg. Ref.* h—k.—*Notes,* ii. 23 —25. viii. 41—47. xv. 22—25.) He was come among them in his Father's name, acting by his authority, bearing his image, fulfilling his word, and seeking his glory, and his mission was abundantly attested ; yet they would not receive him : but when others should come, assuming

the character of the Messiah, without any such attestations, but acting of their own mind and for their own glory, they would readily receive and follow them : for such impostors would pay court to the scribes and rulers, or accommodate their conduct and pretensions to their prejudices and ambition. (*Marg. Ref.* l, m.) Indeed, how was it possible that they could cordially receive his humbling spiritual doctrine, or believe in him as the Messiah, while their hearts were full of pride and vain-glory ? They were accustomed to flatter and compliment each other, and thus to foster self-admiration and false self-importance : and to give reciprocal encouragement to each other's ambition of secular honour, authority, and pre-eminence : but they had no real desire of that honour which God alone confers on the humble and lowly in heart ; (*Marg. Ref.* n—p.—*Note,* xii. 42, 43 ;) and many of them feared the disgrace of being cast out of the synagogue. How then could they welcome a Messiah, who had no worldly preferments to bestow ; whose appearance was as mean as his doctrine was humiliating ; and whose sharp rebukes must needs exasperate their haughty and envious minds?—*In them ye think,* &c. (39) This is a most decided testimony, that the Jews considered eternal life to be revealed and promised in their scriptures ; and that so far they thought right : whatever paradoxes modern learned men may endeavour to support on the subject. (*Note,* 1 *John* v. 11, 12.) ' If ' the Jews did truly think the doctrine of life eternal was ' contained there, and that they by searching might find it ' there ; it must be to them a sufficient rule of faith : if in ' this they erred, it behoved Christ to correct in them an ' error so pernicious.' *Whitby.* This is worthy the serious consideration of all, whether Papists or Protestants, who oppose the circulation of the scriptures *without note or comment.*

Search. (39) Ερευνᾳε. vii. 52. *Rom.* viii. 27. 1 *Cor.* ii. 10. 1 *Pet.* i. 11. *Rev.* ii. 23.—' Metaphora desumpta ' a fossoribus metallorum qui intimas terræ cavernas per- ' scrutantur.' *Schleusner.—Ye will not.* (40) Ου θελετε. " Ye are not willing." vi. 21.—*How can.* (44) Πως δυνασθε. The impossibility was *moral,* not *natural :* the want of *inclination,* or a right state of heart ; not the want of *natural ability.*

V. 45—47. Our Lord concluded by observing, that there was no occasion for him to become the accuser of the unbelieving Jews to his Father ; nor indeed was this

3 s 4

t Gen. iii. 15.
xii. 3. xxii. 18.
xxviii. 14. xlix.
10. Num. xxi. 8.
9. xxiv. 17, 18. Deut. xviii. 18, 19. Acts xxvi. 22. Rom. x. 4. Heb. vii.—x.
would have believed me: 'for he wrote of me.

47 But °if ye believe not his writings, how shall ye believe my words?
u Luke xvi. 29.
31.

the end of his coming among them, though he so sharply reproved them to their faces : for they had another accuser, even Moses, in whom they trusted for salvation. (*Marg. Ref.* q, r.—*Notes*, ix. 27—34. *Jer.* xvii. 5—8. 1 *Pet.* i. 17—21, *v.* 21.) Yet his writings, which were full of types, prophecies, and promises of him, would certainly condemn them for rejecting him, as well as for their other sins. Had they really believed the testimony of Moses, they would certainly have welcomed that Prophet of whom Moses wrote ; but, seeing they treated the predictions of Moses with disregard, and did not really believe them, it would be wonderful indeed, if they had believed in Jesus. (*Marg. Ref.* s—u.—See on *Note*, 39—44. *Note*, *Deut.* xviii. 15—19.)—This whole passage is peculiarly suited to shew us, in what light to consider the writings of Moses and the prophets, or the Old Testament, nearly, if not entirely, as we have it. Our Lord certainly sanctioned the general opinion of the Jews, not only that these books were *authentick*, or *genuine*; but also that they were *divinely inspired*, and as such worthy of the most implicit credence and confidence. And, in particular, he has given his full attestation to the books of Moses, not as compiled from his records, but as written in their present form by Moses himself.—Though our Lord spoke thus openly on this occasion ; yet his persecutors were so overawed, that they for the present proceeded no further against him, for " his time was not yet come."—The open and full declaration of our Lord, that the Jewish rulers, who now sat in judgment on him, would be finally condemned for rejecting him ; and that Moses himself, in whom they trusted, would be their accuser; is inexpressibly dignified and energetick. (*Notes, Matt.* vii. 21—23. xxv. 31—33.)

PRACTICAL OBSERVATIONS.

V. 1—14.

The whole earth appears to a considerate mind, as a " Bethesda," a great hospital, full of those whom sin has made miserable, and to whom the compassion of God affords the means of relief and comfort. As therefore " his mercies are over all his works," and even those, who most deserve misery, experience his goodness during their continuance here ; the mercy of man should also coincide, and we should endeavour to alleviate the sufferings of the vilest, and to do them whatever good we can. Medicines are created and discovered by our offended God, to relieve the diseases of our bodies, which all originate from sin : and we should attempt to render the poor partakers of this benefit by every means in our power. In this view every *in spital*, or *dispensary*, is a " Bethesda :" and would be more completely deserving of that name, if proper means were diligently employed, of doing good to the souls, as well as of healing the bodies, of those who resort to it. Yet alas! how few of these, who in this manner obtain relief, are found in the house of God, " offering the sacri- " fice of thanksgiving " to their great Physician! How few of them live thenceforth to his glory! How few take warning to " sin no more, lest a worse thing should come

" unto them !" (*Notes, Ps.* cvii. 17—22. 31, 32. *P. O.* 1—22. *P. O. Luke* xvii. 11—19.) But the place, where the gospel is preached and divine ordinances are administered, is the true " Bethesda : " thither the poor and helpless should repair ; and hope and wait for a cure, whatever their spiritual maladies be, or however inveterate they have become. Though the multiplied miracles of converting grace, which better ages witnessed, are not generally vouchsafed among us ; yet we still see instances of such as, by washing in " the Fountain which God hath opened," are made whole of their most desperate maladies. All the power indeed is of God ; yet those who would have the benefit must be watchful, earnest, and patient : (*Note, Luke* xiii. 22—30, *v.* 24 :) they must not be supine or dilatory, but make haste to wash and be clean ; and then they should endeavour in their turn to assist others also. Yet, if any seem to meet with reiterated disappointments, they should still wait, hope, and seek ; not neglecting the means of grace, or ceasing to labour and pray for the blessing: for sometimes they, whose case seems most hopeless, and who are ready to give up all for lost, are made partakers of mercy, peace, and spiritual health, when they least expect them.—The Saviour perfectly knows both how long men have been contracting habits of sin, and how long seeking the help and " joy of his salvation :" and he continually attends in his *houses of mercy*, to enquire of sinners, whether they will be made whole. Yet it is a common case, for men to go thither, who are in love with their disease, and only desire to excuse the loathsomeness of it ! But if we earnestly desire to be healed and saved in his way, we shall certainly at length obtain that blessing.—When he speaks, power attends his word : and the ability of believers to perform such duties as are impracticable to others, and once were so to them, will best evidence their cure, and recommend their Physician. (*P. O. Matt.* ix. 1—8.) Though Scribes and Pharisees object and revile ; yet redeemed sinners must obey and honour their Benefactor, and follow the directions of him who has restored health to their souls. By attending on the ordinances of God, they obtain further acquaintance with him ; but without deliverance from the love, power, and allowed practice of known sin, there can be no well grounded hopes of escaping " the wrath to come."—Even in this life, how many hours, days, weeks, months, nay years of pain, do some wicked men endure, through their momentary unlawful indulgences! And if such afflictions are heavy and tedious, whilst year after year men are confined to their beds, and made a burden to themselves and others ; how dreadful beyond all conception will be the everlasting punishment of the wicked!

V. 15—29.

We are still called to trust in him, whom Pharisees and infidels despise. " As the Father worketh hitherto " so does his co-equal Son, especially in carrying on and sustaining his new creation. May those declarations of his eternal power and Godhead, which enrage his enemies, fill our hearts with humble confidence and admiring gratitude.

3 s 5

CHAP. VI.

Jesus feeds five thousand men, with five loaves and two fishes, 1—14. He withdraws from the multitudes, who purpose to make him King, 15. His disciples put to sea without him, and meet with a storm; but he comes to them walking on the sea, 16—21. Being followed to Capernaum by multitudes, he re-

proves their carnal motives even in their diligence about religion; and requires faith in him, 22—29 They demand a sign, like that of the manna, and he speaks copiously of himself as the Bread of life, and of living by faith in him, 30—59. Many are offended, and forsake him, 60—66. Peter, in the name of the twelve, professes stedfast faith in him, as "the Son of God;" but Jesus pronounces one of them to be a devil, 67—71.

Nor ought we at all to regard those, who accuse us of giving the glory of God to another: such objectors do not understand " the mystery of the Father and of the Son;" or perceive that a union of essence, will, and operation, renders it for ever impossible, to honour the one without honouring the other also.—The eternal Son is the adequate and infinite Object of the Father's love: he possesses all his perfections, and performs all his works, he creates or destroys, he raises from the dead and " quickens whom he " will:" " our life is hid in him;" our future judgment is committed to him; and, as dwelling in human nature, he exercises all power and authority throughout the universe, that " all men might honour him, even as they " honour the Father." Unless therefore we can honour the Father too much, we need not fear honouring the Son more than we ought. Here is no danger of excess, but much of defect: all the adoration and worship, rendered to the Son, is directed to the glory of God the Father ; (Note, Phil. ii. 8—11 ;) and they " who honour not the Son" will be condemned, as enemies and despisers of the Father who sent him. May we then hear his voice, and believe his testimony, as he reveals God to man, and invites us to " come to him, and learn of him, and take his yoke upon " us," with promises, that in this way " he will give us " rest," even " rest for our souls." (Notes, Matt. xi. 25 —30.) Thus " our faith and hope will be in God ;" we shall " have everlasting life, and not come into condemna- " tion ;" for in so doing we shall " pass from death to life." And may his voice reach the hearts of those, who are dead in sin, that they may arise from the dead, " repent, and " do works meet for repentance;" and thus prepare for the solemn day of retribution! For the hour will soon arrive, " in which all that are in the graves shall hear his " voice, and shall come forth: they that have done good, " to the resurrection of life, and that they have done evil, " to the resurrection of damnation." May we now live, as those who desire and hope then to be found " a people " prepared for the LORD !"

V. 30—38.

Let none treat the things above stated as assertions, or conjectures, or uncertain speculations : for they are authenticated by the most unanswerable divine testimonies; and they are published, that sinners may hear and fear, believe, and be saved. To the blessed Redeemer all the servants of God bear witness ; but he cannot derive from them any addition to his essential glory. " From his fulness they " have all received : " (Note, i. 16 :) if they be " burning " and shining lights," they glow with his love, and shine by his splendour : he honours them, and they reflect a little of his glory.—Many are willing to hear teachers who are entitled to this character; and are pleased with their

gifts or doctrine ; but they do not obey the word, " they " have no root in themselves, and so in time of tempta- " tion they fall away." Not only the works which Christ finished on earth bore witness to him, as the Son of God ; but those also that he has wrought since his ascension into heaven, in the promulgation and success of the gospel, demonstrate the same truths: and the voice of God, accompanied by the power of the Holy Ghost, has made effectual to the conversion of sinners, still proclaims, that this is " the beloved Son in whom the Father is well " pleased," and that all who would be saved must hear and obey him, as the sole " Author of eternal salvation."

V. 39—47.

When the hearts of men are occupied by pride, ambition, and the love of the world, there is no room for the word of God to abide in them.—Thus many profess to believe, that ." in the scriptures they have eternal life ; " yet they bestow little pains to understand these sacred oracles : others search them with a proud, curious, or prejudiced mind, and so cannot see that they " testify of " Christ : ", others admit this as a doctrine, yet they " are " not willing to come to him, that they may have life." Being destitute of the love of God, they are careless about spiritual and eternal blessings ; or they imagine they shall be able to obtain them in some other way ; or they are proud of their knowledge ; they " seek honour one of " another ; " and they are glad to follow carnal, self-sufficient teachers, who come in their own name, who coincide with their views, flatter their pride, connive at their sins, and seek their own ends by so doing. Alas ! how many trust in their attachment to some form of doctrine, or to some renowned head of a party ; who no more enter into the real meaning of those doctrines, or into the views of the persons whose names they bear, than the Jews believed the words of Moses, or entered into his views of the prefigured and predicted Messiah: Thus the creeds and formularies of many sects and establishments, with suffice for the condemnation of immense multitudes, who glory in belonging to them, as members, as ministers, nay, as rulers ! and it is well, if the sermons many preach, and the books which they publish, do not appear in judgment against them, to accuse them of not believing or practising what they preached or printed. Let us then most diligently search and fervently pray over the scriptures, as men intent on finding eternal life ; let us observe that Christ is the grand Subject of them, and daily apply to him for that life which he bestows; let us seek " that " honour, which cometh from God only," and " not fear " the reproach of men : " and thus " by patient continu- " ance in well-doing, let us seek for glory, honour," and immortal felicity. (Notes, Prov. ii. 1—9. Rom. ii. 7—11.)

AFTER * these things Jesus went over [b] the sea of Galilee, [c] which is the sea of Tiberias.

2 And [d] a great multitude followed him, because they saw his miracles which he did on them that were diseased.

3 And [e] Jesus went up into a mountain, and there he sat with his disciples.

4 And [f] the passover, a feast of the Jews, was nigh.

5 When Jesus then lifted up his eyes, and [g] saw a great company come unto him, he saith unto Philip, [h] Whence shall we buy bread, that these may eat?

6 (And this he said to [i] prove him: for he himself knew what he would do.)

7 Philip answered him, [k] Two hundred [l] pennyworth of bread is not sufficient for them, that every one of them may take a little.

8 One of his disciples, [m] Andrew, Simon Peter's brother, saith unto him,

9 There is a lad here, [n] which hath five [o] barley-loaves, and two small fishes: [p] but what are they among so many?

10 And Jesus said, [q] Make the men sit down. Now there was much grass in the place. So the men sat down, in number about five thousand.

11 And Jesus took the loaves; and [r] when he had given thanks, he distributed to the disciples, and the disciples to them that were set down; and likewise of the fishes as much as they would.

12 When [s] they were filled, he said unto his disciples, Gather up the fragments that remain, [t] that nothing be lost.

13 Therefore they gathered them together, [u] and filled twelve baskets with the fragments of the five barley-loaves, which remained over and above unto them that had eaten.

14 Then those men, when they had seen the miracle that Jesus did, said, [x] This is of a truth that Prophet that should come into the world.

15 When Jesus therefore [y] perceived that they would come, and [z] take him by force to make him a King, [a] he departed again into a mountain himself alone.

16 And when even was now come, his disciples went down unto the sea,

17 And entered into a ship, [b] and went over the sea toward Capernaum: and it was now dark, and Jesus was not come to them.

18 And [c] the sea arose, by reason of a great wind that blew.

19 So when they had rowed about five and twenty or thirty [e] furlongs, they see Jesus [f] walking on the sea, and drawing nigh unto the ship: and they were afraid.

20 But he saith unto them, [g] It is I; be not afraid.

21 Then [h] they willingly received him into the ship: and immediately the ship was at the land whither they went.

NOTES.

CHAP. VI. V. 1—21. 'These things did not immediately follow the preceding discourse: but omitting the things, which Christ had done between the second passover and the approach of the third, and which are recorded by the other evangelists, the apostle John selected this history, because of the copious and most important sermon which followed, and which had been passed over by the other sacred historians.' Beza.—(Marg. Ref.— Notes, Matt. xiv. 13—33. Mark vi. 30—52. Luke ix. 10— 17.)—Philip, &c. (7) Note, 43—46.—Take a little.] 'Much more than this would be requisite to give this multitude a full meal.'—Andrew. (8) Note, i. 35—42, v. 35.—Barley loaves. (9) We find from this evangelist, that the bread multiplied on this occasion, was made of barley, though the promised land abounded with wheat. (Notes, Deut. xxxii. 14. Ps. cxlvii. 12—14. Ez. xxvii. 13—25, v. 17. Acts xii. 20—23, v. 20.)—Gather, &c. (12) The fragments must be gathered up, not only to ascertain the greatness of the miracle; but to prevent waste in any good thing which God has created.—Take, &c. (15) The multitudes expected that the Messiah would be a Prophet, as well as a King: they had a temporary conviction, from the miracle which Jesus had wrought, that he was the Messiah: they concluded that the greatest advantages might be expected under a leader, who was able in this manner to provide food for his adherents: and they probably imagined that he would not be displeased to have a kind of constraint laid upon him, to declare himself the expected King. of

3 B 7

22 ¶ The day following, when the people, which stood on the other side of the sea, saw that there was none other boat there, save that one whereinto his disciples were entered, and that Jesus went not with his disciples

i 15, 17. Matt. xiv. 22. Mark vi. 45. into the boat, ¹ but that his disciples were gone away alone;

_k 24._ 23 (Howbeit ᵏ there came other

· See on 1 boats from ¹ Tiberias, nigh unto the

m See on 11, 12. place ᵐ where they did eat bread, after that the Lord had given thanks:)

24 When the people therefore saw

_n 17. 23._ that Jesus was not there, neither his

o vii. 11. xviii. 4. Mark disciples, ⁿ they also took shipping, and

_5. xx. 16._ came to Capernaum, ᵒ seeking for Jesus.

i. 37. Luke viii. 49.

25 And when they had found him on the other side of the sea, they said unto him, ᵖ Rabbi, when camest thou hither?

26 Jesus answered them, and said, ¶ Verily, verily, I say unto you, ' Ye seek me, not because ye saw the miracles, but because ye did eat of the loaves, and were filled.

27 ˢ Labour not for ᵗ the meat which perisheth, but for that ᵘ meat which endureth unto everlasting life, ᵛ which the Son of man shall give unto you: ʷ for him hath God the Father sealed.

p See on i. 38, 49. 47, 50. iii. 2. ᵇ. ix. 64. li. lxxviii. 87. cvi. 72—14. Ex. xxxiii. 31. Acts viii. 18—21. Rom. xvi. 19. Phil. ii. 21. iii. 12. 1 Tim. vi. Jam. iv. 3, 4. Or, Work not. 26. Ro. Gal. v. 6. Phil. ii. 13. Col. i. 29. 1 Thes. i. 3. s iv. 14, 14. Ps. v. 11—16. vi. 7. Is. lv. 2, 3. Hab. ii. 13. Matt. vi. 19, 20—33. Luke x. 49—42. Cor. vi. 13. vii. 29—31. ix. 24—27. 2 Cor. iv. 18. Col. ii. 22. iii. z. Heb. iv. 11. xiii. 14. Jam. i. 11. Pet. i. 24. 2 Pet. iii. 11—14. t vi. 40. 51. 54. 69. u x. 24. xi. 25, 26. xiv. 6. xvii. 2. Prov. ii. 2—6. Rom. vi. 23. x i. 33, 34. v. 36, 37. vii. 16. x. 37, 38. xi. 42. xv. 24. Is. xi. 1—8. Ish. 1—3. Matt. iii. 17. Mark i. 11. Luke iii. 22. iv. 18—21. Acts ii. 22. x. 38.

Israel. In these designs the apostles perhaps were ready to concur, by reason of their remaining ambition and worldly prejudices.—The language of the sacred writer in the twenty-first verse, implies that the immediate transition of the vessel to the intended harbour was miraculous. —The geography of these regions at that time is so imperfectly known, that several things relative to it, must be left in a measure of obscurity, amidst the discordant opinions of learned writers.

A little. (7) Βραχυ τι sub μερος. Luke xxii. 58. Acts v. 34. xxvii. 28. Heb. ii. 7. 9. xiii. 22.—A lad. (9) Παιδαριον. Matt. xi. 16. Not elsewhere.—A diminutive, from παις puer.—Small fishes.] Οψαρια. 11. xxi. 9, 10. 13. Not elsewhere.—' Omnis cibus, qui pani adjicitur, præsertim coctus, ' et assatus : ...ab οπταω asso.' Schleusner. The word is not properly a diminutive, and the epithet " small" seems improper. Ιχθυας, Matt. xiv. 17.—Take him by force. (15) 'Αρπαζειν. x. 12. 28, 29. Matt. xi. 12. Acts viii. 39. 2 Cor. xii. 2. 4. 1 Thes. iv. 17, et al.—They willingly received. (21) Ηθελον ... λαβειν. " They were willing to " receive him." v. 40. vii. 17.

V. 22—27. Jesus had dismissed the multitudes, before he " went up to the mountain to pray:" but it seems many continued near the place, or returned thither in the morning in expectation of seeing him again: for they had observed that the " disciples went away alone," in the only vessel which was there at that time. Before the next morning, however, several boats came thither: and when the people could not find Jesus, they concluded that by some means he had followed the disciples. They therefore immediately crossed the lake, and resorted to Capernaum to seek for him: and when they found him in the synagogue (59) they expressed their surprise, enquiring of him by what means he had come thither. (Marg. Ref. i—p.) But, instead of resolving their question, he began to blame them for their motives in seeking him. This they did, not because, his miracles having convinced them that he was a divine Teacher of righteousness, they were earnest in seeking instruction in the truths and will of God; but because, having " eaten of the loaves" and fishes, they wanted to make him a King, in order that they might derive secular advantages from him. (Marg. Ref. r.) He therefore warned them, not to " labour for the meat that perisheth, but for

" that, &c." All temporal interests of whatever sort were intended, which only afford a transient support or satisfaction, and will soon perish; so that the possessors will be no better for them. They are of a fluctuating, perishing nature, and are often torn away during life : and if this be not the case, death soon removes men from them, to be without them for ever. The earnestness and diligence of men therefore should not be directed to the acquisition of them ; except in complete subordination to things spiritual and eternal, and according to the rules of the sacred scripture. Moderate attention and industry are every man's duty, and a part of true religion, when employed for the Lord's sake, to his glory, in submission to his will and dependence on his blessing, and in entire subserviency to eternal things ; and not out of covetousness, ambition, or any carnal principle. (Marg. and Marg. Ref. s—u.—Notes and P. O. Matt. vi. 19—34. Col. iii. 1—4.) To obtain and possess the assurance of heaven, to enjoy communion with God, to glorify him, to adorn the gospel and do good, are the Christian's motives to activity, the objects at which he aims: not the desire of living luxuriously, elegantly, or splendidly, or of being applauded or ennobled.—Instead of " labouring " for the meat that perisheth," our Lord exhorted his followers to " labour for the meat which endureth unto ever- " lasting life;" or for all those spiritual blessings which relate to the salvation of the soul. These are of an enduring and incorruptible nature, and terminate in eternal happiness. The greatest application of mind, the utmost earnestness and assiduity in the use of every appointed means, ought to be employed in seeking these important benefits : yet the idea of merit must be entirely excluded ; and men should labour for them, as the " gift of the Son of Man," the incarnate Redeemer, to all true believers: for him God the Father has constituted the absolute Dispenser of these spiritual provisions; and he has sealed his commission, and attested his character, by the miracles which he wrought, and by the other testimonies which he bore to him. (Marg. Ref. x.—Notes, v. 31—44.) These were the advantages, which the Jews should have laboured for, and expected from their Messiah, and not secular honours and emoluments.—" For him hath the Father sealed, even " God." The sentence is complete without the word,

28 Then said they unto him, [r] What shall we do, that we might work the works of God?

29 Jesus answered and said unto them, [s] This is the work of God, that ye believe on him whom he hath sent.

30 They said therefore unto him, [t] What sign shewest thou then, that we may [b] see, and believe thee? what dost thou work?

31 Our [c] fathers did eat manna in the desert; as it is written, [d] He gave them bread from heaven to eat.

(marginal references, left column)
r Deut. x. 27. Jer.
xiii. 3—5. 20.
Mic. vi. 7, 8.
Matt. xix. 16.
Luke x. 25. Acts
ii. 37. ix. 6. xvi.
30.
s 1 John iii. 23.
36. Deut. xviii.
18, 19. Ps. ii. 12.
Matt. xvii. 5.
Mark xvi. 16.
Acts xvi. 31.
xxii. 14—16.
Rom. iv. 4, 5. ix.
30, 31. x. 3, 4.
Heb. v. 9. 1 John
iii. 23. v. 1.
t 1. 18. iv. 48. Ex.
iv. 8. 1 Kings
xiii. 3. Is. vii.
11—14. Matt.xii.
38, 39. xvi. 1—
4. Mark viii. 12.
Luke xi. 29, 30.
Acts ii. 30. 1Cor.
i. 22. Heb. ii. 4.
b W. x. 38. xii. 37. xx. 25—29. Is. v. 19. Mark xv. 32.
Num. xi. 6—9. Deut. viii. 3. Josh. v. 12. Neh. ix. 20. Ps. cv. 40.
Ps. lxxviii. 24, 25. 1 Cor. x. 3. Rev. ii. 17.

32 Then Jesus said unto them, Verily, verily, I say unto you, [e] Moses gave you not that bread from heaven; but my Father giveth you [f] the true Bread from heaven.

33 For the Bread of God is he, [g] which [f] cometh down from heaven, and giveth life unto the world.

34 Then they said unto him, Lord, [h] evermore give us this bread.

35 And Jesus said unto them, [i] I am the Bread of life: [k] he that cometh to me shall [l] never hunger; and he [m] that believeth on me shall never thirst.

(marginal references, right column)
e Ex. xvi. 4. 8. 15.
Ps. lxxviii. 23.
f 33. 35. 41. 50.
55. 58. i. 9. xv.
1. 1 John v. 20.
g 58. 48. 51. iii.
13. vii. 42. xiii.
3. xvi. 28. xvii.
8. 1 Tim. i. 15.
16. 1 John i. 1;
iv. 9.
h 36. iv. 15. Ps.
iv. 6.
i 41. 48—58. 1 Cor.
x. 16—18. xi 23
—29.
k 37. 44. 45. 65. v.
40. vii. 37. Is. iv.
1—3. Matt. xi.
28. Rev. xxii. 17.
l iv. 13. 14. 1s.
xlix. 10. Luke
vi. 25. Rev. vii.
16.

(commentary, left column)

" God," which is added at the end, as explanatory of the preceding clause.

Boat. (22) Πλοιαριον. 23. xxi. 8. *Mark* iii. 9. iv. 36. Πλοιον, 17. 24.—*Had given thanks.* (23) Ευχαριστησαντος. The introduction of this circumstance, in the connexion in which it is here placed, shews that it was thought a more important part of the transaction, by the Evangelist, than it generally is by his readers.—*Labour.* (27) Εργαζεσθε. " Work." *Marg.* 28. 30. iii. 21. v. 17. *Matt.* xxi. 28, et al.—Sealed.] Εσφραγισεν. See on iii. 33.

V. 28, 29. When the people heard our Lord exhort them " to labour," or to *work,* " for the meat, which endureth unto everlasting life " (27); they enquired what they ought to do, that they might " work the works," which God required of them. They seem to have thought of such works, as the Pharisees imposed on their disciples, in addition to the law of Moses. (*Marg. Ref.* y.—*Notes,* iii. 1, 2. *Matt.* xix. 16—22. *Luke* x. 25—29.)—To this our Lord answered, that the work especially required of them, was to " believe on him whom the Father had sent " among them. This may be called the first and great commandment of the gospel to sinners. (*Marg. Ref.* z.—*Matt.* xvii. 5.) The contrariety of genuine faith in the divine Saviour, to the natural pride, self-confidence, self-will, and carnal enmity against God, of fallen man, renders it extremely difficult; and, like obedience to the law, it cannot be exercised without the preventing and assisting grace of God. Much pains must generally be taken in self-examination, and comparing a man's conduct and character with the rule of duty, and his obligations to obedience; in opposing the pride and lusts of his heart; in separating from evil companions and counsellors, and vain pursuits; in redeeming time for religious purposes, and breaking off bad habits, and in using the means of grace; in complying with the call of the gospel, and in " living the life of faith " in the Son of God;" so that it may well be called " a " work." The submission of the understanding to the teaching of God, of the conscience to his righteousness, and of the heart and will to his method of salvation and to his authority, which are implied in it, render it emphatically *an act of obedience.* It honours God in all his perfections, more than any other good work can do: and though it does not justify, *as a good work,* but by receiving Christ for our righteousness; yet without it no other good work can be accepted. So that faith in Christ may especially be called " the work of God;" and it was that act of obedience, to which the Jews were then called, in order to obtain the blessing of eternal life. (*Notes, Matt.* vii. 13, 14. 24—27. *Luke* xiii. 22—30, v. 24.)—' They who seek ' to please God without faith, are diligent to no purpose. ' ...Should any one apply to a physician, and ask him for ' what sum of money he would undertake to cure him, ' and the physician should answer in these words: All the ' money which I require is, that thou wilt confide in me, ' and be fully assured, that I seek nothing but thy reco-' very and established health: ...who would, from such an ' answer, conclude, that this *confidence* was in fact *money,* ' which the physician demanded from the sick man, that ' he might follow his salutary counsels? ... They are there-' fore, evidently ridiculous, who from this passage infer ' that *faith* is a work, and that ... we are justified by our ' works.' *Beza.* (*Notes, Matt.* xi. 28—30. *Heb.* v. 7— 10, v. 9. xi. 4—10. 1 *John* iiii. 18—24, v. 23.)

V. 30—35. When the Jews imagined, that Jesus was about to lead them forth to liberty, victory, and dominion, they were ready to avow themselves his followers; and thought his miracles a sufficient proof that he was the Messiah (14). But when he demanded faith in him, in order to the attainment of " eternal life;" they perceived that his doctrine did not accord with their worldly expectations, their strong attachment to the Mosaick law, the glosses of the Scribes, and traditions of the elders, which indeed made the law itself of none effect; they therefore began to question his divine mission. Some at least demanded, what sufficient evidence he could produce, to convince them that eternal life might be obtained by faith in him; which they seem to have justly considered as a claim to a confidence and dependence unprecedented, and never required by any ancient prophet, or servant of God. (*Marg. Ref.* a, b.—*Notes, Matt.* xii. 38—40. xvi. 1—4.) He had indeed once fed a few thousands with barley-bread and fishes, in a miraculous manner; but what was that in comparison to the wonders performed in the days of their great lawgiver, when two millions of their forefathers had been fed with manna, for the space of forty years; which, both in respect of its excellency, and the manner in which it was given them, might be called " the bread which God " gave them from heaven to eat?" (*Marg. Ref.* c, d.) To this our Lord replied with his usual strong affirmation, that " Moses had not given them that bread:" he had used

36 But I said unto you, ᵐ that ye also have seen me, and believe not.

37 All ⁿ that the Father giveth me shall come to me: and him that cometh to me ᵒ I will in no wise cast out.

38 For ᵖ I came down from heaven, not to do mine own will, but the will of him that sent me.

39 And ᵠ this is the Father's will which hath sent me, that of all which he hath ʳ given me ˢ I should lose no-thing ᵗ but should raise it up again at the last day.

40 And this is the will of him that sent me, that every one, which ᵘ seeth the Son, ᵛ and believeth on him, may

---

no means to obtain it for them, much less did he *create* it; nor did it really come " from heaven," but merely from the upper region of the air. Whereas God, even his Father, who gave their ancestors that typical bread for the temporary sustenance of their natural lives, now gave them " the true Bread " from the heaven of heavens, for the eternal salvation of their souls : for " the Bread of God," emphatically so called, was *that* which descended from heaven, to give life, spiritual and eternal, to perishing sinners all over the world. (*Marg. Ref.* e—g.—Notes, 47—58. iii. 12, 13.)—It is plain that the Jews did not understand the meaning of our Lord : yet many of them had much reverence for him, and supposed that he alluded to some unknown benefit, which he meant to confer on them ; and therefore they *seriously*, though *ignorantly*, desired him to " give them evermore that bread " of which he spoke : for the address is such, that we cannot understand it as used in a deriding manner. (*Note*, iv. 10—15, *v.* 15.) Jesus therefore more explicitly declared, that by " the " Bread of life," he meant himself : and that, by " coming " to him," and " believing on him," they might receive and be sustained by that Bread unto everlasting life.—In his person, atonement, and mediation, he is the suitable and sufficient Sustenance of our souls. The sinner, who in true faith, receiving the sure testimony of God, applies to him, and relies on him, for pardon, grace, comfort, and all things pertaining to eternal life, finds his wants supplied, and his desires satisfied in an adequate manner ; so that he shall never be tortured through hunger and thirst, without having a supply ever ready at hand to relieve and remove them. (*Marg. Ref.* i—l.—Notes, iv. 10—15, *vv.* 13, 14. v. 24—27, *v.*24. 1 *John* v. 11, 12.)—We may here observe that " coming to Christ," and " believing on him," signify the same, in scriptural language ; or rather the former is the never-failing consequence of the latter. (*Note*, i. 10—13.)— ' Our Lord so much insists upon this metaphor, because it ' was familiar to the Jews, and used by their most celebrated ' writers.' *Whitby*. Surely, this was neither his *only* nor his *principal* reason ; for had it not been a metaphor well adapted to convey his meaning, he would have rejected it, and substituted one more apposite.—' It is very usual with ' the sacred writers to represent divine instructions, as the ' food of the soul ; (*Ps.* xix. 10. cxix. 103. *Prov.* ix. 5. ' *Job* xxiii. 12. *Jer.* xv. 16. *Heb.* v. 12. 14 ;) yet I can re-' collect no instance, in which the instructor himself, as ' such, is called *food*, or any are said *to eat him ;* much less, ' in which, as below, they are exhorted to " eat his flesh ' " and drink his blood." So that Dr. Clarke's laboured ' and ingenious criticism on this passage, is far from being ' satisfactory ; and, however clear it may be of any such

' design, I fear it has misled many to a neglect of that ' great doctrine, the atonement of Christ, to which there ' seems in the context so express a reference.' *Doddridge*. —The whole of this discourse has such an inseparable connexion with the real atonement of our Lord's death on the cross, and the life of faith in him and in that atone-ment ; that, if these subjects be kept out of sight, it is impossible to give any clear and satisfactory exposition of the passage. And this is a most conclusive proof of these doctrines, to all who revere the words of Christ ; according to that form of reasoning, which is called *reductio ad absurdum*,—' reducing an opponent to an absurdity, to ' escape the conclusive force of an argument.'—*As it is written,* &c. (31) *Neh.* ix. 15. *Ps.* lxxviii. 24. The varia-tion from the Septuagint, in either place, is immaterial. *Shall never hunger.* (35) Ου μη πεινασῃ.—*Shall never thirst.*] Ου μη διψησῃ πωπστε.—See on iv. 14.
V. 36—40. Our Lord next plainly told the Jews, that though they had seen him and his miracles, and seemed to be his zealous followers, yet they did not truly believe in him. But, if they forsook him, he should not be without disciples ; for all " whom the Father had given him," in his fore-knowledge and choice of them, and by the cove-nant of redemption made with him as their Surety, would " come to him." The event is certain, " they will come," but without any compulsion ; for the discovery of their guilt, danger, and remedy, by the teaching of the Holy Spirit, makes them most willing and glad to come, and to renounce every hope and interest, which interferes with seeking to him for salvation. (*Marg. Ref.* m—o.—Notes, xvi. 8—15. *Ps.* cx. 4.)—At the same time, this purpose and work of God perfectly consisted with the general en-couragements which he gave to all, who desired to come and share these blessings : as it was equally true, that he " would in no wise cast out " one individual who thus came to him ; either at first refusing to admit him into the num-ber of his people, or afterwards casting him out, as Hagar and Ishmael were cast out of Abraham's family. (*Note, Gal.* iv. 21—31.) This implies a promise or engagement of Christ, that no degree of previous guilt, no inveterate habits of vice, no slavery to Satan, no secret decree of God, no involuntary mistake, no feebleness in attempting to come to him, would induce him to reject a single person, who applied to him for the salvation of his soul, with a sincere desire of that blessing, and a believing dependence on his truth, power, and grace, by using diligently and with perseverance the means which he has appointed. In this, the Father's will, which the Son came down from heaven to perform, perfectly concurs : it is his will, that not one of those " given to the Son " should be rejected or lost by

3 T 2

have everlasting life: and I will raise him up at the last day.

41 ¶ The Jews then [a] murmured at him, because he said, [b] I am the Bread which came down from heaven.

42 And they said, [c] Is not this Jesus, the son of Joseph, whose father and mother we know? how is it then that he saith, I came down from heaven?

43 Jesus therefore answered and [d] said unto them, Murmur not among yourselves.

44 No [e] man can come to me, [f] except the Father which hath sent me [g] draw him: [h] and I will raise him up at the last day.

45 It is [i] written in the prophets, [k] And they shall be all taught of God. [l] Every man therefore that hath heard, and hath learned of the Father, cometh unto me.

46 Not that [m] any man hath seen

Margin/reference notes (left column of scripture):
a 43. 12. 60. 66. vii. 12. Luke v. 30. xv. 2. xix. 7. 1 Cor. x. 10. Jude 16.
b 33. 48. 51. 58.
c 33. 42. Matt. xiii. 55, 56. Mark vi. 3. Luke iv. 22. Rom. i. 3, 4. C. Gal. iv. 4.
d 64. xvi.19. Matt. xvi. 8. Mark ix. 33. Heb. iv. 13.

Margin/reference notes (right column of scripture):
e 65. v. 44. viii. 43. xii. 37—40.
Is. xlix. 18—20. Je—. xiii. 23. Matt. xiii. 34. Rom. viii. 7.
f 45. 65. iii. 3—7. Matt. xi. 25—27.
g—10. Phil. i. 29. Col. ii. 12. Tit. iii. 3—5. xii. 32. Cant. i. 4. Jer. xxxi. 3. Hos. xi. 4. h 39. 40. i Mark i. 2. Luke i. 70. xviii. 31. k Is. ii. 3. liv. 13. Jer.xxxi. 33, 54. l 37. 65. v. 38 m i. 18. v.

Mic. iv. 2. Eph. iv. 21, 22. 1 Thes. iv. 9. Heb. viii. 10, 11. x. 16.—40. x. 27. xvi. 14, 15. Matt. xvii. 5. Eph. i. 17. 1 John iv. 1—3. C. viii. 19. xiv. 9, 10. xv. 24. Col. i. 15. 1 Tim. vi. 16. 1 John iv. 12.

---

him, in life or death; but that every one of them should be raised up, to eternal felicity, "at the last day." And it is equally his will, that every one, "who beholdeth the Son," who so contemplates his character and word, and discerns the glory and suitableness of his salvation, as to believe in him, and to entrust his soul in his hands, should have everlasting life, notwithstanding all possible hindrances and objections. (Marg. Ref. p—z.—Notes, 41—46, vv. 44, 45. 60—65, v. 65. x. 26—31, vv. 28, 29. xvii. 11, 12. Ps. xl. 6—8. Heb. x. 5—10.)—These two views of the divine will, his secret will concerning those whom he has "chosen to salvation," and his revealed will concerning the actual salvation of every believer, are perfectly coincident; for no one wills thus to come, till divine grace has subdued, and in part changed, his heart, and therefore no one who comes will ever be cast out. When an awakened sinner is willing to come to Christ, if he finds the doctrines of the divine decrees too dazzling for his feeble eyes, he should look off from them to the general invitations and promises of the gospel: but when he can bear to look at the former, he may find in them the source and reason of his willingness, and be encouraged to hope for the completion of that work which grace has begun in his soul.—But let every one beware of blaspheming or perverting these doctrines, which are so evidently contained in scripture; and which indeed cannot be separated from our ideas of the divine sovereignty and perfections, or from a proper understanding of the entirely free grace of God, in the salvation of his people from their state of sin and death, by regeneration, conversion, faith, justification by grace, and adoption into the family of God.—Giveth, &c. (37) This expression is used by none but our Lord himself, and only in this chapter (39), in the twenty-ninth verse of the tenth chapter, and in the seventeenth chapter of this gospel; so that any diligent enquirer, by comparing the several verses in which it is found, may form a judgment of its real import.—' All ' that the Father graciously chosen to himself, and ' whom he giveth to me in consequence of a peculiar cove- ' nant, to be sanctified and saved by me, will certainly at ' length come unto me. I have given that sense of this ' important text, which on serious and I hope impartial ' consideration, appeared to me most agreeable to the words ' themselves, and to the general tenour of scripture. Mr. ' Le Clerc's gloss upon them appears to me unnatural, and ' Dr. Whitby's frivolous.' Doddridge.—I own myself perfectly unable to understand, what the latter writer means, in his long note on this text; unless it be, that all who believe in Christ will come to him; i. e. all who come, will

come!—' Envy keeps some, covetousness others, and love ' of the praise of men keeps others, from believing. · And ' generally the unbelieving heart is an evil · heart, and a ' reprobate mind, and a hard heart, and a foolish and slow ' heart. ... Meanwhile the better dispositions and prepara- ' tions of the hearts of these here, are to be looked upon; ' as effects wrought by the preventing grace of God, and ' in that respect they are said to be drawn by the Father.' Hammond. (Note, 41—46.) It is not meant, that this learned divine maintains the same views with the author. It is well known, that he contends earnestly for the contrary system. Yet he has here, without perhaps being aware of it, expressed himself in language, suited to the views of all sober Calvinists; and has made a concession of too much importance, to be passed over in the argument; a concession, which it will be difficult for any man, to prove either unscriptural or irrational.—' From the gratuitous election ' in Christ, by the Father, flows the gift of faith, which ' eternal life necessarily follows. Therefore faith in Christ ' is a certain testimony of our election, and consequently ' of our future glorification.' Beza.

I will in no wise cast out. (37) Ου μη εκ©αλω εξω. The double negative is expressed in the translation by the words, " in no wise," which strengthens the negation. The words εκ©αλω εξω certainly imply more, than mere exclusion in the first instance: they rather presuppose admission, and imply the idea of subsequent expulsion, which is so expressly guarded against.—Which seeth. (40) 'Ο θεωρων. 19. 62. ii. 23. iv. 19. Matt. xxvii. 55, et al. Cum attentione video. Θεωρια, Luke xxiii. 48.—Hence the word theory.

V. 41—46. The foregoing declarations of Jesus excited the murmurs, and offended the prejudices, of those who heard them; especially his saying, " I am the Bread which " came down from heaven" (33). Being ignorant of his miraculous conception, they supposed that they were acquainted with his parents; and they thought that he was a mere man born on earth, as other men are: how then could he say, "I came down from heaven?" (Marg. Ref. a—c.—Notes, vii. 40—53, vv. 41—43. Matt. xiii. 54 —58. Mark vi. 1—4. Luke iv. 20—22.) Yet had not our Lord pre-existed in heaven before his nativity, even his miraculous conception would not have removed or answered the objection, "How is it that he saith, I came down " from heaven?" (Notes, iii. 12, 13. xvi. 25—30. Eph. iv. 7—10.) But Jesus required them to suppress their murmurs, and secret whisperings of dissatisfaction; for he must assure them, that " no man can come to him, except " the Father draw him." The ground of this impossibility,

the Father, save he which is of God;
[a] [a] he hath seen the Father.

47 Verily, verily, I say unto you,
[b] He that believeth on me hath everlasting life.

48 I am [c] that Bread of life.

49 Your [d] fathers did eat manna in the wilderness, [e] and are dead.

50 This is [f] the Bread which cometh down from heaven, [g] that a man may eat thereof, and not die.

51 I am the [h] living Bread which came down from heaven. If any man eat of this Bread, he shall live for ever: and the Bread that I will give is [i] my flesh, which I will give for [j] the life of the world.

52 The Jews therefore [k] strove among themselves, saying, [l] How can this man give us his flesh to eat?

53 Then Jesus said unto them, [m] Verily, verily, I say unto you, [n] Except ye

Marginal references (left column):
a vii. 29. viii. 55.
Matt. xi. 27.
Luke x. 22.
b vi. 54. iii. 36. v.
24. xiv. 19. Rom.
v. 9, 10. Col. iii.
3, 4. 1 John v.
12, 13.
p 12, 13.
c 16, 17. xi. 24.
q See on 31.
r Num. xxvi. 65.
1 Cor. x. 3—5.
Jude 5.
s 33. 42. 54. 51. 58.
t ñd. viii. 51. xi.
26, 26. Rom.
viii. 10.

Marginal references (right column):
u iv. 10, 11. vii.
38. 1 Pet. ii. 4.
x 52—57. Matt.
xx. 28. Luke
2. 25. Tit. ii. 14.
Heb. x. 5—12.
20.
y 53. l. 29. 2 Cor.
v. 19. 21. 1 John
ii. 2. iv. 14.
z 41. vii. 40—43.
ix. 16. x. 19.
a 4. 9. iv. 11.
Acts xvii. 32.
1 Cor. ii. 14.
b 26. 47. See on
iii. 3. Matt. v.
c iii. 3, 5. xiii. 8.
xv.4. Matt.xviii.
3. Luke xiii. 3.
5.

lies in the contrariety, which subsists between the proud, worldly, unholy, rebellious, and ungodly nature of fallen man; and the humbling, spiritual, and holy nature of the gospel. This cannot be taken away, except by the energy of divine grace in regeneration. (*Notes,* i. 10—13, v. 13. iii. 3—6.) The Father, " who sent the Son into the world " to save sinners," must draw them to the Son to be saved by him, or they will universally neglect his salvation. The gospel finds none *willing* to be saved from sin and condemnation, in the humbling holy manner revealed in it: none are saved against their will; but the Lord, by his grace, disposes and draws sinners to Christ, and his drawing is the first moving cause of their activity and diligence. (*Note, Phil.* ii. 12, 13.) He cures as it were the fever of the soul; he creates the appetite; he sets the provisions before the sinner; he convinces him that they are wholesome and pleasant, and that he is welcome; and thus the man is drawn to come, and eat, and live for ever. (*Marg. Ref.* d—g.—*Notes,* 60—65. xii. 27—33, v. 32. *Judg.* iv. 6, 7. *Cant.* i. 4. *Hos.* xi. 3, 4.)—Our Lord next reminded his hearers, that this accorded with the doctrine of their prophets, who had declared, that all who received the benefit of the Messiah's kingdom, would be " taught of God." Thus in fact, every man in all ages and places, who " has " learned of the Father " (by hearing and believing his word,) those truths which he teaches concerning his own perfections, his law, the future judgment, the eternal world, the evil of sin, the ruined estate of man, his need of mercy and grace, and the nature and glory of salvation, is infallibly brought to believe in Christ, and count all things but loss in comparison of him; and all who truly believe in him, are thus taught by God himself. The Jews, however, must not hence conclude, that the Father would teach them personally; for none had seen the Father, except his beloved Son, who was of him, and perfectly acquainted with him: they must therefore expect to be taught by his inward influence upon their minds, removing their prejudices, and humbling their pride; by means of his word, and of those ministers whom he sent among them. (*Marg. Ref.* m, n. —*Notes,* i. 18. *Matt.* xi. 27.)—*Draw.* (44) ' That is, as ' Augustin rightly teacheth, whom he shall of *unwilling* ' render *willing.* For it is indeed true, that no one believes ' against his will: ... but we are willing, because it is given ' us, that we should be willing. For it is not from man ' willing, but from God pitying.' *Beza.—Taught,* &c. (45) The texts referred to, (for it cannot be called a quotation.) indisputably relate, not to all the Jews, as some suppose; but to the true Israel, that holy church, of which Israel as a nation was a type. It is the new covenant, of which

Christ is the Surety, (and not the old covenant made with Israel at Sinai,) which engages for this divine teaching, to all those for whose benefit it was formed. (*Marg. Ref.* i—l. —*Notes, Is.* liv. 11—14, v. 13. *Jer.* xxxi. 31—34. *Heb.* viii. 7—13.)

Murmured. (41) Εγογγυζον. 43. 61. vii. 32. *Matt.* xx. 11. *Luke* v. 30. 1 *Cor.* x. 10. Γογγυσμος, vii. 12. *Acts* vi. 1.—*Draw.* (44) Ἑλκυση. xii. 32. xviii. 10. xxi. 6. 11. *Acts* xvi. 19.—*Taught.* (45) Διδακτοι. 1 *Cor.* ii. 13. Not elsewhere N. T.—*Is.* liv. 13. *Sept.*

V. 47—51. After a repeated and most solemn assurance, that faith in him was the only and the certain method of obtaining everlasting life, and that he was " the " Bread of life; " our Lord shewed the Jews the superior excellence of his salvation above the manna, which was but a shadow of so great a blessing. Their fathers had eaten manna in the wilderness, and most of them had died, without entering the promised land, and the rest of them had lived but a short time afterwards: so that the advantage of that food was very small, save to those who saw in it the type of good things to come. (*Marg. Ref.* o. r.—*Notes,* 30—35. v. 24—27, v. 24. *P. O. Ex.* xvi. 22— 36. xvii. 1—7. *Note,* 1 *Cor.* x. 1—5.) But the true " liv- " ing Bread, which came down from heaven," is of so excellent a nature, that the man who feeds on it shall never die: his soul will be nourished by it to everlasting life; and the death of the body will be only a sleep, which will shortly terminate in a glorious resurrection. And this Bread is no other than the flesh of Christ; his human nature which he had assumed into personal union with his Deity, that he might present it to the Father as an expiatory sacrifice for the sins of the world; to redeem sinners of every nation who believe in him, and to obtain for them " all things pertaining to life and godliness." (*Marg. Ref.* s—y.—*Notes,* 52—58. vi. 10—15.)—' The Jews had insi- ' nuated, that feeding a few thousands with the five loaves ' was an inconsiderable thing, when compared with what ' Moses did, when he fed the whole camp of Israel: but ' our Lord here declares the purposes of his grace and ' bounty to be far more extensive, as reaching to the whole ' world, and giving life, immortal life, to all that should ' believe in him.' *Doddridge.*

V. 52—58. The Jews, who were generally ignorant, carnal, and formal, not understanding these declarations, began to dispute among themselves about them. Some took them in one sense, some in another: and probably many derided or censured Jesus, while others vindicated him: yet none of them could conceive how he could " give " them his flesh to eat." (*Marg. Ref.* z, a.—*Note,* iii. 4, 5.)

^d eat the flesh of the Son of man, and drink his blood, ye have no life in you.

54 Whoso ^e eateth my flesh, and drinketh my blood, ^f hath eternal life; and I will raise him up at the last day.

55 For my flesh is ^g meat indeed, and my blood is drink indeed.

56 He that eateth my flesh, and drinketh my blood, ^h dwelleth in me, and I in him.

57 As ⁱ the living Father hath sent me, and ^k I live by the Father; so he that eateth me, ^l even he shall live by me.

58 This is ^m that Bread which came down from heaven: not as your fathers did eat manna, and are dead: he that eateth of this Bread shall live for ever.

But he assured them, in the most decisive manner, that " Except they ate his flesh and drank his blood, they had " not life " (or eternal life) " in them;" but continued dead in sin and under condemnation.—It is here requisite to explain more fully the instruction conveyed by this figurative language. The human nature of " the Word, " who was made flesh," was doubtless intended; (Note, i. 14;) his " flesh and blood" became " meat and drink," when he gave his body to be wounded, and his blood to be shed, on the cross for our sins; and when his soul was made a sacrifice to the divine justice. " The flesh and " blood" of Christ, as separated by death, procured salvation for sinners; and the expressions here employed refer to the intention, efficacy, and benefits of the sufferings of Christ. These are as needful to the life and health of our souls, in our ruined state, as meat and drink are to the life and health of our bodies. The Lord, who, knowing our outward wants, has provided food for our use, in compassion to our perishing misery as sinners has also appointed this nourishment for our souls. Our food does not sustain us by being *prepared;* but by being *received,* digested, and incorporated: so Christ does not give life to our souls, merely by dying for us, or by being exhibited in the gospel; but, as received through faith, digested as it were in humble meditation, and converted into nutriment to hope, love, and other holy affections.—The healthy man hungers and thirsts: nothing but meat and drink can satisfy his appetites; and to obtain these, he will give any thing, or do any thing, which he finds absolutely necessary. Thus the regenerate soul hungers and thirsts for Christ and his salvation, and is prepared to venture, part with, or suffer any thing, rather than come short of an interest in him.—A healthy man also relishes his meat and drink; and the lively Christian delights to feed on Christ, by receiving him for all the purposes of salvation, and living by faith in him.—The food for the body is the gift of God, yet man must labour for it; and our spiritual food must be laboured for, though given us by Christ. (Note, 22—27, v. 27.) The believer feels weariness and uneasiness, and is ready to faint under trials and labours; but, attending on divine ordinances, and receiving Christ by renewed exercises of faith as his daily meat and drink, he finds his spirits recruited, his heart encouraged, and his strength repaired, to run the race, endure the conflict, and perform the work appointed him.—As the flesh and blood of Christ are expressly mentioned here, as well as in the institution of the Lord's supper; numbers have contended, that the external ordinance was intended: in precisely the same way that *baptism with water* has been mistaken for " the new birth of the Spi-

" rit." (Notes, iii. 4—8.) But the Lord's supper was not at this time instituted: and can any one seriously think, that every man continues " dead in sin," and under condemnation, till he has received that sacrament? (which would absolutely and without exception, exclude from salvation all who lived previous to its institution, all infants and young persons dying at that age, and an immense majority of adult professed Christians;) or imagine, that Christ dwells in, and will save, all those who partake of that ordinance, however hypocritically? No doubt it is the general duty of all real Christians, frequently to commemorate the death of Christ at his table: but this is merely the ' outward sign' of the blessing here intended; and those who rest in it will have only the shadow of salvation.—It is also remarkable, that the church, which of all others has most exalted, and even idolized, the Lord's supper, has refused the cup, the emblem of " the blood of " Christ," to the laity; as if they would not allow them to have even the sign of salvation!—We know, however, from scripture, that the justice and holiness of God, and the honour of his violated law, rendered such a sacrifice as that of the death of Christ necessary for us: and unless a man knows and owns his need of that atonement, and habitually lives on Christ for pardon, righteousness, and all things pertaining to salvation, " he hath no life in him." But he, who thus " eats the flesh and drinks the blood of " the Son of man, hath eternal life;" he has the title to it, and the beginning of it: and the resurrection of his soul to spiritual life, is the pledge of the resurrection of his body to everlasting glory. For " the flesh of Christ is " meat indeed," or, *truly,* emphatically, and exclusively; " and his blood is drink indeed;" (Marg. Ref. c—g;) insomuch that when we thus live by faith in the atonement of Christ, and receive from his fulness, we dwell in him, as our Refuge, Rest, and Home; (Marg. Ref. h.—Notes, Ps. xc. 1, 2. xci. 1, 2;) and he dwells in us by his grace and Spirit, as in his temple; so that we are " one with him, " and he with us." (Notes, xiv. 21—24. xvii. 22, 23. Eph ii. 19—22. iii. 14—19. 1 John iv. 9—17, vv. 12, 13. 16.) This mystical union even in some respects resembles that of the incarnate Son of God with the eternal Father: for as his life on earth was sustained by his union with the Deity, and by the indwelling of the Spirit; so believers are united to Christ, and live by that life which is hid in him, and they shall thus live for ever. (Marg. Ref. i. k—m.— Note, Col. iii. 1—4.)—' Whosoever eateth the flesh, and ' drinketh the blood of Christ, in the sense here spoken of, ' " abideth in Christ and Christ in him;" and therefore 'is ' a true and living member of Christ's body: and he small

n 24. xviii. 20. Ps. xl. 9. 10. Prov. l. 20—23. viii. 1—3. Luke iv. 31.

59 These things said he a in the synagogue, as he taught in Capernaum.

o 66. viii. 31.

60 ¶ Many therefore o of his disciples, when they had heard this, said, p This is an hard saying; who can hear n it?

p 41. 42. vii. 43. Matt. xi. 6. Heb. v. 2 Pet. iii. 16.

q 64. ii. 24. 25. xvi. 17. Heb. iv. 13. Rev. ii. 23.

61 When Jesus q knew in himself that his disciples murmured at it, he said unto them, Doth this offend you?

r iii. 13. xvi. 28. xvii. 4. 5. 11. Mark xvi. 19. Luke xxiv. 51. Acts i. 9. Eph. iv. 8. 1 Pet. iii. 22.

62 r What 'and if ye shall see the Son of man ascend up where he was before?

63 It is 'the Spirit that quickeneth; 'the flesh profiteth nothing: "the words that I speak unto you, they are spirit, and they are life.

64 But 'there are some of you that believe not. 'For Jesus knew from the beginning, who they were that believed not, and who should betray him.

65 And he said, Therefore said I unto you, 'That no man can come unto me, except it were given unto him of my Father.

s Gen. b. 7. Rom. viii. 2. 1 Cor. xv. 45. 2 Cor. iii. 6. 1 Pet. iii. 18. t 2. 1 Cor. xl. 27—29. Gal. v. 6. vi. 15. 1 Tim. iv. 8. Heb. xiii. 9. 1 Pet. ii. 21. u 68. xii. 49. 50. Deut. xxxiii. 47. Ps. xix. 7—10. cxix. 50. 93. 130. Rom. x. 8—10. 17. 1 Cor. ii. 9 —14. 2 Cor. ii. 6—8. 1 Thes. ii. 13. Heb. iv. 12. James i. 18. 1 Pet. i. 23. x 66. 61. v. 42. viii. 23. 38—47. y 70. 71. ii. 24, 25. Ps. cxxxix. 2—4. Acts xv. 18. Heb. iv. 13. z 37. 44, 45. x. 16. 26, 27. xii. 37—41. Eph. ii. 8. 9. Phil. i. 29. 1 Tim. i. 14. 2 Tim. ii. 25. Tit. iii. 3—7. Heb. xii. 2. Jam. i. 16—18.

'have eternal life, and be partaker of a happy resurrection: 'and so no person can either be wicked here, or deprived 'of everlasting life hereafter, who, in the sense here men- 'tioned, eats of the flesh and drinketh of the blood of 'Christ. Now this is very true of eating spiritually and by 'faith, as it imports believing in Christ. For "this," saith 'Christ, "is the will of him that sent me, that every one who '"believeth in the Son may have everlasting life, and I will '"raise him up at the last day." But then of sacramental 'eating of Christ's flesh, it is as false: for this was eaten 'by a Judas, and continually is eaten by millions, who are 'both wicked here, and will be damned hereafter. This, 'therefore, cannot be the import of our Saviour's words.' *Whitby.*—Our Lord however, must be supposed to refer to that sacred ordinance, which he intended to appoint, as the memorial of his body broken and his blood shed, for the life of our souls: and as the outward sign of the manner, in which we 'feed on him in our hearts by faith with 'thanksgiving;' as a publick profession of our inwardly receiving his atonement, and as a pledge to all true believers of everlasting life. (*Note, Matt.* xxvi. 26—28.)—Those who suppose, that our Lord meant merely 'the sacra- 'mental eating of his flesh and blood;' whether they graft on this construction, Transubstantiation, Consubstantiation, or any blessing inseparably connected with the act of re- ceiving, independent of the faith or unbelief of the receiver, doubtless pervert the words of Christ, to establish idolatry, superstition, formality, and self-righteousness. While such as speak of 'spiritually feeding on his *words* and *doctrine*,' without explicit reference to "faith in his blood," and 'feeding on him in our hearts, by faith with thanksgiv- 'ing," lead men by another road entirely away from this grand and central part of Christianity. They do not explicitly consider Christ as a High Priest and a propitiatory sacrifice; and they confound him with prophets and apos- tles, on whose doctrine men might feed, but who never spoke of "giving their flesh for the life of the world;" or called on their hearers to "eat their flesh and drink their "blood," as essential to salvation, and as infallibly ensuring it: and thus the most affecting view of that "love of "Christ which passeth knowledge," in giving himself for our sins, and for our salvation, to death upon the cross, is wholly lost sight of, in explaining this most interesting display of it.

Strove (52) Εμαχοντο. *Acts* vii. 26. 2 *Tim.* ii. 24. *Jam.* iv. 2.—The word denotes the eagerness and vehemence of the dispute.—*Whoso eateth.* (54) 'Ο τρωγων, 56, 57, 58. xiii. 18. *Matt.* xxiv. 38.—The word seems to mean *continuance of feeding,* as animals do. (*Gal.* ii. 20.) Τρωγω is used in heathen writers of brutes; εσθιω of men.—*Indeed.* (55) Αληθως, *truly,* 14. i. 48. iv. 42. *Matt.* xxvii. 54. (*Notes,* i. 6—9. xv. 1.)

V. 59. *Marg. Ref.—Note,* 22—27.

V. 60—65. It is not wonderful, that this discourse should astonish our Lord's audience: for though instruc- tion had frequently been spoken of, as *the food of the soul;* yet no prophet, or servant of God from the beginning of the world, had spoken of himself as "the Bread of Life;" and Jesus evidently assumed to himself more than Moses or any other person ever had done, or could have done, without the greatest impropriety. He spake also on the most mysterious doctrines and the most experimental part of religion, with which few of the people were acquainted, and which militated against their strongest prejudices: therefore many, who had hitherto professed themselves "his disciples," concluded that it was "a hard saying," unintelligible, or incredible; and enquired, who could en- dure to hear and receive it, as of divine authority. But Jesus, by his perfect knowledge of their secret thoughts and conversation, was acquainted with their murmurs; (*Marg. Ref.* o—q.—*Notes,* ii. 23—25. viii. 30—36;) and he demanded, whether these sayings stumbled them, and induced them to forsake him. If this now so perplexed them, what would they think of it, if they should "see "the Son of man ascend up where he was before?"—The human nature of Christ had not before been in heaven: but, being God and Man in one mysterious Person, that Person was called either "the Son of God," or "the Son "of man," without exact discrimination; and in virtue of this indissoluble union, the Person called "the Son of "man" might be said to have come down from heaven. (*Marg. Ref.* r.—*Notes,* iii. 12, 13. *Eph.* iv. 7—10.)— This implied, that the Messiah's kingdom was not of this world; for he would at length ascend into heaven, and appear no more personally among them. They were not therefore to understand, what he had said concerning "eating his flesh and drinking his blood," in a gross, car- nal sense; but of spiritually living on him and on his ful- ness by faith: for, as the soul of man gives life to the body, without which the flesh is only a lifeless putrefying lump of clay; so, without the life-giving Spirit of God, or "that which is born of the Spirit, and is spirit," all forms

66 ¶ From that *time* many ᵃ of his disciples went back, and walked no more with him.

67 Then said Jesus unto the twelve, ᵇ Will ye also go away?

68 Then Simon Peter answered him,

Lord, ᶜ to whom shall we go? ᵈ thou hast the words of eternal life.

69 And ᵉ we believe and are sure that thou art that Christ, the Son of the living God.

70 Jesus answered them, ᶠ Have not

---

of religion are dead and worthless. (*Marg. Ref.* s—u.—*Notes*, iii. 6. 2 Cor. iii. 4—6. 17, 18.) Indeed the words which Jesus spake to them were " spirit and life : " they related to spiritual things on which the life of their souls depended ; by believing and meditating on his words, trusting his promises, and thus living in a constant dependence on his atonement and mediation, they would spiritually " eat his flesh and drink his blood ; " and these were *the means*, by which the Spirit of God would nourish their souls unto eternal life. But he spoke these things to them in this figurative manner, because some of them did not believe, and were disposed to make a perverse use of his instructions ; and therefore he had before declared, for their warning, that " none could come to him except " it were given him of his Father." (*Notes*, 41—46. 66 —71.)—' " To be drawn by the Father," and to have " faith ' " given by the Father," are synonymous terms, which ' plainly indicates the interpretation above given.' *Doddridge*.—' My words are spirit and life ; as being the ' means of obtaining the Spirit, and by him this life ; to ' which effects my flesh, if you could eat it, would profit ' you nothing. Had our Lord said, " It is the Spirit that ' " quickeneth, the flesh profiteth nothing ; " therefore the ' flesh, which I will give, shall be joined to my divinity, ' and by the virtue of it, give you life ; he had said ' something like the sense, which others put on the text : ' (namely, the defenders of transubstantiation, and many protestant expositors, who seem rather to lean towards that monstrous opinion !) ' but saying only, " The words ' " which I speak to you, they are spirit ; " we cannot ' doubt but he speaks of eating and of drinking his flesh ' and blood spiritually.' *Whitby*.

Hard. (60) Σκληρος. See on xxv. 24.—*It is the Spirit that quickeneth.* (63) Το πνευμα εστι το ζωοποιουν. *Rom.* viii. 3. 1 Cor. xv. 45. 2 Cor. iii. 6. (See on v. 21.)—' I do ' not here understand το πνευμα, of the Holy Spirit ; for ' πνευμα and σαρξ are evidently opposed to each other. ... ' In like manner, 2 Cor. iii. 6, we have πνευμα opposed to ' γραμμα.' *Bp. Middleton*.—The Holy Spirit, personally, is not meant ; but that spiritual understanding of the words of Christ, " as spirit and life," which are taught by God, through his Holy Spirit, to all who are " born of " the Spirit."

V. 66—71. Many of the professed disciples, who forsook Jesus on this occasion, seem to have no more statedly attended on his personal ministry : but some of them might, after his ascension, when the event had explained his meaning, receive the instructions of his apostles. The multitudes, however, were at this time dispersed ; ' seeing ' he was not such a Messias as they looked for ; and would ' not be content with any kind of following him.' *Hammond*. Their secular expectations also were disappointed ; and their real character detected. (*Marg. Ref.* a.) So

that our Lord, having only his twelve disciples with him, asked them, " Will ye go away also ? " intimating that he would have no unwilling followers. They too were, in many things, greatly prejudiced and mistaken ; and especially they were strangers to the real nature of salvation, through his atoning sacrifice, and by faith in him, as the " Propitiation for sin : " but in general they were teachable, upright believers. (*Note, Matt.* xvi. 21—23.) Peter, therefore, answering in the name of his brethren, enquired " to whom they should go," in case they left him. John, their former master, had directed them to him ; they could get no benefit by becoming the disciples of the Pharisees ; they knew no other, who could be regarded even as a divine teacher ; and they could by no means give up the hope of eternal life, which they were engaged in the pursuit of as their first object ; besides the temporal advantages they might expect by following him : and indeed they believed, and had been fully assured, that he was the promised Messiah, " that Christ, the Son of the " living God ; " and that eternal life could only be found by believing and obeying his words, and observing his instructions. (*Marg. Ref.* b—f.—*Notes, Matt.* xvi. 13— 17.) To this bold and explicit confession Jesus replied, in a manner apparently very abrupt ; observing, that one of the twelve, whom he had chosen to be his apostles, was " a devil." He meant Judas Iscariot, who was a secret enemy, a designing hypocrite, and one who was in every thing of a diabolical disposition, though he had not been suspected by the other apostles ; especially he was a spy, and would prove a traitor, a liar, and a murderer ; like Satan the accuser of the brethren. (*Marg. Ref.* g, h.) Thus Peter, and the rest of them, were taught to be upon their guard, and to answer for themselves alone : they were reminded, while " they thought they stood, to take " heed lest they should fall ; " and Judas was given to understand that his character was well known to his Lord. Probably, he took no notice of it ; and the other apostles would not be able to understand his words till the event explained them, to their great astonishment. (*Marg. Ref.* i—l.)

Will ye also go away? (67) Μη και υμεις θελετε υπαγειν ; " Do ye will," or purpose, " also to withdraw ? "—*Have I not chosen*, &c. (70) Ουκ εγω εξελεξαμην. xiii. 18. xv. 16.—Chosen *to be apostles*, and " chosen unto salvation, by " sanctification of the Spirit unto obedience, and belief of " the truth," are very distinct kinds of election.—*Is a devil.*] Διαβολος εστι, not εσαι, *shall be*. viii. 44. xiii. 2. *Matt.* xxv. 41. 1 *Pet.* v. 8. *Rev.* xii. 9, 10, *et al.*

PRACTICAL OBSERVATIONS.

V. 1—21.

The beneficence of our Lord's miracles concurred with the power of them, to convince the people that he was

b viii. 44. xiii. 2.
21. 27. Acts xiii.
10. 1 John iii. 8.
Rev. iii. 9, 10.
1 1 Tim. iii. 11.
Tit. ii. 3. Gr.

I chosen you twelve, b and one of you is l a devil?

71 He spake of Judas Iscariot, the son of Simon: k for he it was that should betray him, l being one of the twelve.

k Ps. cix. 6—8.
Acts i. 16—20.
ii. 23. Jude 4.
l xviii. 2—6. Ps.
xli. 9. iv. 13, 14.
Matt. xxvi. 14
—16. xxvii. 3—5.

---

sent from God: and the same spirit of love displayed in our conduct, even amidst weakness and poverty, will best adorn the gospel, evince its divine origin and excellency, and conciliate the minds of men. If we copy the example of our Lord, in rendering hearty thanks to the Giver of all our temporal comforts, and in dispensing them liberally to the indigent; our most frugal and homely meals will be far more comfortable and blessed, than the most luxurious feasts of ungodly men. (*Note, Ps.* xxxvii. 16, 17.) But moderation and indifference in respect of our own diet, and a parsimonious care to " gather up the frag- " ments that remain, that nothing be lost," form the very basis of Christian beneficence: and if in opulent cities, all that which is wasted or needlessly consumed, were reserved to feed the hungry; how much more comfortably would the poor be maintained! and how much better would it be both for the souls and bodies of the more affluent! Christians, however, at least, should be willing to fare as Christ did; to obey his commands, and to encounter diffi- culties at his word.—When he is not sensibly present with his people, he is pleading for them; and he will come to them through every intervening obstacle; and, by his power and love, terminate all their sorrows, fears, and hardships. (*P. O. Matt.* xiv. 14—36. *Mark* xi. 30—56. viii. 1—21.)

V. 22—29.

If Jesus were again to appear on earth, feeding and healing men by miracle; he would again be followed by admiring multitudes, who might even desire to have him for their King, in hopes of preferment and secular advan- tages: and indeed many profess his truths and attend on his ordinances, nay minister in holy things, who seek no- thing more than " the loaves and fishes." They call him Rabbi, but will not be taught by him; they speak of him as their Saviour, but they do not rely on him for salvation; they say, " Lord, Lord, but will not do the things which " he says." And though he exhorts all men " to labour, " not for the meat that perisheth, but for that meat " which endureth unto everlasting life:" yet most, even of those who ' profess and call themselves Christians,' labour incessantly, anxiously, and wholly, for perishing vanities, till death convinces them of their folly; and then others succeed them, and copy the example of their in- fatuation. (*Note, Ps.* xlix. 13.) But, to rational crea- tures possessed of immortal souls, nothing is worthy of the chief regard, or to be the object of primary diligence, which will not " endure unto everlasting life," and secure the possessor from final misery and despair. This endur- ing portion " the Son of man " is authorized to bestow on whom he pleases. Let us then direct all our earnestness, and employ all our labour, to secure " the one thing need- " ful;" let us assiduously use every means, perform every duty, oppose every temptation, and seek the mortification of every sinful propensity; and in this way let us " wait " for the mercy of our Lord Jesus Christ unto eternal life." While we daily enquire, what are the works of God, which we are called to perform; let us remember, that an habi-

tual faith in Christ, as our only and all-sufficient Saviour, is the most important, indispensable, and arduous part of the obedience required of us, as sinners seeking salvation. When by his grace we are enabled to " live this life of " faith in the Son of God," all holy tempers follow, and all acceptable services may be performed; but without this no services, however splendid or admired by man, or thought highly of by us, will be regarded by our holy and merciful God. Yet this command, difficult as it is to a proud and carnal heart, only calls on a man who is poor, and deeply in debt, to come that he may be enriched; a malefactor, to accept of pardon and preferment; and a starving wretch, to partake of a feast, or rather of a con- stant, permanent, and eternal supply of all his wants, and of pleasures that always satisfy and never satiate. (*Notes, Rev.* iii. 17—19.)

V. 30—35.

Blessed be our God, that he has given us " the true " Bread from heaven." May he create in us an appetite for it; that we may *intelligently and cordially* say, " Lord, " evermore give us this Bread!" But when we look around us, we see men in general hungering after and feed- ing on husks or ashes: they " spend their money for that " which is not bread, and their labour for that which satis- " fieth not." (*Note, Is.* lv. 1—3.) Some feed on airy speculations, and " philosophy falsely so called:" some aim to satisfy their minds with gold, with fame, or power: some feed more grossly on sensual pleasure: and numbers attempt to allay their cravings after happiness, by dissi- pated mirth, or the pride of life. All these are like " a " hungry man, who dreameth that he eateth, but he " awaketh and his soul is empty:" for at length death comes, and their unsatisfied desires prove their eternal tor- mentors. Nay, many pretending to religion, take plea- sure in superstitions, enthusiasm, notions, forms, contro- versies, or revilings: these also " feed upon ashes; a de- " ceived heart hath turned them aside, that they cannot " deliver their souls, nor say, Is there not a lie in my right " hand?" (*Note, Is.* xliv. 19, 20.) But " the flesh of " Christ is meat indeed, and his blood is drink indeed:" here the soul, which hungers and thirsts for God, for righteousness, and true felicity, and is made sensible of its state and wants, finds a suitable and abundant provision. Here pardon, peace, hope, communion with God, and whatever can calm the conscience, serene and cheer the heart, or promote true holiness, is comprised in one glori- ous Object, a mighty Redeemer, " God manifest in the " flesh," shedding his precious blood to atone for the sins of his rebellious creatures! This is that " living Bread, " which came down from heaven, that we might eat and " live for ever." Oh, how adorable, how stupendous, is this love of our divine Redeemer! May this " love of " Christ constrain us ... to live no longer to ourselves, but " to him who died for us, and rose again." (*Note, 2 Cor.* v. 13—15.)

V. 36—46.

Unhumbled sinners cannot understand spiritual things;

CHAP. VII.

Jesus, when counselled by his unbelieving brethren to shew himself at Jerusalem, at the feast of tabernacles, assigning his reason, refuses to accompany them; but afterwards goes up privately, 1—10. The Jews seek him, and form different opinions of him, 11—13. He teaches in the temple; declares that his doctrine is of God, and answers objections, 14—29. Some seek to take him; others believe; and the Pharisees send officers to apprehend him, 30—32. He foretels his departure to the Father, when the Jews would in vain seek him, 33—36. He invites every one who is thirsty, to come to him and drink; referring to the Holy Spirit, which would be given to believers, 37—39. Divers opinions of him, 40—44. The officers, struck with his discourse, return without him, 45, 46. The Pharisees scornfully reproach them and the common people, and Nicodemus who took his part, 47—52. They are disconcerted, and separate, 53.

(Note, 1 Cor. ii. 14—16;) and therefore, they either object and deride, or they rest in outward forms, instead of " the " power of godliness." He alone who made the provision for our souls, can effectually teach these mysteries, and " draw us " unto Christ that we may live by faith in him. " All that the Father giveth" to the Son, will be thus taught, and will come to him; and he will surely receive and keep them, and " will raise them up at the last day." When therefore sinners are convinced of their need of Christ and his salvation, and that they cannot truly believe in him, except by the teaching and drawing of the Father; let them attend to his word, and pray for his Spirit, and in this way expect his blessing on their souls. For every one, who willingly comes to Christ, will be made welcome, and will on no account whatever be cast out. He has spoken the word, and he will make it good: it is his will, and " the will of the Father who sent him," and it cannot be invalidated. Let sinners then apply with confidence: " let the hearts of them rejoice who seek the " LORD:" let them be thankful that they have discovered their danger and their remedy; and let them seek further instruction, that they may enjoy the comfort, and bring forth the fruits, of " the life of faith " in the incarnate Son of God; and so expect " the last day," in joyful and thankful assurance of a resurrection unto the eternal life and glory.

V. 47—59.

The Jews could not, at the same time when the Lord spake to them, know his meaning; but we may know how Jesus can " give us his flesh to eat." The humble believer can rest in no outward emblem; but, through the sacramental bread and wine, he sees the body and blood of Christ, as truly appropriated by the faith of all acceptable communicants, for every saving purpose. He is convinced, that " except he eat the flesh of the Son of man, and " drink his blood," he has no spiritual life in him, nor any good hope of eternal life: and therefore his great fear is, lest he should be deceived in a matter of such immense importance. He is often ready to faint and be weary, through inward conflicts and outward troubles: but by again receiving Christ, as the Life and Salvation of his soul, he finds his hopes revive, his fears vanish, his strength return, and his graces invigorated; and thus he feeds daily on Christ, and proceeds in his work and warfare with patient alacrity. He finds, that meditation on the cross of Christ, and all the glorious truths connected with it, give life and vigour to his repentance, faith, hope, love, and gratitude; his heart is thus raised above, weaned from the world, and fixed on heavenly things; he is enabled to rejoice in the Lord; he ' dwells in, Christ, and ' Christ in him,' and he learns to live by his beloved Saviour, in some measure as he lived by the Father that sent him, and to his glory. This is the Christian's life: in proportion as he thus lives upon Christ, and thirsts and applies for the blessings procured for us by his precious blood; he copies more and more closely his example, and obeys his commandments, and may rejoice, under all trials, and at the approach of death, " in the hope of the " glory of God." (Notes, Rom. v. 3—11. Gal. ii. 17—21 vi. 11—14, v. 14. 1 Pet. iv. 1, 2.)

V. 60—71.

Many, who are called disciples, dispute against the words of Christ: many attend to the general doctrines of the gospel; but when ministers apply them to their consciences and experience, they are ready to exclaim, " It is a hard " saying, who can hear it?" They form gross conceptions of spiritual things, and argue against their own mistakes and misrepresentations: so that those preachers, who imitate their Master, need not wonder, if their faithful doctrine drives away numbers who for a time seemed zealously attached to them. We must, however, speak the words of Christ, " which are spirit and life," and not like the dead notions of moralists and speculators: (Notes, Jer. xxiii. 28, 29. Matt. vii. 28, 29. Heb. iv. 12, 13:) and we must leave it to him, to " quicken whom he will" by his Spirit, and to determine who are, and who are not, true believers.—Our main business is with ourselves: when many turn back, and walk no more with Christ, he seems to say to us, " Will ye go away also?" But the truly broken-hearted, who can rest satisfied with nothing short of eternal life, will answer, " Lord, to whom shall I go?' Even when discouraged, tempted, and harassed with doubts and fears; he still knows it is vain to think of returning to the world, of seeking salvation by " the works of the " law," of resting in forms and notions, or of going after false teachers: and still he believes, and desires to be fully assured, that Jesus has " the words of eternal life," as " the Christ, the Son of the living God." This faith, in its feeblest exercise, is essentially different from that of the most specious hypocrite, who ever followed the steps of the traitor Judas: such are often near to Christ in external profession and office, yet like Satan in the temper of their hearts and secret conduct; but they are known and will be detected by the heart-searching Judge, however they may impose upon their brethren. May we then be now searched and proved by him; and may our " hearts be " made sound in his statutes," as those, whom he has " chosen unto salvation, through sanctification of the

AFTER these things, Jesus [a] walked in Galilee: for he would not walk in Jewry, [b] because the Jews sought to kill him.

2 Now the Jews' [c] feast of tabernacles was at hand.

3 His [d] brethren therefore said unto him, [e] Depart hence, and go into Judea, that thy disciples also may see the works that thou doest.

4 For [f] there is no man that doeth any thing in secret, and he himself seeketh to be known openly: if thou do these things, [g] shew thyself to the world.

5 For [h] neither did his brethren believe in him.

6 Then Jesus said unto them, [i] My time is not yet come; but your time is alway ready.

7 The [k] world cannot hate you; [l] but, me it hateth, [m] because I testify of it, that the works thereof are evil.

8 Go ye up unto this feast: [n] I go not up yet unto this feast; for my time is not yet full come.

9 When he had said these words unto them, he abode still in Galilee.

10 But when his brethren were gone up, [o] then went he also up unto

---

"Spirit unto obedience, and the belief of his holy truth." (Notes, Ps. cxix. 80. cxxxix. 23, 24. 2 Thes. ii. 13, 14.)

NOTES.

CHAP. VII. V. 1. For a considerable time, our Lord went about Galilee, preaching the gospel; but he did not choose thus to go about preaching in Judea, because he knew that the rulers were determined to put him to death. He did not see good at that time to expose himself to their rage; or to work his miracles and give his instructions amidst such virulent and insidious enemies. It may be supposed, that he attended the passover and other appointed feasts: but he went up privately, and continued only a short time at Jerusalem, or in the neighbourhood. (Marg. Ref.)—The term walked, implies, that he did not continue in the same place, but went from one town or village to another, teaching and healing.—Our Lord was descended from Judah, and therefore a Jew, or Judean, in the strict and literal sense of the word, and the special honour of that tribe in particular, as well as of the nation in general; (Notes, Gen. xlix. 9, 10;) yet his ministry was more favourably attended, in the remote parts of the land where many of the inhabitants belonged to other tribes, than in Judea, which was chiefly occupied by the tribe of Judah. In this sense likewise, "He came to his own, and "his own received him not."

Walked.] Περιεπατει. vi. 66. xi. 54. 1 Pet. v. 8, et al. —Jewry.] Τη Ιουδαια, scil. γη.

V. 2. Notes, Ex. xxiii. 14—18. Lev. xxiii. 34—43. Num. xxix. 12—38. Deut. xxxi. 10—13. Neh. viii. 14—18. Zech. xiv. 16—19.—Of tabernacles.] Σκηνοπηγια. Here only N. T.—Deut. xvi. 16. xxxi. 10. Zech. xiv. 16. 18, 19. Sept. Εκ σκηνη, tabernaculum, et πηγνυμι, figo.

V. 3—10. Perhaps these brethren, or kinsmen, of our Lord were disgusted, because they saw no prospect of secular advantages from their relation to him; which they had expected, in case he was the promised Messiah: and therefore, notwithstanding his miracles, and the holiness of his character and doctrine, they suspected that he was a deceiver, and concluded that he acted from secular motives. They professed friendship, when they advised him to go into Judea, to preach and work miracles, among the rich, powerful, and learned of the nation: and they inti-

mated that he must have many disciples there, who would thus be encouraged openly to espouse his cause; that so the numbers of his adherents being increased, he might proceed openly to assert his claim to the kingdom of the Messiah. They urged, that it was unreasonable, and contrary to all ordinary rules of policy, for him to continue in an obscure part of the country, when his object must be to make himself known: and they concluded, that if he meant to proceed, he ought to stand forth publicly, and " shew himself to the world." (Marg. Ref. d—h.) By this insidious counsel they probably meant to lead him into danger, desiring that the Scribes and Pharisees might examine his pretences; at least they were actuated by merely carnal motives. He therefore told them, that his time for going up to the feast, or of avowing himself amidst his enemies, was not yet arrived: but their time was always ready, and they might go up to Jerusalem with safety whenever they chose. The world could have no enmity against them; as their maxims, principles, and conduct, were congenial with those of other ungodly men, and served to keep them in countenance: but " the world," including the unconverted of every description, must hate him, because he " testified of them that their works were " evil." He not only exposed the heinousness of men's evident immoralities and impieties: but he detected the pride and hypocrisy of the austere and superstitious Scribes and Pharisees; he testified even against their supposed good works, that they sprang from a corrupt source, and were " abomination in the sight of God;" and he shewed, that men of all nations, sects, and external characters, were deserving of the awful wrath and abhorrence of God, for the wickedness of their hearts and lives. These things affronted the pride, disquieted the consciences, interfered with the pursuits, and excited the indignation, of the world in general: thus he was mortally hated by them, notwithstanding the perfection of his character, and the power of his miracles: and the same effects will always be produced by the same cause. (Marg. Ref. i—m.—Notes, xv. 17—21. xvii. 13—16. Is. xlix. 7, 8. Zech. xi. 7—9. 1 John iii. 13—15. iv. 4—6. v. 19.)—It is probable, that these brethren of Christ went up, with many others, some days before the feast: our Lord, however, had his reasons for not going with them, as " his time was not yet fully come." He per-

the feast, ʼnot openly; but as it were in secret.

11 Then ᵗ the Jews sought him at the feast, and said, Where is he?

12 And there was much ʼmurmuring among the people concerning him: for ʼ some said, He ʼ is a good man: others said, Nay; but he ʼ deceiveth the people.

13 Howbeit, no man ᵇ spake openly of him, for fear of the Jews.

14 ¶ Now about ʼ the midst of the feast, Jesus went up into ᵗ the temple and taught.

15 And the Jews ᵘ marvelled, saying, ᵇ How knoweth this man ᵉ letters, having never learned?

16 Jesus answered them, and said, ᵈ My doctrine is not mine, ᵈ but his that sent me.

17 If ᵉ any man will do his will, he shall know of the doctrine, whether it be of God, or *whether* I speak of myself.

---

hays knew that his enemies would have taken umbrage, if he had gone up with the multitude of attendants; therefore he chose to go privately, and just before the feast began. (*Marg. Ref.* n—p.)—ʼ It is not to be doubted, but ʼ that Jesus arrived in time, in order to observe that feast ʼ of seven days most accurately, and indeed without omitʼting so much as one tittle of the law ; ... as bound for the ʼ sake of his people, to keep the whole law most perfectly. ʼ Yet for the same cause,ʼ (that above assigned,) ʼ he did ʼ not openly enter the temple, till the middle of the feast; ʼ that he might, in his Father's house, perform the office ʼ committed to him by his Father.ʼ *Beza.* Attendance on the sacred festivals was a part of the obedience which the law required, to which our Lord willingly subjected himself; and this he perfectly obeyed. This attendance also gave him the opportunity of teaching great multitudes from many different places, and confirming his doctrine by miracles before them. Yet, in availing himself of these opportunities, a wise regard to circumstances was in all respects highly important.—There is reason to conclude that these brethren of our Lord afterwards became his disciples. (*Notes*, Matt. xii. 46—50. *Luke* viii. 19—21. *Acts* i. 13, 14.)

Openly. (4) Εν παρρησια. 13. 26. xi. 14. 54. xvi. 25. 29. xviii. 20. *Mark* viii. 32. 2 *Cor.* iii. 12. *Eph.* iii. 12. vi. 19. 1 *John* ii. 28.—*Shew.*] Φανερωσον. ii. 11. iii. 21. " Manifest " thyself." Φανερως, 10.—*To the world.*] Τῳ κοσμῳ. 7. viii. 23. 26. ix. 39. xv. 18, 19. xvii. 6. 9. 11. 14. In these, and many other places, " the world" especially means, unholy professed worshippers of God, and in particular marks out the chief priests, scribes, and Pharisees. And are not nominal Christians, of the same character, " the world," at this day, as much as either Jews, Gentiles, or Mohammedans? —*Evil.* (7) Πονηρα, " wicked."

V. 11—13. The Jews sought our Lord; which implies that he constantly attended on the three great feasts, though we have not a particular account of it. Some of the people concluded, from his conduct, doctrine, and miracles, that he must be a good and holy man: but others would not allow him even this inferior honour; concluding that he imposed on the people by some artifice, which they were not able to detect: and those who favoured him dared not openly to avow their sentiments, lest the rulers should censure or excommunicate them. Perhaps the Galileans might also fear, lest the Jews should inform against them as his adherents.—ʼ They that thought contemptibly of Christ might ʼ have spoken their minds as freely as they pleased.ʼ *Doddridge.* This has often been the case ; and still is in very many places, even where Christianity is professed.—ʼ An ʼ example of horrible confusion in the very bosom of the ʼ church! The pastors keep the people under oppression ʼ by fear and terror ; the people seek Christ when he does ʼ not appear, and neglect him when he offereth himself to ʼ them. ...Some that know rashly condemn him ; and ʼ very few think rightly of him, and that in secret.ʼ *Beza.* It may be added, that of those who most decidedly favoured him, very few indeed had just views of his person, salvation, and kingdom.

Murmuring. (12) Γογγυσμος. *Acts* vi. 1. *Phil.* ii. 14. 1 *Pet.* iv. 9.—Γογγυζω. See on vi. 41. The word in this place seems to mean no more than a private conversation, in a sort of whisper, or low voice, with difference of opinions, and disputes about those opinions; but without displeasure or irritation against Jesus.

V. 14—17. Our Lord saw good for a time to conceal himself ; not appearing as usual in the courts of the temple : yet he would not lose the opportunity of preaching to the multitudes, who were assembled from distant nations on this occasion. So that about the middle of the feast, which lasted eight days, (*Note*, *Lev.* xxiii. 34 —36,) he went up to the temple, and taught the people. But the inhabitants of Judea enquired, with a mixture of surprise and disdain, how *he* could have sufficient learning, and knowledge of the law, to qualify him as a publick instructor; seeing he had been brought up in an obscure manner, and without any of the advantages of a liberal education. (*Marg.* and *Marg. Ref.* y—b.) To this objection our Lord replied, that his doctrine (or the *instruction* which he delivered) was not his own, as men acquire knowledge by study and tuition, and so teach their own opinions, or those of their master; or as false prophets speak out of their own hearts ; (*Marg. Ref.* c. *Num.* xvi. 28.—*Note, Jer.* xxiii. 25—27 ;) but that it was the message, which he came to deliver from " Him that sent him : " so that it was to be considered as the testimony of God himself brought down from heaven, and declared without any mixture or alteration. And as his doctrine was divine, so the preparation of mind, for understanding it, did not consist in natural quickness or vigour of capacity, or in human learning ; but in a sincere willingness, and earnest desire, to " do the will of God : " insomuch that the man who was brought to this temper, and was determined to obey the command of God, however it might interfere with his interests or prospects, and though it should expose him to persecution, would use proper means for becoming ac-

18 He ' that speaketh of himself seeketh his own glory: but he that seeketh his glory that sent him, the same is true, and no unrighteousness is in him.

19 Did ʰ not Moses give you the law, and ʲyet none of you keepeth the law? ᵏ Why go ye about to kill me?

20 The people answered and said, 'Thou hast a devil: who goeth about to kill thee?

21 Jesus answered and said unto them, ᵐ I have done one work, and ye all marvel.

22 Moses therefore gave unto you ⁿ circumcision, (not because it is of Moses, but of the fathers,) and ye on the sabbath-day circumcise a man.

23 If a man on the sabbath-day receive circumcision, ᵗ that the law of Moses should not be broken; are ye angry at me, because I have ᵒ made a man every whit whole on the sabbath-day?

24 Judge not ᵖ according to the ap-

quainted with the truth, and be enabled to " know of the " doctrine whether it were of God, or whether he spake " of himself," as one who deceived the people.—When the heart is thus disposed " to do the will of God," it rises above the prejudices of pride, self-love, and worldly hopes and fears, which cloud and bias the understanding of others. This state of mind is also the effect of divine grace; and He who has given any one such a measure of seriousness, teachableness, and integrity, will assist him to discern and embrace the truth, and to detect and refuse error. (*Marg. Ref.* d—e.—*Notes,* Ps. xxv. 8, 9. xxxi. 23. *Prov.* ii. 1—9. xxiii. 23. *Is.* xxxv. 8—10. *Jer.* l. 4—6. *P. O.* 1—8. *Notes, Acts* viii. 26—40. x. 1—8.) Indeed every one, who is thus decided to do the will of God, is afraid of being deceived, distrusts himself, and seeks diligently for divine teaching. So that, in every way, he will be guided through all mazes of uncertainty and controversy, to the knowledge of every essential truth; and all, who are fatally deluded, must be allowed to be destitute of this ingenuous upright disposition.—' If any man shall, ' with a simple and honest heart, yield himself over to do ' the will of my Father, according to the measure of that he ' knows, God shall encourage and bless that man with ' further light; so as he shall fully know, whether my ' doctrine be of God, or of myself.' *Bp. Hall.* ' " He shall ' " know of the doctrine," that is, he shall have means ' sufficient to convince him that it is of God.' *Whitby.*— All who hear the word of God ' have means sufficient to ' convince them:' but the person described by our Lord shall actually be convinced. The means to him shall be rendered effectual: otherwise what does the promise amount to?—*Will do his will.* (17) Θελη το θελημα αυτο ποιην.— " Willeth to do his will," or *purposeth.* It is his object and aim, in seeking to *know* the will of God. (*Notes, Matt.* vii. 21—23. xii. 46—50, *v.* 50.)

V. 18. Our Lord added another general rule. The teacher, who is not sent of God, will in one way or other seek his own honour and advancement, having no higher principle than corrupt selfish nature: whereas he, who evidently disregards himself that he may seek the honour of God, proves himself to be truly sent by him; and is free from all ground of suspicion, as if he were an impostor, or acted from any sinister design. Applying this to Christ, who endured poverty, contempt, hardship, suffering, and death, for the glory of God in man's salvation; and who boldly taught those doctrines, which excited the enmity

and rage of the rulers and Pharisees, and yet equally opposed the carnal prejudices of the common people, and so disgusted them; it was evident that he was " true, and " that there was no unrighteousness in him." (*Marg. Ref.* —*Notes,* v. 39—44. 2 *Cor.* iv. 5—7. 1 *Thes.* ii. 1—8, *vv.* 5—8. 2 *Pet.* i. 16—18.)

V. 19—24. It was at least a year and a half (probably longer) since Jesus had healed the man at the pool of Bethesda: (*Notes,* v. 1—9:) yet the Jewish rulers were still desirous of putting him to death for a supposed infraction of the sabbath on that occasion; and he saw proper to refer to their designs in his publick preaching, in order to obviate the people's prejudices against his doctrine. He observed, that they were zealously attached to Moses, their great lawgiver; yet scarcely any of them were conscientiously obedient to the law. For why did they go about to kill him, in direct opposition to the sixth commandment? (*Marg. Ref.* h—k.) To this, some of them, who were ignorant of the designs of the rulers, replied, in a rude and contemptuous manner, that he certainly was possessed by a devil, and was insane: for " who went about " to kill him?" (*Marg. Ref.* l.) To this indecent reflection Jesus meekly answered, that he had wrought one miracle at Jerusalem, which excited their astonishment; not so much by the power and goodness displayed in it, as because he did it on the sabbath-day, and ordered the man to carry his bed in evidence of his cure. (*Notes,* v. 10 —16. 45—47.) But, as to that accusation, they should observe, that Moses had enjoined them the law of circumcision; (though it had been practised long before his time by their fathers;) yet they could not observe that law without deviating from the exact rest, which they supposed to be required on the sabbath: for when the eighth day happened on the sabbath, they used to circumcise the male child, that they might not defer that ordinance beyond the appointed time; nor did they deem this labour any violation of the holy rest. But if this were right, as no doubt it was, why should they blame him for restoring a man, diseased in every part of his body, on that day, to perfect soundness by a word speaking? Surely the law of love was as binding as that of circumcision! and it was as consistent with the design of the sabbath, to restore health to the afflicted, as to administer an external rite. He therefore demanded of them, not to judge by their partial prejudices, or by his external appearance; but to decide on his conduct in an equitable manner, according to the spiritual

pearance, but judge righteous judgment.

25 Then said some of them *of Jerusalem, 'Is not this he whom they seek to kill?

26 But, lo, 'he speaketh boldly, and they say nothing unto him. 'Do the rulers know indeed that this is the very Christ?

27 Howbeit, "we know this man whence he is; but when Christ cometh, 'no man knoweth whence he is.

28 Then cried Jesus in the temple, as he taught, saying, ' Ye both know me, and ye know whence I am: ' and I am not come of myself, but he that sent me ' is true, ' whom ye know not.

29 But ' I know him; ' for I am from him, and he hath sent me.

30 Then ' they sought to take him; ' but no man laid hands on him, because his hour was not yet come.

31 And many of the people ' believed on him, and said, ' When Christ cometh, will he do more miracles than these which this *man hath done?

import of the divine law.—Circumcision was at first given to Abraham, as " the seal of the righteousness of " faith," and of the covenant made with him in Christ; though it was afterwards made a part of the ceremonial law. (Marg. Ref. n.—Notes, Gen. xvii. 7—12. Rom. iv. 9—12. Gal. iii. 15—18. v. 1—6.) Our Lord seems here to have referred to this circumstance, which the Jews generally overlooked, thus confounding together the Sinai-covenant, and that made with Abraham, as indeed numbers still do.

Ye all marvel. Moses therefore, &c. (21, 22.) Παντες θαυμαζετε. Δια τυτο Μωσης, κ.τ.λ.—Some point these words thus, Παντες θαυμαζετε δια τυτο. Μωσης εδωκεν, κ.τ.λ. " Ye " all marvel at this. Moses gave you the law," &c.—This seems the more obvious construction.—Are ye angry, &c. (23) Χολᾶτε. Here only.—A χολη, bilis. Matt. xxvii. 34. Acts viii. 23.—Every whit whole.] 'Ολον ανθρωπον υγιη.—According to appearance. (24) Καῖ οψιν. xi.44. Rev.i.16. Not elsewhere.—The face alone appears, the rest is hid: yet this defective view causes the decision. (Note, vii. 6, 7.) " I have made the whole man sound, on the sabbath-day." The nature of the disease, wholly disabling the man, as well as the completeness of the cure, seems intended.

V. 25—30. While this subject was under consideration, some of the stated inhabitants of Jerusalem, who were acquainted with the designs of the council, (of which they who came from other places were ignorant,) enquired, whether this were not the person, whom the rulers had resolved to put to death as a deceiver: and they were astonished that he was allowed to speak in so open a manner, and met with no interruption. (Marg. Ref. q—t.) Was it possible, that the rulers should at length be persuaded, that he was indeed the promised Messiah? They, however, knew him to be an inhabitant of Nazareth, the son of Mary the wife of Joseph; but when the Messiah came, no man would know whence he was.—Doubtless these persons were ignorant of our Lord's descent from David, of his miraculous conception, and of his nativity at Bethlehem; and they rashly concluded, that his parentage and birth did not answer to those predicted of the Messiah: yet they seem to have had some confused idea of the divine original of that great Redeemer; and thence they decided, that " when he came no man would know whence he " was." Had their prejudices allowed them to examine, 'hey would have found their oblection sufficiently answered,

by the circumstances of our Lord's nativity. Some think, that the Messiah's birth of a virgin was referred to; and others, that a tradition of the Jews, that the Messiah when he came would for a long time be hidden, was meant: but it is more probable, that an erroneous construction of some prophecies, which relate to his eternal Deity, had drawn away their minds from the plainer and more express predictions on the subject. (Marg. Ref. u, x.)—Our Lord, however, knowing their reasonings, though spoken privately, and at a distance, proclaimed aloud, in reproof of their obstinate and ignorant opposition, that they indeed vainly imagined that they both " knew him and whence he " was," and were sure that he was not the Messiah. Yet " he was not come of himself," but was sent by God, who testified of him, and shewed himself true to his promises and prophecies: for, though they professed to be worshippers of God, they did not know his perfections and the glory of them, and had no spiritual or experimental acquaintance with him. But he perfectly and intimately knew him, being from him, and sent by the Father to make him known to men. (Marg. Ref. y—d.—Notes, v. 31—38. viii. 17—20, v. 19. 48—59, vv. 54, 55.)—This declaration, that they knew not God, joined to his claim of such a knowledge of God as was peculiar to himself, exasperated the hearers so much, that they sought an opportunity to apprehend him: but, as " his hour was not yet " come," they were supernaturally restrained from touching him.—Ye both, &c. (28) Or, " Do ye both know me, and " know whence I am?"—He " that sent me is true:" the true God: or, " my real Father," and not Joseph, as ye suppose.

Indeed. (26) Αληθως.—Very.] Αληθως. See on vi. 55. The latter αληθως is wanting in some copies.—Was not yet come. (30) Ουπω εληλυθει. 6. 8.—In the verses referred to, the proper time of our Lord's going up to Jerusalem seems meant: here, the hour when he should be apprehended and put to death.

V. 31—36. The arguments and replies of Jesus convinced many of the people, that he was the Messiah; and they secretly enquired or whispered among themselves, whether that great Deliverer, when he came, could work greater miracles than Jesus did. Some spies, however, carried the report of this to the Pharisees, who were the more exasperated; as they saw that their reputation, authority, and interest must be ruined, if the people received

32 The [i] Pharisees heard that the people murmured such things concerning him; and the Pharisees and the chief priests [k] sent officers to take him.

33 Then said Jesus unto them, [l] Yet a little while am I with you, and then I go unto him that sent me.

34 Ye [m] shall seek me, and shall not find *me*; and where I am, *thither* ye cannot come.

35 Then said the Jews among themselves, Whither will he go, that we shall not find him? will he go unto [n] the dispersed among the [o] Gentiles, [o] and teach the Gentiles?

36 What [p] *manner of* saying is this

that he said, [q] Ye shall seek me, and shall not find *me*; and where I am, *thither* ye cannot come?

37 ¶ In [r] the last day, that great *day* of the feast, Jesus stood [s] and cried, saying, 'If any man thirst, [t] let him come unto me [u] and drink.

38 He that believeth on me, as the scripture hath said, [v] out of his belly shall flow rivers of living water.

39 (But [w] this spake he of the Spirit, which they that believe on him should receive: [x] for the Holy Ghost was not yet *given*; because that Jesus was not yet [y] glorified.)

---

him in this character. Assembling therefore the council, they " sent officers to take him," and bring him before them in a chamber of the temple, where they were convened. (*Marg. Ref.* g—k.) When the officers were come, Jesus observed, that he should continue with them a little longer, notwithstanding their designs against him; but that he should shortly return to the Father who had sent him. Then they might seek him; some of them from malice, and others from a vain desire of help in their extreme distress; but they would not find him: (*Marg. Ref.* l, m.— *Notes, Gen.* v. 21—24. *Heb.* xi. 5, 6:) nor would they ever be able to enter that happy place, whither he was going. (*Note,* viii. 21—26.) This referred to the calamities, which were coming on the Jewish nation for their enmity to Jesus, and to their vain waiting and seeking for the promised Messiah to rescue them. But they could not understand whither he meant to go, having no idea of his ascension into heaven: they therefore enquired, whether he intended to go among the Jews, who were dispersed in other nations; and in case they would not receive him as the Messiah, to become a Teacher of the idolatrous Gentiles themselves? This they would consider as the most despicable and disgraceful employment imaginable. (*Marg. and Marg. Ref.* n, o.)

The *dispersed*. (35) Την διασποραν. *Jam.* i. 1. Not elsewhere.—The *Gentiles.*] Των Ελληνων. Some think, that the dispersion of nations, when God confounded the languages at Babel, is referred to; and that the Gentiles dispersed on that occasion were intended: but the passage seems rather to mean, those countries of the Gentiles into which the Jews were dispersed.—'Ελληνων properly " Greeks." (*Note, Acts* xi. 19—21.)

V. 37—39. As the officers, who came to take Jesus, returned after what is here recorded; it must have been on this day that they were sent to take him. (45.)—On " the last day, the great day of the feast" of tabernacles, there was a holy convocation; (*Notes, Lev.* xxiii. 34—36;) and it is recorded, that the people used to draw and pour out water before the Lord. In allusion, as it is supposed, to this ceremony, Jesus stood forth in a conspicuous situation, and proclaimed aloud, " If any man thirst, let him

" come unto me and drink." Thus he declared himself to be the unfailing Source of salvation to perishing sinners; yea, " the Fountain of living waters," in opposition to the broken cisterns of mere creatures; and in fact he spake as the all-sufficient God. (*Marg. Ref.* r—x.—*Notes, iv.* 10— 15. *Ps.* xxxvi. 5—9. *Is.* lv. 1—3. *Matt.* xi. 27—30. *Rev.* xxi. 5—8, *v.* 6. xxii. 1. 16, 17.) If any man felt himself destitute, exposed to misery, and desirous of true happiness; let him come to Jesus, and his wants would be supplied, his distress prevented or removed, his desires satisfied. If any sinner were disquieted with guilt, and fear of wrath, and experienced fervent desires after the favour of God, communion with him, and recovery to holiness; let him come to Jesus, and his terrors should be dissipated, and the blessings thirsted after be granted. But as this thirst especially means *vehement longing after spiritual blessings*, which nothing can divert, or satisfy except the enjoyment of them; so the sanctifying and comforting influences of the Holy Spirit were particularly intended. For he added, that every one, who believed in him, would be so replenished, that " out of his belly would flow rivers of living " water." This was spoken in reference to several scriptures, rather than as a quotation of any particular passage. (*Marg. Ref.* y.—*Notes, Is.* xliii. 14—21, *vv.* 19, 20. xliv. 3—5. lix. 20, 21. *Ez.* xxxvi. 25—27. *Zech.* xii. 9—14.) The believer would not only have these divine influences communicated to him for his own abiding advantage, but they would be within him " a fountain of living water," whence plentiful streams, yea rivers, would flow forth, for the quickening, sanctifying, and comforting of others also. This holy and fervent affection, as connected with divine knowledge and wisdom, would produce such a tenour of edifying conversation and exemplary practice, and such an improvement of every talent; as would render the man a channel, as it were, by which spiritual blessings would be conveyed to those with whom he associated. (*Notes, Matt.* xii. 33—37, *v.* 35. *Eph.* iv. 29.) This might be especially intended of the apostles, and the preachers of the gospel; but, in a subordinate sense, it is the case of all zealous Christians.—The evangelist here notes, that our Lord spoke this of the Spirit, which believers were afterwards to re-

40 Many of the people therefore, when they heard this saying, said, 'Of a truth this is the Prophet.

41 Others said, 'This is the Christ. But some said, 'Shall Christ come out of Galilee?

42 Hath 'not the scripture said, that Christ cometh of the seed of David, and out of the town of Bethlehem, 'where David was?

43 So 'there was a division among the people because of him.

44 And some of them would have taken him; 'but no man laid hands on him.

45 Then came 'the officers to the chief priests and Pharisees; and they said unto them, Why have ye not brought him?

46 The officers answered, 'Never man spake like this man

47 Then answered them the Pharisees, "Are ye also deceived?

48 Have "any of the rulers, or of the Pharisees, believed on him?

49 But 'this people, who knoweth not the law, are cursed.

50 Nicodemus saith unto them, '(he that came 'to Jesus by night, being one of them,)

51 Doth 'our law judge any man before it hear him, and know what he doeth?

52 They answered and said unto him, 'Art thou also of Galilee? 'Search, and look: for out of Galilee ariseth no prophet.

53 And 'every man went unto his own house.

---

ceive: " for the Holy Ghost was not yet: because Jesus " was not yet glorified." " Holy men of old had indeed " spoken as they were moved by the Holy Ghost;" and all believers in every age had been sanctified and comforted by him: but " the ministration of the Spirit" was not at that time fully introduced; the pouring out of the Holy Spirit either in his miraculous or his sanctifying influences, had not yet taken place; for that signal event was reserved to grace the Redeemer's triumphs, and to attest his resurrection and ascension to heavenly glory. (Marg. Ref. z—b.—Notes, xvi. 7—15. Luke xi. 5—13, v. 13. Acts ii. 14—21. 33—36. 2 Cor. iii. 7—11. Heb. ii. 1—4, v. 4.) Belly. (38) Κοιλιας. (A κοιλος εαυτ.) iii. 4. Matt. xii. 40. Phil. iii. 19.—Prov. xx. 30. Hab. iii. 16. Sept.—All that is within is meant, as distinguished from what is without a man. Mark vii. 21.—Glorified. (39) Εδοξασθη. xii. 16. 23. xiii. 31, 32. xvi. 14. xvii. l. 5. Acts iii. 13.

V. 40—53. This open declaration and invitation of our Lord, with his other publick instructions, excited a fresh debate, and a division, or schism, among the people concerning him: as some deemed him that Prophet who, they supposed, would precede the Messiah; and others the promised Messiah himself. But to this it was objected, that Jesus was of Galilee; whereas the Messiah was to be a descendant of David, and a native of Bethlehem. Thus they remained under the power of prejudice, because they did not make diligent and impartial enquiry concerning him. (Marg. Ref. c—h.) Yet, amidst these disputes, even such of the officers, as were disposed to apprehend him, could not summon resolution to do it: so they returned to the council without him; and, being questioned concerning their conduct, they replied, " Never man spake as this " person does!" His discourses were inimitably powerful and convincing, and delivered with unspeakable dignity and propriety. (Marg. Ref. i—l.—Note, Matt. vii. 28, 29.) This enraged the proud and envious Pharisees, who demanded, whether they likewise were deceived into the opinion of his being the Messiah. And, making their own example the test of truth, they enquired whether any of

the rulers, or even of the Pharisees, the most learned, eminent, and religious men in the nation, " had believed " in him:" for as to the ignorant multitude, who followed him, they knew nothing of the meaning of the scriptures, and were deserving to be despised and execrated of men, as well as accursed of God; being given up as under a curse to judicial blindness. (Marg. Ref. m—o.) To this Nicodemus ventured to reply, by enquiring, whether their law judged and condemned any man unheard, and without examining him concerning the things of which he was accused. (Notes, iii. 1, 2. Deut. xvii. 8—12. xix. 15—21.) This implied a direct answer to their enquiry: here was a ruler, a teacher, and a Pharisee, who at least favoured Jesus. Accordingly they began to revile him, as if he had spoken like a contemptible Galilean; and required him to examine, and he would find, that no prophet arose out of Galilee. This was a rule, for which they had no ground in scripture: for Jonah, at least, was a native of Gath-hepher, or Gittah-hepher, in Galilee (Josh. xix. 13. 2 Kings xiv. 25:) and they could not mean the Messiah exclusively; for this would have implied, that they might oppose and persecute other prophets. They spoke, however, in the heat of irritation; without well considering the import of their own words: yet Nicodemus's interposition disconcerted their measures, and they did not proceed any further in their design at that time. (Marg. Ref. p—t.)—Have any of the rulers, &c. (48, 49.) ' This ' is plainly the popish argument, by which they attempt to ' prove, that private men, Laicks, and inferior priests are ' not to be governed by their own sentiments of Christ's ' doctrine; but must submit to their general councils, and ' to the major part of their church-guides. And ... it is ' as strong in the mouth of the Pharisees, against Christ ' being the true Messiah, as in the mouth of Papists against ' protestants.' Whitby. It is also employed by nominal protestants against such companies, as they choose to brand by some opprobrious name.

A division. (43) Σχισμα. See on Matt. ix. 16.—Accursed (49) Επικαλαρατοι. Gal. iii. 10. 13. Not elsewhere N. T.—

CHAP. VIII.

Jesus teaches at the temple, 1, 2. The Pharisees lay a snare for him, in respect of a woman taken in adultery; but he turns it to their confusion, and warns the woman to sin no more, 3—11. He declares himself to be the Light of the world, 12; justifies his doctrine, shews that his Father bore witness to him, and predicts the doom of unbelievers, 13—29. Many believe, whom he exhorts " to continue in his word; " promising them liberty by the knowledge of the truth, 30—32. He refutes the cavils and detects the vainconfidence of the Jews who opposed him; shewing that they are the slaves of sin, and the children of the devil, 33—47. Being reviled, as a Samaritan and possessed, he refutes the charge, promises life to believers, asserts his dignity, and adds, " Before Abraham was, 1 AM," 48—58. He withdraws from those who attempt to stone him, 59.

Gen. iii. 14. 17. Deut. xxvii. 15, 16, each verse to 26. xxviii. 16, 17, 18, 19. 1 Sam. xiv. 24. Prov. xxiv. 24. Sept. A καθαρα, Gal. iii. 10. 13.

PRACTICAL OBSERVATIONS.

V. 1—10.

No external evidences or advantages can overcome the obstinacy and enmity of the human heart, or secure the sinner's conversion: we need not then be disconcerted by the contempt and opposition of our nearest relations, when we remember that the brethren of the holy Jesus " did not " believe in him."—Worldly men commonly judge of others by themselves; and so ascribe their most unexceptionable actions, however modestly and humbly performed, to ostentation, ambition, spiritual pride, or some selfish motive; knowing that their own most specious conduct springs from no higher principles. They often likewise attempt to give salutary and friendly counsel, with apparent seriousness, to those who are employed in the service of God: yet they can only propose such things, as apparently conduce to their present advantage, and really tend to their injury and disgrace. (Note, 1 Kings xxii. 13, 14.) But the spiritual man sees a variety of reasons for his conduct, and for the time and manner of his proceedings, of which others have no capacity to judge. (Note, 1 Cor. ii. 14—16.) He knows himself to be surrounded with enemies, who hate him, in proportion as his example, conversation, or more publick testimony, exposes the wickedness of men's hearts and lives; protests against the corrupt maxims, pursuits, and fashions of the world; and shews the evil even of their boasted morality, religion, and benevolence, when tarnished by pride, hypocrisy, and enmity to the gospel. He is therefore aware that he needs " the wisdom of the serpent," as well as " the harmless- " ness of the dove:" (Note, Matt. x. 16—18, v. 16:) he consults the word of God, and prays for the teaching of his Spirit: he is decided against carnal advice, and leaves worldly counsellors to possess unenvied that " friendship " of the world which is enmity against God;" (Note, Jam. iv. 4—6;) that he may follow the dictates of heavenly wisdom, and the counsel of an enlightened conscience.

V. 11—18.

The servants of Christ must expect to follow him " through evil report and good report." The most faithful preachers of his gospel must be content to be called by numbers, " deceivers of the people; " though others will " allow them to be good men; and some perhaps think better of them than they deserve, which none ever could do of their Lord and Master. But in general they, who count them deceivers, will speak openly their sentiments: while many who favour them will be afraid of incurring reproach, by avowing their regard to them.—Any plausible objection, the result of ignorance and indolent mistake, will often more than counterbalance the fullest proof of a man's being employed and accepted by God: for the cause is tried before partial judges, who will only hear evidence on one side of the question. Some prejudice, concerning the family, country, or education of the faithful teacher, is employed by Satan, to stop the ears of his servants against the truth: and the charge of ignorant and illiterate is adduced, against the most scriptural preachers, by such as have not yet learned " the first principles of the " oracles of God," however accomplished they may be, in that " wisdom of the world which is foolishness with him." But in an inferior sense, every faithful minister, wherever educated, may humbly adopt the words of Christ. His doctrine is not his own invention, nor does it spring, either from his learning or his ignorance: but it is from God, deduced from his word through the teaching of his Spirit; who commands it to be preached for the glory of his name. All therefore, who presume to engage in this work, should daily study and pray over the scriptures, in order to possess a well grounded confidence, that the grand subjects of their instructions are agreeable to " the oracles of God." They ought likewise to " take heed to themselves, as well " as to their doctrine;" that thus they may always have the " rejoicing in the testimony of their consciences," as not seeking their own glory, the applause of their hearers or any filthy lucre, (as all do, who speak of themselves,) but the glory of God in the salvation of souls. Then it will appear, that " there is no unrighteousness in them," nor any reason to suspect them of bad motives, in the exercise of their ministry. But, amidst the various opinions and controversies about religion, which agitate the world; what a blessed encouragement is it to the honest enquirer to remember, that " if any man," of any nation, " is " willing to do the will of God, he shall know of the doc- " trine, whether it be of God, or whether men speak of " themselves!" The word of the Lord is passed, and cannot be recalled; and all, who desire earnestly and seek diligently to know the will of God, in order to reduce it to practice, shall be guided through every labyrinth of uncertainty, and past every precipice of error, into the ways of truth and peace; and they only shall be given up to strong and destructive delusion, " who hate the truth be- " cause they have pleasure in unrighteousness." (Note, 2 Thes. ii. 8—12.)

V. 19—36.

Unbelievers may be very zealous for their own views of religion, and vehemently persecute those who dissent from them; while at the same time, they are acting in direct

JESUS [a] went unto the mount of Olives.

<sub>a Matt. xxi. 1.
Mark xi. 1. xiii.
1. Luke xix. 37.</sub>

2 And [b] early in the morning he came again into the temple, and all the people came unto him: [c] and he sat down, and taught them.

<sub>b iv. 34. Ec. ix.
10. Jer. xxv. 3,
4 xlix. 4. Luke
xxi. 37, 38.
c Matt. v. 1, 2.
xxvi. 55. Luke
iv. 20. v. 3.</sub>

3 And the Scribes and Pharisees brought unto him a woman taken in adultery; and, when they had set her in the midst,

4 They say unto him, Master, this woman was taken in adultery, in the very act.

5 Now [d] Moses in the law com-

<sub>d Lev. xx. 10.
Deut. xxii. 21—
24. Ex. xvi. 38
—40. xxiii. 47.</sub>

---

opposition to the plain precepts of scripture, and indulging the most diabolical tempers: and when the least check is given them, they revile and abuse others, as if all, not of their party, were unworthy of the least regard. Such men, in their zeal for doctrines, (perhaps true in themselves, though held by them in a perverted manner,) entirely overlook the genuine tendency of them; and are full of pride and rage, in disputing for the most humiliating and conciliatory truths! If external ordinances be their idol, they pervert them to purposes diametrically opposite to their true intention: and they condemn in others things of the same nature with those which they allow in themselves, or undeniably better. But it behoves us to consider matters more candidly and impartially; that we may " not judge " according to appearance, but judge righteous judgment." We should also guard against the folly of opposing our preconceived opinions to such instructions as have the appearance of being from God.—If we would understand religion, we must endeavour, by diligently searching the scriptures, and by fervent prayer to " be taught of God," clearly to understand the glory and harmony of the divine perfections; and we must seek this knowledge of God from the incarnate Son, and by contemplating his character, miracles, life, and death: (*Notes*, xvii. 1—3. 2 *Cor.* iv. 3—6:) otherwise we shall set up a false system in opposition to the truth; and be in danger of being seduced to concur with those who, in every age, have been enraged to persecution by the success of the true gospel of God our Saviour.—For a short time Christ continues, by his word and ministers, among those who reject his salvation: yet the day, both of life and of grace, is of transient and uncertain continuance; and afterwards sinners, in their misery, would be glad of that help which now they despise. But it will soon become in vain to seek him; and where he is, thither shall no unbeliever enter for ever. They may dispute, reason, and murmur about such faithful and alarming sayings at present; but the event will explain them: and in the mean time he will continue to teach his people, who are dispersed throughout the nations; and even us poor sinners of the Gentiles.

V. 37—53.

Still the divine Redeemer proclaims aloud to every man, " Let him, who is athirst, come to me and drink." Happy then is he, whom nothing can satisfy, except the favour, image, and enjoyment of God! Let him come unto Jesus, that this thirst may be allayed, and let him not fear a repulse.—From our smitten Rock the waters of life flow forth abundantly, to follow the true Israelites through this barren wilderness. (*Notes, Ex.* xvii. 5, 6. 1 *Cor.* x. 1—5.) The *miraculous* operations of the Holy Spirit we do not now expect: but for his more ordinary and more valuable *sanctifying* influences we may confi-

dently pray: these will not only be " in us a well of water " springing up into everlasting life;" but they will flow forth in our words and works, to water, fructify, and refresh our fellow-pilgrims in the desert, and to be the means of quickening such as were dead in sin. (*Notes, P. O. Ez.* xlvii. 1—12.)—From our glorified Redeemer these holy streams have flowed, through the medium of the apostles, evangelists, and a succession of believers, down to us in this distant age, and in this remote corner of the earth: may we communicate them to those around us, and to such as shall succeed us, till the whole world be replenished by them.—But alas! how few are thus athirst! Even they, who are for a time impressed and restrained, and who speak highly of the words of Jesus, as more excellent than those of all other teachers, " speaking as " never man spake," often speedily lose their convictions, and go on in their sins: while proud infidels and Pharisees, with carnal Scribes and priests, consider all as deluded, who coincide not with them in opinion. Frequently they revile, as ignorant enthusiasts, or designing hypocrites, such men, as are far more serious, diligent, and impartial in searching for the truth, than themselves; and whose words and works are sober, scriptural, and exemplary: but it seems enough for them to answer by saying, " Have " any of the rulers and Pharisees believed in him?" Whereas the opinions of men of this description have more generally been a *criterion of error*, than *the test of truth*. But if a few of their own rank, education, or description are convinced of the truth, and dare to avow it: they likewise are directly treated with obloquy and contempt, as weak deluded persons, who have suffered themselves to become the dupes of fanaticks and impostors. Thus the wicked from age to age proceed in precisely the same track: yet the Lord gradually brings forward the weak and timid of his sincere disciples, and makes use of them to disconcert the politick designs of his enemies; for " his counsel shall stand, and he will do all his pleasure."

NOTES.

CHAP. VIII. V. 1, 2. It is probable, that our Lord went every evening to Bethany, to the house of Martha, where he was more retired than he could have been in the city: but it is by some supposed, that he spent this night on the mount of Olives, in devotion. He, however, returned early in the morning to the temple, that he might instruct the people there assembled, before they left Jerusalem the day after the conclusion of the feast of tabernacles. (*Marg. Ref.*)

V. 3—11. While our Lord was teaching the multitudes, his enemies concerted a plan for drawing him into a snare. A woman had been taken in adultery, whose guilt was undeniable: they therefore professed a deference to his judgment and authority, and brought the criminal

e Matt. v. 17. xix.
6—8. xxii. 16—
18.
f Num. xiv. 22.
Matt. xix. 3.
Luke x. 25. xi.
53, 54. xx. 20—
23. 1 Cor. x.
9.
g 2. Gen. xlix. 5.
Jer. xvii. 13.
Dan. v. 5.
h Ps. xxxviii. 9.
—14. xxxix. 1?
Prov. xxvi. 17.
Ec. iii. 7. Am.
v. 10. 13. Matt.
x. 16. xv. 23.
xxvi. 63.
i vii. 46. Prov.
xii. 18. xxvi. 4.
5. Jer. xxiii. 29.
1 Cor. xiv. 24,
25. Col. iv. 6.
Heb. iv. 12, 13.
Rev. i. 16. ii. 16.
k Deut. xvii. 6,
7. Ps. i. 16—
20. Matt. vii. 1—5. xxiii. 25—38. Rom. ii. 1—3. 21—20.

manded us, that such should be stoned: [f] but what sayest thou?

6 This they said, [f] tempting him, that they might have to accuse him. [g] But Jesus stooped down, and with his finger wrote on the ground, [h] as though he heard them not.

7 So when they continued asking him, he lifted up himself, [i] and said unto them, [k] He that is without sin among you, let him first cast a stone at her.

8 And again he stooped down, and wrote on the ground.

9 And they which heard it, [l] being convicted by their own conscience, [m] went out one by one, beginning at the eldest, even unto the last: and Jesus was left [n] alone, and the woman standing in the midst.

10 When Jesus had lifted up himself, and saw none but the woman, he said unto her, Woman, [o] where are those thine accusers? hath no man condemned thee?

11 She said, No man, Lord. And Jesus said unto her, [p] Neither do I condemn thee: [q] go, and sin no more.

l Gen. xlii. 21, 22.
1 Kings ii. 44.
xvii. 18. Ps. l. 21.
Ec. vii. 22. Mark
vi. 14—16. Luke
xii. 1—3. Rom.
ii. 15. 1 John iii.
20.
m Job v. 12, 13.
xx. A. 27. Ps. ix.
15, 16. xl. 14,
15. lxvi. 12.
Luke xiii. 17.
n Is. xlii. 11, 12.
13. iii. 17. xviii.
36. Deut. xvi.
18. xxxi. 9.
Luke ix. 56. xii.
13, 14. Rom.
xiii. 3, 4. 1 Cor.
v. 12.
q xxxix. 81? 32.
Prov. xxviii. 13.
Is. i. 16—18. lv.
6, 7. Ez. xviii.
30—32. Matt.
xxi. 28—81.
Luke v. 32. xiii. 3. 5. xv. 7. 10. 32. Rom. ii. 4. v. 20, 21. 1 Tim. i. 15, 16. y Pet. iii. 19. Rev. ii. 21, 22.

to him, that he might decide what punishment should be inflicted on her; as Moses had commanded that such criminals should be stoned. The law doomed both the adulterer and adulteress "to be put to death;" but these scribes and Pharisees shewed their partiality, by prosecuting the woman and letting the man escape. In a case nearly parallel, *stoning* was specified; and probably this had become the general punishment of all convicted of adultery. (*Marg. Ref.* d.—*Notes, Lev.* xx. 10—19. *Deut.* xxii. 13—21. *Ez.* xxiii. 43—49.) The Scribes and Pharisees, however, concluded from many parts of our Lord's doctrine, that he deemed himself authorized to alter or abrogate the appointments of Moses: and therefore they desired his opinion. (*Marg. Ref.* e.—*Notes, Matt.* v. 31, 32. xix. 3—9.) But, if he had ordered them to execute the law, they would doubtless have accused him to the Romans of assuming a judicial authority, independent of their government: had he directed them to set her at liberty, they would have represented him to the people as an enemy to the law, and the patron of the most infamous characters: and had he referred them to the Roman authority, they would have accused him to the multitude, as a betrayer of their liberties. (*Marg. Ref.* f.—*Notes, Matt.* xxii. 15—22.) Indeed they seem to have concluded, that he must, inevitably, either render himself obnoxious to the Romans, or unpopular among the Jews, by his answer to this insidious question: and in either case, it would have facilitated the execution of their purpose in putting him to death. But he saw the wickedness of their hearts; and therefore he stooped down, as if he had not regarded them. Perhaps he wrote with his finger in the dust, the sentence which he afterwards spake. Some think, that he meant to teach them in this manner, that they ought to decide such matters by the written word; and others, that he intimated that such base hypocrites should "be written in the earth." (*Jer.* xvii. 13.) But these are mere conjectures.—'To be willing to be igno-'rant of what our great Master has thought fit to conceal, 'is no inconsiderable part of Christian learning.' *Doddridge.*—His apparent backwardness, however, to interfere, rendered the scribes the more urgent in their demand: and therefore at length, he lifting up himself, abruptly ordered that man, who was "without sin among "them" to begin the execution of the criminal, by first

casting a stone at her. (*Marg. Ref.* g—k.) It was appointed by the law, that the accuser should thus lead the way, in putting the condemned person to death: (*Note, Deut.* xvii. 2—7:) the whole company that brought this woman were her accusers: but it would have been unsuitable for any one of them, who was conscious of secret flagrant wickedness, to have begun this severity; and therefore he required that person to do it, who was conscious of his own innocence.—Our Lord assuredly did not mean, that no man ought to act as judge or witness in a criminal cause, who is not wholly exempt from sin in his own conduct; because that would disannul civil government, which is "the ordinance of God." But he knew the concealed iniquities of these men: and, by thus appealing to their consciences in respect of themselves, he made them sensible of the impropriety of *their* taking an active part in this prosecution. A divine power doubtless attended his word, and a new conviction of guilt seized on them, which for the present disarmed their malice: and, perhaps, fearing lest he should more openly and explicitly mention the particular crimes, of which they severally were conscious; they took the opportunity, whilst he again stooped down, to withdraw silently and singly; the eldest of the company, being most deeply alarmed, departing first, and the others following his example. Thus they were sent away, in disgrace and self-condemned, so that Jesus was left alone: that is, none remained with him of that company, save the woman, who stood in the midst of the court, where the people were assembled to attend on his doctrine; and there she waited to hear what sentence he would pass upon her. But, having baffled the designs of his enemies, he declined all interference with the magistrate's office, and gave her permission to depart; exhorting her at the same time not to repeat her crime, or return to any of her former wickednesses.—There is no decisive proof that she was a true penitent; for our Lord in saying, "Neither do I condemn thee," spake only of condemnation to death according to the *judicial* law; (*Marg. Ref.* l—o.—*Notes,* xviii. 33—36. *Luke* xii. 13, 14;) and the exhortation, " Sin no more," was a direct and strong condemnation of her conduct: (*Marg. Ref.* p.—*Note,* v. 10—14:) yet if these remarkable circumstances were the means of her being converted, pardoned, and saved; it would appear peculiarly suited to the design of him, who

12 ¶ Then spake Jesus again unto them, saying, 'I am the Light of the world: he that followeth me ' shall not walk in darkness, but ' shall have the light of life.

13 The Pharisees therefore said unto him, " Thou bearest record of thyself; thy record is not true.

14 Jesus answered and said unto them, Though I bear record of myself, 'yet my record is true: ' for I know ' whence I came, and whither I go; ' but ye cannot tell whence I come, and whither I go.

15 Ye * judge after the flesh; ᵇ I judge no man.

"came, not to call the righteous, but sinners to repent-" ance."—No conclusive argument can hence be drawn, concerning the punishment of adultery under the Christian dispensation: and doubtless it is absurd, that this crime should escape almost without any legal censure; when theft in many cases is punished with disproportionate severity.—The first eleven verses of this chapter, and the last verse of the preceding chapter, are wanting in many ancient copies and manuscripts; and several learned men have, on that ground, questioned whether the passage be genuine. But others, who have most fully examined the subject, are satisfied that they are indeed a part of the apostolical narrative; and the objections made to it are evidently grounded on prejudice and misapprehension. Some have considered these misapprehensions, (or rather, the expressions which give occasion to them,) as internal evidence against the genuineness of the passage. But it appears to me, that the internal evidence of its being genuine, is sufficient to counterpoise far more external evidence to the contrary, than can be urged against it. Every circumstance is completely in character; and exactly what might have been expected from the Scribes and Pharisees, and from our Lord; and consentaneous with several other snares laid for him, and his method of avoiding them. The manner of the narrative is the plain simple manner of the evangelist; and the answer of our Lord, though perfectly suited to the purpose, would scarcely ever have been thought of by human sagacity. In short, it does not appear to me, that all the criticks who have argued this point, (among whom are some of high respectability and undoubted piety,) could, if combined together, have framed so singular an anecdote, or one so interesting and instructive.—' The notice that Eu-' sebius, and other ancient writers, have taken of the du-' biousness of this passage, with a few other instances of ' a like nature, shews the critical exactness, with which ' they examined into the genuineness of the several parts ' of the New Testament; and so on the whole, strengthens ' the evidence of Christianity.' Doddridge.

Taken. (3) Καὶιλημμενη. 4. i. 5. xii. 35. Mark ix. 18. 1 Cor. ix. 24. Eph. iii. 18. Phil. iii. 12, 13, et al.—In adultery. (4) Μοιχωμενη. Matt. v. 27, 28. xix. 18. Mark x. 19. Luke xvi. 18. xviii. 20. Rom. ii. 22. Jam. ii. 11. Rev. ii. 22. A μοιχεια, 3. Where the law of Moses is referred to, the word always supposes the woman to be the wife of another man; and never denotes the case of a married man lying with a woman neither married nor betrothed to another. But the New Testament rule considers this also as adultery.—In the very act.] Επαυτοφωρω. Here only. Επι, αυτω, et φωραω, furto, a φωρ, fur. As a thief is detected in the act of stealing.—He that is without sin. (7) Ὁ αναμαρτητος.

Here only N. T.—Deut. xxix. 19. Sept.—Peccati expers. ' 'Αναμαρτητος καὶ εξοχην, eum notat, qui est immunis ab adul-' terii et scortationis crimine.' Schleusner.—The eldest. (9) Πρεσβυτερων. "The elders." Probably the elders of the council are meant.

V. 12. After this interruption, our Lord proceeded to instruct the multitudes: and the sun being perhaps at this time just risen, he thence took occasion to declare himself to be "the Light of the world." (Marg. Ref. r.—Notes, i. 4—9. xii. 34—36. 44—50. Mal. iv. 2, 3.) Christ to men in general, as to the concerns of their souls, what the sun is in respect of their temporal life: he is the Source and Fountain of all spiritual knowledge and wisdom, by which any man ever did, or ever shall, obtain the favour of God, acceptably do his will, and enjoy eternal felicity. All other lights must be either typical, derived, or deluding. Those who have taught the same truths, have in their measure reflected his light: they, who have taught opposite opinions, have deceived men, with a false glare of supposed science, into the pit of destruction. (Notes, Is. viii. 20. Matt. vi. 22, 23. Col. ii. 1—9.) He, "the Sun of Righteousness," had with his dawning beams afforded a degree of light to preceding generations: but he was now risen; and he called upon the Jews to make use of his clearer light, in preference to that of the Mosaick dispensation, and in opposition to the instructions of false teachers, or of any of those however distinguished who pretended to illuminate mankind; at the same time he assured them, that no one, who received his doctrine, obeyed his word, and followed him as his true disciple, should continue in ignorance, error, uncertainty, iniquity, or misery; however deeply he had before been involved in this complicated darkness. On the contrary, he should certainly, though in general gradually, be illuminated in the clear knowledge of God, and of every thing pertaining to acceptance, peace, and holiness; that so he might possess that divine light, which guides men safely and comfortably through this world of sin and sorrow, to the everlasting felicity of heaven. (Marg. Ref. s, t.—Notes, Prov. iv. 18, 19. Is. xlii. 13—17, v. 16. Hos. vi. 1—3, v. 3. Acts xxvi. 18—20. Eph. v. 8—14, vv. 8. 14. 2 Tim. i. 10. Rev. xxi. 22—27. xxii. 2—5, v. 5.)—The light of life.] "In him was life, and the life was the "Light of men." (i. 4.)—"With thee is the fountain of "life, and in thy light shall we see light." (Ps. cxxxvi. 9.)—The Messiah had frequently been predicted under this image; (Notes, Is. ix. 2. xlii. 5—7. xlix. 5, 6. lx. 1 —3;) so that this declaration implied an avowal of his character, and also that the Scribes and Pharisees, who opposed him, were blind guides and false teachers.

V. 13—16. Some of the Pharisees, who were among

16 And *yet if I judge, my judgment is true: ᵈfor I am not alone, but ᵉI and the Father that sent me.

17 It is ᵉalso written in your law, ᶠThat the testimony of two men is true.

18 I am ᵍone that bear witness of myself, ʰand the Father that sent me beareth witness of me.

19 Then said they unto him, Where is thy father? Jesus answered, ᶦYe neither know me nor my Father: ᵏif ye had known me, ye should have known my Father also.

20 These words spake Jesus ᶦin the treasury, as he taught in the temple: ᵐand no man laid hands on him; for ⁿhis hour was not yet come.

the multitude, (perhaps indignant at the discomfiture of their brethren, as well as at the intimation of the preceding words,) observed that as " he bare witness to himself," his testimony ought to be considered as false, or invalid, according to the common rule of judgment in such cases. To this he answered, that this rule did not apply to him; as he knew perfectly whence he came, and whither he was about to go; of which they were entirely ignorant.—He had before shewn them, that God had in various ways borne witness to him: (*Marg. Ref.* u—z.—*Note*, v. 31—38:) yet they spake, as if there had been no other proof of his being the Messiah, than his own word; as a mere man, like other men, not giving any adequate proof of his divine mission, or the high claims which he advanced of dignity and authority.—' My coming from heaven on
' an embassy to you, ... and that testified by the Spirit to
' John Baptist, and by John Baptist to you, ... gives a va-
' lidity to my testimony; and joins God the Father him-
' self in the testimony with me. And as the Holy Ghost
' has testified that I am sent by God; so my ascension to
' heaven, (which will sufficiently prove my mission,) being
' known to me beforehand, though not to you; and being
' discoverable by the event to you also; ... it will follow,
' that my testimony of myself is authentick and valid.'
Hammond.—' As I spake from my own certain knowledge,
' and I have already shewn that I come with a divine com-
' mission, my testimony is perfectly true. I well know
' from whence I come, and whither I go; and the most
' evident demonstrations of it have been given to you,
' both in the nature of my doctrine, and in the miracles
' which I have wrought among you: but you are so per-
' verse, that as often as I have hinted or declared it, you
' know not to this day, from whence I come, and whither
' I am going; which is not to be ascribed to the want of
' sufficient evidence, but merely to the force of your own
' prejudices: for you judge according to the maxims of
' flesh and sense, and will believe nothing in opposition to
' those principles which ye have so rashly imbibed; and
' by this means are justly liable to condemnation.' *Dod-
dridge.* The consciousness of our Lord to his own divine dignity, and the foresight of his ascension and mediatorial exaltation, could not be adduced, strictly speaking, as an argument in proof of the validity of his testimony concerning himself, for the conviction of others: but it was proper, that he should speak in this manner concerning his own Deity and authority: and his words being confirmed by miracles, and other sufficient proofs, would not fail to make a deep impression on numbers, leading them to a more careful consideration of the subject, and fully satisfying all who were candid and teachable; while the event would effectually confute gainsayers, and still more

illustrate the great doctrines concerning his person and salvation. As, however, he meant afterwards to recur to this; he seems to have waved the further discussion of it for the present, and only observed that the Pharisees were incompetent judges in such a cause: for they were ignorant of him, as " coming down from heaven," and about shortly to return thither; nay, they were unacquainted even with the place of his nativity as man: and moreover they were so blinded by their carnal prejudices and expectations of a Messiah, that they judged of his pretensions " according to the flesh," without any relish for the spiritual excellency of his character and doctrine, or desire of the real blessings of his kingdom. (*Notes, Matt.* xvi. 21—23. *Rom.* viii. 5—9. 1 *Cor.* ii. 14—16.) He came, however, among them as a Saviour, and did not mean at that time to denounce sentence, or execute vengeance, on any man; of which he had given them a proof in his refusal to pass sentence on the woman taken in adultery. (*Marg. Ref.* a, b.—*Note*, iii. 17, 18.) Yet if he had assumed this character, he should certainly have judged with infallible equity and truth; as his union, of nature, counsel, and operation, with the Father, who sent him and was with him, must exclude all possibility of error or injustice.—Though our Lord did not as a Judge formally pronounce, and so proceed to execute, the sentence of condemnation on the Scribes and Pharisees; yet he had clearly shewn them, what opinion he formed of their character and conduct; which the event, and especially the day of judgment, would prove to have been just and well grounded. (*Marg. Ref.* c, d.)

V. 17—20. The law, of which the Pharisees professed to be so tenacious, admitted the evidence of " two men" as a sufficient proof of any fact; though the scriptures every where described mankind, as prone to deceive and liable to be deceived. (*Marg. Ref.* f.—*Notes, Deut.* xvii. 2—7. xix. 15—21.) Jesus therefore observed, that he was one competent witness concerning his own nature and mission; (for he spake as a prophet declaring his mission, and not as a criminal who might not testify in his own cause;) and his Father was a second unexceptionable witness to him. Doubtless he referred to his own miracles, to the voice from heaven, and the fulfilment of ancient prophecies, by which it was proved that he was " the " Son of God." But the Jews, either did not understand his meaning, or were unwilling fairly to meet the argument; and therefore they enquired who his father was. He did not, however, see good to give them an explicit answer; but only declared that they " did not know either " him or his Father." Indeed, had they acknowledged him in his divine person and mediatorial work, they would have discovered his Father's glory as shining forth in him:

3 x 4

21 ¶ Then said Jesus again unto them, [a] I go my way, and ye shall seek me, [b] and shall die in your sins: [c] whither I go, ye cannot come. 22 Then said the Jews, [d] Will he kill himself? because he saith, Whither I go, ye cannot come. 23 And he said unto them, [e] Ye are from beneath; I am from above: [f] ye are of this world; I am not of this world. 24 I said therefore unto you, That

ye shall die in your sins: [g] for if ye believe not that I am *he*, ye shall die in your sins. 25 Then said they unto him, [h] Who art thou? And Jesus saith unto them, [i] Even *the same* that I said unto you from the beginning. 26 I [j] have many things to say and [k] to judge of you: [l] but he that sent me is true; [m] and I speak to the world those things which I have heard of him. 27 They [n] understood not that he spake to them of the Father.

---

and thus have attained a spiritual and experimental knowledge of the Father also: for, as he afterwards said more expressly, "he who hath seen me hath seen the Father;" and "I and the Father are One." (*Marg. Ref.* g—k.—*Notes*, 54—59, *vv.* 54, 55. 59. i. 18. x. 26—31, *v.* 30. xiv. 7—14, *vv.* 9, 10. xv. 22—25. xvi. 1—3. xvii. 1—3. 1 *Chr.* xxviii. 9. *Matt.* xi. 27. 2 *Cor.* iv. 5, 6.)—This open declaration, that he was the Son of God, was made in that part of the precincts of the temple, where the sacred treasures were collected and deposited: (*Note, Mark* xii. 41 —44:) yet his enemies were so restrained, that they did not apprehend him; because the time of his sufferings and death was not then arrived. (*Marg. Ref.* l, m.—*Notes*, vii. 25—30, *v.* 30. xi. 7—10. xiii. 1—5. *Luke* xiii. 31—33.)

Treasury. (20) Γαζοφυλακιῳ. *Mark* xii. 41. 43. *Luke* xxi. 1.

V. 21—26. (*Note*, vii. 31—36.) Our Lord next warned the unbelieving Jews of their guilt and danger, more plainly than before. He informed them, that he should speedily withdraw from them; and that, in their approaching miseries, they would desire the coming of the Messiah to redeem them; (for he was indeed that great Deliverer, though they would not believe it;) and in this vain expectation they would "perish in their sins;" (or, "in " their *sin*," of rejecting the promised Messiah:) for they would by no means be able to come to that place whither he was going. This appeared so strange to the Jews, who thought of nothing but this present world, that they perversely and scornfully enquired of each other, whether he meant to murder himself, in order to get out of their reach; as he so decidedly declared, that they could not follow him. In answer to this most absurd and malignant reflection, Jesus observed to them, that they were both *earthly* in their original, and *diabolical* in their disposition, and belonged to "this present evil world:" whereas he was "from above," of a heavenly and divine nature, and not at all like the men of the world in his judgment and temper; so that his doctrine, kingdom, and blessings could not suit their mind and heart. (*Marg. Ref.* p—s.—*Note*, iii. 27—36, *vv.* 31, 32.) So long as this contrariety continued, there could be no cordial intercourse between them. (*Note*, *Am.* iii. 1—3, *v.* 3.) He was about to return to heaven, whence he had come down; but it was impossible that they should follow him thither, or even be capable of enjoying its holy pleasures, so long as they retained their present proud and carnal minds, and "enmity " against God:" nor could they escape condemnation, unless they believed him to be the promised Messiah.—Some think that in the expression "I am He," (of which the latter word is not in the original,) our Lord meant to avow himself the great I AM, who spake to Moses. Another passage indeed in this chapter, is unequivocal to this purpose: (*Note*, 54—59, *v.* 58:) but the expression is sometimes applied to others, exactly as in this place: (ix. 9. Gr.) and it would weaken the argument to adduce it in proof of the doctrine; like bringing suspicious witnesses to a fact which is otherwise sufficiently attested.—The Jews however demanded of him who he was, seeing he so peremptorily required them to believe in him; and his answer to this enquiry has greatly embarrassed expositors: but the most obvious meaning, and most naturally conveyed by the original words, seems suggested by our translation; as if he had said, 'At the beginning of this discourse I told you, that I am "the Light of the World;" and if you believe on me as such, you will gradually know more of my person and doctrine.' (*Note*, 12.) This was equivalent to informing them, that he was the Messiah, or the Son of God.—He added, that he had much more to say to them concerning himself and his salvation, as well as about their guilt and danger, and the vengeance which was to be executed on their nation: but his Father, who sent him, being true and faithful, would certainly fulfil all his ancient promises and threatenings respecting them, and attest the doctrine which he taught them: for he only spake to the world, the doctrine which he had received from the Father.—*Die in your sins*. (24) 'As 'wanting that faith in me, which can alone procure the 'pardon of them.' *Whitby.* They scornfully enquired, whether Jesus intended to *murder* himself: and he shewed them, that by rejecting him, they would *murder* their own souls! (*Notes, Prov.* viii. 36. *Ez.* xviii. 25—32.) "To "die in sin " is to die unpardoned, unchanged, under the wrath of God, and a vessel of wrath fitted for destruction (*Marg. Ref.* o.—*Note, Prov.* xiv. 32.)

Sins. (21) Τῃ ἁμαρτια.—Ταις ἁμαρτιαις, 24.—*From be* neath. (23) Εκ των κάτω, scil. μερων. 6. 8.—Καλωτερος, *Eph.* iv. 9.—*From the beginning.* (25) Την αρχην. Scil. κατα την αρχην. *Gen.* xiii. 4. xli. 20. xliii. 18. 20. 1 *Chr.* xxvi. 10. *Sept.*

V. 27—29. Notwithstanding the explicit manner, in which Jesus spake of his Father, the Pharisees, being

28 Then said Jesus unto them, When ye have lifted up the Son of man, then shall ye know that I am he, and *that* I do nothing of myself; but as my Father hath taught me, I speak these things.

29 And he that sent me is with me: the Father hath not left me alone; for I do always those things that please him.

30 As he spake these words, many believed on him.

31 Then said Jesus to those Jews which believed on him, If ye continue in my word, *then* are ye my disciples indeed;

32 And ye shall know the truth, and the truth shall make you free.

33 They answered him, We be Abraham's seed, and were never in bondage to any man: how sayest thou, Ye shall be made free?

34 Jesus answered them, Verily, verily, I say unto you, Whosoever committeth sin, is the servant of sin.

35 And the servant abideth not in the house for ever; *but* the son abideth ever.

36 If the Son therefore shall make you free, ye shall be free indeed.

blinded by their prejudices, did not understand that he meant the God, whom they worshipped as the Father and Creator of heaven and earth, and called their Father (41). He therefore further observed, referring to his crucifixion, that " when they had lifted up " him, " the Son of Man," (*Marg. Ref.* c, d.—*Notes,* iii. 14, 15. xii. 27—33, v. 32,) they would know that he was their promised Messiah, and that he had done and taught nothing of himself, from any motive, or by any will, distinct from that of his Father; (*Note,* v. 19;) who did not leave him alone, but continued to be, and to work, in and with him, as it was evinced by his numerous and beneficent miracles: (*Notes,* iii. 1, 2. v. 31 —38, vv. 36, 37. xiv. 7—14, vv. 10, 11. xvi. 31—33:) for all, which he said and did at last, most perfectly pleased the Father, by fulfilling his eternal purposes, and displaying his glory. (*Marg. Ref.* e—i.)—Numbers who then opposed Jesus, afterwards embraced Christianity, after the pouring out of the Holy Spirit on his apostles and disciples; and very large multitudes were, by the awful judgments of God on the nation, convinced that Jesus was the promised Messiah. " The LORD is known " by the judgment which he executeth." (*Notes, Ps.* ix. 15, 16. *Ez.* xxviii. 21—23. xxxiii. 24—29.)

That please him. (29) Τα αρεστα αυτω. *Acts* vi. 2. xii. 3. 1 *John* iii. 22. Ab αρεσκω, *placeo.* Ευαρεσος, *Rom.* xii. 1, 2, *et al.* Many others have done and do things pleasing to God; but they confess, as with one voice, that " in many " things we offend all." Who, except Jesus, ever did or could truly say, " I always do the things which please " him ?" Of whom else do prophets and apostles speak in such terms? yet this is their uniform testimony to Jesus; who is thus emphatically distinguished from all others of the sons of Adam.

V. 30—36. The dignity and energy, attending the words of our Lord on this occasion, convinced many of his hearers that he was the Messiah, and they professed to believe in him. Directing therefore his discourse to them, he exhorted and encouraged them to " continue in his " word; " or to a persevering attendance on his instructions, belief of his declarations, reliance on his promises, and obedience to his commandments; notwithstanding all the temptations of the world, the flesh, and the devil. (*Marg. Ref.* l.—*Notes,* xv. 3—8. *Acts* xi. 23, 24.) If they did this, they would approve themselves his disciples *truly,* and not only in name and temporary profession : and by the constant teaching of his word and Spirit, their prejudices would be removed, their mistakes rectified, their views enlarged, and their doubts and uncertainties precluded; so that they would know the divine truth and excellency of his doctrine, and be able to distinguish it from every specious delusion. (*Marg. Ref.* m, n.—*Notes,* vii. 14—17. *Prov.* iv. 18, 19. *Hos.* vi. 1—3, v. 3.) Thus they would effectually learn, where their hope and strength lay; and so be made free from the bondage of sin and Satan; from the love of the world and the fear of men; from enslaving attachments to traditional superstitions; from the yoke of the ceremonial law; from legal terrors and the " spirit of bondage; " and from the dread of death, and the condemnation due to their sins. (*Marg. Ref.* o. —*Notes, Rom.* vi. 16—23. viii. 3, 4. *Gal.* v. 1—6, v. 1. 2 *Tim.* ii. 23—26.) In this way they would possess the greatest possible liberty, in the willing delightful service and worship of God, and in the enjoyment of his favour. (*Notes, Is.* lxi. 1—3. *Luke* iv. 16—22. 2 *Cor.* iii. 17, 18. *Gal.* v. 13—15.) His hearers, however, were at that time very far from thus understanding his words: nay, some present asserted, " that they never were in bond- " age to any man." As Abraham's posterity, according to the revelation previously made by God to that patri-arch, had been in the most abject bondage in Egypt; and as afterwards, they had been enslaved to several other nations, especially the Syrians, Assyrians, Chaldeans, Per-sians, and Greeks; and as they were then reduced into subjection to the Romans; it is wonderful, how they could thus flatter themselves into a forgetfulness of their former and present condition. (*Marg. Ref.* p, q.) If they spake of *personal* slavery, they certainly could not ascribe to their descent from Abraham, as many of their brethren had frequently been thus in bondage. If they meant that their political slavery was an unjust usurp-ation, and contrary to their *right,* as Abraham's seed, (which was their constant pretext for rebelling against the

37 I ' know that ye are Abraham's seed : ' but ye seek to kill me, ' because my word hath no place in you.

38 I ' speak that which I have seen with my Father; ' and ye do that which ye have seen with your father.

39 They answered and said unto him, Abraham is our father. Jesus saith unto them, ' If ye were Abraham's children, ye would do the works of Abraham.

40 But ' now ye seek to kill me, ' a man that hath told you the truth, which I have heard of God : this did not Abraham.

41 Ye ' do the deeds of your father. Then said they to him, ' We be not born of fornication; ' we have one Father, *even* God.

42 Jesus said unto them, ' If God were your Father, ye would love me : for I proceeded forth and came from God; " neither came I of myself, but he sent me.

43 Why " do ye not understand my speech ? *even* because ' ye cannot hear my word.

44 Ye ' are of *your* father the devil, and the lusts of your father ye will do : ' he was a murderer from the beginning, ' and abode not in the truth, because there is no truth in him. ' When he speaketh a lie, he speaketh of his own; for he is a liar, and the father of it.

45 And ' because I tell *you* the truth, ye believe me not.

46 Which of you ' convinceth me of sin ? And if I say the truth, ' why do ye not believe me ?

47 He ' that is of God, heareth God's words : ye therefore hear *them* not, because ye are not of God. ·

Romans,) this could not in the least interfere, with the Messiah's restoring them to the possession of *actual* liberty. Our Lord, however, did not see good to refute, or even notice, their vain-glorious boast. Spiritual things were, in his judgment, incomparably most important: and he therefore only reminded them, that the man, who habitually practised any kind of sin, was in fact a slave to that sin, and could have no right to boast of freedom; intimating that this was the case with most of them, especially of those who thus perversely cavilled at his gracious words. (*Marg. Ref.* s.—*Notes, Tit.* iii. 4—7. 2 *Pet.* ii. 18—22.) But if, instead of being so entirely the slaves of sin, they had far more exactly served God according to the letter of the law, depending on it, and rejecting his salvation; they could not on that account abide in the family for ever, as children and heirs; nay, they must at length be excluded, like Ishmael, who was the son of Abraham by a bond-woman. (*Marg. Ref.* t, u.—*Note*, and *P. O. Gal.* iv. 21—31.) But the Son of God, who was also eminently the " Seed " of Abraham," " abideth for ever " in the family as heir: if then he, as the Son and heir, made them free by his power and grace, according to the will of his Father, they would " be free indeed ;" receiving the Spirit of adoption, and the privileges, the liberty, and the inheritance of children. (*Note, Rom.* viii. 15—17.)

If ye continue. (31) Εαν ὑμεις μεινητε. 35. xv. 4. 7. 9, 10. 1 John ii. 27. iii. 6. 24.—*Shall make you free.* (32) Ελευθρωσι ὑμας. 36. *Rom.* vi. 18. 22. viii. 2. 21. *Gal.* v. 1. —Ελευθρος, 33. 36. *Matt.* xvii. 26.—*Were in bondage.* (33) Δεδουλευκαμεν. *Matt.* vi. 24. *Acts* vii. 7. *Rom.* vi. 6. *Gal.* iv. 25. v. 13. *Tit.* iii. 3. 2 *Pet.* ii. 19, et al. Δουλος, 34, 35. *Rom.* vi. 16.—*Committeth sin.* (34) Ὁ ποιων την ἁμαρταν. iii. 21. *Matt.* xiii. 41. 1 *John* ii. 29. iii. 4. 7, 8. 9, 10. (*Notes*, 1 *John* iii. 4—10.)

V. 37—40. Our Lord allowed the external relation of these Jews to Abraham : but he opposed their presumptuous confidence in it ; shewing that this relation could not profit such as were of a contrary spirit to him : (*Marg. Ref.* x, y.—*Notes, Ez.* xvi. 3—5. 44—47. *Matt.* iii. 7—10. *Rom.* ii. 25—29. iv. 9—17. ix. 4—14.) This was certainly the case with those, who were purposing to murder him, because his holy doctrine had no place in their hearts, which were pre-occupied with contrary desires and affections. (*Marg. Ref.* z, a.) Indeed his doctrine and their practice could not but be opposite to each other : for he spake those truths, which he had seen with his Father, and was come from heaven to testify to the world ; and they did those wicked works, which they had seen with their father, or learned from him, acting in concert with him and copying his example. This intimation caused the Jews again to insist upon it, that " Abraham was their " father : " but Jesus shewed them, that if they had been the genuine children of that " father of the faithful," they would have copied his example ; whereas they were seeking to murder him, who certainly had told them the truth, as he had received it from God. This did not at all accord to Abraham's example, who always welcomed every discovery of the truth and will of God, with humble faith and unreserved obedience. (*Marg. Ref.* b—e.—*Notes, Rom.* iv. 18—22. *Gal.* iii. 6—14. 26—29. *Heb.* xi. 8—10. 17—19. *Jam.* ii. 21—24.)

Abraham's seed. (37) Σπερμα Αβρααμ. 33. *Luke* i. 55. *Rom.* iii. ix. 7. *Gal.* iii. 16. 29.—*Gen.* xxii. 18. (*Note*, *Gal.* iii. 15—18.)—*Hath no place.*] Ου χωρει. xxi. 25. See on *Matt.* xix. 11.

V. 41—47. Jesus further observed, that in one sense, it might truly be said, the unbelieving Jews performed " the deeds of their father."—On hearing this, the objectors, perceiving the drift of our Lord's discourse, answered with indignation, that " they were not born of fornication;"

48 Then answered the Jews, and said unto him, ' Say we not well that ª thou art a Samaritan, and hast a devil? 49 Jesus answered, ᵇ I have not a devil : ᶜ but I honour my Father, and ye do dishonour me.

50 And ᵈ I seek not mine own glory : ᵉ there is one that seeketh and judgeth. 51 Verily, verily, I say unto you, ᶠ 'If a man ᵍ keep my saying, he shall never ʰ see death.

---

they were neither the descendants of Gentile idolaters, nor Samaritans, nor apostate Jews, nor themselves the worshippers of idols ; but they had one Father, even God, whose covenanted people and children they were. (Marg. Ref. g—i.—Note, Mal. ii. 10—12.) But Jesus observed to them, that if God indeed were their Father, if they had been born of God and adopted by him, they would certainly have loved him, the beloved Son of God, " the " brightness of his glory and the express image of his Per- " son :" for he " proceeded forth, and came from God;" (which words imply something far beyond his merely coming into the world as Mediator, being wholly different from what are spoken of any other person ;) neither did he come of his own accord, but as sent and commissioned by the Father, to display his glory and make known his truth. (Notes, i. 14—18. vi. 36—40. xvi. 25—30.) Had the Jews therefore either supremely desired the favour of God, or loved his holy perfections, or sought his glory ; they must have loved the character and doctrine of Jesus, and have welcomed him as their Teacher, Saviour, and King. (Marg. Ref. k, l.—Notes, xxi. 15—17. 1 Cor. xvi. 21—24. 1 Pet. i. 8, 9.) As the matter was thus plain, how was it that they did not understand his discourse ? Truly, because their pride and worldly prejudices and passions closed their minds against his holy doctrine; and therefore they were determined not to believe that he was the Messiah, and the Son of God, or even a Teacher sent from him. (Marg. Ref. n, o.) In short they were " the children of the devil," and bore the image of their father: they were therefore resolved to perpetrate those wicked designs, which originated from the lusts in their hearts as moved by Satan, and were the counterpart of his proud and determined enmity to God ; and coincided with his malignant purposes of dishonouring God, opposing true religion, and destroying its friends, as much as possible. From the beginning of the world, or the existence of man, that great adversary of God and of his creation, had been " a murderer," or man-slayer. Having departed from his original love of truth, and his fidelity and loyalty to his Maker and Lord, by his awful apostasy; he proceeded, as soon as possible, to murder the souls and bodies of men. By his lies he tempted Eve, and through her Adam, to eat the forbidden fruit; by which he in a sense murdered the whole human race soul and body at once. Soon after, he instigated wicked Cain to murder his righteous brother Abel ; which was the beginning, and specimen, of all the innocent blood shed by persecutors ever since. (Marg. Ref. p—r.—Notes, Matt. xxiii. 34—36. 1 John iii. 7—15.) He has always been the great tempter of mankind to all kinds of discords and contentions, which terminate in private murder, or in bloody destructive wars, and cruel oppressions and massacres. He prompts men to those excesses, by which multitudes destroy themselves and each other ; and to suicide in all its varied forms. At the same time his suggestions tend

equally to the ruin of men's immortal souls.—All these murders are inseparably connected with lies and deceit : the devil first prevailed over Eve by a lie; (Note, Gen. iii. 4, 5;) all persecutions are excited on lying pretences, by false accusations of the most malignant kind, and in support of false religions. In a word, the Devil is the great promoter of falsehood of every kind throughout the earth, and does all his mischief by it, even as God uses truth as the medium of all good to men. The devil is altogether composed, as it were, of subtlety, dissimulation, and treachery ; so that when he propagates a lie of any kind, he acts in character, and brings forth out of his own inexhaustible treasury; for he is not only a liar, but the original author of all lies, and the father of all liars. (Marg. Ref. r, s.) Now it was evident that these Jews were the children of this great man-slayer and liar ; in that they refused to believe in Jesus, and sought to put him to death, not only though he told them the truth, but " because he did so." Their wicked hearts were diametrically opposite to the truth, which must be holy and humbling : yet if he had taught them any false doctrine, it would have been congenial to their pride and lusts, and they would have been disposed to receive it. (Marg. Ref. t.) But could they convict him of any kind or degree of sin ? If not, how did they excuse their rejection of his doctrine, and their murderous persecution of him, notwithstanding his undeniable miracles ? If indeed he spake the truth of God to them, why did they not believe him ? The reason was obvious : every man, who is born again and belongs to God, has an habitual disposition to hear his words, and to believe and obey them : they therefore did not thus regard them, because they were not the children of God, but the children of the devil ; and, like their father, were at enmity against the truth and holiness of God. (Marg. Ref. u—y.—Note, 1 John iv. 4 —6.)—Ye cannot. (43) ' Men of your tempers cannot ' yield obedience to it. ... The Jews ... wanted not, either ' natural power, or assistance necessary on God's part to do ' this : but only a moral power, or a mind well disposed ' to obey his words.' Whitby. (Notes, Ps. cx. 4. Phil. ii. 12, 13.)

Ye would love me. (42) Ηγαπᾶτε ἂν ἐμέ. 1 John v. 1.—Ye will do. (44) Θελετε ποιειν. " Ye will," or purpose, " to do." —A murderer.] Ανθρωποκτονος. 1 John iii. 15. Not elsewhere. Εξ ανθρωπος et ktεινω occido.—Ανδροκτονος, killer of men, is the epithet given to Mars by Homer. The fabled god of war killed men chiefly : (ανδρας, males, men of war :) but the devil kills men, women, and children, even the whole species.—Convinceth me of sin. (46) Ελεγχει με περι αμαρθιας. xvi. 8, 9. See on Matt. xviii. 15.

V. 48—53. The conclusive arguments, and severe reproofs of our Lord, greatly exasperated his opponents : they therefore now openly declared, what they seem before to have privately whispered, namely, that he was a Samaritan : one of that hated nation, or as great an enemy to them and

3 z 8

52 Then said the Jews unto him, ʲNow we know that thou hast a devil. ᵏAbraham is dead, and the prophets; and thou sayest, If a man keep my saying, he shall never ˡtaste of death.

53 Art ᵐthou greater than our father Abraham, which is dead? and the prophets are dead: ⁿwhom makest thou thyself?

54 Jesus answered, ᵒIf I honour myself, my honour is nothing: ᵖit is my Father that honoureth me, of whom ᵠye say, That he is your God.

55 Yet ʳye have not known him; &c. ˢbut I know him: and if I should say, I know him not, ᵗI shall be a liar like unto you: but I know him, ᵘand keep his saying.

56 Your father Abraham ˣrejoiced to see my day: and he saw it, and was glad.

57 Then said the Jews unto him, Thou art not yet fifty years old, and hast thou seen Abraham?

58 Jesus said unto them, ʸVerily, verily, I say unto you, ᶻBefore Abraham was, ᵃI am.

59 Then ᵇtook they up stones to cast at him: ᶜbut Jesus hid himself, and went out of the temple, going through the midst of them, and so passed by.

---

their religion, as any Samaritan could be; and therefore equally entitled to their contempt and abhorrence. They added, that he had a devil, or was possessed by a demon, and spake by his instigation, being also enabled by him to perform apparent miracles in confirmation of his delusions. (*Marg. Ref.* z, a.—*Note*, vii. 19—24.) But Jesus meekly replied, that he had not a devil; taking no notice of being called a Samaritan, as that reproach did not *so immediately* affect the credit of his divine commission : on the contrary, he honoured God his Father, by his conduct, doctrine, and miracles, the evident tendency of which was to lead men to worship, trust, and obey him: and they dishonoured him by their revilings, as if he were actuated by Satan, which proved that they were enemies to God and his honour. For his part, he sought not his own glory, as distinct from that of the Father, and therefore he disregarded equally their reproaches and their applause. There was, however, One who sought to honour him, and who would call them to account, and execute vengeance on them, for their opposition to him. (*Marg. Ref.* b—e.) He therefore proceeded most solemnly to assure them, that if a " man " keep his saying," cordially embrace, and stedfastly retain, his holy doctrine by obedient faith, " he shall never " see death : " meaning, that *temporal* death, or the separation of the soul from the body, should never do him harm ; and *eternal* death, or the separation of the soul from God, should not come upon him. (*Marg. Ref.* f—h.—*Note*, xi. 20—27, vv, 25, 26.) The Jews, misunderstanding this declaration, openly declared they now were certain that he was possessed : for Abraham and all the prophets had died ; and was he able, not only to escape death himself, but to preserve all his followers from it? and did he openly avow that he was greater than all who ever lived before him? ' Who can promise others shall ' never die, but he who is himself to live for ever? ' *Whitby.* (*Marg.Ref.* i, k. m, n.—*Notes*, xiv. 18—20, v. 19. *Col.* iii. 1—4.)—Jesus had repeatedly shewn them, that he was the promised Messiah, by speaking as " the Son of " God," and " the Light of the world : " and it was evident, even from their own interpretation of the scriptures, that the Messiah was to be far greater, than any one who

had gone before him.—To *see* death, and to *taste of* death, seem only to be figurative expressions of the same import as to die. (*Marg. Ref.* l.)

A devil. (48) Δαιμονιον. 49. 52. x. 20, 21. *Matt.* vii. 22. *Mark* i. 34. 39, et al.—*Notes*, *Acts* xvii. 18. 1 Cor. x. 18—22.—*Ye do dishonour.* (49) Ατιμαζετε. *Luke* xx. 11. *Acts* v. 41. *Rom.* i. 24. ii. 23. Ab α priv. et τιμη honor.—Never. (51) Εις τον αιωνα. 52. iv. 14. vi. 58.—*Taste.* (52) Γευσεται. ii. 3. *Matt.* xvi. 28. *Luke* ix. 27. *Heb.* ii. 9. vi. 4. 1 Pet. ii. 3.

V. 54—59. In reply to the objections of the Jews, our Lord observed, that if he claimed this honour for himself, upon his own testimony alone, " it was nothing," or a *vain* glory like that of ambitious worldly men : but his Father had conferred it on him and testified in various ways that it belonged to him. (*Marg. Ref.* o, p.—*Notes*, v. 31—44.) By his Father he meant the God of Israel, whom they claimed as their God and covenanted Friend, and professed to worship : yet they had no true knowledge of him, nor any of those holy dispositions which spring from that knowledge. (Note, 17—20.) But he knew him fully and perfectly ; and if, to avoid their hatred, he should deny this, he should then indeed be a liar, as they were, when they professed to know, love, and worship him. But he proved his knowledge of God by perfectly keeping his commandments, and executing the commission which he had received from him. (*Marg. Ref.* q—u.) He also assured them, that Abraham had greatly desired to see the day of his appearing upon earth, and rejoiced, and even exulted with triumphant gladness, in the prospect of it. The Patriarch had, by faith in his divine promises and predictions, and through types, looked forward to the appointed season of his coming for the redemption of his people, with the highest satisfaction ; and his hope of salvation was grounded on the same word : but the desperate offspring rejected and hated Him, whom their illustrious ancestor had, at so great a distance, beheld with the utmost reverence and joy! (*Marg. Ref.* x.—*Notes*, *Matt.* xiii. 16, 17. *Luke* x. 23, 24. *Heb.* xi. 13—16. 1 *Pet.* i. 10—12.) The Jews, however, perversely understood him to mean, that Abraham had actually conversed with him, as a man living upon earth at

CHAP. IX.

Jesus gives sight to one who was born blind, 1—7.
The man shews his enquiring neighbours by what

means his eyes were opened, 8—12. He is brought
to the Pharisees, who strictly examine both him and
his parents, 13—23. They are offended at him, for
contending that Jesus is a prophet, and disdainfully
excommunicate him, 24—34. Jesus makes himself

that time. He was not yet fifty years old, and would he avow that he had seen Abraham, who died above one thousand eight hundred years before?—Jesus at this time was not more, on any computation, than thirty-five years of age : but his gravity, joined with his incessant labours, probably, made him look much older than he was.—To their enquiry he answered with his usual most solemn asseveration, " Before Abraham was, I AM." The use of the present tense in this connexion, and the construction of the passage, require us to understand it as a declaration, that, as the great I AM, who appeared to Moses, he possessed an underived and independent existence, before Abraham was brought into being, yea, from all eternity. (*Marg. Ref.* z, a.—*Notes, Ex.* iii. 14. *Heb.* i. 10—12. xiii. 8. *Rev.* i, 8.) Indeed the words do not well admit of any other construction, which can render them intelligible to a man of ordinary capacity. Thus the Jews evidently understood them; and therefore they were about to stone Jesus for blasphemy, without any process of law, or regard to the Roman authority; their indignation was so greatly excited! But by his miraculous power he concealed himself from their view; and, passing through the midst of them without being perceived, he eluded their malice for the present. (*Marg. Ref.* b, c.)—Probably, this discourse left a durable impression on many of the hearers, and prepared their minds for receiving the testimony of his apostles, after the pouring out of the Holy Ghost.— ' Christ here only signifies, that he was before Abraham, ' in the decree of God.' *Grotius.*—' But 1. Christ answers ' to the objection of the Jews, which had no respect to the ' priority of these two persons in the decree of God ; but ' as to actual existence.—2. In this sense even Judas, and ' all the murderers of our Lord, might be before Abraham ' had a being.' *Whitby.*—Some eager but injudicious Calvinists use language similar to this, about *justification*, and other Christian privileges ; and they are justly censured even by their brethren : because the *purpose* of God, and its *accomplishment*, are perfectly distinct ; and should never be thus confounded : but one would not have expected such crude language from the very learned Anti-calvinist, Grotius !

A liar. (55) Ψευτης. 44. *Rom.* iii. 4. 1 *Tim.* i. 10. *Tit.* i. 12. 1 *John* i. 10. ii. 4. 22. iv. 20. v. 10. Ψευδος, 44—*Rejoiced.* (56) Ηγαλλιασατο. See on *Luke* i. 47.—*I am.* (58) Εγω ειμι.—Εγω ειμι 'Ο Ων. ... 'Ο Ων απεσταλκε με. *Ex.* iii. 14. *Sept.*—*Hid himself.* (59) Εκρυβη. " Was hidden," xii. 36.—In what way " Jesus was hidden " from the view of his persecutors, it is not said, nor does it behove us to enquire. (*Notes, Gen.* xix. 11. 2 *Kings* vi. 18. *Luke* xxiv. 13 —24, v. 16.)

PRACTICAL OBSERVATIONS.

V. 1—11.

In the conduct of our Lord we see an example of the strictest attention to retired devotion, connected with the greatest diligence in seizing on every opportunity for publick usefulness : but we must be very careful in redeeming our time, and very moderate in animal recreation, if we would tread in his steps ; and not allow these distinct, and too often detached, parts of our duty to entrench on each other.—Even Jesus himself could scarcely be more active in doing good, than his zealous enemies were, and always have been, in devising and compassing evil ; for malice will convert any thing into an occasion of mischief. The ministers of the gospel, therefore, want divine wisdom and fortitude ; for they will be encountered by subtle, as well as powerful opponents : yet their enemies are seldom more dangerous, than when they assume the appearance of friendship ; and, in the language of respect, attempt to inveigle them, to intermeddle with matters not belonging to them, or to interfere in the peculiar concerns of princes and rulers. (*P. O. Matt.* xxii. 15—22.)—Adultery most certainly merits far severer punishment from the magistrate, than it generally meets with ; and we may sometimes state and explain the law of God respecting these things : but we should not leave our proper employment to direct legislators or magistrates, unless clearly called to that service. If any persuade us openly to intermeddle out of our proper line of duty, we should look upon it as a temptation ; and we may suspect that this is sometimes done, that they may accuse us, either as ambitious men who are enemies to civil liberty, or as turbulent innovators who are disaffected to the authority which God has placed over us. We should, therefore, generally act as though we heard them not ; and answer repeated solicitations by some serious address to men's consciences; thus " studying to " be quiet, and mind our own business."—The prosecution of criminals is in itself a good work : yet it is frequently conducted by such persons and from such motives, that the accusers are in the sight of God the more atrocious offenders. From regard to society they cannot be wholly excluded : nor should we in any sense require too much of those, who concur in the necessary but painful employment, of bringing offenders to justice : yet we may fairly observe, that he, who is concerned in the prosecution of another for a capital offence, and is himself living in the practice of unrepented habitual wickedness, has need to tremble at the prospect of more terrible vengeance from God, than that which he calls for upon a fellow criminal from human justice. He should therefore pause, and prepare for his awful employment, by self-examination, repentance, faith, prayer, and amendment of life ; lest he should " bring upon himself swift destruction." But were such barriers placed around our courts of judicature ; were such rules proclaimed in them, and adhered to, how would they be thinned ! While many, " convicted by their own " consciences, would go out one by one," perhaps beginning at the eldest and greatest persons concerned; the prosecution might be left unfinished, and the criminals be allowed to escape. Nay, if our most solemn religious ordinances could be fenced against those, who are habitually practising secret iniquity, it is to be feared that the small number of our communicants would often be diminished.

known to him, as " the Son of God ;" and he believes in him and worship him, 35—38. Christ declares the design of his coming to be, that the blind

might see, and the seeing be made blind ; with reference to the miracle, and to the proud and wilful blindness of the Pharisees, 39—41.

These reflections may convince us, what little reason men have to object to the doctrine of free salvation : they only, who have always performed a sinless obedience, ought to cast a stone at the preachers of unmerited forgiveness, and eternal life the free gift of God, through faith in Christ : all else should thankfully receive their message. The same considerations may also shew us the readiest way of dealing with pertinacious objectors : an address to their consciences, which calls their sins to remembrance, may render those silent, from fear of detection and recollection of their guilt, whom no arguments can reach. And though we must not excuse crimes, nor object to the infliction of merited punishment ; yet we should hence learn to be gentle and compassionate, even in performing the severest offices ; and ever to shew a disposition to forgive, and be kind to the vilest, as we hope for mercy from God to our own souls. We should, however, strongly urge the admonition, " Sin no more ;" otherwise an escape from temporal punishment can only give an opportunity of " treasuring up wrath against the day of " wrath."

V. 12—29.

Every action of Jesus, as well as his whole doctrine, shews him to us, as " The Light of the world." Let us then no longer look to the schools of philosophy for illumination ; and let us not implicitly follow any man's teaching : on the contrary let us follow Jesus, that we " may " not walk in darkness, but have the light of life." If we have begun to attend on him for instruction ; he has already in some things, " made darkness light before us," and " our path will shine more and more unto the perfect " day." But unbelievers " know not whence he came, " and whither he is gone ;" " they judge after the flesh ;" yet they presume to judge him, before whose righteous tribunal they must shortly stand : whereas, they are incompetent to decide upon the principles and conduct of his meanest disciple. Such men often oppose precepts to doctrines : yet those precepts properly explained condemn their conduct, and bear witness to the doctrines which they oppose : yea, in every way God testifies to his Son, that salvation is by faith in him alone. Those who know not his glory and grace, know not " the Father that sent " him : " but, by the knowledge of the Son, believers attain to the sanctifying and beatifying knowledge of the Father also.—The Redeemer has indeed left this earth, where he was so greatly hated and despised : yet none who truly " seek him shall die in their sins," or be excluded from that place, " whither as our Forerunner he is for us " entered : " but those who continue to deride his warnings, and thus prove themselves " earthly, sensual, and " devilish," will die unpardoned, and perish as " vessels " of wrath fitted for destruction."—But some will say, ' Who is Jesus ? And what are we to believe concerning him ? We allow him to have been a Prophet, a Teacher of most excellent morality, and a bright Example of beneficence and patience : nay, we admit that he was the chief of men, or even of all creatures ; and we would even grant him to be something more than a creature, if we could do

it without acknowledging him as " God over all, blessed " for evermore : " and will not this suffice ?' Let Jesus himself answer this question. Is this to honour him, even as we honour the Father ? Does this answer to his being " the Light of the world," " the Life of men," " the Resur- " rection of the dead," " One with the Father," the ever-lasting I AM ? (58) He, who said such things of himself in the vale of humiliation, will not retract them on the throne of glory : and they who do not believe in him, as being all this, and as more than our words can fully express, will perish in their sins, whatever they object to the bigotry of those who fairly warn them of their danger. For Jesus has much to say and to judge of them : and all shall know, by their conversion, or in their condemnation, that he always spake and did those things which pleased the Father, even when he claimed the highest honours to himself.

V. 30—36.

Many profess the great doctrines of Christianity without saving faith : when we therefore see men convinced that the doctrines, termed evangelical, are indeed divine truths, we should warn them of the temptations and dangers, to which they will be exposed, that they may be excited to guard against them.—By " continuing in the word " of Christ, with an obedient faith, we prove that we are his " disciples indeed," and " have not received the seed in " stony ground." Thus we attain a fuller and more satisfactory knowledge of the truth : and this teaches us the nature, excellency, Author, and means, of true liberty ; and leads us earnestly to pursue, and at length to enjoy, that precious blessing. But as men are capable of imposing on themselves, through self-flattery, in the most unaccountable manner, in respect of their secular concerns ; no wonder, if they mistake their character and state in relation to God and the eternal world. (Note, Jer. xvii. 9, 10.) It is, however, most certain, that he " who committeth " sin is the slave of sin ;" and we may infer safely, that many declaim and dispute about liberty of every kind, and boast of it, nay fight for it, who are themselves base slaves to ambition, avarice, lust, anger, or some other grovelling or malignant tyrant. How highly soever we value freedom, personal or political, civil or religious ; (and when freedom is soberly ascertained, it can scarcely be too highly prized ;) we must recollect that it is a mere shadow to the slave of sin and Satan : and we may well weep to see men, laden with heavy chains, yet glorying in their liberty ; till death terminates their delusion, and makes them know that they must be slaves for ever. From this awful state no maxims of philosophy, no system of ethicks, no inventions of superstition, no external ordinances, can deliver any man : nay, God may outwardly be served from slavish fear, or mercenary hope, and no liberty be obtained or enjoyed ; but " if the Son of God make us free, we shall be free in- " deed," and for ever. While therefore men stand up for freedom, rights, and privileges ; let every one, who would be truly wise, first come to Christ for that real and endur-ing liberty to which he calls us by his gospel. (Note, Matt. xi. 28—30.)

3 Y 3

v. 72. AND as *Jesus* passed by, [a] he saw a man which was blind from *his* birth.

2 And his disciples asked him, saying, Master, [b] who did sin, this man, or his parents, that he was born blind?

3 Jesus answered, [c] Neither hath this man sinned, nor his parents: [d] but that the works of God should be made manifest in him.

4 I [e] must work the works of him that sent me, [f] while it is day: the night cometh, when no man can work.

Margin references (left column):
b 34. Matt. xvi. 14.
c Joh. i. 8—12. iii. 3—6. xxi. 27.
xxii. 4, &c.
xxxii. 3. xii. 7. Ec. ix. 1, 2.
Luke xiii. 2—5.
Acts xxviii. 4.

Margin references (right column):
d xi. 4. 40. viv. 11
—13. Matt. xi.
5. Acts iv. 21.
a iv. 34. v. 19. 36.
x. 32, 37, 38.
xvii. 4. Luke
xiii. 32—34 Acts
iv. 20.
f xi. 9, 10. xii. 35.
Ec. ix. 10. Is.
xxxviii. 18, 19.
Eph. v. 16. Col.
iv. 5.

V. 37—47.

Alas! immense numbers boast of being Christians, as absurdly as the Jews did that they were "Abraham's chil- "dren;" and they suppose that God is their Father, because they have been baptized, even as the Jews did because of circumcision. But which do they resemble most, the primitive Christians, or those who sought to murder Christ, because they could not endure his doctrines and precepts? Are they born again, and made partakers of a divine and holy nature? Do they above all things love Jesus, and his salvation and service? If there is nothing of this kind in their dispositions and conduct, but very many things of a contrary nature, let them not deceive themselves: they are the children of him whose works they do, and whose image they bear; and the pride, rebellion, dissimulation, malice, and malignity of numbers called Christians, shew them to be the offspring of that old apostate, murderer, and liar, the devil. Such affronting applications of evangelical truth, induce men to complain that they cannot understand the words of Christ: no evidence can convince them, that those doctrines are true, which reduce them to the alternative, of renouncing and mortifying every sin, or of perishing for ever in hell. The most unexceptionable conduct of those, who speak the words of God, will not procure them credit, "because they tell them the truth:" but if any improbable report be spread, or any new heresy started; the same persons will embrace it with the most implicit and absurd credulity! The reason is evident; "they are not of God, and therefore they cannot hear his "words."

V. 48—59.

Calumny and reproach must be the recompence of those, who stand up for "the truth as it is in Jesus:" and they may expect to be called the enemies of mankind, of their country, nay, of the church and religion; for, the more they honour God, the more the ungodly and hypocritical will dishonour them. Nor ought we to be disconcerted, at being called enthusiasts and insane, or even branded in more opprobrious terms, by such men, as said to the holy Jesus, "Thou art a Samaritan, and hast a devil." We must, amidst all, still direct men to Jesus, "not seeking "our own glory," but leaving the matter to him "who "seeketh and judgeth:" for we are assured, that they who "keep his saying shall not see death for ever." We should stedfastly profess what we know and believe concerning God and religion; whatever wrong constructions may be put upon our words, by those who falsely claim him as their God, yet know him not; and if we be heirs of Abraham's faith, we shall both trust him for temporal protection, and rejoice with glad exultation in expectation of that day,when the Saviour who said, "Before Abraham "was, I AM," shall appear in his glory to the confusion of his enemies, and to complete the salvation of all who believe in him; while they shall shout in triumphant strains, "Lo, This is our God, we have waited for him, "and he will save us. This is the LORD, we have waited "for him, we will be glad and rejoice in his salvation." (*Notes, Is.* xxv. 9. 1 *Tim.* iv. 6—8. *Tit* ii. 11—15. *Heb.* ix. 27, 28. 2 *Pet.* iii. 10—15.)

NOTES.

CHAP. IX. V. 1—3. Though the first words of this chapter seem connected with the conclusion of the foregoing; yet it is generally thought that some months had intervened: for the events before recorded took place at the feast of tabernacles, but those of this chapter are supposed to have occurred at the feast of dedication, about a quarter of a year afterwards. (*Note,* x. 22—24.)—Jesus passing on the streets of Jerusalem met a man, who was known to have been born blind: and the disciples thence took occasion to ask a question, which seems *in part* to have arisen from the opinion, that men in this world fare better or worse, according to their behaviour in some pre-existent state, of which they have no recollection or consciousness! Many of the Jews at that time had imbibed this absurd sentiment from the heathen: for, not being satisfied with the scriptural account of the entrance of sin and death into the world, they had recourse to this notion to solve the difficulties which they met with in the dispensations of Providence, from observing the extraordinary calamities attendant on some men, more than on others, through the whole course of their lives. The disciples therefore desired to be informed, whether this man's calamity was the punishment of his own misconduct in a pre-existent state, or whether his parents had brought it on him and themselves by some heinous crime? (*Notes,* 27—34, *v.* 34. *Luke* xiii. 1—5.—Many think that the sin mentioned *Lev.* xx. 18, is referred to.) But our Lord assured them, that neither the one nor the other was the real cause of his being born blind; but it was so ordered on purpose, that the powerful operation of God, by his hands, might be openly displayed, in restoring the blind man to sight. No doubt his parents were sinners, and deserved far worse than this affliction; and the man was born in sin as others are: but these were not the *immediate causes* of this singular calamity, which was appointed for another most important and merciful purpose. (*Marg. Ref.*)

Passed by. (1) Παραγων. viii. 59. *Matt.* ix. 9. 27. 1 *Cor.* vii. 31.—*Birth.*] Γεννης. Here only.

V. 4—7. Our Lord next observed, that, notwithstanding the malice of his enemies, it was requisite for him to "work the works," which his Father had sent him to perform, during the short remnant of his life on earth : intimating that his crucifixion would soon take place, which would end his personal labours and miracles; as the night

THE POOL OF SILOAM.

Nehem. iii. 15. Isaiah viii. 6. Luke xiii. 4. John ix. 7, 11.

5 As ᶠlong as I am in the world, I am the Light of the world.

6 When he had thus spoken, ᵍhe spat on the ground, and made clay of the spittle, and he ʰanointed the eyes of the blind man with the clay;

7 And said unto him, ᶦGo wash in ᵏthe pool of Siloam, (which is by interpretation, ˡSent.) He went his way therefore, and washed, ᵐand came seeing.

8 The neighbours therefore, and they which before had seen him that he was blind, said, ⁿ Is not this he that ᵒsat and begged?

9 Some said, This is he: others *said,* He is like him: but he said, I am he.

10 Therefore said they unto him, ᵖHow were thine eyes opened?

11 He answered and said, ᑫA man that is called Jesus made clay, and anointed mine eyes, and said unto me, Go to the pool of Siloam, and wash: and I went and washed, and I received sight.

12 Then said they unto him, ʳWhere is he? He said, I know not.

13 They ˢbrought to the Pharisees him that aforetime was blind.

14 And ᵗit was the sabbath-day when Jesus made the clay, and opened his eyes.

15 Then again ᵘthe Pharisees also asked him how he had received his

---

does the work of the day, or as death terminates the services and fixes the state of every one. (*Marg. Ref.* e, f.—*Notes, Ec.* ix. 10. *Luke* xiii. 31—33.) It was also proper for him, to open this man's eyes, as an emblem of his enlightening the minds of men by the knowledge of divine truth. While he continued on earth, he was " the Light " of the world," by his personal ministry and miracles; and he would be the same, by his doctrine and his Spirit, to the end of time. (*Marg. Ref.* g.—*Notes,* i. 4—9. viii. 12.) He therefore anointed the man's eyes, with clay formed for that purpose with his spittle, which would seem rather suited to close, than to open them: and then he directed him to go and wash at the pool of Siloam, which, signifying *Sent,* might be a type of him whom the Father had *sent* to be " the Light of the world." (*Marg. Ref.* h—m.—*Notes, Gen.* xlix. 10. *Is.* viii. 6—8.) Accordingly the man, having, it may be supposed, heard of the miracles which Jesus performed, and hoping for a cure, obeyed; and thus not only received his sight, but was also enabled to make an immediate and proper use of his eyes, and so returned seeing every object distinctly: for it is a fact now well ascertained, that when sight is given, by a surgical operation, to those who were born blind; they require a considerable time to learn the proper use of the newly acquired sense, as well as great care in preventing any injury to it.—Perhaps our Lord took this method to make trial of the man's faith and obedience; or to shew that the most unlikely means will be efficacious, when he appoints and blesses them.—As far as I can recollect, this is the only instance, in which sight was miraculously given to one born blind: and indeed " opening the eyes of the " blind," strictly speaking, was a miracle peculiar to our Lord himself, and is repeatedly mentioned in the prophecies of his coming. It is neither included in the commission given to the apostles and seventy disciples; nor was it performed, either by them, or by any of the ancient prophets. The removal of Saul's *temporary* blindness by Ananias, is, I think, the only exception.—The same is observable also of opening the ears of the deaf, and the mouths of the dumb. (*Notes, Ex.* iv. 11, 12. *Ps.* cxlvi. 8. *Is.* xxix. 17—19. xxxv. 5—7. *Matt.* ix. 32, 33.)

Of the spittle. (6) Εκ τε πλυσματος. Here only. Πλυω, *Mark* vii. 33. viii. 23.—*He anointed.*] Επιχρισι. 11. Here only. Εκ επι et χριω, *unguo.*—*Pool.* (7) Κολυμβηθραν. See on v. 2.—*Siloam.*] Σιλωαμ. 11. *Luke* xiii. 4.—חלש, from חלש, to *send.*

V. 8, 9. *Marg. Ref.*—*Note, Ruth* i. 19—21.—*Like him, &c.* (9) ' The circumstance, of his having received ' his sight, would give him an air of spirit and cheerfulness, ' and would render him something unlike what he was ' before.' *Doddridge.*

V. 10—12. The simple statement of fact, without any observations on it, in answer to the question proposed, is worthy of notice. (*Marg. Ref.* p, q.—*Note, Jer.* xxxvi. 17, 18.)—*Know not.* (12) ' I have never yet seen him, ' nor ever conversed with him, otherwise than I have just ' told you.' *Doddridge.* (*Marg. Ref.* r.)

V. 13. ' " They brought him to the Pharisees;" that ' is, to the council, which chiefly consisted of this sect; ' whence in this evangelist, the whole council passeth under ' the name of Pharisees. ... This they might do, either out ' of ill-will to Christ, or out of curiosity to know, whether ' they would own the person who had done this signal ' miracle, to be the very man of whom Isaiah had pro- ' phesied, that he should " open the eyes of the blind." ' And surely the providence of God so ordered this, that ' they might hear from the mouth of the blind man, a ' testimony which would either convince them, or render ' their unbelief without excuse.' *Whitby.*—' They brought ' him ... to the Pharisees, in the Sanhedrim, that he might ' be examined by them; that so, if there was any fraud in ' the matter, they might discover and expose it.' *Doddridge.* (*Marg. Ref.* s.—*Note, Acts* iv. 1—3.)

V. 14. It is said, that anointing the eyes with any kind of unguent, or even with spittle, on the sabbath-day, was forbidden by a tradition of the elders: if so, our Lord might use this method of opening the man's eyes, as a protest against their absurd and frivolous traditions. (*Marg. Ref.* t.—*Note,* vii. 19—24.)

V. 15, 16.—*Division.* (16) The council was divided into two parties, which contended with each other, continuing in the same place. It is probable, that

sight. He said unto them, He put
clay upon mine eyes, and I washed,
and do see.

16 Therefore said some of the Pharisees, [x] This man is not of God, because he keepeth not the sabbath-day.
Others said, How can a man that is a
sinner do such miracles? [y] And there
was a division among them.

17 They say unto the blind man
again, What sayest thou of him, that
he hath opened thine eyes? He said,
[z] He is a prophet.

18 But the [a] Jews did not believe
concerning him, that he had been
blind, and received his sight, until
they called the parents of him that had
received his sight.

19 And they asked them, saying,
[b] Is this your son, who ye say was born
blind? how then doth he now see?

20 His parents answered them, and
said, We know that this is our son,
and that he was born blind:

21 But by what means he now
seeth, we know not; or who hath
opened his eyes, we know not: he is
of age, ask him; he shall speak for
himself.

22 These *words* spake his parents,
[c] because they feared the Jews: for the
Jews had agreed already, that if any
man did confess that he was Christ,
[d] he should be put out of the synagogue.

23 Therefore said his parents, [e] He
is of age, ask him.

24 Then again called they the man
that was blind, and said unto him,
[f] Give God the praise: [g] we know that
this man is [h] a sinner.

25 He answered and said, Whether
he be a sinner or no, I know not: [i] one
thing I know, that, whereas I was
blind, now I see.

26 Then said they to him again,
What did he to thee? how opened he
thine eyes?

27 He answered them, [k] I have told
you already, and ye did not hear:
wherefore would ye hear it again? will
ye also be his disciples?

Nicodemus and Joseph of Arimathea, with some others
who privately favoured our Lord, embraced this opportunity of checking the violent proceedings of his
enemies.

Division. (16) Σχισμα. See on vii. 43.

V. 17. (*Marg. Ref.*) ' What opinion of him hath this
' work of power and mercy to thee wrought in thee?'
Hammond.

V. 18—23. *Marg. Ref.* a—c.—*Was Christ.* (22)
' Hence it appears, that though our Lord was cautious of
' professing himself to be the Christ, in express terms, yet
' many understood the intimations he gave; and that most
' of his disciples, by this time, declared their faith in him
' under that character. It also farther appears from hence
' that the parents, and indeed the Sanhedrim, knew who
' it was that opened this man's eyes; though he himself
' was hitherto a stranger to him, and was not yet ac-
' quainted with the dignity of his person. (25. 36.) ' *Doddridge.—Should be put out,* &c.] (*Marg. Ref.* d.) Expulsion from the synagogue was a sort of excommunication, attended with many civil penalties and inconveniences.—We may *account* for the reserve of the man's parents, and their declining to say any thing, which might
bring them into danger of so heavy a punishment; but
their conduct cannot be excused, considering the evidence, which they had
of his power to protect them and do them good.

He is of age. (21) Αυτος ἡλικιαν εχει. 23. See on *Matt.* vi.
27.—*Had agreed.* (22) Συνετεθειντο. *Luke* xxii. 5. *Acts*
xxiii. 20. xxiv. 9.—1 *Sam.* xxii. 13. *Sept.—He should be
put out of the synagogue.*] Αποσυναγωγος γενηται. xii. 42.

xvi. 2.—' *Illum, cui conventibus religiosis in templo et syna-
' gogis interesse non licebat, quem unusquisque ceu pestem
' fugiebat, ut qdeo ab hominum consortio plane exclusus est.'*
Schleusner.

V. 24, 25. Some understand the Pharisees to have
meant, that the man ought to give glory to God, by confessing the collusion, which they supposed to have been
a real miracle; (*Note, Josh.* vii. 19;) for they knew, as they
pretended, that Jesus was " a sinner;" that is, one guilty
of gross violations of the law, and a false prophet. It is
however probable, that, unable to deny the miracle, they
meant to say, ' As by some unknown means God has given
thee sight, render him the praise, without regarding Jesus,
who has nothing to do with the credit of the cure.' But
the man observed, that if Jesus was a sinner, he had no
knowledge of it; and he was fully assured that having
been blind from his birth, he could at present see, and had
obtained sight by attending to his directions. (*Marg. Ref.*
—*Note, Is.* lxvi. 5, 6.)

A sinner. (24) Ἁμαρτωλος. 25. 31. (*Note, Luke* xv.
1, 2.)

V. 26—34. The man, on being again interrogated to
the same effect as before, (10—12,) perceived that the
Pharisees wanted to draw from him some expression, apparently inconsistent with his former testimony; and he
was filled with an honest indignation at their excessive
malice and perverseness: he therefore answered in a manner,
which implied that they could have no good motive for
such repeated questions, unless they were at length disposed to become the disciples of Jesus. Exasperated by

3 Y 6

28 Then ¹ they reviled him, and said, Thou art his disciple; ᵐ but we are Moses's disciples.

29 We ⁿ know that God spake unto Moses: ° as for this *fellow*, ᵖ we know not from whence he is.

30 The man answered and said unto them, Why, ᑫ herein is a marvellous thing, that ye know not from whence he is, ʳ and *yet* he hath opened mine eyes.

31 Now ˢ we know that God heareth not sinners; but if any man be a worshipper of God, ᵗ and doeth his will, ᵘ him he heareth.

32 Since ˣ the world began was it not heard, that any man opened the eyes of one that was born blind.

33 If this man ʸ were not of God, he could do nothing.

34 They answered and said unto him, Thou ᶻ wast altogether born in sins, ᵃ and dost thou teach us? ᵇ And they ᶜ cast him out.

35 Jesus heard that they had cast him out: ᶜ and when he had found him, he said unto him, ᵈ Dost thou believe on ᵉ the Son of God?

36 He answered and said, ᶠ Who is he, Lord, that I might believe on him?

37 And Jesus said unto him, ᵍ Thou hast both seen him, and it is he that talketh with thee.

---

this intimation, which appeared to them rude and insolent, they reviled him as a worthless person, and as the disciple of Jesus, along with others of the ignorant multitude; while they gloried in being the disciples of Moses. (*Marg. Ref.* k—m.—*Note*, v. 45—47. vii. 40—53.) They declared themselves fully assured that Moses spake by authority from God; but they asserted, that they had no evidence whence Jesus was, whom they considered as an impostor of obscure birth and education. Thus they insinuated that the doctrine of Jesus contradicted that of Moses, whereas in fact it established and completed it: and they considered the miracles wrought by Moses, nearly fifteen hundred years before, as undeniable evidences of his divine mission; whereas they treated those of Jesus, which were far more numerous and beneficent, and at least equally astonishing, as unworthy of their notice, though they fell under the cognizance of their own senses! In fact Moses was dead; and they had learned how to explain away his meaning, and to render his writings subservient to their own ambition and interest: whereas Jesus was a living reprover of their hypocrisy, and a formidable rival and adversary to their reputation and authority. (*Note*, *Matt*. xxiii. 29—33.) The man therefore, under all his disadvantages, being free from their prejudices, argued far more conclusively than they. He exposed their obstinate and prejudiced ignorance, by expressing the greatest astonishment, that they could doubt whence that person was, who had wrought such a miracle as had never before been heard of. (*Note*, 4—7.) God did not regard the prayers of notoriously wicked men; much less would he enable an impostor to work so stupendous a miracle, in confirmation of his doctrine: so that if Jesus had not been of God, he could not have done any thing of this kind. (*Marg. Ref.* n—y.—*Notes*, *Deut*. xiii. 1—5. *Matt*. xii. 22 —30.)—This argument, which it was impossible to answer, and which convicted them of malice and folly, excited their most indignant resentment: and, being ignorant of the *scriptural* doctrine, that *all men are born in sin*, they considered the bodily blindness of the man, as a demonstration, that he came into the world under the divine displeasure, and far more depraved than other men; (*Note*, 1—3.) and was it proper that so base and ignorant a wretch should presume to instruct them, who were Pharisees, Scribes, and Rulers assembled in council? Or could such insolence be endured? Thus they disdainfully closed their ears to the truth, and excommunicated the man for his honest and sensible observation. (*Marg.* and *Marg. Ref.* z—b.—*Notes*, 19—23. xii. 42, 43. xvi. 1—3.) —' See here a blind man, and unlearned, judging more ' rightly of divine things, than the whole learned council ' of the Pharisees! Whence we learn, that we are not ' always to be led by the authority of councils, popes, ' and bishops; and that it is not absurd for laymen some- ' times to vary from their opinions.' *Whitby.* (*Note*, *Luke* 54—57, v. 57.)

Wherefore would ye. (27) Τι ... θελίτε.—*Will ye be*, &c.] Θελετε ... γινεσθαι. " Are ye willing to become."—*They reviled.* (28) Ελοιδορησαν. *Acts* xxiii. 4. 1 *Cor*. iv. 12. 1 *Pet*. ii. 23. Λοιδορος, 1 *Cor*. v. 11. vi. 10. Λοιδορια, 1 *Tim*. v. 14. 1 *Pet*. iii. 9.—*A worshipper of God.* (31) Θεοσεβης. Here only N. T.—*Ex*. xviii. 21. *Job* i. 1. 8. ii. 3. *Sept*. Θεοσεβεια, 1 *Tim*. ii. 10. Ex Θεος et σεβω, colo.—*Since the world began.* (32) Εκ τε αιωνος.—The same as απο τε αιωνος. *Luke* i. 70. *Acts* xv. 18.—*Ps*. xc. 2. *Sept*.—*They cast ... out.* (34) Εξεβαλον ... εξω. 35. *Luke* iv. 29. vi. 22.

V. 35—38. ' The condition of those persons is very ' happy, who are thrust out to the greatest distance by im- ' pious persons, (glorying in the name of the church,) ' that Christ himself may approach still nearer to them.' *Beza.* (*Notes*, *Is*. lxvi. 5, 6. *Matt*. v. 10—12. *Luke* vi. 21—23. *Acts* v. 41, 42. 1 *Pet*. iv. 12—16.)—Jesus, knowing what persecution the man endured on his account, found him out, and made himself known to him as " the " Son of God," in order to his further instruction and encouragement; and he, who before considered him as a prophet, now believed in and worshipped him in a far higher character. (*Marg. Ref.* c—h.—*Notes*, i. 47—51, v. 49. iii. 16. iv. 25, 26. vi. 66—71. xx. 24—31.) Without

38 And he said, ᵇ Lord, I believe. And he worshipped him.

39 ¶ And Jesus said, ⁱ For judgment I am come into this world; ᵏ that they which see not might see, and that they which see ˡ might be made blind.

40 And some of the Pharisees which were with him heard these words, and said unto him, ᵐ Are we blind also?

41 Jesus said unto them, ⁿ If ye were blind, ye should have no sin: but now ye say, We see; therefore your sin remaineth.

b xx. 28. Ps. ii. 11. xlv.11. Matt. xiv. 33. xxviii. 9,17. Luke xxiv. 52. Rev. v. 9—14. i lii. 17. v. 22. 27. viii. 15, 16. xii. 47, 48. Jer. i. 9, 10. Luke ii. 34. xiii. 30. 2 Cor. ii. 16. k 25, 26—35. viii. 12. Matt. xi. 5. Luke i. 79. iv. 18. vii. 21. Acts xxvi. 18. 2 Cor. iv. 4—6. Eph. v. 14. l xii. 40, 41. Is. vi. 9, 10. xxix. 10. xlii. 18—20. xliv. 18. Matt. vi. 23. xiii. 13—15. Luke xi. 34, 35. Rom. xi. 7—10. 2 Thes. ii. 10—12. 1 John ii. 11.

m 34. vii. 47—52. Matt. xv. 12—14. xxiii. 16, 17. 19. 24. 26. Luke vi. 39. 40. 41, 44, 45. Rom. ii. 19—22. n xv. 22—24. Prov. xxvi. 12. Is. v. 20, 21. Jer. ii. 35. Luke xii. 47. Heb. x. 26, 27. 1 John i. 8—10.

doubt the worship, which Jesus accepted from him, was at least equal to that which apostles and angels decidedly refused. (*Notes, Acts* x. 24—26. *Rev.* xix. 9, 10. xxii. 8, 9.)

V. 39—41. The preceding address of our Lord to the man might be private; but what here follows must have been more open: for he declared in the hearing of the Pharisees, that, though in secular matters he would not judge or inflict punishment, yet he came into the world on purpose to discover men's secret characters, and to execute spiritual judgment on specious hypocrites. (*Notes, viii.* 13—16, v. 15. *Luke* ii. 33—35.) As, by his miraculous power, the blind received their sight; so, by his doctrine, the poor, the ignorant, and the simple of the Jews, and even the benighted gentiles, would be made wise and discerning in the things of God: and at the same time, those who were proud of their superior knowledge, learning, and wisdom, and most renowned in this respect, would be shewn to be blind in spiritual things, and would have their eyes *judicially* closed. (*Note, Matt.* xi. 25, 26.)—The Pharisees readily perceived that this referred to them; and therefore they disdainfully enquired, whether he meant to insinuate that they were blind also. (*Marg. Ref.* i—l.—*Notes, Luke* xi. 45—48.) To this he replied, that if they had been really blind or ignorant, by misfortune, or through want of capacity or opportunity of instruction; they would comparatively have been free from guilt in their pertinacious opposition to him: but their abundant opportunities, and their high conceit of their own knowledge and discernment, while they wilfully shut their eyes against the light, would leave them without excuse, under the guilt and power of their aggravated wickedness, and under the heavy wrath of God. (*Marg. Ref.* m, n.—*Note,* xv. 22—25.)

PRACTICAL OBSERVATIONS.
V. 1—12.

It becomes us to be very cautious how we ascribe the personal or relative calamities of others to their peculiar sinfulness: (*Notes, Job* ii. 12, 13. iv. 1. *Luke* xiii. 1—5 :) for the Lord may have far other reasons for afflicting them; and those whom he most loves are often long and sharply tried, in order to the display of his grace in supporting and delivering them. But we can never do wrong in applying to Jesus to solve our difficulties; for he is "the Light of the world," from whom we must derive all our knowledge and instruction in the great concerns of eternity. —Let us also learn to copy his perseverance in doing good, amidst discouragements, revilings, and injuries: and let every one seize the present hour, to ensure his own salvation, and to do the work of God; remembering how speedily "the night cometh in which no man can work." (*Note, Ec.* ix. 10.)—Those who confide in their own under-

standings and reasonings, and "trust in their own hearts," are incompetent judges of the Lord's works and ways; for he generally employs such means and instruments as men despise: thus the captious and scornful exclude themselves; while the humble believe, obey, and obtain the blessing.—Those calamities, which are generally thought to be tokens of the divine displeasure, and inseparable from misery, often prove the occasions of special good, and evidences of the Lord's distinguishing favour. The man born blind rejoices, and will rejoice for ever, in having, by means of that heavy affliction, been brought to know and love the holy Jesus; in the honour of his beloved Saviour, which was thus displayed; and in the important benefits, which multitudes, in every subsequent age, have derived from the instructive narrative.—But, on the other hand, what numbers make so perverse and mischievous a use of their limbs, senses, and faculties, even to the end of life; that they might desperately wish for ever, they had been born, and lived all their days, blind, deaf, dumb, lame, nay even idiots or lunaticks!—They whose eyes are opened, and whose hearts are cleansed, by his effectual grace, are the *same men*, yet "new creatures;" and, being known in the *identity* of their persons, and the *newness* of their characters, they live monuments to the Redeemer's glory, and continually recommend his grace to all who desire the same precious salvation. (*P. O. Mark* v. 14—29. *Note, 2 Cor.* v. 17.)

V. 13—23.

How perfect in wisdom and holiness was our Redeemer, when enemies, powerful, sagacious, vigilant, and malignant, as his were, could find no flaw, and were driven to the necessity of renewing against him the repeatedly refuted charge of breaking the sabbath! May we thus be enabled "by well-doing to put to silence the ignorance of "foolish men." (*Note,* 1 *Pet.* ii. 13—17.)—The most illiterate and poor, who are simple-hearted, readily draw proper conclusions from the evidences afforded them of the truth of the gospel: but they whose interests and inclination lie another way, though "ever learning, are "never able to come to the knowledge of the truth."—Religious persecutions can only render men cowards or hypocrites, and suppress investigation, or an avowal of sentiments: and even the censures of the church have too often been levelled against her best friends. But no terror should induce us to conceal our obligations to the Lord: and what men generally term *prudence* and caution,.in this case, is unbelief, ingratitude, and base fear of reproach: and the cross; if not being fatally ashamed of Christ and his cause. (*Note, Mark* viii. 38.)

V. 24—41.

It has often happened, that they profess most zeal for

CHAP. X.

True shepherds enter in by the Door of the sheep-fold, are acknowledged by the sheep, and go before them; being thus distinguished from dishonest and corrupt teachers, 1—8. Christ is the Door, and " the " good Shepherd, who lays down his life for the " sheep," 9—18. Divers opinions are held concerning him, 19—21. He proves his mission by his works; shews the character of his sheep, to whom " he gives eternal life, neither shall any pluck them " out of his hands;" and that " he and the Father are " one," 22—30. The Jews attempt to stone him as a blasphemer; but he justifies his doctrine, and escapes from them, 31—39. He goes beyond Jordan, where many believe on him, 40—42.

VERILY, [a] verily, I say unto you, He that entereth not by the door into the sheep-fold, but climbeth up some

other way, [c] the same is a thief and a robber.

2 But [d] he that entereth in by the door, is [e] the shepherd of the sheep.

3 To him [f] the porter openeth; [f] and the sheep hear his voice: [h] and he calleth his own sheep by name, [i] and leadeth them out.

4 And when he putteth forth his own sheep, [k] he goeth before them, and the sheep follow him: [l] for they know his voice.

5 And [m] a stranger will they not follow, but will flee from him: for they know not the voice of strangers.

the glory of God, who are most assiduous in dishonouring Christ: " but he that honoureth not the Son, honoureth " not the Father that sent him."—When a believer knows not how to answer the objections and arguments of enemies to the truth, he may have recourse to his own experience: " one thing he knows, that whereas he was blind, " now he sees; " and what he has discovered of the glory of God, the evil of sin, the depravity of his own heart, the preciousness of Christ, the beauty of holiness, so evinces to him the truth of the gospel, that no arguments can answer " this witness in himself." (Notes, 2 Pet. i. 19. 1 John v. 9, 10.)—How little ought we to regard the contempt and revilings of the scornful and unbelieving, though most eminent among men; when the holy Jesus was reviled by a convention of Jewish priests and rulers, as a notorious sinner, and " the Lord of glory" was disdained as most base and contemptible! But how unbecoming are such revilings, especially in those who are of superior rank and education!—Plain unlettered sense will commonly go further, in understanding the most important matters, than all the advantages of science, which often render men too self-sufficient to judge aright.—Our God, who heareth the repenting sinner's cry, will not regard those, who go on still in their wickedness: (Note, Ps. lxvi. 18, 19:) but when we desire and aim to do his will, he answers our prayers, and employs us in his service.—When arguments fail pertinacious disputers, they commonly have recourse to railing and abusive language: and many shew their pride and folly, by refusing to hear sober sense and sound argument from their supposed inferiors, and by answering them with contempt and upbraidings. But Jesus will shew himself peculiarly attentive to those, who are suffering for his sake: those who act conscientiously and boldly, according to their present measure of knowledge, shall be led forward; and the more they know of Christ, the greater honour they will render to him. (Notes, Hos. vi. 1—3, v. 3.) Thus the Lord gives eyes to the blind, and closes the minds of haughty boasters. Conscious humble ignorance dwells nearer the porch of wisdom, than arrogant genius and science. If a man be " wise in his own conceit,

" there is more hope of a fool than of him:" and none are in more danger than such as exclaim, " Are we blind " also ? " For numbers of this character will perish under the aggravated guilt of " loving darkness and hating the " light, because their deeds are evil." (Notes, iii. 19—21. Is. viii. 20.)

NOTES.

CHAP. X. V. 1—5. This parable is evidently a continuation of the former chapter: and therefore the false teachers of the Jews, whether Pharisees, scribes, or priests, were primarily intended, by " the thieves and rob-" bers ; " but not exclusively. From Jesus " the Light of " the world," all who are instrumental in illuminating mankind derive their light: and in like manner all true pastors, derive their authority from him, as " the chief " Shepherd." (Notes, Ps. xxiii. lxxx. 1. Is. xl. 9—11. Ez. xxxiv. Zech. xiii. 7. 1 Pet. v. 1—4.) Even before his appearance in the flesh, all the faithful teachers of God's people testified of him, and directed the people to expect salvation, by faith in the Redeemer who was to come. (Notes, v. 39—47. 1 Pet. i. 10—12. Rev. xix. 9, 10, v. 10.) When he was on earth, the priests and scribes, if they had been such shepherds as God approved, would have imitated John the Baptist, and borne testimony to him as " the Son of God," and the Saviour of men. So that in every age of the church a regard to Christ, as the Source of authority, and the Subject and Object of their ministry, has been the grand criterion of faithful pastors.—The priests and scribes demanded of Jesus, by what authority he acted: supposing that he ought to have taken out a commission from them; (Note, Matt. xxi. 23—27 ;) but he here plainly shewed, that they were deceivers, who had received no commission or instructions from him, the great Shepherd and Proprietor of the flock : yet the priests held their office by divine institution; and the Scribes and Pharisees were the acknowledged teachers of the people; though it is doubtful whether they were, by any divine appointment, set apart to that office. (Note, Matt. xxiii. 1—4.) Christ himself, however, is " the Door," by

3 Z

b vi. 5?. 60. vii. 34. viii. 27. 43. Ps. lxxxii. 5. cvi. 7. Prov. xxviii. 5. ix. vi. x. 10. lvi. 11. Dan. xii. 10. Matt. xiii. 13. 14. 51. 1 Cor. ii. 14. 1 J°hn v. 20. e l. 9. xix. 6. Eph. ii. 18. Heb. x. 19—22. p Ps. lxxiii. 13. xcv. 7. c. 3. Is. liii. 6. Ez. xxxiv. 31. Luke xv. 4—6.

6 This parable spake Jesus unto them: but they understood not what things they were which he spake unto them.

7 Then said Jesus unto them again, Verily, verily, I say unto you, I am the Door of the sheep.

q See on 1—14. lvi. 10—12. Ez. xxii. 25—29. xxxiv. 2—4. Zeph. iii. 3, 4. Zech. xi. 4—5. 16, 17. Acts v. 36, 37. r b. 27. l. 7. xiv. 6. Rom. v. 1, 2. Eph. ii. 18. Heb. x. 19—22. s Ps. xxiii. 1—6 lxxx. 1—3. xcv. 7. c. 3. 4. Is. xl. 11. xlix. 9, 10. Ez. xxxiv. 12—16. Zech. x. 12.

8 All that ever came before me, are thieves and robbers: but the sheep did not hear them.

9 I am the Door: by me if any man enter in, he shall be saved, and shall go in and out, and find pasture.

whom all true pastors enter into the church, to exercise their function (9). They believe in him for their own salvation, and receive from him those peculiar dispositions and endowments, which fit them for their work : and they aim to glorify him and to do good to souls; preferring this service to more creditable and lucrative employments, and prepared to suffer hardship of every kind in performing it. Thus they " enter by the Door into the sheepfold " (7) : but all, who intrude into the pastoral office without these views, dispositions, and purposes, (which are so blinded by... no such credentials from Christ, that he has sent the man who possesses them,) " climb up by some other way; " perverting human appointments, though good in themselves, and even divine institutions, in rendering them subservient to their love of ease, wealth, authority, or reputation; and employing the influence of rich and powerful connexions, or that acquired by natural abilities and human learning, as a passport into stations in the church, for which they have not one correspondent disposition or holy qualification. Such men, like the priests, scribes, and Pharisees, in our Lord's time, " are thieves and robbers," who enter the fold in an unauthorized manner, who fleece or butcher, not to feed, the flock; who rob Christ of his honour, and starve the souls of his people, in order to enrich themselves and aggrandize their families, by that which was entrusted to them, to be employed in acts of piety, hospitality, and charity; and for the use of which they are responsible to God. But to them, who enter with a due regard to Christ, and with proper endowments, desires, and intentions, " the Porter openeth; " that is, God, in his providence and by his Spirit, makes way for them successfully to exercise their ministry: and " the sheep of " Christ," his chosen flock, (Notes, 14—18. 26—31. Luke xii. 32,) " hear their voice " and receive the truth from them. And, as in those eastern regions, the sheep, when led forth from the fold to the pasture, follow the shepherd, when they hear his well-known voice, and see him going before them; so these pastors get acquainted with the people committed to their care, and lead them by their instructions into the knowledge of the truth, and into the ways of peace and holiness: they walk before them by their example; and the people follow them with confidence, as they know and experience their doctrine to be good, and their exhortations salutary. But the sheep will not follow those who are strangers to them, to Christ, and to his truth; but will flee from them, fearing lest they should be deceived, and not finding their doctrine suited to their wants and experience, or level to their capacities; and they will seek food for their souls elsewhere. (Marg. Ref.— Note and P. O. Is. lvi. 9—12.—Notes, Jer. xxiii. 1—6. Ez. xxxiv. 2—10. 17—22. P. O. 1—22.—Notes, Zech. xi. 4—11. P. O. 1—11.—Notes, Matt. ix. 36—38. x. 5, 6.)

The sheep-fold. (1) Αυλην των προβατων. 16. Here only

in this sense N. T. Επαυλις, Num. xxxii. 16. 24. 36. Some other way.] Αλλαχοθεν. Here only.—The porter. (3) Ο θυρωρος. See on Mark xiii. 34.—A stranger. (5) Αλλοτριῳ. Matt. xvii. 25. Luke xvi. 12. Acts vii. 6. Rom. xiv. 4. xv. 20. 2 Cor. x. 15, 16. 1 Tim. v. 22. Heb. xi. 34.

V. 6—9. Our Lord evidently meant, by the preceding parable, to expose the ignorant, mercenary, and oppressive rulers and teachers of the Jewish church, and to contrast their character with that of faithful pastors : but the Pharisees and others concerned were so blinded by the prejudice and pride, that they did not understand the drift of his discourse. He was therefore pleased to explain himself more fully, by solemnly assuring them, that he was " the " Door of the sheep." No man ever entered into the true church except by faith in him ; though many others have been externally admitted into the visible church : in like manner, no man ever was a true minister of religion, who was not commissioned and instructed by Christ ; though many have a regular external appointment to the office, who are strangers to him, and pay no suitable regard to him, and whom he does not accept.—By those " who came before him," we must not understand those prophets or faithful teachers, who came before his incarnation ; for these acted by his authority, and were his representatives : but ' all that came under pretence of being their ' King, or their Messiah, as Theudas.' Whitby. Or, all those, who set up themselves above him or against him ; who taught other methods of salvation, and presumed to intrude into his office, and to acquire that authority over the people, which belonged to him only : in short, all such persons, as the hypocritical and ambitious Scribes and Pharisees, who had, before Christ's coming, usurped an absolute dominion over the people's consciences; and when he came, used their influence to oppose and persecute him and his followers. These were, and all such ever have been and are, " thieves and robbers." (Marg. Ref. o—r.) Mankind indeed generally shew some regard to them; but, the remnant of God's chosen people, " the sheep of " Christ," have always turned from them as deceivers. Indeed, as every sinner must enter by " Christ the Door " into the sheep-fold" for safety and sustenance ; how can those be qualified to teach the way of salvation, who are themselves strangers to him, and have never " entered by " the Door into" the ministry, but have " climbed up " some other way ? " All men, whatever be their rank, employment, or character, who have not, by faith in Christ, as the divine Saviour of sinners, passed " from " death unto life," from condemnation and alienation from God, into a state of acceptance, and a life of communion with him, and devoted obedience to him, are still in " the " broad road to destruction." That repentance and conversion, by which men pass, as through " a strait gate,"

3 x 2

10 The "thief cometh not, but for to steal, and to kill, and to destroy: ˣ I am come that they might have life, and that they might have it ʸ more abundantly.

11 I am ᶻ the good Shepherd: the good Shepherd ᵃ giveth his life for the sheep.

12 But ᵇ he that is an hireling, and not the shepherd, whose own the sheep are not, seeth ᶜ the wolf coming, and leaveth the sheep, and fleeth: and the wolf catcheth them, and scattereth the sheep.

13 The hireling fleeth, because he is an hireling, ᵈ and careth not for the sheep.

14 I am ᵉ the good Shepherd, ᶠ and know my *sheep*, ᵍ and am known of mine.

15 As ʰ the Father knoweth me, even so know I the Father : ⁱ and I lay down my life for the sheep.

16 And ᵏ other sheep I have, which are not of this fold : ˡ them also I must bring, ᵐ and they shall hear my voice;

---

from the broad to the narrow way, have special respect to Christ, in all his characters and offices; and every motive and encouragement of those who enter is derived from him. (*Notes, Matt.* vii. 13—20.) Thus men are translated from the kingdom of Satan into the true " church of " the first-born :" (*Notes, Col.* i. 9—14, *vv.* 13, 14. *Heb.* xii. 22—25 :) then they become like the sheep under the tender shepherd's care, which at night are led into the fold, to rest secure from robbers and beasts of prey, and by day are guided to the pasture to feed in quietness and plenty; and find repose, safety, provision, and consolation to their souls, by faith in the good Shepherd's power, truth, and love. (*Marg Ref.* s, t.—*Notes, Ps.* xxiii. 1—3. *Is.* xl. 9—11, v. 11. *Luke* xv. 3—7. 1 *Pet.* ii. 18—25, v. 25.)

Pasture. (9) Νομη. 2 *Tim.* ii. 17. Not elsewhere N. T.—*Gen.* xlvii. 4. 1 *Chr.* iv. 39. *Ps.* lxxiv. 1. *Sept.*

V. 1—13. The transition from viewing Christ, as the Door both of the pastors and the sheep, to the consideration of him " as the good Shepherd," should be carefully noted; because it excludes that confusion of metaphors, which arise from viewing him, at once, as the Door by which the shepherd enters, and yet himself " the good " Shepherd."—Our Lord indeed uses both these figures, in shewing his own authority, and his relation to the sheepfold; yet he does not assume both at once : but, having spoken of himself, as the Door of admission, into the church and into the ministry, he here proceeds to speak of himself as the great and " good Shepherd;" even that Redeemer who had been so often foretold under that character. (*Marg. Ref.* z.—*Notes, Is.* xl. 9—11, v. 11. *Ex.* xxxiv. 23—31. xxxvii. 24—28. *Mic.* v. 1—4.)—The false teachers, before described, sought admission into the church, only that they might enrich and advance themselves; or gratify their pride, ambition, and resentment, by domineering over the people, and persecuting such as refused subjection : (*Marg. Ref.* u.—*Notes,* 1—5. *Ex.* xxxiv. 2—10 :) but Jesus came into the world, that sinners might have spiritual and eternal life through him; that these blessings might be conferred upon them most liberally; and with all possible advantages, even abundantly, and by a surer tenure than that by which the first Adam possessed divine life before the fall; and that the divine life thus communicated might be maintained and continually increased, till perfected in everlasting felicity. (*Marg. Ref.* x, y.—*Notes,* iv. 10—15. *Rom.* v. 12—21.) For " the second Adam," " the Lord from heaven," is the " good Shepherd," eminently and exclusively : from him all pious and useful rulers and teachers derive their authority and ability : him they represent as their Principal ; and resemble him, in proportion to their fidelity, diligence, love, and zeal : but compared with him they are mean, defective, and defiled, and their *goodness* is not only derived, but scanty, and even as nothing. Yet, great and good, just and holy, as he is, he saw his sheep about to perish in their wanderings from God ; and in order to expiate their guilt, and to ransom them from destruction, he not only endured hardship and encountered danger, but he " laid down his life for them," and in their stead ! According to this example, his faithful servants, constrained by love to him and to his ransomed flock, are ready to venture and suffer for their benefit. (*Marg. Ref.* a.— *Notes, Gen.* xxxi. 40. 1 *Sam.* xvii. 34—37. 2 *Sam.* xxiv. 17. *Is.* liii. 4—6. *Zech.* xiii. 7. *Heb.* xiii. 20, 21.) On the contrary, the hireling, to whom the ministry is a mere lucrative trade, not having any real regard to the welfare of the flock, (being like a hired shepherd who regards nothing except his wages,) flees away to secure himself when danger arises, and leaves the people to be misled by seducers or destroyed by persecutors, without giving himself any concern about them. (*Marg. Ref.* b—d.—*Notes, Is.* lvi. 9—12. *Acts* xx. 28—31.)

Giveth his life. (11) Την ψυχην αυτα τιθησιν. " Layeth " down his life." 15. xiii. 37. xv. 13. 1 *John* iii. 16.— *An hireling.* (12) 'Ο μισθωτος. 13. · *Mark* i. 20. Not elsewhere N. T. *Ex.* xii. 45. xxii. 15. *Sept.* Α μισθος, *merces.* He is not *a hireling*, who, faithfully feeding the flock, is maintained by his ministry ; but he to whom the filthy lucre is the great object or inducement. (*Notes,* 1 *Cor.* ix. 7—12. 1 *Tim.* v. 17, 18.)—*Careth not.* (13) Ου μελει αυτη. xii. 6. *Matt.* xxii. 16. *Mark* iv. 38. xii. 14. *Luke* x. 40. *Acts* xviii. 17. 1 *Cor.* ix. 9. 1 *Pet.* v. 7.

V. 14—18. Our Lord again avowed himself to be " the good Shepherd," which has been shewn to be a character appropriated to JEHOVAH, throughout the Old Testament. (*Notes, Ps.* xxiii. lxxx. 1.) " He knows his " sheep :" he distinguishes them from all others ; he values and approves of them ; and he knows their dangers,

[n] and there shall be one fold, *and* [o] one
Shepherd.
17 Therefore [p] doth my Father love
me, because I lay down my life, that I
might take it again.
18 No [q] man taketh it from me, [r] but
I lay it down of myself: I have power
to lay it down, and I have power to
take it again. [s] This commandment
have I received of my Father.
19 ¶ There [t] was a division therefore again among the Jews for these
sayings.
20 And many of them said, [u] He
hath a devil, and is mad; [x] why hear
ye him?

n Ex. xxxvii. 22. Eph. ii. 14. o 2. 11. Ec. xii. 11. Ez. xxxiv. 23. Heb. xiii. 20. 1 Pet. ii. 25. v. 4. p iii. 35. xv. 9, 10. xvii. 4, 5. 24—26. Is. xlii. 1. 21. liii. 10. q xviii. 5, 6. xix. 11. Matt. xxvi. 53—56. r ii. 19—21. Is. liii. 10—12. Acts ii. 24. iii. 15. Tit. ii. 14. Heb. ii. 9. 14, 15. s vi. 38. xiv. 31. xv. 10. Ps. xl. 6—8. Heb. v. 6—9. x. 6—10. t vii. 40—43. ix. 16. Matt. x. 34, 35. Luke xii. 51—56. Acts xiv. 4. xxiii. 7—10. 1 Cor. iii. 3. xi. 18. u vii. 20. viii. 48. 52. Matt. ix. 34. x. 25. Mark iii. 21. Acts xxvi. 24, 25. x vii. 46—52. viii. 47. ix. 28, 29. Is. liii. 3. Acts xviii. 14, 15. xxv. 19, 20. xxvi. 30—32.

difficulties, enemies, weaknesses, and wants: and again, "they know him," by faith and experience; they are so far acquainted with his perfections and offices, as to trust, love, submit to, and obey him. (*Marg. Ref.* f, g.—*Notes*, 26—31. xvii. 1—3. *Ps.* i. 4—6, *v.* 6. *Matt.* vii. 21—23. 2 *Tim.* i. 11, 12. ii. 19.) This mutual knowledge of each other in some degree resembles the knowledge which the Father has of the Son, and the Son of the Father: for it may be rendered, "even as the Father knoweth me, and "as I know the Father." (*Marg. Ref.* h.—*Note, Matt.* xi. 27.) In consequence of his knowledge and love of them, he was also determined to "lay down his life for "them" (11).—Hitherto he had spoken of his people, as of sheep already brought back to his fold; but he next spake of those, who were his by the election and donation of the Father; and especially such of them, as were to be collected from among the Gentiles. Even these were "his sheep," though at that time living in abominable idolatries and iniquities; and "not of that fold," of the commonwealth of Israel. (*Marg. Ref.* l.—*Notes*, xi. 49—53, *v.* 52. *Acts* xviii. 9—11.) In due time, however, through the ransom which he was about to pay for them, he would, by his word and Spirit, bring them forth, cause them to hear his voice, take them under his care, and unite them with the chosen remnant of Israel in one, under himself the one Shepherd and Overseer of their souls. (*Marg. Ref.* m—o.—*Notes, Rom.* xi. 1—6. 1 *Pet.* ii. 9, 10. 18—25.) Thus he plainly predicted the calling of the Gentiles; to shew the Jews, that, though they might continue to despise and reject him; yet he would assuredly have a ransomed flock worthy of so "good a Shepherd." (*Note, Is.* xlix. 5, 6.)—To this he added, that the Father loved him especially for this reason, because he was ready "to lay down his life, in order that he might take it again," to effect the purposes of his gracious undertaking; as this arose from his zeal for the divine glory, and regard to the honour of the holy law of God. But, though he was about to die, in the most cruel and ignominious manner by the hands of wicked men; yet none of them, nor any created being, could by any means take his life from him, against his will; but he would voluntarily lay it down for the ransom of his people. He had assumed human nature voluntarily, and free from pollution. His life was not forfeited by sin, and it was *his own*, so as no other person ever possessed life: he had therefore a right and power to dispose of it as he pleased; and he could, as he saw good, lay it down and then resume it: and so immense was his love to sinful man, that he chose to lay it down with most excruciating sufferings for his redemption! God indeed raised him from the dead, as he was *Man;* yet he rose by his own power as GOD, and as "One with the Father:" but he would exercise this power according to the commandment, which he had, in the capacity of Mediator, received from the Father.—A more decisive testimony to the Deity of our Lord cannot be conceived.—It is *impossible* that a dead man, if no more than man, can do any thing towards restoring himself to life: and even supposing the dead person to have a superior created nature, distinct from manhood; is raising the dead to life the work of an angel, an arch-angel, a created being, however exalted? or is it the work of Almighty God exclusively? And did not *God* raise Christ from the dead? And if he raised himself from the dead; is he not "God over all blessed "for evermore?" (*Marg. Ref.* q—s.—*Note*, ii. 18—22.)

I lay down my life for the sheep. (15) 'Nothing is more 'certain, than that Christ "gave himself a ransom for all." '(1 *Tim.* ii. 6. *Heb.* ii. 9. 1 *John* ii. 2. iii. 16, 17.) ... 'But because the world can no otherwise obtain this sal'vation, than by believing in him, and obeying the voice 'of this Shepherd; therefore he is said to do this more 'eminently for his sheep.' *Whitby.*—*Power.* (18) Εξουσιαν. i. 12. (*Note, Matt.* xxviii. 18.)

V. 19—21. The claims and intimations of the preceding discourse, were so contrary to the prejudices, and above the apprehensions, of many of the Jews; that they deemed them to be the incoherent language of insanity, or the suggestions of an evil spirit; and concluded that Jesus ought no longer to be heard as a publick teacher. (*Marg. Ref.* u, x.—*Notes*, vii. 19—24. viii. 48—53. xv. 17—21. *Matt.* x. 24—26.) But others, who yet probably did not fully understand the doctrine, perceiving that he spake with great propriety, gravity, affection, and consistency, were convinced that these were not like the sallies of a distracted or possessed person: and they enquired, whether a demon, or evil spirit, could possibly open the eyes of a man, who had been born blind. This Jesus had lately done; and this undeniable and unequalled miracle, so contrary to the malignity, as well as beyond the power of an evil spirit, as they rightly concluded, ought to induce more candour and caution in speaking of his doctrine, though very mysterious. (*Marg. Ref.* y.—*Notes, Matt.* ix. 34. xii. 22—30.) The Pharisees ascribed our Lord's miracles to diabolical powers; and modern Jews ascribe them all to enchantment. But these persons supposed it impossible that a demon should open the eyes of a blind man, or one born blind; and the same must be said of many of his other miracles, indeed of them all; but especially of his raising the dead, and commanding the winds and waves into a great calm.

A devil. (20) Δαιμονιον. 21. See on viii. 48.—*Is mad.*] Μαινεται. *Acts* xii. 15. xxvi. 24, 25. 1 *Cor.* xiv. 23.—*Of him that hath a devil.* (21) Δαιμονιζομενε. *Matt.* iv. 24. viii. 16. 28. 33. ix. 32. xii. 22. xv. 22. *Mark* i. 32. v. 15, 16. 18. *Luke* viii. 36.

21 Others said, These are not the words of him that hath a devil: ' can a devil open the eyes of the blind?

22 ¶ And it was at Jerusalem the feast of the dedication; and it was winter.

23 And Jesus walked in the temple ' in Solomon's porch.

24 Then came the Jews round about him, and said unto him, ' How long dost thou ' make us to doubt? ᵇ If thou be the Christ, tell us plainly.

25 Jesus answered them, ᶜ I told you, and ye believed not: ᵈ the works that I do in my Father's name, they bear witness of me:

26 But ye believe not; ᵉ because ye are not of my sheep, as I said unto you.

27 My ᶠ sheep hear my voice, ᵍ and I know them, ʰ and they follow me:

28 And ' I give unto them eternal life; ᵏ and they shall never perish, ' neither shall any pluck them out of my hand.

29 My Father, ᵐ which gave *them* me, ⁿ is greater than all; and none is able to pluck *them* out of my Father's hand.

30 ° I and *my* Father are one.

31 Then ᵖ the Jews took up stones again to stone him.

V. 22—24. "The feast of dedication" seems to have been appointed in the days of Judas Maccabeus, to be annually observed, in commemoration of the purification of the temple, after the persecutions and abominations of Antiochus Epiphanes. (1 *Mac.* iv. 56—59. 2 *Mac.* x. 5 —8.) It is indeed supposed to have been kept all over the land; yet numbers flocked to Jerusalem at that time: our Lord's going up, therefore, at that season must at least have been an intimation, that he did not disapprove of such memorials of special publick mercies, even when appointed by human authority. This was in the month of December; and the portico in which Jesus walked, (probably for shelter from the cold,) bare the name of Solomon; being perhaps situated in the place, where that prince had formerly erected a very splendid one. While he was there, the Jewish rulers came to him, complaining that he kept them in a very painful suspense, by speaking of himself as "the Light of the world," "the Door of "the sheep," "the good Shepherd, &c." and desiring to be told plainly, whether he was the Messiah, or not. (*Marg.* and *Marg. Ref.*) In fact they readily understood his meaning: but they could not form his words into a plausible charge against him before the Roman governor, as they could have done a more explicit declaration, that he was the promised Messiah.

The feast of the dedication. (22) Τα εγκαινια. Here only N. T. *Ezra* vi. 17. *Neh.* xii. 27.—*Dost thou make us to doubt.* (24) Την ψυχην ημων αιρεις. "Hold us in sus-"pense." *Marg. Lift up, or suspend, our soul.*

V. 25. "I said to you, and ye believed not, that the "works, which I do in my Father's name, these bear wit-"ness of me." Thus the verse may literally, and pro-bably ought to be, rendered; as referring to what Jesus had said before: (*Marg. Ref.—Notes,* v. 31—38:) for he had never expressly told them, that he was the Mes-siah.

V. 26—31. The true reason, why the Jews did not be-lieve in Jesus, was the want of that simple, teachable, and inoffensive temper, which characterized his sheep; for they were left to the pride and enmity of their carnal hearts. and therefore no evidence could convince them;

nor was there any proof, that they belonged to that chosen company before mentioned. On the contrary, his sheep, being taught and drawn of God, heard, believed, and obeyed his word: they were known and approved by him, and they followed him as his approved disciples. (*Marg. Ref.* e—h.—*Note,* 14—18. vi. 60—65.) To them he gave eternal life; nor should one of them perish to all eternity, through any outward temptation, or inward evil propensity; neither should Satan, or any enemy "pluck them out of "his hands: (*Note, Deut.* xxxiii. 3:) as "his Father who "gave them to him," (*Marg. Ref.* m, n.—*Note,* vi. 36— 40,) that he might ransom and save them, is greater than any and all the creatures in the universe, so that none can pluck them out of his almighty hands; and as he and "the Father are One," One Being; One in essence, will, and operation. (*Marg. Ref.* o.)—'The sheep of 'Christ are exposed to so great danger from the infernal 'lion, (1 *Pet.* v. 8,) that I doubt not, but this text most 'eminently refers to the care of their Shepherd to guard 'them from his assaults.' *Doddridge.* The conclusion, which our Lord drew from this declaration, that, being One with the omnipotent Father, he was able to defend his sheep against all enemies, sufficiently proves that he meant to claim divine power and perfection, equally with the Father who sent him. (*Notes,* v. 17, 18. xvii. 20, 21.) The Jews well understood the extent of his claim; and there-fore deeming it blasphemy, (as it certainly would have been in any mere man,) they prepared immediately to stone him; and *their* conduct forms a good exposition on *his* words.—The doctrine of the preservation of all true be-lievers, from every enemy, and through all dangers and temptations, to the full enjoyment of eternal life, is taught in these verses, with the greatest decision. "I give them "eternal life," "they shall never perish," or "not perish "for ever." Now, if any of them come short of eternal life, and actually and eternally perish, how can these tes-timonies be true, these engagements faithful? Will not the Saviour's words pass away? (*Note, Matt.* xxiv. 35.)— 'That is, through any defect on my part. ... Or Christ may 'speak here of sheep, *continuing so to the death.*' *Whitby* —This means that they shall not perish, except by their

q 2b 37. v. 10.
20. 36. Matt. xi.
5. Acts ii. 22. x.
36.

32 Jesus answered them, ' Many good works have I shewed you from my Father: ' for which of those works do ye stone me?

s Ps.-n. xiv. 4—
20—22. 1s
xxxv. 17 cix.
i. 5. Ec. iv. 4. 1 John iii. 12.

---

own fault. But if such a condition was implied, in this and similar scriptures, (which must be supposed by those, who deny the doctrine in question,) why is it never once hinted? (*Marg. Ref.* i—l.—*Notes*, v. 24—27. 1 Sam. ii. 9. *Ps.* xxxvii. 27, 28. cxxxviii. 8. *Is.* liv. 15—17. *Jer.* xxxii. 39—41.) In none of these texts is such a condition so much as hinted at; and in some of them, the danger arising from it, and our violating it, is expressly obviated. Can we then reasonably suppose, that a condition was every where implied, a condition of infinite importance to us; and yet that not the smallest intimation of it was given in any one of them? Could this be done by design? Or could it possibly be an oversight? Or was the case so obvious, that no caution or warning was at all requisite? It was indeed of considerable importance for our Lord, in his circumstances, to declare ' his ability and readiness to save all such, as should persevere in believing on him : ' but his words are calculated to convey far more than this assurance; and, ' persevere in believing ' must be *added* to them, before they can be limited to it. (*Notes*, *Deut.* iv. 2. *Prov.* xxx. 5, 6. *Rev.* xxii. 18—21.) And where is the confidence of a believer to be placed, that he shall ' persevere in believing?' Must he trust in the strength of his own resolution? on the constancy of his own will? on his experienced superiority to temptation? That is, shall he " trust in his own heart?" (*Notes*, *Prov.* xxviii. 26. *Jer.* xvii. 9, 10.) For his confidence, as to *perseverance to the end in believing*, must be placed, either on the truth, love, and power of Christ, and on the supposition that he has promised to preserve the true believer; or on his own heart, at least conjointly with Christ, if all the promises to this effect be *conditional*. On the other hand, if we have for a long time persevered in believing, ought we to take the credit of it to ourselves; or ought we to ascribe all the glory of it to the Lord alone?—When Adam fell, it was not *against his will*, or *without his own fault ;* yet he was overcome, enslaved, and ruined, and must have perished with all his race, had not Christ interposed: and could the true believer, though *by his own fault*, thus be plucked out of the hands of Christ, and finally perish; the enemy would triumph over the second Adam, in some respects, as he did over the first. (*Notes*, 1 *Cor.* xv. 45—49. *Col.* iii. 1—4, *vv.* 3, 4.) Indeed, there can be no sin, except where the will consents; or any conceivable way, by which our great enemy, or any of his servants, whether heretics, persecutors, or tempters of whatever description, can " pluck us out of Christ's hand," by an act of violence, or without our own fault. (*Notes*, *Rom.* viii. 28—39. *Jude* 22—25.) It is said, ' Where do we learn this, ' except from such passages as that under consideration?' In fact, we learn it, not so much from any particular text, as from the general tenour of scripture, and our own most obvious notions of right and wrong. Man had not fallen, had he not consented to the temptation ; though it had been possible to have forced the forbidden fruit on him.—When Satan " desired to have Peter to sift him as wheat," our Lord said, " I have prayed for thee, that thy faith fail not." (*Notes*, *Luke* xxii. 31—34, *v.* 32. 1 *Cor.* x. 13. 1 *Pet.* i. 2—

5.) His *perseverance in believing*, therefore, was ensured by Christ's intercession. The event was *certain :* but the exhortation to watch and pray was not superfluous ; for had Peter regarded it, he would have escaped unspeakable anguish. Now if Peter's *perseverance in believing* was secured by our Lord's intercession ; is it not most obvious, with such scriptures before us as that under consideration, to suppose that our *perseverance in believing* is secured in the same way ; and that we are assured of it by express promises, as he was? that is, provided we be true believers. The warnings and exhortations which many object to this doctrine, as if nugatory on the supposition that it is true, are of different sorts. Some are suited to stir up professed Christians to examine, whether they have the true faith or not. This may be distinguished from a dead faith, not only by its other fruits ; but by standing the trials, which cause many to fall away, " having no root in themselves."—" Continue in my word." " Abide in me." " He that " continueth to the end shall be saved." " That on the " good ground are they, which in an honest and good " heart, having heard the word, keep it, and bring forth " fruit with *patience*." (*Notes*, viii. 30—36, *v.* 31. xv. 1—8. *Matt.* xiii. 20—23. *Luke* viii. 4—15, *vv.* 14, 15. 1 *Pet.* i. 6, 7.) These guard the doctrine from perversion, and tend to exclude presumption. Others are suited to stir up believers to " give all diligence to make their calling and " election sure ;" and " to possess the full assurance of " hope unto the end : " that, knowing their own safety and happiness, they may be the more joyful, thankful, and cheerful, in self-denying services and sharp afflictions. (*Note*, 1 *Cor.* xv. 55—58.) There are also such warnings and exhortations as call them to the use of those means, by which it is the will of God to preserve them. Thus the apostle assured his companions in danger, " that there " should be no loss of any man's life : " yet he afterwards said, " Except these abide in the ship, ye cannot be " saved ;" for that was the method, in which it was the will of God to save them. (*Notes*, *Acts* xxvii. 20—32.) And others are intended to put believers on their guard against those temptations, which, if listened to, would not only greatly distress and injure them, but also hinder their usefulness, disgrace their profession, dishonour God, and do unspeakable evil to their brethren and neighbours. Indeed, though a man could be most fully assured, that he should not be killed by falling from a precipice; there might yet be sufficient reason, to warn him to *beware :* for broken bones, and various dreadful effects might follow, should he heedlessly fall down, though by a miracle his life should be preserved.—In fine, it cannot be said to be *impossible*, that Christ should engage, not only to take care of his sheep, while they persevere in believing ; but also to ensure their perseverance, and to secure them from final apostasy, or from dying impenitent and unbelieving. Now, can any man in the world possibly convey this meaning in clearer, and more determinate, and more emphatical language, than that contained in these verses, and the texts referred to ? But, if any be confident that the doctrine is of such a nature, that no words can prove it; do they not

33 The Jews answered him, saying, For a good work we stone thee not, ᵗ but for blasphemy; and because that thou, being a man, ᵘ makest thyself God.

34 Jesus answered them, Is it not written ᵛ in your law, ˣ I said, Ye are ʸ gods ?

35 If he called them gods, ᵗ unto whom the word of God came, and ᵃ the scripture cannot be broken ;

36 Say ye of him, ᵇ whom the Fa-

ther hath sanctified, ᶜ and sent into the world, Thou blasphemest; because I said, ᵈ I am the Son of God?

37 If ᵉ I do not the works of my Father, believe me not.

38 But if I do, though ye believe not me, ᶠ believe the works: ᵍ that ye may know and believe that the Father is in me, and I in him.

39 Therefore ʰ they sought again to take him: but he escaped out of their hand;

" lean to their own understandings," instead of simply crediting the word of God ?

Shall never perish. (28) Ου μη απολωνται εις τον αιωνα. IV. 14. vi. 51. viii. 52. xi. 26.—*Any.*] Τις—*None.* (29) Ουδεις. *Matt.* xi. 27. Any man...no man. Thus it stands in most modern copies, very improperly ; but the oldest copies have it, as it is here printed.—*Pluck.*] 'Αρπασει. 12. 29. vi. 15. *Matt.* xi. 12. xiii. 19, *et al.*—*Are one.* (30) 'Εν εσμεν. xvii. 11. 1 *Cor.* iii. 8. A noun must be understood in each of these places : here perhaps Θειον, *numen* ; in the others σωμα *corpus,* πραγμα *res, negotium.* ' That ' Christ speaks not here of an unity of will and concord ' only, appears, 1. From the reason assigned of the secu-' rity of the sheep : the want of power in any one to snatch ' them out of the hands of Christ, because, the Father being ' greater in power than all, his power could secure them ' from all ; and so could also Christ, he being one in power ' with the Father : for the foundation of this argument is ' not, that the Father's *will,* but that his *power* was above all. ' 2. From the inference of the Jews, that by these words ' " he made himself God," and so was guilty of blasphemy.' *Whitby.* (*Notes,* 32—39. 2 *Tim.* i. 11, 12. 1 *John* iv. 1—4.)

V. 32—39. When Jesus saw the violent conduct of the Jews, he calmly asked them, for which of the numerous and beneficent miracles, " which he had shewed them from " the Father," and wrought in proof of being sent from him, they were about to put him to death ? To this they replied, that it was not for " a good work, but for blas-" phemy," that they meant to stone him : as he, who was evidently a man, spoke as if he were the almighty God. This was a fair inference from his words, and he did not charge them with misrepresenting them. (*Marg. Ref.* q—t.) ' " Jesus," not judging it proper at that time, to bring ' the sublime doctrine of his Deity into further debate, ' " answered them," &c.' *Doddridge.* Viewing his answer in this light, we shall more readily understand it.—Magistrates are in scripture called " gods." (*Marg. Ref.* x—z.—*Notes, Ex.* iv. 16. vii. 1, 2. xxii. 28. *Ps.* lxxxii. l. 6, 7. cxxxviii. 1.) This is commonly explained of their *authority,* by which they were the representatives of God to the people : but the title is not expressly given to any except rulers m Israel, who were the delegates and types of the Messiah, the Lord and King of Israel from the beginning ; and on this account especially they were thus dignified. If then there was any propriety in calling them gods, " to whom the " word of God came," it must arise from their relation to the promised Messiah : and it had a meaning, which could

not be invalidated ; for " the scripture cannot be broken." They were " the LORD's anointed," as types of his great " anointed One :" had he not been *truly* God, they had not *typically* been called gods. What right therefore had the Jews to say to him, whom the Father had separated, and consecrated from the beginning, to be his anointed King upon his holy hill of Zion, and at length had sent into the world ; " Thou blasphemest," because he declared himself to be " the Son of God ?" The Messiah was evidently predicted under this title : (*Marg. Ref.* b. d.—*Notes, Ps.* ii. 7—12 :) Jesus was the Messiah ; and therefore " the " Son of God," and " One with the Father."—It is not to be supposed, that the Jews fully comprehended this reasoning, yet they understood more than they could answer. Nor would it follow from it, as it has been argued, that all who in scripture are called gods were types of Christ : for Satan who is called " the god of this world," and the idols of the Gentiles, were not *dignified* with this title, as the anointed rulers of Israel were ; but *exposed to* execration, as contemptible and hateful usurpers. It cannot be denied, that the most wicked of the high priests were types of Christ our great High Priest : why then should it be doubted, whether the wicked kings and rulers of Israel were types of Christ our King ?—To this our Lord added, that the Jews might have some reason for not believing him, if he did not the works of his Father, that is, such as evinced almighty power : but if he performed such works, though they disregarded his testimony, let them not despise his credentials ; or refuse to believe his union with the Father, and that mutual in-dwelling ot which he spake. (*Marg. Ref.* e—h.—*Notes,* 25. iii. 1, 2. v. 31—38. xiv. 7—14, *vv.* 10, 11.) This again excited the Jews to renew their attempts against him, as it confirmed their former inference from his words ; but he was pleased to evade their malice at that time also. ' When magistrates ' and judges are in scripture called gods, the Holy Ghost ' still addeth something, which excludes them from a true ' divinity ; as that " they shall die like men," (*Ps.* lxxxii. ' 6,) or they are " rulers of the people." (*Ex.* xxii. 28.) ' Whereas, when Christ is called God, it is either with ' some epithet belonging to the supreme God, as..." God ' " over all :" (*Rom.* ix. 5 :) ..." The great God ;" (*Tit.* ' ii. 13 ;)..." The true God :" (1 *John* v. 20 ;) or with ' addition of some operation proper to God, as when it is ' said " The Word was God, and all things were made by ' " him." (i. 1.)' *Whitby.*—*In your law.* (34) The word " law " is in a general sense used for *scripture,* as in some

40 And went away again beyond Jordan, into ' the place where John at first baptized: ᵏ and there he abode.

41 And ' many resorted unto him,

and said, ᵐ John did no miracle; ⁿ but all things that John spake of this man were true.

42 And ᵒ many believed on him there.

---

other places. (*Marg. Ref.* u.—*Note, Ps.* cxix. 1.)—*The scripture cannot be broken.* (35) This is a decisive testimony of our Lord, to the divine inspiration of the Old Testament. —*Sent into the world.* (36) ' It may be said of every man, ' that God " sent him into the world." ' *Campbell.* It is, however, *not said* in scripture of any other man except our Lord, but of him frequently; (*Marg. Ref.* c;) and, it may be questioned, whether it could be said, with propriety, of any other man. God creates men, or brings them into the world; and then sends them, as he sees good: but " to send," applied to rational creatures, presupposes a capacity of being sent, as moral agents; and to " send " into the world," in this sense, evidently implies pre-existence. (*Notes,* vi. 36—40. xvi. 25—30, *vv.* 28—30. 1 *Tim.* i. 15, 16, *v.* 15. *Heb.* ii. 10—15.)

Hath sanctified. (36) Ἡγίασι. xvii. 17. 19. *Heb.* ii. 11. x. 10. 29. xiii. 12. See on *Matt.* vi. 9.—*He escaped.* (39) Ἐξῆλθεν. " He went forth." *Note,* viii. 54—59, *v.* 59.

V. 40—42. (*Marg. Ref.*—*Notes,* i. 19—34. iii. 22—36.) Many, who had formerly heard John's testimony to Jesus, as the " Lamb of God," and " the Son of God," and perhaps had almost forgotten it; now beholding his miracles and hearing his instructions, were convinced that he was the Messiah, and became his disciples.—John was a prophet, and more than a prophet; yet he wrought no miracles: so that miracles are not in all cases necessary to a true prophet. Indeed, it is recorded in scripture of only a few of the prophets, that they confirmed their doctrine by miracles; except as the fulfilment of their predictions might be considered in this light. (*Note, Matt.* xiv. 1, 2.)

PRACTICAL OBSERVATIONS.

V. 1—9.

It is peculiarly incumbent on all, who enter into the sacred ministry, or officiate in it, to scrutinize even with rigour their own motives and principles, and the tendency of their doctrine and example. By whatever external way men obtain admission into this sacred function, unless they enter by " Christ, the Door;" unless their state of mind and heart, their aim and object, their example and instructions authorize the conclusion, that he has sent them; they will have a dreadful account to give of the emoluments and distinctions, which many now so eagerly pursue, or ostentatiously glory in For it will at length be proved, that they have seized on those advantages, to which they had no right; and grown rich and great by an office, in which they had neither knowledge, integrity, humility, nor industry to do good. But happy is that pastor, whom the Saviour teaches and employs; who is himself a true Christian; who regards the honour of Christ, the conversion of sinners, and the edification of believers, more than any secular advantage whatsoever; and who can say to his people, " I seek not your's, but you." To him the Lord will " open a door of utterance;" seals shall be given to his ministry; believers will approve and encourage his labours; and his work will be its own reward: while he gets acquainted with his people, attends to the case of

each of them, leads them forward in the knowledge, experience, and practice of the gospel, and goes before them in every good work.—Every man, who values his own soul, should avoid those who intrude into the ministry, when they are strangers to Christ and the experimental knowledge of his salvation, and when their example and doctrine prove them " hirelings, who care not for the sheep." Indeed the true people of God will flee from teachers of this description; for " they know not the voice of strangers : " and for this they will be reproached by those who, like these Jews, understand not this parable. These very persons would think those men very imprudent, who should trust their health to some ignorant empirick, or their estate to a dishonest lawyer, merely because he happened to live in the same street, town, or village: yet they suppose it incumbent on them to follow the instructions of a man, who neither knows nor cares any thing about vital godliness, if he be the minister of the parish, or of some neighbouring congregation! Alas! how much more sagacious are men, in their temporal than in their eternal concerns! —They will entrust their immortal souls and their eternal interests to such men, as no one of them would employ even to take care of his sheep!

V. 10—21.

Christ himself is, not only the Source of authority to all pastors, but " the good Shepherd," and the perfect model, according to which they ought to be formed, and by which their pretensions must be decided. He came, that sinners " might have life, and have it more abundantly." For their good he became poor, he abased himself, he laboured, he agonized, and died! While we admire and adore his infinite condescension and compassion, and his unspeakable love to such rebels and enemies; let us enquire, which professed pastors of his church are most like him? Are they, who rise from obscurity to wealth, grandeur, and luxury, by the sacred ministry; but who leave the poor of the flock, and every thing that requires labour, condescension, or self-denial, to others; perhaps without much enquiry into their principles or characters, and without knowing whether they too be not " hirelings " of an interior order? Does this procedure, (alas! too common,) resemble the conduct of the good Shepherd? Or rather is it not a perfect contrast to it? But, whatever indignation it may excite, such men must be plainly told that they " are " thieves and robbers:" they only need the character of persecutors to complete their likeness to those, who " came " not, but to steal, and to kill, and to destroy : " and this exemption is in the effect, rather of want of power than of will. But, alas, ' such a minister carries a shoal down ' with him, of those who have perished in ignorance ' through his neglect, or of those who have been hardened ' in sins through his ill example.' *Bp. Burnett.*—Let those, however, be thankful, who have been preserved or recovered from such a state; and let us pray for others, who are still blinded and deluded. Let all who have entered the sacred ministry from worldly motives, and in an

CHAP. XI.

Lazarus, the brother of Martha and Mary, is sick, 1, 2. They send to Jesus, who, declaring his "sickness not unto death, but for the glory of God," abides two days where he is, 3—6. He informs the disciples that Lazarus is dead; and, intimating that he would raise him to life, he proposes going to him : the disciples, fearing the Jews, express their surprise, yet resolve to accompany him, 7—16. Jesus arrives at Bethany, after Lazarus had been dead four days, 17, 18. He assures Martha, that her brother shall rise again, and requires her to believe, that he is the "Resurrection and the Life;" and she confesses her faith in him, as "the Christ, the Son of God," 19—27. She calls Mary, who comes with her, 28—31. Jesus, sympathizing with the mourners, "groans in spirit," and "weeps:" the remarks of the Jews on the occasion, 32—37. He comes to the grave, appeals to God as his Father who sent him, and calls Lazarus out of the grave, 38—44. Many Jews believe; but some inform the Pharisees, 45, 46. They hold a council; and concur with Caiaphas, who instigates them to put Jesus to death ; while, as high priest, Caiaphas was led, beyond his intention, to prophesy concerning the gracious intention and extensive efficacy of his death, 47—53. Jesus retires from places of publick resort, 54. Before the passover, the Jews enquire about him, the rulers having given orders to apprehend him, 55—57.

NOW a certain man [a] was sick, named [b] Lazarus, of [c] Bethany, the town of [d] Mary and her sister Martha.

2 (It was [e] *that* Mary which [f] anointed the Lord with ointment, and wiped [r] his feet with her hair, whose brother [s] Lazarus was sick.)

3 Therefore his sisters sent unto him, saying, Lord, behold, [g] he whom thou lovest is sick.

4 When Jesus heard *that*, he said, [b] This sickness is not unto death, but [i] for the glory of God, [k] that the Son of God might be glorified thereby.

a S. 6. Gen. xlviii.
1. 2 Kings xx. 1
—12. Acts ix. 37.
b b. 11. xii. 2. 9.
17. Luke xvi. 20
—22.
c xii. 1. Matt. xxi.
17. Mark xi. 1.
d Luke x. 38—42.
e xii. 3. Matt.
xxvi. 6, 7. Mark
xiv. 3.
f Luke vii. 37, 38.
r 1.5.xii. 2b. Gen.
xxii. 2. Ps. xvi.
8. Phil. ii. 26,
27. 2 Tim. iv.
20. Heb. xii. 6.
g Jam. v. 14,
15.
h ix. 3. Mark v.
36—42. Rom.xi.
11).
i 40. ix. 24. xii.
28. xiii. 31, 32.
Phil. i. 11. 1 Pet.
iv. 11. 14.
k ii. 11. v. 2b.
vii. 54. xiii. 31,
32. xvii. 1. 5. 10.
Phil. i. 20. 1 Pet.
i. 21.

unholy manner, pause, and consider their awful case ; that, by deep repentance and faith in Christ, becoming his true disciples, they may be commissioned and instructed by him, to exercise their ministry in a far better manner, than they entered upon it. And let all, who desire to be faithful ministers, study and copy Christ's example ; that they may grow more willing to labour and suffer for the good of that flock, for which he shed his precious blood ; that they may mortify every covetous, ambitious, selfish, and sensual desire ; and lay aside all sloth, pride, false delicacy, fear of men, and whatever else can render them unwilling to "spend and be spent for the people."—We all, especially ministers, should likewise have our desires fixed upon those, who are not yet brought into the fold of Christ, but are scattered abroad in this evil world, even to the remotest regions of the globe ; and endeavour, with all our ability, diligence, and influence, that they too may be led to hear the Saviour's voice, and become "the sheep of his pasture:" and if our zeal and earnestness, in so blessed a work, should bring upon us the reproach of being designing hypocrites, ignorant enthusiasts, or even mad fanaticks ; we may remember, that our holy Lord and Master was thus vilified before us.—Let sinners also hearken to him, who says, "I "am the Door." They can now have no access into the favour of God, or hereafter into heaven, except they believe in him. But he will admit all who come to him, and guard and nourish their souls unto everlasting life.

V. 22—42.

The proud, the malicious, and all who are not the sheep of Christ, will be convinced by no evidence, and take no warning : but his sheep, when he comes forth to seek and save them, "hear his voice," and follow his guidance and example ; and thus they become like the harmless, holy, patient Lamb of God. These he knows, and they know him ; they "love him, because he hath first loved them ;" (*Note*, 1 *John* iv. 19;) they seek his glory, and he takes

care of their interests. He "gives them eternal life," and keeps them in his almighty hands to the enjoyment of it ; nor shall any enemy, or any event, ever separate them from his love. "They know whom they have believed;" their "Redeemer is the LORD of Hosts." "God is be-"come their Salvation:" JEHOVAH, Jesus, is their good Shepherd, being One with the Father, and possessing with him all divine power and perfection. They cannot expect too much from him, to whom all the prophets bare witness, of whom the priests and kings of Israel were types and delegates, "whom all angels worship," and "who "upholds all things by the word of his power." (*Notes*, *Heb.* i. 1—4.) His works proclaim him "God over all, "blessed for evermore;" that all men may know and believe, that "he is in the Father, and the Father in him." Modern opposers, who charge us with idolatry for worshipping the Son of God, would doubtless have dared to charge him with blasphemy, had they heard these discourses : but he will refute such charges, and silence all enemies ; who can only deprive themselves of the blessings of his salvation, and provoke him to say to them "De-"part from me," when he shall come to judge the world. —But he continues to send his gospel to others who will receive it. These are frequently the poor, the illiterate, and the obscure of the world ; while the wise, the learned, the wealthy, and the honourable, despise his salvation : and the effects of the testimony, which faithful ministers have borne to him, sometimes do not much appear, till they have entered into their rest ; and then they spring up, and bring forth a blessed harvest, to the glory of God and the salvation of many precious souls. (*Note*, iv. 35—38.)

NOTES.

CHAP. XI. V. 1—6. (*Notes*, x. 40—42. *Luke* x. 36 —42.) Lazarus appears to have been a young man at this time, and to have lived single with his sisters. They formed a very harmonious, pious, and happy family ; and Jesus

5 Now Jesus 'loved Martha and her sister, and Lazarus.

6 When he had heard therefore that he was sick, ^m he abode two days still ^m in the same place where he was.

7 Then after that saith he to *his* disciples, ⁿ Let us go into Judea again.

8 *His* disciples say unto him, Master, ^o the Jews of late sought to stone thee; and goest thou thither again?

9 Jesus answered, ^p Are there not twelve hours in the day? If any man walk in the day, ^q he stumbleth not, because he seeth the light of this world.

10 But if ^r a man walk in the night, he stumbleth, because there is no light in him.

11 These things said he: and after that, ^s he saith unto them, Our friend Lazarus 'sleepeth; but I go that I may "awake him out of sleep.

12 Then said his disciples, Lord, if he sleep he shall do well.

13 Howbeit, Jesus spake of his death; but they thought that he had spoken of taking of rest in sleep.

14 Then said Jesus unto them ^x plainly, Lazarus is dead.

15 And ^y I am glad 'for your sakes that I was not there, 'to the intent ye may believe; nevertheless, let us go unto him.

16 Then said ^z Thomas, which is called Didymus, unto his fellow-disciples, 'Let us also go, that we may die with him.

---

seems to have constantly resorted to their house when he went to Jerusalem.—Bethany is called " the town of " Martha and Mary," because they resided and probably had their inheritance there: but, though they were persons well known and respected, there is not the least probability in the opinion, that the whole village belonged to them. (*Marg. Ref.* a—d.—i. 44.) The evangelist distinguished the Mary of whom he wrote, from others of the same name, by referring to an action of her's, recorded by two of the other sacred historians, and which he was about to mention. (*Notes*, xii. 1—8, v. 3. *Matt.* xxvi. 6—13. *Mark* xiv. 3—9. *Luke* vii. 37—39.)—Lazarus being ill, and supposed to be in danger, his sisters sent word to Jesus, who was at a distance, simply but affectingly saying, " Lord, behold, he whom thou lovest is sick." They knew that this would sufficiently determine whom they meant, and comprize every topick which could be urged for his gracious interposition: and probably they expected that Jesus would come without delay to heal him. When however he heard this message, he said to his disciples, perhaps in the hearing of the messenger, that " this sickness " was not unto death;" (it was not intended finally to remove Lazarus out of the world;) " but for the glory of " God," that is, in a wonderful display of the divine power of his beloved Son, by the miracle to which it would give occasion. (*Marg. Ref.* g—k.—*Notes*, ix. 1—3. *Matt.* ix. 18 —26, v. 24.) This was evidently our Lord's meaning: but the messenger would not so understand it; and the expectation which it might excite would add to the trial of the faith of all concerned, when the death of Lazarus seemed to preclude every hope.—Our Lord loved each person in this favoured family, both as true disciples, and as his most affectionate and intimate friends: yet he remained where he was " two days," after he received the tidings of Lazarus's sickness, nay, his love seems assigned as the reason of the delay: whereas we should have supposed that he would have gone at once to Bethany. But his love was directed by consummate wisdom. (*Marg. Ref.* l, m.—*Note*, 1 *John* iv. 7, 8.)—' When God at any time seems to delay, ' in assisting us, he consults both his own glory, and our

' benefit; as the event shews.' *Beza.*—' Jesus did not ' come to Bethany, till Lazarus had been dead four days; ' not only that the miracle of his resurrection might be the ' greater; but also that all pretence of his being only in a ' *deliquium*' (or apparently dead) ' might be taken away.' *Whitby.*

Wiped, &c. (2) Εκμαξασα. xii. 3. See on *Luke* vii. 38.—*For the glory,* &c. (4) *Notes*, v. 20—23. xiii. 31— 35, *vv.* 31, 32. xvii. 1—3. *Phil.* ii. 9—11, v. 11.

V. 7—10. When our Lord, on the third day, intimated his purpose of returning into Judea, his disciples were surprised. They thought those unworthy of his presence, who had attempted his life; or rather, they doubted whether he would be able to protect himself and them, from the rage of enemies so powerful and so implacable. (*Marg. Ref.* n, o.—*Notes*, x. 32—39.) But his answer implied, that he should certainly be safe, and it was proper that he should be employed, during the appointed period of his life; and when that was expired, he must be delivered into the hands of his enemies: even as men labour and travel securely, while the sun " the light of this world " affords them his light; but are liable to fall into a pit, or down a precipice, if they travel in the night. (*Marg. Ref.* p—r.—*Notes*, ix. 4—7. *Prov.* iv. 18, 19. *Luke* xiii. 31—33. 1 *John* ii. 7—11.)—" Because there is no light " in him;" or in it, that is, the world in which he walks. The Jews divided the time of the sun's being above the horizon into twelve hours; and their days were much nearer the same length in summer and winter, than they are in these northerly regions.—' This alone is the safe ' and right way of life, intrepidly to follow God, calling us, ' and shining on our path, amidst the darkness of this ' world.' *Beza.*

V. 11—16. Our Lord perfectly knew what passed at Bethany: and he spake to his disciples of the death of their *friend* Lazarus, and his being soon restored to life, under the idea of his having " fallen asleep," and being " awaked from sleep." Thus he stated the fact, in language which divested it of its terror; and at the same time, he spake of the miracle which he intended to per-

17 ¶ Then when Jesus came, he found that he had *lain* in the grave ᵈ four days already.

18 Now Bethany was nigh unto Jerusalem, about ° fifteen furlongs off.

19 And many of the Jews came to Martha and Mary, ᵉ to comfort them concerning their brother.

20 Then Martha, ᶠ as soon as she heard that Jesus was coming, went and met him; but Mary sat *still* in the house.

21 Then said Martha unto Jesus, Lord, ᵍ if thou hadst been here, my brother had not died.

22 But I know, ʰ that even now, whatsoever thou wilt ask of God, ⁱ God will give *it* thee.

23 Jesus saith unto her, ᵏ Thy brother shall rise again.

24 Martha saith unto him, ˡ I know that he shall rise again in the resurrection at the last day.

25 Jesus said unto her, ᵐ I am the Resurrection and ⁿ the Life : ° he that believeth in me, though he were dead, yet shall he live ;

26 And ᵖ whosoever liveth and believeth in me shall never die. ᵠ Believest thou this ?

27 She saith unto him, ʳ Yea, Lord, I believe that thou art the Christ, the Son of God, ˢ which should come into the world.

---

form, in the most simple and unostentatious manner· (*Marg. Ref.* s—u.—*Note,* 1 *Thes.* iv. 13—18.) The disciples, however, did not understand him : but, supposing him to mean, that Lazarus was " taking rest in sleep," and thinking this a favourable symptom of his recovery, they seem to have concluded, that there could be no occasion for Jesus to expose himself to his enemies, by going to Bethany. He therefore plainly told them, that " Lazarus was dead ;" and that, instead of regretting that he had not been there, to recover him by a miracle, he rejoiced on their account, as he intended to take occasion from thence greatly to confirm their faith in him : but it was proper for him to go to Bethany without further delay, notwithstanding the malice of the rulers. (*Marg. Ref.* x—a.) Thomas therefore, finding him resolved, proposed to his brethren to accompany him ; though he apprehended they should be called to lay down their lives with and for him. This was the language of cordial affection, and of some faith ; but combined with great ignorance both of the power and salvation of his Lord, and of his own weakness and the deceitfulness of the human heart.—Some interpret this of dying along with Lazarus : but this is very unnatural ; for what special connexion had the death of Lazarus with that of the apostles ? Or what need to go to Bethany, if grief for the loss of their friend would cause their death?—*Thomas,* in Hebrew or Syriack, and *Didymus* in Greek, signify a *twin.*

Sleepeth. (11) Κεκοιμηται. " Hath fallen asleep." 12. *Matt.* xxvii. 52. xxviii. 13. *Luke* xxii. 45. *Acts* vii. 60. xiii. 36. 1 *Cor.* vii. 39. xi. 30. xv. 6. 18. 20. 51. 1 *Thes.* iv. 13, 14, 15. 2 *Pet.* iii. 4.—*May awake him out of sleep.*] Εξυπνισω αυτον. Here only. Εξυπνος. *Acts* xvi. 27.—*He shall do well.* (12) Σωθησεται. " He shall be saved," that is, from death.—*Of taking of rest.* (13) Περι της κοιμησεως. Here only.—*Plainly.* (14) Παρρησια. 54. xvi. 25. 2 *Cor.* iii. 12. *Eph.* vi. 19. *Heb.* iv. 16. x. 24.—*Fellow-disciples.* (16) Συμμαθηταις. Here only.

V. 17—19. It was customary for the Jews to inter the dead very soon after their decease : so that Lazarus was perhaps laid in the grave, on the same day on which he died. (*Acts* v. 6. 10.)—The two days, which passed before Jesus set out on his journey, and the time employed in travelling, prevented his arrival at Bethany, till four days after that event. (39.)—As Bethany was scarcely two miles from Jerusalem, many Jews came from thence to condole with Martha and Mary on the loss of their beloved brother, and to employ the customary methods and topicks of consolation ; and this circumstance was over-ruled to render the miracle more extensively known, and more fully attested, which was evidently one part of our Lord's design. (*Marg.* and *Marg. Ref.*)

Martha, &c. (19) Τας περι Μαρθαν, κ.τ.λ.—This is considered as a Greek idiom, simply meaning as in our version, " Martha and Mary : " yet it seems to imply that they came and joined with the female friends of the afflicted sisters, who, residing at Bethany, were more stately endeavouring to soothe and alleviate their sorrow.—*To comfort.*] Ἱνα παραμυθησωνται. 31. 1 *Thes.* ii. 11. v. 14. Not elsewhere. Παραμυθια, 1 *Cor.* xiv. § Παραμυθιον, 1 *Phil.* ii. 1. Εκ παρα, et μυθεομαι, loquor.

V. 20—27. Martha, hearing of our Lord's arrival, left Mary and the company, that she might meet and welcome him : and some think she also wanted to inform him that many Jews were present ; that he might use his discretion, whether he would go among them or not. She expressed her full assurance, that he both could and would have healed her brother, if he had been on the spot : but she seems not fully to have believed, that he could have healed him at a distance, if he had so pleased. (*Marg. Ref.* g.—*Notes,* iv. 46—54, *vv.* 47. 49. *Matt.* viii. 8, 9. *Mark* v. 21—24.) She also added a confident declaration, that God would grant whatsoever he should then ask of him, for their comfort and support under the affliction : but it is doubtful, whether this did or did not imply some feeble hope of her brother's being restored to life. She, however, considered Jesus as a holy Prophet, who wrought miracles by faith and prayer, in the same manner that the ancient prophets had done ; rather than as the incarnate Son of God, who, being One with the Father, performed his miracles by his own omnipotence.—When he assured

4 ᴀ 3

28 And when she had so said, she went her way, ' and called Mary her sister secretly, saying, " The Master is come, and calleth for thee.

29 As soon ' as she heard that, she arose quickly, and came unto him.

30 Now ' Jesus was not yet come into the town, but was in that place where Martha met him.

31 The ' Jews then which were with her in the house, and comforted her, when they saw Mary that she rose up hastily, and went out, followed her, saying, ' She goeth unto the grave to weep there.

32 Then when Mary was come where Jesus was, and saw him, ' she fell down at his feet, saying unto him, Lord, ' if thou hadst been here, my brother had not died.

33 When Jesus therefore saw her weeping, ' and the Jews also weeping which came with her, ' he groaned in the spirit, and ' was troubled,

34 And said, ' Where have ye laid him ? They said unto him, Lord, come and see.

35 ' Jesus wept.

36 Then said the Jews, ' Behold how he loved him !

37 And some of them said, ' Could not this man, which opened the eyes of the blind, have caused that even this man should not have died ?

---

her, that Lazarus should rise again, she expressed her firm belief that he would, at the general resurrection, arise to eternal life; but intimated, that this could not make up the heavy loss which she had sustained. (*Marg. Ref.* h—l.—*Note*, vi. 36—40.) To enlarge her expectations, and to excite in her more honourable thoughts of him, our Lord declared himself to be " The Resurrection and " the Life." In him, (" the second Adam," " the Lord " from heaven,") and through his mediation, all the dead shall rise again : he is the Author of the resurrection; it will be effected by his power; and his salvation alone will render it a blessing. (*Marg. Ref.* m, n.—*Notes*, v. 28, 29. 1 Cor. xv. 20—28.) In every sense he is " the Resurrec- " tion," the Source, the Substance, the First-fruits, and the efficient Cause of it. He is also the Fountain, the Support, and the Giver of Life, temporal, spiritual, and eternal; and no man can have it, but by and from him. (*Notes*, i. 4, 5. v. 24—27. xiv. 4—6, v. 6. Ps. xxxvj. 5— 9. Col. iii. 1—4, vv. 3, 4.) " He that believeth in me, " though he were dead, yet shall he live; " his soul shall live in heaven, when his body lies in the grave; and his body shall surely rise again to immortal life, by virtue of his union with Christ " the Resurrection, and the Life." (*Marg. Ref.* o.—*Notes*, iv. 10—15, vv. 14, 15. v. 24. xiv. 18—20. Rom. vi. 5—11. viii. 10, 11. 1 Cor. xv. 20— 28. 2 Cor. iv. 13—18. Phil. iii. 20, 21.) On the other hand, " He that liveth and believeth in me, shall never " die," or shall be preserved from dying for ever : that is, the death of the body will be to the believer no more than a peaceful sleep; the soul will continue to live in happiness; and after the resurrection, both body and soul will be preserved from death and every evil to all eternity. (*Marg. Ref.* p.—*Notes*, 1 Thes. iv. 13—18. Rev. xx. 11— 15.) ' Therefore I, who shall hereafter raise all persons to ' life, can raise Lazarus now.' *Whitby.*—The first clause is by some supposed to imply, that the spirits of just men made perfect still believe in Christ, as relying on his truth and power to raise their bodies.—Our Lord then addressing Martha, added " Believest thou this ? " and she answered, by an open confession of her faith in him : she firmly believed that he was the Messiah, " the Son of " God," and the person whom the prophets had foretold should come into the world. (*Marg. Ref.* q—s.—*Notes*, vi. 66—71, v. 69. Matt. xvi. 16—18.) The decision, with which Martha declares her full expectation of " the resur- " rection at the last day," is very remarkable; and shews that this doctrine was firmly maintained among the Jews at that time, the Sadducees alone excepted.—' Grotius ' saith, her faith was weak, because she only believed that ' Christ was prevalent with God; but not that the fulness ' of divine power resided in him.' *Whitby.*

In the last day. (24) Εν τη εσχαλη ημερα. vi. 39, 40. 44. 54.—*Never.* (26) Εις τον αιωνα. iv. 14, *et al.—Which should come.* (27) Ο ερχομενος. Matt. xi. 6. xxi. 9. *Luke* vii. 19. xix. 38.

V. 28—32. Martha, having confessed her faith in Jesus, and probably obtained a measure of comfort and hope from his words, returned to inform her sister, that " the Teacher was arrived " and had asked for her; by which it appears that more conversation passed than is recorded. Accordingly, she went to him without the town, where he saw good to wait for her; this being more proper, we may conclude, than by going to the Jews, to call them forth, as it were, to behold the miracle which he intended to perform. But, as they judged that Mary was going to the grave to indulge her excessive sorrow, they followed her; by which means they became spectators of what ensued. (*Marg. Ref.* t—b.—*Notes*, Gen. xxxvii. 34—36. P.O. 31—36.—*Notes*, 2 Sam. xii. 21—23. Job i. 20—22. 1 Thes. iv. 13—18, v. 13.) Mary prostrated herself before Jesus in the humblest manner; but she expressed herself exactly in the same words which Martha had used (21).

V. 33—40. The very great grief of Mary, and the sympathizing tears of the Jews, joined to a reflection on the miseries which sin has brought on mankind, and a prospect of the ruin which the Jews were bringing on themselves by their unbelief, and perverse opposition to him, may be supposed to have excited this vehement perturbation in our Lord's mind : and, though he was perfectly master of all his passions, he was pleased to give way to them on this occasion : he therefore " groaned in spirit, " and was troubled," or " *troubled himself.*" (*Marg.—Notes*, Gen. xliii. 29—31. xlv. 1, 2.) And when at his re-

38 Jesus therefore again ¹ groaning in himself cometh to the grave. ᵐ It was a cave, and a stone lay upon it. 39 Jesus said, Take ye away the stone. Martha, the sister of him that was dead, saith unto him, ⁿ Lord, by this time he stinketh: for he hath been dead four days. 40 Jesus saith unto her, ° Said I not unto thee, that, if thou wouldest believe, thou shouldest ᵖ see the glory of God? 41 Then they took away the stone from the place where the dead was laid. ᵠ And Jesus lifted up his eyes, and said, ʳ Father, I thank thee that thou hast heard me. 42 And ˢ I knew that thou hearest me always: ᵗ but because of the people which stand by I said it, ᵘ that they may believe ˣ that thou hast sent me.

43 And when he had thus spoken, ʸ he cried with a loud voice, ᶻ Lazarus, come forth. 44 And ᵃ he that was dead came forth, ᵇ bound hand and foot with graveclothes: and his face was bound about with a napkin. Jesus saith unto them, ᵇ Loose him, and let him go. 45 Then many of the ᶜ Jews which came to Mary, and had seen the things which Jesus did, believed on him. 46 But ᵈ some of them went their ways to the Pharisees, and told them what things Jesus had done.

quest they led him to the grave, he vented his inward sorrow and sympathy, by *weeping:* and thus shewed himself in all things like to us, sin alone excepted. (*Marg. Ref.* e—h.—*Notes, Is.* liii. 2, 3. *Matt.* viii. 16, 17.) This the Jews noticed, and expressed their surprise at the greatness of his affection for the deceased: but some of them, taking it for granted, that he would have preserved the life of one whom he so loved, had he been able; and concluding that the same power, which sufficed to open the eyes of the blind, could have healed the sickness of Lazarus, shewed a disposition to infer from his death, that there was no certainty in those apparent miracles. (*Marg. Ref.* i, k.)—Jesus therefore 'again groaning within him,' both on account of the afflictive scene before him, and because of their obstinate unbelief, arrived at the grave, which was a hollow place in the rock, the opening of which was closed with a stone. (*Marg. Ref.* l, m.—*Note, Matt.* xxvii. 57—61, *v.* 60.) This he ordered to be removed; but Martha objected, and thus shewed how low her hopes had fallen respecting her brother. Our Lord therefore reminded her, that he had told her, if she would believe, she should see a wonderful display of the divine glory, in respect of her brother. This was implied, in what Jesus had said of himself, as "the Resurrection, and the Life:" but perhaps he had spoken more explicitly to this purpose; demanding faith from her, and promising a glorious event to her affliction. (*Marg. Ref.* n—p.—*Note,* 20—27.)—*Four days,* &c. (39) The word simply means, that Lazarus had been four days, or till the fourth day, in his present state, without mentioning either his being *dead,* or *buried.* It is not improbable, that he had been dead more than four days. Three days seem, from some frivolous Jewish traditions, to have been the longest term, which they supposed a dead body could subsist, without " seeing " corruption." Our Lord rose on the third day: but he raised Lazarus, after the assigned time was expired, perhaps to give an earnest of that power, by which he will raise the bodies of those unnumbered millions, who have returned, and shall return, to their original dust. (*Notes,* 1 *Cor.* xv. 35—58. *Rev.* xx. 11—15.)

*He groane*d *in spirit.* (33) Ενεβριμησατο. 38. See on *Matt.* ix. 30.—*In spirit.*] Τω πνευμαβι. *Luke* x. 21.—*Was troubled.*] Εταραξεν ιαυτον. (Marg.) See on *Matt.* xiv. 26.—*He stinketh.* (39) Οζει. Here only N. T.—*Ex.* viii. 14. *Ps.* xxxviii. 5.—*Sept.*—*He hath been dead four days.*] Τεβαρταιος εςι. Here only. (*Note,* 17—19, *v.* 17.)

V. 41—46. When the stone had been removed, our Lord, with " eyes lifted up to heaven," openly addressed himself to his Father, in a manner of which we have no other instance attending any miracle wrought by him. The Jews, unable to deny the reality of his miracles, had repeatedly ascribed them to the power of the devil: he was therefore pleased to introduce this most stupendous act of omnipotence, by an appeal to the God of heaven, as his Father: thus making it undeniably evident that he performed it by power from above; and that the Father bore witness to him, and authorized all those declarations of his own dignity and authority, which the Jews considered as blasphemy. (*Notes,* v. 15—18. viii. 54—59, *vv.* 58, 59. x. 32—39.) Accordingly, he praised and thanked the Father, that he had heard him, in respect of the opportunity and circumstances, which had been ordered in providence for the display of his power, by the miracle that he was about to perform. (*Marg. Ref.* q, r.—*Notes,* xii. 27—33, *vv.* 27, 28. *Matt.* xi. 25, 26.) Indeed he was assured, that the Father always accepted and answered the prayers which, as Man and Mediator, he continually presented before him. But he made this publick appeal, for the benefit of the multitudes who stood by; in order to convince them, by the event, that God had sent him as his beloved Son into the world, to perform the works, and to teach the doctrines, which they had seen and heard. (*Marg. Ref.* s—x.—*Note,* v. 20—23.) Having thus spoken, he called aloud, saying, " Lazarus, come forth;" as one who had power in himself, and as " the Resurrection, and " the Life." And by the same energy which created the world, the body which had so long been tending to putrefaction, was at once, in a moment, rendered capable of re-assuming all its suspended functions, and was restored to life, health, and vigour; the immortal soul having been

4 A 5

47 ¶ Then ᵃ gathered the chief priests and the Pharisees a council, and said, ᶠ What do we? for this man doeth many miracles.

48 If ᶠ we let him thus alone, ʰ all men will believe on him; ⁱ and the Romans shall come, and take away both our place and nation.

49 And one of them, named ᵏ Caiaphas, being the high priest that same year, said unto them, ˡ Ye know nothing at all,

50 Nor ᵐ consider that it is expe-

dient for us, that one man should die for the people, and that the whole nation perish not.

51 And this spake he not of himself; but, ⁿ being high priest that year, ᵒ he prophesied ᵖ that Jesus should die for that nation:

52 And ᑫ not for that nation only, but that also he should ʳ gather together in one, ˢ the children of God ᵗ that were scattered abroad.

re-united to it. (*Marg. Ref. y*—a.—*Notes, Matt.* viii. 1—4, *v.* 3. 23—27. *Mark* v. 35—43, *vv.* 41, 42. *Luke* vii.11—17, *vv.* 14, 15. 1 *Cor.* xv. 50—54, *v.* 52.) Immediately, therefore, Lazarus came forth, in his grave-clothes : and Jesus, who would not multiply miracles unnecessarily, ordered the spectators to loose him, and so give him liberty to walk home ; which was done accordingly. The evangelist did not attempt to describe, and it is impossible for us to conceive, the mixed and varied affections of astonishment, gratitude, and joy, which seized on the relatives of Lazarus, and the spectators of this stupendous scene. Many of the Jews were convinced by it, that Jesus was the Messiah, and became his disciples : yet others of them " would not be per-" suaded, though one rose from the dead;" and one named also Lazarus; (*Note, Luke* xvi. 27—31 ;) on the contrary, they went to inform the Pharisees, that they might use proper measures to prevent the increase of his popularity.

Come forth. (43) Δυρο εξω. *Matt.* xix. 22. *Mark* x. 21. *Luke* xviii. 22. *Acts* vii. 3. *Rev.* xvii. 1. xxi. 9.— *Grave clothes.* (44) Κηριαις. Here only N. T.—*Prov.* vii. 16. *Sept.*

V. 47, 48. We can scarcely imagine a more conclusive discovery of " the madness which is in the heart of man," or of his desperate enmity against God, than that which is here recorded. (*Notes,* xii. 9—11. *Ec.* x. 1—3. *Jer.* xvii. 9, 10. *Matt.* ii. 7, 8.) The rulers of the Jews were neither convinced, nor over-awed, by the display of our Lord's astonishing power; which would as readily have effected their destruction, as Lazarus's resurrection, had he so pleased ; (*Note,* xviii. 4—9 ;) but they immediately called the council together, to determine what to do in this emergency. They blamed themselves for hesitating and acting without proper decision in so urgent a case ; for they could not deny that Jesus did many miracles : yet they were determined not to admit them as evidences that he was sent by God. They concluded therefore, that if they did not interpose with their whole authority, men of all ranks would unite in believing in him as the Messiah, and in placing him over them as King ; by which the jealous Romans would be exasperated, and, making war on them, would destroy both Jerusalem and the temple, and so ruin and enslave the nation. (*Marg. Ref.—Notes, Acts* iv. 13—22, *vv.* 16—18. v. 17—25, *v.* 24. 33—39.) Thus they argued from their own erroneous notions of the Messiah's kingdom; as if the establishment of a worldly kingdom had

been the avowed purpose of Jesus! They supposed him able to work miracles, sufficient to convince all the people that he was the Messiah; and yet to be unable to protect them against the Romans! They despised his mean appearance, and were ready to say, " Shall this man save us ? " But hatred of his holy doctrine and example, regard to their own authority, and resentment against him for having exposed his hypocrisy, were at least equally powerful motives of their opposition, as fear of the Romans. These motives, however, were private and personal, and it was not expedient to avow them in the publick council of the nation. They therefore purposed to put him to death, lest the Romans should destroy their city and temple, and ruin the nation : and by so doing, they provoked God to bring these very judgments upon them. ' For this very ' cause, that he did so many miracles, all salutary and ' tending to the good of men, and with such evidence of a ' divine power, as was sufficient to draw all men to the faith, ' they should have owned him as the true Messiah : but ' fear of the Romans induced them rather to cut him off, ' and by that very act they pulled that dreadful vengeance, ' executed by the Romans, down upon themselves. This ' is the just and usual effect of carnal policy, exalting itself ' against the wisdom and the counsel of God.' *Whitby.* (*Note, Matt.* xxvii. 24, 25.)

V. 49—53. Caiaphas seems to have been a Sadducee. (*Acts* iv. 6. v. 17.) He was a bold, profane politician. He arrogantly charged the whole council with total ignorance of the first principles, by which government should be conducted. Whether Jesus deserved death or not, his life ought to be sacrificed to the publick good; as it was evidently expedient, that even an innocent person should be put to death, for the benefit of the whole nation, and to preserve it from destruction. (*Marg. Ref.* k—m.)— ' It would appear, that some of the Sanhedrim were sen- ' sible that Jesus had given them no just or legal handle, by ' any thing he had either done or taught, for taking away ' his life ; and that in their deliberations something had ' been advanced, which made the high priest fear, they ' would not enter with spirit and resolution into the busi- ' ness. ... May we not reasonably conjecture, that this ' must have arisen from some objections made by Nico- ' demus, who ... was not afraid to object to them the ille- ' gality of their proceedings, (vii. 50—52,) or by Joseph ' of Arimathea, ... concerning whom we have this honour- ' able testimony, that he did not concur in their resolu-

53 Then "from that day forth "they took counsel together for to ' put him to death.

54 Jesus therefore ' walked no more openly among the Jews; but ' went thence unto a country near to the wilderness, into a city called ' Ephraim, and there continued with his disciples.

55 And the Jews' ' passover was nigh at hand: and many went out of the country up to Jerusalem ᵈ before the passover, ' to purify themselves.

56 Then ' sought they for Jesus, and ' spake among themselves, as they stood in the temple, What think ye, that he will not come to the feast?

57 Now both the chief priests and the Pharisees ' had given a commandment, that if any man knew where he were, he should shew it, that they might take him.

' tions? (*Luke* xxiii. 50, 51.)' *Campbell.* Perhaps Gamaliel also hesitated.—While, however, Caiaphas deeply disgraced himself, by this most iniquitous and impious counsel; the Lord was pleased to guide his tongue to utter a remarkable prophecy, and thus to honour the office of the high priesthood, notwithstanding the wickedness of him who filled it. For, though he was not aware of it, God by him declared it expedient, that the holy Jesus should be made an atoning sacrifice for the sins of his people; suffering One for all, " the Just instead of the " unjust," that by his death he might save them from perishing. (*Marg. Ref.* n—q.—*Notes,* i. 29. iii. 16. *Is.* liii. 4—6. 1 *John* ii. 1, 2. iv. 9—17, vv. 9. 14.) Thus he died for " that nation," in general, but with particular respect to all of that nation who ever in any age should believe in him, and for all the true Israel, whom that nation typified : and so, " not for that nation only, but for all the " children of God, who were scattered abroad " throughout the earth. This must refer to " the election of grace," by which men are considered, in the purpose of God, as his children, before their conversion, yea before they are brought into existence ; and as such, they are in due season gathered together into his family, and admitted to the privileges of children. (*Marg. Ref.* q—t.—*Notes,* x. 14 —18. *Acts* xviii. 9—11. 2 *Thes.* ii. 13, 14.)—' And not ' for that nation only, but for all mankind, that by the ' virtue of his death, he might gather together his elect ' ones among the Gentiles, and might happily bring them ' to the participation of the same grace and glory.' *Bp. Hall.*—' Note, the Gentiles are here called the sons of ' God, not that they were so at present, but that they were ' by faith to be made such; as our Lord calls them sheep, ' who were to hear his voice. (x. 16.)' *Whitby.*—' They, ' which be endued with so excellent a benefit of God, be ' called according to his purpose, by his Spirit working in ' due season ; they through grace obey the calling ; they ' be justified freely, they be made the sons of God by ' adoption ; they be made like unto the image of his only ' begotten Son Jesus Christ ; they walk religiously in good ' works ; and at length by God's mercy, they attain to ' everlasting felicity.' (*Article* xvii.)—The evangelist here expounds, not the meaning of Caiaphas, but that of the Holy Spirit, who spake by him : and thus this bitter enemy of Christ was constrained to bear testimony to the great doctrine of salvation through his atoning blood ; even as Balaam was constrained to bless Israel, when bent upon cursing them.—The counsel of Caiaphas, however, determined the Sanhedrim to form their plan, and devise suitable measures for putting Jesus to death, without further delay.—*That same year.* (49. 51.) *Notes,* xviii. 10—14. *Luke* iii. 2, 3.—' The high-priesthood still continued in ' the line of Aaron. ... In that year, in which Christ was ' to suffer for the sins of the world.' *Whitby.*

Consider. (50) Διαλογιζεσθε. *Reason, compute, calculate.* —*The children of God.* (52) Τα τεκνα τε Θευ. 1 *John* iii. 10. (*Notes, Rom.* ix. 24—29, v. 26. *Eph.* iii. 3—8, v. 5.) —*That were scattered abroad.*] Τα διεσκορπισμενα. See on *Matt.* xxvi. 31.—By using the *past* tense, the evangelist seems to speak, as one who had lived to witness the fulfilment of the prediction, in some degree, by the success of the gospel among the Gentiles.—*Into one.*] Εις εν. x. 30. xvii. 21, 22, 23. (*Notes,* xvii. 20—23.)

V. 54—57. It was our Lord's purpose to suffer death, at the ensuing feast of the passover : he was pleased therefore to retire, for the present, to an obscure part of the country, where he abode, and conversed privately with his disciples, till within a few days of that solemnity. (2 *Sam.* xiii. 23. 2 *Chr.* xiii. 19.) In the mean while, the Jews, who went up to Jerusalem some time before, to perform such rites as were appointed for their purification, (*Note,* 2 *Chr.* xxx. 16—20,) sought for him, probably from different motives : and they questioned with each other, whether he would have courage to come to the feast, or not : seeing proclamation had been made, requiring any, who knew where he was, to inform the council, that they might apprehend him. (*Marg. Ref.*)

Walked, &c. (54) Περιεπατει. See on *Note,* vii. 1.— *Ephraim.*] *Marg. Ref.* b.—*What think ye ?* (56) Τι δοκει υμιν. *Matt.* xvii. 25. xviii. 12. xxii. 42. *Luke* x. 36. xvii. 9. —*Do you think* " that he will not come to the feast ? " (*Notes,* vii. 11—13. ix. 19—23.)

PRACTICAL OBSERVATIONS.

V. 1—6.

Those families, in which love and peace abound, are highly favoured ; but they whom Jesus loves, and by whom he is beloved, are most happy. Alas ! that this should so very seldom be the case with every individual, even in small families, and still more rarely in large households ! Yet even this privilege cannot exclude sickness and death. It may still be often said, " Lord, he whom thou lovest is " sick ; " and ' they whom thou lovest are mourning over the dying agonies, or the dead bodies, of their dearest relatives :' for Jesus did not come to preserve his people from these afflictions ; but to " save them from their sins " and " from the wrath to come ; " and to convert outward sorrows, and temporal death, into medicines, or means of completing that salvation.—It behoves us, however, to

4 A 7

CHAP. XII.

Jesus is entertained at Bethany, 1, 2. Mary anoints his feet, 3; Judas, from dishonest motives, objects, but Jesus vindicates her, 4—8. The people resort to him, on account of Lazarus; and the rulers consult about putting Lazarus also to death, 9—11. Jesus enters Jerusalem as in triumph, riding on an ass, to the extreme indignation of the Pharisees, 12—19. Certain Greeks desire to see him, 20—22. He pre-

dicts his own death, and its blessed effects, 23—26. Being troubled in spirit, he resigns to the Father, prays, and is answered by a voice from heaven, 27, 28. He signifies the manner of his death, 29—34; and exhorts the people to improve their present advantages, 35, 36. The unbelief of the Jews shewn to be a fulfilment of Isaiah's prophecy, 37—41. Many rulers believe, but dare not confess him, 42, 43. He further warns the people not to reject him, 44 —50.

seek to him, in behalf of our friends and relatives, when sick and afflicted; and if they be true Christians, this will suggest the most encouraging plea in their behalf. But we must leave the event, in humble submission and implicit faith, to his unerring wisdom, without presuming to dictate. In one way or other, the sicknesses of those whom he loves will be " for the glory of God," and for their own good. Indeed we ought to be willing to live or die, to pass through any temporal suffering, or to part with our dearest relatives. when his glory requires it: for that cannot be separated from the real and enduring advantage of those whom he loves; any more than the glory of the Father can be separated from that of his beloved Son. But we cannot judge of his love to us by outward dispensations: " his ways are not as our ways," but infinitely above them; and he sees good to prove the faith of his people by afflictions and delays, when we should think it proper and almost indispensable for him to hasten to their relief. (P. O. xiii. 1—7.—*Note, Is.* lv. 8, 9.) We must therefore learn to " walk by faith," and to wait for him in patience and with persevering faith, and hope, and fervent prayer. (*Notes, Rom.* viii. 24—27. *Heb.* x. 35— 39. xii. 1—3. *Jam.* v. 7—11.)

V. 7—16.

When we follow our Redeemer's example of unwearied diligence in the work of the Lord, we shall experience a similar protection, as far as it is good for us. As long as the appointed but unknown days of our life continue, we may pursue our journey and attend to our duty, without fear of our enemies, who can have no power against us: but when that time is past, we must fall into the grave, and all our precautions to the contrary will be unavailing. (*Notes, Job* vii. 1—6. xiv. 13—15.)—While we therefore have time and opportunity, and the light of the gospel is afforded us, let us endeavour " to do good to all men;" and let us expect death as the end of our labours, and as the entrance of our souls into heavenly rest; nay, the quiet repose of our bodies also, till Jesus shall come, and awake them from sleep to participate our eternal recompence.— But let us remember, that even disciples are dull of apprehension respecting the meaning of their Lord: and that, while he orders every thing in subserviency to the increase of their faith, he deems their transient distress a small matter, compared with the durable good of their souls, and the common benefit of his people. We should therefore be ready to suffer and die with him, if called to it: but many have lively affections, and make confident resolutions, whose views are very dark and erroneous, and who, like Thomas, are in no wise prepared for the day of trial. (*Note,* xx. 24—29, *vv.* 24, 25.)

V. 17—27.

Natural humanity may induce men to sympathize with the afflicted, and attempt to comfort them; and divine grace will always lead us to do so: yet, alas! our compassions and our endeavours are feeble, and generally unavailing: (*Note,* xiv. 27, 28:) but, however the Lord may prove his people, by delaying to appear for their relief; they know that he is their only effectual Comforter, and they will leave all condoling friends, to pour out their complaints before him.—How seldom have we adequate views of his power and love, and suitable expectations of help from him! How constantly is our faith counteracted by alloys of unbelief!—We are indeed assured, that our dear deceased relatives shall " rise again at the resurrection " at the last day," and that all believers shall then appear with Jesus in glory: yet this assurance, comfortable as it is, cannot wholly allay our anguish for the loss of those, who were a daily blessing to us. But we should by no means " sorrow like men without hope, for those who " sleep in him:" neither should we look forward to death with dismay: for our gracious Friend, who gave himself for us, is " the Resurrection and the Life;" and death is now a conquered enemy, or rather converted into a friend to every believer. (*Notes,* 1 *Cor.* iii. 18—23, *v.* 22. xv. 55—58. *Phil.* i. 21—26. 1 *Thes.* iv. 13—18. P. O. 9— 18.) Our pious friends, whose bodies now sleep in the grave, live in heaven, and shall live for ever; and they, who are alive and remain, shall never die; for Jesus " hath " abolished death, and hath brought life and immortality " to light by the gospel." (*Notes,* 2 *Tim.* i. 10. *Heb.* ii. 14, 15.)—But do we indeed believe this? And are we dejected by the troubles of life, and the prospect of the grave? Lord, pardon our unbelief, " increase our faith," and help us assuredly to hope in thee as " the Christ, the " Son of God," who " came into the world to save sin- " ners," by dying on the cross; and " to those that wait " for thee thou wilt appear the second time without sin " unto salvation." (*Note, Heb.* ix. 27, 28.)

V. 28—40.

When Jesus displays his glory and gracious presence to us, as he does not to the world; we should confer with our fellow Christians on the encouragement given us, that we may be " helpers of their joy:" and when he calls us to his ordinances, or his throne of grace, we must not permit any company to detain us. But we should be careful not to limit our faith and hope, by the scanty measures of those with whom we converse; lest we should impede, instead of furthering, each other's " growth in grace."— Our Redeemer was " a man of sorrows." In this world

THEN Jesus, * six days before the passover, came to b Bethany, where Lazarus was, which had been dead, whom he raised from the dead.

2 There c they made him a supper, d and Martha served : but e Lazarus was one of them that sat at the table with him.

3 Then f took Mary a pound of ointment of spikenard, very costly, and g anointed the feet of Jesus, and wiped his feet with her hair: and the house was h filled with the odour of the ointment.

4 Then saith k one of his disciples, i Judas Iscariot, Simon's *son,* which should betray him,

5 Why m was not this ointment sold

---

of affliction, he conformed himself to the situation ; we do not read that he ever laughed ; but " he groaned," he " troubled himself," " he wept." That sensibility, by which many are elated in self-complacency, and self-preference, while they weep for fictitious distress, but are callous to real woe, he never sanctioned. But he wept with the afflicted : and thus both encouraged mourners to trust in him, and expect comfort from him ; and set us an example to withdraw from scenes of giddy mirth, that we may sympathize with the distressed, and counsel them. (*Note, Ec.* vii. 2—6.) Yet proud and prejudiced unbelievers call far more for our compassion and deep concern, than the most afflicted servants of our God. (*Notes, Ps.* cxix. 136. *Jer.* ix. 1, 2. xiii. 15—17. *Luke* xix. 41—44. *Rom.* ix. 1—3.)—It is indeed grievous to hear men pertinaciously dispute against those truths, by the belief of which alone they can be saved from everlasting misery ; and to see the world full of sin and woe, and men rejecting the only remedy with obstinate contempt.—The Lord, however, proceeds with his g a o s plan, notwithstanding the perverseness of mankind r andithout who believe and obey his word, shall experience the displays and efficacy of his glorious power in their behalf. But, while we expect help from him alone ; we must not tempt him by neglecting the means which he has instituted, or by refusing unreservedly to follow his directions to the best of our ability. The sinner cannot " quicken his own soul ;" but he ought to use the means of grace : the believer cannot sanctify himself ; but he ought to " lay aside every weight " and encumbrance : we cannot convert our children, relatives, neighbours, or congregations ; but we should instruct, warn, invite, and exhort them ; and exhibit before them an edifying and conciliating example : seeking a blessing on all by fervent and persevering prayer. (*Note, Ez.* xxxvii. 1—10. *P. O.* 1—14.) Thus we may remove the stone, or loose the grave-clothes, though we cannot raise the dead : and if we would have the Lord do for us and our's, what man *cannot* do ; we must diligently attend to all those things, which we *can* and *ought* to do.

V. 41—57.

Who can express the majesty and condescension of our Redeemer ! For the sake of those, who sought his life, he veiled his glory, and in " the form of a servant," he addressed the Father before he performed that stupendous miracle, which he immediately after wrought by his own power, as " the Resurrection and the Life," as " God manifest in the flesh." If he then shall please to speak, how soon can he rebuke our enemies, new-create our hearts, or answer our prayers for the conversion of those

around us ! How safely may we trust the health and life of our dearest relatives in his hand ! And how cheerfully go down to the grave, in sure hope of a glorious resurrection ! Our sharpest trials will terminate in more abundant comfort, if we indeed believe in him ; and they often are means of promoting his glory in the conversion of our fellow-sinners : so that, if we could foresee all the blessed effects of them, they would be causes of admiring gratitude and joy, and not of sorrow and dejection. But we must wait in faith, hope, and persevering prayer, till these happy effects take place. No outward means can overcome the obdurate enmity of sinners against God : and they, who have engaged their interest and reputation in the unequal contest, become more callous than other men. Sagacious and infidel politicians count all men ignorant and foolish, who hesitate to sacrifice honesty and justice to expediency ; and persecutors deem it a publick calamity, when numbers are converted to Jesus. They think themselves culpable, when not using the most decided or sanguinary methods of opposing the truth : they undertake to crush those with oppressive and overwhelming power, whom they cannot answer: they imagine that the excellency of the end will sanctify all the impieties, frauds, and murders, which are used to compass it : and they deem the life of innocent persons a trivial matter, compared with the peace and *uniformity* of the church ; which too generally consist in gross superstition, usurped authority over men's consciences, and destructive heresies. But, while they seek to avert calamities by such means, they bring them upon themselves in the most tremendous manner.—The Lord will, however, honour his own institutions, notwithstanding man's wickedness ; and extort confessions to his truth from his implacable enemies. Once, and but once, it was expedient that the innocent should suffer for the guilty ; and the divine Saviour willingly died for us, to gather us, as " the children of God," from all our dispersions into his kingdom : may he gather far more and more into his church from every part of the earth ! But no devices of man can derange the purposes of God : while hypocrites amuse themselves with forms and controversies, and worldly men pursue their own projects, Jesus still communes with his disciples, and orders all things in subserviency to his own glory and their salvation.

NOTES.

Lazarus sat at table on this occasion, to shew that he was really alive and m good health ; and Martha waited, to honour Jesus, though the entertainment was made at the house of Simon.—Judas

for ⁿthree hundred pence, ᵒand given to the poor?

6 This he said, ᵇnot that he cared for the poor; but ᵈbecause he was a thief, and had ᵉthe bag, and bare what was put therein.

7 Then said Jesus, 'Let her alone: ᵍagainst the day of my burying hath she kept this.

8 For ʰthe poor always ye have with you; ⁱbut me ye have not always.

9 ¶ Much ʲpeople of the Jews therefore knew that he was there; and they came, not for Jesus' sake only, but that they might see Lazarus also, whom he had raised from the dead.

10 But ᵏthe chief priests consulted that they might put Lazarus also to death;

11 Because that ᵃby reason of him many of the Jews went away, and believed on Jesus.

12 ¶ On the next day, ᵇmuch people that were ᶜcome to the feast, when they heard that Jesus was coming to Jerusalem,

13 Took ᵈbranches of palm-trees, and went forth to meet him, and cried, ᵉHosanna: Blessed is ᶠthe King of Israel, that cometh in the name of the Lord.

14 And ᵍJesus, when he had found a young ass, sat thereon; ʰas it is written,

15 ⁱFear not, daughter of Sion: behold, thy King cometh, ᵏsitting on an ass's colt.

16 These things ˡunderstood not

---

was covetous! this was " his own iniquity:" and neither his professed faith in Christ, nor his apostolical office, had subdued the base propensity; which could be effected by renewing grace alone, and of that he was destitute. (*Note*, 1 Tim. vi. 6—10, vv. 8—10.) Being entrusted with the scanty stock, from which the necessary expenses of our Lord and his company were supplied, he shamefully stole small sums from it; probably accounting for them as given to the poor. (*Note*, xiii. 18—30, v. 29.) And he thought, that if the price of this ointment had been put into the bag, he could have taken a larger sum on the same pretence, without being suspected : or rather, he was forming his plan of treachery, and wished to have the common purse well filled, before he went off with it. More than ten pounds must have appeared a large sum to him, who bargained for about three pounds fifteen shillings, to betray his Lord. (*Note,· Matt.* xxvi. 14—16.)—*Sold, &c.* (5) It is not said, ' Why was it bought?' ' Why was not the ' money rather given to the poor?' Probably, Mary had possessed and used several things, ministering to luxury and indulgence, before she attended decidedly to " the " one thing needful." (*Note*, Luke x. 38—42.) She had at this time, however, no occasion for them; and had doubtless sold many of them, employing the money in charity : but she had been led to keep this box of precious ointment, it is likely, without knowing for what purpose. (*Marg. Ref.* l—t.)—*Day of, &c.* (7) ' If this ointment ' were laid out on a dead body, you would not think ' much of it : you may consider this anointing as an em- ' balming of me.' *Lardner.*—' I am of opinion that Mary ' indeed was not thinking of Christ's death and burial; ' but he testifies, that this had not occurred by chance; ' but that a spectacle, giving a previous intimation of his ' approaching burial, was set before them by divine Pro- ' vidence.' *Beza.*—*The poor, &c.* (8) *Marg. Ref.* u, x.— *Note, Matt.* xxv. 34—40.

That eat at table with him. (2) Των συνανακειμενων. *Matt.* ix. 10 xiv. 9. *Mark* ii. 15. vi. 22. 26. *Luke* vii. 49. xiv. 10. 15.—*A pound.* (3) Λιτραν. xix. 39. Not elsewhere.—

Of spikenard.] Πιστικης. See on *Mark* xiv. 3.—*Very precious.*] Πολυτιμου. *Matt.* xiii. 46. Not elsewhere.—*Odour.*] Οσμης. 2 *Cor.* ii. 14. 16. *Eph.* v. 2. *Phil.* iv. 18.—*Cant.* i. 3. 12. ii. 13. iv. 10. *Sept.*—*He cared.* (6) Εμελεν αυτω. See on x. 13.—*The bag.*] Το γλωσσοκομον. xiii. 29. Not elsewhere N. T.—2 *Chr.* xxiv. 8. 10, 11. *Sept.*—*My burying.* (7) Τω ενταφιασμου μι, *Mark* xiv. 8. See on *Matt.* xxvi. 12.

V. 9—11. Perhaps Lazarus had purposely lived very retired, from the time that Jesus had left Bethany: so that numbers had not been able to gratify their curiosity with the sight of him, till our Lord's return afforded them the opportunity. (*Note*, xi. 54—57.) The undeniable miracle of Lazarus's resurrection naturally induced multitudes, from different motives, to resort to Bethany, to see both Jesus and him at the same time; and many Jews, being convinced that Jesus was the Messiah, and the priests and Pharisees very wicked in opposing him, renounced their party and instruction to attend on his ministry : but the conduct of the rulers, in consulting to put Lazarus to death, that they might prevent the further effect of the miracle, was such a compound of impiety, infidelity, iniquity, malice, and folly, as can never be accounted for, but by deep acquaintance with the desperate enmity of man's heart against God. (See on xi. 47, 48.) They seemed to resolve that the man should die, of whom the Lord had evidently declared that he should live !—' To destroy ' an innocent man, without any crime laid against him, ' only to preserve their own honour and reputation! See ' here the infallible sentence of the rulers of the church.' *Whitby.* (*Marg. Ref.—Note*, xi. 49—53.)

V. 12—19. (*Notes, Matt.* xxi.—11. *Mark* xi. 1—11. *Luke* xix. 28—40.) The testimony of the numerous company of Jews, who were present when Lazarus was called out of the grave, had excited great multitudes, both of the inhabitants of Jerusalem, and of strangers, to go forth and meet Jesus. His disciples had no direct concern in itt nay, they did not understand the meaning of his entering Jerusalem in this manner, till after his ascension and the pouring out of the Holy Spirit, by whose sacred influences

4 B 2

his disciples at the first.: but ⸗ when Jesus was glorified, ⁸ then remembered they that these things were written of him, and *that* they had done these things unto him.

17 The ⁹ people therefore that was with him when he called Lazarus out of his grave, and raised him from the dead, ¹ bare record.

18 For ¹ this cause the people also met him, for that they heard that he had done this miracle.

19 The Pharisees therefore said among themselves, ² Perceive ye how ye prevail nothing? behold, ³ the world is gone after him. .

20 ¶ And there were certain ⁴ Greeks among them that came up ⁵ to worship at the feast :

21 The same came therefore to Philip, which was of Bethsaida of Ga-

lilee, and desired him, saying, Sir, ⁷ we would see Jesus.

22 Philip cometh, and telleth ⁸ Andrew: and again ⁹ Andrew and Philip tell Jesus. ·

23 And Jesus answered them, saying, ¹ The hour is come, that the Son of man should be glorified.

24 Verily, verily, I say unto you, ² Except a ᶦcorn of wheat fall into the ground and die, it abideth alone: but ³ if it die it bringeth forth much fruit.

25 He ⁴ that loveth his life shall lose it ; and he that ⁵ hateth his life in this world shall keep it unto life eternal.

26 If any man ⁶ serve me, ⁷ let him follow me ; and ⁸ where I am, there shall also my servant be: if any man serve me, ⁹ him will *my* Father honour.

---

they recollected the words of the prophet, and perceived their accomplishment in that transaction. (*Marg. Ref.* b—n.—*Notes, Zech.* ix. 9, 10.) But the Pharisees, comparing this conduct of Jesus, and the favour shewn him by the multitude, with their late edict, (xi. 57,) were greatly enraged : they foresaw the entire ruin of their reputation and authority, if he were let alone any longer. Their opposition and proclamation had produced no effect : " the world " seemed to be gone after him; (iii. 26. *Acts* xvii. 6 ;) and while they were more than ever determined to apprehend him, they were afraid to attempt it, lest the multitudes should rise to oppose them. This made way for the treachery of Judas, which otherwise would not have been so necessary. (*Notes,* xi. 49—53. *Matt.* xxvi. 3—5.) —The clause in Zachariah, " Rejoice greatly, &c." is here rendered " Fear not, &c." Had the rulers and people of Jerusalem rejoiced greatly in Christ their King; they would have had no reason to fear, either the Romans or any other enemies—*Glorified.* (16) *Marg. Ref.* q—s.— *Notes,* 23—26. vii. 37—39. xii. 31—35. *Acts* ii. 33—36. iii. 12—16.

Branches. (13) Τα βαΐα. Here only. ‘ *Vocabulum e lingua Coptica ... in linguam Græcam translatum.*’ Schleusner.— *Of palm-trees.*] Των φοινικων. *Rev.* vii. 9. Not elsewhere N. T.—*Judg.* i. 16. iii. 13. *Neh.* viii. 15. Sept.—*A young ass.* (14) Οναριον. Here only. Ab ονος, *asinus.*—Glorified. (16) Εδοξασθη. See on vii. 39.—*Ye prevail.* (19) Ωφελειτε. vi. 63. *Matt.* xv. 5. xvi. 26. xxvii. 24. *Rom.* ii. 25. 1 *Cor.* xiii. 3. xiv. 6, *et al.*

V. 20—22. ‘ By the name of Greeks all were called, ‘ who were neither Israelites nor proselytes, among whom ‘ there were not a few pious men, worshippers of the true ‘ God.’ *Grotius.* The difficulty, which the apostles found about mentioning these " Greeks " to Jesus, as well as the subsequent discourse, strongly implies, that they were uncircumcised persons.—It is supposed that they lived in

the confines of Galilee, and thus got acquainted with Philip. (*Marg. Ref.* t, u.—*Notes,* i. 43—46. *Mark* vii. 24 —30.) They were favourable to the Jewish religion, and came to Jerusalem to worship ; yet it is not said that they ate the passover. They had heard of our Lord's miracles, were desirous of seeing him, and receiving his instructions, and they respectfully applied to Philip for that purpose : but he, perhaps fearing, lest an interview with Gentiles would render his Lord still more obnoxious to the Pharisees, did not make it known to him, till he had previously conferred with Andrew about it. Probably, Jesus ordered them to be introduced to him, and spake what follows in their presence ; though he might see good not to admit them to a private conference.—‘ Because Christ ‘ when he sent them ’ (the apostles) ‘ forth to preach, for- ‘ bade them to go into the coasts of the Gentiles : (*Matt.* ‘ x. 5 :) ... they were in doubt whether such uncircumcised ‘ persons were to be admitted to converse with Jesus ; and ‘ so they consult him first, before they brought them to ‘ him.’ *Whitby.* (*Marg. Ref.* x—a.—*Note, Acts* xxi. 27 —30.)

Greeks. (20) Ἑλληνες. vii. 35. *Acts* xiv. 1. xvi. 1. 3. xvii. 4. xviii. 4. 17. xix. 10. 17. *Rom.* i. 14. 16. *Gal.* iii. 28. *Col.* iii. 11, *et al.* *Notes, Mark* vii. 24—30, *v.* 26. *Acts* xi. 19— 21, *v.* 20.) ‘ In the sacred writings the word Ἑλληνες is ‘ every where opposed to the Jews. Those Jews are called ‘ Ἑλληνισται, who read the Scriptures in the Greek lan- ‘ guage : ... or Gentiles born, but converted to the Jewish ‘ religion, which are called *proselytes.*’ *Leigh.*

V. 23—26. Our Lord, on this occasion, declared openly that the appointed time was at hand, when he should be advanced to his exalted throne, to be glorified as the Saviour and King of both Jews and Gentiles : yet this would not take place, till he had laid down his life for them. (*Marg. Ref.* b.—*Note,* 12—19, *v.* 16.)—A corn of wheat yields no increase, unless it be cast into the ground ; and there

27 Now ¹ is my soul troubled; and ᵐ what shall I say? ⁿ "Father, save me from this hour? ° but for this cause came I unto this hour.

28 ᵖ Father, glorify thy name. ᵠ Then came there a voice from heaven, say-ing, 'I have both glorified it, ˢ and will glorify it again.

29 The people therefore that stood by, and heard it, said that it ᵗ thun-

dered: others said, ᵘ An angel spake to him.

30 Jesus answered and said, This voice came not because of me, ˣ but for your sakes.

31 Now ʸ is the judgment of this world: ᶻ now shall the prince of this world be cast out.

32 And I, ᵃ if I be lifted up from the earth, ᵇ will draw ᶜ all men unto me.

1 xi. 33—35. xiii. 21. Ps. lxix. 1—3. lxxvii. 3. m Is. iii. 8. Matt. xxvi. 38, 39, 42. Mark xiv. 33—36. Luke xxii. 44. 45. Heb. v. 7. n Is. xxxviii. 15. Luke xlii. 49, 50. o xi. 41. Matt. xxvi. 53, 54. p xviii. 37. 1 Tim. i. 15. Heb. ii. 14. q b—c. p xvii. 1. Matt. xxvi. 42. Mark xiv. 36. q Matt. iii. 17. xvii. 5. 2 Pet. i. 17. r ix. 3. xi. 4. 40—44. 6—11. Rev. v. 9—14. Rev. vi. 1. viii. 5. xi. 19. xiv. 2.

s xiii. 31, 32. Is. xlix. 3—7. Eph. ii. 7. iii. 10. 21. Phil. i. t Ex. xix. 16. xx. 18. Job xxxvii. 2—5. xl. 9. Ex. x. 5.

u Acts xxiii. 8, 9. Rev. xviii. 1, 2. x 34. xi. 15. 42. 2 Cor. viii. 9. y 22—27. xvi. 8—10. z xiv. 30. xvi. 11. Gen. iii. 15. 1s. xlix. 24, 25. Matt. xii. 28, 29. Luke x. 17—19. Acts xxvi. 18 2 Cor. iv. 4. Eph. ii. 1, 2. Col. ii. 15. Heb. ii. 14. 1 John iii. 8. Rev. xii. 9—11. xx. 2, 3. a iii. 14. viii. 28. xix. 17, 18. Deut. xxi. 22, 23. b vi. 44. Heb. 2 Sam. xviii. 9, 10. Ps. xxii. 16—18. Gal. iii. 13. 1 Pet. ii. 24. iii. 18. Cant. i. 4. Hos. xi. 4. c i. 7. 29. 1s. xlix. 6. Rom. v. 17—19. ii. 9, 10. 1 John ii. 2. Rev. v. 9. 1 Tim. ii. 6. Heb.

perish, as to its former shape and subsistence: but while this is taking place a blade springs up, which at length produces many grains of the same kind. (*Marg. Ref.* c, d. —*Note,* 1 Cor. xv. 35—38.) In like manner, our Lord might indeed *alone* have possessed his heavenly glory without becoming incarnate; or after his incarnation, he might have entered heaven alone, by his own perfect right-eousness, without suffering or death: but then no sinner of the whole human race could have been saved. His love therefore induced him voluntarily to submit to death, that being laid in the ground, as if about to turn to corruption, he might thence be raised, as the first-fruits of a large in-crease of redeemed sinners, to bear his image, to shew forth his praise, and to participate his glory. As this was his design, and he was about to carry it into effect, his dis-ciples and these Greeks also, should be reminded to "arm " themselves with the same mind:" (*Note,* 1 Pet. iv. 1, 2 :) not loving this present life, when it would endanger that of their souls; but comparatively *hating* it, that they might secure the eternal life which he gave to his faith-ful followers. (*Marg. Ref.* e, f.—*Notes,* x. 26—31. xi. 20 —27. Matt. x. 37—39. xvi. 24—28. Mark viii. 32—37. Luke ix. 18—27, v. 23. xiv. 25—27.) As they called him their Lord, such of them as really meant to devote them-selves to his service should prepare to follow his example in being obedient even unto death, if called to it; for such servants would assuredly be admitted into the same happy place, whither he was going. (*Marg. Ref.* g—k.—*Notes,* xiv. 2, 3. *Ps.* xvi. 8—11. *Matt.* xxv. 19—23. 2 Cor. v. 5— 8. *Phil.* i. 21—26.) Yea, his Father would certainly re-ward, nay honour in the most distinguishing manner, all those who thus served and followed him; however man might despise both him and them.—The clause, " if any " man will serve me, &c." was suited to encourage the Gentiles, and all the hearers, to devote themselves to his service; and to deny themselves for his sake; as well as to shew the nature of his kingdom, and the trials attend-ing his service.

Serve, &c. (26) Διακονη̣. xii. 2. *Matt.* xx. 28. *Luke* xxii. 27, *et al.* Ex διᾳ et κονις, *pulvis.*—*Servant.*] Διακονος. *Matt.* xx. 26. *Rom.* xiii. 4. xv. 8. xvi. 1. *Phil.* i. 1, *et mult. al.*

V. 27—33. The near prospect, which our Lord had of his most tremendous sufferings, excited on this occasion such a perturbation of mind, that he publickly declared that " his soul was troubled; and what should he " say in respect of the scene before him? " Shall I say, Father, " save me from this hour? " Even his holy nature might have dictated this prayer; had he not known that he came

into the world, and had continued so long upon earth, with a special purpose of passing through that season of darkness and anguish; without which all his former la-bours, obedience, and sufferings would be unavailing as to the grand object of his incarnation. He would therefore in perfect acquiescence, say, " Father, glorify thy name :" for he only desired to be supported through the dread-ful scene, to the glory of the divine justice, holiness, mercy, and truth, in the salvation of sinners. (*Marg. Ref.* l—p.— *Notes, Matt.* xxvi. 36—46. *Mark* xiv. 32—36, v. 36. *Luke* xxii. 39—44. Upon this, the voice of the Father from heaven, which had attested him to be his Beloved Son, at his baptism, and when he was transfigured, proclaimed, that he " had both glorified his name, and would glorify it." (*Marg. Ref.* q, r.—*Notes, Matt.* iii. 16, 17. xvii. 5—8.) The life, miracles, and doctrine of our Lord had mani-fested the glory of God; and his death, resurrection, and exaltation would still more extensively and illustriously display it.—Those who heard this voice less distinctly, or the Greeks who did not understand the words spoken, said that " it thundered; " as probably it was attended by thunder: others, who understood what was spoken, sup-posed that an angel addressed him: but none of them seem to have understood, that the Father thus attested his complacency in him and in his whole work. (*Marg. Ref.* t, u.) He therefore assured them, that this voice did not come for his sake, as he had always been fully satisfied of his Father's love; but for their benefit, that they might believe in him as the Son of God. For the " judgment of " this world was come." Its wickedness would be proved, and its condemnation pronounced, in that event which was about to take place. His crucifixion would disclose and aggravate the guilt of man's desperate wickedness, and shew God's abhorrence of sin, and the certain destruction which awaited all unbelievers. His death would make way for the judgment and condemnation of the Jewish nation, and of the whole Gentile world, those excepted who em-braced his gospel. His religion would distinguish men's characters, convict multitudes of hypocrisy, lead others to judge and condemn themselves; and thus, in every way, the judgment of the last day would be anticipated. In con-sequence of his death, resurrection, ascension, the pouring out of the Holy Spirit, and the preaching of the gospel, Satan, the great ruler and prince of this wicked world, whom all idolaters worship as their god, and all uncon-verted sinners obey as their king, would be judged and condemned, with all his subjects; the sentence would begin to be executed in his expulsion from his usurped

33 This he said, ' signifying what death he should die.

34 The people answered him, We have heard out of ' the law, that ' Christ abideth for ever: and how sayest thou, The Son of man must be lifted up? ' who is this Son of man?

35 Then Jesus said unto them, ' Yet a little while is the light with you: ' walk while ye have the light, ' lest darkness come upon you: ' for he that walketh in darkness knoweth not whither he goeth.

36 While ye have light, " believe in the light, that ye may be " the children of light. These things spake Jesus, ° and departed, and did hide himself from them.

37 ¶ But ' though he had done so

many miracles before them, yet they believed not on him:

38 ' That the saying of ' Esaias the prophet might be fulfilled, which he spake, Lord, ' who hath believed our report? and to whom hath ' the arm of the Lord been " revealed?

39 Therefore ' they could not believe, ' because that Esaias said again,

40 He ' hath blinded their eyes, ' and hardened their heart; ' that they should not see with *their* eyes, nor understand with *their* heart, ' and be converted, and I should ' heal them.

41 These things said Esaias, ' when he ' saw his glory, ' and spake of him.

17. Josh. xi. 20. Rom. ix. 18. xi. 7. *marg.* b Deut. xxix. 4. Ps. cxxxv. 16—19. Is. xxvi. 11. xliii. 19, 20. Jer. v. 21. Ez. xii. 2. Mark viii. 17, 18. c Acts iii. 19. xv. 3. Jam. v. 19, 20. d Ps. vi. 2. xli. 4. cxlvii. 3. Is. liii. b. lvii. 18, 19. Jer. iii. 22. Hos. vi. 1. xiv. 4. Luke iv. 18. e Is. vi. 1—5, 9, 10. f. 14. 16. xiv. 9. Ex. xxxiii. 19 —23. 2 Cor. iv. 6. Heb. i. 8. g v. 30. Acts x. 43. 1 Pet. i. 11, 12. Rev. xix. 10.

dominion, by the conversion of sinners, the subversion of the heathen temples, and the destruction of idolatry. Of this, the enquiry of these Greeks was an earnest; and this would progressively be carried on, till the kingdoms of the earth would be subjected to Christ. (*Marg. Ref.* x—a.— *Notes*, xiv. 29—31. xvi. 8—11. *Luke* x. 17—20. 2 *Cor.* iv. 3, 4. 1 *John* v. 19. *Rev.* xii. 7—12.)—In short, " if," or *when*, " he should be lifted up," from the earth, to die on the cross, he would in consequence of his atonement, and by its attractive influence, draw men of all nations and descriptions, to come and put their trust in him, to devote themselves to his service, and to follow him in the way to his eternal glory.—This not only referred to his death, but it was a prediction of the manner in which he was about to die, even by crucifixion; with an evident allusion to the brazen serpent, lifted up in the camp of Israel, that all who looked to it might live. (*Marg. Ref.* b, c.—*Note*, iii. 14, 15.)

Troubled. (27) Τιταρακται. See on *Matt.* xiv. 26.—*It thundered.* (29) Βροντην γεγονεναι. *Mark* iii. 17. *Rev.* iv. 5. vi. 1. viii. 5. x. 3, 4, *et al.*—*The prince of this world.* (31) Αρχων τα κοσμα τατα. xiv. 30. xvi. 11. *Eph.* ii. 2.— *Shall be ... cast out.*] Εκβληθησεται εξω. *Rev.* xii. 9. See on ix. 34.—*Will draw.* (32) 'Ελκυσω. See on vi. 44.

V. 34—36. The people understood our Lord to mean, that he was about to be cut off by a violent death; and they observed, that the law (a general word sometimes used for the whole of the Old Testament,) had represented their promised Messiah as a glorious Prince, whose kingdom was to endure for ever; and from this they had inferred that he would never die: how then could he speak of " the Son of man being lifted up?" (*Marg. Ref.* e— g.) They could not reconcile these things, and they desired to be clearly informed, " who the Son of man was." They knew that he spake of himself by that title; but did he or did he not mean, that he was the Messiah?—Thus they took a part of scripture, and drew erroneous conclusions from it, because they overlooked other parts of · the same holy records: for had they properly adverted to

those prophecies, which explicitly foretold the sufferings and death of the Messiah, (*Notes*, *Ps.* xxii. *Is.* liii. *Dan.* ix. 24—27. *Zech.* xiii. 7,) they must have inferred his resurrection and subsequent glory, from those scriptures which foretold that he should abide and reign for ever. Our Lord, however, did not see good to anticipate their answer to the question, which the event would speedily give them: but he warned them, that the light would continue with them only a little while, and exhorted them to walk in it while they had it, before they were overtaken by the most dangerous and deplorable darkness. He, " the " Light of the World," continued with them a very short time, in respect of his personal ministry: the light of divine truth was soon after withdrawn from the unbelieving Jews, and they have ever since wandered " in " darkness, not knowing whither they go." (*Marg. Ref.* h—n.—*Notes*, iii. 19—21. *Prov.* iv. 18, 19. *Is.* viii. 20— 22. *Jer.* xiii. 15—17. 1 *John* ii. 7—11. *Jude* 11—13.) If then the Jews desired to walk in the light, they must believe in it, and follow its instructions and directions : thus they would become " children of the light," the children of " God, who is Light," and conformed to him in knowledge, righteousness, and felicity; and so be " made meet " for the inheritance of the saints in light," and walk in the light in some measure as they do. (*Notes*, *Eph.* v. 8— 14. *Col.* i. 9—14. 1 *Thes.* v. 4—11.)—Having said this, our Lord retired, and concealed himself from his persecutors, probably by going privately to Bethany. (*Marg. Ref.* o.—*Notes*, x. 32—39, *v.* 39. *Luke* xxi. 37, 38.)

That ye may be the children of light. (36) 'Ινα υιοι φωτος γενησθε. *Luke* xvi. 8. 1 *Thes.* v. 5. Τεκνα φωτος, *Eph.* v. 8. —*Did hide himself.*] Εκρυβη. viii. 59.

V. 37—41. The obstinate unbelief of the Jews, notwithstanding the numerous and stupendous miracles of Jesus, was a most evident accomplishment of an ancient prophecy. (*Note*, *Is.* liii. 1.) It was predicted by Isaiah, as by one astonished, that few in comparison would believe the report of the Messiah's being come : because his external appearance would not coincide with their carnal

4 н 5

h iii. 2. vii. 45. ' *42* Nevertheless, ᵇ among the chief
hl. xi. 45. xxv. rulers also many believed on him:
34.
i Matt. x. 32. but because of the Pharisees ¹ they did
33. Luke xii.
8. Rom. x. 10. 1 John iv. 2, 3. 15.

not confess *him;* ᵏ lest they should be ᵏ vii. 13. ix. 22.
34, xvi. 2. Prov.
put out of the synagogue :　　　　　 xxix. 25. 1s. ii.
7. st lviii. 11. lxvi.
.43 For ¹ they loved the praise of ⁵. Matt. xxvi. 69
—75. Luke vi.
22. Acts v. 41. 1 Pet. iv. 12—16. 1 v. 41. 44. Matt. vi. 2. xxiii. 5—7. Luke xvi. 15.
Rom. ii. 29. 1 Thes. ii. 6.

expectations: · and in the case of these few, " the arm," or
power ;" of the LORD " would be displayed, or made bare,
to subdue their pride, enmity, and worldly prejudices, and
to bring them to believe in their lowly and spiritual Redeemer. Or, the enquiry might be, to whom the despised
Messiah would be made known, as the Arm or Power of
God to salvation. (*Marg. Ref. p. u.*) None of our fallen
race, indeed, are inclined ·of themselves to welcome the
salvation of God; but the Jews of that generation did every
thing which could be conceived to provoke him to withhold it from them, and to " give them up to their own
" hearts' lusts." " Therefore they could not believe," for
the same prophet had also foretold, that " God would
" blind their eyes," &c. (*Marg. Ref.* x—d.—*Notes, Is.* vi.
9, 10. *Matt.* xiii. 14, 15.) They had long that their own
eyes, and hardened their own hearts; and so God would
give up many of them to· that *judicial* blindness, which
would render their conversion and salvation impossible.
The prophecy was not the *motive*, or the *cause*, of their
wickedness; but it was the declaration of the purpose of
God, which could not be defeated: as therefore this prophecy stood in scripture against them, and others of like
character who hated the truth from love of sin, the event
became certain ; in which sense it is ·said,· that ·" they
" could not believe." (*Note, 2 Thes.* ii. 8—12.)—Numbers indeed were given up to judicial blindness; yet others
in the multitude were not : and the preceding exhortations
and warnings would eventually be useful ·to many of these,
as well as manifest the desperate enmity of the others. · In
fact, a large " remnant, according to the election of grace,"
were afterwards converted, while the bulk of ·the nation
was left to be blinded and hardened.·(*Notes, Acts* xxi. 17—
21. *Rom.* xi. 1—10.)—The *unfailing certainty* of predicted
events, must arise, not only from the infallible foreknowledge of God, but also from his fixed decree; unless it can
be thought that he foreknows things over which he has no
power, and which he cannot possibly alter ! But if thousands and ·ten thousands more of the Jews, rulers and
priests among the number, had embraced the gospel, these
prophecies would nevertheless have been accomplished in
all the unbelieving part of the nation : as the prediction and
promise of God, concerning Abraham's seed inheriting
Canaan, were fulfilled; though the generation which came
first out of Egypt perished in the wilderness through their
unbelief. (*Notes, Num.* xiv. 27—30. 34. *Ps.* xc. 13—17.)
So that no hindrance to any man's complying with our
Lord's exhortations arose from the prophecy or purpose of
God; which related only to those who obstinately refuse
to comply with them.—*Could. not.* (39) *Note, Mark* i.
45. " That is,' says Theophylact or Chrysostom, ' they
" ' would not.' ... And yet, if you look to the thing itself, it
' is true, that the reprobate do not believe, because they
' *will not* believe : so that this is the nearest, and most
' direct cause of their unbelief. ... But the Evangelist goes
' deeper, when he says, " They could not believe :" for
' as the reprobate will not believe; so it is certain that
' they *cannot be willing,* because the darkness in which they

' are born, 'cannot· comprehend' the light.' *Beza.* (*Note,
Acts* xxviii. 23—29.)—St.· John ·adds, that· the prophet
" said these things, when he saw *his·* glory and spake of
" him " (41) ; evidently meaning Christ, of whom he
discoursed both before and afterwards. The reference is
made to· that august vision, which· Isaiah had of " the
" glory of the LORD," and the worship of the attendant
seraphim·: and the prophet then saw " the glory of Christ
" and spake of him ;" from which we confidently infer
that Jesus is JEHOVAH.—The. word, in the first verse of
the chapter, referred to, is not JEHOVAH, but Adonai ; but
it is JEHOVAH in the third verse : and the words in the
fifth verse " Thine eyes have seen the King, the LORD of
" hosts," are very remarkable. (*Marg. Ref.* e—g.—*Notes,*
i. 18. *Is.* vi. 1—5.) ' If these words,' " These things said
' " Isaiah, when he saw his glory," are not to be ·under-
' stood of Christ, what use have. they, or to what purpose
' do they serve? There being no. need to tell us, that
' Isaiah then saw the glory of God, the Father, and spake
' of him.' *Whitby.*. . . . . . .
　Who hath believed, &c. (37) The quotation is exactly
from the LXX, and entirely agrees with the Hebrew.—
He hath blinded, &c. (40) Τ*εφλωκεν.* 2 Cor. iv. 4. 1 *John*
ii. 11. Not elsewhere N. T.—*Is.·*xlii.·19. *Sept.*—Hardened.]
Πεπωρωκεν.. ·*Mark* ·vi. 52. viii. 17.·*Rom.* xi. 7. 2 *Cor.* iii.
14.—*Job* xvii. 7. *Sept.*—Πωρωσις, See on *Mark* iii. 5. ·
　V. 42, 43. The resurrection of Lazarus convinced several even of ·the members of the sanhedrim, that Jesus
was the Messiah, and they ·secretly believed in him as such:
but most of them regarded him chiefly as a temporal De-
liverer·. Probably they expected, that he would shortly
appear in that character, and then they might safely acknowledge him. · At present, the Pharisees, and the leading persons, were so violent in their opposition to him,
that these rulers had not courage to confess their sentiments, lest they should be excommunicated : (*Marg. Ref.*
h—k.—*Note,· ix.* 19—23 :) for ambition and regard to
reputation were predominant in their hearts ; and they preferred the esteem and applause ·of their neighbours, and
especially of those in authority, to the favour and approbation of God, which they could not expect while they
acted contrary to their consciences. (*Marg. Ref.* l, m.—
Notes, iii. 1, 2. v. 39—44. *Matt.* x. 32, 33. 37—39. *Rom.*
x. 5—11; vv. 9, 10. 1 *John* ii. 15—17.) Thus they suffered the enemies of Jesus to proceed in· their sanguinary
measures, till they had· him put to death, without making
any opposition or protest against them; nay, they even
sanctioned their conduct by silent concurrence.—Nicodemus and Joseph of Arimathea, though in a measure culpable, can hardly be thought included in this heavy censure.—The *believing* spoken of, seems to have been a persuasion that Jesus was the Messiah, without any clear and
adequate views of his kingdom, or reliance on him for salvation. (*Notes,* ii. 23—25. iii. 16. v. 24—27; v. 24. viii.
30—36, vv. 30, 31.)
　Should be put out of the synagogue. (42) Αποσυναγωγοι
γενωνται. See on ix. 22.—*The praise.* (43) Την δοξαν. 41.

4 B 6

men more than ᵐ the praise of God.

44 ¶ Jesus ⁿ cried and said, ° He that believeth on me, believeth not on me, but on him that sent me.

45 And ᵖ he that seeth me, seeth him that sent me.

46 I ᶜ am come a Light into the world, that whosoever believeth on me should not ʳ abide in darkness.

47 And if any man hear my words, and believe not, ᵗ I judge him not: for I came not to judge the world, but to save the world.

48 He that ᵘ rejecteth me, and receiveth not my words, hath one that judgeth him: ˣ the word that I have spoken, the same shall ʸ judge him in the last day.

49 For ᶻ I have not spoken of myself; but the Father which sent me, he gave me a commandment, what I should say, and what I should speak.

50 And I know that ᵃ his commandment is life everlasting: whatsoever I speak therefore, even as the Father said unto me, so I speak.

---

v. 41. 44. vii. 18. *Rom.* ii. 7. viii. 18. 1 *Thes.* ii. 6. 2 *Thes.* ii. 14. 1 *Pet.* i. 7. v. 1. 10.

V. 44—50. This seems to have been one of our Lord's last addresses to the Jews, before he finally left the temple. (*Note, Matt.* xxiii. 37—39.) He proclaimed in the most publick manner, with a loud voice, saying, " He that believeth on me, believeth not on me," (that is, *only* or *ultimately*,) " but on him who sent me." Thus every true believer has all the divine perfections, for the foundation of his hope of preservation and eternal salvation : (*Marg. Ref.* n, o.—*Notes,* 1 *Pet.* i. 3—5. 17—21.) And he added, " He that seeth me, seeth him that sent me." So that every one, who saw or contemplated him, at the same time contemplated also the Father who sent him. In his holy character the moral perfections of God were displayed; his miracles shewed the divine power, authority, and compassion ; his knowledge of distant events and of the secrets of men's hearts, and his most consummate prudence discovered the divine omniscience and wisdom; and his mediatorial undertaking, obedience, sufferings, and intercession, form the grand exhibition of the glorious justice, holiness, truth, and mercy of God. This was so manifest, that not only believers saw and loved the Father in him; but unbelievers also " saw and hated both him and his Father." (*Marg. Ref.* p.—*Notes,* xiv. 7—14, *v.* 9. xv. 22—25.)— Others indeed had been enlightened, after they came into the world, and so shone for a while, with feeble and reflected beams ; but Jesus was the Light of heaven, and " came a Light into the world," to illuminate it by his doctrine : so that no believer in him would abide in darkness, and every remains of ignorance and error would gradually be dispelled. (*Marg. Ref.* q, r.—*Notes,* 34—36. I. 4—9. viii. 12. *Is.* xlii. 13—17, *v.* 16. *Mal.* iv. 2, 3. *Eph.* v. 8—14. 1 *John* ii. 7—11.) Wicked men hated the Light, and would not hear and believe the instructions of Jesus : but for the present, he did not intend to judge or take vengeance upon them, but would bear their indignities and cruelties with perfect meekness; working no miracles but those of mercy, suited to the character of a gracious Saviour, rather than to that of a terrible Judge and Avenger. (*Marg. Ref.* s, t.—*Notes,* iii. 16—21.) Yet those who " rejected him and his words " should not presume on always escaping with impunity. They would be cited before an impartial Judge: and the words of truth and grace, which he then spake and they despised, would cer-

tainly rise up in judgment against them, to ensure and aggravate their condemnation " at the last day." For he had always spoken the words which he was commanded of the Father to deliver: and they were not only words of truth, purity, and authority, but of abundant mercy and grace; and he assuredly knew them to contain the only and the effectual way, by which sinners might obtain eternal life. He therefore proclaimed them confidently ; and if any rejected them and him, they did it at their peril. (*Marg. Ref.* u—a.—*Note,* 1 *John* iii. 18—24.)—It is plain, that our Lord designed to mark the distinction, between his first coming as a Saviour, and his second coming as a Judge; though he did not see good to speak in so explicit a manner on the subject, as he had on a former occasion. (*Notes,* v. 20—29. *Heb.* ix. 27, 28.)

Cried. (44) Εκραξε. vii. 37. *Matt.* xiv. 30. *Acts* xiv. 14.—*He that seeth.* (45) Ὁ θεωρων. See on vi. 40. (*Notes,* vi. 36—40. 1 *John* i. 1, 2.)—*I am come.* (46) Εληλυθα. xvi. 28. 1 *Tim.* i. 15.—*He that rejecteth.* (48) Ὁ αθετων. See on *Mark* vii. 9.

PRACTICAL OBSERVATIONS.

V. 1—8.

No power or violence of persecutors will deter zealous believers from avowing and expressing their love and gratitude to their gracious Saviour. (*Notes,* and P. O. *Luke* vii. 36—50.)—When the heart is upright, every endeavour to honour him will be accepted ; though men, nay good men, may censure it, as injudicious and unsuitable. But alas! a high profession of religion sometimes covers the most contemptible avarice and dishonesty, or the most consummate wickedness.—Many plead for charity, in opposition to faith, and love to Christ ; not because they " care for the poor," but because it best answers their selfish purposes. And in various ways, one part of religion is pleaded for, in preference to other parts : not that the advocates care for what they recommend, or zealously practise it ; but because they aim thus to discredit what they especially dislike.—It behoves those especially, who are entrusted with money, to be employed in pious or charitable uses, to watch and pray continually against covetousness. " Carrying the bag " has always been a perilous, though generally a coveted service, especially to church-men: and alas! thieves have often been employed in it ! The less men are disposed to suspect, or call us to

CHAP. XIII.

Jesus washes the feet of his disciples ; and requires them to imitate his example of humility and love, 1—17. He declares that one of them would betray him ; and points out Judas as the traitor to John by a token, 18—26. Satan enters into Judas, who leaves the company, 27—30. Jesus speaks of his glorification, as at hand ; and enjoins his disciples to love one another, 31—35. He forewarns Peter, who avowed his readiness to die with him, that before the cock crowed he would thrice deny him, 36—38.

account, in matters of this kind, the more scrupulous should we be in our own conduct ; for if Satan can prevail with ministers, or professors of the gospel, to venture on petty frauds, by pilfering from the poor, or embezzling holy things ; he will soon gain a more decided victory, and expose them to open infamy and complicated ruin.—We should not generally be much moved with the unjust censures which are cast upon us, if we knew the *secret* practices and motives of those who utter them : it is therefore commonly best, while we are careful to keep a clear conscience, silently to leave the Lord to answer for us when blamed or reproached by others.—Whatever other methods we may occasionally take, of honouring Christ with our substance ; the relief of the poor is the stated method, and we have them always with us for that purpose. (*Notes, Deut.* xv. 4—15. P. O.)

V. 9—19.

There is nothing so wicked and infatuated but men, who have once decidedly engaged in persecution, and thus staked their credit and authority in that desperate cause, will attempt, in order to escape a defeat, and the infamy and ruin connected with it. The success of the gospel often enrages them to madness ; and they speak and act, as if they really hoped to obtain a victory over the almighty God himself! (*Note, Matt.* ii. 3—8. P. O. 1—8.) We should hence learn to avoid every measure, which has the most remote tendency to this dreadful evil.—But how miserable must they at length become, who are pained by the honour conferred on Zion's King! All things written of him must be accomplished ; " all nations must bow " down before him ;" " all his enemies must be put " under his feet ;" and the whole world must either submit to him, or be destroyed by him. Yet the more he is glorified, the more exquisite will be the torture of those who hate him, even to all eternity. Happy then are they, and they only, who from their hearts can cry, " Hosanna! " Blessed is the King of Israel, who cometh in the name " of the Lord !" and who can rejoice in the meek and lowly triumphs of his grace on earth, and in the prospect of his universal and everlasting kingdom of glory! (*Notes, 2 Thes.* i. 5—10. *Rev.* i. 7.)

V. 20—26.

Those who are nearest to the means of grace, often ripen the most rapidly for vengeance, while sinners come from afar to enquire after Christ : and it is a joyful sound to hear such as have been ignorant and careless, desiring the instructions and prayers of his ministers, that they may become acquainted with him and his salvation. To receive enquirers of this character in his glory and joy ; and when they approach him, " he sees of the travail of his soul " and is satisfied." (*Note, Is.* liii. 11, 12.)—So great was his love to us poor perishing rebels, that he would not abide alone in his heavenly felicity ; but rather chose to

assume our nature, to submit to death in its most dreadful form, and to be laid in the grave ; that he might rise and return to his glory, and be attended and followed by an innumerable multitude of those, whom he had " redeemed " unto God with his blood ! " While we admire this unspeakably rich and condescending love of our adorable Redeemer, let us enquire whether our conduct and character prove us to be the increase of this " Corn of " wheat." It is obvious that selfish, ambitious, contentious, revengeful, or sensual professors of Christianity, are not the genuine produce from the meek, humble, gentle, self-abasing, generous, patient, and holy Jesus.—Such are doubtless the tares, which the enemy has sown in the field, and which will at last be separated and cast into the fire ; while the wheat, who are conformed by divine grace, in good measure, to their Saviour's likeness, shall be preserved to his heavenly kingdom. (*Notes, Matt.* xiii. 36 —43. 2 *Cor.* iii. 1—6. P. O.) Let us then examine whether " Christ be in us, the Hope of glory ;" and let us beg of him to render us more and more indifferent about this present life and all its trifling concerns ; that we may be ready to relinquish, to venture, or to suffer any thing, in order to obtain eternal life ; and that we may serve the Lord Jesus with a willing mind, and follow his holy example. For where he is, there will all his true servants be for ever, whatever station they have filled in his church on earth ; and they will be honoured by the Father before all his holy angels, and far above the most enlarged of their present expectations.

V. 27—33.

Even temporary pain and suffering are grievous for us to bear ; and the holy Jesus felt a reluctance of nature to the load of anguish, which he endured for our sins. We cannot therefore choose suffering for its own sake : reluctance of mind and inward perturbation will be felt on such occasions. The true believer will sometimes scarcely know what he shall say : his nature will plead, " Father, " save me from this hour ; " (*Note,* xviii. 10—14, v. 11 ;) but grace will enable him to add, " Father, glorify thy " name ;" and, after the example of his crucified Lord, he will be resigned to suffering, that God may be glorified. This state of mind and heart, notwithstanding all its defects, will be graciously accepted through him, who has glorified the Father, and will glorify him, to all eternity.— In the great event of the death of Christ, faith beholds the world judged and condemned ; Satan vanquished and deprived of his usurped dominion ; his slaves liberated, his works destroyed, and his cause eventually ruined : and while we look to Jesus lifted up upon the cross ; we find ourselves impelled by fear to flee from deserved wrath, allured by hope to seek unmerited mercy, and drawn by humble admiration, love, and gratitude, to renounce all other confidences, to break through all impediments, to cast away all our transgressions, and to give up all other

NOW before a the feast of the passover, when Jesus b knew that his hour was come, that he should c depart out of this world unto the Father, d having loved his own which were in the world, e he loved them f unto the end.

2 And g supper being ended, h the devil having now i put into the heart of Judas Iscariot, Simon's *son*, to betray him;

3 Jesus k knowing that the Father had given all things into his hands, l and that he was come from God, and went to God;

4 He riseth from supper, m and laid aside his garments; and took a towel, n and girded himself.

5 After that, he o poureth water into

---

interests; that we may enlist under the Redeemer's banner, be employed in his service, and aspire to a participation of his glory. (*Notes*, i. 29. *Heb*. xii. 2, 3.)

V. 34—50.

Those who have not faith cannot in a right manner behold the Object of faith, even a crucified Redeemer, "Emmanuel, God with us," "purchasing the church with "his own blood;" and must be strangers to its attractive influence, as shewn to the soul by the Holy Spirit: they will therefore find a thousand cavils and objections, in excuse for their unbelief. They often insinuate that the scripture contradicts itself; and then quote the authority of one sacred writer to invalidate the testimony of another: whereas their own partial and prejudiced understanding alone is to blame: for the simplest believer gradually learns to reconcile most of them; as easily as he can the prophecies of Christ lifted up on the cross, and Christ reigning for ever on his glorious throne.—It is however, generally best to avoid disputing with prejudiced objectors; and rather to remind them how short their time may be, to prepare for death and judgment. It behoves us all to "walk in the light while we have" the light; and an obedient faith is far more suited to our case, than frivolous or disputatious speculations. Those who "believe in the "light" will be approved as "the children of the light:" on all others, darkness will speedily come, and they will not know whither they are going, till they fall into "the "blackness of darkness for ever." For while men indulge their proud and infidel prejudices, rebelling against the light of scripture, and of their own consciences, and quenching the motions of the Holy Spirit; the Lord Jesus withdraws in anger, leaves them to reject his salvation, "sends them a strong delusion to believe a lie," and so they are finally blinded, hardened, and ruined. (P. O. 2 *Thes*. ii. 5—12.) Such warnings have always been given by those, who "saw his glory and spake of him:" and the awful denunciations of the word of God will as surely take effect on unbelievers, as his faithful promises will be fulfilled to his people. Every man therefore should be peculiarly careful not to sin against conviction, from fear of reproach and persecution, from love of praise or reputation, or from regard to the friendship of the world. (*Note*, *Jam*. iv. 4—6.) That will not be accounted true faith, which does not overcome this vain ambition, and teach men to value "the praise of God" more than that of the world; and so induce its possessors to confess Christ before his enraged enemies. Chief rulers are especially in danger of prevaricating in these matters: and

thus they may become accomplices in the basest crimes; because the fear of God does not deliver them from the ensnaring fear of men. (*Notes*, *Prov*. xxix. 25, 26. *Matt*. x. 27, 28.) But faith in Christ, and through him, in the power, truth, and love of God, "overcometh the world:" (*Note*, 1 *John* v. 4, 5.) Beholding in Jesus the glory of the Father, we learn to obey, love, and confide in him. By daily looking to him, who "came a Light into the world," we are gradually more and more extricated from the darkness of ignorance, error, sin, and misery; we learn to know the commandment of God our Saviour to be everlasting life; and we enjoy the earnests and foretastes of that blessed inheritance, and at length are admitted to its unalloyed and eternal felicities. (*Notes*, 2 *Cor*. iii. 17, 18. iv. 5, 6. 1 *John* iii. 1—3. *Rev*. xxi. 22—27.) Yet the same word will seal the condemnation of all, who reject and despise it; their present impunity serves only to harden them in incredulity; and the more gracious the truths, promises, and precepts are, which they now despise, the greater will be their confusion, and the severer their punishment, at the last day. 'From all hardness of 'heart, and contempt of thy word and commandment, 'good Lord, deliver us.'

NOTES.

CHAP. XIII. V. 1—5. The transaction, first recorded in this chapter, took place, "before the feast of the pass- "over;" that is, just at the time when the feast of unleavened bread began, and before the pascal lamb was eaten. Some understand it of a supper prepared for our Lord and his apostles, a day or two before the passover: but "the hour was come in which the Son of man should "be glorified;" Judas was, at this supper, marked out as the traitor; Satan entered into him, and he "went out "immediately" (26—30). Before cock-crowing Peter thrice denied his Lord (38): the subsequent discourse and prayer are continued without the least intimation of an interruption, to the end of the seventeenth chapter; and the eighteenth begins thus: "When Jesus had spoken "these words, he went forth with his disciples;" namely, to the garden, where Judas met him with his armed company. (*Note*, xviii. 1—3.) So that the whole narrative must be interrupted, and disjointed in a most violent manner, to admit of that interpretation.—Jesus perfectly knew, that his "hour was come:" the last scene of inexpressible sufferings was immediately to begin; after which he should ascend to his Father, and no longer be personally present with his disciples. (*Marg. Ref*. a—c.— *Note*, xvii. 1—3.) He had loved them, as his chosen and

a bason, and began "to wash the disciples' ° feet, and to wipe *them* with the towel wherewith he was girded.

6 Then cometh he to Simon Peter: and ° Peter saith unto him, ° Lord, dost thou wash my feet?

7 Jesus answered and said unto him, ° What I do thou knowest not now; but thou shalt know hereafter.

8 Peter saith unto him, ° Thou shalt never wash my feet. Jesus answered

him, ° If I wash thee not, thou hast no part with me.

9 Simon Peter saith unto him, Lord, ° not my feet only, but also *my* hands and *my* head.

10 Jesus saith to him, ° He that is washed ° needeth not save to wash *his* feet, ° but is clean every whit: and ye are clean, but not all.

11 For ° he knew who should betray him; therefore said he, Ye are not all clean.

---

immediate friends, with the most endeared affection; and they were to continue in this evil world after his departure. His great concern therefore, even in the immediate prospect of his own sufferings and glory, was about their spiritual good : and he spent this last evening of his life, in instructing and comforting them ; thus shewing his love to them, even " *to the end*". of his days. (*Marg. Ref.* d, e. —*Notes*, xv. 9—11. xvi. 25—30. xvii. 11—16.) When supper therefore was *prepared*, or *begun;* though the devil had already prompted Judas to betray him, and he had made his infamous bargain with the chief priests ; and, though Jesus was fully conscious of his personal dignity, his mediatorial authority, and the speedy approach of his ascension, and glorious exaltation to the right hand of the Father; (*Marg. Ref.* f—k.—*Notes*, iii. 27—36, *v.* 35. v. 20—27. *Matt.* xxviii. 18 ;) he arose from table, (after a customary antepast had been taken, as it is supposed,) and, assuming the habit and office of the lowest menial servant, he spent this last evening of his life, in unpleasing service of washing the feet of his own disciples ! (*Marg. Ref.* o.) This aptly represented him, as laying aside his robes of light and majesty, assuming our nature, and appearing " in the form of a servant;" and his self-abasement, obedience, sufferings, and death, that he might wash our consciences from the guilt, and our hearts from the pollution of sin, in his atoning blood, and by his sanctifying Spirit. (*Marg. Ref.* l—n.—*Notes*, *Phil.* ii. .5—8. *Rev.* i. 4—6.)—*The devil*, &c. (2) The devil, by putting this into the heart of Judas, did not compel him to betray Christ; and God by putting good things into men's hearts does not compel them : in both cases, they act freely according to their prevalent disposition.—*Was come*, &c. (3) 'How can God be said to come from ' God into the world, when he is always in the heavens ? ' Or to leave the world, and go to the Father ? ' *Socinian Objection.*—' As to his divine nature, he is said to descend ' from heaven, not by a local descent, or by quitting ' heaven, but only by the manifestation of himself upon his ' birth. And in this sense God himself is often said to ' descend from heaven, when, by any divine work done on ' earth, he demonstrates his presence there; and he is also ' said to ascend into heaven afterwards. Why therefore may ' not God the Word, be said to descend from heaven, and ' even dwell with men, (as God is said to dwell in the ta- ' bernacle and in the temple,) when the Logos dwelt in the ' human nature upon earth, and manifested his glory? And

' also to " leave the world, and go to the Father," not only ' as properly doing this by the exaltation of his human na- ' ture ; but by doing all his divine works now from heaven, ' where he sits in the majesty and glory of the Father ?' *Whitby*. (Note, iii. 12, 13.)

His own. (1) Τας ιδιας. i. 11. x. 12. xv. 19. (*Note*, xvii. 6—12.)—*To the end.*] Εις τελος. *Matt.* x. 22. *Mark* xiii. 7. 13. *Luke* xviii. 5. 'Εως τελας. 1 Cor. i. 8. Μεχρι τελ ες, *Heb.* iii. 6. 14.—*Supper being ended.*] (2) Δειπνυ γενομενω.—' The reader will observe here, that I have rendered the clause, *supper being come*, which is the sense in ' which the word is often used elsewhere. (xxi. 4. *Luke* ' iv. 42. *Acts* xii. 18. xvi. 35. xxi. 40.) ...It was much ' more natural to wash the feet of guests before, than ' after supper. It was done before the passover: ... part of ' the discourse which John mentions after the feet were ' washed, is mentioned by the other evangelists, as passing at supper; nay, John himself, when he speaks (26) ' of Christ's dipping the sop, and giving it to Judas, after ' this, plainly shews that supper was not ended.' *Doddridge.*—*Having put into.*] Βεβληκοτος—" Having cast " in," &c.—*A towel*. (4) Λεντιον. 5. Here only. *Linteum*, a *linum, flax. A bason.*(5) Νιπτηρα. Here only. A νιπτω, *lavo.—To wipe.*] Εκμασσειν. See on xi. 2.

V. 6—11. It is probable, that Peter was one of the first, whose feet Jesus attempted to wash : so that after what had passed in respect of him, none else made any objection ; and doubtless Jesus washed the feet of Judas the traitor, as well as those of the rest.—Peter, conscious of his own sinfulness, and firmly believing his Lord to be " the Christ, the Son of the living God;" enquired with the utmost amazement, whether He could really mean to wash the feet of one so mean and sinful : intimating that it would be such a degradation, as he could not bear to think of. (*Notes, Matt.* iii. 11—15. xvi. 21—23. *Luke* v. 1—11, *v.* 8.) To this Jesus replied, that though Peter did not then understand the import, or perceive the propriety, of his conduct; yet it would be explained to him in due time, and he would know and approve of his reasons for so doing. (*Marg. Ref.* q.) Peter, however, supposing himself actuated by a humble regard to his Master's honour, earnestly protested, that he should never wash his feet ; thus setting up his own will and wisdom in opposition to those of Christ ! Yet when our Lord declared, that except he washed him, he could have no part in him or his salvation ; Peter suddenly changed his mind, and

12 So after he had washed their feet, and had taken his garments, and was set down again, he said unto them, [b] Know ye what I have done to you? 13 Ye [c] call me Master and Lord: and ye say well; for *so* I am. 14 If [d] I then, *your* Lord and Master, have washed your feet, [e] ye also ought to wash one another's feet.

15 For I have [f] given you an example, that ye should do as I have done to you. 16 [h] Verily, verily, I say unto you, [i] The servant is not greater than his lord; neither he that is sent greater than he that sent him. 17 If ye know these things, [k] happy are ye if ye do them.

b 7. Ez. xxiv. 19. 24. Matt. xiii. 51. Mark iv. 13. e xi. 28. Matt. vii. 21, 22. xxiii. 8—10. Luke vi. 46. Rom. xiv. 9. 1 Cor. viii. 5. Phil. ii. 11. iii. 8. 2 Pet. i. 14—16. d Jer. i. 12. Luke vii. 43. x. 28. Jam. ii. 19. c Matt. xx. 26. 28. Mark x. 43. 44. Luke xxii. 26, 27. 2 Cor. viii. 9. Phil. ii. 5—8. Heb. v. 8, 9. xii. 2. 1 Jn. 19—22.
f Acts xx. 35. Rom. xii. 10. 16. xv. 1—3. 1 Cor. viii. 2 Cor. x. 1. Gal. v. 13. vi. 1, 2. Phil. ii. 3—4. 1 Pet. iv. 1. v. 5.
g Matt. xi. 29. Rom. xv. 5. marg. Eph. v. 2. 1 Pet. ii. 21. iii. 17, 18. 1 John ii. 6. h *See* on iii. 3. 5. i xv. 20. Matt. x. 24. 25. Luke vi. 40. k xv. 14. Gen. vi. 22? Ex. xl. 16. Ps. xix. 11. cxix. 1—5. Ex. xxxvi. 27. Matt. vii. 24, 25. xii. 50. xxiii. 50—41. Luke xii. 47, 48. Jam. i. 22—25. 1 John ii. 3. 29. iii. 22—24.
Gal. v. 6. Heb. xi. 7, 8. Jam. i. 25. ii. 20—24. iv. 17. Rev. xxii. 14.

desired him not only " to wash his feet, but also his hands " and his head." But our Lord intimated, that this was not requisite: for the man who had been in the bath needed not to repeat his washing, except as his feet had contracted some occasional defilement, as in other respects he was every whit clean; and so were all the apostles, except Judas, who was alluded to as being a hypocrite and a traitor. (*Marg. Ref.* z.—*Notes*, vi. 66—71. xv. 3—5.) —This shews, that this action of Christ was an intended emblem of that washing from sin, by his blood and Spirit, without which we can have no benefit from him or part in him. (*Marg. Ref.* s—y.—*Notes*, Ps. li. 1, 2. 7. Ez. xxxvi. 25—27, v. 25. Zech. xiii. 1. 1 Cor. vi. 9—11. Eph. v. 22 —27. Tit. ii. 14. iii. 4—7. 1 John i. 5—7. Rev. i. 4—6. vii. 13—17, v. 14.) The true believer is thus washed, when he first receives Christ for his salvation: all his sins are completely pardoned; the sanctification of the Spirit pervades all his faculties, dispositions, affections, and conduct; and he is graciously considered as " clean every " whit:" yet, by his intercourse with this evil world, he is liable anew to contract guilt and defilement; and in respect of his daily walk, he needs washing continually by Jesus, and learns to apply to him for it, with deep repentance, and by faith and prayer. Thus he is an accepted and sanctified person: but all professed Christians are not thus clean; for some of them are hypocrites, like Judas, and as yet in their sins, in every sense of the word. —' If I do not wash thee, by my blood shed for the ex-' piation of man's sin, and by the sanctifying power of my ' Spirit, (which I would represent unto thee by this wash-' ing,) thou canst have ... no interest in me, no benefit by ' me. ... Alas! I am all unclean, ... wash me therefore all ' over: cleanse thou both my hands, that are guilty of ' many offensive actions, and my head that hath conceived ' many sinful thoughts. ... Ye are my disciples already; ' in respect of the main business of regeneration, washed ' from your sins: yet there are some remains of ... worldly ' affections, which must still be purged away, in the best ' of men. And such is your condition at this time. Ye, ' my disciples, are clean: and yet not all of you.' *Bp. Hall.*

    Part with me. (8) Μερος μετ' εμε.—*Every whit.* (10) Ολος. vii. 23. ix. 34.

    V. 12—17. When our Lord had " taken his garments" and resumed his place at table, he pointed out to the disciples the immediate instruction, which he intended to convey by washing their feet (7). They allowed him very properly the distinction and pre-eminence of being their Lord and Teacher: if then he, who was in every sense so greatly their superior, had condescended to perform this

low and menial service to them his own disciples; " they " ought also to wash one another's feet." There is no ground in scripture for understanding this injunction *literally*, nor any trace of its being observed, as a *religious ordinance*, among the primitive Christians. But the plain meaning is, that the most eminent Christian or minister, by whatever title distinguished, not only if a successor to the apostles, but even an apostle himself, ought readily to perform the lowest, the most laborious, and even the most disgusting act of real charity to the least of his brethren, when there is a proper call to it. ' Not by doing this in a ' literal sense once a year: but in the spiritual, by being ' always ready to do any service, by which we may promote ' the welfare and advance the purity of any member of ' the church: for " the servant is not above his Lord."' *Whitby.* No advancement above others in rank, genius or learning, miraculous endowments, or station in the church, can possibly be comparable to the pre-eminence of our Lord and Master above the greatest of his servants: none therefore can refuse such services, without affecting to appear greater, than the holy and divine Saviour himself. If the disciples attended to and understood these things, they would be happy in his favour; provided they reduced them to practice, and in proportion to the degree in which they copied his example. (*Marg. Ref.* k. —*Notes, Luke* xi. 27, 28. *Jam.* i. 22—27, vv. 25. 27.)— The pride, lordly ambition, ostentation, self-indulgence, indolence, selfishness, and fastidious delicacy, of very many professed Christians, and ministers, and ecclesiastical rulers, form an awful contrast to this example and instruction of our Lord. Such men may literally wash the feet of the poor, when there is no occasion for it, nor any charity in it; and they may be proud of it as a parade of " voluntary humility:" but to enter into the spirit of this exhortation, they " must be born again, and become new " creatures."—Probably, our Lord spake much more to this effect at the same time. (*Marg. Ref.* b—i.—*Notes*, xv. 17—21. *Matt.* xx. 24—28. *Luke* xxii. 24—27.) It did not suit his purpose to speak plainly then, of the emblematical meaning of this action; but in fact the ' thing ' signified' forms the grand example for our imitation. (*Notes*, Phil. ii. 5—8. 1 Pet. ii. 18—25, vv. 21—24.)

    Ye call Master and Lord. (13) 'Υμεις φωνειτε με ὁ διδασκαλος και ὁ κυριος. 14. " Ye call me the Teacher and " the Master."—' The article, in the Greek, prefixed to ' each appellation; and the nominative case employed, ' where, in common language, it would have been the accu-' sative, give great energy to the expression, and shew that ' the words are applied to Jesus, in a sense entirely peculiar. ' The titles here given can only belong to one.' *Campbell.*—

18 ¶ I speak not of you all; ' I know whom I have chosen: but, "that the scripture may be fulfilled, He that eateth bread with me hath lifted up his heel against me.

19 *Now 'I tell you before it come, that when it is come to pass, ye may believe 'that I am he.

20 Verily, verily, I say unto you, *'He that receiveth whomsoever I send receiveth me; and he that receiveth me receiveth him that sent me.

21 When Jesus had thus said, 'he was troubled in spirit, and testified, and said, Verily, verily, I say unto you, 'That ' one of you shall betray me.

22 Then the disciples 'looked one on another, doubting of whom he spake.

23 Now there was ' leaning on Jesus' bosom one of his disciples, 'whom Jesus loved.

24 Simon Peter therefore * beck-oned to him, that he should ask. who it should be of whom he spake.

25 He then lying on Jesus' breast saith unto him, Lord, 'who is it?

26 Jesus answered, ' He it is to whom I shall give a ' sop, when I have dipped it. And, when he had dipped the sop, he gave it to * Judas Iscariot, the son of Simon.

27 And after the sop ᵇ Satan en-tered into him. Then said Jesus unto him, 'That thou doest, do quickly.

28 Now no man at the table knew for what intent he spake this unto him.

29 For some of them thought, ᵈ be-cause Judas had the bag, that Jesus had said unto him, Buy those things that we have need of against the feast: or, ' that he should give something to the poor.

30 He then, having received the sop, ʳwent immediately out: ᶠand it was night.

' Your Master by teaching, and your Lord by com-manding; so Grotius. But ὁ Κυριος ... seems to import " the Lord from heaven," (1) or him who is "Lord of " all," in which sense, to us Christians, there " is but " one Lord." Acts ii. 36. 1 Cor. viii. 2.' Whitby.—(Notes, Matt. xxiii. 8—10. Acts x. 36—43, v. 36. 1 Cor. xv. 45—49.)—An example. (15) Ὑποδειγμα. Heb. iv. 11. viii. 5. ix. 23. Jam. v. 10. 2 Pet. ii. 6.—Ὑποδεικνυμι, Matt. iii. 7.—Happy. (17) Μακαριοι. xx. 29. Matt. v. 3—11. xi. 6. xiii. 16. xxiv. 46. Luke i. 45. xi. 27, 28. Rom. iv. 7, 8. et al.

V. 18—30. (Notes, Matt. xxvi. 20—25. Luke xxii. 21 —23.) Our Lord next shewed the disciples, that he was aware, they were not all upright characters, and would not all be obedient and happy. He perfectly knew what per-sons he had chosen for apostles, as well as which of them were chosen unto salvation. A traitor had indeed been admitted into their company, that the words, which David spake as the type of him, might be accomplished. (Note, Ps. xli. 9.) One, who then was eating bread with him, would treat him with the utmost ingratitude and indignity; as if an animal should lift up his heel, to strike the person who was feeding him. Of this he informed them before it came to pass; that they might not be disconcerted by the event, but rather be confirmed by it in their belief, that he was indeed the Messiah of whom all the prophets wrote. (Marg. Ref. l—o.) And they might be sure, notwith-standing this treachery of one among them, that their labours should still be accepted and honoured; and that they, and all faithful ministers, should be considered as the ambassadors and representatives of him, and of the Father who sent him; and also that those who received them as such would be accepted accordingly. (Marg. Ref. p.— Note, Matt. x. 40—42.) The subject on which our Lord

spoke excited inward perturbation, and " he testified " that one of the company " would betray him."—In the uncertainty and perplexity which this declaration excited, Peter beckoned to John, to ask Jesus, who the traitor was to whom he referred. John was the " beloved disciple," and especial friend of Jesus; and at this time was placed next to him at the table and reclined on his bosom; though he modestly spake in the third person, without mentioning his own name. (Marg. Ref. s—x.—Notes, xix. 25—27. xxi. 1—14, v. 7. 18—23, v. 20. Dan. ix. 21—23, v. 23.) The token by which he shewed that Judas was meant, seems to have been diverse from the " dipping with Jesus " in the dish," mentioned by the other evangelists. (Marg. Ref. y—a.—Matt. xxvi. 23. Mark xiv. 20.) Probably Judas understood our Lord's meaning; though he took the sop given him by Jesus without appearing to notice it: and perhaps the desperate resentment, excited by his being thus detected and exposed, gave Satan his advantage to take full and final possession of him, and to hurry him on in his most wicked course to speedy and awful destruc-tion. However this was, Jesus bade him proceed without delay to execute his designs, seeing he was fully deter-mined on them. (Marg. Ref. b, c.)—It may be supposed, that Judas understood this warning: yet the others did not, but thought that Jesus referred to some orders which he had previously given him, to provide those things which were requisite for the proper solemnization of the festival, during the seven days of its continuance; or to give some-thing to the poor out of their small stock, according to his general custom. But nothing could dismay, retard, or win upon the hardened heart of Judas; and he went out speedily, after he had received and eaten the sop: for it was now night; and he supposed it was time to go to the chief priests, that he might be ready to meet Jesus in the

4 c 4

31 ¶ Therefore, when he was gone out, Jesus said, ^hNow is the Son of man glorified, ⁱ and God is glorified in him.

32 If God be glorified in him, ^kGod shall also glorify him in himself, and shall straightway glorify him.

33 ^l Little children, ^m yet a little while I am with you. ⁿ Ye shall seek me: and, as I said unto the Jews, Whither I go ye cannot come; so now I say to you.

34 A ^o new commandment I give unto you, ^pThat ye love one another; as I have loved you, that ye also love one another.

35 By ^qthis shall all *men* know that ye are my disciples, if ye have love one to another.

garden, to which he concluded that he would in a short time retire. (*Marg. Ref.* d—g.)—' If Christ had marked ' out Judas to John and Peter, as the traitor, a night or ' two before ' (the passover), ' the information must surely ' have reached the rest of the company by this time.' *Doddridge*. The other circumstances, by which Judas was more publickly made known, occurred perhaps some before, and some after, this private intimation.—Many learned men state a variety of particulars from the Rabbinical writers, concerning the customs of the Jews in celebrating the passover, and seem to think that these illustrate the subject. But the customs which they thus record must have been, either mere human traditions, added to the law of God, or warranted expositions of that law. In the former case they are worse than of no value : (*Notes, Matt.* xv. 1—20:) and in the latter, the comment must be judged of by comparing it with the text. The fact indeed is, that these customary observances were at best only *oral traditions*, till long after the passover had ceased to be celebrated, according to the law ; that is, till long after the second temple was destroyed. Whatever the Jews may have observed, or do now observe, in this respect ; they never could celebrate the passover, according to the appointment of God, since Jerusalem was destroyed : for it was to be kept only at the place which the Lord should choose. (*Deut.* xvi. 1—6.) And, as immense superstition (as well as uncertainty) is maintained by the rabbinical writers, and very much which makes void, or contradicts, the law itself as written by Moses ; this may be considered in general as the reason, why the author is so silent on the subject.—The question, whether Judas partook of the Lord's supper, or not, must be decided by the interpretation given to the second verse. If the supper was *ended*, when Jesus washed the feet of his disciples, Judas must have been present, at the institution of the Lord's supper: if the supper was then only prepared, or begun, it is *probable* that Judas retired, before the Lord's supper was appointed : yet even on this supposition, much might be urged on the other side ; and, at last, it is to us of little consequence. No discipline can exclude plausible hypocrites ; and scriptural discipline would exclude openly immoral and ungodly persons and infidels.

He that eateth, &c. (18) Ὁ τρωγων μετʼ εμε τον αρτον, επηρεν επʼ εμε την πτερναν ἀυτε.—Ὁ εσθιων αρτος μυ εμεγαλυνεν επʼ εμε πτερνισμον. *Sept.*—No words, conveying precisely the same ideas, can be more different.—Τρωγων. See on vi. 54.—Πτερναν. Here only N. T.—*Now.* (19) " From hence—" forth." *Marg.* Απʼ αρτι. See on i. 51.—*I am he.*] Εγω ειμι. viii. 58.—' Not only, that I am the Christ ; ... but ' also that I am " He who searcheth the hearts," and ' knows things future and contingent, which is the pro-' perty of God alone : ... and so believing in me, may be-' lieve also in him that sent me.' *Whitby.—Was troubled in spirit.* (21) Εταραχθη τῳ πνευμαλι. xii. 27. See on *Matt.* xiv. 26.—*A sop.* (26) " A morsel." *Marg.* Το ψωμιον. 27. 30. Here only. Ψωμιζω, *Rom.* xii. 20.

V. 31—35. The departure of Judas was, as it were, the signal for the beginning of our Lord's last scene of suffering. This he considered as his *glory* ; seeing it was undertaken from the most honourable motives, would be sustained in so honourable a manner, and would be productive of such blessed and glorious effects : especially as God would be glorified in all his harmonious perfections, by and through him, and his obedience unto the death of the cross. (*Notes*, 2 *Cor.* iv. 3—6. *Eph.* iii. 9—12, v. 10. 1 *Pet.* i. 10 —12, v. 12.) As this must certainly be the effect, in the salvation of innumerable multitudes of sinners ; so God would glorify him, as " the Son of man," in his human nature, by the highest possible exaltation and the nearest possible union with himself : and this he would do in a very short time. (*Marg. Ref.* h—k.—*Note*, xvii. 4, 5.) But with this prospect before him, he looked upon his disciples as his " dear children," yea, as " little children," helpless in themselves, and exposed to manifold dangers and injuries in the world ; and as such he compassionated them, and had their welfare near his heart. (*Notes*, xvii. 6—12.) He should, however, remain but a very little while longer with them ; and it would be in vain for them to seek the com-fort of his personal presence : for it would be true in their case, as well as in that of the unbelieving Jews, (though in a different sense,) that they could not follow him to the place whither he was going, but must be left behind for a time. (*Marg. Ref.* m, n.—*Notes*, 36—38, *v.* 36. vii. 31— 36. viii. 21—26.) Before he left them therefore, he would give them " a *new* commandment." The moral law commanded men to " love their neighbour as themselves ; " and this *implied* that reciprocal and special love of believers to each other, of which he spake : but this was now to be explained with *new* clearness, enforced by *new* motives and obligations, illustrated by a *new* example, and obeyed in a *new* manner. (*Marg. Ref.* o.—*Note*, 1 *John* ii. 7—11.) Thus it might be called " a new commandment," which he peculiarly inculcated upon his disciples. They were required to love each other for his sake, as bearing his image, and in imitation of his compassionate, disinterested, and generous love to them. This implied a regard to each other's interest and comfort, a sympathy in sorrow and joy, and a delight in one another's company : it required the

4 c 5

· 36 Simon Peter said unto him, Lord, ' whither goest thou ? Jesus answered him, Whither I go, thou canst not follow me now; but ' thou shalt follow me afterwards.

· 37 Peter said unto him, Lord, ' why cannot I follow ·thee now ? I will lay down my life for thy sake.

38 Jesus answered him, ' Wilt thou lay down thy life for my sake ? Verily, verily, I say unto thee, ' The cock shall not crow till thou hast denied me thrice.

cultivation of peace and harmony; by reciprocal kindness, candour, forbearance, and forgiveness; by supplying each other's wants, by uniting in prayers and religious exercises, and by concurring to promote the common cause of the gospel, as one body animated by one soul. (*Note, Gal.* vi. 1—5, *v.* 2) We ought to love the *ungodly* with benevolence and compassion, and our enemies with forgiveness and persevering kindness: but believers are to be regarded as the objects of our endeared complacency, our most intimate friendship, and our special and unremitted affection; being brethren in the same family, disciples of the same Lord, soldiers in the same army, travellers in the same journey, heirs of the same inheritance, yea, members of the same body. (*Notes, Ps.* xvi. 2, 3. cxix. 57—63, *v.* 63. 1 *Cor.* xii. 15—26. xiii. 4—7. *Eph.* iv. 1—6. *Phil.* i. 27—30. ii. 1—4. 1 *Pet.* i. 22—25. 2 *Pet.* i. 5—7. 1 *John* iii. 13 —17. iv. 7, 8.) This love must be regulated by the pattern of the Saviour's love to us; and it must even emulate it in degree; for " we ought to lay down our lives for the bre- " thren." ' " As I have loved you," even to the shedding ' of my blood for you and even for mine enemies, not with ' respect to any merit on their part, but out of pure affec- ' tion to their souls. This is the love you are to imitate in ' your affection one to another.' *Whitby.*—This mutual love was appointed by our Lord, as the peculiar distinguishing mark of his disciples, by which men might every where know them from all other persons; perceiving, that while others were selfish, even in their friendship; believers uniformly persevered in giving up their own interest, ease, credit, or pleasure, to promote the welfare of their brethren, in such a manner, and to such a degree as was never before known. (*Notes,* xvii. 20, 21. *Acts* ii. 44— 47. iv. 32—35.)

Little children. (33) Τεκνα. *Gal.* iv. 19. 1 *John* ii. 1. 12. 28. iii. 7. 18. iv. 4. v. 21.

V. 36—38. Peter paid much more attention to what our Lord said about leaving them, than to the " new com " mandment" which he had given them. He desired to know whither Jesus was going, being fully determined, as he thought, to follow him. But Jesus informed him, that he could not follow him at that time ; (for his work was not done, nor had he then the spirit of a martyr;) yet he graciously assured him that he at length should follow him, though he foresaw how shamefully he was about to deny him. (*Marg. Ref.* r—u.) And when Peter still insisted upon it, that he was prepared to die with him; he gave him the solemn warning which has already been considered, (*Marg. Ref.* x.—*Notes, Matt.* xxvi. 30—35. *Mark* xiv. 31. *Luke* xxii. 31—34.)

PRACTICAL OBSERVATIONS
V. 1—11.

Neither the deepest abasement and suffering, nor the highest possible exaltation, rendered our blessed Redeemer,

nor can any thing ever render him, for a moment inattentive to the concerns of his disciples, whom he has chosen, redeemed, and called to be his own for ever. The same love, which induced him to ransom and reconcile them when enemies, still influences him to pity their sorrows, to pardon their sins, to supply their wants, to preserve their souls, and to comfort their hearts, now that he has taught them to trust, love, and serve him : and having " loved them hitherto, he will love them to the end," and for ever. But what can be expected too large for him to do or to give, who came down from heaven, and, " in " the form of a servant," not only washed his disciples' feet,·but shed his precious blood, that he might open a fountain, in which to wash our souls from sin and from uncleanness?—for him, who is continually employed, now that " all things are given into his hands," in thus cleansing the greatest transgressors, who come to him for that inestimable benefit, and in drawing others to come to him ? We may well be amazed at this " love, which passeth know- " ledge ; " but it would evince the grossest ignorance and the most foolish pride, if we should persist in refusing this spiritual washing, without which we cannot be his disciples, or have any part with him. In respect also of those providential appointments, which he orders in subserviency to our sanctification; we should remember, that we often cannot know at the present what he is doing : but as he has promised that " we shall know hereafter," we should confide in his wisdom, truth, and love, when we are most in the dark about his intentions, and when all things seem to be the most entirely against us. Much more then should we submit to his authority in respect of those means of grace, which he has required us to use continually, if we would be cleansed from our filthiness. Yet no outward washing can be more than a sign, or means, of the blessing proposed. Our feet, our hands, our heads, or our whole bodies may be washed, again and again, in any way, or by any form ; and our hearts and consciences may still remain defiled : but if we are truly washed in the blood of Jesus, and are made partakers of his Spirit, through faith; all things will be made clean to us, and we shall be " clean " every whit," according to the gracious dealings of our God with his redeemed people. And, though we cannot but contract defilement in this evil world, our condescending Saviour will daily cleanse us from all sin, till " he pre- " sent us faultless before the presence of his glory with ex- " ceeding joy." (*Notes,* 1 *John* i. 5—10. ii. 1, 2. *Jude* 22 —25.) Even in this sense, how few are there who are cleansed from their filthiness ! In small companies, and among a few communicants or ministers, it may commonly be said, " Ye are clean, but not all," and much self-examination with prayer to the heart-searching God to examine us, with habitual diligence in every means of grace, and every work and labour of love, are requisite, in order that we may obtain and preserve the assurance, that we

CHAP. XIV.

Jesus encourages his disciples to believe in God and in him; and promises them mansions in heaven, 1—3. He shews that he is the Way, the Truth, and the Life, 5, 6; and that he is One with the Father, 7—11. He promises them power to do even greater works than he had done; and that he will grant all the prayers offered in his name, 12—14. He requires obedience as the proof of their love; and promises to give them the Comforter, the Holy Spirit, and much security and comfort, in communion with the Father and with him, as coming and making their abode with those that love him, 15—26. He leaves his peace with them; and shews that his return to his Father was a proper ground for their rejoicing, 27—29: and he informs them of his approaching conflict with the prince of this world, in obedience to the Father, 30, 31.

are partakers of the blessing. (*Notes, Heb.* vi. 9—12. *2 Pet.* i. 5—11.)

V. 12—17.

If we would have the comfort of our acceptance in Christ, we must enquire whether we understand the nature and tendency of what Jesus has done for sinners; and whether we be aiming to copy his example of condescension and active love: whether we be delivered in good measure from self-importance and self-indulgence; and have learned to stoop, to labour, and to deny ourselves, in order to be serviceable to the least of our brethren. (*Notes, Matt.* xx. 24—28. P. O. 24—34. *Note, Acts* xx. 32—35.) But alas! how many are there, who refuse to do as Christ has done before them, even where his example is most clearly given for them to imitate! How many of his professed servants act, as if they were greater than the Lord who sent them! Instead of his lowly deportment, they affect state and consequence; they deem useful employments beneath them: and every troublesome or disagreeable labour of love, such as Jesus delighted in, is intolerable even to their imagination! Nay, among such as seem to be true Christians and sincere ministers, there are but few, who fully enter into the spirit of the example which Jesus has left us; and self-love suggests a thousand excuses and reasons, against many useful and important services, which the Saviour would not have listened to for a moment. Yet only those are and will be happy, who " know these things and do them:" for knowledge, without correspondent practice, will only add to a man's eternal condemnation. (*Note, Luke* xii. 47, 48.)

V. 18—30.

If professed disciples and ministers be found as opposite to Christ, as darkness is to light; if those " who eat bread " with him lift up their heel against him," let us not be discouraged: the scripture has foretold that thus it must be, and its accomplishment may help to confirm our faith and encourage our hope. The Lord " knoweth whom he " hath chosen:" the base behaviour of those who disgrace their sacred profession should render faithful ministers the more valued and respected: and indeed the Lord will take care of them and their reputation, and will bless all those, who " esteem them highly in love for their work's sake." Yet it should trouble us, as it once did our blessed Lord, to find traitors joining in sacred ordinances, and men high in office in his church, selling him, and betraying his cause for filthy lucre's sake. (*Notes* and P. O. *Is.* lvi. 9—12. *Note, Matt.* xxi. 12, 13. P. O. 12—16. P. O. *Rev.* xviii. 9—19.) It does not indeed so much concern us to know exactly who they are that answer this description, as to be sure that we are not of the number, and that we really love the Lord as beloved by him. (*Note,* 1 *John* iv. 19.) But, as some are more near to him than others in union, communion, and endeared affection, we should not envy the privilege of these favoured persons; but avail ourselves of their friendship, to learn more of his mind and will, and to seek increasing nearness and conformity to him.—In process of time, false brethren will be detected; and Satan, having long tampered with them, and put one wickedness after another into their hearts, will at length obtain permission to take full possession: then, perhaps, they will go from the participation of the most solemn ordinances, to perpetrate the most atrocious crimes; and they will separate from the disciples, and make it manifest that they never belonged to them. (*Notes,* 1 *John* ii. 18, 19. *Jude* 17—19.)

V. 31—38.

While hypocrites and apostates " bring upon themselves " swift destruction," the loss is wholly their own: for nothing can prevent the glory of the blessed Redeemer, and that of the Father in him. Even on the cross, the Saviour acquired the most illustrious victories over Satan, the world, sin, and death. (*Note, Col.* ii. 13—15.)—There he magnified the divine law, he paid an inestimable ransom, and rescued unnumbered millions of immortal souls from eternal misery, to the glory of God the Father: and therefore a name and a glory have been given to him, above all the inhabitants of heaven and earth; that " all should ho- " nour the Son, even as they honour the Father that sent " him." (*Notes, v.* 20—23. *Phil.* ii. 9—11.) The thoughts of his glory, and of his love to us, should reconcile us to our distance and trials, while we continue in this world of sin and trouble. We cannot now follow our ascended Lord to his heavenly felicity; yet if we truly believe, we " shall follow him hereafter," notwithstanding our remaining errors, defilements, temptations, and conflicts: but we must await his time, perform our work, and be gradually humbled, proved, and purified for our inheritance.—Who, that seriously contemplates the state of the Christian church, or the spirit of those who seem most zealous for evangelical truth, would suppose, that mutual love, after the example of Jesus, is indeed the appointed criterion, by which all men should know and distinguish his disciples? Had angry zeal for doctrines, forms, and parties, or mutual slanders, revilings, and anathemas rashly denounced, or exactness in the *minutiæ* of a system, or a perverted ingenuity in multiplying *Shibboleths,* still more and more to divide and distract the church; had these, I say, been the test of Christianity, modern appearances might suggest less melancholy reflections, than now obtrude themselves upon the serious and pious mind. But alas! the commandment " to love one another, even as " Christ hath loved us," is still *new* and *strange* to most professed Christians: many seem never to have read it;

LET 'not your heart be troubled: ye believe in God, believe also in me." 2 In 'my Father's house are many mansions: 'if *it were* not *so*, I would have told you. 'I go to prepare a place for you. 3 And if I go and prepare a place for you, 'I will come again, and receive you unto myself; that where I am, *there* ye may be also.

---

few appear to understand, remember, or practise it; and " because iniquity abounds, the love of" these few " waxes " cold." Instead of exercising candour in judging of our brethren, that we may take in all, who appear to hate and repent of sin, to believe in a divine Saviour, and to love and follow after holiness; many seem to think, that a rigorous zeal for an orthodox system, or some external forms ought to swallow up all meekness, candour, and kindness to those, who differ from them even in the smallest particulars! (P. O. 1 *Cor.* xii. 12—26. *Eph.* iv. 1—6.) Men in general notice any of the words of Christ rather than these: and self-preference, boasting, and judging others, supplant humble love which " hopeth all things." (*Note,* 1 *Cor.* xiii. 4—7. P. O. 1—7. *Notes, P. O. Jam.* iii. 13—18.) But this " haughty spirit goes before " a fall ; " and some, whom the Lord loves, are left to feel and to shew their weakness and folly; in order to humble them, to teach them more tenderness to their brethren, as well as more entire dependence on Christ. May we then " endeavour to keep the unity of the Spirit in the bond of " peace ; " to " love one another with a pure heart fer- " vently," and to " walk humbly with our God."

NOTES.

Chap. XIV. V. 1. Our Lord, observing that his disciples were greatly disquieted on account of those things which he had spoken, especially by the prospect of his speedy removal from them, exhorted them not to give place to anxiety or despondency, or to permit trouble to possess and distract their hearts. (*Marg. Ref.* a.—*Notes,* 27, 28. xii. 27—33, v. 27. *Ps.* xlii. 4—11.—P. O. xliii. lxxvii.) They believed in the God of their fathers, and in him, as the Son of God and the promised Messiah: and this faith would be found sufficient to support them, and to secure a happy event to all their trials. (*Marg. Ref.* b.)—The words may be rendered in various ways.—' Ye believe in God, and ye believe also in me; " ' therefore be not troubled, for this faith shall preserve you ' from being overcome.—" Believe ye in God, believe ' " also in me." ... Be not troubled : but how can this be ? ' truly, if ye shall believe in the Father, and in me. ... ' " Ye do believe in God; believe also in me." ...There is ' none of you who does not profess to believe in God : if ' this be indeed so ; believe also in me. Thus indeed you ' will truly believe in God, neither shall ye be cast down ' by any storms.—Or, " Believe in God; and ye believe ' " believe in me." Believe in God ; which if ye do, you ' by the same endeavour believe in me also.' *Beza.*—' Let ' it not suffice you, that ye do believe in one infinite ' and invisible God, ... who hath made you and all the ' world : but repose the whole affiance of your hearts upon ' me, the true and only Son of God, whom ye see clothed ' with flesh. And the rather now fasten your souls on me,

' by a stedfast belief; for that ye shall see this humanity of ' mine subjected to many and great miseries ; and much ' contempt, pain, and insultation, yea, even to an ignomi- ' nious death: but let not your hearts be troubled with ' those heavy things, which ye shall see to befall me, the ' issue whereof ye shall find to be glorious.' *Bp. Hall.*— ' There being no example I can find, where the same word, ' in the same sentence, is used both in the indicative and ' imperative mood; I had rather render these words in ' the same mode thus, " Believe in God, believe also it. ' " me." That is, ' That I may prescribe a remedy to tha. ' trouble, which has seized your hearts from the consider- ' ation of my passion, and my departure from you, and ' of the troubles you must expect in execution of your ' office ; I advise you to believe in God, the Author of that ' doctrine you are to preach, and the Defender of those ' who propagate it; and in me in whose name you preach ' it, as having all power in heaven and earth, and being ' always present with you; and therefore being able to ' assist and preserve you from all dangers, and to reward ' your faithful labours, with that crown of glory I have ' promised.' *Whitby.*—(*Note,* x. 26—31.)—The criticism, with which this quotation opens, is probably well grounded. Dr. Campbell concurs in it, and adds, ' How fre- ' quently, in the book of Psalms, are the people of God, ' in the time of affliction, exhorted to trust in the Lord ? ' Such exhortations, therefore, are not understood to im- ' ply a total want of faith in those to whom they are ' given.'—Yet Bp. Hall's view of the nature and object of that faith in Christ, to which the disciples were exhorted, is most satisfactory : He had just before predicted, that all the disciples would forsake him, and that Peter would thrice deny him : (*Note,* xiii. 36—38:) and therefore, faith in him as a Saviour, and in the mercy of God through him for the pardon of these sins, would be especially requisite to keep them from despair and its awful consequences. (*Notes, Luke* xxii. 31—34. 1 *John* ii. 1, 2.)

Let not your heart be troubled.] Μη ταρασσεσθω ὑμων ἡ καρδια. 27. xii. 27. xiii. 21.

V. 2, 3. Our Lord next assured the disciples, that in heaven, that holy habitation, in which his Father displayed his peculiar presence and glory, many peaceful, enduring, and happy mansions were prepared, for the reception of them, and of all his disciples, however numerous. (*Marg. Ref.* c.—*Notes, Heb.* xi. 8—10. 13—16. xiii. 9—14. 2 *Pet.* iii. 10—13. *Rev.* xxi. xxii. 1—7.) Their expectations indeed of a residence with him, and high preferment in an earthly palace, were about to be finally frustrated : and if their hopes of heavenly felicity had been as groundless and delusory, he would assuredly have undeceived them. (*Marg. Ref.* d.—*Note,* vi. 66—71, v. 68, 69.) But he was about to remove from them, on purpose to prepare a place in heaven for them. It had indeed been

4 And [r] whither I go ye know, [h] and the way ye know.

5 [i] Thomas saith unto him, Lord, [k] we know not whither thou goest; and how can we know the way?

6 Jesus saith unto him, [l] I am the Way, and [m] the Truth, and [n] the Life: [o] no man cometh unto the Father, but by me.

7 If [p] ye had known me, ye should have known my Father also: [q] and from henceforth ye know him, and have seen him.

8 [r] Philip saith unto him, Lord, [s] shew us the Father, and it sufficeth us.

9 Jesus saith unto him, [t] Have I been so long time with you, and yet hast thou not known me, Philip? [u] he that hath seen me, hath seen the Father; [x] and how sayest thou then, Shew us the Father?

10 [y] Believest thou not that I am in the Father, and the Father in me? [z] the words that I speak unto you I speak not of myself: but the Father, [a] that dwelleth in me, [b] he doeth the works.

11 Believe me that I am in the Father, and the Father in me: [c] or else believe me for the very works' sake.

12 Verily, verily, I say unto you, He that believeth on me, [d] the works that I do, shall he do also; [e] and

---

" prepared" for the children of God, " from the found-"ation of the world ;" and for the apostles, in particular, in his counsel and purpose. (Notes, Matt. xxv. 34—40. Luke xxii. 28—30.) Yet the death of the Saviour was necessary to atone for their sins, and to procure them the title to their inheritance : his resurrection would be the earnest of their's: he would enter into heaven as their Fore-runner, to open the way, to remove all hindrances, answer all objections to their admission, and make all things ready for their reception. (Marg. Ref. e.—Notes, Heb. vi. 16—20. ix. 24—28.) He was going from them for this very purpose : he would therefore surely come again, and, having prepared them for that holy inheritance, he would at death receive their souls, and at the last day raise their bodies; that so they might be for ever with him their beloved Friend, in that glorious and happy place to which he was going. (Marg. Ref. f.—Notes, xvii. 24. Acts vii. 54—60, v. 59. 2 Cor. v. 5—8. Phil. i. 21—26. iii. 20, 21. 1 Thes. iv. 13—18.)

Mansions. (2) Μοναι. 23. Here only. A μενω maneo. Μνωσαν πολιν, Heb. xiii. 14.

V. 4—6. Our Lord here intimated, that, after all the instructions which he had given the apostles, they must surely know both the place whither he was going, and the way by which they must follow him : and indeed in a measure they did know these things, though they were not able to apply their principles to their present circumstances. (Marg. Ref. g, h.—Note, vi. 66—71, vv. 68, 69.) But Thomas being weak in faith, greatly attached to the notion of a temporal kingdom, and probably supposing that Jesus meant to retire for a time, before he openly appeared as the Messiah, observed, that as he had not favoured them with any direct information concerning the place to which he was about to go, they could not possibly know by what way they should follow him. (Marg. Ref. i, k.) To this our Lord answered, by saying, " I am the Way, and the Truth, and the Life."—He is our " Way " to the Father, and to heaven ; in his person as " God manifest in the flesh," and as our Surety and

VOL. V.

Mediator, by his perfect obedience and his atoning sacrifice, and by his intercession as our Advocate before his throne. He is our great and only High Priest, who, by his sacrifice on the cross, made propitiation for the sins of the world ; and by his resurrection, ascension, and intercession, gives us access with confidence to God, upon a throne of grace. (Marg. Ref. l.—Notes, x. 6—9. Eph. ii. 14—18. Heb. iv. 14—16. vii. 23—28. x. 19—22.) —He is " the Truth," not only as he is the substance of all typical shadows, and the accomplishment of all the prophecies and promises of a Saviour ; but also as the great Prophet of the church, whose doctrine is that truth, by believing which sinners come, through him " the Way," to the Father and to heaven. (Marg. Ref. m.—Notes, i. 4—9. 17. viii. 12.)—And he is " the Life " also, by whose life-giving Spirit the dead in sin are quickened, and so enabled to believe in him as " the Truth," and to come by him as " the Way," to the mercy-seat of God. (Marg. Ref. n.—Notes, v. 24—27. xi. 20—27, vv. 25, 26. 1 Cor. xv. 45—49. Col. iii. 1—4. 1 John i. 1, 2. Rev. xxii. 1.) Neither can any man, of any age or nation, approach God as a Father, who is not quickened by Jesus as " the " Life," and instructed by him as " the Truth," to come by him as " the Way :" all others will meet God, merely as an offended Sovereign and an avenging Judge. (Marg. Ref. o.—Notes, Matt. xi. 27—30. xii. 29, 30. 1 John ii. 20—25.) Having most clearly stated this, our Lord left Thomas to collect from it the place, whither he was about to remove.

V. 7—14. Had the apostles duly known their Lord, in respect of his person, character, and mediation, they would proportionably have known the Father also : and indeed they had some knowledge of him, which would from that time continually increase, till they more clearly saw the Father in him, " the Brightness of his glory, and the ex-" press character of his substance." (Marg. Ref. p, q.— Notes, Matt. xi. 27. 2 Cor. iv. 3—6. Col. i. 15—17. Heb i. 3, 4.) But Philip, having very confused and defective views of the dignity of his Lord, desired him to discover

4 D

greater *works* than these shall he do; because I go unto my Father. 13 And whatsoever ye shall ask in my name, that I will do, that the Father may be glorified in the Son. 14 If ye shall ask any thing in my name, I will do *it*. 15 ¶ If ye love me, keep my commandments.

16 And I will pray the Father, and he shall give you another Comforter, that he may abide with you for ever; 17 *Even* the Spirit of truth: whom the world cannot receive, because it seeth him not, neither knoweth him: but ye know him; for he dwelleth with you, and shall be in you.

---

the Father to them in some sensible manner; according to those visions, with which holy men of old had been favoured: adding that this would suffice for their satisfaction and comfort, when he should be removed from them. To this our Lord replied by enquiring, (as a gentle rebuke,) whether after he had been so long and intimately conversant with them, Philip could possibly be unacquainted with his divine dignity and glory. He had before told them, that " he who had seen him, had seen the Father:" (*Note*, xii. 44—50:) what need then had he to request any other vision of the Father, when he had been favoured with so many opportunities of beholding him, by that appointed and sufficient method, in which alone the invisible God can be shewn to mortal man? (*Marg. Ref.* r—x. —*Note*, i. 18.) Did not Philip yet believe the essential union and mutual in-dwelling of the Father and the Son, and of the Godhead in his human nature? (*Marg. Ref.* y. —*Note*, xvii. 21—23.) He had frequently spoken to them on this subject; and his words were not " of himself," as distinct from the Father; and therefore they ought to have been more regarded: especially as the Father, dwelling in and working by him, had borne witness to him by so many stupendous miracles. (*Marg. Ref.* z—c.—*Note*, v. 32—39.) If then the displays of his divine truth, purity, knowledge, wisdom, and goodness did not induce their belief of this " great mystery of godliness;" they ought at least to believe him, on account of the works which he performed: these manifestly warranted and attested all the doctrines which he taught, as by the seal of God himself; and the authoritative manner in which he performed them, shewed that he acted by an inherent power, as the incarnate Son of the Father. This proof, however, would gather still greater force, by the powers which were about to be conferred on them who then believed, and for a time on other believers; (*Notes*, Mark xvi. 17—20. Heb. ii. 1—4, v. 4;) as they would be enabled in his name to perform similar works to those which they had witnessed: nay, in some respects they would do still " greater works," than what he had wrought in person. This may refer especially to the multiplied miracles of the apostles after the day of Pentecost; to their communicating the gift of tongues and of working miracles to others also; and above all to the immense multitude of converts, which were made by their ministry. This would be the effect of Christ's ascension to the Father, and his intercession for them in heaven: (*Marg. Ref.* d—f.—*Note*, *Acts* ii. 33—36:) for whatsoever " they should ask in his name," as conducive to these important ends, he would bestow it upon them, *by his own power and authority;* that the Fa-

ther might be glorified in the honour conferred on the Son; by the success of the gospel through their ministry; by the benign effects of it on men's lives and dispositions; and by the display of his justice, mercy, wisdom, truth, and power, in that way of saving sinners. (*Marg. Ref.* g—k.)—' Note also here, that Christ saith, Whatsoever ye ' thus ask, *I will do;* which, as it supposes in him *omni-* ' *science,* enabling him to know the requests of all Christ- ' ians upon earth ; and *omnipotence,* enabling him to assist ' them every where in the performance of the greatest ' works; so must it consequently imply an unity of es- ' sence betwixt the Father and the Son, and so the Fa- ' ther is glorified in the Son. Hence what is here, " I ' " will do it," is, xvi. 23, " the Father will give you." ' Note also, that whereas the Jews used to beg a blessing, ' ... for the sake of Abraham, Isaac, and Jacob; though be- ' ing only mere men, they never prayed to them ; the ' Christians not only prayed to the Father in the name of ' the Son, but invoked the Son also, as being one God with ' the Father: this being a periphrasis of Christians, that ' they were those who called on the name of Christ. (*Acts* ' ix. 14. 21. *Rom.* x. 13.) And this seems here to be men- ' tioned to confirm their faith in him; that he who so loved ' them, had power to do all things for them.' *Whitby.*—What prophet ever used such language as this of our Lord in these verses? " It is not in me: God shall give Pharaoh an an-" swer of peace." (*Gen.* xli. 16. *Dan.* ii. 30. *Acts* iii. 12.) —The answer of the prayer of faith, in working miracles, seems to have been immediately intended; yet not to the exclusion of any other case, in which believers pray to the Father in the name of Christ, for promised blessings. (*Notes*, xvi. 23, 24. *Matt.* xxi. 21, 22.)

It sufficeth us. (8) Αρχει ἡμιν. vi. 7. *Matt.* xxv. 9. *Luke* iii. 14. 1 *Tim.* vi. 8. *Heb.* xiii. 5. 3 *John* 10.—*I am in the Father, and the Father in me.* (10) Εγω εν τῳ πατρι, και ὁ πατηρ εν εμοι εςι. 11. 20. x. 38. xvii. 21. 23.

V. 15—17. Our Lord next reminded the disciples, that, instead of yielding to inconsolable sorrow in the prospect of his removal from them, as if that were the most proper expression of their love to him; they ought to shew their love, by a conscientious and diligent obedience to his commandments: and, while they thus regarded his authority and glory on earth, he, in heaven, would attend to their interests, and, interceding with the Father, obtain for them " another Comforter." The word signifies an *Advocate*, a *Counsellor*, a *Monitor*, and a *Comforter.* Jesus had been their Advocate, to plead their cause on earth ; as he frequently did, against the censures of the Scribes and Pharisees ; and he was going to be their

18 I 'will not leave you ° comfortless; I ° will come to you.

19 Yet ˣ a little while, and the world seeth me no more ; but ye see

me : ʸ because I live, ye shall live also.

20 At that day ᶻ ye shall know that I *am* in my Father, and *ʸ ye in me, and I in you.

Advocate with the Father : (*Note,* 1 John ii. 1, 2.) He had also counselled, admonished, exhorted, and encouraged them with most animating exhortations and promises : but he was about to be removed from them ; and if he should continue on earth, his personal presence must be confined to one place, and was only suited to their state whilst few in number. But another Monitor, Comforter, Counsellor, and Advocate would be given them, in consequence of his return to the Father, who would abide with them collectively and individually during life, yea, for ever ; and with his church to the end of time : (*Note, Matt.* xxviii. 19, 20 :) and his gifts and graces would both encourage their hearts, and make them a comfort to each other, and also plead their cause before the world. This character of " another Comforter," or Advocate, and the language here and elsewhere employed, evidently denote *personality :* and the office itself implies omnipresence, omniscience, omnipotence, and all divine perfections. This other Comforter would be sent by the Father, and through the Son who is " One with the Father : " thus the Trinity of Persons is evidently declared in this, and other parallel passages ; each Person distinct and divine, yet but one God. (*Notes, 25, 26.* xv. 26, 27. xvi. 7.—15.)—This Comforter is called " The " Spirit of truth ; " being essential truth, the Revealer of all divine truth, as the Source of inspiration, and who as sent by Christ " the Truth," is the great Teacher of truth in the hearts of believers.—But the world, or unregenerate men of every nation, name, and religious profession, continuing such, cannot receive him, either as a " Spirit of truth," or as " a Comforter ; " for all his instructions, influences, and consolations are totally contrary to their dispositions, pursuits, and maxims. (*Notes,* 4—6. iii. 3—6. xii. 37—41. 1 *Cor.* i. 17—19. ii. 14—16.) They therefore treat them as foolishness, and reason against them, ridicule them, and blaspheme them, as enthusiasm, delusion, or imposture. But the disciples, being " born of God," were already acquainted with these blessed influences, and the divine Author of them : he even then dwelt with them as " a Spirit of truth," holiness, and consolation ; and, as he had already endued them with some miraculous powers, he would shortly be with them in a more abiding and abundant manner. (*Marg. Ref.* p.—s.)—This promise of the Comforter is made exclusively to those disciples, who loved Christ and " kept his " commandments ; " (*Marg. Ref.* m—o.—*Notes,* 21—24. xv. 9—11 ;) so that it cannot relate to that communication of the Holy Spirit, by which divine life is first given, and the sinner is regenerated. For repentance, faith, love, and obedience flow from this as their source, or as *effects* from their *cause.* It must, therefore, relate to those subsequent influences and consolations of the Spirit, by which " after we have believed, we are sealed ; " and which are " the earnest of our inheritance." (*Notes,* 2 *Cor.* i. 21, 22. *Gal.* iv. 4—7. *Eph.* i. 13, 14.)—Miraculous powers are no doubt included : but these were not *exclusively* confer-

red on those who loved and obeyed Christ : (*Notes, Matt.* vii. 21—23. 1 *Cor.* xiii. 1—3 :) therefore, those animating, comforting influences, which are more immediately connected with love and obedience, must be especially intended.

Comforter. (16) Παρακλητον. 26. xv. 26. xvi. 7. 1 *John* ii. 1.—' Verbale à ... παρακαλητται verbi παρακαλεω, *quod* ' *non solum patrocinium alicujus implorare,* sed etiam, *ex-* ' *hortari, admonere, consolari, solatio reficere, docere, et* ' *instituere* significat.' *Schleusner.*—By some mistake of his prompters, Mohammed seems to have confounded Παρακλητος, a Comforter, with Περικλυτος, *very celebrated.* —His name *Mohammed,* signifies *celebrated ;* another name, which he assumed, *Achmeed,* an adjective from the same root, signifies, *very celebrated.*—He therefore affirmed, that Jesus foretold his coming, as *Achmeed ;* and complains that Christians refused to receive him. Hence the ungrounded notion, that he professed to be the Holy Spirit.

V. 18—20. Jesus was about to be removed from the disciples, as a father is taken away by death from his beloved children ; but he would by no means leave them as deserted and destitute *orphans,* without friend or comforter ; (*Note,* 1 *Thes.* ii. 17—20, *v.* 17 ;) for he would come to them, that is, by the Holy Spirit dwelling in them. (*Marg. Ref.* t, u.—*Notes,* 15—17. 21—24.) The world indeed would soon be deprived of his presence, and would no more see him, so as to contemplate his character and actions, till the day of judgment : but the apostles would see him, not only a few times and for a short space after his resurrection, but continually by faith, and through the influences of the Holy Spirit. (*Marg. Ref.* x.—*Note,* xvi. 14, 15.)—He was about to ascend into Heaven, and as he rose from the dead, and possesses eternal " life in him- " self ; " so they also, and all his true disciples, should certainly live in and by him, till he bring them to be for ever with him. ' As Christ being raised from the dead dieth no ' more : so justified man, being allied to God in Jesus ' Christ our Lord, doth as necessarily from that time for- ' ward always live, as Christ, by whom he hath life, liveth ' always.' *Hooker on Justification.* (*Marg. Ref.* y.—*Notes,* 4—6. v. 24—29. xi. 20—27, *vr.* 25, 26. *Rom.* v. 7— 10. viii. 32—34. 2 *Cor.* iv. 8—12. *Col.* iii. 1—4, *v.* 4.) And in that day, when being ascended into heaven, he should send the Holy Spirit to be their Teacher and Comforter, they would more evidently perceive, and distinctly understand, the in-dwelling of the Father with his incarnate Son ; and their own union with him, as their Head of life and influence, in whom they dwelt by faith as their Rest and Refuge, and who dwelt in them by his Spirit, as his temple and peculiar residence. (*Marg. Ref.* z, a.—*Notes,* vi. 52—58. xvii. 22, 23. *Eph.* ii. 19—22. iii. 14—19.)

Comfortless. (18) " Orphans." *Marg.* Ορφανiς. *Jam.* i. 27. Not elsewhere N. T.—*Ex.* xxii. 22—24. *Deut.* x. 18. *Job* xxix. 12. *Ps.* lxxxii. 3. *Sept.* ' *Liberos pa-*

b 14, 29, 24. xv.
14. Gen. xxvi. 5
—5. Deut. x. 12,
15. vi. 13. xxx.
6—8. Ps. cxix. 4
—6 Jer. xxxi.
33, 34. Ex. xxxvi.
—27. Luke xi.
28. 2 Cor. v. 14,
15. Jam. ii. 23,
24. 1 John iii. 18
—4c. v. 3. 3 John
c Rev. xxiii. 14.
d 23. xv. 9, 10.
s tv. 27. xvii. 23.
Ps. xxxv. 27. 1a.
Zeph. 3—5. Zeph.
iii. 17. 3 Tit.
ii. 16. 1 John iii.
1.
d 16. 22, 23. xvi.
10—11. xxii. 16.
3 Cor. iii. 16. iv.
6. xii. 9, 9.
2 Tim. iv. 17, 18.
3 1 John i. 3
—3. Rev. iii. 17. iii. 20.
Luke vi. 16.

21 He [b] that hath my commandments, and keepeth them, he it is that loveth me; and he [c] that loveth me shall be loved of my Father, and I will love him, [d] and will manifest myself to him.

22 [e] Judas saith unto him, (not Iscariot,) Lord, [f] how is it that thou wilt manifest thyself unto us, and not unto the world?

23 Jesus answered and said unto him, [g] If a man love me, he will keep my words: and my Father will love

him, and we will come unto him, [h] and make our abode with him.

24 He [i] that loveth me not, keepeth not my sayings; [k] and the word which ye hear is not mine, but the Father's which sent me.

25 These things [l] have I spoken unto you, being yet present with you.

26 But [m] the Comforter, which is the Holy Ghost, [n] whom the Father will

h 17. v. 17—19. vi.
56. x. 30. Gen.
i. 26. xi. 7. Ps.
xc. 1. xci. 1. Isa.
lvii. 15. Rom.
viii.
9—11. 1 John 24. iv
4, 15, 16. Rev.
iii. 20, 21. vii.
15—17. xxi. 22,
23. xxii. 3.
i 15. 21—23. Matt.
xix. 21, 22. xxv.
41—46. 3 Cor.
9. 1 John
iii. 16—20.
iv. 16. 26. vii.
29. 26. 38. 42.
xii. 44—50.
12. xvii. 6—8.
l 16. xvi. 1—4, 12,
13. xvii. 6—8.
—30. Acts 1, 2, 8, ii.

m 16. n vii. 39. xx. 22. Ps. li. 11. Is. lxiii. 10, 11. Matt. i. 18, 20. iii. 11. xxviii. 11, 12. 19. Mark xii. 36. xiii. 11. Luke i. 15, 35. 41. 67. ii. 25, 26. iii. 22. xi. 13. Acts i. 2. 5. ii. 4. v. 3. vii. 51. 55. xiii. 2. 4. xv. 8. 28. xvi. 6. xx. 28. xxviii. 25. Rom. v. 5. viii. 17. xv. 13. 1 Cor. ii. 10, 11. vi. 19. xii. 3. 3 Cor. vi. 6. xiii. 14. Eph. i. 13. iv. 30. 1 Tim. i. 3, 6. ix. 8. 2 Tim. i. 14. Tit. iii. 5. Heb. ii. 4. ix. 7. ix. 8. x. 15. 1 Pet. i. 12. 2 Pet. i. 21. 1 John v. 7. Jude 20. o 16. xv. 26. xvi. 7. Luke xxiv. 49. Acts i. 4.

' rente, seu parentibus orbos et destitutos; pupillos.' Schleusner.

V. 21—24. Love to Christ is the principal effect and evidence of union with him, by partaking of his Spirit of life, and truth, and holiness; it was therefore proper again to remind the disciples, that a disposition to receive, remember, and obey his commandments, was the only *decisive* proof of their love to him; without which the highest affections must be mere counterfeit or delusion. (*Marg. Ref. b.—Note*, 15—17.) They, who thus shewed their love to him, would be the objects of the Father's peculiar complacency and affection, both as evidencing his choice of them, and as bringing forth the fruits of his grace: (*Marg. Ref. c.—Notes*, xv. 9—11. xvi. 25—30:) and Jesus would reciprocally shew all love to them, as his redeemed people and genuine disciples; and in consequence of this love, he would manifest his gracious presence, glory, and excellency to them, in a peculiar and encouraging manner. (*Marg. Ref. d.*)—When he had given this intimation, Judas, or Jude, (called also Lebbeus, and Thaddeus, the brother of James; not Iscariot, for he had left them before this;) enquired how this could be, that he would manifest himself to them, and yet the world see him no more. He seems to have perceived, that there would be great and distinguishing condescension and kindness in his Lord, thus to discover himself to his obedient disciples: but he could not conceive how it could be done; or how it could consist with the setting up of his kingdom. (*Marg. Ref. e, f.*) To this Jesus replied by assuring him, that those who received and kept his commandments, thus proving that they truly loved him, would be the special objects of his Father's love; and that he and the Father would come, and take up their abode with them.—The Father and the Son being *personally* distinct, though essentially One, the *plural* number is here used. The presence and special residence of the Father and the Son, in and with the believer, (as " an habitation of God through the Spirit,") are the source of spiritual illumination, intimate communion, and delightful experience of the love of God to the soul; exciting all holy and heavenly affections, and giving an earnest and foretaste of the joys of heaven. These manifestations are perpetual in some of their effects; especially in the abiding sense of the glorious and gracious presence of God with us at all times, and an habitual judgment that he is worthy of all reverence, love, gratitude, and con-

fidence: but they are more realizing and affecting, at one time than another; according as hope, love, gratitude, and admiration, are in more lively exercise, and invisible things are brought near, by the vigorous exercise of faith on the truths and promises of scripture. But this experience must be peculiar to true disciples: for they who do not love Jesus, neither believe nor obey his words, but cast them away with contempt; and thus they not only offend him, but the Father also who sent him and spake by him; and therefore they cannot reasonably expect these discoveries of the divine glory and grace to their souls: nor indeed are they capable of receiving or enjoying them. (*Marg. Ref. g, h.—Notes*, 15—20. *Ps.* xxv. 14. *Rom.* viii. 5—11. 1 *Cor.* iii. 16, 17. vi. 18—20. 2 *Cor.* vi. 14—18, v. 16. *Eph.* ii. 19—22. *Rev.* ii. 17.)—' "We will come to him," by that ' Spirit, whose temple is the body of the saints : (1 *Cor.* iii. ' 16. vi. 13:) and by whose in-dwelling they are made an ' habitation of God. (*Eph.* ii. 22.) Here therefore is no ' express mention made of the Holy Spirit; because by ' him it is, that the Father and the Son dwell in us. And ' so it is in the beginning of the epistles, praying for grace ' and peace from the Father, and our Lord Jesus Christ : ' because this grace and peace were to be conferred on ' men by the Spirit.' *Whitby.*—(*Notes, Rom.* i. 5—7, *v.* 7. *Eph.* i. 1, 2.)

Will manifest. (21) Εμφανισω. *Conspicuum me præbebo.* 22. *Matt.* xxvii. 53. *Acts* xxiii. 15. 22. xxiv. 1. xxv. 2. 15. *Heb.* ix. 24. xi. 14.—*Ex.* xxxiii. 13. 18. *Sept.*—Εμφανης; *Acts* xx. 40. *Rom.* x. 20.—*How is it?* (22) Τι γεγονεν; " What has come to pass ?"—*Abode.* (23) Μονην. 2.

V. 25, 26. The truths, which Jesus had spoken to the disciples in his personal ministry, were fully understood by them: but, when the Holy Spirit, the Author of all holiness, as well as the Teacher of all truth to man, should come to them; he would more efficaciously instruct them, powerfully removing all their prejudices, and assisting all their faculties to receive the truth. (*Notes,* xv. 26, 27. xvi. 7—13.) This indeed, in the case of the apostles, was effected in part by *immediate revelation*, by which they were infallibly preserved from all error, and guided into all truth. Yet even this revelation was principally made by causing them to recollect the doctrines, promises, and precepts, which Jesus had given them; and by enabling them to see the truth, excellency, and glory of them, in the clearest and most convincing manner. Thus our Lord. in

send in my name, [p] he shall teach you all things, [q] and bring all things to your remembrance, whatsoever I have said unto you.

27 [r] Peace I leave with you; my peace I give unto you: [s] not as the world giveth, give I unto you. [t] Let not your heart be troubled, neither let it be [u] afraid.

28 Ye have [x] heard how I said unto you, I go away, and come *again* unto you. [y] If ye loved me, ye would rejoice, because I said, [z] I go unto the Father: for [a] my Father is greater than I.

29 And [b] now I have told you before it come to pass, that when it is come to pass, ye might believe.

30 Hereafter [c] I will not talk much with you: for [d] the prince of this world cometh, [e] and hath nothing in me.

---

his teaching, referred to the Old Testament: and taught nothing but what that ancient revelation, fully understood, had taught men to expect: and the apostles referred to the personal ministry of Christ, and taught nothing but what his words, fully understood, entirely warranted. The same truths, therefore, are taught in every part of scripture; in some more obscurely, in others more clearly: and any *pretended new* revelation, that teaches things contrary to the written word, or manifestly not contained in it, is so palpable an imposture, that not only no authority of bishops, popes, and councils can support it, but even miracles themselves would be insufficient to establish its divine authority. (*Notes, Deut.* xiii. 1—5. *Matt.* xvi. 19. *Acts* xxvi. 19—23. 2 *Thes.* ii. 8—12. 2 *Pet.* iii. 1—4. 1 *John* iv. 4—6.)—The more ordinary teaching of the Holy Spirit is effected in a similar manner: not by any immediate suggestion or new revelation: but by bringing to our remembrance the words of Christ, and of his apostles and prophets; and by enlightening our understandings, and preparing our hearts to receive them in knowledge and love, and to apply them, according to our cases and circumstances, by obedient faith. (*Note*, 2 *Pet.* i. 12—15.)

The Comforter. (26) Παρακλητος. See on 16. (*Notes*, 15—17. xv. 26, 27.)—*He.*] Εκεινος. xv. 26. xvi. 8. 13, 14. —The masculine personal pronoun: surely marking the *personality* of the Holy Spirit.—*Bring to ... remembrance.*] Υπομησει. *Luke* xxii. 61. 2 *Tim.* ii. 14. *Tit.* iii. 1. 2 *Pet.* i. 12. 3 *John* 10. *Jude* 5.

V. 27, 28. Our Lord being about to die, and leave his disciples, bequeathed to them " his peace " as a legacy; or gave it to them as a donation. This comprised peace with God, peace of conscience, a sweet serenity of mind, arising from confidence in God, and submission to him, with the hope of heaven, and a disposition to mutual love and harmony. (*Marg. Ref.* r.—*Notes, Rom.* xiv. 13—18. *Gal.* v. 22—26. *Phil.* iv. 5—9. *Col.* iii. 12—15.) This peace he gave them, not as the people of the world wish peace and prosperity to one another as a mere compliment, without meaning or sincerity; nor yet in that *inefficacious manner*, by which many sincerely desire the welfare of those whom they cannot relieve: but in perfect benevolence, and with divine energy; and it was a far richer legacy, than any other dying friend ever bequeathed. (*Marg. Ref.* s.) They ought, therefore, by no means to give way to sorrow or alarm, because of the afflictions which awaited them. (*Note*, 1.) He had told them that he was about to leave them, and to come again to them; (*Note*, 2, 3;) and if they loved him wisely and properly, they would rejoice on that account; as he was about to leave his present abased and suffering condition, and to return to the Father: for, says he, " my Father is greater than I." It has been already seen, that The Word, as God and with God, is declared to be One with and equal to the Father, the Creator and Lord of all. (*Notes*, i. 1—3. v. 17—29 x. 26—31, *v.* 30.) In this respect Jesus could not say, " My Father is greater than I:" indeed there can be no greater or less in the infinite perfection of Deity. But, as God the Son was manifested in human nature; and as in this sense he was about to finish his work, and to go to receive his merited recompence, in being exalted to the mediatorial throne; the language is evidently proper, not only as to his human nature, but likewise in respect of his mediatorial character and kingdom, in which he acted as the Servant and Apostle of his Father: even as an ambassador, though equal in nature, is inferior in office, to the prince who commissions him. (*Note*, xvi. 7.) In this sense it perfectly accords to all the rest of the scripture; and it behoves all who love him greatly to rejoice in his exaltation to glory, after his voluntary humiliation. (*Marg. Ref.* y—a.—*Notes*, x. 32—39. *Matt.* xxviii. 18.)

Is greater than I. (28) Μαζων με εσι. iv. 12. viii. 53. xv. 20. *Matt.* xi. 11. xxiii. 11. *Rom.* ix. 12. Superiority in *rank*, or *office*, with equality in *nature*, as men, is evidently intended in these and other instances. (*Note*, xvi. 7.)

V. 29—31. Our Lord next shewed the apostles, that he had before-hand told them of his death, resurrection, and ascension into heaven, and the descent of the Holy Spirit; in order that the combined evidence of the prediction, and the miracles attending its accomplishment, might confirm their faith. (*Marg. Ref.* b.—*Notes*, xvi. 1—6, *v.* 4.) But he should have little more opportunity for conversation with them: for Satan " the prince " of this wicked world was coming to assault him with all his power; both by his servants, even Judas, Caiaphas, and the rulers of the Jews, with Pilate and the Romans, who were about to apprehend, condemn, and crucify him; and by his own horrid temptations. (*Notes*, xviii. xix. *Gen.* iii. 14, 15. *Heb.* ii. 16—18. iv. 14—16. v. 7—10.) As, however, there was neither guilt in his actions, nor sin in his heart and nature, that enemy had no part in him, and could obtain no permanent advantage against him: he would find him in every

31 But that the world may know that I love the Father, and as the Fa-ther gave me commandment, even so I do. ᶠArise, let us go hence.

respect invulnerable, and must therefore experience an absolute defeat in the conflict. (*Marg. Ref.* c—e.) To himself it would be inexpressibly severe and terrible, but the event would be most glorious. (*Note, Matt.* xxvi. 36 —39.) Indeed, he should not at all have been exposed to pain or death; if he had not voluntarily subjected himself to it, to manifest his love of the Father, and obedience to him, that he might be glorified in the salvation of his chosen people : ' that the world may know, and knowing imitate ' my obedience to him in the severest precepts.' *Whitby.* As this was his purpose, and the time was at hand, he must call upon them to arise, and go thence to the garden, which was the place of preparation and devotion, and also the spot where his enemies were about to appre-hend him.

Prince of this world. (30) Τω κοσμ κ τ τ αρχ ν. See on xii. 31. (*Notes,* xvi. 8—11. 2 *Cor.* iv. 3, 4. 1 *John* v. 19. *Rev.* xii. 7—12. xx. 1—3.)

PRACTICAL OBSERVATIONS.

V. 1—6.

We cannot help *feeling* trouble and sorrow, under our trials, perils, temptations, and sins; and because of the apostasies and iniquities which we witness : but we should watch against dejection, and that inward prevalence of dismay and disquietude, which excites murmurs and dis-trust, and unfits us for present duty. (*Note, Luke* xxi. 12 —19, *v.* 19.) The vigorous exercise of faith in the pro-mises and perfections of our reconciled God, and in the merits and grace of our heavenly Advocate, forms the proper and the adequate method of keeping trouble from occupying our hearts, and of producing inward joy in the midst of tribulation. For we shall thus be animated, by the prospect of a speedy admission into quiet and delightful mansions in our Father's house above, of which an infi-nite abundance still remain, for the reception of the whole multitude of true believers. This hope will never disap-point us : the promise of the Lord will not deceive us : he has told us, that "in the world we shall have tribula-" tion," and we may know what to expect;' and he would not have permitted us to look for so glorious a felicity hereafter, if he had not intended to give it to us. But " he is gone before to prepare a place for us." He is as much performing the part of a faithful and affectionate Friend, now that he is ascended into the heavens, as when on earth he shed his blood for our sins : and he is as mindful of the concerns of all who look for him, as he will be when he shall " appear the second time without sin " unto salvation." We ought therefore, with all diligence and perseverance to use the appointed means of prepar-ing our souls for the holy inheritance of heaven ; and to wait, in the patience of hope and the obedience of love, till he shall return to " take us to himself, that where he " is, there we may be also." But stubborn unbelievers have no place prepared in heaven, and no friend in the hour of death to receive their departing souls, or to wel-come them at the resurrection of the last day : indeed a far different place, " prepared for the devil and his angels,"

awaits them; and their enemy stands ready to " receive " them to himself, that where he is, there they may be " also;" nor is there any one to prevent the success of his malignant expectations. As therefore all know, that they are liable to be turned out of their present place of resi-dence at an hour's warning; surely, common sense de-mands it of them, to seek admission into those mansions, which Jesus has provided for his redeemed people.—We are indeed far more faulty than Thomas was, if with all our advantages, we know not whither the Saviour is gone, or the way by which we must follow him. Yet ignorance and uncertainty envelope the minds of even professed Christians in general, in this obvious and important matter : and numbers seek to enter heaven by ways of man's de-vising ; while Jesus, " the Way, and the Truth, and the " Life," is wholly, or in great measure, neglected; if not despised and opposed. It will, however, be most certainly known at last, that no one of Adam's fallen race ever found acceptance with God, or admission into the man-sions of felicity, who refused to seek them by faith in the righteousness, atonement, and mediation of our crucified Emmanuel; by reliance on his word, who is essential Truth, and by seeking life to his soul from him, who is the Life itself. It greatly concerns all the opposers and despisers of the grace proposed in the gospel seriously to reconsider this subject ; and all who are beginning to seek the favour of God and eternal life, should especially direct their attention to it, that they may not delay to come in that Way, by which alone sinners can find access to a holy God, and admission into a holy heaven. (*Notes, Is.* xxviii. 12—20. *Jer.* vi. 16, 17. *Matt.* xi. 27—30. *P. O.* 25—30.)

V. 7—14.

In proportion as we know Jesus, we know the Father also. Every true believer has, in a measure, thus known and seen him : the character, doctrine, and cross of Christ form the glass, in which we must contemplate the glory of the invisible God. (*Notes,* xvii. 1—3, *v.* 3. 2 *Cor.* iii. 17, 18. *P. O.* 7—18. *Note,* iv. 5, 6.) It is owing to our inattention to his words and works, that our discoveries are so feeble and so few. Thus we are our own enemies, for this is the only satisfactory good, which can suffice to fill all our enlarged capacities with an adequate felicity. If we sinners could behold God in his essential glory, the discovery would dismay and overwhelm us : in the Person of Jesus alone can we see Him, as " a just God and a " Saviour ;" as glorious in holiness and abundant in mercy; and as the proper Object of our delightful contemplation, our firm confidence, our humble rejoicing, and our thank-ful adoration. May the doctrine and character, the mi-racles and prophecies, the sufferings and glory of our divine Redeemer; the great things, which he personally performed when on earth, and the still greater which he has done by his believing servants, since his ascension into heaven; confirm our faith in him, and assure us, that " He " is in the Father, and the Father in him." Even now, " whatsoever we shall ask in his name," as conducive to our good, and suited to our state, he will give it to us

4 D 6

CHAP. XV.

Jesus, by the parable of himself as the true Vine, and his disciples as the branches, shews the necessity of union and communion with him, in order to fruitfulness; illustrates the conduct of God towards his church; and exhorts his disciples to abide in him,

1—8. *He shews the greatness of his love to them, 9—15; and that he has chosen them, that they may bring forth fruit which may remain, 16. He commands them to love one another; and warns them to expect hatred and persecution from the world, which hates both him and his father, 17—25. He promises the Comforter, to confirm the testimony which they should bear to him, 26, 27.*

(*Notes, Matt.* vii. 7—11. *Jam.* v. 16—18. 1 *John* v. 14, 15 :) that in the renewal of our souls to holiness, our steady and successful resistance of temptation, our patient obedience under trials, and the conversion of sinners by our means, " the Father may be glorified in the Son ; " for these are very great works in the sight of angels and of God himself, however men may despise them. (*Notes*, and *P. O. Luke* xv. 1—10.)

V. 15—24.

We have not indeed been favoured with the Redeemer's personal presence ; but we are encouraged confidently to hope for that of the Holy Spirit, who is sent by the Father, through his intercession, to " abide with us for ever." His miraculous operations are not to be expected, nor are they needful for us : but as a Teacher, a Sanctifier, and a Comforter, he will always continue with his church ; and as the Source of holiness and felicity, he will abide with every believer for ever. (*Note*, iv. 10—15. P. O. 1—15.) " The world " of unconverted men, with all their wisdom and learning, are unable to understand, or to desire and receive, these sacred influences of " the Spirit of truth : " and we can scarcely expect to escape the appellation of enthusiasts or hypocrites, if we profess our faith and hope, and experience in this respect, in the most scriptural manner. But the true believer cannot be unacquainted with that blessed " Comforter, who dwelleth in him ; " nor may he deny his obligations to him and dependence on him, from whose gracious influences all his hopes and joys arise ; and who will for ever dwell in all those, who " love Jesus and keep his commandments." Whatever losses such disciples may sustain, or whatever troubles may await them, they shall not be left destitute and friendless : the absence of their beloved Lord will be short, and his return will be sure ; they see him, whom the world perceives not ; they believe and are assured, that " he is in " the Father, and they in him, and he in them : " in his strength they labour, in his righteousness they are entitled to eternal life ; and " because he lives they shall live also," and be kept by his power through faith to complete salvation. (*Note*, 1 *Pet.* i. 3—5.)—But these privileges do not belong to all who profess, or even are zealous for, the truths of the gospel ; being confined to them, whose " faith " worketh by love," and whose love to Jesus induces them " to keep his commandments : " and they are enjoyed in proportion to the degree of their love and obedience. Such persons are thus evidenced to be the subjects of the Father's electing love, the peculiar purchase of the incarnate Son, and partakers of the Holy Spirit, in his regenerating and new creating grace. The divine image, renewed upon their souls, is beloved and delighted in by the Father and the Son ; their holy affections and obedience are honourable

to the gospel : and their happy experience of near and sweet communion with the Lord in his ordinances, the discoveries of his presence and glory to their souls, the light of his countenance, and the joy of his salvation, will make them know, " how he manifests himself to them as " he doth not to the world : " while their conscious unworthiness will fill them with thankful admiration and adoration of his unspeakable condescension. But those who do not love Jesus, and who keep not his sayings, cannot know what these special manifestations mean : they only proclaim their own folly, if they deny the reality of them, because they never experienced them ; (*Notes*, Prov. xiv. 10. 2 *Pet.* i. 19. 1 *John* v. 9, 10 ;) and if any pretend to them, when living in allowed disobedience to Christ, they must be plainly told that they deceive themselves.

V. 25—31.

Would we know the way of peace, we must fervently pray for the teaching of the Holy Spirit and simply depend on it : thus the words which Jesus has spoken will be brought to our remembrance, and we shall be enabled to understand, believe, and obey them ; and our experience of their truth and goodness will solve those difficulties, which to others are insuperable. Thus we shall receive that legacy, which Jesus has bequeathed to all his disciples, even " His peace," which is " the peace of God " that passeth all understanding ; " and it will contribute more to our present comfort, than the friendship, the applause, or even the possession of the whole world ; for it will garrison our hearts against trouble and terror, in the most afflictive scenes of life, and in the solemn hour of dissolution. (*Note, Phil.* iv. 5—7.) We may distinguish the peace which he gives, from that of Pharisees and hypocrites, by its humbling and sanctifying effects ; and by its enabling us to unite great tenderness of conscience, with sweet affiance in God's mercy, and calm submission to his will. Let us then rejoice, that our beloved Saviour has, in our nature, entered into " the joy set before him," being " ascended to his Father and our Father, to our God " and his God." (*Note*, xx. 11—17, *v.* 17.) Let us compare his words with our experience and observation, for the daily confirmation of our faith. Let us rejoice in his victories over " the prince of this world : " and though the enemy has still a strong party in our souls, yet, depending on the Redeemer's all-sufficient grace, let us prosecute his victories, both by resisting temptation, and opposing the cause of sin and Satan in the world : let us copy the example of the Saviour's love and obedience ; and let us be ready to arise and encounter hardship and danger, with constancy and alacrity ; and to go hence by death, whenever he shall please to summon us away.

4 D 7

I AM the ᵃtrue ᵇVine, and my Father is the ᶜHusbandman.

2 Every ᵈbranch in me that beareth not fruit, he taketh away: ᵉand every branch that beareth fruit he purgeth it, ᶠthat it may bring forth more fruit.

3 Now ᵍye are clean through the ʳord which I have spoken unto you.

4 ʰAbide in me, and ᶦI in you. ʲAs the branch cannot bear fruit of itself except it abide in the vine; no more can ye, except ye abide in me.

5 I am ᵏthe Vine, ye are the branches: he that abideth in me, and I in him, ᵐthe same bringeth forth much fruit; for °without me ᵖye can do nothing.

NOTES.

CHAP. XV. V. 1. The close of the preceding chapter intimates, that our Lord and his disciples then arose from table, as about to leave the house and retire to Gethsemane : yet probably they did not set out, till he had finished this discourse, and the prayer with which he closed it. (xiv. 31. xviii. 1.)—Some however think, that this and the following chapters were spoken by the way, before they passed the brook Kedron.—Perhaps the fruit of the vine, of which they had been partaking, or the sight of a spreading vine, gave occasion to this illustration of that union between Christ and his disciples, which had before been mentioned. (Note, xiv. 18—20.)—The nation of Israel, the worshippers of JE-HOVAH, had frequently been represented as "a vine;" but Jesus declared that he was "the true Vine." (Marg. Ref. a, b.—Notes, Ps. lxxx. 8—13. Is. v. 1—7. Jer. ii. 20, 21.) For that nation had been only a type of the true Israel, the Seed of Abraham ; which consists of Christ, and believers as one with him. (Notes, Rom. iv. 9—17. xi. Gal. iii. 15—29.) He therefore was "the true Vine," the substance of that shadow ; and all the fruitful branches of that vine, which had produced good fruit, had been rendered so by grace derived from him.—His "Father was the Husbandman," who planted, watered, guarded, and took care of this Vine, and of all its branches. (Marg. Ref. c.—Notes, Cant. viii. 11, 12. Matt. xxi. 33—44.) He had appointed the person of Christ as "God manifested in the flesh," and from the beginning had made known his purpose of sending him to redeem sinners. He had determined every thing respecting his mediatorial work, and its happy and glorious consequences. He had constituted him the medium of communication, through which alone he would shew favour, and convey grace, to any of the apostate race of men. He took peculiar delight in his obedience and sacrifice, as man's Surety ; and in "giving him the Spirit without measure," to furnish him for his work ; and also that from his fulness all believers might receive grace sufficient, to render them fruitful and holy ; and he was well pleased with the care of his church, and greatly valued its fruit. (Notes, i. 16. iii. 27—36, v. 34.)—The union of the divine and human nature in the person of Christ, and the fulness of the Spirit in him, resemble the root of the vine, deriving the fertilizing juices from a rich soil ; and his mediatorial work, like the stem, conveys these to all believers, to render them fruitful.—Like the vine, the Redeemer appears to the ignorant, proud, and unbelieving, mean and despicable : while the wise of this world, the learned, the vali-

ant, and the mighty, are counted like the stately cedar or the sturdy oak : but the fruit of this Vine, and of its branches, is far more valuable than all the other productions of the earth. (Notes, Is. iv. 2. liii. 2, 3. Ez. xv. 6—8.\ True.) Aληθινος. i. 9. vi. 32. Rev. iii. 7. 14. vi. 10. See on xvii. 3.

V. 2. In the visible church there are great numbers, who are united to Christ merely by external profession, by attendance on ordinances, or by filling up some station among his disciples, as Judas did. These resemble those luxuriant branches of the vine, which must be pruned away, or they will crowd the others, and prevent the fruit of them from coming to perfection. Every person of this description, the Husbandman will in due time remove. By temptations and persecutions, many are detected, and become apostates ; some are left to turn aside to false doctrines ; and others are cut off by awful judgments, or silently removed by death. Thus Judas was removed from among the apostles, and the unbelieving Jews were cast out of the church. (Marg. Ref. d.—Notes, Matt. iii. 11, 12. vii. 21—23. xiii. 20—22. xxii. 11—14. xxv. 1—4. 1 Cor. xi. 17—22, v. 19. 1 John ii. 18, 19.) On the other hand every one, who is really united to Christ, by partaking of his Spirit, and by true faith in him, and who shews it, in "the fruits of righteousness" which he produces, is pruned and tended by the Husbandman, that he "may bring forth more fruit." The chastisements, temptations, and humiliating discoveries of their own hearts, by which, (in subserviency to his word and sanctifying Spirit,) he purifies them from their idols and worldly attachments, and mortifies their pride and self-confidence, are often very sharp and painful ; but they promote their fruitfulness. (Marg. Ref. e.)

Branch.] Kλημα. 4, 5, 6. Here only N. T.—Ez. xv. 2. xvii. 6, 7. 23. xix. 11. Sept.—He purgeth.] Kαθαιρει. Heb. x. 2. Not elsewhere.—Aιρει, "taketh away;" καθαιρει, "purifieth," or cleanseth ; and καθαροι, "clean," (3) have a relation to each other in the original, which cannot be preserved in a translation.—None but the unfruitful are taken away.

V. 3—5. The apostles, after Judas had left them, were all branches in some measure fruitful : and Jesus, without excepting any of them, declared that they were clean, through the efficacy of the doctrine which he had taught them, and their believing attention and obedience to it ; (Marg. Ref. g.—Note, xiii. 6—11, v. 10.) And, as all their approaching trials were intended for their increasing

6 If a man abide not in me, *he is cast forth as a branch, and is withered; and men gather them, and cast *them* into the fire, and they are burned.

7 If ye abide in me, and *my words abide in you, *ye shall ask what ye will, and it shall be done unto you.

8 Herein *is my Father glorified, that ye bear much fruit: *so shall ye be my disciples.

9 As *the Father hath loved me, so have I loved you: *continue ye in my love.

10 If *ye keep my commandments, ye shall abide in my love; *even as I have kept my Father's commandments, and abide in his love.

11 These things have I spoken unto

---

purity and fruitfulness; he exhorted them " to abide in " him," by faith and continual dependence on him ; thus he would " abide in them," by the efficacious operation of his grace, rendering them fruitful and comfortable. ' " Remain in me," by faith, love, and obedience (10) ... ' " and I will remain in you " by my Spirit.' *Whitby*. (*Marg. Ref.* h, i.—*Notes*, 9—11. viii. 30—36. *Acts* xxiii. 23, 24. 1 *John* ii. 26—29.) For, notwithstanding their present attainments, they could no more perform any spiritual and acceptable obedience, without receiving from him further supplies of grace, than " the branch " could bear fruit, except it remained in union with the vine, and derived continual nourishment from it. As he was " the Vine, " and they were the branches," this illustration would aptly shew them their need of constantly living by faith in him. (*Note, Gal.* ii. 17—21, *v.* 20.) Every believer, thus abiding in him, would " bring forth much fruit : " but as those who were wholly *separated* from him could do nothing good in the sight of God at any time ; so true believers would not be able to do any thing effectual in the service of God, if the exercise of their faith in him should by any means suffer a temporary suspension. (*Marg. Ref.* k—n. —*Notes, Rom.* viii. 10—13. 1 *John* iii. 18—24, *v.* 24.)— ' As this respects all Christians, the sense runs thus : If ye ' abide in me, by that faith which purifies the heart, (*Acts* ' xv. 9,) and works by love ; (*Gal.* v. 6;) and " I in you," ' by that Spirit, without whom none can be a member of ' Christ : (*Rom.* viii. 9. 1 *John* iii. 24. iv. 13 :) you shall ' abound in the fruits of the Spirit. But without my Spirit ' abiding in you, and uniting you to me, your Head, you can ' do nothing acceptable to me, or worthy of my gospel : as ' it respects the apostles, it may further note, that without ' the gifts and powerful assistance of the Holy Spirit, they ' could do nothing to convert the world to the faith ; as ' being not sufficient of themselves for that work, but hav- ' ing their sufficiency from that God who giveth them the ' Holy Spirit. (2 *Cor.* iii. 5, 6.)' *Whitby*.

Abide. (4) Μεινατε. See on viii. 31.—*Without me*. (5) Χωρις εμε. " Severed from me." *Marg.* xx. 7. *Matt.* xiv. 21. *Eph.* ii. 12. A χωριζω, *separo*.

V. 6—8. (*Note, 2.*) Unfruitful professors of the gospel would not " abide in " Christ : their profession would therefore wither, and they would only be fit to be cast into the fire of hell ; even as the withered branches of a vine are of no use, but men gather them and burn them as waste wood. (*Marg. Ref. o.—Notes, Is.* xxvii. 7—11. *Ez.* xv. 1—5. xx. 45—48. *Mal.* iv. 1. *Matt.* iii. 7—10. *Heb.* vi. 7, 8.) But while the apostles and disciples, at that time and in every age, abode in Christ, and maintained

communion with him, while his words dwelt in their understandings, memories, and affections, by obedient faith, they might ask what they would, and their prayers would be assuredly granted ; and this would secure their increasing fruitfulness and usefulness. (*Marg. Ref.* p, q.—*Notes, Ps.* xxxvii. 4. *Col.* iii. 16, 17. 1 *John* v. 14, 15. *2 John* 1—3. 7—11. *Jude* 20—25.) Thus the Father would be glorified, in the abundant fruit produced by them ; as the husbandman would value the produce of his vineyard for the sake of his friends, even though he should not want it for himself : their holy doctrine would thus be recommended and propagated ; the perfections and wonderful works of God made known ; the genuine tendency of the gospel shewn ; sinners converted ; and spiritual worshippers added to the Lord. (*Note,* 12—16.) At the same time this would prove them to be his true disciples, which could not be known by any other evidence, if this were wanting, and they would become more and more worthy of that honourable title. (*Marg. Ref.* r, s.—*Notes,* viii. 30—36, *v.* 31. *Matt.* v. 43—48, *v.* 45. *Gal.* v. 16—26. *Phil.* i. 9—11. *Jam.* ii. 14—26.)

V. 9—11. Our Lord next reminded the disciples, of the exceeding riches of his love to them, which resembled that of the Father to him. (*Note,* xvii. 22, 23.) He indeed is the adequate Object of his Father's love, both on account of his personal dignity and excellency, and his mediatorial righteousness and atonement, and the glory thence redounding to the divine perfections and government : but the love of Christ to his disciples was first placed on them as sinners, and was therefore perfectly unmerited ; though he afterwards loved his own image in them, and delighted in their cordial attachment and obedience to him. His love to them was, however, immense, unchangeable, and everlasting ; and he intended to honour and bless them, according to the purpose and effect of the Father's love to him. (*Note, Eph.* iii. 14—19.) He therefore exhorted them to " continue in his love ; " that is, to persevere in implicit faith and obedience in all things ; thus shewing the sincerity of their love to him, which would conduce to their habitual experience of his love to them, and all its happy effects. For thus he, their Lord and Saviour, had perfectly obeyed his Father's commandments, and so continued in his love. (*Marg. Ref.* t—y.—*Notes,* xiv. 15—24. *Jude* 20, 21.) He had indeed spoken these words unto them, to excite them to this constancy of faith and obedience, that he might have abundant cause to rejoice in them, and their comfort and usefulness ; and that their joy in him, as their unchangeable Friend, might be full and complete, by their uninterrupted communion with him and communications

you, *that my joy might remain in you, and that *your joy might be full.

12 ¶ This is *my commandment, That ye love one another, as I have loved you.

13 *Greater love hath no man than this, that a man lay down his life for his friends.

14 Ye are *my friends, *if ye do whatsoever I command you.

15 Henceforth *I call you not servants; for the servant knoweth not what his lord doeth: but I have called you *friends; *for all things that I have heard of my Father I have made known unto you.

16 Ye *have not chosen me, but I have chosen you, *and ordained you, that ye should go *and bring forth fruit, *and that your fruit should remain: *that whatsoever ye shall ask of the Father in my name, he may give it you.

Marginal references (left): z Is. liii. 11. lxii. 4, 5. Jer. xxxii. 41. xxxiii. 9. Zeph. iii. 17. Luke xv. 5, 6, 7. 10. 23, 24, 32. 1 John i. 4. a xvi. 24. xx. xvii. b Rom. 13. 2 Cor. i. 24. Eph. v. 18. Phil. i. 25. 1 Thes. v. 16. 1 Pet. i. 8. 2 John 12. b xiii. 34. Rom. xii. 10. Eph. v. 2. 1 Thes. iii. 12. iv. 9, 10. 2 Thes. i. 3. 1 Pet. i. 22. id. 6, 8. iv. 8. 1 John ii. 7—10. iii. 11—18. 23. iv. 21. c xx. 11. 15. Rom. v. 6, 8. Eph. v. 11. d viii. 13. 26. 2 Chr. xx. 7. Cant. v. l. Is. xli. 8. Matt. xii. 50. Luke xii. 4. Jam. ii. 23. e ii. 5. xiii. 17. xiv. 21. 1 John v. 3. Gal. iv. 6, 7. Philem. 16. Jam. i. 1. 2 Pet. i. l. Jude l. Rev. i. l.

Marginal references (right): f 14. iv. 19. xvii. 6—8. 26. Gen. xviii. 17—19. 2 Kings vi. 8—12. Ps. xxv. 14. Am. iii. 7. Matt. xiii. 11. Luke x. 23, 24. Acts xx. 27. Rom. xvi. 25, 26. 1 Cor. ii. 9—12. Eph. i. 9. iii. 5. Col. i. 26. 1 Pet. i. 11, 12. i Matt. 10. vii. 70. xix. 28. Luke vi. 13. Acts i. 24. la. ib. x. 41. xxii. 14. Rom. ix. 11—16. 21. 1 John iv. 10. 19. k xx. 21—23. xvi. 13—17. la. xlix. 1—3.

f—3. Jer. i. 5.—7. Matt. xxviii. 18, 19. Mark xvi. 15, 16. Luke xxiv. 47—49. Acts i. 8. Rom. i. 5. xv. 15, 16. 1 Cor. ix. 16—1d. Gal. i. 15, 16. Col. i. 25. 1 Tim. ii. 7. 2 Tim. i. 11. ii. 2. Tit. i. 5. l 6. Prov. xi. 30. Is. xxvii. 6. iv. 10—13. Mic. v. 7. Rom. i. 13. xv. 16—19. 1 Cor. iii. 6, 7. Col. i. 6. Jam. iii. 18. m Gen. xviii. 19. Ps. lxxi. 18. lxxviii. 4—6. cxlv. 4. Zech. i. 4—6. Acts xx. 28—32. Rom. xv. 4. 1 Cor. x. 11. 2 Tim. iii. 15—17. Heb. xi. 4. 2 Pet. i. 14—21. iii. 2. 15, 16. n 7. xiv. 13, 14. xvi. 23, 24. Matt. xxi. 22.

---

from his fulness, and their assured hope of his glory.—Many interpret the words, " my joy, &c." of the joy which Christ conferred on his disciples; but it is most obvious to explain them of the joy which he had in them; and there is abundant scriptural ground for this interpretation. (*Marg. Ref.* z, a.—*Notes, Is.* liii. 11, 12. lxii. 1—5. *Zeph.* iii. 14—17, v. 17. *Luke* xv. 3—7. P. O. 1—10.)—*Continue ye.* (9) Μεινατε. 4. 16.

V. 12—16. (*Note,* xiii. 31—35.) The great commandment, which our Lord, on this affecting occasion, exhorted the disciples to obey, was love of one another, for his sake and after his example. (*Marg. Ref.* b.—*Notes,* 1 *John* ii. 7—11. iii. 16, 17.) This would necessarily imply the highest degree of active, liberal, sympathizing, patient, and self-denying affection.—The greatest love, which had ever been heard of, was expressed, when a man deliberately laid down his own life, to preserve that of his valued friend or benefactor. Many have rushed upon danger in the field of battle, or on a sudden emergency; and thus lost their lives *honourably* in defence of those, who were of superior merit or rank, and to whom their obligations were very great: a few instances are recorded of such as were even deliberately willing to part with life, to preserve whom they greatly loved. But Jesus, " the Lord of glory," was about to lay down his life, in the midst of agony and ignominy, for those who were infinitely inferior to him, utterly undeserving of his esteem, and indeed the meet objects of his indignation and abhorrence. He had fixed his love upon them, when they were enemies, and when the sacrifice of his death was necessary to their deliverance from wrath and reconciliation to God, in consistency with the honour of his law and justice; and he had changed them into his friends by converting grace. (*Notes, Rom.* v. 6—10. 1 *John* iv. 9—12. 19—21.) Thus they had learned to love him, and he had admitted them to the honourable rank of friends: (*Note, Jam.* ii. 21—24:) as such he was now about to die for them, according to his previous engagement; and in doing this, he meant also to shew them in what manner, and to what degree, they ought to love one another.—Notwithstanding his dignity and holiness, and their meanness and sinfulness, he purposed to treat them as his intimate friends, so long as they unreservedly obeyed his commandments; without deviating from any of them, through fear of men, or love of the world. (*Marg. Ref.* c—e.—*Notes,* 9—11. xiv. 15—24.) They were indeed servants; he had a right to exercise all the authority of a Sovereign, and he had often spoken to them as servants; (*Note,* xiii. 12—17;) but from that time he meant still more fully to treat them as his friends. For servants, especially slaves, were seldom informed of their master's intentions and counsels: but he had made known to them all those things, which had been entrusted to him as Mediator, to communicate to his church; and they would soon be instructed, by his Spirit, in a more complete understanding of his whole counsel, and employed to make it known to mankind. (*Marg. Ref.* f—h.—*Notes, Gen.* xviii. 17—19. *An.* iii. 4—8.) But they must recollect, that this marvellous friendship, between " the Lord " of glory " and such poor sinful worms, did not originate from them. They were not, of themselves, disposed to choose him and his service; but he had first " chosen " them to salvation," called them to be disciples, and selected them to the office of apostles: and their choice of him, and love to him, had arisen from his choice of them. (*Marg. Ref.* i.—*Notes, Rom.* ix. 15—18. 2 *Thes.* ii. 13, 14.) He had moreover *ordained,* or *appointed,* them his ministers, in order that they might go forth in his name, into the most distant regions; and that by their holy lives, unwearied labours, patient sufferings, faithful preaching, and fervent prayers, some of them as writers of the sacred scripture, and most of them as martyrs in his cause, " might bring forth fruit," to the glory of God and the salvation of an immense multitude of souls. (*Note,* 6—8.) Nor would this fruit perish when they died, or only remain in the gracious recompence bestowed upon them in another life; but it would also abide, in the continuance and success of the gospel, from age to age, even to the end of the world. So that many millions, who would not come into existence till long after their decease, would arise and bless God for the grace bestowed upon them, and for the gospel transmitted to them through their ministry, and by their writings; even as generous wines are preserved a long time, and prove a cordial to those who live, when both the vines whence they were produced, and they who cultivated them, are removed. (*Marg. Ref.* l, m.—*Note,* 2 *Pet.* i. 12—15. P. O. 12—18.) They were called into this state of friendship, that, their prayers being answered by the Father through his intercession, all blessings might

o ¹2. 1 Pet. ii. 17.
1 John iii. 14—
17.
p 2⁹—2⁹. iii. 20.
vii. 7. 1 Kings
xxii. 8. ia. xllx.
7. iii. 9. Zech.
xi. 8. Matt. v.
11. x. 22. xxiv.
9. Mark xiii. 13.
Luke vi. 22.
Heb. xii. 2, 3.
Jam. iv. 4.
i John iii. 13.
q Luke vi. 32, 33.
1 John iv. 4, 5.
r 16. xvi. 14—16.
Eph. i. 4—11.
2—3. Tit. iii. 8.
—7. 1 Pet. i. 9—12. iv. 3, 4. 1 John iii. 12. v. 19, 20. Rev. xii. 9. xx. 7—9.

17 ¶ These things °I command you, that ye love one another.

18 If ᵖthe world hate you, ye know that it hated me before it hated you.

19 If ye were ᑫof the world, the world would love his own : but ʳbecause ye are not of the world, but I have chosen you out of the world, therefore the world hateth you.

20 Remember ˢthe word that I said unto you, The servant is not greater than his Lord. If they have persecuted me, they will also persecute you : ᵗif they have kept my saying, they will keep your's also.

21 But ᵘall these things will they do unto you for my name's sake, ˣbecause they know not him that sent me.

s v. 16. vii. 32. viii.
59. x. 31. 83. 57.
viii. 16. Matt. x.
24, 25. Luke iii.
54, 55. v. 40.
Acts iv. 27—30.
vii.   Ah—65.
1 Thes. ii. 15,
16.
t Sam. viii. 7.
Is. liii. 1—3. Ez.
iii. 7.
a xvi. 3. Ps. lxix.
7. Is. lxvi. 5.
Matt. v. 11. x.
18, 22, 39. xxiv.
9. Luke vi. 22.
1 Pet. iv. 13, 14.
x vili. 19, 54, 55. Acts xvii. 23, xxviii. 23—27. Rom. i. 28. 1 Cor. ii. 8. xv. 84. 2 Cor.
iv. 3, 4. 2 Thes. i. 8. 1 John ii. 3, 4.

be conferred on them, and all ability and success secured to them, in respect of their most important work. (Marg. Ref. n.—Note, xiv. 7—14, vv. 13, 14.)

Lay down his life. (13) Την ψυχην αυτα ϑη. See on x. 11. 'Christ here saith, he doth ψυχην τιϑεναι, "lay down his '" life for his friends," rather to express the greatness of 'his love, than the merit of his passion ; and when he doth 'so, he uses constantly this phrase : (x. 15. 17. 1 John iii. '16 :) but when the merit of his passion is expressed, the 'phrase used is ὑπερ ἡμων, or ὑπερ ἁμαρτιων, to "die for '" us, or for our sins." (Rom. v. 6. 8. 2 Cor. v. 15. Heb. 'ii. 9. 1 Pet. iii. 18.)' Whitby.—Friends. (14) Φιλοι. 13. 15. iii. 29. xi. 11. Matt. xi. 19. Luke xii. 4. Jam. ii. 23. iv. 4. 3 John 15.—I have chosen. (16) Εξιλεξαμην. 19. vi. 70. xiii. 18. Acts i. 2. 24. 1 Cor. i. 27, 28. Eph. i. 4. Jam. ii. 5. (Note, 17—21, v. 19.)—Ordained.] Εϑηκα. Acts xiii. 47. Rom. iv. 17. 1 Thes. v. 9. Heb. i. 2.

V. 17—21. The apostles and the other disciples of Christ, were engaged in one common cause, for the glory of God and the benefit of mankind ; and it would be peculiarly necessary, that they should be united in the closest bonds of mutual love : especially, as the world would be sure to hate, oppose, and persecute them. (Marg. Ref. o, p.—Notes, Matt. v. 10—12. x. 16—22. 1 Pet. iv. 12—16. 1 John iii. 13—15.) To prepare their minds for this trial, they ought to consider, that the men of the world had " hated him, before it hated them :" they had treated him with the greatest enmity, contempt, and cruelty, notwithstanding the greatest wisdom, holiness, and beneficence of his whole conduct. If then the apostles had been his disciples in name alone, and their principles and conduct had accorded to the maxims, fashions, and pursuits of worldly men ; these would have loved and caressed them, as friends and brethren. (Notes, vii. 3—10. xvii. 13—16. 1 John iv. 4—6.) But he had selected them from among their former worldly companions ; and effectually called them, to preach his humbling doctrine, to copy his holy example, and to promote his cause, in direct opposition to the course of the world : and therefore the same pride, ignorance, and wickedness, which had excited the world to hate him, would induce it to hate them also. (Marg. Ref. q, r.) He had just before reminded them, that the servant was not above his Lord : (Note, xiii. 12—17 :) his apostles, ministers, and zealous disciples therefore could reasonably expect no other, than to be persecuted by such persons as had persecuted him. If men in general had welcomed his doctrine and obeyed it, they might hope that their words also would be thus attended to ; but as the contrary was obvious, it would be vain to indulge such an expectation.

As they would be faithful in their ministry, and holy in their example, the Jews, as well as the Gentiles, would hate, revile, and persecute them, from enmity to him, and his character, doctrine, and authority ; because they knew not that God whom they professed to worship. (Marg. Ref. s—x.—Notes, vii. 25—30, v. 28. viii. 54—59, v. 55. xvi. 1—3, v. 3. Matt. x. 24—26. 34—36. xxiv. 6—8.) For, being ignorant of his perfections, his law, and the spiritual religion which he required and approved, they supposed him to be pleased with their formal services ; and expected him to send a Messiah, to humour their prejudices, to soothe them in their presumptuous confidence, and to gratify their ambition. So that, when Jesus came, in a lowly manner, to call them to repentance, to inculcate his holy religion, and to bestow spiritual blessings ; they hated and crucified him ; and supposed that they pleased God by cleaving to their ceremonies and traditions, and opposing his gospel.—' This seems a strong intimation, 'that even in nations which profess Christianity, if true 'religion fall, as it very possibly may, to a very low ebb ; 'they who exert themselves remarkably for the revival of it, 'must, on the very principle here laid down, expect hatred 'and opposition : and that the passages of scripture relating 'to persecution are not so peculiar to the first ages, or to 'Christians living in idolatrous countries, as some have 'supposed. Would to God, the malignity to be found in 'some of us against our brethren did not too plainly illus- 'trate this remark. Men will probably experience the 'truth of it, in proportion to the degeneracy of those around 'them ; and to the vigour and resolution, with which they 'bear testimony against prevailing errors and vices.' Doddridge.—' They who preached the same doctrine, which 'rendered him' (Christ) 'so hateful to the world, might 'reasonably expect the like treatment from it. ... He being 'not of the world, and they being chosen by him out of the 'world ; the ground of the world's hatred against them must 'be the same.' Whitby.—" The world," which thus hated and persecuted Christ and his apostles, or that part of it especially intended, were the professed worshippers of God, as much as nominal Christians now are : they were the teachers and rulers of the people of God, according to the law ; and they were far more zealous for religion, according to their views of it, than the bulk of professed Christians and ministers are at present. Now, if true religion be the same as it then was ; if it be preached and exemplified in the same manner, and with the same zeal, as in the primitive times ; and if the spirit of the world be the same in every age and nation ; persecution must be the consequence : except as lukewarmness, and indifference about

22 If I had not come, and spoken unto them, *they had not had sin : but now they have no *cloke for their sin.

23 He *that hateth me, hateth my Father also.

24 *If I had not done among them the works which none other man did, they had not had sin : *but now have they both seen *and hated both me and my Father.

25 But *this cometh to pass, *that the word might be fulfilled that is written in their law, *They hated me *without a cause.

26 But *when the Comforter is come, whom I will send unto you from the Father, *even* the Spirit of truth, *which proceedeth from the Father, *he shall testify of me :

27 And *ye also shall bear witness, because *ye have been with me from the beginning.

---

all religion, paralyse the carnal enmity of the heart; or as wise laws bind the hands of those, who would persecute if they might : and even then their tongues and pens will shew their deep and slanderous malignity, against the truth and its zealous friends. The indiscretions and mistakes of the persons concerned, may give the *occasion* and *advantage* to their enemies : but perfect wisdom, meekness, and love would not abate the enmity itself, nay, it would greatly exasperate it.

It hated me before it hated *you.* (18) Εμε πρωτον υμων μεμισηκεν. i. 15. 30. *Matt.* xxii. 38. *Mark* vi. 21. 1 *Tim.* i. 15, 16.—*I have chosen,* &c. (19) Εξελεξαμην. See on 16.—To be " chosen out of the world " must imply far more, than to be chosen as an apostle : for Judas was neither chosen nor called " out of the world," though chosen to be an apostle.

V. 22—25. (*Notes,* iii 19—21. ix. 39—41. *Matt.* xi. 20—24. *Luke* xii. 47, 48.) Doubtless the Jews would in many respects have been chargeable with sin, if Christ had not appeared among them, for even the Gentiles are inexcusable in their ungodliness : (*Note, Rom.* i. 18—20 :) but their sins would have been comparatively small, had he not come among them, published his holy and gracious doctrine, and confirmed it with miracles so varied, multiplied, beneficent, and manifesting omnipotence and sovereign authority, as no other person had ever wrought. (*Notes,* v. 31—38. x. 32—39.) These things, having excited their most virulent enmity, and given occasion to their perpetrating the most atrocious crimes, exceedingly increased their guilt, and left them without the least excuse or palliation of it; for in every respect, Jesus so represented to them the divine glory and character, that in hating him, they manifested the utmost enmity to God : as all others do, who reject and oppose his gospel, when plainly set before them. (*Marg. Ref.* y—a.—*Notes,* viii. 41—47. xiv. 7—14. *Rom.* viii. 5—9. 1 *Cor.* xvi. 21—24. 1 *John* ii. 20—25.) And as the Jews had seen his character and miracles, and observed his ministry, with the most decided enmity; so they had in him seen and hated the holiness, the authority, and the glory of God himself. Thus they fulfilled the words of David, who spake as a type of him, and who was hated without cause by the men of his generation. (*Marg. Ref.* b—e.—*Notes, Ps.* lxix. 4. cix. 2—5.)—The quotation is nearly, but not exactly, from *Ps.* xxxv. 19, *Sept.*

They had not had sin. (22) 'Αμαρτιαν ηκ ειχον. 24. ix. 41. —*Cloke.]* " Excuse." *Marg.* Προφασιν. *Matt.* xxiii. 14. *Mark* xii. 40. *Luke* xx. 47. *Acts* xxvii. 30. *Phil.* i. 18. 1 *Thes.* ii. 5.—*Without a cause.* (25) Δωρεαν. *Marg. Ref.* f. See on *Matt.* x. 8.

V. 26, 27. The apostles, when they saw the contempt and cruelty, with which their Lord was treated, and when they found that they must expect similar ill usage, might be ready to conclude that none would attend to their instructions. He therefore assured them, that " the Comforter," whom he had promised to send them, would testify of him, by his miraculous operations, and by giving success to the gospel : and they also, instructed, emboldened, and encouraged by his influences, would bear testimony to his person and character, his resurrection and ascension, and the glory of his kingdom and salvation ; for which they would be eminently competent, as they had been with him from the beginning of his ministry. (*Marg. Ref.—Notes,* xiv. 15—17. 25, 26. xvi. 7—15. *Mark* xvi. 19, 20. *Acts* i. 4—8. 20—22. ii. 25—36. iv. 5—12. 32—35. v. 32. *Heb.* ii. 1—4.)—The Holy Spirit is here said to proceed from the Father ; and many suppose this to refer, not only to his being sent forth from the Father and the Son, (as the Son was from the Father,) a willing messenger, to apply the salvation of Christ to the hearts of his chosen people ; but to what is called his ' *eternal procession*' from the Father ; by which is meant something in a measure answering to the *eternal generation* of the Son, yet distinct from it. But these are incomprehensible mysteries ; and (though inserted in most of the ancient creeds and formularies,) seem not to be explicitly and evidently revealed : perhaps it is therefore better to adore in silence, than to attempt any explanation of such subjects ; which, not being clearly revealed, cannot otherwise be at all discovered or understood.

Proceedeth. (26) Εκπορευεται. *Matt.* iii. 5. *Mark* vi. 11. x. 46. *Rev.* xxii. 1. (*Note, Rev.* xxii. 1.)—*He.]* Εκεινος. See on xiv. 26.—Πνευμα is neuter ; yet the masculine personal pronoun is joined with it. In these texts, however, Παρακλητος may be considered as the antecedent ; but even this is not the case, xvi. 13, 14. Indeed 'Ο Παρακλητος is as much personal, as εκεινος. (*Note,* 1 *John* ii. 1, 2.)—In fact all the language is manifestly *personal* : " He," " the Comforter," " the Spirit of truth," " is sent," " comes," " bears witness," &c. as in other places he is said to hear, speak, command, forbid, &c.

4 ▲ 4

PRACTICAL OBSERVATIONS.
V. 1—8.

In the person and salvation of Emmanuel, the Lord has made effectual provision for the sanctification, as well as the pardon and justification, of all those who believe in him: but all others must die unreconciled and unholy. He is " the true Vine," whom God has planted, and waters continually. As professed Christians, we appear to belong to this Vine: but woe be to them, who have no other union, no more intimate communion, than what consists in notions, sacraments, and forms. Such branches do not " bear good fruit," perhaps indeed very bad fruit; and one after another of them is taken away, and left as fuel to the fire of divine wrath. But even such branches as " bear fruit " have many remaining hindrances to fruitfulness; and the gracious care of the Husbandman consists in " purging them, that they may bring forth more " fruit : " so that it may reasonably be expected, that true believers will grow in grace under this heavenly culture; and if sharp means be employed to promote their sanctification, they will, when in their right mind, be thankful for them. They also earnestly desire and fervently pray to be enabled to " abide in Christ, that he may abide in " them," by his word and Spirit; and they attend on all instituted ordinances, as means of cementing and preserving this blessed union. They know, that only by persevering faith in Christ can they possess the assurance that they " are clean through his word : " they dread nothing so much, as being found at last among the unfruitful branches, and so left to " wither and be cast into the " fire : " and this fear, and the ardent desire of being made fruitful and useful, ornaments to the gospel and blessings to mankind, dictate such prayers as will surely be answered.— True Christians long to " bring forth more and more fruit," they know that the will and the power must come from Christ, " without whom they can do nothing : " they find by experience, that any interruption in the exercise of faith and the prayer of faith, abates the vigour of every holy affection; makes way for the renewed energy of sinful inclinations; and thus robs them of all spiritual consolation. On the other hand, when they simply " live by faith in the " Son of God," they are made fruitful and joyful; they glorify God, and possess in their own consciences the assurance, that they are the true disciples of the Saviour; and are manifested as such in the consciences of others also. (Notes, 2 Cor. i. 12—14. v. 9—12. 1 John iii. 18— 24.) Let us then indulge a holy ambition, of living more simply on the fulness of Christ, and of growing more and more " fruitful in every good word and work ; " and let us be upon our guard against those, who profess to abide in the living Vine, but produce wild and poisonous grapes, instead of " the fruits of righteousness, which are by Jesus " Christ to the praise and glory of God." (Note, Phil. i. 9—11, v. 11.)

V. 9—16.

While we admire the unspeakable love of Jesus to us, according to the Father's love of him; let us follow his example of obedience, that we may continue in his love: and, as he " rejoices over us to do us good," so may our joy in him and his salvation be full, by near communion with him, and a conscientious walk before him. (Note, 1 John i. 3, 4. 2 John 12, 13.)—Let us often recollect, what a kind and gracious Lord we serve. 'It is his " com- " mandment that we love one another, as he hath loved " us ; " and no love of man, to his dearest friend, ever equalled or even was comparable to his love to us, when strangers and enemies. What admiration must have pervaded the hosts of heaven, when a friendship was proposed, between the Object of their exalted adorations, and poor sinful men on earth! when he assumed human nature, and laid down his life upon the cross for us! when he quickened us by his grace, and so made us willing to become his disciples and his friends! (Note, 1 John iii. 1—3.) and when they observe, how he treats us with the most unreserved affection, makes known to us his gracious purposes, and notices our mean concerns! But let us notice, that they alone are the Redeemer's friends, who " do " whatsoever he commands them." He has stated this evidence, and insisted on this return of friendship; and it is presumption to claim the privilege, while we allow ourselves in any instance of disobedience.—If we indeed do now choose him as our Beloved, we should remember, that this is the effect of his previous choice of us. He has also appointed each of us his place and work; that we may bring forth fruit, in our holy lives, and the faithful and diligent improvement of our several talents: and as the fruit produced by the apostles still remains for our good, so the effect of our feeble endeavours may in some measure conduce to the benefit of others, long after we are gone to our rest. Even in our case, some to whom God has made us useful, may after our decease be useful to others, and they to others, in increasing numbers; as the produce of a few grains of wheat, sown again and again, from year to year, may at length yield an increase which baffles all calculation. Thus faithful ministers, able writers, and zealous champions for the truth, nay apostolical mission, aries may spring from the seed which we have sown : and how far this may extend, or how long it may remain, or what numbers may eventually derive benefit from it, who can tell?—Let us then be " stedfast, unmoveable, always " abounding in the work of the Lord, forasmuch as we " know that our labour is not in vain in the Lord : " (1 Cor. xv. 58:) at the same time " continuing in prayer and " watching thereunto with thanksgiving." (Col. iv. 2.)

V. 17—27.

It is of great importance that all Christians should unite

THESE things [a] have I spoken unto you, that ye should not be offended.

2 They [b] shall put you out of the synagogues: yea, [c] the time cometh, that whosoever killeth you will think that he doeth God service.

3 And these things will they do unto

you, [d] because they have not known the Father, nor me.

4 But these things have I told you, [e] that when the time shall come, ye may remember that I told you of them. And these things I said not unto you at the beginning, [f] because I was with you.

with their brethren in holy love, and in zealous endeavours to promote the cause of the gospel: and let us not be dismayed by the hatred of the world, which can " love only " its own ;" but must dislike those whom Christ " has " chosen out of the world," who bear his image, profess his truth, and obey his commandments. We cannot experience worse usage than our Master before us met with: and we ought not to be offended, or grow weary of welldoing, if we meet with no better. The more we resemble him, the greater enmity will proud and ungodly men feel against us : yet we should be thankful for the restraints which Providence has placed to bloody persecution ; and we ought carefully to avoid exciting needless opposition, by rashness, turbulency, or intermeddling with things not properly belonging to us. But, if we suffer for Christ's sake, and from those who " hate him and the Father that " sent him," we should " rejoice and be exceedingly glad." (Notes, Matt. v. 10—12. Acts v. 41, 42. Phil. i. 27—30. 1 Pet. iv. 12—16.)—Alas! how little do many persons think, that in rejecting and opposing the doctrine of Christ, as our Prophet, Priest, and King, they prove themselves ignorant of that one living and true God, whom they profess to worship ; that they are in fact setting up an idol, the creature of their own imagination and proud reasonings, in the place of " the God and Father of our Lord " Jesus Christ ;" and that their opposition to the scriptural view of the person, atonement, and salvation of the Son of God, springs from determined enmity to the holy character, authority, law, and worship of Jehovah. Thus it was with the Jews, " who saw and hated " both the Son of God, and the Father who sent him : thus it is, at this day, with many who have the scriptures in their hand, the evidences of their divine original clearly set before them, and perhaps the gospel faithfully preached to them; whose built is thus exceedingly aggravated, and " they have no " cloke for their sins," as they evidently hate Christ, " the " Light of the world," because their deeds are evil, and their whole disposition and conduct are diametrically opposite to his holy truths and precepts. But even in these persons the scripture is fulfilled : while, by the conversion of many sinners, and the holy lives of numbers who profess the gospel, " the Comforter, even the Spirit of Truth," still bears testimony to Christ, and confirms that of those faithful ministers, who preach his gratuitous and glorious and holy salvation, after the example and doctrine of those " who were with him from the beginning."

NOTES.

CHAP. XVI. V. 1—3. (Notes, xv. 17—27.) It is probable, that the apostles had expected honour and distinction among men from their relation to Christ: and if this vain hope had been countenanced, their subsequent trials

might have tempted them to conclude that they had been deceived. (Marg. Ref. a.—Note, Jer. xx. 7—9.) Our Lord therefore warned them that persecutions awaited them, that they might not be stumbled or ' disconcerted, as by ' an unexpected and intolerable thing.' Beza. The Jewish rulers would not only excommunicate them ; but they would soon arrive at such a pitch of bigotry and malice, as to deem the murder of them, or any others of his disciples, an acceptable service to God. (Marg. Ref. b, c.—Notes, ix. 18—23. Matt. x. 16—22. Luke vi. 21—23. xxi. 12—19.) They would not only treat them as " sheep for the " slaughter," but as sheep for the altar; and expect to merit the favour of God, by putting them to death, in support of the Mosaick dispensation, and their own traditions ; as if this conduct had been ' of the nature of a sacrifice ' which propitiated for other offences.' Hammond. (Notes, Ps. xliv. 17—22, v. 22. Rom. viii. 35—39.) This was the case with Saul, and many other zealots among the Jews ; and the same has doubtless been the case with many professed Christians, who have been " drunken with the blood " of the saints and the martyrs of Jesus." (Notes, Acts xxv. 9—11. xxvi. 9—11. Rev. xvii. 6.)—The rulers of the Jews had a blind, proud, and obstinate conscientiousness, in what they did : but they persecuted the disciples of Christ, from ignorance of the perfections of God himself; and because, not knowing the Father, they knew not his Son, the promised Messiah, when he appeared among them : and thus they expected to please God by such actions, as could only gratify the malignant prince of darkness ! (Marg. Ref. d.—See on Note, xv. 17—21, v. 21.)—The highest degree of excommunication was supposed to imply the sentence of death : (Notes, Deut. xiii :) and as the magistrate, at this time, had not authority to carry it into execution ; the zealots seem to have made a merit of inflicting it, by assassination, in any way which they could devise. (Notes, ix. 19—23. Acts vii. 54—60, vv. 57—59. xxiii. 12—22.)

Put you out of the synagogue. (2) Αποσυναγωγυς ποιησωσιν υμας. See on ix. 22.—Yea.] Αλλα. Luke xii. 7. See on Phil. ii. 7.—Service.] Λατρειαν. Rom. ix. 4. xii. 1. Heb. ix. 1. 6. Not elsewhere. Λατρευω, Matt. iv. 10. Luke i. 74. Rom. i. 9, et al.

V. 4—6. Our Lord had predicted these things· thus expressly, before he was taken from the disciples, that the remembrance of his words might support them under their trials. He had indeed several times before given them several intimations, both of the hatred which they would incur, and of his removal from them ; but not in so explicit a manner, and as just at hand, as he did at this time : for so long as he continued with them, he was always ready to obviate their misconceptions, and answer their enquiries. (Marg. Ref. e—g.—Notes, xiv. 18—20.

4 E 6

5 But now ᵉ I go my way to him that sent me; and none of you asketh me, ᵇ Whither goest thou?

6 But because I have said these things unto you, ' sorrow hath filled your heart.

7 Nevertheless, ᵏ I tell you the truth; ᶦ It is expedient for you that I go away: for if I go not away, ᵐ the Comforter will not come unto you; ⁿ but if I depart I will send him unto you.

8 And when he is come, ᵒ he will ' reprove the world of sin, and of righteousness, and of judgment:

9 Of ᵖ sin, because they believe not on me;

Matt. x. 16—23. xxiv. 23—25.)—' While I was here, all ' the malice of men bent itself wholly on me, letting you ' alone ; but now the opposition will light on you.' *Hammond.*—Our Lord now declared, that he was about to return to his Father : for since he had first told the disciples, that they could not follow him immediately, and had intimated that he was about to leave the world ; they had not asked him any thing further about the state and place, to which he was going : and therefore, instead of rejoicing in his approaching exaltation, and hoping for important benefits from it, they were overwhelmed with sorrow, as if about to suffer an irreparable loss. (*Marg. Ref. g—i.— Notes,* 16—22. xiii. 31—35. xiv. 1—6.)

Ye may remember. (4) Μνημονητε. 21. xv. 20. Matt. xvi. 9. *Acts* xx. 31. 35, *et al.* Μνημοσυνον, Matt. xxvi. 13.

V. 7. (*Notes,* xiv. 15—17. 25, 26. xv. 26, 27.) Our Lord had before intimated, that his departure from the disciples would prove advantageous to them : but he here solemnly assured them, that what he told them was perfect truth, though they seemed so backward to believe him. It was highly conducive to their benefit that he should leave them : for, unless he passed through his sufferings to glory, the promised Comforter would not come unto them; as this blessing was bestowed, through his atonement and intercession ; and the abundant pouring out of the Holy Spirit would be the immediate effect of his ascension into heaven, and could not take place without it. (*Marg. Ref. —Notes,* vii. 37—39. *Acts* ii. 33—36. *Eph.* iv. 7—10.) When therefore he was gone, he would surely send him to them, according to the counsel and covenant of redemption.—Our Lord not only promised that he would " pray " the Father " to send the Comforter, but also that he " *himself,*" as One with the Father, and as exalted for that purpose to his mediatorial throne, would send him. This certainly does not imply that the Holy Spirit is *naturally* inferior to the Son of God ; neither does the mission of the Son prove that he is *naturally* inferior to the Father. An ambassador is not *naturally* inferior to the prince who sends him ; and his being a subject is a mere circumstance, not essential to his office : but in that office he appears *relatively* inferior ' to his prince, and has, as such, acts by commission and observes his instructions. To this he is bound by the nature of the service, though he might be perfectly voluntary in taking it upon him. This illustration may help our conceptions of the co-equality of the three Persons in the sacred Trinity ; and of the relative and voluntary inferiority of the Son and Spirit, as to their respective offices in man's redemption.—The presence of the Comforter would be far more advantageons to the apostles and the other disciples, than even that of Christ in person could have been. He would be every where present with them, when widely separated from each other ; whereas the bodily presence of Christ could have been only in one place at once. (xi. 21—32.) The teaching, counsels, and consolations of the Holy Spirit would be inward and efficacious ; and his influences would both qualify them for their work, and ensure their success in it.—' The word Παρακλητος ... signifies an *Ad-* ' *vocate,* and a *Comforter.* He did the part of an *Advocate,* ' in respect of Christ and his gospel, by convincing the ' world of sin in not believing on him, and of the right- ' eousness of Christ (9—11) : and by confirming the apos- ' tles' testimony of him, by signs and miracles, and various ' gifts imparted to them ; (*Heb.* ii. 4. 1 *John* v. 6—8 ;) and ' by pleading their cause before kings and rulers, ... and ' against all adversaries. (*Luke* xxi. 15. *Acts* vi. 10.)—In ' respect of the apostles and the faithful, he also did the ' part of a *Comforter,* as being sent for their consolation ' and support in all their troubles, filling their hearts with ' joy and gladness ; and giving them an inward testimony ' of God's love to them, and an assurance of their future ' happiness. (*Rom.* viii.15, 16.)' *Whitby.* (*Notes,* 8—15).

It is expedient.] Συμφερει. xi. 50. xviii. 14. *Matt.* v. 29, 30. xviii. 6. xix. 10. 1 *Cor.* vi. 12. *Heb.* xii. 10, *et al.* —" It is profitable."

V. 8—11. " When He is come, he shall reprove the " world of sin, &c." or rather, " He shall convince the " world concerning sin, concerning righteousness, and con- " cerning judgment." The passage may be interpreted of the miraculous powers communicated by the Holy Spirit, by which the world stood convicted of sin, in rejecting and crucifying the Lord of glory (9) : by which the righteousness of Christ was fully proved, seeing he was returned to the Father, and appeared no more among them : but in proof of his being glorified, he had sent forth his Holy Spirit upon his disciples. (10. *Note,* 1 *Tim.* iii. 16.) Thus it was also evinced, that he would judge the world, as he had declared ; seeing that Satan, " the " prince of this world," would (by the power of the Holy Spirit attesting the apostles' doctrine,) be shewn to be judged and condemned as a criminal, and be gradually expelled from his usurped dominion over mankind. (*Marg. Ref.—Note,* xii. 27—33, *v.* 31.) These miraculous gifts of the Holy Spirit left unbelievers, both Jews and Gentiles, without excuse ; and bound them over to the day of judgment, as determined favourers of Satan's cause in opposition to that of Christ : and doubtless they were the means of conviction to great numbers in different parts of the earth, that Jesus was the Son of God, and the Saviour of the world.—The principal meaning of the words,

¶ la. xiii. 21. xiv. 24, 25. Jer. xxiii. 5, 6. Dan. ix. 24. Rom. i. 17. l14.—21.—26. x. 17 —41. viii. 30, 31. x. 3, 4. 1 Cor. i. 30. xv. 14—28. 2 Cor. v. 21. Gal. v 6. Phil. iii .7—9. 1 Tim. iii. 16. Heb. x. 5—13.

10 Of ᵠ righteousness, because I go to my Father, and ye see me no more;

11 Of ʳ judgment, because ˢ the prince of this world is judged.

ʳ v. 22—27. Matt. xii. 18. 36. Acts xii. 42. xvii. 30, 31. xxiv. 25. Rom. ii. 3, 4. 16. xiv. 10.—12. 1 Cor. iv. 3. vi. 3, 4. 2 Cor. v. 10, 11. Heb. vi. 2. ix. 27. 2 Pet. ii. 4—9. iii. 7. Rev. i. 7. xx. 11—15. ˢ xii. 31. xiv. 30. Gen. iii. 15. Ps. lxviii. 1d. Is. xlix. 24—26. Luke x. 18. Rom. xvi. 20. 2 Cor. iv. 4. Eph. ii. 2. Heb. ii. 14. 1 John iii. 8. Rev. xii. 7—10. xx. 2, 3. 10.

however, doubtless refers to the general *internal* operation of the Holy Spirit, on the minds and hearts of men, in every age and country, when he draws and influences them to believe in Jesus Christ for salvation. He deeply convinces them of many things, concerning the evil and desert of sin, and the great sinfulness of numberless thoughts, words, actions, and omissions, of which before they had scarcely thought: especially he convicts and deteets the sinfulness of their supposed virtues, and of their hearts; by discovering the glory of God to their souls, shewing them their obligations and relations to him, and turning their reflections to the spirituality of the law, to the hateful nature of transgression, as rebellion, ingratitude, and contempt of God, to their own past lives, both as to crimes committed, and duties neglected, to their present behaviour, and to their inward thoughts, desires, and motives, and the imperfection of their best services. (*Notes, Ps.* li. 4. *Rom.* vii. 9—12.) Thus, the veil of ignorance, pride, and self-flattery being removed, they are brought without reserve to condemn themselves, and to plead guilty before God. He convinces them also concerning the nature of righteousness, and the righteousness of God in the sentence denounced against sinners. (*Note, Rom.* x. 1—4.) He leads them likewise to realize and anticipate the day of judgment, and to seek deliverance from the condemnation then to be denounced against ungodly men. But especially the Holy Spirit shews sinners the evil of unbelief, and neglect of Christ and his salvation. Perhaps they once thought this meritorious, at least supposed there was no great evil in it: but now they perceive, that it arises from pride, love of sin, enmity to God, and the most rebellious state of the heart imaginable: they find, that it implies the greatest contempt of the divine authority, justice, truth, wisdom, and mercy, which can be conceived; that it is a rooted aversion to be reconciled unto God: in short, that unbelief is in some respects the source, and as it were the substance, of all other sins; the most affronting and ruinous of all the crimes, of which men are or can be guilty; and ranks all such as deliberately persist in it, with those implacable enemies of God, who hated and crucified the incarnate Redeemer, when he appeared on earth. (*Notes,* iii. 19—21. *Heb.* iii. 7—13. x. 28—31. xii. 22—25, *v.* 25. 1 *John* v. 9, 10.) In connexion with these discoveries, the Holy Spirit discloses to those he thus enlightens, that " righteousness of God " which is revealed to faith, as the ground of a sinner's justification; even the obedience unto death of the divine Redeemer as our Surety. He convinces them concerning the suitableness and sufficiency of this righteousness for the end proposed; he makes them sensible, that in this way God is righteous in justifying sinners, as well as glorious in mercy, and in all other perfections. (*Notes, Rom.* i. 17. iii. 21—26.) He discovers to them how the law is thus magnified, and how real faith, " in the righteousness " of Christ," is inseparably accompanied with hatred of sin, with humility, love of God, and the beginning of all holy affections and dispositions. He convinces them, that

Christ's ascension to the right hand of the Father, fully proves that his ransom is accepted, and the righteousness finished, through which believers are justified; and therefore there is no need for him to appear again on earth, till he shall come to judge the world. (*Notes, Rom.* iv. 23—25. viii. 32—34. *Heb.* vii. 26—28. ix. 24—28. x. 5—10. xiii. 20, 21.) The Holy Spirit likewise gives men a realizing apprehension of a future judgment, (which few so believe, as to be influenced in their daily and hourly conduct by the expectation of it,) and convinces them of many things before unthought of, concerning the nature, rule, and consequences of that solemn season. He shews them, that " the prince of this world," who is already judged and condemned, will then be consigned, with all his angels, and all who adhere to him in opposition to Christ, to " everlasting punishment:" but that all, who truly believe in Christ, and become his disciples and servants, will then be adjudged righteous through his merits; (their good works being adduced as evidences of their faith;) and so be admitted into the regions of everlasting glory and felicity. (*Notes, Matt.* xxv. 31—46. 2 *Cor.* v. 9—12. 2 *Thes.* i. 5—10. *Rev.* xx. 11—15.) Under these realizing convictions, he teaches men to consider their own state, character, and actions; anticipating that decisive season, by daily instituting a judgment upon themselves, whether they belong to Christ, or not; in which they desire to consider all the evidence, then to be adduced; that they may be satisfied on scriptural grounds, that their state is good, and that they are prepared to meet their heart-searching Judge, in the endearing character of a gracious Saviour and Friend.—As these things, with what follows, (*Note,* 14, 15,) evidently contain the substance of the distinguishing work of the Holy Spirit, in illuminating, convincing, converting, comforting, and sanctifying believers, of every age and nation, by which he gives success to the gospel in the world; and as it so aptly answers to the words before us; there can be no doubt but that our Lord had mainly respect to it, and not merely, nor principally, to the miraculous influences of the Holy Spirit, in the days of the apostles.—It is, however, further worthy of notice, that an immense proportion of the human race, have, since the pouring out of the Holy Spirit after our Lord's ascension, been led to form such sentiments " concerning sin, righteousness, and a future " judgment," as the world in general at that time had not the most remote conception of: so that a far higher standard of morals has been fixed, and a far more general and explicit persuasion of a future season of retribution has prevailed, through numerous and populous nations, even among merely nominal Christians, than were at all thought of in any nation, except Israel, nay, than the bulk of the Jews themselves admitted. But were the convictions of all men " concerning sin, righteousness, and " judgment," as deep, abiding, distinct, and efficacious, as those of real believers are; the grand hindrance to their becoming true Christians would be removed. So that these convictions of the Holy Spirit are the very things

448

† xiv. 30. xv. 15. Acts i. k.
a Matt. iii. 1, 2.
Heb. v. 11—14.
x xiv. 17. xv. 26. 1 John iv. 6.
u xiv. 25. 1 Cor. iv. 7—15. 1 John ii. 10—13. Eph.
a iii. 32. vii. 16—
a Joel ii. 28. Acts ii. 17, 18. xi. 28.
x x. 23. xxi. 9—11.
xxviii. 22. 2 Thes. ii. 3, 12. 1 Tim. iv. 1—3. 2 Tim. iii. 1—5. 2 Pet. ii. 1, &c. Rev. i. 1. 19. vi—xxii.

12 I have 'yet many things to say unto you, but 'ye cannot bear them now. 13 Howbeit when he, 'the Spirit of truth, is come, 'he will guide you into all truth: 'for he shall not speak of himself; but whatsoever he shall hear, 'that shall he speak: and 'he will shew you things to come.

b 5. 10. Acts ii. 32—36. iv. 10— 12. 1 Cor. iii. 1— 3. 1 Pet. i. 14.
12. ii. 7. 1 John iv. 1. ii. 3, 14.
c xv. 26. Zech. xii. 10. 1 Cor. ii. 8—10. 2 Cor. iii. 14—18. iv. 6. Gal. v. 5. 1 John iii. 23, 24. iv. 13, 14.
d iii. 35. x. 29, 30. xiii. 3. xvii. 2. 10. Matt. xi. 27. xxviii. 18. Luke x. 22. Col. i. 19. ii. 3, 9.

14 He shall 'glorify me: 'for he shall receive of mine, and shall shew it unto you. 15 All 'things that the Father hath are mine: therefore said I, That he shall take of mine, and shall shew it unto you.

wanting to men in every part of the world; and all that are wanting, as introductory to his rendering Christ glorious in their eyes and precious to their hearts: and the success of ministers and missionaries will bear an exact proportion to the measure, in which "the Holy Spirit "is poured out" on the people, to produce it. This therefore should be the ground of all our hopes, and the subject of our prayers, in every endeavour to win souls. (*Notes, Zech.* xii. 9—14, *v.* 10. *Luke* xi. 5—13. *Acts* ii. 37—40. xvi. 29—34.)

He will reprove. (8) "He will convince." *Marg.* Ἐλεγξει. viii. 9. 46. 1 *Cor.* xiv. 24. *Eph.* v. 11. 2 *Tim.* iv. 2. *Tit.* i. 9. 13, *et al.* See on *Matt.* xviii. 15.—Ελεγχος, *Heb.* xi. 1.—*Of sin.*] Περι ἁμαρτιας. 9—11. 26. vi. 41. ix.17. x. 33. xvii. 9. 20. *Matt.* xvi. 11. *Mark* v. 16. *Luke* xxiv. 47. *Acts* xxviii. 22.

V. 12, 13. Our Lord had many things further to communicate to his apostles, concerning his salvation, the preaching of the gospel to the Gentiles, the abrogation of the Mosaick economy, and the nature of his kingdom and the Christian dispensation. But their minds were not sufficiently freed from prejudices, to receive such instructions, and to make a proper use of them. (*Marg. Ref.* t, u. —*Notes, Mark* iv. 33, 34. 1 *Cor.* iii. 1—3. *Heb.* v. 11—14.) He therefore purposed to leave them to be made known gradually, after his resurrection and ascension, as they became "able to bear them." For "the Spirit of truth" would guide the apostles into every part of the truth, and make known to them many things, which he had not explicitly taught them. (*Marg. Ref.* x, y.—*Note,* xiv. 25, 26.) They were therefore unreservedly to depend on his teaching: for he would punctually adhere to the instructions given him; (even as he, the Son of God, had adhered to the instructions of his Father:) speaking nothing of himself, as if he proposed any separate end or purpose; but teaching exactly those truths, which were appointed by the divine wisdom to be revealed to the church; as being One in nature, counsel, and operation with the Father and the Son. (*Marg. Ref.*—*Notes,* 7.—xv. 9—11. *Acts* i. 1—3. iii. 19—21. xi. 1—18. *Rev.* i. 1, 2.) He would likewise be in them a Spirit of prophecy, to make known to them future events, even to the end of time; that thus the doctrine delivered to them might, in their writings, be handed down to future ages; while the accomplishment of the prophecies, would authenticate the divine original of those writings, to all who should be favoured with them. (*Marg. Ref.* a.—*Notes, Matt.* xxiv. *Luke* xxi. 20—24. *Rom.* xi. 25—32. 2 *Thes.* ii. 3—12. 1 *Tim.* iv. 1—5. 2 *Tim.* iii. 1—5. *Rev.* iv. 1—3.)—'It is certain, 'that the apostles, in compiling the canon of scripture, 'were so assisted by the Holy Spirit, as to write all truths 'necessary for the salvation of believers; and conse-

'quently, that all things necessary to be believed and done 'by Christians, are fully and perspicuously contained in 'the holy scriptures.' *Whitby.*—*All truth.* (13) Πασαν την αληθειαν. "All the truth." "The truth as it is in "Jesus." "The whole counsel of God."

. *Bear.* (12) Βαςαζειν x. 31. xii. 6. xix. 17. xx. 15. *Matt.* viii. 17. xx. 12. *Gal.* v. 10. vi. 2, *et al.*—*He will guide.* (13) Ὁδηγησει. See on *Matt.* xv. 14.—*He will shew.*] Αναγγελει. 14. 15. 25. iv. 25. v. 15. *Mark* v. 14. 19, *et al.*

V. 14, 15. The Holy Spirit when he came, would make the honour of Christ the great end of all his operations and revelations: he would "glorify him," in respect of his person, doctrine, righteousness, atonement, kingdom, and salvation. He would teach men to honour him, by reliance, subjection, and worship: he would exalt the Saviour in their judgment and affections, and lead them to honour him by their profession, preaching, conversation, and conduct. So that, if any persons should profess to have the Spirit of God, and yet dishonour Christ, by their doctrine, or in their conduct, in respect of his Person, or any of his offices; it might be determined without hesitation, that they were influenced by a lying spirit. (*Marg. Ref.* b, c.—*Notes, Acts* ii. 33—36. 1 *Cor.* xii. 1—3. 1 *John* ii. 20—25. iv. 1—3. 2 *John* 7—11.) For the Holy Spirit, accomplishing his great office in the economy of man's salvation, would receive those truths, which related to the person, doctrine, and salvation of Christ, and discover them by his inward and effectual teaching to the minds and hearts of all in whom he resided; that they might see the glory and excellency of them, for every sanctifying and saving purpose: and he would direct and influence the apostles and other faithful ministers, to represent them to mankind, with such energetick language and lively affections, as would lead them also to seek them with all earnestness, and their whole heart. (*Note,* 1 *Pet.* i. 10—12.) Indeed all things which belong to the Father, as the Creator and Proprietor of the universe, belongs to the incarnate Son also, as One with the Father. (*Note,* xvii. 6 —10.) All the perfections and fulness of the Godhead dwell in him bodily, for the benefit of his church, and to effect the purposes of his redemption: the administration of the universal kingdom is vested in him; all judgment is committed to him; and all honour and worship due to him. (*Marg. Ref.* d.—*Notes,* iii. 27—36. v. 20—30. *Matt.* xxviii. 18. 1 *Cor.* xv. 20—28. *Eph.* i. 15— 23. *Phil.* ii. 9—11. *Col.* i. 18—20. ii. 8, 9. 1 *Pet.* iii. 21 22.) So that the Holy Spirit, in glorifying him, shews him to the believer, as "the Lord of all," and coequal with the Father, the Object of all worship, obedience, confidence, love, and praise; and in so doing, the Father also "is glorified in the Son," as One with him: and with reference to this, Jesus said, that the Spirit of truth should

16 ¶ A °little while, and ye shall not see me ; and again ʰa little while, and ye shall see me, ᵉbecause I go to the Father.

17 Then ʰ said *some* of his disciples among themselves, ·What is this that he saith unto us, A little while, and ye shall not see me ; and again a little while, and ye shall see me ; and, Because I go to the Father?

18 They said therefore, What is this that he saith, A little while ? 'we cannot tell what he saith.

19 Now ᵏ Jesus knew that they were desirous to ask him, and said unto them, Do ye enquire among yourselves of that I said, A little while, and ye shall not see me ; and again a little while, and ye shall see me ?

20 Verily, verily, I say unto you, That ye shall weep and lament, ᵐbut the world shall rejoice : and ye shall

be sorrowful, ⁿbut your sorrow shall be turned into joy.

21 A °woman when she is in travail hath sorrow, because her hour is come : but, as soon as she is delivered of the child, she remembereth no more the anguish, ᵖfor joy that a man is born into the world.

22 And ᑫ ye now therefore have sorrow ; ʳbut I will see you again, and your heart shall rejoice, ˢand your joy no man taketh from you.

23 And in that day ye shall ᵗask me nothing. Verily, verily, I say unto you, ᵘWhatsoever ye shall ask the Father in my name, he will give *it* you.

24 Hitherto have ye asked nothing ᵛin my name : ask, and ye shall receive, ʷthat your joy may be full.

take of *his*, and shew it to the disciples, that they might behold, adore, and rejoice. (*Notes,* ii. 6—11, *v.* 11: xiii. 31—35.) When this part of the office of the Holy Spirit is added to the convictions before spoken of, (*Note,* 8—11,) what is wanting to make men established, consistent, joyful, and fruitful Christians ? and which of them is not indispensably necessary for this purpose ?

Of mine. (14) Εκ τυ εμυ. 15. vii. 16. viii. 37. Matt. xx. 15. 23.—*Are mine.* (15) Εμα εσιν.

V. 16—22. Our Lord next intimated to his apostles, that in a few hours he should be removed from their sight by his death and burial : but after a short time they would see him again, as risen from the dead ; because he would visibly ascend to the Father in their presence, that they might testify that event to the world. (*Marg. Ref.* e—g. —*Notes,* Luke xxiv. 50—53. Acts i. 9—12.)—'Because I ' go to eternal glory ; whence I shall be more efficaciously ' present than ever before. For then you shall experi- ' ence who, and how great, I am ; which is a more ade- ' quate view of Christ, than that which relates to his bo- ' dily presence.' *Beza.*—Some explain the passage, of the short space which would intervene before the disciples should see their Lord in glory, having finished their course on earth : but the context seems to determine the mean- ing to the first interpretation.—The disciples, however, did not understand his meaning ; not being yet aware, that he would die, and rise again, and this in so short a time, and then ascend to the Father. But he knew their perplexity ; and therefore declared to them, that indeed the most over- whelming sorrows were coming on them ; while the world, or the multitude of his enemies, would rejoice and exult, as if they had obtained a final victory over him and his cause, when they had nailed him to the cross, and seen him expire upon it. (*Marg. Ref.* h—m.)—Yet the sorrow of/his disciples would soon " be turned into joy : " even

as the woman's pangs of travail are, by the sight of her living child, and her satisfaction in' beholding it. (*Marg. Ref.* n—p.—*Notes, Is.* liii. 9—12. *Luke* xvi. 24—26.) Thus they (as well as he,) " would have sorrow : " but he would certainly " see them again " after his resurrec- tion ; and then they would have have the most cordial, solid, and substantial joy communicated to them ; which would not be destroyed by his ascension into heaven, as the Holy Spirit would be their Comforter : nor would the malice of men or evil spirits, or any of their trials and sufferings in life and death, ever deprive them of it. (*Marg. Ref.* q—s.—*Notes,* iv. 10—15, *v.* 14. *Luke* x. 38—42. *Rom.* viii. 35—39.)

V. 23, 24. When Jesus should ascend into heaven, and the Holy Spirit be poured out on the apostles, their views would be so enlarged, and their faith and hope so confirmed, that they would not have occasion to ask him the meaning of any of his words, as before they had been desirous of doing (19). They would not therefore need his *personal* presence, which they at the present thought indispensably necessary ; for they might be assured that whatever they asked the Father, in his name, would be granted them. (*Marg. Ref.* t, u.—*Notes,* xiv. 7—14, *vv.* 13, 14. xv. 6—8. 12—16, *v.* 16.) Hitherto they had not been used to pray in his name, or through his inter- cession : that way of access had not *explicitly* been esta- blished ; nor had they clearly understood· those types, by which it had been shadowed forth under the old dispensa- tion. They had therefore prayed to the God of Abraham, pleading his mercy, promises, and covenant. But " the " way into the holiest " would soon be thrown open, by the sacrifice, resurrection, ascension, and intercession of Christ : and then they would learn to plead his righteous- ness and atonement, as the ground of their hopes ; and to come through him, as their great High Priest and Ad-

4 F 2

25 These things have I spoken unto you in * proverbs: the time cometh, when I shall no more speak unto you in proverbs, * but I shall shew you plainly of the Father.

26 At that day ye shall ask in my name; and I say not unto you, * that I will pray the Father for you:

27 For ᵇ the Father himself loveth you, ᶜ because ye have loved me, ᵈ and have believed that I came out from God.

28 I ᵉ came forth from the Father, and am come into the world: again, ᶠ I leave the world, and go to the Father.

29 His disciples said unto him, Lo, now speakest thou plainly, and speakest no ᵍ proverb.

30 Now ᶜ are we sure that thou knowest all things, and needest not that any man should ask thee: ʰ by this we believe that thou camest forth from God.

31 Jesus answered them, ¹ Do ye now believe?

32 Behold, ᵏ the hour cometh, yea, is now come, ¹ that ye shall be scattered, every man to his ᵐ own, and shall leave me alone: and ⁿ yet I am not alone, because the Father is with me.

33 These things I have spoken unto

---

vocate, to the mercy-seat of God: and in this way, enlarging and multiplying their petitions, their joy and consolation would be abundant and complete. (*Marg. Ref.* x, y.—*Notes, Rom.* v. 1, 2. viii. 32—34. *Eph.* ii. 14—18. *Col.* iii. 16, 17. *Heb.* ii. 16—18. iv. 14—16. vii. 23—25. x. 19—22. xiii. 15, 16. 1 *Pet.* ii. 4—6. 1 *John* ii. 1, 2.)— To suppose, that Christ meant to forbid them to address him in prayer, when he said " Ye shall ask me nothing," is a direct censure on the apostles and primitive Christians, when acting under the immediate influence of the Holy Spirit. (*Notes, Acts* vii. 54—60, *vv.* 59, 60. 2 *Cor.* xii. 7— 10, *vv.* 8, 9. 1 *Thes.* iii. 11—13. 2 *Thes.* ii. 16, 17.) The disciples had been used to *enquire* of their Lord, as Man, in all their difficulties: but this would speedily and finally be terminated, and they would be taught to apply to God by prayer, through his mediation. But to address the Father in the name of Christ, or to address the Son, as God dwelling in human nature, and " reconciling the " world to himself," must be equivalent, if indeed the Father and the Son are One Deity. (*Notes, x. 26—31, v. 30.)*

Ye shall ask me. (23) Εμε ερωτησετε. 19. 30. viii. 7. xvii. 9. 20. *Luke* xx. 3. 1 *Thes.* iv. 1. v. 12. 2 *Thes.* ii. 1. 2 *John* 5.—*Ye shall ask.*] Αιτησητε. 24. 26. iv. 10. xiv. 13, 14. xv. 7. 16. *Matt.* vii. 7, 8, 9, 10. xx. 20. xxi. 22. *Luke* xi. 9, 10. 1 *John* v. 14, 15, 16.—*May be full.* (24) Η πεπληρωμενη. 6. xv. 11. xvii. 13. *Acts* ii. 28. xiii. 52. *Rom.* xv. 13. 1 *John* i. 4. 2 *John* 12.

V. 25—30. Our Lord had set before the apostles, during his whole ministry as well as in this discourse, the " things pertaining to the kingdom of God," in parables, or " proverbs," in short and weighty sentences, the import of which they did not fully understand: but, after his resurrection, he intended to lay aside all obscurity and reserve; and plainly to instruct them in those things, which related to the perfections, truth, and will of the Father, and the way of access to him. (*Marg.* and *Marg. Ref.* z.) Then they would learn to pray in his name: (*Note,* 23, 24:) but, though they would present their petitions through his *intercession*, as the way in which the Father would grant them " to the praise of his glory;" yet he did not mean, that there would be any need for him to

importune the Father in their behalf, as if he were reluctant to grant their requests, except as thus extorted from him. Seeing the Father also loved them, and delighted to do them good; because, having been drawn and taught by him, they loved and obeyed his only begotten Son, and believed that he came forth from him to be the Saviour of mankind. (*Marg. Ref.* a—d.—*Notes,* vi. 41— 46. 60—65. xiv. 21—24. xv. 9—11.) This was well pleasing in his sight: for indeed Jesus had come forth from the Father, when he assumed human nature; and he was now about to leave the world, and ascend in human nature to the Father, that he might appear in his presence in their behalf.—The apostles, hearing this, declared that he had now spoken plainly, without any proverb: yet, according to the system of some professed Christians, he scarcely ever spoke any thing so abstruse or inexplicable: but it is evident, that those who deny the Deity of Christ do not agree with the apostles in interpreting his words. (*Marg. Ref.* e, f.—*Notes,* iii. 12, 13. vi. 60—65. xiii. 1— 5, v. 3. xvii. 4, 5.)—This declaration of Christ so accorded with the secret thoughts of the apostles' hearts, and answered the enquiries which they desired to make; that it satisfied them of his omniscience; and convinced them, that he was able to answer all their secret doubts; and this served for the present exceedingly to confirm their faith. (*Marg. Ref.* g, h.—*Notes,* i. 47—51. iv. 28—30. xx. 24—29, *vv.* 25. 27, 28. xxi. 15—17.)

In proverbs. (25) " In parables." Marg. Εν παροιμιαις. 29. x. 6. 2 *Pet.* ii. 22. Not elsewhere. Παροιμιαζω, *Matt.* xxiii. 27.—*Prov.* i. 1. xxvi. 7. Sept. Εκ παρα et οιμος, *via.—Plainly.*] Παρρησια. 29. vii. 4. 13. 26. x. 24. xi. 14. 54. xviii. 20. *Mark* viii. 32. 2 *Cor.* iii. 12. vii. 4. *Eph.* vi. 19, *et al.*

V. 31—33. Our Lord foresaw, that, notwithstanding the confident profession which the disciples on this occasion made of faith in him, they would shortly be scattered from him through unbelief; every man seeking some place of concealment, as being afraid or ashamed of being known to belong to him: thus they would shamefully desert him, in his extreme distress, to consult their own safety. (*Marg. Ref.* i—l.—*Notes,* xviii. 4—9. *Zech.* xiii. 7. *Matt.* xxvi. 30—35. 42—46.) Yet he should not be left alone, with-

ᵃ xiv. 27. Ps. lxxxv. you, that ᵇ in me ye might have peace. tion; ᵖ but be of good cheer, ᵠ I have
8—11. Is. ix. 6. 7. Mic. v. 3 Luke ᵒ In the world ye shall have tribula- overcome the world.
ii. 14. xix. 38.

ᵃ xiv. 27. Ps. lxxxv. 8—11. Is. ix. 6. 7. Mic. v. 3 Luke ii. 14. xix. 38. Rom. v. 1, 2. Eph. ii. 14—17. Phil. iv. 7. Col. i. 20. 2 Thes. iii. 16. Heb. vii. 2. xiii. 20, 21. o xv. 19—21. Acts xiv. 22. Rom. viii. 36. 2 Cor. vii. 4. 1 Thes. iii. 4. 2 Tim. iii. 12. Heb. xi. 25. 1 Pet. v. 9. Rev. vii. 14.

p xiv. 1. Acts ix. 31. xvii. 11. xviii. 22. 35. 36. 2 Cor. i. 3. xii. q 11. xii. 31. 1 Sam. xvii. 51, 52. Ps. lxviii. 18 Rom. viii 37. Gal. i. 4. vi. 14. John iv. 4. v. 4.

out any helper, in the midst of his enraged enemies; for the Father would be with him, to support him, to carry him through all his sufferings, and to bring him to the glory reserved for him. (*Marg. Ref. m.—Note, 2 Tim.* iv. 16—18.) But, though he foresaw all their misconduct, he had yet spoken this affectionate parting discourse to them, that they might possess inward peace and tranquility by faith in him; for, in the world, they would surely meet with heavy and virulent persecutions, not only at this time, but to the end of their lives. (*Notes,* 1—3. xv. 17—21.) The world was indeed an enemy, with which they must have many sharp conflicts; while Satan would endeavour, by means of ungodly men, to weary out their patience, or to terrify them into apostasy. But as He, their Surety and the Captain of their salvation, had " over-" come the world," and all the temptations with which it had assaulted him; and as he was about to break through all the remaining opposition of " the prince of this world" and his devoted adherents, and to ascend triumphant to his mediatorial throne; so they, through the power of his grace, and by following his example, would at length obtain a similar victory, and be put in possession of the conqueror's crown. (*Marg. Ref.* n—q.—*Notes,* xii. 27—33, v. 32. xiv. 29—31. *Gal.* i. 3—5. vi. 11—14. 1 *John* v. 4, 5.) They would fight with enemies who had already been vanquished: they might therefore endure the peril and the hardship, with alacrity and constancy, assured of all needful support and comfort; and satisfied, though their faith and patience would be sharply tried, that the event would be unspeakably glorious and happy. (*Note, Rom.* viii. 35—39.)—*His own.* (3.2) " Own home." *Marg.* Τα ἰδια. i. 11. xix. 27. *Acts* xxi. 6.

PRACTICAL OBSERVATIONS.

V. 1—7.

How fallacious is the common opinion, that God will accept every man who is *sincere* in his religion, whatever it may be! For the most bigotted and cruel persecutors, with their anathemas, interdicts, excommunications, prisons, inquisitions, fire and faggots, have often been very *sincere,* in their way; indeed no less sincere, than the more candid and philosophical opposers of " the truth, as " it is in Jesus." They have murdered the true worshippers of God, by thousands, tens of thousands, and verily imagined that they were offering him an acceptable sacrifice! (*Note,* 1 *Tim.* i. 15, 16.) But did these men *sincerely* desire to know the truth and do the will of God? Did they humbly and impartially examine his word, and pray to be taught by his Spirit, that they might know what he would have them to do? Did they *sincerely* embrace and profess the truth, and obey the will of God as far as they knew it; without being at all influenced by temporal interests, or by fear of reproach and persecution? Were they *sincerely* willing to obtain the favour of God, and to devote themselves to his service, at any price, or without regarding consequences?—Without this state of heart and tenour of conduct, what is called *sincerity* may be a

compound of obstinate prejudice, wilful ignorance, proud self-confidence, carnal policy, and malignant passions; and the event will prove, that, after all the pretences of such men, and with all their advantages, they were entire strangers and enemies both " to the Father and the Son; " and " that they hated the light, because their deeds were " evil."—The prophecies of scripture, however, so prepare the attentive believer's mind for these events, that, instead of being stumbled at them, he sees in them a demonstration of the truth of revelation, and an illustration of its doctrines; especially in respect of the " *deceitfulness* " and desperate wickedness of the " human " heart; " the subtlety of Satan, that old liar and murderer of mankind; and the awful justice of God, in giving up his enemies to strong delusions, and leaving them to perish with a " lie in " their right hand." (*Notes,* viii. 41—47. *Jer.* xvii. 9, 10. 2 *Thes.* iii. 8—12. *Rev.* xii. 7—12, *v.* 9. 13—17.)—But let us remember, that humble docility, implicit belief of the scripture, and a disposition unreservedly to do the will of God, are essential to " godly sincerity," even that *sincerity,* which is accepted by him. (2 *Cor.* i. 12.) This will lead men to come to the Father through his beloved Son; and to " set their affections on things above, where Jesus " sitteth at the right hand of God: " and thus they will learn to rejoice in his exaltation, and in the hope of being with him to behold and share his glory.—If this be our character and experience, we should remember, that our hearts are often filled with sorrow at those events, which are highly expedient and advantageous for us. The feeblest believer can see, that this was the case with the apostles: the atonement, the ascension, and intercession of the Redeemer, and the presence of the Comforter were not only more desirable than Christ's personal presence; but they were absolutely necessary to them, and to us all, in order to salvation: yet no removal of a most justly beloved relation, or Christian friend, or faithful minister, can possibly appear to us so much as comparable to that loss, which the apostles supposed that they must inevitably sustain, when their beloved Lord should be removed from them.

V. 8—15.

Every professed Christian ought to enquire, whether the Holy Spirit has " begun a good work" in his heart. Even when about to come as a Comforter, he generally occasions a temporary and poignant sorrow; he always produces deep humiliation; and these are often attended with terror and distress. For, without abasing convictions of sin, and a clear discovery of our guilt and danger, we never understand the value of Christ's salvation: (*Notes, Matt.* v. 3—5:) but when we are brought to a just estimate of our own character, general conduct, and best duties; we perceive the preciousness of the Redeemer's obedience, atonement, and intercession. Then we also discover the sinfulness of unbelief, and neglect of the gospel: and if at any time we are tempted to despair of mercy, through a sense of our own great guilt and depravity; we are aware that this despair would be a more fatal and atro-

CHAP. . XVII.

Jesus prays the Father to glorify him, that he may glorify the Father, and give eternal life, which is found in knowing the Father and the Son, to his disciples, 1—5; to preserve the apostles in unity of faith and love, after his ascension, 6—12; and from the world and all evil, 13—16; and to sanctify them by the truth, 17—19. He intercedes for them, and all who should believe in him through their word; that they might be united in love, admitted to the most intimate communion with the Father and the Son, and be brought to share his glory in heaven, 20—26.

---

cious offence, than all, our other transgressions. Thus we learn to value and rely upon Christ, for righteousness and for sanctification; and to prepare to meet him with comfort and rejoicing hope when he shall come to judgment. At that awful season, the " prince of this " world, and all who continue his servants, will be cast into the lake of fire; and shut up in the blackness of darkness for ever. Every one, in all nations and ages, who is " delivered from the power of darkness, and translated into " the kingdom of God's dear Son," experimentally knows what it is to be thus " convinced of sin, of righteousness, " and of judgment." This is essential to true religion, and to salvation through him, " who was made sin for us, " though he knew no sin, that we might be made the " righteousness of God in him." (Note, 2 Cor. v. 18—21, v. 21.)—If then this be the peculiar work of the Holy Spirit, as the great Agent in applying the redemption of the Son of God; those who are his servants, and " workers " together with him," should use all proper means for producing these needful convictions: they should often and particularly lay open the holy law of God, as " the " ministration of condemnation:" (Notes, 2 Cor. iii. 7— 11. Gal. iii. 10—14.) They should shew the evil of sin, the way of justification by faith in Christ, the guilt and ruinous consequences of unbelief; and the solemn transactions and awful event of " the day of judgment and perdition of ungodly men." On these subjects, all who would be honoured as instruments in converting sinners, should be frequent, copious, alarming, encouraging, and distinguishing. But in matters more disputable and less essential, they would do well, after the example of Christ, not to press them on their auditories, before they are " able to " bear them," or to make a good use of them; and to inculcate them gradually, and as the Spirit of truth removes prejudices and darkness from the mind, and enables it to receive them.—While we attend to the sure word of prophecy, and wait for " the day-dawn and the day-star " to arise in our hearts;" (Note, 2 Pet. i. 19;) we should carefully observe that the Holy Spirit comes forth from the Father, to " glorify Christ" among men. We need not then wonder, that so many deny his Deity and his atonement, or treat his prophetical or kingly authority with neglect or contempt: for they imagine, that the work of the Holy Spirit was confined to the primitive ages, and that all dependence upon his influences at present at least borders on enthusiasm. Could they ascertain this position, it would follow, that Jesus could " be glorified" only in the primitive times.—In proportion as men overlook, or do not trust, expect, and pray for, the influences of the Holy Spirit, Christ is always neglected and dishonoured, even by those who call themselves his disciples.—On the other hand, if men profess to be guided and influenced by the Holy Spirit, and yet do not honour Christ; but either treat his word with contempt, or place their dependence

elsewhere than on his atoning blood, or disgrace him by their unholy lives; it is plain that they are deceivers, or deceived. Where this sacred Teacher and Comforter resides, he shews the Saviour in all his offices, to be glorious and precious; he leads men to depend on him and glory in him; he constrains them by love, to devote themselves to his service, and to honour him, by their lives, and by the improvement of their talents to recommend and promote his cause; he enables them to see, that " all things " which the Father hath " are the Son's also; that in " ho- " nouring him they honour the Father that sent him; ' and that all the power and perfection of Deity are in Christ, for the completion of that design of love for which he suffered on the cross. We should therefore have more admiring views of our glorious Redeemer, and more lively affections towards him, did we more entirely depend on the Holy Spirit, more frequently and earnestly pray to " our heavenly Father, to give us his Holy Spirit," as he has promised; (Luke xi. 13;) and were we more careful neither to grieve him by our sins, nor to quench his sacred influences by our negligence. Thus we should learn to rejoice in Christ Jesus amidst all our tribulations. (Note Rom. v. 3—5.)

V. 16—22.

For a little while, believers must be absent from their beloved Saviour; and they may be often called to mourn for sin, and to pass through manifold tribulations; while the world around them rejoices in carnal mirth, and destructive prosperity, or perhaps in the success of atrocious iniquities! (Notes, Ec. vii. 2—6. Luke vi. 20—26. 2 Cor. vii. 9—11.) But their joys and the believer's sorrows are alike transient: they have their fears and forebodings to damp their mirth; he has his hopes and anticipations to alleviate his afflictions: (Note, Prov. xiv. 10:) and, as a sorrow is coming on them, which none can mitigate or terminate; so the believer is the heir of an unalienable joy. (P. O. Luke xvi. 19—26. Note, 1 Pet. i. 6—9.) Indeed, many of his sorrows are, as a necessary crisis, inseparably connected with everlasting glory, in which all remembrance of grief will be swallowed up in unutterable joy; while, the ungodly man's glimmering " lamp will be put out in " total darkness."—It might have excited in us astonishment and distress, if we had seen the apostles weeping over their crucified Lord, and the enemies of God glorying in their success: but where is now the joy of his murderers, or the sorrow of his friends? These have seen him again. and are filled with consolation. Such will be the event of every believer's trials: may we then " choose that good " part, which can never be taken from us."

V. 23—33.

Blessed be God, we are encouraged to come at all times, especially when depressed with sorrow, to the mercy-seat of our God, in the Redeemer's name; that we may ask

THESE words spake Jesus, ᵃ and lifted up his eyes to heaven, and said, Father, ᵇ the hour is come: ᶜglorify thy Son, that thy Son also may glorify thee:

2 As ᵈthou hast given him power ᵉ over all flesh, that he should ᶠ give eternal life to ᵍas many as thou hast given him:

NOTES

and receive, till our affliction be turned into "the fulness "of joy!" Thus "darkness will become light before us;" those things, which seemed most obscure, will appear plain and satisfactory; we shall have increasing evidence, that the Father himself loves us, as those who, taught and drawn by his preventing grace, love and believe in his incarnate Son. We shall perceive that he knows, and even anticipates, our desires and requests; that he delights to hear and answer our prayers; and that even our manifold infirmities, mistakes, and offences, will not cause him to cease from loving us, and communicating all needful blessings to us.—But "while we think we stand, let us take "heed lest we fall:" we know not how we should act, if we were brought into temptation; we ought therefore to watch and pray without ceasing, that we may not be left to ourselves. (Notes, Matt. vi. 13. xxvi. 40, 41.)—We must seek our peace and comfort in Christ; and not in the world, which we must conflict with as an enemy, in whatever form it appears; an enemy which we must overcome, or we shall fatally be overcome by it: and we should expect tribulation as long as we continue here on earth. But, relying upon our victorious Saviour, and looking constantly to him, we may go forward with confidence; assured of being made more than conquerors, through the love and power of our omnipotent, gracious, faithful, and unchangeable Friend.

NOTES

CHAP. XVII. V. 1—3. ' Jesus Christ, the eternal ' High Priest, being about to offer himself, by solemn ' prayers consecrates himself as the Sacrifice, and us along ' with him, to God the Father. This prayer, therefore, ' has been the foundation of the church of God from the ' creation of the world, is now, and will be, to the con- ' summation of all things.' Beza.—In the preceding chapter our Lord closed his instructions to his apostles, previous to his crucifixion; (except what passed in the garden:) and in this he addressed his Father, in their presence, by a most interesting and affecting prayer; in which his own approaching and most tremendous sufferings seem almost forgotten! Through the whole, he spake as the incarnate Son of God; he supplicated as Man, and as the Mediator of his people; yet he sometimes expressed himself with divine majesty and authority.—In the attitude of reverent devotion, he addressed God, as his Father in a peculiar sense: (Marg. Ref. a.—Notes, xi. 41—46, v. 41. Matt. xi. 25, 26:) and, observing that the important, the decisive, the long expected hour was come, when he should expiate the guilt of his people, by his agonizing sufferings and ignominious death, he prayed, that he, the eternal Father, would " glorify his Son." (Marg. Ref. b, c.—Notes, xii. 27—33, v. 28. xiii. 31—35, vv. 31, 32. xv. 12, 13.)—The Father glorified Christ, by supporting his human nature through his unknown sufferings, and enabling him to exercise perfect meekness, patience, love, and zeal, under

them all; by the appearance of an angel to him in his agony in the garden: by the miracles and prodigies attending his crucifixion; by the conversion of the penitent thief; by the testimonies borne to him by Pilate and the centurion; the fulfilment of ancient types and prophecies in him; the acceptance of his sacrifice; his resurrection and ascension; and his exaltation to the mediatorial throne, " angels, principalities, and powers being made subject to " him." And the Son glorified God the Father, in the display of his justice, holiness, truth, and mercy, and in magnifying his law and government, both in his humiliation, and in the glory which followed it. (Notes, vii. 37—39, v. 39. Ps. lxxii. 17—19. Is. ix. 6, 7. xlix. 5, 6. Acts ii. 33— 36. iii. 12—16, v. 13.)—This petition referred to the power or authority, committed to him as Mediator, to determine the final condition of all the human race; and to give eternal life to all those, who had been " given to him " in the covenant of redemption; (Notes, 6—12. vi. 36—40, v. 37. x. 26—31, vv. 28—30;) for eternal life could not be given to them, unless Christ their Surety both glorified the Father, and was glorified of him. (Marg. Ref. d—f.— Note, v. 20—29.) This eternal life consisted in " the " knowledge of the only true God," as distinguished from all creatures and all idols; and " of his Son Jesus Christ, " whom he had sent " to be the Saviour of the world. God must be known in his perfections, and in the beauty, excellency, glory, and harmony of them. This knowledge must be received from revelation, by faith, and through spiritual illumination, and increased by experience and communion. It cannot be acquired, except by the knowledge of Christ, in his divine Person and mediatorial character and work. (Marg. Ref. g—i.—Notes, Matt. xi. 27. 2 Cor. iv. 5, 6.) In every other view of God, he either appears so just as to exclude the exercise of mercy to the guilty, or so merciful as to interfere with the perfection of justice, holiness, and truth. The glory and the harmony of the divine attributes must be seen " in the face of Jesus Christ:" this knowledge is always attended with reverential fear and confidence; and it produces love, gratitude, submission, obedience, spiritual worship, and conformity to him. (Notes, 1 Chr. xxviii. 9. Jer. xxiv. 7. xxxi. 31—34. Eph. iii. 14—19, vv. 18, 19. Phil. iii. 8—11. 2 Pet. i. 1, 2. iii. 17, 18. 1 John ii. 3—6. v. 20, 21.) This is the sinner's way to eternal life: it evidences his title to it; it is his meetness for it; and the earnest of it; and when this knowledge shall be perfected, holiness and felicity will be experienced. (Notes, xiv. 4—6, v. 6. 2 Cor. iii. 17, 18. 1 John iii. 1—3, v. 3.)

Thou hast given him power. (2) Εδωκας αυτῳ εξουσιαν. iii. 35. v. 22. 26, 27. xiii. 3. Matt. xxviii. 18.—Εξουσιαν. i. 12. v. 22. Note, Matt. xxviii. 18.—The only true God. (3) Τον μονον αληθινον Θεον.—' These words cannot be reasonably ' supposed to exclude him from a true divinity, who is in ' scripture stiled ὁ αληθινος Θεος.... (1 John v. 20.) True ' therefore is the gloss of Grotius, that he is stiled the

3 And ᵉ this is life eternal; that they might know thee ᵇ the only true God, ᶜ and Jesus Christ whom thou hast sent.

4 I ᵏ have glorified thee on the earth: I ˡ have finished the work which thou gavest me to do.

5 And now, O Father, ᵐ glorify thou me with thine own self, with the glory which I had with thee ⁿ before the world was.

6 ¶ I ᵒ have manifested thy name unto ᵖ the men which thou gavest me out of the world: ᑫ thine they were, and thou gavest them me; ʳ and they have kept thy word.

7 Now ˢ they have known that all things, whatsoever thou hast given me, are of thee:

8 For ˣ I have given unto them the words which thou gavest me: and they have ʸ received them, ᶻ and have known surely that I came out from thee, and they have believed that thou didst send me.

9 I ᵃ pray for them: I pray not for the world, ᵇ but for them which thou hast given me; for they are thine.

10 And ᵇ all mine are thine, and

'only true God, in exclusion of those ... whom the false 'persuasion of the Gentiles had introduced.' *Whitby.*—Αληθινος. 1 *Thes.* i. 9. 1 *John* ii. 8. v. 20. *Rev.* iii. 7. 14. xv. 3. xvi. 7. xix. 2. 9. 11. xxi. 5. xxii. 6. See on xv. 1.—*Notes, Is.* xliii. 8—13, *vv.* 10, 11. xliv. 6—8. xlv. 1—6, *vv.* 5, 6. 20—22.

V. 4, 5. Our Lord next stated, that he had " glorified " the Father on the earth." He had glorified him by his perfect obedience, his holy doctrine, and his numerous miracles; and he was about to glorify him by his expiatory sufferings: so that it might be said, that " he had finished " his work" on earth; for he was assured of being carried honourably through that closing awful scene. (*Marg. Ref.* k, l.—*Notes,* iv. 31—38, v. 34. xix. 28—30. *Is.* l. 5—9.) He therefore called on the Father, to " glorify him with " himself," at his right hand, as invested with all authority, exercising all divine perfections, and receiving all adoration; according to that glory, which he had with the Father, before the creation of the world. (*Marg. Ref.* m, n.—*Notes,* i. 1—5. 18. xiv. 25—28. *Prov.* viii. 22—30. 2 *Cor.* viii. 6—9. *Phil.* ii. 5—8. *Heb.* ii. 14, 15.) This glory he had veiled for a time under " the form " of a servant ; " in order that in human nature he might be exalted to it, as the Head and Saviour of his body the church.—To suppose with the Socinians, as some who were far remote from Socinianism, or from being disposed to derogate from the Saviour's glory, have done, that nothing more is here meant, than God's eternal decree of glorifying the man Christ Jesus, not only enervates the language, but induces palpable obscurity and impropriety into it; and sanctions a method of explaining away the scriptures, which is of dangerous, nay pernicious tendency: for thus the elect may be spoken of in similar language, as indeed some have ventured to speak of their eternal justification. (*Note, Rom.* viii. 28—31, v. 30.) —' Bring my human nature into a participation of the ' glory, which I the Λογος had with thee before the begin-' ning of the world.' *Theophylact.*

I have finished. (4) Ετελειωσα. See on iv. 34.—*With thine own self: ... with thee.* (5) Παρα σεαυτω ... παρα σοι. xiv. 17. 23. *Acts* x. 6.—*Num.* xxii. 9. 1 *Sam.* xxii. 3. *Prov.* viii. 30. *Sept.*

V. 6—10. Our Lord, in the greatest part of this prayer

or intercession, had the apostles *primarily* in view, but not *exclusively.* They were the depositaries of his doctrine; and being present on this affecting occasion, were appointed to communicate what they heard, to all other believers, for their instruction and encouragement. Christ had " manifested the name " (or the perfections, purposes, truths, and will) of the Father, to those who had been given to him from among the people of the world, with whom they had associated, before they were called to be his disciples : ' to those peculiar disciples whom thou wast ' pleased by thy grace to fit, and so to bring to me, to ' undertake my discipleship.' *Hammond.* ' To my disciples, ' whom thou hast given to me, by causing them to believe ' in me.' *Whitby.* (*Marg. Ref.* o, p.—See on 1—3, *v.* 2.) They had been the Father's in an especial manner, not only the creatures of his power, but the objects of his choice, even before they were converted; nay, before they were given to the Son to be redeemed and saved by him. At length they had believed, obeyed, and kept his word; and were assured, that all things which Jesus had done, taught, and claimed, (by the gift or commission of the Father to him,) were indeed according to the will, expressive of the perfections, and conducive to the glory of the Father. They had received the words of their Lord with implicit credence, even as he had delivered them from the Father, and were convinced of his divine mission and authority. (*Marg. Ref.* q—y.—*Note,* xvi. 25—30.) He therefore offered this prayer especially for the eleven apostles, but not excluding the seventy disciples, and others who believed in him; and not for the world at large: for unbelievers continuing such, were not, in *this special sense,* interested in his intercession, except as any of them were of that number, who had been " given to him " to be saved by him; as all those had been who had believed in him. Those for whom he prayed were still the Father's, though given to the Son; by reason of the perfect union of essence, counsel, and operation between them. Indeed, not only *the same persons* belong equally to the Father and to the Son, but *the same things* also; so that all things belonging to Christ belong equally to the Father, and all things belonging to the Father, belong equally to the Son. Thus the power and perfections of the Father are the Son's likewise; and the honour and worship of the Son are the

thine are mine; [c] and I am glorified in
them.
11 And now [d] I am no more in the
world; [e] but these are in the world, and
I come to thee. [f] Holy Father, [g] keep
through [h] thine own name those whom
thou hast given me, [i] that they may be
one, as we *are*.
12 While I was with them in the
world, [k] I kept them in thy name: those
that thou gavest me I have kept, [l] and
none of them is lost, but [m] the son of
perdition; [n] that the scripture might
be fulfilled.

13 And now [o] come I to thee; and
these things I speak in the world,
[p] that they might have my joy fulfilled
in themselves.
14 I have [q] given them thy word;
and [r] the world hath hated them, because [s] they are not of the world, even
as I am not of the world.
15 I pray not that thou shouldest
[t] take them out of the world, but that
thou shouldest [u] keep them from the
evil.
16 They [x] are not of the world, even
as I am not of the world.

c v. 23. xi. 4. xii. 23. Acts xix. 17. Phil. i. 20. ii. 9—11. 2 Thes. i. 10. 12. Rev. v. 8—14.
d 13. xiii. 1. 3. xvi. 28. Acts i. 9—11. iii. 21. Heb. i. 3. ix. 24.
e 14—18. xv. 18—21. xvi. 33. Matt. x. 16. Jam. iv. 4. 1 John iii. 12, 13. v. 19.
f 25. Matt. v. 48. 1 Pet. i. 15—17. Rev. iv. 8. xv. 4.
g 12. 15. x. 29, 30. Ps. xvii. 8, 9. Is. xxvii. 3. 1 Pet. i. 5. Jude 1.
h Ps. lxxix. 9. Is. lxiv. 2. Jer. xiv. 7. 21. Ez. xx. 9. 22. 44. Matt. vi. 9. Rom. ix. 17.
i 21, 22. x. 30. xiv. 20. Rom. xv. 5, 6. 1 Cor. i. 10. xii. 12, 13. Eph. iv. 4.
k vi. 37. 39, 40. x. 27, 28. Heb. ii. 13.
l xiii. 18. xviii. 9. Luke iv. 26. 27. 1 John ii. 19.
m vi. 70, 71. 2 Thes. ii. 3.
n Ps. cix. 6—19. Acts i. 16—20. 25.
o 1. xiii. 3. Heb. xii. 2.
p iii. 29. xv. 11. xvi. 22—24. 33. Neh. viii. 10. Ps. xliii. 4. cxxvi. 5. Acts xiii. 52. Rom. xiv. 17. Gal. v. 22. 1 John i. 4. 2 John 12.
q 8.
r vii. 7. xv. 18—21. Gen. iii. 15. Prov. xxix. 27. Zech. xi. 8. Matt. x. 24, 25. 1 Pet. iv. 4, 5. 1 John iii. 12, 13.
s 16. viii. 23. 1 John iv. 5, 6. v. 19, 20.
t Ps. xxx. 9. Ec. ix. 10. Is. xxxviii. 18, 19. lvii. 1. Luke viii. 38, 39. Phil. i. 20—26.
u Gen. xlviii. 16. 1 Chr. iv 10. Ps. cxxi. 7. Matt. vi. 13 Luke xi. 4. Gal. i. 4. 2 Thes. iii. 3. 2 Tim. iv. 18. 1 John v. 18.
x 14.

Father's likewise: and there is no competition between their authority or honour; but the most perfect unity, harmony, and coincidence. (*Notes*, v. 20—23. *Phil.* ii. 9—11.)—And as the disciples were beloved alike by the Son and by the Father; so the Son, equally with the Father, would be glorified in their salvation, and by their holy lives and labours. (*Marg. Ref.* c.—*Thy name*, &c. (6) *Notes*, 25, 26. *Ex.* iii. 14. xxiii. 20—23. xxxiv. 5—7. *Num.* vi. 24—27. *Is.* ix. 6, 7. *Matt.* xxviii. 19, 20.

All mine are thine, &c. (10) Τα εμα παντα σα ετι, και τα σα εμα. See on xvi. 14. *Note*, xvi. 14, 15.

V. 11, 12. Jesus was at the very point of leaving the world, as to his personal presence in human nature. (*Note*, xiii. 1—5, *vv.* 1. 3.) But while he rejoiced in the thought of "going to the Father," he most affectionately regarded his disciples, who were to continue in the world, in the midst of snares, dangers, and tribulations. He therefore interceded with God, as his "Holy Father," (referring to all his moral excellences, as engaged to accomplish the purposes of the new covenant, especially in the sanctification of believers;) that he would "keep them through his "own name," that is, according to his power and perfections, and for the glory of his name; or, *in* the faith, love, and worship of himself: that they might be most intimately united in judgment, affection, doctrine, worship, and labours; even according to the inexplicable union of the Father and the Son in the unity of the Godhead, or of God and man in the Person of Christ. (*Marg. Ref.* d—h. —Note, 20, 21.) He had hitherto, by his presence and instructions, preserved them in this respect: none of those who "had been given to him" had departed from him, or run into the ways of destruction; save that Judas, who was emphatically "a child of wrath," "the son of perdi-"tion," had been left to perish, according to the predictions of the scripture concerning him. (*Marg. Ref.* i—n. —*Notes*, *Ps.* cix. 6—20. *Acts* i. 20—22.)—If we understand "the giving to Christ," in this verse, as before; (6—9;) then Judas is not mentioned as *an exception*, but by way *of opposition, or distinction:* as the woman of Sarepta is distinguished from the widows of Israel, and Naaman the Syrian from the lepers in Israel. (*Note*, *Luke* iv. 23—32.) In the preceding verses, those who were given to Christ are stated to have "kept his word," and "be-"lieved in him:" but Judas had always been a hypocrite, and was now become a traitor and an apostate; and therefore Christ could not mean to include him in that number. (*Note*, vi. 66—71, *vv.* 70, 71. xiii. 18—30, *vv.* 18. 21. 27 —30.) And if in this verse we understand by those "given "to Christ," such, as were given to him to be his apostles, without any reference to faith, or to "the election of "grace;" we cannot explain the preceding verses in that sense, because they are verified in none but true believers, of which number Judas never had been.—*The son of perdition.* (12) *Note*, 2 *Thes.* ii. 3, 4. '"The Son of perdi-'"tion" signifies one, who deservedly perishes: as "a '"son of death," (2 *Sam.* xii. 5,) "children of hell," '(*Matt.* xxiii. 15,) and "children of wrath," (*Eph.* ii. 3,) 'signify persons justly obnoxious to death, hell, and wrath.' *Doddridge.*

I kept them. (12) Eτηρυν αυτυς. 6. 11. 15. *Matt.* xxvii. 36. xxviii. 4. 2 *Cor.* xi. 9. *Eph.* iv. 3. *Jude* 21.—*I have kept.*] Εφυλαξα. xii. 25. *Acts* xii. 4. 1 *John* v. 21. *Jude* 24.—*But.*] Ει μη. *Matt.* xii. 4. *Luke* iv. 26, 27. *Gal.* i. 7. *Rev.* ix. 4. xxi. 27.—*The son of perdition.*] 'Ο υιος της απωλειας. 2 *Thes.* ii. 3.—Απωλειας. *Matt.* vii. 13. *Rom.* ix. 22. 1 *Tim.* vi. 9. 2 *Pet.* ii. 2, 3. Ab απολλυμι, perdo.

V. 13—16. Before Jesus ascended to his glory he spake these things, in his exhortation and intercession, before the apostles, that they and their brethren (and indeed all who should duly regard this record of them,) might "have "his joy fulfilled in them;" that is, the joy which he conferred on them, similar to that, which he possessed in the assurance of his Father's love, and in the prospect of his glory.—'That the joy they had hitherto from my love to 'them, (xv. 11,) my presence with them, and care of 'them, may, in my absence, be increased by the presence 'of that Spirit with them, who will supply my bodily ab-'sence, (xvi. 7,) and whose fruits are joy and peace, (*Gal.* 'v. 22,) yea, by whom I, though absent in body, am 'still present with them. (xiv. 8.)' *Whitby.* (*Marg. Ref.* o, p. *Notes*, xiv. 21—24. xv. 9—11. *Matt.* xxv. 19—23. *Heb.* xii. 2, 3.) They would greatly need this support; as he had "given the word" of the Father to them, that they might boldly profess and zealously preach it before men. The world had already begun to hate them on that account; and would still more hate and persecute them, because they

17 ' Sanctify them through thy truth: ' thy word is truth.

18 As ' thou hast sent me into the world, even so have I also sent them into the world.

19 And ' for their sakes ' I sanctify myself, ' that they also might be ' sanctified through the truth.

20 ¶ Neither ' pray I for these alone, but ' for them also which shall believe on me through their word:

21 That ' they all may be one ; ' as thou, Father, _art_ in me, and I in thee, that they also may be one in us : ' that the world may believe that thou hast sent me.

no longer were of the same character or party with them, but opposite in every thing ; according as he had not been of the world, but contrary to it in his whole doctrine and conduct. (_Marg. Ref._ q—s. x.—_Notes,_ vii. 3—10. xv. 17 —21. _Matt._ v. 10—12. x. 21—26. 1 _John_ iv. 4—6.) He did not pray, however, that the apostles and disciples should be removed out of the world, in order that they might escape the effects of the rage, contempt, and enmity of ungodly men : as they had a great work to do, for the glory of God and the benefit of mankind, which they must continue on earth to finish; at the same time, they must ripen for their exalted state in heaven, by passing through manifold trials and tribulations. (_Marg. Ref._ t, u.—_Notes, Acts_ xx. 22—24. 2 _Cor._ iv. 13—18. _Phil._ i. 19—26. 2 _Tim._ ii. 8—13. 2 _Pet._ i. 12—15.) But he interceded in their behalf, that the Father would preserve them from the evil; that is, from being corrupted by the contagious influence of the world, or tempted by its smiles or frowns to apostatize from him; through the fatal effects of the remains of sin in their hearts, and by the power and subtlety of Satan, that " evil one :" (_Notes, Gen._ xlviii. 16. _Matt._ vi. 13. 2 _Tim._ iv. 16—18 :) that so they might pass safely and honourably through the world, as through an enemy's country, in some good measure as he had done.

My joy, &c. (13) See on xvi. 24.—_From the evil._ (15) Ἐκ τυ πονηρυ. _Matt._ v. 37. vi. 13. xiii. 19, 38, _Luke_ xi. 4. _Gal._ i. 4. 2 _Thes._ iii. 3. 2 _Tim._ iv. 18. 1 _John_ v. 19.

V 17—19. The apostles at this time were truly converted, called out of the ungodly world, and engaged in a work diametrically opposite to all its sentiments, inclinations, and pursuits : (_Notes,_ xvi. 6—11. xv. 3—5 :) but they needed to be far more completely purified, renewed, and consecrated to God, for their distinguished and most important office. Our Lord therefore prayed, that they might be " sanctified through the truth " or revealed word of God, every part of which is holy in its nature and tendency; the means of " sanctification by " the Spirit," and thus of rendering the man of God completely " furnished for every good work." (_Notes,_ 2 _Tim._ iii. 14—17.)—The commandments, doctrines, promises, warnings, and examples of scripture, are suited to discover the evil of sin, and to detect it in all its forms and actings; to impress the mind with fervent affections towards God and holiness; to furnish directions, motives, and encouragements for every thing which is good and excellent; and thus to transform the believer's soul into its own holy nature, and to induce him to that dedication of all his powers to God, in the performance of his proper work, which is here especially intended. (_Marg. Ref._ y, z.) For our Lord immediately referred to his sending forth of his apostles, to publish his gospel in the world : and to

their being wholly consecrated and set apart to that service, and prepared to persevere in it amidst all hardships, perils, and sufferings, unto death itself. In this manner, he had been sent by the Father into the world, and had willingly set apart himself, and his whole human nature, as consecrated by the Holy Spirit, to his most arduous work, and was now about to give himself an atoning sacrifice for sin, for the sake of his apostles and disciples, and for the glory of God in their salvation. (_Marg. Ref._ a—d.—_Notes,_ x. 32—39. _Jer._ i. 5. _Heb._ v. 7—10. x. 28—31.)—In consequence of this, they also would be " sanctified by the " truth," and consecrated to the work of their ministry; that they might promote the same cause in the world, by their labours, writings, example, and patient sufferings; and many of them by becoming martyrs to their testimony to his gospel. (_Note,_ xv. 12—16, _v._ 16.)

Sanctify. (19) Ἁγιασον. 19. _Matt._ vi. 9. xxiii. 17. 19. _Luke_ xi. 2. 1 _Cor._ vi. 11. 1 _Thes._ v. 23.—_Ex._ xxix. 1. 21. 27. 33. _Sept._—See on x. 36.

V. 20, 21. In these verses Christ interceded for all Christians in every age, to the end of the world ; and in this view of them, they are replete with instruction and consolation to us. Doubtless the effectual calling of sinners, to faith in Christ, takes place in answer to his continual intercession in heaven, of which this prayer is a specimen and example : but none are warranted to take encouragement from that consideration, till they in some measure believe his word : he therefore prayed for those " whom the Father had given him " as those " who should " believe on him through the word " of his apostles. (_Marg. Ref._ e, f.—_Notes,_ vi. 36—40. x. 14—18. _Rom._ viii. 28— 31. 2 _Thes._ ii. 13, 14.)—The gospel was especially committed to the apostles, and from them it has been transmitted through succeeding generations to us ; and will be to posterity to the end of the world.—' The true and sav- ' ing faith comes from hearing the doctrine of the apos- ' tles : and that is the doctrine of the apostles, which ' leads us to Christ alone.' _Beza._ This venerable writer had principally in view the additions and alterations, made by popes and councils, and by the prevalence of superstition; but the modern supposed improvements of science, philosophy, and human reasonings, carry large numbers as far from Christ and from the apostolical doctrine, as popery itself does. (_Notes, Col._ ii. 8—10. 18, 19.)— It should also be observed, from our Lord's words, that his religion may certainly be found entire and unadulterated, in the writings of his apostles, and of those who, by their sanction, wrote the other parts of the New Testament. Indeed where else can we look for _the words of the apostles?_ What standard of their doctrine have we, if the New Testament be not that standard? The miracles

k i. 14, xv. 18, 19.
xx.21—24.Mark
vi.7.xvi.17—20.
Luke xxi. 30.
Acts v. 41. Rom.
xv.15—20. 2Cor.
v. 20, vi. 1. Eph.
ii. 20, Phil. i. 29.
Col.i.24. 2Thes.
i. 5—10. Rev.
xxi. 14.
l xiv. 20. 1 John
i. 3, iii. 24.
m vi. 56, xiv. 10.
23 Rom. viii. 10, 11. 1 Cor. i. 30. 2 Cor. v. 21. Gal. iii. 28. 1 John i. 3, iv. 12—16.
n Eph. iv. 12—16. Phil. iii. 15. Col. i. 28, ii. 2, 9, 10. iii. 14. 1 Pet. v. 10.

22 And ᵏ the glory which thou gavest me, I have given them; ˡ that they may be one, even as we are one:

23 ᵐ I in them, and thou in me, that they may be ⁿ made perfect in one ; and ᵒ that the world may know that thou

hast sent me, ᵖ and hast loved them, as thou hast loved me.

24 Father, ᑫ I will that they also, whom thou hast given me, be with me where I am; ʳ that they may behold my glory, which thou hast given me: ˢ for thou lovedst me before the foundation of the world.

p 24. Eph. i. 6, &c.
1John iii.1.iv.19.
q xai. 26. xiv. 3.
Matt. xxv.21 23.
xxvi. 29. Luke
xii.37. xxii. 29—
30.xxiii.43.2Cor.
v. 8. Phil. i. 23.
1Thes.iv.17.Rev.
iii.21.vii.14—17.
Gen. xlv. 18,
1 Cor. xiii. 12.
2 Cor. iii. 18 iv.
6. 1 John iii. 2.
Rev. xxi. 23.
s 5. Prov. viii. 22
—31.

which they wrought proved the *truth* of Christianity: but if they were not inspired infallibly to communicate to the world the true doctrine of that holy religion without addition, adulteration, or omission ; where shall we with certainty learn the *nature* of it ? or how be *sure*, that we are not deluded by some misrepresentation ?—It is peculiarly worthy of observation, that the absurdest claims of popes and councils in this respect, and the more plausible claims of such moderns as want to improve Christianity by human reason, are maintained by the same vain supposition ; namely, that *the scripture of itself is either insufficient, or in some degree uncertain, or too obscure, to answer the purpose.*—In behalf however of all this company of believers, our Lord especially prayed, that they might be united together in the closest bonds of love ; as one Body, under one Head, animated by one soul, according to the incomprehensible union before mentioned, and in virtue of their union with Christ, and the Father in him, through the Holy Spirit dwelling in them. (*Marg. Ref.* g, h.—*Notes*, xiv. 18—24. *Rom.* xii. 3—5. 1 *Cor.* xii. 12 —31. *Gal.* iii. 26—29. *Eph.* ii. 19—22. iv. 1—6. 11— 13.) In some respects this request is granted in behalf of all true Christians, in proportion to the degree of their illumination and sanctification : but the more closely they are united in judgment and affection, and the more entirely they live in peace and harmony, professing the same doctrine, and worshipping God with one heart and one mouth, the clearer evidence do they afford of the divine original and excellency of the gospel, to the conviction of the world around them. (*Notes*, xiii. 31—35. *Jer.* xxxii. 39—41. *Zeph.* iii. 9, 10. *Acts* iv. 32—35. v. 12—16.) On the other hand, the more those who in so many respects are *one*, and who are agreed in the most important matters, differ and dispute about things of inferior moment, the more ambiguous and uncertain do the truth and excellency of Christianity appear. (*Notes*, and *P. O. Eph.* iv. 1—6. *Note*, *Phil.* i. 27—30.) Men are apt to say, ' It will be soon enough for us to embrace the gospel, when its professors are agreed among themselves in what it consists :' and those who are not aware of the advantage, which infidels and ungodly men have made of the divisions and controversies among Christians, against the common interest of our holy religion, must have been very little acquainted with their writings, and made but few observations on the conversation and conduct of mankind. Mere nominal Christians, indeed, give the most extensive occasion to the objections ; but real believers are far from being sufficiently circumspect in this particular.—The union which prevailed among Christians, when the gospel was first propagated, as springing from the communion of the Holy Spirit, the Sanctifier, evidenced to the world the divine original of Christianity, in a manner not much less convincing, than the miraculous powers of the same

Spirit, conferred on them through the laying on of the hands of the apostles. (*Notes*, *Acts* ii. 44—47.) And as believers are mentioned by our Lord, without limitation of age or country ; the evidence to the truth of Christianity, by the miraculous gifts vouchsafed in the primitive church, cannot be particularly intended.—' This ' plainly intimates, that dissensions among Christians ' would ... be the means of bringing the truth and excel- ' lence of the Christian religion into question.' *Doddridge.* (*Notes*, *Matt.* xviii. 7—9. 15—17. *Luke* xvii. 3, 4.)

May be one. (21) 'Εν ωσι. 11. 22, 23. See on x. 30.

V. 22, 23. Our Lord could not here mean his personal or mediatorial glory : but that glory, which was given to him as Mediator, to be by him conferred on his disciples ; or the glory of bearing his image, declaring his truth, working miracles in confirmation of it, labouring and suffering in the same cause, and enduring enmity and opposition from ungodly men, for promoting the honour of God in the world, and finally of sharing his heavenly glory. (*Marg. Ref.* k, l.) Thus he gave to them the glory of concurring in that grand design, for which he became incarnate, and for which he lived and died ; and of being " anointed," in their " measure, by the Holy Spirit," for that service ; (*Marg. Ref.* m, n.—*Notes*, iii. 27—36, v. 34. *Eph.* iv. 7—13 ;) and of being thus made complete, as one body in Christ, and in the Father through him : and all men might see, by their doctrine and behaviour, that they were a holy and happy people ; that their religion was of heavenly original, because of a heavenly nature and tendency ; and that they were the proper objects of the divine love for Christ's sake, and according to the Father's love to his " beloved Son in whom he was well " pleased." (*Marg. Ref.* o, p.)—' Thou, O Father, art ' in me, as Mediator, and I ... am in them by my Spirit, ' working effectually in them, to unite them perfectly in ' one, both in themselves and in us.' *Bp. Hall.*—Whatever differences prevailed in the primitive church ; there is not the smallest trace of any real disunion even in judgment among the apostles ; except for a while, concerning the admission of uncircumcised Gentiles into the church ; and that matter was soon amicably settled. (*Notes*, *Acts* xi. 1—17. xv. 7—21.) They were all along, as far as we can learn, " perfectly joined together in the same mind " and judgment ;" and this by an abundant measure of the illuminating and sanctifying Spirit of God ; as well as by that infallible inspiration, by which they delivered the doctrine of their Lord to mankind. This was an especial honour conferred on them ; and a remarkable accomplishment of this intercession considered as a prophecy. (*Notes*, 2 *Pet.* iii. 1—4, v. 2. 14—16. 1 *John* iv. 1—6. *Jude* 17—19.)

V. 24. The language of this verse has been considered

25 O 'righteous Father, "the world hath not known thee: ˣ but I have known thee, and ʸ these have known that thou hast sent me.

t 11. 1s. xiv. 21. Rom. iii. 26.
u viii.19.55. xv.21. xvi. 8. Matt. xi. 27. Luke x. 22. Acts xvii. 23. xxvi.18. Rom. i. 28, iii. 11. 1 Cor. i. 21. xv. 34.
x i. 18. v. 19, 20, vii. 29. x. 15.
2 Cor. iv. 4. Gal. iv. 8, 9.
y 8. vi. 69. xvi. 27, 30.
2 Thes. i. 8. Heb. viii. 11. 1 John v. 19, 20. Matt. xvi. 16.
Rev. xiii. 8.

26 And ᶻ I have declared unto them thy name, and will declare *it:* ᵃ that the love wherewith thou hast loved me may be in them, ᵇ and I in them.

z See on 6. viii. 50. xv. 15. Ph. ii. 12.
a xiv. 23. xv. 9 Eph. i. 6, 22, 23. ii. 4, 5. v. 30, 32. 2 Thes. ii. 16.
b 23. vi. 56. xiv. 20. xv. 4. Rom. viii. 10. 1 Cor. i. 30. xii. 12. Gal. ii. Col. i, 27. ii. 10. iii. 11. 1 John iii. 24. iv. 15, 14.
Eph. iii. 17.

by many expositors, ancient and modern, as a *claim,* grounded on a covenant, the terms of which would, on the part of Christ, in a few hours be perfectly fulfilled. He does not therefore say, I pray, or *beseech;* but, "I " will;" as acting by authority, and as One with the Father.—It is not, however, certain, that more than a fervent importunate desire was intended: and it is not adviseable to adduce doubtful texts, in proof of a disputed point of doctrine. The language at least implies, that this concluding plea was peculiarly near the heart of the heavenly Advocate, and there can be no doubt, it will infallibly be granted. And what is the import of it? That the whole company which had " been given him," and would in due time believe on him, should at length be safely brought to heaven, the place of his special presence as God, and whither, as man, he was about to ascend; that there they might behold and contemplate his glory, as their beloved Friend and Brother, and in this beatifick vision find their felicity. *(Marg. Ref.* q, r.—*Notes,* 1—3, *v.* 2. 6—12. vi. 36—40. x. 26—31. xiv. 2, 3. *Gen.* xlv. 13. *P. O.* 9—28, *conclusion. Notes,* 2 *Cor.* v. 5—8. *Phil.* i. 19—26. 1 *Thes.* iv. 13—18.) For, in this respect, as well as on account of his divine excellency, the Father " loved him before the foundation of the world;" *(Notes,* 4, 5. *Prov.* viii. 22—30. *Matt.* xxv. 34—40;) because he most perfectly delighted in the mediatorial undertaking and work of the Son, as fully adequate to all the purposes of his glory in the salvation of his people.

They may behold. (24) Θεωρωσι. " Steadily contem- " plate." vi. 40. 62. xiv. 17. 19. xvi. 10. 16, 17. 19.— *Before the foundation of the world.*] Προ καΤαϐολης κοσμω. See on *Matt.* xxv. 34.

V. 25, 26. These last verses primarily related to the apostles.—Jesus addressed God, as his " righteous Fa- " ther," not only because of his essential justice, and the righteousness of his moral government; but as righteous in justifying sinners through his obedience unto death, and in performing the engagements of his everlasting covenant. *(Notes, Is.* xlv. 20—22. *Rom.* iii. 19—26, *v.* 26.) The world, indeed, had not known God, in respect of this righteousness, and his glorious excellences; for it was in a state of rebellion against him, and exposed to his just vengeance on that account. *(Marg. Ref.* u—*Notes,* 1— 3, *v.* 3. viii. 54—59. *Acts* xvii. 22—25. *Rom.* i. 18—23. 28—32. 1 *Cor* i. 20—24. *Gal.* iv. 8—11.) But as he, his beloved Son, had perfectly known him; as the apostles had assuredly believed that the Father had sent him; *(Marg. Ref.* x, y;) and as he had declared, and would still further declare, the name and perfections of God to them, by his doctrine which would be confirmed by his Spirit: so they were, and would be, distinguished from the world, by the knowledge of God and all its happy effects (3); in order that, being One with him, and members of his mystical body, the love of the Father to him might be communicated to them, and abide with them also; and that thus, being joined to him as one

spirit, they might be filled " with all the fulness of God, ' and come as near the Fountain of all felicity as creatures possibly could do. *(Marg. Ref.* z—b.—*Notes,* 6—10. *Eph.* iii. 14—21.)—After all endeavours to explain this chapter, we must allow, that our thoughts are swallowed up, in those depths of wisdom and love, and in those mysteries of the Godhead, with which it is replete; and that the light of heaven alone can fully clear it up to us. *(Note, Rom.* xi. 33—36.)

PRACTICAL OBSERVATIONS.

V. 1—5.

Fervent prayer forms the proper conclusion of religious instructions, and the preparation for approaching trials and sufferings: and our eyes and hearts should habitually be lifted up to our heavenly Father, that he would glorify himself in and by us; prosper our endeavours to honour him; support us in resisting temptations; and carry us through all difficulties to his heavenly kingdom. *(Notes,* 2 *Thes.* i. 5—12, *vv.* 10—12. *P. O.*) But all our supplications must be presented through the intercession of our great High Priest, who " hath power " over all flesh;" and who gives eternal life to all his chosen and believing people, and will consign all unbelievers to everlasting punishment. For, however men may deny, deride, or overlook it, " eternal life" cannot be obtained by any of our fallen race, except through " the " knowledge of God," as revealed in his Son Jesus, and through his meritorious obedience unto death; in which " he glorified the Father on earth," and " finished the " work which was given him to do."—By leaving " the " glory which he had with the Father before the world " was," in his humiliation on earth, by his ascension into heaven to be reinstated in his glory, and by the doctrine which he committed to his holy apostles, he has manifested the name and glory of God to man (6); and all believers " behold that glory as in a glass, till they are " changed into the same image from glory to glory, by " the Spirit of the Lord."—This knowledge however widely differs from those inefficacious notions, which puff up men with pride: for it is humbling, transforming, and sanctifying; the source of all spiritual worship and holy obedience; the hope, the evidence, the earnest of eternal life, and the meetness for heavenly felicity.

V. 6—12.

The special regard of the Saviour to those who were " given to him out of the world," cannot be overlooked by the attentive reader: and the things spoken of them are, not peculiar to the apostles; but they take in all, who receive and keep his word, who are firmly persuaded that his doctrine and his works were from the Father, and who believe in him for the salvation of their souls. For these persons, with particular purpose and design, he " came " into the world;" for them he obeyed and suffered; for them he rose again and reigns; for them he continually in-

CHAP. XVIII.

Jesus retires to a garden; and Judas leads a company thither to apprehend him, 1—3. At the word of Jesus, the officers, soldiers, and company fall to the ground, 4—6 Jesus, yielding up himself, requires that his disciples should be dismissed, 7—9. Peter cuts off Malchus's ear, and Jesus reproves him, 10, 11. Jesus is bound, and led away to Annas, and then to Caiaphas, 12—14. Peter is admitted into the palace, and then denies Christ, 15—18. Jesus is examined by the high priest, and struck by an officer, 19—24. Peter again twice denies him, 25—27. Jesus is brought before Pilate, and declares that his "kingdom is not of this world," 28—37. Pilate testifies to his innocence, and offers to release him; but the Jews prefer Barabbas the robber, 38—40.

tercedes, and not for the world at large: in them he will eternally be glorified with the Father, whose also they are; as " all things that the Father hath are" the Son's likewise. No trembling sinner, however, who desires to approach the Father, and is consciously unworthy to come in his own name, needs to be discouraged; for the Saviour is both able and willing to " save to the uttermost all " them, who come to God by him." These convictions and desires are hopeful tokens: and when they lead a man to the throne of grace, through faith in the word, and reliance on the intercession of Emmanuel; the express promises of God become his security, and the work already wrought in him evidences, that he has been " chosen unto salvation, through sanctification of the " Spirit, and belief of the truth;" nor can any one, whatever he professes or preaches, know his election of God, except by that " faith which worketh by love," and by its evident fruits. (Notes, 1 Thes. i. 1—4, vv. 3, 4. 2 Pet. i. 5—11.)—For many have called Christ Lord and Master, and seemed to be the children and servants of God, who at length proved " sons of perdition," after the example of Judas. Such examples should excite us to serious self-examination, and fervent prayer: but they should not distress the humble believer, who, though he " cannot do " the things that he would," is conscious of integrity in his professed repentance, and faith in Christ, and desire of living to his glory. These are of that number, who, through the intercession of Christ, shall be " kept by the " power of God," to the glory of his name, and in his worship and service, " through faith, unto eternal salva-" tion." (Note, 1 Pet. i. 3—5.) None of them ever were or will be lost: for " the sons of perdition" only seemed to be of them, but they never were one with them in judgment, disposition, and affection. (Note, 1 John ii. 18, 19.)

V. 13—19.

The true disciples of Christ live at present in an ensnaring and evil world, which hates and despises them: yet the recollection of his words, and the experience of his faithfulness, may fill them with holy joy in him and in each other, amidst all their tribulations. They should indeed be willing to die, but not impatiently desire it: for their loving Advocate does not intercede for their immediate removal out of the world, but that they " may " be kept from the evil of it." They must, however, carefully remember, that they are not left here, to pursue any of those objects, which the men of the world are pursuing; but to glorify God, to " serve their generation," to finish their work, and " to be perfected through suffer-" ings," after the example of " the Captain of their sal-" vation." They should therefore hope and pray, that the grace, which has separated them from the world, may preserve them from the evil of it, and from the snares of the wicked one: they should seek to be sanctified more and more through the word of truth, that they may be devoted unreservedly to the service of him, who " through " the eternal Spirit offered himself without spot to God," for their sakes, and " to purge their consciences from " dead works, that they might serve the living God:" (Note, Heb. ix. 11—14, vv. 13, 14:) and they should carefully examine, whether the doctrines which they hold have a sanctifying effect upon their own hearts and lives. For, as all divine truth is of a holy nature, if our religious opinions do not make us hate all sin, and long and pray for holiness, we may be sure, either that they are not divine truths, or that we do not receive them by a living faith, under the teaching of the Holy Spirit.

V. 20—26.

Blessed be God, that we sinners, in these remote regions and distant ages, are interested in this prayer of our Redeemer, if we truly believe in him according to the word of his holy apostles! May we continually recollect, that union and communion with the Father and the Son by the indwelling of the Holy Spirit, and union, peace, and harmony with one another, formed the substance of our Redeemer's prayer for all his disciples, to the end of time. Let us then " endeavour to keep the unity of the " Spirit in the bond of peace:" and let us pray with fervour and without ceasing, for a larger portion of divine illumination, in behalf of ourselves and of all our brethren, that we may all be united " in one mind and judg-" ment." Let us also constantly beseech our God to bestow on us far more abundance of holy love; that we may amicably differ in opinion, where we cannot see things exactly in the same light. Thus a spirit of mutual candour, forbearance, and active self-denying kindness, among " all " who love the Lord Jesus Christ in sincerity," may convince the world, that we are of one heart and soul, though somewhat separated by external circumstances; and that we are all soldiers in one army, though not exactly marshalled and disciplined in the same manner; that we are indeed fighting against sin, the world, and the devil; and that we will not be seduced to turn our arms against each other, as has too often been the case, to the joy and triumph of our insulting enemies. Thus we shall best manifest the truth and excellency of our religion, and the divine authority of its great Author. Thus we shall experience more intimate union of soul, and more sweet and sanctifying communion with the God of our salvation, and with his saints. Thus we shall have a measure of the Redeemer's glory conferred on us, by being conformed to his image, united with his people, and hated by those only, who " hate him and the Father that sent him." Thus at

WHEN Jesus had * spoken these words, ᵇ he went forth with his disciples over ᶜ the brook Cedron, where was ᵈ a garden, into the which he entered, and his disciples.

2 And Judas also, which betrayed him, knew the place; ᵉ for Jesus oft-times resorted thither with his disciples.

3 ᶠ Judas then, having received ᵍ a band *of men,* and officers from the chief priests and Pharisees, cometh thither with lanterns, and torches, and weapons.

4 Jesus therefore, ʰ knowing all things that should come upon him,

went forth, and said unto them, ⁱ Whom seek ye?

5 They answered him, ᵏ Jesus of Nazareth. Jesus saith unto them, I am he. And Judas also, which betrayed him, ˡ stood with them.

6 As soon then as he had said unto them, I am *he,* ᵐ they went backward, and fell to the ground.

7 Then asked he them again, Whom seek ye? And they said, Jesus of Nazareth.

8 Jesus answered, I have told you that I am *he.* If therefore ye seek me, ⁿ let these go their way:

9 That the saying might be fulfilled,

---

length we shall surely be with him for ever, to behold his glory, and enjoy, as one with him, that love with which the Father " loved him before the foundation of the " world;" and shall possess the most complete felicity, in the full knowledge of that glorious God, whom the world has not known; but in knowing whom angels and archangels find blessedness, of which in our present state we can frame no adequate conception. *(Notes,* 1 Cor. i. 6—9. xiii. 8—12. 1 *John* iii. 1—3, *v.* 3.)

NOTES.

CHAP. XVIII. V. 1—3. *(Notes, Matt.* xxvi. 30—56. *Mark* xiv. 26—50. *Luke* xxii. 39—53.)—Cedron, or Kidron, was a small brook to the east of Jerusalem, over which David (the type of Christ) passed weeping, when he fled for fear of Absalom. *(Marg. Ref.* c.—*Note,* 2 *Sam.* xv. 23.) It derived its name from a shady and gloomy valley, through which it ran.—It is probable, that the garden to which Jesus retired, belonged to some friend, who willingly and gladly afforded him and his disciples this quiet retreat. But Judas, knowing his custom and purpose of resorting thither, had procured a cohort of Roman soldiers, as well as the officers of the Jewish rulers, in order to take him: and they came with every preparation, which would have been necessary if they had attempted to apprehend some desperate criminal, attended with numerous armed followers, who would use every method to oppose or to escape them: otherwise lanterns and torches seem not to have been needful, when the moon was at the full. *(Marg. Ref.* a, b. d—g.)—The first Adam fell in a garden; the second Adam began the last scene of his atoning sufferings in a garden likewise.

The brook. (1) Tʋ χιμαρρʋ. Here only N. T.—*Lev.* xi. 9, 10. *Num.* xxi. 14, 15. *Josh.* xiii. 9. *Sept.* Ex χειμα hyems, et ρoos fluxus, a ρɛω fluo.—*The brook Cedron.*] Almost all the manuscripts read " the brook of Cedars:" yet the variation producing this reading is so trivial (τʋν κɛδρʋν for τʋ κɛδρʋν,) and so easily accounted for, and the internal evidence in favour of the reading adopted by our translators so conclusive, that most modern criticks consider it ·as the true one.—*A band.* (3) Tην σπɛιρα. 12. See on *Matt.* xxvii. 27

V. 4—9. John is entirely silent as to our Lord's agony in the garden, which had been fully stated by the three preceding evangelists: *(Notes, Matt.* xxvi. 36—46. *Mark* xiv. 32—42. *Luke* xxii. 39—46:) and he proceeds to mention circumstances, respecting the apprehending of Jesus, which they had passed over. Our Lord, though fully aware of all the inexpressible sufferings which were coming upon him, and every circumstance of them, went forth to meet his rude assailants, with the most perfect serenity and fortitude! *(Marg. Ref.* h.—*Notes,* xiii. 1—5, *vv.* 1—3. *Luke* xxii. 51—56, *v.* 51. *Acts* xx. 22—24. xxi. 7—14.) It is particularly remarked, that Judas stood with the company, when Jesus declared himself to be the person whom they sought; so that he too was constrained to go " backward, and fall to " the ground:" yet he was not dismayed by that further display of the power of his Lord, but dared to proceed with his horrid purpose! *(Marg. Ref.* i—m.—*Note, Ps.* xxvii. 1—3, *v.* 2.) No doubt Jesus could with equal ease have struck the whole company dead in a moment: and it is wonderful, that the scribes, priests, and other Jews did not recollect the companies, which were destroyed by fire from heaven when they came to take Elijah; and that they should venture to renew their attempt after this unexpected repulse. *(Notes,* xi. 47, 48. xii. 9—11. 2 *Kings* i. 9—14. *Luke* ix. 51—56, *v.* 54.) But perhaps they ascribed it to the same power, by which the Pharisees asserted that he wrought his miracles: and if so, they might deem their preservation a peculiar interposition of God in their favour. *(Note, Ec.* ix. 1—3, *v.* 3.) Our Lord, however, was pleased not to proceed any further against them; but only observed, that as they sought him, who was ready to yield up himself, they should let his disciples go away unmolested; and with this they were influenced to comply. This conduct of Jesus accorded to the word, which he had before spoken: *(Marg. Ref.* n, o.—*Note,* xvii. 11, 12:) for he thus not only shewed the most tender concern for their *temporal* safety, as given to him to be his apostles: but he kept them, as true but weak believers, from those temptations, which they were not then prepared to withstand; and this conduced also to their *spiritual* preservation. *(Notes, Luke* xxii. 31 —34. 1 *Cor.* x. 13.)—*Knowing,* &c. (4) ' Our Lord not ' only knew, in general, that he should suffer some great

which he spake, 'Of them which thou gavest me have I lost none.

10 Then ᵖ Simon Peter having a sword drew it, and smote the high priest's servant, and cut off his right ear. The servant's name was Malchus.

11 Then said Jesus unto Peter, ᵠ Put up thy sword into the sheath: ʳ the cup which ˢ my Father hath given me, shall I not drink it?

12 Then ᵗ the band, and ᵘ the captain, and officers of the Jews, took Jesus, and ˣ bound him,

13 And led him away to ʸ Annas first; for he was father-in-law to Caiaphas, which was the high priest ᶻ that same year ᵃ.

14 Now ᵇ Caiaphas was he which gave counsel to the Jews, that it was expedient that one man should die for the people.

15 ¶ And ᵇ Simon Peter followed Jesus, and so did another disciple. That disciple was known unto the high priest, and went in with Jesus into the palace of the high priest.

16 But Peter stood at the door without. Then went out that other disciple, which was known unto the high priest, and spake unto her that kept the door, and brought in Peter.

17 Then saith ᶜ the damsel that kept the door unto Peter, Art not thou also one of this man's disciples? He saith, ᵈ I am not.

18 And the servants and officers stood there, ᵉ who had made a fire of coals, (ᶠfor it was cold,) and they warmed themselves: and ᶠ Peter stood with them, and warmed himself.

' evil, and even death itself; but was acquainted also with
' all the particular circumstances of ignominy and horror,
' that should attend his sufferings. ... It is impossible to
' enter aright into the heroick behaviour of our Lord Jesus
' Christ, without carrying this circumstance along with us.
' The criticks are in raptures at the gallantry of Achilles,
' in going to the Trojan war, when he knew, according to
' Homer, that he should fall there. But, he must have a
' very low way of thinking, who does not see infinitely
' more fortitude in our Lord's conduct on this occasion.'
Doddridge.—Fell to the ground, &c. (6) 'They might
' perhaps ascribe it to the special providence of God, rather
' than to the indulgence of Jesus, that they received no
' further damage. The most corrupt heart has its reason-
' ings, to support it in its absurdest notions, and most cri-
' minal actions.' Ibid.—To the ground. (6) Χαμαι. ix. 6.
V. 10—14. (Marg. Ref. p, q.—Notes, Matt. xxvi. 47
—56. Luke xxii. 47—53.) John alone of the evangelists
mentions Peter and Malchus by name; for probably Peter
had suffered martyrdom before John wrote his gospel.—It
must have been the effect of a secret divine interposition,
that the officers and soldiers permitted the disciples to withdraw quietly, after this violent resistance.—The question
proposed by our Lord, "The cup which my Father hath
" given me, shall I not drink it?" was peculiarly beautiful
and expressive. He did not confine his thoughts to the
malice and injustice of his enemies in his sufferings; but
he received them as a cup put into his hand by his heavenly
Father, who would not afflict him without good reason,
and for the most gracious and important purposes. (Marg.
Ref. r, s.—Notes, Matt. xx. 20—23. ver. 36—39, v. 39.
Mark xiv. 32—36, v. 36.)—Caiaphas seems to have obtained the high priesthood by the interest of Annas, who
possessed it before him. The officers of the council led
Jesus first to Annas, out of deference to his character; but
he sent them back to Caiaphas, to whom Jesus was evidently
brought before the events which are next recorded. (Marg.

Ref. t—a.—Notes, xi. 49—53. Luke iii. 2, 3. ' Of his
' being sent to Annas, the other evangelists say nothing;
' because nothing was done to Christ there; but all was
' performed in the palace of the high priest.' Whitby.
The captain. (12) 'Ο χιλιαρχος. Mark vi. 21. Acts xxi.
31, 32, 33. 37. Rev. vi. 15. xix. 18. Α χιλιας, mille. The
captain spoken of was commander of a thousand men,
though probably only a part of that number was present.
—' At the time of the passover, it was customary for the
' Roman president to send a whole band of a thousand
' men, for a guard to the temple; the captain of which
' band is here called Χιλιαρχος.' Whitby.
V. 15, 16. (Note, Matt. xxvi. 57—62.) Many expositors have supposed, that this other disciple was John the
evangelist: yet, as John was a fisherman of Galilee, it is
not probable that he should be acquainted with the high
priest, and have influence with his servants: and indeed it
is not said, that this disciple was one of the apostles. It
is therefore more likely, that some person residing at Jerusalem, and of rank superior to the apostles, was intended;
that he on this occasion avowed himself the disciple of
Jesus; and, having entered with him into the palace of the
high priest, procured admission for Peter, who had before
been excluded.—Nonnus, an ancient Greek author, renders it, ' and another new friend.' ' He seems not to have
' been John: for he being a Galilean, as well as Peter,
' they might have equally suspected him on that account.'
Whitby.
Was known. (15) Ην γνωστος. 16. Luke ii. 44. xxiii. 49.
—Neh. v. 10. Ps. lxxxviii. 8. Sept.—That kept the door
(16) Τη θυρωρῳ. 17. See on Mark xiii. 34.
V. 17, 18. Marg. Ref.—Note, Matt. xxvi. 57—62. v.
58.—A fire of coals. (18) Ανθρακιαν. xxi. 9. Not elsewhere. Ab ανθραξ carbo.—Cold.] Ψυχος. Acts xxviii. 2.
2 Cor. xi. 27.—They warmed themselves.] Εθερμαινοντο.
25. Mark xiv. 54. 67. Jam. ii. 16. Θερμη, calor. Acts
xxviii. 3.

19 ¶ The high priest then [h] asked Jesus of his disciples and of his doctrine.

20. Jesus answered him, [i] I spake openly to the world; I ever taught in the synagogue, and in the temple, whither the Jews always resort: [k] and in secret have I said nothing.

21 Why askest thou me? [l] ask them which heard me, what I have said unto them: behold, they know what I said.

22 And when he had thus spoken, one of the officers, which stood by, [m] struck Jesus with [n] the palm of his hand, saying, [n] Answerest thou the high priest so?

23 Jesus answered him, [o] If I have spoken evil, bear witness of the evil; but if well, why smitest thou me?

24 Now [p] Annas had sent him [q] bound unto Caiaphas the high priest.

25 And Simon Peter [r] stood and warmed himself. [s] They said therefore unto him, Art not thou also *one* of his disciples? [t] he denied *it*, and said, I am not.

26 One of the servants of the high priest, [u] being *his* kinsman whose ear Peter cut off, saith, [x] Did not I see thee in the garden with him?

27 Peter then denied again; [y] and immediately the cock crew.

28 ¶ Then [z] led they Jesus from Caiaphas [a] unto the [a] hall of Judgment: and it was [b] early; [c] and they themselves went not into the judgment-hall, lest they should be defiled; but that they might [d] eat the passover.

29 Pilate then went out unto them, [e] and said, [f] What accusation bring ye against this man?

30 They answered and said unto him, [g] If he were not a malefactor, we would not have [f] delivered him up unto thee.

31 Then said Pilate unto them, [h] Take ye him, and judge him according to your law. The Jews therefore said unto him, [i] It is not lawful for us to put any man to death:

32 That [k] the saying of Jesus might be fulfilled, which he spake, signifying [l] what death he should die.

Marginal references

[h] Luke xi. 53, 54. xx. 20.
[i] vii. 14, 26. viii. 2. x. 23.—39. Ps. xxii. 22. xl. 9, 10. Matt. iv. 23. Lu. xx. xxi, &c. Luke iv. 15. 16. xix. 45—47. xx. 1, &c. xxi. 37.
[k] vii. 4. Ja. xiv. 9. xlviii. 16.
Matt. xxiv. 26.
[l] Matt. xxvi. 59, 60. Mark xiv. 55—59. Luke xxii. 67, 68. Acts xxiv. 12, 13. 18—20.
[m] Job xvi.10.xxx. 10—12. Is. l. 5—7. Jer. xx. 2. Mic. v. 1. Matt. xxvi. 67, 68. Mark xiv. 65. Luke xxii. 63, 64. Acts xxiii. 2.
[n] Or, a rod.
[o] 2 Cor. x. 1. Matt. v. 39.
[p] 1 Pet. ii. 20—23.
[q] 18. Matt. xxvi. 57.
[r] 18. Mark xiv.67, 68. Luke xxii. 55.
[s] Matt. xxvi. 71, —75. Luke xxii. 58.
[t] Gen. xviii. 15. Prov. xxix. 25. Gal. ii. 11—13.

[u] 10. Prov. xiii. 9.
[x] Matt. xxvi. 73. Mark xiv. 70.
71. Luke xxii. 59, 60.
[y] xiii. 38. Matt. xxvi. 74, 75. Mark xiv. 30. 68, 72. Luke xxii. 4. 60—62.
[z] Matt. xxvii. 1, 2. Mark xv. 1. Luke xxiii. 1. 32. xix. 9.
[a] Luke xxiii. 1.
[b] Prov. i. 16. iv. 16. Rom.
[c] Ps. xxxv. 16. Jer. xli. 8—11. Am. v. 21—23. Mic. iii. 10—12. Matt. xxiii. 2 —28. xi. 30. xxvi. 16. Acts x. 28. xi. 3.
[d] Deut. xvi. 2.
[e] Prov. xxx. 12. 2 Chr. xxx. 21. 24. xxxv. Ez. xiv. 17, 18. Ez. xlv. 21.
[f] Matt. xxvii. 23—30, v. 29. xix. 13—18. 2 Chr. xxx. 21—25. xxxv. 7—19. Ex. xlv. 18—25.
[g] xix. 6, 7. Acts iii. 13, 14.
[h] xix. 6, 7. Acts xxv. 16—20.
[i] Mark x. 33. Luke xviii. 32.
[k] xix. 12. Mark xv. 3. Luke xx. 2.
[l] Mark xxiv. 7.
Luke xxiv. 7.
Acts iii. 13.
[h] xii. 32, 33. Matt. xx. 19. xxvi. 2. Luke xxiv. 7, 8. Acts viii. 89.
[k] iii. 14. x. 31, 33. xii. 32, 33. Matt. xx. 19. xxvi. 2. Luke xxiv. 7, 8. Acts vii. 39.
[l] Deut. xvi. 23. Ps. xxii. 16. Gal. iii. 13.

V. 19—23. (*Notes, Matt.* xxvi. 63—68. *Mark* xiv. 53—59. *Luke* xxii. 63—71.) It is probable, that Caiaphas questioned Jesus concerning the number and rank of his disciples; but to this he answered nothing. He also enquired of him, what doctrine he had taught the people; with reference, either to his assuming the character of the Messiah, or to the contrariety of his doctrine to the traditions of the elders. To this Jesus replied, that he had taught the people in the most frequented places, and the most open manner, and had spoken nothing in private different from his public instructions. It was not therefore proper to require his testimony in his own cause, as they were not disposed to believe it; but that regard to due order, or to law and justice, required them to seek for witnesses among those who had heard him. It is most likely, that some were then present, who had frequently heard his instructions. (*Marg. Ref.* i—l.) This reply was peculiarly suitable to the situation, in which Jesus was at this time placed; for he stood as a prisoner on his trial, before judges who were determined to put him to death, and only sought a pretence for their injustice and murder. An officer, however, of the court, imagining on false grounds that he answered the high priest in a disrespectful manner, contumeliously smote him with the palm of his hand, or rather with a rod, or wand of office. (*Notes, Mic.* v. 1. *Mark* xiv. 60—65, v. 65.) But Jesus meekly replied, by observing, that if on that, or on any other occasion, he had spoken any thing criminal, let him bear witness against him; but if he had answered well, and his words were not faulty, why did he smite him, when he was on his trial in a court, where justice ought to be administered to every one? It was proper, that this man should be rebuked for his illbehaviour, and that the imputation of blame should be done away from our Lord's character; though he was ready to endure every indignity and cruelty, without resistance or menace. (*Marg. Ref.* m—o.—*Notes, Acts* xvi. 35 —40. xxiii. 1—5.)

Struck ... with the palm of his hand. (22) "A rod." *Marg.* Εδωκε ραπισμα. See on *Matt.* v. 39. xxvi. 67.

V. 24—27. *Marg. Ref.*—*Notes*, 10—14. *Matt.* xxvi. 69—75. *Mark* xiv. 66—72. *Luke* xxii. 54—62.

V. 28—32. (*Notes, Matt.* xxvii. 1, 2. 11—18. *Mark* xv. 1—5. *Luke* xxiii. 1—12.) "The hall of judg-"ment," (*Marg.*) or the prætorium, was a part of the Roman governor's palace; in which causes were generally decided, and perhaps some appendages of idolatry were seen there. The Jewish rulers therefore feared, lest they should contract ritual defilement if they went into it; and thus be prevented from eating of the sacrifices offered on the first day of unleavened bread, which were supposed to be an essential part of the feast of the passover. (*Marg. Ref.* a—d.—*Notes*, xiii. 18—30, *v.* 29. xix. 13—18. 2 *Chr.* xxx. 21—25. xxxv. 7—19. *Ex.* xlv. 18—25.) Thus they were scrupulous and zealous in externals; and were purposing to join in sacred ordinances; when they were trampling under foot every obligation of piety, justice, and mercy! (*Notes, Ps.* xxxv. 15, 16. *Is.* i. 10—15. *Matt.* xxiii. 23, 24.)—Pilate, however, condescended to humour them in their scruples; and therefore he went out to them, to demand what accusation they brought against Jesus.

33 Then Pilate entered into the judgment-hall again, and called Jesus, [m] and said unto him, Art thou [a] the King of the Jews?

34 Jesus answered him, [o] Sayest thou this thing of thyself, or did others tell it thee of me?

35 Pilate answered, [p] Am I a Jew? [q] Thine own nation and the chief priests have delivered thee unto me. [r] What hast thou done?

36 Jesus answered, [s] My kingdom is not of this world. If my kingdom were of this world, [t] then would my servants fight, that I should not be delivered to the Jews: but now is my kingdom not from hence.

37 Pilate therefore said unto him, Art thou a King then? Jesus answered,

[u] Thou sayest that I am a King. To this end was I born, and for this cause came I into the world, [x] that I should bear witness unto the truth. [y] Every one that is of the truth heareth my voice.

38 Pilate saith unto him, [z] What is truth? And when he had said this, he went out again unto the Jews, and saith unto them, [a] I find in him no fault at all.

39 But [b] ye have a custom, that I should release unto you one at the passover: will ye therefore that [c] I release unto you the King of the Jews?

40 Then [d] cried they all again, saying, Not this man, but Barabbas. Now Barabbas was a robber.

Marginal references (left column):

m 37. Matt. xxvii. 11. Mark xv. 2. Luke xxiii. 3, 4. 1 Tim. vi. 13.
n 1. 49. xii. 13. 15. ver. 3. 19—22. Ps. ii. 8—12. Is. ix. 6, 7. Jer. xxiii. 5, 6. Zeph. iii. 15. Zech. ix. 9. 1 Luke vii. 38 —40. Acts ii 34
o 36.
p Ezra iv. 12. Neh. iv. 2. Acts xviii. 14—16. xxiii. 20. xxv. 19, 20. Rom. iii. 1, 2.
q 28. ver. 11.
r xix. 6. Acts xxvi. 30. xxiii. 22—24. vi. 18. 19. Ps. xlv. 3—7. Is. ix. 6, 7. Dan. ii. 44. vii. 14. Zech. ix. 9, 10. Rom. xiv. 17. Col. i. 12—14. 1 Ti.

Marginal references (right column):

u Matt. xxvi. 64. xxvii. 11. Mark xiv. 62. xv. 2. Luke xxiii. 3. 1 Tim. vi. 13.
x viii. 14. xiv. 6. Is. lv. 4. Rev. i. 5. iii. 14.
y vii. 17. viii. 47. x. 26, 27. 1 Pet. i. 22, 23. 1 John iii. 14, 19. iv. 6.
z v. 20.
a Acts xvii. 19, 20.
a xix. 4. 6. 21, 22. Matt. xxvii. 24. Luke xxiii. 14. Luke xxiii. 4. 14—16. 1 Pet. i. 19. ii. 22, 23.
b —18. Mark xv. 6—15. Luke xxiii. 17. 20.
c 33.
d Matt. xxvii. 16. 20. Mark xv. 7. 15. Luke xxiii. 18, 19. 25. Acts iii. 13, 14.

He must have known many things respecting the character and reported miracles of Jesus; but he did not wish to interpose. The rulers, therefore, considered his question as an insinuation against their equity; and they replied with a degree of displeasure, that they would not have condemned him, and delivered him to be put to death, if he had not been a malefactor deserving of so heavy a punishment. (*Marg. Ref.* e, f.) Thus they in fact required Pilate to believe Jesus guilty, on their bare word; and without hesitation to give orders for his execution! But he, probably not approving of such a summary method of procedure, and not willing to interfere without necessity, and yet averse to giving them offence, desired them to settle the matter by their own authority, and to judge and punish Jesus by their own law. It is not agreed, how far the authority of the Jewish courts at this time extended: but it seems evident, that they were not allowed, except under some restrictions, to inflict capital punishment, without sanction from the Roman governor; and no other sentence could gratify their virulent malice against Jesus. Nor did they choose to interpret Pilate's permission as a warrant to put him to death; lest he or his successors should afterwards take some advantage of it against them. Thus the words of Jesus, concerning his being lifted up from the earth, and being crucified, were fulfilled: for if the Jews had put him to death, they would have stoned him as a blasphemer. (*Marg. Ref.*—*Notes*, iii. 14, 15. xii. 27—33, vv. 32, 33. *Matt.* xx. 17—19.)

The hall of judgment. (28) To πραιτωριον. 33. See on *Matt.* xxvii. 27.—*Early.*] Πρωια. xxi. 4. *Matt.* xxi. 18. xxvii. 1. Πρωι, xx. 1.—*They should be defiled.*] Μιανθωσι. *Tit.* i. 15. *Heb.* xii. 15. *Jude* 8.—*Lev.* v. 3. xi. 24. 43, 44. xviii. 24. *Sept.*—*A malefactor.* (30) Κακοποιος. 1 *Pet.* ii. 12. 14. iii. 16. iv. 15. Not elsewhere. Κακοποιω, *Luke* vi. 9. 1 *Pet.* iii. 17.

V. 33—36. After the rulers had acknowledged, that they had no authority to put any man to death, Pilate returned into the judgment-hall to examine Jesus more pri-

vately: probably induced by what he had heard of his character and conduct, and what he now witnessed of his meek, calm, and firm deportment. Especially he enquired, if indeed he avowed himself "the King of the Jews;" for this would be adjudged an act of treason against the Roman emperor. And when Jesus asked, whether he made this enquiry from his own opinion of his conduct; or merely because others had informed him, that he laid claim to this character; he replied, that he was no Jew, and knew nothing of their sentiments concerning the expected Messiah, with some disdain of the idea of being a Jew. The priests and rulers of his own nation were the persecutors of Jesus, and therefore Pilate desired to know, by what crimes he had excited their suspicion, or indignation. (*Marg. Ref.* m—x.) Jesus then intimated, that he was a King; but that his "kingdom was not of this world:" it had nothing to do with men's temporal interests or privileges; it left rulers and subjects in the same situation as it found them; and it was therefore no object of jealousy to any government. Had he claimed a kingdom of an earthly nature, he would of course have armed his followers, and they would have fought in his cause: but as his disciples had been few in number, inoffensive in their habits, and forbidden to fight for him, even when he was apprehended; it was evident that his kingdom was not of a secular nature, but related wholly to spiritual and heavenly things, and would be supported entirely by spiritual sanctions and authority. (*Marg. Ref.*—*Notes*, 10—14.)—The multitudes, that followed Christ when he entered Jerusalem, would have readily fought for him, if he had claimed a temporal kingdom: and they seem to have been set against him because he would not. (*Notes*, xii. 12—19. *Matt.* xxi. 1—11. xxvii. 19—23.)

Would ...fight. (36) Αν ... ηγωνιζοντο.—" Would have "striven" or contended. See on *Luke* xiii. 24.

V. 37—40. Pilate next asked, whether Jesus professed to be King in any sense. To which he answered, by assenting to Pilate's proposition, that he was a King, that is, of Israel: and he averred, that he was born for that

CHAP. XIX.

Jesus is scourged, crowned with thorns, and mocked by the soldiers, 1—3. Pilate declaring his innocence, the Jews charge him with calling himself the "Son of God," 4—7. Pilate, after further examination, desires to release him; but overcome with the clamours of the Jews, delivers him to be crucified, 8—16. He is led to Golgotha, and crucified between two robbers, 17, 18. The title placed over his cross, which Pilate refuses to alter, 19—22. The soldiers part his garments, 23, 24. Jesus affectionately commends his mother to the care of John, 25—27; and, receiving vinegar to drink, he expires, 28—30. The legs of the robbers are broken to hasten their death : but Jesus being previously dead, his side is pierced by a soldier, and thus the scriptures are fulfilled, 31—37. Joseph of Arimathea, assisted by Nicodemus, buries him, 38—42.

---

end; that he came into the world to bear witness to the truth of God, in this and every other particular ; and that every one who belonged to the truth, and was disposed to comply with it, heard and obeyed his voice ; though his nation in general rejected and opposed him. (*Marg. Ref.* u, x.—*Note,* 1 *Tim.* vi. 13—16, *v.* 13.)—This reply caused Pilate to exclaim, " What is truth ?" But it is not certain, whether he did it out of curiosity, or in derision, or from some impression of reverence to the character and behaviour of Jesus. As, however, he did not immediately answer ; he went out, declaring to the Jews his full conviction that Jesus was entirely innocent, as to the crimes of which he had been accused. Yet, since they had delivered him up as a malefactor, he proposed by a customary act of grace at that festival, to release to them their inoffensive King ; by which means the people would be satisfied ; and the rulers would be exempted from censure, for the part which they had taken in his prosecution. —But they all, both priests and rulers, and the people who had assembled on this occasion, clamorously preferred the robber Barabbas to him ! (*Marg. Ref. z—d.— Notes, Matt.* xxvii. 19—23. 26—31, *v. 26. Mark* xv. 6— 10. *Luke* xxiii. 13—25. *Acts* iii. 12—16.)—*Came I into the world.* (37) *Notes,* ix. 39—41, *v.* 39. x. 32—39. *v.* 36. xii. 44—50. xvi. 25—30. 1 *Tim.* i. 15, 16.—*Every one, &c.*] *Marg. Ref.* y.—*Note,* 1 *John* iii. 18—24.

Thou sayest, &c. (37) Συ λεγεις ὁτι. See on *Matt.* xxvi. 25.—*What is truth ?* (38) Τι εστιν αληθεια ; " What " thing is truth ? "—Not *What is truth ?* as to different opinions, enquiring which of them is true.—*A custom.* (39) Συνηθεια. 1 *Cor.* xi. 16. Not elsewhere.

PRACTICAL OBSERVATIONS.

V. 1—9.

Even the rancorous malice of our Lord's enemies did not render them more eager to apprehend and crucify him; than his love to perishing sinners made him ready to meet all those sufferings, which he knew were coming on him, that he might effect their salvation ! All the power of earth and hell could not, for a moment, have resisted his omnipotence, if he had seen good to exert it : (*Note,* x. 14—18 :) but he only alarmed, and did not injure, his assailants ; for that was the day of his patience and meekness, as our Surety and Example. Yet " the day of his " wrath " will come, when all who oppose, yea, all who do not obey, his gospel, shall be driven backward and perish for ever. (*Note,* 2 *Thes.* i. 5—10.) In the mean time he spares and warns his adversaries : yet neither his terror, nor his forbearance, will deter men in general from their purpose; or from pursuing worldly things, in contempt of his salvation, and in defiance of his vengeance.—But he most tenderly regards the temporal peace and safety, as

well as the eternal interests, of his faithful disciples : he proportions their trials to their strength ; nor will he ever require them to bear such sufferings for him, as he bare for them, or any at all comparable to them.

V. 10—32.

From the example of our Saviour we should learn, to receive our lighter afflictions, as " a cup which our Father " has given us to drink ; " and to resist every temptation to escape suffering by sin, or to murmur and despond under it ; by asking ourselves, whether we ought thus to oppose our Father's will, or to distrust his love.—Self-confident rashness is very different from the steady courage and patience of faith : and they, who most readily venture into temptation, are often most easily overcome by it.— The company of the profane and wicked men either corrupts or dismays those pious persons who are seduced into it ; and they soon forget their purposes and resolution, and conform to the humour, or try to shun the reproach, of their companions. We should therefore watch and pray against temptation, and get as far out of the way of them as we can : but humiliating experience of our own weakness is commonly necessary to teach us caution and attention to the words of Christ. As he suffered every insult for the sake of Peter, even when Peter was basely denying him ; so he foresaw all our unfaithfulness and ingratitude, at the time when he shed his blood for our sins! This consideration should not only encourage our hope in his boundless mercy, but also shame us out of our base requitals of so gracious a Benefactor.—The most perfect meekness, patience, and wisdom, of the Son of God, only served to increase the outrageous enmity of his persecutors ; and their base usage reciprocally illustrated his consummate excellency. This should teach us what to expect from the wicked, and how to behave towards them. (*Note* and *P. O.* 1 *Pet.* ii. 18—25.)—So blind are men in things pertaining to the acceptable worship and service of God, that they often expect to please him by exactness in externals, while they are deliberately perpetrating the basest iniquities! Nay, they hope to atone for their murders and oppressions, by *hypocritical* forms of godliness !—Those who are most scandalously unjust, frequently expect most credit for their strict regard to justice ; and are greatly affronted to be suspected of the least crime, whilst they are actually committing the greatest. (*Notes,* 2 *Sam.* xx. 8— 10. 20—22.) But the malice even of the worst of men is so over-ruled as to fulfil the words of Jesus, and to accomplish the wise and holy purposes of God.

V. 33—40.

We should always remember, that " the kingdom of " Christ is not of this world : " it cannot then be promoted

THEN *Pilate therefore took Jesus, and ᵇscourged him.

2 And ᶜthe soldiers platted a crown of thorns, and put it on his head, and they put on him a purple robe,

3 And said, ᵈHail, ᵉKing of the Jews! and they smote him with their hands.

4 Pilate therefore went forth again, and saith unto them, Behold, I bring him forth to you, ᶠthat ye may know that I find no fault in him.

5 Then came Jesus forth, wearing the crown of thorns, and the purple robe. And Pilate saith unto them, ᵍBehold the man!

6 When ʰthe chief priests therefore and officers saw him, they cried out, saying, Crucify him, crucify him. Pilate saith unto them, ⁱTake ye him, and crucify him; for I find no fault in him.

7 The Jews answered him, ᵏWe have a law, and by our law he ought to die, ˡbecause he made himself the Son of God.

*Matt. xxvii. 26. Mark xv. 15. Luke xxiii. 16.
ᵇPs. cxix. 3. Is. l. 6. lili. 5. Matt. xx. 19. xxiii. 34. Mark x. 38, 34. Luke xviii. 33. Acts xvi. 22, 23.
ᶜPs. xxii. 16. 2 Cor. xi. 24, 26. Heb. xi. 36. 1 Pet. ii. 24.
ᵈPs. xxii. 6. Is. xlix. 7. liii.
ᵉJohn i. 49.
Matt. xxvii. 27—31. Mark xv. 17—20. Luke xxiii. 11.
ᵈMatt. xxvi. 49.
xxvii. 26.
ᶠ19—22. xviii. 33.
ᵍ6. xviii. 38. Matt. 24. Luke xxiii. 41. 47. 2 Cor. v. 21. Heb. vii. 26. 1 Pet. i. 19. ii. 22. iii. 18. 1 John iii. 5.

ᵍl. 29. Is. vii. 14. xl. 9. xili. 1. Lam. l. 12.
Heb. xii. 2.
ʰ15. Matt. xxvii. 22, 23. Mark xv. 13—15. Luke xxiii. 21—23.
Acts ii. 22, 23. xiii. 27—29.
ⁱxviii. 31. Matt. xxvii. 24, 25.
ᵏLev. xxiv. 16. Deut. xviii. 20.
ˡv. 18. viii. 58. 59. x. 30—33. 36—38. Matt. xxvi. 63—65. xxvii. 42, 43. Mark xiv. 61—64. xv. 39. Rom. i. 4.

by carnal weapons or means of any kind, or by any party; nor accommodated to any temporal interests; and every attempt of this kind is inconsistent, unscriptural, and unholy. For our Saviour and King reigns in the heart and conscience of his true subjects: the princes of this world have nothing to fear from the obedience of Christians to his authority; nor does he need the countenance of their's, though he may see good sometimes to make use of it. His subjects are commanded to "render tribute to whom "tribute is due, and honour to whom honour;" to "sub-"mit to the powers that be;" to "fear God and the king, "and not to meddle with those who are given to change:" though at the same time, they must "obey God rather "than man," when man presumes to interfere out of his own province. It would greatly promote the credit of the gospel, if all the professed subjects of Christ, whilst they stand up for the right of liberty of conscience would be careful to render a conscientious obedience to these plain precepts in this matter. Then they would more resemble him, "who before Pontius Pilate witnessed a good con-"fession;" and prove themselves to be "of the truth," by hearing and obeying his voice.—But many profess to enquire after truth, who are not disposed to wait for an answer or to welcome that which is given by those, who " speak as the oracles of God." Numbers give Jesus and his people a good word, who will not join them, or venture any thing in his cause: numbers commit injustice for fear of their own dependants, and from a desire of popularity; and the majority of all ranks, even of nominal Christians, still in fact prefer Barabbas to Christ; so that it requires more constancy, than unregenerate men possess, to stem the torrent of impetuous wickedness. Let us, however, look to "the Lamb of God," in whom the Roman governor could "find no fault at all:" let us endeavour in the same manner to make all our accusers ashamed: let us never indulge prejudices against persons or doctrines, because multitudes decry them: and let us beware of deliberately sparing our lusts, (those robbers of God, and murderers of the soul,) and thus "crucifying "Christ afresh, and putting him to open shame."

scourged and crowned with thorns, in the exact order of time in which these events occurred. Perhaps Pilate hoped, that by severely scourging Jesus, and allowing the soldiers to treat him with cruel mockery, the rulers of the Jews might be induced to consent to his release: or, that the compassion of the multitude would be excited, and so they might be influenced to prefer him to Barabbas. He therefore brought him forth arrayed in a purple robe, and crowned with thorns, and probably covered with his own blood: and, having repeated his full conviction of his entire innocence, he said to them, "Behold the man:" (Marg. Ref. a—g:) 'Consider whether he be not rather an object of compassion or contempt, than of jealousy, envy, and hatred.' This is not mentioned in the other gospels, in which the next circumstance to that of the soldiers scourging and mocking Jesus is: "They took the " robe off from him, and put his own raiment on him, and " led him away to crucify him."—But the events here recorded, occurred after the mocking of Jesus by the soldiers, and before they took off the robe.—The rulers, however, were too full of enmity and malice to be moved by the spectacle; and perhaps fearing lest it should affect the common people differently, they and their attending officers, became still more clamorous in demanding his immediate crucifixion. This seems to have greatly displeased Pilate; and therefore he bade them take Jesus, "and crucify him:" seeing he found no fault in his whole conduct. 'If you ' will have it so, do it yourselves at your peril; for I cannot ' condemn a man without a fault.' Grotius. This reply induced them to add the charge of blasphemy, to that of rebellion against the Roman authority; that if Pilate would not condemn him as a traitor, he might consent to his death, as justly condemned for blasphemy by their law. (Marg. Ref. h—l.—Notes, v. 15, 16. viii. 54—59. x. 26—31, vv. 30, 31. Lev. xxiv. 10—16. Matt. xxvi. 63—68. xxvii. 54. Mark xiv. 60—65. Luke xxii. 68—71. Rom. i. 1—4.) This was indeed the supposed crime for which he suffered; though they could not but know, that the Messiah was expressly predicted under the title of "the Son " of God." (Notes, x. 32—39. Ps. ii. 7—12, vv. 7. 12. Heb. i. 5—9.)

They smote him with the palms of their hands. (3) Εδίδουν αυτῳ ῥαπισματα. See on xviii. 22. Mark xiv. 65.—Fault. (4) Αιτιαν. 6. xviii. 38. Matt. xix. 3. xxvii. 37. Acts xiii. 28. xxv. 18. 27.

NOTES

CHAP. XIX. V. 1—7. (Note, Matt. xxvii. 26—31. Mark xv. 11—20, v. 20.) John seems to record our Lord's being

4 u 2

8 When Pilate therefore ⁿ heard that saying, he was the more afraid;

9 And went again into the judgment-hall, and saith unto Jesus, ᵒ Whence art thou? ᵖ But Jesus gave him no answer.

10 Then saith Pilate unto him, Speakest thou not unto me? ᵠ knowest thou not that I have power to crucify thee, and have power to release thee?

11 Jesus answered, ʳ Thou couldest have no power *at all* against me, except it were given thee from above: therefore ˢ he that delivered me unto thee hath ᵗ the greater sin.

12 And ᵘ from thenceforth Pilate sought to release him: but the Jews cried out, saying, If thou let this man go, ˣ thou art not Cæsar's friend: whosoever maketh himself a king speaketh against Cæsar.

13 When Pilate therefore ʸ heard that saying, he brought Jesus forth, ᶻ and sat down in the judgment-seat, in a place that is called the Pavement, but in the Hebrew, Gabbatha.

14 And it was ᵃ the preparation of the passover, and about ᵇ the sixth hour: and he saith unto the Jews, ᶜ Behold your King!

15 But they cried out, ᵈ Away with *him*, away with *him*, crucify him. Pilate saith unto them, Shall I crucify your King? The chief priests answered, ᵉ We have no king but Cæsar.

16 Then ᶠ delivered he him therefore unto them to be crucified. And they took Jesus and led *him* away.

V. 8—12. It would be vain, and it is not needful, particularly to enquire what thoughts were excited in Pilate's mind, on this occasion. He seems, however, to have been impressed with an apprehension, that Jesus might probably be some extraordinary person, very high in favour with the superior powers; and that it would be dangerous to proceed further against him : and the mild dignity and gravity of his behaviour, amidst all the insults and cruelties which he experienced, might tend to confirm this opinion. (*Note, Matt.* xxvii. 19—23.) He therefore said unto Jesus, "Whence art thou?" of earthly or of heavenly origin? But our Lord gave him no answer. Pilate was no competent judge in a question of this kind: and his unjust conduct, in allowing such cruelties to be exercised on a person whom he knew to be innocent, rendered him unworthy of further regard. The silence of our Lord, however, seems to have astonished and displeased Pilate; who haughtily enquired how it was that he refused to speak to him, when he knew that he had an unrestrained authority, either to order him to immediate crucifixion, or to release him. (*Note, Matt.* xxvii. 11—18.) Jesus therefore shewed him, that he had this power from above, even from the God of heaven, and would be called to an account for his use of it; nor indeed could he at all have employed it against him, if God had not for wise reasons seen good to permit it. (*Marg. Ref.* m—q.—*Notes,* iii. 27—36, *v.* 27. *Ex.* ix. 13—17. *Ps.* lxii. 11, 12, lxxvi. 10. *Matt.* vi. 13.) There was a peculiar propriety in stating this general truth, when the application of it was made to the Lord of life and glory, now delivered up into the hands of an idolater, who was about to abuse his authority by condemning him to be crucified.—As our Lord suffered for the sins of both Jews and gentiles; it was a special part of the counsel of infinite wisdom, that the Jews should first purpose his death, and that the Gentiles should carry that purpose into execution.—But, though Pilate was about to contract very great guilt by condemning him; Caiaphas, who at the head of the Jewish council had delivered up the promised Messiah into the hands of idolaters, had much deeper criminality: as his situation enabled him to know far more of the true God and his law, as well as to have more acquaintance with the doctrine and miracles of Jesus; and as the conduct of the high priest, and all concerned with him in that prosecution, resulted from far more determinate enmity to the truth, holiness, and authority of God, than Pilate's did. This answer, however, was a solemn warning to Pilate to beware what he did in such a case : and he seems to have understood and felt it in some degree; so that he became the more desirous to release him. (*Marg. Ref.* r—t.)—But the rulers, finding that their last accusation rather obstructed, than forwarded, the completion of their design, endeavoured next to terrify Pilate into compliance, by declaring that he could not be sincerely attached to the interests of the Roman emperor, if he neglected to punish a man, who, -by aspiring to the kingdom, must be deemed Cæsar's competitor and enemy. The jealous tyranny and cruelty of Tiberius Cæsar, who was then emperor, are well known; and Pilate, probably fearing lest some spies should carry an accusation against him to Rome, immediately yielded to their injustice. (*Marg. Ref.* u.)—' Pilate's conscience fighteth for Christ : but ' straightway it yieldeth ; because it is not upholden by the ' singular power of God.' *Beza.* (*Notes, Prov.* xxix. 25, 26. *Matt.* x. 27, 28. 1 *John* v. 4, 5.)—' This chiefly moved ' him, because, as Tacitus and Suetonius observe, Tiberius ' was apt to suspect the worst: and the least crimes with ' him made a man guilty of death, if they related to the ' government. Pilate durst not therefore venture that this ' charge should be laid against him by the Jews.' *Whitby.*

Given from above. (11) Δεδομενον ανωθεν. *Jam.* i. 17. iii. 15. 17. Δεδομενον εκ τη ωρανε, iii. 27.—*Dan.* iv. 17. 25. 32. *Sept.*—*Note, Rom.* xiii. 1, 2, *v.* 1.—*Speaketh against Cæsar.* (12) Αντιλεγει τω Καισαρι. He is Anti-Cæsar. (*Note,* 1 *John* iv. 1—4.)

V. 13—18. (*Notes, Matt.* xxvii. 24, 25. 32—35. *Luke* xxiii. 26—31.) Pilate having ascended his tribunal, which was not in the judgment-hall, but in a more publick place called " the pavement," or " Gabbatha," proceeded to

4 H 3

f Matt. x. 38. xvi. 24. xxvii. 32. Mark viii. 34. x. 21. xv. 21. Luke ix. 23. xiv. 27. xxiii. 26.
g Lev. xvi. 21, 22. Num. xxiv. 14. 1 Kings xxi. 13. Luke xxiii. 33. Acts vii. 58. Heb. xiii. 11—13.
h Matt. xxvii. 33. Mark xv. 21.
i xviii. 32. Ps. xxii. 16. Is. liii. 12. Matt. xxvii. 35—38. Mark xv. 27. Luke xxiii. 32—34. Gal. iii. 13. Heb. xii. 2.
k Matt. xxvii. 37. Mark xv. 26. Luke xxiii. 38.
l 3. 12. i. 45, 46. 49. xviii. 38. Acts iii. 6. xxvi. 9.

17 And he ᶠbearing his cross ᵍwent forth into a place called *the place* of a skull, which is called in the Hebrew ʰGolgotha;

18 Where ⁱthey crucified him, and two other with him, on either side one, and Jesus in the midst.

19 ¶ And Pilate ᵏwrote a title, and put *it* on the cross. And the writing was, ˡJESUS OF NAZARETH THE KING OF THE JEWS.

20 This title then read many of the Jews; for the place where Jesus was crucified was nigh to the city; and it

m 13. v. 2. Acts xxvi. 46. xxii. 9. xvi. 14. Rev. xvi. 16.
n Acts xxi. 37. Rev. ix. 11.

was written ᵐin Hebrew, ⁿ*and* Greek, *and* Latin.

21 Then said the chief priests of the Jews to Pilate, Write not, The King of the Jews: but that he said, I am King of the Jews.

22 Pilate answered, ᵒWhat I have written, I have written.

23 Then ᵖthe soldiers, when they had crucified Jesus, took his garments, and made four parts, to every soldier a part; and also *his* coat: now the coat was without seam, ᵠwoven from the top throughout.

o 12. Ps. lxv. 7. lxxvi. 10. Prov. viii. 29.
p Matt. xxvii. 35. Mark xv. 24. Luke xxiii. 34.
q Or, wrought. Ex. xxxix. 22, 23.

---

pass sentence on Jesus. The Evangelist observes, that "it was the preparation of the Passover," or the day before the solemn sabbath, which occurred on the second day of unleavened bread; (*Marg. Ref.* z.—*Notes,* 31—37. *Lev.* xxiii. 5—8;) for which the people ought to have been making preparation, though many of them were far otherwise employed.—It was also "about the *sixth* hour." As there is no reason to think that St. John computed time in a different manner from the other Evangelists; as six o'clock, (according to the Roman computation,) or soon after sun-rise, must have been much too early for all the events which preceded our Lord's crucifixion to have occurred that morning; as St. Mark has expressly mentioned the third hour, or nine o'clock, for the time of that event, to which the accounts of the other Evangelists accord; (*Note, Mark* xv. 25;) and as the sixth hour or noon, (according to the Jewish computation,) would be too late to agree with the parallel Scriptures: so it seems the most easy way of solving the difficulty, to suppose that *sixth,* instead of *third,* was inserted by some of the early transcribers of this gospel. The mistake would be very trivial, and very easily fallen into; and in a few places it is necessary to allow that something of this kind has happened. Indeed some manuscripts read "the third hour." Pilate, however, again pointed out the suffering Jesus to the implacable Jews, saying, "Behold your King!" perhaps in scorn of them; as if a King crowned with thorns, and covered with stripes, befitted such a people. When they still persisted in demanding his crucifixion; he asked them, whether he should "crucify their King:" and though, on other occasions, they had many doubts and objections, even concerning the lawfulness of submitting, or paying tribute, to the Roman emperor; yet to gratify their malice, they at once exclaimed, that they had "no "king but Cæsar." (*Note, Gen.* xlix. 10.) Upon which Pilate, perhaps deeming this concession, from so turbulent a people, of considerable importance, got over all his scruples, and delivered up Jesus to be crucified. (*Marg. Ref.* b—i.)—'Josephus ... expressly assures us, that Pilate ' having slain a considerable number of seditious Samari-' tans, was deposed from his government by Vitellius, and ' sent to Tiberius at Rome, who died before he arrived ' there And Eusebius tells us, ... that quickly after, (hav-' ing, as others say, been banished to Vienne, in Gaul,) he ' laid violent hands on himself, falling on his own sword

' Agrippa, who was an eye-witness to many of his enormi-' ties, speaks of him in his oration to Caius Cæsar, as one ' who had been a man of a most infamous character. ... ' Probably, the accusations of other Jews, following him, ' had before that proved his destruction.' *Doddridge.*

The pavement. (13) Λιθοςρωτον. Here only N. T.—2 *Chr.* vii. 3. *Esth.* i. 6. *Cant.* iii. 10. Sept. Ex λιθος *lapis,* et ςρωτος à ςρωννυμι, *sterno.* Some think, that it was so called from a curious piece of Mosaick work which adorned it.—*Gabbatha.*] A תג, *altum esse: an elevated place.*

V. 19—22. (*Marg. Ref.* k—n.—*Note, Matt.* xxvii. 37, 38.) The three languages, in which this inscription was written, were more generally understood than any other at that time; and most persons present would be capable of reading it in some one of them: so that this was, in fact, to publish to the nations of the earth that Jesus the Nazarene was the King of Israel, the expected Messiah. It is not therefore wonderful that it gave umbrage to the Jewish rulers; as it seemed to imply, that they had enviously and maliciously persecuted to death their promised Messiah: and probably Pilate intended it as a reflection upon them. He was, however, so put out of humour, by being compelled to condemn an innocent man contrary to his judgment and conscience, that he would not gratify them, in allowing the inscription to be altered; which was doubtless owing to a secret power of God upon his heart, in order that this attestation of our Lord's character and authority might continue.—Perhaps the open insults, which the chief priests and rulers used, as Jesus hung upon the cross, might in part be intended, by ridiculing his pretensions, to counteract the effects of this inscription, on the minds of the people. (*Marg. Ref.* n, o.—*Notes, Ps.* xxii. 11—15. lxix. 16—21. *Matt.* xxvii. 32—44. *Mark* xv. 29—32.)— *Was near the city.* (20) The place of our Lord's crucifixion and sepulture, as shewn to travellers at present, is *within* the city. If then the right place be shewn, as it seems probable, the site of Jerusalem must have been considerably altered in the lapse of so many ages.

V. 23, 24. (*Marg. Ref.*—*Notes, Ps.* xxii. 16—18. *Matt.* xxvii. 35, 36.) It is not, I believe, clearly known, in what way a garment was so formed in the loom, as to need no seam in any part of it. Very probably, this vesture was the work of some of those women, who ministered to our Lord; and it seems to have been considered, as both curious and valuable.

4 υ 4

24 They said therefore among themselves, Let us not rend it, but cast lots for it, whose it shall be: ᵗ that the scripture might be fulfilled, which saith, ʳ They parted my raiment among them, and for my vesture they did cast lots. These things therefore the soldiers did.

25 ¶ Now there stood by the cross of Jesus, ˢ his mother, ᵗ and his mother's sister, Mary *the wife* of ˣ Cleophas, ᵘ and Mary Magdalene.

26 When Jesus therefore saw his mother, and the disciple standing by ˣ whom he loved, he saith unto his mother, ʸ Woman, behold thy son!

27 Then saith he to the disciple, ᶻ Behold thy mother! And from that hour that disciple ᵃ took her unto ᵇ his own *home*.

28 ¶ After this, ᶜ Jesus knowing that all things were now accomplished, ᵈ that the scripture might be fulfilled, saith, I thirst.

29 Now there ᵉ was set a vessel full of vinegar: and they filled a sponge with vinegar, and put *it* upon ᶠ hyssop, and put *it* to his mouth.

30 When Jesus therefore had received the vinegar, he said, ᵍ It is finished: ʰ and he bowed his head, and gave up the ghost.

31 The Jews therefore, ⁱ because it was the preparation, ᵏ that the bodies should not remain upon the cross on the sabbath-day, (for ˡ that sabbath day was an high day,) besought Pilate that ᵐ their legs might be broken, and *that* they might be taken away.

32 Then came the soldiers, and brake the legs ⁿ of the first, and of the other which was crucified with him.

33 But when they came to Jesus,

Marginal references:

ᵗ 24. 36, 37. x. 36. xii. 18, 23.
ʳ Ps. xxii. 18. z. 7. Acts xiii. 27.
ˢ Luke ii. 35. ᵗ Matt. xxvii. 55. Mark xv. 40. Luke xxiii. 49.
ˣ Or, Clopas. Luke xxiv. 18.
ˣ xx. 1. 11—18. Mark xvi. 9. Luke viii. 2. z xiii. 23. xxi. 7. 20. 24.
ʸ Gen. xlv. 8. Gen. xlvi. 12. Matt. xii. 46—50. xxv. Mark iii. 34. 35. 1 Tim. v. 3.
ᵃ 1 John iii. 18. 19.
ᵇ xx. 10. xiii. 1. xvi. 32.
ᶜ 4. 32. Luke ix. 51. xii. 50. xviii. 31. xxii. 37. Acts xiii. 29.

ᵈ Ps. xxii. 15. lxix. 2.
ᵉ Matt. xxvii. 34. 48. Mark xv. 36. Luke xxiii. 36.
ᶠ Ex. xii. 22. Num. xix. 18. 1 Kings iv. 33. Ps. li. 7.
ᵍ 28. Gr. iv. 34. Gen. iii. 15. Ps. xxii. 15. 16. Is. liii. 12. Dan. ix. 24, 26. Zech. xiii. 7. Matt. iii. 15.
ʰ Rom. iii. 25, 26. x. 4. 1 Cor. v. 7, 8. Col. ii. 14—17. Heb. ix. 11—14. 22—28. x. 1—14. xii. 2.
ⁱ x. 11. 18. Matt. xx. 28. xxvii. 50. Mark xv. 37. Luke xxiii. 46. Phil. ii. 8. Heb. ii. 14, 15.
ᵏ Deut. xxi. 22, 23.
ˡ Lev. xxiii. 7—14.
ᵐ Matt. xxvii. 62. Mark xv. 42.
ⁿ 1 Prov. xii. 10. Mic. iii. 3.
ᵒ 18. Luke xxiii. 39—43.

Without seam. (23) Αρραφος. Here only. Ex α priv. et ραπτω, *suo, consuo.—Woven.*] Υφαντος. Here only. Ab υφαινω, *texo.*

V. 25—27. (*Marg.* and *Marg. Ref.* t, u.) The inward anguish, and the conflicting thoughts and affections, with which the mind of Mary must have been agitated, on this most distressing occasion, can never be described or imagined. (*Note, Luke* ii. 33—35.) But, considering all the expectations excited by the conception, birth, and infancy of Jesus, and all the miracles, and other extraordinary circumstances of his publick ministry, she could scarcely doubt, even when she saw him expire on the cross, that he was the promised "Messiah, the King of Israel." (*Notes, Matt.* i. 18—25. ii. *Luke* i. 26—45. ii.) After Joseph's death, and our Lord's entrance on his ministry, it is probable that Mary had generally attended him: and being now present to behold his crucifixion, Jesus, amidst all his own sufferings, was tenderly mindful of her; and by turning her attention to John, the beloved disciple, as one who would be as a son to her, and whom she should love, for his sake, as her own son; and by mentioning her to him as his " *mother*," to whom he was to perform the duty of that relation for *his* sake; he effectually influenced John to take her to him, and to provide for her, and treat her with all respect and affection, as long as she lived. (*Marg. Ref.* x—z.—*Notes*, xi. 1—5. *Matt.* xii. 46—50.) How long that was, or where John from that time resided, we are not informed in Scripture; and history gives us little information, which can be depended on.

Woman. (26) Γυναι. See on ii. 4.—*His own* home. (27) Τα ιδια. See on xvi. 32.

V. 28—30. All our Lord's expiatory sufferings were now on the very point of being finished; but in order to the fulfilment of some other scriptures, he said, " I " thirst:" and his exquisite torture, fatigue, and heat, doubtless caused his thirst to be very intense. (*Notes, Ps.* xxii. 14, 15. lxix. 21.) Probably this was immediately after

he had cried out, " Eli, Eli, &c." for this evangelist generally records other *circumstances* even of the same *events*, than the others do: and so this word, " I thirst," induced some present to offer him vinegar; while others waited to see whether Elias would come to save him. (*Marg. Ref.* c—f.—*Notes, Matt.* xxvii. 32—34. 46—50. *Mark* xv. 34—39. *Luke* xxiii. 44—49.)—When Jesus, by receiving and tasting the vinegar, had accomplished these predictions also, he said, " It is finished." All that the prophets had foretold; all that the types prefigured; all that the justice of God required, as an atonement for sin, in order to the reconciliation of sinners to himself; all that the honour of his law and government demanded; and whatever was necessary for the glory of all the divine perfections, in man's salvation, was now completely finished: and so was the victory over Satan, sin, the world, and death, as far as our Lord's personal obedience and sufferings were concerned.—Probably, the inward darkness and anguish, which began to oppress our Lord's mind in the garden, at this moment were finally dispersed; and thus he expired in the clear perception and full enjoyment of the light of his Father's countenance. (*Marg. Ref.* g, h.—*Note, Matt.* xxvi. 36—39.)

Hyssop. (29) Ὑσσωπῳ. *Heb.* ix. 19. Not elsewhere—*It is finished.* (30) Τετελισται. 28, rendered " were accomplished."—*Matt.* xi. 1. *Luke* xii. 50. xviii. 31. xxii. 37. *Acts* xiii. 29. 2 Tim. iv. 7. *Rev.* xi. 7. xv. 1. 8. xx. 3.—*Gave up the ghost.*] Παρεδωκε το πνευμα. See on *Matt.* xxvii. 50.

V. 31—37. The law of Moses required that the bodies of such malefactors, as were hanged on a tree, should be taken down the same day; (*Note, Deut.* xxi. 22, 23;) and, though the Romans frequently left the bodies of those whom they crucified, upon their crosses, till they were consumed, or devoured by birds of prey; yet they seem to have generally allowed the Jews to bury such as belonged to them, when it was certain that they were dead; which sometimes

4 ᴺ 5

and saw that he was dead already, they brake not his legs.

34 But one of the soldiers with a spear pierced his side, and forthwith came thereout blood and water.

35 And he that saw it bare record, and his record is true; and he knoweth that he saith true, that ye might believe.

36 For these things were done, that the scripture should be fulfilled, A bone of him shall not be broken.

37 And again another scripture saith, They shall look on him whom they pierced.

38 ¶ And after this, Joseph of Arimathea, being a disciple of Jesus, but secretly for fear of the Jews, besought Pilate that he might take away the body of Jesus: and Pilate gave *him* leave. He came therefore and took the body of Jesus.

39 And there came also Nicodemus, which at the first came to Jesus by night, and brought a mixture of myrrh and aloes, about an hundred pound *weight*.

40 Then took they the body of Jesus, and wound it in linen clothes with the spices, as the manner of the Jews is to bury.

41 Now in the place where he was crucified there was a garden; and in the garden a new sepulchre, wherein was never man yet laid.

42 There laid they Jesus therefore, because of the Jews' preparation-*day*; for the sepulchre was nigh at hand.

---

was not till the next day, or even later. But the rulers (though not deterred from their most iniquitous and murderous purpose, by the sacred festival which they were celebrating,) were averse to the bodies continuing on the crosses during the next day; as this was both the first sabbath after the passover, and the second day of unleavened bread, from which the seven weeks till the pentecost were reckoned: and also the day for presenting the first fruits of a sheaf of corn: and so it was a day of peculiar solemnity, which the people were preparing to observe with great exactness. (*Marg. Ref.* i—l.—*Notes*, 13—18. *Matt.* xxvii. 62—66. *Luke* vi. 1.) They therefore besought Pilate, to give orders that their legs might be broken, in order that they might be removed. This was sometimes done, from a sort of compassion, to hasten the death of those who lingered very long in their sufferings; but surely a speedier method of terminating their torture might have been devised! The soldiers, however, broke the legs of the two malefactors, who were still living: and thus they were instrumental to the fulfilment of our Lord's promise to the penitent thief, that he should "that day be with him in " paradise." (*Note, Luke* xxiii. 39—43.) But finding Jesus evidently dead, they broke not his legs: yet one of them, in a contemptuous and inhuman manner, thrust his spear into his side, from whence flowed a stream of blood and water, evidently distinguishable from each other. Probably, the pericardium was pierced; but. however the circumstance may be accounted for, it is allowed to have been a decisive evidence of his being actually dead: and thus the soldier's conduct was over-ruled, to take away all pretences to the contrary, by which his enemies might otherwise have attempted to invalidate the reality of his resurrection. (*Mark* xv. 44.)—The evangelist himself was an eye-witness of this transaction, and he recorded it from his own knowledge as indisputable truth; that all who read his testimony, may believe in the crucified Redeemer. For these circumstances were accomplishments of ancient types and prophecies concerning the Messiah. (*Marg. Ref.* r.—*Notes, Ex.* xii. 46. *Ps.* xxxiv. 19, 20. *Zech.* xii. 9—14, v. 10.) —It can scarcely be doubted, that the only wise God had some special design, in commanding that no bone of the paschal lamb should be broken, though all must of course be dislocated. This had such a special reference to Christ, that St. John marks it as a matter of importance. Perhaps this may intimate, that as the *natural* body of Christ, after all his tortures, was, so preserved by a special providence, that no bone was broken, but the whole was found entire at his resurrection; so the members of the *mystical* body of Christ, whatever sufferings and temptations they pass through, shall be preserved by divine grace from essential detriment; none shall be wanting, but all shall be forthcoming, complete and entire, at " the resurrection of the just." (*Note*, vi. 36—40.)—It is evident likewise, that the apostle considered the blood and water as emblems of the distinct parts of salvation; namely, the pardon of our sins through the atoning blood of Christ, and the cleansing of our hearts by the sanctification of the Holy Spirit, which is conferred on us through the obedience unto death of our divine Saviour; and of which, indeed, the ordinances of Baptism and the Lord's supper are signs, memorials, and pledges. (*Marg. Ref.* o—q.—*Note*, 1 *John* v. 6.)

A bone, &c. (36) Not exactly from the LXX, but agrees with it in meaning.—Εν εξ αυτων ου τριβησεται, *Ps.* xxxiv. 20. *Sept. Note, Ps.* xxxiv. 19, 20.—*They shall look*, &c.] Wholly different from the LXX, but a literal translation of the Hebrew, except as *him* is substituted for *me*.—' What ' the Romans did at the instigation of the Jews, is fitly as- ' cribed to the Jews themselves.' *Whitby.*—*The preparation.* (31) Παρασκευη. (Εx παρα et σκευος, *vas. instrumentum*.) 14. 42. *Matt.* xxvii. 62. *Mark* xv. 42. *Luke* xxiii. 54. Παρασκευαζω, *Acts* x. 10.—*Might be broken*.] Καϊεαγωσιν. 32, 33. *Matt.* xii. 20. Not elsewhere.—*A spear*. (34) Λογχη. Here only.—*Pierced*] Ενυξε. Here only. Καϊανυσσω, *Acts* ii. 37.—*Be broken*. (36) Συνϊριβησεται. *Matt.* xii. 20. *Mark* v. 4. xiv. 3. *Luke* iv. 18. ix. 39. *Rom.* xvi. 20. *Rev.* ii. 27.—*Ex.* xii. 46. *Num.* ix. 12. *Ps.* xxxiv. 20. *Sept.* —*They pierced*. (37) Εξεκυντησαν. *Rev.* i. 7. Not elsewhere.

V. 38—42. *Marg. Ref.*—*Notes, Matt.* xxvii. 57—61. *Mark* xv. 42—47. *Luke* xxiii. 50—56.—*An hundred*

CHAP. XX.

Mary Magdalene goes to the sepulchre, and, discovering that the stone was taken away, runs to tell Peter and John; who hasten thither, and find not the body, but only the grave-clothes in exact order, 1—10. Mary as she weeps sees two angels, and afterwards Jesus, who sends her to inform the apostles, 11—18. Jesus meets them, as assembled in the evening, and speaks peace to them, 19—23. Thomas, who was absent, remains resolutely incredulous, 24, 25. Jesus again meets the assembled disciples, and satisfies Thomas, who confesses him, as " his Lord, and his God," 26—29. " These things were written, that we " might believe, and ... have life through his name," 30, 31.

pound. (39) ' This was an indication, not only of the ' wealth, but also of the great affection of Nicodemus to ' the blessed Jesus. Hence also, they not only anoint ' him, as they commonly used to do others; but bury him ' with so great a mixture of spices, as was done at the ' funerals of great men. So Jacob was embalmed after ' the Egyptian manner, (Gen. l. 2,) and Asa with spices ' and sweet odours. (2 Chr. xvi. 14.)' Whitby. (Notes, iii. 1, 2. vii. 40—53, vv. 50—52.)—' That his grave should ' be appointed with the wicked, (which was the case of ' those who suffered as criminals,) but that he should be ' " with the rich in his death," are circumstances which ' before they happened, were very improbable should ever ' concur in the same person.' Campbell. (Note, Is. liii. 9, 10.)

A mixture. (39) Μιγμα. Here only. Μιγνυμι, *Luke* xiii. 1.—*Pound.*] Λιτραζ. See on xii. 3.—*To bury.* (40) Ενταφιαζιν. See on *Matt.* xxvi. 12.

PRACTICAL OBSERVATIONS.

V. 1—16.

The conflict between convictions and corrupt affections, in unconverted minds, is often strong: but where faith is wanting, the world will get the victory; and the dread of reproach or loss, or the hope of secular advantages will induce them to venture the wrath of God, and all its tremendous consequences. (*P. O. Matt.* xxvii. 19—25. Notes, *Acts* xxiv. 24—27. xxvi. 24—29.)—Every one is inexcusable, who commits known injustice, or deliberately acts contrary to his conscience, on whatever account: but the greater opportunities men possess of knowing the truth and will of God, the more aggravated will their guilt be found, in rebelling against the light. (*Notes, Matt.* xi. 20—24. *Luke* xii. 47, 48.) Yet persons thus favourably distinguished, have often been most desperately engaged in opposing the power of godliness, and persecuting those, whose doctrine and example tended to detect their hypocrisy and usurpations.—All those rulers of every description, who have proudly sat in judgment on Christ and his servants, and condemned them, will soon stand before his tribunal; where they will " know the power of his wrath," and be constrained to confess with terror and anguish, that " Truly this was the Son of God." (*Note, Rev.* i. 7. vi. 15—17.)

V. 17—30.

We cannot wholly pass over this narrative of our Redeemer's crucifixion, without again reflecting, for a moment, on the complicated cruelties and indignities, to which he was exposed, and not for any fault of his own, nay directly contrary to his deservings. But he was wounded and scourged, that we might be healed; he was arrayed with scorn in the purple robe, that he might procure for us sinners " the robe of righteousness and salvation;" he was crowned with thorns, that we might be " crowned with " honour and immortality;" he stood speechless, that we might have an all-prevailing plea; he endured torture, that we might have " a strong consolation;" he thirsted, that we might drink of the waters of life; he bore the wrath of the Father, that we might enjoy his favour; he " was numbered with transgressors," that we might be made " equal to angels;" he died, that we might live for ever!—Let us then often retire to survey this scene, and to admire his immeasurable love; that we may learn to mourn for sin, and hate it, and rejoice in our obligations to the Redeemer; and that we may be " constrained by " love to live no longer to ourselves, but to him who died " for us and rose again." (*Note*, 2 *Cor.* v. 13—15.)—As we ought to hear with thankful exultation, that the ransom and righteousness of our souls were perfected, when Jesus said " It is finished;" so we should be excited to redouble our diligence, that the work of sanctifying grace may be powerfully carried on towards perfection in our hearts. For we should look to him as our King, as well as our High Priest.—In every way, it has been decidedly written, and the writing shall never be reversed, " that Jesus of Naza- " reth is the King" of the church and of the world; and all, who profess his religion, and " will not have him to " reign over them," will be deemed guilty of " crucifying " their King," with indignity and contempt.—We may be encouraged by our Lord's attention to his deeply afflicted mother, when he hung upon the cross, to hope for his condescending pity in all our sorrows and distresses, now that he is exalted to the throne : but we may also learn, that the surest interest in his love will not secure our exemption from the sharpest temporal sufferings. His example likewise teaches all men to honour their parents, in every circumstance of life and death; to provide for their wants; and to promote their comfort, by every means in their power : and we ought also to shew our love to Jesus, by behaving with courteous respect, affection, and liberal kindness to the poorest and meanest of those whom he loves, and who love him. We ought indeed to act towards them as though they were our most honoured and endeared relatives; and we heard Jesus say to us, from his cross, and from his throne of glory, concerning this and the other poor and afflicted believer, " Behold my mother," " my " brother," " my sister;" and, " Whatsoever ye do unto " the least of these, ... ye do it unto me." (*P. O. Matt.* xii. 38—50. xxv. 31—40. Mark iii. 20—35.)

V. 31—42.

The tender mercies of the wicked, and especially of persecutors, are cruel : but the preparation of hypocrites for religious ordinances, by the commission of the most horrible crimes, is the most detestable of abominations. Yet believers, if called to witness such scenes, should pecu-

THE *first *day* of the week [b] cometh Mary Magdalene early, when it was yet dark, unto the sepulchre, and seeth [c] the stone taken away from the sepulchre.

2 Then she runneth, and cometh to Simon Peter, and [d] to the other disciple whom Jesus loved, and saith unto them, [e] They have taken away the Lord out of the sepulchre, and we know not where they have laid him.

3 Peter [f] therefore went forth, and that other disciple, and came to the sepulchre.

4 So they ran both together: and the other disciple did [g] out-run Peter, and came first to the sepulchre.

5 And he, stooping down, *and looking in,* [h] saw the linen clothes lying; yet went he not in.

6 Then [i] cometh Simon Peter following him, and went into the sepulchre, and seeth the linen clothes lie,

7 And the napkin that was about his head, not lying with the linen clothes, but wrapped together in a place by itself.

8 Then went in also that other disciple, which came first to the sepulchre, [k] and he saw, and believed.

9 For as yet [l] they knew not the scripture, [m] that he must rise again from the dead.

10 Then the disciples [n] went away again unto their own home.

11 ¶ But Mary stood without at the sepulchre weeping: and as she wept, she stooped down, *and looked* into the sepulchre;

12 And [o] seeth two angels [p] in white

---

liarly observe, how God over-rules every thing to fulfil his own word. Thus, comparing the sacred oracles with the events which occur in the church and in the world, our faith will be increased even by the most discouraging transactions. May we then continually look to him, whom by our sins we also have, ignorantly and heedlessly, nay sometimes against convictions and mercies, pierced; and who shed from his wounded side both water and blood, that we may have "might be washed, and sanctified, and justified, " in his name, and by the Spirit of our God." (*Note*, 1 *Cor.* vi. 9—11.) Thus our hearts will be habitually affected with penitent sorrow and humiliation for sin, believing hope, and lively gratitude: and prepared for every service to which we are called. In this way, feeble, unestablished, and timorous believers will grow in grace, in knowledge, in stability, and boldness; and so be prepared to avow their relation to Jesus, in the time of extreme danger and difficulty: though they perhaps have formerly hesitated to confess him before men, when it might have been done with comparative safety.

NOTES.

CHAP. XX. V. 1—10. (*Marg. Ref.* a, b.—*Notes*, *Matt.* xxviii. 1—8. *Mark* xvi. 1—8. *Luke* xxiv. 1—12.) Mary Magdalene seems to have arrived at the sepulchre before any of the other women, " when it was yet dark " (1); and finding the stone removed, she hastened back to inform Peter and John, that some persons had " taken " away the Lord out of the sepulchre;" and, as she and her friends knew not " where they had laid him," they were deprived of the opportunity of shewing their respect and affection, by embalming his body. It is very improbable that she should speak thus, if she had seen an angel informing her that Jesus was risen; (*Matt.* xxviii. 5, 6;) and therefore she doubtless was at the sepulchre apart from the other women.—Peter and John, however, hearing her report, set out together to the sepulchre, running as a spee-

dily as they could, in the eagerness of their minds, on this interesting, and to them perplexing occasion; but the latter, probably being the younger man, arrived there first, and, looking in, he saw the linen clothes lie, yet entered not in, perhaps being afraid. Soon after, Peter came up, and, according to the promptitude of his disposition, he entered into the sepulchre without hesitation; and found the grave-clothes laid in such regular order, as evinced that neither friends nor foes had taken away the body in a hasty manner, as fearing interruption or detection. Doubtless this, and several other things connected with our Lord's resurrection, were performed by the ministration of angels. (*Matt.* iv. 11.)—Upon this John also entered in; and, from what he saw, he was inwardly convinced that Jesus was risen; though neither he nor Peter had understood from the scripture, or from the words of Christ, that the Messiah would rise again from the dead. (*Marg. Ref.* c—m.—*Notes*, *Mark* ix. 30—32. *Luke* ix. 45. xxiv. 25—31. 44—49.) The apostles, however, having made their observations, returned to their company, to wait the event of these extraordinary occurrences; John, convinced that his beloved Lord was indeed risen, and Peter full of astonishment and uncertainty.

The Lord. (2) Τον Κυριον. 25. xxi. 7. 12. *Matt.* xxi. 3. xxviii. 6. *Mark* xi. 3. *Luke* ii. 11. *Acts* x. 36. 1 *Cor.* xv. 47.—*Did out-run.* (4) Προεδραμε. *Luke* xix. 4. Not elsewhere.—*Stooping down.* (5) Παρακυψας. 11. *Luke* xxiv. 12. *Jam.* i. 25. 1 *Pet.* i. 12.—*Linen clothes.* (6) Οθονια. 7. xix. 40. *Luke* xxiv. 12.—*The napkin.* (7) Σουδαριον. xi. 44. *Luke* xix. 20. *Acts* xix. 12.—*Wrapped.*] Εντετυλιγμενον. See on *Matt.* xxvii. 59.—*Unto their own home.* (10) Προς εαυτους. To the other disciples, or to some lodging: for their home was in Galilee. Προς τις ιδιας, *Acts* iv. 23.—See on xix. 27.

V. 11—18. Mary Magdalene, who had followed the apostles, oppressed with the most inconsolable sorrow,

sitting, the one at the head, and the other at the feet, where the body of Jesus had lain.

13 And they say unto her, Woman, why weepest thou? She saith unto them, Because they have taken away my Lord, and I know not where they have laid him.

14 And when she had thus said, she turned herself back, and saw Jesus standing, and knew not that it was Jesus.

15 Jesus saith unto her, Woman, why weepest thou? whom seekest thou? She, supposing him to be the gardener, saith unto him, Sir, if thou have borne him hence, tell me where thou hast laid him, and I will take him away.

16 Jesus saith unto her, Mary. She turned herself, and saith unto him, Rabboni; which is to say, Master.

17 Jesus saith unto her, Touch me not; for I am not yet ascended to my Father: but go to my brethren, and say unto them, I ascend unto my Father; and your Father; and to my God, and your God.

18 Mary Magdalene came and told the disciples that she had seen the Lord, and that he had spoken these things unto her.

length looked into the sepulchre, and there saw two angels, probably in the form of young men clothed in white, and they immediately accosted her, enquiring the cause of her excessive sorrow. Yet she seems not to have greatly attended to them, perhaps in her confusion supposing them to have been disciples, who had come to view the sepulchre: and therefore she answered them nearly in the words, which she had used to the apostles (2).—But, as she turned from them, Jesus himself was pleased to appear to her: yet, through excessive weeping, and not all expecting to see him, she did not know him. And, supposing that it was the person employed by Joseph to take care of the garden, it occurred to her, that perhaps he had removed the body to some other place; and therefore she, in very respectful terms, desired, that if he had, he would inform her, and she would take it away, and be at the expense and trouble of the funeral. (Marg. Ref. p—y.)—It is observable, that, though speaking to a supposed stranger, she did not mention the name of Jesus; but merely said " him," as if every body must of course know whom she meant!—Jesus then called to her by name; and his voice and address made him known to her. Turning herself therefore with joy and amazement, she called him " Rabboni," which seems to signify " Teacher," with particular respect and application: but when she was about to spend time in farther expressing her affection, (Note, Matt. xxviii. 9, 10,) or perhaps to satisfy herself that it was not merely an apparition, Jesus prevented her, by saying, " Touch me not, &c." Thus he intimated that she would have other opportunities of expressing her joyful and affectionate regards: for, though he had repeatedly told his disciples, that he was about to go to his Father; yet he was not yet ascended, or about to ascend immediately, but should continue with them a short time on earth, for their satisfaction and comfort. (Marg. Ref. z—c.—Notes, vi. 60—65, v. 62. xiv. 2, 3. xvi. 7—11. 25 —30.) In the mean while she ought, without delay, to carry the joyful news of his resurrection to the disconsolate disciples, whom he acknowledged as his " brethren," notwithstanding they had so lately forsaken him; and she was directed further to inform them that he was risen, in order " to ascend to his Father and their Father, and to

" his God and their God:" for as he, the eternal Son of God, had become their Brother by assuming human nature; so, through the work which he had now finished, they were become the children of God by regeneration and adoption; and his God and Father, as Man and Mediator, was become their God and Father also. (Marg. Ref. d—g.—Note, Heb. ii. 10—15.)—Mary, as instructed, went immediately to inform the apostles: yet even her testimony did not fully satisfy them. (Notes, Mark xvi. 9—13.)—Having now considered separately the different accounts, given by the four evangelists, of our Lord's resurrection, which seem at first sight not easily reconcilable to each other; it may be proper to state very briefly, the most approved method of forming the whole into one consistent narration. (Note, Matt. xxviii. 9, 10.)—It is supposed, that several women agreed to meet at the sepulchre, in order to embalm the body of Jesus; and that Joanna and some others with her, having undertaken to prepare the spices, purposed being there about sun-rising : (Luke xxiii. 55, 56. xxiv. 1—10 :) but Mary Magdalene, the other Mary, and Salome, came to view the sepulchre, as the day " began to dawn." (Matt. xxviii. 1.) Mary Magdalene seems to have arrived some short time before her companions (1); and observing that the stone had been removed, she, without waiting for Joanna and her company, returned back to inform Peter and John. In the mean time the other Mary and Salome came to the sepulchre, and saw the angel, as recorded by Matthew and Mark. While these women returned to the city, Peter and John went to the sepulchre, passing them at some distance, or going another way; but they could not appear to them. After their return Mary Magdalene saw a vision of two angels, and then Jesus himself, as here related : (Mark xvi. 9—11 ;) and immediately after, Jesus appeared to the other women as they returned to the city. (Matt. xxviii. 9, 10.) In the mean while Joanna and her company arrived at the sepulchre, and, entering it, at first they saw nothing, and only observed that the body was not there : but while they were perplexed on that account, two angels appeared to them, and addressed them, as the one angel had done the other women. (Luke xxiv. 1— 10.) They therefore returned immediately to the city,

19 ¶ Then ' the same day at evening, being the first *day* of the week, ᵏ when the doors were shut, where the disciples were assembled, for fear of the Jews, ' came Jesus, and stood in the midst, and saith unto them, ᵐ Peace *be* unto you.

20 And when he had so said, ⁿ he shewed unto them *his* hands and his side. ° Then were the disciples glad when they saw the Lord.

21 Then said Jesus to them again, ᵖ Peace *be* unto you: ᵖ as *my* Father hath sent me, even so send I you.

22 And when he had said this, ⁴ he breathed on *them*, and saith unto them, ʳ Receive ye the Holy Ghost.

23 Whose ' soever sins ye remit, ' they are remitted unto them ; *and* whose soever *sins* ye retain, they are retained.

Marginal references (left column):
i Mark xvi. 14.
Luke xxiv. 36—
49. 1 Cor. xv. 5.
k 26. Neh. vi. 10,11.
l xiv. 19—23. xvi.
22. Matt. xviii. 20.
m 21. xiv. 27. xvi.
33. Ps. lxxxv. 8
—10. Is. lvii. 18.
19. Matt. x. 13.
Luke xxiv. 36.
Rom. xv. 33.
Eph. ii. 14. vi.
23. Phil. i. 2.
2 Thes. iii. 16.
Heb. vii. 2. Rev.
i. 4.
n 27. Luke xxiv.
39,40. 1 John i.1.
o xvi. 22. Is. xxv.
8, 9. Matt.
xxviii. 8. Luke
xxiv. 41.

Marginal references (right column):
p xiii. 20. xvii. 18,
19. xxi. 15—17.
Is. lxi. 1—3.
Matt. x. 16.
xxviii. 18—20.
Mark xvi. 15—
18. Luke xxiv.
47—49. Acts i.
8. 2 Tim. ii. 2.
q Gen. ii. 7. Job
xxxiii. 4. Ps.
xxxiii. 6. Ez.
xxxvii. 9.
r xiv. 16. xv. 26.
4, 26. 16, 8. viii.
15. x. 47. xix.
2. Gal. iii. 2.
s Matt. xvi. 19
xviii. 18. Mark
ii. 5—10. Acts ii. 38. x. 43. xiii. 38, 39. 1 Cor. v. 4, 5. 2 Cor. ii. 6—10. Eph. ii. 20.
1 Tim. i. 20.

and by some means found the apostles, before the other women arrived, and informed them of what they had seen; upon which Peter went a second time to the sepulchre, but saw no angels, only the linen clothes lying. (*Luke* xxiv. 12.) About this time the two disciples set off for Emmaus, having only heard the report of these women, and neither that of Mary Magdalene, nor yet that of the other Mary and Salome. (*Luke* xxiv. 22—24. 33, 34.) These at length arrived, and informed the apostles, that they had seen Jesus himself, and that two of them had been permitted to touch him : and some time after on the same day he appeared to Peter also. There are other ways of reconciling the apparent differences between the evangelists ; but this seems to answer every purpose, as will readily appear to the attentive reader. (See *West, upon the Resurrection*.)

. *Woman.* (13) Γυναι. 15. See on ii. 4.—*The gardener.* (15) Κηπουρος. Here only.—Ex χηπος, (xviii. 1. xix. 41,) et υρος, *custos.*—*Rabboni.* (16) 'Ραββονι, 'Ραββονι, *Mark* x. 51. Not elsewhere.

V. 19—23. On the evening of the day on which our Lord arose, the apostles and other disciples met together, in some room which they had procured ; probably, in order to join in prayer and supplication : though it seems, that they were sitting at meat, when Jesus came among them. (*Notes, Mark* xvi. 14—16. *Luke* xxiv. 36—43.)—The evangelist especially notes, that this was " the first day of " the week : " and this day is afterwards frequently mentioned by the sacred writers ; for it was evidently set apart as the Christian sabbath, in commemoration of Christ's resurrection. (*Marg. Ref.* i.—*Notes, Acts* xx. 7—12. *Rev.* i. 9—11.)—The disciples had shut the doors, for fear of the Jews ; as perhaps they were apprehensive, lest they should be prosecuted, by a false and absurd accusation of stealing the body from the sepulchre. But, when they seem to have had no expectations of the kind, Jesus himself came and stood in the midst of them, having miraculously, but silently, opened the doors of the room, and entered by them.—' Though it be an ancient opinion, that ' Christ made his body p a through the doors ; yet it ' is both groundless and **absurd**, and contrary to the very ' design of Christ in coming to them. It is *groundless* : ' for why might not he, by his power, secretly open the ' doors, his disciples not perceiving it; as the angel opened ' the prison-doors and gates to let out Peter ? (*Acts* xii. ' 10.) It is *absurd :* for since Christ rose in that natural ' body, which was crucified and laid in the grave; philo- ' sophy informs us, that such a body could not penetrate

' through another more solid body. ...And ... this fancy de- ' stroys not only the end of Christ's coming among them, ' but of all that he had said and done to convince them it ' was the same body tbat was crucified, in which he ap- ' peared to them. ...It being as certain, that flesh and ' bones cannot penetrate through a door, as that " a " " spirit hath not flesh and bones." ' *Whitby.*—Before his crucifixion, our Lord had promised the disciples, " his peace ; " (*Note,* xiv. 27, 28 ;) and he now autho- ritatively pronounced and conferred it upon them, as well as assured them that he was entirely reconciled to them after their late misconduct. To convince them also of the reality of his resurrection, he shewed them his wounded hands and side ; which satisfied their doubts and filled them with gladness. (*Marg. Ref.* k—o.) And, having repeated to them the assurance of his peace, he also renewed and confirmed to them their apostolick com- mission, sending them forth to declare his truth to the world, and to be his ambassadors and vicegerents, or re- presentatives, even " as the Father had sent him." (*Marg. Ref.* p.—*Notes,* xvii. 17—19. xxi. 15—17.) And, as an earnest of the approaching descent of the Spirit upon them, as well as to shew that that blessing would be communicated from his fulness, and according to his so- vereign pleasure, " he breathed upon them, and said unto " them, Receive ye the Holy Ghost." (*Marg. Ref.* q, r. —*Note, Gen.* ii. 7.) Thus he shewed them, that their spi- ritual life, and all their ability for their work, as well as their miraculous powers, were derived from him, and ab- solutely depended on him. After this he authorized them to declare the only method, in which sin would be for- given, and the character and experience of those who actually were pardoned, or the contrary. So that to the end of time, the rules and evidences of absolution or con- demnation, which they laid down, and which are con- tained in their writings, infallibly hold good ; and all de- cisions concerning the state of any man, or body of men, in respect of acceptance with God, whether by preaching absolution, or excommunication, or in any other way, are valid and ratified in heaven, provided they accord with the doctrine and rules of the apostles ; but not otherwise. (*Marg. Ref.* s.—*Notes, Matt.* xvi. 19. xviii. 18. 1 *John* i. 5—7.)—*Receive ye the Holy Ghost.* (22) It does not ap- pear, that the apostles, on any occasion, used these words; Peter and John prayed for the disciples in Samaria, that " they might receive the Holy Ghost." ... " Then laid " they their hands upon them, and they received the Holy " Ghost." (*Acts* viii. 15. 17.) The language of authority,

4 E 2

24 ¶ But 'Thomas, one of the twelve, called Didymus, 'was not with them when Jesus came. 25 The other disciples therefore said unto him, 'We have seen the Lord. But he said unto them, 'Except I shall see in his hands the print of the nails, and put my finger into the print of the nails, and thrust my hand into his side, I will not believe. 26 And after 'eight days, again his disciples were within, 'and Thomas with them. Then came Jesus, the doors being shut, and stood in the midst, and said, 'Peace be unto you. 27 Then saith he to Thomas, 'Reach

used by our Lord on this single occasion, seems exclusively appropriate to the great Head of the church, and marks the immense disparity between him and his most eminent servants.—How far the words, ' Receive ye the Holy ' Ghost' in some of the forms of our church, is *scriptural* or *warrantable*, may be worthy the consideration of all persons more immediately concerned in the important transactions referred to. (See *Ordination office of priests*, and *office for consecrating bishops*.)

Side. (20) Πλευραν. 25. 27. xix. 34. *Acts* xii. 7.—*He breathed*. (22) Ενιφυσησι. Here only N. T.—*Gen*. ii. 7. 1 *Kings* xvii. 21. *Job* iv. 21. *Ez*. xxi. 31. xxxvii. 9. *Sept*. —Ex στ et φυσαω, *sufflo*, à φυσα, *follis*, *vesica*.

V. 24—29. (*Marg. Ref. t*.—*Notes*, xi. 11—16. *Matt*. x. 1—4.) It is not known on what account Thomas was absent at this critical time ; perhaps he was even tempted to renounce his hope in Jesus, and to leave the company of the apostles. He, however, positively refused to credit those, who had been satisfied, by the testimony of their senses, that Jesus was risen. With peculiar emphasis, in language which seems to intimate that he had witnessed, and been deeply affected by, all the circumstances of our Lord's crucifixion, yet with determined incredulity, he declared he would not believe, without the combined testimony of his eyes and hands, in different ways : a demonstration, which few of the human race could possibly receive. He might, therefore, most justly have been left in his unbelief, after the rejection of such abundant proof as had already been vouchsafed him. But his gracious Lord was pleased to " deal with him according to the " multitude of his mercies." For, eight days after, or on the eighth day, (that is, " on the first day of the week," *Note*, 19—23,) the disciples were again assembled, perhaps by some intimation from Christ, Thomas being with them ; and Jesus again appeared among them, in the same manner, and with the same condescending and affectionate salutation as before. He then made Thomas sensible, that he knew, without information, all his unbelieving objections and demands, and at the same time offered him the fullest satisfaction which he could desire. It does not appear, whether Thomas actually examined our Lord's hands and side, or not : but his knowledge of his person, the proof of his resurrection, the concurring evidence of Jesus knowing the state of his mind, as well as his tender compassion for him ; joined to a recollection, under the influence of the Holy Spirit, of what Christ had said of his being " One with the Father;" had such an immediate effect upon him, that he at once not only confessed him as risen from the dead, but addressed, nay, in fact, adored him, as " his Lord, and his God ;" " Emmanuel," God in human nature, " God manifest in the flesh ;" and as such entitled to all confidence, love, obedience, and wor-

ship. (*Notes*, i. 1—3. v. 20—23. x. 26—31, *v*. 30. *Matt*. i. 20, 21. 1 *Tim*. iii. 16.)—Nothing can more fully prove, that this was the meaning of Thomas, than the frivolous evasion, to which the Socinians are here driven, as their only refuge from conviction : they pretend that the apostle did not mean to call Jesus his Lord and his God ; but that he exclaimed, " My Lord and my God !" as people sometimes do when greatly astonished. (*Note, Ex*. xx. 7.) Such exclamations are doubtless a violation of the third commandment ; yet this supposes that the apostles were guilty of it in the presence of Christ, and that he approved of it ! Surely such a solution is the most improbable, which can be imagined ! But Thomas evidently addressed these words to Christ, which is decisive against that opinion. " He " answered and said unto him, My Lord and my God :" I acknowledge thee to be my Lord and my God.— Our Lord approved of his present faith and adoration, as justly due to him ; and only with gentleness reproved his former unbelief. He had indeed been convinced by the testimony of his senses, but there had been and were many, and there would be immense multitudes in future ages, who could not have such overbearing evidence ; yet would they be peculiarly blessed in believing in him. It was not said, that they would be more blessed than Thomas : but it intimated, that if others should prove as incredulous as he had been, very few indeed could inherit the blessing ; and it implied, that those, who never saw Jesus, and yet believed in him, would be no losers by that apparent disadvantage ; yea, that believing on competent evidence, without requiring such absolute demonstration, would denote a more teachable frame of mind, and be more honourable to God. (*Note*, 1 *Pet*. i. 8, 9.)

The print. (25) Τον τυπον. *Acts* vii. 43, 44. xxiii. 25. *Rom*. v. 14. vi. 17. 1 *Cor*. x. 6. 11. *Phil*. iii. 17. 1 *Thes*. i. 7. *Heb*. viii. 5. 1 *Pet*. v. 3.—*Am*. v. 26. *Sept*.—*Be not faithless, but believing*. (27) Μη γινη απιτος, αλλα πιτος. " Become not an unbeliever, but a believer." ' Renounce ' not thy former professed faith in me ; but be established ' in faith.'—Απιτος. *Matt*. xvii. 17. *Mark* ix. 19. 1 *Cor*. vi. 6. vii. 12, 13, 14, 15, *et alibi*.—*That have not seen*, &c. (29) Μη ιδοντες, και πιτευσαντες. " Not seeing, yet believing." The indefinite tenses are used, and all, in every age, who have believed, do believe, or shall believe, in an unseen Saviour, are blessed. Our version seems to limit it to the past ; " have believed."

It may here be proper to add a compendious view of the evidence, which *we*, after so many ages, possess of our Lord's resurrection : for this is the grand external demonstration of the truth of Christianity.—It must be premised, that almost all human affairs are conducted on man's testimony : even in the great concerns of life and death, the concurring evidence of two or three persons of good cha-

hither thy finger, and behold my hands: and reach hither thy hand, and thrust ^d it into my side: ^d and be not faithless, but believing.

^{d Matt. xvii. 17.}
^{Mark ix.}
^{Luke ix. 41.}

28 And Thomas answered and said unto him, ^e My Lord and my God.

29 Jesus saith unto him, Thomas, because thou hast seen me, thou hast

^{e 16. 81. ix. 35—38. Ps. xlv. 6. 11. cii. 24—28. cxviii. 24—26. Is. vii. 14. ix. 6. xxv. 9. xl. 9—11. Jer. xxiii. 5, 6. Mal. iii. 1.}

Matt. xiv. 33. Luke xxiv. 52. Acts vii. 59, 60. 1 Tim. iii. 16. Rev. v. 9—14.

racter, sober sense, and competent information, is deemed abundantly sufficient proof of any fact, which is in its own nature credible; especially if it be clear, that they derive no worldly advantage from the testimony which they give. The resurrection of Christ, as connected with the divine authority of Revelation, and the glory of God in the salvation of innumerable multitudes of immortal souls, was an event in itself perfectly credible; as sufficient reasons may be assigned, for the interposition of almighty power to effect it. (*Note, Acts* xxvi. 4—8.) To prepare the way for the testimony to be given of this event, it was expressly foretold by the ancient prophets; (*Notes, Ps.* xvi. 8—11. xxii. 22—31. *Is.* liii. 9—12. *Luke* xxiv. 44—49. *Acts* ii. 25—32. xiii. 24—27;) and even the enemies of our Lord knew, that he had clearly predicted it, and the very time when it would take place. (*Note, Matt.* xxvii. 62—66.) Accordingly, on the day prefixed the body was gone, after all the precautions which those who had procured his crucifixion had taken to secure it: and, though their authority and reputation were in every respect at stake; though they could give no rational account what was become of it; and though they had the whole authority in their hands; they never ventured to bring, either the soldiers who guarded the sepulchre, or the apostles who were said to have stolen the body, to any trial; but chose rather to sit down under the imputation of the basest murder, prevarication, and wickedness, than excite any further enquiry into the transaction. The eleven apostles (to whom a twelfth was shortly after added,) were a sufficient number of witnesses: they were men of plain sense and irreproachable characters; they had been constant attendants on Jesus during some years, and could not but know him, and they unanimously testified, that they repeatedly saw him, conversed, ate, and drank with him, after his resurrection; that they examined the wounds in his hands and side; and that at length they beheld him ascend towards heaven, till a cloud intercepted their view of him. In this testimony they persisted as with one voice, during a series of years; and nothing induced any one of them to vary from it, in the smallest particular. It is evident that they had no previous expectation of the resurrection of their Lord; and, notwithstanding all the miracles which they had witnessed, they were remarkably incredulous about it. They were also exceedingly intimidated by his crucifixion; and they could have no possible temporal motive, to invent and propagate a report of his resurrection: for labour, poverty, reproach, imprisonment, suffering, and death alone could be expected, as their recompence, for thus embracing the cause of one who had been crucified as a deceiver. In every thing else, they appeared to be the most simple, upright, holy, and pious men in the world: yet if in this they falsified; they must have been the most *wicked* and most *artful* persons who ever existed, and that without any prospect of advantage. For they spent all the rest of their lives in propagating the religion of Jesus, as risen from the dead; renouncing every worldly interest; facing op-

position and persecution; enduring all kinds of hardship; prepared at all times to seal their testimony with their blood; and most of them actually suffering martyrdom in the cause, confirming their testimony with their latest breath, and leaving it in their writings as a most valuable bequest to posterity.—Moreover, there were other competent witnesses, who saw Jesus after his resurrection, even to the number of five hundred persons: (*Note,* 1 *Cor.* xv. 3—11, *v.* 6:) these also concurred in the same testimony to their latest breath; and neither terror, nor hope, nor any other motive, ever induced one of them to contradict or dissent from the testimony of the others. If we were to stop here, we could scarcely conceive of a more complete human testimony to any matter of fact. Yet perhaps some may think, that if Jesus had openly appeared after his resurrection to the Jewish nation and their rulers, it might have put the matter beyond all doubt: but it should be considered, that if this measure had been adopted, and the rulers had persisted in rejecting him, as they certainly would, if their hearts had remained unchanged; (*Note, Luke* xvi. 27—31;) the gospel would have had still greater disadvantages to encounter, both among the other Jews, and the Gentiles. On the other hand, if the whole Jewish nation and their rulers had received Jesus as the Messiah, when the gospel had been sent among the Gentiles, it would have appeared as a plan formed for aggrandizing that nation, and as such would probably have been disregarded; and after all, they who lived in after ages could have no further proof of this publick appearance, than the testimony of those individuals who recorded it. In short, if our Lord was not to give ocular demonstration of this resurrection to every man, in every age; (which would have been impossible;) the number of competent witnesses was sufficient, and even preferable to a greater multitude.—But, as if all human testimony was a small matter, in such an infinitely important concern, God himself was pleased to bear witness with the apostles, in a most extraordinary manner; conferring upon them the gifts of tongues and of working miracles, by the Holy Spirit; and enabling them to impart the same to others by the laying on of their hands. (*Notes,* xv. 26, 27. *Acts* viii. 18—24. *Heb.* ii. 1—4, *v.* 4.) Thus the number of unexceptionable witnesses was increased; the testimony to our Lord's resurrection was diffused on every side; and his most inveterate enemies could not deny, that most extraordinary miracles were performed by those who attested that event. (*Note, Acts* iv. 13—22, *v.* 16.) In this manner, the number of the disciples of Jesus was speedily multiplied, by tens of thousands being converted from among those, who had just before demanded his crucifixion: and Christianity got ground rapidly on every side, in opposition to all the wealth, power, learning, superstition, and philosophy of the world; and by unarmed, unlearned, poor, and despised instruments: till at length whole nations embraced the religion of the crucified Nazarene, as the prophets had expressly foretold. (*Notes, Jer.* xvi. 19—21. *Am.* ix. 11, 12.

believed: 'blessed are they that have not seen, and yet have believed.

30 And ' many other signs truly did Jesus in the presence of his disciples, which are not written in this book.

31 But ' these are written, that ye might believe that Jesus is the Christ, the Son of God; and that ' believing ye might have life ' through his name.

Zech. viii. 20—23.) This effect, which could be ascribed to no power but that of God, and the continuance of so humbling and holy a religion in the world to this day, form a demonstration *even to us* of this important fact: nor has any past event since the beginning of the world ever been proved, with such complicated and abundant evidence.— St. Paul's conversion, and the prophecies contained in the writings of those who testified our Lord's resurrection, and which have been accomplishing for almost eighteen hundred years, may be considered as additional complete divine attestations. (*Notes, Acts* ix. 31. 2 *Thes.* ii. 3—12. 1 *Tim.* iv. 1—5. *Preface to the Revelation of St. John.*)

V. 30, 31. (*Marg. Ref.—Note,* xxi. 24, 25.) " The " signs " here spoken of, seem to refer to the evidences of our Lord's resurrection, of which there were far more than it was necessary to record: (*Note, Acts* i. 1—3:) but these were committed to writing, in order that all those who should ever read them, might believe that Jesus was indeed the promised " Messiah," the King of Israel, the Saviour of sinners, and " the Son of God; " that by this faith they might obtain eternal life, through his name, for his sake, and by his mercy, truth, and power. (*Notes,* 24— 29, latter paragraph. iii. 16—18. v. 24—27. 39—44. vi. 66—71. ix. 35—38. xi. 20—27. 1 *John* v. 9—13.)

Signs. (30) Σημεια. iv. 48. *Matt.* xii. 38, 39. xvi. 1. xxiv. 24. *Heb.* ii. 4. *Rev.* xii. 1.

PRACTICAL OBSERVATIONS.

V. 1—10.

They who love the Lord will seek him early and diligently; and, notwithstanding all sorrows, delays, misapprehensions, and discouragements, they will assuredly find him.—External forms and empty notions will no more satisfy the earnest trembling enquirer after salvation, than the sepulchre and the grave-clothes did Mary and the apostles, who sought the Lord Jesus in faith and love.— Under a large proportion of preaching, by men called Christian ministers, we are ready to say, " They have " taken away the Lord, and we know not where they ' have laid him ; " but the broken-hearted disciple cannot be thus contented, though others be filled with admiration of the preacher's eloquence, genius, or learning.—Those who are equally in earnest do not always make equal progress: some men take things more quickly, others investigate more deeply: and they may be mutually helpful, in bringing each other to understand the scripture, and to establishment in the faith. (*Notes, Rom.* xii. 3—8. 1 *Cor.* xii. 12—26. *Eph.* iv. 11—16.)

V. 11—23.

Great love is manifested by proportionable sorrow, when the beloved object is removed : thus the humble believer mourns, when he seeks in vain for the comfort of the Redeemer's presence, or the opportunity of honouring him. At such times, he is apt to imagine that others, as well as himself, must be thinking of his Beloved : and the same state of mind often incapacitates him from perceiving the evidences of the Lord's love to him, or the grounds of his own consolation. Thus he is led to weep, when he should rejoice : but mourners of this character shall be comforted ; (*Note, Matt.* v. 4 ;) angels rejoice over them, and are ready to minister to their comfort ; Jesus will " manifest himself " to them, as he doth not unto the world ; " and in this manner the most disconsolate penitents, and the chief of sinners, become the messengers of peace and comfort to others also.—Our gracious Redeemer, in his highest exaltation, deigns to call his disciples *brethren,* notwithstanding all their falls and ingratitude! and when we consider how low he stooped, and how much he suffered, in order to form the relation and to fulfil the part of a Brother to us sinful worms; we shall not hesitate to expect the greatest honour and felicity from him. (*P. O. Heb.* ii. 5— 18.) He has " ascended to his Father and our Father, to " his God and our God ; " and there he continually manages all our concerns, with the most perfect love and faithfulness: yet when we assemble in his name, especially on his holy day, he will meet with us and speak peace to us; (*Notes, Matt.* xviii. 19, 20; he will assure us of his forgiveness ; counterbalance our sorrows · and alarms from persecuting foes ; and communicate his sacred Spirit of life, love, holiness, and consolation ; according as our services, or our difficulties, require his special assistances, supports, and influences.

V. 24—31.

When disciples are needlessly absent from the assemblies of God's people, they will surely be losers; and their unbelieving fears and sorrows are often prolonged, as a chastisement for their negligence. (*Note, Heb.* x. 23—25.) Indeed unbelief is the source of almost all our sins and disquietudes. We all have too much copied the example of Thomas's incredulity, by refusing to believe the word of God, and to rely on his help, even when our past experience of his care has been abundant; and we are often apt to demand such proof of his truths, and of his will respecting us, as we have no right to expect. But he does not deal with us after our iniquities, and therefore " we are " not consumed." He knows all our difficulties and temptations ; he rebukes and obviates the unbelief of those, whose hearts are upright before him; he will convince them who he is, and what he has done for them ; that they may trust, love, and obey him as " their Lord and " their God." We have not indeed that kind of ocular proof, with which Thomas was favoured, and which infidels still demand ; yet we are equally within the reach of the blessing. We have abundant evidence of the Redeemer's resurrection and glory: some of us, like Thomas, have withheld our credence, till we could no longer " be faith- " less," but were constrained to believe: and these things were written for the benefit of every reader, " that he may

CHAP. XXI.

Jesus appears to some of his disciples, at the sea of Tiberias ; makes himself known by a miraculous draught of fishes ; and eats with them, 1—14. He thrice demands of Peter, whether he loves him ; and thrice requires him to shew his love, by feeding his lambs and sheep, 15—17. He foretels Peter's martyrdom, commanding him to follow him, 18, 19 ; and reproves his curiosity concerning John, who shewed his readiness in the same way to follow him, 20—23. The truth of John's testimony affirmed ; and it is stated that Jesus did many miracles besides, even too numerous to be all recorded, 24, 25.

AFTER [a] these things [b] Jesus shewed himself again to the disciples at [c] the sea of Tiberias ; and on this wise shewed he *himself.*

2 There were together Simon Peter, [d] and Thomas called Didymus, [e] and Nathanael [f] of Cana in Galilee, [g] and the *sons* of Zebedee, and two other of his disciples.

3 Simon Peter saith unto them, [h] I go a fishing. They say unto him, We also go with thee. They went forth, and entered into a ship immediately ; [i] and that night they caught nothing.

4 But when the morning was now come, Jesus stood on the shore ; [k] but the disciples knew not that it was Jesus.

5 Then Jesus saith unto them, [l] Children, [l] have ye any meat ? They answered him, No.

6 And he said unto them, [m] Cast the

net on the right side of the ship, and ye shall find. [n] They cast therefore, and now they were not able to draw it for [o] the multitude of fishes.

7 Therefore [p] that disciple whom Jesus loved saith unto Peter, [q] It is the Lord. Now [r] when Simon Peter heard that it was the Lord, he girt *his* fisher's coat *unto him,* (for he was naked,) and [s] did cast himself into the sea.

8 And the other disciples came in a little ship, (for they were not far from land, but as it were two hundred [t] cubits,) dragging the net with fishes.

9 As soon then as they were come to land, [u] they saw a fire of coals there, and fish laid thereon, and bread.

10 Jesus saith unto them, Bring of the fish which ye have now caught.

11 Simon Peter went up, and drew the net to land full of great fishes, an hundred and fifty and three ; [v] and for all there were so many, yet was not the net broken.

12 Jesus saith unto them, Come *and* dine. And none of the disciples [x] durst ask him, Who art thou ? knowing that it was the Lord.

13 Jesus [y] then cometh, and taketh bread, and giveth them, and fish likewise.

14 This is now [z] the third time that Jesus shewed himself to his disciples, after that he was risen from the dead.

Marginal references:

a ii. 3. Ps. viii. 8. Heb. ii. 6—9.
b xx. 19—29.
b Matt. xxvi. 32. xxviii. 7, 16. Mark xvi. 7.
c vi. 1. 23.
o Acts ii. 41. iv. 4.
p xx. 2. xiii. 23. xix. 26. xx. 2.
q xxi. 20. 28. Ps. cxviii. 23. Mark xi. 3. Luke xix. 31. Acts iii. 36. 1 Cor. xv. 47. Jam. ii. 1.
r Cant. viii. 7. Matt. xiv. 28. Luke vii. 47.
d xx. 28.
e L 45—5.
f ii. 1. 11. iv. 46. Josh. xix. 28. Kanah. 9.
g Matt. iv. 21, 22.
s 2 Cor. v. 14.
t Deut. iii. 11.
h 2 Kings vi. 1—7. Matt. iv. 18—20. Luke v. 10, 11. Acts xviii. 3. xx. 34. 1 Thes. ii. 9. 2 Thes. iii. 7—9.
i Luke v. 5. 1 Cor. iii. 7.
t 1 Kings xix. 6. Matt. iv. 11. Mark viii. 2, 3. Luke xii. 29—31.
k xx. 14. Mark xvi. 12. Luke xxiv. 16, 31. Or. Sirs. l.
l Ps. xxxvii. 3. Luke xxiv. 41—43. Phil. iv. 11—13, 19. Heb. xiii. 5.
u Luke v. 6—8. Acts ii. 41.
m Matt. xvii. 27. Luke v. 4—6.
v Luke xxiv. 42, 43. Acts vi. 41.
x ix. 27. xvi. 19. Gen. xxxii. 29, 30. Mark ix. 32. Luke xii. 11.
y xxi. 19. 26.

"believe that Jesus is the Christ, and that believing he "may have life through his name."

NOTES.

Chap. XXI. V. 1—14. This transaction seems to have occurred, after the disciples had returned into Galilee; and before Jesus had met them on the mountain, according to his appointment. (*Notes, Matt.* xxviii. 9, 10. 16, 17.) —Peter being unemployed, and perhaps in want, proposed to " go a fishing," and his brethren agreed to accompany him : (*Marg. Ref.* a—h :) but, though they laboured during the whole night, the most proper time for fishing, they were entirely unsuccessful. This was a trial of their faith and patience; and also an emblem of the discouragements, which the most able, faithful, and laborious ministers often meet with in their work. (*P. O. Luke* v. 1—15, *vv.* 3—11.) In the morning Jesus stood by the shore, near to the vessel, but he was pleased by some means to prevent their knowing him. (*Marg. Ref.* k.) But when they drew near to land, he accosted them as a stranger, in a very friendly and familiar manner; and asked them whether they had any meat. This might be understood either

with reference to their success in fishing, or as an enquiry whether they had any provisions to dispose of. When they had answered in the negative, he directed them to cast the net on the " right side of the ship," and then they would succeed better : and though he appeared as a stranger, and they, being weary with toiling all night, had probably desisted from fishing ; yet they followed his directions ; and at once inclosed so many fishes, that they were not able to draw the net into the vessel again. This unexpected success convinced John that it was " The Lord ;" (See on xx. 2 :) for probably it brought a former miracle of this kind to his remembrance. (*Note, Luke* v. 1—11.) As soon as he had informed Peter of this, the latter, full of love and gratitude to Jesus, who had so graciously forgiven his late base denial of him, entirely disregarded the net and the fishes; and, girding on his upper garment, (having been stripped for his work,) he leaped into the sea, and swam to shore, as they were not much above a hundred yards distant from it : but the other disciples abode in the vessel to draw the net to land. When this was done, they found that Jesus had already made preparation for their refreshment, after the labour of the night, pro-

15 ¶ So when they had dined, Jesus saith to Simon Peter, Simon, *son of Jonas, *lovest thou me *more than these? He saith unto him, Yea, Lord; *thou knowest that I love thee. He saith unto him, *Feed my *lambs.

16 He saith to him again *the second time, Simon, *son of Jonas, lovest thou me? He saith unto him, Yea, Lord; thou knowest that I love thee. He saith unto him, Feed *my sheep.

17 He saith unto him *the third time, Simon, son of Jonas, lovest thou me? Peter was *grieved, because he said unto him the third time, Lovest thou me? And he said unto him, *Lord, thou knowest all things; *thou knowest that I love thee. He saith unto him, Feed *my sheep.

bably by miracle: but he ordered them to bring also of the fishes which they had then taken; and in doing this they found a great number of very large fishes: yet the net was wonderfully preserved from being broken; and most likely it was borrowed. (*Note, and P. O. 2 Kings* vi. 1—7.) This draught of fishes might be sold for a considerable sum of money, which the apostles would have occasion for, on their return to Jerusalem, before the day of Pentecost.— After they had secured the fishes, Jesus called them to come, and partake of the repast prepared for them; and, in his usual manner, he took the provisions, and gave unto them: but they ventured not to ask him who he was, being satisfied it was the Lord, though he probably assumed for a time a different appearance than usual. (*Marg. Ref.* m— z.)—This was the third time, that he shewed himself after his resurrection, to several of his disciples at once; for he had twice come among them at Jerusalem, when they were met together on the evening of the first day of the week. (*Notes*, xx. 19—29.)—It does not become us to enquire, where or how he spent the rest of his time previously to his ascension.—*Nathanael.* (2) *Note*, i. 47— 51.—It appears here, that Cana had been Nathanael's general residence.—*Dine.* (12) The ancients used to make two principal stated meals; the first of which is generally called *dinner*, and the latter *supper*, in translating the Greek and Latin writers into English; and, I believe, the same method prevails in rendering them into most other modern languages. The first meal was indeed commonly taken much earlier than the dining hours at present. Thus our forefathers used to dine at eleven and sup at five: yet that has not altered the name of the meals.

He shewed. (1) Εφανερωσεν. 14. ii. 11. vii. 4. 2 Cor. v. 10.—*A fishing.* (3) 'Αλιευιν. 'Αλιευς, Matt. iv. 18, 19.—*A ship.*] Το πλοιον. 6. " The ship," viz. which they had borrowed or hired for the purpose. Τω πλοιαριω. 8. —*Children.* (5) Παιδια. 'A word of one mildly, and in a ' friendly manner, addressing others.' *Leigh.* 1 John ii. 13. 18.—*Meat.*] Προσφαγιον. Here only. Εκ προς, et φαγω edo.—*His fisher's coat.* (7) Τον επενδυτην. Here only. Εξ επι et ενδυω induo. An upper garment.—*Naked.*] Γυμνος. Matt. xxv. 36. Jam. ii. 15.—1 Sam. xix. 24. Is. xx. 2—4. Sept. Stripped, as a man who casts off his garment, while at work. —*A fire of coals.* (9) Ανθρακιαν. xviii. 18.—*Fish.*] Οψαριον. 10. 13. See on vi. 9.—*Come.* (12) Δευτε. See on Matt. xi. 28.—*Dine.*] Αριστησατε. 15. Luke xi. 37. Αριστον, Matt. xxii. 4. Luke xi. 38.

V. 15—17. The case of Peter required a more marked notice, than that of the other apostles; in order that both he and others might derive the greater benefit from his

fall and recovery. (*Notes, Matt.* xxvi. 40, 41. 69—75.) Our Lord therefore on this occasion, addressed him by his original name, as if he had forfeited that of Peter through his instability, (*Note*, i. 35—42, *vv.* 41, 42,) saying, " Lovest thou me more than these?" The latter clause might be interpreted of his employment and gains as a fisherman, and be considered as a demand, whether he loved Jesus above all his secular interests; (*Notes, Matt.* x. 37—42. Luke xiv. 25—27;) but Peter's answer determines us to another interpretation. He had, before his fall, in effect, said that he loved his Lord more than any of the other disciples did; for he had boasted, that " though " all men were offended, yet would not he." (*Marg. Ref.* b, c.—*Note, Matt.* xxvi. 30—35.) And Jesus now asked him, whether he would stand to this, and aver that he loved him more than the disciples then present did. To this he answered modestly, by saying, " Thou knowest that I love " thee;" without professing to love him more than the others. Our Lord therefore renewed his appointment to the ministerial and apostolical office; at the same time commanding him " to feed his lambs," even the least of them. This intimated to him, that his late experience of his own weakness ought to render him peculiarly condescending, compassionate, tender, and attentive to the meanest and feeblest believers; and to such as were harassed with temptations, or overtaken with a fault, or who manifested many and great infirmities: as the shepherd takes the greatest care of the most weak and sickly lambs of his flock. (*Marg. Ref.* e, f.—*Notes, Is.* xl. 9— 11. *Ez.* xxxiv. 2—6. 11—16. *Luke* xxii. 31—34, *v.* 34.) —Soon after, our Lord repeated his question: but as Peter had dropped the latter part of it, he urged that no further; which proves the interpretation above given to be the true one: for that is not true love of Christ, which is not decidedly superior to our love of earthly things. When Peter had again appealed to him, that he knew he really did love him; Jesus ordered him to shew that love, by " feeding " his sheep;" or by diligently labouring to promote the edification of every description of believers, as well as to spread the knowledge of his salvation in the world. (*Marg. Ref.* g, h. n.—*Notes,* xiv. 15—17. 21—24. *Acts* xx. 28. 2 Cor. v. 13—15.)—But as Peter had thrice denied Christ; so he was pleased to repeat the same question " a third " time:" this grieved Peter, as it reminded him, that he had given sufficient cause for being thus repeatedly questioned, concerning the sincerity of his love to his Lord. (*Marg. Ref.* i, k.—*Note, 2 Cor.* viii. 6—9.) Conscious, however, of his integrity, he more solemnly appealed to Christ, as knowing all things, even the secrets of his heart,

4 I 7

est that I love thee. Jesus saith unto him, ⁿ Feed my sheep.

18 Verily, verily, I say unto thee, When thou wast young, thou girdedst thyself, and walkedst whither thou wouldest: ° but when thou shalt be old, thou shalt stretch forth thy hands, and another shall gird thee, and carry thee whither ₚ thou wouldest not.

19 This spake he, signifying ᵠ by what death he should glorify God. And when he had spoken this, he saith unto him, ʳ Follow me.

20 Then Peter, turning about, ˢ seeth the disciple whom Jesus loved, follow-

ing; 'which also leaned on his breast ᵗ at supper, and said, Lord, which is he that betrayeth thee?

21 Peter seeing him saith to Jesus, ᵘ Lord, and what shall this man do?

22 Jesus saith unto him, ˣ If I will that he tarry till I come, what is that to thee? follow thou me.

23 Then went this saying abroad among the brethren, that that disciple should not die: yet Jesus said not unto him, He shall not die; but, If I will that he tarry till I come, ʸ what is that to thee?

Marginal references (left column):
ⁿ 15, 16. xii. 8. him.
xiv. 16. xv. 10. Matt. xxv. 40. 2 Cor. viii. 8, 9.
2 Pet. i. 12—15.
iii. 1. 1 John iii. 16—24. 3 John 7, 8.
° Acts xii. 3, 4.
ₚ xii. 27, 28. 2 Cor. v. 4.
ᵠ Phil. i. 20. 1 Pet. iv. 1— 14. 2 Pet. i. 14.
ʳ 22. xii. 26. xiii. 36, 37. Matt. x. 38. xvi. 21—25. Mark viii. 33—38. Luke ix. 23 —26.
ˢ 7. 24. xx. 2.

Marginal references (right column):
ᵗ xiii. 23—26.
ᵘ Matt. xxiv. 3, 4. Luke xiii. 23, 24. Acts i. 6, 7.
ˣ Matt. xvi. 27; 28. xxiv. 3. 27. 44. xxv. 31; Mark iv. 1. 1 Cor. iv. 5. xi. 26. Rev. ii. 25. iii. 11. xxii. 7. 20.
ʸ Deut. xxix. 29. Job xxxviii. 28. xxxiii. 13. Dan. iv. 35.

(*Marg. Ref.* l, m.—*Note*, ii. 23—25,) that he knew he loved him with cordial affection, notwithstanding the grievous inconsistency of his late behaviour. Our Lord then tacitly allowed the truth of this profession, and renewed his charge to him " to feed his sheep."—Two different words (αγαπαω, and φιλεω,) are used in the original, for *to love*. The evangelist twice employs the former, in the question proposed by our Lord, but the latter in Peter's answer; which is also used in the third instance, both in the question and answer. Learned men vary in opinion, concerning the precise difference between these words: but the former seems to denote a more intense affection, than the latter.—The arguments of the papists for the supremacy of the pope, from this passage, only prove their case to be desperate, as to scriptural argument: such a pre-eminence, however, as is here described, would not greatly suit the inclinations of those who are most deeply interested in the controversy. To be more abundantly laborious in feeding the weakest of Christ's flock, with the wholesome food of his pure doctrine, from love to him and his cause ; to submit to any abasement or hardship, and to face any peril or persecution, in this work of compassion and tender care to the poor, the tempted, and afflicted ;—*this* is a pre-eminence, which excites the ambition of very few, compared with the number of those, who aspire after ecclesiastical authority and distinction. (*Note, Matt.* xviii. 1—4. *P. O.* 1—6. *Mark* ix. 33—37, v. 35.) It is indeed true, that one of the words here translated *feed*, may be rendered *rule ;* but then it is the *rule* of a careful shepherd over his valued flock ; and very different from that of those, who, both in opposition to Peter's example and exhortation, have pretended to derive authority from him, " to lord it over God's " heritage." (*Note*, 1 *Pet.* v. 1—4.)

Lovest thou, &c. (15) Αγαπας. 16. iii. 16. 19. 35. xi. 5. xiii. 1. xiv. 15. 21. 23, 24. 28. 31. xv. 9. 12. xvii. 23, 24. 26. *Eph.* v. 2. vi. 24. *Rev.* i. 5, *et al.*—*I love*, &c. (16) Φιλω. 16, 17. v. 20. xi. 3. 36. xii. 25. xv. 19. xvi. 27. xx. 2. 1 *Cor.* xvi. 22. *Rev.* iii. 19.—*Feed.*] Βοσκε. 17. *Matt.* viii. 30. 33. *Mark* v. 11. 14. *Luke* viii. 32. 34. xv. 15.—*Lambs.*] Τα αρνια. *Rev.* v. 6. 8. 12, 13. vi. 1. 16, *et al.*—*Feed.* (16) Ποιμαινε. *Acts* xx. 28. 1 *Cor.* ix. 7. 1 *Pet.* v. 2. *Rev.* ii. 27. vii. 17. xii. 5. xix. 15. See on *Matt.* ii. 6.

V. 18—23. Peter had earnestly professed his readiness to die with Christ ; yet had shamefully failed, when put to

the trial: (*Note*, xiii. 36—38 :) but our Lord next assured him, that he would at length be called on, and enabled, to perform that engagement. In his youth, he had been used to gird himself, (as he had just before girded on his fisher's coat,) and to walk at liberty as he pleased: but in his old age, he would be compelled to stretch out his hands, that others might bind him, and carry him to endure those sufferings, " which he would not ;" and to which nature must be reluctant. This, we are told, signified the death, by which he would " glorify God," as a martyr for his truth. (*Marg. Ref.* p, q.—*Note*, xii. 27— 33.)—It is generally agreed that Peter was *crucified*, nearly forty years after this ; but the circumstances of it are variously related. (*Note*, 2 *Pet.* i. 12—15.)—Jesus next called upon him to signify his readiness to adhere to his cause even unto death, by rising up and following him ; with which Peter complied without hesitation. (*Marg. Ref.* r.) But, turning about, he saw John also, (*Marg. Ref.* s, t,) without any command, silently expressing by his conduct the same willingness to suffer death for the sake, and after the example, of his beloved Lord : and this led Peter to enquire, " What shall this man do?" ' Was he also to be a martyr ?' To this our Lord replied, that if it were his will he should abide on earth till his coming, that was no concern of Peter's, who ought not to indulge a vain curiosity, but to follow him ; as a token of his readiness to adhere to his instructions, to obey his commandments, to copy his example, and to suffer for his sake. (*Marg. Ref.* u. y.—*Note*, *Deut.* xxix. 29.) The crucifixion of Jesus, followed by the glorious resurrection, rendered them far more superior to the fear of men, and far more raised to the hopes and prospects of heavenly glory, even before the descent of the Holy Spirit, than they had been before.—It is most probable, that Jesus meant his coming in power to set up his kingdom, and to execute vengeance on the unbelieving Jewish nation : but the disciples had confused and defective views of this subject, and supposed he meant, that John would live till Christ came to judgment, or that he would at length be translated to heaven, as Enoch and Elijah had been ; or that, being the beloved disciple, he would escape death : but the words had no such meaning.—John lived long after the destruction of Jerusalem, and after the other

a xix. 35. 1 John 24 ¶ This is the disciple which tes-
1 i, 2. v. 6.
3 John 12.   tifieth of these things, and wrote these
b xv. 30, 31. Job
xxvi. 14. Ps. xl. things; and ¹ we know that his testi-
b lxxi. 15. Ec.
xii. 12. Matt.   mony is true.
xi. 5. Acts x. 36.
xv. 35. Heb. xi. 25 And ² there are also many other
22.

things which Jesus did, the which if
they should be written every one, I sup-
pose ᵇ that even the world itself could ᵇ Am. vii 10.
not contain the books that should be   Matt. xix. 24.
written. Amen.

---

apostles ; and, it is probable, died a natural death in extreme old age. (*Preface to this gospel.—Note, Rev.* i. 9—
11.)
  Should not die. (23) Ουκ αποθνησκει. "Dieth not."
  V. 24, 25. We are here informed that the beloved disciple John was the writer of this gospel : and some think
that it was sanctioned, as of divine authority, by the elders
of the churches of Asia; because it is added " We know
" that his testimony is true:" but perhaps it only means
the consciousness and assured confidence of John, and the
other sacred writers, of their own divine inspiration, and
the infallible truth of their testimony.—(*Notes,* xix. 31—
37, *v.* 35. 1 *John* iv. 4—6. v. 19—21. 3 *John* 9—12.) To
this it is subjoined, that the actions of Jesus, which were
worthy of observation, were exceedingly more numerous;
and that but a small part had actually been committed to
writing. The concluding words are generally understood
to be highly *hyperbolical :* but perhaps they also intimate,
that if every one of the actions and words of Jesus had
been written, the books containing them would have been
so voluminous, as to counteract their own intention ; for
men, in the present state of the world, would neither be
able to purchase, peruse, or remember them; and the
men of the world would have even made the multiplicity
of them an additional reason for not *receiving* them.—To
the whole, the evangelist affixes " Amen," as a confirmation of what he had written, and to express his approbation
of the divine conduct in this and in every other particular.
  Contain. (25) Χωρησαι. ii. 6. viii. 37.—See on *Matt.*
xix. 11.

PRACTICAL OBSERVATIONS.

V. 1—14.

  Our blessed Lord is often near us, as to his providential
care and his spiritual consolations, when we are ready to
conclude that he is far off. He does not allow his ministers to " entangle themselves with the affairs of this life,"
or his people to perplex themselves with worldly cares:
but he approves of honest industry, and vouchsafes his
special presence and blessing to those, who conscientiously
attend to their present duty. While he provides for the
souls of his disciples, he kindly enquires into their temporal wants, and allows them to state them to him, as
children to a loving Father : and he will always be mindful to provide for them such " things as are needful."—
None of our labours can prosper without his blessing,
which we ought to seek in all our undertakings : (*Note,*
Prov. iii. 5, 6 :) but our dependence on him is peculiarly
to be recognized in performing the work of the ministry :
and he often permits his servants to labour for a time without visible success ; to prove their faith and patience, to
render them more observant of his directions, or more
simply dependent on his assistance ; and that their usefulness, when vouchsafed, may more evidently appear to be
his work.
  VOL. V.

V. 15—17.

  It is a very blessed effect, when our falls and mistakes
render us more humble, watchful, and zealous.—Our gracious Lord will readily pardon the sins of his believing servants : but he will rebuke them, in one way or other ;
that they may be more sensible, how greatly he abhors
their offences, notwithstanding his tender mercy to their
souls. " The sincerity of our love" to him must at length
be brought to the test; and it behoves us to enquire
seriously, and with earnest and persevering prayer to the
heart-searching God, to examine and prove us, whether we
be able to stand this test : for he says to us, in his word,
as certainly as he did to Peter, " Lovest thou me ? " and
the same will be the grand subject of enquiry at the solemn
day of judgment. (*Notes, Matt.* xxv. 31—46. 1 *Cor.* xvi.
21—24. *Eph.* vi. 21—24.) If we indeed love him ; his
perfections, his truths, his precepts, and his ordinances
will be cordially approved, received, and observed by us;
we shall love those most, who appear most to love and
resemble him ; we shall render him our thankful returns
for his unspeakable mercies, and endeavour to recommend
him to those around us : we shall take pleasure in speaking of him or to him, in hearing him praised, and in promoting his glory ; we shall be ready to labour, venture, or
suffer for his sake : yet after all we shall be grieved and
ashamed, that we love him no more, and serve him no
better. We shall imitate his example, and be gradually
conformed to his image : yet it will be humiliating and
afflicting to us, that we so little resemble him. Those who
thus " love the Lord Jesus in sincerity," have a consciousness of it, notwithstanding all their defects : and, as they
believe and are assured that " he knoweth all things," and
especially that he knows whether they love him or not;
they will apply to him to determine the question for them,
and to enable them to love him, (and that more and more,)
when they cannot confidently aver that they do.—As obedience is the general evidence of our love to Jesus, so the
love of his poor, afflicted, and despised people for his sake,
and an endeavour to be useful to the meanest of his flock,
is that particular expression which he requires of every
one. No man therefore, can be qualified to " feed the
" lambs and sheep" of Christ, who does not love the good
Shepherd more than all secular emolument and preferment:
and all those professed ministers of Christ, without distinction of rank and station, who are too ambitious, haughty,
slothful, delicate, studious of human learning, or occupied
in worldly pursuits and pleasures, to apply themselves earnestly to feed the souls of the people, even the weakest and
poorest of them, with the truth and instructions of God's
word, will be left under an awful condemnation, as utterly
destitute of the love of Christ.—Those who have been
greatly tempted, and have had much humiliating experience of their own frailty and sinfulness, and who have had
much forgiven them ; generally prove the most tender,
  4 K

compassionate, and attentive pastors of weak, bruised, and trembling believers, and the best guides of young converts: and the Lord often leaves those whom he loves, to pass through many painful conflicts with temptation and in-dwelling sin, as well as much experience of his tender compassion, in order to render them more gentle to their weak brethren, and to the lambs of his flock. Thus, when they feel their unworthiness for the least or meanest employment in his service, they become far abler ministers, than they were when they had a much higher opinion of themselves, and of their qualifications for the ministry; and were disposed to look down on those, whom they now " in honour prefer," and look up to.

V. 18—25.

The resolutions which upright young converts rashly form and break, are sometimes at length performed, when in a course of years they have been humbled and proved. They must first learn, that " without Christ they can do " nothing;" and then they will be shewn, that they " can " do all things through him who strengtheneth them." (*Notes*, 2 *Cor.* ii. 14—17. iii. 4—6. xii. 7—10.) Yet sufferings, pain, and death will appear formidable to the most experienced Christian: nor would he be willing to meet them, did he not hope to glorify God by so doing; and were he not desirous of leaving a sinful world, that he may be present with his beloved Lord. (*Note*, 2 *Cor.* v. 1—8.) But with these objects presented to his faith, he becomes ready to obey the Redeemer's call, and to follow him through death to glory; and the more love he had experienced, the readier will he be to tread in his steps.—Curiosity is too apt to interrupt us in our course: a thousand questions are started and discussed, about which Jesus as it were says to us, " What is that to thee? Follow " thou me." If we attend to this voice, even " death itself " will be gain to us," and we shall be ready for his coming: (*Phil.* i. 19—26:) and while here, we must live by faith in the sure testimony of his word, which never fails those who trust in it.—We ought to bless God for all that is written in the scriptures; but we may also be thankful that they are so compendious. It would not suit our situation, our engagements in this life, or our capacities, to have a more copious revelation; and we want no uncertain traditions, or human additions, and should most decidedly protest against them. (*Note*, *Col.* ii. 8—10.) We may, however, anticipate in imagination the joy which we shall receive in heaven, from a far more complete knowledge of all that Jesus did and said; as well as from the conduct of his providence and grace, in his dealings with each of us.—May this be the happiness of the writer and of every reader! Amen, Amen.

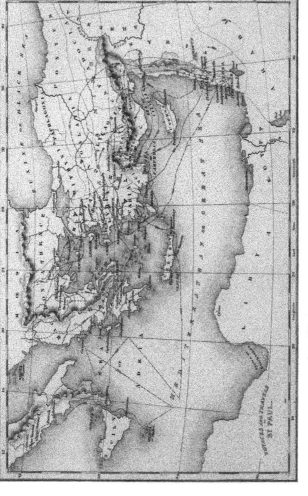

THE ACTS

OF THE

APOSTLES.

LUKE, " the beloved Physician," was undoubtedly the writer of this book ; and, intending it as an appendix to his gospel, he inscribes it likewise to Theophilus. (*Preface to the gospel of St. Luke*.) Indeed the whole may be considered as one publication in two parts: but the convenience of having the four gospels together, seems to have induced Christians in early times to divide it, by inserting St. John's gospel between these two parts. As the history terminates with St. Paul's imprisonment at Rome, during two years, which certainly ended before A. D. 65; it may fairly be concluded, that it was written within thirty or thirty-one years, after our Lord's crucifixion: for it can hardly be supposed, that the sacred writer would have closed his narrative so abruptly, and not have carried it on something further, had he composed it at a later period. The early reception also of this book, as authentick and divine, among the primitive Christians, has been sufficiently proved by learned men, from the testimony of ancient writers. But the circumstance which most of all demands our attention, and should raise our expectations respecting it, is this: it records the fulfilment of the ancient prophecies concerning the kingdom of the promised Messiah, and the manner in which it should be established in the world; and also of those predictions, or promises, which our Lord gave to his disciples, " while he was yet with them," concerning the powers with which they should be endued, the success which would attend their labours, and the persecutions which awaited them ; (*Notes, Matt.* x. 16—23. xxiv. 6—8. *Luke* x. 17—20, *v*. 18. xxi. 12—19. *John* xii. 27—33, *vv*. 31, 32. xiv. 7—14, *v*. 12. 25, 26. xv. 17—21. xvi. 1—3. 7—13.)—It is a fact, which cannot be doubted, that the religion of Jesus the Nazarene, who expired on a cross at Jerusalem, almost eighteen hundred years ago, was soon very extensively propagated among the nations ; that it obtained a permanent establishment, which it preserves to this day; and that the prophets had foretold that this would be the case, as to the kingdom of the Messiah : but the book before us is the only history, which expressly relates the manner in which this religion was at first promulgated.—Here we are informed, that eleven obscure men, whom Jesus had called to be his attendants and apostles, having continued with him till his crucifixion, saw and conversed with him after his resurrection, and afterwards beheld him ascend from them towards heaven, " till a cloud " received him out of their sight." In a few days, having appointed one in the room of the twelfth who had betrayed his Lord and destroyed himself, and being accompanied with a small number of disciples, the Holy Spirit, according to the promise of their Lord, descended upon them, in a most extraordinary manner, enabling them to speak divers languages, and work stupendous miracles ; and in all respects qualifying them for their arduous undertaking.—Accordingly, without further delay, within less than two months from the time when Jesus was crucified ; and at Jerusalem, under the immediate notice of his crucifiers, they began boldly to declare that he was risen from the dead, ascended into heaven, and exalted at the right hand of God; that he was the promised Messiah, " the " Prince of Life," the Saviour and Judge of the world, and as such entitled to all confidence, obedience, and adoration ; and openly to charge the people, the priests, and the rulers, with murdering " the Lord of glory." They were themselves unarmed, and unprotected except by a divine power; they possessed neither human learning, eloquence, nor influence : yet they had all the wisdom and the folly, the learning and the ignorance, the religion and the irreligion, with all the obstinate and varied prejudices, and corrupt passions and habits, of the whole world to encounter; as well as the power of rulers and princes to oppose them : notwithstanding which, they became decidedly and permanently triumphant. They employed no weapons, but simple testimony to the facts which they had witnessed, cogent arguments, affectionate persuasions, holy beneficent lives, fervent prayers, and patient sufferings even unto death.—With the Jews they reasoned from the scriptures of the Old Testament, and shewed how exactly these had been fulfilled in Jesus of Nazareth ; and when they afterwards went among the gentiles, they reasoned with them from such principles as they themselves acknowledged.—Proceeding in this manner, and every where attended by a divine power, both manifested in undeniable miracles, and by inwardly preparing men's hearts to receive the truth ; they had such astonishing success, that many hundreds of thousands, if not millions, not only from among the Jews and proselytes, but also from the grossest and most licentious idolaters, became the avowed disciples of the crucified Jesus, and the devoted worshippers and servants of " the one living and true God." Thus, in ' the Acts of the ' Apostles,' there is given us a history of the manner, in which the most extraordinary revolution that ever took place in the moral and religious state of the world was first begun; the effects of which were afterwards extended far more widely, till Christianity became the religion of powerful and numerous nations, and superseded the idolatries and superstitions, in which they were before enveloped : and if this account be true, the gospel must be divine.

4 K 3

ACTS

Now one most extraordinary circumstance attends this narrative; namely, if the truth of it be not admitted, there is no other history extant in the world, which can be substituted in its place: and thus an event, productive of far more extensive and important consequences, than any other, which ever yet occurred on earth, took place in a manner, of which no account has been transmitted to posterity!—This book is indeed the report of friends to the cause: but there is no counter report, with which we may compare it. Neither Jewish scribes and priests, nor gentile philosophers, historians, or moralists, ever attempted, that we find, to write a history of the first introduction of Christianity, in order to confront the account given by the Christians. The things here recorded " were not done in " a corner." Jerusalem, Cesarea, Antioch, and Ephesus, all great and celebrated cities, nay, Rome itself, the proud capital of the world, were among the places, in which the miracles are attested to have been wrought, and the success attained, in the full view of vehement and powerful opposers, who never ventured to deny the facts, though they could not account for them, without allowing the truth of the gospel.—Indeed the silence of the scribes and priests, who were loudly called upon to vindicate themselves from the charge of the most atrocious crimes; and even that of the heathen writers, in such a cause, is a plain confession, that they had nothing to say.

Some modern scepticks, however, insinuate in a covert manner, that a very different account might be given of the triumphs of Christianity, than that contained in scripture; but all their observations are grounded in misapprehension or misrepresentation. The time for giving another history of these events is long since past, and there are no materials for composing one. And indeed, to suppose, that such a religion as Christianity, which directly opposes every corrupt passion of the human heart, without making the least allowance, either to persons in the highest stations, or to its most zealous friends, could have prevailed in the world as it has done, by such instruments and means, and in the face of such powerful opposition, without the power of God succeeding it; is to assume, without shadow of proof, a fact immensely more incredible, than any of the miracles recorded in scripture, or all of them combined.

We must not, however, here expect a full and particular history of the labours and successes of the apostles and primitive evangelists: a select specimen alone is given. After the pouring out of the Holy Spirit on the day of Pentecost, and the first successes and sufferings of the apostles, little is recorded in the scripture concerning most of them. Indeed the names of more than half of them are never mentioned after the first chapter: yet it cannot reasonably be doubted, that they laboured, suffered, and prospered, as their brethren did; though most of the ancient records and traditions concerning them are so mingled with fiction, as not to be entitled to implicit or indiscriminate credit. Some other labourers are likewise brought forward, as Stephen the first martyr, Philip the evangelist, Barnabas, Silas, and others. But the conversion of Saul the persecutor, with his subsequent labours, sufferings, and triumphs, as the apostle of the gentiles, occupies a large proportion of the book; and the mention of the other apostles, in that part of the history, is occasional and brief. Peter, indeed, the apostle of the circumcision, was chosen to instruct Cornelius and his friends, (the first fruits from among the gentiles,) doubtless to avoid giving needless offence to the Jews; and the martyrdom of James the brother of John is briefly related. Indeed the labours of St. Paul himself are recorded in a very compendious manner. The events of several years are summed up in two or three chapters. And though, after Luke the historian joined the apostle, and became his faithful companion, (which is shewn by his using the first person plural in the narrative,) he is somewhat more circumstantial: yet the epistles of St. Paul prove, that his labours, persecutions, and successes were far greater, and the instructions which he gave his converts, far more particular, than a cursory reading of this history would lead us to suppose. At the same time, the remarkable coincidence, even in minute particulars, of the history and the epistles, is of such a nature, as could never have taken place, had not both been genuine; which will appear more fully, when the epistles come under our consideration.

But the book, on which we now enter, contains also a specimen of true believers, as illustrating the nature and effects of genuine Christianity: and it should be carefully noted, that in every age, all those multitudes who are called Christians, yet bear no resemblance to this specimen, will be driven away as chaff, at the great decisive day: and that the more we are like these primitive believers, when " great grace was upon them all," the more evident it is, that we shall ' be numbered with them in glory everlasting.'—Some intimations are also given of the manner, in which the primitive church was constituted and governed, its ministers were appointed, and its ordinances administered: yet it can hardly be supposed, but that the eager disputants of all those parties, into which the church is at present unhappily divided, must feel considerably disappointed in this respect; and secretly regret, that more particular and explicit information has not been given on these subjects: but this the Lord for wise reasons has seen good to withhold.

CHAP. I.

The sacred writer addresses his narrative to Theophilus, 1. Christ being risen, instructs his disciples; commands them to wait at Jerusalem, for the promise of the Holy Spirit; and ascends towards heaven in their sight, 2—9. Two angels assure them, that he would come again in like manner, 10, 11. The apostles and disciples at Jerusalem continue in prayer, with one accord, 12—14. Peter calls on them to appoint another apostle instead of Judas, in whose awful doom the scripture had been fulfilled, 15—22. Matthias is chosen by lot, accompanied with prayer, 23—26.

THE ᵃ former treatise have I made, O Theophilus, ᵇ of all that Jesus began both to do and teach,

2 Until ᶜ the day in which he was taken up, after that he, ᵈ through the Holy Ghost, had ᵉ given commandments unto ᶠ the apostles whom he had chosen: ,

3 To whom also ᵇ he shewed himself alive after his passion, by many infallible proofs, being seen of them ⁱ forty days, ᵏ and speaking of the things pertaining to the kingdom of God:

4 And, ᵉ being assembled together with *them*, ˡ commanded them that they should not depart from Jerusalem, but wait for ᵐ the promise of the Father, which, *saith he*, ye have heard of me.

5 For ⁿ John truly baptized with water: but ye shall be baptized with the Holy Ghost ᵒ not many days hence.

NOTES.

Chap. I. V. 1—3. Luke began this history by referring his pious friend, Theophilus, to that gospel, which formed the introduction to it. (*Note, Luke* i. 1—4.) He had there given a specimen of the miracles, actions, and doctrine of Christ, and the general scope of all that he did and taught, from his entrance on his publick ministry at .iis baptism by John, till his ascension into heaven, after that he had given proper instructions and injunctions to his chosen apostles. (*Marg. Ref.* c, d.—*Notes, Luke* xxiv. 50 —53.)—The phrase, " began both, &c." simply means, what Jesus had done and taught, from the beginning to the close of his publick ministry.—The use of the word " all " in this connexion, when so many miracles and discourses of our Lord, are recorded by the other evangelists, is a full demonstration, that arguments tending to establish *universal* conclusions, from this *general* term, must be precarious. (*Note, John* i. 6—9.)—The expression " by the " Holy Ghost," may either refer to our Lord's choosing the apostles, or to his giving them commandments after his resurrection : but the latter seems to be intended ; as he " breathed upon them, and bade them receive the Holy " Ghost ; " and as he then " opened their understandings, " that they might understand the scriptures." (*Marg. Ref.* e—g.—*Notes, Luke* xxiv. 44—49. *John* xx. 19—23, *vv.* 22, 23.) All those things which Jesus did and taught, in respect of his human nature, are ascribed to the Holy Spirit ; as well as the endowments which he conferred upon his disciples.—It is also stated, that Jesus " shewed him- " self alive " to his apostles, after his death, by many signs, or evidences, which could not possibly deceive them : (*Note, John* xx. 24—29 :) as he was seen of them, at different times, for the space of forty days, and conversed freely with them concerning those things, which related to the establishment, privileges, and laws of that " kingdom " of God," which was about to be set up on earth, by the preaching of his gospel. (*Marg. Ref.* h. k.—*Note, Matt.* iii. 2.)—' By speaking to, by walking, and by eating with, ' them, he gave them certain indication that he lived ;

' that he was seen and handled by them, was a sure evi- ' dence that he had a true and natural body ; that he per- ' mitted Thomas to view the scars of his hands and feet, ' and put his hand into his side, was a certain token that ' the body raised was the same which was crucified, and ' pierced by the soldier's lance. ... " Concerning the king- ' " dom of God." Namely, Of teaching the doctrine of ' this kingdom to all nations, and receiving them into it ' by baptism, who believed, and professed to own it ; of ' the benefits which were promised to them who cordially ' believed their doctrine, and the condemnation which be- ' longed to them who would not believe it ; of the encou- ' ragements and assistances he would afford them in the ' propagation of it, by his continual presence with them, ' and the assistance of his Spirit ; and by the miracles ' by which their doctrine should be confirmed.' *Whitby.* It is, however, highly probable, that a great deal more passed on these most interesting subjects, between our Lord and his apostles in the course of the forty days preceding his ascension, than is any where recorded.

Treatise. (1) Λογον, *word, account, discourse, narrative.*— *Had given commandments.* (2) Εντειλαμενος. xiii. 47. *Matt.* iv. 6. xv. 4. xix. 7. xxviii. 20. *John* viii. 5. xiv. 31. xv. 14. 17. *Heb.* ix. 20. xi. 22.—*After his passion.* (3) Μδα το παδειν αυτον. *Luke* xxiv. 46.—*Infallible proofs.*] Τεκμηριοις. Here only. ' Aristotle says, that τεκμηριον signifies a certain ' and indubitable sign : from τεκμαρ, *an end*; because it ' puts an end to controversy.' *Leigh.*—*Being seen.*] Οπτα- νομενος. Here only N. T.—1 *Kings* viii. 8. *Sept.*

V. 4—8. The apostles and disciples, no doubt, returned from Galilee to Jerusalem, and assembled there, by their Lord's appointment. (*Notes, Matt.* xxviii. 18. *Luke* xxiv. 50—53.)—He was about to be taken from them, and they might seem to be without employment in that city : yet they were charged " not to depart thence ; " but to wait there for the pouring out of the Holy Spirit, which he had promised to send them from the Father. (*Marg. Ref.* l, m. —*Notes, John* xiv. 15—17. 25, 26. xv. 26, 27. xvi. 7—13.) For it was proper that this extraordinary event should occur in the very place, where Jesus had before been pub-

6 When they therefore were come together, they asked of him, saying, Lord, wilt thou at this time restore again the kingdom to Israel?

7 And he said unto them, It is not for you to know the times, or the seasons, which the Father hath put in his own power.

8 But ye shall receive power, after that the Holy Ghost is come upon you: and ye shall be witnesses unto me, both in Jerusalem, and in all Judea, and in Samaria, and unto the uttermost part of the earth.

9 And when he had spoken these things, while they beheld, he was taken up: and a cloud received him out of their sight.

10 And while they looked stedfastly toward heaven as he went up, behold, two men stood by them in white apparel;

11 Which also said, Ye men of Galilee, why stand ye gazing up into heaven? This same Jesus, which is taken up from you into heaven, shall so come in like manner as ye have seen him go into heaven.

12 Then returned they unto Jerusalem, from the mount called Olivet, which is from Jerusalem a sabbath-day's journey.

---

lickly crucified. This would fully answer to what John had testified concerning him; as it would be a most remarkable baptism by the Holy Spirit, both communicating to them miraculous powers, and more abundantly illuminating and sanctifying their souls. This took place on the tenth day after our Lord's ascension. (*Marg. Ref.* n, o.—*Notes*, ii. 1—4. *Matt.* iii. 11, 12.)—But, notwithstanding all which he had taught them, they still entertained some thoughts of a *temporal* kingdom: (*Marg. Ref.* p, q.—*Notes, Matt.* xviii. 1—4. xxiv. 3 :) perhaps they supposed, that the pouring out of the Holy Spirit would induce the nation, in general, to acknowledge Jesus as the Messiah; and that he would then perform, what they supposed to be the meaning of the ancient prophets in this respect, (*Note*, iii. 19—21, v. 21.) Yet they seem to have feared, lest the base usage, which he had received from the rulers and people of Israel, should deter him from " restoring " the kingdom " to the nation, as in the days of David and Solomon. Our Lord, however, knew that his ascension, and the descent of the Holy Spirit would finally terminate these expectations: he therefore checked their curiosity, by observing, that it was not proper for them to know these matters; which were entirely at the disposal of God, to be managed and effected by his sovereign power and authority, " and according to the counsel of his own " will," with which no one must presume to interfere. (*Marg. Ref.* r, s.—*Notes, Deut.* xxix. 29. *Matt.* xxiv. 36—41, v. 36. *John* xxi. 18—23, v. 22. 1 *Thes.* v. 1—3.) But he assured them, that they would be endued with the Holy Spirit, enabling them to perform many wonderful works; as well as emboldening and strengthening them for their work, and giving them abundant success in it. Thus they would become witnesses of his resurrection, ascension, miracles, and doctrine, in all parts of the earth. (*Marg.* and *Marg. Ref.* t—y.—*Notes, Luke* xxiv. 44—49. *John* xv. 26, 27.)—The apostles seem to have understood, that they were authorized to preach to the Samaritans, who were circumcised, and observed many parts of the ceremonial law, though in many respects both heretical and schismatical: but they were not aware, till long after, that uncircumcised gentiles were to be admitted into the kingdom of their Lord, without any regard to the rites of the Mosaick law. (*Notes*, iii. 19—21, v. 21. viii. 5—8. 14—17. x. 9—23. 36—48. xi. 1—18.) It is, however, not only *difficult*, but perhaps *impossible*, to delineate, with any tolerable precision, the state of the apostles' minds at this crisis; in which darkness and light, hopes and fears, carnal and spiritual views and expectations, were blended so intimately, that almighty power alone could separate them. And this was done, *at once*, and effectually, in most things, by the descent of the Holy Spirit: though in a few particulars, they were left for some time longer, under a degree of error or prejudice.—The change wrought in the minds and hearts of the apostles, on the day of Pentecost, was as truly miraculous as the gift of tongues. They were no longer the same men; nay, in many respects, men of a widely different spirit and character, possessing an enlargement of mind, and a superiority to carnal prejudices, hopes, and fears, beyond what could have possibly been previously conceived.

Being assembled together with them. (4) " Eating to-" gether, &c." *Marg.* Συναλιζομενος. Here only. Ex σvv et αλιζω, *colligo.*—*Commanded.*] Παρηγγειλιν. iv. 18. v. 28. xv. 5. xvi. 23. *Matt.* x. 5. *Luke* v. 14. 1 *Tim.* i. 3. iv. 11. v. 7. vi. 13. 17.—*Wilt thou ... restore again.* (6) Αποκαδι-ςανις;—' Αποκαδιςημι, seu αποκαδισαω, seu αποκαδιςανω, repono, ' restituo, in pristinum locum ... in quo antea fuit reduco, in ' pristinum restituo statum; ex απο et καδιςημι.' Schleusner. *Matt.* xii. 13. xvii. 11. *Mark* viii. 25. ix. 12. *Luke* vi. 10. *Heb.* xiii. 19.—*Hath put.* (7) Εθετο. See on *John* xv. 16.—*The uttermost part of the earth.* (8) Εσχατε της γης. xiii. 47.—*Is.* xlviii. 20. xlix. 6. lxii. 11. Sept.

V. 9—12. The instructions and promises, which have been considered, seem to have been delivered, as our Lord was leading the disciples forth to that part of the mount of Olives, whence he ascended: after which he was gradually raised from the earth, in their sight, till a cloud intercepted their view of him. (*Marg. Ref.* z, a.—*Notes*, 2 *Kings* ii. 11. *Luke* xxiv. 50—53.) And while they looked earnestly after him, with mixed astonishment, regret, and exultation; two angels, in the form of men, accosted them, demanding why they gazed after their ascended Lord, as

13 And when they were come in, they went up into an upper room, where abode both Peter, and James, and John, and Andrew, Philip, and Thomas, Bartholomew, and Matthew, James the son of Alpheus, and Simon Zelotes, and Judas the brother of James.

14 These all continued with one accord in prayer and supplication, with the women, and Mary the mother of Jesus, and with his brethren.

15 ¶ And in those days Peter stood up in the midst of the disciples, and said, (the number of the names together were about an hundred and twenty,)

16 Men and brethren, This scripture must needs have been fulfilled, which the Holy Ghost, by the mouth of David, spake before concerning Judas, which was guide to them that took Jesus.

17 For he was numbered with us, and had obtained part of this ministry.

18 Now this man purchased a field with the reward of iniquity; and, falling headlong, he burst asunder in the midst, and all his bowels gushed out.

if they either desired his present return, or counted him lost to them. For, though he was now ascended to his glorious throne in heaven, to return no more, to reside on earth in his former condition; yet he would assuredly come at length, in a visible manner, in the clouds of heaven, to judge the world, and to gather to himself all his believing people, as he had often promised them. (*Marg. Ref.* b—f.—*Notes, Matt.* xxv. 31—46. xxvi. 63—68. *John* xiv. 1—3. 1 *Thes.* iv. 13—18. 2 *Thes.* i. 5—10. ii. 1, 2. *Heb.* ix. 24—28. *Rev.* i. 7.) Upon this they returned to Jerusalem from mount Olivet.—The place belonging to the village of Bethany, from which Jesus ascended was about a mile distant from Jerusalem: this was called a sabbath-day's journey; probably, because it might generally be necessary to go so far on that day, in order to attend the service of the synagogue.

He was taken up. (9) Επηρθη. *Luke* xi. 27. *John* xvii. 1. 2 *Cor.* x. 5. xi. 20.—*Received.*] Υπελαβεν. ii. 15. *Luke* vii. 43. x. 30.—*Gazing.* (11) Εμβλεποντες. xxii. 11. *Matt.* xix. 26, *et al.*—*Which is taken up.*] Ο αναληφθεις. 2. 22. vii. 43. x. 16. xx. 13, 14. xxiii. 31. *Mark* xvi. 19. 1 *Tim.* iii. 16.

V. 13, 14. Many have supposed, that this " upper " room " was one of the chambers belonging to the temple. But 'these chambers were all appointed for sacred ' things or persons : how improbable therefore is it, that ' poor fishermen, and Galileans, odious for their Master's ' sake, should be permitted to crowd, in such numbers, ' into one of these rooms !' *Whitby.*—The circumstance of the disciples being " continually in the temple," (*Luke* xxiv. 53,) only shews that they resorted from their lodgings or place of assembling, to the temple, at proper hours. (*Notes,* ii. 44—47. iii. 1—11, *v.* 1.) Others have conjectured, that the company met in the house of Mary, mother to John Mark : (xii. 12:) but even this, though far more probable, is altogether uncertain.—' The assemblies of the ' church, to hear the word, and to join in common prayers, ' were first instituted and celebrated by apostolical autho- ' rity, in a private house.'—The brethren, or kinsmen, of our Lord, seem to have been the same, who formerly did not believe in him. (*Notes, Mark* iii. 20, 21. 31—35. *John* vii. 3—10.)—This is the last time, in which Mary, the mother of Jesus, is mentioned in scripture : and it is in a very cursory manner, as one of the company who joined in prayer; but without any peculiar distinction, or the least appearance of her exercising authority over the apostles, or even of giving them counsel, or at all interfering in their measures.—*Peter, &c.* (13) *Marg. Ref.* k—r. —*Notes, Matt.* x. 1—4. *Mark* iii. 13—19.

An upper room. (13) Το υπερωον. " The upper room, &c." ix. 37. xx. 8. Not elsewhere.—*Where abode.*] 'Ου ησαν καλαμενοντες. Here only N. T.—*Num.* xxii. 8. *Josh.* ii. 22. *Sept.* The place in which the disciples assembled for conference and prayer must be meant; for they doubtless lodged in different places.—*Continued.* (14) Ησαν προσκαρτερουντες. ii. 42. 46. vi. 4. viii. 13. x. 7. *Mark* iii. 9. *Rom.* xii. 12. xiii. 6. *Col.* iv. 2.—Προσκαρτερησις, *Eph.* vi. 18.— ' The word signifies, to go on, in performing or enduring ' any thing, courageously, and with a certain invincible ' hardiness and resolution of mind.' *Beza.*—*With one ac-* cord.] 'Ομοθυμαδον. ii. 1. 46. iv. 24. v. 12. vii. 57. viii. 6. xii. 20. xv. 25. xviii. 12. xix. 29. *Rom.* xv. 6. Ex ομως similis, et θυμος, animus.

V. 15. The whole number of disciples, collected together at this time, was about one hundred and twenty. The seventy disciples, probably, were a part of them : but most of the five hundred brethren, who saw Jesus in Galilee before his ascension, had remained there ; and doubtless many others believed in him in different parts of the land. (*Marg. Ref.*)

Names.] Ονομαλα. *Rev.* iii. 4. xi. 13.—*Note, Rev.* xi. 13, 14.—Persons, without special distinction, are evidently meant by Luke.

V. 16—18. While the disciples were continually uniting together in persevering prayer and supplication, it occurred to Peter, to propose the appointment of another apostle, in the place of the traitor Judas, that the number of twelve might be restored. Peter's guilt in denying his Lord had been so great, as at first sight to appear almost like that of Judas : it is therefore most reasonable to suppose, that he was directed by a divine admonition, to take the lead on this occasion ; and the whole transaction shewed, how fully all concerned were satisfied, that he was sincerely and deeply penitent.—In his address he called the disciples " Men and brethren." Our Lord never thus

19 And ¹ it was known unto all the dwellers at Jerusalem: insomuch as that field is called, in their proper tongue, ᵐ Aceldama, that is to say, The field of blood.

20 For it is written ⁿ in the book of Psalms, ° Let his habitation be desolate, and let no man dwell therein: and, ᵖ His ⁹ bishoprick let another take.

21 Wherefore of ʳ these men which have companied with us, all the time ʳ that the Lord Jesus ˢ went in and out among us,

22 Beginning ᵗ from the baptism of John, ᵘ unto that same day that he was taken up from us, must one be ordain-

ed to be ᵛ a witness with us of his resurrection.

23 And they appointed two, Joseph called ˣ Barsabas, who was surnamed Justus, and Matthias.

24 And ʸ they prayed, and said, ᶻ Thou, Lord, which knowest the hearts of all men, shew whether of these two thou hast chosen,

25 That ᵃ he may take part of this ministry and apostleship, ᵇ from which Judas ᶜ by transgression fell, that he might ᵈ go to his own place.

26 And ᵉ they gave forth their lots: and the lot fell upon ᶠ Matthias; and he was numbered with the eleven apostles.

addressed the people; and perhaps it implied an equality, not suitable to the dignity of his character: but the apostles frequently did in speaking to Jews, as well as Christians; yet never in addressing the Gentiles: and it seems to imply, that they recognized a two-fold relation to them, as men of the same nature descended from Adam, and as brethren of the same favoured family as descended from Abraham. (*Marg. Ref.* b.)—Peter reminded the disciples, that the words, not of David, but of the Holy Spirit, speaking by David, concerning Judas, when he prophesied of Christ, or spake as a type of him, had been exactly fulfilled. (*Marg. Ref.* c—e.—*Notes, Ps.* xli. 9. lxix. 22—28. cix. 6—20.) Judas had indeed been numbered with them as an apostle: yet he had deserved his doom, by his treachery and base behaviour, in conducting those who came to apprehend his Lord; but all which he gained, as " the " wages of his iniquity," having been restored by him to the chief priests, had merely served to purchase a field, which in some sense he might be said to have purchased, as he supplied the money which paid for it: and then in despair hanging himself, (perhaps in this very field,) by some accident he fell down, and burst asunder; so that he became a horrid spectacle to the beholders, by the righteous judgment of God upon him. (*Marg. Ref.* f—k.— *Notes, Matt.* xxvii. 3—10.)

Numbered. (17) Καθηριθμημενος. Here only. Ex καλα et αριθμος, *numerus.*—*Had obtained.*] Ελαχε. (Λαγχανω) *Luke* i. 9. *John* xix. 24. 2 *Pet.* i. 1. Not elsewhere N. T.— 1 *Sam.* xiv. 47. Sept.—*Part.*] Κληρον. 25, 26. viii. 21. xxvi. 18. *Matt.* xxvii. 35. *Mark* xv. 24. *Luke* xxiii. 34. *John* xix. 24. *Col.* i. 12. 1 *Pet.* v. 3.—*He burst asunder.*] (18) Ελακησε. Here only. ' Λακεω, ... *disrumpor cum crepitu* ' *quodam.*' Schleusner.—*Gushed out.*] Εξεχυθη. " Were " poured out." ii. 17.

V. 19. This verse seems to come in as a parenthesis, and to be the words, not of the apostle, but of the historian; who informed his readers, that this event became generally known to all the inhabitants of Jerusalem; and that the field, which had been bought with the price of the blood of Jesus, and which cost Judas his life also, was commonly called " the field of blood," at the time when

the history was written.—It is remarkable, that he does not say, in *our*, but *their* proper tongue, and this, I think, shews that the writer was not a Hebrew, but either a Hellenist, or a Gentile. (*Preface to Luke. Note, Matt.* xxvii. 6—10, v. 8.) Some think, that Judas also was buried in this field; if so, he bought a burying-place among strangers for himself, with " the wages of his ini- " quity." (*Notes, Num.* xxxi. 8. 2 *Pet.* ii. 15, 16.)

Aceldama.] Ακελδαμα. ' Vox contracta Syro-chaldaicæ ' linguæ; ex חקל *ager*, et דמא *sanguis.*' Schleusner. V. 20—22. The apostle proceeded to observe, that as the scriptures had been fulfilled in the doom of Judas, so the same scriptures pointed out to them what their present conduct ought to be: for as it was predicted that " his " habitation should be desolate;" so it was directed, that another should take his office and charge. It behoved them, therefore, to take one of their company, who had attended on Jesus with them, from the very beginning of his ministry to his ascension into heaven; that he might be solemnly set apart, to be, with them, a witness of his resurrection, as well as to perform other parts of the apostolical office.—*Let his,* &c. (20) This varies considerably from the LXX, and also from the Hebrew, especially as the plural pronoun is used in both. (*Note, Ps.* lxix. 22— 28, v. 25.)—*His,* &c.] Verbatim from the LXX. *Ps.* cix. 8. —*Went in and out.* (21) *Marg. Ref.* r.

Bishoprick. (20) Επισκοπην. *Luke* xix. 44. 1 *Tim.* iii. 1. 1 *Pet.* ii. 12.—*Ps.* cix. 8. Sept. Επισκοπος, *Acts* xx. 28. *Phil.* i. 1.

V. 23—26. As the other apostles and disciples perceived the propriety of Peter's proposal, they proceeded to select two persons, according to the best of their judgment, for this important service: probably, they had both been of the number of the seventy disciples, and were eminent for wisdom and integrity. But, being unable to decide whether of them was the most proper for the charge, they referred the matter by prayer, and by casting lots, to the Lord's determination. As Jesus had personally appointed the other apostles, many expositors have argued, that this prayer was immediately addressed to him; and the language favours the supposition. (*Marg. Ref.* y, z.)

κ 3

CHAP. II.

The day of Pentecost being come, the Holy Spirit is poured out on the assembled disciples, with "a "sound as of a mighty wind;" while "cloven "tongues as of fire" rest on each of them, 1—3. They speak divers languages, in the hearing of multitudes from many nations, who are come together on the occasion; at which most are amazed, but some deride, 4—13. Peter shews, that this is the fulfilment of a prophecy of Joel, 14—21; that Jesus, whom they had crucified, was risen from the dead, according

to the prophecy of David, 22—32; and that being ascended into heaven, and exalted at the right hand of God, he had poured out the Holy Spirit, to demonstrate that he was the promised Messiah, 33—36. They are pricked to the heart, and enquire what they must do, 37. Peter exhorts and encourages them to repent, and to be baptized in the name of Jesus, 38—40. Three thousand are added to the church, 41. They continue stedfast in the faith, 42. Many miracles are wrought by the apostles, 43. The disciples have all things in common, and abound in love, joy, and praise; while numbers are daily added to them, 44 —47.

They, however, appealed to the Searcher of all hearts, to determine whether of the two he had chosen, to take part of the authority, trust, and labour of the apostleship; from which Judas had fallen by his atrocious crime, to go to that dreadful place of punishment, to which he was righteously condemned. In answer to this appeal, the Lord was pleased that the lot should fall upon Matthias; whom some suppose to have been the same with Nathanael, because both their names signify " the gift of God:" but this is very uncertain. It is remarkable, that Matthias is never mentioned in scripture, except on this occasion, but Barsabas is. (Notes, xv. 22—35, vv. 22. 32.) Yet, no doubt, the Lord had wise and holy reasons for choosing Matthias, though they are wholly unknown to us. (Marg. Ref. a—e. —Note, Prov. xvi. 33.)—The prayer offered on this occasion, was wholly unlike what might have been expected from deceivers. It is dictated by a deep sense of the Lord's perfect acquaintance with all hearts, the importance of the cause in which they were engaged, and their incompetency to decide in it without divine direction. The whole account, when compared with the surprising blindness of the disciples, to the true meaning of the prophecies, before the resurrection of Christ, illustrates the evangelist's words, " Then opened he their understandings, to under- " stand the scripture:" (Note, Luke xxiv. 44—49, v. 44:) for there is a constant recurrence to the sacred oracles, and a clear and sound interpretation of the passages adduced.—It is wonderful, that any persons should have referred to this narrative, in the argument concerning the choice of ministers: when the case was most evidently extraordinary, and one which could never again occur; and when the eleven apostles, with a number of the seventy disciples, probably formed the far greater part of the company present.

Which knowest the hearts. (24) Καρδιογνωτα. xv. 8. Not elsewhere. Ex καρδια, cor, et γνωτης, qui aliquid cognitum habet. Notes, John ii. 23—25. Heb. iv. 12, 13. Rev. ii. 20 —23, v. 23.—*Thou hast chosen.*] Εξιλεξω. 2. Luke vi. 13. John vi. 70. xiii. 18. xv. 16. 19.—*He was numbered with.* (26) Συγκαῖεψηφισθη. Here only. Ex συν, κ αι et ψηφιζω, calculis eligo, Luke xiv. 28. Ψηφος, Acts xxvi. 10.

PRACTICAL OBSERVATIONS.

V. 1—12.

While we thankfully peruse the instructive narrative " of all that Jesus began both to do, and to teach;" let us remember, that all instruction should be reduced to practice; and that ministers should begin *to do,* and then

to teach, that their example may illustrate, confirm, and adorn their doctrine. For these ends, we need a daily supply of that Spirit, by which Jesus " gave command- " ment to his apostles; " that we may be effectually convinced of those truths, which, though authenticated by " infallible proofs," are never cordially and practically believed, till his teaching removes the veil of pride and worldly lusts, from the understanding and the heart. (Notes, 2 Cor. iii. 12—18. iv. 3—6.) Then, and not before, we learn to profit by what Jesus has spoken " con- " cerning the kingdom of God; " and are induced to seek its privileges, and to obey its commandments. We should therefore wait for this " promise of the Father," according to the directions which our Lord has given us. We do not indeed expect the miraculous powers of the Holy Spirit: but we must experience his purifying baptism, or we never can serve God, or be made meet for the inheritance of heaven. In proportion as this is deficient, (for it is communicated in different degrees,) even true believers remain under the influence of carnal prejudices, and cleave to earthly things; by which they are kept in error, or betrayed into curious questions and frivolous speculations. But it behoves us to leave " secret things to the Lord, to " whom they belong; " and to submit to his wisdom, in all the dispensations of his providence and grace. (P. O. Job xxviii. 12—28. John xxi. 18—23.) It is enough, that he has engaged to give his people strength adequate to their trials and services: that, under the influence of the Holy Spirit, they may, in one way or other, be witnesses for Christ on earth; while in heaven he manages their concerns with the most perfect wisdom, truth, and love.—In our affections and hopes, we ought to follow our ascended Saviour, that our conversation and our hearts may be in heaven; and that our expectation of his second coming may be stedfast and joyful, by our " giving diligence to be found of him " in peace, without spot and blameless." (Notes, Col. iii. 1—4. 2 Pet. iii. 10—13.)

V. 13—26.

In order to serve the cause of Christ on earth, we should study to be " of one heart" with all his true disciples; that, by mutual conference, we may encourage and animate each other, and that our united prayers may be more fervent, persevering, and uninterrupted. (Note, 1 Pet. iii. 7.) Thus we may have peace, in communion with God and his saints, notwithstanding the enmity and rage of an ungodly world.—As the church of Christ at first consisted of only few persons, so we ought not to " despise the day

AND when [a] the day of Pentecost was fully come, [b] they were all with one accord in one place.

a xx. 16. Ex. xxiii. 16. xxxiv. 22. Lev. xxiii. 15—21. Num. xxviii. 26—31. Deut. xvi.9—12. 1 Cor. xvi. 8. 1,2. Jer. xxxii.39.
b 46. l. 18—15. iv. 24.,32. v. 12. 2 Chr. v. 13, 14. xxx. 12. Ps. cxxxiii. 1, 2. Zeph. iii. 9. Rom. xv. 6. Phil. i, 27, ii. 2.

2 And [c] suddenly there came a sound from heaven, [d] as of a rushing mighty wind, and [e] it filled all the house where they were sitting.

c xvi. 26, 26. Is. lxv. 24. Mal. iii. 1. d 1 Kings xix. 11. Pe. xviii. 10. Cant. iv. 16. Ex. iii. 12, 13. xxxvii. 9, 10.
John iii. 8.   e iv. 81.

"of small things." (Note, Zech. iv. 8—10.) A little company, united in love, exemplary in their conduct, fervent in prayer, and prudently zealous in promoting the cause of Christ, by every means in their power, will generally increase with rapidity.—We should carefully observe the dispensations of providence, and compare them with the holy scriptures; not only for the confirmation of our faith, but in order to learn our duty: and we ought to point out to our brethren those intimations, which are thus suggested to us; that we may unite our endeavours to do good, as circumstances may require, and occasions may offer.—The crimes and awful end of some ministers, who have been high in rank and reputation in the church, should by no means lead men to despise that sacred calling: but such instances lould[l]y require others, "to look to themselves," to their motives and intentions, as well as to their doctrine and moral conduct. The nearer men approach to Jesus in profession and office, the more detestable is their treachery, if they secretly concur with his enemies, and betray his cause to them. The gain of hypocrites is "the reward of "iniquity," and it will only purchase for them an "Acel-"dama, a field of blood," a more awful condemnation and more notorious infamy: for, if they die impenitent, as it is highly probable they will, in what way soever they leave the world, and whether their habitations be left desolate or flourishing, they must follow Judas to their "own "place," even that prepared for "the workers of ini-"quity," and to each of them according to the degree of guilt contracted by him.—But when mercenary and ungodly men are removed; we should beseech the great Searcher of hearts, to fill their places in the church, with such ministers as have known Christ, and are capable of being witnesses for him, and of declaring to others the efficacy of his sufferings, and "the power of his resurrec-"tion." Those who are entrusted in this matter should be careful to "lay hands suddenly on no man:" but, while they do their best, to select the most able and upright persons for this sacred service, they ought to pour out their most earnest prayers to him, "who knoweth "what is in man," to direct their choice, and to determine for them, who are, and who are not, proper persons. (Notes, 1 Tim. v. 21, 22. 24, 25.) Where this is omitted, or when it degenerates into a form; we need not wonder to see the church crowded with drones, hirelings, blind guides, persecutors, and hereticks; instead of faithful, able, disinterested, and laborious ministers of Christ. Indeed in every thing, when we have gone as far as we can, "according to the wisdom given" to us, we should, in one way or other, refer the decision to the Lord: and surely the lot, which, under both the Old and the New Testament dispensation, has been used and owned, as a solemn and religious appeal to God's providence, to decide doubtful matters for his worshippers, ought not to be used by Christians in such frivolous concerns, or in so irreverent a manner, as it generally is by those who "have

"no fear of God before their eyes." (Notes, Ex. xx. 17. Josh. xiii. 6. 1 Sam. xiv. 36—44. Prov. xvi. 33.)

NOTES.

CHAP. II. V. 1. The word "Pentecost" implies, that this was the *fiftieth* day; that is, from the second day of unleavened bread, whence "the feast of the in-gathering" of the harvest was computed. The Israelites were commanded to bring a meat-offering of the first-fruits of their corn, at this festival: which was observed, as it is generally supposed, in commemoration of the giving of the law from mount Sinai, fifty days after their departure out of Egypt. *(Marg. Ref. a.—Notes, Ex. xix. 1. xxiii. 14—18. Lev. xxiii. 15—21. Deut. xvi. 9.) At this solemnity, the Lord was pleased to "pour out his "Spirit," and thus to consecrate the first-fruits of the Christian church. Multitudes, from all parts of the country, and from distant regions, were constantly collected at Jerusalem on this occasion: and more than usual seem to have attended this year; perhaps from the general expectation which prevailed, that the Messiah would soon appear. Thus numbers, who at the preceding passover had seen Jesus crucified with ignominy, and had carried the report of it to their several places of abode, would now see this remarkable proof of his resurrection and ascension; and this would every where be made known in like manner. —As Jesus arose on the first day of the week, so the Holy Spirit descended on the same, seven weeks, or on the fiftieth day, afterwards. This tended to honour that day, which was soon to be set apart as the Christian sabbath. (Notes, xx. 7—12, v. 7. John xx. 19—29, vv. 19. 26. 1 Cor. xvi. 1, 2. Rev. i. 9—11, v. 10.)—The day of Pentecost, properly speaking, began the preceding evening; so that in the morning it might be said to be "fully come:" and the apostles, and their company, were then collected together in entire harmony and love; probably in the upper room, where they before assembled for prayer and religious conference. (Marg. Ref. b.—Note, i. 13, 14.) No objection to this can properly be made, on account of the room being too small to hold the multitudes that afterwards came together: for we must suppose, that they surrounded the house where the apostles had been, and that these went out to them: as no building, which they could procure, could possibly hold such immense numbers.— Different opinions are maintained, concerning the persons assembled on this occasion; whether the apostles only, or the whole company of disciples: but the language of the sacred writer obviously implies the latter; the pouring out of the Spirit on all the disciples would form a more exact fulfilment of Joel's prophecy (18) and it is plain that others, besides the apostles, were "filled with the Holy "Ghost," at a very early period. (vi. 3. 5. 8.) As afterwards, miraculous powers, and the gift of languages, were conferred on others, by the laying on of the hands of the

4 L 2

3 And there appeared unto them 'cloven tongues, like as of fire, and it sat upon each of them.

4 And they were all filled with the Holy Ghost, and began to speak with other tongues, as the Spirit gave them utterance.

5 And there were dwelling at Jerusalem Jews, devout men, out of every nation under heaven.

---

apostles; so without this, the gift of tongues was now conferred on converts in general. (Notes, viii. 14—17. x. 44—48.) There seems therefore no sufficient reason for supposing, that this first effusion of the Spirit was exclusively bestowed on the apostles. Indeed, either the apostles assembled together *alone*, as if for this special purpose, of which no intimation is given; or else the whole company partook of the blessing: and this certainly accords to the tradition of the church in ancient times.

Of Pentecost.] Πεντηκοστης. xx. 16. 1 Cor. xvi. 8.—Πενθηκοτος, *Lev.* xxv. 10, 11. *Sept. Quinquagesimus.—Was fully come.*] Συμπληρωσθαι. Luke viii. 23. ix. 51. Not elsewhere.—*With one accord.*] Ομοθυμαδον. See on i. 14.—*In one place.*] Επι το αυτο. i. 15. iii. 1. *Matt.* xxii. 34. 1 Cor. vii. 5. xi. 20.—*Ps.* xix. 9. xxxvii. 38. *Sept.*

V. 2, 3. While the assembled disciples were thus waiting the performance of the promise, which their Lord had given them; (i. 4. 8;) there came a sound from heaven, resembling that of an impetuous wind, which rushed in and filled the house, where they were sitting. This was an emblem of the invincible energy, with which the Holy Spirit works upon the minds of men; bearing down all opposition before him; in a manner which cannot be explained, but which is most manifest by its effects. (*Marg. Ref.* c, d.—*Notes, John* iii. 7, 8. 1 *Thes.* i. 5—8.) At the same time, there appeared the form of " tongues," divided at the tip of them, and resembling fire; one of which rested on each of the whole company. This was an emblem of the gift at this time bestowed upon them, of speaking, with fluency and propriety, divers languages which they had never learned; and the appearance " as " of fire," denoted the fervent zeal, with which they were enabled to speak, and the effects which their words produced upon the minds of the hearers. (*Marg. Ref.* f—h. —*Notes, Is.* vi. 6, 7. *Jer.* xxiii. 28, 29. *Matt.* iii. 11, 12.) —The shape of the mitre, worn by bishops, is by some thought to have been derived from the supposed form of these divided tongues; but if they sat on every one present, (as the original determines,) and others besides the apostles were present, the ground of this distinction fails. Indeed it is more likely, that there appeared *several* divisions in the tongues, than merely *two*; as the former would be a more exact emblem of the gift of speaking divers languages, conferred at the same time.

A sound. (2) Ηχος. Luke iv. 37. Heb. xii. 19. Not elsewhere. Ηχεω, Luke xxi. 25. 1 Cor. xiii. 1.—*Mighty.*] Βιαιας. Here only.—Βια, *violentia*, v. 26. xxi. 35.—*Wind.*] Πνοης, xvii. 25. Not elsewhere: A πνω, *flo.* xxvii. 40.— *Cloven.* (3) Διαμεριζομεναι. *Divided.* 45. *Matt.* xxvii. 35. *Mark* xv. 24. *Luke* xi. 17, 18. xii. 52, 53, *et al.*

V. 4. At the time of these extraordinary appearances, the whole company were abundantly replenished with the gifts and graces of the Holy Spirit: (*Marg. Ref.* i:) so that they " began to speak with other tongues," or in languages of which they had before been entirely ignorant; as also with more distinct views and lively affections; even as the Spirit suggested divine truths to their minds, and enabled them to discourse upon them in a suitable manner. (*Marg. Ref.* k, l.) A more stupendous miracle than this can scarcely be imagined; as every one must perceive, who carefully considers the subject; and recollects with what difficulty an adult person acquires the accurate knowledge and pronunciation even of one language, so as to speak it with propriety, and without hesitation. At the same time, it was of the utmost importance to the end designed: for, while it served to confirm the testimony of the witnesses of our Lord's resurrection, it qualified the apostles and first preachers of the gospel for their important service, to which their want of learning would have otherwise been an insurmountable hindrance.—The diversity of languages introduced by the power of God, as a judgment on the presumptuous and rebellious builders at Babel, has always been the great obstacle to the diffusion of useful knowledge, and of true religion. (*Notes, Gen.* xi. 1—9. *Is.* xxv. 6—8.) The persons therefore whom the Lord saw good to employ in propagating the Christian religion among the nations, and who were unacquainted with foreign languages, could have made no progress in their work, without this special gift, or something equivalent to it: for even the Jews dispersed in foreign countries generally spoke the Greek tongue. But, the deficiency being supplied in this miraculous manner, enabled them to shew the credentials of their commission from God, along with their ability for the service to which they were called, in every place whither they went.—' As the confusion of ' tongues in Babel spread idolatry throughout the world, ' and made men lose the knowledge of God and true reli-' gion; so God provided, by the gift of tongues in Zion, to ' repair the knowledge of himself among the nations.' *Whitby.*

Gave them utterance.] Εδιδου αυτοις αποφθεγγεσθαι. 14. xxvi. 25. Not elsewhere N. T.—1 *Chr.* xxv. 1. *Ez.* xiii. 9. *Sept.*—Hence *apophthegm.* Ex απο et φθεγγομαι, iv. 18. 2 *Pet.* ii. 16. 18. ' They are properly said αποφθεγγεσθαι, ' who speak certain sententious and wonderful things. ' So that they speak not so much from themselves, as ' from the inspiration and impulse of the Deity.' *Beza.*

V. 5. Numbers of Jews and proselytes, at that time, were collected in Jerusalem, who had come up to celebrate the feast: (*Note, 1:*) and many took up their residence there more permanently, in order to attend on the worship at the temple, to which they had a devoted affection; and for education and religious instruction. (*Note,* vi. 9—14, v. 9.)—The phrase, " every nation under heaven," is no doubt hyperbolical; and refers to all those nations, among which the people of Israel had been scattered. (*Marg.*

6 Now when this ᵃwas noised abroad, ᵖthe multitude came together, and were †confounded, because that every man heard them speak in his own language.

7 And they were all ᵠamazed, and marvelled, saying one to another, Behold, ʳare not all these which speak Galileans?

8 And how hear we every man in our own tongue, wherein we were born?

9 Parthians, and ˢMedes, and ᵗElamites, and the dwellers in ᵘMesopotamia, and in Judea, and ˣCappadocia, in ʸPontus, and ᶻAsia,

10 ᵃPhrygia, and ᵇPamphylia, in ᶜEgypt, and in the parts of ᵈLibya about ᵉCyrene, and ᶠstrangers of Rome, ᵍJews and proselytes,

11 ʰCretes and ᵏArabians, we do hear them speak in our tongues ˡthe wonderful works of God.

12 And they were all amazed, and were in doubt, saying one to another, ᵐWhat meaneth this?

13 Others mocking, said, ⁿThese men are full of new wine.

14 ¶ But Peter, standing up, ᵖwith

Ref. m. o.—Note, Deut. xxviii. 64.) It is a general, not a universal proposition: and the interpretation of it, which the subject absolutely requires, should render us cautious of deducing conclusions, and attempting to prove doctrines, from single expressions, at least not more energetick; especially when clear testimonies of scripture must be explained, differently than their obvious meaning implies, to establish such conclusions. (Notes, i. 1—3. John i. 6—9. 1 Tim. ii. 3, 4.)

Devout.] Ευλαϐης. viii. 2. See on Luke ii. 25.—Under heaven.] Υπο τον ορανον. iv. 12. Col. i. 23.

V. 6—11. When "this voice was made," (marg.) or, when these extraordinary events were reported abroad; the multitudes came together to the place; and after they had examined the matter, they were thrown into the utmost astonishment, by hearing the apostles and disciples, one after another, address them severally in their own languages. For they understood, either by previous information, or by some circumstances respecting them, that they were all natives of Galilee, persons of mean education and employment, who could not be expected to know any other language, than the dialect of the Hebrew, or the Syriack, which was there generally used: yet they addressed themselves to every one of the company, in that language, which was peculiar to his native country; the same persons also speaking to several of them in succession, in different languages, without the least hesitation or inaccuracy. (Marg. Ref. p—r.)—From the different regions afterwards mentioned, it is computed, that seven or eight distinct languages, and many more different dialects of the same language, must have been thus spoken, that each of this company might hear his native tongue. (Marg. Ref. a—k.) 'The nations here reckoned up, living ' some in Asia, some in Africa, and some in Europe, are ' said, though not without an hyperbole, to be " men of ' " every nation under heaven." (5) ' Whitby.—But the multitude not only remarked the languages, in which the apostles discoursed; but also, that they spake of " the " wonderful works," or " the great things, of God," even those great things, which related to his salvation, and his mercy and truth to his chosen people, as manifested in the events which had recently taken place. (Marg. Ref. l.) —" The strangers of Rome," mean native Jews, and persons proselyted to their religion, who generally resided at Rome, but then sojourned as strangers at Jerusalem.—The gospel was preached, and Christianity established, very early, in many of the countries here mentioned; and no doubt, the events of this important day had a powerful influence, in facilitating its introduction and progress among them.—In Judea, &c. (9) Matt. xxvi. 73.—The peculiar dialect of the Galileans no longer was perceived by the inhabitants of Judea.

When this was noised abroad. (6) Γενομενης της φωνης ταυτης. The " sound of the rushing mighty wind " seems intended, which being heard at a distance brought the multitude to the place whence it was heard. (Note, 2, 3.) —Were confounded.] Συνεχυθη, " troubled in mind." Marg. ix. 22. xix. 32. xxi. 31. Not elsewhere N. T.—1 Sam. vii. 10. Jon. iv. 1. Sept.—Language.] Διαλεκτω. 8. i. 19. xxi. 40. xxii. 2. xxvi. 14.—They were amazed. (7) Εξισταυϐο. 12. See on Mark ii. 12.—Proselytes. (10) Προσηλυτοι. See on Matt. xxiii. 15.—' Centies in versione Alexandrina ' reperitur.' Schleusner.—The wonderful works. (11) Τα μεγαλεια. Luke i. 49. Not elsewhere N. T.—Ps. lxxi. 19. Sept.

V. 12, 13. The strangers, who perfectly understood the words of the disciples, were fully satisfied of the reality of the miracle; though they were in doubt, and great perplexity, as to the meaning and intention of it; but others derided them as a company of drunkards, who, having drunk too freely of the " new " wine prepared for the feast, uttered unmeaning sounds in a confused and clamorous manner, as if they were speaking in other languages. (Marg. Ref.) It is probable, that these were the inhabitants of Judea, who understood no language except their own; and were more prejudiced against Jesus, than those who came from a distance were: yet some of these observed, that the Galileans were no longer distinguishable by their peculiar pronunciation (9).

What meaneth this? (12) Τι αν θελοι τυτο ειναι; What does this forebode? What will be the event of it?—Mocking. (13) Χλευαζοντες. xvii. 32. Not elsewhere. A χλευη, risus, derisio.—New wine.] Γλευκυς. Here only N. T. —Job xxxii. 19. Sept.—γλευκυς, dulcis.

V. 14—21. As Peter is said to have stood up " with " the eleven," we may suppose, that they also spake, to the same effect, to other companies of the assembled multitude; according to the different languages, which their

the eleven, [p] lifted up his voice, and said unto them, [q] Ye men of Judea, and all ye that dwell at Jerusalem, be this [r] known unto you, [s] and hearken to my words:

15 For [t] these are not drunken, as ye suppose, [u] seeing it is *but* the third hour of the day.

16 But this is that which was spoken by [v] the prophet Joel:

17 And it shall come to pass [x] in the last days, (saith God,) [y] I will pour out of my Spirit upon [z] all flesh: and [a] your sons and your daughters shall prophesy, and your young men shall see visions, and your old men shall dream dreams:

18 And [b] on my servants and on my handmaidens I will pour out in those

days of my Spirit, and they shall prophesy:

19 And [c] I will shew wonders in heaven above, and signs in the earth beneath; blood, and fire, and vapour of smoke:

20 The [d] sun shall be turned into darkness, and the moon into blood, before that [e] great and notable day of the Lord come:

21 And it shall come to pass, *that* [f] whosoever shall call on the name of the Lord shall be saved.

22 Ye [g] men of Israel, hear these words; [h] Jesus of Nazareth, [i] a man, approved of God among you, by miracles, and wonders, and signs, [k] which

b I Cor. vii. 21, 22. Gal. iii. 28. Col. iii. 11.

---

several hearers best understood : though the substance of *his* discourse only is recorded for our instruction. He lifted up his voice, and spake with such boldness, and in so audible a manner, that he silenced the mixed conversation, and fixed the attention of the people. He addressed himself especially to the men of Judea, and those who more statedly sojourned at Jerusalem ; and no doubt he spake in the Hebrew or Syriack tongue : and he demanded their serious regard to the highly interesting subject, about which he was about to discourse. He observed, that the opinion, of the company being drunken, was totally groundless, as many present must know : and, as it was no more than " the third hour of the day," or nine o'clock in the morning according to our reckoning, it was very uncandid, to suppose that so many persons had been guilty of excess, on a solemn religious festival, when about to attend on the worship at the temple. (*Marg. Ref.* o—t.) On the contrary, the effects which they witnessed were a fulfilment of a remarkable prophecy of Joel, concerning the pouring out of the Holy Spirit in the last days of the nation, or in those of the Messiah. (*Marg. Ref.* y—b.) This prediction has already been explained. (*Notes, Joel* ii. 28—32.) It may here be observed, that the descent of the Holy Spirit on the day of Pentecost was no more than the beginning of the accomplishment of this prophecy: nor could Peter himself then understand the full meaning of it ; for it related to " all flesh," to men of all nations, Gentiles as well as Jews, as it was afterwards verified in the different Christian churches.—The word, " prophesy," may denote, not only the fluency of the persons in speaking of divine things, for the instruction of others, as the term is sometimes used ; but also their predicting future events, especially those concerning the approaching ruin of the unbelieving Jewish nation: for " the wonders," afterwards mentioned, evidently relate to the prodigies, which preceded and attended the destruction of Jerusalem, and the subsequent devastations ; as these were, in some respects, typical of the terrors and solemnities connected with the end of the world and the day of judgment. (*Notes, Matt.* xxiv. 29—51.) Whether or not we here under-

stand, by " calling on the name of the LORD," an application to the Lord Jesus Christ for salvation, as in a parallel passage ; (*Marg. Ref.* f.—*Note, Rom.* x. 12—17;) the apostle certainly meant to warn the Jews, that none of their prayers would be heard, for deliverance from the approaching miseries, if they continued to reject their promised Messiah, whose coming, resurrection, and exaltation were attested to them by these miraculous operations of the Holy Spirit: and the connexion of the words implies the same warning to all who read them, in respect of deliverance " from the wrath to come."

The quotation, though in general made in the words of the Septuagint, varies from that version, and from the Hebrew text, in nearly the same particulars. Instead of " afterward," or " after these things," we here read, " in " the last days;" the order of the clauses in the seventeenth verse is changed ; " and they shall prophesy," at the end of the eighteenth is added ; as is " above," and " beneath," in the nineteenth. The Septuagint has " no- " table," or *illustrious, (επιφανη,)* instead of *terrible,* (from רֹאֱ, instead of אֲרֶ,) which is here retained.—The conclusion of the prophecy is omitted.

Hearken. (14) Ενωτισασθε. Here only N. T.—*Gen.* iv. 23. *Job* xxxiii. 1. *Is.* i. 2. *Hos.* v. 1. *Sept.* Ab ω et ϣον, auris.—*The last days.* (17) Εσχαταις ἡμεραις. 2 *Tim.* iii. 1. *Heb.* i. 1. *Jam.* v. 3. 1 *Pet.* i. 20. 2 *Pet.* iii. 3.—*Gen.* xlix. 1. *Is.* ii. 2. *Joel* iii. 1. *Sept.* (*Marg. Ref.* x.)—*Shall dream dreams.*] Ενυπνια ενυπνιασθησονται. Ενυπνια, here only—Ενυπναζω, *Jude* 8.—*Judg.* vii. 13. *Jer.* xxiii. 25. *Joel* ii. 28. *Sept.*—*Vapour.* (19) Ατμιδα. *Jam.* iv. 14. Not elsewhere N. T.—*Joel* ii. 30. *Sept.* (*Marg. Ref.* c, d.— *Notes, Matt.* xxiv. 6—8. *Luke* xxi. 7—11, *v.* 11.)—*Shall be turned.* (20) Μεταστραφησεται. *Gal.* i. 7. *Jam.* iv. 9.— Not elsewhere N. T.—*Am.* viii. 10. *Joel* ii. 31. *Sept.*

V. 22—24. The apostle, in connexion with this prophecy of Joel, and its astonishing fulfilment before their eyes, called the attention of his audience more immediately to the grand subject of his discourse. They all had heard or known many things concerning Jesus, who had been despised as " a Nazarene :" yet it was evident, that

God did by him in the midst of you, as ye yourselves also know: 23 Him, being delivered by the determinate counsel and foreknowledge of God, ye have taken, and by wicked hands have crucified and slain; 24 Whom God hath raised up, having loosed the pains of death, because it was not possible that he should be holden of it. 25 For David speaketh concerning

him, 'I foresaw the Lord always before my face; for he is on my right hand that 'I should not be moved: 26 Therefore did my heart rejoice, and "my tongue was glad: moreover "my flesh shall rest in hope: 27 Because thou wilt not leave my soul in hell, neither wilt thou suffer 'thine Holy One to see corruption. 28 Thou hast "made known to me the ways of life; thou shalt "make me full of joy with thy countenance.

---

he was a man, whom God had greatly owned and approved. This appeared from the various, multiplied, and incontestable miracles, which were wrought by him among them, in the most publick manner, as they well knew. (*Marg. Ref.* g—k.) Yet, instead of receiving him as the Son of God, and the Messiah, their rulers had taken him up and condemned him as a malefactor; and so had crucified him " by the hands of the wicked," that is, the hands of the idolatrous Romans: and, as the multitude of the nation had preferred Barabbas to him, and clamorously demanded his crucifixion ; this most atrocious murder was become their own act and deed, as much as if they had performed it with their own hands. (*Notes, Matt.* xxvii. 19—25.)—Indeed all this had been done, " according to the determinate counsel and fore-" knowledge of God ;" who had decreed this great event for the most wise, righteous, and merciful purposes ; and had also predicted it many ages before : yet that was in no degree an excuse for *their* guilt, or an extenuation of it ; as they were influenced by the basest motives in what they did, and " by wicked hands had crucified and slain " him." (*Marg. Ref.* l, m.)—But, though they had murdered this Jesus, as if he had been " a deceiver," God had abundantly vindicated his character and claim, as the promised Messiah ; having raised him up, and liberated him from " the bonds of death," or from those bonds, in which the pains and agonies of his cruel execution had terminated ; (*Note, Is.* liii. 9—12 ;) by which indeed it was impossible that he should be long confined ; whether the dignity of his Person, the nature of his undertaking, the perfection of his work, the purpose of God, or the predictions of scripture were considered. (*Marg. Ref.* n—p.—*Notes, John* ii. 18—22. x. 14—18.)—*Delivered by, &c.* (23) ' Him, being permitted by God to fall into ' your hands, God having withdrawn that protection, which ' was necessary to have preserved him from them ; (and ' this by his decree, that he should lay down his life for ' his sheep, in order to that great design of man's salva-' tion, toward which he did by his foreknowledge discern ' this the fittest expedient;) ye apprehended and crucified ' most wickedly.' *Hammond.* ' In scripture, that is said to ' be done by " the determinate counsel of God," which is ' done according to what he had written and declared in ' his word, all predictions concerning things future, being ' declarations, and determinations that they shall come to ' pass. (*Matt.* xxvi. 24. *Luke* xxii. 22.) …This only

' doth suppose, that God can foresee and foretel, what ' man, not hindered by him, but left to his own inclina-' tions, will do. And if that foresight hath any *influence* ' *on the will,* to make the action necessary, then … all our ' actions must be necessary.' *Whitby.* Did this learned writer suppose, that, according to the doctrine of Calvinists, the *foresight,* or even the *decree,* of God has any *influence on the will* or free agency of man? If either he, or others, who have brought the same objections, suppose this, they are very blameably ignorant of the doctrine which they would confute.—' God foresees and foretels, what man left ' to his inclinations will do;' and God determines to leave him to his inclinations. The permission is enough in such a case : but to determine, by preventing grace, to make the sinner willing to submit, believe, and obey, requires a *positive interposition of a divine and new creating power ;* which none deserves, or, left entirely to himself, desires, and which God bestows or withholds, " according to the " counsel of his own will."—Again, such texts constrain both the above cited learned writers to allow, that the event was certainly foreseen, and could not but take place ; though the persons concerned were under no coercion, and acted according to the lusts of their own hearts. But did God certainly foresee this, as his own all-wise determination and decree ; or as something independent on his decree, which could neither be altered nor prevented ? (*Notes,* iv. 23—28, v. 28. *Matt.* xxvi. 21—24. *Luke* xxii. 21—23.)

Approved. (22) Ἀποδεδειγμένον. *Acts* xxv. 7. 1 *Cor.* iv. 9. 2 *Thes.* ii. 4. Not elsewhere.—*Being delivered.* (23) Ἔκδοτον. Here only.—*The determinate counsel.* Τῃ ὡρισμένῃ βουλῃ.—Ὁρίζω, x. 42. See on *Luke* xxii. 22. Προωρισμω, iv. 28.—Προ, is here prefixed to the noun, προγνωσει ; here to the verb.—Βουλη. iv. 28. v. 38. *Eph.* i. 11. *Heb.* vi. 17. —*Ye have crucified.*] Προσπηξαντες. Here only. Ex προς, et πηγνυμι, figo, affigo.—*The pains.* (24) Τας ωδινας. *Matt.* xxiv. 8. *Mark* xiii. 9. 1 *Thes.* v. 3.—*Ps.* xviii. 5. cxvi. 3. *Sept.*—" The pains of death " would introduce " the pains " of hell," to sinful man. But the sinless Saviour, as our Surety, endured the former, till he could say " It is " finished :" and having done so, it was impossible that he should be holden under the power of the latter ; or that any of his believing people should be subjected to them.

V. 25—32. (*Note,* xiii. 24—37.) David in particular had spoken, expressly and exclusively, of the Messiah in

29 Men *and* brethren, * let me freely speak unto you of the patriarch David, that he is both dead and buried, and his sepulchre is with us unto this day.

30 Therefore, being a prophet, and knowing that God had sworn with an oath to him, that of the fruit of his loins, according to the flesh, he would raise up Christ to sit on his throne;

31 He seeing this before, spake of the resurrection of Christ, that his soul was not left in hell, neither his flesh did see corruption.

32 This Jesus hath God raised up, whereof we all are witnesses.

33 Therefore being by the right hand of God exalted, and having received of the Father the promise of the Holy Ghost, he hath shed forth this, which ye now see and hear.

34 For David is not ascended into the heavens: but he saith himself, The LORD said unto my Lord, Sit thou on my right hand,

35 Until I make thy foes thy footstool.

36 Therefore let all the house of Israel know assuredly, that God hath made that same Jesus, whom ye have crucified, both Lord and Christ.

---

a passage, with which the Jews were well acquainted. (*Marg. Ref.* q—b.—*Note, Ps.* xvi. 8—11.) This, the apostle stated, would be rendered manifest unto them, if they would permit him to speak freely of David, who was one of the venerable patriarchs of their nation, being the progenitor of that numerous and honourable family, from whom the Messiah was to descend: for it was evident, that David "died, was buried, and saw corruption," like other men; and his sepulchre had been preserved, by frequent repairs, even to that day, in honour of his memory. It therefore followed beyond all controversy that he spake not of himself, in the passage which had been cited; but, being a prophet, and knowing that the Messiah would descend from him, in respect of his human nature, to reign upon his throne over the people of God for ever; (*Note, Rom.* i. 1—4. ix. 4, 5;) in the prospect of these events, "he spake of the resurrection of the Messiah," who was indeed to be put to death, but whose soul would not be left in the place of separate spirits, nor would his body be suffered to lie in the grave, till it began in the least to corrupt. In accomplishment of this prophecy God had actually raised up Jesus, whom the Jews had crucified; but who was indeed the promised Messiah, of the family of David, and born at Bethlehem. This event had taken place on the third day after his death, before the body had begun "to see corruption;" (*Lev.* vii. 17;) of this the twelve apostles and all the company present were competent witnesses, as they had seen and conversed with him repeatedly after his resurrection. (*Marg.* and *Marg. Ref.* c—k.—*Notes,* i. 4—8. 20—22. *John* xv. 26, 27. *Heb.* ii. 1—4, v. 4.)—*I foresaw,* &c. (25—28) From the Septuagint, which varies very little from the Hebrew.

I foresaw. (25) Προωρωμην. xxi. 29. Not elsewhere N. T.—*Ps.* xvi. 8. Sept. Προοραω, 'prævideo, ... ante 'me video.' Schleusner. Ex προ, ante, et οραω, video. —The word seems to refer to *place*, not *time.* "I have "set the LORD always before me." *Eng. Version, Ps.* xvi. 8.—*Shall rest.* (26) Κἀλασκηνωσει. *Matt.* xiii. 32. *Mark* iv. 32. *Luke* xiii. 19.—*Ps.* xvi. 9. Sept.—*Thou wilt not leave.* (27) Ουκ εγκαλαλειψεις. *Matt.* xxvii. 46. *Mark* xv. 34. *Rom.* ix. 29. 1 *Cor.* iv. 9. 2 *Tim.* iv. 10. 16. *Heb.* x.

25. xiii. 5.—*Ps.* xvi. 10. xxii. 1. Sept.—*In hell.*] Εις ᾁδυ, (εις ᾁδην, *Ps.* xvi. 10. Sept.) 31. *Matt.* xi. 23. xvi. 18. *Luke* x. 15. xvi. 23. 1 *Cor.* xv. 55. *Rev.* i. 18. vi. 8. xx. 13, 14.—'*Keber,* the Hebrew word for *grave,* is never ' rendered ᾁᾁης' (in the LXX). '*Sheol,* on the contrary, 'is never rendered ταφος, or μνημα, (a tomb, or grave,) ' nor construed with θαπτω, ... to bury, a thing almost ' inevitable, in words so frequently recurring, if it had ' ever properly signified a grave.' *Campbell.* (*Note, Ps.* xlix. 14.)—*Freely.* (29) Μετα παρρησιας. 13. 31. *John* xviii. 20. 2 *Cor.* iii. 12. *Eph.* vi. 19.—*The patriarch.*] Tν πατριαρχν. vii. 8, 9. *Heb.* vii. 4. Not elsewhere.—Tης πατριας αρχων, the head, or beginner of a family.

V. 33—36. The resurrection of Jesus did not rest solely on the testimony of the apostles, and the other disciples. (*Note, John* xx. 24—29.) For, having ascended into heaven, he had been exalted by the power of God, at his right hand, to the highest possible dignity and authority: and, having received, from God the Father, the Holy Spirit, according to the promises of the scripture to the Messiah, he had poured out upon his disciples all those miraculous gifts and divine influences, the effects of which were witnessed at that time, and which could not possibly be accounted for in any other manner. (*Marg. Ref.* l—n. —*Notes, Is.* xliv. 3—5. lix. 20, 21. lxi. 1—3. *Eph.* i. 15 —23. iv. 7—10. *Heb.* i. 3, 4. xii. 2, 3.) For David had not arisen from the dead to ascend into heaven, according to the meaning of the Psalm before cited : but in another place, calling the promised Messiah his Lord, though he was to be his Son ; he had predicted his ascension into heaven, and his exaltation to the right hand of God ; there to be established in supreme authority, till he had subjected all his enemies, and rendered their opposition to him an accession to his own glory. (*Marg. Ref.* o, p.— *Notes, Ps.* cx. 1. *Matt.* xxii. 41—46. 1 *Cor.* xv. 20—28. *Eph.* iv. 11—13.) As therefore the events which the apostles testified, and to which the Holy Spirit poured out upon them also bore witness, accorded so exactly to their ancient prophecies ; the whole house of Israel might be assured, by the most complete demonstration imaginable, that God had constituted Jesus of Nazareth, whom

37 ¶ Now when they heard *this*, they were pricked in their heart, and said unto Peter and to the rest of the apostles, ' Men *and* brethren, " what shall we do?

38 Then Peter said unto them, ' Repent, and ' be baptized every one of you in the name of Jesus Christ, for the remission of sins,' and ye shall receive the gift of the Holy Ghost.

39 For ʰ the promise is unto you, and to your children, ' and to all that are afar off, *even* ⁴ as many as the Lord our God shall call.

40 And ' with many other words

they contemptuously crucified, the Lord and Judge of all worlds; and the anointed Prophet, Priest, and King of his chosen people. So that he was actually possessed of complete authority, both to save and bless those who trusted and obeyed him, and also to crush all who should obstinately refuse to submit to him. (*Marg. Ref.* q, r.— *Notes*, iv. 5—12. *Rom.* xiv. 7—9. 1 *Cor.* viii. 4—6. *Phil.* ii. 9—11.)—The scope of Peter's argument was to shew, that the crucified Jesus was indeed the promised Messiah, and that he was actually risen, ascended, and glorified. When the Jews were convinced of this, and were induced to believe on him in that character; they would readily learn from scripture, and from further instructions, the spiritual nature of his kingdom and salvation, the intent of his sufferings and death, and the various doctrines of his religion.

The promise. (33) Τὴν ἐπαγγελιαν. 39.—*Note*, i. 4—8, v. 4.—*Hath shed forth.*] Εξιχεε. 17. " Hath poured out."—*The Lord said*, &c. (34, 35) Exactly from the Sept. *Ps.* cx. 1.—*Assuredly.* (36) Ασφαλως. xvi. 23. *Mark* xiv. 44.—*Lord.*] Κυριον. 34. x. 36. 1 *Cor.* viii. 6. *Eph.* iv. 5.—*Christ.*] Χριστον. *Messiah.*

V. 37—40. The apostle's arguments were invincibly conclusive, and his application most highly interesting; though in other respects his discourse was peculiarly plain and simple. But if we duly consider the complicated evidence of our Lord's doctrine and miracles, and the obstinate unbelief of the Jews notwithstanding; we shall perceive, that neither Peter's words, nor yet the miracles which the people witnessed, would have produced those effects which followed, had not the Holy Spirit also been communicated, to remove the veil of pride, prejudice, and sinful affections from their minds. " The Comforter being " come, he convinced them of sin, of righteousness, and " of judgment." (*Note, John* xvi. 8—11.) The apostle's words, therefore, attended by the powerful convictions of the Holy Spirit, penetrated their hearts like arrows, or as a sharp sword; and, being filled with terror on account of their enormous guilt, in rejecting and " crucifying the " Lord of glory," they cried out to the apostles in deep distress, as to their friends and countrymen, enquiring with great earnestness, " What must we do?" Was there any hope for them of escaping the vengeance of their exalted Messiah, whom they had so deeply injured? If there were, by what means could it be done? (*Marg. Ref.* s—u. —*Notes*, ix. 3—6. xvi. 29—34. *Matt.* vii. 24—27.) To this the apostle replied, by exhorting them to repent of that, and all their other sins; (*Note, Matt.* iii. 2;) and openly to avow their firm belief, that Jesus was indeed the Messiah, by being baptized in his name. (*Marg. Ref.* r. x —z.—*Note, Matt.* xxviii. 19, 20. *Mark* xvi. 14—16.) In

thus professing their faith in him, all who truly believed would receive a full remission of their sins for his sake; as well as a participation of the sanctifying and comforting graces of the Holy Spirit, and many of them likewise of those miraculous powers, which they saw bestowed upon his disciples. (*Note*, xxii. 14—16.) For " the promise," both the general promise respecting the Messiah, and the blessings of his kingdom, as made to Abraham their father, (*Notes, Gen.* xii. 1—3. xvii. 7, 8,) and the particular promise of the Spirit quoted from Joel; (16—21;) was made, or proposed, " to them and to their children;" and not to those present only, but to all, however dispersed, whom God should call by his gospel. (*Marg. Ref.* a—d.) Peter's words, as suggested by the Holy Spirit, implied the calling of the Gentiles also; yet he could not himself at this time understand them in that sense. (*Notes*, i. 4—8. iii. 19— 21. x. 9—16.)—The promise, as made to Abraham, included also his posterity; and that of the new covenant did the same to those who should be interested in it; and the language here accords with this. (*Notes, Jer.* xxxii. 39—41. *Rom.* xi. 11—21. 1 *Cor.* vii. 10—14.) The male descendants of Abraham were circumcised, as included in the promise, and as a part of the visible church; and this passage may intimate, that the infant-offspring of Christians, being also included in the promise, and in the covenant of their parents, and being a part of the visible church, should be admitted to baptism, which is the outward sign of the same spiritual blessings, as circumcision was. (*Note, Gen.* xvii. 9—12.)—Besides this general address, Peter bore witness to the truth, and in the name of God charged his audience, with very many other words: the substance of which was, that they ought to embrace the gospel, without waiting for the concurrence of their rulers and teachers, or the rest of the people; (*Note, Luke* xii. 54—57;) and, by thus entering into the church and kingdom of Christ, should save themselves from the destruction which impended over that perverse and rebellious generation of Israel, for obstinately rejecting the promised Messiah; as well as that they should " flee for " refuge" to Jesus, " from the wrath to come." (*Marg. Ref.* e—h.—*Notes, Heb.* vi. 13—20.)

They were pricked. (37) Κατενυγησαν. Here only N. T. —*Gen.* xxxiv. 7. *Ps.* cix. 16. Sept. Κατανυξις, *Rom.* xi. 8. Ex καλα, et νυσσω, *John* xix. 34.—*The gift.* (38) Την δωρεαν. See on *John* iv. 10. (*Note, John* iv. 10—15.)—*Did· he testify.* (40) Διεμαρτυρετο. viii. 25. x. 42. xviii. 5. xx. 21. 23, 24. xxiii. 11. xxviii. 23. *Luke* xvi. 28. 1 *Thes.* iv. 6 1 *Tim.* v. 21. 2 *Tim.* ii. 14. iv. 1. *Heb.* ii. 6.—*Save yourselves.*] Σωθητε.—*Untoward.*] Σκολιας. *Luke* iii. 5. *Phil.* ii. 15. 1 *Pet.* ii. 18.—*Deut.* xxxii. 5. *Ps.* lxxviii. 8. *Prov.* iv. 24. *Is.* xxvii. 1. x!. 4. xlii. 16. *Sept.*

^f did he testify and exhort, saying, ^g Save yourselves from this ^h untoward generation.

41 Then they that ⁱ gladly received his word ^k were baptized: and the same day there were ^l added *unto them* about three thousand souls.

42 ¶ And ^m they continued stedfastly in the apostles' doctrine and ⁿ fellowship, and ^o in breaking of bread, ^p and in prayers.

43 And ^q fear came upon every soul: and ^r many wonders and signs were done by the apostles.

44 And all that believed were together, ^s and had all things common;

45 And ^t sold their possessions and goods, ^u and parted them to all *men*, as every man had need.

46 And they continuing ^x daily with one accord in the temple, ^y and breaking bread ^z from house to house, ^a did eat their meat with gladness and ^b singleness of heart;

47 Praising God, ^b and having favour with all the people. And ^c the Lord added to the church daily such as should be saved.

V. 41. The apostle had exhorted " every one " of them to be baptized; and " those who gladly received the word " were baptized. As therefore it is highly improbable, that there should have been none of John's disciples in this large company; we may fairly infer, that Christ's baptism was not precisely the same institution with John's; and that from this time, at least, John's disciples were baptized, when they were admitted into the Christian church, according to the form appointed by our Lord after his resurrection. (*Notes,* xix. 5, 6. *Matt.* iii. 5, 6. xxviii. 19, 20. *John* iii. 22—24.)—Peter exhorted the Jews to be baptized in the name of Jesus Christ, as professing their faith in him, the Messiah; yet there is no reason to doubt that they were baptized, " in," or " into, the name of his " Father, of the Son, and of the Holy Ghost," according to the appointed form.—As so great a number were baptized on this occasion, and as they were not by the river Jordan " where was much water," or near to any other river; but in the midst of a populous city, crowded also with strangers, it is at least highly probable, that they were not baptized by immersion: especially seeing the baptism of the Holy Ghost, represented by it, is constantly, and in several places of the chapter, spoken of, as " poured " out " upon them. (See on 33.)—The numerous converts made on this occasion, though at first " pricked to " the heart," are said to have " *gladly* received " Peter's word. They were deeply convinced of their guilt and danger; and they rejoiced to hear of a free forgiveness, through that Saviour whom they had concurred in crucifying: so that they cheerfully ventured all the consequences of embracing the gospel, and joining themselves, by baptism, to the despised and persecuted disciples of Jesus. (*Marg. Ref.* i.—*Notes,* xvi. 29—34. *John* xvi. 8—11. 14, 15. *Rom.* x. 5—11.)

Gladly.] Ασμενως. xxi. 17. Not elsewhere: *prompte, cum gaudio.*—*Were added.*] Προσετιθηταν. 47. v. 14. xi. 24. xii. 3. xiii. 36. *Luke* iii. 20, *et al.* (*Marg. Ref.* l.)

V. 42, 43. The conversion of this great multitude was *sudden*; yet their profession was not transient or wavering: for they stedfastly attended on the instructions of the apostles, and adhered to their doctrine, though doubtless many efforts would be made to draw them aside, by reasoning,

ridiculing, menacing, or affecting to pity them, as deluded enthusiasts. They also associated with the apostles and disciples in religious conference and worship, joining with them in " breaking of bread," as well as in prayers. (*Marg. Ref.* m—p.) This seems to refer to the administration of the Lord's supper, in remembrance of the atoning sufferings and death of Christ; which evidently took place very frequently in the primitive times. (*Notes,* 1 *Cor.* x. 14—17. xi. 17—28.)—The impression also, which these transactions made upon the spectators and all who heard of them, was very great: for all the people were overawed, and afraid of attempting any thing against the disciples; as they saw evident and signal miracles wrought by the apostles, in confirmation of the resurrection and power of the crucified Jesus. (*Marg. Ref.* q, r. —*Note,* v. 12—16.)

They continued stedfastly. (42) Ησαν προσκαρτερουντες. 46. See on i. 14.—*Fellowship.*] Τη κοινωνια. *Rom.* xv. 26. 1 *Cor.* i. 9. x. 16. 2 *Cor.* vi. 14. viii. 4. ix. 13. xiii. 13. *Heb.* xiii. 16. 1 *John* i. 3. 6, 7, *et al.* Κοινωνος. *Matt.* xxiii. 30. *Luke* v. 10.

V. 44—47. Many of the converts were strangers, who probably were detained at Jerusalem longer than they had intended, in order to get a further insight into the religion which they had embraced; and others were poor: the more affluent therefore of the company were contented to share their abundance, in common with their poorer brethren. (*Marg. Ref.* s—u.—*Notes,* iv. 32—37. *Gal.* vi. 1—5.) This was a remarkable evidence of their indifference about the world; of their joy and confidence in the Lord; in his providential care, as well as in his mercy and grace; of their love and gratitude to him, and of their cordial affection to one another, though just before they had been strangers, and divided from each other. (*Notes,* x. 9—16. *Is.* xi. 6—9. lxv. 24, 25.) Perhaps the predictions which they had heard concerning the approaching desolations of Jerusalem and Judea, might concur in influencing them to sell their estates and possessions, that they might impart to every one of the company, as each had need. (*Note,* 14—21.) This was peculiarly suitable to the state of the church at that time, and the same *disposition* ought always to prevail: yet it is evident, that the

CHAP. III.

Peter and John, at the temple, heal one who had been lame from his birth, 1—8. The people, being astonished, throng around them, 9—11. Peter de-

clares, that this miracle had been wrought by the power, and through faith in the name of Jesus, whom they and the other Jews had delivered to be crucified, but whom God had raised from the dead, 12—16; he supposes that they did it ignorantly, and shews that

---

same way of expressing it is not required, nor would it be in general expedient. (*P. O. Matt.* xxvi. 1—13. *2 Cor.* viii. 10—15.) Indeed, it was done at this time, not by *command* or *constraint*, but voluntarily. (*Note*, v. 1—11, *v.* 4.)—The minds of the new converts were occupied almost entirely with the important concerns of eternal salvation : and as numbers of them were far from home, and probably had not many secular affairs to attend on ; they daily continued in the most harmonious manner, to meet together in the courts of the temple for the worship of God, and in the houses of believers, one after another, as they had opportunity ; where they hospitably entertained each other, as well as joined in sacred ordinances. (*Note, Prov.* viii. 34.) Thus their very meals were sanctified ; as they used the good gifts of God with cheerful gratitude, and in a simple dependence on him, and desire to please him.—They were also greatly occupied in celebrating the praises of God, and blessing him for all his unspeakable benefits : so that even the Jews, who did not join them, held them in great estimation, and shewed great favour to them. (*Note*, iv. 32—35.)—What a lovely exhibition of the effects of genuine Christianity, when applied and blessed by the Spirit of God ! What *excellent* and what *happy* characters does it form !—Thus the Lord, from day to day, inclined the hearts of more and more, to embrace the gospel, and join themselves to the disciples of Jesus : and they did not merely profess to be disciples, but were actually brought into a state of acceptance with God, as penitent believers in Christ. (*Marg. Ref.* b, c.—*Note*, ix. 31.)

Sold. (45) Επιπρασκον. iv. 34. v. 4. *Matt.* xiii. 46, *et al.*—*Continuing with one accord.* (46) Προσκαρτερουντες ομοθυμαδον. See on i. 14.—*With gladness.*] Εν αγαλλιασει. See on *Luke* i. 41.—*Singleness.*] Αφελοτητι. Here only. ‘ *Liberalitas erga pauperes, ex modesto hilarique animo pro-*‘ *fecta.*' Schleusner. 'Απλοτης, *Eph.* vi. 5.—*The church.* (47) Τη εκκλησια. See on *Matt.* xvi. 18.—The word is here used, the first time, for the assembled disciples of Jesus.—*Such as should be saved.*] Τους σωζομενους. *Luke* xiii. 23. 1 *Cor.* i. 18. *2 Cor.* ii. 15. *Rev.* xxi. 24.—*Deut.* xxxiii. 29. *Is.* xlv. 20. lxvi. 19. *Jer.* xliv. 14. *Sept.* (*Note, Rom.* xi. 1—6.)

PRACTICAL OBSERVATIONS.

V. 1—13.

Delays as to the performance of God's promises, till the appointed time is " fully come," are peculiarly advantageous to those, who wait on him in patient faith and fervent persevering prayer. When a company of believers are " of one heart," thus to seek and hope for " the pouring " out of his Holy Spirit," a revival of true religion may reasonably, nay confidently, be expected : for the promise stands sure, that " our heavenly Father will give his Holy " Spirit to them that ask him." (*Notes, Jer.* xxxii. 39—41. *Luke* xi. 5—13, *v.* 13.)—We cannot explain the manner of his operation ; but we may perceive, that with invin-

cible power he bears down all the opposition of pride and worldly lusts and prejudices, as " with a rushing mighty " wind ; " and changes the heart like a vehement fire. Sound judgment, heavenly wisdom and knowledge, fervent affections, holy boldness, and a ready utterance in the things of God, are his gifts to those whom he qualifies for the sacred ministry, or to serve the church of Christ in any important publick situation ; for which all ought simply to depend on him, according to their need. We do not expect such miraculous powers, as were communicated to the apostles on the day of Pentecost ; yet we share the benefit of them ; both in the demonstrative evidence thus given to the truth of the gospel, and in the infallible declaration, which they have authenticated and transmitted to us, concerning the way in which we may be saved.—The remarkable pouring out of the Spirit, even in his ordinary influences and operations, will always produce a measure of the same effects, as this extraordinary communication did. (*Note, Is.* xxxii. 15.) It will soon be " noised abroad ; " many will be excited to examine into it, and to make their observations ; many will be astonished at the change wrought in such persons, as were before known to be careless, ignorant, or illiterate, and at the things spoken by them ; and they will be led to acknowledge, that there is something real and wonderful in it : others will stand in doubt, and not know what to determine about it : nay, some, more ignorant, self-important, malignant, and daring, will, without hesitation or competent information, even pronounce the whole enthusiasm, delusion, hypocrisy, imposture, or perhaps intoxication, and so treat it with scorn and derision ! " But wisdom is justi-" fied by all her children." (*P. O. Matt.* xii. 22—30.)

V. 14—21.

If we are indeed influenced by the Spirit of truth, holiness, and love, we shall meekly bear, or reply to, the most injurious reflections ; assigning the cause of those effects, which excite many and discordant opinions. Thus, even curiosity and malicious reproaches will give the ministers of Christ an opportunity of bearing testimony to the truth, before those who have been strangers and enemies to it. On such occasions, it is peculiarly important for us to shew the agreement of our sentiments, mind, heart, and conduct, with the doctrines, promises, predictions, examples, and precepts of scripture ; clearly and strongly arguing from the sacred word, as undoubted truth ; and applying every subject, as cogently as possible, to the hearts and consciences of our hearers.—To suppose, however, that, now Christianity is publickly professed among us, and we have no longer need of the miraculous gifts of the Holy Spirit, we therefore do not want his sanctifying operations ; is as unreasonable, as it would be to argue from the present improved state of agriculture, that the influences of the sun and rain are become unnecessary : and the state of those congregations, where such notions are maintained, too plainly shew the real tendency

God had thus fulfilled the scriptures, 17, 18 ; he exhorts them to "repent and be converted, that their "sins" may be pardoned, and they made partakers of the promised blessing, 19, 20; and refers them to

Moses and all the prophets, whose predictions were fulfilled in Jesus the Saviour, whom God had sent to bless them, in turning them from their iniquities, 21 —26.

of them. If Peter and Paul should come again on earth to preach the gospel, and to confirm their doctrine with the most undeniable miracles; no saving effects would follow, except the Holy Spirit were given to render the word successful. But, in fact, the whole gospel will seldom, if ever, be faithfully preached, with earnest and faithful application to the heart and conscience; except when the minister is in some good measure enabled to speak, as "the Spirit gives him utterance." Even Peter and the other apostles were manifestly raised above themselves, when thus "filled with the Holy Ghost;" and their singular boldness and liberty, in discoursing concerning the wonderful works of God, as evidently proved that they were supernaturally aided, as the new tongues with which they spake. (Note, Mark xvi. 17, 18.) Such assistance we may expect, and shall experience, from time to time, when called to bear witness to "the truth as it is in Jesus." —It should also be noticed, as the evident doctrine of the sacred oracles, that when God so remarkably pours out his Spirit, in abundance of spiritual gifts and graces, on numbers of every rank and station, as to effect a great revival of true religion; it may also be expected, that he will remarkably punish those, who persist in neglecting and despising his great salvation. Assuredly, at that solemn period which is so often foretold, and prefigured in scripture; when "the sun shall" literally "be turned into "darkness," and the whole visible creation be destroyed by one common conflagration, to introduce "the great "and notable day" of "judgment, and perdition of un- "godly men;" none will escape that dreadful condemnation, and the subseqnent vengeance, except those who have previously called upon the name of the Lord, in and through his Son Jesus Christ, as the only Saviour of sinners and the Judge of mankind. But, on the other hand, whosoever of any age, nation, rank, or character, now calls on the name of the Lord, in this appointed manner, shall then be completely saved, and made an heir of eternal life.

V. 22—36.

The enmity of the human heart against God appears especially in the scornful hatred, generally manifested against those whom he has most evidently owned and approved. The doctrine, miracles, character, and crucifixion of Jesus form the chief proof of this: but instances confirming and illustrating the same conclusion have been multiplied in every age.—The "determinate counsel and "foreknowledge of God" cannot be the motive of men's actions, being wholly unknown by them, or unthought of at the time; and therefore can form no excuse for their sins. In permitting ungodly men to follow their own inclinations, God brings to pass those events, which he has purposed and predicted : but his decrees, and their accomplishment, are most holy, wise, righteous, and good; whereas the instruments by which he works are actuated by the basest motives, and aim at the gratification of their worst passions. (Notes, Gen 1. 20. Is. x. 5—7.) This was most evident in the crucifixion of Christ; which, "as

"appointed of God," was the most glorious display of all the divine perfections, and replete with the richest blessings to mankind ; but, as perpetrated by the Jews, it was the grand discovery of human depravity, and in all its circumstances, the greatest single act of wickedness, which ever was or can be committed. Men of this character aim to counteract the purposes of God, at the very time when they are accomplishing them : and when he has wrought by them, as long as he sees good, he turns his hand against them to their destruction.—As it was "not "possible," that the Redeemer should be held under the power of death, though he endured the pain of it; so it cannot be, that the scripture should be broken, or that his believing people should come short of that blessed resurrection, of which he was the glorious First-fruits. After his example they are taught to "set God always before "them," to walk as in his presence in humble obedience, and in confidence that they "shall not be moved." In proportion to the degree of their faith and hope, their hearts rejoice and dictate praises to their tongues.—They too learn to meet death with a comfortable hope, that, though "their flesh see corruption" in the grave, yet it shall not finally be left there, and that their souls shall never experience the miseries of the place of torment. Through their crucified, risen, and ascended Saviour, "the "ways of life" are made known to them also; and, from present earnests, they are encouraged to expect, that they shall be filled with the joy of God's presence and favour for evermore. (P. O. Ps. xvi.) But all this springs from their assured belief, grounded on prophecies, miracles, and abundant external and internal proofs, and the effectual teaching of the Holy Spirit, by these proofs, that Jesus is indeed ascended into the heavens. Pious kings, patriarchs, and prophets of old looked forward to these events with joyful expectation; and died assuredly believing that the Redeemer would appear to overcome death, and to open the gates of heaven to all that trusted in him. An innumerable company of witnesses testify, that the crucified Jesus was he ; and that, being risen from the dead, "he "is exalted by the hand of the Father," to communicate all blessings to his people, and to put all his enemies under his feet. Therefore "let all men know assuredly," that Jesus is the Lord and Judge of the whole world, and the anointed Saviour of all who obey him. (Notes, Matt. xiii. 16, 17. Luke x. 23, 24. Heb. xi. 13—16. 1 Pet. i. 10 —12.)

V. 37—41.

When the solemn truths of scripture are declared, with plain and direct application to the conscience, attended by the convincing Spirit of God, the proud, stout, and hard heart begins to tremble and be disquieted : nor will the salvation and kingdom of "the Prince of peace" ever be welcome to those, who never were "pricked to the heart," by humiliating convictions of sin, (generally accompanied with alarm also,) so as to be excited to earnest enquiries, "What shall we do?" (Note, Zech. xii. 9—14, v. 10.) But the most desperate enemies, when thus awakened,

4 M 3

NOW [a] Peter and John [b] went up together into the temple at [c] the hour of prayer, *being* the ninth *hour*.

2 And a certain man [d] lame from his mother's womb was carried, [e] whom they laid daily at the gate of the temple [f] which is called Beautiful, [g] to ask alms of them that entered into the temple;

3 Who seeing Peter and John about to go into the temple, asked an alms.

4 And Peter, [h] fastening his eyes upon him, with John, said, [i] Look on us.

5 And he gave heed unto them, expecting to receive something of them.

6 Then Peter said, [k] Silver and gold have I none: [l] but such as I have give I thee: [m] In the name of [n] Jesus Christ of Nazareth, rise up and walk.

7 And [o] he took him by the right hand, and lifted *him* up; and immediately his feet and ancle-bones received strength.

8 And [p] he leaping up stood, and walked, and entered with them into the temple, walking, and leaping, [q] and praising God.

---

should be exhorted to repent, and believe in Jesus, and to prove and profess their faith, in the way prescribed by his holy word. Still repentance and remission of sins are preached to " the chief of sinners," in the Redeemer's name: still the Holy Spirit seals the blessing on the believer's heart: still the encouraging " promises are to us, " and to our children;" who possess manifold advantages and opportunities, through the faith and obedience of their parents: still the same blessings are sent to " all that are " afar off, even as many as the Lord our God shall call." We should therefore embrace this salvation ourselves: and then, as we have opportunity, and as we are able, we should testify, warn, exhort, invite, and persuade sinners to save themselves from the perverse and crooked generation of those who reject the gospel. But if our teachers and rulers, or a large majority of our neighbours, nay, even if our nearest relatives refuse to go with us in the way to heaven, or would hinder us from going; we must stop our ears to their blandishments, persuasions, reproaches, and persecuting opposition, and escape for our lives from the ruin impending over them.—Under the teaching of the Holy Spirit convinced sinners " gladly re- " ceive the word" of salvation, and find " peace and joy " in believing;" they boldly profess the truth which before they despised, renouncing worldly interests, pleasures, and companions; and, joining themselves to the Lord and his people, they delight in attending on his ordinances and in keeping his commandments.

V. 42—47.

When shall we behold the whole company of those, who have been baptized in the name of the Lord Jesus, disposed to copy the example of these first-fruits of the gospel? This specimen of the genuine nature and tendency of Christianity ought carefully to be studied: for unless our views, pursuits, affections, and conduct, in good measure correspond with their's, we have great reason to question whether we be truly believers. Indeed hasty conversions, from one creed or sect to another, are seldom followed by such a stedfastness in faith and practice, " as " becomes the gospel of Christ :" yet these things have been, and will again be united; and we must therefore form no general rules without allowing for exceptions.

Rather let us diligently copy the pattern here exhibited, and pray without ceasing for the " pouring out of the " Spirit," to produce these blessed effects in us and around us : that we too may " continue stedfastly in the apostles' " doctrine," and " in fellowship" with all true believers; that our attendance on the Lord's table may be more frequent, serious, and influential, than it generally is at present; that we may abound more in social prayers and supplications for each other, and for the success of the gospel; that we may delight daily in attending to the word of God, when we have opportunity, and leisure from other duties; that we may " use hospitality without grudging," and communicate liberally to our needy brethren; and that " whether we eat, or drink, or whatever we do, we may " do all to the glory of God," " in gladness and singleness " of heart," at a distance from avarice, selfishness, intemperance, pride, envy, contention, or any of those manifold evils, which corrupt, disgrace, and divide the church of Christ. Thus we shall over-awe our inveterate enemies, even without the power of working miracles : thus we shall " shew forth the praises of him, who hath " called us out of darkness into his marvellous light ;" silence the slanders, and soften the prejudices, of those who are without ; and dispose them to favour us, and attend to " the doctrine of God our Saviour." And when the most unlikely persons, (such as the crucifiers of the Lord Jesus,) are transformed by the gospel into harmless, peaceful, loving, and exemplary worshippers and servants of God, it may be expected, that " the Lord will add to his " church daily such as shall be saved."—Even those who, like Peter, have been overcome by temptation, to act inconsistently with their holy profession ; if indeed they are deeply humbled, and made more bold and zealous for the cause of their gracious Lord; may yet hope to be employed as his instruments in forwarding so blessed a work, for his glory and the salvation of souls. May the Lord then pour out his Holy Spirit on all ministers, Christians, and congregations for these blessed purposes, till " the earth be " filled with the knowledge of his glory!" Amen! and Amen.

NOTES.

CHAP. III. V. 1—11. The events, recorded in this chapter and that which follows, seem to have occurred

9 And all 'the people saw him walking, and praising God.

10 And 'they knew that it was he which sat for alms at the Beautiful gate of the temple: 'and they were filled with wonder and amazement at that which had happened unto him.

11 And as the lame man which was healed " held Peter and John, * all the people ran together unto them * in the porch that is called Solomon's, greatly wondering.

12 ¶ And when Peter saw it, he answered unto the people, ' Ye men of Israel, why marvel ye at this? * or why look ye so earnestly on us, as though by our own power or holiness we had made this man to walk?

13 The ᵇ God of Abraham, and of Isaac, and of Jacob, the God of our fathers, ᶜ hath glorified his Son Jesus; ᵈ whom ye delivered up, and denied him in the presence of Pilate, when he was determined to let *him* go.

14 But ye denied ᵉ the Holy One, and the Just, ᶠ and desired a murderer to be granted unto you;

15 And killed the * Prince of life, ᵍ whom God hath raised from the dead; ʰ whereof we are witnesses.

soon after those which have been considered. (*Note*, ii. 44 —47.)—The apostles and primitive believers generally attended the temple-worship at the hours of prayer; of which the third and the ninth, or nine o'clock in the morning and three in the afternoon, when the morning and evening sacrifices were offered with burning of incense, were the chief. (*Marg. Ref.* a—c.—x. 3—8. *Ex.* xxix. 38—11. xxx. 1—10. *Num.* xxviii. 3—8. *Luke* i. 8—10. *Rev.* viii. 1—6.) The two apostles Peter and John seem, however, on this occasion to have gone up to the temple apart from the others; perhaps to seek an opportunity of preaching to the people, as well as to offer their supplications before God. The lame man, healed by them, was above forty years old, and had been a cripple from his birth. (*Marg. Ref.* d—g.—iv. 22.)—The Beautiful gate of the temple was erected by Herod the Great: it was above fifteen yards high, and about eight yards wide, being formed of Corinthian brass, with the most exquisite workmanship. It is supposed to have separated the court of the Gentiles from the inner court.—The purpose of the apostles to work a miracle in this man's behalf, seems to have arisen from an immediate divine suggestion to their mind.—The declaration of Peter, that he had no silver or gold to bestow, as made after some of the possessions had been sold, and entrusted to the disposal of the apostles, may be considered as a proof, that they were not in the least enriched by the liberality of their brethren.—But, though he could not answer the man's expectations in this way, he was willing to help him, according to the ability committed to him. The circumstances attending this miracle need no comment: we, as it were, see the man making trial of his limbs, and the strength thus unexpectedly communicated to them, in every way which he could imagine; and expressing in the most lively manner his admiring gratitude to God, and his affection for the instruments of this mercy to him. (*Marg. Ref.* h—q.—*Notes*, xiv. 8—10. *Is.* xxxv. 5—7. *Matt.* xi. 2—6.)—Some think, that he held the apostles, as unwilling to part with them, not only from affection, but also from fear, lest when they were gone his lameness should return.—It may be doubted whether, if one, born a cripple, who had never walked, should by ordinary means be immediately restored to perfect soundness, he would be able at once to use his limbs, and to shew his vigour and agility in the manner here described.—As it is probable, that this man had, for a considerable time, been laid at the gate of the temple; he must often have heard concerning Jesus and his miracles, and perhaps he had seen him and heard his instructions. He had not, however, applied for healing; and it had pleased the Saviour to leave him under his malady, that the miracle performed in this extraordinary case, by the witnesses of his resurrection, might " manifest his " glory " more illustriously, than if he himself had wrought it before his crucifixion. (*Note, Matt.* xxi. 14—16.)—The multitudes, drawn together by the report of this miracle, were probably collected, not only from the courts of the temple, but from the adjacent parts of the city. (*Marg. Ref.* r—x.)—*Solomon's.* (11) *Note, John* x. 22— 24.—There is not the least probability in the tradition of the Jews, that this very portico was built by Solomon, and was spared by the Chaldeans, when they burnt the rest of the temple.

Together. (1) Επι το αυτο. See on ii. 1.—*Beautiful.* (2) 'Ωραιαν. 10. *Matt.* xiii. 27. *Rom.* x. 15.—*Fastening his eyes.* (4) Ατενισας. 12. i. 10. vi. 15. vii. 55. x. 4. xi. 6. xiii. 9. xiv. 9. xxiii. 1. *Luke* iv. 20. xxii. 56. 2 *Cor.* iii. 7. 13.— *He gave heed.* (5) Επειχεν. xix. 22. *Luke* xiv. 7. *Phil.* ii. 16. 1 *Tim.* iv. 16.—*Feet.* (7) 'Αι βασεις. Here only.—*Anklebones.*) Τα σφυρα. Here only. ' Α σφυρα, *malleus, ob mallei* ' *similitudinem.*' Schleusner.—*Received strength.*) Εστερεωθησαν. 16. xvi. 5. Α ςτερεος, *robustus, validus.* 1 *Pet.* v. 9.— *Leaping up.* (8) Εξαλλομενος. Here only.— *Leaping.*] 'Αλλομενος. xiv. 10. *John* iv. 14. Not elsewhere.—*Is.* xxxv. 6. Sept.—*Amazement.* (10) Εκστασις. See on *Mark* v. 42. 6. Sept.—*Amazement.* (10) Εκστασις. See on *Mark* v. 42.—*Greatly wondering.* (11) Εκθαμβοι. Here only.—Α θαμβος. 10.—Εκθαμβεομαι. See on *Mark* ix. 15.

V. 12—16. Notwithstanding the multiplied miracles which Jesus had wrought, and the astonishing events which had lately taken place at Jerusalem; the Jews had so little applied their minds to them, that each new miracle excited amazement, as if they had not seen any before, or could not tell what to infer from it. It is indeed probable, that they did not expect to witness any thing of this kind, after Jesus had been put to death. The apostle therefore demanded of them, why they were so astonished at this miracle, when so many others, all combining to prove the

1 8. 1v. 7. 10. 30.
xvi. 18.
k xiv. 9. xix. 13—
17. Matt. xvii.
19, 20. xxi. 21,
22. Mark xi. 22,
23. xvi. 17, 18. Luke xvii. 5, 6. John xiv. 12. 1 Cor. xiii. 2.

16 And [i] his name, [k] through faith in his name, hath made this man strong, whom ye see and know: yea, the faith which is by him hath given him this perfect soundness in the presence of you all.

l 8. iv. 14—16.
Deut. xxxii. 4.
John vii. 23.

same doctrine, had already been performed among them. Or why did they look to him and John, as if they had healed the man by their own power; or as if their own "holiness," or *godliness*, had given them some peculiar interest in the favour of God? (*Marg. Ref.* z, a.) For this was by no means the case: on the contrary, "the " God of their fathers " had wrought this, and all the other wonders which they had witnessed, in order to honour his Son Jesus, " whom he had glorified " at his right hand in heaven. Indeed they had delivered Jesus as a condemned malefactor to Pilate, " because he called himself the Son " of God;" rejecting their promised Messiah, and prevailing with Pilate by importunity to crucify him, when, convinced of his innocence, he " had determined to release him." Nay, at the same time that they thus unanimously and deliberately renounced this righteous Saviour, this " holy One of God;" they had desired the release of a murderer. (*Marg. Ref.* b—f.—*Notes*, ii. 33—36. Matt. xxvii. 19—26. Mark xv. 6—10. Luke xxiii. 13—25.) Thus, they had wickedly preferred a wretch who destroyed men's lives, to " the Prince of life;" the Author of life and salvation, from whom alone spiritual and eternal life could be obtained; and had murdered him by the hands of the Gentiles! But though they had thus atrociously dishonoured the Author of life: (*Note*, John i. 4, 5. v. 24—27. xi. 20—27 xiv. 4—6. Col. iii. 1—4. 1 John i. 1, 2. v. 11, 12:) yet God his Father had raised him from the dead, of which they were witnesses: and the incontestable miracle, which excited their amazement, had been performed by faith in the name of Jesus, and by power derived from him, in confirmation of their testimony to his resurrection and ascension: nor had they done any thing in restoring this cripple to " perfect soundness," except as their faith had relied on the power of Jesus to perform the cure. (*Marg.* and *Marg. Ref.* g—l.)—*Holiness.* (12) ' Here is ' a plain evidence of the variation of the Roman doctrine, ' from that of the apostles, assisted by the Holy Ghost : ' for the apostles here plainly disclaim any excellency or ' piety in them, which might make them worthy to be ' God's instruments, above any others, in working such ' miracles ; but the catechism of the council of Trent plainly ' declares, that God confers on us many benefits by the ' *merits of the saints*; and Lorinus, on the place, declares, ' that innumerable histories, and the practice of the church, ' show that the merits of the saints are prevalent for the ' working of miracles.' *Whitby.*—*Through faith,* &c.] Some expositors interpret this of the faith, which the lame man exercised in the name of Jesus ; and the probability that he had heard and seen Christ himself, as well as the *piety* which apparently accompanied his gratitude to Peter and John for his cure, favours the opinion that he was a believer. Yet it does not appear that he previously expected a cure ; and the texts referred to, will, I think, convince the attentive reader, that the faith of the apostles was intended. (*Marg. Ref.* k.—*Notes*, Matt. xxi. 21, 22. Mark xi, 20—26.) They had used the name of Jesus in faith; and a divine power had, in answer to their expectations, " given perfect

" soundness " to one, who had been a cripple from his birth, who was forty years of age, and who was well known to the people. This was designed to shew, that Jesus was risen ; that he was indeed the Messiah, and as such honoured by the God of Abraham ; and that the apostles were his servants and witnesses.—Every reflecting person must observe the very great difference, which there was in the manner of our Lord's working his miracles, and that of his apostles. His language was that of omnipotence and sovereignty, " I will, be thou clean : " " Peace, be still ; " " Damsel, arise." Nor did he ever, except in the case of Lazarus, which has been considered, (*Notes*, John xi. 41—46, *vv.* 41, 42,) even appeal by prayer to his Father, or give the least intimation of any power exerted, except what was inherent in himself. He never hesitated to receive the greatest honour, which was rendered on these occasions ; he never cautioned any man against supposing that he wrought miracles by " his own power, and to " manifest his own glory." (*Note*, John ii. 6—11, *v.* 11.) But the apostles wrought their miracles expressly " in his " name," and by faith *in him :* they were afraid of receiving any honour to themselves, except as the undeserving instruments in the hands of Jesus: they referred all the honour to their Lord : and they never mentioned the Father; except to shew, that the God of Abraham was fulfilling in " his Son Jesus," the promises made to the patriarchs, and was determined to glorify in every way that Person, whom the Jews had treated with contempt and indignity. No satisfactory reason ever was, or ever can be, given of this manifest difference; but by allowing that Jesus knew himself to be " One with the Father " and coequal to him ; and that the apostles were conscious, that they were weak and sinful men, who depended on Jesus alone for every thing.—*His name,* &c.] His power accompanying the use of " his name," with " faith in his " name : " even " the faith that is by him," effected the cure. (*Notes*, iv. 5—12. xix. 13—20.)

Holiness. (12) Ευσεβεια. 1 Tim. i. 2. iii. 16. iv. 7, 8, *et al.* "Godliness." Ex *ev bene*, et σεδω, *colo.*—*Hath glorified.* (13) Εδοξασε. See on John vii. 39.—*His son.*] Τον Παιδα *αυδε.* 26. iv. 25. 27. 30. Matt. xii. 18.—*Ye denied.*] Ηρνησασθε. 14. iv. 16. vii. 25. Matt. x. 33. Heb. xi. 24, *et al.* " Ye refused."—*When he was determined.*] Κριναντος *αυδε.* " When he judged." Pilate proposed it, as his judgment ; but he was induced by fear to act contrary to his own decision of the cause.—*The Holy One.* (14) Τον 'Αγιον. Rev. iii. 7. See on Mark i. 24. *Marg. Ref.* e.—*The just.*] Δικαιον. vii. 52. xxii. 14. Matt. xxvii. 19. 24. Luke xxiii. 47. Jam. v. 6. 1 Pet. iii. 18. 1 John ii. 1.—*A murderer.*] Ανδρα φονεα. vii. 52. xxviii. 4. Matt. xxii. 7. 1 Pet. iv. 15. Rev. xxi. 8. xxii. 15.—*To be granted.*] Χαρισθηναι. See on Luke vii. 21. Χαρις, *Acts* xxiv. 27. xxv. 3. 9.—*The Prince.* (15) Τον Αρχηγον. v. 31. Heb. ii. 10. xii. 2. Not elsewhere. Ex αρχη, *principium,* et αγω, *duco.*—*Perfect soundness.* (16) 'Ολοκληριαν. Here only N. T.—Ις. i. 6. Sept. Λb ὁλοκληρος, 1 Thes. v. 23. Ex ὁλος, *totus,* et κληρος, *sors.*

17 And now, brethren, I ^m wot that through ignorance ye did *it*, as *did* also your rulers.

18 But ⁿ those things which God before had shewed by the mouth of all his prophets, that Christ should suffer, he hath so fulfilled.

19 ^o Repent ye therefore, and ^p be converted, ^q that your sins may be blotted out, ^r when the times of refreshing shall come from the presence of the Lord;

20 And ^s he shall send Jesus Christ, which before was preached unto you:

21 Whom ^t the heaven must receive until ^y the times of restitution of all things, which God hath spoken by the mouth of all his ^z holy prophets since the world began.

V. 17, 18. The apostle, having shewn the Jews the atrociousness of their crime, was careful not to irritate them needlessly, nor yet to drive them to despair. He was willing candidly to suppose, that both they and their rulers had done this deed in ignorance. This ignorance indeed resulted from pride, prejudice, and many criminal sources; yet " they would not have crucified the Lord of glory, if " they had known him." (*Marg. Ref.* m, n.—*Notes, Luke* xxiii. 32—38, *v.* 34. *John* xix. 8—12. 1 *Cor.* ii. 6—9. 1 *Tim.* i. 12—14. *Heb.* vi. 4—6.) God had, however, in this manner fulfilled the prophecies of the scripture, concerning the atoning sufferings of their promised Messiah: so that, though " they had thought evil against him, yet " God meant it for good."—' Though the ignorance of ' the whole nation, and especially of the rulers in this case, ' was such as took away all just excuse in them, on ac- ' count of their infidelity; (*John* xv. 22—24;) yet, because ' it was occasioned by those prejudices which they had ' contracted, through the meanness of his character, and ' their imagination that Christ should not die, and that his ' kingdom should be temporal, Christ bears with it, till ' the time of the effusion of the Holy Ghost; and then ' calls them again by his apostles to repentance.' *Whitby.* (*Note, Matt.* xii. 31, 32.)—*I wot*, &c. (17) *Marg. Ref.* m. *Before had shewed.* (18) Προκαίηγγειλε. 24. vii. 52. 2 *Cor.* iv. 25. Not elsewhere.

V. 19—21. As the sin of the Jews was so undeniable and aggravated, and as there was yet hope for them in the mercy of God, through the Saviour whom they had crucified; the apostle exhorted them to repent, and turn from that, and all their other sins, to the acceptable worship and service of God, by faith in his Son. (*Marg. Ref.* q, r. —*Notes*, xvii. 30, 31. xx. 18—21. xxvi. 19—23. *Ez.* xviii. 30—32. *Matt.* iii. 2. *Luke* xiii. 1—5. xxiv. 44—49.) Thus, and thus only, all their sins would be blotted out as a cancelled debt, never more to be charged to their account. (*Marg. Ref.* s.—*Notes, Ps.* li. 1, 2. 9. *Is.* xliii. 22 —25. xliv. 22.)—The following words may be rendered, perhaps more clearly, " That seasons of refreshment may " come from the presence of the Lord; and that he may " send Jesus Christ, who hath before been preached unto " you, &c."—' Divine refreshment would no doubt imme- ' diately mingle itself with the sense of pardon, and eternal ' happiness would at length certainly succeed. But the fol- ' lowing clause seems to intimate, that Peter apprehended ' that the conversion of the Jews, as a people, would be ' attended with some extraordinary scene of prosperity and

' joy, and open a speedy way to Christ's descent from hea- ' ven, in order to " the restitution of all things."—I find ' that the learned Vitringa agrees with me in this inter- ' pretation.' *Doddridge.* The prophets in general predicted, not only glorious times to the church under the reign of the Messiah, but to the nation of Israel when converted to him. (*Marg. Ref.* y.) That nation had long been harassed and oppressed in various ways, and was at the time when Peter spoke, under the Roman yoke, which was extremely galling: and the wickedness of the rulers and people, in crucifying the Messiah, might seem to have filled up the measure of their national guilt, and ripened them for destruction. But as Jesus, after his resurrection, had directed his apostles to " preach repentance and re- " mission of sins in his name to all nations, beginning at " Jerusalem;" (*Note, Luke* xxiv. 44—49, *v.* 47;) and as the success of their first attempt had been so signal, and they had hitherto met with no opposition; it is probable, they expected that Christ would soon " restore the king- " dom to Israel," having first brought the nation in general to repent and believe in him; (*Note,* i. 4—8;) and would afterwards, by their means, bring the other nations to embrace the religion of Israel, and so, as proselytes, to seek admission into the kingdom of the Messiah. Then, perhaps, they expected that Jesus would return again from heaven, set up a triumphant kingdom on earth; and, destroying all obstinate enemies, would introduce those glorious days, which all the prophets had foretold.—It is undeniable, that the apostles, for a considerable time after the day of Pentecost, did not clearly understand many things, relating to the calling of the Gentiles, the rejection of the Jews, and the fulfilment of the prophecies. (*Notes,* ii. 14—21. x. 9—16. 44—48. xi. 1—18. xv. 1—21. *Matt.* xxiv. 3.) Their minds were enlightened, and their prejudices dissipated; rapidly indeed, yet gradually, and as their present circumstances and duties required. Thus the ancient prophets were inspired to foretel as much, as it was proper should at the time be known; yet they did not immediately, or certainly, know the meaning of their own predictions; (*Note,* 1 *Pet.* i. 10—12;) and the apostles and primitive Christians after the event understood them far more clearly, than the prophets themselves had done. In like manner, after the conversion of Cornelius, and the council at Jerusalem, Christians in general would understand St. Peter's words, concerning the " pouring out of " the Spirit on all flesh," more distinctly than he did when he uttered them; and after the destruction of Jerusalem,

22 For [a] Moses truly said unto the fathers, [b] A Prophet shall the Lord your God raise up unto you [c] of your brethren, [d] like unto me: [e] him shall ye hear in all things, whatsoever he shall say unto you.

23 And it shall come to pass, [f] that every soul which will not hear that Prophet, shall be destroyed from among the people.

24 Yea, [g] and all the prophets from [h] Samuel, and those that follow after,

as many as have spoken, have likewise foretold of these days.

25 Ye are [i] the children of the prophets, and of [k] the covenant which God made with our fathers, saying unto Abraham, [l] And in thy Seed shall [m] all the kindreds of the earth be blessed.

26 Unto you [n] first, God, [o] having raised up his Son Jesus, [p] sent him to bless you, [q] in turning away every one of y from his iniquities.

Marginal references:
a vii. 37. Deut. xviii. 15—18. b Luke xiii. 33. xxiv. 19. John vii. 12. xii. 46. Rev. i. 1. c Rom. viii. 3. Gal. iv. 4. Heb. ii. 17. d See on Deut. xviii. 18. e Is. iv. 3. Matt. xvii. 4, 5. Mark ix. 4—7. Luke ix. 30—35. John i. 17. v. 24. 39—47. Heb. i. 1, 2. ii. 1, v. 9. f xiii. 38—41. Deut. xviii. 19. Mark xvi. 16. John iii. 18—20. viii. 24. xii. 48. g 19. 21. Rom. iii. 21. h Heb. ii. 3. x. 28—30. xii. 25. h xlii. 20. 1 Sam. ii. 18. iii. 1, 20. Ps. xcix. 6. Jer. xv. 1.

i ii. 39. xiii. 26. Gen. xx. 7. xxvii. 36—40. xlviii. 14—20. k Ps. cv. 8—15. Matt. iii. 9, 16. Gen. xvii. 9, 10. 19. 1 Chr. xvi. 17. Neh. ix. 8. Luke i. 72. Rom. ix. 4, 5. xv. 8. Gal. iii. 29. l Gen. xii. 3. xviii. 18. xxii. 18. xxvi. 4 xxviii. 14. Rom. iv. 13. Gal. iii. 8. 16. m Ps. xxii. 27. xcvi. 7. Rev. v. 9. vii. 9. xv. 6. n 1 Ωⅈ 26. 46, 47. xviii. 4—6. xxvi. 20. xxviii. 23—28. Matt. x. 5, 6. xv. 24. Luke xxiv. 47. Rom. ii. 9, 10. Rev. vii. 4—9. o 15, 22. p 20, 28. Ps. lxviii. 6. 7. lxxii. 17. Luke ii. 10, 11. John i. 16. q Is. lv. 20, 21. Jer. xxxii. 38—41, xxxiii. 8, 9. Ez. xi. 19, 20. xxxvi. 25—29. Matt. i. 21. Eph. v. 26, 27. Tit. ii. 14. 1 John iii. 5—8. Jude 24.

and the abolishing of the Mosaick dispensation, the surviving Christians would more exactly perceive the meaning of the words before us, than Peter himself did at the time. Our Lord had told the apostles: " It was not for you to " know the times and the seasons, which the Father had put " in his own power," (i. 7,) and there is ground to believe, that this, in many respects, was not clearly revealed to them, but left to be discovered by the event. (Note, ii. 14 —21.) Had the nation of Israel, as a body, embraced the gospel, " the times of refreshment would have come from " the presence of the Lord : " and when the nation shall thus turn to their long rejected Messiah, those times will come. But the prophets who foretold these events, predicted also a national rejection of the Messiah, and dreadful desolations to the people, with long continued dispersions. It was not, however, necessary, that the Holy Spirit should on this occasion, make known " the times and sea- " sons " of these dispensations ; and, without such an immediate revelation, the apostle might expect that these happy times for his nation were at hand. Even to the end of the New Testament, such an obscurity is left on these subjects, that diverse opinions still prevail, in respect of the reign of Christ during the millennium, whether it is to be *personal* or *spiritual* ; (Note, Rev. xx. 4—6 ;) and his coming to set up his kingdom all over the earth, has been very generally, even by diligent expositors and other learned writers, confounded with his coming to judge the world : and in various other particulars this obscurity and inaccuracy is found. Now, that which was to be obscurely foretold, a prophet or apostle might but obscurely foresee : and the historian merely records the apostle's discourse.

Repent. (19) Μετανοησατε. ii. 38. viii. 22. xvii. 30, *et al.* See on *Matt.* iii. 2.—*Be converted.*] Επιστρεψατε. ix. 35. 40. xi. 21. xiv. 15. xv. 19. xvi. 18. xxvi. 18. 20. xxviii. 27. *Luke* xxii. 32. 1 *Thes.* i. 9. *Jam.* v. 19, 20. 1 *Pet.* ii. 25. —*Blotted out.*] Εξαλειφθηναι. *Col.* ii. 14. *Rev.* iii. 5. vii. 17. xxi. 4.—*Ps.* li. 1. 9. *Is.* xliii. 25. Sept. Εξ et αλειφω, ungo.—*When.*] Οπως αν. xv. 17. *Luke* ii. 35. *Rom.* iii. 4. --*Ps.* ix. 14. xcii. 7. cxix. 101. *Sept.*—" That they may " come."—*Of refreshing.*] Αναψυξεως. Here only. Αναψυχω, 2 *Tim.* i. 16. *Recovery from fainting.* Εx ανα et ψυχη, anima.—*Which was before preached.* (20) Τον προκεκηρυγμενον. xiii. 24. Not elsewhere. Εx προ et κηρυσσω, prædico. —*Of restitution.* (21) Αποκαταστασεως. Here only. Αποκαθιστημι, *Matt.* xii. 13. *Mark* viii. 25. A restoration to the condition from which any one has fallen.—' The restoration of Israel.'

(*Notes, Is.* xi. 11—16. *Jer.* xxxi. 31—34. xxxii. 37—41. *Ez.* xxxiv. 23—31. xxxvi. 20—32. xxxvii. 20—28. xxxix. 23—29. *Hos.* iii. 4, 5. *Am.* ix. 13—15. *Mic.* vii. 11—20. *Zech.* xii. 6—14. xiii. 1. *Rom.* xi. 11—15. *Rev.* xx. 4—6.) —*Since the world began.*] Απ' αιωνος. xv. 18. *Eph.* iii. 9.

V. 22, 23. (*Note,* vii. 37—43.)—' One cannot imagine ' a more masterly address than this ; to warn the Jews of ' the dreadful consequence of their infidelity, in the very ' words of Moses their favourite prophet ; out of a pre- ' tended zeal for whom they were ready to reject Christianity, ' and to attempt its destruction.' *Doddridge.* (*Note, John* v. 45—47.) The general meaning of the passage is here compendiously given : but it is not a *quotation,* properly speaking, either from the Septuagint, or the Hebrew ; between which there is no material difference.

A prophet, &c. (22) *Note, Deut.* xviii. 15—19.—*Shall be destroyed.* (23) Εξολοθρευθησεται. Here only. Ab εξ et ολο- θρευω, *Heb.* xi. 28. Ολοθρευτης, 1 *Cor.* x. 10.

V. 24—26. Samuel was the first prophet after Moses, who is expressly mentioned as a writer of the sacred oracles ; and from him the schools of the prophets seem to have originated. (*Note,* 1 *Sam.* x. 5, 6.) It is not necessary to prove, that predictions concerning Christ are found in the writings of every one of the prophets, for the words imply a general, not a universal, proposition : yet Jonah and Nahum alone appear to be exceptions ; for Obadiah certainly is not. The book of Jonah is a history, not a prophecy ; and he was a remarkable type of Christ. That of Nahum, is " the burden of Nineveh," and relates expressly as a prophecy to no other subject. (*Note, Nah.* i. 15.)—The persons to whom the apostle spoke, were the descendants of those, to whom the prophets had been sent, and they had inherited from them the deposit of the sacred oracles, as well as the advantages of the covenant first made with their Fathers ; especially that of the Messiah's arising from among them, who was the " Seed of " Abraham, in whom all the nations of the earth would be " blessed." (*Marg. Ref.* i—m.—*Notes, Gen.* xii. 1—3. xxii. 16—18. *Rom.* iii. 1, 2. ix. 4, 5.) Indeed Abraham, Isaac, and Jacob, were prophets ; (*Gen.* xx. 7. *Ps.* cv. 15 ;) and the Jews were their children, and heirs of the covenant made with them ; unless (like profane Esau,) they should despise and refuse their birthright and blessing. (*Notes, Gen.* xxv. 30—34. *Heb.* xii. 15—17.) On this account the first proposal of the gospel was ordered to be made to them. For God, having raised up his Son Jesus, to

CHAP. IV.

The priests and Sadducees imprison Peter and John, 1—3. The signal success of their preaching, 4. When brought before the council, Peter boldly declares, that the late cure had been wrought in the name of Jesus, the only Saviour, whom the rulers had rejected, 5—12. The council, unable to answer, dismiss them with a threatening charge to speak no more in the name of Jesus, which they avow themselves bound to disre-gard, 13—22. They return to their company; and all unite in prayer, for boldness in preaching, and that miracles of mercy might confirm their testimony, 23—30. The house being shaken, they are all filled with the Holy Spirit, and emboldened to speak the word of God, 31. The harmony and charity of the whole company, who had all things in common; the miraculous assistance granted to the apostles; and the pious liberality of Barnabas and others who had possessions, in selling them, to distribute to the needy, 32—37.

---

be a Prophet, Priest, and Ruler, a Mediator of a covenant, the Author of a new dispensation, as Moses had been, but in every respect unspeakably superior to Moses. Having therefore raised him from the dead, and placed him upon his glorious throne, he had sent him, by his gospel and by his Holy Spirit, to render them truly happy : not by advancing them to worldly authority and prosperity, as they had vainly expected; but by teaching, encouraging, and enabling them to turn away from all their sins, that they might walk before him, as his accepted worshippers and adopted children, in the light of his countenance, and the enjoyment of his favour. (*Marg. Ref.* n—q.)—' This chapter furnishes to us additional and very striking views of the admirable spirit, which actuated and fully possessed the apostles, after the day of Pentecost. Behold their *moderation* and their *piety*, still gladly taking part in the Jewish worship (1); their *simplicity*, perfectly willing to be and to pass for poor men (6); their *tenderness* to the afflicted; (6, 7;) their *indifference* to themselves, and *zeal* for their divine Master; (12, 13, &c.) their *boldness*; (13—15;) yet, withal, their *candour* (17); and their *affectionate compassion* for souls (19. 25, 26.),—What do we want as Christians or as ministers, but to be formed to such blessed tempers as these, thus happily blended together? And by what means were the apostles formed to them, but by the influence of that same Spirit, who is so firmly promised, and even urgently offered, to "every one" that asks his presence?—This also repels the suspicion of enthusiasm. Where is the waywardness or self-sufficiency of an enthusiast? On the contrary, moderation, candour, and modesty, are united with most decided courage and most fervent zeal, in the conduct of the apostles.

Families. (25) Πατριαι. *Luke* ii. 4. *Eph.* iii. 15. Not elsewhere. Φυλαι, *Gen.* xii. 3. *Sept.*—*To bless,* &c. (26) Ευλογουντα ὑμας, εν τω αποτρεφειν ἑκαστον απο κ. τ. λ. (Αποτρεφω. *Matt.* v. 42. xxvi. 52. xxvii. 3. *Luke* xxiii. 14. *Rom.* xi. 26, *et al.*) ' Æque commode reddi potest, *ut vos abstraheret ab omni vitiositate,* ac ita, *ut averteret se quisque a pravitate.*' Schleusner.—" Blessing you, in each one turning away from his " wickednesses." Each, who did this at that time, or does it at any time, is blessed by Christ; but none else. This seems the purport of the words.

PRACTICAL OBSERVATIONS.

V. 1—11.

The stated seasons of communion with God, and opportunities of doing good, will be welcomed with alacrity, proportioned to the degree in which we are " spiritually " minded : " (*Notes, Ps.* lxxxiv. 1, 2.10. *P. O. Note,* cxxii.1, 2 :) for the carnal mind alone complains of the tediousness and too frequent returns of these sacred services; as sickly

persons even loathe the sight of the food, which the healthy relish and enjoy.—Piety and charity should always be connected : those who are disabled from labour ought to be supported by benevolence; but too often, the impositions of the slothful and profligate give selfishness an excuse, for turning away from real and known objects of compassion. (*Note, Luke* xviii. 35—43, *v.* 35.)—Poverty and simplicity, and contempt of filthy lucre, in the ministers of Christ, are far better proofs of integrity, than affluence, splendour, and luxury: and, while the Lord employs others as his stewards, in dispensing wealth to relieve the necessities of their brethren; it should not grieve the " steward of the mysteries of God," if he be constrained to say to the expecting poor, " Silver and gold I " have none, but such as I give unto thee." (*Notes, Luke* xvi. 1—13. 1 *Cor.* iv. 1, 2. 1 *Pet.* iv. 9—11.) In every case, we ought to impart to others, according to the ability which is given to us; and " if there be first a wil-" ling mind, it is accepted " by God, " according to what " a man hath, and not according to what he hath not;' and so it ought to be by our brethren. (*Notes,* 2 *Cor.* viii 10—15. ix. 6—11.)—If we would attempt to good pur·pose the healing of men's souls, we must go forth in the name and power of Jesus Christ; calling on helpless sinners to arise, and walk in the way of holiness by faith in him. We should indeed shew affectionate regard to those whom we address : but nothing effectual will be done, till the Lord puts forth his power; and then the most impotent will receive strength to " walk in newness of life," and shew forth the praises of God, by cheerfully joining in his worship, and by cleaving to his ministers and people. Thus the attention of men is excited; facts proclaim the efficacy of the gospel; and every true convert is a monument raised to the honour of the great Redeemer's power and love. (*Note, Is.* lv. 10—13.)

V. 12—18.

Those who are honoured with usefulness should be careful to remind the people, that as the effects are not produced by their power, so they are not wrought for the sake of their holiness or piety, but for the glory of that divine Saviour, whom sinners still deny and despise : He is " the Prince of life," and " the Author of eternal sal-" vation to all them who obey him ; " (*Note, Heb.* v. 7—10;) yet what immense numbers prefer the company and favour of the vilest transgressors, and the indulgence of their ruinous lusts, to him and all his blessings. But whether good have been done, or whether we have been enabled to fight successfully against sin and temptation, it has been effected " by faith in his name : " and we must go forth to all our future labours and conflicts, and our

a 4. vi. 7.12.Matt. **A**ND as they spake unto the people, ‖ Jesus the resurrection from the dead. *f* v. 18. vi. 12.
xxvi. 5. 4. xxvii. ‖ viii. 3. ix. 2. xii.
1. 2. 20. 41. *a* the priests, *b* and the *c* captain of the ‖ 3 And they *f* laid hands on them, 1—3. xvi. 19—
John xv. 20. 24. Matt. x. 16,
xvii. 3. temple, *c* and the Sadducees, came ‖ and put *them* in hold unto the next 17. Luke xxii.
b v. 26. 2 Chr. 52. 54. John
xxiii.4—6. Lu*ke* upon them; ‖ day : for it was now even-tide. xviii. 12.
xxii. 4. g 2 Cor. li. 14—
e Or, *ruler.* 2 Being *d* grieved that they taught ‖ 4 Howbeit, *g* many of them which 17. Phil. i. 12—
c xxiii.5—9.Matt. 18. 2 Tim. ii. 9,
xvii. 12. xxii. 16. the people, and *e* preached through ‖ heard the word believed; *h* and the num- 10.
23. 34. h ii. 41. Gen.
d v. 17. xli. 45. xix. 23. Neh. fl. 10. John xi. 47, 48. e x. 40—43. xvii. 18. 31. ber of the men was about five thousand. xliv. 10. 1a, xiv.
32. xxiv. 14, 15. 21. xxvi. 8. 23. Rom. viii. 11. 1 Cor. xv. 12—20, 23. 2 Cor. iv. 13, 14. 24. liii. 12. John.
1 Thes. iv. 13, 14. xii. 24.

efforts to promote the cause of truth and holiness, by the same faith, engaging his almighty arm to work in us, by us, and for us, that he may have all the glory.—Those who reject, refuse, or deny Christ, do it through ignorance of one kind or another : this can in no case be admitted as an excuse ; but it alleviates the guilt at some times, far more than it does at others. While unbelievers should be reproved and convicted of their sins and all the aggrava- tions of them in the plainest and most faithful manner ; yet we should admit of any extenuation, which can fairly be supposed ; and we should always be careful to shew them, that the mercy of God in Christ Jesus gives them ground of hope, or forgiveness, and eternal salvation, notwithstanding all their crimes. (*Notes,* 1 *Sam.* xii. 20. *Ps.* cxxx. 3, 4.)

V. 19—26.

Blessed be God, that the sins of all, who " repent and " are converted," shall assuredly be blotted out : the con- nexion is inseparable. (*Notes, Matt.* xiii. 14, 15. 2 *Tim.* ii. 23—26. *Heb.* vi. 4—6.) The change is indeed wrought by the grace of God : yet the exhortation to " repent and " be converted," and the assured promise of forgiveness and reconciliation to God, through Jesus Christ, in case they obey the call, should be general to all without distinc- tion ; and all alike should be warned, that except they re- pent and be converted, neither the mercy of God, nor the blood of Christ, will save them from perdition. When sinners are convinced of these things, they will begin to cry to the Lord, " Turn thou me, and I shall be turned ;" " Create in me a clean heart, and renew a right spirit " within me." (*Notes, Ps.* li. 10. *Jer.* xvii. 14. xxxi. 18 —20. *Ez.* xxxvi. 25—27. 37.)—To the penitent, con- verted, and believing, " times of refreshment will come " from the presence of the Lord : " and the day of judg- his judgments on the wicked will be attended with con- solation to the souls of his people ; and the day of judg- ment, when the Lord Jesus shall be revealed to take venge- ance on his enemies, will complete their salvation. (*Note,* 2 *Thes.* i. 5—10.) That solemn period, when the earth shall be burnt up, and the elements shall melt with fervent heat, will be to them " the restitution of all things," " the " manifestation of their adoption, and the redemption of " their bodies : " (*Note, Rom.* viii. 18—23 :) but every soul, who now refuses to hear, believe, and obey that " Prophet like unto Moses," whom God has raised up unto us, will then most certainly be destroyed from among the people.—Though we are not the children of the pro- phets, yet we are of those " kindreds of the earth," who are called on to inherit the blessings procured by the pro- mised Seed of Abraham : to us also are " committed the " oracles of God ; ", to us the glad tidings are preached, that God so loved us as to " send his Son Jesus to bless

" us, in turning every one of us from our iniquities." Let not sinners then imagine, that religion calls them to be uneasy and unhappy ; but rather that it kindly offers to guide them to true felicity. (*Notes, Ps.* i. 1—3. xxxii. 1, 2.) Let none suppose that they can be happy, by continuing in sin ; when God declares that the blessing consists in being " turned from their iniquities." Let none think that they understand and believe the gospel, who seek deliver- ance only from the punishment of sin, but do not expect happiness by salvation from sin itself : and let none expect to be turned effectually from their constitutional or cus- tomary iniquities, except by believing in Christ the Son of God, being " found in him," " who of God is made to " all believers, " Wisdom, and Righteousness, and Sanctifica- " tion, and Redemption." (*Note,* 1 *Cor.* i. 26—31, *v.* 30.)

NOTES.

Chap. IV. V. 1—3. ' Before our Saviour's passion, the ' chief agents against him were the scribes and Pharisees ; ' but now that the apostles do not only assert the re- ' surrection of our Lord, but " preach through Jesus the ' " resurrection of the dead" (2), the Sadducees, who de- ' nied the resurrection of the body, become their fiercest ' adversaries.' *Whitby.*—The Sadducees seem to have ra- pidly increased, among the higher orders, at this time : and as the testimony of the apostles, to the resurrection of Jesus, was subversive of their scheme of infidelity, this was to them an additional reason for opposing their doc- trine. (*Note,* xxiii. 6—10.) It could not therefore be ex- pected, but that, on this and on other accounts, the rulers of the Jews would persecute the apostles, as they had done Jesus himself. Accordingly, under the guidance of the person, who presided over the guard of Levites which constantly attended at the temple, they apprehended Peter and John as they were preaching, and cast them into prison ; being so late in the evening, that they could not then con- veniently proceed against them. (*Marg. Ref.*)—' Over this ' guard,' (of Levites) ' one of the priests was appointed ' captain : and this office, according to Josephus, was next ' in dignity to that of high priest.' *Campbell.* (*Notes,* 2 *Kings* xi. 4—10.)

The captain. (1)   " Ruler."   *Marg.* Στρατηγος. v. 24. 26. See on *Luke* xxii. 52.—*Being grieved.* (2) Διαπο- νημενοι. xvi. 18. Not elsewhere.—Εχ δια et πονεω, laboro. *In hold.* (3) Εις τηρησιν. v. 18. 1 *Cor.* vii. 19. Not else- where.—Α τηρεω, custodio.

V. 4.   Some expositors think, that five thousand per- sons were converted on this occasion ; but it rather seems, that this number of believers was then completed : for it is not likely, that any one day should be honoured with greater success, than that on which the Holy Spirit first descended : nor do the words convey that idea to the

4 ж 2

5 And it came to pass ' on the morrow, that their ᵏ rulers, and elders, and scribes,

6 And ' Annas the high priest, and Caiaphas, and John, and Alexander, and as many as were of the kindred of the high priest, were gathered together at Jerusalem.

7 And ᵐ when they had set them in the midst, they asked, ⁿ By what power, or ° by what name, have ye done this?

8 Then Peter, ᵖ filled with the Holy Ghost, said unto them, Ye rulers of the people, and elders of Israel,

9 If we this day be examined of ᵠ the good deed done to the impotent man, by what means he is made whole;

10 Be it ʳ known unto you all, and to all the people of Israel, ˢ that by the name of Jesus Christ of Nazareth, whom ye crucified, ' whom God raised from the dead, even by him doth this man stand here before you whole.

11 This is ᵘ the Stone which was set at nought of ˣ you builders, which is become ʸ the Head of the corner.

12 Neither ᶻ is there salvation in any other: for there is none other name ᵃ under heaven given among men, whereby we must be saved.

---

mind, but rather that " the number *became* about five " thousand;" yet they imply that the women and children were not included.

Men.] Ανδρων.—*Was.*] Εγενηθη.—Hν, i. 15.

V. 5—12. Caiaphas seems to have performed the ordinary functions of the high priesthood, and Annas to have had the greater influence and authority in the council. (*Notes, Luke* iii. 2, 3. *John* xviii. 10—14.)—The other persons here mentioned were doubtless very considerable at that time; but there seems to be little certainty or importance, in the conjectures which have been formed about them. " The kindred of the high priest," must have been different persons from the heads of the twenty-four courses; as many of these were no more his kindred, than all the other priests were: that is, they were descended from Aaron, either by Eleazar, or Ithamar. (*Notes,* 1 *Chr.* xxiv. 1—6.)—The examination of Peter and John would excite very great attention; as all parties seem to have considered their interest, authority, reputation, and favourite system to be in the most imminent danger. In the question which they asked, they virtually allowed, that an extraordinary cure had been performed: (*Notes, Matt.* xxi. 23—32:) but they enquired, whether it were the effect of a divine power, or of incantation by the use of some " name," according to the notions which then prevailed. Accordingly Peter, " being filled with the Holy Ghost," felt none of those terrors, which had formerly led him to deny his Lord; but spoke before that great assembly, with the utmost courage, liberty, and propriety. (*Marg. Ref.* m—p.—*Notes, Matt.* x. 16—20. *Luke* xxi. 12—19, *v.* 15.) He premised that the action, about which they were cited to answer as criminals, was " a good deed," an act of genuine mercy as well as of divine power: and he would have all the priests, scribes, and rulers, and all the whole nation, to understand, that it had been wrought " by the " name," or power, " of Jesus the Nazarene," who was the promised Messiah. (*Marg. Ref.* q—s.—*Note,* iii. 12 —16.) They had indeed crucified him as a deceiver, for declaring himself to be " the Son of God:" but his resurrection from the dead, by the power of God, had proved his high claim; and the man, who stood before them, miraculously cured of his hopeless lameness, was a

confirmation of their concurrent testimony to that event. Indeed the crucified and risen Jesus was that illustrious person, of whom David prophesied, as of a Stone, designed to be the Cement, Support, and Ornament of the whole spiritual temple; and they were the builders, (by office and authority in the church,) who had set at nought that Stone, and thrown it aside as utterly worthless. (*Marg. Ref.* u—y.—*Notes, Ps.* cxviii. 19—24. *Matt.* xxi. 40—44.)—But, according to that prophecy, he was now exalted to the highest authority in heaven, as the anointed Saviour, and the only Mediator between God and Man: insomuch that there was " no salvation in any other" person, or way, either for the rulers or people; nor " any " other name under heaven given among men," by which either he, or they, or any man might be saved from destruction. This plainly intimated, that no man could be saved, except in a way of God's express appointment; and that the rulers themselves must either be saved by Jesus, or perish for ever. (*Marg. Ref.* z, a.)—Some learned men have laboured to prove, that *healing*, or the cure of bodily disorders, is meant in the concluding verse; and not eternal salvation; because the same original word in some instances signifies *healing*. In fact, it denotes *deliverance*, whether from disease, slavery, death, or damnation; and the context must fix the meaning. But in this place, the miracle of the man who had been healed, was merely adduced as a proof that Jesus was risen from the dead, and consequently the Messiah, the Son of God, and the only Saviour for sinners. The apostles, the rulers, and audience, did not want miraculous cures of bodily diseases; but they all needed a Saviour and salvation: the name of Jesus is given to men of every age and nation, as that by which alone believers are saved from the wrath to come, and " with an everlasting salvation;" not from bodily sickness and temporal death. Indeed every reader must perceive, what energy there was in the address to the consciences of these persecutors, according to the obvious interpretation of it; and how this vain criticism enervates it, and causes all its spirit and vigour to evaporate.—It is observable, that the rulers never mentioned to the apostles, the report of their having stolen the body of Jesus, though they were so fairly called upon to do it;

13 ¶ Now when they saw the boldness of Peter and John, and perceived that they [b] were unlearned and ignorant men, they marvelled; [c] and they took knowledge of them, that they had been with Jesus.

14 And [d] beholding the man which was healed standing with them, [e] they could say nothing against it.

15 But when they had commanded them [f] to go aside out of the council, they conferred among themselves,

16 Saying, [g] What shall we do to these men ? for that indeed [h] a notable miracle hath been done by them, is manifest to all them that dwell in Jerusalem ; [i] and we cannot deny it.

17 But [k] that it spread no further among the people, [l] let us straitly threaten them, that they speak henceforth to no man in this name.

18 And they called them, and commanded them, [m] not to speak at all nor teach in the name of Jesus.

19 But Peter and John answered and said unto them, [n] Whether it be right in the sight of God, [o] to hearken unto you more than unto God, [p] judge ye.

20 For [q] we cannot but speak [r] the things, which we have seen and heard.

21 So [s] when they had further threatened them, they let them go, finding nothing [t] how they might punish them, because of the people: [u] for all *men* glorified God for that which was done.

22 For the man was above [x] forty years old, on whom this miracle of healing was shewed.

---

for they know it to be a mere falsehood, and probably they acted against their own convictions, in professing a full persuasion that Jesus was not risen. (*Note, Matt.* xxviii. 11—15.)—The insertion of *you*, in quoting the prophecy (11), was very pointed. It was saying to each of them, " Thou art the man." (*Note, 2 Sam.* xii. 7.)—*This is the stone,* &c. (11) Nearly from the Sept., which agrees with the Hebrew. *Ps.* cxviii. 22.

The kindred of the high priest. (6) Γενυς αρχιερατικη. Here only.—*Be examined.* (9) Ανακρινομεθα. xii. 19. xvii. 11. xxiv. 8. xxviii. 8. *Luke* xxiii. 14. 1 Cor. ii. 14, 15. xiv. 24.—*The good deed.*] Ευεργησιᾳ. 1 Tim. vi. 2. Not elsewhere. Ex ευ *bene,* et εργον, *opus.*—*The impotent.*] Ασθενης. v. 15, 16. *Rom.* v. 6. 1 Thes. v. 14. *et al.*—*Is made whole.*] Σεσωσται. " Has been delivered."—*Salvation.* (12) Σωτηρια. xiii. 26. 47. xvi. 17. xvii. 34. *Luke* i. 69. 71. 77. *John* iv. 22. *Rom.* i. 16. x. 10. xi. xiii. 11. 2 Cor. vi. 2. Phil. ii. 12. 2 Tim. ii. 10. iii. 15. Heb. i. 14. ii. 3. 10. v. 9. vi. 9. ix. 18. xi. 7. 1 Pet. i. 5. 9, 10. Rev. vii. 10. *et al.*

V. 13—22. " Unlearned and ignorant men." (13) ' This, for three centuries, was the objection against the ' professors of Christianity: ... yet it is a great confirmation ' of the Christian faith; and shews, as Justin Martyr well ' observes, that it was not of human, but divine original ; ' and that being with Jesus was sufficient to make the ig- ' norant and unlearned wise.' *Whitby.* (*Note, John* vii. 14—17.)—It is probable, that the council had hoped to overawe the apostles, into silence and submission: but when they found with what constancy and courage they replied, and with what boldness they charged them with having crucified the Messiah; and when they considered that they were persons of mean education, obscure station, and strangers to the habits of publick life; they were greatly surprised, and recollected that they had seen them with Jesus, when they had laid wait to ensnare him as he taught in the temple, or when he was apprehended.

(*Marg. Ref.* b—d.) And, as the man who had been healed was upon the spot, ready to attest the reality of the miracle ; they could neither object any thing to the incontestable fact, nor deny the conclusion which was drawn from it. To conceal their perplexity, therefore, they ordered the apostles to withdraw for a while : and, having consulted together what they should do in so difficult a case, they agreed that it would be in vain to deny the miracle ; as it was manifest to all men, that it had been wrought by Peter and John, in the name of Jesus the Nazarene. It was, however, necessary to do something effectual to stop the progress of a doctrine, which tended to bring disgrace upon them, to subvert their authority, and, as they imagined, to ruin the nation. (*Notes, John* xi. 47—53. xii. 9—11.) They therefore determined, in defiance of conviction, to forbid the apostles, in the severest terms, on pain of their heaviest displeasure, " to " preach any more at all in the name of that Jesus," whom they had just before punished as a deceiver; which sentence they resolved to justify and support, by prosecuting those who espoused the same cause. (*Marg. Ref.* f—m.) To this, Peter and John replied, with great constancy and propriety, by demanding, whether it was reasonable, or " a *righteous* thing, in the sight of God," to regard the injunctions of men, more than his commandments. They were divinely commissioned and expressly commanded to " preach in the name of Jesus : " and however they might respect the authority, or fear the indignation of the rulers; their inward conviction of the truth and importance of their doctrine, and the remembrance of those things, which they had witnessed concerning their crucified, risen, and ascended Lord, and heard from him, would constrain them to declare his name and salvation to all around them. (*Marg. Ref.* n—r.— *Notes, Is.* xxx. 8—11. *Jer.* xxvi. 12—15. xxxviii. 1—G. *Am.* vii. 10—17. *Mic.* ii. 6, 7. 2 Cor. v. 13—15.)—This bold declaration induced the rulers to add still severer

23 And being let go, [y] they went to their own company, and reported all that the chief priests and elders had said unto them.

24 And when they heard that, [z] they lifted up their voice to God with one accord, and said, [a] Lord, thou *art* God, which hast made heaven, and earth, and the sea, and all that in them is:

25 Who [b] by the mouth of thy servant David hast said, [c] Why did the heathen rage, and the people imagine [d] vain things?

26 The [e] kings of the earth stood up, and the rulers were gathered together, against the Lord, and [f] against his Christ.

27 For of a truth, against [g] thy holy child Jesus, [g] whom thou hast anointed, [h] both Herod [i] and Pontius Pilate, with the Gentiles, and [k] the people of Israel were gathered together,

28 For [l] to do whatsoever thy hand and [m] thy counsel determined before to be done.

---

threatenings; but at the same time, they dismissed them: for, having no plausible reason to alledge, they dared not venture the consequences of punishing them; as the people shewed them great favour, and acknowledged the miraculous cure performed, to be a glorious display of divine power and mercy in the midst of them. Indeed the instantaneous recovery of one born a cripple, and now more than forty years old, was a most astonishing effect of divine power! (*Marg. Ref.* s—u.)—' Not only the energetick and conclusive *discourses* of the apostles are admirable; but " the meekness of wisdom," united with firmness, which distinguish all their replies;—replies often made to persons, whose presence must have been suited to daunt men of their station and their habits. They never shrink, and they are never disrespectful. They refuse to comply with the injunctions of their hostile superiors no further, than they feel themselves compelled to it by the imperious sense of duty. Their coolness, and self-possession, in the presence of persecutors, is not that affected and ostentatious, and of course irritating coolness, which some have displayed; whose conduct has seemed to say, ' See how indifferent we are to you! how much we are your superiors! In fact, how much we despise you!' This invites persecution; whereas the apostles always declined and avoided it, if they could.—This smiling self-complacent coolness may be as very a working of corrupt nature, as fleeing from the cross; and not a much more difficult working in certain circumstances. It lives upon its own admiration, and the admiration which it expects from by-standers; food which will support nothing that " belongs to the Spirit." ' (*Note, Dan.* iii. 16—18.)—It should be remembered, that this was the first time, in which the apostles were called to encounter opponents armed with power. (*Note, Matt.* xxvi. 69—75.) —*Took knowledge.* (13) If John was the " disciple who " was known to the high priest;" this language concerning him, as well as Peter, would scarcely have been used. (*Note, John* xviii. 15, 16.)—*We cannot.* (20) *Notes, Mark* i. 45. *John* v. 39—44, v. 44.

Perceived. (13) Καταλαβομενοι. *John* i. 5. *Eph.* iii. 18. *Phil.* iii. 12, 13. 1 *Thes.* v. 4.—*Unlearned.*] Αγραμματοι. Here only. See *John* vii. 15. Gr.—*Ignorant.*] Ιδιωται. 1 *Cor.* xiv. 16. 23, 24. 2 *Cor.* xi. 6. ' *Qui vitam privatam* ' *agit, nec fungitur munere publico;... plebeius.*' Schleusner. *Say... against.* (14) Αντιπειν. *Luke* xxi. 15.—*A notable.*

(16) Γνωτον. " Known."—*It spread.* (17) Διανεμηθη. Here only N. T.—*Deut.* xxix. 26. Sept. *Divulgetur, dimanet.* —*Let us straitly threaten,* &c.] Απειλη απειλησωμεθα. " Let us threaten them with a threatening." Απειλη. 29. ix. 1. *Eph.* vi. 9. Not elsewhere. Απειλεω, 1 *Pet.* ii. 23. Not elsewhere.—*To speak.* (18) Φθεγγεσθαι. 2 *Pet.* ii. 16. 18. Not elsewhere N. T. *Job* xiii. 7. *Ps.* lxxviii. 2. xciv. 4. Sept.—' Notare videtur *privatim* docere, ' quia a διδασκειν distinguitur.' *Schleusner.*—*At all.*] Καθολω. Here only. Ex καλα, et ὁλος, totus.—*Right.* (19) Δικαιον. See on iii. 14.—*Had further threatened.* (21) Προσαπειλησαμενοι. Here only. See on 17.—*Punish.*] Κολασωνται. 2 *Pet.* ii. 9. Not elsewhere.—Κολασις, *Matt.* xxv. 46. 1 *John* iv. 18.

V. 23—28. It is generally supposed, that the company, to which the apostles returned, consisted of the hundred and twenty persons before mentioned, who probably were assembled to pray in their behalf. (*Marg. Ref.* y.—*Note,* i. 15.) Under the impression of the report made to them by Peter and John, and by the influence of the same Spirit, they all united, as with one heart and soul, in prayer to the Lord, the omnipotent Creator of the world; and in doing this, they introduced with peculiar propriety a prophecy concerning the Messiah, which God had " spoken by the " mouth of his servant David."—Before our Lord's crucifixion, the apostles had overlooked all the predictions of this kind; but now they remembered and clearly understood them. (*Marg. Ref.* z—e.—*Note, Ps.* ii. 1—3.)— The language, used in applying this prophecy to Jesus, may refer to his immaculate conception by the Holy Spirit. Thus he received his human nature perfectly holy: and the unction of the same Spirit preserved that holiness, in full perfection, through all the temptations and trials of his life and death. This aggravated the guilt of those, who hated and opposed the " holy Child" and righteous Servant of God. Yet both Herod the tetrarch or king of Galilee, who professed the Jewish religion, and all the rulers of God's chosen people, and Pilate who was a professed idolater, with the bulk of the Jewish nation, as well as the Gentile attendants on Pilate, had united together to treat him with the utmost cruelty and contempt. (*Marg. Ref.* f—k.—*Notes, Matt.* xxvii. 24—44. *Luke* xxiii. 1— 25.) But they in this were only led to " whatsoever his " hand and counsel had determined before to be done." (*Marg. Ref.*—*Notes,* ii. 22—24. *Luke* xxii. 21—23.)—

29 And now, Lord, ^a behold their threatenings: and grant unto thy servants, ^b that with all boldness they may speak thy word,

30 ^c By stretching forth thine hand to heal; ^d and that signs and wonders may be done by ^e the name of thy holy child Jesus.

31 And when they had prayed, ^f the place was shaken where they were assembled together; and ^g they were all

filled with the Holy Ghost, ^h and they spake the word of God with boldness.

32 ¶ And ⁱ the multitude of them that believed, were of one heart and of one soul: neither said any of them, ^k that ought of the things which he possessed was his own; but they had all things common.

33 And ^l with great power gave the

' The truth is clear, that God decreed that these things
' should be done; although he decreed not that the Jews
' should do them : but only permitted them to do what he
' foresaw they would, if they were thus permitted.' Hammond.
It is then clear, that God, foreseeing this, decreed
to permit them.—' As St. Peter and St. Paul, by calling the
' Jews to repentance for this sin, in crucifying the Lord of
' life, do evidence that their sin was not the less, because
' they did by it fulfil the counsel of God's holy will, and
' kind intentions to mankind; so they consequently evi-
' dence, that God's foreknowledge and determination of a
' thing future, does not impair the liberty of men's wills in
' the accomplishment of it; as all the ancient fathers have
' declared in this particular.' Whitby.—' We must not con-
' sider their work, who were wicked murderers, and profane
' enemies of the truth; but the work of God, which they
' fulfilled, without thinking of any such thing. This dis-
' tinction, rightly observed, will satisfy all moderate men,
' that they should never separate the counsel and decree
' of God, from his decreeing fore-knowledge; and yet that
' they should fix all the blame of crimes on second causes,
' on the devil, for instance, and man. Thus God hardened
' Pharaoh : thus the king of Assyria was a saw, which God
' used : thus God gave to Absalom his father's wives : thus
' God called the revolt of the ten tribes his work : thus the
' wicked, by whom David was troubled, were the hands of
' God : thus Caiaphas prophesied : thus finally, " God
" worketh all things according to the counsel of his own
" will." ' Beza. (Notes, Gen. l. 20. Ex. ii. 5—9. Ps. lxxvi.
10. Eph. i. 9—12, v. 11.)—Why did, &c. (25, 26.) Verbatim
from the LXX. which exactly accord with the Hebrew.
Ps. ii. 1, 2.

Their own company. (23) Τας ιδιας. xxiv. 23. John xiii.
1. xv. 19. 1 Tim. v. 8.—Lord. (24) Δισποτα. See on Luke
ii. 29.—Did ... rage. (25) Εφρναξαν. Here only N. T.—
Ps. ii. 1. Sept. ' Ut equi fremunt et ferociunt.' Schleusner.—
Thy holy child. (27) Τον αγιον Παιδα σε. 30. See on iii. 13.
Note, Luke i. 34—38, v. 35.—Thou hast anointed.] Εχρισας.
x. 38. Luke iv. 18. 2 Cor. i. 21. Heb. i. 9.—Ps. xlv. 7.
lxxxix. 20. Is. lxi. 1. Sept.—Counsel. (28) Βκλη. See on
ii. 23.—Determined before.] Προωρισι. " Predestined," or
" predestinated." Rom. viii. 29, 30. 1 Cor. ii. 7. Eph. i.
5. 11. See on ii. 23. (Notes, Rom. viii. 28—31. Eph. i.
3—12.)

V. 29—31. The disciples were fully persuaded, that the
rage of their persecutors would be restrained, and over-
ruled for good: and they did not pray to be protected;
but to be endued with boldness, to declare their doctrine

openly, and with liberty, energy, and plainness of speech,
at all events; (Marg. Ref. n, o.—Notes, Eph. vi. 18—20.
Col. iv. 2—4 ;) and that it might be confirmed, as of divine
authority, by continued miracles being wrought in the
name of Jesus. Though they had been greatly injured,
and severely threatened; and could not but know, that
those who had crucified their Lord, sought to destroy them
also; they yet prayed that God " would stretch forth his
" hand," not to perform miracles of vengeance, as many
wrought by Moses were; nor yet to defend them; but
" to heal :" for love to the bodies and souls of men had
supplanted their selfish passions, and meliorated their zeal,
since the time when they desired permission to call down
fire from heaven on the Samaritans. (Marg. Ref. p, q.—
Note, Luke ix. 51—56.)—Some expositors have thought,
that this prayer was immediately addressed to the Holy
Spirit; by whose power the human nature of Jesus was
formed in the womb, and who was the immediate Agent
in the miracles performed by the apostles. But this is not
evident : and indeed there are few passages of scripture, in
which the Holy Spirit is expressly prayed to, personally,
separately, and distinctly : perhaps, as prayer is presented
both by and for the Holy Spirit, it may be the less proper to address it to him, except as one with the Father and
with the Son, in the unity of the Godhead.—These petitions, however, were immediately granted : the place, in
which the disciples were assembled, was shaken, probably
as it had been on the day of Pentecost by " the rushing
" mighty wind :" (Note, ii. 2, 3 :) and they were all evidently filled with an abundant communication of the Holy
Spirit, in all his enlivening, sanctifying, and comforting
influences; as well as in respect of the extraordinary
powers imparted to them: so that without delay, they
proceeded to " preach the word with all boldness ;" not
at all dismayed by the menaces of their powerful enemies.
(Marg. Ref. s—u.—Note, Phil. i. 27—30.)

Now. (29) Τα νυν. ' As to the things now occurring.'—
Boldness.] Παρρησιας. 31. John xvi. 25. xviii. 20. 2 Cor.
iii. 12.—Was shaken. (31) Εσαλευθη. ii. 25. xvi. 26. xvii.
13. Matt. xi. 7. xxiv. 29. Luke vi. 38. 48. xxi. 26. 2 Thes.
ii. 2. Heb. xii. 26, 27.

V. 32—35. Not only the company to whom Peter and
John returned, but the whole multitude of believers, were
thus united in judgment and affection, as one body animated by one soul; so that hitherto no controversies, jealousies, or murmurs were known. (Notes, ii. 44—47. vi. 1.
Jer. xxxii. 39—41. Ex. xi. 17—20. John xvii. 20--23.
Eph. iv. 1—6. Phil. ii. 1—4.)—" And great grace was

4 x 6

apostles witness of the resurrection of the Lord Jesus: [a] and great grace was upon them all.

34 Neither [b] was there any among them that lacked: [c] for as many as were possessors of lands or houses sold them, and brought the prices of the things that were sold,

35 And laid *them* down [d] at the apostles' feet: [e] and distribution was made unto every man according as he had need.

36 And Joses, who by the apostles was surnamed [f] Barnabas, (which is, being interpreted, [g]The son of consolation,) a Levite, *and* of the country of [h]Cyprus,

37 Having land, [i] sold *it*, and [k] brought the money, and laid *it* at the apostles' feet.

Margin references (left column):
a ii. 47. Luke ii. 52. John i. 16.
b Deut. ii. 7. Ps. xxiv. 9. 10. Luke xvii. 33. 1 Thes. iv. 12.
c 37. ii. 45. v. 1— 3. Mark x. 21. Luke xii. 33. xvi. 9. 1 Tim. vi. 19. Jam. i. 27.
d xi. 6. v. 2. vi. 1. —6. 2 Cor. viii. 20. 21.
e ii. 45. vi. 1.

Margin references (right column):
f xi. 22—25. 30. xii. 25. xiii. 1. xv. 2. 12. 37.
1 Cor. ix. 6. Gal. ii. 1. 9. 13.
g Mark iii. 17.
h xi. 19. 20. xv. 39. xxi. 16.
i 35. Matt. xix. 29.
k 35.

" upon them all." Some interpret this of the great favour shewn the Christians, by the people in general; but the phrase is different from that before used. (ii. 47. *Luke* ii. 40. 52.) The special favour of God manifested to them; and the powerful effects of his sanctifying grace, in forming them to be such holy, lovely, and happy characters, seem to be especially intended.—The language used, concerning the liberal communication of all the property of the more affluent, with their poor brethren, who were thus exempted from all want; and of their confidence in the disinterested faithfulness of the apostles is suited, as by a specimen, to shew, what Christianity would effect, in meliorating the condition of mankind, if universally and cordially embraced. (*Marg. Ref.* z—e.—*Note, Is.* xi. 6—9. *Notes* and *P. O.* 2 *Cor.* viii. 10—15. *Notes, Gal.* vi. 1—5. *Rev.* xx. 4—6.)

His own. (32) Ἰδιον. *John* x. 3. *Rom.* viii. 32. 1 *Cor.* vii. 2. 4. 7. xv. 38.—*Grace.* (33) Χαρις. ii. 47. xi. 23. *Luke* vi. 32, 33, 34. *John* i. 14. 2 *Cor.* viii. 1. 6, 7. 1 *Pet.* ii. 20.—*Possessors.* (34) Κτητορες. Here only. *Note.* ii. 45. v. 1.

V. 36, 37. Perhaps Barnabas was one of the seventy disciples: he became afterwards so eminent as to be spoken of as an apostle. (xiv. 14.) It is probable, that his name was given him on account of his talent, in exhorting and encouraging sinners to come to Christ, and believers to cleave to him in the midst of persecution. (*Marg. Ref.* g—k.—*Note,* xi. 22—24.) The estate which he sold was an inheritance that he possessed; and not any land which he held as a Levite by purchase, or by inheritance. As Barnabas was born in Cyprus, perhaps the estate lay there: but that is not said. The money, which probably was a considerable sum, was " laid at the apostles' feet," who for a time took the charge of distributing it: but it was soon found expedient to employ others in that service. (*Notes,* vi. 1—7.)

Barnabas. (36) Βαρναβας. Ex בר *filius, et* נבא*, vaticinari.* 1 *Cor.* xiv. 3.—Or נביא, (*Syriack*) *filius consolans.*—*Of consolation.*] Παρακλησεως. ix. 31. xiii. 15. xv. 31. *Luke* ii. 25. vi. 24. *Phil.* ii. 1. *Heb.* vi. 18, *et al.* Παρακλητος, *John* xiv. 16. 26.

PRACTICAL OBSERVATIONS.

V. 1—12.

The zeal of avowed infidels to make proselytes, and their unwillingness that others should believe a future state of retributions, seem at first sight unaccountable: for if *this* be a delusion, it can do men no harm; if *their* sentiments be true, they can do no good. But the honour of being thought wiser than others, and qualified to undeceive a deluded multitude, has abundant charms for the vain-glorious mind. Moreover, infidels have their misgivings, and firmly believe their own reasonings only in proportion as others seem convinced by them: when therefore contrary doctrines are taught with confidence and success; they are secretly alarmed, lest after all they should find themselves mistaken. But, whether the motive be regard to authority, or interest, or reputation, or superstition, or inward quietness, or all combined; ungodly men will be grieved when the gospel is successfully preached, and their vices and errors exposed: and ministers may generally expect contempt and persecution from unbelievers, of discordant principles and parties, in proportion as God honours and prospers them: yet " the gates of hell can never prevail against the church" of Christ.—The harmless and useful servants of God have often been indicted as criminals, for " their work and labour of love," when profligates have escaped with impunity: and ungodly priests and elders, and their connexions, have commonly been most forward in these prosecutions. Nay, to this day, instances are not wanting, in which reading the scriptures, social prayer, and religious conversation meet with frowns and checks; when indolent, and dissipated, profligate, heretical, if not openly infidel churchmen escape uncensured, or are distinguished by preferments! If, however, we observe the instructions and obey the precepts of Christ, he will bear us out; and the teaching of his Spirit will render the most timid bold in his cause.—The despised Redeemer must be confessed before his most malignant enemies, by all who would be owned by him before the assembled world: (*Note, Matt.* x. 32, 33:) and if they, who are builders by office, reject this precious Corner-Stone of the living Temple; we must, when called to it, fairly shew them their folly, guilt, and danger, how much soever they may resent it: for assuredly " there is no salvation in any other; nor any other name given to men," by which any one, " under the whole heaven," can be " delivered from the wrath to come," from sin and Satan, and all evil, and made partaker of eternal glory.

V. 13—22.

Those who boldly declare the truths of scripture, will commonly be considered as " unlearned and ignorant " men;" while they " determine to know nothing but " Christ crucified:" but if they speak and act as those who " have been with Jesus," who have imbibed his instructions and spirit, and learned to copy his example; they will, by well doing and sound argument, put gainsayers to silence. Yet this comes far short of converting them: for when avarice, ambition, or any corrupt passion rules within, men shut their eyes and close their hearts in enmity against the light; and determine to bear down,

CHAP. V.

Ananias and Sapphira, combining to tempt the Holy Spirit by a lie in respect of land sold by them, at Peter's word fall down dead, 1—11. The apostles work many and great miracles, and have much success in their ministry, 12—16. The rulers cast them all into prison, 17, 18. An angel releases them, and directs them to preach openly in the temple, 19, 20. They are at length brought before the council, and, being examined, they boldly bear testimony to Jesus, as exalted to be a Prince and Saviour, 21—32. The rulers, being " cut to the heart," purpose to slay them, but are restrained by the counsel of Gamaliel, 33—39. The apostles are beaten, and dismissed with injunctions, not to speak any more in the name of Jesus, 40. They rejoice in their sufferings, and proceed diligently in preaching Jesus the Christ, 41, 42.

BUT a certain man named Ananias, with Sapphira his wife, sold a possession ;

2 And ^b kept back *part* of the price, ^c his wife also being privy *to it*, and

brought a certain part, ^d and laid *it* at the apostles' feet.

3 But Peter said, Ananias, ^e why hath Satan filled thine heart to ^f lie to the Holy Ghost, and ^f to keep back *part* of the price of the land?

4 Whiles it remained, ^g was it not thine own? and after it was sold, was it not in thine own power? ^h Why hast thou conceived this thing in thine heart? ⁱ thou hast not lied unto men, but unto God.

5 And Ananias, ^k hearing these words, fell down, and gave up the ghost : ^l and great fear came on all them that heard these things.

6 And the young men arose, ^m wound him up, and carried *him* out, and buried *him*.

7 And it was about the space of

if they can, by authority and violence, what, in their consciences, they perceive to bear the stamp of truth and divinity. (*Note, John* iii. 19—21.) But whatever deference be due to rulers, chief priests, and councils ; we must not hesitate to declare, that we will " obey God rather than " man," and venture all consequences in so doing : yet this should always be done with modesty, meekness, and unaffected reluctance to disobey our superiors, in church or state. Indeed, when the heart is powerfully influenced by heavenly love and zeal, and the understanding clearly perceives the importance of the truth and the line of duty, a man " cannot but speak " what he has seen and learned : he has a moral inability to refrain ; his holy principles have a commanding influence over him, superior to the tyrant's frown, or the terrors of persecution ; and as far as God has work for such a man to finish, he will restrain the wrath of his most potent enemies, or turn the tide of popular favour in his behalf, as he sees good. (*Notes, Jer.* xx. 7—9. 2 *Cor.* v. 13—16.)

V. 23—37.

Believers may, in various ways, be confined among those who fear not God : but, " being let go, they will return to " their own company."—Whatever trials we meet with, fervent prayer is our never-failing resource ; and the more we unite in it, as " with one heart," the more signal answers may be expected. All things are alike easy to him, who made the heavens and the earth : vain therefore must be the devices, which princes or people, how powerful or numerous soever they be, can imagine against the Lord, and his anointed Saviour ; for when power, policy, and tumult, have done their utmost, they have but effected what " the hand and counsel of the Lord had determined " before should be done : " in effect, they have only digged a pit for their own destruction ; and rolled a stone, which

will rebound upon them and crush them to pieces.—He knows the power and rage of our foes ; and we should not so much pray for exemption from trials, and protection from dangers, as for grace to enable us steadily to do our duty, and to glorify our God in the midst of them all. Our prayers should especially be presented in love, even for our bitterest persecutors : we should request that the Lord's " hand may be stretched out to heal " and to save, not to avenge and destroy. Thus we may expect to be effectually answered, and to be filled with inward consolation and comfort, amidst all outward tribulations.—But let us carefully consider, the effects produced by the pouring out of the Holy Spirit, in those blessed days, when " great grace " was upon all " the company of believers. They were " all of one heart and soul ; " they had but one common interest to attend on ; their love to the brethren was united with equal contempt of worldly riches, and disregard to worldly interests and indulgences ; so that the poorest had no want, the wealthiest no exclusive possessions. When such dispositions prevail, and are exercised according to the circumstances of the times, the testimony of ministers will have a peculiar energy upon the minds of their hearers ; especially if their own conduct exhibits an example of integrity, disinterestedness, and love : and if it be evident that, like their Master, they deem it " more blessed to " give than to receive." (*Note,* xx. 32—35.)

NOTES.

CHAP. V. V. 1—11. The reputation acquired by those who sold their estates must have been very great : so that it is not wonderful, that the ambition of this honour should, in some instances, over-power the fear of persecution, in the hearts of those who were not upright in the sight of God. But the increase of professed Christians of this character would have disgraced the cause, and spread an in-

three hours after, when his wife, not knowing what was done, came in.

8 And Peter answered unto her, Tell me whether ye sold the land for so much? And she said, Yea, for so much.

9 Then Peter said unto her, ^a How is it that ye ^o have agreed together ^p to tempt the Spirit of the Lord? Behold, ^q the feet of them which have buried thy husband are at the door, and shall carry thee out.

10 Then ^r fell she down straightway

at his feet, and yielded up the ghost: and the young men came in, and found her dead, and, carrying her forth, buried her by her husband.

11 And ^s great fear came upon all the church, and upon as many as heard these things.

12 ¶ And ^t by the hands of the apostles were many signs and wonders wrought among the people; (and ^u they were all with one accord ^x in Solomon's porch:

Marginal references:

a Gen. iii. 9—13.
Luke xvi. 2.
Rom. iii. 19.
o xxiii. 20—27.
Deut. xiii. 6—8.
Prov. xi. 21.
b Mic. vii. 3.
p 3. J. Ex. xvii. 2, 7. Num. xiv. 22. Ps. lxxviii. 18—20, 40, 41, 56. xcv. 8—11. Matt. iv. 7.
1 Cor. x. 9.
q 6. 2 Kings vi.
22. Rom. x. 15.
r 1.

s xix. 17. Ps. lxxxix. 7. Jer. xxxii. 40. 1 Cor. x. 11, 12. Phil. ii. 12. Heb. iv. 1. xii. 7. xiii. 15
2R. 29. 1 Pet. i. 17. Rev. xv. 4.
t ii. 43. iii. 6, 7. iv. 33. xiv. 33, 40.
xiv. 3. 8—11. xvi. 18. Mark xvi. 17, 18. 20. Rom. xv 19. 2 Cor. xii. 12. Heb. ii. 4.
u i. 14. ii 42. 46.
iv. 32.
x iii. 11. John x. 23.

---

fection in the church. The Lord was therefore pleased to check this evil, at the opening of the New Testament dispensation; as he had others, at the promulgation of the law, and the first entrance of Israel into the possession of the promised land. (Notes, Lev. x. 1—11. Josh. vii.)—Ananias and Sapphira, seeing how those persons were respected, who had parted with their whole substance, to supply the wants of their poor brethren, agreed together to sell the land, to secrete a part of the money, and to give the rest to the apostles as the whole price. In doing this, they perhaps expected to have a maintenance from the common stock, and yet to reserve a part of their substance to themselves: but the desire of reputation seems to have predominated. (Marg. Ref. a—d.) Peter however was immediately shewn the deception which they were practising, and charged it upon Ananias in express terms. (Notes, 2 Kings v. 20—27.) His language on this occasion implied, that, whatever Satan might suggest, he could not have " filled the heart" of Ananias with this wickedness, had he not been consenting. (Marg. and Marg. Ref. e—f. —Notes, John xiii. 1—5, v. 2. 18—30, v. 27.) The falsehood, told to the apostles, was a bold attempt to impose upon " the Spirit of truth" himself, who so manifestly spoke and acted by them: and this was to " lie unto God," and not unto men; which is a plain testimony to the Deity and personality of the Holy Spirit. The estate continued Ananias's property, even after his profession of Christianity; the sale of it was not a matter of compulsion, but of voluntary choice; and even the money, after it was sold, was at his own disposal: whence it appears, that this liberality was not expressly required of the primitive Christians, but was the result of their abundant zeal and love. So that the crime of Ananias did not so much consist in retaining part of the price of the land, as in endeavouring in so solemn a transaction, to impose upon the apostles with a deliberate pertinacious lie, the result of avarice combined with ostentation. (Marg. Ref. g—i.)—As his death was the immediate effect of divine power, and merely denounced by Peter, it struck terror into all who heard of it; and he was buried immediately in his own garments, without further preparation or mourning; as Sapphira was afterwards, when, persisting in the same horrid falsehood, she was struck dead by the awful judgment of God. (Marg. Ref. k—s.—Lev. x. 4—6. Notes, 2 Kings i. 10. ii. 23, 24. 2 Cor. xiii. 7—10.)—This apparent severity, on two detected hypocrites, was real mercy to numbers: it excited a reverential fear and a holy jealousy in the whole company; it doubtless brought them to strict self-examination,

prayer, and circumspection, and a dread of hypocrisy, covetousness, or vain-glory: it prevented the increase of scandals in the church, and the intrusion of hypocrites; and thus it conduced to render the gospel honourable in the eyes of the people.—We may also observe, that this event was a divine attestation to the apostles' integrity and veracity, fully intelligible by their enemies. God would never have inflicted such a judgment, at their word, upon inferior dissemblers, if their testimony to the resurrection of Jesus had been a deception: and it shewed that they would not connive at iniquity in those of their own party, or for the sake of their private interest, or that of the society. —Many expositors suppose, that Ananias had made a vow, (either publickly or secretly,) to give his estate for the support of the Christian cause; and that sacrilege was the crime, for which he was visited: but the history never mentions this. He had, from corrupt motives, attempted to impose upon the apostles and upon the Holy Spirit; and his wife had joined him, in this impious and hypocritical attempt.—The papists adduce this passage, as a proof that the successors of Peter (that is, the pope and the ecclesiasticks devoted to him,) are invested with the secular as well as spiritual sword. Let them, therefore, use the weapons of Peter wherever they will, but none else; and let them see whether the same effects will follow.—Tempt, &c. (9) ' As often as any thing is done with an evil con-' science; so often men bring this sentence on themselves, ' and as much as lieth in them provoke God to wrath; as ' if they purposely aimed to make trial, whether he be just ' and almighty or not.' Beza. (Marg. Ref. p.—Notes, Ex-xvii. 1, 2. Matt. iv. 5—7.)—The case, however, of Ananias and Sapphira was very peculiar, and their guilt exceedingly atrocious.—This single example of severity was made, not on avowed enemies and persecutors, but on false friends. Thus Judas, not Caiaphas, was marked out by his awful end, as the first object of divine vengeance on the murderers of Christ. (Note, Matt. xxvii. 3—5.)

Kept back. (2) Ενοσφισατο. 3. Tit. ii. 10. Ananias purloined, or privately stole what he kept back.—Josh. vii. 1. Comp. 11. Sept.—Ex νοσφι, vel νοσφιν, seorsim, separatim.—The land. (3) Τε χωριι. 8. i. 18, 19. iv. 34. xxviii. 7. Matt. xxvi. 36.—After it was sold. (4) Πραθεν. See on n 45.—Gave up the ghost. (5) Εξεψυξε. 10. xii. 23. Not elsewhere N.T.—Ez. xxi. 7. Sept.—The space. (7) Διαστημα. Here only N.T.—Gen. xxxii. 16. Sept.—Ye have agreed together. (9) Συνεφωνηθη υμιν. xv. 15. See on Matt. xviii. 19

V. 12—16. While just punishment was in one instance miraculously inflicted; the power of God, by the hands of

13 And of the rest ʸdurst no man join himself to them: ᶻbut the people magnified them.

14 And ᵃbelievers were the more added to the Lord, ᵇmultitudes both of men and women;)

15 Insomuch that ᶜthey brought forth the sick ᵈinto the streets, and laid *them* on beds and couches, that, at the least, the shadow of Peter passing by might overshadow some of them.

16 There came also a multitude out of the cities round about unto Jerusalem, ᵈbringing sick folks, and them which were vexed with unclean spirits: and they were ᵉhealed every one.

17 ¶ Then ᶠthe high priest rose up, and ᵍall they that were with him, (which is the sect of the Sadducees,) and were filled with ʰindignation,

18 And ʰlaid their hands on the apostles, and put them in the common prison.

19 But ⁱthe angel of the Lord by night opened the prison-doors, and brought them forth, and said,

20 Go, ᵏstand and speak in the temple to the people ˡall the words of this life.

21 And when they heard *that*, ᵐthey entered into the temple early in the morning, and taught. ⁿBut the high priest came, and they that were with him, and called the council together, and all the ᵒsenate of the children of Israel, ᵖand sent to the prison to have them brought.

22 But when the officers came, and found them not in the prison, they returned, and told,

23 Saying, ᵠThe prison truly found we shut with all safety, and the keepers standing without before the doors: but when we had opened, we found no man within.

24 Now when the high priest, and ʳthe captain of the temple, and the chief priests heard these things, ˢthey doubted of them whereunto ᵗthis would grow.

25 Then came one and told them, saying, ᵘBehold, the men whom ye put in prison are standing in the temple, and teaching the people.

---

the apostles, was *continually* exerted in multiplied miracles of mercy. (*Note*, iv. 29—31.) The whole company of believers were as firmly attached to the apostles, and united to each other, as they had been before: and they constantly met, at stated times, " in Solomon's porch," to join in the worship of God; when, probably, the apostles preached and wrought miracles, as opportunity was given them. (*Note*, iii. 1—11, *v.* 11.) But none of those, who were not willing to renounce all things for the sake of Christ, ventured to join them; though they were greatly honoured by the people in general, and numbers of real converts were continually added by baptism to the church, and by faith to the Lord. (*Marg. Ref.* y—b.)—*Join himself*, &c. (13) ' As if he had been a believer, and by way of putting a ' cheat on the apostles. Such unbelievers, as were dis-' pleased with the apostles, and hated the cause, would ' have been glad to put any trick upon them, that they ' might thereby lessen their esteem among the people; yet ' durst not: seeing it might prove no less than fatal for ' any to go about to deceive them.'—Indeed the power of God so evidently attended the apostles, that the people, both in Jerusalem and from the adjacent towns, applied for miraculous cures, by laying their sick in " every " street;" (*Marg.*) that the " shadow of Peter," as he passed along, might fall upon them, from which they expected the benefit: nor were any of them disappointed. (*Marg. Ref.* c—e.—*Note, John* xiv. 7—14, *v.* 12.)—As Peter was the readiest speaker, and stood foremost in every transaction, and as he was one of the first who experienced persecution; it seems that he was more noticed by the people, than any of the other apostles, in these miracles. (*Note*, xix. 8—12, *v.* 12.) ' Hence ' it is ridiculous to argue, that one or the other (Peter or ' Paul) was prince of the apostles, or that the reliques of ' holy men are to be venerated.' *Whitby.*

Join himself. (13) Κολλασθαι. viii. 29. ix. 16. x. 28. xvii. 34. See on *Matt.* xix. 5.—*Might overshadow.* (15) Επισκιασῃ. *Matt.* xvii. 5. *Mark* ix. 7. *Luke* i. 35. ix. 34. Εχ επι et σκια, *umbra.*—*Round about.* (16) Περιξ. Here only. A περι, *circum.* r

V. 17—25. These transactions could not but perplex and enrage the high priest and his party; whether their personal interests and reputation, or religious prejudices, or their political views, were considered: especially that prevailing party, which had adopted the heresy of the Sadducees, must foresee the ruin of their sect, as the consequence of the success of the gospel. (*Note*, iv. 4.)—They therefore imprisoned all the apostles, as disturbers of the publick peace, in the common jail designed for malefactors. (*Marg. Ref.* f—h.) But an angel, unperceived by the keepers, set them at liberty, and ordered them to go boldly into the temple, and proclaim to the people " all " the words of this life;" that is, the whole gospel of him who is " the Way, and the Truth, and the Life;" by which alone sinners can obtain eternal life. (*Marg. Ref.* i—l.) This direction was intended, as an exception to the general rule before given by our Lord, that " when per-" scented in one city they should flee to another;" which

26 Then went the captain with the officers, and brought them without violence: for * they feared the people, lest they should have been stoned:

27 And when they had brought them, ʸ they set *them* before the council: and the high priest asked them,

28 Saying, ' Did not we straitly command you, that ye should not teach in this name? and, behold, ye have filled Jerusalem with your doctrine, ª and intend to bring this man's ᵇ blood upon us.

29 Then Peter and the *other* apostles answered, and said, ' We ought to obey God rather than men.

30 The ᵈ God of our fathers ᵉ raised up Jesus, whom ꜰ ye slew and hanged on a tree:

31 Him ᵍ hath God exalted with his right hand *to be* ʰ a Prince and ' a Saviour, for ᵏ to give repentance to Israel, ' and forgiveness of sins.

Marginal references (left column):
x 13. Matt. xiv. 5.
xxi. 26. xxvi. 5.
Luke xx. 6. 19.
xxii. 2.
y iv. 7. vi. 12.
xxii. 30. xxiii. 1.
Luke xxii. 66.
z 40. iv. 18—21.
a ii. 23. iii. 15. iv.
10. 11. vii. 52.
1 Kings xviii.
17, 18. xxi. 20.
xxii. 8. Jer.
xxxviii. 4. Am.
vii. 10.
b Jer. xxvi. 15.
Matt. xxiii. 35,
xxvii. 25. 1 Thes.
ii. 15, 16.

Marginal references (right column):
c See on ir. 19.—
Gen. iii. 17.
1 Sam. xv. 24.
Mark vi. 7—9.
Rev. xiv. 8—12.
d iii. 13—15. 1 Chr.
xii. 17. xxix. 18.
Ezra vii. 27.
Luke i. 55. 72.
iii. 26. xiii. 33.
ff. 22—24. 32. iv.
10. 11. xiii. 29,
30. Gal. iii. 13.
1 Pet. ii. 24.
ff. 33. 36. iv.
11. Ps. lxxxix.
19. 24. ex. 1, 2.
Ez. xxvi. 24.
Matt. xxviii. 18
Eph. i. 20—22.
Phil. ii. 9—11.

1 Pet. iii. 22.　h iii. 15.　Ps. ii. 6—12.　1a. ix. 6.　Ez. xxxiv. 24. xxxvii. 25.　Dan.
ix. 25. x. 21.　Rev. i. 5.　i xiii. 23.　1a. xliif. 3. 11. xlv. 21.　xlix. 26.　Matt. i. 21.
Luke ii. 11.　Phil. iii. 29.　Tit. i. 4. ii. 10. 13. iii. 4—6.　2 Pet. i. 1. ii. 11. 20. iii. 18.　1 John
iv. 14.　Jude 25.　k xi. 18.　Jer. xxxi. 81—33.　Ez. xxxvi. 25—27.　2 Tim. ii. 25, 26.　Zech. xii. 10.
Luke xxiv. 47.　Rom. xi. 26. 27.　2 Tim. ii. 25, 26.　l ff. 19. xiii. 38, 39.　Mark ii.
10. iv. 12.　John xx. 21—23.　2 Cor. ii. 10.　Eph. i. 7.　Col. i. 14.

---

present circumstances required for the triumph of the gospel, the encouragement of believers, and the confusion of their enemies. (Notes, viii. 1. *Matt.* x. 23.) Accordingly, the apostles obeyed without hesitation; and the report brought to the council evidently shewed, that their deliverance had been miraculous, and that they were not at all afraid of their persecutors. (*Marg. Ref.* m—u.— *Notes,* xii. 18, 19.) The council assembled on this occasion (21), seems to have included many who did not generally attend, and who indeed were not stated members of the Sanhedrim. (*Note,* iv. 1—3.)

The sect. (17) Ἁιρεσις. xv. 5. xxiv. 5. 14. xxvi. 5. xxviii. 22. 1 *Cor.* xi. 19. *Gal.* v. 20. 2 *Pet.* ii. 1.—Αιρετικος, *Tit.* iii. 10.—*Indignation.*] " Envy." Marg. Ζηλω. *Rom.* x. 2. 2 *Cor.* xii. 20. *Gal.* v. 20. *Jam.* iii. 14—16. (*Notes, Rom.* x. 1—4. *Gal.* v. 19—21.—*Jam.* iii. 14—16.)—*The senate.* (21) Την γερωσιαν.—Here only. A γερων, *senes. John* iii. 4.—*The prison.*] Το δεσμωτηριον. 23. xvi. 26. *Matt.* xi. 2.—(Δεσμωτης, xxvii. 1. 42.)—Τηρησει δημοσια. 18.—Δημοσιος. Here only.—*They doubted...whereunto this would grow.* (24) Διηπορουν ... τι αν γενοιτο τουτο. " They " doubted what this thing would become." Διαπορεω. ii. 12. x. 17. *Luke* ix. 7. xxiv. 4.

V. 26. ' Tyrants not fearing God, are constrained to ' fear their own subjects.' *Beza.* (*Marg. Ref.*)—Perhaps the expectation of a temporal kingdom was revived by the miracles of the apostles, among the bulk of the common people: so that, while they neither understood nor embraced the gospel, they favoured the cause, and excited the fears of their persecuting rulers.

V. 27, 28. (*Note,* iv. 13—22, *vv.* 17, 18. 21, 22.) ' It is peculiar to tyrants to obtrude their own commands, ' instead of any reason or argument.' *Beza.*—The rulers feared, lest the success of the apostles in preaching that Jesus, whom they had crucified, was the promised Messiah, should exasperate the people against them as his murderers; and they concluded that they meant to excite an insurrection, in order to deprive them of authority, or to put them to death: at least they charged the apostles with such intentions. (*Marg. Ref.*)

Straitly command. (28) Παραγγελια παρηγγειλαμεν. iv. 18. See on i. 4.—*Intend.*] Βωλεσθε.—Βωλομαι. ' Deli- ' berato consilio aliquid volo, cupio, decerno. Plus enim ' involvit Θελομαι, quam Θελω.—*Matt.* i. 19.' *Schleusner.* A θαος, *consilium.*

V. 29—31. *Marg. Ref.* e—i.—*Notes,* ii. 33—36. iii.

12—26. iv. 5—22, *vv.* 19—21.—*Exalted,* &c. (31) Jesus is exalted to be the Ruler and Judge of all men, and the Saviour of all that believe. " Repent, and believe " the gospel," is the call, exhortation, and invitation to all men; and none but the penitent do truly believe. (*Notes, Matt.* iii. 2. v. 3.) Through this exalted Prince and Saviour, the Israelites, and even the rulers who had crucified him, were encouraged to repent, by the proposal of forgiveness; and suitable instructions, motives, and exhortations were given them. Thus he gave them " place," for repentance; in which sense the phrase, here employed, has it seems been once used by Josephus. Yet it is the evident doctrine of scripture, (*Marg. Ref.* k.—*Notes,* xi. 18. *Jer.* xxxi. 18—20. 31—34. *Ez.* xi. 17—20. *Zech.* xii. 9—14. 2 *Tim.* ii. 23—26,) and likewise of our liturgy, that true repentance is " the gift of God ;" and to exclude this most obvious meaning of the words, as many expositors do, is, in fact, an attempt to improve the language of scripture, and to obscure one evidence of our Saviour's Deity, and of all salvation coming wholly from his fulness of grace. ' Repentance was not indeed actually wrought in Israel, by his efficacious grace ;' that is, not in all Israel; for it certainly was in great numbers : but if any who heard the apostles were convinced that they must repent or perish, yet found their hearts still hard and their wills rebellious ; was it not a most important and seasonable instruction, to be assured, that Jesus was exalted " to give repentance," as well as pardon to the penitent ? that, as one with tears cried to him, " Help my unbelief ;" they might cry to him, " Turn thou me that I may be " turned : " " Pour on me the Spirit of grace and sup- " plications, that I may look unto thee, whom I have " pierced, and mourn" with " that godly sorrow, which " worketh repentance unto salvation."

To obey. (29) Πειθαρχειν. 32. xxvii. 21. Tit. iii. 1. Πειθομαι τω αρχοντι.—Ye slew. (30) Διηχειρισασθε. xxvi. 21. Not elsewhere.—Εx δια et χειριζω, *manu tracto :* a χειρ, *manus.*—*Hanged.*] Κρεμασαντες. x. 39. xxviii. 4. *Matt.* xviii. 6. xxii. 40. *Luke* xxiii. 39. *Gal.* iii. 13.—*Deut.* xxi. 22, 23. 2 Sam. xviii. 9. *Sept.*—*A Prince.* (31) Αρχηγον. See on iii. 15.—*To give repentance.*] Δεναι μετανοιαν. xi. 18. 2 *Tim.* ii. 25.—Μετανοια. xi. 18. xiii. 24. xix. 4. xx. 21. xxvi. 20. *Matt.* iii. 8. 11. ix. 13. *et al.* Μετανοεω. See on *Matt.* iii. 2.—' Μετανοια, when it signifies the awaken- ' ing and change of the mind for the better, is the gift of ' God, of his mere grace.' *Beza.*

4 o 3

32 And ^m we are his witnesses of these things; ⁿ and *so is* also the Holy Ghost, ^o whom God hath given to them that obey him.

33 When they heard *that*, ^p they were cut *to the heart*, ^q and took counsel to slay them.

34 Then ^r stood there up one in the council, a Pharisee, named ^s Gamaliel, ^t a doctor of the law, had in reputation among all the people, ^u and commanded to put the apostles forth a little space;

35 And said unto them, Ye men of Israel, ^x take heed to yourselves what ye intend to do as touching these men.

36 For before these days rose up Theudas, ^y boasting himself to be somebody; ^z to whom a number of men, about four hundred, joined themselves: who was slain; and all, as many as ^a obeyed him, were scattered, and brought to nought.

37 After this man rose up ^b Judas of Galilee, in the days of the taxing, and drew away much people after him: ^b he also perished; and all, *even as* many as obeyed him, were dispersed.

38 And now I say unto you, ^c Refrain from these men, and let them alone: ^d for if this counsel or this work be of men, it will come to nought:

39 But ^e if it be of God, ye cannot

V. 32. *Marg. Ref.—The Holy Ghost,* &c.] *Notes, John* xv. 26, 27. xvi. 12, 13. *Heb.* ii. 1—4, *v.* 4.—' The testimony, arising from this miraculous communication of the Spirit to Christians at that time, entirely removes the objection from Christ's not appearing in publick, after his resurrection. For had there been any imposture, it had been easier of the two, to have persuaded the people at a distance, that he had so appeared to the Jewish rulers, or even to the multitude, and yet had been rejected; than that he had given his servants such extraordinary powers. Since, had this assertion been false, every one might have been a witness to the falsehood of such a pretence, without the trouble and expense of a journey to Jerusalem, or any other distant place.' *Doddridge.* Obey.] Πειθαρχουσιν. See on 29.—' There is no true obedience without faith, or true faith without obedience.' *Beza.*

V. 33—39. (Note, ii. 37—40.) The rulers were *cut* by the words of Peter; they were convicted, tortured, enraged, and alarmed, but not humbled or changed: ' they gnashed their teeth, as if one drew a saw; ' (*Beza;*) and therefore they desperately counselled, or resolved, to put the whole company of the apostles to death. But Gamaliel (whose reputation is very high among the Jews to this day, and who seems to have been a man of great judgment and prudence in secular matters,) cautioned them against so violent a measure. Probably at this time he had some conviction of the truth of the gospel: but, as he was the teacher of Saul, who was a determined persecutor, it may be questioned whether he long retained his tolerating principles. (*Marg. Ref.* r—t.—*Note,* xxii. 1—5.) However, Gamaliel was a Pharisee, and, as such, a decided opposer of the Sadducean system, and so more ready to take this view of the subject: and from some recent instances, he fully proved that the interposition of the council in so decided a manner, was neither needful nor safe. (*Marg. Ref.* u—b.)—' Here Gamaliel affirms two things. First, that before those days, in which that council was assembled, arose Theudas: ... whereas the Theudas, mentioned by Josephus, ... arose, and perished by the hands of Cuspius Fudus, in the fourth year of

Claudius, that is, ten years after the meeting of this council. Secondly, he affirms, that Judas of Galilee arose after him, and yet he arose " in the days of the " taxing," which was under the emperor Augustus, and so thirty-four years before this council, and so this Theudas must have been at least thirty-five years before. ...Origen, who had read Josephus, and declares that he examined things relating to the scripture, ... *out of a love to truth,* speaks thus: ' We say that there was one Theudas before the birth of Christ, who among the Jews declared himself to be somebody.' And again, ' that Judas Galileus, and Theudas *who was before him,* being not of God perished.' And a third time, ' Because they gathered from the scriptures, that the time of the Messiah was come; first Theudas, and after him Judas, tumultuated in the time of the taxing.' Hence do the fathers unanimously say, that those words of Christ, " All that came before me were " thieves and robbers," relate to these two, Theudas and Judas of Galilee; which shews their belief, that both of them were before the time of Christ's preaching. So that it is extremely evident, that the ancient fathers agreed in this, that there was a Theudas pretending to great things, even before the coming of our Lord; though Josephus has taken no notice of him.' *Whitby.* —Dr. Lightfoot supposes, that the Theudas, mentioned by Josephus, was the son of this Theudas; and that he took his name, as engaging in the same enthusiastick attempts. (*Note, Luke* ii. 2.)—St. Luke merely records Gamaliel's speech; and it is indisputable, that he spake of facts well known to his hearers. As to Josephus, his mistakes and omissions are so *numerous* and *palpable,* that his authority ought not to be opposed to other authentick histories; or to facts, which at the time, were known and allowed to have occurred.—From these premises, however, Gamaliel justly inferred, that if the apostles were employed in propagating an imposture, it would at length be detected, and " come to nothing; " without the rulers incurring the hatred and resentment of the people, by contending against it. But, on the other hand, if indeed it were the cause and work of God, which they were not fully sure it was not, they could not possibly prevail against it;

overthrow it; lest haply ye be found even 'to fight against God.

40 And to him they agreed: and when they had called the apostles, and beaten *them*, 'they commanded that they should not speak in the name of Jesus, and let them go.

41 And they departed from the presence of the council, 'rejoicing that they were counted worthy to suffer 'shame for his name.

42 And daily in the temple, and in every house, 'they ceased not to teach, and 'preach Jesus Christ.

---

for if they put the apostles to death, some other persons would be raised up to carry it on: at the same time they would be " found to fight against God," and would thus bring upon themselves his omnipotent vengeance. (*Marg. Ref.* c—f.—*Notes*, ix. 3—6. xxiii. 6—10.)—According to this opinion, which was the verdict of common sense, and supported by the most conclusive arguments, the continuance of Christianity to this day, a religion, neither supported by human authority, nor paying court to any man's corrupt passions; nay, opposed by all the power, wealth, philosophy, false religion, vices, and popular prejudices, of the whole world; and declaring exterminating war against all the corrupt propensities of the human heart, without favouring one more than another; and, also the ruin of the Jewish church and nation, and other persecuting powers, are irrefragable demonstrations, that it was " no work or " counsel of men," but indeed a revelation from God; and, that those who opposed it actually fought against him, and incurred his righteous displeasure for so doing.—How different the introduction of Christianity in the world, and its preservation and continuance to this day, from those of Paganism and Mohammedism!

They were cut to the heart. (33) Διεπριοντο. vii. 54. Not elsewhere.—Ex δια et πριζω, *serra seco* ; *Heb.* xi. 37.— Α πριων, *serra.* 2 *Sam.* xii. 31. 1 *Chr.* xx. 3. *Is.* x. 15. *Sept.—Joined themselves.* (36) Προσεκολληθη. See on *Matt.* xix. 5.—*The taxing.* (37) Της απογραφης. See *Luke* ii. 1, 2.—*It will come to nought.* (38) Καταλυθησεται. 39. vi. 14. *Matt.* v. 17. xxiv. 2. xxvi. 61. 2 *Cor.* v. 1, et al.—*To fight against God.* (39) Θεομαχοι. Here only. Θεομαχεω, xxiii. 9. Ex Θεος et μαχομαι, *pugno.*

V. 40. The whole council, apparently with great reluctance, yielded to Gamaliel's advice, and did not proceed to put the apostles to death: yet, their enmity and rage so far prevailed, that they ignominiously scourged them for disobedience to their former orders, and renewed their prohibition of preaching any more in the name of Jesus. (*Marg. Ref.—Notes*, iv. 13—22, vv. 18—21. *Matt.* x. 16—18. xxiii. 34—36. *John* xix. 1—7. 2 *Cor.* xi. 24 —27.)

They agreed.] Επεισθησαν. 36. " They obeyed" him, or they were persuaded by him.—*Beaten.*] Δειραντες. xvi. 37. xxii. 19. *Matt.* xxi. 35.

V. 41, 42. (*Marg. Ref.—Notes, Is.* lxvi. 5, 6. *Matt.* v. 10—12. *Phil.* i. 27—30. *Jam.* i. 2—4. 1 *Pet.* iv. 12—16.) The apostles went away rejoicing; ' rightly judging, ' that a punishment of this kind, though generally shame- ' ful, became a glory to them, when borne in so excellent ' a cause, and for the sake of Him, who ... had submitted ' not only to stripes, but to death, for them. ...And every day, from morning to night, they ceased not to pursue

---

' this great work ; but took all opportunities to preach in ' the temple, ...and from house to house : and on the ' whole ...it was their constant business to teach and preach ' Jesus as the Messiah.' *Doddridge.* (*Notes, Prov.* i. 21 —23. viii. 34.)—" To publish glad tidings, even Jesus, "'the Messiah." The rulers, however, had been so baffled, and were so conscious that their cause was bad; that, though they rankled with rage and vexation, they were afraid of attempting, at present, any thing further against the apostles.

Were counted worthy. (41) Κατηξιωθησαν. See on *Luke* xx. 35.—*To suffer shame.*] Αλιμασθηναι. See on *Luke* xx. 11.—*Daily.* (42) Πασαν ημεραν.—Every day, or all the day.

PRACTICAL OBSERVATIONS
V. 1—16.

No state of the church has yet occurred entirely free from hypocrites, and other evils resulting from human depravity and the subtlety of Satan : nor is there any thing so excellent, which artful men will not counterfeit, to gratify their avarice, or their love of applause and honour from men. But the conduct of numbers, even in external duties, by doing some things, and shrinking from others, proves their insincerity ; and shews, that they aim to reconcile the service of God and mammon, and the reputation of piety with the interests of the world. (*Notes, Matt.* vi. 1—4. 24. *Jam.* i. 5—8.) When Satan is permitted thus " to fill the hearts" of deceivers with wicked devices ; they attempt, and often successfully, to impose upon the ministers of Christ ; while he, their Judge, " who " hath the keys of death and hell," sees all their secret wickedness, and prepares to expose and punish it.—And does not the narrative, with which this chapter opens, most solemnly warn us, to watch against and subjugate all our passions ; not only the violent and disgraceful, but the plausible likewise, the love of money and of reputation, the ambition, not only of honour from worldly men, but also of consequence in the church?—Deceit and lies are, in all things, hateful to the God of truth ; but most of all, when introduced into the immediate concerns of religion. How then must he abhor those lying professions, subscriptions, and engagements, which numbers continually make at his table, or when they enter into the sacred ministry ! Surely it may be said to every one who acts in this manner, " Why hath Satan filled thine " heart to lie to the Holy Ghost ?" " Why hast thou " conceived this thing in thine heart ? Thou hast not lied " unto men, but unto God." If any of us are conscious of having committed so enormous a crime, let us be thankful, that the doom of Ananias has not been ours, and let us shew our deep repentance, by keeping at the utmost distance from a repetition of the atrocious provo-

CHAP. VI.

On occasion of the murmurings of the Grecians, seven persons, chosen by the church, under the direction of the apostles, are appointed by them to superintend the daily ministration to the poor; that none might be neglected, and that the apostles might

" give themselves to the word of God and to prayer," 1—6. The word of God greatly prevails, 7. Stephen, full of faith and the Holy Spirit, confutes those who disputed against him, 8—10. They suborn witnesses, who, before the council, falsely accuse him of blasphemy against the law and the temple, 11—14. His face shines like the face of an angel, 15.

cation.—Those who combine together, and encourage one another, " to tempt the Spirit of the Lord," may expect to be joined in the same awful punishment: and when notorious criminals escape with present impunity, they are only " reserved to the day of judgment," for more tremendous vengeance. But, on special occasions, the Lord interposes in an extraordinary manner, to detect such offenders, as are about to become a snare to some, and a scandal to others. This righteous severity often proves an important benefit to multitudes; by putting them on their guard against hypocrisy, and exciting them to watchfulness and prayer.—Whatever conduces to the purity and reputation of the church, eventually promotes its enlargement. When unsound professors of the gospel are excluded or detected, the surest method is taken to bring in an increase of true believers: and, if the apparent severity of reproof or censure, which ministers must at some times necessarily exercise, be connected with manifest and enlarged benevolence; that unfavourable impression, which might otherwise be made upon the minds of men, will be prevented; and they will notwithstanding possess confidence and affection. But that power alone, which wrought such astonishing miracles by the hands of the apostles, (though exercised in a different way,) can rescue any of our apostate race from the power of sin and Satan, and add them as believers to the company of spiritual worshippers. God will, in some degree, work by all his faithful servants; and every one, who applies to him in humble faith, shall certainly be healed, as to the dire maladies of his soul.

V. 17—32.

How wretched must they be, whose vexation is increased by the success of the gospel! They may grow more violent in enmity and opposition: but in vain will they attempt to confine those, whom the Lord wills to be at liberty; to slay those whom he wills to live; to disgrace those whom he wills to honour; or even to distress or affright those whom he wills to be joyful and courageous. (Notes, xvi. 25—28. 35—40.) His mighty angels delight to minister to his persecuted servants; and, at the least intimation of his purpose, they are equally ready to destroy their persecutors. (Notes, xii. 5—11. 20—23, v. 23.) As long therefore as we are preserved in life, we should go on with our several duties; and those who are called to " preach the gospel," should be " instant in season and out " of season," without yielding to fear, or self-indulgence, in preaching " all the words of this life" to mankind.—How vain, yet how obstinate, is the contest, which men maintain against their Creator! They see at times, that the word and hand of the Lord are against them, and they tremble for the consequences: yet they will proceed! And, after all their convictions, they are more restrained by the fear of man, than by the " fear of him who is " able to destroy body and soul in hell!" Men of this

character have often opposed their mandates and authority to those of God, and accused the most exemplary and peaceable ministers, of sedition and rebellion; because their doctrines tended to expose the wickedness of their opposers, in its proper colours to mankind. We must, however, adhere to our principles: " We ought to obey " God rather than man ;" and they, who persist in opposing Christ and his cause, must bear the blame. He is a gracious Saviour to all those, who submit to him as a Prince; and he will employ all his power to protect and exalt them likewise. He delights in forgiving the penitent, yea, in " giving repentance and remission of sins " to all the Israel of God; nor will he withhold these inestimable gifts from any who seek to him for them. But he will surely destroy all those, " who will not have him " to reign over them :" this every man will perceive, in proportion as he regards the testimony of his apostles; and of the Holy Spirit whom God has always given as the Teacher, Sanctifier, and Comforter of those who obey his beloved Son.

V. 33—42.

While the convincing arguments of the persecuted, and their own reproaching consciences, increase the rage of determined enemies; the Lord still varies his methods of defeating their malignant purposes. He has all hearts in his hands: and he sometimes uses the candour and sound policy of learned and eminent men, who do not embrace the gospel, to moderate the counsels of outrageous and irrational opposers. Common sense suggests a caution to every considerate man, to take heed to himself what he does, respecting those who so much as appear to be the servants of God. Experience and observation determine, that the success or reputation of religious impostures, not supported by human authority, or by flattering men's vices and corrupt affections, will be short-lived. The abettors of all such designs have recourse to unhallowed means, to gratify their ambition, or to compass their secular designs. Many have drawn the sword in this cause, 'and have perished by it; some have been scattered; and others have exposed their iniquity to the whole world: so that if " every " counsel, or work, which is of men," will in one way or other " come to nought."—But while the teachers of religion are harmless and peaceable members of the community, and appear zealous for the truths and commandments of God, according to their views of them; the caution is universally to be regarded, " Refrain from these men, and " let them alone :" neither deride, revile, molest, nor injure them; from personal dislike, or from political jealousy. If they are insincere or erroneous, they will in time appear to be so; and no other means should be used, except calm discussion and kind usage: but if their cause be that " of God, it cannot be overthrown," and all who attempt it, will be " found to have fought against God."—But when the enmity of the carnal mind is restricted in

AND in those days, [a] when the number of the disciples was multiplied, [b] there arose a murmuring of the [c] Grecians against the [d] Hebrews, because [e] their widows were neglected in [f] the daily ministration.

2 Then [g] the twelve called the multitude of the disciples *unto them*, and said, [h] It is not reason that [i] we should leave the word of God, and serve tables.

3 Wherefore, [k] brethren, [l] look ye out among you seven men of [m] honest

its exercise, and cannot, or dare not, vent itself in bloody persecution; it seeks gratification, by dealing in reproaches, calumnies, menaces, insults, and other injuries. We should, however, " rejoice to be counted worthy" to endure shame and pain, in that cause, in which " Jesus endured the " cross, and despised the shame," and for the sake of so gracious and glorious a Benefactor. (*Note, Heb.* xii. 2, 3.) We should daily endeavour to recommend him, and his salvation, to all around us: and, whether ministers labour in publick, and preach to large congregations, or resort to the houses of their friends and brethren, Jesus, the anointed Saviour of lost sinners, should be the great subject of their instructions, the centre of all their doctrines, exhortations, and encouragements, and the favourite theme of their social conversation.

NOTES.

CHAP. VI. V. 1. " The Grecians," or Hellenists, were Jews, or proselytes, who, having generally resided in other countries, spoke only the Greek language, and used the Greek version of the scriptures in their synagogues; by which they were distinguished from those, who spoke a dialect of the Hebrew.—The accession of numbers to the church, perhaps chiefly from among the poor, might render it more difficult, than at the first to afford them all so plentiful a support, as would have been desirable: (*Marg. Ref.* a.—*Notes*, ii. 44—47.iv.32—35:)and, as the greatest part of the publick stock must have been contributed by the Hebrews; perhaps those who acted under the apostles in this business, thought it right to shew more favour to the poor widows of that description, than to the others: but we may also suppose, that the Grecians were rather too jealous, and suspected more partiality than there actually was. Murmurs, however, and discontents, having been thus excited, the most dangerous disputes and divisions might have ensued, as has frequently happened in great revivals of religion, to the immense detriment of the common cause: and even the apostles themselves might have been exposed to censure or suspicion; but they, being directed by the Holy Spirit, took a most effectual method to prevent these pernicious consequences. (*Marg. Ref.* b—f.)

Was multiplied.] Πληθυνοντων. 7. vii. 17. ix. 31. xii. 24. *Matt.* xxiv. 12. 2 *Cor.* ix. 10. *Heb.* vi. 14. 1 *Pet.* i. 2. 2 *Pet.* i. 2. Jude 2. A πληθος, *multitudo.*—*The Grecians.*] Των Ελληνιστων. ix. 29. xi. 20. (*Note*, xi. 19—21, *v.* 20.)—*The Hebrews.*] Εβραιους. 2 *Cor.* xi. 22. *Phil.* iii. 5. (*Note, Phil.* iii. 1—7, *v.* 5.)—*Were neglected.*] Παρεθεωρουντο. Here only. Ex παρα, et θεωρεω, *aspicio.* " Were overlooked."—*Daily.*] Καθημερινη. Here only. Ex καθα, et ημερα, *dies.*

V. 2—6. (*Notes, Ex.* xviii. 13—26. *Num.* xi. 11—17. *Deut.* i. 12—18.) The apostles stated to the church,

or congregation of believers, whom they called together for that purpose, that it was not reasonable for them to leave their important ministry, to superintend the distribution of their bounty, and see the tables of the poor supplied: and as these murmurs had not arisen through their fault, so they could not consistently attend to the proper means for preventing them. (*Marg. Ref.* g—r.) It would therefore be most proper, for the church to elect suitable persons, to lay out their contributions in the most satisfactory manner; both among the poor, and in other necessary expenses. They therefore counselled them to " look out seven men," (as sufficient for the present,) of known probity and integrity, and " full of the Holy " Spirit;" and they would set them apart for this service, and commit the whole business to their management; that they (the apostles) might have no interruption, in giving themselves up to the preaching of the gospel, and to prayer for its success. This proposal giving them universal satisfaction, the choice was immediately made, and the apostles solemnly set apart the persons chosen for the work, by prayer and imposition of hands.—We read nothing more concerning any of them, except Stephen and Philip; (*Marg. Ref.* s—u.—*Notes*, 8—15. vii. viii. xxi. 7—14;) unless Nicolas (" a proselyte," as distinguished from those who were of Jewish extraction,) were the founder of the heretical sect, called Nicolaitans, which is not at all probable. (*Note, Rev.* ii. 14—16.) All the names seem to be of Greek original; and perhaps they were chosen from among the Hellenists, to give the more entire satisfaction.—It is evident, that they were appointed to take care of the property of the church, and not to the *pastoral office;* and the argument hence deduced to prove that every congregation ought to choose its own spiritual pastors, or for popular elections of ministers in any way, proves nothing. Men are generally careful enough, to entrust their property in the hands of suitable persons; but their souls are seldom more in danger, than when they follow " teachers after their own hearts."—Beza indeed seems to think, that if the apostles would not appoint deacons, except by the choice of the church, much less would they ordain ministers, or spiritual pastors: but this only proves, that scriptural ground for that plan, which he zealously supported, was not easily found, and that arguments were scarce.—Whatever may be said about the expediency or inexpediency of these arrangements; the divine authority of them should be considered as another question. It must, however, be allowed, that matters are far removed from what is reasonable, scriptural, or profitable, respecting the general management of these most important concerns, in almost every part of the visible church, and that pastors should not be *forced* on congregations, against whom they can bring just and reasonable

report, ᵃ full of the Holy Ghost and wisdom, ᵇ whom we may appoint over this business.

4 But we will ᵖ give ourselves continually to ᵠ prayer, and to the ministry of the word.

5 And ʳ the saying pleased the whole multitude: and they chose ˢStephen, a man full of faith and of the Holy Ghost, ᵗ and Philip, and Prochorus, and Nicanor, and Timon, and Parmenas, and Nicolas, ᵘ a proselyte of Antioch;

6 Whom they set before the apostles: ˣ and, when they had prayed, they laid *their* hands on them.

---

objections, whether in respect of doctrine or character.— It has been generally taken for granted, that these seven persons were ordained, or appointed, to the office of " dea- " cons;" yet they are not so called, either in this chapter, or elsewhere : and as the word rendered " deacon" is often translated *servant*, or *minister*, and used concerning Christ himself ; (*Rom.* xv. 8; *Gr.*) some have questioned whe- ther there were such a distinct order in the church, during the times of the apostles. Nothing, however, can be more evident, than that such an order existed, and was well known, when St. Paul wrote his epistle to the Philippians and his first epistle to Timothy. (*Notes, Phil.* i. 1. 1 *Tim.* iii. 8—13.)—' Now if they ' (the deacons,) ' were not in- ' stituted here by the apostles, I desire to know when, ' where, and by whom, they were instituted, and what ' other record we have left us of such an institution of ' them.' *Whitby.* If then, the office of deacons was in- stituted on this occasion ; it seems undeniable, that they were appointed solely to take care of the temporal con- cerns of the church ; and not, as deacons, to preach, or to administer sacred ordinances, except by assisting the elders, presbyters, or bishops, as some think they did, in distributing the bread and wine at the Lord's supper.— ' This is as true of the deacons, mentioned by St. Paul; ' (1 *Tim.* iii ;) there is not a word said of their ministering ' at the altar.' *Whitby.* He might have added, ' or of their preaching.' Yet it is plain, that Stephen did preach, and that Philip both preached and baptized; and he is even called " the evangelist." (xxi. 8.) It therefore occurs to enquire, whether they were preachers of the gospel, before their appointment as deacons, or became preachers afterwards. The following remarks are of some import- ance in this question. ' The choice was committed to ' them;' (the laity;) ' yet this was done 1st, by the parti- ' cular appointment of the apostles, for " the twelve called ' " the multitude, and said unto them, Look ye out seven ' " men." 2dly. They specify the number, and the quali- ' fications, of the persons to be chosen to this office. ' 3dly. They reserve to themselves the appointment of them ' to this work : saying, " Look ye out seven men, whom ' " we may appoint over this business." And, lastly, "they ' " only laid their hands on them." So in the case of the ' rulers over thousands, &c. ... Moses saith, as here, ' " Choose to yourselves men of wisdom and understand- ' " ing, and known to your tribes; ... and I will set them ' " to be your heads." Accordingly he both appointed ' them, and instructed them in the discharge of their ' office. (*Deut.* i. 13—17.) It seems very unlikely, that ' the apostles would have made this one requisite of the ' persons to be chosen, that they should be " full of the " ' extraordinary gifts of the " Holy Ghost ;" ...if their office

' had *confined* them to the ministry of the widows at Jeru- ' salem. ... Being " men full of the Holy Ghost;" and ' of that wisdom which enabled them to teach others ; we ' cannot reasonably conceive, that they were disabled by ' their ordination to this office, from doing that work for ' which they were fitted, and as it were appointed, by these ' gifts of the Spirit conferred on them. In a word, it is ' evident from this history, that before the ordination of ' these deacons, the apostles themselves were engaged in ' this work ; for the treasure of the church was " laid at ' " the apostles' feet, and distribution was made of it to ' " every man according as he had need." This distribu- ' tion, therefore, must be made by them, who had this ' treasure in their hands; and therefore they appoint these ' seven over this business, to ease themselves of this trou- ' ble, that they might " give themselves" more entirely ' " to prayer and to the ministry of the word." ... Now ' surely that work which the apostles personally performed ' for a season, must be consistent with their commission ' to " teach and baptize all nations."' *Whitby.* This statement does not prove, what the learned author seems to have intended, that the deacons, *as such*, were appointed to preach and baptize: but, to me at least, it renders it highly probable, that some of the seven were previously ministers, or evangelists ; and that they spared time from the ministry of the word, for this service, as the apostles had done before the appointment of these assistants. Some of the fathers assert, that they were all of the num- ber of the seventy disciples : but of this there is no other proof. In the abundance of spiritual and miraculous gifts, communicated at this favoured season, it is highly proba- ble, that many were thus qualified for important services, who had not at present a call or opening to perform them. The apostles, in counselling the church, make no distinc- tion between such as had been employed in the ministry, and others: and probably some of each were chosen. Ste- phen and Philip, we may suppose, were of the former ; and when Stephen was martyred, and Philip fully engaged at a distance, others might be chosen as deacons. And it appears to me very likely, that, both at this and future periods, many, who were appointed deacons in the first instance, afterwards became evangelists or pastors; and when they were fully employed, other deacons were ap- pointed. (*Note,* 1 *Tim.* iii. 8—13.)—Let it be especially noted, in this connexion ; that those who claim to be, ex- clusively or particularly, the successors of the apostles, should be more excluded from temporal concerns, and all secular avocations, than even other ministers are, " that " they may more entirely give themselves to prayer and " the ministry of the word."—*Laid their hands,* &c. (6) ' The Christian church observed this rite, both in ordain-

7 And ʳ the word of God increased; ˢ and the number of the disciples multiplied in Jerusalem greatly; and a great company of ᵗ the priests were ᵇ obedient to the faith.

8 ¶ And Stephen, ᶜ full of faith and power, ᵈ did great wonders and miracles among the people.

9 Then ᵉ there arose certain of ᶠ the synagogue, which is called the synagogue of the Libertines, and ᵍ Cyrenians, and ʰ Alexandrians, and of them

' ing ministers, and in conferring the gifts of the Holy
' Spirit.' Beza. (Marg. Ref. x.—Notes, viii. 14—17.
1 Tim. v. 21, 22.)
  Reason. (2) Αρετον. xli. 3. John viii. 29. 1 John iii. 22.
" Pleasing," viz. to God.—To serve.] Διακονειν. xix. 22.
Matt. iv. 11. xx. 28. Rom. xv. 25, et al. Διακονος, Matt.
xx. 26. Phil. i. 1. 1 Tim. iii. 8. 12.—Of honest report. (3)
Μαρτυρομενους. x. 22. xxii. 12. Heb. xi. 2. 4, 5. 39. 3 John
12.—Business.] Χρειας. ii. 45. iv. 35. xx. 34. xxviii. 10.
Matt. iii. 14. Rom. xii. 13. Eph. iv. 28. Phil. iv. 16. 19.
Unus, utilitas, commodum, a χραομαι, Utor aliqua re.—
We will give ourselves up. (4) Προσκαρτερησομεν. See on
i. 14.—The ministry.] Τη διακονια. 1. i. 17. 25. xi. 29. xii.
25. Rom. xv. 31, et al. See on 2.
  V. 7. ' A happy event of a time of trial.' Beza.—
The triumph of divine grace in the conversion of " a great
" company of the priests ; " considering the heavy loss
which they must in consequence sustain, as excluded from
the emoluments of the priesthood ; and the persecution to
which, in an especial manner, they must be exposed from
the unbelieving priests and rulers, in addition to their peculiar prejudices against the gospel ; has appeared to some
expositors too extraordinary to be at all probable ; and
they propose, *without authority*, to alter the text, and to
read, " and a great company, with some of the priests,
" were obedient to the faith." But that divine illumination
and grace, which caused Saul the persecutor " to count
" all but loss for Christ ; " and when " he had suffered the
" loss of all things, to count them but dung that he might
" win Christ," would be sufficient for these priests also.
(*Notes, Matt.* xiii. 44—46. *Phil.* iii. 8—11.) Indeed, the
triumph of the gospel, without this, would in some respects have been incomplete ; and it does not become us,
either to alter the scriptures, or to veil the glory and splendour of divine grace.—There were several thousands of
priests in the days of Ezra : (*Ezra* ii. 36—39 :) and a
great company might embrace the gospel, and yet a large
majority might persist in unbelief.—The abundant proof,
in every way given, that Jesus was the Messiah, could not
fail to convince the understanding of numbers among the
priests and rulers ; and by the grace of God, many of these
acted according to their convictions : " with the heart
" they believed unto righteousness, and with the mouth
" made confession unto salvation." (*Notes*, xxvi. 24—29.
John xii. 42, 43. *Rom.* x. 5—11.)—It seems probable, that
some of these converted priests became ministers of the
gospel ; yet no intimation is given in the New Testament,
of any priest, of the family of Aaron, being employed as a
Christian minister. John the Baptist was a priest ; Barnabas was a Levite : but nothing else, in this respect, is said
either of priests or Levites. It may, then, be a matter of
enquiry, whether this circumstance were not intentionally
ordered, to mark, not a gradual transition, but an imme-

diate and entire change, in the external administration of
the church. (*Notes, Is.* lxi. 4—6. lxvi. 19—23.)
  A great company.] Πολυς οχλος. i. 15. xi. 26. Matt. xxvi.
47.—*Were obedient to.*] Υπηκουον. Matt. viii. 27. Mark i.
27. iv. 41. Luke viii. 25. xvii. 6. Rom. vi. 12. 16. x. 16.
Eph. vi. 1, et al. Εκ υπο, et ακουω, audio.
  V. 8. ' It appears plainly from the foregoing history,
' that it was not as a deacon, that he' (Stephen) ' preached :
' but the extraordinary gifts of the Spirit he received
' eminently qualified him for that work. And no doubt
' many Christians, not statedly devoted to the ministry, and
' whose furniture was far inferior to his, would be capable
' of declaring Christ and his gospel to strangers, in an edi-
' fying and useful manner, and would not fail accordingly
' to do it, as Providence gave them a call and an oppor-
' tunity.' *Doddridge*.—' He that will plead a commission
' from God to preach the gospel, without an ordinary mis-
' sion, must shew the like extraordinary gifts or miraculous
' assistances : God never sending any person to do his
' work, without some testimony from himself, or from
' persons commissioned by him.' *Whitby*.—It is most
likely, that Stephen was previously a preacher : but if he
was not, it can hardly be supposed, that he would undertake that important office, however qualified, at Jerusalem,
and amidst the apostles, *without their sanction* ; or that
others, in such circumstances, would do this. At the
same time, it must fairly be allowed, that extraordinary
cases may arise, which would justify the dispensing with
ordinary rules ; and remarkable persons may be raised up,
though not endued with miraculous powers, who may be
fully warranted to teach the ignorant, not only privately,
but in the most publick manner ; though not expressly appointed to the ministry. It is certain that John the Baptist
wrought no miracles : yet his ministry (as entirely distinct from the priesthood,) was from God, without any
human appointment : and it is far from clear, that all the
prophets wrought miracles, indeed it is recorded of only
a few of them that they did ; and they were not sanctioned,
but opposed, by the stated ministers of religion : yet their
calling was divine. This appeared by the agreement of
their instructions with the scripture, and by *the effects of*
their labours. General rules, however, though they admit of some exceptions, form the measure of our conduct
in all ordinary cases : and it is extremely *dangerous* to give
a kind of unlimited sanction, to all who suppose themselves, or are supposed by their favourers, to be qualified
for the publick ministry, to engage in it, without any appointment from the church and its ministers. (*Marg. Ref.*
—*Notes*, vii. 4. 2 Kings iii. 20. iv. 23. Mark ix. 38—40.
Luke ix. 46—50, v. 50.)
  V. 9—14. There were a number of synagogues at Jerusalem, belonging to different descriptions of strangers residing there ; several of whom were proselytes, and not

of ¹ Cilicia and of ᵏ Asia, ˡ disputing with Stephen.

10 And they were not ᵐ able to resist the wisdom and ⁿ the spirit, by which he spake.

11 Then ° they suborned men, which said, We have heard him speak ᵖ blasphemous words q against Moses, and against God.

12 And ʳ they stirred up the people, and the elders, and the scribes, and came upon him, ˢ and caught him, and brought him to the council,

13 And ᵗ set up false witnesses, which said, This man ceaseth not to speak blasphemous words against this holy place, and the law:

14 For we have heard him say, ᵘ That this Jesus of Nazareth shall destroy this place, and shall ˣ change the ᵛ customs which Moses delivered us.

15 And all that sat in the council, looking stedfastly on him, ʸ saw his face as it had been the face of an angel.

y Ex. xxxiv. 29—35. Ec. viii. 1. Matt. xiii. 43. xvii. 2. 2 Cor. iii. 7, 8. 18.

---

of Jewish extraction. (Marg. Ref. e—k.)—"The Liber- "tines" seem to have been the descendants of persons, who had been slaves, and had obtained their freedom: though some think, that they were Jews, who were admitted to the privilege of Roman citizens; but the word, I believe, is never used in that sense. Each of these synagogues had an academy belonging to it, where students were instructed by some Rabbi: so that these teachers, or their more forward scholars, seem to have challenged Stephen to a disputation concerning his doctrine. But they were baffled by him in argument: for he had not only truth on his side, and eminent abilities; but the Lord had endued him by the Holy Spirit, with such wisdom, judgment, temper, and utterance, as they could not withstand. (Marg. Ref. m.—Notes, Matt. x. 19, 20. Luke xxi. 12—19.) Instead, however, of yielding to conviction, they bribed certain unprincipled persons to accuse him, before the people and the rulers, as an enemy to the Jewish church and nation: so that he was violently apprehended, brought before the council, and charged with blasphemy; for having said that Jesus of Nazareth (whom they mentioned with the utmost contempt,) had declared, that he would destroy the temple, and abrogate the Mosaick law. No doubt Stephen foretold, that Jesus would destroy the city and temple, in case the nation of the Jews persisted in opposition to him: but the apostles did not understand till long after, that the Mosaick law was to be abrogated; so that this was their inference from his doctrine: and as the temple and city had before been destroyed, and yet the ritual law of Moses had not been altered; this inference was precarious, and their testimony false. (Marg. Ref. o—y.—Notes, Is. lxiv. 9—12. Jer. vii. 12—15. xxvi. 9. Dan. ix. 25—27. Mic. iii. 8—12. Zech. xi. 1—3. xiv. —3. Matt. xxvi. 57—62.) There was, however, no blasphemy in the words, if he had really spoken them; for they were literally verified a few years after, according to predictions of the ancient prophets, and the types of the law itself, when rightly understood, as well as the predictions of our Lord. (Marg. Ref. x.—Notes, Is. lxvi. 3—6. 19—23. Jer. xxxi. 31—34. Dan. ix. 24—27. Hos. iii. 4, 5. Zech. xi. 1—3. xiv. 10, 11. Mal. i. 9—11. Matt. xxiv. Heb. viii. 7—13.)—Cilicia. (9) Probably Saul was one of these.

To resist the wisdom. (10) Αντιστηναι τη σοφια. See on Luke xxi. 15.—They suborned. (11) 'Υπεβαλον. Here only: ex υπο, et βαλλω, jucio.—They stirred up. (12) Συνεκινησαν. Here only: ex συν, et κινεω, moveo. "They "moved at once both the people and the elders, &c." They caught.] Συνηρπασαν. xix. 29. xxvii. 15. Luke viii. 29.—Both the people and the rulers concurred in apprehending Stephen: whereas on other occasions, the rulers feared the people.—The customs. (14) "The rites." Marg. Τα εθη. xvi. 21. xxv. 16. xxvi. 3. Luke xxii. 39. John xix. 40. The traditions of the elders, or what was called the oral law, as well as the written institutions of Moses, seem to have been meant.

V. 15. When the members of the council stedfastly looked on Stephen, to observe whether he shewed any signs of guilt or terror, they saw his countenance calm and serene and irradiated, probably in a miraculous manner, as the face of Moses had been when he came down from the mount; so that he appeared more like an angel than a man, as he stood before them. But, as they disregarded all the other miracles, so they remained unmoved even by this divine attestation to his character. It is remarkable, that he who was accused of blaspheming against Moses, should, in the presence of those who "sat in "Moses's seat," be thus honoured; even as that lawgiver had been, when he came down from the mount of God. (Marg. Ref. Ex. xxxiv. 29—35. 2 Cor. iii. 7—18.)

PRACTICAL OBSERVATIONS

V. 1—7.

Unless partial and carnal self-love could be wholly destroyed out of every heart; envies, murmurs, jealousies, and discontents will creep in, and, in some degree, disturb every community on earth, however collected and governed. We need not then be surprised to find such things: they belong to human nature: apostolick administration could not wholly exclude them; and that, even among persons endued with great grace. It is indeed, exceedingly difficult to exclude gross evils, even where the most of those concerned are earnestly desirous of doing it. And as it is not to be expected, that the administration of affairs, either in nations, or in any part of the visible church, will be conducted with apostolick disinterestedness, wisdom, and sanctity; the subject before us may serve to repress our murmurs against governors, and established authorities, though we cannot cordially approve of their measures: for unreasonable expectations always end in bitter disappointments.—We should, however, repress the first risings of selfish passions in our own hearts; and endeavour to pre-

CHAP. VII.

Stephen, being required to answer before the council, shews how God called Abraham, and promised Canaan to him and his seed, 1—8; how Joseph was sold by his brethren, and Jacob with his family went down into Egypt, 9—16; that when they were oppressed by the Egyptians, Moses was born, and brought up by Pharaoh's daughter, 17—22; that attempting to deliver Israel he was rejected, and fled into Midian, 23 —29; that at length he was sent to be their deliverer, 30—36; that he prophesied of Christ, received the law for Israel, and was grieved by their rebellion and idolatry, 37—43; that they had "the tabernacle of "witness," till Solomon built the temple, 44—47; yet, according to the prophets, "the Most High "dwelleth not in temples made with hands," 48—50.

He boldly accuses the council and the nation of imitating the rebellion and persecution of their ancestors, who rejected and slew the prophets; and charges them with murdering Christ, in violation of their own law, 51—53. Being "cut to the heart," they hasten to stone him; while he, favoured with a vision of Christ, and calling on him to receive his soul, and pardon his murderers, falls asleep, 54—60.

THEN said the high priest, [a] Are these things so?

2 And he said, [b] Men, brethren, and fathers, hearken: [c] The God of glory [d] appeared unto our father Abraham, [e] when he was in Mesopotamia, before he dwelt in [f] Charran,

a vi. 13, 14. Matt. xxvi. 61, 62 Mark xiv. 58— 60. John xviii. 19—21. 33—35.
b xxii. 1. xxiv. 7.
c Ps. xxiv. 7. 10. xxix. 3. Is. vi. 3. Matt. vi. 13. Luke ii. 14. John i. 14. xii. 41. 2 Cor. iv. 6—6. Tit. ii. 13 Rev. iv. 11. v. 12, 13.
d Gen. xii. .. Neh. ix. 7. Is. li. 2.
e Gen. xi. 31
f Gen. xxix. 4 Haran.

---

vent them in others, or to remove all occasions of them from others as far as we can : and, if they begin to appear, such concessions and regulations should be made without delay, as may disappoint that enemy, who thus seeks to divide the house and kingdom against itself. (*Notes, Matt. xii. 25, 26. Gal. v. 13—15.*) In general the ministers of Christ should leave to other men, as far as they can, the management of *secular* concerns, even such as belong to the church, or to charitable institutions; that they may keep clear of all suspicion of partiality or injustice, and be more at leisure, and unencumbered in attending to their proper office. But, if it be unreasonable and sinful for them to "leave the word of God," even to superintend the care of the poor, and those secular concerns which have an intimate connexion with piety and charity : how inexcusable must they be, who leave the publick ministry, and even the care of the poor and sick, to others, and waste their times in dissipated pleasures, luxurious indulgence, ambitious and covetous pursuits, or such studies, as are foreign to the clerical profession ! or who spend their time, abilities, and zeal, in political disputes!—If men are not qualified even "to serve tables," or regulate charities, except they be of "honest report," and endued with heavenly wisdom and grace : how pernicious must it be, to commit the important trust of "watching for men's "souls" to such persons, as are evidently destitute of these endowments! It therefore behoves those, who are concerned in choosing, appointing, or ordaining men to any office in the church, to do it with good advice, serious deliberation, and fervent prayer for divine direction. (*Notes, 1 Tim. v. 21, 22. 24, 25.*)—When proper methods have been taken to prevent disputes, and to preserve the peace of the church, and to secure an upright, impartial, and prudent management of all her concerns; and when pastors are left at liberty, and are zealously willing "to give them- "selves continually to prayer, and to the ministry of the "word;" it may be expected that the cause of truth will gain ground, that the number of disciples will be multiplied, and that even the most prejudiced will be won over to embrace the gospel : and when priests, or teachers, or leading persons, who have been blind, prejudiced, or careless, "become obedient to the faith;" it may be considered as a peculiar triumph of divine grace, and a most important advantage to the church.

V. 8—15.

Those who are full of faith will be full of power; not indeed for working miracles, but to resist temptations, to endure hardships, and to perform arduous services : (*Notes, Heb. xi :*) and, when the Saviour calls men forth to contend earnestly for the truth; he "will give them a mouth "and wisdom, which all their enemies shall not be able to "gainsay or resist." But worldly disputants, when thus disconcerted, commonly have recourse to other weapons, to defend their errors and to gratify their deep resentment. In ordinary cases, ridicule and abuse may suffice : but when enmity to the gospel concurs with indignation at being defeated in a vain-glorious contest, a more base and injurious method of revenge will frequently be devised. —How irrational a creature is man! To assert, that an intelligent being is capable of deliberately supporting a system of religion, by subornation, perjury, lying testimony, and murder, might have been deemed a libel on human nature, and on reason itself, had it not been done in numberless instances. But the blame rests not on the *understanding*, so much as on the *heart*, of a fallen creature, "which is deceitful above all things, and desperately "wicked." (*Note, Jer. xvii. 9, 10.*)—Those who prefer human traditions and reasonings to divine revelation, will frequently charge those with blasphemy, who "speak ac- "cording to the oracles of God :" and most injurious false testimony is often borne, through prejudiced conclusions from men's words, or wrong constructions put on them. But the servant of the Lord, possessing a clear conscience, a cheerful hope, and divine consolations, may smile in the face of danger and death; and may appear amidst his most furious persecutors, not only as "a lamb in the midst of "wolves," but even as an angel surrounded with malignant demons.

NOTES.

CHAP. VII. V. 1—8. (*Marg. Ref. a.*) This speech of Stephen may be considered, either as an answer to the accusation brought against him, or as his testimony to Jesus Christ : and the same arguments would serve both purposes. As he was not permitted to conclude; so we have here rather an introduction to his main subject, than the whole of his intended discourse. (*Notes, 51—53. xvii. 30 31. xxiv. 24—27. xxvi. 24—32.*)—There was peculiar wis-

3 And said unto him, [f] Get thee out of thy country, and from thy kindred, and come into [h] the land which I shall shew thee.

4 Then [i] came he out of the land of the Chaldeans, and dwelt in Charran: and from thence, when his father was dead, he removed him into this land, wherein ye now dwell.

5 And [k] he gave him none inheritance in it, no, [l] not so much as to set his foot on: [m] yet he promised that he would give it to him for a possession, and to his seed after him, [n] when as yet he had no child.

6 And God spake on this wise, [o] That his seed should sojourn in a strange land; and that they should bring them into bondage, and entreat [p] them evil [q] four hundred years.

7 And [q] the nation to whom they shall be in bondage will I judge, said God: and after that, shall they come forth, [r] and serve me in this place.

8 And he gave him [s] the covenant of circumcision. [t] And so Abraham begat Isaac, and circumcised him the eighth day; [u] and Isaac begat Jacob; [x] and Jacob begat the twelve [y] patriarchs.

9 And the patriarchs, [z] moved with envy, [a] sold Joseph into Egypt: [b] but God was with him,

10 And [c] delivered him out of all his afflictions, [d] and gave him favour and wisdom in the sight of Pharaoh, king of Egypt; and he made him [e] governor over Egypt and all his house.

11 Now [f] there came a dearth over all the land of Egypt and Canaan, and great affliction: and our fathers found no sustenance.

12 But [f] when Jacob heard that there was corn in Egypt, he sent out our fathers first.

13 And at the second time [g] Joseph was made known to his brethren; and Joseph's kindred was made known unto Pharaoh.

---

dom in referring to the ancient records of the nation, and in speaking honourably of those characters, for which his hearers professed so great a veneration, and so strong an attachment; though they neither understood the general plan of the Lord's dealings with their ancestors, nor entered into their views, nor copied their examples. The animation and beauty of the address must be, in a great measure, lost to us, unless we could place ourselves exactly in the situation of the Jews, and appropriate, as it were, their peculiar sentiments and feelings on these subjects. Stephen was accused of predicting the abrogation of the ceremonial law, as if the intimation of such a change was blasphemous: whereas, in fact, the best and most eminent persons among their ancestors lived before the promulgation of that law; which could not therefore be essential to the acceptable worship of God. This seems to have been covertly insinuated, in the beginning of his discourse, which Stephen opened in the language of respect, deference, and affection. He observed, that " the " God of glory," who is altogether glorious, and the Fountain of glory, and who had shewn his visible glory in the camp of Israel, in the tabernacle, and in the temple, first appeared to Abraham, not in Canaan, to which they thought his peculiar presence limited, but in Mesopotamia. (Notes, Gen. xi. 26—32. xii. 1—3. Josh. xxiv. 2. Heb. xi. 8—10.)—As the history has already been considered, I shall here only advert to those things, which involve difficulty, or form an essential part of Stephen's argument. (Marg. Ref.) Both " Ur of the Chaldees," and Charran, or Haran, were, properly speaking, in Mesopotamia; though Haran was much nearer to the promised land, than Ur was.—It is here peculiarly noticed, that,

when the promise of Canaan to Abraham's posterity was given, he had neither any possession in the land, even so much as to be able to set his foot down, except on the land of others; nor had he any children to inherit, if he had had any possession (5).—From the calling of Abram, to the Exodus, or departure out of Egypt, was four hundred and thirty years. Twenty-five elapsed before Isaac was born; and tradition reports that he was five years old when weaned, and when Ishmael, who was of Egyptian extraction by his mother, mocked him. The apostle considers this as a species of persecution, and many date these four hundred years from that event. (Notes, Gen. xv. 12— 16. xxi. 8—12. Ex. xii. 40.)—" The covenant of circum- " cision," is that covenant, which was sealed by circumcision, above four hundred years before the promulgation of the Mosaick law. (Notes, Gen. xvii. 7—12. 23—27. xxi. 3, 4. Ex. xix. 5. Rom. iv. 9—11. Gal. iii. 15—29.)

Men, brethren, and fathers. (2) Notes, i. 16—18, v. 16. xxii. 1—5, v. 1.—Get thee out. (3) Εξελθε, κ.τ.λ. The words of the LXX, though not the whole of the verse, Gen. xii. 1.—He removed. (4) Μετωκισεν. 43. Not elsewhere N. T.— 1 Chr. v. 26. viii. 6. Sept. Μετοικεσια. Matt. i. 11, 12. Ex μετα et οικος, domus.—Not so much as to set his foot on. (5) Ουδε βημα ποδος. Nec pedis spatium.—When Sarah died, Abraham had no land for a burying place, till he bought it. Notes, Gen. xxiii.—Patriarchs. (8) Πατριαρχας. See on ii. 29.

V. 9—13. Joseph was the peculiar favourite of God, and an eminent type of Jesus; yet his brethren hated and envied him: but they were not able to prevent his exaltation, which was the means of their own preservation. The argument of this passage seems to be, that, as the pa

h Gen. xlv. 9—11. Ps. cv. 23. i Gen. xlvi. 12. 26, 27. Deut. x. 22. 1 Chr. ii. 5,6. k Gen. xlvi. 3—7. Num. xx. 15. Deut. x. 22. xxvi. 5. Josh. xxiv. 4. l Gen. xlix. 33. Ex. i. 6. Heb. xi. 21, 22. m Ex. xiii. 19. Josh. xxiv. 32. n Gen. xxiii. 9—20. xlix. 29—32.

14 Then [h] sent Joseph, and called
his father Jacob to *him*, and all his
kindred, [i] threescore and fifteen souls.
15 So [k] Jacob went down into
Egypt, [l] and died, he, and our fathers,
16 And [m] were carried over into Sychem, and laid in [n] the sepulchre, that
Abraham bought for a sum of money
of the sons of [o] Emmor, *the father* of
Sychem.
17 ¶ But [p] when the time of the
promise drew nigh, which God had
sworn to Abraham, [q] the people grew
and multiplied in Egypt,
18 Till [r] another king arose, which
knew not Joseph.

o Gen. xxxiv. 2, &c. *Hamor. Shechem.* p 6. Gen. xv. 13—16. 2 Pet. iii. 8, 9. q xiii. 17. Ex. i. 7—12. 20. Ps. cv. 24. r Ex. i. 8.

triarchs must have perished, if Joseph, whom they had envied and injured, had not been advanced to authority, and thus enabled to preserve them; so must the Jews and their rulers perish, unless Jesus, whom they had despised and crucified, but whom God had highly exalted, should graciously save them. As therefore Joseph's brethren at length submitted to him, and were forgiven; so ought they to submit, and seek forgiveness from the glorified Messiah. (*Marg. Ref.—Notes, Gen.* xxxvii. xxxix—xlv.) —*Favour.* (10) Many understand this of the courteous and graceful deportment of Joseph, as conciliating the favour of all men, in connexion with his wisdom. (*Notes, Ps.* cv. 17—22. *Prov.* iii. 3, 4. xvi. 7.)

Moved with envy. (9) Ζηλωσαντες. xvii. 5. 1 *Cor.* xii. 31. xiii. 4. xiv. 1. 39. 2 *Cor.* xi. 2. *Gal.* iv. 17. *Jam.* iv. 2.—*Gen.* xxxvii. 11. *Sept.* A ζηλος. See on v. 17.—*Favour and wisdom.* (10) Χαριν και σοφιαν.—*Gen.* xxxix. 4. *Sept.* See on *Luke* iv. 22.—*Sustenance.* (11) Χορτασματα. Here only. A χορταζω. See on *Matt.* v. 6.

V. 14. (*Marg. Ref.—Notes, Gen.* xlvi. 7. 12. 15. 21. 27.) Seventy persons, including Jacob and Joseph, and Joseph's two sons, are reckoned up by Moses; among whom were some grand-children of Benjamin, who was not above twenty-five years of age, when Jacob went down into Egypt. And several grand-children of Joseph are named in Chronicles, who are not mentioned in Genesis. (1 *Chr.* vii. 16. 20.) It is undeniable, that some of the grand-children of Jacob's sons, who afterwards became heads of families in their tribes, were included in the number stated by Moses: and is it not the most obvious way of settling the difficulty, between his account, and that of Stephen from the Septuagint, to include five grand-children of Joseph? Some learned men indeed would make up the number, by the wives of the patriarchs: but it must have been very extraordinary at least that, with so many sons and grandsons, there should have been no more than five women! and, if there were many more, why should five only be here added to the number? Only two females (Dinah, and Serah, a descendant of Gad,) are mentioned in Genesis: and the Septuagint, which Stephen, (who probably was a Grecian, *Notes*, vi. 2—6,) seems to have referred to, may be thus translated: "All the souls which "came with Jacob into Egypt, who came out of his loins, "apart from the wives of Jacob's sons, all the souls were "threescore and six. But the sons of Joseph, who were "born to him in the land of Egypt, were nine. All the "souls of the house of Jacob, who went down with Jacob "into Egypt, were threescore and fifteen souls."—Joseph, and his two sons, and Jacob himself, complete the threescore and ten of our version: and though the Septuagint is not very accurate, or perspicuous in this statement, three things are sufficiently clear: 1. That the additional five mentioned in it were not women. In fact with what propriety could the wives of Jacob's sons be said to come out of his loins? 2. That they were sons, or male descendants, of Joseph. And, 3. That the family of Jacob, containing some born in Egypt, and Joseph who was carried thither long before, as well as Jacob and those who went down with him, are included.—'Reckoning some of the 'children born in Egypt, together with Joseph and his 'sons, and his sons' sons, made up seventy-five persons.' *Hammond.*

V. 15, 16. (*Notes, Gen.* xlvi—xlix.) It appears from this passage, and it is indeed highly probable in itself, and confirmed by ancient tradition, that the bodies of all Jacob's sons were embalmed, and carried up by their descendants, to be interred in Canaan. (*Notes, Gen.* l. 24—26.) Jacob was buried in the cave of the field of Machpelah, with his fathers, Abraham and Isaac. (*Notes, Gen.* xlix. 29—31. l. 1—14.) This Abraham bought of Ephron the Hittite. (*Notes, Gen.* xxiii.) But Joseph, and probably his brethren, were buried at Sychem, or Shechem, in the piece of ground which Jacob bought of the sons of Emmor, or Hamor, the father of Shechem; and which he left as an inheritance to the descendants of Joseph. "Jacob "died, he and our fathers, and they" (our fathers) "were "carried over to Sychem and buried, *he*" (that is Jacob,) "in the sepulchre which Abraham bought for a sum of "money; *and* they" (the other patriarchs,) "in that of "the sons of Emmor, the father of Sychem." This rendering has been proposed by several eminent men, to remove the obvious difficulty of reconciling the passage with the history in the book of Genesis. (*Gen.* xxxiii. 19. *Notes, Gen.* xlviii. 22. *Josh.* xxiv. 29—32, *v.* 32.) But it is rather a paraphrase, than a translation; and not a fair paraphrase of the present text.—'Or we must say, with the great 'Bochart, that some unskilful grammarian, thinking that 'a nominative case was wanting before the word ωνησατο, '*was bought*, wrote in the margin the word Αβρααμ, Abra-'ham, which others put in the text, without which the 'words run thus, with exact truth. "So Jacob went '"down into Egypt, and died" (there), "he and our '"father; and they" (our fathers) "were carried over '"into Sychem, and laid in the sepulchre, that was '"bought for a sum of money of the sons of Emmor, the '"father of Sychem."' *Whitby.*

Were carried over, ... and laid. (16) Μετετεθησαν ... και ετεθησαν. Μετατιθημι. *Gal.* i. 6. *Heb.* vii. 12. xi. 5. *Jude* 4. Not elsewhere. "They were carried over; "..."they were "placed."

V. 17—29. (*Marg. Ref.* p, q. s.—*Notes, Gen.* xv. 12—15. *Ex.* i. 1—22.) The words here rendered, "exceeding "fair," are literally, "fair to God," (*Marg.*) which some have rendered, "Beloved by God;" but this is not a just

19 The * same dealt subtilely with our kindred, and evil-entreated our fathers, so that they cast out their young children, to the end they might not live.

20 In which time 'Moses was born, " and was * exceeding fair, and nourished up in his father's house three months:

21 And * when he was cast out, Pharaoh's daughter took him up, and nourished him ' for her own son.

22 And Moses was ' learned in all the wisdom of the Egyptians, * and was mighty in words and in deeds.

23 And b when he was full forty years old, ' it came into his heart 4 to visit his brethren the children of Israel.

24 And ' seeing one of them suffer wrong, he defended him, and avenged him that was oppressed, and smote the Egyptian:

25 For he supposed his brethren would have understood, how that 'God by his hand would deliver them; ' but they understood not.

26 And h the next day he shewed himself unto them as they strove, and would have set them at one again, saying, Sirs, ' ye are brethren; why do ye wrong one to another?

27 But k he that did his neighbour wrong, thrust him away, saying, 'Who made thee a ruler and a judge over us?

28 Wilt thou kill me, as thou didst the Egyptian yesterday?

29 Then " fled Moses at this saying; and was a stranger in the land of Madian, where he begat two sons.

30 And ' when forty years were expired, * there appeared to him in the wilderness of mount Sina " an Angel of the Lord, " in a flame of fire ' in a bush.

31 When Moses saw it, he wondered at the sight: ' and as he drew near to behold it, the voice of the Lord came unto him,

32 Saying, 'I am the God of thy fathers, the God of Abraham, and the God of Isaac, and the God of Jacob. "Then Moses trembled, and durst not behold.

---

translation. Neither is there any ground to conclude, either that Moses prophesied, as some have supposed, or indeed had true faith and grace, till a short time before he visited his brethren. (Marg. Ref. b, c.—Note, Heb. xi. 24 —26.) The clause " fair to God," seems to refer to the Lord's purposes concerning Moses, which induced him to preserve him, when other children were destroyed; and by means of his extraordinary beauty to accomplish this. (Marg. Ref. u.—Notes, Ex. ii. 2—10. Heb. xi. 23.)— Moses might be " mighty in words," as capable of calm, forcible, and conclusive reasoning; and yet be slow of speech, and destitute of the graces of elocution, as he modestly pleaded concerning himself. (Notes, Ex. iv. 10— 12.)—He had received some general intimation, that he should deliver his people; (as David was assured that he should reign over Israel;) but it does not appear, that he was expressly commissioned to attempt their deliverance at this time. From some general computation, it is probable that he supposed the appointed time was at hand; but forty years more must elapse, before that event actually took place. He also concluded, that when so distinguished a person, as he had been in Pharaoh's court, renounced all his prospects, to join interests with his enslaved people, as the deliverer whom God had raised up; they too, remembering the prediction and promise to Abraham, would readily attach themselves to him: but in this he found himself mistaken. (Marg. Ref. x—l.—Notes, Ex. ii. 11—15. Heb. xi. 24—27.)—' The speech of this single ' person is represented (35) as expressing the sentiments ' of the whole body of the people: as their slowness after-

' wards to believe the mission of Moses, when attested by ' miracles, seems evidently to shew that it was.' Doddridge. (Note, Luke xii. 13, 14.)—Stranger. (29) Marg. Ref. m. —Notes, Ex. ii. 16—21.

Dealt subtilely. (19) Καλασοφισαμενος. Here only N. T. —Ex. i. 10. Sept. Ex καλα et σοφιζω, 2 Tim. iii. 15. 2 Pet. i. 16.—So that they cast out, &c.] Τα ποιειν εκθετα. Here only. Exposita. Εκτιθεντα, 21.—Live.] Ζωογονεισθαι. Luke xvii. 33. Not elsewhere N. T.—Ex. i. 17, 18. 22. Sept.— Fair. (20) Ατειος. Heb. xi. 23. Not elsewhere N. T.—Ex. ii. 2. Sept.—Nourished up.] Ὁς ανετραφη. " Who was " nourished up." 21. xxii. 3. Not elsewhere.—Was learned. (22) Επαιδευθη. " Was educated." xxii. 3. 2 Tim. ii. 25. Tit. ii. 12. Heb. xii. 7, et al. A παις, puer.—He defended. (24) Ημυνετο. Here only.—Him that was oppressed.] Τῳ καλαπονεμενῳ. 2 Pet. ii. 7. Not elsewhere. Ex κατα, et πονεω, laboro.—Would deliver them. (25) Διδωσιν αυτοις σωτηριαν.—As they strove. (26) Μαχομενοις. " Fighting." Διαπλαγκτιζομενος, Ex. ii. 13. Sept.—Sirs.] Ανδρες, men.— Who made, &c. (27, 28) Nearly from the LXX, which rather varies from the Hebrew, especially by adding χθες yesterday.—A judge. (27) Δικαστην. 35. See on Luke xii. 14.—A stranger. (29) Παροικος. 6. Eph. ii. 19. 1 Pet. ii. 11. Παροικια, xiii. 17.

V. 30—36. (Marg. Ref. n.—Ex. ii. 23—25.) " The " Angel of the LORD appeared to Moses, and the voice of " the LORD came to him, saying." (31. 35. Notes, Gen. xlviii. 16. Ex. iii. 2—6.) Some make the expression, that " God sent Moses, by the hand of the angel," an objection to the conclusion, that this was not a created angel.

4 P 6

33 Then said the Lord to him, 'Put off thy shoes from thy feet; for the place where thou standest is holy ground.

34 'I have seen, I have seen the affliction of my people which is in Egypt, and I have heard their groaning, 'and am come down to deliver them. 'And now, come, I will send thee into Egypt.

35 This 'Moses whom they refused, saying, Who made thee a ruler and a judge? 'the same did God send *to be* 'a ruler and a deliverer, 'by the hand of the Angel which appeared to him in the bush.

36 He brought them out, 'after that he had shewed wonders and signs, that he had shewed wonders and signs, in the land of Egypt, and in the Red Sea, 'and in the wilderness forty years.

37 This is 'that Moses, which said unto the children of Israel, 'A Prophet shall the Lord your God raise up unto you of your brethren, 'like unto me; 'him shall ye hear.

38 This is he that was 'in the church in the wilderness 'with the Angel which spake to him in the mount Sina, and *with* our fathers: 'who received the 'lively oracles to give unto us:

39 To 'whom our fathers would not obey, 'but thrust *him* from them, 'and in their hearts turned back again into Egypt,

40 Saying 'unto Aaron, Make us gods to go before us: for *as for* this Moses, which brought us out of the land of Egypt, we wot not what is become of him.

41 And 'they made a calf in those days, and offered sacrifice unto the idol, and 'rejoiced in the works of their own hands.

42 Then God turned, 'and gave them up to worship 'the host of heaven; as it is written in the book of the prophets, 'O ye house of Israel, 'have ye offered to me slain beasts and sacrifices *by the space* 'of forty years in the wilderness?

43 Yea, 'ye took up the tabernacle of Moloch, and the star of your god Remphan, 'figures which ye made to worship them: 'and I will carry you away beyond Babylon.

---

but the "Angel JEHOVAH," the Angel or Messenger of the covenant, the Word and Son of God, by whom he has always been declared unto men. (*Notes, Mal.* iii. 1—4, v. 1. *John* i. 18.) But it only implies the distinct personality of the Father and the Son; and that the Son, having undertaken to become incarnate, always was the medium of communication between the invisible God and sinful man: and though he often appeared in human form, yet was he "the God of Abraham, and of Isaac, "and of Jacob;" being One with and equal to the Father. (*Marg. Ref.* p—t.—*Notes, Matt.* xxii. 23—33, v. 32. *Phil.* ii. 5—11.) Moses was ordered to put off his shoes, and the priests under the law are supposed to have ministered barefoot in the sanctuary: as no shoes or sandals are mentioned, though particular orders are given about all the other garments. This was an expression of reverence, and an emblem of circumspection. (*Notes, Ex.* iii. 4, 5. *Josh.* v. 13—15.)—The example of the Israelites, refusing the help of Moses, was suited to shew the Jews, that it was no new thing for their nation to reject those, whom God had sent to rule over and deliver them; and therefore it was the less wonderful, that they had rejected and crucified their promised Messiah.—(*Marg. Ref.* y—g.) 'It would be too frigid an interpreta-'tion to say that the Lord called Moses by the ministra-'tion of an angel; when, (unless I am deceived,) this 'also is signified, that Moses was armed by his hand and

'power, seeing that Angel, namely Christ, (as the apostle 'explains it, 1 Cor. x. 9,) was the true Deliverer and 'Leader, whose servant Moses was.' *Beza.—I have seen,* &c. (34) This varies considerably from the Septuagint, (*Ex.* iii. 7,) and also from the Hebrew. But it gives the general meaning very clearly.

Trembled. (32) Εντρομος ... γενομενος. Εντρομος. xvi. 29. *Heb.* xii. 21.—*Affliction.* (34) Κακωσιν. Here only. Κακοω, 6. 19. xii. 1. xiv. 2.—*Groaning.*] Στεναγμν. *Rom.* viii. 26. Not elsewhere N. T.—*Ex.* ii. 24. vi. 5. *Sept.*— *They refused.* (35) Ηρνησαντο.—See on iii. 13.—*A de-liverer.*] Λυτρωτην.—Here only. *Redemptor, liberator.* A λυ-τρου, redimo.—The contrast between Δικαστην, and λυτρωτην, is worthy of notice.

V. 37—43. (*Marg.* and *Marg. Ref.* h—o.—*Notes,* iii. 22—26. *Deut.* xviii. 15—22.) Moses had predicted, that God would raise up a Prophet like to him in Israel, to whom the people were commanded to hearken, even in preference to him; and it might be expected, that this Prophet would change some at least of the externals appointed by him. (*Notes,* vi. 9—14. *Matt.* xvii. 5—8.) The Jews whom Stephen addressed, professed a strong attachment to Moses; yet their fathers, even after he had brought them out of Egypt, and when they were daily witnessing the most stupendous miracles, which God wrought by him, were by no means submissive to him. For even "this Moses," for whom they were about to

44 ¶ Our fathers had 'the tabernacle of witness in the wilderness, as he had appointed, ' speaking unto Moses, ' that he should make it according to the fashion that he had seen;

45 ' Which also our fathers ' that came after brought in with ' Jesus into the possession of the Gentiles, ' whom God drave out before the face of our fathers, ' unto the days of David;

46 Who ᵐ found favour before God,

" and desired to find a tabernacle for the God of Jacob.

47 But ° Solomon built him an house.

48 Howbeit, ᵖ the most High ᵠ dwelleth not in temples made with hands; ' as saith the prophet,

49 ' Heaven is my throne, and earth is my footstool: ' what house will ye build me? saith the Lord; or what is the place of my rest?

---

reject the Messiah, when in the church, or congregation, of Israel in the wilderness, attended by the manifested presence of the great " Angel of the covenant," even JEHOVAH, who spake to him from Sinai, and from whom he received those lively oracles, or revelations of the divine will, which contained the way of salvation and eternal life, could not secure their obedience to his authority: on the contrary, they thrust him from them, desired to return to Egyptian bondage, and seduced Aaron to make the golden calf, in contempt of Moses and of the LORD. (Marg. Ref. p—u.—Notes, Ex. xxxii—xxxiv. Neh. ix. 15—17, v. 17.) This had been an earnest and specimen of their subsequent idolatries in after ages, to which God judicially gave them up, till at length he sentenced the nation to captivity under the Assyrians and Chaldeans. (Marg. Ref. x—e.—Note, Am. v. 25—31.) —The name Remphan is here substituted for Chiun in Amos; but little satisfactory has been advanced concerning the demon, or planet, worshipped under this name.— Some conclude from the clause, " took up the tabernacle " of Moloch," that shrines of Moloch, or models of the idol-temple and image within it, were publickly carried in procession by the worshippers. (Note, xix. 23—31.) This however Moses would not allow so long as he lived. They therefore suppose, that God, as a punishment of the idolatry of Israel, in worshipping him under the image of the golden calf, at length gave up the nation to still more open and atrocious idolatry; till they had filled up the measure of their crimes, and were sent into captivity, into Chaldea, Media, and still more distant regions. Many intimations, however, are given by the prophets, that gross idolatries were secretly practised, even in the wilderness. (Notes, Ex. xx. 10—17.)—Stephen observed that this had been the conduct of their ancestors in all former ages, and the Jews had no cause to glory in them : God had before given up the nation to idolatry and captivity; and they had no reason to confide in present external privileges, but rather to fear the terrible judgments of God for crucifying the Messiah. And, as the prophets had formerly predicted the Assyrian and Babylonish captivity, which had come to pass accordingly; so they had no cause to condemn him for predicting the approaching ruin of their city, temple, and nation, if they persisted to oppose the religion of Jesus.—Lively oracles. (38) The law, as given by Moses, considered in itself, was " the ministration of " death; " but as connected with the types, prophecies, and instituted ordinances, which contained the substance

of the gospel, under that dispensation, the way of life eternal was pointed out, and known in a measure by all true believers: and in this sense, even the books of Moses were " living oracles," a revelation by which numbers obtained eternal life, through faith in him of whom Moses in the law, as well as all the subsequent prophets bore witness.—Make us gods. (40) Exactly from the LXX, Ex. xxxii. 1. (Notes, Ex. xxxii. 1. 7—10.)—Ye took up, &c. (42, 43) The LXX have Raiphan and Damascus, instead of Ramphan and Babylon, Am. v. 26, 27. (Note, Am. v. 25—27.)—Some copies here read Damascus. In the church. (38) Εν τη εκκλησια. See on Matt. xvi. 18.—The lively oracles.] Λογια ζωντα.—Λογια. Rom. iii. 2. Heb. v. 12. 1 Pet. iv. 11.—Thrust ... from. (39) Απω-σαντο. 27. xiii. 46. Rom. xi. 1, 2. 1 Tim. i. 19.—To go before us. (40) Οι προπορευσονται. Luke i. 76. Not elsewhere N. T.—Ex. xxxii. 1. Sept.—They made a calf. (41) Εμοσχοποιησαν. Here only. Ex μοσχος, vitulus, et ποιεω, facio. —I will carry you away. (43) Μιλοικιω. See on 4.

V. 44—50. After the giving of the law, the Israelites had worshipped God, not in Canaan, nor at Jerusalem, but in the wilderness; and not at a stately temple, but a moveable tabernacle. This was carried into the promised land by their fathers, under the leading of Jesus, or Joshua; (the type of Jesus the Messiah ;) and, as it witnessed the gracious presence of God with them, and their relation to him, being typical of good things to come, which appeared by the injunction given to Moses about forming it; (Note, Ex. xxv. 40;) so it answered the same purposes, for several hundred years, after their settlement in Canaan. (Marg. and Marg. Ref. f—l.) And though David, having been highly favoured and prospered, desired greatly to build a temple; (Notes, 2 Sam. vii. 1—16. Ps. cxxxii. 1—6;) he was only allowed to make preparation for it; because he had been a warrior, and had shed blood: and therefore the building of the temple was reserved for Solomon, his peaceable son, who was an eminent type of the Messiah. (Marg. Ref. m, n.—Notes, 1 Chr. xxii. 1—12. xxix. 1—19.) Yet when Solomon had finished his magnificent edifice, he considered it merely as a symbol of the Lord's merciful habitation for his true worshippers, and not as a real habitation for the Deity; as if JEHOVAH must needs continue his regard to it and the people, however they behaved : and the language of their prophets, as well as the Babylonish captivity, should have taught the Jews to expect, that the temple would be destroyed, whenever their presumption and rebellion provoked God to turn against

4 T 8

50 Hath *not my hand made all these things?

51 Ye *stiff-necked and 'uncircumcised in heart and ears, ye do always *resist the Holy Ghost; *as your fathers did, so do ye.

52 *Which of the prophets have not your fathers persecuted? and they have slain them *which shewed before of the coming of *the Just One; *of whom ye have been now the betrayers and murderers:

53 Who 'have received the law by

---

them, and be their enemy. (*Notes*, 1 *Kings* viii. 27. ix. 3—9. *Is.* lxvi. 1, 2. *Jer.* vii. 1—15.) The chosen race, Abraham and his seed, had served God above four hundred years, before the law of Moses was promulgated, or the tabernacle erected; and Solomon's temple was not built till four hundred and eighty years afterwards. So that nearly half the time, from the calling of Abraham till the coming of the Messiah, the true worshippers had served God, without the temple: and could those things be essential to true religion, which had not existed during so many ages?—*The tabernacle of witness*. (44) Thus the LXX. translate the Hebrew words, which may signify " the ta-" bernacle of meeting;" namely, the place where the congregation assembled, where they hoped to meet God with acceptance, and where he had appointed to meet them.—*Heaven*, &c. (49, 50) The quotation is not made exactly from the LXX; (*Is.* lxvi. 1, 2;) and it varies both from that and the Hebrew, by putting the last clause as a question: " Hath not?" ' As Stephen had been accused ' of blaspheming the temple; he, with great propriety, ' takes occasion to speak of their sacred places with due ' reverence, as raised by special direction from God; and ' yet corrects that extravagant regard to them, and confi-' dence in them, which the Jews were ready to entertain.' *Doddridge*.

The pattern. (44) Τον τυπον. 43. xxiii. 25. *John* xx. 25. *Rom.* v. 14. vi. 17. 1 *Cor.* x. 6. *Phil.* iii. 17. *Heb.* viii. 5, *et al.—Ex.* xxv. 40. *Sept.—A* tabernacle. (46) Σκηνωμα. 2 *Pet.* i. 13, 14. Not elsewhere. A σκηνη, *tabernaculum.—Made with hands.* (48) Χειροποιητοις. xvii. 24. *Mark* xiv. 58. *Eph.* ii. 11. *Heb.* ix. 11. 24.—*Rest.* (49) Καταπαυσεως. *Heb.* iii. 11. 18. iv. 1. 3. 5. 10, 11.—Not elsewhere N. T. *Ps.* cxxxii. 14. *Is.* lxvi. 1. *Sept.*

V. 51—53. It is conjectured with great probability, that the council, perceiving the scope of Stephen's discourse, and the conclusions which he was about to draw from it in favour of the gospel, as condemning their conduct, and justifying his own doctrine, grew so tumultuous, and shewed such indications of anger and impatience, that he found he should not be allowed to bring his argument to a regular conclusion. He was therefore emboldened and influenced by the Holy Spirit, to apply it in few words, but in the terms of most severe reproof, to the consciences of his furious and malignant judges. He addressed them as an obstinate untractable people, who rested in the outward sign of circumcision, while their hearts were closed by pride, enmity, and unbelief against the truth of God. (*Marg. Ref.* x, y.—*Notes, Lev.* xxvi. 41, 42. *Deut.* x. 16. xxx. 1—10, *v.* 6. *Jer.* iv. 3, 4. ix. 25, 26. *Rom.* ii. 25—29.) Indeed, to resist the Holy Spirit, by rejecting the testimony of inspired prophets, and fighting against them, and him that spake by them,

and by sinning in defiance of convictions, had always characterized the nation. (*Marg. Ref.* z, a.—*Notes, Is.* lxiii. 10. *Heb.* x. 28—31.) Thus their fathers had done in every age: they had opposed and persecuted the prophets, almost without exception, from Moses to Jeremiah, who foretold the captivity; and Ezekiel, and those that arose afterwards; who all, in one way or other, foretold the coming of that righteous Saviour and King, whom they had now traiterously delivered up to Pilate, and thus most basely murdered. (*Marg. Ref.* b—e.—*Notes, Matt.* xxiii. 34—39. *Luke* xi. 46—54.) They had indeed received the law, as given to Moses on mount Sinai, by JEHOVAH, amidst *ranks* of attendant and worshipping angels: and they were proud of that distinction. (*Marg. Ref.* f, g.— *Notes, Gal.* iii. 19—22. *Heb.* ii. 1—4.) But they had never applied their minds to understand, observe, or obey it, in its spiritual meaning, and with reference to " Christ, " the end of the law for righteousness to every believer." (*Note, Rom.* x. 1—4.)—The supposition before mentioned is the more probable, as Stephen began his defence in the most calm and respectful language, and touched on such topicks, as were suited to conciliate and gain the attention of the audience: but nothing can well exceed the marked severity of his conclusion. Had it not been expressly stated that he was " full of the Holy Ghost," when he spake it, many would have been ready to censure him : but probably he was sensible, that the council were determined on his death, out of desperate enmity to his Lord; and he was moved to bear this awful testimony against them, and thus to warn them against that destruction, which they were about to bring upon themselves; without further respect to their rank, or fear of their vengeance; but not without tender compassion for their souls, as his dying prayer evinced. ' Stephen, fired with ' a divine zeal, at length judges those who sat in judg-' ment on him.' *Beza.*—The crucifixion of Christ was the most flagrant violation of the sixth commandment, which ever was committed: and if David, having shed blood in war, or even having shed the blood of Uriah, must not build the temple; could it be supposed that the temple would be continued to those, who had shed the blood of the prophets, and filled up the measure of their crimes by " crucifying the Lord of glory?"

Ye stiff-necked. (51) Σκληροτραχηλοι.—Here only N. T. —*Ex.* xxxiii. 3. 5. xxxiv. 9. *Deut.* ix. 6. *Prov.* xxix. 1. *Sept.* Ex σκληρος, durus, et τραχηλος, cervix. ' Metaphora ' desumpta a jumentis refractariis et jugi impatientibus.' *Schleusner.—Uncircumcised.*] Απεριμητοι.—Here only N. T. —*Ex.* xii. 48. *Jer.* vi. 10. ix. 26. *Ez.* xliv. 7. *Sept.*—Ex α priv. et περιτεμνω, *circumcido.*—*Ye do ...resist.*] Αντιπιπ-τετε.—Here only. Ex αντι, et πιπτω, *cado.*—*Who shewed before.* (52) Τυς προκαταγγειλαντας. See on iii. 18.—*Be-*

4 Q

the disposition of angels, ᵍ and have not kept *it.*

54 ¶ When they heard these things ᵇ they were cut to the heart, and they ˡ gnashed on him with *their* teeth.

55 But he, being ᵏ full of the Holy Ghost, ˡ looked up stedfastly into heaven, ᵐ and saw the glory of God, and Jesus ⁿ standing on the right hand of God,

56 And said, Behold, ° I see the heavens opened, ᵖ and the Son of man ᑫ standing on the right hand of God.

57 Then ᑫ they cried out with a loud voice, and ʳ stopped their ears, and ran upon him with one accord,

58 And ˢ cast *him* out of the city, ᵗ and stoned *him:* ᵘ aud the witnesses laid down ˣ their clothes at a young man's feet, whose name was Saul.

59 And they stoned Stephen, ʸ calling upon *God,* and saying, ᶻ Lord Jesus, receive my spirit.

60 And ᵃ he kneeled down, and cried with a loud voice, ᵇ Lord, lay not this sin to their charge. And when ᵇ he had said this ᶜ he fell asleep.

trayers.] Προδοται. Luke vi. 16. 2 Tim. iii. 4.—*The disposition.* (53) Εις διαταγας. Rom. xiii. 2. Not elsewhere N.T.—Εzra iv. 11. Sept.—' Διαταγαι, a διατασσω: ordines, ' agmina disposita. Εις διαταγας αγγελων, præsente an- ' gelorum choro, seu, adstantibus angelorum agminibus.' Schleusner.

V. 54—60. (*Note,* v. 33—39.) The conclusion of Stephen's address enraged the malignant rulers even to madness; and they seemed like beasts of prey, who were about to devour him: they not only were cut in their hearts, as with a saw, but they gnashed their teeth with fury and anguish. (*Marg. Ref.* h, i.—*Note, Matt.* viii. 10—12.) Stephen, however, was not in the least intimidated by their fury: for, looking up to heaven as appealing to God, and being filled with the Holy Spirit, he was favoured with an extraordinary vision, as the ancient prophets had been. (*Notes, Is.* vi. 1—4. *Jer.* xxxi. 23—26. *Ez.* i. 1—3. viii. 1—4. xi. 22—25. 2 Cor. xii. 1—6. *Rev.* i. 9—11.) In this vision he saw a display of glory, which denoted the presence of God, and Jesus as Mediator " standing at his right hand," that is, in the place °ᶠ pre-eminent dignity and authority. On other occasions, Jesus is spoken of as " *sitting* on his throne:" (*Notes, Ps.* cx. 1. *Dan.* vii. 13, 14. *Matt.* xxii. 41—46. *Rom.* viii. 32— 34. *Col.* iii. 1—4, *v.* 1. *Heb.* xii. 2, 3. 1 *Pet.* iii. 21, 22:) but here he appeared *standing,* to signify his readiness to plead the cause, and receive the soul, of his suffering disciple. Immediately Stephen proclaimed aloud before his enraged enemies, what a glorious scene was now opened to his view: but they, treating it as blasphemy, or determined to hear nothing further, stopped their ears, furiously ran upon him, hurried him out of the city, and stoned him to death. (*Marg. Ref.* k—t.—*Note, Matt.* xxvi. 63—68.) The witnesses, who had accused him of blasphemous words, being required to begin the execution, laid down their clothes at the feet of Saul. (*Note, Deut.* xvii. 2—7.) As he was a native of Cilicia, (vi. 9. xxii. 3,) he had probably heard, or even taken part in, the preceding disputation with Stephen; and thus, the first time we read of this most eminent apostle, we find him consenting and accessary to the death of the first martyr for the faith of Christ!—(*Marg. Ref.* u, x.—*Notes,* viii. 1. xxii. 17—21.) —At length Stephen invoked his incarnate Lord, and committed his departing soul into his hands, in nearly the same words which Jesus had used in addressing the Father,

when he expired on the cross. (*Luke* xxiii. 46. *Note, Ps.* xxxi. 5.) He also calmly kneeled down; and amidst the agonies of this violent death, he copied his Lord's example when he prayed for his crucifiers; beseeching him, not to charge the guilt of this atrocious murder to those who perpetrated it; not to place it to their account; not to impute it to them, but to forgive it: (*Marg. Ref.* y—b.— *Notes, Ps.* xxxii. 1, 2. *Rom.* iv. 6—8. *Luke* xxiii. 32—38, *v.* 34:) and having spoken these words he expired, with the composure of one who falls asleep. (*Marg. Ref.* c.—*Note,* 1 *Thes.* iv. 13—18.)—The early loss of so eminent a minister of Christ, in this manner, must indeed have been a heavy affliction to the church: but how animated was his end! how suited to confirm the faith of the disciples! What an example also were his boldness and his tenderness, even for his murderers! The instruction and encouragement of this single scene might produce the most beneficial effects on multitudes, and that permanently; even far greater, than the long continued labours of many eminent ministers. Such in general has been the event of bloody persecution; and ' the noble army of martyrs' have done more, perhaps, towards the success of the gospel, by their sharp but transient sufferings, than the whole company of those who have professed and preached the truth, in quiet times; and without being called forth, thus to shew, in the fiery trial, the energy of their principles, and the power of divine grace, to the confusion of their enemies, and the encouragement of their brethren.—The prayer of Stephen was a most direct act of divine worship rendered to Jesus, appearing in human nature, as the Son of man, and attended by a vision of the glory of God. The word GOD does not occur in the original. To receive a departing soul to glory, and to pardon the guilt of most aggravated murder, are acts of divine power and authority; and it would be evidently most unreasonable, as well as unscriptural, to make such requests to any mere creature, whether present, or absent. (*Note, Matt.* ix. 2—8.) Indeed the Socinians are most grievously perplexed by this undeniable fact: after many other attempts to evade our inference from it, in which they have been evidently baffled in the argument; some very learned men have lately ventured to say, ' that the example of a man, in an ecstasy of ' devotion, and in the agonies of death, is not proper to be ' imitated by the whole church of God.' As if modern reasoners could better direct our faith and practice, than

this apostolical Protomartyr, when " full of the Holy
" Ghost," when immediately favoured " with the visions
" of God," and when replete with the very light, joy, and
temper of heaven itself!—And let it here be observed, that
we bring a very large number of positive evidences, to
support the truth of this doctrine. If then objectors make
very feeble efforts to invalidate the testimony of each of
them, considered as detached from the rest, so that each
still evinces the point in question; how very powerful
must be the combined proof of the whole! For if twenty,
or forty, or more, such texts were expunged out of the
Bible, we should not want sufficient, yea, unanswerable
evidence of the Deity of Christ.—It is here also enquired,
By what authority did the Jewish council put Stephen to
death? In the case of Jesus, they allowed, that they had
no such authority: and it is probable that their situation
was still the same. (Note, John xviii. 28—32.) Had they
proceeded to pass a legal sentence on Stephen, they would
perhaps have obtained permission from Pilate to execute
it: but they stoned him in a popular fury, without any regular sentence; and the governor might choose to connive
at it, as he did at some of their subsequent persecutions.
(Notes, viii. 1—4. ix. 1, 2.) ' The Jews were more than
' once ready to stone Christ, not only when by their own
' confession they had not power to put any one to death;
' but when nothing had passed which had the shadow of
' a legal trial. (John viii. 59. x. 31. xviii. 31.)' Doddridge.
—When the Jews would afterwards have put Paul to death,
the chief captain and the governor hindered them: yet, if
he had been killed, it is not unlikely that the irregularity
would have been connived at, had it not been discovered
that he was a Roman citizen. The sceptre, however, was
gradually departing from Judah; and the Romans continually intrenched, more and more, upon the authority of
the high priest and council, till the whole was subverted;
for Shiloh was come, and now the gathering of the people
was to Him. (Note, Gen. xlix. 10.)—' If the spirit of a
' man died with his body, no reason can be given, why St.
' Stephen should pray to the Lord Jesus to " receive his
' " spirit," rather than his body.' Whitby. (Notes, John
xiv. 2, 3. 2 Cor. v. 5—8. Phil. i. 21—26.)

They were cut to the heart. (54) Διεπριοντο ταις καρδιαις
αυτων. See on v. 33.—They gnashed.] Εβρυχον. Here
only N. T.—Job xvi. 9. Ps. xxxv. 16. Lam. ii. 16. Sept.
Βρυγμος· See on Matt. viii. 12.—Calling upon, &c. (59)
Επικαλομενον και λεγοντα, Κυριε Ιησυ, κ. τ. λ. ii. 21. ix. 14.
Rom. x. 12, 13. 1 Cor. i. 2.

PRACTICAL OBSERVATIONS.

V. 1—8.

We should be ready to " give a reason of the hope that
" is in us," to enquirers of every description: this ought
indeed to be done in meekness, and with cautious fear of
disgracing a cause, which should be dearer to us than our

lives; but we may confidently rely on the Lord to " give
" us in the same hour what we should speak," if called to
answer for ourselves before the enemies of his truth.
(Notes, Matt. x. 19, 20. 1 Pet. iii. 13—16.)—Whatever
bold and faithful application we may intend or be led to
make, of the doctrines which we inculcate, we should always speak with evident benevolence: and it is proper to
render civil respect and honour even to those superiors,
against whose usurped or abused authority we are constrained to protest.—In all addresses to those who allow
the truth of the scriptures, we should call their attention
to them, lodge our appeal with them, and thence deduce
our arguments.—It is very lawful and expedient to express
approbation of men's opinions, as far as consistent with
truth, and even to avoid the mention of their more harmless prejudices; in order that we may reason with them
from their own principles, and so oppose their erroneous
conclusions and evil practices.—It is also profitable to
recur to the first rise of those usages or sentiments, which
have been warped or perverted.—Would we know the
nature and effects of justifying faith, we should study the
character of " the father of the faithful." " The God of
" glory," to whom he had been a stranger, called him to
leave his country and friends: he ' through grace obeyed
' the calling;' and from that time he walked with God,
as his friend and worshipper. This may teach us the efficacy and freeness of divine grace, the nature of conversion,
and the way to follow the Lord in faith and hope, and to
wait for the fulfilment of his promises in humble patience.
Here too we may see, that external forms and distinctions (though idolized by numbers,) are of small value,
compared with dependence, submission, obedience, separation from the world, and devotedness to God.—The
promised seed are sojourners in a strange land; their inheritance is in reversion, and must be waited for; they
will be evil entreated in this world, and they should leave
it to God to judge their oppressors. Our deliverance from
the bondage of sin and Satan, is an introduction to our
serving the Lord according to his word: and, though the
external seals are not always posterior, in time, to the
grace of the covenant, they are in all cases of immensely
inferior importance, and only valuable as in one way or
other subservient to it: yet exact obedience in these and
all other things is our bounden duty.

V. 9—29.

Those whom God most favours will often be envied
and injured, even by those who are of reputation in the
visible church. But though the troubles of the righteous
man seem grievous and tedious; " the LORD delivereth
" him out of them all:" and wisdom, favour, and preferment are given by God alone. He often renders the
most despised persons the instruments of saving those
who contemned them; even as the insulted and crucified

apostles, having preached in the cities of Samaria, return to Jerusalem, 25. Philip is sent by an angel into the desert of Gaza, 26; where he meets with a eunuch, treasurer of Candace queen of Ethiopia, returning in his chariot from Jerusalem, and reading the prophecy of Isaiah, 27, 28. By a divine monition he joins the chariot, and preaches Jesus to the Ethiopian. 29—35; who, professing faith in him as "the Son "of God," is baptized, 36—38. The Spirit conveys away Philip, who preaches in the cities on the seacoast, till he comes to Cesarea: and the eunuch returns home rejoicing, 39, 40.

Jesus was "exalted to be a Prince and Saviour, to give "repentance and forgiveness to Israel."—All the promises of God will be accomplished in due season, and nothing can retard or hasten that appointed time.—Every earthly friend may fail, or requite our services with black ingratitude; but the Lord will not forsake his people.—In the darkest times of persecution, when treachery and cruelty have combined to destroy the church, the most eminent instruments of its deliverance have been raised up: and when peculiar services are to be performed, God furnishes his servants with suitable qualifications, and sometimes by means of those aliens, against whom they are destined to be employed.—Very useful persons have lived, for many years, among the enemies of God, and have possessed authority, wealth, or reputation in the world: but when he "puts it into their hearts" to join themselves to him and his people; they readily renounce these advantages, and endure reproach, hardship, and affliction for his sake.—Difficulties and perils await the believer, not only from open enemies, but from false or heartless brethren: and they, by whose hands the most extraordinary services have been performed, have found, often during many years, that the people did not understand the Lord's intentions respecting them.—Those who are doing wrong are generally most impatient of rebuke: and Jesus himself is rejected as a Ruler and a Judge, because his commands and decisions run counter to men's lusts and iniquities.—He who labours to persuade the professed people of God, to cease from their disgraceful and pernicious contests with each other, is generally exposed to reproach from those, who especially are most evidently criminal, as if he wanted to usurp authority not belonging to him.— But though men thus prolong their own miseries; the Lord will take care of his servants, and compass his own designs of mercy: and years of retired contemplation, devotion, and humble industry, are as useful to his servants, as those spent in a learned education, or in the active scenes of life: while a humble willingness to labour in obscurity, after having shone in more publick stations, is a happy indication of heavenly wisdom and genuine magnanimity. (Note, Ex. ii. 21. P. O. 11—25. Note, iii. 11.)

V. 30—43.

The best of men have cause to stand in awe, and even to tremble, in the presence of God; though, in infinite condescension, he is pleased to dwell in his church, as in a burning bush; to put honour on it, notwithstanding its meanness; and to preserve it amidst its fiery trials. (Note, Ex. iii. 2. P. O. 1—6.) He sees the affliction and hears the groaning of his people under distresses, oppressions, and persecutions; yea, he often sends his ministers to rescue sinners, when they are disposed to reject them.—If we would have Jesus for a Deliverer, we must submit to him as a Ruler, and wait for him as a Judge; else we shall perish with the Egyptians, and not be saved with the Is-

raelites. He is the great "Angel of the covenant," who brings his people from bondage, through the wilderness to their promised rest; and all the scenes exhibited in Egypt, at the Red Sea, at Sinai, and in Canaan, shadowed forth his excellences and his glorious salvation. But as Israel thrust Moses from them, and purposed to return to their bondage; so men in general will not obey Jesus, because they love this present evil world: and any kind of false religion, or irreligion, however absurd, by which men rejoice in their own works and imaginations, is more suitable to the carnal mind, than the spiritual truth and worship set before us in the sacred scriptures. (Notes, Ex. xxxii. 1—6. P. O. 1—14.) On this account, God is provoked to give men up to their lusts and delusions, and so they fill up their measure of sin, and perish without remedy.

V. 44—60.

Every review of the history of the world, of the church, or of our own hearts and lives, tends to "exclude boast- "ing," and to cover us with shame: and the whole scripture proclaims man to be a proud ungrateful rebel against God. He works by various means and instruments, and men are almost universally guilty of neglecting or of idolizing them. But as heaven is his throne and the earth his "footstool," none of our services can profit him, who "made all these things:" and next to the human Nature of Christ, the broken and spiritual heart is his most valued temple. (Note, Is. lvii. 15, 16.)—The plainest arguments, and the most incontestable facts, only irritate those, whose interests and passions have engaged them against the truth: and it is proper, that they should be shewn, in the most explicit manner, their guilt and danger, who with determined obstinacy "resist the Holy Spirit;" who are 'baptized infidels;' who tread in the steps of those that betrayed and murdered the just and gracious Saviour; and who habitually violate those very precepts, which they substitute in the place of his righteousness and atonement.—The application is generally the most useful, and often the most offensive, part of a discourse; without which the rest will have but a transient impression: but when sinners are convicted, and not humbled, they will be exasperated; and the greatest wisdom and grace cannot mollify them.—Though we are not favoured with prophetick visions, we may by faith stedfastly fix our thoughts and affections on heavenly things: thus we shall see the glory of God, and Jesus ever appearing in the Father's presence for us, enthroned in power, pleading our cause, and prepared to help us in all our distresses, and at last to receive our departing souls. We must not then refuse to confess his name, to declare his glory, and to avow our obligations to him, even in the presence of his most furious enemies. If we be called to suffer for his sake, we should the more earnestly call on his name, to support us under our trials, and to bring us to his glory; never forgetting to beseech him to forgive and bless our enemies

AND [a] Saul was consenting unto his death. And at that time [b] there was a great persecution against [c] the church which was at Jerusalem; [d] and they were all scattered abroad throughout the regions of Judea and [e] Samaria, [f] except the apostles.

2 And [g] devout men carried Stephen *to his burial.* [h] and made great lamentation over him.

3 As for [i] Saul, he made havock of the church, entering into every house, and haling men and women, committed *them* to prison.

4 Therefore [k] they that were scattered abroad went every where preaching the word.

---

and persecutors. Thus may we follow those, " who " through faith and patience now inherit the promises ;" that while we live, we may glorify Him ; and whenever we die, we may fall asleep in the arms of his power, truth, and love; to be received into " his presence, where is " fulness of joy," and to share " the pleasures that are " at his right hand for evermore."

NOTES.

CHAP. VIII. V. 1. The word "consenting," is much too feeble: the original implies complacency, and cordial approbation. (Note, xxii. 17—21.)—As the rulers had compassed the death of Stephen, without exciting an insurrection of the people, or the resentment of the governor, they ventured to carry on the persecution with increasing violence.—The whole subsequent history shews, that a great number of believers continued at Jerusalem : though it is probable, that the most of those, who commonly resided in other countries, returned home at that time : and many others doubtless fled from the storm. But the preachers of the gospel were particularly aimed at, and were especially scattered. The apostles, however, though principally obnoxious, stood their ground : they were satisfied that their presence was still necessary at Jerusalem : and their enemies were so restrained or overawed, that they did not venture to assault them—though no doubt, they zealously and diligently laboured to promote the gospel. (Marg. Ref. a. f.—Notes, Neh. vi. 10 —14. 1 Cor. xvi. 5—9, v. 9.)—' It is a very ancient ' tradition ... that our Lord assigned twelve years after his ' ascension, for the conversion of the unbelieving Jews in ' Judea, ... saying to his apostles, Go ye out into the ' world after twelve years. ... It shews the reason, why the ' apostles continued at Jerusalem, while the rest of the ' disciples were scattered abroad.' *Whitby.* As the scripture says nothing of this, it is far more probable, especially after the command before given, (v. 20,) that the apostles, considering the importance of their station at this crisis, and the necessity of shewing both friends and enemies, that they were not to be intimidated ; and, depending on special protection, acted as Daniel did on a similar occasion, and left the event to God. (Notes, Dan. vi.)—As the disciples had before lived in much harmony and comfort together; they would not perbaps have thought of separating so soon, if this storm had not arisen : thus the efforts of Satan and his servants were over-ruled for the promulgation of the gospel; while the apostles were competent for all the work which was to be done in Jerusalem, and the persecution would not prevent, but forward their success.

Was consenting.] Ην συνευδοκων. xxii. 20. *Luke* xi. 48. *Rom.* i. 32. Ex συν, et ευδοκεω, *Matt.* iii. 17. xvii. 5. Ευδοκια· See on *Matt.* xi. 26.—*Death.*] Αναιρεσει. xxii. 20. Not elsewhere. ' *Interfectio, cædes, internecio.*' Schleusner. —*Were scattered abroad.*] Διεσπαρησαν. 4. xi. 19. Not elsewhere. *Dissemino, semina spargo.* Were sown like seed.

V. 2. Even in the prospect of this rising storm, some of the devoted servants of Christ ventured to give an honourable interment to the mangled body of Stephen ; and to lament their own loss, and that of the church, in the premature removal of so able and faithful a minister, from whose continued labours so great things might have bee. expected. (Note, Is. lvii. 1, 2.) Thus honourably and publickly to bury one stoned by the council, as a blasphemer, and as such *accursed,* was a very courageous display of faith, zeal, and confidence in God. It must also have greatly offended the persecutors ; and perhaps served as a pretence for their subsequent violence. (*Marg. Ref.*)

Devout.] Ευλαβεις. See on *Luke* ii. 25.—*Carried ... to his burial.*] Συνεκομισαν. Here only. ' *Præparo mortuum ' ad sepulturam.*' Schleusner. Ex συν, et κομιζω, *fero, porto.*

V. 3. Saul, having distinguished himself at Stephen's martyrdom, was judged a suitable agent in the service of the persecutors ; and he furiously engaged in it, like a savage tiger or wolf, making havock among the defenceless sheep!—The circumstance of Saul's entering every house of the disciples, and dragging away, not only men, but women also, and casting them into prison, should be carefully noted. He " was exceedingly mad against them." —Doubtless many were cut off at this time : yet Pilate seems to have connived at it. (*Marg. Ref.—Notes,* vii. 54 —60. ix. 1, 2. xxvi. 9—11.)

He made havock.] Ελυμαινετο. Here only. ' Verbum ' proprium de feris, viz. leonibus, apris, lupis, &c. A ' λυμη, exitium, noxa.' Schleusner.

V. 4. *Marg. Ref.—They that were scattered,* &c.] ' Not ' the whole church of Jerusalem, or the body of the laity; ' ... for what authority had they to preach the word? but ' the hundred and eight that were " full of the Holy ' " Ghost." ' *Whitby.*—The whole company, after our Lord's ascension, was about one hundred and twenty, that is, one hundred and eight besides the twelve apostles : but it clearly appears from the history, that the women formed a part of this number. After so great an increase of the church, as had since that time taken place, it may well be supposed, that many had been set apart for the ministry before the martyrdom of Stephen. So that, even allowing that none were scattered, except the ministers ;

5 Then [l] Philip went down to [m] the city of Samaria, [n] and preached Christ unto them.

6 And the people [o] with one accord gave heed unto those things which Philip spake, hearing and seeing the miracles which he did.

7 For [p] unclean spirits, crying with loud voice, came out of many that were possessed *with them:* and many taken with [q] palsies, and that were [r] lame, were healed.

8 And [s] there was great joy in that city.

l 1. 14, 15. 40. vi. 5. xxi. 8.
m i. 8. Matt. x. 5, 6.
n 35—37. v. 42. ix. 20. xvii. 2, 3. John iv. 25, 26. 1 Cor. i. 23. ii. 2. iii. 11.
o xiii. 44. 2 Chr. xxx. 12. Matt. xx. 15, 16. John iv. 41, 42.
p v. 16. Matt. x. 1. Mark ix. 26. xvi. 17, 18. Luke x. 17. John xiv. 12. Heb. ii. 4.
q ix. 33, 34. Mark ii. 3—11.
r iii. 6, 7. xiv. 8—10. Is. xxxv. 6. Matt. xi. 5. xv. 30, 31.
s xiii. 48. 52. Ps. xcvi. 10—12. xcviii. 2—4. Is. xxxv. 1, 2. xlii. 10—12. Luke ii. 10, 11. Rom. xv. 9—12.

(which is extremely improbable;) it is incongruous to limit the number in this manner.—'There is no room to 'enquire where these poor refugees had their orders. They 'were endued with miraculous gifts; and if they had not 'been so, the extraordinary call they had to spread the 'knowledge of Christ, wherever they came, among those 'who were ignorant of him, would abundantly justify 'them in what they did.' *Doddridge.*—Were then all the Christians endued with miraculous powers? or might none, who were not, declare, what they had seen and heard?—'Some difference may perhaps be here observed between 'ευαγγελιζεσθαι, ... and κηρυσσειν: ... not in respect of the 'matter of their preaching, but of the manner of it. The 'latter ... doth generally signify a publick solemn pro-'claiming of Christ, as when a ... herald or crier doth ... '*by way of office* proclaim any thing: but the former im-'ports no more, than the telling it, making it known; as 'good news is published, without the voice of a herald or 'crier, by all that have heard it, to all they meet with. ... 'Not that ευαγγελιζεσθαι is never used of that publick, au-'thoritative proclaiming; for it is sometimes used of the 'apostles: and the word ... Evangelist is the name of 'an office in the apostles' times. ... But, I say, that some-'times, and particularly in this place, it may belong to 'whatsoever publishing the gospel of Christ; and by 'whomsoever, that is, by those who have no calling to it. 'For when the doctrine of Christ was first preached by the 'apostles, ... and a multitude of ... Jews and proselytes 'received the faith, and for doing so professedly, were 'presently persecuted and driven out of Jerusalem; it is 'not to be imagined, but that all, wheresoever they came, 'both men and women, published what they knew, both 'of the doctrine, and the miracles by which it was con-'firmed, and of their own sufferings for it. ... When of 'Philip, who was a deacon ... it is related, ... that "he '"preached Christ," it follows that he baptized also.—'But of these other disciples, there is no more said, but 'that they passed along ... *publishing this good news*, the 'gospel which they had received; but no mention of 'gathering disciples, or baptizing. Accordingly ... when 'there is mention ... of these very men, that being scat-'tered by the persecution, ... they spake the word, or pub-'lished the gospel, ... the phrase used is observable: (xi. '19. Gr:) the word λαλειν being known to belong to any 'way of reporting, or relating, by talk or discourse. ... 'And upon the success of this, through God's prospering 'hand, and many receiving the faith, it follows, that ... 'the church of Jerusalem ... sent Barnabas to visit and 'confirm them. ... Thus Apollos (xviii. 25) spake and 'taught exactly the things concerning the Lord, knowing 'only the baptism of John.' *Hammond.*—It appears to me, that the remarks contained in this quotation, are suited to throw much light on a difficult and disputed subject. Whether the learned author's criticism on the original words be exact, or not; the difference between statedly and authoritatively, as a herald, and by office and authority, preaching to regularly convened congregations; and simply declaring what a man knows of Christ and salvation, among relations, juniors, ignorant neighbours, or ignorant persons of any sort, without assuming any authority, seems of great importance. No doubt, in this way, a man's sphere will often gradually enlarge, till he appears something like an authoritative preacher: but would it not then be proper, that pastors and rulers should send some Barnabas, to confirm what has been done, and to confer the due authority? and would it not be right, in this case, for the person himself to seek, from the pastors and teachers of the church, their regular sanction to his labours, now become more publick, than he at first either expected or intended?—To authorize all who choose, without any human appointment, and in ordinary cases, to become authoritative preachers, seems a dangerous extreme: and to suppose that no man, in an ignorant family, or among poor children, or illiterate neglected persons, may expound a chapter of sacred scripture, or talk to them about their souls, except previously ordained to the ministry; appears suited to destroy all zeal in the laity for the success of the gospel, and to prevent all communication of knowledge to a deluded and perishing world; except by those, who are so fully employed in their own several charges, as to have little opportunity of attempting any thing further; and who are often restricted, by peculiar circumstances, from every exertion out of their own line and department. (*Note,* vi. 8.)—*Scattered abroad.*] *Notes, Ps.* lxxii. 16. *Hos.* ii. 21—23. *Zech.* x. 5—12.

Preaching the word.] Ευαγγελιζομενοι τον λογον. 12. 25. 35. 40. v. 42. x. 46. xiv. 7. 15. 21. xv. 35. xvi. 10. xvii. 18. *Luke* ii. 10. *Rom.* x. 15. 1 *Cor.* i. 17. *Eph.* iii. 8. See on *Matt.* xi. 5.

V. 5—8. It is evident, that Philip the apostle was not here meant, for he continued at Jerusalem; and the mission of Peter and John to Samaria evinces the same: (*Note,* 14—17:) and as Philip, one of the seven, was the only person of that name, whom the historian had mentioned, he was doubtless here spoken of. (*Marg. Ref.* l.—*Note,* vi. 2—6, *v.* 5.)—As Jesus had stayed two days among the Samaritans, and had mentioned them among those, to whom the apostles were to preach; (*Notes,* i. 4—8. *John* iv. 39—42;) the apostles do not seem to have hesitated about the admission of the Samaritans into the church, notwithstanding the bigoted enmity of the Jews against them. Probably, Philip went to the same city, (Sychar) where Christ had preached: and, though the impressions made by his word might, in many instances, have been effaced: yet when Philip preached Jesus to them, as the promised Messiah, and wrought many signal mira-

9 ¶ But there was a certain man called Simon, which before-time in the same city ' used sorcery, and bewitched the people of Samaria, " giving out that himself was some great one;

10 To whom ˣ they all gave heed, from the least to the greatest, saying, ʸ This man is ˮ the great power of God.

11 And to him they had regard, because that of long time ª he had bewitched them with sorceries.

12 But when ᵇ they believed Philip preaching the thiugs ᶜ concerning the kingdom of God, and the name of Jesus Christ, they were baptized, ᵈ both men and women.

13 Then Simon himself ᵉ believed

also: and when he was baptized, he continued with Philip, ᶠ and wondered, beholding the ˮ miracles and signs which were done.

14 ¶ Now ʳ when the apostles, which were at Jerusalem, heard that Samaria ʰ had ʰ received the word of God, they sent unto them ¹ Peter and John:

15 Who, when they were come down, ᵏ prayed for them, that they might receive the Holy Ghost.

16 For as yet ¹ he was fallen upon none of them: ᵐ only they were baptized in the name of the Lord Jesus.

17 Then ⁿ laid they *their* hands on them, ° and they received the Holy Ghost.

---

cles in proof of his resurrection from the dead; they with one consent attended on his ministry, and expressed great joy throughout the çity, that this blessed " gospel of sal-" vation" had been sent to them, and that they were invited and admitted to share the blessings of the Messiah's kingdom. (*Marg. Ref.* m—s.—*Notes, John* iv. 5—9. 16—18.)

To the city, &c. (5) Εις πολιν της Σαμαρειας. Or, " to a city of Samaria."—*Preached Christ.*] Εκηρυσσεν τον Χριστ. ix. 20. Mark xvi. 15. 20. 1 Cor. i. 23. xv. 11, 12. —See on *Matt.* iii. 1.

V. 9—13. It is evident that Simon actually used sorcery, and produced many extraordinary effects by satanical influence, and not merely by human imposture: (*Marg. Ref.* t.—*Notes, Ex.* vii. 11, 12. 22, 23. xxii. 18:) and, while he boasted, " that he was some great one," (*Note,* 2 *Pet.* ii. 18, 19,) the Samaritans were so exceedingly astonished at his sorceries, that they were even fascinated into a belief, that he was a man by whom the great power of God was most signally displayed and exerted : perhaps he avowed himself, or was supposed, to be the promised Messiah. (*Marg. Ref.* u—a.—*Note, Gal.* iii. 1 1 *Cor.* i. 20—24. *Gal.* iii. 1—5, *v.* 1.) Ecclesiastical historians have given us strange accounts of the horrid blasphemies, which this man propagated ; but these seem to have been subsequent to the events here recorded.—The evident and beneficent miracles of Philip, however, confirming his doctrine concerning the kingdom of God, and the salvation of Jesus Christ, being attended by a peculiar blessing, effectually rescued many of the people from the infatuation, and prevailed on them to profess faith in Christ, by being baptized : and, as in Christ there is no distinction of male or female, both men and women were thus received into the church. (*Marg. Ref.* b—d.—*Note, Gal.* iii. 26 —29, *v.* 28.) Perhaps Philip exposed the nature and tendency of Simon's magical arts. At length, however, that sorcerer professed himself a believer, and probably had a strong conviction in his mind and conscience of the truth of the gospel : accordingly he too was baptized, and continued to attend on Philip with great assiduity ; being ᴀ much astonished by beholding Philip's miracles, as the

Samaritans had been by *his* sorceries.—Perhaps Simon deemed Philip a magician of superior skill and attainments, and hoped to get acquainted with the secret of his art, by which he produced effects, far exceeding all that he himself had been able to perform. (*Marg.* and *Marg. Ref.* e, f. —*Notes,* xix. 13—20. *Ex.* vii. 22, 23. *Num.* xxii. 5.)— " Simon believed also," ' that this Jesus, who enabled ' Philip to do these things, was some power superior to ' any he conversed with.' *Whitby.*

Used sorcery. (9) Μαγευων. Here only. Μαγος, *Matt.* ii. 2. (Note, *Matt.* ii. 1, 2.)—*Bewitched.*] Εξιρων. 11. 13. See on *Mark* iii. 21.—*Some great one.*] Τινα μεγαν. See v. 36. Gr.—*The great power of God.* (10) 'Η·δυναμις τε Θεε ἡ μεγαλη. *Rom.* i. 16. 1 *Cor.* i. 18. 24. 2 *Thes.* ii. 9. 2 *Pet.* ii. 11. *Rev.* xiii. 2.—*Sorceries.* (11) Μαγειαις. Here only. —Simon was first a magician, and then he aspired to be a prophet and an apostle. (Note, *Num.* xxii. 5.)—*He continued.* (13) Ην προσκαρτερων. See on i. 14.

V. 14—17. The apostles acted in concert, as a collective body; no one arrogating authority over the others, but every one paying a great regard to the determination of the whole company. Peter, therefore, who was in every thing the most forward to speak and to act, and John the beloved disciple, were " sent " by their brethren to confirm the converted Samaritans in the faith. When they came to the city, and saw the effects of Philip's ministry ; they, by prayer and imposition of hands, obtained for the converts the Holy Spirit ; that is, his miraculous gifts und operations. For though, as believers, they partook of his regenerating, sanctifying, and comforting influences ; yet they had not before been favoured with these extraordinary communications. ' Without doubt, Peter and John were ' sent by the other apostles, partly that they might con-' firm the doctrine of Philip the deacon; and partly that ' they might establish a church in that city by apostolical ' authority.' *Beza.* (*Marg. Ref.* g—m.)—Some expositors maintain, that none received the miraculous gifts of the Holy Spirit, except such as were marked out by God himself, to be pastors and teachers : and others seem to think, that the whole company of Christians partook of them. This, however, is unlikely ; (1 *Cor.* xii. 29, 30;) yet it is

4 q 7

18 ¶ And when Simon saw that through laying on of the apostles' hands, the Holy Ghost was given, ᵖ he offered them money,

19 Saying, ᵠ Give me also this power, that on whomsoever I lay hands, he may receive the Holy Ghost.

20 But Peter said unto him, ʳThy money perish with thee, because ˢthou hast thought that ᵗthe gift of God may be purchased with money.

21 Thou ᵘhast neither part nor lot in this matter: ˣfor thy heart is not right in the sight of God.

22 ʸRepent therefore of this thy wickedness, ᶻand pray God, ᵃif perhaps ᵇthe thought of thine heart may be forgiven thee.

23 For I perceive that thou art in ᶜthe gall of bitterness, and in ᵈthe bond of iniquity.

plain, that others, besides the ministers, were thus favoured. It is probable, that many received the gift of the Holy Spirit, by the laying on of the apostles' hands; and that from among these persons, the ministers were generally selected, by those who were entrusted with that important concern. (Notes, xiii. 1—3. xiv. 21—23. xix. 1—7. 2 Tim. ii. 1, 2. Tit. i. 5—9.)—It may be supposed, that Peter and John ordained ministers in this city of the Samaritans. But it does not appear, that their laying of hands on some, " that they might receive the Holy " Spirit," after having prayed for the company in general that they might partake of these benefits, implied previous ordination.—The rite of confirmation, as practised by many Christian churches, has often been, and still is, spoken of, as a continuation of this apostolical imposition of hands, for the confirmation of new converts, by the Holy Spirit thus given to them. But it is far from evident, that this was done universally by the apostles, or by those who immediately succeeded them. As, however, miraculous powers, rather than *sanctifying grace*, were thus conferred; unless miraculous powers were now connected with that rite, the parallel must wholly fail. How far something of this kind, properly regulated and conducted, may be rendered subservient to the edification of young persons, descended from Christian parents, and baptized when infants, is another question: but to advance this observance into a sacrament, and even above a sacrament, (as it certainly is advanced, when the Holy Spirit is supposed to be conferred by imposition of hands, and by using words in prayer like those of Peter and John,) puts the subject in a very different light. Doubtless it was at first thus magnified, in order to exalt the episcopal order, to whom the administration of it was confined, as if they were entrusted with apostolical authority: but as miracles are out of the question; so to follow the apostles in faith, humility, diligence, in " preaching in season, out of " season," in piety, and self-denial, is the only scriptural or adequate method of magnifying either the episcopal or the clerical office. Assuredly, as this matter is very often conducted, it must be allowed to be an evil; and it ought either to be attended to in another manner, or not at all. —It appears indisputable that Philip was, before these transactions, a regularly ordained minister, or evangelist. (Note, vi. 2—6.)

V. 18—24. Many teachers, and probably private Christians, wrought miracles, and spake with tongues, " as " the Spirit gave them utterance:" but the honour of communicating those gifts, by imposition of hands and prayer, was, generally at least, restricted to the apostles. When Simon, therefore, saw the effects which followed from the laying on of their hands; he concluded, that they could, if they chose, impart to him a similar power, supposing that the whole power was at their disposal. (Note, 2 Cor. xiii. 7—10.) This he supposed would admirably subserve his purpose, of obtaining honour and wealth : for by enabling men at his own will to speak foreign languages, without the trouble of learning them; and to cure diseases by a word, he should not only carry on a most lucrative trade, but be almost adored as a deity. Judging therefore of the apostles by himself, and seeing that they were very poor men; he supposed that they would willingly confer this power on him for a sum of money, and he ventured to make this infamous proposal to them. (Marg. Ref. p, q.) His ambitious mind could not be satisfied with the power of working miracles himself; (though indeed this seems not to have been conferred on him;) but he aspired to the unrestricted power of communicating the Holy Spirit, for the same purposes, to whom he pleased. Instead of deeming the very lowest place, among the people of God, too great an honour for one, whose sorcery, impiety, and blasphemy had been so atrocious; as he certainly would have done, if he had been truly converted: he aspired, with horrible pride and ambition, at equality with the apostles in power and authority; while he meant to prostitute the sacred operations of the Holy Spirit, to gratify his love of filthy lucre and of human applause, and attempted to seduce the apostles to concur in the detestable sacrilege!—Whatever miraculous power of discerning men's spirits Peter might possess, and on some occasions exercise, he had no need of it in this case : but, perceiving the extreme wickedness and hypocrisy of Simon, he expressed his abhorrence of his money and of his crime, in the most decided manner. Let him take his treasure with him, if he could, into that perdition, to which he was evidently hastening; for Peter would have none of it. This was not a wish that Simon might perish; but an awful warning that he was in most extreme danger of perdition, which he could not escape if he proceeded further in his present course. Peter added, that he made this proposal, because, being utterly ignorant of God and spiritual things, and awfully blinded by Satan, he had blasphemously thought, that the free and most precious gift of God's Spirit might be bought and sold by a mercenary traffick. (Marg. Ref. r—t.) He was, therefore, evidently destitute

GAZA.

Josh. xv. 47. Judges i. 18; xvi. 21. Jerem. xlvii. 5. Zeph. ii. 4. Zech. ix. 5. Acts viii. 26.

24 Then answered Simon, and said,
[e] Pray ye to the Lord for me, that none
of these things which ye have spoken
come upon me.
25 And they, [f] when they had testified and preached the word of the Lord,
returned to Jerusalem, and preached
the gospel in many [g] villages of the
Samaritans.
26 ¶ And [h] the angel of the Lord
spake unto Philip, saying, [i] Arise, and
go toward the south, unto the way
that goeth down from Jerusalem unto
[k] Gaza, which is [l] desert.
27 And [m] he arose and went: and,
behold, [n] a man of Ethiopia, an eunuch
of great authority under Candace
[o] queen of the Ethiopians, who had the
charge of all her treasure, [p] and had
come to Jerusalem for to worship,
28 Was returning, [q] and sitting in
his chariot read [r] Esaias the prophet.

e Gen. xx. 7. 17. Ex. viii. 8. x. 17. xii. 32. Num. xxi. 7. 1 Sam. xii. 19. 23. 1 Kings xiii. 6. Ezra vi. 10. viii. 23. Job xlii. 8. Jam. v. 16.
f i. 8. xviii. 5. xx. 21. xxvi. 22, 23. xxviii. 23. 28. 31. John xv. 27. 1 Pet. v. 12.
g Luke ix. 52—56.
h v. 19. x. 7. 22. xii. 8—11. 23. xxvii. 23. 2 Kings i. 3. Heb. i. 14.
i 1 Chr. xxii. 16. Is. lx. 1, &c.
k Josh. xiii. 3. xv. 47. Zech. ix. 5.
l Matt. iii. 1—3. Luke iii. 2—4.
m Matt. xxi. 2—6. Mark xiv. 13—16. John ii. 5—8. Heb. xi. 8.
n Ps. lxviii. 31. lxxxvii. 4. Is. xliii. 6. xlv. 14. lx. 3—6. lxvi. 19, 20. Jer. xiii. 23. xxxviii. 7. xxxix. 16. Zeph. iii. 10.
o 1 Kings x. 1. Matt. xii. 42.
p 1 Kings viii. 41—43. Ps. lxviii. 29. Is. lvi. 3—8. John xii. 20.
q xvii. 11, 12. Deut. vi. 6, 7. xi. 18—20. xvii. 18, 19. Josh. i. 8. Ps. i. 2, 3. cxix. 99. 111. Prov. ii. 1—6. viii. 33, 34. John v. 39, 40. Col. iii. 16. 2 Tim. iii. 15—17.
r xxviii. 25. Is. i. 1. *Isaiah.* Luke iii. 4. iv. 17.

of true faith, and "had neither part or lot" in the blessings of the gospel; as "his heart was not right in the "sight of God," nor was his profession of Christianity sincere. If he would then escape perdition, let him deeply repent of this most horrid wickedness, and pray earnestly to God, that this blasphemous thought of his depraved heart might be pardoned. For though "all manner of "sin and blasphemy shall be forgiven" to the true penitent; yet Simon's crime came *at least* so near to that against the Holy Spirit, which never can be pardoned, that it was a very doubtful case, whether God would ever give him true repentance. (*Marg. Ref.* u—b.—*Notes, Matt.* xii. 31, 32. 2 *Tim.* ii. 23—26.) Indeed he was, as it were, so plunged and drenched in impiety, as in the bitterest gall; that he must be most loathsome in the sight of God, and exposed to the most dreadful punishment; and he was, evidently, so bound in the chains of sin and Satan, that the almighty power of God alone could deliver him. (*Marg. Ref.* c, d.)—Nothing can be more evident, than that the apostle here exhorted an unconverted sinner to repentance and prayer; yea, one who he feared had committed the unpardonable sin, though he did not look upon his case as absolutely hopeless.—When Simon heard this awful warning, denunciation, and exhortation, he desired the apostles to "pray for him:" not that he might be delivered from his ambition, avarice, and impiety; but that he might be exempted from the punishments, which they had mentioned. Perhaps he feared a doom similar to that of Ananias and Sapphira: or he hoped, that by inducing the apostles to conceal his crime, he might escape infamy, and have an opportunity of carrying on his delusions. For he does not seem to have professed any repentance, or to have prayed for himself. (*Note,* 1 *Sam.* xv. 30, 31.)—Credible historians inform us, that he retained a sort of profession of Christianity, which he distorted by the most horrible and senseless blasphemies; and thus he became the founder of a most multifarious sect of hereticks, who were long the trial and the scandal of the church. (*Marg. Ref.* e.)—From his infamous attempt, to bargain for the power of conferring the Holy Spirit, all mercenary contracts for church-benefices, and other methods of turning the concerns of religion into a lucrative trade, are called *Simony;* of which there have been, and are, a great variety of *species;* and will be, so long as men continue covetous and ambitious, and verily suppose that "gain is godliness." It is therefore much easier to expose and declaim against such impious practices, than to find an effectual remedy for them.—Alas, Simon Magus has left far more indisputable successors, than Simon Peter has done: especially in that church which grounds its claims on succeeding to St. Peter's authority; but not in that church alone. (*Notes* and *P. O. Is.* lvi. 9—12. *P. O. Rev.* xviii. 9—19.)—'It' (the sin of Simon) 'struck at the very foun-'dation of the Christian faith; supposing that the apostles, 'and other Christians, did their miracles, by some higher 'art of magick, than that which he had learned; and so 'they by the same art could teach others to do the same 'works for any other end.' *Whitby.* (*Notes, Ex.* vii. 13. 22, 23.)—'They who buy and sell sacred things are the 'successors, not of Simon Peter, but of Simon Magus.' *Beza.*

Laying on. (18) Της επιθεσεως. 1 *Tim.* iv. 14. 2 *Tim.* i. 6. *Heb.* vi. 2. Not elsewhere. Επιτιθημι, 17. 19.—*Perish with thee.* (20) Συν σοι ειη εις απωλειαν. xxv. 16. *Matt.* vii. 13. *John* xvii. 12. *Phil.* iii. 19. 2 *Pet.* ii. 1, 2, 3. iii. 7. 16. *Rev.* xvii. 11. *Notes, Is.* xxxiii. 15, 16. *Matt.* xxvi. 14—16. xxviii. 3—5. 1 *Tim.* vi. 6—10, *vv.* 9, 10. 2 *Pet.* ii. 15, 16.—*The gift of God.*] Την δωρεαν τυ Θευ. See on *John* iv. 10. Note, *Matt.* x. 7, 8.—*Right.* (21) Ευθεια. ix. 11. xiii. 10. *Matt.* iii. 3. *Luke* iii. 4, 5. Note, *Ps.* cxxv. 4, 5, *v.* 5. —*The gall of bitterness.* (23) Χολην της πικριας. Χολη. *Matt.* xxvii. 34. Not elsewhere N. T.—*Deut.* xxxii. 32. *Ps.* lxix. 21. *Prov.* v. 4. *Sept.*—Πικρια. *Rom.* iii. 14. *Eph.* iv. 31. *Heb.* xii. 15.—*Ps.* x. 7. *Jer.* ii. 21. *Sept.*—*The bond.*] Συνδεσμον. *Eph.* iv. 3. *Col.* ii. 19. iii. 14.—1 Kings vi. 10. *Is.* lviii. 6. *Dan.* v. 6. *Sept.* *Note,* 2 *Pet.* ii. 4—9, *v.* 4.

V. 25. The apostles, having performed the service on which they had been sent; and having "testified, and "preached the word of the Lord" in this city of Samaria, set out to return to Jerusalem, and in their journey they preached the gospel with success (for so the word implies,) in many villages of the Samaritans. John was one of those, who formerly asked leave to call for fire from heaven, to consume certain of that nation; but his Lord had now taught him better things. (*Marg. Ref.*—*Note, Luke* ix. 51—56.)

Had testified.] Διαμαρτυραμενοι. See on ii. 40.—*Preached the gospel in many villages,* &c.] Πολλας τε κωμας ευηγγελισαντο. See on 4.

V. 26—31. Philip seems to have continued some time among the Samaritans, after the return of the apostles: at length an angel was sent to order him immediately to go to a part of the road, between Jerusalem and Gaza, which lay through a desert: and he obeyed without demurring; though it must have appeared strange to be sent a journey

29 Then ᵃ the Spirit said unto Philip, Go near, and join thyself to this chariot.

30 And Philip ʳ ran thither to *him*, and heard him read the prophet Esaias, and said, ᵘ Understandest thou what thou readest?

31 And he said, ˣ How can I, except some man should guide me? ʸ And he desired Philip that he would come up and sit with him.

32 The place of the scripture which he read was this, ᶻ He was led ᵃ as a sheep to the slaughter; ᵇ and like a lamb dumb before his shearer, so ᶜ opened he not his mouth:

33 In ᵈ his humiliation his ᵉ judgment was taken away; ᶠ and who shall declare his generation? ᶠ for his life is taken from the earth.

34 And the eunuch answered Philip, and said, I pray thee, ᵇ of whom speaketh the prophet this? of himself, or of some other man?

35 Then Philip ⁱ opened his mouth, and ᵏ began at the same scripture, and ˡ preached unto him Jesus.

Left margin references:
a x. 19. xi. 2. xiii.
2—4. xvi. 6, 7.
xx. 22, 2ᵌ.
1 Cor. xii. 11.
Tim. iv. 1.
r Ps. cxix. 32.
Ec. ix. 10. John
iv. 34.
u Matt. xiii. 19.
23. 51, xv. 10.
xxvi. 15. Mark
xiii. 14. Luke
xxiv. 44, 45.
John x.30. 1 Cor.
xiv. 19. Rev.
xiii. 18.
x Ps. xxv. 8, 9.
lxxiii. 16, 17. 22.
Prov. xxx. 2, 3.
Is. xxix. 18, 19.
xxxv. 8. Matt.
xviii. 3, 4. Mark
x. 15. 1 Cor. iii.
18. viii. 2. 1 ix.
36, 37. Jam. i.
10. 21. 1 Pet. ii.
1, 2.
y 2 Kings x. 9. 26. x. 15, 16.
xxii. 8. ii. 40. Rom. viii. 36.
z Is. liii. 7, 8.
b John i. 29.
a Ps. xliv. 11, 22. Jer. xi. 19.
1 Pet. i. 19. ii. 21—24.

Right margin references:
so c Ps. xxxii. 2, 9.
Matt. xxvi. 62,
63. Luke xxiii.
34. John xviii. 9
—11.
d Phil. ii. 8, 9.
e Job xxvii. 2.
xxxiv. 5. Is. v.
23. x. 2. Hab. i.
4. Matt. xxvii.
12—26. John
xix. 12—16.
f Ps. xxii. 30. Is.
liii. 8. 12.
g Ps. xxii. 15. Is.
ini. 10. 12. Dan.
ix. 26. Zech.xiii.
7.
h Matt. ii. 2—4.
xiii. 36. xv. 15.
i x. 34. Matt. v. 2.
2 Cor. vi. 11.
k xviii. 28. xxvi.
22, 23. xxviii.
23. Luke xxiv.
44—47.
l iii. 20. ix. 20. xl.
1 Pet. i. 1. ii, 12.

20. xvii. 3. 18. xix. 13. 1 Cor. i. 23. ii. 2. Eph. iv. 21. 1 Pet. i. 1, 12.

---

of many miles, into an uninhabited place, without being told what he was to do when he came thither. (*Marg. Ref.* h—m.—*Notes, John* ii. 1—11, *vv.* 5—8. *Heb.* xi. 8—10.) But just when he arrived at the spot, a chariot, passing on the road, began to shew for what end he had been sent. In this sat an Ethiopian eunuch, or chief officer, who was the high treasurer of Candace, the queen of Ethiopia in Africa, and possessed great authority in the management of all publick concerns. That country seems to have been generally governed by queens, and Candace was a name commonly given to them. (*Marg. Ref.* n—p.)—As Cornelius the Centurion is supposed to have been the first Gentile convert, it must be concluded, that this man was a proselyte to the whole Jewish religion; and not merely a favourer of some of its grand doctrines and precepts. He had, however, taken a very long journey, in order to worship at Jerusalem; where it cannot be supposed, that he had heard any thing favourable concerning Jesus, from the priests, scribes, and rulers. Yet his heart was prepared to receive the truth: and, as he rode in his chariot, he employed his time in reading the scriptures; and that *aloud*, as it is evident from the narrative, probably that his servants might hear. By an immediate suggestion from the Spirit of God, Philip was ordered to approach the chariot: and, conscious of a divine mission, he without hesitation enquired of the eunuch, whether he understood the things which he read: who, sensible of his disadvantages, and humbly desirous of instruction, was not offended with the question, though proposed by a stranger of inferior rank. On the contrary he allowed, that he could not discover the prophet's meaning, without an interpreter: and, concluding from Philip's address, attire, or appearance, that he could give him information on the subject, he took him up to him into the chariot. (*Marg. Ref.* q—y.)

Which is desert. (26) This may be understood either of *Gaza*, or of the road: but the latter is the more obvious interpretation, as more immediately connected with the context.—*A man of Ethiopia.* (27) Ανηρ Αιθιοψ. Here only. Ab αιδομαι *uror*, et ωψ *facies*. A negro.—*Jer.* xiii. 23. Sept.— *Of great authority.*] Δυναστης. See on *Luke* i. 52.—*Understandest*, &c. (30) Αραγε γινωσκεις. "Dost thou indeed " understand, &c."—*Gen.* xxvi. 9. Sept.—The passage of scripture was a difficult prophecy; and the question seems to imply surprise, that he should understand it, or select it.—*Guide.* (31) 'Οδηγηση. See on *Matt.* xv. 14.

V. 32—35. The passage here quoted has been fully considered. (*Notes, Is.* liii. 7, 8.)—The Greek translation of the Old Testament was first begun at least in Egypt; thence it had found its way into Ethiopia. Greek was understood by superior persons there; and from this translation, it is highly probable, that without any other teacher, this Ethiopian obtained the knowledge of the true God; and thus became first a proselyte to Judaism, and then a convert to Christianity: what an abundant encouragement to translating, and dispersing translations of the sacred oracles!—The chief difficulty, which the eunuch found in the prophecy, related to the person of whom the sacred writer spoke. 'Was Isaiah thus inhumanly put to death 'by the Jews? Or did he foretel the sufferings of some 'future and greater person?' *Doddridge.*—This is a question which, it might be thought, would force itself on every attentive reader of this extraordinary prophecy. And it gave Philip an opportunity of instructing the Ethiopian in the grand truths of the gospel, to the greatest advantage. We may suppose, that he shewed him the circumstantial and exact accomplishment of the prediction, in the Person, doctrine, conduct, sufferings, death, resurrection, and ascension of the Lord Jesus; concerning whom it is most likely, that he had heard many disadvantageous reports, whilst at Jerusalem: and also the necessity and nature, the benefit and efficacy of faith in him, as the Saviour of the lost. 'It is probable, that it was in the familiar way of 'dialogue, ... that Philip continued to instruct this stranger 'in the doctrine of Christ.' *Campbell.* (*Note,* 4.) 'Who 'can be named either of kings or prophets, to whom these 'things agree? No one truly.' *Grotius de veritate.* Yet in his notes on the chapter, this learned writer endeavours to interpret the words concerning the prophet Jeremiah!—*He was led,* &c. (32, 33.) From the LXX: the variations from the Hebrew do not materially alter the meaning.—Bp. Lowth translates the Hebrew of the clause here rendered " In his humiliation his judgment was taken " away," " by an oppressive judgment he was taken off." —Man's oppressive judgment was, in our Lord's " humi- " liation," suffered to take effect, and God did not interpose to hinder it.

The place. (32) 'Η ... περιοχη. Here only. *Sectio, portio.* —*His generation.* (33) Την γενεαν αυτης. 'Generatio, ge- ' nitura, proles natales, id. quod γενεσις' ... *tempus, seculum,* ' aetas.' Schleusner.—Who shall declare the age · of him,

4 A 2

CÆSAREA.

Acts viii. 40; ix. 30; x. 1, 24; xi. 11; xviii. 22; xxi. 8; xxiii. 23, 33; xxv. 1, 4, 6, 13.

36 And as they went on *their* way, they came unto a certain water: and the eunuch said, ^mSee, *here is* water; what doth hinder me to be baptized?

37 And Philip said, ⁿIf thou believest with all thine heart, thou mayest. And ^ohe answered and said, ^pI believe that Jesus Christ is the Son of God.

38 And he commanded the chariot to stand still: and they went down both into the water, both Philip and the eunuch; ^qand he baptized him.

39 And when they ^rwere come up out of the water, ^sthe Spirit of the Lord caught away Philip, that the eunuch saw him no more: ^tand he went on his way rejoicing.

40 But Philip was found ^uat Azotus: and, passing through, ^xhe preached in all the cities, till he came to ^yCæsarea.

Margin notes (left column):
m x.47. 8r. xxxvi. 28. John iii. 5. 24. Tit. iii. 5, 6. 1 John v. 8.
a 12, 13, 21. ii. 38. 39. Matt. xxviii. 19. Mark xvi. 16. Rom. x. 10.
o 1 Pet. iii. 21.
p xx. 28. Matt.xvi. 16. John vi. 69. ix. 35—38. xi. 27. xx. 31. 1 John iv. 15. v. 1. 5. 10—13.

Margin notes (right column):
q John iii. 22, 23. iv. 1.
r Matt. iii. 16. Mark i. 10. Gr.
s 1 Kings xviii. 12. 2 Kings ii. 16. Ez. iii. 12—14. viii. 3. xi. 24. 2 Cor. xii. 2—4.
t 8. xiii. 52. xvi. 34. Is. xxxv. 1, 2. Iv. 12, 13. lxi. 10. lxvi. 13, 14. Matt. xiii. 44. Rom. v. 2. xv.
u 10—13. Phil. iii. 3. iv. 4. Jam. i. 9, 10. iv. 16. Josh. xv. 46, 47. 1 Sam. v. 6. Zech. ix. 6.

Ashdod.   x Luke x. 1, 2. Rom. xv. 19.   y x. 1. xxi. 8. xxiii. 23, 33. xxv. 4.

" whose goings forth have been from of old, trom ever-
" lasting ?" *Mic.* v. 1 : His race, who is the Father of
the age, or world to come ? *Is.* ix. 6 : His eternal generation ?—*Preached*, &c. (35) Ευηγγελισατο ... τον Ιησυν. See
on 4.

. V. 36—40. The discourse of Philip, no doubt com-
prising abundant instruction, with animated exhortations
and persuasions; and the prophecy as shewn to coincide
with its accomplishment in so wonderful a manner; fully
convinced the eunuch, through the concurrent teaching
and illumination of the Holy Spirit, that Jesus was the
promised Messiah: and he was enabled to understand the
nature of his kingdom and salvation. Accordingly, he desired to be numbered among his disciples. Doubtless
Philip had shewn him the nature of baptism, as the initiatory ordinance of Christianity: when therefore they came
to water, he desired to be baptized; of which he was not
likely, for a long time, to have any other opportunity; and,
stedfastly professing faith in Jesus as " the Messiah, the
" Son of God," he was baptized by Philip.—Men will form
their conjectures, concerning the mode in which Philip baptized him, according to their different sentiments on that
subject. (*Marg. Ref.* m—r.—*Notes*, ii. 41. *Matt.* iii. 5, 6.
xxviii.19, 20, v. 19. *Mark* i. 4—11, v. 5. 1 *Pet.* iii. 21, 22,
v. 21.) As soon as the eunuch was baptized, the Spirit of
God miraculously conveyed Philip away, so that he saw
him no more; (*Marg. Ref.* s.—*Notes*, 1 *Kings* xviii. 12—
16. 2 *Kings* ii. 16—18. *Ex.* iii. 12—15:) but this rather
served to confirm the faith of the Ethiopian: and he went
on his way home, " rejoicing," not in his baptism, (for in
that Simon Magus might have rejoiced also,) but in Christ
and in his glorious salvation. (*Marg. Ref.* t.)—History informs us, that this eunuch became a preacher of the gospel, in Ethiopia and the adjacent regions; and there
founded a flourishing church, which continued for several
ages afterwards; and it is supposed, on very probable
grounds, that he was endued with the miraculous power
of the Holy Spirit, to qualify him for that service.—Philip
being conveyed to Azotus, or Ashdod, proceeded to preach
in the several cities on the sea-coast, as Joppa, Lydda, and
Saron, till he came to Cæsarea, where he afterwards generally resided. (*Marg. Ref.* u—y.—*Notes*, ix. 32—43. x. 1,
2. xxi. 7—14. xxiii. 23, 24. 34, 35.)

Into the water. (38) Εις το υδωρ. vii. 3. 5. 26.—*Out of the
water.* (39) Εκ τε υδαιος. vii. 3, 4. 10. 37. 40.

PRACTICAL OBSERVATIONS.

V. 1—8.

The death of eminent ministers and Christians ought to be lamented as a publick loss to survivors, though it is
their own greatest gain; and we should honour their me-
mory, however men may disgrace them, or hate us for
our regard to them. But the Lord does not want the services of the most eminent men: (*Note*, *Matt.* xiv. 8—11:)
if he permit them to be cut off, when they seem scarcely
to have begun their work, or if persecution " make havock
" in the church;" he can over-rule these events to the
glory of his name, and the more extensive promulgation
of his gospel. At the same time the most furious enemies
cannot touch, or even terrify, those who are most obnoxious to them, unless he permit them.—The glory of his
grace often shines forth with peculiar lustre in our view,
when we are informed of the manner, in which his most
honoured servants spent the years preceding their conversion. Who, that witnessed Saul, ready to embrue his hands
in the blood of Stephen, and wasting the church like a
beast of prey, could have expected, that he would at
length prove the most eminent of all, who ever laboured
to promote the Redeemer's cause ?—Wherever the true believer is driven, he carries with him his knowledge of the
gospel, as an inestimable treasure, not only for his own
benefit, but to make others also truly rich; (*Note*, 2 *Cor.*
iv. 7;) and in one way or other he will make known the
preciousness of Christ in every place : for when a simple
desire of doing good influences the heart, it will be found
impossible to exclude a man from all opportunity of usefulness.—Facts authenticate the truth of the gospel, when
it is faithfully preached : and though miracles are no longer
wrought, yet sinners are converted; and unclean spirits
reluctantly quit possession of those, over whom they have
long reigned with uncontrouled sway: and the gospel
brings with it substantial and permanent joy to every
heart, house, village, city, or country, in which it is cordially received.

V. 9—13.

When the ministers of Christ labour with success, the
servants of Satan will endeavour to counteract them. The
magicians of Egypt appeared to do the same things with
their enchantments, which Moses did with his rod; yet
the men of God shall in due time obtain a decided victory.
(*Notes*, *Ex.* vii. 11, 12. 22, 23. viii. 7, 8. 18, 19. ix. 11.
2 *Tim.* iii. 6—9.) Human artifice and satanical influence
may effect strange things, to astonish and fascinate the deluded multitude. Thus wicked men may give out that
they are " some great ones;" and many, " from the least
" to the greatest," may give heed to them, as if they " were
" the great power of God:" but when " the things con-
" cerning the kingdom of God, and the name of our Lord

4 R 3

CHAP. IX.

Saul, having sought and obtained letters from the high priest, sets out for Damascus, to persecute the disciples, 1, 2. Drawing near the city, he is surrounded by a light from heaven, and, falling to the earth, hears Jesus expostulating with him, 3—5. He submits, and is led blind to Damascus, where he continues three days, without sight or food, 6—9. Ananias is directed in a vision to go to him ; by whom he is re-

stored to sight, and baptized, 10—18. Immediately he preaches in the synagogue, with great boldness, 19 —22. The Jews seek to kill him, but he escapes from them, 23—25. He goes to Jerusalem, and is by Barnabas introduced to the apostles, 26—28. Preaching boldly in the name of Jesus, his life is in danger, and he is sent to Tarsus, 29, 30. The church has rest, and is edified and multiplied, 31. Peter heals Eneas at Lydda, 32—35 ; and at Joppa raises Tabitha from the dead, 36—43.

" Jesus Christ," are powerfully brought home to men's hearts, the charm is dissolved, and the truth rendered triumphant. Indeed, whoever compares the juggles and ambiguous pretences to miracle, or extraordinary operation, that shrink from investigation, which every age produces and fosters, and then detects and despises ; with the open, beneficent, incontestable, and disinterested miracles of Christ and his apostles, will easily discern the most manifest difference, or rather the most entire contrariety. The one can only subserve the credit or interest of designing men, and abet delusion, hypocrisy, or immorality ; the other evidently tended to promote the best of all causes, even that of truth and holiness : the former have ever sunk into neglect, in proportion as they have been dispassionately examined ; the other have been despised by superficial and self-conceited enquirers alone : while men of superior wisdom, piety, and diligence, searching deeply into these matters, have always decidedly borne testimony to their reality and importance. But when impostors have exhausted their ingenuity, in devising schemes for deceiving mankind, they sometimes assume a profession of true religion, as their last resource. They avowedly embrace the gospel ; they attend on the ordinances of God ; they attach themselves to his ministers, as greatly impressed and affected by their words and works : and thus they aspire to a character for sanctity, in subserviency to their selfish designs. Nor should we hastily censure those servants of God, who are thus imposed upon : the Lord alone " searches the heart ; " we know that his grace is sufficient for the chief of sinners ; we ought to hope the best of professed believers, till any of them discover their hypocrisy ; and men of this description often carry matters very plausibly, till some suitable temptation puts them off their guard, and then they are made manifest in their true character.

V. 14—25.

The abundant unction of the Holy Spirit divests men of their narrow and selfish prejudices, and teaches them to own all as brethren, who receive the word of God, and to impart to them some spiritual good as they have opportunity and ability : for in these things, there is no room for competition, as no man is impoverished by others being enriched. Yet the carnal mind converts even spiritual gifts into nutriment for ostentation, envy, and ambition : (P. O. 1 Cor. xiv. 26—40 :) selfish hypocrites judge of others by themselves ; and covetous men deem a large sum of money an irresistible allurement, and a valuable consideration for the most sacred offices and endowments. Plausible hypocrites are often detected by their desire of pre-eminence, and by devising to render religion subservient to worldly interest. (Notes, 2 Pet. ii. 12—19. 3 John,

9—12.) But if men attempt to put " filthy lucre " in competition with the truths, ordinances, precepts, gifts, and glory of God ; we must abhor their favours and bribes, and warn them that they are in the way of perdition. Indeed, many high and plausible pretensions are sufficiently detected to be base impostures, by the mercenary spirit of those who boast of them ; and then set the pretended gift of God to sale, and dispose of it for ready money. (P. O. Ez. xiii. 17—23.) But, though simoniacal practices are every where exclaimed against, they almost universally insinuate themselves into all things relative to religion !— Commonly those who aspire to be the chief, have " neither " part nor lot in the matter ; " for a proud and covetous heart cannot be " right in the sight of God." But when we most plainly perceive, that men are " in the gall of " bitterness and in the bond of iniquity ; " and when we most solemnly warn them of their guilt and danger ; we should still exhort them to repent of their wickedness, and to pray to God, if peradventure it may be forgiven.—Men often imagine that their thoughts are free, and have no sin in them ; yet " the thought of the heart " may possibly be so atrocious, as to exclude a man from repentance and forgiveness. Many desire others to pray for them, who do not humbly pray for themselves ; and many at some times dread punishment, who yet resolutely proceed to commit the most horrible impieties. The ministers of Christ, however, must testify against such persons ; and preach the gospel of Christ, in cities or villages, and in every place as they have opportunity, and then leave the event with the Lord.

V. 26—40.

We ought not to be discouraged, when called to minister in obscure places, or to few hearers : seldom was more effectual and extensive good done in the most numerous assembly, than followed Philip's preaching to one stranger in a desert : and implicit obedience and submission became the servants of God. He " knows whom he has chosen ; " and a thousand incidents, apparently casual, form a part of his great plan, for bringing them to the knowledge of his salvation. In this view nothing can be decidedly deemed little, or unimportant ; as we know not what vast effects may be connected with it.—The Lord will have some of all ranks, nations, and complexions among his redeemed people, to shew the power and largeness of his grace. Where he has implanted a desire after himself, he will in due time satisfy it : though such enquirers may go to places, and among persons, where the most religion might be expected, and yet learn nothing of Jesus ; and even come away more prejudiced or bewildered than before. (P. O. Matt. ii. 1—8.) Those who seek the truth will improve their leisure time in searching the scriptures ;

4 R 4

DAMASCUS.

Gen. xiv. 15; xv. 2. 2 Sam. viii. 5, 6. 1 Kings xi. 24; xv. 18; xix. 15; xx. 34.
Isaiah vii. 8. Acts ix. 3; xxii. 5.

AND [a] Saul, yet [b] breathing out threatenings and slaughter against the disciples of the Lord, went unto the high priest,

2 And [c] desired of him letters to Damascus to [d] the synagogues, that if he found any [e] of this way, whether they were men or women, he might bring them bound unto Jerusalem.

3 And [f] as he journeyed, he came near Damascus; and suddenly there shined round about him [g] a light from heaven:

4 And [h] he fell to the earth, and heard a voice saying unto him, [h] Saul, [i] why persecutest thou me?

5 And he said, [k] Who art thou, Lord? And the Lord said, [l] I am Jesus whom thou persecutest. [m] It is hard for thee to kick against the pricks.

Marginal references:
a 11—13. 19—21. vii. 58. viii. 3. xxii. 3, 4, xxvi. 9—11. 1 Cor. xv. 9. Gal. i. 13. Phil. iii. 6. 1 Tim. i. 13.
b Ps. xxvii. 12.
c 14. vii. 19. xxii. 5. xxvi. 12. Esth. iii. 8—13.
d Ps. lxxiii. 7.
e vi. 9. xiii. 14, 15. xxii. 17—21.
Gr. *of the way.* xix. 9, 23, xxii. 4.
f 17. xxii. 6. xxvi. 12, 13. 1 Cor. xv. 8.

[Right column references:]
f Ps. civ. 2. 1 Tim. vi. 16. Rev. xxi. 23. xxii. 5.
g v. 10. Num. xvi. 42. John xviii. 6. Rom. xv. 22. 1 Cor. iv. 7.
h Gen. iii. 9. xvi. 8. xxii. 11. Ex. iii. 4. Luke x. 41. John xx. 16. xxi. 15.
i xxii. 7, 8. xxvi. 14, 15. Is. lxiii. 9. Zech. ii. 8.
k Matt. xxv. 40, 45. 1 Cor. xii. 12. Eph. v. 30.
l 12. Eph. v. 30.
m k 1 Sam. iii. 4. 16. 1 Tim. i. 18. xxvi. 9. xiv. 9. 1 Cor. xv. 22.
m v. 39. Deut. xxxii. 15. Job ix. 4. xi. 9, 10. Ps. ii. 12. Is. xlv. 9. 1 Cor. x. 22.

---

even when they have but small advantages for understanding it. But alas! how few of our nobles, and ministers of state, study that sacred volume, as they ride in their chariots! or willingly take long journeys to enquire after God, or worship him! Surely this Ethiopian will rise up in judgment against them, and condemn them!—Should any one, on some special occasion, be found reading the scriptures; and should a minister of Christ, in the most grave, courteous, and modest manner, enquire of him, whether he understood what he read; it is to be feared, he would resent the question as impertinence. But humility is teachable, and leads to wisdom: and when we are conscious of our ignorance, and willing to gain information even from an inferior or a stranger; we shall not be left without instruction. When God, by means of the Bible alone, excites serious enquiries after the truth; he will send an expositor to obviate difficulties and perplexities: for while many things, and those the most essential, are so plain, that any honest reader may understand them; others require the aid of teachers and interpreters. Thus, while one society disperses the sacred scriptures, another sends missionaries: both are needful, and there should be no competition between them, but most cordial concurrence in their most excellent designs.—In reading the word of God, we should pause to enquire, of whom, and of what, the sacred writers spoke. But we should especially employ our thoughts about that meek and holy, that patient and suffering Redeemer, who was "led as a sheep to the "slaughter, and was dumb as a lamb before the shearer." In his humiliation his "judgment" and his life "were "taken away:" but he is now exalted at the right hand of the Father; his generation as the Son of God is abundantly declared, the generation of the righteous own him as their spiritual Progenitor, and all judgment is vested in him.—Such prophecies are excellent texts, from whence to preach Jesus to sinners; for they at the same time explain and demonstrate his doctrine: and as this is the substance of all our preaching, so we may expect that it will be crowned with peculiar success. If we "believe "with all our heart, that Jesus is the Christ, the Son of "God," and profess that such methods as we can, we shall surely be accepted in attending divine ordinances. And when the enquirer after salvation becomes acquainted with Jesus and his precious gospel, he will "go on his "way rejoicing," to fill up his station in society, from other motives, and in another manner, than before: and thus the conversion of one man may prove a blessing to vast multitudes.—'The communion of saints' on earth, though pleasant, is commonly transient: their different employments and services call them into different places; but under the influence of the same Spirit, they all "serve "their generation," and then they will meet before the throne, to part no more, but to join in unceasing and joyful praises to their common Lord and Saviour.

NOTES.

CHAP. IX. V. 1, 2. It is not certainly known, in what year Saul was converted: perhaps it might be two or three years after our Lord's ascension. (vii. 58. *Philem.* 9.) He, however, persisted in persecuting the disciples for a considerable time, with increasing violence: and he menaced the whole multitude with slaughter and extirpation; as if he could not breathe without uttering threatenings against them, or would, if able, have "slain them with the breath "of his lips." (*Marg. Ref.* a, b.—*Notes,* viii. 1—4. *Is.* xi. 2—5, v. 4. xxx. 27, 28.) Probably, the diligence and success of those, whom he had driven from Jerusalem, in propagating the gospel, increased his rage and animosity. Being a zealous volunteer in the service, he devised plans for fully exterminating the religion of Jesus, and was ready to carry them into execution, to the utmost of his ability: and with this view he proposed to the high priest, (probably Caiaphas,) that he should give him letters from the council and chief priests, to the rulers of the synagogues in Damascus; authorizing them to apprehend those who believed in Jesus, and to send them bound to Jerusalem to be punished. (*Marg. Ref.* c, d.—*Notes,* xxii. 1—5. xxvi. 9—11.)—The sanhedrim had no doubt an ecclesiastical authority over the Jewish synagogues in other countries: yet they could not exercise it in many respects without the concurrence of the synagogues themselves, and the connivance of the civil rulers. Damascus had long been the capital city of Syria: it was still very large and populous, and numbers of Jews resided there. It does not clearly appear under whose authority it was at this time; but probably the ruling powers were disposed to concur in the execution of the commission, granted by the high priest and council of the Jews.—Perhaps some of the persons, who had been converted on the day of Pentecost, or soon after, had first carried the gospel thither; and those who had been scattered by the preceding persecution, seem to have laboured successfully among the Jews of that city.

Breathing out. (1) Εμπνεων. Here only. *Of this way.* (2) "Of the way." *Marg.* xix. 9. 23. xxii. 4. xxiv. 14.— Τῆς ὁδοῦ ουσας.

V. 3—6. The disciples at Damascus, when they heard of Saul's commission from the chief priests (14), would doubtless unite in prayer for deliverance: but it may be

6 And he ⁿtrembling and astonished said, ° Lord, what wilt thou me to do?　And the Lord *said* unto him, ᵖ Arise, and go into the city, ᵠ and it shall be told thee what thou must do.

7 And ʳthe men which journeyed with him stood speechless, hearing a voice, but seeing no man.

8 And Saul arose from the earth: and when his eyes were opened, ˢ he saw no man: but they led him by the hand, and brought *him* into Damascus.

9 And he was ᵗthree days without sight, and neither did eat nor drink.

Marginal references (left column):

n xvi. 29. xxiv. 25, 26. 1 Sam. xxviii. 5. lxvi 2. Hab. iii.
16. Phil. ii. 12.
o ii. 37. xvi. 30. xxii. 10. Luke iii. 10. Rom. vii. 9. x. 3. Jam. iv. 6.
p 15. xxvi. 16.
Matt. xvi. 6—9. Rom. v. 20. Ps.
16—24. x. 20. Gal. i. 15, 16. 8, 9, 12. xcv. 12.

1 Tim. i. 14—16.
1e. lvii. 18.
q x. 6. 22, 32. 31. 13, 14. Ps. xxv.
r xxii. 9. xxvi. 13, 14. Dan. x. 7. Matt. xxv. 40, 41.

Marginal references (right column):

18. xiii. 11. xxii. 11. Gen. xix. 11.
Ex. iv. 11. 2 Kings vi. 17—20.
t I., 12 2 Chr. xxxiii. 12, 13. 1d. 19. Esth. iv. 16. Jon. iii. 6—8.

---

questioned, whether one of them thought of that method of deliverance, by which the Lord intended to rescue them. (*Notes*, 10—14. xii. 12—17.) For when Saul drew near to the city, and doubtless pleased himself with thinking of the consternation which he was about to excite ; he was at once surrounded with a dazzling splendour, like lightning, brighter than that of the meridian sun : and, falling to the ground with terror and amazement, he heard the voice of one calling to him by name repeatedly, and saying, "Why persecutest thou me?" (*Marg. Ref.* e—i.—10. *Gen.* xxii. 1. 11. xlvi. 2. *Ex.* iii. 4. 1 *Sam.* iii. 10.) Saul had imagined, that he was attempting to extirpate a company of deluded and obstinate hereticks, or sectarians ; and that he was doing service to God, by his zeal for the law of Moses and the traditions of the elders, against a worthless company of dangerous innovators : but it now appeared that he was persecuting "the Lord of glory," who considered the cause of the disciples as his own. (*Notes*, xxvi. 9—11. *Gen.* xii. 1—3. *Zech.* ii. 6—9. *John* xv. 17—25. xvi. 1—3.) And why did he this ? Had they done him any harm ? or was there no evidence that Jesus was the Messiah, after all the miracles wrought by him and his apostles ? Saul, astonished by this most alarming expostulation, enquired who that glorious Lord was, who thus appeared and spake to him : to which it was answered, that he was Jesus, the Nazarene, whom he had no doubt often derided and blasphemed under that title, and compelled others to blaspheme, and whom he now persecuted in his disciples. (*Marg. Ref.* k, l.—*Notes*, xxvi. 12—18.) But, as it would be hard, or painful, for a man "to kick against the *spikes*," by which he could only wound himself ; thus Saul could only injure and ruin himself, by contending with One, who possessed "all "power in heaven and earth." On hearing this, Saul was exceedingly terrified and astonished ; probably he dreaded the immediate vengeance of that glorious Lord, whom he had so deeply offended : his guilt was undeniable, his pleas were all silenced ; and the concurring influence of the Holy Spirit enlightening, convincing, and humbling his heart, he submitted without reserve, and only asked "Lord, what wilt thou have me to do." If mercy could be extended to him, he was prepared for any submission, or self-denial, which might be required of him. Accordingly, he was directed to go into the city, and there to wait for further orders. (*Marg. Ref.* n—p.)—Kick, &c. (5) ' This is a proverbial expression, signify-' ing the damage and hurt, they are like to receive, who ' resist and fight against those, who are superior to them, ' and especially against God. ' I will rather offer sacrifice ' to him, than, being a mortal man, be angry with God, ' and kick against the goads.' So *Euripides.*' Whitby. (*Marg. Ref.* m.)

Shone round about. (3) Περιηστραψεν. xxii. 6. Not elsewhere. Εκ περι et αστραπτω, *fulguro :* αστραπη, xxvi. 13.—*It is hard.* (5) Σκληρον. xxvi. 14. See on *Matt.* xxv. 24.—*To kick.*] Λακτιζειν. xxvi. 14. Not elsewhere. Αλαξ adv. *calce, calcibus.*—*The pricks.*] Κεντρα. xxvi. 14. 1 *Cor.* xv. 55, 56. *Rev.* ix. 10. Not elsewhere—' *Quicquid' pungit,* aut *vim* ' *pungendi habet:* a κεντεω, *pungo.*' Schleusner:—*Calcar : stimulus, quo boves concitabantur.*—*What wilt,* &c. (6) Τι θελεις με ποιησαι ; "What willest thou me to do ? "

V. 7.　Saul's attendants, who at first fell to the ground as well as he, having recovered themselves, rose up, and stood speechless with terror and amazement. They indeed heard a voice, though they understood nothing of what was spoken ; (*Note,* xxii. 6—13, *v.* 9. *John* xii. 27—33, *v.* 29;) but they saw no man : (*Marg. Ref.*—*Note, Dan.* x. 4—9 :) whereas, Saul in vision saw Jesus in human form, as Stephen had done : (*Note,* vii. 54—60 :) and we find from the account, which he afterwards repeatedly gave of this transaction, that much more passed between the Lord and him, than is here recorded. (*Notes,* xxii. 14—16. xxvi. 16—18. 1 *Cor.* xv. 3—11.)

Speechless.] Ενεοι. Here only.—*Prov.* xvii. 28. *Is.* lvi. 10. *Sept.*

V. 8, 9.　Saul now arose from the earth : but, when his eyes were opened, he found that the splendour, with which he had been surrounded, had blinded him. This effect proved the whole transaction to have been a reality, and not merely an illusion of the imagination. (*Marg. Ref.* s.)—He was therefore led to Damascus ; and he entered that city a harmless lamb, though he set out to journey thither with the fierceness of a tiger ! We are not informed, whether his attendants were, or were not, converted ; but this silence seems to indicate that they were not. After his arrival in the city, terror, remorse, anxiety, self-examination, and prayer, with earnest desires of mercy, so occupied his mind, and his body also was so disordered, that he took no sustenance of any kind for three days ; for it pleased the Lord to leave him so long to his reflections, before he sent him any relief, or further instruction. (*Marg. Ref.* t.)—It is impossible to describe what Saul thought, felt, and experienced, during this awful and important interval. There is, however, abundant reason to conclude, that the Holy Spirit enlightened his mind at this time, with a just view of the divine law, in its spirituality and excellency ; and thus shewed him the worthlessness of his pharisaical righteousness ; and his exceedingly heinous guilt, not only in persecuting the Messiah in his followers, but also in his whole conduct, and the state of his heart.　This seems to be intimated in some parts of his epistles ; and indeed was essentially necessary to a right understanding of that gospel, which he was to spend the rest of his life in preaching. (*Notes, Rom.* vii. 9—12.

10 ¶ And " there was a certain disciple at Damascus, named Ananias; " and to him said the Lord in a vision, " Ananias. And he said, ' Behold, I am here, Lord.

11 And the Lord *said* unto him, " Arise, and go into the street which is called Straight, and enquire in the house of Judas for *one* called " Saul of Tarsus: ' for, behold, he prayeth;

12 And " hath seen in a vision a man named Ananias, coming in, and putting *his* hand on him, that he might " receive his sight.

13 Then Ananias answered, ' Lord, I have heard by many of this man, ' how much evil he hath done to thy saints at Jerusalem:

14 And " here he hath authority from the chief priests, to bind all that " call on thy name.

15 But the Lord said unto him, 'Go thy way: for he is " a chosen vessel unto me, ' to bear my name before the

---

Gal. i. 11—24. ii. 17—21.)—With this narrative in view, can we wonder, that one, thus " saved by grace," and made an apostle at the very moment when he might most justly have been sent down " quick into hell," should especially delight in expatiating on the divine sovereignty, and on the riches and freeness of " the grace of our God " and Saviour," in saving his chosen people? The same doctrines may be distinctly traced in the other parts of scripture, and abundantly proved from them: but this apostle, snatched as a brand from the burning, and rejoicing with most grateful exultation in his stupendous deliverance and astonishing felicity, with a noble, but highly rational enthusiasm, delights in recurring to the source of all his hopes and joys, and in calling on his brethren, to ascribe unreservedly all the glory of their salvation to God alone. Were our humiliation equally deep, and our views of the way in which we have been " called " out of darkness into marvellous light," as distinct as his were; few objections to these doctrines, or difficulties concerning them, would trouble our minds: and we should soon perceive the holy tendency and efficacy of them.

They led him by the hand. (8) Χειραγωγουντες. xxii. 11. Not elsewhere N. T. A Χειραγωγος, xiii. 11. Εκ χειρ, *manus*, et αγω, *duco.* This seems to imply, that they were on foot, and not riding, as generally pictured.

V. 10—14. Ananias had previously been a " devout " person, according to the law of Moses; and was now become a disciple of Christ, and probably a preacher of the gospel: though it is not likely that he was one of the seventy disciples. (*Notes,* xxii. 6—16, *vv.* 12—16.) To him the Lord Jesus appeared " in a vision," and addressing him also by name (4), he directed him to go to Saul of Tarsus; who was employed in prayer, and was prepared, by a coincident vision, for his coming to restore his sight, of which he had lately been bereaved.—Saul had been a strict Pharisee, and doubtless had made long, formal, and constant prayers before this. (*Notes,* Matt. vi. 5—8. xxiii. 14:) but he now prayed as a sinner for salvation, and doubtless to that Saviour whom he had before persecuted. (*Marg. Ref.* x. z. c.) It was indeed most wonderful, that he, who before " breathed out threaten- " ings and slaughter against the disciples of Jesus," should now pour out humble prayers to him; and it was a sufficient proof, that he had submitted, and was changed, and therefore ought to be encouraged.—Ananias, however, was astonished at hearing the name of Saul, in this connexion:

he considered the message on which he was sent, as replete with peril; and he spake, as if forgetful that Jesus had fully known of Saul's previous conduct, or the intent of his journey to Damascus. (*Marg. Ref.* e, f. h.)—" To " call on the name of Jesus," is here used as the distinguished characteristick of a believer.—' The unbelieving ' Jews say of him, preaching Christ in their synagogues, ' " Is not this he who wasted those, who called on that ' " name in Jerusalem?" (21.) Thus St. Paul writes to ' saints, ... under the title of " all that call upon the name ' " of the Lord Jesus Christ in every place;" (1 *Cor.* i. 2:) ' and then in the very next verse, he himself prays, that ' " grace and peace may be derived on them from God the ' " Father, and from the Lord Jesus Christ." ... And he bids ' Christians " follow after peace with all those that call ' " upon the Lord with a pure heart;" that is, with all ' believers; it being the same thing to believe in, and to ' call upon, the name of the Lord Jesus. Hence St. ' Paul saith, " He that believeth in him shall not be ' " ashamed, because it is written, Whosoever shall call ' " on the name of the LORD shall be saved." (*Joel* ii. ' 32.) And hence we learn, who that Lord is, whom ' Ananias bids St. Paul invoke, when he saith, " Arise ' " and be baptized, calling upon the name of the Lord," ' even the Lord Jesus who appeared to him; (xxii. 16;) ' ... and what is meant by that phrase, namely, " Profess ' thy faith, by being baptized in, and by calling on, his ' name.' This was a thing so continually practised by the ' first Christians, that Pliny mentions it in his epistle to ' Trajan, telling him, that it was the custom of the ' Christians to sing a hymn to Christ, as God. For, St. ' Paul, in his thirteen first epistles, prays for " grace and ' " peace from God the Father, and from our Lord Jesus;" ' and St. John in his second epistle, *ver.* 3, doth the same.' *Whitby.* Some indeed would render the clause, " are " called by thy name:" but the direct meaning of the original, the repetition of the same language in different connexions, and the remarks contained in the quotation just made, are sufficient to shew, that this translation is absolutely inadmissible. (*Notes,* ii. 14—21, *v.* 21. Rom. x. 12—17, *v.* 12. 14.)

Straight. (11) Ευθειαν. See on viii. 21.—*Thy saints.* (13) Τοις αγιοις σε. 32. Rom. i. 7.—' Ananias ... calls ' Christians his (the Lord's) saints.' *Whitby.*—*That call,* &c. (14) Τως επικαλαμενως. See on vii. 59.

V. 15, 16. Our Lord at once silenced Ananias's objec-

Gentiles, and kings, and the children of Israel:

16 For I will shew him how great things he must suffer for my name's sake.

17 And Ananias went his way, and entered into the house; and putting his hands on him said, Brother Saul, the Lord, even Jesus that appeared unto thee in the way as thou camest, hath sent me, that thou mightest receive thy sight, and be filled with the Holy Ghost.

18 And immediately there fell from his eyes as it had been scales; and he received sight forthwith, and arose, and was baptized.

19 And when he had received meat he was strengthened. Then was Saul certain days with the disciples which were at Damascus.

20 And straightway he preached Christ in the synagogues, that he is the Son of God.

21 But all that heard him were amazed, and said, Is not this he that destroyed them which called on this name in Jerusalem, and came hither for that intent, that he might bring them bound unto the chief priests?

22 But Saul increased the more in strength, and confounded the Jews which dwelt at Damascus, proving that this is very Christ.

tion, and commanded him to go without delay: as this violent persecutor was "a vessel of election," whom the Lord had fore-known, and meant to employ; that, being filled with the treasure of the gospel, he might convey his name and doctrine among the nations of the earth, and even to their kings, as well as to his people the "children of Israel."—It should be noted, that this precedes in the history the admission of any uncircumcised Gentiles into the church. (Marg. Ref. k—m.—Notes, Rom. ix. 22, 23. 2 Cor. iv. 7. 2 Tim. ii. 20—22.) At the same time, he would "shew him, how great things he should suffer for his name's sake," according to the sufferings which he had inflicted on others. (Marg. Ref. n, o.)—Some think, that a distinct representation was made in a vision to Saul's mind of all the various persecutions, which he afterwards underwent: at least he had such a discovery made of them, as rendered his subsequent ministry a lively copy of Christ's own example, who foresaw every thing that he was to endure from the very first. He did not, however, fully know the particulars, as many subsequent passages prove. (xx. 22. xxvii. 24. Rom. xv. 23—28.)

A chosen vessel. (15) Σκευος εκλογης. Σκευος, Rom. ix. 21. 2 Tim. ii. 20, 21. Εκλογη, Rom. ix. 11. xi. 5. 7. 28. 1 Thes. i. 4. 2 Pet. i. 10.

V. 17—22. Ananias, thus admonished, obeyed Jesus without further hesitation. He no longer considered Saul as a persecutor, but as a disciple; and, laying his hands upon him, he called him "Brother Saul;" while he informed him that he was sent to him by the Lord, (even that Jesus, whom he had seen by the way, surrounded with awful glory,) in order that he might miraculously be restored to sight, and then made partaker of the Holy Spirit. (Marg. Ref. p—r. t.)—'Ananias, who at most is only 'supposed to have been one of the seventy disciples, only 'laid his hands on him, "that he might receive his sight;" 'and ... he was replenished with the Holy Ghost by the 'immediate gift of Christ; he being an "apostle not of 'man, nor by man, but by Christ alone." Gal. i. 1.' Whitby. This appears to have been the case; especially as the conferring of the Holy Spirit, in his miraculous

gifts, seems in all cases, previous to that of Cornelius and his friends, to have taken place after baptism. (Note, x. 44—48.)—'It is more probable, that Ananias did not 'lay hands on him a second time; as we do not elsewhere 'find, that any but the apostles had the power of confer-'ring the Holy Spirit.' Doddridge.—At the words of Ananias, however, "there fell from the eyes" of Saul, "as it were scales," which had occasioned his blindness. These had been an emblem of the benighted state of his soul, amidst the full light of the gospel; as the recovery of his sight, by the power and mercy of Christ, was of his spiritual illumination. (Note, 2 Cor. iv. 5, 6.) When this token of reconciliation had been granted him, he arose, and, by being baptized, professed himself a disciple of the Lord Jesus; and having thus obtained hope and peace, he took proper refreshment, and found his vigour and strength of body restored to him. These extraordinary events being then made known by Ananias to his brethren, Saul was received among them, and continued some time with them at Damascus: but, instead of delivering his letters to the persons to whom they were addressed, he boldly went to the synagogues, and preached Christ to the Jews there assembled; shewing that Jesus was indeed the promised Messiah, and "the Son of God." As his character was well known, and the intent of his journey to Damascus: this change excited the amazement of all men, and probably, in many instances, gave energy to his testimony; though others were offended by it. (Marg. Ref. b—g.—Note, 10—13.) But he grew more strong in faith, and more powerful in argument: so that the Jews could by no means answer his reasonings from "the scripture," proving that Jesus was the promised Messiah, and that all the ancient prophecies had been fulfilled in him.—From his own account, it appears that he received his complete knowledge of the gospel, immediately by revelation from Jesus Christ. (Note, Gal. i. 11—14.)

Brother Saul. (17) Marg. Ref. q.—Notes, Gen. xlv. 4, 5. Luke xv. 25—32. Philem. 12—16.—That appeared.] Ὁ οφθεις. "Who was seen." 1 Cor. xv. 5—8.—Scales. (18) Λεπιδες. Here only N. T. Lev. xi. 9, 10. Num.

4 A 8

23 ¶ And after that many days were
fulfilled, [i] the Jews took counsel to kill
him:
24 But [k] their laying await was known
of Saul: and they watched the gates
day and night to kill him.
25 Then the disciples took him by
night, [l] and let *him* down by the wall
in a basket.
26 And [m] when Saul was come to
Jerusalem, [n] he assayed to join himself
to the disciples: [o] but they were all
afraid of him, and believed not that he
was a disciple.
27 But [p] Barnabas took him, and
brought *him* to [q] the apostles, and declared unto them [r] how he had seen
the Lord in the way, and that he had
spoken to him, [s] and how he had
preached boldly at Damascus in the
name of Jesus.
28 And he was with them, [t] coming
in and going out at Jerusalem.
29 And [u] he spake boldly in the
name of the Lord Jesus, [x] and disputed
against the [y] Grecians: but they went
about to slay him.
30 *Which* [z] when the brethren knew,
they brought him down to [a] Cæsarea,
and sent him forth to [b] Tarsus.
31 Then had [c] the churches rest
throughout all Judea, and Galilee, and
Samaria, and [d] were edified; [e] and walking in the fear of the Lord, [f] and in
the comfort of the Holy Ghost, [g] were
multiplied.

i 16. xiii. 50. xiv. 2. 19. xxii. 21—23. Josh. x. 1—6. Matt. x. 16—23. 2 Cor. xi. 26. 1 Thes. ii. 15, 16.
k 29, 30. xiv. 5, 6. xvii. 10—15. xxiii. 12—21. xxv. 3. 11. Judg. xvi. 2, 3. 2 Cor. xi. 32.
l Josh. ii. 15. 1 Sam. xix. 11, 12. 2 Cor. xi. 33.
m xxii. 17. xxvi. 20. Gal. i. 17—19.
n 19. iv. 23.
o Matt. x. 17—19. xxiv. 10 Gal. ii. 4.
p iv. 36. xi. 22. 25. xii. 25. xiii. 2. xv. 2. 25, 26. 35—39. 1 Cor. ix. 6. Gal. ii. 9. 13.
q Gal. i. 18, 19.
r 17. 1 Cor. xv. 8.
s 20—22. iv. 13. 29. Eph. vi. 19, 20.
t i. 21. Num xxvii. 16, 17 2 Sam. v. 2 1 Kings iii. 7. Ps. cxxi. 8. John x. 9.
u 20—22. 27.
x vi. 9, 10. xvii 17. xviii. 19. xix 8. Jude 3, 9.
y vi. 1. xi. 20.
z 24, 25. xvii. 10 15. Matt. x. 23
a viii. 40. or, Matt. xvi. 13.
b 11. xi. 25.
c viii. 1. Deut xii. 10. Josh xxi. 44. Judg iii. 30. 1 Chr xxii. 9. 18. Prov. xvi. 7. Is. xi 10. Heb. iv. 9.
d 1 Cor. iii. 9—15. xiv. 4, 5. 12 26. 2 Cor. x. 8. xii. 19. xiii. 10. Eph. iv. 12. 16. 29. 1 Thes. v. 11. 1 Tim. i. 4. Jude 20.
e Neh. v. 9. 15. Job xxviii. 28. Ps. cxi. 10. Prov. i. 7. viii. 13. xiv. 26, 27. xvi. 6. xxiii. 17. Is. xi. 2, 3. xxxiii. 6. 2 Cor. vii. 1. Eph. v. 21.
f John xiv. 16—18. Rom. v. 5. viii. 15—17. xiv. 17. xv. 13. Gal. v. 22, 23. Eph. i. 13, 14. vi. 18, 19. Phil. ii. 1. 2 Thes. ii. 16, 17.
g vi. 7. xii. 24. Esth. viii. 16, 17. Zech. viii. 20—23.

xvi. 38. *Deut.* xiv. 9. *Sept.—He that destroyed.* (21) 'Ο πορθησας. *Gal.* i. 13. 23. Not elsewhere.—*Increased ... in strength.* (22) Ενεδυναμȣτο. *Rom.* iv. 20. *Eph.* vi. 10. *Phil.* iv. 13. 1 *Tim.* i. 12. 2 *Tim.* ii. 1. iv. 17. *Heb.* xi. 34. —*Confounded.*] Συνεχυνε. ii. 6. xix. 32. xxi. 31.—*Proving.*] Συμϐιϐαζων. xvi. 10. 1 *Cor.* ii. 16. *Eph.* iv. 16. *Col.* ii. 2. 19. (Ex συν, et βιβαζω, *ascendere facio.*) *Copulo, compingo:* taken from mechanics.—Proving by quotations from scripture, skilfully arranged, and compared together, and connected with each other. (*Note*, xvii. 1—4.)

V. 23—30. When Saul had preached a while at Damascus, he went into Arabia, and laboured there for a considerable time: and after his return to Damascus, the Jews enraged at his supposed apostasy, and his pertinacity in preaching that Jesus was the Messiah, took counsel to slay him. (*Gal.* i. 17, 18.) It seems that Aretas, an Arabian king, had got possession of Damascus at this time; and that the governor appointed by him favoured and abetted the designs against Saul. (2 *Cor.* xi. 32, 33.) The Jews either preferred this method of proceeding against him, to sending him bound to Jerusalem; or they had been deprived of that power by a change of the government. Saul, however, providentially discovered and eluded their malice, which was very active, vigilant, and sanguinary, as they had assassins stationed at every gate of that large city, ready to murder him, as soon as ever he approached. (*Marg. Ref.* i—l.—*Notes*, xxiii. 12—22. xxv. 1—5.) Having escaped that danger he went from thence to Jerusalem. This was three years after his conversion: yet when he would have joined the Christians there, they questioned his sincerity, and suspected that his enmity to them had only assumed another form; aiming to do them that mischief by subtlety, which before he had effected by violence. (*Marg. Ref.* m—o.) Damascus was not much above a hundred and fifty miles from Jerusalem; but modern conveniences for a regular correspondence between distant places were then unknown; and some wars in the neighbourhood are supposed to have greatly obstructed the communication. Saul had spent a considerable part of his time in Arabia, in an obscure situation; and the former perils, alarms, and sufferings, which the disciples had experienced from him, had rendered them unreasonably suspicious. But Barnabas, who by some means had obtained fuller information, and had contracted an acquaintance with Saul, introduced him to the apostles Peter and James; the other apostles being absent at that time, no doubt preaching the gospel in different places; and, having given them a satisfactory account of the manner and effects of his conversion, he was admitted to communion with the disciples, both publick and private, and soon began to preach among them. (*Marg. Ref.* p—t.—*Note*, *Gal.* i. 15—24.) He especially disputed with the Grecians or Hellenists, whom he had before joined against Stephen; (*Note*, vi. 9—14;) and his unanswerable arguments so exasperated them, that they purposed to kill him likewise. He therefore retired to Tarsus, his native city, and preached there and in the adjacent places for some time, till at length Barnabas went, and brought him to Antioch. (*Note*, xi. 25, 26.)—It is supposed that the apostle went by land to Tarsus, and that Cæsarea Philippi is meant in the thirtieth verse. (*Gal.* i. 21.—*Note*, *Matt.* xvi. 13—16.)

Took counsel. (23) Συνεϐȣλευσαντο. *Matt.* xxvi. 4. *John* xi. 53. xviii. 14. *Rev.* iii. 18. Ex συν, et βȣλη, *consilium.* —*Laying await.* (24) 'Η επιϐȣλη. xx. 3. 19. xxiii. 30. —*They let him down.* (25) Χαλασαντες. See on *Mark* ii. 4.—*In a basket.*] Εν σπυριδι. See on *Matt.* xv. 37.—*He had preached boldly.* (27) Επαῤῥησιασατο. 29. xiii. 46. xiv. 3. xviii. 26. xix. 8. xxvi. 26. *Eph.* vi. 20. 1 *Thes.* ii. 2. A παῤῥησια, *libere, palam, aperte.*—*The Grecians.* (29) Τȣς Έλληνιστας. See on vi. 1.

V. 31. When Saul, the grand instrument of persecution, was become a zealous preacher, and was removed out of the reach of his enemies, the persons concerned seem to have been disheartened. Other causes likewise concurring, the persecution was suspended, and the churches were left in peace. This opportunity they diligently improved, to edify one another in knowledge, faith,

32 ¶ And it came to pass, [b] as Peter passed throughout all *quarters*, he came down also to [i] the saints which dwelt at [k] Lydda.

33 And there he found a certain man named Eneas, [l] which had kept his bed eight years [m] and was sick of the palsy.

34 And Peter said unto him, Eneas, [n] Jesus Christ maketh thee whole: [o] arise, and make thy bed. And he arose immediately.

35 And [p] all that dwelt in Lydda and Saron saw him, and [p] turned to the Lord.

36 ¶ Now there was at [q] Joppa a certain disciple named Tabitha, which by interpretation is called [r] Dorcas: this woman was [s] full of good works and [s] alms-deeds which she did.

37 And it came to pass in those days that [t] she was sick, and died: whom when they had washed, they laid *her* [u] in an upper chamber.

38 And forasmuch as [x] Lydda was nigh to Joppa, and the disciples had heard that Peter was there, they sent unto him two men, [y] desiring *him* that he would not [t] delay to come to them.

39 Then Peter arose, and went with them. When he was come, they brought him into the upper chamber:

---

and every good thing; and to settle all the concerns of the several churches, in order to the regular administration of divine ordinances. The disciples likewise " walked in the " fear of the Lord," or habitually conducted themselves, with reverential regard to the authority of God, as his upright worshippers; and enjoyed much comfort, and were animated in obedience, by the power of the Holy Spirit, in the hope and peace of the gospel: and thus many others were won over to them, and their numbers were continually increased in each church, and churches were formed in other places.—' Their shining piety above others, ' and their great joy in the Holy Ghost attracting others ' to the faith.' *Whitby*. (*Note*, Zech. viii. 20—23.)— ' The edification of the church is the event of persecu- ' tion, provided the Lord be patiently waited for.' *Beza*. (*Marg. Ref*.)—The conversion of Saul, from a furious and most active persecutor, to a zealous, unwearied, and self-denying preacher of the gospel, and his subsequent labours and sufferings in the cause, for a long course of years, is an undoubted fact, which ought to be accounted for by all, who have the least doubt of the divine original of Christianity. If his own narrative be admitted, Christ- ianity is without doubt divine, and the only true religion; and those who hesitate to admit his testimony in its full latitude, are required, in support of their cause, to give some other rational and probable account of so unpa- ralleled an event.

Were edified.] Οικοδομημεναι. *Matt*. vii. 24. 26. xvi. 18. *Rom*. xv. 20. 1 *Cor*. viii. 1. 10. x. 23. xiv. 4. 17. *Gal*. ii. 18. 1 *Thes*. v. 11. 1 *Pet*. ii. 5. 7. Ex οικος, *domus*, et in- usitato δομεω, *struo*. (*Notes*, 1 *Cor*. iii. 10—15. *Eph*. ii. 19—22. iv. 14—16. *Jude* 20, 21.)

V. 32—35. Little has been thus far recorded concern- ing the labours of the apostles, except at Jerusalem; though doubtless they incessantly endeavoured to propa- gate the gospel in every way which they could. Here, however, we find that Peter made a circuit through various parts of the land of Judea, and the adjacent parts, proba- bly to visit the places where the gospel had been planted, by those whom the persecution had scattered: and coming to " the saints," or believers, at Lydda, a town near the shore of the Mediterranean Sea, he wrought a miracle, " in the name of Jesus," and by his power, which was the means of convincing and converting to the faith of Christ many of the inhabitants of that and the adjacent country: so that they believed him to be " the Lord," the Messiah, and became his disciples. (*Marg. Ref*.) . " Eneas, Jesus, " the Christ, healeth thee" (34). ' It is worth our while ' to observe the great difference that there is, between the ' manner in which this miracle was wrought by Peter, and ' that in which Christ performed his works of divine power ' and goodness.' *Doddridge*. (*Notes*, iii. 1—11, *v*. 6. 12 —16.)—*Eight years*, &c. (33) iv. 22. xiv. 8. *Mark* v. 25. *Luke* xiii. 16. *John* v. 5.—Saron (35) is supposed to have been a plain, or valley, extending from Cesarea to Joppa.—The success of the gospel, on this occasion, seems to have been very great; for it is supposed, that the neighbourhood was populous.—Philip preached in the cities, from Azotus (or Ashdod) to Cesarea; and Lydda and Saron doubtless were among them. (viii. 40.) It is highly probable, that the gospel was introduced at Lydda by his ministry: and that Eneas was made known to Peter, as an afflicted person favourable to the gospel.

Throughout all quarters. (32) Δια παντων. ' Through ' all the forementioned places of Judea, Samaria, and Ga- ' lilee (31).' *Whitby*.—*And turned unto the Lord*. (35) 'Οιτινες επιτρεψαν επι τον Κυριον· " Who turned unto the " Lord." See on iii. 19. They turned to the Lord Jesus Christ: they had previously been worshippers of God and not idolaters. (43. 1 *Thes*. i. 9.)

V. 36—43. The words Tabitha, and Dorcas, the one Syriack, and the other Greek, signify a *hind*, or *doe*; but whether this pious woman was thus named for any par- ticular reason, or not, is uncertain. (*Marg*. and *Ref*.)— '.The reason why St. Luke gives this interpretation of her, ' Syriack name, seems ... to be this, that she being a græciz- ' ing Jewess, was called by the first name by the Jews, and ' by the second among the Greeks.' *Whitby*.—She was a peculiar ornament to the gospel, which she had embraced: for she so abounded in good works and alms-deeds, that her whole life was a continued succession of them; as a tree is full of fruit, when every branch is loaded with it.'

JOPPA.

2 Chron. ii. 16.   Ezra iii. 7.   Jonah i. 3.   Acts ix. 36—43; x. 5—23.

^a and all the widows stood by him weeping, ^a and shewing the coats and garments which Dorcas made ^b while she was with them.

40 But Peter ^c put them all forth, ^d and kneeled down ^a and prayed; and turning *him* to the body, said, Tabitha, arise. And ^f she opened her eyes: and when she saw Peter, she sat up.

41 And ^e he gave her *his* hand, and lifted her up; and when he had called the saints and ^h widows, ⁱ he presented her alive.

42 And it was known throughout all Joppa; ^k and many believed in the Lord.

43 And it came to pass, that he tarried many days in Joppa, with ^l one Simon a tanner

---

(Marg. Ref. r, s.—*Notes, John* xv. 6—8, *v.* 8. *Phil.* i. 9—11, *v.* 11.) She not only gave away her substance; but she employed her time and skill in labouring diligently and constantly, for the poor widows and other believers; so that her death was considered as a publick loss. The principal persons therefore among the disciples, having heard of Peter's miracle at Lydda, which was but about six miles from Joppa, (*Marg. Ref.* q.x,) sent for him, in hopes that he would be enabled to restore her to life again; which evinced very strong faith, as it does not appear, that any apostle had hitherto wrought a miracle of this kind. When he came, and had witnessed the deep mourning of those, who expressed at once their gratitude and their loss, by shewing the garments which Dorcas had made for them, " while she was with them;" he went alone into the room where she lay, and there prevailed by prayer for her restoration to life. (*Marg. Ref.* y—b.) In performing this miracle Peter used words, in some respects like what Jesus had employed on similar occasions; but he had prefaced it with humble prayer upon his knees. (*Notes,* 1 *Kings* xvii. 20—24. 2 *Kings* iv. 33—35. *John* xi. 41—46.) He was doubtless assured, that this request was granted, before he addressed Dorcas. His words were not, " I say unto thee, Arise," in the language of authority, but simply, " Tabitha, arise," as an intimation that Jesus had restored her to life: and it should also be remembered that there was no witness to the transaction.—This miracle was not only a high gratification and valuable benefit to the admiring thankful company of believers; but it was the means also of converting very many to the faith. Peter therefore, finding an opening for usefulness at Joppa, continued there for some time, lodging at the house of one Simon a tanner, and not with Tabitha; perhaps, lest he should *seem* to receive a recompence for the exercise of his miraculous powers. (*Notes,* viii. 18—24. *Matt.* x. 7, 8.)—It is remarkable, that there is no instance in scripture of a prophet, or eminent minister of religion, being raised from the dead; (for it does not appear, that St. Paul was entirely dead, when he had been stoned at Lystra; *Note,* xiv. 19, 20;) and but few of their miraculous recoveries from sickness: though we should perhaps have thought, that these were the most proper cases for a divine interposition.

A disciple. (36) Μαθητρια. Here only.—*An upper chamber.* (37) Ὑπερωω. 39. See on i. 13.—*Would not delay.* (38) " Be grieved." *Marg.* Μη οκνησαι. Here only N. T.—*Num.* xxii. 16. *Judg.* xviii. 9. *Sept.* Οκνηρος, *Matt.* xxv. 26. *Rom.* xii. 11 : ab οκνος, *pigritia.*—*A tanner.* (43) Βορσει. x. 6 32. Not elsewhere. A Ϛυρσα, *corium, pellis,* *Job* xvi. 15. *Sept.*

PRACTICAL OBSERVATIONS.

V. 1—9.

The power of doing evil has seldom been adequate to the inclination, even in those who have been most successful persecutors and destroyers in the church, or in the world: for could scourges of God execute their threatenings, as readily as they utter them, their very breath would be fatal to mankind, and especially to the disciples of the Lord.—The restraints providentially imposed upon us, previous to our conversion, prevent much mischief; or the deplorable history of our past lives would have been still worse.—Even when sinners are most eager to execute their rebellious purposes, the Lord sometimes discovers his designs of mercy towards them: and thus the extremity of their wickedness illustrates the infinite riches and power of his grace.—While we are praying, in imminent dangers or overwhelming troubles, we are apt to be discouraged, if we can see no way by which we may be delivered : but he, who in a moment is able to change furious persecutors into zealous preachers, can perform his promises by various methods, of which we have not the least conception.—The manifested light and glory of the divine justice, holiness, and power, would sink the stoutest rebel on earth to despair at once, if it were not accompanied with some indications of mercy and grace : but the Lord sends convictions and terrors to abase men in the dust, that their hearts may be prepared for " peace and " joy in believing."—No man can have a good or even a plausible reason for rebellion against the authority of God : he has given no cause for it, nor can any good come of it, but directly the contrary : for " it is hard to kick against the " pricks."—Little do proud Pharisees and despisers of the gospel imagine, while indulging their contempt and hatred of those whom they deem wild enthusiasts or obstinate sectaries, that they are persecuting the Lord himself, and that he will resent it accordingly. He is One with his disciples, and they with him : he will requite every favour done to them, as if done to himself; and whoever injures them touches " the apple of his eye." But opposers of the gospel do not generally believe, that Jesus is " the " Lord of glory;" and that all their hard speeches and strenuous endeavours against him, are a direct attack upon the Lord of Hosts himself. (*Note, Jude* 14—16.) When he shall therefore appear, in far more terrible majesty, than he did to Saul of Tarsus; they will tremble with astonishment at the awful consequences of that conduct, in which they now perhaps imagine there is much merit, or by which they seek renown.—When a sinner is brought to a proper sense of his own state, character, and

CHAP. X.

Cornelius, a devout centurion in Cæsarea but a gentile, being directed by an angel, sends for Peter to instruct him, 1—8; who in the mean time is prepared by a vision, 9—16; and, being commanded by the Spirit, he, attended by certain disciples, accompanies the messengers, 17—23. Cornelius renders undue

honour to Peter, who declines it, 24—26; and shews the occasion of his sending for him, avowing the readiness of himself and his friends to receive the word of God from him, 27—33. Peter preaches to them Jesus, and salvation by faith in him, 34—43. The Holy Spirit is poured out on the company, as on the apostles on the day of Pentecost; and Peter commands them to be baptized, 44—48.

conduct, he will submit without reserve; allowing that he might justly be left to perish; casting himself wholly on the mercy of the divine Saviour, and enquiring what he would have him to do. This will thenceforth be the language of his heart and prayers continually: 'What must I do to be saved? In what way must I come? What means shall I use? What method shall I take to obtain assurance of my reconciliation? What return can I make for thy mercy? How shall I recommend thy salvation to others? Shall I enter upon this or the other business, or not? How shall I behave in these circumstances, or manage this matter?' These, and such like questions, the believer will have daily to propose to the Lord, in faith and prayer; desiring to be taught, inclined, and enabled to know and do his will. (*Note, Col.* iii. 16, 17, *v.* 16.) When this submission has been made, the Lord takes the humbled penitent under his direction, and teaches him what he would have him to do: yet he does not shew him the whole at once, but gradually, as it becomes necessary: and he uses his servants as instruments in this work; that his appointments may be honoured, and 'the com- 'munion of the saints' may be promoted. Nor does he generally bring transgressors to "peace and joy in believ-"ing," without such previous rebukes, sorrows, and distresses of conscience, as may evince the atrociousness of their crimes, and lay a foundation for their future humility, gratitude, patience, and meekness.—Under great remorse of conscience, and when the soul is deeply engaged about eternal things, a man loses his desire after animal recreation: so that fasting in such circumstances is often a matter of course, rather than an imposed duty. But happy are they, who thus sow in tears, that they may reap in joy! (*Note, Ps.* cxxvi. 5, 6. *P. O.—Notes, Matt.* v. 4. 2 *Cor.* vii. 9—11.)

V. 10—22.

"Behold he," the proud Pharisee, or the prouder infidel, "prayeth;" in that manner which the Saviour notices with cordial approbation! Behold the licentious profligate, the iniquitous publican, the unmerciful oppressor, or the daring blasphemer, "prayeth!" What happy tidings are these, when well authenticated, to such as understand the nature and efficacy of prayer; of such prayer, as the humbled sinner presents before a merciful God, for the blessings of eternal salvation!—Yet, even eminent disciples are sometimes staggered at the commands of their gracious Lord, though they express their readiness to obey: and while they allow, in general, the infinite sufficiency of his mercy, they are apt to assign limits to it in particular instances, according to their several prejudices and passions! But the Lord is peculiarly glorified in far exceeding all our limitations, and scanty expectations; and in shewing that *they* are "the chosen vessels of his mercy," whom we are ready to consider as the objects of his most

righteous vengeance: nay, that perhaps, he intends them to do and to suffer more in his cause, and for his sake, than those who stand highest in our estimation. This was the case with him, who had done so "much evil to the "saints" of the Lord Jesus at Jerusalem, and was preparing to do all he could against those, who called on his name at Damascus; and in more obscure instances, the same is taking place continually.—He expects implicit obedience from his servants: all their objections arise from unbelief; and when they are in a right frame of mind, they would go even into the lion's den, should their obedience require it, assured that he will be with them, to support or deliver them.—Converting grace renders believers the children of the same Father, abolishes their former distinctions, and terminates their enmities: and, when the bitterest foe, or the vilest malefactor, becomes a real disciple, we are required to own and to love him as a "brother," without any upbraidings, prejudice, or resentment; and we should rejoice to be useful to him, either in his temporal or spiritual concerns.—The efficacious teaching of the Holy Spirit causes "the scales" of ignorance, prejudice, and pride to fall from the eyes of the understanding, which before excluded the clear light of the gospel: then the sinner receives his sight, and professes the faith which once he despised: then he passes from the kingdom of Satan to that of God; (*Notes, Eph.* i. 15— 23, *vv.* 15—18. *Col.* i. 9—14;) and, being a new creature, he lives in a new element, and joins himself to new companions: (*Note,* 1 *Sam.* x. 10—13:) and, as he has opportunity and ability, he endeavours to recommend Jesus, the anointed Saviour and the Son of God, to the attention of his former associates in iniquity or infidelity: and this is often done with an energy of argument and persuasion, which confounds those, who are the most hardened against the truth.

V. 23—31.

While many, who witness the effects of the gospel, are *amazed,* only a few in comparison are effectually convinced by them. Even Saul's conversion, though it is, at this day, a real demonstration of the truth of Christianity, a fact that can neither be doubted, nor accounted for upon any other principle; even when it first took place, and when it concurred with his convincing arguments, and most stupendous miracles, could not of itself effect the conversion of one enemy to the gospel: for nothing can produce true faith, but that power which new creates the heart. (*Notes and P. O. Luke* xvi. 27—31.) Thus the Jews, both at Damascus and Jerusalem, rejected Saul's unexceptionable testimony, and sought to kill him; as he had sought the destruction of those who had been Christians before him!—True believers are apt to carry their suspicions too far, in respect of those against whom they have imbibed strong prejudices, and from whom they have

a viii. 40. xvi. 8 **THERE** was a certain man ᵃ in Cæ-
xxiii. 23. 33.
b xxv. 1. 13. sarea, called Cornelius, ᵇ a centurion of
Job xxii. 2h. xvii.
l. 31. 43. Mart the band called the ᶜ Italian *band*,
vii. 5, &c. xxvii.
54 Luke vii. 2 2 *A* ᵈ devout *man*, ᵉ and one that
c xxvi. 1.
d 7. 22. ii. 5. viii. 2. xiii. 50. xvi. 14. xxii. 12. L⸺e ii. 25.   e 35. ix. 31. xiii. 16. 26.
I Kings viii. 43. 2 Chr. vi. 33. Job i. 1. Ps. cii. 13. Is. lix. 19. Dan. vi. 26. Rev. xv. 4.

feared God ᶠ with all his house, ᵍ which ᶠ 7. xvi. 15. xviii.
8. Gen. xviii.
gave much alms to the people, ᵇ and 19. Josh. xxiv.
15. Job i. 5. Ps.
prayed to God alway. cl. 6—8.
g 4. 22. 31. ix.
35. 1x. leiii. 7, 8. Luke vii. 4, 5. ᵇ Rom. xv. 26, 27. 2 Cor. ix. 8—15.   h ix. 11.
Ps. xxv. 5, 8, 9. iv. 17. lxxxvi. 3. morg. lxxxviii. 1. Prov. ii. 3—5. Dan. vi. 10. 16. 20.
Mart. vii. 7, 8. Luke xviii. 1. Col. iv. 2. 1 Thes. v. 17. Jam. i. 5.

received great injuries. Indeed the world is so full of deceit, and the visible church of hypocrisy, that it is hard
for us to be sufficiently cautious, without verging to the
extreme. The Lord, however, will clear up the characters of the upright; he will bring them acquainted with his
people; and give them opportunities of bearing testimony
to his truth, perhaps before those, with whom they once
concurred in enmity and opposition to it. He sees good
to prove his churches by tribulations and persecutions:
but by taking off their enemies, converting some and dismaying others, or finding them other employment, he
gives seasons of rest and peace; in which we should diligently edify ourselves and each other, that we may be prepared for future trials, in case they should be allotted us.
—When believers walk conscientiously, "in the fear of
" the Lord, and in the comfort of the Holy Spirit," they
appear to be an excellent and happy people, and are generally multiplied: and it behoves us to watch against dejection or melancholy, as much as against known sin; for
it prejudices the minds of unbelievers against the truth,
and renders them afraid of it, as only productive of dejection and discomfort.

V. 32—43.

The unwearied labours of the primitive preachers of
the gospel, should be studied and imitated, by all their
successors in the ministry: and the displays of the power
and grace of Christ should encourage us, in all our difficulties. He can heal our bodies or our souls, of the most
inveterate maladies, whenever he pleases: his long delays
do not prove that he never intends to deliver us; and he
can make our tedious afflictions or temptations, and our
merciful deliverances, the means of saving the souls of
those around us, and of greatly displaying the glory of his
power, mercy, and truth.—While we live upon the fulness
of Christ, for our whole salvation, we ourselves should
desire to be " full of good works and alms-deeds," for the
honour of his name and the benefit of his saints. Then
those who go before us will be witnesses in heaven, and
they who survive us will testify on earth, to the reality of
our faith and love. (*Note, Luke* xvi. 9—13. *Notes* and
P. O. 2 Cor. ix. 8—15.)—Many seem to think, that none
can glorify Christ, or help to promote his gospel, except ministers: but such persons as Tabitha are as much wanted,
and are as useful in their places, even as able faithful
preachers: for while the latter proclaim the truths of the
gospel by their word; the other substantiate, illustrate,
and demonstrate the excellency of them, in their lives.
How mean then is the grovelling ambition of those numerous females, who aspire to no higher distinction, than that
of external personal decoration and accomplishment, and
who waste their lives in trifling pursuits; when multiplied
charities and labours of love, might have rendered them,
at less xpense of time and treasure, a blessing to multitudes, and an ornament to Christianity! When such
triflers die, all dies with them, and their loss is not greatly

either felt or lamented: while even such as have had little
in their power, and have " laboured, working with their
" own hands," that they might relieve the poor and needy,
will be substantially useful through life, and " sincerely
" lamented at death; and" their " works follow them," and
will be graciously rewarded in heaven. We cannot expect,
nor should we desire, the return to life of those who have
thus " served their generation, and are fallen asleep:"
yet the presence, conversation, and prayers of faithful
ministers may be a benefit to the survivors; and they
should ever be ready to embrace opportunities of comforting the mourners, and giving a salutary turn to their sorrows. The Lord can make up every loss; he over-rules
every event for the good of those who trust in him, and
for the glory of his own name: and unostentatious piety,
disinterested diligence, and indifference about outward
accommodations, should mark the whole conduct of those,
who preach the gospel of God our Saviour.

NOTES.

CHAP. X. V. 1, 2. Hitherto none had been admitted,
by baptism, into the Christian church, but Jews, Samaritans, and proselytes; who all were circumcised persons,
and observed the ceremonial law: but the time was now
come, when the gentiles were to be openly called, to share
all the privileges of the people of God; without being
proselyted to Judaism, either before, or after their conversion to Christianity.—The character of the person whom
God was pleased to select, as the first-fruits of this harvest
from among the Gentiles, was suited (as much as any
thing could be,) to abate the prejudice of the Jewish converts against the alteration. Cornelius was a centurion,
or the commander of a hundred men, in " the Italian
" band," or cohort, of Roman soldiers, which attended the
governor, who at this time generally resided at Cæsarea.
(*Marg. Ref.* a. c.) It may be supposed, that Cornelius,
if a native of Italy, would think it a trial, to be sent so far
from his country and all his connexions: for the *Cornelii*
were an illustrious family at Rome. Yet in Judea, he became acquainted with the true God; and, renouncing
idolatry, he worshipped him with reverence and obedient
attention. He taught his family to do the same, and was
a liberal friend to the poor Jews among whom he resided;
he was constant in his devotions, probably with his family,
as well as in secret; and he set apart seasons for fasting
and prayer, as it is reasonable to conclude, to seek further
directions from God respecting his truth and will. (*Marg.
Ref.* d—h.—*Notes,* xiii. 1—3. *Dan.* ix. 2, 3. x. 1—3. *John*
i. 47—51, *v.* 48.) He was in some measure acquainted
with the scriptures, and the promises of a Messiah by
means of the Greek translation, as it is most probable:
though it may be questioned whether he had learned to
rely on him, as a spiritual Redeemer who was to come.—
Many writers are very full and exact, about two sorts of
proselytes to the Jewish religion; and others argue against

3 He ¹ saw in a vision evidently about the ninth hour of the day, ¹ an angel of God coming in to him, and saying unto him, ᵐ Cornelius.

4 And when he looked on him ⁿ he was afraid, and said, ° What is it, Lord? And he said unto him, ᵖ Thy prayers and ⁱ thine alms are come up for a memorial before God.

5 And now ʳ send men to Joppa, and call for one Simon, ˢ whose surname is Peter:

6 He lodgeth with ᵗ one Simon a tanner, whose house is by the sea-side : ᵘ he shall tell thee what thou oughtest to do.

7 And when the angel which spake unto Cornelius was departed, he called ˣ two of his household servants, ʸ and a

that distinction : but the nature of the case, and the facts recorded in scripture render it evident, that some of the Gentiles were circumcised, professed obedience to the whole Mosaick law, and were completely incorporated among the native Jews; and, that others became worshippers of the true God, and professed obedience to the moral precepts, who were not circumcised, nor observant of the ceremonial law. Of this latter description Cornelius was ; and therefore considered entirely as a Gentile, though of good report among the Jews.—'The Jews ac-' counted them unclean as well as the other Gentiles : ... 'yet ... they deemed the alms they gave to the Jews clean; '... and because Cornelius was free in giving to the Jews 'of Cæsarea, he was a man of good report among them 'all. (22)' Whitby. (Notes, Matt. viii. 5—13. Luke vii. 1—10.) The promised Saviour, however, was now come, and the way of salvation by him was openly preached : it was therefore proper, that all "who feared God" should explicitly believe in him, and profess themselves his disciples. There was evidently a preparation in the heart of Cornelius, for the reception of the gospel ; he had doubtless a true faith in the word of God, as far as he understood it, though he had not an explicit faith in Christ. (Note, viii. 26—31.) This preparation and faith were the fruits of the regenerating Spirit of God, who was given to him through the mediation of Jesus, even before he knew him; and this indeed is the case with every man, when "God who is rich in mercy, for his great love "wherewith he loved him, even when dead in sin," at first "quickens him together with Christ." (Note, Eph. ii. 4—10, vv. 4, 5.) Had it been possible for Cornelius, in this state of mind, to have refused the salvation of Christ when proposed to him ; he would not have been saved by his works : but this could not be, for God had prepared and inclined him to welcome the gospel, because he intended to call him to believe it ; so that he could neither be saved without faith in Christ, nor could he perish through want of it. It is mere trifling to enquire, as many have done, what his state would have been, had he died after his prayers were heard, and before he had believed in Christ ; for it goes upon the absurd supposition of the Lord's beginning a work, and not bringing it to the intended completion. It is a universal rule, that whatever is from God, of a spiritual and holy nature, will for Christ's sake be accepted by him : but it may be doubted whether he ever communicates regenerating grace to an adult person, where he has not given, or does not mean to send, some measure of the light of his word : though it does not behove us to limit his mercy ; nor can we tell how small a portion of divine truth may be the seed or

the food of divine life in the soul. This we may know certainly, that no regenerate man will finally reject the gospel, when proposed to him.—Many objections and reasonings, and much perplexity on this subject, among persons of contrary systems, seem to arise from inattention to this truth ; that nothing spiritually good, or acceptable to God, can be produced from the heart of fallen man, except by the regenerating Spirit of Christ : where that is communicated, all things necessary to salvation will in due time follow ; yet when, or in what order, cannot be previously ascertained. (Notes, John i. 10—13, vv. 12, 13. iii. 3—8.) But many things good, in the estimation of man, and many specious appearances of evangelical religion, are as distinct from spirituality and holiness, or the choice and love of the holy excellency of God and heavenly things; as polished brass, in its highest perfection, is different from pure gold. (Note, Luke xvi. 14, 15.) Perhaps these observations may assist the reader, in understanding this interesting chapter ; which cannot easily be made to accord with the exactness of systematical writers of different creeds, on these subjects.—The Italian band. (1) 'Many, 'with Grotius, have explained this, as if the meaning 'were, that Cornelius was a centurion of one of the co-' horts belonging to the Italian legion. ... But I refer the ' reader to the many learned and judicious things, which ' Mr. Biscoe has said, (Boyle's Lectures,) to shew that the ' Italian legion did not exist at this time. ... I think it ex-' ceedingly probable, for the reasons which he urges, that ' this was a cohort different from any of the legionary ' ones; and consequently that Luke has here expressed ' himself with his usual accuracy ; and that the mistake ' lies, as it generally does, in those who think they have ' learning enough to correct him. It is probable, that this ' was called the Italian cohort, because most of the sol-' diers belonging to it were Italians.' Doddridge. Instead of generally, always would have been more proper. Band. (1) Σπειρης. See on Matt. xxvii. 27.—A devout man. (2) Ευσεβης. 7. xxii. 12. 2 Pet. ii. 9. Ευσεβεια· See on iii. 12.—One that feared God.] Φοβεμενος τον Θεον. 22. 35. xiii. 16. 1 Pet. ii. 17. Rev. xix. 5.—Gen. xxii. 12. xlii. 18. Ex. i. 17. Ps. cxii. 1. cxv. 13. cxlvii. 11.—With all his house.] Συν παντι τω οικω αυτη. xi. 14. xvi. 31. xviii. 8. 1 Cor. i. 16.—Not πανοικι· See on xvi. 34. (Note, Josh. xxiv. 15.)—Prayed ... alway.] Δεομενος ... διαπαντος. iv. 31. Luke xxi. 36. Δεομαι, xxi. 39. Matt. ix. 38. Luke viii. 28. 34. xxii. 32, et al. Διαπαντος, ii. 25. xxiv. 16. 2 Thes. iii. 16. Heb. ii. 15. ix. 6. xiii. 15.—Ps. xvi. 8. Sept.

V. 3—8. Cornelius, influenced by divine grace, was acting conscientiously, and waiting for clearer discoveries of the will of God : and, when he was keeping a solemn

devout soldier of them that waited on him continually;

8 And when he had declared all *these* things unto them, ' he sent them to Joppa.

9 ¶ On the morrow, as they went on their journey, and drew nigh unto the city, ª Peter went up upon the house-top to pray, about ᵇ the sixth hour:

10 And ª he became very hungry, and would have eaten; but while they made ready, ᵈ he fell into a trance,

11 And ª saw heaven opened, ᶠ and a certain vessel descending unto him, as it had been a great sheet, knit at

the four corners, and let down to the earth;

12 Wherein ᵍ were all manner of four-footed beasts of the earth, and wild beasts, and creeping things, and fowls of the air.

13 And there came a voice to him, ʰ Rise, Peter; kill and eat.

14 But Peter said, ¹ Not so, Lord; ᵏ for I have never eaten any thing that is common or unclean.

15 And the voice *spake* unto him again the second time, ¹ What God hath cleansed, *that* call not thou common.

16 This was done ᵐ thrice: and the vessel was received up again into heaven.

---

fast, and praying at the hour of the evening-sacrifice, as one of the stated hours of prayer; (*Marg. Ref.* i, k. 30. —*Notes*, iii. 1—11. *v.* 1. *Dan.* ix. 21—23;) he saw, in a vision, an angel in human form and shining garments, who addressed him by name as he entered his apartment. Being greatly alarmed at the vision, (as probably his doors were fastened,) and aware that this was a heavenly visitant, he desired in the language of reverence, to know what was the meaning of his coming. The angel then assured him, that "his alms and prayers were come up before God" with acceptance; who was, as it were, reminded by them of his promises and purposes to do him good. (*Marg. Ref.* l—p.—*Notes*, *Ps.* x. 17, 18. *Prov.* ii. 1—8. *Is.* lxii. 6, 7. *Luke* i. 11—17. *John* i. 47—51, *v.* 48. *Rom.* viii. 24 —27.) He therefore was come, not to be his instructor, but to direct him to send for Peter to Joppa; who would shew to him the way of truth and salvation, about which he was earnestly enquiring. (*Note*, xi. 4—17, *vv.* 13, 14.) Thus the angel left it to the apostle to preach the gospel to Cornelius, that the sacred ministry might be honoured, and that he might become acquainted with the disciples of Christ for his future benefit. Peter, the apostle of the circumcision, by whose preaching the foundation of the church of converted Jews was laid, on the day of Pentecost, was chosen on this occasion, rather than Paul the intended apostle of the Gentiles; probably, that the unprecedented admission of uncircumcised persons, into the church, might give as little offence to the Jewish converts as possible.—Philip, the evangelist, seems to have been at Cæsarea at this time; yet it did not please God to employ him in the case of Cornelius, as he had done in that of the Ethiopian treasurer. (*Notes*, viii. 26—40.) Cornelius receiving these directions, and having pious servants and soldiers, through the influence of his example and instructions, immediately sent three messengers to Joppa, to enquire for a man, of whom he had probably never heard, before the angel made him known to him, with special directions where to find him. (ix. 43. *Marg. Ref.* u—z.) It does not appear, that Cornelius had the least acquaintance with the Christians at or near Cæsarea.—His intercourse with the unbelieving Jews was suited rather to increase than remove his prejudices: and, as far as it can

now be judged, the reading of the Greek translation of the scriptures was the principal and almost sole *means*, by which effects so beneficial and excellent had been produced. (Note, viii. 32—35, *v.* 32.)

Evidently. (3) Φανερως. *Mark* i. 45. *John* vii. 10.— *For a memorial.* (4) Εις μνημοσυνον. *Matt.* xxvi. 13.— *Lodgeth.* (6) Ξενιζεται. 18. 23. 32. xvii. 20. xxi. 16. xxviii. 7. *Heb.* xiii. 2. Ξενια, xxviii. 23. *Philem.* 22.—*Household servants.* (7) Οικετων. *Luke* xvi. 13. *Rom.* xiv. 4. 1 *Pet.* ii. 18. Not elsewhere.—*Waited on him continually.*] Προσκαρτερουντων. See on i. 14.

V. 9—16. ' Peter, after he had received the Holy ' Spirit, needed to make daily proficiency, in the know-' ledge of the benefit of Christ.' *Beza.* (*Note*, iii. 19— 21.) The prejudices of Peter were so strong against uncircumcised persons, that the report of Cornelius's vision would not have satisfied his mind, as to the propriety of going to him, unless the Lord had likewise by other means prepared him for the service. (*Notes*, xi. 1—18.)—When the messengers drew near to Joppa, Peter had retired for prayer to some convenient solitude, which he had upon the top of the house, it being then about noon; for, like David and Daniel, he prayed at least three times a day. (*Marg. Ref.* a, b.—*Notes*, *Ps.* lv. 16, 17, *v.* 17. *Dan.* vi. 10, 11.) While he was there, he became uncommonly hungry, and would gladly have eaten; but, before his ordinary repast was ready, he fell into a trance, or *ecstasy;* in which his senses were closed to external objects, but invisible things were presented to his mind, as if he saw them with his eyes. (*Marg. Ref.* c, d.—*Notes*, vii. 54—60. xxii. 17— 21. 2 *Cor.* xii. 1—6.) In this state there appeared to him a great vessel, resembling a very large sheet, or wrapper, of which the four corners were fastened together: this seemed to come down from heaven to the earth; and upon further observing it, he found that it contained all kinds of living creatures, especially, if not exclusively, all those animals, which were unclean according to the law. At the same time he heard a voice directing him to satisfy his hunger, by immediately killing and eating whatever he chose. To this he decidedly objected, though he supposed it to be the voice of the Lord; as he had always observed the ritual law, in this matter, with the most scrupulous

417

a 19. 11. 12. v. 24.
xxv. 20. John
vii. 12. 1 Pet. i.
11.
● 7.—16.

17 ¶ Now ª while Peter doubted in himself what this vision which he had seen should mean; behold, ª the men which were sent from Cornelius had made enquiry for Simon's house, and stood before the gate,

p 5, 6. xi. 11.

18 And called, ª and asked whether Simon, which was surnamed Peter, were lodged there.

19 While Peter thought on the vi-

q viii. 29. xi. 12.
xiii. 2. xvi. 6, 7.
xx. 13. 1 Cor.
xvi. 11. 1 Tim.
iv. 1.
r viii. 26. iv. 15.
xv. 7. Mark
xvi. 13.
s ix. 17. xiii. 4.
Is. xlviii. 16.
Zech. ii. 9—11.

sion, ª the Spirit said unto him, Behold, three men seek thee.

20 Arise, therefore, ª and get thee down, and go with them, doubting nothing; ª for I have sent them.

21 Then Peter went down to the

men which were sent unto him from Cornelius; and said, ª Behold, I am he whom ye seek: ª what *is* the cause wherefore ye are come ?

22 And they said, ª Cornelius the centurion, ª a just man, and one that feareth God, and ª of good report among all the nation of the Jews, was warned from God by an holy angel to send for thee into his house, ª and to hear words of thee.

23 Then called he them in, ª and lodged *them*. And ª on the morrow Peter went away with them, ª and certain brethren from Joppa accompanied him.

t John i. 36, 39.
xvii. 4—6.
u 29. Mark x. 51
x 1—5.
y xxvr. 15. Hos.
xiv. 9. Hab. ii.
4. Matt. v. 9.
Mark i. 2A.
Luke xi. 2A.
z xxiii. 50. Rom.
ii. 17. Heb. x.
38. xii. 25.
vi. 3. xxii. 12.
Luke vii. 4, 5.
1 Tim. iii. 7.
Heb. xi. 2.
3 John 12.
6 33. xi. 14.
John v. 24. vi.
45. 68. viii. 20.
xvii. 8, 20. Rom.
x. 17. 18. 2 Cor.
v. 16—20. 2 Pet.
iii. 2.
b Gen. xix. 2, 3.
xxiv. 31, 32.
21. Heb. xiii. 2.
1 Pet. iv. 9.
c 29. 33. Ec. ix.
10.
d 45. ix. 38. 42.
xi. 12. 2 Cor
vii. 21.

exactness. To this objection, it was replied, "What God "hath cleansed," that "call not thou common," or polluted. (*Marg. Ref. g.*—l.) To impress his mind more deeply, and to shew the certainty of the inference to be drawn from it, the transaction was thrice repeated, and then the whole vision disappeared. (*Gen.* xli. 32. *John* xxi. 17. 2 *Cor.* xiii. 1.)—The same law, which established the distinction between clean and unclean meats, had also marked the distinction, between Jews and Gentiles, and restricted their intercourse with each other: but the pride and bigotry of the Jews had carried the separation further than the law required; and had even produced a contempt of the Gentiles, however friendly or conscientious. The law also concerning the distinction of meats and of animals had both been an emblem of the distinction between clean and unclean persons, and a means of preserving it. (*Notes, Gen.* vii. 2, 3.—viii. 20—22. *Lev.* i. 1, 2. xi. 1—8. *Rom.* xiv. 13—18. 1 *Tim.* iv. 1—5.)—' Being thus sepa-' rated by this precept,' (concerning clean and unclean meats,) ' from all familiar converse with other nations,' ' hence they came to look on them, who did not use this ' abstinence as unclean, because they did freely eat of ' those things, which the law made unclean to them; and ' to say the unclean beasts did signify the people of the ' world.' *Whitby.*—*Call not thou common.* (15) ... " Do " not thou pollute." Gr. ' It was the priests' office, in ' case of leprosy, and other matters of a like nature, to ' pronounce the thing or person under examination, clean ' or unclean. In the Hebrew it is thus expressed, " The ' " priest shall cleanse,"..." The priest shall pollute him." ' ...What God hath cleansed, that is by this vision and ' command declared to be clean, do not thou pollute, that ' is, pronounce not thou unclean.' *Whitby.* To inform a Jew, that God had cleansed those animals, which before had been declared unclean, that they were no longer to be deemed common, or rejected as such, was in fact to announce the abrogation of the Mosaick law, and the introduction of another and more enlarged dispensation; and it plainly intimated, that uncircumcised Gentiles, whom God cleansed by faith and grace, were to be received into the church, without regard to the ceremonial law, or to their uncleanness according to it. (*Notes,* xv. 7—11. *Eph.* ii. 14—18. *Col.* ii. 13—15.)—This great

vessel might therefore signify the Christian church, as living under the full revelation of the new covenant of grace, the origin of which is from heaven, though its place is on earth. Its security, by the promise, oath, and covenant of God, and the engagements of his unchangeable wisdom, power, truth, and love, may also be intimated by the vessel being knit at the four corners. The animals of various species may represent sinners of every nation, description, and previous character, as gathered into the church by the preaching of the gospel, and by faith and grace: (*Note, Is.* xi. 6—9 :) and the voice, repeatedly addressing Peter, evidently meant, that he should thenceforth associate with converts to Christ, from among the Gentiles, and make no distinction between them and the Jewish disciples, for God had cleansed them; and that he should preach to the Gentiles, even as to the Jews, for God intended to cleanse them also. (*Notes,* 27—33. xi. 1—3. *Gal.* ii. 11—16.)

As they went on their journey. (9) 'Οδοιπορουντων εκεινων. Here only. 'Οδοιπορια See on *John* iv. 6.—*Very hungry.* (10) Προσπεινος. Here only.—*A trance.*] Εκτασις. xi. 5. xxii. 17. See on *Mark* v. 42.—*A vessel.* (11) Σκευος τι. 16. xi. 5. xxvii. 17. *Matt.* xii. 29. *Luke* xvii. 41. See on ix. 15.—*Four-footed.* (12) Τετραποδα. xi. 6. *Rom.* i. 23.—Εχ τετρας, quaternarius, et πυς, pes.—*Common.* (14) Κοινον. See on *Mark* vii. 2.—*Call not ... common.* (15) Μη κοινα. See on *Matt.* xv. 11.

V. 17—23. Peter did not readily understand the import of this vision ; though he knew that it contained some weighty instruction, which he diligently applied his mind to discover. (*Marg. Ref.* n.) Whilst he was thus engaged in deep reflection, the messengers of Cornelius arrived and enquired for him: but to satisfy his mind more fully, in a case that implied in its consequences the abolition of the ritual law, which God himself had given to Israel, this fact was immediately revealed to him ; and he was ordered to go with the messengers without scruple or hesitation.—God had directed Cornelius by the angel, to send these messengers, yet " the Spirit said to Peter, " I have sent them :" this is the language of Deity and personality. (20. *Marg. Ref.* q—s.) Accordingly Peter, having heard their report concerning Cornelius's character and vision, (*Notes,* 1, 2. *Job* i. 1,) hospitably entertained

4 a 8

24 ¶ And 'the morrow after, they entered into Cæsarea. And Cornelius waited for them, 'and had called together his kinsmen and near friends.

25 And as Peter was coming in, Cornelius met him, 'and fell down at his feet, and worshipped *him*.

26 But Peter took him up, saying, 'Stand up; I myself also am a man.

27 And as he talked with him, he went in, 'and found many that were come together.

28 And he said unto them, Ye know how 'that it is an unlawful thing for a man that is a Jew, to keep company, or come unto one of another nation: 'but God hath shewed me, that I should not call any man common or unclean.

29 Therefore came I *unto you* without gainsaying, 'as soon as I was sent for: ''I ask therefore for what intent ye have sent for me?

30 And Cornelius said, 'Four days ago 'I was fasting until this hour; and at the ninth hour I prayed in my house, 'and, behold, a man stood before me in bright clothing,

31 And said, Cornelius, 'thy prayer is heard, and thine alms 'are had in remembrance in the sight of God.

32 Send 'therefore to Joppa, and call hither Simon, whose surname is Peter; he is lodged in the house of *one* Simon a tanner, by the sea-side; who, when he cometh, shall speak unto thee.

33 Immediately therefore I sent to thee; and thou hast well done that thou art come. Now therefore 'are we all here present before God, to hear all things that are commanded thee of God.

them till the next day, and then went with them. But he took with him some of the believers, who dwelt at Joppa; that they might witness, and be ready to attest, the whole of what passed on this unprecedented occasion. (*Notes*, xi. 1—18.)

Doubted. (17) Διηπορει. See on *Luke* ix. 7.—*Thought*, &c. (19) Ενθυμουμενε. *Matt.* i. 20. ix. 4. Ενθυμησις· See on *Matt.* iv. 4.—*Doubting*. (20) Διακρινομενος. xi. 2. 12.—See on *Matt.* xxi. 21.—*Of good report.* (22) Μαρτυρεμενος. See on vi. 3.—*Was warned from God.*] Εχρηματισθε. *Matt.* ii. 12. 22. See on xi. 26.

V. 24—26. Cornelius, expecting a satisfactory discovery of the divine will from Peter, had collected his relations and intimate friends, (who, though Gentiles, were previously disposed to receive instruction, even as he was,) that they might share the benefit. (*Marg. Ref.* f. 33.) Peter had been made known to him in so extraordinary a manner, that Cornelius seems to have supposed, he must be something more than man: perhaps he thought that he was the Messiah, of whom he had read such glorious things in the writings of the prophets. He, however, prostrated himself before the apostle, and rendered him such homage, as Peter deemed improper to be received by any one, who was only a man like himself; and therefore he resolutely rejected it: yet Jesus continually accepted of the very same. (*Marg. Ref.* g, h.—*Notes, Matt.* xiv. 33. xv. 25—28. *Mark* v. 21—24.)—' If the worship, intended ' and given by Cornelius, was religious worship, ... Peter ' declares such worship was not to be given to a mere ' man : if it *was* only civil worship; he who thought it ' not fit to receive that, would much less have received re- ' ligious worship.' *Whitby.* ' Religious worship belongs ' to God alone; but civil and immoderate must not be ' rendered even to apostles, when present, much less when ' absent, and dead; and much less to their tombs. ...If ' Cornelius had desired to kiss Peter's toe, would Peter have

VOL. V.

' allowed him? Yet truly it is Peter's vicegerent, who re- ' quires kings to kiss his slipper!' *Beza.* (*Notes, Rev.* xix. 9, 10. xxii. 8, 9.)

Waited. (24) Ην προσδοκων. iii. 5. xxvii. 33. xxviii. 6. See on *Matt.* xi. 3—*Near friends.*] Τες αναγκαιες φιλες· xiii. 46. *Phil.* i. 24. ii. 25. *Tit.* iii. 14.—' Αναγκαιοι di- ' cuntur, qui Latinis *necessarii*, ...omnes qui sunt affinitatis ' et familiaritatis vinculis, arctissimè inter se conjuncti.' *Schleusner.*—*Worshipped.* (25) Προσεκυνησεν. vii. 43. viii. 27. xxiv. 11. See on *Matt.* viii. 2.

V. 27—33. When Peter had entered the house, in which so many uncircumcised persons were collected; he observed to them, that they knew it to be contrary to the law of Moses, for a Jew to associate with those of another nation; but God had shewed him, that this distinction was no longer to be strictly adhered to. (*Marg. Ref.* i—l.) He had therefore come to them without saying any thing to the contrary; and he now desired to be more particularly informed, on what account he had been sent for. Upon which Cornelius repeated the substance of his vision; (*Marg. Ref.* o—s.—*Note*, 3—8;) expressed his satisfaction in his having come to them so readily; and assured him that he and his friends were met together, as in the immediate presence of God, and prepared to give an implicit assent and a cordial welcome to the divine message which he was about to deliver, whatever it might be. (*Marg. Ref.* u.—*Notes*, xvii. 10—15. *Jer.* xlii. 1—6. 20—22.) The circumstances, preceding Peter's coming to Cornelius and his friends, rendered an implicit faith in his words most reasonable and proper, even previous to a comparison of them with the sacred oracles, the standard and test of truth.—*Unlawful.* (28) *Note*, 9—16.—The unlawfulness of the Jews associating with uncircumcised persons, and those who did not observe the ritual law, seems to have been generally inferred from the restriction laid on such intercourse, by the distinction of meats

4 T

34 ¶ Then Peter [x] opened *his* mouth,
and said, [y] Of a truth I perceive that
God is no respecter of persons:
35 But [z] in every nation he that
[a] feareth him, and worketh righteousness, [b] is accepted with him.
36 The [c] word which *God* sent unto
the children of Israel, [d] preaching peace
by Jesus Christ; ([e] he is Lord of all;)
37 That word, *I say*, [f] ye know,
[g] which was published throughout all
Judea, and began from Galilee, [h] after
the baptism which John preached;
38 How [i] God anointed Jesus of Nazareth with the Holy Ghost, and with
power; [k] who went about doing good,
and healing all that were oppressed
of the devil: [m] for God was with him.
39 And [n] we are witnesses of all
things which he did, both in the land
of the Jews, and in Jerusalem; [o] whom
they slew, and hanged on a tree:
40 Him [p] God raised up the third
day, and shewed him openly;
41 [q] Not to all the people, but unto

x vii. 8. Matt. v. 2. Eph vi. 19, 20. y Deut. x. 17. xvi. 19. 2 Chr. xix. 7. Job xxxiv. 19. Ps. lxxxii. 1, 2. Matt. xxii. 16. Luke xx. 21. Rom. ii. 11. Gal. ii. 6. Eph. vi. 9. Col. iii. 11. 25. Jam. ii. 4. 9. 1 Pet. i. 17. z xv. 9. Is. lvi. 3—8. Rom. ii. 25—29. iii. 22. 29, 30. x. 12, 13. 1 Cor. xii. 13. Gal. iii. 28. Eph. ii. 13—18. iii. 6—8. Phil. iii. 3. Col. i. 6. 23—27. iii. 11. a 2. ix. 31. Job xxviii. 28. Ps. xix. 9. lxxxv. 9. cxi. 10. Prov. i. 7. ii. 5. iii. 7. xvi. 6. Ec. xii. 13. 2 Cor. vii. 1. Eph. v. 21. 1 John ii. 29. b Gen. iv. 5—7. Hos. viii. 13. Luke i. 28. *marg.* Eph. i. 6. Heb. xi. 4—6. c ii. 38, 39. iii. 25, 26, xi. 19. xiii. 46. Matt. x. 6. Luke xxiv. 47. d Ps. lxxii. 1—3, 7. lxxxv. 9, 10. Is. ix. 6. xxxii. 15—17. lv. 12. lvii. 19. Luke ii. 10—14. 2 Cor. v. 18—21. Eph. ii. 13—18. Col. i. 20. Heb. vii. 2, 3. xiii. 20. e ii. 36. v. 31. Ps. ii. 6—8. xlv. 6. 11. cx. 1, 2. Is. vii. 14. xlv. 21—25. Jer. xxiii. 5, 6. Dan. vii. 13, 14. Hos. i. 7. Mic. v. 2. Mal. iii. 1. Matt. xi. 27. xxii. 44—46. xxviii. 18. John iii. 35, 36. v. 23—29. Rom. x. 11—13. 1 Cor. xv. 27. 47. Eph. i. 20—23. iv. 5—12. Phil. ii. 11. Col. i. 15—18. Heb. i. 2. 6—12. 1 Pet. iii. 22. Rev. i. 5. 18. xvii. 14. xix. 16. f ii. 22. xxvi. 26. xxviii. 22. g Luke iv. 14. xxiii. 5.

h i. 22. xiii. 24, 25. Matt. iii. 1—3. iv. 12, &c. Mark i. 1—5. 14, 15. John iv. 1—3. i ii. 22. iv. 27. Ps. ii. 2. 6. *marg.* xlv. 7. Is. xi. 2. xlii. 1. lxi. 1—3. Matt. xii. 28. Luke iii. 22. iv. 18. John iii. 34. vi. 27. x. 36—38. Heb. i. 9. k 2 Chr. xvii. 9. Matt. iv. 23—25. ix. 35. xv. 21—31. Mark i. 38, 39. iii. 7—11. vi. 6. 54—56. Luke vii. 10—17, 21—23. ix. 56. 1 Pet. v. 8. l Mark v. 13—15. vii. 29, 30. Luke iv. 33—36. ix. 42. Heb. ii. 14, 15. 1 John iii. 8. m John iii. 2. x. 32. 38. xvi. 32. n 41. i. 8. 22. ii. 32. iii. 15. v. 30—32. xiii. 31. Luke i. 2. xxiv. 48. John xv. 27. o ii. 23, 24. iii. 14, 15. iv. 10. v. 30. vii. 52. xiii. 27—29. Gal. iii. 13. 1 Pet. ii. 24. p xiii. 30, 31. xvii. 31. Rom. i. 4. iv. 24, 25. vi. 4—11. viii. 11. xiv. 9. 1 Cor. xv. 3, 4. 12—20. 2 Cor. iv. 14. Heb. xiii. 20. 1 Pet. i. 21. q 39. i. 2, 3. 22. xiii. 31.

and other ceremonies: for it is not forbidden by any express law.

As he talked with. (27) Συνομιλων. Here only.—Ex συν et ὁμιλεω, xxiv. 26. See on *Luke* xxiv. 14.—*Unlawful.* (28) Αθεμιτον. 1 *Pet.* iv. 3. Not elsewhere. Ex α priv. et θεμις, *jus.*—*To keep company.*] Κολλασθαι. v. 13. viii. 29. ix. 26. xvii. 34. *Luke* x. 11. xv. 15.—*Of another nation.*] Αλλοφυλῳ. Here only. Ex αλλος, et φυλη, *tribus.*—*Without gainsaying.* (29) Αναντιρρητως. Here only. Αναντιρρητος, xix. 36.—Ex α priv. αντι, *contra*, et ῥεω, *dieo.*—*As soon as I was sent for.*] Μεταπεμφθεις. 5. 22. xi. 13. xxiv. 24. 26. xxv. 3.—*Num.* xxiii. 7. *Sept.*—*That are commanded.* (33) Τα προστεταγμενα. 48. *Matt.* i. 24. viii. 4. xxi. 6. *Mark* i. 44. *Luke* v. 14.

V. 34, 35. The circumstances of this transaction so impressed the apostle's mind, that he opened his discourse by allowing, that he had been erroneously prejudiced, in favour of the Jews, and against the Gentiles: for he was now convinced, that "God was no respecter of persons."—"To respect persons," is entirely different from *discriminating characters*, or *conferring unmerited favours on one man, and not on another.* A judge *respects persons*, if he condemns one and acquits another, or decides in favour of the injurious party, from partiality to his friend, or to one of his own nation, sect, or party: (*Marg. Ref.* y.—*Notes, Deut.* x. 17. *Matt.* xxii. 15—22, *v.* 16:) yet in private life, he may send a present to what friend he pleases, or dispense his alms to what poor persons he chooses, without giving others a ground for charging him with "*respect of* "*persons.*" (*Note, Matt.* xx. 1—16, *v.* 15.) If God had accepted a man's worship because he was a Jew, and rejected that of another man, of exactly the same dispositions and character, because he was a Gentile; there would have been some reason to assert, that he was "a respecter of persons:" but if he had favoured a proud, wicked, or hypocritical Jew, merely on account of his circumcision, or relation to Abraham; and rejected a humble, pious, believing, sincere worshipper, because of his uncircumcision, or his gentile extraction; there would have been an evident ground for the charge. Yet the Jews in general carried their ideas of God's special favour to their nation so far, as fully to involve these consequences. It does not however follow that God will accept from any man that service, which is destitute of *spiritual* good; or that any man will do what is *spiritually* good, without 'regenerat-'ing grace;' or that God is bound in justice to give his special grace to an unconverted man, because of his external decency of character, or formal services; or that he may not confer this unmerited favour on any one, as he sees good, *without* "respecting persons;" or that the fruits of grace can claim, or meet acceptance, on any other ground, than that of the covenant of mercy, through the righteousness and atonement of our divine Surety. In short, where the essence of true religion is found, God graciously accepts it without regarding names, forms, or sects. So that, "in every nation, he that feareth God "and worketh righteousness is accepted of him:" for this, when genuine, comprises the substance of true religion, and constitues the evidence, though not the meritorious cause, of a man's acceptance; and, whatever may yet be wanting in his explicit knowledge and faith, will in due time be communicated. (*Marg. Ref.* z, a.—*Notes, Job* xxxiv. 16—19. *Gal.* ii. 6—10. 1 *Pet.* i. 17—22.)—'I think 'this text proves that God would sooner send an angel to 'direct pious and upright persons to the knowledge of the 'gospel, than suffer them to perish by ignorance of it. 'But so far from intimating that such persons may be 'found among those that reject Christianity, ... it deter-'mines nothing as to their existence in every nation.' *Doddridge.* (*Notes, Rom.* ii. 7—16.) Does universal history, ancient and modern, bring to our knowledge one person, who without revelation, in some way or degree, was a humble penitent, a spiritual worshipper of God, a conscientious worker of righteousness, in his habitual conduct; in one word a Cornelius? If it do not, all advanced from this passage about virtuous heathens is wholly foreign to the purpose. Their virtue was not and is not good 'be-'fore God.'

I perceive. (34) Καταλαμβανομαι. iv. 13. *John* i. 5. *Eph.* iii. 18. *Phil.* iii. 12, 13.—*Respecter of persons.*] Προσωποληπτης. Here only.—Προσωποληψια, *Rom.* ii. 11. *Eph.* vi. 9. *Col.* iii. 25. *Jam.* ii. 1. A προσωπον, *persona, facies,* et λαμβανω, *accipio.*—*Accepted.* (35) Δεκτος. *Luke* iv. 19. 24. 2 *Cor.* vi. 2. *Phil.* iv. 18.

V. 36—43. The apostle next proceeded to state the substance of the instruction, which he was sent to com-

r Luke xxiv. 30.
41—43. John
xxi. 13.
e 1 & iv. 19, 20.
v. 28. 29—32.
Matt. xxviii. 19.
20. Mark xvi.
15, 16. Luke
xxiv. 47, 48.
John xxi. 21, 22.
t xvii. 31. Matt. xxv. 31—46. John v. 22—29. Rom. xiv. 9, 10. 2 Cor. v. 10. 2 Tim. iv. 1, 8. 1 Pet. iv. 5. Rev. i. 7. xx. 11—15. xxii. 12.

witnesses chosen before of God, ' even to us, who did eat and drink with him after he rose from the dead.

42 And ' he commanded us to preach unto the people, and to testify 'that it

u xxvi. 22. See on
Luke xxiv. 29—
27. 44—46.—
John i. 45. v.
39, 40. 1 Pet. i.
11. Rev. xix. 10.
x iii. 16. iv. 10—
12. John xx. 31.
23. Heb. xiii. 20.
y xiii. 38, 39. xv.
9. xxvi. 18.

is he which was ordained of God *to be* the Judge of quick and dead.

43 To " him give all the prophets witness, that * through his name, * whosoever believeth in him, shall receive remission of sins.

Mark xvi. 16. John v. 24. Rom. viii. 1. 34. x. 11. Gal. iii. 22. Eph. i. 7. Col. i. 14.

---

municate. This indeed would scarcely have been necessary, if Cornelius had been so " accepted" for his good works, as not to need the righteousness and atonement of Christ; or if, as numbers argue, every man might be saved by his own religion, if sincere in it. But his prayers for instruction, being accompanied by obedience and good fruits, according to his present light, were accepted, and in consequence, the only way of salvation was made known unto him, and his heart was prepared to welcome it. (*Notes,* 1, 2. xi. 4—18.)—Peter, in calling the attention of the company to his subject, observed that they had doubtless known something about the preaching of " Jesus of Nazareth," and the reports which had been circulated concerning him; though their information had been imperfect and unfavourable. Now these reports, properly understood, contained that very instruction which God had sent him to deliver; even the word, which he had some time before sent to the Jews, preaching reconciliation to himself, and peace with each other, by this Jesus, who was the promised Messiah, the anointed Saviour and King of Israel; yea, " the Lord of all" men, whether Jews or Gentiles; of all creatures whether men or angels, and of all worlds, even of all things in heaven, earth, and hell; both in respect of his divine nature, as the incarnate Son of God, and as the Mediator between God and man, the Law-giver, Governor, and Judge of all: for so the words, " this Person is Lord of all," evidently mean. (*Marg. Ref.* e.—*Notes, Matt.* xxviii. 18. *Rom.* xiv. 7—12. 1 *Cor.* xv. 45—49. *Eph.* i. 15—23. ii. 14—22. *Phil.* ii. 9—11. 1 *Pet.* iii. 21, 22.) The apostle declared, that he came to confirm that doctrine, which they knew had been published throughout all Judea; though it was first more statedly preached in Galilee, after John had prepared the way for it by his ministry and baptism. This doctrine implied, that God had " anointed Jesus with the " Holy Spirit," in an evident manner, at his baptism, when he had declared him to be his " beloved Son in " whom he was well pleased;" (*Marg. Ref.* f—i.—*Note, Matt.* iii. 16, 17;) and had endued him, as Man, with that divine power, which he exercised " in going about " doing good," and performing all kinds of miraculous cures; especially delivering those who were oppressed by evil spirits, as an emblem of his rescuing sinners from the yoke and service of Satan: for God was evidently with him, as appeared by the authority and beneficence of his miracles. (*Marg. Ref.* k—m.—*Notes, Luke* iv. 16—19. *John* iii. 1, 2. v. 31—38.) To this, Peter and the other apostles were appointed to bear witness; as they had been his constant attendants, and the spectators of these interesting scenes: till at length, the Jewish rulers, hating the holy doctrine, and envying the reputation of Jesus, had seized him, and condemned him to death as a deceiver; and had procured the execution of their sentence from Pilate: so that he had been most cruelly and ignomini-

ously crucified as a malefactor. (*Marg. Ref.* n, o.—*Notes,* ii. 22—24. iii. 12—16. iv. 5—12.) But, though it had pleased God, for most wise and gracious purposes, to permit their malice to proceed thus far; he had yet raised him from the dead, and " shewn him openly" after his resurrection: not indeed to all the people, whose conduct had rendered them unworthy of such a favour; neither would that method have been so convincing and satisfactory to all those, in every age and nation, who were concerned in this event; (*Note, John* xx. 24—29, *latter part;*) but to a competent number of witnesses, whom he had before chosen for that purpose; even to the twelve apostles, and many others, who had seen, conversed, eaten, and drunk with him, after he arose from the dead. (*Marg. Ref.* p—r.—*Notes, Luke* xxiv. 36—43. *John* xxi. 1—14.) He had also commanded them to preach these things to mankind: and to assure them, that he, who was then proposed to them as a Saviour, was ordained by God, to be the Judge of those, who should at the last day be found living on earth, and of the innumerable multitudes which would then be raised from the dead. (*Ma_{r}g. Ref.* s, t.—*Note,* xvii. 30, 31.)—These things indeed were no other, than what had been predicted in the scriptures, with which Cornelius and his friends were become in some measure acquainted: and in due time they would see, that the several particulars relating to the person, character, miracles, doctrine, life, death, resurrection, and ascension of Jesus, were an exact accomplishment of ancient prophecies; and that all the prophets, in one way or other, bore witness to him, and directed mankind to expect remission of any nation or description believed in him, should receive a free and complete remission of all his sins. (*Marg Ref.* u—y.—*Notes,* iii. 24—26. *Luke* xxiv. 25—31. 44—49. *John* v. 39—44. *Rev.* xix. 9, 10.) This should be considered as only an abstract of Peter's discourse; and as he was interrupted in it by the descent of the Holy Spirit, we need not wonder, that various points of Christian doctrine are not explicitly stated in it; for they were left to be communicated afterwards, and by degrees. (*Notes,* vii. 1—8. 51—53. *Matt.* xxviii. 19, 20, *v.* 20.)

Preaching peace. (36) Ευαγγελιζομενος ειρηνην. *Rom.* x. 15. *Eph.* ii. 17.—*Is.* lii. 7. Sept.—*He is Lord of all.*] 'Ουτος εςι παντων Κυριος. *Rom.* x. 12. *Phil.* ii. 11.—*Doing good.* (38) Ευεργετων. Here only. Ευεργεσια· See on iv. 9. Ευεργετης, See on Luke xxii. 25.—*That were oppressed.*] Τας καλαδυναςευομενας. *Jam.* ii. 6. Not elsewhere N. T.—*Ex.* i. 13. Sept. Εx καλα et δυναςευω, princeps sum. Δυναςης· See on Luke i. 52.—*Whom they slew,* (39) Ανειλον κριμασαντες. See on v. 30.—*Shewed him openly.* (40) Εδωκεν αυτον εμφανη γενεσθαι. Εμφανης, *Rom.* x. 20. Not elsewhere.—*Chosen before.* (41) Τοις προκεχειροτονημενοις. Here only. Εx προ et χειροτονεω, xiv. 23. 2 Cor. viii. 19.—Εx χειρ, manus, et τεινω, extendo. Our Lord " called whom he would...and he

44 ¶ While Peter yet spake these words, [a] the Holy Ghost fell on all them which heard the word.

45 And [a] they of the circumcision which believed, were astonished, as many as came with Peter, because that on [b] the Gentiles also was poured out the gift of the Holy Ghost.

46 For they heard them [c] speak with tongues, and magnify God. Then answered Peter,

47 Can [d] any man forbid water, that these should not be baptized, which have received the Holy Ghost as well as we ?

48 And [e] he commanded them to be baptized [f] in the name of the Lord. [g] Then prayed they him to tarry certain days.

" ordained twelve." (Mark iii. 13, 14.) Thus they were " chosen of God : " for says Jesus " I and the Father are " One."—*To testify.* (42) Διαμαρτυρασθαι. viii. 25. xx. 21. 23, 24. See on ii. 40.—*Which was ordained.*] Ὁ ὡρισμενος. See on ii. 23.

V. 44—48. (*Note,* xi. 4—17.) It does not appear that the descent of the Holy Spirit, on this occasion, was accompanied by the same circumstances, as on the day of Pentecost : but the effects were evident, and similar to those which were then produced. (*Notes,* ii. 2—4.) The Gentile converts were immediately enabled to speak in languages, which they had not previously learned ; and to magnify God, and celebrate, with adoring gratitude, the glory displayed in the work of redemption. (*Marg. Ref.* z— c.) As they were thus undeniably filled with the Holy Spirit, poured out upon them ; not only by his illuminating, sanctifying, and comforting influences, but by his miraculous gifts also ; Peter justly concluded, that it would be unreasonable to refuse them the baptism of water : and when none of his companions could say any thing against it, he ordered them to be baptized, by some of those who attended him. (*Marg. Ref.* d—f.—*Notes,* i. 4—8. *Matt.* iii. 11, 12.)—*Forbid water,* &c. (47) ' These words contain a ' plain and convincing demonstration of the falsehood of ' the Quaker's doctrine, that water-baptism is unnecessary ' to them, who have received the inward baptism of the ' Spirit : since the apostle here not only declares, that ' water-baptism ought therefore to be administered to these ' persons, because they had already been baptized with the ' Holy Ghost ; but also commands them to be baptized ' upon that account.' *Whitby.*—It was not necessary for the sacred historian, on such occasions, to repeat the *appointed form* of Christian baptism ; and therefore the special confession of Jesus, as the Messiah, the Son of God, is alone noticed. But there seems no ground to doubt, that the form also was adhered to. Some learned men *conjecture,* that when Jews, who had before believed in the Father and in the Holy Spirit, were baptized, it was only in the name of the Son : but that the Gentile converts were baptized " into the name of the Father, the Son, and " the Holy Spirit." This, however, is merely *conjecture,* and very improbable : for not the least trace of it is found in scripture ; nor any difference marked, between the *form* of baptizing Jewish and gentile converts. It is rather taken for granted, that the apostles and primitive teachers, adhered to the instruction of their Lord just before his ascension ; and it was therefore needless to mention that circumcision in the narrative. (*Note, Matt.* xxviii. 19, 20, v. 19.)—It is not said that the brethren who accompanied Peter, were pastors ; but it is probable, that some of them were. There had been Christians at Joppa for a consider-

able time : and either those who first collected a church in that city, appointed pastors ; or Peter, when he went thither, " set in order this which was wanting." (*Note,* Tit. i. 5—9.) Now it is most natural to suppose, that on so interesting an occasion, Peter would take with him, as witnesses, some of the pastors of the church, and not exclusively private Christians. Ananias is not said to have been a minister, or pastor ; yet it can scarcely be doubted that he was.—The apostle, however, seems to have devolved the service of baptizing the Gentile converts on his attendants ; perhaps for the same reasons, which the apostle Paul assigned, on an occasion in some respects similar. (*Notes, John* iv. 1—4. 1 *Cor.* i. 10—19.)—*To tarry,* &c. (48.) It cannot be supposed, but that Peter lived with these converted Gentiles, according to their usual habits, as to eating, and other things of that nature, after all which had preceded his going among them, without any special regard to the ceremonial law. This may be of use, if recollected, in forming our judgment on some other portions of this history. (*Notes,* xxi. 17—26. 1 *Cor.* ix. 19—23. *Gal.* ii. 11—16. iv. 12—16.)

Fell upon. (44) Επεπεσε. 10. viii. 16. xi. 15. *Mark* iii. 10. Εκκεχυται 45. Thus they were " baptized with the " Holy Ghost." xi. 16.—*Magnify.* (46) Μεγαλυνοντων. See on *Luke* i. 46.

PRACTICAL OBSERVATIONS.

V. 1—8.

Pure and undefiled religion is sometimes found, where it might least have been expected : (*P. O. Matt.* viii. 5— 13 :) and " the vessels of mercy " are often brought acquainted with God, by means of which at the time they know not the consequence, and which perhaps thwart their inclinations, and disappoint their schemes of future life.—" The saving grace of God teaches " men to " wor- " ship him with reverence and godly fear," to serve him conscientiously, to unite justice and charity, and to pray with constancy and perseverance. It leads men to order their households in the fear of God ; and commonly they become instrumental to the good of those around them. (*P. O. Gen.* xviii. 16—22. *Josh.* xxiv. 14—33.) This Roman soldier was more like " a son of Abraham," even before he became a Christian, than most of that patriarch's lineal descendants were ; and doubtless he will rise up in judgment against numbers of nominal Christians, and even professors of evangelical truth. Yet all this diligence, liberality, equity, piety, and self-denial, could not have saved him, without the atonement of Christ : even *he* must be accepted, and admitted into heaven, in the same way with Saul the persecutor, with the converted jailor, and the thief upon the cross ; " that no flesh should glory in " the presence of God." What then will become of those

474

CHAP. XI.

Peter is blamed by those of the circumcision, for going among the Gentiles, 1—3. He satisfies them, by relating the whole transaction; and they "glorify "God, who had given to the Gentiles repentance unto "life," 4—18. The gospel having spread to Phenice, Cyprus, and Antioch, 19—21; Barnabas is sent to Antioch, who rejoices over the converts, and exhorts them to persevere, 22—24. He goes to fetch Saul from Tarsus, and many are instructed at Antioch, where the disciples are first called Christians, 25, 26. Agabus foretels a famine; and the disciples at Antioch send relief to their brethren in Judea, by Barnabas and Saul, 27—30.

who, without one tenth of the external appearance of his piety and charity, presume that they shall go to heaven on the score of their good works, and reject the way of salvation by faith in Jesus Christ? But where these things are genuine, they are always attended with a humble, teachable, and enquiring disposition: and those who practise what they know, without being proud of it, or trusting to it, and who at the same time wait upon God for further teaching, by faith and prayer, shall never perish for want of instruction. (*Note, John* vii. 14—17.) Should the Lord create such a disposition in the heart of an inhabitant of China, Japan, or the unexplored parts of Africa; he would sooner send an angel from heaven, or a minister from the uttermost part of the earth, to shew him the way of salvation, than leave him destitute of that knowledge, for which he longs and prays without ceasing. The aims and supplications of such persons spring from right principles and motives, and go "up as a memorial before God;" not to merit his favour, but to plead with him to fulfil his gracious promises.—The sublime subjects, which pertain to redemption through the blood of the Son of God, seem more proper for the tongues of angels to proclaim, than for us poor worms of the earth. Doubtless in many respects, they could preach them unspeakably better: yet our humiliating and thankful experience may balance something on the other side. In that case, however, it would not be so evident, that "the excellency of the power," which makes the word successful, is wholly "of God:" nor would their presence and language be so suited to man's weakness, or so conducive to his comfort.—The Lord knows where, and about what, his servants are employed; and when he has further work for them, he will surely by one means or other shew it to them.—Implicit obedience tends to increasing light and comfort: and pious servants or attendants are a great blessing, which we should seek from God, use proper means to obtain, and express a proper value for when they are granted to us.

V. 9—23.

The thoughts and ways of the Lord are far above our's: the best of men are seldom entirely free from some remaining prejudices; even those who were infallibly guided by the Holy Spirit, to declare the doctrine of Christ to mankind, were gradually let into the secret designs of God, and delivered from their mistakes and prejudices, as it became needful. How absurdly then do they act, who aim and expect to put the new convert, at once, into full possession of that whole system, which perhaps they themselves have been learning for years!—The Lord may command his servants, without assigning his reasons: but he generally satisfies them, about the propriety of those services to which he calls them; and their constancy and fervency in prayer very much conduce to it. (*Note, John* xv. 12—16.)—When pious persons conscientiously deny themselves, in obedience to what they deem the command of God, without self-righteousness or spiritual pride; their conduct may evidence their sincerity, and exhibit to others a very useful example; even should it appear that they were mistaken. in their scruples: and in this view, the apostle's readiness to endure hunger rather than eat forbidden food, and his scrupulous exactness in this respect, during his whole past life, convey to us important and humiliating instructions. (*Notes, Dan.* i. 8—16. *P. O.* 8— 20.)—The company of those, who are collected together into the church of God, and secured by the covenant of grace, are previously of very different characters and dispositions; yet all alike estranged from God and holiness. But when they are truly converted, they become all of "one mind and judgment," in the grand concerns of religion: they have the same faith, hope, and love, and the same motives and distinguishing principles; and their several natural dispositions, being corrected, regulated, and moderated by sanctifying grace, render them more quali fied in different ways to serve the common cause of the gospel. (*P. O. Is.* xi. 1—9.) Let us then learn "not to "call those common" whom God has cleansed, or to despise those whom he has received; and not to neglect or despair of those, whom he may yet call to the knowledge of himself.—If we diligently endeavour to discover the meaning of his word; the dispensations of his providence, and our own experience will often throw light upon it; and, without any immediate revelation, we shall be directed and encouraged to proceed in the path of duty, "nothing "doubting." But how strong must prejudice be, when so many divine monitions were requisite, to induce an apostle to attend on a man of fair character and good report, who by the warning of an angel had sent for him, that he might receive the instructions of life from his lips!

V. 24—43.

Those who love the truth will desire to bring their friends, and especially their relations, acquainted with it, and will diligently use their influence with them for that purpose.—While numbers despise the servants of God, some will honour them in an improper manner: and it becomes them decidedly to refuse undue and excessive respect; for humility and modesty are the peculiar ornaments of piety.—Alas! how seldom are we called to speak to auditories, however small, in which it may be said, that "they are all present in the sight of God, to hear all things "that are commanded us of God!"—Whatever men may assert or object, it will be found, "that God is no Re- "specter of persons:" and if any do not see the consistency of this with evangelical truth, or the sovereignty of his dispensations; let them learn to admit, that it is wholly

AND [a] the apostles and brethren that were in Judea, heard that [b] the Gentiles had also received the word of God.

2 And when Peter was come up to Jerusalem, [c] they that were of the circumcision contended with him,

3 Saying, [d] Thou wentest in to men uncircumcised, and didst eat with them.

4 But Peter [e] rehearsed *the matter* from the beginning, and expounded *it* by order unto them, saying,

5 I [f] was in the city of Joppa, praying: and [g] in a trance I saw a vision, A certain vessel descend, as it had been a great sheet, let down from heaven by four corners; [h] and it came even to me:

a viii. 14, 15. Gal. i. 17—22.
b x. 34—38. xiv. 27. xv. 3. Gen. xlix. 10. Ps. xxii. 27. xcvi. 1—10. Is. xl. 10. xxxii. 15. xxxv. 1, 2. xliii. 1, 6. xlix. 6. lii. 10. liv. 3. lxii. 19. Jer. xvi. 19. Hos. ii. 23. Am. ix. 11, 12. Mic. iv. 7. Zeph. ii. 11. iii. 9. Zech. viii. 20—23. Mal. i. 11. xv. 1. b xvi. 20—23. Gal. ii. 12—14. 11. 2 John 10.
Matt. viii. 11. Mark xvi. 5. Luke ii. 32. Rom. xv. 7—12. c x. 45. xv. 1. d x. 23. 28. 48. Luke xv. 2. 1 Cor. v. 11.
e xiv. 27. Josh. xxii. 21—31. Prov. xv. 1. Luke i. 8.
f See on x. 9—16.
g xxii. 17. 2 Cor. xii. 1—5.
h Jer. i. 11—14. Ez. ii. 9. Am. vii. 4—7. viii. 2.

owing to their narrow capacities, and the proud and carnal self-love of their own hearts. For God does not limit his conduct by the rules, or according to the systems of bigotted or prejudiced persons: he gives grace to whom he pleases, and as he sees best; and the fruits of that grace always meet with his acceptance, through the mercy of the covenant and the merits of the great Mediator. When he begins, he will carry on his work: and by whatever way he leads sinners to heaven, they will be prepared to join the chorus of the Redeemed, in singing " salvation to God " and the Lamb." That preventing grace, which leads men to fervent prayer and conscientious obedience, is not given to supersede the gospel, but to render men willing to embrace it. The minister of Christ must therefore declare to sinners of every character, that word, which God has sent to men, " preaching peace by Jesus Christ," " the Prince of peace " and " the Lord of all;" by whom alone they can be saved, and to whom they must at length submit, in one way or other. Many serious enquirers hear reports of this doctrine, but these come to them, so distorted and misrepresented, that they are for a long time set against it: and they are astonished, when, in answer to their prayers, the Lord leads them to hear and receive his truth, from the very persons against whom they have been so greatly prejudiced; and when they find their doctrine so different in its nature and tendency from what they supposed, and so exactly suited to their wants and desires. —While we consider the effects of our Redeemer's immeasurable unction by the Holy Spirit; let us endeavour to copy his example, being unwearied in doing good, and in promoting the deliverance of our fellow-sinners from the oppression of Satan, by all the means which we can devise: thus it will appear that " God is with us," whatever men may say of us or do to us.—Receiving the testimony of apostles and prophets to the efficacy of his sacrifice, and the free remission of our sins through faith in his name; let us daily prepare to meet him, as the constituted Judge of the living and of the dead; and " be diligent to " be found of him in peace without spot and blameless." (*Note*, 2 *Pet*. iii. 14—16. P. O. 14—18.)

V. 44—48.

When we endeavour to mix faith with the word of God, and to yield obedience to it; we may expect to be more fully illuminated, sanctified, and comforted, by the gift of the Holy Spirit: that, through " the love of God " being " shed abroad in our hearts," we may use our tongues to celebrate his praises. This inward baptism of the Spirit is especially to be valued; yet outward ordinances should not be neglected: and those who conclude that they have

no occasion for the external signs, because they have received the internal grace of the covenant, speak and act in a very unscriptural manner, and give reason for suspecting that they deceive themselves: yet if we have both the ' outward sign and the inward and spiritual grace,' it is not of much importance, in what order we have received them. Those who have learned and experienced the things of God, will desire the further company of his ministers, to build them up in their most holy faith.—But surely, we sinners of the gentiles should read this chapter with peculiar gratitude and admiring praise: thus the partition-wall was broken down, the law of ordinances that was against us was abolished, the door of mercy was opened to us; that we might become fellow heirs with the ancient people of God, in all the blessings of his covenant and salvation. (*Notes* and *P. O. Eph.* ii. 11—22.) May the Lord speedily recall the Jews into the church, and bring in " the fulness " of the Gentiles;" that " his name may be hallowed," his kingdom established, and " his will done," throughout the whole earth, as it is by all the angels and saints in heaven!

NOTES.

CHAP. XI. V. 1—3. The dissatisfaction of the believers, who "were of the circumcision," when they heard of Cornelius's conversion, and Peter's conduct respecting him, emphatically illustrates the degree, in which the Jews were prejudiced against the Gentiles, even when they appeared to worship God alone, and were exemplary in their general conduct; unless they were circumcised, and became obedient to the Mosaick law. If the believers from among the Jews, were so alarmed and offended at Peter, for eating, on such an occasion, with persons of so good a report as Cornelius and his friends; what must have been the thoughts of the Jews in general, concerning the state of the idolatrous and licentious Gentiles? (*Note*, x. 34, 35.)—It is not said that " the apostles con- " tended " with Peter on this account: yet, if the general opinion had not been unfavourable to his conduct, none would have publickly called him to an account, or have warmly contested the point with him.—This fact is likewise an unanswerable proof, that the primitive church had no idea of Peter's supremacy and infallibility: indeed, the persons concerned by no means rendered due respect to his apostolical authority.

Contended. (2) Διεκρινοντο. 12. See on x. 20.—*Uncircumcised*. (3) Ακροβυσιαν εχοντας. *Rom*. iii. 30. iv. 9—11. 1 *Cor*. vii. 18. *Gal*. ii. 7. v. 6. *Col*. iii. 11. Ex ακρος, *ex* tremus, et Ϛυω, *vel* Ϛυζω, tego.

V. 4—17. Peter, when thus called upon, pleaded no

6 Upon the which when I had ¹fastened mine eyes, I considered, and saw four-footed beasts of the earth, and wild beasts, and creeping things, and fowls of the air.

7 And I heard a voice saying unto me, Arise, Peter: slay and eat.

8 But I said, Not so, Lord: for nothing ᵏ common or ¹ unclean hath at any time entered into my mouth.

9 But the voice answered me again from heaven, ᵐ What God hath cleansed, *that* call not thou common.

10 And this was done ⁿ three times: and all were drawn up again into heaven.

11 And, behold, ᵒ immediately there were three men already come unto the house where I was, sent from Cæsarea unto me.

12 And ᵖ the Spirit bade me go with them, ᑫ nothing doubting. Moreover, ʳ these six brethren accompanied me, and we entered into the man's house:

13 And ˢ he shewed us, how he had seen an angel in his house, which stood and said unto him, Send men ᵗ to Joppa, and call for Simon, whose surname is Peter ;

14 Who shall tell thee ᵘ words, whereby thou and ˣ all thy house shall be saved.

15 And ʸ as I began to speak, ᶻ the Holy Ghost fell on them, ᵃ as on us at the beginning.

16 Then ᵇ remembered I the word of the Lord, ᶜ how that he said, John indeed baptized with water, ᵈ but ye shall be baptized with the Holy Ghost.

17 Forasmuch then ᵉ as God gave them the like gift as *he did* unto us who believed on the Lord Jesus Christ, ʳ what was I, that I could withstand God ?

18 When they heard these things, ᵍ they held their peace, ʰ and glorified God, saying, Then ¹ hath God also to the Gentiles ᵏ granted repentance unto life.

---

exemptions; but with a becoming candour and frankness, stated the whole transaction to his brethren, and thus vindicated what he had done, beyond all possibility of objection. (*Marg. Ref.—Notes*, x. 9—48.)—*Not so*, &c. (8) It has been argued from this, that only unclean animals were seen in this vision : but that is not determined in the text; and the apostle's objection may have been made against the *general* proposal to him, of slaying and eating whatever animal he chose. (*Note*, x. 9—16, *v.* 14.)— *Thou*, &c. (14) This is far more full and explicit than the narrative in the preceding chapter : Cornelius must himself be saved, not by his prayers and alms, his piety and equity and charity; but by the words which Peter would speak to him, and by faith in those words; and thus also salvation would come to his family. (*Notes*, ii. 37—40. xvi. 13—15. 29—34. *Gen.* xvii. 7, 8. *Jer.* xxxii. 39—41. *Luke* xix. 1—10. 1 *Cor.* vii. 10—14.)—*Baptized*, &c. (16) *Notes*, i. 4—8. *Matt.* iii. 11, 12.—*Did unto us.* (17) The Spirit was poured out on Cornelius and his friends immediately, without imposition of hands, and even previously to baptism, or a direct confession of faith in Jesus; and this, following all the preceding declarations of the will and purpose of God, removed all doubt, as to Peter's conduct respecting them.

Were drawn up. (10) Ανεσπασθη. *Luke* xiv. 5. Not elsewhere.—*All thy house.* (14) Πας ὁ οικος σου. See on x. 2.—*The like gift.* (17) Την ισην δωρεαν—ἰσος, *æqualis, par. John* v. 18. *Phil.* ii. 6. Δωρεαν. See on *John* iv. 10.— *Withstand.*] Κωλυσαι. viii. 36. x. 47. xvi. 6. xxiv. 23. *Mark* ix. 38, 39.—"ᶜ Forbid God."

V. 18. The clear discovery of the express purpose of God, which appeared in all the circumstances of the transaction, overpowered the prejudices of the objectors; and they could not but admire and adore his grace, which had opened a way even to the gentiles to obtain eternal life, when they repented, and forsook idolatry and wickedness, and "turned to God" and his worship and service ; and which had given to some of them " repentance " unto life." (*Marg. Ref.—Notes*, x. 24—26. xv. 7— 11.)—It may hence be inferred, that even the disciples did not before consider the professed repentance of a gentile, however attended with "works meet for repentance," to be acceptable with God, unless it led him unreservedly to embrace the religion of the Jews. This proves, that many things, which learned men have stated concerning the proselytes of the gate, and their privileges, rather shew what ought to have been the case, than what it really was. —Dr. Whitby has here a long note, to evince, that the language of this verse and of similar passages, which state, that repentance and faith are the gift of God, does not imply that they are not *conditional*, and that they give encouragement to those alone, who perform the *conditions;* in which important truths are contained, but blended, as it appears to me, with much error.—That repentance and faith, and every kind of obedience, are the duties of every man; that means should be used, by such as desire to perform these duties ; and that none receive the gift and grant of God, who live and die in the neglect of the appointed means of grace ; are propositions not in the least to be contested. But this learned divine, and many others, seem to forget, that "the heart of stone," " the uncir- " cumcised heart," " the carnal mind which is enmity " against God," effectually prevents every man from doing these duties, or properly using those means, or even

viii 1—4.

19 ¶ Now ¹ they which were scattered abroad, upon the persecution that arose about Stephen, travelled as far as ᵐ Phenice, and ⁿ Cyprus, and ° Antioch, preaching the word ᵖ to none but unto the Jews only.

20 And some of them were men of Cyprus and ᵠ Cyrene, which, when they were come to Antioch, spake unto 'the Grecians, ˢ preaching the Lord Jesus.

21 And ᵗ the hand of the Lord was with them; ᵘ and a great number believed, and ˣ turned unto the Lord.

22 Then ʸ tidings of these things came unto the ears of the church which was in Jerusalem: ᶻ and they sent

(marginal references: m xv. 3. xxl. 2. n iv. 36. xiii. 4. xv 39. xxi. 16. o 24. xv. 22. 35. p iii. 26. xiii 46 John vi. 37. q ii. 10. vi. 9. xiii. 1. Matt. xxvii. 32. r vi. 1. ix. 29. viii. 5. 35. ix. 20. xvii. 18. 1 Cor. i. 22. 33. iii. 2. Eph. ii. 2. s 2 Chr. xxx. 12. Ezra vii. 9. viii. 18. 22. Neh. ii. 8. 18. Is. liii. 1. iiv. 1. Luke i. 66. t 24. ii. 47. iv. 4. v. 14. vi. 7. 1 Cor. iii. 6. 7. 1 Thes. i. 5. x ix. 35. xxvi. 18. 20. 1 Thes. i. 9, 10. y 1. viii. 14. xv. 2. 1 Thes. iii. 6. z iv. 36. 37. ix. 27. xiii. 1—3. xv. 22. 35—39.

---

heartily *desiring* spiritual blessings, till it be removed by regeneration. (*Notes*, vii. 51—53. *Deut.* xxx. 1—10. *Jer.* iv. 3, 4. *Ez.* xi. 17—20. xxxvi. 25—27. *Rom.* viii. 5 —9. *Eph.* ii. 4—10. *Phil.* ii. 12, 13.) Hence it is " God, " who worketh in us to *will*," as well as to do. ' We have ' no power to do good works, pleasant and acceptable to ' God, without the grace of God by Christ preventing us, ' that we may have a good will, and working with us when ' we have that good will.' *Art.* x.—' They blessed God, ' ... that he had afforded the same mercy to the gentiles, ' as to the Jews, that if they will return and amend, and ' receive Christ, they shall be saved ; and that he had given ' them the grace to do so.' *Hammond.*—' He has not ' only made them the overtures of it ; but has graciously ' wrought it in some of their hearts.' *Doddridge.*—The inseparable connexion of repentance and eternal life should not pass unnoticed, in this place. (*Marg. Ref.*— *Notes*, iii. 19—21. v. 29—31. 2 *Cor.* vii. 9—11. 2 *Tim.* ii. 23—26. *Heb.* vi. 4—6.)

V. 19—21. (*Marg. Ref.* l—s.) The words here translated " preaching," do not necessarily imply a publick and authoritative proclamation. (*Notes*, viii. 4. 32—35.) " Speaking the word to none, but unto the Jews only." " They spake unto the Grecians, declaring the glad tidings " concerning the Lord Jesus."—' As in this place the ' Hellenists are opposed to the Jews ; and as the church ' of Antioch was, as it were, a new Jerusalem for ' gentiles ; it appears, that under this term, those were ' included, ... who had so far profited by their acquaintance ' with the dispersed Jews, that, condemning idolatry, they ' acknowledged God, who had spoken by Moses and the ' prophets, though they remained uncircumcised ; of which ' description Cornelius was, as it is evident from the pre- ' ceding history.' *Beza.*—' Instead of 'Ελληνιϛας, Hel- ' lenists, the Alexandrian manuscript, which is favoured ' by the Syriack and some other ancient versions, reads ' 'Ελληνας, Greeks; which common sense would require us ' to adopt, even if it were not supported by the authority ' of any manuscript at all. For as the Hellenists were ' Jews, there would, on the received reading, be no op- ' position between the conduct of these preachers, and ' those mentioned in the preceding verse. Here undoubt- ' edly we have the first account of preaching the gospel to ' the idolatrous gentiles : for it is certain, there is nothing ' in the word 'Ελληνας, to limit it to such as were worship- ' pers of the true God. ... As the Greeks were the most ' celebrated of the gentile nations near Judea, the Jews ' called all the gentiles by that general name. (*Rom.* x. 12. ' *Gal.* iii. 28. *Col.* iii. 11.)' *Doddridge.*—It would, in my mind, be far preferable to leave the point undecided, or even to adopt Beza's exposition ; than to alter the text, ' without the authority of any manuscript :' for who can say, how far men may proceed in altering the scriptures by conjectural criticisms, pleading at the same time, that ' common sense requires it ?' This, however, is not here the case, for there is good ground to conclude, that *Greeks* is the genuine reading.—The distance of Antioch and Cyprus from Jerusalem renders it probable, that no worshippers of God, according to the law, except " Grecians," or Jews using the Greek and not the Hebrew or Syriack language, and reading the Greek translation of the scriptures in their synagogues, resided in those parts : (*Note*, vi. 1 :) and if there were synagogues of Jews, who used the Hebrew or Syriack, no good reason can be assigned, why the word of God should be spoken to them only, and not to their brethren, who differed from them in nothing but language. It is, therefore, highly probable, that the persons spoken of, for a considerable time, addressed none but Jews and circumcised proselytes : but that at length, the report of Cornelius's conversion having reached Antioch, which cannot be shewn to have been even impro- bable ; some of them were encouraged to preach to un- circumcised persons also : and their great success, by the immediate power of the Lord, accompanying the word, gave a divine sanction to their proceedings. Upon the whole it is most likely, that at Antioch, and about this time, the gospel was first preached to idolatrous gentiles. —Was not the extraordinary success of the word, and the holy effects which followed by " the hand of the Lord," as real a sanction, both to the mission of the preachers, and to their conduct in preaching to the gentiles, as out- ward miracles would have been ?—*Hand, &c.* (21) *Marg. Ref.* t.—No miracles are mentioned, and the inward power of divine grace, teaching, inclining, and aiding the hearers to believe, seems exclusively meant.—*Believed, &c.*] *Marg. Ref.* x.—*Notes*, 18. iii. 19—21. xiv. 24—28, v. 27. xxvi. 16—23. 1 *Thes.* i. 9, 10.

Which were scattered. (19) 'Οι ... διασπαρεντες. See on viii. 1.—*Grecians.* (20) 'Ελληνιϛας. See on vi. 1.—*Turned unto the Lord.* (21) Επεϛρεψεν επι τον Κυριον. See on ix. 35.

V. 22. (*Marg. Ref.*) ' The apostles do not rashly ' condemn the extraordinary vocation, but judge of it by ' its effects.' *Beza.* Barnabas was sent by the apostles, as it may be supposed, to examine on the spot into the na- ture and effects of that success, which had attended the gospel at Antioch ; and to set in order such things as re- lated to the appointment of pastors, and the administra- tion of sacred ordinances to the new converts ; perhaps to baptize them, and so " add them to the church." (24. *Note*, viii. 14—17.)

4 т 8

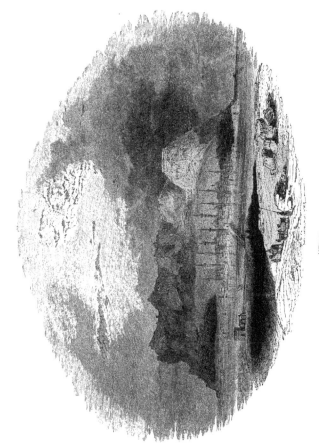

ANTIOCH, IN SYRIA.

Acts xi. 19—30 : xv. 22—41.

forth Barnabas, that he should go as far as Antioch;

23 Who when he came, and had seen the grace of God, was glad, and exhorted them all, that with purpose of heart they would cleave unto the Lord.

24 For he was a good man, and full of the Holy Ghost, and of faith: and much people was added unto the Lord.

25 Then departed Barnabas to Tarsus, for to seek Saul:

26 And when he had found him he brought him unto Antioch. And it came to pass, that a whole year they assembled themselves with the church, and taught much people. And the disciples were called Christians first in Antioch.

27 ¶ And in these days came prophets from Jerusalem unto Antioch.

28 And there stood up one of them, named Agabus, and signified by the Spirit, that there should be great dearth throughout all the world: which came to pass in the days of Claudius Cæsar.

29 Then the disciples, every man

V. 23, 24. Barnabas "saw the grace of God," in its happy effects, on the conduct and spirit of these converts; and this greatly rejoiced his benevolent mind. (*Marg. Ref.* a.—*Notes*, Mark ii. 3—12, *v.* 5. 1 *Thes.* i. 1—4, *vv.* 3, 4.) But he was aware that their faith would be assaulted by manifold temptations and persecutions; and that those who had been gentiles would be discouraged, through the prejudices of their Jewish brethren: he therefore exhorted, encouraged, and besought them, by every argument and motive which he could devise, "to cleave to " the Lord" Jesus, or *abide with him*, by a continued exercise of faith, a bold profession of his name, and implicit obedience to his commandments; whatever they might be called to renounce or suffer for his sake. (*Marg. Ref.* b—d.—*Notes*, xiv. 21—23. *John* viii. 30—36. xv. 3—11.) For " he was a good man," a person of remarkable affection, philanthropy, and genuine candour; as well as eminent for the miraculous gifts of the Holy Spirit, and the exercise of a vigorous faith in the midst of danger and persecution. So that, through his labours, and those of the other teachers, great accessions were made to the number of Christians at Antioch; and a flourishing church was planted there, from which preachers were afterwards sent forth to evangelize the nations. (*Marg. Ref.* e, f.—*Notes*, iv. 36, 37. xiii. 1—3. xv. 30—41.)

With purpose. (23) Τη προθεσει. xxvii. 13. *Rom.* viii. 28. ix. 11. *Eph.* i. 11. iii. 11. 2 *Tim.* i. 9. iii. 10.—*They would cleave to.*] Προσμενειν. xviii. 18. *Matt.* xv. 32. *Mark* viii. 2. 1 *Tim.* i. 3. See on *John* viii. 31.—*Were added.* (24) Προσετιθη. ii. 47.

V. 25, 26. As so large and encouraging a sphere of usefulness was unexpectedly opened, in this great and populous city, Barnabas went from thence to Tarsus, that he might procure the assistance of Saul: (*Note*, ix. 23—30:) and, having prevailed with him to accompany him, they laboured together at Antioch for a whole year, in further instructing the numerous converts, and in reducing the church to order and regularity, as well as in preaching the gospel to the unconverted inhabitants. (*Marg.* and *Marg. Ref.* i.)—Nothing is recorded of the apostle's success at Tarsus. (*Note*, *Matt.* xiii. 54—58.) There were, however, churches in Cilicia. (*Note*, xv. 36—41.)—*Were called Christians.* (26) " It came to pass that they" (Paul and Barnabas) " called the disciples Christians." This is indisputably the natural construction of the verse.—But the word implies that this was done by divine revelation: for it has generally this signification in the New Testament, and is rendered " warned from God," or " warned " of God," even when there is no word for GOD in the Greek. ' The believing Jews and Gentiles, being made ' one church, that the name of Jew and heathen might no ' more continue the distance that was betwixt them, this ' new name was given to them both; as some conceive ' according to the prophecy mentioned, *Is.* lxv. 15.' *Whitby.* Their enemies had hitherto called them Nazarenes, or Galileans: and if they had devised some other opprobrious name, they would, probably, have derived it from the word JESUS, rather than from CHRIST, or the MESSIAH, which they would never allow the crucified Nazarene to be. On the other hand, the disciples had called each other " brethren," " believers," and " saints," which names were not sufficiently distinguishing: but the word Christian, aptly denoted their reliance on that anointed Prince and Saviour, who was generally rejected with disdain by Jews and Gentiles: it also implied, that they were partakers of an *unction* by the Holy Spirit. Doubtless it was afterwards used as a term of reproach by their persecutors, though it was so honourable in its meaning and original. At present it is applied promiscuously to so vast and heterogeneous a multitude, that it scarcely implies either honour or reproach: and those who seriously profess to believe and obey Christ are generally distinguished by other names, whether they are spoken of with respect, or in derision. (*Marg. Ref.* k.—*Note*, 1 *Pet.* iv. 12—16.)

It came to pass, that ... the disciples were called Christians. (26) Εγενετο αυτοις ... χρηματισαι ... τες μαθητας Χριστιανους.—Χρηματισαι is infinitive active, and needs another verb to govern it, and an accusative case after it. Χρηματιζω. x. 22. *Matt.* ii. 12. 22. *Luke* ii. 26. *Rom.* vii. 3. *Heb.* viii. 5. xi. 7. xii. 25. (*Notes*, *Is.* lxii. 1—5, *v.* 2. lxv. 13—15, *v.* 15.)—Χριστιανους. xxvi. 28. 1 *Pet.* iv. 16.

V. 27—30. These prophets were evidently endowed by the Holy Spirit, with the power of foretelling future events; and were a superior order of extraordinary ministers, however the word may sometimes be used. (*Marg. Ref.* l.—*Note*, xxi. 7—14.)—The scarcity predicted by Agabus was to extend " throughout all the world," as the

q ii. 44, 45. iv. 34, according to his ability, determined ⁴ to send relief unto the brethren which dwelt in Judea:

30 Which also they did, and sent it ʳ to the elders ˢ by the hands of Barnabas and Saul.

Roman empire was ostentatiously called. (*Note, Luke* ii. 1.) Some indeed would explain it of the land of Judea and Galilee : but the expression is incapable of that meaning : and the famine might be very general, and severely felt in the various provinces of the empire ; though some places might be less straitened than others.—' *Eusebius* ' saith of this famine, that it oppressed almost the whole ' empire ; and that it was recorded by historians most ' averse to our religion ; viz. by Suetonius, in the Life ' of Claudius, who saith, it happened (*ob assiduas steri-* ' *litates*) through a long barrenness. Josephus saith that it ' raged so much in Judea, ... that many perished for want of ' victuals : and Dion Cassius, that it was a very great fa- ' mine.' *Whitby.*—The believers at Antioch, which was a rich and trading city, were more affluent than those in Judea ; who had also impoverished themselves, by selling their estates after the day of Pentecost. For these reasons, and probably because the Gentile converts wished to conciliate the affections of their Jewish brethren ; they determined to make a collection, in proportion to their gain in trade, or from their estates, and to send a sum of money to relieve the poor Christians in Judea. (*Marg. Ref.* p, q. —*Notes, Rom.* xv. 22—29. 1 *Cor.* xvi. 1, 2.) Barnabas and Saul were entrusted to carry these first-fruits, of the faith and love of the gentile converts, to Jerusalem : and as, probably, most of the apostles were absent, preaching the gospel in other places, they delivered the money to the " elders," that they might entrust it to the deacons to be distributed. This is the first time " elders " are mentioned in the church of Christ ; but we shall have more favourable opportunities, of considering several questions relative to their office : (*Note,* xx. 17 :) without doubt they were pastors of the Christian church ; and as both Peter and John call themselves *Elders,* (1 *Pet.* v. 1, 2. 2 *John* 1,) it is not clear that the apostles were not included. (*Marg. Ref. r.*)

All the world. (28) 'Ολην την οικουμενην. See on *Luke* ii. 1.—*According to his ability.* (29) Καθως ηυπορειτο. Here only. Ευπορια, xix. 25 : ex ευ, bene, et πορος, lucrum.—*Relief.*] Διακονιαν. 2 *Cor.* ix. 12.—*The* elders. (30) Τας πρεσβυτερυς. xiv. 23. xv. 2. xx. 17. *Presbyteros,* whence comes presbyter, and by contraction *præster :* hence the English word *priest ;* which by no means signifies a *sacri-* *ficer,* (ιερευς,) as many suppose.

PRACTICAL OBSERVATIONS.

V. 1—18.

The imperfection of human nature, even in its best estate, appears, when pious persons are offended and grieved at those things, which should excite in them the most lively joy and gratitude. Sometimes true believers are displeased to hear, even of the word of God being preached and received, because the peculiarities of their own church, sect, or system, have not been adhered to : and they are ready to find fault with the Lord's plan of bringing sinners to repentance, and faith in Christ, and with those who execute it ; because their own plan and pre'udices have

been broken in upon. (*Notes, Jon.* iv. 1—4. *Mark* ix. 38— 40. *Luke* ix. 46—50, *v.* 50.) Hence it is, that the zealous servant of God may expect to be censured, on account of those very things, in which his Master has peculiarly prospered him, and by those whom he most esteems and loves ! We should, however, meekly bear with the infirmities of our brethren : and, instead of taking offence, or answering with warmth, we ought candidly to explain our motives, and shew the nature of our proceedings, in order to satisfy and conciliate their minds.—It behoves every one to remember who and what he is : and while men are very zealous for their own regulations, they should take care, that they do not " withstand God," or prescribe other terms of admission among them, than he has appointed for admission into his church ; lest they should reject and grieve those who have believed in Christ, and received the gift and the baptism of the Holy Spirit, even as they have.—Men of piety and candour, though they have been prejudiced, will be satisfied with a proper answer, and a sufficient explanation and reason : and those who love the Lord will glorify him, when they are certified that he " hath given repentance unto life," even to the most abject of their fellow-sinners. (*Notes* and *P. O. Luke* xv. 1—10. 25—32.)

V. 19—30.

When the Lord Jesus is preached in simplicity, and according to the scripture ; his power will attend the word to give it success : and when sinners are brought " to " believe, and turn unto the Lord ;" " good men," who are " full of faith and of the Holy Ghost," will discern, admire, and rejoice in the grace of God bestowed upon them ; and exhort all, who profess the gospel, " to " cleave to the Lord" Jesus " with purpose of heart," knowing how many efforts Satan and his servants will employ to draw them aside. Where a prospect of great usefulness appears, they will bestow pains, to procure the assistance of the most able and zealous ministers, though themselves should be thus eclipsed : and while such men proceed with one heart in the work, believers will be encouraged in assembling together, in order to their edification and establishment.—We, at this day, are called by the name given to these ancient disciples: may we be anointed with the same Spirit, and walk in their steps ! A Christian is a member of Christ's mystical body, a temple of the Holy Spirit, an adopted child of God, an anointed king and priest unto him, and an heir of everlasting glory. (*Note,* 1 *John* ii. 20—25.) May we be ambitious of these honours, which belong to all his saints ! may we " walk worthy of this vocation, wherewith we are " called !" and may " all, who call themselves Christians, ' be led into the way of truth, and hold the faith, in unity ' of spirit, in the bond of peace, and in righteousness of ' life !' Such Christians will sympathize with their brethren in all their afflictions: the various dispensations of Providence will give them opportunity of shewing their love, by distributing according to their ability to " the " necessity of the saints :" thus God will be glorified, the

CHAP. XII.

King Herod persecutes the church; kills James, the brother of John; and imprisons Peter, 1—4; who, in answer to unceasing prayer, is delivered out of prison by an angel, 5—17. Herod puts the keepers to death; and leaving Jerusalem goes to Cæsarea, 18, 19. Proudly receiving the honour due to God alone, he is smitten by an angel, and dies miserably, 20—23. The word of God prospers, 24. Barnabas and Saul return to Antioch, 25.

a Or, *begun.*, iv. 30. ix. 31. Luke xix. word
a Matt. x. 17, 16. xxiv. 9. John

NOW about that time, Herod the king *a* stretched forth *his* hands *b* to vex certain of the church.

2 And he killed *b* James the brother of John *c* with the sword.

3 And because *d* he saw it pleased the Jews, *e* he proceeded further to take Peter also. *f* Then were the days of unleavened bread.

b Matt. iv. 21, 22. xx. 23. Mark x. 35—38.
c 1 Kings xix. 1, 10. Jer. xxvi. 23. Heb. xi. 37.
d xxiv. 27. xxv. 9. John xiii. 43. Gal. i. 10. 1 Thes. ii. 4.
e ii. 14. iv. 18. Ps. lxxvi. 10. John xix. 11.
f Ex. xii. 15—20. xiii. 3—7. Lev. xxiii. 6—14. Matt. xxvi. 17. 1 Cor. v. 7, 8.

4 And when he had apprehended him, *g* he put *him* in prison, *h* and delivered *him* to four quaternions of soldiers to keep him: *i* intending after Easter to bring him forth to the people.

5 Peter therefore was kept in prison; but *k* prayer was *k* made without ceasing of the church unto God for him.

6 And when Herod would have brought him forth, *l* the same night Peter was sleeping between two soldiers, *m* bound with two chains: *n* and the keepers before the door kept the prison.

7 And, behold, *o* the angel of the Lord came upon *him*, *p* and a light

g iv. 3. v. 18. viii. 3. Matt. xxiv. 9. Luke xxi. 12. xiii. 33. John xiii. 36—38. xxi. 18.
h xvi. 23, 24. Matt. xxvii. 64—66.
i iv. 28. Esth. iii. 6, 7. 13. Prov. xix. 21. xxvii. 1. Lam. iii. 37. Matt. xxvi. 5. Or, *instant prayer was made.*
k 12. ia. lxii. 6, 7. Matt. xviii. 19.
k Luke xviii. 1. 1 Cor. xii. 26. 2 Cor. i. 11. Eph. vi. 18—20. 1 Thes. v. 17. Heb. xiii. 3. Jam. v. 16.
l Gen. xxii. 14. Deut. xxxii. 36. 1 Sam. xxvi. 24. 27. Ps. iii. 5, 6. iv. 8. Is. xxvi. 3. 8, 4. Phil. iv. 6.
m vii. Heb. xiii. 6.
n xxi. 33. xxviii. 20. Jer. xi. 4. xxxix. 19. xl. 30. xxvii. 25, p ix
more. 2 Tim. i. 16.   *n* v. 23. Matt. xxvii. 4.   *o* 23. v. 19. xx. 30. xxvii. 25,
74. 1 Kings xix. 5. 7. Ps. xxxiv. 7. Is. xxxvii. 36. Dan. vi. 22. Heb. i. 14.
2. 2 Sam xxii. 29. Ex. xliii. 2. Mic. vii. 9. Hab. iii. 4. 11. Rev. xviii. 1.

---

harmony among believers promoted, the faith and hope of the poor encouraged, their prayers and praises excited; and fruit brought forth, which will abound to the account of those by whom it is produced. (Note and *P. O. 2 Cor.* ix. 8—15.) The wisdom of this world indeed would earnestly plead, in the prospect of a famine, the propriety of hoarding for ourselves and families, against the emergency; and doubtless frugality, as distinguished from avarice, is not only prudent, but an incumbent duty: yet " the wis- " dom from above" will teach us, in such circumstances especially, to " lend to the LORD" by giving liberally to his needy servants, and to trust him, when the time comes, to provide for us and our's, in his own manner and measure. (*Notes* and *P. O.* ii. 42—47.—*Note, Jam.* iii. 17, 18.)

NOTES.

CHAP. XII. V. 1—4. This Herod, surnamed Agrippa, was grandson to Herod the Great, by Aristobulus; nephew to Herod Antipas who slew John the Baptist; brother to Herodias his incestuous paramour; and father to king Agrippa, of whom we shall read hereafter. (*Notes,* xxv. 13—27. xxvi. *Matt.* xiv. 1—5.) The emperor Caligula made him tetrarch of Galilee; and Claudius afterwards made him king of Judea, because he had been serviceable to him in obtaining the empire. Judea had been before, and was again soon after, under the dominion of a Roman governor. Herod being invested with his new dignity, endeavoured by all means to ingratiate himself with the Jews: and this probably combined with his hereditary enmity to the gospel, in exciting him to persecute the church. He seems to have harassed the Christians for some time, before he attacked the apostles: but at length he seized on James, the son of Zebedee, and immediately ordered him to be beheaded. (*Marg. Ref.* a—c.) Thus was he baptized with the baptism of his Lord, as it had been predicted; (*Note, Matt.* xx. 20—23, v. 23;) and received the crown of martyrdom, before any of the other apostles. As Herod found that the Jews were much

pleased with this measure, he apprehended Peter also; (*Marg. Ref.* d, e.—*Notes,* xxiv. 24—27. xxv. 9—11;) and probably he intended to put the other apostles to death, when he could get them into his power: but, as the passover and the feast of unleavened bread were then celebrated, he meant to defer his proceedings against Peter, till these solemnities were over. (*Marg. Ref.* f—i.—*Note, Matt.* xxvi. 3—5.) He therefore committed him to sixteen soldiers, who were appointed to guard him in prison, night and day, four at a time by rotation; intending as soon as the feast was ended, to gratify the Jews by his publick execution. (*Marg. Ref.* h.)—Even if Easter were observed at that time, in the Christian church, of which nothing is mentioned in the sacred records; Herod would certainly pay no regard to it: it is therefore surprising, that the venerable translators of the Bible should have used that word, instead of " the passover," in this connexion!— This Herod ' was a great zealot for the Mosaick law, dwelt ' much at Jerusalem, and was fond of all opportunities of ' obliging the Jews. ...This early execution of one of ' the apostles, ...would illustrate the courage of the rest in ' going on with their ministry; as it would evidently shew, ' that all their miraculous powers did not secure them from ' dying by the sword of their enemies.' *Doddridge.*
To *vex.* (1) Κακωσαι. vii. 6. xiv. 2. Κακωσις, vii. 13.— *It pleased.* (3) Αρεσον εστι. See on vi. 2.—*Of unleavened bread.*] Των αζυμων. xx. 6. 1 Cor. v. 7, 8. Αb α, priv. et ζυμη, *fermentum.*—*Quaternions.* (4) Τετραδιοις. Here only. Α τεσσαρες, quatuor.—*Easter.*] Το πασχα. The passover, including the days of unleavened bread. *John* xviii. 28.

V. 5—11. The time of Peter's imprisonment gave the church an opportunity, not of concerting measures for his rescue, but of pouring out their fervent prayers for the preservation of his useful life. Probably they met together in different places for that purpose; and one company succeeding to another, there was literally no intermission of their prayers for him, day or night. Yet he was free from anxiety about the event: and the night be-

4 U 3

shined in the prison: and he smote Peter on the side, and raised him up, saying, ⁴Arise up quickly. ʳAnd his chains fell off from *his* hands.

8 And the angel said unto him, Gird thyself, and bind on thy sandals: and so he did. And he saith unto him, Cast thy garment about thee, and follow me.

9 And ʰhe went out, and followed him; ʲand wist not that it was true which was done by the angel, but thought he saw a vision.

10 When they were past ᵘthe first and the second ward, they came unto the iron gate that leadeth unto the city, ˣ which opened to them of his own accord: and they went out, and passed on through one street, and forthwith the angel departed from him.

11 And when Peter ʸ was come to himself, he said, Now ᶻI know of a surety, ᵃthat the Lord hath sent his angel, ᵇand hath delivered me out of the hand of Herod, and *from* ᶜall the expectation of the people of the Jews.

12 And when he had considered *the thing*, ᵈ he came to the house of Mary, the mother of ᵉ John whose surname was Mark, ᶠ where many were gathered together, praying.

13 And as Peter ᵍ knocked at the door of the gate, a damsel came to ʰhearken, named Rhoda.

14 And when she knew Peter's voice, ʰ she opened not the gate for gladness, but ran in, and told how Peter stood before the gate.

15 And they said unto her, ʲThou art mad. But she constantly affirmed that it was even so. Then said they, ᵏIt is his angel.

16 But Peter continued knocking: and when they had opened *the door*, and saw him, they were astonished.

17 But he, ˡbeckoning unto them with the hand to hold their peace, ᵐdeclared unto them how the Lord had brought him out of the prison. And he said, Go shew these things unto ⁿJames, and to the brethren. ᵒAnd he departed, and went into another place.

fore his intended execution, while others were earnestly praying for his life, he went to sleep with the utmost composure; though his posture must have been very uneasy, being chained with two chains, one on each hand, to the two soldiers between whom he lay. Even the strong light, which attended the angel's entrance into the dungeon, did not awake Peter; but when the angel, gently smiting his side, caused him to arise, he found his chains immediately loosed. (*Marg. Ref.* k—p.) Yet, neither the voice of the angel, the light in the prison, the falling of the chains, nor the preparation of Peter to depart, was noticed by the keepers, who were supernaturally thrown into a deep sleep. Nay, Peter himself supposed, that he only saw a vision, as he had sometimes done before; and that it was not a reality. (*Marg. Ref.* q—t.—*Note*, x. 9—16.) The wards or watches here mentioned seem to have included the stated guard of the prison, as well as the soldiers especially appointed to keep Peter: and these too were rendered insensible to the whole transaction. "The great iron "gate" separated the environs of the prison from the city, and was doubtless barred in the strongest manner: yet it opened of its own accord. (*Note*, John xx. 19—23.) When the angel had led Peter out of the reach of his keepers, and into a part of the city which he knew; he departed from him, and then he became sensible of the reality of his deliverance. (*Marg. Ref.* u, x.—*Note*, v. 17—25.)—The people, as Peter well knew, eagerly longed to see him put to death, as a special gratification; notwithstanding the numerous miracles of mercy, which had been performed by him! (*Marg. Ref.* z—c.—*Note*, John xv. 17—21.)

Without ceasing. (5) Εκτενης. See on *Luke* xxii. 44. 'The word εκτενης primarily signifies *extended*, but because 'the fervency of our desire is usually the cause, that we 'pray much or long, for any thing; therefore to pray 'εκτενως, is also to pray fervently and importunately.' *Whitby.—Would have*, &c. (6) Εμελλεν. "Was about, &c." *Luke* xxi. 7.—*Of his own accord*. (10) Αυτομάτη. See on *Mark* iv. 28.—*Come to himself*. (11) Γενομενος εν αυτῳ.— 'When, recovering from his surprise, he tranquilly exercised 'his understanding.' (*Note*, *Luke* xv. 17—19.)—*Expectation*.] Προσδοκιας. See on *Luke* xxi. 26.

V. 12—17. This Mary was the sister of Barnabas. (*Col.* iv. 10.)—It is probable, that it had been customary, for some of the believers in Jerusalem to assemble at her house for religious worship; though it can scarcely be supposed that Peter knew that they were then joining in prayer for him. He, however, judged it best to go thither. But either their hopes were sunk very low, or they expected their prayers to be answered in some other way: for they were utterly indisposed to believe the report of the damsel, who informed them that he stood at the gate: and when she insisted upon it that it was Peter, for she knew his voice; rather than suppose, that he had actually obtained his liberty, they concluded, "that it was his "angel." (*Marg. and Marg. Ref.* d—k.) They seem to have spoken according to the notion, true or false, which has generally prevailed; that when people are near death, or have actually expired, a spirit, or angel, in their exact form, and speaking with their voice, sometimes appears to their friends or acquaintance; which notion perhaps first arose from the opinion, that every man has his

4 U 4

18 Now as soon as it was day, ᵖ there was no small stir among the soldiers, what was become of Peter.

19 And when Herod had ᵗ sought for him, and found him not, ʳ he examined the keepers, and ˢ commanded that *they* should be put to death. And ᵗ he went down from Judea to Cæsarea, and *there* abode.

20 ¶ And Herod ᵘ was highly displeased with them of ˣ Tyre and Sidon: ʸ but they came with one accord to him; and, having made Blastus ᶻ the

† *Gr. that was over the king's bed chamber.*

king's chamberlain their friend, desired peace; ᶻ because their country was nourished by the king's *country*.

21 And upon a set day, Herod, arrayed in royal apparel, sat upon his throne, and made an oration unto them.

22 And the people gave a shout, saying, 'It is the voice of a god, and not of a man.

23 And immediately ᵇ the angel of the Lord smote him, ᵇ because he gave not God the glory: ᶜ and he was eaten of worms, and gave up the ghost.

Luke xII. 47, 48.   2 Thes. ii. 4.   c 2 Chr. xxi. 18, 19.   Job vii. 5. xix. 26.   Is. xiv. 11.
II. 8. lxvi. 24.   Mark ix. 44—48.

---

guardian angel appointed to take care of him. For to suppose, that they only meant that it was a messenger from him, is absurd; as a messenger could not speak with his well-known voice, though he might use his name.—When, however, Peter at length obtained admission, their transport of surprise was so great, that he could hardly obtain a hearing, when he desired to inform them, how the Lord had answered their prayers in his deliverance. (*Marg. Ref.* l, m.—*Notes*, Job ix. 14—21. *Is.* lxv. 24, 25.) The other apostles seem to have been absent from Jerusalem: but James, the son of Alpheus, who wrote the epistle, was in some place of concealment in the neighbourhood; and Peter desired especially that he should be informed of his deliverance, for his encouragement. Having thus given proper directions to the disciples, he deemed it his duty to retire to some place of greater safety. (*Marg. Ref.* n, o.) —' It is utterly incredible, that he now went to Rome, ' and made an abode of twenty-five years, which the popish ' writers pretend.' *Doddridge.* It would be easy to multiply similar instances, in which the legends of the Romish church as much contradict the sacred history, as its traditions make void both the commandments and testimonies of God. (*Notes*, Matt. xv. 1—14.)

Were gathered together. (12) Ησαν συνηθροισμενοι. xix. 25. Luke xxiv. 33.—*She constantly affirmed.* (15) Διισχυ-ριζετο. See on *Luke* xxii. 59.—*Beckoning.* (17) Κατασεισας. xiii. 16. xix. 33. xxi. 40. Ex καλα, et σειω, moveo.

V. 18, 19. The astonishment of the soldiers, when they found Peter was gone; their endeavours to throw the blame from themselves upon each other, and their dread of Herod's vindictive rage, may easily be conceived. Indeed they had cause to tremble: for that tyrant, exasperated at his disappointment, and unwilling it should be thought that Peter had been miraculously delivered, ordered them to immediate execution; alledging, no doubt, that Peter's escape was owing to their negligence and sleeping upon guard. (*Marg. Ref.* p—s.—*Note, Matt.* xxviii. 11—15.) Yet, it is highly probable, that he himself perceived that Peter had been rescued in a supernatural manner, as all the apostles had before been; (*Note*, v. 17 —25;) and we may suppose, that this intimidated him, and induced him to suspend the persecution. Perhaps the chagrin, at being thus baffled, might hasten his departure to Cæsarea, and influence him to continue there: though Josephus informs us, that he went thither to celebrate

certain heathenish games, in honour of the Roman emperor.

That they should be put to death. (19) Απαχθηναι. ' Ad ' supplicium eos rapi jussit.' Schleusner.—xxiv. 7. Matt. xxvii. 31. Luke xxiii. 6.

V. 20—23. The Tyrians and Zidonians, being engaged in extensive commerce, depended almost entirely on Judea and Galilee for corn and other provisions. (*Notes*, 1 *Kings* v. 2—9. *Ez.* xxvii. 13—25 \ But Herod. having taken great offence at some part of their conduct, purposed to declare war against them; and by cutting off their supplies he could soon have reduced them to distress. This consideration led them to pay court to the king's favourite, by whose good offices they renewed their peace with him; having made the needful concessions and submissions. (*Marg. Ref.* u—y.) This gave occasion to Herod, on an appointed day, to display his magnificence in a most ostentatious manner, of which Josephus has given a particular account: and, having from his throne delivered a speech, with much affectation of eloquence, and boastings of his equity and clemency; the people, either impressed with the splendour of the scene, and by the graces of his elocution, or courting his favour by the most abominable flattery, exclaimed that " it was the voice of a God, and " not of a man!" (*Marg. Ref.* z.) Many heathen princes had received, nay, arrogated to themselves, divine honours: but it was far more horrible impiety in Herod, who was acquainted with the word and worship of the living God, to accept, and be pleased with, such idolatrous and sacrilegious adorations, without rebuking the blasphemy, and giving God the glory. Immediately therefore an angel smote him with an incurable disease; so that his bowels bred worms, which consumed them: and, after lying for some time, a most abject and loathsome spectacle, in excruciating pain, he died in the most degraded and wretched manner that can be conceived. (*Marg. Ref.* a—c.) Josephus ascribes his miserable end to the judgment of God on him, for the impiety here recorded, and introduces him, as owning it in very strong language: but he suppresses some circumstances, probably from regard to his family; and it was reserved for an inspired writer to inform us, that his disease arose from a stroke inflicted by an angel. (*Notes*, 2 Sam. xxiv. 17. 2 Kings xix. 35—37.) It is however remarkable, that the sacred historian does not represent the awful death of Herod, as a judgment on

d A ᴎ. vi. 7. xi.
ii. xix. 20. Prov.
xxviii. 28. Je.
vii. 19—13. liv.
14—17. lv. 10.
11. Dan. ii. 24,
25. 44, 45. Matt. xvi. 18. Col. i. 6. 2 Thes. iii. 1.

24 ¶ But ^d the word of God grew and multiplied.

25 And ^e Barnabas and Saul returned

e xi. 29, 30. xlii. 1—5.

from Jerusalem, when they had fulfilled *their* * ministry, and took with them ^f John whose surname was Mark.

* Or, charge.

f See on 12.—1 Pet. v. 13.

him for persecuting the church, though he had so inviting and so just an occasion of doing it; but assigns another cause of that event. This is a striking contrast to the usual practice of enthusiasts; who generally, without any adequate reason, take pleasure in representing all the calamities which befal those who even in a slight degree oppose them, as divine judgments on them for so doing.—Many persecutors have ended their days by a similar disease, which has rendered them more loathsome while alive, than a putrid corpse can be: as well as filled them with the most intolerable pains. (*Notes, Zech.* xiv. 12—15. *Matt.* ii. 19—23.)

Was highly displeased. (20) " Bare a hostile mind " intending war." *Marg. Ην...θυμομαχων.* Here only. Ex θυμος, mens, ira, et μαχομαι, pugno.—*Having made Blastus their friend.*] Πεισαντες Βλαστον. " Persuading " Blastus."—*The...chamberlain.*] Τον επι τω κοιτωνος. Here only. Κοιτη, bed, *Luke* xi. 7.—*On a set day.* (21) Τακτη... ημερα.—Here only. Α τεταχται, from τασσω. See on xiii. 48. —*Made an oration.*] Εδημηγορει. Here only. Ex δημος, populus (22), et αγορευ, concionem in foro habeo.—*Eaten of worms.* (23) Σκωληκοβρωτος. Here only. Ex σκωληξ, vermis, et βρωσκω, edo.—*Gave up the ghost.*] Εξεψυξεν. See on v. 5.

V. 24. After the death of Herod, " the word of God " continued to grow and multiply; like seed, the produce of which is sown again the next year, and so on from year to year. (*Notes, Is.* lv. 10, 11. *Matt.* xiii. 18—23. 36—43. *John* xv. 12—16, v. 16.) Thus the believers, who sprang up from the first preaching of the word, still further diffused the knowledge of the gospel; and the cause of Christ got ground on every side, notwithstanding the opposition which was excited against it; and even by means of that opposition. (*Marg. Ref.*—*Note,* 1—4.)

V. 25. (*Note,* xi. 27—30.) Probably Barnabas and Saul left Jerusalem, after a short continuance there, and perhaps before the beginning of this persecution: but the narrative, as it concerns them, is here resumed.—John Mark was nephew to Barnabas, and was taken by him and Saul, that he might be trained up for future usefulness; and, in the mean time, be serviceable to them in the multiplicity of their engagements. (*Notes,* xiii. 13—15. xv. 36—41. *Preface to the Gospel according to Mark.*)

PRACTICAL OBSERVATIONS.

V. 1—17.

The enmity of the human heart against God, and the instigations of Satan, concur in exciting opposition to the church from time to time: and when wicked rulers find, that the vexation and murder of pious Christians and zealous ministers are agreeable to their subjects, they are encouraged to proceed in that diabolical work. Thus, some of the saints, having finished their testimony, are removed to their rest: their pains are transient, and mitigated by divine consolations, and their subsequent felicity is unspeakable and eternal. (*Notes,* vii. 54—60. *Is.* lvii. 1, 2. *Rev.* xi. 7—12.) But amidst the " many devices, which

" are in the heart of man, the counsel of the LORD shall " stand." (*Notes, Ps.* lxxvi. 10. *Prov.* xix. 21.)—When time is given for prayer, and great numbers are excited to join in it, as with one heart and soul; it may be regarded as an indication, that God intends to grant their desires. (*Note, Jam.* v. 16—18.) He is reluctant to refuse the petitions of his children; and therefore he sometimes suddenly executes his purposes, without giving them the opportunity of interposing their requests to the contrary. But the lives of eminent saints are more desired by their brethren, than by themselves. (*Note,* xx. 22—24.) A peaceful conscience, a lively hope, and the consolations of the Holy Spirit, produce the most entire composure in the immediate prospect of death, even in those very persons, who have at other times been the most distracted with terrors on that account. (*Note, Matt.* xxvi. 69—75.) —When the Lord sees good to deliver, all obstructions are insignificant: his angels gladly visit the dungeons or cells, where his poor and afflicted children lie: even *they* can defeat or suspend all the powers of men; and they delight to minister comfort to the heirs of salvation. (*Notes, Luke* xvi. 22, 23. *Heb.* i. 13, 14.)—Whether we be waiting for deliverance from the bondage of sin, or for the termination of our trials and sorrows, while the Lord affords us his light, and puts forth his power, to excite our attention and expectation; we should implicitly follow his directions, and wait his will. Thus will he lead us forth to liberty and safety, and deliver us from the power and expectation of our strongest enemies.—He sometimes answers prayer in so unexpected a manner, that his people can scarcely believe it a reality: nay, their fears and misapprehensions may for a time exclude the joy, to which he calls them; and even that joy, when excited, being accompanied with other tumultuous passions, may unfit them for the employment of the present moment; but the whole will surely terminate in adoring and rejoicing praises and thanksgivings.—It is our duty to take care of our lives, so long as the Lord sees good to preserve us; to shelter ourselves from the violence of furious enemies; and likewise to give encouragement from our experience, to those who are exposed to similar dangers; as well as to excite them to praise God in our behalf.

V. 18—25.

The instruments of persecution are exposed to the most imminent danger: (*Notes, Dan.* iii. 19—23. vi. 24:) the wrath of God is suspended over all, who engage in this hateful work; and the tyranny of persecutors, when obstructed in its course, is apt to burst forth on every one who comes in its way, without regard to equity and mercy. But those who thus " fight against God," ripen apace for more signal vengeance; while they are buoyed up, with success and flattery, into the most extravagant pride and arrogance.—We may, however, learn wisdom from the policy of the Tyrians and Zidonians: for we have *justly* offended the almighty Lord with our sins; we entirely depend on him for " life, and breath, and all things:" it

4 υ 6

CHAP. XIII.

Barnabas and Saul, by the command of the Holy Spirit, are set apart from among other teachers at Antioch with fasting and prayer, and sent forth to preach the gospel, 1—3. Attended by John Mark, they arrive at Cyprus, and preach at Salamis, 4, 5. At Paphos, Elymas the sorcerer, opposing them, is smitten with blindness, and the deputy, Sergius Paulus, believes, 6—12. They pass through Pamphylia (where Mark leaves them) to Antioch in Pisidia, 13, 14. Saul, now named Paul, preaches in the synagogue, shewing that Jesus is the Messiah, through whom all believers are pardoned and justified; and warning his hearers not to reject him, 1d—41. The Gentiles desire to hear the word again; and some Jews and proselytes join Paul and Barnabas, 42, 43 Almost the whole city throng to hear the word, 44 The envious Jews gainsay and blaspheme; and the apostles turn to the gentiles, of whom many believe, 45—49.

The Jews raise a persecution, and drive Paul and Barnabas away, who go to Iconium, 50, 51. The disciples are filled with joy and with the Holy Spirit, 52.

N OW there were [a] in the church, that was at Antioch, certain [b] prophets and teachers; as [c] Barnabas, and Simeon that was called Niger, and [d] Lucius of Cyrene, and Manaen, [e] which had been brought up with [f] Herod the tetrarch, [f] and Saul.

2 As [g] they ministered to the Lord, [h] and fasted, [i] the Holy Ghost said, [k] Separate me Barnabas and Saul for [l] the work whereunto I have called them.

a xi. 22—34. xxv. 26, 27.
b xi. 25—27. xv. 36. Rom. xii. 6
7. 1 Cor. xii. 28, 29. xiv. 24, 25. Eph. iv. 11. 1 Thes. v. 20.
c iv. 36. xi. 22—30. xii. 25. 1 Cor. ix. 6. Gal. ii. 9, 13.
d xi. 20. Rom. xvi. 21.
e Herod's foster-brother.
f Matt. xiv. 1. Luke iii. 1. 19, 20. xiii. 31. 54. xviii. 28. Phil. iv. 22.
g ix. viii. 1—3. ix. 1, &c.
h xi. 4. Deut. x. 8. 1 Sam. ii. 11. 1 Chr. xvi. 4. 37, &c. Rom. xv. 16. Col. iv. 17.
i 2 Tim. i. 11. iv. 5. 11.
k ix. 15. xxii. 21. xxvi. 17, 18. Rom. i. 1. Gal. i. 15. 2 Tim. i. 11.
l ix. 20. Dan. ix. 3. Matt. vi. 16. ix. 14, 15. Luke ii. 37.

1 Cor. vii. 5. 2 Cor. vi. 5. xi. 27. i x. 19. xvi. 6, 7. 1 Cor. xii. 11.
21. Num. viii. 11—14. Rom. l. 1. x. 15. Gal. i. 15. ii. 8, 9. 2 Tim. i. 2. 1 ix. 15.
xiv. 26. Matt. ix. 38. Luke x. 2. Eph. iii. 7, 8. 1 Tim. ii. 7. 2 Tim. i. 11. Heb. v. 4.

---

surely then behoves us to humble ourselves before him, that, through the appointed Mediator, who is ever ready to befriend us, we may be reconciled to him, before "wrath come upon us to the uttermost;" as it did upon proud Herod, who, while others trembled at his impotent rage, would not fear the almighty God! But, "a haughty "spirit is before a fall:" "God resisteth the proud" as his rivals and enemies; angels gladly vindicate his glory, by crushing the sacrilegious competitors; the whole creation stands ready to avenge its Creator's cause upon those, who refuse to give him the glory; and the most contemptible insects or vermin are able to degrade, vilify, and torment those haughty rebels, who affect to be worshipped as deities. (Note, Ex. viii. 16, 17.) "The triumphing of "the wicked is short:" the word of God, and the cause of the gospel, have stood their ground against many such boasting persecutors and opposers as Herod; their destruction has made way for its more abundant success; and the ruin of every one, who shall hereafter engage against the cause of Christ, will introduce its still further progress. (Notes, Rev. xix. 11—21.) But they, who labour to promote it, shall "go from strength to strength," and proceed from one service to another, till their work is finished: and then they shall enter into those glorious mansions, from which their eyes shall behold, and only behold, the destruction of the workers of iniquity.

NOTES.

Chap. XIII. V. 1—3. The first considerable church of converts, consisting chiefly of the Gentiles, seems to have been collected at Antioch in Syria: so that it was the principal place of residence for those teachers, who went forth to preach among the Gentiles, even as Jerusalem was in respect of the Jewish converts. Several eminent persons were, at the time to which this chapter relates, resident there, (besides their stated pastors,) who were well qualified as teachers, and endowed with the gift of prophecy.—The surname of Niger, or "Black," by which Simeon was known, seems to have been given him on account of his complexion; perhaps he was a negro. Some have conjectured that this was Simon the Cyrenian,

who was compelled to bear the cross after Jesus: and if so, Lucius was of the same country.—Manaen, who was educated along with Herod Antipas, the tetrarch, had probably renounced considerable prospects for the sake of the gospel. (Marg. Ref. a—f.)—While these persons were employed in devotional exercises, in the intervals of their sacred ministry, and were observing a day of solemn fasting and prayer, probably in order to seek a blessing on their labours, and direction concerning their future progress; they were ordered, by an immediate revelation of the Holy Spirit, to "separate Barnabas and Saul for the "work, unto which he had called them." (Marg. Ref. g—l.) This language evidently implies the personality and Deity of the Holy Spirit. (Note, x. 17—23. John xiv. 15 —17. xvi. 7—13. 1 Cor. xii. 4—11.) The work intended was the preaching of the gospel to the gentiles at large, of which Saul had some previous information when he was converted. (Notes, xxii. 17—21. xxvi. 16—18.) —The prophets and teachers, in laying their hands on them, with fasting and prayer, acted by immediate order from the Holy Spirit; thus giving a publick testimony to their assured confidence, that they were divinely appointed to that service, and expressing fervent desires for their success in it. (Marg. Ref. m, n.) Accordingly, they are said to have been "sent forth by the "Holy Ghost." (4)—Barnabas and Saul had, for a considerable time, been ministers of the word: so that this imposition of hands could not be for the purpose of ordaining them; nor does it appear, that any spiritual gift, or new authority, was conferred by it. (Note, viii. 14—17.)—St. Paul was "an apostle, not by man:" (Note, Gal. i. 1, 2:) his apostolical office could not then be conferred at this time; but his appointment by the Lord Jesus himself, as the apostle of the gentiles, might thus be publickly acknowledged, in the principal church of gentile converts. Barnabas also is afterwards spoken of as an apostle. (xiv. 4. 14.) Perhaps he was appointed by the Holy Spirit to that office, on this occasion; with some reference to the martyrdom of James, by which the number of the apostles was diminished. (Note, xiv. 24—28.)

Teachers. (1) Διδασκαλοι. 1 Cor. xii. 29. Eph. iv. 11.

3 And when ᵐ they had fasted and prayed, and laid their hands on them, ⁿ they sent them away.

4 So they, ° being sent forth by the Holy Ghost, departed unto Seleucia; and from thence they sailed to ᵖ Cyprus.

5 And when they were at Salamis, ᑫ they preached the word of God ˢ in the synagogues of the Jews: and they had also ʳ John to ˢ their minister.

6 ¶ And when they had gone through the isle unto Paphos, they found a ᵗ certain sorcerer, ᵘ a false prophet, a Jew, ˣ whose name was Barjesus;

7 Which was with ʸ the deputy of the country, Sergius Paulus, ᶻ a prudent man; who called for Barnabas and Saul, and desired to hear the word of God.

8 But Elymas the sorcerer (ᵃ for so is his name by interpretation,) ᵇ withstood them, seeking to turn away the deputy from the faith.

9 Then Saul, ᶜ who also is called Paul, ᵈ filled with the Holy Ghost, ᵉ set his eyes on him,

10 And said, ᶠ O full of all subtlety, and all mischief, ᵍ thou child of the devil, thou enemy of all righteousness; ʰ wilt thou not cease to pervert ⁱ the right ways of the Lord?

11 And now, behold, ᵏ the hand of the Lord is upon thee, ˡ and thou shalt be blind, not seeing the sun for a season. And immediately there fell on him ᵐ a mist and a darkness: and he went about seeking some to lead him by the hand.

12 Then ⁿ the deputy, ° when he saw what was done, believed, ᵖ being astonished at the doctrine of the Lord.

Jam. iii. 1. (Notes, 1 Cor. xii. 27—31. Eph. iv. 11—13. Jam. iii. 1, 2.)—Niger.] Νιγερ. A Latin word. Hence Negro. —Which had been brought up with Herod.] "Herod's "foster-brother." Marg. Συντροφος. Here only.—A συντροφω, simul nutrio.—As they ministered. (2) Λειτουργουντων αυτων. Rom. xv. 27. Heb. x. 11. Not elsewhere.—Λειτουργια See on Luke i. 23.—Separate.] Αφορισατε. See on Matt. xxv. 32.

V. 4, 5. Selucia was a sea-port, about fifteen miles from Antioch. It does not appear that Saul and Barnabas preached there: but thence they passed into the island of Cyprus, the native place of Barnabas, (iv, 36,) and they had an opportunity of preaching in the synagogues at Salamis, the first city to which they came.—If the sentence of excommunication, which had been published against those who confessed Jesus to be the Christ, was still in force: (John xi. 57:) it is evident, that it was little noticed at a distance from Jerusalem: for the apostles were not refused admission into the synagogues, and were constantly allowed to preach in them. (Marg. Ref. p, q.)— John Mark accompanied Paul and Barnabas, to perform such services by their direction, as he was capable of: with a view no doubt of his being employed more and more, as a´ preacher of the gospel. (Marg. Ref. r, s.— Notes, 1 Kings xix. 19—21. 2 Kings iii. 11, 12.)

Sent forth by the Holy Ghost. (4) Note, xx. 28.—Minister. (5) Υπηρετην. 22. 26. xxvi. 16. Matt. v. 25. Luke i. 2. iv. 20. 1 Cor. iv. 1.

V. 6—12. The apostles went through the large and populous island of Cyprus, preaching in the cities as they had opportunity; doubtless with some success, both among the Jews and the Gentiles; till they arrived at Paphos, on the opposite side of it. This city was celebrated for the temple there dedicated to Venus, and infamous for the licentiousness practised at it. Here they met with a noted sorcerer, or magician, named Bar-jesus, that is, "the son "of Jesus." This man, being a Jew, pretended to be a prophet, and, confirming his pretensions by magical arts, was endeavouring to gain the attention of the proconsul of Cyprus, or the Roman governor appointed by the senate. (Marg. Ref. t—y.) The proconsul, however, was an intelligent and considerate person, who desired to know the truth in these highly interesting concerns; and having heard of Saul and Barnabas, he invited them to come, and declare the word of God unto him. But Bar-jesus, (who was also called "Elymas," from an Arabick word signifying a sorcerer,) foreseeing the ruin of his own character and influence, in case the proconsul should embrace the gospel; did all that he could to oppose the apostles, and to prejudice him against their doctrine. It may be supposed, that he disputed against the truth of the facts which they testified; misrepresented the nature and tendency of their doctrine; insinuated many things, in a subtle and malicious manner, against their intentions and to their disadvantage; and perhaps he performed some of his "lying "miracles" to support his own pretensions against them. (Marg. Ref. z—b.) But Saul, under the immediate influence of the Holy Spirit, "set his eyes upon him," as expressing his abhorrence of his crimes; declared him to be a man, "full of subtlety," malignity, and mischief; "a "child of the devil," who bare his image and supported his cause; and "an enemy of all righteousness," notwithstanding his plausible pretences: at the same time sharply expostulating with him, for thus pertinaciously misrepresenting and speaking evil of "the right ways of the Lord," that he might countenance his own vile impostures. He then denounced sentence upon him, as in the name of God, that he should be struck blind; so that, "for a season," he should be unable to see the light of the sun; though, in case he repented, the calamity might at length

13 ¶ Now when Paul and his company loosed from Paphos, they came to Perga in Pamphylia: and John departing from them returned to Jerusalem.

14 But when they departed from Perga, they came to Antioch in Pisidia, and went into the synagogue on the sabbath-day, and sat down.

15 And after the reading of the law and the prophets, the rulers of the synagogue sent unto them, saying, Ye men and brethren, if ye have any word of exhortation for the people, say on.

16 Then Paul stood up, and beckoning with his hand, said, Men of Israel, and ye that fear God, give audience.

be removed, as a similar one had been in the case of Saul himself. (*Notes*, ix. 8, 9. 17—22.) This sentence was immediately executed by the power of God: and, being enveloped in darkness, and filled with horror and confusion, he sought some person to lead him out of the place: an apt emblem of the benighted state of his soul. (*Marg. Ref. d—m.*) This decided victory of the apostles over their opponent, being connected with the other clear evidences of the truth of the gospel, and made effectual by the power of the Holy Spirit, induced the proconsul to embrace and profess Christianity: for " he was astonished," both at the energy of the doctrine upon his heart and conscience, and at the power of God by which it was confirmed. (*Marg. Ref. o, p.*)—Some think that he was the first idolatrous Gentile, who was converted to Christ: but it is not probable, that all the gentile converts at Antioch had previously been proselyted from idolatry; or that Saul and Barnabas had made no converts from idolatry in their progress through Cyprus. The conversion, however, of so eminent a person was a very memorable event: probably he continued for some time in his high station, serving the Lord Jesus in the use of his authority, and countenancing the professors and preachers of the gospel by his influence and example.— Saul is here said to have been " also called Paul " (9); and henceforth he bears that name. As this is the same with the proconsul's surname; some have thought that he assumed it on account of the conversion of this ruler: but it is more probable, that before this the Greeks had called him Paul, and the Hebrews Saul; and that, from this time, being generally conversant with the Gentiles, he was commonly known by the former name.—Dr. Lardner has, with great learning, vindicated the accuracy of St. Luke, in calling the governor *a proconsul;* and shewn, that those who governed the provinces by the appointment of the senate, were called proconsuls, though they had never been consuls; and that Cyprus was at this time a province of that description.

A ... sorcerer. (6) Μαγον. 8. See on viii. 9. Matt. ii. 1. —*The deputy.* (7) Τῳ ανθυπατῳ. 8. 12. xix. 38. ' Ex ανti loco, vice, et ιπατος, (id. quod ινιρτατος *summus consul.*' Schleusner. Ανθυπατιω, xviii. 12.—*Mischief.* (10) 'Ραδιυργιας. Here only. 'Ραδιυργημα, xviii. 14: *flagitium scelus.* A ραδιυργιω quod ex ραδιος, *facilis,* proclivus, et εργον opus. Always used in a bad sense.—*To pervert the right ways.*] Διαστρεφων τας οδυς ... τας ευθειας. Διαστρεφω. 10. xx. 30. Matt. xvii. 17. Luke ix. 41. xxiii. 2. Phil. ii. 15. To make crooked, what is straight.—Ευθεια. See on viii. 21.—*A mist.* (11) Αχλυς. Here only. *Caligo aeris. Nebula.*—*Some to lead him by the hand.*] Χειραγωγος. Here only. Χειραγωγεω See on ix. 8.

V. 13—15. It does not appear, whether Paul and Barnabas had or had not any opportunity of preaching the gospel at Perga, or in Pamphylia: but John Mark by this time grew weary of the fatigue and hardship of the journey; and, foreseeing that they should meet with many perils and persecutions in their future progress, he consulted too much his own ease and inclinations; and so leaving them he returned to Jerusalem. (*Marg. Ref. r, s.* —*Notes*, Matt. viii. 21, 22. Luke ix. 57—62. Phil. ii. 19— 23.) This indicated an inconstancy of mind, unbecoming one, who was engaged in so important a service; and the consequences resulting from this conduct are repeatedly mentioned, in the subsequent part of the sacred volume. (*Notes*, 4, 5. xv. 36—41. Col. iv. 9—14, v. 10. 2 Tim. iv. 9—13, v. 11.)—Paul and Barnabas, however, proceeded to Antioch in Pisidia, a province of Asia Minor, which was at a great distance from Antioch in Syria, whence they set out. There they went into the synagogue on the sabbath-day: and after the sections, from the law of Moses and from the writings of the prophets, had been read, the rulers of the synagogue invited them to speak to the congregation. (*Marg. Ref. z, a.*—*Note*, xv. 21. Luke iv. 16—19.) Either they had previously heard of them, or from them; or something in their conduct indicated their desire to be heard.—The apostles frequented the synagogues on the sabbath-days, in order to find an opportunity to preach: but the disciples in general observed the first day of the week, for their assembling together. (*Note*, xx. 7—12, v. 7.) Yet the Jewish converts seem also to have kept the sabbath for some time: and this change, as well as some others, appears to have been brought about gradually, to avoid giving needless offence to the Jews.—*If ye have any,* &c. (15) Literally, " If any word of exhortation be in " you." ' There is some emphasis in this Hebraism; by ' which it is understood, that whatever there is in us of ' divine grace, is derived to us from God, that we may ' carry it about as a treasure shut up in earthen vessels.' Beza. (*Notes*, 2 Cor. iv. 7. Eph. iii. 8.)

Paul and his company. (13) 'Οι περι τον Παυλον. See on John xi. 19.—*When (they) loosed.*] Αναχθεντες. xii. 4. xvi. 11. xxi. 1. xxvii. 12. Matt. iv. 1. Luke iv. 5.—*The rulers of the synagogue.* (15) 'Οι αρχισυναγωγοι. xviii. 8. 17. Mark v. 22. *Note*, Matt. ix. 18—26, v. 18.—*Of exhortation.*] Παρακλησεως. ix. 31. xv. 31. Rom. xii. 8. 1 Cor. xiv. 3. 2 Cor. vii. 7. viii. 4. 17. Phil. ii. 1. 1 Thes. ii. 3. 1 Tim. iv. 13. Heb. xii. 5. Παρακλητος See on John xiv. 16.

V. 16—19. The apostle perhaps observed, that some present were indisposed to attend on his discourse: he therefore beckoned with his hand, to intimate his desire of a candid hearing; (xii. 17;) and then introduced his

4 X

17 The 'God of this people of Israel chose our fathers, ' and exalted the people when they dwelt as strangers in the land of Egypt, ʰand with an high arm brought he them out of it.

18 And ' about the time of forty years ᵐ suffered he their manners in the wilderness.

19 And ᵏ when he had destroyed seven nations in the land of ' Chanaan, ᵐ he divided their land to them by lot.

20 And after that ⁿ he gave unto them judges, about the space of four

main subject by such a reference to the history of Israel, as was suited to conciliate their minds and to fix their attention. (*Marg. Ref.* b—d.—*Note*, vii. 1—8.)—Some explain the expression, " Ye that fear God," of the religious proselytes (43) : but it is plain, that there were Gentiles, as well as proselytes, in the synagogue (42) ; perhaps some place was allotted to them, in hopes that they would soon embrace the Jewish religion, as others already had done.—The apostle reminded them, that the God of Israel had of old chosen their fathers ; and likewise had formerly raised their nation from a state of deep depression in Egypt, to great honour and prosperity in Canaan. He had with mighty power delivered them from bondage, graciously borne with their provocations, for forty years in the wilderness, destroyed the Canaanites, and then divided the land by lot among them.—These events were both an accomplishment of the promises made to Abraham, Isaac, and Jacob, in whose " Seed all the nations of the earth would be blessed," and a type of a better and more spiritual redemption. (*Marg. Ref.* e—i.—*Notes*, *Deut.* vii. 6—8. *Neh.* ix. 7. *Is.* xli. 8, 9. li. 1—3. *Ex.* xvi. 6—8. xx. 5, 6. 1 *Pet.* ii. 9, 10.)

Suffered he their manners. (18) Ετροποφορησεν. Here only N. T. Ex τροπος, *mores*, *Heb.* xiii. 5, et φορεω, *fero*. See *Marg.*—The present reading contains an important meaning ; and it is not desirable *needlessly* to alter the text, though but in a single letter, without clear authority of ancient manuscripts, which is not in this case adduced.—*He divided ... by lot.* (19) Κ͞αθεκληροδοτησεν. Here only. N. T.—*Josh.* xix. 51. *Sept. Alex. Ed.* Ex κατα et κληροδοτεω, *sorte divido :* a κληρος, *sors*, et δοδις, *ille qui dat.*

V. 20. This verse has peculiar difficulties connected with it. The time, which elapsed from the departure of Israel out of Egypt, to the building of Solomon's temple, was no more than four hundred and eighty years. (*Note*, 1 *Kings* vi. 1.) But, on the lowest computation, fifty-seven years elapsed, from the passage of the Red Sea to the death of Joshua ; and eighty-four years, during the days of Samuel, Saul, and David, and till the fourth year of Solomon : and this leaves only three hundred and thirty-nine years, from the death of Joshua to the times of Samuel. So that, without adverting to the difficulties of computing the years during the judges ; (*Notes*, *Judg.* iii. 11. xi. 25, 26 ;) it is evident that this general calculation cannot possibly allow four hundred and fifty years for that part of the history, even continuing it to twenty years after the death of Eli. Some alteration, therefore, seems unavoidably needful either in this narrative, or in the general statement in Kings. On this ground some think that three hundred and fifty years, should be read, in this place, instead of four hundred and fifty : and it is evident, that the error might easily be made by a transcriber. This would

bring the computation within about ten or eleven years : and, as the historian says, " *about* the space, &c." it might be improper to expect greater accuracy. There is, however, no authority, which warrants such a change in the text.—' Josephus saith, that Solomon began to build ' the temple ... five hundred and ninety-two years after the ' children of Israel's departure out of Egypt. Now if you ' make the time of the Judges four hundred and fifty years, ' the computation is exactly five hundred and ninety-one ' years. He' (Paul) ' therefore here, ... accords with the ' computation of his nation, at that time, that so they ' might not except against his words. Wilderness 40, ' Joshua 17, Judges 450, Samuel and Saul 40, David 40, ' Solomon 4 :—591. ... St. Luke continually follows exactly ' the computation of the Septuagint and of the Jews, as ' we learn from his inserting Cainan ; (Luke iii. 36 ;) his ' making Saul to reign forty years (21) ; and from this ' verse, where he accords exactly with Josephus.' *Whitby.* —Perhaps this learned writer did not recollect, that this computation of Josephus alters the whole system of biblical chronology. For the chronology of the Hebrew scripture to the Exodus, and from the building of the temple till the coming of Christ, is founded on grounds sufficiently firm : but if one hundred and twelve years, more than the general computation, passed between the Exodus and the building of the temple ; then the birth of Christ took place, in the year of the world 4115, instead of 4004. It is well known, or at least generally acknowledged, that the chronology, both of the Septuagint and of Josephus, is erroneous and perplexed, in no ordinary degree : but how far the apostle, and Luke in recording his discourse, took these unimportant matters, as they found them, is another question : and if they did so, the circumstance of learned men in their studies having discovered that those generally admitted calculations were inaccurate, has, in my view, nothing to do with the divine inspiration, of either the preacher or the historian. For they were inspired, to deliver divine truth to mankind, unsophisticated and unmutilated : not to correct genealogies, or give ebronological calculations. Even, on the supposition, that the apostle was aware of the inaccuracy ; it would have obstructed his grand object, to advance any new opinion, or to go out of his way to correct the current one.— ' Grotius and Usher note here, that other copies read thus ; ' " He divided to them their land about four hundred and ' fifty years, and after that he gave them judges : " and ' they begin the time of this computation from the birth of ' Isaac, ... and to the end of seven years, (in Canaan,) when ' the land was divided to them, was about four hundred ' and fifty years.' *Whitby.* I agree with this writer, that this is not the natural or obvious construction of the

412

hundred and fifty years, [o]until Samuel
the prophet.
21 And afterward [p]they desired a
king: and God gave unto them [q]Saul
the son of [r]Cis, a man of the tribe of
Benjamin, by the space of forty years.
22 And [s]when he had removed him,
[t]he raised up unto them David to be
their king; [u]to whom also he gave testimony, and said, [x]I have found David
the *son* of Jesse, a man after mine own
heart, which shall fulfil all my will.
23 Of [y]this man's seed hath God,
according to *his* promise, [z]raised unto
Israel a Saviour, Jesus:
24 When [a]John had first preached
before his coming, the baptism of repentance to all the people of Israel.
25 And as John [b]fulfilled his course,
he said, [c]Whom think ye that I am? I
am not *he*. But, behold, there cometh
one after me, whose shoes of *his* feet I
am not worthy to loose.
26 Men *and* brethren, [d]children of
the stock of Abraham, [e]and whosoever
among you feareth God, [f]to you is the
word of this salvation sent.

o 1 Sam. iii. 20. p 1 Sam. viii. 5—22. xii. 12—19. q 1 Sam. x. 1. 21—26. xi. 15. xv. 1. r 1 Sam. ix. 1, 2. x. 21. *Kish*. s 1 Sam. xii. 25. xiii. 13, 14. xv. 11. 23. xvi. 1. xxviii. 16, 17. xxxi. 6. 2 Sam. vii. 15. 1 Chr. x. 13, 14. Hos. xiii. 10, 11. t 1 Sam. xvi. 1. 13. 2 Sam. ii. 4. v. 3—5. vii. 8. 1 Chr. xxviii. 4, 5. Ps. ii. 6. lxxviii. 70—72. lxxxix. 19, &c. Jer. xxxiii. 21. 26. Ez. xxxiv. 23. xxxvii. 24, 25. Hos. iii. 5. u xv. 8. Heb. xi. 4, 5. x vii. 46. 1 Sam. xiii. 14. 1 Kings xv. 3. 5. y ii. 30. 2 Sam. vii. 12, 13. Ps. lxxxix. 35—37. cxxxii. 11. Is. vii. 13, 14. xi. 1. 10. Jer. xxiii. 5, 6. xxxiii. 15—17. Am. ix. 11. Matt. i. 1. xxi. 9. xxii. 42. Luke i. 31—33. 69. John vii. 42. Rom. i. 3. Rev. xxii. 16. z ii. 32—36. iii. 26. iv. 12. v. 30, 31. Is. xliii. 11. xlv. 21. Zech. ix. 9. Matt. i. 21. Luke ii. 10, 11. John iv. 42. Rom. xi. 26. Tit. i. 4. ii. 10—14. iii. 3—6. 2 Pet. i. 1. 11. ii. 20. iii. 2. 18. 1 John iv. 14. Jude 25. a i. 22. x. 37. xix. 3, 4. Matt. iii. 1, &c. Mark i. 2—8. Luke i. 76. iii. 3, &c. John i. 6—8, 15, &c. iii. 25—36. v. 32—36. b 34. xx. 24. Mark vi. 16—28. John iv. 34. xix. 28—30. 2 Tim. iv. 7. Rev. xi. 7. c xix. 4. Matt. iii. 11. Mark i. 7. Luke iii. 15, 16. John i. 20—28. 26, 27. 29. 34. 36. iii. 27—29. vii. 18. 2 Cor. iv. 5. d 15. 17. 46. iii. 25. 2 Chr. xx. 7. Ps. cv. 6. cxlvii. 19, 20. Is. xli. 8. xlviii. 1. li. 1, 2. Matt. iii. 9. x. 6. Luke xxiv. 47. e 16. 43. x. 35. f xvi. 17. xxviii. 28. Is. xlvi. 13. Luke i. 69. 77. Rom. i. 16. 2 Cor. v. 19—21. Eph. i. 13. Col. i. 5.

27 For they that dwell at Jerusalem, and their rulers, [g]because they
knew him not, [h]nor yet the voices of
the prophets, [i]which are read every
sabbath-day, [k]they have fulfilled *them*
in condemning *him*.
28 And [l]though they found no cause
of death *in him*, yet desired they Pilate
that he should be slain.
29 And [m]when they had fulfilled all
that was written of him, [n]they took
him down from the tree, and laid *him*
in a sepulchre.
30 But [o]God raised him from the
dead:
31 And [p]he was seen many days of
them which came up with him from
Galilee to Jerusalem, [q]who are his
witnesses unto the people.
32 And [r]we declare unto you glad
tidings, [s]how that the promise which
was made unto the fathers,
33 God hath fulfilled the same unto
us their children, in that he hath raised
up Jesus again: as it is also written in
the second psalm, [t]Thou art my Son,
this day have I begotten thee.
34 And as concerning that he raised
him up from the dead, [u]*now* no more

g iii. 17. Luke xxiii. 34. John viii. 28. xv. 21. xvi. 3. Rom. xi. 8—10. 25. 1 Cor. ii. 8. 2 Cor. iii. 14. iv. 4. 1 Tim. i. 13. h Matt. xxii. 29. Luke xxiv. 25—27. 44, 45. i 14, 15. xv. 21. k xxvi. 27, 28. xxviii. 23. Gen. l. 20. Matt. xxvi. 54—56. Luke xxiv. 20. 44. John xix. 28—30. 36, 37. l iii. 13, 14. Matt. xxvii. 19. 22—25. Mark xv. 13—15. Luke xxiii. 4, 5. 14—16. 22—25. John xviii. 38. xix. 4. 12—16. m 27. ii. 23. iv. 28. Luke xviii. 31—33. xxiv. 44. John xix. 28. n Matt. xxvii. 57—60. Mark xv. 45, 46. Luke xxiii. 53. John xix. 38—42. 1 Cor. xv. 4. o ii. 24. 32. iii. 15. 26. iv. 10. v. 31. x. 40. xvii. 31. Matt. xxviii. 6. John ii. 19. x. 17. Heb. xiii. 20. p i. 3. x. 41. Matt. xxviii. 16, 17. Mark xvi. 12—14. Luke xxiv. 36—42. John xx. 19—29. xxi. 1, &c. 1 Cor. xv. 5—7. q i. 8. 22. ii. 32. iii. 15. v. 32. x. 39. Luke xxiv. 48. John xv. 27. Heb. ii. 3, 4. r 38. Is. xl. 9. xli. 27. lii. 7. lxi. 1. Luke i. 19. ii. 10. Rom. x. 15. s ii. 39. Gen. iii. 15. xii. 3. xxii. 18. xxvi. 4. xlix. 10. Deut. xviii. 15. Is. vii. 14. ix. 6, 7. xi. 1. Jer. xxiii. 5. Ez. xxxiv. 23. Dan. ix. 24—26. Mic. v. 2. Hag. ii. 7. Zech. vi. 12. ix. 9. xiii. 1. 7. Mal. iii. 1. iv. 2. Luke i. 54, 55. 68—73. Rom. iv. 13. Gal. iii. 16—18. t Ps. ii. 7. Heb. i. 5, 6. v. 5. u Rom. vi. 9.

passage: but could it stand without any alteration of the text, it might be admitted.—"And after these things *which* "took *up* about four hundred and fifty years, he gave them "judges, &c." This would require no change in the text: but I doubt whether it be not wholly inadmissible; and if so, we must recur to the solution above given.

V. 21. (*Marg.* and *Marg. Ref.*—*Notes*, 1 *Sam.* viii—xii.) 'David was but thirty years of age, when he began 'to reign over Judah, which was not till after Saul was 'slain: (2 *Sam.* v. 4:) and Samuel did not only anoint 'him, (at which time we cannot suppose David to have 'been less than fifteen years old,) but lived a consider-'able time after. ...The authority of Josephus is urged:... 'for he says,...that Saul reigned eighteen years during 'Samuel's life,...and twenty-two after his death:...but 'this is utterly incredible; for then David could not be 'eight years old when Samuel anointed him.' *Doddridge.* —Indeed, as many subsequent events, which must have occupied several years, took place, between the anointing of David and the death of Samuel; (*Notes*, 1 *Sam.* xvi—xxv. 1;) it is certain, according to the scriptural history, that Saul survived Samuel but a short time; and every circumstance combines to prove, that all the years during which Samuel judged Israel, and Saul reigned, are here intended 'I suppose, that the years of Samuel also are 'added to the reign of the king, by Paul:' *Sulpitius Severus:* 'as doubtless they were, they making together 'just forty years.' *Whitby*.

V. 22. *Marg. Ref.*—*Notes*, 1 *Sam.* xiii. 13—15. xv. 26—28. xvi. 1—3. 13. 1 *Kings* viii. 15—21. ix. 4—6. *Ps.* lxxviii. 70—72. lxxxix. 19—37.—*When he had removed.*] Μεταστησας. xix. 26. *Luke* xvi. 4. 1 *Cor.* xiii. 2. *Col.* i. 13. —*My will.*] Τα θεληματα. "The wills." Implying the several particulars, in which David, a prophet, a king, and a type of Christ, accomplished the commands and purposes of God.

V. 23. The mention of David gave the apostle an occasion of introducing his grand subject: for the Messiah was foretold, as "the son of David;" and Paul was prepared to prove, that Jesus was the Messiah, "the Son of "David." (*Marg. Ref.*—*Notes*, ii. 25—32. 2 *Sam.* vii. 12—17. *Ps.* cxxxii. 17. *Is.* vii. 13, 14. ix. 6, 7. *Jer.* xxiii. 5, 6. *Matt.* i. 20, 21. xxi. 8—11. xxii. 41—46. *Luke* i. 26—33. ii. 8—14.)

V. 24—37. 'He indicates that John was the herald of 'Christ, who did not foretel his coming as a distant event; 'but pointed him out as already come.' *Beza.* (*Note, Matt.* xi. 13—15.)—The Jews, who were present, had doubtless heard of John's ministry; and of his declaration that he was not the Messiah, but his fore-runner; and probably

to return to corruption, he said on this wise, *I will give you 'the sure mercies of David.

35 Wherefore he saith also 'in another *psalm*, Thou shalt not suffer thine holy One * to see corruption.

36 For David, after he had † served his own generation by the will of God,

‖ fell on sleep, *and was laid unto his fathers, *and saw corruption:

37 But *he whom God raised again saw no corruption.

38 Be 'it known unto you therefore, men *and* brethren, *that through this man is preached unto you the forgiveness of sins.

---

some report had reached them of his testimony to Jesus. (*Marg. Ref.* a—c.—*Notes, Matt.* iii. 1—12. *John* i. 6—9. 19—42. iii. 27—36.) The apostle therefore referred them to that testimony, while he pressed them all, both the descendants of Abraham, and all others who worshipped God, to believe and embrace "the word of salvation" which had been sent to them. He then obviated the prejudice, which would arise in their minds against his doctrine, from the conduct of the rulers at Jerusalem: observing, that the indeed had not known their Messiah, when he appeared in the midst of them : (*Marg. Ref.* f—k. —*Notes, John* xvi. 1—3. 1 *Cor.* i. 6—9 :) nor had they understood the scriptures, which were publickly and constantly read among them. (*Note,* 13—15.)—Thus they had ignorantly fulfilled them, by judging and condemning Jesus, and procuring his crucifixion from Pilate ; though they could allege no crime against him, except that he declared himself to be "the Son of God." And when they had, without designing it, fulfilled the various predictions of the prophets, concerning his sufferings and death ; they allowed him to be taken down from the cross and buried, and then guarded the sepulchre with all care to prevent any imposition. (*Marg. Ref.* l—n.—*Notes,* ii. 22—24. *Matt.* xxvii. 57—66.) But "God had raised him from "the dead;" which was testified by a great number of most unexceptionable witnesses. (*Marg. Ref.* o—q.— *Note, John* xx. 24—29.) Accordingly, they (even Paul and Barnabas) had travelled as far as Antioch to declare to their brethren "the glad tidings," that God had fulfilled in their days the promise made to Abraham, Isaac, Jacob, and David, in raising from the dead the Lord Jesus, and thus attesting him to be his only begotten Son, according to the prophecy of the Messiah contained in the second Psalm. (*Marg. Ref.* r—t.—*Note, Ps.* ii. 7—9.) The passage here quoted shews that the Messiah was "the "Son of God," in a peculiar sense ; and the decree there mentioned was *confirmed,* when he was "declared to be "the Son of God with power, by his resurrection from the dead." (*Note, Rom.* i. 1—4.)—In respect of that event, it might be inferred from the words of the Lord by his prophet, declaring that he would give to believers "the sure "mercies of David." (*Marg. Ref.* u, x.—*Notes,* 2 *Sam.* xxiii. 5. *Is.* lv. 1—3.) These "sure mercies" especially referred to the promised Messiah, and his kingdom and salvation : but the prophet predicted also the sufferings and death of the Messiah in the strongest terms ; (*Notes, Ps.* xxii. lxix. *Is.* liii. *Dan.* ix. 24—27. *Zech.* xiii. 7 ;) so that these "sure mercies" could not be conferred, but through his resurrection and exaltation. Accordingly David had prophesied in another Psalm, that "God would not

"suffer his holy One to see corruption." (*Notes,* ii. 25— 32. *Ps.* xvi. 8—11.) This could not be understood of David himself : for, having served the interests of Israel, during that generation in which he lived, "according to "the will of God, he fell on sleep;" and, being laid to his fathers, "he saw," or turned to, "corruption." But Jesus, his Descendant and Antitype, having arisen on the third day, "saw no corruption;" nor was he again to die and return to the grave, the scene of corruption ; but to live for ever in heavenly glory: and it does not appear, that any other person, since the world began, actually died, and yet did not eventually see corruption. Enoch and Elijah were "translated that they should not see "death." Those whom the prophets, and Jesus, and the apostles, raised, afterwards died and returned to dust ; and those who rose after Christ's resurrection, it is probable, had "seen corruption." Every part therefore of the doctrine accorded to the predictions of the prophets ; which concurred with the testimony of the apostles to the resurrection of Jesus, and with the miracles wrought by him and them, to demonstrate that he was the promised Messiah. The several quotations are nearly in the words of the Septuagint, which accord with the Hebrew.—*The second Psalm.* (33) The Psalms were arranged in the same order as they are at present.

Had first preached. (24) Προκηρυξαντος. See on iii. 20.— *His course.* (25) Τον δρομον. xx. 24. 2 *Tim.* iv. 7. Not elsewhere.—*Think ye.*] Ὑπονοειτε. xxv. 18. xxvii. 27. Ex νοω, et νοω, *cogito.*—*Of the stock.* (26) Γενος. iv. 36. vii. 13. 19, *et al.*—*The...mercies.* (34) Τα ὁσια. Marg. 35. ii. 27. 1 *Tim.* ii. 8. *Rev.* xv. 4.—*Is.* lv. 3. Sept.—*Having served.* (36) Ὑπηρετησας. xx. 34. xxiv. 23. Not elsewhere. Ὑπηρετης· See on 5.—*His own generation by the will of God.*] Ἰδια γενεα ...τῃ τοῦ Θεου βουλῃ. As there is no preposition to either clause, the words may be rendered "Having served," or "ministered unto the will," or counsel, "of God, in his "own generation, he fell asleep, &c" And this seems the more exact view of the subject. "The counsel of "God," to which David ministered, related to many generations: but he fulfilled his service during his life : whereas Christ fulfils a most important part of his office, subsequent to his death as risen and ascended and glorified.

V. 38—41. The apostle here applied the doctrine, which he had stated and proved. It was of the utmost importance to the people, to be assuredly convinced, that through this person, even Jesus the incarnate Son of God, forgiveness of sins was preached to them, by his atoning sacrifice, and as the gift of his mercy ; and that none could possibly obtain that benefit, save by faith in him.

39 And ᵇ by him all that believe are justified from all things, ᶠfrom which ye could not be justified by the law of Moses.

40 ᵏ Beware therefore lest that come upon you ˡ which is spoken of in the prophets;

41 Behold, ᵐ ye despisers, and wonder, and perish: ⁿfor I work a work in your days, a work which ye shall in no wise believe, though a man declare it unto you.

42 ¶ And when the Jews were gone out of the synagogue, ˣthe Gentiles besought that these words might be preached to them ° the next sabbath.

43 Now when the congregation was broken up, many of the Jews ᵖ and religious proselytes ᑫ followed Paul and Barnabas: who, speaking to them, ʳpersuaded them to continue in 'the grace of God.

44 And the next sabbath-day ᶠcame

almost the whole city together, to hear the word of God.

45 But when the Jews saw the multitudes, ˢthey were filled with envy, and ˣspake against those things which were spoken by Paul, contradicting and blaspheming.

46 Then Paul and Barnabas ʸwaxed bold, and said, ᶻIt was necessary that the word of God should first have been spoken to you; but ᵃseeing ye put it from you, and judge yourselves unworthy of everlasting life, lo, we ᵇ turn to the Gentiles:

47 For ᶜ so hath the Lord commanded us, saying, ᵈI have set thee to be a Light of the Gentiles, ᵉthat thou shouldest be for salvation unto the ends of the earth.

48 And when the Gentiles heard this, ᶠthey were glad, ᵍand glorified the word of the Lord: ʰ and as many as were ᶦordained to eternal life believed.

(Marg. Ref. f, g.—Notes, ii. 37—40. Luke xxiv. 44—49, rv. 46, 47.) But all that believed would be completely justified from every charge, brought against them on account of their sins; and in such a manner, as could not be done according to the Mosaick law. (Marg. Ref. h, i.) There were several crimes, for which no sacrifices were appointed, but to which the sentence of death was annexed, by that law: (Note, Ps. li. 16:) nor could the legal sacrifices take away guilt from the conscience; except as the penitent offender, through them, had a believing dependence on the promised Redeemer and his atoning sacrifice. (Notes, Heb. ix. 8—28. x. 1—18.) That whole dispensation also was now virtually abolished; having lost all its efficacy; and could not profit those who rejected the salvation of Jesus. (Note, Heb. x. 26, 27.)—It therefore behoved them to beware, lest the awful denunciations of the prophets, against the despisers of the mercy and justice of God, should come upon them.—"The work" here spoken of, may be that of redemption by the blood of Christ; or rather, that of approaching vengeance on the Jews for their contempt of him, and the admission of the Gentiles to their forfeited privileges. (Marg. Ref. k, l.— Notes, ii. 14—21. vi. 9—14.) All these were fully testified, authenticated, or predicted; but the scornful men of that age and nation would not believe them, and therefore they would be filled with astonishment, and so perish. (Notes, Is. xxviii. 12—22. Hab. i. 5.)—The prophecies referred to seem primarily to have related to the Babylonish captivity; but they were still more awfully accomplished in the destruction of Jerusalem, and the rejection of the

Jews, with tremendous judgments, for their opposition to the gospel. (Marg. Ref. m, n.)—This discourse, and the subsequent verses, are worthy of particular consideration; especially for the representation which it gives of the apostle's message; and as it enters so explicitly, in the way of the epistles, into the doctrine of justification by Christ. (Notes, Rom. iii. 19—26. iv. 1—8. v. 1, 2.)—The gospel which the apostle brought, was the fulfilment of the great promise made to the fathers. (23. 29. 32.) It was the word of God. (44. 46.) It related to a Saviour and salvation, "the word of this salvation." (23. 26. 47.) Repentance was the great preparation (24); the forgiveness of sins and full justification its primary blessings; (38, 39;) and its great scope, its ultimate blessing, "everlasting life;" (46. 48;) and these blessings were restricted to believers in Jesus, and extended to all of them without exception.—Behold, &c. (41) From the LXX, with some variation: but it varies more from the Hebrew. (Hab. i. 5.)

Is preached. (38) Καταγγελλεται. iv. 2. xvii. 23. xxvi. 23. Καταγγελευς, xvii. 18.—Be justified. (39) Δικαιωθηναι. Matt. xi. 19. xii. 37. Luke x. 29. Rom. ii. 13. iii. 4. 20. 22. 24. 28. 30, et al.—Ye despisers. (41) Οι καταφρονηται. Here only N. T. Hab. i. 5. Sept. Καταφρονευ. Matt. vi. 21. xviii. 10.—Perish.] Αφανισθητε. See on Matt. vi. 16. Αφανισμος, Heb. viii. 13.

V. 42—48. When the congregation were leaving the synagogue, the Jews in general did not express a desire of hearing the apostles any more; but the Gentiles intreated that these words might be spoken again to them the next

k vt. 7. ix 42.
xii. 24. xix. 10.
26. Phil. i. 13,
i 4.
i 45. vi. 12. xlv.
2. 19. xvii. 13.
xxi. 27. 1 Kings
xxi. 25.
m 45. ii. 5. Rom.
x. 2.
n 1 Cor. i. 26
—29. Jam. ii.
5, 6.   o viii. 1.   Matt. x. 23.   2 Tim. iii. 1.

49 And the word of the Lord [k] was published throughout all the region.

50 But [l] the Jews stirred up the [m] devout and [n] honourable women, and the chief men of the city, [o] and raised persecution against Paul and Barnabas,

p xvi. 37—39.
lxvi. 5. Am. 1ji.
12. Mark v. 17.
q xviii. 6. Matt.
x. 14. Mark vi.
11. Luke ix. 5.
r xiv. 1. 19. 21.
xvi. 2.
s ii. 46. v. 41.
Matt. v. 12.
Luke vi. 22, 23.
John xvi. 22.
t ii. 4. iv. 81. Gal. v. 22. Eph. v. 18.—50.

[p] and expelled them out of their coasts.

51 But [q] they shook off the dust of their feet against them, and came unto [r] Iconium.

52 And the disciples [s] were filled with joy, and [t] with the Holy Ghost.

39. Rom. v. 3. xiv. 17. xv. 13. 2 Cor. viii. 2. 1 Thes. i. 6. Jam. i. 2. 1 Pet. i. 6—8. iv. 13.

---

sabbath-day. Some render the words, " in the interven-" ing week;" (Marg.) but the concourse of people on the ensuing sabbath establishes the sense of our translation; though it is probable, that the private labours of Paul and Barnabas, during the week, concurred in bringing together so great a multitude on the next sabbath-day. Several Jews and religious proselytes, however, followed Paul and Barnabas, professing faith in Jesus; whom they exhorted and persuaded to continue in attendance on the gospel, and in dependence on the mercy and grace of God revealed in it; and not to suffer themselves to be discouraged or perverted by any of the reasonings, revilings, or persecutions, which were used to turn them aside from the truth. (Marg. Ref. r, s.—Notes, xi. 23, 24. xiv. 21—23.) On the ensuing sabbath, almost all the inhabitants of the city, idolaters as well as others, were drawn together, by various motives, to hear what the apostles had to communicate. This, instead of rejoicing the Jews, filled them with envy and indignation; because the blessings of the Messiah's kingdom, and the peculiar privileges belonging to the people of God, were thus set before the Gentiles, and enquired after by them: and their prejudices against the gospel being thus increased; they set themselves to contradict the testimony and doctrine of the apostles, reviling them as impostors; and, it is probable, blaspheming the Lord Jesus, and his miracles and authority. (Marg. Ref. t—x.) When therefore Paul and Barnabas saw the inveteracy of their malice, they took courage to testify against them; observing, that it was indeed necessary, according to the promises of the scripture, and the express command of Christ, that the gospel should first be proposed to them; (Note, Luke xxiv. 44—49, vv. 47, 48:) but since they decidedly rejected it, and were condemned out of their own mouths, as unworthy of eternal life, and improper persons to receive so infinitely valuable a gift; (Marg. Ref. y—a.—Notes, Prov. viii. 35, 36. Ez. xviii. 30—32, v. 32;) those who were sent to preach it would unreservedly make the same proposal to the Gentiles, and associate with them. For this, they had not only the command of the Lord Jesus, but the authority of their scriptures; which had declared that the Messiah was to be set for " the Light of the Gentiles, and " for salvation to the ends of the earth." (Marg. Ref. b —e.—Note, Is. xlix. 5, 6.)—This declaration rejoiced the Gentiles, who honoured and respected the word of God, while the Jews opposed and perverted it: and though it is not probable that all, who were thus affected at first, did at that time "believe unto salvation;" yet many did, even " as many as were ordained to eternal life." (Marg. Ref. f—h.)—Some interpret the word here used, of the internal disposition of the heart of the hearers: those who were in earnest to obtain eternal life at all adventures, believed the gospel. This indeed does not seem the meaning of the word; yet as such a disposition is the effect of pre-

venting grace, it still leads us back to that humiliating doctrine, which so much labour is employed in vain to obscure or exclude. (Notes, Phil. ii. 12, 13. Jam. i. 16 —18. See Art. x. of the Church of England.) ' O God, ' from whom all holy desires, all good counsels, and all ' just works do proceed, &c.' Col. ' The translators of ' the English Testament give many words a predestinarian ' sense, which there is no reason for.' Gilpin. The justice of this remark may fairly be disputed: but it shews at least, what even an opponent allows to have been the creed of the translators; for men do not generally, in translating or commenting, give words a meaning contrary to their own decided opinions, without very strong reasons for so doing.—It is indeed useless, and highly improper, and quite unnecessary, to rest the argument on a word, which may perhaps admit of some other meaning: but the laboured discussions of those, who are greatly afraid lest the doctrine of gratuitous personal election to eternal life should be collected from it, leave this impression on my mind, that these writers would themselves have carefully avoided a term, which needs so much guarding against misconstruction.—I have set, &c. (47) Nearly but not exactly from the LXX, who well translate the Hebrew. (Is. xlix. 5, 6.)

When the congregation was broken up. (43) Λυθεισης της συναγωγης. Here συναγωγη is used for the congregation, and not for the place of worship; which accords to the original use of it.—Λυθεισης. 25. ii. 24. Matt. v. 19. John ii. 19.—To continue.] Επιμενειν. x. 48. xii. 16. xv. 34. Col. i. 23, et al.—Προσμενειν. xi. 23.—Envy. (45) Ζηλου. See on v. 17. (Notes, Rom. x. 1—4, v. 2. Jam. iii. 13—16.)—Spake against.] Αντιλεγον αλλλεγοντες, contradicting. xxviii. 19. 22. See on Luke ii. 34.—Ye put it from you. (46) Απωθεισθε. See on vii. 39.—Were ordained. (48) Ησαν τεταγμενοι. Marg. Ref. i. Gr. Where all the places in which this verb occurs, are referred to.— Τασσω. ' Statuo.' ... certo ordine colloco ac dispono: et est ' vox e re militari ducta, ubi milites τεταγμενοι dicuntur, ' qui loco et ordine ducis jussu collocati et dispositi sunt.' Schleusner. Luke vii. 8. Rom. xiii. 1.—1 Sam. xxii. 7. 2 Sam. vii. 11. Sept. ' Οσοι ησαν τεταγμενοι εις ζων αιωνιαν. ' Quotquot destinati erant à Deo felicitati Christianorum ' æternæ.' Schleusner.

V. 49—52. The indefatigable and successful labours of the apostles, exasperated more and more the unbelieving Jews: and they, being themselves destitute of authority, excited some women of rank, who had embraced and were peculiarly zealous for the Jewish religion; and by their means the magistrates were stirred up against the apostles: so that an edict was obtained, banishing them from the city and its adjacent territory, as disturbers of the publick peace. They, therefore, having solemnly warned their persecutors, in the way which Jesus had commanded, that they were thus exposing themselves to the

CHAP. XIV.

Paul and Barnabas preach with success at Iconium; and, being driven thence by the Jews, they preach at Lystra, 1—7. They heal a man who had been a cripple from his birth, 8—10. The priests and people attempt to sacrifice to them as gods, and are hardly restrained by their most earnest expostulations, 9—18.

Paul is stoned, at the instigation of the Jews from Antioch and Iconium, and left for dead; but reviving, he goes with Barnabas to Derbe, 19, 20. They return to Lystra, Iconium, and Antioch, confirming the churches, and ordaining elders in each of them, 12 —23. Passing through Pisidia, Pamphylia, and Perga, they sail to Antioch in Syria, and rehearse to the church what things God had wrought by them, 24—28.

---

wrath of God, (*Marg. Ref.* m—p.—*Notes*, xviii. 1—6. *Matt.* x. 11—15,) went to Iconium, a city to the northeast of Antioch. But the new converts, whom they left behind, instead of being discouraged by this opposition, were filled with holy joy; having been made partakers of the extraordinary gifts, as well as the graces and consolations, of the Holy Spirit. (*Marg. Ref.* r—t.) This indicates a continuance at Antioch, and success in its vicinity, much greater than is generally noticed.

Stirred up. (50) Παρωτρυναν. Here only. Ex παρα, et θρυνω, *extimulo, instigo.*—*Devout.*] Σεβομενας. 43. xvi. 14. xvii. 4. 17. xviii. 7. 13. xix. 27. *Matt.* xv. 9.—*Honourable.*] Ευσχημονας. xvii. 12. See on *Mark* xv. 43.

PRACTICAL OBSERVATIONS.

V. 1—12.

The Lord raises up instruments for his work, and brings them forth from various places and situations in life: and that zeal for his glory, with which he inspires their hearts, induces them to renounce the most pleasing connexions, and flattering prospects, that they may be employed in promoting his cause.—Whatever means are used, or rules observed, for ordaining ministers; the Holy Spirit alone can fit them for their important work, and call them forth to it: but "fasting and prayer" are highly proper attendants on their separation to that sacred service.— Those who 'are moved by the Holy Ghost to take this 'office upon them,' and "are sent forth by him," will find opportunities of exercising their ministry. The ignorance, carelessness, and profligacy of numbers will indeed obstruct their usefulness: yet false teachers, and vain pretenders to religion, are the most pernicious opposers of the gospel: for they prejudice the minds of enquirers by their misconduct; or induce them, through misrepresentations and perversions, to embrace some vain delusion, instead of "the truth as it is in Jesus." "Prudent men," however, who know the value of their souls, and the importance of eternal things, will desire to hear the word of God, and to give it a fair and careful investigation, whatever be their rank in life.—It does not behove us, who have no miraculous powers, or infallible guidance of the Holy Spirit, to use such decided language, in reproving opposers and deceivers, as Paul did to "Elymas the sorcerer:" yet we may plainly expose the hypocrisy, disingenuity, malice, and enmity, of those children and servants of "the wicked one," who shew themselves to be "enemies to all righteousness," by deliberately "pervert-" "ing the right ways of the Lord," and the evident truths of the gospel, to promote their own credit and interest. Assuredly "their end will be according to their works:" their *wilful* blindness will expose them to *judicial* blindness, and this will terminate "in the blackness of dark-

"ness for ever;" unless they repent during the season of the Lord's long-suffering towards them: and the truth of God will be established and made successful, by the ruin and confusion of all its opposers.

V. 13—22.

Those "who put their hands to the plow, and look back, "are not fit for the kingdom of God." If we are not prepared to face opposition, and to endure hardship, we are not properly qualified for the work of the ministry. Yet some, who at first disappointed the expectation of senior ministers, have afterwards been recovered and made useful. —The reading of the scriptures, in the publick assemblies of God's people, is an ancient and excellent usage; and they, who are called to preach the gospel, will find a peculiar advantage, in laying their credentials and instructions in this manner before the people. Yet alas! many both read and hear the word of God, who do not understand or believe it; and the scriptures are, alas, very often so read in our churches, that it might be supposed, the readers did not desire to be heard and understood by the congregation!—The gospel should be "preached to every "creature:" yet with an especial address to those "who "fear God," and enquire after the way in which his favour may be obtained. On some occasions, it is adviseable to put the case most favourably, in respect of the dispositions and profession of our hearers; that we may thence take occasion to reason with them from their own principles, and to exhort them to behave consistently with their characters.—Every transient view of the dealings of God with his church reminds us of his mercy and long-suffering, and of man's ingratitude and perverseness: but when he grants our inordinate desires, we may expect a scourge instead of a comfort. He will however remove those who rebel against him; that he may raise up others in his church, who may act more "according to his own "heart, to fulfil all his will." May this be done, both in respect of rulers and ministers of religion, all over the earth, and that speedily. Amen.

V. 23—37.

The most honoured servants of God have discovered or been conscious of great imperfection; and have confessed themselves unworthy to perform the meanest service to the divine Saviour. They call men to repentance, and direct their attention to Jesus: yet they soon fulfil their course, and are gathered to their fathers; but "he ever liveth to "save to the uttermost all them, who come to God through "him." (*Note, Heb.* vii. 23—25.) Still this "word of "salvation is sent to us;" and every one who truly fears God will accept of it. But too many fulfil the scriptures, by opposing the truth, through ignorance and unbelief;

AND it came to pass [a] in Iconium, that they [b] went both together into the synagogue of the Jews, and so spake, [c] that a great multitude, both of the Jews, and also of the [d] Greeks, believed.

2 But [e] the unbelieving Jews stirred up the Gentiles, and made their minds evil affected against the brethren.

3 Long time [f] therefore abode they [g] speaking boldly in the Lord, [h] which gave testimony unto [i] the word of his

grace, [k] and granted signs and wonders to be done by their hands.

4 But [l] the multitude of the city was divided: and part held with the Jews, and part with the [m] apostles.

5 And [n] when there was an assault made, both of the Gentiles, and also of the Jews, with their rulers, to use them [o] despitefully, and to stone them,

6 They [p] were ware of *it*, [q] and fled unto [r] Lystra and Derbe, cities of [s] Lycaonia, and unto the region that lieth round about:

---

after the example of those who " crucified the Lord of " glory." May we then look to him, as " declared to be " the Son of God with power, by his resurrection from " the dead," " now no more to return to corruption," as testified to by prophets and apostles, and as the substance and repository of " the sure mercies of David;" that, by faith in him, we may walk with God, and " serve " our generation according to his will;" and when death comes, may fall asleep in him, with a joyful hope of a blessed resurrection.

V. 38—52.

Forgiveness of sins through Jesus Christ, and him alone, should be preached to all men; for this is the most needful blessing for every sinner, and an introduction to all others; " and by him all that believe are justified from all their " sins," be they ever so numerous and aggravated; a privilege which no law or institution besides could ever confer. (*Notes*, *Ps.* xxxii. 1, 2. *Rom.* iv. 6—8. *P. O.* 1—8. *Note*, v. 1—5.) But woe to those despisers, who will not believe the testimony of God, either concerning the redemption which he has wrought, or concerning the judgment which he has appointed; but treat the declaration of them with self-righteous, worldly, or infidel contempt, or with careless indifference! With what astonishment will they at length hear the despised Jesus denounce on them the sentence of everlasting condemnation! But, while immense numbers thus " judge themselves unworthy " of everlasting life;" others, and those often the most unlikely persons, desire to hear more of the glad tidings of salvation: thus the prodigal " comes to himself," returns home, and is welcomed and feasted; whilst the elder brother is filled with indignation and envy, and begins to oppose, contradict, and blaspheme. (*Notes, Matt.* xxi. 28—32. *Luke* xv. 20—32. *P. O.* 17—32.) We must not, however, be satisfied with hopeful appearances: but exhort such as are thus seriously impressed, to " con- " tinue in the grace of God," and instruct them in what manner to resist the temptations, to which they will be exposed. (*Notes, John* viii. 30—36. xv. 3—11.)—As many as are " ordained to eternal life" will believe: but we know not previously who these are: we should therefore declare, that " Jesus is placed for a Light of the " Gentiles, and for Salvation to the ends of the earth:" and we should publish his truth as extensively as we can; and bear our testimony against those who oppose and reject it, however honourable or devout they may appear.

Thus the word of God will be glorified in the midst of persecution: and Jesus will fill his disciples with grace, peace, and " joy in the Holy Ghost," to support them under tribulations, and to render them triumphant over all the power and subtlety of the enemy of their souls.

NOTES

CHAP. XIV. V. 1. *Marg. Ref.*—*Greeks.*] Ελληνων. *John* xii. 20. *Greeks*, or *Gentiles*. Some of these were perhaps before favourable to the religion of the Jews, and frequented the synagogue; (*Note*, xiii. 16—19;) but probably others were idolaters, who on that occasion had been induced to attend.

V. 2. *Marg. Ref.*—*Unbelieving.*] Απειδωντες. xvii. 5. xix. 9. *John* iii. 36. *Rom.* ii. 8. x. 21. xi. 30, 31. xv. 31. *Heb.* iii. 18. xi. 31. 1 *Pet.* ii. 7, 8. iii. 1. 20. iv. 17. It is often rendered *disobey.* Απειθης, xxvi. 19. Ab α, priv. et πειθω, suadeo.—*Stirred up.*] Επηγειραν. xiii. 50. Not elsewhere.—*Made ... evil affected.*] Εκακωσαν. vii. 6. 19. xii. 1. xviii. 10. 1 *Pet.* iii. 13.

V. 3, 4. The apostles judged it necessary to continue at Iconium for a considerable time, notwithstanding the persecution which was gathering against them; and boldly to fulfil their ministry in dependence on the Lord; in order to encourage and establish the new converts, that opposition and danger might not subvert them: and God was pleased at this time " to give testimony to the word of his " grace," to enable them to work many miracles, which perhaps they had not done at Antioch. (*Note*, iv. 29—31.) Thus a considerable part of the inhabitants either embraced the gospel, or favoured the cause: and these counteracting the machinations of their opponents, the apostles were for a time protected. (*Marg. Ref.*)—' Our con- ' stancy ought to equal the obstinate perverseness of the ' wicked. ... We should not give place, because of ' threatenings, no, nor even of open violence, except there ' be an evident necessity; and then, not for the sake of ' enjoying quiet, but that the gospel may be more exten- ' sively propagated.' *Beza.* (*Note*, viii. 1.)

Gave testimony, &c. (3) *Notes, Mark* xvi. 19, 20. *John* xv. 26, 27. *Heb.* ii. 1—4, v. 4.—*Was divided.* (4) Εσχισθη. See on *Matt.* xxvii. 51. Σχισμα· See on *Matt.* ix. 16.

V. 5—7. The rulers of the synagogue, and the principal persons among the Jews, seem to have gained over to their party the magistrates of the city, who were Gentiles. Thus a plan was formed, and an attempt made,

7 And 'there they preached the gospel.

8 ¶ And there sat a certain man at Lystra, "impotent in his feet, "being a cripple from his mother's womb, who never had walked:

9 The same heard Paul speak; 'who stedfastly beholding him, and perceiving that 'he had faith to be healed,

10 Said with a loud voice, "Stand upright on thy feet. And he leaped and walked.

11 And when the people saw what Paul had done, they lifted up their voices, saying in the speech of Lycaonia, 'The gods are come down to us in the likeness of men.

12 And they called Barnabas, 'Jupiter; and Paul, Mercurius, because he was the chief speaker.

13 Then the priest of Jupiter which was before their city, brought oxen and garlands unto the gates, 'and would have done sacrifice with the people:

14 Which when 'the apostles Barnabas and Paul heard of, 'they rent their clothes, and ran in among the people, crying out,

15 And saying, 'Sirs, "why do ye these things? 'we also are men 'of like passions with you, 'and preach unto you, that ye should turn "from these vanities unto 'the living God, 'which made heaven and earth, and the sea, and all things that are therein;

16 Who in times past 'suffered all nations to walk in their own ways.

17 Nevertheless, 'he left not himself without witness, 'in that he did good, 'and gave us rain from heaven, and fruitful seasons, filling our hearts with food and gladness.

18 And with these sayings 'scarce restrained they the people, that they had not done sacrifice unto them.

violently to apprehend Paul and Barnabas; and, having disgraced and insulted them, as disturbers of the city, to stone them as blasphemers. But this conspiracy was discovered by some at the very crisis of danger: and thus the apostles escaped, and went first to Lystra, and afterwards to Derbe (20), where, not at all discouraged by perils or ill usage, they boldly " preached the gospel." (*Marg. Ref.—Note,* 1 *Thes.* ii. 1—8.)—The situation of these cities may be far better understood by a good map, than by any description in words.

An assault. (5) Ὁρμη. *Jam.* iii. 4. Not elsewhere N. T. *Prov.* iii. 25. *Jer.* xlvii. 3. *Sept.* Ὁρμαω, vii. 57. *Matt.* viii. 32.—*They preached the gospel.* (7) Ησαν ευαγγελιζομενοι. " They were declaring glad tidings."

V. 8—10. The apostle perceived that the cripple " had " faith to be healed," or, " faith of being healed," or, " of being saved." (*Marg. Ref.* z.—*Notes, Matt.* ix. 18 —26, *v.* 22. 27—29.) It is probable, that by a divine suggestion St. Paul knew, that the man expected a cure from the power of the Lord Jesus, and that it was a proper occasion for him to perform a miracle. He therefore called to him with a loud voice, to stand upright on his feet; and be was enabled at once to use his limbs with an entire ease, agility, and vigour, as though he had never been lame. (*Marg. Ref.* a—*Note,* iii. 1—11.) In some manuscripts and ancient versions, it is added, after " a " loud voice," and before " Stand," " I say unto thee, in " the name of the Lord Jesus Christ."

Impotent. (8) Αδυνατος. *Matt.* xix. 26. *Rom.* viii. 3. xv. 1. *Heb.* vi. 4. 18. x. 4. xi. 6. Αδυνατεω, *Matt.* xvii. 20.—*Faith to be healed.* (9) Πιστιν τε σωθηναι.

V. 11—18. When the idolaters saw this astonishing v.

effect follow upon the speaking of a few words by Paul, they concluded, according to the fabulous traditions of their priests and poets, that two of their deities had become visible in human form. The age and gravity of Barnabas suggested to them the opinion, that he was Jupiter, their supreme deity; and Paul's promptitude in speaking, joined perhaps to his personal appearance, led them to suppose that he was Mercury, the patron of eloquence; and as they imagined the interpreter of the gods. And so firmly were they persuaded of these things, that the priest of Jupiter, of whom there was a temple, or statue, near the gates of the city, was induced to bring bulls and garlands, either to decorate the sacrifices, or the intended objects of their worship; and they were about immediately to seek the favour of the apostles, by divine honours and a propitiatory offering! But Paul and Barnabas discovering their intention, were more discomposed by it, than by all the persecution which they had experienced; and to express their detestation of their idolatry, and especially that themselves were become the objects of it, they rent their clothes, and ran in among the people, expostulating with them about their conduct, protesting against the sacrilegious honours intended them; declaring that they were mere men like themselves, liable to the same infirmities, sufferings, and death; and reminding them that they came to preach to them, that they should relinquish " these vanities" and delusions, and worship the great Creator of the universe. (*Marg. Ref.* f—o.) This was very bold and decided language to zealous idolaters, with their priests at the head of them, in such a critical juncture; and may be very properly contrasted with the temporizing conduct of heathen philosophers, who, being
4 Y

19 ¶ And *there came thither cer-tain Jews from Antioch and Iconium, who 'persuaded the people; and 'hav-ing stoned Paul, 'drew him out of the city, 'supposing he had been dead.

20 Howbeit 'as the disciples stood round about him, he rose up, and 'came into the city; and the next day he departed with Barnabas to 'Derbe.

21 And when they had preached the

---

convinced of the folly and falsehood of the vulgar super-stitions, not only conformed to them, but instructed their disciples to do the same, as a part of their duty to the re-public. Thus they made hypocrisy, and dissimulation in so important a matter, an essential part of their instruc-tions, confirmed it by their example, and perpetuated as much as they could, the most stupid idolatry, connected with the most abominable vices; from generation to gene-ration!—Let the intelligent reader compare this conduct and declaration of the apostles towards the worshippers of Jupiter, with some modern admired effusions of expanded candour, in which the worship of God, whether men call him JEHOVAH, Jove, Lord, or by any other name, is sup-posed to be equally acceptable to him. Is it then of no consequence whether JEHOVAH, or Jupiter, or Baal be God? Surely either the prophets and apostles were bigots, or these men have renounced Christianity. (Note, 1 Kings xviii. 21. P. O. 17—29.)—Paul and Barnabas further added, that God had, in his unsearchable wisdom, justice, and long-suffering, hitherto suffered all nations to walk in their own ways; and therefore idolatry had generally prevailed. (Marg. Ref. p.—Notes, xvii. 22—31. Rom. i. 18—27.) Yet the idolaters were without excuse, as God had " not " left himself without witness:" seeing he still had done them good in his providence; and afforded them many temporal benefits, which both satisfied their bodily neces-sities, and conduced to the joy and gladness of their hearts. (Marg. Ref. q—s.—Notes, Jer. xiv. 19—22. Matt. v. 43 —48.) By these discourses, they with difficulty restrained the people from proceeding with their sacrifice: yet it seems that they were by no means disposed to hear their doctrine at this time; but rather were displeased with their refusal of the honours intended them. (Notes, Matt. xxi. 8—11. xxvii. 19—23.)—' As a friend, in sending us fre-' quent presents, expresses his remembrance of us and ' affection to us, though he neither speaks nor writes, so ' all the gifts of the divine bounty, which are scattered ' abroad on every side, are so many witnesses sent to attest ' the divine care and goodness.' Doddridge.—' ' Here see,' saith Chrysostom, ' the devil's malice! He would have ' brought in ... divine worship of men, by those very per-' sons who were sent to convert men from it! persuading ' them again to esteem men as gods, as formerly they had ' done! And how fully he hath done this in the Roman ' church, where innumerable men are worshipped with in-' vocation, and even mental prayers, which suppose them ' to know the hearts of the supplicants, and so to have ' the property, ascribed to God alone in the scriptures, I ' have fully shewed.' ... Cicero ... proves, the gods must be ' of human shape, because they never appeared in any ' other!' Whitby.—Like passions. (15) ' The pagans ' never denied, that their gods were beings of like passions ' with themselves; but they attributed to them a total ex-' emption from mortality and disease. ... Indeed this was ' not only the principal, but, I may almost say, the sole

' distinction they made between gods and men. ... We ' are your fellow mortals, as liable as you to disease and ' death.' Campbell. This appears the direct import of the apostle's words; yet liability to other infirmities and pas-sions of human nature, needs not to be excluded: but certainly they pervert the expression, who explain it of the prevalence of sinful passions. (Note, Jam. v. 16—18.)

In the speech of Lycaonia. (11) Λυκαονιστι.—It is not agreed whether this was a dialect of the Greek, or of the Syriack.—Jupiter. (12) Δια. 13. Used accus. as from Ζευς. Ζευπατηρ, Jupiter, Jovis, corrupted from Jehovah. —Mercury.] Ἑρμης. ' Nuntius et legatus reliquorum ' deorum habebatur: απο τε ειρειν, dicere, nuntiare.' Schleus-ner.—The chief speaker.] Ὁ ἡγεμενος τε λογε. He who took the lead in discourse.—Ran in. (14) Εισπηδη-σαθ. xvi. 29. Not elsewhere.—Sirs. (15) Ανδρες.—Of like passions.] Ομοιοπαθης. Jam. v. 17. Not elsewhere. Ex ομοιος, similis, et παθος, affectus. A πασχω, patior.—Preach unto you.] Ευαγγελιζομενοι ὑμας.—In times past. (16) Εν ταις παρωχημεναις γενεαις. " In the past generations." Παροι-χομαι. Here only. Ex παρα, præter, et οιχομαι, eo, discedo. —All nations.] Παντα τα εθνη· all the nations, or Gentiles, as distinguished from Israel. (Note, Num. xxiii. 9.)—Without witness. (17) Αμαρτυρον. Here only. Ex α, priv. et μαρτυς, testis.—In that he did good.] Αγαθοποιων See on Luke vi. 9. 33.—Restrained. (18) Κατεπαυσαν Heb. iv. 4. 8. 10. Not elsewhere. Ex καθα, et παυω, ces-eare aliquem facio.

V. 19, 20. The apostles still continued at Lystra, in order to improve the advantage, which the miracle they had wrought seemed to produce them. But when the Jews of Antioch and Iconium heard of their success and repu-tation, they followed them to Lystra, and by their insinu-ations induced the people to treat them as impostors, and disturbers of the peace. Accordingly they first assaulted Paul, whose activity rendered him peculiarly obnoxious both to the Jews and the idolaters; and, stoning him till they supposed he had been dead, dragged him out of the city with the utmost indignity. Thus he who had con-curred, with full approbation in stoning Stephen, was re-minded of that great sin, by enduring the tortures of being stoned. But though he was bereft of sense and motion for a time, yet his life was in him: and whilst the disci-ples stood around him, probably intending to bury him, (Note, viii. 2,) it pleased God to restore him miraculously to his strength, and to heal his bruises; so that he was able to travel the next day with Barnabas to Derbe. It is indeed intimated, that he was not dead: yet without a miracle, he could not, after being stoned and left for dead, have been able to travel, probably on foot, the very next day. (Marg. Ref.—Notes, ix. 36—43. xx. 7—12. 2 Cor. xi. 24—27. 2 Tim. iii. 10—12.)

V. 21—23. After the apostles had published the glad tidings of salvation, and " made many disciples" in Derbe, they revisited the several cities, whence they had been

gospel to that city, and had taught many, they returned again to Lystra, and to Iconium, and Antioch,

22 Confirming the souls of the disciples, and exhorting them to continue in the faith, and that we must through much tribulation enter into the kingdom of God.

23 And when they had ordained them elders in every church, and had prayed with fasting, they commended them to the Lord, on whom they believed.

24 And after they had passed throughout Pisidia, they came to Pamphylia.

25 And when they had preached the word in Perga, they went down into Attalia;

26 And thence sailed to Antioch, from whence they had been recommended to the grace of God, for the work which they fulfilled.

27 And when they were come, and had gathered the church together, they rehearsed all that God had done with them, and how he had opened the door of faith unto the Gentiles.

28 And there they abode long time with the disciples.

driven by persecution; to instruct, encourage, and establish the new converts: "exhorting them to continue in "the faith;" and shewing them, that the kingdom of God and his heavenly felicity, must be entered, through many afflictions, trials, and persecutions. (Marg. Ref. f—k.—Notes, xi. 23, 24. xiii. 42—48. 1 Thes. iii. 1—5.) They also appointed elders over them in every church. These elders were their stated pastors, who presided in the worship of God, and preached his word to them. (Marg. Ref. l, m.) In respect of the manner in which these elders were selected, it cannot be supposed, that the apostles, in their present circumstances, would appoint any to the sacred ministry, who were not acceptable to the people; or that they would ordain any, without their own full satisfaction that they were proper persons, whatever the people might be inclined to. There seems to have been the most perfect harmony in the management of this important concern: yet it can scarcely be doubted, that both the apostles, and those to whom, in some sense, they afterwards delegated this part of their authority, interfered with their judgment and influence, in the nomination of proper persons to the ministerial office; as well as set them apart by imposition of hands and prayer. In all such questions, the middle, between the extreme points contended for by the zealots of opposite parties, seems to be the nearest to the true state of the case.—As the churches increased, deacons were doubtless chosen, under the superintendence of the elders: but it does not appear that the apostles appointed any at this time.—After this was settled, the apostles, by prayer and fasting, commended the new converts to the gracious keeping of the Lord Jesus, in whom they had believed. (Marg. Ref. n, o.) It is probable, that the apostles, and those employed by them, selected the presbyters, or pastors, from such as were more signally made partakers of miraculous gifts, by the Holy Spirit; yet, as these endowments might be possessed by those who had not true faith and grace; and, as eminent and intelligent believers do not seem always to have been endowed with them; it appears unscriptural to suppose that all such were appointed to the pastoral office, and none else.—No impartial person can (as it appears to me,) read this passage, without being convinced, that stated resident pastors of each church, and not preachers of the gospel at large, are here intended: but whether these stated resident pastors were, as some argue, "bishops," according to the modern acceptation of the word, is a subject which will hereafter come under our consideration. (Notes, xx. 17. Phil. i. 1. 1 Tim. iii. 1.)

Had taught. (21) "Made many disciples." Marg. Μαθητευσαντες. Matt. xxviii. 19. See on Matt. xxvii. 57.—Confirming. (22) Επιστηριζοντες. xv. 32. 41. xviii. 23. Not elsewhere N.T.—2 Sam. i. 6. Sept. Ex στι, et τηρικω, stabilio, Luke xvi. 26. xxii. 32. 1 Pet. v. 10.—To continue.] Εμμενειν. Gal. iii. 10. Heb. viii. 9. See on xiii. 43.—When they had ordained. (23) Χειροτονησαντες. 2 Cor. viii. 19. Not elsewhere. Ex χειρ, manus, et τεινω, extendo.—Προχειροτονεω. See on x. 41.—"They" (Paul and Barnabas) "ordained them" (the Christians) "elders, &c." —If an election by holding up hands be intended, Paul and Barnabas were the sole electors. It may then be fairly asked, whether this is the only scriptural authority, for the people choosing their own spiritual pastors? or whether any other can be adduced? If no other, then surely, whatever may be said on the ground of expediency, the divine authority of this method stands on a very slender foundation!—They commended them.] Παρεθεντο. xx. 32. Luke xxiii. 46. 1 Tim. i. 18. 1 Pet. iv. 19.

V. 24—28. After some other labours in the regions of Asia Minor, the apostles returned to Antioch in Syria; (Marg. Ref. p, q;) whence they had been recommended, by the prayers of their brethren, "to the grace of God" for the work, in which they had been so remarkably prospered. (Marg. Ref. r, s.—Notes, xiii. 1—5. xv. 36—41.) To them they related their success; and shewed how God had, by their ministry, "opened the door of faith," by which great numbers of the poor Gentiles had entered into the church: (Note, xi. 18:) and, finding much work at Antioch, they continued there a long time among the disciples. (Marg. Ref. t—y.)—The thirteenth and fourteenth chapters contain the first history of a mission among the Gentiles. The missionaries were prepared and selected by the Holy Spirit: they were "recommended to the "grace of God," and helped forward by their brethren; leaving country, friends, and comforts, to face dangers and endure hardships, from love to Christ, and to the souls of their unknown perishing fellow sinners: they

CHAP. XV.

Dissensions having been excited, in the church at Antioch, about circumcising the gentile converts; Paul and Barnabas are sent to Jerusalem, to consult the apostles and elders on the question, 1, 2. They arrive at Jerusalem, and the apostles and elders assemble, 3—5. Peter declares his opinion, 6—11. Paul and Barnabas report what God had done by them among the gentiles, 12. James decides against circumcising the gentile converts, but proposes some rules for their conduct, 13—21. Letters are sent by messengers, accompanying Paul and Barnabas, to the churches, with the determination of the council, and that of the Holy Spirit also; which are received with joy, 22—31. Judas and Silas, the messengers, abide at Antioch, and labour there, 32—35. Paul and Barnabas purpose to revisit the churches which they had planted; but are separated by a sharp contention about John Mark; and set out to preach the gospel in different directions, 36—41.

suffered much tribulation, but were supported, comforted, and preserved: and they prospered greatly in their "work " and labour of love;" and returning to gladden the hearts of their brethren, and to rejoice with them, they ascribed all the glory to God, who had granted the prayers offered in their behalf, and had wrought by them and with them.—*Had been recommended.* (26) Ησαν παραδεδομενοι. xv. 26. 40. *Rom.* vi. 17. 1 *Pet.* ii. 23. 2 *Pet.* ii. 21.

PRACTICAL OBSERVATIONS.

V. 1—10.

Perseverance in doing good, amidst dangers, hardships, ingratitude, and persecution, is a blessed evidence of grace, an expression of "the mind which was in Christ," and a distinguishing mark of his faithful ministers.—The Lord will enable his true and zealous followers "so to speak," and he will so bless their word, that some in every place, and of divers descriptions, will be brought by their labours to "the obedience of faith." But great success commonly causes vehement opposition: and envious and malicious unbelievers excite the minds of those who are more moderate, and render them "evil affected against the bre- "thren." This, however, should not discourage those who are prospered in their ministry: on the contrary, they should labour the more boldly and diligently, depending on the Lord to promote his own cause, and leaving it to him to "bear testimony to the word of his grace," in such ways as he sees good.—In all cities, towns, and villages, where the gospel is effectually preached, a division takes place among the people: some decidedly favouring, and others earnestly opposing the persons employed: and generally some unconverted persons, for a time, take part with the preachers and professors of the truth, by means of whom the Lord restrains the fury of his enemies, till his own purposes are effected.—Wherever his servants are driven, they should seek opportunities of making known his truth, without being intimidated by former perils or sufferings.—None should be considered as having derived benefit from the power and grace of Christ, by means of his ministers and ordinances, till they have "faith working " by love," and shew an unreserved obedience: but " all " things are possible to those that believe." When we receive this most precious gift of God, we shall be delivered from that impotency in which we were born, and from the dominion of those inveterate habits, which we have ever since been contracting; and be enabled to walk with cheerfulness and thankful constancy in the ways of the Lord.

V. 11—18.

The servants of God might often obtain undue honour to themselves, if they would connive at men's errors and vices; with far greater ease, than they can prevail with them to honour God, by renouncing their vanities, believing his truth, and worshipping his name. But they dread and detest all such sacrilegious homage, more than any reproaches or injuries whatever. They ought never to allow their hearers to think of them, in any other light, than " as men of like passions with themselves;" who, having been taught the knowledge of God and of his salvation, are sent to preach it to those who have hitherto been left to " walk in their own ways."—We should show the greatest affection to the persons of men, and bear with many of their mistakes and prejudices, in a candid spirit: but we must not spare decidedly to protest against their delusions and superstitions, which are as ruinous to the soul as the grossest immoralities.—The Lord saw good for a long time to " suffer all nations to walk in their own " ways;" and he still is pleased to leave innumerable multitudes to follow lying vanities: this should lead us to thankfulness for our peculiar advantages, and to adore the depth of his unsearchable wisdom and justice; but it should not induce us to palliate the idolatries or impieties of our apostate race; or to neglect doing all that we can to communicate " the Light of life" unto them. God never " left himself without witness," in any place or in any age: his long-suffering, and the exuberant bounty of his providence, towards enemies and rebels, are very wonderful; and they proclaim how worthy he is of universal love and adoration, and how inexcusable man is in his forgetfulness of him, and enmity against him.—The most cogent arguments, the most earnest and affectionate address, nay, the most stupendous miracles, are scarcely sufficient to restrain men from the greatest absurdities, or the vilest abominations: much less can they, without his special grace, convert the hearts of sinners to God and holiness.

V. 19—28.

They, who are not established by the grace of God in faith and holiness, are liable to be seduced by ill-designing men from one extreme to another: and to treat those as the worst of malefactors, whom just before they were ready to honour as more than men. This should warn us not to desire or value popularity, or human applause; but to " seek that honour alone, which cometh from " the unchangeable " God." Safety, life, breath, and comfort are entirely at his disposal: and if we have experienced his protection and consolation, in the midst of perils and afflictions; we shall be the better able to " confirm the " souls" of weak believers, to exhort them " to continue " in the faith," and to animate them to press forward in the way to heaven; though they must pass thither through much tribulation. (*Note, Rev.* vii. 13—17.)—

AND [a] certain men, [b] which came down from Judea, taught [b] the brethren, and said, [c] Except ye be circumcised [d] after the manner of Moses, [e] ye cannot be saved.

2 When therefore [f] Paul and Barnabas had no small dissension and disputation with them, [g] they determined that Paul and Barnabas, and [h] certain other of them, [i] should go up to Jerusalem unto [k] the apostles and elders about this question.

3 And, being [l] brought on their way by the church, they [m] passed through

Phenice and Samaria, [n] declaring the conversion of the Gentiles: [o] and they caused great joy unto all the brethren.

4 And when they were come to Jerusalem, they were [p] received of the church, and of the apostles and elders; and they declared [q] all things that God had done with them.

5 But there rose up certain of [r] the sect of the Pharisees which believed, saying, [s] That it was needful to circumcise them, and to command them to keep the law of Moses.

6 And [t] the apostles and elders came together for to consider this matter.

When proper means have been used, and regulations made, for the edification of new converts, and infant churches; we may confidently commend them, with fasting and prayer, to that faithful, gracious, and powerful Lord, " in " whom they have believed," in case we be compelled to leave them, either by removing to another situation, or by death.—If zealous ministers are made useful to souls, they think little of hardships and trials.—Those who have joined in prayer for a blessing on their labours, will be glad and thankful, to hear them rehearse all which God has done with them: and all, who love the Lord Jesus and their fellow-sinners, will rejoice to hear, that he has " opened the door of faith " to those, who before were strangers to him and his salvation.—But, if this meeting of the messengers of salvation with those by whom " they " had been recommended to the grace of God, for the " work which they fulfilled," was a season of lively joy and gratitude; what will be that meeting, when apostles, evangelists, missionaries, and all who concurred in sending them, or helped them forward, or prayed for them, with all those who eventually derived benefit from their labours, shall assemble before the throne, with unalloyed love, gratitude, and joy, to render praises to their gracious Lord, for all that he has done by them, for them, or in answer to their prayers.

NOTES.

Chap. XV. V. 1—6. It is probable, that the events recorded in this chapter took place about seventeen years after St. Paul's conversion; but some expositors date them three years earlier. (Note, Gal. ii. 1—5.)—The persons, who taught the Gentile converts at Antioch, that they " could not be saved," unless they were circumcised and observed the whole ceremonial law, came from Judea, and professed to speak the sentiments of the apostles and church at Jerusalem: but they were " false brethren, who " came in privily to spy out" and destroy Christian liberty. Their confident decision on the subject could not but prove a great discouragement and temptation to the Gentile converts, and an immense hindrance to the success of the gospel: at the same time, it tended to false sentiments concerning justification, and would eventually have been subversive of genuine Christianity. (Marg. Ref.

a—d.—Notes, Gal. i. 6—10. iii. 1—5. y. 1—6.) For these and similar reasons, Paul and Barnabas vigorously opposed them, and used all their authority, and every proper argument to satisfy the minds of the people, and to silence the false teachers: yet this did not suffice. It was therefore determined, that they should go up to Jerusalem, and refer the matter to the apostles and elders; that by their authority and influence, the controversy might be terminated, and the peace of the church preserved. (Marg. Ref. f—h.) The apostle informs us, that " he " went up, by revelation;" the Lord having made it known to him, or to some of the prophets residing there, that he would have him do so. (Notes, Ex. xviii. 17—26.) Accordingly, he and Barnabas set out on their journey, being attended part of the way by the pastors, or principal persons, of the church; who thus shewed their respect to them, and the pleasure which they took in their company, and who probably bore their expenses: and as they passed through Phœnicia and Samaria, they gave a particular account, to the Christians there, of the conversion of the Gentiles, both at Antioch and in the provinces of Asia, which greatly rejoiced them. (Marg. Ref. l—o.) In like manner when they came to Jerusalem, the church, with the apostles and elders, welcomed them; and there they declared, more fully than they had before heard, what " God had done" by their ministry. But though these glad tidings gave general satisfaction; yet some of the Pharisees, who had embraced the gospel, but who still retained an undue regard for the ceremonial law, contended that they ought to comply with its precepts. As therefore there was not an entire agreement upon the subject, it was judged expedient for the apostles, elders, and others of the church to meet together, and to give the important subject a full discussion, in order that it might be finally determined to the satisfaction of all concerned in it. (Marg. Ref. p—t.)—' I know not any reason to conclude, that their ' inspiration ' (that of the apostles,) ' was always so in- ' stantaneous and express, as to supersede any deliberation ' in their own minds, or any consultation with each other.' Doddridge.—This has commonly been called " The first " general council;" and it seems to have also been the last, where it could properly be said, " It seemed good to " the Holy Ghost, and to us, &c.". (28)

4 Y 5

7 And when there had been ª much disputing, Peter rose up, and said unto them, Men *and* brethren, ˣ ye know how that a good while ago ʸ God made choice among us, that the Gentiles ᶻby my mouth should hear the word of the gospel, and believe.

8 And God, ᵃ which knoweth the hearts, ᵇ bare them witness, ꜀ giving them the Holy Ghost, even as *he did* unto us;

9 And ᵈ put no difference between us and them, ᵉpurifying their hearts by faith.

10 Now therefore ᶠ why tempt ye God, to ᵍ put a yoke upon the neck of the disciples, ʰ which neither our fathers nor we were able to bear ?

11 But we believe, ⁱ that through the grace of the Lord Jesus Christ, we shall be saved even as they.

12 ¶ Then all the multitude kept silence, and gave audience to Barnabas and Paul, ᵏ declaring what miracles and wonders God had wrought among the Gentiles by them.

Dissension, (2) Στασεως, xix. 40, xxiii. 7. 10. xxiv, 5. See on *Mark* xv. 7.—*Disputation.*] Συζητησεως. 7. xxviii, 29. Συζητητης; 1 *Cor.* i, 20. Ex συν et ζητησις, xxv. 20.—*Question.*] Ζητηματος, xviii. 15, xxiii, 29. xxv. 19. xxvi. 3.—*Being brought on their way.* (3) Προπεμφθεντς. xx. 38. xxi, 5. *Rom.* xv. 24. 1 *Cor.* xvi, 6, 11. 2 *Cor.* i. 16. 19. *Tit.* iii. 13. 3 *John* 6.—*The conversion.*] Την επιστροφην. Here only. Ab επιστρεφω, xxvi. 18. *Jam.* v. 19.—See on iii. 19.—*The sect,* (5) Της αιρεσεως.

V.—7—11. It is probable, that several of the elders on both sides, spoke with great earnestness on the subject, before the apostles gave their sentiments, and brought the matter to a determination. Indeed, it is not certain that any of the apostles were present, except Peter, James, and John: perhaps the rest were employed in preaching the gospel at a distance. (*Note, Gal.* ii. 6—10, *v.* 9.) Those present, however, chose rather to hear the arguments of their brethren, and to shew the ground on which their own conclusions rested, than to decide the question merely by apostolical authority. But at length Peter arose, and reminded the assembly, that some years before, God had expressly chosen him, from among the whole company, and directed him to preach the gospel to Cornelius and his company, that they might be brought to believe in Christ: and the heart-searching God had borne witness to the truth and acceptableness of their faith, by the gift of the Holy Spirit; even as he had done to the believing Jews; putting no difference between them, " having purified " their hearts by faith." (*Marg. Ref.* u—d.—*Notes,* x, 3 —16. 44—48. xi. 1—18. 1 *Chr.* xxviii. 4—6. *Matt.* xvi. 19.)—" The heart" may here signify the soul, with all its faculties and powers; and the expression may refer, not only to the sanctification of the soul by the Holy Spirit, but also to the purifying of the conscience through the blood of Christ from the guilt of sin. (*Marg. Ref.* e. —*Note, Heb.* ix. 11—14. 1 *Pet.* i. 22.) Having received this internal purification, through faith in Christ, they did not want the legal purifications, which were types and shadows of these substantial blessings: and as God had, in this first extraordinary case, decided the question; why should his ministers again put it to the trial, as if they would tempt him, to impose so heavy a yoke on the Gentile converts? This did not relate merely to circumcision, but to the whole ceremonial law; which, though proper and useful for the time, required so many distinctions,

burdensome purifications, expensive sacrifices, long journeys, and other things of a similar nature; that it was a very uneasy yoke, in every age, even to the inhabitants of the promised land, and still more to those Jews who resided in other countries: and, while it served to prevent idolatry from being universal, it also tended exceedingly to prevent the general diffusion of true religion, (*Marg. Ref.* f—h.)—" Though these words are by most interpreters ' applied to the numerous ritual precepts, the costly sacri- ' fices, and the frequent tedious Journeys up to Jerusalem; ' required by the law, which made the observance of it ' difficult and irksome; I would rather refer them to that ' defect, that the apostle hath observed in it, that it could ' " not purge the conscience from the guilt of sin;" (*Heb.* ' ix. 9. x. 1;) that it " could not give life," (*Gal,* iii. 21;) ' that it was a killing letter, leaving them under condem- ' nation; (2 *Cor,* iii. 6—9;) and so making it necessary ' for them to believe in Christ, that they might be justi- ' fied, (*Gal.* iii. 16,) and redeemed from the curse of the ' law; (*Gal.* iii. 13;) according to those words of the ' apostle, xiii, 38, 39. ...For to this sense the following ' words incline; " we could not bear this yoke; for we ' " believe that by the grace of our Lord Jesus Christ we ' " shall be saved." ' *Whitby.—*There was, however, no occasion to impose this yoke upon the Gentiles, as even the Jewish converts did not expect to be saved, in any degree, by observing the Mosaick law, but merely by faith in Christ, exactly in the same manner with their Gentile brethren; though they deemed it a part of their present duty to observe it. (*Marg. Ref.* i.—*Note, Gal.* ii. 11—16.) Our believing fathers in old times were saved by faith in a Messiah that was to come, of which the ceremonies were types, sacramental signs, and means of grace : but Christ being come, we shall be saved by him, without those ceremonies.

A good while ago. (7) Αφ' ημερων αρχαιων. xv. 21. xxi. 16. 2 *Cor.* v. 17. 2 *Pet.* ii. 5. *Rev.* xii. 9.—*Ps.* lxxix. 8. lxxxix. 49. *Sept.* As a short time only had passed since the conversion of Cornelius; may not this remarkable language relate rather to the antecedent purpose of God, than to the fulfilment of it by Peter (18).—*Which knoweth the hearts.* (8) 'Ο καρδιογνωστης. See on i. 24. (*Notes, Jer.* xvii, 9, 10. *Heb.* iv. 12, 13. *Rev.* ii. 20—23, *v.* 23.)

V. 12. (4) It is expressly said, that " the apostles and " elders came together for to consider of this matter".

4 Y 6

13 And 'after they had held their peace, "James answered, saying, 'Men and brethren, hearken unto me.

14 'Simeon hath ' declared how God at the first did visit the Gentiles, 'to take out of them a people for his name.

15 And 'to this agree the words of the prophets; as it is written,

16 After 'this I will return, and will build again the tabernacle of David, which is fallen down; and I will build again the ruins thereof, and I will set it up;

17 That 'the residue of men might seek after the Lord, and all 'the Gentiles upon whom my name is called,

saith the Lord, 'who doeth all these things.

18 ' Known unto God are all his works from the beginning of the world.

19 Wherefore my sentence is, 'that we trouble not them, which from among the Gentiles are 'turned to God:

20 But that we write unto them, that they abstain 'from pollutions of idols, and *from* 'fornication, and *from* 'things strangled, and *from* blood.

21 For Moses of old time hath in every city them that preach him, 'being read in the synagogues every sabbath-day.

---

(6); and on another occasion the apostles and elders are distinguished from the company of believers. (Notes, xxi. 17—26.) "All the multitude," must therefore be here restricted to the whole of the assembly convened for this special purpose, (perhaps including select persons who were not elders,) the determination of which assembly was afterwards made known to the church at large, who concurred in it. (Note, 22—29.)—The miracles, which God wrought by the apostles, when they were preaching to the Gentiles, attested his approbation of their conduct, and proved that they did right, in not requiring the converts to be circumcised. (Marg. Ref.—Notes, xiv. 3, 4. 8 —10. Gal. iii. 1—5.)

All the multitude.] Παν το πληθος. 30. iv. 32. v. 14. 16. vi. 2. 5. xiv. 1. 4. xix. 9. xxi. 22.

V. 13—18. When Paul and Barnabas had concluded their narrative, the apostle James closed the conference. He first referred them to the account given by Simeon, (2 Pet. i. 1. Gr.) or Simon Peter, of the manner in which God first visited the Gentiles in mercy, to take from among them a people, to worship and glorify his name: and he shewed them, that, though this was contrary to the prejudices of many among them, yet it accorded with the predictions of the prophets, as, for instance, of a remarkable prophecy by Amos. (Marg. Ref. 1—r.—Note, Am. ix. 11, 12.) It was there foretold, that the tabernacle of David would fall and long lie in ruins: but afterwards God promised to raise it up, and build again those ruins. Then all the enemies of the church, represented by Edom, would be subjected; and a remnant of men, even of all the nations, would seek the Lord, and "his name would "be called upon them."—This the Lord had undertaken to perform: and as all his works were "known to him "from the beginning of the world;" he was now evidently accomplishing his plan, which he had before arranged, and of some parts of which he had given previous intimations. (Marg. Ref. s—z.—Notes, ii. 22—24. iv. 23 —28. xvii. 26—29.)—After this, &c. (16, 17) The quotation varies from the LXX, and still more from the Hebrew. The grand outline, however, of the prediction is in all the same. (See on Note, Am. ix. 11, 12.)

A people for his name. (14) Notes, Hos. i. 8—10. ii. 21—23. Rom. ix. 24—29. 1 Pet. ii. 9, 10.—*The ruins.* (16) Τα καθεσκαμμενα. Rom. xi. 3. Not elsewhere N. T. 1 Kings xix. 10. Am. ix. 11. Sept. Ex καθα et σκαπτω, Luke vi. 48.—*I will set it up.*] Ανθρθωσω. See on Luke xiii. 13.—*The residue.* (17) 'Οι καθαλοιποι. Here only N. T.—Am. ix. 12. Sept. Ex καθα et λοιπος, Luke xviii. 11.—*Upon whom my name is called.*] Εφ' ους επικεκληται το ονομα με επ' αυτως. Jam. ii. 7.—Is. xliii. 7. Am. ix. 12. Sept.—*From the beginning of the world.* (18) Απ' αιωνος. iii. 21. Luke i. 70. John ix. 32. Col. i. 26.

V. 19—21. On the ground before stated, James gave it as his decided opinion, that the Gentile converts ought not to be molested about circumcision, or the ritual law; but that it might be expedient and proper, to point out to them some particulars, which they would do well to observe. He then proposed to write to them, that they should abstain from meats, which had been offered to idols, and polluted in that worship, that they might decidedly shew their entire renunciation and abhorrence of idolatry; (Marg. Ref. a—c.—Notes, 1 Cor. viii. 7—13. x. 18—33;) and also to caution them against fornication. This was by no means held in such abhorrence among the Gentiles, as it ought to have been; nay, it was generally considered as a trivial matter: and as it was very closely connected with their idolatrous feasts, the new converts might be in peculiar danger of being seduced into it; to the dishonour of their profession, the injury of their own souls, and the great detriment of domestick comfort, and union in the worship of God. (Marg. Ref. d.) This was no doubt a moral injunction, independent of the ceremonial law. So was likewise the prohibition to eat of things sacrificed to idols as connected with its consequences; being in reality communion with idolaters in idolatry: and no doubt it is in force at this day, as a command of the moral law; and must be charged on the consciences of all such as live among idolaters.—The subsequent injunctions are of another nature, and enforced by other reasons. The law of Moses had long been published in the several cities, where the gospel was then planted, being "read in their "synagogues every sabbath;" the people therefore every

22 ¶ Then it pleased it the apostles and elders, with the whole church, to send chosen men of their own company to Antioch, with Paul and Barnabas; namely, Judas, surnamed Barsabas, and Silas, chief men among the brethren:

23 And they wrote letters by them after this manner; The apostles, and elders, and brethren, send greeting unto the brethren which are of the Gentiles in Antioch, and Syria, and Cilicia:

24 Forasmuch as we have heard, that certain which went out from us have troubled you with words, subverting your souls, saying, Ye must be circumcised, and keep the law: to whom we gave no such commandment:

25 It seemed good unto us, being assembled with one accord, to send chosen men unto you, with our beloved Barnabas and Paul;

26 Men that have hazarded their lives, for the name of our Lord Jesus Christ.

27 We have sent therefore Judas and Silas, who shall also tell you the same things by mouth.

28 For it seemed good to the Holy Ghost, and to us, to lay upon you no greater burden than these necessary things;

29 That ye abstain from meats offered to idols, and from blood, and from things strangled, and from fornication: from which, if ye keep yourselves, ye shall do well. Fare ye well.

---

where knew, that the eating of blood was prohibited very strictly. This prohibition was given from reverence to the blood of the sacrifices, which, being the life of the animal, was the essence of the atonement, as typical of that of Christ. It would then have needlessly grieved and stumbled the Jewish converts, and prevented their friendly intercourse with their brethren, and further prejudiced the unconverted Jews against the gospel; if the Gentile converts had shewn so open a disregard to the solemn sacrifices, which were still offered at the temple. This seems to have been the reason of this restriction. (Marg. Ref. e, f.) As long as the sacrifices continued to be offered, we may suppose it was observed: but " as " every creature of God is good, and nothing to be re- " fused;" as there is no intimation to this effect in the apostolical epistles; and as the reason of it, which is here annexed, has long since ceased; so we must conclude that we are left as free in this, as in other similar matters. (Note, 1 Tim. iv. 1—5.) The permission given to the Israelites to sell the bodies of animals which died of themselves, to their heathen neighbours; shews, that the restriction of eating blood was ceremonial, not moral. They would not have been allowed to tempt the Gentiles to immorality. (Notes, Lev. xvii. 10—16. Deut. xiv. 21.)—It has been observed by several persons, that if Peter, instead of James, had said, " My sentence is," it would have given a more plausible argument for Peter's supremacy, than any which the Papists can adduce.

My sentence is. (19) Εγω κρινω. " I judge," or " decide." —We trouble not.] Μη παρενοχλειν. Here only N. T.— Judg. xiv. 17. 1 Sam. xxviii. 15. Mic. vi. 3. Sept. Ex παρα et οχλος, turba. Ενοχλεω, Heb. xii. 15.—Pollutions. (20) Αλισγηματων. Here only. Αλισγεω, Dan. i. 8. Mal. i. 7. Sept.—Fornication.] Της πορνειας. 29. 1 Cor. vii. 2.—It seems used as a general word for all sins of that kind.—From things strangled.] Τε πνικτε. 29. xxi. 25. Α πνιγω, strangulo.—Of old time. (21) Εκ γενεων αρχαιων.—See on 7.

V. 22—29. In order to authenticate their decision more fully, the apostles, and elders, and brethren, thought good to select two eminent or leading persons among them, to go with Paul and Barnabas to Antioch. By them they wrote circular letters, not only in the name of the apostles and elders, but of the whole church, to whom the decision of the assembly was made known, and in which all concurred, to the Christians at Antioch, and Syria, and Cilicia; in which they doubtless meant to include all those churches, that were established in other cities. In these, they acknowledged the Gentile converts as " brethren;" and by this term saluted them; and they disowned those persons who had gone out from them, to trouble them with their doctrine, and to subvert the foundations of their faith and hope. (Marg. Ref. l—o.—Notes, 1—6. Gal. i. 6—10. ii. 1—5. v. 1—12. vi. 11—16.) They had therefore unanimously agreed, when met together, to send two other brethren, namely, Barsabas, and Silas, or Silvanus, leading men in the church, (Marg. Ref. i, k,) along with Paul and Barnabas, (whom they greatly loved and honoured, as men who had ventured their lives for the name of Christ,) to inform them of the same things by word of mouth, and to explain them more fully if requisite. For, being warranted to declare themselves directed by the immediate influence of the Holy Spirit; they were assured, that " it " seemed good to him," as well as to them, to impose on them no other burthen, than the things before-mentioned; which were indeed necessary, either on their own account, or in respect of present circumstances; and in attending to them they would do well and be accepted of God. (Marg. Ref. p—f.)—Many suppose, that the determination of God, in the case of Cornelius, was exclusively referred to: but it can hardly be supposed, that the apostles and council, were left without a satisfactory consciousness, in a matter of such peculiar importance, that they were guided in the decision, by the immediate inspiration of the Holy Spirit. We may suppose from the harmonious conclusion of the business, that those who at first were of another opinion were at length convinced; and made no

30 So when they were dismissed, they came to Antioch: and when they had gathered the multitude together, they delivered the epistle;

31 Which when they had read, they rejoiced for the consolation.

32 And Judas and Silas, being prophets also themselves, exhorted the brethren with many words, and confirmed them.

33 And after they had tarried there a space, they were let go in peace from the brethren unto the apostles.

34 Notwithstanding, it pleased Silas to abide there still.

35 Paul also and Barnabas continued in Antioch teaching and preaching the word of the Lord, with many others also.

36 ¶ And some days after, Paul said unto Barnabas, Let us go again and visit our brethren in every city where we have preached the word of the Lord, and see how they do.

37 And Barnabas determined to take with them John, whose surname was Mark.

38 But Paul thought not good to take him with them, who departed from them from Pamphylia, and went not with them to the work.

39 And the contention was so sharp between them, that they departed asunder one from the other: and so Barnabas took Mark, and sailed unto Cyprus;

40 And Paul chose Silas, and departed, being recommended by the brethren unto the grace of God.

41 And he went through Syria and Cilicia, confirming the churches.

---

further opposition to the general determination of this question. (*Note*, xvi. 4, 5.)

Chief. (22) Ἡγουμενος. See on xiv. 12. (*Note*, Heb. xiii. 17.)—*Have troubled*. (24) Εταραξαν. xvii. 8. See on Matt. xiv. 26.—*Subverting*.] Ανασκευαζοντες. Here only. (Ατοσκευασαμενοι. xxi. 15.)—Rendering their souls unfit for their work and warfare; as an army would be, if deprived of its baggage.—*Gave commandment*.] Διεστειλαμεθα. Matt. xvi. 20. Mark v. 43. vii. 36. viii. 15. ix. 9. Heb. xii. 20.—*That have hazarded*. (26) Παραδεδωκοσι.—"Who have given up," or devoted. See on xiv. 26.—*Meats offered to idols*. (29) Ειδωλοθυτων. xxi. 1 Cor. viii. 1. 4. 7. 10. x. 19. 28. Rev. ii. 14. 20. Ex ειδωλον, *idolum*, et θυω, *macto*. See on 20.—*Fare ye well*.] Ερρωσθε. xxiii. 30. " Be ye strong," or *in health*.

V. 30—35. This epistle, when read at Antioch, settled the dispute in that city, and rejoiced the hearts of the disciples: and the ministry of Judas and Silas, who were prophets, of considerable authority in the church, and of eminent gifts, and spake fully and freely on the subject, conduced greatly to establish them in the faith. (*Marg. Ref.* g—m.—*Notes*, i. 23—26, v. 23. xi. 27—30.) So that Silas, having formed an intimate friendship with Paul, and being delightfully employed, did not choose to return with Judas; having a prospect of greater usefulness at Antioch, and perhaps having an eye to that service, which be afterwards performed. (*Marg. Ref.* n, o.)—*Being prophets*, &c. (32) ' That is, saith Dr. Hammond, being ' two bishops of Judea: but if so, why " pleased it Silas ' " to abide there still;" " rather than go back to his ' " charge ? " Yea, why after so long a stay at Antioch, ' doth he go along with Paul in his travels, through Syria ' and Cilicia, " confirming the churches ?" (41) Why ' do we find him still with Paul; (xvi. xvii. xviii;) and ' preaching at Thessalonica, Corinth, and other places; ' but not at all returning to his see ?' *Whitby*.

The epistle. (30) Την επιστολην. ix. 2. xxii. 5. xxiii. 25.

33, *et al*. Ab επιστελλω. 20.—*The consolation*, (31) " Exhortation." Marg. Τη παρακλησει. See on xiii. 15.—*Confirmed*. (32) Επεστηριξαν. 41. See on xiv. 22.—*Preaching the word*. (35) Ευαγγελιζομενοι ... τον λογον. (*Marg. Ref.* q.)

V. 36—41. The primary view of Paul, in proposing to Barnabas another journey into those distant regions, was, to revisit the churches which they had planted, and see whether they went on prosperously, and to confirm and edify them: but doubtless he meant also to seek further opportunities of spreading the gospel. (*Marg. Ref.* r—t.)—Barnabas seems to have been too partial to his nephew; and perhaps Paul was too severe with him. (*Note*, xiii. 13—15.) Doubtless they were both betrayed into undue warmth and pertinacity; which shews the remains of human depravity in the hearts of the best of men: and the impartiality of the inspired historian, in recording it, is worthy of notice. (*Marg. Ref.* u—y.)—It has indeed been maintained, that, though both were angry, neither of them sinned: but if the one was angry without cause, or above cause, or expressed his anger unduly, he sinned; and if the other gave him just cause, he doubtless sinned. Certainly this never could have occurred, if both had been perfect.—Thus these two fellow-labourers parted, probably to meet no more on earth: neither of them, however, remitted any thing of his zeal and diligence, on account of this disagreement; or said any thing, that we know of, to disparage the other: so that two missions were sent forth instead of one, both of which it is probable were " recommended to God," by the prayers of the brethren; yet the language here used seems more directly applicable to Paul, whose conduct on this occasion was most approved. (*Marg. Ref.* b—d.) We read nothing further in the history concerning Barnabas; who went first to Cyprus, where he and Paul first preached, when they set out from Antioch. (*Notes*, xiii. 4—12. 1 Cor. ix. 6. Gal. ii. 6—10.) Doubtless he laboured and prospered to the end of his life; but

4 Z

CHAP. XVI.

Paul and Silas come to Derbe and Lystra, and Paul, having circumcised Timothy, takes him for an assistant, 1—3. They deliver the apostolick decree to the churches, which are established, and increased in numbers, 4, 5. Having gone through Phrygia and Galatia, the Spirit forbids them to preach in Asia and Bithynia, and they come to Troas, 6—8. A vision directs them to go into Macedonia, and they arrive at Philippi, 9—12. Lydia, being converted, entertains them, 13—15. Paul casts out a spirit of divination, 16—18; and, in consequence, he and Silas are seized, scourged, imprisoned, and put in the stocks, 19—24. They pray and sing praises; and an earthquake opens the doors of the prison, and looses their bonds, 25, 26. The jailor, prevented by Paul from killing himself, is converted, with his family, 27—34. Paul and Silas, being set at liberty, refuse to leave the prison, till requested by the magistrates, 35—39. They comfort the brethren and depart, 40.

the rest of this book relates primarily to the ministry and sufferings of St. Paul and his companions.—*And Cilicia.* (41) This and the twenty-third verse contain the only intimation of any church being found in Cilicia, the native country of St. Paul. (*Note,* xi. 25, 26.)

Determined. (37) Εζωλυσατο.—*To take with them.*] Συμπαραλαβειν. 38. xii. 25. *Gal.* ii. 1.—*The contention was so sharp.* (39) Εγινετο παροξυσμος. *Heb.* x. 24. Not elsewhere N. T.—*Deut.* xxix. 28. *Jer.* xxxii. 37. *Sept.* A παροξυνω, acuo, acutum reddo; ab οξυς, acutus. Hence *Paroxysm.*

PRACTICAL OBSERVATIONS.

V. 1—11.

The great enemy of God and man is continually devising measures for obstructing the success of the gospel. For this purpose, he endeavours to make divisions among those who preach and profess it; (*Notes and P. O.* vi. 1—7;) and to corrupt its purity, and obscure the glory of divine grace in it, by plausibly substituting another foundation; or by introducing such alterations or appendages, as are calculated to mislead or discourage unestablished enquirers. (*Notes,* 1 *Cor.* iii. 10—15. *Gal.* i. 6—10.) In these attempts he avails himself of the errors, bigotry, and prejudices of well-meaning persons, and of the ambition and selfishness of false brethren.—Wise and good men will avoid disputation as far as they can; yet they should not determine against all controversy, or condemn it indiscriminately: for when false teachers " come in unawares" to " subvert men's souls;" when the fundamental truths of the gospel are opposed or perverted, and the principles of men are poisoned by pernicious tenets; we ought to " contend earnestly " (though in meekness) " for the faith " once delivered to the saints:" and to decline controversy in these circumstances, argues luke-warmness and cowardice, rather than meekness and wisdom. (*Note, Jude* 3, 4.) —When fair argument and scriptural evidence fail to convince gainsayers; we must be careful, that we be not seduced to use improper means of conducting the disputation: and if any method of preserving peace and truth can be suggested, we should submit to very great personal inconvenience, or apparent degradation, to accomplish so desirable an end. Sometimes the *opinion* of those, " who " seem to be pillars," will go further than *arguments:* and we may fairly, in such circumstances, appeal to their judgment, in order to " stop the mouths" of those, who profess to speak *their* sentiments; and to satisfy such as have imbibed prejudices, which close their minds to the most conclusive reasoning. But we ought never to be so engaged about any single question, as to neglect opportunities of declaring what God has done for or by us, or of

being helpers to the joy of our brethren in every place.— It may be useful for the ministers and disciples of Christ, to meet together, to consider any controverted subject, in order that they may form the more accurate and decided judgment upon it: yet great humility, prudence, temper, candour, and integrity are requisite, to prevent such contentions from degenerating into party-cabals, or scenes of contention and confusion. This has brought ecclesiastical councils and synods into general disrepute: and indeed little good can be expected from them, when they are very numerous; or when they are so constituted, as to give an opening for political contests, or party interests. Yet, select companies meeting in the fear of God, and in the spirit of humble prayer for divine teaching, may help each other to investigate truth, and to decide difficult and important questions. We should, however, remember that the apostles themselves assigned the reasons of their determinations; and did not require the elders and churches to submit to their authority, without knowing the grounds on which they went: and in such discussions, we shall generally, if not always, find, that by examining the source of the subject in question, it will appear to have been already decided by the Lord himself; and that it would be " tempting " him to debate the matter any further.—We " sinners of the Gentiles" have great cause to bless God, that we have heard the gospel. May we have that faith, which the great Searcher of hearts approves, and attests by the seal of the Holy Spirit! Then our hearts and consciences will be purified from the pollution and guilt of sin; and we shall not want any of those burdensome superstitions, which many have attempted to impose " on the necks of " the disciples," instead of the abrogated ceremonial law. Those ordinances which God has appointed as means of grace to our souls, and of rendering him the worship due to his name, we shall delight in attending on: accounting his service perfect freedom, and the Redeemer's yoke easy and pleasant: and we shall adopt or reject merely circumstantial regulations, as they appear to promote edification, or the contrary. We shall however place no dependence on any of these things; believing that " we shall be " saved by the grace of the Lord Jesus," even as these primitive Christians were.

V. 12—31.

That is undoubtedly the way of eternal life, to which God of old affixed the seal of miracles, which he confirms to us by the testimony of prophets and apostles, and which he blesses for the conversion of sinners in every age and nation. Thus he at first " visited the Gentiles, to take a " people from among them" for the honour of " his

THEN came he [a] to Derbe and Lystra; and, behold, a certain disciple was there, [b] named Timotheus, the son of a certain woman, [c] which was a Jewess, and believed; [d] but his father was a Greek;

2 Which [e] was well reported of by the brethren that were at Lystra and [f] Iconium.

3 Him [g] would Paul have to go forth with him; [h] and took and circumcised him, because of the Jews which were in those quarters: for they knew all that his father was a Greek.

" name:" and thus is he building the tabernacle, and setting up the kingdom, of "the Son of David," in every part of the earth. He, " who doeth all these things," carries on his work according to " the counsel of his own will;" (Note, Eph. i. 9—12, v. 11;) for " known unto him are " all his works, from the beginning of the world:" his providential dispensations illustrate and fulfil his word; and it does not behove us to attempt to modify his operations, in conformity with our limited or prejudiced apprehensions. We should not therefore " trouble" those about forms or notions, who are evidently turned unto God; much less ought we to impose on them by authority, or as necessary to salvation, such things as never, at any time, could plead a divine sanction. It may, however, be proper to warn them to keep at a distance from all *occasions*, or *appearances*, of those evils, to which they were before most addicted, or to which they are now most likely to be tempted; and strenuously to caution them to use their Christian liberty, with such moderation and prudence, as the good of their brethren, their friendly intercourse with them, and the success of the gospel may render expedient. (Notes, Rom. xiv. 1—6. 13—23. xv. 1—3. Gal. v. 13—15. 1 Pet. ii. 13—17.)—Those who possess influence and authority should support their faithful brethren, whose usefulness may be hindered by the prejudices gone forth against them: they should embrace opportunities of decidedly speaking in commendation of upright characters; and against those, " who trouble" the church, and " subvert " men's souls:" and, if other things are equal, those persons, who have ventured and suffered the most for the name of the Lord Jesus, are entitled to the most respect and affection from their brethren.

V. 32—41.

Unanimity among ministers and Christians gives great weight to their determinations: what they do with one accord, may often be considered as the mind and work of the Holy Spirit; especially when their counsels and measures are evidently consonant to scripture, and conducive to the peace and purity of the church; and when the whole is managed in the spirit of unassuming love: but arbitrary injunctions, and vindictive anathemas, have long distinguished the proceedings of antichristian councils, from those of this Christian synod.—Instructions, arguments, and exhortations are the proper means of producing conviction and obedience, and of confirming men in the faith: and Christian liberty, soberly explained and used, is conducive to consolation and gratitude.—While we approve and imitate the zeal, love, and indefatigable diligence and courage of the apostles, in proposing to revisit the churches, where they had been so persecuted; we must also note the effects of human imperfection in the best of men; that we may watch and pray against all

occasions of contention, and all sharpness and pertinacity in contending with our brethren. Yet we should also admire the wisdom of God, in disappointing the devices of the enemy, and over-ruling even the infirmity of apostles, to promote the cause of the gospel: and we should copy their example, in not allowing any personal differences, to take us off from the work, to which the Lord has severally called us; to render us negligent or unfaithful in it; or induce us to say or do any thing, to lessen the character, or obstruct the usefulness, of those faithful, and zealous labourers who, in some things, differ from us.

NOTES.

CHAP. XVI. V. 1—3. Barnabas having sailed to the island Cyprus, Paul and Silas journeyed by land, through Syria, into Asia Minor; exercising their ministry as they passed along, both in Syria and Cilicia. (Notes, xv. 36—41.) At length they arrived at Derbe, and Lystra, where they found Timothy, who was already a disciple. He had been piously educated, and made acquainted with the scriptures from his youth; (Notes, 2 Tim. i. 3—5. iii. 14 —17;) and he had been brought to believe in Christ, when Paul and Barnabas were before at Lystra. (Marg. Ref. a, b.—Notes, xiv. 19, 20. 1 Tim. i. 1, 2.)—" Being " well reported of" by his Christian brethren, and endowed with very promising abilities, Paul purposed that he should accompany him in his travels and labours: but, as his father was an uncircumcised Gentile, it was known, that he had not been circumcised in his infancy; and he therefore judged it expedient for him to receive circumcision, previous to his entrance on his publick ministry. (Marg. Ref. d—h.) Not that this was at all needful for him as a Gentile convert; or that the apostle thought the Jewish believers were bound to observe the ceremonial law: but lest the knowledge of his father, as a Gentile, should prejudice the Jews in the adjacent cities against Paul and his ministry; if they had supposed that he had taken an uncircumcised person, to be his intimate companion and assistant: and it would likewise exclude Timothy from preaching in the synagogues, for which he seems to have been peculiarly qualified. He therefore thus far condescended to the prejudices of the Jews: though some time before at Jerusalem, he would not agree to the circumcision of Titus, when it was considered as requisite for salvation. (Notes, Gal. ii. 1—5.)—' After this, Paul laid ' his hands upon him, and set him apart for the ministerial ' office, conferring on him extraordinary gifts, (2 Tim. i. ' 6,) which were attended with prophecies of his future use- ' fulness. (1 Tim. i. 18. iv. 14.) ...He' (the apostle) ' al- ' ways openly avowed, that the gentiles were free from the ' yoke of the Mosaick ceremonies, and that the Jews were ' not to expect salvation by them; and he also taught that

4 2 3

4 And as they went through the cities, ' they delivered them the decrees for to keep, that were ordained of the apostles and elders which were at Jerusalem.

5 And ᵏ so were the churches established in the faith, ' and increased in number daily.

6 Now when they had gone through-out ᵐ Phrygia, and ⁿ the region of Galatia, and were ° forbidden of the Holy Ghost to preach the word in ᵖ Asia,

7 After they were come to Mysia, they assayed to go into ⁴ Bithynia: but the Spirit suffered them not.

8 And they, passing by Mysia, came down to ' Troas.

9 And ˢ a vision appeared to Paul in the night: There stood a man of ᵗ Macedonia, and prayed him, saying, ᵘ Come over into Macedonia, and help us.

10 And after he had seen the vision, ˣ immediately we endeavoured to go into Macedonia, assuredly gathering that the Lord had called us for to preach the gospel unto them.

11 Therefore loosing from Troas, we came with a straight course to Samothracia, and the next *day* to Neapolis;

12 And from thence to ʸ Philippi, which is ˢ the chief city of that part of Macedonia, *and* ᵃ a colony: and we were in that city abiding certain days.

' they were not in conscience bound to observe them at ' all, except in cases where the omission of them would ' give offence.' *Doddridge.*—Grotius observes, that this was probably the beginning of Luke's acquaintance with Timothy, ' though Paul knew him long before.'—The apostle's manner, in speaking of the persecutions which he endured " at Antioch, Iconium, and Lystra, &c.;" though, before he wrote it, he had gone through very many others; implies that Timothy had witnessed his sufferings in that neighbourhood, and would be peculiarly affected by recollecting them. (*Note*, 2 *Tim.* iii. 10—12.)

Came he. (1) Κατηντησε. xviii. 19. 24. xx. 15. xxi. 7. xxv. 13. *Phil.* iii. 11, *et al.*—Ex κατα et ανταω, *obviam eo.* —*Was well reported of.* (2) Εμαρτυρειτο. See on vi. 3.

V. 4, 5. (*Note*, xv. 22—29.) ' As they passed through ' the several cities of those regions, that peace might be ' secured among the brethren, and no unnecessary burden ' laid upon the gentile converts, they delivered to their ' custody an exact and attested copy of the decrees, which ' were determined as a rule for their direction by the apos-' tles and elders, that were assembled lately in full council ' at Jerusalem. The several churches therefore, where ' they came, being watered by such faithful labourers, and ' encouraged with so favourable a decision of the grand ' point in question, were much confirmed in their adher-' ence to the Christian faith, and increased more and more ' in numbers daily.' *Doddridge.* (*Marg. Ref.*—*Notes*, vi. 7. ix. 31.)

The decrees. (4) Τα δογματα. xvii. 7. See on *Luke* ii. 1. —*Were ordained.*] Κεκριμενα. See on xv. 19. " The apos-" tles and elders " alone are mentioned, as ordaining the decree. *Notes*, xv. 12. 22—29.—*Were established.* (5) Εστηριωντο. iii. 16. Στερεωμα, *Col.* ii. 5.—*Increased.*] Επερισσευον. *Matt.* v. 20. xiii. 12. xv. 37. See on *Mark* xii. 44.

V. 6—12. It seems to have been at this time, that Paul preached so successfully at Galatia, as to found those flourishing churches, to which he afterwards wrote his epistle. (*Marg. Ref.* n.—*Notes*, xviii. 18—23. *Preface* to *Galatians.*) He probably intended to go regularly from place to place in that neighbourhood, planting the gospel as he proceeded; but, by an immediate revelation, the Holy

Spirit forbad him to preach in the province of Asia, or in Bithynia; these were distinct parts of Asia Minor, in which the several cities and regions, mentioned in the preceding chapters, were situated. (*Marg. Ref.* o—q.—*Notes*, xix. 8—12, *v.* 10. 1 *Pet.* i. 1, 2.)—It was the will of God, that the apostle and his companions should proceed to a still greater distance from Judea: in the mean time the gospel would be gradually diffusing its influence in those parts, by other means; and we find, that soon after, flourishing churches were established in those very places, where the apostle and his fellow-labourers were at that time forbidden to preach. They therefore went on to Troas, on the coast of the Egean Sea: and, while they were waiting at that city, to know the will of God concerning them; Paul had a vision, of a Macedonian who, as a humble suppliant, said, " Passing over into Macedonia, assist us;" from which it was assuredly concluded, that they were commanded to cross the sea into Europe, in order that they might preach the gospel to the inhabitants of Macedonia. Accordingly, they took ship, and passed by the usual course to Philippi, which was a principal city, if not the *chief* city, in that division of Macedonia; and a Roman colony, being chiefly inhabited by Roman citizens, who had various privileges, and were governed by their own laws. (*Marg.* and *Marg. Ref.* r—y.)—The historian on this occasion begins to speak in the first person plural, saying, " *We* endeavoured, &c. " (10): hence we learn that he attended Paul in this voyage, and probably in most of his subsequent labours; though he modestly avoided mentioning any thing particular concerning himself.—*The Spirit*, &c. (7) Some manuscripts, and many ancient versions and citations read, " the Spirit of Jesus." The language used, in speaking of the Spirit, is personal and authoritative.—*A man*, &c. (9) Some think that the apostle knew the person, who appeared to him in vision, to be a Macedonian, by his dress or language; and others suppose, that he resembled some one with whom Paul was acquainted.—It does not appear from the history, that any of the Macedonians were previously enquiring after salvation, (as Cornelius had been,) or disposed to seek direction and help. But the Lord purposed to call many of them by his

13 ¶ And * on the * sabbath we went out of the city by a river side, [b] where prayer was wont to be made, [c] and we sat down, and [d] spake unto the women which resorted *thither.*

14 And a certain woman named [e] Lydia, a seller of purple, of the city of [f] Thyatira, which [g] worshipped God, heard *us :* [h] whose heart the Lord opened, that she attended unto the things which were spoken of Paul.

15 And [i] when she was baptized, and her household, she besought *us,* saying, [k] If ye have judged me to be faithful to the Lord, [l] come into my house, and abide *there.* [m] And she constrained us.

16 And it came to pass, [n] as we went to prayer, a certain damsel, [o] possessed with a spirit of [r] divination, met us, [r] which brought her masters much gain by soothsaying:

17 The same followed Paul and us, and cried, saying, [q] These men are [r] the servants of [s] the most high God, which shew unto us [t] the way of salvation.

18 And this did she many days. But Paul, [u] being grieved, turned and said to the spirit, [x] I command thee in the

grace, and directed his servants, by this vision, to the proper means of accomplishing his gracious designs. (*Note,* xviii. 9—11.)—*Colony.* (12) ' The criticks were long puzzled to find any mention of Philippi, as a Roman colony: ' but some coins (dug up, I think, within the last century,) ' shew, that a colony was planted there by Julius Cæsar, ' and afterwards much augmented by Augustus.' *Doddridge.*

Help. (9) Βοηθησον. xxi. 28. *Matt.* xv. 25. *Mark* ix. 22. 24.—*Assuredly gathering.* (10) Συμβιβαζοντες. See on ix. 22.—*Loosing.* (11) Αναχθεντες. See on xiii. 13.—*We came with a straight course.*] Ευθυδρομησαμεν. xxi. 1. Not elsewhere.—*A colony.* (12) Κολωνια. *Colonia.* A Latin word.

V. 13—15. This is the first account, transmitted to us, of the gospel being preached in Europe : though the church at Rome, it is probable, was planted considerably before this time. (*Preface to Romans.*)—There were Jews residing in most if not all of the cities, which the apostles and evangelists visited ; though they appear to have been only a few at Philippi. It seems they had not a *synagogue,* with rulers : but there was a small oratory without the city, by the river-side, where a few people were accustomed to assemble, for the worship of God, on the sabbath-days. (*Note, Luke* vi. 12.) Thither the apostle and his friends went, and took the opportunity of discoursing to " the " *women* who resorted thither," concerning the gospel of Christ : for, it does not appear, that there were any other *men* in the assembly. (*Marg. Ref.* a—d.)—Among the rest, there was a native of Thyatira, a city of Asia, who at this time resided at Philippi, to traffick in purple cloths, which were then in great estimation. She seems to have been of Gentile extraction, but proselyted to the Jewish religion : and the Lord was pleased to " open her heart " to attend unto the things which were spoken of Paul, and to believe his doctrine. This implies, that pride, prejudice, the love of sin, and the love of the world, close the heart against the truths of God ; till his grace makes way for admission of them into the understanding and affections. (*Marg. Ref.* e—h.—*Notes, Ps.* cxix. 18. *Luke* xxiv. 44—49, *v.* 44.) Thus she was led to embrace the gospel, and was baptized, with her household ; the adult part of which no doubt were instructed in Christianity, along with her. There is no proof that there were any children in her family, though

it is probable there were : the Syriack version indeed renders it, " the children of her house ; " but this only shews the sentiments of those, who made that early translation : and the language here used seems not capable of being consistently used in the narratives of those, who reject infant baptism. (*Note,* 29—34.)—After this Lydia besought the apostle and his company, if they really considered her to be a true believer, to lodge in her house ; for, probably, they had before been very poorly accommodated : and by her urgent invitations she overcame their reluctance, to put her to so much trouble and expense. By this it appears that she was a person rather in affluent circumstances. —Many others seem, about this time, or soon after wards, to have been converted. (*Preface to Philippians.*)— *Opened.* (14) ' By the grace of God she received the faith. *Hammond.*—' To open the ear, or the heart, is a phrase ' used to signify the rendering any person willing or in- ' clined to do any thing. *Ps.* xl. 7.' *Whitby.* (*Note, Phil.* ii. 12, 13.)

Prayer was wont to be made. (13) Ενομιζετο προσευχη ειναι. 27. vii. 25. viii. 20. xiv. 19. See on *Luke* iii. 23.—*A seller of purple.* (14) Πορφυροπωλις. Here only.—*She constrained.* (15) Παρεβιασατο. See on *Luke* xxiv. 29. *Marg. Ref.* m.

V. 16—18. As the apostle and his friends went from the house of Lydia, to the oratory above mentioned ; (*Note,* 13—15 ;) they were met by a female slave, who was instigated and enabled by an evil spirit to utter ambiguous predictions, or divinations, after the manner of the priestesses of the Pythian Apollo. Thus she had acquired great reputation, as a kind of oracle, or fortune-teller, for making wonderful discoveries ; which were probably accompanied by various agitations and distortions of body, and a peculiar kind of voice and articulation : for these were common on such occasions. By this practice she brought her masters a considerable gain, and became very valuable to them. (*Marg. Ref.* n—p.) But being excited by the evil spirit, who desired to discredit, and bring into suspicion, the ministry and miracles of the apostle and his coadjutors, she cried aloud, " These are the servants of the most High " God, who shew to us the way of salvation." For some days Paul waited, perhaps to see in what manner the Lord would silence so disgraceful a testimony to his truth : at length, being grieved by the damsel's perseverance, he cast

name of Jesus Christ to come out of her. And he came out the same hour.

19 And when her masters saw that ʸ the hope of their gains was gone, ᶻ they caught Paul and Silas, and drew them into the ᵃ market-place unto the rulers.

20 And brought them to the magistrates, saying, These men, ᵃbeing Jews, ᵇ do exceedingly trouble our city,

21 And teach ᶜ customs, which are not lawful for us to receive, neither to observe, being Romans.

22 And ᵈ the multitude rose up together against them; ᵉand the magistrates rent off their clothes, and commanded to beat them.

23 And when they had laid many stripes upon them, ᶠ they cast them into prison, charging the jailor ᵍ to keep them safely;

24 Who having received such a charge, thrust them into ʰ the inner prison, ⁱ and made their feet fast in the stocks.

Marginal references (left): y ver. 25, 26. 1 Tim. vi. 10. z ix. 16. xiv. 5. 15. xv. 26. xviii. 12, 13. xxi. 30. Matt. x. 16. 17. xxiv. 9. Mark xiii. 9. *Or, court.* a xviii. 2. xix. 34. Ezra ix. 12—15. Esth. iii. 8, 9. xviii.—8. xxviii. 22. 1 Kings xviii. 17, 18. Matt. ii. 3. John xv. 18—20. Rom. xii. 2. Jam. iv. 4. c xxvi. 3. Jer. x. 3.

Marginal references (right): d xvii. 5. xviii. 12. xix. 29, &c. xxi. 30, 31. xxii, 22, 23. e 37. v. 40. xxii. 24—26. Matt. x. 17. xxvii. 26. 2 Cor. vi. 5. xi. 23—25. 1 Thes. ii. 2. Heb. xi. 36. 1 Pet. ii. 24. f 18. xii. 4. Luke xxi. 12. g xii. 17. Eph. iii. 1. iv. 1. 2 Tim. i. 8. Philem. 9. Rev. i. 9. ii. 10. h v. 28. xii. 16. 1 Sam. xxiii. 22. 23. Matt. xxvi. 48. xxvii. 65—66. h 1 Kings xxii. 27. Jer. xxxvii. 15. 16. xxxviii. 26. i Job xiii. 27. Lam. iii. 53—55. xx. 2. xxix. 20. i 2 Chr. xvi. 10. Heb. Job xiii. 27. xxxiii. 11. Ps. cv. 18. Jer.

---

out the evil spirit by the power of Christ; and she returned to the full possession of her faculties, so that she could utter no more divinations: perhaps she was converted to Christianity. (Marg. Ref. q—x.—Notes, Mark i. 23—28. 34.)—This transaction demonstrates, beyond all controversy, that such pretensions are not always human impostures, but are sometimes real satanical operations. Had this damsel's divination been a mere juggle between her and her masters, the command of the apostle could not have detected it, or prevented them from carrying on the deception: nor could he at once, or indeed at all, have convinced the whole multitude, and the city in general, that it was a mere imposture; for men are by no means easily undeceived in matters of this nature. And if mere jugglers had been convinced, that Paul and his friends were indeed " the servants of the true God," and teachers of the way of salvation; they would never have ventured to address them in this manner.—But, as the woman was really instigated, and in a sense inspired, by an evil spirit; and as, in the paroxysms of her distraction, and amidst strange and wild actions and gestures, she actually uttered such things, as were apparent prophecies and wonderful discoveries; such as Satan could at any time make, by his foresight, and conjectural knowledge, if God would permit him; (Note, Deut. xiii. 1—5;) the change was manifest, when the dispossession took place; and all concerned were fully satisfied, that she could divine no longer, and that it was in vain to apply to her for that purpose.

To prayer. (16) Εις προσευχην: not την προσευχην, as it would have been, had the place, and not the worship been exclusively meant. Luke vi. 12.—A spirit of divination.] Πνυμα Πυθωνος. Marg. Here only. From Apollo Pythius.—Gain.] Εργασιαν. 19. xix. 24' 25. Luke xii. 58. Eph. iv. 19.—By soothsaying.] Μαντευομενη. Here only N. T.—Deut. xviii. 10. 1 Sam. xxviii. 8. Ez. xii. 24. Sept.—Being grieved. (18) Διαπονηθεις. See on iv. 2.

V. 19—24. The owners of this damsel, being sensible that no further lucre could be made by her, and that her value, if offered to sale, was greatly diminished, were exceedingly exasperated by their loss: and when they had seized on Paul and Silas, and accused them before the magistrates as disturbers of the peace, and teachers of unlawful customs; the multitude also, being enraged at the loss of their prophetess, joined in the tumultuous accusation. (Marg. Ref. y—d.) Whereas, had the apostle satisfactorily detected an artful impostor; they who had been convinced of the cheat, would have been enraged at those who had duped them of their money, and not at him who had undeceived them.—It does not appear, that the Jews were forbidden to exercise their religion at Philippi, or in other cities of the Roman empire, at this time; so that the accusation was altogether malicious and groundless. Yet the magistrates, concurring with the popular fury, violently rent off the garments of Paul and Silas; and, having severely scourged them, without any previous trial, they cast them into prison and charged the Jailor to keep them safely; as if they had been dangerous and artful criminals, who would certainly effect their escape if possible. And he, being probably a man of a severe temper, and desirous of pleasing his employers, and perhaps despising them on account of their religion, cast them into the inner prison, or the darkest and most noisome part of the dungeon; and there fastened their feet in the stocks, which must have rendered their situation very painful. (Marg. Ref. e—i.) Thus they were left, with their wounds undressed, in the cold and dark dungeon, without any refreshment, to wear away the night, expecting the next day to be further proceeded against. (Note, 1 Thes. ii. 1—8.) But neither they, nor any of the persons concerned, thought of that most gracious design, for which the Lord had permitted these sufferings to come on them.—Timothy, and Luke, and the rest of the company, as less noticed, were exempted from this severe trial.—Gone. (19) The same word is used, as before, when the evil spirit went out; ' as ' if the hope of their gains had removed from them, along ' with the unclean spirit.' Beza.—Being Jews. (20) The Christians were here confounded with the unconverted Jews, as both protested against the Pagan worship. But, had the worship of JEHOVAH been contrary to any Roman law, then in force, and actually carried into execution, no Jews could have remained in any of the cities where colonies were planted. It appears, that some statutes to this effect had been enacted; but doubtless it was generally found impracticable to execute them; and so they became obsolete, except when an occasion was sought of gratifying malice and cruelty by persecution.

The market-place. (19) Την αγοραν. xvii. 17. Matt. xx. 3: xxiii. 7, et al. Note, xvii. 16, 17.—The magistrates. (20) Τοις τρατηγοις. 22. 35, 36. 38. iv. 1. v. 24. 26. These were the chief military officers, who generally acted also as magistrates, in places subject to the Romans. Ex ρςαδος, exercitus, et ηγεομαι, dico, dux sum.—Exceedingly trouble.]

25 And *at midnight Paul and Silas prayed, and ^m sang praises unto God: ⁿ and the prisoners heard them.

26 And ^o suddenly there was a great earthquake, so that the foundations of the prison were shaken: and immediately all the doors were opened, ^p and every one's bands were loosed.

27 And ^q the keeper of the prison awaking out of his sleep, and seeing the prison-doors open, ^r he drew out his sword, and would have killed himself, supposing that the prisoners had been fled.

28 But Paul ^s cried with a loud voice, saying, ^t Do thyself no harm; for we are all here.

29 Then he called for a light, and sprang in, ^u and came trembling, ^x and fell down before Paul and Silas,

30 And ^y brought them out, and said, ^z Sirs, ^a what must I do to be saved?

31 And they said, ^b Believe on the Lord Jesus Christ, and thou shalt be saved, ^c and thy house.

32 And ^d they spake unto him the word of the Lord, and to all that were in his house.

33 And he took them the same hour of the night, ^e and washed *their* stripes; ^f and was baptized, he and all his, straightway.

34 And ^g when he had brought them into his house, he set meat before

Εκταρασσουσιν. Here only. Ex εκ et ταρασσω, turbo.—Rent off. (22) Περιρηξαντες. Here only. Ex περι, et ρηγνυμι, vel ρησσω, rumpo, frango.—To beat.] Ραβδιζειν. 2 Cor. xi. 25. Not elsewhere. A ραβδος, verga, baculus.—The jailor. (23) Δεσμοφυλακι. 27. 36. Here only. A δεσμον, vinculum, 26, et φυλαξ, custos.——Made ... fast in the stocks. (24) Ησφαλισατο εις το ξυλον. " He made safe unto the wood." It is not agreed among learned men, in what way this was done; but doubtless the posture of Paul and Silas was very painful. Ησφαλισατο. See on Matt. xxvii. 65. Ασφαλως, "safely." 23.

V. 25—28. It might have been expected, by those who know not the consolations of God, that Paul and Silas would have vented their feelings, in bitter lamentations, and exclamations against the cruelty and injustice of the treatment which they had received. Yet " at midnight," when their wounds and bruises would naturally become doubly painful, they first poured out their hearts in prayer; and doubtless remembered their persecutors, especially the jailor: and, being thus filled with divine consolation, they joyfully sang praises to God, so loudly that the other prisoners heard them. (Marg. Ref. k—n.—Note, Jam. v. 13.) At this very time, the Lord was pleased to bear testimony to their innocency, by an extraordinary earthquake, which probably was felt all over the city; but which especially shook the foundations of the prison, burst open all the doors, and in a wonderful manner brake off the bonds and fetters of all the prisoners: and yet no person was hurt by it! Nor does it appear, that any of the prisouers attempted to escape! This tremendous concussion awakened the jailor, who supposing, from the doors being open, that the prisoners, especially Paul and Silas, had fled, was about to murder himself. For he expected to be called to a severe account, and to be disgraced, or put to an ignominious death, for allowing them to escape: (Notes, xii. 5—11. 19, 19:) and therefore, according to the false notions of honour which then prevailed, and in a mixture of infidelity, pride, and desperation, he was about to plunge himself into eternity, with all his unrepented sins upon his head, by another act of most daring contempt of God and rebellion against him. But Paul discovering, either by his exclamations, or by a divine monition, what he was about to do, cried out aloud, (being in earnest to save him from destruction, even as if he had been a friend, or brother,) intreating him " to do himself no harm," for he and the other prisoners were there; not having attempted to take advantage of these awful events, nor purposing to do it.

At midnight. (25) Κα̣α το μεσονυκτιον. xx. 7. See on Mark xiii. 35.—Prayed and sang praises.] Προσευχομενοι υμνευν. " Praying they sang praises."—Υμνεν. Matt. xxvi. 30. Mark xiv. 26. Heb. ii. 12. Υμνος, Eph. v. 19. Col. iii. 16. —Heard them.] Επηκρουντο. Here only. Ex επι et ακροαομαι, exaudio.—A great earthquake. (26) Σεισμος ... μεγας. See on Matt. viii. 24.—Awaking out of his sleep. (27) Εξυπνος γενομενος.—Εξυπνω. Here only. Εξυπνιζω, John xi. 11.—He would have killed, &c.] Εμελλον ιαυτον αναιρειν. " He was " about to kill himself."—Harm. (28) Κακον, " evil, " wicked."

V. 29—34. The friendly address of Paul and Silas to the jailor, connected with the extraordinary interposition of God in their favour, seems to have been made effectual by the Holy Spirit, at once to convince him, that these were indeed " the servants of the most high God;" though probably, he had before derided that pretension, and concurred with those who persecuted them on that account. (Note, 16—18.) Thus he was led to a conviction of his guilt, in treating them with cruelty and contempt, as well as to a sense of his former sins: and he trembled, lest he should immediately be destroyed by the righteous vengeance of God, and sink into misery in another world. Yet remembering, that they came to " shew men the way " of salvation," he seems to have conceived hopes of that deliverance. Calling therefore " for a light," in great haste and terror, he came in and fell down before Paul and Silas; and first (as a proof that he began to relent and be sorry for his sin,) bringing them out of the stocks and the inner prison, he addressed them in the most re-

them, [h] and rejoiced, believing in God with all his house.

35 ¶ And [i] when it was day, the magistrates sent the serjeants, saying, Let those men go.

36 And the keeper of the prison told this saying to Paul, The magistrates have sent to let you go: now therefore depart, [k] and go in peace.

37 But Paul said unto them, [l] They have beaten us openly uncondemned, being Romans, and have cast us into prison; and now do they thrust us out

privily? Nay, verily; but [m] let them come themselves and fetch us out.

38 And the serjeants told these words unto the magistrates: [n] and they feared, when they heard that they were Romans.

39 And they [o] came and besought them, [p] and brought them out, [q] and desired them to depart out of the city.

40 And they went out of the prison, [r] and entered into the house of Lydia: [s] and when they had seen the brethren, [t] they comforted them, and departed.

---

spectful manner, " saying, Sirs, what must I do to be " saved ?" By being saved, he doubtless meant deliverance from present death, and from future condemnation. (Marg. Ref. u—a.—Note, xxiv. 24—27.)—' He spake ' thus to them, as knowing, or conceiving, from the words ' of the Pythoness, that they were appointed to shew to ' others the way of salvation.' Whitby. Nor were they reluctant, on account of past injuries, immediately (though an unseasonable hour, and themselves greatly in need of case and rest) to give instruction and encouragement to him ; or led to despair of his salvation, or to prescribe harder terms to him than to others, because of his atrocious crimes : on the contrary, they exhorted him to " be- " lieve in the Lord Jesus Christ," and assured him that in doing this he would certainly be saved. (Marg. Ref. b.) This faith implied a belief of their testimony concerning Jesus, as the promised Messiah, and concerning his person, character, sufferings,' death, resurrection, and ascension ; and a reliance on him for all things pertaining to salvation.—They also included his household in this assurance : not that their faith could save them : but his example might lead them to believe in Christ also ; and with him they would become a part of the visible church, and have the benefit of the means of grace for their salvation. (Marg. Ref. c.—Notes, ii. 37—40. xi. 4—17, v. 14. Gen. xvii. 7, 8. Jer. xxxii. 39—41. Luke xix. 1—10, v. 9.)—They then instructed him and all his family more fully in the doctrine of the gospel : and the Lord so blessed the word, that he was immediately humbled, softened, and changed from a lion as it were into a lamb : so that he first compassionately washed and dressed their stripes, and then professing faith in Christ, he was baptized in his name ; though he might fear the heavy displeasure of the magistrates, for thus embracing the cause, which they had set themselves to oppose: and at the same time all his household was baptized likewise. (Marg. Ref. d—f.) Now, therefore, regarding Paul and Silas with the greatest respect and most endeared affection, he brought them into his house, and entertained them at his table. (Marg. Ref. g.—Notes, Matt. x. 40—42. xxv. 34—40. Gal. v. 1—6, v. 6. 1 John iii. 13—15.) At the same time his trembling was turned into joy.—" He rejoiced with all his house," " having believed in God." (Note, 13—15, v. 15.)—When a Gentile householder was converted to the Jewish religion, all the males in his family, including infants, were circumcised with him, unless any of the adults, after instruc-

tion, refused to be so : it is therefore obvious to suppose, that the same rule was observed, in the baptism of those households, of which we read in the New Testament ; for it has already been shewn, that the covenant sealed to Abraham, was the same as the Christian covenant ; and that circumcision was the sign of the same blessings, of which baptism now is. (Note, Gen. xvii. 9—12.) And the language, concerning the baptism' of believers and their households, so much accords to that concerning the circumcision of Abraham and his household ; that, in connexion with other scriptures ; with the general and early use of infant-baptism in the primitive church ; and with the consideration that we do not read in the New Testament of one single instance, in which the children of Christian parents were baptized adult ; it must be allowed strongly to countenance the sentiments and practice of pœdo-baptists : though we suppose, that the change of the initiatory ordinance, as far as infants were concerned, was silently and gradually ; like that respecting the sabbath : the Jewish converts still circumcising their male children, to avoid giving needless offence to the unconverted Jews. (Note, 1—3.)—It seems also most probable, to me at least, that Paul and Silas, in their painful condition, and in the jailor's house, did not baptize him and his family by immersion.

He sprang in. (29) Εισεπηδησε. See on xiv. '4.—Came trembling.] Εντρομος γενομενος. vii. 32. Heb. xii. 21 —Sirs. (30) Κυριοι. This implies an acknowledged superiority. 16. 19. Eph. vi. 5. 9.—What must I do to be saved ?] Τι με δει ποιειν ινα σωθω ; " What does it " behove me to do, in order that I may be saved ? "—Rejoiced, believing in God with all his house. (34) Ηγαλλιασατο πανοικι πεπιστευκως τω Θεω.—" He rejoiced through all " his house, having believed in God."—Ηγαλλιασατο· See on Luke i. 47.—Πανοικι. Here only N. T.—Εx. i. 1. Sept.—Εx πας, omnis, et οικος, domus. Πεπιστευκως Sing. denoting the jailor alone.

V. 35—40. Perhaps the earthquake, and the reports of what had taken place at the prison, concurred in dismaying the magistrates from proceeding further against Paul and Silas : they were, however, no doubt conscious that they had done more than they could justify : and they therefore sent their serjeants, or beadles, to give orders to the jailor to release them ; which he delivered to them with great joy and affection. (Marg. Ref. k.) But the apostle, though willing to suffer for the cause of Christ, and not at

CHAP. XVII.

Paul preaches at Thessalonica; and some, both Jews and Greeks, believe. 1—4. The unbelieving Jews raise disturbances, and trouble the rulers, 5—9. Paul and Silas are sent by night to Berea, 10. The Bereans ingenuously attend to the word, and "search

" the scriptures daily: therefore many believe," 11, 12. The Jews of Thessalonica follow Paul and Silas to Berea, to stir up persecution, 13; Paul is conducted to Athens, 14, 15. His zeal is excited by the excessive idolatry of that city; and he disputes in the synagogue, and in the forum with the philosophers, 16—18. He is brought before the Areopagus, 19—21.

---

all disposed to avenge himself; judged it proper to remind these iniquitous magistrates, that they had acted illegally, and might be severely punished for it: because this would tend to procure more equitable treatment for the Christians, and indeed for the other citizens, in future. In the tumult of the proceedings against him and Silas, the day before, they had not thought it expedient to plead their privilege as Romans, or no notice had been taken of their plea: but Paul now charged the magistrates with scourging them publickly and imprisoning them in a cruel and ignominious manner, though they had not been condemned of any crime, and though they could prove themselves Roman citizens. And now they meant to set them at liberty, in an underhand manner, that they might conceal their own injustice. He and Silas, however, did not choose to go away, under the imputation of having deserved such punishment: if therefore the magistrates desired that they should depart, they must come themselves, acknowledge their fault, and dismiss them in a more honourable manner. (*Marg. Ref.* l, m.) This reply might well alarm them: for, as no man could claim the privilege of a citizen falsely, without exposing himself to the severest punishment; so a prosecution for such illegal treatment of Roman citizens would have subjected the magistrates to heavy penalties, and incapacitated them from ever again exercising authority; if not to capital punishment. They therefore came, and submissively intreated Paul and Silas to leave the city, lest further commotions should be excited, in which they might not be able to protect them: and, as the apostle by no means intended to require reparation for the injury, he and Silas went to the house of Lydia, and, having visited and encouraged the other new converts, they departed.—The epistle to the Philippians, shews, what a flourishing church was at this time planted; and in what a happy manner these troubles terminated. (*Marg. Ref.* n—s.—*Notes, Is.* lx. 10—14. *Rev.* iii. 8, 9.) —*Being Romans.* (37) Having been admitted to the privileges of Roman citizens; or being the children of such as had been thus admitted.—This was the case with numbers in the colonies, who were, from other nations, thus incorporated among the Roman citizens. (*Note,* xxii. 22—30.)

The serjeants. (35) Ῥαβδουχος. 38.—Here only. A ῥαβδος, *virga, et εχω, habeo.*—" The lictors;" the same persons, who had scourged Paul and Silas.—*Uncondemned.* (37) Ακαλαχριτας. xxii. 25. Not elsewhere.

PRACTICAL OBSERVATIONS.

V. 1—12.

" 'The wisdom that is from above" is peculiarly requisite, that we may know when, and how far, we may bear with men's prejudices, in order to their edification; and when we must resolutely protest against them. (*Note,* l *Cor.* ix. 19—23.) But if a man have it at heart to carry his

point, as far as possible; and if he be delivered from the prevalence of pride, selfishness, obstinacy, and moroseness; he will be directed by circumstances, under the influence of the Holy Spirit, to act according to the word of God: yet his conduct will often appear incongruous and inconsistent, to the superficial observer. (*Note,* 1 *Cor.* ii. 14—16.)—The greatest precaution should be used, that the ministers of Christ be men of good report: lest prejudices against individuals should be added to the carnal enmity of the human heart against the gospel, to prevent their success; and that such as " are of the contrary part " may have no evil thing to say of them." Scriptural regulations, therefore, in this and similar concerns, tend exceedingly to the establishment of believers in the faith, and to the increase of the church in numbers. (*Notes,* 1 *Tim.* iii. 7. *Tit.* ii. 7, 8.)—We have no ground to expect to be directed by immediate revelation, in the various actions of our lives: but, while we act according to the best of our judgment, in obedience to the word and dependence on the Spirit of God; we shall find circumstances, apparently casual, operate as prohibitions and directions, subverting our plans, and substituting others in their stead. —" He that holds the stars in his right hand," directs his ministers to the several places, where he means to employ them; and often contrary to their own plans and expectations.—When we are, by any means, satisfied of the Lord's will respecting us; we should prepare for obedience, to whatever hardship, labour, and peril it may expose us: and those who go in simplicity, faithfulness, and affection, to preach the gospel among ignorant or careless sinners, do the most for their help and benefit that man can do: though it seldom happens, that persons of this character are forward to invite them. The deplorable condition, however, of our fellow creatures, in very many parts of the world, and even their insensibility to their own danger and misery, ought to stimulate our exertions, to carry or send them effectual help; and to aid, by our labours, contributions, and prayers, every scriptural attempt for that purpose. Nor should we forget, that it was this generous and tender compassion for the inhabitants of this quarter of the globe, without any desire or request from us, or our ancestors, or even from those to whom they were sent, which induced the apostles and evangelists to " put their " lives in their hands," and come over into Europe to help us. And could they now address us, it would probably be in these few but emphatical words, " Go thou " and do likewise."

V. 13—24.

While the servants of Christ wait upon him in his ordinances; he will find them some opening to speak in his name: nor should the most eminent minister be averse to preach to a very small number of the most obscure persons.—The Lord alone can " open the heart" for the reception and belief of his word; (*Note,* 1 *Cor.* iii. 4—9:)

5 A

He preaches the living God, the Creator and Lord of all, as hitherto unknown to the Athenians, 22—29. He calls on them to repent; because God will judge | the world by Jesus, whom he has raised from the dead, 30, 31. Some mock, others purpose to hear him again, and a very few believe, 32—34.

and true faith is always attended by love shewn to the servants of Christ: his genuine disciples desire to approve themselves faithful stewards, to " use hospitality without ' grudging," and to employ their substance in supporting and promoting the gospel; and they commonly prove a blessing to their households also.—The powers of darkness vary their methods, of prejudicing the minds of men against the light of the gospel, or drawing off their attention from it.—Lying miracles, and useless divinations, are far more valued, in this evil world, than the truths and precepts of God are: men readily incur expense for the former; but refuse the latter, even when freely communicated: they are much more desirous of being told their *fortune*, than their *duty*, or even " the way of salvation !" and impostures, in endless variety, have been used to deceive mankind, and to set them against true religion.— Satan, the father of lies, can declare the most important truths, when it subserves his purpose of deception and murder: and, if he were permitted, he could do more mischief, by ingeniously connecting the doctrines of the gospel, with pernicious errors and immoral practices, than by any species of superstition, persecution, and infidelity. Much he actuates effects in this way, by means of antinomian, enthusiastical, and scandalous preachers; who, being confounded with the real servants of Christ, bring them also into contempt and abhorrence, with thousands, nay millions of superficial observers. But we must strenuously disclaim such coalitions: and commendations, from bad and suspicious characters, should more excite our grief and indignation, than all their calumnies and reproaches. —The conversion of sinners, " from the power of Satan " unto God,". often deprives those connected with them, of the gains which they made by their vices: thus the gospel interferes with the worldly interests of those, who will do any base thing for money, and prefer the gain of unrighteousness to the lives or souls of those employed by them: and this concurs with other principles, in exciting their rage and persecution. (*Notes*, xix. 23—31. *P. O.* 21—31. *Note*, 1 *Tim.* vi. 6—10, *vv.* 9, 10.) So that those who do more good than others, by drawing sinners off from the service of the devil, may expect to be reviled as men, who " exceedingly trouble the city:" and while they teach men to fear God, to repent of sin, to believe in Christ, and to live sober, righteous, and godly lives; they will be accused of teaching customs, which are illegal, impracticable, or ruinous to the community ! Too often indeed the laws of the state interfere with those of God, and the customs of the world contradict the wisdom and holiness of his service: yet, interested opposers frequently make these things a mere pretence for persecution, while they are actuated by avarice, ambition, or revenge alone. The vilest of malefactors may, therefore, expect more favourable treatment than zealous ministers, who will not let sinners go on unmolested in the ways of destruction.— Pride, cruelty, contempt, and enmity, often concur in uniting the mob and the magistrates against them. And if we, in this happy land, escape abuse, stripes, dungeons, the stocks, and the stake; we should bless God for our mild government, and that equitable constitution by which he

secures us: and shew our gratitude, by praying earnestly for our rulers, and by turning away our ears from those innovators, whom nothing but licentiousness can satisfy.

V. 25—34.

The consolations of God are neither few nor small to his suffering servants: he gives them, in answer to their prayers, songs in the darkest night of tribulation, and in the most painful and dreary situation.—What different persons are true Christians, from what they are supposed to be ! They are happier than their most prosperous foes, who do their worst to make them miserable: they need not to be strictly guarded, when God requires them to lodge in a prison; and walls, bolts, fetters, and keepers are as nothing, when he wills them to be at liberty. In the most destitute state they have an omnipotent Friend; all nature stands ready to plead their cause; they are capable of becoming the best of benefactors, in their most abject penury; and they are ready to do good to their most cruel enemies.—How wonderful also are the varied methods of divine grace! and how unlikely the objects of it! The Lord sometimes brings sinners acquainted with himself, by occasion of their own crimes; and frequently through the sufferings of his servants. He gently, and by degrees, leads some into the knowledge and experience of his truth: others he alarms by most tremendous dispensations, and snatches them by a gracious violence from the jaws of destruction. (*P. O. Luke* xix. 1—10.) Some are brought as near to hell, as can be conceived; and then are suddenly rescued and made heirs of heaven. Under the influence of their mad passions, many have been powerfully instigated by Satan, to plunge themselves into the bottomless pit by their own hands; just at the time, when God was about to lead them into the ways of peace and felicity. Thus he illustrates and demonstrates the sovereignty and efficacy of his grace; and gives occasion to praises and thanksgivings, which will be varied almost infinitely to all eternity.—Whatever men have been, or have done to us, we ought not to " render evil for evil;" but, if possible, to prevent them from doing harm to themselves: and We should be as earnest in this, on proper occasions, with respect to our greatest enemy, as if he were our brother and friend.—When sinners begin to enquire, under terror and distress of conscience, with earnestness, and a desire of immediate instruction, " what they must " do to be saved;" especially when their conduct shews any disposition to relent, and " to do works meet for re- " pentance;" they should all be answered in the same manner, whatever their previous character has been: " Believe in the Lord Jesus Christ, and thou shalt be " saved." None can be saved in any other way: none are excluded from salvation who seek it in this way. Yet it is not enough merely to state this unexplained truth, we should further instruct men, in respect of the object, nature, and effects of this faith, as we have opportunity: and when sinners are converted, they will soon learn to love and honour those, whom they before despised and hated; they will alleviate the sufferings, which before they derided and augmented; they will supply the wants

5 A 2

NOW when they had passed through Amphipolis and Apollonia, they came to ᵇThessalonica, ᶜwhere was a synagogue of the Jews: 2 And Paul, ᵉas his manner was, ᵈwent in unto them, and three sabbath-days ᵉreasoned with them out of the scriptures; 3 ᶠOpening and alledging that

'Christ must needs have suffered, and risen again from the dead: and that ʰthis Jesus, ⁱwhom I preach unto you, is Christ. ·4 And ¹ some of them believed, and consorted with Paul and ᵏSilas; and of ¹ the devout Greeks a great multitude, ᵐand of the chief women not a few.

of the indigent servants of God, and join themselves to them, by professing their faith in Christ, and venturing reproach and persecution for his sake; and they will desire, that all who belong to them, may be devoted to the Lord, and trained up in his service. When such fruits of faith begin evidently to appear, we need not be surprised, if terrors are speedily succeeded by confidence and joy in God: and thus the events which menaced the most fatal consequences, often terminate in mutual congratulations and thanksgivings; and the richest of blessings on the families to which they belong.

V. 35—40.

The servants of Christ should suffer persecution peaceably, and forgive injuries readily: yet there may be cases, in which it will be proper for them to claim the protection of the laws, and to protest against the flagrant injustice of oppressive magistrates; especially when they violate the laws of their own country which they are commissioned to execute, in vehement zeal against the objects of their contempt and aversion. This (which is far different from resisting the execution of the law itself, when deemed unreasonable,) may conduce to publick justice, the peace of the church and of the community, and the credit of their profession. (Notes, xxiii. 1—5. Rom. xiii. 1—5.) But when proper concessions are made by those who have acted illegally, Christians should never express personal resentment, or insist strictly,upon reparation; but manifest a disinterested publick spirit in every thing. Thus their enemies will be ashamed, silenced, or conciliated; the Lord will make them "more than conquerors" in every conflict; and, instead of being cast down by their sufferings, they shall even become the comforters of their brethren, who have been exempted from so large a share of tribulation. (Note, 2 Cor. i. 1—7, vv. 3—6.)

NOTES.

CHAP. XVII. V. 1—4. Either no Jews resided at Amphipolis and Apollonia, or the apostle had no opportunity of preaching among them; at least no mention is any where made of his labours or success in those cities. He therefore journeyed on to the west, till he arrived at Thessalonica, the city in which the Roman governor of Macedonia resided. (Marg. Ref. a.) And there, according to his custom, he went to the Synagogue, and reasoned from the scriptures, to the Jews and the other worshippers there assembled, for three successive sabbath-days: adducing many passages from the prophets, explaining their meaning, and thence evidently shewing, that according to the prophets the promised Messiah was to suffer death and to

rise again; and proving, from the exact fulfilment of these predictions, that Jesus was indeed the Christ, or the Messiah. (Marg. Ref. d—h.) These reasonings did not convince the Jews in general, for their hearts were set upon a temporal kingdom : yet some of them believed, or were persuaded, and united themselves to Paul and Silas; and a great many of the worshipping Gentiles believed; and among the rest, several of the principal women in the city. (Marg. Ref. i—m.) From the Epistles to the Thessalonians it is evident, that the apostle was remarkably successful among the idolatrous Gentiles also; and that he continued here a considerable time: but after the first three sabbaths, it is probable, he left the Jews, and preached chiefly to the Gentiles.—As the historian says they, not we; it is conjectored that Luke stayed behind at Philippi, and did not join the company till some time after.—'Upon inspecting ' the history, I see nothing in it which negatives the sup-
' position, that St. Paul pursued the same plan at Thes-
' salonica, which he adopted in other places; and that,
' though he resorted to the synagogue only three sabbath-
' days; yet he remained in the city, and in the exercise of
' his ministry among the Gentile citizens,"much longer ;'
' and until the success of his preaching had provoked the
' Jews to excite the tumult and insurrection, by which he
' was driven away. ... The Alexandrian and Cambridge
' manuscripts read των σεϐομενων και 'Ελληνων πολυ πληθος' ("of
" the worshippers, and of the Greeks a great multitude.")
' ... If we be not allowed to change the present reading, ...
' may not the passage ... be considered as describing the
' success of St. Paul's discourses, during the three sabbath-
' days, in which he preached in the synagogue ?' and ... that
' his application to the Gentiles at large, and his success
' among them, was posterior to this ? ' Paley.—It appears
from the epistles to the Thessalonians, that the church at
Thessalonica was chiefly formed of converted idolaters;
and that St. Paul and his companions entered very particularly into the several parts of Christian doctrine and
duty, in their practical instructions of the new converts,
before they left the city: and in writing to the Philippians,
the apostle observes, that they had sent twice to supply his
wants, when at Thessalonica. (Notes, Phil. iv. 14—20.
1 Thes. i. 9, 10. iv. 1—5.) These things shew that he laboured in this city much longer, than the three sabbath-
days here mentioned.

When they had passed through. (1) Διοδευσαντες. Luke viii. 1. Not elsewhere.—Ex δια, et οδυω, iter facio.—As his manner was. (2) Κατα ... το ειωθος. Luke iv. 16. Ειωθει, Matt. xxvii. 15. Mark x. 1.—Reasoned.] 'Διελεγετο. 17. xviii. 4. 19. xix. 8, 9. xxiv. 12. 25. Mark ix. 34.—Opening. (3) Διανοιγων. xvi. 14. Mark vii. 34, 35. Luke ii. 23.

5 But the Jews which believed not, * moved with envy, ° took unto them certain lewd fellows of the baser sort, and gathered a company, ° and set all the city on an uproar, and assaulted the house of ° Jason, and sought to bring them out to the people.

6 And when they found them not, ° they drew Jason and certain brethren unto the rulers of the city, crying, ° These that have turned the world upside down are come hither also ;

7 Whom Jason hath received : ° and these all do contrary to the decrees of Cæsar, saying, That there is another king, *one* Jesus.

8 And ° they troubled the people, and the rulers of the city, when they heard these things.

9 And when they had taken security of Jason, and of the other, they let them go.

10 ¶ And ° the brethren immediately sent away Paul and Silas by night unto ° Berea: who, coming thither, ° went into the synagogue of the Jews.

11 These were ° more noble than those in Thessalonica, in that ° they received the word with all readiness of mind, ° and searched the scriptures daily, whether those things were so.

12 Therefore ° many of them believed ; also of ° honourable women which were Greeks, and of men, not a few.

13 But when ° the Jews of Thessalonica had knowledge that the word of God was preached of Paul at Berea, they came thither also and ° stirred up the people,

14 And ° then immediately the brethren sent away Paul, to go ° as it were to the sea : ° but Silas and Timotheus abode there still.

15 And they that conducted Paul brought him unto ° Athens: and ° receiving a commandment unto Silas and Timotheus for to come to him with all speed, they departed.

---

xxiv. 31, 32. 45.—*Alledging.*] Παραθεμενος. xiv. 23. xvi. 34. xx. 32. Luke ix. 16. x. 8, *et al.* Εκ παρα, et τιθημι, *pono.* ° Placing it before their eyes ; that is, so manifestly ° expounding it, that we perceive the things which are pro-° posed to be seen.' *Beza.—Believed.* (4) Επεισθησαν. xiii. 43. xiv. 19. xviii. 4. xix. 8. 26. xxvi. 26. 28. xxviii. 23. *Matt.* xxvii. 20. *Luke* xvi. 31.—*Consorted.*] Προσεκληρωθησαν. Here only. Εκ προς, et κληροω, *Eph.* i. 11.—A κληρος, *sors.*
V. 5—9. The unbelieving Jews were enraged, and filled with envy, or fierce zeal, because the apostle preached to the Gentiles that they might be saved. (*Marg. Ref.* n. —*Notes*, xiii. 42—48. xiv. 2. 1 Thes. ii. 13—16.) They therefore raised a mob, from among the lowest and most licentious people in the city, who threw every thing into disorder ; and then they violently assaulted the house, where the apostle and his company generally lodged, in order to drag them before the people as publick disturbers. —Jason, the owner of this house, seems to have been a relation of Paul, and a Jew. (*Rom.* xvi. 21.)—Paul and his friends were absent or concealed at this time : the multitude therefore dragged Jason, and some other of the new converts, before the magistrates, or rulers of the city ; exclaiming, that the men, of whom they had heard many reports, as having excited great confusion in every place, and who attempted innovations, tending to " turn " the world upside down," and subvert the established order in religion and civil government, were at length come thither also ; and that Jason had lodged them in his house, and had embraced their doctrine, as many others had done. (*Marg. Ref.* o—s.) They had all, however, broken the edicts of the Roman emperor, and rebelled against his

authority : for they avowed that there was another King, one Jesus who had been crucified ; who, they averred, was risen again, and was exalted to a dominion far superior to that of Cæsar, and entirely independent on him. (*Marg. Ref.* t, u.) This accusation gave great disquietude both to the magistrates, and the assembled multitudes : as they feared the displeasure of the emperor, if they should neglect such a charge ; and yet they knew not how to proceed upon it. At present, however, they only required Jason and his friends to give security for their peaceable behaviour, and to make their appearance if further called on.
Who believed not. (5) Οι απειθυντες. See on xiv. 2.— *Moved with envy.*] Ζηλωσαντες. See on vii. 9. (*Note, Jam.* iii. 13—16.)—*Lewd fellows.*] Ανδρας πονηρους. " Wicked " men."—*Of the baser sort.*] Των αγοραιων.—Here only, in this sense. Αβ αγορα, *forum.* The persons who performed the lowest offices, in the markets.—Αγοραιος, differently accented, xix. 38.—*And gathered a company.*] Οχλοποιησαντες. Here only. Εκ οχλος, *turba*, et ποιεω, *facio.* —*Assaulted.*] Επισταντες. iv. 1. vi. 12. xxii. 13. 20, *et al.*— *The rulers of* the city. (6) Τας πολιταρχας. 8. Here only. —Εκ πολις, *civitas*, et αρχων, *princeps.*—*Turned the world upside down.*] Οι την οικουμενην αναστατωσαντες.—'Η οικουμενη' See on *Luke* ii. 1.—Αναστατου. xxi. 38. *Gal.* v. 12.—*The decrees.* (7) Τα δογματα. See on xvi. 4.—*Security.* (9) Το ικανον. ° Formula forensis, το ικανον λαμβανειν ... satis ° accipere, satis dandum sibi curare: ... *fidejussores.*' Schleusner.
V. 10—15. The Christians at Thessalonica judged it to be no longer safe, for Paul and Silas to continue among them ; and therefore they secretly sent them to Berea; an

5 ᴀ 4

a Ex. xxxii. 19.
20. Num. xxv.
&—11. 1 Kin. xix. 10. 14. Job xxxii. 2, 3, 18—20. Ps. lxix. 9. cxix. 158. Jer. xx. 9. Mic. iii. 8.
b Mark iii. 5. John ii. 18—17. 2 Pet. ii. 7, 8.
c Or, full of idols. 23. marg.

16 ¶ Now while Paul waited for them at Athens, [a] his spirit was stirred in him, when he saw the city [c] wholly given to idolatry.

17 Therefore [b] disputed he in the synagogue with the Jews, and with

[p] the devout persons, and in the market [q] daily with them that met with him.

18 Then certain [r] philosophers of the Epicureans and of the Stoicks [s] encountered him. And some said, What will this [t] babbler say? other some, he

p v. 2. xiii. 16.
q Prov. i. 20—22.
viii. 1—4, 34.
Jer. vi. 11.
r Matt. v. 1, 2.
Mark xvi. 15.
s Luke xiii. 3. 2 Tim. iii. 8.
Rom. i. 22. 1 Cor. i. 20, 21.
Col. ii. 8.
vi. 2. Mark ix. 1 Cor. iii. 18, 19.

14. Luke xi. 53.　† Or, base fellow. Prov. xxiii. 9. xxvi. 12.

adjacent city: and when they came thither, they, without delay, fear, or resentment, proceeded to make known the joyful tidings, concerning the Messiah, to the Jews assembled in the synagogue. (*Marg. Ref.* x—z.) These proved to be of a more ingenuous, candid, liberal, and teachable disposition than the Jews of Thessalonica; and more deserving of the honourable distinction of Abraham's seed, in which the nation in general gloried: for they applied their minds, with all readiness and seriousness, to the word which the apostle preached to them; and though they did not *implicitly* receive his doctrine, or submit to his arguments; they impartially and diligently investigated the subject. They not only heard him preach on the sabbath-days, or at other times; but they "every day" employed themselves in searching the scriptures, and comparing its predictions with the facts attested to them. (*Marg. Ref.* a—c.—*Notes, Matt.* xiii. 23. *Luke* viii. 4—15, *v.* 15.) Thus many of them were led to a full conviction of the truth; and with these Jews several religious proselytes, and some of the most affluent and honourable women of the city, embraced Christianity. (*Marg. Ref.* d, e.) But the envious Jews of Thessalonica, hearing of this success, followed Paul and Silas to Berea, and there excited a storm of popular fury against them. And, as Paul was most obnoxious to them, it was judged necessary for him to recede from the danger: they therefore conducted him towards the sea-coast, that it might be supposed he was about to embark for Asia. But he at length changed his course, and arrived at Athens, the most renowned city of Greece; having left his fellow-labourers behind him, to regulate the affairs of the church at Berea; and, having sent word to them to come as soon as they could to him, he waited for them there.—It does not appear, that Silas came to him, while at Athens: and Timothy, when he arrived, was sent from Athens back to Thessalonica, as we learn from the first epistle to the Thessalonians: and both he and Silas again joined the apostle at Corinth. (*Marg. Ref.* f—m —xviii. 5.—*Note,* 1 *Thes.* iii. 1—5.)

More noble. (11) Ευγενεσεροι. *Luke* xix. 12. 1 *Cor.* i. 26. Not elsewhere. Ex ευ, *bene,* et γενος, *stirps, familia,* xiii. 26. 1 *Pet.* ii. 9. (*Note,* 1 *Pet.* ii. 9, 10.)—' St. Luke ' shews them wherein their true nobility consisted, viz. in ' such a disposition of the soul, as inclined them to attend ' to the doctrine of the gospel.' *Whitby.* (*Notes, Jam.* i. 16—18. iii. 17, 18.)—*And stirred up.* (13) Σαλευοντες, ii. 25. iv. 31. xvi. 26. *Matt.* xxiv. 29. *Luke* xxi. 26, *et al.*

V. 16, 17. It is probable, that the apostle did not at first intend to enter on his ministry at Athens, till Silas and Timothy joined him: perhaps, he had not determined whether he should attempt to publish the gospel there, or pass over into Asia. While, however, he continued in this renowned city, the centre of polite learning, philosophy, and the fine arts, and, as it were, the university of the Roman empire, and of the world; he took little notice of

the sculpture and edifices, the fragments of which to this day are considered as the most perfect models of their kind; or of their paintings and exhibitions, and other curiosities of this sort. Paul is generally allowed to have been a man of fine taste and cultivated genius; but his thoughts were too much occupied about more sublime and interesting subjects, to make observations on these elegant or magnificent trifles: (*Note, Luke* xxi. 6:) for his spirit was agitated, grieved, sharpened, and filled with zeal, indignation, and astonishment, to see a city, which was thought to be so peculiarly enlightened, wholly devoted to the most stupid idolatry. (*Marg. Ref.* n.)—It has been asserted that there were more idols at Athens, than in all the rest of Greece: the Athenians always imported the deities and superstitions of every nation, along with their arts and learning; so that a satyrist ludicrously observed, 'It was ' easier to find a god, than a man, in that city.' This fact most completely demonstrates the insufficiency of science and philosophy to guide men in matters of religion. The barbarous Scythians, the wild Indians, nay, the stupid Hottentots, have never deviated further from truth, or sunk into grosser darkness, in respect of God and religion, than the ingenious and philosophical Athenians did!—The apostle, however, was thus excited to begin his labours without delay: and first in the synagogue he proposed his doctrine to the Jews and proselytes; and, reasoning with them from the scriptures, he earnestly endeavoured to convince them that Jesus was the Messiah: (*Note,* 1—4, *v.* 2:) but he does not appear to have had great success among them. This was probably on the sabbath-day.— He also argued and reasoned every day in the market-place, or forum, with such of the philosophers, students, or others, as he could meet with: (*Marg. Ref.* o—q:) for there these men were used to converse and debate concerning their different opinions: and the forum was as much the place in which they met for this purpose, as the change is the place of meeting for the merchants in London.

Was stirred. (16) Παρωξυνετο. 1 *Cor.* xiii. 5. Not elsewhere N. T. *Num.* xiv. 11. 23. *Deut.* ix. 18. xxxii. 41. *Sept.* Παροξυσμος· See on xv. 39.—*Wholly given to idolatry.*] "Full of idols." *Marg.* Κατειδωλον. Here only. Ex καλα, et ειδωλον, *idolum.—In the market.* (17) Εν τη αγορα. xvi. 19. *The forum.—Them that met with him.*] Τις παραλυγχανοντας. Here only. Ex παρα, et τυγχανω, *sum, existo, adipiscor.*

V. 18. In the forum, the apostle was encountered by certain philosophers of different sects. The Epicureans were gay and superficial infidels, who amused themselves and others with various curious speculations. They ascribed the original of all things to chance: they professed to allow the existence of the gods; yet they contended, that they did not interfere in the creation or government of the world, but indolently satisfied themselves with their

seemeth to be a setter forth of strange gods: because he preached unto them *Jesus and the resurrection.

19 And they took him, and brought him unto *Areopagus, saying, "May we know what this * new doctrine, whereof thou speakest, is?

20 For thou bringest certain 'strange

things to our ears: we would know therefore ' what these things mean.

21 (For all the Athenians and strangers which were there, ' spent their time in nothing else, but either to tell or to hear some new thing.)

22 Then Paul stood in the midst of 'Mars' hill, and said, Ye men of

---

own undisturbed felicity: they deemed the enjoyment of this present world the supreme good, and they denied a future state of rewards and punishments. The Stoicks allowed the existence of the gods, but supposed them to be bound by eternal and irresistible fatality; they affected almost to extinguish their own feelings and passions; they were most extravagantly proud and obstinate; they judged a virtuous man, according to their notions of virtue, to be independent of their deities, and in some respects superior to them; and spoke as if he might defy fate itself: they maintained that virtue was its own reward, and expressed themselves very obscurely about a future state of retributions. (*Marg. Ref.* r, s.)—These two sects of philosophers, being alike opposite in their tenets to the doctrines of the gospel, and being full of the pride of superior learning, encountered Paul, and thought of silencing him in the argument: and some of them despised him as a babbler, or a man who had picked up a few scraps of learning in different places, of which he wanted to make a shew; and as one who was fond of hearing himself speak, even among those who had studied so much more than he had. But others concluded, that he meant to introduce some new deities under their notice: for, being accustomed to deify virtues, vices, health, diseases, &c. they supposed that he preached to them Jesus as a God, and *Anastasis*, or the Resurrection, as a goddess, whom they ought to worship in preference to any of their present idols. (*Marg. Ref.*)

Encountered.] Συνεϐαλλον. iv. 15. xviii. 27. xx. 14. *Luke* xiv. 31.—*Babbler.*] Σπερμολογος. Here only. Εχ σπερμα, *semen*, et λεγω, *colligo.* ' Σπερμαλογος signifies a parasite ' or a beggar, who prates and carries about stories, for the ' sake of getting a maintenance. The deadliest term that ' Demosthenes there, (at Athens,) above three hundred ' years before, bestowed on Æschines.' *Broughton* in *Leigh.* Æschines was an orator, the most eager and decided rival and antagonist of Demosthenes.—*A setter forth.*] Καταγγελευς. Here only. Καταγγελλω, 3. .13. 23.—*Of strange gods.*] Ξενων δαιμονιων. Ξενος, 21. *Matt.* xxv. 35. 38, et al. Δαιμονιον, 1 *Cor.* x. 20, 21. 1 *Tim.* iv. 1. *Jam.* ii. 19. *Rev.* ix. 20. 'The Gentiles used it for the objects of their ' worship in a good sense, not as we Christians use it at ' present, invariably in a bad sense.' *Campbell.* Ought Christians to use a word in a good sense, which, in its best meaning, signifies the objects of abominable idolatries? Holy angels are never called *demons* in scripture: but either evil spirits, or the supposed invisible objects of idolatrous worship; and this, with every object of it, is especially " an abomination to the Lord." (*Notes, Deut.* xxxii. 17. 1 *Cor.* x. 18—22. 1 *Tim.* iv. 1—5.)—*He preached.*] Ευηγγελιζετο.—*The resurrection.*] Την αναστασιν.

V. 19—21. As a multitude seems to have collected around the apostle and his opponents, the latter conducted him, not as a criminal, (according to the opinion of some expositors, which is contrary to the whole narrative, but as a philosophising speculator, to the Areopagus, or principal senate pf Athens: and before that renowned body, and a number of philosophers, and other citizens and strangers, they civilly requested him to shew them more accurately, what was the new doctrine which he taught; for in all their reading and enquiries, they had never met with the sentiments, which he had delivered. (*Marg. Ref.* u—z.) This enquiry was merely the result of vain curiosity: for all the Athenians, and the strangers who came thither to study, from every part of the world, ocenpied themselves almost entirely in devising, learning, or propagating some new sentiment or speculation, having no *leisure* for any thing else. (*Marg. Ref.* a.) The word signifies *newer:* the new imagination, or system, of the preceding year, month, or week, soon became like an almanack out of date: it was the taste of the age and place to discard and antequate every hypothesis, as soon as it became vulgar; and to substitute some *newer* scheme in its place: and lively ingenious students, especially in metaphysicks, commonly run into this humour. If Paul there fore could start some *newer* speculation, than the *newest* fashion of philosophy among them, his doctrine would at least gratify and amuse them.

Areopagus. (19) " Mars' hill." *Marg.* Αρειον παγον. 22. Αϐ Αρης, *Mars*, et παγος, *collis.*—Αρεοπαγιτης, 34. Some learned men think, that the word *Areopagus* is not properly translated " Mars' hill," or the hill of Mars, as it does not appear, that a temple was built to Mars, in the place where the Areopagus convened. They argue, that the name was derived from the trial of murderers by the court there held. (See on *Matt.* v. 44.) The nature and functions of this court, or senate, which was highly celebrated in those ages and countries, must be learned from the Greek antiquaries; being far too complicated a subject for this publication.—The contemptuous neglect, and the interruption, which the apostle's admirable address met with from it, constrains the impartial enquirer to question, how far such a court, or council, deserved the encomiums so lavishly bestowed upon it.—*Strange things.* (20) Ξενιζοντα. 1 *Pet.* iv. 4. 12. Α ξενος, 18. 21.—*Spent their time.* (21) Ηυκαιρουν. *Mark* vi. 31. 1 *Cor.* xvi. 12. Ευκαιρος, *Mark* vi. 21. *Heb.* iv. 16.—*Some new thing.*] Τι καινοτερον. 19. *Matt.* ix. 17.

V. 22—25. The apostle being thus called on to declare his doctrine, and placed in a convenient situation for being heard by the senators, philosophers, and people, entered on his subject with very different views from those

Athens, [b] I perceive that in all things ye are too superstitious.

23 For as I passed by, and beheld your [c] devotions, I found an altar with this inscription, [d] TO THE UN-KNOWN GOD. Whom therefore ye [e] ignorantly worship, him declare I unto you.

24 God [f] that made the world, and all things therein, [g] seeing that he is Lord of heaven and earth, [h] dwelleth not in temples made with hands;

25 Neither [i] is worshipped with men's hands, as though he needed any thing, [k] seeing he giveth to all life, and breath, and all things;

26 And [l] hath made of one blood all nations of men for to dwell on all the face of the earth, [m] and hath determined the times before appointed, and the bounds of their habitation:

27 That [n] they should seek the Lord, if haply they might feel after him, and find him, though [o] he be not far from every one of us:

28 For [p] in him we live, and move, and have our being; [q] as certain also of your own poets have said, For [r] we are also his offspring.

29 Forasmuch then as we are the offspring of God, [s] we ought not to think that the Godhead is like unto gold, or silver, or stone, [t] graven by art and man's device.

of his curious auditors. He observed to them, that he perceived them to be in all things exceedingly addicted "to the fear of demons," or the worship of invisible beings. The word is ambiguous, and might be understood either as a commendation or a censure; and doubtless he chose it for that reason, to convey the implied censure, in the most inoffensive manner. Xenophon uses the word, when commending one as a religious man. The Athenians were indeed very religious in their way; but that was altogether superstitious and idolatrous. In surveying the city, and especially the temples, and the manner and objects of their worship, he had met with an altar inscribed "To the unknown God." (*Marg. and Marg. Ref.* b—d.) It is attested by many writers that there was such an altar: and some think, that, having imported the deities and worship of most other nations; they had erected this altar to the God of the Jews, who was always spoken of as invisible and incomprehensible, and whose names the Jews themselves scrupled to mention. Various other conjectures have been formed: but perhaps, after multiplying their deities to the utmost, some of them suspected, that there was one God superior to all their idols, of whom they yet had no knowledge; and therefore they prevailed to have an altar dedicated to him also. Either way it suited the apostle's purpose, to make this inscription the motto of his discourse; and he informed his learned audience, that he came to declare to them this "unknown God," of whom they confessed themselves ignorant, even while they professed to worship him. Indeed, he was the great Creator of heaven and earth, which neither existed from eternity, nor were produced by *chance*, or by *necessity*, as some of their philosophers had imagined; but were formed by the One living, self-existent, eternal, almighty God: and as he was the Proprietor and Governor of heaven and earth, he could not be supposed to inhabit temples, as their idols did; nor could he be served with the workmanship or oblations of men's hands, as if he wanted something to consummate his felicity: seeing he himself was the universal Bene-'actor, and the Source of being, life, breath, and all things

to all creatures; and they were on that account required to worship him and acknowledge their obligations to him, their dependence on him, and their grateful devoted subjection to him. (*Marg. Ref.* e—k.—*Note*, xiv. 11—18, vv. 15—17.)

Too superstitious. (22) Δεισιδαιμονεστερυς. Here only. Εκ δειδω, *timeo*, et δαιμων, *dæmon*, *numen*. Δεισιδαιμονια, xxv. 19.—*And beheld.* (23) Αναθεωρων. Heb. xiii. 7. Not elsewhere. '*Fixis oculis intueor et specto.*' Schleusner. Εκ ανα, et θεωρεω, *contemplor.*—*Devotions.*] Τα σεβασματα. 2 Thes. ii. 4. Not elsewhere. Α σεβαζομαι, *colo, veneror. Omnia quæ venerantur.—An altar.*] Βωμον. Here only.— *To the unknown.*] Αγνωςω. Here only. Γνωςος, Rom. i. 19. Αγνωσια. 1 Cor. xv. 34. 1 Pet. ii. 15.—*Ignorantly.*] Αγνοουντες. xiii. 27. 1 Tim. i. 13.

V. 26—29. This glorious God had formed the whole race of men of one family, in that one man and woman, from whom they were all descended; that they might dwell upon the face of the earth as brethren, without injuring each other: and neither blind chance, nor invincible necessity, but God, the sovereign Lord of all, had, in his infinite wisdom and justice, appointed the different ages of the world for the accomplishment of his predetermined counsels and decrees; and had allotted to every one the period in which he should live, and "the bounds of his "habitation." (*Marg. Ref.* l, m.—*Note, Deut.* xxxii. 9.) All this was intended to lead them to seek after him and his favour, and after the knowledge of his perfections, his works, his truth, and will, which was shewn to them in the visible creation: if by any means, in their present state of error and ignorance, they might grope after him, as men in the dark, and find him; without which all other science would be of no real value. (*Marg. Ref.* n.—*Notes, Rom.* i. 18—23. *Heb.* xi. 5, 6.) Yet the difficulty of knowing the true God did not arise from distance, or his unconcern about human affairs, as the Epicureans vainly supposed; but from very different causes : for in fact "he "was not far from every one" of them; as in him all lived, moved, and existed, and must perish without his upholding power. This even some of their own poets had allowed,

u alt. 16. Ps. l.
21. Rom. i. 28.
x iii. 19. xi. 19.
xx. 21. xxvi. 17
*20. Matt. iii.
2. iv. 17. Mark
vi. 12. Luke
xiii. 5. xv. 10.
xxiv. 47. Rom. ii. 4. 30 And *the times of this igno-rance God winked at; *but now com-mandeth all men every where to re-pent: 2 Cor. vii. 10. Eph. iv. 17, &c. v. 6.—8. Tit. ii. 11, 12. 1 Pet. i. 14, 15. iv. 3.

31 Because *he hath appointed a day, in the which he will judge the world in righteousness, by *that* man whom he hath ordained; *whereof* he hath *given assurance unto all *men*, y x. 42. Matt. xxv.
31, &c. John v.
22, 28. Rom. ii.
5, 16. xiv. 9, 10
1 Cor. iv. 5.
2 Cor. v 10.
2 Tim. iv. 1.
2 Pet. iii 7.
Jude 14, 15.
* Or, offered faith.

being in this matter far wiser than the philosophers: for one of them, (called Aratus,) had said, " We are also his " offspring," and others had expressed nearly the same sentiment. If then men were the offspring of God, the absurdity of representing the Deity himself, by gold, or silver, or stone, however exquisitely fashioned and carved, must be evident ; as nothing of this kind could do more than form an imperfect resemblance of man's exterior form, without at all representing even the functions of animal life, or the operations of his mind. (*Marg. Ref.* o—t.— *Notes, Ex.* xx. 4. *Is.* xliv. 9—20.)

Hath determined. (26) Ὁρισας. 31. .See on ii. 23.— *Before appointed.*] Προτεταγμενας. Here only. Ex προ, ante, et τασσω, constituo. See on xiii. 48.—*The bounds.*] Τας ὁροθεσιας. Here only : θεσις τε ὁρε, positio termini.— *Habitation.*] Κατοικιας. Here only. Κατοικησις, Mark v. 3. A κατοικεω, 24. Ex κατα, et οικος, domus.—*If haply they might feel after.* (27) Ει αρα γε ψηλαφησειαν. *Luke* xxiv. 39. *Heb.* xii. 18. 1 *John* i. 1.—*Poets.* (28) Ποιητων. Here only, in this sense.—" A doer ;" *Rom.* ii. 13. *Jam.* i. 23. 25. iv. 11.—*The Godhead.* (29) Το Θειον. Here only. Θειος, adj. 2 *Pet.* i. 3, 4. Θειοτης, *Rom.* i. 20. See on *John* x. 30.—*Graven.*] Χαραγματι. *Rev.* xiii. 16, 17. xiv. 9. 11. xv. 2. xvi. 2. xix. 20. xx. 4. A χαρασσω, sculpo.

V. 30, 31. God had indeed long borne with men's apostasy, ignorance, and idolatry: he had acted, as if he would not look upon their provocation, in giving his glory to abominable idols : and, while he continued his provi-dential kindness, he sent no prophets to the nations in general, to call them off from idolatry to the worship of his name. But " the times of this ignorance" were ex-piring ; and by his servants he now " commanded all men, " every where to repent" of their idolatry and all other sins, and not to attempt any excuse or vindication of their conduct. (*Marg. Ref.* u, x.)—This was a most bold de-mand on the self-wise and self-admiring stoicks ; and as opposite to their notions of virtue and of fatality, as to the epicurean sentiments of chance and pleasure.—The apostle further added, that though they should at present escape with impunity ; yet God had " appointed a day," when he would summon all the inhabitants of the earth to his tri-bunal, and judge them in perfect righteousness, rendering to every man according to his work. This he would do, by that extraordinary Person, " the Man Christ Jesus," who was constituted the universal Lord and Judge of the whole human race. Of this, God " had given" the fullest " assurance to all men," by raising him from the dead, which was proved by most unexceptionable testimony. (*Marg. Ref.* y, z.)—Thus far the apostle was permitted to proceed in *introducing* his subject; for much more he certainly intended to say, had not the latter end and pe-tulance of his audience constrained him to desist.—' Con-trast this address with the speculations of the Greek phi-losophers; with those of the Epicureans and the Stoicks 'n particular. In this contrast, it appears dignified, ra-tional, sublime. It asserts the Being and Unity of God ;

that he created the world, and all things in it ; his uni-versal providence ; the intimate relation of men, all over the world, to each other ; (though his hearers, the *Greeks,* had been accustomed to call the rest of mankind *bar-barians ;*) the palpable folly of idolatry, and its criminality, with calls to repentance : and it sets before them a future judgment, and a life beyond the grave : all this in the compass of a few verses, in which not a word seems re-dundant, yet nothing is defective! Whoever reflects on the endless mazes, in which these wise philosophers of Athens, and indeed all those of the ancient world, were wandering, on all these subjects, so awfully interesting ; and compares the solid rationality of the sentiments, here so simply proposed, with their vain but ostentatious wisdom, must be very much struck indeed.—Then with regard to *evidence.* They had nothing to offer, but ab-struse and bewildering reasonings, which were perfectly incomprehensible by the mass of mankind, and which brought home no effectual conviction to the mind of any one. All was among *them* without certainty, and without authority But the apostle was able to confirm his doc-trine, by arguments intelligible to all ; the conclusiveness of which human nature *feels,* and cannot but feel. He would have appealed to miracles, (particularly the resur-rection of Christ,) and to various other proofs ; but his tired audience refused to hear him out.'—The manner of the apostle likewise, in addressing these idolaters and phi-losophers who were strangers to the ancient scriptures, and his reasoning with them on such principles as they allowed or could not deny, should be compared with his addresses to the Jews, who professed to believe the scrip-tures, and with whom he argued on the ground of that profession. Christianity might indeed be established by proofs, wholly independent of the Old Testament : yet it called men to believe nothing, as actually accomplished, but what had been predicted, typified, or promised. Of this the inspired preachers never failed to avail themselves, in addressing the Jews ; both as a most conclusive proof that their doctrine was from God, in addition to all mira-cles and other internal and external evidences : and also, as peculiarly interesting to those who possessed, and professed to reverence, the sacred oracles. But to have brought proofs, from scripture, to idolatrous or philoso-phizing gentiles, would have been highly irrational : and St. Paul's example especially, in this particular, cannot be too carefully studied and copied by all, who are called to address infidels, or idolaters, or persons totally ignorant and careless in the concerns of religion.

Of this ignorance. (30) Της αγνοιας. iii. 17. *Eph.* iv. 18. 1 *Pet.* i. 14. See on 23.—*Winked at.*] Ὑπεριδων. Here only. Ex ὑπερ, et ειδω, video.—*Every where.*] Πανταχη. xxi. 28. xxiv. 3. xxviii. 22. *Mark* xvi. 20. *Luke* ix. 6. 1 *Cor.* iv. 17.—*Given assurance.* (31) Πιστιν παρασχων.— Πιστις, *Rom.* i. 17. Here used from the *ground* and *evi-dence,* on which faith rests in confidence. (*Note, Rom.* i. 17.) Παρασχων, xvi. 16. xix. 24. xxii. 2.—See *Marg.*

5 A 8

^a in that he hath raised him from the dead.

32 And when they heard of the resurrection of the dead, ^z some mocked: and others said, ^b We will hear thee again of this *matter*.

33 So Paul departed from among them.

34 Howbeit ^c certain men clave unto him, and believed: among the which *was* Dionysius ^d the Areopagite, and a woman named Damaris, and others with them.

V. 32—34. It is probable, that the Epicureans led the ridicule, by deriding "the resurrection of the dead," as an impossibility or absurdity: the rest of the company, however, found the apostle's doctrine too solemn, alarming, and practical, for their vain and curious minds; and therefore they declined hearing any more on such subjects, till another time. (*Marg. Ref.* a, b.—*Notes,* 19—21. xxiv. 24—27.) The apostle was indeed treated at Athens with more exterior civility, than in some other places: but none despised or neglected his doctrine with more supercilious indifference, than these speculating philosophers; and this, as it appears, proved the worst soil, in which he ever attempted to sow " the good seed of the kingdom." Yet even here grace triumphed over the prejudices of one senator, and a woman of considerable note, with a few others; who believed the gospel, and further attended on the apostle for instructions: but there is no proof or intimation, that a church was founded at Athens. (*Marg. Ref.* c, d.)

Mocked. (32) Εχλευαζον. See on ii. 13.

PRACTICAL OBSERVATIONS.

V. 1—9.

It is most evident from this history, that the zealous servants of Christ must be despised and hated, by all kinds of unconverted persons for his sake. Nothing, however, shall in any wise hurt them; and nothing should dismay them, or deter them from publishing the glad tidings of salvation.—We ought to " reason " with our hearers, and to prove our doctrines with conclusive arguments; and not merely to address their imaginations and affections: but our reasonings should be deduced from the word of God, or grounded on it, or suited to call men's attention to it; otherwise we shall lose ourselves in empty speculations, or go beyond our depth. But when we clearly open and explain the scriptures, and support our conclusions by testimonies of holy writ; when we thus evidently lay before men those truths, which relate to the person, sufferings, resurrection, and kingdom of Jesus Christ; and then apply these subjects to their hearts and consciences, by pathetick addresses, warnings, and persuasions; we use the proper means of bringing them to " the obedience " of faith," and may expect to see our labours blessed to many souls.—But how strange is it, that men should grudge and envy others, those privileges, of which they will not themselves accept! and that zeal for religious creeds or systems should induce them " to take to them-" selves wicked men of the baser sort," to set cities in an uproar, to assault and destroy men's houses, and to lay wait for their lives! Such proceedings disgrace and betray every cause which they are brought to support: and the friends of truth and piety must mourn and lament, if any of their professed associates, take weapons of this kind

from the enemies of God and his people, and use them to their annoyance. Mobs are always incompetent judges of liberty and privileges: and how egregiously absurd is it, for them and their leaders, to exclaim against others, as disturbers of the peace and order of the community!— Indeed the gospel is intended, in a certain sense, " to turn " the world upside down: " for sin and Satan have inverted the right order of things; and when the kingdom of God is established in the hearts of men, an entire revolution takes place, in their judgment, maxims, affections, conduct, and conversation. (*Note,* 2 *Cor.* v. 17.) In this respect we should all desire and endeavour " to turn the " world upside down; " and should pray that ministers may be sent to every part of the earth, whom the Lord will employ in effecting this blessed revolution among men.—But the kingdom of Christ it not of this world: and his most faithful servants will be the most peaceable subjects to that authority, which Providence places over them; they will be ready to obey the decrees of Cæsar, unless he command them to break the laws of their other and more exalted " King," even " Jesus " " the Prince of " the kings of the earth; " and then they will meekly endure persecution for conscience' sake. In general, they will leave it to the children of this world, to contend about civil liberties and immunities; except when called on to perform a constitutional duty as members of the community, or when required to act in a publick station. So that neither rulers nor people need be troubled, at the increase of real Christians: though many turbulent spirits, making religion the pretext, will ambitiously join in faction and rebellion, and thus bring a disgrace upon the gospel. Of such we should beware; from such we should withdraw; that we may give all reasonable *security* for our good behaviour in civil society, while we claim the undoubted right of worshipping God according to our consciences.

V. 10—15.

True dignity and nobleness of spirit greatly consist in an enlarged and unprejudiced mind, open to conviction, willing to investigate the truth, to examine the evidence adduced in support of men's opinions, and to treat religious enquiries with candour, seriousness, and diligence. Such an ingenuous and teachable disposition comes from above: (*P. O. Jam.* i. 9—18, *vv.* 16—18. iii. 13—18 :) those who possess it cautiously avoid a blind credulity, an obstinate bigotry, and a heedless conceited incredulity: they receive the word of sober teachers " with all readi-" ness of mind ; " and, knowing their need of divine instruction, they " daily search the scriptures, to see whe-" ther things be so, or not : " impartiality, humility, and industry combine in their researches, and the truth requires no more. Men of this character will gradually rectify their mistakes, obtain solutions of their difficulties,

CHAP. XVIII.

Paul goes to Corinth, meets with Aquila and Priscilla; works with them as a tent-maker; and preaches, first to the Jews, 1—5; and, when they opposed and blasphemed, to the Gentiles with more success, 6—8. Encouraged by a vision, he remains there a long time,

9—11. The Jews bring him before Gallio, the pro consul, who refuses to attend to such questions, 12—17. Paul returns by Ephesus to Jerusalem, goes from. thence to Antioch, and revisits the churches which he had planted, 18—23. Apollos preaches at Ephesus. and being more fully instructed by Aquila and Priscilla, he goes to Achaia, where he labours very successfully, 24—28.

find answers to their objections, and be led into a solid understanding and firm belief of the gospel. (*Notes, Hos.* vi. 1—3, v. 3. *John* i. 47—51. vii. 14—17.) And when this "noble" disposition is found in those, who are also honourable in society, it forms a distinction peculiarly valuable and useful. But nothing can be more ignoble and base, than bigotry and persecution ; and many, who appeared devout in their way, have in every age and place, been most inveterate against the truth, and most active in stirring up others to oppose it.

V. 16—21.

The spiritual mind, however ingenious or cultivated, can take little delight in contemplating the most admired productions of science and genius, while it observes, that the persons concerned are wholly enslaved to sin, or given up to impiety and infidelity.—Not only do unlettered savages "sit in darkness, and the region and shadow of "death," but even those cities and persons, that are most renowned for civilization and science, are often enveloped in the deepest ignorance, in the things of God and eternity. Indeed, none are more childish in their superstitions, more impious in their speculations, or more credulous of absurd impostures, than some of the most eminent persons for genius and learning have been and are. Thus "God hath made foolish the wisdom of this world :" he has "taken the wise in their own craftiness ;" and has made way for the display of his glory, in saving sinners "by the foolishness of preaching." (*Notes,* 1 *Cor.* i. 17 —31.) The consideration of the state of the world, both wise and unwise, should deeply affect our hearts ; while we avow our belief of the sacred scriptures, and contend for the doctrines revealed in them. Yet, if in "the meek- "ness of wisdom," we should venture to start such topicks "as Jesus and the resurrection," either in the busy resorts of commerce, in the courts of justice, in the schools of the philosophers, or in polite company, even in this Christian land ; numbers would frown, deride, or exclaim : while Epicureans, and Stoicks, and speculators of jarring tenets, would unite in "encountering" us with their arguments, or shewing their contempt of us, as vain babblers, or as innovators in religion. And should any seem to pay a more respectful and civil attention to our discourse ; it would probably be in order to gratify a vain curiosity, and to hear 'the new doctrine,' as they would call it. For though the truths of the gospel are, in some respects, as old as the fall of man ; yet they are often "strange things" in the ears even of the learned : and they, whose lives have been almost entirely spent in studying, hearing, or telling "some new thing," are frequently totally unacquainted with "the good old way" to heaven ; and talk about it in the most obscure and perplexed manner. Indeed, every thing is *new* to him, who has never heard it

before ; as the letters of the alphabet are to children, when first taught to read : thus men's deep *ignorance* is the real cause, why the gospel is stigmatized by them as "a new "doctrine !" But modern speculators seldom shew so much respect to the preachers of the gospel, as the Athenians did to Paul ; for they are aware that the doctrine of the cross will afford little gratification to curiosity and vain-glory ; and that conclusions may be drawn from it, very inimical to their carnal pursuits and sinful lives.

V. 22—29.

In addressing mankind about their souls and eternal salvation, or its awful reverse, we should study their peculiar dispositions and opinions ; and enquire what truths they admit, and what errors they maintain. Thus we may be able to combat them, from their own principles, and gradually point out the absurdity of their tenets, and the inconsistency of their conduct : and we may often graft the truth on such sentiments as they allow.—Alas ! how many are there to this day, who have their devotions and superstitions, and are exceedingly zealous for them ; yet the great Object of all worship is to them "an unknown "God !"—They are not acquainted with the mysterious manner of his subsistence, the glory and harmony of his perfections, or the way in which he will be approached and served. If such men allow the truth of the scriptures, we may reason with them from those sacred oracles : otherwise, we should lead them, from self-evident principles, or such as admit of the most obvious proof, to see their need of a revelation, to attend to the evidences of its divine original, and to the beneficial tendency of the things contained in it. Thus we may declare unto them "that "God whom they ignorantly worship ;" and gradually lead them, from the works of creation to the great Creator ; and from his providential care and bounty, to their obligations to love and worship him, and their criminality in ungratefully neglecting him. From a view of his perfections and authority as the great Proprietor and Lord of all, we may expose the vanity of superstition and idolatry : and of all mere outward forms, oblations, and services, by which men have sought to recommend themselves to God ; as if they could benefit him, "who giveth to all life, and "breath, and all things." We may also infer, that the end and design of God in our creation, and of all his appointments towards us, and of our special advantages, is, to lead us to seek and serve him "in spirit and truth," that we may find him, and true happiness in his favour. Hence we may shew how men grope in the dark, and proceed amidst bewildering doubts and uncertainties, in this most important matter, though the Lord is near unto us, and "we live, move, and exist in him ;" and thus prove their need of his word and Spirit, to lead them into a spiritual acquaintance with him. From the rational na-

5 B 2

CORINTH.

Acts xviii. 1—18.

^a xvii. 32, 33
^b xix. 1. 1 Cor. i. 2 Cor. i. 23. 2 Tim. iv. 20.

AFTER these things, Paul ^a departed from Athens, and came to ^b Corinth ;

^c 26. Rom. xvi. 3.
^d 1 Cor. xvi. 19. 2 Tim. iv. 19.
^d ii. 9. 1 Pet. i. 1.
^e xi. 26.

2 And found a certain Jew, named ^c Aquila, born in ^d Pontus, lately come from Italy with his wife Priscilla, (because that ^e Claudius had commanded all Jews to depart from Rome,) and came unto them.

^f xx. 34, 35. 1 Cor. iv. 12. 1 Cor. ix. 6—12. 2 Cor. xi. 9. 1 Thes. ii. 9. 2 Thes. iii. 8, 9.
^g xiii. 14, &c. xiv. 1. xvii. 1—3, 11. 17. xix. 8. Luke iv. 16.

3 And because he was of the same craft, he abode with them, ^f and wrought : for by their occupation they were tent-makers.

4 And ^g he reasoned in the synagogue every sabbath, and ^h persuaded the Jews and the Greeks.

5 And when ⁱ Silas and Timotheus were come from Macedonia, Paul ^k was pressed in the spirit, ^l and testified to the Jews, that Jesus ^a was Christ.

6 And when ^m they opposed themselves, and blasphemed, ⁿ he shook his raiment, and said unto them, ^o Your blood be upon your own heads ; I am clean : ^p from henceforth I will go unto the Gentiles.

^h 13. xiii. 43. xix. 26. xxvi. 28. xxvii. 23. Gen. ix. 27. marg.
ⁱ Chr. xxxii. 11. Luke xvi. 31. 2 Cor. v. 11.
^k xvii. 14, 16. 1 Thes. iii. 2.
^l xvii. 3. xx. xvii. 16. Job xxxiii. 18— 20. Jer. vi. 11.
^m xx. 9. Ex. iii. 14.
ⁿ Mic. iii. 8. Luke xii. 50.
^o 2 Cor. v. 14.
Phil. i. 24. Gr. 28. ii. 36. lx. 22.
x. 42. xvii. 3.
xx. 21. John xv. 27. 1 Pet. v. 13.
Or, is the Christ. Dan. ix. 25, 26.
John i. 41. iii. 28. x. 24.

^m xiii. 45. xix. 9. xxvi. 11. Luke xxii. 65. 1 Thes. ii. 14—16. Jam. ii. 6, 7. 1 Pet. iv. 4, 14. xxii. 51. Neh. v. 13. Matt. x. 14. Luke iv. 5. x. 10, 11. o xx. 26, 27. Lev. xx. 9. 11, 12. 2 Sam. i. 16. Ez. iii. 18, 19. xviii. 13. xxxiii. 4. 6, 9. 1 Tim. v. 22. x xiii. 46, 47. xxx. 9, 10. xxvi. 20. xxvii. 28. Matt. viii. 11. xxi. 43. xxii. 10. Rom. iii. 29. ix. 25, 26. 30—33. x. 12, 13. xi. 11—15.

ture of man, who is in this respect " the offspring," and bears the image of God, we may infer the absurdity of many established customs and sentiments, which degrade the infinite God even beneath the level of his creatures. Sometimes we may produce the testimony of poets and prophets of their own, in confirmation of our sentiments : and if a man have acquired classical learning and general knowledge, he may thus make a good use of them ; yet it is scarcely advisable for those, who are intended for the ministry, to spend any very great proportion of their valuable time, about those indecent fables and corrupt principles and practices, which must engross much attention, from those who aspire to proficiency in this kind of learning.

V. 30—34.

Notwithstanding all the renown of Athens, and of ancient Greece, God deemed those " the times" and places " of ignorance :" and though he connived at the dishonour there put upon him, yet he did not excuse the impiety and iniquity of the inhabitants. He commanded them, yea, he commands us, and " all men every where to repent :" nor will any proud pretensions to virtue, or vain reasonings about necessity or contingence, or any philosophical or theological system, excuse men in neglecting this call. All men every where need repentance, and must perish without it : all, who repent and believe the gospel will be saved ; and this is every man's duty, though no one is disposed to perform it without the grace of God. (Notes, Luke xiii. 1—5.) But the sins, committed in the time of a man's ignorance, will be far less severely punished, than those which are perpetrated, in defiance and contempt of the light of the gospel.—In calling men to repentance, we should always direct their attention to that " appointed " day, when God will judge the world in righteousness ; " and to Jesus and his authority, salvation, death, and resurrection : and whatever introduction we use, all our discourses must lead to him, and centre in him.—But even the most consummate wisdom and address, united with the purest zeal and simplicity, in the teacher, will often leave the hearers under the deeper condemnation. Some reject the word with supercilious contempt and mockery ; and others from indolence, levity, and procrastination. Of all subjects, that gains the least attention which deserves the most : men profess an intention some time to

hear it again ; but this time never arrives to numbers. It shall, however, be brought to their remembrance at the great tribunal, to seal their condemnation.—No persons are more likely to fall into these snares of Satan, than self-conceited scholars, and scoffing scepticks and infidels. But " if they scorn, they alone must bear it." The minister must be satisfied with having faithfully delivered his message ; nay, even if he be interrupted by the petulance of despisers, before he can conclude his subject. The word of God, however, will never be absolutely useless : some Athenians, and some senators, as well as others, " will cleave to the Lord" and his faithful servants ; and these may be useful to others in due time. So that we should go on with our labours, in patience and hope, " whether men will hear, or whether they will forbear."

NOTES.

CHAP. XVIII. V. 1—6. The apostle seems to have had so little prospect of success at Athens, that he left it as soon as he well could : though it does not appear, that he was in any degree persecuted. Accordingly, he went to Corinth, in Achaia, (within the peninsula called Peloponnesus,) a city remarkable for opulence, elegance, luxury, and licentiousness. Here he met with Aquila, a Jew, who was a native of Pontus in Asia, but had resided for some time at Rome, where it is probable, that he was converted to Christianity, with his wife Priscilla. They had, however, lately been expelled from that city, as Jews, by the edict of the Roman emperor ; who was induced to treat all of that nation, as seditious and dangerous persons. Some think that the preaching about this time at Rome, that Jesus was the promised Messiah, and " the King of Israel," gave occasion to this severity : but this is very uncertain. (Marg. Ref. a—e.)—Paul, however, being acquainted with the character of these two excellent persons, went to lodge with them ; and, having in his youth learned their trade of making tents, which were much used in those warm climates, he wrought at it for his livelihood.—It was an excellent custom in those days, for such persons as received a liberal education, to be also instructed in some mechanical trade : this served them as an amusement in prosperity, and was a certain resource in case all other prospects failed.—Whatever assistance Paul received from the churches at Antioch, or Philippi, or other cities ; he was

7 And he departed thence, and entered into a certain *man's* house, named q Justus, *one* that r worshipped God, whose house joined hard to the synagogue.

8 And s Crispus, t the chief ruler of the synagogue, u believed on the Lord, with all his house: and many of the Corinthians x hearing, believed, and were baptized.

9 ¶ Then y spake the Lord to Paul in the night by a vision, z Be not afraid, but speak, and hold not thy peace:

10 For a I am with thee, b and no man shall set on thee to hurt thee; c for I have much people in this city.

11 And d he e continued *there* a year and six months, teaching the word of God among them.

Marginal references (left): q Col. iv. 11 ; r x. 2. 22. xiii. 42. xvi. 14. xvii. 4. t 1 Cor. i. 14. † 17. xiii. 15. Mark v. 35. u x. 2. xvi. 14. 15. 34. Gen. xvii. 27. xviii. 19. Josh. xxiv. 15. x x. 43. 37—41. viii. 12. 35—38. Matt. xxviii. 19. Mark xvi. 15, 16. Rom. x. 14—17. 1 Cor. i. 13—17.

Marginal references (right): y xvi. 9. xxii. 18. xxiii. 11. xxvii. 23—25. 2 Cor. xii. 1— z Is. lviii. 1. Jer. i. 17. Ez. ii. 6— 8. iii. 9—11. Jon. iii. 2. Mic. iii. 8. Eph. vi. 19, 20. 1 Thes. ii. 2. a Ex. iv. 12. Josh. i. 5. 9. Judg. ii. 18. Is. viii. 10. xli. 10. xliii. 2. Jer. i. 18, 19. Matt. i. 23. xxviii. 20. 2 Cor. xii. 9. 2 Tim. iv. — b Is. liv. 17. Jer. xv. 20, 21. Matt. x. 30. Luke xxi. 18. c xv. 14. 18. John x. 16. xi. 52. Rom. x. 20, 21. 1 Cor. vi. 9—11. d xiv. 3. xix. 10. xx. 31. * Gr. *sat there.*

17. 22.   10. xx. 31.

---

often reduced to great necessity, by the expenses of his journeys: and we learn from many intimations in his writings, that he frequently wrought with his own hands for his subsistence, lest he should be chargeable to his converts. (*Marg. Ref.* f.—*Notes,* xx. 32—35. 1 Cor. iv. 9—13. 1 Thes. iv. 9—12. 2 Thes. iii. 6—9.)—On the sabbath-days, however, as usual, " he reasoned " with the Jews at Corinth in the synagogue, concerning the kingdom and salvation of Christ; and endeavoured to " persuade " both them, and the Gentiles who joined in their worship, to believe in Jesus as the Messiah. But when Silas (who perhaps had staid some time at Berea,) and Timothy were come to him, to confirm his testimony, and most solemnly to obtest, that Jesus was indeed the predicted Messiah ; he was inwardly excited by the Holy Spirit to still greater vehemence of mind, in bearing testimony to his Lord: and when the Jews opposed his doctrine, and even blasphemed the name of Jesus, " he shook his raiment " as renouncing all fellowship with them : and, to add emphasis to his warnings, he declared, that they were likely to perish in their sins by their own default, as murderers of their own souls; but that he, having faithfully delivered his message, was pure from the guilt of their ruin; and would therefore go and preach the gospel to the Gentiles. (*Marg. Ref.* g—i. 1—p.—*Notes,* xiii. 49—52. xx. 25 —27. Ez. iii. 17, 18. xxxiii. 2—9. 1 Tim. v. 21, 22.) —*Pressed in spirit.* (5) ' Either his own, or the Holy ' Spirit, so powerfully urged and constrained him, that he ' could not refrain from speaking.' *Whitby.* It is not to be supposed, that the apostle was excited, or constrained, by a vehemence of natural temper, to act improperly on this occasion : and if the ardour of his own spirit was holy, no doubt it was excited by the Holy Spirit. On the other hand, how can it be supposed, that the Holy Spirit urged and constrained him, except by exciting and invigorating holy affections in his heart ? (*Marg. Ref.* k.—*Notes,* Jer. xx. 7—9. Ez. iii. 12—15. 2 Cor. v. 13—15.)—*He shook his raiment.* (6) ' The command of our Saviour was, " to " shake off the dust from their feet ; " and so Paul and ' Barnabas do : (xiii. 51 :) but here Paul also shakes it off ' from his raiment, as a testimony unto them, that he had ' now renounced any further dealings with them : adding ' that now their blood would be upon their own heads, ' that is, they only would be guilty of it. (xx. 26. Matt. ' xxvii. 24, 25.) ' *Whitby.*

Departed. (1) Χωρισθεις. 2. See on Matt. xix. 6.— *Lately.* (2) Προσφατως. Here only. Προσφατος, Heb. x. 20.—*Had commanded.*] Διατεταχεναι. vii. 44. xxiii. 31. xxiv. 23. Matt. xi. 1. Ex δια, et τασσω. See on xiii. 48.

—*Of the same craft.* (3) 'Ομοτεχνον. Here only. Ex ὁμος, *similis,* et τεχνη, *ars.*—*Tent-makers.*] Σκηνοποιοι. Here only. Ex σκηνη, *tentorium,* et ποιεω, *facio.*—*He was pressed.* (5) Συνειχετο. vii. 57. xxviii. 8. See on Luke xii. 50.—*Testifying.*] Διαμαρθυρομενος. See on ii. 40.—*When they opposed themselves.* (6) Αντιτασσομενων δε αυτων. Rom. xiii. 2. Jam. iv. 6. v. 6. 1 Pet. v. 5. Ex αντι, *contra,* et τασσω, *dispono.*—*Prov.* iii. 34. *Sept.*—*He shook.*] Εκλιναξαμενος. xiii. 51. Matt. x. 14. Mark vi. 11. Ex εκ, et τινασσω, *quatio.*

V. 7, 8. It is probable, that the apostle continued to lodge and work with Aquila and Priscilla : though he no more preached in the synagogue ; but used the house of a Gentile, who had renounced idolatry before his conversion to Christianity, and perhaps had been circumcised. This circumstance might tend to give the Jews, who desired it, an opportunity of still attending his preaching. Indeed several of them had already embraced the gospel ; especially the chief ruler of the synagogue, with all his family: and many afterwards were converted, and received into the church by baptism, both of the Jews and Gentiles. (*Marg. Ref.*— *Note,* 1 Cor. i. 10—16.)

Joined hard.] Ην συνομορυσα. Here only. ' Ex συν ' et ὁμορος, *confinis, conterminus :* Hocque ex ὁμυ, *una,* et ὁρος, ' *terminus.*' Schleusner.

V. 9—11. The apostle at this time seems to have been greatly discouraged in respect of his ministry, by the virulent enmity of the Jews, and the dissolute character of the Gentiles ; and especially by a consciousness of his own insufficiency, and manifold infirmities. (*Notes,* 1 Cor. ii. 3—5. 2 Cor. x. 7—11. xii. 7—10. Gal. iv. 12—16.) The Lord Jesus, therefore, condescended to appear to him in vision, to obviate his fears, to embolden him in his labours, to assure him of his protecting presence, and to inform him that he had " much people in that city." (*Marg. Ref.* y—c.—*Notes,* xxiii. 11. xxvii. 20—26.) In this he evidently spake of those, who were *his* by election, the gift of the Father, and the purchase of his atonement, though at that time in an unconverted state ; (*Notes,* John vi. 36—40. x. 14—18. xi. 49—53 ;) and what sort of persons these at Corinth then were, the apostle has in another place informed us. (1 Cor. vi. 9—11.)—Thus encouraged, he fixed his abode at Corinth for a year and a half, during which time he planted a very numerous and flourishing church. (*Marg.* and *Marg. Ref.* d.)—*People,* &c. (10) ' So they are called, who are still heathens, not because of ' any absolute decree of their election to eternal life ; but ' because Christ saw that they were *disposed* to believe, ' and by faith become his people ; as elsewhere (*John* x.

5 D 4

f xiii. 7. 12.
f 27. Rom. xv. 26.
xvi. 5. 1 Cor.
l. l. ix. 2. xi. 10.
1 Thes. l. 7, 8.
g xiii. 50. xiv. 2,
19. xvii. 5. 13.
xxi. 27, &c.
h 16, 17. xxv. 10.
John xix. 13.
Matt. xxvii. 19.
Jam. ii. 6.
i 4. vi. 13. xxi.
24. xxiv. 5, 6.
xxv. 8.
k xxi. 39, 40. xxii.
l. 2. xxvi. 1, 2.
Luke xxi. 12—
15. 1 Pet. iii. 14.
15.
l xxiii. 27—29.
xxv. 18—20. 26.

12 ¶ And when Gallio was 'the deputy of 'Achaia, 'the Jews made insurrection with one accord against 'Paul, and brought him to 'the judgment-seat,

13 Saying, 'This *fellow* persuadeth men to worship God contrary to the law.

14 And 'when Paul was now about to open *his* mouth, Gallio said unto the Jews, 'If it were a matter of wrong

or wicked lewdness, O *ye* Jews, reason would that I should 'bear with you:

15 But if it be 'a question of words and names, and *of* your law, 'look ye to it; 'for I will be no judge of such matters.

16 And 'he drave them from the judgment-seat.

17 Then all the Greeks took 'Sosthenes 'the chief ruler of the synagogue, and beat *him* before the judg-

m xiii. 18. Mark
ix. 19. 2 Cor.
xi. 1. 4 Heb. v.
2.
n xxvi. 3. 1 Tim.
l. 4. vi. 4. 2 Tim.
2.
o xxiii. 29.
l. 29. Tit. iii. 9.
p Matt. xxvii. 4.
24.
p xxiv. 6—8. John
xvii. 31.
q Ps. lxxvi. 10.
Rom. xiii. 3, 4.
Rev. xii. 16.
r 1 Cor. i. 1.
s 1 Cor. i. 1. &

' 16) he calls those his sheep who should hereafter believe ' in him.' *Whitby.* Thus, in opposing the doctrine of God's decrees, and predestination, the original depravity and carnal enmity of the human heart, and the necessity of regeneration, are virtually denied, or at best, totally lost sight of. " Except a man be born again, he cannot " see the kingdom of God."—" God who is rich in mercy, " for his great love, wherewith he loved us, even when we " were dead in sins, hath quickened us together with " Christ; by grace are ye saved." (*Notes,* xiii. 42—48, v. 48. *John* iii. 3—8. *Eph.* ii. 4—10. *Tit.* iii. 3—7.)—Were such persons as the idolatrous licentious Corinthians *disposed* of themselves, independently of divine grace ' pre-' venting them,' to embrace the humbling pure gospel of Christ; and to change their jovial and sensual rites, for the spiritual worship of the heart-searching holy God? Does this doctrine accord with the ninth and tenth articles of our church? And would it not have been called *Pelagian,* before the term *Arminian* was known?

V. 12—17. Gallio is supposed to have been the brother of Seneca, the renowned pagan moralist; and he bears a fair character in history.—As the Jews were allowed the free exercise of their religion at Corinth, they supposed that he would exert his authority against those, who innovated on their ancient customs: they therefore tumultuously seized on Paul, and dragged him to the Roman tribunal; and, with much contempt, accused him of inducing men to worship God, in a manner contrary to their law. But when the apostle was about to plead his own cause, and to embrace the opportunity of declaring the gospel before Gallio; that magistrate refused to take any cognizance of such matters. He declared, that if any person had been defrauded or oppressed, or if any mischievous licentiousness had been committed; it would have been reasonable for him to attend to the fact, notwithstanding the irregularity and clamour of their proceedings: but, as their dispute related only to their religious peculiarities, the names of Jesus, and the Messiah, or the obligations of the Mosaick law, on all that worshipped the God of the Jews; they should decide for themselves, for he would not trouble himself about such subjects. With this answer he dismissed them, and ordered them away from the judgment-seat, with apparent sternness. And when the Greeks violently assaulted and beat Sosthenes, even in Gallio's presence, he took no cognizance of this breach of the peace, for he " cared for none of those " things."—It is not agreed who Sosthenes was: some think that he was the same person as Crispus, before men-

tioned (8); others, that he succeeded him as chief ruler of the synagogue, when Crispus embraced Christianity. Some think that he was the leading person in the prosecution of Paul, and that he was contemptuously and cruelly treated by those Greeks, who favoured the apostle: others conjecture, that he was a Christian, and that the Jews excited the Greeks to abuse him, when they could not prevail to wreak their malice on Paul. We afterwards read of Sosthenes, among the apostle's chief friends: (1 *Cor.* i. 1 :) if this was the same person, as it is probable from the manner in which Luke mentions him; the latter opinion is favoured by it: for the conversion of a leading persecutor would scarcely have been passed over in silence.— The Alexandrian manuscripts and some ancient versions read *Jews,* instead of *Greeks;* and it has been conjectured that παντες (*they all*), was the original reading, and that some transcribers took the liberty of inserting *Greeks,* and others *Jews,* in the copies which they wrote. This indeed would remove the difficulty, and clearly shew that Sosthenes was a christian; but the authority for the alteration, is scarcely sufficient to warrant the conclusion. See *Paley's Horæ Paulinæ.*—Gallio's conduct in this transaction has been considered in very different lights; some having severely condemned it, and others having highly approved it. Doubtless he acted properly, in refusing, *as a magistrate,* to give any assistance to persecutors, or to interfere with the determination of religious controversies: but there evidently was a contemptuous disregard of all such topicks, as wholly unworthy of his notice: he probably deemed both Jews and Christians to be ignorant and deluded fanaticks; and concluded that it was of no consequence who was right or wrong, in disputes of this nature. A mixture of philosophical scepticism, and of political contempt of religious concerns, compared with affairs of state, seems to have influenced his conduct. (*Notes,* xxiii. 25—30. xxv. 19. xxvi. 24—32.) As he would not use his authority against Paul; so he would not protect Sosthenes, or punish the injury done to him: and the historian evidently blames him, because, " he cared for none of these things."— ' This profane man thought this a controversy rather of ' words than of things; and considered the dóctrine of ' God as vain words.' *Beza.*

Was the deputy. (12) Ανθυπατευοντος.—Here only.— See on xiii. 7.—' Dr. Lardner justly observes, …that this ' is another instance of the exact propriety with which St. ' Luke expresses himself. For, though the province of ' Achaia, which comprehended all the rest of Greece, had ' a more various fortune than that of Cyprus, and fre-

ment-seat: ' and Gallio cared for none of those things.

18 ¶ And Paul *after this* tarried *there* yet a good while, and then took his leave of the brethren, and sailed thence into " Syria, and with him * Priscilla and Aquila, ' having shorn *his* head in * Cenchrea: for he had a vow.

19 And he came to * Ephesus and left them there: ᵇ but he himself entered into the synagogue, and reasoned with the Jews.

20 When they desired *him* to tarry longer time with them, ᶜ he consented not;

21 But ᵈ bade them farewell, saying, *I must by all means keep this feast that cometh in Jerusalem : but I will return again unto you, ᶠ if God will. And he sailed from Ephesus.

22 And when he had landed at ᵍ Cæsarea, and ʰ gone up, and saluted ' the church, ᵏ he went down to Antioch.

23 And after he had spent some time *there*, he departed, and went over *all* ' the country of Galatia and Phrygia in order, ᵐ strengthening all the disciples.

24 ¶ And a certain Jew named * Apollos, born at * Alexandria, ᵖ an eloquent man, *and* ᑫ mighty in the scriptures, came to Ephesus.

25 This man was ' instructed in the way of the Lord; and, being ˢ fervent in the spirit, he spake and taught diligently the things of the Lord, ᵗ knowing only the baptism of John.

26 And he began ᵘ to speak boldly in the synagogue: whom when * Aquila

he purposed, for reasons which are not here specified, to be at Jerusalem at the ensuing passover: but he promised to return to them, if the Lord would permit him. (*Marg. Ref.* a—f.—*Note, Jam.* iv. 13—17.)—The voyage and circuit here briefly stated must have taken up a long time: yet they are related in very few words; which shews, that the design of the narrative is not so much to gratify curiosity, as to give an instructive specimen of the manner, in which Christianity was at first propagated. The travels, labours, and success of the apostle also were far greater, than a superficial reader would suppose; for the events of years, and the conversion of thousands, are sometimes recorded in a few verses. The apostle sailed from Ephesus to Cæsarea ; from thence he travelled by land to Jerusalem : (*Note*, xxiii. 23, 24:) and having shewn his affection and respect to the Christians there, and finished the business which he had in view, he went down thence to Antioch in Syria. After a while, he set out a third time from that city, to preach the gospel in Asia Minor ; and so he passed again through the several cities and regions, where churches had before been planted : among the rest, through the churches of Galatia, (*Note*, xvi. 6—12,) encouraging and animating the disciples, regulating their affairs, and doubtless making numerous converts. (*Marg. Ref.* g—l.)

Took his leave. (18) Αποταξαμενος. 21. See on *Mark* vi. 46.—*Sailed.*] Εξεπλει. xv. 39. xx. 6. Not elsewhere.— *Having shaved.*] Κειραμενος. viii. 32. 1 *Cor.* xi. 6. Not elsewhere.—*He consented not.* (20) Ουκ επενευσεν. Here only. Ex επι, et νευω, *nuto, assentior.*—*I will return.* (21) Ανακαμψω. *Matt.* ii. 12. *Luke* x. 6. *Heb.* xi. 15. Ex ανα et καμπτω, *flecto, Rom.* xi. 4. xiv. 11.

V. 24—28. While Paul was making the extensive circuit above stated, Apollos, a native of Alexandria in Egypt, a person of a ready and graceful elocution, and of great acquaintance with the scriptures of the Old Testament, arrived at Ephesus. (*Marg. Ref.* n—q.—*Note*, 1 *Cor.* xvi. 12.) He had acquired some knowledge of the way of salva-

---

' quently changed its form of government; yet A. D. 44, ' (which is generally supposed to have been about eight ' years before this event,) it was restored to the senate, ' and so became proconsular.' *Doddridge.—Persuadeth.* (13) Αναπειθει. Here only. Ex ανα, et πειθω, *suadeo.— Lewdness.* (14) 'Ραδιουργημα. Here only.—'*Admodum* ' grave scelus.' Schleusner. 'Ραδιουργια' See on xiii. 10. —*I should bear.*] Ηνεσχομην. See on *Matt.* xvii. 14. —*Gallio cared for none of those things.* (17) Ουδεν τωτων τω Γαλλιωνι εμελεν. " None of these things was any con- " cern to Gallio." *Mark* iv. 38. Gr.

V. 18—23. Notwithstanding the tumultuous enmity of the Jews, the Lord Jesus continued to protect his servant, while he abode a considerable time longer at Corinth. (*Note, Rom.* xvi. 1, 2.)—At length, however, he took a pious and affectionate farewell of the new converts, and set sail for Syria ; being accompanied by Aquila and Priscilla, who intended to settle for a time at Ephesus. But before he embarked, he cut off his hair at Cenchrea, the port of Corinth, on account of a vow which he had taken, respecting some of his multiplied deliverances. (*Marg. Ref.* u. y.) Probably, this was of the nature of the Nazarite's vow : but when the distance prevented a person from going to Jerusalem, at the expiration of the term ; it seems, that he was customarily dispensed with, in cutting off his hair in another place, and not at the sanctuary. Perhaps some casual defilement made it necessary for the apostle to cut off his hair, and begin again the appointed term : and being at so great a distance, it might be judged allowable to do this at Cenchrea ; and to offer the required sacrifices when he came to the temple. It is not indeed recorded, that he did offer them ; but this by no means proves that he did not. (*Note, Num.* vi.)—When the apostle arrived at Ephesus, where he left his friends Aquila and Priscilla ; he took the opportunity of setting before the Jews, in that city, the substance and evidences of his doctrine : yet he would not be prevailed upon to stay longer with them ; as

and Priscilla had heard, they took him unto them, and ᵗ expounded unto him the way of God more perfectly.

27 And when he was disposed to pass into Achaia, ᵘ the brethren wrote, ˣ exhorting the disciples to receive him:

who when he was come, ᵇ helped them much which had ᶜ believed through grace:

28 For he mightily ᵈ convinced the Jews, *and that* publickly, shewing by the scriptures that Jesus ᵉ was Christ.

---

tion, by faith in the Messiah; as far as it could be learned from the ministry of John the Baptist, and his testimony to Jesus, whom he pointed out, as "the Lamb of God," "the Son of God," the "Bridegroom of the church," and the promised Messiah. (*Marg. Ref.* r—t.—*Notes, John* i. 29—34. iii. 27—36.) It does not however appear, that he had ever been among the Christians; nor is it known when, and by whom, he received Christian baptism: and there is no proof, that he had at this time any miraculous powers. But, being very zealous and "fervent "in spirit," for the honour of God, and the interests of true religion; he went from place to place, diligently teaching the Jews what he knew concerning the necessity of "repentance, and fruits meet for repentance," as a preparation for the blessings of the Messiah's kingdom. On these subjects he boldly preached in the synagogue at Ephesus, in the hearing of Aquila and Priscilla: and they perceiving his ability, zeal, and piety, said nothing to his disadvantage, though they found that he had very imperfect views of those subjects on which he spoke. On the contrary, they formed an acquaintance with him, and shewed him more completely the doctrine of the gospel, and the things which had taken place in respect of Jesus Christ: and he, with the most amiable humility, received their instructions, and so obtained more adequate qualifications for his important work. (*Marg. Ref.* u—y.) At length, he determined to go into Achaia, and to Corinth: and, by their recommendatory letters, he was introduced to the Christians there; and proved exceedingly useful to *them*, and successful in convincing the Jews, in the most publick manner, that Jesus was indeed the promised Messiah. (*Marg.* and *Marg. Ref.* z—b. d.—*Note*, 1 *Cor.* xvi. 12.)—*Believed through grace.* (27) ' That is, through the ' gospel, says Dr. Hammond, or through the favour of God ' in vouchsafing them the knowledge of it.' *Whitby*. (*Marg Ref.* c.—*Notes*, 9—11. *John* i. 10—13. *Eph.* ii. 4 —10. *Tit.* iii. 4—7.)—' The best comment on these words ' is what we are told elsewhere: " Paul planted, Apollos ' " watered; but God gave the increase." ' *Doddridge*. (*Note*, 1 *Cor.* iii. 4—9.)

Eloquent. (24) Λογιος. Here only. Λογια, vii. 38. —*Was instructed.* (25) 'Hr καληχημενος. See on *Luke* i. 4. —*Being fervent in the spirit.*] Ζεων τῳ πνευματι. *Rom.* xii. 11. Not elsewhere. ' Ζεω, *ferveo de fervore ignis vi exci-* ' tato.' *Schleusner*. Hence ζηλος.—*Diligently.*' Ακριβως. —*More perfectly.* (26) Ακριβεστερον. Luke i. 3. *Eph.* v. 15. 1 *Thes.* v. 2.—*Exhorting.* (27) Προïρεψαμενοι. Here only.—Εx τοα, et πρετω, *verto.* Προτρεπω, *propello, impello, adhortor.*—*Through grace.*] Δια της χαριτος. *Rom.* xii. 3. 1 *Cor.* xv. 10. *Eph.* iii. 7, 8.—*Mightily.* (28) Ευτονως. *Luke* xxiii. 10. Not elsewhere.—Εx ευ, et τεινω, *tendo.*— *He ... convinced.*] Διακαλῃλεγχετο. Here only.—Εx δια, καλια, et ιλεγχω, *John* xvi. 8.—*Publickly.*] Δημοσια. xvi. 37. xx.

20. Δημοσιος, v. 18. A δημος, *populus.*—' Palam falsas ' eorum de Jesu opinionesrefutabat.' *Schleusner*

PRACTICAL OBSERVATIONS.

V. 1—8.

While the zealous ministers of Christ carefully shun whatever may entangle them in the affairs of this life; they will submit to any hardship or labour, which may be rendered subservient to their usefulness, or remove obstacles out of their way: and to work at a trade, for daily bread, in order to preach the gospel without charge, differs exceedingly from carrying on lucrative business, in order to grow rich, and live in abundance, in connexion with the office of an evangelical preacher.—The knowledge of any thing, by which an honest living can be earned, is a very valuable acquisition: it never can prove injurious to any man; it cannot be taken from him; and it may, on one occasion or other, be peculiarly useful to him.—Even among affluent persons, the ministers of Christ are more likely to do good, by shewing an entire indifference to all those things which wealth can purchase; than by affecting a style of living, which emulates that of the very persons, from whose liberality it requires and almost demands support.—The love of Christ is the best bond of friendship; and the communion of the saints sweetens labour, contempt, and even persecution.—Cogent arguments and affectionate persuasions should concur, in our endeavours to lead sinners to faith in the Saviour; but when great neglect or contempt is manifested; we should be " pressed " in spirit" to testify to the truth with greater vehemence, even though it may excite more virulent opposition: and we must warn those who " contradict and blaspheme," that they will perish, and " their blood will be upon their " own head," if they reject that faithful testimony, by which we keep ourselves pure from the guilt of their destruction. When some oppose the gospel, we must turn to others; (*Note, Heb.* vi. 4—6;) and our regret, that so many persist in their unbelief, should not prevent our *gra-* titude for the conversion of some to the faith of the divine Saviour. (*Notes*, and *P. O. Luke* xv. 1—10.)

V. 9—23.

The most eminent, useful, and courageous ministers experience seasons of dejection and anxiety, through consciousness of their own unworthiness and defects, the prospect of perils and difficulties in their work, and the determined enmity and opposition of many among whom they labour. But the Lord Jesus knows, and will obviate all their fears: he will encourage them " to speak, and " not hold their peace;" and he will teach them to trust in his protection amidst all dangers; while he gathers in his chosen flock from those places, in which they are scattered before their conversion. Even the irreligion and in-

CHAP. XIX.

Paul, arriving at Ephesus, finds disciples who knew only John's baptism; and, having instructed them, and baptized them in the name of Christ, he confers on them the miraculous gifts of the Holy Spirit, 1—7. He preaches, first in the synagogue; and then very successfully in a school for two years, God confirming his word by miracles, 8—12. Certain Jewish exorcists, attempting to cast out a devil in the name of Jesus, are driven away naked and wounded, 13—17. Many, who had used magical arts, are converted, and burn their books, 18—20. Paul purposing to go into Macedonia, and then to Jerusalem, and afterwards to Rome, sends friends before him, 21, 22. Demetrius, and the silversmiths at Ephesus, raise a mob against him, to support their gainful traffick and the worship of Diana; and this is attended with great uproar and confusion, 23—34. The town-clerk, with great difficulty and address, appeases it, 35—41.

AND it came to pass, [a] that while Apollos was at Corinth, [b] Paul having passed through the upper coasts, [c] came to Ephesus; and finding certain disciples,

2 He said unto them, [d] Have ye received the Holy Ghost since ye believed? And they said unto him, [e] We have not so much as heard whether there be any Holy Ghost.

3 And he said unto them, [f] Unto what then were ye baptized? And they said, [g] Unto John's baptism.

4 Then said Paul, [h] John verily baptized with the baptism of repentance, saying unto the people, That they should believe on him which should

[Marginal references, right column:]
a xviii. 24—28.
I Cor. i. 12. iii.
b 4—7. xvi. 12.
b xviii. 23.
c xviii. 19—21.
d 6. n. 17. 38. 39.
viii. 15—17. 9.
44. xi. 15—17.
Rom. i. 11, 12.
e 1 Sam. iii. 7.
John vii. 39.
1 Cor. vi. 19.
xii. 1, &c. Gal.
iii. 5.
f Matt. xxviii. 19.
1 Cor. xii. 13.
xviii. 2b. Matt.
iii. Luke iii.
g L 5. x. 16. xiii.
25—2b. Matt.
iii. 11, 12. xi.
3—6. Luke 2b—
32. Mark i. 1—
12. Luke i. 76—
79. iii. 16—18.
John i 29—34.
iii. 2b—36. v. 33
—35.

---

fidelity of rulers, though exceedingly criminal in itself, has often been over-ruled for the protection of the disciples of Christ. Whatever be their motives, such magistrates us take care to prevent, or impartially to punish, those crimes which are injurious to the welfare of the community; and who refuse to use their authority in persecuting one religious sect at the instance of another, or in imposing doctrines, forms, and modes of worship on men's consciences; certainly best understand and perform the duties of their office. Yet, indifference to all religion, and to the infinitely momentous interests of eternity, is no necessary concomitant of toleration, but rather a disgrace to 't; as it shews that rulers, of this description, are actuated merely by indolence and worldly policy, and not by a regard to the rights of conscience, or by a sense of their duty to God: and their toleration or protection of his worshippers, will often be partial and contemptuous, and attended by improper connivance at those who violate the peace of society; as well as a total and systematical neglect of the due improvement of the talents entrusted to them. We should, however, be thankful for security, thus continued to us, in Providence; and we must not forget to pray for those who seem more to regard the liberties of mankind, than the salvation of their own souls.—We ought simply to promote, in our several places, the cause of Christ; forming such plans as seem to us most proper for that end, and relying on the Lord, to enable us to accomplish them, if he see good. But alas! how immensely short do we come, in active zeal, diligence, and patience, to the indefatigable " apostle of the Gentiles!" And with what earnestness and alacrity, did he proceed from city to city, and nation to nation, to strengthen the disciples, and make known the salvation of Christ to perishing sinners!

V. 24—28.

When natural talents for argument and elocution unite with great diligence in studying the scriptures; and when they are attended with fervent zeal, piety, and humility; they qualify a man for doing much good by " teaching diligently " and accurately " the things of the Lord." And even, if persons thus qualified and disposed, are at

present in many things mistaken or ignorant; the Lord will provide them teachers, as well as hearers, and lead them forward in the knowledge of his truth and will.— Experienced Christians, when they hear ministers, who seem earnest and pious, though not fully acquainted with the gospel, should by no means despise them, or teach others to undervalue them: they ought rather to endeavour, privately and meekly, to point out this and the other truth to their attention; and so to lead them on to a greater competency of knowledge, and exactness of judgment. And if faithful counsel and instruction are taken in good part, and duly improved; and popular young men are thus open to conviction, and willing to learn from those, who in some respects may be deemed their inferiors; they will make a rapid progress in knowledge, and maturity for usefulness: and they may soon be recommended as useful helpers to those " who have believed through grace; " as well as able defenders of the gospel, against those who set themselves to oppose it.

NOTES.

CHAP. XIX. V. 1—4. After Apollos was gone to Corinth, Paul, having travelled over the upper or inland parts of Asia Minor, establishing the believers and promoting the gospel, arrived at Ephesus, a rich and famous city on the coast of the Egean Sea; where he had before left Aquila and Priscilla, who had privately been making way for his preaching the gospel to the Jews residing in that city. (Marg. Ref. a—c.—Notes, xviii. 18—28.) There he found some religious persons, who expressed a regard to Jesus, as the Messiah; and he enquired of them whether, having believed, they had received the Holy Spirit, in respect of his miraculous gifts. To this they replied, " We have not so much as heard, whether there " be any Holy Ghost; " by which they must at least have meant, that they had never been led to expect his miraculous powers, or informed of any thing respecting the extraordinary communication of them to believers, at that time; or about the gospel being especially " the ministra- " tion of the Spirit." (Marg. Ref. d, e.—Notes, John vii. 37—39 2 Cor. iii. 7—11.) [i] As Apollos had left Jerusa-

come after him, that is, on Christ Jesus.

^{i H. 38. viii. 12.}
^{16. Rom. vi. 3.}
^{4. 1 Cor. i. 13.}
^{ib. x. 2.}
^{k vi. 6. viii. 17.}
^{19. ix. 17. 1 Tim.}
^{v. 22. 2 Tim. i.}
^{6.}
5 When they heard *this,* ¹ they were baptized in the name of the Lord Jesus.

6 And when Paul had ᵏ laid *his* hands upon them, ¹ the Holy Ghost came on them; and they spake with tongues, and prophesied.

^{l ii. 4. x. 45, 46.}
^{xiii. 2. 1 Cor.}
^{xii. 8—11. 28—}
^{30.}

7 And all the men were about twelve.

8 ¶ And he ᵐ went into the syna-

^{m xiii. 14. 46. xiv.}
^{1. xxvi. 22, 23.}

'lem, and gone to Alexandria, before the miraculous effu-
'sion of the Holy Ghost on the apostles, at the day of
'Pentecost: so had they also done, and had been travel-
'ling into other parts of the world, where the gospel had
'not yet been planted.' *Whitby.* This is not improbable:
nd perhaps, like Apollos, they endeavoured to communicate to the Jews in different places what they had
learned from John the Baptist, concerning Jesus, the Mes-
"siah, the Lamb of God," "the Son of God," and "the
"Bridegroom" of the church; and, having just before
arrived at Ephesus, they had not become acquainted with
Aquila and Priscilla. But hearing of Paul, it is probable
they introduced themselves to him, as persons who believed
in Jesus as the promised Messiah: and, perhaps being regarded as teachers of this doctrine, the apostle might
suppose that they had received the Holy Spirit, at the day
of Pentecost, or by the laying on of the hands of the
apostles; till their answer shewed that they had very imperfect views of the Christian doctrine. He therefore,
further enquired, "unto what they had been baptized:"
and their answer introduced his remarks, concerning the
ministry and baptism of John, as the forerunner and witness to the Messiah. (*Marg. Ref.* f—h.—*Notes, Matt.* iii.
11, 12. *Luke* i. 76—79. iii. 15—20. *John* i. 6—9. 19—
42. iii. 27—36.)

The upper coasts. (1) Τα ανωτερικα μερη. Here only.
Ab ανωτερος, *superior.* The upper parts of Asia Minor,
which were more remote from the Mediterranean Sea.

V. 5, 6. Several learned criticks, of different sentiments
concerning baptism, have argued that these are the words
of Paul, shewing the disciples, that when John baptized
those who heard his doctrine, he virtually baptized them
in the name of Jesus; and not the words of the historian,
relating the baptism of these persons, subsequent to the
apostle's instruction of them. Some of those, who first
contended for this interpretation, did it out of zeal against
such as they called *Re-baptizers,* lest they should adduce
this example in support of their practice. Yet, by maintaining the baptism of John, and the baptism of Christ,
to be *entirely* the same, they have furnished their opponents with a far more plausible argument, than that which
they wanted to wrest from them. But, however that may
be, I cannot think, that any impartial man, who never
heard of these controversies, would, either from reading
the original, or our version, put this construction on the
words. If John could, in any sense, be said to "bap-
"tize his disciples in the name of the Lord Jesus;"
Jesus himself must have been baptized virtually in his own
name. (*Note, John* iii. 22—24.) Even St. Paul's question, "Unto what then were ye baptized?" implies a distinction between different kinds of baptism; and denotes,
that, while he understood they had been baptized, he also
concluded that they had not received Christian baptism,
having never heard of the Holy Spirit, in whose name

VOL. V.

Christians were baptized. (*Note, Matt.* xxviii. 19, 20,
v. 19.)—'This is visible even in the words of St. Paul
'here: John said to those that came to his baptism ἱνα πισ-
'τευσωσιν (4), not that they *did,* but that "they *should,*
'"believe in him that was coming after him;" now they
'were not to be baptized in the name of Jesus Christ, till
'they did actually believe in him, which they who had re-
'ceived John's baptism were so far from doing, that they
'were "musing whether John himself were not the
'"Christ."' *Whitby.* After Christ's ascension no enquiry
was made, that we read of, whether the converts had been
baptized by John, or not: and if but one of the three
thousand, who were baptized on the day of Pentecost, had
been John's disciple, (and probably numbers were such,)
the baptism of John, and that of Jesus, must have been
distinct ordinances. (*Note,* ii. 41.) The difference between that introductory institution to the Christian dispensation, and the initiatory external seal of that dispensation,
has been already considered. (*Notes, Matt.* iii. 5, 6.)—
Some have indeed said, that 'if John's baptism and Christ's
were different, our Lord had no communion with the New
Testament church in baptism, as he had with the Old Testament church in circumcision.' But "he was made under
"the law" to fulfil its righteousness, as our Surety; and
must therefore, both on that account, and as our example,
obey every command, and attend on every institution of
God, then in force: whereas, there was not the same
reason for his joining in the ordinances of the gospel,
which he appointed merely as our Lord and King. Doubtless he ate the passover with his disciples, yet it does not
appear that he partook of the eucharist: (*Notes, Matt.*
xxvi. 26—29. *Luke* xxii. 14—18:) it is not probable that
he did; neither can it be supposed, that he was "bap-
"tized into the name of the Father, of the Son, and of
"the Holy Ghost," which is essential to Christian baptism. I apprehend therefore, that these persons, having
been further instructed by Paul, were admitted into the
church by baptism; previously to the communication of
the Holy Spirit to them, by the imposition of the apostle's
hands, in his miraculous powers and gifts. (*Notes,* viii.
14—17. x. 44—48.)

V. 7. 'The opinion of Bishop Stillingfleet is very pro-
'bable, that St. Paul designed these twelve men for a nur-
'sery of the churches in Asia, or persons to be sent from
'Ephesus to preach among them.' *Whitby.* Thus these
persons continued in the church of Ephesus, waiting for
opportunities of acting as evangelists; as the pastors and
teachers had before done at Antioch in Syria. (*Note,* xiii.
1—3.)—The case of these disciples seems to have been,
in all respects, the same with that of Apollos, though
they were less eminent in the church. (*Note,* xviii. 24
—28.)

V. 8—12. The apostle proceeded after the same method, and met with the same opposition from the Jews, at

5 C

gogue, and spake boldly for the space of three months, * disputing and persuading the things concerning the kingdom of God.

9 But when °divers were hardened, and believed not, ° but spake evil of that way before the multitude, ° he departed from them, and separated the disciples, disputing ' daily in the school of one Tyrannus.

10 And * this continued by the space of two years; so that all they which dwelt in ' Asia, heard the word of the Lord Jesus, ° both Jews and Greeks.

11 And * God wrought special miracles by the hands of Paul;

12 So ' that from his body were brought unto the sick handkerchiefs or aprons, and the diseases departed from them, and the evil spirits went out of them.

13 Then certain of the ° vagabond Jews, ° exorcists, ° took upon them to call over them which had evil spirits the name of the Lord Jesus, saying, We ° adjure you by Jesus, whom Paul preacheth.

14 And there were seven sons of one Sceva a Jew, and chief of the priests, which did so.

15 And ° the evil spirit answered and said, Jesus I know, and Paul I know; but who are ye ?

Ephesus, which he had done in other places. (Marg. Ref. m, n.—Note, xviii. 18—23.) Many obdurately rejected the gospel, and openly reviled " the way" of seeking acceptance with God, by faith in Jesus: (Marg. Ref. o, p. :) so that the apostle deemed it proper to separate the disciples from among them, lest they should perplex or subvert them. And, leaving the opposing Jews, he preached the gospel, and argued in behalf of his doctrine, without intermission, "daily," in a publick school, before all, both Jews and Gentiles, who would attend him. It is not known whether Jewish divinity, or heathen learning and philosophy, had before been taught in this place: but it is probable, that Tyrannus was converted to Christ, and his school afforded the apostle a commodious place, in which to publish his doctrine ; which he did with such success for two years together, that in that time, men of all places and descriptions " in " Asia had heard the word of the Lord Jesus." At the same time he was enabled to work most extraordinary miracles, in confirmation of his doctrine. (Marg. Ref. q—y.—Notes, v. 12—16. John xiv. 7—14.) The handkerchiefs, and aprons (probably such as both men and women, at their work, wore to save their other clothes) could not convey any virtue from the apostle, but were mere tokens of the Lord's omnipotent operation, as the waving of the rod of Moses had been. No doubt the apostle was enabled to confirm his doctrine by miracles, in other places, even though we have no information about it.—' These cures wrought upon absent persons, some of ' them a considerable distance from Ephesus, might con-' duce greatly to the success of the gospel among those, ' whose faces Paul himself had not seen.' Doddridge. It may likewise be supposed, that the apostle sent forth some of his assistants, to preach the gospel in the adjacent cities, while he was labouring at Ephesus ; and it is not unlikely that the twelve persons before mentioned were thus employed.—' Asia, throughout the Acts of the apostles and ' the Epistles of St. Paul, does not mean the whole of ' Asia Minor, or Anatolia, nor even the whole of the pro-' consular Asia, but a district in the anterior part of that ' country, called Lydian Asia, divided from the rest, much

' as Portugal is from Spain, and of which district Ephesus ' was the capital.' Paley.—Two years. (10) The apostle preached three months in the synagogue, and two years in the school of Tyrannus. But in his address to the elders of Ephesus, he mentions three years; (xx. 31 ;) and most commentators date the beginning of these three years from his first coming to Ephesus. (xviii. 19—21.) Nine months, however, seem far too short a time for his voyage and journey to Jerusalem, and his circuit, by Antioch, and through Galatia and Phrygia, and the upper regions of Asia. The circuit itself could not be made, without travelling perhaps a thousand miles, probably on foot, besides the voyage from Ephesus to Cæsarea; and the stay in each place, in order to answer the intended purposes, must have been considerable. Neither does it appear, how he could say, " Remember, that by the space of three years, " I ceased not to warn every one of you night and day with " tears;" if he had been absent from them nine months of the time. It is therefore most natural to conclude, that after he had preached two years in the school of Tyrannus, he continued at Ephesus some months longer, before he went into Macedonia.

Disputing. (8) Διαλεγομενος. 9. See on xvii. 2.—We're hardened. (9) Εσκληρυνοντο. Rom. ix. 18. Heb. iii. 8. 13.—Ex. iv. 21. vii. 3. 22. viii. 19. ix. 12. x. 20. 27, xi 10. xiv. 4. 8. 17. Sept. A σκληρος, durus, ix. 5. Matt. xxv, 24. John vi. 60.—Believed not.] Ηπειθων. See on xvii. 5.—The school.] Σχολη. Here only. Proprie otium.— Body. (12) Χρωτος. Here only. Lev. xiii. 2—4. 11. 13. Sept. A χροα, color.—Aprons.] Σιμικινθια. Here only. ' Vox est origine Latina, ex semi ac cingo : ... semicinctium, ' hoc est tegumentum, quo anterior pars corporis, a cingulo ' et lumbis usque ad pedes præcingitur, et quo opifices fere ' uti solent.' Schleusner.

V. 13—20. (Note, Num. xxii. 5.) It was common in those days for persons to exorcise such as were possessed with evil spirits, especially among the Jews ; and, whatever methods they employed, they seem to have, in one way or other, expressed a dependence on God, and at some times at least to have succeeded. (Note, Matt. xii. 27, 28.)—The persons here mentioned made a trade of

5 c 2

Mark v. 3. 4. 15. Luke viii. 29. 33.

16 And *the man in whom the evil spirit was, leaped on them, and overcame them, and prevailed against them, so that they fled out of that house naked and wounded.

17 And this was known to 'all the Jews and Greeks also, dwelling at Ephesus; *and fear fell on them all, and the name of the Lord Jesus was magnified.

18 And many that believed came,

and 'confessed, and shewed their deeds.

19 Many of them also which used curious arts, brought their books together, and burned them before all men: and they counted the price of them, and found it fifty thousand pieces of silver.

20 So mightily grew the word of God, and prevailed!

such exorcisms, and travelled from place to place to carry it on. When they were at Ephesus, the superior efficacy of the name of Jesus in the mouth of Paul, above all their adjurations, determined them to adopt his manner, in hopes of increasing their gain: as if the words had operated in some unaccountable manner, as a charm, in producing the effects, to which the miracles wrought, on the application of the handkerchiefs and aprons from the body of Paul to the diseased and possessed, might give some occasion. (*Marg. Ref.* a—c.—*Notes,* viii. 9—24.) Thus without regard to the authority, salvation, or honour of Jesus, they attempted to cast out evil spirits, by adjuring them in his name to depart: and seven sons of one man, a chief priest, (probably the head of one of the twenty-four orders of the priests,) combined together in such an attempt. But the evil spirit, by the mouth of the demoniack, answered, that he " knew Jesus, and un-" derstood Paul," when he charged them in the name of Jesus; but who were they? The words are ambiguous; and might imply a confederacy with Jesus and Paul, in consequence of which the evil spirit would have gone out, had Paul thus spoken to him: and Satan might intend to bring the gospel into suspicion by the insinuation. (*Marg. Ref.* d.—*Notes, Matt.* xii. 22—30.) Yet they may signify that the evil spirit knew the power and authority of Jesus, and the efficacy of the apostle's faith, to engage that power by his word; so that if Paul had commanded, he must have yielded. But he knew not them, and would not obey their command. On the contrary, the possessed man, instigated by the evil spirit, assaulted the exorcists with supernatural force and fury, overcame them all, tore off their clothes, and drove them out of the house naked and wounded.—A man must himself be " possessed with " a spirit" of incredulity, who can doubt of this having been a real possession, and maintain that this event was merely the effect of insanity. (*Marg. Ref.* e.—*Notes,* xvi. 16—18. *Matt.* viii. 28, 29.)—This extraordinary transaction was soon known all over Ephesus, both to Jews and Gentiles; and clearly proved, that the effects in the miracles of the apostle, were produced by the power of Christ, and through faith in his name; thus obviating any false conclusions which might have been drawn from the extraordinary nature of them; (*Note,* iii. 12—16;) and men became afraid to revile or speak contemptuously of the name of Jesus, or to use it for selfish purposes: so that it was in consequence had in great honour. Many, therefore, who had embraced the gospel before, or who were then led to believe it, came and confessed the sins which they had committed, especially in practising magick

and sorcery; and shewed the arts which they had employed. Many also of those, who had been more eminent for these impious and wicked arts, brought the books which treated on such subjects, and which were highly esteemed at Ephesus; and, being determined no more to use them, or to make gain of them, or to throw temptation in the way of others; but rather desirous of expressing their abhorrence of these practices, they publickly burned them. The sum, at which they were valued, upon the lowest computation, amounted to about fifteen hundred pounds: some reckon it to have been almost seven thousand; the one supposing drachmas to be meant, the other shekels of four times the value. (See *Tables.*) This was a mighty triumph of the gospel over men's prejudices, favourite pursuits, and love of money; when they were thus at once induced to commit to the flames, books, which might have been sold for so large a sum, lest they should do further mischief to mankind. (*Marg. Ref.* i—l.)—I think it evident, that these books did not merely contain an account of the tricks, by which jugglers of any description imposed on men's senses: for in that case, the persons concerned might have used the books, to detect the artifices of such impostors. They contained the rules and forms of those abominable incantations, by which an intercourse with evil spirits has continually been attempted, or conducted. These being in reality the regulations of the worship of the devil, the devised means of worshipping him, and of seeking help and information from him, ought by all means to be destroyed, and forgotten if possible: though the attempt to revive these practices, by publishing books on such subjects, forms one of the bad effects which attend on the manifold advantages of the liberty of the press in this *Christian* age and nation. (*Notes, Ex.* vii. 9—12. ix. 11. xxii. 18. *Num.* xxiii. 23. *Deut.* xiii. 1—5.)

Vagabond. (13) Περιερχομενων. xxviii. 13. 1 *Tim.* v. 13. *Heb.* xi. 37.—' Περιερχομαι, *circumeo ;* ... *circumforaneus* ' *sum, pervagor varias regiones. Ex* περι, *et* ερχομαι, *venio.*' Schleusner.—*Exorcists.*] Εξορκιςων. Here only. ' Εξορ-' κιςης, *an exorcist,* is one who impels another, as in the ' name of God, to the confession of the truth, or to any ' action. 'Ορκιζω, *I adjure,* is used for commanding any ' thing, interposing the authority of God, *numinis divini,* ' *Mark* v. 7. 1 *Thes.* v. 27.' Leigh. Εξορκιζω· See on *Matt.* xxvi. 63.—*We adjure.*] 'Ορκιζομεν. See on *Mark* v. 7.—*Jesus I know, and Paul I know.* (15) Τον Ιησυν γινωσκω, και τον Παυλον επιςαμαι. Επιςαμαι, x. 28. xviii. 25. *Mark* xiv. 68.—*Leaped on.* (16) Εφαλλομενος. Here only. Ex επι, et αλλομαι, *salio.*—*Overcame.*] Κατακυριευσας. See on *Matt.* xx. 25.—*Wounded.*] Τετραυματισμενυς. See on *Luke*

21 ¶ After a these things were ended, Paul b purposed in the spirit, c when he had passed through Macedonia and Achaia, d to go to Jerusalem, saying, After I have been there, e I must also see Rome.

22 So he sent into f Macedonia two g of them that ministered unto him, Timotheus and h Erastus; but he himself stayed in Asia for a season.

23 And the same time i there arose no small stir about k that way.

24 For a certain man named Demetrius, a silversmith, which made silver shrines for l Diana, m brought no small gain unto the craftsmen;

25 Whom he called together, with the workmen of like occupation, and said, Sirs, n ye know that by this craft we have our wealth:

26 Moreover ye see and hear, o that not alone at Ephesus, but almost throughout all Asia, this Paul hath persuaded and turned away much people,

saying, p That they be no gods which are q made with hands:

27 So r that not only this our craft is in danger to be set at nought: but also that the temple of the great goddess Diana should be despised, and her s magnificence should be destroyed, t whom all Asia and the world worshippeth.

28 And when they heard these sayings, u they were full of wrath, and cried out, saying, Great is Diana of the Ephesians.

29 And x the whole city was filled with confusion: and, having caught y Gaius and z Aristarchus, Men of Macedonia, Paul's companions in travel, they rushed with one accord into a the theatre.

30 And when b Paul would have entered in unto the people, c the disciples suffered him not.

31 And certain of d the chief of Asia which were his friends, sent unto him,

---

xx. 12.—*Used curious arts.* (19) Τα περιεργα πραξαντων. 'Qui magicas artes exercuerant.' *Schleusner.* 1 Tim. v. 15. Περιεργαζομενος, 2 Thes. iii. 11. Ex περι, et εργον, opus. —*They counted.*] Συνεψηφισαν. Here only. Ex συν, et ψηφιζω, calculis computo, Luke xiv. 28.—*Mightily.* (20) Καλα κρατος. Col. i. 11. "According to power," viz. that of God.

V. 21, 22. After these long-continued labours at Ephesus, the apostle purposed to go into Macedonia; either, under the immediate guidance of the Holy Spirit, or in the zeal and fervency of his own spiritual mind: but as he did not exactly accomplish his plan, according to the manner which he intended, some prefer the latter interpretation.—He, however, designed to sail westward into Macedonia; and, having visited the churches there and in Achaia, to go south-east as far as Jerusalem: and afterwards to return to the north-west, further than he had ever before been, that he might preach the gospel at Rome also. (*Marg. Ref.* p—r.) Thus he had laid the plan of his voyages and journeys, backward and forward, of some thousands of miles, as if it had been no more than a progress through a single province!—One part of his design, was to collect money in the different churches which he had planted, and to carry it to Jerusalem for the relief of the poor Christians there. For this purpose he sent before him Timothy, and Erastus, who had been the chamberlain of Corinth, (Rom. xvi. 23,) to prepare the minds of the Thessalonians, Philippians, Bereans, and Corinthians; but he continued some time longer at Ephesus, before he went into Macedonia. (xxiv. 17. *Notes, Rom.* xv. 22—29. 1 Cor. xvi. 1—12. 2 Cor. viii. ix.)

Purposed in the spirit. (21) Εθετο εν τω πνευματι. xx. 22. It does not appear, that πνευμα with the article, and with-

out the possessive pronoun, or something to fix the application of it, is used in the New Testament, except for the Holy Spirit. (*Marg. Ref.* o.—*Note,* xx. 22—24.)
V. 23—31. In this interim an alarming and perilous disturbance was excited " about that way" of worshipping the God of Israel. (*Marg. Ref.* y.) Demetrius, a principal silversmith, carried on a large trade for silver models of the renowned temple of Diana at Ephesus, with a little image in each of them; which were in great request, both as curious and beautiful ornaments, and for idolatrous purposes; and in this manufacture he employed a great number of workmen, highly to their emolument, as well as his own. Having therefore convened them, and all others whose occupations were connected with the support of the popular and prevalent idolatry: he reminded them, that they got their wealth by making these silver shrines, or temples, and similar articles of commerce: and he then shewed them, that Paul's preaching was likely to disgrace and ruin their trade, by persuading the Ephesians and all the Asiaticks, " that they were no gods, which were made " with hands:" a most heretical tenet, in the judgment of those who grew rich by manufacturing deities! (*Marg. Ref.* z—d.—*Notes, Is.* xli. 5—7. xliv. 9—20. *Jer.* x. 3—16. *Hos.* viii. 5, 6.) So that, not only were they likely to be impoverished, and the workmen to be deprived of employment and means of subsistence, the business itself falling into disgrace; but their religion likewise was at stake, (about which, in subserviency to his lucre, Demetrins would be thought very zealous,) and the splendid temple and magnificent apparatus, with which the great goddess Diana was worshipped, by persons from all parts of the world, were likely to sink into contempt and neglect, to the great injury of their renowned city.—This address

5 c 4

desiring *him* that he would not adventure himself into the theatre.

f 29. xxi. 34. 32 Some therefore ' cried one thing, and some another ; for the assembly *a 40. Matt. xi. 7 —9. Luke vii. 31—35.* was confused, ' and the more part knew not wherefore they were come together.

t 1 Tim. i. 20. 2 Tim. iv. 14 33 And they drew ' Alexander out of the multitude, the Jews putting him *u xii. 17. xiii. 16. xxi. 40. xxiv. 10. Luke i. 22.* forward. And Alexander " beckoned with the hand, and would have made *x xxii. 1. xxvi. 1, 2. Phil. i. 7.* " his defence unto the people.

y 26. xvi. 20. Rom. ii. 22. 34 But when ' they knew that he *z 1 Kings xviii. 26. Matt. vi. 7.* was a Jew, ' all with one voice, about the space of two hours, cried out, *a 28. Rev. xiii. 4.* ' Great *is* Diana of the Ephesians.

35 And when the town-clerk had appeased the people, he said, *Ye* men of Ephesus, what man is there that knoweth not, how that the city of the Ephesians is " a worshipper of the great *Gr. the temple-keeper.* goddess Diana, ᵇ and of the *image b 26. 2 Thes. ii. 10, 11. 1 Tim. iv. 2.* which fell down from ᶜ Jupiter ? *c xiv. 12, 18.*

36 Seeing then that these things cannot be spoken against, " ye ought *d v. 36—39. Prov. xiv. 29. xxv. 8.* to be quiet, and to do nothing rashly.

37 For ye have brought hither these men, ' which are neither robbers of *e xxv. 8. 1 Cor. x. 32. 2 Cor. vi. 3.* churches, nor yet blasphemers of your goddess.

38 Wherefore if ⁱDemetrius and the *r 24.* craftsmen which are with him, ' have a *g xviii. 14. Deut. xvii. 8. 1 Cor. vi. 1.* matter against any man, ' the law is open, and there are deputies ; let them *h Or, the court-days are kept.* implead one another.

39 But if ye enquire any thing con-

---

to the interest, idolatry, pride, and resentment of the company, was calculated to inflame their passions. Accordingly, in most furious indignation against Paul and the Christians, and with immense zeal for their lucrative religion, they began to exclaim as with one voice, " Great " is Diana of the Ephesians." This soon brought a mob together, and threw the whole city into an uproar : and as Paul was not met with, the ringleaders of the riot seized upon two of his companions in his travels ; and rushed with them into the theatre, where the publick games are supposed to have been then celebrating ; probably intending to throw them to the wild beasts, which slaves and condemned malefactors used to fight, for the cruel diversion of the spectators. (*Marg. Ref.* f—m.) When the apostle understood this, he was desirous of entering into the theatre, to speak to the people ; being willing to venture himself, in hopes of preserving his friends : but the disciples, knowing that the enraged mob would not scruple to tear him in pieces, interposed to hinder him. Indeed, some of the Asiarchs, or officers appointed from the different cities of Asia, to superintend the publick games, being friendly to him, sent to intreat that he would not thus expose himself, as they could by no means undertake to protect him. (*Marg. Ref.* o—q.)—*No gods,* &c. (26) ' This plainly shews that the contrary opinion ' generally prevailed, namely, that there was a kind of di- ' vinity in the images of their supposed deities, ... though ' some of them ... learned to speak of them just as the ' papists now do ; who indeed may seem to have borrowed ' some of their apologies from the heathens.' *Doddridge.* —The vulgar, both among pagans and papists, always have supposed, that there is some kind of divinity in the image : but the more learned and philosophical palliate the absurdity, by considering the image as the visible representation of the invisible deity or saint. It might also be easily shewn, that the processions, and very many other observances of the papists, are copied from pagan customs ; and far more clear illustrations of these pompous ceremonies may be made from Virgil, Horace, Ovid, Juvenal, and other classical writers, than from the holy scriptures, or even the Apocrypha.

Stir. (23) Ταραχος. xii. 18. Not elsewhere. A ταρασσω, concutio, turbo.—*That way.*] Της οδ̄ε. See on ix. 2.—*A silversmith.* (24) Αργυροκοπος. Here only N. T.—*Jer.* vi. 29. Sept. Εξ αργυρος, argentum, et κοπτω, tundo, cudo. —*Shrines.*] Ναος, templa.—*Gain.*] Εργασιαν. 25. See on xvi. 16.—*The craftsmen.*] Τοις τεχνιταις. 38. Heb. xi. 10. *Rev.* xviii. 22.—*Deut.* xxvii. 15. 1 *Chr.* xxii. 15. *Jer.* x. 9. xxiv. 1. *Sept.* A τεχνη, xvii. 29. xviii. 3.—*He called together.* (25) Συναθροισας. See on xii. 12.—*Workmen of like occupation.*] Περι τα τοιαυτα εργαιας. " Workmen about " such things." Those who wrought the work devised by " the craftsmen."—*Wealth.*] 'Η ευπορια. Here only. Ευπορεω, xi. 29. Εξ ευ, et πορος, transitus.—*Craft.* (27) Μερος. 1. v. 2. *John* xiii. 8. *Rev.* xx. 6. xxi. 8. *Portio, pars, negotium opificium.*—*To be set at nought.*] Εις απελεγχον ελθειν. Here only. Ab απελεγχω, refuto. Εξ απο, et ελεγχω. See on *John* xvi. 8.—*Diana.*] Αρτεμιδος. 28. 34, 35. Here only. Ab αρτεμης, incolumis, integer.—*Magnificence.*] Μεγαλειοτητα. See on *Luke* ix. 43.—*Of confusion.* (29) Συγχυσεως. Here only. A συγχυνω, 32. xxi. 31.—*Companions in travel.*] Συνεκδημος. 2 *Cor.* viii. 19. Not elsewhere. Εξ συν, et εκδημος, peregrinus.—*The theatre.*] Το θεατρον. 31. 1 *Cor.* iv. 9. Θεατριζομαι, *Heb.* x. 33. A θεαομαι, intentis oculis aspicio, et intueor.—*Of the chief of Asia.* (31) Των Ασιαρχων. Here only. Εξ Ασια, et αρχος, præfectus. ' Fuerunt *Asiarchæ principes sacerdotum totius Asiæ.*' Schleusner.—*Adventure.*] Δωναι.

V. 32—41. As Paul did not appear among the people, and the ringleaders of the tumult could not make the multitude generally acquainted with their intentions ; some cried one thing and some another : and, as it is usual on such occasions, the greater number of them knew not the cause, for which the tumult had been excited. At length, one Alexander was singled out from the multitude, who made signs with his hand, that he wanted to speak in his own behalf before them. Many think that this was Alexander the coppersmith, who afterwards became an apostate from Christianity ; but this is uncertain. (*Marg. Ref.* s— u.—*Note,* 2 *Tim.* iv. 14, 15.) It is not agreed, whether he was a convert to Christianity, or an unbelieving Jew : some think that he desired to declaim against the gospel,

cerning other matters, it shall be determined in a *lawful assembly.

40 For ᵇ we are in danger to be called in question for this day's up-

roar, there being no cause whereby we may give an account of this concourse.

41 And ᵏ when he had thus spoken, ʰe dismissed the assembly.

Or, ordinary.
ᵇ xx. l. xxi. 31.
38. 1 Kings i.
41. Matt. xxvi.

ᵏ Prov. xv. l. 2
Ec. ix. 17.
1 Ps. lxv. 7. 2 Cor.
i. 10.

---

and thus to avert the odium from the Jews; and that the Jews put him forward for this purpose, thus joining with the idolaters, though it tended to undermine their own cause: others conclude, that, being seized on, he meant to plead for Christianity and against idolatry, and that the Jews were desirous of his being heard, from an apprehension that this tumult was excited against them, as well as against the Christians. The multitude, however, would not hear him, because they knew him to be a Jew, and an enemy to their idolatry; but, in contempt of all the worshippers of JEHOVAH, and in order to magnify their favourite idol, they with one consent most vociferously cried out, for two hours together, "Great is the Ephesian "Diana." (*Marg. Ref.* y—a.—Note, 1 Kings xviii. 26—29.) Having spent their rage, and wearied themselves in this senseless manner, they were thus kept from greater outrages: till at length the Town-clerk, or Scribe, some magistrate of great authority, was enabled to appease the tumult; after which he spoke to the people with consummate address and ingenuity. He seemed to allow the truth and importance of their absurd traditions and idolatries; though it may be doubted, whether he really believed a word of them. He observed, that it was universally allowed, that their city thought it her chief honour, to support the temple and worship of Diana, and to preserve the image of her, which immemorial tradition declared to have fallen down from Jupiter: and was not therefore "made "with hands." As these things were undeniable, they ought to behave more quietly and cautiously. They had indeed apprehended two men, and were about to wreak their vengeance upon them: yet they had neither sacrilegiously robbed the temple of Diana, nor the temple of any other of their deities; nor had they uttered any blasphemies against their goddess. The apostle was not present, yet doubtless he too was meant: but, while his doctrine undermined the foundations of idolatry, we may suppose, that he never went out of his way to rail at any particular idol.—The town-clerk, or scribe, proceeded to shew, that if any persons were injured in their property, or business; they might bring the matter before the proconsuls, in a regular course of law, and thus obtain satisfaction. But, if the complaint related to matters of religion, or other publick interests; they ought to be decided in a regular meeting of the citizens, or in the accustomed manner, and not before the populace. So that, in fact, the law had been violated that day, by these riotous proceedings; and the city and magistrates were liable to be called into question by the Romans for it; as they could assign no sufficient cause for the insurrection. By this politick harangue, the multitude were prevailed with to disperse; and Paul and his friends were preserved from the most imminent danger.

The town-clerk. (35) 'Ο γραμματευς, *scribe, secretary, recorder.—Had appeased.*] Καθαστειλας. 36. Here only. 'In primis de velis usurpatur quæ contrahuntur; ex καλω, 'et στελλω, *contraho.*' Schleusner.—*A worshipper.*] "The "temple-keeper." *Marg.* Νεωκορον. Here only. 'Ex

'νεως, *pro* ναος, *templum, et* κορεω, *purgo, verro.*' Schleusner. —*The image that fell down from Jupiter.*] Τε διοπετης. Here only. Ex διος, *Jovis,* xiv. 12, et πιτω, *pro* πιπτω, *cado.* —*Cannot be spoken against.* (36) Αναντιρρητων οντων. Here only. Ex α *priv.* αντι, *contra,* et ρεω, *dico.* Αναντιρρητως, x. 29.—*Rashly.*] Προπετης. 2 Tim. iii. 4. Not elsewhere. Ex προ, et πιθω, *pro* πιπτω, *cado.*—*Robbers of churches.* (37) 'Ιεροσυλης. Here only. Ex ιερον, *sacrum,* et συλαω, *spolio. Sacrilegos.—The law is open.* (38) Αγοραιοι αγονται. 'Dies 'forenses, seu judiciales habentur.' Schleusner.—*Deputies.*] Ανθυπατοι. See on xiii. 7. xviii. 12. The office of proconsul of Asia was at this time divided between two magistrates, commonly called *procurators,* but who might properly be called *proconsuls.—Let them implead.*] Εγκαλειτωσαν. 40. xxiii. 28, 29. xxvi. 2. 7. Rom. viii. 33. 'Causam 'inter se disceptent.' Schleusner.—*In a lawful assembly.* (39) Εν τη εννομω εκκλησια. Εννομος, 1 Cor. ix. 21. Εκκλησια, See on Matt. xvi. 18.—*Uproar.* (40) Στασεως. xxiii. 7. 10.—*Concourse.*] Συστροφης. xxiii. 12. Not elsewhere. Συστρεφω, xxviii. 3.

PRACTICAL OBSERVATIONS.

V. 1—12.

We do not at present expect miraculous powers to be conferred on us by the Holy Ghost: yet all, who profess themselves to be the disciples of Christ, should be called upon to examine, whether they have received "the seal of "the Holy Spirit," in his sanctifying influences, to the sincerity of their faith. (*Notes, Rom.* viii. 14—17. *2 Cor.* i. 21, 22. *Eph.* i. 13, 14. iv. 30—32.) Alas! many seem not to have "heard, that there is a Holy Ghost!" and many regard all that is spoken concerning his graces and consolations, to be enthusiasm and delusion! But it may properly be enquired of them, "Unto what then were ye "baptized?" For they evidently know not the meaning of that external sign, on which they place so great dependence. Where, however, men are conscientious and teachable, they will receive increasing light: repentance and its genuine fruits prepare the heart for the comforts and blessings of faith in Christ, and for the witness and earnest of the Holy Spirit: and we should not "despise the day of "small things."—When convincing arguments, and affectionate persuasions, only harden men in unbelief, and excite them to blasphemy; we must "separate ourselves," and such as we can influence, from their contagious company; and we should endeavour to find out more teachable persons, to whom we may communicate the glad tidings of salvation.—The power, which attends the word of the Lord Jesus, will eventually distinguish it from other doctrines: he uses divers instruments and means, in exerting his power; but the work of healing our souls, or pulling down the kingdom of Satan, is wholly his own.

V. 13—20.

The enemy of souls does not greatly regard those, who use the name of Jesus, without faith or love, for the sake of their temporal interest or reputation. He and his as-

CHAP. XX.

Paul and his friends go into Macedonia and Greece, and return to Troas, 1—6; where, as Paul preaches long, Eutychus falls from a window, and is taken up dead: but he is restored to life; and the apostles and disciples break bread, and converse till day-break, 7 —12. Paul and his friends sail to Miletus, 13—16.

He sends for the elders of Ephesus, 17. He states to them his ministry, conduct, and prospects; exhorting, warning, and instructing them with great fervency, and faithful love, and " commending them to God and " the word of his grace," 18—35. He prays with them; and takes a most affectionate farewell, leaving them in great sorrow, because they should see his face no more, 36—38.

sociates know the work of the divine Saviour, and the efficacy of his word in the mouth of his faithful servants; but they despise hireling preachers, and hypocritical professors of the gospel, whom they will overcome to their destruction. But all the efforts of the devil and his servants, to disgrace or oppose the cause of Christ, eventually redound to its honour, and to the credit of his faithful ministers.—The name of Jesus is magnified, when deceivers are detected and disgraced; when sinners are brought to confess and forsake their evil deeds; when they renounce their curious arts, and iniquitous or impious gains, in obedience to the gospel; and when they make expensive sacrifices to the truth, in the presence of all men.—It would by no means be proper, that all books which have no relation to matters of religion, or are not altogether favourable to it, should be destroyed: but surely such as are indecent and licentious, scornfully infidel, or heretical in essential matters, would be condemned to the flames, if " the word of God grew mightily and prevailed" among us; not indeed by the sentence of the inquisitor, but by the voluntary choice of the possessors. Men would, in that case, neither read such books themselves, nor keep them in their houses, to poison the principles and morals of their children or dependents; nor sell them to contaminate the minds and murder the souls of others. Were all such books destroyed in this kingdom, their price would be found immensely more than " fifty thou- " sand pieces of silver!" Will not then these Ephesian converts rise up in judgment against such professors of the gospel especially, as trade in pernicious books and pamphlets; and who encourage such publications for lucre's sake, as they must know are likely to do great mischief in the world? And is it not a proof, that the word of God declines in its influence and authority, when books pretending to teach, and persons professing to exercise, forbidden and curious and magical arts, are publickly advertised among us? But let no friend of the gospel countenance any pretensions of this kind; whether they be human impositions, or diabolical delusions.

V. 21—31.

The enterprizing spirit and unwearied diligence of conquerors, navigators, and others, are generally admired: but the same endowments, when directed by love to Christ and to the souls of men, commonly meet with neglect, if not ridicule and contempt! Yet surely our apostle " la- " boured more abundantly, than all " the admired heroes of the world, or those who explore undiscovered regions; as well as more than any other preacher of the gospel: and happy and honourable are all they, who have been influenced by the same motives, to tread in some good measure in his steps. But when they are most active and successful, they may assure themselves of most opposition from

the worshippers of mammon, and the bigots of idolatry and superstition. Indeed the distinct principles of avarice and superstition naturally coalesce: nor would idolatry, delusion, or vice, though congenial to the human heart, meet with so firm and general a support, did they not conduce to the temporal advantage of numbers, who grow rich by them. Abuses in ecclesiastical systems, absurdities in creeds, and superstitions in religious worship, will be sure to engage many zealous supporters; while they encourage the elegant arts, with manufactures and commerce, and bring no small gain to the craftsmen and to other parties concerned. The immense encouragement which Popery has always given to painting, sculpture, musick, architecture, and other ingenious arts, attaches great multitudes to its splendid forms; and greatly impedes all attempts for reformation. " Sirs, ye know, that by this craft " we have our wealth," is often the private argument of men one among another: while the honour of the great Diana, or of the system, the church, or sect, is the ostensible pretence. Nay, the devotees of mammon and superstition not only impose on others, but on themselves; and imagine that they really love their religion, while they only value the affluence and splendour and honour, derived from it! Their selfishness increases their bigotry; and their interested opposition to the gospel clokes its malignity under zeal for some forms or observances: their indignation and resentment and envy are expressed in furious zeal for the honour of their idol; and the servants of God are hated and persecuted, because they draw men off from those sins, by which lucrative trades are supported. Such persons would " eat up the sin of the people, and set their " hearts upon their iniquities;" whilst they vehemently contend " for the vain conversation delivered by tradition " from their fathers." (Notes, xvi. 16—24. Hos. iv. 7— 11. 1 Pet. i. 17—21. Rev. xviii. 11—19. P. O. 9—19.) Ecclesiastical history continually furnishes the student with instances of these combinations: and we can scarcely look around us in the world, but we see the part of Demetrius and the workmen, acted over and over again, even to the filling of cities with tumult and confusion. It is as safe to contend with wild beasts, as with men who are thus enraged by bigotry and disappointed avarice; or who think that all arguments are answered, when they have shewn that they grow rich by those measures which the ministers of truth, and the friends of genuine reformation oppose: and whatever side in religious controversies, or whatever name this spirit assumes; it is antichristian, and should be strenuously discountenanced by all the friends of truth and piety. —Zeal for the honour of Christ, and love to the brethren, will induce consistent believers to venture into any danger, where these are concerned: but those who value the lives of useful persons may sometimes properly interpose to moderate their zeal: and friends will often be raised up to

AND [a] after the uproar was ceased, Paul called unto him the disciples, [b] and embraced them, and departed for [c] to go into Macedonia.

2 And when he had gone over [d] those parts, and had [e] given them much exhortation, he came into [f] Greece,

3 And there abode three months. And when [g] the Jews laid wait for him, as he was about to [h] sail into Syria, he purposed to return through Macedonia.

4 And there accompanied him into Asia, [k] Sopater of [l] Berea; and of the Thessalonians, [m] Aristarchus and Secundus; and [n] Gaius of [o] Derbe, and [p] Timotheus; and of Asia, [q] Tychicus and [r] Trophimus,

5 These going before, tarried for us at [s] Troas.

6 And we sailed away from [t] Philippi, after [u] the days of unleavened bread, and came unto them to Troas in five days; where we abode [x] seven days.

them, from those who are strangers to vital religion, but have observed their integrity and consistent behaviour.

V. 32—41.

A confused mob can never effect any thing, but mischief and madness. Like a wild beast, it sometimes turns against and destroys those, who meant to govern its operations, or to derive advantage from them: and generally the greater part of riotous multitudes know not for what purposes they are come together. (Note, 2 Cor. i. 8—11.) It is well, when their fury evaporates in senseless clamour; for it is commonly most cruel and destructive. Yet he, who "ruleth the waves of the sea," can also "still the "madness of the people:" and in him we should trust ourselves and all belonging to us, when perils alarm us.—Worldly policy and sagacity often abound, where piety is utterly wanting: and prudent worldly men, by cajoling the deluded multitudes in their follies and absurdities, prevail far more with them, than the most eminent servants of God possibly could by truth and argument. What senseless fables have they implicitly credited, who would not believe the report of the gospel! And how ridiculous have they often been, in their religious opinions and worship, who have discovered the most consummate good sense upon every other subject! For "the god of this "world blinds the minds" of unbelievers. Let us, however, be thankful for prudent magistrates, who can by any means keep the peace, and afford us protection, while we quietly worship God according to our consciences, and endeavour to promote the knowledge of his great salvation.

NOTES.

CHAP. XX. V. 1—6. The apostle probably concluded, that it would be imprudent for him to continue at Ephesus, lest some other insurrection should be excited on his account: he therefore, not long after, affectionately took leave of the disciples in that city, and set out to travel into Macedonia. He went through Troas, and had then a favourable opportunity of preaching the gospel: but not meeting Titus, whom he expected from Corinth, he was so desirous of visiting that city, that he proceeded on his journey without further delay. (Marg. Ref. b—d.—Note, 2 Cor. ii. 12, 13.) The first epistle to the Corinthians seems to have been written before he left Ephesus; (Note, 1 Cor. xv. 31—34;) and the second, when he was in Ma-

cedonia on his progress to Achaia, which probably took up more time than he had expected. (Prefaces to the first and second epistles to the Corinthians.) In the several churches of Philippi, Thessalonica, and Berea, he exhorted, instructed, and encouraged the disciples very copiously, concerning all things relating to their faith and practice, and the management of the common concerns of each church. (Marg. Ref. e.) He was especially employed also, in making collections for the poor Jewish converts at Jerusalem. (Note, xix. 21, 22.) When he had thus passed through Macedonia, he came into Greece, where he spent three months, at Corinth and the adjacent places: and being then about to sail into Syria, he understood, that some Jews had formed a conspiracy to meet him by the way, either to rob him of the money which he had collected, or to murder him: he therefore returned through Macedonia, and revisited the churches in that region.— The persons here mentioned seem to have been the messengers appointed by the several churches, to accompany him with their contributions to Jerusalem. (Marg. Ref. i—q.—Note, 2 Cor. viii. 16—24.) Timothy had gone before the apostle into Macedonia; we find him here attending on him, and he was with him when he wrote the second epistle to the Corinthians: (Note, 2 Cor. i. 1—7, v. 1:) yet elsewhere he says, that he desired him to tarry at Ephesus, when he went into Macedonia. (1 Tim. i. 3, 4.) It is probable, that the first epistle to Timothy was written, when the apostle was in Macedonia, soon after he left Ephesus: so that we must conclude that Timothy returned thither before Paul came away; and that he staid there only a short time, before he, on some account, came to Paul in Macedonia. But he might return thither, and take up his stated residence there afterwards, for some time, according to the statement of ecclesiastical writers. —The historian here again speaks in the first person plural, whence we may conclude, that he had now rejoined the company; and he continued with St. Paul, while some of the others went before to Troas, where a Christian church had before been founded; and thither after a short time the apostle followed them. (Marg. Ref. s—x.)

The uproar. (1) Τον θορυβον. xxi. 34. xxiv. 18, See on Matt. xxvi. 5.—And embraced.] Ασπασαμενος. xviii. 22. xxi. 6, 7. 19. xxv. 13. Matt. v. 47. x. 12. Rom. xvi. 5, et al. —Greece. (2) Ελλαδα. Hence Ελληνες and Ελληνισαι.—

7 ¶ And upon *the first *day* of the week, when *the disciples came together *to break bread, Paul preached unto them, ready to depart on the morrow; *and continued his speech until midnight.

8 And there were many lights *in the upper chamber where they were gathered together.

9 And there sat in a window a certain young man named Eutychus, *being fallen into a deep sleep: and as Paul was long preaching, he sunk down with sleep, and fell down from *the third loft, *and was taken up dead.

10 And Paul went down, *and fell on him, and embracing *him*, said, *Trouble not yourselves; for his life is in him.

11 When he therefore was come up again, *and had broken bread, and eaten, and talked a long while, *even till break of day, so he departed.

12 And *they brought the young man alive, and *were not a little comforted.

13 ¶ And we went before to ship, and sailed unto Assos, there intending to take in Paul: for so had he appointed, *minding himself to go afoot.

Laid wait for him. (3) Γνομενης αυτω επιβελης. 19. ix. 24. xxiii. 30.—Ex επι, et βελη, *consilium.—He purposed.*] Εγενετο γνωμη. 1 Cor. i. 10. vii. 25. 40. 2 Cor. viii. 10. *Philem.* 14. *Rev.* xvii. 13. 17.

V. 7—12. It is not said, that the disciples were *called* together, as on a special occasion; but that they came together, as it seems according to their general practice. Hence it is evident, that Christians were accustomed to assemble for religious worship, " on the *first* day of the " week;" but the change, from the seventh to the first, appears to have been gradually and silently introduced, by example rather than by express precept. *(Marg. Ref. y.— Note, John* xx. 19—23.) Their principal time of assembling appears to have been in the evening : either for fear of enemies ; or because many servants in heathen families, and other poor persons, could not obtain liberty of meeting them at an earlier hour.—" Breaking of bread," or commemorating the death of Christ in the eucharist, was one chief end of their assembling. *(Marg. Ref. z, a.)* This ordinance seems to have been constantly administered every Lord's day : and probably no professed Christians absented themselves, after they had been admitted into the church; unless they lay under some censure, or had some real hindrance. It may be gathered from the narrative, that the apostle hastening to Jerusalem, spending seven days at Troas, and departing the next morning, staid on purpose to spend one Lord's day with them : and, preaching to them on this occasion, as he had seldom spoken to them before, and being about to leave them, not knowing that he should ever see them again, his fervent affection led him to continue his discourse even till midnight. *(Marg. Ref. b.)* His audience no doubt in general attended to his exhortations with eagerness and delight; but one young man was overcome with sleep, and, falling from the third story, was taken up dead. He had, probably, been previously wearied with labour; and perhaps was not duly attentive to the important topicks, on which the apostle was discoursing.—The enemies of the Christians accused them, of holding nocturnal meetings in the *dark;* but the sacred historian informs us, that there were many lights in the room. And as it was most likely very much crowded, the windows seem to have been open to admit the air.— The fall of Eutychus interrupted the religious exercises of the company, and excited in them much sorrow and

anxiety : Paul, however, went down, and, embracing his body, exhorted them not to disquiet themselves, for his life was in him. It is probable that Eutychus had been dead : but the apostle was assured of his restoration to life, which perhaps took place at the moment when he spoke; and he afterwards gradually recovered health and strength. *(Marg. Ref. c—h.)* Accordingly, the company returned to their sacred services : and, after the Lord's supper had been celebrated, and the company had taken some refreshment; the apostle, instead of apologizing for the length of his discourse, resumed the subject, and continued to converse with them till the day dawned, and it was time for him and his friends to set out on their journey. At this time the young man was brought among them alive and well ; so that the whole concurred in giving them no ordinary degree of encouragement and consolation. *(Marg. Ref. i—m.)*—We may easily conceive how many things would be said at Troas, about a night spent altogether in preaching, religious conversation, and devotion : and had Eutychus lost his life, it would have given the enemies of the gospel some plausible ground for exclaiming against *unseasonable hours, long sermons, and enthusiastical irregularities.*

Upon the first day of the week. (7) Εν τη μια των σαββατων. *Luke* xxiv. 1. *John* xx. 1. 19. 1 Cor. xvi. 2.— *Preached.*] Διελεγετο. 9. See on xvii. 2.—*He continued.*] Παρετεινε. Here only N. T.—*Ps.* xxxvi. 10. *Sept.* Ex παρα, ct τεινω, *extendo.—In a window.* (9) Επι της θυριδος. 2 Cor. xi. 33. Not elsewhere.—*Being fallen.*] Καταφερομενος. xxvi. 10. Not elsewhere.—*The third loft.*] Το τριστεγον. Here only. Ex τρις, *ter*, et ςεγη, *tectum;* a στεγω, *tego.— Embracing him.* (10) Συμπεριλαβων. Here only. Ex συν, περι, *circum*, et λαμβανω, *capio.—Trouble not yourselves.*] Μη θορυβεισθε. xvii. 5. *Matt.* ix. 23. *Mark* v. 39.—*And talked.* (11) Ομιλησας. xxiv. 26. See on *Luke* xxiv. 14.—*Not a little.* (12) Ου μετριως.—Here only. A μετρον, *mensura.*

V. 13—16. Assos, Trogyllium, and Miletus were cities of Asia, on the sea-coast: Mitylene was a city in the Isle of Lesbos, which, with Chios and Samos, was situated near the Coast of Asia, in what is now called the Archipelago. Paul chose " to go *afoot*" from Troas to Assos; probably for the sake of retirement and private devotion, as his publick work left him little to be alone. But he

14 And when he met with us at Assos, we took him in, and came to Mitylene.

15 And we sailed thence, and came the next *day* over against Chios; and °the next *day* we arrived at Samos, and tarried at Trogyllium; and the next *day* we came to °Miletus.

16 For Paul ° had determined to

*o 17. 2 Tim. iv.
20. Miletum.
p IR. xviii. 21.
19. xxiv. 12,
13. xxiv. 17
Rom. xv. 24—
28.*

sail by Ephesus, because he would not spend the time in Asia; for he hasted, if it were possible for him, to be at Jerusalem ᵠ the day of Pentecost.

17 ¶ And from Miletus he sent to Ephesus, and called ʳ the elders of the church.

18 And when they were come to him, he said unto them, Ye know

*q li. 1. Ex. xxxiv.
22. 1 Cor. xvi. 8.*

*r 28. xi. 30. xiv.
23. xv. 4. 6. 23.
xvi. 4. 1 Tim. v.
17. Tit. 1. 5.
Jam. v. 14.
1 Pet. v. 1.
2 John i. 3 John
1.*

might also intend to call on some friends, or transact some business, unknown to us. When he had joined his company, he determined not to stop at Ephesus, as he knew that he should not easily get away from his beloved people there; and therefore they sailed past Ephesus to Miletus, a city about thirty miles further to the south.—The apostle seems to have had the direction of the vessel, which he could not have had, if merely a passenger: it is therefore probable that it belonged to some of his friends.—His purpose was, to make what haste he could to Jerusalem, that he might spend the feast of Pentecost there: (*Marg. Ref.* o—q :) perhaps hoping for some opportunity of usefulness among the Jews and proselytes who came to the feast, or of softening their prejudices against him: especially he might deem this the best time for dispensing the contributions which he carried, in such a manner as to promote the friendly communion between the Jewish and Gentile converts.—The historian continues to speak in language which shews that he was one of the company.

Had he appointed. (13) Ην διατεταγμνος. vii. 44. xviii. 2. xxiii. 31. xxiv. 23, *et al.* Ex δια, et τασσω, *ordino.* See on xiii. 48.—*Minding ... to go afoot.*] Μελλων πεζευιν. Here only. Πεζη, *Matt.* xiv. 13. *Mark* vi. 33.—*To sail past.* (16) Παραπλευσαι. Here only. Ex παρα, et πλεω, *navigo.* Αποπλευσαντες, 15.—*Spend the time.*] Χρονοτριβησαι. Here only. Ex χρονος, *tempus,* et τριϐω, *tero.*

V. 17. The apostle could not, with propriety, visit Ephesus: but he desired to give some further instructions and admonitions to "the elders of the church," which he had there planted; and accordingly he sent for them to come to him at Miletus.—The same persons are in this chapter called "elders" or *presbyters,* and "overseers" or *bishops;* (28. Gr.) it must therefore be allowed, that these were not distinct orders of ministers in the church at that time. Probably, when the apostles founded a church they appointed pastors over it; according to the numbers to be superintended, or the field of usefulness which was opened in the neighbourhood: these were at first called either "elders," or "overseers," that is, *presbyters,* or *bishops,* indifferently; and no one had any direct authority over the rest. By degrees the number of converts would increase, other churches would be planted in the neighbourhood, and more pastors chosen. In the mean time the senior ministers, and such as were most eminent for wisdom, ability, piety, or usefulness, would acquire a measure of influence and authority: and their juniors, both in their own church, and in others which had been planted from it, would naturally look up to them. Thus they would be expected to take the lead in every business: especially in the ordination of ministers, in directing their labours, and in animadverting on such as turned aside to

heretical doctrines, or immoral practices. Hence the name of "Bishop," or *Overseer* or *Inspector,* seems gradually to have been appropriated to one principal minister, to whom a measure of authority and distinction was insensibly annexed; and the title and rank of "Presbyters" were continued to the rest. (*Note,* xi. 27—30.) It is evident that episcopacy prevailed, generally and early, in the primitive church; and it seems to have been gradually introduced. There were many elders in the church at Ephesus at this time; yet Christ afterwards addressed his epistle "to the "*angel* of the church of Ephesus;" which seems to mean the superintending pastor, who was an inspector over the elders. (*Note, Rev.* ii. 1.) It appears, to me at least, that neither episcopacy, nor any other species of church-government, can be proved from *scripture,* to be *exclusively* of divine authority. But a moderate episcopacy has many and great advantages to recommend it: and the high claims and excessive authority, which soon began to be advanced and exercised by bishops and lordly prelates, of different titles; and all the abuses of antichristian tyranny, supply the best arguments to those, who would entirely exclude that order from the church. In this, however, as well as in other things, very much remains to be remedied and rectified, among every description of Christians, before matters can be reduced to the scriptural standard.—Every impartial man must allow, that if Timothy had been at this time bishop of Ephesus, in that sense for which some contend; the apostle would have given these elders some exhortation, to pay a proper deference to his episcopal authority.—To assert, as some have done, (Dr. Hammond especially,) that these elders of Ephesus were indeed the diocesan bishops of all the Asiatic churches, only exposes the cause which it is meant to support: for, besides the inexcusable liberty taken with the words of scripture; how could these bishops have been got together, at so short a notice? Unless it be supposed, that they all resided at Ephesus, and left the charge of their dioceses to others, according to the too common custom of later times! The statement would also shew, that there were no presbyters; and consequently *a parity of ministers, in the primitive church,* directly contrary to the sentiments of those who make it. (*Marg. Ref.—Notes, Phil.* i. 1. 1 Tim. iii. 1. v. 19, 20.)

V. 18—21. 'Paul, a diligent imitator of Christ, hast 'ening to bonds by a continued course, first as it were 'makes his will; in which he gives some account of his 'manner of life, defends the doctrine which he had 'taught, and exhorts the pastors of the church to perse-'verance.' *Beza.*—The apostle first called the attention of these elders, to the methods which he had pursued, and the conduct which he had manifested, among them, since his

from the first day that I came into Asia, after what manner I have been with you at all seasons,

19 Serving the Lord with all humility of mind, and with many tears and temptations which befell me by the lying in wait of the Jews;

20 And how I kept back nothing that was profitable unto you, but have shewed you, and have taught you publickly, and from house to house;

21 Testifying both to the Jews, and also to the Greeks, repentance toward God, and faith toward our Lord Jesus Christ.

22 And now, behold, I go bound in the Spirit unto Jerusalem, not knowing the things that shall befall me there:

23 Save that the Holy Ghost witnesseth in every city, saying, that bonds and afflictions abide me.

24 But none of these things move me, neither count I my life dear unto myself, so that I might finish my course with joy, and the ministry which I have received of the Lord

---

first coming into Asia; that is, the district so called, of which Ephesus was the capital. (Note, xix. 8—12.) He had, at all seasons, however circumstanced, devoted himself to the service and worship of the Lord, in a humble, gentle, unassuming, and self-abasing manner: without aspiring at the honour which came from man, or being ambitious of distinction or authority. (*Marg. Ref.* t—x.—*Notes, Matt.* xviii. 1—4. xx. 24—28. 1 *Thes.* ii. 1—8. 1 *Pet.* v. 1—4.) His services had been attended with many tears of fervent affection, and with great sorrow of heart; on account of the obstinate unbelief of the Jews, the blind idolatry of the Gentiles, the afflictions, temptations, and misconduct of the Christians, and his own manifold infirmities. He had also encountered many hardships, and been exposed to many perils, from the insidious malice of the Jews and the conspiracies which they laid against him: these were a great trial to him, and might have tempted him to decline the service, or to be unfaithful in his ministry. Yet the elders knew, that he had not " shunned," from any motive, to give them, not only instructions, true as far as they went, but all such counsels, warnings, and encouragements, as could conduce to their spiritual advantage; this he had simply consulted without greatly regarding, whether they or others were pleased or displeased with him. What he had taught publickly, he had also discoursed of privately; going " from house to house," among the converts and such as were willing to receive him, to admonish, counsel, and instruct, every one in particular, as his case required. (*Marg. Ref.* y—e.) He had, especially, with the utmost earnestness, insisted upon the absolute necessity of repentance towards God, the great Creator and Governor of the world, whose holy laws all had broken, and whose righteous displeasure they had incurred; before whom they ought therefore to humble themselves with godly sorrow, confessing their sins, and shewing their sincerity by works meet for repentance. With this he had connected his unwavering testimony, to the necessity of " faith toward our Lord Jesus Christ;" or a belief of those divine testimonies, which relate to his Person, righteousness, atonement, and mediation; and a reliance on him, as the divine Surety and Saviour of sinners, for all the blessings of salvation.—This repentance

and faith, when considered in connexion with man's need of them, the source from which they spring, and the invariable effects of them, on the heart and life of him, who continually exercises them; may be considered as the substance of Christianity, the religion of a sinner under a dispensation of mercy and grace. (*Marg. Ref.* f—h.—*Notes,* xxvi. 19—23. *Matt.* iii. 2. *Luke* xv. 8—10. 17—21. *P. O.* 17—24. *Note,* xxiv. 44—49.)

I came. (18) Επιϭην. xxi. 2. 6. xxv. 1. xxvii. 2. *Matt.* xxi. 5.—*Serving.* (19) Δουλευων. vii. 7. *Matt.* vi. 24. *John* viii. 33. *Rom.* vi. 6. *Gal.* v. 13, *et al.* A δουλος, *servus.*—*Humility of mind.*] Ταπεινοφροσυνης. *Eph.* iv. 2. *Phil.* ii. 3. *Col.* ii. 18. 23. iii. 12, 1 *Pet.* v. 5.—Ex ταπεινος, *humilis,* et φρην, *mens.*—*The lying in wait.*] Ταις επιϭουλαις. See on 13.—*I kept back.* (20) Υπεϭειλαμην. 27. *Gal.* ii. 12. *Heb.* x. 38. Not elsewhere N. T.—*Ex.* xxiii. 21, *Deut.* i. 17. *Sept.* Ex υπο, et τελλω, *mitto.* See on 27.—*Testifying.* (21) Διαμαρτυρομενος. 23, 24. xviii. 5. See on ii. 40. The word signifies, to give a most solemn and urgent charge, as in the sight of God.

V. 22—24. The apostle next informed the elders, that under the impulse of the Holy Spirit, which constrained him to proceed by the *bonds* of zeal and love, he was going up to Jerusalem, not knowing what persecutions or trials he might meet with there: save that the Holy Spirit testified in every city, where the gospel was planted, by the mouth of some of the prophets there raised up, " that " bonds and afflictions awaited him." (*Marg.* and *Marg. Ref.* i—l.) This, however, did not in the least deter him from the service which he had undertaken, or so discompose his mind, as to unfit him for his important duties: because " he made no account of these things;" indeed he did not value life, for his own sake; having no desire to live, except the glory of God and the benefit of the church required it. (*Notes, Phil.* i. 19—26.) For his grand object was, to finish his Christian race, with joyful assurance of meeting the approbation of his Lord, and of receiving " the prize of his high calling;" and, in order to this, to execute faithfully, till death, the important ministry which the Lord Jesus had committed to him; and to testify to sinners of every nation, the glad tidings of the abundant mercy and grace of God, for the complete

Jesus, ⁿ to testify ˢ the gospel of the grace of God.

25 And now, behold, ᵗ I know that ye all, among whom I have gone preaching the kingdom of God, shall ⁿ see my face no more.

26 Wherefore ˣ I take you to record this day, ʸ that I *am* pure from the blood of all *men* ;

27 For ᶻ I have not shunned to

declare unto you ᵃ all the counsel of God.

28 ᵇ Take heed therefore unto yourselves, and to ᶜ all the flock, ᵈ over the which the ᵉ Holy Ghost hath made you ᶠ overseers, ᵍ to feed ʰ the church of God, ʰ which he hath purchased with his own blood.

salvation of their souls. (*Marg. Ref.* m—r.—*Notes,* Luke ix. 51—56. John iv. 31—34. xvii. 4, 5. 1 Cor. ix. 24—27. 2 Tim. iv. 6—8. Heb. xii. 2, 3.)

Bound in the Spirit. (22) Perhaps the bonds and imprisonment, which the Holy Spirit, by the prophets, constantly predicted, as awaiting the apostle, were intended by this expression. (23. *Note,* xix. 21, 22.) Δεδεμενος τω πνευματι.—‘ This resembles συνειχετο τω πνευμαθι, xviii. 5. ‘ In both places I understand το πνευμα not of the Holy ‘ Spirit, but of the spirit and mind of Paul.’ *Bp. Middleton.*—See on xviii. 5. (*Notes,* xviii. 1—6, *v.* 5. John iii. 6.)—*None of these things move me.* (24) Ουδενος λογου ποιουμαι. “ I make account of nothing.” (*Note,* Rom. viii. 18—23, *v.* 18.)—*So that I might finish my course.*] ʼΩς τελειωσαι τον δρομον μυ. 2 Tim. iv. 7. Τελειοω See on John iv. 34. Δρομος᾽ See on xiii. 25.

V. 25—27. An immediate revelation seems to have been, about this time, made to the apostle, that he should no more revisit Ephesus, or see any of these elders, or those in that neighbourhood to whom he had preached, any more on earth. This made him the more earnest in his exhortations and admonitions ; and he therefore, testified to them, and called on them to bear witness for him, that he was guiltless of the blood (that is, of the eternal ruin) of those, who might perish among them or their flocks : as he had not declined, either from fear, or desire of their applause, or friendship, to “ declare unto them the whole “ counsel of God,” respecting the way of salvation by Christ for all true believers, and the certain destruction of all who neglect so great salvation ; and respecting all things pertaining to the doctrine, practice, and discipline of the church. (*Marg. Ref.*—*Notes,* 18—21. xviii. 1—6. Ez. iii. 17—19. xxxiii. 2—9.) As he had been wholly preserved from ignorance or mistake, about the truth and will of God, in these things ; so he had been kept from all unfaithfulness in respect of them.—‘ Hence we learn, that it is necessary ‘ for a pastor, to declare to his people all, that is necessary ‘ for them to believe and do, in order to salvation, in order ‘ that the guilt of their ruin may not lie upon him.’ *Whitby.* It is probable, that the apostle went, after this, into the neighbourhood of Ephesus: (*Note,* 2 Tim. iv. 9—13, *v.* 12. Philem. 22—25:) and, on this ground, some learned men think, that in saying, “ I know that ye all ... shall see “ my face no more ;” he only meant to draw this conclusion from the predictions, which were given of the sufferings that awaited him. The elders, however, understood him, as speaking with certainty of what he knew by revelation : nor did he attempt to undeceive them, though he

saw them overwhelmed with grief. (*Note,* 36—38. *Preface* to 1 Timothy.

I have not shunned. (27) Ουκ ὑπεϛειλαμην. See on 20. ‘ A military word from soldiers who recoil, and leave their ‘ standing.’ *Leigh.*—‘ The proper import of the word ‘ ὑποϛελλω, in such a connexion,’ (as used by Demosthenes and Lucian,) ‘ is, to *disguise* any important truth, ‘ and at least to *decline* the open publication of it, for fear ‘ of displeasing those, to whom it ought to be declared.’ *Doddridge.*—*The counsel.*] Την Ϛωλην. Eph. i. 11. Heb. vi. 17. See on ii. 23.

V. 28. In imitation of the example which he had set them, and in expectation of that great and awful account which they must give of their ministry, the apostle next warned the elders “ to take heed to themselves,” to their state, spirit, conduct, and doctrine ; and to all the flock, over which the “ Holy Ghost had made them overseers.” (*Note,* 1 Tim. iv. 11—16.) Their qualifications for the ministry had been derived from the Divine Spirit ; he had disposed them to undertake that service ; he had directed those who selected and ordained them ; and he had confirmed that appointment by his gifts and endowments. (*Marg. Ref.* b—d.—*Note,* 1 Cor. xii. 4—11, *v.* 11.)—Some think, that the twelve men before spoken of were especially intended, and that the gift of the Holy Spirit, by the laying on of the hands of Paul, was referred to. (*Note,* xix. 7.)—The great end of the pastoral office to which they were appointed was, that they might “ feed the church of God, “ which he had purchased with his own blood : ” that they might continually dispense those pure and wholesome truths, which are the proper nutriment of the soul : and which, when regenerated, it desires, relishes, feeds on, and grows by, in knowledge, faith, hope, and holiness. The conversion of sinners, as part of this chosen flock, is implied in this commission. (*Marg. Ref.* e—h.—*Notes,* John xxi, 15—17. Eph. iv. 11—13. 1 Pet. ii. 1—3. v. 1—4.)—The most able criticks have shewn, that the present is the genuine reading of the verse ; though a few copies have “ the church of the Lord,” a phrase not used in the New Testament. The passage is a most decisive testimony to the deity of Christ. The atonement and ransom of our souls, is the blood of Jesus, who is as truly God, as man : and thus in his mysterious Person, as God and man, he “ purchased the church with his own blood.” This gave the infinite value to his sacrifice ; and it suggests to his ministers the most powerful motives to faithfulness, diligence, patience, and fortitude in their work.—The personality and deity, and sovereignty likewise, of the Holy

29 For I know this, that after my departing shall grievous wolves enter in among you, not sparing the flock.

30 Also of your own selves shall men arise, speaking perverse things, to draw away disciples after them.

31 Therefore watch, and remember, that by the space of three years I ceased not to warn every one night and day with tears.

32 And now, brethren, I commend you to God, and to the word of his grace, which is able to build you up, and to give you an inheritance among all them which are sanctified.

33 I have coveted no man's silver, or gold, or apparel.

34 Yea, ye yourselves know, that these hands have ministered unto my necessities, and to them that were with me.

35 I have shewed you all things, how that so labouring ye ought to support the weak; and to remember the words of the Lord Jesus, how he said, It is more blessed to give than to receive.

Spirit, are clearly shewn, in the words, " Over which the " Holy Ghost hath made you overseers."

Take heed ... unto yourselves.] Προσεχετε εαυτοις. *Luke* xii. 1. xvii. 3. xxi. 34. See on xvi. 14.—*The flock.*] Τῳ ποιμνιῳ. 29. *Luke* xll. 32. 1 Pet. v. 2, 3.—*Hath made.*] Εθυτο, *ordained, constituted. John* xv. 16.—*Overseers.*] Επισκοπης. Phil. i. 1. 1 Tim. iii. 2. Tit. i. 7. 1 Pet. ii. 25. Επισκοπη* See on i. 20. Ab επισκοπεω, Heb. xii. 15.—*Hath purchased.*] Περιεποιησατο. 1 Tim. iii. 13. Not elsewhere N. T.—*Gen.* xxxi. 18. xxxvi. 6. Sept. Περιποιησις, Eph. i. 14. 1 Thes. v. 9. 1 Pet. ii. 9. Ex περι, et ποιεω, *facio.*

V. 29—31. To enforce these things still more, the apostle assured his brethren, the pastors of the flock, that he certainly knew, by the Spirit of prophecy, that after he was gone from them, grievous, strong, and cruel wolves would break into the fold, and devour the sheep: these may either mean seducing teachers from other countries, intruding among them and usurping authority, so as to fleece, scatter, or oppress the flock, for the gratification of their own avarice or ambition: or cruel persecutors, by whom many believers were put to death, and many professed Christians were tempted to apostatize. (*Marg. Ref.* i.—*Notes, Ez.* xxxiv. 2—6. *Matt.* vii. 15—20.) Besides these, others would spring up from " among themselves," devising and propagating heretical doctrines; corrupting the purity of the faith; disturbing the harmony of the church; drawing off the people from their faithful pastors on various pretences; attaching many to themselves as their disciples; and thus forming scandalous sects and schisms. (*Marg. Ref.* k—m.—*Notes,* 1 Tim. i. 18—20. 2 Tim. i. 15. ii. 14—18. 2 Pet. ii. 1—3. Rev. ii. 6, 7.) As " the enemy sows these tares in the field," while men sleep; (*Notes, Is.* lvi. 9—12. *Matt.* xiii. 24—30. 36—43;) Paul exhorted the elders on this account to watch, and be vigilant to observe and check the first appearance of all these evils: remembering that for three years together he had constantly warned them, one by one, by night as well as by day; bereaving himself of rest and refreshment, that he might seize on every opportunity for these admonitions; and that his earnest affection for their souls, joined with his foresight of these perversions, had caused him to mingle his warnings with many tears. (*Marg. Ref.* n—r. —*Notes,* 19—21. xix. 8—12, v. 10.)

Departure. (29) Την αφιξιν. Here only. Ab αφικνεομαι,

Rom. xvi. 19.—*Perverse things.* (30) Διεστραμμινα. " Per- " verted things." xiii. 8. 10. *Matt.* xvii. 7. Phil. ii. 15.— *By the space of three years.* (31) Τριετιαν. Here only. —*To warn.*] Νεθετων. *Rom.* xv. 14. *Col.* i. 28. 1 Thes. v. 12. 14. 2 Thes. iii. 15. Ex νες, *mens,* et τιθημι, *pono. To place before the mind.*

V. 32—35. Having endeavoured to impress these pastors with a deep sense of the arduousness and importance of their work, the apostle concluded by " commending " them to God;" earnestly calling on them to rely wholly on his guidance, assistance, protection, and blessing; and calling on God to take their souls, and those of the flock, into his almighty and gracious keeping. He also commended them to the " word of his grace," as the ground of their hope, rule of their conduct, and the source of their consolation; seeing that the Lord was able, according to his word, to build them up in faith and holiness, amidst all the temptations, trials, and delusions, to which they might be exposed; and at length to " give them an " inheritance" in heaven, among all those whom he had set apart for himself, and made meet by his sanctifying Spirit for their holy felicity. (*Marg. Ref.* s—y.—*Note,* xxvi. 16—18.) There he expected again to meet them, as " kept by the power of God, through faith unto salvation." (*Notes,* 1 Pet. i. 3—5. Jude 22—25.)—He could appeal to them, that he had acted disinterestedly among them : though many of the Ephesians were rich, yet " he had " not coveted," or in any way sought for, any man's wealth, or secular advantages: nay, he had not accepted of that maintenance, to which he was fairly entitled ; but had laboured at a manual employment to maintain himself and his fellow-labourers. (*Notes,* 1 Cor. ix. 4—12.) Thus he had shewed them, by his example, the tendency of his doctrine; that from him they might (even the " presbyters," or " bishops,") might learn, that it was their duty to *labour,* after the same manner, in order to maintain themselves, and to contribute to the support of their poor brethren, when weak and sick, or otherwise unable to maintain themselves. (*Marg. Ref.* z—c.—*Notes,* 1 Thes. v. 12 —15. 2 Thes. iii. 6—9.) They ought also to remember the words, which the Lord Jesus had commonly used, as an important aphorism, " It is more blessed to give than " to receive." It is more happy to be able to give, than to be obliged to receive ; and therefore better to labour and

c vii. 60. xxi. b.
2 Chr. vi. 13.
Dan. vi. 10.
Luke xxii. 41.
Eph. iii. 14.
Phil. iv. 6.
f 1 Sam. xx. 41.
2 Sam. xv. 30.
2 Kings xx. 3. Ezra x. 1. Job li. 12. Ps. cxxvi. 5. 2 Tim. i. 4. Rev. vii. 17. xxi. 4.

36 ¶ And when he had thus spoken, [e] he kneeled down, and prayed with them all.

37 And they all [f] wept sore, and fell on Paul's neck, [g] and kissed him;

38 Sorrowing most of all for the words which he spake, [h] that they should see his face no more. [i] And they accompanied him unto the ship.

g Rom. xvi. 16.
1 Cor. xvi. 20.
2 Cor. xiii. 12.
1 Thes. v. 26.
h 20.
i xv. 3. xxi. 5. 16.
1 Cor. xvi. 11.

be frugal, than to indulge sloth and expense: there is more comfort and pleasure in giving than in receiving; there is more of grace, of love, of heaven, and of the divine image, in giving, than in receiving. This traditional speech, so suited to the character of him, " who, being rich, for our " sakes became poor, that we through his poverty might " be rich," would not have been preserved for our use, if it had not thus been committed to writing. (*Marg. Ref.* d. —*Notes, 2 Cor.* viii. 6—9.)—With this example, instruction, and admonition to labour, disinterestedness, and liberality, the apostle closed his address to these elders; and his words could not but make a deep and durable impression on their pious minds.

I commend. (32) Παρατιθημαι. See on xiv. 23.—*To build up.*] Επσικοδομησαι. 1 *Cor.* iii. 10. 12. 14. *Eph.* ii. 20. *Col.* ii. 7. *Jude* 20. Ex επι, et οικοδομεω, *Matt.* xvi. 18. *John* ii. 20. See on ix. 31.—*Which are sanctified.*] Τοις ἡγιασμενοις. xxvi. 18. 1 *Cor.* vi. 11. *Jude* 1.—*I have coveted.* (33) Επεθυμησα. *Rom.* vii. 7. See on *Matt.* v. 28.—*To support the weak.* (35) Αντιλαμβανεσθαι των ασθενωντων. Αντιλαμβανω See on *Luke* i. 54. Ασθενεω, ix. 37. xix. 12. *Matt.* x. 8. xxv. 36. *John* v. 3. 7. xi. 1, 2, 3. 6, et al. Ex α priv. et σθενος, robur.

V. 36—38. (*Note,* xxi. 1—6.) The solemn and affectionate address, which has been considered, was concluded with humble and fervent prayer; and the whole company were so affected with the mingled passions of love and sorrow, that they wept much: especially they were exceedingly grieved to hear, that they were no more to behold the face of so faithful and affectionate a friend and instructor. ' This, which is St. Luke's own explication, ' leaves no room for ambiguity, which might be imagined ' in the expression used before (25),' *Doddridge.* (*Marg. Ref.*)—It does not appear that there was a church at Miletus; for none are spoken of, but the elders of Ephesus and St. Paul's companions.—It is probable, that Timothy went to Ephesus with these elders, and resided there for some time; as we do not find that he accompanied the apostle to Jerusalem, or was with him before he arrived at Rome. (*Preface* 1 Tim.)

He kneeled down. (36) Θεις τα γονατα αὑτω. vii. 60. ix. 40. xxi. 5. *Luke* xxii. 41.—*Sorrowing.* (38) Οδυνωμενοι. *Luke* ii. 48. xvi. 24, 25. Ab οδυνη, *Rom.* ix. 2. 1 *Tim.* vi. 10.—*They accompanied.*] Προεπεμπον. See on xv. 3.

PRACTICAL OBSERVATIONS.

V. 1—12.

Tumults and opposition may constrain a Christian or minister to remove from his station, or to alter his purpose: but his employment and pleasure will be the same wherever he goes.—Even believers need " much exhorta- " tion," to render them habitually stedfast, zealous, prudent, and persevering in every good work, and to animate faith and prayer to be enabled to do this.—Christians should always delight in commemorating their Lord's death at his table, and his resurrection by observing his holy day: but the general contempt and profanation of the Christian sabbath by the professed disciples of Jesus, and the withdrawing of so great a majority of the congregation, even where the gospel is preached, when the Lord's supper is about to be administered, evince the low state of vital religion among us, and tend to reduce it still lower. —It shews a carnal state of mind, when people are soon wearied in the worship of God, and are in haste to close it, for the sake of animal recreation, or vain conversation. Doubtless it is inexpedient, on ordinary occasions, to lengthen out religious ordinances much beyond the usual time: yet surely Paul would be displeased, surprised, or grieved, to hear the professors of his doctrine complain of an instructive sermon, because it was *an hour long;* or of the length of the service, when it scarcely exceeded *two hours!*—If we cannot wholly excuse Eutychus, for yielding to sleep at midnight, during the apostle's copious exhortations; how inexcusable are they, who in the middle of the day, and during a service of a moderate length, make a practice of sleeping, as if best pleased when most composed to rest! Infirmity or weariness, indeed, requires tenderness: but such an indulged habit of contempt should be treated with decided severity. They who thus offend have cause to tremble, lest some sudden judgment should cut them off in their sin, and leave them to perish without remedy: and such as desire to get the better of this temptation should join earnest prayers, with all other methods of keeping themselves awake; for when this is neglected, they need not wonder that they are unsuccessful.—Should a company of believers among us, on some remarkable occasion, spend a whole night in the exercises of religion, what exclamations, revilings, and derision would it excite! Yet little is said, when the devotees of festive indulgence, fashionable dissipation, or more vulgar revels, employ their nights in the most irregular manner: as if time spent in devotion broke in upon the order of families, or the peace of society, far more than when dedicated to vain amusement, or bacchanalian riot! Or as if more earnestness were allowable in any thing else, than in the service of God!—Nay, many of us, who now count religion our chief joy, can remember a time, when we entrenched upon the hours of rest, for our frolicks and pleasures, with far less reluctance, than we now should for the purpose of secret or social worship. So hard is it for spirituality to flourish in the heart of a fallen creature, under any culture! and so naturally and spontaneously do carnal affections grow and thrive there!—The Lord, however, will take care of the concerns, and pardon the infirmities, of his people: and he will comfort them under all their tribulations, even when called to separate from those, whom they have most loved.

V. 13—21.

No Christian can be comfortable or prosperous, without retirement. Popular ministers may preach, converse, or pray in company, to the edifying of others: and yet de-

CHAP. XXI.

Paul and his friends leave Miletus, and arrive at Tyre; where, finding disciples, they stay seven days, and part from them with prayer, kneeling down on the sea-shore, 1—6. They proceed to Cæsarea, to the house of Philip the evangelist, whose four daughters prophesy, 7—9. Agabus foretels that Paul will be bound at Jerusalem: he is not however dissuaded from going thither, 10—16. Arriving at Jerusalem, he reports, to James and the elders, the success of his labours among the Gentiles, 17—19. He is persuaded to purify himself at the temple, with four men who had a vow, 20—26; where he is set upon by some Jews from Asia, and in danger of being slain in a tumult, but is rescued by the chief captain; who binds him with chains, and leads him to the castle, 27 —36. He requests, and is permitted, to speak to the people, 37—40.

cline in their own souls, for want of self-examination, humiliation, and secret prayer, suited immediately *to their own case:* nay, the most able preachers will generally cease to be very useful, if their personal religion is neglected, or hurried over in a formal manner. This the fervent Christian knows; he will therefore redeem time for retirement, at the expense of many inconveniences: and the friends of popular ministers should consider this, and not too much intrude upon the regular and needful hours for retirement of those persons in whose company they most delight.— In prosecuting the work of God, our own inclinations and those of our beloved friends must often be thwarted: we must not " spend our time " with them; when duty calls us another way, or when a prospect is before us of doing more essential good.—As the office of ministers is of the highest importance and difficulty; to instruct, encourage, animate, or admonish those, who now are or hereafter may be employed in it, is a service of very great moment. To do real good to a pastor of the flock, is eventually to profit numbers: and those who have a talent for this service, and a proper call to it, should deem themselves highly honoured, and be satisfied sometimes to omit more public lick services, for the sake of it. But they, who are thus employed, in instructing such as are to instruct others, should themselves be most unexceptionable characters, and be able to appeal to them respecting their own conduct at all seasons.—All those who are employed in the sacred pastoral service, whether favoured with living monitors, in some degree resembling St. Paul, or not, should consider this charge of the apostle as addressed to them, even as really as to the Ephesian elders; and as thus setting before them the proper conduct, spirit, and principles of a true minister of Christ. A proud, ambitious, selfish, and unfeeling heart, is peculiarly opposite to the service of God, in the pastoral office, or to the proper filling up of eminent stations in the church. Unless a man be " clothed with " humility " and softened into love and compassion; his very abilities, zeal, and diligence, will be disgusting and odious. Except we are ourselves deeply affected with the subjects on which we treat, how can we expect to affect others? and how can we convince them, that we indeed mean any thing by our exhortations, unless we persevere in our labours amidst temptations and opposition? We must not be " men-pleasers; " nor may we " keep back " any thing that is profitable," whatever offence may be taken, or however well some persons would reward us, for conniving at their errors and conformity to the world. (*Notes, Gal.* i. 6—10. 1 *Thes.* ii. 1—8.)—Indeed the omission of " what is profitable," because not *pleasing*, is the grand *temptation*, and *sin*, of many who teach no false doctrine, but " shun to declare the whole counsel of God : "

and omissions in this respect, though less *disgraceful*, are often equally *criminal* and *pernicious* with false doctrine.— What we preach publickly we should also be ready to inculcate privately, from house to house, as far as we have access to our hearers, or any prospect of doing them good : and ordinary visits should be thus improved, as well as opportunities of this kind purposely sought for. Thus we shall get acquainted with the state of our people's souls : a private address to an individual will often set a man right, extricate him from some perplexity, remove some difficulty, or stir him up to some duty, about which he had long hesitated : and we also shall thus learn to exercise our publick ministry to better effect.—Every part of divine truth ought, at one time or other, to be set before our congregations; and every duty inculcated : but the great essentials, without which there can be no salvation, should be testified most earnestly and frequently : nor can we have a better summary of them, than this of the apostle, even " repentance towards God, and faith towards our Lord " Jesus Christ," with their genuine fruits and effects : without these no sinner can escape destruction, and with these none will come short of eternal life. (*Note, Heb.* vi. 9, 10.)

V. 22—31.

The powerful influences of the Holy Spirit bind the zealous Christian or minister to his duty, in a manner perfectly consistent with the greatest conceivable liberty : even when he expects persecution and affliction, " the love of " Christ constraineth him " to proceed. (*Note,* 2 *Cor.* v. 13 —15.) When he is satisfied respecting his state and duty, he is not moved with the prospect of difficulties or sufferings; he values his life chiefly that he may glorify the Lord with it; nor is it dear to him, for the sake of any of those things which carnal men pursue. His great desire is " to " finish his course with joy," and to be welcomed by his Lord with " Well done, good and faithful servant ; " and if he has received from the Lord Jesus the office of the ministry, to testify to sinners the glad tidings of the grace of God ; he will desire to live no longer, than he can execute it honourably and usefully : that when the time shall come, when all " those, among whom he hath gone preach- " ing the kingdom of God, shall see his face no more; " he may be able to " take them to record, that he is pure " from the blood of all men, having never shunned to de- " clare to them all the counsel of God ; " according to the measure in which he was enabled by diligently searching the scriptures, and prayer for divine teaching, to become acquainted with it.—Our Lord Jesus knew perfectly what should befall him at Jerusalem ; which exceeded all that any other can possibly suffer or imagine : yet he " sted- " fastly set his face to go thither." (*Note, Luke* ix. 51—

5 D 7

AND it came to pass, that after [a] we were gotten from them, [b] and had launched, we came with a straight course unto Coos, and the *day* following unto Rhodes, and from thence unto Patara:

2 And [c] finding a ship sailing over unto [d] Phenicia, we went aboard, and set forth.

3 Now when we had discovered [e] Cyprus, we left it on the left hand, and sailed into [f] Syria, and landed at [g] Tyre: for there the ship was to unlade her burden.

4 And [h] finding disciples, [i] we tarried there seven days; who [k] said to Paul, through the Spirit, that he should not go up to Jerusalem.

5 And when we had accomplished [l] those days, we departed, and went our way; [l] and they all brought us on our way, [m] with wives and children, till *we were* out of the city: and [n] we kneeled down on the shore and prayed.

56.) The apostle did not " know what should befall him ;" nor do we : but let us be " followers of him as he was of " Christ."—Behold in St. Paul the Christian hero! No man was ever celebrated as a *hero*, who had any reserves in the pursuit of his main object; who could say, I will venture and labour so much, and no more, to attain it. None, who could not say, " Neither count I my life dear " to myself," in this grand concern. But only few can say with the apostle, My salvation is sure; this pursuit leads to heaven : " To me to live is Christ, and to die is " gain."—When affectionate and faithful pastors are called away from those, to whom they have been useful; they will be doubly earnest, that they may be succeeded by those who will " take heed to themselves, and to all their " flock ; " such as have indeed been made " Overseers by " the Holy Ghost," and who will feed them with the wholesome doctrine of divine truth. And what ought we to shrink from, when the benefit of that beloved company, " the church of God, whom he hath purchased with his " own blood," requires it at our hands ?—It cannot but lie heavy upon the mind of the faithful minister, when about to be removed from his beloved charge, to reflect upon the various perils, to which they will be exposed, from the subtlety and malice of Satan; from cruel persecutors, and crafty seducers; and from such as cause divisions, and " speak perverse things to draw away disciples after them." However, he can only warn them and their teachers, to watch : for if the enemy and his servants are so vigilant and indefatigable, we ought by no means to be heedless and indolent : and if a minister, in this case, can take the people to witness, that he has been " instant in season, " out of season," by day and by night, warning and exhorting them with all earnestness and affection; it will give emphasis to his parting admonitions, and confidence to his own heart when he is constrained to leave them.

V. 32—38.

When we part from our friends and brethren, we should " commend each other to God, and the word of his grace, " as able to build us up," and put us in possession of our holy inheritance : and ministers and their people ought to commend themselves and each other to God and his word, in the same manner; that they may be kept by his power, according to his promise, and in obedience to his precept, " through faith unto " eternal " salvation." But none obtain that inheritance, except those whom the Lord has sanctified.—It is peculiarly incumbent on all, who teach others to aspire after a heavenly treasure, to be themselves indifferent about earthly things, and free from all suspicion of " coveting any man's gold, or silver, or apparel." But alas ! few who claim the honour of being ' the successors ' of the apostles,' in office and authority, are disposed to affect an equality with them in self-denial, and a willingness to labour night and day without emolument, and in circumstances of comparative poverty! It is indeed probable, that their authority, as successors to the apostles, would be far less questioned, if this were their conduct and spirit. The zealous and prudent minister of Christ, however, who is " wise to win souls," will not tenaciously demand even his *due maintenance*, when it would interfere with his usefulness; but will " suffer all things rather than " hinder the gospel of Christ." Should peculiar circumstances require or admit of it ; his own hands would minister to his necessities, and those of his family or friends : that he might shew the people all his principles reduced to practice ; and teach even the poor of the flock thus to labour, that they might be able to assist in supporting the weak ; and that every one might learn to enquire, not what gain he shall make, but what good he can do ; according to the words of our gracious Lord, who has taught us, that " it is more blessed to give than to receive :" a sentence, that should be written on every heart, especially on that of every minister of the gospel. " This " mind was in Christ Jesus ; " may it be in us also !— Those who thus exhort and pray for one another, may have many weeping seasons, and painful separations ; (*Note*, 2 *Tim.* i. 3—5 ;) but " their sorrow shall be turned " into joy," and they will soon meet before the throne to part no more. May the Lord supply his whole church with bishops, presbyters, and pastors of every description, who drink deep into this spirit, and who closely follow the steps of this blessed apostle, and these Ephesian " overseers of that flock, which he purchased with his own " blood ! " Amen, and Amen.

NOTES.

CHAP. XXI. V. 1—6. " And it came to pass, that " embarking, having been torn from them, &c." So the first clause may be literally rendered : and the language was evidently intended to convey the idea of that powerful reciprocal affection, which cemented together the hearts of these Christian friends, and rendered their final separation at the call of duty exceedingly painful, and the effect of a very violent effort. (*Marg. Ref.* a, b.—*Note*, xx. 3

6 And when we had [o] taken our
leave one of another, we took ship;
[p] and they returned home again.
7 And when we had finished *our*
course from Tyre, we came to Ptolemais, [q] and saluted the brethren, and
[r] abode with them one day.
8 And the next *day* [s] we that were
of Paul's company departed, and came
unto [t] Cæsarea; and we entered into
the house of [u] Philip [x] the evangelist,
which was *one* of the seven, and
abode with him.
9 And the same man had four daughters, [y] virgins, [z] which did prophesy.
10 And [a] as we tarried *there* many
days, there came down from Judea a
certain prophet named [b] Agabus.
11 And when he was come unto
us, [c] he took Paul's girdle, and bound
his own hands and feet, and said, [d] Thus
saith the Holy Ghost, [e] So shall the
Jews at Jerusalem bind the man that
owneth this girdle, [f] and shall deliver
him into the hands of the Gentiles.
12 And when we heard these
things, both we, and they of that place,
[g] besought him not to go up to Jerusalem.
13 Then Paul answered, [h] What
mean ye [i] to weep, and to break mine
heart? [k] for I am ready not to be bound
only, but also to die at Jerusalem, for
the name of the Lord Jesus.
14 And when he would not be persuaded, we ceased, saying, [l] The will of
the Lord be done.

o 2 Cor. ii. 13.
p John i. 11. Gr. vii. 53. xvi. 32. xix. 27.
q 19. xviii. 22. xxv. 13. 1 Sam. x. 4. xiii. 10. Matt. v. 47. Heb. xiii. 24.
r 10. xxviii. 12.
s xvi. 10. 13. 16, 17. xx. 6. 13. xxvii. 1, 2. xxviii. 11. 16.
t viii. 40. ix. 30. x. 1. xviii. 22. xxiii. 23.
u vi. 5. viii. 5—13. 26—40.
x Eph. iv. 11. 2 Tim. iv. 5.
y 1 Cor. vii. 25—34. 38.
z ii. 17. Ex. xv. 20. Judg. iv. 4. 2 Kings xxii. 14. Neh. vi. 14. Joel ii. 28. 1 Cor. xi. 4, 5. Rev. ii. 20.
a 4. 7. xx. 16.
b xi. 28.
c 1 Sam. xv. 27, 28. 1 Kings xi. 29—31. 2 Kings xiii. 15—19. Jer. xiii. 1—11. xix. 10, 11. Ez. xxiv. 19—25. Hos. xii. 10.
d xiii. 2. xvi. 6. xx. 23. xxviii. 25. Heb. iii. 7. 1 Pet. i. 12.
e 33. xxii. 25. xxiv. 27. xxvi. 29. xxviii. 20. Eph. iii. 1. iv. 1. vi. 20. 2 Tim. ii. 9. Heb. x. 34.
f xxviii. 17. Matt. xx. 18, 19. xxvii. 1, 2.
g 4. xx. 22. Matt. xvi. 21—23.
h 1 Sam. xv. 14. Is. iii. 15. Ez. xviii. 2. Jon. i. 6.
i xx. 37. 1 Sam. i. 8. Phil. ii. 26. 2 Tim. i. 4.
k xx. 24. Rom. viii. 35—37. 1 Cor. xv. 31. 2 Cor. iv. 10—17. xi. 23—27. Phil. i. 20, 21. ii. 17. Col. i. 24. 2 Tim. ii. 4—6. 2 Pet. i. 14. Rev. iii. 10. xii. 11.
l Gen. xliii. 14. 1 Sam. iii. 18. 2 Sam. xv. 25, 26. 2 Kings xx. 19. Matt. vi. 10. xxvi. 39. 42. Luke xi. 2. xxii. 42.

—38.)—Coos and Rhodes were well-known islands in the Egean Sea: Patara was a city of Lycia, upon the continent of Asia. Perhaps the ship, in which Paul and his friends had sailed thus far, was bound to this port. They however met with another, which was about to sail directly into Phenicia, in which they embarked; and, leaving the island of Cyprus on their left hand, they sailed directly to Tyre, where the ship was to unlade her freight. (*Marg. Ref.* e—g.—*Note*, xxvii. 4, 5.) Here they sought out the disciples of their Lord: and, as the most dangerous part of their voyage was past, and time enough remained for their journey to Jerusalem before the Pentecost, they continued a week at Tyre; in order, probably, to spend one Lord's day with their brethren, as well as to confer together on the interesting subject of their common faith. Some disciples here also cautioned Paul not to go up to Jerusalem: they were shewn by the Spirit of prophecy, that he would meet with great sufferings and trials, if he went thither; and they supposed that he might lawfully decline the journey and avoid the danger: but he judged otherwise. 'Does the Spirit of God then oppose 'himself? By no means. ... But they, understanding, by 'the revelation of the Spirit, what danger awaited Paul, 'out of love, and not by any special command of the 'Spirit, intreated him not to go up to Jerusalem; being 'ignorant of what the same Spirit had commanded Paul.' *Beza.* (*Marg. Ref.* h—k.—*Notes*, 7—14. xx. 22—24.) When they therefore departed, the whole company of the disciples, with their families, attended them to the seashore, with the greatest expressions of respect and affection; and there they all kneeled down in the most solemn and humble manner, and united in fervent prayer for each other's protection and felicity. (*Marg. Ref.* l—p.)—Should a company of believers, in this Christian country, and in the environs of one of our great commercial cities, imitate this example; they would doubtless be derided, as a *fanatical* or *hypocritical* set of people.—It is most evident, from this circumstance, that *kneeling* was the general posture for publick and social prayer, in the primitive church; otherwise this company would scarcely have used it in so inconvenient a situation.

Were gotten from them. (1) Αποσπασθεντας. '*Avulsos* '*ab iis.*' Schleusner. xx. 30. *Matt.* xxvi. 51. *Luke* xxii. 41. Ex απο, et σπαω, *traho.*—*Had launched.*] Αναχθηναι. 2. See on xiii. 13.—*We came with a straight course.*] Ευθυδρομησαντες. See on xvi. 11.—*When we had discovered.* (3) Αναφανεντες. *Luke* xix. 11. Not elsewhere. Ex ανα, et φαινομαι, *appareo.*—*Landed.*] Καταχθημεν. xxii. 30. xxviii. 12. *Luke* v. 11.—*To unlade.*] Αποφορτιζομενον. Here only. Ex απο, et φορτος, *onus.*—*Her burden.*] Τον γομον. *Rev.* xviii. 11, 12. Not elsewhere N. T. A γεμω, *onustus sum.* —*Accomplished.* (5) Εξαρτισαι. 2 *Tim.* iii. 17. Not elsewhere. Ab εξ, et αρτιος, *integer.*—*Home again.* (6) Εις τα ιδια. *John* xvi. 32. xix. 27.

V. 7—14. The apostle and his friends finished their voyage when they had sailed from Tyre to Ptolemais, a city on the sea-coast of Galilee, so called, because rebuilt by Ptolemy, king of Egypt; having before been called Accho. (*Judg.* i. 31.) Here too they met with disciples, with whom they spent only one day; and on the next they journeyed by land to Cæsarea. (*Marg. Ref.* q. s, t.)—Philip, one of the seven first deacons, whose usefulness as an evangelist is before recorded, now resided in this city; and probably he had laboured there and in the adjacent parts, during the intervening years. (*Notes*, vi. 2—6. viii. 5—13. 26—40.) He had the peculiar honour of having four daughters, all endued with the gift of prophecy: (*Marg. Ref.* y, z.—*Notes*, ii. 14—21. *Judg.* iv. 4—9. 2 *Kings* xxii. 14. 1 *Cor.* xi. 2—16:) and perhaps they gave intimations to Paul of his approaching trials. As, however, he and his friends stayed at Cæsarea several days, Agabus, of whom we read before, (*Note*, xi. 27—30,) came from Judea, properly so called; (for Cæsarea lay in that part of the land, which belonged to the kings of Israel, not in that belonging to the kings of Judah;) and, with a significant emblem, he certified Paul, by the Holy Spirit, that at Jerusalem he would be seized as a malefactor by the Jews, who would cause him to be bound,

15 And after those days we took up our carriages, "and went up to Jerusalem.

16 There went with us also *certain* of the disciples of Cæsarea, and brought with them one Mnason of Cyprus, an old disciple, with whom we should lodge.

17 And when we were come to Jerusalem, the brethren received us gladly.

18 And the *day* following Paul went in with us unto James; and all the elders were present.

19 And when he had saluted them, he declared particularly what things God had wrought among the Gentiles by his ministry.

20 And when they heard *it*, they glorified the Lord, and said unto him, Thou seest, brother, how many thousands of Jews there are which believe; and they are all zealous of the law;

---

hand and foot, and delivered to the Gentiles, as the Lord Jesus had been. (*Marg. Ref.* c—f.) This prediction induced both the apostle's companions, and the Christians of Cæsarea, earnestly to dissuade him from his intended journey out of love to him, and the value which they set on his useful life and labours. (*Marg. Ref.* g.) But he considered himself bound in duty, to accomplish the service with which he had been entrusted, of conveying the oblations of the Gentile converts to the church at Jerusalem; and, on this and other accounts, he was stedfastly purposed to proceed, whatever persecutions might await him. The prospect indeed of bonds and imprisonment could not move him; yet the affectionate intreaties of his friends exceedingly distressed his feeling mind: and he earnestly expostulated with them, for thus weeping, and " breaking his heart" with their ill-timed sorrows; which unfitted him for his duty, when they ought to have encouraged him in it: (*Marg. Ref.* h—k.—*Notes*, 1—6. xx. 22 —24. *Matt.* xvi. 21—23 :) for, by the grace of God, he was ready to be bound, or even put to death as a martyr, for the honour of his beloved Saviour, either now at Jerusalem, or whenever he should be called to do it. When therefore they saw him fixed in his purpose, they no more attempted to dissuade him from it; but acquiesced in the will of God as to the event, being satisfied that he could and would over-rule it for good. (*Marg. Ref.* l.)—It was not long after, that the apostle was conveyed back to Cæsarea, a prisoner; and, as he had liberty to see his friends, they would again have the opportunity of conversing with him. (*Notes*, xxiii. 31—35. xxiv. 22, 23.)— *Evangelist.* (8) 'Evangelist is the name of an office, in ' the apostles' times.' *Hammond.* 'This word occurs only ' thrice in the New Testament: *Acts* xxi. 8. Secondly, ' in the Epistle to the Ephesians, where evangelists are ' mentioned after apostles and prophets, as one of the ' offices, which our Lord, after his ascension, had appointed ' for the conversion of infidels, and the establishment of ' order in his church; *Eph.* iv. 11: and lastly, 2 *Tim.* iv. ' 5. ... This word has also obtained another signification, ' which, though not scriptural, is very ancient.' *Campbell.* (*Notes, Eph.* iv. 11—13. 2 *Tim.* iv. 1—5.)—*So shall,* &c. (11) ' Not so as to the girdle; for he was only bound ' with chains : nor so as to the binding of his feet; for ' Paul seems only to have had the chains fastened to his ' hands : but so as to be as truly and as much bound as ' Agabus was; not personally by the Jews, but by the Ro-' mans at their instigation, and on their account.' *Whitby.* *When we had finished* our course. (7) Τον πλουν διανυσαν-

---

τες.—Πλουν xxvii. 9, 10. Not elsewhere. A πλεω, *navigo*. Διανυω. Here only. ' Id. quod τελεω.' *Schleusner.—We came.*] Κατηντησαμεν. See on xvi. 1. " Finishing our " voyage, we arrived at Ptolemais."—*The evangelist.* (8) Ευαγγελιςυ. *Eph.* iv. 11. 2 *Tim.* iv. 5. (*Notes, Eph.* iv. 11—13, *v.* 11. 2 *Tim.* iv. 1—5, *v.* 5.)—*They of that place.* (12) Οι εντευιοι. Here only. Εκ εν, et τοπος, *locus.*— *What mean ye?* (13) Τι ποιειτε; " What are ye doing ?" —*To break.*] Συνθρυπτοντες. Here only. Εκ συν, et θρυπτω, *frango.*

V. 15, 16. When the time allotted for the stay of the apostle and his companions at Cæsarea was expired, " they " collected and prepared for carriage those things, which " were to be taken with them," and went up to Jerusalem. It is probable they travelled on foot : and some think that they carried their luggage themselves; others that they laded beasts of burden with it. (*Note,* 1 *Sam.* xvii. 22.) Perhaps it had been conveyed by sea from Ptolemais to Cæsarea, though they journeyed by land : but, as they were now travelling the interior part of the country, it became necessary to make some other preparation for the conveyance of it. For they carried with them a considerable sum of money from the Gentile converts, to the poor brethren at Jerusalem. (xxiv. 17.)—In this journey, they were attended by some of the disciples of Cæsarea, who " brought them to one Mnason," a native of Cyprus, who then lived at Jerusalem, at whose house the apostle and his company might be conveniently lodged, during the feast. He was " an old disciple :" perhaps he had been a disciple of Jesus, during his abode on earth ; or he had joined the church, soon after the day of Pentecost ; and had all along maintained (as it must be supposed,) a consistent character, and was now matured in wisdom and grace. (*Marg. Ref.* p.)

We took up our carriages. (15) Αποσκευασαμενοι. Here only. ' *Colligere vasa et sarcinas, sibi sumere res ad iter faci-' endum necessarias.*' *Schleusner.* Εκ απο, et σκευος, *vas, instrumentum.—Brought with them one Mnason ... with whom we should lodge.* (16) Αγοντες παρ ῳ ξενισθωμεν, Μνασωνι. " Conducting us to one Mnason, ... with whom " we might lodge."—*An old disciple.*] Αρχαιῳ μαθητῃ. See on xv. 7.

V. 17—21. The Christians at Jerusalem gladly welcomed the apostle ; rejoicing in the success of his ministry, and in the fruits of the faith and love produced by the Gentile converts. The next day he introduced " the mes-" sengers of the churches," to the apostle James ; who seems to have been the only one of the twelve then resid-

5 κ 2

21 And they are informed of thee, ^a that thou teachest all the Jews which are among the Gentiles to forsake Moses, saying, That they ought not to circumcise *their* children, neither to walk after the customs.

22 What is it therefore? ^b the multitude must needs come together: for they will hear that thou art come.

23 Do therefore this that we say to thee: ^c We have four men which have a vow on them;

24 Them take, ^d and purify thyself with them, and be at charges with them, ^e that they may shave *their* heads: and all may know that those things, whereof they were informed concerning

thee, are nothing; ^f but *that* thou thyself also walkest orderly, and keepest the law.

25 As touching the Gentiles which believe, ^g we have written and. concluded, that they observe no such thing, save only that they keep themselves from things offered to idols, and from blood, and from strangled, and from fornication.

26 Then Paul took the men, and the next day purifying himself with them ^h entered into the temple, ⁱ to signify the accomplishment of the days of purification, until that an offering should be offered for every one of them.

---

ing at Jerusalem, and who peculiarly superintended the concerns of the church in that city: but all the elders were convened on the occasion. After affectionate salutations, Paul proceeded to relate to them particularly, what God had done by his ministry, since he last saw them ; (*Notes*, xv. 1—6. xvi—xx ;) at which they rejoiced and glorified God. (*Marg. Ref.* q—u.) They however intreated him to recollect how many " tens of thousands" of Jewish converts to Christ were now assembled at Jerusalem, who were all zealous for the Mosaick ceremonies, and greatly prejudiced against him for his supposed opposition to them. For they had been informed, and had generally imbibed the opinion, that he every where instructed the Jews to *apostatize* from Moses ; inculcating it as a matter of bounden duty, that they should not circumcise their children, or observe any of the customs of the ritual law. (*Marg. Ref.* x—a.) In this they had been misinformed : for, though the apostle had shewn, that none were bound to observe the ceremonial law, and that they must by no means place any dependence on such obedience for justification ; he had never forbidden the Jewish converts to observe it, as a matter of expediency, when their communion with their Gentile brethren would admit of it. (*Note*, xvi. 1—3.)—*Elders*. (18) ' All the bishops ' of Judea, saith Dr. Hammond, without one word to ' prove it.' *Whitby*. That learned writer's zeal for episcopacy leads him frequently to express himself in a manner, which seems to imply that there were no presbyters in the primitive church : perhaps he was not aware, that this supposition would reduce all ministers, above deacons, to an entire parity of order, as effectually as either the presbyterian or the independent plan could do.—*How many thousands*. (20) Or, " How many tens of thousands." *Gr.* This can hardly mean less than forty or fifty thousand : and, though a considerable part of this large number might come from other places to keep the feast; yet it can scarcely be doubted, but that there were so many Christians, statedly residing at Jerusalem, as to form several distinct congregations; yet the whole is spoken of as one church.

Gladly. (17) Ασμενως. See on ii. 41.—*How many thousands.* (20) Ποσαι μυριαδες. xix. 19. Luke xii. 1. Heb.

xii. 22. Jude 14. Rev. v. 11. ix. 16.—*Zealous.*] Ζηλωται. i. 13. xxii. 3. Luke vi. 15. 1 Cor. xiv. 12. Gal. i. 14. Tit. ii. 14.—Α ζηλος. (*Note*, Jam. iii. 13—16.)—*They are informed.* (21) Κατηχηθησαν. 24. See on Luke i. 4.—*To forsake.*] Αποςασιαν. 2 Thes. ii. 3. Here only. Ex απο, et ἱςημι, sto.

V. 22—26. Disadvantageous reports had been circulated concerning Paul. His coming would soon be known ; the multitude would certainly come together, to enquire into the reasons and motives of his conduct : and much disturbance might arise from their prejudices, if nothing were done to satisfy them. James, therefore, and the elders, enquired what was proper to be done, to counteract their prejudices. And as they had among them four persons, who were under a Nazarite's vow, the term of which was nearly expiring : they proposed to Paul to join with them as one of the company ; that he might purify himself, and bear a part in the expenses of the customary sacrifices, when the time came for them to shave their heads upon the completion of their vow. (*Notes, Num.* vi. 1—21.) As this would be a publick transaction, his concurrence in it would soon be known : and thus the whole multitude would at once be convinced, that they had been misinformed ; and that the apostle himself " walked " orderly," according to the prescriptions of the law. (*Marg. Ref.* c—f.)—This conclusion seems to have been rather stronger than the real case would admit of. The apostle had before performed a vow of a similar nature ; (*Note*, xviii. 18—23 ;) and he doubtless paid some regard to the Mosaick law, as a matter of expediency : but he does not appear to have habitually observed it, as it may be inferred from his own words. (*Notes*, 1 Cor. ix. 19—23. Gal. ii. 11—16. iv. 12—16.) They probably meant, that he attended to the legal ceremonies, as far as his intimate communion with uncircumcised persons would permit him : but it may be questioned, whether this, if it had been fully explained, would have satisfied the persons concerned. James and the elders at the same time avowed, that they intended nothing contrary to their former determination, concerning the gentile converts: (*Note*, xv. 22 —29 :) and the apostle, complying with their counsel, took the necessary steps, for joining with the Nazarites in their purifications and oblations. (*Marg. Ref.* g—i.)—It

27 And when the seven days were almost ended, ^k the Jews which were of Asia, when they saw him in the temple, ^l stirred up all the people, ^m and laid hands on him,

28 Crying out, ⁿ Men of Israel, help: ^o this is the man that teacheth all *men* every where against the people, and the law, and this place: and

further, ^p brought Greeks also into the temple, and hath polluted this holy place.

29 (For they had seen before with him in the city, ^q Trophimus an Ephesian, whom they supposed that Paul had brought into the temple.)

30 And ^r all the city was moved, and the people ran together; ^s and

---

has been questioned whether on this occasion he and his advisers acted in strict consistency with Christian simplicity: and it should be remembered, that, though the apostles were infallibly preserved from mistaking, corrupting, or mutilating the doctrine, which they were entrusted to communicate to the church; yet they were not rendered infallible in their personal conduct: in many things, they acknowledged, and it is evident, they all offended, and were to be blamed. (*Note, Gal.* ii. 6—10.) Perhaps it would be found very difficult wholly to defend the apostle from the charge of temporizing, accommodating, or refining too much in this matter. His deference to the judgment of his brethren, his desire of " becoming all " things to all men," and his willingness to conciliate the Jewish believers, seem to have carried him rather too far: and he was led to hold out a greater degree of regard to the Mosaick law, than he shewed in his general conduct. The concession, however, by no means answered the intended purpose; on the contrary, it was the immediate occasion of his predicted sufferings.—" To be at charges " with Nazarites was both a common and a very popular ' thing among the Jews. ... Maimonides ... asserts, that a ' person who was not himself a Nazarite, might bind him- ' self by a vow to take part with one in his sacrifice.' *Doddridge*.—This, however, not being mentioned in the law, was rather complying with custom and tradition, than shewing a regard for the ceremonies of Moses.—' James ' and the brethren thought it was most regular and con- ' venient, that the Jewish ritual should still be observed, ' by those of the circumcision who believed in Christ. And, ' considering what tribulation the church at Jerusalem ' must otherwise have been exposed to by the sanhedrim, ' who no doubt would have prosecuted them to the utmost ' as apostates; and also how soon Providence intended to ' render the practice of it impossible; ... it was certainly ' the most orderly and prudent conduct to conform to it; ' though it were looked upon by those, that understood ' the matter fully, (which it was not necessary that all ' should,) as antiquated and ready to vanish away.' *Ibid.* —The Jewish Christians at Jerusalem and in Judea might comply with the law far more easily and exactly, than their brethren could in other countries, who were joined in the same churches with the Gentile converts.—Does not the epistle to the Hebrews, probably written by the apostle when a prisoner at Rome, shew, that he thought it of great importance, even to the Christians in Judea, to understand that the Mosaick law had no longer any validity; and that he considered their attachment to it, as exceedingly unfavourable to their proficiency in true religion? (*Preface to Hebrews.*)

The multitude. (22) Πληθος. vi. 2. xv. 12. The mul-

titude of Christians are here distinguished from James and the elders, who concert measures to obviate the effect of their prejudices. "The multitude must needs come to- " gether:" not as regularly convened to join and vote in the consultation, or as by *right*; but as drawn together by the reports concerning Paul. (*Notes,* xv. 1—6, *vv.* 4 —6. 12.)—*Purify thyself.* (24) 'Αγνισθητι, 26. xxiv. 18. —*Be at charges.*] Δαπανησον. *Mark* v. 26. *Luke* xiv. 14. 2 *Cor.* xii. 15. *Jam.* iv. 3. Δαπανη, *Luke* xiv. 28.—*They may shave.*] Ξυρησωνται. 1 *Cor.* xi. 5, 6. Not elsewhere. —*Thou walkest orderly.*] Στοιχεις. *Rom.* iv. 12. vi. 16. *Gal.* v. 25. *Phil.* iii. 16. A ςοιχος, ordo militum in acie. —*Things offered to idols,* &c. (25) Ει δωλοθυτων. See on xv. 29.—*Of purification.*] Τω αγνισμω. Here only N.T. —*Num.* vi. 5. xxxi. 23. *Sept.*

V. 27—30. As the apostle could not enter on his purification, till the third day after his arrival at Jerusalem; (17, 18. 26;) and as he made his defence before Felix, (which seems to have been seven or eight days after he came to Jerusalem; (*Note,* xxiv. 10—21;) the first clause should certainly be rendered, " when the seven days were about " to be accomplished;" that is, the seven days which had been fixed on, and mentioned to the priests as the term at the end of which the sacrifices would be offered, and the vow performed. (*Note,* 22—26.) -At this time, some Jews from Asia, (*Note,* xix. 8—12,) who had known Paul when he preached there, saw him in the inner court of the temple, whither he went to the priests, about the sacrifices to be offered: and, being actuated by a furious and bigoted zeal, they excited a tumult, and seized upon him, as a profaner of that sacred place: calling earnestly on all true Israelites to assist them in a cause, in which their religion and national honour were at stake. For this was the very man, who had every where taught men to disregard their title to be the peculiar people of God; to violate the law of Moses, as abrogated; and to despise the temple as about to be destroyed: (*Marg. Ref.* m—o.—*Note,* vi. 9 —14:) and to shew his contempt and enmity the more, they averred, that he had brought uncircumcised Gentiles into the holy place to profane it. In this they were mistaken: for, having seen Paul walking in the city with Trophimus, a Gentile convert, they took it for granted, that he had also brought him into the temple. (*Notes,* xix. 23 —31. 32—41, *vv.* 32—34.) This out-cry, however, soon brought the multitudes from every part of the city; and Paul was dragged as a criminal, to be put to death without the sanctuary, lest it should be defiled with his blood: at the same time the doors were shut, that he might not escape to the horns of the altar for refuge, and that no other Gentiles might enter. (*Marg. Ref.* q—s.)—There was a

they took Paul, and drew him out of the temple: and forthwith the doors were shut.

31 And ᵗ as they went about to kill him, tidings came unto the ᵘ chief captain of the band, ˣ that all Jerusalem was in an uproar;

32 Who immediately ʸ took soldiers and centurions, ᶻ and ran down unto them: and when they saw the chief captain and the soldiers, they left ᵃ beating of Paul.

33 Then the chief captain came near, and took him, and commanded him to ᵇ be bound with two chains; ᶜ and demanded who he was, and what he had done.

34 And ᵈ some cried one thing, some another, among the multitude: and when he could not ᵉ know the certainty for the tumult, he commanded him to be carried ᶠ into the castle.

35 And when he came upon the stairs, so it was, that he was borne of the soldiers ᵍ for the violence of the people.

36 For the multitude of the people followed after, crying, ʰAway with him.

37 And as Paul was to be led into the castle, he said unto the chief captain, ¹ May I speak unto thee? Who said, Canst thou speak Greek?

38 Art not thou that Egyptian, ᵏ which before these days madest an uproar, and leddest out into the wilderness four thousand men that were murderers?

39 But Paul said, ˡ I am a man *which am a Jew of Tarsus, a city* in ᵐ Cilicia, ⁿ a citizen of no mean city: and I beseech thee, ° *suffer me to speak unto* the people.

40 And when he had given him licence, Paul stood ᵖ on the stairs, ᵠ and beckoned with the hand unto the people. And when there was made ᵠ a great silence, he spake unto *them* in the ˢ Hebrew tongue, saying,

Marginal references (left column)

t xxii. 77. xxvi. 9.
16. John xvi. 2.
u xxiii. 17. xxiv. 23.
7. 22. xxv. 23.
x 38. xvii. b. 13.
40. 1 Kings l. 41.
Matt. xxvi b.
Mark xiv. 2.
y xxiii. 23, 24.
z xviii. 2.. xxix.
7.
a v. 40. xviii. 17.
xxii. 19. 24. 25.
15.
b 11. xii. 6. xv.
23, xxi. 2b. 26.
xxviii. 20 Judg.
xv. 13. xvi. 8.
12. 71.
c xxii. 24. xxv.
16. John xviii.
29, 30.
d xix. 32.
e xxii. 30. xxv.
20.
f 87. xxii. 24
xxiii. 10. 16.

Marginal references (right column)

g Gen. vi. 11, 13
Ps. iv. 9. lviii.
2. Jer. xxiii. 10.
Hab. i. 2, 3.
h vii. 54 xxii. 22.
Luke xxiii. 18.
John xix. 15.
i 19. xix. 30.
Matt. x. 18—20.
Luke xxi. 15.
k v. 36, 87. Matt.
1. 11. 1 Cor. iv.
3.
l iv. n. 30. xxii.
3. xxiii. 34.
m ix. 2. xv. 23. 41.
—27. xxiii. 16.
E. 1 Pet. ii. 15.
iv. 15, 16.
p 35. 2 Kings ix.
13.
q xii. 17. xiii. 16.
xix. 33.
r xxi. 2.
s vi. 1. xxvi. 14.
Luke xxiii. 38.
John v. 2. xix.
13. 17. 20. Rev.
ix. 11. xvi. 16.

---

court appropriated to the Gentiles, in which Trophimus might legally have worshipped: but the insurgents supposed, that Paul had taken him into the courts, which none but Jews and circumcised proselytes might enter.

When the seven days were almost ended. (27) Ὡς ἐμελλον αἱ ἑπτα ἡμεραι συντελεισθαι.—" As the seven days were " about to be ended."—Συντελεω, *Matt.* vii. 28. *Mark* xiii. 4. *Rom.* ix. 28. *Heb.* viii. 8.—*Stirred up.*] Συντχεον. Here only N. T.—*Gen.* xi. 7. 9. Ex συν et χεω, *fundo.* Idem ac συγχνω, 31. See on xix. 32.—*They had seen before.* (29) Ησαν προεωρακοτις. See on ii. 25.—*The people ran together.* (30) Εγενετο συνδρομη τε λαω. Here only. Ex συν, et δεδρομα, pret. med. verbi συντρεχω.

V. 31—36. It has been asserted, that the Jews claimed the liberty of putting to death, without any legal process, such uncircumcised persons as entered the inner courts of the temple: yet even this could not be applicable to Paul. In the fury of their zeal, however, they were about to kill him: but Lysias, the commanding officer of the Roman forces at Jerusalem, being also the tribune, or captain over a thousand men, hearing of the riot, immediately took the centurions and soldiers under his command, or part of them, and hastened to quell it. His presence induced those who were beating Paul, (intending to put him to death by blows with stones or staves,) to suspend their violence: and Lysias, from their rage, concluding that he must be some desperate malefactor, ordered him to be " bound with two chains;" and asked who he was, and of what crime he had been guilty. But, not being able to learn any thing, from the incoherent clamours of the mob, he ordered him to be conveyed to the castle; which stood on an eminence near the temple, being the station of the Roman soldiers who kept guard there. When the soldiers had brought Paul to the stairs, which led to the entrance of the castle, they were obliged to carry him, to prevent the people from violently rushing upon him, and killing him: for they all furiously followed after, exclaiming, " Away with him," or " Kill him;" for certainly this was their meaning. (*Marg. Ref.*—*Notes*, vii. 54—60; xxii. 22—30.)

Tidings. (31) Φασις. Here only.—Ab inusitato φαω, dico, aio.—*The chief captain.*] Τῳ χιλιαρχῳ. 33. 37. *John* xviii. 12. See on *Mark* vi. 21.—*Was in an uproar.*] Συγκεχυται. See on 27.—*Cried.* (34) Εξοων. 17. xvii. 6. *Matt.* iii. 3. *Mark* xv. 34.—*The castle.*] Την παρεμ-βολην. 37. xxiii. 10. 16. 32. *Heb.* xi. 34. xiii. 11. 13. *Rev.* xx. 9.—A παρεμβαλλω, immitto, interjicio. Ex παρα, εν, et βαλλω, jacio.—*The stairs.* (35) Τες αναβαθμες. 40. Here only N. T.—*2 Kings* ix. 13. xx. 11. Αναβαθμιον, *Ex.* xx. 26. Sept. Ab αναβαινω, ascendo.—*Away with him.* (36) Αιρε αυτον. See on *Luke* xxiii. 18.

V. 37—40. When the apostle had been conveyed into the environs of the castle, out of the reach of the multitude, he desired permission from the chief captain to speak to him: who was surprised to hear his prisoner so readily use the Greek language. He indeed supposed him to have been an Egyptian, who, some time before, had made an insurrection in the city, and, leading forth a numerous banditti, had done extensive mischief. For, as that insurgent had escaped, when his followers were destroyed or dispersed, it was natural for Lysias to suppose Paul to be the same person, attempting to excite new disturbances. The apostle however assured him, that he was " a Jew," and a native of Tarsus, and a citizen of no inconsiderable city: he therefore begged of him, that he might be permitted to address the multitude in order to silence their

CHAP. XXII.

The apostle declares, before the people, the place of his birth, his education, his zeal against the gospel; his conversion, and his commission from Jesus to preach to the gentiles, 1—21. At the mention of the gentiles, the people furiously exclaim against him; and the chief captain orders his soldiers to examine him by scourging, 22—24: which he avoids, by pleading the privilege of a Roman citizen, 25—29. He is brought before the council, 30.

clamours, and rectify their misapprehensions; by which Lysias also would learn who he was, and what he had done. Accordingly, having obtained permission, he placed himself on the top of the stairs, and made a signal with his hand to the multitude, that he desired to speak to them: and, curiosity concurring with other motives, they observed a profound silence, whilst he addressed them in the Hebrew tongue, at least in that dialect of it which was generally used.—*Four thousand*, &c. (38) Josephus mentions thirty thousand men, whom this Egyptian, (whose name is not known,) had collected together: but it is probable that he " led forth " only four thousand, and that the rest came to him in the wilderness; or only four thousand of the company were *murderers*. (*Marg. Ref.*)

Canst thou speak Greek? (37) 'Ελληνιϛι γινωσκεις; *John* xix. 20.—Greek was spoken by numbers in Egypt, especially where Greek colonies had been planted. The Jews also in Egypt spake Greek, and used the Greek translation of the scriptures. But the native Egyptians spoke another language.—*Modest an uproar.* (38) Αναϛατωσας. See on xvii. 6.—*Murderers.*] Των σικαριων. Here only.—' Vox ' origine Latina, orta a *sica* h. e. *gladiolo.*' Schleusner.—A short sword, which they concealed under their garments, till an occasion was afforded them, of assassinating the objects of their vindictive cruelty.—*Of no mean city.* (39) Ουκ αϲημου πολεως. Here only. Εκ α priv. et ϲημα, *signum.* —*In the Hebrew tongue.* (40) Τη Εϲραϊδι διαλεκτψ. xxii. 2. See on ii. 6.—It is decidedly agreed among the learned, that the Syriack or Chaldee dialect is meant. No doubt many Chaldee words and phrases came into use among the Jews, who returned from the Babylonish captivity. Yet those parts of the Old Testament, which were written after that event, are in Hebrew, except a few passages in Ezra, which are Chaldee, for special reasons. This creates a difficulty, as to the current opinion taken in its full extent. Nor does the language of the New Testament favour it: and several of the arguments used in support of it, are inconclusive. (*Notes*, Ezra iv. 7—9. vii. 11, 12. *Neh.* viii. 8. *Jer.* x. 11. *Dan.* ii. 4.)

PRACTICAL OBSERVATIONS.

V. 1—16.

Wherever zealous Christians travel, they will enquire after their brethren in the Lord, and get acquainted with them; because they delight in their company, and desire to do them good, and to derive benefit from them. (*Note, Ps.* cxix. 57—63, *v.* 63.) But, even this sweet and endeared ' communion of the saints ' must not induce them to prolong their continuance together, beyond what other duties admit of.—Fervent social prayer abates the poignancy of our sorrow, when constrained to separate from those whom we love: and this is peculiarly seasonable, when sharp afflictions or important services lie before us. Our children too should be admitted to such scenes of affection and devotion; that their tender minds may be early im-

pressed with a sense of the excellency and importance of religion: (*Note, Gen.* xlviii. 1. *P. O.* 1—8.) Thus we may hope, that when they grow up, they will be evidently partakers of the blessing, and endued with spiritual gifts, for the edification of others also; which should be considered as the greatest favour God can bestow on us, with respect to our offspring.—The path of duty will eventually be that of safety: yet it often leads into many apparent, or temporary, dangers and difficulties; the prospect of which may induce those, who value the useful lives of eminent persons, to dissuade them from the services allotted to them: but, if they are satisfied of their call in Providence; they should not turn aside, out of concern or affection for their friends, any more than from fear of their enemies. It is, however, an extraordinary attainment, for the same man to be so firm and inflexible, in following the dictates of his own conscience, as to be habitually ready to endure bonds, or face death for the Lord's sake; and yet so full of tenderness and sympathy, as to be more affected by the sorrows of his friends, than by the prospect of his own perils and sufferings. (*Note, Phil.* ii. 24 —30.)—When we have given the best counsel we can, to those who conscientiously desire to know the will of God; and yet find that they are not convinced, or persuaded, by what we have urged; we should desist, and acquiesce in the will of the Lord, who can educe good from those measures and events, which seem to us undesirable or inexpedient.—In our endeavours to do good to our brethren, we should introduce them to the acquaintance of those, who have been a comfort or benefit to us: and " old disciples" should be *accessible;* as well as careful to set their younger brethren an example of humility, spirituality, stedfastness, zeal, prudence, candour, and enlarged love; which may evince, that their dependence on the Lord, and devotedness to him, have increased, according to the years during which they have known him. (*Notes, Heb.* v. 11—14. *Rev.* ii. 2—5. *P. O.* 2—7.)

V. 17—26.

What a striking proof is it of the weakness and depravity of human nature, that so large a proportion of the disciples of Christ, even in the days of the apostles, were exceedingly disaffected to the most eminent minister, probably, who ever lived! Neither his extraordinary conversion, his blameless and holy character, his peculiar endowments, his extensive labours and usefulness, or his patient sufferings in the cause of Christ; nor yet the oblations which he bestowed so much pains to collect, and bring from the Gentile converts to their Jewish brethren, could conciliate their esteem and affection: because he would not render that respect to the antiquated Mosaick ceremonial, with which they had been used to regard it! Nor could even the authority of James and the pious elders pacify their minds, or prevent their tumultuously assembling together; when they heard that he was come

5 κ 6

a vii. 2. xiii. 26.
xxiii. 1. 6.
xxviii. 17.
b *Greek alii.* xix.
33. xxiv. 10.
xxv. 8. 16 xxvi.
1, 2. 24. Luke
xii. 11. xxi. 14.
Rom. ii. 18.
1 Cor. ix. 3.
2 Cor. vii. 11.
xii. 19. Phil. i.
7. 17. 2 Tim. iv.
16. 1 Pet. iii. 15.

MEN, brethren, and fathers, hear
ye ᵇmy defence *which I make* now
unto you.

c *See on* xxi. 40.
d xxi. 39. Rom.
xi. 1. 2 Cor. xi.
22. Phil. iii. 5.
e ix. 11. 30. xxi.
39.
f vi. 9. xv. 23. 41.
xviii. 24. Gal. i.
21.
g Deut. xxxiii. 3.
Luke ii. 46. viii.
35. x. 39.

2 (And when they heard that he
spake ᶜin the Hebrew tongue to them,
they kept the more silence: and he
saith,)

3 I am verily a man *which am* ᵈa
Jew, ᵉborn in Tarsus, ᶠ*a city* in Cilicia, yet brought up in this city ᶠat the
feet of ʰGamaliel, ⁱ*and* taught according to the perfect manner of the law of

h v. 34. i xxiii. 6. xxvi. 5. Gal. i. 14. Phil. iii. 5.

the fathers, ᵏand was zealous toward
God, as ye all are this day.

4 And ˡI persecuted ᵐthis way unto
the death, binding and delivering into
prisons both men and women.

5 As ⁿalso the high priest doth bear
me witness, °and all the estate of the
elders: from whom also I received letters unto ᵖthe brethren, and went to
Damascus, to bring them which were
there bound unto Jerusalem, for to be
punished.

k xxi. 20. 2 Sam.
xxi. 2. Rom. x.
2. 3. Gal. i. .7.
13. Phil. iii. 6.
l ix. 2, 14. xxii.
4, 5. vii. 58.
viii. 1—4. 1x. 1.
2. 13, 14. 21.
xxvi. 9—11.
1 Cor. xv. 9.
1 Tim. i. 13—15.
m xvi. 17. xviii.
26. xix. 9. 23.
n ix. 1. 2. 14.
o v. 21. Luke
xxii. 66.
p 1. Rom. ix. 3.

---

to Jerusalem! How watchful then should we be against
prejudices of every kind; and against those misrepresentations of men's principles and conduct, from which prejudices commonly originate! And how patient should we
be, if called to have fellowship with the great apostle of
us Gentiles in this affliction; and to endure the suspicions
and coldness, of those whom we most esteem and love!
We ought indeed to use all proper methods of rectifying
the judgments and conciliating the affections of our
brethren, as far as their misapprehension can interfere
with our usefulness: yet we should watch against the
temptation of conniving at those errors or evils, which are
the general source of prejudices, and which cannot consistently be countenanced. When accommodation is allowed to infringe upon our "simplicity and godly sin-
" cerity," it will seldom produce any good effect. Our
brethren will not be satisfied, unless we go to the full
length of their sentiments; others will begin to suspect
our integrity, and to hesitate concerning us; and it is in
vain to attempt conciliating the favour of graceless bigots,
and furious zealots of any party, from whom we shall
commonly do well to keep at a distance. But much wisdom, integrity, and humility are requisite, to guide us in
the middle way, between an uncomplying inflexibility in
things of small consequence, and a temporizing spirit in
respect of important truth. (*P. O.* 1 *Cor.* ix. 19—27.) Yet,
the Lord will preserve his upright servants from fatal mistakes; though he may see good to leave them to err, in matters of less importance, and in some particular instances.

V. 27—40.

Those who idolize notions, or "the form of godliness,"
while they hate the power of it, will misrepresent or condemn that conduct, which God most approves and blesses:
thus, if part of the truth be misrepresented, but not rendered sufficiently odious, to exasperate a sect, or a mob,
against the objects of their detestation; some false accusation will be devised more fully to effect the purpose:
and, as the cause of God is supposed to be at stake, all
means are sanctified, by which the help and concurrence
of multitudes can be ensured. On these occasions, the
professed worshippers of God too often copy the example
of the most infuriated idolaters: (*P. O.* xix. 21—31:) and
innocency or excellency is no security to any man's life:
for, in popular tumults, all discrimination of character, and
distinction between truth and error, are confounded. Pro-

fessed attachments to this or the other party or church
among Christians, will readily give energy to the clamour.
"Men of Israel, help, &c." The church is in danger!
Our religious liberties are in danger! And the groundless
outcry may affect the lives or characters, even of the most
prudent, benevolent, and pious servants of our God! He,
however, is at all times a Refuge for his people: and he
sometimes over-rules the fury of their enemies to raise them
up friends among such as are strangers to him; who become favourable to them, because they find that they are
not those vile characters, which they have been represented,
or suspected to be. And, if he gives us an opportunity
of pleading our own cause before those who are prejudiced
against us; we should always prepare to speak decidedly
and boldly in behalf of the truth, and earnestly to recom
mend the gospel of Christ to their most serious attention.

———

NOTES.

CHAP. XXII. V. 1—5. The apostle addressed the
enraged multitude, in the customary stile of respect and
goodwill, as "men and brethren;" and, seeing many
principal persons present, he also added "fathers," to denote, that he was ready to render them all due honour and
obedience, consistent with the will of God, notwithstanding their indignation against him. (*Marg. Ref.* a.—vii. 2.
Note, i. 16—18.) When therefore they found, that he
spoke so composedly to them, in the Hebrew dialect, they
observed a strict silence; and he proceeded to shew, that
he was a Jew, and not a Gentile or a proselyte; and though
born at Tarsus, that he had been educated in Jerusalem by
Gamaliel, the most eminent of their Rabbies. (*Note,* v. 33
—39.) At his feet he had been used to sit: according to
the custom of those times, when the scholars sat on the
ground, or on low seats near the teacher, who was raised
above them on a sort of throne. (*Notes, Deut.* xxxiii. 3.
Mark v. 14—20. *Luke* x. 38—42.) Paul had therefore
been instructed after the most accurate manner, in the
law of Moses, and in the traditions of the elders; and was
a zealot for their manner of worshipping God; as he knew
them to be zealots at that time. Of this he had given
abundant proof, by persecuting those who sought the
favour of God, in the "way" of the gospel; doing all in
his power, to get them put to death, or cast into prison,
without distinction, whether men or women. (*Marg. Ref.*
d—m.—*Notes,* viii. 3. ix. 1, 2. xxvi. 9—11. *Gal.* i. 11—
14.) *Phil.* iii. 1—7. 1 *Tim.* i. 12—16.) To this the high

6 And it came to pass, ⁱ that as I made my journey, and was come nigh unto ʳ Damascus, ʲ about noon, suddenly there shone from heaven a great light round about me.

7 And I fell unto the ground,ᵗ and heard a voice saying unto me, ᵗ Saul, Saul, ᵘ why persecutest thou me ?

8 And I answered, Who art thou, Lord ? And he said unto me, ˣ I am Jesus of Nazareth, ʸ whom thou persecutest.

9 And they that were with me ᶻ saw indeed the light, and were afraid ; ᵃ but they heard not the voice of him that spake to me.

10 And I said, ᵇ What shall I do, Lord ? And the Lord said unto me, Arise, and go into Damascus ; ᶜ and there it shall be told thee of all things which are appointed for thee to do.

11 And ᵈ when I could not see for the glory of that light, ᵉ being led by the hand of them that were with me, I came into Damascus.

12 And ᶠ one Ananias, ᵍ a devout man according to the law, ʰ having a good report of all the Jews which dwelt there,

13 Came unto me, and stood, and said unto me, ⁱ Brother Saul, receive thy sight. And the same hour I looked up upon him.

14 And he said, ᵏ The God of our fathers ˡ hath chosen thee, that thou shouldest know his will, ᵐ and see ⁿ that Just One, and shouldest ᵒ hear the voice of his mouth.

15 For ᵖ thou shalt be his witness unto all men ᑫ of what thou hast seen and heard.

16 And now, ʳ why tarriest thou ? ˢ arise, and be baptized, and wash away ᵗ thy sins, ᵘ calling on the name of the Lord.

s. Heb. x. 22.　1 Pet. iii. 21.　　*t* Il. 21. ix. 14.　Rom. x. 12—14.

---

priest, who was then in authority, could bear witness, as well as the other members of the Sanhedrim ; for he had received letters from them to the brethren, or the Jews, at Damascus, against the Christians in that city. But he would now relate to them the manner, in which he had since that time, been induced to embrace and preach that doctrine which he then so furiously persecuted.

Defence. (1) Or, *Apology.* The sacred writers never use this word, or the correspondent verb, except when the person spoken of defended himself from some charge brought against him. They never in one instance call the authoritative preaching of the gospel *an apology.* (*Marg. Ref.* b.) And, whatever may be urged in favour of the word, in this age of *apologies,* it indisputably conveys the idea of a cautious defensive war against impiety and infidelity, rather than of that boldness and decision, with which the cause of God and truth ought to be supported.—Aπoλoγιας. xxv. 16. 1 Cor. ix. 3. 2 Cor. vii. 11. 1 *Phil.* i. 7. 17. 2 *Tim.* iv. 16. 1 *Pet.* iii. 15. Aπoλoγιoμαι· See on *Luke* xii. 11. It does not appear, that the Greek Classicks use the term in any other sense. *Plato* in *Phædo,* 7 Sect. thus employs it.—*Brought up.* (3) Aνατεδραμμενος. See on vii. 20.—*Taught.*] Πεπαιδευμενος. See on vii. 22.—*The perfect manner.*] Aκριβειαν. Here only. Aκριβης, xxvi. 5. Aκριβως. See on xviii. 25.—*The law of our fathers.*] Tε πατρωε νoμω. xxiv. 14. xxviii. 17. Παlρικος, *Gal.* i. 14.—*Zealous.*] Zηλωτης. See on xxi. 20.—*The estate of the elders.* (5) Tε πρεσΰυτεριον. *Luke* xxii. 66. 1 *Tim.* iv. 14.—*For to be punished.*] Ἵνα τιμωρηΣωσιν. xxvi. 11. Not elsewhere. Tιμωρια, *Heb.* x. 29.

V. 6—13. (*Marg. Ref.*—xxvi. 12—15. *Notes,* ix. 3—22.) It is evident, that the apostle considered his extraordinary conversion, as a most complete demonstration of the truth of Christianity : and when all the particulars of his education, his previous religious principles, his zeal, his

enmity against Christians, and prospects of secular honours and preferments by persecuting them, are compared with the subsequent part of his life, and the sudden transition from a furious persecutor to a zealous preacher of the gospel, in which he laboured and suffered to the end of his life, and for which he died a martyr ; it must convince every candid and impartial person, that no rational account can be given of this change, except that which he himself assigns : and if that be true, Christianity is divine. (*Note,* ix. 31.)—*Heard not the voice,* &c. (9) The persons attending the apostle heard a sound, but did not distinguish that articulate voice, in which the Lord Jesus addressed Saul by name. (*Note,* ix. 7.)

The ground. (7) To εδαφος. Here only N. T.—*Num.* v. 17. 1 *Kings* vi. 15. *Sept.* Eδαφιζω, *Luke* xix. 44.—*Appointed.* (10) Tέlαxlαι. See on xiii. 48.—*Devout.* (12) Euσεΰης. See on x. 2.—*Having a good report.*] Mαρτυρεμενος. See on v. 3.

V. 14—16. The God of Abraham had chosen Saul the persecutor, as the object of his special love : in consequence of this, he had also purposed, that he should know his will ; and " see that Just One," who came to save sinners ; and also hear, believe, and obey his voice, as speaking immediately to him. (*Marg. Ref.* k—o.) This purpose he had begun to effect, as Saul journeyed to Damascus : and he would have further visions of him, and revelations of his will ; that he might be fully qualified to be his apostle, a witness of his resurrection, to men of all nations, and likewise of all that he himself had seen and heard. As he had therefore such full proof of the Lord's abundant and gratuitous love to him, notwithstanding his most aggravated crimes, and of his purpose to employ him as his minister ; why should he doubt any longer, or hesitate to profess his faith by being baptized, as an outward sign of the washing away of his sins, and the seal, to him

3 E 8

17 And it came to pass, that *when I was come again to Jerusalem, even *while I prayed in the temple, I was in a trance;

18 And 'saw him saying unto me, *Make haste, and get thee quickly out of Jerusalem: *for they will not receive thy testimony concerning me.

19 And I said, Lord, *they know that I imprisoned, and beat in every synagogue, them that believed on thee:

20 And when the blood of thy *martyr *Stephen was shed, I also was standing by, *and consenting unto his death, and kept the raiment of them that slew him.

21 And he said unto me, 'Depart; *for I will send thee far hence unto the Gentiles.

22 ¶ And they gave him audience unto this word, and *then* lifted up their voices, and said, *Away with such *a fellow from the earth; for it is not fit that he should live.

23 And as they cried out, 'and cast off *their* clothes, and threw dust into the air,

24 The *chief captain commanded him to be brought into the castle, and bade 'that he should be examined by scourging; that he might know wherefore they cried so against him.

25 And as they bound him with thongs, Paul said unto *the centurion that stood by, *Is it lawful for you to scourge a man that is a Roman, and uncondemned?

26 When the centurion heard *that,* he went and told the chief captain, saying, *Take heed what thou doest; for this man is a Roman.

27 Then the chief captain came,

---

and to all true believers, of that blessing, and of " the right-"eousness of faith," as circumcision had been to Abra-ham? *(Marg. Ref.* p—t.—*Note,* ii. 37—40. *Rom.* iv. 9—12.) In doing this, he must " call on the name of the " Lord," even the Lord Jesus, as the expression generally means : for this invocation of him, as the son of God, seems to have been one principal part of the required profession of faith in his name. (*Notes,* ii. 14—21. *Joel* ii. 28 —32. 1 *Cor.* i. 1, 2.)—* The inference of Chrysostom from ' this place is this, that by these words he shews that ' Christ was God ; because it is not lawful to invoke any ' but God.' *Whitby.* The invocation of saints and angels had not, it seems, at that time, (near the end of the fourth century,) received the sanction of the most eminent Christian ministers.

Hath chosen thee. (14) Προεχειρισατο. xxvi. 16. Not else-where N. T.—*Josh.* iii. 12. Sept. Εκ προ, et χειρ, *manus.*—*That just One.*] Τον δικαιον. See on iii. 14.—*Why tarriest thou ?* (16) Τι μελλεις ; *Quid moraris aut cunctaris ?* Here only in that sense.—*Calling on.*] Επικαλεσαμενος. " Having " called, &c." " Washing away thy sins," is rather con-nected with " having called on the name, &c." than with " be baptized." (*Note,* Rom. x. 12—17, *vv.* 12—14. See on ix. 14.)

V. 17—21. The apostle, having shewn his hearers, in what manner he was induced to become a Christian, and how he was appointed a preacher of the gospel, proceeded to declare the way, in which he had been led to exercise his ministry chiefly among the Gentiles ; as this was the principal cause of their peculiar rage against him. A con-siderable time after his conversion, he came up to Jerusa-lem ; and, while worshipping in the court of the temple, he was thrown into a trance, or ecstasy, in which he, even the Lord Jesus, appeared to him in vision, and commanded him speedily to leave that city, for the Jews would not receive his testimony concerning him. (*Marg. Ref.* a—d. *Note,* ix. 23—30.) To this he ventured to object, that

as they were in general acquainted with the severities which he had exercised against the Christians, and especi-ally his concurrence in the martyrdom of Stephen ; he had a confidence, that they would regard his testimony as to the manner of his conversion, and attend to the gospel as preached by him. But the Lord silenced this plea, and directed him to depart without delay, as he had purposed to employ him at a great distance among the Gentiles. (*Marg. Ref.* g.—*Notes,* xxvi. 16—18.)—Doubtless many who heard the apostle, on this occasion, could well re-member the facts to which he referred, and attest them to others. He therefore hoped to convince the multitude, that his labours among the Gentiles were not the result of his own choice, as he earnestly desired to have been useful to his countrymen : but at the same time this mis-sion intimated the approaching rejection of the Jewish nation, as well as the calling of the Gentiles into the church.

A trance. (17) Εκςασει. x. 10. xi.　See on Mark v. 42. Note, x. 9—16.—*I imprisoned.* (19) Εγω ημην φυλακιζων. Here only. A φυλακη, *custodia, carcer.* Note, viii. 3.—*Martyr.* (20) Τυ μαρτυρος. xxvi. 16. *Heb.* xii. 1. *Rev.* xvii. 6. Μαρτυς, *Rev.* ii. 13.—*Consenting.*] Συνευδοκων, " Concurring " with hearty good will." See on viii. 1.—*Death.*] Αναιρεσει. See on viii. 1. " Murder." ' Rightly ; for Stephen was ' slain, without any precedent sentence of law, by mani-' fest violence, as by robbers ; when it was not allowed to ' the Jews capitally to condemn any one, even accord-' ing to the laws.' Beza. *Note,* vii. 54—60.—*Those that slew.*] Των αναιρουντων. ii. 23.

V. 22—30. The Jews patiently attended to the apostle's account of his own conversion : but when he declared that he was sent by Jesus himself to preach to the Gentiles ; this was so contrary to their bigoted self-preference, their contempt of other nations, and all their religious preju-dices, that they would endure no more ; so that, in the most furious rage, they cried out, that such a fellow ought to

and said unto him, Tell me, art thou a Roman? He said, Yea.

28 And the chief captain answered, With a great sum obtained I this freedom. And Paul said, But I was *free* born.

29 Then straightway they departed • Or, tortured Aim. 24. Heb. from him which should have * exa- xi. 55. P 5ih, 25. xvi. 38, mined him: ' and the chief captain also &c.

was afraid, after he knew that he was a Roman, and because he had bound him.

30 On the morrow, ' because he would have known the certainty wherefore he was accused of the Jews, he loosed him from *his* bands, ' and commanded the chief priests and all their council to appear, and brought Paul down, and set him before them.

q xxi. 11. 33. xxvi. 29. Matt. xxvii. 2.

r h. v. 21. xxiii. 15. Matt. x. 17.

be dragged away to immediate death, for it was " not fit " for him to live " on the earth: seeing he thus openly preferred uncircumcised idolaters to the covenanted people of God. (*Marg. Ref.* h.—*Note*, 1 *Thes.* ii. 13—16.) Amidst these exclamations they cast off their clothes, either as preparing to stone him to death if they could get hold of him, or to express their abhorrence of his supposed blasphemy: and they threw dust into the air, as frantick with rage; or that it might fall and cover them, to denote the greatness of their horror at what had been said. (*Marg. Ref.* i.) This conduct might well astonish the tribune, who could not possibly understand, what had wrought them up to such an excess of fury: he indeed concluded, that Paul had certainly committed some peculiarly atrocious crime with which he was not acquainted. He would not however give him up to their resentment: but, according to the barbarous and irrational practice, in use even among the Romans, (as it is in many nations to this day,) he ordered him to be examined by severe scourging; till the anguish of the stripes inflicted on him, should extort from him a confession of his guilt. When the soldiers were binding him with thongs to a pillar, or block, for that purpose, he demanded of the centurion, whom the tribune had charged with this service, whether it were lawful for them thus to scourge a Roman citizen, who had not been condemned for any crime. (*Marg. Ref.* m, n.—*Note*, xvi. 35—40.) A Roman might not be punished before he was legally condemned, nor scourged in *this manner* at all; which was far more severe, than the scourging with rods: and, as it was even unlawful to bind him with thongs, in order to examination by torture, though not to put fetters upon him in order to confine him; the centurion was led by this question, to caution the tribune to take care what he did; who came to the apostle to enquire whether he really were a Roman. He had himself purchased this valuable privilege for a great sum of money: and, as Paul was a Jew, apparently in very low circumstances, he questioned him how he had acquired it: but the apostle informed him, that he was free born. He had before mentioned his being a citizen of Tarsus, yet the tribune had not thence inferred, that he was entitled to the privilege of a Roman citizen: so that it is probable, all the citizens of the Roman colonies had not this privilege; or that Tarsus was not a colony. Paul, however, satisfied the tribune that he was a Roman; and so the design of torturing him by scourging, to make him confess some crime which could not be proved, was given up; and the tribune feared lest he should be called to account for having bound him. Instead therefore, of using this method to discover his guilt, he, on the morrow, summoned the council, and brought Paul, freed from his fetters, before

them to be examined. Hence we may infer, that a great number of the principal persons in the nation had joined with the multitude, in their vehement and outrageous zeal against the apostle.

Fit. (22) Καθηκον. *Rom.* i. 28. Not elsewhere.—*They cried out.* (23) Κραυγαζοντων αυτων. *Matt.* xii. 19. xv. 22. *John* xi. 43. xviii. 40. xix. 6. 15. Κραυγη, xxiii. 9.—*Cast off.*] 'Ριπτουντων. *Matt.* ix. 36. xv. 30. xxvii. 5.—*Examined.* (24) Ανθαζεσθαι. 29. Here only. Εx ανα et ιαζω, exploro.—*By scourging.*] Μαςιξιν. *Mark* iii. 10. v. 29. 34. *Heb.* xi. 36. Μαςιξιν, 25.—*They bound.* (25) Προετεινεν. Here only. "He," or "one extended."—*With thongs.*] Τοις ιμασιν. *Mark* i. 7. *Luke* iii. 16. *John* i. 27.—*Uncondemned.*] Ακαλακριτον. See on xvi. 37.—*A sum.* (28) Κεφαλαιν. *Heb.* viii. 1. Not elsewhere. ' Subaudiendum est χρημα.... Capi- ' tulum; a κεφαλη, caput.' Schleusner.—*Freedom.*] Πολιτειαν. *Eph.* ii. 12. Not elsewhere. Πολιτευμα, *Phil.* iii. 20. A πολις, civitas.

PRACTICAL OBSERVATIONS.

V. 1—5.

The honour of the gospel requires its advocates to speak with temper, benevolence, and respect to their superiors; as well as with boldness and constancy, in the midst of all the ill usage, to which they may be exposed.—A simple narration of the Lord's dealings with us, in bringing us from opposing, to profess and promote, his gospel, when it is delivered with modesty and caution, will generally make more impression on the minds of men, than laboured arguments or rhetorical declamations. Indeed, the conversion and experience of some individuals have been so remarkable, that the recital of them has great force of argument in it: though it seldom, if ever, amounts to that complete demonstration of the truth, which arose from the change wrought in the character and conduct of the apostle. —Natural abilities, the advantages of education, proficiency in learning, exactness in a system, and a fervent religious zeal according to that system, may be either valuable or mischievous; as they are directed, under the influence of divine grace, in support of the truth, or as employed by men's selfish passions in defence of error. Zeal, especially, is an ambiguous attainment: it may be a violent, cruel, and dreadful flame, kindled from beneath, and destroying all around it with fatal vehemence; or it may be a gentle, active, kind, and heavenly principle, powerfully influencing the possessor to every thing excellent and beneficial, in the persevering use of the most unexceptionable means of obtaining the most important ends. (*Note, Jam.* iii. 13—16.)

V. 6—21.

Many, who for a time have devoted their talents to the service of delusion and error, have afterwards been induced

5 т 2

CHAP. XXIII.

Paul, pleading his conscientiousness before God, is smitten at the command of the high priest, whom he reproves for his injustice, 1—3. Being censured for it, he excuses the sharpness of his language, 4, 5. Declaring himself a Pharisee, in respect of the resurrection, a division in the council is excited, 6—9. The chief captain, fearing lest he should be torn in pieces, conveys him back to the castle, 10. The Lord favours him, by a most encouraging vision, 11. Forty Jews conspire to murder him; binding themselves by oath, not to eat or drink till they have done it, 12, 13. They avow their purpose to the chief priests, and secure their concurrence, 14, 15. The conspiracy is discovered to Paul, and from him to the chief captain, 16—22; who sends Paul, under a strong guard, and with a letter, to Felix the governor at Cæsarea, 23—35.

AND Paul, [a] earnestly beholding the council, said, [b] Men and brethren, [c] I have lived in all good conscience before God until this day.

2 And the high priest [d] Ananias commanded them that stood by him, [e] to smite him on the mouth.

3 Then said Paul unto him, God shall smite thee, [f] thou whited wall: [g] for sittest thou to judge me after the law, and commandest me to be [h] smitten contrary to the law?

4 And they that stood by, said, Revilest thou God's high priest?

5 Then said Paul, [i] I wist not, brethren, that he was the high priest: for

[margin notes:
a d. vi. 15. xxiii. 1. Prov. xxviii. 1.
b xxii. 1.
c Acts. 16. 1 Cor. iv. 4. 2 Cor. i. 12. iv. 2. 2 Tim. i. 3. Heb. xiii. 18. 1 Pet. iii. 16.
d xxiv. 1.
e 1 Kings xxii. 24. Jer. xx. 2. Mic. v. 1. Matt. xxvi. 67. John xviii. 22.
f Matt. xxiii. 27, 28.
g Lev. xix. 35. Ps. lviii. 1, 2. lxxxii. 1, 2. xciv. 20. Ec. iii. 16. Am. v. 7. Mic. iii. 8—11. h Deut. xxv. 1, 2. John vii. 51. xviii. 24.
i xxiv. 17.]

---

to consecrate them to the cause of Christ. The Lord having chosen the sinner, " that he should know his will;" he is awakened, humbled, illuminated, and brought acquainted with Jesus and his blessed gospel. Being acknowledged as a " brother," by those who were disciples before him, he makes profession of his faith, calls on the Redeemer's name, receives the comfort of being " washed " from his sins," and testifies to others, what he has heard and learned of the Saviour's glory and grace. Thus he passes from Satan's kingdom to that of Christ, and begins to seek its peace and prosperity; while his former associates are surprised, offended, or enraged, at the revolution which has taken place. When a man is thus admitted among the servants of Christ, he is often employed in such services, as disconcert all his own plans and purposes. Not being wholly weaned from " leaning to his own under- " standing," he is sometimes reluctant to renounce his favourite plan, even after he has been praying for direction respecting the will of God! A person in these circumstances often imagines, that his former friends, having known his contempt and enmity against the truth, will pay the more attention to his testimony on that account; and that his former zeal for some form or party, and against those tenets which he deemed enthusiastical and erroneous, will induce them to enquire into the grounds of the change which has taken place. Perhaps he thinks that their opposition arises mainly from misinformation; and that if the truth were fairly set before them, they could not resist the evidence of it. Thus he may practically forget, that nothing can reconcile the heart of fallen man to the gospel, execpt the special grace of God; that " a prophet is " not without honour save in his own country;" and that a servant of Christ may expect a more favourable hearing from entire strangers, than from prejudiced neighbours, relatives, and acquaintance; who commonly treat his attempts to convince them, as a usurpation of authority to which he is not entitled. (Note, Matt. xiii. 54—58. P. O. 51—58.)

V. 22—30.
When the servants of Christ, in obedience to his express command, turn from those who reject their testimony, and seek for more favourable hearers; those whom they leave

will sometimes be highly displeased.—Bigotry and spiritual pride are commonly connected with furious wrath and intolerant malice: and it is well for mankind, that the power of persecutors is often inadequate to their rage; otherwise they would drive all the servants of Christ out of the earth, as unfit to live upon it. (Note, Heb. xi. 35—38.) But the Lord mercifully restrains their madness, by subjecting them to more moderate men. For, though many iniquities have been practised by magistrates, not professing any great regard to religion, even in civilized nations; yet their severity is commonly tender mercy, compared with the cruelty of enraged bigots, when advanced to authority: and their haste in punishing is deliberation and caution, compared with the fury of a licentious mob, when excited by frantick persecutors.—But how great a privilege is it to be governed according to a written law! that if a magistrate is about to act unjustly, it may be demanded of him, whether this be lawful; and suggested to him, to take heed what he does, lest he should expose himself to a judicial rebuke. Christians are allowed to avail themselves of these privileges: our birth-right as Britons (who are far more favoured in Providence, than even the Roman citizens were,) is not forfeited by our becoming the subjects of Christ; though we should insist upon our privileges, with great modesty, prudence, and quietness.—We should, however, most of all value that freedom, to which all the children of God are born; and which the largest sums of money cannot, in any measure, purchase for such as remain unregenerate. (Note and P. O. Gal. iv. 21—31.)

NOTES.

Chap. XXIII. V. 1—5. When the apostle was placed before the Sanhedrim, he stedfastly viewed it, to observe of what persons it now consisted; and, as confidently looking at those, who formerly employed him in persecuting the Christians: and he then solemnly protested, that he had " to that day lived," or acted as a member of the community, " in all good conscience towards God." The rulers, priests, and people were ready to condemn him as a most atrocious criminal, for embracing the gospel, and preaching it to the Gentiles: but he declared, that in these things he had not acted from sinister motives, but out of

5 v 3

k Ex. xxii. 28. Ec.
x. 20. 2 Pet. ii.
10, 1. Jude 8,
9.

it is written, ᵏ Thou shalt not speak
evil of the ruler of thy people.

l Matt. x. 16.

6 But when ˡ Paul perceived that the
one part were Sadducees, and the other
Pharisees, he cried out in the council,

m xxvi. 5. Phil.
iii. 5.
n xxiv. 15, 21.
xxvi.　6—8.
xxviii. 20.

Men *and* brethren, ᵐ I am a Pharisee,
the son of a Pharisee: ⁿ of the hope
and resurrection of the dead I am called
in question.

o xiv. 4. Ps. lv. 9.
Matt.　x. 34.
John vii. 40—
43.

7 And when he had so said, ° there
arose a dissension between the Pharisees and the Sadducees; and the multitude was divided.

p iv. 1. Matt. xxii.
23, 24. Mark xii.
18. Luke xx. 27.

8 For the ᵖ Sadducees say that
there is no resurrection, neither angel

nor spirit; but the Pharisees confess
both.

9 And there arose a great cry: and
the scribes *that were* of the Pharisees'
part arose, and strove, saying, ᑫ We
find no evil in this man: but ʳ if a
spirit or an angel hath spoken to him,
ˢ let us not fight against God.

q xxv. 25. xxvi.
31. 1 Sam. xxiv.
17. Prov. xvi. 7.
Luke xxiii. 4.
r 14, 15. 22.
s viii. ix. 4. xxii. 7.
17, 18. xxvi. 14
—19. xxvii. 23.
John xii. 29.
v. 39. xi. 17.
1 Cor. x. 22.

10 And when there arose a great
dissension, the chief captain, ᵗ fearing
lest Paul should have been pulled in
pieces of them, commanded the soldiers to go down, ᵘ and to take him by
force from among them, and to bring
him into the castle.

t 27. xix. 29—31.
xxii. 30—36. Ps.
vii. 2. l. 22. Mic.
iii. 2, 3. Jam. i.
19, 20. iii. 14—
18. iv. 1, 2.
u xxii. 24.

---

a conscientious regard to his duty, in the sight of God, in
which he had persevered amidst many trials to that very
time.—He had indeed acted according to his conscience,
when he persecuted the Christians: but this was the result
of pride, ignorance, inattention, and obstinate self-will;
and it can hardly be supposed, that he could call this " a
" good conscience before God." The council, however, would have given him credit for that part of his
life: his object therefore evidently was, to shew that he
had acted conscientiously and on good grounds, in those
things, which they deemed deserving of death; and he
doubtless meant more fully to have explained his reasons
and motives, if the council would have heard them. (*Marg.
Ref.* a, c.) But the high priest, being a leading person
in this prosecution, and aware that Paul's protestation of
innocence implied a charge of malice and injustice against
his virulent enemies, ordered him to be " smitten on the
" mouth," for pleading ' not guilty,' when they were determined to condemn him! This was oppressive, iniquitous,
and illegal in the extreme: and the apostle immediately
denounced the judgment of God upon him for it, and for
his other crimes; and declared him to be " a whited wall,"
or a hypocrite, who might be compared to a wall formed
of the meanest materials, but whited over and made to
have a fair outside. (*Notes, Matt.* xxiii. 25—28.) This
appeared, in that he, when sitting in the council to judge
him according to the law of God, instead of enquiring into
the merits of his cause, had ordered him, by a direct violation of that law, to be smitten, before he was proved
guilty of any fault, or even impropriety in his behaviour.
(*Marg. Ref.* g, h.—*Notes,* 1 Kings xxii. 24, 25. Jer. xx.
1—6. John xviii. 19—23.)—' Ananias carried it very plausi-
' bly towards the citizens, and stood high in their favour :
' yet he impiously and cruelly defrauded the inferior priests
' of their legal subsistence, so that some of them even
' perished for want. And God did remarkably smite him:
' for after his own house had been reduced to ashes, in
' a tumult begun by his own son, he was besieged and
' taken in the royal palace; where, having in vain at-
' tempted to hide himself in an old aqueduct, he was
' dragged out and slain.' *Doddridge.*—But though the answer of Paul contained a just rebuke, and an evident prediction; yet he seems to have been too much carried away
by indignation at the base usage which he had experienced:

being therefore censured for " reviling God's high priest;"
he pleaded, that he was not aware that Ananias was the
high priest. It seems unreasonable to suppose, that the
apostle would, in such circumstances, question his title to
his office, though the scripture referred to rather points
out Ananias's office as supreme magistrate, than his sacred
function. (*Note, Ex.* xxii. 28.) It is however probable,
that the apostle meant to allow, that, in the warmth of his
spirit, he had not adverted to the person who had given
the orders, or was not aware that he was the high priest.
Perhaps the high priest in the Sanhedrim was not always
to be known by his seat, or his garments; and Ananias
did not fill that office, when Paul had been more intimately
conversant with that assembly. But it is not very clear,
whether the apostle intended by this concession to wave
the question concerning his speaking by " the Spirit of
" prophecy," as not choosing to insist on it; or whether
he allowed that he had spoken too sharply, and could not
justify the whole of his answer, or propose it to the imitation of others. (*Marg. Ref.* k.)

I have lived. (1) Πεπολιτευμαι. Phil. i. 27. Not elsewhere. " I have performed the duty of a citizen." Πολιτεια·
See on xxii. 28.—*Good conscience.*] Συνειδησει αγαθη. 1 Tim.
i. 5. 1 Pet. iii. 16. 21. Συνειδησις, xxiv. 16. John viii. 9.
Rom. ii. 15. ix. 1. 1 Cor. x. 27. 29. 2 Cor. i. 12. 1 Tim. iv.
2. Tit. i. 15. Heb. ix. 9. 14. x. 2. 22. xiii. 18. 1 Pet. ii. 19.
A συνειδω, Conscius sum, v. 2. 1 Cor. iv. 4.—*Shall smite.* (3)
Μελλ. τυπτειν. " Is about to smite thee : " evidently the language of prediction, not of imprecation.—*Thou whited wall.*]
Τοιχε κεκονιαμενε. See on Matt. xxiii. 27.—*Contrary to the
law.*] Παρανομων. Here only. Παρανομια, 2 Pet. ii. 16. Ex
παρα, contra, et νομος, lex.—*Revilest thou*, &c. (4) Λοιδορεις;
John ix. 28. 1 Cor. iv. 12. 1 Pet. ii. 23. Λοιδορια. 1 Tim.
v. 14. 1 Pet. iii. 9.—*I wist not.* (5) Ουκ ηδειν. " I knew
" not."—*Speak evil.*] Ερεις κακως. This shews what is
meant by λοιδορεις. See John xviii. 23.—*Ex.* xxii. 28. Lev.
xix. 14. xx. 9. Sept.

V. 6—10. The apostle personally knew many members of the Sanhedrim; and he was aware, that there were
two parties among them of opposite principles, and very
vehement in their contests with each other; though they
were now agreed in persecuting him. (*Notes, Matt.* xxii.
15—22. *Luke* xxiii. 6—12.) Seeing, therefore, they would
pay no impartial attention to reason, or facts however au-

x ii. 25. xvii. 9.
xxvii. 23, 24. Ps.
xlvi. 1, 2. cix.
31. Is. xli. 10.
14. xlili. 2. Jer. xv.
22. 2b. Matt. ix. 2. xiv. 27. 11 And the night following ᵇ the Lord stood by him, and said, ⁷ Be of good cheer, Paul; ⁸ for as thou hast testified of me in Jerusalem, so ᵃ must thou bear witness also at Rome.

18-21, Matt. xxviii. 20. John xiv. 18. 2 Cor. i. 8-10. y xxvii.
Joan xvi. 33. xix. 21, xx. 22. xxii. 18, xxviii.
23-29. Rom. i. 15, 16. Phil. i. 13. 2 Tim. iv. 17.
a Is. xlvi. 10. John xi. 8-10.

thenticated; he attempted to divert their violence from himself upon each other. Accordingly, he cried aloud, "I am a Pharisee, and the son of a Pharisee;" he had been educated in the opinions of that sect, and still maintained the principal doctrines, which were controverted between them and the Sadducees: (*Marg. Ref.* m, n.—*Notes*, xxvi. 4—8. *Phil.* iii. 1—7, *v.* 5:) nay, indeed he was called in question at that time, for professing the hope, and bearing testimony to the reality, of the resurrection of the dead. The principal fact, which he attested as the apostle of Christ, was his resurrection from the dead to be the first-fruits of his people; and all the doctrines of the gospel were intimately connected with that fundamental principle. The first persecution of the church was excited by the testimony of the apostles to the resurrection of their crucified Lord; and the Sadducees took the lead in it, because "they preached through Jesus the resurrection of "the dead." (*Note*, iv. 1—3.) The enmity also of many in the council against Paul, at this time, was increased by their consciousness, that his doctrine was wholly subversive of their favourite sentiment: so that in every way, he was called to account for preaching Jesus as risen, and the hope and doctrine of a future resurrection. This was therefore an evident truth: he was not obliged to bring forward all the doctrines which he professed, when not interrogated about them: and it seems to have been entirely justifiable in him, by this seasonable profession of his faith on this controverted point, to draw off the Pharisees from the side of his persecutors; and to induce them to afford him some protection amidst all this illegal violence. At the same time he shewed a most consummate sagacity, and a deep acquaintance with the human heart, and of that universal disposition, which continually manifests itself, of favouring those, who take our part in any contested point. ' Grant me discernment, I allow it you.' *Cowper.* Accordingly, this declaration was so pleasing to the Pharisees, that their rage was for the time disarmed: and the Sadducees being proportionably exasperated, the two parties began eagerly to dispute about "the resurrection of the dead," and the existence of angels, and of separate spirits; the one contending for these doctrines, and the other arguing against them, with the greatest violence. (*Marg. Ref.* o, p.—*Notes, Matt.* iii. 7—10. xxii. 23—33.) At length those scribes, who espoused the party of the Pharisees, (being sharpened against their antagonists, and perceiving that the apostle's doctrine and narrative tended to establish their tenets, and to subvert those of the Sadducees,) declared that they could not find him guilty of any crime: and, though they did not believe what he said concerning Jesus of Nazareth; yet if an angel, or the spirit of some deceased person, had spoken to him; (as doubtless this had often been done, for thus they assumed the point in contest;) it did not become them " to fight against God," by punishing him. (*Marg. Ref.* q—s.)—There is a great similarity between this speech, and the counsel which Gamaliel had formerly given; and perhaps there was a reference to it, though it is probable, that he died before

this time. (*Note, v.* 33—39.)—The contest, however, at length became so fierce between the parties, that Lysias, who seems to have been present, began to apprehend, they would tear Paul in pieces in their fury; and therefore he ordered him to be taken from them by force, and conveyed into the castle. (*Marg. Ref.* t, u.)—What must this heathen have thought of the worshippers of JEHOVAH, when he saw this assembly of chief priests, learned scribes, and rulers of Israel, forgetful of what became their rank, profession, and sacred character; and carried away by an unbridled rage, in their religious contests, to those excesses, which the Roman senators and magistrates, or principal persons, would have been ashamed of, even in their eager competition for pre-eminence and dominion?

I am called in question. (6) Κρινομαι. " I am judged," as an accused person on his trial.—*A dissension.* (7) Στασις. 10. —*Was divided.*] Εσχισθη. See on xiv. 4.—*Strove.* (9) Διεμαχοντο. Here only. Εκ δια, et μαχομαι, *pugno.*—*Let us not fight against God.*] Μη θεομαχωμεν. Here only. Θεομαχοι. See on v. 39.—*Fearing.* (10) Ευλαβηθεις. *Heb.* xi. 7. Not elsewhere. Ευλαβεια, *Heb.* v. 7. xii. 28. Ευλαβης, viii. 2.—*Should have been pulled in pieces.*] Μη διασπασθη. See on *Mark* v. 4.—*The soldiers.*] Το στρατευμα. *Matt.* xxii. 7. *Luke* xxiii. 11. *Rev.* ix. 16. xix. 14. 19. *Exercitum.*

V. 11. (*Notes, xviii.* 9—11. xxvii. 20—26.) The apostle had been repeatedly delivered from the most imminent danger: but he was still confined in prison; and knew that the desperate malice of his numerous enemies would leave nothing unattempted, in order to take away his life. He might therefore, perhaps, be under some discouragement in respect of his situation: but his gracious Lord was pleased to appear before him, assuring him that he accepted of his testimony concerning him in Jerusalem; and that his desire, of attesting his truth at Rome also, would certainly be granted. (*Note*, xix. 21, 22.) This ensured his protection against all his enemies, who might " fight with him, but could not prevail against him." (*Marg. Ref.*—*Note, Jer.* i. 17—19.)—' Here is an instance ' of a divine appointment, without any necessity laid on ' the will of Paul.' *Whitby.* This erroneously supposes, that they, with whom this learned writer meant to contend, held that the divine decrees laid a necessity on the human will! (*Notes,* ii. 22—24, *v.* 23. iv. 23—28, *v.* 28.) In fact the instance proves, beyond all controversy, that an event may be certainly determined by almighty God, and infallibly come to pass; though all parties concerned exercise the utmost free-agency, of which the rational nature is capable. Some argue from this vision, that the Lord approved of the apostle's conduct: but, though this is undoubtedly true as to the grand outline, yet the vision no more proves that the conduct of the apostle was free from all mixture of infirmity, than the vision, with which Jacob was favoured at Bethel, proves that he had not sinned in fraudulently obtaining the blessing. (*Notes, Gen.* xxvii. 6—14. xxviii. 16, 17.) The actions of men must be judged of by the law of God; and not by the event, or by any special instances of the Lord's unmerited kindness to them.

3 F 3

12 ¶ And when it was day, [b] certain
of the Jews banded together, [c] and
bound themselves [*] under a curse, saying, [d] That they would neither eat nor
drink till they had killed Paul.
13 And they were more than forty
[e] which had made this conspiracy.
14 And [f] they came to the chief
priests and elders, and said, We have
bound ourselves under a great curse,
that we will eat nothing until we have
slain Paul.
15 Now therefore ye with the council signify to the chief captain, [g] that he
bring him down unto you to-morrow,
as though ye would enquire something
more perfectly concerning him: and
we, or ever he come near, are ready to
kill him.
16 And [h] when Paul's sister's son
heard of their lying in wait, he went
and entered into the castle, and told
Paul.
17 Then Paul called [i] one of the centurions unto him, and said, Bring this
young man unto the chief captain; for
he hath a certain thing to tell him.

[b] 21. 30. Ps. ii. 1—3. lxiv. 2—6. Is. viii. 9, 10. Jer. xi. 19. Matt. xxvi. 4.
[c] 1 Kings xix. 2. 2 Kings vi. 31. Matt. xxvii. 25. Mark vi. 23—26.
[*] Or, with an oath of execration. Lev. xxvii. 29. Josh. vi. 26. vii. 1. 15. Neh. x. 29. Matt. xxvi. 74. Gr. 1 Cor. xvi. 22. Gal. iii. 13.
[d] 1 Sam. xiv. 24. 27, 28. 40—44.
[e] 2 Sam. xv. 12. 31. John xvi. 2.
[f] Ps. iii. 1, 2. Is. iii. 9. Jer. vi. 15. viii. 12. Hos. iv. 9. Mic. vii. 3.
[g] xxv. 3. Ps. xxxvii. 32, 33. Prov. i. 11, 12. 16. iv. 16. Is. lix. 7. Rom. iii. 14—16.
[h] Job v. 13. Prov. xxi. 30. Lam. iii. 37. 1 Cor. iii. 19.
[i] 23. xxii. 26. Matt. viii. 8, 9.

18 So he took him, and brought
him to the chief captain, and said,
[k] Paul the prisoner called me unto him,
and prayed me to bring this young
man unto thee, who hath [l] something
to say unto thee.
19 Then the chief captain [m] took
him by the hand, and went *with him*
aside privately, and asked *him*, [n] What
is that thou hast to tell me?
20 And he said, The Jews have
agreed to desire thee, that thou wouldest bring down Paul to-morrow into
the council, [o] as though they would
enquire somewhat of him more perfectly.
21 But do not thou yield unto them:
[p] for there lie in wait for him of them
more than forty men, which have
bound themselves with [q] an oath, that
they will neither eat nor drink till they
have killed him: and now are they
ready, looking for a promise from thee.
22 So the chief captain *then* let the
young man depart, and charged *him*,
[r] *See thou* tell no man that thou hast
shewed these things to me.

[k] xvi. 25. xxvii. 1. xxviii. 17. Gen. xl. 14, 15. Eph. iii. 1. iv. 1. Philem. 9.
[l] Luke vii. 40.
[m] Jer. xxxi. 32. Mark viii. 23. ix. 27.
[n] Neh. ii. 4. Esth. v. 3. vii. 2. ix. 12. Mark x. 51.
[o] 15. Ps. xii. 2. Dan. vi. 5—12.
[p] 12—14. ix. 23, 24. xiv. 5, 6. xx. 19. xxv. 3. 2 Cor. xi. 26. 32, 33.
[q] 14. Rom. ix. 3.
[r] Josh. ii. 14. Mark i. 44.

V. 12—22. The Jews, perceiving that Lysias was resolved to protect Paul, unless legally convicted of some crime, began to fear that their malice would be disappointed. Therefore forty of the most zealous of them, (probably not members of the council, nor yet persons of a low rank,) supposing that they should do God service by murdering his minister, (*Notes*, xxvi. 9—11. *John* xvi. 1—3,) conspired together, engaging by a solemn oath, and an anathema, or imprecation of divine vengeance on themselves, if they tasted either meat or drink till they had slain Paul. So far indeed from being ashamed of this most atrocious intended assassination, they gloried in it as highly meritorious! and, knowing that many of the priests and the elders of the council would favour the design; (for the Sadducees seem to have been the more numerous in that assembly;) they informed them of their whole plan, and assigned them the part, which they should perform in order to accomplish it; while the guilt or odium of the measure, if there were any, would rest wholly on the conspirators. (*Marg. Ref.* b—g.—*Note*, xxv. 1—5.) It is not known, by what means Paul's nephew discovered this conspiracy: but as so many persons were privy to it, and as the conspirators aimed to conceal it from Lysias and his friends alone, till it was executed; they might not all be very cautious in speaking of it. Providence, however, took this method of detecting and disappointing it. Paul, though assured of protection, deemed it his duty to use every proper means for his own safety: (*Notes*, 11. xxvii. 28—32:) and the conduct of Lysias towards the young man shewed much affability, good sense, generosity, and regard to truth and equity; which, in a heathen, formed a striking contrast to the insidious, violent, cruel, and iniquitous conduct of the Jewish priests and rulers, who were evidently ripe for vengeance. (*Marg. Ref.* h—r.)—'Such execrable vows as these were not unusual among 'the Jews, who challenged to themselves a right of punish- 'ing those, without any legal process, whom they con- 'sidered as transgressors of the law; and in some cases 'thought, that they were justified in killing them....It is no 'wonder, therefore, that these Jews should make no scruple 'of acquainting the chief priests and elders with their con- 'spiracy against the life of Paul; who were so far from 'blaming them for it, that not long after they renewed the 'same design themselves. (xxv. 2, 3.) ... Dr. Lightfoot has 'shewn from the Talmud, that if they were prevented 'from accomplishing such vows as these, it was an easy 'matter to obtain an absolution from their Rabbies.' *Doddridge*.—The Rabbies, however, could not deliver them from the curse of God, which they had imprecated on themselves; though they gave them leave to eat and drink, notwithstanding their vow.

Banded together. (12) Ποιησαντες ... συστροφην. See on xix. 40.—*Bound themselves under a curse.*] "With an "oath of execration." (*Marg.* and *Ref.*) Ανεθεματισαν ἑαυτες. *Mark* xiv. 71. Καθαναθεματιζω· See on *Matt.* xxvi. 74.—*Conspiracy.* (13) Συνωμοσιαν. Here only. Ex συν, et ομνυμι, vel ομνυω, *juro.*—*Under a great curse.* (14) Αναθεματι. *Rom.* ix. 3. 1 *Cor.* xii. 3. xvi. 22. *Gal.* i. 8, 9.—*Deut.* vii. 26. *Josh.* vi. 17, 18. vii. 1. 12, 13. *Sept.* See on 12.—*Signify.* (15) Εμφανισατε. 22. See on *Matt.*

23 And he called unto him ' two centurions, saying, Make ready two hundred soldiers to go to Cæsarea, and horsemen threescore and ten, and spearmen two hundred, 'at the third hour of the night;

24 And provide *them* ° beasts, that they may set Paul on, and bring *him* safe unto ° Felix ' the governor.

25 And he wrote a letter after this manner:

26 Claudius Lysias unto ' the most excellent governor Felix *sendeth* ° greeting.

27 This man ᵇ was taken of the Jews, and should have been killed of them: then came I with an army and rescued him, ° having understood that he was a Roman.

28 And ᵈ when I would have known the cause wherefore they accused him, I brought him forth into their council:

29 Whom I perceived to be accused of ° questions of their law, ' but to have nothing laid to his charge worthy of death or of bonds.

30 And when ° it was told me, how ᵍ that the Jews laid wait for the man, I sent straightway to thee, ʰ and gave commandment to his accusers also, to say before thee what *they had* against him. ' Farewell.

31 ¶ Then the soldiers, ᵏ as it was commanded them, took Paul, and brought *him* by night to Antipatris.

32 On the morrow they left the horsemen to go with him, and returned to the castle;

33 Who, when they came to Cæsarea, and ' delivered the epistle to the governor, ᵐ presented Paul also before him.

34 And when the governor had read *the letter*, ⁿ he asked of what province

xxvii. 53.—*Lying in wait.* (16) Ενεδρον. Not elsewhere. Ενεδρενω, 21. See on *Luke* xi. 54.

V. 23, 24. The desperate measures of the Jews, no doubt, confirmed Lysias in his determination to protect his prisoner; but, by keeping him at Jerusalem, insurrections might have been excited, and some opportunity might have been afforded to his vigilant enemies, of murdering him. He therefore resolved to send him to Felix, the Roman governor, who resided at Cæsarea, which is computed to have been about seventy miles from Jerusalem. The body of Roman soldiers, appointed to escort him, consisting of two hundred legionary soldiers, two hundred light-armed foot-soldiers, and seventy horsemen, would have sufficed to repel any tumultuary assault of the Jews: but to prevent bloodshed, they were ordered to set off about three hours after sun-set, that they might be out of the reach of the zealots before morning. This prudent precaution was accompanied by one equally humane: Paul was not required to walk with the soldiers, who had been accustomed to long and speedy marches; but they were ordered to provide beasts, mules, or horses, changing them when necessary; that he might be conducted safely and conveniently to Cæsarea. (*Marg. Ref.*)

Spearmen. (23) Δεξιολαβως. Here only. Ex δεξιος, *dexter*, et λαμβανω, *capio*. Learned men are far from agreed as to the precise meaning of the word.—*Beasts.* (24) Κτηνη. *Luke* x. 34. 1 *Cor.* xv. 39. *Rev.* xviii. 13.— *Bring him safe.*] Διασωσωσι. xxvii. 43, 44. xxviii. 1. 4. *Matt.* xiv. 36. *Luke* vii. 3. 1 *Pet.* iii. 20. Ex δια, et σωζω, *salvum præsto, servo.*

V. 25—30. This epistle, which is a good specimen of the Roman method of writing letters, may be considered as a model of brevity, simplicity, and perspicuity. The customary title of respect to a superior, and expression of good-will, are *once only* made use of: and in this it differs exceedingly from modern epistles, to persons of high rank

and authority; which are generally encumbered with multiplied compliments, and ascriptions of honour.—Lysias, however, was careful not to intimate to Felix, that he had bound Paul, in order to scourge him: and, as we suppose this to have been an exact copy of the letter, it appears, he was willing Felix should conclude, that his interposition in Paul's favour arose from a *previous* knowledge that he was a Roman citizen; though it is evident this was not the case. (*Notes,* xxi. 31—40. xxii. 22—30.) In other respects, the account was fair and candid; and we cannot wonder that a heathen should state his conduct in that light, which was most favourable to his own reputation and advancement, and not likely to injure any man. (*Marg. Ref.* a, b. e, f. h.)

After this manner. (25) Περιεχουσαν τον τυπον τουτον. Περιεχω, *Luke* v. 9. 1 *Pet.* ii. 6. Περιοχη· See on viii. 32. Τυπος, vii. 43, 44. See on *John* xx. 25.—*The most excellent.* (26) Τω κρατιςω. See on *Luke* i. 3.—*Greeting.*] Χαιρειν. See on *Matt.* xxviii. 9.—*Laid to his charge.* (29) Εγκλημα. xxv. 16. Not elsewhere. Εγκαλειν, 28, 29. See on xix. 38.—*Laid wait.* (30) Επιβουλης μελλειν εσεσθαι. xx. 24. xx. 3. 19.—*Accusers.*] Κατηγοροις. 35.—*Farewell.*] Ερρωσο. See on xv. 29.

As it was commanded. (31) Καθα το διατεταγμενον. See on xviii. 2.

V. 33—35. *Marg. Ref.*—*Herod's,* &c. (35) This was not the common jail; but part of a palace built by Herod the Great; who had re-built Cæsarea, which was before called Straton's tower; and had given it a new name, in honour of the Roman emperor, by whose favour he ob-

he was. And when he understood that
° xv. 41. xxi. 39. he *was* of °Cilicia;
p 90. xxix. l. 19.
72. 24—27. xxv.
16.   35 I will hear thee, said he, ' when

thine accusers are also come. And he
commanded him to be kept ⁹ in Herod's ⁹ Matt. il. l. 3
16.
'judgment-hall.   ᵛ Matt. xxvii. 27
                                            John xviii. 28.

---

tained the kingdom. Paul was lodged in this place, as
more favoured than prisoners in general were.

Province. (34) Επαρχιας. xxv. 1. Not elsewhere. Ex
επι, et αρχω, impero.—*Judgment-hall*. (35) Πραιτωριω.
See on *John* xviii. 28.

PRACTICAL OBSERVATIONS.

V. 1—5.

To rejoice in the testimony of a good conscience before
God, amidst calumnies and persecutions, is an invaluable
blessing: but this cannot be habitually possessed, except
by the constant exercise of faith in Christ, and an upright
obedience to his commandments. (*Note,* 2 *Cor.* i. 12—14.)
—No rank, learning, authority, religious profession, or
sacred function, can change the pride and selfishness of
the human heart: but iniquity and oppression are most
hateful, when committed in courts of justice, and masked
with pretensions to piety. (*Notes, Ps.* xciv. 20, 21. *Is.* x.
1—4.) The actors, in such atrocious. hypocrisy, are
" whited walls" and " painted sepulchres," whom God
will smite with distinguished vengeance.—The best of men
are liable, when greatly injured and insulted, to be put off
their guard: and even that zeal and faithfulness, which the
Holy Spirit dictates, in warning sinners of approaching
ruin, will sometimes be mingled with the remains of our
sinful passions, and prompt us to " speak unadvisedly
" with our lips." But, whether in reality, or only in appearance, we speak or act inconsistently with the divine
precepts; it is in general adviseable to decline a strenuous
justification of ourselves, and to admit that our conduct
was in some respects unfit for imitation: and in no ordinary circumstances should we by any means " speak evil "
of our rulers; whatever their characters may be, or however they may have injured us; for the Christian's maxims
are, to honour those in authority, and " to overcome evil
" with good." (*Notes, Rom.* xiii. 1—5 *Tit.* iii. 1, 2.
1 *Pet.* ii. 13—17. 2 *Pet.* ii. 10, 11. Jude 9, 10.)

V. 6—11.

" The wisdom of the serpent," as well as " the harm-
" lessness of the dove," is necessary for us, amidst " un-
" reasonable and wicked men." It is useless to urge the
most conclusive arguments, when we know that our cause
is already prejudged: and it is lawful, on some occasions,
to seek the protection of one party against the violence of
another, by declaring that we agree with them in many
important doctrines; provided this can be said consistently
with exact truth. Thus we may sometimes divert the
storm which we could not repress, and divide the counsels of the enemies of the gospel.—Among those who
oppose spiritual religion, some come nearer to the truth
than others: and though self-righteous Pharisees are to be
warned and shunned; yet Sadducees and infidels, who
deny all the doctrines of revealed religion, should be still
more strenuously opposed.—In every controversy, especially relating to religion, an appeal to men's passions and
prejudices, and an avowed preference of their tenets to
those of their opponents, will generally go further, than

either sound arguments, or exemplary conduct, in softening their resentment, and securing their esteem. Allow
them to have truth on their side, and they will be disposed
in some measure to grant you the same: for man is a
vain-glorious creature, who courts flattery, and would have
his own opinion considered as the standard of truth! A
practical uniform attention to this characteristic of our
fallen nature seems the grand device for managing mankind; whether among the giddy multitude, or in the great
councils of nations, or in ecclesiastical conventions. But
it is a delicate operation, which requires great skill and caution; and there is imminent danger of deviating from strict
" simplicity and godly sincerity," into carnal policy, whenever we have recourse to it: though we may avail ourselves
of it on some great emergency; and when it may evidently be done, without at all receding from our principles, and to the advantage of the truth.—But what a
scandal is it, when the professors and ministers of true
religion are so furious in their contests, that idolatrous and
ungodly men cry shame of their violence, and are constrained to interpose authority, or military force, to quell
the riot, and prevent more fatal consequences! or when
national and ecclesiastical assemblies more resemble a
meeting of furious assassins, than a convention of legislators, or the servants of God! Yet this has often been
the case, and the fury of controversy is not yet extinct.—
But the Lord Jesus will be the comfort and refuge of his
faithful servants, amidst all dangers and troubles, till their
testimony and work be finished: and did their enemies
know, how sweet their secret consolations are, they would
be far less surprised at their fortitude and patience in publick.

V. 12—35.

The corruption of the best things becomes the worst:
erroneous religious principles, zealously espoused by carnal
men, dictate such enormities, as others seem scarcely capable of; and thus the most horrid villanies have been perpetrated, not only without remorse, but with exultation.—
How careful should we be not to vow and to bind ourselves,
to what is criminal, or may be impracticable; and not to
trifle with oaths and imprecations! For, through neglect
of such precautions, men are drawn into wickedness, and
expose themselves to vengeance, which way soever they
turn themselves: nor will evasions or dispensations from
whatever quarter extricate them from the snare. All that
in this case can be done, is to repent, and seek forgiveness of so great a wickedness. The Lord with perfect
ease disappoints the best concerted schemes of iniquity,
and detects the most secret devices of his enemies. He
has instruments for every work: the natural abilities, or
cultivated minds, and moral virtues of heathens, have
often been employed, in the protection of his persecuted
servants: for they can discern between the unaffected conscientiousness of upright believers, and the zeal of false
professors; though they disregard or do not understand
their doctrinal principles.—Nothing *spiritually* good can
indeed be found in our fallen nature, except as the fruit of
renewing grace: yet a regard to truth, equity, and hu.

5 ʏ 8

Christ, according to the scriptures, 19—23. Festus exclaims that he is mad, but he mildly denies the charge, 24, 25; and addresses Agrippa, who owns himself "almost persuaded to be a Christian," 26—28. Paul expresses his earnest desire, that every one present were altogether Christians, 29. Agrippa and the company agree with Festus, that Paul is innocent, 30—32.

THEN Agrippa said unto Paul, ᵃ Thou art permitted to speak for thyself. Then Paul ᵇ stretched forth the hand, and ᶜ answered for himself:

2 I think myself happy, king Agrippa, because I shall answer for myself this day before thee, touching all the things whereof I am accused of the Jews;

3 Especially, ᵈ *because I know* thee to be expert in all customs and questions which are among the Jews: wherefore I beseech thee ᵉ to hear me patiently.

4 My ʳmanner of life from my youth, ᶠ which was at the first among mine own nation at Jerusalem, know all the Jews;

5 Which knew me from the beginning, ʰ if they would testify, ⁱ that after the most straitest ᵏ sect of our religion I lived a Pharisee.

6 And now I stand, and ˡ am judged, for the hope of ᵐ the promise made of God unto our fathers:

7 Unto which *promise* ⁿ our twelve tribes, ᵒ instantly serving *God* ᵖday and night, ᵠ hope to come: ʳ for which hope's sake, king Agrippa, I am accused of the Jews.

8 Why ʳ should it be thought a thing incredible with you that God should raise the dead ?

NOTES.

Chap. XXVI. V. 1—3. Agrippa having signified to Paul, that he was allowed to plead his own cause, in order that a more authentick account of his case might be made to the emperor; he stretched out his hand, with a decent action, to give emphasis to his words, according to the manner of the most celebrated ancient orators; and proceeded to state his subject in that manner, which was most suited to impress the audience with a conviction of its truth and importance. (*Marg. Ref.* a, b.)—The subsequent speech has generally been allowed to be peculiarly pertinent, convincing, and suited to the circumstances in which, and the splendid company before whom, it was delivered. He addressed himself immediately to Agrippa, declaring that he deemed it a happy incident, that he was permitted to defend himself from the accusations of the Jews, before one, whose education, and subsequent enquiries and studies, had rendered him so accurately acquainted with all the customs and rites of the Jewish religion, and all the questions controverted among the different sects among the Jews; as he would be far more competent to form a judgment of his cause, than any stranger could be. He therefore besought the favour of a candid and patient hearing, whilst he went through the several particulars, which he had to state on the subject. (*Marg. Ref.* d.—*Note*, xxiv. 10—21, *vv.* 10, 11.)

Answer. (2) Απολογεισθαι. 1. See on Luke xii. 11.—*I am accused.*] Εγκαλιμαι. 7. See on xix. 38.—*To be expert.* (3) Γνωςην οντα. Here only. Γνωςος, xix. 17.—*Patiently.*] Μακροθυμως. Here only Μακροθυμεω. See on Matt. xviii. 26. Ex μακρος, *longus*, et θυμος, *animus*.

V. 4—8. ' Paul, dividing the narrative of his life into ' two parts, cites his adversaries themselves as witnesses ' of the former part, and the fathers and prophets to attest ' the latter part.' *Beza.*—After a brief account of his reli-

gion, as a Pharisee, which was the strictest and most exact sect of the nation; and an appeal to the Jews themselves, that he had acted in consistency with that profession, from his youth to the time when he became a Christian; the apostle declared that he stood as a criminal to be judged, on account of his professed hope in the promise made by God to their ancestors. Some commentators suppose the apostle to mean, almost exclusively, that the resurrection to eternal life, was " the promise made unto " the fathers: ' but it is manifest, beyond all doubt, that the promise of a Saviour was the most prominent part of the revelation made to Abraham, Isaac, and Jacob, and the grand subject of prophecy; (*Marg. Ref.* m —*Notes*, Luke xxiv. 44—49. *John* v. 39—44. *Heb.* xi. 39, 40. 1 *Pet.* i. 10—12. *Rev.* xix. 9, 10;) while the doctrine of the resurrection was not so fully and plainly revealed in the Old Testament, as it is in the New. (*Note*, 2 *Tim.* i. 10.) St. Paul says elsewhere, " We declare unto you glad tidings, " how that the promise which was made unto the fathers, " God hath fulfilled the same unto us their children; in " that he hath raised up Jesus again." (*Notes*, xiii. 24—37. *Rom.* i. 1—4, *v.* 4.) Thus the resurrection of Jesus demonstrated that he was the promised Messiah, against all the unbelieving Jews; and the doctrine of the resurrection, against the Sadducees. The latter were instigated to persecute the apostles, for " preaching through Jesus the re-" surrection of the dead;" (*Notes*, iv. 1—3. xxiii. 6—10;) the former, for preaching the very person whom they had crucified, as the Messiah, and as risen and " exalted to be " a Prince and Saviour." Yet the whole nation expected a Messiah; and all, except the Sadducees, professed to believe the doctrine of the resurrection. In general, all that remained of the twelve tribes, wherever dispersed, hoped for the accomplishment of the promise concerning the Messiah, and a resurrection to eternal life through him: and their constant worship at the temple, morning and

9 I verily thought with myself, ' that I ought to do many things contrary to ' the name of Jesus of Nazareth.

10 Which thing "I also did in Jerusalem: and many of ' the saints did I shut up in prison, ' having received authority from the chief priests; and when they were put to death, I gave my voice against *them*.

11 And I punished them oft ' in every synagogue, ' and compelled *them* to blaspheme: and, being exceedingly ᵇ mad against them, I persecuted *them* even unto strange cities.

12 Whereupon, ᶜ as I went to Damascus, ᵈ with authority and commission from the chief priests,

13 At ᵉ mid-day, O king, I saw in the way a light from heaven, ᶠ above

the brightness of the sun, shining round about me and them which journeyed with me.

14 And when we were all fallen to the earth, I heard a voice speaking unto me, and saying ᶠ in the Hebrew tongue, ʰ Saul, Saul, why persecutest thou me ? *It is* ' hard for thee to kick ᵏ against the pricks.

15 And I said, Who art thou, Lord ? ' And he said, ᵏ I am Jesus, whom thou persecutest:

16 But ' rise, and stand upon thy feet: for I have appeared unto thee for this purpose, ᵐ to make thee ⁿ a minister and a witness, both of these things which thou hast seen, and of ° those things ° in the which I will appear unto thee;

---

evening, as well as their other frequent and incessant religious observances, implied the same hope. (*Marg. Ref.* o—q.) And, as the resurrection of Jesus was proved, by most unexceptionable and abundant testimony, and might be shewn to be the fulfilment of ancient prophecies; what reason could be given, why it should not be credited?—"Why should it be thought a thing incredible with you, " that God should raise the dead ?"· Is not the great Creator able to restore the dead to life again ? And cannot sufficient reasons be assigned for his omnipotent interposition, that his truth may be attested, his worshippers encouraged, and his name glorified? (*Marg. Ref.* r.—*Note, John* xx. 24—29.) Thus the apostle makes a natural and easy transition, from the hope of their fathers, and the doctrine of the resurrection, to that which was his principal subject; namely, the proof, which he intended to adduce, that Jesus was indeed risen, and was the promised Messiah.—Some render the eighth verse thus, " What ! " Is it a thing incredible with you, if God raises the dead ?" and this indeed gives a peculiar animation to the question. (*Notes,* 1 *Kings* xvii. 21, 22. 2 *Kings* iv. 33—35. xiii. 20, 21. *John* xi. 41—48. 1 *Cor.* xv. 12—19.)

My manner of life. (4) Την ζιωσιν μν. Here only. A ζιος, *vita.*—*Who knew me from the beginning.* (5) Προγινωσκοντες μι ανωθεν.—Προγινωσκω, *Rom.* viii. 29. xi. 2. 1 *Pet.* i. 20. 2 *Pet.* iii. 17. Ανωθεν· See on *Luke* i. 3. *John* iii. 3.—*The most straitest.*] Ακριθεστατην. See on xxiv. 22.—*Sect.*] 'Αιρεσιν. xxiv. 5. 14. See on v. 17.—*Religion.*] Θρησκειας. *Col.* ii. 18. *Jam.* i. 26, 27. Θρησκος, *Jam.* i. 26. Not elsewhere.— *Twelve tribes.* (7) Δωδεκαφυλον. Here only. Ex δωδεκα, duodecim, et φυλη, *tribus.*—*Instantly serving God.*] Εν εκτενια λατρευον. Here only. Εκτενης· See on xii. 5. *Luke* xxii. 44. Λατρευον, xxiv. 14. See on *Luke* ii. 37.—*A thing incredible.* (8) Απιςον. *Matt.* xvii. 17. *John* xx. 27. 1 *Tim.* v. 8, et al. Ex a priv. et πιςις, *fides.* ' Quod omnem fidem superat.' Schleusner.

V. 9—11. The apostle acknowledged that he himself had formerly been extremely prejudiced against the gospel, and had thought it his duty to do many things " contrary

" to the name of Jesus," who was usually in contempt called " the Nazarene." (*Marg. Ref.* s, t.) Accordingly he had at Jerusalem, by the authority of the chief priests, imprisoned many of those excellent persons, whom he now knew to be " the saints" and holy servants of God: and when any of them were condemned to death by the council, he had approved and applauded the sentence, and promoted its execution. He had also, by means of scourging and other severities, in all the synagogues, and by threatening death, compelled many professors and favourers of Christianity, to deny and revile the Saviour as a deceiver, in language which he now thus publickly declared to be blasphemy: and in every respect he was enraged against them to a degree, which might justly be regarded as the excess of madness and insanity. (*Marg. Ref.* u—a.—*Notes,* 24 —29. vii. 54—60, *v.* 58. viii. 3. xxii. 1—5. *John* xvi. 1— 3. 1 *Tim.* i. 12—14.)

Did I shut up. (10) Κατεκλεισα. *Luke* iii. 20. Not elsewhere N. T.—*Jer.* xxxii. 3. *Sept.* A καθα, et κλειω, claudo. —*I gave my voice.*] Κατηνεγκα ψηφον. *Rev.* ii. 17. Not elsewhere. Ψηφιζω· See on *Luke* xiv. 28.—*I punished.* (11) Τιμωρων. See on xxii. 5.—*Being exceedingly mad.*] Εμμαινομενος. Here only. Εκ εν, et μαινομαι, 24, 25. xii. 15.

V. 12—15. *Marg. Ref.*—*Notes,* ix. 1—22. xxii. 6— 16.—*Commission.* (12) Επιτροπης. Here only. Επιτροπος, *Matt.* xx. 8. *Luke* viii. 3. *Gal.* iv. 2. Ab επιτρεπω, xxi. 39, 40.—*From heaven.* (13) Ουρανοθεν. xiv. 17.—*Above the brightness of the sun.*] Υπερ την λαμπροτητα το ηλιυ. This is not mentioned elsewhere. Λαμπροτης. Here only. A λαμπρος, splendidus, x. 30. *Rev.* xxii. 16.

V. 16—18. It is evident, that this commission was given to Paul by our Lord, at the time of his conversion ; though not mentioned in the compendious narrative of that event. (*Note,* ix. 15, 16.)—' The words make a part ' of the sentence, in which Christ bids him rise from his ' astonishment, into which his appearance to him, in the ' way to Damascus, had thrown him.' *Doddridge.*—Jesus called on him to arise from the earth, as prepared to receive and execute his mandates. He had appeared to him,'

17 * Delivering thee from the people, and *from* * the Gentiles, unto whom now I send thee,

18 To * open their eyes, * *and* to turn *them* from darkness to light, * and *from* the power of Satan unto God, * that they may receive forgiveness of sins, * and inheritance among them which are * sanctified, by * faith that is in me.

19 Whereupon, * O king Agrippa, * I was not disobedient unto the heavenly vision:

20 But shewed * first unto them of Damascus, * and at Jerusalem,' and throughout all the coasts of Judea, * and *then* to the Gentiles, that they should * repent and * turn to God, * and do works meet for repentance.

21 For these causes ' the Jews caught me in the temple, and went about to kill *me*.

22 Having therefore * obtained help

---

not to destroy him, but to appoint him a minister of his gospel, and a witness to all men; not only of this vision, but of many other things, which he would afterwards reveal to him from time to time. (*Marg. Ref.* l—o.) For executing this ministry, the Jews would indeed seek to kill him; but Jesus promised to deliver him from them, and from the Gentiles, to whom he now gave him a commission to preach his salvation. (*Marg. Ref.* p, q.) The end and effect of his ministry among them, through the power of the Holy Spirit accompanying his word, would be "to "open their eyes:" for, though their bodily eyes were open, and their intellectual powers, in secular matters, might be very penetrating; they had notwithstanding been hitherto spiritually blind, through the influence of the devil, and the depravity of their carnal minds; so that they could see nothing of the glory of God, of his truth and will, or of the way of acceptance and holiness. But, oy the change to be wrought in their minds by divine grace, and the instructions of his word, they would be turned from the darkness of ignorance, error, and wickedness, to the light of divine knowledge, truth, and holiness; and from those idolatries and vices, by which they worshipped and served Satan, as his bond slaves, to the holy worship and service of the living God; that, through the gospel, they might receive a full pardon of all their sins, and be made heirs of that heavenly inheritance, to which all those who are renewed to holiness will be admitted, by faith in him, as the Saviour of lost mankind. (*Marg. Ref.* r—z. —*Notes, Is.* xlii. 5—7. 13—17. xlix. 5—13. *Matt.* iv. 12 —17. *Luke* i. 76—79. iv. 16—19. *Eph.* v. 8—14. *Col.* i. 9—14. 1 *Pet.* ii. 9, 10.)—The distinction between " open-" ing their eyes, and turning them from darkness to light," should be particularly noticed. Had the eyes of the ignorant gentiles been opened by divine grace, and no light of scriptural instruction given them; they must still have groped in the dark, as a seeing man does in a dark room: had the light of truth been sent, but the illumination of the Holy Spirit withheld; their condition would have resembled that of blind men in the full light of day. But adequate instruction was given them by the gospel, and their minds and hearts were prepared to receive it by regeneration. Paul received this commission to the Gentiles, at the time when he was converted; yet he did not

preach to any but Jews and proselytes, till after Cornelius had been converted by the ministry of Peter: for he waited for farther intimations of the Lord's will, as to the time and manner, in which he was to set about that important service; and perhaps he did not fully understand, at first, the import and extent of his charge.—To interpret the language of this passage, as if it were exclusively applicable to idolaters, implies an opinion that nominal Christians are of a better nature than other men; or that pride, covetousness, and all the other vices, by which men are enslaved to Satan, are not so heinous in professed Christians, as they are in heathens! Gross idolatry indeed has been, in this part of the world, exchanged for irreligion, infidelity, superstition, formality, and hypocrisy, among *nominal* Christians: but the hearts and minds of the unregenerate and unconverted are as much blinded by aversion to spiritual religion, and by the love of the world and of sin, as those of the ancient gentiles were. ' Those ' who call themselves Christians, because they happen to ' be born in a Christian country; but attend neither to the ' doctrines, nor the duties of the gospel, seem to differ ' but little, with respect to the point under consideration, ' from those to whom the gospel was first preached: the ' process in both must be nearly the same.' *Bp. Tomline's Refutation of Calvinism.*—May it not be added, ' Because ' they have been baptized with water?'—*By faith,* &c. (18) ' This may be referred to *sanctified;* ... but the sen-' tence is much fuller, if we join it with the word *receive.*' *Beza.* No doubt we are " sanctified," as well as " justi-" fied," by faith in Christ; but the words under consideration seem to shew, that all the blessings mentioned are received by faith in Christ, and not one of them only.

To make thee. (16). Προχειρισασθαι σε. xxii. 14. Not elsewhere.—*Delivering.* (17) Εξαιρουμενος. vii. 10. 34. xii. 11. xxiii. 27. *Matt.* v. 29. xviii. 9. *Gal.* i. 4.—*The power of Satan.* (18) Της εξουσιας τε Σατανα. Εξουσια, *Luke* xxii. 53. *Col.* i. 13. *Note, Matt.* xxviii. 18. Σαλανας, v. 3. *Matt.* iv. 10. xii. 26. xvi. 23. *Rev.* xii. 9, *et al.* A צֹרֵר, *Odi, odio habere.*—*Inheritance.*] Κληρον. See on i. 17.—*Which are sanctified.*] Τοις ηγιασμενοις. See on xx. 32.

V. 19—23. The apostle next intimated to king Agrippa, that it could not be supposed he would refuse obedience to a vision, which was so evidently from heaven. Accord-

of God, I continue unto this day, ' witnessing both to small and great, saying "none other things, than those which ª the prophets and Moses did say should come;

23 That ° Christ should suffer, *and* that he should be ᵖ the first that should rise from the dead, ᑫ and should shew light unto the people, and to the Gentiles.

24 ¶ And as he thus ' spake for himself, ' Festus said with a loud voice, ' Paul thou art beside thyself; much learning doth make thee mad.

25 But he said, ᵘ I am not mad, ˣ most noble Festus; but speak forth

ᵗ the words of truth and soberness.

26 For ª the king knoweth of these things, before whom also I speak freely: for I am persuaded that none of these things are hidden from him; for ª this thing was not done in a corner.

27 King Agrippa, ᵇ believest thou the prophets? I know that thou believest.

28 Then Agrippa said unto Paul, ° Almost thou persuadest me to be a Christian.

29 And Paul said, ᵈ I would to God, ° that not only thou, but also all that hear me this day, were both almost and altogether such as I am, ᶠ except these bonds.

---

ingly, he began to preach first to the Jews at Damascus whither he went to persecute the Christians, and then in other places, and at length to the Gentiles; calling on them to repent of all their sins, to turn to the worship and service of God, and to live holy lives, as became true penitents; and thus to expect the mercy and favour of God through Jesus Christ. (*Marg. Ref.* b—h.—*Notes,* xx. 18—21. *Matt.* iii. 7—10. *Luke* iii. 7—14.) " For " these causes the Jews," being exasperated with him, for declaring that Jesus whom they had crucified was the Messiah, and for preaching to the Gentiles, seized on him in the temple, and would have murdered him, if they had not been prevented; but, having obtained help from God, by means of Lysias, Felix, Festus, and others, his life had hitherto been preserved; and he had employed it in testifying, to the poorest of mankind, as well as to the rich and honourable, with equal plainness and faithfulness, the grace of the gospel. In doing this he had said nothing, but what entirely accorded to the types and predictions of the law, as well as to the express and repeated language of the prophets, and even of Moses their great lawgiver. As these foretold, that the promised Messiah would suffer and die, and yet that he would reign in a most glorious manner: and consequently that he should rise from the dead, as the first-fruits of the resurrection; and that he was to shew the light of salvation, not only to the people of Israel, but to the Gentiles also. (*Marg. Ref.* i—q.— *Notes,* xiii. 42—48. *Luke* xxiv. 25—31. 44—49, vv. 44— 46. *John* v. 45—47.)

Disobedient. (19) Απειθης. *Luke* i. 17. *Rom.* i. 30. 2 *Tim.* iii. 2. *Tit.* i. 16. iii. 3. Απειθεω· See on *John* iii. 36.—*Vision.*] Οπτασια. *Luke* i. 22. xxiv. 23. 2 *Cor.* xii. 1. Ab οπτομαι, *video.*—*Turn.* (20) Επιςρεφειν. 18. See on iii. 19.—*Went about to kill me.* (21) Επειρωντο διαχειρισασθαι. " Attempted to murder me with their own hands." See on v. 30. (*Notes,* xxi. 27—36.) Εκ δια, et χειριζω. A χειρ, *manus.*—*Help.* (22) Επικυριας. Here only.— *That Christ should suffer.* (23) Ει παθητος ὁ Χριςος. Here only. A πασχω, *patior.*—' Ει being put for ὁτι, *that,* saith ' *Oecumenius.* ... 1 *Tim.* v. 10. *Heb.* iii. 11.' *Whitby.*

V. 24—29. While Paul was confirming his testimony

to the resurrection and glory of Jesus, by the predictions of scripture; and probably was preparing to adduce more particular proof, from the prophets, to each part of his doctrine; he was suddenly interrupted by Festus. He had never heard any thing before on these subjects; the resurrection of Jesus, and the vision of Paul, appeared to him incredible, or visionary in the highest degree. Probably he was astonished to hear him speak of his doctrine as of universal concernment; and aver that one, who arose among the despised Jews, was appointed to be " the Light " of the Gentiles," even of the philosophical Greeks and Romans. He therefore said in a loud voice, audible by the whole assembly, " Paul, thou art beside thyself, &c." He perhaps had observed, that the apostle spent much time in retirement, study, and reading; and he supposed that, having studied very closely about certain abstract and visionary matters, his over-attention had deranged his intellects : so that he could not deem him fit either to be blamed or credited; but to be an object of mere compassion. (*Marg. Ref.* s, t.—*Notes,* 9—11. 2 *Kings* ix. 11. *Jer.* xxix. 24—32. *Mark* iii. 20, 21. 2 *Cor.* v. 13—15.) To this rude interruption before so large and splendid an audience, the apostle calmly and gravely replied, addressing the governor by the customary title of " most noble," or " most excellent;" assuring him, that he " was not " mad ;" and that he declared nothing but what was altogether true, of the highest importance, and able to stand the test of the most deliberate investigation. Indeed " king Agrippa" was acquainted with these subjects : the events respecting the miracles, doctrine, death, and reported resurrection of Jesus, and the subsequent promulgation of Christianity, could not have been hid from one, who was so well informed in all the affairs of the Jews ; for these things had not been transacted in an obscure " corner," but in the most publick manner imaginable. (*Marg. Ref.* u, x. a.) He would therefore enquire of Agrippa, whether he did indeed believe, that the old prophets spake by divine inspiration, and that their predictions would be certainly fulfilled. He however knew that he would answer in the affirmative, for he doubted not but he did in this respect believe them: and he only desired

30 ¶ And when he had thus spoken, *the king rose up, and the governor, and Bernice, and they that sat with them :

31 And when they were gone aside, they talked between themselves, say-ing, ᵇ This man doeth nothing worthy of death or of bonds.

32 Then said Agrippa unto Festus, This man might have been set at liberty, if he had not ˡ appealed unto Cæsar.

Agrippa to examine, whether they had not exactly been fulfilled in Jesus of Nazareth.—This appeal to the scriptures, joined to the apostle's other arguments, had so great an effect upon Agrippa's mind, that he could not conceal his convictions; but openly declared, that Paul had " almost persuaded him to be a Christian." His understanding and judgment were for the time convinced, but his heart was not changed : (*Note*, 2 Cor. iv. 1, 2 :) and he must have been aware, that the sacrifices to be made, and the cross to be sustained, would in his case be very great. So that while he was more candid, and just in his government, than others of his family ; his conduct and temper were widely distant from the spirituality and humility of the gospel. The apostle, however, desirous to fix the impression upon his mind, replied, in the genuine spirit of Christian love, that he earnestly wished and prayed that not only he, but every one in that large and splendid assembly, might not only " almost," but " alto-" gether," embrace and be established in the faith of the gospel, and partakers of all its substantial blessings and consolations ; and in short, entirely like himself in every thing, except in his bonds and imprisonment, which he would wish to bear alone. This most benevolent wish implied his full conviction of the truth of the gospel ; the absolute necessity of faith in Christ in order to salvation ; his own happiness as a Christian, even in his bonds ; his opinion that Agrippa, Festus, and others present, did not then believe ; and his fear that they would reject the gospel to their final condemnation.

Thou art beside thyself. (24) Μαινη. 25. xii. 15. John x. 20. 1 Cor. xiv. 23. See on 11.—*Doth make thee mad.*] Εις μανιαν περιτρεπει. Περιτρεπω. Here only. Εκ περι, et τρεπω, verto. Μανια. Here only. Hence μαινομαι.—*Speak forth.* (25) Αποφθεγγομαι. See on ii. 4.—*Soberness.*] Σωφροσυνης. 1 Tim. ii. 9. 15. Not elsewhere. Σωφρων, 1 Tim. iii. 2. Tit. i. 8. ii. 2. 5. Α σως, sanus, et φρην, mens.—*Freely.* (26) Παρρησιαζομενος. ix. 27. 29. ⅲ. 46. xiv. 3. xviii. 26. xix. 8.— *A corner.*] Γωνια. iv. 11. Ma't. vi. 5, et al.—*Almost.* (28) Εν ολιγω. (Και εν ολιγω και εν πολλω, 29.) *Within a little.*— *To be a Christian.*]' Χριςιανον γινεσθαι. "To become a Christ-" ian." See on xi. 26.—*I would to God.* (29) Ευξαιμην αν. xxvii. 29. Rom. ix. 3. 2 Cor. xiii. 7. 3 John 2. See on Rom. ix. 3.—*Except.*] Παρεκτος. Matt. v. 22. 2 Cor. xi. 28.

V. 30—32. Agrippa, like Felix, seems to have been made very uneasy, and even alarmed, by St. Paul's convincing and impressive address : he was therefore the first to dismiss the subject, and to retire from the place of hearing. (*Note*, xxiv. 24—27.) His opinion, that Paul was innocent, and might have been liberated, had " he " not appealed unto Cæsar," would give Festus a more favourable opinion of him : but it does not appear, that either of them, or any of those present, enquired further after Christ and his salvation ; and this most admirable speech of the apostle seems to have been peculiarly unsuccessful, as to the event of it at that time. (*Note*, xvii. 32—34.)—Learned men have shewn, that no laws against the Christians had at this time been enacted by the Roman legislature.

PRACTICAL OBSERVATIONS.

V. 1—11.

The Lord will never fail to give those, who for his cause are called to appear before kings, and rulers, and councils, " a mouth and wisdom, which none of their ad-" versaries shall be able to gainsay or resist." (*Notes*, vi. 9—14, v. 10. Matt. x. 19, 20. Luke xxi. 12—19, v. 15.) —When Christian love abounds in the heart, it dictates a *sincere* language, far surpassing all compliment and worldly politeness ; and teaches us to " render honour to " whom honour is due," without flattery or fear of man. —That religious knowledge which unconverted men acquire, and their " expertness" about customs and questions in divinity, in general lie dormant, as mere learned lumber, in the understanding : yet, when attended with a measure of candour, they are thus rendered more accessible to truth, and more competent to judge of the evidence adduced in support of it. Nor is it any flattery to give such men the credit of their attainments ; or improper to intreat a " patient" hearing, when the subject might demand the most reverent attention. (*Note*, Philem. 8— 11.)—A moral conduct, and a form of godliness, are often connected with a bigoted aversion to the gospel ; and this leads to many other heinous crimes : yet it is a mercy to be preserved, during our unconverted years, from those vices, which might afterwards disgrace our characters among worldly people, and so prevent the influence of our testimony : and this is greatly corroborated, when they, who " knew our manner of life from our youth," could testify, that we then acted consistently with our principles, and according to what we thought right ; for they may thence infer, that our change of sentiment and conduct also originated from a regard to duty.—Men are often censured and persecuted for professing their hope in the express promises of God, and for a consequent expectation of the resurrection, and future state of righteous retributions : and numbers repeat creeds, subscribe doctrines, and join in forms of worship, habitually, and with apparent earnestness ; and yet condemn others for explicitly professing the truths contained in them ! Many things are " thought incredible," because the infinite nature and perfection of that God, who has revealed, performed, or promised them, are overlooked ; and because men will not see how his power and glory are concerned in them. (*Note*, Matt. xxii. 23—33, v. 29.)—Those who have been most strict in their conduct, previous to conversion, will afterwards see abundant cause for deep humiliation, even on account of things, which at the time they " verily thought they

CHAP. XXVII.

Paul, attended by some friends, sails as a prisoner towards Rome, and is kindly used by the Centurion sent with him and other prisoners, 1—8. He foretels the danger of the voyage, but is not credited, 9—11.

Sailing against his advice, the company are exposed to a most violent and long continued tempest, and are in extreme danger, 10—20. Paul, encouraged by an angel, assures them that all their lives shall be preserved, but that the ship shall be wrecked, 21—26; the whole of which exactly comes to pass, 27—44.

" ought to do:" their contemptuous or injurious treatment of the saints, their opposition to the gospel, and endeavours to seduce, reason, or terrify others into a neglect of it, will often sit very heavily on their minds; and they will condemn those words, as impious and blasphemous, which they once uttered, or excited others to utter, without remorse; and allow that conduct to be *madness*, in which they once gloried.

V. 12—23.

The true convert can give "a reason of his hope;" and a good account of the change which has taken place in him, even when there is nothing extraordinary in his experience. (*Note*, 1 *Pet.* iii. 13—16.) Having been convinced of his guilt and danger, as a transgressor of God's law, and a stranger to his grace, or a despiser of it; he was led to seek for mercy, and to believe in the Lord Jesus; and, being encouraged with the hope of acceptance, of increasing light, and of continued protection, he began to employ himself in his service. Thus the Lord reconciles sinners to himself, and sometimes "commits to them " the word of reconciliation:" he sends them to their fellow sinners, to "beseech them in his stead to be recon- " ciled to him;" (*Notes*, 2 *Cor.* v. 18—21. vi. 1, 2;) and, by his power attending their word, he "opens their eyes, " turns them from darkness to light, delivers them from " the kingdom and power of Satan," forms them spiritual worshippers of God, forgives their sins, adopts them into his family, sanctifies them by his grace, and brings them to his heavenly inheritance, by faith in his name. (*Note*, 1 *Thes.* i. 9, 10.)—Those who are thus enlightened and favoured will not be "disobedient" to the commands of the Redeemer: and all who understand and preach the gospel will perceive, that it contains directions, motives, and encouragements, to "repent, and turn to God, and " to do works meet for repentance," addressed to men, as sinners, without discrimination; and, that it has no saving efficacy on the heart, where these fruits do not clearly appear in the life. (*Notes, Tit.* ii. 11—14. iii. 4— 8.) Yet, for calling on men thus to "repent and be con- " verted;" and for "witnessing none other things," than what are evidently contained in the holy scriptures; what numbers have been execrated, persecuted, and slain, even by the professed worshippers of God! So that it is owing to the peculiar help and protection of God, when zealous and laborious preachers of the gospel are preserved from the violence of the wicked, and have their lives, and opportunities to bear their faithful testimony, continued to them: but let who may be the instruments, they should give the whole glory, both of their protection, and of their persevering faithfulness and diligence, to God alone.

V. 24—32.

The persons, whom God employs to protect his servants, often despise them as visionaries or madmen, for being so zealous about invisible objects, for believing subjects so

mysterious, crediting facts of so extraordinary a nature; and relating their experience of the way in which the Lord brought them to trust in his grace, and embrace his gospel; and for attesting that the same faith and diligence, and an experience in many respects similar, are indispensably necessary to all men, both small and great, in order to their salvation. Indeed few ascribe the madness of modern teachers to deep study, or much learning: but they rather impute it to weakness of intellect, or contemptible ignorance; whatever evidences they give of good sense, enlarged minds, and extensive knowledge in other subjects. But as apostles and prophets, nay, the Son of God himself, were exposed to this obloquy; let us not be moved, if those who deemed us sober and intelligent, when we were "exceedingly mad," should set us down for *insane*, when divine grace has brought us to ourselves, and made us wise unto salvation. (*Note, Luke* xv. 17—19.) Yet let us be careful, in these circumstances, to speak with temper; that we may disprove the charge by a dispassionate conduct, as well as by "the words of truth and sober- " ness." We should likewise cautiously avoid all real enthusiasm, and whatever is ambiguous or incapable of being supported by appropriate evidence; whilst we deny, and attempt to refute, the charge of being visionaries and fanaticks.—It is highly important for us to lead men's attention, by clear instructions, conclusive arguments, and well authenticated facts, to the sacred oracles, as the standard of truth; and, while we enquire, whether our hearers do indeed believe the scriptures, we should, as much as may be, take it for granted that they do: for many assent to the truth of the Bible, and pay a respect to testimonies from it, who have not yet understood or received the doctrines or salvation there revealed. Arguments and testimonies of this kind "almost persuade" numbers to be Christians, who yet are never *wholly* induced to leave all for Christ. When this is the case, they often grow weary of hearing the truth, and sin away conviction: and their own confessions eventually increase their condemnation for rejecting the gospel, out of love to the world, and sinful pleasures. While we beware of this fatal hesitation and irresolution in our own conduct; and recollect how far being "almost persuaded to be a " Christian" is from being altogether such a one as Paul was, or even as every true believer is; we should endeavour to impress still more deeply the minds of those, who are under serious convictions of the truth. In doing this, the language of fervent, disinterested affection is peculiarly becoming: and we should sincerely desire and pray, that others may participate all our hopes and comforts; and be exempted from our crosses and trials. Yet even this beautiful philanthropy, when expressed in the most graceful and conciliatory language, will fail to recommend the holy gospel to the carnal hearts of worldly men. They will grow weary of subjects and reflection so humiliating and solemn; and even, when they deem the preacher a

5 u 6

AND [a] when it was determined that we should sail into [b] Italy, they delivered Paul, and certain other prisoners, unto one named Julius, [c] a centurion of [d] Augustus' band.

2 And entering into a ship of Adramyttium, [e] we launched, meaning [f] to sail by the coasts of Asia; one [g] Aristarchus, a Macedonian of Thessalonica, being [h] with us.

3 And the next *day* we touched at [i] Sidon. And [k] Julius courteously entreated Paul, and gave *him* liberty to go unto his friends to refresh himself.

4 And when we had launched from thence, we sailed under [l] Cyprus, because [m] the winds were contrary.

5 And when we had sailed over the sea of [n] Cilicia and [o] Pamphylia, we came to Myra, *a city* of Lycia.

6 And there [p] the centurion found a ship of [q] Alexandria sailing into Italy; and he put us therein.

7 And when we had sailed slowly many days, and scarce were come over against Cnidus, the wind not suffering us, [r] we sailed [s] under [t] Crete, over against Salmone;

8 And, hardly passing it, came unto a place which is called The Fair Havens; nigh whereunto was the city *of* Lasea.

9 Now when much time was spent, and when sailing was now dangerous, because [u] the fast was now already past, Paul admonished *them*,

---

man of integrity, and cannot but think he has truth on his side, they will not allow his " saying to be worthy of " all acceptation ;" or faith in Christ, producing prompt obedience to his precepts, to be *absolutely necessary to their salvation.* Alas! how many such persons have been " almost persuaded to be Christians," who nevertheless at .ast perished in their sins ! God grant that none who read these observations may be found in that unhappy number!

NOTES.

CHAP. XXVII. V. 1, 2. ' Paul, among prisoners in-' deed, and through various forms of death, yet distin-' guished by many splendid testimonies, is led to Rome, ' as by the hand of God himself.' *Beza.*—It was determined, by Festus and his council, to send Paul, with some other prisoners, to Italy ; that at Rome he might be judged by the emperor, to whom he had appealed : and he was, according to the general custom, committed to the care of a centurion with soldiers under him. As this centurion belonged to the emperor's own 'cohort, or regiment, it is probable that he was going to Rome on other business. (*Marg. Ref.* a—d.)—Adramyttium was a city of Mysia, on the coast of Asia; this ship therefore, if only returning thither, could convey the company but a small part of their long voyage.—Aristarchus, of whom mention has repeatedly been made, is called by the apostle, his " fellow " prisoner ;" yet it is likely, that this was rather by choice than compulsion. (*Marg. Ref.* g, h.—*Note,* Col. iv. 9— 14, *v.* 10.)—The historian himself likewise attended the apostle, and so speaks in the first person plural, in many parts of the narrative. This was a singular instance of the great affection of Luke and Aristarchus for the apostle, and a great solace to him under all his trials: and they would be in many ways assistant to him, in all his plans for usefulness, both during the voyage and after he arrived at Rome.

Should sail. (1) Τυ αποπλειν. xiii. 4. xiv. 26. xx. 15. Ex απο, et πλεω, 2.—*Prisoners.*] Δεσμωτας. 42. Not elsewhere. Δεσμιος, xxv. 14. 27.—*Augustus'.*] Σεβασης. See on xxv. 21.

V. 3. It may be supposed, that the opinion of Festus, and the concessions made by king Agrippa, had induced this centurion to treat Paul with attention and kindness ; regarding him perhaps as an injured man, and bearing some degree of respect for his integrity and talents.—It is probable, that there were Christians at Sidon at this time, though nothing further is recorded concerning them. (*Marg. Ref.*)

Courteously entreated.] Φιλανθρωπως χρησαμενος. Here only. Φιλανθρωπια, Tit. iii. 4. Ex φιλος, amicus, et ανθρωπος, homo.—Χρωομαι, 17. 1 Cor. vii. 21. ix. 12. 2 Cor. iii. 12.— *To refresh himself.*] Επιμελειας τυχειν. Here only. Επιμελομαι, Luke x. 34, 35.

V. 4, 5. The wind being contrary, the mariners found it necessary to sail between Cyprus and the Continent of Asia ; and then, turning to the west, to pursue their voyage near the southern shore of Asia Minor, till they came to Myra. But, had the wind been favourable, they would have sailed to the west of Cyprus, by a direct course to the same place. (*Marg. Ref.*)

We sailed under. (4) Υπεπλευσαμεν. 7. Here only. Ex υπο, et πλεω, *navigo.*—*Had sailed over.* (5) Διαπλευσαντες. Here only.—*The sea.*] Το πελαγος. See on .Matt. xviii. 6.

V. 6. Very large quantities of corn were sent to Rome from Alexandria in Egypt, and it is probable, this ship was employed in that trade. (*Note,* 33—38.)

V. 7. *Crete.*] (*Marg. Ref.*) A large island in the Mediterranean, now called Candia. (*Note,* Tit. i. 5—9.)—*Under,* &c.] Between the island and the continent of Asia. (*Note,* 4, 5.)

Sailed slowly.] Βραδυπλοουντες. Here only. Ex βραδυς, tardus, et πλεω, *navigatio.*

V. 8. *Hardly passing it.*] Μολις παραλεγομενοι. Μολις, 7: 16. xiv. 18. Rom. v. 7. 1 Pet. iv. 18. Παραλεγομαι, 13. *Prope littus navigo.* " Scarcely coasting it ;" that is, with danger, as well as difficulty. (*Note,* 1 Pet. iv. 17—19, v. 18.)

V. 9. (*Marg. Ref.*—*Notes,* Lev. xvi. 29—31. Jer. xxxvi. 6, 7.) The fast, or great day of atonement, was in the seventh month, or the latter end of September, when sailing

10 And said unto them, Sirs, "I perceive that this voyage will be with hurt and much ° damage, not only of the lading and ship, but also of our lives.

11 Nevertheless the centurion ° believed the master and owner of the ship, more than those things which were spoken by Paul.

12 And because ⁷ the haven was not commodious to winter in, the more part advised to depart thence also, if by any means they might attain to Phenice, *and there* to winter; which is an haven of ° Crete, and lieth toward ₇. the south-west and north-west.

13 And when ° the south wind blew softly, supposing that they had obtained *their* purpose, loosing *thence* they sailed close by Crete.

14 But ᵇ not long after there ᵗ arose against it ° a tempestuous wind, called Euroclydon.

15 And when the ship was caught, and could not bear up into the wind, ᵈ we let *her* drive.

16 And running under a certain

---

was thought dangerous : for, in that imperfect state of navigation, the mariners commonly kept within a moderate distance from the shore, and seldom put to sea during the winter-season.—Some commentators suppose, that the Michaelmas-flows, which are peculiar to the Mediterranean sea, are referred to : but, I apprehend, that at present the Mediterranean is navigated at Michaelmas and in winter, as well as other seas.

Dangerous.] Επισφαλης. Here only. Ex επι et σφαλλω, *everto, labefacto.* Opponitur τω ασφαλης, xxv. 26.—*Admonished.*] Παρηνει. 22. Here only. Ex παρα, et αινεω, *laudo.*

V. 10. The apostle doubtless had an intimation from God of the approaching storm : and foresaw that much damage would be sustained by it, and their lives exposed to great danger ; though the particular event of it was not as yet made known to him. (*Marg. Ref.* u.—*Note,* 20—26.) The centurion, and all on board the ship, must have had some general knowledge of Paul's character and principles ; and the religious converse and worship of him and his friends, as well as their whole behaviour, must have excited attention : yet they probably regarded them as deluded men ; entitled indeed to civil usage, being very inoffensive and well meaning, yet not worthy of notice as to their religious opinions. But it was the Lord's purpose to exhibit Paul among them, as a most extraordinary person ; that they might learn to enquire after his principles, and receive his instructions.

Sirs.] Ανδρες. 21.—*Hurt.*] Υβρεως. 21. 2 Cor. xii. 10. Υβριζω, xiv. 5.—*Damage.*] "Injury." *Marg.* and *Ref.* Ζημιας. 21. Phil. iii. 7, 8. Ζημιοω᾽ See on Matt. xvi. 26.—*The lading.*] Φορτω, or φορτιω, Matt. xi. 30. xxiii. 4.

V. 11. ' Men, by following their own prudence, rather ' than the word of God by the mouth of his servants, rather ' their own will run themselves and one another into in- ' finite dangers.' *Beza.*—The centurion judged that he who navigated the vessel, and the owner of it, understood such matters, far better than the prisoner Paul. (*Marg. Ref.*)

Believed.] Επειθετο. xvii. 4. xviii. 4. Luke xvi. 31.—*The master and owner of the ship.*] Τω κυβερνητη και τω ναυκληρω. Κυβερνητης, Rev. xviii. 17. ' *Gubernator navis, qui ad clavum* ' *sedet, et navis cursum dirigit :* a κυβερναω ... *rego navem.*' *Schleusner. The helmsman,* or *pilot.*—Ναυκληρος. Here only. Ex ναυς, *navis,* et κληρος, *sors.*—*The owner,* or *supercargo.*

V. 12. *Phenice.*] This harbour seems to have been situated on the west side of Crete ; and to have been defended from the fury of the winds, by a high and winding shore, forming a kind of semicircle, and perhaps by some small island in front ; leaving two openings, one towards the south-west, and the other towards the north-west. Some think that it was sheltered from the winds, which blew from those quarters.

The haven.] Λιμενος. Here only N. T.—*Ps.* cvii. 30. *Sept.*—*Not commodious.*] Ανευθετω. Here only. Ex α priv. et ευθετος, *appositus,* Luke ix. 62. xiv. 35. *Heb.* vi. 7. Ex ευ, *bene,* et θετος, *positus.*—*To winter in.*] Προς παραχειμασιαν. Here only. Παραχειμαζω, xxviii. 11. 1 Cor. xvi. 6. *Tit.* iii. 12. A χειμα, seu χειμων, *hiems.*—*The south-west.*] Λιβα. Here only N. T.—*Ps.* lxxviii. 26. *Sept.*—*North-west.*] Χωρον. Here only. ' *Nomen venti inter occidentem et sep-* ' *tentrionem spirantis.*' *Schleusner.*

V. 13. (*Marg. Ref.*) *Sailed close, &c.*] The mariners kept as near within shore, as they safely could, that they might not be driven out to sea. (*Note,* 8.)

The south-wind.] Νοτω. xxviii. 13. Matt. xii. 42. Luke xii. 55.—*Blew softly.*] Υποπνευσαντος. Here only. Ex υπο, et πνεω, *spiro, flo.*—*Their purpose.*] Προθεσιν. See on xi. 23.—*Sailed.*] Παρελεγοντο. See on 8.—*Close.*] Ασσον, *proprius, juxta.* Here only.

V. 14, 15. This tempest came from the east, as its name imports : yet it violently and frequently shifted its direction, and thus excited so tremendous an agitation of the waves, that the ship could not in any way be managed, during the storm. The mariners were therefore constrained to let her drive before it, (finding all efforts to the contrary entirely useless,) though at the hazard of being dashed upon the rocks, or otherwise wrecked. (*Marg. Ref.*—*Note, Ps.* cvii. 23—30.)

Tempestuous. (14) Τυφωνικος. Here only. A τυφων, *ventus procellosus.*—*Euroclydon.*] Ευροκλυδων. Here only. Ex ευρος, *eurus,* et κλυδων, *fluctus.*—*Was caught.* (15) Συναρπασθεντος. vi. 12. xix. 29. Luke viii. 29.—*Bear up.*] Ανθοφθαλμειν. Here only. Ex αντι, et οφθαλμος, *oculus.* " Could not face the wind."

V. 16. *Boat, &c.*] The seamen laboured to secure the boat, (and with great difficulty succeeded,) as a resource in case the ship should be wrecked : but it pleased God not to make any use of the boat in their deliverance (32).

Running under.] Υποδραμοντες. Here only. Ex υπο, et τρεχω, *curro.*—*We had much work to come by.*] Μολις ισχυσαμεν περικρατεις γενεσθαι. Μολις᾽ See on 8. Περικρατης. Here only. Ex περι, et κρατεω, *teneo.*—*The boat.*]

CHAP. XXIV.

The high priest and elders go to Cæsarea; and, by Tertullus, accuse Paul before Felix, 1—9. Paul makes his defence, refutes the charges brought against him, and gives an account of his own conduct, 10—21. Felix defers the matter, and shews favour to Paul, 22, 23. Paul reasons before Felix, and Drusilla his wife, concerning "righteousness, temper-" ance, and judgment to come;" till "Felix "trembles," and postpones the subject to a convenient opportunity, 24, 25. He hopes in vain for a bribe to release Paul; and at length, being superseded in his government, he leaves him in prison, to please the Jews, 26, 27.

a 11. xxi. 27. b xxiii. 2. 30. 33 xxv. 2.

AND after ᵃ five days ᵇ Ananias the high priest descended with the elders, and with a certain ᶜ orator named Tertullus, who ᵈ informed the governor against Paul.

2 And when he was called forth, Tertullus began to accuse him, saying, ᵉ Seeing that by thee we enjoy great quietness, and that very worthy deeds are done unto this nation by thy providence;

3 We accept it always, and in all places, ᶠ most noble Felix, with all thankfulness.

4 Notwithstanding, ᵍ that I be not further tedious unto thee, I pray thee that thou wouldest hear us of thy clemency a few words.

5 For ʰ we have found this man a pestilent fellow, ⁱ and a mover of sedition among all the Jews throughout the world, and a ring-leader of ᵏ the sect of the ˡ Nazarenes:

6 Who also hath ᵐ gone about to profane the temple; ⁿ whom we took, ° and would have judged according to our law.

7 But ᵖ the chief captain Lysias came upon us, and with ᑫ great violence took him away out of our hands;

8 ʳ Commanding his accusers to come unto thee: ˢ by examining of whom, thyself mayest take knowledge of all these things whereof we accuse him.

9 And ᵗ the Jews also assented, saying. That these things were so.

---

manity in social life, is often met with in those, who know not God; and indeed is seldom totally overcome, except by false principles, or long habits of vice. This greatly conduces to keep the world in order, and by means of it the Lord fulfils his word to his persecuted people: for all hearts are in his hand, and they are indeed blessed who put their trust in him. (*Note, Ps.* lxxxiv. 11, 12. *P. O.*)

NOTES.
CHAP. XXIV. V. 1—9. The high priest, and elders, considered the prosecution of Paul as so important a national concern, or rather they were so indignant against him and Lysias, that they lost no time in going to Cæsarea: so that they arrived there five days after Paul left Jerusalem.—Some think that this was only five days from the time of his being apprehended; and consequently they suppose that more days were spent in his purification: but this is not likely. (*Note,* xxi. 27—30.)—In order to render their cause more specious before the governor, they retained a noted orator as their counsel: but disingenuity and falsehood are far more prominent in his speech, than oratorical abilities. He, however, well understood the art of flattery; and lavished high encomiums on Felix, who bore a very bad character. (*Note,* 24—27.) He panegyrized him, as the author of peace and prosperity to the nation; and as if the Jews had been deeply indebted to his wise foresight, beneficent plans, and prudent administration: and this in language, which at least implied such a profane disregard to divine Providence, as was not customary, in the publick discourses of the most eminent persons among idolaters. (*Marg. Ref.* c. e, f.) Yet we

read of no benefit whatever, resulting from Felix's oppressive government, except that he freed the country from some daring gangs of robbers.—' All historians agree, that ' he was a man of so bad a character, that his government ' was a plague to all the provinces, over which he presided. ' And as for Judea, its state under Felix was so far from ' being what Tertullus here represents, that Josephus ' (besides what he says of the barbarous and cowardly ' assassination of Jonathan the high priest by his means,) ' declares that the Jews accused him before Nero of insuf-' ferable oppressions; and had certainly ruined him, if ' his brother Pallas had not interposed in his favour.' *Doddridge.*—Tertullus however intimated, that he would have enlarged still more in encomiums on Felix, had he not feared being tedious to him; and therefore he intreated him, according to his known clemency, to hear him speak a few words concerning the prisoner. For they had found him to be "a pestilence," a man who infected every one with his pernicious principles, and so became a publick nuisance. He had excited the Jews to sedition all over the world; being a ringleader of a most dangerous sect, who professed allegiance to Jesus the Nazarene, and who could not therefore be supposed loyal subjects to the Roman emperor. (*Marg. Ref.* h—k.) But, waving other particulars, he had just before ventured to profane the temple, by bringing Gentiles into it: and when, according to the allowance of the Roman authority, they had apprehended him, and were about to proceed against him, *in a legal manner;* Lysias had interposed with a military force, taken the matter out of their hands, and required his accusers to come thither; by whose testimony Felix

10 Then Paul, after that the governor ⁿ had beckoned unto him to speak, answered, Forasmuch as I know that thou hast been of many years ᵃ a judge unto this nation, I do the more cheerfully answer for myself:

11 Because that thou mayest understand, that there are yet ʳ but twelve days since I went up to Jerusalem for ᵇ to worship.

12 And they ᶜ neither found me in the temple disputing with any man, neither raising up the people, neither in the synagogue, nor in the city:

13 Neither ᵇ can they prove the things whereof they now accuse me.

14 But this ᵉ I confess unto thee, that ᵈ after the way which they call ᵉ heresy, so worship I ᶠ the God of my fathers, ᵍ believing all things which are written ʰ in the law and in the prophets;

15 And ⁱ have hope toward . God, which they themselves also allow,

ᵏ that there shall be a resurrection of the dead, both of the just and unjust.

16 And ˡ herein do I exercise myself, to have always a conscience void of offence toward God, and *toward* men.

17 Now after many years I came ᵐ to bring alms to my nation, ⁿ and offerings.

18 Whereupon ᵒ certain Jews from Asia found me purified in the temple, neither with multitude, nor with tumult:

19 Who ᵖ ought to have been here before thee, and object, if they had ought against me.

20 Or else let these same *here* say, if they have found any evil doing in me, while I stood before the council,

21 Except it be for this one voice, that I cried standing among them, ᵠ Touching the resurrection of the dead I am called in question by you this day.

might be certified of the truth of all these allegations. (*Marg. Ref.* m—q.)—Almost every clause, in this speech, contained a palpable falsehood, as every one who compares it with the narrative must perceive: yet the abandoned high priest and elders, did not hesitate to attest the truth of it! (*Marg. Ref.* t.)—The high priest, the chief magistrate of the Jews, was known to be one of Paul's accusers: yet the tribune, a subordinate officer under the Roman governor, *commanded* these accusers to go to Cæsarea. This shews to what entire subjection the Jews were at this time reduced. And was not then " the seep-" tre departed from Judah" because Shiloh was come? (*Note, Gen.* xlix. 10.)—The disciples long before had been named Christians; yet Tertullus still calls them Nazarenes; which shews that the disciples were not first called Christians by their enemies. (*Note,* xi. 25, 26, v. 26.) .

A certain *orator.* (1) 'Ρήτορος τινος. Here only. A ρεω, *dico*—*Informed.*] Ελφανισαν. See on xxiii. 15.—*Very worthy deeds.* (2) Καιορθωματων. Here only. ' A καιορθοω, ' *quod Græcis est, res bene et præclare gerere, felici* ' *successu uti, maxime in bello.*' Schleusner. Ex καλα, et ορθος, *rectus.*—*Providence.*] Προνοιας. *Rom.* xiii. 14. Not elsewhere. A προνοεω, *Rom.* xii. 17. 2 *Cor.* viii. 21. 1 *Tim.* v. 8.—*Thankfulness.* (3) Ευχαριςιας. 2 *Cor.* ix. 12. *Eph.* v. 4. 1 *Tim.* iv. 3, 4. *Rev.* vii. 12. Ex ευ, *bene,* et χαρις, *gratia.*—*I be not ... tedious.* (4) Μη ... εγκοπω. *Rom.* xv. 22. *Gal.* v. 7. 1 *Thes.* ii. 18. 1 *Pet.* iii. 7. *Clemency.*] Επιεικεια. 2 *Cor.* x. 1. Not elsewhere. Επιεικη, *Phil.* iv. 5. *Tit.* iii. 2.—*A few words.*] Συντομως. Here only. A συντεμνω, *concido* ; quod ex συν, et τεμνω, *seco.*— *A pestilent fellow.* (5) Λοιμον. *Matt.* xxiv. 7. *Luke* xxi. 11. Not elsewhere N. T.—1 *Sam.* ii. 12. *Ps.* i. 1. *Prov.* xxi. 24. xxii. 10. . *Sept.*—*A ring-leader.*] Πρωτοςατην.

Here only. Ex πρωτος, *primus,* et ιςημι, *sto.*—*The sect.*] 'Αιρεσεως. 14. See on v. 17.—*Hath gone about to profane.* (6) Επειρατε Ϛεϐηλωσαι. "Hath attempted to profane." Βεϐηλοω· See on *Matt.* xii. 5.—*Assented.* (9) Συνεθιντο. See on *John* ix. 22.

V. 10—21. ' Tertullus, by a diabolical rhetorick, begins ' with flatteries and ends with lies: but Paul, relying on a ' divine eloquence, having made a simple introduction, ' repels from him, by a true denial, the crime of sedition ' which had been brought against him.' *Beza.*—Felix fully knew the disposition and character of these accusers ; and, though lavishly flattered, he seems to have paid little regard to their representations. He therefore gave Paul leave to speak in his own defence ; who, without seeking to conciliate favour by any compliment, began with observing, that he spake the more cheerfully before Felix, as he had been for some years a judge of that nation ; (about seven years, and longer than several of his predecessors ;) and so was more competent to ut derstand questions of this nature than a stranger would have been. The apostle then observed, that only twelve days before, he had come up to Jerusalem to keep the feast of Pentecost, and to worship according to the law : that he had neither entered into any disputation in the temple, nor excited any insurre tion in the synagogues or the city ; nor could the least evidence be adduced in proof of the allegations of his accusers, respecting the profanation of the sanctuary. (*Marg. Ref.* u—b) Indeed he was free to confess, that he worshipped the God of his fathers, in a way which they branded as a heresy or sect (5) ; as if it were grounded on pernicious principles, or implied an unlawful separation : but, in fact, he believed the doctrines and promises, both of the law and the prophets, concerning the Messiah ; and thus

5 G 2

22 ¶ And when Felix heard these
r 10. 24. xxvi. 3. things, ' having more perfect knowledge of that way, he deferred them,
s 7. xviii. 20. xxv. and said, 'When Lysias the chief cap-
26. Deut. xix.
18. tain shall come down, I will know the
uttermost of your matter.

23 And he commanded a centurion to
t 26. xxvii. 3. keep Paul, ' and to let him have liberty,
xxviii. 15. 31.
Prov. xvi. 7. and that he should forbid none of " his
u xxi. 8—14. acquaintance to minister or come unto
him.

24 ¶ And after certain days, when

Felix came with his wife Drusilla, x xxvi. 22. Mark
which was a Jewess, ᶻ he sent for Paul, 3. xxiii. 8.
y xvi. 31. xx. 21.
and heard him concerning ⁷ the faith in Gal. i. 16. 20.
iii. 2. 1 John v.
Christ. 1. Jude 4. Rev.
13.

25 And as ᵃ he reasoned of ᵃ right- xvii. 12.
z xvii. 2. 1 Sam.
eousness, ᵇ temperance, ᶜ and judg- xii. 7. 1s. 1. 18.
xii. 21. Rom.
ment to come, ᵈ Felix trembled ; and 15.
a ii. 25. 2 Sam.
xxiii. 3. Job xxix. 14. Ps. xl. 7. xlv. 7. lviii. 1, 2. lxxii. 1—4. Prov. xvi. 12.
Ec. iii. 16. 1s. i. 21. xvi. 5. lxi. 8. Jer. xxii. 3. 15—17. Ez. xiv. 9. Dan. iv. 27. Hos.
x. 4. 12. Am. v. 24. vi. 1. 1 John iii. 7. 10. b Prov. xxxi. 3—5. Ec. x. 16. 17.
1s. xxviii. 6. 7. Dan. v. Hos. vii. 5. Mark vi. 18—24. Gal. v. 23. Tit. ii. 11,
12. 2 Pet. i. 6. c x. 42. xvii. 31. Ec. iii. 17. v. 8. xi. 9. xii. 14. Matt. xxv. 31
—46. Rom. ii. 16. xiv. 12. 1 Cor. iv. 5. 2 Cor. v. 10. 2 Thes. i. 7—10. 2 Tim. iv. 1.
Heb. vi. 2. ix. 27. 1 Pet. iv. 5. Rev. xx. 11—15. d ii. 37. ix. 6. xvi. 29. 1 Kings
xxi. 27. 2 Kings xxii. 19. Ezra x. 3. 9. Ps. cxix. 120. 1s. lxvi. 2. Jer. xxiii. 29. Rom.
iii. 19, 20. 1 Cor. xiv. 24, 25. Gal. iii. 22. Heb. iv. 12. xii. 21. Jam. ii. 19.

he hoped for the acceptance of God, and expected a future
" resurrection both of the just and the unjust," as the
Jews in general allowed: for the Sadducees, though high
in rank and power, bore but a small proportion in numbers to the rest of the nation. (Marg. and Marg. Ref.
c—k.) In this faith and hope, the apostle daily exercised
himself, after the most careful and diligent manner, to
keep his conscience free from all offence, in his whole
conduct towards God and man ; even as a painter touches
and retouches his piece continually, in order to bring it to
a more exact resemblance to the objects delineated.—
Accordingly, after many years' absence, he had come to
Jerusalem, not as an enemy to his nation, but in a most
friendly manner, bringing a sum of money, which he had
collected among the Gentiles, to relieve the necessities of
his poor brethren ; as well as oblations to offer at the
temple: and some Jews from Asia had found him in the
temple, " purified " according to the law, and neither attended by a multitude, nor making a tumult. These persons ought to have been produced against him, if his prosecutors meant to prove, that he had profaned the sanctuary: but, as they had not thought proper to bring them,
knowing that they could testify nothing against him in this
respect ; let the high priest and elders declare, whether
any crime had been alleged against him, when he stood
before the council ; except it were criminal to profess his
belief of the resurrection, and to assert that he was pro-
seented on that account. (Marg. Ref. l. n—q.)—Mayest
understand. (11) As knowing, that the feast of Pentecost
was observed at that time.—God of my fathers. (14) Had
Paul worshipped some other god, than the God of Israel,
he would not have been entitled to protection by the Roman
laws, made in favour of the Jews.—Just and unjust.
(15) ' The doctrine of the Pharisees, according to Jose-
' phus, restrained the resurrection to the just, condemn-
' ing the unjust to perpetual torments without any resur-
' rection.' Whitby. (Note, Matt. xxii. 23—33.)—Alms, &c.
(17) This purpose, of Paul's journey to Jerusalem, is not
before mentioned in the history ; but it appears evidently in
his epistles: and this shews how little the historian aimed
to enhance the credit of his principal character. (Marg.
Ref. m.—Note, Rom. xv. 22—29.)—The apostle's answer
refers distinctly to the three charges brought against
him, namely, sedition, heresy, and profanation of the temple.
The more cheerfully. (10) Ευθυμοτερον. xxvii. 36. Not
elsewhere. Ευθυμεω, xxvii. 22. 25. Jam. v. 13. Ex ευ,
bene, et θυμος, animus.—Answer.] Απολογουμαι. See on Luke
xii. 11. Απολογια, See on xxii. 1.—Raising up, &c. (12)

Επιστασιν ποιυντα. 2 Cor. xi. 28. Not elsewhere. Ex επι,
et συν, et ςασις, seditio, 5.—Prove. (13) Παραςησαι. xxiii.
24. xxvii. 24. 2 Tim. ii. 15.—' Παραςησαι est idem quod
' αποδειξαι, xxv. 7.' Schleusner.—Heresy. (14) 'Αιρεσιν. See
on 5.—Of my fathers.] Πατρωω. See on xxii. 3.—I exercise myself. (16) Αντος ασκω. Here only.—' In eo
' equidem omnibus viribus meis elaboro.' Schleusner.—A
conscience.] Συνειδησιν. See on xxiii. 1.—Void of offence.]
Απροσκοπον. 1 Cor. x. 32. Phil. i. 10. Not elsewhere. Ex
α priv. et προσκοπτω, impingo, Matt. iv. 6.—Purified. (18)
'Ηγνισμενον. See on xxi. 24.

V. 22, 23. The defence of Paul was simple and convincing ; the charges brought against him by Tertullus
were clearly refuted ; and, probably, Felix concluded that
the prosecution was merely a party matter. Having also
more acquaintance with the reports, which had been dispersed, concerning Jesus and his doctrine, than Lysias had,
he was more aware of the motives and intentions of the
Jews: he therefore deferred the further hearing of the
cause, till Lysias came down. He would not gratify the
Jewish rulers by condemning a Roman citizen, or delivering him up to their malice ; neither would he affront them
by releasing him. He, however, allowed him more liberty
than he had before ; and by his permission the Christians
of Cæsarea and others might have access to him, which
would be comfortable to him and profitable to them.
(Marg. Ref. t.—Notes, xxi. 7—14.)—' It seems to me evi-
' dent, that these words,' (22) ' cannot admit the expli-
' cation of Grotius and others, that Felix deferred them,
' that he might have a more exact knowledge of Christianity ;
' but, that having his residence at Cæsarea, where Cor-
' nelius the centurion and his friends were converted,
' where Philip the evangelist dwelt, and where there were
' many disciples ; (xxi. 8. 16 ;) he became thus acquainted
' with the way of Christianity.' Whitby.
Having more perfect knowledge. (22) Ακριβεςερον ειδως.
xviii. 26. xxiii. 15. 20. xxvi. 5.—Of that way.] Της οδω.
See on ix. 2.—I will know the uttermost.] Διαγνωσομαι.
See on xxiii. 15.—Liberty. (23) Ανεσιν. 2 Cor. ii. 13. vii.
5. viii. 13. 2 Thes. i. 7.

V. 24—27. Felix seems to have been absent from
Cæsarea for a time ; and on his return he brought Drusilla
with him. She was daughter to that Herod, who beheaded James the brother of John ; (xii. 1, 2 ;) and sister to
king Agrippa, who is afterwards mentioned. (xxv. 13—
27.) She was married to Azizus, king of the Emesenes,
who had been circumcised in order to obtain her : but she
had left her husband to cohabit with Felix, being a very

e xvi. 30—34.
xxvi. 28. 1 Kings
xxi. 26, 27. Jer.
xxxvii. 17—21.
xxxviii. 14—28.
Matt. xiv. 5—
10.
f xvii. 32. Prov.
vi. 4, 5. ix. 6.
Hag. i. 2. Luke
xiii. 24, 25. xvii.
q 2, 3. Ex. xxiii.
8. Deut. xvi. 19.
Ps. xxvi. 9, 10.
27. xxxiii. 31.
v. 5, 6. 1 Tim. answered, ' Go thy way for this time;
' when I have a convenient season I
will call for thee.

26 He ᶠ hoped also that money
should have been given him of Paul,
26—29. 2 Cor. vi. 2. Heb. iii. 7, 8, 13. iv. 11. Jam. iv. 13, 14.
1 Sam. viii. 3. xii. 3. 2 Chr. xix. 7. Job xv. 34.
Prov. xvii. 8. 23. xix. 6. xxix. 4. Is. i. 23. xxxiii. 15. lvi. 11. Ez. xxxi.
Hos. iv. 18. xii. 7, 8. Am. ii. 6, 7. Mic. iii, 11. vii. 3. 1 Cor. vi. 9. Eph.
vi. 9, 10. 2 Pet. ii. 3. 14, 15.

that he might loose him: ʰ wherefore
he sent for him the oftener and communed with him.

27 But after ' two years ᵏ Porcius
Festus came into Felix' room: and
Felix, ˡ willing to shew the Jews a
pleasure, left Paul bound.
h 24.
i xxviii. 30
26. 31.
k xiii. 3. xxv. 9.
14. Ex. xxiii. 2.
Prov. xxix. 25.
Mark xv. 15.
Luke xxiii. 24,
25. Gal. i. 10.

profligate woman.—Felix had heard many things concerning Jesus and Christianity: (Note, 22, 23:) but he was
curious to learn a more authentick and complete account
of these matters from Paul; as Drusilla also seems to have
been. The apostle was therefore sent for, that he might
speak before the governor, concerning the " faith in
" Christ."—What he said concerning the Person, miracles,
life, death, resurrection, salvation, and kingdom of Jesus,
we know not: but, in order to shew his noble auditors the
tendency of the gospel, and its importance to them, as
well as to others; he reasoned about the nature and obligations of justice, equity, sobriety, temperance, and a
proper government of the appetites and passions: and concerning a future judgment assuredly about to take place,
when every man, without distinction, must " give an ac-
" count of himself to God;" and, if found guilty, be punished for his crimes in a most tremendous manner.
(Marg. Ref. x—c.)—This was a most suitable, bold, and
faithful address of the prisoner, to this powerful, oppressive,
iniquitous, and adulterous judge, and his licentious paramour; and a proper method of shewing them their need
of the repentance, forgiveness, and grace of the gospel.
While the licentious Jewess seems to have remained wholly
obdurate; Felix was so convicted in his own conscience,
that he trembled before his prisoner, from dread of the
wrath to come; but, instead of enquiring, " What must I
" do to be saved?" he abruptly ended the conference,
intimating that he was too much engaged at that time to
consider the subject any further; but that when he had
leisure, he would again send for Paul, and hear his doctrine. (Marg. Ref. d—f.) Thus his terrors and convictions soon subsided; his avarice, and other corrupt passions, retained their full dominion: and, knowing that the
Christians were eminently liberal, by general report, as
well as by what he had heard of the alms and oblations
sent by the apostle to Jerusalem; he hoped that they
would buy his liberty with a considerable sum of money.
(Marg. Ref. g.) He therefore kept Paul in prison, and
frequently sent for him, and talked with him, but not concerning the faith of Christ: and at length, when succeeded
by another governor; he left the apostle bound, in order
to please the Jews by this act of injustice, and so prevent
them from accusing him before the emperor. (Marg. Ref.
k, l.—Note, and P. O. Mark vi. 14—29.) But in this he
was disappointed; for they accused him of extortion and
oppression, and he narrowly escaped punishment on that
account. Neither the apostle, nor his friends, would purchase his liberty, by becoming accessary to the bribery and
extortion of Felix: they would not " do evil, that good
" might come."—' It was during the two years of Paul's
' imprisonment here that many contentions arose between
' the Jews and Gentiles, as to their respective rights in
' Cæsarea, which, after many tumults and slaughters of

' the Jews, were inflamed, rather than appeased, by the
' hearing at Rome, and did a great deal towards exasperat-
' ing the Jewish nation to that war, which ended in its utter
' ruin. ... She (Drusilla) was afterwards ... consumed,
' with the son she had by Felix, in a terrible eruption of
' mount Vesuvius.' Doddridge.—' It is no wonder that
' Felix trembled; and that Drusilla did not so also was an
' argument of her Jewish confidence, that she might then'
(in the day of judgment), ' escape by being a daughter of
' Abraham.' Whitby.—The conduct of the trembling jailor
at Philippi and that of Felix, should be carefully and mi-
nutely compared; for the contrast is in every particular
striking and instructive. (Note, xvi. 19—34.)—Go thy
way. (25) That is, ' Go back to prison.' (Note, 1 Kings
xxii. 26, 27.)

Concerning the faith in Christ. (24) Περι της εις Χριστον
πιστεως. xx. 21.—As he reasoned. (25) Διαλεγομενα αυτα.
12. See on xviii. 4.—Temperance.] Εγκρατειας. Gal. v.
23. 2 Pet. i. 6. Εγκρατης, Tit. i. 8. Εγκρατευομαι, 1 Cor.
vii. 9.—' Inprimis, moderationem, quæ circa venerem versa-
' tur, seu castitatem significat. ... Huic virtuti opponitur
' ακρασια.' Schleusner. 1 Cor. vii. 5.—Trembled.] Εμφοβος
γενομενος. x. 4. xxii. 9. Luke xxiv. 5.—For this time.]
Το νυν εχον subaudi πραγμα. iv. 29. Matt. xxiv. 21. Luke i.
48. Rom. iii. 26.—Communed. (26) 'Ομιλει. xx. 11. See
on Luke xxiv. 14.—Came into Felix' room. (27) Ελαβε
διαδοχον ὁ Φηλιξ. " Felix received a successor." Here only.
A διαδεχομαι, succedo.—To shew ... a pleasure.] Χαριτας
καλαθεσθαι. xxv. 3, 9.—" To lay up favours," or " obliga-
" tions to gratitude."

PRACTICAL OBSERVATIONS.

V. 1—21

The selfish and malignant passions of mankind are too
commonly the spring of that prompt and persevering activity, which generally prevails: and the graces of language
and elocution have very commonly been tarnished by falsehood and flattery; and employed rather to mislead men,
and prejudice them against the truth, than to influence
them to favour and embrace it.—The persecutors of the
Lord's people have commonly been the panegyrists of his
open enemies: and deviations from truth, by compliments,
inure the mind to dissimulation; and thus prepare the way
for the most direct slander and false testimony.—In how
different a light will the characters of Paul and Felix,
appear, at the day of judgment, than they do in Tertullus's
harangue! Let us not then value the applause, or b ?
troubled at the revilings of ungodly men: as the basest
and most criminal of the human race have been almost
deified by encomiums, and the excellent of the earth have
been treated as " pestilences," as " movers of sedition,"
and deserving of universal execration; and this by professors of the true religion! by priests, elders, and persons of

CHAP. XXV.

The Jews accuse Paul to Festus, first at Jerusalem, and then at Cæsarea, 1—7. He answers for himself, and appeals to Cæsar, 8—11. His appeal is admitted, 12. Festus be ng visited by king Agrippa, opens the matter to him, who desires to hear Paul, 13—22. Paul is brought forth before a most splendid assembly; and Festus states his case to them, 23—27.

ᵃ xxiii. 34.
l. 5, xviii, 22, xxi.
15.
c 15, xxiv, 1, Job
xxxi, 31. Prov.
iv. 16. Rom. iii.
12—19.

NOW when Festus was come ᵃ into the province, after three days ᵇ he ascended from Cæsarea to Jerusalem.

2 Then ᶜ the high priest, and the chief of the Jews, informed him against Paul, and besought him,

3 And ᵈ desired favour against him, that he would send for him to Jerusalem, ᵉ laying wait in the way to kill him.

4 But Festus answered, that Paul should be kept at Cæsarea, and that he himself would depart shortly *thither.*

5 Let ᶠ them therefore, said he, which among you are able, go down with *me*, and accuse this man, ᵍ if there be any wickedness in him.

ᵈ iv. 2. 1 Sam.
xxiii. 19—21.
Jer. xxxviii. 4.
Mark vi. 23—25.
Luke xxiii. 8—
24.
e xxiii. 12—15,
xxvii. 3—11. Ps.
xxxvii. 32, 33,
lxiv. 2—6, cxl.
1—5. Jer. xviii.
18. John xvi. 3.
Rom. iii. 8.

ᶠ 16. xxiii. 30.
xxix. 8.
g 18, 19, 20, xxiii.
14. 1 Sam. xxiv,
11, 12. Ps. vii. 3
—5. John xviii.
29, 30.

---

chief authority in the visible church!—But the servants of God must not attempt, by flattery, to conciliate the favour of those, who seem to have the most absolute power over them: nor should they retort on their accusers, further than is necessary for the refutation of their slanders. They should also be ready to confess their faith when called upon, and the foundation of their hope, though they be deemed heretical and sectarian by their enemies; and take occasion to shew the agreement of their principles with the word of God, and with the doctrines professed in his church; especially to call men's reflection to the resurrection of the dead, and the future season of righteous retribution. But they have never rightly understood the doctrines of St. Paul, and are not proper persons to plead for them, who do not " exercise themselves to have a conscience void of " offence towards God and man." (*Note*, 1 *Pet.* iii. 13—16.) In a continual application of the blood of Jesus, and an habitual dependence on his grace, we should daily seek to have our conduct and temper more and more conformed to his holy precepts, as the rule of our duty. Thus our actions will recommend our principles; our kindness even to those who injure us will expose the malignity of our accusers; and a sober, righteous, and godly life will prove the most effectual refutation of all their calumnies.

V. 22—27.

Those who are openly irreligious, and even immoral, often shew more favour to zealous believers, than hypocritical bigots do: yet their selfish designs commonly prevent them from doing impartial justice.—Many curiously enquire after the faith in Christ, who are utterly averse to its holy tendency. We should not therefore amuse enquirers of this description with speculation, or even bare unapplied scriptural truths; but we ought to " reason with them con-" cerning righteousness, temperance, and judgment to " come;" and to level the word of God against the pecu-liar vices of their conduct, without fear of their displea-sure, how powerful soever they may be. This alone can make them sensible of their need of " faith in Christ," and prepare them to understand the doctrine of the gospel; and such opportunities ought not to be lost.—So great is the power of divine truth, that it can overawe the con-sciences of the most potent and profligate, and can make a prince tremble before his prisoner. How then will the wicked be able to stand before the judgment-seat of God? —But many, when thus affected, will hear no more: they will in effect say to the minister or the book that alarms

them, nay, to their own consciences, " Go thy way at " this time:" they will pretend business, engagements. and impediments, at present; and they hope to be here-after more favourably circumstanced, or better disposed; and then they will attend to the concerns of their souls. Thus, through procrastination, the hopeful impression wears off: iniquity retains its dominion in their hearts; and the evident love of worldly gain, or some other corrupt indulged propensity, clearly explains the reason of their rejection of the divine message. (*Note, John* iii. 19—21.) —Thus " the convenient time " never arrives; they con-tinue to sin on to the end of life against their better know-ledge; and the faithfulness of their reprovers serves only to aggravate their future condemnation. Hence also it is that wicked professors of religion are the most hardened of all sinners; because they have so often and so resolutely done this violence to their own consciences, that they at length become totally callous. (*Note*, 1 *Tim.* iv. 1—5.) " To day " therefore, let all that would be saved, attend to the voice of God; " lest he swear in his wrath, that " they shall never enter into his rest." (*Notes, Luke* xiii. 22—30, *vv.* 25—28. *Heb.* iii. 7—13. *P. O.* 7—19.)

NOTES

CHAP. XXV. V. 1—5. The implacable malice of the high priest and the rulers against Paul, whose long impri-sonment could not soften them; and their dark design of assassinating him, mark the horrible wickedness of the Jews, a short time before their final ruin, of which Jose-phus gives a most awful account.—It was very wonderful that Festus should refuse to gratify the great men of the nation, which he was appointed to govern, by sending for Paul to Jerusalem; as he staid in that city long enough to have heard his cause there. But God was pleased thus to influence his mind, in order to Paul's preservation. (*Marg. Ref.* c—e.)—' When we consider, how much edification to ' the churches depended on Paul's life, and how evidently, ' under God, his life depended on this resolution of Fes-' tus; it must surely lead us to reflect, by what invisible ' springs the blessed God governs the world; with what ' silence, and yet at the same time with what wisdom and ' energy!' *Doddridge.*—*Able.* (5) That is, *able* to sub-stantiate an accusation; or, *able*, without material detri-ment, to take the journey to Cæsarea, for this purpose. (*Marg. Ref.* f, g.)

The *province.* (1) Τη ιπαρχια. See on xxiii. 34.—*In-formed.* (2) Ενεφανισαν. See on xxiii. 15.—*Laying wait.* (3)

6 And when he had tarried among them *more than ten days, he went down unto Cæsarea; and the next day, sitting in the judgment-seat, commanded Paul to be brought.

7 And when he was come, the Jews which came down from Jerusalem stood round about, ¹ and laid many and grievous complaints against Paul, which they could not prove;

8 While he answered for himself, ᵏ Neither against the law of the Jews, neither against the temple, nor yet against Cæsar, have I offended any thing at all.

9 But Festus, ¹ willing to do the Jews a pleasure, answered Paul, and said, Wilt thou go up to Jerusalem, and there be judged of these things before me?

10 Then said Paul, ᵐ I stand at Cæsar's judgment-seat, where I ought to be judged: to the Jews have I done no wrong, ⁿ as thou very well knowest.

11 For ° if I be an offender, or have committed any thing worthy of death, I refuse not to die: but, if there be none of these things whereof these accuse me, ᵖ no man may deliver me unto them. �q I appeal unto Cæsar.

12 Then Festus, when he had conferred with the council, answered, Hast thou appealed unto Cæsar? ᵗ unto Cæsar shalt thou go.

13 ¶ And after certain days, ᵏing Agrippa and Bernice came unto Cæsarea, ᵗ to salute Festus.

14 And when they had been there many days, Festus declared Paul's

Marginal notes left column:
ᵃ Or, as some copies read, no more than eight down
ᵇ 10. 17. xviii. 12
—17. Matt. xxvii.
19. John xix.
13. 2 Cor. v. 10.
Jam. ii. 6.

i 24. xxi. 28
xxiv. 5, 6. 13.
Ezra iv. 15.
Esth. iii. 8. Ps.
xxvii. 12. xxxv.
11. Matt. v. 11,
12. xxvi. 60—
62. Mark xv. 3, 4.
ᵏ Luke xxiii.
2. 10. 1 Pet. iv.
14—16.
k 12. xiii. 13, 4.
xxiii. 1.
ᵏ. 12. 17—21.
xxviii. 21. Gen.
xl. 22. Jer.
xxvii. 18. Dan.
vi. 22. 2 Cor. i.
12.
l 3. 20. xii. 3.
xxiv. 27. Mark
xv. 15.

Marginal notes right column:
m xvi. 37, 38. xxii.
25—28.
n 25. xxiii. 29.
xxvi. 31. xxviii.
18. Matt. xxvii.
18. 23, 24.
2 Cor. iv. 2.
o Josh. xxii. 22.
1 Sam. xii. 3—5.
Job xxxi. 21, 22.
1 Sam. iii. 17.
Rom. xiv. 7, 8.
Phil. i. 12—
14. 20.
p xvi. 37. xxii. 25.
1 Thes. ii. 15.
q 10. 25. xxvi. 32
xxviii.
19.
r 21. xix. 21. xxiii.
11. xxvi. 32.
xxvii. 1. xxviii.
16. Ps. lxxvi. 10.
Is. xlvi. 10, 11.
Lam. iii. 37.
Dan. iv. 35.
Rom. xv. 28,
29, 28.
t 1 Sam. xiii. 10.
xxv. 14. 2 Sam.
viii. 10. 2 Kings
x. 13. Mark xv.
18.

Ενεδραν ποιουντες. See on xxiii. 16.—*Accuse.* (5) Κατηγο-ρειτωσαν. 11. 16. xxii. 30, et al. Κατηγορια, Luke vi. 7. John xviii. 29. Tit. i. 6.—*Wickedness.*] Ατοπον. (Wanting in many MSS. &c.) xxviii. 6. See on Luke xxiii. 41.

V. 6—8. *Marg. Ref.* h—k.—*Notes,* xxiv. 1—21.—*Against Cæsar.* (8) The epistle to the Romans, in which submission to the existing powers, without excepting the most faulty characters, is decidedly enforced, was written before this time. (*Notes,* Rom. xiii. 1—5.)

More than ten days. (6) *Marg.*—*Grievous.* (7) Βαρεα. xx. 29. Matt. xxiii. 4. 23. 2 Cor. x. 10. 1 John v. 3.—*Complaints.*] Αιτιαματα. Here only. Ab αιτιαομαι, accuso. —*Prove.*] Αποδιξαι. ii. 22. 1 Cor. iv. 9. 2 Thes. ii. 4. See on παραιτησαι, xxiv. 13.—*While he answered for himself.* (8) Απολογουμενου αυτου. See on xxiv. 10.

V. 9—11. Festus, though doubtless more and more convinced of Paul's innocence, being very desirous of acquiring favour with the principal persons among the Jews, proposed to Paul, that he should "go up to Jerusalem," and be judged there before him, in the presence of the council. This proposal renders it the more wonderful, that he did not before send for him to Jerusalem, at the request of the same persons. (*Marg. Ref.* l.—*Note,* 1—5, vv. 4, 5.)—It may be supposed that Festus was not aware of a conspiracy formed against his life: but probably the apostle was fully informed of it; or at least was assured, that no kind or degree of violence or deceit would be wanting to murder him. And, though assured by the Lord himself, that he should "bear testimony to "him at Rome," he used all proper means for his own preservation: so far was he from thinking, that the divine decrees and man's free agency were incompatible; or that the purposes of God, *even when known,* render the use of means needless or useless. (*Notes,* ii. 22—24. iv. 23—28. xxiii. 11. xxvii. 29—32.)—The Roman governors were the emperor's representatives: the apostle, therefore, as a Roman citizen, when standing at the tribunal of Festus, was in the place where "he ought to be judged;" but, should he be sent to Jerusalem to be tried under the in-

fluence of the Jewish rulers, he would, independently of plots and conspiracies, be deprived of his privilege. Had any crime been charged upon him, which deserved death, he might have waved this privilege; but as Festus well knew that this was not the case, yet was ready to give him into the hands of his enemies, as a special favour by which he hoped to conciliate them, which no man had a right to do; the apostle felt himself authorized, and thought that Festus must see that he did right, in "appealing to "Cæsar," and demanding that the emperor himself should decide his cause. (*Marg. Ref.* m—q.—*Notes,* xvi. 35—40. xxii. 22—30.)—Nero, who is still infamous for his excessive cruelty, was at that time the Roman emperor.

To do ... a pleasure. (9) Χαριν καταθεσθαι. 3. See on xxiv. 27.—*Thou very well knowest.* (10) Συ καλλιον επιγινωσκεις. The comparative for the superlative.—*I refuse not,* &c. (11) Ου παραιτυμαι. 'I do not request to be ex-'cused.' Παραιτυμαι: See on Luke xiv. 18.—*May deliver.*] Δυναται ... χαρισασθαι. Δυναται, can. Note, Mark i. 45. Χαριζομαι, 16. Luke vii. 21. Χαρις, 3. 9.—*I appeal.*] Επικαλουμαι. 12. 21. 25. xxvi. 32. xxviii. 19. See on vii. 59.

V. 12. *Marg. Ref.* r.—*Council.*] Not of the Jews; but of the principal persons, who attended the courts of the Roman governors.

V. 13. Agrippa was son to that Herod, who beheaded James and imprisoned Peter. (*Note,* xii. 1—4.). He had received the title of king from the Roman emperors, and dominion over several districts, without the boundaries of the promised land; and also over a part of Galilee. He had also considerable authority at Jerusalem, over the concerns of the temple; yet in subordination to the Roman governors. Bernice was his sister, a woman of a licentious character, who was suspected of living in incest with him. In other respects Agrippa bore a good character; being equitable in his administration, of a generous disposition, and paying a strict attention to the externals of religion. (*Marg. Ref.*)

V. 14, 15. (*Marg. Ref.*) 'The judgment, which they 'demanded against Paul, was not a *trial,* but a *sentence*

cause unto the king, saying, "There is a certain man left in bonds by Felix; 15 About whom, 'when I was at Jerusalem, the chief priests and the elders of the Jews informed *me*, desiring *to* have judgment against him.

16 To whom I answered, 'It is not the manner of the Romans to deliver any man to die, before that he which is accused have the accusers face to face, 'and have licence to answer for himself, concerning the crime laid against him.

17 Therefore, when they were come hither, 'without any delay on the morrow I sat on the judgment-seat, and commanded the man to be brought forth;

18 Against whom, when the accusers stood up, they brought none accusation of such things as I supposed:

19 But had 'certain questions against him of their own 'superstition, and of one Jesus 'which was dead, whom Paul affirmed to be alive.

20 And because I 'doubted of such manner of questions, 'I asked *him* whether he would go to Jerusalem, and there be judged of these matters.

21 But when Paul 'had appealed to be reserved unto the 'hearing of 'Augustus, 'I commanded him to be kept till I might send him to Cæsar.

22 Then 'Agrippa said unto Festus, I would also hear the man myself. Tomorrow, said he, thou shalt hear him.

23 And on the morrow, when Agrippa was come, and Bernice, 'with great pomp, and was entered into the place of hearing, with the chief captains and principal men of the city, at Festus's commandment Paul was brought forth.

' upon a previous conviction, which they falsely and wickedly pretended : and, probably, it was the knowledge that ' Festus had of Paul's being a Roman citizen, that engaged him to determine to try the cause himself.' Doddridge. (Note, 1—5.)

Left. (14) Καταλελειμμενος. xviii. 19. xxi. 3. xxiv. 27.—*Judgment*. (15) Δικην. xxvii. 4. 2 Thes. i. 9. Jude 7. *Supplicium*, ultionem.

V. 16. *To deliver any man to die*.] Or, ' to give up any man to destruction, by way of gratifying or obliging others.'—*Licence to*, &c.] Or, " Place for an apology," or of pleading his own cause. (*Marg. Ref*.)

To deliver ... to die.] Χαριζεσθαι εις απωλειαν. Χαριζεσθαι· See on 11. Απωλειαν, viii. 20. Matt. xxvi. 8. John xvii. 12.—*Accusers*.] Κατηγορας. 18. xxiii. 30. 35. xxiv. 8. John viii. 10. Rev. xii. 10. Κατηγορεω· See on 5.—*Licence to answer*.] Τοπον απολογιας. ' Opportunitatem seu concessionem se defendendi.' Schleusner. See on xxii. 1.—*The crime laid against him*.] Τε εγκληματος. See xxiii. 29.

V. 17—19. *Superstition*. (19) As Festus entertained Agrippa with great respect; so it cannot be supposed, that he would have used the word, here translated *superstition*, if it had implied any harsh censure of his religion : we must therefore conclude that it was of a doubtful signification ; to be understood in a good or evil sense, according to its application. (*Note*, xvii. 22—25.)—Festus seems to have regarded Paul as a credulous visionary, in affirming that Jesus was alive : but he thought his opponents far more criminal, in persecuting him so virulently on that account; for the matter in contest was in his judgment of no importance !

Delay. (17) Αναβολην. Here only. ' Ab αναβαλλομαι, ' differo : in perfecto, αναβεβολα.' Schleusner.—*Superstition*. (19) Δεισιδαιμονιας. Here only. Δεισιδαιμον· See on xvii. 22.

V. 20. (*Marg. Ref*.) It is evident that Festus gave a very partial account of his own conduct; for, being convinced of Paul's innocence, and of the malice of his enemies, he was yet desirous of gratifying the Jews, by giving them every advantage against the object of their vengeance ; nor is it probable, that the apostle would have appealed to Cæsar, had he not perceived this to be the drift of the proposal, which Festus made to him.

I doubted.] Απορημενος. John xiii. 22. 2 Cor. iv. 8. Gal. iv. 20. Απορια· See on *Luke* xxi. 25. " I hesitated," as needing advice or direction.—*Of such manner of questions*.] Εις την περι τυτε ζητησιν. " As to the question about this," thing or person.

V. 21. *Marg. Ref.—Augustus. ... Cæsar*.] These were different *titles* of the Roman emperor; Nero was his name.

Augustus.] Τε Σεβαςε. 25. xxvii. 1. Σεβαζομαι, Rom. i. 25.

V. 22. ' No doubt, but Agrippa had learnt from his ' father, ... and from many others, something of the nature and pretensions of Christianity : so that he would ' naturally have a curiosity to see, and discourse with, so ' eminent a Christian teacher as Paul was ; who, on account of what he had been in his unconverted state, was ' to be sure more regarded, and talked of among the Jews, ' than any other of the apostles.' Doddridge. (*Note*, 13.) —' Festus, thinking of no such thing, exposes the wickedness of the Jews, and shews the innocence of Paul, even ' in the presence of kings ; and thus marvellously assists ' the church of God.' Beza. (*Marg. Ref*.)

V. 23. Perhaps this was as magnificent an assembly, as ever was brought together to hear the truths of the gospel : though none present meant any thing more, than to gratify their curiosity by attending to the defence of Paul the prisoner.

With great pomp.] Μετα πολλης φαντασιας. Here only.

24 And Festus said, King Agrippa, and all men which are here present with us, ye see this man, ¹ about whom all the multitude of the Jews have dealt with me both at Jerusalem, and ᵐ *also* here, crying ᵐ that he ought not to live any longer.

25 But when I found that he had ⁿ committed nothing worthy of death, ᵒ and that he himself hath appealed to Augustus, I have determined to send him.

26 Of whom I have no certain thing to write unto my lord. Wherefore I

have brought him forth before you, and ᴾ specially before thee, O king ᴾ ˣˣᵛⁱ· ²· ˢ Agrippa, that, after examination had, I might have somewhat to write.

27 For it seemeth to me unreasonable to send a prisoner, and not withal to signify the crimes *laid* against him.

CHAP. XXVI.

Paul, before Agrippa, Festus, and their attendants, declares his manner of life and his hope as a Pharisee, 1—8; his zeal in persecuting the church, 9—11; his wonderful conversion, and call to the apostleship, 12—18; and his subsequent preaching and testimony to

---

Λ φανταζω, (Heb. xii. 21,) ' *Apparere facio; ... phantasiæ,* ' seu *vi imaginativæ aliquid propono.*' Schleusner. Ostentation, affectation of magnificence.—*The place of hearing.*] Το ακροατηριον. Here only. Ακροατης, *Rom.* ii. 13.

V. 24—27. (*Marg. Ref.* m, n.—*Note,* xxii. 22—30.) The motive of Festus, in bringing Paul before this splendid company, evidently was, that he might collect something from Agrippa and those present which would enable him to write to the emperor, in a manner more creditable to himself, and less unreasonable or absurd, than it seemed to him in present circumstances practicable for him. But God had far other and higher reasons for influencing his mind to a measure, in various respects leading to most important consequences. (*Note, Phil.* i. 12—14.)—*My lord.*] Or, The lord and ruler of the vast Roman empire; a pompous title, then generally given to the emperors.

I have no certain thing. (26) Ασφαλες; τι ουκ εχω. xxi. 34. xxii. 30. *Phil.* iii. 1. *Heb.* vi. 19. Ασφαλιζομαι· See on *Matt.* xxvii. 65.—*Unreasonable.* (27) Αλογον. 2 *Pet.* ii. 12.—*Ex.* vi. 12. *Sept.* Ab α, priv. et λογος, *sermo, ratio.*

PRACTICAL OBSERVATIONS.

V. 1—12.

The malignant enmity of hardened persecutors cannot be worn out by length of time, or satisfied with any sufferings of those against whom they are enraged, unless terminating in their violent death. They deem it a *peculiar favour*, when rulers will gratify their malice; and they have no scruples about conspiracies, assassinations, or massacres, when legal forms fail of effecting their purposes. We cannot therefore too much watch against the feeblest risings of that principle, which may be matured into such dire excesses.—But God limits the rage of the most unprincipled men, by the intervention of others, not at all more conscientious, in many things, than themselves: (*Note, Ps.* lxxvi. 10:) and sometimes he influences them *unaccountably* to act contrary to their own general purposes, in such particulars as form a part of his plan.— Happy will it be for us, when " many and grievous com- " plaints are brought against us," if our accusers can prove none of them; and if we can shew, that we have conscientiously obeyed the civil magistrate, behaved peaceably in the community, and attended to the ordinances and worship of God. (*Note,* 1 *Pet.* iv. 12—16.) When

these things are evident, a man may have great boldness before his judges, in appealing to their consciences with respect to his innocence; or in claiming the protection of the law, against the iniquity of those who long to be gratified by his punishment. But how scandalous is it to the professors and ministers of religion; when the true, exemplary, and zealous servants of God are compelled to appeal from their bigotted malice, to the decision of idolaters, and even to that of the most cruel tyrants, as more likely to do them justice than they are!

V. 13—27.

The most important questions, which relate to the worship of God, the way of eternal salvation, and the grand truths of the gospel, appear dubious and uninteresting to the politicians and wise men of the world. They can see, however, and condemn the mismanagement, into which men are betrayed by an indiscreet or furious zeal; and this confirms them in their sceptical disregard of religion in general. Yet the day is at hand, when Festus and the whole world will know, that all the temporal concerns of the immense Roman empire were frivolous, as the toys and sports of children, compared with the single question, whether Jesus the crucified was risen from the dead, according to the doctrine of the apostle, or was not risen. Then those who have had the means of instruction, and have despised them, will be most awfully convinced of their sin and folly. But alas! many, who seem to desire information on such questions, only want to gratify a vain curiosity, and not to learn the way to heaven : " and the " great pomp," with which some of the rich and honourable of this world, attend at " the places of hearing the " word of God," nay, at the Lord's table, shew, that they are actuated by the same motives as Paul's splendid auditory was, though in a far more aggravated manner.—Ministers indeed do not commonly now stand in fetters, as prisoners, to make their defence before their hearers; yet numbers affect rather to sit in judgment on them, as " offenders " for a word," than to learn from them the truth and will of God, for the salvation of their own souls : and alas, too many preachers'seem far more anxious to collect together and to please their genteel and *splendid* congregations; than to " declare the whole counsel of God," and to " keep themselves pure from the blood of all men." (*Notes,* xx. 18—21. 25—27. *P. O.* 13—31.)

island, which is called Clauda, we had much work to come by the boat:

17 Which when they had taken up, they used helps, undergirding the ship; and [c 29. 41.] * fearing lest they should fall into the quicksands, strake sail, and so were driven.

18 And we being exceedingly tossed with a tempest, [f] the next *day* they lightened the ship;

19 And the third *day* [g] we cast out with our own hands the tackling of the ship.

20 And when [h] neither sun nor stars in many days appeared, [i] and no small tempest lay on *us*, [k] all hope that we should be saved was then taken away.

21 But [l] after long abstinence, Paul stood forth in the midst of them, and said, Sirs, [m] ye should have hearkened unto me, and not have loosed from Crete, and to have gained this harm and loss.

22 And now [a] I exhort you to be of good cheer: [b] for there shall be no loss of *any man's* life among you, but of the ship. [c]

23 For [d] there stood by me this night the angel of God, [e] whose I am, [f] and whom I serve,

24 Saying, 'Fear not, Paul; [g] thou must be brought before Cæsar: and, [h] lo, God hath given thee all them that sail with thee.

25 Wherefore, sirs, be of good cheer: for [i] I believe God, that it shall be even as [k] it was told me.

26 Howbeit, we must be cast upon [l] a certain island.

Τῆς σκαφης. 30. 32. Here only. 'Α σκαπτω, fodio, excavo, 'quia cavatur ex una arbore, seu trabe.' *Schleusner.*— *Boats* in general seem originally to have been *canoes;* which retained the name, when formed in another manner.

V. 17. *Quicksands.*] These are supposed to have been the greater and lesser Syrtes, towards the coast of Africa, which were extremely formidable to ancient navigators.

Helps. (17) Βοηθειαις. *Heb.* iv. 16. Not elsewhere. A Conθηναι, xxi. 28.—*Undergirding.*] Ὑποζωννυντες. Here only. Ex ὑπο et ζωννω, vel ζωννμι, cingo.—*Quicksands.*] Συρτιν. Here only. Α συρω, traho, attraho.—*Strake sail.*] Χαλασαντες το σκευος. Χαλαζω, ix. 25. See on Mark ii. 4. Σκευος, 'Vela navis, cum rudentibus et antennis.' Schleusner.

V. 18, 19. Note, *Jon.* i. 4—6.—*Tackling.*] Those things needful for navigating the ship, which were carried for future use, in case they should be wanted. In this perilous emergency, the mariners cast every thing overboard, which could possibly be spared, as the only method by which they could hope to keep the ship from sinking. (*Marg. Ref.—Notes, Phil.* iii. 1—11, *vv.* 7, 8.)

Being exceedingly tossed with a tempest. (18) Σφοδρως χειμαζομενων ἡμων. Σφοδρως. Here only. Χειμαζω. Here only. Α χειμα, hyems. See on 12.—*They lightened the ship.*] Εκβολην εποιουντο. Here only. Ab εκβαλλω, ejicio. They cast out the lading of the ship.—*With our own hands.* (19) Αυτοχειρες. Here only. Ex αυτος, et χειρ, manus.—*The tackling.*] Την σκευην. Here only N. T.—*Jon.* i. 5. Sept. 'Omne id, 'quo navis instrui, armari, ac onerari solet.' Schleusner.

V. 20—26. The mariners could not make any usual observations, because the sun and stars were totally hidden by clouds; they were not able, therefore, to discover to what part of the sea they had been driven: and, as the tempest still lay hard upon them, and allowed them no respite to repair their shattered vessel, they gave up all for lost; and expected every moment to go to the bottom, or to be dashed upon the rocks. (*Marg. Ref.* h—k.) This prepared them to regard the words of Paul, which in other

circumstances they probably would have contemptuously neglected. As he had before been assured of bearing testimony to Jesus at Rome, he was probably composed during the whole tempest; but the Lord was pleased to send him further assurances, respecting his own preservation, and that of all the company. (*Note,* xxiii. 11.) After they had all neglected, for some time, to take proper sustenance, through the terror of immediate death; and after Paul and his friends had, perhaps, spent some time in prayer; he stood forth before the mariners, and reminded them of the divine admonition he had before given them, which they ought to have unreservedly obeyed: (*Marg. Ref.* l, m.—*Note,* 10:) and by neglecting of which they had "gained" nothing of what they had expected, but only exposed themselves to great injury and disgrace. He, however, exhorted them to be of good courage, for he was authorized to assure them of the preservation of all their lives. For that God, whose he was in an especial manner, whom he worshipped continually, and whom he served with all his powers and capacities, by preaching the gospel of his Son, (*Marg. Ref.* n—r.—*Notes, Dan.* vi. 10 —23. *Rom.* i. 8—12,) had sent his angel, (who knew where to find him, though they knew not where they were,) and by him God had assured him of being preserved to stand before the Roman emperor; and also had informed him, that he had granted his prayers and fervent desires, and for his sake, and as a special favour to him, would save the lives of all those who sailed with him. He therefore exhorted them to be cheerful, and hope amidst their perils; for he believed assuredly that God would fulfil his word, as he knew him to be always faithful to his promises. (*Marg. Ref.* s, t.) The ship, however, would certainly be wrecked, and they would be cast "upon an island," and not on any part of the continent, either of Europe, Asia, or Africa: by which circumstance it would be manifested that he spake by revelation from God. (*Notes,* xxviii. 1, 2. *Gen.* xviii. 23—33. xix. 27—29.)

27 ¶ But when 'the fourteenth night was come, as we were driven up and down in Adria, about midnight 'the shipmen deemed that they drew near to some country;

28 And sounded, and found *it* twenty fathoms: and when they had gone a little further, they sounded again, and found *it* fifteen fathoms.

29 Then fearing lest they should have 'fallen upon rocks, they cast four 'anchors out of the stern, 'and wished for the day.

30 And as the shipmen were about to flee out of the ship, when they had let down 'the boat into the sea, under colour as though they would have cast anchors out of the 'foreship.

31 Paul 'said to the centurion and to the soldiers, 'Except these abide in the ship, ye cannot be saved.

32 Then 'the soldiers cut off the ropes of the boat, and let her fall off.

33 And 'while the day was coming on, Paul besought *them* all to take meat, saying, 'This day is the fourteenth day that ye have tarried and continued fasting, having taken nothing.

34 Wherefore I pray you to take *some* meat; "for this is for your health: 'for there shall not an hair fall from the head of any of you.

35 And when he had thus spoken, he took bread, 'and gave thanks to God ' in presence of them all: and when he had broken *it*, he began to eat.

36 Then were 'they all of good cheer, and they also took *some* meat.

37 And we were in all in the ship 'two hundred threescore and sixteen ' souls.

38 And when they had eaten enough, 'they lightened the ship, and cast out the wheat into the sea.

Tempest. (20) Χειμωνος. See on *Matt.* xvi. 3.—*Was taken away.*] Περιηρειτο. 40. 2 *Cor.* iii. 16. *Heb.* x. 11. *Undiquaque aufero.* Ex περι et αιρεω, capio—*Abstinence.* (21) Ασιτιας. Here only. Ex α priv. et σιτος, cibus. Ασιτος, 33.—*Ye should have hearkened.*] Εδει ... πειθαρχησαντας. See on v. 29.—*Loss.* (22) Αποβολη. *Rom.* xi. 15. Not elsewhere. Ab αποβαλλω, abjicio, *Mark* x. 50.—*Hath given.* (24) Κεχαρισαι. See on xxv. 11. *Luke* vii. 21.—*Be cast.* (26) Εκπεσειν. 17. 29. 32. *Gal.* v. 4. 2 *Pet.* iii. 17. *Rev.* ii. 5.

V. 27. *Marg. Ref.—Adria.*] This name was not then confined to what is now called the Adriatick Sea, but was extended to a much larger part of the Mediterranean.

Adria.] Αδρια. Here only. ' Ab Adria, urbe ... Italiæ ' nobili, in agro Picenorum.' *Schleusner.*

V. 28—32. The mariners, finding by the line, that the depth of the water decreased on every sounding, were afraid of being driven, in the dark, on the rocks or sands, which are found near the shore, and therefore used their utmost endeavours to bring the ship to anchor: waiting with earnest longings for day light, that they might discover where they were, and what methods could be used for their preservation. (*Marg. Ref.* c, d.—*Note, Ps.* cxxx. 5, 6.) They were fully sensible of the extreme danger, to which the ship was exposed; but they hoped to save themselves in the boat, thus leaving the passengers to perish. This selfish purpose, however, they endeavoured to conceal: but the apostle, perceiving what they were about to do, assured the centurion and the soldiers, that they could not be preserved, unless the mariners remained with them; and they paid so much regard to his judgment, as immediately to cut the ropes, by which the boat was fastened, and to give her up to the sea. (*Note,* 16.) It was the purpose of God to save the lives of the company by means of the mariners, and they must not tempt him, by neglecting the proper method of self-preservation. (*Marg. Ref.* h, i. —*Note, Matt.* iv. 5—7.)—Nothing could be more absolute than the promise above given (24): yet neither the centurion nor the soldiers charged Paul with inconsistency, in what he now said to them. If the end was absolutely decreed, the means of attaining it were so likewise; and the case is the same, in concerns of still higher importance.—' God hath indeed assured me, that none of all our ' lives shall miscarry in this danger; but that God, who ' hath ordained our preservation, hath also ordained the ' means thereof, and therefore hath appointed, that these ' mariners shall continue in the ship, if we will hope for ' safety.' *Bp. Hall.* (*Notes,* xxiii. 12—22, *vv.* 16—18. xxv. 9—11.)

Sounded. (28) Βολισαντες. Here only. A βολις. ' 1. *Jaculum. Heb.* xii. 20.—2. *Perpendiculum nauticum, seu funis ' cui plumbum est alligatum.*' *Schleusner.—Fathoms.*] Οργυιας. Here only. *Mensura sex pedum.*—*Rocks.* (29) Τραχεις τοπους. See on *Luke* iii. 5. *Loca saxosa.*—*Anchors.*] Αγκυρας. 30. *Heb.* vi. 19. Not elsewhere.—*The stern.*] Πρυμνης. 41. *Mark* iv. 38. Not elsewhere.—*Wished.*] Ηυχοντο. See on xxvi. 29.—*The shipmen.* (30) Των ναυτων. 27. *Rev.* xviii. 17. Not elsewhere. A ναυς, *navis.*—The *sailors,* as distinguished from the *passengers.*—*The foreship.*] Πρωρας. 41. Here only. Ex προ et οραω, *video.*

V. 33—38. Till day-light should make way for using proper means of preservation, the apostle shewed the whole company, that they might make a most important use of the time, by taking seasonable food. During a fortnight, the tremendous violence of the tempest had kept them from making any regular meal, or taking even needful sustenance: so that they were greatly weakened, not only by fatigue and terror, but also by abstinence. This seems the most natural and obvious meaning of the language here used, which was no doubt in some degree

39 And when it was day, they knew not the land: but they discovered a certain creek with a shore, into the which they were minded, if it were possible, to thrust in the ship.

 40 And when they had ⁹ taken up the anchors, they committed *themselves* unto the sea, and loosed the rudder-bands, ° and hoised up the main-sail to the wind, and made toward shore.

41 And falling into a place where two seas met, ° they ran the ship aground; and the forepart stuck fast, and remained unmoveable, but the hinder part was ' broken with the violence of the waves.

42 And ° the soldiers' counsel was to kill the prisoners, lest any of them should swim out and escape.

43 But the centurion, ° willing to save Paul, kept them from *their* purpose; and commanded that they which could swim, should cast *themselves* first *into the sea*, and get to land:

44 And the rest, some on boards, and some on *broken pieces* of the ship. And so it came to pass, ° that they escaped all safe to land.

Marginal refs (right):
y 1 Kings xxii. 48. 2 Chr. xx. 37.
Ez. xxvii. 26.
84. 2 Cor. xi. 25, 26.
Ps. lxxiv. 20.
Prov. xii. 10. Ec. ix. 3. Mark xv. 15—20.
Luke xxiii. 41.
a b. 11. 31. xviii. 10. 24. Prov. xvi. 7.
b 22. 34. Ps. cvii. 30. Am. ix. 9.
John vi. 39, 40.
2 Cor. i. 8—10.
1 Pet. iv. 18.

---

hyperbolical: but some think, that they were put on short allowance, as the voyage was likely to be much longer than had been expected. St. Paul therefore, whose influence no doubt continually and rapidly increased, urged them to take adequate refreshment; that they might be strengthened for the arduous struggle, which would be necessary, in order to their deliverance from such perilous circumstances; and that their health might not be impaired, seeing that God would certainly preserve their lives. (*Marg. Ref.* m.) Having, therefore, with all the boldness and confidence arising from a clear conscience and a well grounded hope in God, "given thanks" to him, in the most publick manner, for the food afforded them, and the promise vouchsafed them; he, by his own example, led them to take a regular and cheerful meal: and being fully satisfied with food, and knowing that a few hours must terminate their perils, they cast the remainder of their provisions, as well as of the lading, (for probably the ship was freighted with wheat,) into the sea, as a measure conducive to their preservation. (*Marg. Ref.* o—t.)—*An hair,* &c. (34) *Marg. Ref.* n.—The number stated to have been aboard this *merchant-ship*, is very large; and, I believe, not generally equalled in vessels of that description, even at present, except employed as transports, in the freight of convicts, or in the slave-trade.

Fasting. (33) Ασιτοι. See on 21.—*Health.* (34) Σωτηριας. See on iv. 12.—*He gave thanks.* (35) Ευχαριςησε. xxviii. 15. *Matt.* xv. 36. xxvi. 27. *John* vi. 11. 23, *et al.*—*Of good cheer.* (36) Ευθυμοι. See on xxiv. 10. Ab ευθυμεω, 22. 25.—*When they had eaten enough.* (37) Κορεσθεντες τροφης. 1 *Cor.* iv. 8. Not elsewhere.—*They lightened.*] Εκυφιζον. Here only. A κυφος, *levis.*

V. 39. The island, Malta, on which the ship was wrecked, is known to be almost surrounded with rocks. But the mariners discovered a bay of the sea, running up a little way within land, where was a *beach*, or convenient landing place; and thither they endeavoured to steer the vessel. Had these things been left to men, unskilled in navigation, the ship must in all probability have been dashed to pieces on the rocks; and the lives of the passengers could not have been preserved, without the most extraordinary miraculous interposition.

A ... creek.] Κολπον. *Luke* vi. 38. xvi. 22, 23. *John* i. 18.—*Metaph. sinus maris.* A bay of the sea.—*With a shore.*] Εχοντα αιγιαλον, 40. xxi. 5. *Matt.* xiii. 2.—' Interdum,

' *littus opportunum appellandæ navi.*' Schleusner.—*To thrust in.*] Εξωσαι. vii. 45.

V. 40. *Taken up,* &c.] Or, as some think, having cut the cables, and left the anchors. (*Marg.*)—*Rudder-bands.*] It is probable, that the rudders were made fast during the tempest, to prevent injury to those on board, by their useless and vehement motion: but at this crisis they were loosened, as it was hoped some use might be made of them, in steering the ship.—Learned men have shewn, that it was not uncommon among the ancients to have two rudders, one on each side of the ship.

They committed, &c.] Ειων. v. 38. xiv. 16. *Matt.* xxiv. 43. *Luke* iv. 41. 1 *Cor.* x. 13.—*The rudder-bands.*]Ζευκτηριας των πηδαλιων, Ζευκτηρια. Here only. A ζευγνυμι, conjungo. Πεδαλιον, *Jam.* iii. 4. Not elsewhere.—*The mainsail.*] Αρτεμονα. Here only.—*They made toward shore.*] " They used their utmost efforts to reach the shore." Κατειχον εις τον αιγιαλον. See on 39.—Κατεχω, *Luke* iv. 42. The multitude used their utmost efforts to keep Jesus among them. (*Philem.* 13.)

V. 41. *Where two,* &c.] A portion of land, on a sandbank from the shore, ending in a point, (called by sailors, *a spit,* from its sharp ending,) divided the channel in the midst, on each side of which was deep water. On this point, which had not been perceived, the ship was forcibly driven, and fixed; the head or foreship being immoveable, and the stern at liberty: and thus it was soon dashed to pieces by the fury of the waves. (*Marg. Ref.*)

A place where two seas met.] Τοπον διθαλασσον. Here only. Εκ δις et θαλασσα, mare.—*They ran ... aground.*] Επωκειλαν. Here only. Ab επι et οκιλλω, *appello.*—*Stuck fast.*] Ερεισασα. Here only.—*Unmoveable.*] Ασαλυτος. *Heb.* xii. 28. Not elsewhere. Ab a priv. et σαλευω, *agito.*

V. 42—44. The soldiers, perceiving that all must shift for themselves; and supposing, that if any of the prisoners should escape, the survivors of their guards would be called to account for it, advised the immediate execution of the whole company, though yet uncondemned. This could not have been thought of, had not the Roman laws allowed it, or had it not been sometimes done. So that this cruel and unfeeling policy disgraced the jurisprudence of the renowned Romans! Indeed the centurion himself seems not to have been at all shocked by the proposal: and he was induced, rather by a personal regard to Paul, than by general principles, either of humanity or justice,

CHAP. XXVIII.

The whole company, having escaped to the island Melita, are humanely entertained by the inhabitants, 1, 2. A viper fastens on Paul's hand, which he shakes off into the fire, without harm; and the people, who at first supposed he was a murderer, believe that he is a god, 3—6. Publius, the chief man of the island, entertains them all three days, 5—7. Paul heals the father of Publius, and many other sick persons; and they meet with much respect and kindness, 8—10.

Paul and his company depart; and having arrived within some miles of Rome, they are met by brethren from that city, 11—15. Paul is entrusted to a soldier, and dwells in his own lodging, 16. He sends for the chief of the Jews, and shews them the occasion of his coming, 17—22. He proves to a large company, from the scriptures, that Jesus is the Christ, 23. Some believe, and others do not, 24. He solemnly warns the unbelievers, and shews that the Gentiles would receive his word, 25—29. He continues during two years, to preach the gospel in his own hired house, without interruption, 30, 31.

to negative the counsel; and this at a time too, when his own life and that of the soldiers were in as much peril, as the lives of the prisoners! (*Marg. Ref.* z, a.)—Thus the apostle, in this respect also, proved a blessing to his companions in suffering: (*Note, Gen.* xii. 1—3, *v.* 3 :) and by the special interposition of Providence, every one of the numerous company got safe to shore.—It is highly reasonable to suppose, that these extraordinary incidents were over-ruled to the conversion and salvation of many of their souls. (*Marg. Ref.* b.)

Should swim out. (42) Εκκολυμβησας. Here only. Εκ εκ et κολυμβαω, 43. Here only.—*Boards.* (44) Σανισιν. Here only.—*On broken pieces of the ship.*] Επι τινων των απο τα πλοιν. " Some of the things belonging to the ship," whether as parts of it, or on board of it.—*They ... escaped safe.*] Διασωθηναι. 43. xxiii. 24. xxviii. 1. 4. 1 *Pet.* iii. 20.

PRACTICAL OBSERVATIONS.

V. 1—20.

The Lord provides kind friends, and adequate consolations, for his faithful servants, in all their multiplied and varied trials: and even such persons, as might previously have been expected to be inimical to them, are sometimes induced to entreat them courteously, and to minister to their refreshment; nor shall these fail of receiving a suitable reward.—Zealous and able ministers cannot, in any situation, be wholly excluded from usefulness: and their gracious God often causes them to pass through troubles, to manifest the power of his consolations in supporting them, and the excellency of their principles and character; in order to excite the attention of the careless, the ignorant, and the prejudiced, to their example and instructions. Their admonitions, however, will generally be at first slighted, even by those worldly men, who behave in a friendly manner: for, while persons of this description give them credit for *good meaning*, they generally have a very mean opinion of their sagacity. Thus, in hopes of avoiding difficulties, or obtaining conveniences and advantages, the counsels of heavenly wisdom are slighted: and, when Providence seems to favour men's carnal projects, they are sanguine in concluding that they have gained their purpose. But disobedience to the counsel and command of God however made known, will surely lead men into troubles and dangers; and the event will convince them, that their hopes were vain, and their conduct foolish.— What labour do almost all men employ, and what sacrifices do they readily make, in order to preserve their lives, when in imminent danger! Yet how few are willing to labour, or to renounce temporal interest or pleasure, to escape

impending and eternal destruction! (*P. O. Is.* ii. 10—22. *Notes, Matt.* x. 27, 28. xvi. 24—28. *P. O.* 21—28.)— Groundless hopes are often succeeded by desponding fears; but when sinners renounce all hope of saving themselves, they are prepared to understand the word of God, and to trust in his free mercy through Jesus Christ.

V. 21—44.

It is an unspeakable advantage, when the distressed, and those who draw near to death, have some persons at hand, to direct them to the true Foundation of hope and Source of consolation: and opportunities of this kind should be diligently improved. (*Notes, Job* xxxiii. 19—30. *P. O.* 14 —33.)—It may be proper to remind the afflicted, that they have brought their troubles on themselves, by neglecting good counsel, and by disobeying the commandments of God: but we must also encourage them to hope in his mercy, and in his gracious promises.—" The Lord knoweth " them that are his;" and holy angels are ready to minister to them, wherever they go. If we can truly say, " His I am, and him I serve," the whole scripture says to us, " Fear not;" and he frequently spares the lives, and in numerous instances even saves the souls, of others, for the sake, and in answer to the prayers, of his redeemed and devoted servants. So that they are " a blessing," to every family and neighbourhood in which they reside, and in all places to which they travel.—The comfort of God's precious promises cannot be enjoyed, without a believing dependence on them; and the fulfilment of them must be waited for, in a diligent attendance on the appointed means of grace.—If he have " chosen us in Christ " to eternal salvation; he has also determined, that we shall obtain it in the way of repentance, faith, prayer, watchfulness, and diligent persevering obedience: and it is the most fatal presumption to expect it in any other way. (*Notes, and P. O.* 2 *Thes.* ii. 13—17.)—Men in general are so selfish, that they are ready to provide for their own preservation, even by such measures as directly conduce to the destruction of those, with whom they are most intimately connected! No peril or sufferings can subdue human depravity: so that soldiers and sailors, who experience more hardships, dangers, and evident deliverances than other men; and who it might be thought, would be more careful than others to be always prepared for death and judgment; are too commonly peculiarly regardless of religion and morality!—We must, however, endeavour to accommodate ourselves, as far as we conscientiously can, to those among whom we are placed; and to excite, encourage, and instruct them, by our example and conver-

AND when they were escaped, then they knew that [a] the island was called Melita.

2 And the [b] barbarous people [c] shewed us no little kindness: for they kindled a fire, and received us every one, [d] because of the present rain, and because of the cold.

3 And when Paul had gathered a bundle of sticks, and laid *them* on the fire, there [e] came a viper out of the heat, [f] and fastened on his hand.

4 And when [g] the barbarians saw the *venomous* [h] beast hang on his hand, they said among themselves, [i] No doubt this man is [k] a murderer, whom, though he hath escaped the sea, yet vengeance suffereth not to live.

5 And he shook off the beast into the fire, and [l] felt no harm.

6 Howbeit they looked when he should have swollen, or fallen down dead suddenly: but after they had looked a great while, and saw no harm come to him, they changed their minds, and [m] said that he was a god.

7 ¶ In the same quarters were possessions of [n] the chief man of the island,

---

sation, to trust in the Lord, to thank him for all their comforts, to obey his commands, and to use the proper means of securing their own interest and happiness.—The promises of God cannot be frustrated by the most formidable dangers, nor can his purposes be defeated by any endeavours of his creatures: it is therefore our part, to attend on our present duty, and to leave events with him. —All true believers will certainly obtain eternal life and happiness, even as all this company obtained temporal deliverance. Their difficulties, perils, alarms, temptations, and distresses may be many, and of various kinds. They will sometimes have such hair-breadth escapes, as to remind them of the apostle's words, " the righteous scarcely " are saved ;" and their preservation and victories will be effected in different ways, beside and beyond their expectation. (*Notes, Rom.* viii. 28—39. 1 *Pet.* iv. 17—19.) They will often, under dark and gloomy dispensations, be required to wait for some token of the Lord's favour, (when they have no light or comfort day after day,) with more earnestness, than these mariners wished for the dawn. It will, however, at length, so come to pass, that by one means or another, they will all escape safe to heaven, where mutual congratulations and admiring praises and thanksgivings, will succeed their present trials and distresses, and will not be terminated or interrupted to all eternity.

NOTES.

Chap. XXVIII. V. 1, 2. The small island of Melita, lies to the south of Sicily. It is now called Malta : for many ages it belonged to the knights of Malta, and recent events have made its name familiar to most readers. Probably, it was peopled by a colony of Phœnicians: and the inhabitants were called " barbarians " by the Greeks and Romans, who gave this name to all the rest of the world. The islanders however, were noted for their humanity and kindness to strangers; and their conduct to the shipwrecked company, in their urgent distress, corresponded with that character. As they were all wet, cold, destitute, and almost ready to perish ; they kindled a large fire in some place sheltered from the weather, which was cold and rainy, and there entertained and refreshed them, in the best way they could. (*Marg. Ref.* c, d.)

Melita. (1) Μελιτη· a μελι, *mel apum*, *Matt.* iii.—The island abounded with honey.—*The barbarous people.* (2) Οι βαρβαροι. 4. *Rom.* i. 14. 1 *Cor.* xiv. 11. *Col.* iii. 11.—*Ps.* cxiv. 1. *Sept.*—*Kindness.*] Φιλανθρωπιαν. *Tit.* iii. 4. See on xxvii. 3.—*Cold.*] Ψυχος. *John* xviii. 18. 2 *Cor.* xi. 27. Ψυχομαι, *Matt.* xxiv. 12.

V. 3—6. The apostle knew how to accommodate himself to any circumstances: and, as the situation of the company required it, he readily assisted in making the fire. But in doing this, he was exposed to a more imminent danger, even than that which he had just escaped. The bite of a viper was supposed to be fatal; and as this viper was irritated by the heat, it might be expected, that it would immediately bite him. When therefore the islanders, who had some general notions of a superior power engaged to punish atrocious criminals, saw this fierce and destructive animal fasten on his hand, they looked on him as a dead man : and, perceiving that he was a prisoner, they concluded that he had committed murder, and so had exposed himself to divine vengeance; and that he had escaped from the sea, only that he might be punished in a more exemplary manner. (*Marg. Ref.* f. h—k.—*Notes, Luke* xliii. 1—5.) But when, after a considerable time, they saw that no harm followed, they went into the opposite extreme, and concluded that he was one of their deities, thus become visible among them. (*Marg. Ref.* l, m.—*Notes,* xiv. 11—20. *Mark* xvi. 17, 18. *Luke* x. 17 —20. *Rom.* xvi. 17—20, *v.* 20.) They did not indeed, at this time, know any thing of the true God, whose invisible power had thus preserved the life of his servant; but the impression, which these events made on their minds, would conduce to render them afterwards more observant of the apostle's conversation and behaviour.

Had gathered. (3) Συρρεψαντος. Here only. Ex συν et ρρεψω, *verto.*—*A bundle of sticks.*] Φρυγανων πληθος. Here only. A φρυγω, vel φρυσσω, *torreo, torrefacio.*—*A viper.*] Εχιδνα. *Matt.* iii. 7. xii. 34. xxiii. 33. *Luke* iii. 7.—*The venomous beast.* (4) Το θηριον. 5. x. 12. xi. 6. *Mark* i. 13. *Tit.* i. 12. *Jam.* iii. 7. *Rev.* vi. 8. xi. 7, *et al.* A θηρ, *fera.* —*Vengeance.*] Ἡ δικη. See on xxv. 15.—*Should have swollen.* (6) Μελλειν πιμπρασθαι. Here only.—*No harm.*] Μηδεν ἀτοπον. See on *Luke* xxiii. 41.

V. 7—10. It had been providentially ordered, that the ship should be wrecked, near the house and estate of the governor of the island, who courteously and hospitably

whose name name was Publius; ° who received us, and lodged us three days courteously.

8 And it came to pass, that ° the father of Publius lay sick of a fever and of a bloody flux: to whom Paul entered in, and ° prayed, and ° laid his hands on him ° and healed him.

9 So when this was done, ° others also, which had diseases in the island, came, and were healed:

10 Who also " honoured us with many honours; and when we departed, they ˣ laded us with such things as were necessary.

11 ¶ And after three months, we departed in ʸ a ship of Alexandria,

which had wintered in the isle, ° whose sign was Castor and Pollux.

12 And landing at Syracuse, we tarried *there* three days.

13 And from thence we fetched a compass, and came to Rhegium: and after one day ° the south wind blew, and we came the next day to Puteoli:

14 Where ᵇ we found brethren, ° and were desired to tarry with them seven days: and so we went toward Rome.

15 And from thence, ° when the brethren heard of us, they came to meet us as far as Appii forum, and The three taverns; whom when Paul saw, ° he thanked God, and took courage.

---

entertained the whole company three days, till they could be conveniently accommodated elsewhere. Thus Paul became acquainted with the sickness of the governor's father, who was confined by a most painful and dangerous disease; and when he had (doubtless by his own proposal) prayed for him, and laid his hands on him, he was immediately healed. This must have been a very acceptable return to Publius for his liberal courtesy; and would also excite general attention towards the apostle and his instructions. Accordingly, sick persons from every part of the island were brought to him, and were healed. (*Marg. Ref.* p—t.) No doubt Paul and his companions zealously improved these opportunities of preaching the gospel; and probably they had considerable success during the three months of their continuance in the island. (11) So that at length they were greatly honoured, as highly favoured by the Lord, and as having abundantly requited the kindness shewn them. The whole company were treated with respect, chiefly on the apostle's account; and all their wants were liberally supplied when they departed. (*Marg. Ref.* u, x.) It is, however, reasonable to conclude from this compendious narrative, that the conduct and discourses of St. Paul and his friends, and all the events of the shipwreck and deliverance, had made a deep impression on the minds of the soldiers, sailors, and passengers; and that they too had behaved so well at Melita, as to conciliate the esteem and favour of the inhabitants.—' No one will ever ' repent of having entertained a servant of God, however ' wretched and indigent.' *Beza.*

The chief man. (7) Τῳ πρωτῳ. ' Grotius has produced ' an ancient inscription, by which it appears, that the title ' of πρωτος, or chief, was given to the governor of this island; ' and so it is used here by St. Luke, with his usual pro-' priety of expression.' *Doddridge.—Lodged.*] Εξενισεν. x. 6. 18. xvii. 20. xxi. 16. *Heb.* xiii. 2.—*Courteously.*] Φιλοφρονως. Here only. Φιλοφρων, 1 *Pet.* iii. 8. Ex φιλος, *amicus,* et φρην, *mens.*—*A bloody flux.* (8) Δυσεντερια. Here only. —Εx ὁυς, et εντερον, *intestinum.* Dysentery.'—*Such things as were necessary.* (10) Τα προς την χρειαν. n. 45. iv. 35. vi. 3. xx. 34. *Rom.* xii. 13, *et al.*

V. 11—14. When the winter was over, the centurion and his soldiers, with the prisoners, and their companions,

embarked as passengers on board an Alexandrian vessel. Castor and Pollux, according to the heathen fables, were twin sons of Jupiter by Leda; and, as a subordinate kind of deities, were supposed to be concerned in the protection of mariners. The images, therefore, of these brothers were placed at the head or the stern of the ship; or, as some think, on both. The apostle had no option, whether he would sail in a ship thus stamped by idolatry: but it is probable, that most ships were, in one way or other, distinguished by some things connected with the prevalent idolatrous sentiments and observances: and, as merely a passenger, he would not have regarded it, had he been at liberty.—Syracuse was the capital city of Sicily, Rhegium was a town on the southern extremity of Italy, and Puteoli a sea-port on the south-west side of it. At Puteoli the company landed; and, finding some Christians, the apostle and his friends were desired by them, and allowed by the centurion, to spend a week with them. The centurion's regard to Paul evidently increased during the whole voyage; but it is not said, whether he at length became a Christian, or not. (*Marg. Ref.*)

Which had wintered. (11) Παρακιχι.μακοτι. See on xxvii. 12.—*Whose sign.*] Παρασημα. Here only. Ex παρα, et σημα, *signum.*—Castor and Pollux.] Διοσκουροις.—Here only. Ex Διος, et κυρος, pro κορος, *puer.* (See on xiv. 12.)—*The next day.* (13) Δευτεραιοι. Here only. Pro τη δευτερα ἡμερα, *secundo die.*

V. 15. The apostle's approach towards Rome having been known, some of the Christians, who resided in that city, came to meet and welcome him though in bonds. They knew him especially as ' the apostle of the gentiles;' and the epistle, which he had some time before written to them, had no doubt impressed them with the highest veneration for his character. (*Marg. Ref.* d. *Preface to Romans. Notes, Rom.* i. 8—12. xv. 22—29.)—Appii forum is computed to have been fifty-one miles from Rome, and The three taverns, thirty-three.—This testimony of respect appears to have been very seasonable: for the circumstances in which the apostle was about to make his first visit to this renowned city, compared with the expectations which he had before expressed, concerning visiting the church there, were suited to damp his hopes of being

16 And when we came to [f]Rome,
[g]the centurion delivered the prisoners
to the [h]captain of the guard: [i]but
Paul was suffered to dwell by himself
with a soldier that kept him.
17 ¶ And it came to pass, that after
three days, Paul called the chief of the
Jews together: and when they were
come together, he said unto them, Men
and brethren, [k]though I have committed nothing against the people or
customs of our fathers, yet [l]was I delivered prisoner from Jerusalem into
the hands of the Romans:
18 Who, [m]when they had examined
me, would have let *me* go, because
there was no cause of death in me.
19 But when the Jews spake against
it, [n]I was constrained to appeal unto
Cæsar; [o]not that I had ought to accuse
my nation of.

f ii. 10. xviii. 2. xix. 21. xxiii. 11. Rom. i. 7—15. xv. 22—29. Rev. xvii. 9. 18.
g xxvii. 3. 31. 43.
h Gen. xxxvii. 36. 2 Kings xxv. 8. Jer. xl. 2.
i 30, 31. xxiv. 23. xxvii. 3. Gen. xxxix. 21—23.
k xxiii. 1. xxiv. 10—&c. xxv. 8. 10. Gen. xl. 15.
l xxi. 33. xxiii. 33.
m xxii. 24, 25. 30. xxiv. 10. 22. xxv. 7, 8. xxvi. 31.
n xxv. 10—12. 21. 25. xxvi. 32.
o Rom. xii. 19—21. 1 Pet. ii. 22, 23.

20 For [p]this cause therefore have I
called for you, to see *you*, and to speak
with *you*: because that [q]for the hope
of Israel I am bound with [r]this chain.
21 And they said unto him, [s]We
neither received letters out of Judea
concerning thee, neither any of the
brethren that came shewed or spake
any harm of thee.
22 But we desire to hear of thee
what thou thinkest: [t]for, as concerning this [u]sect, we know that every
where it is spoken against.
23 ¶ And when they had appointed
him a day, there came many to him
into *his* lodging; to whom [x]he expounded and testified the kingdom of
God, persuading them concerning
Jesus, [y]both out of the law of Moses,
and *out of* the prophets, [z]from morning till evening.

p 17. x. 29. 33.
q xxiii. 6. xxiv. 15—*See on* xxvi. 6, 7.
r xxvi. 29. Eph. iii. 1. iv. 1. vi. 20. Phil. i. 13. Col. iv. 18. 2 Tim. i. 16. ii. 9. Philem. 10 13.
s Ex. xi. 7. Is. xli. 11. liv. 17.
t xvi. 20, 21. xvii. 6, 7. xxiv. 5, 6. 14. Luke ii. 34. 1 Pet. ii. 12. iii. 16. iv. 14—16.
u v. 17. xv. 5. xxvi. 5. 1 Cor. xi. 19. *marg.*
x xvii. 2, 3. xviii. 4. 28. xix. 8. xxvi. 22, 23.
y *See on* xxvi. 6. 22. Luke xxiv. 26, 27. 44.
z xx. 9—11. John iv. 34.

countenanced, or made useful; but God was pleased to use this promising appearance to inspire him with gratitude and confidence. (*Marg. Ref.* f.)

Courage.] Θαρσος. Here only: θαρσεω, xxiii. 11. *Matt.* ix. 2. 22.

V. 16. When the company arrived at Rome, the other prisoners were committed to the custody of the captain of the imperial guards, to be lodged in prison: but, through the account sent by Festus, and the report of Julius, Paul was exempted from this hardship, and was allowed to dwell in a lodging apart from other prisoners; and only guarded by a soldier, to whom it is supposed that he was chained. (*Marg. Ref.*—*Note*, 30, 31.)

The captain of the guard.] Στρατοπεδαρχῃ. Here only. Ex στρατοπεδον, *exercitus*, et αρχω, *impero*.

V. 17—20. 'Paul every where remembers that he is an 'apostle.' *Beza.*—When the apostle and his friends had arranged their private concerns, and settled themselves in some lodging, as well as they could; he lost no time in sending for the principal persons of his nation to come to him, as he could not go to them. When they were come, he stated to them, that though he had not injured any of his people, or committed any offence against their laws and customs; yet he had been apprehended at Jerusalem, and delivered as a criminal into the hands of the Romans; and at length had been constrained in his own defence to appeal to the emperor. In this statement, he carefully avoided all mention of the violent attempt which had been made on his life, and the subsequent plots which had been formed to assassinate him. (*Notes*, xxv. 1—12.) He desired to satisfy his countrymen, that he had no ill will to his nation, or resentments against individuals, or intention of accusing them before the Romans. (*Marg. Ref.* k—o.) It was, however, a fact, that he had not committed any crime, for which he ought to be thus prosecuted; but that he was a prisoner, entirely on account of professing that hope in the Messiah, which was common to the nation; only that he held it with respect to Jesus, who had been crucified and was risen from the dead. (*Note*, xxvi. 4—8.) His address was the language of candour, caution, and benevolence; and he spake of his chain with great indifference, being willing to wear it for Christ's sake. (*Marg. Ref.* p—r.—*Notes*, *Gen.* xl. 14, 15. *2 Tim.* i. 6—13.)

Spake against it. (19) Αντιλεγοντων. 22. See on *Luke* ii. 34.—*I am bound.* (20) Περικειμαι, *circumdatus sum.* *Mark* ix. 42. *Luke* xvii. 2. *Heb.* v. 2. xii. 1.—*With this chain.*] Την αλυσιν ταυτην. xxi. 33. *Eph.* vi. 20. *2 Tim.* i. 16. See on *Mark* v. 3.

V. 21, 22. The leading persons of the Jews replied to the apostle, that they had received no account by letters, publick or private, concerning him from Judea; nor had they heard any of those who came to Rome, accuse him of any crime: but they desired to hear his sentiments concerning Jesus, seeing "this sect," or *heresy*, of the Nazarenes, or Christians, was every where spoken against, as destructive of the religion of their ancestors, the source of many disorders, and injurious to mankind. (*Marg. Ref.* t, u.—*Notes*, xxiv. 1—21. xxvi. 4—8.) This answer shews, that the Jews in Judea despaired of success in following up their accusations at Rome; and that immense pains had been taken to misrepresent the Christians, in every part of the world.

We desire. (22) Αξιουμεν. xv. 38. 'Αξιοω. 1. *Dignum* '*habeo.* *Luke* vii. 7. 2. *Dignum reddo.* *2 Thes.* i. 11. '3. *Cupio, volo, opto.*' Schleusner.—*Sect.*] 'Αιρεσεως. xxiv. 5. See on v. 17.

V. 23—29. The apostle proceeded in the same manner, with the Jews in his lodgings, as he had before been used to take in their synagogues; explaining the nature and privileges of the Redeemer's kingdom and salvation; "testifying" to the facts by which it was introduced; proving from the scriptures of the prophets, that Jesus was the promised Messiah, and persuading them to believe

24 And *some believed the things which were spoken, and some believed not.

25 And when they b agreed not among themselves they departed, after that Paul had spoken one word: ' Well spake the Holy Ghost by Esaias the prophet unto our fathers,

26 Saying, d Go unto this people, and say, e Hearing ye shall hear, and shall not understand; and seeing ye shall see, and not perceive:

27 For the heart of this people is waxed gross, and their ears are dull of hearing, and their eyes have they closed; lest they should see with *their* eyes, and hear with *their* ears,

and understand with *their* heart, and should be converted, and I should heal them.

28 Be f it known therefore unto you, that g the salvation of God is h sent unto the Gentiles, and *that* they will hear it.

29 And when he had said these words the Jews departed, and had i great reasoning among themselves.

30 ¶ And Paul k dwelt two whole years in his own hired house, and received all that came in unto him,

31 l Preaching the kingdom of God, m and teaching those things which concern the Lord Jesus Christ n with all confidence, no man forbidding him.

in him. (*Marg. Ref.* x, y.) Thus, in the earnestness of his zealous and benevolent soul, he spent the whole day : and though some were won over to the faith, yet it appears that most present rejected his testimony and even disputed against such as believed. Therefore the apostle parted from them, by observing, that the Holy Spirit had well described their disposition, and awfully denounced their doom, by the prophet Isaiah. The passage has already been considered. (*Marg. Ref.* c—e.—*Notes, Is.* vi. 9, 10. *John* xii. 37—41.) ' As for the quotation from ' Isaiah, which he applies to them, I would observe, that ' it is quoted oftener than any other text from the Old ' Testament, (that is, six times,) in the New : (here and ' *Matt.* xiii. 14, 15. *Mark* iv. 12. *Luke* viii. 10. *John* xii. ' 40. *Rom.* xi. 8 :) yet in such a variety of expression ' as plainly proves, the apostles did not confine them- ' selves exactly, either to the words of the original, or ' of the Greek version.' *Doddridge.* St. Paul had observed, during the whole of his ministry, that the nation in general thus closed their eyes and ears to the truth; and he foresaw with great concern, that God was about to give them up to *judicial* blindness and obduracy for their sins. He would, however, assure them, that the Gentiles, to whom the salvation of God was sent by his ministry, would hear and obey his word. The Jews being thus warned, had, when departing, much reasoning and disputation among themselves in consequence of what they had heard; and probably afterwards some of them embraced the gospel. (*Marg. Ref.* f—i.—*Go unto,* &c. (27, 28) See *Note, Matt.* xiii. 13—15. The rendering here is exactly the same. *When they had appointed.* (23) Ταξαμενοι. See on xiii. 48.—*Believed.* (24) Επειθοντο. 23. xvii. 4. xviii. 4. xix. 8.—*Believed not.*] Ηπιςων. *Mark* xvi. 11. 16. *Luke* xxiv. 11. 41.—*When they agreed not.* (25) Ασυμφωνοι οντες. Here only. Ex α, priv. et συμφωνος, *consonus.* See on *Matt.* xviii. 19.

V. 30, 31. The rulers of the Jews did not follow up their prosecution of Paul, on his appeal to the emperor, who at the present took no notice of the matter : thus the apostle remained two years longer a prisoner at Rome. He was, however, allowed to hire a house, and there openly to exercise his ministry, proclaiming " the king-

" dom of God," the reign of the Messiah ; (*Note, Matt.* iii. 2 ;) and teaching all things that related to the Lord Jesus, shewing that he was indeed the Messiah. This he did without meeting with the least interruption, which shews that Nero's persecution was not begun at this time. (*Marg Ref.* m, n.) With this remark Luke closed his history : probably the apostle was soon after set at liberty ; though it is generally agreed that he afterwards suffered martyrdom at Rome. (*Preface to the second Epistle to Timothy.*)—Doubtless Luke, Aristarchus, and others who attended on the apostle, or came to him, being themselves at liberty, laboured diligently to make the gospel known in the city and its vicinity, during all the time of the apostle's imprisonment ; though the historian, by a modesty almost unprecedented, is wholly silent concerning his own labours and sufferings.—Several of St. Paul's epistles were written during this imprisonment. (*Prefaces to the Ephesians, Philippians, Colossians, Philemon, Hebrews.*)

No man forbidding him. (31) Ακωλυτως. Here only. Ex α, priv. et κωλυω, *prohibeo.*

PRACTICAL OBSERVATIONS.

V. 1—10.

Those who are despised for their rude and uncultivated manners, are often more hospitable, and shew more genuine philanthropy than their more polished neighbours : and *heathens,* or reputed *barbarians,* will rise up in judgment against many persons, in this *civilized* Christian nation, who do not scruple to embezzle the property, or injure the persons, of such as are cast upon our shores.—True dignity has no need of affected stateliness ; and pride or sloth alone deems that beneath any man, which the present exigency requires for personal or social advantage. —We are always in danger in ourselves, and always safe when under God's protection : and he leads his servants through perils to illustrate their characters, or to shew his power in their deliverance.—Even uninformed and barbarous people have a horror of " murder," and an apprehension of divine vengeance on those who commit it : but this may give rise to erroneous judgments ; as it is not so generally considered, that the wicked are often reserved,

518

for future and more terrible punishment. (*Note*, 2 *Pet.* ii. 4—9.)—They, whose minds are destitute of due information, are peculiarly apt to pass from one extreme to the other; and to decide on men's characters rather by their success, than by their actions.—The Lord raises up friends to his people, in every place whither he leads them; he rewards, or enables *them* to requite, their benefactors in a suitable manner; and he renders them a blessing to all who are connected with them.—The cure of diseases, though valuable, is far more so when united with the means of grace and salvation; and the friends, who are raised up to a pious man by his good behaviour and usefulness, will be above all others affectionate and liberal; as far as this is needful and consistent.

V. 11—31.

The ordinary transactions of travelling are seldom worth a recital: but the comfort of ' communion with the saints,' and the kindness shewn us by our friends, are deserving of a more particular mention.—The respect and love, which lively Christians bear to faithful ministers, even though they have never seen them, will induce them sometimes to go far to converse with them: nor should they esteem them the less, on account of their sufferings for the gospel. This conduct is the more incumbent upon them; as the most eminent servants of God are liable to discouragements, and need somewhat to refresh their hopes under long continued trials and temptations.—The Lord moderates the afflictions of his people, as it is best for them; and he can render them easy under their remaining troubles. They should therefore be prompt to every service in their power: they also ought to obviate prejudices, which hinder their usefulness, as far as they can; and in refuting the charges brought against them, they should be candid, and express good-will towards their enemies.—Should we be called to wear a chain for Christ's sake, we ought not to be ashamed of it, but to glory in it: and though real Christians are every where, and at all times, in this deluded ungodly world, " spoken against," as a precise, troublesome, or fanatical sect; yet we may so behave, that none can speak any *personal* harm of us.—We should ever be ready to declare our sentiments of Christ and the gospel, to those who desire to hear them: and if the audience did not grow weary, there are times when a zealous minister could expound, and " testify the " kingdom of God," and " persuade men concerning " Jesus, from morning till evening." Yet at last we must be thankful, if some believe, though far more reject our testimony with pertinacious contempt. But we must shew those who disbelieve, what the Holy Spirit has spoken concerning them, and how the scriptures are fulfilled in them: and warn them not to close their hearts in obstinate unbelief, lest God should *judicially* leave them to be blinded and hardened to their destruction.—While we mourn on account of despisers, we should rejoice that " the salvation of God is sent" to others, who will receive it; and, if we ourselves be of this number, how thankful should we be to him who has made us to differ!—If under reproach and persecution, the true minister can obtain leave and liberty to preach the gospel, and is favoured with success; he will think his sufferings amply compensated: and be reconciled to his own want of liberty, if he finds that " the word of God hath free course, and is glorified.' (*Note*, 2 *Tim.* ii. 8—13.)

END OF VOL. V.